ISBN 978-1-5280-3137-0
PIBN 10927937

1 MONTH OF
FREE
READING

at

www.ForgottenBooks.com

By purchasing this book you are eligible for one month membership to ForgottenBooks.com, giving you unlimited access to our entire collection of over 1,000,000 titles via our web site and mobile apps.

To claim your free month visit: www.forgottenbooks.com/free927937

English
Français
Deutsche
Italiano
Español
Português

www.forgottenbooks.com

(AMERICAN)

Appleton's

ANNUAL CYCLOPÆDIA

AND

REGISTER OF IMPORTANT EVENTS

OF THE YEAR

1874.

EMBRACING POLITICAL, CIVIL, MILITARY, AND SOCIAL AFFAIRS; PUBLIC DOCU-
MENTS; BIOGRAPHY, STATISTICS, COMMERCE, FINANCE, LITERATURE,
SCIENCE, AGRICULTURE, AND MECHANICAL INDUSTRY.

VOLUME XIV.

NEW YORK:
D. APPLETON AND COMPANY,
549 & 551 BROADWAY.
1875.

PREFACE.

THE year 1874 was remarkable for the novel spectacle which it presented of the earnest and extensive conflict of principles, with the entire absence of military strife, except in certain localities where hostile factions were contending for the possession of the civil government. Thus in the northern provinces of Spain, in Cuba, in Western and Eastern Asia, the disturbances were local, and small forces were engaged. But this conflict of principles, without interference with the quiet pursuits of industry, is one of the fruits of diffused intelligence and education. The most extensive of these conflicts existed between some of the governments of Europe and the Roman Catholic Church. In Germany, in Switzerland, in Italy, and in Austria, the supremacy of the State in antagonism to the independence of the Church was asserted and maintained by the most energetic and decisive measures. In France the republic remained entirely tranquil, and the progress of popular principles was unchecked. In Spain the strongest political factions have transferred the authority to the heir of the late Queen. All these leading public subjects, and the various relations arising out of them, with the views of governments and people, are set forth in these pages with fullness and completeness.

In no year since the war have the internal affairs of the Southern States caused more earnest discussion than during 1874. From some of these States came reports of disorders as conflicting as they were exciting. The alleged marching of negroes upon Vicksburg not only spread alarm throughout Mississippi, but riveted public attention. An appeal to arms was made, to decide a question of State politics in Arkansas, and an apparent civil war, after more than a month's duration, was only ended by the interference of the Federal Government. The exciting events in Louisiana during the latter part of the year, and the beginning of 1875, mark an epoch in the constitutional history of the nation. All of these events, not alone the public acts, but the constitutional questions and political issues involved, and whatever tends to throw light upon the cause of the difficulties, and the solution of the problems presented, are recorded in these pages with official accuracy, impartiality, and with a fullness and clearness that leave nothing to be desired. In the preparation of the record, official documents alone, where such existed, were used; while in disputed matters, both sides were accorded a full hearing, and, as far as possible, in the official acts and language of their respective representatives.

The details of the affairs of the United States embrace the finances of the Federal Government; the operation and results of its system of revenue and taxation; the banking system; the financial and industrial experience of the country; its commerce, manufactures, and general prosperity; the finances of the States; their debts and resources; the various political conventions assembled during the year, with their nominations and platforms; the results of elections; the movements to secure cheap transportation from West to East; the action of Congress on the subject, and the debates and action on civil rights and national finances, specie payments, and other important public questions; the proceedings of State Legislatures; the progress of educational, reformatory, and charitable institutions; the extension of railroads and telegraphs, and all those matters which are involved in the rapid improvement of the country. These are contained, with ample details, in these pages.

The important diplomatic correspondence of the Federal Government, derived from the most authentic sources, is presented, and the existing relations with foreign nations.

Every country in the civilized world is noticed in these pages, and whatever of public interest has transpired in them is here recorded. Under the title of Great Britain, will be found the most complete account of her colonial possessions existing in print.

The advance in the various branches of astronomical and chemical science, with new and valuable applications to various purposes, is extensively described.

The narrative of the geographical discoveries in the different parts of the earth, with their results, is very full and interesting.

The record of literature and literary progress in the United States, and in each of the countries of Europe, is as important as during any previous year. The titles of the more able works of various classes are given, with remarks on the nature of their contents.

The statistics of the religious denominations of the country, with their conventions, conferences, progress of opinions and arrangements for future union and coöperation, are here fully presented.

Biographical sketches of living men noted during the year, and notices of deceased persons of distinction in every rank of society, find a place in these pages.

All important documents, messages, orders, and letters from official persons, have been inserted entire.

A General Index, in one volume, is nearly prepared, and will form an addition to this series of volumes as soon as it can be printed.

THE
ANNUAL CYCLOPÆDIA.

A

ABBOT, Rev. GORHAM DUMMER, LL. D., an eminent scholar and teacher, a son of Rev. Jacob Abbott, and younger brother of the prolific and popular writers, Messrs. Jacob and John S. C. Abbott; born in Brunswick, Me., September 3, 1808; died at South Natick, Mass., August 3, 1874. Mr. Abbot was educated, like his brothers, at Bowdoin College, from which he graduated in 1826, and pursued a partial theological course at Andover with the class which graduated there in 1831. He was next settled as a Congregationalist minister at New Rochelle, N. Y., where he remained for three years, doing at the same time some literary work for the American Tract Society. He then established a female seminary, first in Lafayette Place, then on Washington Square, then the Spingler Institute on Union Square, where he remained for thirteen years, and subsequently remodeled the Townsend Mansion on Fifth Avenue, which for a time he conducted in connection with the Spingler Institute, and finally his school was removed to the Suydam Mansion on Park Avenue. During much of the more than thirty years he was thus engaged in teaching, his seminary occupied high rank not only in New York but throughout the country. Mr. Abbot was not only a skillful and successful teacher, but he was an excellent judge of character and possessed great executive ability. He retired from his seminary in 1869 or 1870 with an ample competence, which subsequent unfortunate investments materially diminished. But Dr. Abbot (he received the honorary degree of LL. D. from Ingham University in 1860) was not a teacher only, he had also achieved a good reputation as an author. His "Family at Home," "Nathan Dickerman," "Mexico and the United States," and other works, were creditable alike to his thorough research and his rhetorical ability. He was greatly interested in Biblical study, and imported at his own expense a set of the plates of the Annotated Paragraph Bible of the London Tract Society, and published several editions of that admirable work, at a low price, to facilitate Biblical instruction.

ADVENTISTS. I. SEVENTH-DAY ADVENTISTS.—The statistical returns of this denomination show it to have fifteen State Conferences, three hundred churches, seventy-five ordained ministers, sixty licentiates, and fifteen thousand members. Meetings of the General Conference were held at Battle Creek, Michigan, in November, 1873, and August, 1874. At the former meeting, November 14, 1873, the treasurer reported his receipts to have been, including the balance on hand at the time of making his previous report in March, 1873, $9,039.63, and his expenditures, $4,879.88; showing a balance still on hand of $4,159.75. A committee, appointed at the previous General Conference for that purpose, reported that several families holding the views of the denomination had been induced to remove to Battle Creek, where the Conference was endeavoring to establish a strong centre of influence. This committee were requested to continue their efforts for another year. Fifty-two thousand dollars had been pledged to the fund for the establishment of a denominational school. Resolutions were adopted by this Conference declaring the denomination to be intrusted with two great truths, which it was its duty to set before men, viz.: "The doctrine of the near advent of Christ, and that of the commandments of God and the holy Sabbath;" expressing regret at the opposition of many of the Advent people "to the Sabbath and the law of God;" but disavowing the existence toward them of a spirit of contention or bitterness, and uttering the hope "that with many of them a more candid spirit toward these great truths might yet prevail." The Seventh-Day Baptists were recognized as "a people whom God has highly honored in making them in past ages the depositaries of his law and Sabbath;" and the desire was expressed, "so far as practicable, to coöperate with them in leading men to the conscientious observance of the commandments of God." A declension was noticed from both the health and dress reforms, and the people were entreated "to arouse and make these subjects matters of conscience." Increased confidence was professed in the gift of the "spirit of prophecy which God has so mercifully placed in the third angel's message;" the endeavor was resolved upon "to maintain an affectionate regard for its presence and its teachings;" and the Executive Committee were requested to prepare, or cause to be prepared, a work giving the reasons for believing the testimonies of a Sister White to be the teachings of the Holy Spirit. The Executive Committee were advised to take steps for the speedy publication of tracts and periodicals in other languages. Measures were taken to secure the consolidation of the systems of the Tract and Missionary Societies by some general organization, and for the formation of an Educational Society.

The meeting of the General Conference in August, 1874, was held in connection with the National Camp-meeting of the denomination, which continued from the 6th to the 17th of the month. The organization of the General Tract and Missionary Society was completed. Reports from about one-half of the local Tract and Missionary Societies connected with the State Conferences showed that sixteen million pages of tracts had been distributed and sold during the year. · Elder J. N. Andrews was commissioned as a missionary to Europe, with instructions to look after the Swiss Mission and other points of interest on the Continent. Progress was reported in the efforts to establish a denominational school. The school had been opened, under the care of Mr. S. Brownsberger, a graduate of the Michigan University. A fine brick building for its use was nearly completed, on a lot of twelve acres' extent. The report of the Seventh-Day Adventist Publishing Association, made at its fourteenth annual meeting, November 17, 1873, showed the amount of its assets to have been then $119,707.51, and its debts $37,319.12, leaving $82,388.39 as the value of its net assets.

II. ADVENT CHRISTIAN ASSOCIATION.—The National Advent Camp-meeting of the Advent Christian Association was held at Springfield, Massachusetts, August 6th to 8th. A meeting of ministers was held just before the camp-meeting, to consult on topics involving the interest of the work of the Association "in spreading the knowledge of the speedy coming of the Lord," at which a congregational form of government was devised. Each organized church, with its members and officers, will remain an independent body, but the formation was recommended of quarterly, State, and

General Conferences, as "advisory and suasive bodies for the more perfect work of producing harmonious and efficient labor in all parts of the country."

The annual meeting of the American Advent Missionary Society was held in connection with the camp-meeting, August 12th. The treasurer reported his total receipts to have been $5,112.74, and his total expenditures $4,692.99. This Society was organized in 1865; since which, to the time of the present meeting, it had received and expended for its work $33,000.

III. EVANGELICAL ADVENTISTS.—The American Evangelical Advent Conference was held at the Hebron Camp-ground, Hebronville, Massachusetts, August 20th and 22d. The Committee on Worship reported an order of service. The Committee on Systematic Benevolence reported that the action of the Conference of the previous year had been carried out, and that preparations had been made to continue the prosecution of their work. The Committee on Ordinations reported that no cases for ordination had been presented.

The annual meeting of the American Millennial Association, which has charge of the business and publishing interests of the denomination, was held at Hebronville, August 20th. The treasurer reported his receipts for the year ending July 1, 1874, to have been, including the balance and cash on hand at the beginning of the year, $7,657.10, and his expenditures, $6,689.01.

IV. LIFE AND ADVENT UNION.—The annual camp-meeting of the American Life and Advent Union was held at Springfield, Massachusetts, beginning August 1st. The eleventh anniversary of the Union was held August 6th. Leonard C. Thorne, of New York, was chosen president. The treasurer reported his receipts for the year just ended to have been $4,216.87, and his expenses $4,484.31. A balance was also due him, on the previous year's account, of $1,297.32. The sum of $2,299 was pledged on an effort to raise $3,200, for the purposes of the Union for the ensuing year, to be devoted to the publication of its paper, pamphlets, and books.

·AFGHANISTAN, a country in Central Asia, bounded north by Toorkistan, east by British India, south by Beloochistan, and west by Persia. In an official correspondence between the cabinets of St. Petersburg and London, especially in the dispatches of Lord Granville, dated October 17, 1872, and of Prince Gortchakoff, dated January 31, 1873, England and Russia agreed upon the regulation of the northern frontier of Afghanistan. According to this new agreement, Afghanistan is in future to embrace—1. Badakshan with the dependent district, Wakhan, from Siripul in the east as far as the confluence of the river Koktcha with the Oxus (Amu-Darya), which constitutes the northern frontier of this province in its entire extent; 2. Afghan Toorkistan, which embraces the districts of Kunduz, Khulum. and Balkh, and is bounded north by the Oxus in its course from the mouth of the Koktcha as far as Khodja Sala, a post-station on the road from Bokhara to Balkh. The Emir of Afghanistan can claim nothing on the left bank of the Oxus below Khodja Sala; 3. The interior districts of Akhshee, Siripul, Maymene, Shibergan, and Andjai, the latter of which is the extreme possession of Afghanistan in the northwest, while the desert beyond it belongs to the independent Toorkoman tribes; 4. The west frontier of Afghanistan between the territories of Herat and the Persian province of Khorassan has not undergone any change.

Since the new regulation of the frontier, the area of Afghanistan is estimated at 278,-647 square miles. The population is estimated at upward of 4,000,000. The population of the provinces into which Afghanistan is divided is given by a Russian military periodical as follows: Caboolistan, 900,000; Hasareh, 195,000; Khorassan with Herat, 1,654,000; Seistan, 280,000; Kunduz, 400,000; Khulum, 300,000; Balkh, 64,000; Andjai and Shibergan, 60,000; Aktcbe, 10,000; Maymene, 100,-000; in all, 3,963,000. In this report, no statement is made of the population of the provinces of Badakshan and Wakhan. The population of the former is estimated by E. Schlagintweit from 100,000 to 150,000. To the territory of Maymene, Vámbéry now assigns a population of 300,000.

Afghanistan was again, in 1874, the scene of serious dynastic difficulties, which attracted great attention from the fact that both Great Britain and Russia appeared, as usual, to take a profound interest in them, and to use them with a view to establishing their ascendency in this region. Russian and English accounts of these troubles widely differ, and in many cases it is at present impossible to ascertain the truth. The recent disturbances arose in consequence of the appointment of Abdallah Jan, the younger son of Shere Ali, the present ruler, as heir-apparent to the throne, with the exclusion of Yakoob Khan, the eldest son, who for some time had been governor of the important province of Herat. The latter at once prepared to enforce his claims to the throne by a resort to arms, and to reopen the civil war among the members of the dynastic family, from which the country has already suffered so much. As all the living members of the ruling family who had taken a part in the former civil wars of the country may be expected to appear again on the scene, a brief retrospect of the former family quarrels will help to elucidate the present complication. Shere Ali, the present ruler of Afghanistan, had been preferred by his father, Dost Mohammed, in the same manner in which he now favors his youngest son. When, on the death of his father, he assumed the reins of the government, his elder brothers, Afzool and Azim, at once rose against him. Afzool placed himself at the head of the rebellion in Balkh, while Azim fought in the east, and finally a younger brother, Emin, raised the standard of revolt in Candahar. The latter was killed in the battle of Kelat-il-Ghilzie, in which Shere Ali also lost his beloved eldest son. Soon the sons of the rivals took a prominent part in the war. The eldest surviving son of Shere Ali, Ibrahim, is a weak and insignificant man, while the second son, Yakoob, who, when a boy, had detected the disguise in which the Hungarian traveler, Vámbéry, traversed these countries, soon gained great renown for his sagacity and bravery. Rhaman Khan, the oldest son of Afzool, is likewise a brave warrior, and the two cousins fought many hotly-contested battles against each other. After many vicissitudes, Afzool Khan was overtaken by death, while advancing at the head of his victorious columns. His brother Azim, who by his misgovernment had become extremely unpopular, died soon after. The brave Rhaman, after several crushing defeats, was driven by Yakoob Khan out of the country, and Shere Ali recognized as ruler of the Afghans. But, although Shere Ali was indebted for the throne to his son Yakoob, he soon began to favor his younger son, Abdallah Jan (born in 1862), the child of his favorite wife. This preference was shown in an ostentatious manner when Shere Ali, in 1869, had an interview with the Viceroy of India. Lord Mayo by no means encouraged the plan, and, when Yakoob Khan attempted to secure his right of succession, he used his whole influence to bring about a reconciliation between Shere Ali and his disaffected son. The latter was appointed governor of the province of Herat, and until 1874 the relation between father and son continued of a peaceable nature. It was, however, expected all the time that, whenever Shere Ali should officially proclaim Abdallah Jan as his presumptive successor, Yakoob Khan would again rise in rebellion, and that in such a case Rhaman Khan would also appear on the scene. As Rhaman Khan had closely allied himself with the Russians, the British statesmen have looked forward with considerable anxiety to the time when civil war might once more reign in Afghanistan.

The province of Herat is situated in the northwestern corner of Afghanistan, and is bounded by Persia, Khiva, and Bokhara. The great distance from the capital of Afghanistan made it possible for Yakoob Khan, not only to be virtually the independent ruler, but also to prepare for another war against his father. He appears to have had secret diplomatic correspondence with the governments of the neighboring countries, but the character of the negotiations is not yet fully known. He is believed, however, to have courted the friendship of Russia, which, according to the papers of British India, has of late built two roads leading to the frontier of Afghanistan — one from Urgentsh to Herat, and the other from Urgentsh to Meshid.

The policy of the British authorities with regard to the civil troubles in Afghanistan, if we are to believe their official professions, has been one of non-intervention. They claim to have been willing, all the time, to recognize the victor, whoever he might be. During the wars following the death of Dost Mohammed, both Shere Ali and Afzool Khan received letters from Lord Lawrence, who, in one of those to Afzool Khan, expressly declared that as long as Shere Ali held possession of Herat, and desired friendly relations with England, he would recognize him as Emir of Herat, while at the same time he felt no hesitation in recognizing Afzool Khan as Emir of Cabool and Candahar as long as he held those places. Toward the end of the civil war between Shere Ali and his rivals, the Government of India appears, however, to have taken a very active interest in the success of Shere Ali. After the battle of Mainmanah, in 1868, and after the victorious entrance of Shere Ali into Cabool, the Indian Government sent him £60,000 sterling, to enable him to fully conquer his opponents. At the durbah of Amballah, Lord Mayo is reported to have promised to Shere Ali an annual subsidy of £120,-000. From the English Blue-Book it appears that in November, 1869, Prince Gortchakoff remarked to the British embassador in St. Petersburg that the Indian Government was supporting the Emir of Afghanistan with regular subsidies. In 1873, shortly before the proclamation of Abdallah Jan as heir to the throne, a Mohammedan was sent by the Government of India as special envoy to Cabool, and it was surmised that he was to assure Shere Ali of the approval of the proposed change in the succession by the viceroy, and to promise him support in case of war.

In September, the hostilities between Shere Ali and Yakoob Khan actually commenced. The latter was supposed to have the entire sympathy not only of Russia, but Persia, which has been hankering after Herat ever since she lost it. In November, a report was received in Calcutta that Yakoob Khan had been treacherously arrested and imprisoned in his own capital. He was charged with the design to surrender Herat to the Persians. It was expected that this arrest would be followed by serious complications.

AFRICA. The growth of Egypt stands from year to year more conspicuously forth as the prominent feature of the recent history of Africa. A new expedition under Colonel Gordon has been sent into the regions of Central Africa, which in 1873 were explored by Sir Samuel Baker, and it now appears more probable than ever that immense tracts of land extending southward to the equator may soon be permanently incorporated with Egypt. A war with the Sultan of Darfur resulted in a complete victory for Egypt, and may lead to the annexation of this country also to the dominions of the Khédive. While thus in point of extent the country will probably become one of the largest empires of the world, great reforms continue to be introduced in all the branches of public administration. (*See* EGYPT.)

The war of England against the Ashantees, which began in 1873, was a brilliant success. One of the worst native governments of Africa was thoroughly humbled, another powerful blow dealt to the slave-trade, and a new road paved for the steady progress of civilization in Western Africa. (*See* ASHANTEE.)

A war between the English colony of Natal and the Zulus, under their chief, Langalobele, which also began in 1873, ended early in 1874, by the capture of the Zulu chief, who on February 9th was sentenced to banishment for life. An appeal against this sentence was moved by Bishop Colenso, on the complaint of several members of the tribe, and was allowed.

The new Emperor of Morocco, though just, is reported to be severe and energetic. Toward the close of the year he set out on an expedition to punish several rebellious tribes. The imposition of a gate-tax at Mogador was considered by the foreign consuls of that town as a violation of the commercial convention between Morocco, Great Britain, and Spain. (*See* MOROCCO.)

The trade of the eastern coast of Africa, which is chiefly in the hands of East Indians, has assumed much larger dimensions since the opening of the Suez Canal. In January, 1873, a monthly steamship-line was opened between Aden, Zanzibar, and Madagascar; the vessels belong to the British Indian Steamship Company. The revenue of the company in December, 1873, from goods shipped from Zanzibar to Aden, was about $20,000; and their vessels were not large enough to satisfy all demands.

The diamond-fields in South Africa continue to attract large crowds of natives from the interior, who find it easy to be employed by the diggers, and who returning to their homes diffuse among the native population a general acquaintance with the progress of civilization. New extensive gold-fields were discovered in September on the Blyde River.

The new British possession in South Africa, Griqualand West, which on October 27, 1871, was annexed to the Cape Colony, has been organized by a royal decree, dated February 7, 1873, and proclaimed by the governor of the Cape Colony, on July 5, 1873. It has received the official name, Province of Griqualand West, and will have a lieutenant-governor, and a Legislative Assembly, consisting of four members, elected by the three districts, Kimberleg (2), Barkly (1), and Hag (1), and four members appointed by the crown.

The total area of Africa is now estimated (*see* Behm and Wagner, "Bevölkerung der Erde," II., Gotha, 1874) at 11,555,855 square miles; population, 203,300,000. This includes the island of Madeira and the Canary Islands, which often are considered a part of Europe.

The following table gives the population of the large geographical divisions of Africa, and their political subdivisions:

GEOGRAPHICAL DIVISIONS.	Population of Divisions.	Population of Subdivisions.
NORTHERN AFRICA................	15,260,000	
Morocco......................		6,000,000
Algeria......................		2,414,218
Tunis.......................		2,000,000
Tripoli and Fezzan...........		848,000
Bara........................		302,000
Sahara......................		3,700,000
NORTHEASTERN AFRICA..........	34,500,000	
Egypt.......................		8,400,000
Territory of the Kabdi.......		68,000
Territory of the Coomana....		150,000
Abyssinia...................		3,000,000
Gallas......................		7,000,000
Soumali (peninsula)..........		8,000,000
Countries east of the White Nile......................		7,840,000
Mohammedan countries of the Middle Soudan...............	38,800,000	
Western Soudan..............	17,600,000	
Upper Guinea................	26,000,000	
Equatorial territory..........	45,500,000	
SOUTH AFRICA.................	20,285,000	
Territories on the eastern coast, between the equator and the Portuguese possessions...............		3,500,000
Portuguese · { Eastern coast..		300,000
Possessions. { Western coast.		9,000,000
Balunda countries....´......		4,730,000
Damara Gr. Namaqua........		50,000
West Bechuanas.............		160,000
Transvaal Republic..........		275,000
Orange Free State...........		57,000
British Territory............		952,000
Kaffres, districts of.........		1,210,000
ISLANDS......................	5,343,000	
Madeira....		118,379
Canary Islands..............		283,859
Cape Verd Islands...........		67,347
Guinea Islands..............		54,300
Ascension, St. Helena........		6,444
Tristan da Cunha		53
Madagascar, and adjacent islands........................		4,000,000
Other islands in the Indian Ocean.....................		813,000
Total, Africa.............	203,300,000	

AGRICULTURE. The year 1874 was not especially favorable to the husbandman, but one of the great crops being above the average, and the protracted drought of the months of July and August, and the first half of December, having seriously reduced the crops of corn and fodder, as well as the root-crops and the pasturage, throughout the States of the Atlantic slope. In the States beyond the Mississippi, over a tract nearly 600 miles in length from north to south, and varying in width from about 100 miles at the north to 250 miles in Southern Kansas, the grasshoppers, or more properly the locusts, made almost a clean sweep of every green thing, in some cases making a partial devastation at first, and then a second invasion a few weeks later, and destroying grass, corn, the later cereals, and buckwheat, potatoes, beets, and indeed all vegetable crops not harvested. It has usually been the fact that, when our crops were not excessive, there has been a large export demand, produced by short crops in Great Britain, France, Portugal, etc., so that a crop below the average has often proved

as profitable as a larger one in consequence of the higher prices obtained. But this has not been the case the past year. The wheat and barley crop in Great Britain was exceptionally large, and that of France much better than for many years previous, and consequently the export demand which in the year ending June 30, 1874, was 60,551,181 bushels for Great Britain alone, and 71,039,928 for all foreign countries, has fallen off heavily for the new crop, and every effort to increase shipments has resulted in a reduction of price both in England and the United States, which has rendered the export nearly or quite unremunerative. The export of barley and oats, never very large, has been decreased from the same causes, while the crop of Indian-corn was so much below the average, and much of it so poor in quality, that there was comparatively little to send abroad; and our export, which in 1872-'73 was more than 38,500,000 bushels, or about one-thirtieth of the crop, will not probably in 1874-'75 reach 20,000,000 bushels. The export demand for cotton was insufficient, even with the diminished crop, to maintain the price, and there was a steady reduction in values, even in the old crop. The tobacco-crop was, in the States most largely engaged in its production, almost an entire failure. Still, so wide is the extent of our territory, and so varied the climate, soil, and productions of different sections, that the losses and deficiencies of one section are made up by the more ample productions of another, and though there may be somewhat less to export, or a diminished demand for our products from abroad, a general famine is hardly possible. There is in one part or another of our country "bread enough and to spare." The lateness of the autumn in this as in the preceding year was very favorable to the gathering of cotton, corn, and the fruits and root-crops generally.

The *Wheat* crop was in condition and yield per acre about 2 per cent. below that of the previous year, but the increased acreage, amounting to 7 per cent., makes the entire crop somewhat larger than that of 1873. It may, we think, be safely estimated at 305,000,000 bushels, being a little larger than in any previous year. On the Pacific coast, as well as in portions of the Mississippi Valley, the yield was considerably above the average, but the great wheat-growing States of Indiana, Illinois, Wisconsin, Minnesota, Iowa, and Kansas, produced not quite their average amount.

Indian Corn.—This crop was materially injured by the drought of July and August in all the States which produce the largest quantities of it. The number of acres planted was considerably in excess of 1873, but the production was decidedly less to the acre even where it was not destroyed by the grasshoppers. The Agricultural Department early in the season estimated the yield at 812,000,000 bushels, but the favorable weather in September and October secured the ripening of the entire crop, and the latest returns show that not less than 854,000,000 bushels were harvested. The crop of 1873, which was not thought to exceed 870,000,000 bushels, actually turned out to be 920,000,000.

The *Rye* crop is about 8 per cent. below the average, but probably does not differ materially from that of last year. We should put it at 14,891,000 bushels, or 98 per cent. of the crop of 1873.

Oats are very nearly an average crop in quantity, a larger acreage than usual having been devoted to them. In New England and on the Pacific coast the yield was very large and the quality excellent. In the central and Southern States, drought, rust, the chinch-bugs, and the grasshoppers, have done extensive injury to the crop. The estimate of the Agricultural Department is 240,000,000 bushels, which is probably very near the truth.

Barley.—This crop, though early in the season reported as slightly below the average, has yet, from increased acreage, been probably larger in amount than in any previous year. The Agricultural Department estimate it (probably slightly below the truth) at 32,704,000 bushels, or 1 per cent. advance on the largest previous crop.

Buckwheat is never a very large crop, and is confined to a few States. In New England it was an average crop; in the Middle States about 8 per cent. short; in the Northwest its condition was unsatisfactory; and in portions of Kansas the grasshoppers destroyed it. It is only cultivated, in the Southern States, in West Virginia, Tennessee, and very slightly in North Carolina, and in these it was a fair crop. It is seldom grown for two successive years on the same land. The yield may possibly reach 9,000,000 bushels.

Potatoes (Solanum tuberosum). — In New England the crop was more than an average. Elsewhere drought, Colorado beetles, chinch-bugs, a fly, said to be a *cantharis*, and, above all, the grasshoppers, made sad havoc with the crop, except on the Pacific coast, where it was an average crop. The rot was not as severe as usual. The crop is estimated at 106,000,000 bushels. The Colorado beetle (the ten-lined spearman) has appeared in considerable numbers east of the Mississippi, and a few have been seen in Pennsylvania, New Jersey, and New York.

Potatoes, Sweet (Batatus edulis).—Owing to the drought, the crop was from 8 to 10 per cent. below the average. It probably reached 46,000,000 bushels.

Hay.—The protracted drought materially injured the pasturage, and rendered the early feeding of cattle necessary, and prevented in most sections the cutting of the aftermath, but the first growth was not affected, and the quality was, for the most part, excellent. The Agricultural Department estimate the crop at 25,500,000 tons; and later reports may show that it exceeded this amount. On the Pacific coast, where our ordinary grasses do not succeed well, the hay is mostly from alfalfa, lucerne, and the wild-rice. The quantity in California was said to be one-third larger than ever before. The alfalfa is cut four or five times in a season. In the South, pea-vine hay has been found very nutritious for cattle, and in South Carolina and Georgia is largely cured.

Tobacco.—The tobacco-crop in all the leading tobacco States, was almost a failure. In Kentucky the product was reported as only 24 per cent. of the usual average; in Missouri 55 per cent., and this reduced late in the season by the ravages of the chinch-bug, a new enemy; in Virginia, the product would not exceed 58 per cent.; Tennessee yields only 19 per cent., and North Carolina but 54 per cent. The seed-leaf tobacco of the Connecticut Valley did better, yielding 75 per cent.; and the Pacific coast, where it is becoming an important crop, was 2 or 3 per cent. above the average in quantity, and the quality was excellent. The entire production did not probably exceed 200,000,000 pounds.

Cotton.—As usual, the aggregate amount of the cotton-crop of 1874 has been hotly and somewhat angrily discussed; one party contending that the early heavy rains, the later droughts, the ravages of the caterpillar and boll-worm had reduced the crop so much, that it would not be half that of the previous year, which slightly exceeded, according to actual returns, 4,100,000 bales; the other arguing that, notwithstanding these drawbacks, the weather, late in the season, had been so very favorable, and the cultivation of the crop so much more careful and thorough than usual, that the crop would not vary more than 8 or 10 per cent. from that of the preceding year. The views of the latter party seem to have been justified by the returns so far as they have been received, and the estimate of the crop, which places it at 3,748,000 bales, is not, probably, far from the truth. The only States in which there was any considerable falling off from the product of the preceding year were —Texas, about 12 per cent.; Arkansas, over 35 per cent; and Tennessee, about 38 per cent. On the other hand, Florida had increased her production about 7 per cent. over the previous year, while South Carolina, Georgia, Alabama, Mississippi, and Louisiana, were but slightly, if at all, below the previous year's production.

The following table, giving the average number of pounds of ginned cotton produced to the acre in 1870, 1871, 1873, and 1874, indicates, even in the States having the highest average, either that the cotton-land had become impoverished by the constant repetition of the same crop, or that the lack of manure and of careful tillage had reduced the yield far below its fair and legitimate amount. At the same time it is but just to say that there are some indications of a determination to improve both in the quality and quantity of the crop. Still the fact remains that the land which will not yield in average years at least half a bale (200 lbs.) to the acre is either very poor land or very badly tilled.

STATES.	Average Number of Pounds of Ginned Cotton per Acre, 1870.	Average Number of Pounds of Ginned Cotton per Acre, 1871.	Average Number of Pounds of Ginned Cotton per Acre, 1872.	Average Number of Pounds of Ginned Cotton per Acre, 1874.	REMARKS.
Virginia..........	165	172	...	168	Crop very uniform, but lands poor.
North Carolina...	175	143	150	172	Cotton-lands generally sandy.
South Carolina...	170	117	188	194	Some improvement. Increased manuring.
Georgia..........	173	120	184	136	Best lands not sown to cotton, and little or no manure.
Florida...........	165	85	126	100	Generally sandy land, and no manure.
Alabama..........	155	130	151	139	Lands unproductive from constant cropping.
Mississippi	205	150	172	139	Gradual deterioration of cotton-lands.
Louisiana........	252	150	180	173	Rich soil, but imperfect tillage.
Texas............	275	180	221	170	Highest average in the South.
Arkansas.........	255	215	195	108	Rich lands, but poor tillage.
Tennessee........	190	180	190	143	Poorer lands, but better tillage.

Sugar-Cane.—The sugar-crop was unusually good in Louisiana, Texas, and Southern Alabama, which are the areas of the largest production, and very nearly an average in Georgia, Florida, and Mississippi. A little is grown in Arkansas and Tennessee, but it is an uncertain crop in both States. The yield is fully 175,000 hogsheads and perhaps more. *Sorghum* is reported as a crop in twenty-one States, and in those States where it is most largely grown the yield was much above the average. It is mainly used in the form of syrup or molasses, and the production must have been somewhat more than 16,000,000 gallons. *Beet-Sugar* is becoming a production of considerable importance in California, and the year was unusually favorable for the manufacture of sugar from the *maple*, an industry which is largely followed in the Eastern and Middle States.

Flax.—Returns from only fifteen States are given, but of these those most largely engaged in its culture, Indiana, Wisconsin, Minnesota, Iowa, and Kansas, all report an excess over last year's abundant crop, while the other States are nearly up to last year's production, except Kentucky, where, for some cause, there is only two-thirds of a crop. The product is probably not far from 28,000,000 lbs.

Peas and Beans were not quite an average crop, though probably amounting to nearly 15,500,000 bushels.

There are no satisfactory returns of the *Rice* crop. It is cultivated as a crop only in North and South Carolina, Georgia, and Florida, and perhaps to a small extent in the Gulf States. The usual production is now about 88,000,000 pounds.

Fruits.—In all the Northern, most of the Western, and all the States on the Pacific coast, the year was an exceptionally fine one for fruit. In the Southern States the protracted drought, and in some sections insect destroyers, impaired the crop from 10 to 30 per cent. The grape is becoming one of our most important fruits, not only for table-use, but for the manufacture of wine and brandy, which is every year assuming a greater magnitude, and within the next decade will probably diminish our importation of these articles to a very small amount. Both in quality and quantity the grapes of 1874 in the principal wine-growing districts, East and West, were greatly superior to ordinary vintages. In this crop California takes the lead, having now nearly 100,000,000 vines in full bearing, including all the best species and varieties of Europe, as well as all the native and cultivated varieties of all parts of our own country. The *Apple* crop was very abundant throughout a part of the Eastern, and all of the Middle States, most of the Northwestern, and all of the Pacific States. In the Southern and Southwestern, as well as in the Northeastern States, it was less than an average. The quality of the fruit was not, however, equal to the quantity, the winter apples rotting early and fast. *Pears* were much below the average in quantity, except in New England and on the Pacific coast, but for the most part the quality was good. The *Peach* crop was below the average, especially in Delaware and Maryland, but the quality of the fruit was generally very good. The Northwestern and the Pacific peach districts did not yield so largely as in some seasons. The early small fruits, *strawberries, raspberries, blackberries,* and *cherries*, were very plentiful, strawberries especially being lower in the great markets than for several years.

On the next page we give, instead of our usual table of statistics of the number and value of live stock in each State and the Territories, at the beginning of 1875 a table showing the aggregate numbers, prices, and total values of each kind of live-stock for the whole country for the ten years 1866–1875 inclusive.

In the ANNUAL CYCLOPÆDIA for 1873 attention was called to the diminishing yield of wheat per acre, even in our newest wheat-growing States, as an alarming fact, and the experiments of an English farmer, Mr. J. B. Lawes, on the beneficial effects of different kinds of manures, experiments running through a series of years, were detailed as demonstrating that there was no necessity for such a diminution. We present this year another series of experiments, approaching the subject in an entirely different direction, that of the quality and quantity of the seed sown. Major

YEAR.	HORSES.			MULES.			MILCH-COWS.		
	Number.	Average Price.	Total Value.	Number.	Average Price.	Total Value.	Number.	Average Price.	Total Value.
1866..	5,503,912	$81 10	$446,367,263	908,632	$93 05	$84,082,958	....	......	....
1867..	5,276,514	79 46	429,271,818	822,470	92 52	76,094,954	....	......	....
1868..	5,757,000	75 16	432,696,226	855,763	77 61	66,415,769	8,120,898	$39 77	$322,968,141
1869..	6,332,798	84 16	533,024,787	921,662	106 74	98,386,359	9,247,714	39 11	361,752,676
1870..	8,249,170	81 38	671,319,461	1,179,570	109 01	128,584,796	10,095,622	39 12	394,940,745
1871..	8,701,701	78 52	683,257,587	1,242,271	101 53	126,127,786	10,023,549	37 33	374,179,093
1872..	8,990,900	73 37	659,707,916	1,276,300	94 82	121,027,316	10,803,500	31 97	329,408,983
1873..	9,222,470	74 21	684,443,957	1,310,000	95 15	124,658,085	10,575,900	29 72	314,358,982
1874..	9,333,800	71 45	666,927,406	1,339,350	89 22	119,501,859	10,705,300	27 99	299,609,302
1875..	9,520,476	71 05	675,429,820	1,392,324	88 10	122,716,604	10,919,406	27 01	294,933,159

YEAR.	OTHER CATTLE.			SHEEP.			SWINE.		
	Number.	Average Price.	Total Value.	Number.	Average Price.	Total Value.	Number.	Average Price.	Total Value.
1866..	*26,985,662	$24 70	$665,310,851	41,253,652	$3 45	$142,325,099	28,845,008	$5 70	$164,416,517
1867..	11,570,844	21 55	249,351,682	39,400,000	3 37	132,774,660	24,698,236	5 43	134,111,424
1868..	11,943,940	20 86	249,144,599	39,050,718	2 52	98,407,809	24,344,234	4 55	110,766,266
1869..	12,185,385	25 12	306,211,473	37,724,279	2 17	82,139,979	23,316,476	6 26	146,188,755
1870..	15,391,590	22 54	346,926,440	40,949,312	2 28	93,364,433	26,779,900	6 79	187,191,502
1871..	16,211,484	22 82	369,940,056	31,911,999	2 82	74,035,837	29,452,000	6 20	182,602,352
1872..	16,389,800	19 61	321,568,693	31,679,300	2 80	88,771,197	31,796,800	4 86	155,733,828
1873..	16,413,800	20 06	329,298,755	33,002,400	2 96	97,922,350	32,632,050	4 09	133,729,615
1874..	16,218,100	19 15	310,649,803	33,938,200	2 61	88,690,569	30,860,900	4 86	134,565,526
1875..	16,220,000	19 00	308,180,000	33,598,818	2 65	89,636,868	28,083,419	4 30	120,753,702

F. F. Hallett, of Manor-Farm, Kemptown, England, has been for more than twenty years a highly-intelligent, practical wheat-grower, and has devoted much time and study to the nature and habits of the wheat-plant and the best means of developing it. He found that where wheat had the opportunity (from sparse or thin sowing) to expand, "tiller," or "stool," i. e., to spread out its joints and eventually its stems from a single grain, it always availed itself of the opportunity, and that each of these offshoots produced a stem, and an ear or head of wheat. He discovered further that by a proper selection of grains for sowing, and then planting (by drill) at a sufficient distance apart, this tillering and spreading process could be greatly increased, so that he exhibited at the Exeter meeting of the British Association a plant of wheat from a single grain, which had 94 stems, each crowned with its ear of wheat; a plant of barley from a single grain with 110 stems, and a plant of oats from a single grain with 87 stems. These results were obtained, not by the use of any manure or by any new process of tillage, but by the following means: His seed was selected on the following plan: choosing the best and most productive plant, of either wheat, barley, or oats, viz., the one which had tillered the most and formed the best heads, he planted the grains from it in rows, twelve inches apart every way, and so arranged that the grains from each head or ear should be in a row by themselves. At harvest he selected from these, after careful study and comparison, the finest plant—that which had tillered most and produced the finest, largest, and fullest ears. This process he repeated for four or more years, the improvement being at first rapid, but after a series of years having apparently reached its limit. The following table shows the results of four or five years' repetition of this process:

* This includes milch-cows, the enumeration not having been made separately.

Table showing the Importance of each Additional Generation of Selection.

YEAR.	EARS.	Length.	Containing.	No. of ears on finest stool.
		Inches.	Grains.	
1857...	Original ear........	4¾	47	..
1858...	Finest ear........	6¼	79	10
1859...	Finest ear	7¾	91	22
1860...	Ears imperfect from wet season...... .	..	..	39
1861...	Finest ear........	8¾	123	52

Thus, by means of repeated selection alone, the length of the ears has been doubled, their contents nearly trebled, and the "tillering" power of the seed increased fivefold. The wheat used for this series of experiments was the original red; experiments subsequently made with Hunter's white wheat increased the number of grains from 60 in the original ear to 124 in the fourth year's best ear; with the Victoria white, from 60 to 114; with the Golden Drop, from 32 to 96 grains; with Grace's white, still more remarkable results. Major Hallett thus gives his seed-wheat a "pedigree," as he terms it, growing always from the best and producing the wonderful results stated above and the more wonderful ones which follow. He deduces from his observations and experiments the following laws of the development of cereals:

1. Every fully-developed plant, whether of wheat, oats, or barley, presents an ear superior in productive power to any of the rest on that plant.

2. Every such plant contains one grain, which upon trial proves more productive than any other.

3. The best grain in a given plant is found in its best ear.

4. The superior vigor of this grain is transmissible in different degrees to its progeny.

5. By repeated careful selection the superiority is accumulated.

6. The improvement, which is at first rapid, gradually, after a long series of years, is dimin-

ished in amount, and eventually so far arrested that, practically speaking, a limit to improvement in the desired quality is reached.

7. By still continuing to select, the improvement is maintained, and practically a fixed type is the result.

But there are two other conditions necessary to the highest success in these experiments, viz., that the grains should be sown sparingly, in order to give ample room for tillering or spreading; and uniformly, that there may be no alternation of crowded and thin patches; and that it should be sown early, that it may have the advantage of the autumnal growth, and spread out its stools ready for early growth in the spring.

The yield of wheat per acre in England, in favorable seasons, is much greater than with us, averaging, Major Hallett says, 34 bushels; and he has taken the pains to count the average number of heads on ears per acre, which he states to vary very slightly from 1,000,000. Of ordinary No. 1 wheat there are 700,000 grains to the bushel. Of the "pedigree" wheat there are, in consequence of its superior size, but 460,000 grains to the bushel. The usual practice in England has been to sow from a bushel to two bushels of wheat to the acre. Major Hallett asserts, from many years' experience and careful counting and manuring, that five pints of his pedigree wheat, drilled in by single grains 12 by 12 inches apart, to the acre, will produce more than 1,000,000 heads or ears to the acre; and that from these ears, in consequence of their great yield and size, the product will be not less than 70 bushels to the acre of the very best wheat, and more than this quantity if the wheat is sown the last of August or the first of September, and is hoed or cultivated when it first comes up, to prevent its being smothered by weeds. Major Hallett states that in average seasons (in England) wheat sown by or before September 1st comes up in 7 days; on or about October 1st, in 14 days; on or about November 1st, in 21 days; and on or about December 1st, in not less than 28 days. The earlier the sowing the smaller the quantity of seed required, the more perfect and extensive the tillering, the better the resistance to the winter, and the earlier and larger the crop. From five pints to six or eight quarts are ample seed if sown on the last of August or the first of September; from the middle to the end of September three or four quarts should be added for each week's delay. He claims that by his method there will be a great saving of seed, amounting, if it were carried out in England, to 8,000,000 bushels of wheat, or one-eighth of the largest amount ever imported from this country; a great increase of production, amounting to a doubling of their present crop, which would effectually prevent any necessity for importation of grain; the quality of the wheat would be improved; the power to withstand frosts and injurious insects would be greatly in-

creased; the farm-work would be materially forwarded; the crop would never be "winter-proud;" the harvest would be from two to three weeks earlier, and would be far less liable to be affected by unfavorable seasons in its ripening. Of course, comparatively few of our farmers can afford the time or trouble to obtain their seed-wheat, barley, or oats, on the "pedigree-plan," but in every wheat-growing district there are one or two who will be willing to raise seed-wheat or other grains on this principle, and who will in four or five years have a supply, not only for themselves but for their neighbors; and meanwhile, the Agricultural Department is procuring a small supply to test it; but the early sowing and the use of the drill, planting the single grains far enough apart to permit them to tiller well, and also the hoeing or cultivating, is possible for every wheat-grower. The same principle of selection, too, may be tried here, as it has been in England, with root-crops, hops, strawberries, cotton, rice, etc.

We are sometimes met with the objection from the farmer, that it is of no use to increase the production of grains, corn, cotton, etc., because that the market being glutted, the price falls so low that production is unprofitable, and the farmer is the poorer for his great crop. There is some truth in this view, but not in the inference those who take it would draw from it. In favorable years, cotton, wheat, Indian-corn, and perhaps some other articles, are produced beyond the demand for exportation, or perhaps the existing home demand; but the remedies for this condition do not lie in restricting the production, but in enlarging the market; not in half-tilling 200 acres to get twelve or fifteen bushels of wheat or 125 pounds of cotton to the acre, but in such thorough and careful cultivation of forty or fifty acres as shall bring from fifty to seventy bushels of wheat or 500 pounds of cotton to the acre, and devoting the rest of the land to other and needed crops; not selling cotton at whatever price it will bring, to buy corn for fattening hogs, but growing the corn; not buying hay, but raising it; not buying sugar, or cloth, or linen, but making them, or at least growing the sorghum, keeping the sheep, and raising the flax, of which they are made. The remedy for this difficulty of over-production is moreover in great part removed by creating a home-market; wherever manufactures prosper, there a permanent market for agricultural produce, at good prices, is established; one infinitely better than a foreign one, because it is not dependent on so many chances of failure. On this subject the words of Mr. J. R. Dodge, Statistician of the Agricultural Department, in an address delivered before the National Agricultural Congress in May, 1874, are worthy of consideration, and are to the following effect:

When we consider that less than a third of the area of the States, and less than a fifth of the entire domain of the United States, is mapped into farms, and remember that of this farm-area only one-fourth is tilled or mowed; and when we further reflect that the average yield per acre could be doubled if the many could be brought up to the plane of the few in the practice of intensive culture, then we begin to realize what numbers our country is capable of feeding, and what waste of toil and effort comes from neglect of the economic lessons taught by the statistics of scientific agriculture.

We now know that our wheat occupies an area less than the surface of South Carolina; and, if the yield should equal that of England, half of that acreage would suffice. We know of our national crop, maize, which grows from Oregon to Florida, and yearly waves over a broader field than all the cereals besides, that it covers a territory not larger than the Old Dominion, and might produce its amplest stores within narrower limits than the present boundaries of Virginia. The potato-crop could grow in the area of Delaware, though yielding less than a hundred bushels per acre; the barley for our brewing requires less than the area of a half-dozen counties; and the weed of solace, sufficient to glut our own and European markets, is grown on the area of a county twenty miles square.

The average farmer of the Eastern States disregards the logic of facts which reveals success only in high culture. His brother of the West has cheap lands, very fertile, easily worked, without obstructions interfering with the most varied employment of agricultural machinery. His own lands may be low in price, because poor in plant-food; his sons have gone into trade and manufactures, and to virgin soils toward the sunset; his surplus earnings have gone to the savings-bank, or to Illinois or Kansas, as a loan at ten per cent., until, rheumatic, and declining with age, he finds production also declining, his herds and flocks decreasing, and the conclusion inevitable that "farming does not pay." Labor is scarce and high because in demand by other industries, which in turn offer high prices for farm-products; fertilization is needed everywhere, draining in many situations, and irrigation in some others. But these things cost money, and he has neither the ambition nor the confidence for its expenditure, and, worse still, in many instances the money is lacking. These may be potent reasons for discouragement, but they do not prove that farming there, with money, youth, enterprise, and skill, may not be highly profitable. And the teaching of statistics, in examples of high success with high culture, disproves the current assumption of unprofitableness. There are numerous cases in which the gross return per acre has been hundreds of dollars instead of tens. I know an instance there in which a common vegetable, usually known in field-culture rather than in gardening, returned in 1873 $12 for every day's labor expended on it. The lesson of statistics of Great Britain, of Holland, of all countries of dense population, proves success to be only possible by enriching the soil and increasing the yield. Though Massachusetts farmers constitute but one-eighth of the aggregate of all occupations, there is no reason why they should not be able to feed all, if Great Britain, with one-sixteenth of her population, can furnish more than half her required food-supplies. And if, in the present state of Massachusetts agriculture, the value of her annual product be $442 to each farmer, while the cultivator of the rich prairie State, Illinois, earns but $560 (and in point of fact it is probable that unenumerated products of the former State would swell the total to the latter figures), then the results of intensive culture throughout the Commonwealth would be comparatively munificent. This is a valuable lesson which New England will ultimately learn from statistics, far more thoroughly than is now known and practised by a few of her best cultivators.

The West has also much to gain from the teachings of statistics. Iowa, vigorous and ambitious, too young for despondency, is in a spasm of indignation against monopoly and an excess of middlemen, and yet in trade and transportation she has but eight per cent., or little more than half the proportion of the Middle States. She may have too many and too greedy go-betweens, and she needs justice in the transportation of her products; but these evils remedied, the burden of her trouble would still remain. The great difficulty is, her corps of industry has sixty-one per cent. of farmers instead of twenty-five. Double-track railroads, canals vexed with steam-propellers, grange-association, free trade, and every other fancied boon obtained, she will still remain in comparative poverty and positive discontent while she continues to have less than fourteen per cent. of her people engaged in manufacturing and mechanical industry. History does not point to a permanently prosperous people having such preponderance of population in agricultural pursuits.

Minnesota is only happy when the people of Great Britain are supposed to be in danger of starvation. That danger is greatly over-estimated. Statistics will show that in some years but three per cent. of our wheat-export, and but a trifling proportion in any season, can be sold to any except subjects of Great Britain. On one-sixteenth the area of that island is grown in a good year 100,000,000 bushels of wheat; in an average season 90,000,000; and in fifteen years, from 1858 to 1872 inclusive, the deficiency made good by importation was a fraction less than 66,000,000 per annum. Could home-culture be extended to meet this demand, the total breadth required would be equal to one-ninth the surface of Minnesota. An increase in the average yield of wheat in France from fifteen bushels to eighteen, by a small advance in culture, would fully equal the British deficiency, as was recently stated by the well-known statistician, Mr. James Caird. Russia, with her broad and cheap acres, also stands near to compete for this deficiency. Minnesota, meanwhile, as her crop is maturing, can never ascertain whether the want will be 40,000,000 or 90,000,000, or whether the home price will be fifty cents or $1, or the ultimate result debt or competence. And yet seventy per cent. of the cultivated area of Minnesota is put in wheat, and fifty-seven per cent. of her people are engaged in its cultivation; eight per cent. in sending it to market; a large proportion of its fourteen per cent. of mechanics and manufacturers are building mills and grinding wheat; and its twenty-one per cent. of professional men expect much of their income from wheat. There are reasons why wheat should be temporarily grown there, but dependence upon foreign markets, evidently felt by many, for a permanent and increasing demand, is shown by statistics to be foolish and futile. The home-market is the only reliable and permanently valuable one for this cereal, and the nearer to the place of growth the surer and larger the benefit derived.

The cotton States have been especially persistent in disregarding the teachings of statistics and defying the laws of political economy. Every intelligent publicist knows that a certain amount of money, say a present average of $300,000,000, may be derived from cotton. If the average quantity is increased the price diminishes, and vice versa. If fluctuations are frequent the speculator or manufacturer, and not the producer, derives an advantage. If you choose to produce 5,000,000 bales, you obtain ten cents per pound and lose money; if you grow but three, you get twenty cents and obtain a profit. Now it is better for the world, and in a series of years better for the grower, to produce regularly enough to supply the current wants of the trade at a medium and remunerative price, or as near a regular supply as possible, for the vicissitudes of the season will inevitably cause injurious fluctuations despite the highest effort of human wisdom and foresight. As the uses of cotton increase, and markets are extended throughout the world, its manufacture will be enlarged, and its culture should obtain corresponding enlargement. To overstep the boundary of current demand and glut the market, may be pleasing to the speculator and to the manufacturer, so far as he combines speculation with weaving, but it is death to the grower.

There is much false reasoning on this matter. A planter may truly affirm that he obtains $30 per acre for his cotton and but $25 for his corn, and he thereupon and therefore declares that he will plant no more corn. Let all act upon this suggestion, and instead of $55 for the acre of cotton and that of corn, the total return of the two acres of cotton will be but $30. A surplus of corn may be put into meat, and wool, and whiskey, or used to eke out a scarcity of some kind of forage for animals; but a surplus of cotton must wait for the slow grinding of the mills of the fabricating gods, usually until disgust at low prices reduces production correspondingly.

Thus, while cotton is and long will be the leading product and the most profitable field-crop at fair prices, its prominence in the list has kept, and is now keeping these States in comparative poverty, which is unnecessary as it is inconvenient and injurious. It does not produce money enough to give wealth to a population of 9,000,000. The other crops, instead of barely equaling in the aggregate the receipts from this, should represent at least $4 for every one of cotton. The census-record of production in these States is but $558,000,000; the record should be made to read $1,500,000,000. With three-fourths of the people of ten States employed in agriculture, the value of agricultural products exceeds but little that of the States of New York and Pennsylvania, where only one-fourth are so employed. The averages for each person engaged in agriculture in those States are respectively, as deduced from the census, $677 and $707, while those of Georgia and Mississippi are $239 and $282. For the ten States the average is $267; for the four populous Middle States, $686. Even the States producing cheap corn show a large return, the average for one man's labor in the five States between the Ohio River and the lakes being $498, while the six sterile Eastern States produce $490 for each farmer. It may be the census is less complete in the cotton States, but it is undeniable that agricultural industry makes a smaller aggregate return there than in any other section. Nor is the reason wanting; it is due to the prominence of cotton, the return for which is substantially a fixed quantity, and the neglect of all other resources.

Let us glance at the topography and capabilities of this section. The area occupied by cotton, allowing 10 per cent. addition to usual estimates, is less than one-fortieth of the surface of these States; it is but one-thirteenth of the proportion actually occupied as farms. Forty-six per cent. of the census crop was grown in 81 counties, which are all that produce as much as 10,000 bales each; and 77 per cent. grew in 215 counties, making not less than five bales each. The total acreage in cotton is scarcely more than one-sixteenth of the surface of Texas. What is to be done with the other fifteen-sixteenths? A very large proportion of the area of these States is unadapted to cotton, either by reason of elevation or of soil. There is no other section of the country with resources so varied; none presenting such a field for new and promising enterprise. Competition is possible with the sea-islands in oranges and bananas and other fruits in Florida, and with New York and Michigan in apples and other fruits, on the table-lands of the Alleghanies. More than half the value of all cotton exports is paid for imports of sugar, which could and should all be grown in these States. But one pound in ten of the required supply is now made, upon a smaller surface than half of a single county twenty miles square. The demand of the world for oils—cotton, rape, *palma christi*, and many

other—is large and prices are remunerative, and this section is peculiarly adapted to their production. A hundred million pounds of cheese, to compete with an equal quantity in New York, without danger of glutting the market, could be made from grasses of the glades that grow on lands costing one-twentieth the value of Empire-State pastures. More than two hundred million acres of these States are covered with wood, and the axe is still brought into requisition to girdle the monarchs of the forest, and await a slow decay for replacing fields worn out by a wasteful culture, while a timber-famine threatens other sections of the country, and a thousand forms of woody fabrication can readily be transmuted into gold—at least into greenbacks, which seem to be preferred to gold in certain districts. Even the forest-lands, certainly those of the coast-belt, are covered with wild grasses, only partially utilized, which, in connection with the herbage of the prairie sections, are worth, in flesh and wool, at a meagre estimate, half the value of the cotton-crop. The list might be increased indefinitely. With the introduction of the best machinery, the most economical methods, and the most efficient means of fertilization, with well-directed and persistent labor, adapted to the wants of all classes of workers, the present population is amply sufficient to double the gross product of agricultural industry, and far more than double its profits.

I have hitherto only spoken of agricultural industry. The suggestions relative to the necessity of other productive industries in the West apply with augmented force to the South. While the proportion engaged in them ranges from 14 per cent. in Iowa to 24 in Ohio, it only runs from 3 per cent. in Mississippi to 6 per cent. in Georgia. The intelligent planter of Georgia knows perfectly well, by the test of local experience, that the manufacture of cotton in his State is far more remunerative than the same business in Massachusetts, not only on account of saving freights and commissions, both on raw material and manufactured goods, but in the greater abundance and cheapness of labor. It might be considered a fair division of the crop, and certainly a generous one on the part of the South, to keep one-third for home manufacture, to send a third to the North for manufacture into finer goods, and the remaining third to Europe. This would insure a steady and imperative demand, and a great enlargement of net profits.

There is no good reason why Virginia should not equal Pennsylvania in manufacturing and mining production, as she now does in resources of mine and forest. There is no sufficient cause why 25 per cent. of the people of Pennsylvania should produce in agriculture a value of $52 annually for each inhabitant of the State, while 59 per cent. of the people of Virginia should only divide $42 per head of total population. The influence of home markets on prices, with the reflux influence of prices on fertilization and culture, is sufficient to answer for all this difference. I ask, in all sincerity and deference, if it is manly or just to decry others who take advantage of opportunities enjoyed in equal fullness by ourselves, while we utterly refuse to use them? In this connection permit me to repeat what I said years ago, in the sincerest and most friendly spirit, of the unsurpassed facilities for mining and manufacturing enjoyed by the southern portion of the Atlantic slope: "This path of progress has been equally open to all; laws supposed to favor a diversified industry have been applicable to all States alike; the best water-power and the cheapest coal are in States that make no extensive use of either; milder climates and superior facilities for cheap transportation have furnished advantages that have not been transmuted into net profits; and yet such communities, daily inflicting irreparable injuries upon themselves by neglecting the gifts of God and spurning the labor of man, are wont to deem themselves injured by the prosperity flowing from superior industry and a practical political economy."

ALABAMA. During the latter part of 1874 the condition of affairs in this State attracted much attention. The reports, however, have been so conflicting that it is impossible to determine which are correct, or what the actual facts have been. On the one side it has been reported that the most flagrant outrages have been perpetrated in certain counties, especially Sumter, Greene, and Pickens; that a bitter war has been waged upon the negroes, who have been secretly threatened and murdered; that diabolical deeds have been committed by the Ku-klux, or other disguised assassins; and that generally there has been a reign of terror. On the other side these reports have been denounced as false, and as having been circulated for political purposes; and it has been declared that the peace of the State has not been disturbed by political crimes. This conflict of testimony has existed both among correspondents and the editors and public men of the State. Of the many statements that have been made, two opposing ones may be selected as carrying the greatest weight of authority. The first of these was made in a letter, dated September 7, 1874, written by Hon. Charles Hays to Hon. Joseph R. Hawley. Mr. Hays was the Representative in Congress of the Fourth Congressional District of Alabama, in which most of the disorders are alleged to have occurred. In a note to Mr. Hays requesting this written statement of facts for publication, Mr. Hawley says: "I know you as a native and life-long resident of Alabama, engaged largely in planting, formerly the largest slaveholder in the State, and a soldier in the Confederate army throughout the war. Please give me in writing, as compactly as clearness will permit, the substance of what you have told me. I want to publish it at home, and give it to my neighbors and constituents as the account of a gentleman of unimpeachable honor." Mr. Hays in his letter recites numerous instances of foul deeds, giving the names of the victims, and the times and places of the outrages, which he alleges were inflicted upon orderly negroes by their political opponents. He prefaces this enumeration with the following general statement:

I am anxious that the true condition of affairs in the State of Alabama should be known as soon as possible to the whole country, in order that they may begin to realize the fact that the spirit of rebellion against the laws and Government of the United States, to extinguish which so many brave and gallant men laid down their lives, still exists in the hearts of many misguided people. They embrace every opportunity to commit deeds of lawlessness and crime, that are everlasting stigmas upon the fair name of the nation, and an open insult to the flag of our country, which many of your people are vainly patriotic enough to believe is an ægis of protection, wherever it floats. I had fondly hoped that the "reign of terror" in the South was over, and that peace, good-will, and prosperity, might henceforth reign supreme. In this hope I am sadly disappointed, for candor compels me to say that to-day riots, murders, assassinations, and torturings, for the purpose of terrorizing the true friends of the Gov-

ernment are more common than they have been at any hour since Lee surrendered to Grant, and unless the strong arm of Federal power can avert the calamity I can see nothing in the future save gloom and despair to the loyal men of the South, ruin to the material interests of the country, and death to those of us who uphold the honor and integrity of the nation, and counsel submission to the laws of the United States. But I need make no appeals to the patriotism or the sympathy of the Northern men, who, like yourself, have bared their breasts to the battle-storm in the dark and bloody past. The bare recital of proved facts shall be my only appeal. That will cause the heart to shudder, the cheek to blanch, and the mind to wonder how such dastardly outrages, such unprovoked murders, and such fiend-like conduct, can be tolerated for an hour. I shall be particular to narrate no rumors, to color no atrocity, to "set down naught in malice," but simply to give you well-authenticated facts, with dates, names, and localities, so that every man in the land may himself verify the accuracy of my statements, if he deems it necessary. These, then, I proceed to give you, with the deliberate opinion on my part that the half cannot be told, and that to-day many victims of hellish murder are sleeping in unknown spots and secluded places, from which they will never be wakened until the final judgment-day.

The first case mentioned by Mr. Hays was that of Captain W. P. Billings, a former resident of Brooklyn, N. Y., who he alleges was "brutally murdered," on about the 1st of August, in Sumter County, about one mile from his residence, on the Gainesville branch of the Mobile & Ohio Railroad:

When discovered he and his horse were both lying dead in the public road, his body pierced with buck-shot, and that of his horse riddled with bullets. The "hiding-place" of the assassins was found, but the coroner's jury returned the usual verdict, "that he came to his death by gunshot-wounds, and that the parties firing were unknown." Captain Billings was a Republican, and had that day addressed a Republican meeting at Abraham's plantation, some fifteen miles distant from the spot where he fell. He had about a twelvemonth since purchased a cotton-plantation in the county, was a man of unimpeachable character, and did not know he had an enemy in the world.

"The next example," says Mr. Hays, "is, perhaps, one of the most atrocious, unprovoked, and terrible, that has ever stained the pages of Southern desperation." This was the case of Thomas L. Ivey, "an inoffensive, intelligent, honest, and hard-working colored man, appointed a United States mail agent on the Alabama & Chattanooga Railroad, running between Meridian, Miss., and Livingston, Ala." On the 29th of August, near Livingston, in Sumter County, the train was signaled by a man standing on the track, and when it stopped "the report of a number of guns or pistols was heard, and Ivey was found shot to pieces." After mentioning other instances of outrages in Sumter County and in Mississippi, near the Alabama line, Mr. Hays says:

Not only are murders and whippings resorted to, to effect a change in the politics of the negroes, but other means also, as will be seen from the following "notice," which was taken from a sign-board on the cross-roads near Livingston, Ala., and handed me by a Democrat. It is one of many of like import, and is evidently intended to appeal to the well-known superstitious dread of the most ignorant colored people:

"WARNING!

[A picture of a coffin.]

The invisible monarch rules in Sumter, and watches the doings of his people from a little star above you. All 'niggers,' white and black, will take warning from the fate of Billings and Ivey. They were killed by unknown hands, which will never be known. Those hands will destroy again. Colored men, who want to live in peace and be protected, can do it by inquiring where they can sign the white man's constitution. 'Inquire,' and our monarch will send a man to you, who will have the 'roll.' Never vote the Radical ticket again. Sign, and live. Refuse, and die. Signed at the Spirit-Land, at the hour of death, and by the graves of the dead.

V. V... V."

Mr. Hays cites two cases in Pickens County, where he declares outrages are frequent, but, "from the terrorism existing in that locality, only an occasional murder leaks out." He says:

In Carrollton, Pickens County, four colored men, who were supposed to be "emissaries," sent to post the negroes on their rights, were taken the third week in August from their cabins and hung by three roadside. This deed was perpetrated in open daylight by a body of unmasked white men. On August 20, 1874, the bodies of three men, two colored and one white, were discovered floating down the Tombigbee River, lashed to some logs. When found the bodies were badly decomposed, and their personal identity to this day remains undiscovered. The white man had a placard pinned to his neck saying, "This is the way we treat Dutch niggers," evidently alluding to the nativity of the man, who seemed to be a German. The other two were placarded, "To Mobile, with the compliments of Pickens County."

Instances are given of peaceable meetings of colored persons having been broken up in Hall, Russell, and Coffee Counties, resulting in the last-named county in the death of two, and the wounding of six colored persons. The disorders in Choctaw County are thus specified:

On or about the 1st of August the newspapers of Alabama were filled with accounts of large bodies of armed negroes congregating in Choctaw County for the purpose of commencing a war upon the whites. Of course the excitement was intense. Hundreds of whites from different sections swiftly hurried to the scene of the supposed conflict, but when they arrived no armed negroes could be found. Yet something must be done to make an example. So a company of whites ambushed a party of negroes returning from church, killed ten and wounded thirteen. Again, Green Lewis, colored route agent on the Selma & Meridian Railroad, was warned that if he continued to run on that road they would murder him. I had his route changed to save his life. Again, Hon. Joseph H. Speed, Superintendent of Public Instruction, was attacked and beaten by a mob at Marion, Ala., because he had that day made a Republican speech in the town. Hons. Adam C. Felder and William H. Seawell, two prominent white Republicans, were shot at in Greenville, Ala., some night in July last, on their return from the courthouse, where they had been making Republican speeches. They were also "rotten-egged" and otherwise insulted. Full particulars of this outrage were published at the time. W. A. Lipscomb, belonging to one of the most reputable families in the

South, was found dead in the public road in Marengo County last week. He was shot to death, and was an earnest Republican.

In concluding his statement, Mr. Hays says:

These, my dear sir, are a few of the "troubles" in Alabama, for the suppression of which I, in company with others, have asked the intervention of the Federal Government. No one regrets that such action has been deemed necessary more than myself. Born, educated, and living all my life in the South, I thought I knew the feelings and the passions of our people. Up to this time not a single white Democrat has been murdered, outraged, or otherwise maltreated in any way in the State of Alabama. The killing has all been on one side. The reports even of our sufferings have been held back and kept back from the people of the North. The agents of the Southern Associated Press alone furnish news to your papers. Every agent of this association in Alabama (and in the South generally) is a rebel and a Democrat. Our views, speeches, platforms, writings, and actions generally, are garbled and missent to deceive the people of the North, and convince them that the South is being plundered by adventurers; that corruption and infamy stalk forth with monstrous iniquity in all our public places, and that every man who dares to raise his voice for the principles of Republicanism is a felon, and unworthy to walk the earth on which he lives. All these things, and more, too, have we borne in silence.

This statement of Mr. Hays was bitterly denounced by the opposition press. In regard to some of the outrages specified, it was denied that they were committed, while it was stoutly maintained that politics had nothing to do with any of them. On the 1st of October the Democratic and Conservative State Executive Committee issued an address intended as a reply to the statements made by Hays, and "for the purpose of repelling the slanders circulated against the good people of this State for political purposes." Before proceeding to notice specifically the allegations made by that gentleman, the committee say:

1. That we were selected as the Executive Committee of our party in a full convention assembled here on the 29th day of July last, and thus we are the legitimate representatives of our party.

2. That the Republican or Radical party in Alabama is composed of about nine-tenths negroes and one-tenth whites.

3. That the Democratic and Conservative party is composed almost exclusively of the white people of the State, embracing a majority of the people.

4. That, to show the spirit which governed and now governs our party, we quote a paragraph from the address of our Executive Committee issued on the 27th day of August, 1874:

"We especially urge upon you carefully to avoid all injuries to others while you are attempting to preserve your own rights. Let peace not only prevail, but let our people avoid all just cause of complaint. Turmoil and strife, with those who oppose us in this contest, will only weaken the moral force of our efforts. Let us avoid all personal conflicts; and, if these should be forced upon us, let us only act in that line of just self-defense which is recognized and provided for by the laws of the land. We could not please our enemies better than by becoming parties to conflicts of violence, and thus furnish them plausible pretexts for asking the interference of Federal power in our domestic affairs. Let us so act that all shall see, and that all whose opinions are entitled to any respect shall admit, that ours is a party of peace, and that we only seek to preserve our rights and liberties by the peaceful but efficient power of the ballot-box.''

The speeches of our candidates and our other public speakers in this canvass have reflected, encouraged, and illustrated the sentiments thus urged, as essential to good order, obedience to law, and to the complete triumph of our party in the coming election—and we here declare that we do not believe that in a single instance has any authorized speaker of our party departed from the line of conduct above recommended.

But notwithstanding these peaceful, law-abiding declarations and conduct of our party, the public press of the Republican party North and the Republican press of Alabama have teemed with the vilest slanders of our people; slanders concocted, we fully believe, by the leaders of the Republican party in Alabama, for the express purpose of misleading the public mind, and against law, justice, and honesty, to secure to themselves another lease of ill-gotten power, heretofore used to wrong and oppress the good people of this State.

We recognize the fact that a large proportion of the most worthy and respectable people in the North, East, and West, are to be found in the ranks of the Republican party, and that their party associations are dictated by an honest judgment and true patriotic feeling.

But with us in Alabama the case is widely different. The negroes, forming nine-tenths of the party here, are of course as a body ignorant, and from their recent condition of slavery a low order of morality prevails among them.

The remainder of the party is made up chiefly of professional politicians and their hangers-on, who live by office, and a few worthy people who have been induced heretofore to act with the Republican party. This little army of office-holders, with a few honorable exceptions, feel that the contest is one for their daily bread, and, though "work they will not," yet they are not ashamed to "beg," to steal, or to lie.

We assert on our word as men of character who have something to lose by asserting a falsehood, that no unprejudiced man of either party in the North, East, or West, who knows any thing of the facts, or of the character of those by whom the charges are made, can come to any other conclusion than that they are made without foundation in fact, were known by those who made them to be unfounded, and were made for the vile purpose of obtaining for themselves and their associates a continuance of their power to be exercised for purposes of plunder.

That Governor Lewis, who has some character to lose and who must be informed of all the facts, has failed to give any official sanction to the complaints against our people, is of itself suggestive of their utter falsehood.

And, in order the more easily, as they supposed, to secure their purposes, the leaders of the Republican party have represented to the President of these United States that our party is opposed to the Government of the United States, and in favor of a new rebellion, when they well know that our opposition is not to the Constitution or Government of the United States, but only to the persons who have abused the public trust, squandered the people's money, bought and sold our public offices, and who have in every conceivable manner violated the principles of a just and pure government.

The greater portion of the address consists of affidavits, cited to show that there was "little foundation in truth" for that portion of Mr. Hays's statement concerning a general war between the whites and blacks of Choctaw County. In one of these affidavits the deputy-sheriff of Choctaw County, E. O. Glover, gives

the particulars of going in August with a *posse* of 150 men to arrest Jack Turner and about thirty other negroes for having attempted to lynch one Huff Cheney. The negroes disbanded and scattered, and were not found at that time; but eleven of them were subsequently arrested without any disturbance. The deputy-sheriff concludes his affidavit, which is dated September 26th, by saying, "I have not heard of a negro being killed or wounded in this county during the time I have been acting as sheriff, now nearly seven months." Other affidavits are adduced to corroborate these statements. The address then concludes as follows:

These affidavits not only show that this charge is false in fact, but that Mr. Hays must have known it to be false when he wrote his letter to General Hawley.

All the other charges contained in the letter of Mr. Hays, except the fact of the killing of Billings and Ivey, are equally destitute of any foundation in truth, and are admitted to be untrue by every intelligent and unprejudiced man in this State.

That Billings and Ivy were killed, is true; but there is not one scintilla of evidence to show that either was killed by Democrats, or for party purposes. But the facts as they have been developed tend strongly to show that other than political causes produced the death of Billings and Ivey.

The general charges made against our people, by Hays, White, Spencer, Martin, Stokes, and Pelham, to the effect that there is a reign of terror in this State, through intimidation practised by our party to control the voters and to prevent the free expression of opinion, are untrue, particularly and generally. Letters and affidavits of Republicans of respectable standing have been published in the counties where such terrorism is particularly alleged to exist, showing that no such terrorism and no such intimidation have been practised. The fact that there are, to-day, two negroes, nominated by the Republican party, the one in this district, and the other in the Mobile district, daily traveling through these two most southern districts, and making speeches, unmolested, is proof positive that the peaceful disposition of our people has been basely slandered. From the beginning of the canvass, there has never been a disturbance of a Republican speaker, or of a Republican audience, by any member of our party, according to the best of our knowledge, information, and belief.

Yet, upon such charges as these, with no better foundation than we have shown, United States troops have been sent to the State of Alabama, and they are now engaged in arresting and handcuffing white citizens of this State, and dragging them from their families, and incarcerating them in the dungeons, under the leadership of deputy United States marshals, members of the Republican party. And this is done when there is no obstruction to the full execution of the laws of Alabama, or of the United States, and while there are hosts of officers willing to execute the law in every nook and corner of this State, and when there is not a just shadow of pretext that the officers or people of this State are either unwilling or unable to enforce the law.

We call especial attention to the fact, that the chief executive officer of this State belongs to the Republican party, and he has never asked for troops of the United States to aid in the execution of the laws.

As a significant fact, showing the *animus* of those who have thus slandered the people of our State, it is now notorious that the fund appropriated by Congress for the overflowed districts in this State has been and is now distributed for electioneering purposes, by Republican instrumentalities, generally in the State, without reference to overflowed localities, among those whom they suppose can be corrupted. We here avow, that we have long resided in this State, and are generally acquainted with the people, and we declare that, to the best of our knowledge, information, and belief, there does not exist in this State any White League, or any secret political association of our party. And we further declare that we believe that the charges made against our people and party have no real foundation in fact; and they were known to be untrue when they were first published, and they have been published and circulated for wicked and corrupt purposes.

On account of these reported outrages, and the consequent state of the public feeling, the political campaign was attended with unusual excitement. The Democratic Conservative party assembled in convention in Montgomery on the 29th of July, and adopted the following platform:

The Democratic and Conservative people of Alabama, in convention assembled, do resolve and declare:

1. That the radical and dominant faction of the Republican party in this State persistently, by false and fraudulent representations, have influenced the passions and prejudices of the negroes, as a race, against the white people, and have thereby made it necessary for the white people to unite and act together in self-defense, and for the preservation of civilization.

2. That the rights of all classes of men under the Constitution and laws of the land must be respected and preserved inviolate, but we deny that Congress can constitutionally enact rules to force the two races into social union or equality.

3. That the so-called civil-rights bill recently passed by the Federal Senate, and now pending in the House, is a flagrant and dangerous invasion of the ancient conservative principles of personal liberty and free government, and presents an issue of vital moment to the American people, and calls upon them to decide at the ballot-box whether they will or will not be coerced to absolute, social as well as political, equality of the negro race with themselves. We view with abhorrence the attempt on the part of the Federal Government to take control of schools, colleges, hotels, railroads, steamboats, theatres, and graveyards, for the purpose of establishing negro equality, and enforcing it under numerous penalties of fines, damages, and imprisonment.

4. Civil remedies for the protection of civil rights are adequately provided by the common law to all races of men in this State, and added to these are social remedies for social wrongs, which every race and class of men are perfectly left free by the laws to adopt for themselves; so that the negro race has the same means of protecting itself against the invasion of its civil rights under the law, and against intrusion upon its so-called rights and privileges by the white race, that we have to preserve and protect ourselves and families against the intrusion of the negro race. Under these laws, the race to which in the providence of God we belong has achieved an eminence among the people of the world, which is our proud inheritance, and has become to us a trust we cannot resign without dishonor. We therefore denounce as a violation of the letter and spirit of our Constitution, and as dishonoring to the genius of our race, all legislative enactments which attempt to convert into crimes the rules and maxims of our social intercourse, to which we are indebted for the excellence and glory of our civilization, or to punish with degrading penalties our refusal to admit an ignorant and barbarous race to equal participation with our families in our social institutions.

5. That we extend to all our race, in every clime, the right hand of fellowship, and a cordial invitation to come and settle among us, and unite their destiny with us.

6. That proper laws should be enacted by the Legislature to secure to the employés of railroad corporations liens upon the property of such corporations for the payment of wages.

7. The exigencies of the times and the impoverished condition of the people render it imperative that the State government should return at once to that system of economy in public expenditures which conduced so much to the successful and satisfactory administration of the government and the prosperity of the people before the war. Through radical legislation and misgovernment new and unnecessary offices and agencies have been created, with large salaries, and every other service conceivable to our enemies and oppressors resorted to, until our State government, no longer under the control of the people, has in its practice and precepts reversed, abrogated, and annulled the democratic maxim that governments are based upon the consent of the governed. Retrenchment in the number of offices, in official salaries, and in the fees or commissions of agents, is necessary and indispensable to the public welfare, and we pledge ourselves to reduce every public expenditure, and abolish and dispense with every office demanded by an economical administration of the government.

8. The Democratic and Conservative party of Alabama is pledged, so soon as it shall be placed in power by being intrusted with the State administration, to cause to be made such speedy and thorough investigation as shall, by its result, make known to the people of the State and the world our true financial condition, and, by its representatives here assembled, it resolves that every dollar justly owing by the State shall be faithfully paid when it is able to do so. At the same time, it is firmly determined that the welfare of the people of the State and the interests of its honest creditors shall not be put in jeopardy by the payment of unlawful or fraudulent claims of any kind.

The ticket nominated was as follows: Governor, George S. Houston; Lieutenant-Governor, Robert F. Ligon; Justices of Supreme Court, Thomas J. Judge, Robert C. Brickell, Amos R. Manning; Attorney-General, John W. A. Sanford; Secretary of State, Rufus K. Boyd; Treasurer, Daniel Crawford; Superintendent of Public Instruction, John M. McKleroy.

The Republican State Convention assembled in Montgomery on the 20th of August, and after a session of three days adopted the following platform:

The Republican party of Alabama, in State Convention assembled, again declares its unshaken confidence in, and its unalterable devotion to, the great principles of human liberty which called it into existence, namely, the civil and political equality of all men, without distinction of race or color.

2. In the practical application of these principles we have neither claimed nor desired the social equality of different races or of individuals of the same race, neither do we claim or desire it now, and all assertions to the contrary are without the slightest foundation. In point of fact, we reject the issue of race against race, which is tendered us by the Democratic party, as fraught with incalculable evils to our whole people, which sows the seeds of ruin to all our national, social, and political interests, and which, if persisted in by that party, will plunge us again into a war with the Government of the United States.

3. We have not made a race-issue in the past, neither do we make or tender such an issue. What we demand for one man we demand for all, with-

out distinction of race or color, and we point with pride and confidence to every line of our political record in proof of this declaration, and we denounce the assertions that have made it necessary for a whole people to unite and act together in self-defense and for the preservation of white civilization as untrue, and an emanation of that selfish spirit which in the past demanded every thing for one race and was unwilling to concede any thing to the other; that the race-issue tendered by the Democracy of Alabama is but the outcropping and is the natural sequence of the ambitious spirit which led a peaceful people into a war with their Government in 1861; which during that war rode rough-shod over the people of the South, and after the war perpetuated its carnival of blood by a career of crime in the Ku-klux Klan, which in the extent of its organizations, the numbers involved in it, the multiplicity and heinousness of its crimes, and the manner of their commission, finds no parallel on the rolls of human history. It is now, as it was then, each in its different mode, for resistance to the Constitution and law of the land. Again they will commit the same acts, with vengeance sharpened and envenomed by continued and repeated persistence in wrong.

5. That we neither desire nor seek the invasion of the rights of the white people by the colored; we only ask equal advantages in matters of public and common rights. This we consider to be all that is embraced in what is known as the civil-rights bill, and in order that we may be understood, and no false charges made against us, we hereby declare that the Republican party does not desire or seek mixed schools or mixed accommodations for the colored people, but they ask that in all these advantages they shall be equal. We want no special equality enforced by law. We recognize the fact that every home is sacred from intrusions, and that in a free country every one can dictate for himself the line of social exclusion that society gave us by laws more inexorable than statute or common law, and opens or closes its door to whomsoever it will, and that no civil law can or should invade it.

6. We hold that governments are instituted among men for the protection of life, and liberty, and property, and we demand a rigorous execution of the laws of this State and of the United States for that purpose, and we call on the Governor of this State to take all legal means at his command for the purpose of discovering and bringing to trial all persons offending against the laws. Murder by lying in ambush, whether by one or many, must be put an end to, and the peace and security of the humblest home must be respected and protected.

7. The good faith and the credit of the State were well sustained, and the price of its bonds, when the government passed from the hands of Governor Smith to his Democratic successor in November, 1870, is unmistakable evidence of the fact; and we pledge ourselves to use the means of the State for the payment of all its just debts, and to provide for the proper adjustment of what is called the railroad indebtedness of the State, and to put an end to the further indorsement of the bonds of all private corporations. These results can be achieved by an economical use of our resources without oppressing the people. Good faith, economy, and retrenchment of all unnecessary expenses in the use of our resources, will secure the result.

8. That the seizure of the Alabama & Chattanooga Railroad by the Democratic administration has resulted in greatly impairing the value of the allotted security held by the State to provide for the payment of the State liability thereon, and we are of the opinion that, instead of seizing the road and thereby destroying the security it furnished to protect the State from loss on the bonds it has indorsed, the plainest principles dictate that the road should be managed by those most interested in it.

A convention of the colored voters of the State was held in Montgomery on the 25th, 26th, and 27th of June. An address to the people of the State was published, in which, after reciting the constitutional provisions that had been framed to secure the rights of colored citizens, they say :

We are denied the facilities of traveling upon the public highways of the country, unless we submit, as we are compelled to do, to the most inconvenient and sometimes filthy accommodations which the public carriers may think proper to furnish, while others are accommodated with comfortable and cleanly quarters, and fully protected from intrusion and insult, to which we are often subjected, notwithstanding the same fare is exacted of us that is paid by those who are more favored.

We are denied accommodation in the public inns and eating-houses in the country while traveling from place to place, and are therefore placed at great trouble and inconvenience without any fault on our part.

Notwithstanding the constitutional guarantees hereinbefore referred to, there is a political party in this State, known as the Democratic and Conservative party, which, regardless of the constitutional oath to which its members have subscribed, is engaged in a ruthless crusade against us as a race, with the avowed purpose of not only preventing us from exercising the constitutional rights which have been secured to us, but of abridging these rights to the fullest extent of its ability, should it obtain power in this State. To this end it is engaged in exciting the baser prejudices and passions of the white men against us as a race, and is openly threatening us with a civil and relentless war of extermination, falsely charging us with being enemies of the white man because we have heretofore refused to support and sustain that party.

The position of this class of voters in the politics of Alabama is indicated by the following resolutions adopted by this convention:

Whereas, It is charged by the organ of the Democratic white man's party in Alabama that the colored people of Alabama are trying to force an issue of race in said State, for the purpose of creating dissension and strife among the people; and—

Whereas, It is evident that the white man's party means the alignment of all the white people of the State against the colored people :

Resolved, That the colored people of Alabama are in favor of free schools, free churches, freedom of speech and thought and action by all men ; that we are in favor of the civil and political rights of all men as embodied in our constitution and our free institutions.

Resolved, That the colored people of Alabama, while according to all men those inalienable rights born of American citizenship, demand that the same shall be guaranteed to them, and that they favor such legislation as will secure them fully in these rights, and place them beyond the control of the "white man's party," or any other party.

Resolved, That we are opposed to bringing strife and discord in this State between the people; that we are in favor of every measure of legislation which tends to protect our people from the enmity and hatred of the so-called white man's party ; and we will use all honorable means to secure by legislation every right due us as a people which comes within the province of legislation and which can be enforced in the courts.

Resolved, That the Republican party having exhibited its fidelity to the cause of human rights and to the best interests of the colored people, we hereby pledge that party our continued support and adherence.

Resolved, That, in order to bring about the success of the Republican ticket in November next, we encourage our people everywhere to the adoption of that great statesmanlike idea upon which parties never fall but may ever stand, the great idea that the office should seek the man and not the man the office; that we impress upon the members of the Republican party in the State of Alabama, that they nominate none for office save those they know to be true to the principles of the party, and who can bring to the support of our State ticket the greatest number of voters for our district, county division, congressional and State candidates.

Resolved, That the members of the Republican party everywhere be urged to see to it that our conventions be fairly and patriotically assembled, and assembled solely for the purpose of advancing the interests of the party, and not the interests of individuals.

Resolved, That the convention through its State Representatives impress upon the legislative body of the State of Alabama, at its next session, the importance and urgent necessity of their creating a compulsory school bill, feeling assured that, without such a bill as is here asked for, the rising generation will be (intellectually speaking) but little superior to generations gone before, and our Government grow weaker and weaker, for the want of an educated, intelligent class of citizens.

After a very exciting contest, the election was held on the 3d of November, and resulted in the success of the Democratic Conservative ticket, the vote being as follows:

Governor—George S. Houston, 107,118; D. P. Lewis, 93,928.

Lieutenant-Governor—R. F. Ligon, 107,-109; H. McKinstry, 93,532.

Attorney-General—J. W. A. Sanford, 106,-923; George Turner, 93,493.

Secretary of State—R. K. Boyd, 106,882; N. H. Rice, 93,612.

Treasurer — Daniel Crawford, 106,575; Arthur Bingham, 93,455.

In a total vote, therefore, of 201,046, Houston's majority was 13,190. At the previous election of 1872, the total vote for Governor was 171,239, of which Lewis received 89,868, and Herndon 81,371, giving the former a majority of 8,497. President Grant's majority in the same year was 10,828, the total vote for President being 169,716.

After the election the Executive Committee of the Democratic party, which had now come into power for the first time in several years, issued an address, in which the future policy of the party was indicated as follows

The party we represent is firmly pledged, by all that is sacred among men, to use its utmost endeavors to bring the blessings of good government to all the people of this State, and, under the providence of God, it remains to be seen whether our party is equal to the responsible and arduous duties it has undertaken to perform. These duties require of us, that justice must be fairly administered according to the laws of the land; that the rights of all the people of Alabama, both of person and of property, must be preserved inviolate; that there must be no oppression of any race or class of men; that the credit and good name of this State must be restored; that harmonious relations of mutual confidence and good-will must be cultivated and adjusted, among all the conflicting interests represented among the people of this State; that yielding a cheerful obedi-

ence to the laws of the United States, and promptly bearing our share of the burdens of the General Government, whether in war or in peace, we must also cultivate such other relations that the citizens of every State composing our great Union who may from time to time have business with us, or come into our midst, shall receive that justice and hearty welcome at our hands due to brethren of the same great household, without regard to difference of political opinion. If we fail to accomplish substantially these results, just so far will we disappoint the hopes and expectations of a large majority of the people of Alabama. A bright future is before us, and we feel that, with proper exertions on our part, there can be no reasonable doubt they will speedily result in prosperity to all the people of our beloved State.

George Smith Houston, the successful candidate for Governor, was born in Tennessee, in 1809. At the age of twelve he went with his parents to Alabama, and settled in Lauderdale County. In 1831 he was admitted to the bar, and in the following year was elected to the Legislature. In 1834 he removed to Limestone County, and in 1837 was elected to the office of Solicitor. He continued in this office until 1841, when he was elected to Congress on the Democratic ticket. He was reëlected in 1843, '45, '47, '51, '53, '55, '57, and 1859. But before the expiration of the last term he withdrew from Congress, when Alabama seceded from the Union. In 1860 he was a "Douglas Democrat," and opposed secession, but subsequently went with his State when it seceded. After the war he was elected to the United States Senate, but was refused admission, when he retired to private life and there continued until the campaign of 1874.

The Legislature assembled on the 16th of November, and continued in session till December 17th, when it adjourned until January 13, 1875. The most important act passed was the bill authorizing the Governor to appoint two commissioners, citizens of Alabama, who with the Governor shall constitute a board to adjust and liquidate the bonded liabilities of the State. The Governor at once complied with the law by appointing, for the required term of two years, L. W. Lawler, of Talladega, and J. B. Bethea, of Montgomery, who are said to be able financiers. The commissioners are required to report their action to the Governor, by whom it must be communicated to the Legislature. The powers and duties of the commission are set forth in the second section of the act as follows :

SECTION 2. *Be it further enacted*, That it shall be the duty of said commissioners, and they are hereby authorized and empowered to take charge and ascertain, liquidate, and adjust the subsisting legal liabilities of the State of Alabama on the bonds issued and the bonds indorsed by the State of Alabama and the coupons on the same in such manner as the interests of the State may require, and by negotiation to provide for the payment of such amount of the said several legal liabilities as may be arranged for under the powers hereby conferred, and the interest that may be agreed to be paid upon the principal so negotiated, in such a manner and at such times as to them may seem advisable; and for this purpose said Commissioners shall, by advertisement or otherwise, at as early a day as practicable, require the presentation of all claims of the character aforesaid to them, with the amount claimed, and may inquire into the consideration alleged to have been paid or given to the State therefor, or that is alleged in support of the liability claimed against the State: *Provided*, however, that no adjustment of said alleged liabilities, or any part thereof, or an arrangement for the payment of any sum in discharge thereof, shall be binding on the State unless and until approved and ratified by the General Assembly thereof.

The total receipts into the State Treasury during the year ending September 30, 1874, amounted to $1,870,757, and the disbursements to $1,624,363. The aggregate direct indebtedness of the State is reported by the Treasurer at $10,452,593. This includes the bonds issued for State purposes to the amount of $6,619,800 due at different times from 1886 to 1894, and on which the annual interest amounts to $411,896. The nature of this indebtedness is indicated in the following exhibit:

Total bonded debt, as above stated......... $6,619,800 00

EDUCATIONAL FUND INDEBTEDNESS.

University fund..............	$300,000 00
Sixteenth section fund.......	1,740,200 29
Valueless sixteenth section fund......................	97,091 21
Surplus revenue fund........	669,086 80
Total educational fund indebtedness..	2,806,378 30
Outstanding State certificates per Treasurer's report...........................	81,525 00
Outstanding obligations...................	944,880 00
Aggregate direct indebtedness........	$10,452,593 30

(Annual interest on trust funds, $224,510.25.)

The contingent liabilities of the State, under acts approved in 1867 and 1870, are reported at $15,051,000, as follows:

Indorsement of Railroad Bonds, etc., to September 30, 1874.

NAME OF ROAD.	Miles.	Amount.
Alabama & Chattanooga..............	295	$4,720,000
Alabama & Chattanooga, reported excess issued......................	...	580,000
East Alabama & Cincinnati..........	25	400,000
Mobile & Alabama Grand Trunk.....	55	880,000
Mobile & Montgomery...............	...	2,500,000
Montgomery & Eufaula..............	80	1,280,000
Selma & Gulf.......................	40	640,000
Selma, Marion & Memphis..........	45	720,000
South & North......................	183	391,000
Savannah & Memphis................	40	640,000
Total......................	763	$12,751,000
State Bonds for Railroad Purposes.		
Alabama & Chattanooga..............	......	$2,000,000
Montgomery & Eufaula..............	......	300,000
Total......................	......	$2,300,000
Aggregate....................	......	$15,051,000

The present condition of the Alabama & Chattanooga Railroad is of the greatest importance to the credit of the State, as its liability for the indorsed debt of that corporation is the only obstacle to the resumption of the payment of interest on the State debt. The liability of the State as indorser under the acts of the General Assembly of Alabama for $4,720,000 of the bonds of that corporation has never been questioned by any department of the State. On that liability the State paid, during the

administration of Governor Lewis, in interest, the sum of about $834,000, and there are now in arrears $944,000 as interest, and it is believed that this is short by $110,000. The State also became responsible for $312,000, as purchase-money bid by Governor Lindsay at bankrupt sale, and has paid large sums as fees to attorneys; $140,000 have been paid to the employés of the road, under the receivership of the State when first seized by Governor Lindsay.

On the 9th of September Governor Houston sent a special message to the Legislature concerning this corporation, in which he said:

Since entering upon the discharge of the duties of Governor, I find the complications connected with the Alabama & Chattanooga Railroad, and its company, so numerous and extensive, that fear may be properly entertained that the important interests of the State, arising out of the indorsement of the bonds of the Company for the construction of that road may be seriously endangered. I regard it of the highest importance to the State that it shall not in any sense become a party to any of the suits pending in the Federal courts touching the interest of that road. Nor should the State submit its interest, or rights secured by statute, to the jurisdiction of those courts, or do any act tending to defeat or impair its statutory lien. With the view that the true condition of the road and the State's interests therein may be ascertained, and the future policy of the State for the protection of its interests in this regard be determined, I invite your early attention to the subject, assuring you of my purpose to co-operate with you in your efforts to protect the rights of the State.

The South & North Alabama Railroad has complied with the act of the General Assembly, approved April 21, 1873, and has surrendered her indorsed bonds to the amount of $3,635,000, and received from the State bonds to the amount of $341,000, under said act of the Legislature.

The Savannah & Memphis Railroad has made no default in payment of its interest, and has completed twenty miles of additional road, for the examination of which commissioners have been appointed, but have not yet reported.

The other railroads for which the State has indorsed bonds are in default in the payment of interest on their bonds, and those which are incomplete are doing nothing in the construction of their roads.

ALASKA. This Territory of the United States, which was formerly known as Russian America, comprises all that portion of the North American Continent lying west of the 141st parallel of west longitude, together with a narrow strip of land between the Pacific Ocean and the British dominions. The Territory also includes all the islands near the coast and the whole of the Aleutian Archipelago, except Behring and Copper Islands, on the coast of Kamtchatka. The area of Alaska, including the islands, is 580,107 square miles. The population in 1870 was 29,097, of whom 26,843 were natives of the Territory, 1,421 half-breeds, 483 Russians, and 350 were natives of the United States and foreigners, not Russians. There are not more than 1,500 completely civilized inhabitants. Sitka, or New Archangel, is the capital, and only considerable town of the Territory; it is situated on a small but commodious harbor on Baranov Island, in latitude 57° 3' north and longitude 135° 17' west. It was long the headquarters of the Russian-American Fur Company, though the natural centre of the fur-trade is the island of Kodiak, south of the Aliaska peninsula. At the time of the transfer of the Territory to the United States in 1867, Sitka, although founded in the last century, was little better than a collection of log-huts, about one hundred in number, with a few superior buildings occupied by government officers. St. Paul, the principal settlement on Kodiak Island, is the main depot of the seal-fisheries, and is surrounded by the best farming-land in the Territory. Next in importance as a settlement is Captain's Harbor, on the island of Unalashka, where is found the best anchorage in the Aleutian group. The remaining civilized places in Alaska consist for the most part of small trading-posts scattered throughout the country, the principal of them being Fort Yukon, near latitude 66° north, the most northerly station of the Hudson Bay Company. The interior of Alaska has been but little explored, and our knowledge of the country is confined mainly to the islands, the coasts, and a few of the larger rivers. The entire coast line of the Territory, without including the smaller indentations, measures 4,000 miles in length, and is bounded by three seas, the Arctic Ocean on the north, Behring Sea on the west, and the North Pacific on the south.

The climate is by no means as severe as that of corresponding latitudes on the eastern coast of North America. In regard both to climate and agriculture, the Territory is naturally divisible into three regions: the Yukon district, comprising all the country north of the Alaskan Mountains; the Aleutian district, comprising the islands of that name and the peninsula; and the Sitka district, comprising the remainder of the Territory. In the Yukon district the mean annual temperature is about 25° Fahr., and the ground remains frozen to within two or three feet of the surface throughout the summer. The amount of rainfall is not accurately known. In winter the ice on the Yukon, which is the chief river of Alaska, averages five feet in thickness, and, where there is sufficient water, it has been known to freeze to a depth of nine feet. The summer is short, dry, and hot. May, June, and July constitute the pleasant season; then the rainy weather begins and lasts till October. The lowest temperature ever recorded in this region was −70° Fahr. The climate of the Aleutian district is warmer, the mean annual temperature being from 36° to 40° Fahr. The average annual rainfall is about 40 inches, distributed among 150 rainy days in each year. January, February, and June, are the pleasantest months.

A still warmer and moister climate is characteristic of the Sitka district. The town of Sitka is said to be the rainiest place in the world outside of the tropics. From 60 to 90 inches of rain fall annually, and the number of rainy days in each year varies from a minimum of 190 to a maximum of 285. The mean annual temperature is 44°; but the average temperature in winter is proportionately much higher than in summer, being only a little below the freezing-point; while the excessive rains in summer make that season unduly cold. Ice fit for consumption scarcely ever forms at Sitka.

The agricultural resources of Alaska are practically confined to the Aleutian and Sitka districts. The abundant growth of rich perennial grasses in the valley of the Yukon affords excellent fodder for cattle, but no grain has ever been raised there, and the only vegetables which have succeeded are radishes, turnips, and lettuce. The most fertile land is found at Cook's Inlet on Kodiak Island, and among the Aleutians, where good oats, barley, and root-crops, can be raised without much difficulty. Whether the potato can ever be successfully cultivated in Alaska, is doubtful. In the most favored farming districts the agricultural production can scarcely ever exceed the local demand.

The leading industries of Alaska are the fisheries and the fur-trade. In 1870, the product of the fisheries, in salted codfish alone, was 10,612,000 pounds. The great source of wealth of the Territory, and its commercial importance, is the production of fur-seal skins. The total annual catch of fur-seals throughout the world has been estimated, by high authority, at 160,000, of which 100,000 are taken from the waters of Alaska. The value of the entire fur-products of Alaska has been stated at upward of $1,200,000 per annum. Prior to 1867, the large fur-products of this country were collected by the Russian-American Fur Company of St. Petersburg, through its agents in Alaska, and, being concentrated annually at Sitka, were forwarded by ship to London and St. Petersburg. The furs are mainly those of the fur-seal taken in two small islands in Behring's Sea; the sea-otter skins taken mostly along the shores of the Aleutian or Fox Islands; and, general furs, such as beaver, fox, marten, bear, etc., found in the forests of the main-land. These are nearly all collected by the natives of the Territory, and by them traded off for the necessities of their mode of life. The fur-sealing on the two islands of St. Paul and St. George, situated three hundred miles from any other land, is a special branch of the trade. These islands are the summer home of these peculiar animals, to which they resort from May to November in each year, for the purposes of reproduction, rearing of their young, and shedding their coats of hair. As winter approaches they all migrate, and are not seen again until the following spring. During the summer millions of these animals line the shores for miles, and, notwithstanding that thousands are killed each year, they continue to multiply and increase. The demand for this particular fur having increased very largely in recent years, it is a matter of national importance to preserve the race of fur-seals. In 1868 parties from San Francisco, California, and New London, Connecticut, visited the islands of St. George and St. Paul, and secured large numbers of these skins. As the fur-bearing seal had been nearly exterminated in other parts of the world, the Congress of the United States extended special jurisdiction over the islands of St. Paul and St. George, forbade any one to go there without authority, and in due time passed a judicious law to govern the taking of the animals; sent proper persons to enforce the same, leased the islands, and laid a tax upon the skins taken, which is producing an annual revenue to the Government of over $300,000. The law wisely provides that none but male seals shall be killed. The breeding females, the young, and old bulls, are not molested. The proper season for killing is strictly observed, and thus the animals are likely long to continue to supply their beautiful fur.

The seal-islands of Alaska are leased by the United States Government to the Alaska Commercial Company of San Francisco, a corporation organized under the laws of California. The number of fur-seal skins which this company are allowed to take is now limited to 100,000 per annum; this entire product is sent to London, and there sold at the great semi-annual auctions. The company are under heavy personal bonds to the Government, faithfully to observe all laws of Congress relative to the time and mode of killing the animals, and the treatment of their native employés. They have the exclusive right to capture the fur-seal at St. George and St. Paul Islands, but all other kinds of fur-bearing animals may be taken by any persons, and the general fur-trade is open to free competition. The company have from sixteen to twenty trading-posts on the main-land and islands of Alaska, at which are gathered every year large numbers of furs and skins. They employ about a dozen vessels, and a corps of traders or factors, and concentrate their gatherings annually at San Francisco, whence they are forwarded to the best markets. The extent of the fur-trade of Alaska is indicated in the following approximative statement of the number of skins annually brought to San Francisco:

Fur-seal, 100,000; hair-seal, 150; sea-otter, 3,700; land-otter, 1,500; silver fox, 475; blue fox, 3,400; cross fox, 1,200; red fox, 6,400; white fox, 575; beaver, 17,600; marten, 10,700; sable, 600; mink, 6,700; bear, 425; musquash, 4,000; lynx, 250; ermine, 1,350; squirrel, 100; bird-skins, 100; reindeer-skins, 100; moose-skins, 200.

Under the provisions of the act of April 22, 1874, authorizing the Secretary of the Treasury to appoint a person qualified by experience and education to visit the trading-stations and Indian villages in the Territory of Alaska, Seal Islands, and the large islands in Behring's Sea, to collect authentic information relating to the varied interests of the Government in that Territory and the adjacent regions, Mr. Henry W. Elliott was designated as a special agent for that purpose. The report presented by him to the Treasury Department as the result of his labors contains a comprehensive statement of the character of the country, the condition of the natives, the present state of the seal and other fisheries, and the trade of the Territory, with minute descriptions of the haunts and habits of the seal and other fur-bearing animals, as also many valuable suggestions in regard to the management of the natives, the preservation of the seal-fisheries, and the economical collection of the revenue. No more satisfactory exhibit of the condition of the Territory and of its probable resources has hitherto been presented to the Treasury Department.

The Government has derived an income from the tax on seal-skins and from the rent of the fur-seal islands, since the acquisition of the Territory, as follows:

Tax on seal-skins	$1,150,219 75
Rent of fur-seal islands	170,480 75
Sale of seal-skins taken by Government agents, under section 6, act July 1, 1870	29,529 17
Making a total income of	$1,350,229 67

ALEXANDER, WILLIAM COWPER, LL. D., a distinguished lawyer, scholar, and political leader, of New Jersey, for fifteen years past the President of the Equitable Assurance Society of New York, born in Virginia in 1806; died in New York City August 23, 1874. He was the second son of Rev. Archibald Alexander, D. D., the celebrated pulpit orator and theological professor, and a brother of James W. Joseph Addison, Henry M., Samuel D., and Archibald Alexander, Jr., all eminent in their several professions. William C. Alexander graduated from Princeton College in 1824, and was admitted to the bar in 1827, when he soon attained distinction both for his profound legal attainments and his remarkable and commanding eloquence as an advocate. He early took an active part in political matters, never seeking, and often peremptorily declining office, but ever striving to maintain principle, integrity, and honor. He was for several years President of the State Senate of New Jersey; and, sorely against his will, was the nearly successful candidate for the governorship of the State. He would have been chosen United States Senator from the State by a large majority, but he prohibited the use of his name. He was a delegate to the Peace Congress in 1861. It was while thus esteemed and honored that he withdrew almost entirely from political life, to devote himself, as he has done with great assiduity and zeal, to the interests of life assurance. He was chosen President of the Equitable Life Assurance Society at its organization in 1859, and remained in that office till his death; and, by his commanding influence, and his rare executive ability, won for it an unprecedented success. Though an elegant and forcible writer, and an eloquent speaker, he had published very little beyond occasional addresses and arguments. He took a deep interest in education generally, and especially in the prosperity of Princeton College. He made the address of welcome to President McCosh on his inauguration, which was an eloquent and enthusiastic greeting, although he had but a few hours for its preparation. He received the honorary degree of LL. D. from Lafayette College, Easton, Pa., in 1860.

AMERICA. The progress of affairs in the States of North America was attended with no unusual event. A favorable summer resulted in large and abundant harvests. In the United States some disturbances arose with small parties of Indians, and in Louisiana the dissatisfaction with the State government continued, and required the presence of a small force of the United States troops. A disturbance also arose at Vicksburg, between blacks and whites (*see* MISSISSIPPI). The question of mixed schools of white and black children was extensively discussed in the Southern States, in anticipation of the passage of a "civil rights" act by Congress. Financial affairs throughout the country continued in an uncertain state, and a general embarrassment prevailed. The relations with foreign governments have been of the most peaceful character.

With the exception of the Plate provinces, where absolute tranquillity has been unknown since the Paraguayan War, the whole of South America has enjoyed a year of profound peace; and it would seem as if political turmoils and internecine strifes had at last ceased to be the normal occupation of the people, and were about to give place to the development of those inexhaustible natural resources which rank the South-American states among the richest and most beautiful in the world. Industrial enterprise is carried on with unabating energy in Chili and Peru, and commercial intercourse is rapidly extending between all the countries and the United States and Europe. Railways and telegraphs are multiplying in Brazil, Uruguay, Peru, Chili, and the Argentine Republic; and a concession was granted in the course of 1874, for the construction of a line of railway to unite the Atlantic and Pacific seaboards, bringing Buenos Ayres within sixty hours of Valparaiso. The completion of the submarine cable from Lisbon to Pernambuco has put almost all of South America in direct connection with the great telegraphic net-work of our globe; and local lines are fast extending the links to every corner of the country. Education is the object of much zeal in all the states; and in

this respect Mexico is among the foremost; nor are the five Central-American states, spite of their endless international disputes, forgetful of the happy results to be obtained by the diffusion of useful knowledge. Large appropriations have been made during the year for the construction of school-houses, and the importation of books and teachers, for which purpose agents have already been dispatched to the United States by more than one of those little republics.

An alliance between the republics of the Pacific and Atlantic had been suggested for the avowed purpose of protecting republican principles in all of them; but, notwithstanding some diplomatic steps already taken, it is not probable that the project will receive much serious consideration.

ANGLICAN CHURCHES. *The Public Worship Regulation Act.*—On the 20th of April the Archbishop of Canterbury introduced in the House of Lords a bill for the better administration of the laws respecting the regulation of public worship. He supported it with a strong argument, showing the necessity for additional legislation to suppress irregularities in ritual, and preserve the peace and harmony of the Church. The bill was long and fully discussed in the House of Lords, and passed its third reading toward the end of June. In the House of Commons, it was again subjected to a rigorous scrutiny. Of the speeches made in this House, that of Mr. Gladstone against the bill, on the 9th of July, and that of Mr. Disraeli in favor of it, on the 16th of July, received the most attention. The bill passed the House of Commons on the 3d of August, having received some amendments which were concurred in without delay by the House of Lords, and it became a law on the 7th of August. It is commonly cited by its shorter title, as "The Public Worship Regulation Act, 1874." It provides that the Archbishops of Canterbury and York may, with the approval of her Majesty, or that her Majesty may, if the archbishops fail to act, appoint a suitably-qualified person to be, during good behavior, a judge of the Provincial Courts of Canterbury and York. In case of a vacancy in the office of official principal of the Arches Court of Canterbury, or of official principal or auditor of the Chancery Court of York, or of Master of the Faculties to the Archbishop of Canterbury, this judge shall become *ex officio* such official, principal, auditor, or Master of the Faculties. The judge, before entering upon his office, must file a declaration that he is a member of the Church of England. It is further provided that "if the archdeacon of the archdeaconry, or a church-member of the parish, or any three parishioners within which archdeaconry or parish any church or burial-ground is situated, or for the use of any part of which any burial-ground is legally provided, or in case of cathedral or collegiate churches, any three inhabitants of the diocese," being members of the Church of England, male persons of full age, and qualified by residence, "shall be of the opinion—1. That in such church any alteration in or addition, to the fabric, ornaments, or furniture thereof has been made without lawful authority, or that any decoration forbidden by law has been introduced into such church; or, 2. That the incumbent has within the preceding twelve months used or permitted to be used in such church or burial-ground any unlawful ornament of the minister of the church, or neglected to use any prescribed ornament or vesture; or, 3. That the incumbent has within the preceding twelve months failed to observe, or caused to be observed, the directions contained in the Book of Common Prayer relating to the performance, in such church or burial-ground, of the services, rites, and ceremonies ordered by the said Book, or has made or permitted to be made any unlawful addition to, alteration of, or omission from such services, rites, and ceremonies," such person or persons may represent the same to the bishop: *Provided*, that no proceedings shall be taken concerning any alteration in, or addition to, the fabric of a church which has been completed five years before making complaint. The bishop on receiving the representation may, with the consent of the parties, hear the case, and pronounce such judgment and issue such monition as he may think proper: "*Provided*, that no judgment, so pronounced by the bishops, shall be considered as finally deciding any question of law so that it may not again be raised by the parties." If the parties do not give their consent to the hearing by the bishop, he shall forthwith transmit the representation to the archbishop of the province, and the archbishop "shall forthwith require the judge to hear the matter of the representation at any place within the diocese or province, or in London or Westminster." Failure by the person complained of to answer the representation is to be regarded as a denial of its truth or relevancy. The judge is given the usual powers of a court of record, and is authorized to pronounce judgment, issue monitions, and make orders for costs. An appeal lies from his judgment or monition to her Majesty in council. Obedience to the monition or order of the bishops or judge "shall be enforced, if necessary," by an order inhibiting the incumbent from performing any service of the Church, or otherwise exercising the cure of souls within the diocese for a term not exceeding three months; which inhibition shall not, however, be relaxed until the incumbent shall have undertaken in writing to pay due obedience to the monition or order, or the part thereof which shall not have been annulled. If, however, the inhibition shall remain in force for more than three years from the date of issuing the monition, or if a second inhibition in regard to the same monition shall be issued within three years from the relaxation of an inhibition, the benefice or preferment held by

the incumbent complained against shall become void, and the patron may make a new appointment; but he shall not reappoint the person who has been the subject of the proceedings. In case the bishop is the patron of the benefice, the incumbent of which is proceeded against, or is unable to act in the case, the archbishop of his province is authorized to act in his place; if the archbishop is the patron or is disabled, it is provided that the Queen shall appoint an archbishop or bishop to act in his stead. In cases in which a cathedral or collegiate church is involved, the duties otherwise assigned in the act to the bishop of the diocese are to be performed by the visitor. Complaints concerning the fabric, ornaments, furniture, or decorations of such cathedral or collegiate church must be made against the dean and chapter thereof; complaints concerning the ornaments of the minister, or the manner or form of conducting the services must be made against the clerk in holy orders who is alleged to have offended in the matter complained of; and the visitor shall have the same powers as to the infliction and execution of penalties as are given to the judge and bishop in the case of other ministers. This act is to go into force on the 1st of July, 1875.

The Convocation of Canterbury met for organization March 6th, in St. Paul's Cathedral. The Bishop of London presided at the opening meeting, in the absence of the archbishop, who was ill. The Latin sermon was preached by Dr. Merivale, Dean of Ely. The venerable R. Bickersteth, D. D., Archdeacon of Buckingham and Vicar of Aylesbury, was elected prolocutor of the Lower House. He made an opening address, in which he reviewed the work of convocation during the previous five years. He regarded the question of the Athanasian Creed as set at rest, at least for a generation, by means of the synodical declaration which had been adopted in 1873. The revision of the English version of the Holy Scriptures would, he thought, unless the existence of this Convocation were cut prematurely short by some political convulsion, be presented by it to the critical judgment of Biblical students. He trusted that the work would be found to be worthy of a place by the side of the present authorized version, and in time come to occupy the position that incomparable volume now held. He expressed the hope that some legislative action would be taken to give power to the Queen to subdivide unwieldy dioceses; and he thought that by this means the subject of the reform of convocation might be satisfactorily settled. He hoped that the movement which had been begun in convocation for intercommunion with the Churches of the East would tend to promote the union of the universal Church. After effecting their organization, both Houses were adjourned to April 28th.

On the 29th of April the Bishop of Lichfield, in the Upper House, presented a number of petitions on the subject of a second Pan-

Anglican Council. He referred to addresses which had come from Canada, from the West Indian bishops, from the Protestant Episcopal Church in the United States, and from the Church in Australia, on the subject; and expressed himself convinced that so general a call for a conference indicated that the time had come when the Anglican communion should have an acknowledged head. He moved for the appointment of a joint committee of both Houses of Convocation to consider a report as to what was the exact position that the Archbishop of Canterbury held with regard to the different branches of the Church scattered throughout the world, and that his Grace should be requested to convene a general conference of the Anglican communion in continuation of that of 1867. The archbishop, in speaking upon this motion, remarked that, with regard to the former conference of bishops at Lambeth, his predecessor had distinctly disavowed any claims of authority, and that it was still more necessary to do so now, on account of the changes which had taken place in the status of colonial churches. By the act of the home Government each of these churches was now an independent and voluntary communion, possessing, as in the act of forming, a definite constitution. They did not recognize their bishops as alone representing the Church, and did not give them power to decide upon laws and doctrines. The motion of the Bishop of Lichfield was amended by the addition of a clause directing that its provisions be communicated to the Primate of the Northern Provinces, and was adopted. The Bishops of London, Winchester, Lichfield, Gloucester and Bristol, and Peterborough, were appointed to act on the committee. The committee made a report in the Upper House on the 10th of July, recommending that a second meeting of the Lambeth Conference be convoked by his Grace the archbishop, for the year 1876; that then the work begun in 1867 be continued, and the reports of committees be taken into consideration; also, that the relation of the Archbishop of Canterbury to the other bishops of the Anglican communion be that of primate among archbishops, primates, metropolitans, and bishops.

On the 28th of April petitions, influentially signed, in relation to the bill introduced in the House of Lords by the Archbishop of Canterbury for the regulation of public worship, were presented in the Upper House of Convocation by the Bishop of Peterborough, and in the Lower House by the Dean of St. Paul's. In offering the memorials, the Bishop of Peterborough made an address, the tone of which was in favor of restraining lawlessness, but against permitting infringements of the just rights and liberty of the clergy. The Bishop of Lincoln spoke in favor of toleration. In the Lower House a message was received from the Upper House asking whether it still adhered to its action of 1869 on the subject of

Church discipline, and inviting it to give its opinion regarding the inhibition of practices affecting the ritual of the Church declared unlawful by the courts (as presented in the new bill), and the relation of such inhibition to the liberty of the clergy. The reply of the Lower House was conveyed in the following declaration:

The Lower House of the Convocation of Canterbury, in answer to the two questions submitted to it by his Grace the president, on April 28, 1874, respectfully answers:

1. (a.) That the Lower House does adhere to all the resolutions on the subject of "clergy discipline" passed by the late Lower House, in the sessions of June, 1869; but that the Lower House would object to their partial application for the correction of a particular class of offenses; as the resolutions of the late Lower House were intended by the Lower House to be applied to the general reformation of all procedure in all cases tried in ecclesiastical courts. (b.) That the Lower House "recommends, as a particular mode whereby such resolutions can be made effective," the immediate preparation of a plan for the purpose with a view to an application to the crown for "assent and license" to enact it, and also with a view to obtain such statutable aid from Parliament as may be found needful.

On the 1st day of May, the Lower House resolved:

That this House, recognizing the necessity of speedy legislation in the matters involved in the question proposed to this House by his Grace the President, regrets its inability to approve the provisions of the bill recently introduced into the House of Lords for the purpose, and now requests that his Grace will be pleased to direct the appointment of a committee of this House to consider the provisions of the said bill; and further to request that his Grace will be pleased to summon Convocation at an early date, to receive such report.

(a.) And also that his Grace will be pleased to direct that it be an instruction of the committee to inquire whether the particular mode of action for the purposes in question, and especially for facilitating the proceedings in the Ecclesiastical Courts of Appeal, would be the proper "canonical drafts" with a view to application to the crown for "assent and license" to enact them; and (b) further to inquire into the measure of statutory aid which it may be needful to obtain from Parliament.

The archbishop replied in behalf of the Upper House to these resolutions, that the Lower House, by adhering to the resolutions of 1869, appeared to agree in the principles embodied in the proposals which were then before the public for the discipline of the clergy, including morals and doctrine. Their lordships (the bishops) were quite ready to consider all the matters, but they regarded it as desirable that the various subjects should not be unnecessarily united together, and were anxious to separate those relating to public worship. The appointment of the committee as asked for was agreed to. The committee appointed under the resolutions cited above made a report to the Lower House, May 7th, suggesting that further regulations respecting the conduct of the service according to the use of the Church of England should be by canon rather than by statute, and suggesting a number of objections to the archbishop's bill. They recommended several specific amendments to the bill, and professed that, even with these modifications, they were unable to recommend legislation in the manner proposed by the bill. They further expressed the opinion that if the "Church Discipline Act" were repealed, and the existing consistory courts were reformed, there would be little difficulty in dealing expeditiously with such cases as were contemplated by the bill. The House resolved to transmit this report to the Upper House, with the request that their lordships would consider the objections it presented, and the amendments it proposed. The Upper House replied, through the archbishop: "We have given such consideration as we well can to the report which has been placed in our hands. There are in it certain proposed amendments of the present system of clergy discipline recommended by the committee, and some worthy of serious consideration, and they will receive very serious consideration, probably both here and elsewhere. There are other recommendations, too, worthy, no doubt, of no less serious consideration than the others, but which do not approve themselves to the majority of this House; but perhaps, on further consideration, these objections may disappear. There are things in the report which do, and partly there are things which do not, commend themselves to our minds, and this difference of opinion was naturally to be expected." The Public Worship Bill was also discussed incidentally at the meeting of the Convocation in July. A gravamen was presented against it in the Lower House; and in the Upper House the archbishop made an explanation respecting it, and the Bishop of Lincoln made some criticisms of it.

The Convocation proceeded, at its session in July, to discuss the fourth or final report of the commission on ritual. A committee was appointed to consider and report on the previous action of the Lower House on the subject of ritual, with instructions to report as early as convenient upon the "Ornaments Rubric" and the position of the celebrant. The recommendations of the commissioners with regard to a daily service were adopted, as follows:

The directions concerning the daily use of the Church services are retained, not as an indispensable rule, but as a witness to the value put by the Church on daily prayers and intercessions, and on the daily reading of the Holy Scriptures.

The Committee of the Whole on the Ornaments Rubric, which had been in session in the interval since the last meeting (in May), reported in the Upper House the following resolution, which was adopted:

Resolved, That the Ornaments Rubric is of doubtful and difficult interpretation, and that it is most desirable that it should be replaced by a rubric which shall clearly define what dresses and ornaments of the ministers shall be permissible in the Church of England.

The Bishop of Lichfield offered the following resolution, which was seconded by the Bishop of Peterborough:

Whereas, In the 34th Article it is affirmed that every national Church has authority to retain, change, and abolish ceremonies or rites of the Church ordained only by man's authority: And whereas, In the Preface to the Book of Common Prayer it is affirmed that rites and ceremonies, being in their nature "things indifferent," may be changed upon weighty and important considerations, according to the various exigencies of times and occasions: And whereas, A large number of the clergy and of the faithful laity of the Church of England are of opinion that the use of distinctive dress in ministering the Holy Communion of the Body and Blood of Christ would tend to reverence and edification: And whereas, It would tend to peace that the desire of the clergy and laity should be granted: Resolved, That it is desirable that the use of a distinctive dress be permitted in ministering the Holy Communion, but only at such places and upon such conditions as shall be hereafter approved by lawful authority.

The Bishop of Lincoln proposed as an additional clause:

Provided it be distinctly understood nothing is symbolized by such Eucharistic vestments as is in any way at variance with the doctrines of the Church of England, as contained in the order of the Holy Communion in the Book of Common Prayer.

The resolution and amendment were referred to the committee of the whole House.

The report of the Committee on Intercommunion with the Eastern Churches was presented in the Lower House of the Convocation on the 8th of May. A resolution was passed expressing gratitude for the directions issued by the Patriarch of Constantinople to his metropolitans, instructing their clergy to perform the rites of Christian burial for deceased members of the English Church. A resolution calling on the Archbishop of Canterbury to use his endeavors to secure intercommunion between the two Churches, and especially to enable members of the English Church residing within the jurisdiction of the Eastern Church to avail themselves of the rites and sacraments of that Church, was, after discussion, withdrawn.

Measures were taken during the earlier sessions of the Convocation for the preparation of a Manual of Private Prayers for members of the Church of England, to be submitted for consideration; for the preparation of a Form of Prayer to Almighty God, in behalf of the ministers of the Church, to be used on suitable occasions, with the sanction of the archbishop and bishops; and for an inquiry into the expediency of the appointment of a day of public intercession on behalf of the missions of the Church once in each year, or at such intervals as may be deemed expedient.

The Convocation of York met for organization March 6th. An address to her Majesty was unanimously adopted, praying that Parliament would maintain and improve the laws upon the subject of intemperance. At a subsequent meeting, May 22d, the following resolution was adopted in reference to the bill introduced in the House of Lords by the Archbishop of Canterbury for the regulation of public worship: "That while some legislation is expedient for the better administration of the laws respecting the regulation of public worship, it is most desirable that, simultaneously with such legislation, the rubrics, canons, and general laws of the Church, be revised, with a view to their being more clearly defined, and that the existing ecclesiastical courts be reformed."

The Church Congress.—The English Church Congress met in its fourteenth session at Brighton, October 6th. At the beginning, sermons were preached in St. Peter's Church by the Bishop of Ely, and in St. Nicholas's Church by the Bishop of Salisbury. The Bishop of Chichester, as bishop of the diocese in which the Congress was held, presided, and delivered the opening address. After giving counsel in regard to the temper in which the deliberations of the meeting should be conducted, he called attention to the subjects introduced by the committee of arrangements, which had not been brought forward at any previous Congress, of which the most important was the Old Catholic movement on the Continent. He characterized this movement as a phenomenon of the deepest interest to the English people, as the beginning of a reformation in the Roman Catholic Church, the principles of which were not unlike those which had governed the reformation in their own Church. He trusted that the Conference would show that it thoroughly sympathized · in the struggles of the leaders in this movement to free themselves from connection with the Roman Church. The discussion of this subject was opened formally in a paper read by the Bishop of Winchester. He gave a brief account of the history and character of the Old Catholic movement, and spoke favorably of the Conference just held at Bonn, which he had attended. Prof. Meyer followed, with an account of the persecutions which he represented the friends of the Old Catholic movement to have had to suffer in Roman Catholic countries. The subject was further discussed by the Bishop of Melbourne and Dr. Littledale. A paper was read by the Rev. M. H. Banning, on "Foreign Missions, especially in Reference to Modern Judaism," in which the number of converts from Judaism to Christianity at the present day was spoken of as encouraging to further efforts among the Jewish people. The subject was continued in a paper by the Rev. Dr. Barclay, who claimed that mission-stations had been established in the chief centres of the Jewish population in all the nations of Europe except Russia, on the north coast of Africa, in Western Asia, and in Jerusalem. He estimated that one-half of the Jewish population of ten million souls were reached directly or indirectly by missionary efforts, and that twenty thousand Jews had been baptized into Christianity. The subject of "Foreign Missions in Relation to Mohammedanism and other Oriental Systems of Religion" was discussed in papers and addresses on "Mohammedanism," by the Earl of Chichester; "Buddhism in Ceylon," by Bishop

Claughton; and "China," by Bishop Horden. The discussion of the subject of "Church Patronage" was opened with a paper prepared by the Bishop of Lincoln, and read by Mr. Walter Phillimore. Canon Ashwell read a paper on the same subject, which was continued, with addresses by Mr. Walter Phillimore, the Earl of Harrowby, J. G. Hubbard, M. P., Canon Gregory, and the Rev. E. Garbet. All of · the essayists agreed in condemning the abuses practised in the sale of livings and advowsons, and various suggestions were made of measures of reform. On the subject of the "Convocations of the Church of England," papers were read by Lord Alwyne Compton and Canon Ryle, in which the admission of laymen to the Convocation was favored; and others by Canon Trevor and Canon Parr, in which it was opposed. The discussion was continued by Colonel Bartlett, M. P., and Canon Freemantle. Several points involved in the controversy between the Ritualistic and Evangelical parties were touched upon, and much excitement, and even disorder, resulted. The "Adaptation of the Fabrics and Services of the Church to the Wants of the Times" was considered in papers and addresses by Mr. Beresford Hope, M. P., the Rev. W. Cadman, Prof. Donaldson, Mr. G. E. Street, the Rev. J. W. Perry, the Dean of Manchester, Canon Rawlinson, and other persons. A variety of views were offered. The subject of "Skepticism, Critical, Scientific, and Popular," was introduced with a paper by Canon Westcote, on "Skeptical Criticism." Prof. Pritchard read a paper on "Scientific Skepticism," in which he dealt prominently with the atomic theory of Prof. Tyndall. Prof. Birks read a paper on the same subject. The Rev. Dr. Hersey, the Rev. J. W. Tidcombe, the Rev. Dr. Hayman, the Rev. Dr. Wright, and the Bishop of Edinburgh, took part in the discussion which followed. Papers were read on "The Spiritual Life; its Helps and Hinderances," by the Dean of Norwich and the Rev. G. H. Wilkinson; on "The Education of Women," by the Rev. C. Bigg, the Rev. J. L. Davis, Mr. W. E. Hubbard, and the Rev. Prof. Plumtre; and on "Church Music," by the Rev. Dr. Stainer. A meeting for working-men was held during the sessions of the Congress, at which the Dean of Chichester presided. Addresses were made by Canon Miller, Canon Ellison, Mr. Gorst, and the Rev. Mr. Wainright, and the subject of "The Influence of Social and Sanitary Conditions on Religion" was discussed. On Saturday, October 10th, a special service was held in Chichester Cathedral. A dispatch was received from the Congress of the Protestant Episcopal Church in the United States, sitting in the city of New York, conveying the hearty greetings of that body, and was suitably answered. The Patriarch of Syria and the Bishop of Jerusalem, of the Eastern Church, were presented to the Congress at one of its sittings. Private meetings of the Ritualistic party were held during the session, at which it was decided to present a petition to the Convocations of Canterbury and York in favor of such action as should insure the "retention of such ornaments of the Church and of the ministers thereof as were prescribed by and used under the Prayer-book of 1549." At similar meetings of the Evangelical party, resolutions were adopted pledging resistance to all attempts at a revision of the rubrics in " an anti-Protestant" direction, and more particularly to all proposals to legalize vestments and the Eastward position. The Congress was regarded as a very successful one. The attendance was so large as to make necessary a division into two sections. The various schools of opinion in the Church were well represented in most of the discussions.

A Church Congress was held at Edinburgh May 18th, 19th, and 20th. The programme embraced papers and discussions upon the following topics: " The Past and Present Condition of the Episcopal Church in Scotland; " " The Evangelizing Work of the Church ; " " Foreign Missionary Work," on which subject a paper was assigned to Bishop Callaway, of Independent Kaffraria; " Church Finance," papers by Messrs. W. Mitchell and Lordson Walker ; " Diocesan, Parochial, and Congregational Organization," papers and addresses by the Rev. J. Erskine Clarke, of Battersea, Canon Humble, of Perth, Dr. Mackness, of Broughton Ferry, and the Rev. F. Sandford, of Edinburgh ; " Christianity in Relation to Modern Unbelief," papers and addresses by Provost Cazenove, of Cumbral, Provost Powell, of Inverness, Prebendary Clark, of Taunton, Dr. McCann, of Glasgow, and the Rev. Gedart Jackson, of Leith ; " The Training and Supply of Clergy," discourse by Canon Barry, of King's College, London, Prof. Lorimer, of Edinburgh University, and the Rev. J. Cowper, of Aberdeen ; " On Quickening and Strengthening Spiritual Life in the Church," the Rev. W. D. Maclagan, of Newington ; " The Relation of the Church to Education," discussed by the Rev. W. Percy Robinson, of Trinity College, Glenalmond, the Rev. Julius Lloyd, of Greenock, the Rev. F. Teesdale, of Inverness Grammar-School, and Mr. G. Auldjo Jameson, of Edinburgh ; " The Ecclesiastical Architecture of Scotland," Sir G. G. Scott; " The Cathedral Organization of Scotland," Rev. Mackenzie E. C. Walcott, Precentor and Prebendary of Chichester.

The Exeter Reredos Case.—The questions of the lawfulness of images in churches and of the power of the bishop over the cathedral were partly involved in a case known as the " Exeter Reredos Case," which engaged the attention of the ecclesiastical courts in the summer of 1874. The Dean and Chapter of Exeter Cathedral, in repairing the cathedral building, had determined to erect a reredos, containing figures sculptured in *alto-rilievo* and arranged in groups to represent the Ascension,

the Transfiguration, and the Descent of the Holy Ghost. The spot where it was intended to set it up had been occupied by tablets containing the ten commandments. The bishop opposed the erection, but, his authority to forbid it having been disputed, proceedings were instituted before Mr. Justice Keating to test the legal points. It was held on behalf of the bishop that the work was illegal from the beginning, having been commenced without his faculty, and that the images were forbidden by the rubrics. The dean and chapter pleaded that in matters of cathedral decoration their authority was quite independent of that of the bishop; that the images, being in relief, and not statues, were not of the class forbidden in the rubrics ; and that, by being arranged in groups to represent events, they were not liable to the objection attached to single images. Justice Keating affirmed the power of the bishop in the premises, and sustained his decision that the images were unlawful. The bishop pronounced a judgment in accordance with the opinion of Justice Keating. An appeal was taken by the dean and chapter to the Court of Arches, by whom a decision was given in August, reversing those of Justice Keating and the bishop.

In order to meet a supposed emergency requiring the provision of facilities for enlarging the episcopate in India, the Judicial Committee of the Privy Council, at the suggestion of the Christian Knowledge Society, early in the year recommended the passage of an enabling act empowering the bishops in India to rearrange their existing dioceses, to constitute new dioceses, and to consecrate additional bishops. They suggested the appointment of coadjutor bishops for the missions of Southern India, as a temporary expedient, and even went so far as to suggest the amount of income that should be allotted to each bishop.

The report of the joint committee on the new canons and constitutions was presented to the convocations of Canterbury and York during the year. It proposed a reduction of the one hundred and forty-one canons of 1603 to ninety canons.

A society has been formed in England, of which the Bishop of Winchester has been chosen president, with the object of bringing about the union with the Anglican Church of Nonconformist bodies that hold the fundamental tenets of Christian faith, such as the doctrine of the Trinity, the Incarnation, and the Atonement. The society purposes to avoid carefully compromising in any way the creeds and the constitution of the Church. It intends, however, to advocate freedom of action in matters of secondary importance. Its plan of work is : 1. To diffuse, by means of lectures, public meetings, and other instrumentalities, a better knowledge of the history, principles, and formulas of the Established Church ; 2. To promote kindly feelings between Churchmen and Nonconformists by means of friendly intercourse and such acts of united worship as ecclesiastical law allows; 3. To remove the obstacles to the admission of properly-qualified Nonconformist ministers to orders in the Church of England. The headquarters of the Society will be in London; branch associations are to be formed throughout the kingdom.

The annual festival of the Confraternity of the Blessed Sacrament was held on the day of Corpus Christi. The occasion was observed with special service in about fifty churches. The society in England is about twelve years old. Its especial objects are: 1. To promote "the honor due to the presence of the Lord" in the Sacraments; 2. "Mutual and special intercession;" 3. "The promotion of fasting communion."

From statistics given in *Mackeson's Guide to the Churches of London and its Suburbs* for 1874, it appears that there are 759 churches in London. Information is given as to the mode of conducting the services in 745 of these churches. The Holy Communion is observed weekly in 240 of them, and daily in 26; "Early Communion" is held in 310 churches; Saints'-day services are held in 316, and daily service in 181 churches. No week-day services are held in 126 churches; 265 churches have surpliced choirs; 185 churches pay their choristers partly or wholly; 331 churches have weekly offertories; the seats are appropriated in 110, and are free in 130 churches; floral decorations are used in 153 churches; altar-lights in 36, and Eastward position is taken on Holy Communion in 74 churches.

Society for the Propagation of the Gospel.— The receipts of the Society for the Propagation of the Gospel in Foreign Parts for 1873 were $551,000. The Society had provided wholly or in part for the support of 484 ordained missionaries, who were thus distributed: In America and the West Indies, 220; in Africa, 94; in Asia, 125; in Australia and the islands of the Pacific Ocean, 44. Among the missionaries enumerated were included 49 native ministers in India. The Society employed also about 822 catechists and lay teachers, most of whom were natives of the countries in which they were laboring, and had 141 students enrolled in its colleges.

Church Missionary Society.—The seventy-fifth anniversary of the Church Missionary Society was held May 5th. The "ordinary income" for the year was reported to have been £127,720, while the "total income" had reached £261,-221. At the previous annual meeting a deficit of nearly £12,000 was reported in the account of receipts and expenditures. This deficit had been made good during the current year, and a surplus remained, after meeting all claims, of £10,407. A legacy of £22,800 had been received from the estate of Mr. T. W. Hill, of Bristol, and a gift of £20,700 had been made to the Society by Mr. Walter Jones, of Manchester. The contributions for the Henry Venn Memorial Fund, for aiding in the internal

development of native churches, had reached the sum of £8,544. The report of the Society sketched the progress of missionary work carried on under its direction at Sierra Leone, Yoruba, the Niger Mission, the Mediterranean Mission, Northern and Western India, Southern India, Ceylon, Mauritius, and Madagascar, China, Japan, New Zealand, Northwest America, and on the North Pacific coast. The number of principal stations under the care of the Society was stated to be 157; of ordained missionaries employed, 354, of whom 142 were native ministers; of unordained laborers, 34; of teachers, 2,244; of native communicants in the mission churches, 22,555; of native Christians, 107,268. In consequence of the action of the Society for the Propagation of the Gospel in Foreign Parts, in appointing a bishop for Madagascar, the Society had withdrawn its missionaries from that country, in order that it might not be made a party to interference with the work of the London Missionary Society.

The Irish Church.—The report of the Representative Body of the Church of Ireland for 1874 states that that board had agreed to purchase all the glebes except three. The sum of £144,877 10s. 7d. had been paid in part payment on this account to the Church Temporalities Commissioners. Of this amount £86,942 11s. 8d. were contributed by the parishes, and £6,310 18s. 2d. were received for sales to the public. The receipts from the clergy on account of rents, after allowing four per cent. interest on the balance of £51,614 0s. 9d., had produced a surplus of £9,318 17s. 5d. The number of commutants on the 31st of December, 1873, was 2,058, or 102 less than the whole number of annuitants. The amount granted for composition up to the same date was £968,500, the commutation capital of the annuitants being £1,974,500. The amount advanced under Table III. was £933,000, extinguishing annuities to the amount of £84,300. The balance arising from commutation of church offices was £206,226. The balance of the general sustentation fund amounted to £155,781 19s. 11d., the interest on which, at four per cent., was £8,360 7s. To this fund had been added the unappropriated subscriptions to the 31st of December, 1873, amounting to £11,335 4s. 11d. A list was given in the report of the amounts allotted to the various parishes entitled to claim a portion of the £500,000 granted on account of private endowments. The total sum allocated on account of the Boulter and Robinson funds was £140,222 17s.; and on account of general endowments £78,764 3s. 5d. The total estimated cost of glebes directed to be purchased out of this fund was £18,122 3s. 8d., and the sum set apart to provide an indemnity for unsettled cases, and to meet other contingencies, was £17,890 15s. 11d. The balance remaining unappropriated was £150,000, for which, together with £15,000 of accrued interest, the report proposed a definite schedule of allocation.

The fourth meeting of the General Synod of the Church of Ireland was held at Dublin, beginning April 9th. The Lord Primate presided. But little progress was made during the session in the work of revising the Prayerbook. A large proportion of the amendments proposed by the revision committee, and approved by the laity, were defeated upon a division of orders by failing to receive the requisite two-thirds vote of the clergy. Thirty-three petitions were presented in favor of the revision and eight against it. Among the adverse memorials were an address signed by 550 of the clergy, and one signed by more than 800 gentlemen of rank and position, 200 clergy, and 6,600 members. A number of amendments to the ritual, relating to the Form for the Consecration of Bishops, to the Form of Prayer for June 30th, and to various prayers, thanksgivings, and collections, were agreed to without opposition, and with but little discussion. A proposition to omit from the answer to the second question of the Catechism the words, "whereby I was made a member of Christ, a child of God, and an inheritor of the kingdom of Heaven," was negatived on a division of orders, as were also several other alterations of the Catechism proposed by the revision committee. A new question and answer were, however, approved, to be introduced into the Catechism before Communion, in the following terms : " Question.—After what manner are the body and blood of Christ taken in the Lord's Supper? Answer.—Only after a heavenly and spiritual manner, and the means whereby they are received and taken is faith."

A motion for leave to introduce a bill requiring the reordination of Reformed Roman Catholic priests seeking admission into the Church of Ireland was defeated by a vote of the clergy. A motion to substitute another form for the Commination service held on Ash-Wednesday was also rejected. The proposition to remove the so-called "damnatory clauses" of the Athanasian Creed was carried with the laity by a large majority. The clergy refused concurrence. A strong division of opinion was manifested upon the subject. Both houses finally concurred in an arrangement by which the Creed should be inserted entire and without change in the latter part of the Prayerbook, and should also be printed in the morning services with the "damnatory clauses" omitted, for recitation in place of the Apostles' Creed on the occasion of the festivals, when it is directed to be substituted for that article. It was the intention of this adjustment to leave it optional with the clergyman whether the Creed in question should be read entire or without the "damnatory clauses."

Provincial Synods of Canada, Australia, and the West Indies.—On account of its close connection with the Established Church in England, synodal action in the Episcopal Church in Canada was of doubtful legality before 1857. In that year an act was passed

providing that the several dioceses in the Province of Canada might, by their respective bishops, clergy, and laity, meet to frame constitutions and make regulations for their own government. The same act further authorized them to meet in general assembly within the province, by such representatives as might be determined upon, to frame a constitution and make laws for the general management and good government of the Church. Under this act diocesan synods were formed in the dioceses of Quebec, Toronto, Montreal, Huron, and Ontario. When confederation took place, the Episcopal Churches in the Eastern provinces naturally desired to enjoy the benefits of a similar union. Accordingly, acts were passed by the Parliament of the Dominion extending the provisions of the Provincial Act to Nova Scotia in 1870, and to New Brunswick in 1870. These acts prescribed the manner in which the dioceses in the provinces named could be admitted to the Provincial Synod, and enjoy in that body the same standing as the Canadian Synods possessed. Application for such admission was made by the diocese of Nova Scotia in 1871, but, on account of a fatal defect in form, it could not be granted. The application was renewed in 1874 by an almost unanimous vote of the Synod, in proper form, and deputies were chosen to represent the diocese in the Provincial Synod. The Diocesan Synod of Fredericton (New Brunswick), which met June 30th, on the second day of its session, also resolved, by a vote of fifty to forty-six, to enter the Provincial Synod, and appointed deputies to represent it there. The Provincial Synod is pledged to continue an integral portion of the United Church of England and Ireland; to take the Holy Bible, "as set forth by that Church, on the testimony of the Primitive Catholic Church," as the rule and standard of faith ; and, under the supremacy of the Queen, to receive and maintain, and transmit unimpaired to posterity, its Book of Common Prayer and its " Scriptural and Apostolic form of government and doctrine." It purposes for itself to deal chiefly with matters of discipline, government, and Church extension throughout the Dominion. By its constitution it consists of two Houses ; the first, or Upper House, comprising all bishops having sees or officiating as assistant or missionary bishops under its jurisdiction; and the second, or Lower House, which is composed of twelve clerical and twelve lay delegates from each diocese united with the Synod. The Houses meet separately. The Metropolitan is President of the Upper House. The Lower House, at the beginning of each session, elects a prolocutor from among its own members. The Synod meets at Montreal every third year, on the second Wednesday of September.

The Provincial Synod of Canada met at Montreal September 9th. The meeting was opened by the metropolitan in a joint session of the two Houses, after which the Rev. J.

Gamble Geddes, of Hamilton, was chosen prolocutor of the Lower House. The delegates from the dioceses of Halifax and Fredericton were introduced and welcomed. Among the questions that received most attention was one in reference to the mode of appointing the metropolitan. The Queen, in nominating the first Bishop of Montreal, had selected that city as the seat of the Metropolitan See. The bishops were, however, not willing to accept as their prince, or the province as its metropolitan, a bishop in whose election they and the province had had no choice; on the other hand, the Diocese of Montreal could not be expected to consent to be deprived of its suffrage in the choice of a bishop. In order to meet these difficulties, the Provincial Synod at its previous meeting, in 1871, adopted a canon to be carried into effect if confirmed by the present Synod, providing that, on the occurrence of the next vacancy in the Diocese of Montreal, that diocese should cease to be the fixed Metropolitan See; that then, and subsequently on the avoidance of the Metropolitan See, the bishops of the Ecclesiastical Province should meet under the presidency of the senior bishop, and elect one of their own. number to be president of the House of Bishops, and that the bishop so elected should become, *ipso facto*, metropolitan, and his See, the Metropolitical See of the Province; that the city of Montreal should continue to be the place of meeting of the Provincial Synod. The following canon was enacted: "No alteration or addition shall be made in the Book of Common Prayer and Administration of the Sacraments and other rites and ceremonies of the Church, the Articles of Religion, or the form and manner of making, ordaining, and consecrating bishops, priests, and deacons, or the version of the Scriptures authorized to be read in the Churches, unless the same shall be enacted at one session of the Provincial Synod and confirmed at another session of the same; provided their confirmation be approved by two-thirds of the House of Bishops and two-thirds of each order of the Lower House. Nevertheless, any alteration in or addition made to the Prayer-Book or articles by the Church of England in her convocation and authorized by Parliament may be accepted for use in this Ecclesiastical Province when passed by the Provincial Synod in one session only, without the necessity of future confirmation."

A conference of West Indian bishops was held near the beginning of the year, at Georgetown, Demerara. It determined upon the confederation of the West Indian dioceses into a separate province, of which the bishops would style themselves "Bishops of the West Indian Church." The establishment of a Provincial Synod, to consist of bishops only, and of a synod, or Church council, in each diocese, to consist of the bishop, clergy, and representatives of the laity, was decided upon. The organization of a bishopric endowment fund

and a general sustentation and endowment fund was considered favorably.

At the meeting of the assembly of the Church of England in the Diocese of Melbourne, bills were passed creating a province in the colony, constituting the Diocese of Ballarat; regulating the appointment of future bishops of Melbourne; and making provision for the systematic religious instruction of the youth of the colony from moneys to be derived from "the selling or letting of school lands." The Bishop of Melbourne will be metropolitan of the newly-formed province.

ARGENTINE REPUBLIC (Repúblioa Argentina), an independent state of South America, lying between latitude 22° and 41° south, and longitude 53° and 71° 17′ west; and bounded north by Bolivia; east by Paraguay, Brazil, Uruguay, and the Atlantic; south by that. ocean and the Rio Negro, which forms the boundary-line with Patagonia; and west by Chili, from which it is separated by the Andes Mountains. The boundary question with Paraguay is still unsettled; numerous proposals have been exchanged with Brazil during the year, but that empire, persisting in affirming the injustice of the Argentine claim to the Chaco territory, north of the Rio Pilcomayo, war has been regarded as imminent; and the Argentine press severely censured the hostile policy and attitude of its Government toward Brazil. The vexed question of title to Patagonia is still the subject of angry discussion between the republic and Chili; but here the arbitrary policy of the latter elicited little sympathy, and, should war have followed, public opinion would have regarded the Santiago Government as chiefly to blame. Report represented Chili as about to take formal possession of the entire territory from the Santa Cruz River southward to the Straits of Magellan, which would seem to be a breach of the compact between the two countries—that neither should exercise jurisdiction over any portion of the territory until a mutually satisfactory solution should be reached; but Chili is said to have alleged, in its own defense, that the Argentines were the first to violate the agreement by erecting a fort on the southern bank of the river alluded to. It would, however, appear that the Argentine Government proposed to leave the matter to arbitration, as in the case of previous treaties.

The Argentine territory is divided into fourteen provinces, for which, with their area and population, according to the census of 1869, *see* Annual Cyclopædia, 1872. Some of the provinces doubled their population between 1849 and 1869, others in somewhat less than thirty years. Among those whose population increases most rapidly are Buenos Ayres, Entre-Rios, Santa Fé, Corrientes, Salta, and San Juan, which are the chief centres of immigration. The aggregate population of the republic very nearly doubled from 1849 to 1869, and the ratio of increase per decade has been approximately the same during the same period, according to the annexed official returns, the first two being only estimates:

YEARS.	Population.
1849	985,000
1859	1,304,000
1869	1,827,334

There are in the province of Buenos Ayres eight individuals to the square mile; in Tucuman, five; in Córdoba, three; in some of the upper provinces there is but one; and in the whole republic there are only three, or about fifty times less than in most European countries.

In 1873 the number of immigrants exceeded 79,000, or almost double the number of the previous year; and it would appear that the class of settlers shows a marked improvement—thanks to the superior condition and accommodations of the steamers now used in that service. Sailing-ships are almost entirely super-

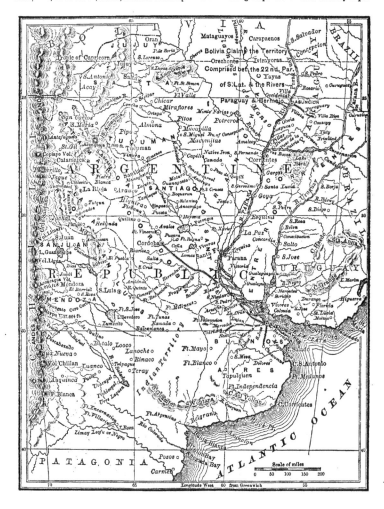

seded, and twenty steamers monthly keep up a constant stream of emigration from Italian, French, Spanish, German, Belgian, and English ports.

The following is a comparative table of the arrivals in the six years, 1868–'73 :

YEARS.	Arrivals.	YEARS.	Arrivals.
1868.................	29,234	1872.................	41,002
1869......	37,934	1873.................	79,712
1870.................	41,058		
1871.................	21,758	Total in 6 years..	250,698

A statistical table, compiled from auctioneers' books, notaries' registers, and banking-houses in the city, shows that the value of property purchased by foreign settlers and of moneys remitted in small drafts to their friends at home reached the enormous figure of £2,600,000, or $13,000,000, viz. :

Public lands bought....................	£45,460
Returns of 24 auctioneers...............	1,280,000
Foreign investments at Rosario........	240,300
Remittances to Italy....................	405,000
" to Spain....................	302,600
" to France.................	182,400
" to Gt. Britain and Ireland.	84,200
" to Switzerland...........	89,500
" to Germany..............	24,000
	£2,603,460

Mr. Wilcken, the director of the immigration department, regards these figures as far below the truth ; but it is, nevertheless, wonderful that the yearly savings of a hundred thousand families in Buenos Ayres. and Santa Fé should average $1,300, or an aggregate sum equivalent to the revenue of not a few second-rate European monarchies. There is an interesting fact in real estate immediately traceable to the large numbers of immigrants referred to. The province of Buenos Ayres has an area of 70,000 square miles, and a population of 521,653, or eight inhabitants to the square mile approximately, 30 per cent. of whom are foreigners ; while Santiago del Estero has an area of 35,000 square miles, and but four inhabitants to the square mile, only one per 1,000 of whom are foreigners. Now, in the former province, a single building-lot costs, in the suburbs of the capital, as much as one square league, or 6,660 acres of land in the latter. Mr. Wilcken ingeniously calculates in the following manner the accretion to the public wealth resulting from the immigration of 1873, adopting the United States basis of $1,000 per individual arrived :

79,712 immigrants, at $1,000.........	$79,712,000
Capital of immigrants on arrival.....	7,014,656
Increase of revenue at $12...........	956,544
Salaries at $200 each.................	15,942,000
	$103,725,200

This estimate, however enormous it may appear, is affirmed to contain no exaggeration ; nor is it, after all, so very wonderful, if we are to accept as accurate the $13,000,000 of savings above cited for the same year. Little variation is noticeable in the proportion of nationalities, the Italians still standing for a full half of the arrivals. The sum appropriated in 1873 for the expenses of the department

was $178,724, and these really amounted to but $105,784, leaving a surplus of $72,940. It may be curious to mention that the forwarding immigrants' letters to Europe free of charge is regarded as a most successful means of encouraging immigration ; and an expenditure of $28,620 for free passages to Europe in favor of 100 deserving colonists was the means of securing 402 new settlers. Some 18 per cent. of the total outlay of the department is for the remuneration of fourteen agents in Europe.

It was estimated that the arrivals in 1874 would amount to 100,000.

The President of the Republic is Dr. Don Nicolás Avellaneda, elected in 1874 ; Vice-President, Dr. M. Acosta, elected in the same year ; Minister of the Interior, Dr. Simon de Iriondo ; of Foreign Affairs, Dr. Félix Frias ; of Finance, Don Santiago Cortines ; of Justice, Public Worship, and Public Instruction, Dr. Onésimo Leguizama ; of War, Dr. Adolfo Alsina. Argentine minister to the United States, Sr. Don Manuel R. Garcia (in Europe since 1872) ; chargé d'affaires, Sr. Don Cárlos Carranza. The Governors of the fourteen provinces are as follows :

Buenos Ayres (pro tem.)........	Colonel Barrios.
Minister of the Interior......	Dr. A. Alcorta.
Minister of Finance..........	L. Basavilbaso.
Catamarca........................	Gen. O. Navarro.
Córdoba..........................	E. Rodriguez.
Corrientes........................	M. V. Gelabert.
Entre-Rios........................	L. Echague.
Jujuy.............................	A. Mas-Oller.
La Rioja..........................	R. Ocampo.
Mendoza..........................	H. Civit.
Salta.............................	P. Sanavria.
San Juan..........................	M. Gómez.
San Luis..........................	L. L. Quiroga.
Santa Fé..........................	S. Bayo.
Santiago..........................	A. Ibarra.
Tucuman..........................	B. Lopez.

In the estimated budget for 1875, the various items of revenue and expenditure stand as in the following tables :

REVENUE.

Import duties.............................	$14,900,000
Additional duties.........................	3,596,000
Export duties.............................	2,300,000
Additional duties.........................	1,300,000
Public warehouse fees....................	800,000
Stamped paper............................	430,000
Post-Office...............................	200,000
Telegraphs................................	110,000
Dividend of Central Argentine Railway Co...	116,620
Rio Cuarto and Port Ruiz Railways.........	130,000
Interest on Varela loan fund...............	100,000
Light-dues................................	80,000
Sundries..................................	234,373
	$23,996,893

EXPENDITURE.

Finance :	
Interest on public debt..................	$7,762,229
Customs officials, etc...................	1,516,179
Discounting bills........................	500,000
Contaduria...............................	131,632
Salaries, etc............................	243,209
Interior :	
Post-Office..............................	610,789
Congress.................................	493,400
Immigration..............................	400,224
Public works, railways, etc..............	809,428
Telegraphs...............................	256,560
Provincial subsidies.....................	225,000
Engineers' department....................	91,800
Gran Chaco government....................	42,000
Public salaries, etc.....................	190,128

Expenditure brought forward.............. $13,297,578

Army and Navy:
Army.................................... 4,684,472
Navy.................................... 302,781
Indians................................. 223,556
Extra appropriations.................... 544,000

Justice, Public Worship, and Public Instruction:
Federal judges.......................... 166,512
Bishops and churches.................... 289,924
Public instruction...................... 1,661,763
Observatory............................. 39.140
Free libraries.......................... 22,776

Foreign Affairs:
Foreign office.......................... 25,716
Legations, etc., abroad................. 22,148

$21,348,366

The liberal appropriations for public works, public instruction, telegraphs, and the Post-Office Department, as they appear in the first table, are unequivocal signs of the financial prosperity of the country; but it should be observed that the Post-Office and telegraphs are still a heavy item of expense to the Government, inasmuch as they cost $867,349, and yield but $310,000. In the high estimated cost of the Post-Office, $610,789, are comprised the new Buenos Ayres Post-Office, and some new offices in the interior. The Central Argentine Railway dividend on 17,000 shares held by the Government makes up two-thirds of the sum required as guarantee; but since May, 1872, the line has paid no dividend, although there has been no interruption in the payment of the guarantee. The Rio Cuarto, Gualeguay, and Port Ruiz lines are not estimated to do more than cover expenses in 1875. The item light-dues, in the revenue table, is a new tax of six cents per ton for sea-going and one cent per ton for coasting vessels, to be collected commencing from January, 1875. It is presumed that this tax will produce upward of $120,000 per annum. It is also proposed to derive some $60,-000 from dock-fees, at the rate of ten cents per ton on all merchandise landed at the Boca.

The interest on the public debt represents more than one-third of the total expenditure; the army and navy department stands for somewhat less than one-fourth, in spite of an increase of $22,868, and a proposed appropriation of $48,000 for the purchase of army stores; and the expenses of the foreign department do not amount to one hundredth of the national outlay, notwithstanding the establishment of two new legations, one in Peru and the other in Bolivia. The collection of customs costs 7 per cent.

The annexed table shows the growth of the revenue in the course of the ten years, 1863-'73, as compared with that of the Chilian revenue:

YEARS.	Argentine Revenue.	Chilian Revenue.
1863	$6,478,683	$6,700,659
1864	7,005,328	6,574,918
1865	8,295,071	7,301,043
1866	9,568,554	6,197,111
1867	12,046,287	9,756,888
1868	12,496,126	10,694,974
1869	12,676,680	11,484,806
1870	14,833,905	11,587,781
1871	12,683,155	11,681,032
1872	18,172,379	13,843,000
1873	20,160,380	15,392,557

The annual salaries of Argentine officials are expressed in the subjoined table:

President	$20,000	Chief of Agricultu-	
Vice-President	10,000	ral Department..	$8,000
Cabinet minister	9,000	Envoy ext'rdinary.	12,000
Sub-secretary	2,500	Sec'y of legation	3,750
Archbishop	5,000	Receiver of customs	5,000
Bishop	3,500	Captain of port	5,000
Canon	1,100	Admiral	2,500
Federal Judge	8,500	Colonel	2,400
Sectional " $3,000 to 6,000		Lieutenant-colonel.	1,400
Brigadier-general	3,250	Major	1,000
General	3,000	Captain	750
Senator	3,500	Lieutenant	500
Deputy	3,500	Rector of National	
Postmaster-general	3,750	College	1,600
Inspector of Tele-		Professor.. $1,050 to	1,350
graphs	3,750	Navy-captain	1,200
Chief of Engineer		Army-surgeon	3,000
Department	5,000	Port doctor. $1,250 to	3,000

The national debt amounted in January, 1874, to $71,031,081.50, comprising two branches, namely: the home debt, $20,933,976.50, and the foreign debt, $50,097,105.

The items of the home debt stood as follows:

	Emissions.	Paid off.	Balance.
Buschenthal	$2,674,823 50	$1,007,059	$1,667,764 50
National bonds	21,714.000 00	3,968,388	17,746,212 00
Bonds & bridges.	1,248,000 00	86,000	1,162,000 00
National Bank	358,000 00	....	358.000 00
Total	$25,995,423 50	$5,061,447	$20,933,976 50

In the course of eleven years interest was paid to the amount of $8,853,924.

The following table sets forth the elements of the foreign debt:

London loan of 1826.................. $8,850,500
   "   " of 1865.................. 11,045,500
   "   " of 1871.................. 28,443,490
Foreign claims...................... 1,757,615

Total........................... $50,097,105

Notwithstanding this heavy indebtedness—little less than $35 for each inhabitant of the republic—Argentine stocks, within a very few years, reached par, for the first time it is true, on the London exchange.

The subjoined table presents a view of the distribution of foreign capital in public debts and joint-stock companies in the Argentine Confederation:

CENTRAL GOVERNMENT.

Riestra loan, 1865 .... £2,138,000
Public works. 1871................ 5,716,100
Hard dollar loan, 1872........... 1,224,000
                                          £9,078,100

BUENOS AYRES GOVERNMENT.

Six per cent. loan, 1824....... £819,400
Three per cent. loan, 1824....... 888,200
Six per cent. loan, 1870....... 1,001,800
Six per cent. loan, 1873.......... 2,040,800
                                          4,750,200

ENTRE-RIOS GOVERNMENT.

Seven per cent. loan, 1872.... 214,900

SANTA FÉ GOVERNMENT.

Seven per cent. loan, 1874................... 300,000

Total amount due on March 1, 1874... £14,343,200

By reference to the table given above of the estimated budget for 1875, it will be observed that of the $23,996,893 of revenue, no less than $22,596,000 are derived from the customs department; that is to say, from export and import duties, and warehouse fees or storage. It appears, from official returns, that the province of Buenos Ayres stands for 82 per cent. of that branch of the revenue; Santa Fé, for 11 per cent.; Entre-Rios, for 5 per cent., and the remaining eleven provinces, for 2 per cent.

Books, paper, printing materials and apparatus, plants, fruits, ice, tobacco (for sheep), gold, silver, church utensils, etc., scientific instruments, steamboat machinery, machinery for new industries, furniture, and immigrants' baggage and other effects, are admitted into the republic free of duty. Ploughs, coal, iron, lumber, salt, silk, wrought silver or gold, and steam thrashing and reaping machines, pay a duty of 15 per cent. *ad valorem.* Precious stones pay 8 per cent. *ad valorem.* All other commodities pay 25 per cent. *ad valorem.* On wines, etc., from Europe, an allowance of 10 per cent. is made for leakage. Hides, sheep-skins, wool, beef, tallow, feathers, and bone-ash, pay an export duty of 6 per cent. *ad valorem.* All other articles exported are free of duty.

In the budget for 1874, the revenue is set down at $20,432,000, and the expenditure at $23,421,392, the deficit of $2,989,392 being covered by treasury bills.

In 1873 there was a surplus of nearly $5,-000,000, the revenue having been considerably greater, and the expenditure less, than the estimates. The revenue for that year was in advance of that of 1872 by $2,044,852.

The municipal revenue and expenditure of Buenos Ayres City were as follows in 1873:

REVENUE.

Weights and licenses.................	$189,059 40
Street-lighting........................	141,379 24
Markets............................	48,840 00
Funerals and graves.................	21,337 20
Abattoirs..........................	14,699 96
Hackney-coach stands...............	21,220 00
Fines, fees, etc.....................	39,576 20
Total...................	$431,112 00

EXPENDITURE.

Hospitals...........................	$89,654 33
Scavengers..........................	134,397 60
Free schools........................	68,596 64
Prisons, Board of Health, etc........	112,516 36
Public works........................	137,370 48
Lighting, etc.......................	124,200 60
Total...................	$659,736 00
Deficit.................	$238,624 00

The army of the republic consists of 9,000 regulars, and 150,000 National Guards; in all, 159,000 men. The regulars are, for the most part, stationed on the Indian frontiers at Mendoza, Rio Quinto, Rojas, Azul, etc.; and there is a small number garrisoned at the national capital. Of the National Guards, 40,000 are in the province of Buenos Ayres.

The navy is composed of a few old steamers, and a small number of iron-clads of recent construction.

Through the unremitting energy of ex-President Sarmiento, and the zealous coöperation of Dr. Avellaneda, then Minister of Public Instruction, and now President of the Republic, education is in a very prosperous condition. The number of public schools has

almost doubled since 1868. According to official returns, there are 1,645 of these schools in the fourteen provinces, with an aggregate attendance of 103,000—the largest, in proportion to the population, in South America. The census of 1869 registered 312,011 individuals, or one-fourth of the adult population, who could read and write.

The figures given above for the agregate attendance at the schools include 400 youths receiving education at the national colleges.

A prize of $10,000, offered by Congress to any province one-tenth of whose population should attend school, has been successively awarded to Mendoza and San Juan.

There are 120 free libraries in the republic, exclusive of the State Library and the *Biblioteca Nacional* in Buenos Ayres. The sum of $22,776 is appropriated for their support.

Although the civil war in the province of Entre-Rios has sensibly checked the general prosperity, its hurtful influence has by no means extended to the foreign commerce of the nation, which is rapidly increasing, both in imports and exports, from year to year.

The trade with the various countries in 1873 is shown in the subjoined table:

COUNTRIES.	Imports.	Exports.
Belgium	$2,967,586	$13,891,508
Brazil....................	2,968,953	769,464
Chili....................	1,444,182	2,365,475
England.................	19,344,143	9,894,007
France..................	18,255,138	8,677,819
Germany.................	3,228,015	449,557
Holland.................	1,611,616	226,204
Italy....................	3,784,384	1,487,925
Spain...................	2,952,600	1,231,697
United States............	5,167,616	3,032,949
Uruguay.................	2,735,299	992,949
Other countries..........	1,999,341	2,100,515
Total.....	$66,458,873	$45,122,105

In regard to the balance of trade, there was a marked and progressive improvement from 1870 to 1872, viz.:

YEARS.	Imports.	Exports.	Ratio.
1870............	$46,624,776	$26,753,203	As 9 to 5
1871............	39,398,000	23,442,543	" 5 to 3
1872............	60,229,143	45,743,192	" 4 to 3

(The decline in 1871 is to be attributed to the yellow fever, which prevailed at Buenos Ayres in the early months of that year.)

But, on reviewing the trade of 1872 and 1873, a difference of 33½ per cent. in the imports over the exports is observed:

ARTICLES EXPORTED.	Quantities.	Value.
Wool...................	363,725,000 lbs.	$38,530,000
Tallow.................	205,902,000 "	12,872,000
Ox and cow hides.........	5,661,000 "	12,322,000
Horse-hides, bones, metals, etc..................		12,322,000
Sheepskins,..............	123,000,000 "	9,916,000
Jerked-beef.............	181,300,000 "	4,120,000
Total.................		$90,082,090
Imports for the two years.......		$121,093,900
Excess of imports..............		$30,011,810

England and France stand foremost among the countries exporting to the Argentine Republic, but the imports from the first, in the first five months of 1874, showed a decline of no less than 50 per cent. as compared with the corresponding period of the year before:

ARTICLES.	Value in 1873.	Value in 1874.
Cotton fabrics..............	$2,186,235	$1,197,925
Woolen "	582,175	238,805
Linen "	228,490	107,380
Clothing....................	654,890	257,520
Hardware..................	488,705	274,670
Total................	$4,090,495	$2,076,300

The principal imports from the United States are lumber (70,000,000 feet in 1873), kerosene-oil, lard, starch, marine stores, agricultural implements, street and railway cars, hardware, and tobacco; and the trade is decidedly on the increase; but, until direct steam communication is established between the two countries, the commercial exchanges must of necessity remain restricted.

Belgium takes the largest quantity of Argentine produce, most of the wool being sent to Antwerp; next in order is Great Britain, which, like the United States (but more extensively), receives hides and tallow; then comes France, taking sheepskins, partly in exchange for fancy wares, silks, wines, etc.; the jerked-beef goes to Brazil and Cuba; and live cattle are driven over the Andes into Chili.

Wool, hides, jerked-beef, and tallow, are the staple articles of export. The farms of the province of Buenos Ayres alone have an aggregate stock of 60,000,000 sheep, yielding some 200,000,000 pounds of wool annually, which is in advance of the total clip of Australia. The farming stock of the fourteen provinces is estimated at 15,000,000 horned cattle, 4,000,000 horses, and 80,000,000 sheep, valued at $150,000,000 approximately, and yielding in exported produce about $45,000,000 per annum.

The exports to the United States in the year ending September 30, 1873, were as follows:

ARTICLES.	Quantities.	Value.
Dry ox and cowhides...	388,177	$1,989,454 00
Salted ox and cowhides.	1,000	7,241 00
Horse-hides.............	100	257 00
Wool....................	8,237 bales.	1,089,406 00
Sheep skins...........	2,975 "	409,515 00
(loose)......	74,719	89,992 00
Horse-hair............	660 bales.	204,324 00
Goat-skins...........	581 "	220,532 00
Nutria-skins..........	170 "	87,203 00
Water-hog skins......	15,376	3,488 00
Deer-skins.............	18,600	7,237 00
Feathers...............	203 cases.	133,187 00
Horns	381,076	33,293 00
Hide-cuttings	320 bales.	16,917 00
Bone-ash...............	636 tons. }	15,491 00
Shin-bones (loose).....	94,065 }	
Tallow.................	12 hhds.	516 00
Junk....................	1,137 tons. }	26,747 00
Rags...................	74 bales. }	
Sundries...............	....	7,774 32
Total value........	....	$4,392,574 32

There are thirteen lines of steamers which ply regularly between Buenos Ayres and European ports, viz.:

Lines.	No. of Steamers.
Royal Mail (British)........................	6
Lamport & Holt (British)....................	26
Glasgow....................................	2
Belgian....................................	12
French....................................	25
Genoa....................................	12
Hamburg..................................	5
Total number of steamers...............	88

Rosario, now the second city in importance in the republic, with respect to population, geographical position, commerce, and industry, has fairly entered upon a career of prosperity not equaled by any town in the Southern Continent. It is the natural key to the whole interior north of the province of Buenos Ayrès to the Bolivian frontier, and west of the Paraná to the Chilian Andes. Although 350 miles from the ocean, it can be reached by the largest vessels, which can moor close to the town, and are discharged and reloaded with great facility. The Central Argentine Railway, opened to traffic between this place and Córdoba in 1870, and shortly to be completed to Tucuman, was the first element of good fortune for Rosario, and the feature mainly instrumental in placing it in direct contact with the Atlantic world.

The direct foreign commerce for this port in the three years 1870-'72, is officially reported as follows:

YEARS.	Exports.	Imports.
1870......................	$1,402,124	$4,661,793
1871......................	1,841,774	6,541,990
1872......................	2,756,001	7,181,726

From the foregoing statistics it is seen that both exports and imports have wellnigh doubled in the course of the triennium referred to. The following table presents the direct foreign shipping movement (including entries and clearances) for the same period:

YEARS.	Steamers.	Sailing-Vessels.
1870......................	27,832 tons.	51,100 tons.
1871......................	103,490 "	51,534 "
1872......................	159,200 "	71,009 "

The value of the trade between Rosario and other Argentine ports, in 1872, was $6,498,287, of which $3,629,531 were for imports; the carrying was accomplished by 1,372 vessels entered, with an aggregate of 111,797 tons, and 1,379 cleared, with 117,990 tons. These vessels are small craft manned and owned by Italians, and sailing under the national colors; and packet-steamers, one of which, the Edward Everett, flies the United States flag, by special permission from the Argentine Government.

Railway interests are fast advancing in the Argentine Republic; the following lines are already open to public traffic:

Lines.	Length in Miles.
Buenos Ayres Western, to Chivilcoy	101½
Branch to Lobos	44
Buenos Ayres Northern, to Tigre	20
Buenos Ayres Great Southern, to Dolores	130
Branch to Las Flores	75
Central Argentine, Rosario to Córdoba	246
Villa Maria to Rio Cuarto	82
Buenos Ayres to Ensenada	37
East Argentine, Concordia to Federacion	36
Total	769

The lines expressed below are in process of construction:

Lines.	Length in Miles.
Buenos Ayres to Rosario	185
Branch to Rojas, Pergamino, etc.	240
Buenos Ayres to Fort Campana	40
Central Northern, Córdoba to Tucuman	333
Andine, Rio Cuarto, to Rio Quinto	76
East Argentine, Federacion to Caseros	55
Western, Chivilcoy to Bragado	30
Total	1,262

Most of these are to be finished by 1876, and all of them in 1877.

Of the projected or conceded lines, the following are the principal:

Lines.	Length in Miles.
Transandine, Buenos Ayres to Mendoza, San Juan, and Valparaiso (about)	900
Bragado and Planchon to Chili	650
Rioja to Copiapó (Chili)	300
Totoralejos to Rioja (branch of Great Northern)	200
Paraná to Concepcion	155
Santa Fé to Swiss Colonies	17
Great Southern, Las Flores to Azul and Tandil	130
Corrientes to Mercedes	138
Caseros to Mercedes	91
Bahia Blanca to Tandil	140
Lobos line, Las Heras to 25 de Mayo	75
Total	2,796

By far the most important line in the whole republic, and one of the most so in the South American Continent, will be the International Railway, 935 miles long (or 840 exclusive of the branch from Mendoza to San Juan), as it will open up much-needed means of communication between the chief producing centres of the interior and the ports of Valparaiso and Buenos Ayres, passing Santa Rosa on the Chilian side of the Andes, and bringing Buenos Ayres and Valparaiso within from forty to sixty hours' transit of each other. The gauge is to be 39½ inches, as on the Tucuman line; the concession has already been obtained by Clark & Co. (who so successfully established the Transandine Telegraph); and their estimate of the cost is $29,325,000, being at the rate of $25,000 per mile from Buenos Ayres to San Juan, and $50,000 per mile across the Andes. This estimate would appear extremely moderate if compared with the $27,000,000 expended on the railway from Vera Cruz to Mexico, but 263¾ miles in length, though presenting perhaps greater difficulties for the engineers to surmount than the Argentine and Chilian route. The steepest grade, says Mr. Clark, by the Uspallata Pass would be 1 in 25 for a short distance, and a tunnel nearly two miles long would have to be opened through hard rock; by the Patos route, two tunnels and a viaduct would be necessary; so the contractors prefer the first route. The fare from Buenos Ayres to Valparaiso would be $50, or one-fourth the passage by steamer; and the contractors' estimate of the annual passenger traffic on the line is:

	Receipts.
Through-passengers (10,000)	$500,000
Way-passengers (40,000)	200,0.0
Total receipts	$700,000

The Argentine share in the cost of the line would be somewhere about four times that of the Chilian share. The guarantee on the total cost of construction is 7 per cent.

There are now 4,146 miles of telegraph-wires in the republic, 2,618 of which are government property; and extra wires from the capital to Córdoba and Santa Fé were contracted for at $75,000, the work to be completed by the end of 1874. The messages transmitted in 1872 reached the number of 181,773, the receipts being $78,528; and in 1873 they numbered only 170,823, but the receipts were larger by $3,300. The returns for the first quarter of 1874 were nearly double those of the year preceding. The uniform rate is 25 cents per message of 20 words, on the government lines. The line from Montevideo to the Brazilian frontier being completed, and the submarine cable between Lisbon and Pernambuco successfully laid, the Argentine Republic is now connected by telegraph with the old continent.

The returns for the Post-Office Department were as follows for the two years expressed:

ITEMS.	1872.	1873.
Letters, newspapers, etc.	5,769,966	6,787,430
Receipts	$150,380	$173,108
Expenses	$189,492	$211,459

The new general post-office, at a cost of $90,000, is to be completed in March, 1875.

A postal treaty with Brazil was ratified on December 26, 1873.

The insurrection in Entre-Rios up to December, 1873, had undergone no sensible modification, nor was it deemed probable that the spirit of rebellion could be permanently crushed until the Government should resolve to dispatch an adequate force to the disturbed province. This decisive step was ultimately taken, and Colonel Gainza, at the head of a powerful army, completely overthrew Jordan's troops, then mustering about 6,000 horse and foot, with eight pieces of cannon. The rebel chief narrowly escaped capture, all his artillery fell into the hands of the Government troops, and the number of the killed was estimated at 1,000. Thus ended a petty struggle which, had prompt measures been adopted, might have been terminated immediately after it began, but which indecision permitted to be prolonged until a series of futile attempts to bring it to a close had cost the country no less a sum than $16,000,000. Industry, in the mean time, was not interrupted within the province; and the value of the wool, hides, lime, and other produce locked up in the interior, and released only upon the reëstablishment of tranquillity, was estimated at $7,500,000. According to report, the principal officers who had served under Jordan tendered their submission to the national Government after the defeat. Gainza was rewarded with immediate promotion to the rank of general.

The most important event of the year was the electioneering campaign, which was to decide who should succeed Señor Sarmiento in the executive office. The three candidates were Mitre, Alsina, and Avellaneda: the first had already been President of the Republic, was brigadier-general in the army, and had been intrusted with diplomatic missions to Brazil, particularly after the termination of the Paraguayan War, in all which capacities he had gained much popularity; the second was at the time Vice-President, and had been Governor of Buenos Ayres; and the third, an able statesman and Minister of Public Instruction, was universally esteemed as the stanch friend of education. Shortly before the elections, Señor Alsina retired from the contest, and devoted his energies in favor of Señor Avellaneda, who was ultimately elected, and was proclaimed by Congress as the fortunate candidate on August 6th. The elections passed over with relatively little disturbance; but on October 1st a rebellion broke out at Buenos Ayres, headed by General Mitre, who urged, as a plea for the step, that fraud had been practised at the polls. The republic was declared in a state of siege, the National Guards called to arms, and some battles fought with varying success. Numerous arrests were made; Mitre tendered his resignation as general, and received the support of the navy; the press was clamorous for the confiscation of the property of the insurgents; commercial houses were closed, and commercial credit postponed by a Government decree; newspapers were suspended; banks closed; wealthy citizens fled to Montevideo, and foreigners hurried to their consulates for passports, to protect them from the universal conscription. The Government demanded of the Chambers an appropriation of $2,000,000 to defray the expenses of the war; and, to enhance the general excitement, tidings were received that Entre-Rios was in revolt, and that Jordan, at the head of the insurgents was hurrying toward Buenos Ayres to join Mitre. All public works were stopped, and thousands thrown out of employment. On November 6th the insurgent flotilla was near Buenos Ayres, but no action of importance had taken place. Mitre was the favorite candidate in Buenos Ayres, and the inhabitants of that province were determined to have him replaced in power.

About the middle of December Mitre declined to pursue the contest, and came to terms with the new administration. This ter-

minated the civil war. President Avellaneda entered upon the executive functions on the 12th of October.

ARIZONA. This Territory was separated from that of New Mexico, and organized by act of Congress passed February 24, 1863. No complete survey of the Territory has been made. Its area is estimated at 113,000 square miles, and the Territory contained, according to the census of 1870, 9,658 inhabitants, exclusive of Indians. Tucson, in Pima County, is the capital, and largest town. Arizona City, in Yuma County, is a prosperous business place, situated at the junction of the Gila and Colorado Rivers. Prescott, the former capital, is situated in Central Arizona, and is the headquarters of the Military Department of Arizona. The number of Indians is about 32,000, of whom about 5,000 are on reservations, and the remainder are nomadic. Many of these Indians are friendly to the whites, but the greater number are hostile. Of the friendly Indians the Pimas and the Maricopas rank first in numbers and civilization. They occupy a reservation on the Gila River, about 200 miles east of Arizona City. The Papagos live south of the Gila, along the line of Sonora. The Mohaves and the Yumas live along the Colorado, the Utes on the Upper Colorado, and the Moquis and Navajos in Northeastern Arizona. These tribes are engaged in stock-raising and agriculture. Of the hostile Indians, the Apaches are the most powerful and warlike. They comprise several tribes, distributed over the greater portion of Middle and Eastern Arizona. All of the hostile tribes are becoming more peaceable than formerly.

The mountains of Southern and Central Arizona are nearly all mineral-bearing, and contain lodes of gold, silver, copper, and lead. Mining will doubtless constitute one of the leading industries of the Territory. But this source of wealth has not been developed to any considerable extent, owing to the lack of men and capital. What is most needed in the Territory is a large immigration of good, sturdy, industrious men with their families. Reports from the Territory say that such men can find or make plenty of work, at about the following wages: Blacksmiths, per day, $4 to $5, and board; carpenters, $5 to $8 per day; cooks, per month, with board, $40 to $60; farm-hands, with board, $30 to $60 per month; herders, $40 to $50 per month, and board; masons and bricklayers, per day, $5 to $8; miners, $3 to $5; laborers, $2.50 to $3; teamsters, $50 to $60 per month, and board.

The prices of provisions are moderate, being reported about as follows, at Prescott: Flour, $10 per hundred; bacon, 30 cts. per lb.; ham, 30 cts.; beans, 10 cts.; coffee, 60 cts. to $1; sugar, 25 to 35 cts.; beef, 20 to 30 cts.; pork, 25 cts.; mutton, 15 cts.; venison and antelope, 20 cts.; potatoes, by the ton, 3 and 4 cts. per lb., but retailing at 5 cts. per lb.; beets, turnips, onions, and cabbage, 5 cts. per lb. Lumber is

$40 to $60 per M., according to quality. Board is $10 per week.

Persons desiring to reach Arizona from the Atlantic States, and to settle in Northern or Central Arizona, will find the road *via* Albuquerque, New Mexico, the best and shortest. Grass, wood, and water, are plenty, except in one or two places; but, with a little care, no trouble need be encountered.

The distances are as follows: From Granada, or Las Animas, Colorado (railroad towns), to Prescott, about 615 miles; from St. Louis to either of these places by railroad is 850 miles. Persons who may desire to go to the southern portion of the Territory, can take the old overland road, *via* Mesilla, to Tucson, which is 835 miles from Trinidad, Colorado. Both of the above are excellent natural roads.

Immigrants coming from the Pacific coast to Northern or Central Arizona will find two roads from San Bernardino, California: one *via* Hardyville and the Hualpai mines to Prescott; the other *via* Ehrenberg and Wickenburg to Prescott or Phœnix, the chief town of Salt River Valley. The distance from San Bernardino to Prescott by either of these routes is about 400 miles. On the road *via* Ehrenberg is a semi-weekly line of stages. The fare from San Bernardino to Prescott is $75, currency. Immigrants desiring to go to the southern part of the Territory can take the road from San Diego, *via* Yuma, to Tucson, on which there is a tri-weekly line of stages. The fare to Tucson is $90; the distance about 450 miles.

The Colorado Steam Navigation Company run a line of steamers from San Francisco to the mouth of the Colorado River, a steamer leaving San Francisco every twenty days. River-steamers run up the river to Yuma, Ehrenberg, Mohave, and Hardyville. Fare from San Francisco to Yuma: Cabin, $40; steerage, $25. Most of the freight comes this way.

Freight by wagons from Los Angeles to Prescott, *via* Ehrenberg or *via* Hardyville, is 12 cents per pound; the same from San Diego to Tucson, *via* Yuma.

There are eight military posts in the Territory, as follows: Fort Whipple, and department headquarters, near Prescott; Camp Verde, 30 miles east of Prescott; Camp Mohave, on the Colorado River; Camp McDowell, on the junction of the Verde and Salt Rivers, some 20 miles above Phœnix; Camp Lowell, near Tucson; Camp Bowie, in Apache Pass; Camp Apache, 200 miles northeast of Tucson; and Camp Grant, at the foot of the Graham Mountains.

Lines of telegraph connect Prescott, Wickenburg, Phœnix, Maricopa, Wells, Florence, Tucson, Yuma, and other points, with San Diego, California, and it is believed that there will soon be direct telegraphic communication with points in Utah and New Mexico.

The climate of Arizona is mild and generally healthful. In the southern part of the Terri-tory the temperature ranges from 34° to 118° Fahr. The atmosphere is dry, and this region is singularly free from malarious diseases. Snow falls in Central Arizona, but, excepting in the higher mountains, disappears in a few hours. The temperature in summer rarely exceeds 90° and seldom falls below zero in winter. Rain falls mainly in the months of July and August, but there are frequent showers in April and May, as well as in the winter months. The climate of Arizona is said to be highly beneficial to those afflicted with bronchial or lung diseases.

The Territory has special advantages for stock-raising and the production of wool; for, not only is the climate favorable, but on the hills and mountain-sides a rich and abundant pasturage is found.

Arizona has three newspapers: the *Sentinel*, a weekly, published in Yuma; the *Citizen*, also a weekly, issued at Tucson; and the *Miner*, daily and weekly, published at Prescott. The government is administered by a Governor, Secretary, Treasurer, and Auditor, who are appointed by the President of the United States. The Legislature and Delegate to Congress are elected by the people. The judicial power is vested in a Supreme Court, consisting of three judges, appointed by the President, and probate courts. The Supreme Court holds one session annually, at Tucson. The present Governor is Hon. A. K. P. Safford.

ARKANSAS. In no State in the Union, excepting perhaps Louisiana, have there been such stirring events and such public excitement during 1874 as in Arkansas; and in no State, with the exception named, have public affairs called for such earnest consideration on the part of the General Government, or claimed a larger share of public attention throughout the country. An appeal to arms was made to decide a determined contest for the Executive office, which had been pending for nearly two years. This was followed by a Constitutional Convention, called under extraordinary circumstances, and which in a brief period caused the entire organic law of the State to be changed, and led to another contest between opposing factions for possession of the State government.

The contest between Brooks and Baxter for the governorship had its origin in the bitter political campaign of 1872; and, in order to present the facts of the controversy more intelligibly, it will be necessary to trace the record briefly from that time.

In the spring of 1872 a division in the Republican State Committee led to the calling of two conventions, and the nomination of two State tickets. One of these conventions nominated Joseph Brooks for Governor, and declared in favor of Greeley and Brown, and the Cincinnati platform; the other, after indorsing the Administration of President Grant, chose Elisha Baxter as their candidate for Governor. Owing to this division in the Republican ranks, the Democrats nominated no

State ticket, but favored the election of the Brooks wing. The election was held on the 5th of November. On the 6th of January, 1873, the General Assembly convened, and at once canvassed the returns of the recent election, pursuant to section 19 of Article VI. of the constitution, which provides:

That the returns of every election for Governor, Lieutenant-Governor, Secretary of State, Treasurer, Auditor, Attorney-General, and Superintendent of Public Instruction, shall be sealed up and transmitted to the seat of Government by the returning-officers, and directed to the presiding officer of the Senate, who, during the first week of the session, shall open and publish the same in presence of the members then assembled. The person having the highest number of votes shall be declared elected, but, if two or more shall have the highest and an equal number of votes for the same office, one of them shall be chosen by joint vote of both Houses. Contested elections shall likewise be determined by both Houses of the General Assembly in such manner as is or may hereafter be prescribed by law.

As it appeared that 41,784 votes had been cast for Elisha Baxter, and 38,673 for Joseph Brooks, the former was declared by the General Assembly to be the duly-elected Governor of the State, and was at once installed in the office. Meantime, on the 4th of January, Mr. Brooks, alleging that fraud had been practised at the polls by the supporters of Baxter, and that a majority of the legal votes had been cast in favor of himself, petitioned the Circuit Court of the United States to enjoin Baxter from exercising the functions of Governor. A similar suit was also brought before the same tribunal by William M. Harrison, who had been a candidate on the Brooks ticket for Associate Justice of the Supreme Court against Marshall L. Stevenson, his successful opponent, on the Baxter ticket. A decision was rendered in this case on the 13th of January, to the effect that a court of the United States had no jurisdiction in the premises. As the facts and principles of law were the same in this as in Brooks's case, no further proceedings were had in the latter.

On the 19th of April Brooks applied to the Legislature for permission to contest the election of Baxter, but his petition was rejected by a vote of 63 to 9. Application was then made, June 2d, by the Attorney-General, in behalf of Brooks, to the Supreme Court of the State for a writ of quo warranto, to try the validity of Baxter's title to the office of Governor, which, it was alleged, he had usurped. After elaborate arguments by counsel, this application was denied by the court, which held that, "under the constitution the determination of the question, as to whether a person exercising the office of Governor is duly elected or not, is vested exclusively in the General Assembly of the State, and neither this nor any other State court has jurisdiction to try a suit in relation to such contest, be the mode or form what it may; whether at the suit of the Attorney-General, or on the relation of a claimant through him, or by an individual

alone claiming a right to the office. Such issue should be made before the General Assembly. It is their duty to decide, and no other tribunal can determine the question."

Brooks now brought suit against Baxter in the Circuit Court of Pulaski County, under section 525 of the Civil Code of Arkansas, which provides that, "whenever a person usurps an office or franchise to which he is not entitled by law, an action by proceedings at law may be instituted against him, either by the State or party entitled to the office or franchise, to prevent the usurper from exercising the office or franchise." His petition stated that he had received more than 45,000 votes for Governor, while less than 30,000 had been cast for Baxter, and prayed that the latter might be ousted as a usurper, and that the office of Governor, with $2,000 emoluments which had been received by Baxter, might be judicially awarded to himself.

It should also be recorded here that a similar suit, embodying the same facts and principles of law, was begun in the same court by Berry, who had been the candidate for State Auditor on the ticket with Brooks, against Wheeler, who had been declared elected by the General Assembly. But the Supreme Court, on the application of Wheeler, issued a writ of prohibition restraining the proceedings of the Circuit Court, on the ground that the latter had no jurisdiction. In pronouncing the opinion of the court, Chief-Justice McClure said: "As to all matters of contested election for the offices of Governor, Lieutenant-Governor, Secretary of State, Auditor, Treasurer, Attorney-General, and Superintendent of Public Instruction, I am of the opinion that it can only be had before the General Assembly."

Governor Baxter interposed a plea of want of jurisdiction in the Brooks suit, but, apprehending that a decision would be rendered in favor of his opponent at the October term, and that the latter would gain possession of the State government before an appeal could be taken to the Supreme Court, he sent a communication dated September 4, 1873, to the President of the United States, reciting the essential facts of the controversy, and asking that Federal troops be sent to Little Rock, "as the course of events may compel me to resort to the extreme remedy of martial law, as the only means by which an effectual stop can be put to the proceedings of those men who are now disturbing the peace and good order of the State." This application was refused by President Grant, on the ground that it was not made in accordance with the Constitution of the United States.

Nothing more was heard of the controversy till the spring of 1874. On the 15th of April, the Circuit Court of Pulaski County, in the absence of Governor Baxter's counsel, issued a judgment of ouster in favor of Brooks against Baxter. The former immediately took forcible possession of the Governor's office, and placed a strong guard around the State-House. The following dispatch was now sent to the President of the United States:

EXECUTIVE OFFICE, LITTLE ROCK, *April 15th.*
U. S. GRANT, *President, Washington, D. C.:*

Having been duly installed as Governor of Arkansas by the judgment of a court, I respectfully ask that the commanding officer of the arsenal be instructed to deliver the arms belonging to the State, now in his custody, or hold the same subject to my order. JAMES BROOKS.

Governor Baxter having established his headquarters at St. John's College, sent the following communication to Washington:

LITTLE ROCK, ARKANSAS, *April* 15, 1874.
To the President of the United States:

I have been advised by public rumor that in the State Circuit for this county, in a long-pending case brought by Joseph Brooks for the office of Governor of this State, a demurrer to the complaint was overruled and an immediate judgment of "ouster" against me given. This was done in the absence of counsel for me and without notice, and immediately thereafter the Circuit Judge adjourned his court. The claimant has taken possession of the State buildings and ejected me by force. I propose to take measures immediately to resume possession of the State property, and to maintain my authority as rightful Governor of the State. Armed men acting under this revolutionary movement are now in charge of the Government Armory and Capitol buildings. I deem it my duty to communicate this state of affairs to the President. I trust the revolutionary acts may be settled without bloodshed, and respectfully ask the support of the General Government in my efforts to maintain the rightful government of the State of Arkansas, and that the commander of the United States arsenal at this post be directed to sustain me in this direction. I respectfully request a reply to this communication at an early moment.

ELISHA BAXTER, Governor of Arkansas.

The application of Brooks for the State arms in the arsenal was refused by the President, who was not advised that Brooks's "right to hold the office of Governor has been fully and finally decided by the courts of Arkansas;" and on the same day the following communication was sent to Mr. Baxter:

DEPARTMENT OF JUSTICE, WASHINGTON, *April* 16th.
The Hon. ELISHA T. BAXTER, *Little Rock:*

I am instructed by the President to say, in answer to your dispatch to him of yesterday, asking for the support of the General Government to sustain you in the efforts to maintain the rightful government in the State of Arkansas, that in the first place your call is not made in conformity with the Constitution and laws of the United States; and in the second place, that as the controversy relates to your right to hold a State office, its adjudication, unless a case is made under the so-called Enforcement Act of Federal Jurisdiction, belongs to the State courts. If the decision of which you complain is erroneous, there appears to be no reason why it may not be reversed and a correct decision obtained from the Supreme Court.

GEORGE H. WILLIAMS, Attorney-General.

On the afternoon of the 16th Brooks issued the following proclamation:

EXECUTIVE OFFICE, LITTLE ROCK, *April* 16, 1874.
To the People of Arkansas:

As you will recollect, I was a candidate for the office of Governor at the November election of 1872.

That I received a majority of the votes cast for that office has never been denied, even by the friends of Elisha Baxter. I appealed to the Legislature and asked to be allowed to contest the election for the office of Governor, and my petition, at the instance and by the connivance of Elisha Baxter, who corruptly used his official patronage to bribe members of the Legislature, was rejected, and I was denied not only the right of petition which the Constitution guarantees to every citizen, but the right to have the question of election investigated and passed upon. The Attorney-General asked the Supreme Court for a writ of *quo warranto* against Elisha Baxter, for the purpose of compelling him to show by what warrant and authority he assumed to discharge the duties of the office of Governor. That tribunal declared it had no jurisdiction to hear and determine a contest for the office of Governor, and the cause was dismissed for want of jurisdiction.

I then commenced an action against Elisha Baxter, under the provisions of the code, in the manner prescribed by law for the recovery of the office and the salary received by Elisha Baxter during the time he wrongfully withheld the same from me. I served notice on Elisha Baxter that I would, at certain times and places named in said notices, take testimony in support of my claim. Elisha Baxter, for reasons best known to himself, neglected and failed to appear at the times and places mentioned, and treated the court proceedings with derision and contempt, openly boasting in public and private speeches and conversation that he would resist the execution of the judgment of any court of the State with the militia if it attempted to interfere with his discharge of the duties of the office of Governor. Notwithstanding his threats, I continued to take testimony and prosecute a suit for the purpose of asserting my own rights and vindicating your choice at the ballot-box. On yesterday the Circuit Court rendered a judgment in my favor for the office and the salary, and I at once took the oath of office and took possession of the same.

Elisha Baxter no longer holds the Executive office, and it is to be hoped that you will join your voice with mine, rejoicing that the man you chose for Governor has at last been duly installed into office. Being in office, it is but fair that I, to some extent, define my future policy, which the adherents of Elisha Baxter will no doubt misrepresent for the purpose of advancing their personal interests and gratifying their own ambition.

For my political tenets, I respectfully refer you to the platform of the Reform party, on which I was a candidate in 1872. From the principles therein enumerated I have not departed, and, God helping me, never will. No one man in the State has felt the power of ballot-box stuffers and political thimble-riggers to the extent that I have. I say to you that, so far as in me lies, the ballot-box and election machinery of the State shall never again be made an engine of fraud and oppression, as it was in 1872. This is a republican form of government, where the voice of the people should rule, and so far as I am concerned it shall rule from this time henceforth, and so long as I occupy the Executive chair every man shall have the free and undisturbed right to vote as to him shall seem best, and that vote once cast shall be counted as the man that cast it intended it should be.

Efforts no doubt will be made by designing men to convey the impression that it is the duty of the people to rally to the standard of a man who, no doubt, will claim he is Governor of Arkansas, who you all know was not elected, and who has no more right or claim to the office than any one of you has, for the purpose of placing that man again in the Executive office. I say frankly to you that all such attempts will lead to strife and bloodshed, for I shall resist and suppress the action of all mobs that may assemble together under the banner or at the call of

Elisha Baxter. No man in the State can regret strife and bloodshed more deeply than myself; but feeling as I do that self-government rather than self-aggrandizement is in the issue, I shall employ every means at my command to maintain its supremacy. Elisha Baxter forced me from the Legislature to the courts, and thus far I have patiently borne with the law's delay at all times, feeling that justice would be done me by the judgment of a court of competent jurisdiction. I am in the Executive office. When it is adjudicated that I am not there legally I will bow my head in silence to the decree of the court, be it what it may. The power that Elisha Baxter used to force me into the court I will use to make him respect and abide its decrees.

To one and all I say, keep quiet and pursue your different vocations. Your services are not needed at the capital to preserve either peace or good order. Should the time come when they will be needed, you will be notified in due time through the proper channel.

JOSEPH BROOKS, Governor of Arkansas.

Governor Baxter now began movements for regaining possession of the State government. On the evening of the 16th he issued the following proclamation, declaring martial law in Pulaski County:

Whereas, An armed rebellion exists in the county of Pulaski, against the State government, and it becomes necessary to employ all the force at my disposal to suppress it: therefore, by the authority vested in me by law, I hereby proclaim the existence of martial law within said county, and command all persons capable of military duty to assist in the putting down of the said rebellion. During the time that martial law shall thus prevail, every infringement of the right of peaceable and well-disposed persons will be severely punished by whomsoever it may be committed. The utmost respect shall be paid by all persons to citizens not in arms, and to their property, and to that of the Federal Government. In testimony whereof, I, Elisha Baxter, Governor of the State of Arkansas, do hereby set my hand, the private seal of said State being now not accessible to the Governor of the State. Done at Little Rock, this 15th day of April, 1874.

ELISHA BAXTER,
Governor of Arkansas and Commander-in-Chief.

Having issued this proclamation, the Governor marched from St. John's College with his force of about two hundred men, down into the heart of the city, and established his headquarters at the Anthony House. Guards were placed along the principal streets, completely surrounding the State-House with a cordon of sentinels. Baxter's forces, which were rapidly receiving additions from other counties, also took possession of the telegraph-office. The State-House was held by between one hundred and one-hundred and fifty men, who were well armed and had two cannon. Governor Baxter now issued the following proclamation to the people of the State:

EXECUTIVE OFFICE, }
LITTLE ROCK, *April* 16, 1874. }
To the People of Arkansas:

An insurrection, organized in the interest of certain parties disappointed in an attempt to secure the influence of the Executive for proposed frauds in the approaching election, has effected the seizure of the Capitol, and now attempts to usurp the functions of government. The momentary success of this insurrection, so far as regards the occupation of the building, has been owing to that security which

the political traditions of the American people give to legitimate government, in time of peace. The armed sentries and loaded cannon which, for the moment, support the usurpation within the precincts of the State-House, had not been deemed requisite to the maintenance of a recognized government; the unexpected and forcible occupation of the building could not, at the instant, be successfully resisted: aversion to unnecessary bloodshed has for a few hours withheld the arm of the State government from immediate vindication of its rights and dignity. Forbearance has seemed only to embolden the impudence of the handful of insurgents. Forbearance, therefore, is at an end.

General orders No. 1, from headquarters of the militia of Arkansas, of date correspondent with that of this proclamation, declares martial law in the county of Pulaski. It is due to the people of the State that the circumstances which have rendered necessary this course of action be published.

At the election of 1872, I was returned Governor of Arkansas. At a late stage of the session of the Legislature chosen at the same time, my opponent, Joseph Brooks, Esq., sought his sole, legitimate, and constitutional method of redress (had he been injured in the decision of the election), by an appeal to the representatives of the people. The appeal was summarily rejected.

Application was then made to the highest judicial authority of the State—the Supreme Court—for a writ of *quo warranto*, which should determine my right to the office of Governor. In that case, as in the suit instituted for the office of Auditor of State, the highest judicial tribunal of Arkansas decided that, under the supreme organic law of the State, the determination of the question of election of State officers is exclusively vested in the Legislature.

Public excitement was allayed. The State settled itself to quiet, under an administration which, I trust, has not been unfaithful to its professions, or obnoxious to the people.

Meantime, a proceeding had been instituted before a circuit court of a county for the possession of the office of Governor. I do not care, at present, to comment upon the question of authority of such a court to adjudicate a matter, from the decision of which the Supreme Court of the State had, upon constitutional grounds, not merely shrunk but affirmatively denied its own jurisdiction. The Pulaski Circuit Court did clandestinely assume upon a demurrer filed in court, but never submitted to the court for its action, to render judgment of ouster, against the officer who, for fifteen months, had exercised the functions of chief magistrate of the State. The judgment was rendered, upon the call of the contestant's attorney, in violation of the express agreement of counsel, that the case should not be taken up in the absence of the representatives of either party. It was rendered, therefore, in point of fact, without the knowledge, or even the suspicion, of the Governor or of his counsel.

In pursuance of a plot already matured, in anticipation of the decision of the Circuit Court, the conspirators—forgetting, in their haste, that *no writ of ouster had ever been issued*—betook themselves to the room where the Chief-Justice of the State (the sole dissenter from the decision of the Supreme Court in the matter) awaited them, by previous appointment; and then, armed with the Chief-Justice's attestation to Mr. Brooks's oath of office, proceeded forcibly to eject from the State-House the chief magistrate of the Commonwealth.

An appeal lies, of course, to the Supreme Court of the State. That Supreme Court has already, in a case involving the point at issue, determined that no court has the authority to decide the validity of election of any executive officer of the State. It need hardly be remarked that, pending an appeal, the effect of the judgment of the Circuit Court of Pulaski County is suspended, and that the undertaking to sustain the enforcement of that judgment, pending the appeal, is without color of law, or moral palliation.

The forcible ejection of the chief magistrate from the premises was followed by prearranged and prompt summons to armed desperadoes to bar all access to the State-House of its legitimate occupants. Mr. Brooks has issued a paper entitled a proclamation, in which he distinctly announces his intention of bloodshed.

The Executive of the State has but one obligation to perform—that to which he is bound alike by his duty as a citizen and his official oath. The authority of the law will be immediately and effectively asserted, peaceably, if it may be, but asserted in any event. The government proposes to occupy the Capitol. As Governor of Arkansas, I appeal to the people of the State to support the government of the State against shameless usurpation. Under the solemn obligations of my oath of office, I renew my promise to be true to them. I ask from them the support which they owe to their chief magistrate.

ELISHA BAXTER, Governor of Arkansas.

On the following day, April 17th, Captain Rose, being in command of the barracks at Little Rock, and having received instructions from Washington to "take no part in the political controversy in the State of Arkansas, unless it should be necessary to prevent bloodshed or collision of armed bodies," sent the following communication to Baxter, and a copy to Brooks.

HEADQUARTERS, LITTLE ROCK BARRACKS, }
LITTLE ROCK, *April* 17, 1874. }

SIR: I am informed by the United States Marshal of this district that there is danger of a collision between the forces under your command and those of certain forces under the command of Joseph Brooks. I therefore have the honor to enjoin upon you that you make no movement with your forces in any direction in the city of Little Rock, Arkansas, or its vicinity, with a view to bring about such a collision, or that may bring on such a collision, or to make any movement that may possibly bring about a collision with the United States troops under my command, or to impede any movement I may wish to make with the troops of my command to prevent the shedding of blood and the collision of armed forces.

Very respectfully, your obedient servant,

T. E. ROSE,
Captain 16th Infantry, commanding post.
General ELISHA BAXTER, commanding forces in the State of Arkansas.

Baxter at once replied that he would not advance his lines that night toward the enemy, and added, "I trust that your request or injunction does not extend to the prohibition on my part of any military operations." Brooks replied that he did not intend to move any portion of his command from the State-House grounds, and that his force would "only be used to repel any attack that may be made by the forces under the command of Elisha Baxter, having for its object the custody or control of the State-House and State-House grounds. Any and all such attacks will be resisted with all the force at my command." A communication was now addressed by the Mayor of Little Rock to Attorney-General Williams, asking that the officers in command of the arsenal be instructed "to aid the city police in making the arrest of men who are openly violating the law and setting the same at defiance." The

mayor added that with such aid he could preserve the peace of the city without being compelled to take sides with either of the contending factions, and wanted to know "if the Federal Government is powerless to protect the lives and property of twenty thousand inhabitants who are situated as we are." To this communication the Attorney-General sent the following reply:

DEPARTMENT OF JUSTICE, }
WASHINGTON, *April* 18, 1874. }

FREDERICK KRAMER, *Mayor of Little Rock, Ark.:*

You must be aware that the President cannot interfere in the domestic difficulties of a State, except in conformity with the Constitution and laws of the United States. He cannot recognize a call made upon him for military aid by the mayor of a city. He has instructed the officer commanding the United States troops at Little Rock to prevent bloodshed. That is all he can do under the existing circumstances. I will ask in answer to your inquiry whether the United States are powerless to protect 20,000 people situated as the citizens of Little Rock, if the people of Arkansas have not patriotism enough to allow a question as to who shall hold a State office to be settled peaceably and lawfully, and not bring upon their State the disgrace and ruin of civil war?

GEORGE H. WILLIAMS, Attorney-General.

A difficulty having arisen as to communications by mail and telegraph, since Baxter's forces held possession of the telegraph-office, and both contestants for the Executive office claimed the letters addressed to the Governor of Arkansas, the following instructions were issued to Postmaster Pollock and Captain Rose:

WASHINGTON, D. C., *April* 17, 1874.

Postmaster, Little Rock, Arkansas:

Letters addressed to Governor E. Baxter or Elisha Baxter, Governor, should be delivered to said Baxter. Letters addressed to Governor Brooks, or Brooks, Governor, should be delivered to said Brooks. Letters addressed "Governor of Arkansas," you will withhold until further orders.

JOHN A. J. CRESWELL, Postmaster-General.

EXECUTIVE MANSION, }
WASHINGTON, D. C., *April* 18, 1874. }

Colonel ROSE, *Commanding U. S. Troops, Little Rock, Arkansas.*

I have a dispatch from the Acting President of the Western Union Telegraph Company saying that Baxter's officers now inspect all messages at Little Rock before transmission, and will allow no messenger to pass out with any message for the Brooks party, whether from the United States officials or otherwise. Under these circumstances it will be seen that this company is unable at present to maintain the sanctity of telegraphic correspondence. While the Government takes no part in the unhappy state of affairs existing in Arkansas at this time, you will see that official dispatches of the Government, whether from the military or civil departments, are transmitted without molestation by either of the contestants for the gubernatorial chair. Report to the Secretary of War the situation of affairs. U. S. GRANT.

After Captain Rose had taken possession of the telegraph-offices in obedience to the above instructions, Governor Baxter sent the following dispatch to President Grant:

LITTLE ROCK, ARK., *April* 19, 1874.

To the President of the United States:

A few days since, in the absence of my counsel, and at a time wholly unexpected, the Circuit Judge of this county, a court of inferior jurisdiction, rendered judgment in favor of Mr. Brooks against me for the office of Governor of this State, and without notice to me or my counsel I was at once forcibly put out of my office, and that without any pretense of a writ being served on me. All that was done, too, after the Supreme Court of this State had twice decided that no court in the State had jurisdiction of the case at all, and the Legislature alone had jurisdiction. At once, on being ejected from office, I took steps to restore myself, to get possession of office, and to carry on the government. The people are coming to my aid, and are ready to restore me at once. In making this organization I am obstructed by the interference of United States troops in displacing my guards from the telegraph-office, and now it is apprehended that there will be further interference. Such interference breaks me down, and prevents any effort on my part to restore the State government and to protect the people in their rights. I beg of you to modify any order to the extent of such interference, and leave me free to act in this way to restore law and my place as the legitimate Governor of the State. Such interference does not leave me any chance to assert my claim to the office of Governor.

In the interests of peace and of these people who are flocking here to my support by hundreds, I beg of you to remove the United States troops back to the arsenal, and permit me to restore legitimate government by my own forces, which I will do promptly if the United States will not interfere. There is an armed insurrection against the legal State government here, and I call upon you to aid in suppressing it; but if you will not, then leave me free to act, and order the United States troops, without an hour's delay, to their own ground, and keep them out of my way. I have been thwarted and delayed thus long and, in fact, ejected from my office because of the fact that I had heretofore disbanded the militia of the State.

I make this earnest demand to repress insurrection and prevent domestic violence under my sense of duty to the Constitution and laws of the United States, as well as the State of Arkansas, and I rely confidently, as I have all the time, upon the assurance contained in your letter of September 15, 1873, to prevent the overthrow of my official authority by illegal and disorderly proceedings. An immediate answer is requested; otherwise bloodshed may be the result. ELISHA BAXTER,
Governor of the State of Arkansas.

On the following day application was made for Federal aid by Brooks, as follows:

LITTLE ROCK, ARK., April 20, 1874.
His Excellency U. S. GRANT, *President of the United States.*

SIR: I hereby inform you that one Elisha Baxter, a private citizen, pretending to be Governor of Arkansas, without warrant or authority of law, assumed to declare martial law in the capital county of the State, and to appoint a pretended military governor of the city of Little Rock, the seat of government; that he called out armed bodies of men for the avowed purpose of attacking and capturing the Capitol of the State by military force and installing himself as Governor of such State; that large bodies of armed men have assembled, and are continually assembling, under said Baxter's proclamation of martial law, and are in close proximity to the State-House, and have this day actually advanced on the State-House and confronted a body of Federal troops stationed in front of the State-House, under order from their commanding officer, acting under command to preserve the peace, and were only prevented from making the attack by the presence of Federal troops; that these armed bodies have seized and appropriated private property, and are hourly seizing and appropriating private property, without compensation; have conscripted and are continually conscripting private citizens, and compelling them to aid and abet them

in their insurrectionary purposes, and have seized and are daily seizing railroads in the State, and appropriating them to the same illegal and insurrectionary purposes; that there are armed bodies at this moment assembled within a few hundred yards of the State-House, and threaten an immediate attack upon it; that the Legislature adjourned *sine die* in April last; has not since been convened; is not now in session, and cannot be convened in time to prevent the threatened attack; that domestic violence now actually exists in this State and at the seat of government which the civil and military authorities under my control are powerless to prevent or suppress. Therefore I, Joseph Brooks, Governor of the State of Arkansas, in pursuance of the Constitution and laws of the United States, hereby make application to your Excellency to protect the State capital and the State of Arkansas against domestic violence and insurrection.

In testimony whereof I have hereunto set my hand and caused the great seal of the State to be affixed at Little Rock this 20th day of April, A. D. 1874.
JOSEPH BROOKS, Governor.
By the Governor:
EDWARD CURREY, Secretary of State *ad interim.*

Little Rock now had the appearance of a military camp. The troops on both sides were being constantly reënforced. Great excitement prevailed throughout the city, and business was almost entirely suspended. On the 21st a body of colored troops, under Colonel White, marched to the Metropolitan Hotel, where they were addressed by Governor Baxter and their commander. Amid the cheers which followed these speeches, a shot was fired from the crowd which had collected around, into the body of Baxter's adherents. This led to an indiscriminate firing on both sides, which resulted in the wounding of several persons. The disturbance was quelled by the Federal forces.

On the next day the following telegraphic correspondence in relation to a settlement by the Legislature passed between Governor Baxter and President Grant:

LITTLE ROCK, ARK., April 22, 1874.
To the President of the United States, Washington:
As I cannot move with my troops to assert my claims to the office of Governor without a collision with the United States troops, which I will not do under any circumstances, I propose to call the Legislature together at an early day, and have them to settle the question, as they alone have the power. But to do this the members of the Legislature must have assurance of protection from you, and a guarantee that they may meet in safety. This will be a peaceable solution of the difficulty, and I will readily abide by the decision of the Legislature.
ELISHA BAXTER, Governor of Arkansas.

EXECUTIVE MANSION, WASHINGTON, } April 22, 1874. }
The Hon. ELISHA BAXTER, *Little Rock, Arkansas:*
I heartily approve any adjustment peaceably of the pending difficulties in Arkansas by means of the Legislative Assembly, the courts, or otherwise. I will give all the assistance and protection I can under the Constitution and laws of the United States to such modes of adjustment. I hope that the military on both sides will be disbanded.
U. S. GRANT.

Upon receipt of the President's reply, Governor Baxter issued the following proclamation, convening an extraordinary session of the Legislature:

EXECUTIVE OFFICE, LITTLE ROCK.

To members of the Senate and House of Representatives of the General Assembly of the State of Arkansas:

Events of the most extraordinary character, involving the peace and welfare of the people of the State, having recently transpired, as Executive of the State I communicated these matters to the Executive of the nation, stating to him that I had been forcibly ejected from the Executive office, and was prevented by the intervention of Federal troops from asserting by force my claims to said office. At last, on this 22d day of April, I sent the following dispatch to the President:

[Here follows a copy of the dispatch, and of the President's reply.]

Now, therefore, during the present occasion, one of sufficient magnitude, and after such assurances received from the Executive of the nation, I deem myself warranted in the exercise of the power vested in me by the constitution of the State, to convene the Legislature of the State of Arkansas, to meet at Little Rock, the capital of said State, on Monday, May 11, 1874, at twelve o'clock. In testimony whereof I have hereunto set my hand and affixed my private seal, the seal of the State not being at present accessible.

Done at the capital, this 22d April, 1874.

ELISHA BAXTER, Governor of Arkansas.

By the Governor:

J. M. JOHNSON, Secretary of State.

On the 27th of April formal application for Federal aid was again made by Governor Baxter, as follows:

LITTLE ROCK, *April* 27, 1874.

U. S. GRANT, *President:*

On the 19th day of this month, as Governor of this State, I telegraphed you there was an armed insurrection against the legal government of this State, and made a requisition upon you for aid to suppress it, and to prevent domestic violence. I have just now been advised that you never received the requisition. I now take occasion to say that an armed insurrection exists in this State against the lawfully constituted authority thereof, and, as the Legislature cannot meet until the 11th day of May, I call upon you for aid to protect the State against domestic violence.

ELISHA BAXTER, Governor of Arkansas.

Up to the close of the month the position of affairs had continued about the same as at the beginning of the difficulty. Brooks still held possession of the State-House, while Baxter's headquarters had remained at the Anthony House. The excitement throughout the city had not diminished, nor had business been resumed. Disturbances were frequent, and arrests were made on both sides, but there had been no general collision between the opposing forces. On the 30th, however, an action occurred at New Gascony, in Jefferson County, between a body of Brooks's troops, reported at two hundred strong, and a portion of Baxter's force, stationed at Pine Bluff, under General King White. The number of the Brooks party killed was variously reported from five to eleven, the wounded from twelve to twenty, and the captured from twenty to sixty. None of General White's troops were reported to have been killed, but seven were wounded. Different reports were given of the origin of this collision: one, to the effect that General White had marched against the Brooks troops because they were threatening

Pine Bluff; and another, because they were committing depredations in Jefferson County.

On the 3d of May two of the judges of the Supreme Court, John E. Bennett and E. J. Searle, while on their way to attend a session of the court in Little Rock, were arrested at Argenta, opposite that city, and taken from the train by parties claiming to act under the authority of Elisha Baxter. The latter, however, disclaimed any knowledge of the arrest or of the disposition that had been made of the judges. For several days the whereabouts of the prisoners was unknown to the public, and it was even rumored that they had been assassinated. The public excitement, therefore, was very high. It subsequently appeared, however, that the captured judges had been taken by a military guard to Benton, in Saline County. While in custody at this point, Judge Bennett sent the following communication to Captain Rose:

BENTON, SALINE COUNTY, ARK., *May* 5, 1874.

Colonel ROSE, *commanding United States Troops, Little Rock, Arkansas.*

COLONEL: On last Saturday evening, as Judge Searle and myself were quietly seated in the cars at Argenta, opposite Little Rock, we were forcibly ejected and arrested by an armed body of men, numbering, I suppose, about twenty-five. We asked by what authority we were arrested, and were answered it was by order of Governor Baxter. We then demanded to know for what crime, or supposed crime, we were restrained of our liberty. They told us they would not tell, but said we should be immediately taken before Governor Baxter; but we have not been so taken, but have been forced to come to this place, where we now are, twelve o'clock, M. On yesterday I addressed a letter to Governor Baxter, narrating the above facts, and demanding that we should be informed of the nature of the accusations against us; but as yet he has not done so, nor do I believe he will do so. The premises considered, allow me to say we are American citizens of the State of Arkansas, have always been true and loyal to the government of both. We were both soldiers in the Federal army, Judge Searle a major and lieutenant-colonel; I have held all ranks from a sergeant to colonel of the Seventy-fifth Illinois Infantry; have been a first-lieutenant in the regular army. We have always been peaceful and quiet citizens; are at present holding the honorable positions of associate justices of the Supreme Court of the State of Arkansas; have never violated any laws of God or man for which we are amenable to any tribunal in the State of Arkansas or the United States, that we are aware of; but, notwithstanding all this, we are now restrained of our liberty—held by main force in a country not under martial law—not where we can demand our rights as citizens of this great republic—not where we can get the benefit of the writ of *habeas corpus*, or any other nominal writ known to the civil law. Therefore, we appeal to you for assistance for our liberation. Can we have it?

Respectfully, your obedient servant,

JOHN E. BENNETT,

Associate Justice Supreme Court.

Upon receipt of this note, troops were sent toward Benton by Captain Rose; but the two captured judges escaped on the 6th, and soon reached Little Rock.

On the 7th of May a session of the Supreme Court, attended by four of the five judges, was held in Little Rock, and an opinion delivered in the case of Joseph Brooks against Henry Page, State Treasurer, which was an application for a mandamus to compel the Treasurer to pay a warrant drawn by Brooks as Governor. The chief question before the court had reference to the validity of Brooks's title to office as established by the judgment of the Circuit Court of Pulaski County. Chief-Justice McClure and Associate Justices Bennett, Searle, and Stephenson, concurred in the opinion "that the Circuit Court had jurisdiction of the subject-matter, and its judgment appears to be regular and valid."

In communicating this decision to President Grant, Brooks again made an urgent appeal for Federal interference in his favor.

As the time for the meeting of the Legislature drew near, activity seemed to increase on both sides. On the 7th the steamer Sallie, carrying about twenty-five Baxter men, was fired upon twenty miles above Little Rock, by a body of Brooks troops. Several were killed and wounded. A sharp skirmish occurred on the 9th between the opposing forces in Little Rock. The streets of the city were barricaded, and communication by telegraph and railroad was greatly interrupted.

At this juncture of affairs the representatives in Washington of the contesting parties were making strenuous efforts to compromise the difficulties. Finally, on the 9th of May, the following compromise was agreed upon, and copies telegraphed by the Attorney-General to Brooks and Baxter for their acceptance:

It is agreed this May 9, 1874, at Washington, D. C., between the respective attorneys and agents of Joseph Brooks and Elisha Baxter, claimants for the office of Governor of the State of Arkansas, that on account of the conflicting claims of the parties, and the division of sentiment among the people of said State, the Legislature of the State shall be called by the said Brooks and Baxter, to meet in extra session on the fourth Monday of May, A. D. 1874, at twelve o'clock, noon, at the usual place of meeting in the State-House, each to put a separate call forthwith for that purpose, and the Legislature so called shall be permitted to meet without molestation or hinderance by either of said parties or their adherents ; that they shall receive and entertain a communication from Mr. Brooks, setting forth specifically the grounds for his claim to the office of Governor, as well as his reasons for contesting Baxter's right thereto ; that they shall investigate the facts and allegations so set forth by Brooks, and such investigations shall be conducted in the manner prescribed by the constitution and laws of the State, giving to both parties a full and fair hearing upon such competent and relevant testimony as either party may offer ; that the Legislature shall determine, in the manner provided by law, which of the contestants received at the November election, 1872, a majority of the legal votes, and declare the result ; and the parties shall abide by that action. Brooks and Baxter shall each relieve from duty and send home all his troops, retaining only as many as each may think necessary as a body-guard at Little Rock, not exceeding one company. All warlike demonstrations are to forthwith cease, and both parties are to keep absolute peace, and refrain from any interference with each other or their adherents until the contest is finally decided by the Legislature or the national Government has taken action thereon. That

until the determination of the General Assembly as to who was legally elected Governor in a contest to be made before that body by Joseph Brooks, the question as to which of the contestants has the legal right to exercise the functions of the office of Governor may at his discretion be determined by the President on the applications heretofore made to him by the respective contestants. That the Legislature shall receive from each claimant to the office such communications as either may send to it until the contest for the office is finally decided by the General Assembly.

I submit the foregoing plan of adjusting the difficulties in Arkansas to the respective claimants to the office of Governor, it having been agreed to by all their friends and attorneys here, subject to approval ; and I have to say that the President earnestly desires its adoption by both parties.

GEORGE H. WILLIAMS, Attorney-General.

This proposition was rejected by Baxter and accepted by Brooks, in the following terms :

LITTLE ROCK, ARK., May 9, 1874.
To the Hon. GEORGE H. WILLIAMS, Attorney-General of the United States.

SIR : Yours of this date, submitting a proposition for the settlement of the trouble in Arkansas, is received and fully considered. A similar proposition in all respects, except so far as relates to the joint call of the Legislature, was submitted by me some two weeks since, and rejected by Brooks. I cannot consent to any thing that will, in whole or part, recognize Brooks as Governor. Either I am Governor, or I am not Governor. The Legislature has been called together for the 11th of this month. The members are rapidly assembling, with nearly a quorum present now. With the belief that they will receive the protection of the General Government in their meeting and deliberations, I could not lawfully disperse them if I would ; nor have I any means of compelling a Legislature that might be convened under the joint call to confirm the terms proposed. The Legislature might as well meet now and act under my call, because it might not return two weeks hence, and in the mean time we are in confusion, with no recognized Governor, and in a state of war. To dispose of all these matters, I have called the Legislature for the 11th inst., under the conviction that it would assemble and be protected by the General Government. I now renew my appeal to the President to protect the Legislature now called. If the Legislature meets now, the question may be submitted to it finally, and I will abide its decision fully. I am therefore constrained to decline the terms proposed.

ELISHA BAXTER, Governor of Arkansas.

BARING CROSS, ARK., May 10, 1874.
To Attorney-General WILLIAMS, Washington :

Your dispatch submitting a proposition to submit the question of who was duly elected Governor, and to refrain from warlike demonstrations until the contest is finally decided by the Legislature or the national Government, as proposed in your dispatch, is accepted. My claims to the governorship of Arkansas have already been adjudged in the Circuit Court, and the right to exercise the office declared by the Supreme Court in a proceeding where the main question at issue was, "Who is the Governor of Arkansas ?" I feel so confident of my election and the justice of my claims that I am willing to submit the question to any other tribunals you have named, and peacefully abide the determination, at all times asserting that the only tribunal that can have or has the right to construe the Constitution is the Supreme Court of the State, which, in its late decision in the case of Brooks against Page, determined that the Circuit Court had both the power and jurisdiction to adjudicate my right to the office.

JOSEPH BROOKS, Governor of Arkansas.

On the 11th, the day appointed for the meeting of the Legislature, thirty-seven members of that body had arrived in the capital. This number, however, was not sufficient for a quorum. On the same day the following propositions, made by President Grant, for a short adjournment of the Legislature, were received by Brooks and Baxter:

WASHINGTON, D. C., *May* 11, 1874.

To the Hon. JOSEPH BROOKS, *Little Rock, Arkansas:*

I have suggested to Mr. Baxter that the members of the General Assembly, now in Little Rock, adjourn for a reasonable time, say ten days, to give you an opportunity to call in those members who may not respond to his call, so that there may be a full Legislature. The United States will give all necessary protection to the Legislature in meeting and transacting its business, as usual, at the State-House, and prevent, as far as practicable, all violence and disturbance of the public peace. I urgently request that the military of both parties be at once disbanded, which is the first step toward a peaceable settlement. Answer. U. S. GRANT.

To the Hon. ELISHA BAXTER, *Little Rock, Arkansas:*

I recommend that the members of the General Assembly, now at Little Rock, adjourn for a reasonable time, say for ten days, to enable Brooks to call to the body his supposed adherents, so that there may be a full Legislature. Any hasty action by a part of the Assembly will not be satisfactory to the people. Brooks's friends here agree that if this course is pursued no opposition will be made to the meeting of the Assembly in the State-House as usual, and that he will at once dismiss his forces if you will do the same. I urgently request that all armed forces on both sides be disbanded, so that the General Assembly may act free from any military pressure or influence. The United States forces will give all necessary protection to the Legislature, and prevent, as far as practicable, all violence and disturbance of the public peace. Answer.

U. S. GRANT.

Baxter replied that he would agree to this proposition upon the conditions expressed in the following:

LITTLE ROCK, ARK., *May* 11, 1874.

To U. S. GRANT, *President, Washington, D. C.:*

There is almost a quorum of both Houses of the Legislature present, and they have power, under the constitution, to adjourn from day to day, until they have a quorum, and they can adjourn no longer than until they have a quorum. I am in favor of their adjourning as long as they please, until every supposed Brooks adherent is present. With this understanding, I will disband my troops in proportion as Brooks disbands his, but for the meeting of the Legislature at the usual place Mr. Brooks must get as far from it west as I am east, and deposit the State arms in the State Armory, and let the State-House and public buildings be turned over at once to J. M. Johnson, the Secretary of State, to whom, under the law, they belong.

ELISHA BAXTER, Governor of Arkansas.

The President considered this a "fair and reasonable" proposition, and in communicating it to Brooks, through Attorney-General Williams, expressed the opinion that his "interests require its immediate acceptance." Mr. Brooks, however, entertained a different opinion, and gave his reasons in the following reply:

EXECUTIVE OFFICE, STATE OF ARKANSAS, BARING CROSS, ARK., *May* 12, 1874.

The Hon. GEORGE H. WILLIAMS, *Attorney-General, Washington, D. C.:*

The members of the General Assembly here, even if there were a quorum, and there is not, do not constitute a Legislature, unless convened by the Governor. If you recognize this assemblage as a Legislature you recognize Baxter as Governor, for no one but the Governor can convene the Legislature in extraordinary session. If it is not a Legislature called by the proper authority, its adjournment is a matter of no consequence. So far as the Secretary of State is concerned, if any of his prerogatives are interfered with, the courts of the State, and not the President, is the proper tribunal before which to redress his grievances. I have answered the President's dispatch at length. I shall not disband any troops under my command until the question of "Who is Governor of Arkansas?" is settled, unless required to do so by the direct command of the President. I have no proposition to submit, and will entertain none on the subject other than that proposed by yourself, sanctioned by the President, and agreed to by the agents and attorneys of Baxter and myself. The case made on the papers requires the President to recognize either Baxter or myself as Governor of Arkansas. The settlement of the question, either before the courts or the Legislature, is one that in my opinion does not require the intercession of the President on Baxter's behalf. He must act on the papers before him and not upon what a Legislature may or may not do in the future. Upon a majority of the votes of the legal voters of this State, and upon the judgments of the Supreme and Circuit Courts, I am willing to stand or fall. But, if these are to be held for naught by the President, until such time as he can ascertain the opinion of the Legislature to guide him in determining who is Governor, and during the pendency of the question to allow the State and citizens to be plundered and robbed by an armed mob, which has already fired on the Federal troops and commenced an indiscriminate slaughter of colored men, to avoid a further sacrifice of life and loss of property, I am impelled by a sense of duty to submit my case as it now stands, and abide the President's determination.

JOSEPH BROOKS, Governor of Arkansas.

The opinion seems to have been general that the refusal of Brooks to act upon the suggestions made by the Government at Washington worked unfavorably for his cause. Moreover, there appeared to be a growing anxiety on the part of President Grant to reach a speedy settlement of the difficulty. The forces on either side were being augmented, collisions between members of the opposing parties were becoming more frequent, and the general aspect of affairs was growing more threatening. On the 13th the Legislature organized, with a quorum of each branch present. On the ensuing day the following joint resolution, invoking the interposition of the Federal Government, was passed and telegraphed to Washington:

Whereas, The Legislature of the State of Arkansas has convened, a quorum of each House being present; and—

Whereas, The capital of our State is occupied by armed and contending forces; and—

Whereas, The State-House is now in possession of armed troops: therefore, be it—

Resolved, By the General Assembly of the State of Arkansas, That the President of the United States be and is hereby requested to put this Legislature in possession of the Legislative Halls, and that the public property on State-House Square be placed under the supervision and control of this body, the legal custodians thereof while in session, and that he make such order for the disposition of said armed contending forces as will more perfectly protect the State against domestic violence and insure this body protection; and that a duly certified copy of this resolution be at once transmitted to the President of the United States.

Upon receipt of this communication from the Legislature, President Grant issued the following proclamation, recognizing Baxter as the legal Governor of the State, and ordering the forces of Brooks to disband and return home

Whereas, Certain turbulent and disorderly persons, pretending that Elisha Baxter, the present Executive of Arkansas, was not elected, have combined together with force and arms to resist his authority as such Executive, and other authorities of said State; and—

Whereas, Said Elisha Baxter has been declared duly elected by the General Assembly of said State, as provided in the constitution thereof, and has for a long period been exercising the functions of said office into which he was inducted according to the constitution and laws of said State, and ought by its citizens to be considered the lawful Executive thereof; and—

Whereas, It is provided in the Constitution of the United States that the United States shall protect every State in the Union on application of the Legislature, or of the Executive when the Legislature cannot be convened, against domestic violence; and—

Whereas, The said Elisha Baxter, under section 4 of Article IV. of the Constitution of the United States, and the laws passed in pursuance thereof, has heretofore made application to me to protect said State and the citizens thereof against domestic violence; and—

Whereas, The General Assembly of said State convened in extra session at the Capitol thereof on the 11th instant, pursuant to a call made by said Elisha Baxter, and both Houses thereof have passed a joint resolution applying to me to protect the State against domestic violence; and—

Whereas, It is provided in the laws of the United States that in all cases of insurrection against the laws thereof it shall be lawful for the President of the United States, on application of the Legislature of such State, or of the Executive, when the Legislature cannot be convened, to employ such part of the land and naval forces as shall be judged necessary for the purpose of suppressing such insurrection, so causing the laws to be duly executed; and—

Whereas, It is required that whenever it may be necessary, in the judgment of the President, to use the military force for the purpose aforesaid, he shall forthwith, by proclamation, command such insurgents to disperse and retire peaceably to their respective homes within a limited time: now, therefore—

I, Ulysses S. Grant, President of the United States, do hereby make proclamation and command all turbulent and disorderly persons to disperse and retire peaceably to their respective abodes within ten days from this date, and hereafter submit themselves to the lawful authority, to the said Executive, and the other constituted authorities of said State, and I invoke the aid and coöperation of all good citizens to uphold law and preserve the public peace.

In witness whereof I have hereunto set my hand and caused the seal of the United States to be affixed.

Done at the City of Washington, this 15th day of May, in the year of our Lord 1874, and of the Independence of the United States the ninety-fifth.

U. S. GRANT.

By the President:

HAMILTON FISH, Secretary of State.

The announcement of this action on the part of the General Government caused the greatest rejoicing in Little Rock. Brooks now disbanded his troops and retired from the State-House, and Baxter took possession. The expenses incurred on account of military operations during these disturbances were reported to Governor Baxter at $250,000, by Adjutant-General McCanary, and $300,000 by T. J. Churchill, major-general commanding.

As the action of the Federal Government in this important controversy was based upon the opinion of Attorney-General Williams, that document is here given in full, not only as being an authoritative exposition of vital questions of constitutional law which are frequently arising, but also as affording a precedent to be followed by the Government hereafter in similar cases.

DEPARTMENT OF JUSTICE, }
WASHINGTON, *May* 15, 1874. }

The President.

SIR: Elisha Baxter, claiming to be Governor of Arkansas, having made due application for Executive aid to suppress an insurrection in that State, and Joseph Brooks, claiming also to be Governor of said State, having made a similar application, and these applications having been referred by you to me for an opinion as to which of these persons is the lawful Executive of the State, I have the honor to submit: That Baxter and Brooks were candidates for the office of Governor at a general election held in Arkansas on the 5th day of November, 1872.

Section 19, of Article VI. of the constitution of the State provides that the returns of every election for Governor, Lieutenant-Governor, Secretary of State, Treasurer, Auditor, Attorney-General, and Superintendent of Public Instruction, shall be sealed up and transmitted to the seat of government by the returning officers, and directed to the presiding officer of the Senate, who, during the first week of the session, shall open and publish the same in the presence of the members there assembled. The persons having the highest number of votes shall be declared elected, but, if two or more shall have the highest and equal number of votes for the same office, one of them shall be chosen by joint vote of both Houses.

Contested elections shall likewise be determined by both Houses of the General Assembly, in such manner as is or may be prescribed by law.

Pursuant to this section, the votes for Governor at the said election were counted, and Baxter was declared to be duly elected. Said section, as it will be noticed, after providing for a canvass of the votes, specially declares: "Contested elections shall likewise be determined by both Houses of the General Assembly, in such manner as is, or may hereafter be, prescribed by law." When this constitution was adopted, there was a law in the State which continues in force, prescribing the mode in which the contest should be conducted before the General Assembly, the first section of which is as follows:

All contested elections of Governor shall be decided by the joint vote of both Houses of the General Assembly, and in such joint meeting the President of the Senate shall preside.

Brooks accordingly presented to the Lower House of said Assembly his petition for a contest, but by the decisive vote of 68 to 9 it was rejected by that body. Subsequently the Attorney-General, upon the petition of Brooks, applied to the Supreme Court of the State for a *quo warranto* to try the validity of Baxter's title to the office of Governor, in which it was alleged that Baxter was a usurper, etc. That court denied the application, upon the ground that the courts of the State had no right to hear and determine the question presented, because exclusive jurisdiction in such cases had been conferred upon the General Assembly by the constitution and laws of the State.

Brooks then brought a suit against Baxter in the Pulaski Circuit Court, under section 525 of the Civil Code of Arkansas, which reads as follows:

Whenever a person usurps an office or franchise to which he is not entitled by law, an action by proceedings at law may be instituted against him, either by the State or the parties entitled to the office or franchise, to prevent the usurper from exercising the office or franchise.

Brooks states in his petition that he received more than 45,000 votes, and that Baxter received less than 30,000 votes for Governor at the said election, and, after declaring that Baxter has usurped the office, prays that it may be given to him by the judgment of the court, and that he may recover the sum of $2,000, the emoluments of said office withheld from him by Baxter. This presented to the court a simple question of a contest for the office of Governor. Baxter demurred to this petition on the ground that the court had no jurisdiction of the case, and afterward, on the 15th of April, the court, in the absence of the defendant's counsel, overruled the demurrer, and without further pleadings or any evidence in the case, rendered judgment for Brooks in accordance with the prayer of his petition. Brooks, within a few minutes thereafter, without process to enforce the execution of said judgment, and with the aid of armed men, forcibly ejected Baxter, and took possession of the Governor's office. On the next day after the judgment was rendered, Baxter's counsel made a motion to set it aside, alleging, among other things as grounds therefor, that they were absent when the demurrer was submitted to the final judgment thereon rendered; that the judgment of the court upon overruling the demurrer should have been that the defendant answer over, instead of which a final judgment was rendered without giving any time or opportunity to answer the complaint upon its merits; that the court assessed the damages without any jury or evidence; and, finally, that the court had no jurisdiction over the subject-matter of the suit, but the next day this motion was overruled by the Court.

Section 4, Article IV., of the Constitution of the United States, is as follows: "The United States shall guarantee to every State in this Union a republican form of government, and shall protect each of them against invasion, and, on application of the Legislature, or of the Executive (when the Legislature cannot be convened), against domestic violence."

When, in pursuance of this provision of the Constitution, the President is called upon by the Executive of a State to protect it from domestic violence, it appears to be his duty to give the required aid, and especially when there is no doubt about the existence of the domestic violence; but where two persons, each claiming to be Governor, make calls respectively upon the President under said clause of the Constitution, it of course becomes necessary for him to determine, in the first place, which of said persons is the constitutional Governor of the State. That section of the constitution of Arkansas heretofore cited, in my opinion, is decisive of this question, as between Baxter and Brooks. According to the constitution and laws of the State, the votes for Governor were counted and Baxter declared elected, and at once was duly inaugurated as Governor of the State. There is great difficulty in holding that he usurped the office into which he was inducted under these circumstances. Assuming that no greater effect is to be given to the counting of the votes in the presence of the General Assembly than ought to be given to a similar action by any board of canvassers, yet when it comes to decide a question of contest, the General Assembly is converted by the constitution into a judicial body, and its judgment is as conclu-

sive and final as is the judgment of the Supreme Court of the State on any matter within its jurisdiction. Parties to such a contest plead and produce evidence according to the practice provided in such cases, and the controversy is invested with the forms and effect of a judicial procedure. When the people of the State declared in their constitution that a contest about State officers shall be determined by the General Assembly, they cannot be understood as meaning it might be determined in any Circuit Court of the State. To say that a contest shall be decided by decision, and then to say, after the decision is made, that such contest is not determined, but is as open as it ever was, is a contradiction in terms. Can it possibly be supposed the framers of this constitution, when they declared contested elections about State officers, including the Governor, should be determined by the General Assembly, intended that any such contest should be just as unsettled after as it was before such determination of it? Manifestly, they intended to create a special tribunal to try claims to the high offices of the State. But the tribunal is not special if the courts have concurrent jurisdiction over-the subject. Brooks appears to claim that when a contest for Governor is decided by the General Assembly, the defeated part may treat the decision as a nullity, and proceed *de novo* in the courts. This makes the constitutional provision as to the contest of no effect, and the proceedings under it an empty form. When the House of Representatives dismissed the petition of Brooks for a contest, it must be taken as a decision of that body on questions presented in the petition. But it is not of any consequence whether or not the General Assembly has in fact decided the contest, if the exclusive jurisdiction to do so is vested in that body by the constitution and laws of the State.

Section 14 of Article V. of the constitution of Arkansas, like most other constitutions, declares that each House of the Assembly shall judge of the qualifications, election, and returns of its members, and it has never been denied anywhere that these words confer exclusive jurisdiction. But the terms, if possible, are more comprehensive by which the constitution confers upon the Legislative Assembly jurisdiction to judge of the election of State officers. Doubtless the makers of the constitution considered it unsafe to lodge in the hands of every Circuit Court of the State the power to revolutionize the Executive Department at will, and their wisdom is forcibly illustrated by the case under consideration, in which a person who had been installed as Governor, according to the constitution and laws of the State, after an undisturbed incumbency of more than a year is deposed by a Circuit Judge, and another person put in his place upon the unsupported statement of the latter that he had received a majority of votes at the election.

Looking at the constitution alone, and it appears perfectly clear to my mind that the courts of the State have no right to try a contest about the office of Governor, but that exclusive jurisdiction over that question is vested in the General Assembly. This view is confirmed by judicial authority. Summing up the whole discussion, the Supreme Court of Arkansas say in the case of the Attorney-General against Baxter, above referred to under this constitution, that the "determination of the question, as to whether the person exercising the office of Governor has been duly elected or not, is vested exclusively in the General Assembly of the State, and neither this nor any other State court has jurisdiction to try a suit in relation to such contest, be the mode or form what it may, whether at the suit of the Attorney-General or on the relation of a claimant through him, or by an individual alone claiming a right to the office. Such an issue should be made before the General Assembly; it is their duty to decide, and no other tribunal can determine that question. We are of opinion that this court has no jurisdiction to hear and determine a writ of *quo warranto* for the purpose of rendering a judgment of *ouster* against the chief Executive of this State, and the right to file an information and issue a writ for that purpose is denied." Some effort has been made to distinguish this case from that of Brooks against Baxter, in the Circuit Court, by calling the opinion a *dictum*, but the point presented to and decided by the Supreme Court was that in a contest for the office of Governor the jurisdiction of the General Assembly was exclusive, which of course deprived one court as much as another of the power to try such contest. There is, however, another decision made by the same court upon the precise question presented in the case of Brooks against Baxter. Berry was a candidate for State Auditor on the same ticket with Brooks. Wheeler, his competitor, was declared elected by the General Assembly. Berry then brought a suit under said section 525 in the Pulaski Circuit Court to recover the office. Wheeler applied to the Supreme Court for an order to restrain the proceedings, and that court issued a writ of prohibition forbidding the said court to proceed, on the ground that it had no jurisdiction in the case as to the question of law involved. The cases of Berry and Brooks are exactly alike. That this Circuit Court should have rendered a judgment for Brooks under these circumstances is surprising, and it is not too much to say that it presents a case of judicial insubordination which deserves the reprehension of every one who does not wish to see public confidence in the certainty and good faith of judicial proceedings wholly destroyed. Chief-Justice McClure, who dissented in the case of the Attorney-General against Baxter, delivered the opinion of the court in the Wheeler case, in which he uses the following language: "The majority of the court in the case of the State against Baxter, the decision of the *quo warranto* and a contested election proceeding being convertible remedies having one and the same object, decides that neither this nor any other State court, no matter what the form of action, has jurisdiction to try a suit in relation to a contest for the office of Governor as an abstract proposition of law. I concede the correctness of the rule, and would have assented to it if the question had been before us. The question now before this court is precisely one of contest and nothing else. As to all matters of contested elections for the offices of Governor, Lieutenant-Governor, Secretary of State, Auditor, Treasurer, Attorney-General, and Superintendent of Public Instruction, I am of the opinion that it can only be had before the General Assembly."

He then adds, in conclusion: "I think a writ of prohibition ought to go to prohibit the Circuit Court from entertaining jurisdiction of Berry against Wheeler that has for its object a recovery of the office." All five of the judges heard this case, and there was no dissent from these views as to the question of jurisdiction. To show how the foregoing decisions are understood in the State, I refer to a note by the Hon. H. C. Caldwell, Judge of the District Court of the United States for the Southern District of Arkansas, upon Section 2379 of a digest of the Statutes of the State, lately examined and approved by him, which is as follows:

By the provisions of Section 19 of Article IV. of the constitution, the jurisdiction of the General Assembly over cases of contested election for the officers, in said section enumerated, is exclusive.—Attorney-General on the relation of Brooks against Baxter, manuscript opinion, 1873; Wheeler against Whylock, manuscript opinion, 1873.

It is assumed in the argument for Brooks that the judgment of the Pulaski Circuit Court is binding as well upon the President as upon Baxter until it is reversed, but where there are conflicting decisions as in this case, the President is to prefer that one which, in his opinion, is warranted by the constitution and laws of the State. The General Assembly has decided that Baxter was elected. The Circuit Court

of Pulaski County has decided that Brooks was elected. Taking the provisions of the Constitution which declares that contested elections about certain State officers, including the Governor, shall be determined by the General Assembly, and that provision of the law heretofore cited which says that all contested elections of Governor shall be decided by the Legislature, and the two decisions of the Supreme Court affirming the exclusive jurisdiction of that body over the subject, and the conclusion irresistibly follows that said judgment of the Circuit Court is void. A void judgment binds nobody. Said section 525, under which this judgment was rendered, must be construed with reference to the constitution and other statutes of the State, and is no doubt intended to apply to county and other inferior officers for which no provision elsewhere is made. But the constitution takes the State officers there enumerated out of the purview of this section and establishes a special tribunal to try these contested election cases, to which they are parties. The jurisdiction of this tribunal is exclusive. (Ohio against Grisell and Menlon, 15 Ohio, 114; Attorney-General against Garrugues, 28 Pennsylvania, 9; Commonwealth against Baxter, 35 Id., 263; Commonwealth against Leech, 44 Id., 332.)

Respecting the claim that Brooks received a majority of the votes at the election, it must be said that the President has no way to verify that claim. If he had, it would not, in my opinion, under the circumstances in this case, be a proper subject for his consideration. Perhaps if every thing about the election was in confusion, and there had been no legal count of the votes, the question of majorities might form an element of the discussion; but where, as in this case, there has been a legal count of the votes, and the tribunal organized by the constitution of the State for that purpose has declared the election, the President, in my judgment, ought not to go behind that action to look into the state of the vote. Frauds may have been committed to the prejudice of Brooks; but, unhappily, there are few elections where partisan zeal runs high in which the victorious party, with more or less of truth, is not charged with acts of fraud. There must, however, be an end to the controversy upon the subject. Somebody must be trusted to count votes and declare elections. Unconstitutional methods of filling offices cannot be resorted to because there is some real or imagined unfairness about the election. Ambitious and selfish aspirants for office generally create the disturbance about this matter, for the people are more interested in the preservation of the peace than in the political fortunes of any man. Either of the contestants, with law and order, is better than the other with discord and violence. I think it would be disastrous to allow the proceedings by which Brooks obtained possession of the office to be drawn into a precedent. There is not a State in the Union in which they would not produce a conflict, and probably bloodshed. They cannot be upheld or justified upon any ground, and in my opinion Elisha Baxter should be recognized as the lawful Executive of the State of Arkansas.

Since the foregoing was written I have received a telegraphic copy of what purports to be a decision of the Supreme Court of Arkansas, delivered on the 7th instant; from which it appears that the Auditor of the State, upon a requisition of Brooks, drew his warrant on the Treasurer for the sum of $1,000, payment of which was refused. Brooks then applied to the Supreme Court for a writ of mandamus upon the Treasurer, who set up, by way of defense, that Brooks was not Governor of the State, to which Brooks demurred, and thereupon the court say:

The only question that we deem it necessary to notice is, did the Circuit Court have jurisdiction to render the judgment in the case of Brooks against Baxter? We feel some delicacy about expressing an opinion upon the question propounded, but under the pleadings it has to be passed upon incidentally, if not absolutely, in determining whether the relator is entitled to the relief asked, for his right to the office, if established at all, is established by the judgment of the Circuit Court of Pulaski County. We are of opinion that the Circuit Court had jurisdiction of the subject-matter, and its judgment appears to be regular and valid. Having arrived at these conclusions, the demurrer is overruled, and the writ of mandamus will be awarded, as prayed for.

To show the value of this decision it is proper that I should make the following statement : On the 20th of April Brooks made a formal application to the President for aid to suppress domestic violence, which was accompanied by a paper signed by Chief-Justice McClure and Justices Searle and Stephenson, in which they stated that they recognized Brooks as Governor, and to this paper, also, is appended the name of Page, the respondent in the above-named proceeding for mandamus. Page, therefore, did not refuse to pay the warrant of the Auditor because he did not recognize Brooks as Governor, but the object of his refusal evidently was to create such facts as were necessary to make a case for the Supreme Court. Accordingly, the pleadings were made up by the parties, both of whom were on the same side in the controversy, and the issue so made was submitted to judges virtually pledged to give the decision wanted, and there, within the military encampment of Brooks, they hurriedly but with delicacy, as they say, decided that he is Governor, a decision in plain contravention of the constitution and laws of the State, and in direct conflict with two other recent decisions of the same court deliberately made. I refrain from comment. More than once the Supreme Court of the United States has decided that it would not hear argument in a case made up in this way, and a decision obtained under such circumstances is not recognized as authority by any respectable tribunal. No doubt this decision will add to the complications and difficulties of the situation, but it does not affect my judgment as to the right of Baxter to the office of Governor until it is otherwise decided upon a contest made by the Legislature of the State.

On the 11th instant the General Assembly of the State was convened in session upon the call of Baxter, and both Houses passed a joint resolution pursuant to Section 4, Article IV. of the Constitution of the United States, calling upon the President to protect the State against domestic violence. This call exhausts all the means which the people of the State have under the Constitution to invoke the aid of the Executive of the United States for their protection, and there seems to be, under the circumstances of the case, an imperative necessity for immediate action. I have the honor to be, with great respect,

GEO. H. WILLIAMS, Attorney-General.

The Legislature continued in session until May 28th, when it adjourned. The most important measure passed was a bill providing for the assembling of a Constitutional Convention, on the 14th of July, and the election of delegates, to be held June 30th.

At the election held on the 30th of June, 80,259 votes were cast for, and 8,607 against holding a convention ; the majority for the convention being 71,652. At the same time, 91 delegates were chosen. On the 14th of July, the convention assembled in Little Rock. This was the fifth Constitutional Convention which had been convened in the State, the others having been held in 1836, 1861, 1864, and 1868. The new constitution was voted upon by the people on the 13th of October, and was ratified by a majority of 53,890 votes, 78,697 votes having been cast for, and 24,807 against it.

This large majority in favor of the new constitution indicates the dissatisfaction, among the people, in reference to the old one, which was adopted in 1868, before the State had fairly recovered from the effects of the war. One of the most marked defects in the constitution of 1868 was the almost unlimited appointing power vested in the Governor, the extent of which is indicated by the following language of one of the public men of the State: "The Governor of Arkansas has more official patronage than any Governor in the Union ; he appoints a chief-justice, sixteen circuit judges, sixteen prosecuting attorneys, one chancellor, six criminal judges, three supervisors in each of the eighty counties of the State, six circuit court clerks, eighty county treasurers, eighty county assessors, eighty coroners, all the justices of the peace, constables and notaries public, a land-commissioner, a commissioner of public works, a State geologist and insurance agent, with perhaps some others, besides having power to fill all vacancies in elective offices." Under the new constitution, the choice of all civil officers is vested in the people, thereby depriving the Executive Department of the power of appointment. With the old constitution, disappear all its disfranchisements. The distinguishing features of the new constitution, as compared with that of 1868, consist in submitting the election of all officers of the government to the popular vote ; in diminishing the number of officers to such limit as is necessary to an economical and successful administration of the government; in limiting the rate of taxation by the Legislature on the assessed value of all property ; in protecting the public credit, by expressly prohibiting the Legislature from contracting any debt, save for certain specified purposes ; and in prohibiting all local and special legislation.

The Bill of Rights declares that no distinction shall be made in the rights of citizens on account of race or color ; that the privilege of the writ of *habeas corpus* shall not be suspended except by the General Assembly; that no person shall be imprisoned for debt in any civil action, on mesne or final process, unless in cases of fraud; that monopolies shall not be allowed ; and that no distinction shall be made between resident aliens and citizens in regard to property. The power of declaring martial law is taken from the Governor and vested in the Legislature by Section 12 of the Bill of Rights, which says that "no power of suspending or setting aside the law or laws of the State shall ever be exercised, except by the General Assembly."

The right of suffrage is extended to every male citizen of the United States, or male person who has declared his intention of becoming a citizen, of the age of twenty-one years, who has resided in the State twelve months, in the county six months, and in the voting precinct, or ward, one month previous to the election. It is provided that no law shall be enacted " whereby the right to vote at any election shall be made to depend upon any previous registration of the elector's name." The general elections shall be held biennially on the first Monday of September; but the General Assembly may fix a different time. The number of Representatives is fixed at not less than 73 nor more than 100, and of Senators at not less than 30 nor more than 35.

Representatives are to be chosen for two and Senators for four years. The sessions of the Legislature are made biennial, and are limited to sixty days, but may be extended by a two-thirds vote of each House. This limitation, however, does not apply to the first session under the new constitution, or when impeachments are pending. No member shall, during the term for which he has been elected, receive any increase of pay for his services, under any law passed during such term. The limitations contained in the following sections of Article V. are placed upon the powers of the Legislature.

SECTION 31. No State tax shall be allowed, or appropriation of money made, except to raise means for the payment of the just debts of the State, for defraying the necessary expenses of government, to sustain common schools, to repel invasion and suppress insurrection, except by a majority of two-thirds of both Houses of the General Assembly.

SEC. 32. No act of the General Assembly shall limit the amount to be recovered for injuries resulting in death, or for injuries to persons or property, and, in case of death from such injuries, the right of action shall survive, and the General Assembly shall prescribe for whose benefit such action shall be prosecuted.

SEC. 33. No obligation or liability of any railroad, or other corporation, held or owned by this State, shall ever be exchanged, transferred, remitted, postponed, or in any way diminished by the General Assembly; nor shall such liability or obligation be released, except by payment thereof into the State Treasury.

The Executive term of office is reduced from four to two years, and the office of Lieutenant-Governor is abolished, the functions of it devolving upon the President of the Senate. The provisions in Article VI. in regard to the elections of State officers and contested elections— the point upon which the exciting gubernatorial controversy of this year turned—are substantially the same in the new constitution as they were in the old.

All judges are to be elected by the people; those of the Supreme Court for eight years, of the Circuit Courts for four years, and of the county courts and justices of the peace for two years. Sheriffs, assessors, coroners, county treasurers, and surveyors, are also elected by the people for two years. The General Assembly is required to " provide, by general laws, for the support of common schools by taxes, which shall never exceed, in any one year, two mills on the dollar on the taxable property of the State; and by an annual per capita tax of one dollar, to be assessed on every male inhabitant of this State over the age of twenty-one years: Provided, The General Assembly may,

by general law, authorize school districts to levy, by a vote of the qualified electors of such district, a tax not to exceed five mills on the dollar in any one year for school purposes: Provided further, That no such tax shall be appropriated to any other purpose, nor for any other district than that for which it was levied." A system of free schools is to be maintained, " whereby all persons in the State, between the ages of six and twenty-one years, may receive gratuitous instruction." The creation of school offices is left to the Legislature, and, until otherwise provided by law, the Secretary of State is required to discharge the duties of Superintendent of Public Instruction.

For the encouragement of manufactures and mining, the General Assembly is authorized to exempt, by general law, from taxation, for the term of seven years from the ratification of the constitution, the capital invested in any or all kinds of mining and manufacturing business in the State.

Railroads and canals are declared public highways and the companies common carriers; the directors are required to make annual reports under oath to the Auditor of Public Accounts; and the rolling-stock and all other movable property are considered personal estate, and liable to execution and sale in the same manner as the personal property of individuals. The General Assembly is required to " prevent by law the granting of free passes by any railroad or transportation company to any officer of this State Legislature, executive or judicial;" and also "to pass laws to correct abuses and prevent unjust discrimination and excessive charges by railroad, canal, and turnpike companies, for transporting freight and passengers, and shall provide for enforcing such laws by adequate penalties and forfeitures."

Executive and judicial officers are prohibited from receiving fees; the amount of their salaries is to be fixed by the General Assembly, but shall not exceed annually the following sums: Governor, $4,000; Secretary of State, $2,500; Treasurer of State, $3,000; Auditor of State, $3,000; Attorney-General, $2,500; Commissioner of State Lands, $2,500; Judges of the Supreme Court, each, $4,000; Judges of the Circuit Courts, and Chancellors, each, $3,000; prosecuting attorneys, $400.

The constitution provided that an election for State officers and members of the Legislature should be held on the same day on which the vote on the constitution was taken, viz., October 13th, and that the Legislature then elected should assemble on the 10th of November. In view of this provision the Democratic Convention assembled in Little Rock, September 9th, to nominate a State ticket. Governor Baxter was twice chosen as the candidate for Governor, but declined the nomination. The following nominations for State officers were then made:

Governor, A. H. Garland; Chief-Justice, E.

H. English; Associate Supremo Justices, David Walker, William M. Harrison; Secretary of State, B. B. Beavers; Auditor, Wm. R. Miller; Treasurer, T. J. Churchill; Attorney-General, S. P. Hughes; Commissioner of State Lands, J. N. Smithee; Chancellor, John R. Eakin.

The platform adopted was as follows:

Whereas, The Constitutional Convention, recently assembled at Little Rock, framed a constitution for the State of Arkansas, and the same has been submitted to the people for ratification on the 13th day of October, A. D. 1874; and—

Whereas, In the opinion of this convention the constitution so submitted is just, liberal, and wise, and will secure to the State peace and prosperity, if properly enforced: therefore be it—

Resolved, That the people be, and they are, earnestly requested and advised to use their best efforts to secure the ratification of such constitution, and to have the same carried into effect and enforced according to its letter, meaning, and spirit.

Resolved, That in this movement all persons within the State desiring her future welfare, regardless of past issues and differences, are cordially invited to secure the equality of all men before the law, honesty and capability in the administration of every public duty, the speedy and just punishment of every crime, the purity and freedom of the ballot, the advancement and perpetuity of public education, economy in every department of the government, and the rightful use of every prerogative of power to the end that the protection of the rights of the whole people shall be complete.

Resolved, That this convention pledges its unabated exertions to secure the adoption of such constitution, as well as the election of the persons nominated by it for the different offices on the State ticket.

A State Convention of the Republican party met in Little Rock, September 15th. There was a strong feeling among the delegates against the course pursued by Baxter and the Constitutional Convention. Resolutions were passed pledging fidelity to the Republican party, denying the authority of Elisha Baxter as Governor, pronouncing in favor of Joseph Brooks, and declaring all the acts of Baxter, subsequent to the decision of the Circuit Court, null and void; and that the Constitutional Convention was a conspiracy of members of the White League, Ku-klux, and leaders of the lost cause, to overthrow the reconstructed government.

The convention further declared "that the late so-called Constitutional Convention recently assembled, having been called by a revolutionary Legislature, without warrant or authority of law, and in violation of the existing constitution of the State, all acts had and done by that convention, as well as those of the Legislature which called it, are revolutionary, null, and void, and it would be both improper and impolitic for the Republican party to place men in nomination as candidates for any of the offices provided for by said so-called convention."

And "that the officers, whose election is provided for in the constitution of 1868, and the laws passed thereunder, be nominated and voted for at the general election to be held on Tuesday, the 3d day of November next."

No nominations, therefore, were made to

be voted upon at the election of October 13th. This resulted in the success of the Democratic ticket—Garland, as candidate for Governor, having received 76,453 votes, and the other candidates about the same number.

The congressional election was held on the 3d of November, and resulted in the choice of Democrats in all of the districts, viz.: I. Lucian G. Ganse; II. William F. Slemons; III. William W. Wilshire; IV. Thomas M. Gunter.

On the 10th of November the new Legislature assembled, as provided by the new constitution, and soon after Governor Garland and the other State officers recently elected entered upon their official duties. Another contest now arose for the possession of the Executive office. V. V. Smith, who had been elected Lieutenant-Governor on the ticket with Baxter in 1872, and had since held that office, issued a proclamation to the people of the State on the 13th of November, in which he declared that the recent Constitutional Convention had not been called in accordance with the supreme law of the State; that its proceedings were therefore illegal, and the constitution which it framed null and void; that the election held under such constitution was unlawful, and the officers chosen were usurpers; that the office of Governor had been abandoned by Baxter and usurped by Garland; that in 1872 he himself had been elected Lieutenant-Governor for four years; and that, according to the constitution he was entitled to succeed to the office of Governor, rendered vacant by Baxter. After these declarations, and the assertion that "the attempt to seize and the seizing of the legislative, executive, and judicial offices of the State" was "revolution, and nothing but revolution," the proclamation ended as follows:

Now, therefore, I, V. V. Smith, Lieutenant-Governor of the State of Arkansas, by virtue of the authority vested in the Lieutenant-Governor by the tenth (10th) section of Article VI. (6) of said constitution (Elisha Baxter having abdicated and abandoned the office of Governor), do hereby command all persons claiming to derive political authority under and by virtue of the so-called constitution of October 13, 1874, to desist and refrain from the exercise of all official authority thereunder, and all persons that may have assumed to act under the authority of said pretended constitution, whether executive, legislative, or judicial, are hereby commanded to relinquish and surrender said offices to the persons entitled thereto, under the constitution of 1868, and the laws passed thereunder, within five (5) days from the date hereof, or I shall take such measures as will, in my opinion, result in the observance and enforcement of this command.

In testimony whereof I have hereunto set my hand, and caused the seal of the State to [L. s.] be affixed, at Little Rock, this, the 13th day of November, A. D. 1874.

V. V. SMITH, Governor of Arkansas.

By the Governor:

EDWARD WHEELER, Secretary of State.

On the same day Smith made application to President Grant to guarantee to the State a republican government, and protect it from domestic violence.

Governor Garland at once caused warrants to be issued for the arrest of Smith and Wheeler for conspiring to overthrow the government, but those persons could not be found.

During the excitement caused by the Brooks-Baxter contest, and before the adjournment of Congress, a select committee of five was appointed, with Luke P. Poland as chairman, to investigate the condition of affairs in Arkansas, and "whether said State had now a government republican in form, the officers of which are duly elected, and, as now organized, ought to be recognized by the Government of the United States." This committee proceeded to Little Rock, and took testimony during the summer.

President Grant declined to interfere in behalf of Smith, on the ground that the affairs of the State were under investigation by Congress. Garland, therefore, remained in possession of the executive office unmolested at the close of the year.

On the 18th of December the Senate, in Committee of the Whole, adopted a bill creating a State Board of Finance, with authority to issue $25,000,000 in bonds for the purpose of taking up the floating indebtedness of the State and procuring money to pay the current expenses of the Government during the ensuing year. The State lands are to be mortgaged as security for the payment of the bonds.

The following is a statement of all outstanding bonds of this State, up to October 1, 1874.

State Bank bonds. ....:............	$240.000
Real Estate Bank bonds...........	621,000
Arkansas funded bonds......................	3,050,000
Memphis & Little Rock Railroad bonds.......	1,200,000
Mississippi, Ouachita & Red River Railroad bonds....................................	600,000
Little Rock, Pine Bluff & New Orleans Railroad bonds................................	1,200,000
Little Rock & Fort Smith Railroad bonds....	1,000,000
Arkansas Central Railroad bonds.............	1,350,000
Bonds to supply deficits....................	300.000
Total.................................	$9,561,000

The treasurer is not required, by law, to keep a record of the levee bonds; therefore they do not appear in this list.

ARMY OF THE UNITED STATES. The expenditures and estimates of the War Department, as submitted in the annual report of the Secretary to the President at the close of the year, were as follows.

The actual expenditures of the War Department for the year ending June 30, 1873, including river and harbor improvements, were.....................	$46,325,308 21
The same for the last fiscal year, ending June 30, 1874............................	42,326,314 71
Showing a reduction of.............	$3,998,998 50
The estimates for the Military Establishment for the fiscal year ending June 30, 1875, were...........................	$34,410,722 89
Those submitted for the ensuing fiscal year are.................................	32,488,969 50
Showing a reduction of.............	$1,921,753 39
The estimates of the Chief of Engineers for fortification, river and harbor improvements, and public buildings and grounds, and Washington Aqueduct, for the fiscal year ending June 30, 1875, were	$20,459,396 00

Brought forward..........................		$20,459,396 00
His estimates for the fiscal year ending June 30, 1876, are as follows, viz.:		
Fortifications and other works of defense.........	$2,108,70 000	
Geographical and military surveys..................	399,000 00	
Improvement of rivers and harbors.................	13,285,509 00	
Public build'gs and grounds, and Washington Aqueduct......................	678,410 50	
		16,471,610 50
Showing a reduction of.............		$3,987,785 50
The total estimates of the War Department, for all purposes, for the fiscal year ending June 30, 1875, were........		$60,180.923 89
The same for the ensuing fiscal year are..		53,144,499 00
Showing a reduction in favor of those for the ensuing year of...........		$7,036,424 89
The estimates for the military establishment for the fiscal year ending June 30, 1876, are.................................		$32,488,960 50
The appropriations for the current fiscal year were...............................		28,582,392 00
Excess of next year's estimates over this year's appropriations........		$3,906,577 50

By the operation of the fifth section of the act of June 20, 1874, all unexpended balances of appropriations which had remained on the books of the Treasury for two fiscal years prior to July 1, 1874, excepting such amounts as were required to meet unfulfilled contracts at the time of the passage of the act, were carried to the surplus fund of the Treasury. This necessitated estimates by the War Department for various objects, the appropriations for which have always been available at any time. Therefore, certain items, for which estimates have not been heretofore required, are now included in the aggregate estimates of the department.

The strength of the army, October 15th, was reported at 26,441 enlisted men. In the report of the General of the Army to the Secretary of War, General Sherman says on this point: "I have no doubt that by the 1st of January, 1875, the number of enlisted men will be reduced, by ordinary casualties, discharges, and deaths, to the number limited by law—namely, 25,000, and will venture the expression of opinion that this limit forces the companies to so small a standard that the efficiency of the service is greatly impaired thereby. It is utterly impossible to maintain the companies at remote stations up to the very small legal standard, because months must necessarily elapse after discharges and deaths before recruits can be be sent from the general rendezvous."

In the act making appropriations for the support of the army, approved June 16, 1874, $105,000 was allowed for recruiting purposes, and it was provided that "no money appropriated by this act shall be paid for recruiting the army beyond the number of 25,000 enlisted men, including Indian scouts." In commenting upon this measure, Secretary Belknap says:

This prohibition fell in an unfortunate time and

manner. The demands for the service of United States troops have been increased, and have been imperative for Indian and other service, ever since the adjournment of Congress, and serious consequences might easily have attended the manifest want of any considerable reliable force. There was no margin for emergencies, such as have arisen in connection with Indian affairs and the troubles in the South. I was opposed to the reduction at the time it was made, and have since had no reason to change the opinion then formed. The reduced appropriations for army purposes have been too heavily taxed by the necessity of movement of troops; for, when obliged to be scattered at points on sudden emergencies, they have been moved from other points where their presence was needed, and had to be returned at the earliest possible moment. The reduction proposed and insisted on by Congress would, when it was accomplished, save alone the pay, subsistence, and clothing, of five thousand men; but this amount cannot all be considered as having been saved, for, when troops were needed at points where the force was found, in consequence of the reduction, to be too small for real service, other troops from other points were required to be transported at an expense almost large enough to equal in amount the saving from the sources named. Besides, the number of posts was not reduced; the necessities of the service required that they should be garrisoned, and, although they were occupied by very small forces, yet the expense incident to the retention and operation of the posts existed to almost as great an extent as it would have done had the number on duty been larger. In my judgment, if a reduction of the army is to be made, it can only be made by reducing the number of officers and men; in other words, by reducing the number of regiments. How that can be done in the present interests of the service, with the condition of affairs which requires the retention of the posts now in existence, and indeed the establishment of others, is a problem which must be determined if the reduction is insisted on. Reflection as to the amount necessary to be appropriated for the ensuing fiscal year satisfies me that the appropriation for clothing, pay, and subsistence, should be made for the army upon a basis of 30,000 men. This would most certainly prevent any deficiency, and, should appropriations to that extent be made, whatever surplus might remain on hand would be, under existing laws, turned into the Treasury.

The most important of the military divisions is that of the Missouri, commanded by Lieutenant-General Sheridan, which embraces substantially all the territory east of the Rocky Mountains to the Mississippi River, and includes the States of Illinois and Minnesota. Within this immense area are grouped most of the Indian tribes who are in a transition state from that of savages to a condition of comparative civilization. Here, the contact between the frontier settler and the aboriginal savage has resulted in chronic hostilities. General Sherman reports that "during the past year, by the extraordinary activity of the troops, and the good sense of our military officers, the frontier has been comparatively safe. On the northern line of Texas and southern line of Kansas, the untamed savages—Kiowas, Comanches, Cheyennes, and Arapahoes—began this season their usual raids, and, as the Indian agents confessed their utter inability to manage their respective tribes by the usual humane and Christian treatment, the whole

subject was turned over to the War Department, and committed to the management of Lieutenant-General Sheridan, who has laid hold of it with his accustomed energy. He is at this moment down in the Indian country near Fort Sill, giving his personal attention to the subject, and I have no doubt before the winter is over these Indians will learn a lesson which will enable the civil agents to bring them within the sphere of humanization, if not of civilization."

Within the limits of the Military Division of the Missouri are 76 established posts and camps garrisoned by 8 regiments of cavalry, 17 regiments of infantry, and a small detachment of engineer troops, aggregating, at the last official report, 17,819 commissioned officers and enlisted men.

Notwithstanding the occurrence of a few cases of yellow fever at Forts Jefferson and Barrancas during the summer of 1874, the army enjoyed unusually good health during the year. There has, however, been a large death-rate from accidental causes. The ratio of deaths and discharges from wounds, accidents, and injuries, is more than twice as great as in the British Army. Thus, in the past six years, it has averaged about 5 per 1,000 of strength in the American Army, while in the British Army the average has been 2.37 per 1,000 of strength. The mortality statistics of the army during the year are thus reported by the Surgeon-General:

White troops on sick-list	45,911
Average per 1,000 of strength	1,790
Entries per man on sick-list	2
Sick of disease	38,827
Average number of cases per 1,000 of strength	1,514
Sick of wounds, accidents, etc	7,084
Average per 1,000 of strength	276
Average number constantly on sick-list	1,190
Average per 1,000 of strength	46
Constantly under treatment for disease	938
Average per 1,000 of strength	36
Constantly under treatment for wounds, accidents, etc	252
Average per 1,000 of strength	10
Whole number of deaths	341
Average per 1,000 of strength	13
Died of disease	229
Average per 1,000 of strength	9
Died of wounds, accidents, etc	112
Average per 1,000 of strength	4
Proportion of deaths from all causes to cases treated	1 in 135
White soldiers discharged for disability	874
Number of cases among colored troops	4,535
Average per 1,000 of strength	1,816
Cases of disease	3,843
Average per 1,000 of strength	1,539
Cases of accidents, wounds, etc	692
Average per 1,000 of strength	277
Average number constantly on sick-list	130
Average per 1,000 of strength	52
Constantly under treatment for disease	101
Average per 1,000 of strength	40
Constantly under treatment for wounds, accidents, etc	29
Average per 1,000 of strength	12
Number of deaths from all causes	37
Average per 1,000 of strength	15
Died of disease	25
Average per 1,000 of strength	10
Died of wounds, accidents, etc	12
Average per 1,000 of strength	5
Total number of colored soldiers discharged for disability	59
Average per 1,000 of strength	24

Under the act appropriating $1,000,000 for placing head-stones at the graves of soldiers interred in the national military cemeteries, contracts have been made for the whole work, which is now in progress. There are 76 national cemeteries, in which are interred 139,962 unknown, and 162,079 known soldiers.

Under the Chief of Engineers, the works for the defense of the coast have been prosecuted with vigor, and as rapidly as the appropriations would permit; and in several of the important harbors the works are approaching completion. Generally, the works are modifications of existing defenses, constructed for less powerful armaments than those now used. The rapid advances that have been made in power of modern ordnance render it essential, in the opinion of the Secretary of War, that these works should be pushed forward to completion, and properly armed.

The survey of the lakes has been carried on during the year with its accustomed energy and success. The connection of the triangulation of Lakes Superior and Michigan, the in-shore and off-shore hydrography and topography, have been finished; the Wisconsin triangulation has been carried southward to the vicinity of Chicago, and the Keweenaw base has been measured. The surveys of the Detroit River and River St. Lawrence, from the forty-fifth parallel, have been completed, and a map of the lower half of the former has been published; the determination of several points in the interior of Michigan has been made in aid of surveys by the State; the survey of Lake Ontario has been commenced, and much of the field-work has been reduced. The preparation of Chart No. 1 of the St. Lawrence, of Sandusky Harbor, and of the mouth of the Detroit River, has been completed, and put into the hands of the engravers. It has been stated that a single survey made last year, viz., the survey of the mouth of the Detroit River, will save from $50,000 to $100,000 to commerce this year.

The geographical surveys and explorations west of the 100th meridian in California, Nevada, Utah, Arizona, Colorado, New Mexico, Wyoming, and Montana, have been carried on successfully. At the commencement of the fiscal year the three main parties engaged in this work had left their rendezvous at Salt Lake, Utah, Denver, Colorado, and Santa Fé, New Mexico. They moved south into Arizona, connecting with the work of former years, and covering during the surveying season about 75,000 square miles of territory. In addition to its topographical work proper, the survey embraced the fixing of many points astronomically, and investigations in geology, mineralogy, natural history, and the natural resources of the country traversed. It is expected that a large part of the results of this survey will be ready for the press during the coming year.

Among the more important results accomplished by the corps of engineers during the year may be mentioned the discovery of a new wagon-route from the line of the Union Pacific Railway to the Yellowstone Park and Montana; a reconnoissance in the country of the Ute tribe of Indians; the construction of a wagon-road from Santa Fé to Taos, New Mexico; and a survey of the Black Hills of Dakota by the engineer officer attached to the military expedition which was sent into that interesting country during the summer of 1874.

The board of ordnance officers appointed to consider the expediency of reducing the number of arsenals and the construction of a grand arsenal on the Atlantic seaboard, have submitted a report, which "strongly recommends the retention of the Springfield Armory and the Frankford Arsenal, and the establishment of a grand arsenal in the vicinity of New York City for manufacturing purposes; retaining also the Indianapolis Arsenal, Indiana; Kennebec Arsenal, Maine; Fortress Monroe Arsenal, Virginia; and Augusta Arsenal, Georgia, as places for storage and repair. It recommends the sale of the Alleghany, Columbus, Detroit, Pikesville, Watervliet, Watertown, and Washington Arsenals, the sales to be made as rapidly as circumstances will permit, the proceeds to be devoted to the purchase of a site and the erection of buildings for the grand arsenal. These seemingly large reductions by sale will, when accomplished, leave thirteen arsenals and the armory; and all this can be effected from the sales of arsenals, and without the expenditure of a dollar out of the national Treasury."

The work done by the Signal-Office has been of the highest value to the agricultural and commercial interests of the country, as well as to the cause of science.

During the year twenty-three stations of observation have been added to those from which reports are deemed necessary to enable proper warnings to be given of the approach and force of storms and of other meteoric changes for the benefit of agricultural and commercial interests. The daily exchange of telegraphic reports with the Dominion of Canada has been maintained, and warnings of threatened danger have been regularly sent, to be displayed at the ports of the Dominion. A series of daily telegraphic reports has been received from stations in the West Indies, extending from Cuba, by Jamaica, to Barbadoes and the Windward Islands. The most eastern station thus established, and in the course of possible cyclones, lies 2,300 miles to the southward and eastward of Washington. The issue of the official deductions had at the office of the Signal-Officer, from the reports there received, has continued during the year. A minute examination of these deductions, and a comparison with the meteoric changes afterward occurring within the time and within the district to which each has had reference, have given the average percentage of 84.4 as verified. With a more scrutinizing form of analysis the percentages have improved upon those of the preceding year. The wide diffusion given these reports may be judged from the fact that they appear in almost every newspaper published daily in the United States.

The display of cautionary day and night signals upon the lakes, and at the great ports of the United States, upon the Atlantic and Gulf coasts, has been made systematically on occasions of supposed especial danger at forty-two different stations, sea and lake ports, and cities. Of the total number of cautionary signals thus displayed, seventy-five per cent. have been afterward reported as justified. In no case has any great storm swept over the ports of the United States without preannouncement.

By an arrangement with the Post-Office Department, 6,286 printed "farmers' bulletins," on which appear the daily reports of the Signal-Office, have been distributed and displayed in frames, daily at as many different post-offices in different cities, villages, and hamlets, in different States, for the use of the agricultural population of the country, and they have been so displayed, on an average, within ten hours from the time they have left the Signal-Office in Washington.

The river reports, giving the average depth of water in the different great rivers of the interior, and notice of dangerous changes, for the benefit of river commerce and the population in the vicinity, have been regularly made, telegraphed, bulletined in frames, and published by the press at the different river ports and cities, and, in cases of great floods, special river reports have been issued.

By the great diffusion given the reports of this office through the press, the display of the different office bulletins and forms of report, the maps and regular publications, it is estimated that the statements based upon the information gathered upon the files of the office and issued for the public use reach daily at least one-third of all the households in the United States.

The publications of the office, the *Weekly Weather Chronicle* and the *Monthly Weather Review*, have been regularly issued during the year. A number of valuable charts have been prepared. A single atlas condenses into twelve charts results as to the average courses of movements of areas of disturbance in the United States, derived from the studies of the 3,375 charts charted at the Signal-Office in the period from March, 1871, to April, 1874.

As in the preceding years, a very considerable number of observations have, at the request of the Department, been taken on vessels at sea, to complement the synchronous reports of the service, and forwarded. Their utility is evident in the study of storms approaching our coasts, or which endanger vessels sailing from our ports.

At the Congress of persons charged with meteorological duties, assembled at Vienna in 1873, a proposition, to the effect that it is desirable, with a view to their exchange, that at least one uniform observation of such character as to be suitable for the preparation of synoptic charts be taken and recorded daily and simultaneously throughout the world, was adopted.

Special correspondence had by the Signal-Officer, by authority of the department, with scientists and chiefs of meteorological services representing the different countries, has resulted in arrangements by which a record of observations to be taken daily, simultaneously with the observations taken throughout the United States and the adjacent islands, is exchanged semi-monthly. These reports are to cover the territorial extent of Algiers, Austria, Belgium, Great Britain, Denmark, France, Germany, Italy, the Netherlands, Portugal, Russia in Europe and Asia, Sweden and Norway, Spain, Switzerland, and Turkey. Requests for similar coöperation are proffered to other nations as rapidly as practicable. The results had from this report are considered of especial importance, combining a coöperation thus already extending around the northern hemisphere to aid in the solution of questions upon which the United States has entered, and preparing for an exchange of telegraphic reports when that may be deemed advisable. Thus it has been left to the youngest nation to organize, and in a great measure perfect, a system of weather observations and meteorological studies which will soon encircle half the globe.

The sea-coast service of the Signal-Corps, in connection with the life-saving service, has been continued during the year. Telegraphic lines reaching from Barnegat to Cape May and from Norfolk to Cape Hatteras have been constructed, the stations upon them occupied, and the telegraphic lines operated by the officers and enlisted men of the signal-service. The telegraphic wires connect each station directly with the War Department.

The chief Signal-Officer earnestly recommends a more permanent organization of the signal-service, as necessary for the interests of the United States.

In June, 1874, $15,000 was appropriated by Congress "to enable the Secretary of War to begin the publication of the official record of the late war, both of the Union and Confederate armies." This work has been commenced with a determination to spare no pains to make the arrangement of the records simple and complete, and at the same time to omit all irrelevant matter.

One of the most important military changes during the year was, the removal of the headquarters of the commanding general from Washington to St. Louis. This change took place October 1st. "Here," says General Sherman, "I am centrally located, and, should occasion arise, I can personally proceed to any point of this continent where my services are needed."

ARNOTT, NEIL, M. D., F. R. S., F. G. S., an eminent British physician, physicist, and philanthropist, born in Arbroath, Scotland, in 1788; died in London, March 4, 1874. He was a member of a family somewhat noted in the annals of Scotland, his family home being at Dysart, near Montrose, Scotland. He was educated at the Aberdeen Grammar-School, and subsequently at Marischal College, in the University of Aberdeen, and, after taking the medical course in the university, went to London in 1806, and became the pupil of Sir Everard Home, Surgeon of St. George's Hospital. After passing his medical examination, he spent some years as a surgeon in the naval service of the East India Company, and in 1811 settled in London as a physician, where he soon attained a very large practice. In 1815 he was appointed physician to the French embassy, and soon afterward to the Spanish embassy. In 1823–'24, Dr. Arnott was induced to deliver a course of lectures on natural philosophy in its applications to medicine, a subject to which he had given great thought. These lectures formed the basis of his valuable and popular work, first published in 1827, " Elements of Physics; or, Natural Philosophy, General and Medical." This work was for forty years the standard work on physics, but the professional duties of the author were so engrossing that it was not until 1864 that he was able to find time to prepare the concluding chapters on electricity and astronomy. In 1836 he was named a member of the Senate of the University of London, and soon afterward a Fellow of the Royal Society, and still later a Fellow of the Geographical Society. In 1837 he was gazetted physician extraordinary to the Queen. In 1838 he published a treatise on " Warming and Ventilating ; " and, in 1855, one on " The Smokeless Fire-place, Chimney-Valves, etc." He was a man of great mechanical genius, and invented the Arnott stove, the Arnott ventilator, a water-bed of great excellence for invalids, and other valuable contrivances to increase human comfort and relieve suffering. With characteristic disinterestedness, he refused to patent any of these, lest the cost of them should be enhanced to the poor. In 1861 he published a " Survey of Human Progress." In 1869 he gave to each of the Universities of Aberdeen, Edinburgh, Glasgow, and St. Andrew's, a donation of £1,000 ($5,000) for the promotion of the study of experimental physics among the medical students. He also placed at the disposal of the Senate of the University of London £2,000 ($10,000) to found a scientific scholarship.

ASHANTEE.* Even before the arrival of Sir Garnet Wolseley, October, 1873, on the Gold Coast, the commanding general of the Ashantees, Amantaquia, had received from the King of the Ashantees the order to retreat. Violent rain-showers and epidemics had carried off many of their warriors. Before retreating, the Ashantee general made an attempt to possess himself of Abrakrampa, the capital of Abra, and formerly the capital of the kingdom of Fantee. The place was defended by Major Baker Russell, at the head of about 600 men, mostly natives, and gallantly withstood the onset of the Ashantees, who, on November 6th, abandoned the siege, and continued their retreat. At the beginning of December they fully evacuated the British territory, after having occupied it for nearly a year, and thoroughly devastated the Denkera and Fantee districts. The Ashantees, in their retreat, did not stop short of their capital, Coomassie. Here, according to their custom, the soldiers were received with military salutes and other honors. Of the 40,000 warriors who had taken the field, only 20,000 returned home. Seventy-nine coffins, containing the remains of the fallen nobles, were carried through the streets. The army was assembled by the King on the large market-place, and treated to roast-lamb and brandy. The general, the princes, and nobles, who had taken part in the expedition, were invited by the King to a council, where it was resolved to continue the war.

As General Wolseley considered the number of troops he had under his command entirely insufficient to finish the war, he soon after his arrival demanded new reënforcements. At the beginning of December the new troops arrived, consisting of the Forty-second Regiment, Royal Highlanders, called the Black Watch, a regiment which in the eighteenth century during

* For a geographical description of the kingdom of Ashantee, see ANNUAL CYCLOPÆDIA for 1873.

the Jacobite disturbances had become famous as coast watch, the Rifle Brigade, the Twenty-third Regiment, Royal Welsh Fusileers, some volunteers of the Seventy-ninth Regiment, a battalion of marine infantry, and the First Regiment of West Indians (negroes). As the preparations for transporting the troops into the interior were far from being finished, they had to remain in their ships for about one month. As a sufficient number of beasts of burden was not at hand, a large corps of carriers had to be organized. As the Fantee generally showed themselves unwilling and untrustworthy, the organization of this branch of the service encountered unexpected difficulties ; the West Indian negroes, and even the Highlanders and the riflemen, had for some days to serve as carriers. At last, Lieutenant-Colonel Colley, to whom the task of organizing the army had been assigned, succeeded in organizing a sufficient number of Fantee women, who were hired at one and a half shilling a day, and had to carry fifty pounds each. In the mean while, Major Home, of the Engineers, had constructed a good military road from Cape-Coast Castle to Prahsu on the Prah. Eight barrack-stations were established on this road, seven of which afforded shelter for half a battalion each ; while at Prahsu, accommodations had been prepared for the entire English army. Electric wires connected Cape-Coast Castle with Mansu, and Mansu with Prahsu. These two villages, as well as Donqua, Yankomasi, and the other villages on the road from Cape-Coast Castle to Prahsu, had been destroyed at the time when the Ashantees invaded the territory. At Mansu and Prahsu post and telegraph offices were established, and Mansu and Donqua were fortified by means of intrenchments, palisades, and ditches. Prahsu, which was more strongly fortified than any of the other stations, had the appearance of a city of soldiers' huts. The army was attended by seventy physicians and surgeons.

On December 27th, General Wolseley, with the Naval Brigade under Captain Blake, left for the Prah. The plans of operation provided that the regiments were to begin their march on January 6, 1874, that they were to arrive a week later at Prahsu, and to cross the Prah on January 15th. On the same day, Captain Glover and Captain Butler were to cross the Prah with the native corps they were to raise in Western Assin, and Captain Dalrymple in the west with the Wassaws. This plan was, however, but partly executed ; the efforts of Butler and Dalrymple to raise native corps were an entire failure. The Ashantees were first followed by the native troops under command of Wood and Russell, who suffered less than the English troops from want of provisions, and therefore were prepared the first to cross the Prah. This river is considered the frontier of the Ashantees, but Ashantee proper begins at the Adansi

Mountains. The country lying between, called Ashantee Assin, is the northern portion of Assin, and was at this time but thinly peopled, as the inhabitants had mostly emigrated into the southern districts, which belong to the English dominions. As the Ashantees did not consider their country invaded so long as the Adansi Mountains were not occupied by the enemy, they did not oppose the crossing of the Prah, and the English army marched the first thirty miles, or about one half of the distance between the frontier and Coomassie, without encountering any serious resistance. All the villages had been abandoned by the inhabitants. They were found to be better built than those in the English dominions, and afforded good shelter to the troops. On the 6th, Lord Gifford, who commanded the scouts, was pushing on as far as the village of Essiaman, twelve miles beyond the Prah. He saw smoke in the village in front of him, let his men load, and advanced hoping to surprise those within; but the men he had sent round to intercept the rear of the few holding the village were fired on, and he was obliged to return the fire. Only eight Ashantee scouts occupied the village. One was killed, the rest escaped, leaving two women prisoners. One of the English scouts was wounded, five slugs being put into or through him. The women said there were no Ashantees nearer than Quisab. The Ashantee scouts had, according to their evidence, been down to the Prah on the 2d of January. They had, in fact, accompanied the envoys, who on that day came to Sir Garnet Wolseley with letters from the King of Ashantee, which were addressed to Colonel Harley. The envoys were kept till the 6th, on which day the bridge over the Prah was completed. On the 4th they were allowed to see the practice with the Gatling guns. That night one of the Ashantee scouts shot himself. Afterward it appeared that he had been so frightened by the Gatling shot that he had said if white men had those weapons resistance was useless. The other envoys said they would report him to the King of Ashantee, and the fear of death by torture made him kill himself. He was buried on the farther side of the river, to the great delight of the envoys, who were most anxious to have him buried in his own land. Each man threw dust on the body, as in a Jewish funeral.

At this time the difficulty about the carriers had come to an end. Thanks almost entirely to the vigorous steps taken by Colonel Colley, and to the admirable management of that officer, eight thousand carriers were now working steadily upon the road. Here the concentration of the troops was to take place. The troops were moving by three stages, each about eleven miles long, from Prahsu to Monsi, at the southern foot of the Adansi Hills. First, from Prahsu to Essiaman; second, from Essiaman to Acrowfumu; third, from Acrowfumu to Monsi. The headquarters, with the Naval

Brigade, and the First Battalion of the Rifle Brigade, reached Monsi on the 20th. The other battalions followed in succession. The road had been admirably made, and every stream bridged completely to Fommanah, situated a mile and a half on the farther side of the Adansi Hills, by the engineers. The road, with the exception of the three miles nearest the Prah, was better than that between Cape Coast and the Prah, along which the general's carriage, drawn by natives, moved the whole distance. Even the portion for three miles this side of the Prah had been well covered with a sort of bastard, but very bad, corduroy. It was terribly swampy all along the line. At Atobiasi, Essiaman, Acrowfumu, Monsi, Quisah, Fommanah, and at two points between Acrowfumu and Monsi, not marked on home maps, intrenchments had been made to be held by small forces and protect the stores. Storehouses had been also made, and some huts. Those who could not thus obtain shelter had large tents, under which wattle-beds, keeping the men well off the ground, were constructed. The Adansi Hills fell into the hands of the English on the 16th. Lord Gifford pushing up with his scouts found the Ashantees in possession, but succeeded in frightening them into falling back by surrounding them and threatening an attack. On the 8th Major Russell, finding Quisab, half a mile on the farther side of the Adansi Hills, unoccupied, entered it with his regiment, and intrenched it. Wood's regiment and Rait's artillery were pushed up together on the 15th in support. Colonel Colley's vigor and success with the native carriers elicited universal praise. He undertook the task when it had just become a serious difficulty, and by a combination of energy and care for the men succeeded in placing it on a proper footing. The whole matter was put in his hands. He redressed all grievances, chiefly due to the carelessness of native guides, saw that the men had proper food, and intervals of rest. Then he surrounded with West Indian sentries villages to which deserters resorted, and thus made escape impossible. After the return of his embassadors the King secretly determined to continue the war vigorously; at the same time, however, he sent the captive missionaries to General Wolseley to assure him of his desire to make peace. Missionary Kühne arrived at Prahsu on January 13th to deliver the message of the King. General Wolseley replied that the King must set free all the European captives, pay an indemnity to the amount of £200,000, and sign a treaty of peace in the presence of the British army which would secure the protectorate and its allies against future attacks. On January 24th, the general with the Naval Brigade marched to Fommanah and established his headquarters in the palace of the King of Adansi. Now the King also liberated the missionary Ramseyer, his wife, and the Frenchman Bonnat. Ramseyer delivered to General Wolseley a letter from the King in which he notified the English general that he had instructed Amanquatia to pay the indemnification, on condition that General Wolseley remained in Fommanah. General Wolseley now believed the war to be at an end, and sent an express steamer to England to notify his government. The captives informed the English, however, that in every house in Coomassie slaves were busy making slugs out of stones. Of the liberated captives, Mr. and Mrs. Ramseyer were sent to Cape-Coast Castle, while Bonnat remained with the expedition. The Ashantee messengers were sent back by General Wolseley on the afternoon of January 26th. During the negotiations for peace, the regiment of Russell had advanced farther, and Lord Gifford, by extensive reconnoissances, had found that the villages on the road were strongly occupied by Ashantee warriors, and that the women and children had been removed from them. Major Russell summoned these garrisons to evacuate the villages, and, when they refused, attacked one of the villages and set it on fire. General Wolseley, still believing in the sincerity of the King's propositions for peace, gave orders to Major Russell hereafter not to burn any village, nor at any future encounter with the Ashantees to open fire. Soon after Lord Gifford intercepted a powder-convoy which was sent from Coomassie to Borborasi; at the same time he learned that the Ashantee general Essamanquatia and the Prince of Adansi were there with a considerable force. Colonel McLeod, who had been appointed brigadier of the native forces, received orders to march to Borborasi, first to open negotiations and, in case resistance should be made, to attack the enemy, but not to destroy the place. Captain Nicol, who led the van, stopped in front of the village, but, when on the point of beginning negotiations, was treacherously shot through the heart. Colonel McLeod then took the village, but, in accordance with his instructions, did not destroy it. On January 28th, other Ashantee messengers came to Fommanah, but immediately returned. The English soldiers were officially informed that the negotiations had been broken off, and that the war would go on. The Ashantee general Amanquatia had concentrated his new strong army and taken position at Amoaful, twenty miles from Coomassie. The van of the Ashantees occupied the village of Egginasi, half a mile from Amoaful. The latter is a place of about 2,000 inhabitants, situated on a high hill, while Egginasi lies on a lower hill; between both is a marshy valley crossed by a turbid creek. The slopes of both hills were densely wooded. Here Amanquatia had an army of 20,000 men, while the English only numbered 3,000. The English van, embracing the regiments of Wood and Russell, on January 30th, occupied Quarman, a village situated half a mile south of Egginasi; in the afternoon Major Home widened the road to Egginasi, and during the night Lord Gifford reconnoitred the enemy's position. The

bulk of the English army was at Jusarfu, four miles south of Quarman. It consisted of the Forty-second Regiment, the Black Watch, under Major Duncan McPherson; the Rifle Brigade, under Lieutenant-Colonel Warren; and one hundred men of the Twenty-third Regiment, under Lieutenant-Colonel Moslyn. Together, these troops formed the White Brigade, commanded by Brigadier Sir Archibald Alison, son of the English historian; to this were added the Naval Brigade under Captain Grubbe, a company of the Second West Indians, under Lieutenant Jones, and the Houssa with seven-pounders and rockets, under Captain Rait.

As General Wolseley saw that the small English army would be encircled by the overwhelming numbers of the enemy, as soon as it would reach Egginasi, he formed his army into a large square, in order to front the enemy on all sides, and to keep the inclosed ground free from all hidden enemies. Brigadier Alison, with the Forty-second Regiment, Gifford's skirmishers, Home's sappers, and Rait's artillery, was to advance and take Amoaful. Lieutenant-Colonel Moslyn commanded the right flank, and Colonel McLeod the left. General Wolseley, with his staff and Commodore Hewett and a company of the Twenty-third Regiment, took his place behind the front column. Quarman was occupied by Lieutenant Jones and the Second West Indian; the rear was commanded by Lieutenant-Colonel Warren. On January 31st, early in the morning, the Black Watch marched through Quarman and Egginasi into the woods, where, at about eight o'clock, they were most vehemently attacked by the Ashantees. The battle lasted until nearly twelve o'clock, when the end of the wood was reached, the hill taken, the fire of the Ashantees silenced, and Amoaful occupied. The Ashantees had lost a large number of killed and wounded, but the losses of the Black Watch were likewise severe. Nine officers and one hundred and five men were severely wounded; one officer and two men killed. The three other columns of the English army had also encounters with the Ashantees, who even destroyed a part of the baggage; but, at last, the Ashantees had to fall back on all sides. After the battle at Amoaful, there was a comparative lull for one day; though, even on that day, February 1st, some of the troops which had been most hotly engaged in the battle had to attack the village of Becquah, on the left flank of the English position. But on the second day, when the general moved forward as far as Agimmamu, the enemy disputed every mile of ground. Again, on February 2d, the enemy was in great force, opposing the advance of the English, and hanging round their flanks. The King on that day sent to Sir Garnet a characteristic letter, alleging, perhaps with unconscious truth, that "your Excellency's very rapid movements put me into confusion," and offering compliance if he were given time. Sir Garnet, in reply, demanded hostages in the persons of the King's mother and brother, and, in the event of their not being sent that day, announced that on the 4th of February he would march on Coomassie. They were not sent; and that evening the British force halted on the banks of the Ordah. A heavy rain fell during the night, and drenched the troops in their bivouac; and early the next morning they crossed the Ordah for their final advance. Here, however, the enemy made their last stand. They did not, according to Sir Garnet, fight with the same courage as at Amoaful. Their fire was wild, and they did not venture to attack the English at such close quarters. But their resistance was none the less most determined, and they maintained a general action for six hours. The village of Ordahsu was soon carried; the Ashantees, nevertheless, maintained the attack all around; but the baggage and ammunition were passed through the troops into the village, and then the force was massed there. At length, after some hours' incessant fighting, a panic seems to have seized the enemy, and they fled to Coomassie in complete rout, leaving behind them the umbrellas and other symbols of their chief's authority. Sir Garnet then called on his troops to make their final effort; and, notwithstanding their two days' work, and their lack of rest the night before, they pushed on upon the very heels of their retreating foe, and, at six o'clock in the evening, they formed up in the main street of Coomassie, and gave three cheers for the Queen. Sir Garnet Wolseley soon found that the King was adopting the same policy of gaining time by promises of negotiating. If Sir Garnet had been able to wait, he would, no doubt, have tried further measures to induce the King to come to terms; but this, he found, would be impossible. The rain which had fallen on the eve of the battle of Ordahsu was but the commencement of a succession of tornadoes, and he knew that with every day's delay the streams would become dangerously swollen, and the swamps more impassable. It was imperative that he should return at once, whether with or without a treaty. In these circumstances Sir Garnet determined, by burning the city, "to leave such a mark of our power as shall deter from future aggression a nation whom treaties do not bind." He accordingly prepared for the return-march with the same skill which had marked his advance. In the morning of the 5th he had sent off, under escort, all the wounded who were unable to march, and he gave orders to be ready for the return of his army on the morning of the 6th. Early on that day the town was set on fire, and the mines in the palace exploded, and as a rearguard of the Forty-second Highlanders left the capital its destruction was complete.

A writer who was present at the entry of the troops into Coomassie gives a description of the interior of the King's palace. He says there was a court-yard of some ten yards square in the inner yard and twenty yards exterior. The court-yard was open. Upon one side was a staircase leading to the upper story, upon the other were open store-rooms, in which the royal umbrellas, the canes used in processions, etc., were kept. The upper rooms were used as store-rooms. Here was an infinite variety of articles, for the most part mere rubbish, but many interesting and valuable. Silver plate, gold masks, gold caps, clocks, glass, china, pillows, guns, cloth, caskets, an olla-podrida, which resembled the contents of a sale-room. The rest of the palace was built in the native manner, and exactly resembled that of the King of Fommanah, but multiplied, not magnified, many times. In one were the war-drums, all ornamented either with human skulls, or thigh-bones; others were quite empty, while in two or three was simply a royal chair, upon which his Majesty used to sit to administer justice or decree vengeance. Signs of the latter were not wanting. Several stools were found covered with thick coatings of recently-shed blood, and a horrible smell of gore pervaded the whole palace, and indeed the whole town. That ghastly odor was everywhere perceptible, indeed, we could never get rid of it; occasionally it might have been fancy, but every one was of opinion that a sickly smell of blood was ever present. Part of this was no doubt due to a charnel-place, some twenty yards from one of the fetich-trees, hidden from sight of all who walked, by a fringe of rushes. Here were the bodies of some of the victims of fetich. Five or six were only two or three days old, while of others nothing but the skulls remained, and there were scores of others in various stages of putrefaction. The palace was full of fetich-objects. The King's private sitting-room was, like the rest, an open court, with a tree growing in it. This tree was covered with fetich-objects, and hung with spiders'-webs. At each end was a small, but deep alcove, with a royal chair, so that the monarch could always sit upon the shady side. Along each side of the little court ran a sort of veranda, beneath which was an immense assortment of little idols and fetiches of all kinds. From one of these a door opened into the King's bedroom, a room about ten feet by eight. At one end was the royal couch, a raised bedstead with curtains, and upon a ledge by the near side—that is to say, the King had to step over the ledge to get into bed—were a variety of weapons, together with an English general's sword, bearing the inscription, "From Queen Victoria to the King of Ashantee." Upon the floor, at the end opposite the bed, was a couch upon which the King could sit and talk with his wives. The room was very dark, being lighted only by a small window, about a foot square, opening into the women's apartments. In this part of the palace all sorts of stuffs, some of European, some of native manufacture, were found scattered about in wild confusion. General Wolseley, after burning Coomassie on the 6th of February, prosecuted his return-march with the utmost practical speed. On the 8th he reached Amoaful, the scene of his first difficult struggle with his enemy nine days before. On the 9th he dispatched a telegram from Detchiasu, a little way to the north of the Adansi Hills, saying that messengers had just arrived from the King, requesting peace, and that he intended halting with the troops north of the hills until the 13th or 14th, to allow time for negotiations. It was at first feared that the King's old policy of treacherous procrastina-tion was being revived; soon, however, it was ascertained that it was the approach of a sec-ond English force which prompted the King to tender his submission in earnest.

This English force was under command of Captain Glover, formerly administrator of Lagos, who, being in England at the outbreak of the Ashantee War, had asked for and re-ceived permission to organize, in the eastern districts of the Gold Coast, with the aid of a well-disciplined regiment of Yoruba and Houssa, on which he could rely, a native army of from 10,000 to 15,000 men, which was to coöperate with Wolseley. Lord Kimberley, the Colonial Minister, provided Glover with money, arms, and provisions, and obtained for him from the Minister of War and the Admi-ralty the permission to choose his own officers. Having arrived on the Volta, Captain Glover succeeded, by means of liberal distributions of money, muskets, and rum, in collecting a con-siderable army of Accras, Kroboes, and Krippies. But, as soon as they saw themselves in posses-sion of these things, they declared that Captain Glover, before they would follow him against Coomassie, must first destroy the Awoonahs and Aquamoo, otherwise these enemies during their absence would cross the Volta and plunder their country. Captain Glover considered it necessary to accede to the demand, and to march first against these two tribes which lived outside of the protectorate, and were at peace with the English. He went to Adda, on the Volta, where he established a force, and had to wait several weeks for the Accra, who were not yet ready. On December 23d, 24th, and 25th, he at length crossed the Volta with 800 Houssa and Yorubas and 20,000 na-tive allies, consisting of Aquapims, Accras, Ad-dahs, Kroboes, Krippies, etc., to attack the Awoonahs on the east bank of the Volta. The passage was effected by means of the Lady of the Lake, three steam-launches, and a number of canoes. The loss of the English was small, and the enemy was driven from all his posi-tions. On Christmas-night Captain Glover received urgent dispatches from Sir Garnet Wolseley directing him to proceed without a day's delay to the Prah, with all his disciplined forces, leaving the native allies to settle the Awoonah and Aquamoo affairs. Consequent-ly, on the 26th, the Houssas and Yorubas were taken back across the river, and Mr. Golds-worthy (the deputy commissioner), with Lieu-

tenant Mooro, Royal Navy, was left with the native allies, with orders to finish off the work to the east of the Volta, and to follow Captain Glover to the Prah with as many of the levies as he could bring, with as little delay as possi-ble. Meanwhile, the Houssas and Yorubas were pushed on as rapidly as possible for Akim, Captain Glover's instructions being to cross the Prah on the 16th of January, on which date Sir Garnet Wolseley would cross with the European regiments, and Captain Butler, be-tween Sir Garnet and Captain Glover, with the western Akims. By the greatest exer-tions, the Houssas and Yorubas, with a certain amount of provisions and ammunition, were moved from the Volta to the Prah, by way of Akapong and Kebbe, over six or seven moun-tain-ranges, and through dense forests with only small bush-paths, and on the night of the 14th the main body of the English force biv-ouacked within a few miles of the Prah. The Houssas and Yorubas marched admirably, do-ing long twenty-mile marches over precipitous mountain-passes, and reaching the Prah fresh and in the best possible spirits. The percent-age of sick was wonderfully small. On the morning of the 15th of January the advanced guard crossed the Prah at half-past ten o'clock, without any signs of an enemy. The Prah is a very rapid stream, with the bed of the river exceedingly rocky, the banks being steep and thickly wooded. Captain Glover crossed with the main body about noon. In the afternoon reconnoissances were made, but nothing was seen of the enemy. On the 16th, Obogoo, a large village, about fifteen miles distant in a northwesterly direction, was occupied. After waiting several days at Obogoo for ammuni-tion and receiving reënforcements of Akims and Kroboes, he continued his advance on Coo-massie, and finally reached a point fourteen miles northeast of it. He there heard of its occupation by Sir Garnet, and he dispatched to join his superior officer a little force which deserves the credit of one of the most gallant actions during the war. Captain Sartorius, with no more than twenty men, marched to Coomassie. He found the ruins still smoking. He passed through them without seeing a hu-man being, and on the 12th of February he reached Sir Garnet at Fommanah after having marched with his twenty men through the enemy's land over a distance of fifty-one miles. King Koffee having sent 1,000 ounces of gold as a first installment of indemnity with the request of peace, General Wolseley received his envoy at Fommanah on February 13th, and through him sent a draft of peace to Coo-massie for signature. The following are the particulars of the terms of peace agreed upon:

1. The King of Ashantee is to pay an in-demnity of 50,000 ounces of gold.

2. He renounces all claim to Adansi, Assin, Akim, Denkera, and Wassaw.

3. He binds himself to withdraw his forces

from Apollonia, Dix Cove, and all other parts of the coast belonging to Great Britain.

4. He undertakes the responsibility of keeping a road, fifteen feet wide, clear of bush, from Coomassie to the Prah.

5. He engages also to protect goods and merchandise in transit between the Prah and Coomassie.

6. The King is to prohibit human sacrifices.

7. Finally, he promises to be at peace with England forever.

Captain Glover followed Sartorius to Coomassie and Fommanah. General Wolseley, on February 16th, recrossed the Prah, and on February 19th made his triumphal entry into Cape Coast Castle, where the European merchants and the natives had erected grand triumphal arches. The Ashantee women, painted black and white, swung green branches, and sang triumphant hymns as each regiment entered. Prahsu, which had been strongly fortified, received a garrison of West-Indians, and remained in telegraphic communication with Cape Coast Castle. The English regiments soon after embarked, and were at the beginning of March welcomed in England by grand ovations. According to a return, issued in July, the total strength of the force (exclusive of native levies and West-Indian regiments) engaged in the prosecution of the war in Ashantee was 2,507 of all ranks: 297 officers, and 2,290 non-commissioned officers and men. The casualties from disease numbered 511, and from engagements with the enemy 202, and after arrival at home, up to the 31st of May last, there were ten deaths from wounds or diseases contracted in Africa. The total number who died was eighteen officers and fifty-three non-commissioned officers and men.

The native allies with whom Captain Glover had to deal are thus described by him:

Sakety, chief of the eastern Kroboes, was the only chief of the whole eastern protectorate whom I found always ready, willing, and able to carry out the orders he received, and I trust her Majesty's Government may be pleased to mark its sense of his most exceptional conduct. The chief of Abude, in Aquapim, marched with me to Coomassie, and rendered great assistance in providing carriers. His conduct is exceptional also, and should be noticed. The King of Eastern Akim, one or two chiefs, and perhaps some hundred of his men, are the exception that I am about to report, viz., that the eastern Akims are the most abject cowards it is possible to conceive. They would neither scout, patrol, reconnoitre, carry, nor fight. At Conomo I threatened to burn their camp and drive them back to their women across the Prah, and only spared them for the sake of their king, a young man of twenty-one or twenty-two years. Among the cowards of the protectorate I should consider them preëminent. The natives of the different tribes of the eastern district of the protectorate I must report as truculent, disobedient, and unreliable. That they can be got to fight on some occasions I have seen; but, where there is neither pride nor shame, you have no sense of feeling to work upon, save one—their fear. There has been one bright exception to this distressing report of the eastern tribe of the protectorate. Two companies of Christians, one of Akropong and the other of Christiansburg, numbering about one hundred each, under their two captains, accompanied by Bible-readers of the Basle Mission, attend a morning and evening service of their own daily, a bell ringing them regularly to prayers. In action with the enemy at Adidumé, on Christmas-day, they were in advance, and behaved admirably, since which they have garrisoned the depot at Blappah. Their conduct has been orderly and soldier-like, and they have proved themselves the only reliable men of the large native force recently assembled on the Volta.

The success of the English expedition proved a powerful blow to the rule and influence of the Ashantee King. To understand the events which followed the English expedition, it must be remembered that, about two hundred years ago, the Ashantees were a small tribe, vassals of Denkera, then a powerful state, now part of the English protectorate. The Ashantees being ill-treated, rebelled, gained their independence, and founded Coomassie. They were surrounded by small kingdoms—Becqua, Kokofo, Mampon, Adansi, and Djuabin—all of which they conquered; but these states still remained under their own kings, who paid tribute to the King of Ashantee, contributed soldiers when he went to war, attended the capital at certain festivals, and were summoned, as occasion arose, to councils, at which each chief or king spoke in turn, according to his rank. Thus the Ashantee nation was not homogeneous, but composed of various kingdoms, which cherished the traditions of their independent sovereignty, which were held together merely by the fear of punishment, and which were prepared at any time to secede from tyranny and taxation should any misfortune befall the imperial tribe. This seceding or separating process commenced before the English troops were out of Ashantee. The chief of Adansi and his people had been much oppressed by Ashantee. He resisted the white men, but, as soon as Coomassie had been taken and the struggle decided, he determined to throw off his ancient yoke and place himself in the hands of the stronger and also more merciful power. He met Sir Garnet Wolseley in the ruins of Fommanah, his own capital, and there made arrangements for migrating into the protectorate. At the same time a rumor reached the general that the chief or King of Becqua desired to follow the example of Adansi. Becqua is a powerful state, and its capital, which the English troops destroyed, was not much smaller than Coomassie. Finally, the King of Djuabin sent in his submission to Glover, and afterward began negotiations with the King of Eastern Akim, with a view to migration to that country. Subsequently Becqua and Djuabin determined to hold their own territory, to cast off their allegiance, and to resist any attempt that Cal-Calli might make to subdue them. Becqua was supported by Denkera, and Djuabin by Akim. Coomassie and its territory lie just between the rebellious states, and if Kokofo and Mampon refused to assist the Ashantees, the latter kingdom would be likely to be reduced to its former elements, viz., a small tribe, the city of Coomassie, and a few plantation villages.

On July 10th a messenger arrived from the King of Ashantee to the administrator of the protectorate, to inform him that the Kings of Djuabin and Becqua were in revolt, and refused to ·attend Cal-Calli's summons to view his return to the capital, and further, that they threatened to attack him if he attempted to use force. The King of Ashantee therefore sent down to the administrator, asking for his interference, as peace was what he wanted, and the attack, if carried out, would possibly lead to a lengthy war, and effectually destroy trade. The administrator questioned the embassadors, and, after a good deal of fencing on their part, drew from them that which led him to think the King of Ashantee had been endeavoring to put some pressure on Djuabin and Becqua, thus bringing about the present crisis. The administrator at once sent Captain Lees to Coomassie to act as peace-maker between the tribes, and so prevent the threatened outbreak.

Shortly before being sent to Coomassie, Captain Lees had convoked a very important " palaver " to induce the Awoonahs to sign a treaty of peace with the Accras and Addahs. The former had been the allies of the Ashantees in the late war, but it was now thought desirable to establish cordial relations between all the tribes of the coast. A meeting having taken place between the hostile parties for this purpose, the interpreter standing forth delivered the administrator's message to the Awoonahs, and said : " You have not now the Ashantees to protect you, and we want you to be our allies. If such does not please you, there is no need to conceal the fact that we think it necessary for us to take an active part in protecting our interests, and showing that we intend to maintain our rights and enforce our power. Do you doubt there are Ashantees present? for I will call them, and you will hear what they have to say." Then there stood in the open space an Ashantee messenger, bearing his emblematic two-handed sword, who told the Awoonahs his people were at peace with the English, and to be their friends forever. After some trouble, "fetich " was eaten by those who had lately been foes, and a binding peace was effected between them.

·Interesting information, on the introduction of slaves by Ashantee traders to the British protectorate on the Gold Coast, is contained in dispatches published by the English Government in August, 1874. The first is dated as far back as the beginning of 1866, and is from Mr. Cardwell to Governor Blackall, then recently appointed. In it the Secretary for the Colonies notifies the disallowance of the colonial ordinances which recognized the existence of slavery within the British colony at Lagos and the towns of Badagry, Palma, and. Leckie ; suggests the prescription of a punishment for subsequent violence on compulsory deten-

tion, and gives instructions to warn the neigh-. boring chiefs against permitting their slaves to enter British territory, lest they should be liberated or prevented from returning. The second dispatch was sent by the Earl of Kimberley, in the beginning of 1872, to the Governor of the West-African settlements, and briefly indicated the difficulty of dealing in a mere protectorate with people who are not British subjects ; but at the same time urges that every means should be taken to induce the natives to desist from their nefarious practices. At the same time it was suggested that the proper course would be to endeavor to come to an understanding with the chiefs of the protected tribes to forbid the slave-trade within their separate districts, and to persuade them to enter into agreements with the Gold-Coast government to this effect, when the government would be in a position to enforce these semi-treaty agreements. The Earl of Kimberley specially called attention to the fact that any slave imported into what was strictly British territory must at once be set free, and requested the West-African governor to forward his ideas as to the best mode of giving effect to the propositions which he had made. A note stated that no reply was received to this dispatch.

During the presence of Captain Lees at Coomassie, the King of the Ashantees made the utmost efforts to obtain the support of the English for the reunion of the tribes which since his defeat had rebelled against him. Captain Lees, however, refused to interfere, and it was, therefore, believed probable that the kingdom of the Ashantees would fall to pieces.

On November 3d an important meeting of all the kings and chiefs of the western and central positions of the Gold Coast was held at the Castle of Cape Coast, in the Palaver-hall. Governor Strahan made an address to them, in which he reviewed at·length the former relations of their districts to the Ashantees, the wrongs which had been inflicted upon them by the Ashantee kings, and the aid and benefits they had received from England. He then announced to them, that now the Government of England, in return for these benefits, requested their aid in putting an end to a thing the Queen and her people abhorred.

Governor Strahan said : " This thing is against a law which no King or Queen of England can ever change. I have pointed out to some of you that the English people buy sheep, fowls, and other live-stock, but not men, women, and children. The Queen is determined to put a stop at once to the buying and selling of slaves, either within or without the protectorate, in any shape, degree, or form ; and she will allow no person to be taken as a pawn for debt." (This last passage was repeated with considerable emphasis.) "The Queen desires to make you as happy as her own people. This buying, selling, and pawning of men, and women, and children, is wrong, and no country where it exists can be happy. The Queen does not desire to take any of your people from you; those of them who like to work for, and with, and to assist you, can remain with you. If they are happy, and continue to live with you on the same terms as now, no change will be forced upon you; but any person who does not desire to live with you on those terms can leave, and will not be compelled by any court, British or native, to return to you. The Queen hopes to make you happy in many ways, as happy as those in her other dominions. It is right that I should tell you distinctly that, if you desire her protection, you must do as she wishes—as she orders. This is the Queen's message. When the Queen speaks in this way, it is not a matter for palaver, question, hesitation, or doubt, but she expects obedience and assent. I will only say that, without the Queen's money and troops, you would have been slaves of a blood-thirsty people. The Queen has paid a great price for your freedom. You and those near and dear to you would have been dragged hence to form a portion of the thousands who are decapitated and sacrificed by this savage race for their customs. Your homes would have been homes full of misery. I see you to-day enjoying peace, and I call on you all to join with me in the prayer, 'God save the Queen.' My message is delivered."

When the governor ceased speaking, the chiefs for a short time consulted among themselves what answer to give. At last King Edoo, of Mankessim, solicited permission from the governor to retire till the next day, so that they, the kings, might consult together as to what answer they could give. This, however, the governor refused, and referred them to that portion of his speech or message wherein he had stated that when the Queen expressed her wishes it remained only for them to obey; but, if they wished it, he would retire for a short time, and leave them to their deliberations. The governor then left the Palaver-hall, and, upon his return, in about one hour, the kings and chiefs informed him that they were willing to cease from buying or selling slaves, but raised objection to the slaves being permitted to go free if they chose, without there being any cause shown, and likewise to pawns not being allowed. After some discussion, it was decided that no slave could leave his or her master or mistress, unless there was proof of cruelty or maltreatment, when such slave would be entitled to his or her freedom. And the question of pawns was settled by the debtor being held liable for the amount that the pawn had been given as security for, and that the amount should be recovered on the pawn leaving. This concluded the meeting in the castle, but the governor invited all the kings and chiefs to go over to Government House to drink long life to her Majesty.

Reports from Coomassie, received at Cape Coast Castle, in November, confirmed the rumor that King Koffee had been deposed, and had retired to the villages beyond Coomassie. Guacoo Duah had been proposed as his successor. A palaver had taken place at Accra about the household-slave question, and the natives had agreed that their slaves should be under British protection, in accordance with the governor's proclamation. At Cape Coast Castle the different chiefs were willing to open trade further into the interior than had yet been done. (*See* H. Brackenbury, Captain Royal Artillery, Assistant Military Secretary to Sir Garnet Wolseley, "The Ashanti War: a Narrative prepared from Official Documents, by permission of Major-General Sir Garnet Wolseley." Edinburgh, 1874.)

ASIA. While the Russian Government, by the treaty concluded near the end of the year 1873, with the Khan of Bokhara, ceded a part of the territory obtained from the conquered Khan of Khiva, to Bokhara, it regulated, early in 1874, the permanent organization of that part of its new acquisitions which it intends to retain, under the name of trans-Caspian territory. The dependence of the khanates of Bokhara, Khiva, and Khokand, upon Russia, becomes every year more complete, and, though they remain nominally independent countries, they are virtually governed by the Russian authorities of the neighboring provinces. (*See* RUSSIA and KHOKAND.)

In Afghanistan, the Ameer Shere Ali announced the son of his favorite wife, young Abdullah Jan, as his heir, to the exclusion of his eldest son, Yakoob Khan, the Governor of Herat. As Yakoob Khan did not conceal his intention to vindicate his claims to the throne by force of arms, a new civil war was regarded as imminent. Toward the close of the year, Yakoob Khan, while visiting his father at Cabul, was suddenly imprisoned, a measure which it was thought would precipitate rather than retard the outbreak of hostilities. England and Russia are well known to counteract each other's influence in Afghan affairs, but both are working as much as possible in secret, and much that belongs to the current history of these countries will only be cleared up in the future. (*See* AFGHANISTAN.)

In Kashgar, the country ruled by Yakoob Kushbegee, the influence of Russia and England is likewise at conflict. An English embassy, in February, 1874, succeeded in concluding a new treaty with the Ameer of Kashgar, which it was hoped would open for the trade of British India new markets in Central Asia, and enable the English to compete with the Russians, who had previously established treaty relations with Kashgar, and were already driving a thriving trade with the Kashgarees. The rumored intentions of the Chinese Government to send out an expedition for the reconquest of Kashgar, which was formerly a Chinese dependency, may lead to new complications. (*See* KASHGAR.)

The disposition of the Chinese Government toward foreign nations remained wavering and doubtful. Among the mass of the people the hatred of every thing foreign seemed far from being on the decline, and the degradation, of Prince Kung, the chief representative of a friendly foreign policy, was looked upon as a victory of the anti-foreign party. An expedition of Japan against the pirates of Formosa, an island which China claims as a dependency, for a time interrupted the friendly relations between the two great eastern Asiatic countries, and even threatened a war. Toward the close of the year the difficulty was, however, peaceably adjusted. (*See* CHINA.)

Japan, on the contrary, continues to advance resolutely on the road of progress. Several insurrectionary movements were promptly put down, and the outrages committed by the pirates of Formosa against shipwrecked Japanese led to an expedition of Japan against Formosa, which, notwithstanding the protest of the Chinese Government, proved an entire success. The results of the first census were published by the government, and great reforms were introduced into the department of Public Instruction. (*See* JAPAN.)

British India, as was expected at the close of the year 1873, was again visited by an extensive famine, and for several months the number of persons assisted by the government was estimated at 3,000,000. The energetic and timely preparations made by the government carried the population of the suffering districts safely through the great ordeal, and about October this famine was declared to be at an end. Toward the close of the year, a resolution was issued by the Viceroy in council, announcing that a campaign against the Duffla had become unavoidable for the rescue of captives carried off by this tribe from British territory. (*See* BRITISH INDIA.)

Persia is agitated by severe conflicts between the liberal lay party, represented by Mirza Husseïn, and the ecclesiastical party of the Mohammedan priests; and the vacillation of the Shah makes it doubtful whether the reform party will command sufficient influence to improve the wretched condition of the country. New difficulties sprang up between Persia and Turkey, which were, however, peaceably adjusted. (*See* PERSIA.)

The war of the Dutch against the sultanatè of Acheen, on the island of Sumatra, was continued throughout the year 1874. Though not a complete failure like the first expedition in 1873, it was marked by slow progress and severe losses. The Dutch announced their intention to annex Acheen to their dominions, and to extend their rule over the entire island of Sumatra. (*See* NETHERLANDS.)

The complications between France and the Emperor of Anam, arising out of the bloody persecutions of the native Christians in the latter country, were terminated by a new treaty, which promised to the Christians of Anam entire religious liberty, and conceded to France a greater influence than she had ever had before. (*See* FRANCE.)

The grand project of a Central Asian railway, which, if realized, could not fail to exercise an extraordinary influence upon the destiny of the interior of Asia, is declared by M. Victor de Lesseps to be feasible. With respect to the material obstacles in carrying a railway over the mountains, De Lesseps is of opinion that neither the Karokaram Passes nor the Bolan Pass need terrify modern engineers. The Karokaram Mountains are much higher than any yet surmounted, but the gradients are much easier than others that have been successfully crossed by railways. There are several alternative routes. The traffic expected would, in his opinion, suffice to pay interest on the capital required for the construction of the railway.

ASTRONOMICAL PHENOMENA AND PROGRESS. *Minute Structure of the Solar Photosphere.*—Prof. S. P. Langley, of the Alleghany Observatory, communicates to the *American Journal of Science* the results of his repeated and careful examinations of the sun's surface. In exceptionally favorable atmospheric conditions the so-called "rice-grains" of the photosphere have been resolved into very minute points of light, which Prof. Langley calls *granules.* These intensely bright, circular bodies, which are less than three-tenths of a second in diameter, are irregularly distributed, and tend evidently to collect in clusters. They constitute the properly luminous area, or, in other words, are the chief source of solar light. Those results of Mr. Langley's telescopic studies which seem to have escaped the notice of other observers, are thus briefly recapitulated:

The ultimate visible constituents of the solar photosphere being, not the rice-grains, but smaller bodies which compose them, and the size of these latter being valuable at not over $0''.3$: from a comparison of the total area covered by them with that of the whole sun, we are entitled to say that the greater part of the solar light comes from an area of not over one-fifth of its visible surface, and which may be indefinitely less.

We must then greatly increase our received estimates of the intensity of the action to which solar light (and presumptively its heat and solar light (and presumptively its heat and actinism) are due, on whatever theory we form them. (There is a presumption from observation that there is a drift of all the photosphere in a direction approximately parallel to its equator, while the evidence as to this point is not yet conclusive.)

In the penumbræ there are not only numerous small cyclones, and even right- and left-handed whirls in the same spot, but probably currents ascending nearly vertically, while the action of superposed approximately horizontal currents is so general that they must be considered a prominent feature in our study of solar meteorology.

A study of the outer penumbral edge leads to the conclusion that it is formed by rupture.

The Transit of Venus.—Some account of the arrangements made by different governments for observing the transit of Venus, on the 8th of December, 1874, has been given in previous volumes. Complete reports from all the expeditions sent out to observe the phenomenon have not yet been received, and hence the resulting value of the solar parallax remains undetermined. It can only be stated that the observations were successful at Tschita, latitude 52° north; at Hobart Town, latitude 43° south; at Wladiwostok, Peking, Teheran, Thebes, Sydney, and more than twenty other intermediate stations. It is obvious, however, that considerable time will be required for an exhaustive discussion of all the observations.

Asteroids.—Six minor planets were discovered during the year, bringing the known number up to 140. Hertha, the 135th of the group, was discovered by Dr. Peters, of Clinton, N. Y., on the 18th of February. This is the twentieth asteroid first seen by the Director of the Litchfield Observatory. No. 136 was detected by Palisa, at Pola, on the 19th of March, and No. 137 by the same observer on the 21st of April. M. Perrotin, of Toulouse, discovered No. 138 on the 19th of May. The 139th of the cluster was found by Prof. Watson, at Peking, China, on the 10th of October. This being the first planet discovered in that empire, it was named Ne-Wha, from a Chinese goddess. It is the seventeenth asteroid first detected by Prof. Watson. M. Palisa, of Pola, discovered No. 140 on the 13th of October. Of these asteroids, No. 137 is of the twelfth magnitude, No. 138 between the eleventh and twelfth, and the remaining four of the eleventh.

The minor planet Æthra, No. 132, was discovered in 1873, but trustworthy elements of its orbit were first published in the *Astronomische Nachrichten* of August 11, 1874. This asteroid is distinguished by the great eccentricity of its orbit, as shown by the following comparison with the orbits of other bodies:

NAME.	Eccentricity.
Mercury	0.2056
Polyhymnia	0.3397
Æthra	0.3819
Second comet of 1867	0.5075
Faye's comet	0.5560

There is thus seen to be less difference in form between the orbits of Æthra and the second comet of 1867 than between the former and the orbit of Mercury. It is noteworthy, moreover, that the aphelion of Mars differs in longitude but one degree from the perihelion of Æthra, and that the greatest distance of the former exceeds the least of the latter. These facts indicate the possibility of so near an approach of the two bodies that the disturbing influence of Mars on the asteroid may materially modify the elements of its orbit.

Comets.—Dr. Winnecke, of Strasburg, discovered the first comet of 1874 on the 20th of February, and the second on the 12th of April.

Neither became visible to the naked eye, and their elements had no special resemblance to those of any comet previously known. The third was first observed by M. Coggia, at Marseilles, on the 17th of April. It was first seen by the naked eye about two months after the date of its discovery, and early in July it had become a conspicuous object in the northern heavens. It passed its perihelion on the 9th of July; its least distance from the sun being 62,000,000 miles. About the 20th of July its tail was sixty-eight or seventy degrees in length. The period of this comet, according to Geelmuyden, is 10,445 years.

Spectroscopic observations of Coggia's comet indicated the presence of carbon. Dr. Huggins inferred from numerous examinations that the nucleus was solid, heated by the sun, and throwing out matter which formed the coma and tail. Part of this was in a gaseous form, giving the spectra of bright lines. The other portion existed probably in small incandescent particles; the polariscope showing that certainly not more than one-fifth of the whole light was reflected solar light.

The fourth comet of the year was discovered by M. Borelly, of Marseilles, on the 26th of July. Its perihelion passage occurred on the 27th of August, its least distance from the sun being 91,000,000 miles. The fifth was detected by M. Coggia, of Marseilles, on the morning of August 20th, and the sixth by M. Borelly, of the same observatory, on the 7th of December.

Meteors.—The display of August meteors was observed by Prof. Daniel Kirkwood, at Bloomington, Ind. The night of the 9th—when the maximum generally occurs—was so cloudy as to prevent observations. The evening of the 10th, however, was perfectly clear. Two observers counted sixty-four meteors from $11^h.\ 16^m.$ to $12^h.\ 16^m.$ As one person can notice but a fifth part of the whole number, the observations indicated a fall of 160 meteors per hour. The usual characteristics of the *Perseids* were distinctly noticed. Their apparent brightness, for instance, generally increased from their first appearance till the moment before extinction.

In the *Astronomische Nachrichten*, No. 2,014, Herr Nicolaus von Konkoly gives some highly interesting spectroscopic observations of the August meteors. From the 7th to the 11th of the month he observed the spectra of 130. The nucleus gave, in every instance, a continuous spectrum. The trains of *all* gave sodium lines; those of the red meteors gave also strontium or lithium; and those of the green magnesium. The spectrum of some of the largest also indicated iron. The observations of the November swarm entirely failed, not only in this country but also in Europe. No return of this shower, in considerable numbers, can now be expected till near the close of the century.

On the 27th of July—a well-known meteoric epoch—Prof. Tacchini, of Italy, observed four fire-balls which entered our atmosphere at the same time, and passed through it in parallel lines. They continued visible about forty seconds. A meteorite composed in part of iron, nickel, and sulphur, fell in Turkey on the 20th of May.

The Zodiacal Light.—Prof. Arthur W. Wright, of Yale College, communicates to the *American Journal of Science and Arts* (May and July, 1874) some interesting researches in regard to the nature of the zodiacal light. The results of the investigation are briefly stated as follows:

1. The zodiacal light is polarized in a plane passing through the sun.
2. The amount of polarization is, with a high degree of probability, as much as 15 per cent., but can hardly be as much as 20 per cent.
3. The spectrum of the light is not perceptibly different from that of sunlight, except in intensity.
4. The light is derived from the sun, and is reflected from solid matter.
5. This solid matter consists of small bodies (meteoroids) revolving about the sun in orbits crowded together toward the ecliptic.

The *theory* that the zodiacal light is produced by the reflection of the sun's rays from innumerable asteroids interior to the earth's orbit, and too small to be separately observed, was proposed by Cassini two hundred years since. Its *demonstration*, however, was first announced in the memoirs above quoted. Prof. Wright, in a third paper, which was read before the American Association for the Advancement of Science, in August, 1874, gives reasons for regarding the orbits of the reflecting bodies as very eccentric.

The Inner Satellites of Uranus.—The question of priority in the discovery of the inner satellites of Uranus has been recently examined by Prof. Edward S. Holden, of the Washington Observatory. After discussing the original observations, together with those of Lamont, Struve, and Lassell, Mr. Holden concludes that not only Titania and Oberon, but also the inner satellites, Ariel and Umbriel, were really discovered by Sir William Herschel, and that the observations of Lassell in 1847 were but rediscoveries of the same bodies. The justice of this conclusion is called in question by Mr. Lassell, who ably vindicates his own exclusive claim to the original discovery. "From a less distinguished authority," he remarks, "than that of an astronomer writing from the Washington Observatory, the assertion might have passed unnoticed, from a conviction that it would not obtain credence; but Prof. Holden's conclusions will probably be held to have an importance or prestige, which compels me at some length to prove how perfectly erroneous they are. I myself claim to be the original and only discoverer of these inner satellites, Ariel and Umbriel, single-handed and unassisted, without coadjutor, rival, or competitor."

Among the reasons assigned by Mr. Lassell for concluding that none of the stars noticed by Sir William Herschel in the vicinity of Uranus could have been Ariel and Umbriel, is the fact that the means at his disposal "did not suffice to reveal to him the existence of these most minute bodies."

Stellar Parallaxes.—Dr. Brunnow, the Astronomer Royal for Ireland, has devoted special attention for several years to the determination of the parallaxes of certain fixed stars. The star known as No. 1,830 of Groombridge's catalogue was supposed, from the fact of its having a large proper motion, to be comparatively near us. The observations of Prof. Brunnow, however, have shown its annual parallax to be only nine-hundredths of a second—a parallax which corresponds to a distance ten times greater than that of Alpha Centauri. From a series of observations on Sigma Draconis, the same distinguished astronomer obtains a parallax of one-fourth of a second; for No. 3,077 of Bradley's catalogue, seven-hundredths of a second; and for the double star No. 68, Pegasi, five-hundredths of a second. The distance corresponding to the last would not be traveled by light in less than sixty years.

Periods of Binary Stars.—M. Flammarion, of Paris, has redetermined the periods of the following double stars:

Zeta Herculis	34.57 years.
Eta Coronæ Borealis	40.17 "
Xi Ursæ Majoris	60.60 "
Gamma Virginis	175.00 "

The first of these periods, it will be observed, is somewhat greater than that of Saturn, while the last is a little greater than the period of Neptune. M. Flammarion remarks that the large number of observations used in the calculation renders his conclusions entirely trustworthy.

Distribution of the Bright Fixed Stars.—A paper on "The Number and Distribution of the Bright Fixed Stars" was read before the American Association for the Advancement of Science, in August, 1874, by Dr. B. A. Gould, Director of the Cordoba Observatory. In this memoir the existence of a zone or great circle of very bright stars, intersecting the Milky-Way at an angle about equal to that between the equator and the ecliptic, is, for the first time, distinctly recognized. Dr. Gould remarks:

It has been generally assumed that the number of visible stars of any given magnitude, whether brighter or fainter, diminishes as their distance from the Milky-Way increases. In the elevated position and pure atmosphere of Cordoba, this nebulous circle is seen with a vividness far surpassing that to which we are accustomed here; and, moreover, most of that portion which lies in the Southern Hemisphere is intrinsically brighter than the northern half; so that its position is far more clearly defined than I have ever seen it elsewhere. And few celestial phenomena are more palpable there than the existence of a stream or belt of bright stars, including *Canopus, Sirius,* and *Aldebaran,* together with the most brilliant ones in *Carina, Puppis, Columba, Canis Major, Orion,* etc., and skirting the Milky-Way on its preceding side. When the opposite half of the Galaxy came into view, it was equally manifest that the same is true there also, the bright stars likewise fringing it on the preceding side, and forming a stream which, diverging from the Milky-Way at the stars *Alpha* and *Beta Centauri*, comprises the constellation *Lupus* and a great part of *Scorpio*, and extends onward through *Ophiucus* toward *Lyra*. Thus a great circle or zone of bright stars seems to gird the sky, intersecting with the Milky-Way at the Southern Cross, and manifest at all seasons, although far more conspicuous upon the Orion side than on the other. Upon my return to the North, I sought immediately for the northern place of intersection; and, although the phenomenon is by far less clearly perceptible in this hemisphere, I found no difficulty in recognizing the node in the constellation *Cassiopeia*, which is diametrically opposite to *Crux*. Indeed, it is easy to fix the right ascension of the northern node at about 0ʰ· 50ᵐ·, and that of the southern one at 12ʰ· 50ᵐ·; the declination being in each case about 60°, so that these nodes are very close to the points at which the Milky-Way approaches most nearly to the poles. The inclination of this stream to the Milky-Way is about 25°, the Pleiades occupying a position midway between the nodes.

Dr. Gould, after noticing this remarkable circle and commencing the preparation of data in statistical form to demonstrate its existence, found that he had been partially anticipated by Sir John Herschel. The British astronomer, however, " does not appear to have recognized the fact that this zone of bright stars may be traced with tolerable distinctness through the entire circuit of the heavens, forming a great circle as well defined as that of the Galaxy itself." These interesting researches, a detailed account of which is given in the paper referred to, may have an important bearing on the great problems of determining the position of our sun in the cluster to which it belongs, the form of the cluster itself, and the relative distances between the stars of which it is composed.

The Companion of Procyon.—It is well known that the star Procyon has manifested considerable irregularity in its motion, and that the celebrated Bessel ascribed the phenomenon to the disturbing influence of an undiscovered companion. In 1851 Prof. O. Struve commenced a series of observations on this star with the view of obtaining, if possible, materials for the confirmation of Bessel's theory. These researches were without any positive result till the 19th of March, 1873, when, under exceptionally favorable atmospheric conditions, a faint point of light was detected at a distance of about twelve seconds from Procyon. Prof. Struve immediately concluded that the newly-discovered star was a satellite, whose orbital motion had but recently brought it so far out of the rays of the bright star as to render it separately visible. Unfortunately, however, before any definite conclusion could be reached, the apparent ·relative positions of the sun and Procyon had so far changed as to render further observations of the small star impossible. The beginning of the year 1874 was singularly unfavorable for telescopic researches, and it was not till the 21st of March that Struve succeeded in rediscovering the point of light which he had detected in March of the previous year. In April he obtained a number of satisfactory observations; the distance of the com-

panion, as well as the position-angle, being carefully measured. The interesting results are thus stated by Struve himself :

It is well known that Prof. Auwers, as soon as he had received my observations of last year, repeated his investigations into the variable proper motion of *Procyon*, availing himself of the observations of this star which have been made since 1862. From this he concluded that it was doubtful whether the object observed by me was really the sole body disturbing the proper motion of *Procyon*, but that the doubt would be removed if it appeared this spring that the position-angle had undergone an increase of from 9° to 10°. And this increase has really shown itself in the most remarkable manner. I consider it, therefore, to be decisively established .that the object I have observed is actually the companion whose existence has been theoretically proved by the calculations of Auwers ; and hope that the astronomical world will rejoice with me in the triumph thus obtained for the labors of my honored friend, and through them for our common science. In order to remove any exception that might be taken, that the wished-for result had in any degree been itself the cause of the recognition, and affected the measurement of the place of so difficult an object, I will just remark that I had not looked again at the paper of Auwers in question since its first receipt last summer, and had totally forgotten the data of its direction, and the mutual relation of the two stars. I did not again take it up until after I had succeeded in making the first observation, and the results of that paper were even less present to the mind of my assistant, Herr Lindemann, whose younger eye appears generally to have seen the companion even better than mine.

According to Prof. Auwers, Procyon completes a revolution in forty years. Its orbit is nearly circular, and its plane perpendicular to the line of sight. Taking its parallax at one-fourth of a second, he finds the mass of the principal star to be eighty times that of the sun, or more than eleven times that of Struve's satellite.

The Nebula near Eta Argûs.—The results of further observations on the star *Eta Argûs* and its adjacent nebula were reported by Mr. R. J. Ellery, of the Melbourne Observatory, under date of January 28, 1874. Marked changes had been noticed during the six months preceding that date. The great bay of the lemniscate had nearly filled up with dense nebula, leaving a dark sigmoid inlet. Nebula apparently less dense had also formed from side to side ·of the opening in which Eta is situated —threatening to completely involve the star. These rapid variations, where it was supposed until recently that cycles of immense duration would be required for any sensible change, are regarded by astronomers with no ordinary interest.

Mr. Burnham's Catalogue of New Double Stars.—S. W. Burnham, Esq., of Chicago, has communicated to the Royal Astronomical Society of London five catalogues of new double stars, amounting in all to 300. A number of these are naked-eye stars which have been frequently examined by other observers. In some cases the components of binary stars have themselves been found double. *Alpha Delphini*, which had been known as a triple star, is found by Mr. Burnham to be sextuple. The double star No. 263 of South and Herschel's Catalogue has five very minute stars in the immediate vicinity of the two bright components. The system consists, therefore, of seven known members.

The Extended Nebulæ of Sir John Herschel's General Catalogue.—In a paper read by Cleveland Abbe, Esq., before the Philosophical Society of Washington, June 4, 1874, the author, after referring to his previous researches on the distribution of the nebulæ in space, proceeds to inquire whether any definite relation exists between the planes of rotation of the elongated or extremely elliptical nebulous masses. He states the problem as follows:

We have thus far studied the distribution in space of the centres of the nebulæ—are there not planes that have a definite relation to these bodies? Among the stars we have the Milky-Way and the orbits of binary stars; among the planets we have their orbits and equators, and the orbits of their satellites; among the nebulæ we may expect to find analogous planes, whose relations to each other and to those already known cannot but be highly instructive. As yet, we have but very few double nebulæ, nor can we for a long time hope to determine the planes of the orbits of any binary nebulæ, if such exist; on the other hand, in regard to the axes of rotation of nebulæ or the planes of their equators, there is more room for study. It is a plausible hypothesis, that some nebulæ are in rotation about their respective axes, and only in the case of an irregular nebula do we find presumptive evidence of numerous centres of aggregation and rotation; this latter class will not now further claim our attention. Those nebulæ whose whole mass is rotating about a single axis must appear to us either circular or elliptical, according to our position in relation to that axis; we might then at once assume that every well-defined circular nebula has its axis of rotation directed toward us, and might thus determine the position of the plane of its equator; this, however, would be hazardous, since not only do we thus assume the fact of a rotation, but also assume that the average rotation of all nebulæ is so rapid that, when viewed from any other direction, they would present a sensibly elliptical outline; moreover, often globular clusters of stars are recorded as circular or globular nebulæ. I have, therefore, for the present, passed by the circular and the ordinary elliptical nebulæ, and have confined myself to those described in Herschel's Catalogue as exceedingly or very much extended. In regard to them it may be remarked that, if these nebulæ are gaseous and without rotation, we can only explain their apparent shape by supposing them to be endowed with a motion of translation—to be, in fact, wisps, like comets' tails; if, on the other hand, they be in a state of rotation, they must be flat rings or disks, or extended flattened ellipsoids, and we are authorized to consider that the planes of their equators do sensibly pass through the position of the observer; similarly, if the nebulous appearance be due to the presence of lenticular or ring-shaped clouds of asteroids, or of meteoric dust, we shall be able to make a determination of the plane of the orbits of these bodies.

Having computed the right ascensions and declinations of the south-poles of the fifty-nine nebulæ in question, I have also plotted them upon equal surface charts similar to those used by Messrs. Proctor and Waters, on which also have been drawn the limits of the Milky-Way as given by those same gentlemen, according to Heis and Herschel. Owing to the fact that the unresolved nebulæ are, as a rule, far more numerous near the poles of the Milky-Way than elsewhere,

it follows at once that the greater number of the nebulæ now under consideration are near these poles, and therefore our poles of rotation, if we may presume to use that term, lie near the Milky-Way itself; but a careful enumeration shows us that in the Northern Hemisphere these poles lie to the southward of the central portion of the Milky Way, while in the Southern Hemisphere the reverse holds good; in fact, there exists a medial plane about which the poles of these nebulæ cluster, and which is itself inclined to the plane of the Milky-Way at an angle of about 30°, so that if the north-pole of the Milky-Way be in right ascension 12ʰ· 45ᵐ· and declination 30°, the pole of the plane near which the rotation axes of the nebulæ lie will have about the same right ascension, but a declination of about 60°. Numerically expressed, this latter plane is so situated that of fifty-nine nebulæ twenty-nine have their axes inclined to it by less than 10°, and forty-two have their axes inclined less than 20°.

It is, I conceive, quite desirable that we should, on the one hand, have more accurate determinations of the position-angles of these extended and ray-like nebulæ, and that, on the other hand, the reversion spectroscope of Zöllner should be applied to determine whether or not they be really in a state of rotation.

Mr. Abbe concludes:

It may then in general be stated that, so far as we are able to determine the position of planes of rotation among the nebulæ, they do not show any such tendency to agree with each other as is shown in the orbits and equators of the major planets of the solar system; that, on the contrary, they are inclined at all possible angles to each other, but have this remarkable feature, that their mutual nodes cluster about a point in right ascension 12ʰ· 45ᵐ·, and north inclination 60°.

Results of Spectroscopic Observations.—1. Dr. Huggins's observations of different nebulæ have shown conclusively that these bodies are not moving with the same velocity as some of the fixed stars. 2. The observations of Mr. Lockyer have added zinc and aluminium to the list of known solar metals. 3. The researches of Secchi and Rutherfurd have shown that there are three classes of stars: the spectra of the first giving only hydrogen lines very thick, and metallic lines exceedingly thin. This class includes Sirius. The spectra of the second class (which includes our sun) differ only in degree from those of the first; having medium brightness and many lines. The third class is distinguished by banded spectra, indicating the existence of compounds.

The Gold Medal of the Royal Astronomical Society.—At the annual meeting of the Royal Astronomical Society on the 13th of February, 1874, their gold medal was awarded by the Council to Prof. Simon Newcomb, of the Washington Observatory, for his researches on the orbits of Neptune and Uranus, and other contributions to mathematical astronomy. The president, Prof. Cayley, in his address before the Society explaining the grounds of the Council's decision, reviewed in brief the principal works of Prof. Newcomb, particularly those on the orbits of the two outer planets. He concludes as follows:

In what precedes I have endeavored to give you an account of Prof. Newcomb's writings: they exhibit all of them a combination, on the one hand, of mathematical skill and power, and on the other hand of good hard work—devoted to the furtherance of astronomical science. The "Memoir on the Lunar Theory" contains the successful development of a highly-original idea, and cannot but be regarded as a great step in advance in the method of the variation of the elements and in theoretical dynamics generally; the two sets of planetary tables are works of immense labor, embodying results only attainable by the exercise of such labor under the guidance of profound mathematical skill—and which are needs in the present state of astronomy. I trust that, imperfectly as my task is accomplished, I shall have satisfied you that we have done well in the award of our medal.

The President then, delivering the medal to the foreign secretary, addressed him in the following terms:

MR. HUGGINS: I request that you will have the goodness to transmit to Prof. Newcomb this medal, as an expression of the opinion of the Society of the excellence and importance of what he has accomplished; and to assure him at the same time of our best wishes for his health and happiness, and for the long and successful continuation of his career as a worker in our science.

The Planetary Researches of Leverrier.—The *Comptes Rendus* of December 21, 1874, contains an interesting account of Leverrier's researches on the theories of the principal planets, Mercury, Venus, the Earth, Mars, Jupiter, Saturn, Uranus, and Neptune. When those investigations were commenced, more than thirty years since, none of the tables intended to represent the planetary motions accorded rigorously with the observations. To discover the unknown causes of these systematic errors was the principal object of Leverrier's researches. His theory of Uranus was published in 1846, and led to the discovery of Neptune. This work has been recently revised and extended, and the final results were communicated to the Academy of Sciences on the 15th of November, 1874. The theory of Neptune was given in December; those of Jupiter and Saturn had been previously presented.

In the case of Mercury M. Leverrier has shown that all the anomalies are included under a simple law, and that it "is sufficient to increase the motion of perihelion by thirty-one seconds in the century, to bring every thing into order. The displacement of the perihelion thus acquires in the planetary theories an exceptional importance. It is the surest index, when it has to be increased, of the existence of cosmic matter as yet unknown, and circulating, like other bodies, round the sun. The consequence is very clear. There exists in the neighborhood of Mercury, doubtless between the planet and the sun, a matter as yet unknown. Does it consist in one or more small planets, or in more minute asteroids, or even in cosmic dust? The theory tells us nothing on this point. On numerous occasions trustworthy observers have declared that they have witnessed the passage of a small planet over the sun, but nothing has been established on the subject."

M. Leverrier continues: "The discussion of the observations of the sun led us at once to an important result connected with the great question which agitates at this moment the scientific world, a result which surprised us ourselves, so great was the false confidence inspired by the determination of the parallax of the sun deduced by the Director of the Berlin Observatory from the transits of Venus in 1761 and 1769. I arrived at the conclusion that the parallax of the sun, 8.″57, should be increased by the twenty-fifth part of its value.

"Soon afterward the comparison of the theory of Venus with the observations led to the same result, the necessity of augmenting by $\frac{1}{25}$ the parallax of the sun.

"Again, the theory of Mars led in its turn to an equally precise conclusion. It was established that it was impossible to satisfy the totality of the observations of Mars except by increasing the motion of its perihelion by about one-eighth.

"This was the reproduction of the same fact as for Mercury, and the consequence to be derived was the same, viz., that the planet Mars must be subjected to the action of a quantity of matter as yet neglected, and which had to be estimated at about one-eighth of the mass of the earth.

"But then two hypotheses were possible: either the hitherto neglected matter resided in the totality of the ring of the small planets, or else it had to be added to the earth itself. In the second case, and as a consequence, the parallax of the sun had to be increased by about one twenty-fourth part of its received value; that is to say, we are led to the result already obtained from the theories of the sun and Venus.

"Jupiter and Saturn have given rise to a theoretical work, the extent of which has been considerable, on account of the very large mutual perturbations of the two planets. The comparison of the theory of Jupiter with the observations has presented, after suitable modifications of the elements, a complete accordance."

Recent Changes in the Form and Position of Nebulæ.—The *Monthly Notices* of the Royal Astronomical Society for December, 1874, contains a letter from R. J. Ellery, Esq., Director of the Melbourne Observatory, in which he states that he is engaged in a systematic series of observations of Sir John Herschel's figured nebulæ. Many of these objects appear to have greatly changed since Herschel's drawings were made at the Cape of Good Hope, between 1834 and 1838. These changes are found, according to the observer, not only in the form and character of the nebulæ, but also in their position with respect to the adjacent fixed stars as figured by Herschel. Whether such transformations are real, or merely apparent, can only be decided by further observations.

AUSTRALIA AND NEW ZEALAND.—

The area and population of the British colonies in Australia and of New Zealand were, according to the latest official accounts, as follows:

COLONIES.	Area.	Population.	Year.
New South Wales.....	308,560	539,190	Dec., 1872
Victoria...............	88,451	790,488	Dec., 1873
South Australia.......	380,602	198,257	Dec., 1873
Queensland............	668,259	133,553	Dec., 1872
Western Australia.....	975,834	25,724	Dec., 1872
Northern Territory....	526,531	201	....
Tasmania	26,215	104,217	Dec., 1873
New Zealand..........	106,259	279,560	Dec., 1872
Total.............	3,077,701	2,070,819	

Not included in the figures given above for the population of the several colonies are the natives, whose number is rapidly decreasing. In Victoria they numbered about 5,000 when the colony was first settled; in 1851, their number was reported as 2,693; in 1863, as 1,908; in 1873, as 859—516 males and 343 females. In South Australia they numbered, in 1871, 3,369; in Tasmania, one; in Queensland, 2,235. The natives of New Zealand, or Maories, consist of 18 tribes, numbering about 36,359. By the census of 1864, they numbered 55,970—31,667 males, 24,303 females. They are represented in the Legislature of New Zealand by four members. The colonial "Blue-Book," issued in 1874, contains a dispatch from the Governor of New Zealand, Sir J. Ferguson, addressed to the Earl of Carnarvon, in which the author states that of late there had been decided indications of a desire on the part of the "Hau-hau" party among the Máories to put an end to their estrangement from the Government, and that they and their people may share in the advantages which the loyal tribes enjoy. A loyal chief of the Waikato has twice waited upon the Governor and declared his belief in the willingness of the separated tribes to come under subjection, provided they are permitted to manage their own affairs under their own chiefs; upon which basis they would be ready to permit communications through their districts, and provide for the surrender of criminals. It remained to be seen whether the "Hau-hau" chiefs are really disposed to surrender their independence, a step which would be distasteful to many of their followers. The Governor goes on to say: "With the exception of the danger of incursions of some turbulent members across the boundary, against which due precautions are taken, there is no disturbing element in connection with the native population. Europeans are constantly becoming more intermixed with them, and they are more habituated to, and dependent upon, the comforts of European products, and the money derived by the sale or lease of their land. There is, however, much cause for regret in the demoralizing influences which invariably accompany the influx of Europeans. Few natives of any class can resist the temptation to drink habitually and to excess while they have the means of indulging in it. There are chiefs who

set an example of sobriety or total abstinence, but it cannot be doubted that the frequent excess in ardent and often bad spirits by both sexes, and their inordinate use of tobacco from a very early age, are prominent causes of the rapid and almost general diminution of the numbers of this fine and capable race, which is presented alike by the paucity of the births and the mortality among the children, rather than among the infants. At the same time there is reason to hope that a remnant will be saved, and that the considerable number of children receiving instruction upon the English system in our schools may raise up a certain number so educated as to resist the temptations which have proved fatal to so many. The full capacity both of Maories and half-castes to acquire and employ all branches of knowledge induces the belief that there will long survive in New Zealand representatives of the Maori race." The Governor adds: " I wish that some systematic effort were made to fit the children of chiefs, by higher education, for their proper work among their people, and even for taking a part in the future government and business of the country. In spite of the comparative failure of some former attempts, I hope, through private association, if not by the action of the Government, to set on foot some definite organization for this purpose."

The colonies, being independent of each other, each colony has its own educational system. That of New South Wales consists of primary schools, the grammar-school, and the university. The former exist all over the colony. The grammar-school is intended partly as a preparatory step to the university. It has ten teachers, 237 pupils, and several scholarships of the yearly value of £20, open to all pupils below twelve. The University of Sydney employs five tutors to forty-five students. The course of instruction is somewhat similar to that of English colleges. Affiliated with it are two colleges, St. Paul's, Anglican, one tutor and five students; and St. John's, Roman Catholic, two teachers to one and nine to the other. In connection with it there are also several public and "In Memoriam" scholarships of the annual value of £50, which are awarded to successful candidates. The University is presided over by a chancellor, the government being in the hands of a senate. The total number of schools, in 1872, was reported as 1,464, with 106,691 pupils. Of these schools, 878 were under the Council of Education; the number of denominational schools, under the board, was 223, of which 104 belong to the Church of England, 86 to the Roman Catholics, 18 to the Presbyterians, 14 to the Wesleyans, and one to the Jews. The Government, in 1871, contributed to the support of the educational institutions £143,198, and £56,019 was received in the shape of fees and voluntary contributions.

In Victoria, the number of day-schools, including state schools, private educational establishments, colleges, and grammar-schools, was

2,050, with an average attendance of 165,276 scholars, who were instructed by 4,429 teachers. Of these schools, 988 were common-schools, with 2,317 teachers and 71,247 boys and 59,898 girls upon the rolls. The local receipts for the maintenance of these schools, arising from school fees and other sources, were £107,190; this amount was supplemented by a Government grant of £167,194, making a total of £274,384. There were seven colleges and grammar-schools, two in connection with the Church of England, three with the Presbyterian Church, one with the Wesleyans, and one with the Roman Catholic Church. They had an aggregate number of 74 masters and 1,142 students. The Melbourne University, during the year 1871, was attended by 122 students, of whom 116 were matriculated. The total number of students matriculated since the establishment of the university, up to 1871, was 526. During the year ending May, 1873, 428 candidates presented themselves for the matriculation examination, of whom 229 passed, 13 passing with credit, among whom were two ladies. The library of the university contained 9,000 volumes. Under the New Education Act, the instruction in the state schools is free, secular, and compulsory. The governing power is in the hands of a Minister of Education, assisted by a secretary. Each school is under periodical inspection. The teachers, who are required to pass an examination, are paid by fixed salaries; they also receive the fees of the scholars, and have a further allowance according to the progress made by the scholars under their charge.

In *South Australia*, the educational system, as far as relates to the schools receiving aid from the Government, is under the control of a Central Board of Education, consisting of seven members. The principal officers are a chief and a second inspector and secretary. The total number of licensed schools open, at the close of 1872, was 307, which had 299 teachers and 15,123 scholars. The annual average cost of each scholar was about £1 18s.; the annual stipend of each teacher, £97 18s. The schools held in trust by the board numbered 98; they have been commenced by private subscription, supplemented by the state funds. Recent efforts have been made for the establishment of an Adelaide University.

In *West Australia*, the Legislative Council, during the session of 1870, passed an Education Act, based upon the principle of Foster's act, now in operation in England. Schools are divided into elementary and assisted. The former are maintained wholly at the cost of the colony; the latter are private, but can receive a capitation grant on condition of submitting to Government inspection for secular results, and to the observance of a strict conscience clause during the four hours of secular instruction insisted upon by the act. The elementary schools are under the control and supervision of a central board and local dis-

trict boards. The central board, consisting of five members, is appointed by the Governor, and the local district boards are chosen by the general body of electors. Compulsory attendance of children can be enforced by the local boards. In the elementary schools four hours a day are devoted to secular instruction, and one hour, under the provisions of a conscience clause, to reading the Bible, or other religious books approved of by the board; but no catechism or religious formulary of any kind may be used; and the Bible, if read, may be read without note or comment. The average annual attendance of scholars was 2,338, an excess over 1871 of more than 600. A Government inspector makes periodical visits to the schools, and the salaries of teachers are dependent upon their report of regularity of attendance and proficiency on the part of scholars. In Perth there is a Church of England collegiate school, under the patronage of the bishop.

The educational system of *Queensland* is under the control of the Board of Education, which consists of six members, appointed by the Government, one of the ministry being chairman. It has been assimilated to the national system, as in operation in Ireland. Fees have been abolished, and education is free. The property of the schools, and the land granted for school purposes, are vested in this board, which has the control of the money voted for education, and the power to make by-laws and regulations in connection with these schools, which must be in accordance with the national system of education as established here, and approved by the Governor. Aid is granted to schools not established by the board, on their complying with certain regulations; these are known as non-vested schools. The Government also aids in the establishment of a grammar-school whenever the inhabitants of a district raise by subscription the sum of £100, and supplements this sum by double the amount for the erection of the necessary buildings; and if the sum of £250 per annum be guaranteed for three years as school-fees by responsible parties, the Government gives £500 per annum for the salaries of masters and current expenses. As yet only Brisbane and Ipswich have availed themselves of this grant. For 1872, the school statistics were as follows: schools in operation, 150; schools opened, 17; schools closed, 3; increase in number of schools, 14; vested schools, 95; non-vested schools, 38; provisional schools, 20; number of teachers and pupil-teachers, 373; aggregate attendance of children, 21,482; average attendance of children, 10,779. The parliamentary vote for educational purposes was £40,000; the local subscriptions being £1,753. The total expenditure for all purposes was £39,315, the value of property vested in the board, £52,562.

In *New Zealand* each province has its own school acts and regulations. In some cases state aid is given to both national and denominational schools; in others, it is limited to the national schools. There is a university at Dunedin. The number of schools is 397; of these 24 are for boys, 13 for girls, and 360 are mixed schools. The teachers number 602; 379 males, 223 females. The average attendance of pupils is 16,510; on register, 21,034.

Tasmania has a school board, under whose supervision is the distribution of all moneys voted by the Parliament for the purpose of public education. In 1872, 139 schools were in operation; the average attendance was 5,224; number of scholars on the roll, 9,979; number of male teachers, 105; of female, 111; of pupil-teachers and paid monitors, 31; average cost of each scholar, £2 6s. There are four superior schools, Horton College, High School, Hutchinson's School, and the Church Grammar-School. The attendance of children at school is compulsory, under a fine of £2, unless it can be shown that the child is privately educated, or is prevented by sickness or other valid cause from being present. In the census of 1870 the state of education among the population was as follows: persons able to read and write, 56.32 per cent.; persons able to read only, 14.04 per cent.; persons not able to read, 29.64 per cent. At the date of the previous census, in 1861, it was found that only 42.62 per cent. could read and write, that 14.60 per cent. could read only, and that 31.75 per cent. were totally uneducated.

The population connected with the leading religious denominations of Australia and New Zealand was, in 1874, estimated as follows:

Episcopalians...... 750,000 | Methodists......... 225,000
Roman Catholics... 460,000 | Independents...... 50,000
Presbyterians...... 280,000 | Baptists............ 40,000

The Episcopal Church, at the beginning of 1874, had ten bishops in Australia—Sydney, Newcastle, Bathurst, Goulborn, Grafton and Armidale, Melbourne, Perth, Brisbane, Adelaide, Tasmania—the Bishop of Sydney bearing the title of Metropolitan; and six bishops in New Zealand—Auckland, Christ Church, Nelson, Wellington, Waiapu, Dunedin—one of whom (in 1874, the Bishop of Christ Church) holds the title of Primate. In 1874 an assembly of the Diocese of Melbourne resolved to make the church in the colony of Victoria an independent province, with the Bishop of Melbourne as Metropolitan. An Episcopal See was established at Ballarat, and others will soon be established at other places.

The Catholic Church in Australia, from the foundation of the ecclesiastical province of Australia in 1842, until 1874, had only one archbishop, at Sydney. In May, 1874, the Pope divided it into two provinces, the Bishop of Melbourne being raised to the dignity of an archbishop. At the same time two new bishoprics were established at Ballarat and Sandhurst. Besides the bishops of these two new dioceses, those of Adelaide, of South Australia, Perth, of West Australia, and Hobart Town, of Tasmania, will be suffragans of the new Arch-

bishop of Melbourne; while six bishops, namely, those of Bathurst, Maitland, Goulbourn, and Armidale, in New South Wales, Brisbane in Queensland, and Port Victoria in North Australia, will continue to be under the Archbishop of Sydney. The foundation of the Catholic Church in Australia was laid in 1820, when two priests settled in the colonies, the one in Tasmania, the other in New South Wales. In 1832 the Vicar Apostolic of Mauritius, to whose diocese Australia belonged, sent his Vicar-General, Ullathorne, into the colonies, who found there three priests, one unfinished church, two unfinished chapels, and four free schools. In 1835, the connection of Australia with the Vicariate Apostolic of Mauritius was abolished, and Dr. Polding, an English Benedictine, appointed Vicar-Apostolic of Australia. In consequence of the immigration from Ireland, the Church made rapid progress, and in 1842 Pope Gregory XVI. appointed Dr. Polding Archbishop of Sydney, and erected the two Dioceses of Adelaide and Hobart Town. In 1845 the Church numbered fifty-six priests, twenty-five churches and chapels, and thirty-one schools. New dioceses were established in 1845 at Perth; in 1847, at Melbourne; in 1849, at Port Victoria, or Port Effington; in 1859, at Brisbane; in 1865, at Bathurst and Maitland; in 1866, at Goulbourn; in 1869, at Armidale. The bishops of Australia have thus far held two Provincial Councils. The first took place at Sydney in September, 1844, and was attended by the Archbishop of Sydney, two bishops, and thirty-three missionaries; the second was held in 1869 at Melbourne, and was attended by nine bishops and a large number of priests.

The revenue, expenditure, and public debt of the colonies were, in 1872, as follows:

COLONIES.	Revenue.	Expenditure.	Debt.
New South Wales......	£2,794,274	£2,362,482	£10,606,080
Victoria (1873–'74)......	3,883,650	4,171,688	12,134,800
South Australia (1873)..	t33,000	783,000	2,167,700
West Australia.........	135,800	98,248	35,000
Tasmania..............	234,608	241,100	1,455,900
Queensland............	825,000	809,051	5,253,826
New Zealand (1873–'74.)	1,730,500	1,128,000	8,900,991

The following table exhibits the imports and exports in 1872:

COLONIES.	Imports.	Exports.
New South Wales......	£9,609,508	£11,245,082
Victoria...............	13,689,629	18,871,194
South Australia...	2,801,780	3,524,075
West Australia.........	226,656	209,196
Tasmania.............	807,182	866,181
Queensland............	2,434,486	2,560,383
New Zealand...........	4,078,193	5,190,665

The latest data concerning railroads and telegraphs are as follows:

COLONIES.	Railroads.	Telegraph-Wires.
New South Wales....	405	6,114
Victoria..............	440	3,472
South Australia......	190	3,723
West Australia......	16	600
Tasmania.............	45	291 (lines).
Queensland...........	218	1,811
New Zealand.........	105	4,011

The latest statistics of live-stock are as follows:

COLONIES.	Horses.	Horned Cattle.	Sheep.	Hogs.
New South Wales.	304,100	2,014,888	16,278,697	213,198
Victoria	181,643	921,673	10,002,381	177,447
South Australia...	82,215	169,154	4,900,687	98,436
West Australia....	25,203	44,550	688,290	19,749
Tasmania	24,344	104,594	1,395,358	55,927
Queensland.......	93,910	1,168,235	7,408,334	82,707
New Zealand.....	81,028	436,592	9,700,639	151,460

AUSTRO-HUNGARIAN MONARCHY, an empire in Central Europe. Emperor, Francis Joseph I., born August 18, 1830; succeeded his uncle, the Emperor Ferdinand I., on December 2, 1848. Heir-apparent to the throne, Archduke Rudolphus, born August 21, 1858. Area of the monarchy, 240,348 square miles; population, according to the census of 1869, 35,901,435. The area of cis-Leithan Austria (the lands represented in the Reichsrath) is 115,908 square miles; population at the end of 1874, officially estimated at 21,169,341. The estimate is based upon the census of December 31, 1869, by adding the average percentage of increase, as it results from the census of 1869 and that of 1857. It was distributed among the different crown-lands as follows:

Countries.	Inhabitants in 1874.
Austria below the Enns	2,087,980
Austria above the Enns.................	741,918
Salzburg	153,386
Styria	1,164,512
Carinthia	338,045
Carniola..............................	468,065
Trieste...............................	132,274
Görtiz and Gradisca...................	212,349
Istria................................	266,303
Tyrol.................................	787,494
Vorarlberg............................	103,341
Bohemia	5,287,344
Moravia..............................	2,056,081
Silesia...............................	544,459
Galicia...............................	5,8.7,798
Bukowina........	537,815
Dalmatia.............................	460,327
Total.........................	21,169,341

Of the total population, 10,303,437 were of the male, and 10,865,904 of the female sex. The number of marriages in 1873 was 193,836, of births 829,947 (429,324 males, 400,623 females). Of the children born alive, 712,109 were legitimate, and 98,727 illegitimate; of those still-born, 15,420 were legitimate, and 3,691 illegitimate. The number of twins was 18,530. The number of deaths was 679,396 (354.333 male, and 325,063 female).

The ministry for the common affairs of the empire consisted, at the beginning of the year, of Count Andrassy, Minister of Foreign Affairs and of the Imperial House (appointed 1871); Baron von Holzgethan, Minister of the Finances of the Empire (appointed January, 1872); and Baron Kuhn von Kuhnenfeld, Minister of War (appointed January, 1868).

The ministry of cis-Leithan Austria was composed of Prince Adolf von Auersperg, President; J. Lasser Baron von Bollheim, Interior; C. von Stremayr, Public Works and Instruction; Glaser, Justice; Banhans, Commerce and

Political Economy; J. Ritter von Chlumecky, Agriculture (all appointed November, 1871); Baron von Pretis-Cagnodo, Finances (January, 1872); Colonel Horst, Defense of the Country (appointed pro tem. November, 1871; definitely, March, 1872); J. Unger (November, 1871), and Fl. Ziemialkovski (April, 1873), ministers without portfolio.

According to the common budget of the whole empire for the year 1874, the amount required for the ordinary branches of administration was 116,364,502 florins; the receipts for the same branches were estimated at 5,-815,125 fl.; the receipts from customs at 17,-500,000 fl.; leaving 93,049,378 to be distributed among Austria Proper and Hungary (the former contributing 70 per cent. and the latter 30 per cent.). The cis-Leithan budget for 1873 estimates the revenue at 393,677,697 fl., and the expenditures at 389,929,292 fl. The common debt in 1872 amounted to 412,001,964 fl.; the debt of cis-Leithan Austria at 2,693,-495,790 fl. The army on the peace-footing numbered, in August, 1873, 283,125, and on the war-footing 1,093,979 men. The navy numbered 68 vessels; tonnage, 107,470.

The total number of savings-banks, at the end of the year 1873, was 259 (against 211 in 1871); the number of depositors, 1,207,688; ditto of deposits, 482,763,132. They are very unequally distributed among the several provinces, and, in some of them, are barely known, as appears from the following table:

PROVINCES.	Savings Banks.	Depositors.	Deposits.
Lower Austria............	49	366.848	168,669,604
Upper Austria............	25	100,758	34,901,535
Salzburg	2	13.368	4,306,184
Styria...................	40	170,781	58,273,439
Carinthia................	6	26,374	9,046,395
Carniola.................	2	25,266	9,055,683
Trieste, Göritz, Gradisca, and Istria..........	2	7,563	2,502,512
Tyrol and Vorarlberg......	12	60,588	12,292,883
Bohemia	67	311,453	147,089,897
Moravia.................	27	62,713	21,137,573
Silesia..................	12	20,785	4,132,840
Galicia..................	12	38,710	10,183,197
Bukowina................	1	2,130	1,018,248
Dalmatia................	2	351	143,612
Total...............	219	1,207,688	482,763,132

The universities of Austria had, during the summer of 1873, the following number of professors and students:

UNIVERSITIES.	Professors.	Students.
Vienna......................	253	3,440
Grätz.......................	83	925
Innspruck...................	73	640
Prague......................	154	1.811
Lemberg	46	932
Cracow......................	69	570
Total......................	678	8.318

Of the students, 7,637 were Austrians, and 681 were foreigners. With regard to their nationality, 3,599 were Germans, 1,656 Czechs, 1,219 Poles, 489 Ruthenes, 513 Slovens, Croats, and Serbians; 389 Italians, Ladinians, and

Friulians; 51 Roumanians, 313 Magyars, and 89 others. The number of technical high-schools is eight, which, in 1873, had the following number of professors and students:

HIGH-SCHOOLS.	Professors.	Students.
Vienna	86	1,076
Grätz	44	315
Prague (German)	39	451
" (Czechic)	45	713
Brünn	28	156
Lemberg	23	353
Cracow	26	357
Total	291	3,421

Among the other special high-schools there were 2 for agriculture, 2 for mining, and 4 commercial academies. Of special theological schools, exclusive of the theological faculties of the universities, the Roman Catholic Church had 40, with 189 professors and 1,449 students; the Greek Catholic Church, 1, with 3 professors and 21 students; the Armenian Catholic, 1, with 2 professors and 5 students; the Oriental Greek Church, 2, with 8 professsors and 55 students; the Evangelical Church, 1, with 25 professors and 1,530 students. The number of gymnasia was 93, with 1,635 professors and 22,669 students; that of Real-gymnasia, 53, with 658 professors and 8,182 students; that of Realschulen, 67, with 1,210 professors and 21,187 students.

The total number of periodicals published in cis-Leitban Austria, in 1872, was 835, of which 259 were devoted to politics, 97 to political economy, 53 to agriculture and forestry, 43 to industry, 34 to medicine and natural science, 14 to law, 52 to pedagogy (including 12 devoted to stenography), 22 to theology and religion, 8 to history, 8 to military affairs, 13 to literature, 53 to belles-lettres, 33 to humor, 22 to the theatre, music, and art; 12 to fashion, 10 to the entertainment of children, 9 to sport, hunting, gymnastics, rifle associations, and fire-companies; 51 were local non-political newspapers, and 42 commercial and advertising sheets. More than two-thirds of all the papers were published in the German language, 189 in Slavic dialects (110 in Czechic, 50 in Polish, 14 in Slavonic, 11 in Ruthenian, and 4 in Illyrian); 43 in Italian, 5 in French, 2 in Greek, 1 each in English, Hungarian, and Roumanian; 10 in Hebrew, some of which, however, were printed in German letters. Ninety-eight papers were issued daily (14 twice a day), 274 weekly, 52 twice a week, 28 three times a week, 45 three times a month, 172 twice a month, 152 once a month, 2 from six to ten times a year, and 12 four times a year. The largest number of periodicals is published in the crown-land of Lower Austria (370, of which 357 belong to the city of Vienna), the smallest in the Bukowina (2).

The agricultural produce in 1872 was estimated at 1,434,860,248 florins. The chief products were wheat, 11,226,139 hectolitres, valued at 108,149,467 florins; rye, 23,490,765

hectolitres, valued at 146,361,414 florins; barley, 17,367,828 hectolitres, valued at 102,648,-327 florins; oats, 34,934,608 hectolitres, valued at 107,502,277 florins; potatoes, 75,227,410 hectolitres, valued at 135,376,420 florins; hay, 7,437,676,111 kilogrammes, valued at 188,533,-868 florins. The money value of the mining produce was estimated, in the same year, at 41,693,087 florins, and the number of persons employed in the mining industry was 86,728; the money value of the produce of the smelting-houses was 30,994,464 florins, and the number of persons employed was 12,173. The number of beet-sugar manufactories, in 1872, was 233, and the number of beets used 31,865,287 zollcentner. Of the 2,337 breweries, the largest number (956) was in Bohemia; Upper Austria had 269; Moravia, 249; Galicia, 245; Carinthia, 137; Tyrol and Vorarlberg, 133; Lower Austria, 112. The number of distilleries was 44,047, of which 11,613 were in Tyrol and Vorarlberg, 9,790 in Styria, 5,614 in Lower Austria, 4,359 in the Littoral, 3,705 in Salzburg, 3,543 in Carinthia, and 3,017 in Carniola.

The commerce of the Austro-Hungarian monarchy, in 1872, was as follows:

	Imports.	Exports.
	Florins.	Florins.
Austro-Hungarian Customs Union without precious metals	613,726,357	387,963,537
Austro-Hungarian Customs Union—precious metals	36,500,769	66,143,689
Customs Territory of Dalmatia	9,246,931	6,879,921

The First Danube Steam Navigation Company had, in 1872, 156 steamers and 574 towing-boats: income, 13,261,918 florins; expenditures, 12,697,746 florins; surplus, 564,172 florins. The Steam Navigation Company of the Austrian Lloyds had, in 1872, 69 steamers: income, 10,551,014 florins; expenditures, 9,-287,579 florins; surplus, 1,263,417 florins.

The commercial navy, at the end of the year 1872, was composed as follows:

NAVY.	Vessels.	Tonnage.	Men.
Trieste and Territory	461	88,989	4,135
Göritz and Gradisca	135	1,007	419
Istria	1,522	92,588	6,096
Dalmatia	4,505	94,346	14,384
Total	6,623	276,980	25,084

The number of new vessels built, in 1872, was 479, tonnage, 12,138; of vessels repaired, 214, tonnage, 7,986.

The movement of shipping in the Austrian ports, during the year 1872, was as follows:

No. of Ports.	PROVINCES.	ENTERED.		CLEARED.	
		Vessels.	Tons.	Vessels.	Tons.
2	Trieste and Territory	9,208	1,001,739	9,090	986,840
4	Göritz and Gradisca	1,179	22,993	1,199	19,409
38	Istria	18,905	1,628,467	19,186	1,618,016
56	Dalmatia	12,983	1,125,195	12,984	1,124,232

The number of post-offices, at the end of the year 1872, was 3,824; the number of private letters forwarded to places in Austria, 122,-397,073; of official letters, 18,082,190; of newspapers sent, 55,758,088; number of private letters sent abroad, 32,445,099; of official letters, 2,014,341; of postal cards, 15,549,700.

The Austrian Government is beginning to bestow close attention upon the development of the Landwehr. Regimental schools of instruction already exist for the improvement of non-commissioned officers of the various battalions during their eight weeks of annual training; but to extend the period for these would, of course, involve heavy expense, and the chief object of the new measures introduced is, therefore, to improve the instruction of the better class who are to officer the force. For this purpose a central school is established at the headquarters of each of the seven great Landwehr districts, with a staff of instructors chosen by the commandant, who is to give the preference to officers of the regular army, should such present themselves, who have been employed already in instruction. He is also to do his utmost to make the objects of the school and its advantages known to the proper classes of his district. At each there is to be a regular daily course of theoretical study, chiefly in military subjects, and lasting from the 1st of January to the 31st of July, followed by two months of practical instruction. But, in addition, there are to be regular evening classes for those candidates who have occupations of their own in the daytime, who may then go through the whole course without interfering with their civil pursuits. Young men who have been under training in the Landwehr, and are specially reported on as apt soldiers, are eligible as candidates, as are those who have been made non-commissioned officers, and done well in the regimental school. But others who have not been out for training, and desire to qualify for Landwehr commissions, are also to be admitted, a moderate educational test being in all cases provided by proper school certificates where they can be produced, or by direct qualifying examination where none such are forthcoming. There is no limit fixed to the number of pupils; but those who have not served in training can only be admitted entirely at their own expense, which is also the rule for any Landwehr officer who may attend on his own application for the purpose of self-improvement. These last, of course, are subject to no examination at the close of the course; but the others have then to appear before a jury composed in part of Landwehr officers of standing and in part of professors. According to the result of the final examination, the pupils are to be either rejected altogether, recommended to come up again for another annual course, or noted to receive a commission in the order in which they stand on the successful list.

The provincial Diets of Austria which were in session at the opening of the year 1874 finished their labors on January 17th, with the exception of that of Trieste. Several of the Diets were occupied with a new regulation of school affairs, and the Conservatives and Liberal parties, as might be expected, had severe conflicts, the general result of which was not to the satisfaction of the Liberal party. In the Moravian Diet, the Government was vehemently attacked by several Czechic deputies, but supported by the majority.

The Reichsrath reassembled in Vienna on January 23d. The Catholic party entered the year with the hope that the influence of the Church upon the court was still sufficiently strong to defeat the four liberal church laws, which the ministry, in compliance with the request of the Liberal majority of the Reichsrath, was known to have prepared. The hope was strengthened by the fact that the Emperor, when the ministry submitted to him the first draft of the laws, referred it to Bishop Kutscher, who holds an appointment in the Ministry of Instruction, for an elaborate report, and that the bishop strongly advised the Emperor not to sanction the ministerial draft. The ministerial Council, at a meeting held under the presidency of the Emperor on January 18th, prevailed, however, upon the Emperor to allow the laws to be laid before the Reichsrath. The four laws were: 1. A law for the regulation of the external legal relations of the Catholic Church, embracing the formal abolition of the Concordat of 1855, and the co-operation of the Government in the appointments made by the bishops for ecclesiastical benefices, defining the limits of ecclesiastical jurisdiction, regulating the right of the state with regard to the faculties of Catholic theology at the universities, regulating the ecclesiastical corporations, the ecclesiastical patronage, the superintendence of the state over the administration of the Church; 2. A law for regulating the external legal relations of monastic communities, and vindicating for the state the right to allow or to forbid the establishment of monasteries, and to inspect them, and for all the members of such communities to leave them at any time after notifying the civil magistrate of their intention; 3. A law for taxing ecclesiastical property for the purpose of improving the revenue of the lower clergy; 4. A law regulating the legal recognition of religious denominations. The Reichsrath, on February 6th, referred the four laws to a subcommittee of seven members, and appointed another committee of five members to draft a law for reforms in the state laws concerning marriage. The discussion of the laws in the Reichsrath began on March 5th. The opponents of the laws, Count Hohenwart, Greuter, Prince Czartoryski, who spoke in the name of most of the Poles, Weiss von Starkenfels, and many others, warned against arousing an opposition of the Church against the Government, which was already endangered by political and national conflicts. The new laws, they urged, would only redound to the honor and the glory of Prussia, and were of an illiberal and despotic character. The chief speakers in support of the proposed laws were Prof. Suess, of Vienna, the Minister of Public Worship, Dr. Stremayr, and the prime-minister, Prince Auersperg. Prof. Suess announced an amendment which demands that the bishops of Austria must take an oath of loyalty to the constitution. Dr. Stremayr denied any intention on the part of the Government to carry on a war against the Church, but insisted that no well-regulated Government could allow religion to be made the pretext for dangerous schemes against the state. He called the laws the result of legislative necessity for guarding the freedom of religion and averting dangers, which from the zeal of misguided ecclesiastics might arise for the state. The prime-minister declared emphatically, in view of threats that the law could never be enforced, that the Government would possess sufficient energy to see the law respected. The Emperor, by telegraph, declared his approval of the speeches made by the two ministers, and at the close of the general discussion on the Reichsrath, by 224 against 71, received the ministerial draft, which on March 16th, after a discussion on the several articles, was adopted without any change. In the Herrenhaus the discussion of the new laws began on April 10th. The cardinal-archbishops, Rauscher, of Vienna, Tarnoczy, of Salzburg, and Prince Schwarzenberg, spoke against them, and declared, in a memorial which they handed in, that they adhered to the conviction which they expressed in the year 1868 relative to the existing legality of the Concordat, while, besides several ministers, Count Anton Auersperg, better known under the *nom de plume* of Anastasius Grün, as one of the greatest German poets, warmly defended them. After a motion of the Catholic party to pass over the laws to the order of the day had been negatived, by 77 against 43 votes, all the archbishops and bishops left the House, and the law was adopted in the form in which it had come from the Lower House. The Pope, in an Encyclical Letter, addressed to the Austrian bishops, and dated March 7th, had denounced the laws as being of the same stamp and character as the new Church laws of Prussia, and and as involving the same danger for the Church. The prime-minister, Count Andrassy, in his reply to the circular, said that it exaggerated facts, and that the Holy See might rest assured that the laws in question were not intended as an act of hostility toward it, or as a curtailment of its rights in questions of religion, their object being solely to regulate material questions, and more especially to remove stipulations which were obstacles to imperial legislation. The Government did not publish the reply of Count Andrassy, but in the great meeting of the Austrian and Hungarian delegations held at Pesth, Count An-

drassy, in reply to a question, gave a sketch of his note. He stated that his note does not question the Pope's right to communicate his opinion to the bishops on ecclesiastical matters, but expresses regret that the Encyclical should have pronounced a condemnation of things which are in no way of a dogmatic character, but belong to the sovereign domain of state legislation. The note adds that the Government will, nevertheless, endeavor to avoid a conflict with the Church, but will only do so if, in contradiction with the Encyclical Letter, the bishops are advised to obey the laws of the state. In conclusion the note says that if the clergy do not obey the laws which have been enacted and sanctioned, the Government will consider itself bound to protect the rights of the state, and is in any case convinced that it will be able to compel respect for the law. Count Andrassy added that no reply had been received, but since that time a certain appeasement appeared to have supervened.

The Reichsrath adjourned on March 24th for three weeks, and, immediately after resuming its sessions on April 14th, referred (on April 15th) a motion, introduced by Deputy Fux, relative to the expulsion of the Jesuits and all affiliated orders from Austria, to the Committee on the new Church laws. The three other Church laws were all adopted by the Reichsrath, which also adopted Liberal amendments to the law on the monastic communities which the ministry refused to accept, and to which the Herrenhaus had not yet given its consent, when on May 7th the eighth session of the Reichsrath was adjourned. From November 5, 1873, the day of opening, to its close, the House of Deputies had held sixty-three, and the House of Lords twenty-one meetings. Soon after, the first two of the confessional laws received the sanction of the Emperor, and were promulgated as laws of the empire.

At the beginning of the year, Dr. Glaser, the Minister of Justice, in a circular addressed to all officials concerned, announced the complete introduction of the system of trial by jury, as about to come into effect, in accordance with last year's act. The officials are reminded in this circular that the spirit of the new legislation is that they are to attach equal importance to the vindication of the law to the protection of the innocent. Crime is to be prosecuted in the interests of the community with all the more energy since the peculiar powers of public prosecutors in originating proceedings as hitherto practised in Austria will no longer exist. Confidence must be created in the readiness of the representatives of the states to follow up the complaints of individual persons against those who have wronged them, irrespective of rank or person. In particular the minister finds it necessary to warn those he addresses, that the power of preliminary detention for purposes of prosecution must be exercised in future with the greatest circumspection.

In February, the Emperor Francis Joseph paid a visit to the Emperor of Russia at St. Petersburg, where he was received with marked honors. The conferences of Austrian and Russian ministers held on this occasion appear to have chiefly concerned commercial questions, as a mixed commission was appointed by the two Governments to meet in March in St. Petersburg. Complaints of the Russian mode of levying duties on goods crossing the frontier have been frequent in Austro-Hungary for some time. With a view to obtain, if possible, a removal of the grievance, the Austrian Government, not long ago, requested the Chambers of Commerce to set forth their several views in written memorials, stating what the present grievances are, and how they may be remedied. Copies of these memorials, illustrated by established facts, were submitted to the Russian Government by the Austrian legation at the time of the Emperor's visit to St. Petersburg, and the propositions therein contained were at the same time warmly advocated by the Austrian diplomatists assembled at the Russian capital. The Russian authorities met the Austrian suggestions in a friendly and sympathetic spirit, offering to coöperate in the proposed reforms to the best of their endeavor. The Austrian negotiators took care to prove that the advantage would be mutual, and that Russian interests cannot possibly suffer from the alterations. Semi-officially it was also stated that "the happy issue" of the journey of Francis Joseph "protects Austria against a disturbance of her internal development by the bugbear of Panslavism."

On June 14th, the Minister of War, J. von Kuhn, resigned, and the Governor of Bohemia, General von Koller, was appointed in his place. Kuhn had asked for his dismission twice before, the last time when the general staff was separated from the Ministry of War, and an independent chief of the staff appointed. The Emperor at that time declared to Kuhn that no competent man had yet been found to carry through the organization of the army. It is no secret that the old military party, at the head of which is Archduke Albrecht, was the cause that Kuhn's resignation was formerly offered and this time accepted.

A visit made by the Emperor, in September, to Bohemia, called forth a number of addresses. The Czechic towns had sent a number of deputations which were to express the wishes of the Czechic population for a decentralization of the empire, and the restoration of Bohemian autonomy. The Emperor was, however, careful in his answers not to give any encouragement to the hopes of the Czechs. When the Town Council at Prague, in its address, demonstratively declared that it offered the expression of its confidence exclusively to the person of the monarch, the Emperor replied by expressing the hope that Prague would continue to grow under the protection of the laws and the institutions given by him. Those deputa-

tions which intended to present addresses of outspoken federalistic tendencies were not admitted at all to the audience. While the attitude of the Emperor with regard to the Czechic federalists was, on the whole, satisfactory to the Liberal party, they were less pleased with the position he took with regard to the new Church laws in his intercourse with the bishops. In a private audience given to the Cardinal-Archbishop of Prague, Prince Schwarzenberg, he was reported by Catholic papers to have expressed his regret that up to the present time he had been prevented by circumstances from doing what he desired to do for the Church; and, on the other hand, his satisfaction in having averted from her some evils which otherwise would have befallen her, and his determination to protect the Church so far as the present circumstances would allow. The Liberal papers did not deny that remarks like these had been made, though they claimed for them an entirely private and unofficial character.

All the provincial Diets of cis-Leitban Austria were opened on September 15th. The Czechs in Bohemia are divided as to whether their representatives shall take part in the proceedings of the Bohemian Diet or not. The Old Czechic party persists in its refusal to attend the Diet, while the "Young Czechs" (Liberals) are of the contrary opinion. The latter had been successful in electing seven of their candidates, who were present on the opening of the Diet. All the Diets closed their sessions by October 17th. In order to avoid the simultaneous meeting of the provincial Diets and the Reichsrath, the former will in future be held in the spring.

The Reichsrath reassembled on October 20th. The Minister of Public Worship, to the great disappointment of the Catholic party, had previously announced that the Government would strictly carry out the new Church laws. The same minister had made another concession to the Liberal party by the appointment for the theological faculty of the University of Inspruck of two professors not belonging to the order of the Jesuits which hitherto had filled all the chairs of this faculty. The preliminary statement of the budget for 1875, which the Minister of Finance read to the Reichsrath in October, did not give satisfaction, as it showed a decrease in the direct revenue.

The joint annual meeting of the legislative delegations of Austria and Hungary took place this year in April at Pesth. In reply to a question relative to Austria's foreign relations and the present state of Europe, Count Andrassy positively denied the existence of any immediate danger of war. Austria in her intercourse with neighboring and other states had greatly contributed, and would continue to contribute, to the preservation of peace. The best means of rendering this line of conduct effective in the future consisted in continuing to maintain the strength of the monarchy at such a point as to enable Austria to preserve peace as long as possible, but her own interests under all circumstances. Referring to the recent meetings of European sovereigns, the minister remarked that the exclusive object of the exchange of views which had passed between their Majesties and their ministers was the guaranteeing of peace. He denied and refuted the assertion made by some newspapers of political conventions having been entered into at the last meeting for making a division of the East and giving a new direction to the foreign policy of Austria. Herr Scrinsez, a member of the delegation, having pointed out that Austria's maritime commerce was retrograding, Count Andrassy said the conclusion of commercial and navigation treaties had always led to an extension of intercourse with foreign countries in the interest of commerce. On the occasion of the Emperor of Austria's visit to Russia, he had been especially guided by the conviction that the most intimate possible commercial relations afforded the best guarantee of peace. Herr Czartoryski suggested that the Red-Book should not in future be issued, but Count Andrassy refuted his arguments and described the Red-Book as one of the guarantees of constitutionalism. Herr Grass moved that the expenditure for the post of embassador at the Vatican should be struck off the charges for the diplomatic service. This motion was, however, rejected, Count Andrassy having opposed it, stating that Austria had no small interest in possessing the right

of being diplomatically represented at the court of the head of the Catholic Church, a right which no other power had renounced. He alluded to the process now going on throughout Europe of separating the temporal from the ecclesiastical power, and said that, not only the interests and rights of twenty-eight million Catholic subjects, but the rights of the state and of the Emperor and Apostolic King, which could not be abandoned, must continue to be represented. The amalgamation of the embassy to the Vatican with the legation at the Italian court would be absolutely impracticable, considering the notoriously unfriendly relations subsisting between the latter and the Roman Curia.

An exhibition of great interest was opened in October at Vienna, in the building erected for the International Exhibition, comprising all the chief articles of produce and manufacture which enter into the existing trade between Europe and the East. China, Japan, Turkey, Egypt, the East Indies, and Tunis, were all efficiently represented. This effort to utilize the great building of the International has for its object to bring together in one centre all that can illustrate the importance of Eastern commerce, and afford the most recent and valuable information both as to the raw produce and the manufactured articles hitherto in demand, their prices at different places, and the relative rates ruling in those Oriental centres for European manufactured goods of every kind.

B

BACHMAN, Rev. JOHN, D. D., LL. D., a venerable Lutheran clergyman, naturalist, and author; born in Dutchess County, N. Y., February, 1790; died in Charleston, S. C., February 24, 1874. He received a thorough classical education, and entered the ministry of the Lutheran Church in 1813, and in 1815 was settled as pastor of the Lutheran Church in Charleston, S. C., and retained that position till his death. He early became an intimate friend and associate of J. J. Audubon, and, being a zealous and careful student of zoology, rendered him great assistance in the preparation of his "Ornithology," and wrote nearly the whole of the work on the "Quadrupeds of America," which was so admirably illustrated by Audubon and his sons. His other works on natural science were: "Catalogue of Phænogamous Plants and Ferns growing in the Vicinity of Charleston, S. C.;" "The Doctrine of the Unity of the Human Race, examined on the Principles of Science" (1850); "Notice of the Types of Mankind (by Nott and Gliddon), with an Examination of the Charges contained in the Biography of Dr. Morton" (1854); "Examination of Prof. Agassiz's Sketch of the Natural Provinces of the Animal World, and their Relation to the Different Types of Men" (1855); "The

Characteristics of Genera and Species, as applicable to the Doctrine of the Unity of the Human Race" (1854). He also contributed to the *South Carolina Medical Journal* a series of papers discussing the bearing of modern science upon revealed religion. His relations with the great naturalist Agassiz were very cordial and tender. He welcomed him to Charleston in 1852, and was very loath to hear of his return to the North. But while Dr. Bachman was thus active as a naturalist, he did not forget his duties as a Lutheran clergyman and pastor. He was indefatigable in the performance of his clerical duties, and won for himself, during his long pastorate of almost sixty years, the undivided love of his people. Among his theological writings were, "A Sermon on the Doctrine and Discipline of the Evangelical Lutheran Church" (1837); "Design and Duties of the Christian Ministry," 1848; "A Defense of Luther and the Reformation" (1853), etc., etc. In all the relations of life Dr. Bachman was earnest, active, and courteous. His efforts for the promotion of the systematic study of zoology in the United States were untiring, and attended with remarkable success.

BACON, Rt. Rev. DAVID W., D. D., Roman

Catholic Bishop of the Diocese of Portland, Me.; born in Brooklyn, N. Y., in 1814; died in St. Vincent's Hospital, New York, November 5, 1874. He received an excellent classical training in the New York Catholic schools, whence he proceeded to Mount St. Mary's College and Seminary, Emmettsburg, Md., and having completed his course returned to New York, where he was ordained by Bishop Dubois in 1838. He was a man of remarkably fine personal presence, an accomplished scholar and gentleman, and, soon after his settlement as pastor of the Church of the Assumption in Brooklyn, he had attained to a greater popularity than any Catholic clergyman in Brooklyn. He was unwearied in his efforts for the extension of the Catholic Church in that city, and, though his own congregation was the largest by far in Brooklyn, he was not satisfied until he had purchased the land and erected the Church of St. Mary, Star of the Sea, at the corner of Court and Luqueer Streets, the largest and most commodious church edifice in the city, where he was pastor during the last years of his residence in Brooklyn. In 1855 he was consecrated bishop of the newly-created Diocese of Portland, Me., which embraced the two States of Maine and New Hampshire. His labors here were unremitting, and attended with great success. At the commencement of 1874 there were in the diocese 58 churches, and 6 were in course of erection, 52 priests, 20 ecclesiastical students, 4 female religious asylums, 2 male asylums, 6 female academies, and 20 free schools, with a Catholic population estimated at 80,000. When he took charge of the diocese the number of churches was very small, and there were no charitable institutions. His constant labors had so thoroughly impaired his health, that in August, 1874, he found it necessary to make a voyage to Europe for its restoration, but it was too late for him to be benefited. On his arrival in France he was obliged to go immediately into the hospital at Brest, where he remained until he was carried on board ship to return, and, on his arrival in New York, November 4th, was carried at once to St. Vincent's Hospital, where he died the next evening.

BAILEY, Rev. SILAS, D. D., a Baptist clergyman and college president; born in Massachusetts about 1812; died in Paris, June 11, 1874. Dr. Bailey was educated at Brown University, whence he graduated with distinction in 1834, and, after taking a theological course at Newton Theological Seminary, was for a time a pastor in Massachusetts. He was called from this duty to become Principal of Worcester Academy, about 1840, and, after several years of active service there, was elected President of Granville College (now Dennison University), Granville, Ohio, where he remained for about ten years of severe labor, complicated by the lack of sufficient endowment for the college. From Granville he went to Franklin, Ind., and soon after became president of the young col-

lege there. He was measurably successful in building up this college, attracting to it many students by his ability as a teacher, but the same difficulty—insufficiency of endowment—confronted him there as at Granville, and, finding his health failing, he resigned and accepted the pastorate at Lafayette, Ind., where he remained for three years, winning golden opinions from all who knew him. But teaching was his true vocation, and, being called to the professorship of Theology at Kalamazoo College, Mich., he embraced the opportunity, in the hope of training up young men for the ministry in the West. After four or five years of teaching there, his health again failed, and he returned to Lafayette, where a wealthy friend and admirer gave him a life-lease of a beautiful home and grounds near the city for one dollar rental per annum. Here he recovered his health, and engaged in some literary labors; but the death of his wife and only daughter, in quick succession, broke up his home. Some months later, he received the intelligence of the death of a brother who had left him a large property, and he determined to go to Europe, having married a second time. He had but just arrived in Paris when he was taken suddenly ill, with a return of his old malady, and died in about a week. Dr. Bailey (he received the degree of D. D. from Madison University in 1849) was a profound scholar, a most diligent student, a vigorous and elegant writer, an impressive speaker, and a man of rare executive ability. Though he had written much, he had published but little—a few sermons, addresses, baccalaureates, orations, essays, and reviews. He had accumulated a fine library, which he left to Franklin College, Indiana, the scene of his former labors, together with $13,000 for its care and increase.

BALLEVIAN, ADOLFO, President of the Republic of Bolivia; died at Oruro, February 14, 1874. Señor Ballevian had been, for many years, prominent in political life in Bolivia, and was greatly esteemed as one of the purest and best of the Bolivian statesmen. The long succession of revolutions which had made the state notorious, and which had been promoted by ambitious generals, who, backed by their troops, seized the supreme power, in defiance of the Constitution, had ceased with the death of Melgarejo in 1871; and General Morales, who succeeded Melgarejo, was the first regularly-elected President for some years. On his death, in February, 1873, Señor Ballevian was elected, and commenced his administration in April, 1873, in such a way as to win the approval and confidence of the citizens of the republic, but his sudden death, after an administration of ten months, caused wide-spread regret, and excited great alarm lest a revolution should be precipitated, and anarchy again prevail.

BAPTISTS. The *American Baptist Year-Book* gives the following statistics, for 1873, of the Baptists throughout the world:

COUNTRIES.	Associations.	Churches.	Ordained Ministers.	Total Membership.
NORTH AMERICA:				
Canada	12	327	238	17,541
Grand Ligne Mission	....	10	6	369
Mexico	....	8	3	151
New Brunswick	2	136	73	10,516
Nova Scotia	3	163	94	18,021
Prince Edward Island	1	14	6	820
United States	890	20,520	12,598	1,633,939
West Indies:				
Bahamas	...	5	3	2,887
Hayti	...	1	1	100
Jamaica	...	94	36	20,509
Trinidad	...	2	1	434
Total	908	21,285	13,059	1,705,287
EUROPE:				
Denmark	...	17	17	1,902
England	31	1,973	1,740	177,321
France	...	12	8	574
Germany	3	103	270	19,393
Greece	...	1	1	...
Holland	...	1	4	91
Ireland	1	40	25	1,492
Italy	...	7	7	277
Norway	1	12	6	300
Poland	...	2	2	1,162
Russia	...	5	5	1,439
Scotland	1	104	76	7,096
Spain	...	4	4	200
Sweden	10	221	157	9,336
Switzerland	...	8	8	350
Turkey	...	1	1	109
Wales	9	522	374	54,004
Total	56	3,033	2,705	275,046
ASIA:				
Assam	...	8	21	493
Burmah	1	17	20	1,039
Ceylon	...	3	3	655
China	...	16	23	860
Hindostan	...	40	41	4,085
Japan	...	...	3	10
Karen	...	330	79	16,183
Shans	...	1	1	14
Siam	...	4	2	154
Teloogoos	...	6	15	2,861
Total	1	425	208	26,354
AFRICA:				
Cape Colony	...	6	5	369
Camaroons	...	4	3	120
Liberia	...	20	16	1,250
St. Helena	...	1	1	200
Total	...	31	25	1,930
AUSTRALASIA:				
New South Wales	1	24	15	812
New Zealand	...	9	7	519
Queensland	...	12	7	250
South Australia	1	45	26	1,620
Tasmania	...	6	4	120
Victoria	1	48	32	1,800
Total	3	144	91	5,112
Grand total	968	24,918	16,092	2,013,729

It appears from this table that about four-fifths of the Baptist associations, their churches, ministers, and members, are in the United States. The total number of baptisms reported in 1873, in all countries, was 77,767.

I. REGULAR BAPTISTS IN AMERICA.—The American Baptist Year-Book for 1874, gives the following statistics of the Baptist churches in the United States: Number of associations, 890; of churches, 20,520; of ministers, 12,598; of members, 1,633,939.

The number of baptisms reported during 1873 was 70,162. The number of Sunday-schools was 9,222. The total amount of be-nevolent contributions of the churches and Sunday-schools, reported in 1873, was $3,988,-909.31. Ten theological seminaries reported for 1873: instructors, 45; students, 441; value of property, $1,125,000; amount of endowments, $1,001,000; volumes in libraries, 43,000. Thirty-five colleges and universities reported: instructors, 291; students, 5,056; total value of property, $5,519,688; amount of endowments, $3,012,000; volumes in libraries, 149,-634. Sixty academies, seminaries, institutes, and female colleges, reported: instructors, 339; students, 5,478; total value of property, $2,029,000; amount of endowments, $262,185.

According to the American Baptist Year-Book for 1875, the statistics of associations, churches, ministers, and members, were in the preceding year as follows:

STATES AND TERRITORIES.	Associations.	Churches.	Ordained Ministers.	Total Membership.
Alabama	50	1,210	631	75,614
Arkansas	36	907	490	44,901
California	6	100	84	4,158
Colorado	2	18	13	677
Connecticut	6	114	123	19,882
Dakota	1	14	10	273
Delaware	...	10	7	367
District of Columbia	1	24	29	8,152
Florida	14	251	163	17,092
Georgia	95	2,367	1,354	170,354
Idaho	...	1	1	20
Illinois	41	1,056	782	68,313
Indiana	30	563	333	39,352
Indian Territory	3	61	47	3,910
Iowa	21	371	252	20,784
Kansas	17	242	162	8,860
Kentucky	59	1,367	723	147,031
Louisiana	21	576	296	35,313
Maine	13	260	166	19,303
Maryland	1	44	33	5,652
Massachusetts	15	282	316	44,679
Michigan	16	296	233	20,583
Minnesota	7	177	106	6,293
Mississippi	45	1,206	588	88,269
Missouri	67	1,425	831	88,662
Nebraska	7	90	46	3,052
Nevada	...	3	8	50
New Hampshire	7	85	85	8,855
New Jersey	5	169	178	28,296
New Mexico	...	1	.....	20
New York	46	831	746	108,964
North Carolina	56	1,392	831	116,528
Ohio	40	735	487	49,447
Oregon	5	59	47	2,052
Pennsylvania	20	536	429	56,914
Rhode Island	3	59	66	10,080
South Carolina	27	759	434	93,922
Tennessee	50	1,179	779	104,312
Texas	43	995	604	54,019
Utah	...	1	1	16
Vermont	7	110	72	8,615
Virginia	80	1,107	541	146,586
Washington	2	12	9	224
West Virginia	16	334	199	24,747
Wisconsin	12	179	132	11,262
Wyoming	...	2	2	47
Total	943	21,570	13,354	1,761,171

The anniversaries of the Northern Baptist societies of the United States were held at Washington, D. C., beginning with that of the Bible and Publication Society, on May 22d. The occasion was the completion of the fiftieth year of the society's existence, and was marked by the observance of special jubilee services. The Hon. James L. Howard, of Connecticut, presided. The report of the board reviewed the history and work of the society for the preceding fifty years. The receipts during the period of its existence had been: in the business department, $3,162,038.85; in the missionary department, $799,224.86; making a total of $3,961,263.71. Its annual receipts had grown from $372.80 in its first year to $430,854.93 in the year just completed. For the first sixteen years the society had limited itself to the printing and circulation of tracts. In 1840 its constitution was so amended as to make its work embrace also volumes, particularly Sunday-school books. It had now on its list 1,136 publications of all kinds. It published also five periodicals. The number of pages embraced in the publications of fifty years was 3,324,104,466. The receipts of the society for the last year were reported to have been: in the business department, $360,696.10; in the benevolent department, $71,240.15; total, $431,936.25. Its disbursements had been $414,246.39. At the request of the board, a committee of seven persons was appointed to report at the next annual meeting of the society whether any improved method can be adopted in the management of its affairs.

The anniversary of the *American Baptist Home Mission Society* was held at Washington, May 23d. The total receipts of the society for the year were reported to have been $257,257.36, and its expenditures, $247,427.74. Of these amounts $50,374.86 had been received, and $43,228.17 expended on account of the Church-Edifice fund. Contributions had been received from forty-six States and Territories. It was shown in the report that, in 1859-'60, only nineteen, and in 1868-'69 only thirty-two States and Territories had contributed to the treasury of the society. Three hundred and eighty-five missionaries had been employed, under whose labors one hundred and thirteen new Baptist churches had been organized, and 2,264 persons had been baptized. The churches under their care had contributed $18,500 to the cause of home missions. The reports from the freedmen's schools were favorable. Applications had been received in the church-building department, for aid in building houses of worship, from one hundred and twenty churches, and had been granted in the cases of sixty of them. The whole amount appropriated in these instances was nearly $50,000. A resolution was passed by the society favoring coöperation with the Baptist Historical Society. A resolution was also unanimously adopted, expressing the wish that the remembrances of the recent civil conflict in the United States might be blotted out, and that the exchange of correspondence and of fraternal delegates with the Southern Baptist Convention might be continued.

The thirteenth anniversary of the *American Baptist Historical Society* was held in Washington, May 27th. The report of the corresponding secretary showed that 447 books, 739 pamphlets, and 62 manuscripts, had been

added to the library of the society during the year. The library now contained 6,302 volumes, and about 14,000 unbound pamphlets. The society had received bequests amounting to $14,000, and an annuity of $500. The monetary receipts for the year had been about $400. The Rev. Howard Malcolm, D. D., was re-elected president of the society.

The annual meeting of the Board of Councilors of the *American Baptist Educational Commission* was held at Washington, May 23d. The Rev. Alvah Hovey, D. D., presided. The commission had made appeals to the public in behalf of the Southern Baptist Theological Seminary, and William Jewell College, Missouri. During the year the Rochester Theological Seminary and Dennison University had been endowed. An appeal was made to the commission in behalf of Snake Forest College, N. C., whose endowment of $100,000 had been swept away by the war, and of the Columbian University. Addresses were made on the proposed movement to enlarge the endowments of all the Baptist educational institutions in the United States as a centennial celebration, to be completed in 1876.

The fiftieth anniversary of the *American Baptist Missionary Union* was held at Washington, May 26th. The receipts of the Union for the year ending March 31, 1874, were reported to have been: from regular donations of churches and individuals, $165,313.46; from special "thank-offerings," $20,243.84; from legacies, $28,754.77; from woman's societies, $33,378.27; from miscellaneous sources, $13,840.57; making a total of $261,530.91. This amount was larger than that of the preceding, or of any previous year, by $45,430.21. The year had begun with a balance against the treasury of $42,069.64. The appropriations for the expenses of the year were $247,240.07, making in all $289,309.71 to be provided for. A special effort was made in June to meet the deficit by what were called "thank-offerings." By the close of the year the balance against the treasury had been reduced to $27,778.80. Sixteen new missionaries had been sent out during the year, four of whom were under the auspices of the Woman's Baptist Missionary societies, and eight missionaries had returned to their fields after visits to the United States. The report of the board raised a question whether the progress of the work in some parts of the field would not be advanced by adopting a policy of appointing unmarried men as missionaries. The subject was referred to a committee, who reported: 1. That the question was one to be determined by circumstances; 2. That, in general, the chief personal interests to be relied upon in the missionary work were the married man and his household; 3. That, when special circumstances seemed to call for such action, the board should be free to employ unmarried men.

Two women's missionary societies work in coöperation with the American Baptist Missionary Union : the *Woman's Baptist Mission-ary Society*, whose chief support comes from New England and New York, and the *Woman's Missionary Society of the West.* The receipts of the Eastern society for the year were $26,061, and those of the Western society were $8,154. The Eastern society had supported eleven woman missionaries, thirteen Bible-women, and one native preacher, had paid the expenses of four other missionaries, and had aided in the support of twenty-two schools, with 1,151 pupils.

The last session of the *Burmah Baptist Missionary Convention* was attended by fourteen male missionaries, five female missionaries, thirteen ordained native ministers, twenty-five unordained ministers, and eighty other persons. The sessions occupied five days, including Sunday. The proceedings were conducted in three languages—the Burmese, the Karen, and the English. Favorable reports were received from nearly all the stations. The work had been pushed with vigor at most of them, and encouraging progress had been made. The summary of the returns gave a total of 375 churches, 88 ordained and 338 unordained preachers, 19,307 members, with 1,044 baptisms during the year, and 144 schools with 6,179 pupils. The contributions of the churches had amounted to 52,639 rupees, or about $25,000.

The thirty-seventh anniversary of the *American and Foreign Bible Society* was held in the city of New York, May 14th. The report of the treasurer showed the receipts for the year to have been $8,282, and the expenditures $8,194.77. The society had received about $1,500,000 since its beginning, and had sent out nearly 5,000,000 copies of the Scriptures, most of them entire, in many languages. During the past year it had given to the destitute in the United States 2,665 Bibles and Testaments, and had sold 872 Bibles and Testaments. A committee, appointed to confer with a similar committee of the American Bible Union with a view to the consolidation of the two societies, reported that a plan of union had been approved by the boards of both societies. The society voted to authorize the plan to be carried out. The new society is to be called the "American and Foreign Bible Union."

The twenty-fifth anniversary of the *American Bible Union* was held in New York City, October 14th. The Rev. Thomas Armitage, D. D., presided. The report of the treasurer showed the receipts of the Union for the year to have been $64,217, and its expenditures $69,509. The entire receipts since the society was organized were shown to have been $872,928. The proposition and plan of the board for a consolidation with the American and Foreign Bible Society were accepted, and committees were appointed to coöperate with similar committees from the other body to complete the union. It was expected that the consolidation would be perfected in May, 1875.

The *Southern Baptist Convention* met at Jefferson, Texas, May 7th. The Rev. James P. Boyce, D. D., of South Carolina, was re-elected president. The Foreign Mission Board reported that, in all, the sum of $32,770.13 had been received into the treasury for general missionary purposes, or about $4,000 more than had been received during the previous year, and $10,000 more than the average annual receipts of the preceding six years. Practically, the board was free from debt. Applications for appointment to missionary work had been received from eight States. Lack of means, however, had made the board unable to employ all those who offered themselves. The work on the African missions had been temporarily suspended. The convention favored its resumption, and decided that an effort should be made to raise for it during the year the sum of $5,000. The appointment of colored missionaries in preference to white, but with a white superintendent, was recommended. Thirty missionaries and three native assistants had been employed in China. The need of suitable residences for the missionaries was set forth. The prospects of the mission in Italy were regarded as hopeful. One American missionary, the Rev. George B. Taylor, D. D., and five Italian evangelists, were at work in this field. A plan was adopted for the future support of the Foreign Mission Board. It contemplates the submission of careful annual estimates by the board; the apportionment of the amount to be raised among the States; the appointment of an executive committee in each State; the distribution of "mite-boxes" to every Baptist family; the presentation of the mission-work by the pastors to the attention of the churches; the payment of the missionaries quarterly in advance, the money to be borrowed on the credit of the board if it is not on hand. The estimates for carrying on the Foreign Mission work during the ensuing year were fixed at $50,602.

The receipts of the Domestic and Indian Mission and Sunday-school Board during the year had been $32,465, but had been exceeded by the expenses $11,400. Fifty-five missionaries had been employed, twenty-five of whom, however, had been dismissed before the end of the year for the lack of funds. Nineteen other missionaries had been in service among the Indians. The Sunday-school department was $8,374 in debt. One hundred and sixty-six new Sunday-schools had been organized, in which were 5,001 scholars and teachers. Two colored students had been aided. The debt of the Domestic and Indian Mission department remained the same as it was the year before, viz., $11,411.24. The name of the board was changed to the Home Mission Board, and it was relieved from all Sunday-school work as a specialty, and directed henceforth to limit its operations to the support of ministers of the gospel. The convention ordered all receipts for Sunday-school work to be applied to the liquidation of debts, and all other available funds to be applied for the same purpose as fast as consistent. It was estimated that it would require $75,000 to be raised during the year to sustain the work of the board and pay its debts. The trustees of the Southern Baptist Theological Seminary were seeking to raise the sum of $75,000 for the support of the seminary pending the completion of its endowment and its removal to its permanent seat at Louisville, Ky. Forty thousand dollars had already been pledged to this purpose. Upon the presentation of the case to the convention, $20,000 more were contributed.

The *Eastern Conference of German Baptist Churches* and ministers met at Tavistock, Ontario, September 10th. Reports from the churches reported the whole number of their members to be 3,792. Four hundred and seventy-eight baptisms had been made. The *Western Conference* met at Green Garden, Hill County, Ill., September 10th. The several churches reported a total membership of 3,498 souls, with 453 Sunday-schools and 3,192 scholars. The total amount of money raised for the expenses of the churches and for benevolent causes and other enterprises was $40,051. The Sunday-schools had also contributed the sum of $2,285. The dividing line between the two conferences corresponds with the eastern boundary-line of the State of Ohio. The *German Baptist Union Association*, or "Bundes Conference," is composed of messengers of all the churches included in the Eastern and Western conferences, and meets every three years. Its fourth meeting was held in Chicago, Ill., September 16th to 23d. Delegates were present from Canada West, and the States of Connecticut, New York, Pennsylvania, Ohio, Indiana, Kentucky, Missouri, Iowa, Wisconsin, and Minnesota. The Rev. G. Schulte, of New York, was elected moderator; Prof. A. Rauschenbusch spoke in behalf of the German department of Rochester Theological Seminary. Twenty-two young men had received instruction in this department, and a large number were expected the next year. The receipts of the German Baptist Publication Society for the year ending January 1, 1874, were reported to have been $19,973.15. It was publishing three periodicals : the *Sendbote*, weekly, with 4,300 subscribers; a child's paper, with 8,500 subscribers; and the *Sunday-school Lessons*, with two thousand subscribers. This society is established at Cleveland, Ohio. It was organized in 1865. From its beginning to the 1st of January, 1874, it had published 79,-500 copies of sixty-eight distinct works.

The Baptist Convention of *Nova Scotia, New Brunswick, and Prince Edward Island*, held its twenty-ninth annual meeting at St. John, N. B., beginning August 22d. Judge M. Culley was chosen president. The statistical reports furnished by the minutes of the associations gave the following results :

ASSOCIATIONS.	Churches.	Baptisms.	Members.
Nova Scotia.			
Western Association........	67	1,124	9,469
Central "	47	975	6,593
Eastern "	57	283	3,843
	171	2,382	19,905
New Brunswick.			
Western Association........	72	146	4,962
Eastern "	66	389	5,846
	138	485	10,828
Prince Edward Island	14	154	960
Total...................	323	3,021	31,696

The net increase for the year had been nearly eight per cent., a higher rate than had been attained in any year since the formation of the convention. The number of baptisms also exceeded that of any previous year. Twelve ministers had been ordained during the year. The educational interest of the convention is confined chiefly to Acadia College. The endowment fund of this institution amounted to $43,357.22 paid and invested, and $21,854.25 of notes. The college had thirty-seven students. The following resolutions were recommended by the Committee on Education, and were unanimously adopted by the convention :

Resolved, That the convention tender its hearty congratulations to the friends of free education in New Brunswick, on the success which has crowned their zealous and united efforts, whereby the designs of the advocates of sectarian education at the public expense have been defeated.

Resolved, That in view of the avowed determination of certain organs of ultramontane opinions, in defiance of the will of the people, to effect the overthrow of the non-sectarian school systems of the maritime provinces, as well as in view of the alleged fact that in some parts of Nova Scotia the school law of that province is openly disobeyed, a committee be appointed, to watch the proceedings of the opponents of free education, and to take such steps as may tend to the exposure and removal of abuses.

A meeting in the interest of foreign missions was held August 25th. The total receipts for the mission funds for the year were reported by the treasurer to have been $7,771.27. The societies had three missionaries at Bangkok, Siam, two at Rangoon, and three at Tavoy, Burmah.

The anniversary of the *Nova Scotia Baptist Home Missionary Union* was held at Parrsborough, July 10th and 11th. The total receipts for the year were reported by the general agent to have been $6,251.22, and the payments $5,292.27. Fifty-six missionaries had been employed for longer or shorter periods during the year. Application was made from the association of Prince Edward Island to be received into the Union Home Missionary work.

The annual meeting of the *Baptist Home Missionary Convention East, of Canada*, was held in Montreal in September. The jurisdiction of the convention extends from Belleville to Quebec. It comprises twenty-six churches. The treasurer submitted a report showing his annual expenditures since 1870 to have been as follows: 1870, $800; 1871, $1,062; 1872, $1,912; 1873, $2,670; 1874, $4,098.94. His receipts for 1874 had been $3,783.24, leaving a balance due him of $213.70. The convention urged the churches to increased interest in the department of missionary work recently established in Calcutta, India, by the Rev. J. McLaurin and his wife.

II. FREE-WILL BAPTISTS.—The following are the statistics of the Free-will Baptist Church, as given in the *Free-will Baptist Register* for 1874:

YEARLY MEETINGS.	Number of Churches.	Ordained Preachers.	Number of Communicants.
New Hampshire	124	125	8,659
Maine Western	67	61	4,409
Maine Central	105	97	6,395
Penobscot	110	72	4,016
Vermont	63	53	3,203
R. Island and Massachusetts	47	54	4,986
Holland Purchase	33	38	2,111
Genesee	26	27	1,451
Susquehanna	37	21	1,464
New York and Pennsylvania	43	31	1,104
St. Lawrence	17	15	783
Union	13	11	640
Central New York	43	25	2,197
Pennsylvania	13	10	557
Ohio and Pennsylvania	40	32	1,574
Central Ohio	26	19	1,401
Ohio	10	9	631
Ohio River	54	33	3,135
Indiana	7	4	360
Northern Indiana	19	10	604
Michigan	89	81	3,286
St. Joseph's Valley	20	11	823
Illinois	47	40	1,652
Southern Illinois	66	48	3,003
Wisconsin	66	65	2,645
Minnesota	24	17	627
Minnesota Southern	34	19	665
Iowa	32	25	1,303
Iowa Northern	41	28	1,259
Kansas	13	9	249
Virginia F. B. Association	12	5	703
Louisiana	21	13	591
Ontario, P. Q.	16	4	664
Orissa	5	7	371
Shelby Association	14	9	578
Liberty Association	27	16	1,605
Nine quarterly meetings not connected with any yearly meeting	36	25	659
Churches not connected	11	2	306
Total, 36 yearly meetings.	**1,471**	**1,173**	**70,629**

The number of quarterly meetings given in the tables of the *Register* is 163, and the number of licensed preachers 121. The tables show an increase from 1873 of two quarterly meetings, twenty-five ministers, and fifty-three members, and a decrease of thirty-three churches. The *Register* gives a list of twenty-one colleges, academies, and other literary institutions under the care or patronage of the Free-will Baptists. There are a number of associations of Baptists in America, which, in doctrine and polity, are in general agreement with the Free-will Baptists. From the best information received respecting them, they are supposed to number in the aggregate not less than twenty-five thousand members.

The twenty-second triennial General Conference of the Free-will Baptists in the United States met at Providence, R. I., October 7th. The Rev. D. W. C. Durzin, of New Hampshire, was chosen moderator. The Committee on Doctrine and Church Polity made a report, on certain questions which had been submitted to them, of which such parts were adopted as expressed the views of the Conference, to the following effect: To the question, "What course should be pursued by our churches with those who join other churches without asking a letter from us?" answer was returned: "Such a course is contrary to our church covenant;" in answer to the question, "When members are received from Pedo-Baptist Churches by letter, and ask for baptism and receive it, how are they to be returned—as received by baptism or by letter?" the direction was given that they be returned as received by baptism. It was decided not to be a violation of the usages of the denomination to send women as delegates to quarterly and yearly meetings, and to the General Conference. It was declared that "whereas the rite of communion is by the New Testament left wholly to the discretion of the applicant," therefore "the Church may not presume to pass upon the fitness of any Christian to participate in the sacrament of the Lord's Supper." In answer to various resolves and queries, relative to the reception of members by letter from Pedo-Baptist Churches, it was resolved: "That we believe Christian baptism to be a personal act of public consecration to Christ, and not the door into the Christian Church; that believers' baptism, and immersion only as baptism, is a fundamental doctrine of our church;" and that, as a general principle, it is not consistent with the doctrine and polity of the Free-will Baptist denomination to admit persons to full membership who have not been baptized (immersed), but merely sprinkled, or poured, but that "persons presenting letters from other evangelical churches may be received by assenting and conforming to the doctrines and usages of our Church in the future." It was declared destructive of all order to receive and accredit a properly-expelled minister without a full conference with the body expelling him, and not in accordance with the policy of the church, "for a ministerial council, however called or organized, to assume to expel a minister from the denomination, who is a member in good standing in one of our churches." It was also decided that a person may be a delegate to the General Conference who is not a member of the yearly meeting he represents, provided he be chosen by the body he represents.

The Rev. A. H. Merrill made a report of his action as a corresponding messenger to the Church of God in Pennsylvania. He had attended the East Pennsylvania Elderships, the principal body of this denomination, and had been well received. There seemed to be a general feeling, among those whom he saw, that the two denominations were essentially one in principle, and should be more closely identified. The members of the Church of God were, however, tenacious in regard to the name of their denomination. Fraternal greetings were exchanged with the American Christian Conference, which was in session at the same time at Stanfordville, N. Y., and a committee was appointed to confer with a committee of that body as to the propriety and means of uniting the two bodies into one conference. The fact was observed that the Free-will Baptists had no representative at the meeting of the Evangelical Alliance held in New York, in October, 1873. That such an omission might not again occur, a resolution was passed directing "the consummation of the ordinary denominational relationship" between the Conference and the Evangelical Alliance, and the Rev. G. T. Day was appointed a delegate to attend the next session of the Alliance; delegates were also received from the General Missionary Convention of the Disciples of Christ, and from other religious bodies. Resolutions were passed pledging the denomination to the principle of total abstinence from the use, manufacture, and sale of intoxicating liquors, favoring the policy of prohibitory laws and the support of friends of temperance for office, and expressing sympathy with the efforts of the women in behalf of temperance.

The report of the *Sunday-School Union* to the General Conference showed its work to have been conducted with great vigor. Detailed reports were given from 387 out of 1,504 churches, representing 56 out of 161 quarterly meetings, which showed the number of scholars in schools connected with reporting churches to be 29,950, and the number of teachers 2,646. The report of the treasurer of the *Education Society*, made at its annual meeting held during the session of the General Conference, showed his receipts for the year to have been $7,703.62, and his expenditures $6,752.29. The total receipts of the *Printing Establishment* at Dover, N. H., for the preceding three years, were reported to the General Conference to have been $137,065.42. The assets of the establishment were valued at $74,032.72, and its liabilities were reported to be $3,489.26. The receipts of the *Home Mission Society* for the year were reported at the annual meeting, held October 9th, to have been $9,110.82, and its expenditures $8,290.81. The permanent fund amounted to $4,594.97. The liabilities of the society were $7,336.30, and its assets $6,261.80, leaving a balance against it of $1,074.50. More than 2,800 members had been added to the Church through the agency of the society in the South, during the preceding year.

The report of the *Foreign Missionary Society*, made at the anniversary held during the meeting of the General Conference, showed the balance in the treasury, August 30, 1873, to have been $4,201.33; that the receipts dur-

ing the year had been $14,968.65, and the expenditures $16,055.24, and that a balance remained in the treasury, August 30, 1874, of $3,112.74. The year's receipts for the Bible and Tract cause had been $39.27, and the expenditures $35.27. One hundred dollars had been added to the permanent fund, and that fund now amounted to $7,303.02. The society had the charge of five missionary churches, with 371 members and 643 Sunday-school scholars. Two quarterly meetings had been formed in India (those of Balason and Midnapore), and they had united in a yearly meeting known as the Orissa Yearly Meeting. Five male and eight female missionaries, three ordained and three licensed preachers, twelve native lay preachers, and several girls employed as teachers, were engaged in the work of the society. A printing-office was in operation at Midnapore.

The General Conference of the *Free Baptists in New Brunswick* met October 12th. The number of churches was reported to be 138, of which 43 had regular pastoral oversight; the number of ordained ministers was 41, of whom only 28 were regularly engaged with churches. Five hundred and thirty-three additions by baptism had been made during the year.

The *Free Baptist Conference in Nova Scotia* numbers thirty churches, fourteen ordained ministers, of whom thirteen are reported as in active service, and 3,000 communicants. One hundred and fifty persons were added to the churches by baptism in the last ecclesiastical year.

III. SEVENTH-DAY BAPTISTS.—At the meeting of the General Conference of this body, September 23d, the clerk reported that there were 83 churches on the roll, from 62 of which reports had been received. Including the statistics of the other churches as given in the minutes of the year before, the whole number of members in the denomination appeared to be 8,237. The net increase of membership reported during the year was 298. Contributions of $3,217.10 to benevolent enterprises were reported from thirty churches.

The receipts of the *Seventh-Day Baptist Educational Society* were reported at its anniversary, September 25th, to have been $1,755. The policy of organizing and conducting schools on a denominational basis was insisted upon.

The receipts of the *Seventh-Day Baptist Tract Society*, for the three years ending with its anniversary in 1874, were $9,577.44, and its expenditures $7,257.80, leaving a balance in its treasury of $2,319.64.

The receipts of the *Seventh-Day Baptist Missionary Society* were reported at its anniversary, September 24th, to have been $4,030.-99. A balance of $811.48 over the expenditures was carried to a new account. The receipts of the society for the meeting-house fund had been $32.53, and those for the special fund $3,349.28. The foreign mission of the society was at Shanghai, China, where two missionaries and three native preachers had been employed. Seventeen missionaries had been employed in the home-field.

The sixtieth session of the *Seventh-Day Baptist General Conference* was held at De Ruyter, N. Y., beginning September 23d. The Rev. George E. Tomlinson, of Westerly, R. I., was chosen moderator. A report from the reorganization of the conference was presented, and was adopted. It provided that the body should be called the "Seventh Day-Baptist General Conference;" that representation in it should be fixed on the basis of two delegates from each church, and one additional delegate for each twenty-five members of the church; churches to be allowed to appoint as delegates members of other churches. The General Conference was declared to possess powers and prerogatives as follows: "1. The prerogative in appeal, of an ordinary council, in all matters appertaining to doctrine or discipline, faith and practice, as between the churches, and between the churches and their respective members; and the power of exclusion of churches from membership in the conference, for the want of harmony either of faith or practice with the denomination. 2. It shall have power to receive such trusts as either societies or individuals may, from time to time, confide to its keeping, and to make all necessary provision for the same; to promote the cause of missions, Sabbath-schools, Sabbath observances, academic, collegiate, and theological education, and all the interests of religion as embodied and expressed in the denomination, by such measures as may be deemed best by the denomination in conference assembled."

The following resolution was adopted: " *Whereas*, Several years have passed since an *exposé* of Christian doctrine has been publicly announced by this conference; and whereas, many of the younger church-members would thus be much assisted in apprehending the full, explicit, and orthodox system of Christian doctrine: therefore *resolved*, That this conference now convened appoint a committee of seven of the most aged Seventh-Day Baptist ministers present, and five of the most aged Seventh-Day Baptist deacons present, twelve in all, to draft such an *exposé* and present the same to this conference at its next anniversary." Such a committee was accordingly appointed.

Resolutions were also adopted, declaring, "that copartnerships in which we allow our capital to be used on the Sabbath are a violation of the spirit of the fourth commandment;" condemning the use of liquors and tobacco, and expressing sympathy with the woman's temperance movement; and reaffirming the former expressions, by the General Conference, of disapproval of secret societies, and urging ministers to present the subject before the people and churches, to consider what is their duty in reference to it.

A communication was received from the Seventh-Day Baptist Church of Mill Yard, London, relating to the progress of the Sabbath cause in Great Britain, and was suitably acknowledged. A petition was adopted to be presented to Congress against the proposed so-called religious amendment to the Constitution of the United States. A petition was adopted for presentation to the Legislature of Pennsylvania, asking for a modification of the Sunday laws of that State, so that keepers of the seventh day might be exempted from the penalties imposed for the infraction of Sunday.

An account was given to the conference by the Rev. N. V. Hull of an informal meeting, called a biennial meeting, which was held in the old meeting-house at Newport, R. I., on the 16th of September, 1873. About one hundred and fifty "Sabbath-keepers" visited this church, which was regarded as the birthplace of the Seventh-Day Baptist denomination in America, and observed the occasion with appropriate addresses, the relation of reminiscences, and the pledging of subscriptions to the missionary and tract causes of the Church. The conference adopted a resolution in favor of repairing the old church at Newport. A committee was appointed to consider upon the organization of a Woman's Missionary Society.

IV. TUNKERS. — The National Convention of Tunkers met at Girard, Ill., May 24th. It was described as the largest meeting of believers, who are popularly called by that name, ever held in the United States. It was estimated that 10,000 persons were present, of whom about 2,000 were delegates. The conference resolved to send out ministers on missionary work. A special committee was appointed to have the minutes of previous conferences compiled and published. A question arose as to the proper manner of wearing the beard. It was decided, that while it had ever been the rule of the Church to wear the full beard, the wearing of mustaches alone was not permitted. The voice of the conference was given against allowing members to engage in banking, as it was liable to lead to covetousness, litigation, and usury. The sending of children to college was discountenanced, and it was determined that the name of the Church should not be used in the establishment of high-schools. The question, whether colored brethren should be saluted with the holy kiss, was left to be settled by each church making its own rules on the subject. It was decided to be inconsistent with the religion of the sect for members to join farmers' clubs; and, that the keeping and use of "the ungodly piano," and other musical instruments, was improper, although it could not be prohibited.

V. PARTICULAR BAPTISTS IN ENGLAND. — The anniversary meeting of the English Baptist Union was held in London, April 27th. The reports of the Union showed that during the year there had been a clear increase in the membership of the churches, of 2,652 souls. The increase in five years had been only 9,444 souls, or less than one per cent. a year.

The autumnal meetings of the Union were held at Newcastle-on-Tyne. They were opened on the evening of October 5th, with a sermon by the Rev. A. Mursel, on "The Lamp of Faith," in which a reply was made to some of the views advanced by Prof. John Tyndall, in his address delivered a few days previously before the British Association. The formal session of the Union was opened October 7th, with an address by the Rev. C. Stovel, president. Reports were received from several societies. That of the *Education Board* returned the receipts for the year at £842 19s. 8d., of which £234 10s. 7d. were still on hand. Forty-four children were under the patronage of the board. The receipts of the *Pastors' Income Augmentation Fund* had been £2,340 19s. 6d. The amount of income and the number of churches receiving the advantages of the fund had multiplied fivefold since 1870.

VI. GENERAL BAPTISTS IN ENGLAND.—The Association of General Baptists in England met at Loughborough, June 23d. The Rev. Thomas Barrass, of Peterborough, presided, and delivered an opening address. He spoke particularly of the unveiling of the statue of John Bunyan, at Bedford, which had taken place a short time before, and of the circumstance that on this occasion a duke and a dignitary of the Church of England had attended to do honor to the memory of a man whom nobles and clergy of the time of the Restoration had acquiesced in imprisoning. The statistical returns showed the number of members in the churches to be 22,086. The work of the *Foreign Missionary Society* was described as presenting an unusually hopeful aspect. Numerous additions had been made at the Orissa Mission. Canon Grassé, a convert from the Roman Catholic Church, had been enrolled as an agent for the society in Italy.

VII. BAPTISTS IN RUSSIA.—For a period of about twenty years, by means of the preaching of the Rev. Mr. Oncken, of Hamburg, Baptist principles have been extended through Prussia, and into parts of Poland and Southern Russia. The Russian Government offered no interference with their spread within its territory, so long as the conversions were confined to foreigners, and to persons not considered members of the Orthodox Church. So soon, however, as it was found that native Russians, and persons claimed as members by the Church, had joined the Baptists, the law against proselytism was put in force. In the course of 1872, thirteen persons, inhabitants of the district of Tarashavsky, government of Kiev, were arrested and imprisoned for apostatizing from the faith. As the imprisoned converts were Russian subjects, no notice of the case could be taken through diplomatic channels of communication. The sub-ject was brought to the attention of the World's Conference of the Evangelical Alliance, which met in the city of New York in October, 1873. A committee was appointed by the American branch of the Alliance, with the Rev. Dr. Sampson as chairman, who presented a memorial to the Russian minister, and an argument on the subject. These papers were politely returned. A gentleman, a member of the Baptist Church, who was in St. Petersburg, afterward brought the subject to the attention of several members of the imperial court, among whom was the Baron de Rosen. This nobleman interested himself actively in behalf of the imprisoned religionists. He advocated their cause before Count Sievers, and secured his promise to make the necessary inquiries about the legal proceedings to be observed in the case. He also wrote to Prince Dondonkoff-Korsakoff, Governor-General of Kiev, claiming his good offices for the liberation of the prisoners. The prince replied, April 9th, that the prisoners had all been released but one, who was at Odessa, beyond the jurisdiction of the government, and that they had all been acquitted by the civil courts of Kiev. He added a pledge that he could guarantee to the Baptists safety and peace so long as they did not try to make proselytes, in opposition to the present laws of the empire, and so long as they did not by action or manner attack the Orthodox Church in their unauthorized public meetings, "which," he remarked, "they have, however, done repeatedly." He repeated this pledge, promising again that, so long as they observed the conditions named above, "they will have positively nothing to fear from the local administration which is intrusted to me for this country."

The following memorandum, embodying an official report of the action of the court in the case, was attached to the letter of Governor-General Prince Dondonkoff-Korsakoff:

From the correspondence of the bureau of the governor-general relative to the Stundists, it appears that the indictment for belonging to that sect embraced fifty-three persons, of whom twelve were put under arrest—the prosecution calling for other persons as accessories. Further investigation of the civil court at Kiev demonstrated that, although they were implicated in following a heresy, to such a heresy cannot be applied the provisions of the section 203 of the code "Penalties and Fines." Consequently the following of such a heresy cannot be made punishable. Accordingly, then, the chamber court at Kiev acknowledged the said persons cannot be considered guilty of disseminating a heresy among the people.

At present none of the accused is under arrest except a leader of the Stundists in the district of Taraska, by the name of Jerome Balaban, who was exiled to the government of Cherson, as he was considered guilty of disseminating a false doctrine.

With Balaban's expulsion from the district of Taraska, the Stundists became more calm, and less vehemently opposed to the Orthodox Greco-Russian creed. They now even bring their children to be baptized by the Orthodox priests.

BEKE, CHARLES TILSTONE, Ph. D., F. S. A., F. R. G. S., etc., an English traveler, geologist, geographer, and ethnologist, born in London, October 10, 1800; died in London, September 2, 1874. He was from an ancient family long settled in Bekesburne, East Kent. He received a commercial education, and afterward studied law in Lincoln's Inn; but eventually resumed mercantile pursuits, residing for a short time in Saxony, whence he returned to London, and eventually sailed for the Mauritius, where he remained for several years. Having devoted much attention to ancient history, geography, philology, and ethnography, he published the results in "Origines Biblicæ; or, Researches in Primeval History," London, 1834, a work of great labor and study, which brought him, from the University of Tübingen, the diploma of Ph. D. His historical and geographical studies of the East led him to consider the great importance of Abyssinia for commercial and other intercourse with Central Africa; but his proposals to undertake an exploring journey were declined by the Government. Supported by private individuals, he proceeded to Shoa, in Southern Abyssinia, which country he reached in the beginning of 1851, several months before the party under Major Harris. Shortly after the arrival of the latter, Dr. Beke quitted Shoa, and went alone into the interior, where he explored Godjam and the countries lying to the west and south, previously almost entirely unknown in Europe. The results of these researches appeared partly in several journals, and in "A Statement of Facts," etc. (first edition, London, 1845; second edition, 1846). Having returned to Europe, he excited the attention of geographers by his publications: "An Essay on the Nile and its Tributaries" (London, 1847); "On the Sources of the Nile in the Mountains of the Moon" (1848); "On the Sources of the Nile" (1849); and by his "Mémoire Justificatif en Réhabilitation des Pères Paez et Lobo," Paris (1848). He became involved in a controversy with M. d'Abbadie; and in a "Letter to M. Daussy" (1849), and "An Inquiry into A. d'Abbadie's Journey to Kaffa" (1850), he declared this journey for the alleged discovery of the sources of the Nile (1843–'44) to be a mere fiction. In addition to many essays on ethnography and geography, Dr. Beke has published a treatise "On the Geographical Distribution of Languages in Abyssinia" (Edinburgh, 1849); and while in Mauritius he wrote "The Sources of the Nile, with the History of Nilotic Discovery" (London, 1860), in which work he has incorporated the results of his previous labors on that particular subject. On his return from his Abyssinian travels, the Geographical Societies of London and Paris gave him their gold medals. From 1836 to 1838, being then resident at Leipsic, Dr. Beke was acting British consul in Saxony, and from 1849 to 1853, in London, acted as secretary of the National Association for the Protection of British Industry and Capital. In 1861 Dr. and Mrs. Beke undertook a journey to Harran,

near Damascus, which place he had identified, in his "Origines Biblicæ," with the residence of the patriarch Abraham, as mentioned in the books of Genesis and Acts; and they thence traveled over Mount Gilead into the Holy Land, in the footsteps of the patriarch Jacob. In 1865, Mrs. Beke, with the coöperation of her husband, published a narrative of this journey, under the title of "Jacob's Flight, or a Pilgrimage to Harran." Dr. and Mrs. Beke again left England November 4, 1865, on a fruitless mission to obtain the release of the Abyssinian captives, and, on his return, he published a second edition of "The British Captives in Abyssinia," London, 1867. In 1870 Dr. Beke received a civil-list pension of £100 ($500), in consideration of his geographical researches, and especially of the value of his explorations in Abyssinia. But, though he had passed the limit of threescore and ten, his zeal for geographical exploration did not cease. Several months, in 1871 and 1872, were passed in a careful reëxploration of the Sinaitic Peninsula, especially with reference to the true site of Mount Sinai; and, in 1873, he followed this investigation with the startling announcement, in an elaborate memoir, that Jebel Musa was not the true Sinai, but that "the Mount of God" lay at a considerable distance from it, and was the only mountain which fulfilled all the required conditions. He maintained this position by plausible and perhaps conclusive arguments, but it involved him in a protracted controversy, which only terminated at his death.

BELGIUM,* a kingdom of Europe. Leopold II., King of the Belgians, son of King Leopold I., former Duke of Saxe-Coburg, was born April 9, 1835, ascended the throne at the death of his father, December 10, 1865; was married August 22, 1853, to Marie Henriette, daughter of the late Archduke Joseph of Austria, born August 23, 1836. Offspring of this union are three daughters. Heir-apparent to the throne is the brother of the King, Philipp, Count of Flanders, born March 24, 1827, Lieutenant-General in the service of Belgium; married April 26, 1867, to Princess Marie of Hohenzollern-Sigmaringen, born November 71, 1845; offspring of the union is a son, Baldwin, born July 3, 1869.

The area of the kingdom is 11,373 square miles; population, according to the last census, taken in 1866, 4,727,833; according to an official calculation of December, 1872, 5,175,037. Of this population, 54 per cent. belong to the Flemish and 44 to the Walloon-French nationality. The following table exhibits the population of each province of the kingdom on December 31, 1872, as well as the number of arrondissements and communes into which each province is divided:

* See ANNUAL CYCLOPÆDIA of 1873 for latest information on the army, navy, commerce, and movement of shipping.

PROVINCES.	Number of Arrondissements.	Number of Communes.	Population, Dec. 31, 1871.
Antwerp.........	3	150	503,599
Brabant.........	3	340	903,381
Flanders, East...	6	250	674,912
" West..	8	295	846,043
Hainault.........	6	435	914,756
Liége	4	335	611,723
Limburg.........	3	206	201,337
Luxemburg......	5	205	204,568
Namur...........	3	351	314,718
Total........	41	2,567	5,175,037

The number of births, in 1872, was 85,750 males and 81,627 females; the number of legitimate births was 155,528; of illegitimate, 11,848; the number of deaths, 40,084; the number of still-born children, 7,558; the number of deaths, 62,041 males, and 58,088 females. The number of marriages in 1871 was 37,538; the number of divorces, 75.

The following table shows the immigration into and the emigration from Belgium from 1841 to 1871:

	From 1841 to 1850.	From 1850 to 1860.	From 1861 to 1870 (about).	1871.
Immigration..	33,466	60,206	107,490	16,708
Emigration....	45,470	88,607	103,490	13,170

Excess of emigration over immigration, 1841–1850.. 12,004
" " " " " 1851–1860.. 28,401
" "immigration over emigration, 1861–1870 (about).................................. 4,000
" "immigration over emigration, 1871...;... 3,537

The following cities had, on December 31, 1871, a population of upward of 20,000 inhabitants:

1. Cities with 100,000 inhabitants and more.

Brussels........ 175,634 | Ghent............ 125,070
Antwerp........ 133,853 | Liége........... 109,686

2. Cities with from 25,000 to 100,000 inhabitants:

Bruges.............. 48,027 | Molenbeck St.-Jean. 30,974
Malines............ 36,985 | Jaclles.............. 26,786
Verviers........... 35,558 | Schaerbeck......... 26,714
Louvain............ 31,716 | Namur.............. 25,600
Tournay .... 31,313 | Courtrai............. 25,426

3. Cities with from 20,000 to 25,000 inhabitants:

Saint-Nicolas........ 24,021 | Mons 23,251
St.-Josse-Ten-Noode 24,080 | Séraing............. 23,758

The Legislature consists of two Chambers, a Senate and a Chamber of Representatives, both of which are elected by the people. The Chamber of Representatives had, from 1831 to 1839, 102 members; from 1839 to 1847, 95; from 1847 to 1859, 108; from 1859 to 1866, 116; since 1866, 124. The Senate always consists of one-half the number of members composing the Chamber of Representatives. The members of both Chambers are elected by the same class of citizens; those of the Chamber of Representatives for a term of eight and those of the Senate for a term of eight years. The former must have attained the twenty-fifth, the latter the fortieth year of their age: the latter have also to pay direct taxes to the amount of 2,116 francs 40 centimes. The electors must have completed their twenty-first year of age, and pay direct taxes to the amount of 42 francs 31 centimes. The number of electors was, in 1840, 46,894 (1.15 per cent. of the population); in 1850, 78,228 (1.76 per cent.); in 1860, 97,311 (2.05 per cent.); in 1865, 104,362 (2.09 per cent.); in 1870, 110,589 (2.17 per cent.); in 1872, 106,-928 (2.06 per cent). The number of voters who availed themselves of their right of suffrage varied, from 1843 to 1872, from 86 per cent. in 1843, to 62 in 1868. The number of persons eligible for the Senate was, in 1873, 49 in the province of Antwerp, 96 in Brabant, 84 in East Flanders, 56 in West Flanders, 66 in Hainault, 37 in Liége, 12 in Limburg, 4 in Luxemburg, and 47 in Namur: total in the whole kingdom, 451, or 0.0087 per cent. of the population. The number of persons entitled to take part in the election of members of the Provincial Councils was, in 1872, 211,708. According to the law of 1872, the Provincial Councils of the several provinces consisted of the following number of members: Antwerp, 58; Brabant, 73; East Flanders, 80; West Flanders, 69; Hainault, 76; Liége, 67; Limburg, 40; Luxemburg, 41; Namur, 55: total, 559. The aggregate receipts of the provincial administrations, in 1871, were 11,164,386 fr.; the expenditures, 9,864,355 fr.: surplus, 1,300,034.

Of the four universities of Belgium, the free Catholic University of Louvain had, in 1872, the largest number of students (901); the free (Liberal) University of Brussels had 583, the State University of Liége 436, and the State University of Ghent 210; the Royal Academy of Fine Arts at Antwerp, 1,576 students. There were, besides the Antwerp Academy, 72 other academies of design, and drawing schools, with 9,447 pupils; a Conservatory of Music at Brussels, with 675, and another at Liége with 789 pupils.

Nearly the entire population of Belgium is nominally connected with the Roman Catholic Church, at the head of which is the Archbishop of Malines, and five bishops. The other ecclesiastical benefices consisted, December 31, 1872, of 156 deaneries, 233 cures (parishes of the first class), 2,772 succursales (parishes of the second class), 180 chapels, 1,730 vicariates, 110 coadjutors, 29 annexes, 706 oratories and chapels of hospitals, colleges, etc. The number of religious communities of men, in 1866, was 178, with 2,991 inmates; that of religious communities of women, 1,144, with 15,205 inmates. The number of mutual aid societies recognized by the state was 98; their aggregate revenue, 207,203 fr.; expenditures, 180,447 fr.; capital, December 31, 1871, 475,895 fr.; number of mutual aid societies not recognized by the state, 466,806 fr.; capital, December, 1871, 511,692 fr.

In the budget for 1873, the receipts were estimated at 205,985,000 francs; the expenditures at 201,412,211; the public debt on May 1, 1873, amounted to 760,114,664 fr.

In January, in the Chamber of Representa-

tives, M. Bergé, addressed an interpellation to
the Minister of Foreign Affairs concerning a
note which the Belgian Government was reported to have received from the Government
of Germany on account of the anti-German
spirit of the ultramontane press of Belgium
and the attitude of the Catholic priesthood.
M. Bergé deplored the violent language used
by some papers against Germany, but insisted
that the Belgian constitution guaranteed freedom of the press, and that the Government
could not be held responsible for the language
of newspapers. The minister, in reply, stated
that no note on the subject under discussion
had been received from Germany, but took occasion to recommend to the Belgian papers
to observe a moderate and impartial attitude
with regard to foreign affairs, in order that the
friendly relations now existing between Belgium and all foreign powers might be strengthened.

Toward the close of the session, in May, the
Liberal members, especially the former minister, Frère-Orban, made a violent attack upon
the Minister of Finance, M. Malou. He endeavored to prove that the financial administration of the ultramontane ministers had always been injurious to the country, and in
support of his assertion gave the following official figures: from 1841 to 1847 (ultramontane
ministry), excess of expenditure, 36,584,000 fr.;
from 1848 to 1854 (liberal ministry), excess of
revenue, 38,584,000 fr.; from 1855 to 1857
(ultramontane ministry), excess of expenditure, 3,059,000 fr.; from 1858 to 1869 (liberal
ministry), excess of revenue, 34,803,000 fr.
From 1870 to 1873 (ultramontane ministry),
probable excess of expenditure, 29,292,000 fr.
Besides, the public debt had been increased
since 1870 by 338,000,000 fr. The minister, in
defense of his administration, stated, that the
ordinary budget from 1871 to 1873 showed an
excess of expenditure; and that the excess of
expenditure over revenue in the extraordinary
budget, as well as the increase of the public
debt, was solely caused by the large number
of public works undertaken by the Government.

The results of the elections held in June for
the two Chambers of the Belgian Legislature
were in so far favorable to the Liberals, that the
Catholic party lost a few seats in the Senate as
well as in the House of Representatives. The loss
was, however, not sufficiently large to change
the complexion of either of the Chambers, or to
endanger the continuance of the Catholic ministry. The new Senate had a Catholic majority of four, and the Chamber of Representatives
of fourteen. The defeat most keenly felt was
that of the Minister of Public Works, Beer-
naarts, who, in Soignies, had to give way to
a Liberal candidate. (He was subsequently
chosen at a supplementary election.) Other
places, where the Liberals defeated the candidates of the Catholic party, were Verviers,
Thuin, and Charleroi. On the other hand,

however, the Catholic party defeated the Liberals in one of the largest cities of the kingdom, Ghent, where the excitement ran very
high, and as many as ninety-five per cent. of
the inscribed voters took part in the election.
As in former years, the Liberal party maintained its ascendency in the Walloon, and the
Catholic party in the Flemish districts.

In compliance with an invitation from the
Russian Government, an International Congress, composed of representatives of all the
governments of Europe, met at Brussels on
July 27th, to discuss a number of questions relating to warfare. On the proposal of one of
the members, the Congress decided that absolute secrecy should be observed respecting its
proceedings. The presidency of the Congress
was offered to the Belgian Minister of Foreign
Affairs, and, on his declining to accept it, Baron
Jomini, the Russian delegate, was nominated
president. M. Borchgrave, of the ministry of
Foreign Affairs, was appointed secretary to
the Congress. The Congress was closed on August 28th, when the protocols were signed by
all the delegates except those sent by England
and Turkey. It appears from the protocols,
that most of the sections were agreed to with
but slight modifications. At the second sitting,
Baron Lambermont declared that, if Belgium
were invaded, she would resist to the last extremity, and thus, he said, he would vote for
no resolution which might tend to diminish
the means of national defense, or restrain the
citizens in their duty toward their country.
Subsequently, Sir A. Horsford, the British delegate, read an abstract from his instructions,
ordering him to abstain from discussing any
point that would concern such general principles of international law as are not yet universally recognized and accepted; and Baron
Jomini, on the part of Russia, said he would
not consent to restrain in any way the right
of self-defense. With regard to the military
authority on an enemy's territory, the Russian
scheme proposed that an army occupying an
enemy's country might insist on the public officials continuing to exercise their functions under its control, and also on their taking an
oath. This proposal was considered by the
committee on August 12th, and, finding no support, was superseded by a clause providing that
functionaries invited and consenting to continue in office should enjoy the protection of
an invader, and should not be removed unless
they violated the obligations they had undertaken. The scheme also proposed, that the
army of occupation should have the right of
collecting taxes already existing. General
Voigts-Rhetz, one of the German delegates,
suggested that, in case of inability to collect
existing taxes, equivalent imposts might be
raised, and that the army might suspend some
taxes and impose others. After some discussion, the committee adopted, subject to further consideration of its terms, a clause empowering the levy of existing taxes and the

imposition, in the event of this being impossible, of new taxes as far as possible conformable to existing customs and forms, such taxes to be applied to the expenses of administration to the extent to which the native Government was bound to apply them. At the sitting of the 18th, the Portuguese delegate adhered to the reservation of Belgium, Spain, Holland, and Switzerland, as to any proposal impairing its means of defense. On the clause authorizing the invader to seize the Government funds, arms, and provisions, a question was raised as to the meaning of funds, and, on the suggestion of General Voigts Rhetz, it was agreed that all property belonging to individuals or corporations, though in the public treasury, should be respected. As to the seizure of railway plant and private armories, it was resolved that railway material, telegraphs, arms, and vessels not belonging to the state, should be restored, and compensation given on the conclusion of peace. It was likewise agreed that public buildings, real property, forests, and lands belonging to the state, should be guarded from permanent injury, and that ecclesiastical, corporate, and charitable property, as also that of artistic or scientific institutions, should be treated as private property. On the proposal of General Voigts Rhetz, it was agreed that civil contracts concluded during the occupation should remain valid on its termination, and that the Governments should lend their assistance to securing justice by the competent tribunals for those having rights dating from the occupation. There were strong protests against this last decision, as designed to legitimatize bargains between the invader and natives; in other words, acts of treason.

The new session of the Belgian Chambers was opened on November 10th. The Senate by 48 against one vote elected the Prince de Ligne President, and De Tornaco and D'Anethan Vice-Presidents. In the Chamber of Deputies, Thibaut was elected President, and Tack and Schollaert Vice-Presidents. While the Catholic party retained control of both Chambers, the differences between the Old Liberals and Young Liberals became wider than ever. The questions which widened the breach already existing were chiefly the immediate reform of the primary instruction and the extension of the suffrage. The Association Liberale of Ghent split on these questions as those of Brussels, Liége, Mons, and Verviers, had done before.

Brussels is being rapidly transformed into one of the finest and healthiest capitals of Europe. The new boulevard which traverses the city in about the same way as the Boulevard de Sevastopol de Paris, was nearly completed during the year 1874. The principal building on it, the New Exchange, was opened on December 27, 1873. Another fine building on the new boulevard, the new Central Market, was opened on September, 1874, by an exhibition of productions of Belgian industrial art. The

King and the entire royal family took an active part in the opening exercises. The exhibition was quite successful and attracted a large number of visitors to Brussels, The transept of the building was decorated with specimens of Belgian carpet-manufacture, remarkable for good design and warmth of color. The whole breadth of the end of the building north of the transept was occupied by an immense stalactite grotto. Belgian skill in this respect has evidently been stimulated by the many remarkable caves, such as those of Rochefort, to be found in the country. The making of these grottoes for ornamental purposes is now carried on on a large scale at Brussels. In the building were to be found specimens of Belgian coach-making and architectural work of all kinds in stone, marble, and iron. Belgian wood-carving was represented by a magnificent church pulpit, terminating in a spire, and by minor work. All varieties of musical instruments, collections of garden furniture and flower-stands, arms, highly-finished locksmiths' work for iron safes, mosaic-work, stationery and book-binding, and saddlery, testified to the comprehensiveness of Belgian art-industry. The famed Belgian lace-manufacture was worthily represented. The bronze objects, of which there was a large collection, were not inferior to the best manufactured elsewhere; and the exhibition of glass of all kinds and of marble chimney-pieces was worthy the reputation enjoyed by Belgium in these branches of manufactures.

In point of municipal organization, Brussels, alone among the large capitals in Europe, resembles London. The town itself comprises only one-half of the inhabitants of what, in administrative language, is called the Brussels agglomeration. The suburbs, some of them very large and important, have their own municipal administrations, totally independent of that of Brussels. As such a state of things creates many inconveniences, the burgomaster of Brussels invited the burgomasters of the suburban communes to a conference, and proposed to them, as the annexation of their communes to Brussels is impossible, to form with Brussels a municipal federation so as to secure a better and more expeditious execution of all affairs of common interest. The proposal has been favorably received. A new Protestant church, erected for the sole use of the English and American communities, was opened in 1874. The total cost of the building is about £6,000.

BENEDICT, Rev. DAVID, D. D., an eminent Baptist clergyman, historian, and author, born in Norwalk, Conn., October 10, 1779; died at Pawtucket, R. I., December 5, 1874. He had learned the shoemaker's trade, and entered into business in Stratford, Conn., when he became interested in religion, and, having united with the Baptist Church in that place, he prepared for college, entered the junior class of Brown University in 1804, and graduated with high honors in 1806. While in college he preached in Pawtucket, R. I., and, soon after his graduation, was ordained pastor of the First Baptist Church in that town, which relation he sustained for twenty-five years with great success; but his tastes for historical study and research were so strong that much of his time was spent in this class of studies. In 1813 he published his "History of the Baptists," in two volumes, 8vo; in 1817, an "Abridgment of Robinson's History of Baptism;" in 1820, an abridgment of his own "History of the Baptists," comprising, however, considerable new matter. In 1824 his "History of all Religions," a thick 12mo, appeared; in 1848, a new and enlarged "History of the Baptist Denominations in America and all Parts of the World," in two thick volumes, 8vo, was published. In 1860, at the age of eighty-two, he issued his "Fifty Years among the Baptists." He had been engaged for the past twenty years in collecting the materials for a new and greatly enlarged edition of his "History of the Baptists." He had also prepared "A Compendium of Ecclesiastical History," and "A History of the Donatists," both of which were left ready for the press at his death. Among his earlier works were a humorous poem entitled "The Watery War;" another poem delivered at Trenton, July 4, 1807, and published by the town authorities; and a "Conference Hymn-Book," which had a very large circulation. During the greater part of the sixty-nine years of his ministerial life, he had been engaged in preaching regularly, though not at all times a pastor; and he retained his faculties in nearly their full vigor till within a few months of his death. A sermon preached on his ninety-second birthday, October 16, 1870, is said to have been remarkable for its ability and clearness, and the force and vigor with which it was delivered. He received the degree of D. D. from Shurtleff College in 1851. Dr. Benedict, though not in general a graceful or brilliant writer, was remarkable for his painstaking accuracy, and his zeal in the collection of historic material; and, in private life, was a man of great social powers, and of a most genial and sunny temper.

BLACK, ADAM, M. P., a distinguished publisher and political leader of Edinburgh, born in that city in 1784, died there, January 25, 1874. He was the son of a wealthy builder, and received his education at the university of his native city. After serving his apprenticeship, he went into business as a bookseller and publisher, and, among other important books, brought out two editions of the "Encyclopædia Britannica," one of which was begun in 1830, and the other in 1853. He was also the proprietor by purchase of the copyright of the "Waverley Novels," and, after the failure of his rivals, Constable & Co., he became publisher of the Edinburgh Review, and was thus brought into close relations with many eminent men of the Whig party. He held and

avowed liberal opinions at a time when they were unpopular, and aided in securing parliamentary and municipal reform. He was Lord Provost of Edinburgh from 1843 to 1848, and in February, 1856, succeeded Mr. Macaulay as member for that city in the House of Commons. He continued in Parliament until 1865, and was a consistent supporter of the leading Liberal measures. He declined, while Lord Provost of Edinburgh, the honor of knighthood offered him by Queen Victoria at the suggestion of Lord Russell.

BOLIVIA.(REPÚBLICA DE BOLIVIA), an independent state of South America, lying between latitude 10° and 24° south, and longitude 57° 25' and 70° 30' west. It is bounded north and northeast by Brazil, south by the Argentine Republic and Chili, and west by the Pacific Ocean and Peru. (The territorial divisions, area, and population of the republic, are given at length in the ANNUAL CYCLOPÆDIA for 1872.)

The President of Bolivia is Dr. Tomás Frias, installed on February 14, 1874.

The new cabinet is composed of the following ministers: Interior and Foreign Affairs, Señor Don M. Baptista; Finance and Public Works, Señor Don Pantaleon Daleuce; Justice and Public Worship, Señor Don D. Calvo; and War, General Hilarion Daza.

The metropolitan archbishop is Dr. P. J. Puch y Solona, elevated in 1861; with the following bishops: La Paz, Dr. Juan de Dios Bosque (1874); Santa Cruz de la Sierra, F. X. Rodriguez (1870); and Cochabamba, F. M. del Granado, titular Bishop of Troy in part.

The Bolivian consul-general in New York is Señor Don T. Pol.

The standing army is composed of eight generals; 359 superior and 654 subaltern officers; and, at most, 2,000 soldiers.

The annual expenditure of the armed force amounts to about $2,000,000.

The following tables exhibit the details of the estimated budget for 1873-'74.

REVENUE.

Customs Duties:	
At Arica, $405,000 ; at Cobija, $250,000.... =	$655,000
Export duty on silver......................	193,696
Guano-sales.................................	300,000
Stamped paper,..............................	27,268
Duty on cattle from the Argentine Republic	20,880
Church (Colonel) loan.......................	650,000
Contributions from Indians.................	686,307
Departments................................	396,423
Total.............	$2,929,574

EXPENDITURE.

Ministry of the Interior,...................	$597,458
Ministry of Foreign Affairs................	153,940
Ministry of Finance (includ'g the home debt)	2,072,013
Ministry of Justice, etc	399,167
Ministry of War............................	1,126,916
Expenses extraordinary	156,010
Total......................	$4,505,504

By comparing the sums of these two tables, there appears a deficit of no less than $1,575,-930, or rather more than one-half of the entire revenue—a deficit which it was pronounced advisable to cover, as usual, by borrowing.

It is, however, objected that in the table of the revenue certain items do not figure, which would tend to reduce the deficit very materially. Among these items are enumerated the interest on $1,250,000, advanced by the present lessee of the Caracoles silver-mines, and the export duty on silver at the custom-houses of Arica and Cobija.

An official report, the accuracy of which has been questioned, showed the national debt to amount, in June, 1873, to $16,428,329, including Colonel Church's loan of £1,700,000, negotiated in London in 1871, at 68, and at the rate of six per cent. interest, the whole of which was to be applied for the construction of railways.

The balance-sheet presented to Congress in December, 1873, represented the national debt at $24,757,072.88, of which $20,115,898.24 formed the foreign debt.

Financial agents of the republic submitted to the bond-holders a statement of the financial situation, in which they set down the revenue at $3,142,429, and the expenditure at $1,464,794. The surplus which would result here is said to be applied upon the payment of the interest on the national debt, as follows:

To the loan of 1872 (1871 ?), with sinking-fund..	$680,000
To the loan of Valdeavellano	90,000
To the Bolivian Bank (loan to the Government)	283,000
To the Chilian Bank of Guarantees	234,408
To Melgs	205,192
To Mejillones Railway	118,125
Balance	66,910
Total	$1,677,635

In the foregoing report, it is affirmed that the Mejillones Railway is in course of construction (that is to say, that the works have not been suspended), and will be completed by March, 1876.

It is difficult to obtain positive information concerning the foreign trade. The chief staples of export are guano, silver coin and bullion, Peruvian bark, tin, and hides. The value of the imports through Tacna and Arica is estimated at $5,500,000; and that through Cobija at $2,000,000.

Notwithstanding the loans effected for the purpose of carrying on the works on the Madeira & Mamoré Railway, and the great benefits to be derived from that line, opening up as it would an easy route for the transport of Bolivian products to the Atlantic, and bringing the republic into contact with the great marts of the Eastern world, the enterprise appears to be almost completely abandoned. The only signs of life or decision in this matter of such vital importance are the intermittent harangues in the Assembly upon the necessity of completing the road. As for the line from Mejillones to Caracoles, the works were suspended for want of funds to prosecute them, and they are likely to remain so indefinitely. Not so, however, the Antofagasta Railway, leading to Salar del Cármen, which was to be completed by July, 1874.

It may here be remarked that advantages from the Madeira Railway would not accrue solely to Bolivia; they would be largely shared in by the neighboring empire of Brazil, to which country the line would be of considerable importance as well in a strategic as in an economic point of view. If the eastern regions of the republic would be enabled to pour their products through the Amazon into the great mercantile circulation, and to receive their supplies from Brazil and the outer world, the empire will thereby be brought into closer commercial and political alliance with Bolivia, and be placed in possession of elements of development and security for the vast regions of Western Brazil, now virtually and practically inaccessible and indefensible. The Madeira Railway once completed, but a few hundreds of miles of iron way would be necessary to bring the line, and consequently the whole Amazonian Valley, into connection with the littoral region of the Pacific, and render Bolivia independent of her powerful neighbor, Peru, to whom she is now indebted for a port on the Pacific, and over whose territory merchandise, inward or outward bound, has to be transported. Those whose commercial interests are centred in the Pacific-coast region, foreseeing that the turning the tide of Bolivian foreign trade through Brazilian channels, will materially enhance the prestige of the empire among South American nations, have determined to use all their financial power to prevent the construction of the Madeira & Mamoré line of railway. A concession has been granted for a railway from Tacna to the Bolivian frontier, to Messrs. Hainsworth & Co., of that port, and Messrs. Emile Erlanger & Co., of Paris. The line will be 108 miles in length, and is to cost 18,000,000 of soles, or about $16,200,000, gold. This line will be advantageous to Bolivia, inasmuch as it will facilitate the transport of her productions to the coast, but the advantage will cease as soon as she can build a railway of her own, over her own territory, and the political and economic ends of the Tacna road will remain virtually defeated.

In the mean time, the Mollendo & Puno Railway is finished, and will shortly be extended to La Paz, which will then be but a short distance from the Pacific. A complementary branch of the Puno line is also to be constructed, connecting La Paz and Yungas.

A contract has been made with Messrs. Montero Brothers for a railway from Neria to Oruro, a rich mining district, where the mines cannot, however, be efficiently worked for want of powerful machinery, and this it is impossible to introduce with the existing means of transport.

In the Assembly extraordinary, whose sessions closed on December 7, 1873, some important measures were resolved upon. Among these may be mentioned a still further increase of imposts, the reduction of the salaries of government officials, the decision to carry out in every respect Colonel Church's plans rela-

tive to the Madeira & Mamoré Railway enterprise, and the authorizing the Government to
negotiate a loan of £1,000,000. The Committee of Finance was earnest in its appeal to
the Government for the prompt liquidation of
the national debt, as indispensable to the financial welfare of the country.

The illness of General Ballevian, the late
President of the republic, rendered it necessary
for him to withdraw from public affairs, leaving Dr. Frias to occupy the presidential chair
ad interim. But the ministry, already very
unpopular, became ere long altogether insupportable by their arbitrary measures; the
country, though quiet, that is to say not in absolute warfare, was uneasy, and no confidence
was inspired by the Government. Such was
the position of affairs at the beginning of the
year. But a real calamity, the death of Ballevian, which occurred on February 14th,
heightened the disordered state of the country.
Revolutions raged for a time in the coast region, and the supreme power was disputed by
a number of unscrupulous chieftains whose
only right was the sword and the bayonet.
Dr. Frias still continues to hold the reins of
government.

An industrial exhibition was inaugurated in
February, at Cochabamba.

BORDEN, GAIL, a skillful inventor and philanthropist, born in Norwich, N. Y., in 1801;
died in Borden, near Columbus, Colorado County, Texas, January 11, 1874. His parents were
New-Englanders, and in December, 1814, they
followed the popular tide of emigration, and
removed westward to Covington, Ky., opposite Cincinnati, and a year and a half later to
the vicinity of Madison, in the then Territory
of Indiana. At the age of twenty-one, young
Borden, finding his health impaired, migrated
to the pine-district in Mississippi, where for a
time he was engaged in teaching. Here he was
appointed County Surveyor, and also Deputy
U. S. Surveyor. Having married, he removed
to Texas in 1829, his father and father-in-law,
with their families, preceding him thither. His
abilities soon brought him into prominence. In
1833 he was elected delegate to the convention held at San Felipe, to define the position
of the colonists, and to petition the Mexican
Government for separation from the State of
Coahuila. He was also appointed by General
Austin to superintend the official surveys, and
compiled the first topographical map of the
colony; and, up to the time of the Mexican
invasion, had charge of the Land-Office of San
Felipe, under direction of Samuel M. Williams,
then Colonial Secretary. In 1835 he and his
brother, Thomas H., now of Galveston, established the *Texas Telegraph* at San Felipe, the
same paper which, subsequently transferred to
Houston, was given up a year or two since.
The office was burned by Santa Anna in 1836,
but the paper, after the victory of San Jacinto,
was revived. This was the only newspaper
issued in Texas during the war which led to

the separation of Texas from Mexico. The Republic of Texas being founded, Mr. Borden was
appointed by President Houston first collector
of the port of Galveston, which city, up to
1837, had not been laid out. Mr. Borden made
the first surveys of the city, prior to taking
charge of the customs, in June of that year.
In 1839 he was appointed agent of the Galveston City Company, a corporation holding several thousand acres, on which the city is built.
He held this position for over twelve years.
Toward the close of this period his attention
was drawn to the need of more suitable food-
supplies for emigrants crossing the Plains, and,
experimenting with this end in view, he produced the "pemmican," which Dr. Kane made
use of in his polar expeditions. He next produced a "meat-biscuit," which was exhibited
at the London World's Fair, in 1851, and gained
for him the "Great Council Medal," and led to
his election as an honorary member of the
London Society of Arts, in 1852. He manufactured this "meat-biscuit" extensively in
Texas, with the view of supplying good and
portable food for emigrants crossing the plains;
but, meeting with the opposition of army-con-
tractors, he lost heavily, and emerged penniless from the unequal contest he had maintained. Coming North, he turned his attention to the preservation of milk, and in 1853
claimed a patent for "producing concentrated
sweet milk by evaporation *in vacuo*, the same
having no sugar or other foreign matter mixed
with it." Commissioner Mason was not convinced that this process had any special merits, contending that the same results might be
obtained by evaporating milk in the open air;
and it was not till reënforced by scientific opinions that Mr. Borden, in 1856, received a patent. The development of the invention was
now a source of fresh embarrassments. The
inventor had parted with all but three-eighths
of his interest in the patent, when, after two
unsuccessful attempts to establish works, the
New York Condensed Milk Company was
formed, and began business on an extensive
scale at Wassaic, Dutchess County, N. Y. This
was in 1860, soon after which the civil war
caused the product to become quickly and extensively known, as it became an essential article in military and naval supplies. The business of milk-condensing rapidly expanded, and
works were built at Brewster's Station on the
Harlem line, and at Elgin, forty-two miles from
Chicago, in both of which Mr. Borden owned
one-half. During the war, when the soldiers
needed meat-juices in a condensed form, Mr.
Borden resumed his experimental labors, and
produced an extract of beef of superior quality.
Finding, during late years, that its cost retarded the sale of this article, he devoted much
time and money to establishing its manufacture in Texas, where it could be made cheaply and well. Mr. Borden also made excellent
preparations, in a condensed form, of tea, coffee,
and cocoa, prepared pemmican for use upon

Dr. Kane's polar expeditions, and succeeded in condensing juices so as to retain all that constitutes the peculiar value of the fruit from which they were made. Mr. Borden made liberal use of the great wealth which he had acquired. In person, he was tall and spare. His temperament was nervous, and his enthusiasm unbounded. With keen, critical and appreciative powers of observation, his habits were active, and his faculty of adapting means to ends most remarkable. His varied career, with its disappointments, trials, and successes, had given him a fund of anecdotes and reminiscences ready at call and freely used.

BRAZIL (IMPERIO DO BRAZIL), the only empire in the New World, a vast country of South America, extending from latitude 4° 30' north to 33° south, and from longitude 35° to 78° west. Its boundaries are as follows: North, the United States of Colombia, Venezuela, British, French, and Dutch Guiana, and the Atlantic Ocean; east, the ocean just named; south, Uruguay, the Argentine Republic, and Paraguay; and west, Bolivia, Peru, Ecuador, and Colombia. The territory of the empire is divided into twenty provinces and one *municipio neutro* (neutral municipality), which with the population and capital of each, as published in the official returns of the Minister of the Interior in 1874, are as follows:

PROVINCES.	Population.	Capitals.
Amazonas...................	76,000	Manaos.
Pará	320,600	Belem, or Pará.
Maranhão...................	500.000	São Luiz.
Piauhy.....................	184,156	Therezina.
Ceará......................	550,000	Fortaleza.
Rio Grande do Norte.......	240,000	Natal.
Parahyba..................	300,000	Parahyba.
Pernambuco...............	1,250,000	Recipe.
Alagôas......	341,816	Maceió.
Sergipe...................	280,000	Aracajú.
Bahia.....................	1,400,000	São Salvador.
Espirito Santo............	70,597	Victoria.
Rio de Janeiro............	1,100,000	Nictheroy.
São Paulo.................	850,000	São Paulo.
Paraná....................	120,000	Curitiba.
Santa Catharina..........	140,000	Desterro.
Rio Grande do Sul........	440,000	Porto Alegre.
Minas Geraes.............	1,500,000	Ouro Preto.
Goyaz....................	160,000	Goyaz.
Matto Grosso.............	64,000	Cuyabá.
Municipio Neutro.........	274,972	Rio de Janeiro.
Total................	10,161,041	

By comparing this table with that published in the ANNUAL CYCLOPÆDIA for 1872, a difference of 248,041 will be observed, which can scarcely be attributed to an absolute growth of population, but is more probably due to discordant estimates made at different times. It appears evident, nevertheless, that the number of inhabitants is sensibly larger now in Alagôas, Rio Grande do Sul, Paraná, and Rio de Janeiro, than it was in 1872; but the apparent diminution of 36,000 in Matto Grosso and of 176,000 in the Municipio Neutro can only be satisfactorily accounted for in the way already suggested. A like observation may be made concerning the area of the empire, which,

in the report cited above is set down at 12,-676,744 square kilometres, or 4,855,885 square miles. There are in the empire 209 cities, 433 towns, and 1,473 parishes.

The government consists of a constitutional and hereditary monarchy, based upon the fundamental law of March 25, 1824, modified by amendments bearing date August 12, 1834, and May 12, 1840. Emperor, Dom Pedro II., born December 2, 1825; proclaimed April 7, 1831 (regency from the last date to July 23, 1840); crowned July 18, 1841; and married September 4, 1843, to Theresa Christina Maria, daughter of the late king Francis I. of the Two Sicilies.

The Minister of the Interior is Dr. J. A. Corrêa de Oliveira, Deputy; Minister of Justice, Dr. M. A. Duarte de Azevedo, Deputy; Foreign Affairs, Viscount de Caravellas, Councillor of State; War, J. J. de O. Tunqueira, Deputy; Navy, J. D. Ribeiro da Luz, Senator; Public Works, Commerce, and Agriculture, J. P. da Costa Sereiva, Jr., Deputy; and Finance, Viscount do Rio Branco, President of the Council of State and of the Tribunal of the National Treasury.

The Council of State is composed of the following members in ordinary: Viscount do Rio Branco, President; Princess Imperial Donna Izabel; Prince Gaston d'Orléans, Count d'Eu; Senators, Viscount d'Abaeté; Marquis Sapucahy; Viscount B. de Souza Franco; Marquis of São Vicente; J. T. Nabuce d'Aranjo; Viscount de Muritiba; and of the seven members extraordinary: Viscount Inhomirim; Viscount de Bom Retiro; Viscount Jaguary; Viscount de Caravellas; Duke de Caixas; Viscount de Nictheroy, Senators; and Viscount d'Araxá.

The President of the Senate, which is composed of 58 members elected for life, is Viscount Jaguary; Vice-President, Viscount de Camaragibe.

The Chamber of Deputies consists of 122 members, elected for four years. The President is Councillor M. P. Corrêa; Councillor A. J. Henriques; J. P. M. Portella; A. G. de Paula Fonseca.

The provinces are administered by presidents, aided by legislative assemblies. They are enumerated in the following list:

Provinces.	Presidents.
Alagôas...................	Dr. J. V. d'Aranjo.
Amazonas.................	D. Monteiro Seixoto.
Bahia....................	Dr. V. J. d'Oliveira Lisboa.
Ceará....................	Baron d'Ibiapaba.
Espirito Santo...........	Dr. L. F. Horta Barboza.
Goyaz....................	A. C. d'Assiz.
Maranhão.................	Dr. A. O. Gomez de Castro.
Matto Grosso.............	M. da Silva Reis.
Minas Geraes.............	J. L. da Costa Belem.
Pará.....................	J. V. de Azevedo.
Parahyba.................	D. S. E. Carneiro da Cunha.
Paraná...................	F. G. C. d'Aranjo Abranches.
Pernambuco	H. P. de Lucena.
Piauhy...................	Dr. A. Lemenha Lins.
Rio Grande do Norte......	J. C. Bandeira de Melho.
Rio Grande do Sul (or São Pedro).............	J. P. de Cavalho Moraes.
Rio de Janeiro...........	M. J. de Freitas Travassos.
Santa Catharina..........	Dr. J. Thomé da Silva.
São Paulo................	J. F. Xavier.
Sergipe..................	Dr. A. Dos Passos Miranda.

The Archbishop of Bahia is the Primate of Brazil, and there are 11 bishops: those of Pará, São Luiz, Olinda, Rio de Janeiro, São Paulo, Porto Alegre, Marianna, Diamantina, Goyaz, and Cuyabá.

The Supreme Court of Justice (at Rio de Janeiro) is composed of a president, a councillor, and 17 members.

The eleven Courts of Appeals throughout the empire have each a president; that of Rio de Janeiro has 17 members; that of Bahia, 11; that of Pernambuco, 15; those of Maranhão, Pará, Ceará, Minas Geraes, São Paulo, and São Pedro do Sul, 7 each; and those of Matto Grosso and Goyaz, 5 each. There is a Tribunal of Commerce at Rio de Janeiro, Bahia, Pernambuco, and Maranhão; and a Supreme Tribunal of War and Justice at Rio de Janeiro, the president of which is the Emperor.

The army in time of peace comprises a special corps of 401 men; twenty-one battalions of infantry, 10,259 strong; five regiments of horse, 2,495 strong; and three regiments and one battalion of artillery, with one battalion of engineers, 3,381. Total strength of the army, 16,536. The Brazilian army of occupation in Paraguay is made up as follows: Special corps, 21 men; infantry, 1,326; horse, 274; and artillery, 776; making in all, 2,397 men.

By virtue of a new law, the strength of the army in time of war is to be 32,000. The National Guard was disbanded, to be organized anew after the census has been completed.

The police force comprises 6,476 men, of whom 483 were in Rio de Janeiro.

The present naval force of the empire is as follows: 17 iron-clad steamers, 9 steam corvettes, 24 steam gunboats, 6 steam transports, and 4 sail-of-the-line—the total armament being 218 guns, and the total horse-power of the steamers, 7,217. There are besides one school-ship and a brig for midshipmen, both without armament; and also 2 steam iron-clads, 2 steam corvettes, and 1 transport, in process of construction. There are in the navy 15 general staff-officers, 418 first and 152 second class officers, a sanitary corps of 67 men, 27 almoners, 215 accountants, 223 cabin boys, etc., 42 engineers, 2,897 imperial marines, a naval battalion of 945, and 961 apprentices: total strength of the navy, 5,962 men.

From the foregoing remarks it has been observed that the whole of the Brazilian troops have not yet been withdrawn from Paraguay, nor will they completely evacuate the territory of that republic until the pending question of boundaries shall have been settled between the Governments of Ascencion and Buenos Ayres.

The constant and progressive increase in the foreign commerce of Brazil, notwithstanding the multifarious circumstances which not only militate against, but seem to threaten to impede its development, can only be attributed to a patient and ambitious energy on the part of her agriculturists—an energy as surprising as it is real, if it be remembered that the most

productive portions of the empire are almost entirely comprised within the tropics.

The value of the coffee-exports alone for the year 1872–'73 surpassed by more than twenty-five per cent. that of the entire exports from the Argentine Republic in the same period. Of the whole coffee-crop nothing need be said, nor could any remarks thereupon enhance the eloquence of the figures just given.

Cotton statistics are no less surprising than those of coffee, the exports of that article having been so prodigiously extended since 1860 as to rank, at the present time, second only to those of the United States.

In the following table are exhibited the total exports from Brazil during the triennium 1870–'73, and the value of each of the principal commodities:

COMMODITIES.	Value, 1870–'71.	Value, 1871–'72.	Value, 1872–'73.
Coffee...............	$41,857,524	$35,111,209	$57,642,783
Cotton...............	11,965,149	23,392,804	13,412,180
Sugar...............	8,928,567	13,961,574	13,862,526
Hides...............	5,495,713	6,295,036	7,443,042
India-rubber	5,036,885	5,245,429	5,032,683
Tobacco............	3,264,502	3,403,117	3,417,403
Mate	1,870,805	2,013,793	1,668,802
Diamonds..........	1,470,898	567,998	795,757
Rum...............	541,190	465,960	283,243
Timber............	421,689	671,198	561,856
Wool..............	255,858	269,571	154,688
Hair...............	228,908	311,942	260,401
Brazil-nuts........	161,514	162,423	221,864
Gold...............	154,055	416,824	219,631
Sundries..........	2,081,856	3,112,395	2,353,744
Total..........	$83,234,993	$95,261,268	$107,310,868

The general increase resulting from the foregoing figures may be summarized as follows:

Increase in 1871–'72, as compared with 1870–'71, $12,026,275
" " 1872–'73, " " 1871–'72, 12,049,600
" " 1872–'73, " " 1870–'71, 24,075,875

Mean annual increase................... $16,050,583 50

The subjoined table shows the value of the exports from the different provinces in the three years above referred to:

PROVINCES.	1870–'71.	1871–'72.	1872–'73.
Rio de Janeiro.....	$39,082,346	$33,088,834	$51,044,391
Pernambuco........	7,543,179	14,174,393	12,730,878
Bahia..............	9,090,880	11,265,955	8,981,818
Rio Grande do Sul.	4,744,752	5,496,671	5,916,950
Pará...............	6,018,175	6,322,680	6,290,600
Maranhão..........	2,199,966	2,678,604	1,917,173
São Paulo..........	6,406,203	8,941,225	10,738,056
Parahyba..........	409,362	1,574,308	1,292,281
Ceará..............	2,635,562	2,897,823	2,517,284
Alagôas...........	1,909,837	4,592,799	2,317,130
Sergipe............	369,960	1,089,300	1,680,424
Paraná............	1,803,390	1,934,288	1,592,397
Santa Catharina....	118,480	251,631	141,759
Rio G'de do Norte.	575,672	844,314	564,937
Espirito Santo.....	....	....	....
Piauhy	255,709	233	434,810
Amazonas..........	....	....	....
Matto Grosso......	....	....	....
Total..........	$83,234,993	$95,261,268	$107,310,868

A fact worthy of remark is, that Rio de Janeiro, though the smallest of all the provinces save four, and though about two-thirds of the commodities shipped therefrom proceed from other provinces, has still by far the largest exports, these being on an average fifty per cent. larger than those of Pernambuco, and double those of Bahia.

The great Brazilian staple of export, as is seen by the first table, is coffee, of which 276,-835,873 lbs. were shipped in 1870-'71; 301,-347,790 lbs. in 1871-'72; and 461,510,836 lbs. in 1872-'73. Of the quantity shipped in 1872-'73, no less than 379,389,553 lbs. were from Rio de Janeiro, or about one-third more than the total exports for the whole empire in 1870-'71.

After coffee the two most important commodities of export are cotton and sugar, both of which are most extensively shipped from Pernambuco, although the province of Bahia likewise sends large quantities of sugar to foreign countries.

The total shipments of these two articles from all the ports of the empire in the three years already referred to were as follows:

ARTICLES.	1870-'71.	1871-'72.	1872-'73.	Total.
	Pounds.	Pounds.	Pounds.	Pounds.
Cotton.....	102,342,781	183,795,297	98,159,742	388,297,810
Sugar......	257,363,966	379,558,806	404,765,392	1,041,687,364

ENTERED	Sea-going vessels.	Foreign........ 9,403 Brazilian....... 415	} 9,818, with an aggregate of 5,254,000 tons.
	Coasting-vessels....................		19,985, with an aggregate of 4,350,000 tons.
CLEARED	Sea-going vessels.	Foreign........ 8,573 Brazilian....... 398	} 8,971, with an aggregate of 5,254,000 tons.
	Coasting-vessels....................		19,525, with an aggregate of 4,241,000 tons.

At the end of 1873, there were in Brazil 715 miles of railway in operation,* and 3,319 miles of telegraph.

The submarine telegraph from Pará to Rio de Janeiro, touching at Pernambuco and Bahia, was successfully laid, and was opened to the public service on December 23, 1873.

The completion of this line extends telegraphic communication over an extent of 2,-300 miles on the Brazilian coast.

The submarine cable between Lisbon, Madeira, St. Vincent, and Brazil, was opened for service in June, and the cable between Rio Grande do Sul and Montevideo was inaugurated on August 7, thus placing Brazil, the Plate Provinces, and Chili, in telegraphic communication with the Eastern Hemisphere.

The number of letters which passed through the post-office in 1872-'74 was 12,059,081, of which 6,502,684 by way of Rio de Janeiro.

The growth of the national revenue is prodigious. On the accession of the present Emperor in 1832, the entire income of the empire did not exceed $5,500,000; by 1864 it had more than quintupled; and in 1871, though comparatively low—$48,994,892—as compared with the year preceding—$49,708,46—still showed an increase almost tenfold.

The chief source of the revenue is the import and export duties, especially the former, which usually amount to more than one-half of the total income.

The following tables show the items of the national finances for the year 1871-'72:

* For the names and particulars of the lines, see the ANNUAL CYCLOPÆDIA for 1872 and 1873.

VOL. XIV.—7 A

The average price of the cotton of the foregoing table was rather less than 18 cents per lb., and that of the sugar somewhat over 8½ cents per lb.

Next in importance are hides, the value of the exports of which in 1872-'73 was $7,443,-023, the province of Rio Grande do Sul alone standing for $5,037,316.

Immediately after, and almost coördinate with, hides is India-rubber, of the total value of the exports of which—$5,032,883—the province of Pará furnished rather more than nine-tenths, or $4,864,023.

Foremost among the tobacco-producing provinces stands Bahia, the value of the quantity shipped therefrom in the triennium 1870-'73 having averaged $2,500,000, while the total exports from all the provinces in the same period did not reach a mean value of $3,500,-000.

The value of the imports for the year 1872-'73 reached $75,500,000.

The shipping movements at the various ports of the empire, in the year 1872-'73, were as follows:

REVENUE.

Import duties................................	$29,299,792
Shipping duties...........................	250,230
Export duties..............................	8,614,676
Interest on railway shares..................	58,078
Receipts—the Dom Pedro II. Railway......	2,443,203
Post-Office................................	393,346
Telegraphs................................	58,580
Stamp-duties..............................	1,745,404
Mutation duties............................	1,903,388
Taxes on industries, trades, etc...........	1,525,855
Lottery taxes..............................	731,551
Mines....................................	19,737
Receipts extraordinary.....................	1,208,436
Deposits..................................	1,399,539
Slave liberation fund......................	525,093
Income-tax...............................	252,916
Real-estate tax............................	1,066,059
Sundries..................................	1,092,144
Total	$52,570,157
From the provinces......................	10,174,908
Municipal taxes...........................	2,141,261
Total revenue...........................	$64,886,326
Amount of estimated revenue for same year*	52,324,920
Surplus................................	$12,561,406

EXPENDITURE.

Ministry of the Interior :	
Civil list.......................$400,000	
Princes, etc................... 257,500	
Legislative Chambers........... 868,740	
Public worship............... 471,427	
Public instruction.............. 442,959	
Sundries................... 572,484	
	$2,513,100
Ministry of Justice...................	1,890,284
Ministry of Foreign Affairs..............	417,986
Ministry of Navy.........................	7,389,885
Ministry of War.........................	7,765,639
Ministry of Finance.....................	19,701,355
Ministry of Commerce...................	10,912,107
	$50,790,386
Estimated expenditure for same year †	59,952,181
	$9,161,795

* See ANNUAL CYCLOPÆDIA for 1873. † Ibid.

Thus it is observed that the revenue exceeded the estimate by $12,561,406 ; and that the expenditure was likewise inferior to the estimated sum by $9,161,795. But a more prosperous state of things is observable in the excess of $14,095,940 in the revenue over the expenditure.

The estimated budget for 1873–'74 was : revenue, $51,064,940 ; expenditure, $45,331,370 ; leaving a surplus of $5,733,570.

That for 1875–'76 stands as follows :

REVENUE.

Receipts ordinary and extraordinary	$53,000,000
Slave liberation fund	566,535
	$53,566,535

EXPENDITURE.

Ministry of the Interior	$3,777,762
Ministry of Justice	2,861,495
Ministry of Foreign Affairs	596,780
Ministry of the Navy	5,799,903
Ministry of War	7,862,297
Ministry of Finance	21,561,206
Ministry of Commerce	8,847,582
	$51,307,025
Surplus	$2,259,510

During the decade, 1864–'73, the revenue has been uniformly in advance of the sums estimated for the respective years.

The paper-money in circulation at the beginning of the year was as follows :

National (March 31, 1874)	$74,773,315
Bank-notes (January 31, February 28, and March 31)	16,774,062
	$91,547,377

These notes are of the following banks and issues :

Bank of Brazil (March 30)	$15,960,000
Bank of Bahia (February 28)	695,587
Bank of Maranhão (January 31)	118,475
Total, at 5 per cent. interest	$16,774,062

The customs receipts for the whole empire in 1872–'73 amounted to $40,705,708, being an increase of $1,567,962, as compared with the years 1871–'72.

The custom-house of Rio de Janeiro alone yielded no less than $19,358,792, against $17,448,679 in the previous year.

All kinds of machinery going into the empire are now free of duty, as are, likewise, the following articles : live trees, shrubs, and plants, of whatever species they may be; soda, roots, bulbs, and in general every thing useful in horticulture and agriculture.

Mr. Partridge, the United States minister to Brazil, had several conferences with the Minister of Foreign Affairs on the subject of duties on American products, representing how desirable it would be to have these relieved of all imposts, as was Brazilian coffee at American ports. But when the new tariff was published (March 31st), the only article on which the duty had been even lightened was found to be kerosene, which is extensively imported. Flour is subject to a duty of 54 cents per barrel; lumber, to about $7 per 1,000 feet; turpentine

pays some 9½ cents per gallon ; rosin, $1.15 per barrel; and the impost on lard was positively advanced rather more than ¾ cent per pound, the duty on that article being now 4¾ cents.

The foreign debt on December 31, 1872, stood at	$68,723,111
The installments paid thereon in 1873 amounted to	1,820,000
Amount of the foreign debt on Dec. 31, 1873.	$66,903,111

The following table exhibits the state of the home debt :

Debt at four, five, and six per cent	$142,954,200
Debt prior to 1827	171,446
Orphans' fund and deposits	15,589,838
Treasury notes (two, four, and six months)	8,052,000
Paper-money	74,773,315
	$241,540,799
Total amount of the national debt	$308,443,910

A new loan was contracted in October for £5,000,000, issued at 98, with five per cent. interest.

The debt of the Argentine Republic to the empire, reduced to $10,308 in December, 1873, was paid off in June; while that of Uruguay amounted, with interest, to £1,245,092.

The chief banks in the empire, eighteen in number, are, with their capitals, etc., in 1872, enumerated in the following table :

BANKS.	Capital.	Remarks.
Bank of Brazil	$16,500,000	Emission, $20,000,000.
London & Brazilian	7,500,000	Branches at Bahia, etc.
English	5,000,000	Branches at Bahia, etc.
Rural	4,000,000	Deposits, $10,000,000.
Commercial	6,000,000	One-sixth paid up.
Campos	500,000	11 per cent. dividend.
Bahia	4,000,000	Emission $900,000.
Bahia Reserve	2,000,000	Half paid up.
Bahia Mortgage	600,000	7 per cent. dividend.
Bahia Savings	1,500,000	7 per cent. dividend.
Bahia Commercial	2,800,000	7½ per cent. dividend.
Bahia Economy	310,000	7½ per cent. dividend.
Pernambuco		In liquidation.
Alagôas	150,000	12 per cent. dividend.
Maranhão	500,000	13½ per cent. dividend.
Maranhão Commerc'l	1,000,000	Half paid up.
Pará Commercial	400,000	Deposits, $1,000,000.
Rio Grande do Sul	500,000	11 per cent. dividend.

The postal treaty, provisionally concluded with the Argentine Republic in 1870, was ratified in December, 1873.

The Bishop of Olinda, whose arrest was ordered on January 2, 1874, was conducted to Rio de Janeiro and arraigned for trial before the Supreme Tribunal of Justice on a charge of contempt and usurpation of the imperial authority. Having been convicted, he was sentenced to four years' imprisonment with labor, and to pay the costs of the legal proceedings. The sentence was afterward (March 12th) commuted to simple imprisonment for four years in the fortress of Santa Cruz. On being informed that the order for his arrest emanated from the Supreme Tribunal of Justice, he denied the competency of that or any other civil court to take cognizance of acts asserted by him to be of a purely spiritual character, and consequently amenable to the pontifical authority only.

The rumor that a hostile alliance of South American powers was a subject of debate in a secret session of the Argentine Congress, was contradicted by the Argentine Minister of Foreign Affairs in a note addressed to the Brazilian envoy, declaring that the government would enter into no alliance importing a war with the empire, and that, while differing with the Rio de Janeiro Government in the Paraguay question, it would confine itself to the execution of the remainder of the agreement of November 19, 1872, leaving the boundary question to the action of time.

On July 1, 1874, Secretary Fish handed to Senhor R. F. Torreão de Barros, of the Brazilian legation at Washington, the sum of $96,-406.73, in refundment of the payment made by Brazil on September 30, 1867, upon the reclamation of the United States Government, as an indemnity in the matter of the brig Caroline. This spontaneous act of justice elicited the encomiums of the Petropolis Court and of all the diplomatic agents at Rio de Janeiro.

The sanitary state of many portions of the country was very unsatisfactory; yellow fever, small-pox, and typhoid fever, raged, now simultaneously, now alternately, especially at Rio de Janeiro, where the mortality reached an alarming proportion; but the sufferings of the people were materially alleviated by the prompt and efficacious assistance procured by public and private benevolence.

The terms of a consular convention with Great Britain, and of a treaty of extradition with Belgium, were ratified; but the all-absorbing topic in political circles during the year was the organization of the military force, and of the police, to which subject attention was particularly called by the Emperor in his speech at the opening of the Legislative Chambers in May.

BRISTED, CHARLES ASTOR, an American author and man of letters, born in New York City in 1820; died in Washington, D. C., January 15, 1874. He was the only son of an Episcopal clergyman of New York City, but of English birth, and his mother was the eldest daughter of the late John Jacob Astor. He graduated from Yale College with high honors in 1839, and soon after sailed for Europe, and spent five years in Trinity College, Cambridge, whence he graduated in 1845, taking numerous prizes, and being made foundation scholar of the college. He married in 1847, and, possessing an ample fortune, traveled extensively in Europe, amusing himself by writing for newspapers, periodicals, and magazines, on social and ephemeral topics, generally over the nom de plume of "Carl Benson." In this way he was a frequent and welcome contributor to Fraser's Magazine, the Knickerbocker, the Whig Review, New York Spirit of the Times, Clipper, Galaxy, and New York Evening Post. There was, nevertheless, a cynical tone to his writings, which increased as he grew older. He did not hesitate to discuss any topic, great or small, which struck his fancy, and his wide culture and profound scholarship made his essays always attractive to readers of light literature. At times he essayed the severer labor of book-making. His published works comprise an edition of "Selections from Catullus" by an Eton assistant master, which he revised, adding notes of his own; a "Letter to the Hon. Horace Mann," a reply to his tract entitled "Thoughts for a Young Man;" a series of sketches of New York society life, first printed in Fraser's Magazine, which appeared in book-form in 1852, under the title of "The Upper Ten Thousand;" and what was probably the most useful as well as the most extended of his works, "Five Years in an English University," which told the story of university-life in an entertaining and instructive way. To this last volume were added, in an appendix, his college orations and essays, together with specimen examination papers, the whole making a work of considerable interest to scholars, as the interior movement of an English university was then even more novel to American readers than now. A new edition of this work was published, with considerable additions, in 1873. Mr. Bristed was one of the trustees of the Astor Library from its origin. After spending many years in Europe, at its gayest capitals and resorts, where he was the associate of many of the most eminent men of the time, he returned, a few years since, to this country, and latterly made his home in Washington, where he was constantly in society. He suffered much from ennui during the latter years of his life.

BROWN, JOHN CARTER, a wealthy and benevolent citizen of Providence, R. I., a liberal patron of education, born in Providence, in 1797; died there June 10, 1874. He was a descendant of Rev. Chadd Brown, a Baptist minister, who fled from persecution in Massachusetts in 1636, and was the son of the late Nicholas Brown, the liberal benefactor of Brown University, and the grandson of the first Nicholas, who aided in its organization. Mr. Brown graduated from Brown University in 1816 in the same class with Mr. Robert H. Ives (subsequently his partner), Bishop Smith, of Kentucky, Dr. J. Mauran, Rev. Dr. Solomon Peck, and others. The year of his graduation he entered his father's counting-house, and in 1832 became a partner in the firm, which has continued to bear the same title—Brown & Ives—for more than eighty years. But, though an active business-man, and deeply interested in great enterprises of commerce and manufactures, Mr. Brown never relinquished his scholarly habits. He was a man of remarkable intellectual culture, and kept himself constantly informed on all scientific topics of the time. He early commenced the collection of a library, at first of the Aldine and other rare editions of the classics, and early copies of the Bible in all languages; but soon drifted into the specialty of American history, general and local, and of the early voyages of discovery to this continent. With ample resources and a most commendable zeal he prosecuted this work for more than forty years, and had accumulated nearly all the publications extant in any language relating to America, his collection being, in the opinion of those best qualified to judge, by far the most complete in the world. This magnificent library was freely placed at the service of scholars, and in at least three instances he sent to eminent historians across the Atlantic books which, if they had been lost, could not have been replaced. One of these, Sir Arthur Helps, has in one of the volumes of his "Spanish Conquest in America" made a graceful and glowing acknowledgment of this unexampled courtesy. But Mr. Brown was also liberal in his gifts to educational purposes. To Brown University he gave during his life and by his will $160,000; to the Redwood Library at Newport, $5,000; considerable sums to the Providence Athenæum; large sums during his life to the Insane Asylum, and $5,000 at his death; and $25,000 to the Rhode Island Hospital.

BURT, NATHANIEL C., D. D., an eminent Presbyterian clergyman, author and scholar, born in 1825; died in Rome, Italy, March 4, 1874. We have no knowledge of Dr. Burt's early life, but he graduated from Princeton College in 1846, and from Princeton Theological Seminary in 1849. He was ordained at Springfield, Ohio, June 1, 1850, and, after a pastorate of five years there, was called to the Franklin Street Presbyterian Church in Baltimore in 1855, and in 1860 to the Seventh Presbyterian Church in Cincinnati. The condition of his health was such that he was compelled

to spend a year or more abroad, and he accordingly visited Europe in the summer of 1866, and, after spending some months in the south of Europe, in the winter of 1866–'67 made the tour of Egypt, and in the spring and early summer of 1867 went over every portion of the Holy Land. He had carefully prepared himself for this exploration by a critical study of every thing extant on the geography and history of Palestine; but his investigations added much to our knowledge of the localities and sites of places mentioned in the Scriptures. The results of this tour were given to the public in 1868 and 1869 in his "The Far East;" "Hours among the Gospels;" and his ablest and most valuable work, "The Land and its Story." Compelled by continued ill-health to relinquish the pastorate in 1869, he was for a short time President of the Ohio Female College, a position for which his extensive and varied culture eminently fitted him. Finding, however, that he could only enjoy tolerable health in the mild climate of Southern Europe, he undertook the care of young ladies, who desired to finish their education in Europe, and enjoy a sight of its leading capitals. He spent his winters with his family in Rome, Dresden, or Nice, and made excursions with his pupils, of whom he usually had ten or twelve under his charge, to the principal cities of the Continent, keeping up their instruction meantime. It was on one of these excursions from Nice to Rome that he was suddenly attacked with hæmorrhage from the lungs, and died in a few minutes. In addition to his works already mentioned and some manuals for his pupils, Dr. Burt had written much for the religious periodicals and reviews.

C

CALIFORNIA. Public affairs in this State during the past year have been unusually quiet. No general election was held, and there was consequently no political campaign. The Legislature, which assembled on the first day of December, 1873, continued in session till March 30, 1874. Much legislation was accomplished during this time, but it was chiefly of local interest. In respect to the important measures which consumed much time, the session is perhaps more marked for what was not accomplished than for the bills that became laws. One of the most important subjects considered by the Legislature had reference to the railroads of the State. Early in the session the "Freeman bill," intended to regulate the rates for passengers and freight on those railroads, and to prevent unjust discrimination, was introduced in the Assembly, where it met with much favor, and was passed. It was not passed by the Senate, however, and failed, therefore, to become a law. A bill having the same object in view as that of the

"Freeman bill" was passed by the Senate only a day or two before the final adjournment of the Legislature; but this also failed to become a law. During the session acts of incorporation were passed for constructing railroads from Colfax to Nevada City, Los Angeles to Independence, Marysville to Knight's Landing, and San Luis Obispo Bay to Santa Maria. In each act of incorporation there are limitations and regulations as to fares and freights. There is also a prohibition as to freight or passenger discriminations, and as to granting free passes. The nature of this prohibition will be seen from the following provision contained in the act incorporating the Colfax & Nevada City Railroad:

No discrimination shall be made between persons, parties, or localities, as to fares and freights, or the transportation of goods; and no free passes shall be issued or given to any person or party to travel the road, except those who are actually engaged in the business of the road: any violation of this section shall be deemed a misdemeanor.

Numerous amendments to the constitution—

so numerous as to present an almost new constitution—were agreed upon by the General Assembly, and referred to the Legislature next to be chosen. The Legislature also published a recommendation to the people of the State to vote, at the next general election for members of the Legislature, "for or against calling a convention to revise and change the constitution of this State." Among other measures of some importance were acts reapportioning the senatorial districts, and fixing the number of Senators and members of the Assembly from each; providing for a system of irrigation in Los Angeles County; regulating the sale of mineral lands belonging to the State, and fixing the price at $2.50 per acre; appropriating $175,000 for the construction of a branch State-prison near the town of Folsom, in Sacramento County; and $600,000 for the completion of the Napa State Asylum for the Insane.

An important work done by the Legislature was the revision of the school laws. Under the amended school system, the State Superintendent of Instruction is elected by the people for four years. He is required, among other duties, to collect and compile the school statistics of the State, report annually to the Controller, before the 10th of August, the number of children in the State between five and seventeen years of age, and to apportion the school-fund. The State Board of Education comprises the Governor, Superintendent of Public Instruction, Principal of the State Normal School, and the School Superintendents of San Francisco, Sacramento, Santa Clara, Alameda, Sonoma, and San Joaquin Counties. Boards of education are elected in cities under the provisions of special statutes. County superintendents are elected for two years, and, besides other duties, apportion the school moneys of each district, and make annual reports to the State Superintendent. There is a State Board of Examination, composed of the State Superintendent and four teachers appointed by him, which grants life-diplomas, State-diplomas for six years, and State-certificates respectively for four, three, and two years; also a County Board of Examination, comprising the County Superintendent, and not less than three teachers appointed by him, which grants certificates of three grades. County or City Boards of Examination grant certificates only upon actual examination. The law requires all schools to be classified into first, second, and third grades, unless otherwise provided by special statute. Separate schools must be provided for children of African or Indian descent; otherwise, such children must be admitted into the schools for whites. The statute contains this important provision concerning female teachers: "Females employed as teachers in the public schools of this State shall in all cases receive the same compensation as is allowed male teachers for like services when holding the same grade-certificate." Women over twenty-one years of age, and citizens of the United States and of California, are eligible to all educational offices within the State, except those from which they are excluded by the constitution.

The school-fund amounts to $1,417,500. The amount in the State Treasury in March, subject to apportionment, was $316,630, of which $33,244 was derived from interest on school-lands; $44,280 from bonds held in trust; and $239,631 from property-tax. In addition to this, a school-tax is levied by the counties. The "Tuttle bill," which became a law in 1874, provides for an expenditure for school purposes of $1,000,000, or nearly four times as much as the schools received during 1872 or 1873. The compulsory-education law of 1874 requires all children between eight and fourteen years of age to be sent to school two-thirds of the time during which a public school may be taught, under a penalty of not more than $20 for the first, or $50 for each subsequent violation.

The total receipts for school purposes in 1873–'74 amounted to $2,551,799; total expenditures, $2,113,356; total teachers' salaries, $1,434,367; school libraries and apparatus, $29,245. There were 1,462 school districts, and 1,868 schools; 882 male and 1,454 female teachers; 97,681 pupils in the public schools, with an average attendance of 72,972, and 12,507 in private schools.

The "local-option" law passed by the Legislature at this session led to an important decision in the Supreme Court, which held the statute to be unconstitutional. The act had been passed "to permit the voters of every township or incorporated city to vote on the question of granting licenses to sell intoxicating liquors." Pursuant thereto an election was held in the fourth township of Contra Costa County, at which a majority of the votes were cast against license. The petitioner was afterward convicted of an alleged violation of the law, as declared by the statute, and sentenced to imprisonment in the county jail. The opinion of the court, written by Mr. Justice McKinstry, and concurred in by Chief-Justice Wallace and Mr. Justice Niles, held:

1. This statute is void, because it did not become a law when it left the hands of the Legislature; but was to take effect only when it should be approved by a majority of the people of a township, and then only in the township where thus approved.

2. That this statute is not a law conferring upon towns any governmental or police powers.

Justices Rhodes and Crockett dissented. The grounds upon which this decision was based were, that the power to make laws, conferred by the constitution on the Legislature, cannot be delegated by the Legislature to the people of the State, or to any portion of the people. Our Government being a representative republic, and not a simple democracy, an act, in order to become a law, "must be passed through both Houses of the Legislature, be signed by the Speaker of the Assembly, and be approved by the Governor; or, if vetoed by the Executive, must again be passed by the constitutional majority. Thus, and thus only, can a general statute be enacted." It being urged that it was not a delegation of the law-making "power when the Legislature enacted that a law should take effect provided the people of the State or of a district should ratify it, the court remarked that this position had been upheld by courts of high character, but thought that the decisions in which it had been denied were sustained by better reasons. The court admitted that a statute might be conditional, its taking effect being sometimes made to depend upon a subsequent event. This last proposition was illustrated by the case of The Cargo of the Brig Aurora *vs.* The United States (7 Cranch, 382), in which the validity of a provision of the "non-intercourse law" was upheld. The provision was to the effect that in case Great Britain or France should revoke or modify its edicts previously issued—so that they should cease to violate the neutral commerce of the United States—the trade suspended by the law should be renewed. It will be observed that in this instance the members of Congress exercised their own judgment, and simply determined that trade should be suspended while the Orders in Council or edicts should continue in operation.

In drawing the distinction between a statute being made dependent upon a condition of this kind and the one at bar, the court said:

But it does not follow that a statute may be made to take effect upon the happening of a subsequent event which may be named in it. The event must be one which shall produce such a change of circumstances as that the law-makers—in the exercise of their own judgment—can declare it to be wise and expedient that the law shall take effect when the event shall occur. The Legislature cannot transfer to others the responsibility of deciding what legislation is expedient and proper, with reference either to present conditions or future contingencies. To say that the legislators may deem a law to be expedient, provided the people shall deem it expedient, is to suggest an abandonment of the legislative function by those to whose wisdom and patriotism the constitution has intrusted the prerogative of determining whether a law is or is not expedient. Can it be said in such a case that any member of the Legislature declares the prohibition or enactment to be expedient? A statute to take effect upon a subsequent event, when it comes from the hands of the Legislature, must be a law *in presenti* to take effect *in futuro*. On the question of the expediency of the law, the Legislature must exercise its own judgment definitely and finally. If it can be made to take effect on the occurrence of an event, the Legislature must declare the law expedient if the event shall happen, but inexpedient if the event shall not happen. They can appeal to no other man or men to judge for them in relation to its present or future propriety or necessity; they must exercise that power themselves, and thus perform the duty imposed upon them by the constitution. But in case of a law to take effect, if it shall be approved by a popular vote, no event affecting the expediency of the law is expected to happen. The expediency or wisdom of the law, abstractly considered, does not depend on the vote of the people. If it is unwise before the vote is taken, it is equally unwise afterward. The Legislature has

no more right to refer such a question to the whole people, than to a single individual. The people are sovereign, but their sovereignty must be exercised in the mode pointed out by the constitution. (Barto *vs.* Himrod, 8 N. Y., 483; Rice *vs.* Foster, 4 Harr., 479.)

In support of the validity of the law, it was urged that the general statute which prohibits the sale of intoxicating liquors without license, and the "local-option" statute, should be read as one law, and that, so reading them, it was not left to the popular vote to give effect to the law, but only to determine whether licenses should be issued under it. To sustain this position, a decision of the Supreme Court of New Jersey was cited, in which this distinction seems to have been recognized. In that State a statute was sustained, which, in itself, contained a prohibition of sales without license, and then left to the people in *town-meeting* to say whether licenses should be granted. The court, however, not only questioned the soundness of this decision, but also pointed out an essential difference between the circumstances of that case and the one under consideration. For, in the New Jersey case, the determination of the question was referred by the Legislature to the town-meetings; while, in the California case, it was submitted not to the voters of a town, but to those of the territorial subdivision of a county; and the court pointed out that a wide distinction existed between the system of town government and that of a city, county, or subdivision of a county. "The marked and characteristic distinction," in the language of Chief-Justice Shaw, of Massachusetts, "between a town organization and that of a city, is, that in the former all the qualified voters meet, deliberate, act, and vote; whereas, under a city government, this is all done by their representatives." In pointing out the fact that, although the constitution made it imperative for the Legislature to "establish a system of county and town governments," such a system of "town governments" had, nevertheless, never been established, the court says:

The Legislature of California has never established a "system of town governments." The word "town" is nowhere used in the statutes in the sense in which it is employed in the constitution. The supervisors are authorized (Pol. Code, § 4056) to divide the counties into "townships," as they are authorized to divide them into election, school, road, and supervisorial districts; but the territory included in any one of the districts last named need not be the same as that included within the limits of a township. No township governments have been established. The only officers mentioned in the general laws as township officers are justices of the peace and constables. The townships have neither been given personality nor any other of the attributes of corporation; no official has been named empowered to call the inhabitants or voters together for the purpose of consultation and joint action; no act has been passed providing for any presiding officer, or regulating the mode of conducting business, or of declaring the result of the action of the inhabitants or voters when assembled; and neither the voters themselves, nor any boards of officers elected by the voters, have ever been constituted a deliberative assembly for the purpose of adopting prudential rules or regulations in respect to matters placed under the control of the town governments.

The exercise by the town governments, when they shall be established, of the power to make local rules will coexist with the power of the State Legislature to make general laws, and will apparently (but apparently only) constitute an exception to the rule, that the power to make laws, placed by the constitution in the Senate and Assembly, cannot be delegated. When the mandate of the constitution shall have been obeyed, and a "system of town governments" shall have been established, and when local legislatures shall have been organized under that system, the State Legislature may confide to members of such local legislatures the task of deliberating and acting upon matters purely local in their nature. The Legislature may give to the town governments, when formed, the right to make local rules; but the Legislature has no more right to delegate to the people living within certain territorial limits, but who have no distinctive political character or governmental organization, the power to make laws, than it can delegate the same power to all the people of the State.

The statute of March 18, 1874, under the provisions of which the prisoner was convicted, does not itself establish any system of town government. The only officers who are directed to perform any acts are county officers; the election is to be ordered by, and the returns made to, the supervisors. There is no provision for an assemblage of the people of the town for deliberation; the vote to be taken can in no way be said to express the result of such deliberation. The constitution intended that the opinion of a majority should govern as to town matters, but that it should be an "organically expressed" opinion. The power to enact laws must be employed by the State Legislature; that to make by-laws for a town by the local legislature; to become law or by-law it must first be considered by the appropriate deliberative body. The statute under consideration simply permits a species of *plebiscitum* with reference to a particular subject, in which the only option of the people of a township is to say "yes" or "no" to a complicated project. After the spasmodic effort at the polls, the "town government" (if this can be called one) subsides into inaction, without any form or power of self-vitalization, until again aroused to the exertion of its single function by the supervisor of the county. The statute furnishes neither a system nor a government.

When M. de Tocqueville, and other writers, who have studied our institutions in a philosophical spirit, have expressed their admiration for the system of town governments existing in New England, as affording an excellent school of preparation for the discharge by the citizen of his duties to the State, it was in view of the public discussions in reference to affairs of local, but sometimes absorbing interest, at which all the qualified inhabitants of the town could be present, and in which all were authorized to take part. To substitute for such local legislation, where measures receive the sanction of the law only after public interchange of opinions, the machinery of a "primary election" would be to degrade the whole system. That cannot be called a system of town government in which no deliberative assemblage is provided for, and in which a local law is adopted by the ballots of perhaps a bare majority, who vote secretly, and without consultation with the rest of the voters; who are actuated by motives which need not be publicly avowed, or controlled by reasons the weakness of which would be exposed by a public discussion.

On the 19th of November a State Temperance Convention was held in San Francisco, the object of which was the formation of a political temperance party. The convention was largely attended. The views of the delegates were expressed in the following resolutions:

Resolved, That no liquor shall be sold where other merchandise is sold, and no merchandise shall be sold where liquor is sold; and that all those who sell liquor shall be held responsible for its effects upon the individuals purchasing it.

Resolved, That the local option law has been indorsed by the popular sentiment of California, and therefore that this convention desire the embodiment of some form of legislative enactment of the principle of that law, *in presenti* and not *in futuro*.

Resolved, That the education of the masses is the safeguard of American freedom; therefore we are in favor of mingling labor with our common-school system, so as to train the mind of the youth to appreciate industry and ingenuity.

Resolved, That the national and State laws creating an agricultural, mechanical, and mining college in the University of California, are necessary for the development of the resources of the country, and we insist upon their theoretical and practical introduction into the university, with all the rights and privileges accorded to the other departments in the college of letters.

Resolved, That we approve of the eight-hour system of labor as a social and national blessing, and regard the eight-hour law of the State and nation as a progressive step in civilization, whereby we shall secure a more intelligent and patriotic citizenship, and more energetic and ingenious mechanics.

Resolved, That it is wrong in principle to so employ convict-labor as to come in competition with the occupations of honest men and women; therefore we demand reform in the management of the penitentiary of this State, so as to give prisoners employment that will not in any way injure the producing population.

Resolved, That we are decidedly in favor of the immigration of the Caucasian race, but look upon the introduction of the Chinese into this country as injurious to those of our people who work for a living, and nationally unsafe and socially demoralizing to the present and coming generations.

Resolved, That associations having influences in favor of the masses have our decided approval, and we look upon the Trades Unions and Grangers as common educators of the mechanics and farmers, whereby we form a greater degree of social progress and equality among the working-classes.

A resolution was also adopted recognizing the coöperation of women in the cause of temperance, and calling upon the women of the State to unite in the work.

Also, a resolution providing for the formation of a State Central Committee to work with a quorum of fifteen members.

The territory between the Gulf of California and the southern boundary of the State has been recently explored by private enterprise, and valuable facts acquired. This is the region of the Great Desert. The Cocopah Mountains extend over this desert for about 50 miles, and are about 1,000 feet high. They are supposed to be rich in gold, silver, and copper. On the northwesterly side of this range is Lake Maquata, a considerable body of salt-water, which is fed sometimes by the high tides from the gulf, and at other times by the overflow of the Colorado River. On the southerly side of the Cocopah Mountains is a large body of land, having an alluvial soil, and is every way suitable for agricultural purposes. In this district are a great number of mineral springs and volcanoes, and a lake of fresh water (Lake Chapman), whose waters flow northward down New River. North of what is known as the Colorado Desert is the Mohave Desert, and, farther on, the Amargosa or Death Valley. The two latter are below the level of the sea, and both are really connected with the greater one, and constitute one desert.

The engineer making the survey found that New River, a branch of the Colorado, could be turned into the desert so that all the lower levels, embracing the barren and worthless part, would be covered with water, leaving the mountains and the fertile districts above water. The theory is that this great desert furnace can be cooled by covering a large and now worthless area with water, at comparatively small expense. This theory is indorsed by the engineer, who holds that were the desert a sea it would send up a column of atmosphere charged with moisture, which, meeting the colder currents from the ocean, would precipitate frequent showers, and thus change large tracts of country from barrenness to fertility. The rain-currents moving from the southeast toward the northwest, cross the desert, the moisture falling to the upper edge, at which point the rain disappears, it having been absorbed by the heated air of the plains. The engineer observed this phenomenon for nearly a month, including parts of July and August of the present year.

Death Valley, in California, has also been explored recently by the United States Government Survey, sent out to explore the Western Territories. From reports made by officers of this expedition, it appears that Death Valley, in California, is a detrital sink of unique physical characteristics. This whole region presents a series of valleys or detrital plains, each entirely inclosed by the ridges of Cordilleras that are more or less distinct as a series of mountain-masses. The "Death Valley" proper is one of the most remarkable of all known interior continental depressions, and has portions near the centre of its axial line below the level of the sea, although far inland, and lying much to the north of the lower border of the great Interior Basin. It is the sink of the Amargosa River, which has its source in the areas of drainage formed to the south and east of Belmont, Nevada, and traverses the desert of that name while passing southward, until, reaching latitude 35° 41' 5", it makes an abrupt angle to the west, and thence, at right angles to the north, reaches the point of greatest depression, a little less than three hundred feet below sea-level, in the heart of Death Valley proper. This valley, of the ordinary oval form, is fully seventy miles in length, varying from five to fifteen miles in width, surrounded by frowning mountains of volcanic and sedimentary origin, the Telescope Range, rising higher than 10,000 feet. The line crossing this dismal area from the mouth of Death Valley Cañon to the thermal springs in Furnace Creek, presenting a labyrinthine maze of efflorescent saline forms, creates at the level of vision a miniature ocean, the vibration of whose contorted waves has a sickening effect upon the senses. The lurid glare, horizoned by the bluish haze radiated from the mountain-sides, appears focused to this pit, though broad in expanse. It seems, coupled with the extreme heat, to call for the utmost powers of mental and physical endurance.

The journey through the Valley of Death occasioned the utmost apprehension evinced through the entire season. To this were added the effect of the fearful cloud-burst experienced while among the Telescope Mountains, to the west, and the absence of the guide, who had ventured toward the northwestern arm of the valley, it was feared, to return no more. The transit of forty-eight hours in a temperature that remained at 117° Fahr. at midnight, so exhausted both men and animals, that further travel was rendered precarious.

The coinage at the United States Mint in San Francisco for the years ending June 30, 1873 and 1874, is shown in the following statement:

GOLD COINAGE.	1872-'73.	1873-'74.
Double eagles.............	$16,612,000	$21,960,000
Eagles.....................	140,000	120,000
Half-eagles.................	200,000	155,000
Quarter-eagles.............	15,000	67,500
Total gold...	$16,967,000	$22,302,500
SILVER COINAGE.		
Trade-dollars.............	$9,700	$2,122,000
Half-dollars...............	18,500	241,000
Quarter-dollars...........	16,000	129,000
Dimes......................	16,000	59,500
Half-dimes................	34,300	....
Total silver............	$94,500	$2,550,500
Add gold..:...........	16,967,000	22,302,500
Total gold and silver...	$17,061,500	$24,853,000

The coinage of trade-dollars is comparatively a new feature. Notwithstanding the large amount of coin turned out, the mint had to close for the annual settlement with orders unfilled. During the fiscal year of 1871-'72 the total coinage at the mint was $18,745,500, of which $955,500 was in silver, and the remainder in gold, against $18,616,775 for the year 1870-'71, including $751,775 in silver.

CARLTON, Rev. THOMAS, D. D., a Methodist clergyman, long connected with the publishing interests of his denomination, born in New Hampshire in 1808; died in Elizabeth, N. J., April 16, 1874. In early childhood his parents removed to Lockport, Niagara County, N. Y., where he enjoyed good educational advantages. He united with the Methodist Episcopal Church in early youth, and in 1829 was received on trial as a preacher by the Genesee Conference, in which he continued to labor for the next twenty-three years. Of these, thirteen were spent in the pastorate, seven as presiding elder, and three as agent for the Genesee Wesleyan Seminary. In this time he developed remarkable business and financial abilities in

·church matters, as well as in the more direct labors of the ministry. In 1848 he was a member of the Quadrennial Conference, and was then made a member of the book committee at New York. In 1852, he was elected by the General Conference principal or senior book agent of the Book Concern, and by repeated reëlections was retained in that position for about twenty years. During the years of his administration, the Concern grew steadily in all its financial interests, enlarging its operations, and nearly doubling its capital, besides paying for objects entirely outside of itself not less than $800,000. During all the time of his book agency Dr. Carlton was also the treasurer of the Methodist Missionary Society; and while in that office more than $8,000,000 passed through his hands, for all of which service he received no compensation. Nor was there ever a note or other paper of the Society dishonored at maturity, though to preserve its honor it sometimes became necessary to borrow large amounts, for which not infrequently his own personal securities were pledged. His accounts, though carefully audited at each year's end, never showed any discrepancies; and at his retirement, a little more than a year before his death, the Missionary Board bore a hearty testimony to his ability and conscientious fidelity in their service. He was much honored and esteemed in Elizabeth, where he had been active in building up a strong Methodist interest, had been twice a member of the City Council, and had been elected, a few months before his death, city treasurer. He was also a member of the Board of Managers of the Methodist Missionary Society, a director in the Shoe and Leather Bank, and in the Home Life-Insurance Company. To high abilities he joined rare social powers. He received the degree of D. D. from Wesleyan University.

CHANG and ENG, the well-known Siamese twins, born at Bangesau, Siam, April 15, 1811; died near Mount Airy, N. C., January 17, 1874. Their father was Chinese, and their mother Chino-Siamese. The connection of the two was by a fleshy and partly cartilaginous band extending from the ensiform cartilages of the breast-bones down to a point below the umbilicus, or navel, of each. There had been but a single umbilical cord attached to the middle of the under side of this band, and while the band (which was eight or nine inches in length, about eight in circumference, and two and a half in diameter—its upper or outer surface being convex, and the under or inner concave) was cartilaginous and nearly insensible except at its median point, there was evidently some intercommunication through it to the viscera of both. The breast-bones were so nearly joined that they were naturally face to face, and could never have occupied the position of back to back. What this connection was was a disputed point, which could not be settled until a careful *post-mortem* examination was made. It was then found that there were no

direct blood-vessels or nerves connecting either the circulation of the blood or the nervous fluid through both bodies, but that the peritonæum or membrane covering the bowels was extended in *two* pouches from the abdomen of Chang passing through the band into the abdomen of Eng, and that *one* similar pouch from the peritonæum of Eng passed through the band lying between the two from Chang, into the abdomen of Chang. These pouches contained small blood-vessels coming from the livers of each (which were in both close to the cord), and these blood-vessels were covered with a thin layer of genuine liver-tissue. A separation or division of the cord would therefore have been almost certainly fatal to both. The twins differed considerably in size and strength as well as in disposition, Chang being considerably the larger and stronger, but also more irritable and intemperate, while Eng was smaller, but sober and patient. They came to this country in 1829, and were publicly exhibited in America and Europe for nearly twenty-five years. Having accumulated a joint fortune of about $80,000, they settled down as farmers in North Carolina, and at the age of forty-four or forty-five married two sisters, by whom they had a number of children (Chang six, and Eng five), of whom eight with the two widows survive them. Two of the children were deaf and dumb; the rest had no malformation or infirmity. They lost a part of their property, which consisted partially of slaves, by the war, and were very bitter in their denunciation of the Government in consequence. After the war they again resorted to public exhibitions to regain their lost wealth, but were not very successful. Their lives were embittered by their own quarrels, and the bickering of their wives; and they returned home, after a decision by the most eminent European surgeons that the severing of the band (which both desired) would prove fatal, with their tempers much soured, and their spirits depressed. It should be said, however, that they had always maintained a high character for integrity and fairness in dealing, and were much esteemed by their neighbors. In 1870 Chang had a paralytic stroke, and was subsequently weak and ill, while Eng's health was much improved. Chang died first, probably from acute laryngitis, or congestion of the lungs, the result of a ride in extreme cold weather, and Eng, about two and a half hours later, probably from nervous shock at his brother's death, and perhaps, also, from some mysterious influence resulting from their connection. The bodies were brought to Philadelphia and carefully examined by a corps of eminent physicians. There are but five or six cases of these "double monsters" on record; none of them united just as these were, and none who had attained such an age.

CHEMISTRY. *Influence of Color on Reduction by Light.*—This subject has been investigated with great thoroughness by Mr. M.

Carey Lea, of Philadelphia, and the results published in the *American Journal of Science and Arts.* In those metallic salts which suffer reduction under the action of light, the nature of the acid has much to do with the facility of reduction ; thus ferric oxalate and citrate are much more easily reduced than ferric sulphate. Further, the reducibility of a salt is, as a rule, influenced by the substances in contact with it: thus silver chloride, when alone, changes rather slowly to violet; more rapidly, and to a deeper violet, when in contact with silver nitrate ; on certain sorts of organic matter being added, the change is still more rapid, and the color produced may be intense black. It is affirmed by Dr. Hermann Vogel that in the case of silver bromide such contact not only affects its general sensitiveness to light, but also modifies its impressibility to rays of different refrangibilities. According to Vogel, this change follows a definite law, viz.: the colored substances, absorbing certain rays, increase the impressibility of the bromide to those rays which they absorb. Thus a colored substance which absorbs the yellow rays and radiates the rest of the spectrum, increases the sensitiveness of silver bromide to the yellow rays. The existence of this law Mr. Lea was unable to verify. Below is an abridged account of his experiments.

1. *Ferric Salts.*—Strips of paper were first strongly colored with aurine, with aniline blue, and with aniline green, and then impregnated with ammonia *ferric oxalate* and exposed, side by side with ordinary white paper similarly impregnated, to a spectrum (an artificial spectrum made by coating strips of glass with suitable transparent pigments). After exposure both papers were plunged into a solution of ferridcyanide of potassium, which produced Turnbull's blue in the reduced portions, the remainder continuing white. The result of three experiments was to show the aniline blue to be without influence. The aniline green slightly diminished the impressibility, but not more in one part than in another. The aurine produced this effect more strongly. Neither coloring matter exerted any specific influence on the impressibility by any particular portion of the spectrum.

2. *Potassium Bichromate.*—In contact with *aurine* this salt showed no change of action in its behavior to white, blue, or violet light, nor in the orange or the red. In the yellow it was less impressed than the bichromate strip of paper without aurine. Papers colored with aniline blue and green acted like the plain bichromate, but were perhaps a trifle less sensitive to the whole spectrum.

3. *Potassium Ferridcyanide.*—Papers colored with aurine, coralline, aniline red, blue, and green, and mauveine, were exposed, the reduction being brought about with ferric ammonia oxalate. All these six colors diminished the impressibility of the ferridcyanide throughout the whole range of the spectrum, and no relation could be traced between the color used and the impression of particular rays.

4. *Uranic Nitrate.*—The same coloring-matters used. With short exposures to violet and white light only the mauveine appeared to give a slight increase of sensitiveness ; but as the increase extended equally to white and violet, no conclusion could be drawn as to influence on specific rays. The coralline diminished the general sensitiveness a good deal, the aurine nearly destroyed it, and the three aniline colors diminished it a little.

5. *Silver Chloride.*—Here coralline, rosaniline, and

red litmus-paper, increased the sensitiveness to blue and violet; mauveine and aniline green were without effect, and aurine diminished sensitiveness to all six.

6. *Silver Iodide.*—Here a violet-blue aniline color increased the sensitiveness to yellow and green rays; but also had a similar effect upon the violet. Aniline green increased the sensitiveness to violet, blue, green, and yellow rays, but not to the orange and red (the colors approximating to its own color), while, on the contrary, coralline increased the sensitiveness to the rays most different from its own color. Hence no definite law appears.

7. *Silver Bromide.*—Here colorless substances as well as those possessing color were placed in contact with the salt to be reduced. The result was that none of the many substances used exerted a more discriminating action on the sensitiveness to individual rays than salicine, a perfectly colorless substance: it rendered the silver bromide as sensitive to the red ray as to the green. The author's conclusion is, that "there is no general law connecting the color of a substance with the greater or less sensitiveness which it brings to any silver haloid for any particular ray."

The Centennial of Chemistry.—The celebration of the hundredth anniversary of the discovery of oxygen gas was one of the notable events of the year 1874. The idea of this centennial originated with Prof. H. C. Bolton, of Columbia College, New York, who, in a communication to the *American Chemist*, enumerated the many important discoveries in chemistry which signalized the year 1774, and which mark that period as the starting-point of modern chemical science. The project was favorably received, and, at the suggestion of Prof. Rachel L. Bodley, Northumberland, Pa., where Priestley lived after coming to this country, and where he is buried, was selected as the place of meeting. In answer to the call, nearly one hundred chemists assembled at Northumberland on July 31st. Dr. C. F. Chandler was chosen president of the meeting, and was conducted to the chair by Priestley's grandson, Dr. Joseph Priestley. The more prominent features of this interesting celebration were, an address on the "Life and Labors of Dr. Priestley," by Prof. Henry H. Croft, of University College, Toronto ; the reading of several of Priestley's letters written while residing in this country; an address, "A Century's Progress in Theoretic Chemistry," by Prof. T. Sterry Hunt ; a memorial tribute at the grave of Priestley, delivered by President Coppee, of Lehigh University ; a "Review of the Century's Progress in Industrial Chemistry," by Prof. J. Lawrence Smith, of Louisville, Ky.; and an address of Prof. Benjamin Silliman, on "American Contributions to Chemistry." A visit to the house which Priestley built, and in which he died ; an inspection of his "shed," or laboratory, in which he did his scientific work ; and the exhibition of apparatus, manuscripts, and pictures, relating to Priestley, contributed in large measure to the interest of the proceedings.

Composition of the Water of Great Salt Lake.—In the *Chemical News*, H. Bassett gives an analysis of the water of the Great Salt Lake. He finds the total solid residue in

100 parts by weight to amount to 13.42, distributed as follows, viz. : .

Chlorine	7.86
SO₃	0.88
Sodium	3.83
Potassium	0.99
Calcium	0.06
Magnesium	0.30

The water has a slight alkaline reaction, and a specific gravity of 1.102 at 17° Centigrade.

Agricultural Chemistry.—In a report to the Connecticut State Board of Agriculture on the value of brewers' refuse barley-grains as manure, and as food for milch-cows, Prof. S. W. Johnson states that—

As a *fertilizer*, these grains most nearly compare to stable-manure. Like the latter, they are a refuse product, or residue of a kind of digestive process. I give here the comparative composition of the two substances :

SUBSTANCES.	Brewers' Grains, fresh.	Stable-Manure, fresh.
Moisture	78.5	71.0
Organic matter	20.4	24.6
Ash	1.1	4.4
Nitrogen	0.75	0.45

The analysis of stable-manure is an average of several analyses. It is seen that the grains contain 7½ per cent. more water, 4 per cent. less organic matter, more than 3 per cent. less ash. Nitrogen is ⅔ more in the grains, but it exists exclusively as gluten or similar albuminoid, and not at all as ammonia compound. The less activity of the nitrogen in the grains is compensated by its greater quantity. The ash consists chiefly of phosphates of lime and magnesia, as is to be inferred from the treatment the grains have received, and as Soheven found in analyses of the ash of similar grains. In fact, the phosphate of these grains is about the same as that of stable-dung, or one-third of one per cent. The soluble ash ingredients of stable-manure, especially potash, must be nearly lacking in the grains. Considering their low price, the grains must be regarded as a cheap manure, but they are deficient in alkalies and sulphates, as compared with stable-dung.

As *cattle-food*, these grains have a higher value than for manure. This will be evident from the following analyses and remarks :

SUBSTANCES.	Brewers' Grains.	Meadow-Grass before Bloom.	Maize-Fodder in August.
Moisture	78.50	75.0	82.2
Ash	1.07	2.1	1.1
Cellulose (crude fibre)	3.11	7.0	4.7
Albuminoid	4.68	3.0	1.1
Starch, sugar, fat, etc. (by difference)	12.64	12.0	10.9

The grains are seen to surpass corn-fodder in every respect, and to contain four times the percentage of albuminoid, or flesh-forming matters, of the green maize-stalks. They contain also well with grass before blossom, and have but one deficiency, viz., that of potash and sulphates. The proportion of albuminoids in brewers' grains exceeds that of any kind of green fodder grown in this country, young clover not excepted.

The condition of the nutritive matters in these grains is doubtless adapted for rapid digestion, and they must be regarded as an excellent adjunct to the farmer's resources.

Estimation of Phosphoric Acid in Superphosphates.—In a series of valuable papers, published in the *Moniteur Scientifique*, on the "Estimation of Phosphoric Acid in Superphosphates," the author, H. J. Joulie, reaches the following conclusions:

1. The superphosphates are not, as was at first supposed, mixtures of acid phosphate and of sulphate of lime, but they also contain free phosphoric acid, acid phosphate of lime, bicalcic phosphate, and unattacked tribasic phosphate.

2. The retrogradation they undergo in ageing is due to a slow formation of bicalcic phosphate at the expense of the free phosphoric acid, which seizes on the unattacked carbonate and phosphate of lime, and of acid phosphate, which breaks up into free phosphoric acid and bicalcic phosphate.

3. As the assimilability of the superphosphates depends on the sum of the phosphoric acid which they contain under the first three forms, it is increased rather than lessened by drying and by age.

4. The determination of the phosphoric acid soluble in water gives only a very inadequate idea of the assimilability of the superphosphates, as it does not take account of the phosphoric acid which they contain in the shape of bicalcic phosphate, which is at least as assimilable as the soluble phosphoric acid.

5. The determination of the phosphoric acid soluble in the alkaline citrate of ammonia, under the conditions here described, is a precise measure of the positive assimilability of the phosphates contained in manures and superphosphates.

6. The adoption by analysts of this method will bring about an improvement in the manufacture of superphosphates, will develop the precipitated phosphate industry, and improve the production of compound manures, wherein the assimilable phosphates will of necessity be substituted for the fossil phosphates so soon as the analysts have ceased to confound the two.

Nitre-producing Plants.—Upward of a year ago a communication from A. Boutin to the French Academy of Sciences called attention to the large amount of nitre found in the ash of the plant *Amaranthus blitum*. During the past year M. Boutin analyzed two other plants of the same genus, viz., *Amaranthus atropurpureus* and *A. melancholicus ruber*, both of them exotics, cultivated in gardens for the sake of their beautiful foliage. The author finds that the *A. ruber*, desiccated at 100° C., contains 16 per cent. nitrate of potash—equal to 22 grammes of nitrogen per kilogramme of the dried plant, and 72 grammes of potash. The *A. atropurpureus* contains, in the dry state, 22.77 per cent. nitrate of potash ; consequently 1 kilogramme contains 31 grammes nitrogen and 103.5 grammes of potash. Having been dried for some time in the open air, the stems of the plant are covered with an efflorescence of nitrate of potash, in fine, needle-shaped crystals. The author thinks that sooner or later this family of plants will be cultivated for the sake of the nitrogenous fertilizing materials they produce.

The Nitrogen of the Soil.—Prof. Armsby, of Millbury, Mass., read, in the chemical section of the American Association, a paper on this subject, detailing a series of experiments which he had made to determine the loss and gain of nitrogen in the soil. His method was to allow organic matter containing a known amount of nitrogen to decay, under circumstances in which all the nitrogen given off or accumulated could be measured. The organic matter consisted of dried and sifted barn-yard manure, mixed with one-fourth its weight of dried and pulverized flesh. The experiments marked I. in the following tables were conducted in purified air; those marked II., in purified nitrogen. The exposure to air in the first set of experiments was kept up for more than two months; the exposure to nitrogen was for a shorter period; the temperature varied from 50° to 80°, averaging 70° Fahr.

The apparatus was exposed to diffused daylight.

QUANTITIES AND MATERIALS USED.

No. of Experiment.	Organic Matter: grammes.	Gypsum: grammes.	Potash (KOH): grammes.	Water c.c.	Total Nitrogen: grammes.
I. 1.......	15	..	....	6	0.486
I. 2.......	15	..	0.798	6	0.486
I. 3.......	15	15	....	6	0.486
I. 4.......	15	15	0.798	6	0.486
II. 1.......	15	..	....	6	0.453
II. 2.......	15	..	0.798	6	0.453
II. 3.......	15	15	....	6	0.453
II. 4.......	15	15	9.798	6	0.453

NITROGEN AFTER DECOMPOSITION (IN GRAMMES).

No. of Experiment	Substances.	Gain of Ammonia expressed as Nitrogen.	TOTAL GAIN OF NITROGEN		TOTAL LOSS OF NITROGEN	
			Weight.	Per cent.	Weight.	Per cent.
I. 1..........	Organic matter..................................	0.0118	......	....	0.054	11.11
I. 2..........	Organic matter and potash....................	0.0301	0.074	15.22	......	....
I. 3..........	Organic matter and gypsum..................	0.1631	......	....	0.0302	6.21
I. 4..........	Organic matter, potash, and gypsum..........	0.0907	......	.	0.0686	13.09
II. 1..........	Organic matter	0.0614	0.0007	1.48	......	....
II. 2..........	Organic matter and potash....................	0.0255	0.0876	19.34	......	....
II. 3..........	Organic matter and gypsum..................	0.0784	......	....	0.0052	1.14
II. 4..........	Organic matter, potash, and gypsum..........	0.0479	......	....	0.0088	1.94

These results show a loss of nitrogen in all cases except I 2 and II 2; the small gain of II 1 being within the errors of experiment. The loss is very much less in the second than in the first series of experiments. This cannot be attributed to shorter duration, since the gain of II 2 is greater than that of I 2. It confirms the deductions of Lawes, Gilbert, and Pugh, that the loss of nitrogen is caused by a process of oxidation. Gypsum seems to prevent in part the loss of nitrogen. The relation of the formation of ammonia to the experiments is not obvious. A considerable gain of nitrogen is effected in the experiments where potash alone is mixed with organic matter. No trace of nitric acid was found, and there is no reason to suppose it was formed during the experiments. The gain of nitrogen cannot be ascribed to nitrification. The fact of the fixation of nitrogen is demonstrated; the method is as yet open to question. The following conclusions sum up our present knowledge. 1. The loss of free nitrogen during the decomposition of nitrogenous organic matter is generally due to oxidizing action. 2. An increase of combined nitrogen in soil may take place by oxidation of free nitrogen to nitric acid. 3. Some organic substances in the presence of caustic alkali are able to fix free nitrogen without the agency of oxygen or the formation of nitric acid.

Estimation of Nitrates in Potable Water.—A method for the estimation of nitrates in potable waters, presented by Mr. W. F. Donkin, of the British Chemical Society, is worthy of note, as affording a ready means of ascertaining the purity of water. A nitrate, in the presence of chlorides, when treated with phenol and sulphuric acid, gives a reddish solution which, on the addition of an excess of ammonia, changes to a more or less decided blue. On this reaction the process depends. The water under examination is compared with a standard solution of potassium nitrate containing a known quantity of the salt; these are treated in a precisely similar manner. The process is capable of accurately determining the amount of nitrates present to within one part in four million parts of water.

Proportion of Carbonic Acid in the Air.—The amount of carbonic acid in the atmosphere has been newly investigated by Truchot. In a communication to the Paris Académie des Sciences he says that his method of analysis consisted in passing a known volume of air through a graduated solution of barium hydrate, allowing the barium carbonate to be precipitated, and then re-titrating the solution. His results are as follows: 1. At Clermont-Ferrand (where he made his experiments) the amount of carbonic acid in the air is greater at night than during the day. 2. The proportion is not sensibly greater in the city than in the country. 3. In the vicinity of green-leaved plants the proportion of carbonic acid varies considerably, according as the green parts of the plants are exposed to the direct solar rays or to diffused light, or exist in the shade, the amounts for these cases respectively being 3.54, 4.15, and 6.49 per 10,000 parts of air. 4. The mean amount of carbonic acid in the air is 4.09 parts per 10,000. 5. This proportion of carbonic acid bears an inverse ratio to the altitude; thus at Clermont-Ferrand (altitude 395 metres) it is 3.13; on the Puy-de-Dôme (altitude 1,446 metres), 2.03; on the Pic de Sancy (altitude 1,881 metres), 1.72 per 10,000 volumes of air.

Composition of Cosmic Dust.—The Norwegian explorer Nordenskiöld on many occasions discovered on the snow in high northern latitudes minute particles of a black substance to which he gave the name of cryoconite. Since his return from the polar regions he has analyzed this dust, comparing it with a substance of the same nature found by his brother on the snow in remote regions of Norway. In neither case was it possible that these particles could have had a terrestrial origin, and hence Nordenskiöld regards them as associated with meteors. The substance is a silicate having the formula $2RSi + AlSi_2 + (H)$. It also contains metallic particles (iron, nickel, and cobalt), and about two per cent. of organic matter.

An Improved Cement.—A very slow-setting stucco or cement, which becomes extremely hard, is prepared by the addition of a small quantity of alum to plaster of Paris. A still finer cement—one which sets with equal slowness and acquires the same hardness—is obtained by simply plunging the dehydrated gypsum for a few minutes into water containing slightly more sulphuric acid than suffices to transform into sulphate all the carbonate of calcium which may be present in the gypsum. After the liquid has been drained off, the plaster is submitted to a heat approaching redness for two or three hours.

Solvent Action of Water on Lead.—The discussion in the French Académie des Sciences on the action of water on lead (a summary of which was given in the volume for 1874) was the occasion of Sir Robert Christison making a very thorough investigation of the subject. His results agree in the main with those attained by the majority of the French *savants*. They may be summed up as follows: 1. The purest waters act the most powerfully on lead, corroding it, and forming a carbonate of peculiar and uniform composition. 2. All salts impede this action, and may prevent it altogether, some of them when in extremely minute proportions. 3. The proportion of each salt required to prevent action is nearly in the inverse ratio of the solubility of the compound which its acid forms with the oxide of lead. The first of these three propositions is often called in question, but all the experiments made by the author invariably confirmed it. A sample of very pure spring-water was sent to him, with the assurance that it had been found incapable of attacking lead; but on trial it was·found to corrode the lead with as much energy as distilled water. An interesting fact, first observed by Dr. Nevins, is confirmed by the author's researches, viz., that some salts seem to allow of a certain action going on when they are largely present in water, though when they exist in very small quantities they prevent action.

This curious circumstance might well excite alarm in the minds of those who receive their water-supply through leaden pipes: according to Sir Robert Christison, however, "there is reason to suppose that the proportion required to *permit* action is greater than is ever likely to occur in waters applicable to household use." Doubtless this excess of salts is found in some mineral waters, and the passage of such waters through leaden pipes may have the effect of corroding the latter. Oftentimes the corrosive action of *water* has been confounded with the corrosive action of other agents; for example, when a lead pipe has been surrounded with fresh mortar, which is frequently or permanently moistened, or when lumps of fresh mortar have fallen upon the bottom of a lead cistern. Again, the effect of galvanic action has been mistaken for the effect of corrosion by water. If a lead pipe be soldered with pewter solder and not with lead, erosion takes place near the line of junction of the solder with the lead. The same is to be said of the contact of the pipe with bars of other metals, or bits of such metals lying on it; and some facts seem to indicate the existence of the same property in certain stony and earthy substances. Other investigations of this general subject by Fordos, Robierre and Champouillon, Maralo, Mayençon and Bergeret, and Dumas Belgrand and LeBlanc, have been published during the year.

Ozone.—The statement of Schönbein, that ozone is produced by the action of light upon oil of turpentine, is negatived by the later researches of Kingsett. He first endeavored to ascertain the rate of absorption of oxygen by a given amount of turpentine and similar bodies, and found that the former, in sunshine, absorbed 36.6 cubic centimetres of oxygen daily, but in the shade only 0.6 c.c. Oil of caraway absorbed 3 c.c. daily; oil of bergamot, 3 c.c.; oil of juniper, 2.5 c.c.; oil of cubebs 2 c.c.; oil of lemon, 1.2 c.c.; naphtha, 0.7 c.c.; ether, 0.19 c.c; benzole showed no absorption during forty days. On agitation then with potassium iodide and starch solution, the well-known blue coloration was more or less quickly developed, though the color did not appear at once, and, in the case of the bergamot, required several minutes. On testing the substance formed for ozone, neither lead nor manganese paper was affected, nor were their solutions changed by actual contact with the oil; a mixture of.sulphuric and chromic acids, however, became violet. Further experiments were made with the oil of turpentine. Thus a quantity of this substance was placed in a bottle with an equal volume of water, air was slowly drawn through it for many hours, and it was allowed to stand several days in a shallow dish exposed to the air. The water on examination colored starch-paper blue, precipitated manganese dioxide from potassium permanganate and gave a violet color with chromic and sulphuric acids, but caused no change either in lead acetate or manganese sulphate. The oil, even after washing, gave both the starch and the chromic-acid tests. Hence it appears that, even after washing, oxidized oil of turpentine contains a body with the reactions of hydrogen dioxide. Still it cannot be either ozone or hydrogen dioxide, but a body derived from the turpentine by the action of air and water upon it. If it be the hydrate of terpene oxide, $C_{10}H_{16}O.H_2O$, zinc chloride must destroy it. Active turpentine was therefore distilled with zinc chloride, and the active properties were entirely destroyed. The conclusion that the active agent in turpentine exposed to light is hydrate of terpene oxide receives confirmation from sundry other of its reactions.

Do Plants liberate Ozone?—The supposed liberation of ozone by plants was tested by J. Belluci in a series of experiments which are given in detail in the *Comptes Rendus*. M. Belluci passed air containing $\frac{1}{100}$ of its volume of carbonic anhydride for six hours, in the daytime, through a glass tube, part of which was covered with black paper, into a receiver inclosing living plants, whence it issued by a second tube. In each of the tubes were placed two ozonoscopic papers. Now, it appears that the papers in the dark parts of both tubes were quite unaltered; and the change in the others could only be produced by ozone existing in the air which traversed the apparatus. The intensity of coloration of the paper exposed to light in the second tube almost exactly corresponded to that of the paper in the illuminated part of the first tube; thus excluding the supposition that the chemical activity of the air was due to ozone produced by the plants. The author thinks M. Cloëz's view confirmed, according to which the combined action of humid oxygen and solar light accounts for the coloration of iodized starch-paper, independent of ozone.

Experiments made by Emanuel Schöne, of the Berlin Chemical Society, on the relations of ozone to water, gave the following results: 1. Ozone is partially destroyed by passing through water. If dry, ozonized oxygen is simply collected over water, the ozone present is diminished by about 25 per cent. If passed through water for a longer time the loss of ozone is greater. The loss is the more considerable the longer the gas is in contact with the water, and the greater the surface exposed. 2. Ozone is absorbed by water in a considerable degree, even at the ordinary temperature of the atmosphere. 3. On passing dry ozonized oxygen through water much more ozone disappears than is absorbed by the water. The decrease of the proportion of ozone is, therefore, only very slightly determined by absorption, but must be considered as a consequence of the destructive action of water. 4. Ozone does not convert water into peroxide of hydrogen. As regards the loss of ozone in ozonized oxygen gas on standing for a longer or shorter time in contact with water, the author concludes: 1. If ozonized oxygen is left in contact with water, the ozone is gradually converted into ordinary oxygen. In three days the original proportion of ozone is reduced to one-half, and in fifteen days mere traces of ozone remain. 2. The transformation of ozone into oxygen in contact with water, and at common temperatures, is attended with an increase of bulk.

Regarding the production of ozone by the agency of phosphorus, R. Lamont states that

when phosphorus oxidizes in air, forming the pentoxides, it combines with 1 molecule of oxygen and part of another, splitting up the latter so that 1 of its atoms combines with a molecule (0-0) forming ozone (0-0-0).

Improved Process in Calico-Printing.— Owing to the expense attending the use of specially prepared back-cloths in calico-printing, a cheap substitute in the shape of unbleached pieces of cloth, rejected for printing after the singeing process, is now commonly employed. But with the introduction of aniline black it was found that these could be used but once, the color soiling the piece so as to prevent its being completely cleansed by the subsequent bleaching operation, and also injuring the strength of the cloth. To meet these difficulties, A. Kielmeyer resorts to the following course of procedure:

I have used now for some time with advantage the aluminate of soda, which is to be obtained easily and cheaply, and I use it thickened to a pap with dark-burnt starch to print aniline black. The alkaline portion of this print-color acts with aniline black as an etching-ground, for, with the alkaline reaction, a development of the black is impossible; at the same time, where the black and aluminate of soda come in contact, solid hydrate of alumina separates out and acts thus as a preservative by cutting off any direct contact of the black with the cotton-fibres. It is evident that this preservative with aniline black, under proper combination and treatment, may perform a third function—that of a red mordant. But I confine myself now to pointing out how the above considerations on aluminate of soda may be utilized on a large scale for preparing the unbleached calico to serve as back-cloth for imprinting aniline black; while I add, at the same time, that experiments for printing such goods with carbonate or acetate of soda have not served the purpose. Both salts act by their alkalinity as a check upon the development of aniline black, but they cannot act also as preservatives; they cannot prevent a portion of the color which penetrates through the print from being deposited on the cotton-fibres of the underlayer, and developing to a full black.

The unbleached goods destined to serve as backing for aniline black, after the singeing process, are passed twice through a cold solution of aluminate of soda at 4° to 5° Baumé. The goods are allowed to lie unrolled for two hours, so that the aluminate of soda may be spread as uniformly as possible through the texture, and then dried on the cylinder. A piece of 50 metres consumes 5 kilos. of aluminate of soda, and, for such as shirt-patterns, may serve two or three times as underlayer. Then it is washed with the remaining unbleached pieces which have served as backing for other print-colors before the actual bleaching, placed in muriatic acid at 2° Baumé, and once more washed. After this procedure, for the remainder has been for a long while adopted in manufactories, only the operation of priming still remains to be estimated, and this should certainly not amount to more than the various manipulations of cleaning the old expressly woven. For heavy patterns, such as stripes, the prepared cloth can only serve once as backing, and for very heavy goods, such as cloths with aniline black ground, the priming liquid should be taken at 10° Baumé.

After bleaching these pieces, not the slightest mark of the black pattern is seen, to which they served as underlayer, not even on the borders; the white is as clear as on other bleached pieces, and my first fear, that hydrate of alumina might remain behind on the texture, and afterward produce some coloring, has by no means been confirmed. On the contrary, the goods may be used for any desired article of manufacture. I have also made another observation, that aniline black with white goo s, printed on backing thus prepared, was much less developed on the under-side of the texture, than when printed with unprepared underlayers, while at the same time the black was fully developed on the upper side. Every aniline black, even when prepared from the best instructions, must affect the strength of the thread, and all the more so in proportion as it can act upon it on all sides; but here the damp underside of the print comes into close contact with the aluminate of soda of the underlayer, and takes up a portion of the latter, by which this side of the thread is guarded against any perilous exposure to chemical reaction. At the same time, also, a guarantee is obtained for the relative strength of the whole texture.

Alizarin as a Test.—Prof. A. R. Leeds gives, in the *American Chemist*, an account of his experiments on the value of alizarin as a reagent. By digesting for a short time with alcohol of 95 per cent., a solution was obtained holding in one cubic centimetre 0.00425 gramme alizarin. One cubic centimetre of this solution imparted a bright-yellow color to a litre of water. By the addition of 2.25 cubic centimetres of a solution containing 0:000198 gramme potash per cubic centimetre, the yellow changed to a distinct rose-color, indicating the presence of one part of potash in more than 2,000,000 parts of water. A similar change of tint was produced by 0.00032 gramme soda dissolved in a litre of water, or one part in more than 3,000,000. The addition of 6 milligrammes of potash and 4 milligrammes of soda, to a litre of water containing 0.00425 gramme alizarin, changed the yellow into a rose-color so dark that any further deepening of the color was too inappreciable to be used as a means of detecting an increase in the percentage of alkali. On instituting a comparison between litmus and alizarin, it was found that a litre of water containing 0.0066 gramme of the latter with 0.0008 gramme of the acid H_2SO_4 underwent the same change of color as a litre of water containing 0.02 gramme litmus and 0.0024 gramme H_2SO_4.

A number of samples of drinking-waters gave a strongly alkaline reaction with alizarin, those of Hoboken and New York changing the color to a dark red. A litre of Croton water, drawn from a hydrant in the lower part of New York, January 2d, gave a bright cherry-color with 0.0066 gramme alizarin, and acquired the same tint as that imparted by 0.0016 gramme soda to a litre of distilled water containing 0.0066 gramme alizarin. The yellow color was restored to the latter by 0.004 gramme H_2SO_4, to the former by 0.03 gramme H_2SO_4. In this way the alkalinity of a number of samples of drinking-water may be rapidly compared, and the total amount of acid required to neutralize the bases may be determined without previous condensation.

In all the above cases extremely dilute solutions were employed, and no change of tint and no precipitation of the coloring-matter was observed even after standing a number of hours. But, when larger amounts of coloring-matter and an excess of acid were present, the alizarin was partly precipitated and rendered the liquid turbid.

The distilled water in common use at the Stevens Institute, condensed in a worm of block-tin and

collected in stone-ware jugs, was invariably alkaline: collected in bottles of white glass, it had a neutral reaction. Snow-water measuring 50 c.c., obtained by melting the snow which fell on December 27th, of last year, and titrated at the temperature of the room, was neutral. Some precautions are necessary for the preparation of test-paper with this reagent. Thin unsized white paper, which had been customarily employed in the preparation of litmus-paper, was turned red by the alizarin solution, and it was necessary to have recourse to fine Swedish filtering-paper. The commoner Swedish paper turned the yellow to a brownish-yellow color. Even the best French gelatin could not be employed to size the paper used for testing, since it manifested a slightly alkaline reaction. Alizarin test-paper, as above prepared, when moistened with a drop of saliva, is strongly reddened, and should be employed by physicians in place of litmus. I have likewise employed white silk and silk thread dyed with alizarin, and this mode of applying the test may in some cases be found useful.

New Method of assaying Lead-Ores.—According to the method proposed by A. Mascazzini, the ore or other substance is oxidized, and its metals converted into sulphates before reduction. The best agent for this purpose is sulphate of ammonia. The ore is mixed with an equal or double weight of the sulphate, according as it supposed to be poorer or richer, and the mixture is ignited in a small porcelain crucible, covered to prevent spirting. When cold, the mass is treated with boiling water, acidulated with sulphuric and muriatic acid; thus the sulphates and oxides of iron, copper, etc., are dissolved, the lead and silver remaining insoluble.

This portion is washed by decantation, the washings being passed through a filter. This filter is next dried and its ashes added to the dried insoluble portion. It is then mixed with muriatic acid and powdered zinc, in order to reduce the sulphate of lead and the chloride of silver. The metallic deposit is washed with water which has been boiled, or acidulated with sulphuric acid, and is then pressed into a compact mass.

This is dried and heated with from 1½ to 2 parts its own weight of a flux composed of 13 grammes of carbonate of potassa, 10 grammes carbonate of soda, 5 grammes of melted borax, and 5 grammes of farina. The whole is covered over with dried chloride of sodium, and the heat is raised by degrees to redness. When the whole is in a state of quiet fusion, it is submitted for a moment to a higher temperature. This process serves for determining lead and silver in white-lead, red-lead, ores rich in gold and silver, also antimony, tin, and copper. If, in the assay of ores of gold and silver, the amount of lead is insufficient, pure oxide of lead is added.

Extraction of Vanadium.—R. Boettger has found vanadium in variable proportions in pisolithic iron in larger quantities than it was hitherto supposed to exist. The ore, well-powdered, is heated for a long time to redness with nitre and soda. It is extracted with boiling water, and neutralized with nitric acid free from nitrous vapors, the reaction being left feebly alkaline. The bulk of the alumina and silica is thrown down. The filtrate yields, on the addition of nitrate of baryta, a precipitate, vanadiate of baryta, ·from which the vanadic acid is easily separated. To make fine vanadic ink, one part of pyrogallol is ground very fine with three parts of gum-arabic and three parts vanadiate of ammonia, with the addition of rainwater.

Preservation of Wine.—M. Paul Bert has discovered that wines may be kept for an indefinite length of time without becoming sour, if they be subjected to the action of compressed air, or, what is the same thing, so far as the prevention of acetification is concerned, to superoxygenated air. He put some spores of *Mycoderma vini* and of *M. aceti* in new wine which had been subjected to the action of air superoxygenated to a degree equal to a pressure of thirty atmospheres. The bottle containing the wine was then carefully sealed. Later, when the cork was drawn, the wine was found to be perfectly free from acidity ; it had ·preserved all its bouquet ; was but* slightly bitter, and was flatter, less alcoholic, than wine not treated with oxygenated air. There was no trace left of the *Mycoderma*. Thus these ferments had been killed by the excess of oxygen. At the same time the organic matters had been slowly oxidized, and the wine resembled wines that have grown too old. Possibly, by the use of oxygen, new wine might acquire some of the qualities of wines that have remained in cellars for a number of years.

Experiments on the Cultivation of the Sugar-Beet.—Prof. C. Anthony Goessmann, of the Massachusetts Agricultural College, communicates to the *American Chemist* the following notes of his experiments on the cultivation of the sugar-beet. A piece of land, 287 feet long and 150 feet wide, running from north to south, and consisting of a brown, sandy loam, which had been well manured with stable-manure two seasons previous, was divided into six plats of equal size. These plats ran from east to west across the main field ; from two to three feet of space was left between adjoining lots. Each lot was separately manured ; all manures were applied at the same time, about two weeks before planting the seeds. The various kinds of sugar-beets were planted in rows running from north to south, passing thus through all the plats treated with different fertilizers.

Plat No. 1 received no fertilizer.

No. 2 received crude potassium sulphate from Stassfurt, at the rate of 300 lbs. per acre. This potash fertilizer contained 54 per cent. of potassium sulphate, or 29.3 potassium oxide.

No. 3 was treated with kainite and superphosphate of bone-meal, at the rate of 300 lbs. each per acre. The former contained 28 per cent. of sulphate of potassa (equal to 15.2 potassium oxide), and the latter from 10 to 11 per cent. of soluble phosphoric acid.

No. 4 was manured with a blood-guano containing potash at the rate of 1,200 lbs. per acre.

No. 5 received at the rate of 1,200 lbs. of blood-guano (per acre) without potash.

No. 6, which represented the most northern portion of the experimental field, was manured on the 7th of May, 1878, with fresh horse-manure at the rate of 14 tons per acre.

All the seeds were planted on the 16th of May, 1873. Four kinds of seed were turned to account ; they consisted of the two kinds of seeds—Vilmorin and Electoral—raised during the previous year upon the College farm ; a white sugar-beet received from Freeport, Illinois ; and Sutton's improved English sugar-beet. The examination of the roots was begun on the 6th of October, 1873, and carried on for two successive weeks. The roots selected for testing were of a corresponding size, and their weight from twelve ounces to two pounds apiece.

Percentage of Cane-Sugar found in the Juice of the Roots raised from the following Seeds:

THE KIND OF FERTILIZER.	Freeport, Illinois	Sutton's English	Electoral, College Farm	Vilmorin, College Farm
Fresh horse-manure	11.96	9.71	9.42	7.8
Blood-guano without potash..	10.99	9.17	10.10	10.20
Blood-guano with potash......	12.55	10 01	13.24	10.50
Kainite and superphosphate of bone-meal..............	13.15	10.91	12.16	10.50
Sulphate of potassa...........	14.52	12.42	14.32	12.78
No manure; second year after stable-manure..............	13.49	.....	12.78	12.19

The influence of fresh stable manure in the first year is too striking to be passed over without recognizing its decidedly injurious character. Even a light sandy loam cannot entirely destroy its peculiar reaction on the composition of the roots.

New Process for measuring the Alcohol in Wines.—If, to a known volume of water, larger and larger quantities of alcohol are added, the density and the superficial tension of the mixtures obtained are simultaneously diminished, and consequently there is an increase in the number of drops which they form if allowed to flow slowly from a given aperture. If this aperture has constant dimensions, the number of drops corresponding to each alcoholic mixture is constant also. The difference between the numbers thus found is large enough to furnish a basis for a very sensitive alcoholometric method. The instrument proposed is a pipette holding 5 c.c. It is filled with the alcoholic liquid under examination, and the number of drops escaping is counted. From this number the proportion of alcohol is calculated by the aid of tables which the author has drawn up. Slight traces of liquids more diffusible than alcohol, such as acetic ether, greatly increase the number of drops.

Spontaneous Combustion of Charcoal.—When the charcoal intended for use in the manufacture of gunpowder is taken from the iron cylinders in which it is prepared, it is first placed in iron coolers provided with tight-fitting lids, and allowed to stand for twenty-four hours before it is put into the store-bins. But if, says A. F. Hargreaves, of the London Chemical Society, the charcoal is ground twenty-four hours after burning, and is placed in iron coolers with the lids off, the temperature gradually rises, and in less than thirty-six hours afterward it takes fire. If ground, however, after an interval of three days, there is no perceptible rise of temperature. From a series of experiments made by Mr. Hargreaves, it would appear that charcoal continues to absorb oxygen for thirty-six hours after it has been burnt, and the full amount of hygroscopic moisture is only attained after exposure to the air for about two weeks.

Poisons in Colored Tapers.—The presence of poisonous coloring-matters in green and red wax-tapers has been proved by Mr. James McFarlane. Green tapers owe their color to arsenite of copper (Scheele's green). The alliaceous odor evolved during the combustion of these tapers left no doubt as to the presence of arsenic. The quantity was estimated to be 0.60 per cent., equal to 0.35 gramme of arsenious acid in each 2-gramme taper—quite enough to poison two people if taken directly in the solid form. The red tapers weighed, on the average, 8.94 grammes, and the ash, weighing 3 milligrammes, was totally devoid of metallic appearance. Mercury, existing as vermilion, was found by Reinsch's process, and its quantity was carefully determined. The amount of mercuric sulphide ultimately collected, washed, and dried, was 1.66 per cent. White, yellow, and blue tapers were found to be harmless, the blue being colored with ultramarine, and the yellow with chromate of lead.

Silicon in Pig-Iron.—Having observed that silica, instead of silicon, is obtained in the insoluble residue when pig-iron containing a large quantity of silicon is dissolved by dilute sulphuric acid, E. Handfield Morton, of the London Chemical Society, was led to call in question the received theory of the silicon being *intimately mixed* with the pig-iron.

To determine this point he made a number of experiments with a No. 1 Bessemer iron, containing 4.612 per cent. of silicon. Weighed quantities of this pig-iron were placed in sealed tubes with Nordhausen sulphuric acid, in atmospheres of carbon dioxide and hydrogen, and also *in vacuo;* the tubes were then heated in an air-bath by two Bunsen burners for twenty-four hours, but in every case the silicon contained in the pig-iron had been converted into silica, and a small quantity of sulphur dioxide found in the tube, which occasioned sufficient pressure to blow the top off the tube when cracked with a file. On examining the insoluble residue from these experiments, under the microscope, perfectly transparent crystals of silica were observed, interspersed with opaque pieces of the same substance. When these insoluble residues were treated with hydrofluoric acid, complete solution was effected. The next attempt to isolate the silicon in this pig-iron was made by heating weighed quantities of the latter with an excess of pure iodine in sealed tubes, all air being first displaced by carbon dioxide; the same heating arrangement being used as in the sulphuric-acid experiments. At the end of twenty-four hours, all iodine-vapor having disappeared, one of the tubes was opened and the contents analyzed, with the following results:

Iodine	76.432 per cent.	
Iron	20.013 " "	
Silica	1.709 " "	
Carbon	0.759 " "	
Total	98.913	

Directly the tube was cracked, the pressure of gas blew the top off. The contents consisted of dull-red lumps, the whole of the iron having been converted into the ferrous iodide, as the above figures correspond to the formula, FeI₂. There can be little doubt but that the silica which was formed in this experiment was due to a slight decomposition of the carbon dioxide, with which the tube was filled; the greatest part of the silicon having been converted, in all probability, into an iodine compound; for, although iodine-vapor is without action upon silicon under ordinary conditions, it is highly probable that, when silicon in the nascent state is presented to iodine-vapor, a compound of iodine and silicon may be formed. These results were confirmed by several other similar experiments. This pig-iron was also carefully tested for graphitoidal silicon, by treating the iron with hydrofluoric acid: the insoluble residue was filtered off, and ignited to get rid of the carbon, when a mere trace of a dark powder remained, which proved to be iron.

From these results it may fairly be concluded that the silicon contained in pig-iron does not exist in a state of mechanical mixture, but exists combined with a portion of the iron as a cilicide of iron, in the same manner that carbon exists as a carbide of iron, only differing from carbon in so far that it does not exist in a graphitoidal form in pig-iron. If the pig-iron used had contained any uncombined silicon, it would have been found in the insoluble residue from the experiments with Nordhausen sulphuric acid and hydrofluoric acid, as it is insoluble in even the latter acid after having been strongly heated; and, as any uncombined silicon must have been heated intensely in the blast-furnace, there can be little doubt that, as a rule, pig-iron does not contain any uncombined silicon.

The author then experimented to ascertain whether or no the supposition of the combination of the silicon with the iron was correct, and the result proved a confirmation of his hypothesis. Experiments with white pig-iron gave identical results.

New Method of separating Calcium from Magnesium.—For the complete separation of these two substances, which, by the ordinary method, is a very difficult operation, E. Sonstadt proposes the following process:

In the course of recent experiments on the iodates, I have found that iodate of calcium is not sensibly soluble in a saturated solution of iodate of potassium, whereas iodate of magnesium is not precipitated from solution in any degree by iodate of potassium. If to 10 or 12 c.c. of a saturated solution of iodate of potassium a few drops are added of solution of sulphate of calcium, and after two hours the liquid is filtered, and oxalate of ammonium added to the filtrate, a slight opalescence appears after a while, due to the presence of a trace of calcium. But if the iodate of potassium solution to which the calcium salt was added is allowed to stand twenty hours, and is then filtered, and oxalate of ammonium added to the filtrate, not the slightest opalescence appears even after many hours. A slight crystallization takes place, owing to a diminution of the solubility of the iodate of potassium by the presence of oxalate of ammonium, but the crystals entirely disappear, leaving the solution perfectly limpid, on addition of a very small proportion of water. The precipitation of calcium by saturation of the solution with iodate of potassium does not appear to be affected by the presence of alkali and magnesium salts, in whatever proportion these may be present. If, for instance, a small quantity, as a decigramme, of ordinary Epsom salts is dissolved in the least possible quantity of water, and four or five times its bulk of a saturated solution of iodate of potassium is added, after a few hours a crystalline precipitate forms, which may be collected on a filter, washed with solution of iodate of potassium, dissolved off the filter with dilute hydrochloric acid, and, minute as the quantity of calcium present is, it may be shown immediately by the precipitate falling on addition of ammonia and oxalate of ammonium to the strongly acid filtrate.

In separating calcium from magnesium, by precipitation of the former by iodate of potassium, it is obviously important, in view of the subsequent determination of the magnesium, to know if the presence of iodate of potassium hinders the precipitation of magnesium as magnesium-ammonium phosphate. So far from this being the case, I find that the double phosphate is even less soluble in a saturated solution of iodate of potassium containing some free ammonia than it is in a mixture of two parts ordinary "liquor ammoniæ" with one part of water. Thus, the addition of solution of iodate of potassium to the ordinary liquid containing phosphate of an alkali and much free ammonia, over precipitated magnesium-ammonium phosphate, renders the fluid at once opalescent, and occasions an additional precipitation of magnesium salt.

I may mention here that I have never met with a specimen of any magnesia or magnesium salt in commerce, although sold as chemically pure, that did not contain a very sensible proportion of calcium. I believe the only available source of a magnesium salt that shall be free from calcium is distilled magnesium; in this, I have never found any trace of calcium.

Colophthaline and Coloph-Alumina.—Under the above names Mr. Paul Curie describes a solid hydrocarbon and a new organic base which he has obtained from common resin (colophony). By a process of distillation at high temperatures, he obtains from this source a much larger proportion of colophthaline than by the ordinary method, and in a form which admits of easy purification. *Colophthaline* is easily soluble at the ordinary temperature in benzol, naphtha, spirits of turpentine, carbon bisulphide, and ether; it is dissolved by alcohol and glacial acetic acid at their boiling-point only, and is deposited again on cooling. The liquid products with which colophthaline is mixed being much more easily soluble in alcohol, this substance can by this means be completely freed from them. Thus purified, colophthaline is a flocculent white body, possessing a slight balsamic odor. Its melting-point is at 70° C., and, when melted, its color becomes brown; it boils at about 400° C. It is composed of carbon, 93; hydrogen, 7—total, 100, which numbers correspond to the formula $C_{22}H_{10}$.

Oxidizing agents, chlorine, and nitric acid, attack colophthaline with the greatest facility, forming compounds that undergo a most remarkable reaction when fused with hydrate of potassium. They are transformed into a white amorphous body of decided basic properties, having so nearly exactly the appearance of alumina that it might be easily mistaken for that metallic oxide. For this reason I claim for this new substance the name of *Coloph-alumina*, and I will now proceed to enumerate some of its extraordinary characteristics.

Coloph-alumina having been prepared in the manner above described, the fused alkaline mass is dissolved in dilute hydrochloric acid, in which solution ammonia forms a voluminous precipitate of hydrate of coloph-alumina; this white gelatinous precipitate being washed, and left to dry spontaneously, loses the greater part of its water, and shrinks gradually into a compact, hard, stony-looking mass, which still retains 1 equivalent of water, and only loses it at a high temperature. Coloph-alumina is insoluble in all neutral liquids—water, spirits, ether, etc.; it is infusible and non-volatile; it resists the action of all oxidizing agents, though at a high temperature, and *is not decomposed even at* 1000° C. by chlorate or nitrate of potassa! Owing to the difficulty of decomposing coloph-alumina, it has been found impracticable to effect its analysis by any direct method; its chemical composition, however, as deduced from the mode of its formation, appears to be represented by $C_{20}H_6O_4$.

The basic properties of coloph-alumina are not very energetic. Nevertheless hydrochloric, nitric, acetic, and oxalic acids dissolve the base with ease, but the salts thus formed have not been obtained otherwise than in solutions, as by concentrating the liquor the base and the acid are too easily dissociated.

Concentrated sulphuric acid does not merely *dissolve* coloph-alumina; heated to about 200° C., it substitutes SO_3 to H, and forms a compound which is amorphous and nearly insoluble in water—*Sulpho-coloph-alumina*, probably $C_{23}H_4(SO_3)_2O_{42}(HO)$; a red heat merely regenerates coloph-alumina from this.

Artificial Vanillin.—The following is a condensed description of the process by which vanillin is obtained from the sap of pine or other coniferous trees: Take, 1. Coniferin; or, 2. The sap of plants mentioned above which has been purified or liberated from albumina or other impurities; or, 3. An extract of all those parts of the just-mentioned plants containing coniferin; or, 4. The products obtained from coniferin by means of fermentation, putrefaction, or similar action; and treat one or other with oxidizing agents, or such agents of similar action, such as bichromate of potassium and sulphuric acid, or any other peroxide, oxide, or acid, or salt, which produce the same effect. The product of the reaction in all these cases is artificial vanillin, which has been proved to be identical in all physical and chemical properties with the aromatic principle obtained by the extraction, etc., of the natural vanilla-beans.

A New Synthesis of Glycocoll.—A new synthesis of glycocoll, that is of interest as illustrating certain fundamental points in chemical theory, has been effected by Emmerling. Hydrogen iodide exerts upon organic bodies a double action; it not only reduces them from which they are derived, but also causes them, by assimilating water, to break up into two or more molecules.

It is from this fact that Emmerling advances to his synthesis. His method is to pass cyanogen gas through a concentrated solution of hydrogen iodide. One of the cyanogen atoms in the molecule, by hydrogenation, becomes the methylamine residue CH_2NH_2; while the other, by exchanging its nitrogen for the elements of water, gives rise to a carboxyl group OOOH. Therefore the formation of glycocoll takes place according to the following equation:

$$\begin{matrix} CN \\ | \\ CN \end{matrix} + (HI)_6 + (H_2O)_2 = \begin{matrix} CH_2NH_2 \\ | \\ COOH \end{matrix} + NH_4I + I_4$$

The yield is considerable, and the properties of the glycocoll are identical with those of glycocoll of organic origin. According to the author, this result goes far to prove that the reason why uric acid yields glycocoll by treatment with HI is, because it contains a cyanogen molecule.

Formation of Black Phosphorus.—It has been discovered by Ritter that black phosphorus can be uniformly obtained when the melted phosphorus, from which it is prepared, contains arsenic. Hence, the property of becoming black may be communicated to phosphorus by placing it for a short time in an arsenical solution, preferably acidified with hydrochloric acid. The quantity of arsenic phosphide necessary to produce this effect is very small—one-half of one per cent., or even less.

Properties of Eucalyptol.—The hydrocarbon called by Cloëz eucalyptol, and constituting the chief portion of the ethereal oil of *Eucalyptus globulus*, has been critically examined by Faust and Homeyer. It was prepared by fractional distillation from this oil, 3 kilogrammes yielding 600 grammes, boiling between 174° and 180° Cent. In general behavior, as in odor, it resembles a terpene. It is turned brown and dissolved by sulphuric acid, and water again sets it free. Nitric acid of specific gravity 1.4, diluted with two parts of water, converts it into paratoluic and terephthalic acids. Elementary analysis gave 88.74 of carbon and 11.48 of hydrogen. Suspecting an associated hydrocarbon poorer in hydrogen, the eucalyptol was polymerized and distilled after dilution. An oil was obtained boiling constantly at 173°-174° Cent., and having the composition of cymol; and conversion into the barium salt of the sulpho-acid confirmed this conjecture. Hence, Cloëz's eucalyptol is a mixture of cymol with a terpene, which may be called eucalyptene.

Relation of the Alkalies to Putrefactive Changes.—According to experiments made by Dr. Dougall, of Glasgow, the alkalies and alkaline earths and their salts—with a few exceptions—hasten decomposition when present in small proportion in fluids containing organic matter. This is the case with domestic soap-suds, spent lye, and all more or less alkaline liquids. Ammonia, permanganate of potash, biborate of sodium, among chemical waste-substances, do not accelerate putrefaction, but at the same time they do not retard it. Soda, potash, nitrate, and chlorate of potassium, and lime, are especially vigorous as purifiers. In regard to the antiseptic powers of different volatile bodies, the chloride of lime appears to be efficient in nearly all cases.

Chrysenine.—Under this name Phipson publishes an account of a new base which he has obtained from chrysene. It is a solid, of a bright-yellow color, strongly alkaline, has a hot, acrid, pungent taste, like piperine, is soluble in alcohol, and is affected by the action of light. It may be volatilized, yielding a vapor that is irritating to the eyes, and that forms dense fumes with vapor of hydrochloric acid.

New Method of obtaining Nitric Oxide.—Berthelot gives the following improved process for readily obtaining nitric oxide : Monohydrated nitric acid, cooled by a freezing mixture, is mixed with pulverulent phosphoric oxide in small portions at a time, taking care to avoid any elevation of temperature; the temperature of the mass should never exceed 0° C. When a little more than its weight of phosphoric oxide has been added to the nitric acid, the mass assumes the consistence of jelly; it is then placed in a roomy tubulated retort and distilled very slowly, the products being condensed in receivers with ground stoppers, immersed in ice. Perfectly pure nitric oxide in very large, brilliant crystals is thus obtained. It is non-explosive, either as a solid or a vapor, but decomposes very readily at common temperatures with nitrogen, tetroxide, and oxygen. It should not be preserved in hermetically-sealed vessels. It keeps well in good glass-stoppered bottles placed under a bell-glass with sulphuric acid.

Restoration of Deteriorated Chloroform.—According to Mr. E. B. Shuttleworth, chlorine and hydrochloric acid are by far the most general and injurious products of the decomposition of chloroform. Traces of sulphuric acid quickly induce this change. When sulphuric acid is employed as the purifying agent, and is not completely removed by repeated washing and rectification, the product very soon gives clear indications of chlorine, or some of its acid compounds. For the restoration of spoiled chloroform, Mr. Shuttleworth recommends that it be agitated with a dilute solution of hyposulphite of soda. It should then be separated by means of a glass funnel from the supernatant liquid, and again washed ; this time with simple water. After being separated, the chloroform should be passed through filtering-paper, to free it from traces of moisture, when it will be found much improved and comparatively sweet ; at least, good enough for external use. In the manufacture of chloroform, one washing with hyposulphite of soda is more effectual than three with simple water. The quantity of hyposulphite used may be so small as to be of no injury to the succeeding charges of chloroform. Of course, there are other impurities which the hyposulphite will not remove; these are of a more stable character, and, as they possess a higher boiling-point than chloroform, they may be separated by distillation, or by treatment with sulphuric acid in the usual manner.

Etching on Copper.—A new process for engraving on copper consists of the following steps: 1. The copper-plate is covered with a layer of adherent silver, on which a colored varnish is spread. 2. The design is sketched upon this with a dry paint. 3. Perchloride of iron is then applied, which bites in the lines of the design.

Formation of Urea in the Organism.—Though it has been supposed by many chemists that urea is a direct product of the gradual oxidation of albumin, all attempts at its artificial production have hitherto failed. The products obtained by the use of oxidizing agents have been ammonia, benzoic acid, and aldehydes of the fatty series, while those obtained by the use of acids and alkalies have been ammonia and amido-acids of the fatty and aromatic series (glycocine, leusine, and tyrosine). In the living organism, whenever albumin is decomposed and oxidation is hindered by the absence of hæmoglobin, as in the case of pus, much leusine and tyrosine are found, but little or no urea. So, too, when the oxidizing power of the organism is diminished these principles appear in the urine, but hardly any urea. Two German chemists, Messrs. Schultzen and Nencki, reasoning from these facts, were led to believe that the amido-acids of the fatty series, and perhaps tyrosine, are the intermediate links between albumin and urea. To test this hypothesis, they fed dogs on a diet containing a constant but small amount of nitrogen, and thus got a constant and small amount of nitrogen in the urine. Then they administered a quantity of leusine and glycocine, the result being a large increase of urea, the nitrogen in this additional urea corresponding with that of the glycocine and leusine. Thus it was proved that these bodies are converted into urea. Tyrosine also increased the urea, though not to so great an extent, and part of it remained unchanged in the urine and fæces. Acetamide was excreted unchanged. As amido-compounds analogous to acetamide are not excreted normally, they probably are not formed during the decomposition of albumin in the body. Since amido-acids contain only one atom of nitrogen and urea contains two, it must be formed from them by synthesis, and the authors think it likely that bodies from the cyanogen group form the intermediate links. It is supposed that the albuminous substances contained in food take up water under the influence of the digestive ferments, and are split up, partly in the alimentary canal but chiefly in the circulation, into amido-acids and non-nitrogenous bodies. The latter undergo combustion, yielding carbonic acid and water, while the amido-acids form urea. The

authors think it not improbable that ammonia is liberated from albumin simultaneously with cyanic acid and unites with it to form urea, or with cyanogen to form cyanamide, which is then transformed into urea.

Tempering Steel.—An improvement in this process, suggested by H. Caron, consists in heating the water into which the steel is plunged. A temperature of about 55° C. is sufficient to give to the spiral springs of the needle-gun an elasticity and resistance corresponding to the best ordinary tempering followed by the usual drawing. Steel containing from .002 to .004 of carbon, tempered in boiling water, has its tenacity and elasticity greatly increased, without sensibly altering its softness. For regenerating burned iron, Caron employs a boiling solution of chloride of sodium. A bar of burned iron, which, before this tempering, broke without bending, was, after the bath, capable of being bent double in the cold.

New Coloring-Matters.—A process for converting certain organic bodies into coloring-matters has been patented in France by Messrs. Croissant and Brétonnière. The substances employed are mostly of little intrinsic value, such as sawdust, humus from old trees, mosses, cellulose, horn, etc. Starch, horn, tannin, and aloes, are also among the substances which are converted into coloring-matters. The principle involved is the dehydrogenation of these bodies by the action of sulphur at a high temperature, the sulphur being supposed to replace the hydrogen. If, for instance, it be required to convert bran into coloring-matter, it is placed in a small sheet-iron tank fitted with a lid. Caustic soda and flowers of sulphur are added in certain proportions, and the whole is made up into an homogeneous paste. The vessel is then placed in a furnace where it can be heated to from 256° to 300° C. Sulphuretted hydrogen is given off in abundance. When the mixture is dry, we find in the boiler, after cooling, a black, friable matter, perfectly soluble in water, to which it imparts a fine sap-green. The solution has a strong affinity for fibres, which it dyes without mordant. One and the same body gives various tones of color, according to the temperature and the proportions of the mixture. Certain substances, such as extracts of dye-woods, aloes, etc., are converted at boiling-point; while lignine, bran, etc., require a higher temperature. The following examples are added:

(1.) Aloes.......................... 3 kilogrammes.
Caustic-soda lye at 40° Beaumé. 10 litres.
Water.......................... 10 " '
Flowers of sulphur............. 3 kilogrammes.

The mixture is boiled, and yields a lilac-gray. At higher temperatures a deep brown is produced.

(2.) Humus.......................... 20 kilogrammes.
Normal sulphide.........,...... 40 litres.

This "normal sulphide" contains 70 litres sodá-lye at 40° Beaumé, 65 litres of water, and 30 kilogrammes of sulphur. To dye cotton, a sufficient quantity of the product is dissolved in water at 60° C., and the goods are worked in this in the usual manner. They are then passed through boiling bichromate of potash, which fixes the color. The following additional particulars are taken from a pamphlet issued by the "Patent-Farben-Fabrik" of Gottingen—an establishment devoted to the manufacture of the new colors:

The Société Industrielle of Mühlhausen has found that these colors attach themselves permanently to the fibre, by the mere evaporation of the water in which they are dissolved—a circumstance of great importance in calico-printing. All the colors are soluble in water, and are precipitable by mineral as well as organic acids and metallic salts. The colors have a remarkable affinity for both animal and vegetable fibres, upon which they have no injurious action.

The new colors dye wool, silk, linen, and cotton, equally well. When mixed, goods can be dyed in one operation without appearing checkered, the color producing one and the same tone of equal intensity, both upon the weft and the warp. In dyeing, after the color and the chrome baths, the goods are passed through a boiling soda-bath, and washed in abundance of water. Animal fibre may require the addition of a little acetic acid to remove the last traces of alkali. Other metallic salts may be used instead of chrome, according to the particular effect desired.

Cyanogen in Bromine.—Dr. T. L. Phipson states that he has found in what purported to be pure bromine, prepared for medicinal uses, a notable amount of cyanogen. It has been known for many years that, in the manufacture of iodine, a certain quantity of that dangerous compound, iodide of cyanogen, sometimes finds its way into one of the glass condensers; and a similar compound with bromine may occur in this liquid element—a more serious case than the other, since it is dissolved and masked in the liquid. Its presence in bromine, says Dr. Phipson, may be detected in the following manner: Take an equal weight of iron-filings (say half an ounce) to that of the bromine, and add to the iron-filings four or five times their weight of water; mix in the bromine very gradually, and stir all the time, filter rapidly while warm from the reaction, place the filtered liquid in a partially-closed bottle, and in the course of some hours a deposit of ferricyanide of iron (Berlin blue) will have formed, and may be collected on a filter. In the course of two days (with the above quantity) the whole of the cyanogen is thus eliminated.

Soluble Starch.—According to Musculus, the best mode of preparing soluble starch is as follows: Put 400 grammes of starch in a flask containing two litres of a solution of sulphuric acid of $\frac{1}{25}$. Heat until the solution is effected. Then add chalk to arrest the action of the acid, filter, and evaporate to a syrupy consistence; filter again to separate the calcic sulphate, and set aside in a cool place. After twenty-four hours have elapsed, the solution begins to cloud, and finally gives a bulky, white deposit of soluble starch, which may be separated and washed. If left for some time in contact with water, it slowly dissolves, a little sugar being produced.

Its rotatory power is nearly four times that of anhydrous glucose. Alcohol precipitates it from its solution in an insoluble state.

Value of Chloralum as a Disinfectant.—In the (German) *Quarterly Journal of Practical Pharmacy*, Prof. D. N. Fleck discusses very fully the value of the various chloralum preparations—chloralum liquid, chloralum powder, chloralum wool and wadding. A translation of this paper appeared in the *American Chemist* for July. To determine the value of chloralum as a disinfectant, equal volumes of liquid sewage were treated with that and five other disinfecting agents, and the clear supernatant liquid tested with alkaline silver solution for its percentage of putrefying matter. It was thus found that—

Chloride of lime disinfects	100.0 %	putrefying matter.		
Caustic lime	"	84.6	"	"	"
Alum	"	80.4	"	"	"
Sulphate of iron	"	76.7	"	"	"
Chloralum	"	74.0	"	"	"
Chloride of magnesium	"	57.1	"	"	"

From the data set forth in this paper, the author concludes that—

1. Chloralum preparations are chiefly mixtures of chloride of aluminum.
2. They contain chlorides of lead, copper, and arsenic, which render them dangerous, especially as internal medicaments, or as astringents for fresh and suppurating wounds.
3. The price of chloralum preparations is exorbitant, considering their composition and efficacy. Where, as in case of the liquid chloralum, a net profit of at least 700 per cent., or, as in the case of the wadding, a clear profit of at least 4,000 per cent., can be easily calculated, the limits of sound and solid business are transgressed.
4. Chloralum and the preparations thereof belong to that class of unworthy secret preparations which the public should be warned decidedly against buying.

Effect of Acid on Iron Wire.—At a meeting of the Massachusetts Philosophical Society, some iron and steel wire was exhibited, on which certain curious effects had been produced by the action of sulphuric acid. The soft charcoal wire had become short and brittle, its weight increased. More remarkable still, when the wire was broken, and the face of the fracture wetted, it frothed as though the moisture acted as a powerful acid. Exposure to the air for a few days, or to radiant heat of a fire for a few hours, caused these effects to disappear. Prof. Osborne Reynolds having undertaken the investigation of these phenomena, soon observed that, on breaking off a short piece from the end of the wire, the two fresh surfaces behaved very differently: that of the long piece, on being wetted, frothed for some seconds, while that of the short piece was nearly inactive. This seemed to imply that the gas was not generated on the fresh surface, but that it came from a considerable depth beneath it. Prof. Reynolds hence concluded that the effect was due to hydrogen having entered into combination with the iron during its immersion in the acid; when the iron was exposed, the hydrogen gradually passed off.

To test this conclusion, a piece of wrought-iron pipe six inches long and ¼ inch external diameter, and rather over ⅛ inch thick, was used; this was cleaned in a lathe both outside and inside. Over one end was soldered a piece of copper, so as to stop it, and the other end was connected with a glass tube by means of a tube of India-rubber. The glass and iron tubes were then filled with olive-oil, and the iron tube immersed in cold dilute sulphuric acid. After five minutes bubbles began to pass up the glass tube, which were caught at the top, and subsequently burnt, proving to be hydrogen. But the evolution of gas was extremely slow. Warm, freshly-diluted acid, however, caused the hydrogen to come off much more quickly. A lamp was then placed under the bath, and when the dilute acid was on the point of boiling, as much hydrogen was given off in five seconds as had previously come off in ten minutes. After having been in acid for some time, the tube was taken out, well washed with cold water and soap, so as to remove all trace of the acid; it was then plunged into a bath of hot water, upon which gas came off so rapidly from both the outside and inside of the tube as to give the appearance of the action of strong acid. This action lasted for some time, but gradually diminished. It could be stopped at any time by the substitution of cold water in place of the hot, and it was renewed again after several hours by again putting the tube in hot water. The volume of hydrogen which was thus given off by the tube after it had been taken out of hot acid was about equal to the volume of the iron. With regard to the frothing of the wire when broken and wetted, this was due to warmth caused in the wire by the act of breaking. This was proved by the fact that the froth appeared on the sides of the wire in the immediate neighborhood of the fracture, when these were wetted, as well as the end; and by simply bending the wire it could be made to froth at the point where it was bent. If, as is probable, the saturation of iron with hydrogen takes place whenever oxidation goes on in water, then the iron of boilers and ships may at times be changed in character and rendered brittle in the same manner as Mr. Johnson's wire; and this, whether it can be prevented or not, is at least an important point to know, and would repay a further investigation of the subject.

CHILI (REPÚBLICA DE CHILE), an independent state of South America, comprised between the 24th and 56th parallels of south latitude, and longitude 70° and 74° west; and bounded north by Bolivia, east by the Argentine Republic and Patagonia, with which the great chain of the Andes serves as boundary, south by Cape Horn, and west by the Pacific Ocean. The vexed question of title to Patagonia is still the subject of angry discussion between this republic and the Argentine; but here the arbitrary policy of Chili elicited little sympathy, and, should war have followed, public opinion would have regarded the Santiago Government as chiefly to blame. Report represented Chili as about to take formal possession of the entire territory from Santa Cruz River southward to the Straits of Magellan, which would seem to be a breach of the compact between the two countries—that neither should exercise jurisdiction over any portion of the territory until a mutually satisfactory solution should be reached; but Chili is said to have alleged, in its own defense, that the Argentines were the first to violate the agreement by erecting a fort on the southern bank of the river alluded to. It would, however, appear that the Argentine

Government proposed to leave the matter to arbitration, as in the case of previous treaties.

The territory, which comprises an area of 133,223 square miles, or 248,813 including the 115,590 square miles of Patagonian territory to which Chili urges a claim, is divided into sixteen provinces (that of Linares having been formed by a law promulgated on December 11, 1873, from a portion of the province of Maule). The provinces, as they now stand, with their population in 1872, are as follows:

Provinces.	Population.
Aconcagua	135,323
Arauco	90,158
Atacama	84,074
Chiloé	64,148
Colchagua	155,778
Concepcion	157,860
Coquimbo	160,701
Curicó	102,281
Llanquihue	44,339
Maule	} 214,323
Linares	
Ñuble	128,182
Santiago	380,419
Talca	109,344
Valdivia	28,928
Valparaiso	146,729
Magellan Colony	749
Total	2,083,046

Hence it would appear that the population has increased by nearly 31,000 from 1870 to 1872. The foreign population in Chili amounts to some 20,000, chiefly English, Germans, and French.

The President of the Republic is Señor F. Errázuriz, inaugurated on September 18, 1871.

The Minister of the Interior is E. Altamirano (September 18, 1871); Foreign Affairs and Colonization, A. Ibañez (December 9, 1871); Justice, Public Worship, and Public Instruction, J. A. Barceló; Finance, R. Barros Luco; and War and the Navy, A. Pinto (September 18, 1871).

The Council of State, the president of which is the President of the Republic, is composed of two members from each of the courts of justice, one church dignitary, one general, the director-in-chief of one of the Departments of Finance, two ex-ministers, and two ex-intendants.

The President of the Supreme Court of Santiago is Señor Montt. There is a Court of Appeals at Santiago, Concepcion, and La Serena. The Postmaster-General is Señor J. M. Riesco.

The present Archbishop of Santiago is the Rt. Rev. R. N. Valdivieso; the Bishop of La Serena is M. Orrego; of Concepcion, J. H. Salas; and of San Cárlos de Chiloé, Señor de Paule Solar.

The Chilian chargé d'affaires ad interim at Washington is Señor F. G. Errázuriz; and the consul at New York, Mr. Rogers.

The regular army is composed of nine generals, 10 colonels, 34 lieutenant-colonels, 57 majors, 138 captains, 266 lieutenants, 2,000 infantry, 712 horse, and 804 artillery; total 3,516 men. Of the 514 officers, 41 field and 125 subaltern belong to the National Guard.

The National Guard is made up as follows:

NATIONAL GUARD.	Horse.	Infantry.	Artillery.	Total.
Commanding officers.	12	47	11	70
Subaltern "	147	1,034	121	1,802
Men..................	4,137	28,296	2,659	35,092
Total	4,296	29,377	2,791	36,464

The navy is composed of nine vessels, with an aggregate of 1,400 horse-power, 84 guns, and 661 sailors. Two corvettes, built in England, were to arrive at Valparaiso by the end of 1874.

There are in the navy two rear-admirals, three first-class and 10 second-class captains, 44 lieutenants, 21 midshipmen, and 15 cadets; one battalion of marine artillery, with 600 men, commanded by one colonel, one lieutenant-colonel, four captains, and 18 lieutenants. There is, besides, at Valparaiso, a battalion of marine artillery, forming a part of the *guardia civil* (police force), under the command of one colonel, one lieutenant-colonel, six captains, and 25 lieutenants, and comprising 794 men.

The total value of the exports in 1872 and 1873, and of those to the countries which usually take Chilian products, is shown by the following table:

COUNTRIES.	1872.	1873.
France..................	$4,755,371	$1,194,469
England..................	18,864,179	19,398,289
Germany..................	198,036	483,307
Belgium	158,737	80,887
Italy..................	33,732	....
Australia..................	9,917	....
Portugal..................	650	....
Cape of Good Hope	36,336	67,786
Polynesia..................	36,529	88,571
United States..............	580,981	1,887,140
Falkland Isles..............	86,078	111,713
Central America............	111,460	20,702
Colombia..................	111,460	126,216
Ecuador..................	308,100	165,650
Peru..................	7,516,657	7,493,399
Bolivia..................	345,808	5,850,683
Brazil.	112,969	187,612
Uruguay..................	189,756	190,418
Argentine Republic.......	48,735	87,094
Ship-stores..................	618,434	152,635
Total..................	$37,122,460	$38,810,271

From the foregoing table it is observed that the value of the exports was greater by more than $1,500,000 in 1873 than in 1872. The subjoined table sets forth the value of each of the principal commodities exported in the same biennial period:

COMMODITIES.	1872.	1873.
Agricultural products......	$14,946,407	$14,277,318
Home manufactures	734,184	466,393
Mining produce...........	17,820,993	16,291,028
Gold and silver coin.......	445,147	1,849,952
Bank-notes................	599,545	4,019,246
Total..................	$34,545,276	$36,903,937
Foreign goods reëxported..	2,577,184	1,906,334
Total exports..........	$37,122,460	$38,810,271

Here it is seen that the increase in 1873 was owing to larger shipments of coin and bank-notes, for in almost all the other articles there was a marked falling off in that year. The

extensive circulation of Chilian money abroad dates from the establishment of the National Bank of Bolivia.

The principal native manufactures sent out of the country are lamp-oil, boots and shoes, ox and horse carts, flour, matting, furniture, launches, sailcloth, etc.; boots and shoes being sometimes exported to the extent of $10,000 per annum, and carts to about the same amount.

The growth of the imports is still more striking than that of the exports, as will be seen in the annexed table, in which is also expressed the value of the imports from various countries in 1872 and 1873:

COUNTRIES.	1872.	1873.
France..................	$7,851,014	$6,742,790
England..................	15,453,466	18,475,116
Germany..................	3,815,133	4,167,926
Belgium..................	818,347	756,555
Holland..................	11,391	8,350
Spain..................	192,498	290,383
Portugal..................	2,296	9,425
Italy..................	209,409	268,957
China..................	19,845	127,644
Australia..................	22,986	......
Polynesia..................	111,425	67,561
United States..............	1,573,645	2,094,348
Central America..........	171,687	148,489
Colombia..................	1,792	21,199
Ecuador..................	85,005	84,716
Peru..................	3,088,040	216,344
Bolivia..................	62,725	221,346
Brazil..................	837,063	777,543
Uruguay..................	59,995	4,043
Paraguay..................	47,346	36,412
Argentine Republic.......	1,193,910	1,396,892
Fisheries	31,108	64,439
Total..................	$34,657,928	$37,928,427

The imports for the two years above referred to may be classified as follows, with the value of each class:

ARTICLES.	1872.	1873.
Fancy goods, includ'g wearing apparel, manufactured goods, etc., etc...........	$4,765,732	$5,311,013
Raw material, and articles, machinery, etc., for industrial purposes........	6,467,740	7,010,635
Articles used for food.....	6,052,423	6,535,607
Other articles, not included in either of the foregoing categories................	17,372,033	19,171,172
Total..................	$34,657,928	$37,928,427

In 1873 the increase in the commodities more extensively imported was about 12 per cent., while in others it was only 10 per cent. The figures of the preceding tables indicate an improvement of rather more than 7 per cent. in the imports for 1873, and of a fraction less than 5 per cent. in the exports. But a noticeable fact is, that the annual increase of exports has been in about the same ratio (5 per cent.) during the thirty years 1844–'73; and while they not only did not begin to preponderate until the middle of that period, but were, in the mean, fully one per cent. less than the imports, they have, since 1859, in which year they were considerably greater than the imports, steadily and progressively kept the lead, and their relative increase as compared to these has been as 7 to 5, approximately, viz.:

YEARS.	Imports.	Exports.	Total.
1844.........	$8,596,674	$6,087,023	$14,683,697
1845.........	9,104,764	7,601,523	16,706,287
1846.........	10,149,136	8,115,288	18,264,424
1847.........	10,068,849	8,442,085	18,510,934
1848.........	8,601,357	8,253,595	16,954,952
1849.........	10,722,840	10,603,447	21,326,287
1850.........	11,788,193	12,426,269	24,214,462
1851.........	15,884,972	12,146,391	28,031,363
1852....... ..	15,347,332	14,087,556	29,434,888
1853.........	11,553,696	12,138,779	23,692,475
1854.........	17,428,299	14,527,156	31,955,455
1855.........	18,433,287	19,180,589	37,613,876
1856.........	19,804,041	18,159,522	37,963,563
1857.........	20,196,968	19,778,150	39,975,118
1858.........	18,186,292	18,335,442	36,521,734
1859.........	18,395,654	19,559,254	37,954,908
1860.........	22,171,506	25,451,279	47,622,785
1861.........	16,676,314	20,349,634	37,025,948
1862.........	17,226,655	21,994,432	39,221,087
1863.........	20,487,517	20,118,852	40,606,369
1864.........	18,867,365	27,242,853	46,110,218
1865.........	21,240,976	25,712,623	46,953,599
1866.........	18,757,345	26,680,510	45,437,855
1867.........	24,863,473	30,686,930	55,550,403
1868.	25,839,801	29,518,817	55,358,618
1869.........	27,232,218	27,725,778	54,957,996
1870.........	28,224,139	26,975,819	55,199,958
1871.........	26,631,880	31,981,693	58,613,573
1872.........	34,657,928	37,122,460	71,780,388
1873.........	37,928,427	38,810,271	76,738,698
Total......	$565,067,898	$599,914,020	$1,164,981,918

A review of this last table likewise shows the increase of the entire foreign trade of the republic in the first fifteen years to have been in the ratio of 2½ to 1, and of about 2 $\frac{1}{16}$ to 1 in the other fifteen years; and that the mean annual increase during the latter half was nearly 8 per cent.

It is, however, to be kept in view that the great excess of the exports over the imports is due to the immense quantities of money—gold and silver coin, and bank-notes, especially the last—sent out of the country. The value of the coin exported in 1844 was $155,370; in 1854, $945,317; in 1864, $936,844; and in 1873, $1,849,956; and, in the thirty years 1844–'73, $19,883,992, or an average of $666,356 per annum. The total value of the mining produce of every description exported during the same thirty years, reached $369,440,092, of which $135,983,641 was for copper in bars.

The decline in the exportation of agricultural produce in 1873 is not attributable to any dwindling in the productiveness of the country, but to a decreased demand in the markets hitherto chiefly dependent on Chili, and now drawing their supplies from other foreign sources or from home industry. For instance, in 1868, the Argentine Republic and Uruguay took Chilian wheat to the amount of $235,-695, and flour to $649,734; while in 1873 they imported but $33,443 worth of the former, and $119,153 of the latter article. Both of those Plate republics now export wheat, Uruguay having sent wheat and flour to Brazil of the value of $151,200 in 1872.

Besides the causes of depression just referred to, there were others of a different character, such as the financial crisis, which proved so disastrous in the United States in 1873, and whose effects were sensibly felt in every mercantile community on the globe.

Notwithstanding the abundant yield of the coal-mines of Coronel and Lota, which in 1872 reached 3,087,000 metrical quintals, prodigious quantities of that article are still brought from England to Chili. The imports, in 1872, amounted to $418,483, and to $1,006,529 in 1873, spite of the enhanced price of coal in that year—23, 33, and even 45 shillings per ton. What more convincing proof could be adduced of the industrial prosperity of the republic, of the development (unprecedented in South America) of her manufactures, foundries, and railways, and of steam navigation on her coasts?

Respecting exports, the following changes are to be noted: Those to France decreased 2.18 per cent.; to Belgium, 10 per cent.; to Ecuador, 86 per cent.; and others too unimportant to be mentioned. Those to Great Britain increased 3 per cent.; to Germany, 1.57 per cent.; to the United States, 2.25 per cent.; to the Argentine Republic, 79 per cent.; to Bolivia, 70 per cent.; to Brazil, 66 per cent.; and to the Cape of Good Hope, 87 per cent. Peru, Polynesia, Colombia, and Uruguay, received, with but slight difference, the same amounts as in 1872.

Interior maritime commerce is still increasing rapidly, the excess of last year over 1872—$7,010,598, an increase of 20 per cent.—being superior to all its predecessors. During the first quinquennium, 1864–'68, the total value of the coasting-trade amounted to $149,150,720; and during 1869–'73 to $183,628,799, an increase of 23 per cent. This trade amounted, in the decade 1864–'73, to $332,779,519.

Here follows a statement of the shipping movements at all the Chilian ports:

FLAGS.	ENTERED.		CLEARED.	
	No. of Vessels.	Tons.	No. of Vessels.	Tons.
British............	2,625	2,811,678	2,599	2,800,290
French............	173	145,216	175	145,268
German............	154	78,861	152	77,290
Italian...	135	49,448	130	45,327
Russian............	2	1,255	2	1,255
Swedish	10	3,852	9	3,320
Norwegian........	9	3,395	12	5,951
Belgian............	4	2,459	6	3,647
Danish............	7	3,678	7	3,572
Dutch............	9	3,423	9	3,423
United States.....	429	123,584	411	121,262
Polynosian........	4	701	3	229
Salvadorian.......	24	9,102	19	8,282
Colombian.........	3	1,710	3	1,710
Guatemalan.......	390	136,743	397	133,035
Nicaraguan.......	484	130,855	477	126,614
Peruvian..........	46	19,011	44	17,670
Bolivian...........	2	275	1	140
Uruguayan........	134	28,098	134	28,098
Chilian............	1,293	501,450	1,280	492,593
Total.........	5,937	4,059,809	5,860	4,018,976

The movement of the port of Valparaiso may be thus stated:

		Vessels.		Tons.
Entered	{ Sailing-vessels...	989,	aggregating...	432,945
	Steamers.........	595	"	541,581
Cleared	{ Sailing-vessels...	980	"	421,494
	Steamers.........	596	"	540,249
Total................		3,160		1,536,318

The Chilian merchant navy comprised, in

1878, 52 sailing-vessels of all rigs, 28 steamers, and 2 steam-tugs; total tonnage, 19,164.

The sources and amount of the national revenue for 1872, about one-half of which is commonly derived from customs, are shown in the following table:

REVENUE.

Customs...	$7,875,768
State railways......................................	1,975,677
Monopolies (tobacco, playing-cards, etc.).....	1,524,857
Tax on the sale of real estate...................	689,463
Real-estate tax.....................................	648,035
Patent-rights.......................................	375,855
Sale of guano.......................................	300,000
Post-office..	38,346
Telegraphs..	25,473
Sundries...	643,986
	$13,594,410

Here follow the items of the national

EXPENDITURE.

Ministry of the Interior...........................	$4,895,089
Ministry of Foreign Affairs, etc................	305,893
Ministry of Justice, etc..........................	2,123,193
Ministry of Finance................................	6,080,561
Ministry of War....................................	2,171,810
Ministry of the Navy..............................	1,033,137
	$16,609,183

The deficit of $3,014,773 is to be accounted for probably by an increased outlay for railways. The estimated budgets for 1873 and 1874 were respectively:

Revenue......For 1873, $14,000,000; for 1874, $14,260,810
Expenditure..For 1873, $13,364,450; for 1874, $16,009,183

The following table exhibits the state of the public debt on January 1, 1873:

DEBTS.	Capital.	Interest.	Appropriation, 1871.
HOME DEBT.			
Three per cent., 1865...	$3,150,775	$94,523	$34,600
Eight per cent., 1865...	2,323,000	196,784	135,900
Meiggs loan, at 6 pr. ct..	1,472,000	93,840	92,000
Garland loan, at 6 pr. ct.	1,288,000	78,540	21,000
On real estate, 3@5 p. c.	7,925,247	345,219	......
Other debts	757,000	......	......
Total............	$16,916,022	$808,906	$283,500
FOREIGN DEBT.			
Loan of 1842, at 3 pr. ct.	1,704,000	54,360	108,000
Loan of 1848, at 4½ "	6,122,000	275,585	165,500
Loan of 1870, at 5 "	4,797,500	245,400	110,500
Loan of 1867, at 6 "	8,872,500	547,500	252,500
Loan of 1866, at 7 "	4,785,000	346,220	161,000
Total............	$26,281,000	$1,469,015	759,500
Loan of 1873, at 3 pr. ct.	10,700,000	....	......
Total public debt..	$53,897,022	$2,277,921	$1,081,000

The following is a comparative statement of the receipts of the custom-house at Valparaiso during the first ten months of 1872 and 1873:

MONTHS.	1872.	1873.
January......................	$298,572 06	$353,417 17
February...................	506,000 89	467,674 78
March......................	545,950 89	684,085 56
April......................	524,472 27	737,134 89
May........................	514,361 10	605,911 72
June........................	498,501 17	601,494 28
July........................	522,859 52	588,153 37
August.....................	244,875 19	848,886 25
September.................	496,677 06	542,346 87
October....................	460,427 85	559,608 55
Total................	$5,112,697 51	$5,981,982 94
Increase in favor of 1873..	....	$876,285 43

The Senate refused to grant a subsidy of $100,000 for the Transandine Telegraph.

The lines of railway in operation at the beginning of 1874 were the same as those enumerated in the ANNUAL CYCLOPÆDIA for 1873, page 112. (For details of the projected Transandino railway from Valparaiso to Buenos Ayres, *see* page 34 of this volume.)

There are 3,177 miles of telegraph open in the republic, of which 1,951 miles, with 52 offices, belong to the state.

The post-office returns for 1871 and 1872 show the following statistics:

MAIL MATTER.	1871.	1872.
Letters...................	4,367,218	4,807,589
Samples..................	10,398	9,977
Printed matter............	7,171,559	5,614,858
Total................	11,549,175	10,432,424

A new penal code, submitted to Congress for approval toward the end of 1873, was reported to be of a nature to completely revolutionize the criminal law of the republic. One important feature therein, providing for the peaceful exercise of religious worship by all sects, and deciding the clergy to be amenable to the civil authority, greatly alarmed the clerical party, and a petition against the sanctioning the law, signed by the archbishop and two of his bishops, was presented to the Senate. Indeed, the spirit of discord caused by the Ultramontane party in Europe, followed by the attempt to override the supremacy of the law in Brazil, has extended itself to Chili. Public feeling, however, appears to be too strong for the clerical party, and it is expected the bill will pass, after which there will probably be more peace and quietness in the community. Chili has long suffered from this infliction, being in every other respect liberally and quietly governed. It was only after the achievement of independence that the right of sepulture was allowed to foreigners.

An archiepiscopal pastoral was issued in October, excommunicating *latæ sententiæ* the voters for the amendments in the denounced code, and extending to all magistrates who might enforce the new law.

The President's message to Congress was exceedingly brief, being merely the announcement that peace reigned undisturbed in all parts of the republic, and the expression of the hope that the question of separation of Church and state might soon be disposed of, to the interest of the country.

Few states in South America more quietly pursue the even tenor of their way than Chili; and yet it is proverbial for its steady progress in all industrial enterprises, for the absence of political perturbation, and for its punctuality in meeting its financial engagements. Its securities rank among the foremost on the London Stock Exchange, being usually held for investment; it builds its own railways and its own telegraphs without much foreign help;

and the money it borrows for such purposes is secured by national and private bonds.

An excellent sign of the times for Chili is the general tendency manifested by the people to abandon mining, and devote their attention to agriculture.

Spite of very unfavorable weather, the crops were, in most of the provinces, very abundant; but the general health has been unusually bad. A treaty of limits has been entered into by the representatives of Chili and Bolivia, by the terms of which the boundary fixed between the two states is the 24th parallel of south latitude; with an understanding that, should any question arise as to the exact position of Caracoles, or any other mining region, it shall be determined by a commission of surveyors appointed by both Governments. It is further stipulated that Chili shall receive indemnification for any loss sustained by this arrangement, the amount of which to be determined by arbitration. As respects the interest of Chili, jointly with Bolivia, in the customs up to the date of the contract, it is to be determined in the same manner, the arbitrator being the Emperor of Brazil. Bolivia renounces, for its part, all claims to the possession of mines lying to the south of latitude 24°, and undertakes not to increase its export duties, but to allow the free entry of Chilian products. Chili will, further, be entitled to half of the proceeds derived from the sale of Mejillones guano.

These are, briefly, the principal stipulations of the treaty, and it will be seen that they are clearly of the nature of a compromise. Neither party has insisted on theoretical rights, but has sensibly arrived at a settlement in view of substantial and practical considerations, an example worthy of imitation by the other republics, in the solution of similar boundary difficulties, and it may reasonably be hoped that, in the case of Chili and the Argentine Republic, the same spirit of cordiality will be manifested with reference to the conflicting claims to sovereign jurisdiction in Patagonia.

The railway had worked a wonderful change in the city of Concepcion. New buildings were springing up in all directions, and a new face was being put upon old ones. Extraordinary activity, in comparison to that of prerailway times, was everywhere observable.

CHINA, an empire in Asia; reigning Emperor, T'oung-chê, formerly called Ki-tsiang, "High Prosperity," born April 27, 1856, the eldest son of the Emperor Hieng-fun, "Perfect Bliss;" succeeded to the throne at the death of his father, August 21, 1861; became of age, and assumed the government in 1873. He was married on October 16, 1872, to Alootay, daughter of the Vice-rector of the Peking Academy, Chungchi.

The area and the population of China cannot at present be accurately stated, as parts of the western dependencies have successfully established their independence, while other portions,

especially the district of Kooltsha, have been incorporated with Russia. Although the new frontiers cannot, as yet, be accurately defined, it is assumed that at least 500,000 square miles of the former possessions of China were, in 1873, entirely lost to the imperial Government. Another large tract of land, in the southwestern part of China proper, which for many years had been in the hands of the Mohammedan Panthays, was, in the latter months of the year 1872, and in the beginning of 1873, entirely recovered. The total area of China is now roughly estimated at 3,970,000 square miles, of which 1,553,000 belong to China proper, and the remainder to the several dependencies. China proper is very densely peopled, the population amounting in 1812, according to an official census, to 367,000,000; in 1842, to 414,000,000; and in 1852, to 450,000,000, or 347 inhabitants per square mile. Since 1852, the population is believed to have somewhat decreased in consequence of the bloody civil wars and famines; and in 1874 it was estimated (Behm and Wagner, "Bevölkerung der Erde," II., 1874) at 404,000,000. The dependencies of China, embracing Mantchooria, Mongolia, Thibet, and Corea, though their area largely exceeds that of China proper, have a population of only about 20,200,000.

The population of the ports which, in virtue of the treaties concluded with foreign nations, were opened to the foreign trade, were, according to the latest dates, as follows:

CITIES.	Population.	Foreigners.
Peking..........................	1,648,814	....
Canton	1,000,000	806
Tien-tsin..........................	930,000	127
Hankow..........................	800,000	130
Foochow	600,000	206
Ningpo..........................	400,000	140
Shanghai..........................	276,640	2,074
Takao..........................	230,000	....
Amoy..........................	300,000	157
Chinkiang..........................	130,000	....
Newchuang..........................	70,000	....
Tamsui..........................	50,000	....
Kiukiang..........................	50,000	....
Swatow..........................	45,000	128
Cheefoo....	......	157

According to the official reports of the Chinese Government in 1872, the number of foreigners in the several treaty-ports was as follows:

British	1,771	Swedes	34
Americans	541	Italians............	24
Germans.....	481	Austrians............	22
French............	239	Belgians	5
Spaniards............	59	States without a treaty	346
Dutch	56		
Russians............	48		3,661
Danes	35		

The two highest boards of state officers are the Board of Secretaries of State, and the Council of State. The former has six members, four of whom have the title of Actual Secretaries of State, and two of Under-Secretaries. One-half of each class are Mantchoos and one-half Chinese. It is the duty of this board to consult on the administration of the country, to proclaim the imperial will, to regulate the laws of the state, and, in general, to assist the Emperor in the administration of the country. Of late, this board has lost much of its former influence, and the administration of the empire is chiefly conducted by the Council of State. This board is composed of the imperial princes, the Secretaries of State, the Presidents of the Ministries, and the chiefs of other branches of administration. It has the duty of drawing up the imperial decrees and decisions, and adopting such resolutions as are necessary for an effective and well-regulated administration. Subordinate to the Secretaries of State, and the Council of the Empire, are six ministries or executive departments, at the head of each of which are two presidents and four vice-presidents (one-half Mantchoos and one-half Chinese). Some departments, like those of War, of Justice, and of Public Works, have, moreover, a chief president. Other boards, dependent upon the Secretaries of State and the Imperial Council, are, the Colonial Ministry, the Board of Censors, and the Peking or Imperial Academy. The Colonial Ministry is charged with the administration of Mongolia and other Chinese dependencies. The Board of Censors consists of two chief censors, of four assistants, and from forty to fifty censors. It is a kind of Court of Revision and Appeal. Its members have the right to bring to the knowledge of the Emperor any remonstrances against administrative measures, and even to criticise imperial decrees. A department of Foreign Affairs was established in 1860, and consists of the Presidents of the Executive Departments.

The public revenue is mostly derived from three sources, namely, customs, licenses, and a tax upon land. The aggregate revenue of the Government is estimated at $200,000,000 taels (1 tael = $1.61). The receipts from the customs of the treaty-ports have been regularly published since 1861. The customs duties fall more upon exports than imports; their total produce at the treaty-ports amounted, in 1871, to 11,216,000 Haikuan taels; in 1872, to 11,678,636; in 1873, to 10,977,082. China has, as yet, no foreign debt; it is not known

whether the Government has raised or is responsible for loans contracted at home.

The foreign commerce of China, from 1870 to 1873, was as follows (value expressed in taels):

YEAR.	Imports.	Exports.
1870	71,000,278	61,990,235
1871	78,190,033	74,860,550
1872	74,826,130	83,719,857
1873	73,992,063	77,540,919

The foreign commerce of the year 1872 was thus divided among the several foreign countries (value expressed in taels):

COUNTRIES.	Imports.	Exports.
Great Britain	29,186,000	43,022,000
Hong-Kong	23,364,000	13,441,000
East Indies	18,489,000	458,000
United States	410,000	13,280,000
Japan	3,148,000	1,461,000
European Continent	890,000	4,849,000
Australia	496,000	2,387,000
Singapore	808,000	459,000
Siam	455,000	165,000
Philippines	225,000	207,000
Java	239,000	382,000
Cochin-China	510,000	127,000
Amoor Territory	214,000	44,000
Siberia	15,000	1,899,000
Russia Codessa	39,000	1,017,000
Other countries	178,000	463,000
Total	78,066,000	83,720,000
Reëxported	3,240,000	
	74,826,000	

The principal articles of imports and exports were, in 1872 and 1873, as follows (value expressed in taels):

IMPORTS.	1872.	1873.
Opium	27,653,000	29,030,000
Cotton goods	25,407,000	21,540,000
Woolen goods	4,795,000	5,950,000
Raw cotton	2,329,000	
Metals	3,611,000	3,100,000
Coal	1,229,000	
Rice	1,093,000	
Sea-grass	1,084,000	
Black tea	33,504,000	52,500,000
Green tea	10,276,000	
Silk, raw	27,719,000	27,780,000
Silk goods	2,607,000	
Sugar	1,505,000	

The movement of shipping in the Chinese ports, from 1871 to 1873, was as follows (entrances and clearances combined):

FLAG.	Vessels.	Tons.	Vessels.	Tons.	Vessels.	Tons.
British	7,160	3,380,881	8,360	3,954,130	6,955	3,645,557
American	4,600	3,187,648	5,14	3,471,293	5,001	3,483,203
German	1,480	428,747	1,976	607,948	1,702	492,033
French	277	135,829	225	164,316	189	151,233
Siamese	115	45,456	146	56,857	147	60,980
Danish	273	59,371	221	51,367	195	51,448
Swedish and Norwegian	218	45,884	209	50,346	131	29,368
Chinese	474	30,013	545	36,117	865	207,118
Russian	86	34,340	81	33,068	69	49,693
Spanish	50	18,454	79	23,959	48	16,727
Netherlands	203	59,791	82	21,672	55	12,368
Other	25	5,148	42	15,370	81	27,526
Total	14,963	9,381,557	17,090	8,486,473	15,381	8,227,754

The Peking *Gazette* of December 15, 1873, contains imperial decrees which confirm the report that had been current of a success obtained by the troops under Tso Tsung-tang, over the Mohammedan insurgents in Kansuh. The achievement turns out to be no less than the capture of the city of Su-chow, in the extreme northwest of Kansuh, which has for ten years past been in the hands of insurgents. It is the last remaining stronghold hitherto occupied by the Mohammedans " within the wall," and its recovery therefore is a matter of great importance to the Imperial Government.

In the southwestern province of Yunnan the Mohammedan rebellion of the Panthays had been fully suppressed in 1873. A weak remainder, which had survived the downfall of the empire, was crushed out in the course of the year 1874. The chief, Yahsakon, when the Chinese had surrounded Usar, the last place held by the Panthays, fled with about 200 companions into a pagoda, where he was compelled by hunger to surrender. He was executed, with the majority of his companions, and his head carried about in the province as a warning. The Chinese rule in the province of Yunnan is now fully reëstablished.

The efforts of the Chinese Government in behalf of a suppression of the coolie-trade obtained toward the close of the year 1873 an important success. The Portuguese Governor of Macao, Count de San Januario, on December 27, 1873, announced in the official gazette of Macao that, in virtue of a new treaty between Portugal and China, the shipment of Chinese coolies from Macao would be forbidden from and after January 27, 1874. The measure caused great excitement in Macao, as the coolie-trade has been for many years the most important business of this city, and more than 195,000 coolies have been shipped from it since 1852. The *China Mail* stated that many brokers who had received advances had their agreements canceled. The "fantan" houses, with one or two exceptions, closed their doors, and many of the barracoon-men were dismissed. It was expected that upward of 300 houses were to be vacated, and some 40,000 persons would be thrown out of employment. The Chinese Government present-

CITY OF HONG-KONG.

ed the Governor of Macao, the master of the port, and the deputy of Macao in the Portuguese Cortes, with gold medals as a mark of its recognition. The stoppage of the coolie-trade at Macao compelled the Government of Peru, which cannot do without coolie-labor, to negotiate with the Government of China a treaty for the regulation of the voluntary emigration of coolies. Aided by the representative of England in Peking, the envoy of Peru, Garcia, succeeded in prevailing upon the Chinese Government to order the Governor-General of Tien-tsin, Li Hung Chang, as superintendent of the commerce with foreign nations, to conclude a treaty with Peru. The treaty was completed and signed by the representa-

tives of the two Governments on June 26th. It consists of a convention deed of a treaty proper. In the former Peru concedes to China the right to send a commission to Peru for the protection of the coolies, and promises to this commission protection by the Peruvian authorities. The coolies now in the service of Peruvians are notified by official proclamations that they may bring forward any complaints against their employers. These complaints are to be investigated by the court in open session. If they prove to be well founded, the employers are informed that, unless they redress the complaints, their contract with the employés will be annulled. The coolies whose contract expires are called upon to declare whether they desire to return to China or not. To those coolies who desire to return, the Government guarantees a free passage, either compelling those employers who engaged to send the coolies back to China, to fulfill their contracts, or in the other cases defraying itself the necessary expenses. The treaty proper consists of nineteen articles; the first five regulate the mutual diplomatic representation at Peking and Lima, the appointment of consular agents in the treaty-ports, the tariff, etc. The emigration of Chinese to Peru is to be entirely voluntary, and every kind of force and fraud is to be punished. Peru promises to appoint official interpreters in all working districts, and to deal out impartial justice to all Chinese complainants in case the Chinese consuls in Peru are unable to adjust the difficulty. The Peruvians in China are under the jurisdiction of Peruvian consuls. The treaty is drawn up in Spanish, Chinese, and English; and in cases of doubtful meaning the English text is to be regarded as decisive. The treaty is to remain in force for ten years; if changes are then to be made, they must be announced six months before the expiration of the treaty; if no such announcement is made, the treaty remains in force for ten years more.

In October a dangerous conspiracy was discovered among the Chinese soldiery at Tientsin. Rumors of the most alarming character were in circulation among the foreign community, and a general feeling of insecurity was everywhere manifest. The district of Tientsin, since in 1873, has been the scene of great military activity. It is estimated that ever since that time there have been from 20,000 to 60,000 troops within two days' march of Tien-tsin. These troops are principally from Honan, and constitute the flower of the army of the Governor-General, Li Hung Chang. They are strangers in this province, but none the less masters of the soil, and they live on the fat of the land. It was not, then, a matter of surprise that these vagabonds, weary of inactivity, corrupted by idleness and lust, and restrained by no power but their own will, should engage in any game, however desperate. The leader of the revolt was supposed to be General Whang, who was thought to possess the confidence of large numbers of officers and southern troops at present without employment. A number of the rebels were arrested by order of Li Hung Chang, whose fidelity to foreigners was not doubted. One of the rebels confessed that the object of their attack was to plunder Tien-tsin, and to kill all the foreigners. The Chinese said that the organization was not political, being got up by a band of bad characters for purposes of looting. The local authorities professed ignorance of the movement. Three gunboats were at the time at Tien-tsin, and the consuls asked for reenforcements.

The expedition undertaken by the Government of Japan against the native tribes of the island of Formosa (*see* JAPAN), in order to punish them for acts of piracy against Japanese subjects, led to serious complications between Japan and China, as Formosa is claimed by the Government of China as a part of its dominions. It belongs to the province of Fuhkien, has an area of 14,982 square miles, and a population of about 3,000,000. The western and most fertile part of the island is inhabited by Chinese colonists, who have emigrated to the island in large numbers during the last two or three centuries. The eastern and mountainous part is virtually independent of Chinese rule, and is inhabited by a copper-colored race of barbarians, who number only about 20,000, but have thus far defied the Chinese authorities. They were in the habit of killing all the shipwrecked crews thrown on their shores. Thus, in 1867, the captain and crew of the American vessel Rover * were killed, and, as the Chinese authorities failed to give the desired satisfaction, Admiral Bell, the commander of the United States squadron in the Chinese waters, sent an expedition against the savages, which, however, did not meet with the expected success. Subsequently General Legendre, United States consul at Amoy, had an interview with Toketok, the head-chief of the southern savages of Formosa, and concluded with him a kind of treaty, in which the savages promised to spare in future the lives of shipwrecked persons and to surrender them for ransom. For several years the treaty seems to have been adhered to; but, of late years, Japanese fishers were repeatedly massacred by them. Thus, in 1873, fifty natives of a group of islands belonging to Japan were killed by them. An envoy was sent to China to demand satisfaction. He was admitted with the representatives of the European powers to an audience with the young Emperor, but was unable to obtain the redress demanded, as Prince Kung, the head of the Foreign Department, replied that the Chinese Government had not sufficient control of the southern portion of Formosa to be able to reach and punish the guilty. The Japanese Government then concluded to take the punishment of the savages into its own hands, and in May, 1874, sent against Formosa an expedition, which was a brilliant success. As the Japanese showed an inclination to occupy part of the island permanently, the Chinese Governor of Formosa issued a proclamation, in which he said: "The Japanese have come into our land to make war against the tribe of the Bootans for having murdered some of the natives of the Lieuchew Islands. They have taken revenge; but, as the army of invasion does not appear willing to leave the island, the Emperor has sent two high officers to command the Japanese to go home. While the negotiations with the Japanese general are pending, they have commanded the native tribes to lay down their arms." At an interview held in Formosa, in June, between

* *See* AMERICAN ANNUAL CYCLOPÆDIA for 1867, Art. CHINA.

the Japanese General Saigo and a Chinese envoy, Shen-pao-Chen, the latter, apparently upon ample authority, acceded to the requirements of the Japanese general. On his return home his action was repudiated by the Peking Government, and the attitude of China became very threatening. The governors-general of the Chinese provinces made preparations for war, and would have carried out their plans if Prince Kung, by opening direct diplomatic negotiations, had not got the further treatment of the Formosa difficulty into his own hands. The prince seemed to fear that an unsuccessful war might raise the turbulent elements in the country against the Mantchoo dynasty. He was aware that China was any thing but prepared for a serious war. The army was in a most disorderly state, the coolies sent to be trained in the use of Krupp guns simply asked for their pay and then went back again, the ships-of-war would probably be unable to leave their harbors, and the soldiers refused to go on board the transports which were to take them to Formosa. Moreover, the Chinese feared the Japanese iron-clads, especially since the failure of the negotiations for the purchase of the Danish monitor Rolf Krake. The purchase of arms and the appointment of two Frenchmen as military advisers could not at once make the army efficient, at least so far as the men and the system were concerned.

At one time the war party appeared to be in the ascendant. An imperial decree of September 10th declared Prince Kung to have forfeited the title of the First Prince of the Empire, on the ground that, in the interviews with the Emperor, he had neglected the respect due to the person of the Emperor. An edict of September 11th revoked, however, that of September 10th, but adds that it was hoped that Prince Kung would heed the warning. Negotiations for peace were resumed, and terminated in October in the conclusion of a convention between the two Governments, which fully secured the continuance of peace.

The first bona fide Chinese telegraph has at length been commenced. The Viceroy of Fuh-kien, in July, began (with the assistance of the Great Northern Telegraph Company) a line from Pagoda anchorage to Foochow.

On May 3d a serious riot took place at Shanghai against the French. It was occasioned by a resolution of the Municipal Council of the French residents to build a street through a piece of land containing a former cemetery of natives of the province of Ningpo.* The mob set fire to several houses, plundered, committed acts of violence against several persons, and finally attacked the hall of the French municipality, in which a large number of foreigners had assembled. To the great dissatisfaction of the majority of his countrymen and of the

* It is common for the natives of the several provinces of China to have in each of the large cities special clubs, religious meeting-houses, and cemeteries in which the poor are interred, the corpses of the wealthy being generally sent to their birthplaces.

other foreigners, the French consul not only took no steps for the protection of his countrymen, but at once yielded to the representations of the Chinese authorities in the dispute relative to the road interfering with the Ningpo graves. The rioters, who had been arrested, were surrendered to the Chinese authorities for punishment, and quiet was restored.

A request of the Embassadors of England and France, that Messrs. Wade and Geoffroy be admitted on the Chinese New-Year's day to another solemn audience with the Emperor, was refused. The English press, in the Chinese treaty-ports, was all the more indignant at this refusal, as on May 20th the representative of Russia, Bützov, was admitted to an audience, which was moreover officially announced in the Peking Gazette. A request from the Government of the United States for a removal of the sand-bank near Wosung, which debars large vessels from entering the Yang-tse River, was also refused.

According to reports from Corea, a great political change has taken place in this vassal-kingdom. The Regent Li, who had married the widow of the deceased King and seized all power, who had repulsed the invasions of the French and American expeditions, derided the Japanese, and shown himself decidedly opposed to any intercourse with foreign nations, has been deposed in consequence of a revolution. The young King is reported to be more liberal, and even to be favorable to opening a port to the foreign trade.

The English projects for establishing a direct trade-road and a railway between the south-western province of Yunnan and Burmah have, according to the well-known Chinese traveler, Baron F. von Richthofen, but little prospect of success. On the other hand, the efforts of the Frenchman Dupuis (see ANNUAL CYCLOPÆDIA, 1873, p. 120), to use the Songha, or river of Tongkin, as a trade-road to Yunnan, promise, in his opinion, a better result. The best route for establishing railroad connection between China and Europe is, according to Richthofen, a road from Shanghai, via Singan-fu and Hami, to Kooldja. (See "Verhandlungen der Gesellschaft für Erdkunde zu Berlin," 1873, pp. 58–67, and 1874, pp. 115–126.)

CHRISTIANS. .I. CHRISTIAN CONNECTION. —The statisticians of the Christian Connection declare that the reports of conference clerks are so different in character, and often so imperfect, that it is impossible to harmonize them in a tabulated statement, or to make any item complete. Instead of such statement, the following general summary is given in the Christian Almanac for 1875: Number of ordained ministers, 1,197; number of unordained ministers, 210; number of members reported during the year 1873, 64,760; number of members not reported in 1873, 903; number of members added during the year, 4,038; total numbers reported, 69,701. It was thought that full returns from all the conferences, if they could be had, would show the increase of member-ship during the year to have been not less than 12,000. Fifteen churches had been dedicated, and thirteen churches remodeled and repaired, during the year. One of the leading clergymen of the Christians, in answer to the inquiries of the officers of the census, has given the following estimate for the denomination as a whole in the United States: church organizations, 1,100; church edifices, 1,050; sittings in the churches, 100,000; value of church property, $735,000.

It is estimated that the Christians and Disciples of Christ together have 3,578 church organizations, 2,822 church edifices, 865,602 sittings and $6,425,137 of church property.

The biennial session of the Christian Publishing Association was held in Dayton, Ohio, June 23d and 24th. The treasurer reported his receipts to June 23, 1874, to have been $15,544.94, and his disbursements, $16,064.02; leaving a balance due him of $519.08. He estimated the value of the assets of the Association under his control to be $33,383, and the amount of its liabilities, $11,469.08. The office agent reported the value of the stock, accounts, and cash, under his control, to be $11,-684.45, and the liabilities of the office to be $4,325.19. The receipts of the office to June 22d had been $12,148.67. Combining the reports of the two officers, the auditing committee found the entire assets of the Association to be $42,123.93, and its liabilities, $15,794.19, leaving a balance over indebtedness of $26,-329.74.

The institution formerly known as the Wolfborough Christian Institute, at Wolfborough, N. H., has been removed to Andover, N. H., and renamed the Proctor Academy.

The report on Sunday-schools made to the Quadrennial Convention, October 6th, showed that about 150,000 scholars were attending the Sunday-schools connected with the church, and that about 40,000 copies of the *Sunday-school Herald* were taken.

The quadrennial session of the *American Christian Convention* began at Stanfordville, Dutchess County, N. Y., October 6th. The Rev. J. H. Coe, of New Bedford, Mass., presided. Visiting delegates were received from the Disciples of Christ, and a strong feeling was shown on the occasion in favor of a closer union of Christian bodies. A prominent feature of the proceedings was the dedication of the Biblical Institute at Stanfordville. This institution was formerly situated at Eddytown, Yates County, N. Y. It had been removed two years before the present meeting of the convention to Stanfordville, where sixty acres of land had been bought for it, at a cost of $18,000. The Institute building and a students' home had been erected by the Hon. David Clark, of Hartford, Conn., at a cost stated to have been between $20,000 and $30,000, and were presented to the Convention as his free gift. The Institute was organized and in oper-

ation, with a full faculty and a respectable body of students. The trustees have adopted a rule prohibiting the smoking or chewing of tobacco within any of the buildings or upon the premises. The advantages of tuition, the use of class-books and the library, and, in the case of students without families, the occupancy of a lodging-room and study-room in the students' home, are offered in this institution free "to any worthy man or woman devoted to the gospel ministry."

The following resolutions on the subject of Christian union were unanimously adopted by the convention:

Resolved, That we urge our ministering brethren, so far as possible, to become associated with, or to organize branches of the Evangelical Alliance, and to attend general or branch conferences of the Alliance.

Resolved, In regard to our relations with other denominations seeking union with us, or our union with them, that we reaffirm our faith in Christ as the Great Head of the Church, in the Bible as the only authoritative standard of faith and duty, and in vital Christian piety as the true test of Christian fellowship, and that the very principles of union forbid any discrimination against conscientious followers of the Lord Jesus, because of differences of opinion concerning speculative theology, or the purpose and practice of Christian ordinances, or any interference with the liberty of individual churches in faith or fellowship, and demand constant and well-directed effort for harmony and union among all God's children.

Resolved, That recognizing the difficulties attending formal church union arising from present denominational affiliations, variations of church government, and the possession of vested property, we recommend our ministers to arrange frequent exchanges of pulpits, and to cultivate association and acquaintance with ministers of all denominations.

Resolved, That we cordially greet those churches which, casting off denominational affiliations, and resolving themselves into independent organizations, have made their fellowship Christian fellowship.

A resolution was also adopted extending sympathy and encouragement to the editors, publishers, and contributors of the *Church Union*, a religious journal published in the city of New York, and to other workers in the same cause, in their efforts to secure the unity of the Church. The subject of adjusting a basis of representation in the convention was discussed, but was deferred till the next quadrennial meeting. A new constitution was adopted for the ministerial Life Assurance Association.

II. CHRISTIAN CHURCH.—The General Convention of the *Christian Church* held its fourth quadrennial session at Graham, N. C., beginning May 1st. The Rev. W. B. Wellons presided. A special committee, consisting of the Rev. J. T. Whitley, Rev. John N. Manning, and Mr. John M. Moring, was appointed to consider and report upon the general subject of Christian union. The committee presented a report, recommending the adoption and circulation of a manifesto, setting forth the views and aims of the denomination as an organization. The report was unanimously adopted. The manifesto is as follows:

I. It is the steadfast belief of this body that Christ established but *one* Church, designing that all his followers, as members of that one body, should harmoniously work together for the salvation of the world. We are of opinion that the present division of the Church into sects, and the attitude of these sects toward each other, are offensive to God, detract from the glory of the Saviour, and impede the reformation of the world.

II. It is our belief that entire unanimity of opinion upon matters of theological doctrine and ecclesiastical polity is unattainable, so long as "we see through a glass darkly;" but that a unity of love, forbearance, and coöperation, is fully within the reach of all true Christians.

III. We hail with joy the wide-spread and increasing desire among God's people to come into a closer relationship with one another, manifested in such meetings as those of the Evangelical Alliance, and represented by many periodicals of the day. It pleases us to know that churches are springing into existence in various localities, composed of Christians who are tired of sectarian intolerance, and desire to manifest their essential unity; and that "doubtful disputations" are sinking into disuse, while the great points of faith, common to all Christians, are rising into due prominence.

IV. As an organization, it is the chief object of the Church we represent to bring together all true Christians upon a platform of mutual forbearance, common sympathies, and fraternal love. We therefore offer the hand of fraternal greeting to all true followers of our blessed Redeemer, assuring them of our profound interest in their welfare, and soliciting their kindly sympathies and prayers. Holding these views and aims, we hereby declare our desire to coöperate with any and all those who love our Lord Jesus Christ, in performing the great work he has assigned his Church. We have formed an organization merely to make our labors more effective; and we are ready to form a corporate union with any body of Christians upon the basis of those great doctrines which underlie the religion of Christ; clinging only to those fundamental truths without which Christianity could not exist, we are ready to submit all minor matters to the decision of the individual conscience.

V. We suggest that something like the following be adopted as a

BASIS OF UNION:

1. *Belief.*—1. In God, as our Creator and Law-Giver; 2. In Christ, as our Divine Mediator and Redeemer; 3. In the Holy Spirit, as our Comforter and Sanctifier; 4. In the Bible, as inspired by God, and the supreme standard of appeal in all matters of religion; 5. In the sinfulness and lost condition of man; 6. In the doctrine that salvation is a free gift of God, through Christ, and can be received and enjoyed only by faith; 7. That love to God and men is the whole duty of man; 8. That those who accept and obey the gospel in this world will be happy in the world to come—while those who reject the gospel in this life will be miserable forever.

2. The right to hold and express opinions not conflicting with the above articles of belief is freely conceded to each individual member of the Church.

3. Nothing more ought to be demanded as a prerequisite to admission into the Church than a credible profession of "repentance toward God and faith in our Lord Jesus Christ."

4. The body should be called by some name sanctioned by Scripture usage; either Christian Church, Church of Christ, or some other equally significant and appropriate.

VI. With a view to forming and cultivating fraternal relationships with all Christians who are likeminded with ourselves, we hereby invite correspondence from individual Christians, independent local churches, and other religious organizations.

III. CHRISTIAN CHURCH IN CANADA.—The Conference of the *Christian Church in Canada* met at Burnham, Ontario, September 16th. Nineteen ordained, and seven unordained ministers, were engaged in the work of the conference. Twenty churches were reported, with 900 members. The number of members was more than 100 less than were reported the previous year. The falling off was accounted for by the fact that one church had withdrawn from the connection, and one other church failed to make a report. It was thought that between 4,000 and 5,000 people in the Province of Ontario were in "full sympathy" with the denomination. The reports from the Sunday-schools showed a total of nearly 1,500 officers, teachers, and scholars.

CHRISTIAN UNION. I. CHURCH OF CHRIST OF THE CHRISTIAN UNION.—The following statistics of this denomination were presented at the meeting of the General Council in May: Number of preaching-places, 1,500; of churches, 1,000; of Sunday-schools, 500; of Sunday-school scholars, 25,000; of church homes, 300; value of church property, $150,000; number of protracted meetings held during the year, 1,600.

The fifth General Council of the Christian Union met near Wesley, Ind., May 27th. The Rev. J. V. B. Black, of Missouri, was chosen president or moderator. The following minute on fraternal relations was adopted:

Whereas, There is a tendency on the part of Protestant Christendom to set aside useless and dangerous dogmas and denominational hatreds, and to come closer together upon the essential principles of Christ: therefore—1. Be it known that we hail with glad hearts these signs of unity, and behold in them the hand of God leading men from darkness into the light. 2. We also discover, on the part of the leading clergymen of the United States and Europe, a ready and willing tendency toward a union of all who dwell in Christ. 3. We also hail with grateful emotions the expressions of prominent journals throughout the land, in which we find a manifest desire for the union of all Christians, as the Word of God provides. 4. We stand ready to fraternize with all who receive Christ as their only head; the Bible as their only rule; and good fruits as the only test of membership in the Church of Christ; pledging ourselves, through Christ who strengtheneth us to keep and observe these great principles of heavenly truth. 5. We extend greeting and cheer throughout Christendom to all who have engaged with us in this great reformation, and pray earnestly that God may hasten the time when all his children shall be one.

The Committee on the "State and Wishes of the Churches" reported that an encouraging degree of success had attended the labors of the Union through the churches of the different States, "to develop the oneness of the Church of Christ." They presented the "hope and object" of the free and sovereign churches represented in the Union to be—

1. To abate many of the evils now existing, by virtue of the encroachments upon the natural and gracious rights of conscience exhibited on the part of a professed church authority, existing outside of and above the Church, as founded and transmitted by Christ and his inspired apostles. 2. To exhibit

the practicability of maintaining a state of Christian order and effort inside of *Bible* authority and precedent. 8. To develop extended and general union, communion, and coöperation among all God's children upon the simple, soul-saving faith of the Gospel of Christ, without associating with it the necessity of an arbitrary concurrence in matters of opinion or speculative theology, about which Christians will, do, and may differ, without prejudice to their Christian standing or usefulness. 4. To recognize but one Church—the Church of Christ; having but one head—Christ, "whom God hath given to be head over all things for the church;" having but one rule of law and order—*the inspired Scriptures;* and but one condition of fellowship—"good fruits."

Resolutions were adopted declaring the circulation of the Word of God to be of paramount importance; advising the churches to coöperate with the American Bible Society in extending the circulation of the Scriptures without note or comment; giving a special warning "touching those translations made in the interests of certain sectarian dogmas;" and recommending "the use of, and adherence to, the common translation known as 'King James's.'"

The ministers were exhorted to urge upon the people the duty of living in accordance with the principles of temperance in all things, and themselves to set an example of temperance "by abstaining from all practices and habits that tend to intemperance in eating and drinking."

Sunday-schools were commended, while disapproval was expressed "of the worldly amusements practised by many of the Sunday-schools of the day, in order to render them attractive." It was declared a duty of all Christians to encourage and assist in giving a liberal education to children and youth. The Council also expressed its interest in the education of the ministry, particularly in the Holy Scriptures and Christian truth.

II. UNION CHRISTIAN CHURCHES.—The Ohio State Council of the Christian Union, at its annual meeting, held at Liberty Chapel, Hancock County, Ohio, in September, took the following action;

Whereas, It is very desirable that the mutual recognition and visible union of all genuine Christian Union people should be effected: therefore, to this end we recommend that this Council invite the Rev. J. B. Wellons, of the Christian Church South, to attend and bring with him two of his co-laborers; the Rev. George E. Thrall, editor of the *Church Union,* to attend and bring with him two of his co-laborers; the Rev. Thomas J. Mellish, of the Baptist denomination, to attend and bring with him two of his brethren; the Rev. W. McCune to attend and bring with him two of his Presbyterian brethren; to meet in the city of Cincinnati on the 21st of October, 1874, three delegates to be appointed by this Council to confer with them, in arranging, if possible, a union on the Bible as the common platform of a common Christianity.

The meeting was held at the appointed time and place, there being present as delegates the Rev. Messrs. J. W. Durant and P. P. Wolf and Mr. Virgil E. Shaw, on the part of the State Council of the Christian Union of Ohio; the Rev. George E. Thrall, the Rev. Thomas J.

VOL. XIV.—9 A

Mellish, with the Rev. John G. Fee, the Rev. W. McCune, with the Rev. J. A. P. McGaw, and Mr. J. W. Barber and the Rev. J. B. Wellons, D. D., the Rev. J. N. Manning, and Solomon Apple, of the Christian Church South; the Rev. W. McCune was chosen president of the convention. The meeting continued three days. A paper was adopted, entitled the "Basis of the Union Christian Churches of America." It begins with a preamble, declaring that—

In love to God, in faith unfeigned in Christ, in dependence upon the guidance of the Holy Spirit, in charity toward all Christians of every name, in obedience, as we believe, to the requirements of the New Testament, and in order to make manifest the always existing spiritual oneness of believers, and to promote the conversion of the world unto God, we submit to all Christians the following basis of visible Christian union:

Basis.—The Scriptures of the Old and New Testaments are an infallible revelation from God, and a sufficient rule of faith and practice.

This is followed by a list of "great truths of Scripture, held substantially in the same sense by evangelical ministers and churches, always and everywhere," each of which is supported and further defined by two or more texts quoted from the Bible. The points of doctrine thus announced and defined in the language of the Scriptures alone, are:

The unity of God; the nature, works, and attributes of God; Jesus Christ is God; Christ's incarnation and humanity; concerning the Holy Spirit; the universal sinfulness of man; Christ's death for sinners; justification by faith; regeneration and sanctification; repentance; obedience to the Gospel; good works necessarily grow from true faith; the law of love; the law of Christian forbearance; the right of private judgment; death and the resurrection; the judgment; endless rewards and punishments; the Church universal; the church of a city or place; qualifications of bishops or elders; qualifications of deacons; the duty of confessing Christ before men; baptism; the Lord's Supper; religious worship and the Sabbath, or the Lord's Day; discipline; a duty to try the spirit and to reject false teachers.

The following declaration was made respecting the reception of ministers, and appended to the *Basis:*

As evangelical ministers of the various orthodox denominations cordially recognize each other as ministers of Christ, notwithstanding denominational differences, so do we recognize them.

And inasmuch as Christ receives as his ministers those who are not of one mind concerning Calvinism or Arminianism; or as to Episcopal or Methodist Episcopal, or Congregational, or Presbyterian church government; or as to infant baptism or believer's baptism only; or as to immersion or sprinkling, or any other denominational peculiarity, neither do we require an assent to any denominational peculiarity as a condition of fellowship.

Whoever gives us scriptural evidence that Christ has received him as his minister, we will also receive to cordial and unrestricted fellowship in cheerful obedience to Christ.

But as Christ requires that his gospel shall be committed to "faithful men who shall be able to teach others also," and that his ministers shall "be able by sound doctrine both to exhort and to convince the gainsayers," we will require all ministers of the gospel asking our recognition and fellowship, whether called bishops or elders, and whether proposing to exercise the functions of pastors, evangelists, or teachers, to give satisfactory evidence that they receive substantially in their plain, evangelical sense the above-cited passages of Scripture.

We distinctly disclaim all intention to require an assent to any human modification of these Scriptures or any human inferences therefrom, and we affirm it to be our purpose only to acquire an assent to God's own truth expressed in God's own language, as it has been commonly received by Christ's ministers and people in all times and in all places.

A rule was adopted providing that ministers asking to be received shall be required, after a satisfactory conference, to answer affirmatively three questions, by which they will be committed to receive " the whole of the Scriptures of the Old and New Testaments as an infallible revelation from God, and as a sufficient rule of faith and practice ; " to receive the portions of the Scriptures cited in the *Basis* "in their plain and obvious meaning as received by the great body of evangelical believers in all ages, and not in any rationalistic or anti-evangelical sense ; " and to a promise to endeavor to discharge all the duties of the gospel ministry that are required of them in the Scriptures.

A declaration was adopted concerning the qualifications of church-members, that " Christian Churches should receive into their fellowship all who make a creditable profession of repentance toward God and faith toward our Lord Jesus Christ," and that " we will receive all into the fellowship of the Church who give Scriptural evidence that they believe in Christ as their Saviour." In connection with these declarations a number of Scriptural texts were cited, illustrative of the doctrines that " Christ saves all who believe on him," of repentance and the new birth, and of the duties of keeping the commandments and of loving the Lord Jesus Christ and the brethren. Candidates for membership will be required to answer affirmatively questions expressing their principles.

The convention further declared :

All members and churches adopting the basis will be recognized and enrolled as Union Christian ministers and churches, to be known as the "Union Christian Churches of America."

Any minister who has adopted the basis, but who does not deem it expedient to sever existing denominational relations, shall at his request be enrolled notwithstanding.

Ministers are requested to signify their adoption of the Basis by a letter addressed to Rev. W. B. Wellons, D. D., Suffolk, Va.

Churches desiring to take action concerning the Basis are requested to give public notice of a meeting for that purpose.

When the church is convened it is suggested that the Basis be read, and that then a vote be taken on the two following questions :

1. Do you approve the "Union Christian Basis?"
2. Do you adopt the "Union Christian Basis?"

The Secretary of the meeting is requested to signify the result in a letter addressed to Rev. W. B. Wellons, D. D., Suffolk, Va.

All churches either approving or adopting the Basis are requested to appoint one or more delegates to attend a general convention of the "Union Christian Churches" at Suffolk, Va., on the first Wednesday of May, 1875. All ministers adopting the Basis,

including those who may not have severed heretofore existing denominational relations, are also invited to attend this convention, to take counsel concerning the promotion of Christian union and the conversion of the world.

It was recommended provisionally that any single church, or the several church organizations which may adopt the basis of union, should continue their respective forms of church organization, or such forms as they may adopt, until such time as a permanent plan for the fellowship and coöperation of the Union Christian Churches may be adopted. A committee of five persons, consisting of the Rev. Messrs. Thomas J. Mellish, W. B. Wellons, W. C. McCune, and George E. Thrall, and Mr. V. E. Shaw, was appointed to take into consideration the whole subject of a plan for the organization and coöperation of the churches and ministers adopting the basis of union, with instructions to report at the first General Convention of the churches. The same committee was appointed an Executive Board to consider all matters pertaining to the union movement, and was directed to issue an address to the Churches of America in connection with the basis of union.

CLANRICARDE, Most Noble ULICK JOHN DE BURGH, Marquis and Earl of, Baron Somerhill, K. P., a British and Irish peer, born County Galway, Ireland, December 20, 1802 ; died in London, April 11, 1874. At the age of six years he succeeded his father as fourteenth earl, and was educated at the University of Dublin. He was addicted to manly sports, was a skillful horseman, but never a very close student. A passion for gambling had also taken possession of him. While yet young (in 1825) he turned his attention to politics, and the same year married the only daughter of George Canning, then Premier. In anticipation of this marriage, Mr. Canning appointed him Under-Secretary of State, from 1825 to 1827. He performed his duties indifferently well, and was raised to a marquisate, the title having been anciently in the family, and, in 1826, made a Peer of Great Britain, under the title of Baron Somerhill. He would have been promoted to the cabinet by Mr. Canning, had not some gambling transactions placed him in an unfavorable light. In 1838, however, he was nominated embassador to St. Petersburg by Lord Melbourne, and served there for three years creditably, and under Earl Russell's first administration was Postmaster-General until 1852. Soon after this he was a party in a very grave scandal, and under such circumstances that the public were greatly incensed against him. He offered to resign the lord-lieutenancy of County Galway, but the offer was declined. In 1857, Lord Palmerston appointed him Lord Privy Seal, and the appointment raised such a storm of indignation as led to the overthrow of the cabinet. From that time Lord Clanricarde took no part in public affairs, except an occasional participation in the debates in the Lords. He was an able speaker, well informed on many points, and, through the influence of his wife, a woman of remarkable talent and very exalted character, he was enabled to maintain a position in society which his reputation would have otherwise rendered impossible. He had vast estates in Ireland, and was very popular there.

COCHISE, a famous Indian chief, the head of the Coyotero Apaches in Arizona; died in the White Mountain district in Arizona, June 9, 1874, at the supposed age of sixty years. Cochise had been for some years friendly to the Mexicans and the few white settlers of Arizona, when his hostility was aroused by a very treacherous and criminal massacre of Indians in Arizona by United States troops under the direction of Colonel (afterward General) Harney. Thenceforward he was a bitter enemy of the whites, and his band of Coyoteros was the most daring and destructive of all the Apaches of the Territory. No efforts were made to quiet or pacify them for a number of years, it being supposed that all efforts to that end would prove ineffectual. In 1870 General Safford entertained a different opinion. He visited the Coyoteros in the White Mountains, and became convinced that by judicious management they might be pacified, and urged upon Congress the necessity of providing men and means to aid them. Nothing was done, however, and they became more restless and predatory than before. In the autumn of 1871 Mr. Jefferds, the Indian Agent of Arizona, made an effort to open negotiations with Cochise. Penetrating to his stronghold, he found him in a favorable mood for a treaty, but afraid to go to the Indian agency, lest he should be seized and put to death. Subsequently General Crooke succeeded in having an interview with him and effected a complete reconciliation. Since that time Cochise has been exerting a powerful influence for good over his tribe, and there has been no further trouble with the Coyoteros. His sickness was long and distressing, but he manifested his friendly spirit in his dying speech to his people, telling them to come to the agencies, men, women, and children, and to live at peace forever with the white people. His son Taza, or Tuch-la, succeeded him.

COLOMBIA (ESTADOS UNIDOS DE COLOMBIA), an independent republic of South America, occupying the territory formerly known as the Republic of New Granada, which formed the central part of old Colombia, a nation founded and liberated by Bolivar, and comprising besides Venezuela and Ecuador. The territory of the republic extends from the isthmus of Panama (one of the nine States of the Union) to the peninsula of Goajira, on the Atlantic coast, and to 2° 30' south latitude on the Pacific coast, and thence to the banks of the Orinoco, which separates it from Venezuela, and to the Amazon, which separates it from

the empire of Brazil. The area of the territory of new Colombia has been estimated at rather more than 500,000 square miles; of these, 400,000 square miles lie to the north and the remainder to the south of the equator.

The great height attained by the Andes (which in some parts rise to the region of perpetual snow) gives to the country a variety of climate, from the biting cold of the arctic seas to the burning heat of Senegal. Between these two extremes, in the superandine plateaus and the slopes of the Cordilleras, are to be found all the mild climates of the temperate zone.

The valley of the lower Magdalena, around which is grouped the population of seven States, comprises the vast region of the central part of the country, having a length of 500 miles, and a width varying from 70 to 100, till it finally loses itself in the plains that border on the Atlantic. This valley is covered with dense forests, rich in all sorts of timber, cabinet woods, resinous and medicinal plants of the tropics. In those places where the forest has been cleared and the soil brought under cultivation, its fertility has proved equal to the best in the world.

The Atrato Valley is generally similar to that of the Magdalena in its physical aspect.

The Cauca Valley is, on the contrary, an elevated plain covered with spontaneous and artificial pasturage at a height of 5,200 feet above the level of the Pacific Ocean. Its average temperature is 25° Cent. (77° Fahr.), and it is peopled by 435,000 civilized inhabitants. The general aspect of this valley is uniform in its physical constitution. On a bird's-eye view from the south, the country presents the appearance of a narrow plain wedged between the western and central ranges of the Andes, and extending northward as far as the eye can reach. Its soil, remarkably suited for pasturage, produces cacao, coffee, sugar-cane, rice, tobacco, cotton, and indigo, without counting the plantain, maize, and mandioca, which grow luxuriously in every part of that fertile country.

The towns and villages lying along the Cordilleras enjoy alternately the advantages of both heat and cold, situated as they are among the numerous breaks, slopes, and plateaus formed by the spurs of the Colombian Andes.

The Magdalena, which runs northward between the central and eastern ranges of the Andes to its embouchure in the Atlantic, is the great fluvial highway of the country, through which is conducted all the foreign traffic of the five central States, and the greater part of those bordering on the Atlantic. This traffic is so important that, for more than twenty years, the river has been navigated by steamboats of fifty to two hundred tons, without any pecuniary aid from the Government. During that period from eight to twelve steamers, the property of private companies, have been constantly employed in the service, each carrying a mean aggregate of 50,000,000 lbs., or 25,000 tons, annually, from Barranquilla to Honda, a distance of 160 leagues, or rather more than 500 miles.

The mouths of the Magdalena being obstructed by bars upon which there is too little water to admit vessels of deep draught, it was found necessary to construct a railway to connect the bay of Sabanilla with the town of Barranquilla, the lower limit of the navigable portion of the river. This railway, fifteen miles long, was built in 1871, by a German company, with seven per cent. guarantee on the estimated capital of $600,000, but its returns have gone on gradually increasing, so that the Government has not been called upon to pay any part of the stipulated guarantee for the last year. The traffic of said railway consisted of 261,561 bales imported and 345,217 bales exported in 1873. The town of Barranquilla, the third in commercial importance in Colombia, contains a population of 11,000 souls, possesses an excellent dock-yard, and is the entrepot for the imports and exports of almost the whole commerce of the country.

The population of Colombia, according to the last census (1870), was 3,000,000, distributed, as regards the territory, in the following geographical zones: 235,000 in the beautiful and fertile valley of the Cauca, bordering on the Pacific, whose interior traffic is partly carried on through the rivers Cauca and Atrato; 1,300,000 on the table-lands and slopes of the eastern Cordillera, forming the States of Cundinamarca, Boyacá, and Santander, on the eastern banks of the Magdalena; 366,000 in the mining State of Antioquia, embracing the labyrinth of mountains formed by the spurs of the central Cordillera, opposite the State of Santander, on the western banks of the river; 327,000 in the two Atlantic States of Bolivar and Cartagena, comprising flat plains under a burning climate, at the level of the sea. The agriculture of the last two States, so favorably situated for foreign commerce, with a soil as fertile as that of Cuba, but possessing the advantage of good facilities for inland navigation by numerous navigable canals, has entered upon an era of rapid development; their products representing at the present two-thirds of the total agricultural exports of the republic: 206,000 in the isthmus of Panama; 231,000 in the valley of the Upper Magdalena, where the river is still navigable above Honda, for a space of 100 miles. This State, Tolima, on a flat country at the level of the river, was, until lately, the most extensive exporting State in Colombia.

A bill before the House of Representatives for colonizing the territories of Casanare and San Martin passed its second debate. It makes important provisions for reduction of the Indians who inhabit those territories, and for the purpose of keeping at a distance by pacific means the fierce tribes living beyond the Guaviare.

The revenue for the year 1872-'73 was about $4,000,000, distributed as follows:

Customs	$2,775,450
Salt-works	799,213
Panama Railway	250,000
Postal service	67,609
State property	73,595
Mint (about)	18,000
Telegraphs	10,627
Public lands	8,507
Total	$4,002,001

The expenditure during this time was $3,150,000, leaving a balance in favor of the Treasury of $852,001. The custom-houses yielded $2,775,450.38.

The laws promulgated by Congress during the year, for the purpose of creating a separate fund to be set apart for the redemption and payment of interest on such loans as may be contracted for the construction of railways, were to take effect on September 1st.

These laws established an increase of 25 per cent. in the import duties on four of the five classes of the customs tariff, and of 20 cents in the price of each arroba, or 25 lbs., of the salt which is sold in the government works.

The customs tariff is very simple; it only recognizes five classes for the valuation of goods for duty, which latter is collected uniformly on the gross weight of the merchandise as follows:

First class, articles free of duty, in which are comprised articles of food unprepared by cooking, vessels put together and in pieces, and all machinery exceeding 1,000 kilogrammes in weight.

Second class, paying 2 cents per kilogramme. In it are comprised machinery of all classes, not exceeding 1,000 kilogrammes in weight, hydraulic pumps, paper for printing, agricultural implements, printing-presses, photographs, lithographs and apparatus for the same.

Third class, 10 cents per kilogramme, including printed books, letter-paper, paper for hangings, kitchen-utensils, nails of all sorts, safes, wines and distilled liquors, furniture, drugs and medicines, perfumery, matches, china, earthenware and glass, paints and varnishes.

Fourth class, 24 cents per kilogramme, comprising cotton fabrics of one color, metals made into articles of good quality, dressed skins, cutlery, manufactured India-rubber, watches and clocks.

Fifth class, duty on which was not increased, but which pays and contributes to pay 45 cents per kilogramme, embracing ready-made boots, shoes, and clothing, fabrics of silk, wool, and flax, fabrics of cotton, figured or stamped, jewelry, and in general all fine commodities not comprised in the preceding classes.

From the 1st of September, classes 2, 3, and 4, were to increase in a progression of 5 per cent. per month until the 1st of January, 1875, when they will pay respectively 2½, 12½, and 30 cents.

As this duty is moderate, since it is scarcely equivalent to an *ad valorem* charge of 15 per cent. on articles of the second class, of 35 per cent. on those of the third, of 27 per cent. on those of the fourth, and of 25 per cent. on those of the fifth, it is not feared that the increased duty will act unfavorably upon the consumption or reduce the amount of the revenue.

With regard to the salt, as the duty is levied on an article which is a monopoly and also one of prime necessity, the increase in the price must equal, almost with mathematical exactitude, a proportionate rise in the income derived therefrom. And thus it has happened in the other instances in which the Government has been compelled to raise the price of the article. In 1867 the salt-works produced $1,066,- 614. With the increase included, salt was to be sold at the offices at the following prices: Rock or native salt at 50 cents the 12½ kilogrammes; the granulated in the boiler or simply evaporated, not calcined, at 60 cents; and the calcined, 80 cents. As the average consumption of salt is 5 lbs. per annum for each inhabitant, even admitting that the half of the price of the article represents the highest value of the monopoly, the tax is barely equal to 30 cents per inhabitant. It is upon these bases that Congress calculated that the estimated revenue for the fiscal year (from 1874-'75) would be as follows:

Customs.....................................	$3,400,000
Salt-works..................................	1,100,000
Panama Railway.............................	250,000
Postal, telegraphs, mints, and sundry other branches..................................	173,728
Total............................	$4,923,728

And as the ordinary expenditures of the Government, including the payment of the dividends on the foreign and home debts, do not exceed from $3,500,000 to $3,800,000, the Administration can reckon, from the first year of the increased duties, upon a surplus of much more than $500,000, which, added to a balance of another half-million, now in the general Treasury, will form, during the year 1875, a secure minimum-fund of $1,000,000 to meet any engagements which may be incurred for the construction of the projected railroads. Indeed, these estimates are already corroborated by the results obtained since the arrangements made for the public credit both at home and abroad during the year 1872, which have been the point of departure for Colombian financial affairs. Without reducing the surplus of half a million dollars now in the Treasury, the Government has been able to meet, in the course of the last two years, expenses extraordinary of more than $800,000 for the construction of telegraphic lines, the purchase of a Remington armament, of a steam revenue-cutter, and to make at the same time an unusually large payment on account of the home debt, and of the loan of 1863.

The tranquillity of the last ten years has made itself felt in so favorable a manner in the prosperity of the country that the revenue from the customs has doubled in the course of that period. In 1865 they produced $1,300,000; and in 1873, $2,775,000.

Supposing an increase of only seven per cent. in each year, and the amount derived from the customs to be $3,000,000 instead of $3,400,000; and even regarding all other branches of revenue as stationary, and calculating that all ordinary expenditures will increase at the rate of five per cent. per annum on $3,500,000: the financial position of the Colombian Government, should peace be preserved, will be as follows, during the eleven years, 1875-'85:

YEARS.	Revenue.	Expenses.	Surplus.
1875.................	$4,500,000	$3,500,000	$1,000,000
1876.................	4,710,000	3,675,000	1,035,000
1877.................	4,934,000	3,858,750	1,075,250
1878.................	5,175,129	4,051,687	1,123,442
1879.................	5,432,388	4,254,271	1,168,117
1880.................	5,707,655	4,466,985	1,240,670
1881.................	6,002,190	4,690,334	1,311,856
1882.................	6,317,343	4,924,851	1,392,492
1883.................	6,654,557	5,171,094	1,483,463
1884.................	7,015,375	5,429,648	1,585,727
1885.................	7,401,451	5,701,131	1,700,320

The financial capacity of the country cannot be measured by the amount of revenue actually collected, because, in countries where taxes are voted by the representatives of the people, public opinion does not allow their increase with the mere view of expending their product in the payment of public salaries. But when it becomes necessary to appeal to new taxes for works of public utility, the construction of new means of communication, no one can doubt that the country will readily support one or two millions of contributions. The salt-mine revenue alone may produce, if necessary for this object, twice as much as it does at present.

The institutions of credit begin to be established and to work with perfect security. There exists in the capital a good bank of issue and discount, established in 1871, and which gave the following results in 1873:

Deposits................................	$700,000
Discount bills...........................	2,000,000
Bank-notes in circulation...............	560,000

The general movement of the bank amounts to $39,000,000.

The national expenditure for the fiscal year ending August 31, 1873, was as follows:

Civil service...........................	$2,100,000
Foreign debt...........	570,000
Interior debt...........................	480,000
Total............................	$3,150,000

These figures, compared with those of the revenue, show a surplus of $850,000.

The national debt stood as follows:

Home debt...........................	$10,000,000
Foreign debt...........................	11,000,000
Total............................	$21,000,000

Up to the 30th of June last more than one-half of the bonds of New Granada were converted into Colombian 4½ per cent. bonds, in accordance with the agreement approved of by Congress on the 4th of March preceding. Bonds were presented for £3,845,350, for which others were issued to the value of £2,- 589,148 ($12,945,740).

The foreign debt, contracted for the war of independence, will bear interest at 4½ per cent.

per annum until the end of the year 1877, and 4¼ per cent. from 1878 forward; but, should the import duties in the year produce $3,000,000 net, the interest is to be increased to 5 per cent. The amortization of this debt will begin from the said year 1878, by means of an accumulating fund of $125,000 per annum.

The general Treasury of the republic hands over every month to the agent of the creditors the twelfth part of the sum necessary to cover the annual interest. This interest is paid every three months, and the payments are made with rigorous punctuality.

For the payment of interest and for the amortization of the capital of the foreign debt arising from the loan of 1863, the republic has to deliver, every month, $10,000; and it is the endeavor of the Government to make further appropriations, with a view to hasten the extinguishment of the debt.

The Bank of Santander, in one of its ordinary sessions held in Bucaramanga in October, found that it had gained, by discounts, premiums, interest, and commission, the sum of $6,602.76.

On January 31st the banks of Bogotá decided to pay a dividend of $37.50 per share.

An attempt is being made to establish an insurance company at Bogotá, which, besides guaranteeing the mercantile movements of Colombia, will leave to the commerce of the country an immense sum now sent abroad to foreign companies. It is calculated that commerce pays in premiums to foreign insurance companies about $100,000 annually, or in fifty years a sum of $5,000,000 lost to the country.

The foreign commerce for the year 1873 was represented by $23,000,000, distributed as below:

EXPORTS—

Coffee.........................	$1,900,000
Indigo.......................	400,000
Cotton.......................	260,000
India-rubber........	150,000
Hides	500,000
Gold and silver.............	2,560,000
Bark....................	1,800,000
Panama hats.................	260,000
Tobacco	2,000,000
Sundries......................	730,000
	$10,500,000
IMPORTS.................................	12,500,000
Total trade...........................	$23,000,000

It says a good deal for the increasing trade of the east coasts of Colombia that a Hamburg steamer brought to the port of Sabanilla 1,600 packages on the 11th of August, and left on the 18th for Hamburg and intermediate ports with 5,965 packages of exports and $243,628 in specie.

The removal of the custom-house from Sabanilla to Barranquilla had not yet been determined, it being apprehended that the advantage to be obtained thereby would be counterbalanced by greater facilities for smuggling.

The production of coffee is on the increase in many districts, but especially in the State of Cundinamarca, where four plantations contain above 500,000 trees, which were expected to yield 2,000 quintals, or 200,000 pounds.

Jesuit-bark of good quality is, on the other hand, becoming scarce in the forests of the eastern Cordilleras.

The statistics of Bolivar for 1874 showed the quantity and value of the live-stock in that State to be as follows: Asses, 13,027; horses, 7,388; goats, 7,439; mules, 2,402; sheep, 260; cattle, 139,009: total value, $2,557,100.

The Government of the State of Cundinamarca offers premiums for the introduction of an improved race of horses, sheep, and cattle, into the State.

The foreign trade in the year ending August 31, 1873, was carried on in 739 sailing-vessels with an aggregate of 46,697 tons, and 271 steamers with 14,499 tons, exclusive of the transit trade over the isthmus of Panama, where there is no custom-house.

Señor Parra, the Minister of Finance and Public Works, in an interesting report to Congress, accounts for the decay of trade at Santa Marta and the river port of Mompos in the following terms: "The railroad of Bolivar now offering to commerce from abroad a better and safer route than that by Los Caños, has had the effect of attracting away from the port of Santa Marta, notwithstanding its excellence, vessels of large tonnage, and therefore the latter port has now scarcely any trade with the interior, just as it formerly happened to Cartagena, and as it will happen sooner or later to Sabanilla, if, as is generally expected, the entrance by the Bocas de Ceniza should become navigable for large sea-going vessels. Barranquilla will then no longer be the principal fluvial port of the Colombian Union, as has already happened to Mompos; but some point higher on the banks of the Magdalena will be the anchoring-place of ocean-vessels, and the seat of a great city. The inhabitants of cities like Santa Marta and Mompos, from which the currents of trade have been turned aside by changes in the direction of commercial routes, must then turn their attention to agriculture, cattle-raising, or the extraction of natural products, as those of Cartagena are now doing."

The report also contains some curious remarks on customs, salt-works, the emerald mines of Muzo, the mint and railways, together with important observations on immigration, the conversion of Indian tribes, navigation by the Bocas de Ceniza, and the necessity of light-houses along the coasts.

A new contract was made with Mr. Alexander Weekbehr, modifying that of November, 1872, for the navigation of the Upper Magdalena by steam.

A London house deposited $10,000 as security for the fulfillment of a contract with the President of Bolivar to establish steam navigation along the dike of Cartagena.

A steam-tug company was established at Buga to improve the navigation of the river

Cauca, and the required amount of capital subscribed.

In view of the peculiar topography of the country, hurriedly sketched at the commencement of the present article, it will not be wondered at that the chief subject of deliberation with the Colombian Government is that relating to the construction of railways to connect the valley of the Cauca with the Pacific Ocean, and open up for the 1,600,000 inhabitants of the States of Cundinamarca, Boyacá, Santander, and Antioquia, rapid and convenient communication with the steamers navigating the Magdalena. The prompt and favorable resolution of this problem is the great economical question of the country, and the whole nation has so well understood the necessity of carrying on these works that four successive Legislatures, from that of 1871 to the last in 1874, conferred on the Executive, by unanimity of votes, plenary powers to contract for the construction of the "Cauca & Pacific Railway," and the "Cundinamarca, Boyacá, Santander & Magdalena River Railway," generally known as the Northern Railway. It may, then, be officially stated that in the execution of these two works the aspirations of the country are at present centred. The absence of good roads to place the densely-populated portions of the country in cheap, safe, and rapid communication with the commercial centres of the world, is the chief cause why the industry of the country has not yet received the development proportionate to the number and activity of its inhabitants, the fertility of its soil, and the abundance of its mineral products. The principal towns of the inter-Andine States are situated at an average distance varying from forty-five to sixty miles from the banks of the Magdalena; goods are transported on mules in loads of ten arrobas, 250 lbs., divided into two bales of five arrobas each, and at a cost of from $6 to $9 each load. The bales that exceed this weight are transported on men's backs, or rather women's, for most of the carriers are women, thus condemned to take the place of beasts of burden, traffic which contributes to debase and degrade this part of the population. The largest packages transported in this way are pianos, mirrors, paintings, crystal, and other articles of luxury or art, requiring delicate handling. As for boilers, cylinders, and all other machinery, whose weight exceeds half a ton, they are usually impossible of transportation, since the mountain-roads do not admit the employment of sledges. The carriage of an ordinary piano over the forty-two miles from the river to the plain of Bogotá costs $160. The heaviest loads lately brought to Bogotá were the following: A steam-boiler, of 4-horse power, for the sulphuric-acid factory, the carriage of which cost $830; and one mechanical printing-press, weighing 5,000 lbs., or 200 arrobas, the carriage of which cost $1,000.

Steam machinery for agricultural and mining purposes, fire-engines, coaches, and carriages, iron boats, suspension bridges, and in general all pieces exceeding the weight of half a ton, are objects impossible of introduction into the interior of the country.

It is not, therefore, to be wondered at that the material development, laboring under such disadvantages, should have been so far, and must of necessity continue to be tardy, until suitable means of transport shall have been established between the populous producing regions of the republic and the navigable rivers.

According to a recent estimate presented to the Government, the Northern Railway would cost the nation $24,175,000.*

There was a keen discussion in Congress, which prolonged its sessions to June 15th, between S. C. Roldan and the Minister of Finance, concerning the proposed railway to the north of the republic, Roldan regarding it as ruinous to the country, and Señor Parra maintaining that the enterprise would be quite the contrary.

The constructors of the Buenaventura Railroad had deposited in the Bank of Bogotá $25,000, as a guarantee that they would go on and finish the road. One of the contractors was expected in Bogotá, with $1,800,000 in bonds, to be legalized by the national Government.

The Government undertook the construction of telegraphs in 1864, and at present there are about 700 miles of wires in actual service. These lines connect the capital with the principal towns of the north of the republic, and also with the port of Buenaventura on the Pacific, where it will unite the submarine cable to be laid along the southwestern coast of America, from Peru and Chili, and to join at Panama the transatlantic cable connecting Europe and America. During the year 1873 the number of telegrams dispatched was 50,000, yielding $14,000. A line of telegraph between Bogotá and Neiva was in course of rapid construction.

The coinage of gold and silver money amounted to $533,671. The emission of silver coin has diminished, because the mines of Santa Ana, which were the most productive of this metal, have ceased working. To make up for this want, the Bank of Bogotá ordered from Europe $200,000 of silver coin, and the value of $100,000 in bars of the same metal, to be coined at the mint in Bogotá. In the month of June last, there were exported from Medellin, in the State of Antioquia, $189,000 in the precious metals. The mines suffered a good deal from the heavy rains of the season, which, by causing the rivers to overflow, seriously affected the mines of Barbosa and others. A land-slide completely covered up the Cristales mines. Mining is nevertheless progressing favorably; certain mining establishments are now worth $1,000,000 which formerly were only valued at $200,000. The Zancudo mine has, since 1866, produced 28,050 lbs. of silver-ore,

* For particulars of direction, stations, etc., of the railway, see the ANNUAL CYCLOPÆDIA for 1873.

valued at $1,333,800, exclusive of the gold from the mills. According to a recent estimate, the Zancudo mine is valued at $6,000,000. The Cristales mine yielded in sixteen months 766 lbs. of gold, which, at $147 per lb., gives $112,602. The Frontina mine yielded 7½ lbs. gold from the grinding-mill after thirteen days' work. There are, in the State of Antioquia, 206 mines with metallic veins, and 355 with alluvial washings, giving occupation to 16,000 laborers. The value of the machinery employed is estimated at $240,000, and the net product at $2,300,000. During the present century the mines of Antioquia have yielded $100,000,000 approximately. The yield of gold since 1869 is set down at $8,585,247.09½, and of silver, at $1,346,907.74. Since 1868 the State has derived (from taxes, imposed on denouncements, titles, and preservation of mines) the sum of $40,359,27.

The latest reports received from the gold gravel-washing enterprises in Tolima were still of a promising character, and confidence continued to be felt that the eventual results would be satisfactory. The Malpaso was at work with an increased supply of water; and, as a very large quantity of good pay-dirt was passing through the sluice, a good return from the next clean-up was expected. The future of this undertaking would appear to be assured, the waste having been traversed, and the monitor now operating upon extensive and rich deposits. A slide of gravel had occurred, causing the clean-up to be postponed. It would seem that a considerably supply of water can be brought to the Rica deposits; and, as regards the Malabar, washing was directed toward the high banks, on reaching which it was believed that large profits would be realized. The operations so far attempted were stated to be only of a preliminary nature.

As the present lease of the famous emerald-mines of Muzo and Cascuez is to expire on April 1, 1875, the Government has published proposals for a new contract. These are the mines which yield the emeralds erroneously called in Europe "emeralds of Peru," probably because Peru is considered the great source of the mineral riches of America. From them was extracted the precious emerald specimen so much admired at the Exhibition in 1867, where it was somewhat capriciously labeled "French Industry."

The attention of the Government has of late been directed to the encouragement of national industry; and some now and important branches have been introduced. Since 1870 the following establishments have been inaugurated at Bogotá: The Bank of Bogotá, with a large capital; a sulphuric-acid factory; establishments for the distillation of alcohol and other spirituous liquors; a factory for making glass, with a capital of $400,000; a cigar-factory, where some 60 women are at work. These women, when they learn the business, get from 50 to 70 cents per day. This factory

was succeeding so well that it was expected there would soon be work for 500 women. Gas-works are now about to be put in operation. Besides these, an insurance company, with a capital of $2,500,000, was about to be organized, the number of shareholders to be 200.

A bill was laid before Congress for the establishment of an agricultural bureau, the duty of whose members would be to study and use every means to forward agriculture in Colombia in all its branches; collect and preserve specimens of vegetables, foreign and national, seeds and roots; and to publish all the information to be had, bearing on the subject. Besides the chief of the bureau, at a salary of $2,400 per annum, there are to be appointed also a meteorologist and entomologist for the special study of the natural history of insects prejudicial to agriculture, receiving $1,200 each, with a staff of other sub-officials.

Another bill was read in the House of Representatives for the establishment of a vast iron-manufactory in some central locality, to furnish the various tools, machinery, etc., necessary for the different branches of industry, and particularly for agriculture.

The Executive power of the nation had offered to the London Company for the Constructing of Public Works a guarantee of seven per cent. per annum profit on $500,000 in order to have introduced into the country Hindoo "laborers and colonists." Judging from the opinion expressed by the Minister of Public Works, spontaneous immigration into Colombia is not likely to take place for a long time; but Señor Parra is in favor of the introduction of Asiatics. He regrets to have to confess that in Colombia at present no industry is taken up unless it promises immediate returns; the desire is, to have every thing to-day, even if nothing be left for the morrow. Whatever be the causes of this peculiar idiosyncrasy, the example of the English is pointed out, with whom it is customary to plant oak-trees, and wait fifty years for them to be suitable to be made into planks. They send out to America and procure the young cinchona-trees of the Andean regions, in order to plant them in the English colonies in the East, so that they may possess forests from which they can always supply themselves with quinine. "In Colombia," says the secretary, "we hesitate even about planting coffee, and have almost abandoned the cultivation of cacao."

There was a project on foot for the water-supply of Bogotá by aqueduct, at a cost of $200,000, the municipality to take one-half of the shares.

Various improvements had been undertaken in Cartagena, such as a hospital for measles, a public clock and park, a new theatre, repairs of the College of the State and the prison establishment, and the lighting of the city by petroleum-gas.

In Mompos a monument was to be erected to commemorate the 6th of August, 1810; and in Barranquilla a hospital and general cemetery.

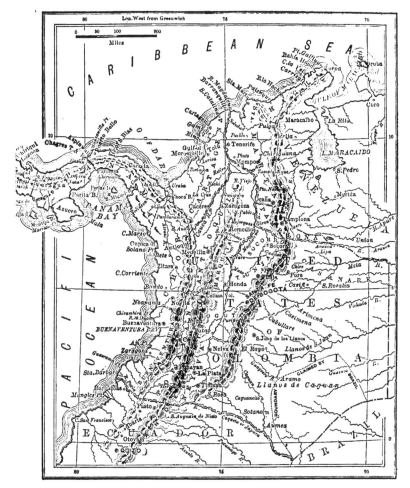

The present Constitution of Colombia dates from May 8, 1863. The executive power is vested in a President, elected for a term of two years by the people; and each new President enters upon his official functions on the 1st of April. Señor Santiago Perez was inaugurated April 1, 1874.

The cabinet is composed of four ministers or secretaries, as follows: the Minister of the Interior and of Foreign Affairs, Señor Jacobo Sanchez, vice Señor Justo Arosemena, who declined to accept the appointment; Minister of the Treasury and of Credit, Señor N. Ezquerra;

Minister of Finance and Public Works, Señor A. Parra; and Minister of War and Marine, Señor R. S. Vila. The legislative power resides in a Senate with 27 members, and a Chamber of Representatives with 61 members.

The chief magistrate of each of the nine States has the title of Governor, save in Panamá, where he is called President.

The State Governors, etc., in 1874, were as follows: Antioquia, Señor J. M. Berrio; Bolivar, Señor R. S. D. Vila; Boyacá, Señor V. Rueda; Cauca, Señor T. C. Mosquera; Cundinamarca, Señor J. Barriga; Magdalena, Señor

J. M. Campo Serrano; Panamá, Señor Miró; Santander, Señor N. Cadena; Tolima, Señor J. N. Leiva. The Colombian consul-general in New York is Señor M. Salgar.

The old question of limits between Colombia and Venezuela, which has never yet been settled since the dismemberment of the first Colombian republic, comprising New Granada, Venezuela, and Ecuador, still frequently gives place to stormy altercations between the Governments of Carácas and Bogotá. The past year was marked by one of these disputes, and the tenor of the press of the Colombian capital seemed to indicate that a waywardness or indiscreet management on either side might result in a rupture of the comparatively cordial relations existing between the sister republics. A note was dispatched to the Venezuela Government by the Secretary of Foreign Affairs of Colombia in consequence of certain events that had occurred in the State of Zulia, which intervenes between Colombia and the shores of Lake Maracaybo, claiming from Venezuela satisfaction for damages caused and persevered in by the local authorities of that republic, regarding goods in transit between the two nations by way of the river Zulia, and requesting that measures should be adopted to put an end to said vexations. Proofs were offered on the part of Colombia, that her respective frontier authorities have done every thing in their power to prevent, within territories under her jurisdiction, all movements hostile or disagreeable to a neighboring republic. It is difficult to see how this can be altogether prevented without a modification of the line of limits understood to separate Venezuela from Colombia in the region referred to, and which, if rigidly observed, would deprive the latter republic of the right of way on the waters of the Maracaybo Lagoon, free access to which should redound to the convenience and interests of both countries.*

With the exception of intermittent bickerings of the nature of those just alluded to, peace reigns undisturbed in Colombia; the republic has not, for now twelve years, been at war with any foreign nation; and internecine strife seems to have come to an end forever.

The last civil war, that of 1860-'62, terminated in the reorganization of the country under the constitution of 1863, which still exists. This constitution adopted the federal form, similar to that of the United States of America, giving to each of the nine States, into which the Union is divided, the full extent of power necessary for its internal government; but even as far back as 1853 the country had secured in its institutions the most precious conquests of human liberty. Foreigners enjoy in Colombia the same civil rights as natives; and, in case their property be taken for public use, they are entitled to a pecuniary indemnification therefor...

There is no state Church in Colombia; natives and foreigners enjoy unbounded liberty of conscience and worship; and there are Protestant churches in Bogotá, Barranquilla, Panama, and other towns.

Nearly all the States of the Union have adopted the trial by jury for felony and other great crimes.

Imprisonment for debt has been abolished. The exercise of all professions, including law and medicine, is completely free.

The only monopolies now existing are those of the salt-mines, which belong to the General Government, and the distilleries of spirits in some of the States.

Brigandage is and has always been unknown in Colombia.

Among the more important proceedings of the Congress during the year may be enumerated the following:

I.—PUBLIC ORDER.

ARTICLE I. The organization of a government, such as is required by the Constitution. Section 1 of Article VII. ceases to exist in any of the States in the following cases:

2. When a President, governor, or supreme chief, dissolves the Legislative Assembly or impedes its reunion; 2. When, without due faculty, new elections for deputies are ordered or a constituent convention called; and 3. When obedience to the Assembly is refused, and the latter has no power to compel it.

2. The individual who, either as President, governor, or the highest authority of a State, executes any of the afore-mentioned acts in this article, commits the crime of treason to the institutions, and shall suffer the punishment of expulsion from the territory of Colombia for ten years.

ART. II. When, in any of the States, any of the infractions treated of in the preceding article takes place, the Executive power of the Union shall inform the Attorney-General of the same, forwarding him such documentary proofs as can be obtained. The Attorney-General shall then transmit them to the Supreme Court of the Union, which, within three days, shall give its opinion on the existence of the acts, and whether they are or are not such as are expressed in Article I.

The Supreme Court shall decide regarding these same points within eight days after being furnished with the documents in the case. Its resolution will be a decree that declares whether there is or not ground for preferring against the person of the magistrate referred to an accusation of treason.

ART. III. If the sentence of the court declares that there are grounds for accusation against the individual, who, either as President, governor, or superior authority of a State, has committed any of the transgressions above expressed, the Executive power of the Union, at the request of the Legislature, or of the same State, at the request of the Legislature, or of the president, governor, or superior authority of the same State, will furnish an armed force for the defense of its government and the establishment of the latter, if overturned by sedition.

II.—PENAL CODE.

A bill to reform the penal code was presented by Señor Correosa, and passed its first reading.

III.—CIVILIZATION OF INDIANS.

A bill for the conversion and civilization of the savage Indian tribes of the republic passed its first reading.

IV.—POLYGLOT JOURNAL.

The House of Representatives, by unanimity of votes, approved of the following proposition: "Let the President of the Chamber name a committee of

---

* See the ANNUAL CYCLOPÆDIA for 1872, page 109.

two representatives to bring forward a project of law for the purpose of establishing a periodical, to be published in Europe, in the French, English, and German languages, for the purpose of making known the United States of Colombia in the great mercantile centres of Europe, in an industrial, political, mercantile, and geographical point of view." Señors Restrepo and Araujo S. were named as a committee.

Additional testimony to the prosperous condition of the republic is presented in the summary hereafter transcribed from President Murillo's message to Congress, dated February 1, 1874:

The President congratulates the assembled Senators and Representatives on the highly-satisfactory and flattering condition of the republic in general. The elections for members of Congress and for the next President of the Union have been effected without any disturbances, which, with the confidence of the people in peace and progress, have shown that Colombia marches on firm ground, that liberty is secure, and industry remunerative and increasing on every side.

The satisfactory condition of the national finances at the present time places it beyond a doubt that the Treasury will be quite able, from this time henceforth, to meet the interests of a capital of not less than $15,000,000, which will enable the country easily to initiate the construction of the railways proposed as parts of a great line of communication from ocean to ocean, and all of which, faithfully and honestly carried out, cannot fail to place Colombia in a distinguished posititon as a contributor to the general productions of the world.

With respect to the railway from Buenaventura to Cali, it as yet has gone on slowly. The contractor, Mr. Smith, was daily expected at Buenaventura with every requisite to go on with the road. The task of building this line is a gigantic one, and excuses for its delay are found in the great obstacles to be overcome. The railway from Sabanilla to Barranquilla continues profitably and satisfactorily. Telegraph-lines are of daily construction, so that before long the territory of the republic will be crossed by wires from the port of Buenaventura on the Pacific to the Venezuelan frontier and near to Lake Maracaybo on the Atlantic, making in all 969 miles of telegraph.

Primary instruction continues to diffuse knowledge, notwithstanding the opposition of the Church. Religious teaching not being now recognized as a function of the Government, the schools and other establishments supported by it are warned to abstain from being in any way accessory to religious propagandism. The people in this question have sided with the Government.

All the foreign relations of the republic, especially with Great Britain, are on the most friendly footing.

The Government of Venezuela still refuses to continue the negotiation of treaties for the arranging of the commercial relations and territorial limits between the two countries.

General Bueventura Correosa, as minister from Colombia to Costa Rica, succeeded in concluding with that republic a treaty of amity, commerce, and navigation, a postal convention, and one respecting the literary copyright, all of which are to be submitted for the approval of Congress.

The treaty of commerce with Peru, approved by Congress, has been found beneficial to both countries. Señor Vallenzuela, who negotiated this treaty, is now occupied in negotiating with a company that has undertaken to lay a telegraphic cable between Panama and the coasts of Peru, for the establishment of a telegraph-station of this cable at the port of Buenaventura, in exchange for the permission to land one of its extremes on the coast of Colombia. In order to secure the station at Buenaventura, it has been found necessary to revoke a former permission

of which advantage has been taken, but the continuation of which would tend to prevent the certainty of getting the above-mentioned acquisition. The relations of Colombia with Ecuador are as friendly as possible.

In Pasto were collected $643.50 to assist in printing copies of the Bible.

By virtue of a decree, issued on November 1, 1870, public instruction ceased to be an exclusively clerical charge, and was placed under the immediate direction of the Government, under whose auspices the entire school system was reformed; competent teachers were brought from Europe—principally from Germany. Schools multiplied in every direction; and, to insure the full measure of happy results fairly to be expected from a work inaugurated by dint of patient labor and the liberal expenditure of public funds, Colombia was first among the nations of the New World to adopt the measure of compulsory education.

The beneficent influence of the school-reform is already apparent, as is eloquently attested by the extracts here transcribed from an official report, dated October 16, 1874.

In the State of Antioquia there were, in December, 1873, the following schools:

Primary public schools for males			97
" " "	"	females	47
Grammar "	"	" males	38
" "	"	" females	13
Private schools for males			135
" "	"	females	155
Normal School			1
	Total		486

The attendance at these schools, exclusive of the Normal School, was 21,416; and the total expenditure for instruction, $121,455.

In Bolivar there were but 44 schools open, against 119 in 1872; but this decadence was attributed to causes foreign to a lack of interest in the education of youth.

Boyacá possessed 208 public schools, 36 of which were for females, with a total attendance of 9,000. The amount annually contributed by the various districts for the support of these schools was $38,531.

The schools in Cauca numbered 158 public, 22 of which were for females; and 71 private, 35 being for females. The total attendance was 9,925; and the annual outlay for the support of the establishments, $77,298.

Cundinamarca had in 1873 the following:

Public schools for males			130
" "	"	females	88
Private "	"	males	50
" "	"	females	58
Schools for both sexes			12
	Total		338

The number of scholars enrolled at these schools was 16,489; and $76,000 were expended for teachers' salaries alone.

In Magdalena there existed 49 public and 51 private schools, attended by 2,968 scholars, and supported at an expenditure of $15,974, contributed by the several departments.

Santander had 300 schools, 279 of which

were public; the total attendance was 11,974; and the appropriations for their support, $81,-470, of which $58,010 were from the State, and the remainder contributed by the various districts. There were 100 schools of all kinds in Tolima, with 3,640 scholars.

As for Panama, public instruction is reported to be in as forward a state there as circumstances permit. At the beginning of the year 1874 there were no public schools on the isthmus; and in September sixteen had been established.

The actual progress attained in this important branch will be better seen by comparing the attendance at the schools in Santander in each of the seven years (1869–'74), as follows:

Years.	Attendance.	Years.	Attendance.
1868	5,631	1872	13,207
1869	6,608	1873	11,974
1870	6,625	1874	13,295
1871	12,238		

The advantage of the new system is manifested by the increase in the number of scholars from 1870 to 1871: the attendance having almost doubled immediately. The expenditure in Santander, at the end of 1874, for public instruction, was—

From the national Treasury	$6,200
From the State	81,470
From the districts	46,357
Total	$134,027

The increase in the attendance at school in the State of Cundinamarca from January to August, 1874, was nearly 6,000, or almost fifty per cent.; that from July, 1872, to August, 1874, was 14,515; and 26 new schools were opened in the year 1873–'74. Out of the State revenue in Cundinamarca, $164,664 per annum are expended on the schools.

The national Treasury devotes $317,120 yearly to the development of public instruction, as follows:

Subsidies to the States	$200,000
Subsidy to the National University, the Vasquez Academy, and other colleges	117,120
Total	$317,120

And this, besides the *renta nominal privilegiada* recognized by the Treasury in favor of public instruction, and amounting to $1,680,-000, which is punctually paid.

In almost all the States there are colleges in which higher instruction is given, and which are supported out of private incomes, amounting in the aggregate to about $1,000,000 per annum.

There are in Bogotá schools of engineering, natural sciences, arts, and trades; and five teachers of painting, music, architecture, sculpture, and engineering, for the Vasquez Academy, were to be brought from Europe. Normal schools for females, and several new common schools, were to be established in each State.

From the foregoing statistics it would appear that each State in the Colombian Union devotes nearly one-half of its entire revenue to the cause of education, and that alone affords sufficient proof that the present administration of the republic, and the two immediately preceding it, have not been ignorant of the maxim that the education of the people is the groundwork of prosperity.

COLORADO. The officers of this Territory are as follows: Governor, Edward M. McCook; Secretary, John W. Jenkins; Judges of Supreme Court, Moses Hallet (Chief-Justice), James B. Belford and E. T. Wells (Associate Justices); United States Attorney, H. C. Alleman; United States Marshal, M. A. Schaffenburg; Assayer U. S. Mint, J. F. L. Schirmer; Surveyor-General, T. B. Searight. Colorado is fast becoming a popular resort for invalids, especially those afflicted with pulmonary complaints. In respect to climate, the Territory may be divided into two parts, viz., mountains and plains. The former, comprising about one-half of the area of the Territory, and forming its western portion, consists of a succession of perpetually snow-clad ranges and peaks, separated by beautiful and fertile valleys and parks, which are from 7,000 to 9,000 feet above sea-level, while many of the peaks attain an altitude of nearly 15,000 feet. It is well watered by clear, cold rivers and streams, which are rapid in their course, and abound with speckled trout. The forests are composed principally of pine and fir, which give a delightful and healthful aroma to the air. Hot and cold mineral springs, possessing a great variety of medicinal virtues, are found in many localities. The atmosphere is a little moister than that of the plains, and is rare, clear, cool, and charged with an unusual amount of electricity. This region is unsurpassed, in its endless variety of grand and beautiful natural scenery, by any place in America. Persons desiring to escape the fatal diseases incident to large towns and cities in the summer months, may here gain not only health and comfort, but pleasure; those who are fond of botany may find in the abundant flora many rare and most beautiful plants and flowers; while those who have a taste for mineralogy may also here find deposited every variety of the base and precious metals, from the crude iron-ore to the delicate frosted wire-gold.

The second climatic division of Colorado embraces the eastern portion, which extends from the foot of the mountains to the boundary-line. It is an open prairie, or plateau, which varies in altitude from 3,000 to 6,000 feet above the level of the sea. It is watered by streams rising in the mountains, which are all swift in their courses. The soil is dry and alkaline, free from boggy and marshy places, and "blossoms as the rose" with a great variety of flowers during the spring months, but is principally covered with a short, thick herbage, called buffalo-grass, which usually dries into sweet and nutritious hay during the month of August. Trees are only found along the river or creek bottoms. This portion has a pure, rare, dry air, bracing and exhilarating in its effects, warmed and softened by the rays of a genial sun, which is seldom shaded by clouds or hidden by storms, subject to frequent changes of temperature, but nearly free from dampness at all seasons, fogs and dews being almost unknown.

Although many diseases are mitigated or cured by residence in Colorado, the climate is peculiarly favorable to those relating to the air-passages. The malady called the hay-asthma has never been known, and those who suffer annually from this distressing disease in other climates may here escape every symptom of it. Persons suffering from spasmodic asthma here find speedy relief. The most desirable place of residence for consumptives is upon the plains, within twenty miles of the foot-hills, for this portion is protected from the dry north winds by spurs or divides from the main range; and furthermore, there is daily an interchange of currents of air between the plains and mountains, similar to the land and sea breezes upon the beach. The mountain air is moister, and, mingling with the dry atmosphere of the plains, relieves it of any harshness it may possess.

The chief source of wealth of Colorado is found in its mines. Recently new mining districts have been opened, and promise to add largely to the material resources of the Territory. Probably the most productive of the new districts is that known as "Mount Lincoln," on whose lofty and precipitous slopes untold wealth has been unearthed by the exertions of the restless prospector. The deposits are essentially different from any of those elsewhere made known among the mountains of Colorado, and form a valuable and most interesting feature of its mineral resources. The ores are found in limestone formations which compose the exterior crust of the mountain, and in layers, or strata (dipping to the east and into the mountain at an angle of twenty degrees), making the process of extraction easy, and, from their great extent and richness, highly profitable. The principal mine, and one highly characteristic of the limestone region, is the "Moose" mine. This mine, discovered in the fall of 1871, has produced an enormous quantity of high-grade ore, which has given a desirable impetus to the mining interest of Park County. The character of the ore is an argentiferous galena with copper pyrites.

The Territory has an efficient system of public schools. The Superintendent of Public Instruction is appointed by the Governor for two years, and receives an annual salary of $1,200. There are 25 county superintendents. Nearly all of the public school-houses have been built since 1869. In 1874 there were 243 school districts, 180 schools, and 125 school-houses; number of persons from five to twenty-four years of age, 14,417; enrolled in the public schools, 7,456; average cost of tuition per month for each pupil, $3.12; average monthly salary paid male teachers, $62; female, $51; value of school-houses, $260,183; average rate of taxation for school purposes, 3.77 mills; total school-fund, exclusive of bonds issued for building purposes, $137,557.

The following railroads are now in operation:

	Miles.
Kansas Pacific, connecting Northern Colorado with St. Louis and Chicago, within our territorial boundary	210
Denver Pacific, forming a connection with the Union Pacific Continental Railway	106
Denver & Rio Grande (narrow gauge) on its way to the Mexican coast, connecting Northern and Southern Colorado	102
Colorado Central, opening up the great gold and silver region	41
Kansas Pacific, Kit Carson & Fort Lyon, opening up the old overland Santa Fé and Arkansas River trail, and the rich country of Southern Colorado	54
Denver & Boulder Valley, from Denver to Erie, Valmont, and Boulder, opening the rich mineral region of Caribou and Gold Hill	39
Golden & Julesburg, completed to Longmont, traversing the fine farming valleys of Northern Colorado	30
Total	642

COMMERCE OF THE UNITED STATES.

The number of merchant-vessels and amount of tonnage belonging to the several customs districts and ports of the United States, June 30, 1874, are shown in the following statement. By the act of April 18, 1874, canal and other boats employed on inland waters, with few exceptions, are exempt from enrollment and license:

STATES.	Vessels.	Tons.
Maine	3,221	565,842.59
New Hampshire	62	11,370.18
Massachusetts	2,563	458,373.10
Rhode Island	274	36,265.55
Connecticut	836	96,317.44
New Jersey	1,124	94,699.24
New York	5,051	1,026,023.56
Pennsylvania	2,985	363,542.18
Delaware	197	13,533.88
Maryland	1,998	142,267.65
District of Columbia	472	28,196.50
Virginia	892	22,623.54
North Carolina	279	7,408.91
South Carolina	195	8,142.43
Georgia	63	9,291.84
Florida	237	9,588.76
Alabama	99	7,909.41
Mississippi	94	3,368.56
Louisiana	572	50,961.71
Texas	306	11,998.27
Total on the Atlantic and Gulf coasts	21,465	2,967,715.30
Total on the Western rivers..	1,564	373,464.59
Total on the Northern lakes..	4,833	758,838.84
Total on the Pacific coasts...	1,125	164,418.99
	28,987	4,264,437.72
Unrigged vessels not reported	2,936	331,446.00
Aggregate in 1874	31,923	4,595,883.72
Aggregate in 1873 (including unrigged vessels).	31,684	4,468,046.81
Increase in 1874 over 1873	239	127,836.91

The value of the total imports from and of total exports to the various foreign countries for each of the three years, ending June 30th, was as shown in the following table. (For further details, *see* FINANCES OF THE UNITED STATES, in this volume.)

COUNTRIES.	1872.	1873.	1874.
1. GREAT BRITAIN AND IRELAND:			
Imports	$249,325,957	$237,796,788	$198,595,830
Domestic exports	313,195,069	363,509,205	373,566,508
Foreign exports	8,490,972	11,708,694	7,587,544
2. CANADA AND OTHER BRITISH NORTH AMERICAN POSSESSIONS:			
Imports	40,961,482	43,809,070	38,158,004
Domestic exports	27,774,091	34,368,811	42,505,914
Foreign exports	4,984,989	4,203,745	4,589,242
3. BRITISH WEST INDIES, INCLUDING BRITISH GUIANA AND HONDURAS:			
Imports	9,550,847	7,016,574	5,024,911
Domestic exports	8,658,637	9,118,399	9,473,948
Foreign exports	138,429	239,509	210,441
4. BRITISH EAST INDIES AND AUSTRALIA:			
Imports	15,220,665	19,998,165	15,929,841
Domestic exports	3,325,985	4,082,747	4,268,906
Foreign exports	55,388	66,695	68,844
5. BRITISH POSSESSIONS IN THE MEDITERRANEAN AND AFRICA:			
Imports	4,634,480	4,257,862	2,023,281
Domestic exports	4,045,010	4,304,866	4,060,794
Foreign exports	160,183	52,870	26,516
6. FRANCE:			
Imports	43,164,206	33,977,524	51,771,109
Domestic exports	31,752,011	33,637,270	48,729,429
Foreign exports	541,812	575,286	739,094
7. FRENCH POSSESSIONS IN AMERICA:			
Imports	2,290,963	1,208,022	1,444,940
Domestic exports	1,460,746	1,339,242	1,385,356
Foreign exports	40,414	27,170	19,060
8. FRENCH POSSESSIONS IN AFRICA:			
Imports	441,159	68,422	149,339
Domestic exports	714,557	133,847	135,560
Foreign exports	47,133	....	29,390
9. SPAIN:			
Imports	4,426,436	4,962,431	4,598,204
Domestic exports	9,445,705	10,056,724	11,643,715
Foreign exports	20,861	16,909	9,423
10. CUBA, PORTO RICO, AND OTHER SPANISH POSSESSIONS:			
Imports	86,890,515	91,663,997	99,468,498
Domestic exports	16,140,625	17,336,509	21,861,834
Foreign exports	1,779,811	1,528,897	2,164,758
11. NORTH-GERMAN UNION (PRUSSIA, HAMBURG, BREMEN, ETC.):			
Imports	46,245,817	61,497,954	44,074,252
Domestic exports	40,144,642	61,767,997	64,344,622
Foreign exports	1,074,542	1,764,099	1,369,088
12. HOLLAND:			
Imports	2,547,715	2,943,077	2,516,693
Domestic exports	11,010,391	10,842,840	13,712,846
Foreign exports	165,541	367,408	202,573
13. DUTCH WEST INDIES:			
Imports	1,067,564	1,192,313	1,634,960
Domestic exports	789,255	954,852	992,001
Foreign exports	24,946	43,359	40,730
14. DUTCH EAST INDIES:			
Imports	7,325,202	7,556,954	3,857,706
Domestic exports	111,328	255,184	451,452
Foreign exports	....	....	122
15. DENMARK AND DANISH WEST INDIES:			
Imports	780,215	478,840	457,390
Domestic exports	1,799,898	2,487,506	2,430,791
Foreign exports	68,116	86,623	22,156
16. RUSSIA AND RUSSIAN POSSESSIONS:			
Imports	1,965,893	2,212,293	1,257,170
Domestic exports	6,917,709	11,764,256	10,284,803
Foreign exports	4,076	20,545	15,937
17. AUSTRIA AND AUSTRIAN POSSESSIONS:			
Imports	1,012,066	781,402	488,642
Domestic exports	1,460,348	1,608,612	1,682,949
Foreign exports	34,474	62,544	5,972
18. PORTUGAL:			
Imports	461,013	579,075	506,135
Domestic exports	1,508,481	1,180,187	1,553,042
Foreign exports	8,939	5,450	25,819
19. PORTUGUESE POSSESSIONS:			
Imports	196,432	127,126	51,607
Domestic exports	211,193	178,000	215,293
Foreign exports	2,225	2,877	....
20. SWEDEN AND NORWAY, AND SWEDISH WEST INDIES:			
Imports	1,770,586	2,598,052	2,037,914
Domestic exports	742,055	2,542,330	2,385,088
Foreign exports	....	....	1,386
21. BELGIUM:			
Imports	5,580,461	5,711,077	5,727,441
Domestic exports	13,054,186	15,280,437	20,197,515
Foreign exports	328,755	462,802	620,710

COUNTRIES.	1876.	1878.	1874.
22. ITALY AND SICILY:			
Imports	$7,592,191	$7,974,542	$8,499,204
Domestic exports	5,438,718	7,241,097	8,378,606
Foreign exports	18,468	54,559	4,019
23. GREECE:			
Imports	307,761	413,604	484,168
Domestic exports	71,700	51,379	82,609
Foreign exports	....	....	....
24. TURKEY:			
Imports	866,719	1,184,018	786,877
Domestic exports	1,209,443	1,542,002	2,549,493
Foreign exports	6,995	10,983	9,058
25. MEXICO:			
Imports	8,507,124	10,480,225	13,239,905
Domestic exports	3,445,658	4,084,816	4,073,079
Foreign exports	2,132,931	2,345,347	1,920,691
26. CENTRAL AMERICAN STATES:			
Imports	1,609,044	1,981,322	2,896,012
Domestic exports	1,406,855	1,279,329	1,350,515
Foreign exports	71,060	68,220	82,916
27. HAYTI AND SAN DOMINGO:			
Imports	1,517,951	2,860,425	1,933,177
Domestic exports	3,326,747	4,854,246	4,760,389
Foreign exports	244,232	416,967	201,401
28. UNITED STATES OF COLOMBIA:			
Imports	6,589,449	6,410,964	7,749,428
Domestic exports	4,495,258	5,317,001	5,123,545
Foreign exports	181,501	298,685	235,499
29. BRAZIL, ARGENTINE REPUBLIC, URUGUAY, AND VENEZUELA:			
Imports	42,701,742	49,717,247	56,426,680
Domestic exports	8,809,946	11,915,269	13,540,546
Foreign exports	308,983	437,210	476,695
30. PERU AND CHILI:			
Imports	2,398,304	2,276,258	1,922,846
Domestic exports	10,665,692	6,649,516	5,349,021
Foreign exports	279,591	227,690	186,875
31. SANDWICH ISLANDS:			
Imports	1,285,320	1,316,270	1,017,172
Domestic exports	620,295	654,103	628,280
Foreign exports	43,469	43,088	26,348
32. CHINA AND JAPAN:			
Imports	35,927,778	36,445,314	*24,648,852
Domestic exports	12,077,224	15,000,751	†10,508,072
Foreign exports	1,845,212	2,775,493	‡2,875,777
33. ALL OTHER COUNTRIES:			
Imports	5,236,759	6,824,940	1,463,585
Domestic exports	3,390,262	3,843,193	918,254
Foreign exports	164,801	295,704	2,218
TOTAL IMPORTS	$640,338,766	$663,617,147	$595,861,248
TOTAL DOMESTIC EXPORTS	$549,219,718	$649,132,563	$693,089,054
TOTAL FOREIGN EXPORTS	$22,769,749	$28,149,511	$23,780,388

* Including Hong-Kong, $449,230.   † Including Hong-Kong, $7,070,800.   ‡ Including Hong-Kong, $2,810,205.

CONCHA, Don MANUEL DE LA, Marquis of Douro and the Havana, a Spanish general and statesman, born at Madrid in 1794; died from wounds received in battle before Estella, at Martemuro, June 28, 1874. He first saw service in the War of Independence under Napoleon I., and in 1816 sailed for the Spanish South American colonies, which were then in revolt, and in that troublesome and difficult conflict distinguished himself as a skillful soldier under Espartero. Returning to Spain in 1824, he engaged in the Carlist War on the side of Queen Maria Christina. He was successively commissioned brigadier and major-general in the campaign, and at its close was elected a deputy to the Cortes from the city of Cadiz. In the Cortes he was at first a supporter of Espartero, but after his defeat he advocated the adminis-

tration of Narvaez. In June, 1843, he was made commandant of Valencia and Murcia, and, by his rapid movements, compelled the insurgents of Saragossa to capitulate, and occupied Barcelona in the name of the Queen. In February, 1844, he suppressed a new insurrection at Cartagena so promptly and wisely that he was appointed Captain-General of Catalonia. He put down the Carlists with a strong hand, and proclaimed both Don Carlos and the Prince of the Asturias traitors and outlaws. In 1847, on the occasion of the differences with Portugal, he proceeded to the frontier with 6,000 picked troops and occupied Oporto. The same year he accompanied Queen Maria Christina to Paris, and, returning to Madrid, took his seat in the Cortes among the ultra-Conservatives. In 1849 he went to Italy with the Spanish troops designed to aid the Pope, and on coming back was reinvested with the captain-generalcy he had formerly held. General Concha next took a leading part in the insurrection of 1854. He signed the address, which was the signal for that outbreak, and was ordered into exile in the Canary Isles. The wily soldier, however, preferred going to France, whence he was soon enabled to return by the progress of the popular uprising. Arriving at Saragossa he was placed by the Junta in command of the insurrection, which speedily resulted in the exile of Queen Maria Christina, the downfall of Narvaez, and the triumph of Espartero. His friends being now in power, General Concha was restored to all his former honors, made Director-General of the Artillery, and finally marshal. He continued in the enjoyment of his titles after O'Donnell overthrew Espartero in 1856, but he was deprived of them by Narvaez, who forced him to live aloof from politics. The veteran was living in retirement when, during the troubles of 1868, Queen Isabella II. called him to form a ministry. The revolution was meanwhile making progress, but he believed that it might be suppressed if the Queen would return to Madrid and send away her friend Marfori. This she refused to do; and Marshal Concha handed her his resignation at the frontier, after instructing the officers of the Madrid garrison to oppose no longer the popular movement. After the revolution of 1868, Marshal Concha, already in his seventy-fifth year, had remained in retirement until the spring of 1874, when the successes attained by the Carlists had alarmed Serrano so greatly that he summoned the veteran soldier, though in his eightieth year, to take command of the army and lead them to battle against his old foes. Bilbao, which had been for some time invested by Don Carlos, was first to be relieved, as its garrison was reduced to the greatest straits. Taking command as promptly as of old, Marshal Concha left Madrid April 11th, and, arriving at the seat of war, advanced with 20,000 men against the enemy. Acting with masterly skill, he assailed the enemy in the rear while Serrano attacked him in front, and at the same time succeeded in joining his forces with those of that commander. The Carlists fought bravely, but were overmatched by this strategy and hastily abandoned their positions. Marshal Concha entered the beleaguered city, as he had promised to do, on the national festival of the 2d of May, amid the acclamations of the people. Being placed in supreme command of the Northern Army, Concha now determined to follow up his successes, and by driving the Carlists to a small district destitute of resources place them entirely in his power. Leaving Bilbao, May 11th, he reached Portugalete the same day and stopped there for the night. On the 12th he entered Somorrostro, then infested by Carlist bands which collected customs duties and levied contributions in rations and money. On the 13th he marched to Sopuerta, which is

situated on the Valmaseda road, at the foot of the Galdames Heights, and on the 17th he was at Orduna. On arriving at the latter place he had a slight skirmish with the Carlists, who it seems were taken by surprise. On the 18th the marshal arrived at the little town of Espejo, and informed the inhabitants that if a shot was fired he would not leave one stone standing in the place, which threat, together with the presence of the army, proved effectual. On the 19th he reached Vittoria, the scene of Wellington's victory, and on the 6th of June gained Logrono. Marshal Concha continued marching into Navarre with the view of establishing a fortified line which would prevent the Carlists advancing beyond that province, while he protected the roads to the capital. His strategy had so far forced the Carlists to abandon Durango and to retire to Estella, where they established three intrenched lines. The roads being impracticable for heavy artillery, Marshal Concha was obliged to suspend operations for a time against Estella, which he constantly menaced. His force numbered 38,000 men, with eighty-seven pieces of artillery, while that of the enemy was estimated at 24,000, commanded by Don Carlos in person. On the 25th of June he began the attack on Estella, and on the 28th, while encouraging his troops to resist the bold defense of the Carlists, he was shot just as he was mounting his horse, and was borne by a gallant lieutenant of hussars to an inn at Abarzuza, where he died in a few minutes. A brave soldier, and humane as brave, his errors of former years were covered by the halo of glory which surrounded him in his last hours.

CONGREGATIONALISTS. At the meeting of the National Council of the Congregational Churches in the United States, held in October, 1874, the Secretary presented a comparative summary of the statistics of the churches for that year, and of those of 1871, when the last National Council was held. It showed a net increase, in three years, of 204 churches. The number of churches organized during the period was 413, but 209 churches once on the list had been dropped. Nearly all of the churches dropped were in the recently-settled but not in the most recently-settled States, and the loss was occasioned by changes in population. The existing churches might be grouped by locality thus: In the New England States, 1,451; in New York, New Jersey, and Pennsylvania, 340; from the eastern boundary of Ohio to the Mississippi River, 853; west of the Mississippi (excluding the Pacific States), 552; in the Pacific States and Territories, 75; in the Southern States (exclusive of Missouri), 54. More than one-half the increase of churches (124 churches) had been gained in the four States of Iowa, Kansas, Nebraska, and Wisconsin. The gain in the Southern States (not including Missouri) had been twelve churches. The net gain in church-members had been 17,161, an annual average of 5,720. The annual average increase for the preceding fifteen years had been 6,554. The present report did not include the additions made in the revivals of the previous winter. The additions by profession of faith during the three years had been 40,432. The gain in members was distributed geographically as follows: In New England, 1,245; in New York, New Jersey, and Pennsylvania, 3,358; from the eastern boundary of Ohio to the western boundaries of the first tier of States beyond Missouri, 10,092; in the Southern States (not including Missouri), 1,245; in the Western and Pacific States and Territories, 1,232. The number of Sunday-school scholars had increased 11,089. The benevolent contributions had been imperfectly reported. The estimates did not include the large amounts given by individuals. The report of 1874 showed an increase of $259,260.24 over that of 1871. The amounts raised for the home expenses of the churches were not included in the calculation. Of $1,213,816 of contributions, reported in 1873, $856,833.19 had come from the New England States. The State of Arkansas had been dropped from the rolls, and the States of Nevada and West Virginia and the Territory of Idaho had been added. The number of theological seminaries in 1874 was seven (or the same as in 1871). In 1871 they had thirty-two professors; in 1874, thirty-five; in 1871 they had eleven lecturers; in 1874, sixteen; in 1871 they had 272 students; in 1874, 327.

A Council of Congregational Churches met in the city of Brooklyn, N. Y., March 24th, to consider questions which were submitted to it concerning the nature and terms of membership and the principles of fellowship in the Congregational churches. The occasion for summoning the Council was given in certain action of Plymouth Church, Brooklyn, in a case of discipline, to which two neighboring churches took exception on the ground that it was not according to the principles of Congregational church government and usage. A member of Plymouth Church had ceased to unite with it in worship and to attend its meetings in 1869. He claimed that he had thereby withdrawn himself from the jurisdiction of the church. About four years afterward, charges were brought against him for conduct unworthy a church-member. They were not pressed for trial; but at the annual meeting of the church, October 31, the name of this member was called in examining the rolls of the church, and the fact of the existence of the charges was announced. The explanation was made to the meeting that he was no longer a member of the church. Although this was the first public notice that had been given of his withdrawal, the case was dropped without further proceedings, and the member's name was stricken from the rolls. The attention of the neighboring churches was called to this action as presenting novel and singular features. It was discussed at meetings of the Church of the

Pilgrims and of the Clinton Avenue Congregational Church. An address, expressing the views of these meetings, and their objections to the principle of action adopted by Plymouth Church, was sent to that church. Plymouth Church objected to the tone of the address, and made a reply to it, in which it was intimated that the remonstrating churches had passed judgment and condemnation upon the case without fairly examining it. The remonstrating churches replied with a letter, explaining their motives, repelling the imputation that they were offensive, and making inquiry as to the position which Plymouth Church held in the case. Plymouth Church replied, embodying in its letter an extract from its manual, first published in 1848, in which was affirmed in substance its entire independence of all other churches "in regard to its faith, order, and discipline." It was held by the remonstrating churches that such independence had never been claimed by the Congregational Churches of America. Further correspondence was had, with a view of discussing by fraternal conference, or by a council, in the call of which the complaining churches and Plymouth Church should join, the following questions:

1. Does the order and usage of Congregational churches permit a member, who has entered into public covenant with a church, to terminate his relations with that church by his own volition or act, so that no action on the part of the church is requisite to such termination of membership?

2. Was the action of Plymouth Church on the 31st October, 1873, in dropping a member against whom grave and specific charges had been formally presented, an action in accordance with the usages of Congregational churches, and with their understanding of the rule of Christian discipline?

Plymouth Church was also invited to give its adhesion to the following declaration on church-fellowship, to the principle of which it was considered to have committed itself in one of its letters: "Whenever any church shall openly and avowedly change the essential conditions upon which it was publicly received into the fellowship of neighboring churches, it is their right, either by individual action, or by council, to withdraw their fellowship." Plymouth Church asked for modifications in the statement of the points to be submitted to the Council, and the imposition of conditions to the calling of it, which the other churches did not feel at liberty to grant. The remonstrating churches, therefore, determined to call the Council alone. Invitations to attend the Council were sent out to seventy-nine churches and seventeen ministers not settled over churches. The Council met in the Clinton Avenue Congregational Church, Brooklyn, and was constituted by the election of the Rev. Leonard Bacon, D. D., of New Haven, Conn., as moderator; Judge Charles J. Walker, as assistant-moderator; the Rev. Alonzo Quint, D. D., of New Bedford, Mass., as scribe; and the Rev. J. C. Meserve, of Brooklyn, N. Y., as assistant-scribe. Two of the churches invited had declined to be represented. The delegates who were present had gathered from fourteen States. Plymouth Church was invited to declare its views orally before the Council on the questions presented by its pastor and such committee as it might appoint, and by the same committee to convey such information concerning the action referred to in those questions as the Council might request. It declined to appear, "lest," as it replied in its letter, "by our acceptance we should seem to renounce our conscientious convictions and to withdraw our solemn testimony against the violation of Christian liberty, courtesy, and equity, which has characterized the calling of this Council and the steps which led to it, and lest we should establish a precedent full of danger to smaller churches, as encouraging irregular and unwarrantable proceedings on the part of strong churches, which the weaker party might afterward, by the force of our example, be compelled to condone." In the same letter, the church made some explanations of its position on the subject of church-fellowship, which were subsequently referred to in the decision of the Council as having, to a certain extent, influenced its action. The first business was to determine whether the Council was a mutual, an *ex-parte*, or an advisory one. It was decided to be an advisory Council. Its discussions were conducted for the most part in secret session.

The decision of the Council was embodied in a formal document. It reviewed the circumstances which led to the calling of the Council, and the preliminary correspondence which took place between the churches calling it and Plymouth Church. In respect to that part of the correspondence in which a reference of the points of difference to the advice of a Council was sought, it said:

We find on the part of Plymouth Church no definite expression either of consent or refusal. Yet, inasmuch as the Plymouth Church did not distinctly refuse to unite on a reference to a Council, we cannot but regret that the complaining churches did not urge their request till a refusal or an evasion should have become unequivocal.

On the main questions on which advice was sought, it pronounced the following judgment and opinions:

We say distinctly that the idea of membership in a Congregational Church is the idea of a covenant between the individual member and the church; that by virtue of that covenant the member is responsible to the church for his conformity to the law of Christ, and the church is responsible for him; and that this responsibility does not cease till the church, by some formal and corporate act, has declared the dissolution of the covenant. The covenant may be broken by the member. He may offend, and, when duly admonished, may give no satisfactory evidence of repentance. In that case, he is cut off from communion; the Church having given its testimony is no longer responsible for him, and he can be restored only by the removal of the censure. Voluntary absence of a resident member from the communion of the Church, and from its public worship, does not dissolve the covenant, but is a reasonable ground of admonition, and, if persisted in, of final censure.

When a regular complaint is made against such a member that in some other respect he violates the laws of the Church, and especially when the complaint is that he has circulated and promoted scandals derogatory to the Christian integrity of the pastor and injurious to the reputation of the Church, the consideration that he has long ago forsaken the Church is only an aggravation of his alleged fault.

In regard to the future relations between these churches and Plymouth Church, we express our hope that the very extraordinary proceeding which gave occasion for the correspondence and for this Council will not be a precedent for the guidance of that Church hereafter. Could we suppose that such proceedings will be repeated, we should feel that the disregard of the first principles involved in the idea of church-membership and the idea of the fellowship of churches with each other, would require the strongest possible protest. But the communication from the Plymouth Church to this Council makes professions and declarations which justify the hope that such deviation from the orderly course of discipline will not be repeated. The accused person in that case has not been retained in the church, nor commended to any other church.

We recite some of those declarations from the Plymouth Church which encourage the hope we have expressed: "We rejoice," says the Plymouth Church, "to live in affectionate fellowship with all churches of the Lord Jesus, and especially with those who are in all things like-minded with us, holding to the same faith and order, not only in things fundamental but in things less essential yet dear to us by conviction or association. * * * * We cheerfully admit that whenever any church shall openly and avowedly change the essential conditions upon which it was publicly received into the fellowship of neighboring churches, or shall by flagrant neglect exert a pernicious and immoral influence upon the community, or upon sister churches, it is their right either by individual action or by council to withdraw their fellowship. We hold that preceding disfellowship in all such cases there should be such affectionate and reasonable inquiry as shall show that the evil is real, that the causes of it are within the control of the church, that the evil is not a transient evil, such as may befall any church, but is permanent and tending to increase rather than diminish."

While it is not to be forgotten that this communication from Plymouth Church is entirely subsequent to the case as it stood upon the convening of this Council, when the Plymouth Church, by its action of December 5th, had declared itself responsible for no other church, and no other church for it, in respect to doctrine, order, and discipline, which action, as interpreted in the circumstances then existing, implied a withdrawal to the ground of total independency, yet that church is to be fraternally judged by its latest utterance.

These professions on the part of Plymouth Church may be accepted by other churches as indicating its intention to maintain an efficient discipline, and to regard the mutual responsibility of churches. At the same time, the Council feels constrained to declare that these declarations seem to us inconsistent with the resolution of interpretation adopted by Plymouth Church, December 5, 1873, and with other acts and statements appearing in the published documents. We think that the action of that church, as presented in these documents, if unmollified, would justify these churches in withdrawing fellowship. Yet, inasmuch as the Plymouth Church seems to us to admit, in its communication to us, the Congregational principles of discipline and fellowship, we advise the churches convening this Council to maintain with it the relations of fellowship as heretofore, in the hope that Plymouth Church may satisfy these churches of its acceptance of the principles which it has been supposed to disavow.

' The sixth *National Council of the Congregational Churches in the United States* (or the second, counting from the organization of the Council as a permanent body at Oberlin, O., in 1871), met at New Haven, Conn., September 30th. The Hon. Lafayette S. Foster, of Connecticut, was chosen moderator, and the Rev. George F. Magoun, D. D., and the Rev. I. E. Dwinell, D. D., were chosen assistant-moderators. Attention was given chiefly to the consideration of the report of the committee appointed at the preceding meeting on the consolidation of the benevolent societies supported by the Congregational churches. The main provisions of the plan supported by the committee were adopted as follows :

I. That for the work of foreign missions the American Board of Commissioners for Foreign Missions be earnestly commended to the churches; and that it is advised that the funds which formerly were contributed by our churches to the operations in papal lands, through the American and Foreign Christian Union, be added to the contributions ordinarily made to that board.

II. That for the work among the freedmen of our land, heretofore carried on with so much efficiency and success by the American Missionary Association, that organization be commended to the continued support of our churches.

III. That the Council heartily approve of the consolidation already effected between the American Education Society and the College Society, and commend the new organization to the generous support of the churches.

IV. That for the ordinary home missionary work the American Home Missionary Society is deserving of vigorous support, and that in the judgment of the Council it is desirable that it so far enlarge its operations as to comprehend and supervise all that work of the churches which is properly related to the idea and plan of home evangelization in the special fields which it occupies ; that the now separate enterprises of church erection and missionary Sunday-school work be incorporated with the work of the American Home Missionary Society, and be provided for by the establishment of district bureaus or otherwise, at the discretion of the Executive Committee, and that separate annual collections be taken for the special work of church-building and missionary Sunday-schools.

V. That we advise that the Congregational Publishing Society be disembarrassed of all work incongruous with a strictly business enterprise, and that every possible effort be made to promote its prosperity in its special field by securing through its agency the publication and sale of denominational and Sunday-school literature of a high order.

VI. That in the judgment of this Council the consolidation into one of our various missionary and benevolent magazines is desirable, and that the officers of the different societies are respectfully requested to consider the practicability of such a consolidation.

The report of the committee also contained recommendations that the missions of the American Board among the North American Indians be transferred to the care of the American Home Missionary Association, and the foreign missions of the latter organization be transferred to the American Board and kindred societies ; and that the congregations be advised to transfer to the denominational boards representing kindred enterprises their present contributions to union societies. These propositions were not approved by the Council.

A resolution was adopted, commending all the benevolent societies to the continued confidence and support of the churches, and declaring " that no proposal of union, necessarily in the future, need, in the intermediate time, lessen the contributions to their various objects." A paper, by the Rev. D. B. Coe, D.D., on " Christian Comity between Denominations in the Home Field," called attention to an agreement which had been made a short time before between the Presbyterian Board of Home Missions and the Executive Committee of the American Home Missionary Society, for the purpose of avoiding rivalry in establishing churches in sparsely-populated districts. It had often happened that the agents of different denominations had undertaken to build up two or more churches, in neighborhoods which could, at most, competently support but one. Thus, several weak congregations, constantly dependent upon the missionary organizations for help, had been started in places where a single congregation, of either denomination, might have sustained an independent existence, and flourished. In their agreement, the Presbyterian Board of Home Missions and the Executive Committee of the American Home Missionary Society had consented that they would mutually exert their influence to prevent interference of this kind with each other's work ; that, so far as they could control operations, neither board should hereafter enter a field requiring help which was already occupied by the other ; that, in places where the two societies were already represented by different churches dividing energy and resources that ought to be united, they would counsel mutual forbearance and yielding, and the withdrawal of one or the other church in favor of the one which should seem best fitted for the work there ; and that, in selecting new fields, they would take care to prevent interference. This paper was ordered to be printed with the proceedings of the Council. A special committee was appointed to address other evangelical bodies on the subject to which it related, and solicit them to appoint committees for a general conference in regard to the evils against which it was intended to provide. In case the conference is held, this committee will also represent the council in it.

The first General Council of the Congregational churches was held at Cambridge, then called Newtown, Mass., in 1637. The second was held at Cambridge in 1646. Adjourned sessions of the same body were held in 1647 and 1648, and the result of their deliberations was embodied in the so-called "Cambridge Platform." The third council was held at Albany, N. Y., in 1852, and considered plans for carrying on missionary operations in the West. The fourth council was held at Boston in 1865, and held an adjourned session at Plymouth. The fifth council was held at Oberlin, Ohio, where the National Council was organized as a permanent body, to meet every three years. The present session, although only the second meeting of the council as a permanent body, was, by including all the previous meetings of general councils, counted as the sixth.

The twenty-first anniversary of the *American Congregational Union* was held in the city of New York, May 14th. Mr. A. S. Barnes presided. The trustees reported that grants had been made during the year to forty-six churches. The receipts for the year ending May 1, 1874, were $61,184.64, which, with the balance on hand at the beginning of the year, made the available resources of the Union $67,044.19. The expenditures for the same period were $60,580.40, leaving a balance at the close of the year of $6,463.79. The usual social reunion was held in the evening, and was addressed by the Rev. Dr. Post, of St. Louis, the Rev. H. M. Gallaher, Baptist, the Rev. Dr. John Hall, Presbyterian, and by other persons.

The forty-eighth anniversary of the *American Home Missionary Society* was held in New York City, May 13th. The receipts for the year were reported to have been $290,120.34, and the expenditures $287,662.91. The sum of $12,652 was still due to missionaries for labor performed, but not yet reported, and further appropriations had been made to the amount of $106,979, making the total amount of moneys pledged $119,632. Nine hundred and sixty-nine missionaries had been employed, of whom three had preached to congregations of colored people, and thirty-two had preached in foreign languages. The number of congregations and missionary stations supplied was 2,195, fifty more than supplied during the previous year, and twenty more than the largest number occupied in any former year. The receipts were $22,429 more than those of the previous year, and had been exceeded by those of only one year in the history of the society.

The sixty-fifth annual meeting of the *American Board of Commissioners for Foreign Missions* was held at Rutland, Vt., October 6th. The Rev. Mark Hopkins, D. D., LL. D., presided. The treasurer, according to the orders of the board, made separate statements of the receipts and expenditures for the ordinary missionary work among the heathen, and for the work in "nominally Christian lands." The total receipts for the general work had been $443,925.29. The expenditures on the same account had been:

Cost of missions....................	$399,681 96
Cost of agencies....................	9,247 63
Cost of publications................	10,666 80
Cost of administration.............	16,904 93
Total expenditures...........	$436,590 82

For the work in "nominally Christian lands," the receipts had been $33,981.22, the expenditures as follows:

Cost of missions....................	$43,886 88
Cost of agencies....................	2,133 63
Total.................	$46,020 51

The board was reported in debt to the amount of $30,441.07.

Several events had occurred to impede the progress of the missionary operations: among them were named the famine which had prevailed in some parts of Turkey; the murder of the Rev. Mr. Stephens in Mexico; the intrusion of English High-Churchmen into the Mahratta mission, in India; the attempts of the Turkish Government to suppress the circulation of the Scriptures among the Moslems; and the financial stringency at home. Nevertheless, an increased interest in the cause, and a healthy growth in most of the missions, were reported. The board resolved to endeavor to raise the sum of $400,000 among the churches for the payment of its debt and the prosecution of its work during the coming year, expecting to secure $100,000 more from legacies and other sources, and fixing the whole amount sought at $500,000. Twenty-five hundred dollars were pledged during the meeting toward the establishment of an institution of Christian learning in Japan.

The twenty-eighth annual meeting of the *American Missionary Association* was held at Clinton, Iowa, October 28th. The treasurer's report showed the total receipts for the year to have been $319,728.75, and the aggregate expenditures $344,004.05. Of the latter sum, $280,833.87 had been expended in the South. The expenditures in the foreign missionary work had been $9,034.16 for Africa, $4,156.29 for the Jamaica mission, $2,967.61 for Siam, and $92.67 for special purposes in the Sandwich Islands.

The *Congregational Union of Ontario and Quebec* held its meeting in June. The Rev. Joseph Unsworth, of Georgetown, was elected chairman for the year. The receipts of the Congregational Missionary Society for the year had been, including a balance of $1,200 from former years, $8,082, of which sum $4,900 had been actually raised among the Canadian churches. The Colonial Missionary Society of England had given during the previous year £400 toward the operations in Ontario and Quebec, and would give £350 for the current year.

The forty-fourth annual meeting of the *Congregational Union of England and Wales* was held in London, May 11th. The total income of the Union for the year was reported to have been £7,311 12s. 4d. A Conference on church finance had been held in December, 1873, at Birmingham, at which the conclusion was reached that the stipends of Congregational ministers were, as a rule, insufficient to such a degree as to limit the usefulness of their ministry. The Conference had estimated that no stipend in the country districts should be lower than £150, and had sketched a plan of operations, the object of which was to bring the subject more directly before the churches, and to secure greater liberality and promptness in the collections for this object.

'The following resolution was unanimously adopted in reference to the relations of church and state :

Resolved, That this Assembly recognizes the gravity of the political difficulties and perils arising from the doctrines and pretensions of the Ultramontane party, now supreme in the Roman Catholic Church, and believing that these difficulties are greatly aggravated by the existence of organic relations between churches, whether Catholic or Protestant, and civil governments, desires to express its deliberate judgment that the civil supremacy of the state, which it is the duty of nations and governments to defend against all ecclesiastical encroachments, and the rights of conscience, which it is the duty of nations and governments to respect, can be secured and permanently maintained only by the dissolution of all organic relations between the church and state.

In reference to the growth of ritualism in the Church of England, the following resolution was also unanimously adopted :

Resolved, That, in view of the prevalence and rapid growth in the Church of England of doctrines and practices closely resembling those of the Church of Rome, this Union earnestly calls upon Protestant Nonconformists to meet the danger to which the spiritual life of the nation is exposed by increased activity in inculcating Scriptural truth. In particular, it suggests to pastors and Sunday-school teachers the desirableness of such elementary teaching—whether in the form of sermons, lectures, or catechetical instruction—as may serve to protect the people from being misled by religious teachers who misuse the authority and influence with which they have been invested.

The autumnal meeting of the Congregational Union of England and Wales was held at Huddersfield, beginning October 8th. The Rev. J. G. Rogers presided, and delivered an address on " The Age, and our Work in it." He criticised the utterances of Prof. Tyndall in his address before the British Association, and expressed disapproval of the schemes of the Episcopal High Churchmen for the reunion of Christendom. The most important subjects considered by the meeting were those of finance and ministerial support. The present arrangements of the churches for supplementing the stipends of ministers were declared, in the opinion of the Union, to be insufficient. The assembly expressed its appreciation of the importance of the work carried on by the Home, the Irish Evangelical, and the Colonial Missionary Societies, and invited increased contributions to their funds. A resolution was adopted recognizing " the great service which the Sunday-schools of England have rendered in promoting religious knowledge among the young, and in leading many, whom probably no other agency would have reached, to the obedience of faith ; " regarding the stimulus which recent legislation had given to the cause of education, " as rendering it only the more imperative that the Sunday-school system should be maintained, and that efforts should be put forth to raise it to the highest point of efficiency ; " and suggesting a closer pastoral oversight of the schools, preparatory instruction of the teachers, coöperation in the management of the

schools, periodical examinations of them, and special services for their benefit.

The eightieth annual meeting of the *London Missionary Society* was held in London, May 14th. The treasurer's balance-sheet showed the total receipts for general purposes to have been £99,954 16s. 10d. ; contributions and dividends for special objects, £12,986 4s. 1d. ; total income, £115,909 10s. 10d. The expenditures had been £114,061 19s. 8d. The number of English missionaries engaged by the society was stated to be 155 ; but beyond these were an increasing number of fairly qualified native agents engaged as pastors and teachers. During the year thirty-three offers of service had been received by the directors, and nine of them had been accepted. The results of the foreign work of the year were spoken of in the report of the directors as " both numerous and important."

The annual meeting of the *Congregational Union of Scotland* was held in April, the Rev. Dr. Russell presiding. The report of the widows' fund showed that it had increased £480 during the year.

The following are the statistics of the Congregational Churches in the United States and British America, as given in the *Congregational Quarterly* for January, 1875 :

STATES, ETC.	Churches.	Ministers.	Church-Members.
Alabama	8	7	335
California	66	68	2,949
Colorado	9	6	303
Connecticut	296	377	50,011
Dakota	10	6	244
District of Columbia	1	13	413
Georgia	11	7	600
Idaho	1	...	12
Illinois	239	221	20,877
Indiana	24	19	1,253
Iowa	224	198	12,803
Kansas	115	97	3,999
Kentucky	5	9	369
Louisiana	12	13	983
Maine	238	178	19,329
Maryland	3	1	190
Massachusetts	508	617	82,479
Michigan	196	162	13,287
Minnesota	86	66	4,165
Mississippi	3	5	107
Missouri	71	45	3,406
Nebraska	65	48	1,613
Nevada	1	1	12
New Hampshire	188	181	18,356
New Jersey	20	28	2,558
New York	252	219	26,487
North Carolina	6	5	168
Ohio	214	191	18,930
Oregon	9	9	525
Pennsylvania	75	50	5,358
Rhode Island	25	32	4,442
South Carolina	1	1	243
Tennessee	8	11	522
Texas	6	7	263
Utah	1	1	99
Vermont	198	197	17,920
Virginia	2	2	99
Washington Territory	5	3	76
West Virginia	2	1	47
Wisconsin	198	176	12,978
Wyoming	1	...	21
Total	**3,403**	**3,278**	**330,391**
Ontario and Quebec	89	76	4,658
New Brunswick	5	4	369
Nova Scotia	10	7	852
Jamaica	6	3	521
Total in North America	**3,513**	**3,368**	**336,811**

CONGRESS, UNITED STATES. The first session * of the Forty-third Congress commenced on December 1, 1873. (For the Message of the President, *see* PUBLIC DOCUMENTS, ANNUAL CYCLOPÆDIA, 1873.)

The Vice-President, Henry Wilson, of Massa-

* The following is a list of members at the first session of the Forty-third Congress.

SENATE.

Alabama—George Goldthwaite, George E. Spencer.
Arkansas—Powell Clayton, Stephen W. Dorsey.
California—John S. Hager, Aaron A. Sargent.
Connecticut—William A. Buckingham, Orris S. Ferry.
Delaware—Thomas F. Bayard, Eli Saulsbury.
Florida—Abijah Gilbert, Simon B. Conover.
Georgia—Thomas M. Norwood, John B. Gordon.
Illinois—John A. Logan, Richard J. Oglesby.
Indiana—Daniel D. Pratt, Oliver P. Morton.
Iowa—George G. Wright, William B. Allison.
Kansas—James M. Harvey, John J. Ingalls.
Kentucky—John W. Stevenson, Thomas C. McCreery.
Louisiana—J. Rodman West, ————.
Maine—Hannibal Hamlin, Lot M. Morrill.
Maryland—William T. Hamilton, George R. Dennis.
Massachusetts—Charles Sumner,* George S. Boutwell.
Michigan—Zachariah Chandler, Thomas W. Ferry.
Minnesota—Alexander Ramsey, William Windom.
Mississippi—Henry R. Pease, James L. Alcorn.
Missouri—Carl Schurz, Lewis V. Bogy.
Nebraska—Thomas W. Tipton, Phineas W. Hitchcock.
Nevada—William M. Stewart, John P. Jones.
New Hampshire—Aaron H. Cragin, Bainbridge Wadleigh.
New Jersey—John P. Stockton, Frederick T. Frelinghuysen.
New York—Reuben E. Fenton, Roscoe Conkling.
North Carolina—Matt. W. Ransom, Aug. S. Merrimon.
Ohio—Allen G. Thurman, John Sherman.
Oregon—James K. Kelley, John H. Mitchell.
Pennsylvania—John Scott, Simon Cameron.
Rhode Island—William Sprague, Henry B. Anthony.
South Carolina—Thos. J. Robertson, John J. Patterson.
Tennessee—William G. Brownlow, Henry Cooper.
Texas—Joseph W. Flanagan, Morgan O. Hamilton.
Vermont—George F. Edmunds, Justin S. Morrill.
Virginia—John F. Lewis, John W. Johnson.
West Virginia—Arthur I. Boreman, Henry G. Davis.
Wisconsin—Matthew H. Carpenter, Timothy O. Howe.

HOUSE.

Alabama— Frederick G. Bromberg, James T. Rapier, Charles Pelham, Charles Hays, John H. Caldwell, Joseph H. Sloss. At Large, Alexander White, Christopher C. Sheets.
Arkansas—Asa Hodges, Oliver P. Snyder, Thomas M. Gunter. At Large, William J. Hynes.
California—Charles Clayton, Horace Frank Page, John K. Luttrell, Sherman O. Houghton.
Connecticut—Joseph R. Hawley, Stephen W. Kellogg, Henry H. Starkweather, William H. Barnum.
Delaware—James R. Rofland.
Florida—Josiah T. Walls, William J. Purman.
Georgia—Andrew Sloan, Richard H. Whiteley, Philip Cook, Henry R. Harris, James C. Freeman, James H. Blount, Pierce M. B. Young, Alexander H. Stephens, Hiram P. Bell.
Illinois—John B. Rice, Jasper D. Ward, Charles B. Farwell, Stephen A. Hurlbut, Horatio C. Burchard, John B. Hawley, Franklin Corwin, Greenbury L. Fort, Granville Barrere, William H. Ray, Robert M. Knapp, James C. Robinson, John McNulta, Joseph G. Cannon, John R. Eden, James S. Martin, William R. Morrison, Isaac Clements, Samuel S. Marshall.
Indiana—William E. Niblack, Simeon K. Wolf, William S. Holman, Jeremiah M. Wilson, John Coburn, Morton C. Hunter, Thomas J. Cason, James N. Tyner, John P. C. Shanks, Henry B. Sayler, Jasper Packard. At Large, Godlove S. Orth, William Williams.
Iowa—George W. McCrary, Aylett R. Cotton, William G. Donnan, Henry O. Pratt, James Wilson, William Loughridge, John A. Kasson, James W. McDill, Jackson Orr.
Kansas—David P. Lowe, Stephen A. Cobb, William A. Phillips.
Kentucky—Edward Crossland, John Young Brown, Charles W. Millikin, William B. Read, Elisha D. Standeford, William E. Arthur, James B. Beck, Milton J. Durham, George M. Adams, John D. Young.
Louisiana—J. Hale Sypher, Lionel A. Sheldon, Chester B. Darrall, George L. Smith, Frank Morey. At large (vacancy).
Maine—John H. Burleigh, William P. Frye, James G. Blaine, Samuel F. Hersey, Eugene Hale.
Maryland—Ephraim K. Wilson, Stevenson Archer, William J. O'Brien, Thomas Swann, William J. Albert, Lloyd Lowndes, Jr.

* Deceased. Wm. B. Washburne elected to vacancy.

Massachusetts—James Buffinton, Benjamin W. Harris, Henry L. Pierce, Samuel Hooper, Daniel W. Gooch, Benjamin F. Butler, Ebenezer R. Hoar, John M. S. Williams, George F. Hoar, Alvah Crocker, Henry L. Dawes.
Michigan—Moses W. Field, Henry Waldron, George Willard, Julius C. Burrows, William B. Williams, Josiah W. Begole, Omar D. Conger, Nathaniel B. Bradley, Jay A. Hubbell.
Minnesota—Mark H. Dunnell, Horace B. Strait, John T. Averill.
Mississippi—Lucius Q. C. Lamar, Albert R. Howe, Henry W. Barry, Jason Niles, George C. McKee, John R. Lynch.
Missouri—Edwin O. Stanard, Erastus Wells, William H. Stone, Robert A. Hatcher, Richard P. Bland, Harrison E. Havens, Thomas T. Crittenden, Abram Comingo, Isaac C. Parker, Ira B. Hyde, John B. Clarke, Jr., John M. Glover, Aylett H. Buckner.
Nebraska—Lorenzo Crounse.
Nevada—Charles W. Kendall.
New Hampshire—William B. Small, Austin F. Pike, Hosea W. Parker.
New Jersey—John W. Hazleton, Samuel A. Dobbins, Amos Clark, Jr., Robert Hamilton, William Walter Phelps, Marcus L. Ward, Isaac W. Scudder.
New York—Henry J. Scudder, John G. Schumaker, Simon B. Chittenden, Philip S. Crooke, William R. Roberts, Samuel S. Cox, Thomas J. Creamer, John D. Lawson, Richard Schell, Fernando Wood, Clarkson N. Potter, Charles St. John, John O. Whitehouse, David M. Dewitt, Eli Perry, James S. Smart, Robert S. Hale, William A. Wheeler, Henry H. Hathorn, David Wilber, Clinton L. Merriam, Ellis H. Roberts, William E. Lansing, R. Holland Duell, Clinton D. MacDougall, William H. Lamport, Thomas C. Platt, H. Boardman Smith, Freeman Clarke, George O. Hoskins, Lyman K. Bass, Walter L. Sessions. At large, Lyman Tremain.
North Carolina—Clinton L. Cobb, Charles R. Thomas, Alfred M. Waddell, William A. Smith, James M. Leach, Thomas S. Ashe, William M. Robbins, Robert B. Vance.
Ohio—Milton Sayler, Henry B. Banning, John Q. Smith, Lewis B. Gunckel, Charles N. Lamison, Isaac R. Sherwood, Lawrence T. Neal, William Lawrence, James W. Robinson, Charles Foster, Hezekiah S. Bundy, William E. Fink, Milton I. Southard, John Berry, William P. Sprague, Lorenzo Danford, Laurin D. Woodworth, James Monroe, James A. Garfield, Richard C. Parsons.
Oregon—James W. Nesmith.
Pennsylvania—Samuel J. Randall, Charles O'Neill, Leonard Myers, William D. Kelley, Alfred C. Harmer, James B. Biery, Washington Townsend, Hiester Clymer, A. Herr Smith, John W. Killinger, John B. Storm, Lazarus D. Shoemaker, James D. Strawbridge, John B. Packer, John A. Magee, John Cessna, R. Milton Speer, Sobieski Ross, Carlton B. Curtis, Hiram L. Richmond, Alexander W. Taylor, James S. Negley, Ebenezer McJunkin, William S. Moore. At Large, Lemuel Todd, Charles Albright, Glenni W. Scofield.
Rhode Island—Benjamin T. Eames, James M. Pendleton.
South Carolina—Joseph H. Rainey, Alonzo J. Ransier, L. Cass Carpenter, Alexander S. Wallace. At Large, Richard H. Cain.
Tennessee—Roderick R. Butler, Jacob M. Thornburgh, William Crutchfield, John M. Bright, Horace H. Harrison, Washington C. Whitthorne, John D. C. Atkins, David A. Nunn, Barbour Lewis. At Large, Horace Maynard.
Texas—Wm. S. Herndon, William P. McLean, De Witt C. Giddings, John Hancock. At Large, Roger Q. Mills, Asa H. Willie.
Vermont—Charles W. Willard, Luke P. Poland, George W. Hendee.
Virginia—James B. Sener, James H. Platt, Jr., J. Ambler Smith, William H. H. Stowell, Christopher Y. Thomas, Thos. Whitehead, John T. Harris, Eppa Hunton, Rees T. Bowen.
West Virginia—John J. Davis, J. Marshall Hagans, Frank Hereford.
Wisconsin—Charles G. Williams, Gerry W. Hazelton, J. Allen Barber, Alexander Mitchell, Charles A. Eldredge, Philetus Sawyer, Jeremiah M. Rusk, Alexander S. McDill.

DELEGATES FROM TERRITORIES.

Arizona—Richard C. McCormick.
Colorado—Jerome B. Chaffee.
Dakota—Moses K. Armstrong.
District of Columbia—Norton P. Chipman.
Idaho—John Hailey.
Montana—Martin Maginnis.
New Mexico—Stephen B. Elkins.
Utah—George Q. Cannon.
Washington—Obadiah B. McFadden.
Wyoming—William R. Steele.

chusetts, presided in the Senate, and James G. Blaine, of Maine, was elected Speaker of the House.

In the Senate, on December 1st, Mr. Sumner, of Massachusetts, submitted the following resolutions:

Whereas, By international law and existing custom war is recognized as a form of trial for the determination of differences between nations; and—

Whereas, For generations good men have protested against the irrational character of this arbitrament, where force instead of justice prevails, and have anxiously sought for a substitute in the nature of a judicial tribunal, all of which was expressed by Franklin in his exclamation: " When will mankind .be convinced that all wars are follies, very expensive and very mischievous, and agree to settle their differences by arbitration?" and—

Whereas, War once prevailed in the determination of differences between individuals, between cities, between counties, and between provinces, being recognized in all these cases as the arbiter of justice, but at last yielded to a judicial tribunal, and now, in the progress of civilization, the time has come for the extension of this humane principle to nations, so that their differences may be taken from the arbitrament of war, and, in conformity with these examples, submitted to a judicial tribunal; and—

Whereas, Arbitration has been formally recognized as a substitute for war in the determination of differences between nations, being especially recommended by the Congress of Paris, where were assembled the representatives of England, .France, Russia, Prussia, Austria, Sardinia, and Turkey, and afterward adopted by the United States in formal treaty with Great Britain for the determination of differences arising from depredations of British cruisers, and also from opposing claims with regard to the San Juan boundary; and—

Whereas, It becomes important to consider and settle the true character of this beneficent tribunal, thus commended and adopted, so that its authority and completeness as a substitute for war may not be impaired, but strengthened and upheld, to the end that civilization may be advanced and war be limited in its sphere: Therefore—

Resolved, That in the determination of international differences arbitration should become a substitute for war in reality as in name, and therefore coextensive with war in jurisdiction, so that any question or grievance which might be the occasion of war or of misunderstanding between nations should be considered by this tribunal.

Resolved, That the United States, having at heart the cause of peace everywhere, and hoping to help its permanent establishment between nations, hereby recommend the adoption of arbitration as a just and practical method for the determination of international differences, to be maintained sincerely and in good faith, so that war may cease to be regarded as a proper form of trial between nations.

They were ordered to be printed, and referred to the Committee on Foreign Relations.

Mr. Ferry, of Michigan, offered the following resolutions:

Resolved, That the Committee on Finance be instructed to consider the expediency of providing for a national system of banking and currency in lieu of the present one, which shall embody the substantial features following, to wit:

1. Banking to be open and free to all individuals and associations without limitation of capital.

2. The maximum currency circulation to be $800,-000,000 exclusive of fractional, and to be issued and authenticated solely by the Government, of uniform character, with " United States Currency" imprinted on its face, made lawful money and a legal tender for all public and private dues except duties on imports and interest on the public debt, and convertible on demand into Government bonds bearing interest at 3 65-100 per cent. per annum in currency.

3. The Government to issue bonds stamped " currency bonds," of denominations of $1.00 and multiples bearing interest at the rate of 3 65-100 per cent. per annum, convertible into currency on demand, and to be exempt from taxation by Federal, State, municipal, and local authority.

4. Substitution of the United States currency for national currency to be done at the convenience of the Government, without diminishing the volume of current circulation, and the bonds held for the security of the national currency to be adjusted with the banks by purchase or surrender; substitution of United States currency for other existing forms, bringing about uniformity of currency, to likewise be done without lessening the current circulation.

5. For immediate relief to existing monetary stringency the forty-four millions Treasury reserve to be issued without delay in the purchase of Government bonds bearing the higher rates of interest, and as fast as practicable additional purchases of like bonds to be made with United States currency, until the maximum circulation be reached.

6. Preparatory to withdrawal of the fractional currency the Secretary of the Treasury is required to make public designation of a period after which to begin the redemption in silver of denominations of twenty-five cents, and under also a second period designated at which to commence like redemption of the remaining fractional currency then in circulation, and all when so redeemed to be destroyed; and that the committee report at as early a day as practicable by bill or otherwise.

The resolution was referred to the Committee on Finance.

———

In the House, on December 8th, the special committee on increased salaries reported a bill to repeal the increase of certain salaries adopted March 3, 1873, and to restore the former rates, to wit, for members of Congress, etc. On December 9th the bill was considered.

Mr. Wilson, of Indiana, said: " Mr. Speaker, the subject now under consideration is one which has attracted much public attention. The action of the Forty-second Congress, in passing the act by which the salaries of Senators and Representatives were increased, which it is now proposed to repeal, and especially that feature of it whereby the increased pay was made to date from the beginning of the Congress, has met with the fiercest denunciation. Not only those who voted for it, but those who voted against it, yet received its benefits, have been stigmatized as thieves and robbers.

" It matters not how many years of faithful service had been devoted to the country, nor how exalted a character for integrity had been builded up; this one act has been deemed an unpardonable sin, and treated as an unmitigated criminality. While indulging in this wholesale denunciation, no one stopped to consider the circumstances under which any member happened to be placed, and which to him, and to any reasonable man, might seem to make it his duty to vote for the measure; no difference of opinion was permitted as to its justice; no appeal to reason would be listened to. My distinguished friend from Ohio (Mr. Garfield), who struggled against it until, in a conference report which he had resisted to the last, it was brought before the House attached to one of the most important appropriation bills, and then, as all of us who are familiar with the facts must confidently believe (and it is but justice to him to say so here), voted for it in the conscientious discharge of his duty to the country, has fared no better than any one else.

"I do not doubt that this unstinted abuse has been indulged in by many honest, conscientious men, who, in my judgment, came to hasty conclusions; and certainly by many who thought they could see in it their opportunity for preferment, hoping for official honors upon some demerit of others, rather than upon any merit of their own.

"Mr. Speaker, I may be mistaken, but I have thought that I could see, in what has transpired here since this question came before the House, a disposition upon the part of some gentlemen to seek to gain popularity for themselves by trying to cast reproach upon their fellow-members.

"Now, sir, it is not my purpose to argue against the repeal of that act, nor that it did not fix the salaries too high, but to show that there is nothing in it that is immoral or dishonest; that a man might vote for it, or receive its benefits, and still be the peer in integrity and conscience of the very best of all the multitude of his detractors. The limit fixed to this debate will not permit me to enter into an elaborate consideration of this subject in its various aspects, and I must necessarily treat it briefly. As the Constitution now is, the power is granted to each Congress to fix its own compensation. This power was granted for the reason that it was not deemed wise to allow one Congress to fix the compensation of its successor; it was recognized as a delicate duty for members to fix their own salaries, but, after weighing all the arguments pro and con, it was deemed best that it should be so. A great many newspaper articles have been published, and speeches made, in which it has been assumed that, when a Senator or a member of Congress is elected, it is a contract to serve, during the period for which he was elected, for the compensation provided for at the time of his election. But, sir, nothing is plainer than that the assumption is without foundation. On the contrary, as before remarked, for reasons which the framers of the Constitution regarded as outweighing those that were urged against it, it was provided that each Congress might judge of its own compensation. Such is not only the plain letter of the Constitution, but there is history which shows that so the people themselves desired it to be.

"Now, Mr. Speaker, five Congresses have increased the salaries, and each time dated the increase back to the beginning of the Congress,

or, in other words, have embodied in the law this feature, which the gentleman from Ohio (Mr. Lawrence), a short while ago, so earnestly objected to as 'back pay.'

"The Constitution was purposely framed so as to allow each Congress to fix its own salary, and, acting within its express constitutional power, the Forty-second Congress, in passing the act to which I have referred, has followed an unbroken line of precedents, and has trodden in the footsteps of many illustrious predecessors.

"Having the right to fix its own compensation, it is of course wholly immaterial on what day of the Congress it is done. The merit or demerit does not in any way depend upon whether it is done on the first, or the last, or any intervening day. It might be done on the first day, and then it would all be 'front pay,' to use the language of some of the newspapers; but the effect upon the Treasury would be precisely the same as if fixed upon the last day. The merit or demerit, the good or bad qualities of the act, depends, therefore, not on the time in the session when it is done, but altogether upon the amount. If the amount fixed would have been right if it had been fixed at the beginning of the Congress, it is equally right if fixed at any later day in the Congress to date from the beginning. Upon this question of amount it is but natural that there should be a diversity of opinion, and that difference may exist between honest men.

"I shall not argue the question whether or not the action of the Forty-second Congress was ill-timed or indiscreet, although it would possibly not be difficult to convince a thinking man that it is never ill-timed nor indiscreet to do what is right; but this would involve the single question, and it is the only question involved, as the gentleman from Ohio (Mr. Lawrence) now admits, whether or not the amount fixed by that Congress was in excess of a fair compensation. Those who had experience here would differ in regard to it, and those who have had no opportunity to know to what expenses Senators and Members are subjected are not in a good condition to form a correct opinion.

"It is sufficient for us to know that the people, whether wisely or unwisely, are unwilling to pay the amount fixed by that Congress. We cannot now argue that they are wrong. They have a right to dictate what they will pay. They have a right to demand that it shall be repealed. They have made that demand, and we are now about to accede to it. When repealed we must once more fix salaries; and that, also, we are about to do. Whatever we may do will be criticised; but we must do something, and perhaps the best guide to us in disposing of the matter is the law as it was before, and I trust that the House will place the bill upon that basis."

Mr. Townsend, of Pennsylvania, said: "The people of the country are willing to compensate their Representatives fairly and equitably. They are neither unjust nor ungenerous. They are willing that we should have a fair salary for the services we are rendering them here. I think, Mr. Speaker, that the popular indignation during the past summer was not directed so much against the increase of pay as it was against what has been called the back pay. The people felt indignant that in the last hours of the last day of the session, after we had signed our receipts monthly, acknowledging that we had been paid in full for our services here, we should pass a law taking immediately out of the Treasury $5,000 each, which we had acknowledged we had not earned. It was for this that people called members to a stern account.

"I thought on that occasion, when the bill was before the House, that it was injudicious, and I thought that it was wrong. I thought that the people had had no opportunity to pass upon the bill. And I am very sure that, if the bill had been brought into the House at the first session of Congress, before the county, and district, and State conventions met, that bill increasing the pay and giving back pay never would have passed, in the form and at the figures at which it did eventually pass. If it had been passed at that earlier session, however, if the people had had a chance to express their sentiments with regard to it, in their different constituencies, they would have made no complaint. They could have dealt with their Representatives as they thought best. But they had no such opportunity. On that occasion I advocated the bill extending the pay to $6,000 a year. I did it because I saw there was a determination to increase the pay, and I felt that $6,000 a year, as I proposed at that time, would be about a just compensation for what we would lose, in the shape of stationery, mileage, and obligation to pay postage on public documents, under the bill that finally passed.

"Therefore it was that I voted against the bill, and never touched the back pay, but turned it over to the Treasurer, who receipted for the same."

Mr. Poland, of Vermont, said: "Mr. Speaker, I should not have occupied any of the time of the House on this subject had it not been that I have introduced a substitute for the bill reported by the committee, for which, and in behalf of which, I desire to say a word or two. A few days since I was in company with a considerable number of gentlemen—I think over a hundred—when the subject of the salary bill and what ought to be done with it was the sole topic of conversation, and a number of them expressed their views in relation to it. They all concurred in saying that it had been utterly condemned by the public judgment of the whole people of the United States; that the thing had been discussed, and considered, and adjudicated, by the sovereign people, that authority to which we all owe allegiance,

whose commands and whose judgments we are bound to obey. Gentlemen declined to discuss the question whether or not the bill was itself wrong, whether the provision for raising salaries from $6,000 to $7,500 was right or wrong. They said it was a non-essential question, now that the people had considered it and had passed judgment upon it, from which there was no appeal, and by which judgment we were bound; that our sole duty now was to execute that judgment. They said it was as idle now to discuss whether it was right or wrong as to discuss what a man might have proved in a case that had already been tried and gone to final judgment. And, Mr. Speaker, such has substantially been said by almost every gentleman who has discussed the question before the House.

"My friend from Indiana (Mr. Wilson), while maintaining here that the increase was just, and right, and proper to be made, and justifying his vote in favor of it, says it is too late to stand upon that; that it has been decided the other way, and decided by a tribunal that we are all bound to obey. Now, Mr. Speaker, I owe as much allegiance and obedience to the public judgment upon this and upon all subjects as any gentleman upon this floor; but I do not agree in the conclusion that is to be drawn. The people have decided that this increase of salary—increased in amount, and going back and making it apply to that Congress which had almost expired—was wrong. So, gentlemen, all say. Now, what does the bill that has been reported by your committee propose to do? Why, it proposes that that bill shall be left to stand; that all the increased pay that was received by members of the Forty-second Congress, they shall be allowed to keep; and that all the increase of pay which the members of this Congress have so far received they shall be allowed to keep. Now, Mr. Speaker, let me ask you, and ask the gentlemen on the floor, whether that is conforming to the public judgment on this subject? Is that what the people have decreed?

"Is this going to satisfy the demands of the people on this subject? When the people have resolved in conventions, and when they have said through the public press, that the law is to be repealed, what did they mean by it? That we were merely to change the law now and take a different and lower rate of compensation hereafter? Not at all; what the public judgment has demanded and now demands on this subject, if it demands any thing, is that this thing shall be utterly wiped out. That no benefit or advantage that any man has derived under it shall be kept and retained by him. That, and that alone, will satisfy the public demand and the public judgment on this subject; and, sir, it was for that purpose and with that view that I introduced a substitute for the report of the committee. Why, those very gentlemen who said, upon the occasion that I refer to, that the public judgment had so pronounced against this thing that nobody was at liberty to say a word in favor of it, now come in here with this lame and impotent conclusion.

"Mr. Speaker, while I agree with these gentlemen in their premises, I utterly disagree to their conclusions. I propose for one to vote for a bill which shall carry out the decision of the people upon this subject, and utterly wipe out all the effects, consequences, and benefits, that have been derived by members of Congress under that bill. And, Mr. Speaker, I must do upon this subject as many gentlemen have done, because we are all personally interested; I must state my own personal experience on the subject and how I stand in reference to it. I voted against the bill. In reference to whether it was right or wrong as to the amount, I was governed, I suppose, in my vote very much as other gentlemen were. I voted to retain the $5,000 because it was enough for me. Before I came to Congress, I had been for a considerable time in public office in my own State, where salaries are very small, and had become accustomed to live upon a very small salary, and habits of simple and plain economy that I had acquired in that way I could well enough preserve here. Five thousand dollars was an ample compensation for my services, and furnished me ample means to live in the manner in which I chose to live. Therefore, so far as I was personally concerned, that was the consideration that affected my vote.

"But more than that, Mr. Speaker, I considered it an exceedingly unfortunate time to make this increase. Various things that had taken place last winter had greatly excited the public mind with reference to corruption in public office; the whole country was agog upon that subject, and I knew that this increase of salary at that time, and especially the retroactive feature, would excite public condemnation, and draw down the censure of the people upon it, as it has done, and therefore, sir, I voted against it. But, notwithstanding my vote, it passed, and then came the question of what was to be done. The press of the country immediately began to say that every man who took that pay, that was given to him by law, was a grabber and a thief. The idea that I held an office, the salary of which was fixed by law, and was to be called a thief for taking that salary, was not one that was very palatable to me. It did not commend itself to my judgment nor to my conscience; nor did I propose to be actuated or influenced by any threat of that sort, and therefore, sir, I took the money and still retain it. Other gentlemen's consciences were more tender and susceptible than mine. They began to be affected differently, and one after another they returned this back pay into the Treasury. Well, what was the result of that? Why, people immediately began to say they were cowards and hypocrites, and that they did it merely for the purpose of pacifying the press; making a show of honesty they did not possess; courting public favor,

and commending themselves in that way to the people. That brought me to commune with myself, with my own judgment and conscience, in relation to what I ought to do; whether I were more amenable upon the one side to be called a grabber and thief, or whether, by pursuing a different course, I should subject myself to be called a coward and a hypocrite, who was, by false pretenses, endeavoring to curry public favor. Well, now, the result of my communing with myself was—(and I do not intend by this to cast any reflection on the motives of other members)—the result of my own reflection and judgment was, that I should be altogether more amenable to the latter charge. That in point of fact it would be much better proved, so far as I was concerned, than the opposite charge, that, by keeping the money thus given me by law, I was a grabber and a thief. Therefore, Mr. Speaker, I chose to retain what I received under the law, and make my endeavor here to have the law so modified and changed that I may be allowed to return the money to the Treasury, if that is the will of the people, without subjecting myself to the charge of being a hypocrite and a coward, and of doing it because of the clamor of the public press upon the subject.

"And inasmuch as I found my conscience upon this subject was a little obtuse, and not easily moved by the threats and denunciations of some portions of the press, and that a majority of the gentlemen who stood in the same position with myself had consciences equally as torpid as my own, and equally, perhaps, needed the quickening of law to help them, I propose that we regulate this thing by law : that by law we wipe out all the consequences of that act by which the salary was raised and given to members of the Forty-second Congress and to members of the Forty-third Congress.

"Now, this is an important question to be decided. If we have not the legal power to do this, if there is any thing in the Constitution, either expressed or implied, that prohibits our doing it, then we ought not to attempt to do it. But I insist that there is not any thing in the Constitution against it; I say that we have a perfect right to do it. We cannot, of course, go back and regulate the salaries of the members of the Forty-second Congress. But we have full power over the salary of every member of this Congress, a perfect right to regulate it by law as we choose.

"Now, the bill that was reported by the minority of the committee, and which has been proposed as a substitute for that of the majority, goes to the extent of saying that members of the Forty-third Congress shall account for what they have received since the 4th of March last. Nobody has questioned, and I think nobody can successfully question, the power of the House to compel them to account for what they have received under the law since the 4th of March last. Now, is not the question of our power precisely the same in relation to what they have received as members of the Forty-second Congress?"

Mr. Stephens, of Georgia, said: "Mr. Speaker, I wish to make a few remarks upon this subject now under debate. For, as little as members of the House may think of this subject, in my judgment it involves a great principle; and I shall speak mainly to the principle.

"As was remarked by the gentleman from New York, who opened the debate yesterday with so much eloquence (Mr. Tremain), I am utterly disconnected with that branch of the subject, the 'back-pay grab,' as it is called, which has so entered into and pervaded this discussion, but upon that branch I have something to say. Therefore my remarks will be confined, first to the moral principle involved in the question, and then to the political expediency and policy of the increase of salaries adopted by the last Congress. Sir, I was utterly astonished the other day when some gentleman undertook to speak of this question as a party question. In my opinion neither party is responsible for the measure of the increase of salary at the last session. I believe that the Democracy, in the proportion of votes, according to the analysis I have seen, are as much responsible for it as the Republicans. Perhaps some of our Republican friends at the time the bill was passed were a little shy—a little timid —anxious to have the measure pass, but at the same time not wishing to take what they deemed the risk of popular disfavor by voting in accordance with their personal convictions.

"But, sir, to come at once to the gist of the morality of the act. The gentleman from New York (Mr. Tremain) yesterday made some important admissions which cover the whole case. He admitted that, by the Constitution of the United States, each Congress for itself is empowered to fix the pay of its own members. This, sir, is a wise provision of the Constitution, which the States, after its ratification, refused to change. This provision of the Constitution has been acted on from the beginning of this Government. Congress has repeatedly increased the pay, and at every such increase the *back* pay was considered as legitimate as the *front* pay. This the gentleman also admitted. This saves me from going into historic details. I therefore confine myself to principle. If it was not immoral to take it on all former occasions, how can it be on this? The principle is the same. Whenever the pay has been increased, it was necessarily retroactive and extra. Were the men who did this thing in the last century and in the early part of this century—the brightest ornaments in our history for intellect, for talents, and for virtue —were they 'salary-grabbers?' Were they 'thieves' and 'robbers,' for doing just what was their constitutional right to do?

"Now, sir, if there is any thing wrong, any thing immoral, any thing dishonest, any thing which would reflect disgrace upon a man's memory for taking this legal appropriation, I must confess I do not see it. One gentleman said that he returned it because it was too much pay, and the inquiry was promptly made, how much he thought would have been admissible.

"If it is wrong to take the whole, it was wrong to take a single cent of it. The principle is the same; and, if it is wrong for the present House to take what the law allows them to take, where are we to make the distinction between right and wrong? During my life I have endeavored to pursue the right, and, whenever I am acting in pursuance of the right, I do not consider I am committing any offense whatever which would subject me to the charge of 'grabbing' what did not rightfully belong to me.

"I say, Mr. Speaker, when Congress passed the retroactive law at its last session it was their right to do it—their constitutional right. I am not now saying whether it was expedient to do it, but I do say that no blot should rest upon the name of any man or be cast upon that of his children or upon his memory if, after it passed, even against his vote, he took what the law gave him. I have nothing to say of those who, after taking it, returned it, for that is a matter with themselves. All that I mean to say is, that if I had been here, whether I voted for it or not, I would have taken it, and I should have felt I was justly entitled to it, just as though it were eight dollars a day or one dollar a day, if the Congress voted it.

"It was a constitutional law, constitutionally passed, and those who are entitled to it are as much entitled as at any other time to the pay then fixed. If there were those who thought it was too much, it was, of course, their right to refuse to take it. I would not attempt to cast a slur upon any gentleman who saw fit to return it; I am only speaking for myself. So much for the morality view. It is well known that every Congress which has ever increased the pay increased it from the beginning; and I think I may say that every Legislature in the United States which has increased its pay increased it from the beginning. There is not a single case of exception that I know of; and therefore I trust that the press, that the men who attempt to lead the masses of the people, will perceive where the right is, and not attribute wrong where there was none. If they think it was inexpedient let them discuss it from that point, and not allege there was any immorality.

"This brings me to the second view which I propose to present to the House. I am not going to state what I deem my services here worth, but I do intend to state what I think the services of a representative of any people in any district in the United States ought to be worth; and perhaps I will go far above the figure of any law which has ever been passed upon the subject. I will say this: that reprosentatives in this hall ought to be men of that mental calibre, that moral calibre, that information, that education, that virtue, of that trustworthiness—of all the qualities that make men fit for the highest pursuits of life. The representative ought to be of that character which would entitle him to the highest amount of wages, if you choose to call it so, which is given to the highest grades of skilled labor in the country. There are, Mr. Speaker, various kinds of labor, skilled and unskilled, and there are various kinds of power — water - power, steam-power, muscle and mind or brain-power.

"My standard of wages for a member of this House would be that amount which the higher grades of skilled labor, combined with brain - power and virtue, usually commands. And I am satisfied that, when the people of this country understand the nature of the duties and proper character of a member of Congress, when they understand the importance of government, and good government, and wise government, there are none throughout the length and breadth of the country who will dispute this proposition.

"Why, sir, the salaries of managers of railroads reach $25,000. There is hardly a master-mechanic in any of the machine-shops which does not receive $10,000 as a compensation for his skilled labor, his brain-labor. There is hardly a town in which there are not merchants who make from $10,000 to $15,000. There is hardly a district in the United States, I suspect, where there are not one or more lawyers whose income is not as much as $10,000 or $15,000. There is hardly any place or district where the most eminent physicians do not make $10,000 or $15,000. There is hardly any business of life requiring skilled labor or brain-labor which does not command that compensation; the income of many journalists greatly exceeds it.

"Now, sir, when you teach the people what government is, the science of government, the nature of the duties of a member of Congress, the interest that everybody in the community feels and every member of society has in good government, in the laws we pass here within the sphere of Federal limited power, touching more or less the interest and the pocket of the humblest human being now within the jurisdiction of these States, they will say that legislation should be in the hands of men of character, of virtue, and integrity, who understand their duties—men who understand the science of government. This requires study, it requires labor, it requires an immense deal of thought; and, therefore, if the government is maintained rightly in the Senate and in the House, the rule of fixing the pay under the Constitution should be such as to afford an arena in these halls for the virtue and talent of the highest grade in our country.

"Some sham, would-be leader of the people may go to the poor man driving the plane or the plough and tell him 'he is getting only a pit-tance for his daily toil, while a member of Congress is getting $16 a day;' and he may induce that man, in the humblest but honest walks of life, to vote for him on his promise to reduce the pay. But that same man, if he were ill, would send for a skilled physician in preference to a quack, though the former was making twice as much as the latter. So with the other learned professions; and, when the people properly understand the importance of good legislation, they will have as little use for a cheap Congressman as for a cheap doctor or a cheap lawyer.

"What, Mr. Speaker, is the motive power of all humanity that prompts action—I mean that inward force which stirs honest, virtuous action? It is a desire for status. It is a desire for honorable position, with its attendants. It is the desire of a man not only to provide for himself, but for his family. Status in society is the great object. What are the elements of status? Income and honor. Honest acquisitions and meritorious deeds.

"Now, sir, to return to the question before the House, in fixing a salary of a member of Congress, of a President of the United States, of the judges of the Supreme Court, and of all your diplomatic and foreign servants, the basis on which the whole should be placed is, as I have said—the standard of salary should be, in my opinion, upon the basis stated and according to the grade of service. The Government in all its departments should offer fair competition for the highest virtue and intelligence with all the other vocations in life. The youth of the country in selecting pursuits should not be driven from the political field for want of those inducements offered by other kinds of employment. The political arena, with just compensation, affords the broadest, widest, and grandest field for intellectual action. With that view it is necessary that the Government should offer the highest inducements to skilled and brain labor in all its departments. But the idea I wish to impress upon the House is a general principle. Let the salary be fixed upon a principle that will enable the Government service to come in fair competition with the other enterprises of this age of progress, as it is termed.

"I will state another thing. It so happened that one of the last things I ever said upon this floor, fourteen years ago, was upon this matter of salary. It grew out of a debate on a proposition to increase the salary of the judge of, I think, the western district of Virginia. I was, so to speak, delivering my valedictory to the then members of this House, never expecting to return here again, and therefore I could speak disinterestedly. I gave it as my opinion then, and I will give it to you now. At that time the expenditures of the Government were about $80,000,000 per annum, and the expenses for the whole civil, diplomatic, judicial, and legislative departments of the country were not exceeding, I think, $3,000,000. I gave it as my opinion that if the salary of members of Congress was $10,000, and of Senators $15,000, and of the Chief-Justice $50,000, and of the President $100,000, and of the associate justices of the Supreme Court $25,000, and of our foreign ministers twice or three times what it was, the expenditures of the Government would be $60,000,000 instead of $80,000,000. Sir, no man —I feel almost reluctant to say it—no man, it is well known, who has not a fortune himself, can hope to represent the United States at any foreign court, even with the increased salary, and maintain the dignity of the Government. I gave that as my opinion then. It is the brain part of the Government that you should nourish; the legislative, judiciary, and executive parts of it form that brain-power that is to conduct you safely, if you attain high success in the future. In the human body the brain is the one-eleventh part of the body, and it is the brain portion that you should nourish. Sir, if we had spent more upon this department of the Government, statesmanship would have been more studied—more a matter of science.

"Now, I am not going to say what the salary of members ought to be. You have heard my ideas on the principle, and also on the expediency. Certainly I shall not vote for the bill as reported by this committee. What shape this thing may take I do not know; but my opinion is that the bill of last session, of which you have heard so much complaint, is really a reduction in fact. I know it will be to me, because of the postage on what I anticipated to do in the distribution of knowledge among the constituents that I represent. I think the amount of postage will cover $2,500, and therefore, unless gentlemen wish to reduce the pay to below what it was before, they will not reduce it. My own judgment is, that the unwisest part of the legislation of last Congress was the repeal of the franking privilege. One word upon that. Ours is a Government founded upon the enlightenment of the people. No representative government can last except where the people understand its nature, are devoted to its principles, and have the patriotism to maintain it. Those three elements are essential to the existence of all representative governments; in other words, they must depend upon the virtue, the intelligence, and the patriotism of the people. Light, political light, they must have. The Constitution declares that our public proceedings, our journal, shall be published, or given to the people."

Mr. Garfield, of Ohio, said: "Mr. Speaker, there was so much to admire in the speech to which the House has just listened, that it may seem ungracious to say any thing in conflict with the doctrines announced. And yet the distinguished gentleman (Mr. Stephens) has said some things so strikingly different from the views generally entertained by the American people, that I venture to offer a few suggestions by way of reply, while the subject is still fresh in the minds of his hearers.

"All that the gentleman said in regard to the relation of public opinion to representative men will, I presume, be cordially concurred in by those who heard him. The real leaders of the people—they who give voice to the best thoughts or aspirations of their countrymen—are immeasurably above those who consult public passion only to cater to its worst tendencies. It is a high and worthy work to study public opinion, for the purpose of learning how best to serve the public good; but to study to learn how best to serve ourselves is base. But it is important that we understand what we mean by public opinion. It is not an infallible standard of right; for it is sometimes wholly wrong. Its judgments are frequently revised and reversed by its own consent. But it is true that, after a full hearing, public opinion finally adjusts itself on a basis which will be practically just and true. He greatly errs who calls all the passing and changing moods of the public mind the fixed and final verdict of public judgment.

".The public opinion that teaches its most valuable and impressive lessons resembles the ocean—not when lashed by the breath of the tempest—but when seen in the grandeur of its all-pervading calm. The men who shall take the dash and roar of its wild waves on the rocks as their symbol of public opinion will not only fail to learn its best lessons, but may find themselves wrecked on its breakers. But the sea in its hour of calm, when the forces that play upon it are in equipoise—when its depths are unvexed by tempests—is the grand level by which all the heights and depths of the world are measured. And so public opinion, though it may at times dash itself in fury against events and against men, will at last settle down into broad and settled calm, and will mark the level on which we gauge our political institutions, and measure the strength and wisdom of opinions and men.

"While recognizing, thus, the general justness and the almost omnipotent power of public opinion in a government like ours, it is equally important that the individual man should not be the servile and unquestioning follower of its behests. We may value it as a guide, we may accept its lessons, but we should never be its slaves.

"There is a circle of individual right within which every man's opinions are sacredly his own, even in defiance of public opinion, and which his manhood and self-respect demand that he shall never surrender. But there are public questions like that which we are to-day considering, on which the voice of public opinion has a right to be heard and considered by every Representative in the national legislature.

"Now, if we were legislating for the ideal republic of Plato, I do not know that a wiser plan of compensation could be found than that proposed by the distinguished gentleman from Georgia (Mr. Stephens). If we lived in a world where the highest power was the best paid, his scheme would be perfect and his argument unanswerable. But, so far as I have studied life, exactly the reverse is the accepted rule. The things that have the highest marketable value in the world, as we find it, are not the things that stand highest in the intellectual or moral scale.

"One of the brightest and greatest men I know in this nation, a man who, perhaps, has done as much for its intellectual life as any other, told me not many months ago, that he had made it the rule of his life to abandon any intellectual pursuit the moment it became commercially valuable; that others would utilize what he had discovered; that his field of work was above the line of commercial values; and when he brought down the great truths of science from the upper heights to the level of commercial values, a thousand hands would be ready to take them and make them valuable in the markets of the world."

(A voice: "Who was he?")

Mr. Garfield: "It was Agassiz. He entered upon his great career, not for the salary it gave him, for that was meagre compared with the pay of those in the lower walks of life; but he followed the promptings of his great nature and works for the love of the truth and for the instruction of mankind. Something of this spirit has pervaded the lives of the great men who did so much to build up and maintain our republican institutions. And this spirit is, in my judgment, higher and worthier than that which the gentleman from Georgia (Mr. Stephens) has described.

"To come immediately to the question before us, I agree with the distinguished gentleman that we should not be driven or swayed by that unjust clamor that calls men thieves who voted as they had the constitutional right to vote, and accepted a compensation which they had the legal and constitutional right to take. I join in no clamor of that sort; nor will I join in any criminations against those who used their right to act and vote differently from myself on this subject. It is idle to waste our time now in discussing the votes of the last Congress in relation to the salary bill. We are called upon to confront this plain, practical question, 'Shall the salary bill of the last Congress be repealed?' I shall argue it on two grounds: first, the just demands of public opinion; second, the relation of this repeal to the Government and its necessities; and I shall confine my remarks to these two points. I think it cannot be doubted that public opinion plainly and clearly demands the repeal; and on a subject like this the voice of the people should have more than even its usual weight.

"When the public says to me, and to those associated with me, that we have under constitutional law given ourselves more pay than that public is willing to grant us, it would be indelicate and indecent in us on such a question to resist that public opinion.

"It does not compromise the manhood, the independence, or the self-respect of any Representative to say that he will not help to keep on the statute-book a law which allows him more pay than public opinion thinks he ought to have. Even if he believes public opinion wrong, he ought to yield to it in a matter of such delicacy.

"That is all the argument I make on the score of public opinion.

"I now come to the other point, the necessities of the Government. Gentlemen must remember that only seven years ago our expenditures had risen to a volume that was simply frightful, in view of the burdens of the country. We were then paying out over the counter of our Treasury $1,290,000,000 a year as the cost of sustaining the Government and meeting the great expenses entailed by the war. What was the duty of this national Legislature? Manifestly to bring the expenditures of the Government down as rapidly as possible from the high level of war to the normal level of peace.

"If, therefore, the Forty-third Congress intends to go forward in the work of economy and retrenchment, if it has any hope of making further reductions in the expenditures of this Government, we must, before undertaking to carry out that work, give ourselves the moral power that will result from a reduction of our own pay to the old standard. As the case stands to-day, our own salaries are the master-key in our hands by which, and by which alone, we can turn the machinery that will bring about a further reduction of expenses in the Government.

"Mr. Speaker, I say all this on the theory that we are to run the Government as our fathers who made it intended it should be run —not on the principle of the gentleman from Georgia (Mr. Stephens), a principle that would make this the most expensive Government on the globe, but on the old principle that there is something due to the honor of the service we perform."

The bill was subsequently recommitted with instructions, and on December 16th the committee reported the following bill:

A Bill (H. R. No. 793) to repeal the increase of certain salaries and to establish the rate of the same.

SECTION 1. *Be it enacted*, That all provisions in an act entitled "An act to provide for the legislative, executive, and j i ia expenses of the Government for the year ending June 30, 1874, and for other purposes," approved March 3, 1873, that increase the salary or compensation of Senators, Representatives, or Delegates in Congress, or of any officer or employé, are hereby repealed, except so far as the same relate to the judges of the Supreme Court, and to the President of the United States, during his present term of office.

SEC. 2. Hereafter the compensation of Senators, Representatives, and Delegates in Congress shall be at the rate of $5,500 per annum ; and this shall be in lieu of all allowances except the actual and necessary individual traveling expenses in coming to and returning from the national capital once each session, which shall be paid to each Senator, Representative, and Delegate, on the same being certified by him to the proper accounting officer; and the salary or compensation of all officers and employés of the Government, subject to the exceptions named in section 1 of this act, shall hereafter be the same that they were prior to the passage of the act named in said section.

Sec. 3. That the Secretary of the Treasury is required to cover into the Treasury all sums that may remain undrawn, or which have been received as increased compensation under the provisions of said act, approved March 3, 1873, and which shall have or may come into his possession by the return thereof.

Mr. Hale, of Maine, said: "Members will see that very little scope was left to the committee. The bill itself in some particulars does not suit me; in some regards it will not suit others. On that point I may speak for members of the committee. But what the committee did was to follow out the spirit of the instructions, and that was to lump the whole mileage, and then distribute it as salary among the members. The matter was confined to the Forty-first Congress, in making the reckoning, by the terms of the instructions moved by the gentleman from Indiana (Mr. Orth), and adopted by the House. The committee, not trusting to any thing less than an official report, obtained from the Register of the Treasury a complete and accurate list, which I hold in my hand, of the mileage paid to every member of the Forty-first Congress, and also to every Senator, which I also hold in my hand, upon another sheet. The list is in detail, showing what each member and each Senator received. That, of course, was not needed; but the office wished to make their reply to my request exhaustive. The committee took simply the aggregate of the mileage to the members of the Forty-first Congress, which amounted to $209,542.40, paid to two hundred and sixty-five members in all. The mileage to the Senate was $71,382.40, paid to seventy-two Senators. The aggregate of the two amounts was $280,924.80. We of course have divided that amount by the aggregate number of Senators, Representatives, and Delegates, making as the average for the whole Congress $833.60 for two years, or for one year $416.80. To that the committee, acting under instructions, added $125 for stationery allowance, making an average of allowance for mileage and stationery, the franking privilege being excluded by the terms of the instructions, of $541.80. Under the instructions to report a bill as near this as practicable, the committee took the responsibility of fixing an even sum, and they took the nearest hundred dollars, being $5,500, cutting off $41.80, which I presume no gentleman will object to. The bill is therefore reported under the instructions, fixing the salary at the rate of $5,500 hereafter for members of Congress, and is made in terms as distinct as the committee could make them, to be in lieu of all allowances whatever, except—and there the language of the instructions is followed—actual individual necessary expenses of Senators, Members, and Delegates, in coming from their residences to the national capital and returning to them, to be duly certified to the accounting officers. The bill is amended, also, according to the instructions, so as to embrace all officials, with the exceptions referred to in the instructions, to wit, the justices of the Supreme Court and the President of the United States during his present term of office. After fixing the salaries of members of Congress, all other salaries, in accordance with instructions, are put back at the rate that they were under the law previous to the passage of the act of March 3, 1872, all that part of it which is commonly known as the salary bill.

"Now, the committee in doing this have endeavored to follow strictly the instructions of the House, and have presented this bill in accordance with those instructions."

Mr. Kasson, of Iowa, said: "I offer the following amendment to come in at the close of the second section of the bill:

Provided, That Senators, Representatives, and Delegates, in the Forty-third Congress who shall have received their compensation since the 4th of March, 1873, in accordance with the provisions of the act hereby repealed, shall hereafter be paid only such equal monthly installments as shall in the aggregate make their compensation severally from the 4th of March, 1873, to the close of the present Congress equal to the amount of salary herein provided.

"I suppose, Mr. Speaker, that that amendment explains itself. I offer it in order that the entire compensation of members of Congress for this Forty-third Congress shall only amount to the figure provided for in this bill."

Mr. Eldredge, of Wisconsin, said: "Mr. Speaker, I have no idea of making a speech at this time, but I desire to say a few words, mostly personal to myself. I am one of those who have been subjected to most malicious and malignant assaults on account of voting for the salary bill of the last Congress. It is, I believe, the first and only vote of mine since I have been a member of this House that has been challenged or criticised by my constituents, though I have never ' dodged ' a vote, and never been absent from the House except from unavoidable necessity.

"I have voted and spoken on most or all the great questions that have come before Congress growing out of the war, being forced too many times to vote under the operation of the previous question without opportunity for discussion or reflection. For the first time I am charged with sinister motives in casting my vote. Though, up to this time, I have said nothing in vindication of it, I have by no means ignored the fact or been indifferent to the epithets that have been uttered against me in common with others, or the unjust charges made. *I voted for the bill.* I will not deny it or shrink from the responsibility of the vote. I voted for it, believing in my soul that it was right, and that it was for the best interest of the country that it should be passed. *I believe so now.* Neither the clamor of the press, the so-called voice of the people, nor the arguments of the present discussion, have convinced me to the contrary. I shall not now attempt to answer. I cannot, in the time I shall have allowed me, even refer to the objections which have been made to the law of 1873, nor will I retort in invective upon those who have maligned me. I repeat only what is no longer denied, that the Congress had the constitutional power and the legal right to enact the law. There was, therefore, no moral wrong or vice in it. It was not ' *theft*,' '*robbery*,' nor any other crime. There was never, in fact, any question of any real importance involved except the sum at which the salary should be fixed. Was the sum in the law too much or too little? Was it reasonable or unreasonable, just or unjust? No fault was ever found with the amount at which the salary was established by the law of 1866. And yet I assert, what I most solemnly believe, and what no honest man can, after a full consideration and understanding of the subject, doubt, that the old law giving a salary of $5,000, with the perquisites then provided for, and the franking privilege as it then existed, was, in a pecuniary point of view, more desirable, *better*, for the members of Congress than the salary as now provided by law. I cannot go into the figures; I have not time to show this; but the gentleman from Nevada (Mr. Kendall), and the gentleman from Missouri (Mr. Comingo), and others, have demonstrated this beyond cavil or doubt. I do claim, therefore, and if time permitted could show and satisfy all honest men, that the pay of members is not too high.

"I have been in Congress more than ten years. If there be any ten years of life better than any *other ten*, they are those when we are most mature; and in that sense I have been in Congress the best ten years of my life. I have never taken from any man during my life a dollar that did not belong to me, or that I did not believe I had honestly earned. I would not do it now. I am an economical man, reared in poverty and accustomed to live upon small means. I have indulged in no extravagances, and have not even felt myself able, in view of the support of my family and the education of my children, to return or reciprocate the social courtesies and compliments that have been extended to me. And yet I now and here declare I have not been able to lay up any thing or add one dollar to what I had when elected to Congress, and have not now of this world's goods as much as when first elected. My own case I supposed to be that of all those who have attended to their duties honestly and faithfully, and who were not blessed with large wealth. *I suppose so now*. I have conversed with many members, and found their experience the same as mine. The sessions of Congress have been longer and the expenses of members far more for the last ten years than ever before. The cost of living everywhere has been greater, and especially in Washington.

"Mr. Speaker, I have listened attentively to this whole debate. I have waited for arguments, *for reasons* to be given why this law should be repealed. It is intimated by some that it provides for the payment to members of too large a salary. And yet when it is asserted here, and demonstrated by those who have spoken, *demonstrated by figures*, that the pay and perquisites, including the franking privilege, as it is called, under the old law were as much or more than the present pay, no answer is made, no denial even is put in.

"But it is said the whole question has been before the bar of public opinion and has there been decided, and Representatives are here predicating their action, their votes, upon this decision—*bowing*, as they call it, *to public opinion*. Now, sir, I have as much respect for public opinion as any man. I believe, too, when the people have a fair chance, when they have had the opportunity to examine, to know and understand all the facts, that their judgment is very likely to be right. I bow with reverential awe to such judgment—to the judgment of the people so formed. But, in order to be right, it is absolutely essential that the subject should have been fairly and truthfully presented, and candidly and calmly considered. When this is not the case, *public opinion* is quite as apt to be wrong as right. The masses can be no better judge—are no more likely to be right without deliberation, without consideration, without knowledge of all the facts and circumstances—*than an individual*. The voice of the people is only the aggregation of the voices of individuals. If the individuals are wrong, if they are moved by caprice, or passion, or error, there is no safety or propriety in following or obeying their demands. It is the duty of the representative to examine for himself, to weigh the whole subject, to ascertain the *right*, and act accordingly as duty and conscience dictate. It is not true statesmanship, it is not the duty of the representative, to bow to the storm, to yield to the passion or the caprice of the multitude, and surrender his individual judgment and conscience, his honest convictions, to inconsiderate clamor. There can be no government, no individual representation, no freedom or liberty even, in such case. The power that would elect a President one day would crown a king the next. I do not argue that the representative must stand with his fingers on the public pulse and bow down or rise up according as it shall beat high or low. He is the *representative*, not the *slave* of the people. He is one of the people at the same time that he represents the people. He is chosen a representative not because he has *no* views or opinions of his own, but *because of his views and opinions*, known and understood beforehand, and because he is known to be reliable in the hour of danger and trial. There is, if you please, a '*higher law*' than the people speaking through the press—the mere echo of the hour; an unorganized and unrecognized force, appreciated only because of its noise or the good it might do. I was elected under the Constitution, hold my office, receive my instructions, and learn my duty, from the people — my constituents — through that instrument. *It is the supreme law to me.* They expect me—my constituents expect me—to bow in absolute submission to its requirements, and I will obey them in that or resign. I was not, I never was chosen because I was the weakest and most submissive of my people, but rather because I was believed to be able to withstand a storm. I have stood here on this floor in opposition to the public, the general opinion of this House, of the country, resisting some of the most popular measures of the time, assaults, as I believed then and still believe, upon the Constitution, when there were only twenty-five or thirty to stand with me and share with me the taunts and jeers of the overwhelming majority, some of whom—the gentleman from Massachusetts (Mr. Dawes), for one—admit now that they were wrongs so flagrant they will not do for precedents. The storm of public opinion does not blow now as it blew then. I remember when it was claimed that public opinion demanded the impeachment of your President, and some were foolhardy enough to insist that it ought to be done because the people demanded it, whether he was guilty or not; and there is not a statesman throughout this broad land who does not now know, if that popular clamor had been obeyed, it would have shivered your Constitution and Government to atoms.

"Public opinion! what sacrifices has it not demanded? What crimes has it not committed? Inexorable, unrelenting, and unreasoning, it hung upon the cross the Saviour of man, and has more than once since demanded the crucifixion of the innocents. Once moved, what reason, what argument, what consideration of justice or humanity ever satiated its thirst for blood?

"It is needless to multiply or suggest instances; thousands rush to the recollection of us all—both ancient and modern—where humanity, duty, and true statesmanship required, demanded the representative should resist, and not pander to, public opinion. 'The voice of the people is the voice of God,' is as absurd as it is irreverent and profane.

"But, whether right or wrong, this question of the salaries of members, as provided for under the old law and the law of 3d of March, 1873, has never to my knowledge or belief been even fairly stated in a half-dozen newspapers in the United States. Why is it that it has never been candidly discussed? Why is it that it has received only denunciation? Why have the facts been suppressed or outrageously misrepresented? It was because truth and fairness would not subserve the purpose."

Mr. Hale, of New York, said: "Mr. Speaker,

this debate seems to have taken a somewhat remarkable turn. The provisions of that law were condemned by popular clamor, if gentlemen choose to call it so; but it was a popular clamor based on sufficient grounds, and commending itself, in my judgment, to the mind of every upright man in this House or out of it. The complaint made against the statute increasing the pay of members of this House was, as I understand, first and last, in regard to the amount, as being excessive. I believe that the sentiment of the better class of the community was that the amount fixed by that bill was larger than it ought to be, irrespective of every other consideration; and I for one especially believe that it was larger than it ought to be in proportion to the other official salaries paid by the people of this country in the administration of their State and national Governments. But that, as I have said, was the least of the considerations weighing with the people in this matter. The second, and a greater consideration, was that the members of the Forty-second Congress constituted themselves the judges in their own case, increasing at the end of their term their pay for the entire term, and that to an amount which the people believed excessive. The third proposition on which this popular condemnation rested, and, in my judgment, the weightiest of all, relates to the manner in which the act was done. It was not done by square, manly, honest legislation. This House in the Forty-second Congress repeatedly by large majorities voted down the proposition for an increase of their pay when presented as a bold and naked proposition, and then by trick and subterfuge and evasion ingrafted the increase upon a bill on which they could have some excuse for saying, 'We vote ourselves increased pay purely as a matter of necessity, because we must do it or defeat the appropriations for the support of the Government.' Each and every one of these objections I claim to be well founded, ranking in weight according to the order in which I have stated them.

"And, therefore, sir, I am unqualifiedly in favor of the repeal of that bill so far as the salaries of members of both Houses of Congress are concerned, and the return directly to the old compensation, salary, and mileage."

The Speaker: "The question now is upon the amendment of the gentleman from Iowa" (Mr. Kasson).

The question was taken as follows:

YEAS—Messrs. Albright, Archer, Arthur, Ashe, Atkins, Banning, Barrere, Barry, Bass, Beck, Berry, Bowen, Bright, Brown, Buckner, Bundy, Burchard, Burleigh, Burrows, Benjamin F. Butler, Cannon, Cason, Amos Clark, Jr., John B. Clark, Jr., Clements, Clymer, Stephen A. Cobb, Coburn, Conger, Cook, Corwin, Cotton, Cox, Crittenden, Crocker, Crutchfield, Curtis, Danford, Dawes, De Witt, Dobbins, Donnan, Dunnell, Eames, Eden, Fort, Foster, Frye, Garfield, Gooch, Gunkel, Eugene Hale, Hamilton, John T. Harris, Hatcher, Hathorn, Havens, John B. Hawley, Gerry W. Hazelton, John W. Hazleton, Hendee, Hereford, E. Rockwood Hoar, George F.

Hoar, Holman, Hoskins, Hunter, Hyde, Jewett, Kason, Killinger, Knapp, Lawrence, Lawson, Leach, Loughridge, Lowe, Luttrell, Magee, Marshal, Martin, McCrary, James W. McDill, McDougall, McJunkin, McLean, McNulta, Mellish, Merriam, Mills, Monroe, Moore, Morrison, Neal, Negley, Nesmith Niblack, O'Brien, Orr, Orth, Packer, Page, Hosea W. Parker, Isaac C. Parker, Pendleton, Perry, Phillips, Pierce, Pike, Thomas B. Platt, Poland, Potter, Pratt, Rainey, Ransier, Read, Richmond, Robbins, Ellis H. Roberts, William R. Roberts, James W. Robinson, Ross, Rusk, Henry B. Sayler. Milton Sayler, Scofield, Henry J. Scudder, Isaac W. Scudder, Sessions, Sheldon, Sherwood, Lazarus D. Shoemaker, Smart, A. Herr Smith, John Q. Smith, Southard, Speer, Sprague, Stanard, Starkweather, Stone, Storm, Strait, Swann, Taylor, Todd, Tremain, Tyner, Vance, Waldron, Walls, Jasper D. Ward, Marcus L. Ward, Wells, Wheeler, Whitehouse, Whitthorne, Wilber, Charles W. Willard, George Willard, Charles G. Williams, John M. S. Williams, William B. Williams, Ephraim K. Wilson, James Wilson, Jeremiah M. Wilson, Wolfe, Wood, Woodford, Woodworth, John D. Young, and Pierce M. B. Young—172.

NAYS—Messrs. Adams, Albert, Averill, Barnum, Bell, Biery, Blount, Bradley, Bromberg, Buffinton, Roderick R. Butler, Cain, Caldwell, Cessna, Clayton, Clinton L. Cobb, Crossland, Crounse, Davis, Durham, Eldredge, Elliott, Freeman, Giddings, Glover, Robert S. Hale, Hancock, Harmer, Benjamin W. Harris, Henry R. Harris, Harrison, Joseph R. Hawley, Hays, Herndon, Houghton, Hubbell, Hunton, Hurlbut, Hynes, Kellogg, Lansing, Lewis, Lofland, Lowndes, Lynch, Maynard, Milliken, Myers, O'Neill, Packard, Parsons, Pelham, Purman, Rawls, Ray, Rice, Sawyer, John G. Schumaker, Sener, Shanks, Small, H. Boardman Smith, J. Ambler Smith, Snyder, Standeford, Stowell, Strawbridge, Sypher, Thornburgh, Townsend, Waddell, Wallace, White, Whitehead, Wm. Williams, and Willie—76.

Not VOTING — Messrs. Barber, Begole, Bland, Freeman Clarke, Comingo, Creamer, Crooke, Darrall, Duell, Farwell, Field, Hersey, Hooper, Howe, Kelley, Kendall, Lamar, Lamison, Lamport, Alexander McDill, McKee, Mitchell, Morey. Niles, Nunn, Phelps, James H. Platt, Jr., Randall, Rapier, James C. Robinson, Sheats, Sloss, George L. Smith, William A. Smith, Stephens, St. John, and Thomas—37.

So the amendment was agreed to.

Several amendments were offered and rejected, or adopted, and on December 17th Mr. Hurlbut, of Illinois, offered the following substitute to the bill:

Be it enacted, etc., That from and after the passage of this act the compensation of Senators, Representatives, and Delegates, shall be at the rate of $6,000 per annum, payable monthly; and in addition thereto the actual individual expenses of each Senator, Representative, and Delegate, in coming to and returning from the seat of Government once in each session, to be certified in writing by each.

SECTION 2. That the compensation of the Speaker of the House of Representatives shall be at the rate of $2,000 in addition to his pay as Representative, amounting in all to $8,000. And that of the Vice-President shall be the same amount, with the same allowance for traveling expenses as hereinbefore provided.

SEC. 3. That all laws and parts of laws inconsistent with the provisions of this act are hereby repealed.

SEC. 4. That the Secretary of the Treasury is required to cover into the Treasury all sums which may remain undrawn, or which have been received as increased compensation under the provisions of said act, approved March 3, 1873, and which shall have or may come into his possession by the return thereof.

Mr. Hurlbut: "On that substitute I demand the previous question."

The Speaker: "The first question is upon the substitute moved by the gentleman from Illinois (Mr. Hurlbut) for the bill as amended by the House."

The question was taken, as follows:

YEAS — Messrs. Adams, Albert, Archer, Ashe, Atkins, Averill, Barrere, Barry, Beck, Begole, Biery, Bowen, Bradley, Bright, Buffinton, Burrows, Benjamin F. Butler, Roderick R. Butler, Cain, Cessna, Amos Clark, Jr., Clayton, Clements, Clinton L. Cobb, Comingo, Cook, Creamer, Crocker, Crooke, Crossland, Crutchfield, Darrall, Davis, De Witt, Dobbins, Duell, Durham, Eldredge, Elliott, Farwell, Field, Freeman, Giddings, Robert S. Hale, Hamilton, Haucock, Harmer, Benjamin W. Harris, Harrison, Hathorn, Havens, Hays, John W. Hazleton, Herndon, E. Rockwood Hoar, George F. Hoar, Houghton, Howe, Hubbell, Hunton, Hurlbut, Hynes, Kelley, Lamar, Lamport, Lansing, Leach, Lewis, Lofland, Lowndes, Lynch, Alexander S. McDill, McJunkin, McKee, Mellish, Milliken, Morey, Myers, Negley, Nesmith, Nunn, O'Brien, O'Neill, Packard, Page, Isaac C. Parker, Parsons, Pelham, Phelps, James H. Platt, Jr. Thomas C. Platt, Rainey, Randall, Ransier, Rapier, Rawls, Ray, Rice, Richmond, Sawyer, John G. Schumaker, Henry J. Scudder, Isaac W. Scudder, Sener, Shanks, Sheldon, Sloss, Smart, George L. Smith, H. Boardman Smith, J. Ambler Smith, Snyder, Stanard, Standeford, Storm, Stowell, Strawbridge, Swann, Sypher, Taylor, Thomas, Thornburgh. Townsend, Vance, Waddell, Waldron. Wallace, Walls, Jasper D. Ward, Marcus L. Ward, Wheeler, White, Whitehead, John M. S. Williams, William Williams, Willie, Ephraim K. Wilson, Wood, and Pierce M. B. Young—139.

NAYS—Messrs. Albright, Arthur, Banning, Barber, Bass, Bell, Berry, Blount, Bromberg, Brown, Buckner, Bundy, Burchard, Burleigh, Caldwell, Cannon, Cason, Freeman Clarke, Clymer, Stephen A. Cobb, Coburn, Conger, Corwin, Cotton, Cox, Crittenden, Crounse, Curtis, Danford, Dawes, Donnan, Dunnell, Eames, Eden, Fort, Foster, Frye, Garfield, Glover, Gunckel, Eugene Hale, Henry R. Harris, John T. Harris, Hatcher, John B. Hawley, Joseph R. Hawley, Gerry W. Hazleton, Hendee, Hereford, Holman, Hoskins, Hunter, Hyde, Jewett, Kasson, Killinger, Knapp, Lawrence, Lawson, Loughridge, Lowe, Luttrell, Magee, Marshall, Martin, Maynard, McCrary, James W. McDill, McDougall, McLean, McNulta, Merriam, Mills, Monroe, Moore, Morrison, Neal, Niblack, Niles, Orr, Orth, Packer, Hosea W. Parker, Pendleton, Perry, Phillips, Pierce, Pike, Poland, Potter, Pratt, Read, Robbins, Ellis H. Roberts, William R. Roberts, James W. Robinson, Ross, Rusk, Henry B. Sayler, Milton Sayler, Scofield, Sessions, Sherwood, Lazarus D. Shoemaker, Small, A. Herr Smith, John Q. Smith, Southard, Speer, Sprague, Starkweather, Stone, Strait, Todd, Tremain, Tyner, Whitehouse, Whitthorne, Wilber, Charles W. Willard, George Willard. Charles G. Williams, William B. Williams, James Wilson, Jeremiah M. Wilson, Wolfe, Woodford, Woodworth, and John D. Young—130.

Not VOTING — Messrs. Barnum, Bland, John B. Clark, Jr., Gooch, Hersey, Hooper, Kellogg, Kendall, Lamison, Mitchell, Purman, James C. Robinson, Sheats, Wm. A. Smith, Stephens, and St. John—16.

So the substitute of Mr. Hurlbut was agreed to.

The Speaker: "The question is now in ordering the bill as amended to be engrossed and read a third time."

Mr. Hale, of Maine, said: "I shall be careful not to trespass upon the indulgence of the

House; but I have certain privileges, and those privileges I shall surely claim. I shall not be cried nor howled down.

"Everybody, Mr. Speaker, I think, will admit that the passage of the salary bill on last March was unfortunate and inopportune. If there had been any doubt upon that question, the almost unanimous voice of the people settled it. And, sir, it was a matter upon which the people might well pass—it was the voting of money from the public purse to pay public servants. Now, there can be no question as to that being a subject-matter which the people might consider. There can be no question as to what was the result of that consideration. It was sharp, swift, and immediate condemnation, and it was so marked and so undoubted that I see no humiliation on the part of any gentleman here following that direction of the people on this subject-matter. I, of course, feel no humiliation. I have no back-track to take, no new record to make; but I do not, from this comfortable stand-point, gloat over the gentlemen who have changed their views, because there was the best reason for change. The people passed upon the subject they had a right to pass upon! The contract for pay, and this is the fair formula to put it in, was a two-sided contract, and the party paying the money vetoed the bill involving the increase. The public stamped its disapproval upon it, and, therefore, I see no inconsistency on the part of gentlemen like the gentleman from Massachusetts (Mr. Butler) taking ground now in favor of substantial repeal as that gentleman here assures us he does.

"He has been instructed on a matter where he originally voted as he pleased, subject to the disapproval of the other contracting party, and, therefore, I repeat again there is no humiliation here in responding on this question to the people's voice.

"Now, sir, I cannot vote for the proposition which is at present before the House, because I believe that it is an evasion of the public demand. It evades our instructions from our constituencies, whose money we are passing upon. The people have decided in favor of substantial repeal. There have been gentlemen enough here who, within the last ten days, have reiterated this proposition to carry it if they will vote as they have talked. But the proposition before the House is not repeal simon pure. This House has already passed upon it that it is not. Less than a week ago —on the motion of the gentleman from Indiana (Mr. Orth)—this whole matter was committed to the special committee, with instructions to report a repeal of the salary increase, so far as the same was practicable under the Constitution, and to go back to the old salary and allowances; but instead of these allowances being unfairly distributed, as was the case under the mileage law, to lump the mileage and average it among the members as salary. The committee reported such an equalizing bill to

this House. It involved substantial repeal. It took no more money from the Treasury than the old law. It equalized mileage, not as I would rather have seen it done, from the pockets of members who draw excessive mileage, into the Treasury, but from the pocket of one member into that of another. But, so far as that goes, it was one kind of equalization. I, for one, was willing to stand to it, and the committee reported a bill fixing the salaries at $5,500, the $500 over the old law being the average amount of mileage and stationery allowances.

"I tried to bring the House to vote upon that proposition. I was in favor, as I have been from the beginning, of not incumbering bills that carried repeal on their forefront with any thing that would clog them. But I could get no direct vote on the proposition, though members enough would talk for it.

"And now, sir, after the House has voted first upon one thing and then another, after it has instructed its committee to fix our salaries at $5,500, right in the face of the report of the committee a proposition is put in here by which at the end of a fortnight's hard fighting, with the eyes of everybody upon us, we seek to get out of the fray by increasing our salaries in the sum of $500.

"Sir, it is not the amount that the people will care about. It was not, as has been often stated in this discussion, any particular sum that awakened the country last spring, but it was the conduct of the business that roused the people; and to-day, sir, this House cannot afford, as the upshot of all this agony for 'repeal,' to again increase our salaries over the old figure and negative the idea of repeal. Sir, the people do not expect that from us. They expect us to go back to the old law or to its equivalent. Is there any gentleman here that can give us a reason why we should add $500 to what we formerly received? And, what is the worst of it, no option is given us in voting. The gentleman from Illinois who springs this proposition refuses to allow me to move an amendment inserting $5,500 for $6,000, and refuses to allow the gentleman from Massachusetts (Mr. Dawes) to offer as a substitute the bill reported by the select committee."

The Speaker: "The question now is, will the House order that the bill as amended by the substitute of the gentleman from Illinois be engrossed and read a third time."

The question was taken as follows:

YEAS—Messrs. Adams, Albert, Archer, Ashe, Atkins, Averill, Barrere, Barry, Bass, Beck, Begole, Bell, Biery, Bowen, Bradley, Bright, Buffinton, Burchard, Benjamin F. Butler, Roderick R. Butler, Cain, Cannon, Cessna, Amos Clark, Jr., Clayton, Clements, Clinton L. Cobb, Stephen A. Cobb, Comingo, Cook, Creamer, Crocker, Crooke, Crossland, Crounse, Crutchfield, Darrall, Davis, De Witt, Duell, Durham, Eldredge, Elliott, Farwell, Field, Freeman, Garfield, Giddings, Glover, Robert S. Hale, Hamilton, Hancock, Harmer, Benjamin W. Harris, Henry R. Harris, Harrison, Hathorn, Havens, John B. Hawley,

Joseph R. Hawley, Hays, John W. Hazleton, Herndon, E. Rockwood Hoar, George F. Hoar, Hoskins, Houghton, Howe, Hubbell, Hunton, Hurlbut, Kelley, Kellogg, Lamar, Lamport, Lansing, Leach, Lofland, Lowe, Lowndes, Lynch, Magee, McCrary, Alexander S. McDill, McJunkin, McLean, McNulta, Mellish, Merriam, Milliken, Mills, Meyers, Negley, Nesmith, Nunn, O'Brien, O'Neill, Packard, Page, Isaac C. Parker, Parsons, Pelham, Pendleton, Phelps, Phillips, James H. Platt, Jr., Thomas C. Platt, Rainey, Randall, Ransier, Rawls, Ray, Rice, Richmond, Ellis H. Roberts, Ross, Sawyer, John G. Schumaker, Henry J. Scudder, Isaac W. Scudder, Sener, Shanks, Sheldon, Sherwood, Sloss, Smart, A. Herr Smith, George L. Smith, H. Boardman Smith, John Q. Smith, Snyder, Stanard, Standeford, Storm, Stowell, Strawbridge, Swann, Sypher, Taylor, Thomas, Thornburgh, Townsend, Tremain, Vance, Waddell, Waldron, Wallace, Jasper D. Ward, Marcus L. Ward, Wheeler, White, Whitehead, John M. S. Williams, William Williams, Willie, Ephraim K. Wilson, Wood, and Woodford—158.

NAYS — Messrs. Albright, Arthur, Banning, Barber, Berry, Blount, Bromberg, Brown, Buckner, Bundy, Burleigh, Burrows, Caldwell, Cason, John B. Clark, Jr., Clymer, Coburn, Conger, Corwin, Cotton, Cox, Crittenden, Curtis, Danford, Dawes, Donnan, Dunnell, Eames, Eden, Fort, Foster, Frye, Gooch, Gunckel, Eugene Hale, John T. Harris, Hatcher, Gerry W. Hazelton, Hendee, Holman, Hunter, Hyde, Hynes, Jewett, Kasson, Knapp, Lawrence, Lawson, Luttrell, Marshall, Martin, Maynard, James W. McDill, McDougall, Monroe, Moore, Morrison, Neal, Niblack, Niles, Orr, Orth, Packer, Hosea W. Parker, Perry, Pierce, Pike, Poland, Potter, Pratt, Read, Robbins, William R. Roberts, James W. Robinson, Rusk, Henry B. Sayler, Milton Sayler, Scofield, Sessions, Lazarus D. Shoemaker, Small, J. Amber Smith, Southard, Speer, Sprague, Starkweather, Stone, Strait Todd, Tyner, Wells, Whitehouse, Whitthorne, Wilber, Charles W. Willard, George Willard, Charles G. Williams, William B. Williams James Wilson, Jeremiah M. Wilson, Wolfe, Woodworth, John D. Young, and Pierce M. B. Young—104.

NOT VOTING.—Messrs. Barnum, Bland, Freeman Clarke, Dobbins, Hereford, Hersey, Hooper, Kendall, Killinger, Lamison, Lewis, Loughridge, McKee, Mitchell, Morey, Purman, Rapier, James C. Robinson, Sheats, William A. Smith, Stephens, St. John, and Walls—23.

So the bill, as amended, was ordered to be engrossed and read the third time.

The question was put upon the passage of the bill, and on a division there were—yeas 122, nays 74.

So the bill was passed.

In the Senate, on January 5, 1874, the bill of the House was considered. The Committee of Civil Service reported in favor of striking out the three sections of the bill and inserting in lieu thereof the following:

That so much of the act of March 3, 1873, entitled "An act making appropriations for legislative, executive, and judicial expenses of the Government for the year ending June 30, 1874," as provides for the increase of the compensation of members of Congress and Delegates, and the several officers and employés of either House of Congress, or both, be and the same is hereby repealed, and the salaries and compensation of all said persons shall be as fixed by the laws in force at the time of the passage of said act.

SECTION 2. That the compensation of the several heads of Departments shall be each $8,000 per annum.

The amendment to the amendment offered by Mr. Pratt, of Indiana, was to insert at the end of line 10 of the amendment of the committee the following:

Provided, however, That the Senators, Representatives, and Delegates of the Forty-third Congress who have received their compensation since the 4th day of March, 1873, at the rate of $7,500 per year, in accordance with the act of March 3, 1873, shall hereafter be paid only such monthly installments as shall, in the aggregate, make their compensation for the whole Congress equal to the sum of $5,000 per year, exclusive of mileage allowances.

Mr. Logan, of Illinois, said: "Mr. President, I should like to ask the Senator from Indiana a question, inasmuch as he is reputed to be a very fine lawyer, and doubtless is. He is aware of the provision of the Constitution which declares that Senators and Representatives shall receive a compensation for their services, to be ascertained by law and paid out of the Treasury of the United States. When that compensation is ascertained by law and paid out of the Treasury of the United States, has this Congress any power to reclaim it or require them to pay any portion of it back?"

Mr. Pratt, of Indiana, said: "I suppose that we have the control of this question during the entire term of Congress; that we could provide now that those who had received the limit of $5,000 should receive nothing further for their services during the residue of this Congress. I suppose we could dispense with the salary entirely if we thought proper. But this bill with my amendment makes the compensation precisely equal for all—$5,000 apiece."

Mr. Logan: "Now, Mr. President, the Senator says that he supposes that we could abolish the salary entirely. That is very probably true; but that is not the question. I put the question to him whether this Congress has any power to reclaim a salary that has been paid out of the Treasury to a member of Congress, under a law which has fixed such salary? Is there any difference between doing that directly and providing that a Senator or member of Congress shall have his future salary reduced by debiting against it that which he has drawn before, under the law? Is not that a taking back part of that which he has drawn under the law, when the Constitution expressly provides that his compensation shall be fixed by law and paid out of the Treasury of the United States? This is the compensation fixed by law, and it has been paid out of the Treasury of the United States, and you have no power to touch it any more than you have any other of his private property; and, as a lawyer, it seems to me that the Senator from Indiana will so say."

Mr. Pratt: "It seems to me that that question does not arise here. It could only arise in case the whole $5,000 provided by this bill as compensation for each member of Congress had been in fact already paid, and, more than that, had been paid and an attempt was made to recall it. Such is not the case here. No one has yet been paid, under the law of March last, $5,000."

Mr. Logan: "That is dodging the question again. I certainly do not desire to discuss this question at length. I expect I have received my portion of the odium of this law of March last. I do not say that we have not made a mistake in the eyes of the people; but, because the country does not believe in the amount of salary we provided, that is no reason why reasonable men should demand of us to do that which we have no power as a Congress to do; nor do they.

"I am willing to yield to the demands of the people as readily as any other man in this chamber, when reasonable. I may not satisfy my constituents, but am willing to yield in my official capacity to their demands or their requests. But to go further than that, and beyond reason and law and the dictates of common-sense, to satisfy the unreasonable demands of Senators who are playing a *rôle* for themselves, we are not called upon to do it. No demand has been made to go beyond our constitutional power by the people. Sir, the demand made by the people on the Congress is this—the repeal of the law of March 3, 1873.

"What effect does the amendment have? It has the effect to charge every member of Congress for the next year to come with what he has already received in excess of the rate of $5,000 a year—to debit him with so much, and only allow him to draw enough hereafter to bring him down to $5,000. I suppose I should not get any thing for the next three months under this, because my conscience has not prevented me from drawing my salary under the law. I guess I shall have to stay here without any money. The conscience of my friend from Indiana probably being a little more sensitive, he may not have drawn his amount, and hence he will be permitted to receive some pay. There is the distinction this amendment makes between Senators—between the consciences of Senators.

"But it goes further. Here are our cabinet ministers, here are our heads of bureaus, here are all the men who are incorporated in the increased salary bill, and you provide that the members of Congress who are now here having seats shall return their pay, but everybody else may keep his. Is that honest? Is that what the people want? Is that what they demand? Do they mean that we shall perpetrate a fraud upon them; that we shall by clipping our own wings impose upon them and hide the increase of salary as it affects other officers? They demand no such thing.

"Now, I do not claim that I am so versed in the law as my friend from Indiana; but what little law I do know suggests to me at least that we have no power to do that which he asks by his amendment. I am aware that, when we decide questions here, sometimes our legal knowledge is overriden by outside pressure; sometimes our views are changed very

much by the popular verdict, though the law is just as plain as it can be written, and we are willing to violate it merely to say before the country that we rushed to the rescue. I do not believe in such legislation."

Mr. Thurman, of Ohio, said: "I wish to say a word upon the legal question suggested by my friend from Illinois, because I think if he comes to understand it perfectly he will find there is not the difficulty in this amendment of the Senator from Indiana that he supposes to exist. If the amendment be adopted, it creates no inequality whatsoever in the payment of members. They will all be paid precisely the same sum. Nor is it any violation of vested right. The amendment proposes that the excess over $5,000 provided by the act of March last, when received by members, shall be taken into account in settling with them in the future until the expiration of the year; the whole effect of which, if carried out, would be that each member of the Forty-third Congress would receive for the year the sum of $5,000.

"But the objection that this is in violation of vested rights of members, or will produce any inequality between them, I submit to my friend from Illinois is not well taken. It does not destroy the equality between the members at all, nor does it destroy vested rights. Let us see how that is. In regard to the compensation of Senators and Representatives the Constitution provides:

The Senators and Representatives shall receive a compensation for their services, to be ascertained by law, and paid out of the Treasury of the United States.

"There is no provision as to when it shall be paid, or how it shall be paid, except that it shall be paid out of the Treasury of the United States. But, when we come to the compensation of the President, the Constitution reads:

The President shall, at stated times, receive for his services a compensation, etc.

"And the same provision in regard to the judges of the courts:

The judges both of the Supreme and inferior courts shall hold their offices during good behavior, and shall, at stated times, receive for their services a compensation which shall not be diminished during their continuance in office.

"The first difference, then, between members of Congress, whether Senators or Representatives, and the President and the judges, is that the Constitution is obligatory in respect to the President and the judges, that their compensation shall be paid at stated times; whereas there is no such provision in regard to that of Senators and Representatives.

"There is then another material difference between the two, and that is, that the salary of the President and the salaries of the judges cannot be diminished during, in the case of the President, the period for which he shall have been elected, and as to the judges, during the term they shall hold office; whereas the compensation of members of Congress may be increased or diminished during the very term of their office. We may increase our own salaries, or we may diminish them; and that being the case, as we have complete power over that subject to increase or diminish the salary, if now at this moment each member of Congress had already received precisely the sum of $5,000 for the year commencing on the 4th day of March last, I say, as the Senator from Indiana has already said, if we thought he had received enough for this year, we might say he should be paid no more than the $5,000 that he had already received. We may increase our own salary or diminish it, and we might diminish it for the succeeding three months down to a dollar a day, and no one could dispute that that would be a constitutional law, although the effect of it might be to make the whole compensation for the year just $5,000. I will suppose such a case as that. So we might say that it should be nothing for the next three months because we have already received enough.

"I do not find, therefore, any constitutional difficulty in the adoption of the amendment of the Senator from Indiana; and I shall vote for it for this, if no other reason, that I feel myself bound by the instructions of my Legislature to undo, as far as it is in my power to do, the effect of the act of 3d March last."

Mr. Logan: "I ask the Senator whether, when the individual receives the money under the law payable monthly, it does not vest in him and become his private property?"

Mr. Thurman: "I will answer the question of my friend. That question would arise provided you required the member to pay it back; but the amendment of the Senator from Indiana does not require anybody to pay back."

Mr. Ferry, of Connecticut, said: "Does not the amendment of the Senator from Indiana require that this shall be charged to the member of Congress?"

Mr. Thurman: "Yes; and, if the effect of charging it is to take away any right to any more compensation for that year, he will get no more; but, if the excess should be more than his compensation at the rate of $5,000 a year would be for the remainder of the year, he is not required to pay back the excess."

Mr. Logan: "On this point, because it is the point of controversy, I want the Senator—for he is a very good lawyer—to answer me this question: Has Congress any power to deprive you of your property after it is once vested in you?"

Mr. Thurman: "The Senator, being a very good lawyer himself—and I say that not to bandy compliments—does not need to be told that private property cannot be taken without making just compensation, under the Constitution of the United States."

Mr. Logan: "Very well. The question then is, whether, if a man receives his salary, it does not become private property. Does it not? I know I cannot put questions to the Senator that he cannot answer, but I should like to know whether or not it does not become private property. If it does not, is it real estate? It is something. I should like the Senator to tell me, after he receives his salary, what kind of property it is."

Mr. Thurman: "Certainly when a member has drawn his pay and got it in his pocket it is his private property, and is liable for his debts; and if he goes into bankruptcy it can be taken by the assignees."

Mr. Logan: "Now, following that, I will ask this question: Suppose it is private property, and it is liable for his debts, by what process can Congress divest him of it, without making just compensation?"

Mr. Thurman: "It does not divest him of it."

Mr. Logan: "Yes, it does. You do not divest a man of what he is to get, but of what he has got, by refusing to pay the amount due to him monthly until it is equalized to the $5,000 per annum. That is exactly what you do. Now I should like to ask the adroit Senator another question. Suppose this bill should become a law to-day. I have drawn several thousand dollars of my pay; I do not remember how much. The law passes to-day, and is signed by the President, requiring that money which I have drawn to be charged over on my account in future, and in that way the Government of the United States is to obtain the money back. Now, suppose I resign to-morrow, can the Government recover that money from me? That is the question I ask."

Mr. Thurman: "I am afraid the Senator will resign in order to keep his money." (Laughter.)

Mr. Logan: "There is no danger of that; but I should like the Senator to answer me that question, inasmuch as his legal mind controls him in voting for this bill. He thinks it is legal and proper, because he has been so instructed."

Mr. Scott, of Pennsylvania, said: "The amendment proposes equalization, as I understand it; that it proposes to take all the members of the present Congress—the Forty-third Congress—who have drawn the increased rate of compensation since the 4th of March last, and to deduct from their compensation in the future an amount which will bring them down to the $5,000 per year fixed in this bill.

"Now, if equalization is the purpose, if you intend to make the salary of the members yet under congressional control as nearly equal as possible, why not go farther back? Here are a large number of Senators who were in the Forty-second Congress; there are many members of the House who were in the Forty-second Congress; and, if there be any feature in the legislation of last March which was considered objectionable, it is what has been popularly baptized as the back-pay feature of the bill. If the Forty-third Congress has power to defalcate against the coming salary what has been received in the months since March last, why has it not the power to defalcate against the members who took the back pay in the Forty-second Congress? Why does the amendment of the Senator from Indiana stop there? I can understand no difference. If my friend from Ohio takes the ground that Congress has the power now to open accounts, and to defalcate against the coming salary the excess that has been received since the 4th of March last, why have we not the power to go back into the Forty-second Congress?"

Mr. Thurman: "That would be a discrimination between members."

Mr. Scott: "Between what members?"

Mr. Thurman: "Between those who belonged to the Forty-second Congress and those who did not."

Mr. Scott: "Not at all. It makes no discrimination among the present members; it reduces them all to $5,000. The only discrimination it makes is in favor of those who were in the Forty-second Congress and are not in the Forty-third. They have got the money, and you cannot reach them; but, if you can reach members from the 4th of March last, you can reach every member of the Forty-third Congress who was a member of the Forty-second, and this amendment falls short of its highly-patriotic purpose."

Mr. Stockton, of New Jersey, said: "I understood the Senator from Ohio to say that he could see nothing unconstitutional, he could see no invidious distinction in an amendment which provided that those Senators who, since the 4th of March, have been drawing pay at the rate of $7,500, should have charged up to them that sum, so that they would draw now a less sum than those who did not receive the increased pay under the salary bill. To that proposition the Senator from Ohio, impelled, as he says, by the action of his Legislature to speak on the subject, has given the weight of his authority, than which there is no greater in this Senate.

"Mr. President, the Constitution says that the Senators and Representatives shall receive a compensation to be ascertained by law. It must be the Senators each and all of them alike. It must be ascertained, namely, made certain as to amount. It must be by law that it is made certain; that is, by a general rule applying to all. If I understand this question, a Senator of the United States, a member of the Congress of the United States, under the Constitution and the law passed thereunder, may receive the sum ascertained by law. He has no option about it. If it is nothing, he has no right to any thing; if it is a larger sum than it was when his constituents elected him, he must receive that sum and no other. It is the sum 'ascertained by law.' Those are the words of the Constitution. That that law was unconstitutional; that that law was improper or illegal—I speak not now

of motives, nor of the propriety or wisdom in its passage—but simply that it has never been claimed that there was any defect in that law by which it was not an operative law. This has never been suggested. So it has never been whispered that a Senator of the United States had a right to receive more or less than that sum. When it was received it was his own. Of course, no Senator was bound to draw it. A man may let his money that is due him pile up in the Treasury of the United States. or in the office of the Secretary of the Senate, to any amount he pleases, as he may in a bank or anywhere else. There it piles up; there it goes to his credit; it is credited to him. The day the bill became operative the amount due to each was payable; and the man who did not go to the office the day he was entitled to it and draw the sum, the average of which, it was said in this debate, was about $8,000, was just as much entitled to it as those who did, and his administrators were just as much entitled, by the laws of this land, to collect it if he died as if he had taken it during his life. That position cannot be controverted. It is impregnable.

"Now, Mr. President, how would it be in case it appears that any Senator has not received this pay? No such case can exist under the law. Every member of Congress received his pay—back pay, increased pay, and all. Take the case of the gentleman who devoted the back pay, which was his legal right, to building the Washington Monument; or of the gentleman who divided among the poor of his district, kind and charitable as he was, the money so taken from the Treasury; and are they, with their charitable and generous disposition of it, embraced in the clause of this amendment, or are they excluded as those that did not take the increase? If they are included because they did with it what their good and charitable hearts suggested, nevertheless they took it. The United States Government did not make an appropriation to assist in the building of the Washington Monument. Money cannot be taken out of the Treasury to be distributed among the poor of a congressional district except by law. No, Mr. President, they took it; and a Senator who wrote a letter to the Secretary of the Senate telling him to cover the pay which was due him back into the Treasury of the United States took that money. He could only convey a title to it, because it was their property. He disposed of it where his conscience, where his means, where his disposition led him in the exercise of that right which it was his duty to exercise, where they told him it had better go; but it was nevertheless his act. It was covered into the Treasury by no law of Congress, but by the act alone and solely of that individual; and if that individual had died before he made that disposition it would have belonged to his estate, and could have been claimed by his executors. He was generous with his own, not with the public money. So that, Mr. President, whether a Senator, receiving it as all did, devoted it to pay his debts, or whether in the exercise of a noble generosity, claiming the right to do what he would with his own, he gave it for such purposes as he thought convenient and proper, or whether he did it without taking any action on the matter, still in contemplation of law this sum was to his credit; and it required his act, his conveyance, to divest himself of it; or, in case of death, the act of his representative. So it has been in every case; and in such instances, if there be such where the voluntary disposition of it has not been made by the individual, it stands there as his property now, subject to an action in case of his death by his administrator or executor."

Mr. Thurman : " Mr. President, I should not say a word more on the point immediately under consideration, but that I must have been extremely unfortunate in the expression of my views, or else I must be exceedingly mistaken in my view of what is the Constitution, for I find that I am criticised all around and told that I am wrong in my views. But yet, sir, I cannot see it. What is considered back pay in popular parlance was the additional sum of $5,000, less mileage, which was paid to each one of the members of the Forty-second Congress for his services in that Congress. That was the back pay. It amounted to different sums to the different members, according to the amount of their mileage. To the Senators from Ohio it amounted to about $4,300, or between $4,300 and $4,400. To the Senator from Oregon, who liberally contributed his share to finish the Washington Monument, it amounted to the sum of one hundred and forty-odd dollars; and so on. It was a very different sum, according to the amount of mileage that a member was to receive. That is not in this bill, nor is it in the amendment offered by the Senator from Indiana farthest from me (Mr. Pratt). But the act of March 3, 1873, provided that the salary of members of Congress should thenceforth be at the rate of $7,500 per annum, payable monthly. It made an annual salary, just as the previous act had made; an annual salary just as the act of 1856, which established $3,000, had made. So this act of March last provided that in the future the compensation of a member of Congress should be $7,500 per annum.

" Now, it is agreed on all hands that that act is to be repealed, and we are to go back to $5,000 per annum; and, inasmuch as that is done in deference, as it is said, to public opinion, which condemns the act, the Senator from Indiana farthest from me proposes to give full effect to that public opinion and make it apply to this Congress just as fully as if the salary had not been raised at all *quoad* this Congress.

" Now I want to go on and state what this amendment of the Senator from Indiana is. It

is simply to say in effect that the pay of members of the Forty-third Congress shall be $10,-000 for this Congress, and in computing their pay $10,000 you take into account what has already been paid. I put it to any one here if this amendment, read in these words—' that the compensation of members of the Forty-third Congress, for the Congress, shall be $10,-000 '—if that was the simple amendment and nothing more, and not a word was said about charging up to them what they have received —would not the necessary effect be that all they have received would be taken out, and they would only receive the balance of the $10,000; and is there anybody who would say that was not constitutional ?

" Or suppose you take it in another way and provide that the bill shall take effect from the 4th day of March next, leaving you to receive pay at $7,500 up to the 4th day of March next, and then provide that for the succeeding year your pay shall be only $2,500 a year, would anybody say that that would be unconstitutional ? And yet that would be precisely the effect of the amendment of the Senator from Indiana. It would make your pay for the Congress $10,-000 and no more, and his amendment makes it $10,000 and no more, and this objection is a mere objection to the form of the thing, to what is called the charging up, the debiting members with what they have received over and above at the rate of $5,000 a year; and as we have power to decrease our compensation as well as to increase it, as we may do it at any time whatsoever, as we may take into consideration what we have received heretofore in determining what we shall receive in the future, I, for the life of me, cannot see, with the utmost respect for those who think otherwise, where is the difference between the proposition of the Senator from Indiana and either one of the propositions that I have suggested ; for instance, the proposition that the pay of the Forty-third Congress shall be $10,-000 for the Congress, or that this act shall take effect on the 4th day of March next, and the pay for the next year shall be at the rate of $2,500.

" Inasmuch as you might plainly provide that this law should take effect on the 4th of March next, and that then for the next succeeding year we should receive only $2,500 a year, or inasmuch as you might provide that the compensation of members for the two years ending the 3d of March, 1875, should be $10,-000, and that would leave you to be charged up with all you had received before this time, so you may take it in the form in which it is expressed in the amendment of the Senator from Indiana.

" Now a word as to the back pay. The Senator from Pennsylvania says, Why may you not charge up the back pay ? For this reason : that that would make an inequality in the pay of members of Congress, paying some men one salary, and others another and different salary.

I do not go into the question whether or not there must be equality; whether there must be uniformity. I know that there are some persons who think there need not be uniformity."

Mr. Wright, of Iowa, said: "I trust that the vote will be taken upon this amendment at once, as also upon all other amendments that may be offered, though I trust none will be offered, and that we shall get to a vote on the bill in a very short time.

"Upon this measure, as upon all others, while I have a seat upon this floor I propose, as far as I can, to look to practical results. In other words, I think a vast deal more of a practical certainty than I do of theoretical perfection. I know that we may remain here and discuss this and other questions day after day, whereas if we would come down to the real question before us, and decide it on the judgment of each Senator, we should be more likely to reach such practical results as would be beneficial to the country as well as to ourselves.

"So far as the amendment offered by the Senator from Indiana is concerned, if it stood alone and aside from its effect on this bill, I certainly am not prepared to say that I should oppose it. I think my course upon this question last session, as well as this, is sufficient to indicate how I would stand upon the general proposition. In other words, I think that in justice and in right, and in view of all the considerations that obtain, it is but proper that this bill, so far as Senators and members are concerned, should relate back to the 4th of March last. But, as I have already said, while that is my opinion, I nevertheless am as well of the opinion that, if this amendment shall be carried, it perhaps will result in the defeat of the bill—if not here, that it perhaps may fall as between the two Houses."

Mr. Carpenter, of Wisconsin, said: "The amendment as it is now drawn discriminates from this time forth as to the pay of Senators in this Chamber. That cannot be done constitutionally, in my opinion. We can figure on this question; we can ascertain just what every Senator has received; we presume that they have received all that they are entitled to; if they have not, they have but to go to the office and draw the money; it is there for them; they have received, or may to-day obtain, $6,250. Now, then, let us fix the pay of all Senators from this time out at $3,750, if that is the proper amount."

Mr. Pratt: "Mr. President, I do not share the constitutional scruples of my learned friend from Wisconsin; but, sir, to return to the objections which have been made against the pending amendment, the first proposition which I make in answer to all of the objections which have been urged against it is this: in now changing the compensation of members of Congress from $7,500 a year to $5,000 a year we do so in obedience to the will of the people, to the pronounced popular judgment. So my friend from Wisconsin has just announced to the Senate. He says that despite his own convictions on the subject he is going to vote for this reduction because the people, his masters, demand it. Now, sir, the point I make is this, that if it was wrong on the 3d of March, 1873, to raise the salary from $5,000 to $7,500 a year, it has been wrong every day since, and we are wrong-doers in having received compensation under that law, and should either return it to the Treasury or else it should be deducted from our compensation in future. I do not see how we can escape from that conclusion. The whole argument of my friend from Wisconsin is this: He yields to this demand because the people have willed it; because they have determined that this increase of salary was wrong. I submit to him that the same people likewise demand that this bill which we are now considering should relate back to the 4th of March, 1873, so that at no period should we be in the receipt of more than $5,000 a year. The second proposition which I make is, that, upon every increase which has been made by Congress of the compensation of its members, the increase has related back uniformly to the beginning of the Congress when the increase was made. The compensation has been changed some five or six times, and I repeat that, wherever that increase has been made, it has related back to the beginning of that Congress. If that be correct as a principle, why should not the decrease of compensation be governed by the same principle, and the decrease relate back to the beginning of the Congress?

"Now, let us take our legislation from 1789 down to the present time. The first compensation was an allowance of six dollars per day. The first increase was from six dollars to seven dollars per day; the next increase was to eight dollars a day; the next to $1,500 a year; the next to $3,000; and then, in 1866, an increase was made to $5,000, and in 1873 to $7,500. There has been but one instance, I believe, since the institution of this Government, when the compensation of members of Congress was decreased, and that took place in the year 1818. The previous Congress had increased the compensation from six dollars or eight dollars a day, whatever it was, to $3,000 for the Congress, or $1,500 a year. There was great complaint made of that increase, and the succeeding Congress promptly repealed the law, decreasing the compensation to eight dollars a day, and made that decrease relate back to the commencement of that Congress. I have the act here by me if any Senator has any question upon that subject.

"There is but one consideration more, then, Mr. President, which I wish to submit to the Senate; and that is in reply to the objections of my friends from Illinois and Wisconsin. They complain that there will be inequality between the compensation of members of Congress; they complain that they will have to refund money which they have already received under the existing law, and the complaint is that it is violative, if not of the letter, at least of the spirit, of the Constitution, as impairing the obligation of the contract under which the money was paid.

"This position would have great force in case it were well founded; but the amendment which I have offered is prospective in its operation; it compels no Senator, no member of the House of Representatives, to refund a dollar of the money which he has received under the act of March 3, 1873. Under that law the compensation for the entire Congress would be $15,000. Up to the 4th day of January in this present year the compensation under the law amounts to the sum of $6,250. That, subtracted from the compensation established by this bill ($10,000 per Congress), leaves $3,750 yet to be paid to members of Congress, to be distributed over the fourteen months remaining of the Forty-third Congress; and, according to my calculation, that will leave $268 per month to be paid to each member of Congress in the future. Nothing is to be returned whatever; so that I think that objection is not well taken. This amendment contemplates no return to the Treasury of any dollar that has been received under an existing law, but fixes the compensation in the future so that those who have received under the existing law $625 a month will hereafter, during the remaining fourteen months of this Congress, receive but $268 a month. That is the whole of it."

Mr. Sherman, of Ohio, said: "The committee, after a careful consideration of this subject, with the House bill and with all the debates in the House before them, concluded that it was better from this time forth, from the passage of this bill, to restore the salary of $5,000 a year and the ordinary allowances and mileage. It is true that objections were at once made that the old mileage system was objectionable, was unequal, by giving to members from remote States a greater portion than was their due. On the other hand, it was insisted that men who come from a great distance, from their business and from their families, ought to have some additional compensation, more than the mere expense of traveling from their remote place of residence to this point. Other considerations operated. At any rate, this was a long-established system, that had not given rise to much complaint; and if there was any gross injustice in it, that might at any time be corrected by a reduction of the rate of mileage. If twenty cents a mile is now too high, owing to the cheapness of transportation, it can at any time, by a mere amendment of the law, be reduced to ten cents a mile. The committee thought it was better simply to restore the law as it was on the 3d of March, 1873; and there are grave and serious reasons why this system of mileage ought to be maintained, but perhaps at a lower rate than that now fixed by law.

"In regard to other allowances, as to which so much complaint has been made, what are they? They are fixed and ascertained. We were allowed under the old law $125 per annum apiece to pay for the ordinary stationery and the incidents connected with the ordinary discharge of our duty. It is true that the newspapers say that five or ten thousand knives are supplied to members of the Senate. If so, they are paid for by members of the Senate. The whole amount of our allowance as fixed by law is $125 to each member, and that is not more than sufficient for the purpose. What other allowances are given? None other. No member of Congress can by any possibility draw from the public Treasury under the old law any thing but his compensation, the $5,000 a year, the mileage allowed by law, and this allowance for stationery. The franking privilege being repealed, as a matter of course, we are relieved in a great measure from the burden of franking public documents. The amount of postage that may be paid by any of us probably would range somewhere in the neighborhood of two or three hundred dollars a year. That may or may not be provided for, as Congress may hereafter deem wise. I say, therefore, Mr. President, that the amendment reported by the committee is substantially correct.

"As to the proposition now offered by the Senator from Indiana, I certainly would not vote for it. I have no more power and we have no more right to take from members of Congress money which they have earned and received in pursuance of law than we have the right to take your house, or your farm, or confiscate your property. It is their property, and although it is in the form of money, as exhibited here yesterday by my friend from Texas (Mr. Flanagan), what he has received is property—his property—and no man has a right to take it from him. With all due deference to my friend from Indiana, who I know would never like to do any thing by indirection, I do say that the legal effect of his amendment is by indirection, by a device, to take money from the pockets of the men who earned it, and hold it, and have it now by law. Why, sir, what is the proposition? Senators are discussing the various forms in which the proposition may be put. They say if it is framed in such and such words it is constitutional, but if framed in other words it is unconstitutional. Sir, I care not in what form you put it, it is unjust, and therefore I will not vote for it. I would not vote for it under any demand.

"Mr. President, there are one or two other points that have been made on which I desire to say a word, because I do not wish to speak on this bill again. When the committee reported this bill they considered other questions, which, I see from the amendments prepared all around me, are to be presented, and we have got to debate them over again; and I wish now in advance to give, as near as I can, the reasons why we did not do so and so.

"In the first place, it is said that the President of the United States had the benefit of this increase-of-salary act, it raising his salary from $25,000 up to $50,000 a year, and that if we are now disposed, either in deference to public opinion or because we think it is right, to go back to the old salary, we ought to put the President in the same position. I could not answer that argument if we had the power to do it. If the same public opinion which controls the votes of some members—it does not control mine, because I think the salary of $5,000 is enough—and induces them to go back to $5,000 a year, is to apply to members of Congress, it may be asked, why not go back to $25,000 for the President? The answer at once is that the Constitution of the United States forbids us to do so.

"But, they say, let us do it any way; let us repeal the law of March 3, 1873, and not say any thing about the President. Well, sir, if we do that, we do what we know we have not the constitutional power to do.

"But, they say, the courts will set aside our action. I trust in God the Congress of the United States will never allow the courts to set aside our action in passing a law that we know to be unconstitutional; and no man now can touch the salary of the President of the United States, during his term of office, in the slightest degree, without violating the oath which he took at your desk, sir, and which ought to be sacred to him at every hour of his life. It is utterly impossible for him to do it; and we ought not to pass a law which by any construction would assert the power to do what the Constitution forbids us doing. Therefore it was that the committee omitted from the operation of this bill the President of the United States, whose salary is now protected by the Constitution; and we cannot touch it to the amount of five cents.

"The same observation would apply to the judges of the Supreme Court of the United States. But it is said that there is a vacancy in the Supreme Court which may be filled after the passage of this act; other vacancies may occur from time to time, and let us pass an act that will operate upon future judges. That would be manifestly unfair. There ought to be one equal rule, applying to all the existing judges and those to be appointed in the future. Therefore you cannot make a discrimination there.

"But there is another reason. I would not reduce the salary of these judges if I had the absolute power to do it, because I believe the judges of the highest tribunal of the United States are not too highly paid when they receive $10,000 a year. They are secluded; they are excluded from all other employment; they are separated from the mass of the people nearly to hold even the scales of justice. That is not our position. We are members of

Congress, representatives of States. We are at liberty to pursue nearly all the vocations of life. We can engage in our professions during the time that we are not here employed in the public service. We are not cramped and crippled by those rules of propriety which guard and protect the Supreme Court of the United States. Therefore, in measuring our compensation, we are not to be governed by the same rules and the same principles that we would be governed by in fixing the compensation of the judges of the Supreme Court. I do not think their compensation is too high. As far as my constituents are concerned, I never have heard any one complain about the reasonable increase of the salaries of the judges of the Supreme Court of the United States.

"In regard to the President of the United States, heretofore, while his salary was fixed at $25,000 a year, it was supported and aided by direct appropriations made by Congress, so that, instead of $25,000 a year, the President has for many years, away back into the time of Andrew Jackson, and thence down, been paid for certain matters which ordinarily enter into the private expenses of every citizen, in order to add to his salary of $25,000 a year. If, then, we think the salary now fixed by the Constitution and the law is too high at $50,-000, we have it in our power, to the extent that we desire, to the extent we think is fair and right, to cut off those additional appropriations that have been made from time to time in addition to the salary of the President of the United States; so that we are not beyond remedy to reduce the incidental expenses of the Executive office if we think the compensation is sufficient to enable the President to pay these things out of his own salary."

The President *pro tempore:* "The question is on the amendment proposed by the Senator from Indiana (Mr. Pratt) to the amendment of the committee."

The amendment to the amendment was rejected.

Mr. Morrill, of Vermont, said: "I offer the following amendment, to come in after line 10 of the first section of the amendment of the committee, as a proviso:

Provided, That the allowance for mileage hereafter to be paid to each Senator, Representative, and Delegate, for going to and returning from the seat of Government once in each session shall be one-half of the sum allowed and paid prior to the act of March 3, 1873.

"I desire to say that one of the strongest arguments that was made use of in order to carry the increase of salaries, and to defend it after it had been carried, was that it rectified the great abuse of the mileage system, by which we paid for travel four, five, or six times as much as the cost thereof. It would suit me, perhaps, better than any mileage at all, to have a fixed sum; but as it is not perhaps practicable to introduce a measure in relation to that matter here, or is not as practicable as it would be to reduce it, I propose to fix the same amount that we allow our military officers—that is, ten cents per mile—reducing it from what it is now—twenty cents a mile—to ten cents a mile, which is the same we allow our military officers to have for traveling expenses. That will be in most cases twice the amount of the cost, and it is amply sufficient."

Mr. Stevenson, of Kentucky, said: "I should like to inquire of the Senator from Vermont why he desires in his proposed reform to adhere in his amendment to the inequality and alleged injustice of the former system of mileage. If he seeks to reach an exact standard of justice, why not pay every member of Congress exactly what it costs him to travel to and from the capital? The Senator remarked that the bill to increase pay at the last session derived its greatest strength from the injustice and inequality of the mileage system which that compensation bill dispensed with. It does not occur to me that his amendment removes that injustice. It is true that those who receive mileage will, by the amendment, only get one-half as much as they did under the old law, but still the mileage will be unequal, and the injustice of the measure would seem to me to run just in the same ratio as it did before, though the amount of mileage would be lessened. For instance, a Senator from the Pacific coast, who can come here for $300, would, under the Senator's pending amendment, get $800; while a Senator living in the vicinity of Washington would only get one-half of the mileage he would be entitled to, which, perhaps, might not, under the reduction, pay him what he had absolutely expended. Now, if the object of the Senator be to reduce it down to a proper standard, why not fix the amount at the precise sum which it costs every member by the most direct route of travel to reach Washington? Why go back to the principle of inequality in mileage which must always discriminate so unequally between members of Congress, and which it was one object of the present law to get rid of?"

Mr. Morrill, of Vermont: "I have already admitted that this amendment does not remedy the abuse wholly, but it does remedy it to the extent of one-half, and it leaves that amount in the Treasury. It gives us precisely the same mileage that we allow the officers of the Army and Navy when they are compelled under military or naval orders to travel over the country; and that sum is deemed to be a just one. If we are to have any mileage at all, it strikes me that ten cents a mile is amply sufficient. We all know that it is much more than the actual cost of travel.

"Then, when you come back to the proposition of the Senator from Kentucky, as I said before, the idea of giving an account of our traveling expenses is to me offensive and rather repugnant. Shall I, when I make out my bill of expenses, if I happen to smoke cigars—as I do not—give an account of how many cigars I have smoked? When I travel, shall I come on night and day, or shall I be allowed for the expense of a day at a hotel in New York, or at Springfield? I do not know precisely what is legitimate. If I come with my family, part of the expenses, perhaps, may be mingled up with those of my family. I hardly know how to separate them. Suppose I stop a day in New York, and require a parlor for my family, am I to charge that to the Government? Therefore I would much prefer to have a fixed sum for us all. If, perhaps, the total salary had been fixed at $5,500, it might have been acceptable; but in the absence of any such provision I do propose to remedy the gross abuse that exists in the mileage system; and I therefore propose that we shall be paid, what we allow our military officers, ten cents a mile—that is to say, to reduce the former mileage allowances from twenty cents a mile to ten cents a mile."

The President pro tempore: "The question is on the amendment proposed by the Senator from Vermont (Mr. Morrill) to the amendment of the committee."

The question being taken by yeas and nays, resulted—yeas 30, nays 33; as follows:

YEAS—Messrs. Anthony, Bogy, Boreman, Buckingham, Cameron, Carpenter, Conkling, Crozier, Davis, Edmunds, Fenton, Ferry of Connecticut, Ferry of Michigan, Frelinghuysen, Hamlin, Ingalls, Morrill of Maine, Morrill of Vermont, Morton, Norwood, Oglesby, Pratt, Ramsey, Ransom, Saulsbury, Schurz, Scott, Sherman, Sumner, and Thurman—30.

NAYS—Messrs. Allison, Bayard, Boutwell, Brownlow, Chandler, Clayton, Conover, Cooper, Cragin, Dennis, Dorsey, Flanagan, Gilbert, Goldthwaite, Hamilton of Maryland, Hitchcock, Howe, Kelly, Lewis, Logan, McCreery, Merrimon, Mitchell, Patterson, Sargent, Spencer, Sprague, Stevenson, Tipton, Wadleigh, West, Windom, and Wright—33.

ABSENT—Messrs. Alcorn, Ames, Gordon, Hamilton of Texas, Johnston, Jones, Robertson, Stewart, and Stockton—9.

So the amendment to the amendment was rejected.

Mr. Cragin, of New Hampshire, said: "I move to add at the end of the first section of the committee's amendment the following:

Provided, That mileage shall not be allowed for the first session of the Forty-third Congress.

"There cannot be any objection to that, I think, as we have received our actual traveling expenses."

The President pro tempore: "The question recurs on the amendment proposed by the Senator from New Hampshire (Mr. Cragin) to the amendment of the committee."

The amendment to the amendment was agreed to.

The President pro tempore: "The question now recurs on the amendment proposed by the Senator from Maryland (Mr. Hamilton)."

The Chief Clerk read the amendment to the amendment, which was to strike out the first and second sections of the amendment of the committee, and insert the following:

That so much of the act of March 3, 1873, entitled "An act making appropriations for the legislative, executive, and judicial expenses of the Government for the year ending June 30, 1874," as provides for the increase of the salaries of the President, Vice-President, members of Congress, and Delegates, and all other officers therein named, be, and the same is hereby, repealed ; and the salaries and compensation of all said officers, and clerks of every name and description, shall be and remain as fixed by the laws in force at the time of the passage of the act the provisions of which are hereby repealed: *Provided*, That this repeal, so far as it relates to the salary of the President, shall not take effect until the 4th day of March, 1877, on and after which date said repeal, as to the salary of said officer, shall have full force and effect, and as to all other officers from and after the taking effect of this act: *And provided further*, That this repeal shall not relate to or affect the salaries of the Chief and other justices of the Supreme Court of the United States as now established by law.

The President *pro tempore:* "The question is on the amendment proposed by the Senator from Maryland (Mr. Hamilton), upon which the yeas and nays have been ordered."

The question being taken by yeas and nays, resulted—yeas 32, nays 29 ; as follows:

YEAS—Messrs. Allison, Bogy, Boreman, Carpenter, Clayton, Conkling, Cooper, Davis, Dennis, Edmunds, Fenton, Ferry of Michigan, Goldthwaite, Gordon, Hamilton of Maryland, Hitchcock, Kelly, Lewis, McCreery, Merrimon, Norwood, Oglesby, Patterson, Pratt, Ramsey, Ransom, Saulsbury, Schurz, Stevenson, Thurman, Windom, and Wright —32.

NAYS — Messrs. Anthony, Bayard, Boutwell, Brownlow, Buckingham, Cameron, Conover, Cragin, Crozier, Dorsey, Flanagan, Frelinghuysen, Gilbert, Hamlin, Howe, Ingalls, Mitchell, Morrill of Maine, Morrill of Vermont, Morton, Sargent, Scott, Sherman, Spencer, Sprague, Sumner, Tipton, Wadleigh, and West—29.

ABSENT—Messrs. Alcorn, Ames, Chandler, Ferry of Connecticut, Hamilton of Texas, Johnston, Jones, Logan, Robertson, Stewart, and Stockton—11.

So the amendment to the amendment was agreed to.

The President *pro tempore:* "The question now is on the amendment of the committee as amended in the Senate."

Mr. Conkling, of New York, said: " I now offer the amendment which I have sent to the desk."

The Chief Clerk : "It is proposed to strike out the following words:

That so much of the act of March 3, 1873, entitled "An act making appropriations for the legislative, executive, and judicial expenses of the Government for the year ending June 30, 1874," as provides for the increase of the salaries of the President, Vice-President, members of Congress, and Delegates, and all other officers therein named, be, and the same is hereby, repealed ; and the salaries and compensation of all said officers and clerks of every name and description shall be and remain as fixed by the laws in force at the time of the passage of the act the provisions of which are hereby repealed: *Provided*, That this repeal, so far as it relates to the salary of the President, shall not take effect until the 4th day of March, 1877, on and after which date said repeal, as to the salary of said officer, shall have full force and effect, and as to all other officers from and after

the taking effect of this act: *And provided further*, That this repeal shall not relate to or affect the salaries of the Chief and other justices of the Supreme Court of the United States as now established by law.

"And in lieu thereof to insert the following:

That so much of the act of March 3, 1873, entitled " An act making appropriations for the legislative, executive, and judicial expenses of the Government for the year ending June 30, 1874," as provides for the increase of the compensation of public officers and employés, whether members of Congress, Delegates, or others (except the President of the United States and the justices of the Supreme Court), be, and the same is hereby, repealed ; and the salaries, compensation, and allowances, of all said persons (except as aforesaid) shall be as fixed by the laws in force at the time of the passage of said act: *Provided*, That mileage shall not be allowed for the first session of the Forty-third Congress. That all moneys appropriated as compensation to the members of the Forty-second Congress in excess of the mileage and allowances fixed by law at the commencement of the said Congress, and which shall not have been drawn by the members of the said Congress respectively, or which having been drawn have been returned in any form to the United States, are hereby covered into the Treasury of the United States, and are declared to be the moneys of the United States absolutely, the same as if they had never been appropriated as aforesaid.

Mr. Morton: "Will it be in order, if this amendment is adopted as an entirety, to move to strike out any portion of it ? "

The President *pro tempore:* " It will not. It will be in order to add to it, but not to strike out any portion of it."

The Secretary proceeded to call the roll, and the result was announced as follows :

YEAS—Messrs. Allison, Anthony, Boreman, Boutwell, Buckingham, Cameron, Carpenter, Chandler, Conkling, Conover, Crozier, Edmunds, Ferry of Michigan, Frelinghuysen, Hitchcock, Howe, Ingalls, Logan, McCreery, Merrimon, Mitchell, Morrill of Maine, Morrill of Vermont, Morton, Oglesby, Patterson, Pratt, Ramsey, Robertson, Sargent, Scott, Sherman, Stockton, Wadleigh, West, Windom, and Wright—37.

NAYS—Messrs. Bogy, Brownlow, Clayton, Fenton, Flanagan, Gilbert, Goldthwaite, Gordon, Hamilton of Maryland, Kelly, Lewis, Norwood, Schurz, Sprague, and Tipton—15.

ABSENT—Messrs. Alcorn, Ames, Bayard, Cooper, Cragin, Davis, Dennis, Dorsey, Ferry of Connecticut, Hamilton of Texas, Hamlin, Johnston, Jones, Ransom, Saulsbury, Spencer, Stevenson, Stewart, Sumner, and Thurman—20.

So the amendment of Mr. Conkling was agreed to.

The President *pro tempore:* "The question recurs on the amendment proposed by the committee as amended, which is to substitute what has been read for three sections of the House bill."

The amendment was agreed to.

The Chief Clerk read the fourth section of the House bill, as follows:

SEC. 4. That the Secretary of the Treasury is required to cover into the Treasury all sums that may remain undrawn or which have been received as increased compensation under the provisions of said act approved March 3, 1873, and which shall have or may come into his possession by the return thereof.

Mr. Conkling: " I move to strike it out."

The President *pro tempore:* "The question is on the amendment of the Senator from New York."

The amendment was agreed to.

The bill was read the third time.

The question being taken, resulted as follows:

YEAS—Messrs. Allison, Anthony, Bayard, Bogy, Boreman, Boutwell, Buckingham, Cameron, Carpenter, Chandler, Clayton, Conkling, Crozier, Davis, Dorsey, Edmunds, Fenton, Ferry of Michigan, Frelinghuysen, Goldthwaite, Hamilton of Maryland, Hamlin, Hitchcock, Howe, Ingalls, Logan, McCreery, Merrimon, Mitchell, Morrill of Maine, Morrill of Vermont, Morton, Oglesby, Patterson, Pratt, Ramsey, Robertson, Sargent, Saulsbury, Schurz, Scott, Sherman, Spencer. Stevenson, Stockton, Sumner, Wadleigh, West, Windom, and Wright—50.

NAYS—Messrs. Brownlow, Conover, Flanagan, Gordon, Lewis, Norwood, Sprague, and Tipton—8.

ABSENT—Messrs. Alcorn, Ames, Cooper, Cragin, Dennis, Ferry of Connecticut, Gilbert, Hamilton of Texas, Johnston, Jones, Kelly, Ransom, Stewart, and Thurman—14.

So the bill was passed.

On motion of Mr. Conkling, the title of the bill was amended so as to read: "A bill repealing the increase of salaries of members of Congress and other officers."

In the House, on January 13th, the amendments of the Senate were considered.

The Speaker: "The first bill upon the Speaker's table is a bill to establish the compensation of Senators, Representatives, and Delegates, returned from the Senate with amendment."

Mr. Hurlbut, of Illinois, said: "It was my fortune, sir, to introduce the bill which comes back amended by the Senate. I believe the bill which I introduced was just and fair as a measure of future compensation. I believed then, and believe now, that mileage was injudicious, discriminating, and unfair. But, sir, the Senate of the United States has sent back to us practically a new bill, restoring the status not only of the members of the House and of the Senate, but of all other officers and employés of the Government whose salaries were increased by the act of March 3, 1873, with the exception of the President of the United States and the judges of the Supreme Court, who are covered and protected by a constitutional provision. I propose to accept that measure as a measure looking to economy and as a settlement, so far as I am concerned, of this vexed question."

Mr. Hale, of Maine, said: "I move, Mr. Speaker, that the House concur in the Senate amendment; and upon that I call the previous question."

The question was taken; and the tellers reported—yeas 126, nays 57. The previous question was seconded and the main question was ordered, which was on concurring in the Senate amendment.

The question was taken; and it was decided in the affirmative, as follows:

YEAS—Messrs. Albright, Archer, Arthur, Ashe, Atkins, Banning, Barber, Barnum, Bass, Beck, Be- gole, Bell, Berry, Biery, Bland, Blount, Bowen, Bradley, Bright, Bromberg, Brown, Buckner, Buffinton, Bundy, Burchard, Burleigh, Burrows, Benjamin F. Butler, Roderick R. Butler, Cain, Caldwell, Cannon, Cason, Cessna, Amos Clark, Jr., John B. Clark, Jr., Clayton, Clements, Clinton L. Cobb, Stephen A. Cobb, Coburn, Comingo, Conger, Cook, Corwin, Cotton, Crittenden, Crooke, Crounse, Crutchfield, Curtis, Danford, Davis, Dawes, De Witt, Dobbins, Donnan, Dunnell, Durham, Eames, Eden, Elliott, Farwell, Field, Fort, Foster, Frye, Garfield, Giddings, Glover, Gooch, Gunckel, Eugene Hale, Robert S. Hale, Hamilton, Hancock, Harmer, Benjamin W. Harris, Henry R. Harris, Harrison, Hatcher, Hathorn, Havens, John B. Hawley, Joseph R. Hawley, Gerry W. Hazelton, John W. Hazelton, Hendee, Hereford, Herndon, Hersey, E. Rockwood Hoar, George F. Hoar, Holman, Hoskins, Houghton, Howe, Hubbell, Hunter, Hunton, Hurlbut, Hyde, Kasson, Killinger, Knapp, Lamport, Lansing, Lawrence, Lawson, Leach, Lewis, Loughridge, Lowe, Luttrell, Lynch, Magee, Marshall Martin, McCrary, Alexander S. McDill, James W. McDill, MacDougall, McKee, McNulta, Mellish, Merriam, Milliken, Mills, Mitchell, Monroe, Moore, Morrison, Myers, Neal, Nesmith, Niblack, Niles, Nunn, O'Brien, O'Neill, Orr, Orth, Packard, Packer, Page, Hosea W. Parker, Isaac C. Parker, Parsons, Pelham, Pendleton, Perry, Phelps, Pierce. Thomas C. Platt, Poland, Potter, Pratt, Purman, Rainey, Rapier, Rawls, Read, Rice. Richmond, Robbins, Ellis H. Roberts, James W. Robinson, Ross, Rusk, Sawyer, Henry B. Sayler, Milton Sayler, John G. Schumaker, Scofield, Isaac W. Scudder, Sener, Sessions, Sheats, Sheldon, Sherwood, Lazarus D. Shoemaker, Small, Smart, A. Herr Smith, H. Boardman Smith, J. Ambler Smith, John Q. Smith, William A. Smith, Southard, Sprague, Stanard, Starkweather, Stone, Strait, Strawbridge, Swann Thornburgh, Townsend, Tyner, Vance, Waldron. Wallace, Walls, Jasper D. Ward, Marcus L. Ward, Wells Wheeler, Whitehead, Whitehouse, Whitthorne, Wilber, Charles W. Willard, George Willard, Charles G. Williams, John M. S. Williams, William B. Williams, Willie, Ephraim K. Wilson, James Wilson, Wolfe, Wood, Woodford, Woodworth, John D. Young; and Pierce M. B. Young—225.

NAYS—Messrs. Albert, Averill, Barry, Clymer, Cox, Crossland, Hays, Hynes, Kelley, Kendall, Lamison, Morey, Negley, James H. Platt, Jr., Randall, Shanks, Sloss, Standeford, Storm, Stowell Todd, Waddell, White, Whiteley, and William Williams—95.

NOT VOTING—Messrs. Adams, Barrere, Freeman Clarke, Creamer, Crocker, Darrall, Duell, Eldredge, Freeman, John T. Harris, Hooper, Jewett, Kellogg, Lamar, Lofland, Lowndes, Maynard, McJunkin, McLean, Phillips, Pike, Ransier, Ray, William R. Roberts, James C. Robinson, Henry J. Scudder, George L. Smith, Snyder, Speer, Stephens, St. John, Sypher, Taylor, Thomas, Tremain, and Jeremiah M. Wilson—36.

So the amendment of the Senate was concurred in.

The question recurred upon the following amendment of the Senate to the title of the bill:

Amend the title so as to read: "An act repealing the increase of salaries of members of Congress and other officers."

The amendment was concurred in.

In the House, on January 7th, the bill to establish an educational fund, and to apply the proceeds of the public lands to the education of the people, was considered.

Mr. Hoar, of Massachusetts, said : "Mr. Speaker, after the excited discussions which have taken place in the House during the whole of the present session, I suppose it is not disagreeable to all of us to address ourselves to a measure intended purely for the benefit of the country, containing nothing which can appeal to partisan or sectional ambition, interest, or desire.

"One-fourth of the voters of the country to-day are unable to read or write. For the next ten years thirty-two Senators and one hundred and four Representatives, constituting, when voting compactly, a power which will be able to control on very important measures of legislation of the country, are to be chosen by States one-half of whose voting population have not knowledge enough of reading or writing to make either of practical advantage in receiving or conveying information. This condition of things, disclosed by the census of 1870, is, in the opinion of those persons most capable of judging, growing worse instead of better. And if a census were to be taken of the illiterate portion of the population of the country to-day, it would disclose a very much larger number unable to derive any information in the discharge of their duties as citizens from reading, and unable to convey such information to others by writing. It is true I ought to say that a sentiment has grown up in many, and perhaps all, of the States which promises better things in that respect; that is an encouraging symptom. It is true, also, that the State of Virginia is a most conspicuous and honorable exception to the general statement that I have made. But, with the exception of the fact that men are waking up in the southern portion of the country to labor in this matter, and with the exception of the State of Virginia, to whose Democratic authorities I desire to pay a tribute of respect which their recognition of this great work deserves, this condition of things is rapidly growing worse.

"Now, there are two main objects which are intended to be reached by this bill. The first is to consecrate forever to the purpose of the education of the people this vast national domain, so far as it may be considered the property of the nation. Of course, whatever policy may commend itself to Congress as necessary for furthering the interests of the settler, to that the legislation which treats of the public lands as mere property must give way. The interests of the great States which in the future are to cover this domain, the interests of the people that are to compose their population, must of course be paramount to every other interest whatever.

"But at the present time the policy of the country is to sell for reasonable prices these lands, and the proceeds are received into the public Treasury. This bill proposes to make an annual distribution among the States of one-half the amount of those proceeds, for the purpose of aiding in the endowment of public schools in the different States. It is proposed that for the first five years this distribution shall be made on the basis of illiteracy ; that is, of the need of the particular States. It is true that this distribution will create a certain inequality among the States for the first five years. But I think every gentleman who remembers, looking now at the interests of his own State, that the vote of an illiterate and uneducated person in another State affects all national questions, affects the policy of the country as much as the vote of the most educated and instructed citizen of his own State, that the humble black laborer in the rice-swamp by his vote affects the national policy of the country with exactly the same power that Agassiz, or Eliot, or Barnard does, will see that it is for the interest of each State that the distribution should be made for the present in proportion to the needs of the several States.

"Heretofore, in discussing this question, I have presented to the House some statistics, with the view of showing the need of different States, growing out of the number of persons therein who are unable to read or write. When I presented those statistics, some gentlemen, representing States where the number of illiterate was large, seemed to suppose that it was done for some purpose of exciting reproach against their States, or of vaunting in some way the superiority of my own. Sir, it was with no such purpose that these statistics were presented to the attention of the House and of the country. I am perfectly aware that the State which I have the honor to represent, if it has any advantage in this respect over any other State, owes that advantage largely to its wealth, its compactness of population, and the length of time which it has been settled. And I am not here, in discussing a question of this kind, to make any claims to any special merit or credit on account of any thing that may have been done by my people or by my forefathers in this respect. I am aware that other States, new, with populations scattered over a large territory, which have had, whether by their fault or the fault of others, the great burden of slavery, which have been devastated by war, have been unable, even if willing, to supply this want for themselves.

"But I will beg of the representatives of the States now to be affected, not to reject this olive-branch which is held out to them by the people of the wealthier and more densely populated States, which offers them not merely national aid in the establishment of their institutions of education, but offers to give them for the first five years, subject to extension by Congress hereafter, if at the end of five years such a condition continues to exist, this great advantage in the distribution of a common fund.

"I have prepared, and shall have printed as a part of my speech, a table showing the amount of the fund which will be received by different States under this distribution. Let me refer to the manner in which the distribution will operate as respects two or three States.

"The whole net proceeds of the sale amount to about $2,000,000 annually. Of this sum one-half is proposed to be distributed annually, while the other half is to constitute a permanent fund, the income of which shall be distributed in the same way. Under this distribution the State of Alabama, with a population of 996,992, would receive as its share of $1,000,000 the sum of $67,689.71 ; while the State of Connecticut, with a population of 537,454—a little more than half the population of Alabama—will receive only $5,234.03. The State of Kentucky, with a population of 1,321,-011, would receive $58,705.46 ; while the State of Massachusetts, with a population of 1,457,351, would receive only $17,273.94.

"Now, Mr. Speaker, this bill in its mechanism is exceedingly simple; but I believe (and in the expression of this belief I am fortified by the unanimous testimony of educators in all parts of the country) that its protection of the Government against the waste or misapplication of these funds is absolute and complete. It requires of the States just two conditions, and declares that every State which shall, within one year, comply with those two conditions shall, in the next year, receive its share of this distribution. Those two conditions are: first, the establishment of a system of free public schools for all its citizens, leaving all the details of that system to its own discretion ; and, secondly, a report that it has established such a system, and that it has applied the money in accordance with the provisions of the bill, and a report of the number of children that have been in attendance at those schools during the previous year. A great many other conditions have been suggested as desirable to be added ; but it seems to me that the performance of these conditions will be sufficient for the end proposed.

"Many gentlemen say, 'Why, how is it possible that a gift of $50,000 to a State of a million and a half of inhabitants, one-half of whom cannot read or write, can suffice to produce the result which this bill aims to accomplish?' But, Mr. Speaker, the history of education in this matter answers that question, and answers it to the surprise as well as the satisfaction of persons who have not previously investigated the subject. I am informed by the distinguished agent of the Peabody fund, Dr. Sears, perhaps the highest authority in this country on this special subject, that the expenditure of $30,000 a year from this fund (I believe that is the amount, though I may not have it precisely in my memory) causes probably an expenditure of from ten to twenty times that amount in the localities where this slight expenditure has been made ; and not only that, but that the results proceed in a vastly increasing ratio. When you say to a town, or a parish, or a neigh-

borhood, 'We will give you $5,000 for the establishment of schools,' not only is the proposition readily accepted—for any community dislikes to see such an offer go by unimproved —but every town or community within the circuit of forty miles around comes in and says, 'Why can you not do the same for us?'

"The bill contemplates that there shall be made to the General Government a report setting forth the number of schools in each State, and the number of pupils actually attending therein.

"That list will be tabulated and reported to Congress, and the result will be if in any State it appears, either that the State has refused to get its share of the bounty of Congress, or that the State stands lowest in rank in these particulars which are reported, somebody in that State will set its rivers on fire until that state of things is changed. It was that stimulant, and that stimulant alone, giving a few dollars only to each town, by which Horace Mann created anew the common-school system of Massachusetts, and raised it from its degraded condition, thereby making his name immortal among the benefactors of mankind. On this point the authority of the various school superintendents as given by Dr. Sears, to which I have alluded, is decisive.

"Then, Mr. Speaker, that will leave the other million dollars to be deposited in the national Treasury, and invested in Government bonds, the interest only to be distributed, leaving the principal to accumulate as a national educational fund.

"It seems to my mind the vast public domain we are rapidly disposing of in one way or another ought not to be used up for the necessities of a single generation. The people of the country, and especially the laborers of the country, take a deep interest in the public lands. They will not consent to any disposition of the proceeds of the sale of these public lands ; and this bill gives no public lands, but simply disposes of the proceeds of their sale when paid into the Treasury—they will not consent, I say, to the disposition of them to any purpose less sacred than that of the education of the people.

"It does not seem just that the entire proceeds of this vast national heritage should be disposed of for the necessities of a single generation, and nothing left for the future."

Mr. Dunnell, of Minnesota, said: "Mr. Speaker, I desire to make some remarks upon this bill, but shall not long occupy the attention of the House. I think there are very grave questions involved in the measure—some that we ought not to forget or overlook in the discussion of it. While it is not agreeable for me ever to vote against any measure that looks toward public free schools, yet I am constrained to present a few considerations in opposition to the passage of this bill, and give some of the reasons why I shall vote against it. In the first place, it is a new departure ; it is the adoption of a new policy—a policy which has never hitherto been pursued since the formation of the Government. Ever since there have been public schools in any State of the Union, those public schools have relied wholly and entirely on State support and State appropriations. Never before has a direct attempt been made to go to the Treasury of the United States and take out money and parcel it among the several States for educational purposes. I have, sir, in past years of my life, had some little connection with public education, and I have been a firm believer that that kind of interest which is needed for a happy, full, and successful development of the common-school system must be close at home.

"It is utterly impossible to rely upon the general Government to foster and keep alive that kind of spirit that is needed for a successful free-school development; and most certainly I do not think we should go to the Treasury this year—and I say this to the chairman of the Committee on Ways and Means (Mr. Dawes)—to a Treasury wellnigh depleted, and take out of it the sum of $2,000,000 and scatter it through the Union, even for so good a purpose as free education.

"Now, my great objection to this bill lies in this: what are these public lands of ours which we propose practically to tax in order that we may get money, and get ' net proceeds,' wherewith to pay out and create this fund? We must recollect that we will get no 'net proceeds' unless we tax these lands. We have had a great deal said here about these lands belonging to the people. If these lands are to be taxed in order that we may get a fund that shall be worthy of the name, who are to be taxed?

"We have two policies: the homestead and the preëmption policy. Where do we get the most of the proceeds of our public lands? We get them under the operation of the preëmption law. Both Houses of Congress, however, at the last session, voted to repeal the preëmption laws, and henceforth and forever open up the entire public domain to the homestead principle. The homestead principle has been adopted by both of the great national parties of the country; it is the popular sentiment of the country to-day. Nor is it proposed insidiously to keep on the statute-book a preëmption law that shall give us 'net proceeds.' Without that law we shall have only the income that shall arise from the sale of the mineral and pine lands, and very few of these now remain. Therefore I say that, as legislators here, we ought to remember that these public lands are, as it were, our outlying opportunities for national development. What are we going to do with the poor man coming over from Europe to settle in this country? Whither shall we direct him? We wish to direct him to the great prairies—the public lands of the West. Shall we tell these men that these lands are open to be entered under the homestead law? Yes. We should let that word go to Europe in advance, and let the people there understand that this is our policy. But pass this bill, and its friends will inevitably, naturally, and logically, oppose the repeal of the preëmption laws.

"Then you must inform every person in the East, in the older States, who desires a home in the West, every incoming settler upon our public domain, that he must pay $1.25 or $2.50 an acre. Will it pay thus to burden the public lands? I say not. We will be taxing those who are the poorest and yet the best people in the country; we will be taxing the men who wish a home, the poor men who come into the country; for, unless we sell them these lands, we will get no 'net proceeds.'

"The Committee on the Public Lands has already before it a bill to repeal the preëmption law. It ought to be repealed. The gentleman from Massachusetts (Mr. G. F. Hoar) talked about speculators. Sir, where does the speculator in public lands get the chance to defraud and carry on his business? It is under that identical preëmption law. Abolish that, and every man may have a free home. Give us the homestead-law alone. The preëmption is where the fraud comes in; it is where the fearful swearing takes place; it is where the speculator thrives and flourishes."

Mr. Kasson, of Iowa, said: "I wish to call the attention of the House particularly to this fact, that we are endeavoring by this bill to move further in the direction which was rendered necessary by the war, but which has ceased to be necessary with the declaration of peace. Sir, in this Congress we have fought many battles in which, under the so-called war-power of the Union, we have assumed powers of a very dangerous character, but also of a very necessary character at the time. During the continuance of the war we gathered great powers into this body, and, to secure the fruits of the war, we amended the Constitution so as to get still further powers for a condition of peace. I ask gentlemen now whether, when the Constitution has been amended as thoroughly as any gentleman desires, and when we are in a condition of peace and restored Union, there is a man upon this floor who desires in any respect to further centralize the Government at this time? I ask what clause of the Constitution can bring us into connection with the school districts of the different States of this Union? I wish some member of the committee would point me to a clause of the Constitution, or to any amendment of the Constitution, that brings the Congress of the United States into contact with subdivisions of States of this Union, known as school districts, and with teachers' wages therein? I know of none. I know of no power in that instrument by which we can touch the school districts of this Union in the manner of regulation; and yet this bill provides for the payment of the salaries of the teachers of a certain class of school districts in the several States; it provides for a certain class of scholars that shall be entitled to the benefits of the fund appropriated from the people's Treasury, to the exclusion of others.

"Sir, I say it is a stretch of power which, as a member of the Republican party, I repudiate as not being within the range of the powers of the Congress of the United States. I have stood upon this floor in times of danger, and have advocated the use of all the powers that could be gathered to strengthen the hands of the Government; but I am here to-day to protest with all my force against taking away one solitary State or municipal right that exists now in this free Union.

"Sir, the great pendulum of the clock of history is moving ever to and fro. After reaching one extremity it is bound to go back toward the other extremity. We reached the extreme in one direction during the war, and now the pendulum has commenced sweeping in the other direction. If gentlemen on this floor are not wise, we shall find ourselves now, with the views we entertain as the majority, imploring Heaven to come to our help to prevent these powers being turned against us and our dearest home interests. Can no gentleman on this side of the House imagine such a political revolution in the future as shall take from men of our views the power on this floor, and at the other end of the Capitol?

"Can they not see, then, that the principles established in this bill will put us, perhaps, under a majority here who do not appreciate our municipal organizations of the North, our school-district system and its value; who may, as we are doing now, put the strong hand of the Federal Government upon the dearest rights which we cherish in the States to which we belong and which we love? Everybody, sir, who looks at all to the philosophy of history, must see that the time has come when we must heed the swinging of this great constitutional pendulum, when we must guard against the extreme to which we shall inevitably drift, unless we commence early to apply the steadying powers of a more wise, and constant, and peaceful judgment."

Mr. Phillips, of Kansas, said: "The gentlemen defending the measure have claimed that this bill interferes with nothing; that it leaves the preëmption and homestead laws intact; that it interferes with no new legislation; that it only takes moneys formerly derived from public lands and applies them as a school fund in the way specified. In taking this position, I believe the gentlemen are honest; in expressing it, I am sure they are candid; I feel equally sure that they are mistaken.

"On the American land question the public mind is deeply stirred; and the settlers, who are, after all, the interested parties, are determined on reform. An indignant protest has gone up against permitting the lands to go into the hands of corporations and speculators,

great or small. The public lands left have little or no value save that which the labor of the settler gives them. That this value should not be taxed to sustain other interests, is demanded. And while these demands are being made, while the few good steps already taken are sought to be blended with better ones still to be taken, while the Committee on the Public Lands is engaged in preparing measures to properly dispose of the public domain, this bill comes in from the Committee on Education and Labor to settle the question effectively and ruinously, and to bar the avenues to land reform forever. Do not tell me that legislation hereafter may do what it pleases. Pass this bill, and you create a great interest, which will forever fight all questions of land reform, and which will be here, whenever a bill is pending to aid the struggling settlers, to argue that all lands are consecrated to education, and the ghost of religion and morals will be conjured up to make this bill a finality, and to seal and foreclose all the blunders of American land legislation.

"I think it high time that the land question be considered apart from all such propositions. It is the foundation-stone of American politics. The time is surely coming when the hardy pioneers will no longer be asked to develop the country and maintain outside benevolence. I would a thousand times rather vote money from the Treasury. The last thing Congress should part with is the public domain."

Mr. Cox, of New York, said: "Mr. Speaker, I am opposed to this bill for several reasons. First, on economic ground; secondly, because I am opposed to the enactment by Congress of the civil-rights bill as reported and recommitted; thirdly, because the bill itself augments Federal power, is unjust in the distribution of the funds, and is a part of a pernicious system of 'over-legislation.'

"First, as to economy: Whether we stop prodigal expenditure or husband legitimate resources, it is alike wise; in fact, it is necessary in this emergency of the Treasury. I have before me the President's message. Last year, he says that there were 1,626,266 acres of public lands sold for cash. This was some 300,000 more than the year before. By the Land-Office Report of October 20, 1873, it appears that there were cash gross receipts, under various heads for lands sold, for the year ending June 30, 1873, amounting to $3,408,515.50. Under this head are certain scrip not strictly cash. These are to be deducted, together with the expenses of sale. The appropriation for land-sales ending June 30, 1873, was $772,000.

"Without being too nice, therefore, I may take the calculation of the gentleman who reports the bill (Mr. G. F. Hoar), and reckon the proceeds of the lands for each year, as from one to two millions net cash, the mean being one million and a half. Of this, under the bill, for five years the more illiterate sections, as where the negroes predominate, will get the most in proportion. New York gets $63,429.54, on a basis of one million and a half—being nearly sixty cents *per capita* of her illiterate school-children. These children, of ten years and over, number in New York 239,271 in a population of 4,382,759; while the next State on the list—North Carolina—gets nearly twice as much money ($105,425.63), because she has more illiteracy, or 397,690 children of ten years and over in a population of 1,071,361. If these figures are inducement enough for North Carolina and other States to vote for this bill and 'mixed schools,' they are not inducement enough for one member from New York, at least, to divert one million and a half at this time from an imperiled Treasury. I say nothing now of the imminent disturbance it will bring upon the most admirable school system of the United States.

"Secondly: I am opposed to this bill, next, because I am opposed to the congressional enactment of the civil-rights bill, as it was when recommitted.

"Whoever opposes the civil-rights bill on account of the mixed-school system must oppose this bill, which furnishes funds for such a system. It is now very relevant, therefore, to discuss the civil-rights bill. This I do not propose to do, except so far as to show its consequences, if passed, as affecting this bill and the probability of its passage. It does not follow, however, that all who favor the civil-rights bill must vote for this; although it is singular to me how so sound a reasoner on this matter as the eminent and eloquent member from Iowa (Mr. Kasson) can aggrandize Federal power by voting mixed schools, and oppose this bill, as he does, because he would restrain this centralizing tendency. He seems to swing with the pendulum, and describes the oscillating arc he so happily represented.

"Nor does it follow that the colored advocates who have enraptured the galleries on the former bill will vote this. Can they do it if the House should 'proscribe' them from the common use of the schools? Is it not irrefragable that if the right to the inn, railroad, theatre, and cemetery be conceded to the black to the same extent as to the white, to enjoy them (though the enjoyment of the graveyard is perhaps a melancholy hilarity), that the same right should be extended to them as to the schools? The colored members are correct in their reasoning, assuming these premises. Indeed, all the *amis des noirs* who have spoken are right in demanding equality alike in school and inn, in cemetery and car. When you debar them from the school you as much keep up the bar sinister as by keeping them from the play-house. Would it not be a craven logic, unworthy of the struggling blacks and their admirers, to insist on the one and not the other? Is it not, therefore, nonsense to pretend that this bill does not have in it, indirectly, a colored element? '*Hic niger est, nunc tu, Romane, caveto!*'

"Mr. Speaker, without invidious reflection upon any one, may I not commend the calm and statesmanlike way in which the gentleman from Massachusetts (Mr. Hoar) presented this bill? He did not appeal to the clamor of the House or to the claqueurs of the gallery. He did not seek to question that body up yonder, which, like the African Sphinx, sits an insoluble riddle until its sensibility is tickled by allusions to its industry, education, and heroism! If, however, its plaudits serve to grace the noble fervor of the gentleman from South Carolina (Mr. Elliot), who spoke so well for his race, or the chartered liberties of debate who tumble about in bellicose drollery, I am content to praise and enjoy this novel mode of deliberation.

"But I do not refer to the civil-rights bill merely to mark the difference in the manner of debate. This act consecrates the net proceeds of the public lands for education, and provides the mode of their application. The civil-rights bill provides for mixed schools; and if it becomes a law the funds thereby dedicated will be thus applied.

"'But,' it is said, 'the civil-rights bill is recommitted, and may be reported back without the mixed schools.' I do not know as to that. I will give three or four reasons why I think 'civil rights' and mixed schools will return to us again for our action: first, partisan reasons; second, the speech and oath of the gentleman from Massachusetts (Mr. Butler), the champion of the measure; and, third, the attitude of the colored people as to mixed schools since the recommittal of the bill."

The bill was subsequently discussed on several occasions, but failed to become a law.

In the Senate, on December 16th, the resolution offered by Senator Sherman, of Ohio, on specie payments and the currency, was considered.

The resolution was read, as follows:

Resolved, That it is the duty of Congress during its present session to adopt definite measures to redeem the pledge made in the act approved March 18, 1869, entitled "An act to strengthen the public credit," as follows:

"And the United States also solemnly pledges its faith to make provision at the earliest practicable period for the redemption of the United States notes in coin."

And the Committee on Finance is directed to report to the Senate at as early a day as practicable such measures as will not only redeem this pledge of the public faith, but will also furnish a currency of uniform value always redeemable in gold or its equivalent, and so adjusted as to meet the changing wants of trade and commerce.

Mr. Ferry, of Michigan, said: "I offer the following as a substitute for the resolution:

Strike out all after the word "resolved," and insert:

That the Committee on Finance is directed to report to the Senate at as early a day as practicable such measures as will restore commercial confidence and give stability and elasticity to the circulating medium, by making banking free to all, by providing for an increase of currency of $100,000,000 (including the $44,000,000 reserve), by making the whole currency of Government issue and lawful money by the issue of currency bonds bearing 3.65 per cent. interest.

Mr. Pratt, of Indiana, said: "Mr. President, I wish to submit some remarks upon the resolution reported by the chairman of the committee. Before doing so I will ask that the views of the minority be read by the clerk."

The Presiding Officer: "The Clerk will report the views of the minority."

The Chief Clerk: "The resolution reported as the views of the minority, by Mr. Bayard, is as follows: "

Whereas a just regard for the interests of every class of the community demands that the national basis of finance shall consist of a uniform standard and intrinsic value: therefore—

Resolved, That the Committee on Finance be, and they are hereby, instructed to report to the Senate measures which will secure at the earliest practicable day a return to specie payments.

Mr. Pratt: "Mr. President, there is just this difference between the resolution submitted by the chairman of the Committee on Finance and that submitted by the Senator from Delaware, on the part of the minority of that committee: The one declares it the duty of Congress during its present session to adopt definite measures for the redemption of the United States notes in coin, but also declares it to be its duty to furnish a currency of uniform value, always redeemable in coin or its equivalent, and so adjusted as to meet the changing wants of commerce and trade; while the other instructs the committee to report to the Senate measures which will secure at the earliest practicable day a return to specie payments.

"The one contemplates legislation in respect to the currency, while the other looks solely to measures for the redemption of the existing currency in coin, and that too at the earliest practicable period.

"To be sure, these resolutions are not legislation. They do not bind Congress to do any thing upon the subject-matter, nor do they undertake to define *when* the earliest practicable day for the resumption of specie payments shall be.

"It is now nearly five years since Congress made a memorable pledge to the same effect. I read from the act of March 18, 1869:

And the United States also pledges its faith to make provision at the earliest practicable period for the redemption of the United States notes in coin.

"What could sound fairer to the ear? What could be more explicit? What could the United States pledge, possessing higher guarantee to the holder of its notes, than its faith? Well, that 'earliest practicable period' when this redemption should take place has not come yet; and yet, as everybody is aware, the intervening years have been marked by a higher degree of prosperity than this nation has ever known. Never, during all our national life, has there been such diversified industrial activ-

ity; never for the same period of time have the products of labor been so large, or our commerce, foreign and domestic, so great; never was labor better paid. In fine, in agriculture, mining, and manufactures especially, in commerce at home and abroad, in the increased acreage of the land cultivated, in the founding of new communities, in the extension of railways and the development of our great natural resources, the nation never exhibited greater signs of prosperity. During all this time we proudly pointed to our paper currency as the best the country had ever possessed. We boasted of its uniformity in value in all parts of the United States, of the excellence of its engraving, rendering counterfeits the next thing to impossible, and, above all, our pride was that it rested upon the wealth and credit of the country for ultimate redemption. We read upon the face of every greenback the promise of the United States to pay the bearer so much money, and upon the face of every bank-note the promise of the bank to pay in money or greenbacks on presentation. So that, while the bank-note might be redeemed in a United States note or greenback, we knew that the greenback could be redeemed in nothing but coin. It was not a promise as in the case of a national-bank note to redeem in another promise, but to pay the bearer so many dollars. And that was interpreted, and rightly too, to mean metallic dollars—gold or silver—the money of the Constitution, the recognized standard of value of the world.

"Indorsing this view, came first the declaration by Congress in March, 1869, in the act to strengthen the public credit, and then the decision of the Supreme Court. There is nobody, I take it, that denies at this day this interpretation of the nation's obligation written upon the face of every greenback. The promise is to pay the bearer so many dollars, either at Washington or at the office of the assistant treasurer in New York. That means that they shall be paid on the demand of the holder. They are not post-notes, but demand-notes, due whenever presented at the place where payable for payment. If they were the notes of an individual or a bank, no one would doubt the nature of the obligation nor the effect of a refusal to pay. The notes would go to protest, the individual into bankruptcy, and the bank into the hands of a receiver.

"While this is the strict legal view of the obligation of the greenback, I know it is urged that greenbacks were issued at a time of great national necessity because there was very little specie in the country at the time, inadequate entirely to the wants of Government, and not available on account of the suspension of the banks, and because there was an absolute necessity for a larger volume of currency which possessed the functions of money. The Government, at that time in close grapple with the rebellion, needed money to carry on the war. The soldiers and sailors must be paid; they must be fed and clothed, and supplied with arms and munitions of war and transportation. A great deal of money was needed; at first a million a day; then two millions, and finally three. Congress, driven to its wit's end to devise the ways and means to procure it in such amounts as were needed, devised in a happy moment of inspiration the greenback scheme, which has accomplished such a wonderful success. But it was in its nature a forced loan. You compelled soldiers, contractors, and every creditor of the Government, to accept as money, and in full discharge of the debt, the promissory notes of the Government. It was as if a man deeply embarrassed, but with plenty of property, should call his creditors around him and say, 'Gentlemen, I owe you and haven't the money to pay. Take my due-bills with my blessing. When I am able to pay, I will take them all up.' There was just this difference in the two cases: Congress compelled the creditor to accept the due-bills. The citizen debtor had no such power. The debtor in the one case could be sued on his due-bills if not paid on presentation, while the United States could not be. The due-bill of the citizen was a simple evidence of debt; the greenback possessed the function of paying debts.

"When the act of Congress passed creating greenbacks and imparting to them the qualities of money and making them a legal tender for all debts public and private, except duties on imports and interest on the public debt, its constitutionality was questioned all over the country. It was regarded and treated as a war measure necessary for the exigencies of the times and justified only by that necessity. When we looked into the Constitution for the power, we found these words, and no more, in the enumeration of the powers of Congress:

To coin money, regulate the value thereof, and of foreign coin.

"We found the States prohibited from coining money, emitting bills of credit, and from making any thing but gold and silver coin a tender in payment of debts. Thus stood the Constitution.

"The objectors argued that money could not be coined from paper, leather, or any other material than metals, and that the framers of the Constitution intended from the clause I have quoted, and from the context, to confer upon Congress the simple power of coining money from gold, silver, and copper, the only metallic currency then in use in the world, and that this was all the power conferred on it.

"On the other hand, it was urged that as the States were prohibited from making any thing but gold and silver coin a tender in payment of debts, there was in the very terms of that prohibition an implication that Congress might do what the States could not, that is to say, make something else than coin a legal tender in the payment of debts. This view, as we know, prevailed, and it is too late now to draw in question the constitutionality of that legislation on which the greenback issues rest.

"But the law, as originally passed, was as just as the necessities of the case allowed. Congress had provided as to the bonds, which had a long time to run, that the interest should be paid semi-annually in coin, and those holding greenbacks were allowed to fund them in these bonds so as to compensate them for any damage or loss in being kept out of the promised coin when the Treasury could not or would not redeem them upon presentation.

"I repeat that the holder of the greenbacks could at his option, at any time, convert them into the time obligations of the Government bearing six per cent. interest, which contained explicit guarantees for the payment of both principal and interest. Upon these obligations the Government has never made default, but scrupulously has observed its promises; and we have seen, as the gratifying result of its good faith, these obligations constantly rising in value, until they now are, and for some time past have been, worth their face in gold both at home and abroad, and even command a premium.

"But Congress, in an evil hour, as I think, repealed that portion of the law allowing the conversion of greenbacks into bonds at the option of the holder, the repeal to take effect after the 1st of July, 1863. As at first issued there was this indorsement upon them:

This note is a legal tender for all debts public and private, except duties on imports and interest on the public debt, and is exchangeable for United States six per cent. twenty year bonds, redeemable at the pleasure of the United States after five years.

"The act of March 3, 1863, which destroyed this option after the 1st day of July following, was an act of injustice, because it was a breach of the plighted faith of the United States to those who had taken them in good faith, relying upon this guarantee that they could at pleasure exchange them for bonds. From that time forth the greenbacks have been at a discount as compared with the bonds, and must continue so until Congress shall take measures either to allow their conversion into interest-bearing bonds or compel their redemption in coin.

"As the matter stands now, we have $356,-000,000 of this legal-tender issue afloat, circulating as money, without any power in the holders to get the promised coin, or to exchange them for bonds. They are dishonored promises to pay, or, as my friend from Vermont the other day styled them, 'engraved falsehoods.' This state of things has continued for ten years, and is likely to continue for ten years to come unless Congress takes measures to wipe away the dishonor.

"But how shall this be done? If we count the $44,000,000 United States notes retired while Mr. McCulloch was Secretary of the Treasury, and until recently supposed to be redeemed and canceled notes, as a part of the valid greenback issue, it will require $400,000,-

000 of coin to redeem them. When redeemed, of course, the national banks will be compelled to redeem their circulation in coin, which will require $354,000,000 more.

"But suppose that the Government after redeeming them continues to treat them as lawful money and pay them out in discharge of its debts and in the payment of current expenses: They must in that case be redeemed again, and as often as they are issued, if the holder of them prefers coin. Thus it will be seen that Congress when it enters upon the work of redemption must take measures not only to redeem them once, but as often as they are reissued. And right here comes the difficulty. While no doubt it is practicable to borrow $400,000,000 of gold to redeem the entire issue once, yet if we are to maintain redemption we must be prepared to supply ourselves with the requisite amount of coin not only to resume, but to maintain resumption.

"I repeat, sir, where is the coin to come from? If the Treasury, in addition to what is in its vaults now, could command all the coin in the country, in the hands of the banks and individuals, nobody supposes that there is enough at this time to redeem one-half of the outstanding greenbacks. There has been ever since the war a constant drain of the precious metals abroad. We are paying about $100,000,000 of coin a year in the shape of interest upon our national bonds, and probably more than one-half of them are held in Europe, where the interest must go. In addition to this there is a large volume of indebtedness of the States, cities, mining and manufacturing companies, and railway corporations, held abroad, amounting in the aggregate to a greater sum than the national bonds, which are in the hands of foreign capitalists and on which we pay interest. The whole product of our mines, large as it is, is insufficient to pay this interest account. More than this, and worse than all, the balance of trade every year for the last ten years has been against us, and this balance has to be adjusted in coin or its equivalent. Until recently there has been a constant outflow of specie from this country to pay these balances. We cannot discharge them in our greenbacks or national-bank notes. They can be paid only with money, such money as is recognized by the commercial world; that is, gold and silver.

"I should not omit to say in this connection that it is estimated that American citizens traveling in Europe spend $75,000,000 a year, of course in gold.

"Mr. President, it is mournful to study those monthly reports emanating from the Treasury Department, which exhibit the state of our commerce with foreign countries. On the one hand, what we export is in the main the necessaries of life—such things as people must have to subsist on and clothe themselves with. To be sure, they are comprehensively classed as commodities, the growth, produce, and manufactures of the United States; but when you come to analyze the tables you find what is exported is chiefly raw material, the products of the soil, the mines, the quarries, and the forests; but where are the manufactures? Leaving out the oils, mineral and animal, a few sewing-machines, mowers, and reapers, a little leather, and certain classes of machinery, and our tables of exports present a dreary barrenness of the products of skilled labor. Thus, last year, we exported over $227,000,000 in value of unmanufactured cotton, while all the manufactures of every kind, produced from that material, exported by us, amounted to less than $3,000,000 in value. We exported last fiscal year in gold and silver bullion, and in gold and silver coin, $76,905,546. That exhausted and more than exhausted the entire products of our mines, whose yearly income is rated at, I believe, about $58,000,000

"In the mean time, what have we been importing during the last fiscal year? Here again we must turn to the tables. The total of those imports, including both those dutiable and free of duty, was the startling sum of $663,410,597. I embrace in this statement all commodities entered for immediate consumption and those entered for warehousing, which mostly go into consumption ultimately.

"Now, sir, contemplate a few of the items. I want to show in this connection what we recklessly and needlessly import, to the detriment of our domestic industries, which could just as well have furnished to our hand most of the articles we have run in debt to buy, or which we were better off to do without entirely.

"I begin with the manufactures of wool. We imported—

Cloths and cassimeres	$16,000,000
Shawls, a little short of	3,000,000
Carpets, about	4,833,000
Dress-goods, about	19,500,000
Hosiery, shirts, and drawers	613,000
Other manufactures of wool not specified	7,500,000
Total manufactures of wool	$50,946,000

"We imported of—

Leaf-tobacco	$6,500,000
Cigars	3,330,300
Perfumery and cosmetics, a little over	1,000,000
Precious stones, a fraction short of	3,000,000
Printing-paper, writing-paper, paper hangings, papier maché, and other manufactures of paper, upward of	2,000,000
Paintings, chromo-lithographs, and statuary, say	1,330,300
Musical instruments	1,000,000
Leather of all kinds	6,750,000
Gloves of kid, and all other, of skin or leather, say	3,500,000

"We imported of—

Pig-iron	7,203,769
Bar-iron	5,288,481
Railroad bars or rails of iron	10,541,036
Hardware	6,643,512
Machinery	1,693,966
Muskets, pistols, rifles, and sporting-guns	822,119
Steel ingots, bars, sheets, and wire	4,155,234
Railroad bars or rails of steel	9,199,666
Cutlery	2,234,347
Total of iron and steel and their manufactures	$47,782,130

"I have omitted other varieties of iron and

steel manufactures imported, exceeding in value $10,000,000.

"I spoke a moment ago of the amount of raw cotton exported, while the entire manufactures of cotton exported by us were less than $3,000,000 in value. Let us now again turn to the tables, to ascertain the amount of cotton manufactures imported into the country during the last fiscal year:

The amount of the bleached and unbleached

was	$3,865,558
Of printed, painted, or colored.	5,028,256
Of hosiery, shirts, and drawers	5,449,301
Of jeans, denims, drillings, etc	536,893
Of other manufactures of cotton	20,321,909
Total	$35,201,317

"We imported—

Of earthen, stone, and china ware	$6,015,906
Of fancy goods	4,861,199
Of household and personal effects and wearing-apparel	16,248,421
Our importation of human hair and its manufactures was	932,026
Our importation of jewelry exceeded	1,000,000

"Looking at this list, who shall say that we have not been the most improvident and extravagant people under the sun, trampling under foot all wise economic laws? This country ought, upon its thousand hills and boundless prairies, to raise sheep enough to clothe our bodies, and we should have skill and enterprise enough to manufacture the wool into its various forms of usefulness. Yet I have enumerated manufactures of wool imported into this country in a single year amounting in value to upward of fifty million dollars.

"The exhibit I give of the imports of iron and steel manufacture is more startling still, amounting to nearly sixty million dollars, while our imports of the manufactures of cotton, as I have shown, is upward of thirty-five millions. We sent our raw cotton to England, France, and Germany, and here it comes back to us, after traversing the ocean twice, with foreign labor and skill added, to the extent of many millions.

"Sir, no country on earth is blessed with richer deposits of iron-ore than ours; none can be more accessible by water and railroad routes; and yet, here I present you with the manufactures from that ore imported within a single year from foreign countries, mounting up to nearly sixty million dollars. What a blind ignoring is this of our natural mineral resources, and our labor and skill!

"But what I want in this connection to call the attention of the Senate to is the extravagant importation of mere luxuries, which minister only to pride and extravagance, such as jewelry, fancy goods, gloves, musical instruments, carpets, shawls, precious stones, dress-goods, cosmetics and perfumery, and many other articles I will not pause to enumerate, amounting in the aggregate to many millions. I have not enumerated the silk goods and laces, and foreign liquors, of which we import so largely.

"While this extravagance of importation continues, of things which, as I have said, we do not need and were better off without, or which we could as well produce at home, giving variety to our industry and profitable employment to our own mechanics and manufacturers, I see no prospect of a speedy return to specie payments.

"It is a very evident proposition to me, Mr. President, that if we export all the specie extracted from our own mines or brought into the country, in paying the excess of imports over exports year by year, we are in no condition to maintain specie payments, although by a spasmodic effort we might, by borrowing coin, redeem our legal-tender notes once.

"What, then, is the actual condition of our circulating medium, having the properties of money, and which this resolution commits Congress to provide for redeeming?

"The recent report of the Treasurer of the United States shows that on the 30th of June last the outstanding amount of the national currency was as follows:

Legal-tender notes issued	$356,000,000 00
Deducting amount on hand	6,392,771 00
Left in circulation	349,607,229 00
The fractional currency outstanding was	44,799,365 44
Deduct amount on hand	6,709,847 71
Which left in circulation	$38,089,517 73

"The sum total of legal-tender notes and fractional currency in circulation on that day was $387,696,746.73.

"But this expresses only a part of our currency.

"On November 1, 1873, there were 1,980 national banks in existence, having an authorized circulation of $354,000,000, and an actual circulation of $348,360,149; the sum of $5,649,051 being still due to banks organized or in process of organization.

"The paper currency of all kinds in circulation, it will thus be seen, is $736,056,895; greater by two-thirds than the entire paper circulation of the United Kingdom of Great Britain and Ireland in August last. To this should be added whatever sum has been drawn from the forty-four million greenback reserve, so called. The actual paper circulation at this time, including the bank reserves, is not probably far from $750,000,000; making nearly $19 per capita to our population, estimated at forty millions.

"By the census of 1870 the entire wealth of the country was estimated at about thirty thousand million dollars, so that the currency of the country as compared with its wealth is not far from four per cent.

"Now, it is important to understand what relation the present volume of our currency bears to that furnished by the banks of the several States before the war. That circulation in the year 1860 amounted to $207,102,000. So that it will be seen that the national bank notes and the legal-tender notes now constituting our circulation amount to more than three and a half times the entire circulation authorized in 1860 by all the States of the Union.

"The bank circulation of the States in 1862, previous to the greenback issue, had increased somewhat over that of 1860, being $238,671,-210; and the amount *per capita* at that time was $7.59, and the ratio of this circulation to the wealth of the country was at that time 1½ per cent. I know that gold and silver constituted in 1860 and 1861 no inconsiderable part of the circulating medium of the country, but I am not able to state the exact ratio it bore to the paper currency—probably not greater, however, than one-third or one-half at most.

"I have given these statistics to the Senate to show that, whether we measure the present volume of our currency by the wealth or population of the country, the percentage is largely in excess of the paper currency, gold, and silver, which constituted the circulating medium of the country in 1860 and 1862.

"I have not adduced the facts I have given in respect to the amount of our currency, nor instituted the comparison that its volume bears to that which we had in 1860 and 1862, for the purpose of showing that no more currency is needed at this time to carry on the business, trade, and commerce of the country. Indeed, sir, it is quite evident that at certain seasons of the year, in the fall and winter months especially, there is great stringency in the money market—more money being required to purchase and move the crops to market than can be commanded. The President, in his last message to us, has very plainly said so, and it is very clearly implied in the reports laid upon our desks of those gentlemen managing the national finances, whose opinions command our respect. I refer to the Secretary of the Treasury, the Treasurer, and Controller of the Currency; all of. them qualified, by the positions they hold and their means of information, to speak to us with authority upon this question.

"The voice of the entire West, if I except capitalists and bankers, who have money to loan, is emphatic that we require more currency. There is one test which I regard as demonstrative that we have too little money. I refer to the extraordinary high rate of interest which prevails throughout the Western country. There must be a real scarcity when for legitimate purposes money commands 12 per cent.

"But, Mr. President, I did not rise to discuss this precise question, nor the merit of the many schemes offered to graduate the currency to the wants of production and trade at different seasons of the year. That is a deep and very difficult question—I mean the adjustment of our currency to the legitimate wants of business, by a plan comprehensive enough to embrace the present and future, which shall relieve the present distress, and which shall look forward steadily to a return to specie payments, when all the currency now passing as money and all we shall add to it shall be money in fact, in its ready convertibility into gold and silver. In voting for the resolution submitted by the Committee on Finance, I wish it to be distinctly understood I do it in the expectation that the committee will furnish to the Senate a plan by which the volume of the currency may be increased at needed seasons without undue inflation. But we must constantly guard against doing any thing which shall disturb the present system of values, derange prices, or affect materially existing relations between creditors and debtors. Any legislation which shall cause these results—will be vicious and disastrous."

Mr. Fenton, of New York, said: "I do not concur with a prominent Senator on this floor, as reported at a recent lecture by him in New York, that an unfavorable balance of trade is the prime cause of our financial evils. It is bad enough, but, more strictly speaking, an unfavorable balance is rather the effect than the cause. While, therefore, a more favorable state of trade to us is altogether desirable, we shall best promote such a condition by making our currency equivalent to gold. The immense expansion of 1836 carried the consumption of foreign commodities up to $10.93 *per capita* under the medium tariff; while under a still lower one, in 1840, the expansion was but $5.21. In this connection, it is not out of place to refer to a coincident increase of trade in the two most notable periods of currency expansion in our previous history. I embrace the year just mentioned, and come forward to another which is still fresh in our recollection. I do not here dwell upon the effects of the tariff, because it does not bear upon my argument upon this point. I only ask that it be kept in mind that taxation not only fails as a remedy for such a condition, but may even aggravate the difficulty.

YEAR.	Amount of Currency.	Amount of Imports.	YEAR.	Amount of Currency.	Amount of Imports.
1835	$186,000,000	$149,895,742	1855	$377,000,000	$261,468,520
1836	255,000,000	189,980,035	1856	408,000,000	314,639,942
1837	276,000,000	140,989,217	1857	445,000,000	360,890,141
1838	200,000,000	113,717,404	1858	341,000,000	282,613,150

."In the amount of currency here given I embrace both the circulation and deposits. The affinity observable in this table is broken, as will be seen, only in a single instance, and that is capable of a special explanation, as of

a condition somewhat similar during the last three or four months. If we were to examine the statistics of reports for the same periods, we should perceive a corresponding tendency to decline, though not as certain and uniform as the increase of imports. It will not do to congratulate ourselves on the past full trade as a real change in our favor. Whatever there is of it may be traced to transient and extraordinary causes. If it were otherwise, our case would be even more critical, in that it would be evidence of a disturbed condition in Europe, which might tend to weaken confidence in our securities which are held there. Our indebtedness over the sea is so great and our commercial relations are so intimate and dependent that trouble there would increase our embarrassment here.

"Here I am naturally led to the inquiry as to the amount of gold in the country and its supply. The amount in the States east of the Rocky Mountains in 1861 has been given by competent authority at $165,000,000. The annual productions of the mines average about $60,000,000, making a total for the thirteen years beginning with the fiscal year which closed June 30, 1861, and ending June 30, 1873, of about $780,000,000. The imports of coin for the same period were $248,459,652. On the other hand, the exports of coin and bullion amounted to $922,641,003. Allowance must also be made for a portion of the production of the mines which have been employed in the arts. What amount has been devoted to this use cannot be accurately determined; but if I fix it at $120,000,000 for the thirteen years it will be low enough. Treating the amount brought into the country by immigrants as offset by the amount taken away by travelers, the balance will stand thus:

Coin in 1861...............................	$165,000,000
Production of mines for thirteen years....	780,000,000
Imports for same time	244,459,652
Total................................	$1,189,459,652
Exports for thirteen years.... $922,641,003	
Used in the arts............:...... 120,000,000	
	$1,042,641,003
Coin in Atlantic States, 1873...............	$146,816,649

"I have no doubt this sum is equal to the present amount of specie, notwithstanding the larger importations during the fall months—a sum about equal to the annual interest upon our indebtedness held abroad. To state the case another way: The average amount in the Treasury during the past few years has been about $80,000,000. The banks hold also possibly $25,000,000, and $40,000,000 would be a liberal estimate for all that may be found in other hands; making not far from $145,000,000, or less than one dollar of specie to every five of the paper issues. How are specie payments to be maintained with such a disproportion? Gold, if left free, will tend in the direction where there is the greatest demand. It may accumulate from temporary causes for a brief period, even when there is a redundancy of paper currency, but it will surely flow away again to other countries where it will have employment as a standard of value. We have, as matters now stand, little reason to hope for any permanent accumulation here. This posi-

tion is fortified by the movements of specie during the last six years:

IMPORTS.		EXPORTS.	
YEAR.	Amount.	YEAR.	Amount.
1868.........	$14,188,168	1868........	$93,784,192
1869.........	19,807,876	1869........	57,138,280
1870.........	26,419,179	1870........	58,155,666
1871.........	21,270,024	1871........	98,441,988
1872.........	13,743,689	1872........	79,877,534
1873.........	21,480,987	1873........	84,608,571

"It thus appears that during these six years the net exports of specie amounted to $355,-096,268, while the whole production of the mines for the corresponding period has been $360,000,000.

"This leads me to repeat that for a resumption by the Government there must be a reduction of paper, so that paper and specie shall bear a recognized relation to each other."

Mr. Morton, of Indiana, said: "Mr. President, I do not desire to make a speech on this subject, but before voting on this resolution I wish to give some reasons for my vote. In the first place, I desire to call the attention of the Senate to what this resolution is. It contains two propositions, and I will now read the first one:

That it is the duty of Congress during its present session to adopt definite measures to redeem the pledge made in the act approved March 18, 1869, entitled "An act to strengthen the public credit," as follows:

And the United States also solemnly pledges its faith to make provision at the earliest practicable period for the redemption of the United States notes in coin.

"The question first presented is, whether it is the duty of Congress at this session to take definite measures for the redemption of the United States notes in coin, for that is the pledge given in the act of 1869. I agree that the faith of this Government is pledged to redeem what are called greenbacks in coin. I agree to that as fully and as strongly as anybody; and I further agree that we are to keep steadily in view what is called a return to specie payments; but the question is, whether it is our duty at this session of Congress, at this time, in the present condition of the country, to look to and adopt such measures; and at this point I differ with the committee. There is a wrong time to do a right thing; and in my opinion this is not the time in which we should adopt definite measures—to redeem these notes in coin—unless the time be put off so far that it will not increase the present embarrassment or intensify the effects of the panic upon the country.

"The Senator from Massachusetts (Mr. Sumner) has repeatedly declared before the Senate, and I think in substance the other day, and that declaration was made very strongly this morning by the Senator from Wisconsin (Mr. Howe), that every day we failed to redeem the legal-tender notes the faith of the public was broken; that we were 'lying,' and that the country was deceived. I desire to enter my protest against that language. The Government is not liable to that charge. The Senator from Massachusetts said the other day in his argument that it was a promise to pay coin upon demand, and that is the literal effect of that promise; and yet when that promise was made it was understood by everybody that it was to be broken for an indefinite length of time. If it was to be redeemed literally and at that time, there would have been no use in issuing greenbacks. The understanding of the country was, and nobody can be deceived upon that point, that the Government was to redeem those notes in coin when it was practicable to do so, and not before; and the question may be fairly presented, Has it up to this time been practicable?

"Mr. President, is this the time (and that is the main question I rose to discuss) to adopt definite measures to return to specie payments? I submit that we should come to specie payment in prosperous times, and not in adversity; that any definite measures now to return to specie payment in a short time will create a further shrinkage of values. Everybody understands that. And now, when we want relief, when we want to come out from under the load that is upon us, it is proposed that we shall adopt measures that will increase that burden, and diminish the general prices of property and labor.

"Mr. President, let me ask another question. It is said, and that has been the argument, that this is a good time to return to specie payments. I have heard it said by able men, 'We have got pretty nearly down to the bed-rock now; it is time to return to specie payments.' I ask this question: Has this panic increased or does the present condition of things increase the facility of returning to specie payments? I say no. Why? Because, while property has decreased in value and there has been a vast shrinkage in the price of property and in every thing, still the same difference exists between greenbacks and gold that existed before the panic. Gold has now an average premium of ten per cent. So it had before the panic took place. Therefore, if you still go down to gold value you must go down ten per cent. So that the panic has not increased the facility of returning to specie payments, for you will have an additional shrinkage on the top of the shrinkage you have now.

"Sir, the panic was not caused by the depreciation of the currency; and if it was not caused by that, I ask how you are to relieve the effects of the panic by taking steps to come to specie payments? The good physician always looks to the character of the disease, and what brought it about, before he attempts to prescribe; and when we look to the cause of this panic we find that it was not caused by any defect in the currency. The people have faith in our currency, more than they have ever had in any paper currency this nation has had heretofore. While we may abuse greenbacks, I tell you the nation has faith in them. The great body of the people love them, and nearly all of them want more. What was it that caused this panic? Why, sir, it was just such a cause as operates in countries where they have no currency but gold and silver; and I make the statement that panics occur quite as frequently where the currency is gold and silver as where it is paper convertible into coin. They have had two panics in England when their currency was upon a gold basis since we have had one in this country. Panics are just as likely to occur in countries where they have nothing but gold and silver as in other countries. Panics do not spring out of the character of the currency generally, but out of some sudden and unexpected event. A panic in finance is just like a panic in the army. It is generally caused by some sudden event that confuses the minds of men and destroys confidence, and it has nothing to do with the character of the currency.

"Then, Mr. President, I desire to meet the idea that this panic was brought about by a defect in our currency; and I assume that it was not, and, assuming that proposition to be incontrovertible, I will pass on a little further.

"Money is scarce—made scarce by a want of confidence. It is all in the country. Men have it, but they are hoarding it; and they are hoarding paper-money as it was never hoarded before, showing the confidence the people have in this currency. They are hoarding our paper-money just as they hoarded gold and silver in other times. Men were willing to convert every thing they could into your greenbacks, national bank notes, and bonds. Money became scarce by the panic, because it was not in circulation.

"Now, sir, what is the real remedy for a panic? I ask that question, and I should like at some time for the distinguished chairman of the Committee on Finance to answer it. Is it by the resumption of specie payments? When before was it ever proposed as a remedy for a panic? I should like to know the single time that it was ever proposed before as a remedy for a panic. Why, sir, a suspension of specie payments has generally been the remedy—not the resumption. I call the attention of the Senate to the experience of banks and governments in every country, and I maintain the proposition that so far from resumption being regarded as a remedy for a panic, suspension has often been the remedy. In 1837, when that panic took place, the solvent banks of the country were saved only by suspending specie payments. Take a single illustration: The State Bank of Indiana, one of the best banks at that time in the country, was hard run and could not discount a dollar. The Legislature came together and authorized the banks to suspend for five years. Relief was at once obtained; the bank began to discount freely;

money became plenty; and when the period for resumption came around, people seemed to have forgotten all about it.

"In 1857—and my friend from Connecticut (Mr. Buckingham) will remember it well—the panic bore down with crushing force until the banks of New York and all the Eastern States, by common consent, determined to suspend, and from that time there was ease; from that time discounts became free. No, sir; suspension is the remedy for panics, and resumption is a thing for times of prosperity. That is experience.

"I lay down this as a general proposition, to be established by reference to the history of panics for the last one hundred and fifty years, that the true relief for a panic, to bring about a restoration of confidence, has been, not resumption, not contraction, but by making additions to the currency at the time. This is a very important proposition, if it is true.

"The remedy has been by making a small—I use the word 'small'—addition to the volume of the currency at the time.

"One word in regard to the action of the Government. The Government, when this panic took place, authorized the purchase of bonds to the amount of the currency balance in the Treasury at that time, about $44,000,000, if I remember correctly. It was said that that was taken up by the savings-banks in New-York, Philadelphia, and Boston, and so it was. It was said that it was unwise, because the money did not go into circulation. It was the very wisest thing that could be done, and in my opinion prevented great mischief and circumscribed the evil effects of the panic at once.

"Mr. President, instead of following theory in a matter of this kind, let us follow rather the lights of experience. And now what is being done by the Treasury Department? Acting on that principle—whether they are doing it for that purpose or not, that is what they are doing. The Government is to-day, by the disbursement of the $44,000,000 reserve, adding to the volume of the currency; and those small additions which are being made, of which the whole country is aware, are doing much to-day toward removing the effect of this panic. So that this falling off in the revenue, while it is a great misfortune, is not an unmixed one; it is carrying some benefit to the people. The Government is not responsible for this panic. Why, sir, this panic was an accident, just as much as the explosion of a boiler of a steamboat, or a collision upon a railroad—an accident, the result of an event that nobody could foresee. It had no connection with our Government system of finance or any thing in our currency. It was an accident that might have happened just as well in a country that had nothing but gold and silver as a currency. It was an accident, and shall not relief be provided for this accident? Our Government is now relieving against it. I was very sorry when the panic commenced that our Government did not see

its way clear to put into circulation at once the whole $44,000,000 reserve. I believe, if the Government had been able to do that, this panic would have stopped at once; it would not have lasted three weeks; but the President was not at liberty to do that, the Secretary of the Treasury did not feel safe in doing that. Why? He anticipated, and with a sagacity that he, perhaps, has not got credit for—he anticipated, as did the President, that there might be a falling off in the revenues, and that that falling off would require this $44,000,000 reserve to carry on the ordinary operations of the Government; and those anticipations have turned out to be correct to the very letter."

Mr. Frelinghuysen, of New Jersey, said: "Mr. President, what plan should we adopt to render the legal tenders convertible into gold? In attempting to answer that inquiry I realize that we are entering upon a dangerous sea. It is easier, much easier, to theorize and criticise than to act affirmatively; but I will suggest a measure rather for the purpose of seeing whether our excellent Committee on Finance will not by placing it in its crucible evolve from it gold, than because I imagine that there is not much of alloy in my suggestion.

"The Secretary of the Treasury should be authorized to issue bonds of the United States, bearing six per cent. interest, payable in United States specie-paying notes, or in gold; and these bonds should be issued in exchange, at not less than par, for gold, from time to time, as the opportunity occurred, or be issued and sold, and the proceeds used from time to time in the purchase of gold, such gold to be held in the Treasury until enough was accumulated wherewith to commence the redemption of the outstanding United States notes in specie.

"That there be no unnecessary issue of these bonds in obtaining the requisite amount of gold wherewith to commence the redemption, and that a sufficient supply of gold may be continuously in the Treasury, the Secretary should have the right to reissue the redeemed Treasury notes in exchange for coin at par, and for no other purpose, the aggregate amount of such notes which may be outstanding and those which may have been redeemed and held at no time to exceed the amount that shall have been lawfully issued at the date of the passage of the proposed act.

"And to put it beyond question that when the redemption is commenced it will not be discontinued, the Secretary should be authorized, in the event of the supply of gold being unequal to the redemption, and in that event only, to redeem the said notes in sums of $1,000 with such of the six per cent. bonds as have not been issued.

"To this plan (as to any other) plausible, perhaps grave, objections can be urged. Let us briefly consider those objections. The first objection is, that we could not get the gold; that any great accumulation of gold in our Treasury would, to a degree, disturb the finances of the world; that the price of gold would rise, and thus the effort at redemption defeat itself; and that to prevent its flow to us, various devices and hostile legislation would be resorted to by other nations. All this is probably true, if the proposal was to secure this accumulation in a short period of time. And to meet that difficulty the proposed plan avoids fixing any period within which the accumulation shall be made, or the gold purchased, and it fixes no specific time when the redemption shall commence. The proposed act leaves that necessarily to the discretion of the Secretary, who would act in view of the price of gold from time to time, and would avail himself of those products of our own mines, which have never yet constituted a portion of the circulating medium of the world—a product which, I understand, is estimated to amount this year to $60,000,000.

" We at one time had in our Treasury $100,-000,000 ; and if we had that amount now, with the power in the Secretary to reissue the redeemed notes at par for gold, and in default of gold to redeem with six per cent. bonds, we could, without risk of suspension, commence to redeem in coin to-day.

" 2. The next objection is, that the plan proposed would create a too sudden transition in the modes of business, and would produce a shock injurious to the country. I agree that resumption should not be sudden ; and such is not the purpose of the bill. Due notice would be given by the passage of the act that the Government was moving slowly, though irresistibly and inevitably, to the fulfillment of its provisions and to resumption. The act would fix no time when the resumption would commence ; that would depend on what success the Secretary had in obtaining the coin on sufficiently favorable terms, and when, in view of the situation of the money market, it was wise to commence the payment of coin ; of all which the public, week by week, would have full notice.

" Thus the objection as to impossibility of at once obtaining the gold, and the objection that the plan would be a shock to business, are met by having no arbitrary and definite time fixed for resumption, but having taken the firm resolve to redeem, having conferred on the Secretary the power to obtain the means wherewith to redeem, it is left to the Secretary, fully informed as to all the circumstances in his discretion, exercised in full view of the nation, to fix the day to commence resumption.

" 3. Another objection to the plan is, that combinations would be made to drain the Treasury of gold, and resumption would be a failure—that it would be followed by suspension.

" The one important point in any attempt at resumption, a consideration in importance overshadowing all others, is, that when we commence to redeem, the impossibility of defeat or failure must be apparent.

" It must come so slowly as to produce no jar, and so inevitably as to disarm opposition. The Secretary of the Treasury should have the power to issue $225,000,000 of these six per cent. bonds. He should have the right to reissue the redeemed United States notes in exchange for coin at par ; to avoid possible failure he should have the right to redeem the United States notes in sums of $1,000 with such of the bonds as remained unissued. With such powers and resources, it would be apparent that resumption could not be defeated, when the Secretary, selecting the opportune time, should say the resumption would begin. That time he would select in view of the accumulation of gold he had made, in view of the condition of the money market, and in view of the permanent approximation in value the United States notes had made to gold. The passage of the proposed act, rendering it certain that at some time the United States notes were to be redeemable, would do much to raise their value in the market, and a much less gold reserve in the Treasury would be required for redemption than I would be willing now to state. Perhaps few would agree with me as to the amount."

Mr. Schurz, of Missouri, said : " I shall now approach the question of financial policy. Is there any one among us who, under ordinary circumstances, when we had a metallic currency in the country, would have thought of substituting for that metallic currency an irredeemable Government paper-money ? If there is any one I have not heard of him. We all know that there was a time when the great leaders of public opinion in the United States—a large majority of them at least—considered it unconstitutional to make any thing a legal tender save the precious metals. I might quote for hours from the sayings of the great men of the past, whose names are mentioned only with respect. I state this not for the purpose of reviving a discussion on the constitutional point, which would now be too late, as it has been otherwise decided, but to give a specimen of the old-fashioned way of thinking which quite generally prevailed before the war, and which was disturbed only by its extreme necessities. Leaving the constitutional question entirely aside, certainly no consideration of financial policy was then advanced to urge the substitution of irredeemable legal-tender paper currency for gold dollars. Nobody thought of such a thing.

" The reasons why the precious metals were considered the most reliable measure of value and the best available tool of exchange were so generally accepted then, and are in fact so little called in question now, in this debate at least, that I do not feel called upon to go into an elaborate defense of a position which is virtually not attacked. Even the opponents of the resolution under debate on this floor seem to recognize them as valid, for they admit that only actual distress has forced us to give up the specie basis, and that at some time we must return to it. I think even the honorable Senator from Indiana on my left (Mr. Morton), and the honorable Senator from Michigan on my right (Mr. Ferry), want to be considered hard-money men in a certain sense.

"I am well aware that in the country all sorts of schemes are broached by which an irredeemable paper currency is to be made a perpetual institution. Every one of us is fairly flooded with pamphlets from all sides, setting forth the wildest conceptions, which pretend to be new discoveries, but, in fact, wittingly or unwittingly, are only repetitions of schemes which have always appeared in the same way in every country when an irredeemable currency had entangled a nation in great embarrassments which it was difficult to overcome. Most of them only show that a disturbed condition of things is apt to throw the minds of men out of balance; and that while an irredeemable currency was but recently looked upon as a disease, patients may sometimes become so afraid of a cure that they positively fall in love with their ailment. I will not spend any time in discussing any of these schemes now, but shall take them up when they come before us. I merely mention them to point out to the inflationists on this floor in what direction they are tending.

"Now, sir, have we any inflationists on this floor? Those who oppose the resolution repel the name. They do not like it. There is a certain odious flavor about it. They say that they are not opposed to resumption, but want to put it off to a better time. But what do they propose now? There is the Senator from Indiana (Mr. Morton), who proposes an increase of our currency at least to the amount of $44,000,000. There is the Senator from Michigan (Mr. Ferry), proposing an increase of our irredeemable currency to the amount of at least $100,000,000. Now, gentlemen, I call this by its right name—inflation. Whatever circumlocution they may use to disguise the fact, it remains after all what it is.

"Thus we have the alternative plainly before us—resumption or inflation. The inflationists all speak of our business embarrassments as the reason why resumption should be put off and inflation resorted to.

"Now we come to the second question—the remedy to be applied to the difficulties surrounding us. At an early stage in this debate the Senator from Indiana and the Senator from Michigan were ready with their answer. The Senator from Indiana says: not resumption, but suspension of specie payments has always with good effect been used as a cure for panics. When listening to him I wondered how the panic could have occurred at all here at this time, since we were already in a decidedly suspended condition, and since the remedy had been applied for eleven years constantly without interruption before the disease broke out. Now, what does the Senator from Indiana want? Does he want to cure this crisis by suspending us still more? He may by his advice suspend us more, but certainly he will not cure the crisis.

"Thus the relief sought by an inflation of our currency turns out to be a mere delusion, as anybody who had given any attention to the subject always knew it must; but there are people who seem to be clinging with a childlike faith to the ridiculously absurd notion that by printing and issuing more Government promises to pay we shall increase the wealth of the country. We might call it a ludicrous form of superstition, if not insanity, were it not so serious and sad. Now, suppose for a moment we could, by some sort of witchery, wipe out all existing engagements in which money is involved, such as debts, contracts, and so on, and then multiply all the greenbacks and national-bank notes in the possession of the people by ten, so that, waking up one beautiful morning, every individual in the United States would find ten greenback dollars in his pocket, or safe, where the day before he had only one. What a jubilee there would be among fools! But what a disappointment as soon as the true state of the case became generally understood! Does any sane man think that by such multiplication the wealth of the country would be increased one farthing? It is evident that it would not.

"Now, since all Senators admit that ultimately we must come back to a specie basis, the only question to be discussed in that respect seems to be that of method and opportunity. The difficulties which stand in the way of redemption I see clearly enough. In considering them I have at once to enter my protest against two plans suggested, which, as I believe, involve dangerous delusions. The first is that proposed by the Senator from Michigan (Mr. Ferry), that we should first expand the currency in order to revive prosperity, which revived prosperity would then enable us to return to specie payments with greater ease and facility. The second is that proposed by the Senator from Massachusetts (Mr. Boutwell), to do nothing, but let things remain as they now are, and to wait until the business of the country will have grown so much that its necessities will bring gold and paper to a par by a natural process of development.

"I approach now the proposition of the Senator from Massachusetts (Mr. Boutwell), that we should sit still, do nothing with the currency, waiting patiently and quietly for the development of the resources of the country and the increase of business to bring greenbacks and gold together in value, as he said in his speech a few days ago. When in his opinion that period is likely to arrive the Senator did not tell us, and yet an answer to just that question would be a very valuable piece of information, coming from the principal champion of that policy.

"Now, I repeat I do not under-estimate the difficulties that stand in the way of resumption; but I declare as my candid opinion that since the first year after the close of the war, when our irredeemable currency system had not so deeply eaten its way into the whole economic life of the nation, and when the business of the country had to adapt itself from the ways of war to the ways of peace—a moment which unfortunately we missed — the present time is the most opportune for the inauguration of a resumption policy; and if we lose that opportunity again we shall have to wait for another and perhaps more disastrous revulsion to see it return. And it is just from the present crisis in our economic affairs that the new opportunity springs. The reason is very simple. Many of the difficulties which, it was feared, would accompany and follow resumption have already been anticipated by the crisis. Much of that preparation which must precede resumption in order to avoid disastrous embarrassment has already been performed by the crisis.

"As to the resolution now under discussion, I shall vote for the amendment of the Senator from Delaware (Mr. Bayard), in which I find the simplest and clearest statement of the object I pursue. If that should fail, the resolution introduced by the honorable chairman of the Committee on Finance will of course have my support. Let me express the hope that at an early day a bill embodying a method of a return to specie payments will be laid before us."

Mr. Sherman, of Ohio, said: "Mr. President, at the outset of my remarks I wish to state some general propositions established by experience, and the concurring opinions of all writers on political economy. They may not be disputed, but are constantly overlooked. They ought to be ever present in this discussion as axioms, the truth of which has been so often proved that proof is no longer requisite.

"The most obvious of these axioms, which lies at the foundation of the argument I wish to make to-day, is that a specie standard is the best and the only true standard of all values, recognized as such by all civilized nations of our generation, and established as such by the experience of all commercial nations that have existed from the earliest period of recorded time. While the United States as well as all other nations have for a time, under the pressure of war or other calamity, been driven to establish other standards of value, yet they have all been impelled to return to the true standard; and even while other standards of value have been legalized for the time, specie has measured their value as it now measures the value of our legal-tender notes.

"This axiom is as immutable as the law of gravitation or the laws of the planetary system, and every device to evade it or avoid it has, by its failure, only demonstrated the universal law that specie measures all values as certainly as the surface of the ocean measures the level of the earth.

"I purpose now to pursue the argument further, and to prove that we are bound both by public faith and good policy to bring our currency to the gold standard; that such a result was provided for by the financial policy adopted when the currency was authorized; that a departure from this policy was adopted after the war was over, and after the necessity for a depreciated currency ceased; and that we have only to restore the old policy to bring us safely, surely, and easily, to a specie standard.

"First, I present to you the pledge of the United States to pay these notes in coin 'at the earliest practicable period.' In the 'act to strengthen the public credit,' passed on March 18, 1869, I find this obligation:

And the United States also solemnly pledges its public faith to make provision at the earliest practicable period for the redemption of the United States notes in coin.

"Without renewing the discussion in regard to the nature of these notes, or quoting the decision of the Supreme Court of the United States, or the declaration of the various acts of Congress from 1862 down, I rest upon this pledge of the public faith. Under what circumstances was it made? The condition of our currency, the obligation of our bonds, the nature of our promises, had been discussed before the people of the United States in the campaign of 1868; various theories had been advanced; and the result was that those who regarded the faith of the nation as pledged to pay not only the bonds of the United States, but the notes also, in coin, prevailed, and General Grant was elected President of the United States. On the eastern portico of the Capitol, on March 4, 1869, he made this declaration:

A great debt has been contracted in securing to us and our posterity the Union. The payment of this, principal and interest, as well as the return to a specie basis, as soon as it can be accomplished without material detriment to the debtor class or to the country at large, must be provided for. To protect the national honor every dollar of Government indebtedness should be paid in gold, unless otherwise expressly stipulated in the contract. Let it be understood that no repudiator of one farthing of our public debt will be trusted in public place, and it will go far toward strengthening a credit which ought to be the best in the world, and will ultimately enable us to replace the debt with bonds bearing less interest than we now pay.

"The Congress of the United States, in order to put into form its sense of this obligation, passed the act 'to strengthen the public credit,' and the last and most important clause of this act is the promise which I have just read, that these notes should be paid 'at the earliest practicable period' in coin.

"Mr. President, we see, then, the effect of this promise. And I here come to what I regard as a painful feature to discuss—how have we redeemed our promise? It was Congress that made it, in obedience to the public voice; and no act of Congress ever met with a more hearty and generous approbation. But I say to you, with sorrow, that Congress has done no single act the tendency of which has been to advance the value of these notes to a gold standard; and I shall make that clearer before I get through. Congress made this promise five years ago. The people believed it and business men believed it. Four years have passed away since then, and your dollar in greenbacks is worth no more to-day than it was on the 18th of March, 1870; and no act of yours has ever tended to advance the value of that greenback to par in gold, while every affirmative act of yours since that time has tended to depreciate its value and to violate your promise.

"Mr. President, these are simple facts, although it may be painful for us to discuss them. I do not say that Congress, in this matter, disregarded the will of the people, because there was a public feeling against any measure which tended to advance the value of the greenbacks to the gold standard. I am not complaining of Senators or Members who represent their constituents, but I do say that the fact stands out as clear as light, that the Congress of the United States which made this promise has done no single act the tendency of which even leads one to suppose that it will ever redeem its promise.

"Sir, let us see what has been done. We have paid $400,000,000 of the public debt, and we boast of it—of debt not due for years. We have paid to redeem that debt a premium of $40,000,000. In other words, we have paid $440,000,000 to redeem four hundred millions of debt not yet due, and we have not redeemed a single debt that was due in March, 1869; but, on the contrary, we have increased the kind of debts then due more in proportion than the increase of our population. And, sir, while our promise did advance the credit of our bonds and of our notes alike, and while the execution of that promise as to our bonds has advanced our bonds to above par in gold, yet we have done nothing whatever to redeem the second clause of that pledge; but, on the other hand, all we have done has been done with the intention and with the effect of depreciating the value of our notes.

"Mr. President, I am not here to find fault with individuals; but I do say that the Congress of the United States in the measures which have been adopted has not done what it ought to have done to redeem the pledge of the public faith to pay these notes in coin 'at the earliest practicable period.' Why, sir, at this moment we are living in daily violation of this pledge. I said a moment ago that instead of adopting measures looking toward specie payments we have increased the volume of our currency in every branch of it. Now let us see if this be true. I have here a statement, taken from the official report of the Secretary of the Treasury, of the amount of the currency on the 30th of June, 1869. I cannot find a statement for the 1st of March, 1869, but it

was the same, because it was fixed by law. I find on the 30th of June, 1869, we had three hundred and fifty-six millions of greenbacks, the same amount that we had on the 18th day of March. That was the maximum amount, as it was supposed, fixed by law. When the act of the 18th of March, 1869, was passed, no one dreamed that there existed a power to issue forty-four millions more.

"Our greenbacks were then $356,000,000. On the 1st of January, 1874, according to the last statement of the public debt, they were $378,481,339. We had, then, increased this form of our currency $22,481,000. And that is not all. Since that time, and up to the 10th of January, according to a New York newspaper—and I suppose it is correct—I find that the amount of legal-tender notes outstanding was $381,891,000, or an increase since the 1st of January of something like $3,400,000, or at the rate of $400,000 a day. Every dollar of this new issue of paper-money directly tended to depreciate that outstanding and was in violation of the spirit and the provision of the law of 1869. I am not now speaking of the legal power of the Secretary of the Treasury to make this issue, because I have already given my opinion fully on this subject in an official report, but only call your attention to the fact that by our acquiescence we have actually watered, debased, and depreciated by new issues the very notes we promised to pay in coin at the earliest practicable period.

"Nor is this all. Under authority clearly conferred by law to the Secretary of the Treasury, we have increased the fractional currency from $27,508,928, at which it stood on the 30th of June, 1869, to $48,554,792, or an increase of fractional currency of $21,036,000. Again, sir, driven by a local demand which we could not resist, founded upon a palpable injustice growing out of the mistake of an officer of the Government long ago in the distribution of the national-bank circulation, we did authorize by law an increase of the bank circulation to the South and West to the amount of $54,000,-000. The amount of bank-notes issued at the time we made this pledge was $299,789,000; and to-day the amount outstanding is $339,081,-000, showing an increase in this kind of notes of $39,300,000, or an increase of the currency since the promise to pay it in coin at the earliest practicable period, and all legal tender in effect, of $82,317,000; and now this process of inflation is going on daily—first, by the issue of the balance of the forty-four million reserve; and, second, by the issue of new bank-notes as banks are organized under the act of July, 1870; and yet there is a cry for more, more.

"My honorable friend asked me a while ago what was the nature of the pledge made by the act of March, 1869, as to the time of payment of United States notes in coin. If I was defending a person charged as a criminal for violating this law, or one like it, I would claim, as the Senator from Indiana does, that as no time was fixed, no man could be convicted for a penitentiary offense for a violation of the law. But what is this pledge? Let me read it again:

And the United States also solemnly pledges its faith to make provision at the earliest practicable period for the payment of the United States notes in coin.

"What is the meaning of that? Does it not mean that the United States shall apply its means, its power, its energies, its revenue, its money, to redeem these notes? Does it mean a vague promise, such as party platforms sometimes use to deceive and mislead the people? Does it mean only a vague, indefinite promise by which business men are to be gulled and deluded into basing their contracts upon an artificial standard? No, sir; it is the promise of a great, proud, and rich people, who mean what they say—that every practicable means shall be used to that end.

"Now, sir, I ask, has it been practicable at any time in the last four years to advance in some degree these notes toward the specie standard? My honorable friend from Indiana says that for the last four or five years we have had a time of unbounded plenty and great prosperity; we have built thousands and tens of thousands of miles of railroads; we have built furnaces; we have expanded our enterprises and proved our energy. Yes, sir; all this we have done. We have gone through a period of prosperity almost unexampled; but it seems we never were prosperous enough during all this time, according to the Senator from Indiana, to fulfill any part of this obligation which we made on the 18th of March, 1869. Sir, when will it be practicable?

"But now let us come to the specific question of the time for resumption. Shall the redemption of this pledge be postponed until the public debt is paid? Why, sir, one-tenth of the money we have used to pay the public debt not due would have brought us to a specie standard. No one supposes that under an ordinary state of affairs the currency of the country—the greenbacks—need be reduced below three hundred millions in order to bring us to a specie standard. I have heard some of the ablest and most experienced business men of the country declare that, whenever the right to convert greenbacks into gold or its equivalent was secured so that prudent men would see that the Government had the power to maintain its specie standard, there would be no reduction of the currency to any appreciable extent. But whether that be so or not, no one has claimed that the amount of greenbacks need be reduced below three hundred millions in order to bring that remaining three hundred millions up to the standard of gold. That would be a reduction of $56,000,000. Fifty-six millions of the money that we have applied to the payment of debt not yet due would have brought all the remaining greenbacks up to par in gold, would have made our bank-notes convertible into the

standard of gold, and we would have had, without knowing it, specie payment—a solid, safe, and secure basis. The forty millions of greenbacks we paid as premium for our bonds would have accomplished this result. Thousands of men who have been ruined by the false ideas that sprung from this fever-heated, depreciated paper-money would be now useful, able, and successful business men, instead of being ruined by bankruptcy.

"Sir, we gain nothing by postponing the fulfillment of our promise with a view to reduce the public debt. We have to pay the debt in coin any way, and the same coin that pays it now would pay it after our currency had been restored to par. If the old idea of Mr. Pendleton had prevailed, that these bonds should be paid in greenbacks, then there would be a motive for us to depreciate the greenbacks in order to pay off our bonds at the cheapest rate. But this promise to pay in coin extended to the bondholder. We promised to pay the bondholder gold for his bond and the people gold for their greenbacks. We have fulfilled our promise to the bondholder. We have paid him in gold. We have bought the gold. We have paid him at a premium of ten per cent. on our currency. Not a single effort, not a single measure, has succeeded in either House of Congress that looks to the redemption of the promise to the people who hold these greenbacks, and which measure their daily toil in their productive avocations. We cannot postpone this obligation until the payment of the public debt, because, although we have rapidly advanced in the payment of the public debt, it will be many long years before that 'consummation most devoutly to be wished' will be reached.

"Shall we postpone the redemption of our greenbacks until we can accumulate enough gold in our Treasury to pay them? We know the effect of that policy. Any attempt to accumulate great masses of gold in the Treasury will not only excite popular opprobrium, by holding idle in the vaults of the Treasury money that ought to draw interest, but it will create a stringency in the gold-market. It will advance the value of every thing we wish to get. Accumulate gold in great masses, and it will advance the price of gold all over the world. We could not now, with all our teeming productions, draw to this country $200,000,000 in gold without disturbing the Bank of France, the Bank of England, and all the money centres in the world. Therefore the idea of postponing the day of specie payments until we can accumulate enough gold to redeem the greenbacks would be the idlest, vainest delusion and the most foolish hope.

"Mr. President, I have gone into this argument to show, first, that we are bound by the obligation that we assumed on the 18th of March, 1869, to resume specie payments, or to do something to advance our notes to the par of gold. I have endeavored to show that such was the legal and established policy of the Government when the notes were first issued. Now, I have only to say, very briefly, that there are various modes, to none of which do I intend to commit myself until the whole subject is finally discussed, by which this can easily, without trouble, without difficulty, be accomplished. There are three modes that have been proposed in debate in the Senate, and a multitude come to us from the people, but I will group them into three classes.

"There is, first, the proposition to accumulate gold in the Treasury with a view to the actual redemption of our notes in coin. That is supported by two bills now before the committee: one introduced by the Senator from Vermont (Mr. Morrill), and the other by the Senator from New Jersey (Mr. Frelinghuysen). What are the objections to this plan? They seem to me to be these: In the first place, any attempt to accumulate large masses of gold in the Treasury, lying idle to await some future event not fixed by act of Congress, would not be a wise use of the public moneys. In the next place, I entirely object to conferring upon the Secretary of the Treasury the power of issuing one hundred millions or any lesser sum of six per cent. bonds with a view to buy gold to hoard it in the Treasury to maintain resumption. I believe that it is impossible, in the very nature of things, to maintain the resumption of specie payments ·at all times and under all circumstances; and if any thing has been established by modern experience, it is that all a nation can do that issues paper-money is to maintain it at a specie standard in ordinary times; but, in times of panic, such as by periodical revulsions come over every country, specie payments cannot be maintained. They can scarcely be maintained in England, and are not now maintained in France, although they approach them. Therefore, every plan for specie payments ought to have some provision for the temporary suspension of specie payments, or some means by which in times of great panic and financial distress there may be a temporary departure from the specie standard. I say this not that it ought to be so, but simply as a matter of demonstrated experience shown by the history of almost all commercial nations in Europe.

"The second plan is the actual payment of the United States notes and their cancellation; in other words, the plan of contraction. In the first place, this plan while it operates does so with such severity as, in a popular government like ours, to cause its suspension and repeal. Undoubtedly, the most certain way to produce specie payments is by retiring the notes that are dishonored, paying them off, taking them out of circulation. But the trouble is, the process of contraction is itself so severe upon the ordinary current business of the country that the people will not stand it; and in this country the people rule. The policy of Mr. McCulloch, already commented upon, if it

had been continued further, would have undoubtedly brought us to a specie standard, but with great distress, great impoverishment, and with more difficulty than was really necessary to accomplish the object in view.

"These are the difficulties that occur to me as against these two policies. There is a third plan. This plan, which in my judgment presents the easiest and best mode of attaining specie payments, is to take some bond of the United States which in ordinary times, by current events, is shown to be worth par in gold in the money-markets of the world, where specie is alone the standard of value, and authorize the conversion of notes into that bond.

"I again appeal to the Senate to now firmly take its stand against any inflation of paper-money under any circumstances, under any provocation, or any plea. This alone will do a great good to the country. But if it will go further—if the Senate will lead the way to some wise and practical measure, looking to a redemption of the pledged faith of the United States, the people we represent will have cause to be proud of the political body which they have so long honored. I believe, sir, that no act of the Senate would so much inspire confidence, give strength to our business men, revive our industry, as by a decided vote on these propositions to show that our firm purpose is to take the road that leads to specie payments and a restored currency."

Mr. Logan, of Illinois, said: "Mr. President, if a return to specie payments will cure all our financial evils, why not come to it at once? If the doctrine advanced by its advocates be true, the evils resulting will only be temporary. When our personal health is at stake we swallow the medicine presented by the physician that we may regain our vigor and strength.

"If the doctrine advanced by specie-payment theorists be correct, why not give the medicine at once? We have the power in our hands: repeal all laws which make any thing but gold and silver legal tender, and restore these metals to their former functions of standard value. Government will have a little trouble, perhaps, to take up her greenbacks, and commerce will certainly have to pass through some narrow straits; but, according to the theory advanced by learned Senators, the clear and open sea is just a little distance ahead.

"But, sir, the admission which the advocates of specie payment make here and elsewhere, either directly or indirectly, in regard to the supply of the precious metals, seems to me to be fatal to their theory.

"How many are there who will contend that the supply is sufficient to meet the wants of trade? How many are there among our national legislators ready to face the storm which would result from a shrinkage of prices so as to correspond with the amount of gold and silver which can be brought into circulation. Why, sir, in a 'Memorial of the Chamber of Commerce of New York' which lies before me, and which leads the van in favor of specie payment, I find this admission, which they are forced to make:

Whatever policy might have been judicious before, it is vain to talk of contraction now, when three hundred and fifty millions of greenbacks and three hundred millions of national-bank notes are employed unceasingly to keep the wheels of an extended commerce in motion (page 8).

"This, it seems to me, is almost if not entirely fatal to their theory, and contradicts all the arguments they have advanced to sustain their position. It is an open admission on the part of those thoroughly acquainted with all the intricacies of the money-market that there is not a sufficient amount of the precious metals for use. This is virtually admitting the whole question at issue. If the gold and silver in circulation, or that can be brought into circulation by legislative action, is not sufficient in amount for the business of the country—and the advocates of specie payment generally admit it is not—then it is evident it does not represent the value of the commodities of trade or products of labor, and therefore can neither answer the purpose of a standard of value alone within our country, nor a sufficient medium of exchange. If the demands of commerce are such that as it expands in volume it requires a corresponding increase in the amount of currency or medium of exchange in use, then it is apparent that there is something in the very nature of trade and laws of exchange which will not allow a continual shrinking in the nominal value while the volume is actually increasing. In other words, there is a strong tendency in the natural laws of trade and commerce to maintain a comparatively uniform price of products, even when it requires a strong pressure upon the amount of the circulating medium afloat. The theory of the contractionists or advocates of specie payment, when reduced to a nutshell, is this, that there is no reason why twenty-five cents may not represent the value of a bushel of wheat in New York as well as $1.50, provided the prices of all other articles of trade and commerce are reduced to the same standard. I hope they do not desire this, yet if their logic is true, then theoretically the iron money of Lycurgus, or the 'cowries' of the Africans, may answer all the purposes of money; but practical facts, and not theories, are the things we are called to deal with at present.

"Apply the theory, then—no matter how correct it may appear on paper—to the case as it stands, and tell me what would be the result. Suppose that by a reduction of the currency wheat was reduced in New York to twenty-five cents per bushel, and other things to a corresponding value, when would the national, State, county, city, and individual debts be liquidated? Does any one fail to see that we would be involved in financial ruin and bankruptcy? Sir, the evil effect would not stop even here, for our civilization would feel

the shock, our system of education and means of spreading and increasing intelligence would be crushed, and we would soon be gliding backward toward a state of ignorance and superstition.

"I am aware that the advocates of specie payment do not propose any such extreme measure as this, but I do maintain that whenever we contract below that point which experience has shown to be the true and healthy standard, we are so far cramping our energies, and retrograding in a corresponding degree.

"What inference, then, are we to draw from these facts which experience is constantly presenting? Most undoubtedly that a healthy and vigorous commerce requires an amount of currency uniformly proportioned to the amount of trade.

"Having now discussed these points which have a general bearing upon the subject of a metallic basis, I approach directly the question before us, which may be stated thus: 'Is it sound financial policy to take such action at present as shall tend to a moderate increase of our currency?'

"One point in this question I think ought to be universally conceded, and that is, that we cannot reach specie payment by a further forced contraction without bringing great distress and probable bankruptcy upon our people. Another point made evident by the late panic is, that the amount of currency, as at present arranged, fails to meet the wants of the country, and that some change is necessary to meet the present necessity.

"To attempt a review of all the remedies proposed would require more time than I can at present devote to it; therefore I shall confine my remaining remarks to the discussion of but one or two leading propositions.

"If 'taking action looking to a speedy resumption of specie payment' means any thing, it means displacing a portion of the paper currency that gold may be induced to flow in by the consequent increase in the value of the remaining paper; or, it means fixing a day, not far distant, by positive enactment, when the Secretary of the Treasury shall commence to pay gold for legal-tender notes. All other methods proposed are but shifts to avoid the responsibility of meeting the issue fairly and squarely, and, although doubtless presented in good faith, yet they are in effect schemes which tend to ease the pain without assisting in the least to cure the disease. There are but three methods open before us: increase, contraction, or resumption of specie payment by simple operations of law; and if we act at all we must proceed in one or the other of these plans. Any thing short of this is only shifting the burden from one shoulder to the other. It is admitted that contraction is impracticable under the present state of affairs; therefore we may dismiss this from the discussion, for to argue that we can contract by expanding is simply a perversion of terms. If expansion is what we need at present, let it be admitted plainly and unreservedly, and let us at once proceed to take such action as will bring about this result as speedily as the nature of the case will admit of.

"If the way to contraction is blocked, then there are but two paths open before us—resumption by direct operation of law, or expansion.

"Without attempting to follow out the various plans presented for returning to specie payment, I select the memorial first alluded to as the best and perhaps clearest exponent of this theory. It says (page 8): 'We have reached the verge of success in bringing gold and currency to a par with each other, and it apparently needs but an announcement by the Secretary of the Treasury that legal-tender notes will be paid in gold at an early day, to annul the present differences between the two;' and suggests that the redemption of legal-tender notes be commenced the 4th of May next, but that the power to issue be continued.

"This is the money-holders' side of the question, presented in plain and unequivocal language, and is the theory of those who advocate a return to a specie basis reduced to a nutshell.

"Suppose, Mr. President, we pass a law requiring the Secretary of the Treasury to commence redeeming legal-tender notes on the 4th of May next, or even the 1st of January, 1875: how is this to bring relief? Will it increase the volume of currency, or unlock any considerable portion of that which is now hoarded up? For each dollar of gold put into circulation a dollar of legal tender will be withdrawn; and there will be no increase in the amount of currency in circulation, unless we assume, as is done in this memorial, that all legal tenders will at once come to par, and thus increase the total value of the currency by the amount of the present difference between these and the same nominal amount of gold. Suppose it to be true that the promise to redeem would, without the presentation of a single dollar, bring the entire amount of the legal-tender issue to a par with gold, would this afford the relief demanded? Would this place more money in circulation than there is at present? Sir, go further: suppose the utmost that the most sanguine advocate of the theory can possibly claim—that the reaction of this policy upon the national-bank notes, by transferring the required reserve for their redemption into gold or its equivalent, would also bring them up to a par with gold—would even this meet our financial demands? Would this supply the wants of the commerce and business of our country? Would this start our mills and manufactories again into full and active operation? Would it unlock the storehouses of the West, and pour the grain, beef, and pork, into the Eastern market? Is there some talismanic power in a dollar of gold that will render it so much more effective in trade than a sound and secure paper dollar?

"Would this loosen the grasp of those who now cling so firmly to their greenbacks and hide away their national-bank notes? No, sir; they would hold them the firmer, as the ten per cent. would be made to them by holding on and not by letting them out. There would be no more dollars in circulation then than now; the volume of the currency would be just the same then as now. But even this supposition every one knows to be impracticable, for to come to specie payment there must be contraction; the amount of gold and paper must be brought nearer together.

"And right here we have revealed to us the two parties to this question, the opposing forces in this contest; those who hold the funds, and those who need them; those who live by interest and percentage, and those who live by labor and traffic.

"The same contest arose in England about twenty years ago, when the gold of California and Australia began to flow into the European markets. The money-lenders, annuitants, and those having fixed incomes, sent forth pamphlets and treatises on currency containing warnings of the danger threatened by this extraordinary influx; they plied Parliament, with all the sophistry and arguments of which they were masters, to enact such laws as should maintain their advantages over the producing class and business men of the country.

"In one of these pamphlets, which I have here before me, I find this remarkable statement:

"I read from 'Financial Pamphlets,' vol. xvi., page 28:

Those who are in debt, or those who think themselves likely to have to borrow money, see a manifest advantage in a state of affairs which promises to alleviate the burden of their present and future incumbrances. The trading classes, in addition to their share of these advantages, expect a great extension of trade—all expect a reduction in taxation, and exclaim against any interference with a natural event which offers these advantages, for the sake of a few capitalists. It seems hopeless to attempt to meet such an array of opponents by arguments on the abstract propriety of maintaining a steady currency, yet it is very much to be wished that they should be met on this ground.

"This, sir, is a confession of the very principle for which we who advocate a moderate increase of the currency are now contending. And when the Chancellor of the Exchequer (as you will find on page 30 of the same pamphlet), wisely looking to the welfare of the great mass of the people of England, announced in his financial statement that 'the discovery of gold has established credit in this country in a manner which no political economist could ever have imagined; that it has increased and confirmed credit, and immensely increased the employment of the people'—those who had been striving to limit the standard of value to silver alone felt all their sophistry scattered to the winds by the announcement of these facts. The struggle now, sir, is the same in principle as then; the results which flowed from the increase of currency then by the influx of gold will follow the moderate increase of our currency now."

Mr. Boutwell, of Massachusetts, said: "If I am, as I am, in favor of the resumption of specie payments, with such limitations as were set forth in the annual report of the Secretary of the Treasury for 1872, I may be asked, Why not come at once to specie payments? The statement has been made here that during four years no progress has been made toward resumption. I am incapable of comprehending the value of facts if considerable progress has not been made. In 1868 the average premium on gold was 39½ per cent.; in 1869 it was 32½; in 1870 it was a trifle less than 15; in 1871, a little less than 12; in 1872 it was 12.4; and in 1873 it was 13.84. Consider, if you please, four years.. In 1869 the premium on gold was 32½, and in 1873 it was 13.84.

"Do not these facts, in themselves considered, open to explanation of whatever sort, demonstrate conclusively that in these four years we have made an advance toward resumption, unless the delusion has taken possession of men's minds that it is of no consequence whether, commercially considered, paper and coin are substantially at the same value or not when we consider the ability of the country to resume specie payments? If the theory be abroad that it is of no consequence whether the premium on gold be much or little, that the ability of the country to resume specie payments is substantially the same in each case, then I can only say that those who entertain that opinion are beyond the reach of any argument which I can present."

Mr. Morton: "Will the Senator allow me in this connection to ask him a question?"

Mr. Boutwell: "Yes, sir."

Mr. Morton: "I ask him to give his opinion, if he will, to the Senate as to the cause of the decline in the price of gold from March, 1869, to March, 1873, and how much of that decline does he attribute to the influence of the act respecting the public credit passed in March, 1869?"

Mr. Boutwell: "I attribute great importance to that act, because it was an initial step in a policy by which the public credit was established—a policy by which up to this time the public credit has been maintained. When that act was passed the credit of the United States in Europe was substantially that of Italy, Spain, Turkey, and the dishonored countries of Europe that for a generation have been struggling under the weight of heavy debt, and have not received those ideas by which the resources of nations are developed.

"From the passage of the act of March 18, 1869, which declared the purpose of the country, followed as it was by the collection of the public revenues and the appropriation of the surplus to the payment of the public debt, the credit of the country steadily and rapidly advanced, until in all the markets of Europe it

has been the equal of any other nation. For three years our bonds have been sold in more markets of Europe than the bonds of any other state, and commanded as high a price as any. But the depreciation in the price of gold, due largely to that fact, was not due exclusively to it. It was due also to the fact that the business of the country increased, that the uses for money were enlarged, that the field in which money circulated was extended; and it is to further similar progress, which is a natural progress, supported, as I should hope it might be, by such legislation as would develop the resources and increase the business of the country, especially with reference to its commercial marine, that I look to the ultimate and not distant equalization, commercially, in the value of paper and coin.

"Until that time arrives, I say advisedly, until that time arrives, any policy looking to a resumption of specie payments by direct and specific legislative action is fraught with the greatest danger to public and private interests.

"There are two ways of securing specie payments. One is by a contraction of the currency. By contracting the currency you can diminish the volume, so that a dollar in paper, commercially, shall be of the value of a dollar in coin. But that process of force will prostrate the business of the country, close up our factories and workshops; not only reduce the wages of labor, but drive hundreds and thousands of men from employment in every part of the land. Believing this, I of course cannot consent to any policy by which the power of the Government is to be directly applied in the contraction of the currency. Not apprehending merely, but believing, knowing even, as far as I can know any thing in the future that is not capable of absolute demonstration, that results like those which I have stated, or results kindred to them, are sure to follow, I cannot take the responsibility imposed by a policy of direct specific contraction. On the other hand, I am certain that the development of the resources of the country, the increase of its business, the addition of uses to which currency can be applied, will certainly and without great delay close the slight difference that exists between the value of paper and the value of coin." .

The formal debate on the resolution was here suspended.

Subsequently, on March 23d, Mr. Sherman, of Ohio, from the Committee on Finance, reported to the Senate a bill "to provide for the redemption and reissue of United States notes, and for free banking." On March 24th the bill was considered.

Mr. Sherman said: "Mr. President, some complaint has been made in the Senate and in the country at the delay in the presentation by the Committee on Finance of some bill covering the financial question; but a moment's reflection will, I am sure, convince every Senator that there has been no fault on the part of that committee. From the beginning of the session to this hour that committee, under the direction of the Senate, has been studying and discussing the various plans and propositions which were referred to the committee; and I may say that over sixty different propositions, either coming in the form of petitions or in the form of bills, have been sent to the committee, all of them suggesting different plans and ideas. It was impossible to consider all these and to agree upon any comprehensive measure until within a day or two.

"There was another consideration. The committee found themselves divided in opinion, precisely as the country is, and precisely as the Senate is, into as many as three different classes of opinion. There were, first, those who desired to take a definite and positive step toward the resumption of specie payments. There were, second, those who desired an enlargement of the currency, or what we commonly call an inflation of the currency. There were, third, those who, while willing to see the amount of bank-notes increased and the question of the legal tenders settled in some form, were also desirous that some definite step should be taken toward a specie standard. There were these differences of opinion.

"For the purpose of ascertaining the views of the Senate, and not involving ourselves in reporting a bill that would be defeated as the bill of the last session was, we presented early in the session resolutions of a general character which stated these three ideas: First, the resolution of the majority of the committee that some definite step should be taken toward specie payments. Then there was' the amendment offered by the gentleman who now occupies the chair (Mr. Ferry, of Michigan) that there ought to be an increase of the currency without reference to any plan of redemption. Third, there was the proposition made by the Senator from Delaware (Mr. Bayard) that measures should be taken at once looking to the resumption of specie payments.

"These propositions were discussed, and the committee were enlightened by that discussion; at least they obtained the opinions of members of the Senate. Subsequently, in the course of our investigation, a question about the $25,000,000 section (section 6 of the act of July 12, 1870) came up, and the committee deemed it right, by a unanimous vote, to ascertain the sense of the Senate as to whether they wished this section carried into execution. As it stood upon the statute-book it was a law without force. It was a law so expressed that the Controller said he could not execute it. Therefore the committee reported a bill which would have provided the necessary details to carry into execution that section of the existing law. But in the present temper of the public mind in the Senate and in the country that bill was discussed, and has been discussed day after day, without approaching the question at all. During all this time the commit-

tee have been pursuing their inquiries, and finally they have reported the bill which is now before us.

"The measure that is reported is not a satisfactory one to any of us in all its details. Probably it is not such as the mind of any single member of the Senate would propose. It is in the nature of a compromise bill, and therefore, while it has the strength of a compromise bill, it has also the weakness of a compromise bill. There are ideas in it which, while meeting the views of a majority, taken separately will be opposed by others. I am quite sure that I say nothing new to the Senate when I say it does not in all respects meet my own views. But there is a necessity for us to yield some of our opinions. We cannot reconcile or pass any measure that will be satisfactory to the country unless we do so. Any positive victory by either extreme of this controversy will be an absolute injury to the business of the country. Therefore, any measure that is adopted ought to be so moderate, pursuing such a middle course, such a middle ground, that it will give satisfaction to the country. It must be taken as a whole; and therefore the effect of amending this proposition will be simply to destroy it. If an amendment in the direction of expansion is inserted, it will drive away some who would be willing to support it as it is. If an amendment in the way of contraction is proposed and carried by a majority of the Senate, it will drive away those who might be willing to take this measure as a compromise. The only question before the Senate now is, whether this is a fair compromise between the ideas that have divided the people of this country and the members of the Senate; whether it will surely improve our currency while giving the relief that is hoped for by a moderate increase of the currency. Now I ask the Secretary to read the bill."

The Chief Clerk read as follows:

Be it enacted by the Senate and House of Representatives of the United States of America in Congress assembled, That the maximum limit of United States notes is hereby fixed at $382,000,000, at which amount it shall remain until reduced as hereinafter provided.

On March 26th Mr. Merrimon, of North Carolina, offered a substitute for the entire bill. The discussion continued for some days, as in Committee of the Whole. On the question of agreeing to the amendment proposed as a substitute, Mr. Sherman, of Ohio, said: "I simply want to call attention to the fact that the only difference between the substitute and the bill as pending is in one section with regard to the increase of the public debt. That is the only difference between the two. They are *in hæc verba* the same except as to that one section. The substitute now pending offered by the Senator from North Carolina, differs only from the text of the bill now before the Senate in omitting that one section."

Mr. Conkling, of New York, said: "So that those who vote for the amendment vote that there may be an increase of the public debt, and those who vote against it that there shall not."

The roll-call having been concluded, the result was announced—as follows:

YEAS—Messrs. Allison, Bogy, Boreman, Cameron, Carpenter, Clayton, Dorsey, Ferry of Michigan, Goldthwaite, Gordon, Harvey, Hitchcock, Ingalls, Johnston, Lewis, Logan, McCreery, Merrimon, Morton, Oglesby, Patterson, Pease, Pratt, Ramsey, Robertson, Spencer, Tipton, West, and Windom—29.

NAYS—Messrs. Anthony, Bayard, Chandler, Conkling, Cragin, Davis, Fenton, Frelinghuysen, Hager, Hamilton of Maryland, Hamilton of Texas, Hamlin, Howe, Jones, Kelly, Morrill of Vermont, Sargent, Saulsbury. Schurz, Scott, Sherman, Stewart, Thurman, and Wadleigh—24.

ABSENT—Messrs. Alcorn, Boutwell, Brownlow, Buckingham, Conover, Cooper, Dennis, Edmunds, Ferry of Connecticut, Flanagan, Gilbert, Mitchell, Morrill of Maine, Norwood, Ransom, Sprague, Stevenson, Stockton, and Wright—19.

So the substitute of Mr. Merrimon, as modified, was agreed to.

The bill was reported to the Senate as amended.

The President *pro tempore:* "The Senate, as in Committee of the Whole, having made one amendment to the bill, the question now is on concurring in that amendment made as in Committee of the Whole."

Mr. Conkling: "This is inflation, utter and hurtful. Spasmodic relief may come from it, temporary and apparent prosperity may come from it, but it takes no heed of the future except to smoothe the way to degradation, disaster, and distress.

"Without necessity or even sore temptation to extenuate it, such a policy spurns the experience of all epochs, tramples on reason and right, and violates the pledged faith of the nation as attested by solemn and repeated acts of the American people in Congress assembled, by the avowals of every department of the Government, and by the declarations in national convention of the political party which chose most of us to the seats we hold, and chose also a Chief Magistrate bound by his word against every scheme and device of repudiation and dishonor. I mean so to vote that by my act the record of Congress shall not palter in a double sense, and shall not be stained by a trace of bad faith."

Mr. Stewart, of Nevada, said: "I can add nothing to this debate. I simply wanted to indicate that this was the beginning of a struggle in which there is nothing but disaster until we finally get back to money that has a real purchasing value, a real measure of value that the world recognizes. Until we get back to solvency and honesty the struggle will be severe. It looks as if it would be protracted, because after ten years' talk of gradual resumption we find ourselves taking a leap—not a step, but a leap—in the other direction, refusing to say that we mean any thing but expansion, refusing to say that we mean any thing but repudiation of our solemn obligation that we would redeem

the greenbacks at some time, refusing to say any thing, but starting off in the direction of repudiation; and it will be hard to come back gradually. You will come back with a crash; you will come back with such a crash as this country has never seen. You will come back through struggle. The day will be long remembered by the American people when this vote is cast, taking the step we are about to take."

Mr. Anthony, of Rhode Island, said: "Mr. President, I have taken no part in this discussion, and I do not propose to delay this vote a moment. I have voted steadily according to my judgment, which accords with the judgment and the interests of those whom I have the honor in part to represent.

"We are now about to do an act which has the quality of novelty. In a time of profound peace, with all the elements of prosperity and productiveness in as great abundance as they have ever been, with money exceptionally plentiful, with only that stagnation and hesitation of business which is caused by the apprehension of what we are now about to do, we are proposing to add largely to the paper currency of the country; and in doing that we refuse to take any, the slightest, measure looking to its present or its ultimate redemption or reduction at any time whatever. We are going against all the lessons of history, against all the teachings of experience, and against all the laws of political economy which have been evolved by the observation and the practice of life. I can only enter against it the protest of my vote."

Mr. Thurman, of Ohio, said: "Upon the measure itself I have a word to say. It simply means that no man of my age shall ever again see in this country that kind of currency which the framers of the Constitution intended should be the currency of the Union; which every sound writer on political economy the world over says is the only currency that defrauds no man; it means that so long as I shall live, and possibly long after I shall be laid in the grave, this people shall have nothing but an irredeemable paper currency with which to transact their business, that currency which has been well described as the most effective invention that ever the wit of man devised to fertilize the rich man's field at the expense of the poor man's brow. I will have nothing to do with it, sir."

The roll-call having been concluded, the result was announced—as follows:

YEAS—Messrs. Allison, Bogy, Boreman, Cameron, Carpenter, Clayton, Dorsey, Ferry of Michigan, Goldthwaite, Harvey, Hitchcock, Ingalls, Johnston, Lewis, Logan, McCreery, Merrimon, Morton, Norwood, Oglesby, Patterson, Pease, Pratt, Ramsey, Robertson, Spencer, Tipton, West, and Windom—29.

NAYS—Messrs. Anthony, Chandler, Conkling, Cooper, Cragin, Davis, Fenton, Frelinghuysen, Hager, Hamilton of Maryland, Hamilton of Texas, Hamlin, Howe, Jones, Kelly, Morrill of Vermont, Sargent, Saulsbury. Schurz, Scott, Sherman, Stewart, Thurman, and Wadleigh—24.

ABSENT — Messrs. Alcorn, Bayard, Boutwell, Brownlow, Buckingham, Conover, Dennis, Edmunds, Ferry of Connecticut, Flanagan, Gilbert, Gordon, Mitchell, Morrill of Maine, Ransom, Sprague, Stevenson, Stockton, and Wright—19.

So the bill was passed.

Mr. Wright: "I move to amend the title of the bill so as to make it read: "

A bill to fix the amount of United States notes and the circulation of national banks, and for other purposes.

The motion was agreed to.

On April 14th the bill passed the House by the following vote:

YEAS—Messrs. Albright, Arthur, Atkins, Averill, Barber, Barrere, Begole, Bell, Biery, Bland, Blount, Bowen, Bradley, Bright, Brown, Buckner, Bundy, Burchard, Burrows, Benjamin F. Butler, Roderick R. Butler, Caldwell, Cannon, Cason, Cessna, Amos Clark, Jr., John B. Clark, Jr., Clements, Clinton L. Cobb, Stephen A. Cobb, Coburn, Comingo, Conger, Cook, Corwin, Crittenden, Crossland, Crounse, Crutchfield, Curtis, Darrall, Davis, Dobbins, Donnan, Dunnell, Durham, Farwell, Field, Fort, Foster, Hagans, Harmer, Henry R. Harris, John T. Harris, Harrison, Hatcher, Havens, John B. Hawley, Hays, Gerry W. Hazelton, Hereford, Hodges, Houghton, Howe, Hubbell, Hunter, Hunton, Hurlbut, Hyde, Hynes, Jewett, Kasson, Killinger, Knapp, Lamison, Lewis, Loughridge, Lowe, Martin, Maynard, McCrary, Alexander S. McDill, James W. McDill, Mo-Junkin, McKee, McNulta, Milliken, Monroe, Morey, Myers, Neal, Nunn, Orr, Orth, Packard, Packer, Isaac C. Parker, Pelham, Phillips, Pratt, Purman, Rapier Ray, Richmond, Robbins, James W. Robinson, Ross, Rusk, Sawyer,· Milton Sayler, Sener, Shanks, Sheats, Sheldon, Sherwood, Lazarus D. Shoemaker, A. Kerr Smith, George L. Smith, Snyder, Southard, Sprague, Stanard, Standiford, Stowell, Christopher Y. Thomas, Tyner, Vance, Wallace, Jasper D. Ward. Wells, White, Whitehead, Whiteley, Charles G. Williams, William Williams, Wilshire, James Wilson, Jeremiah M. Wilson, Woodworth, and Pierce M. B. Young—140.

NAYS—Messrs. Adams, Albert, Banning, Barnum, Bass, Beck, Bromberg, Buffinton, Burleigh, Clayton, Clymer, Cotton, Cox, Creamer, Crooke, Danford, Dawes, DeWitt, Eames, Eden, Eldredge, Frye, Garfield, Gooch, Gunckell, Eugene Hale, Robert S. Hale, Hamilton, Hancock, Benjamin W. Harris, Hathorn, Joseph R. Hawley, Herndon, E. Rockwood Hoar, George F. Hoar, Holman, Hooper, Hoskins, Kelley, Kellogg, Kendall, Lamar, Lawson, Lofland, Lowndes, Magee, Marshall, MacDougal, McLean, Mellish, Merriam, Mills, Mitchell, Moore, Niblack, Niles, O'Neill, Page, Hosea W. Parker, Parsons, Pendleton, Perry, Phelps, Pierce, Pike, James H. Platt, Jr., Thomas C. Platt, Poland, Potter, Rainey, Randall, Read, Rice, Ellis H. Roberts, William R. Roberts, John G. Schumaker, Scofield, Isaac W. Scudder, Sessions, Small, Smart, H. Boardman Smith, John Q. Smith, Speer, Starkweather. St. John Stone, Strawbridge, Swann, Tremain, Waldron, Wheeler, Whitehouse, Wilber, Charles W. Willard, George Willard, John M. S. Williams, Willie, Ephraim K. Wilson, Wood, and Woodford—102.

NOT VOTING—Messrs. Archer, Ashe, Barry, Berry, Cain, Freeman Clarke, Crocker Duell, Elliott, Freeman, Giddings, Glover, John W. Hazelton, Hendee, Hersey, Lamport, Lansing, Lawrence, Leach, Luttrell, Lynch, Morrison, Negley, Nesmith, O'Brien, Ransier, James C. Robinson, Henry B. Sayler Henry J. Scudder, Sloan, Sloss, J. Ambler Smith, William A. Smith, Stephens, Storm, Strait, Sypher, Taylor, Charles R. Thomas, Thornburgh, Todd, Townsend, Waddell, Walls, Marcus L. Ward, William B. Williams, Wolfe, and John D. Young—48.

On April 22d the following veto message was received in the Senate from President Grant:

To the Senate of the United States:

Herewith I return Senate bill No. 617, entitled "An act to fix the amount of United States notes and the circulation of national banks, and for other purposes," without my approval.

In doing so, I must express my regret at not being able to give my assent to a measure which has received the sanction of a majority of the legislators chosen by the people to make laws for their guidance, and I have studiously sought to find sufficient arguments to justify such assent; but unsuccessfully.

Practically, it is a question whether the measure under discussion would give an additional dollar to the irredeemable paper currency of the country or not, and whether by requiring three-fourths of the reserves to be retained by the banks, and prohibiting interest to be received on the balance, it might not prove a contraction. But the fact cannot be concealed that theoretically the bill increases the paper circulation $100,000,000, less only the amount of reserves restrained from circulation by the provision of the second section. The measure has been supported on the theory that it would give increased circulation. It is a fair inference, therefore, that if, in practice, the measure should fail to create the abundance of circulation expected of it, the friends of the measure, particularly those out of Congress, would clamor for such inflation as would give the expected relief.

The theory, in my belief, is a departure from the true principles of finance, national interest, national obligations to creditors, congressional promises, party pledges—on the part of both political parties —and of personal views and promises made by me in every annual message sent to Congress, and in each inaugural address.

In my annual message to Congress in December, 1869, the following passages appear:

"Among the evils growing out of the rebellion and not yet referred to, is that of an irredeemable currency. It is an evil which I hope will receive your most earnest attention. It is a duty, and one of the highest duties, of government to secure to the citizen a medium of exchange of fixed, unvarying value. This implies a return to a specie basis, and no substitute for it can be devised. It should be commenced now, and reached at the earliest practicable moment consistent with a fair regard to the interest of the debtor class. Immediate resumption, if practicable, would not be desirable. It would compel the debtor class to pay beyond their contracts the premium on gold at the date of their purchase, and would bring bankruptcy and ruin to thousands. Fluctuations, however, in the paper value of the measure of all values (gold) is detrimental to the interests of trade. It makes the man of business an involuntary gambler; for in all sales where future payment is to be made both parties speculate as to what will be the value of the currency to be paid and received. I earnestly recommend to you, then, such legislation as will insure a gradual return to specie payments and put an immediate stop to fluctuations in the value of currency."

I still adhere to the views then expressed.

As early as December 4, 1865, the House of Representatives passed a resolution, by a vote of 144 yeas to 6 nays, concurring "in the views of the Secretary of the Treasury in relation to the necessity of a contraction of the currency, with a view to as early a resumption of specie payments as the business interests of the country will permit," and pledging "co-operative action to this end, as speedily as possible."

The first act passed by the Forty-first Congress on the 18th day of March, 1869, was as follows:

"An act to strengthen the public credit of the United States.

" *Be it enacted, etc.,* That in order to remove any doubt as to the purpose of the Government to discharge all its obligations to the public creditors, and to settle conflicting questions and interpretations of the law, by virtue of which such obligations have been contracted, it is hereby provided and declared that the faith of the United States is solemnly pledged to the payment in coin, or its equivalent, of all the obligations of the United States, and of all the interest-bearing obligations, except in cases where the law authorizing the issue of any such obligations has expressly provided that the same may be paid in lawful money, or in other currency than gold and silver, but none of the said interest-bearing obligations not already due shall be redeemed or paid before maturity, unless at such times as the United States notes shall be convertible into coin at the option of the holder, or unless at such time bonds of the United States bearing a lower rate of interest than the bonds to be redeemed can be sold at *par* in coin. And the United States also solemnly pledges its faith to make provision at the earliest practicable period for the redemption of the United States notes in coin."

This act still remains as a continuing pledge of the faith of the United States " to make provision at the earliest practicable moment for the redemption of the United States notes in coin."

A declaration contained in the act of June 30, 1864, created an obligation that the total amount of United States notes issued, or to be issued, should never exceed $400,000,000. The amount in actual circulation was actually reduced to $356,000,000, at which point Congress passed the act of February 4, 1868, suspending the further reduction of the currency. The forty-four millions have ever been regarded as a reserve, to be used only in case of emergency, such as has occurred on several occasions, and must occur when, from any cause, revenues suddenly fall below expenditures ; and such a reserve is necessary, because the fractional currency, amounting to fifty millions, is redeemable in legal tender on call.

It may be said that such a return of fractional currency for redemption is impossible. But let steps be taken for a return to a specie basis, and it will be found that silver will take the place of fractional currency as rapidly as it can be supplied, when the premium on gold reaches a sufficiently low point. With the amount of United States notes to be issued permanently fixed within proper limits, and the Treasury so strengthened as to be able to redeem them in coin on demand, it will then be safe to inaugurate a system of free banking with such provisions as to make compulsory redemption of the circulating notes of the banks in coin, or in United States notes, themselves redeemable and made equivalent to coin.

As a measure preparatory to free banking, or for placing the Government in a condition to redeem its notes in coin " at the earliest practicable moment," the revenues of the country should be increased so as to pay current expenses, provide for the sinking fund required by law, and also a surplus to be retained in the Treasury in gold.

I am not a believer in any artificial method of making paper-money equal to coin when the coin is not owned or held ready to redeem the promises to pay ; for paper-money is nothing more than promises to pay, and is valuable exactly in proportion to the amount of coin that it can be converted into. While coin is not used as a circulating medium, or the currency of the country is not convertible into it at par, it becomes an article of commerce as much as any other product. The surplus will seek a foreign market as will any other surplus. The balance of trade has nothing to do with the question. Duties on imports being required in coin, creates a limited demand for gold. About enough to satisfy that demand remains in the country. To increase this sup-

ply I see no way open but by the Government hoarding through the means above given, and possibly by requiring the national banks to aid.

It is claimed by the advocates of the measure herewith returned that there is an unequal distribution of the banking capital of the country. I was disposed to give great weight to this view of the question at first ; but, on reflection, it will be remembered that there still remains $4,000,000 of authorized bank-note circulation assigned to States having less than their quota not yet taken. In addition to this, the States having less than their quota of bank circulation have the option of twenty-five millions more to be taken from those States having more than their proportion. When this is all taken up, or when specie payments are fully restored, or are in rapid process of restoration, will be the time to consider the question of " more currency."

U. S. GRANT.

EXECUTIVE MANSION, WASHINGTON, *April 22,* 1874.

On April 28th the message was considered in the Senate.

The President *pro tempore:* " The bill (S. No. 617) to fix the amount of United States notes and the circulation of national banks, and for other purposes, is now before the Senate ; and the question is, Shall the bill pass, notwithstanding the objections of the President of the United States? upon which question the Constitution requires that the yeas and nays shall be taken. Senators in favor of passing the bill, notwithstanding the objections of the President of the United States, will, as their names are called, answer ' yea,' those opposed ' nay,' and the Secretary will call the roll."

The question being taken by yeas and nays resulted—yeas 34, nays 30 ; as follows :

YEAS—Messrs. Allison, Bogy, Boreman, Cameron, Carpenter, Clayton, Conover, Dennis, Dorsey, Ferry of Michigan, Goldthwaite, Gordon, Harvey, Hitchcock, Ingalls, Johnston, Lewis, Logan, McCreery, Merrimon, Mitchell, Norwood, Oglesby, Patterson, Pease, Pratt, Ramsey, Robertson, Spencer, Sprague, Tipton, West, Windom, and Wright—34.

NAYS—Messrs. Anthony, Bayard, Boutwell, Buckingham, Chandler, Conkling, Cragin, Davis, Edmunds, Fenton, Ferry of Connecticut, Flanagan, Frelinghuysen, Gilbert, Hager, Hamilton of Maryland, Hamilton of Texas, Hamlin, Howe, Jones, Kelly, Morrill of Vermont, Sargent, Scott, Sherman, Stevenson, Stewart, Stockton, Thurman, and Wadleigh—30.

ABSENT—Messrs. Alcorn, Brownlow, Cooper, Morrill of Maine, Morton, Ransom, Saulsbury, and Schurz—8.

The President *pro tempore:* " Upon this question the yeas are 34 and the nays are 30. Two-thirds of the Senators present not having voted in the affirmative, the Senate refuses to pass this bill."

An act was finally passed by Congress which increased the legal-tender notes $26,000,000, and abolished the reserve on bank-note circulation. Other sections were expected to produce an equal amount of contraction.

In the House, on December 18, 1873, Mr. Butler, of Massachusetts, from the Committee on the Judiciary, reported a bill to protect all citizens in their civil and legal rights. The bill provided that whoever, being a corporation or natural person and owner, or in charge of any public inn, or of any place of public amusement or entertainment for which a license from any legal authority is required, or of any line of stage-coaches, railroad, or other means of public carriage of passengers or freight, or of any cemetery or other benevolent institution, or any public school supported in whole or in part at public expense or by endowment for public use, should make any distinction as to admission or accommodation therein of any citizen of the United States because of race, color, or previous condition of servitude, should, on conviction thereof, be fined not less than $100 nor more than $5,000 for each offense; and the person or corporation so offending should be liable to the citizens thereby injured in damages to be recovered in an action of debt.

The second section provided that offenses under this act, and actions to recover damages, might be prosecuted before any territorial, district, or circuit court of the United States having jurisdiction of crimes at the place where the offense was charged to have been committed, as well as in the district where the parties might reside, as now provided by law.

Mr. Butler, of Massachusetts, said: "I desire briefly to explain to the House the thesis on which this bill proceeds. It is perhaps sufficiently explained in the title—'A bill to protect all citizens in their civil and legal rights.' The bill gives to no man any rights which he has not by law now, unless some hostile State statute has been enacted against him. He has no right by this bill except what every member on this floor and every man in this District has, and every man in New England has, and every man in England has by the common law and the civil law of the country. Let us examine it for a moment. Every man has a right to go into a public inn. Every man has a right to go into any place of public amusement or entertainment for which a license by legal authority is required. He has a right to ride in 'any line of stage-coaches, railroad, or other means of public carriage of passengers or freight,' and to be buried in any public cemetery; or he has a right in any 'other benevolent institutions or any public school supported in whole or in part at public expense or by endowment for public use'—that is, while he behaves himself and pays the requisite cost, charges, and fees; and he has a right of action now against every man who interferes with that right unless there is some state of hostile legislation.

"Now, then, we propose simply to give to whoever has this right taken away from him the means of overriding that state of hostile legislation, and of punishing the man who takes that right away from him. This is the whole of that bill. There is an amendment offered by the gentleman from Louisiana (Mr. Morey) which I am inclined to accept, or, at least, to permit a vote of the House to be taken upon

it; and that is applying the remedies and penalties under those transactions of the civil rights bill of 1866.

"Now, then, who shall say that this bill ought not to pass? What is the ground of possible opposition to it? Whether right or wrong, whether for good or ill, the result of the late war has been that every person born on the soil, or duly naturalized, is a citizen of the United States, entitled to all the rights, privileges, and immunities of a citizen. All legislation, therefore, that seeks to deprive a well-behaved citizen of the United States of any privilege or immunity to be enjoyed, and which he is entitled to enjoy in common with other citizens, is against constitutional enactment. But I am not unmindful of the great point to be taken against this bill by its opponents. They will say that it is an invasion of State rights; that the citizens ought to be left to regulate their own domestic affairs in their own way; that that is in accordance with the resolutions of 1798, and that it is in accordance with the well-understood doctrines upon which this confederation of States was founded.

"I know, I think, as well as I know any other portion of human knowledge, the length, breadth, and extent of State rights, and I am content to uphold them everywhere; but I am not content to uphold State wrongs, and there is the distinction I take. No State has a right to pass any law which inhibits the full enjoyment of all the rights she gives to her citizens by discriminating against any class of them provided they offend no law; and while from my teaching and from my belief I am an old State-rights Democrat, yet State rights are one thing and State wrongs are another, and State wrongs must yield to the Constitution of the United States.

"Why, sir, if a citizen of the United States, black or white, places his foot on the soil of a foreign country, say England, for instance, and is there deprived of his common rights by force, the whole power of the United States, the Army and Navy, can be brought to bear, and ought to be brought to bear, and will be brought to bear to protect him. 'I am an American citizen' is now a prouder cry than was 'I am a Roman citizen,' when it was uttered by the apostle Paul in his defense against unjust imprisonment. A greater power than Rome is behind him with men, money, and political power, and civil and religious liberty, and with the determination to enforce all in his behalf.

"Now, shall it be said that it is only on the soil of the United States where a citizen cannot have that power exerted in his behalf? All over the world he is entitled to the protection of that power, except where? Except if a State can inhibit it on the soil of the United States, and under the flag which he or his father or his children have shed their blood to defend and perpetuate as a symbol of the glory, the honor, and the power of his country. I say, sir, that, the Constitution having given equal rights to all men, no State, no man, no power, no potentate on earth, has a right to take away or abate one jot or tittle of those rights. Whether it was wise or not to have given these equal rights is a question which no man can answer to-day, because we are trying an entirely new experiment in government. Rome threw her laws all over the world, but kept her citizenship in Latium. She held by force her colonies and gave them her laws, but she held on to the birthright of citizenship, and it was sold only by corrupt emperors at a great price. We are trying the other experiment of a republic. Rome failed; we may fail; but ours is the other and correlative experiment. We take in nations or parts of nations; we take in peoples or parts of peoples wholly diverse from us; and instead of throwing our laws over them and holding them by force, we have always given to them equal rights of citizenship with us and rights of self-government; and not only the right of governing themselves, but of assisting in governing us. This great experiment, for the first time tried in the history of the world, has not yet been concluded so that any man can say with certainty that it is the very summit of human wisdom. Certain it is, however, that it is the best emanation of human wisdom yet shown in government, with the best results, and it is going forward as the missionary idea of liberty and equality in the world with the high hopes of every patriot and every well-wisher of his country for its success. It is incumbent upon us to do every thing we may that that success shall be achieved, that no prejudice against race or color shall prevail for a moment in any quarter of the country. When a man is a citizen he springs up to the high plane of citizenship; and standing upon that plane he is the equal of every other citizen, whatever may have been his former condition of nationality, race, or color, and he must have all his rights secured to him inviolate. This is the ground on which we present this bill to the House and the country, and we insist that whatever there may have been in State rights in olden times, there is now no right in any State to baffle or abate one jot or tittle any constitutional right of equality in the civil and legal privileges of the meanest citizen of the republic."

Mr. Beck, of Kentucky, said: "Mr. Speaker, I do not believe that any man on this side of the House opposes this bill because he wants the negro race oppressed, because he desires to see them deprived of education or of any other right guaranteed to them by the Constitution and laws. But many of us do object, and I for one, to the usurpation by Congress of authority over matters that belong exclusively to the States, prescribing severe penalties to be enforced by the courts of the United States; to enforce laws which are violative, as I believe, of the rights of the States and the people thereof. We are approaching consolidation fast enough. We are drifting into centralism step by step so rapidly and steadily that it will not be many years before the States will occupy the same relation to the General Government that the counties bear to the States. Ten years ago that suggestion met with ridicule only from men of all parties.

"I object further to this bill, because this coercive legislation, which seeks to put the colored population of the States of the South into the common schools with the white children, will not only be no advantage to them, but will be a positive injury, and will only be available when men who are seeking to drive party politics at the point of the bayonet will make disturbances there, and will seek to enforce martial law because the behests of Congress are not obeyed, and thus carry the elections at the point of the bayonet for the man they want to elect against the popular will.

"I object to this bill because the Constitution of the United States and all its amendments are violated by its provisions. This question has been carefully examined by the Supreme Court of the United States; and that tribunal, as I read the decision, has decided in the late case from New Orleans, that these rights pertaining to the rights of corporations, and inferentially to common schools, are not embraced in the powers confided to Congress by the constitutional amendments. Under the authority to enforce the amendments by appropriate legislation, these are not rights guaranteed by them, or rights about which Congress has authority to legislate.

"Massachusetts, to-day, does not allow a man to vote in the State unless he can read the constitution in the English language and write his name. If the people of Kentucky, in the exercise of their constitutional authority, should do as Massachusetts has done—should amend their constitution by incorporating such a proposition—not one negro in a hundred in the State of Kentucky could go to the polls and vote. We have not done so; we have not thought of doing it, because we have endeavored, in good faith, to give those negroes, ignorant as they are, the rights conferred upon them by the fifteenth amendment. Under such a provision ninety-nine out of every hundred of the negroes, who were slaves in my State seven years ago, would be excluded from the polls. We could, if we saw fit, prescribe other qualifications for the exercise of suffrage or the qualification for office.

"The Supreme Court of the United States, as I before remarked, very recently considered these questions in the slaughter-house cases; it carefully examined the bearings of the constitutional amendments on this subject. The fourteenth amendment, as is well known, did not allow to colored men the right to vote, and that was controlled by State laws, notwithstanding all the rights conferred by former amendments, and therefore it was necessary to pass the fifteenth amendment. The fourteenth amendment provides as follows:

SECTION 1. All persons born or naturalized in the United States, and subject to the jurisdiction thereof, are citizens of the United States and of the State wherein they reside. No State shall make or enforce any law which shall abridge the privileges or immunities of citizens of the United States; nor shall any State deprive any person of life, liberty, or property, without due process of law; nor deny to any person within its jurisdiction the equal protection of the laws.

"Now, what does the court say in commenting upon the amendment?

"Let me read a few paragraphs from the opinion:

The next observation is more important in view of the arguments of counsel in the present case. It is that the distinction betweeen citizenship of the United States and citizenship of a State is clearly recognized and established. Not only may a man be a citizen of the United States without being a citizen of a State, but an important element is necessary to convert the former into the latter. He must reside within the State to make him a citizen of it, but it is only necessary that he should be born or naturalized in the United States to be a citizen of the Union.

It is quite clear, then, that there is a citizenship of the United States and a citizenship of a State which are distinct from each other, and which depend upon different characteristics or circumstances in the individual.

We think this distinction and its explicit recognition in this amendment of great weight in this argument, because the next paragraph of this same section, which is the one mainly relied on by the plaintiffs in error, speaks only of privileges and immunities of citizens of the United States, and does not speak of those of citizens of the several States. The argument, however, in favor of the plaintiffs rests wholly on the assumption that the citizenship is the same, and the privileges and immunities guaranteed by the clause are the same.

The language is, "No State shall make or enforce any law which shall abridge the privileges or immunities of citizens of *the United States.*" It is a little remarkable, if this clause was intended as a protection to the citizen of a State against the legislative power of his own State, that the term "citizen of the State" should be left out when it is so carefully used, and used in contradistinction to "citizens of the United States," in the very sentence which precedes it. It is too clear for argument that the change in phraseology was adopted understandingly and with a purpose.

Of the privileges and immunities of the citizen of the United States, and of the privileges and immunities of the citizens of the State, and what they respectively are, we will presently consider; but we wish to state here that it is only the former which are placed by this clause under the protection of the Federal Constitution, and that the latter, whatever they may be, are not intended to have any additional protection by this paragraph of the amendment. If, then, there is a difference between the privileges and immunities belonging to a citizen of the United States as such, and those belonging to the citizen of the State as such, the latter must rest for their security and protection where they have heretofore rested, for they are not embraced by this paragraph of the amendment. * * * But when, as in the case before us, these consequences are so serious, so far-reaching and pervading, so great a departure from the structure and spirit of our institutions; when the effect is to fetter and degrade the State governments by subjecting them to the control of Congress in the exercise of powers, heretofore universally conceded to them, of the most ordinary and fundamental character; when, in fact, it radically changes the whole theory of the relations of the State and Federal Governments to each other and of both these governments to the people, the argument has a force that is irresistible, in the absence of language which expresses such a purpose too clearly to admit of doubt.

"The whole spirit and bearing of the decision is against the constitutionality of the law now proposed, matters of regulation as to education, local corporations, and their rights and privileges, being subjects which bear only on the individual as a citizen of the State, and not as a citizen of the United States.

"But it is now proposed to legislate in Congress as to matters such as the regulation of corporations, inns, endowed seminaries of learning, and how school funds shall be distributed, and to compel all children, white or black, to attend school together. That is a matter for State legislation, and Congress has no right to interfere with it. Surely, sir, the people could establish schools in any of the States which none but white females should attend or that none but white males should attend, and might do the same for colored males and females. That would not at all interfere with the colored population having their proportion of the taxes collected to be expended in the education of colored children. We in Kentucky have a right, I say, to arrange separate schools for them, wherein they will get their equal rights. I suppose no man will contend that in any school in my State, established expressly for the education of females, any male negro shall have the right to force himself where no white male can go. The principle may be extended even that far hereafter if Congress enters upon this character of legislation. The effect of trying to force the colored children among the whites will not be of any benefit to the negro, but, on the contrary, will be of positive injury. Men make a mistake when they think coercion is the appropriate and legitimate province of legislation. Something is due even to the prejudices of men; something is due to the views which State Legislatures may entertain; and whenever Congress undertakes to take control of the States and to deprive them of power, either from spite or any other cause, it is acting unwisely, because it tends to destroy whatever is valuable in the common-school system by making people loathe and despise instead of love and cherish it.

"When you undertake, by your legislation here, to force white and black, male and female, into the same school, the men who have wealth will not send their children; but the poor man will be compelled to send his or let them grow up in ignorance and vice, which will be the alternative chosen in most instances. You will force, in all the States where there is a large colored population, all the skilled industry of other parts of the world away from us, because men who are poor and desire to come among us will not, when they see their richer white neighbors sending their children to private schools or to other States, where they can send their children nowhere but to be with the colored children. You will destroy the public schools altogether, and will not benefit the colored people by doing it. If there was no question as to your power—if the Constitution of the United States gave to you the authority—it would be impolitic and unwise to force it to that extent. It is this question in regard to schools that I look at with the most serious apprehension, though the other provisions of the bill are equally vicious in principle. Does any gentleman upon this floor think that any intelligent man representing a Southern State wants to keep the colored people of the South in ignorance? If he does he is grievously mistaken.

"No, sir; if he had no higher motive than his own interest, he would endeavor by every means in his power to improve them mentally and morally; and the States are rapidly developing means to do so, as rapidly as can be expected. They are straining every nerve to furnish them the means of education, to make them industrious, to make them honest, to make them understand the great duties imposed on them by the amendments to the Constitution in their altered condition. No matter what may have been his views of the policy of those changes, now that they are the fundamental law, no man desires to restore the former state of things. Every man is desirous of seeing that the interests of the colored people are promoted; that their intelligence shall be increased; and that all the elements which will make them more virtuous citizens than they were shall be given them in abundance.

"Why, sir, if Congress takes this step, it is the entering wedge to take absolute control over education everywhere. Your courts will have to watch the States, and will have to punish the wrongs done, and the colored people will be driven on and on as demagogues arise wanting their votes, and they will be brought here to hold conventions and make demands of Congress, until there is no telling where the strife will end.

"I suppose there are gentlemen on this floor who would arrest, imprison, and fine a young woman in any State of the South if she were to refuse to marry a negro man on account of color, race, or previous condition of servitude, in the event of his making her a proposal of marriage, and her refusing on that ground. That would be depriving him of a right he had under the amendment, and Congress would be asked to take it up, and say, 'This insolent white woman must be taught to know that it is a misdemeanor to deny a man marriage because of race, color, or previous condition of servitude;' and Congress will be urged to say after a while that that sort of thing must be put a stop to, and your conventions of colored men will come here asking you to enforce that right."

Mr. Rainey, of South Carolina, said: "Mr. Speaker, I did not expect to participate in this debate at this early period; and I would have preferred to wait until I should have had a full exposition of the opinions entertained by the other side of the House. I know, sir, that gentlemen on the other side have professed a great deal of friendship for the race to which I belong; and in the last presidential election they pledged themselves that they would accord to the negroes of this country all the rights that were given to other citizens. I am somewhat surprised to perceive that on this occasion, when the demand is made upon Congress by the people to guarantee those rights to a race heretofore oppressed, we should find gentlemen on the other side taking another view of the case from that which they professed in the past. The gentleman from Kentucky (Mr. Beck) has taken a legal view of this question, and he is undoubtedly capable of taking that view. I am not a lawyer, and consequently I cannot take a legal view of this matter, or perhaps I cannot view it through the same optics that he does. I view it in the light of the Constitution—in the light of the amendments that have been made to that Constitution; I view it in the light of humanity; I view it in the light of the progress and civilization which are now rapidly marching over this country. We, sirs, would not ask of this Congress as a people that they should legislate for us specifically as a class if we could only have those rights which this bill is designed to give us without this enactment. I can very well understand the opposition to this measure by gentlemen on the other side of the House, and especially of those who come from the South. They have a feeling against the negro in this country that I suppose will never die out. They have an antipathy against that race of people, because of their loyalty to this Government, and because at the very time when they were needed to show their manhood and valor they came forward in defense of the flag of the country and assisted in crushing out the rebellion. They, sir, would not give to the colored man the right to vote or the right to enjoy any of these immunities which are enjoyed by other citizens, if it had a tendency to make them feel their manhood and elevate them above the ordinary way of life. So long as he makes himself content with ordinary gifts, why, it is all well; but when he aspires to be a man, when he seeks to have the rights accorded him that other citizens of the country enjoy, then he is asking too much, and such gentlemen as the gentleman from Kentucky are not willing to grant it."

Mr. Stephens, of Georgia, said: "I am opposed to the passage of this measure, or any one kindred to it, even if any of the rights proposed to be secured by it were properly just in themselves, because of the want of the necessary power, under the Constitution, on the part of Congress to apply the appropriate remedy by the enactment of any such law as this bill proposes. I presume that it will not be assuming too much to take it for granted that it will be admitted by every member of the House that the powers of Congress are specific as well as limited, and that all the powers which Congress can, legislatively or otherwise, rightfully exercise are held by delegation from the people of the several States of the Union. Where, then, in the Constitution is to be found the power which authorizes the passage of this measure? The power under which it is claimed, as I understand it, is derived chiefly from the first and fifth sections of the fourteenth article of amendment. It is true, in this connection, I have frequently seen reference made, also, to the fifteenth article of amendment. To see how far the power is sustained by the claim, we must therefore look into the purport and meaning of both these articles of amendment as they stand, without any consideration at this time as to their history, or how they became incorporated into the organic law of the Union.

"The two sections of the fourteenth article referred to are in the following words:

ARTICLE XIV. *Section* 1. All persons born or naturalized in the United States, and subject to the jurisdiction thereof, are citizens of the United States and of the State wherein they reside. No State shall make or enforce any law which shall abridge the privileges or immunities of citizens of the United States; nor shall any State deprive any person of life, liberty, or property, without due process of law; nor deny to any person within its jurisdiction the equal protection of the laws. * * *

Sec. 5. The Congress shall have power to enforce, by appropriate legislation, the provisions of this article.

"Sections 2, 3, and 4 of this article embrace a number of different subjects, not at all germane to the one under consideration.

"The fifteenth article is in the following words:

ARTICLE XV. *Section* 1. The right of the citizens of the United States to vote shall not be denied or abridged by the United States, or by any State, on account of race, color, or previous condition of servitude.

Sec. 2. The Congress shall have power to enforce this article by appropriate legislation.

"The reading of the fifteenth amendment shows it has no application whatever to the subject. Its main object was to deny to both Congress and the States the exercise of a certain power.

"And as to the first section of the fourteenth, all I have to say here is that it very clearly appears from its words that it has but two objects. These were, first, to declare the colored race to be citizens of the United States, and of the States, respectively, in which they reside; and, secondly, to prohibit the States, severally, from denying to the class of citizens, so declared, the same privileges, immunities, and civil rights which were secured to the citizens of the several States, respectively, and of the United States, by the Constitution as it stood before citizenship to the colored race was declared by this amendment.

"As to the fifth section of the fourteenth

amendment and the second section of the fifteenth, so far as they relate to the subject-matter of the body of each amendment, respectively, their clear meaning and import are to provide security to the colored race in the enjoyment of the privileges, immunities, and rights so declared, in the same way and in like manner as was provided for the security of like privileges, immunities, and rights of the citizens of the several States, respectively, by the Constitution before this amendment, and that no other remedy for a violation of the prohibitions on State action in either of these amendments was contemplated than such as existed for like violations of like prohibitions anterior to the amendments. The exercise of no new power was conferred by either of these new amendments. The denial of the exercise of any number of powers by the United States, severally, does not, most certainly, confer its exercise upon the Congress of the States. Neither of these amendments confers, bestows, or even declares, any rights at all to citizens of the United States, or to any class whatever. Upon the colored race they neither confer, bestow, nor declare civil rights of any character; not even the right of franchise. They only forbid the States from discriminating in their laws against the colored race in the bestowment of such rights as they may severally deem best to bestow upon their own citizens. Whatever rights they grant to other citizens shall not be denied to the colored race as a class. This is the whole of the matter. The question then is, how can Congress enforce a prohibition of the exercise of these powers by a State? Most assuredly in the same way they enforced or provided for violations of like prohibitions anterior to these amendments.

"The proper remedies before were, and now are, nothing but the judgments of courts, to be rendered in such way as Congress might provide, declaring any State acts in violation of the prohibitions to be null and of no effect, because of their being in violation of this covenant between the States as set forth in the Constitution of the United States. No new power over this matter of a different nature or character from that previously delegated over like subjects was intended to be conferred by the concluding sections of either the fourteenth or fifteenth article of amendment. No such thing as the tremendous power of exercising general municipal as well as criminal legislation over the people of the several States could have been dreamed of by the proposers of these amendments. Such a construction would entirely upset the whole fabric of the Government, the maintenance of which in its integrity was the avowed object of the war. If the construction upon which this bill rests be a true construction, then you have power to prosecute and punish all those in Georgia and other States, numbering not only thousands but hundreds of thousands, who are seeking to avail themselves of the benefit of relief acts passed by their States, which acts the Supreme Court of the United States have declared, in the way properly provided by Congress, to be in violation of that clause of the Constitution prohibiting the States, severally, from passing any law impairing the obligation of contracts. ' The prohibition against the States in the one case is the same in words and effect as in the other. To what monstrous consequences would not such a construction lead ? It is my purpose, sir, to show, beyond the power of refutation, the correctness of all these propositions or positions.

" First, then, that the chief object of the first and fifth sections of the fourteenth amendment was, as stated, to make citizens of this class of persons there can be no doubt, or if there was any doubt before, it seems that there ought to be none any longer; for the Supreme Court, in the case before cited, said in direct terms of these parts of the fourteenth amendment just quoted, 'that its main object was to establish citizenship of the negro can admit of no doubt.' So that proposition may rest there.

" Next, as to the correctness of the other propositions, I prefer to rely upon the same high authority rather than to indulge in any process of reasoning myself. I therefore shall cite extensively from the same decision in sustainment of all the positions taken.

" In speaking of that clause of the Constitution as it stood before this amendment, in reference to the privileges and immunities of citizens of the several States secured by it, this court distinctly assert:

Its sole purpose was to declare to the several States that, whatever those rights, as you grant or establish them to your own citizens, or as you limit or qualify, or impose restrictions on their exercise, the same, neither more nor less, shall be the measure of the rights of citizens of other States within your jurisdiction.

" And in relation to the powers of Congress to enforce such rights under the Constitution, as it stood before, by municipal laws operating over the people of the States, the court further assert:

It would be the vainest show of learning to attempt to prove, by citations of authority, that up to the adoption of the recent amendments, no claim or pretense was set up that those rights depended on the Federal Government for their existence or protection, beyond the very few express limitations which the Federal Constitution imposed upon the States—such, for instance, as the prohibition against ex post facto laws, bills of attainder, and laws impairing the obligation of contracts. But, with the exception of these and a few other restrictions, the entire domain of the privileges and immunities of citizens of the States, as above defined, lay within the constitutional and legislative power of the States, and without that of the Federal Government.

" The court, then, in reference to the powers of Congress to pass municipal laws as a proper remedy against the exercise of powers prohibited to the States by the Constitution, with great point and potency put the question:

Was it the purpose of the fourteenth amendment, by the simple declaration that no State should make or enforce any law which shall abridge the privileges and immunities of *citizens of the United States*, to transfer the security and protection of all the civil rights which we have mentioned from the States to the Federal Government ? And where it is declared that Congress shall have power to enforce that article, was it intended to bring within the power of Congress the entire domain of civil rights heretofore belonging exclusively to the States ?

" They answer it, too, with equal emphasis and power, in these words :

All this and more must follow if the proposition of the plaintiffs in error be sound. For not only are these rights subject to the control of Congress whenever, in its discretion, any of them are supposed to be abridged by State legislation, but that body may also pass laws in advance, limiting and restricting the exercise of legislative power by the States in their most ordinary and usual functions, as in its judgment it may think proper on all such subjects. And still further, such a construction, followed by the reversal of the judgments of the Supreme Court of Louisiana in these cases, would constitute this court a perpetual censor upon all legislation of the States on the civil rights of their own citizens, with authority to nullify such as it did not approve as consistent with these rights as they existed at the time of the adoption of this amendment.

" Further on, in the same decision, in speaking of the fourteenth and fifteenth amendments and the heat and excitement of popular sentiment when they were before the people, the court gives forth certain other most important utterances on this subject, to which I call special attention. They say :

Under the pressure of all the excited feeling growing out of the war, our statesmen have still believed that the existence of the States, with powers for domestic and local government, including the regulation of civil rights—the rights of person and of property—was essential to the perfect working of our complex form of government, though they have thought proper to impose additional limitations on the States and to confer additional power on that of the nation.

"Additional prohibitions imposed on the States severally and additional powers conferred on the General Government, but none of a new nature or character. It is here judicially affirmed that all the essential features of our original complex Federal system are still preserved. In substance it amounts to this, that these amendments (whether rightfully or wrongfully incorporated into the Constitution) do not change the nature and character of the Government. Soul-inspiring words are these! So long as an incorruptible judiciary shall sustain the pillars of the Constitution in their stately position, and the grand old Federal arch unbroken in any of its parts, no serious apprehension need be indulged in as to our future safety from the batteries of legislative demolition or reconstruction of the temple of our liberties, if the people of the several States shall continue equally true to themselves. The United States still exist as a Federal republic, and are not yet merged into a centralized empire. It is true the court here speaks of the States in union as a nation.

This is also eminently correct as the word was here doubtless intended to be used. The United States is indeed, and ever has been, a nation, and a nation of the highest type. It is a Federal republic — a republic of republics. Hence, the armorial motto stamped upon the great seal, as it was in the beginning: '*E pluribus unum*'—a nation of nations!

"But to proceed. I wish to call special attention to another decision, made by the same tribunal at the same term (*see* 16 Wallace, 138, 139), giving additional light upon the true construction of the fourteenth amendment, which very clearly shows that the power claimed under it, even as it stands, cannot justify the passage of this bill, and that the rights embraced within its provisions are not of that character which can be rightfully legislated for by congressional enactment. I quote extensively, for nothing I could say could impart either force to the argument or clearness to its conclusion. They say:

In regard to that amendment (the fourteenth) counsel for the plaintiff in this court truly says that there are certain privileges and immunities which belong to a citizen of the United States as such, otherwise it would be nonsense for the fourteenth amendment to prohibit a State from abridging them; and he proceeds to argue that admission to the bar of a State of a person who possesses the requisite learning and character is one of those which a State may not deny.

In this latter proposition we are not able to concur with counsel. We agree with him that there are privileges and immunities belonging to citizens of the United States in that relation and character, and that it is these and these alone which a State is forbidden to abridge. But the right to admission to practice in the courts of a State is not one of them. This right in no sense depends on citizenship of the United States. It has not, so far as we know, ever been made in any State, or in any case, to depend on citizenship at all. Certainly many prominent and distinguished lawyers have been admitted to practice both in the State and Federal courts who were not citizens of the United States or any State. But on whatever basis this right may be placed, so far as it can have any relation to citizenship at all, it would seem that, as to the courts of a State, it would relate to citizenship of the State; and as to Federal courts, it would relate to citizenship of the United States.

The opinion just delivered in the Slaughter-house cases (16 Wallace, page 36) renders elaborate argument in the present case unnecessary; for, unless we are wholly and radically mistaken in the principles on which those cases are decided, the right to control and regulate the granting of license to practise law in the courts of a State is one of those powers which are not transferred for its protection to the Federal Government, and its exercise is in no manner governed or controlled by citizenship of the United States in the party seeking such license.

It is unnecessary to repeat the argument on which the judgment in those cases is founded. It is sufficient to say they are conclusive of the present case.

"If it is within the reserved powers of a State to deny the right of admission to the bar to any who may be held to be her citizens, or citizens of the United States, is it not much more one of her reserved rights to say who may, or who may not, be admitted into her public schools or other institutions?

"Here I leave the question, so far as our powers over the subject-matter are concerned. I consider it as settled by the highest judicial tribunal of the country, so far as that tribunal is competent to settle any question of constitutional law.

"But, in the second place, among the reasons for my opposition to this bill, I oppose it because of its inexpediency. Even if the power were, without question or doubt, vested in Congress to pass municipal regulations of this sort to operate over the people of the several States of the Union, I think it would be exceedingly injudicious and unwise to exercise it. Better leave all such matters to the States. In point of fact, I do not believe the colored people of Georgia have any desire for mixed schools, and very little, indeed, for mixed churches, as contemplated by this measure. The tendency on their part, throughout the State, in all their religious denominations, except the Catholic, is to separate from the whites in church association and organization. In all instances, within my knowledge, the whites have been perfectly willing, and even solicitous, for them to remain and worship in the same houses and before the same altars; but they preferred to go by themselves. So with the schools. They have no desire or wish for mixed schools composed of white and colored children. All they want is their right and just participation in the common-school fund in schools of their own. This they now have in Georgia. They also have a university for themselves at Atlanta, aided by the State; as the State University for whites is in like manner aided by the State. They have no desire for any thing partaking of the character of social rights; and if the people, colored and white, in the several Southern States, shall be left to themselves to work out their own destiny under the present system, subject alone to the controlling law of justice, as before stated, without external interference of any sort, it will, in my judgment, be infinitely better for both races. Reciprocal duties will soon, of themselves, bring about as much harmony and concord as are usually found in any State or country.

"Interference by the Federal Government, even if the power were clear and indisputable, would be against the very genius and entire spirit of our whole system. If there is one truth which stands out prominently above all others in the history of these States, it is that the germinal and seminal principle of American constitutional liberty is the absolute, unrestricted right of State self-government in all purely internal municipal affairs.

"Let us not do by the passage of this bill what our highest judicial tribunal has said we have no rightful power to do. If you who call yourselves Republicans shall, in obedience to what you consider a party behest, pass it in the vain expectation that the republican principles of the old and true Jeffersonian school are dead, be assured you are indulging a fatal delusion.

The old Jeffersonian, democratic, republican principles are not dead, and will never die so long as a true devotee of liberty lives. They may be buried for a period, as Magna Charta was trodden under foot in England for more than half a century; but these principles will come up with renewed energy, as did those of Magna Charta, and that, too, at no distant day. Old Jeffersonian, democratic, republican principles dead, indeed! When the tides of ocean cease to ebb and flow, when the winds of heaven are hushed into perpetual silence, when the clouds no longer thunder, when earth's electric bolts are no longer felt or heard, when her internal fires go out, then, and not before, will these principles cease to live; then and not before will these principles cease to animate and move the liberty-loving masses of this country."

Mr. Elliott, of South Carolina, said: "While I am sincerely grateful for this high mark of courtesy that has been accorded to me by this House, it is a matter of regret to me that it is necessary at this day that I should rise in the presence of an American Congress to advocate a bill which simply asserts equal rights and equal public privileges for all classes of American citizens. I regret, sir, that the dark hue of my skin may lend a color to the imputation that I am controlled by motives personal to myself in my advocacy of this great measure of national justice. Sir, the motive that impels me is restricted by no such narrow boundary, but is as broad as your Constitution. I advocate it, sir, because it is right. The bill, however, not only appeals to your justice, but it demands a response from your gratitude.

"The honorable gentleman from Kentucky, always swift to sustain the failing and dishonored cause of proscription, rushes forward and flaunts in our faces the decision of the Supreme Court of the United States in the Slaughter-house cases, and in that act he has been willingly aided by the gentleman from Georgia. Hitherto, in the contests which have marked the progress of the course of equal civil rights, our opponents have appealed sometimes to custom, sometimes to prejudice, more often to pride of race, but they have never sought to shield themselves behind the Supreme Court. But now, for the first time, we are told that we are barred by a decision of that court, from which there is no appeal. If this be true, we must stay our hands. The cause of equal civil rights must pause at the command of a power whose edicts must be obeyed till the fundamental law of our country is changed.

"Mr. Speaker, I venture to say here in the presence of the gentleman from Kentucky, and the gentleman from Georgia, and in the presence of the whole country, that there is not a line or word, not a thought or dictum even, in the decision of the Supreme Court in the great Slaughter-house cases which casts a shadow of doubt on the right of Congress to pass the pending bill, or to adopt such other legislation

as it may judge proper and necessary to secure perfect equality before the law to every citizen of the republic.' Sir, I protest against the dishonor now cast upon our Supreme Court by both the gentleman from Kentucky and the gentleman from Georgia. In other days, when the whole country was bowing beneath the yoke of slavery, when press, pulpit, platform, Congress, and courts, felt the fatal power of the slave oligarchy, I remember a decision of that court which no American now reads without shame and humiliation. But those days are past. The Supreme Court of to-day is a tribunal as true to freedom as any department of this Government, and I am honored with the opportunity of repelling a deep disgrace which the gentleman from Kentucky, backed and sustained as he is by the gentleman from Georgia, seeks to put upon it.

"What were these Slaughter-house cases? The gentleman should be aware that a decision of any court should be examined in the light of the exact question which is brought before it for decision. That is all that gives authority to any decision.

"The State of Louisiana, by act of her Legislature, had conferred on certain persons the exclusive right to maintain stock-landings and slaughter-houses within the city of New Orleans, or the parishes of Orleans, Jefferson, and Saint Bernard, in that State. The corporation which was thereby chartered was invested with the sole and exclusive privilege of conducting and carrying on the live-stock-landing and slaughter-house business within the limits designated.

"The Supreme Court of Louisiana sustained the validity of the act conferring these exclusive privileges, and the plaintiffs in error brought the case before the Supreme Court of the United States for review. The plaintiffs in error contended that the act in question was void, because, first, it established a monopoly which was in derogation of common right and in contravention of the common law; and, second, that the grant of such exclusive privileges was in violation of the thirteenth and fourteenth amendments of the Constitution of the United States.

"It thus appears from a simple statement of the case that the question which was before the court was not whether a State law which denied to a particular portion of her citizens the rights conferred on her citizens generally, on account of race, color, or previous condition of servitude, was unconstitutional because in conflict with the recent amendments, but whether an act which conferred on certain citizens exclusive privileges for police purposes was in conflict therewith, because imposing an involuntary servitude forbidden by the thirteenth amendment, or abridging the rights and immunities of citizens of the United States, or denying the equal protection of the laws, prohibited by the fourteenth amendment.

"On the part of the defendants in error it

was maintained that the act was the exercise of the ordinary and unquestionable power of the State to make regulation for the health and comfort of society—the exercise of the police power of the State, defined by Chancellor Kent to be 'the right to interdict unwholesome trades, slaughter-houses, operations offensive to the senses, the deposit of powder, the application of steam-power to propel cars, the building with combustible materials, and the burial of the dead in the midst of dense masses of population, on the general and rational principle that every person ought so to use his own property as not to injure his neighbors, and that private interests must be made subservient to the general interests of the community.'

"The decision of the Supreme Court is to be found in the 16th volume of Wallace's Reports, and was delivered by Associate-Justice Miller. The court hold, first, the act in question is a legitimate and warrantable exercise of the police power of the State in regulating the business of stock-landing and slaughtering in the city of New Orleans and the territory immediately contiguous. Having held this, the court proceed to discuss the question whether the conferring of exclusive privileges, such as those conferred by the act in question, is the imposing of an involuntary servitude, the abridging of the rights and immunities of citizens of the United States, or the denial to any person within the jurisdiction of the State of the equal protection of the laws.

"That the act is not the imposition of an involuntary servitude the court hold to be clear, and they next proceed to examine the remaining questions arising under the fourteenth amendment. Upon this question the court hold that the leading and comprehensive purpose of the thirteenth, fourteenth, and fifteenth amendments was to secure the complete freedom of the race which, by the events of the war, had been wrested from the unwilling grasp of their owners. I know no finer or more just picture, albeit painted in the neutral tints of true judicial impartiality, of the motives and events which led to these amendments. Has the gentleman from Kentucky read these passages which I now quote? Or has the gentleman from Georgia considered well the force of the language therein used? Say the court, on page 70:

The process of restoring to their proper relations with the Federal Government and with the other States those which had sided with the rebellion, undertaken under the proclamation of President Johnson in 1865, and before the assembling of Congress, developed the fact that, notwithstanding the formal recognition by those States of the abolition of slavery, the condition of the slave race would, without further protection of the Federal Government, be almost as bad as it was before. Among the first acts of legislation adopted by several of the States in the legislative bodies which claimed to be in their normal relations with the Federal Government, were laws which imposed upon the colored race onerous disabilities and burdens, and curtailed their rights in the pursuit of life, liberty, and property to such an extent that their freedom was of little

value, while they had lost the protection which they had received from their former owners from motives both of interest and humanity.

They were in some States forbidden to appear in the towns in any other character than menial servants. They were required to reside on and cultivate the soil, without the right to purchase or own it. They were excluded from any occupations of gain, and were not permitted to give testimony in the courts in any case where a white man was a party. It was said that their lives were at the mercy of bad men, either because the laws for their protection were insufficient or were not enforced.

These circumstances, whatever of falsehood or misconception may have been mingled with their presentation, forced upon the statesmen who had conducted the Federal Government in safety through the crisis of the rebellion, and who supposed that by the thirteenth article of amendment they had secured the result of their labors, the conviction that something more was necessary in the way of constitutional protection to the unfortunate race who had suffered so much. They accordingly passed through Congress the proposition for the fourteenth amendment, and they declined to treat as restored to their full a a ion in the government of the Union the States which had been in insurrection until they ratified that article by a formal vote of their legislative bodies.

Before we proceed to examine more critically the provisions of this amendment, on which the plaintiffs in error rely, let us complete and dismiss the history of the recent amendments, as that history relates to the general purpose which pervades them all. A few years' experience satisfied the thoughtful men who had been the authors of the other two amendments that, notwithstanding the restraints of those articles on the States and the laws passed under the additional powers granted to Congress, these were inadequate for the protection of life, liberty, and property, without which freedom to the slave was no boon. They were in all those States denied the right of suffrage. The laws were administered by the white man alone. It was urged that a race of men distinctively marked as was the negro, living in the midst of another and dominant race, could never be fully secured in their person and their property without the right of suffrage.

Hence the fifteenth amendment, which declares that "the right of a citizen of the United States to vote shall not be denied or abridged by any State on account of race, color, or previous condition of servitude." The negro having, by the fourteenth amendment, been declared to be a citizen of the United States, is thus made a voter in every State of the Union.

We repeat, then, in the light of this recapitulation of events, almost too recent to be called history, but which are familiar to us all, and on the most casual examination of the language of these amendments, no one can fail to be impressed with the one pervading purpose found in them all, lying at the foundation of each, and without which none of them would have been even suggested: we mean the freedom of the slave race, the security and firm establishment of that freedom, and the protection of the newly-made freeman and citizen from the oppressions of those who had formerly exercised unlimited dominion over him. It is true that only the fifteenth amendment in terms mentions the negro by speaking of his color and his slavery. But it is just as true that each of the other articles was addressed to the grievances of that race, and designed to remedy them, as the fifteenth.

"These amendments, one and all, are thus declared to have as their all-pervading design and end the security to the recently-enslaved race, not only their nominal freedom, but their complete protection from those who had formerly exercised unlimited dominion over them. It is in this broad light that all these amendments must be read, the purpose to secure the perfect equality before the law of all citizens of the United States. What you give to one class you must give to all; what you deny to one class you shall deny to all, unless in the exercise of the common and universal police power of the State you find it needful to confer exclusive privileges on certain citizens, to be held and exercised still for the common good of all.

"Such are the doctrines of the Slaughterhouse cases—doctrines worthy of the republic, worthy of the age, worthy of the great tribunal which thus loftily and impressively enunciates them. Do they—I put it to any man, be he lawyer or not; I put it to the gentleman from Georgia—do they give color even to the claim that this Congress may not now legislate against a plain discrimination made by State laws or State customs against that very race for whose complete freedom and protection these great amendments were elaborated and adopted? Is it pretended—I ask the honorable gentleman from Kentucky or the honorable gentleman from Georgia—is it pretended anywhere that the evils of which we complain, our exclusion from the public inn, from the saloon and table of the steamboat, from the sleeping-coach on the railway, from the right of sepulture in the public burial-ground, are an exercise of the police power of the State? Is such oppression and injustice nothing but the exercise by the State of the right to make regulations for the health, comfort, and security of all her citizens? Is it merely enacting that one man shall so use his own as not to injure another's? Are the colored race to be assimilated to an unwholesome trade or to combustible materials, to be interdicted, to be shut up within prescribed limits? Let the gentleman from Kentucky or the gentleman from Georgia answer.

"But each of these gentlemen quotes at some length from the decision of the court to show that the court recognize a difference between citizenship of the United States and citizenship of the States. That is true, and no man here who supports this bill questions or overlooks the difference. There are privileges and immunities which belong to me as a citizen of the United States, and there are other privileges and immunities which belong to me as a citizen of my State. The former are under the protection of the Constitution and laws of the United States, and the latter are under the protection of the constitution and laws of my State. But what of that? Are the rights which I now claim—the right to enjoy the common public conveniences of travel on public highways, of rest and refreshment at public inns, of education in public schools, of burial in public cemeteries—rights which I hold as a citizen of the United States or of my State? Or, to state the question more exactly, is not the denial of such privileges to me a denial to me of the equal protection of

the laws? For it is under this clause of the fourteenth amendment that we place the present bill, no State shall 'deny to any person within its jurisdiction the equal protection of the laws.' No matter, therefore, whether his rights are held under the United States or under his particular State, he is equally protected by this amendment. He is always and everywhere entitled to the equal protection of the laws. All discrimination is forbidden; and while the rights of citizens of a State as such are not defined or conferred by the Constitution of the United States, yet all discrimination, all denial of equality before the law, all denial of the equal protection of the laws, whether State or national laws, are forbidden.

"The distinction between the two kinds of citizenship is clear, and the Supreme Court have clearly pointed out this distinction, but they have nowhere written a word or line which denies to Congress the power to prevent a denial of equality of rights, whether those rights exist by virtue of citizenship of the United States or of a State. Let honorable members mark well this distinction. There are rights which are conferred on us by the United States. There are other rights conferred on us by the States of which we are individually the citizens. The fourteenth amendment does not forbid a State to deny to all its citizens any of those rights which the State itself has conferred, with certain exceptions, which are pointed out in the decision which we are examining. What it does forbid is inequality, is discrimination, or, to use the words of the amendment itself, is the denial 'to any person within its jurisdiction the equal protection of the laws.' If a State denies to me rights which are common to all her other citizens, she violates this amendment, unless she can show, as was shown in the Slaughter-house cases, that she does it in the legitimate exercise of her police power. If she abridges the rights of all her citizens equally, unless those rights are specially guarded by the Constitution of the United States, she does not violate this amendment. This is not to put the rights which I hold by virtue of my citizenship of South Carolina under the protection of the national Government; it is not to blot out or overlook in the slightest particular the distinction between rights held under the United States and rights held under the States; but it seeks to secure equality, to prevent discrimination, to confer as complete and ample protection on the humblest as on the highest.

"Sir, I have replied, to the extent of my ability to the arguments which have been presented by the opponents of this measure. I have replied also to some of the legal propositions advanced by gentlemen on the other side; and now that I am about to conclude, I am deeply sensible of the imperfect manner in which I have performed the task. Technically this bill is to decide upon the civil status of the colored American citizen; a point disputed at the very formation of our present Government, when by a short-sighted policy, a policy repugnant to true republican government, one negro counted as three-fifths of a man. The logical result of this mistake of the framers of the Constitution strengthened the cancer of slavery, which finally spread its poisonous tentacles over the southern portion of the body politic."

Mr. Butler, of Massachusetts : "Mr. Speaker, if these are rights, again let me ask, why should they not be given to all citizens of the United States, if we have the constitutional power to do so? If the States give them and execute them, then there will be no longer any need for this statute. It will not be enforced, and will do no harm. Where a State will do its duty, there this statute will be inoperative. Where the State does not do its duty in this behalf, then the flag of the United States, and the power of the United States, and the judiciary of the United States, should protect the citizens against all unfriendly State legislation, or against the want of legislation. And I have the authority of the gentleman from Virginia (Mr. Harris) for saying that 'no State has legislated on the subject.'

"And it is because of the very prejudice which has prevented such legislation that I claim the passage of the bill.

"Is it a prejudice at all? Was there any objection in the South to consorting with the negro as a slave? Oh, no; your children and your servants' children played together; your children sucked the same mother with your servants' children; had the same nurse; and, unless tradition speaks falsely, sometimes had the same father.

"Would you not ride in first-class cars with your negroes in the olden time? What negro servant accompanying a mistress or master, and administering to his or her health, was ever denied a first-class passage in a first-class car in the South before the war? What negro girl, being the nurse or servant of a lady, was not allowed to sit by that lady and that child in a first-class car? What negro servant, accompanying a lady or a gentleman, was ever denied admittance to a first-class hotel? My friend from Tennessee, I think it was, told us that in the olden time the master and his slave always used to worship together in the same churches, but that now there are separate churches, and the negroes prefer to worship by themselves.

"But how was it before the war? You talk about your prejudices against social equality! I put this question to the minds and consciences of every man of you. Who is the highest in the social scale, a slave or a freeman? You associated with the slave in every relation in life. He now has become your freeman, and now you cannot associate with him; he has got up in the scale, and you cannot stomach him. Why is this? It is because he claims that as a right which you accorded him always freely as a boon. It is because the laws of your land,

the Constitution of your country, gave all men equal rights in accordance with the fiat of God Almighty which has made some of them your equal in all things, and therefore he is no longer to be associated with or tolerated! This is not a prejudice against the negro in any personal objection to him—it is a political idea only.

"I had, sir, to deal with this question early in the war, and I cannot better explain the operations of this kind of prejudice than by stating the exact fact which happened on board one of the boats upon Chesapeake Bay, between Baltimore and Fortress Monroe. A member of the Christian Commission went North after two school-teachers, and brought back two ladies, one of whom had some colored blood in her veins, but so much more white that it took a connoisseur to find the color. The women bought first-class tickets, and took their state-room, sat down at the table, and paid for their supper. A Virginian, who was on board, being able to know a negro from long use whenever he saw one, smoked out the fact that one of them, a lady in dress, a lady in culture, a lady in manners, had some negro blood in her veins, and he complained to the clerk of the boat that he could not eat at the table in the saloon with her, and the clerk ordered her forward among the deck-hands and servants. The lady and her companion, frightened, ran to their state-room, and locked themselves in. The Virginian insisted on her being taken out of that. But a provost passenger on board was roused to his duty, and insisted that all that should be stopped. Next morning complaint was made to me as commanding general, and I sent for the clerk—an inoffensive old gentleman, who looked as if he would not harm anybody. I said, 'What is all this?' He said, 'I was only carrying out the rules of my boat.' I said, 'Do you not recognize the fact that the war has made a difference in these things?' He answered, 'Not in the rules of our boat.' I asked, 'What were the rules of your boat before the war? Could not a colored nurse go with the children of her mistress, and occupy a state-room with them?' 'Yes, sir.' 'Could she come to the table with them?' 'Yes, sir.' 'Which do you think, Mr. Clerk, is the highest in the social scale, a freeman or a slave?' 'Oh, a freeman, general, of course.' 'Very well, Mr. Clerk; I think I can make a rule for your boat now that will be easy of enforcement. Do not go away and say that the commanding general says that the negro is as good as a white man. I am not going to say any such thing. But hereafter let this be your rule: Let no free person ever be deprived of any privileges on your boat that were ever accorded to a slave person. Do this, and there will be no trouble hereafter.' And there was none.

"That tells the whole story and covers the whole argument of prejudice. It is not a prejudice, gentlemen. You make a mistake.

A prejudice is where you do not like the thing itself. We in the North had somewhat of this prejudice against the colored. You of the South had none. From the rarity, they were offensive to us. But we are getting used to the negro, and are getting free from our former mode of feeling and speaking on the subject. That was a prejudice. But you had not any such feeling of dislike or offensiveness at the South. Now I am getting over that feeling, and you are getting it. And it is a political idea you are getting, and not a prejudice at all.

"Now, sir, you will allow me to state how I got over my prejudices. I think the House got over theirs after the exhibition we had yesterday. I think no man will get up here and say he speaks only to white men again. He must at first show himself worthy before he can speak to some colored men in this House after what occurred yesterday.

"I got over my prejudices from the exhibition of like high qualities of the negro, but in a different manner from that in which, I have no doubt, many a prejudice was removed against the negro in the House yesterday. In Louisiana, in 1862, when our arms were meeting with disasters before Richmond, I was in command of the city of New Orleans with a very few troops, and those daily diminishing by the diseases incident to the climate, with a larger number of Confederate soldiers paroled in the city than I had troops. I called upon my Government for reënforcements, and they could not give me any, and I therefore called upon the colored men to enlist in defense of their country. I brought together the officers of two colored regiments that had been raised by the Confederates for the defense of the city against us—but which disbanded when we came there because they would not fight against us, and staid at home when their white comrades ran away—and I said: 'How soon can you enlist me one thousand men?' 'In ten days, general,' they answered; and when the thousand men were brought together in a large hall; I saw such a body of recruits as I never saw before. Why, sir, every one of them had on a clean shirt, a thing not often got in a body of a thousand recruits. I put colored officers in command of them, and I organized them. But we all had our prejudice against them. I was told they would not fight. I raised another regiment, and by the time I got them organized, before I could test their fighting qualities in the field, the exigencies of the service required that I should be relieved from the command of that department.

"I came into command again in Virginia in 1863. I there organized twenty-five regiments, with some that were sent to me, and disciplined them. Still all my brother officers of the regular army said my colored soldiers would not fight; and I felt it was necessary that they should fight to show that their race were capable of the duties of citizens; for

one of the highest duties of citizens is to defend their own liberties and their country's flag and honor. On the 29th of September, 1864, I was ordered by the commanding general of the armies to cross the James River at two one in the centre of their line, and attack the enemy's line of works; one in the centre of their line, Fort Harrison, the other a strong work guarding their left flank at New Market Heights; and there are men on this floor who will remember that day, I doubt not, as I do myself. I gave the centre of the line to the white troops, the Eighteenth Corps, under General Ord, and they attacked one very strong work and carried it gallantly. I went myself with the colored troops, to attack the enemy at New Market Heights, which was the key to the enemy's flank on the north side of James River. That work was a redoubt built on the top of a hill of some considerable elevation; then running down into a marsh; in that marsh was a brook; then rising again to a plain which gently rolled away toward the river. On that plain, when the flash of dawn was breaking, I placed a column of three thousand colored troops, in close column by division, right in front, with guns at 'right shoulder shift.'

"I said: 'That work must be taken by the weight of your column; no shot must be fired;' and to prevent their firing I had the caps taken from the nipples of their guns. Then I said, 'Your cry, when you charge, will be, "Remember Fort Pillow!"' and as the sun rose up in the heavens the order was given, 'Forward!' and they marched forward, steadily as if on parade —went down the hill, across the marsh, and as they got into the brook they came within range of the enemy's fire, which vigorously opened upon them. They broke a little as they forded the brook, and the column wavered. Oh, it was a moment of intensest anxiety, but they formed again as they reached the firm ground, marching steadily on with closed ranks under the enemy's fire, until the head of the column reached the first line of abattis, some one hundred and fifty yards from the enemy's works. Then the axe-men ran to the front to cut away the heavy obstructions of defense, while one thousand men of the enemy, with their artillery concentrated, from the redoubt poured a heavy fire upon the head of the column hardly wider than the clerk's desk. The axe-men went down under that murderous fire; other strong hands grasped the axes in their stead, and the abattis was cut away. Again, at double-quick, the column goes forward to within fifty yards of the fort, to meet there another line of abattis. The column halts, and there a very fire of hell is pouring upon it. The abattis resists and holds, the head of the column seemed literally to melt away under the rain of shot and shell, the flags of the leading regiments go down, but a brave black hand seizes the colors; they are up again and wave their starry light over the storm of battle; again the axe-men fall, but strong hands and willing hearts seize the heavy sharpened trees and drag them away, and the column forward, and with a shout which now rings in my ear they went over that redoubt like a flash, and the enemy never stopped running for four miles!

"It became my painful duty, sir, to follow in the track of that charging column, and there, in a space not wider than the clerk's desk and three hundred yards long, lay the dead bodies of five hundred and forty-three of my colored soldiers, slain in defense of their country, and who had laid down their lives to uphold its flag and its honor as a willing sacrifice; and as I rode along among them, guiding my horse this way and that way lest he should profane with his hoofs what seemed to me the sacred dead, and as I looked on their bronzed faces upturned in the shining sun to heaven as if in mute appeal against the wrongs of that country for which they had given their lives, and whose flag had only been to them a flag of stripes on which no star of glory had ever shone for them —feeling I had wronged them in the past and believing what was the future of my country to them—among my dead comrades there I swore to myself a solemn oath, 'May my right hand forget its cunning and my tongue cleave to the roof of my mouth if I ever fail to defend the rights of these men who have given their blood for me and my country this day and for their race forever!' and, God helping me, I will keep that oath.

"From that hour all prejudice was gone, and an old-time States-right Democrat became a lover of the negro race; and as long as their rights are not equal to the rights of other men under this Government I am with them against all comers; and when their rights are assured, as other men's rights are held sacred, then, I trust, we shall have what we ought to have, a united country North and South, white and black, under one glorious flag, for which we and our fathers have fought with an equal and not to be distinguished valor.

"Now, Mr. Speaker, these men have fought for their country; one of their representatives has spoken, as few can speak on this floor, for his race; they have shown themselves our equals in battle; as citizens they are kind, quiet, temperate, laborious; they have shown that they know how to exercise the right of suffrage which we have given to them, for they always vote right; they vote the Republican ticket, and all the powers of death and hell cannot persuade them to do otherwise. They show that they knew more than their masters did, for they always knew how to be loyal. They have industry, they have temperance, they have all the good qualities of citizens, they have bravery, they have culture, they have power, they have eloquence. And who shall say that they shall not have what the Constitution gives them—equal rights?"

The Speaker: "The pending motion is that made by the gentleman from Massachusetts (Mr. Butler), that the pending bill and proposed amendments thereto be recommitted to the Committee on the Judiciary."

The motion to recommit was agreed to.

Mr. Vance of North Carolina, said: "Mr. Speaker: Having been unable to obtain the floor on the civil-rights bill, I propose to devote a portion of my time to the discussion of that subject; and I think I can do so without prejudice and without subjecting myself truthfully to the charge of hatred toward the colored race. In the will of my grandfather (who was one of those who struggled for liberty upon the heights of King's Mountain) he enjoined it upon his children and his grandchildren to treat kindly the colored people upon the plantation. I hope never to forget a sentiment so noble and so worthy of obedience. In fact, as a Southern man, as one who has sympathized from my earliest time of knowledge with the South in all the great principles and struggles which have interested her, I have felt it my duty to advance in every laudable way the interests of the colored race in this country. I have even taught a colored Sunday-school of one hundred and fifty scholars. I have endeavored in every way possible to advance the interests of that race. I feel, therefore, that I can speak upon this subject without prejudice.

"The charge has been made against the people of the South that their opposition to such measures as the civil-rights bill has arisen from prejudice and hatred. This charge is unfounded; it is untrue. Before the war—in the days past and gone—in the days when there were 4,000,000 slaves in the South, the churches of the South sent missionaries into the cotton plantations, and down into the orange-groves, and out upon the rolling prairies of Texas. Into all parts of the country where great numbers of colored people were collected the churches sent their missionaries, and held up there the standard of the Cross, instructing them in the sublime principles which relate to questions vastly more important than mere earthly things

"I have yet to meet the Southern man (and I thank God for it) who does not in his heart rejoice that the colored man is free. In my intercourse with the people of my own land, in my travels through the 'sunny South,' I have found the feeling everywhere one of gratitude and thankfulness that the chains of the colored man have been broken; that he is now permitted to walk the earth a free man.

"Sir, the people of the South were not to blame for the introduction of slavery among them. It came from elsewhere, and became incorporated as a part of our institutions. The old colored women nursed the white children of the South, while kindness and friendship were maintained between the two races. Such an institution could not be readily abolished. It could probably only be done by the shock of arms.

"Every Southern man who will call to mind the fact that after the thunder of artillery had ceased, when the clang of arms was no more heard in the country, the Southern people rallied and took the oath to support the proclamations of Mr. Lincoln, in order that the colored man might be free. Those proclamations, Mr. Speaker, were regarded at the time as unconstitutional; yet the Southern people were willing that the colored man should enjoy his freedom, and all over the South they came forward and took the oath to support those proclamations.

"Following hard upon that, the conventions of the Southern States assembled, and by a solemn act ratified the freedom of the colored man, confirming it forever by statute upon the records of their governments.

"What else did they do? They went to work and secured the colored man in all his civil rights, or what may properly be termed civil rights. The people there consented that he should vote; they consented he should hold office; they, consented he should serve upon juries; they consented that he should hold property, and that he should be a witness in court. All the real rights properly known as civil rights were guaranteed to the colored man in that section; and the charge cannot justly be made against this people that they are opposed to according civil rights to the colored man on account of any prejudice or hatred, for it is not in their hearts.

"Why, then, do we oppose the civil-rights bill? That is the question; and speaking as I do, and feeling as I speak, without prejudices, I will show what is the real objection to the bill known as the civil-rights bill. I think gentlemen of the committee will bear me out when I say the title of the bill we had before us ought to be changed, and made to read thus: 'A bill to protect the colored people in their social rights.' That is the way it should read.

"Now, Mr. Speaker, the distinguished gentleman from Massachusetts (Mr. Butler) laid down the law, and it has not been controverted, that all men are entitled under the law to the right to go to an hotel, to ride in a public railway-carriage, to interment, and to be taught in the public school sustained by moneys raised by taxation.

"It is laid down as the common law of the land. Now, let us see for a few minutes, Mr. Speaker, how the case stands. There is no railway-car in all the South which the colored man cannot ride in. That is his civil right. This bill proposes that he should have the opportunity or the right to go into a first-class car and sit with white gentlemen and white ladies. I submit if that is not a social right. There is a distinction between the two. Now, there is not an hotel in the South where the colored man cannot get entertainment such as food and lodgings. That is his civil right. The bill of the committee provides that there shall be no distinction. Even if he is allowed to go into the dining-room, and is placed at a separate table because of his color, it will be a violation of

this law. Placing him, therefore, at the table with the whites is a social right.

"Now, sir, provision has been made for free schools in my own native State of North Carolina. We have cheerfully taxed ourselves there for the education of our people, including the colored race; but separate schools are organized for the instruction of the latter. One of the civil rights of the colored man undoubtedly is the right to be educated out of moneys raised by taxation. His children, under the law, have that right; but this bill goes further, and provides that colored children shall go into the same school with white children, mixing the colored children and the white children in the same schools. I submit to the committee whether that is not a social right instead of a civil right. Therefore it is I say this bill ought to be changed, or rather its title ought to be changed. The real objection, then, to civil rights, so called, is that it is not best for both races; that in fact it will be detrimental to the interests of both races.

"Now, Mr. Speaker, I propose to show briefly how that will be. In the first place, the true policy in regard to the intercourse of mankind all over this broad earth is in the recognition of the fact that such intercourse is one made up of mutual interests. It is the interest of the hotel-keeper to entertain his guests, it is the interest of the railway company to transport passengers; the interests are mutual; and that is the true policy all the world over. But whenever you undertake to force persons of color into their social rights, then, in my judgment, you have done the colored man a serious damage. Let the people of the South alone, sir, and this thing will adjust itself. It will come out all right. In coming to this city the other day, colored men were sitting in first-class cars with their wives, where they were admitted by the managers of the road; and I am told in this city one of the first hotels admits colored men as guests. It will adjust itself if let alone; but if you undertake to coerce society before it is ready, you will damage the colored man in all his interests, and at the same time do damage to the white race.

"There are between four and five millions of colored people in the South, whose interests are intimately and closely connected with those of the white people. The one cannot well do without the other. Where does the colored man get his place to live, where does he obtain employment? In a great measure from the white men of the country, and almost entirely from those opposed to this bill. And I tell the committee now, through you, Mr. Chairman, that the great majority of the people of the Southern States, of all political shades of opinion, are opposed to any thing like force in this matter.

"This bill, Mr. Speaker, will, more or less, bring about an antagonism of the races; and that state of things would not be best for the colored man. I submit it in good faith, that if the question is ever presented in the South, 'Shall this country be ruled by white men or ruled by colored men?' the colored man is not able to stand any such antagonism as that; he will necessarily, sir, go down. I ask, What race has ever been able to stand before the Caucasian? Look at the history of the world. Where is the Indian? Why, sir, less than two centuries ago on this spot the Indian reared his wigwam and stood upon these hills and looked upon the broad, beautiful Potomac, or his eye swept over the hunting-grounds of the West; and he had the title to this magnificent country. Where is he now? He has gone back, step by step, before the advancing march of the white man. No race, sir, in the world has been able to stand before the pure Caucasian. An antagonism of races will not be good for the colored man."

Meantime the subject was taken up in the Senate, and the bill presented on the first day of the session by Mr. Sumner, of Massachusetts, was considered and referred to the Committee on the Judiciary.

On April 30th the Committee on the Judiciary reported the bill with an amendment, which was to strike out all after the enacting clause, and in lieu thereof to insert the following:

That all persons within the jurisdiction of the United States shall be entitled to the full and equal enjoyment of the accommodations, advantages, facilities, and privileges of inns, public conveyances on land or water, theatres, and other places of public amusement; and also of common schools and public institutions of learning or benevolence supported, in whole or in part, by general taxation; and of cemeteries so supported: subject only to the conditions and limitations established by law, and applicable alike to citizens of every race and color, regardless of any previous condition of servitude.

SECTION 2. That any person who shall violate the foregoing section by denying to any citizen, except for reasons by law applicable to citizens of every race and color, and regardless of any previous condition of servitude, the full enjoyment of any of the accommodations, advantages, facilities, or privileges in said section enumerated, or by aiding or inciting such denial, shall, for every such offense, forfeit and pay the sum of $500 to the person aggrieved thereby, to be recovered in an action on the case, with full costs; and shall also, for every such offense, be deemed guilty of a misdemeanor, and, upon conviction thereof, shall be fined not less than $500 nor more than $1,000, or shall be imprisoned not less than thirty days nor more than one year: Provided, That the party aggrieved shall not recover more than one penalty; and when the offense is a refusal of burial, the penalty may be recovered by the heirs at law of the person whose body has been refused burial: And provided further, That all persons may elect to sue for the penalty aforesaid or to proceed under their rights at common law and by State statutes; and having so elected to proceed in the one mode or the other, their right to proceed in the other jurisdiction shall be barred. But this proviso shall not apply to criminal proceedings, either under this act or the criminal law of any State.

SEC. 3. That the district and circuit courts of the United States shall have, exclusively of the courts of the several States, cognizance of all crimes and offenses against, and violations of, the provisions of this act; and actions for the penalty given by the preceding section may be prosecuted in the territorial, district, or circuit courts of the United States wherever the defendant may be found, without regard to the other party. And the district attorneys, marshals and deputy-marshals of the United States, and commissioners appointed by the circuit and territorial courts of the United States, with powers of arresting and imprisoning or bailing offenders against the laws of the United States, are hereby specially authorized and required to institute proceedings against every person who shall violate the provisions of this act, and cause him to be arrested and imprisoned or bailed, as the case may be, for trial before such court of the United States or territorial court as by law has cognizance of the offense, except in respect of the right of action accruing to the person aggrieved; and such district attorneys shall cause such proceedings to be prosecuted to their termination as in other cases: Provided, That nothing contained in this section shall be construed to deny or defeat any right of civil action accruing to any person, whether by reason of this act or otherwise. And any district attorney who shall willfully fail to institute and prosecute the proceedings herein required shall, for every such offense, forfeit and pay the sum of $5,000 to the person aggrieved thereby, to be recovered by an action on the case, with full costs, and shall, on conviction thereof, be deemed guilty of a misdemeanor, and be fined not less than $1,000 nor more than $5,000.

SEC. 4. That no citizen possessing all other qualifications which are or may be prescribed by law shall be disqualified for service as grand or petit juror in any court of the United States, or of any State, on account of race, color, or previous condition of servitude; and any officer or other person charged with any duty in the selection or summoning of jurors who shall exclude or fail to summon any citizen for the cause aforesaid shall, on conviction thereof, be deemed guilty of a misdemeanor, and be fined not more than $5,000.

SEC. 5. That all cases arising under the provisions of this act in the courts of the United States shall be reviewable by the Supreme Court of the United States without regard to the sum in controversy, under the same provisions and regulations as are now provided by law for the review of other causes in said court.

The amendment was agreed to.

The bill was reported to the Senate as amended.

The president pro tempore: "Will the Senate concur in the amendment made as in Committee of the Whole?"

Mr. Frelinghuysen, of New Jersey, said: "Mr. President, the Committee on the Judiciary have devolved on me, on whom it should not have been imposed, the duty of presenting and explaining this bill, which I shall do in the most concise manner, even pruning from my remarks such comment as a measure having for its object the civil rights of all might naturally inspire in the councils of a free people.

"I invoke for the bill a calm, impartial, and unpartisan consideration, and ask its adoption only as it commends itself as consistent with the permanent interests of the nation, with the Constitution, and with justice to all classes of citizens. Would that the author * of the measure was here to present and defend it! To our views it would have been becoming that he who was in the forum the foremost leader of the grandest victory of the nineteenth century

* Mr. Sumner, deceased.

in the Western Hemisphere, the victory of freedom over slavery, should have placed the cap-stone on the structure he was permitted to be an efficient instrumentality in aiding to erect. But it was otherwise decreed.

"I call the attention of the Senate to but two sections of this measure—the first section and the fourth section of the amendment; the other parts of the bill being mere machinery to carry those into effect. The first section provides:

That all persons within the jurisdiction of the United States shall be entitled to the full and equal enjoyment of the accommodations, advantages, facilities, and privileges of inns, public conveyances on land or water, theatres, and other places of public amusement; and also of common schools and public institutions of learning or benevolence supported, in whole or in part, by general taxation; and of cemeteries so supported: subject only to the conditions and limitations established by law, and applicable alike to citizens of every race and color, regardless of any previous condition of servitude.

"The fourth section provides: ·

That no citizen possessing all other qualifications which are or may be prescribed by law shall be disqualified for service as grand or petit juror in any court of the United States, or of any State, on account of race, color, or previous condition of servitude; and any officer or other person charged with any duty in the selection or summoning of jurors who shall exclude or fail to summon any citizen for the cause aforesaid shall, on conviction thereof, be deemed guilty of a misdemeanor, and be fined not more than $5,000.

"It is the one purpose of this bill to assert, or rather to reassert, 'freedom from all discrimination before the law as one of the fundamental rights of United States citizenship.' If, sir, we have not the constitutional right thus to legislate, then the people of this country have perpetrated a blunder amounting to a grim burlesque over which the world might laugh were it not that it is a blunder over which humanity would have occasion to mourn. Sir, we have the right, in the language of the Constitution, to give ' to all persons within the jurisdiction of the United States the equal protection of the laws.'

"This bill when enacted, it is believed, will be a finality, removing from legislation, from politics, and from society, an injurious agitation, and securing to every citizen that proud equality which our nation declares to be his right, and which is a boon in defense of which most men would die.

"The colored citizens ask this legislation, not because they seek to force themselves into associations with the whites, but because they have their prides and emulations among themselves, and wish there in those associations to feel that there is no ban upon them, but that they are as fully enfranchised as any who breathe the air of heaven.

"I ask you, should the colored citizens be content to demand less than full and equal enfranchisement; should they say, 'We are content that we and our children shall wear forever the badge of political inferiority,' would

they not thereby prove themselves to you to be unfit for the high dignity to which the nation has called them? Let us not doubt the foundation principle of our Government; it has always proved true. Give equality to all. Our confidence will not be abused.

"This bill applies alike to the white citizen and to the colored citizen.

"I am aware that the majority of the Supreme Court in the Slaughter-house case (16 Wallace), giving construction to the thirteenth, fourteenth, and fifteenth amendments in the light of the history which called them into being, make them apply especially, though not exclusively, I think, to the enfranchisement of the colored race. There can be no doubt they apply equally to all races.

"The court, in the case of The Live-stock Association vs. The Crescent City Live-stock Company (1 Abbot, page 88), undoubtedly give the true construction to the amendments as to their application. The court say:

It is possible that those who framed the articles were not themselves aware of the far-reaching character of their terms. They may have had in mind but one particular phase of social and political wrongs which they desired to redress. Yet if the amendment as framed and expressed does in fact bear a broader meaning, and does extend its protecting shield over those who were never thought of when it was conceived and put in form, and does reach social evils which were never before prohibited by constitutional enactment, it is to be presumed that the American people in giving it their imprimatur understood what they were doing, and meant to decree what has in fact been decreed.

"This bill therefore properly secures equal rights to the white as well as to the colored race.

"Again let me say that this measure does not touch the subject of social equality. That is not an element of citizenship. The law which regulates the tastes and affinities of the mind; its law is the arbitrary, uncontrolled human will. You cannot enact it.

"This bill does not disturb any laws, whether statute or common, relating to the administration of inns, places of public amusement, schools, institutions of learning or benevolence, or cemeteries, supported in whole or in part by general taxation (and it is only to these that it applies), excepting to abrogate such laws as make discrimination on account of race, color, or previous servitude.

"Inns, places of amusement, and public conveyances, are established and maintained by private enterprise and capital, but bear that intimate relation to the public, appealing to and depending upon its patronage for support, that the law has for many centuries measurably regulated them, leaving at the same time a wide discretion as to their administration in their proprietors. This body of law and this discretion are not disturbed by this bill, except when the one or the other discriminates on account of race, color, or previous servitude.

"As the capital invested in inns, places of

amusements, and public conveyances, is that of the proprietors, and as they alone can know what minute arrangements their business requires, the discretion as to the particular accommodation to be given to the guest, the traveler, and the visitor, is quite wide. But as the employment these proprietors have selected touches the public, the law demands that the accommodation shall be good and suitable, and this bill adds to that requirement the condition that no person shall, in the regulation of these employments, be discriminated against merely because he is an American or an Irishman, a German or a colored man.

"I have called attention to inns, places of amusements, and public conveyances, separately from schools, institutions of learning and benevolence, and cemeteries, supported in whole or in part by general taxation, because the condition of the existence of the former, to wit, inns, places of amusements, and public conveyances, differs from that of the latter, to wit, schools, institutions of benevolence, and cemeteries. I assume that no one can question that schools, institutions of learning and benevolence, and cemeteries, which are supported by the taxation of all, should be subject to the equal use of all. Subjecting to taxation is a guarantee of the right to use. Even as to these institutions, which are the fruit of taxation, the bill does not disturb the established law, statute or common, or the discretion of their managers, except so far as the one or the other, in violation of the fundamental principles of our Government, discriminates against some one under our jurisdiction because of his blood, because of his complexion, or because of the cruel wrong of slavery which he may have suffered.

"Uniform discrimination may be made in schools and institutions of learning and benevolence on account of age, sex, morals, preparatory qualifications, health, and the like. But the son of the poorest Irishman in the land, who has sought our shores to better the condition of his offspring, shall have as good a place in our schools as the scion of the chief man of the parish. The old blind Italian, who comes otherwise within the regulations of an asylum for the blind supported by taxation, shall have as good a right to its relief as if he were an American born.

"There is but one idea in the bill, and that is, the equality of races before the law.

"The inquiry may arise whether this bill admits of the classification of races in the common-school system; that is, having one school for white and another for colored children. That subject has been discussed somewhat in the courts. In a case in 24 Iowa Reports, page 267, it was directly considered. There the court held that—

The constitution and statutes in force effectuating it provide for the education of all the youths of the State, without distinction of color; and the board of directors have no discretionary power to require

colored children to attend a separate school. They may exercise a uniform discretion, operative upon all, as to the residence or qualification of children to entitle them to admission to each particular school, but they cannot deny a youth admission to any particular school, because of his color, nationality, religion, or the like.

"The law of Iowa goes further than the law proposed in this bill. Here there is no prohibition as to a discrimination on account of religion or of morals. It does not say that all youths shall have this right. The only prohibition in this bill is one which prevents discrimination on account of race. The same subject was considered in the case of The State on the relation of Garnes vs. McCann and others, in 21 Ohio Reports, page 198. There the court held:

That the act authorizing such classification on the basis of color does not contravene the constitution of the State, nor the fourteenth amendment of the Constitution of the United States, and that colored children residing in either of the districts for white children, are not, as of right, entitled to admission into the schools for white children.

"The constitution and laws of Iowa provide for the 'education of all the youths of the State without distinction of color.' In Ohio the statute expressly provided for separate schools for white and colored children. Therefore the decisions of those courts afford no precedent for the construction of this bill when enacted. The language of this bill secures full and equal privileges in the schools, subject to laws which do not discriminate as to color.

"The bill provides that full and equal privileges shall be enjoyed by all persons in public schools supported by taxation, subject only to the limitation established by law, applicable alike to citizens of every race and color, and regardless of previous servitude.

"The bill does not permit the exclusion of one from a public school on account of his nationality alone.

"The object of the bill is to destroy, not to recognize, the distinctions of race.

"When in a school-district there are two schools, and the white children choose to go to one and the colored to the other, there is nothing in this bill that prevents their doing so.

"And this bill being a law, such a voluntary division would not in any way invalidate an assessment for taxes to support such schools.

"And let me say that, from statements made to me by colored Representatives in the other House, I believe that this voluntary division into separate schools would often be the solution of difficulty in communities where there still lingers a prejudice against a colored boy, not because he is ignorant, or untidy, or immoral, but because of his blood.

"It is claimed that the enactment of the bill would be in violation of the Constitution, because the regulation of inns, public conveyances, and places of amusement, common schools, institutions of learning and benevolence, and cemeteries, supported by taxation, are under the regulation of the States, and not of the General Government. The bill proposes to leave them under State control, and expressly says that all persons are to have the full and equal enjoyment of inns, etc., subject to the conditions and limitations established by law—State statutes and common law—with the exception that such laws must be applicable alike to citizens of every race and color, and regardless of previous servitude.

" Is it constitutional for the General Government to legislate to prevent discrimination on account of race, etc. ? We maintain that the General Government has this right under three different grants of power :

" 1. Under the thirteenth, fourteenth, and fifteenth amendments, considered together and in connection with the contemporaneous history ;

" 2. Under the provision of the fourteenth amendment, which prohibits a State from enforcing any law which abridges the privileges and immunities of citizens of the United States ; and also,

" 3. Under the provision of article fourteen, which requires a State to give to every person within its jurisdiction the equal protection of the laws ; and under the general power given Congress to enforce these provisions by appropriate legislation.

" I cannot more forcibly nor with greater brevity show that these amendments were intended to do away with slavery—to wipe out every consequence of it ; to prevent State legislation of every kind that discriminated on account of race, color, etc., and make the race formerly in servitude equal in all respects to other citizens—than by reading a portion of the opinion of the majority of the court in the Slaughter-house cases (16 Wallace, 67, 68, and 69) :

But within the last eight years three other articles of amendment of vast importance have been added by the voice of the people to that now venerable instrument.

The most cursory glance at these articles discloses a unity of purpose, when taken in connection with the history of the times, which cannot fail to have an important bearing on any question of doubt concerning their true meaning.

Nor can such doubts, when any reasonably exist, be safely and rationally solved without a reference to that history ; for in it is found the occasion of the necessity for recurring again to the g en source of power in this country, the people of the States, for additional guarantees of human rights ; additional powers of the Federal Government ; additional restraints upon those States. Fortunately, that history is fresh within the memory of us all, and its leading features, as they bear upon the matter before us, free from doubt.

The institution of African slavery as it existed in about half the States of the Union, and the contests pervading the public mind for many years between those who desired its curtailment and ultimate extinction and those who desired additional safeguards for its security and perpetuation, culminated in the effort, on the part of most of the States in which slavery existed, to separate from the Federal Government, and to resist its authority. This constituted the war of the rebellion, and, whatever auxiliary causes may have contributed to bring about this war, undoubtedly the overshadowing and efficient cause was African slavery. In that struggle slavery, as a legalized social relation, perished. * * *

The proclamation of President Lincoln expressed an accomplished fact as to a large portion of the insurrectionary districts, when he declared slavery abolished in them all. But, the war being over, those who had succeeded in reestablishing the authority of the Federal Government were not content to permit this great act of emancipation to rest on the actual results of the contest or the proclamation of the Executive, both of which might have been questioned in after-times, and they determined to place this main and most valuable result in the Constitution of the restored Union as one of its fundamental articles. Hence the thirteenth article of the amendment of that instrument. Its short sections seem hardly to admit of misconstruction, so vigorous is their expression, and so appropriate to the purpose we have indicated :

1. Neither slavery nor involuntary servitude, except as a punishment for crime, whereof the party shall have been duly convicted, shall exist within the United States or any place subject to their jurisdiction.

2. Congress shall have power to enforce this article by appropriate legislation.

To withdraw the mind from the contemplation of this grand yet simple declaration of the personal freedom of all the human race within the jurisdiction of this Government—a declaration designed to establish the freedom of four millions of slaves—and with a microscopic search endeavor to find in it a reference to servitudes, which may have been attached to property in certain localities, requires an effort, to say the least of it.

" You see that the court hold that slavery caused the war ; that the war in fact destroyed slavery ; that in order that its permanent destruction might not be questioned in after-times, the thirteenth amendment was adopted ; and that this is a fact so apparent, that you need not, to see it, look with a microscope.

" If the discrimination against that race for whose benefit chiefly the amendments were adopted is because of their having recently been slaves—and as the discrimination is confined to that race, is not that the cause of it? —then we are authorized to pass all laws appropriate to efface the existence of any consequences or residuum of slavery.

" The fourteenth and fifteenth amendments are stated by the court to have had the same origin.

" How is the United States, how are we, to protect the privileges of citizens of the United States in the States? We cannot deal with the States or with their officials to compel proper legislation and its enforcement ; we can only deal with the offenders who violate the privileges and immunities of citizens of the United States.

" By so doing, so far as this bill goes, we do not interfere with the States passing and enforcing just such laws as they see proper as to inns, public conveyances, schools, institutions of learning and benevolence, places of amusement, and cemeteries—they may modify or abolish them at pleasure ; but, as no State under the old Constitution could discriminate in law against a citizen of another State as to fundamental rights to any greater degree than it did against a citizen of its own State, of the same class, so now no State must discriminate against a citizen of the United States merely on account of his race."

Mr. Thurman, of Ohio, said: "I do not believe that there is one-third of the Senate who, untrammeled by any outside pressure or any intrinsic consideration, would be found to vote for it. I think I am very liberal in supposing that even a third of the Senate would, if untrammeled, give it their support. But there are about eight hundred thousand colored voters in the United States, and they are essential to the maintenance of the power of the Republican party, and their demands, or what are supposed to be their demands, have more power in this Chamber than the Constitution of the country or the welfare of the colored race itself. That is the trouble, sir; that is what produces all the trouble we have about this matter. If this question were to be decided solely by the provisions in the Constitution, notwithstanding the bold and unqualified language of the Senator from Indiana (Mr. Pratt), notwithstanding his bold and positive assertions, I, humble as I am, would venture to achieve in this Senate such a victory over his constitutional interpretation as would settle that question at least in this body. Furthermore, if the fate of this measure were to be determined by its intrinsic merits, by its policy or impolicy, it would require but very little ability to show that it ought never to pass. And yet further, if its fate were to be determined by the interest of the colored race, there is nothing more capable of demonstration than that the very best interests of that race require that it should be defeated. And again, if its adoption or rejection depended upon principles of eternal justice recognized in all civilized communities, its rejection would be certain.

"I do not know but that it is considered almost ridiculous here to speak of the principles that once were universally admitted in regard to this Government and in regard to our Constitution. There was a time when no human being in the United States, of whatever political party, denied the proposition that the Government of the United States is a government of delegated powers, and that it possesses no powers but such as are expressly conferred upon it by the Constitution, or such as result by necessary implication from those which are thus expressly conferred. I say there was a time when no man in all the length and breadth of this land disputed that proposition; and perhaps there are very few now who openly deny it; and yet in practice it is utterly disregarded, and instead of that a wholly different mode of interpreting the Constitution and powers of this Government has acquired complete dominion in its legislative department. The old doctrine, which had the sanction not only of the fathers of the

Constitution, but of nearly three generations after them, has come to be totally supplanted in practice by the dogma that Congress may do whatever it is not expressly forbidden to do in the Constitution; so that, instead of the old doctrine that where you cannot find a delegated power, the power does not exist, the theory upon which Congress now acts is that it may exercise every power of Government whether it can be found in the Constitution or not, unless it is expressly prohibited. Upon no other foundation whatsoever can much of the legislation of the last eight or nine years be maintained for a moment. And I regret to say, Mr. President, that not only here, but in a judicial tribunal that I need not name, this doctrine has the apparent sanction of one of its most distinguished judges. A doctrine from which Marshall himself, strong as he was in his devotion to Federal power, would have shrunk in horror, is now avowed in effect, not in the seat that he occupied, but so close to it that it cannot but excite remark.

"Now, sir, what is the Constitution of the United States? It consists of certain delegations of power to the Federal Government apportioned among the departments of that Government, and of certain prohibitions. It is thus affirmative in its provisions and negative in its provisions. It grants power to the Government and to the several departments thereof, and then it contains prohibitions for the greater security of the States and of the people; prohibitions against the exercise of power by the Federal Government. Those prohibitions are to be found especially in the ninth section of the first article and in the first eight amendments. Then it contains another set of prohibitions upon the powers of the States, and those prohibitions are in every instance prohibitions upon the States as States; not prohibitions upon individuals, but prohibitions upon the States in their sovereign capacity as States.

"In the course of time the people proceeded to further amend the Constitution by articles thirteen, fourteen, and fifteen, and now I ask the particular attention of the Senate to what the prohibitions in these articles are in order to show that they are precisely of the same nature as the prohibitions in the original Constitution and in the first eight amendments thereof; prohibitions some of them upon the Federal Government as a Government, and the others prohibitions upon the States as sovereign States, and nothing else, nowhere prohibitions upon individuals as individuals, nowhere treating individuals as mere members of the community, but everywhere, in every line and sentence of the amendments, treating the States as corporations, as sovereign States, and acting upon them as States, and treating the Federal Government in its sphere as a sovereign Government, and acting upon it in its sovereign capacity. What is the thirteenth article of amendment?

Neither slavery nor involuntary servitude, except as a punishment for crime whereof the party shall have been duly convicted, shall exist within the United States, or any place subject to their jurisdiction.

"There is a prohibition upon both the Federal and the State governments. It is not directed against an individual, for how could any individual constitute slavery? Slavery can only exist by operation of law, and law could only be enacted by either the Federal or the State governments. The prohibition then is upon these governments as governments, and in no other sense whatsoever.

"Now, let us come to article fourteen, section 1:

All persons born or naturalized in the United States, and subject to the jurisdiction thereof, are citizens of the United States and of the State wherein they reside.

"That is mere definition. Then comes the prohibition:

No State—

"Not 'no individual,' but 'no State'—

shall make or enforce any law which shall abridge the privileges or immunities of citizens of the United States.

"An individual cannot make law; it is the State alone that can make law, and it is the State alone that can enforce law; and therefore the prohibition is directly upon that sovereign being, the State, that it shall neither make nor enforce any law that 'shall abridge the privileges or immunities of citizens of the United States;' and proceeding, it says:

Nor shall any State deprive any person of life, liberty, or property, without due process of law; nor deny to any person within its jurisdiction the equal protection of the laws.

"Mr. President, is not that plainly a prohibition directed to the States in their capacity as States? Is that provision a mere statute of murder, etc.? Is that merely a provision that no man in the United States shall commit murder, that no man in the United States shall kidnap, that no man in the United States shall unlawfully arrest and detain? Is that it? In other words, is this great provision of the Constitution degraded to the mere office of an ordinary criminal code? No, sir; but it is a limitation on the power of the States, and its prohibition is addressed to the States.

"What next? I need not speak of sections 2, 3, and 4 of that article, because they are not necessary to illustrate what I am endeavoring to prove. I therefore proceed to article fifteen; and what is that?

The right of citizens of the United States to vote shall not be denied or abridged by the United States or by any State on account of race, color, or previous condition of servitude."

Mr. Morton, of Indiana, said: "The Senator states that the prohibitions in the first section of the fourteenth amendment are addressed to the States as corporations and not to individuals. Calling his attention to the fact that the last section provides that Congress may en-

force the amendment by appropriate legislation, I ask him how Congress may enforce the prohibitions against a State?"

Mr. Thurman: "Just precisely as it enforces the prohibition against a State that it shall not pass any law impairing the obligation of contracts, contained in the original Constitution. It enforces it by providing for the making of a case for the judicial tribunals of the United States, in which that law impairing the obligation of contracts may be declared to be null and void. So, too, any law which any State may pass or enforce in violation of the thirteenth, fourteenth, or fifteenth amendments may be declared void in precisely the same way; and the only proper and constitutional mode in my judgment for Congress to adopt, is to provide for bringing any such cases that it seems proper to provide for decision before the judicial tribunals of the Federal Government. That was the mode under the Constitution before these amendments were adopted; and it is the proper mode yet.

".The Constitution is not so imperfect an instrument as some seem to suppose. It provides not simply for an executive and legislative department, but also for a judicial department, and provides that the judicial power shall extend to all cases arising under this Constitution or the laws and treaties made in pursuance thereof. That gives the judicial power ample cognizance of every case that can possibly arise that brings into discussion the validity of any State law which is said to be in contravention of the Constitution of the United States, or the laws of Congress passed in pursuance thereof.

"And now, in regard to this clause that 'Congress shall have power by appropriate legislation to enforce this article,' Congress would have exactly the same power if that clause were not in the Constitution at all. That does not add one iota to the power of Congress.

"The section is.

The Congress shall have power to enforce this article by appropriate legislation.

"That does not add, as I say, one iota to the power of Congress; and if it were stricken out of each of the thirteenth and fourteenth and fifteenth amendments, the power of Congress would be precisely what it now is. For what is 'appropriate legislation?' It is the very same thing that is provided for by the eighth section of article one, as construed by the Supreme Court in McCulloch vs. Maryland, the well-known and familiar provision as to the power of Congress to make necessary laws, and which reads:

The Congress shall have power to make all laws which shall be necessary and proper for carrying into execution the foregoing powers, and all other powers vested by this Constitution in the Government of the United States, or in any department or officer thereof.

"That provision covers the amendments

adopted afterward, just as much as it covers the powers conferred by the original Constitution.

"The judicial power extends to 'all cases' —you must have a case made before you can have a decision that a State law or a State decision is unconstitutional. The function of Congress is to provide by law for the making of the case, and then the judicial power intervenes and decides upon the validity or invalidity of the State law.

"The provision at the close of section eight of article one, 'that Congress shall have power to make all laws,' etc., applies to all provisions of the Constitution that may be in it in all time to come. It is a standing, speaking power that continues for all time as long 'as the Constitution shall endure, and reaches every particle of it, however it may be added to by amendment. We all know perfectly well that that provision 'to make all laws which shall be necessary and proper for carrying into execution the foregoing powers,' and so on, is wholly and absolutely unnecessary. It was so declared—and no man ever contradicted it—in the *Federalist*, and proved to be wholly unnecessary, and it was put in only out of abundant caution. In no debate whatever, either in the Federal Convention or in the conventions of the States, have I ever seen, nor do I believe that it has ever been found, the position that that was a substantive, independent power of Congress. It was nothing but putting in words, in the form of an express grant, that power which would have resulted by necessary implication even if those words were stricken out of the Constitution; and so it is expressly stated in the *Federalist.* There is no question about that.

"Now, whence come these words, 'appropriate legislation?' They come from the language of Marshall in deciding the case of McCulloch *vs.* The State of Maryland. It had been argued that Congress could not pass laws under this provision 'which may be necessary and proper for carrying into execution the foregoing powers,' etc., unless the measure adopted by Congress was one that was 'absolutely necessary,' and by 'absolutely necessary' was meant one which if it were not enacted would leave an express power without execution; that it was one which must be enacted in order that the express power could be executed at all, and therefore it must be one upon which the very existence of the express power in practice must depend. Otherwise it was not necessary legislation. We know with what power Marshall reasoned that down; and, going perhaps to the other extreme, he said that it was sufficient that the legislation was a natural and proper mode of effecting the end to be accomplished; that if the end was within the competency of Congress under the Constitution, then Congress had the power to adopt any means which are 'appropriate' and proper. 'Appropriate' was

the very word he used, and it was from that decision, using that word, that Congress had the power to adopt any legislation which was in its judgment appropriate, that the last section in each of the thirteenth, fourteenth, and fifteenth amendments was derived. It was taken right from that decision, showing conclusively that nothing more was meant by this clause, 'Congress shall have power to enforce by appropriate legislation the provisions of this article,' than was meant by the last clause in the eighth section of the first article of the Constitution, which says that Congress may make all laws which shall be necessary and proper for carrying into execution the foregoing powers, etc. They mean precisely the same thing; and therefore if this provision upon which so much has been based, and which the Senator from Indiana over the way (Mr. Pratt) seems to think overrides every thing in the Constitution and allows us to legislate whatever we please, whatever we may deem to be appropriate on the subjects provided for in these amendments to the Constitution, were stricken out of these articles, their provisions would not be weakened one single particle; not by the weight of a hair would they be weakened; they would be precisely the same. Nay, if the last clause were stricken out of section 8 of article 1, the Constitution would be precisely what it is.

"I have said that these are prohibitions upon the powers of the States. But what does this bill undertake to do? Does this bill undertake to treat with laws made or enforced by States that deprive any citizen of the United States of any privileges or immunities of a citizen of the United States, or that deny him the equal protection of the laws? Does it do any such thing as that? Let us see. Mark it, this bill must rest, if it have any constitutional warrant at all, upon these words: 'No State shall make or enforce any law which shall abridge the privileges or immunities of citizens of the United States.' And again: 'Nor shall any State deprive any person of life, liberty, or property, without due process of law; nor deny to any person within its jurisdiction the equal protection of the laws.'

"'No State shall make or enforce any law which shall abridge the privileges or immunities of citizens of the United States.' Does this bill deal with any such law of a State? No, sir; it does not profess to do so. It is not aimed at any law of a State. It is aimed against the acts of individuals; it is aimed against keepers of theatres, keepers of circuses, keepers of hotels, managers of railroads, stage-coaches, and the like. There is not one single sentence in the whole bill which is leveled against any law made or enforced by a State. The Constitution says that no State shall make or enforce any such law. This bill says to a State: 'Although you do not make any such law, although you do not enforce any such law, although your law is directly the opposite, although you punish every man who does any one of the acts mentioned in this bill, and punish him never so severely, yet the Congress of the United States will step in and under that clause of the Constitution which says that you, the State, shall not make or enforce any such law, we, the Federal power, will seize the man whom you have punished for this very act, and will punish him again ; we will treat the keeper of a theatre as the State; we will treat the hotel-keeper as the State ; we will treat the railroad conductor as the State ; we will treat the stage-driver as the State ; and although you may have punished each and every one of these men for the very acts enumerated in this bill, we, under the pretense that the States do make or enforce a law which deprives a citizen of his equal privileges and immunites, will seize that citizen again and subject him to a double punishment for the offense for which he has already suffered.' That is what this bill is; and no sophistry can make it any thing else.

"Take the case of Louisiana. If I am rightly informed—and if I am not the Senator from Louisiana can correct me—there is not one single act or omission in this bill which is not already punishable in Louisiana under her State statute. And now, sir, you are to go with the Federal power into the State of Louisiana and under pretense that that State has made and enforced laws which violate the fourteenth amendment, when every law that she has made and every law that she does enforce is in strict consonance and accordance with that amendment, you are to go there and seize her citizens who have already been punished by the State authority and punish them a second time by the Federal arm !

" Why, sir, if it is constitutional reasoning that supports this bill, then I confess that all my studies of the Constitution have been wholly in vain. If this is justice, then I confess that forty years and more of study of the law have all been thrown away upon me. If this is not monstrous, if this is not inhuman, if it is not a violation of the first principles of right, if it is not a violation of the spirit of that provision in the Constitution that no man shall be put in jeopardy twice for the same offense, if it is not legislation utterly disgraceful to a civilized people, then I confess, Mr. President, that I am not able to see correctly what is the scope or purpose of this legislation, or what are the principles of right and justice that should prevail under a civilized government."

Some verbal amendments were made to the report of the committee, after which it was adopted as a substitute for the original bill, and passed by the following vote :

YEAS—Messrs. Alcorn, Allison, Boutwell, Buckingham, Conkling, Edmunds, Flanagan, Frelinghuysen, Hamlin, Harvey, Howe, Ingalls, Mitchell Morrill of Vermont, Oglesby, Patterson, Pease, Pratt, Ramsey, Robertson, Sargent, Scott, Spencer, Stewart, Wadleigh, Washburn, West, Windom, and Wright—29.

NAYS—Messrs. Bogy, Boreman, Carpenter, Coop-
er, Davis, Hager, Hamilton of Maryland, Johnston, Kelly, Lewis, McCreery, Merrimon, Norwood, Ransom, Saulsbury, and Stockton—16.

ABSENT—Messrs. Anthony, Bayard, Brownlow, Cameron, Chandler, Clayton, Conover, Cragin, Dennis, Dorsey, Fenton, Ferry of Connecticut, Ferry of Michigan, Gilbert, Goldthwaite, Gordon, Hamilton of Texas, Hitchcock, Jones, Logan, Morrill of Maine, Morton, Schurz, Sherman, Sprague, Stevenson, Thurman, and Tipton—28.

In the House, the bill was considered and referred to the Committee on the Judiciary, where it remained, together with the House bill, at the close of the Session.

In the Senate, on March 4th, the bill to restore the rights of the State of Louisiana was considered.

Mr. Carpenter, of Wisconsin, said : " Mr. President, I shall endeavor to show that the admitted facts warrant the passage of the bill now under consideration. Those facts are summed up in the preamble to this bill, which I will ask the Clerk to read."

The Chief Clerk read as follows :

Whereas, There is no Governor, Lieutenant-Governor, Secretary of State, Attorney-General, Auditor of Public Accounts, or Superintendent of Education in the State of Louisiana, holding said offices, respectively, under an election by the legal voters of the State of Louisiana, in pursuance of the constitution and laws of said State ; and whereas there is not in said State any Legislature elected by the legal voters of said State, according to the constitution and laws thereof ; and whereas there is no provision in the constitution or laws of said State for the election of a Governor, Lieutenant-Governor, Secretary of State, Attorney-General, Auditor of Public Accounts, or Superintendent of Education, until the next regular election, to be held in November, A. D. 1876 ; and whereas the offices of Governor, Lieutenant-Governor, Secretary of State, Attorney-General, Auditor of Public Accounts, and Superintendent of Education are now filled *de facto* by persons claiming the right to hold said offices in virtue of a pretended canvass of the votes given at the last general election in said State, on the 4th day of November, A. D. 1872, by John Lynch and others, but which canvass has been shown to be fraudulent and void ; and whereas a body of men in said State now claim to be the members of, and to constitute, the Legislature of said State, and were organized as a Legislature in pursuance of illegal orders issued by a judge of the Circuit Court of the United States for the District of Louisiana ; and whereas the President of the United States, in May, A. D. 1873, did issue his proclamation recognizing the person now holding *de facto* the office of Governor of said State as legal Governor of said State, and the persons now holding *de facto* the offices of Lieutenant-Governor, Secretary of State, Attorney-General, Auditor of Public Accounts, and Superintendent of Education in said State as legal officers of said State government, which proclamation was issued upon representations made by said persons holding said offices, or on their behalf, but it now appears that said persons holding said offices are not legal officers of said State ; and whereas said pretended Legislature is now in session, pretending to enact laws for said State, which said pretended Governor is pretending to approve, under which pretended laws it will be claimed rights have vested, so that the people of said State may be oppressed and involved in vexatious and expensive litigation before the next general election, under the constitution and laws of said State, in A. D. 1876 ; and whereas the public peace in said State is at present preserved, and can only be preserved during the existing state of things in said State, at the expense of the United States, and by retaining a part of the army in said State: Therefore, to quiet the discontent and restore the State to its full rights, and give it officers of its government which shall be chosen by the legal voters of said State.

Mr. Carpenter: "This preamble sets forth the general propositions which I claim result from the facts of this case either conceded or clearly established by the evidence. My first purpose is to establish this, and, if I succeed in doing so, I think it will not be very difficult to satisfy the Senate that Congress ought to apply some remedy. I shall then contend that a new election is the only adequate remedy for such a case; that, when the people of a State have been defrauded of the result of an election, and all the State officers and the Legislature are usurpers, the proper remedy is to give the people another opportunity to elect their officers.

"In the first place, let it be borne in mind that the general election in that State, for the election of presidential electors, Governor and other State officers, half of the Senate, and all the members of the lower House of the Legislature, was held on the 4th day of November, 1872.

"I ask the attention of the Senate to the fact that, at this election, electors of President and Vice-President ought to have been elected, because I claim that the decision of both Houses of Congress rejecting the vote of the electors of that State, and denying Louisiana any voice whatever in the election of President and Vice-President, is an adjudication by Congress that no result was accomplished by the pretended election of November 4, 1872. If any thing was accomplished at that election, then presidential electors, a Governor and other State officers, and a Legislature, were elected. But, if no presidential electors were elected, then no election of Governor and other State officers and members of the Legislature was effected. Congress having decided that the election was void as to presidential electors, it follows that the election of State officers and members of the Legislature held at the same time, and subject to the same objections, must be void also.

"Let us consider this election, the canvass of votes, and the subsequent determination of Congress in the premises.

"The election passed off quietly; no riots or violence interfered with its progress; and the returns were generally made to the Governor of the State in conformity with the statute law of the State. But these returns were never canvassed, except by the De Periet board, appointed by Governor Warmoth under the act of November 20, 1872, and the Foreman board, appointed by the pretended McEnery Legislature. The result of both these canvasses was to declare that McEnery and his associates on the State ticket were elected by about 9,906 majority.

"The Lynch board never made a canvass of the returns, because they never had the returns before them; but, in a manner wholly unwarranted by any law, and in open defiance and flagrant violation of the law under which they pretended to act, entered into an investigation at large to estimate the result of the election. This board certified that a certain number of persons, who may be designated the Grant electors, were duly elected; that Kellogg and his associates on the State ticket were elected; and that members now constituting the Kellogg Legislature were also duly elected at that election.

"The validity of the election as respects presidential electors was necessarily involved in the question whether their votes for President and Vice-President should be counted. The subject was referred to the Committee on Privileges and Elections; and I shall refer the Senate to the unanimous report of that committee, made by its chairman, the Senator from Indiana (Mr. Morton), as bearing upon that subject. Before doing so, however, permit me to refer to the objections which I have made against the validity of the canvass by the Lynch board, the only canvass relied upon to establish the right of Kellogg and his associates to hold the offices of that State:

"1. I showed that the Lynch board, so called, never had a legal existence; that Longstreet and Hawkins, who pretended to be members of that board, never were elected; and that Bovee was disqualified, because he was a candidate at that election.

"2. That the persons claiming to be members of this board were enjoined from canvassing any thing but the official returns.

"3. That the board was abolished by the act of November 20, 1872.

"4. That this board never had the returns before them.

"5. That they had no warrant of law, even conceding that they were a legal board, for doing what they pretended to do—that is, inquire at large into the result of the election; that all that even the legal board could do was to canvass the legal returns.

"6. That, if the board had been duly elected, had not been enjoined, and if it had not been abolished, and had the official returns, and had been authorized by law to depart from the returns and inquire at large to ascertain the result of the election, still their proceedings were corrupt and fraudulent, as admitted and sworn to by the members of the board, to such extent as to invalidate their proceedings; to such an extent as would nullify the effect of the judgment of a judicial court clothed with jurisdiction to make such inquiry.

"Now let me refer to the report of the committee, drawn and presented by the Senator from Indiana (Mr. Morton), to see how far it sustains the objections I have made to the canvass by the Lynch board. The subject being considered was the result of the election as to presidential electors. After setting out the election law of 1870, and the circumstances under which it is claimed the Lynch board and the Warmoth board were elected and organized, the report proceeds as follows:

The election for presidential electors, members of Congress, State officers, and members of the Legislature, was held in Louisiana on the 4th of November, and the returns of the election in the various parishes were sent to the Governor by the Supervisors of Registration, as required by law. The Governor refused to act with the board known as the Lynch board, or to open and lay before that board the returns of the election from the various parishes; but opened them and prepared to make the count before what is known as the Wharton board, which was then enjoined from further proceedings by Judge Durell. The official returns which had been sent to the Governor were by him withheld from the Lynch returning board, and never at any time came into the possession or under the examination of that board. The Legislature of Louisiana, at its session in the winter of 1872, passed an act abolishing the returning or canvassing board, as created by the act of 1870, and authorizing the State Senate to elect a returning board, to have the same powers as the former, and making other changes in the mode of conducting the elections; and on the 20th of November, 1872, the Governor, who had not signed this act, but kept it in his possession during the pendency of these proceedings in the Circuit Court of the United States, and also proceedings of a like character commenced in the eighth district court of the State, signed the bill and published it as a law.

" This is the act which abolished the Lynch board. Again the report says:

Some two or three days preceding the 4th of December, the Lynch board officially declared that M. F. Bonzano, J. Lanabere, C. H. Halstead, L. C. Croudanez, A. R. Johnson, Milton Morris, J. Taylor, and John Ray, whom we shall designate as the Grant electors, had received a majority of all the votes in the State for electors of President and Vice-President, and the Secretary of State de jure, Mr. Bovee, not then in possession of the office of Secretary of State or the State seal, but who had been decided by the Supreme Court of the State a few days before to be the lawful Secretary, made a certificate of election to the persons so declared chosen as electors, and on the 4th of December they met and cast their votes for President and Vice-President, according to the requirements of the act of Congress. They did not, on that day, however, seal up their vote, but kept it open for several days until Mr. Bovee, the Secretary of State, got possession of the State seal, so as to attach it to their certificates of election. The Secretary of State had no right, under the law, to make any certificate upon the subject, unless for the information of the Governor, and his certificate constitutes no legal evidence of the election of the persons therein named—the Lynch board.

" And I call attention to the language of the Senator from Indiana in this his first report from the committee, which was unanimous:

The Lynch board, in making the count and declaration as to the election of electors, did so without having before them any of the official returns of the election as made out by the officers of the election under the laws of the State, and had no legal evidence before them at all upon which they could count the votes, but their count was made upon documents, affidavits, and statements, ex parte in their character, having no legal validity, and which could not, in the nature of things, form the basis of an accurate and reliable declaration of the result of the election.

" There, Senators, is the judgment passed by the Senator from Indiana upon the validity of the canvass by the Lynch board.

" Mr. President, bearing in mind that the Senator, in this report, was speaking of the election of November 4, 1872, for the election of presidential electors, State officers, and Legislature, and that the same objections exist to the validity of the election of State officers and Legislature as in regard to presidential electors; that the election for all was held at the same time, under the same election laws, and that the returns for all these officers were made in the same way; that the canvass by the Lynch board was made in the same manner as to all these officers, and that, if one is invalid, so also is the other, am I not justified in saying that the Senator from Indiana, by this report, in effect determined that the election failed as to State officers and Legislature, as well as in regard to presidential electors? What we call an election consists of several parts. There is, first of all, a registration of voters. Secondly, the casting of ballots. Thirdly, the counting and canvassing of votes. Each step in this process must be performed according to law to secure the legal result which we call an election.

" It will be seen, by carefully examining this report, that the fact that the votes were not legally canvassed and certified was regarded as conclusive that the election as to presidential electors was void.

" The two Houses of Congress adopted, or at least acted upon, the doctrine of this report, and decided that the so-called Grant electors had not been duly elected, and therefore the votes cast by them for President and Vice-President could not be counted.

" Now, Mr. President, it is clearly established that the election of the Kellogg government was subject to all the objections and afflicted with all the infirmities which both Houses of Congress held conclusive against the election of presidential electors. It will bear repetition that the election of the Kellogg government was, at the same time, in the same manner, surrounded by the same circumstances, canvassed by the same board, and in the same manner, and, in every particular affecting its validity, identical with the election of the Grant electors, which both Houses of Congress have declared to be absolutely void.

" Therefore, am I not warranted in declaring that Congress has already, in effect, declared that the Kellogg government never was elected?

" In connection with this report, I should add that the decision of the Supreme Court of Louisiana was made before that report.

" Notwithstanding the decision of that court, now relied upon by the Senator from Indiana to establish the validity of the election of the Kellogg government, because it held that the Lynch board was the legal returning board, the Senator from Indiana regarded the pretended canvass by that board as absolutely void, in consequence of the irregularity of their proceedings, and the fact that the returns never were before them; which objections exist in full force, and must be equally fatal, in regard to the election of the Kellogg government.

"Let me say that, although this report was made as a preliminary report by the committee, yet all the testimony subsequently taken by the committee tends to increase rather than lessen the objection to the validity of that election.

"Congress will stand in an unenviable attitude before the country if in regard to an election for several officers, held at the same time and conducted in the same manner as to all, it shall decide that as to one it is void and as to the other valid; if it shall hold that as to presidential electors it was void, and yet as to State government it was valid.

"Assuming the case as I claim it to be, two questions arise in regard to the bill now under consideration for holding a new election in that State under Federal authority: first, has Congress the power to pass such a bill? and, second, if it has the power, is it expedient to exercise it?

"I shall first consider the question whether Congress possesses such power. Many of our friends, for whose judgment I have great respect, doubt its existence; and we all agree that, if the power does exist, it is one of the most delicate attributes of this Government, and ought not to be exercised except in case of necessity. But I maintain that, if the necessity exists, it is our imperative duty to exercise this power discreetly, prudently, but so as fully to meet the existing case and remedy the existing evil.

"The Constitution makes it our duty to guarantee to the State of Louisiana a republican form of government. What does the phrase, 'republican form of government,' mean? I answer, it means a republican kind of government, or a republican government; and that the essential element of a republican government is that its offices shall be held by persons chosen for that purpose by the people; that no government is republican, within the meaning of the guarantee clause, the powers of which are administered by persons not chosen by the people. To construe the Constitution so as to hold that as long as a State government observes the form it may depart from the reality of republican government, is to render the guarantee clause utterly worthless. The Supreme Court has often declared that the Constitution must be so construed as to secure the substantial results contemplated by its framers; that forms and fictions are not enough.

"All history demonstrates that the greatest danger to free government is from the usurpation of rulers and the perversion of forms. The cunning hypocrisy of Augustus established a despotism in Rome after the sword of Julius Cæsar had failed. Augustus established the empire in the name of the republic; and long

after his power was complete, and the imperial government in full operation, maintained republican *forms*; that is, it was 'republican in form,' but imperial in fact. Napoleon, the first consul, gradually ripened into the emperor. We have recently seen the Republic of Spain, without any change of form, assuming and exercising imperial power. The pretended election of Napoleon III. was, in form, republican; in fact, a fraud. And illustrations might be multiplied indefinitely. If republican governments on this continent are ever overthrown, it will be accomplished by employing the forms of a republic to mask departure from its substance. The literature of 1789 shows that our fathers were keenly alive to this fact; and it would be strange, indeed, if in framing a constitution designed, as its preamble declares, to insure domestic tranquillity and secure the blessings of liberty to themselves and their posterity, and in establishing a government to preside over and protect the States, no provision was made to guard them against the greatest and the most common danger that besets free institutions; and yet it will be conceded that no such provision was made unless it is contained in the clause under consideration.

"If I am right in saying that it is the vital element of republican government that its rulers are chosen by the people, it follows that the present government of Louisiana, lacking this, is not a republican government. And in regard to the *power* of Congress to interfere at this time, it is evident that, if such power does not exist, it would not if in 1876 Kellogg and his associates should run again and be defeated by 20,000 majority, and Durrell should set them up; and in 1880 the same thing should take place, and be repeated in 1884, and so on during Kellogg's natural life. These repetitions would make the outrage more manifest, but would not increase the power of Congress. If Congress cannot interfere in the first year of such a usurpation, it cannot in the fiftieth; because our power is derived from the Constitution, which is the same at all times; and what we cannot do at once, we cannot do ultimately. If Kellogg and his associates should be thus continued in power for twenty years, and avow the purpose of remaining during their lives by the use of the same means, would it be contended that the State had a republican government? It might, indeed, be said that the State had a government republican in form, but it would be true that the form was used to continue a despotism. There is nothing in the Constitution, taken as a whole, nor in the literature of that day, which will justify us in saying that the framers of the Constitution were sticklers for form, and intended to provide that in usurping the functions of free government, and transforming the States into despotisms, in fact the usurpers should be confined to a particular method of accomplishing that result, namely, an observance of the forms of a republican government. It was intended to preserve not the form merely, but the reality; not the fiction, but the fact of free government, republican government, a government elected by the people; and that, too, not occasionally, and after long interruptions, but at all times. And if Congress ascertains that at any time such government does not exist in a particular State, its duty is imperative to take the proper steps to give such a government to the State. And what laws may Congress pass in such a case? The Constitution answers this question. 'The Congress shall have power to make all laws which shall be necessary and proper for carrying into execution all the powers vested by this Constitution in the Government of the United States'—one of which is the power to guarantee to every State a republican form or kind of government.

"Now, in the case before us, what law is necessary and proper to confer upon the State of Louisiana a government chosen by its people? Evidently a law which shall authorize the people of that State to fill the State offices with persons of their own choice in place of the present usurpers. The constitution of that State is republican, the judges of the Supreme Court are properly in their places, but the political department of the government is held by usurpers. The extent of our legislation in a given case should be measured by the evil to be corrected. In 1865 you found that State without any government whatever, and then you took the proper steps to establish a republican government there. You provided for a convention to frame a State constitution. You provided for an election by the people to fill the State offices and the Legislature. It was necessary at that time to do these things, because there was no government and no part of a government intact in that State. Now it is necessary to do only a part of these things. It is not necessary to frame a constitution, for the State has one adopted by the people. It is not necessary to provide for the election of judges, because the judicial department of that government has not been usurped. But it is necessary to provide for the election of State officers and a Legislature, because those places are held by usurpers, and because the government is not republican in kind, unless its political department, its law-making power, is held by persons who have been elected by the people. I do not see how any one who supported the reconstruction acts of Congress can question the constitutionality of this bill. As certainly as the whole includes its parts, so certainly, if Congress has the power to set up a whole government, and authorize an election to fill all its offices, it has the power to reclaim one department of the government from usurpers and restore it to the people.

"It is said that this bill is in conflict with the theory of State rights; but what right can be dearer to a State than the right of self-government? The people have been deprived of

this right, and this bill proposes to restore it. The people of every State have a right to demand that the United States shall guarantee to them a government, and a whole government, of their own choosing, and shall rid them of a government which exists only by usurpation. They secured this right by the adoption of the Constitution of the United States, vesting the power in us, and thereby casting the duty upon us, to do this thing. And if any State, at any time, is compelled or permitted to submit to a usurping government, it is because we fail to perform the duty imposed upon us. And whether we fail from timidity, or from party prejudice or policy, it is equally a disregard of our duty.

"If I am right in asserting that it is the duty of the United States to guarantee a republican government to every State, and right in saying that a government held by usurpers is not a republican government, then it is impossible to deny the constitutionality of this bill; because, if we have the power to interfere at all, the manner of interference is a matter entirely within the discretion of Congress. The powers conferred upon this Government are sovereign powers; that is, powers unlimited, save as the Constitution regulates their exercise; and they override all State constitutions and laws. This power to guarantee a republican government to the States is an absolute and sovereign power, and its exercise wholly unrestricted by the Constitution. Congress is authorized to do a certain thing, and the mode of doing it is committed entirely to the discretion of Congress. We may do in every case just what the case requires; and in this case it is evident that what this bill proposes is the only remedy, the only way, to give that State for the next two years a government of its own choosing."

Mr. Ferry, of Connecticut, said: "I do not wish to interrupt the Senator, but I should like to ask a question. Who is to decide whether the officers exercising the governing power in a State have been chosen by the people of that State?"

Mr. Carpenter: "Ultimately, no doubt, we must decide it."

Mr. Ferry: "Then I understand that in all cases where the officers exercising the governing power of a State have not been elected, or are alleged not to have been elected by the people of that State, Congress has the right to inquire, decide, intervene, and order a new election?"

Mr. Carpenter: "I say undoubtedly, as a question of power. My friend is seeking to force me upon what he thinks the great objection to this power; but let me suggest to him that I am discussing the power itself, and not the propriety of exercising it in every case; and that the objection suggested by his question is more properly directed against the exercise of the power improperly than against its existence. It is undoubtedly true that this power might be abused; but the same is true of every power conferred upon the Government. The principal arguments I have heard and seen against the existence of this power are designed to show, and do conclusively show, that the power, if abused, would lead to disastrous results; and the fear is always expressed that if the power were conceded it would be abused. But why is there more danger of the abuse of this than of many other powers of the Government? No one will question, I presume, that, as regards mere power, Congress might to-day decide the existing government of Connecticut not to be republican in form, and take steps to supplant it by another. This would of course be a scandalous abuse of the power. But does any one fear that it will be so abused? There is no doubt of the existence of the power, nor that it was wisely conferred. The safeguard against its abuse lies in the fact that the proceeding might be taken in regard to any other and every other State; and Senators are not likely to vote proceedings against another State which they would be unwilling to have applied to their own. Everybody, in the discussion of this question, refers to the election in New York when Griswold was elected, but Hoffman was canvassed in as Governor of that State; and it is asked triumphantly, Is it the duty of Congress to interfere in such a case? I say no ; not because Congress did not possess the power, but because such a case would not justify the exercise of it. There is no parallel between that case and this.

"The Senator from Connecticut must be aware that extreme cases are not proper tests of general principles. There are cases in which Congress should interfere. There are cases in which it should not. There may be other cases of which it would be difficult to say to which class they belong; and where Congress should be in doubt, prudence would dictate that no action should be taken."

Mr. Frelinghuysen: "In New York they had a republican form of government, and that is all the Constitution guarantees."

Mr. Carpenter: "This suggests again the question I have already discussed in regard to the meaning of the phrase 'republican form.' If you merely mean the form of government fixed by the State constitution—"

Mr. Frelinghuysen: "I was using the words of the Constitution."

Mr. Carpenter: "The words of the Constitution must be construed; and the same word is used in different senses in the Constitution. The constitutional phrase is, the State shall have a 'republican form of government;' which I claim means a republican kind of government, or a republican government. If the Senator from New Jersey can maintain that while the constitutional structure of the government is republican it is immaterial whether it be administered by those who were elected or by those who were defeated by the people, then, in Wisconsin, which has a republican constitution, and where at the last election the

Democrats carried their State officers and the Legislature, while Republicans enough to have changed the result staid at home and did not vote, if Governor Washburn had said to his successor, 'True, you were elected, but I think I will stay in;' and the members of the old Legislature had said, 'We don't like to see Democrats in our place; we will hold over,' the government thus administered would have been republican in form, if the Senator from New Jersey is right, and would have satisfied the requirements of the Constitution. If this be so, the States of this Union are the legitimate prey of fraud and violence, and the guarantee of the Constitution is utterly worthless. A construction of that instrument which gives the people of a State over to the usurpation of their rulers, and denies them all remedy, is, to say the least of it, not wisely devised to insure the domestic tranquillity or to secure the blessings of liberty to ourselves and our posterity."

Mr. Frelinghuysen: "I think that the Senator from Wisconsin strikes out of the Constitution the word 'form,' and makes the Constitution read that there shall be a republican government. I think that word 'form' has great significance. I think the two things that were guaranteed are a republican form of government, and tranquillity, peace, government. If the people of a State have a republican form of government, and if the United States maintain order and peace and tranquillity so that the people can correct their own errors, their own mistakes, I think that then we have done all that we ought to do; and that for the United States to intervene and force an election upon them is taking from them a republican form of government."

Mr. Carpenter: "The word 'form' is in the Constitution, but the question is, What does it mean? I think it is synonymous with 'kind' or 'class,' and the phrase is equivalent to 're-publican government.' There is no doubt that the objection intended to be secured by this provision was to compel the States to remain republics, and prevent their becoming monarchies; to perpetuate government in which the people should enjoy the right of self-government by electing their officers, and to forbid governments in which the people should be governed either under the pretext of divine right or by usurpation; and any construction of the Constitution under which it fails to accomplish this end must be a misconstruction. Such a construction does injustice to the memory of the fathers; it is trifling with the whole subject to say that so long as usurpation and despotic power observe republican forms in administration they are protected by the Constitution."

Mr. Thurman: "Will the Senator allow me to interrupt him for a moment?"

Mr. Carpenter: "Certainly."

Mr. Thurman: "I wish to make this suggestion: There is nothing in the Constitution of the United States that requires that a State shall have a written constitution. Its constitution may be like that of Great Britain, without one word of writing. Now if the word 'form' be taken in its most narrow sense, pray what is the guarantee worth in a case where there is no written constitution of a State ? "

Mr. Carpenter: " That well illustrates what I was trying to illustrate in another way, and it comes back to this : the question is, whether by that article of the Constitution it was intended to guarantee something to a State, or nothing; whether it was meant to deal with the reality of the thing, or with the mere fiction and form ? "

Mr. Norwood, of Georgia, said : " Before the Senator passes from that point, I wish to ask him a question; and I will state in advance to the Senator that my object is to get light on this subject: because it is in my opinion the main point in the case, and the one in regard to which I have felt greatly embarrassed. I wish him to state whether he thinks there is but one remedy where a republican form of government has been destroyed or overthrown ? The remedy he proposes is, by act of Congress to order a new election. Does he consider that a better remedy than for Congress, if it ascertains, as he says it can, by a review of an election in the State, that a minority has overthrown the majority and taken possession of the government, to determine that the majority shall have control of the government; and, if necessary, to authorize the Executive to see that the majority shall be installed ? "

Mr. Carpenter: " The Senator, of course, is aware that I do not think that McEnery was in fact elected, although the returns show that he was."

Mr. Norwood: " I understand that. I am merely asking the Senator whether he thinks it is better to order a new election than to have those put in power who the returns show were elected."

Mr. Carpenter : " If I believed that McEnery was in fact elected at that election, the logic of the situation would dictate that Congress, if that were necessary, should recognize his government. But in the first place I do not believe that the McEnery government has any more right than the Kellogg government. In the second place the McEnery government never had an existence in fact.

" Mr. President; these interruptions (of which I do not complain) have drawn me somewhat away from the line of argument I intended to pursue, compelled me to interrupt the order in which I intended to discuss the topics involved, so that in returning to my subject I may repeat some things I have said. But I will resume, as well as I can, the thread I had in hand when I was interrupted.

" In the first place, if the present state of things in Louisiana amounts to a usurpation, then Congress may prescribe a remedy, or it can prescribe no remedy in case of any usurpation in a State. I had supposed that it was universally conceded that this article of the Constitution was intended to vest this power in the General Government, that the guarantee of republican government was intended to protect the people against usurpation, and that the guarantee against domestic violence was intended to protect the State government against turbulence within the State; and that the jurisdiction to determine whether the state of things existing in a State authorized the General Government to interfere for the purpose of executing the first of these guarantees was vested exclusively in the General Government, not in the State; and I have read from the writings of Mr. Calhoun, the great champion of State rights, in support of this view.

" And when it is conceded, as it is by the Senator from Connecticut, that the only existing government in Louisiana is, 'root and branch, a usurpation,' I supposed Congress had the power, and was obliged, to provide some suitable remedy; and the bill under consideration seems to me to provide the only suitable remedy.

" But what seems to me a very important element of this case is, that we are not now considering in the first instance whether the Federal Government ought to interfere. The fact is, the Federal Government has already interfered through its judicial department. A Federal judge acting not only without jurisdiction, but in confessed violation of an act of Congress, has organized this usurpation; and the question is whether Congress has the power to undo the wrong he has done, by restoring to the people of that State the right of which he has deprived them. Can it be maintained that a Federal judge, in open defiance of Federal law, may take a State government from the hands of the people, confer it upon usurpers, and that Congress is powerless in the premises ? It may be said the judge might be impeached. This would punish him, but would not redress the wrong. The Kellogg government would still exist, protected by Federal troops, unless Congress should interfere; and I can imagine no form of interference that would redress the wrong, except to restore to that people, as this bill proposes, the right they have been deprived of, to choose their own rulers. And I shall be curious to hear the Senator from Connecticut point out any other remedy. For that, however, I must wait until he shall see fit to reveal it.

" I understand that the Supreme Court of the State is in collusion with Kellogg, has already corruptly decided many cases in his favor, and will continue in the same course. There can be no judicial remedy in that State, and the remedy of force is forbidden by the Constitution of the United States. This State government will not inaugurate any movement to overthrow itself. The people of the State cannot; because, first, the Constitution of the United States forbids it; and, second, because, if they should attempt it, they would be confronted with Federal bayonets. Now, sir, what is the device locked up in the mind of the Senator from Connecticut which will meet this case?

"Let me return once more to this question of power, from which I have been so often drawn to answer the questions that have been put to me. The Constitution provides that the United States shall guarantee to every State a republican government. The State of Louisiana has not such a government at present. What remedy may we employ? I answer, in the language of the Constitution, any proper and necessary remedy; and we are the exclusive judges of the means proper to be employed, provided we possess the power to do any thing in the premises. I deny that any power conferred by the Constitution upon the United States is subject to the consent, or falls by the dissent, of any State. The powers conferred upon this Government are sovereign powers; they are unlimited, except where the Constitution itself has regulated their exercise. Where the Constitution confers power over a given subject, and does not regulate the exercise of the power, the power of this Government is as absolute as the power of the Czar of Russia. Take the power to declare war. Has not this Government as much power in that respect as the Czar of Russia or the Sultan of Turkey? Take the power of taxation. In certain particulars it is restricted by the Constitution; but, excepting those restrictions, it is an unlimited and arbitrary power. We may declare war to-morrow, with or without cause, against any nation or all mankind. We may, by the power of taxation, withdraw the last dollar from the pockets of the people and place it in the Treasury. We may put every man, woman, and child, into the army. Take the power to establish post-offices and post-roads. This is one of the unlimited powers conferred by the Constitution, and Congress may establish as many or as few as it pleases, and provide such method as it pleases for carrying the mails.

"The Constitution of the United States was intended to classify and distribute the powers of sovereignty between the General and State governments. It enumerates the powers which shall be possessed by the General Government, but does not, like a code of procedure, prescribe the mode, manner, or extent of their execution. All that is committed to the discretion of Congress. What is proper to be done within the limits of reason is for Congress to determine. The Constitution says nothing about a military academy; but it authorizes Congress to raise and maintain armies. How they shall be raised, whether by encouraging volunteering or by draft, how they shall be armed, disciplined, and regulated, all that is committed to Congress by that provision of the Constitution which empowers Congress 'to make all laws necessary and proper' to raise and maintain armies. Congress has deemed it advisable to establish

a school of instruction at West Point as a means of securing suitable officers of the army.

"Now, take this power to guarantee a republican government to a State, and assuming, as the Senator from Connecticut agrees, that the existing State government is a usurpation, and assuming, as I maintain, that a republican government is a government by the people, and that a government by usurpation is not a republican government, and that the United States are bound to correct this evil, no man can deny the constitutionality of this bill, because it provides one, if not the best, remedy for the evil. In other words, if the United States have the power to interfere in this case, the mode in which that interference shall be made is entirely within the discretion of Congress; and by passing this bill we shall determine that this is a proper mode. Those who deny the power of Congress to pass this bill deny the power of Congress to interfere at all; deny—if they concede, as my friend from Connecticut does, that this is a case of usurpation—the power of Congress to interfere in case of any usurpation of a State government. If this be a sound doctrine, then the Constitution of the United States secures to the people of a State not 'the blessings of liberty,' but the evils of usurpation and despotism. The people cannot by force overthrow such usurpation, because the government de facto will appeal to the President, as this government has done, and will be supported by him, as this is. It must be presumed that the clause of the Constitution under consideration was inserted for some purpose; and if not for a case like this, for what purpose was it inserted? To deny that it authorizes Congress to interfere in the most flagrant case of usurpation, is to deny that it has any effect whatever; and if it applies to a flagrant case of usurpation, it applies to every case of usurpation.

"But the great objection which this bill encounters is as to its expediency. It is said that to pass this bill would be a dangerous precedent. What is meant by saying that this would be a dangerous precedent? It is a dangerous precedent to hang a man, and it might be argued that if a government were clothed with power to hang a murderer, it might abuse that power, or make a mistake, and hang a man for murder who had not committed that offense. Calomel is a dangerous remedy, and it might be argued that to allow physicians to administer it would set a precedent for them to administer it where it was unnecessary. But all this class of argument merely tends to show that, if the power to pass this bill were conceded, it might encourage the passage of a similar bill in a case where it was unnecessary; in other words, the power might be abused. But if this is a satisfactory argument against this power, it would be against every other power conferred by the Constitution. Chief-Justice Marshall said, in a case long ago, that there was no power conferred upon the Government that might not be abused; therefore, that a particular power might be abused was no argument against its existence. This power is undoubtedly one of the most delicate of those conferred upon this Government, and its abuse would be attended with wide-spread and disastrous results; but it was thought necessary to confer it in order to prevent revolutions in the States, which would be likely to result in monarchy. It was said in the *Federalist* the existence of such a power would in most cases render its exercise unnecessary. And so it has proved. For nearly a century no other case has arisen that called for its exercise. But, now that the case has arisen, to deny the existence of this power would encourage the repetition of such wrongs to an extent that cannot be foreseen. We may well wish the necessity for our decision had not arisen; but it has without our fault. If you were crossing Long Bridge, prudence would dictate that you should avoid running off on the right-hand side; but if to avoid this accident you should drive so far from that side as to go off on the other, your very prudence would cause your calamity. So here it is as dangerous not to act when the case calls for action as it is to act when the case does not call for it. And I cannot resist the unpleasant conclusion that for Congress to refuse to act in a case like this, and to deny its power to do so, would be setting a precedent to be followed by fatal results."

Mr. Sherman, of Ohio, said: "Every Senator in the whole body will admit that the Senator from Wisconsin has redeemed his pledge faithfully, eloquently, and ably. No one will gainsay that; but I think it is equally clear, if any one will read not only the newspapers but the indications that we have from persons from Louisiana—and I have also been on the ground in Louisiana and heard from both sides —that a large majority of the people of Louisiana have acquiesced in the existing condition of affairs. It is as plain, as palpable to me as the light of day, that it is wise that they have so acquiesced. They will have an opportunity at the next election in November to redeem their State government, if it has fallen into the hands of usurpers. The power will be again restored to them, and I think it is the wisest thing in the world to pass in silence all that has occurred in Louisiana, with the certainty that the people themselves will correct any evils that have been done there.

"I sympathize with my friend from Wisconsin, but at the same time I do not believe he is pursuing the course best for the people of the United States or for the people of Louisiana. I believe Congress had better attend to their ordinary legitimate business, leaving matters in Louisiana to right themselves, and they are now being rapidly righted, and at the next election we may probably have a Legislature elected by the consent of the governed, ready to pass laws to suit their wishes without difficulty. The very election law now pend-

ing has been passed, perhaps by the general consent of all, and is declared to be a fair law. There is no practical difficulty in the Louisiana matter. If we let things alone in Louisiana, the popular will as expressed in a legal election will undoubtedly prevail. The only result of this movement now to overthrow the government of Louisiana will be to derange and disorder the condition of affairs there, and turn out of office two or three State officers whose terms happen to extend beyond next fall."

Mr. Saulsbury, of Delaware, said: "Mr. President, I do not know that I shall vote for the bill of the Senator from Wisconsin when it comes before the Senate; but I think it is right that he should have the privilege of bringing that question before the Senate whenever he sees proper to do so. I concur with him that no more important question can be presented at the present session of Congress than the question involved in the condition of affairs in Louisiana. I am surprised at the enunciations of Senators on this floor that there has been a general acquiescence on the part of the people of Louisiana in the present condition of affairs in that State. Why, sir, it is known to every Senator on this floor that if the Federal power was withdrawn, if the troops of the United States were removed from Louisiana and a proclamation made that the people of Louisiana should settle this matter for themselves, the Kellogg government would vanish out of existence in less than one month. The people of Louisiana have protested against such proceedings in every way that it was possible for them to resort to. They have been before the Committee on Privileges and Elections at the present session protesting; they have appealed to the President of the United States, but have been turned away; and now are they to be turned away from this Hall of Congress? Are we to spurn their appeals for relief simply on the ground that because they do not resist the Federal authority they are supposed to acquiesce in the present condition of affairs?"

Mr. West, of Louisiana, said: "I will say one word to those gentlemen who are crying about the people of Louisiana, who are here beseeching Congress to come to their relief. Who are they? The disappointed office-holders, the disappointed expectants of office; and the men who have countenanced assassination and murder in my State. Sir, the opportunity will come to reply to these men. I do not shirk it. I shall not move to lay the Louisiana bill on the table, but I shall stand here and I shall show to this Senate, if I have the power, that the rightful government of the State is now exercised there.

"Sir, it is a fallacy to suppose that Mr. Kellogg cannot maintain himself. Where are the United States troops in Louisiana to-day, and how many have you got? Less than five hundred men there, and less than you have had there for the last ten years—five hundred men distributed all throughout that State to preserve tranquillity there, in a State where lawlessness has predominated to the extent that we all know of, and where lives almost innumerable have been sacrificed by the men who are now here seeking to get another chance to have possession of that government.

"I only desired to say that much to the men who claim that the people of Louisiana are here asking for relief. The people of Louisiana are quietly pursuing their industrial avocations, and the government of their choice exercises the functions that they have conferred upon it. The Senate and the House are in possession of no information that will at all warrant action. But let the question come up and let it be debated whenever the Senate is ready."

Mr. Frelinghuysen: "Mr. President, having rather incidentally than by deliberate purpose taken some subordinate part in the discussion of this question when it was before the Senate on a former occasion, I propose now to submit concisely my views on two propositions: First, that the President of the United States was authorized by the Constitution, standing alone, and that he was also authorized by the statutes of the country, to send armed protection to Louisiana; and second, that Congress is not authorized to order a new election in that State.

"And I may here say that while I cannot agree with the conclusions of the Senator from Wisconsin (Mr. Carpenter), I trust I do not violate delicacy in stating that I admire the marked ability with which he has presented his views. He has so presented the case that he may properly demand and not petition for it a serious and careful consideration. It is to the labors of that Senator and the Senator from Indiana (Mr. Morton) that we and the country are indebted for an understanding of this somewhat complicated subject.

"I submit that the President was authorized by the Constitution, standing alone and not enforced by any statute, to send the protection he did to Louisiana. Mr. Kellogg was the Governor *de facto* of that State. The President told us that he had so recognized him, and that he would continue so to do unless Congress directed to the contrary, and we purposely did nothing. Kellogg was therefore Governor *de facto*, recognized by the President and by the silent acquiescence of Congress; and on the 13th of May, 1873, he sent the President this communication:

Sir: Domestic violence existing in several parishes of this State which the State authorities are unable to suppress without great expense and danger of bloodshed, and the Legislature not being in session, and it being impossible to convene the Legislature in time to meet the emergency, I respectfully make application, under the fourth section of article four of the Constitution of the United States, for a sufficient military force of the United States Govern-

ment to enable the State authorities to suppress insurrection and domestic violence.

Very respectfully, your obedient servant,
WM. P. KELLOGG, Governor of Louisiana.
To his Excellency U. S. GRANT, President of the United States.

"If the President was satisfied that domestic violence existed, on being called upon by the Governor for a force to suppress it, he was bound under the provisions of the Constitution to do so, whether there was or was not any statute imposing that duty upon him. That disorder existed in that State cannot be questioned, because the preamble of the bill introduced for a new election truly declares in these words:

Whereas, The public peace in said State is at present preserved and can only be preserved during the existing state of things in said State at the expense of the United States and by retaining a part of the army in said State.

"That the demand upon the President was made according to the constitutional requirements (whether in compliance with the statutes or not) cannot be questioned, after reading the foregoing application.

"Sir, the Constitution carefully distributes the powers of government into three branches, the legislative, judicial, and executive. Article one, section 8, declares the powers of Congress in eighteen different clauses. Article three, section 1, declares that the judicial power shall be vested in one Supreme Court and in such inferior courts as Congress may ordain and establish; and article two, section 1, declares that the executive power shall be vested in the President of the United States. This distribution of power is essential to republican liberty. The aggrandizement of all power in one body, whether it consists of many individuals or of a unit, is despotism. The question is, to which of these three divisions of government the duty under the Constitution attaches to protect a State from domestic violence? The Constitution says that it is 'the United States' that is to give this protection. We are here told that saying the 'United States' shall give the protection is equivalent to saying that Congress shall give it. To that I cannot agree. If the Constitution had intended that Congress, as contradistinguished from the Executive or judiciary, should give this protection, it would have enumerated this power among those conferred upon Congress in the eighth section of the first article. In that enumeration of the powers of Congress it is provided that Congress may suppress insurrection and repel invasion; but a general insurrection is a very different thing from domestic violence in a State. That term includes insurrection, but it comprehends much more that does not amount to insurrection. Neither can it be claimed that this power is given to Congress by the last clause of the eighth section of the first article, which says Congress shall have power 'to make all laws necessary and proper to carry into execution the foregoing powers,' because this protection against domestic violence is not a foregoing power, not being mentioned until we come to the fourth section of the sixth article, while this provision as to making all laws, etc., is found in the eighth section of the first article; and besides, where the question is whether the President's power is restricted to the execution of a statute, rather than to the execution of the Constitution, it does not settle any thing to say that Congress may make laws when necessary and proper. That is the very question. When not necessary they need not, and when not proper they may not pass the law. I say that Congress need not pass a law to give authority to the President to afford this protection; not that they may not.

" The term ' United States ' includes all three of the divisions of the Government, and that division of the Government is to act to which the duty appropriately belongs. If a State should pass a law tending to create an aristocracy, as that a State judgeship should be hereditary, then it would be the province of the judiciary to fulfill the guarantee and to declare such law void. In that case the judicial power is ' the United States.' If all law and all form of government in a State have been destroyed by a rebellion, so that it is necessary to have a new organization of government, then it is the legislative power that must fulfill this guarantee by setting up new governments, and then Congress is ' the United States.' And here is where Andrew Johnson violated his duty and departed from his proper and legitimate powers, by undertaking as the Executive to exercise legislative functions. If there exist domestic violence, disorder, and obstruction to the laws, then it is the province of the Executive on being called upon to fulfill the guarantee of the Constitution, and the Executive is ' the United States.'

" Mr. President, this provision of the Constitution contemplates a sudden emergency, when violence has subjected and trampled down the law, and when, without waiting for the Legislature, the Governor is to call upon the President for protection. Every other year Congress is for nine months not in session, and when in session the introduction of a bill, its reference to a committee, its report upon it, its being three times read and thus passing each House, and then to be subjected to the approval of the President, is a process inconsistent with the demands of the emergency as contemplated by the Constitution. I know Congress may delegate some of its powers; but when the duty is such that Congress cannot perform and that the Executive must, and the power is omitted in enumeration of the powers of Congress, and the power is carefully stated to belong not to Congress but to the United States, then we are to infer that the Constitution intended to confer the power on the Executive, and not that the duty was to be performed either by the President, or by any one else, by virtue of a delegation of power from Congress.

" Again, the President of the United States is by the Constitution invested with all the power necessary to perform this duty. He is, by article two, section 2, made the Commander-in-Chief of the Army and Navy; and then the Constitution, having given him this power, expressly declares that ' the President shall take care that the laws be faithfully executed,' and requires him to swear ' that he will faithfully execute the office of President.' There has never been any act passed requiring him to perform this constitutional duty. The Constitution need not be enacted into law to be enforced. It is itself the highest law. There might or there might not be an act of Congress authorizing the President to repel invasion; that is merely accidental. His duty is the same. If a fleet should come up the Potomac, is the President to stand like a cowardly dotard, with the Army and Navy at his control, until the White House is in ashes and the Capitol in ruins, waiting for a declaration of war by Congress, or authority to act from them? The Constitution has made him the custodian of the nation, the protector of its laws; it has given him the means to execute his high office, and he must perform it.

" We claimed that the Rio Grande was the western boundary of Texas. Mexico disputed it; and President Polk sent General Taylor there in 1845 to protect our interests, and war existed for months before it was declared by Congress.

" We obtained possession of Louisiana in 1803; of Florida in 1819; and there were frequent occasions when the President sent our fleet to guard the disputed territory between the Mississippi River and the Perdido.

" It is true that it is the laws of the United States, and not of the States, that the President, under the Constitution, is to see are faithfully executed; but under our system of government the laws of the United States and the laws of the States are in their execution so inseparably interwoven and interlaced that it is impossible that the former can be executed and enforced in a State where anarchy exists; and consequently, under the provision that the President is to see the laws of the United States faithfully executed, he must see to it that anarchy does not exist in the State.

" I do not see that we have on this question any thing to do with the propriety of Durell's decisions. The President is intrusted with the Army, not to enforce any man's views or opinions; he is intrusted with the duty of enforcing the laws; he enforces the writ which speaks in the name of the United States, and is tested by the Chief-Justice, and must be obeyed. To hold the President responsible for unjust decisions because he insists that the process of the United States shall be respected, would be to hold that he must sit in judgment to approve or disapprove the findings of the Federal courts, and would be a commingling of the executive with the judicial functions of greater absurdity,

CONGRESS, UNITED STATES.

perhaps, than the merging of the powers of Congress with those of the Chief Magistrate as insisted on in this case.

"I then submit, Mr. President, that protection from ' domestic violence' under the fourth section of the fourth article appeals to the arm, the force, of the nation in an emergency, and is an appeal to the President, because the executive power is vested in him and it is executive power that is required; and because he is Commander-in-Chief of the Army and Navy, he is bound to see the laws faithfully executed; and because it is the United States and not ' Congress' that guarantees against domestic violence, Congress cannot take that power from the President. It is his. Congress may regulate it, may say he shall or shall not use the militia, he shall or shall not use the Army or the Navy; it may take from him all means of performing his constitutional duty, but when he has the means he must perform it.

"I do not dispute that Congress may also execute this guarantee. There is, under the Constitution, a mixture as well as a division of powers. The President acts legislatively when he approves or vetoes a bill; the Senate acts judicially in impeachments; the House of Representatives acts as an inquest in its presentation of an impeachment; and the Senate shares the executive power in the matter of appointments and treaties; but the President in his sphere is as independent of Congress as Congress is of him. He may nominate, and with the advice of the Senate appoint, to office; he may convene Congress, and under certain circumstances may adjourn it; he may receive public ministers; he may make treaties, subject to ratification by the Senate; he must see to it that the laws are executed, and he must fulfill the guarantees of the Constitution when that duty appropriately belongs to him.

"These powers cannot be taken from him.

"Congress has sometimes attempted to encroach upon these powers. It tried to limit the pardoning power, but the Supreme Court sustained the President. In the case known as *Ex parte* Garland, found in 4 Wallace, 380, the court says:

Congress can neither limit the effect of *his* pardon, nor exclude from its exercise any class of offenders. The benign prerogative of mercy cannot be fettered by any legislative restriction.

"And again in 13 Wallace, 128, in a case arising under what is known as Drake's amendment, the court holds a similar doctrine. The House of Representatives, in 1796, attempted to limit the President's power to make treaties, and by a resolution declared that where a treaty depended for the execution of any of its stipulations on an act of Congress, it was the right of the House to deliberate on the expediency or inexpediency of carrying such treaty into effect. The case in question was a treaty with Great Britain.

"Washington, in a message of March 80, 1796, denies such power; and Kent (volume i.,

page 286) says: 'The House of Representatives is not above the law, and has no dispensing power. The argument in favor of the conclusive efficacy of every treaty made by the President and Senate is so clear and palpable as to carry conviction throughout the community.' We must be careful, if we intend to preserve this Government, how the legislative branch, which is by far the most powerful, encroaches on the executive or on the judiciary.

"Governor Kellogg was right in making his application for aid to rest on the Constitution rather than upon any statute.

"But I submit that it is perfectly clear that the President was by statute also authorized to afford this protection. The statute of 1795 authorizes the President to use the militia in case of an insurrection in any State against the government thereof on the application of the Governor or Legislature.

"The act of 1807 substitutes the Army for the militia, and goes further than the act of 1795, and authorizes the President to use the Army not only in cases of 'insurrection,' but in cases of 'obstruction of the laws either of the United States or of any individual State.' This certainly was a case of obstruction of the laws of an individual State. I have that confidence in the legal judgment of the Senator from Wisconsin, that I am induced to believe that he will agree with me that the statute of 1807 applies directly to this case.

"Now let me consider the second proposition, namely, that the United States is not authorized to order a new election in Louisiana. The Constitution provides that the United States shall guarantee to each State government peace, tranquillity, freedom from anarchy, and disorder; second, its guarantee is that each State shall have a government in form republican; that it shall not be in its framework an aristocracy, where authority is vested in a privileged order; that it shall not be a democracy, where the people in person exercise the sovereign power; the government shall not be a despotism, where the absolute power is exercised by a man or men without constitutional restraint; but that the government shall be in form republican, where the supreme power is intrusted to representatives elected by the people.

"The Constitution says—and whether right or wrong we are controlled by it, and it is beyond all argument—that we are only to guarantee a republican form of government with order and tranquillity; and when we insist that full and accurate significance shall be given to the word ' form' as it occurs in this provision of the Constitution, we are not sticking in the bark, we are not superficial, but we are going to the very root of the matter. We are claiming that the Federal Government only has to do with the form, leaving the substance, the administration of the form of government, to the people of the States. Those who would ignore this word ' form' from the restricted grant of power given by the States under the constitutional compact to the Federal Government would usurp the very substance to the Federal Government, and leave only the 'form' or shell of republican government to the States.

"The Senator from Wisconsin submitted this well-considered sentence to the Senate:

If I am right in saying that it is the vital element of republican government that its rulers are chosen by the people, it follows that the present government of Louisiana, lacking this, is not a republican government.

"I do not object to his definition. Republican government is one the vital element of which is that rulers are elected by the people. Ten years ago a majority of the people of Louisiana had no voice in electing the rulers. Was it a republican government? I do not say that it was. It certainly was not, under the definition stated. But as Congress had no right except over the form of government, it was never claimed that under the guarantee clause of the Constitution Congress could give the right to vote to the disfranchised majority of the people of that State. It required an amendment to the Constitution before that could be effected.

"This word 'form' is not a matter of chance as it occurs in this Constitution. The people of the Southern States, when they entered into this compact, knowing that large portions of their populations were disfranchised, and not intending that they should have a voice in the election of rulers, would never have agreed to insert in the Constitution that the Federal Government should see to it that their State governments should not only be republican in form, but also should see to it that the rulers were elected by the people. They stipulated that all the people should be considered and counted in the apportionment of representation, but not so in the election of rulers."

Mr. Carpenter: "I want not to answer the Senator, but simply to ask him a question, as he did me, so that I may distinctly understand him. Does he maintain that in case the three branches of government in Louisiana to-day, that is, the men holding those three branches of government, shall collude together, the court to decide all questions in favor of the other two, the other departments to administer every thing in their common interest, to keep themselves in power under the present existing republican constitution of that State during their natural lives, and they should do so for fifteen years, would Congress have any power to interfere, the form—that is, the constitution—being conceded to be republican."

Mr. Frelinghuysen: "That is not a case before us."

Mr. Carpenter: "It is two years before us."

Mr. Frelinghuysen: "I think I will show the case supposed is not before us at any time. It is difficult to solve questions put in this manner out of the order of debate; but my answer is: That if after repeated trials in a State

where we have performed our duty of giving them order and government, and of seeing to it that it is republican in form, it should turn out that the people were so depraved, ignorant, and degraded, so unfit for the blessings of republican government, that they abused all their privileges, I suppose it would then be incumbent upon us to fulfill that guarantee of the Constitution *pro tanto*, to fulfill it just as far as we could, and to give them government, even if it was under a military commission. But, sir, we will never be called upon to resort to that extreme measure, unless the extreme case which my friend has supposed, of the executive, legislative, judicial branches of government, and the people themselves, all combining in one dire conspiracy to destroy themselves."

Mr. Carpenter: "Let me correct my friend as to the effect of my question. My question meant this: Where the judges of the Supreme Court, the members of the Legislature and the executive department, the Governor and the other officers, should combine among themselves to hold the people under their government, and the people should be of course resisting that, and the government should apply to the President to sustain it, and the President should interfere, and then the question should be presented to us whether, after that thing had continued for ten years, and they had avowed their purpose of continuing for life, we should have any power whatever to interfere? The particular case is only put to test the Senator's argument of the distinction between our guaranteeing a republican government and what he calls a republican form of government."

Mr. Frelinghuysen: "I think I have answered that question. I say that we are bound to carry out the guarantee of the Constitution. If the people are so entirely unfit for a republican government, we must still give them government, even if it is a military commission. But no such state of things will exist. You can suppose a condition of things which will prove that any government is inefficient and unfit for the purposes for which it is inaugurated.

"Mr. President, if the Federal Government can, in the exercise of its arbitrary discretion —a discretion from which there is no appeal, and to which there is no review, not even by the people, for we are not responsible to the people of Louisiana for the votes given here— if the Federal Government can, in the exercise of its arbitrary power, set aside the election of Governors and Legislatures of the States, then there is an end of the independent government of the States. I submit that the procedure here contemplated is without precedent in the General Government, and without analogy in any of the State governments.

"As a matter of necessity, deliberative assemblies must be the judges of the qualifications of their own members. We judge of the qualifications of Senators, and the House of those of Representatives. But, further than this necessity extends, was it ever heard of that an election of a State officer, a Governor, a State Treasurer, a controller, was set aside by a political body? An election is never set aside even by the judiciary. It is submitted to a dispassionate and impartial tribunal of justice, not to set aside an election, but to determine whether the claimant was ever elected.

"Order a new election in Louisiana, and you have established a precedent that must impair elective government. Excited parties enter upon a strongly-contested election; the one party in harmony with the dominant party in Congress (perhaps a Senator is to be elected by the Legislature); that party seeks by violence and fraud to obtain success, and when it fails comes to Congress and makes that very fraud and violence the pretense for covering their defeat and for having the election set aside, and for having a second trial with the adverse party who were successful damaged and disgraced by having their victory set aside. No, sir; better far let the States suffer for their own misdeeds, even the innocent with the guilty; their suffering will lead them to cure the evil. Admonished by the evil results of a vicious election, in the calm periods that intervene between elections all parties will unite in devising and adopting safeguards to secure honest elections. Registry laws, poll-lists, proper places for the polls, police regulations, and severely penal statutes, will be adopted as the means of preventing the repetition of the evil. We had better adhere to the Constitution and do what it says, which is that we shall guarantee to the several States government—which we did with Louisiana when we sent our troops there preserving order and tranquillity—and that we shall guarantee to them a republican form of government, which we did when we approved the constitution of Louisiana, under which form that government is now carried on.

"If there are frauds in elections or usurpations in office, let the remedy be found in the courts of the States or by means of impeachment, or by the frequently-recurring popular elections. But let us adopt the theory that we are under the guarantee clause of the Constitution to interfere with States further than to secure to them order and tranquillity and a republican form of government, and that we are to see to it that the proper persons are in power, still I insist that Congress is not to order a new election in Louisiana. If Congress is to interfere, and there is one who we know has been duly elected and who under the constitution of Louisiana is entitled to the office of Governor, Congress surely is not to interfere by ordering a new election, but by placing the one entitled to the office by election and by the Louisiana constitution in power."

Mr. West, of Louisiana, said: "The only conclusion that Congress has come to in regard to the vote of Louisiana is the conclusion that I want to hold you to to-day, that you do not know how the election has gone in Louisiana, and until you do know you have no right to interfere with it.

"We are told that the Kellogg government is a gross usurpation, and that dire consequences are to result to the dominant party in Congress, and in the country, and that we as Senators will be grossly derelict of our duty unless we apply a remedy which it is alleged exists under the instruction of the Constitution that the United States *shall* guarantee to every State in this Union a republican form of government.

"This proposition has so far mainly been urged upon us by the Senator from Wisconsin. In the bill which he has introduced to restore the rights of the State of Louisiana he has assumed an existing state of facts in regard to affairs there from which I totally dissent, and which assumption I contend and shall endeavor to show to the Senate is not at all warranted by the information in its possession.

"In the first place, let me ask what is our right of interference? That right must be based upon two general grounds: first, whether it is conferred upon us by the Constitution upon any given state of facts; and, second, whether that state of facts exists.

"I shall leave the argument on the first of these propositions to the more experienced members of this body, whose views will interest, instruct, and enlighten the Senate to a degree that I should be entirely without expectation of equaling, and I shall confine myself altogether to the proposition that the Senate has not been informed, nor attempted to inform itself, as to whether a state of facts exists growing out of the election of 1872 in Louisiana that either requires or even justifies Congress in interfering. I assert and maintain that the Senate does not know that William P. Kellogg was not elected Governor at that time; that the information laid before the Committee on Privileges and Elections of the Forty-second Congress related entirely to what was done by certain returning boards, to what occurred through an order issued by a judge of a Federal court, and that the examination held by that committee scarcely touched upon what, if we are to exercise our right of interference, is the true subject of inquiry: *How did the people of Louisiana vote on the 4th of November, 1872?* for which person of the two then seeking their suffrages for the office of Governor on that day did they actually vote? With the exception of myself, and I do not know that I ought even to except myself, nobody has given greater attention to this matter than the Senator from Wisconsin. He, after spending these weeks elaborating his report and studying that testimony, admits in the Senate that he does not believe Mr. McEnery was elected. Now, we know perfectly well that there were two men voted for on that day. The Senator from Wisconsin says:

I do not think that Mr. McEnery was in fact elected. "Now, can there be an election without a result? If he does not think that in fact Mr. McEnery was elected on that day, he must think in fact the other man was. That is the question for Congress to determine, it seems to me, before it is called upon to determine whether it has the right constitutionally to interfere.

"In a case somewhat analogous, the New Jersey case of 1840, known most generally as the Broad Seal case, Congress took a direct and thorough method of ascertaining the facts connected therewith, as my friend from California (Mr. Hager) very well knows, for he was counsel in the case. It may with some truth be contended that neither the acts of a returning board nor the order of a Federal judge can impose a government upon the people of a State, and that a government established by either of such means is no more republican in form than were it established by force of arms, however it might subsequently rigidly comply with the written form of a republican constitution.

"It is the voice of the people alone that constitutes a government under our institutions. That 'governments derive their just powers from the consent of the governed' is an axiom too familiar to be forgotten, and I contend that Congress has not in its possession any evidence worthy of regard that Mr. Kellogg is Governor in violation of the consent of the governed; and until it is so informed, it can do no greater wrong, can in no manner more widely depart from its obligation as one of the coördinate branches of the Government of the United States to *guarantee* to Louisiana a republican form of government, than unjustifiably to set aside the present government in that State and impose upon her people the necessity of making another choice through the bill of the Senator from Wisconsin.

"William P. Kellogg is to-day Governor of the State of Louisiana. He is recognized as such by your Chief Executive, by your coördinate branch of Congress who have admitted to seats upon their floor members properly certified by him to have been elected. He is recognized as such also by the Supreme Court of that State, and Congress ought to be satisfied, before it undertakes to overthrow him as the Governor of one of the sovereign States of the Union, that he holds the office contrary to the desires, contrary to the expressed wish and intention of the people governed. They should know that, and they should know what the people of Louisiana willed in 1872, and what their wish is to-day, before they undertake to interfere with him. There is not a particle of evidence of that kind here. : If he holds the office by the wish and according to the intention of the people governed, then his government is republican in form under the constitution of that State, and as all the evidence goes to show that he does so hold it, those who would oust him from

his position are compelled to show proof to the contrary."

Mr. Bayard, of Delaware, said: "Mr. President, in rising to discuss so grave and important a question as the one now before the Senate, I must confess myself oppressed by the scene the Senate-Chamber now presents. We have just heard a most sincere, a most feeling and able speech by a member of this body upon a subject which he has truly declared to be second in importance to none which could be brought before the Senate. He has truly said it not only involves the present and the prospective welfare and happiness of a large body of our own fellow-citizens, but the questions involved in the consideration of their case enter into and affect the existence of our federal form of government; and yet we have seen upon the Administration side of the Chamber scarce as many Senators as there are fingers upon a single hand, and even upon this side of the Chamber but few interested auditors. Nevertheless it is not the part of a true man to hesitate for want of success. Duty and duty alone should he consider, and leave the consequences to that Higher Power who in his own good time will cause the right to prevail.

"Mr. President, in the amendment which I have offered to the bill introduced by the Senator from Wisconsin (Mr. Carpenter) I have recited a series of facts relating to that community which we term the State of Louisiana. To recapitulate these facts—not to take the time of the Senate by having the amendment read again, as it is fresh in our memory—I will merely state them, as follows: First, that an election was held in the State of Louisiana on November 4, 1872, in accordance with the constitution and laws of that State, whereby certain named persons comprising what was known as the fusion or McEnery ticket were elected to the offices which constitute the government of the State of Louisiana, according to the actual count and the official returns of all the votes cast at that election; second, that the persons so elected did organize in their respective official capacities and did assume the functions of office so devolved upon them according to the constitution and laws of Louisiana and the election held thereunder; third, that the defeated candidates at this election did by the unauthorized and illegal interference of the Federal authorities, civil and military, obtain and hold armed possession of the State-House of the State of Louisiana and dispossess and exclude the rightful officers therefrom; fourth, that this usurpation by force of Federal power continues in defiance of the will of the people of Louisiana, as expressed at their election, and in violation of the constitution and laws of the State of Louisiana and of the United States. And the deduction from these recitals is that it is the duty of the Congress of the United States to repair, so far as is possible, the wrong and injustice done aforesaid to the people of Louisiana, and protect that people against this usurpation, and to maintain them in the enjoyment of their chosen government.

"These are the recitals of facts which I will simply say are thoroughly sustained by the reports of the committee to whom this question was submitted, and who by a voluminous report accompanied by more than a thousand pages of testimony have stated to the Senate the result of the investigation, elaborate and thorough, of the proceedings in that election. I do not propose to reiterate, prove anew, these allegations. I simply content myself by saying they are reported to the Senate by indubitable authority. But one member of the committee has been found in his report to deny the existence of these facts, and even he—I refer to the honorable Senator from Indiana (Mr. Morton) admits that the action of the United States court under which the government of Kellogg was placed in possession of the offices of Louisiana was an act of flagrant usurpation. So far even he goes. But the rest of the committee, the four Senators who signed the majority report, the Senator who drew that report whose able and thorough demonstrations of the facts on which that report was based is so fresh in our memories, the able statesman who unfortunately is no longer a Senator, Mr. Trumbull, of Illinois, and the then Senator from Georgia (Mr. Hill), all concurred in stating as true the facts which I have alleged in the preamble to this amendment.

"I do not desire to weary the Senate by recapitulating their proof, but simply aver that they are all sustained by the debates, by the report, by the testimony taken. The Senate is spared any further necessity of examining into these facts. We have had as careful an inquiry into them, as full a report upon them, as any one could desire for the elicitation of truth. The speech we had from the Senator from Kentucky (Mr. McCreery) was memorable for its ability, for that mingling of logic, wit, and truth, which marked his utterances. The speech of the Senator from Wisconsin (Mr. Carpenter) and that of the Senator from Maryland (Mr. Hamilton), within a few days, all have gone to substantiate these facts as recited in the amendment, and to render it a work of supererogation for me to introduce new authority further to sustain these recitals of fact.

"Mr. President, the issue before the Senate of the United States is no mere question of party triumph. We are not sitting here as a court to hear and try the contested election of Kellogg or of McEnery. In my opinion, we have and can have no such jurisdiction, and our decision, even if backed by the military force of the United States, would be void in law and without authority in morals. The issue before the people of the United States in this case of Louisiana is nothing less than the preservation of our form of government, whether it now is or whether it is to be a Federal Union of equal States or a consolidated power of unlimited rule by a central government over outlying provinces.

"This question is all-important to Louisiana to-day. It may be equally important to New York to-morrow, or to Massachusetts or to Indiana. Let no man suppose that the violation of a great constitutional principle of government can be committed, can become a precedent, without its evils reaching those who set it on foot. This is no claim simply for the right to hold and enjoy the powers and emoluments of an office. It is the cry of a sister State for relief from a foul usurpation set on foot and maintained by unlawful exercise of power by Federal authorities, civil and military. Let the people of Louisiana speak for themselves, they who are before the Senate for relief, whose petitions are signed by thousands, whose language is entirely respectful, nay, in my opinion, almost too humble for American citizens to use in addressing their public representatives. The people of Louisiana in whose behalf the measure which I have proposed is offered are not office-holders. They are not interested in the emoluments of office under the government of Louisiana. They truly describe themselves as follows:

They take the liberty to say that they have had no connection with these suits as parties or attorneys—

"That is to say, the suits in the courts of Louisiana, or the Federal courts, for possession of the various offices in the State of Louisiana—neither do they claim any of the offices in dispute. They have not heretofore been concerned in the controversies among the political classes which have endangered the peace of, and brought scandal upon, the State. They affirm that, during the last four years, there has not been good government in Louisiana. There have been extravagance, prodigality, dishonesty, and waste in the public expenditures. The public debt has been enormously increased, with but little corresponding benefit. The credit of the State has been given to speculating corporations, for personal aims. The taxes on property have assumed such proportions that they might appropriately be called rents paid by the proprietors to the State for its occupation and use. The taxes upon business oppress the commercial and laboring classes. The laws to control elections, corporations, and public institutions, stimulate these excesses of office-holders, and the consequence is universal depression and discontent. The State needs an honest, faithful, and responsible government, conducted to attain public objects, and not to enrich its members or to perpetuate their power. There was an earnest effort to obtain such a government at the last election, but a political conspiracy has unfortunately defeated it.

"That is why they are here. Nay, further, I prefer to let these people speak by their own voice—the report of a committee of two hundred citizens of the resident population of New Orleans, made in March, 1873, states—

That the people of the United States are divided among States, and the humiliation and degradation of a State of the Union to the level of a province, deprived of the rights of self-government, can only be the harbinger of similar woes to themselves.

We have asked nothing of the American people, of their President, Congress, or judges, in any intemperate, immodest, or minatory form of address.

We have not asked them to execute any vengeance upon any person or party in our behalf. We have submitted to them whether it is not proper for them to uphold their own Constitution, to require fidelity and honor from their own officers in performance of duties they have imposed upon them, and whether it does not behoove them to maintain the covenants of union among the States, and to maintain the stability of State governments and the privileges of local self-government, so that tranquillity, justice, and liberty, be maintained.

"These, Mr. President, are the demands of our fellow-citizens, of Louisiana, not a low squabble for official emolument or power, but a demand for the exercise of those principles upon which our Government was founded, and upon the existence and perpetuation of which we alone can expect its honest and happy continuance.

"I do not propose that, so far as I can prevent it, either the people of the United States or the Senate should be misled by the specious statements of the Senator from Indiana, who has inveighed against the measure proposed by the Senator from Wisconsin, on the ground that it would invade the rights of a State. Sir, the Senator from Wisconsin well said that when we heard the Senator from Indiana pleading for the rights of the State of Louisiana it was difficult to listen to him with a grave countenance. What, sir, after this State has been trodden to the earth by the foot of Federal power; after the Senator is willing, nay, anxious, that foot should be kept there; after this State has been throttled on the highway by Federal power aiding and backing up the footpads who are called the present government of Louisiana, and it is proposed that relief should be given, the Senator from Indiana assures us that it would be invasion of the rights of a State! Sir, he is no fit guardian of the rights of a State. I lately saw a picture of a wolf who had killed the shepherd, had possessed himself of his garments, his hat, cloak, and crook, and' was employed in watching the unwary lambs who soon were to become his prey ; and when I have heard the Senator from Indiana, turning to those of us in this Chamber who do profess to regard the rights of the States and who follow our profession by practice, warn us against interference in this case lest the rights of a State might be endangered, then, sir, again does that picture rise before my mind's eye, and I recognize what manner of shepherd the Senator from Indiana is where State rights are concerned.

"Mr. President, the issue for the people of the United States to consider is, shall this conspiracy, as the people of Louisiana have justly termed it, this conspiracy to overthrow a State, be successfully accomplished? Can an Attorney-General of the United States concoct and carry into effect a scheme with his party confederates to invade a State, ride rough-shod over her constitution and laws, prearrange with a corrupt and reckless judge of a district court of the United States for a violation of

law, an unwarranted usurpation, an assumption of jurisdiction which was known to the Attorney-General and known to the judge and known to all men to be unwarranted in law and to be a usurpation, and to use this dishonestly-assumed power as a pretext for the use of the armed forces of the United States Government to thrust down and keep down the lawful government of a State?

"Sir, this is a case beyond mere technical pleadings and mere forms. Law is silent before arms. Law disappears and the constitution of the State and of the United States disappears before the breath of the Attorney-General and his associates in this business. The pretense of law by Kellogg is a mockery ; it is a bold, shameless, unmitigated fraud from beginning to end. The whole history of the means whereby even the forms of government were followed in Louisiana—the installation of Pinchback, the instant abolition of the courts of the State, the supply of the bench with new men and interested candidates to whose sole jurisdiction of these very questions was by special statutes given—all these things are such a tangled web of fraud that pretense of law or fair dealing nowhere can be found among them."

Mr. Merrimon, of North Carolina, said : "Mr. President, the Senator from Wisconsin (Mr. Carpenter), who introduced the pending bill, has labored earnestly in its support, and his ability and zeal command my cordial respect and admiration. But, with all due respect for him, I cannot support his bill—because, in the first place, as I have shown, McEnery is Governor ; because, in the second place, if, as he says and insists, there was no election in 1872, then Warmoth, by the express words of the Constitution, is Governor ; and because, in the third place, even if there were no State authorities there, the bill goes a bow-shot, in providing for an election, beyond what I think Congress has power to do under the Constitution and our system of government. There is, in my judgment, no power in Congress arising by express provisions of the Constitution, by reasonable construction or by necessity, under our system of government, State and Federal, which authorizes it to pass the pending bill.

"And I wish I had time to enlarge somewhat on this point. I am willing to concede that in one contingency Congress may pass a law authorizing the people to reorganize a State. If by possibility (and there is such a possibility) a State government in the Union should be absolutely deprived of State officers, so that the government of the State shall be left without officers to operate its government, in that case I contend that Congress could grant the people relief. But how? Simply by passing a law authorizing the people of the State to hold an election *according to their own constitution and laws*. That is all that Congress can do ; it is all that Congress is bound to do ; and it has that power by the tenor and spirit of the Constitution, not by its express letter. The power arises by the tenor of the Constitution and by the nature and theory of our Government; and I wish I had time to enlarge upon this idea. I repeat, in the contingency I have mentioned, Congress could pass a law authorizing the people of a State thus deprived of State officers to hold an election in pursuance of their own constitution and laws, under the auspices of their own local authorities, to supply officers to the State government until the next regular election.

"This bill, however, provides that an election shall be held under the auspices of the United States, and provides in all respects an election law without reference to the laws of the State. It proposes to send a military Governor into the State of Louisiana, and virtually to reconstruct the State of Louisiana after the manner of the reconstruction acts. I cannot subscribe to that doctrine, and I have many reasons why I cannot, upon which time will not allow me to enlarge now.

"I can support the proposition of the honorable Senator from Delaware (Mr. Bayard). I do not like that proposition as well as I might some others. In my judgment the proper course for Congress to take in this case is to pass a joint resolution declaring that according to the constitution and laws of the State of Louisiana McEnery and his associates are the properly ascertained officers of the State of Louisiana and recognizing them as such, and that it is the duty of all the authorities of the United States to uphold and sustain them according to the Constitution and laws of the United States. If Congress should pass such a resolution as that, I have no doubt the President would approve it and be governed by it. I do not suppose that he has any motive to keep Kellogg there longer than he can ascertain the will of Congress. If he withdraws the troops and McEnery is acknowledged to be Governor, it will be easy for him to make a requisition on the President to prevent domestic violence, if need be, and the destruction of that State and the whole machinery of its government. If such a resolution were passed the Louisiana troubles would be settled in twenty-four hours, constitutional government would be restored, and law and right would triumph over faction and usurpation."

The bill was discussed at considerable length without any final action upon it in the Senate.

In the House, on May 27th, Mr. Poland, of Vermont, from the Committee on the Judiciary, reported a bill, conferring jurisdiction upon the Criminal Court of the District of Columbia, and for other purposes, which was read a first and second time.

The bill provides that the Criminal Court of the District of Columbia shall have concurrent jurisdiction with the police court of the District, of all crimes and misdemeanors committed in the District.

The second section provides that the provisions of the thirty-third section of the judiciary act of 1789 shall apply to courts created by act of Congress in the District.

Mr. Poland: "I will take no time in explaining this bill unless some gentleman desires it."

Mr. Speer, of Pennsylvania, said: "Does the bill apply to pending cases? It should not do so."

Mr. Poland: "It has no effect upon pending cases in any way. I will state in a word the necessity for this bill. Three or four years ago Congress established a police court in this District, giving it exclusive jurisdiction over certain classes of crimes and misdemeanors. Very grave doubts are entertained as to the constitutionality of that law; and it is understood that the Supreme Court of the District has made a decision which squints in the direction of deciding that the police court has constitutionally no such jurisdiction. If that should be so held, there would be no criminal court in this District having jurisdiction over those offenses. Therefore we provide in this bill that the Criminal Court of the District of Columbia shall also have jurisdiction over the same cases."

Mr. Speer: "Does this bill affect the Buell libel case in any way?"

Mr. Poland: "Not in the slightest degree."

The bill was ordered to be engrossed and read a third time; and, being engrossed, it was accordingly read the third time, and passed.

Mr. Poland moved to reconsider the vote by which the bill was passed; and also moved that the motion to reconsider be laid on the table. The latter motion was agreed to.

In the Senate, on June 16th, Mr. Frelinghuysen, of New Jersey, said: "I will ask the Senate to pass a bill providing for a criminal court in this District. It has been examined carefully by the Committee of the Judiciary, and it is very necessary that it should pass."

There being no objection, the bill conferring jurisdiction upon the Criminal Court of the District of Columbia, and for other purposes, was considered as in Committee of the Whole.

An amendment was reported by the Committee on the Judiciary to strike out in line four of section 1 the word "concurrent" before the word "jurisdiction," and, after the word "jurisdiction" in the same line, to strike out the words "with the police court of said District," and, at the end of the section, to insert "not lawfully triable in any other court, and which are required by law to be prosecuted by indictment or information."

The amendment was agreed to.

The bill was reported to the Senate as amended, and the amendment was concurred in.

The amendment was ordered to be engrossed, and the bill to be read a third time. The bill was read the third time, and passed.

In the House on June 20th, the amendments

of the Senate were concurred in, two-thirds voting in favor thereof.

The bill, as passed, was as follows:

" *An act conferring jurisdiction upon the Criminal Court of the District of Columbia, and for other purposes.* Be it enacted by the Senate and House of Representatives of the United States of America in Congress assembled, That the Criminal Court of the District of Columbia shall have jurisdiction of all crimes and misdemeanors committed in said District, not lawfully triable in any other court, and which are required by law to be prosecuted by indictment or information.

" Section 2. That the provisions of the thirty-third section of the judiciary act of 1789 shall apply to courts created by act of Congress in the District of Columbia."

The question of "transportation" was a prominent subject at this session of Congress. It related to increased facilities and reduced prices for the transportation of agricultural products from the fertile fields of the Western States to the seaports on the Atlantic coasts. Vast quantities of these products were practically without a market, owing to the cost of transportation. In the Senate the subject was referred to a special committee, of which Mr. Windom, of Minnesota, was chairman. The committee made a very lengthy report, of which the substance is stated in a speech of Mr. Windom, delivered in the Senate on April 24th. It presents such a complete view of the whole question, with such a variety of important facts, that it has been inserted in this volume under the title of Public Documents, to which the reader is referred.

This session of Congress was closed, by adjournment, on June 23d.

CONNECTICUT. The Democratic party of this State assembled in convention at New Haven on the 3d of February, 1874, for the purpose of nominating their candidates for Governor and the other State officers, at the general election in April. A considerable proportion of the delegates were Liberal Republicans, who made common cause with the Democrats. Charles R. Ingersoll was nominated for Governor, and the incumbents of the other State offices were renominated.

The following platform was unanimously adopted by the convention:

Resolved, That this convention does hereby declare and make known the following to be its principles of action; and to the support of them it invites the hearty coöperation of all honest men:

1. We declare our unfaltering devotion to the Constitution of the United States and to the Union of the States thereby established; and we affirm that the people of the several States have the sole and exclusive right of governing themselves as free, sovereign, and independent States, subject only to the limitations of the Constitution; and all the powers not therein expressly granted to the national Government are reserved to the States respectively.

2. We affirm that the greatest danger with which we are now threatened is the corruption and extravagance which exist in high official places; and we do declare as the cardinal principle of our future political action, that retrenchment, economy, and reform are imperatively demanded in all the governments of the people—Federal as well as State and municipal—and we here proclaim ourselves the uncompromising foes of all salary-grabbers, ring-politicians, and land-monopolists, whoever they may be, and wherever they may be found, whether they are in office or out; and we appeal to honest men everywhere, without regard to past political affiliations, to join us in branding as they deserve these corrupt leeches on the body politic, and in assisting us to purge official stations of their unwholesome and baneful presence.

3. The present Federal Administration—by its utter inability to comprehend the dignity or responsibilities of the duties with which it is charged; by its devotion to personal and partisan interests; by its weak and incompetent management of the national finances; by its unwarranted interference with the local self-government of the people, by its support of the corrupt governments which it has imposed, by its power, upon several of the States of the Union; by its complicity with corrupt practices and scandals in various quarters; and by its appointment of notoriously incompetent men to high official positions—has justly brought upon itself the condemnation of the American people.

4. The procuring of *money* from a notoriously corrupt "ring" of Washington politicians, for use in this State, in controlling our elections, is so marked an evidence of political corruption, that it deserves the severest rebuke; and we call upon the people of Connecticut in the coming election to enter such a protest against so gross an abuse of official trust as will secure punishment for the present, and afford adequate protection for the future.

5. We recognize in the present stringency of the money-markets—the panic which led thereto—the general prostration of business, and the consequent suffering of the working-classes, the direct fruits of that policy which, while it pretends to advance the interests of the country, is in reality plunging us into national and individual bankruptcy and ruin. And as an offset to this policy, we demand, and we call upon the people to inaugurate, a speedy return to *specie payments*, as called for alike by the highest considerations of commercial morality and honest and economical government.

6. While we are in favor of all just and equal taxation necessary to sustain our Government and our public institutions, we are opposed to all unjust and unequal systems of taxation which tend to favor one class at the expense of other classes of the people.

7. The public domain of the United States is the property of the people, and as such should be preserved for the people; and we condemn the policy of wholesale grants to speculative corporations for the benefit of the few to the exclusion of the many.

8. We are opposed to all monopolies, which operate for the especial benefit of privileged persons or classes, and to all combinations or corporations made to effect purposes hostile to the best interests of the people.

9. That we recognize the grievances of which the industrial classes complain, and we favor a governmental policy that shall impose such restraints and prohibitions upon grasping corporations and stock-gamblers as will prevent those financial fluctuations which have ever resulted in a debased currency, official defalcations, bankrupt employers, and starving working men and women.

10. That we are in favor of such action by the Legislature of our State as will bring the question of calling a Constitutional Convention directly before the sovereign people of this State, for their adoption or rejection, as they shall deem best.

11. We point with pride to the manner in which the affairs of this State have been administered during the past year; to the watchful economy with which all departments of the State government have been conducted; to the dignity and impartiality with which the Executive duties have been performed;

and we pledge ourselves to use our most earnest efforts to secure the reëlection of the men who have so worthily and capably discharged the important trusts confided to them.

The Republicans held their State Convention at Hartford, on the 11th of February, 1874. The attendance was large. Henry B. Harrison, of New Haven, was nominated as the Republican candidate for Governor, by acclamation. The candidates for the other State offices were, respectively, as follows: for Lieutenant-Governor, John T. Wait, of Norwich; for Secretary of State, John G. A. Stone, of Killingly; for Controller, E. Perry Parker, of Coventry; for State Treasurer, David P. Nichols, of Danbury.

The following resolutions were reported from the appropriate committee:

The Republican party of the State of Connecticut, in convention assembled, declare that the true end of government is to secure equal and exact justice to all its citizens, with as little infringement as possible upon individual freedom; that the government of the people by the people and for the people, interpreted and foreshadowed by the Declaration of Independence, is the true American idea; that this idea can only be realized by the election of honest and capable men to public office, and by conducting public affairs with strict prudence and in accordance with the sound and approved maxims of business and political economy.

Resolved, That, in accordance with these principles, the States should be left to regulate their own internal affairs without interference, and this convention gladly indorses the course of the national Administration in reference to the recent election in Texas.

That good administration and freedom from temptation to official dishonesty can be best secured by such an organization of the civil service as shall insure a competent body of civil officers who shall be undisturbed by the changes and temptations of active politics.

That there ought to be no further increase of the paper currency of the country, and that the people expect from the present Congress the adoption of such measures as will forward the early resumption of specie payments.

That there should be no more subsidies of public lands in the interest of private corporations; that taxation should be equal, and be laid in such a manner as least to interfere with the general prosperity, and so as to encourage the various industries.

That we expect of our State Legislature and State officers the strictest integrity and economy, the largest possible relief from the burden of taxation, the maintenance of public education, the preservation of the purity and freedom of the ballot-box, the continuance of such registration laws as shall invite all who are entitled to the precious right of suffrage to participate in it, and shall at the same time exclude all from fraudulent voting.

That the sessions of the General Assembly should be short, and its legislative acts few and general.

That in making judicial and other legislative appointments, character and capacity should be the only qualifications considered, and that all bargains and trades for these appointments are abusive of the health of the Commonwealth and destructive of the interests of the people.

That the rightful interests of labor, in view of the present condition of the industrial classes, and their relations to capital and the great corporations of the country, demand the careful solicitude and attention of the Legislature.

That we recognize the wisdom and necessity of obtaining reliable statistics in regard to the condition of the laboring classes, upon which to base proper legislation, and we believe that an impartial bureau for that purpose is demanded alike by humanity and the best interests of the State.

That party organizations are useful and necessary, but that, while we are proud of the birth and history of the Republican party, we recognize no such allegiance to political associations as shall prevent our fair and candid criticism of the acts of all public men; and, that every case of negligence, wastefulness, or dishonesty, on the part of any having control of public moneys, ought to be promptly and severely punished without fear or favor.

That the question, whether or not a convention should be submitted by the General Assembly to the people of the State for their decision.

With these declarations we present to the people of Connecticut the names of the Hon. Henry B. Harrison for Governor, and of his associates upon the ticket for their several offices, with pride.

The resolution concerning a revision of the organic law of the State gave rise to a lengthy discussion, in which several delegates took part; some of them arguing for the removal of that plank from the platform, others for its retention. The sentiment of those who were in favor of passing the resolutions as reported by the committee finally prevailed, and the platform was adopted in full.

At the election, on the 6th of April, 1874, the candidates on the Democratic ticket were reëlected by considerable majorities. The whole number of votes polled for Governor was 91,578; which is 4,716 more than the aggregate votes cast for Governor in 1873. Of that number, 46,689 were given to the Democratic candidate, 40,011 to the Republicans, and 4,859 to the candidate presented by the Temperance party. On the one-capital question, all of the votes cast had been 67,529—yeas, 36,781; nays, 30,298. The political complexion of the Legislature was as follows: In the Senate—Democrats 17, Republicans 4; in the House of Representatives, Democrats 142, Republicans 97, Independent 2; which gave the Democrats a majority of 13 votes over the Republicans in the Senate, of 45 in the Lower House, and of 58 on joint ballot.

The Legislature assembled at New Haven on the 6th of May, 1874.

The financial condition of the State appears to be remarkably prosperous. Her bonded debt, which at the close of the late civil war amounted to $10,000,000, is now reduced to $5,014,500; the rate of interest to be paid on it being six per cent. per annum. Its reduction during the last fiscal year was $207,210.27. The amount of State bonds purchased within the same period was $81,000; and at the end of it there was in the Treasury a balance on hand of $863,988.33; which is $126,000 in excess of the balance on hand one year before. No floating debt exists.

The public revenue, collected during the last fiscal year on account of the civil list, amounted in the aggregate to $1,762,427.96, derived almost entirely from the following four sources:

From the one-mill tax on the towns, $422,953.-
56; tax on savings-banks, $507,103.30; tax on
railroad companies, $298,421.04; and tax on
mutual-insurance companies, $327,020.08.

The entire value of all taxable property in
Connecticut amounts at present to $354,099,-
707; showing an increase of more than $5,000,-
000 over the amount in the preceding year.

It is estimated that the current income of
the State, notwithstanding the reduction of
the State tax from two mills to one mill, will
be sufficient to meet all the ordinary expenditures of the government, and cover also the
extraordinary appropriations required for the
new State-House now in course of erection at
Hartford.

The capital of the public-school fund in
Connecticut amounts to $2,044,190.81. Of
the interest which annually accrues on it, and
which is devoted to educational purposes, a
corresponding portion is distributed among the
children of school-age *per capita*, at the rate
of one dollar each.

Seventy-nine savings-banks were in operation in the State on the 1st of January, 1874,
the total sum of their deposits amounting to
$70,769,407,95; showing an increase of very
nearly two and a quarter millions over their
total at the beginning of the previous year.
The assets of these banks had an increase of
$2,406,187.85 within the last year. In their
loans and investments in personal property
during that period, there was a decrease of
about $2,000,000; while the amount of their
loans on real estate increased by some $4,000,000
within the same time. This result is attributed
to the reduction of the tax on loans secured
upon property of the last-named description.

The whole number of persons who severally
owned the money deposited in the savings-
banks at the beginning of 1874 was 204,741;
their classification in respect to the amounts
belonging to them, respectively, being as follows: Depositors of sums less than $500 num-
bered 158,371, the total amount of their deposits being $21,896,685; depositors of sums
between $500 and $1,000, 28,324, all their deposits amounting to $15,907,016; and deposit-
ors of sums exceeding $1,000, 18,046, their ag-
gregate deposits making a total of $32,965,706.

The owners of these larger sums represent
less than one-eleventh part of all the depositors in regard to number, yet absorb nearly
one-half of the amount of all the deposits
taken together. Governor Ingersoll called the
attention of the General Assembly to that fact,
saying that "in this the true idea of a savings-
bank seems to have been lost sight of, and the
institutions, to that extent, operated as trust
companies for the investment of surplus capital;" adding that "the very large number of
small depositors shows that the mass of the
public, dealing with these institutions, have
done so upon the faith that they are what they
were only chartered to be, institutions for savings." Upon which he says that ".any legisla-

tion in regard to them should, in the first place,
and before any other consideration, be directed
to the security of the deposits there made."
The better to guard the interests of those small
depositors against loss, he suggested that the
General Assembly should keep a watchful eye
upon the operations of the savings-banks, and
surround them with such salutary restraints
by legislative enactments as were best calculated "to keep that fact constantly before the
eyes of their officers."

A special commission was appointed by an
act of the Legislature at the previous session
to examine into the condition of the savings-
banks in the State. The report presented by
this commission recommended the restriction
of the loans by savings-banks on personal security to forty per cent. of their deposits on
hand.

Public instruction seems to progress very
satisfactorily. As regards the number of persons who partake of its benefits in proportion
to the population, Connecticut is claimed to
stand first among the States in the Union. The
number of children who attended schools of all
kinds during the last year was 123,386; and
all of them, except 8,329, attended the public
schools. There are 1,648 public schools in
the State, and the number of teachers employed was about 2,500.

In the Normal School there were 43 graduates during the year, the whole number of
students in attendance, from April 1, 1873, to
the same date in 1874, having been 210.

In the Sheffield Scientific School there are
30 free scholarships at the disposition of the
State, which are said to be now eagerly sought
after, and have all been granted in accordance
with the requirements of the statute. Under the
acts previously passed by the Legislature, the
income of the fund held by the School Fund
Commissioner under the Federal land grant,
for the promotion of scientific education,
amounting to $8,100, is paid to the Sheffield
Scientific School.

The aggregate receipts from all sources, for
the support of the public schools in 1873, exceeded $1,500,000, derived from the following
sources:

From district and town taxes	$1,098,428 63
From State tax	199,272 00
From school fund	132,848 00
From town deposit fund	45,452 58
From local funds	12,196 45
From voluntary contributions	7,172 42
From other sources	47,119 12
Total	$1,542,489 20

The various charitable institutions of the
State are well provided for, although the Hospital for the Insane, at Middletown, is the only
one of these institutions that is under the absolute control of the State. The better to secure
the efficiency of their management, and realize
from them the objects for which they have
been severally established, an act was passed
by the General Assembly at the last session,
creating a State Board of Charities, composed

of six members, to be appointed by the Governor, three gentlemen and three ladies, whose duty it is personally to visit such institutions, inspect the manner in which they are conducted, and ascertain their condition in all respects, with a view to provide for their wants, and report to the Legislature on the result of its operations. This board has accordingly been organized, and presented its first report to the General Assembly.

The whole number of patients under treatment in the Hospital for the Insane, at the beginning of May, 1874, was 394; of whom 35 only were regarded as curable. This is said to be due in a great measure to the chronic condition of that large number of patients who have been removed to the institution from the almshouses of the towns, where the treatment necessary to their cure could not be had; their recovery having been rendered by long delay more difficult, if not impossible. As these chronic patients cannot be discharged to make room for new ones, the necessity of enlarging the hospital-building at no distant day is apparent, although it is capable at present of accommodating some 50 patients more than it actually contains. Of 896 patients admitted to the hospital since its beginning, 799 have been beneficiaries of the State. The income of the hospital last year amounted to about $92,000, and the expenditures to $87,000.

The number of pupils at the School for Imbeciles, at Lakeville in Salisbury, is 64. Twenty-nine of these are State beneficiaries, all orphans except two.

At the American Asylum for the Deaf and Dumb, at Hartford, 66 scholars have received State aid during the year; the expense for that purpose having been $9,279.23. The State has also aided 15 blind children at the Perkins Institute in Boston.

The number of discharged soldiers who have been under medical and surgical treatment at the hospitals of New Haven and Hartford was 182, at a total cost to the State of $18,000; the services rendered for that purpose by the medical profession in either city having been gratuitous.

For the support of soldiers' children in the different towns, the State appropriated last year nearly $90,000. About $2,700 were also appropriated for the support of such paupers as do not belong to any town.

The inmates of the Industrial School for Girls, at the end of April, 1874, numbered 76, sent thither from forty-three towns in the State. Henceforward, these girls will be not unprofitably occupied in the details belonging to a box-factory which has recently been established in connection with the school. It is anticipated that the institution will thereby become financially independent.

In the State Reform School there were 311 boys kept under correction. During the year 200 of them had been received into the school, and 190 discharged.

With reference to persons arrested for drunkenness and kindred offenses, the General Assembly, at the last session, passed an act appointing a commission to inquire into their penal treatment, and also into the expediency of establishing a State Asylum for Inebriates. The report of this commission was made.

A bill was also passed by the Legislature at the session of 1874, incorporating the State Inebriate Asylum, to be called "The Connecticut Reformatory Home." An additional bill has also been passed, entitled "An act concerning inebriates, dipsomaniacs, and habitual drunkards," approved July 25, 1874, which provides for their reception into the asylum, their treatment, and discharge; its first section being as follows:

SECTION 1. Whenever any person shall have become an habitual drunkard, a dipsomaniac, or so far addicted to the intemperate use of narcotics or stimulants as to have lost the power of self-control, the Court of Probate for the district in which such person resides, or has a legal domicil, shall, on application of a majority of the selectmen of the town where such person resides, or has a legal domicil, or of any relative of such person, make due inquiry, and if it shall find such person to have become an habitual drunkard, or so far addicted to the intemperate use of narcotics or stimulants as to have lost the power of self-control, then said court shall order such person to be taken to some inebriate asylum within this State, for treatment, care, and custody, for a term not less than four months, and not more than twelve months; but if said person shall be found to be a dipsomaniac, said term of commitment shall be for the period of three years: *Provided, however,* That the Court of Probate shall not, in either case, make such order without the certificate of at least two respectable practising physicians, after a personal examination, made within one week before the time of said application, or said commitment, which certificate shall contain the opinion of said physicians that such person has become, as the case may be, a dipsomaniac, an habitual drunkard, or has, by reason of the intemperate use of narcotics or stimulants, lost the power of self-control, and requires the treatment, care, and custody of some inebriate asylum, and shall be subscribed and sworn to by said physicians before an authority empowered to administer oaths.

In the State penitentiary there were 181 convicts in confinement at the beginning of May, 1874; all males except two—one white, and one colored woman. Twenty-nine of the whole number were foreign-born. The convicts are employed in remunerative work. Notwithstanding a reduction in the price of prison-labor, necessitated by the prostration of business during the winter of 1873–'74, a net income of $2,114.30 has been received into the Treasury from the prison.

The General Assembly of 1874 continued its session eighty-two days, and was adjourned on the 25th of July. A large number of acts were passed on subjects not only of a local or private interest, but more of a general character and importance. Among these last named are the following: The license law already existing has been so amended that, while its general features have suffered no change, alterations have been made in it calculated to secure an impartial and thorough enforcement of its provisions. The usury-law, which was enacted in 1872, has also been revised and amended "by striking out the word *six* in the said act wherever it occurs, and inserting in lieu thereof the word *seven;*" this being now fixed as the limit of the annual rate of interest to be paid or received on money loans in Connecticut.

The greatest importance appears to have been attached by the people to the acts passed this year in regard to elections and naturalization. The two previously existing laws on these subjects had been enacted in 1868, when both bills were vetoed by Governor English, and both passed over his objections by the Legislature. At the present session both of them have been repealed, or rather considerably modified, by great majorities, though not without considerable opposition. Concerning elections, all the provisions of the former law calculated to protect the freedom of voting and guard the integrity of the ballot-box against abuse or fraud, have been retained in the new. Those portions of it which might seem to have a tendency to restrict the right of the electors to vote, or put obstacles in the way of its lawful exercise, have been repealed.

With a view to accommodate the working-classes by enabling them to exercise their right of suffrage with the least inconvenience, a provision has been inserted in the new law, compelling the boards of selectmen to hold evening sessions for the admission of votes; thus relieving workmen from the necessity of losing, for that purpose, any portion of their working-hours during the day.

With regard to naturalization, the authority of receiving applications and issuing certificates for it was confined by the law of 1868 to one court in the state—the Superior Court. The new law generalizes that authority, by empowering the courts of Common Pleas and the city courts—all the courts of record in the State, except the Courts of Probate, to make records of naturalization, and issue certificates of it.

Early in the session the Legislature elected William W. Eaton United States Senator for the term of six years from March 4, 1875, in the place of Wm. A. Buckingham. Three vacant seats on the benches of the Supreme and Superior Courts in the State were also filled by this Legislature. Besides the usual appropriations, the General Assembly appropriated $10,000 "for a triangulated survey of the State."

The number of fire, fire and marine, and marine insurance companies, doing business in Connecticut, is 120; representing a cash capital of about $30,000,000, with gross assets of $77,000,000.

The life and accident insurance companies are 29; of which 10 are home companies. The assets of these last-named companies amount in the aggregate to nearly $65,000,000, the assets of the other State companies being about $191,000,000. There was a total increase of about $25,000,000 over the assets of the preceding year.

There are 22 railway companies in the State. Their aggregate length measures 1,197 miles, of which 896 are within the State. Twenty-eight of these have been built during the last year.

Some details respecting these roads are exhibited in the following official statement:

They have transported during the year 10,542,821 passengers, being an increase over the preceding year of 408,188, without fatal injury to any passenger, except in two instances, resulting from incaution of the passenger on leaving a train. Other instances of injury, to the total number of 110, have occurred, of which 59 resulted in death. Of the whole number of cases of injury, except of passengers or employés, almost two-thirds were of persons walking or lying on the track.

The total cost of these roads and equipment was $54,659,029.82, represented by a total nominal capital of $44,690,700, of which $36,068,694.62 has been paid in.

The gross earnings of all the companies for the year ending September 30, 1873, were $12,037,986.33, of which about one-half was received from passengers. The total net income amounted to $2,586,463, of which all but about $50,000 has been paid in dividends by nine corporations.

The work of the State Board of Fish Commissioners, to whom the care of this interest has been committed since 1865, when that board was created, appears to have been crowned with success. From June 21 to August 21, 1873, 44,000,000 shad were hatched at Holyoke. Forty millions of these were put into the Connecticut River. In four years the shad, of good size, will reappear in the Connecticut. The catch of shad in 1873 was not so large as in the previous year, because none were planted in 1869. The black bass has been introduced into 37 ponds and reservoirs in different parts of the State. From 1868 to 1871 inclusive, 2,981 of these fish were placed in the ponds and reservoirs, and the commissioners find that they have increased and done so well that they deem it best not to distribute any more of them. Two hundred and forty-four thousand young salmon were placed in the various rivers of the State last year, 115,000 of them in tributaries of the Connecticut. The commissioners have concluded to unite with the commissioners of Massachusetts, Vermont, and New Hampshire, in stocking the Connecticut river with salmon—all their efforts for the present being devoted to that river. Eight hundred and fifty thousand young salmon will be placed in the tributaries of the Connecticut this year. About 50,000 California salmon have also been placed in the rivers of the State. Some thousands of the fresh-water, or land-locked salmon, have been hatched at the hatching-houses in Westport, where the young fish are at present.

In compliance with the act passed by the Legislature of 1873, for the establishment of a Bureau of Labor Statistics, consisting of a chief and his deputy, both of these officers were appointed by Governor Ingersoll in October of that year.

The whole number of births which took

place in Connecticut during the year 1873 was 14,087, or 282 more than in 1872, and 42½ per cent. in excess of the births returned in 1863. Of the 13,984 births, in which the sex was stated, the proportion was 110 males to 100 females. The illegitimate births numbered 152. Of colored children there were 247 births.

The entire number of deaths in the State was 9,822, which is 148 less than in 1872. The deaths in the colored population were 207, or 40 less than the births.

The marriages contracted in 1873 were 4,841, or 182 less than in the preceding year. The marriages, where both parties were of American birth, numbered 2,768; where both were foreigners, 1,313; and where one party was American the other foreigner, 575.

The marriages contracted among the colored population were 141, including one mixed.

The number of divorces granted in 1873 was 457. The applications for divorce were made, in 274 cases, by the wife, and in 183 by the husband.

The construction of the new State-House at Hartford has been steadily progressing.

At the election on October 5th the constitutional amendment was approved by a large majority.

STATE-HOUSE, HARTFORD.

CORNELL, EZRA, a philanthropist and benefactor of education; born at Westchester Landing, Westchester County, N. Y., January 11, 1807; died at his home in Ithaca, N. Y., December 9, 1874. His father, who belonged to the Society of Friends, was engaged in the making of pottery, and the son worked at this occupation at Tarrytown, and afterward in Madison County, his laborious youth limiting his educational opportunities. He had no more than a common-school education, but in addition to native shrewdness and sound judgment manifested at an early age a desire for knowledge and a mind liberal in the reception of new ideas. In 1826 he left home and obtained employment at Homer, whence, two years after, he removed to Ithaca, where he obtained a place, at rather scanty wages, in the machine-shop attached to the cotton-mill of Otis Eddy, which stood on the site now occupied by one of the stately buildings of Cor-

nell University. Mill-work and agriculture took up his time by turns for fifteen years, when in 1843 he became connected with the construction of the first telegraphic line established in this country. He formed the acquaintance of F. O. J. Smith, Representative from Maine, and chairman of the Committee of Commerce of the House, who was owner of one-fourth interest in the invention of Prof. Morse; and also of Prof. Morse himself. The plan of laying the telegraphic wires in pipes underground was determined upon for the experimental line between Baltimore and Washington—as this method had been used successfully in England—and Mr. Cornell, who had an inventive turn of mind, had devised a machine for laying the pipes. He was engaged to superintend the work at the modest salary of $1,000 per year. The wires were covered with cotton and imperfectly insulated with bitumen. It soon became known to Prof. Morse that the plan would not succeed, and Mr. Cornell, to afford the opportunity for a change of plans, purposely disabled his machine, and subsequently put up the wires on poles as is now done. Mr. Cornell now devoted his whole attention and energy to the prosecution of the telegraphic business, being more than once reduced to great straits from the want of means. After the Government relinquished its connection with the telegraph as unprofitable, in 1845, it took a new start as a private enterprise, and began to prove profitable. When the line was extended to New York in 1845, Mr. Cornell was appointed to superintend it, and also to supervise the construction of lines from New York to Philadelphia. In 1846 he constructed a line to Albany, and another in the following year from Troy to Montreal. Being confident of the success of these projects, he invested extensively in telegraphic stocks, and realized large profits from them. His good fortune did not end with his business successes, for in 1863 he was elected member of the Assembly from his district, and in the year following of the State Senate, and was reëlected for the next term. In 1862 he was chosen President of the State Agricultural Society, and while in London that year he sent several soldiers from England to this country to join our army, paying all their expenses. He had some years before made his home at Ithaca, and finding that there was a need of a public library there he erected a fine building for it, and gave it an endowment of $25,000, which he subsequently increased to $50,000, and finally to $100,000, for the purchase of books and the support of the librarian. His wealth was now rapidly increasing, and having tasted the luxury of giving, he began to plan larger benefactions. In 1862, Congress had passed the Agricultural Land Grant Act, giving to the States, under certain conditions and restrictions, 30,000 acres of government lands for each Senator and Representative of the State in Congress. Certain parties in the State of New York had been instrumental in procuring the passage of this act, and when it was passed, and New York was found to be entitled to 990,000 acres of land, those parties, who had founded the People's College at Ovid, N. Y., and the Agricultural College at Havana, N. Y., asked for this landed endowment to be granted by the State to their institutions. It was granted to them under the conditions required by the act, but both institutions found themselves utterly unable to fulfill these conditions, and consequently the grant lapsed. Meantime, Mr. Cornell, then a member of the State Senate, had been an attentive observer of their efforts, and had formed the purpose of founding a university that would not fail. In 1865 he asked of the Legislature a charter for a university which he proposed to found and endow with the sum of $500,000. The charter was passed, but with two stipulations not greatly to the credit of the lobby or the Legislature in that

stage of the proceedings. One was that, as a condition of receiving this charter, he should pay over to Genesee College, Lima, N. Y., over and above his endowment of Cornell University, $25,000. This was subsequently refunded to Mr. Cornell by a Legislature which had the grace to be ashamed of the acts of its predecessor, and by him immediately donated to Cornell University. The other stipulation was that provision should be made for the free tuition of one student from each Assembly district in the State. Mr. Cornell complied with both, and immediately put into the hands of the designated trustees of the new university securities to the amount of $500,000. The next year, the People's College and the Agricultural College having both collapsed, Mr. Cornell made application for the land grant for his university, which he had further endowed with $260,000 more in land, money, and a valuable mineralogical and geological collection. He obtained the grant, and, taking counsel of judicious friends, he laid the foundations of his university course broad and deep, and proceeded to erect the buildings for it. He also contracted with the State for the purchase of the entire Agricultural College land-scrip, in order to locate it more advantageously for the university. The buildings were so far completed at Ithaca that, on the 7th of October, 1868, the university was formally opened, nearly 500 students being in attendance. Many other liberal gifts were made to the university subsequently, and it is now one of the most prosperous seats of learning in the country, with a prospect, when its lands are all sold, of being, perhaps, the richest of American colleges. It accomplishes the union of liberal and practical education contemplated by its founder as well as by Congress when public lands were granted to the States. It has also realized Mr. Cornell's idea of offering instruction to any person in any study ; and, added to all these advantages, it allows the fullest freedom of religious belief among its Faculty as well as among its students. The pressure to sell agricultural college land-scrip by so many States at the same time had materially depreciated its value, and made the location of these lands proportionately more difficult. Mr. Cornell had been very successful in locating the scrip, purchasing largely timbered lands, but the sales of these lands were delayed by the financial condition of the country, and other causes, and some persons were ready to attribute to Mr. Cornell the design to enrich himself at the expense of the university. He demanded an investigation, which was made as thorough and searching as possible, and resulted in his triumphant vindication. He had been infirm for several months, owing to an attack of pneumonia in the spring of 1874, but his final illness was brief, and his death sudden. Few men have been so widely and sincerely mourned.

COSTA RICA (República de Costa Rica), one of the five independent states of Central

America, situated betweeen latitude 8° and 11° 5' north, and longitude 81° 20' and 85° 53' west; and bounded on the north by Nicaragua, on the east by the Caribbean Sea, on the south-east by the United States of Colombia, and on the south and west by the Pacific Ocean. The question of limits, still pending with Nicaragua, will probably be amicably disposed of before the end of the present year, both Governments evincing a readiness to come to terms. A more difficult question is that with Colombia, a boundary-line with which republic was proposed by the Colombian minister, but rejected by the Costa Rica Congress, who did not see fit to surrender the whole of Admiral's Bay on the Caribbean Sea. The Government, apparently aware of the exaggerative proportions of the estimate of 1873, now estimates the population of the republic at 185,-000, comprising 5,000 civilized and 10,000 uncivilized Indians, 120 Africans, and some 600 Chinese. It has been remarked that Costa Rica possesses a larger number of inhabitants of unmixed European blood than any of the Hispano-American states. The territory, which comprises an area of 21,493 square miles, is divided into the five provinces of Alajuela, Cartago, Guanacaste, Heredia, and San José, with the two districts of Limon and Puntarenas. The President is General Tomás Guardia, who had resigned for a time in favor of Señor Salvador Gonzales.

The first *Designado* (first Vice-President) is Señor Rafael Barroeta; and the second, Dr. Vicente Herrera, whose functions embrace also those of the Departments of the Interior, Justice, War, and the Navy, and who is provisional Minister of Foreign Affairs and Public Instruction; Minister of Public Works, Señor Salvador Lara; and Minister of Finance and Commerce, Señor Joaquin Lizano.

The national Congress, by the terms of the Constitution of 1871, is composed of a single Chamber, the members of which (deputies) are elected for four years. Speaker, Señor Manuel A. Borrilla.

The president (*regente*) of the Supreme Court is Señor Vicente Saenz.

The commander-in-chief of the army is the President of the Republic.

The consul-general of Costa Rica in New York is Señor J. M. Muñoz.

The armed force comprises 16,370 militia, being the number of male inhabitants between the ages of eighteen and thirty years; 900 of whom perform active service and may be said to constitute the regular army; and a reserve corps, 18,819 strong, made up of the male inhabitants between the ages of thirty and fifty-five years: total military strength, 35,189.

The main sources of the national revenue are the customs receipts, amounting to about one-third and sometimes to nearly one-half of the entire income, and the tobacco and spirit monopolies. The following tables exhibit the income and expenditure for the year 1873–'74:

INCOME.

Proceeds of the National Bank	$141,746 00
State lands	19,239 00
Customs receipts	1,151,865 00
Spirits monopoly	831,279 00
Tobacco monopoly	421,420 00
Gunpowder monopoly	8,741 00
Sale of salt	4,698 00
Stamp-duties	23,719 00
Licenses	22,003 00
Court of Justice fees	25,146 00
Post-Office	25,522 00
Telegraphs	5,616 00
Fines	2,745 00
Proceeds of loans	18,293 00
Deposits	34,000 00
Sundries	79,552 95½
Total	$2,812,584 95½

EXPENDITURE.

Ministry of the Interior	$191,972
Police	22,956
Ministry of Finance, etc	138,719
Ministry of Justice, etc	72,529
Ministry of War, etc	350,005
Ministry of Public Works	173,711
Public Instruction	73,188
Public Worship	17,698
Charities	3,000
Navy	30,532
Foreign Affairs	33,036
Custom-houses	30,365
Administration of monopolies	403,625
Deposits	59,960
Commissions, etc., on loans	179,360
Exchange, etc	131,281
Instalments on preferred notes	73,375
Expenses of Costa Rica Railway	2,127,380
Interest and instalments on six per cent. loan	114,450
Subsidies to various municipalities	27,119
Sundries	76,886
Total	$4,328,597

Here, then, is a deficit of no less than $1,-516,010, or considerably more than one-half of the entire revenue of the republic; a state of affairs rather at variance with the recent calculations of a native economist, who affirms that "with good management the revenue could easily be raised to leave a surplus of $200,000 per month outside of the expenses of the administration, or, in other words, to bring the total income to $4,000,000 per annum." Without attempting to disprove the feasibility of such an increase, it is only necessary to observe that, even in the event of its realization, there would still be a yearly deficit of from $500,000 to $1,000,000 (as is shown by the foregoing table), at least while the outlay on the railway continues at the rate above registered—$2,127,380. The revenue for the fiscal year above referred to is, however, some $300,-000 in advance of that of the preceding year.

Important reforms, tending to secure more economical management in the customs department, were recommended, and the transferring the customs office of the south to the capital, where it would be under the immediate supervision of the Government.

A steady growth in the receipts of this department is attested by the following figures:

Years.	Receipts.	Years.	Receipts.
1868–'69	$210,294	1871–'72	$623,185
1869–'70	278,595	1872–'73	921,758
1870–'71	332,436	1873–'74	1,151,865

Other progressive branches are the spirits and tobacco monopolies, which show, in 1873–

'74, as compared with, the year before, an increase of nearly $200,000 and $100,000 respectively.

The national debt of Costa Rica amounts, as stated in the ANNUAL CYCLOPÆDIA for 1873, to $23,100,000, made up as follows: British loans, $17,000,000; indebtedness to Peru, $100,000;[*] and home debt, $6,000,000 (inclusive of floating obligations). That is to say, this, one of the smallest states in America is burdened with onerous liabilities at the rate of about $125 to each inhabitant, a proportion much larger than that of the indebtedness of England, France, or Holland; and, worst of all, she now finds that, in spite of her natural resources, she has been borrowing too fast. When, in 1871, her commerce was in a prosperous condition, and promised to become still more so with improved means of transportation for her products from the interior to the coast, and the construction of piers in her seaports, a first loan of £500,000 was ventured upon; shortly afterward, in the same year, another loan of £500,000 was offered for public subscription, and was floated at the rate of 74, with interest at six per cent. By May, 1872, the first loan had reached a high premium, and the credit of the republic seemed to be satisfactorily established at the London Stock Exchange, so that a third and much larger loan of £2,400,-000, brought out at so favorable a juncture and under the auspices of influential bankers, was received with full confidence, and bonds for the whole amount save £173,000 were at once applied for. This loan was to bear interest at seven per cent., with a sinking-fund of but one per cent.; to the payment of the coupons were hypothecated the spirit, tobacco, and coffee taxes; and, for the final extinguishment of the loan, the year 1903 was fixed upon. The first two payments were duly made; the bondholders were quite satisfied, and some of the stock actually went to a premium; but not so the third coupon, and Costa Rica is registered in default since April 1, 1874, in the sum of £2,-362,800. At a meeting of bondholders, held on August 7th, at London, a resolution was adopted for the appointment of agents in Costa Rica to receive the proceeds of the revenues forming the special guarantee of the loan, confidently regarded as adequate to cover the entire claim. No doubt was entertained of the willingness of the Government to redeem the credit of the republic rather than allow its name to figure side by side with those of Honduras, Venezuela, Santo Domingo, and others hopelessly insolvent.

The item standing for public instruction in the table of expenditure shows that the cause of education is receiving more attention than heretofore; some of the school-buildings in process of building in 1873 have been completed, and a few others have been commenced.

The commerce still continues steadily on

* Incorrectly set down at $136,000 by a statistical publication for 1874.

the increase. The total value of the imports in 1873 was $3,500,000, and that of the exports $3,775,196; of which $3,933,181 was for coffee (25,167,975 lbs); $48,576 for hides; $17,753 for India-rubber; $12,920 for deerskins; and $37,872 for mahogany, cedar, and other woods.

The coffee-crop is reported as having been very small; but the deficiency in quantity was compensated for by an unprecedented rise in price, as much as $23 and even $24 per 100 lbs. having been obtained at Puntarenas. The following crop was likely to be very abundant; the total yield was calculated at 400,000 quintals—60,000,000 lbs.—and the probable price at Puntarenas at $20 per quintal. The shipping at the port of Puntarenas was 95 vessels entered, with an aggregate of 15,464 tons; while at Limon the number entered was 82, with 11,221 tons; and the number cleared 79, with a total of 10,054 tons. Puntarenas was visited besides by 91 mail-steamers and one whaler, and Limon by 10 mail-steamers.

The railway progresses steadily and, it is said, satisfactorily, though rather slowly, and a new contract with Meiggs which has been talked of would at once dispel all doubt as to the ultimate completion of the line.

Trains already run from Alajuela, the inland terminus, to Cartago, a distance of 26¼ miles; and from Limon, on the Atlantic, to near the Rio Matina, say 21 miles, there are 38 miles more in course of preparation; and it was expected that, with the number of workmen employed, and the appliances at their disposal—500 men, and machine-shops and machinery sufficient for a road 1,000 miles in length—the track would, by the end of the year, be completed to Pacuaré, about 45 miles from Limon. There are at the latter port, besides the machine-shops, a car-shop, a government-house, storehouses, and dwelling-houses for officials, and several frame buildings were to be put up before the end of the year. Indeed, since the Government took charge of the railway, no effort has been omitted to secure dispatch and the utmost economy in the construction of the line. The sum monthly expended for keeping the road in good condition is $3,233.75.

No new telegraph has been constructed during the year; but it is now proposed to submerge a cable from Limon to Aspinwall, and to establish telegraphic communication between Costa Rica and Nicaragua, San Salvador, and Guatemala.

In January occurred one of those massacres of coolies which commonly mark the building period of railways in the Spanish-American republics of the Pacific coast.

The only event to really disturb the public peace during the year was an abortive attempt to overthrow the Government. The leader of the outbreak, which took place at Puntarenas in October, was one Joaquin Fernandez. The President declared the republic in a state of siege, and decreed that all who should take part with the rebel should be tried and sentenced according to the *ordenanzas*, and that persons aiding the rebel cause would have their property confiscated.

After an unsuccessful attempt to seize the government buildings, Fernandez and his followers embarked for the province of Guanacaste, carrying with them $11,000 plundered from the National Bank. The town of Bagaces, however, remained faithful, and in Puntarenas the authorities had taken all the measures required by the circumstances. General Guardia set out for the latter place on October 21st.

The Congress was opened on May 1st, with the customary message from the President, the tenor of which reveals a state of prosperity at home, and friendly relations abroad. "Respecting the Central-American republics, sisters of Costa Rica," says General Guardia, "the Government could encourage no sentiment not tending to cement and extend those cordial relations which ought to unite those peoples who so long formed one nation."

Political factions in the interior, whose discontent with the administration had been manifested in attempts at insurrection, were put down by the strong arm of the law, and the only encouragement they received were frowns from the majority of the people. The condition, history, and prospects of the railway—"which is to make or mar the republic"—were referred to at length ; as were also the resolve on the part of the Government to carry on the work under its own guidance, and in spite of all pecuniary or other difficulties that might stand in the way, and its determination to submit to any sacrifice rather than let the national credit suffer abroad.

A public library was to be established at San José.

The port of Limon was gradually taking on the aspect of a lively and flourishing town.

COTTON. According to the annual report of the cotton-crop of the United States for the year ending September 1, 1874, made by the *Commercial and Financial Chronicle*, of New York (and the work which is thus performed each year by this journal is of the highest value to the public), the production of 1874 is one of the three largest crops ever raised in the United States; the total number of bales being 4,170,388, while the yield of 1871 was 4,352,317, and that of 1860 4,669,770 bales. In 1874, 2,840,981 bales were exported, and 1,305,943 were taken by home-spinners, leaving a stock on hand, at the close of the year (September 1st), of 108,152 bales. The tables which follow show the whole movement for the twelve months. The first table indicates the stock at each port, September 1st of 1874 and 1873, the receipts at the ports for each of the last two years, and the export movement for the past year (1873–'74) in detail, and the totals for 1872–'73 :

PORTS.	Receipts Year ending		Exports, Year ending September 1, 1874.				STOCK.	
	September 1, 1874.	September 1, 1873.	Great Britain.	France.	Other Foreign.	Total.	September 1, 1874.	September 1, 1873.
Louisiana..............	1,221,608	1,240,384	633,429	249,980	263,914	1,147,314	15,959	7,177
Alabama................	299,578	332,457	89,714	7,245	40,408	182,367	3,962	5,802
South Carolina........	438,194	374,476	166,322	39,667	41,877	247,866	4,150	4,123
Georgia	620,857	614,089	238,786	42,588	148,197	429,571	4,579	1,224
Texas.................	389,045	343,450	202,426	22,578	49,385	274,383	4,505	4,589
Florida...............	14,185	14,068	35	....	800	835	....	....
North Carolina........	57,895	61,576	5,965	....	368	6,333	232	289
Virginia..............	505,876	433,586	14,375	....	6,346	20,721	2,293	1,602
New York..............	200,689*	165,605*	446,354	8,738	30,514	485,596	56,043	47,746
Boston................	24,680*	26,875*	25,110	....	289	25,399	8,000	9,500
Philadelphia..........	16,404*	21,209*	24,461	....	3,787	28,248	6,545	7,250
Baltimore.............	6,431*	17,663*	25,103	65	16,295	41,528	1,944	1,387
Portland..............	3,755*	5,961*	352	....	....	352	....	....
San Francisco.........	....	....	454	14	....	468	....	....
Total this year.....	3,804,290	....	1,867,936	370,865	602,180	2,840,981	108,152	....
Total last year.....	....	3,651,346	1,905,566	252,903	521,517	2,679,986	....	90,989

By the above it will be seen that the total receipts of the Atlantic and Gulf shipping-ports this year have been 3,804,290 bales, against 3,651,346 bales last year. If, now, are added the shipments from Tennessee and elsewhere—

* These figures are only the portion of the receipts at these ports which arrive overland from Tennessee, etc. The total receipts at New York, Baltimore, Boston, and Philadelphia, for the year ending August 31, 1874, are given elsewhere.

where direct to manufacturers, the result is the following crop-statement for the two years:

	Year ending September 1, 1873-'74.	Year ending September 1, 1872-'73.
	Bales.	Bales.
Receipts at the shipping-ports.	3,804,290	3,651,346
Add shipments from Tennessee, etc., direct to manufacturers..	237,572	141,500
Total.............	4,041,862	3,792,846
Manufactured South, not included in above..............	128,526	137,662
Total cotton-crop for the year..	4,170,388	3,930,508

Of the total exports (2,840,981 bales) above given, 1,807,584 bales were shipped to Liverpool, 368,577 to Havre, and 200,705 to Bremen; 1,147,314 were exported from the port of New Orleans, 132,367 from Mobile, 274,383 from Galveston, 247,866 from Charleston, 429,-571 from Savannah, 485,596 from New York, 41,528 from Baltimore, and 82,350 from other ports.

The greater portion of the crop was shipped in vessels directly from Southern ports, but no small amount was sent North by railroad. The total amount thus carried overland was 497,083 bales, while the overland movement direct to manufacturers reached 237,572 bales. This latter amount was doubtless increased in consequence of the Southern floods, which forced some cotton over Northern routes, which would otherwise have passed through a Southern port. The details of the entire overland movement are shown in the following statement:

	Bales.
Shipments for the year from St. Louis...........	92,196
Carried North over Illinois Central Railroad from Cairo, etc................	4,600
Carried North over Cairo & Vincennes Railroad.	18,783
Carried over the Mississippi River above St. Louis................	6,148
Carried North over St. Louis & Southeastern, less deductions................	6,604
Carried North over Evansville & Crawfordsville, less reshipments................	27,749
Carried North over Jeffersonville, Madison & Indianapolis Railroad.............	134,097
Carried North over Ohio & Mississippi Branch..	82,630
Shipped through Cincinnati by Louisville, Cincinnati & Lexington Railroad.............	81,775
Receipts at Cincinnati by Ohio River...........	51,501
Shipped to mills adjacent to river and to points above Cincinnati................	21,000
Total carried overland..................	497,083

Deduct—Receipts overland at New York, Boston, Philadelphia, etc..... 251,962
" Shipments from Mobile and other outports by rail.................. 140,112
Less deducted at New Orleans.................. 107,188
Less deducted at Savannah. 21,508
Less deducted at Charleston.................. 3,917 132,583 7,549

| Total to deduct............. | 259,511 |

Leaving the direct overland movement not elsewhere counted................ 237,572

The distribution of the crop by States, together with the estimated weight of the bales, is given in the table below. According to this statement, it will be seen that the total gross weight of the latest crop reaches 1,956,742,297

pounds, and that the average weight of the bales is 469 pounds.

CROP OF—	Number of Bales.	Weight, lbs.	Average Weight.
Texas................	389,045	186,352,535	479
Louisiana.............	1,221,698	564,424,476	462
Alabama.............	299,578	147,991,582	494
Georgia.............	625,857	294,126,983	469
South Carolina.......	438,194	205,074,792	468
Virginia.............	505,876	238,298,836	461
North Carolina........	57,895	25,879,063	447
Tennessee.............	632,245	299,684,130	474
Total crop 1873-'74..	4,170,388	1,956,742,297	469
Total crop 1872-'73..	3,930,508	1,824,920,023	464

The following statement will afford a comparison between the crop of this year and those of former years:

Years.	Bales.	Years.	Bales.
1873-'74..........	4,170,388	1847-'48..........	2,347,634
1872-'73..........	3,930,508	1846-'47..........	1,778,651
1871-'72..........	2,974,351	1845-'46..........	2,100,537
1870-'71..........	4,352,317	1844-'45..........	2,394,503
1869-'70..........	3,154,946	1843-'44..........	2,030,409
1868-'69..........	2,499,039	1842-'43..........	2,378,875
1867-'68..........	2,593,993	1841-'42..........	1,683,574
1866-'67..........	2,019,774	1840-'41..........	1,634,945
1865-'66..........	2,193,987	1839-'40..........	2,177,835
1861-'65..........	no record.	1838-'39..........	1,360,532
1860-'61..........	3,656,086	1837-'38..........	1,801,497
1859-'60..........	4,669,770	1836-'37..........	1,422,930
1858-'59..........	3,851,481	1835-'36..........	1,360,752
1857-'58..........	3,113,962	1834-'35..........	1,254,328
1856-'57...... ...	2,939,519	1833-'34..........	1,205,394
1855-'56..........	3,527,845	1832-'33..........	1,070,438
1854-'55..........	2,847,339	1831-'32..........	987,487
1853-'54..........	2,930,027	1830-'31..........	1,038,848
1852-'53..........	3,262,882	1829-'30..........	976,855
1851-'52..........	3,015,029	1828-'29..........	870,425
1850-'51..........	2,355,257	1827-'28..........	727,593
1849-'50..........	2,096,706	1826-'27..........	957,281
1848-'49..........	2,728,596		

The crop of Sea-Island cotton this year amounted to 19,912 bales, of which 8,825 were the production of Florida, 1,408 of Georgia, 8,759 of South Carolina, and 920 of Texas. Including the 1,667 bales on hand at the beginning of the year, the total supply of this kind of cotton was 21,577 bales. As the stock on hand at the end of the year, September 1st, was 593 bales, the total amount distributed was 20,986 bales, of which 18,873 were exported to foreign ports, leaving 2,113 bales as the amount consumed (or otherwise to be accounted for) in the United States. The total crop of Sea-Island cotton, in 1873, was 26,289 bales.

Full returns of the cotton-manufacturing industry of the United States for the year ending July 1, 1874 were also presented in the Chronicle. These results were formerly obtained and published by the "National Association of Cotton Planters and Manufacturers," an organization which existed during the years of 1868, 1869, and 1870, and which published the first authentic statement of the actual consumption of cotton by the mills of this country. This association has not been in existence since 1870, but the statistics published this year have been prepared by its former secretary. The annual consumption of cotton by American mills in recent years has been as follows:

NORTHERN AND SOUTHERN MILLS.	1869-'70.	1870-'71.	1871-'72.	1872-'73.	1873-'74.
	Bales.	Bales.	Bales.	Bales.	Bales.
Taken by Northern mills.............................	806,860	1,088,056	977,540	1,063,465	1,177,417
Taken by Southern mills...:	90,000	91,240	120,000	137,662	128,526
Total takings from crop.........................	896,860	1,100,196	1,097,540	1,201,127	1,305,943
Added to mill-stock during year......................	....	80,750	....	....	85,000
Reduction of mill-stock during year....................	33,876	....	40,000	50,000	....
Total consumption of mills..................	930,736	1,019,446	1,137,540	1,251,127	1,220,943

These totals show a decrease in actual consumption this year of 30,184 bales, while they also indicate the rapid progress which this industry has made within the past five years.

In the following tables of the capacity and consumption of the cotton-mills of the United States, only those mills are included which *spin* cotton. In New York, Pennsylvania, and other States, there are many mills which only weave the yarns which other mills have spun; they, therefore, consume no cotton. The number of spinning-mills, with the number of looms and spindles, the amount of cotton consumed, and other items of importance, for the year ending July 1, 1874, was as follows:

STATES.	Number of Mills.	Number of Looms.	Number of Spindles.	Average Size of Yarn.	Average Running-time.	Average Consumption of Cotton per Spindle.	Quantity of Cotton used.	Quantity of Cotton used.
				No.	Weeks.	Pounds.	Pounds.	Bales.
NORTHERN STATES:								
Maine....................	24	12,415	609,808	25.98	50.71	59.07	36,473,547	78,607
New Hampshire.............	42	20,422	855,150	23.43	51.46	69.89	59,759,468	128,792
Vermont....................	0	1,274	58,948	29.75	46.84	46.34	2,734,167	5,895
Massachusetts	194	71,202	3,769,692	28.55	49.89	58.93	208,325,299	488,201
Rhode Island...............	115	24,706	1,336,842	35.20	48.10	43.51	58,146,985	125,317
Connecticut................	104	18,170	908,222	31.40	48.45	53.48	48,514,613	104,557
New York..................	55	12,476	580,917	32	47.70	42.22	24,536,349	52,880
New Jersey.................	17	2,070	150,968	29.30	51	53.50	8,078,647	17,411
Pennsylvania...............	60	9,772	452,064	17.51	42.80	84	37,969,726	81,872
Delaware..................	8	796	47,076	22.94	49.66	65.14	3,174,174	6,841
Maryland..................	21	2,299	110,260	11.50	47.85	174.34	19,222,703	41,438
Ohio......................	5	236	20,410	11.83	36.80	86.48	1,826,304	3,936
Indiana...................	4	618	22,988	14.56	47.44	159	3,671,227	7,912
Minnesota.................	1	24	3,400	3	52	99.41	338,000	728
Total Northern.........	650	176,480	8,927,754	28.56	49.83	56.86	507,790,099	1,094,387
SOUTHERN STATES:								
Alabama..................	16	1,860	57,594	10.50	48.37	112.33	6,490,079	13,772
Arkansas.................	2	28	1,956	19	51	121.69	136,000	293
Georgia..................	42	2,934	197,330	12.71	47.77	133.57	18,529,899	39,920
Kentucky.................	4	42	10,500	6.26	49.24	178.86	1,878,020	4,047
Louisiana................	3	300	15,000	12	47.02	86.31	1,294,560	2,790
Mississippi..............	11	348	15,150	11.33	39.29	75.17	1,138,804	2,545
Missouri.................	4	382	18,656	10.75	49.66	183.25	3,481,573	7,388
North Carolina...........	30	1,055	55,498	12.08	46.54	123.10	6,832,673	14,726
South Carolina...........	18	1,288	62,872	13.36	39.67	113.25	7,134,558	15,376
Tennessee................	42	1,014	47,058	12.89	51.10	133.38	6,272,458	13,518
Texas....................	4	230	10,225	12	47.02	127.80	1,278,125	2,755
Virginia.................	11	1,564	56,490	16	47.57	95.23	5,334,025	11,496
Total Southern.........	187	10,495	487,629	12.5	47.02	122.53	59,798,774	128,526
RECAPITULATION.								
Total Northern..........	660	176,480	8,927,754	28.56	49.33	56.86	507,790,099	1,094,387
Total Southern...........	187	10,495	487,659	12.5	47.02	122.53	59,798,774	128,526
Grand total..............	847	186,975	9,415,383	27.73	48.26	60.29	567,583,873	1,222,913

The cost of manufacturing varies from four and a half mills to six and a half mills per number per pound in different mills, according to their organization, condition, and management. The rate of four and a half mills is extremely low, and is reached by very few factories; while six and a half mills is an extravagantly high cost. The mean or average is probably five and a fourth or five and a half mills per number. Including the cost of the cotton, and two per cent. for selling, the cost of printing-cloth is 5.02 cents per yard; light sheeting, 7.41 ; and standard sheeting, 8.94. From the above table it appears that the number of spinning-spindles in the United States on the 1st of July, 1874, was 9,415,383, against 7,114,000 at the same date of 1870, and 6,763,557 at the same date of 1869, as follows:

LOCATION.	Looms.	Spindles.	Yarn, Average.	Av. per Spindle.
North, 1874.........	176,480	8,927,754	28.56	56.86
South, "	10,495	487,629	12.05	122.53
Total, 1874......	186,975	9,415,383	27.73	60.29
North, 1870......	147,682	6,851,779	28¼	50.87
South, "	5,852	262,221	12¾	134.23
Total, 1870......	153,534	7,114,000	28¼	52.93
North, 1869......	....	6,538,494	28	60.70
South, "	....	225,068	12¾	138.12
Total, 1869......	....	6,763,557	27½	64.88

The above records a very rapid progress since 1870, being about 33 per cent. in the number of spinning-spindles.

The kinds and quantities of goods produced during the year ending July 1, 1874, were as follows:

KINDS OF GOODS.	New England States.	Middle and Western States.	Total Northern States.	Total Southern States.	Total United States.
Threads, yarns, and twines (lbs.)..........	32,000,000	99,000,000	131,000,000	18,000,000	149,000,000
Sheetings, shirtings, and similar plain goods (yards)............................	520,000,000	90,000,000	610,000,000	97,000,000	707,000,000
Twilled and fancy goods, osnaburgs, jeans, etc. (yards)............................	204,000,000	80,000,000	284,000,000	22,000,000	306,000,000
Printed cloths (yards)........................	481,000,000	107,000,000	588,000,000	....	588,000,000
Ginghams (yards)............................	80,000,000	3,000,000	83,000,000	....	83,000,000
Ducks (yards)................................	14,000,000	16,000,000	30,000,000	....	30,000,000
Bags (number)................................	5,000,000	1,000,000	6,000,000	....	6,000,000

Besides the above, there is a large production of hosiery and knit goods, made of cotton by itself, or mixed with wool, of which we are able to give no satisfactory statement.

A review of prices and actual cost of production shows that the year under consideration was not a profitable one to American spinners. This is the result not mainly of the panic, but of some of the causes that produced the panic. Our figures are peculiarly instructive, as shedding special light on one part of this subject. It has been shown that the productive power of our mills has increased one-third since 1870. Then they were reported at 7,114,000 spindles; now they have reached 9,415,383 spindles.

Nor have these spindles been idle. Each year they have been producing at a pretty full rate, augmenting the cotton consumption of the mills at about the same ratio. This would seem to be an excessive or unnatural increase, unless there has been some change going on during the same time in our foreign trade. That is to say, our own consumption of goods could not increase to that extent in the four years; and therefore an over-production was a necessity, unless a demand (outside our own country) would absorb a portion. No such foreign outlet has existed. The following statement shows the imports and exports of manufactured goods at all the ports of the United States each year of the period referred to:

EXPORTS OF COTTON MANUFACTURES.

YEAR ENDING JUNE 30.	1874.	1873.	1872.	1871.	1870.
Colored goods, yards.............	4,600,447	3,585,629	2,843,888	5,083,928	6,064,715
" " Value........................	$660,262	$596,912	$458,998	$724,841	$1,035,469
Uncolored goods, yards.................	13,237,510	10,187,145	8,859,191	14,832,931	8,276,384
" " Value....	$1,680,297	$1,655,116	$1,317,719	$1,776,694	$1,345,988
Other manufactures of, value..............	$744,773	$695,500	$527,613	$1,056,601	$1,405,825
Total value of cotton-manufactures exported..............	$3,091,332	$2,947,528	$2,304,330	$3,558,136	$3,787,282

IMPORTS OF COTTON MANUFACTURES.

YEAR ENDING JUNE 80.	1874.	1873.	1872.	1871.	1870.
Bleached and unbleached, square yards.....	26,361,866	31,152,540	41,700,373	36,938,026	29,506,154
" " value............	$3,083,933	$3,865,558	$5,316,877	$4,883,622	$3,925,266
Printed, painted, or colored, square yards..	23,380,205	33,355,661	36,578,465	28,975,876	30,027,259
" " value............	$3,155,494	$5,028,256	$4,975,624	$3,634,315	$4,003,087
Jeans, denims, drillings, etc., square yards.	2,220,599	3,685,477	6,483,461	5,386,146	5,338,611
" " value........	$328,296	$536,893	$878,580	$737,251	$818,506
Hosiery, shirts, and drawers, value........	$4,621,259	$5,449,208	$5,411,523	$5,085,993	$4,734,475
Other manufactures of, value..............	$16,994,896	$20,321,909	$18,684,843	$15,535,459	$9,898,769
Total value of cotton-manufactures imported..............	$28,183,878	$35,201,324	$35,307,447	$29,876,640	$23,380,053

It appears that no material change has taken place in the foreign movement. Our exports have remained almost nominal, while at the same time our imports, instead of decreasing, have increased largely. The last year's figures (1874) are exceptional, because the evil we have referred to had then begun to assert itself—we produced somewhat less and imported less, while we increased our exports slightly. It was an effort under natural laws to correct an over-supply; and even had the panic been averted, the goods-trade must have been unsatisfactory.

What, then, is the remedy for this unfavorable condition of prices, as compared with the cost of production? Most certainly it can be found alone in the removal of the cause—that is, production must either be decreased or our own circle of consumers enlarged. We cannot accept of the former alternative—we have not too many spindles; we should have twice as many, considering our favorable situation for manufacturing. But it is evident we have too many for our home market, and our goods cost too much for competition with other manufacturing peoples in markets common to both. This ought not to be with our cheaper and better cotton, and would not be, but for our own high cost of living, rent, fuel, provisions, and supplies to mills. We have not the space now to point out the causes of these unfavorable conditions; they are easily determined, and it becomes our manufacturers to see that the proper remedies are applied, so that our field for seeking customers may be enlarged by permitting us to compete with England and Holland in the markets of the world. There is no reason why, in all but the finest goods, this much-desired end should not be reached. Turning to the period before the war, the comparison is not at all favorable. Notwithstanding our experience, and knowledge and capabilities for manufacturing cheaply are now so much greater than then, we exported in 1874 of our cotton manufactures only a value of $3,000,000 currency, against about $11,000,000 gold in 1860, the movement for 1860 and 1859 being as follows:

EXPORTS OF COTTON MANUFACTURES.

YEAR ENDING JUNE 30.	1860.	1859.
Printed, painted, or dyed...	$3,856,449	$2,320,890
White and other duck	1,403,506	1,302,381
Duck..................	382,089	215,855
Other manufactures........	5,792,752	4,477,096
Total value..........	$10,934,796	$8,316,222

Even these totals are small, but they show progress, and suggest the direction in which we are to look for the relief we now need; always remember-

ing that the great lesson which our investigation has taught is, that if we would have a healthy, rapid development of our cotton manufactures in the future, the cost of production must be lessened until foreign customers can take our surplus.

The following tables, compiled with the greatest exactness by M. Ott-Trümpler, of Zurich, show the imports and consumption of cotton in Europe, in thousands of bales, for 1874, and afford valuable comparisons with preceding years :

EUROPE.	America.	India.	Brazil.	Egypt.	Sundry.	Total.
GREAT BRITAIN.						
Stock in the ports October 1, 1873...............	191	508	85	23	43	550
Imports during the season (including 11,000 bales from Continent)	1,858	1,067	511	318	114	3,668
Total.......	2,049	1,575	596	341	157	4,718
Exports to the Continent........	116	509	34	9	31	699
	1,933	1,066	562	332	126	4.019
Stock in the ports September 30, 1874...........	232	405	149	47	36	870
Total deliveries........	1,701	660	413	285	90	3,149
CONTINENT.						
Stock in the ports October 1, 1873...........	147	177	19	1	26	370
Imports of the season (direct from countries of production) at Havre, Marseilles, Bordeaux, Nantes, Antwerp, Rotterdam, Amsterdam, Bremen, Hamburg, Trieste, Genoa, Venice, and Naples........	716	857	90	77	121	1,861
Export from England to the Continent, deduction being made for 11,000 bales reëxported to England........	113	505	30	9	31	688
Total........	976	1,039	139	87	178	2,419
Stock in the ports September 30, 1874........	169	167	16	4	23	379
Total deliveries........	807	872	123	83	155	2,040

YEARS.	DELIVERIES—ENGLAND.						DELIVERIES—CONTINENT.					
	America.	India.	Brazil.	Egypt.	Sundry.	Total.	American.	Indian.	Brazil.	Egypt.	Sundry.	Total.
1873-'74......	1,701	660	413	285	90	3,149	807	872	123	83	155	2,040
1872-'73......	1,654	737	509	396	129	3,315	669	795	144	87	189	1,884
1871-'72......	1,412	658	668	239	155	3,132	501	703	198	49	190	1,641
1870-'71......	1,925	558	879	241	119	3,222	919	733	140	96	158	2,046
1869-'70......	1,304	834	361	168	93	2,760	608	693	165	58	173	1,627
1868-'69...	877	913	493	175	129	2,587	545	850	191	61	209	1,916
1867-'68......	1,197	799	533	183	111	2,822	588	723	175	69	277	1,782
1866-'67......	1,018	815	298	160	135	2,414	582	777	152	55	217	1,783
1865-'66......	846	878	259	186	150	2,319	391	755	164	69	237	1,616
1864-'65......	187	850	203	285	348	1,873	49	637	121	89	286	1,182
1863-'64......	178	620	134	219	414	1,565	64	543	74	106	246	1,033
1862-'63......	99	905	111	163	54	1,332	34	559	49	64	108	814
1861-'62......	804	675	101	122	15	1,217	258	415	21	42	40	776

The receipts at the ports of Spain, Sweden, and Russia, and the consumption in Italy of native cotton, are not included in the above statement. Although the American crop of this year has exceeded the previous one by 240,000 bales, and although the European receipts from other countries amount to 159,000 bales more than in 1873, the estimated stock in European ports has increased only 29,000 bales. While the total deliveries in Europe are only 30,000 bales less than in 1873, there has been a decrease in England of 186,000 bales, and, for the Continent, an increase of 156,000 bales. In the opinion of M. Ott-Trümpler, this shows that the actual consumption in England in 1873-'74 must have exceeded the apparent consumption, while the contrary was the case on the Continent.

CROSBY, Rev. ALPHEUS, A. M., an eminent scholar, professor, and author, born in Sand-

wich, N. H., October 13, 1810 ; died at Salem, Mass., April 17, 1874. He received his early training for college at Gilmanton and Phillips (Exeter) Academies, and entered Dartmouth College at the early age of thirteen. He graduated in 1827, and after teaching for a year was recalled to Dartmouth as a tutor, where he remained for three years, and then entered on his theological course at Andover. In 1833 he was licensed to preach, and the same year chosen Latin and Greek Professor at Dartmouth. Four years later, the professorship was divided, and Prof. Crosby took the Greek Language and Literature, and retained it till 1849, when he resigned, to devote himself to the preparation of collegiate text-books. Dartmouth did herself honor in retaining his name on her Faculty as *Emeritus* Professor. For the next six or seven years his leisure time was devoted to the promotion of popular education as a lecturer at the teachers' institutes, and from 1854 to 1857 as agent of the Massachusetts Board of Education. In 1857 he became Principal of the Massachusetts State Normal School at Salem, where he continued till 1865, being remarkably successful. From 1865 to 1867 he edited as a recreation a weekly paper called *The Right Way*, but the engrossing character of his studies led him to abandon every thing else for them. He had published a "Greek and General Grammar," "Greek Tables," "Greek Lessons," an edition of "Xenophon's Anabasis," "Eclogæ Latinæ," "First Lessons in Geometry," and had been engaged for ten years or more on a Greek Lexicon on a different plan from those already published, and to which he was devoting all the resources of his thorough and profound scholarship. His excessive intellectual labors brought on the disease of the brain which caused his death.

CRUVEILHIER, JEAN, M. D., a French physician, professor, and author, born at Limoges, February 9, 1791; died in Paris, March 11, 1874. After obtaining a good classical education in his native city, young Cruveilhier came to Paris to study medicine, where he was a pupil of Dupuytren, and devoted himself to the study of his profession with great assiduity and enthusiasm. He received his medical degree in 1816, reading on the occasion a thesis of remarkable originality and ability on pathological anatomy. He returned for a time, from family reasons, to Limoges, and practised his profession there. As soon as possible, however, he came back to Paris, and in a public competition achieved the first place among the teacher-pupils. About 1820 he was called to Montpellier, to be a professor in the famous medical school there. In 1822 he published the first volume of his "Treatise on Operative Surgery, illustrated by Anatomy and Physiology." In 1825 M. Frayssinous, the Grand-Master of the University of France, wishing a successor to Beclard, who had just died, made choice of M. Cruveilhier, and he was thus called back to Paris. In his new position he devoted himself with the utmost zeal to the study of anatomy, and in 1826 reorganized the old Anatomical Society. His course of lectures on anatomy and physiology to his classes was the result of almost incredible labor and research, and it attracted a very large attendance. Under his vivid and accurate descriptions these usually dry sciences assumed a new and deep interest. This "course" was published in four volumes, 8vo, 1834–1838. Meanwhile the immense resources of material which were opened to him in the great hospitals of La Maternité, La Salpêtrière, and La Charité, constantly drew his attention more and more to the subject of his earlier studies, pathological anatomy. Sparing no labor or research, he prepared in the course of eleven years (1829–1840) the crowning work of his life: "The Pathological Anatomy of the Hu-

man Body; or, a Description, with Colored and Lithographic Illustrations, of the Various Morbid Alterations of which the Human Body is susceptible" (two thick and large folio volumes, with 233 plates). This great work demonstrated his fitness to fill the chair of Pathological Anatomy, founded by Dupuytren, and he was installed as professor in August, 1835. M. Cruveilhier's other published works were: "An Address upon the Duties and the Morals of the Physician," 1837; "Life of Dupuytren;" "The Anatomy of the Nervous System of Man," illustrated by plates of life-size, folio, 1845; "A Treatise on Descriptive Anatomy," 1851; "A Treatise on General Pathological Anatomy," 5 vols., 8vo, 1849–1864; and numerous papers and memoirs in the bulletin of the Academy of Medicine, of which he was one of the most distinguished members. He was made a commander in the Legion of Honor in 1863.

CURTIS, BENJAMIN ROBBINS, LL. D., an eminent jurist, for six years one of the Associate Justices of the Supreme Court of the United States, born in Watertown, Mass., November 4, 1809; died in Newport, R. I., September 15, 1874. He entered Harvard College in 1825, and was one of the most accomplished scholars of the famous class of 1829, graduating with high honors, and immediately entered the law-school, where his great abilities were speedily recognized. Admitted to the bar in 1832, he began the practice of law at Northfield, Mass., but soon removed to Boston, where he attained eminence in his profession and acquired extensive business. In early life he was a member of the Whig party, and throughout Mr. Webster's career he was a devoted follower of that statesman. In September, 1851, Justice Woodbury being dead, Mr. Curtis was appointed by President Fillmore to fill his place on the bench of the United States Supreme Court. In the case of Dred Scott he dissented from the decision of the court, and made a powerful argument in support of his conclusions. He upheld the right of Congress to prohibit slavery, and declared his dissent from "that part of the opinion of the majority of the court in which it is held that a person of African descent cannot be a citizen of the United States." On this memorable occasion only one other justice of the seven coincided with the opinion of Judge Curtis. Finding his salary insufficient, Judge Curtis retired from the Supreme Court in the autumn of 1857, and resumed the practice of his profession in Boston.

In 1854 Judge Curtis published "Reports of Cases in the Circuit Courts of the United States." This was followed by a more important work containing the decisions of the Supreme Court of the United States, with notes and a digest comprising the cases reported by Dallas, Cranch, Peters, and Howard. The plan of this valuable compilation, the old series of which filled fifty-eight volumes, was approved by Chief-Justice Taney and the other Justices of the Supreme Court. This book was succeeded by another entitled "A Digest of the Decisions of the Supreme Court of the United States from the Origin of the Court to the Close of the December Term, 1854." As the title indicates, this was a work of the first importance, requiring great patience as well as ability for its completion.

The impeachment of President Johnson brought Judge Curtis again into national prominence. Associated with Messrs. Stanbery, Evarts, Nelson, and Groesbeck, he defended the President with great ability and zeal. The answer to the articles of impeachment, a document of nearly six columns, was read by him, and was largely his work. He opened the case in a masterly speech of ten columns, which occupied two days in delivery. Although his voice was feeble and his delivery unimpressive, he received the homage of respectful attention from the Senators as well as from the public who thronged the galleries. His forcible argument concluded with an able summary of the whole case, and a calm appeal to the sense of equity of the senatorial court, reminding it of the great responsibility devolving upon it. As a jurist, he was remarkable for the vast extent of his legal attainments, the clearness and accuracy of his statements, and the vigorous grasp of his logic. Justly proud of his profession, he resisted every inducement to engage in party strife, and, save as member for one or two terms of the Massachusetts House of Representatives, he never held a legislative or political office. His law practice has been one of the most lucrative in New England. He was the Democratic candidate in the protracted senatorial contest of 1874, and no candidate found a more unwavering support. He was also a member of the commission on the new charter. His name was frequently mentioned in connection with the chief-justiceship before the appointment of Judge Waite.

CUSHING, WILLIAM B., commander U. S. Navy, a gallant and daring naval officer, born in Wisconsin, November 24, 1844; died in the Hospital for the Insane, Washington, D. C.,

December 17, 1874. He was appointed to the Naval Academy from New York, September 24, 1857, and resigned in 1858; but in May, 1861, was reappointed acting-midshipman, and immediately went into service at Hampton Roads, and on the day of his arrival captured and brought into port a tobacco-schooner, the first prize of the war. In November, 1862, he was ordered in the steamer Ellis to capture Jacksonville, Fla., and destroy the salt-works at New Juliet. He accomplished both tasks, but his steamer being aground, he fired her, and escaped in a small boat. At Fort Fisher he proceeded, under a constant and heavy fire, to buoy out the channel in a small skiff, and continued the work for six hours till he had completed it. At the final assault on Fort Fisher, he accompanied the force of sailors and marines, in a "forlorn hope" attack on the sea-front of the fort, and amid an unceasing fire at short range, which cut down his men in windrows, he crossed a hundred yards of the bare and glittering sand, unharmed and apparently unconcerned, rallied his men and lent such efficient assistance to the struggling troops, that before midnight the fort was surrendered. His most remarkable exploit, and the most remarkable and daring act of the whole war, was the destruction of the Confederate ram Albemarle at her wharf at Plymouth, N. C., while she was carefully guarded and many miles within the enemy's lines. The gallant officer received for this daring feat a vote of thanks from Congress, and a complimentary letter from the Secretary of the Navy, as well as a prompt promotion to the rank of lieutenant-commander. Since the close of the war Lieutenant-Commander Cushing had served in the Pacific and Asiatic Squadrons, being in command of the steamer Lancaster in 1866–'67, and of the Maumee, in the Asiatic Squadron, in 1868–'69. On the return of the Maumee to the United States, Lieutenant-Commander Cushing was advanced to the rank of commander, being much the youngest officer of that rank in the navy. He was allowed leave of absence, and his health, which had been impaired by his over-exertions, failed completely in the last few months.

D

DAKOTA. No little attention was attracted to this Territory, during the past year, by the military reconnoitring expedition to the country in Southwestern Dakota, known as the Black Hills. The expedition was organized for the purpose of exploring the unknown territory in this region, with the view of discovering practicable military routes between Fort Lincoln, in the Department of Dakota, opposite the terminus of the Union Pacific Railroad, and Fort Laramie, in the Department of the Platte.

The expedition, which was under the command of General Custer, consisted of ten companies of the Seventh Cavalry, one company of the Twentieth Infantry and of the Seventeenth Infantry, with a battery of three Gatling and one 3-inch Rodman gun, and a detachment of Indian scouts, guides, etc. The scientific men accompanying the expedition comprised, among others, William Ludlow, Captain of Engineers, U. S. A., and Chief-Engineer of the Department of Dakota; Prof. N. H. Winchell, of the University of Minnesota, as geologist; Mr. G. B. Grinnell, as paleontologist and zoologist; and Dr. Williams, as chief medical officer.

The expedition left Fort Lincoln July 2d, and returned to that place August 30th, with a loss of four men—three from sickness, and one killed in a quarrel. During this trip of nearly 1,000 miles, no hostile Indians were met. The route pursued led up the south side of Heart River, thence in a west-southwest direction, across the Cannonball, and up the north fork of Grand River; thence southwesterly to a point which was named Prospect Valley, in about latitude 45° 30', and longitude 103° 40'; thence up the east side of the Little Missouri River; and southerly to the north fork of the Cheyenne River, Belle Fourche. This point was reached on July 18th, in about longitude 104°, after sixteen marches and 300 miles of travel. Hitherto the country had much resembled other portions of Dakota—an open prairie; wood scarce, and only found in river valleys; water not always to be met with in sufficient quantity, and frequently impregnated with salts, making it both disagreeable and injurious; but still, a fair amount of grass, and no serious difficulties were presented. All the country bordering on Heart River is good, that on Cannonball is fair; Grand River country is poor, as well as that near the head-waters of the Moreau or Owl River.

All the streams flow eastward, and head close up to the Little Missouri, which, running northward at right angles to the others, has but a narrow and barren belt tributary to it on the east side. Its main support is from its branches heading in the Powder River range of hills. The expedition came in view of Slim Butte (which is rather a high steep coteau than a butte), of Slave and Bear Buttes, and many others not hitherto located. The Black Hills, as they were approached, looked very high and dark under their covering of pine-timber.

The expedition crossed the Belle Fourche on July 20th, and found themselves in a new country. The whole character of the surroundings was changed. There was an abundance of grass, timber, small fruits, and flowers, and what perhaps was better appreciated than all, an ample supply of pure cold water. These advantages, with a few exceptions, were enjoyed until the Black Hills were left for the return-journey. The course now lay up the valley of the Redwater—a large branch of the Belle Fourche—to Inyan Kara, thence easterly and southeasterly into the heart of the hills. Valley leads into valley, to the beautiful park country, always until now marked "unexplored" on the maps. After arriving near Harney's Peak—a lofty granite mass, over 8,000 feet above the sea, and surrounded with craggy peaks and pinnacles—a rapid reconnoissance was made to the south fork of the Cheyenne, nearly due south, with five companies of cavalry, and the exit from the interior was ascertained to be not difficult on that side.

Returning, the course lay northerly and northeasterly, looking for an exit near Bear Butte. From Bear Butte the return-journey led back past Slave Butte, touching the head-waters of the Moreau, crossing the down trail in Prospect Valley, thence tapping the head of Grand River and following roughly the east side of the Little Missouri northward and eastward to where the trail of the Yellowstone expedition crosses it, and thence into Lincoln, on the north side of Heart River. The return-route was a much better one for a large force than the other. There was no difficulty in finding good camps, with plenty of water and grass. The country passed over, tributary to the Moreau, is barren, but the river valley itself is more favorable, and at the head of Grand River is much better country than lower down. From Grand River to above Heart River the grass had been thoroughly burned by the Indians.

The limited time occupied in the exploration gave little opportunity for study. The preliminary reports made represent the Black Hills as a region admirably adapted to settlement, abounding in timber, in grass and flowing streams, with springs of pure cold water almost everywhere. The valleys of South Slope are ready for the plough, the soil of wonderful fertility, as evidenced by the luxuriance of the grass and the profusion of flowers and small fruits; the climate entirely different from that of the Plains, giving evidence of being much more agreeable—cooler in summer, and more moderate in winter; not subject to drought, for the nightly dews are very heavy; not liable to excessive snow-fall, for, in narrow valleys containing a large creek, no indications of overflow could be detected.

No coal was found. Extensive deposits of iron-ore of good quality exist. Immense beds of gypsum were met with. Specimens of gold were washed from the soil in the vicinity of Harney's Peak, and quartz in bed and bowlder was visible in large quantities. Plumbago also was found in small quantities. Large amounts of excellent building-stone, limestones, sand-stone, and granite, were present. Some of the limestones, particularly in the vicinity of Inyan Kara, were fine enough for marbles and handsomely colored. The timber is mainly red pine and spruce of large size. Oak, ash, and elm, are found on the exterior slopes. Game is abundant; bear, elk, and deer of two kinds were found, and many killed. On the prairies, antelopes were found in large numbers.

The complete report, accompanied by the reports of Prof. Winchell, Mr. Grinnell, and Dr. Williams, will be prepared, together with a map showing the route pursued, with bordering country, from Fort Lincoln and return, and a special map on a larger scale of the Black Hills proper.

As a game-region, the Black Hills will compare very favorably with any locality in the country. Deer of two species are most abundant, the white-tailed deer especially being so numerous about the head-waters of Elk Creek that 100 were killed by the command in a single day. Elk, from indications, are numerous, although only a few were killed. Several bears were secured, and not a few exciting incidents occurred during their capture. No mountain-sheep were obtained, although there were many indications of their presence, and a single female was seen. Almost all the streams which were passed were dammed in many places by beaver, and fresh tracks and signs were very plenty.

Game-birds are well represented by several species of geese and ducks, which are to be found along the various water-courses in and about the Hills, and by at least two species of grouse, the sharp-tailed and the ruffed. The former are numerous along the open valleys and in the sparsely-wooded hill-sides, and the latter among the dense pines of the higher land. Altogether, the Black Hills offer to the sportsman an abundance and variety of game, and, if opened to the white man, will be as much esteemed as a hunting-ground by him as they now are by the Indian.

The visit of the expedition caused great excitement among the Sioux Indians. The accounts of rich mines and agricultural lands created an eagerness among many persons to proceed to the favored land in search of gain, and exploring and mining expeditions were formed for this purpose; but measures were taken by the War Department to prevent any intrusion into the Territory. Notwithstanding this prohibition, private expeditions were fitted out at Yankton, Bismarck, and other points, with the purpose of proceeding to the Black Hills. Some of them were driven back by the Indians with loss of life and property.

DELAWARE. The Republican State Convention met in Georgetown, July 28th, and after nominating Dr. Isaac Jump, of Dover, for Governor, and renominating Hon. James R. Lofland for Representative in Congress, adopted the following platform:

The Republican party of Delaware, in State Convention assembled, congratulating the people of this State upon the assuring prospect which the coming canvass presents of relief from the mismanagement, abuses, and extravagance, which the Democratic party, for years past, have entailed upon us, and of obtaining such practical and important reforms, and such wise and judicious economy, as the spirit of the times and the present necessities of our people demand in the governmental policy of our State, do resolve:

1. That we reiterate and reaffirm our adherence to the principles of the Republican party of this State, as heretofore officially announced, and our confidence in it as the only party that will give us retrenchment and reform.

2. That we regard representation according to population, coupled with a district system, as a cardinal principle of republican government, and that we are in favor of adopting such measures as will speedily and substantially effect the practical application of this principle to the legislative department of our State government, to remedy the unjust and unequal provisions of our present system.

3. That as a means of securing the reforms that are so much needed in the organic law of the State, and of keeping pace with the enlightened progress of the age, and with our sister States, a Constitutional Convention is imperatively demanded, and we hereby declare our intention, if invested with the power, to provide for the early organization of such a convention.

4. That the laws of this State allowing the wages of labor to be attached for debt are oppressive upon those whose daily sustenance is dependent upon their daily toil, and we are in favor of their repeal, and that, in harmony with the liberal policy of other States, we are further in favor of exempting from execution a reasonable portion of the property of a debtor, not only as affording relief to his family, but as better securing the creditor, and tending to elevate all classes of a common citizenship.

5. That we are in favor of repealing the laws passed by a Democratic Legislature which lay heavy burdens of taxation upon our people in compelling them to pay taxes upon the wages of productive labor, mortgages, and upon savings and houses, acquired through the commendable medium of building and loan associations.

6. That we regard the law, passed by the last Democratic Legislature in reference to the duties of assessors and collectors, as a base attempt to disfranchise that class of our voters and citizens who are not owners of real estate, in order to accomplish party purposes, and as a measure which, unless prevented by the vigilance of good citizens, will cheat the counties out of their taxes, and the people out of their votes; and further as an unjust discrimination against the poorer classes, by giving improper influence to property alone.

7. That the Delaware volunteers, having been among the first in the field and among the last to leave, during the late war, and with few exceptions having received no bounties, we hereby instruct our Representative in Congress to use his influence in favor of the law now pending in Congress, providing for the equalization of bounties.

8. That while we do not advocate mixed schools for the education of the children of this State, we do contend that the party in power here has demonstrated its opposition to public education by its constant refusal to adopt and legalize measures looking to the improvement of our school system; that it has committed itself thoroughly against popular education; and a reform in this direction which shall place the blessings of good schools within the reach of all can only come through the success of the Republican party.

9. Recognizing the rightful claim of labor to equal chances with capital, we assert the right of the laborer to such remuneration for his labor as shall guarantee the comfort of himself and family and the education of his children, and we declare our opposition to the present property tests for holding office in Delaware, as repugnant to the spirit of the age, and insulting to the working-men of the State.

10. That the proper measure of taxation is the sum necessary to an economical administration of the government; that this principle has been grossly violated by the Democratic party of this State; that under its administration the public burdens have become odious and oppressive, that reform is imperatively demanded, and experience has shown that it can only be accomplished by displacing those who have abused the trusts confided to them, and substituting in their stead others who will have a proper regard for the rights of the people.

11. That we recognize in our able representative in Congress, Hon. John R. Lofland, a faithful public servant, whose attention to the wants and interests of our people, and whose constant and unassuming performance of his duties, deserve our unqualified commendation.

The Democracy assembled in State Convention in Dover, August 27th, and nominated John P. Cochran for Governor, and James Williams for Congress. The resolutions adopted were as follows:

The Democratic party of the State of Delaware, in convention met, renew their ancient and unbroken allegiance to the constitutions of their State and General Governments, and point with pride and satisfaction to the just, honest, economical, and reputable administration of the affairs of the State of Delaware under Democratic rule, whereby safety to person and property has been maintained, and the financial and political credit of the State sustained upon an equality with the best governed and most favored of her sister States.

Resolved, That the welfare of all classes of our population, the rich and the poor, the white and the black, in the future as in the past, can and will be best conserved by a continuance of that strict obedience to constitutional limitations upon official power; that respect for established laws; that absence of class-influence and legislation; that due regard for the rights of the community as a whole, which have characterized the administration of government by the Democratic party, and which formed the chief guarantees of a free and stable government.

Resolved, That the continued example of utter and flagrant disregard of the most sacred and essential rights of local self-government by President Grant and his associates, as established in the wanton invasion and overthrow of the lawful government of the State of Louisiana, the retention in office and personal favor of the guilty officials through whose action, aided by the army of the United States, this gross outrage was perpetrated, fills us with indignation and alarm, and that against it all we utter our solemn protest.

Resolved, That the course of the radical administration has brought great loss and sorrow to our people, and shame and discredit to the name of republican government, by the encouragement shown to the delegation of public robbers from the State of South Carolina, and the rudeness exhibited to her most meritorious and suffering citizens by the selection and retention in office, all over the country, of men notoriously dishonest, corrupt, and unworthy; by allowing the lowest and most virulent partisanship to control appointments to the highest offices; by a refusal to punish dishonesty in office where exposed; by issuing and maintaining an unconstitutional currency without intrinsic value, whose fluctuations are the constant profit of speculators in the cost of the laboring-classes, and which demoralizes and unsettles commerce in all its branches.

Resolved, That the lamentable condition of the States of South Carolina, Mississippi, and Louisiana, continues to excite our kindest and strongest sympathies for the men of our own race who, by the lawless exercise of armed Federal power, are placed and kept under the galling rule of ignorance and crime, and we fervently hope that an awakening sense of the whole people of the Union may soon relieve these evils of radicalism and negro government.

Resolved, That we denounce the wild, cruel, and reckless measure called the Civil Rights Bill, as grossly violative of the letter and spirit of the Federal and State constitutions, and only calculated to sow new seeds of discord between the States and people; that it is an undisguised attempt to enforce a social equality between negroes and white people, and to encourage, if not compel, an intermingling of those races whose essential differences have been marked and established by Almighty God.

Resolved, That the course of Hon. Jas. R. Lofland, as a Representative in Congress from this State, in relation to this Civil Rights Bill, has been in defiance of the intelligence and decency of the entire community, and deserves and will receive the scorn and opposition of any right-thinking inhabitant of Delaware.

Resolved, That the act passed at the last session of Congress, enlarging the jurisdiction of the Federal Courts of the District of Columbia, is a base attempt to muzzle the public press, and to shield the corrupt and unscrupulous officers of the Government from just criticism.

Resolved, That we contemplate with just pride the national reputation and commanding rank and influence won for our State in the Senate of the United States, and that we hereby extend our grateful thanks to our faithful Senators, Hons. T. F. Bayard and Eli Saulsbury, for their constant opposition to the infamous Civil Rights Bill, and every other pernicious and tyrannical radical measure, and for their manly defense of constitutional government, the freedom of the press, the cause of the oppressed, and the rights and honor of their race and native State.

Resolved, That we cordially invite all honest citizens to unite with us in the election of the worthy candidates whom we this day present for their suffrages, believing that good private and public character are inseparable, and that just, economical, and honest rule can only be expected from those whose private lives have given such assurance.

The election, held on the 3d of November, resulted in the choice of Cochran for Governor by a majority of 1,239, and Williams as Representative in Congress by a majority of 1,646. The total vote in the several counties was as follows:

FOR GOVERNOR.

NAMES.	New Castle.	Kent.	Sussex.	Total.
Cochran................	5,796	3,178	3,514	12,488
Jump	5,615	2,751	2,883	11,249
Majority for Cochran...	181	427	631	1,239

FOR CONGRESS.

NAMES.	New Castle.	Kent.	Sussex.	Total.
Williams...............	5,891	3,244	3,558	12,693
Lofland...............	5,498	2,683	2,846	11,027
Majority for Williams..	393	561	712	1,666

In 1872 James R. Lofland was elected to Congress by a majority of 362 in a total vote of 22,392, he having received 11,377 votes.

John P. Cochran, who is now Governor of Delaware, is a citizen of Middletown, about sixty-five years of age. He is an extensive farmer and land-owner in New Castle County, and has one of the largest peach-orchards on the peninsula. He is of Dutch descent, and has always been a Democrat. Hon. James Williams, who was elected as Representative, is a farmer of Kent County, has been a Representative in the State Legislature for several terms, and also Speaker of that body.

The entire public debt, January 1, 1875, was $1,250,000. A large portion of this was created for the payment of volunteers, and the relief of persons drafted into the military service during the war; but more than $500,000 was incurred in aid of the construction of the Junction & Breakwater and the Breakwater & Frankford Railroads. In reference to the future policy of the State in extending aid to these or other railroad companies, Governor Ponder says:

Without intending to express any opinion upon the propriety of the action of the Legislature in aiding the construction of these roads, I respectfully suggest that no further increase of the public debt, for similar purposes, ought to be authorized by the General Assembly. The credit of the State ought not to be placed in jeopardy by any further issue of bonds, nor should the revenues derived from taxation, or otherwise, be applied to any other purposes than the ordinary expenses of the government and the reduction of the present liabilities of the State.

I do not know that any application will be made to the Legislature, at its present session, for aid in the construction of railroads or other works of internal improvement; but from a firm conviction that any policy which would further connect the State with railroad improvements would be hazardous to its credit, I deem it an imperative duty to urge the necessity of guarding carefully against any augmentation of the State debt, and the consequent increased measure of taxation which such augmentation would necessarily entail upon the people of the State.

Whatever local advantages might be anticipated from the construction of additional railroads, it is certain that they would not justify an increase of present liabilities, or compensate for the injury which would be inflicted by additional taxation rendered necessary thereby.

It is to be hoped that a sincere desire to preserve untarnished the credit of the State, and to protect our citizens from further taxation, will prevent the Legislature, at its present session, or hereafter, from authorizing any further issue of State bonds for any purpose whatsoever.

The whole sum of the assets of the State, including investments appropriated to the school-fund, amounts to $1,123,189. The amount of liabilities over all assets is $100,-811, and over assets not appropriated to the school-fund, $576,950. This latter amount may be regarded as the real debt of the State over available assets. The revenues under existing laws are ample for any present or anticipated demands upon the Treasury. The ordinary expenses of the government have been met, the interest on the public debt promptly paid, and the principal of that portion of the debt created by the exigencies of the war reduced $388,000 within the last four years. This has been accomplished from the ordinary receipts of the Treasury, without postponing the payment of any claim against the Treasury.

The annual receipts into the Treasury from all sources average about $207,872; and the expenditures, including $75,000 interest on the public debt, an appropriation of $3,000 to Delaware College, and one-half of the biennial expenses of the Legislature, about $111,025. A large part of the revenue is derived from taxes paid by railroads and other corporations, and from fees for licenses granted by the State.

Within the past year an important case, in which Delaware, though not nominally, was in reality a party, has been decided in the Supreme Court of the United States. The case was that of William Minot, Jr., a stockholder in the Pacific Western & Baltimore Railroad Company, against William J. Clarke, late State Treasurer, and William M. Ochletree, a collector of State taxes under the law of 1869. The bill filed in the Circuit Court prayed for an injunction to restrain such officers from proceeding to collect from the railroad company certain taxes imposed by said law upon railroad corporations in this State, upon the assumed ground that the law was unconstitutional and void for various reasons, and among others that it impaired the obligation of a contract alleged to exist between the State and the company, exempting the latter from taxation.

The decree of the Circuit Court sustained the constitutionality of the law and the right of the State to tax the corporation, and, upon an appeal from the decree, taken by complainant, was affirmed by the Supreme Court.

It would be difficult to over-estimate the value of this decision to the State. It disposes effectually of the claim on the part of the principal railroad corporation existing within its limits to exemption from taxation, and, by maintaining the constitutionality of the law referred to, relieves the State from any possible liability for the amount of taxes paid by the company under protest.

The school system of Delaware is substantially the one adopted forty-five years ago. The State has no Superintendent of Public Instruction. All questions relating to schools are left in the hands of the inhabitants of the school districts into which the State is divided. They decide whether there shall be a school or not; a certain amount of school-tax must, however, be raised by each district in order to entitle it to its *pro rata* share of the school-fund. A superintendent for each county is annually appointed by the Governor; the former, however, has exceedingly limited powers, and receives no pay other than traveling expenses. The State law makes no provision for the education of colored children. Material aid, however, for the instruction of this class is rendered by "The Delaware Association for the Moral Improvement and Education of the Colored People," and the Freedmen's Bureau. In 1873 a bill was introduced into the Legislature, providing for a thorough supervision of the schools, for annual reports to the Governor or Legislature, and for giving to the colored population their *pro rata* share of the school-fund. This, however, failed to become a law. The State school-fund is derived from the income of Delaware's share of the "surplus revenue" distributed by the United States to the several States, together with a portion of the proceeds accruing from certain State fees and licenses. A portion of the fund is apportioned equally among the counties, and the balance according to the white population.

The peach season of 1874 closed about the 1st of October. The net receipts of the crop are estimated at $669,775. The season was very little shorter than usual, it beginning about as early and continuing about as late, but the daily shipments were much below the average of the several preceding years, and the aggregate of the crop was considerably lessened thereby. The bulk of the crop was moved to market by rail, the region of growth being mostly confined to a small area lying on both sides of the Delaware Railroad, and extending about twenty or thirty miles with its length. Only a limited quantity of peaches for market was grown along the bays and numerous water-courses of the peninsula, and the shipments from some of them were very meagre indeed. The aggregate of the shipments (by baskets) both by rail and water was as follows:

By rail, northward 620,000
By rail, from Middletown to Dover 7,669

Total by rail................................ 627,669
By water, to Baltimore....................... 54,550
By water, to Philadelphia.................... 155,000

Aggregate shipment by water and rail.... 837,219

The shipments of strawberries were estimated at 667 car-loads, containing 186,760 crates, or 7,470,400 quarts. This is the heaviest crop yet sent to market from the peninsula, and will in all probability be the largest for years to come. It exceeds the estimated crop of last year (5,000,000 quarts) 2,470,400 quarts, but it is very doubtful if this year's crop has brought to the peninsula the amount of money of last year, which was estimated at $500,000.

DENMARK, a kingdom in Northern Europe. Reigning sovereign, Christian IX., fourth son of the late Duke William of Schleswig-Holstein-Sonderburg-Glücksburg, and of Princess Louise of Hesse-Cassel; appointed to the succession of the Danish crown by the Treaty of London, of May 8, 1852, and by the Danish law of succession of July 31, 1853; succeeded to the throne on the death of King Frederick VII., November 15, 1863; married, May 26, 1842, to Louise, daughter of Landgrave William of Hesse-Cassel. Heir-apparent, Prince Frederick, born June 3, 1843; married, July 28, 1869, to Princess Louisa, only daughter of the late King Charles XV. of Sweden; offspring of the union are two sons, Christian, born September 26, 1870, and Charles, born August 3, 1872. The King has a civil list of 500,000 rigsdalers, and the heir-apparent 60,000 rigsdalers. The new ministry, appointed on June 14, 1874, consisted of the following members: President of the Council and Minister of Finance, C. A. Fonnesbech; Minister of War, General P. F. Steinmann; Minister of the Interior, F. C. H. E. Tobiesen; Minister of Public Education and Ecclesiastical Affairs, J. J. A: Worsaae; Minister of Justice and for Iceland, C. S. Klein; Minister of the Navy, N. F. Kavn. The area of Denmark proper, inclusive of lakes, is 14,753 square miles; of European dependencies (Faroe Islands and Iceland), 40,268 square miles; of American possessions (Greenland, St. John, St. Thomas, and St. Croix, 759,900 square miles. In the following table we give the population of the kingdom and its dependencies according to the latest dates:

	Census of 1870.	Official Calculation, 1874.
DENMARK.		
City of Copenhagen.............	181,291	193,000
Islands........................	815,331	842,000
Jutland........................	788,119	826,000
	1,784,741	1,861,000
DEPENDENCIES.		
Faroe (17 inhabited islands)....	9,992	10,500
Iceland (inhabitable)...........	69,763	70,900
Greenland (exclusive of the glaciers)......................	9,825	9,800
St. Croix, St. Thomas, } in the W. Indies.. St. John, }	37,821	37,700
	127,401	128,900

Nearly the entire population of Denmark proper, namely, 1,769,583, or 99.15 per cent., is connected with the Lutheran Church; of the remainder, 1,433 are Reformed; 1,857 Catholics; 3,223 Baptists; 1,211 Free Congregationalists; 2,128 Mormons; 4,290 Jews; 260 Methodists; 849 Irvingites; 74 Anglicans; 28 Friends; 12 Greek Catholics; 88 of various other sects; 205 without definite creed. The number of emigrants from Denmark was, in 1873, 7,200; in 1872, 6,893; in 1871, 3,906; in 1870, 3,525; in 1869, 4,360: nearly all the emigrants went to the United States. The actual revenue and expenditure of the state for the two years 1871-'73 (the financial year ending March 31st) were as follows:

	Revenue—Rigsd'ls.	Expenditure—Rigsd'ls.
1871-'73............	22,516,916	20,565,183
1872-'73............	24,944,985	23,678,013

In the budget for the year 1874-'75 the revenue was estimated at 23,024,226; the expenditures at 22,799,200; the surplus, 225,026 rigsdalers. The public debt, on March 31, 1873, amounted to 110,425,552 rigsdalers, of which 81,032,889 were home debt, and 29,392,663 foreign debt. The state assets were 53,227,148, leaving 57,198,404 as the real amount of the indebtedness of the state. The debt has been in the course of reduction since 1866, when it amounted to 132,000,000 rigsdalers. It was expected that in the spring of 1875 this debt would be reduced to 93,000,000 rigsdalers, and that when, on March 31, 1875, the English loans would be paid off, the foreign debt would only amount to 13,000,000 rigsdalers. Five and a half million rigsdalers of the foreign debt were again to be paid in 1877.

The commerce of Denmark, which is mainly carried on with Germany and Great Britain, was, from 1869 to 1873, as follows (value expressed in rigsdalers):

YEAR.	Imports.	Exports.
1869-'70..................	20,100,000	9,040,000
1870-'71..................	21,740,000	11,890,000
1871-'72..................	23,600,000	9,720,000
1872-'73..................	21,380,000	11,080,000

The precise amount of the commercial transactions is not known, as the official returns since 1863 have not given the declared or real value of the imports or exports, but only their weight.

The movement of shipping in 1871 and 1872 was as follows:

HOME NAVIGATION.

YEAR.	Vessels.	Tons.	Foreign vessels.
1871-'72	46,110	599,157	1,007
1872-'73	48,071	638,938	1,085

OUTWARD NAVIGATION.

YEAR.	Vessels.	Tons.	Foreign vessels.
1871-'72	89,341	1,214,582	21,588
1872-'73	42,612	1,276,575	24,088

The commercial navy, on March 31, 1873, was composed of 2,629 sailing-vessels, with an aggregate of 175,657 tons, and 109 steamers, with 21,602 tons; total, 2,738 vessels, with 197,259 tons.

The army, in time of peace, numbers 15,258 men; and on the war-footing, 52,656. The navy, in 1874, comprised 32 steamers, 7 of which are iron-clads, and 2 sailing-vessels. It was manned by 800 men, and officered by 1 admiral, 15 commanders, 34 captains, 47 lieutenants, and 20 sub-lieutenants.

On January 1, 1874, there were 5,567 miles of railroad in operation. A new railroad on the island of Laaland was opened on June 24, 1874. The length of telegraph-lines, in 1873, was 4,370 miles; that of the wires, 1,578 miles. The post-office forwarded, in 1872-'73, 14,958,-402 letters, and 13,781,803 newspapers.

The Folkething (lower branch of the Legislature) had closed the year 1873 by the adoption of an address to the King, expressing the wish that the administration of the country be changed. When the Folkething, after the expiration of the Christmas vacation, reassembled, on January 6, 1874, a reply to the address was received, which declared that, however much the misproportion between the length of the session and the accomplished work was to be deplored, and however desirable a solution of the conflict between the Government and the Legislature, and the removal of the agitation prevailing throughout the country, might be, the Government must decline a change of administration, but must rather appeal to the patriotism of the parties, and expect from them the work of reconciliation. The official *Berling Gazette*, which, on January 1, 1874, entered its one hundred and twenty-sixth year, published on that day a warning article on the serious condition of the country, which, according to the issue of the pending conflict, might either expect a quiet and gradual development of its material and spiritual interests, or an imminence of the trials and dangers so indissolubly connected with the absolute rule of elective majorities. The ministry, immediately after the adoption by the Folkething of the address to the King, expressing want of confidence in the administration, had offered its resignation, but the King, in a letter dated January 2, 1874, replied that the ministry must remain in office, as it consisted

of the best men in the country, who possessed his entire confidence, and whose character was a guarantee that the fundamental law would be defended against any encroachment. The United Left now adopted the course of referring all drafts laid before it to a committee instead of passing them to a second reading. The army bill was thus disposed of by a vote of 47 against 40 votes. After a debate which lasted several days, an order of the day, with preamble, was adopted by 57 votes against 31, condemning the publication by the ministry of the autograph letter written by the King on the 2d of January, in reply to an address passed by the Folkething in December. The resolution protests against the course taken by the ministry, on the ground that the King is thereby drawn into party conflicts. During the discussion the Government declared that the adoption of this order of the day would have no practical results. As, according to the fundamental law, an electoral district is not to have more than 16,000 inhabitants, and as the electoral districts of Copenhagen, owing to the rapid increase of population, exceeded this number, the Government proposed the creation of four new electoral districts. As the United Left, which has its chief strength in the country, fears that the increase of city districts will add to the strength of the Liberal party, it rejected the proposition of the Government, as it had already rejected a similar bill two years ago. A motion to forbid the manufacture of phosphor-matches was adopted by both Houses. A Government bill for raising the salaries of Government officers was rejected in the Folkething by 52 against 42 votes. The Landsthing, which does not agree with the Folkething, declined, by 31 against 11 votes, a bill passed by the latter to establish in the provincial towns special dwellings for the houseless poor. The Landsthing granted and the Folkething denied the Danish indigenate to the grandchildren of the late Danish state minister, Count Carl von Moltke (died in 1866) on the ground that their father, Count Adam von Moltke, had until recently resided in Austria, and had, in 1864, belonged to the Austrian army operating against Denmark; that, therefore, no guarantee was given that the children, who were born in a foreign country (a daughter ten years old, and a son four years old), would be educated as patriotic Danes. The merits of the grandfather were not taken into account, on the ground that, as Danish minister, he was a representative of Holstein. The Folkething, in discussing the budget estimate, rejected the proposed construction of a new iron-clad, as well as the construction of new barracks in Odense, for which the Government had demanded an allowance of 51,300 rigsdalers. On the other hand, the pay of private soldiers in the army and navy was raised at the rate of two shillings a day. With the modifications moved and carried by the opposition, this budget was, at length, unanimously passed. The election of the Minister of Justice, Klein, in the district of Aalborg (by 850 against 841 votes) was declared by the Folkething invalid (by 58 against 26 votes). On April 1st, the Diet was closed.

On April 26th the Minister of Justice, Klein, whose election as member of the Folkething has been declared by the Folkething invalid, was reëlected over the candidate of the Left, by 1032 votes against 894.

In June the Minister of Finance, Krieger, offered his resignation, and after a protracted ministerial crisis, lasting for several weeks, the offered resignation of the entire ministry was accepted, and a new cabinet formed, under the presidency of Fonnesbech, hitherto Minister of the Interior. Of the members of the old cabinet, the Minister of Foreign Affairs, Baron von Rosenörn-Lehn, the Minister of Justice, Klein, and the Minister of the Navy, Ravn, remained. Tobiesen, hitherto president of a section in the ministry of the Interior, was appointed, in place of Fonnesbech, Minister of the Interior; Privy Councillor Worsaae, a celebrated writer on antiquities, Minister of Instruction and Public Worship; and the Minister of the Navy, Ravn, assumed, pro tempore, the ministry of War. Subsequently, General Steinmann was appointed for this position. General Steinmann is a native of Schleswig, who has never taken an active part in politics; he was commander of the troops on Alsen when this island was occupied by the Prussians.

The relations of Denmark to Germany appeared to be, on the whole, of a friendly character. In May, the public funeral of Herr Günther, a German engineer at Copenhagen, who had lost his life in an attempt to rescue a drowning man, called forth a grand demonstration, several ministers and other high authorities, with an immense crowd of people of all classes, taking part in it. The German minister had an audience of the King to convey to his Majesty the thanks of the Emperor of Germany for the sympathy evinced on the occasion. He has also thanked the Danish authorities, in the name of the Emperor, for their presence at the funeral. Subsequently, the good understanding between the two Governments seemed to be somewhat disturbed by the expulsion of some Danish subjects from Schleswig. The *National Gazette*, of Berlin, admitted that Danes had been expelled from North Schleswig, and explained that this was due to the continuous system of agitation carried on by certain Danish electors. The measure, it added, was not general, but individual, in its application, and could not give rise to diplomatic negotiations, it being lawful for Germany to expel foreigners from her territory without explanation. It was intimated, moreover, that the relations between the two Governments were of the most friendly character.

On October 5th King Christian opened the new session. In his speech from the throne

his Majesty said that he had felt himself bound personally to convey to the members the greetings of the inhabitants of Iceland and the Faroe Islands. He expected that the new cabinet and the Parliament would harmoniously coöperate in their deliberations upon the proposed reforms. To carry out the measures necessary for the defense of the kingdom and the improvements of the public service, fresh grants would be required. With foreign powers the relations were amicable. The political situation would not yet allow of a settlement of the North-Schleswig question, but the Government still maintained the hope that a satisfactory solution would be arrived at, which was the desire of both himself and the Danish people. The Queen of Denmark, the Crown Prince and Princess of Denmark, the Princess of Wales, and the Princess Thyra, were present at the ceremony. The hope of the new ministry to effect a reconciliation with the United Left was disappointed, and at a large political meeting J. A. Hansen, in the name of the United Left, announced that the new ministry would be opposed by his party as much as the old, especially on account of the finance law and a ministerial bill on preachers' salaries. In the North-Schleswig question the party deprecated a hostile attitude toward Prussia, but expected more from the Prussian sense of justice. On November 10th, the Folkething, after a debate lasting five hours, by a vote of 54 against 28, expressed its continuing want of confidence in the ministry, on the ground that the police had interfered with the right of meeting by suppressing an assembly of Mormons. A motion to express want of confidence in the Minister of Public Instruction for having reproved a school-teacher who had used toward the King the words " the man who calls himself King," was almost unanimously negatived. A motion, by one of the prominent leaders of the United Left, Berg, deputy for the town of Kolding, to abolish all diplomas of nobility, titles, and orders, was, notwithstanding the protests of the ministers, passed by 55 against 11 to a second reading. On January 18th the Diet adjourned to January 6, 1875.

On January 5th the King sanctioned the new Constitution of Iceland, which substantially agrees with the fundamental law of Denmark. A special minister will in future be responsible for guarding the Constitution of Iceland. The Governor of the island is appointed by the King. The Althing will consist of 6 members appointed by the King and of 30 elected by the people.

On July 15th the King, attended by his son, Prince Waldemar, the Minister of Justice Klein, and the Minister of Public Instruction Worsaae, left Copenhagen in order to embark for Iceland, where a millennial anniversary of the settlement of the island was to be celebrated with unusual solemnities. On his voyage to Denmark he also visited the Faroe Islands, where he was received with great en-

.thusiasm. An appalling incident occurred in connection with this visit. The King, on landing, was received on the pier by the governor of the town, M. Finsen, and the local officials, who delivered to his Majesty a loyal address in the name of the people of the Faroe Islands. The royal party then proceeded up the pier, a short distance beyond which a triumphal gateway was erected, where the president of the municipality received his Majesty, and presented an address on the part of the townspeople of Thorshavn. The concluding words of the address had hardly been spoken when the greatest consternation was caused among those present by the president dropping down dead on the spot. It was ascertained that he had been in feeble health for a long time, and a fatal termination was hastened by the excitement of the occasion. This untoward event cast a gloom over the King's visit to the Faroe Islands, and created a painful impression.

Immense enthusiasm welcomed the King when he landed, on July 30th, in Iceland, where the celebration of the anniversary was a grand success (*see* ICELAND). On August 10th the King reëmbarked to return home by way of England, where, on his landing at Leith, in Scotland, on August 16th, he was received by his daughter, the Princess of Wales, who accompanied him to Edinburgh.

The President of the Folkething, J. A. Hansen, received, on his sixty-eighth birthday, from his many friends, a villa near Copenhagen, called "The People's Gift," as a recognition of his great merits in behalf of ameliorating the condition of the peasantry.

The aggregate national wealth of Denmark is estimated at 2,000,000,000 rigsdalers.

In January, the socialist Pihl, who in November, 1873, had avowed an intention to march at the head of the socialistic laborers to the royal palace, and to extort from the King an amnesty for three imprisoned socialists, was sentenced to eight months of forced labor.

In February, the Supreme Court of Denmark suppressed the International Workingmen's Union throughout the kingdom.

On August 15th, the new port of Esbjerg, in Jutland, was opened to commerce.

DE WITT, Rev. THOMAS, D. D., a venerable, accomplished, and eloquent clergyman of the Reformed (Dutch) Church, born in Kingston, Ulster County, N. Y., September 13, 1791; died in New York City, May 18, 1874. He was of pure Dutch and Huguenot stock, and of the best blood in New York. He was a cousin of the late Governor De Witt Clinton. He graduated from Union College in 1808, before he completed his seventeenth year; studied theology with Rev. Dr. Freligh, of Schraalenburgh, N. J., and Rev. Dr. Brodhead, of Rhinebeck, and entered the first class of the Theological Seminary at New Brunswick in 1810, graduating there in 1812. The same year he was ordained as pastor of the combined congregations of Hackensack and Hopewell, Dutchess

County, N. Y., where he remained until 1827, when he accepted a second call (having rejected the first) to the Collegiate Dutch Church of New York City, of which he was the senior clergyman for nearly forty-seven years. He was a man of faith, of learning, and of power; thoroughly indoctrinated in the theology of his Church, and believing it with his whole soul; yet having no trace of bigotry or exclusiveness in his nature; possessing a fluent and eloquent delivery, great clearness in argument, an unblemished purity of life, and a gentle, modest, and genial manner, which won all hearts. He was for many years a zealous student, especially in historical matters, was Vice-President and President for many years of the New York Historical Society, and an active director of the Bible, Colonization, Tract, and Sunday-school Societies, as well as the boards of his own church. He had published very little, even his sermons being generally unwritten, yet he wrote with great vigor, force, and elegance.

DIPLOMATIC CORRESPONDENCE AND FOREIGN RELATIONS.

The relations of the United States with other nations have been peaceful during the year, and the correspondence with their representatives contains few points of importance.

The rights of naturalized citizens of the United States when returning to their native country are subject to some conditions, as appears by the following letter, dated October 5th, from Acting-Secretary J. L. Cadwalader to Mr. Jay, at the capital of Austro-Hungary:

The right to enjoy such privileges as may attach to a citizen of the United States is properly proved by the production of a passport legally issued.

In every case where the action of a diplomatic or consular officer of the United States is invoked, on behalf of a person claiming to be a citizen of the United States, it is incumbent on such officer not only to carefully and zealously guard and protect the rights of all *bona-fide* citizens, but also to carefully abstain from committing this Government to a demand for protection on behalf of a person presenting a false or fraudulent claim to citizenship.

Naturalized citizens, who have become such solely to avoid the duties and burdens attached to a residence in and allegiance to their own country, and who have returned to their native country without intention to reside in the United States, or to assume the duties or burdens common to its citizens, who, in other words, are desirous of enjoying all the benefits and immunities common to citizens of each country, and of avoiding all corresponding duties in each, may be held to have forfeited all right to the protection of the United States. Particular instructions will be found on these questions in section 30 of the personal instructions lately issued.

The attention of the Department has also been called, on several occasions, to applications for passports in foreign countries, founded on certificates of naturalization, which, upon their face, bear conclusive evidence that they have been illegally or fraudulently obtained. In such cases a passport should be refused and the fraudulent certificate forwarded to this Department.

Relative to American citizens enlisting in the military service of foreign nations, Mr. Williams, at Peking, writes to Secretary Fish, under date of May 29th, stating the particulars of a conversation with the Chinese officials, of which the following is an extract:

They then inquired if, in the event of hostilities arising between China and Japan, Americans who were engaged in the ranks of the enemy should be killed by Chinese troops, what notice would be taken of it by their own Government?

I answered that all Americans who entered the military service of the Japanese did so at their own risk, and that the American Government would take no notice of their death under such circumstances; all persons composing a hostile force could only be regarded as enemies by China.

The reply of Secretary Fish, under date of July 29th, was as follows:

You state in your dispatch that you had informed certain officials in this conversation that the Americans entering into the military service of China or Japan did so at their own risk, and that the Government would take no notice of their death under such circumstances. Your answer goes further than the Department feels justified in approving.

In case such American citizens should be killed in battle, in the ordinary course of civilized warfare, no notice would be taken thereof; but the United States will expect that no unusual or inhuman punishment be inflicted upon any of its citizens who may be taken prisoners, but that they shall be treated according to the accepted rules of civilized warfare.

Where the exercise of a commission or the enlistment in a foreign service is not prohibited by law, the fact that a war arises between the country in whose service a citizen of the United States may be and another nation, with which the United States are at peace, does not, in the opinion of this Department, create an obligation "to refuse to serve or to leave the flag thus employed."

Such fact is of not infrequent occurrence. Citizens of all nationalities were engaged on both sides during the rebellion, and such has frequently been the case with European nations.

I fail to perceive that the doctrine of exterritoriality affects the question of the rights of citizens of the United States to engage in the service of foreign powers when not prohibited by law, or that it becomes unlawful because of the engagement being made with a non-Christian power. China has not infrequently availed herself of the services of Americans, as in the case of Ward and Burgevine, and it is not for her to take exception against this Government that it refuses to interfere to prevent its citizens from entering into foreign military service which may not be prohibited by law.

On January 9th Mr. Bancroft writes from Berlin to Secretary Fish, denying the desire of the Government of Germany to obtain the island of St. Thomas. He says:

As to St. Thomas, Germany does not want it, would not accept it as a gift; has no hankering after that or any other West India colony; from principle avoids them; wishes at most a coaling-station in Asiatic seas, and that only in case it can be enjoyed in security without being made a military post. This statement I have had often from every member of the government that could by any possibility have charge of any negotiation made for the acquisition of territory. They have said it to me over and over again. This much in answer to a telegram received night before last through General Schenck.

Again, on January 12th, he writes:

Further, in time past I am very certain that the idea has never been entertained on either the side of Denmark or of Germany to transfer St. Thomas to the latter power. As to the present, I cannot find the slightest reason to believe that any such negotiation is on foot or even in contemplation.

The decisions in the Alabama case respecting the extent to which a neutral power may furnish coals to a war-ship of a belligerent have naturally brought home to the German Navy Department a sense of the feebleness of their position in foreign seas in the event of a war, and so may have given rise to the wish for the possession of coaling-stations, especially in the Eastern Asiatic seas. But it does not change their general policy not to hold in foreign seas posts that would but be new points for attack for a fleet in time of war.

Mr. Fish replies:

DEPARTMENT OF STATE,
WASHINGTON, *February* 11, 1874.

SIR: Referring to your No. 562, of the 16th ultimo, relating to the final denial by the proper authorities of reports concerning negotiations between Germany and Denmark respecting the cession of the Danish West Indies, I have to request you to be watchful in case any negotiation of that character should occur.

I am, etc., HAMILTON FISH.

The mission of Mr. George Bancroft to Berlin was closed during the year by his resignation. Mr. J. C. Bancroft Davis was appointed minister to fill the vacancy. The following letter is the last official act of Mr. Bancroft:

AMERICAN LEGATION, BERLIN, *June* 30, 1874.

SIR: My last act of public duty before leaving Berlin shall be to ask you to express to the President my grateful sense of the honor which he has done me in the language which he used in granting me my discharge from the public service. I can receive it with a good conscience, for I have never, so far as I know, missed an opportunity of carrying out the instructions of the Department, and promoting, to the best of my ability, the honor and the welfare of the country. You in Washington can hardly conceive the degree of comfort secured to our German fellow-citizens by the peaceful security which they obtain for their visits in Germany by the treaty of naturalization. From 10,000 to 15,000 of them come yearly to their mother-country now, without suffering the least anxiety, where before many of them, in order to see their friends, were obliged to remain on the other side of the frontier or come into Germany stealthily, running the risk of arrest every hour.

During the war between Germany and France, great efforts were made to turn the current of opinion and the feeling of the German Government against the United States on account of sales of arms to one of the belligerents. It was to me a very great source of satisfaction that complaints were happily prevented. Our happy coöperation in the San Juan arbitration led to the most pleasing and satisfactory results. Take it for all in all, my mission to Berlin has rounded off in the pleasantest manner the years of my life that have been devoted to the public service, and I may say that my unsolicited appointment by Mr. Johnson and my new commission from Mr. Grant have made to me the years of my great old age the flower of my life.

Yours, etc., GEORGE BANCROFT.

The vagrancy of Italian children, which attracted attention in the United States during the year, has been made the subject of special legislation in the Italian Parliament. The Italian minister at Washington thus speaks of the law, in a letter addressed to Secretary Fish:

LEGATION OF ITALY,
WASHINGTON, *April* 27, 1874.

SIR: Your Excellency is aware that public attention in the United States has for some time been seriously occupied with the subject of foreign vagrancy in this country, especially that of children, who are induced by false promises to leave their native land, and who are subsequently reduced to a condition of the utmost wretchedness. The Italian Parliament long since took this state of things into consideration, with a view to the complete suppression of this odious traffic. It has now just passed a law which was promulgated December 21, 1873, whereby a number of acts connected with the matter are made criminal offenses, and corresponding penalties are provided therefor. It hopes by this means to prevent, or at least considerably to diminish, the traffic in question.

The efficacy of this law would, however, be considerably increased if foreign governments would coöperate in its execution.

I am aware of the difficulties which present themselves to these states when it seems desirable to extend the powers of the central Government. I nevertheless feel confident that your Excellency will be pleased to g e some attention to this subject, in order to see if there is any means of coming to an agreement in relation to the matter. The Government of the King would be happy to take into serious consideration any proposition that the Government of the United States might think proper to make to it, either for the adoption of additional articles to the extradition treaty now in force between the two countries, or for any thing else.

I have, to this effect, the honor to inclose to your Excellency the text of the law in question, and I beg you to accept the assurances of my very high consideration. L. CORTI.

During the year Mr. Daniel E. Sickles resigned as minister to Spain, and Mr. Caleb Cushing was appointed as his successor. The instructions to Mr. Cushing were given in the following letter from Secretary Fish:

DEPARTMENT OF STATE,
WASHINGTON, February 6, 1874.

SIR: Whatever general instructions you may need at the present time for your guidance in representing this Government at Madrid have reference entirely to the actual state of the island of Cuba and its relation to the United States as well as to Spain.

It is now more than five years since an organized body of the inhabitants of that island assembled at Yara, issued a declaration of independence, and took up arms to maintain the declaration. The movement rapidly spread, so as to occupy extensive regions of the eastern and central portions of the island, and all the resources of the Spanish Government have been exerted ineffectually to suppress the revolution and reclaim the districts in insurrection to the authority of Spain. The prosecution of the war on both sides has given rise to many questions, seriously affecting the interests and the honor of the United States, which have become the subject of diplomatic discussion between this Government and that of Spain.

You will receive herewith a selection, in chronological order, of the numerous dispatches in this relation which have passed between the two Governments. From these documents you will derive ample information, not only respecting special questions, which have arisen from time to time, but also respecting the general purposes and policy of the President in the premises.

Those purposes and that policy, as indicated in the accompanying documents, have continued to be substantially the same during the whole period of these events, except in so far as they may have been modified by special circumstances, seeming to impart greater or less prominence to the various aspects of the general question, and thus, without producing any change of principle, yet, according to the particular emergency, to direct the action of the United States.

It will suffice, therefore, on the present occasion, first, briefly to state these general views of the President; and, secondly, to show their application to the several incidents of this desperate struggle on the part of the Cubans to acquire independence, and of Spain to maintain her sovereignty, in so far as those incidents have immediately affected the United States.

Cuba is the largest insular possession still retained by any European power in America. It is almost contiguous to the United States. It is preëminently fertile in the production of objects of commerce which are of constant demand in this country, and, with just regulations of reciprocal interchange of commodities, it would afford a large and lucrative market for the productions of this country. Commercially, as well as geographically, it is by nature more closely connected with the United States than with Spain.

Civil dissensions in Cuba, and especially sanguinary hostilities, such as are now raging there, produce effects in the United States second in gravity only to those which they produce in Spain.

Meanwhile our political relation to Cuba is altogether anomalous, seeing that for any injury done to the United States or their citizens in Cuba we have no direct means of redress there, and can obtain it only by slow and circuitous action by way of Madrid. The Captain-General of Cuba has, in effect, by the laws of Spain, supreme and absolute authority there for all purposes of wrong to our citizens; but this Government has no adequate means of demanding immediate reparation of such wrongs on the spot, except through a consul, who does not possess diplomatic character, and to whose representations, therefore, the Captain-General may, if he chooses, absolutely refuse to listen. And grievous as this inconvenience is to the United States in ordinary times, it is more intolerable now, seeing that, as abundantly appears, the contest in Cuba is between Peninsular Spaniards on the one hand and native-born Spanish-Americans on the other; the former being the real representatives of Spanish force in Cuba, and exerting that force, when they choose, with little, if any, respect for the metropolitan power of Spain. The Captain-General is efficient to injure, but not to redress, and, if disposed to redress, he may be hampered, if not prevented, by resolute opposition on the part of the Spaniards around him, disobedient alike to him and to the supreme Government.

In fine, Cuba, like the former continental colonies of Spain in America, ought to belong to the great family of American republics, with political forms and public policy of their own, and attached to Europe by no ties, save those of international amity, and of intellectual, commercial, and social intercourse. The desire of independence on the part of the Cubans is a natural and legitimate aspiration of theirs, because they are Americans. And while such independence is the manifest exigency of the political interests of the Cubans themselves, it is equally so that of the rest of America, including the United States.

That the ultimate issue of events in Cuba will be its independence, however that issue may be produced, whether by means of negotiation, or as the result of military operations, or of one of those unexpected incidents which so frequently determine the fate of nations, it is impossible to doubt. If there be one lesson in history more cogent in its teachings than any other, it is that no part of America, large enough to constitute a self-sustaining state, can be permanently held in forced colonial subjection to Europe. Complete separation between the metropolis and its colony may be postponed by the former conceding to the latter a greater or less degree of local autonomy, nearly approaching to independence. But in all cases where a positive antagonism has come to exist between the mother-country and its colonial subjects, where the sense of oppression is strongly felt by the latter, and especially where years of relentless warfare have alienated the parties, one from another, more widely than they are sundered by the ocean itself, their political separation is inevitable. It is one of those conclusions which have been aptly called the inexorable logic of events.

Entertaining these views, the President at an early day tendered to the Spanish Government the good offices of the United States for the purpose of effecting by negotiation the peaceful separation of Cuba from Spain, and thus putting a stop to the further effusion of blood in the island, and relieving both Cuba and Spain from the calamities and charges of a protracted civil war, and of delivering the United States from the constant hazard of inconvenient complications on the side either of Spain or of Cuba. But the well-intentioned proffers of the United States on that occasion were unwisely rejected by Spain, and, as it was then already foreseen, the struggle has continued in Cuba with incidents of desperate tenacity on the part of the Cubans, and of angry fierceness on the part of the Spaniards, unparalleled in the annals of modern warfare.

True it is that now, when the war has raged for more than five years, there is no material change in the military situation. The Cubans continue to occupy, unsubdued, the eastern and central parts of the island, with exception of the larger cities or towns, and of fortified points held by the government, but their capacity of resistance appears to be undiminished, and with no abatement of their resolution to persevere to the end in repelling the domination of Spain.

Meanwhile this condition of things grows, day by day, more and more insupportable to the United States. The Government is compelled to exert constantly the utmost vigilance to prevent infringement of our law on the part of Cubans purchasing munitions or materials of war, or laboring to fit out military expeditions in our por s ; we are constrained to maintain a large naval force to prevent violations of our sovereignty, either by the Cubans or the Spaniards ; our people are horrified and agitated by the spectacle, at our very doors, of war, not only with all its ordinary attendants of devastation and carnage, but with accompaniments of barbarous shooting of prisoners of war, or their summary execution by military commissions, to the scandal and disgrace of the age ; we are under the necessity of interposing continually for the protection of our citizens against wrongful acts of the local authorities of Spain in Cuba; and the public peace is every moment subject to be interrupted by some unforeseen event, like that which recently occurred, to drive us at once to the brink of war with Spain. In short, the state of Cuba is the one great cause of perpetual solicitude in the foreign relations of the United States.

While the attention of this Government is fixed on Cuba, in the interest of humanity, by the horrors of civil war prevailing there, we cannot forbear to reflect, as well in the interest of humanity as in other relations, that the existence of slave-labor in Cuba, and its influence over the feelings and interests of the Peninsular Spaniards, lie at the foundation of all the calamities which now afflict the island. Except in Brazil and in Cuba, servitude has almost disappeared from the world. Not in the Spanish-American republics alone, nor in the British possessions, nor in the United States, nor in Russia—not in those countries alone, but even in Asia, and in Africa herself—the bonds of the slave have been struck off, and personal freedom is the all but universal rule and public law, at least to the nations of Christendom. It cannot long continue in Cuba, environed as that island is by communities of emancipated slaves in the other West India Islands and in the United States.

Whether it shall be put an end to by the voluntary act of the Spanish Government, by domestic violence, or by the success of the revolution of Yara, or by

what other possible means, is one of the grave problems of the situation, of hardly less interest to the United States than the independence of Cuba.

The President has not been without hope that all these questions might be settled by the spontaneous act of Spain herself, she being more deeply interested in that settlement than all the rest of the world. It seemed for a while that such a solution was at hand, during the time when the Government of Spain was administered by one of the greatest and wisest of the statesmen of that country, or indeed of Europe, President Castelar. Before attaining power, he had announced a line of policy applicable to Cuba, which, though falling short of the concession of absolute independence, yet was of a nature to command the approbation of the United States.

" Let us," he declared, on a memorable occasion, " let us reduce to formulas our policy in America.

" 1. *The immediate abolition of slavery.*

" 2. Autonomy of the islands of Porto Rico and Cuba, which shall have a parliamentary Assembly of their own, their own administration, their own government, and a federal tie to unite them with Spain, as Canada is united with England, in order that we may found the liberty of those states, and at the same time conserve the national integrity. I desire that the islands of Cuba and Porto Rico shall be our sisters, and I do not desire that they shall be transatlantic Polands."

I repeat, that to such a line of policy as this, especially as it relates to Cuba, the United States would make no objection ; nay, they could accord to it hearty coöperation and support, as the next best thing to the absolute independence of Cuba.

Of course, the United States would prefer to see all that remains of colonial America pass from that condition to the condition of absolute independence of Europe.

But we might well accept such a solution of present questions as, while terminating the cruel war which now desolates the island and disturbs our political intercourse, should, primarily and at the outset abolish the iniquitous institution of slavery, and, in the second place, should place Cuba practically in the possession of herself by means of political institutions of self-government, and enable her, while nominally subject to Spain, yet to cease to be the victim of Spanish colonial interests, and to be capable of direct and immediate relations of interests and intercourse with the other states of America. * * *

In these circumstances, the question what decision the United States shall take is a serious and difficult one, not to be determined without careful consideration of its complex elements of domestic and foreign policy, but the determination of which may at any moment be forced upon us by occurrences either in Spain or in Cuba.

Withal the President cannot but regard *independence*, and emancipation, of course, as the only certain, and even the necessary, solution of the question of Cuba. And, in his mind, all incidental questions are quite subordinate to those, the larger objects of the United States in this respect.

It requires to be borne in mind that, in so far as we may contribute to the solution of these questions, this Government is not actuated by any selfish or interested motive. The President does not meditate or desire the annexation of Cuba to the United States, but its elevation into an independent republic of freemen, in harmony with ourselves and with the other republics of America.

You will understand, therefore, that the policy of the United States in reference to Cuba at the present time is one of expectancy, but with positive and fixed convictions as to the duty of the United States when the time or emergency of action shall arrive. When it shall arrive, you will receive specific instructions what to do. Meantime, instructed as you now are. as to the intimate purposes of the Government, you are to act in conformity therewith in the absence of any specific instructions, and to comport yourself accordingly in all your communications and intercourse, official or unofficial, with persons or public men in Spain.

In conclusion, it remains to be said that, in accordance with the established policy of the United States in such cases, as exemplified in the many changes of government in France during the last eighty years, and in the Mexican Republic since the time of its first recognition by us, and in other cases which have occurred in Europe and America, you will present your credentials to the persons or authorities whom you may find in the actual exercise of the executive power of Spain.

DISCIPLES OF CHRIST. The *General Christian Missionary Convention* met at Cincinnati, Ohio, October 20th. About six hundred delegates were present; Isaac Essett was chosen president. A quarter-centennial address was delivered by W. K. Pendleton, in which was given an historical sketch of the convention. Progress was reported by the general secretary in the organization of Sunday-schools in the States of Kentucky, Missouri, Ohio, Indiana, New York, Pennsylvania, Virginia, West Virginia, Illinois, Iowa, Wisconsin, and Michigan. Seventy-five Sunday-schools had been organized in Kentucky since November, 1873. A normal Sunday-school institute had been held in Ohio, and a great Sunday-school convention in Indiana. The committee to whom the report of the general secretary was referred, recommended that his work be continued, and that each State desiring his services be asked to become responsible for the expense of the work done within its bounds. An essay was read on the subject of home missions; it elicited a general discussion: the conviction was expressed that efforts should be made to furnish the churches with better pastoral care, to give assistance to weak and declining churches, to look more carefully after the freedmen, to secure the preaching of the gospel to the foreign population coming into the country, and to build up the cause of the denomination in the cities. The general board were instructed by the convention: 1. To employ four evangelists to work wherever the board might suggest. 2. To endeavor to receive and appropriate moneys as follows: to the establishment of missions among the freedmen, $3,000; for the Bible-school at Louisville, Ky., $1,000; for missions in Nebraska, $2,000; for missions in Kansas, $2,000. 3. To have personal appeals for funds made through the corresponding secretary, and to appoint such other agents as may be necessary to promote the foregoing objects. The committee appointed at the previous meeting of the General Convention to make arrangements to have the Disciples of Christ appropriately represented at the celebration of the centennial anniversary of American Independence, in 1876, reported that to set forth in a proper manner the various features which it would be desirable to have represented on the part of the Disciples, embracing their literature, their history, the statistics of their churches, colleges, and their journalism, would cost not less than $25,000. The subject was laid on the table.

The report of the Board of Missions presented an encouraging view of the work of the yea just passed in Ohio, Kentucky, Nebraska, Michigan, Indiana, Kansas, Illinois, Virginia, West Virginia, Pennsylvania, New York, Colorado, Wisconsin, and Missouri. Sixty-four new places had been visited, thirty-seven churches organized, 288 weak churches helped, 4,497 persons added to the churches, and the sum of $64,045.97 contributed to the purposes of the board. The board represented that a chief obstacle to their more complete success lay in a provision of the constitution which authorized donors to disburse their own contributions. The operation of this rule was regarded by the board as such as practically to destroy "church coöperation," and they recommended such amendment as would obviate its objectionable features. The board advised that some measure be adopted by which the State treasurers should be enabled to pay regularly whatever may be due to the general board; that each county in a State be made a district, with an advisory committee of three to promote Sunday-school institutes, to make provision for churches desiring ministerial labor, to hold mass meetings, to see that contributions are promptly forwarded to the general board, and to act as a medium of communication between the county and State boards. The convention instructed the general board to establish one or more foreign missions. A meeting of women was held during the session of the convention at which a "Woman's Christian Missionary Society" was organized. Delegates were present from nine States. The announcement was made that the society started with a fund of $391 in its treasury. A formal reception was given it by the convention, when addresses were made by Mrs. Goodwin on the "Undeveloped Talent of the Church," and by Mrs. S. E. Pearre on "Woman's Board Missions." The convention gave recognition and approval to the new society, and pledged coöperation with it. A committee who had been commissioned to bear the friendly greetings of the convention to the General Conference of Free-will Baptists at Providence, R. I., made a report of their proceedings. The Rev. C. M. Graham, of Chicago, visited the convention as a fraternal delegate from the Free-will Baptists. He asked the appointment of a committee to confer with a similar committee of that denomination on the subject of union. He represented that the Free-will Baptists were quite favorable to union. A committee of conference on the subject was appointed, consisting of five members.

The general annual meeting of the churches of the *Disciples of Christ, in England, Scotland, Ireland, and Wales*, took place August 11th, at Carlisle. The reports of the stations were incomplete. Eighty-two out of one hundred and nine churches made returns. Sixty-one churches reported an increase of one hundred and twenty-nine members since 1873. The treasurer's statement showed his receipts to have been £813 13s. 6d. and his expenditures £931 16s. 4d.

DISTRICT OF COLUMBIA. In January, petitions were introduced into the Senate of the United States and the House of Representatives, signed by the citizens of the District of Columbia, praying that an investigation into the affairs of the District be ordered. The chief cause of complaint was directed against the action of the Board of Public Works, which had entered upon an extensive system of public improvements which was bringing financial embarrassments upon the District, and grievous burdens upon the inhabitants. It was further alleged that the proceedings of the board had been attended with irregularities and corrupt practices.

Congress proceeded at once to appoint a joint committee, consisting of Senators Thurman and Boutwell (the latter, in consequence of illness, was succeeded by Senator Allison), and Messrs. Stewart, Wilson, Hubbell, Bass, Jewett, and Hamilton, of the House of Representatives. The first meeting of the committee was held on February 11th, and on the 5th of March the investigation was begun. After an immense amount of testimony had been taken, a report was made on the 16th of June. The committee reached the following conclusion:

Your committee are of opinion that the present embarrassments of this District, and the serious complications which now environ its finances and affairs, are primarily chargeable to the attempt early made by the authorities placed over it to inaugurate a comprehensive and costly system of improvements to be completed in a brief space of time, which ought to have required for its completion several years.

A system of improvements, covering more than a hundred miles of streets, contemplating a system of sewerage and of other expenditures which were to extend over almost every street and avenue in the cities of Washington and Georgetown, as well as of the roads in the county, and to be undertaken at a single stroke, without the preliminary organization of the various details of engineering work, and plats, plans, and estimates, in a community situated as was this at the time, could not well be otherwise than pernicious. It made but little difference in some respects what plan of letting contracts was adopted; any plan under these circumstances would have been found defective. And in contemplation of the fact that, when the Board of Public Works entered upon the execution of this plan of improvements which, as it was originally designed, involved the expenditure of not less than $6,000,000, it, from one cause or another, so changed and enlarged the plan as to involve an expenditure of $18,000,000 instead, it is not surprising that we find that the difficulties and embarrassments which might be expected to attend the lesser scheme were proportionately increased; and while your committee join in the general expression of gratification at beholding the improved condition of the national capital, the embellishments and adornments everywhere visible, they cannot but condemn the methods by which this sudden and rapid transition was secured.

Taking into consideration the expense involved in the comprehensive plan before referred to, and enlarged as stated, your committee are of opinion that the board adopted an erroneous and, in its results, a vicious method of letting contracts for this work, viz., without competition open to the public; and that the method adopted by the board resulted in the payment of an increased price over and above what would have been paid if open, fair, and free competition had been invited.

After the passage of the loan act of $4,000,000, the Board of Public Works invited proposals and bids for work to be done in pursuance of said plan, and on the 1st of September opened all these various bids, giving notice afterward to the bidders that none of the bids would be accepted, but that the board would fix a scale of prices for the various classes of work, and let contracts at their discretion, upon this scale of fixed prices. This opened the way for favoritism in the letting of contracts, and for a system of brokerage in contracts which was demoralizing in its results, bringing into the list of contractors a class of people unaccustomed to perform the work required, and enabling legitimate contractors to pay large prices in order to secure contracts, and, in the opinion of your committee, was the beginning of nearly all the irregularities disclosed in the testimony in the letting of contracts. Any system which would enable an adventurer to come from a distant city, and, in the name of a contracting firm, make proffers of fifty cents per yard to any person having, or supposed to have, influence with the board, whereby a paving contract could be secured, and, after persistent effort, succeed in securing a contract, and actually binding his principals, the contractors, to pay $97,000 for a contract of 200,000 yards of pavement, after an effort of five months to secure it, the gross amount to be received being only about $700,000, in its nature must be vicious, and ought to be condemned.

The committee called attention to discrepancies in the measurements for work done as made by an engineer appointed by the committee contrasted with those certified to by the board, and criticised the absolute power vested in the vice-president, Shepherd, and also the reckless manner in which the functions of treasurer and auditor had been performed. The committee "unanimously arrived at the conclusion that the existing form of government of the District is a failure; that it is too cumbrous and too expensive; that the powers and relations of its several departments are so ill-defined that limitations intended by Congress to apply to the whole government are construed to limit but one of its departments; that it is wanting in sufficient safeguard against maladministration and the creation of indebtedness; that the system of taxation it allows opens a door to great inequality and injustice, and is wholly insufficient to secure the prompt collection of taxes; and that no remedy short of its abolition and the substitution of a simpler, more restricted and economical government will suffice."

As the session of Congress was near its close, the committee recommended the appointment of a commission to manage the affairs of the District under limited and restrained powers; and that a committee should be appointed to devise a new frame of government to be submitted to Congress at its next session.

In accordance with this recommendation, a

bill was passed by Congress, and approved June 20th, providing for the appointment of commissioners to wind up the affairs of the District, and of a committee comprising two Senators and two members of the House, to prepare a suitable form of permanent government. The report of the committee was submitted to Congress December 7th, through the chairman, Senator Morrill. The plan submitted was, that Congress should exercise that exclusive legislation over the District with which it is invested by the Constitution, and provide for the general superintendence of its affairs, and the enforcement of the laws through officers and agents directly amenable to the supreme executive authority of the United States. The form of government recommended by the committee was as follows:

As to a frame of government, observing their instruction and the constitutional limitations on the appointing power, and having regard to proper efficiency of administration and of official responsibility, the committee have deemed it necessary to make the new government for the District a department in the Government of the United States strictly limited to the affairs of said District. At the head of this department shall be a board of general control, designated " a Board of Regents," of three persons, to be appointed by the President and confirmed by the Senate, with a certain tenure of office, and removable only for cause, who are to exercise the chief executive authority, always acting as a public body and with limited and defined powers. Within this department and subject to its supervision are distinct subdivisions of bureaus, the head of each of which is a Board of Coöperative Control, whose duties and powers are also defined, and whose doings are open to proper inspection. These boards are appointed by the regents, except as to the Board of Education, a portion of the members of which are to be elected by the inhabitants, and except, also, as to the Bureau of Public Works, the head of which is to be detailed by the President from the Engineer Corps of the army, have a certain tenure of office, and are removable by the regents for cause. They relate to and embrace the entire civil service of the District, except such as falls under the executive departments and the courts, and are denominated the Boards of Health, Education, Police, Excise, Public Works, Fire, and Buildings.

With the view of relieving Congress of embarrassing details of strictly municipal affairs, it has been thought desirable to present a framework of government that could be administered with as infrequent appeals to its authority as the nature of the case would allow. To accomplish this it was necessary to confer sweeping, ill-defined, discretionary authority, or to enter into details as to the extent and manner of exercising authority, and accordingly the latter course has been adopted, and, the committee trust, will be found to have secured thereby a desirable publicity of official action, certainly as to method, responsibility for abuses, efficiency in the public service, and protection to individual rights. Authority to make suitable and necessary ordinances and regulations in harmony with the laws of Congress has been conferred upon those charged with the executive administration as extensive as the local interests are likely to require.

The militia system has been revived, and a limited and comparatively inexpensive force provided for, deemed adequate, however, to any demands for its service which may be anticipated.

The judicial courts, standing upon the basis of statutes of the United States, quite independent of local control, are not deemed necessarily to fall within the scope of the authority of the committee, and have received no share of its attention, except as to the Police Court, in regard to which certain provisions are made with the view of efficiency and dispatch in the transaction of its business. The establishment of a Municipal Court is also provided for, having exclusive civil jurisdiction of matters noncognizable by justices of the peace, and thus superseding the office and jurisdiction of said justices ; and in addition thereto it is provided that any Judge of said Municipal Court may, under such regulations as may be prescribed by the Supreme Court of the District, be designated by the Chief-Justice of said court to hold a term and sessions of the Police Court, with the view of facilitating the business therein.

Provision is made for the assessment and collection of a tax upon the real and personal estates of the inhabitants of the District, except such as are exempt by law, at the supposed medium rate of $2 on the $100, the valuation for such taxation being the true value thereof, as upon a just appraisement between debtor and creditor. The assessors are to be appointed by the regents, and may be by them removed for cause. The taxes are to be payable to the Collector of Internal Revenue for the District, collected by him and paid into the United States Treasury, and all sums provided for from any source whatever are to be collected and paid into the Treasury of the United States in like manner, and all payments for salaries and compensations and for other purposes are to be made by the Treasurer of the United States upon appropriations by Congress, and all vouchers and accounts are to be audited by, and all warrants and requisitions are to pass under the control of, the proper officers of the Treasury of the United States.

Annual reports are to be made by the regents to the President, to be transmitted to Congress with a particular statement of the public service for the past year, the application made of all public moneys, with detailed statements of the expense of each bureau and separate office of said government.

The net debt of the District of Columbia, less securities on hand and available, was thus reported by President Grant in his annual message at the opening of Congress : Bonded debt issued prior to July 1, 1874, $8,883,940 ; 3.65 bonds, act of Congress, June 20, 1874, $2,088,-168.73 ; certificate of the Board of Audit, $4,-770,533.45 ; total, $15,742,667.61—less special improvement assessments chargeable to private property in excess of any demand against such assessments, $1,614,054.37 ; less Chesapeake & Ohio Canal bonds, $75,000, and Washington & Alexandria Railroad bonds, $59,000 ; in the hands of the sinking-fund, $1,748,054.37, leaving the actual debt, less said assets, $13,-994,613.24. In addition to this, there are claims preferred against the government of the District amounting in the estimated aggregate reported by the Board of Audit to $3,147,-787.48, of which the greater part will probably be rejected. This sum can with no more propriety be included in the debt account of the District government than can the thousands of claims against the General Government be included as a portion of the national debt, but the aggregate sum thus stated includes something more than the funded debt chargeable exclusively to the District of Columbia. The act of Congress of June 28, 1874, contemplates an apportionment between the

United States Government and the District of Columbia in respect to the payment of the principal and interest of the 3.65 bonds. Therefore, in computing with precision the bonded debt of the District, the aggregate sums above stated as respects the 3.65 bonds now issued, the outstanding certificates of the Board of Audit, and the unadjusted claims pending before that board, should be reduced to the extent of the amount to be apportioned to the United States Government.

DOMINION OF CANADA. Since our last extended notice of this Confederation, it has been further enlarged by the admission of the old British colony of Prince Edward's Island, situated in the Gulf of St. Lawrence, southern portion, and separated from the main-land by the Northumberland Straits. It is a fertile island, 130 miles long by 34 wide, devoted chiefly to agriculture; but its fisheries are valuable, and ship-building is also prosecuted with some enterprise. Its population, according to the latest census, is 103,000. For some time the inhabitants of the island were more unwilling than otherwise to enter the Union; but serious financial embarrassment arose, and the public mind naturally turned toward Ottawa for relief. In addition to the benefit which Prince Edward's will enjoy in common with the other provinces forming the Confederation, it was provided that the railroad, of 200 miles in length, which the local government had undertaken to construct at a cost of $3,250,000, should become the property of the Dominion. Further exceptional advantage was conferred in the form of aid to steamboat and telegraphic communication with the main-land.

To complete the union of provinces as authorized by imperial authority in 1869, it only remains now to obtain the assent of Newfoundland; and, doubtless, means to that end will soon present themselves.

This being accomplished, the Dominion of Canada will extend from the last-mentioned possession, on the Atlantic Ocean, to Queen Charlotte's Island on the Pacific, extending across the continent in its broadest part, a distance of 80° of longitude, but in high latitude, and occupying the whole of the country north of the territory of the United States. This space appears large on the map, but we are told that "the greater part of it is beyond the limit of the growth of trees, and much of the residue is too cold to constitute a chosen residence for Europeans." Its geographical configuration is also remarkable; denied expansion on the one side by the frozen ocean, and on the other by the United States, it somewhat resembles a mathematical line, having length without breadth.

Recent political proceedings in the Dominion have been of a grave character, arising in the main from what may, in a country of such limited resources, be considered a gigantic railway policy. It will be remembered that, in the parliamentary session of 1872, an act was passed authorizing the construction of a Pacific Railway by a private company, to be subsidized by the Government. On the 5th of February, 1873, a charter was granted for this purpose to Sir Hugh Allan and others, and almost immediately arose suspicions of questionable prearrangements between the Government and Sir Hugh. Charges were accordingly formulated, a parliamentary investigation, and, subsequently, an inquiry by royal commission, were entered into, resulting in such disclosures of monetary transactions between the leader of the Government, Sir John, and the leader of the company, Sir Hugh, as finally caused the complete overthrow of the Macdonald administration. A short time previous to this event Sir Hugh Allan relinquished the charter, having been unable to obtain in England the necessary capital to commence the construction of the road. Alexander Mackenzie, Esq., the leader of the opposition to the government of Sir John A. Macdonald, became the prime-minister of the succeeding administration, formed under command of the Governor-General, the Earl of Dufferin, in November, 1873,

The immediate and pressing question which the new Government had to deal with was the construction of the Pacific Railway, to which, undoubtedly, the Dominion had been pledged by the previous Executive, and in an address to his constituents, the electors of the county of Lambton, issued immediately upon his acceptance of office, Mr. Mackenzie is thus explicit:

We must meet the difficulty imposed on Canada by the reckless arrangements of the late Government with reference to the Pacific Railway, under which they pledged the honor and resources of this country to the commencement of that gigantic work in July, 1873, and to its completion by July, 1881. That compact has already been broken. Over a million has now been spent in surveys, but no part of the line has yet been located, and the bargain is, as we always said it was, incapable of literal fulfillment. With a view to obtain a speedy means of communication across the continent, and to facilitate the construction of the railway itself, it will be our policy to utilize the enormous stretches of magnificent water communication which lie between a point not far from the Rocky Mountains and Fort Garry, and between Lake Superior and French River on the Georgian Bay, thus avoiding for the present the construction of about 1,300 miles of railway, estimated to cost from $60,000,000 to $80,000,000, and rendering the resources of the country available for the prosecution of those links of the Pacific Railway which are necessary in order to form a complete line of rail and steamboat communication from east to west.

Recent official reports show that the surveys for this work are rapidly advancing; that the Pembina branch of the road is already under contract; that tenders for the line from Nipissing to Georgian Bay have been called for; the telegraph and wagon-road through British Columbia commenced; and that the premier, availing himself of the favorable state of the markets, has purchased 40,000 tons of steel rails for the purposes of this great national undertaking.

The legislation of the Dominion parliamentary sessions of 1873-'74 has been eminently practical and progressive. An act of the former session, cap. 33, confirms a contract between the Postmaster-General and Sir Hugh Allan (who has been engaged in this service for many years), for a weekly mail-service between Quebec or Montreal and Liverpool in summer, and Portland and Liverpool in winter, for the sum of $126,533.33 per annum—either party having power to end the contract upon giving one year's notice, and the Postmaster-General having said power at any time for non-performance. A stringent law was passed, in which, besides dealing severely with "corrupt practices," is prescribed against the party wrongfully elected, not only the loss of the seat, but incapacity to sit during that Parliament. The ballot has also been introduced, and, so far, has worked successfully. Cases of controverted elections are by another law transferred from parliamentary committees to the Supreme Courts. The operation of this law has been observed to be prompt and effective, it being evident that the grosser forms of bribery must certainly disappear under its strictness and influence. A source of much difficulty between the governments of Ontario and Quebec has been removed by the act, cap. 30, under which the Dominion Government assumes the total debt of those provinces at the time of the Union, viz., $73,006,088, instead of $62,000,000, as laid down in the Act of Confederation (1867). As this change disturbed the monetary arrangements generally, under which the Union took place, proportionate concessions have been made to the other four provinces.

The Minister of Finance, in his official statement, April 1, 1873, gave a good account of the material prosperity of the Dominion. Deposits in banks had increased in five years nearly $37,000,000; the exports in that time had nearly doubled; the increase of imports was still larger. Notwithstanding, he said, the large outlays in constructing the Intercolonial Railway, in purchasing the Northwest Territory, in assuming the debt of British Columbia, and the expenditure on the Pacific Railway survey, the Dominion debt did not amount to one cent more per head than when the provinces were confederated. The revenue of the fiscal year was $20,714,813; the expenditure $17,559,468. By another arrangement of figures, however, the successor to this gentleman, the present Finance Minister, satisfied Parliament that a deficit of not less than $3,000,000 existed when he came into office, to meet which he obtained its consent to raising the duty on general imports from 15 to 17½ per cent., to reimposing a small amount on tea and coffee, to a limited increase of the excise duties, and in other particulars to a readjustment of the tariff.

The railways of Canada, on the 1st of October last, extended over 4,022 miles; the traffic returns, from July to December, amounted to $8,633,759, of which $4,903,759 is set down to the Grand Trunk Company.

The progress of telegraphy has also been rapid in proportion to the population. The position of the Montreal Telegraph Company, on the 17th of October last, will be seen by the following table:

Miles of poles	12,001
Miles of wire	20,267
Miles of cable	12½
Number of offices	1,288
Sets of instruments	1,612
Messages for the year ending November, 1873	1,784,752
Words to newspapers, nearly	9,000,000

Of the Dominion Telegraph Company it is reported:

Number of offices	300
Miles in operation	6,000
Number of employés	400
Sets of instruments	500

The increase of tonnage and the steady advance of marine and fishery interests in the Dominion are also observable. The official reports of the Department of Marine show ample appreciation, on the part of the responsible minister, of the duties devolving upon him. In the Quebec division, for instance, extending to the coasts of Labrador and Newfoundland, there were, at the close of navigation, 35 lighthouses, 5 light-ships with steam fog-whistles, 52 buoys, and 35 beacons. The fisheries of the Dominion are also reported to be much on the increase. A protective system has been adopted in favor of the estuary, river, and inland fisheries. About 1,000 decked vessels, and 17,000 open boats, with not less than 42,000 men, are computed to be engaged in the several provinces. The latest official statement estimates the value of the catch of the year as $9,570,116, showing an increase of thirty-three per cent. in two years.

Much and increased interest is now manifested in Canada in favor of immigration. In the year 1872 the combined expenditure of the Dominion and Provincial Governments for this purpose amounted to $261,963,003. The vote of the Dominion Parliament, alone, last year was nearly $300,000. The return of the numbers settling in the early part of the year 1873 shows 42,000, including a large number of French Canadians who had returned from the United States—a movement which is still continuing, and is being much encouraged. During the past year (1874) the number of immigrants is less than that of the previous report, but it is stated that as a class, consisting chiefly of English agricultural laborers, they are desirable.

The Dominion obituary of the last two years contains many honored names, including those of Sir George E. Cartier, baronet, for many years a distinguished French-Canadian statesman ; Hon. Joseph Howe, long known as one of the ablest and most patriotic of the public men of Nova Scotia, and the Governor of that province at the time of his demise; Right Rev. John Farrell, Catholic Bishop of Hamilton, Ontario; Hon. Henry Black, Judge of the Admiralty Court of Quebec, and an able jurist; Hon. J. W. Johnston, Judge of Nova Scotia; Lady Hincks, wife of Sir Francis Hincks; and Judge Armstrong, of Ottawa.

DUPLEX TELEGRAPHY. The progress of the inventions of the method for passing counter-messages simultaneously over a telegraph-wire, which has been brought to perfection and practical availability by Mr. Stearns, an American, is described as follows by the London *Engineer:*

The aim of the duplex system is to send messages in contrary directions at the same moment along the same line without causing any interruption to the transmission in either direction. Of course, it is well known that two currents cannot pass each other on a wire; but, by the various means which will be described below, the effects on the sending and receiving instruments at either end of the line are exactly the same as though the currents really passed one another. It was in 1853 that the first practical application of the duplex system was made by Dr. Gentl, a director in an Austrian telegraph company. By using a second battery, which he called his equating battery, he was enabled to send dispatches in contrary directions at the same time. He employed a relay, the coils of which were wound with two separate wires in contrary directions, one wire being in circuit with the line battery and the other with the equating battery, so that when the key was depressed and the whole current of the line battery passed through the relay it remained perfectly unaffected, since the magnetic effect on either coil was equal and opposite. This is of course true for both stations, so that either can send to the other without the relay of the sending station being in any way affected: and thus the first great difficulty in duplex telegraphy is overcome. The key that Dr. Gentl used was a double-current key with six contacts. In the circuit of the outer coils of the relay are inserted the equating battery and the front and middle contacts of the right side of the key. The inner coils are connected with the middle contact of the left side of the key and the line wire, the front contact on the same side being connected with line battery, and the back contact being to earth. Thus, the circuit of the line battery is through the two back contacts of the left side of the key, the interior coils, and the line wire to the farther station, where it goes through the interior coils and the two front contacts of the left side of the key to earth, and by earth back to the — pole of the line battery. The current from the equating battery at the same time passes through the two back contacts of the right side of the key, the outer coils of the relay, and back to the — pole of the same battery. It will be seen that the only use of the equating battery is to neutralize the effect of the line battery on the relay. If now both stations send currents at the same instant, one current will go as above described through the key and inner coils to the farther station's relay, which records the signal, as the equilibrium maintained by the second battery has been destroyed, and the other current will go by earth to the farther's station's relay, which will also be affected. In short, if A's line current destroys B's, B's equating current registers the signals, and *vice versa.*

This arrangement, which seems so perfect in theory, was found sadly deficient in practice; as it was found quite impossible to keep the currents of the line and equating batteries equal; for the local circuit being so much shorter than the line circuit, and the outer coils of the relay being always thicker and

shorter than the inner ones, the tension of the line batteries remained almost constant, while that of the equating ones fell rapidly. Another fault of this arrangement was that, when contact is broken at the middle contacts of the key and made at the back ones, the circuit is for a moment interrupted at the front contact, and thus some signals are lost. Dr. Gentl afterward applied his principle to a chemical telegraph with somewhat better results.

The next system, which was invented by Messrs. Frischen and Halse in the following year, certainly did away with the above faults, as no equating battery nor double key was used. Their method was what may be called a "differential" one. The arrangement was very much the same as that of an ordinary Morse circuit. The relay is constructed in the same way as in the former arrangement; it is connected with the lever of an ordinary Morse key, one of the coils leading to the line and the other through a resistance to earth. This resistance is made equal to the resistance of the other portion of the circuit—viz., the other coils, the line, and one branch of the relay at the distant station—so that when the key is depressed the current has two paths open to it, each possessing equal resistance. Consequently, by the law that "if two circuits are open to a current it will divide itself between them in the inverse ratio of their resistance," half of it will flow through one set of coils, and the resistance, to earth; neutralizing the effect on the home relay of the other half of the current, which will flow through the other coils and line to the farther station. Thus, no signals will be given on the home relay. At the farther station, after producing the signal, the current will pass to earth, either through the earth contact of the key, or else, if the key is depressed, through the other branch of the relay and the resistance above mentioned. If, now, both stations be sending to one another at the same time, one current goes by line to the distant station, and the other current goes by earth.

But, perfect as this system seemed, it did not answer, owing to our defective knowledge of electromagnetic induction and bad insulation, and nothing was heard of it for many years. Its revival is chiefly due to Mr. Stearns, an American, and it is now much more popular in that country than the old system. To such perfection has it been brought that on one of the most successful lines—that between New York and Chicago—it is stated that as many as 1,600 messages have been got off in ten hours. On this line there is a repeater half-way.

Mr. Stearns's system is also based on the differential arrangement, though slightly different from the last-mentioned plan, as it is based on the difference of potentials and not on the difference of currents. The relays are wound with two coils so arranged that, equal currents being passed through both, equal magnetization will be produced; but if those currents be passed through in opposite directions the relays will remain unaffected. By means of the keys —ordinary Morse—the line is always kept in contact with the earth or battery, except when the key is first depressed, when the battery is for a moment short-circuited. But contact is immediately after broken, which allows the current to flow through two circuits—one through the line and the other through the inserted resistance to earth. A condenser is inserted in the shortest circuit, of such capacity, that the condenser and the resistance coils are equivalent to the whole line. If, now, one circuit be sending, and not the other, a current is sent through both coils of the home relay in opposite directions, so that the instrument remains unaffected. Thence it passes through the line round the inner coils of the distant relay, which causes the instrument to record the signals, and to earth by the earth contact of the key. If both stations be sending at the same time, the line currents neutralize each other; but a current is sent round the outer coils of each relay, through the artificial line composed of the resistance coils and condenser, and through earth to the distant station, where it passes through the inner coils of the relay, and records the signals. The particular advantage of this last system is, that any instrument, however delicate, may be worked by it.

It may be here remarked that a number of small condensers are better than one large one, as small electro-magnetic coils may be inserted between the plates, provided with movable centres, by which the magnetic retardation may be increased or lessened.

E

EASTMAN, Rev. ORNAN, A. M., a Presbyterian clergyman, for forty-nine years an officer, and for forty-two years Secretary of the American Tract Society, born at Amherst, Mass., March 27, 1796; died in New York City, April 24, 1874. He pursued his preliminary studies at Amherst Academy, afterward Amherst College, and entered Yale College, whence he graduated in 1821 with honor. After completing his theological studies at Andover in 1824, he was for a year an efficient agent of the American Board of Commissioners of Foreign Missions; he entered the service of the American Tract Society in Boston, where he remained from 1825 to 1828, when he was transferred to the New York Society, first as General Agent for the Mississippi Valley, and from 1832 as Finance Secretary. In 1870 he withdrew from his more laborious duties, but was continued as Honorary Secretary till his death. Mr. Eastman was a man of wide and thorough culture, of an exceedingly retentive memory, of remarkable financial ability, of a simple but effective eloquence, and of great skill in the presentation of his cause. Few men in this country were more widely known; he had traversed almost every State and Territory of the Union, not only once but many times, and so genial were his manners, and so winning his address, that where he came oftenest he was most heartily welcome. He died after only five or six days' illness, his health all through life having been remarkably good.

ECUADOR (REPÚBLICA DEL ECUADOR), a country of South America, comprised between latitude 1° 5′ north and 5° 30′ south, and between longitude 59° 52′ and 80° 35′; and bounded north by Colombia and Brazil, east by the empire just mentioned, south by Peru, and west by the Pacific Ocean. According to a new estimate, published in 1873, the area is 277,885 square miles, including 29,509 square miles of the insular province of Galápagos; and the population 1,308,082, of whom 200,-000 are uncivilized Indians in the province of Oriente. The population of the capital, Quito, is now set down at 76,000. The President of the Republic is Señor Garcia Moreno, and the ministry is the same as that noted in the ANNUAL CYCLOPÆDIA for 1873.

The army is reported to comprise 1,500 men, notwithstanding that, in 1868, when it was but 1,200 strong, the Government announced the intention of taking into consideration plans for its reduction, and perhaps even its ultimate

extinction. That the only measure hitherto taken in reference to the armed force of the country has been to increase its numbers will not be a matter of surprise to any who are aware that Señor Moreno's government is essentially a military one.

The financial situation of Ecuador is one of the least promising among all the South American states, save, perhaps, that of Uruguay and Paraguay; this last, however, owes its poverty to a disastrous war, which drained its life-blood almost to the last dregs; but the strenuous efforts of a wise government are directed to improve the condition of the country and re-establish the national credit abroad, and meet the hearty coöperation of the people. Not so in Ecuador, where the public revenue scarcely ever exceeds $1,500,000, while the expenditure is seldom below $2,000,000, though but a small fraction is devoted to the development of that very branch which is the main source of income to the nation, namely, foreign commerce, or more directly the customs.

It may not be out of place to give here a statement of the yield of this latter department during the six years 1868–'73:

Years.	Receipts.
1868	$502,783 61
1869	588,729 36
1870	902,792 69
1871	973,792 69
1872	1,180,128 80
1873	1,187,586 47
Total in United States gold	$5,283,812 92

By comparing the figures of this table with those stated above for the revenue, it will be seen that considerably more than two-thirds of the latter are derived from that source.

The progressive annual increase indicated in the table is attributable to the energy of the merchants of Guayaquil, through which port nearly all the foreign commerce is carried on, and whose mercantile community enjoys, and has ever enjoyed, an enviable reputation abroad.

At the commencement of 1870 the national liabilities were stated to be $16,370,000, made up as follows: British loan, contracted in 1855, $9,120,000, and a home debt of $7,250,000.

Nothing has been done for several years toward the liquidation of this debt, nor have any payments been made on account of interest since 1867, a chronic insolvency which led to the insertion of the name of Ecuador in a list of defaulting republics, published in London last summer, under the title "black-sheep."

It seems somewhat incredible, in the face of such circumstances, that President Moreno attempted to borrow $5,000,000 in February last. Something still more incredible is the ostensible profit of the *Banco del Ecuador*, apparently substantiated by the balance-sheet of that institution, which we here transcribe:

ASSETS.

Cash, in gold and silver coin................	$494,939 82
Debts in accounts-current..................	566,414 77
Bills receivable............................	493,255 88
Inventory.................................	60,826 43
Government of Ecuador....................	247,589 90
Shareholders.............................	800,000 00
Loans to the Goverument..................	681,341 70
Government, for tithes....................	59,027 21
Conversion of coins.......................	309,173 41
Branch Bank at Quito.....................	263,946 02
Branch Bank at Cuenca...................	239,515 96
Shares in the "Banco Hipotecario"........	1,700 00
Yaguachi Railway.........................	7,130 61
Suudries.................................	459,252 90
	$4,134,114 11

LIABILITIES, ETC.

Capital...................................	$1,000,000 00
Notes in circulation.......................	2,040,773 00
Credit in accounts-current................	187,882 99
Deposits on demand.......................	31,108 19
Interest on transactions not at maturity....	5,446 84
Credits...................................	576,527 54
Deposits on time..........................	42,408 61
Profit and loss............................	124,456 20
Sundries..................................	125,510 84
	$4,134,114 11

This profit of $124,456.20 (in Euadorian money*) the directors of the bank proposed to apply as follows:

Public works, as per contract with the Government...............................	$10,000 00
For account of inventory....................	9,456 20
Dividend of 15 per cent. on $700,000 effective capital................................	105,000 00
	$124,456 20

At a cursory glance, the condition of the institution looks favorable; but a careful analysis of the various items of the balance-sheet shows that all is not gold that glitters.

The item, "interest on transactions not at maturity," $5,446.84, is either due or not due the bank; if due, it should go into the profit-and-loss sheet; and, if not due, it should not figure at all, unless it be for display.

The item $309,173,41, under the title "conversion of coins," which figures as a debt to the bank, loses its virtue by the explanation, that the government of Señor Moreno, desirous to withdraw from circulation a quantity of depreciated coin, directed the bank to effect the redemption, which was done at the current nominal rates of the coins; but which coins, when realized as old metal, left a net loss of $309,173.41. This deficit, or loss, if bearable by the Government, should be incorporated in the account of the Government, else it will be understood that the Government is not responsible for its liquidation. It ought, therefore, to be treated as a profit-and-loss item, and, viewed thus, the statement would stand as follows:

* The *peso* of Ecuador is equivalent to 71 cents.

Conversion of coins.....................	$309,173 41
Less the putative profit in the account......	124,456 20
Less in reality..........................	$184,717 21

The nominal capital of the bank is displayed as..................................	$1,000,000 00
But the amount owed by the chief shareholders (*socios*).......................	300,000 00
The effective capital is really but..........	$700,000 00

On which the 15 per cent. dividend is computed. On the basis of this capital the bank contracts liabilities thus:

Notes in circulation......................	$2,040,773 00
Credits (foreign).........................	576,527 54
Credits in accounts, etc..................	187,882 99
Sundries................................	125,510 84
Total...................................	$2,930,694 37

—more than quadruple the amount of the capital.

The Yaguachi Railway is indebted to the amount of $7,130.61, and the enterprise, being a Government one, the indebtedness should be classed as a Government debt.

According to one of the Guayaquil journals, a loan or credit for £80,000 had been furnished the Government for this railway, on the responsibility of the bank. This sum does not appear in the foregoing balance-sheet, but may in part be hidden in the item *sundries*. If, however, it be nowhere in the statement, it is more than likely that, in the present state of depletion of Señor Garcia Moreno's treasury, it may be set down as an additional liability of the bank.

Among the following assets of the bank, some are justly regarded as of doubtful solidity:

The Government of Ecuador....	$247,589 90	
Loans to the Government.......	681,341 70	
The Government, for tithes.....	59,027 21	
Conversion of coins............	309,173 41	
Branch Bank of Quito..........	263,946 02	
Cuenca........	239,515 96	
Yaguachi Railway..............	7,130 61	
Sundries......................	459,252 90	$2,216,977 71
Which, deducted from the gross assets.....		4,134,114 11
Leaves..............................		$1,917,136 40

To meet the following liabilities:

Notes in circulation...........	$2,040,773 00	
Accounts-current.............	187,882 99	
Deposits on demand..........	31,108 19	
Credits......................	576,527 54	
Deposits on time.............	42,408 51	
Sundries....................	125,510 84	3,004,211 07
Deficit..............................		$1,087,074 67

The accounts above stated as due by the Quito and Cuenca branches of the bank may possibly be available, unless the operations of those branches with Señor Moreno's government have been proportionately extensive with those of the present bank at Guayaquil.

Of the assets enumerated in the preceding statement, the Government owes no less than $945,089.42, or nearly one-third more than the entire capital of the institution.

No words could be given that would throw more light upon the present financial situation of the Euadorian Republic than the hurried sketch here drawn of the chief, if not the only, public institution in the country.

The injurious effects of the unfortunate state of the finances were so visibly felt in commercial circles, that the mercantile community of

·Guayaquil addressed a petition on the subject to the Executive, on the 18th of July. The appeal met with an immediate response, the bank having at once exchanged its notes without any restriction whatever, and drawn bills at 40 per cent.

A Guayaquil paper, evidently echoing the public voice, presented the following complaint : " The monetary crisis, which, for some time back, has been assuming colossal proportions, has sunk the republic into a very painful condition; commerce is uncertain; public expenses are limited ; and social ruin is threatened."

The following decree relating to the national debt was sanctioned by the Congress about the beginning of 1874 :

ARTICLE 1. In future will belong to the inscribed debt : Notes issued by the offices of public credit, whatever the source of the obligation legitimizing the same; the amounts in arrears for salaries and pensions, whether civil, military, diplomatic, or financial, during the legitimate administrations of the republic, or recognized by the capitulation of the 26th of September, 1861 ; and the interests for loans decreed and exacted by the Government prior to 1869. Special paragraph : For the amortization of these credits it will be requisite to exchange the documents representing the same against notes of public credit.

ART. 2. The inscribed debt will be amortized (with distinction as to origin) with the product of the tax on the transfer of properties, as established by decree of February 29, 1869. Special paragraph : Dating from January 1, 1874, it will be paid in cash only, at the rate of 4 per cent., until the amortization referred to in the present law is effected. The rate will be reduced to 2 per cent. in cash from the first day of the year following the entire amortization.

ART. 3. Every six months the creditors included in the inscribed debt will be called together; the sum available for distribution among them will then be announced; and paid to those offering the best terms to the Treasury. No proposal exceeding 10 per cent. to be received.

ART. 4. ·This decree modifies the 1st and 2d Articles of the decree of February 20, 1869, and Articles 2 and 5 of the Law of Public Credit of June 15, 1861.

This decree was followed shortly after by another :

ARTICLE 1. Ten per cent. of the part of the Church revenue (diezmos) belonging to the state shall be remitted annually by the Executive to our Holy Father during the embarrassing circumstances with which he is now afflicted, and as an offer of justice, loyalty, and reverence, that the Ecuadorian people make to the head of the Church.

ART. 2. That the present decree shall be considered in force as from the beginning of the present year.

The President, in justification of the decree, adduced the following reasons : " That the Catholic population should contribute to the sustenance of the universal Government of the Church ; that this duty is more required at present, when our Holy Father finds himself despoiled by iniquitous usurpations of his lands and incomes, and when no Catholic Government should fear to comply ; and that the circumstances of the republic permit it to give in some manner a solemn testimonial of their adhesion to the Holy See."

The chief articles of export, with their value and the quantities thereof shipped in 1873, were as follows :

ARTICLES.	Quantity.	Value.
Cacao......................	25,181,203 lbs.	$3,021,744
India-rubber...............	1,636,543 "	654,617
Coffee.....................	729,522 "	182,385
Peruvian bark..............	1,113,632 "	389,768
Hats......................	254,000	178,678
Precious metals............	....	267,068
		$4,694,280
Equivalent in U. S. money.	....	$3,332,938 80

EGYPT, a country of Northeastern Africa, nominally a pashalik of the Turkish Empire, but virtually an independent state since 1811. The ruler of Egypt, who has the name of Khedive, is Ismail Pasha, born at Cairo in 1830, second son of Ibrahim, the son of Mehemet Ali, succeeded to the government at the death of his uncle, Saïd Pasha, January 18, 1863 ; heir-apparent is the eldest son of the Khedive, Mechmed Tefwick. The territories under the rule of the Khedive are estimated at 659,100 square miles; the Egyptian statistician De Regny (in his work, " Statistique de l'Egypte d'après des Documents officiels," vol. iv., 1873) claims 927,000 square miles. . Since then Sir Samuel Baker has proclaimed the annexation of a large portion of Central Africa, extending to the southward as far as the equator, to the dominions of the Khedive ; and Colonel Gordon, in 1874, has been sent there at the head of a new expedition, to confirm the Egyptian rule. In addition to these immense tracts of land, the entire kingdom of Darfour was, toward the close of the year 1874, incorporated with the dominions of the Khedive. If, as appears to be probable, the incorporation of these territories with Egypt should be permanent, the Khedive will rule over an empire extending over an area of at least 1,500,000 square miles, with a population of some 20,000,000. At all events it seems probable that Egypt will not only remain as it now is, the most prominent among the native states of Africa, but will become, ere long, one of the largest empires of the globe. The population of Egypt proper is given by Regny as 5,251,757 in 1872 ; that of the entire Egyptian Empire is estimated at about 8,700,000. The population of Egypt proper was in 1872 divided as follows :

DIVISIONS.	Natives.	Foreigners.	Total.
Cairo, and other sea-ports...............	569,047	74,216	643,263
Lower Egypt........	2,637,536	4,480	2,642,016
Middle Egypt........	604,774	1,000	1,966,478
Upper Egypt.........	1,360,704		
Total.........	5,172,061	79,696	5,251,757

The following table shows the strength of the several nationalities to which the foreign population in 1873 belonged :

Greeks..............	34,000	English..............	6,000
French..............	17,000	Germans.............	1,100
Italians.............	13,906	Other nationalities...	1,390
Americans..........	6,800		

The population of the large cities in 1872 was as follows: Cairo, 349,883 (19,120 foreigners); Alexandria, 212,054 (47,316 foreigners); Damietta, 29,383 (50 foreigners); Rosetta, 15,002 (10 foreigners); Suez, 13,498 (2,400 foreigners); Port Saïd, 8,671 (4,210 foreigners); Tanta, 60,000; Zagazig, 38,000 to 40,000; Syoot 27,470; Damanhoor, 25,000.

The public debt, in 1873, amounted to £44,204,000, of which £19,149,000 were consolidated, and £25,055,000 floating debt. The consolidated private debt of the Khedive was, in 1873, £8,910,000; and his floating debt was estimated by the *Economist* at £6,513,000. Early in 1874 the Khedive caused to be prepared a tabular statement of the receipts and expenditures of the last ten years. From a summary of this statement it appears that the revenues of Egypt steadily increased from £4,813,970 in 1864, to £10,571,048 in 1873 (an exceptional rise in 1872 having been consequent on a partial redemption of the land-tax), and that the proceeds of the loans raised during the entire term amounted to £26,949,000, making an aggregate of receipts in the ten years of £98,102,720. On the other hand, the expenditures during the period have been £112,561,784, leaving a deficiency in the shape of floating debt amounting to £14,359,064, which will have to be provided for out of the new loan lately issued, and which loan will cause the total debt of Egypt to stand at £49,000,000 in 7 per cent. stock, requiring annually for interest £3,430,000. Of the receipts during the ten years, sixteen millions sterling are stated to have been absorbed directly or indirectly in the Suez Canal; 900 miles of railway have cost nearly ten millions; two millions and a half have been devoted to improve the steam, postal, and commercial service; five millions have been paid to sufferers by the cattle-plague; and half a million has been the cost of the expedition of Sir Samuel Baker to the White Nile. The Egyptian Government in 1874 concluded to publish full particulars of the actual income in the last financial year, for which the accounts were closed, as well as other details of its financial condition. These particulars are set out in full accounts, which show with great minuteness the sources of the gross and net income from customs, the railway administration, etc., while the details as to the direct taxes specify the yield of each tax per province, as well as the varying yield per head or acre, according to the mode in which the tax is levied. The result is that Egypt, from being a country respecting whose financial position very little was published, already ranks among those which are best known. The general facts are that the revenue at present amounts in round numbers to nearly £10,000,000 annually, against an expenditure of rather less than £9,000,000, including in this latter sum all the interest and charge for the debt, of which a considerable portion is for the sinking-fund. The sources of

the revenue are such as to be susceptible of considerable increase. The customs and the railway administration yielded £600,000 and £878,000 respectively in 1872–'73—in both instances an advance upon the previous year; and while a further advance, it is understood, has also taken place in the current year, a large additional sum has been obtained from customs by a new duty on tobacco, estimated to return £500,000. The direct taxes, again, yielded £6,500,000 in 1872–'73, of which £5,500,000 were taxes upon land of various kinds. The cultivated land of Egypt extends to 4,715,000 acres, on which the Government taxes on the average thus amount to about 23s. per acre; the average gross produce being estimated at between £5 and £6 per acre. The tax or rent paid to the state is very moderate; in fact, about a third part of the lands is subject only to what are called tithes, and from this portion the yield is about one-third of the above average, so that they are very much under the maximum of what they could afford to pay. About £1,500,000 of the present land taxes—viz., the Moultabala—constitute a terminable charge, but this is set off by the constant diminution of the capital of the debt through the agency of the sinking-fund, while in a question of the real resources of a country the fact that a certain portion of the taxes which can be easily paid legally expires at a certain date does not show that any such loss of revenue need actually ensue. In addition, a quantity of new land is annually brought under cultivation, the increase being from 4,297,000 acres in 1863 to 4,712,000 acres in 1873, or nearly 10 per cent. Altogether the land revenue of Egypt, like the customs and railway receipts, is of a progressive character, and susceptible of considerable increase, so that the actual present surplus of revenue over current expenditure, great as it is, is no sufficient indication of the financial strength of the country.

The foreign commerce of the port of Alexandria during the period from 1863 to 1872 was, on an average, as follows:

COUNTRIES.	Imports.	Exports.
	Piasters.	Piasters.
Great Britain............	236,100,000	874,000,000
France...................	60,400,000	118,600,000
Austro-Hungarian Monarchy..	44,200,000	62,700,000
Turkey..................	72,100,000	17,000,000
Italy....................	33,600,000	33,900,000
Syria...................	32,900,000	10,000,000
Barbary.................	24,500,000	2,600,000
Belgium.................	3,700,000	1,900,000
Russia..................	1,300,000	3,700,000
United States...........	1,300,000	600,000
Other countries.........	13,900,000	2,300,000
Average, 1863–1872.....	514,000,000	1,127,300,000
Total, 1872.............	590,300,000	1,330,500,000
Total, 1871.............	560,900,000	999,500,000

The exports from Egypt during the years 1853–1872 were as follows, according to official statements (1 piaster = 5 cents):

Year.	Piasters.	Year.	Piasters.
1853	191,000,000	1863	865,000,000
1854	187,000,000	1864	1,404,000,000
1855	275,000,000	1865	1,317,000,000
1856	330,000,000	1866	1,052,000,000
1857	237,000,000	1867	1,003,000,000
1858	208,000,000	1868	1,059,000,000
1859	215,000,000	1869	1,623,000,000
1860	212,000,000	1870	1,028,000,000
1861	291,000,000	1871	1,201,000,000
1862	506,000,000	1872	1,472,000,000

The following table shows the movement of shipping, in the principal ports, in 1872:

ENTERED IN	Mail-Steamers	Steamers	Sailing-vessels	TOTAL. Vessels.	TOTAL. Tons.	War-vessels.
Alexandria	516	366	2,023	2,905	1,238,000	48
Port Said	270	512	596	1,378	856,800	65
Suez	189	400	205	794	666,470	64

The commercial navy, in 1872, consisted of 555 sailing-vessels, of 30,909 tons, and 30 steamers, of 28,965 tons; in all, 585 vessels, of 59,-874 tons.

The commerce of Egypt continues to derive great advantages from the construction of the Suez Canal, connecting the Mediterranean with the Red Sea, opened for navigation November 17, 1869. The total expenditures for the construction of the canal and the first arrangements amounted, up to the close of the year 1873, to 458,400,065 francs. The value of the buildings and the inventory belonging to the company was estimated at 21,473,474 francs. The income of the company was, in 1871, 13,-276,000 francs; in 1872, 18,325,000; in 1873, 24,831,127. The expenditures were, in 1871, 15,918,000 francs; in 1872, 16,253,000; in 1873, 17,346,109. Surplus in 1872 (the first year which showed a surplus), 2,071,279 francs; in 1873, 7,485,077. The number of vessels passing through the canal from 1870 to 1873 was as follows:

YEAR.	Vessels.	Tons.
1870	486	435,911
1871	765	701,467
1872	1,082	1,439,169
1873	1,173	2,085,073

The following table exhibits the nationality, number, and tonnage of the vessels passing through the Suez Canal in the year 1873:

NATIONALITIES.	Vessels.	Tonnage.
English	813	1,499,792
French	83	221,811
Austro-Hungarian	70	90,967
Netherlandish	36	72,593
Italian	98	59,121
German	28	35,619
Spanish	17	31,299
Turkish	26	20,116
Russian	9	14,361
Norwegian	5	9,299
Belgian	4	6,912
Others	24	20,971

The strength of the Egyptian army, which is raised by conscription, is about 14,000 men, consisting of 8,000 infantry, 3,000 cavalry, artillery, and engineers, and 3,000 negro troops. In 1873 the aggregate length of the railways

which were in operation was 1,193 kilometres (1 kilometre = 0.62 English miles). The telegraph-lines had an aggregate length of 6,480 kilometres, the telegraph-wires of 13,750.

A new railroad to the Soudan has been projected, and is to be built by the engineer John Fowler. Its length is to be about 880 kilometres; it is to be completed within five years, and to cost £1,400,000. About one-half of the expense is to be paid by the revenue derived from the Soudan territory.

Education in Egypt is still backward and limited. The number of those attending primary schools in 1873 was 90,000 (of whom only 3,018 were girls), which, in a population of 5,250,000, represents a proportion of 17 per 1,000, a proportion smaller than in any European country except Russia. The prejudices, difficult to overcome, existing among the Mohammedans as to the education of females, are a great obstacle to the progress of general education. In giving, therefore, a proportional estimate of the number educated, it is fair only to reckon the male population. This would give a proportion of at least 34 per 1,000 who attend school; and though the education given may not be of a high class, nor the previous training and qualification of the teachers up to the European standard, yet the fact that of the whole number only 8,000 are educated at the sole cost of Government, the cost of the others being wholly borne by the parents, without the inducement of food or clothing, shows that there is no unwillingness to benefit by such education as is within their reach. The Khedive is attempting to combat the prejudice regarding female education, and has established a large girls' school at Cairo, where, besides an elementary education, sewing, washing, and dress-making, are taught.

The Khedive has offered the people of Syria generally to receive twenty-five students, irrespective of race or religion, into the Egyptian Medical College, to be educated gratuitously in medical science for the benefit of their native places. Crowds of candidates have offered themselves, some of whom have been admitted, and the remainder directed to stand over till the college should receive them. "We had hoped," writes the editor of the al Jawaib, "that some of our Moslem brethren would have availed themselves of the opportunity thus offered to send their sons to this college, but we have been sadly disappointed, for all the candidates were Christians. Does it not occur to the Moslems to remember the apostolical tradition: 'Strive to acquire knowledge, even though you may have to go to China seeking it?'"

Immediately after the return of Sir Samuel Baker from the expedition into the interior of Africa, a new expedition was planned by the Khedive. It started early in March, in 1874, under command of Colonel Gordon. As the mission was intended to be of a pacific character, and the design of further conquest was disavowed, Colonel Gordon took with him only a small escort, but the governor of Khartoum was ordered to support him if called upon. His artillery force consisted of one mitrailleur, as being more portable than any field-gun. He was accompanied by two young Englishmen, J. Russell, son of Dr. William H. Russell, the well-known correspondent of the London *Times*, and Mr. Anson, son of the English admiral and a relative of Colonel Gordon. The immediate object of the new expedition was believed to be not so much the suppression of the slave-trade, which would be an impossible task in the present condition of the interior, as to obtain a more complete knowledge of that immense territory which may be designated as the district of the head-waters of the Nile. The opening up of this country, the utilization of its resources, and commercial union with or annexation to Egypt, are the grand objects in view, in the carrying out of which the Khedive is more inclined toward conciliatory measures than arbitrary force, and trusts to judicious management rather than to the sword. The disappearance of the slave-trade will be a natural consequence of the enterprise if successful, for, as the country becomes better known, and is brought into more direct communication with the civilized world, so, in a like measure, will the pursuit of the slave-hunter grow more and more precarious, until eventually, when the whole length of the Nile is the scene of busy traffic,' it will die away altogether. Colonel Gordon, accompanied by his chief-of-staff, Colonel Long, an American, Lieutenant Hazzan Effendi Wafti, both of the Egyptian army, and a small party —in all less than a score of persons—left Cairo by special train for Suez, whence he embarked on board a private Government steamer for Suakim, at which point he entered Africa and pushed across the Suakim Desert to Khartoum, where he organized his forces and awaited the arrival of the luggage, stores, and ammunition, which left Cairo a few days later in charge of Mr. W. J. Kemp, an English engineer. Including the persons named, the expedition under command of Colonel Gordon consisted of one American and three Egyptian officers, two English engineers, three interpreters, a native doctor for the soldiers, and 250 Egyptian soldiers. The aim of Colonel Gordon was to launch, on the lake Albert N'yanza, one or more of the steamers which were brought up for the purpose by Sir S. Baker, but left by him in the neighborhood of Gondokoro, where they have remained ever since. It was feared they would be found to have suffered considerably from the effects of damp and of marauding natives—more particularly as they were lying in detached pieces at different points of the route—and that much time and trouble would have to be expended to render them again fit for the work for which they were designed. The bulk of the men constituting the expedition, as well as stores,

were sent in advance to Gondokoro. In July, Mr. Anson, one of the two young Englishmen accompanying Colonel Gordon, succumbed to the murderous climate. According to reports received by the Egyptian Government in the month of September, Colonel Gordon was then engaged in gaining a firm footing at the mouth of the Sobat, and in securing the control of the navigation on the Sobat, Bahr-el-Gebel, and Bahr-el-Ghasal. The Egyptian Government prepared to send to Colonel Gordon a number of boats made in sections, and to be transported in cases on camels, for the exploration of the lakes Albert N'yanza and Victoria N'yanza, and the final solution of the problem as to the sources of the Nile. The trial of the first of these boats was made in September, at Kasr o' Nil Palace, in presence of the Khedive and a numerous attendance of ministers and officials. This little vessel is made of teak, and consists of sixty-four pieces; she is constructed to be packed in four cases. The boat was constructed in Alexandria, under the direction of Captain McKillop, R. N., who, together with Colonel Gordon's agent, Mr. Curzon Thompson, sailed the little craft across the Nile. The Khedive was much pleased with the result, for this boat was designed entirely by himself, and is an evidence of the deep interest he takes in the Gordon expedition. Some larger boats, built on the same principle, are to follow, one of them a steamer. The little craft, after her trial, was taken to pieces and repacked in her cases (which can be formed into a useful pontoon). The Egyptian Government expects that certain positions through which all trading parties to the interior are obliged to pass will be secured by Colonel Gordon, and that, as the sale of arms and ammunition is forbidden under penalty of death, and none can trade or hunt elephants without a Government license, a very short time may give the Egyptian authorities perfect control in those regions.

The most important event in the history of Egypt during the year 1874 was the war against the Sultan of Darfour, which resulted in the annexation of another large country to the dominions of the Khedive. A full account of the origin of this conflict between the two countries, giving also interesting information on the Sultan and the people of Darfur, is contained in a letter from the celebrated traveler Dr. Nachtigal to Prof. Bastian of Berlin, dated El Obeid, in Kordofan, August 20, 1874.* Dr. Nachtigal had just arrived at El Obeid after his visit to Darfour. The ruler of this country, Sultan Brahim, had been prepared for his arrival in Darfour by letters from Khartoum, which the Egyptian Government had sent at the request of the German consul-general in Alexandria. The Sultan received Dr. Nachtigal kindly, but denied to him the permission to travel in the country, on the ground that the

* Published in Verhandlungen der Gesellschaft für Erdkunde zu Berlin, 1874, No. 8.

inhabitants hated the foreigners, Christians and Turks. During a longer stay in the town of Fasher, Dr. Nachtigal found that the fear of the Sultan was well founded. In none of the many African countries which he had visited had he to suffer so much from the fanaticism of the inhabitants as in Darfour, and even in the very house of the Sultan he was not safe from it. Their hostility to all foreigners, kindled by their religious fanaticism, had become still more intense by the fear of an imminent invasion of their country by the Turks. Many occurrences in the districts south of their country justified this fear. There a certain Zabir had established his rule, and, though he still respected the frontier of Darfour, had subjected or plundered the dependent districts of the Arabic Rézegat and the pagan districts of Telkauna, Kutuváka, Hofva-t-m-nehas, Shale, and Bina. Zabir is a Djalee by descent, and a man of considerable learning, who several years ago had left Khartoum, where he was employed as a clerk, in order to associate with the Bakara in the slave-trade. He entered the services of Ali Abu Omori, and subsequently worked for his own account in the vicinity of the Bahr-el-Ghasal, gathering, in the course of time, a large number of fire-arms, and gradually extending the sphere of his activity. In the same territory, another adventurer soon established himself, called the Bulaláwi Mohammed, who was a native of the tribe of the Abu Simmim, the original inhabitants of the Fittri, and also had lived for some time in Egypt. The Bulaláwi Mohammed had insinuated to the Egyptian authorities in Cairo and Khartoum that he was able to conquer the states of the eastern Soudan, between the Nile and the Tsade Lake, and to incorporate them with Egypt. He had consequently received from the Egyptian Government soldiers, arms, ammunition, and money, and it was generally known that he was in the service of Egypt. As the country between the southern frontier of Darfour and the Bahr-el-Ghasal was soon utterly exhausted, a conflict between the two rival adventurers became inevitable. In this conflict the Bulaláwi Mohammed succumbed and was killed. This happened in 1872. The Egyptian Government, which regarded the Bulaláwi Mohammed as being in its employ, desired to punish Zabir, but could not reach him, as he was too far away from Kordofan. Zabir, in his turn, endeavored to conciliate the Egyptian Government by refunding to it the expenses incurred in fitting out the expedition of the Bulaláwi Mohammed, and by giving to it an account of the conflict, which was intended to show its true origin, the absurd character of the plans of his rival, and the utter incompetency of the latter to carry out his plans. He also asserted that he was willing to carry out the plans of the Bulaláwi, so far as they were practicable, if he were placed at the head of the expedition. It seems that at the time it was only promised to incorporate with Egypt the districts south of Dar-

four; but it is probable that the raising of complications with the Government of Darfour and the annexation of the entire country were already taken into consideration. Zabir also engaged to support the troops confided to him by the Egyptian Government at his own expense, while the latter Government would engage to furnish to him every thing necessary at cost price. Zabir continued, after the death of the Bulaláwi, to cultivate the friendship of the Rézegat Arabs, through whose territory he received men and arms from Kordofan, and exported slaves and elephants' teeth. The tribe of Rézegat Arabs had been for several years under the rule of Darfour, and during the reign of the late King, Mohammed-el-Hassim, they had almost been annihilated. With Zabir they had for some time lived in peace; but, instigated by Darfour, they suddenly became treacherous, and toward the close of 1873 they plundered, at Shegga, a caravan belonging to Zabir, murdering nearly all the persons belonging to it. This act of treachery was soon followed by condign punishment. Zabir surprised Shegga, established there his headquarters, and subjected the greater part of the Arab tribe to his rule. He offered to Egypt the establishment of a new Egyptian mudirate (province) of Shegga, was appointed colonel and mudir, and now received openly the command of Egyptian soldiers. To the Sultan of Darfour he wrote that he had punished the Rézegat for their treason, but had no intention to attack Darfour proper. At the same time he established a military post at Kálaka, a centre of the Habbania, another Arab tribe living west of the Rézegat and subjected to Darfour. If at this time the young King had applied at Cairo or Constantinople for peace, he might have been successful. He preferred, however, to lead an army against Zabir, under command of his vizier, Ahmed Shetta. A lieutenant of Zabir was defeated by Ahmed Shetta; but, three days later, Zabir obtained a complete victory, Ahmed Shetta even losing his life. The Sultan suspected that the Egyptian Government was backing Zabir, and sent an embassador to Cairo to treat for peace.

While on his way from Darfour to El Obeid, in Kordofan, Dr. Nachtigal learned that the Governor-General of the Egyptian Soudan staid at El Obeid, and was on the point of going to Shegga for the purpose of inspecting the new mudirate. When he arrived, however, at El Obeid, he found the Governor-General ready to march at the head of an army against Darfour. His army was but small, numbering about 1,500 men, of whom 1,000 were infantry and 500 cavalry, and three guns; 500 other cavalry troops were expected from Khartoum. Zabir had under his command 8,000 men, with six cannon, and in July had informed the Egyptian authorities that he did not need any more men or cannon, but believed himself strong enough to defeat the Darfourians, and that he was on the point of marching upon Dara, which is situated from four to five days' journey northwest of Shegga. The Governor-General of Soudan left El Obeid on August 17th, and expected to establish his headquarters in the beginning of September at Omshanga, the chief place of the extreme east of Darfour, situated about six days' journey north-northeast of Shegga, and about seven days east of Fasher. The accounts of the progress of the expedition given in the Egyptian papers slightly differ from the above report, and supplement it in some details. The Egyptian reports state that the hostile attitude assumed by the Darfourians toward the Government of the Khedive, the exactions practised by the Sultan of Darfour on Egyptian subjects, and also his tyranny over his own subjects, had long been a subject of annoyance to the Egyptians. Moreover, Zabir Beg, the mudir over the whole district of the Bahr-el-Ghasal, wrote a letter to Ba-Bakr, his brother-in-law, informing him that the Sultan Ibrahim of Darfour, having collected together an army of 12,000, with horses, fire-arms, and all appliances of war, had placed it under the command of a sultan named Abuna, who had marched to a spot called El Kúlaka, the principal station of the Egyptian troops, with the design of attacking them. The threatened attack was made on July 2d by a fierce onset on the part of the Darfourians, the Egyptians standing fast to receive them. The battle soon waxed hot; but the order, discipline, and steadiness of the latter soon told to their advantage, for in less than an hour their antagonists were vanquished and put to flight. The Sultan Abuna was slain, and his sons and a number of his nobles were taken prisoners. One hundred and ten other prisoners were made, some of whom are officers. Among the spoil captured was the horse on which the Sultan rode, his arms and dress, which were forwarded to Egypt. When the Sultan Ibrahim, the sovereign of Darfour, heard of this defeat, and the death of his commander, Abuna, he was greatly chagrined, and went about collecting together his nobles, and collecting another army of 50,000 men and horse, which he divided into 50 troops of 1,000 each, and placed it under the command of a renowned general. After supplying them with 65 banners, and distributing muskets and ammunition among them, he ordered that they should fall upon the Egyptian troops in a body. They did so, but were doomed to a disastrous defeat, for the Egyptians again routed the wretched Berbers, capturing 25 flags, 500 muskets, 600 Arab slaves, besides horses and war-material. On hearing of this second repulse, the Sultan of Darfour began levying the remainder of the troops, intending to take the command in person. A telegram, dated Cairo, December 11th, from the Governor-General of the Soudan, announced that the entire kingdom of Darfour accepted annexation to Egypt. The only dissentients were the family of the ex-Sultan, who had fled to the mountains and

proclaimed the Emir Hassaballah as Sultan. The Egyptian troops were pursuing the fugitives. The annexation of Darfour to Egypt will cut off one main source of the slave-trade; for, Darfour being close to Wadai, which is one great slave-preserve, its people are the greatest slave-dealers in Central Africa, many of their caravans even making their way across the Sahara, through Fezzan to Tripoli, Bengazi, and the ports on the Mediterranean, and so *via* Malta—it is said—or along the African coast to the different slave-markets. The routes followed by the caravans pass through the oases of the Libyan Desert. Many routes are known only to the Bedouins, but every now and then a party falls into the hands of the Egyptian authorities. It is, however, almost impossible thoroughly to watch the long Nile frontier and prevent slaves from being smuggled into the country. On this subject an Egyptian journal says: "It is indisputable that, if annexed to Egypt, Darfour will become one of the most prosperous and flourishing of countries, for the Khedive will introduce into it colleges and schools, and railroads and telegraphs, arts, science, and commerce, and will rule over it with kindliness, justice, and good-will, so that in the course of a few years it will acquire a high name among states, and become a great field for European commercial enterprise."

The extraordinary rising of the Nile in 1874 created a profound sensation and panic in Egypt, but owing to the personal energy and perseverance of, and the wise precautions taken by, his Highness the Khedive, a great national calamity was averted. Though the commencement of the rising of the Nile is anxiously looked forward to by the Egyptians, as begetting hope of good crops and abundance, yet it is not by any means a criterion of a good Nile, which alone can realize that hope. Thus the Nile of 1873 commenced to rise as early as the 17th of June, and rose fairly well for about twenty days, and then stopped for fifteen days, and ultimately finished off at a rise of 19¾ feet only on the 11th of September, and made a bad Nile. Again, the Nile is subject to make false starts—the Nile of 1869 made five such false starts, and that of 1872 three, both commencing their serious rise on the 1st of July respectively. To show the uncertain and capricious nature of the Nile at the commencement of the rise, that of 1868 commenced on the 1st of July; 1869, on the 10th of June; 1870, on the 30th of June; 1871, on the 7th of July; 1872, on the 15th of June; 1873, on the 17th of June; 1874, on the 15th of June; or between the earliest and latest days a period of twenty-seven days. On the 27th of July, 1874, a very high Nile was foreshadowed; at that date the rise was double that of 1868, nearly one-third more than that of 1873, and in excess of that of 1869, when the Nile rose 29 feet 2½ inches in the Rosetta branch of the Nile, in about the middle of the Delta. It was fortunate that the Khedive this year remained in Egypt during the summer. The danger was seen, and the Khedive immediately undertook the responsibility and directed the works. Every available boat and steamer was at once pressed into service on the Nile ; 200,000 kantars of stones were ordered to be quarried forthwith and sent to various places; while the railway and other boats brought poles and timber from Alexandria. The officers of the army, mounted, kept guard on the banks night and day, in addition to the ordinary watchmen at every hundred yards; and it may safely be stated that eight-tenths of the whole male population of Egypt have been employed for three months watching and strengthening the banks of the Nile, which had been raised in many places from six feet to ten feet, and proportionately thickened and strengthened with the poles at the bends of the river, where the momentum was great, by stones being thrown in, and by being faced with stones where they exhibited any signs of weakness. Boats and large barges were kept ready filled with stones for instant use. About noon one day the Nile was seen to have worked its way through the base of the bank—probably followed the tree-roots which were growing there; in one minute 5,000 men were on the spot, like wasps, basketing earth, and in five minutes ten boatloads of stones were alongside, and in two hours all danger was over. Had the water found its way through in the middle of the night instead of the middle of the day, and a breach been made, no human power could have saved the district between there and the sea, with the Nile 12 feet, 15 feet, and in some places 20 feet, above the adjacent ground, and with a force or fluid pressure of 100 pounds per square foot at the surface of the river. When all danger was over, the attention to the banks was not withdrawn for ten or fifteen days, as they were highly saturated, and had been subject to the force and saturation of the current of a full Nile for forty days. The Nile of 1868 attained its maximum height of 19 feet on the 28th of August; 1869, 29 feet 2¼ inches, 14th of October; 1870, 25 feet 6 inches, 14th of October; 1871, 23 feet 9 inches, 28th of September; 1872, 25 feet 4 inches, 22d of October; 1873, 19 feet 9 inches, 11th of September; 1874, 29 feet, 7th of October.

In August, great consternation arose throughout Egypt in consequence of plague having broken out at Leet, and other places near Jeddah, brought on, as was reported, by water used for domestic purposes being allowed to filter through an old burial-ground. Quarantine of twenty-one days was imposed at Suez upon all vessels touching at any of the Arabian ports, including Aden and also El Wedgi, where vessels were sent instead of being allowed to remain out their time at Suez, and whither a considerable quarantine force was dispatched. Orders were issued forbidding

any ships belonging to the Egyptian Government to call at Jeddah, or any of the neighboring ports, and trade between them and ports on the Egyptian side was temporarily suspended. Thanks to the stringent measures promptly taken by the Egyptian Government, this threatening danger was averted.

At the beginning of December two expeditions, each consisting of eight European and twelve Egyptian officers and sixty-three soldiers, were sent out by the Government to the Soudan. They were instructed to explore the country between the Nile and Kordofan and Darfour, and the country south of the equator and west of the Albert N'yanza.

On December 8th, the European residents of Alexandria sent a delegation to Cairo to present to the Khedive an address, in which he was thanked for having averted the overflowing of the Nile and thus prevented a terrible misfortune. In remembrance of this important event the Europeans of Alexandria were desirous to erect a monument to the Khedive, and had already collected for the purpose £13,000. In his reply to the address the Khedive referred to the war against Darfour, which country, containing a population of about 5,000,000, had now been incorporated with Egypt, and would, within five or six years, be connected with Egypt by a railroad. He declined the erection of a monument, but preferred to devote the moneys raised for the monument to the establishment of a school open to all creeds and nationalities.

The long preparations for the establishment of new international tribunals were not yet quite finished at the close of the year 1874. The new courts will be presided over by foreigners, and foreigners will constitute a majority of the judges, numbering four out of seven in the Court of Original Jurisdiction, and five out of eight in the Appellate Court. The judges will be irremovable, and will be chosen by the European Governments, unless the latter remit the appointment to the Egyptian Government. These tribunals will decide all cases in which one or both parties are foreigners. International will thus be substituted for consular jurisdiction. As to penal proceedings, France has insisted on the privileges conferred by treaties, and has simply agreed to modify their application. All crimes, except those directed against the tribunals themselves or connected with the execution of their sentences, will continue under the jurisdiction of their respective consuls. The new tribunals will have authority to issue declarations of bankruptcy, but these will not affect the civil status of the bankrupts like declarations issued in their own country.

Nubar Pasha in March notified the foreign consuls that, in consequence of the completion of the breakwater outside of Alexandria harbor, dues at the rate of fourpence per Turkish ton will be levied on all vessels with cargoes entering or leaving the port of Alexandria after the 1st of June. Vessels in ballast will have to pay twopence per ton. War-vessels will be exempt.

ELLIOTT, Rev. DAVID, D. D., LL. D., a Presbyterian clergyman, college president, and theological professor, born in Sherman's Valley, Perry County, Pa., February 6, 1787; died at Allegheny City, Pa., March 18, 1874. He was of Scotch-Irish parentage, and after receiving such advantages as the village schools afforded, he was sent in his fourteenth year to Mifflin County, where he fitted for college under the tuition of Rev. Messrs. Coulter, Russell, and Brown. He entered Dickinson College in the Junior Class, and graduated in 1808; studied theology for three years, was a home missionary for one year, and was settled at what is now Mercersburg, Pa., where he remained for eighteen years, when he was called to Washington, Pa., as pastor, and was also for nearly two years President of Washington College. In 1835 he was called to the professorship of Ecclesiastical History and Church Government in the Western Theological Seminary at Allegheny, Pa. He declined, but the following year, at the urgent solicitation of the directors, he accepted the chair of Systematic Theology in the seminary. He held this position for nearly thirty-five years, and retired in 1870 as Professor Emeritus. He received the degree of D. D. in 1835 from Jefferson College, and that of LL. D. from Washington College in 1847. In 1837, the year of the disruption, he was Moderator of the Presbyterian General Assembly, which divided that year, but lived to see and rejoice in the reunion of 1870–'71, and took part in the exercises of the occasion.

ESPARTERO, Don JOAQUIN BALDOMERO, Duke of Vittoria, Marshal, Grandee of Spain, Senator, and from 1841 to 1843 Regent of Spain, a Spanish soldier and statesman, born at Granatula in La Mancha, in 1792; reported as having died at Logroño, December 21, 1874. He was of humble origin, his father being a poor cartwright, with nine children, of whom Joaquin was the youngest and feeblest, and hence was intended, in accordance with the Spanish proverb, for the priesthood, and in 1806 went with this object to the University of Almagro; but two years later, when the French invaded Spain, he entered the corps of students called the Sacred Battalion, and acquired a knowledge of the art of war. Continuing in the military service, though unable to pass the examination for the corps of engineers, into which he desired to enter, he received a commission in the infantry, and rose rapidly. He went to South America in 1814, where he fought against the insurgents until the Spaniards were expelled in 1824, when he returned to his native land, in company with Narvaez, Maroto, Alaix, Laserna, and others, all of them destined afterward to take a prominent part in Spanish politics. He brought home a considerable fortune, and soon after married a lady of wealth at Logroño. He was

stationed for seven years with his regiment on the island of Majorca, but in 1832 declared himself openly in favor of the succession of Isabella II., daughter of Ferdinand VII., and played a leading part in the hostilities which followed the King's death. In August, 1836, he succeeded in saving the city of Madrid from the Carlists, and became successively general-in-chief of the Army of the North, Viceroy of Navarre, and Captain-General of the Basque Provinces. When the army of Don Carlos appeared before Madrid on the 12th of September, 1837, Espartero had again the glory of saving the capital. His successful campaign of 1839 resulted in the expulsion of Don Carlos, and won for him the titles of Grandee of Spain and Duke of Vittoria. In 1840 the Queen-mother Christina was compelled to resign her office of Regent, and on the 8th of May, 1841, Espartero was appointed to supply her place until Queen Isabella should have reached her majority. Espartero governed the country with energy, firmness, and ability, but in 1843 a combination of the Republican and Moderados parties brought about his overthrow. His rival, General Narvaez, came into power, and he retired to England, where he resided for four years, Narvaez having caused him to be declared as a traitor and deprived of all his titles and dignities. In 1848, this decree having been annulled and his rights restored, he returned to Spain, and for a short time resumed his place in the Senate, but soon withdrew and lived quietly at Logroño till 1854, when dissatisfaction with the court caused an insurrection of the people, resulting in the expulsion of the Queen-mother from Spain. In this emergency Espartero was called to the head of the Government and conducted the affairs of the nation for two years. In 1856 he was supplanted by General O'Donnell, and since then had taken no part in political agitation, although it has often been suggested that his services were needed at times in the eventful period which has since elapsed. In 1857 he resigned his dignity as Senator. At the revolution of 1868 General Espartero gave his hearty adhesion to the provisional government, although he took no active part in the events of the period. In May, 1869, during the debates on the policy of reëstablishing the monarchical form of government, Señor Garido, one of the deputies, suggested that Espartero should be chosen King of Spain, but this proposal found no echo from the Cortes. In the subsequent changes he gave King Amadeus a passive support, and regarded the administration of Marshal Serrano with a moderate degree of favor. Though, like all the Spanish leaders, Espartero was found at some times supporting and at others opposing the Queen and Queen-mother, it must be admitted that his career was one of more honesty, integrity, and patriotism, than that of any of his rivals or compeers. He seems to have sought always, though perhaps not in all cases by the most judicious meas-

.ures, what he believed to be for the best interests of Spain.

EUROPE. A remarkable feature of the history of Europe during the year 1874 is the absence of grave international complications. The political horizon was hardly darkened by any war-cloud, and wherever one appeared to rise it was speedily dispersed. The commanding influence which the new German Empire has obtained in the international relations of the European states has thus far been of a decidedly peaceable character, and has manifestly tended to strengthen the basis of a lasting peace. The Parliaments paid but little attention to international questions, which were, on the contrary, more than in former years, attended to by the cabinets. The rapid progress of railroads and telegraphs in every country of Europe greatly strengthens the commercial relations of the several nations, and the more universal study of foreign languages and the better knowledge of foreign literatures more and more produce the feeling of a brotherhood of nations. The international congresses for literary, sanitary, humanitarian, and commercial purposes, are increasing every year, both in numbers and importance, and begin to take a very prominent place in the history of civilization.

One of the most important international congresses of the year met at Brussels, in pursuance of an invitation from the Russian Government, and had for its object the mitigation of the horrors of war by a revision of the general rules and customs of war. It was generally admitted and agreed upon that the legitimate aim of war was only the weakening of the enemy; that no unnecessary sufferings should be imposed upon the population of the hostile country, and that the war should be limited within as narrow boundaries as possible. At the close of the year the resolutions passed by the congress had not received the sanction of the several governments, but intimation had already been given that a new conference would be called to complete the work of that held at Brussels. A considerable reluctance to take part in the work of this congress was shown by England, which feared for its ascendency at sea in case the negotiations should be extended to naval warfare. It did not send its representatives until it had received assurances that the negotiations should be limited to land operations, and when the congress had completed its labor the representatives of England did not sign the protocol. (*See* BELGIUM.)

An international postal congress, which met at Bern in compliance with an invitation from the Prussian Government, called into life a postal convention embracing a large portion of the globe. The congress was attended by the representatives of nineteen states, and the convention as proposed by the congress was adhered to by all the states of Europe except France, which made it dependent upon its ratification by the National Assembly, by

Egypt, and the United States of America. The international postal association is to last for three years, and every third year a new international congress is to meet to revise and develop the terms of the convention. The chief object of the convention is to introduce a uniform postage for all mailable matter. (*See* SWITZERLAND.)

The attention of the governments and the people of Germany was chiefly directed to a consolidation of the new empire. The greatest obstacle to the rapid progress of the work of consolidation must be found in the continuing conflict between the governments of Prussia and other German states and the Roman Catholic Church. The determined refusal of the Prussian bishops to submit to the new laws concerning Church affairs led to the arrest of several of them, but at the close of the year neither the bishops nor the governments showed the least inclination to recede from the position taken. The extraordinary excitement which the continuance of this conflict produced in the Catholic districts led to an attempt upon the life of Prince Bismarck by Kullmann, a young Catholic mechanic. The deed was promptly and energetically denounced by all organs of the German Catholics, but widened the breach already dividing the Catholics from the remainder of the population. The German Reichstag, in which the National Liberals had a large plurality, lacking only a few votes of an absolute majority, vigorously supported most of the bills introduced by the Imperial Government for promoting the consolidation of the empire. A determined opposition was, however, made by the majority of the Reichstag to the army and press laws proposed by the Government; but in either case, the ministerial crisis produced by the clash of opinion was soon ended by a compromise. Prince Bismarck continued to direct the affairs of the empire, supported by the confidence of the Emperor and the majority of the Reichstag, and one of his foremost opponents, Count Arnim, who was German ambassador in France, had dared to disobey the instructions of the imperial chancellor, to counteract his policy, and to take official documents from the archives of the embassy, was promptly brought to trial and sentenced to three months' imprisonment. In Alsace-Lorraine the opposition to a permanent union with Germany remained unsubdued, and the majority of the delegates whom the new Reichsland had elected for the German Parliament returned home after having entered their protest against the reunion with Germany. The Imperial Government feels, however, confident that the reorganization of the public schools, and the obvious advantages of the commercial union of the Reichsland with the other German states, will ere long overcome all opposition. The confidence of the Imperial Government in the final reconciliation of the population of Alsace-Lorraine is so great that it complied with the petition of the three district diets of the Reichsland for the establishment of a provincial committee, which in future will be consulted in all questions relating to the administration of the country. (*See* GERMANY.)

The adoption of the new Federal Constitution in Switzerland by the requisite majority of the cantons and of the people, marks a turning-point in the history of the oldest European republic. The new constitution greatly strengthens the jurisdiction of the Federal authorities, especially in all questions relating to the Church and schools. The legislation concerning the Catholic Church continued to be much more stringent than in Germany, and in several cantons the utmost efforts were made by the cantonal governments to put the administration of all the Catholic congregations in the hands of Old Catholics. The new laws required for the execution of the Federal Constitution were, at the close of the year, in the course of preparation. (*See* SWITZERLAND.)

In Austria, the new electoral law has as yet not produced the results which the Liberal party expected from it. The difficulties arising from the nationality conflict and the financial distress of the country continued, and the Reichstag is divided into so many small parties warring against each other that it proved unable to carry any measure against the ministry. The latter continued, in all questions relating to Church matters, to waver between the two parties, not gaining the entire confidence of either. Hungary has the same difficulties to surmount as Cisleithan Austria, and its Diet was even more powerless than that of the other half of the monarchy. (*See* AUSTRIA and HUNGARY.)

The relations between Turkey and Austria, which were formerly of the most friendly character, were greatly changed in 1874. The Sublime Porte suspected the Austrian Government of encouraging the struggle of Roumania and Servia for independence, with a view to the annexation of Bosnia and Herzegovina to the Austrian dominions. It therefore opposed the conclusion of a commercial convention between Austria and the Danubian Principalities, but had finally to abandon its opposition, as Russia and Germany took sides with Austria. The financial embarrassments of Turkey have at length prevailed upon the Government to establish a great banking institition, with the aid of which extensive reforms are to be introduced. For the present, however, the country is at the mercy of the foreign bankers, and a radical improvement cannot be expected until the absolute form of government shall be abolished. (*See* TURKEY.)

The Government of Russia, which is growing in extent with marvelous rapidity, is chiefly intent upon consolidating all the discordant nationalities of the empire into an homogeneous population. It makes, therefore, extraordinary efforts to improve the system of public instruction and to force upon all the use of the Russian language. It finds, moreover, that the

difficulties in the way of carrying through this plan are much greater than had been imagined, and are for the present insurmountable. There are many indications that all the branches of administration are utterly corrupt, and the frequent conspiracies, in which sometimes persons of the highest rank are involved, are therefore all the more dangerous. (*See* RUSSIA.)

The financial condition of France has greatly improved in consequence of an excellent harvest and the revival of commerce, but the political future of the country is as uncertain as ever. At the supplementary elections held in several departments, the Republicans gained a number of new seats, but nothing as yet indicates that the majority of the French people really wants the permanent establishment of the republic. Among the monarchical parties, the Bonapartists are steadily gaining ground. The foreign relations of France were of a thoroughly peaceable nature as far as Germany is concerned; this was officially recognized by the German Government, while the withdrawal of a French man-of-war from Civita Vecchia, where it had been stationed for the protection of the Pope, greatly improved the relations with Italy. Only Spain had repeatedly to complain of the indirect encouragement which the French Government afforded to the Carlists, and it needed the support of the Spanish remonstrances by Germany to put an end to the partiality of the French for the Carlists. (*See* FRANCE.)

At the beginning of the year 1874 the administration of the honest Castelar was overthrown by a conspiracy of generals, who were believed to plan a restoration of the monarchy. The authors of this *coup d'état* placed Marshal Serrano at the head of a new ministry, whose attention throughout the year was absorbed by the war against the Carlists, who, favored by several governments of Europe, made at times considerable progress, and seriously endangered the existing Government. In the last days of December, the preparations for the restoration of the Bourbons had been completed, and the son of Queen Isabella was proclaimed King of Spain, under the name of Alfonso XII. (*See* SPAIN.)

In Italy, a new Parliament was elected, the second since the completion of Italian unity. The majority of the new Parliament belonged, like the ministry, to the moderate Liberals, but the opposition, consisting of Radical and Republican deputies, was strong enough to obstruct in many ways this administration. The conflict with the Pope remained in full force, and the Government appeared to be at a loss as to the policy which it would be safest to pursue. (*See* ITALY.)

The vast British Empire was again enlarged in 1874 by the annexation of the Feejee Islands, and a new district in Western and South Africa. At home the Liberal ministry, which had been in power for several years, was gradually losing ground, and Mr. Gladstone therefore resolved to dissolve the Parliament and make an appeal to the country for a new proof of its continuing confidence. The general elections resulted, however, in a complete victory of the Conservative party and the appointment of a Tory ministry. Toward the close of the year the country was thrown into great excitement by a pamphlet published by Gladstone on the Vatican Decrees. (*See* GREAT BRITAIN.)

The new elections which took place in Belgium somewhat reduced the majority of the Catholic party in the two Chambers of the Legislature, without, however, destroying it in either. The advantage thus gained by the Liberals was, however, more than neutralized by the widening breach between the more moderate wing of the Liberals and the Radicals. (*See* BELGIUM.)

The Government of the Netherlands did not succeed in bringing the war against the sultanate of Acheen to a close. The Craton, the stronghold of the Achinese on the coast, was occupied, and the commanding general of the Dutch issued a proclamation of annexation, but the brave Achinese, stimulated by religious fanaticism, persisted in a stubborn resistance and compelled the Dutch Government to fit out a third expedition. The thorough discussion of the policy pursued by the Government in the East Indian colonies convinced the Dutch Chambers of the indispensable necessity of sweeping reforms in the administration of the colonies. (*See* NETHERLANDS.)

In the three Scandinavian kingdoms a current of friendly feeling toward the kindred people of Germany appears to have set in and to gather strength. The expulsion of some Danish agitators from Schleswig, by order of the Prussian Government, gave for a time new fuel to the irritation of the Danes who still complain of the non-compliance on the part of Germany with the fifth article of the Peace of Prague, which provides for taking a vote of the inhabitants of Northern Schleswig on the question whether they will belong to Germany or to Denmark. The statistics of the votes cast in Northern Schleswig at the last elections for the German Reichstag show, however, that the German nationality is making rapid progress, and it is likely to be soon in the ascendency. The long conflict between the people of Iceland and the Danish Government was terminated by the royal assent to the new liberal Constitution of Iceland. In the Danish Diet the uncompromising opposition of the majority of the Folkething to the policy of the ministry continued. The principles of the opposition assume more and more a republican character, and may ere long lead to serious complications. (*See* DENMARK and SWEDEN.)

The population of Europe at the close of 1874 was estimated at about 300,921,000 against 301,281,000 in 1873. The apparent decrease is due to a more accurate statement of the population of Turkey, which, according to the con-

current opinion of the best authorities, is not so large as had formerly been assumed. The following table exhibits the area and population of the countries of Europe, arranged according to the number of inhabitants, the indented countries being either dependencies or tributary states so small as to be only nominally independent, and virtually dependent upon the larger country, the name of which precedes theirs:

COUNTRIES.	Square Miles.	Inhabitants.
Russia............................	1,924,897	69,883,852
Finland.......................	142,368	1,832,138
Germany........................	208,739	41,060,095
France...........................	204,091	36,102,921
Austria...........................	240,954	35,904,435
Lichtenstein..................	68	8,320
Great Britain and Ireland......	121,607	32,412,010
Malta, Gibraltar, and Heligoland....................	145	176,213
Italy............................	114,295	26,801,154
San Marino.................	22	7,303
Monaco....................	6	3,127
Spain (inclusive of Balearic and Canary Islands).............	195,774	16,835,506
Andorra....................	144	12,000
Turkey...........................	142,957	8,397,529
Roumania..................	46,710	4,500,000
Servia.....................	16,817	1,338,505
Montenegro...............	1,701	120,000
Sweden..........................	171,761	4,297,972
Norway..........................	122,280	1,763,000
Belgium..........................	11,373	5,113,000
Portugal (inclusive of Azores and Madeira)................	35,813	4,367,882
Netherlands......................	12,680	3,716,002
Luxemburg................	999	197,528
Switzerland......................	15,992	2,669,147
Denmark.........................	14,738	1,861,000
Faroe and Iceland.........	40,268	81,400
Greece...........................	19,358	1,457,891
Total.....................	3,806,051	300,921,000

The number of Catholics is estimated at 147,500,000, or 49.1 per cent. of the total population; the number of Protestants at 71,760,000, or 23.9 per cent.; the number of Greek Catholics at 69,350,000, or 23.1 per cent.; the number of Jews at 5,000,000; the number of Mohammedans at 6,400,000. Included in the number of the Catholics are about 100,000 Old Catholics.

The area and population of the foreign colonies of European states were estimated, at the close of 1874, as follows:

COUNTRIES.	Area.	Inhabitants.
Great Britain..............	7,983,006	203,618,250
Turkey.....................	1,793,316	24,736,000
Netherlands................	675,069	24,401,000
Russia.....................	5,942,039	11,490,000
Spain......................	117,210	8,093,610
France.....................	457,606	5,640,000
Portugal...................	739,871	3,258,140
Denmark...................	46,892	47,500
Sweden....................	9	2,900
Total.................	17,755,018	281,217,400

EVANGELICAL ALLIANCE. The British Secretary of the Evangelical Alliance visited the French and the Italian branches of the organization during October, for the purpose, chiefly, of obtaining an expression of their preferences as to the place in which the next General Conference of the Alliance should be held. He visited Lyons, October 3d; Turin, October 6th; Milan—where a new branch of the Alliance was then formed—October 8th; Venice—where a committee was then formed—October 10th; Rome, October 14th; Florence, October 17th to 19th; Geneva, October 23d; Paris, October 27th. The general opinion of the members of the Alliance at these several places was in favor of holding the next general meeting (which will take place in 1876) in Rome. A meeting, composed of eighteen evangelical clergymen and laymen, was held in Rome in connection with the visit of the British Secretary, October 14th, at which it was decided to form a branch of the Alliance at once. A resolution was passed, declaring that "the time has come when, with the full religious liberty enjoyed in this land, a conference, under wise arrangements, of Christians from different countries, held in the city of Rome, would be not only expedient and practicable, but of the deepest interest, and likely to be largely blessed. The testimony that would be given to the doctrines of evangelical truth, and to the union of all the followers of our Lord, notwithstanding national and ecclesiastical differences, would, in our judgment, eminently serve the cause of truth in this land, and greatly encourage those who seek the increase of the kingdom which is righteousness and peace and joy in the Holy Ghost." The active support of the Christians of Rome was promised, and an invitation was cordially extended to members of the Alliance everywhere to make the city of Rome the seat of the next conference.

THE DOMINION BRANCH.—The idea of the organization of a branch of the Evangelical Alliance for the Dominion of Canada was first mooted in the city of New York during the great Conference of the Evangelical Alliance which was held there in October, 1873. The Canadian delegates met under the presidency of the Rev. Anson Green, D. D., of Toronto, when it was proposed, and agreed to unanimously, "that the various branches of the Evangelical Alliance in the Dominion be constituted into an organization; that the head office be in Montreal, and the office-bearers be selected so as to secure a general representation of the Dominion; and that the first general meeting of the Canadian branch be held in Montreal, on some day in October, 1874." The necessary arrangements for the meeting thus provided for was left in the hands of the Montreal branch, whose officers were requested to act as provisional officers on behalf of the *Dominion Evangelical Alliance* until the meeting should take place. In the spring of 1874, invitations to take part in the meeting were sent to distinguished·clergymen and laymen in Great Britain, the United States, and the Dominion of Canada. The officers of the Montreal branch, under whose care the provisions for holding the conference were made, consisted of the Rev. Principal Wilde, D. D., President; the Rev. Garin Lacey, Corresponding Secretary; Mr. Ernest

Taylor, Recording Secretary; Principal J. W. Dawson, LL. D., F. R. S., Vice-President; Mr. William Clendenning, Honorary Treasurer; and about twenty-three clergymen and other gentlemen who were associated with them as a committee of arrangements.

The conferences were opened on the 1st day of October, by a meeting of welcome, held in the American Presbyterian Church, Montreal, at which Principal J. W. Dawson, of McGill College, presided. An address of welcome was made by the Rev. John Jenkins, D. D., and replies and other addresses were made by several delegates. The Rev. Donald Fraser, D. D., and Major-General Burroughs, R. A., represented the British Branch Alliance; Rev. Mr. Dobbs, of Kingston, Ont., and the Rev. G. Patterson, of Pictou, N. S., spoke for their respective local organizations; and addresses were made by the Rev. Dr. Bliss, of the Syrian branch, the Rev. John Hull, D. D., and the Rev. Philip Schaff, D. D., of New York City, and Mr. H. Thane Miller, of Cincinnati.

The regular discussions of the Alliance began on the second day, Friday, October 2d. At the opening of the meeting on this day, ex-Governor L. A. Wilmot, of New Brunswick, was chosen President of the Conference, and the Rev. Dr. Taylor, of Montreal, Vice-President. A resolution was then adopted that "this Conference does now form a Dominion Branch of the Evangelical Alliance." Letters, responding to invitations to attend the conference, were read from numerous persons, to whom they had been sent, in Great Britain, the United States, and the Dominion. The subject assigned for the discussion of the day was "Christian Union, and Allied Topics." The first paper was read by the Rev. Dr. John Hall, of New York, and was on "The Present Demands on the Pulpit—just and unjust." The Rev. Dr. Philip Schaff then opened the discussion of the regular subject with a paper on "The Doctrinal Consensus of Evangelical Christendom." At the afternoon session, the Hon. James Ferrier presiding, papers were read on "Christian Union," by the Very Rev. Dean Bond, of Montreal; on "The Scriptural Idea of the Visible Church of Christ as constituted of Denominations of.Christians," by the Rev. Dr. R. L. Dabney, of Virginia; on "The History and Principles of the Evangelical Alliance," by the Rev. R. Beems, D. D.; and on "The Work of the Evangelical Alliance," by Major-General Burroughs. An evening meeting was held in the St. James Street Wesleyan Church, at which Principal Dawson presided. The Rev. Dr. Bliss, of the Syrian Branch Alliance, delivered an address on "Education in Syria;" and Mr. H. Thane Miller, of Cincinnati, spoke on the subject "How to win Young Men to Christ."

On the third day, Saturday, October 3d, the general subjects for discussion included "The Church's Work and Worship, and Allied Topics." Papers were read on "The Relation of Art to Church-Worship," by the Rev. Donald Fraser, D. D.; on "The Hymns of the Church, a Bond of Unity," by the Rev. John Latham, of Halifax; and on "Confessions of Faith, their Use and Abuse," by the Rev. Prof. MacKnight, of Halifax. In the evening a reception was held in the Convocation Hall of McGill College. Addresses were made by Principal Dawson, of McGill College; the Rev. Dr. McCosh, President of Princeton College, N. J.; Prof. Daniel Wilson, LL. D., of Toronto University; the Rev. Dr. Black, of Inverness, Scotland; and general remarks were made by other persons.

Sunday, October 4th, a united communion service was also held in the afternoon at St. Paul's Church. The Anglican Church, the Church of Scotland, the Canadian Presbyterian Church, the Free Church of Scotland, the Wesleyan Methodist Church, the English Presbyterian Church, the Presbyterian Church in the United States of America, and the Congregational and the Baptist Churches, were represented by ministers or laymen participating in the services.

Mass-meetings were held during a part of the day at several churches. One at the First Baptist Church was addressed by the Rev. Dr. Cramp, of Wolfville, N. S., the Earl of Cavan, and Mr. H. Thane Miller. At the St. James Wesleyan Church, the Rev. Dr. Dabney and the Rev. Dr. Fraser spoke. The Rev. Dr. McCosh, Major-General Burroughs, and the Rev. Dr. Black, of Inverness, addressed a meeting at the Zion Church. At a meeting in the Erskine Church addresses were delivered by the Rev. Dr. Bliss, President of the Syrian Protestant College, and ex-Governor Wilmot, of New Brunswick. At a meeting in the Lagauchetierre Street Wesleyan Church, the speakers were the Rev. Mr. Wilson, the Rev. Mr. McEwen, and the Rev. Mr. Grant. Addresses were made before a meeting in the Ottawa Street Wesleyan Church by the Rev. James Bennett, of St. John, N. B., the Rev. D. M. Gordon, D.'D., of Ottawa, and the Rev. Mr. Patterson, of Nova Scotia. Another meeting was held at the Cote Street Canada Presbyterian Church, where Mr. Gibson made an address on the subject of "Spiritual Life," and was followed in addresses by Mr. Henry Varley and Prof. Wilson. A meeting of the French-speaking delegates to the conference was held Sunday evening in the French Protestant Church, Monday, October 5th; several papers were read which had been assigned to Saturday, but had not been reached on that day. They were: "The Church of Canada—can such a Thing be?" by the Rev. G. M. Grant, M. A., of Halifax; "The Teaching of our Lord regarding the Sabbath and its Bearing on Christian Work," by the Rev. George Patterson, of Pictou, N. S.; "Reasons why the. Distinctive Principles of Protestantism should be inculcated," by the Rev. Dr. Cramp, of Wolfville, N. S.; "Ultramontanism," by the Rev. C. Chapman; and "French Canadian

Missions," by Mr. James Court. An address was also made by the Earl of Cavan.

A mass-meeting was held in the evening of this day at the St. James Street Wesleyan Church; addresses were here delivered on "Sunday-school Work," by the Rev. J. H. Vincent, D. D., of New York; on "Spiritual Life—what is it?" by Mr. Henry Varley; and on "God's Work in Scotland during the Last Twelve Months," by the Rev. Dr. Black, of Inverness, Scotland.

A meeting of the French-speaking branch of the Alliance was held at Association Hall on this day (Monday, October 5th). The Rev. J. G. Tanner presided. The following papers were read: "On the French Evangelical Schools of Lower Canada in 1874," by the Rev. Charles Roux; "French Missions among the Roman Catholics of Canada," by the Rev. T. Lafleur; and on "Evangelical Missions among the French Canadians," by the Rev. C. Doudiet. At a public meeting held in connection with the French branch, the Rev. Mr. Tanner made an address on the objects of the Alliance, and a general discussion took place, in the course of which the Rev. R. P. Duclos, of St. Hyacinthe, Pastor Vernon, Prof. Coussinet, the Rev. M. Coté, Pastor Lafleur, and Pastor Doudiet, spoke.

The general subject of "Science, Philosophy, and Literature, in Relation to Christianity," was assigned for Tuesday, October 6th. The discussion was opened by the Rev. Dr. James McCosh, of Princeton, N. J., with a paper on "Grand Truths in Nature, overlooked by Prof. Tyndall." Other papers were read in the morning session, on "Modern Philosophy in Relation to Christianity," by Prof. J. C. Murphy, LL. D., of McGill College, Montreal; and on "Evangelical Rationalism," by the Rev. J. M. Gibson, of Chicago.

In the afternoon the sessions of the conference were held in two sections The first section met in St. Andrew's Church. Papers were read on "French Canadian Missions," by the Rev. Theodore Lafleur; on "An Investigation of the Relations of the Comparative Study of Religions to Christianity," by Prof. Campbell; on "Efforts to meet Skepticism and Infidelity," by Major-General Burroughs, and on "Inspiration," by the Rev. Principal Mac-Vicar, LL. D.

The second section met in the First Baptist Church. Papers were read on "Creation and Development," by the Rev. James Bennett, of St. John, N. B.; on "The Attitude of Religion toward Science," by Prof. Daniel Wilson, LL. D., of the University of Toronto; on "Modern Christianity, from the Stand-point of Modern Science," by Principal J. W. Dawson, LL. D., of McGill College; and on "Modern Literature in its Relation to Christianity," by President Noah Porter, of Yale College, New Haven, Conn.

After the reading of the papers was concluded, a business meeting was held. The basis laid down by the parent Alliance as the bond of union of the members and branches of the general body was adopted as the constitution of the Dominion branch. The formation of local branches throughout the Dominion was recommended, a report of which should in each case be forwarded to the general secretary. The Hon. L. A. Wilmot, D. C. L., of Fredericton, N. B., was chosen President for the ensuing year, and Vice-President, secretaries, and members of the General Committee were appointed. The latter body were authorized to appoint an Executive Committee out of their number.

The conference closed on Tuesday evening, October 6th, with a farewell meeting in the St. James Street Methodist Church. Short addresses were delivered by President Wilmot, the Earl of Cavan, the Rev. Dr. Black, of Inverness, Scotland, the Rev. Dr. Ryerson, of the Methodist Church of Canada, Mr. Henry Varley, Mr. H. Thane Miller, the Rev. Mr. Grant, of Halifax, N. S., the Rev. Mr. Morton, missionary from Trinidad, Major-General Burroughs, and the Rev. Dr. Fraser, and the benediction was pronounced by the Rev. George Douglas.

EVANGELICAL ASSOCIATION. The following are the statistics of the Evangelical Association for 1874:

CONFERENCES.	Itinerant Preachers.	Local Preachers.	Members.	Churches.
East Pennsylvania....	94	87	14,401	186
Central Pennsylvania..	77	62	10,829	151
New York.............	35	10	3,962	60
Pittsburg.............	55	36	7,008	113
Kansas...............	24	11	1,694	16
Canada...............	32	13	3,856	67
Michigan.............	38	22	3,660	46
Illinois..............	75	71	8,749	101½
Iowa.................	64	26	5,260	50
Wisconsin............	56	27	8,739	107
Ohio.................	67	58	7,593	138
Minnesota............	31	7	2,790	29
Indiana *............	55	42	6,053	100½
Germany.............	31	4	5,445	12
California and Oregon,	3	..	145	3
Total.............	737	476	90,249	1,184

The number of members was 7,054 greater than in 1873. The churches were valued at $2,777,070. Number of parsonages, 330; value of the same, $374,605; number of Sunday-schools, 1,441½; of officers and teachers in the same, 16,406; of scholars, 82,047; number of children baptized, 6,994; of adults baptized, 1,238; of members "newly received," 16,731. Amount of "conference contributions," $4,-702.71; of contributions for missions, $72,-526.91; of contributions for the Sunday-school and Tract causes, $2,330.97.

The anniversary of the *Missionary Society* of the Evangelical Association was held in October. The receipts for the year were reported to have been $70,584.20, and the ex-

penditures $62,897.65. The receipts showed a ratio of contributions of about 80 cents per member of the Church. The debt of the society had been diminished during the year by $2,546.50, and has now $4,121.20. Cash bequests had been received to the amount of $7,132.07. The corresponding secretary reported that $24,000 were in the treasury for the mission among the heathen, and recommended that the question of the place where such a mission should be established be referred to the next General Conference. The number of home and foreign missions was reported to be 270. Twenty-six missions had been struck from the list of missions at various conference sessions, and converted into self-sustaining charges, or connected with such charges. An actual increase of 48 missions had taken place. A resolution was adopted, "that Japan be considered our heathen mission-field; that the bishops and the corresponding secretary be constituted a committee in reference to the men who are willing to be sent; and that we request the General Conference at its next session to appoint two or three missionaries to this field."

EVANGELICAL SYNOD OF THE WEST. The general meeting of the Evangelical Synod of the West commenced at Indianapolis, Ind., on October 8th. Seventy-five ministers and lay delegates were present, representing five synods, and about three hundred ministers. The Rev. A. Balzer presided. A new division was made into seven synods. The original aim in the formation of the synod was to reproduce in the United States the essential features of the United Evangelical Church of Germany; hence it was called "Evangelical," and denominational peculiarities were held of little account. Its confessional basis is founded upon the *consensus* of the confessions of the Lutheran and Reformed Churches. Either Luther's or the Heidelberg Catechism may be used in the churches, as the majority of the members may prefer. The synod stands in intimate relations with many mission institutions of Germany, as those of Dr. Wickern, and the Missionary or Emigrants' Associations of Berlin, Barmen, Langenberg, and Basle. The synod of Wisconsin was founded under the auspices of the Association at Berlin. Pastor Krummacher manifested a great interest in this body during his visit to the United States. The Evangelical Synod appears to be gradually assuming a more distinctly denominational form. It has now its own hymn-book, catechism, church and Sunday-school papers, educational institutions, and, almanac. Its principal publications are the *Friedensbote*, semi-monthly, the *Theologische Zeitschrift*, monthly, and a Sunday-school paper. Its leading educational institutions are a teachers' seminary at Elmhurst and a theological seminary at St. Charles, Mo. The Rev. A. Balzer, President of the General Conference, is also editor of the principal paper, superintendent

* From the report of 1873.

of the publication interests, and director of all the synodical machinery. The particular synods meet every year, and the General Conference every three years. A delegate from the General Synod, South, of the Lutheran Church, attended the present meeting. The Evangelical Synod of the West consists exclusively of German-speaking congregations, and numbered, in 1874, 276 clergymen, 250 congregations, and about 40,000 communicants.

EVANGELICAL UNION. The thirty-seventh annual conference of the Evangelical Union of Scotland was held in Glasgow, in September. The conference is composed of the ministers of the several churches and two lay delegates from each church. The Rev. George Gladstone, of the Evangelical Church, was chosen president. Two ministers were reported to have died during the year. Two churches—one in Wishard, with one hundred and eighty-five members, and one in Motherwell, with ninety-seven members—were re-

ceived into the Union. Two ministers were also received. The report of the Home Mission showed that nineteen churches of the Union were without settled pastors. Several legacies and gifts to various connectional institutions were announced. Favorable reports were made of the condition of the chapel debt and building-fund, of the ministers' augmentation fund, and of the worn-out ministers and ministers' widows' fund. The last fund is supported by contributions from the churches, and the payment by those who become entitled to its benefits of one pound sterling each annually. Such persons, on failure of their health, become entitled to an allowance of at least £40 a year. The widow of a member dying receives a grant of £40. The Union supports an institution called the Academy, at which the theological students are trained. Eighteen such students had been attending the institution at the time the conference met.

F

FAIRBAIRN, Rev. PATRICK, D. D., a clergyman of the Free Church of Scotland, and for twenty years principal of the Free Church College at Glasgow, born in Edinburgh in 1805; died at Glasgow, August 6, 1874. He was educated at the University of Edinburgh, was settled over one of the parish churches of the Scottish Kirk, followed Chalmers and Guthrie and their associates in the Disruption of 1843, and was, of course, obliged to give up his parish and his manse. He became soon after minister of the Free Church parish of Salton, whence he was called, in 1853, to the Free Church College at Glasgow, first as professor, and later as principal. A man of great and varied learning, and one of the ablest writers in the Free Church, he was yet one of the most accessible, simple-hearted, and genial of men, but withal a man of the most untiring industry. His published works have nearly all come to be regarded as standards, for their profound research and their careful accuracy of statement. The following are those best known: "The Typology of Scripture," 2 vols., 8vo (this has passed through many editions); "Exposition of the First Epistle of Peter," 2 vols., 12mo (1836); "Hengstenberg's Commentary on the Psalms," translated by Dr. Fairbairn, 3 vols., 8vo (1845-'48); "Jonah: his Life, Character, and Mission," 12mo (1849); "Ezekiel, and the Book of his Prophecy," 8vo (1851); "Hengstenberg's Revelation of St. John," a Commentary, translated by Dr. Fairbairn, 2 vols., 8vo (1851); "Prophecy," etc., 8vo (1856); "Hermeneutical Manual," 8vo (1858). He was also the editor of the "Imperial Bible Dictionary," not yet quite completed. He was a powerful and eloquent speaker, and had taken a deep interest in the revival work in progress

VOL. XIV.—19   A

in Scotland, as a result of the American evangelists, Messrs. Moody and Sankey. His death was attributed to heart-disease.

FAIRBAIRN, Sir WILLIAM, Bart., C. E., LL. D., F. R. S., an eminent British civil engineer and iron-worker, born in Kelso, Scotland, in 1789; died at Manchester, England, August 18, 1874. Having learned the rudiments of education at a parish school, and received some instruction from an uncle, he was apprenticed to an engine-wright at a British colliery. When his apprenticeship terminated, he wrought two years in London, and then visited many places in England, Wales, and Ireland, working a short time in each, in order to acquire a general knowledge of mechanical engineering. Eventually, he began business on his own account at Manchester, in 1817, and persevered in it despite many discouraging circumstances. The first important improvement which he introduced was the general substitution of iron for wood in the shafting of cotton-mills, and the use of lighter shafting where metal was already in use. This change reduced the cost of machinery, and enabled the motion to be speeded from forty to one hundred and sixty revolutions per minute. Mr. Fairbairn afterward directed his attention to iron ship-building, and was the first in England to construct an iron ship. The construction of iron vessels eventually became one of the principal branches of his business, his firm having built more than a hundred, varying from the smallest size to the war-frigate of 2,600 tons. In 1834-'35, Mr. Fairbairn and Mr. E. Hodgkinson were invited by the British Association to seek out the cause of certain supposed defects in the iron produced by hot-blast furnaces. He and his associate accordingly investigated the subject, and submitted a valuable report thereon, printed in the "Transactions" of the Association. He also, at the instance of scientific bodies, or for his own information, tested the strength of various kinds of British iron, determined the tenacity of boiler-plates of different thicknesses, and made a long series of experiments on the resistance of hollow tubes or cylinders to outside pressure, leading to valuable practical results. Mr. Fairbairn coöperated with Robert Stephenson in designing and constructing the great tubular bridge across the Menai Strait, the success of which led to the building of many others on the same principle. Stephenson suggested a circular tube supported by chains; but this plan was modified at the instance of Mr. Fairbairn, who made a long series of experiments upon model tubes, and found that a rectangular structure, strengthened by a series of cells at the top and bottom, and suspended without chains or any other support from pier to pier, was best adapted to the stipulated conditions. Sir William (he was knighted in 1869), who was one of the founders and earliest members of the British Association, wrote many able papers on subjects connected with his profession, and published several important works, among which may be noticed "Mills and Mill-Work;" "Iron—its History and Manufacture;" "Application of Iron to Building Purposes;" "The Conway and Brittannia Tubular Bridges;" "The Strength of Hollow Globes and Cylinders when exposed to Pressure from without;" "On Canal Steam Navigation;" "Iron Ship-building," and First, Second, and Third Series of "Useful Information for Engineers." He was a corresponding member of the National Institute of France, of the Royal Academy of Turin, and a Chevalier of the Legion of Honor. He had been President of the British Association in 1861-'62, and had received the honorary degree of LL. D. from the University of Edinburgh.

FEEJEE (FIJI, OR FIDJI) ISLANDS, a group of islands in the South-Pacific Ocean, which, until 1874, were an independent country, when they were annexed to the British dominions. The islands occupy the central portion of Western Polynesia. They lie about midway between Tongan Islands and the French colony and island of New Caledonia, between the meridians of 177° east and 178° west longitude, and between the parallels of 15° 30' and 20° 30' south latitude. The number is variously stated, but it is believed to be about 225. They are dotted over an area of ocean extending nearly 300 miles from east to west, and 200 miles from north to south, and it is computed that their aggregate superficies is about 8,034. The principal islands are Viti Levu and Vanua Levu, each of which has a circumference of about 250 miles; in these two islands the principal planters reside. Next in importance and size to these are Kandavu, Taviuni, Rambi, Koro, Ngau, and Ovalau.

The Feejee Islands have been divided into eight groups or divisions, viz.: The Ono Group, comprising Ono, Ndvi, Mana, Undui, Yannya, Tuvana-i-tholo, and Tuvana-i-ra; the Lakeba Group, including Vatoa, Tiwutha, Thithia, and thirty-three islands and islets; the Exploring Isles, among which are Mango, Kanathea, Naitumba, Vatuvara, Yathata, and a number of smaller islands; Middle Feejee, containing Matuku, Totoya, Moala, Ngau, Nairai, Koro, Ovalau, and some others; the Vanua Levu Group, comprising Vanua Levu, Taviuni, and the adjoining islands, in number about fifty; Viti Levu, or Great Feejee, in whose boundaries about other fifty islands are encircled; the Kandavu Group, numbering in all about thirteen islands; and the Yasawas Group, including about thirty islands, most of them of small area. Viewed from the ocean, the islands have been described as presenting pictures of almost fairy-like loveliness. The navigation among the islands is not easy, but landing as a rule can be effected safely. The reefs stretch out their arms in all directions, needing great care in their avoidance.

The white population was estimated in December, 1871, according to the official *Feejee Gazette*, at 2,040 persons, the majority of whom are British subjects; some 200 or so are Americans. The native population is believed to be about 146,000, though some think it to be not far short of 200,000. These numbers are distributed over about 140 of the islands, the remainder being, so far as is known at present, altogether uninhabited. The official returns give the following numbers and distribution of the native and European population: Ovalau (in which is situated the port of Levuka)—whites, 450; natives, 2,000. Islands of the Eastern group—whites, 1,000; natives, 10,000. Kandavu—whites, 46; natives, 12,-000. Taviuni—whites, 150; natives, 1,000. Vanua Levu—whites, 500; natives, 33,000. Viti Levu—whites, 450; natives, 70,000. Central Islands—whites, 160; natives, 9,000. Yassawas—whites, 58; natives, 8,000. Other islands of the Feejeean Archipelago—whites, 126; natives, 1,000—making a total of 148,-040. In 1871 the number of white persons who arrived in the group numbered 887; the departures were 562, leaving a net increase in the population of 325; 2,275 foreign laborers arrived, being 570 in excess of the number of the previous year. The aborigines or Feejeeans are described as a well-made and handsome race of men, of different shades of color, the predominant hue being a dark olive. In character they are described as being full of contradictions, sometimes kind and tractable, at other times relentlessly cruel and obstinate. They are not a brave people, are very unforgiving and ungrateful, are lazy and treacherous, but may withal be managed with tact and firmness. Their dress is of a simple character, and consists of a length of cloth or white *taypa*, called a *sulu*, wound round the waist.

They anoint their bodies with cocoa-nut oil, and beyond this peculiarity are said to be clean in their persons, though not particularly so in their habits.

Cotton is the principal production, other trees and plants being the breadfruit-tree, orange, lemon, banana, plantain, and cocoa-nut tree; the sugar-cane, nutmeg, guava, ginger, turmeric, arrow-root, tea-plant, and yams, grow in great profusion; the latter is the favorite edible of the natives. The growing of sugar, coffee, and maize, is now being attended to, and the results are very promising. To cotton, however, Feejee owes much of the importance to which it is now arriving. It is only a few years since the plant was introduced, the merit of this being due to Dr. Brower, the American consul at the time, and Mr. J. B. Smytherman. The planting-season is from September to February. The seed is sown in rows, and appears above-ground in about three days. In two or three months it expands into a bush, bearing a beautiful flower of a delicate yellow color. In three months more the tree has grown to the height of three to five feet; the blossoms give way to bolls which mature, ripen, and burst, and in a short time are ready for picking. Numerous natives are imported from the New Hebrides, Sandwich Islands, and other groups, the native supply of labor being insufficient. The bulk of the population (about 120,000) professes Christianity, only the tribe of the interior of Viti Levu still holding out against any advance of Christianity and civilization. It is only thirty-six years ago since the first missionaries, the Revs. W. Cross and Cargill, landed at Lakeba. They found the Feejeeans at nearly the lowest depth of degradation—blood-thirsty, and addicted to cannibalism and all manner of vice. The introduction of Christianity has brought about a great change. Cannibalism has ceased since 1854; polygamy is abolished, and the idols all destroyed; divine worship is general, and peace abounds.

The following are the returns of the Wesleyan Church in Feejee and Rotomah for the year 1872: Chapels, 634; other preaching places, 354; missionaries (including the return of two to the group), 13; English school-master, 1; native assistant missionaries, 52; catechists, 883; day-school teachers, 2,372; Sabbath-school teachers, 2,620; local preachers, 814; class-leaders, 2,828; full and accredited native members, 24,413; native members on trial, 4,377; Sabbath-schools, 1,121; Sabbath scholars, 46,732; day-schools, 1,414; day-scholars, 46,732; catechumens, 1,764; members died during the year, 412; attendants on public worship, 109,250. There has been an increase of members in nearly every circuit—in one at the rate of 8 per cent., in another 10 per cent., and in a third 52 per cent. The Roman Catholics have for some time had a mission in the islands, in the hands of French priests, but their influence, and the body itself, are small, compared to that of the Wesleyans. The number of English connected with the Wesleyan Society at Feejee is 40.

During the year 1871, the arrivals at Feejee were: At Levuka, 1 ship, 11 steamships, 23 barks, 10 brigs, 100 schooners, and 84 cutters; in all, 179. At the Eastern group, 32 vessels of various kinds; making a total of 211. The aggregate tonnage of the arrivals was 30,806 tons; of the departures, 30,693 tons. For the financial year ending September 30, 1872, the entrance in the port of Levuka was 128 vessels (1 American); tonnage, 22,778. The imports were valued at $27,000, the exports at $368,000. The value of the exports in 1871 was as follows: Sea-island cotton, $381,860; kidney and short-staple ditto, $19,327; cocoanut-oil, $17,820; tortoise-shell, $1,150; bêche-de-mer, $500; fungus, $600; wool, $750; cotton-seed, $5,000; copra, $5,400; candlenuts, $400; sundries, '$20,000—making a general total of $452,807. Imports: Drapery, cotton and woolen, $100,535; ironmongery and cutlery, $92,020; wines, beer, and spirits, $71,160; groceries and provisions, $21,045; ship-chandlery, $35,770; furniture and timber, $9,670; tobacco and cigars, $15,685; books and stationery, $2,390; drugs and medicines, $2,470; machinery, $34,000; crockery and glassware $5,065; fancy goods, $6,110; horses and cattle, $10,000; sheep, $5,000; total value of imports, $412,920. The estimated revenue for the financial year ending June 30, 1872, was £23,593, the expenditure being computed at £20,431, leaving a surplus of £3,400. The principal receipts are derived from the sale of land, the estimated returns of which for the year are £18,400. The estimated receipts for the year ending June 30, 1873, were $121,324; expenditure, $127,020. The postal service was first organized by the proprietor of the Feejee Times, who established an organization called the Feejee Times Express, which also included an insular-parcels delivery. It subsequently passed into the hands of the Government. There is irregular communication between the various islands, by means of small craft, but arrangements are now in progress for superseding these by the employment of a steamer. There is frequent, though not regular, communication with Melbourne and Sydney, and a monthly service has been arranged between Feejee and Auckland; sailing vessels, too, frequently ply, and the missionary-ship John Wesley also affords a means of reaching the islands. The principal town in the Feejee Islands is Levuka, which may be deemed the commercial capital of the group. It is situated on the east coast of the island of Ovalau, and is distant 2,160 miles from Melbourne, 1,730 from Sydney, and 1,180 from Auckland. The island itself is of no magnitude, being but eight miles long by about seven miles in breadth. It lies about 15 miles due east of Viti Levu. The town, consisting of North and South Levuka, is not by any means desirably located, being walled in on two sides, and backed by lofty mountains, that render an extension of the boundary difficult for practical purposes. The town is supplied by water procured from Totoga Creek, and is under the control of a municipal council consisting of a mayor and aldermen. The resident population consists of about 306, and there is a floating population of 400 more. The harbor is formed by a barrier reef, peculiar to the South-Sea Islands, which acts as a natural breakwater; inside the reef is good anchorage. Loading and discharging accommodation is afforded by three jetties. Levuka is, and has been for some time, the principal port of the Feejee Islands. It has one Wesleyan, one Anglican, and one Roman Catholic church. Schools are connected with the two former.

The Feejee Islands were, till lately, ruled by two principal chiefs, Thakombau and Maafu, and others of secondary importance, Tui Thakau Ritove, Tui Mbau, Ratu Kini. Thakombau bore the title of King of Feejee, and had the largest territories. He professes Christianity now. Maafu is also a convert, and stands high as a preacher; he is spoken of as being a superior man.

The whole of the group was, some years ago, erected into a kingdom—Thakombau, or Cakombau, as he is now more generally called, being the supreme head, Maafu and also Tui Cakau acknowledging his sovereignty. After the definite refusal by the British Government of the sovereignty of Feejee, an attempt was made by the white settlers, principally for their own protection, to initiate a form of government by which law and order might be maintained. These efforts, however, did not result very successfully, owing to the difficulty of reconciling conflicting interests. About this time the ocean postal service to California was started. The Feejean settlers made application for the islands to be called at by the steamers. The Australian Steam Navigation Company agreed to this on condition that the port of Levuka should be surveyed, buoyed, and lighted. A meeting of the leading merchants and planters was held, and this condition was unanimously accepted, and a marine surveyor sent for from New Zealand. Lieutenant George Austin Woods undertook the survey, and promptly executed the work. In the course of his labors he was brought into contact with Cakombau, who, highly impressed with his energy and abilities, sent him an autograph letter, asking him to make a government for his people and the white people; at the same time requesting him to mention the names of any gentlemen whom he might wish to be associated with him. To this communication Mr. Woods returned answer he would try, and after a time submitted to Cakombau the names of Messrs. Hennings, Smith, Logan, and Burt. Eventually, the last-named gentleman became the leader of the Feejean cabinet.

This attempt to form a government was, on the whole, favorably received by the white men, and support generally accorded to the King and ministry. The latter thereupon took steps to construct the government. Circulars were issued to the various districts, calling upon them to elect delegates; and in the early part of 1871 elections took place through the islands for delegates to meet in congress, to discuss and frame a constitution. In August, 1871, these delegates met in solemn convention, and, after much deliberation, agreed to a constitution for the creation of the kingdom of Feejee, and to regulations and conditions under which the government of the kingdom should be carried on. The House of Delegates having performed its function, it was in due course dissolved. Returning officers were next appointed, and writs issued for the election of members to serve in the Assembly of Feejee. These elections were duly carried out, and the first Feejean Parliament met under the speakership of Mr. Butters, formerly Mayor of Melbourne. The Constitution Act, framed by the House of Delegates, provided for a government of the whole group, and the establishment of a Constitution from October 1, 1871. It also provided that the form of government should be executive, legislative, and judicial: the Executive to consist of the King and the ministry; the legislative of a Privy Council and a House of Representatives. The judicial was vested in a Supreme Court, consisting of a Chief-Justice and two Associate Judges, one of whom is a native, whose decisions are final. The Privy Council was composed of the native governors of the provinces into which the Constitution Act directed that the kingdom should be subdivided. The House of Representatives was formed of European delegates from the electoral districts proclaimed throughout the islands, the members being elected by white men, from whom the government must be chosen. All measures passed by the House of Representatives were to be submitted to the Privy Council and the King's cabinet, who have not, however, the power of vetoing any measures not meeting with their approval, but simply of referring them back to the Assembly from which they originated. The number of representatives was limited to forty, and not less than twenty. The qualifications of an elector were manhood, payment of taxes, and six months' residence.

The nominal constitution of the kingdom of Feejee was, however, unable to prevent the administration from falling into a most deplorable condition. The finances, especially, appeared to be in hopeless disorder, and, at the beginning of the year 1874, the Treasury was without a farthing to discharge debts. Members of the Feejean civil service received in payment "certificates of indebtedness," which were held in such disfavor that the Banking Company refused to discount them at any price, while private individuals charged 20 to

25 per cent. for doing so. The desire for the annexation to the British dominion gained, therefore, steadily in strength. The English Government being informed of the unanimous wishes of the white settlers, which were shared by thousands of natives, sent Consul Layard and Commodore Goodenough as commissioners to examine the islands and make a report on the question of annexation. The commissioners addressed the following letter to the King and chiefs:

Commodore Goodenough and Consul Layard are the two chiefs sent out by her Britannic Majesty, the Queen of England to visit Feejee, to inquire and consult with the King of Feejee and the chiefs respecting the government of Feejee. These two chiefs desire to consult with the King and chiefs of Feejee fully and clearly, that they may know what they (the chiefs) desire or prefer—whether the King of Feejee shall govern Feejee, or whether her Britannic Majesty, the Queen of England shall govern Feejee; they (the commissioners) desire to know their (the chiefs') minds. Should it be their true minds (the King and chiefs of Feejee) to give Feejee to England—that it should become the Queen of England's to govern—there is but one object and design sought—Feejee's peace and welfare in all time; that the King and chiefs, with all their people and all the inhabitants of the land, may live in peace and prosperity. This, and this only, is the desire and object. It is no new thing for England to govern islands like Feejee. She owns and governs in several parts of the world a great number of similar islands to Feejee, and it will be very easy for her to govern Feejee also, and preserve its peace and promote the welfare and prosperity of its people. But England will never take Feejee by force or stealth; if the King and chiefs do not wish to give it, if they think they can, and are willing, to govern the land themselves; if the King of Feejee retains the government for himself, that is well, and England will only require of him and place before him one thing—that he shall govern wisely and righteously, with equal j s e to natives and British subjects resident in Feejee, at all times. But there is one matter to be considered by the King and chiefs of Feejee; they must know that the number of foreigners in Feejee will greatly increase from year to year, as well as their property, and for these reasons the King and chiefs must think and study well over the matter, whether they will be able to conduct their government in the future under more difficult circumstances or not. There is but one desire on the part of the Government of England respecting Feejee, which is, that its peace, welfare, and prosperity, may be secured, and that each and all of its inhabitants, of both races, may be able to obtain and secure their individual and just rights, whether they be native-born or foreigners—that, and that only.

The King was easily prevailed upon to consent to annexation, when the commissioners declared a readiness to accept it, subject to the ratification of the home government. The Governor of New South Wales, Sir Hercules Robinson, visited the islands, accepted the unconditional cession, and established in them a provisional government complete in all its administrative and judicial details. Subject always to a prudent and economical management, his estimate of revenue was not unfavorable. He imposed taxes, and a tariff based upon that of New South Wales; and he formed a code of civil and criminal law sufficient for present circumstances; and, pending further orders,

he retained in his own hands the general supervision of the provisional administration. King Thackombau had his favorite war-club elaborately ornamented in silver, with emblems of peace, and sent it to the Queen with a dutiful message, confiding the interests of his people unreservedly to the justice and gene os of her Majesty. Soon after the ex-King, with his sons, visited Sydney, where, in December, the incorporation of the islands with the British dominions was celebrated by a great banquet.

The Feejee Islands were discovered by the Dutch navigator Tasman, on February 6, 1643, who called them Prince William's Islands, but effected no landing. Captain Cook, by whom they were later sighted, but not touched, named the island now called Vatoa, Turtle Island. In 1789 they were closely passed by Lieutenant Bligh. In 1796 the missionary-ship Duff touched at the islands, and would have landed missionaries but for the hostile attitude of the natives. Perhaps the earliest known settlement made by Europeans was by a party of convicts who escaped from New South Wales in the year 1804 in an open boat, and succeeded in making the islands, where they were received kindly by the natives. Additions to the white population were made from time to time by shipwrecked seamen and by deserters from the whaling-ships, who frequently touched at the islands for water and fresh provisions. About the year 1835 some small traders succeeded in effecting a lodgment on the beach at Levuka.

The American Exploring Expedition, under Lieutenant Wilkes, 1838-'42, first excited the interest of civilized nations in the Feejee Islands. The first British consul was appointed in 1858. The number of white settlers was gradually augmented by other traders and planters, till, in the year 1859, it was estimated that the white population was not far short of 100. In 1866, 26 British and 3 foreign ships were entered, their gross tonnage amounting to 4,314. In the following year the population had nearly quintupled itself; the imports during the year had increased £29,000, and the exports, consisting of cotton, cocoa-nut oil, bêche-de-mer, etc., to £39,969. Much land, too, began to be brought under cultivation, and numerous plantations were opened up in various parts for the culture of Sea-island cotton, for which the soil and climate are eminently fitted. From 1867 to the present time a steady tide of immigration, principally from Victoria, has been setting in. In 1868, 52 ships, of the aggregate tonnage of 6,560, were entered; in the succeeding years 93 ships, of 7,920 tonnage, were entered; and during the years 1870 and 1871 it is estimated that these numbers have been almost doubled. The exports during this time were as follows: In 1868, £45,167, of which cotton alone was valued at £30,915, the next and largest being tortoise shell, £8,009. In 1869 the exports were £57,020, cotton again being the staple export, amounting to £45,000.

Since then the exports have been steadily rising in value.

The "Polynesian Company" was projected at Melbourne, for taking up the offer of cession of 200,000 acres of land made by King Thakombau to the British Government, on consideration of an indemnity being paid to the American consul for alleged damage done to the consulate. In addition to the land, other special concessions were also offered. The company was formed, and the transaction carried out; but the success of the company is not favorably spoken of, though they have plenty of good land, with fine harbors.

The first proposition for the annexation of the Feejee Islands to Great Britain was made in 1859, and the well-known English consul, Pritchard, took an active part in it. Lord John Russell was at that time Secretary of State, and declined the offer. Soon after the friends of annexation sent Colonel Smythe to the islands to report on the question. His report was unfavorable, and the scheme of annexation failed a second time. In 1870 the question came up again, and very favorable opinions concerning it were expressed at the conference of Australian colonies held in that year, but the new offer, made in 1871, was once more declined by the Colonial Secretary, Earl Kimberley. Owing, however, to the pressure brought upon him, the Colonial Secretary, in 1873, sent two commissioners to the islands to examine the question again in all its aspects. Their reports were published in 1874. They found throughout the islands indescribable misery and disorder, and strongly favored annexation, which, as already stated, was now accepted by the British Government.*

FILLMORE, MILLARD, LL. D., thirteenth President of the United States, an American statesman; born at Summer Hill, in the town of Locke, Cayuga County, N. Y., January 7, 1800; died in Buffalo, N. Y., March 8, 1874. He was of Puritan stock, his ancestors having been among the early settlers of Ipswich, Mass. His father had migrated to Cayuga County, N. Y., when it was a mere wilderness, and was hence unable to give more than a very slender education to his children. Millard Fillmore had never seen a grammar or geography until his nineteenth year. He was sent at an early age to Livingston County, then a very wild region, to learn the clothier's trade, but, four months later, was apprenticed to a wool-carder in the town in which his father lived. . The boy had a passion for books, and every leisure moment was spent in devouring such books as the village library furnished, and in endeavoring to add to his meagre stock of learning. At the end of four years, Judge Wood, of Cayuga County, perceiving his thirst for education, and his capacity for higher pursuits than wool-

carding, offered him a place in his law-office, and advanced him the means to prosecute a preliminary course of study. These advantages were promptly and gratefully accepted, and, by teaching during the winter, he was able to repay the judge's advances. In the autumn of 1821 he removed to the county of Erie, and the following spring entered a law-office in Buffalo; was admitted to the bar in that city in 1823, and commenced practice in Aurora, Erie County. He was married, in 1826, to a daughter of Rev. Lemuel Powers. He removed to Buffalo in 1830, and went into partnership with Hon. Nathan K. Hall, afterward his Postmaster-General, who died one week before him. In 1829 Mr. Fillmore was elected to the Assembly of New York from Erie County, and reëlected in 1830 and 1831. Though in a minority, he distinguished himself by his advocacy of the act to abolish imprisonment for debt, a measure which he succeeded in having passed. In the fall of 1832 he was elected to the Twenty-third Congress on the anti-Jackson ticket, and took his seat during the stormy session succeeding the removal of the deposits from the United States Bank. After serving one term, he renewed the practice of his profession till the fall of 1837; he had been again elected to Congress in November, 1836, and took his seat in December, 1837. As a member of the Committee on Elections, in the famous New Jersey "broad seal" case, he established his reputation in the House. The agitation of this election case was among the prominent causes that determined the overthrow of the Democratic party and the Whig triumph in the presidential election of 1840. Mr. Fillmore was reëlected to the Twenty-seventh Congress, and there obtained the arduous and responsible position of chairman of the Committee of Ways and Means. The session continued during a period of nine months, during which he was not absent from his duties in the House a single hour. The financial affairs of the Administration were in great disorder, and the public reputation of Mr. Fillmore was largely advanced at this time by his unwearying industry and the tact and judgment he brought to bear upon national affairs. He was regarded as the author of the Tariff of 1842. One of the most noted measures passed during that session, and through his advocacy, was that which required the departments, in submitting estimates of expenses, to accompany them with references to the laws which authorized them. At the close of the first or long session of the Twenty-seventh Congress Mr. Fillmore declined a reëlection to Congress, and, in the spring of 1841, returned to Buffalo, and devoted himself again to his profession. In the National Whig Convention of 1844 Mr. Fillmore was one of the candidates for the vice-presidency, but his name was withdrawn at his own request. In the fall of the same year he was nominated for Governor of New York, but was defeated by Silas Wright. In

* See Williams and Calvert, "Fiji and the Fijians" (new edition, London, 1870); Goodenough and Layard, "Report on the Offer of the Cession of the Fiji Islands to the British Crown" (published in "Foreign Relations of the United States," 1874). .

.1847 he was elected Controller by a very large majority, and removed to Albany to enter upon the duties of the office. In the summer of 1848 he was nominated, and in the following November elected Vice-President of the United States on the ticket of General Zachary Taylor. As President of the Senate, he won for himself a high reputation for dignity, impartiality, and fairness. It was the period of the long and angry discussions of the several propositions for the organization of the Territories, and the consideration of the compromise measures introduced by Mr. Clay, in what was known as the "Omnibus Bill." During all these heated debates in the Senate, extending over many months, Vice-President Fillmore gave no indication to any one, except the President, which side he favored.

On the 9th of July, 1850, President Taylor died, and on the 10th Mr. Fillmore took the oath of office as President and entered upon his duties. In the selection of a new cabinet, that of President Taylor having resigned, Mr. Fillmore showed his judgment. Daniel Webster, Thomas Corwin, and John J. Crittenden, were the foremost characters in the new cabinet, and each was, in his way, a representative man. It was a critical period in the national history. Mr. Clay's compromise measures, which were still pending, were intended to prevent collisions between the North and the South, and to quiet the angry and bitter feelings then existing. They provided for the admission of California as a free State; defined the boundaries of Texas, paying her $10,000,000 for relinquishing all claim to jurisdiction outside those limits; organized the Territories of New Mexico and Utah, by bills which were silent on the subject of slavery; prohibited the slave-trade in the District of Columbia; and granted more summary and effective provisions for the recovery of fugitives from slavery. President Fillmore, by constitution a conservative, yet a truly patriotic citizen, had been in favor of this bill from the first, and believed that by it the North and South would be pacified, and the horrors of a civil war averted, and he consequently used his efforts for its passage, promptly approved it when passed, and by his proclamations endeavored to enforce the most odious and difficult provisions of it—those relating to the rendition of fugitive slaves. No one can doubt the purity of his motives, the conscientiousness which led him to undertake its enforcement, or the patriotism which prompted his conduct. But he and his cabinet had failed to comprehend the real feelings of the people on these questions. The compromises were unsatisfactory to both parties. The South had been defeated on the main question—the extension of slavery to the Pacific—and did not regard the fugitive slave law as adequate compensation for this great loss, and were not disposed to acquiesce in it. The fugitive slave law had set the North on fire, and could not be enforced except at the

point of the bayonet, and thus the "Omnibus Bill" brought speedy destruction upon all its advocates. Mr. Webster, long the idol of his party in the North, was cast overboard, and the disappointment and chagrin which was the result of his signal defeat unquestionably hastened his end, as it probably did Mr. Clay's also. The party which had elected Taylor and Fillmore by such majorities in 1848 was so overwhelmingly defeated at the next presidential election that it hardly attempted to rally again, and disappeared from public view before 1856. The two sections, North and South, were thenceforward arrayed in more bitter hostility toward each other than before, and the strife which, ten years later, culminated in a terrible civil war, was greatly aggravated. President Fillmore came in for a large share of denunciation, both from the North and the South; and, after the close of his presidential term, never held any other public office. In other respects, President Fillmore's Administration of two years and eight months was deserving of honorable remembrance. He gave countenance and aid to several important exploring expeditions, especially to that of Commodore Perry to Japan; that to the La Plata River; that of Lieutenant Lynch to the Dead Sea; that of Ringgold to the Chinese Sea; and that of Herndon and Gibbon to the Amazon. An invasion of Cuba by lawless citizens of the United States being threatened, he issued his proclamation prohibiting it, and when the expedition sailed, through the connivance of the collector of the port of New Orleans, caused its capture and the punishment of those engaged in it; removed the collector, and caused the vessel to be seized and condemned for violation of the neutrality laws. The foreign policy of Mr. Fillmore's Administration was dignified and self-respecting; and, by the character of its representatives abroad, as well as by its manly independence, did much to give the Government position and influence with other nations.

After the expiration of his term of office, Mr. Fillmore returned to Buffalo, where he led a quiet life, enjoying a consulting practice, with his old-time partner, and greatly esteemed for his integrity and courteous manners. In 1855 he visited Europe, and made a tour of nearly two years' duration. While thus absent from the country he was nominated for the presidency in 1856, by the "American" or Know-nothing party, and polled a respectable popular vote, but received only the electoral vote of Maryland. The degree of D. C. L. was tendered to him by the University of Oxford, but he declined the honor. He had received the honorary degree of LL. D. from an American college during his presidency. True to his conservative views, ex-President Fillmore took no active part in the late civil war, though his sympathies were, it is believed, with the Union. Of late years, he had frequently presided over large commercial conventions and other public gatherings, being admirably qualified for the control of such assemblages by his thorough parliamentary ability, his widely-extended knowledge, his broad views, and a personal urbanity which nothing could disturb.

FINANCES OF THE UNITED STATES.

The financial embarrassment which commenced in the last quarter of the year 1873 continued during 1874. Meantime, the question of expansion or contraction of the currency became prominent in the minds of the people, as involving the remedy demanded. The Government practically maintained a neutral position, and the volume of the currency continued without any important change.

In the annual report of the Secretary of the Treasury, made December, 1873, there was presented a statement of the receipts and expenditures of the Government for the first quarter of the fiscal year ending June 30, 1874, and an estimate of the same for the remaining three-quarters of the fiscal year. The receipts and expenditures of the first quarter above mentioned, ending on September 30, 1873, which is the first of the fiscal year ending June 30, 1874, were as follows:

Customs...............................	$43,195,403 68
Sales of public lands..................	573,768 07
Internal revenue......................	25,640,454 41
Tax on circulation, etc., of national banks...........................	3,490,713 66
Repayment of interest by Pacific Railways...........................	193,970 56
Customs' fines, etc....................	431,514 21
Consular, patent, and other fees.......	503,941 12
Proceeds of Government property.......	303,765 32
Miscellaneous sources.................	1,507,931 21
Net ordinary receipts................	$81,853,492 24
Premium on sales of coin..............	2,350,818 34
Government of Great Britain—payment for the award of the tribunal of arbitration at Geneva..........................	15,500,000 00
Total receipts....................	$99,704,310 58
Balance in Treasury, June 30, 1873......	$131,192,028 50
Total available..................	$230,896,339 08

The expenditures during the same period were as follows:

Civil and miscellaneous expenses, including public buildings, light-houses, and collecting the revenues............	$17,372,293 60
Indians................................	2,008,715 19
Pensions...............................	8,698,156 58
Military establishment, including fortifications, river and harbor improvements, and arsenals................	13,795,053 48
Naval establishment, including vessels and machinery, and improvements at navy-yards.........................	9,792,451 57
Interest on the public debt, including Pacific Railway bonds..................	37,051,907 79
Total, exclusive of the principal and premium on public debt..................	$88,718,578 21
Premium, purchased bonds. $1,301,946 78	
Award by Geneva Tribunal, investment account...... 15,500,000 00	
Net redemption of the public debt................. 32,986,823 91	49,788,775 69
Balance in Treasury, September 30, 1873.	92,388,985 18
Total..........................	$230,896,339 08

For the remaining three-quarters of the same fiscal year, ending June 30, 1874, it was estimated that the receipts would be as follows:

Customs...............................	$111,000,000
Sales of public lands.................	1,500,000
Internal revenue.....................	66,000,000
Tax on national banks................	3,200,000
Pacific Railways......................	800,000
Customs' fines, etc....................	800,000
Consular, patent, and other fees......	1,300,000
Sales of public property..............	1,000,000
Miscellaneous sources................	2,000,000
Total.........................	$187,100,000

It was estimated that the expenditures for the same period would be as follows:

Civil expenses........................	$15,250,000
Foreign intercourse....................	1,100,000
Indians................................	6,590,000
Pensions...............................	21,780,000
Military establishment................	34,000,000
Naval establishment...................	18,000,000
Miscellaneous, civil, including public buildings..............................	34,000,000
Interest on the public debt...........	70,000,000
Total.........................	$200,680,000

But the moneys received and covered into the Treasury by warrants during the fiscal year ending June 30, 1874, were as follows:

From customs.........................	$163,103,833 69
From internal revenue................	102,409,784 90
From sales of public lands............	1,852,428 93
From tax on circulation and deposits of national banks......................	7,030,038 17
From repayment of interest by Pacific Railway Companies....................	1,028,895 56
From customs' fines, penalties, etc......	651,271 76
From labor, drayage, storage, etc.......	741,435 23
From sales of Indian trust-lands........	903,439 50
From fees—consular, letters-patent, and land................................	1,898,189 74
From proceeds of sales of Government property............................	1,699,017 63
From marine-hospital tax..............	352,379 98
From steamboat fees...................	274,490 91
From profits on coinage, etc..........	447,970 73
From tax on seal-skins................	356,610 42
From miscellaneous sources...........	1,691,303 70
Total ordinary receipts...........	$284,441,090 84
Premium on sales of coin..............	5,037,665 22
Total net receipts, exclusive of loans....	$289,478,756 66

Payment by the British Government of the award of the tribunal of arbitration at Geneva..........	$15,500,000 00	
Excess of net receipts from certificates of deposit of legal tenders, etc., over redemptions.............	17,207,475 23	32,707,475 23
Total net receipts.................		$322,186,231 29
Balance in Treasury, June 30, 1873......$131,192,028 50		
Amount since received from late depositary, Cincinnati, Ohio........	1,033 78	
	$131,193,067 28	
Deduct unavailable balances with depositaries carried to their debits on books of the Register, and to the credit of the Treasurer of the United States..........	13,730 18	
		$131,179,337 10
Total available cash...............		$453,365,568 39

The net expenditures by warrants during the same period were:

For civil expenses..........................	$17,627,115 09
For foreign intercourse..................	1,508,064 27
For Indians..............................	6,092,462 09
For pensions.............................	29,038,414 66
For military establishment, including fortifications, river and harbor improvements, and arsenals...............	42,313,927 22
For naval establishment, including vessels and machinery, and improvements at navy-yards.......................	30,932,587 42
For miscellaneous, civil, including public buildings, light-houses, and collecting the revenue....................	50,506,414 25
For interest on the public debt...........	107,119,815 21
Total net ordinary expenditures, exclusive of the public debt,..................	$283,738,800 21
Premium on bonds purchased............	1,395,073 55
	$287,133,873 76
Award of Geneva Tribunal, investment account..................................	15,500,000 00
Total net disbursements...........	$302,633,873 76
Balance in Treasury, June 30, 1874.......	150,731,694 63
Total...............................	$453,365,568 39

It will be seen by this statement that the

net revenues for the fiscal year were...	$289,478,756 06
And the ordinary expenses...............	287,133,873 76
Leaving a surplus revenue of........	$2,344,882 30

During the months of July, August, and September, on the first quarter of the fiscal year 1874, bonds to the extent of $12,936,450 were purchased.

The receipts during the first quarter of the fiscal year ending June 30, 1875, were as follows:

From customs	$46,651,200 10
From internal revenue...................	26,314,615 33
From sales of public lands...............	391,465 88
From tax on circulation, etc., of national banks...................................	3,596,148 23
From repayment of interest by Pacific Railways.................................	217,941 97
From customs' fines, etc.................	80,540 81
From consular, patent, and other fees....	451,257 11
From proceeds of sales of Government property................................	522,546 77
From miscellaneous sources.............	1,255,339 57
Net ordinary receipts...............	$79,431,048 27
From premium on sales of Coin..........	1,453,237 72
Total net ordinary receipts.........	$80,884,285 99
Receipts from certificates of deposit of legal tenders and Coin certificates in excess of redemptions...................	5,247,068 24
Balance in Treasury, June 30, 1874.......	150,731,694 63
Total available.....................	$236,863,048 86

The expenditures during the same period were as follows:

For civil and miscellaneous expenses, including public buildings, light-houses, and collecting the revenues............	$20,838,410 77
For Indians..............................	3,032,752 93
For pensions.............................	8,913,407 18
For military establishment, including fortifications, river and harbor improvements, and arsenals...............	11,618,290 99
For naval establishment, including vessels and machinery, and improvements at navy-yards.......................	8,122,728 14
For interest on the public debt, including Pacific Railway interest...............	32,787,899 38
Total ordinary expenditures.......	$85,313,489 42
Balance in the Treasury, September 30, 1874....................................	151,549,559 44
Total...............................	$236,863,048 86

For the remaining three-quarters of the same fiscal year, ending June 30, 1875, it was estimated that the receipts would be:

From customs	$115,350,000 00
From internal revenue....	78,784,000 00
From sales of public lands...............	1,000,000 00
From tax on national banks.............	3,300,000 00
From Pacific Railways...................	500,000 00
From customs' fines, etc.................	200,000 00
From consular, patent, and other fees....	1,200,000 00
From sales of public property............	1,000,000 00
From miscellaneous sources.............	2,100,000 00
Total...............................	$203,434,000 00

For the same period, it was estimated that the expenditures would be:

For civil and miscellaneous, including public buildings......................	$48,060,000 00
For Indians..............................	5,000,000 00
For pensions.............................	21,442,000 00
For military establishment...............	28,500,000 00
For naval establishment..................	17,000,000 00
For interest on the public debt...........	70,000,000 00
Total...............................	$190,002,000 00

Thus, for the fiscal year ending June 30, 1875, from the foregoing account of actual receipts and expenditures for the first quarter, and of the estimates of the same for the remaining three-quarters, the estimates being based on the assumption that Congress would not increase the expenditures by deficiency or other appropriations, it was expected that the revenues would amount to $284,318,285.99, and that the ordinary expenses would be $275,315,489.42; which would leave a surplus revenue of $9,002,796.57 to be applied to the sinking-fund.

The sum of $31,096,545 would be required under the law for this fund; and, therefore, unless the revenues shall increase beyond the amount anticipated, there would be a deficiency in the sinking-fund account for this year of $22,093,748.43.

During the fiscal year the public debt was reduced by the sum of $5,762,447.65, as will appear by the following statement:

Principal of the debt July 1, 1873.......	$2,234,482,993 20
Interest due and unpaid, and accrued interest to date.......................	42,356,652 82
Total debt.......................	$2,276,839,646 02
Less cash in the Treasury...........	131,179,337 10
Debt, less cash in the Treasury....	$2,145,660,308 92
Principal of the debt July 1, 1874.......	$2,251,690,468 43
Interest due and unpaid, and accrued interest to date.......................	38,939,087 47
Total debt.......................	$2,290,629,555 90
Less cash in the Treasury...........	150,731,694 63
Debt, less cash in the Treasury....	$2,139,897,861 27
Showing a decrease during the year, as above stated, of......................	$5,762,447 65
This decrease is represented by the excess of receipts over expenditures....	$2,344,882 30
The interest due and unpaid June 30, 1874, was less than June 30, 1873, by..	3,417,565 35
	$5,762,447 65

In the following table is given a statement of the outstanding principal of the public debt of the United States on June 30, 1874:

STATEMENT OF THE OUTSTANDING PRINCIPAL OF THE PUBLIC DEBT OF THE UNITED STATES, JUNE 30, 1874.

TITLE.	Length of Loan.	When redeemable.	Rates of Interest.	Selling Price.	Amount authorized.	Amount Issued.	Amount outstanding.
Old debt................	....	On demand........	5 & 6 p. ct.	....	....	....	$57,665 00
Treasury notes prior to 1846..................	1 and 2 years.	1 and 2 years from date.	1 mill to 6 per cent.	Par.	....	....	82,575 35
Treasury notes of 1846...	1 year....	1 year from date...	6 per cent.	Par.	$10,000,000	....	6,000 00
Mexican indemnity.......	5 years...	April and July, 1849	5 per cent.	Par.	350,000	$303,573	1,104 91
Treasury notes of 1847...	1 and 2 years.	After 60 days' notice.	6 per cent.	Par.	23,000,000	....	950 00
Loan of 1847.............	20 years..	January 1, 1868.....	6 per cent.	Par.	23,000,000	28,207,000	1,250 00
Bounty-land scrip.......	Indefinite	July 1, 1849.........	6 per cent.	Par.	Indefinite.	....	3,400 00
Texan indemnity stock..	14 years..	January 1, 1865......	5 per cent.	Par.	10,000,000	5,000,000	174,000 00
Treasury notes of 1857...	1 year....	60 days' notice......	5 & 5½ p. c.	Par.	20,000,000	20,000,000	2,000 00
Loan of 1858.............	15 years..	January 1, 1874......	5 per cent.	Par.	20,000,000	20,000,000	394,000 00
Loan of 1860.............	10 years..	January 1, 1871......	5 per cent.	Par.	21,000,000	7,022,000	10,000 00
Loan of February, 1861 (1881's).............	10 or 20 y's	January 1, 1881.....	6 per cent.	Par.	25,000,900	18,415,000	18,415,000 00
Treasury notes of 1861...	2 years. 60 days.	2 years after date. 60 days after date.	6 per cent.	Par.	22,468,100 12,896,350	35,364,450	3,150 00
Oregon war debt........	20 years..	July 1, 1881........	6 per cent.	Par.	2,800,000	1,090,850	945,000 00
Loan of July and August, 1861 (1881's)...	20 years..	July 1, 1881........	6 per cent.	Par.	250,000,000	50,000,000 139,321,200	189,321,350 00
Old demand notes.......	....	On demand........	None......	Par.	60,000,000	60,000,000	76,732 50
Seven-thirties of 1861....	3 years...	August 19 and October 1, 1864.	7 3-10 p. c.	Par.	140,094,750	140,094,750	19,200 00
Five-twenties of 1862....	5 or 20 y'rs	May 1, 1867........	6 per cent.	Par.	515,000,000	514,771,600	169,516,150 00
Legal-tender notes.......	....	On demand........	None......	Par.	450,000,000	915,420,031	382,000,000 00
Temporary loan........	Not less than 30 days.	After 10 days' notice.	4, 5, and 6 per cent.	Par.	150,000,000	....	78,560 00
Certificates of indebtedness.............	1 year....	1 year after date....	6 per cent.	Par.	No limit..	561,753,211	5,000 00
Fractional currency.....	....	On presentation....	None......	Par.	50,000,000	223,025,663	45,881,295 67
Loan of 1863.............	17 years..	July 1, 1881........	6 per cent.	Pre'm of 4.13	75,000,000	75,000,000	75,000,000 00
One-year notes of 1863...	1 year ...	1 year after date....	5 per cent.	Par.	400,000,000	44,520,000	74,775 00
Two-year notes of 1863..	2 years...	2 years after date...	5 per cent.	Par.	400,000,000	166,480,000	52,850 00
Coin certificates........	....	On demand........	None......	Par.	Indefinite.	562,776,400	22,825,100 00
Compound int'st notes..	3 years...	June 10, 1867, and May 15, 1868.	6 per cent. compound.	Par.	400,000,000	266,595,440	415,210 00
Ten-forties of 1864.......	10 or 40 y's	March 1, 1874.......	5 per cent.	Par to 7 per ct. pr.	200,000,000	196,117,300	194,567,300 00
Five-twenties of March, 1864.................	5 or 20 y'rs	November 1, 1869...	6 per cent.	Par.	....	3,882,500	946,600 00
Five-twenties of June, 1864.................	5 or 20 y'rs	November 1, 1869...	6 per cent.	Par.	400,000,000	125,561,300	58,046,200 00
Seven-thirties of 1864 and 1865.............	3 years...	August 15, 1867. June 15, 1868... July 15, 1868...	7 3-10 p. c.	Par.	800,000,000	829,992,500	228,450 00
Navy pension fund......	Indefinite	....	3 per cent.	Par.	Indefinite.	14,000,000	14,000,000 00
Five-twenties of 1865....	5 or 20 y'rs	November 1, 1870..	6 per cent.	Par.	203,327,250	203,327,250	152,534,850 00
Consols of 1865........	5 or 20 y'rs	July 1, 1870........	6 per cent.	Par.	332,998,950	332,998,950	202,663,100 00
Consols of 1867.........	5 or 20 y'rs	July 1, 1872........	6 per cent.	Par.	379,602,350	379,616,050	310,624,400 00
Consols of 1868.........	5 or 20 y'rs	July 1, 1873.......	6 per cent.	Par.	42,539,350	42,539,350	37,474,000 00
Three per ct. certificates.	Indefinite	On demand........	3 per cent.	Par.	75,000,000	85,150,000	5,000 00
Certificates of indebtedness of 1870.............	5 years...	September 1, 1875..	4 per cent.	Par.	678,362	678,362	678,000 00
Funded loan of 1881.....	10 years..	May 1, 1881........	5 per cent.	Par.	500,000,000	200,000,000	315,800,750 00
Certificates of deposit...	Indefinite	On demand........	None......	Par.	No limit..	137,675,000	58,760,000 00
							$2,251,690,468 43

With regard to refunding the national debt, the Secretary of the Treasury makes the following statement:

On assuming charge of this Department, June 3, 1874, the Secretary found the balance of the five per cent. loan authorized by the acts of July 14, 1870, and January 20, 1871, then unissued, to be $178,548,300.

On the 2d day of July a circular was issued by the Secretary, inviting proposals, and in response thereto bids from various parties, at home and abroad, were received, the aggregate amount of which was $75,933,550. Of this amount, $20,933,550 comprised the domestic bids, and $55,000,000 the joint proposal of Messrs. N. M. Rothschild & Sons, of London, and Messrs. J. and W. Seligman & Co., of New York, The domestic bids at par and above, which were accepted by the Department, aggregated $10,113,550, and those at less than par, which were rejected, amounted to $10,820,000.

The proposal for $55,000,000 excluded the acceptance of all other bids, and provided that the parties should purchase $10,000,000 on or before August 1, 1874, and the remaining $45,000,000 at their pleasure, in several successive installments, prior to February 1, 1875; also that they should have the option of the entire balance of the five per cent. loan, $122,688,550, until the expiration of six months from January 31, 1875, and that the Secretary should keep an agent in London to deliver new fives and receive payment therefor. This proposition was modified, and on the 28th day of July a contract was entered into between the Secretary and Messrs. August Belmont & Co., of New York, on behalf of Messrs. N. M. Rothschild & Sons, of London, England, and associates, and Messrs. J. and W. Seligman & Co., of New York, for themselves and associates, for the negotiation of $45,000,000 of the five per cent. bonds, the contracting parties having deposited with the United States Treasury two per cent. of the amount subscribed for, as a guarantee for the fulfillment of their agreement. The conditions of the contract were substantially as follows:

The contracting parties to have the option of the balance of the loan, viz., $122,688,550, until January 31, 1875; to be allowed one-quarter of one per cent. commission upon the amount taken; they agreeing to subscribe for $15,000,000 of the before-mentioned amount—$45,000,000—on the 1st day of August, 1874, and to subscribe for the remaining amount—$30,000,000—at their pleasure, in amounts of not less than five millions each, prior to the 31st day of January, 1875. The contract also allows the parties the exclusive right to subscribe for the remainder or any portion of the five per cent. bonds authorized by the acts of Congress aforesaid, by giving notice thereof to the Secretary of the Treasury prior to January 31, 1875.

The agreement, on the part of the Secretary of the Treasury, with the parties before mentioned, was to issue calls of even dates with their subscriptions for the redemption of an equivalent amount of six per cent. five-twenty bonds, as provided by the act of July 14, 1870. The subscribers agreed to pay for said five per cent. bonds, par and interest accrued to the date of maturity of each call, in gold coin, United States coin coupons, or any of the six per cent. five-twenty bonds called for redemption; they also agreed to defray all expenses incurred in sending bonds to London, upon their request, and in transmitting bonds, coin United States coupons, or gold coin, to the Treasury Department at Washington, D. C.

On account of the subscriptions of Messrs. Rothschild and Seligman, and their associates, and those of home subscribers, calls for six per cent. five-twenty bonds of the loan of February 25, 1862, were made as follows:

August 1, 1874	$25,000,000
September 1, 1874	15,000,000
October 1, 1874	10,000,000
November 2, 1874	5,000,000
Total	$55,000,000

The excess of subscriptions over calls—viz., $113,550—has been provided for by uncalled bonds which have been received by the Department in payment for that amount.

The larger portion of the bonds subscribed for has thus far been negotiated in Europe, where exchanges are still being made.

· Such being the amount and condition of the public debt, the next feature of the finances of the Government to be considered is its revenue. The largest amount of this revenue is collected at the custom-houses. But, during the fiscal year ending June 30, 1874, the decline in these receipts was nearly $25,000,000. The receipts for the last half of the year 1874, being the first two quarters of the fiscal year 1875, were $2,500,000 less than for the corresponding period of the previous year.

The act of June 6, 1872, admitted large classes of manufactures to a reduction of ten per cent. of the duties prescribed by previous statutes, without designating specifically the articles to which the reduction should apply, leaving much room for construction in the practical application of the act to articles of new design or of particular combinations of materials. This act was followed by a system of extreme pressure for reduction, claimed through changes of classification of articles, and advantage was sought to be taken of every doubtful construction of all parts of the act.

During the years 1873 and 1874 there was a good deal effected in the way of reduction of duties through changes in form or component materials of merchandise, intended to answer the same purpose in consumption that articles and fabrics charged with a higher rate of duty had previously answered. Very large substitutions of materials other than wool have been made for fabrics previously paying the duty charged on woolens. Silks, linens, and cottons, have been similarly imitated, while the true rate of duty was avoided in some cases, and sought to be avoided in others, by claiming them as subject to rates of duty prescribed in the acts of 1861–'62 as manufactures of mixed materials.

Some portions of the reductions thus claimed were admitted in the revision of the statutes of 1874, while others were rejected as not properly authorized. It has been ascertained, as the result of careful calculation, that a concession of the reduced classifications claimed in the large number of appeals made to the Secretary during the year 1874 would have reduced the revenues so far as to seriously embarrass the Treasury. This urgency for reduction diminished, and more general acquiescence in reasonable and proper construction of the statutes by those who would at any time be content with an equal administration of such laws followed.

The general depression of business resulting from the panic of September, 1873, was followed by unusual delay in forwarding crops. Prices in all the markets, foreign and domestic, were not sufficiently high to induce shippers to make the usual investment in moving the crops, and the result was that the demand for consumption of foreign merchandise usual in the West and interior in the fall was held in reserve. As a consequence of this absence of demand for foreign merchandise, purchases for the interior and the West were greatly restricted, and with reasonable caution importers avoided assuming the burden of stocks of goods not likely to be readily taken off their hands for consumption. In what manner or at what time this constraint will be entirely relieved, it is not easy to say; but it would be wholly without precedent to find such abundant production as has marked the year 1874 without remunerative demand for consumption, for any considerable time. It is a reasonable inference that this state of things will yield as the wants of Europe for our surplus crops are developed in the year 1875, and that general commerce, with the revenues to be received from it, will revive accordingly. For the present, it is of the highest importance to protect the revenue provided by law in the most faithful manner.

It is certain that the aggregate amount now received from this source is necessary to revenue to meet demands, which cannot be safely stated at less than $160,000,000 in gold, besides the receipts from internal revenue and other sources. The impost statements for 1872-'73 show how heavily the revenues from customs were depleted by the reduction of 1872, coffee alone having yielded $10,969,098.77 in 1871, and $7,192,074.91 in 1872. On the importations of coffee, in 1873, the rate of three cents per pound would have yielded nearly $9,000,000, and two cents per pound almost $6,000,000.

The following table exhibits the annual imports of coffee and tea from 1871 to 1874, inclusive, with the total value thereof, and the average price per pound in the countries of their production:

STATEMENT OF IMPORTS OF COFFEE AND TEA DURING THE FOUR FISCAL YEARS (ENDING JUNE 30), 1871 TO 1874, INCLUSIVE.

FISCAL YEARS ENDING JUNE 30.	COFFEE.		Average Cost per Pound at Place of Shipment.	TEA.		Average Cost per Pound at Place of Shipment.
	Pounds.	Aggregate Cost at Place of Shipment.		Pounds.	Aggregate Cost at Place of Shipment.	
1871	317,992,048	$30,992,869	9.74 cents.	51,364,910	$17,254,617	33.60 cents.
1872	298,805,946	37,942,225	12.69 "	63,811,003	22,943,575	36.00 "
1873	293,297,271	44,109,671	15.00 "	64,815,136	24,466,170	37.74 "
1874	285,171,512	55,048,967	19.34 "	55,811,605	21,112,234	37.82 "

This record of foreign prices for coffee tends strongly to the conclusion, making due allowance for the effect of short crops on prices, that the duty repealed by the act of 1872 was added to the selling price abroad, with no advantage to consumers here, while the country, as a whole, has paid more than before for the entire stock. The repeal of the duty on tea caused little or no reduction of prices to consumers here, but an increase of prices abroad.

The decrease from each source of internal revenue for the year ending June 30, 1874, as compared with the fiscal year 1873, appears from the following statement:

SOURCES.	1873.	1874.	Decrease.
Spirits	$52,099,371 78	$49,444,089 85	$2,655,281 93
Tobacco	34,386,303 09	33,242,875 62	1,143,427 47
Fermented liquors	9,324,937 84	9,304,679 72	20,258 12
Banks and bankers	3,771,031 46	3,387,160 67	383,870 79
Penalties, etc.	461,653 06	364,216 34	97,436 72
Adhesive stamps	7,702,376 85	6,136,844 64	1,565,582 21
Back taxes under repealed laws	6,329,782 00	764,880 14	5,564,901 86
Total	$114,075,456 08	$102,644,746 98	$11,430,709 10

The decrease in the receipts from spirits is due to the small production of brandy in 1874, in consequence of the partial failure of the fruit-crop in 1873; the earlier collection of special taxes in 1874 than in 1873; the reduction in the value of warehouse, rectifiers', and dealers' stamps by act of June 6, 1872, which reduction operated during the whole of the fiscal year 1874, but during only eleven months of 1873; and the smaller collections from repealed taxes relating to spirits in 1874 than in 1873.

The falling off in the receipts from tobacco is owing chiefly to the abolition of the system of bonded warehouses, under act of June 6, 1872, by which large quantities of manufactured tobacco were placed upon the market during the fiscal year 1873, and to the increased activity given during the early part of the same year to the movement of plug-tobacco by the reduction in the rate of tax from 32 to 20 cents per pound.

The act of June 6, 1872, so far as it relates to a reduction of taxation on banks and documentary stamps, did not go into full operation prior to the last fiscal year.

The number of brewers engaged in the production of fermented liquors during the fiscal years 1873 and 1874, was as follows: In 1873, 3,554; in 1874, 2,524—a decrease of 1,030.

During the fiscal year 1873, over $5,000,000 were collected from income as back taxes, and $500,000 from gas, items no longer taxable, and collections of past-due taxes, under repealed statutes, are of course constantly decreasing.

The receipts from internal revenue for the first quarter of the fiscal years ending June 30, 1874 and 1875, were as follows:

First quarter of 1874 .... $25,640,454 41
First quarter of 1875 .... 26,314,615 33

Increase 674,160 92

The aggregate receipts for the months of October and November, 1873, were $13,863,029.97, and for the same months of 1874 they were $17,476,202.99.

The comparative coin value of the exports and imports of the United States for the last fiscal year, as appears from official returns to the Bureau of Statistics, may be exhibited as follows:

Exports of domestic merchandise $569,433,421
Exports of foreign merchandise 16,849,619

Total exports $586,283,040
Imports 567,406,342

Excess of exports over imports $18,876,698

Exports of specie and bullion $66,680,405
Imports of specie and bullion. 28,454,906

Excess of exports over imports $38,175,499

Total excess of exports of merchandise, specie, and bullion, over imports of same..... $57,052,197

While these returns are believed to be reasonably accurate as regards the exports by sea, it has been found impracticable to obtain complete statements of our exports to Canada, owing to the fact that manifests, containing the quantities and values of merchandise exported in railway-cars, are not legally required. Detailed statements have been received, however, from the Commissioner of Customs of the Dominion of Canada, from which it appears that the coin value of our exports to Canada during the last fiscal year was $10,200,059 in excess of that returned by the United States customs officers, which would increase the exports for the last fiscal year as above stated, by that amount.

Merchandise of the value of $17,878,225 was withdrawn from bond for consumption, in excess of that entered for warehouse, during the year.

The export of coin and bullion was $24,952,188 less than for the preceding year, while the exports of domestic merchandise have increased $63,803,118.

There appears to have been a decrease in importations for the last year of $74,729,868, as compared with the previous fiscal year, and of $59,188,735, as compared with the fiscal year ended June 30, 1872.

The following imports show an increase in value, respectively:

Coffee, $10,941,570; molasses, $1,046,773; salt, $556,127; flaxseed, $147,229; brass and other metals, $475,439; medicinal barks, $418,436; coal, $410,762; hair, $408,826; raw hemp, $328,994; indigo and cochineal, $353,474; unmanufactured wool, $384,810; articles exported, and returned, $1,287,622; opium, $561,726; spices, $586,642; barley, $2,838,672; dress-goods, $1,714,838.

Those exhibiting a decrease in importation are principally unmanufactured wool, $12,183,632; manufactures of wool, $4,149,298; raw silk, $2,606,613; manufactures of silk, $5,893,253; fine linen, laces, and other manufactures of flax, $2,955,636; cotton goods, $7,007,455; kid gloves, leather, and manufactures of leather, $1,107,528; furs, $379,427; hides and skins, $1,281,565; jute and jute butts, $1,471,727; paper-stock, $1,058,297; paper and paper hangings, $734,872; horse-hair, $792,675; old and scrap iron, $5,148,370; copper ingots, $2,347,626; manufactures of copper, $887,836; pig and bar lead, $1,094,240; tin plates, $2,000,727; watches, $900,531; jewelry and precious stones, $876,997; fancy goods and perfumery, $468,986; tobacco, snuff, and cigars, $1,304,002; wines and liquors, $622,000; fruit and nuts, $1,392,044; sugar, $829,490; tea, $3,353,860; dutiable chemicals, $873,711; chemicals, drugs, and dyes, $1,444,919; dye-woods, madder, argols, bleaching-powder, and nitrate of soda, $713,083; soda-ash, $928,448; earthen, stone, and china-ware, $1,133,570; common window-glass, and glassware, $1,399,341; lumber, $2,-

694,327; crude India-rubber and gutta-percha, $703,821.

There was a falling off in the importation of iron and steel and their products of $20,866,536 in value, upon the following articles: Rails, $8,982,267; steel and manufactures of steel, $3,324,513; pig-iron, $3,915,747; bar-iron, $2,266,170; sheet, hoop, and band iron, $1,169,308; machinery, $400,192; anchors, cables, chains, castings, and hardware, $308,339.

There was also a decrease in the importation of live animals of $702,381, and of provisions of $849,331 in value.

Of domestic products exported, the following articles show an increase in value, in currency: Wheat, $49,969,205; wheat-flour, $9,876,430; rye and rye-flour, $1,440,999; corn and corn-meal, $1,029,829; cheese, $1,400,985; butter, $139,462; pork, $801,677; beef and tallow, $1,576,044; fish, $603,712; leaf-tobacco, $7,710,046; oil-cake, $487,798; horned cattle, $454,900; hogs, $838,435; agricultural implements, $503,839; timber, wood, and manufactures of wood, $2,233,919; coal, $909,675; manufactures of hemp, $691,021; iron and manufactures of iron, $846,197; fire-arms, $1,158,269; sailing-vessels sold to foreigners, $371,407.

The decrease in the exportation of domestic products appears principally in the following articles: Raw cotton, $16,016,489; bacon, hams, and lard, $3,576,025; hides, $1,044,641; furs and fur-skins, $391,185; leather and manufactures of leather, $518,976; sewing-machines, $556,424; crude mineral-oil, $910,354; crude turpentine and resin, $585,565; and silver ore, $969,303.

The most important question relating to the finances which was before the country during the year was on the expansion or contraction of the currency and the payment of specie. The views and action of Congress will be found in the debates on the currency, under the title of Congress, in this volume. The brief veto message of the President to Congress, resisting inflation, will be found in the same part of this volume. The views of the President were still further expressed in a memorandum prepared by himself and made public through the following correspondence:

UNITED STATES SENATE-CHAMBER,
WASHINGTON, June 4, 1874.

To the President:

I was so deeply impressed by the clearness and wisdom of the financial views, some of which you have fortunately reduced to writing, recently expressed by you in a conversation in which I had the honor, with a few others, to be a participant, that I cannot dismiss them from my mind. The great diversities of ideas throughout the country upon this subject, and the fact that public opinion concerning the same is still in process of formation, lead me to believe that the publication of these views would be productive of great good. I venture, therefore, to request of you that I may have a copy of the written memorandum to which I have alluded, with your permission that it may be made public.

I have the honor to be, very respectfully, your obedient servant, JOHN P. JONES.

The President replied as follows :

EXECUTIVE MANSION,
WASHINGTON, D. C., *June* 4, 1874.

DEAR SIR: Your note of this date, requesting a copy of a memorandum which I had prepared, expressive of my views upon the financial question, and which you, with others, have heard read, is received, but at too late an hour to comply to-night. I will, however, take great pleasure in furnishing you a copy in the morning, as soon as I can have it copied.

It is proper that I should state that these views were reduced to writing because I had been consulted on this question, not only by some of the members of the Conference Committee, but by many other members of Congress. To avoid any and all possibility of misunderstanding, I deemed this course both justifiable and proper.

With this explanation I inclose you herewith the memorandum referred to.

Very respectfully, U. S. GRANT.
To Hon. J. P. JONES, United States Senate.

The memorandum inclosed was as follows :

MEMORANDUM OF VIEWS ENTERTAINED ON THE SUBJECT OF DESIRABLE LEGISLATION ON THE FINANCES.

I believe it a high and plain duty to return to a specie basis at the earliest practicable day, not only in compliance with legislative and party pledges, but as a step indispensable to lasting national prosperity. I believe, further, that the time has come when this can be done, or at least begun, with less embarrassment to every branch of industry than at any future time after resort has been had to unstable and temporary expedients to stimulate unreal prosperity and speculation, on basis other than coin as the recognized medium of exchange throughout the commercial world.

The particular mode selected to bring about a restoration of the specie standard is not of so much consequence as that some adequate plan be devised, the time fixed when currency shall be exchangeable for coin at par, and the plan adopted rigidly adhered to. It is not probable that any legislation suggested by me would prove acceptable to both branches of Congress ; and, indeed, a full discussion might shake my own faith in the details of any plan I might propose. I will, however, venture to state the general features of the action which seems to me advisable, the financial platform on which I would stand, and any departure from which would be in a spirit of concession and harmony in deference to conflicting opinions :

1. I would like to see the legal-tender clause, so called, repealed, the repeal to take effect at a future time, say July 1, 1875. This would cause all contracts made after that date, for wages, sales, etc., to be estimated in coin. It would correct our notions of values. The specie dollar would be the only dollar known as the measure of equivalents. When debts afterward contracted were paid in currency, instead of calling the paper dollar a dollar and quoting gold at so much premium, we should think and speak of pa e as at so much discount; this alone would add greatly in bringing the two currencies near together at par.

2. I would like to see a provision that at a fixed day, say July 1, 1876, the currency issued by the United States should be redeemed in coin, on presentation to any assistant treasurer, and that all the currency so redeemed should be canceled and never reissued. To effect this it would be necessary to authorize the issue of bonds, payable in gold, bearing such interest as would command par in gold, to be put out by the Treasury only in such sums as should from time to time be needed for the purpose of redemption. Such legislation would insure a return to sound financial principles in two years, and would, in my judgment, work less hardship to the debtor interest than is likely to come from putting off the day of final reckoning. It must be borne in mind, too, that the creditor interest had its day of disadvantage also when our present financial system was brought in by the supreme needs of the nation at the time.

I would further provide that, from and after the date fixed for redemption, no bills, whether of national banks or of the United States, returned to the Treasury to be exchanged for new bills, should be replaced by bills of less denomination than $10, and that in one year after resumption all bills of less than $5 should be withdrawn from circulation, and in two years all bills of less than $10 should be withdrawn. The advantage of this would be strength given to the country against time of depression resulting from war, failure of crops, or any other cause, by keeping always in the hands of the people a large supply of the precious metals. With all smaller transactions conducted in coin many millions of it would be kept in constant use, and, of course, prevented from leaving the country. Undoubtedly a poorer currency will always drive the better out of circulation. With paper a legal tender and at a discount, gold and silver become articles of merchandise as much as wheat or cotton. The surplus will find the best market it can. With small bills in circulation there is no use for coin except to keep it in the vaults of banks to redeem circulation. During periods of great speculation and apparent prosperity there is little demand for coin, and then it will flow out to a market where it can be made to earn something, which it cannot do while lying idle. Gold, like every thing else, when not needed, becomes a surplus, and, like every other surplus, it seeks a market where it can find one. By giving active employment to coin, however, its presence can, it seems to me, be secured, and the panics and depressions which have occurred periodically in times of nominal specie payments, if they cannot be wholly prevented, can at least be greatly mitigated. Indeed, I question whether it would have been found necessary to depart from the standard of specie in the trying days which gave birth to the first legal-tender act had the country taken the ground of no small bills as early as 1850.

Again, I would provide an excess of revenue over current expenditures. I would do this by rigid economy and by taxation where taxation can best be borne. Increased revenue would work a constant reduction of debt and interest, and would provide coin to meet demands on the Treasury for the redemption of its notes, thereby diminishing the amount of bonds needed for that p pose. All taxes, after redemption begins, should be paid in coin or United States notes.

This would force redemption on the national banks. With measures like these, or measures which would work out such results, I see no danger in authorizing free banking without limit.

The views of the Secretary of the Treasury respecting the resumption of specie payments were briefly expressed in his report, as follows :

While it seems to be very generally conceded that resumption of specie payment is essential to the honor of the Government and to the general welfare, the views of intelligent and well-informed persons as to the best method of resumption are so widely divergent, and the plans that have been suggested so multifarious, that the Secretary feels embarrassment in suggesting a plan, the details of which will commend themselves to Congress. But there are one or two fundamental ideas underlying the subject which, it is believed, must be the basis of any practicable plan for resumption, and are, therefore, submitted for the consideration of Congress.

It is obvious that there can be no resumption by the Government so long as the volume of paper currency is largely in excess of the possible amount of coin available for that purpose which may come into the Treasury in any year, and while no provision is made for the conversion of this paper-money into any thing having a near relation to coin; nor is it possible for the banks or people to resume so long as the large amount of irredeemable paper now in circulation continues to be by law legal tender for all private debts with reference both to the past and the future. While this state of things lasts gold will continue to flow from us, and find employment where the natural laws of trade, unobstructed by restraining legislation, make its daily use indispensable.

The Secretary, therefore, recommends Congress to provide by law that after an early and fixed day United States notes shall cease to be legal tender as to contracts thereafter made. But this provision should not apply to official salaries or to other ordinary expenditures of the Government under then existing contracts or appropriations. Between the day thus to be fixed and the time of final resumption a sufficient period should elapse to enable the people and banks to prepare for the latter by such gradual processes in business as will neither lead to violent contraction in credit and values, nor suddenly increase the obligations of debtors. The sudden and immediate appreciation of the paper dollar to its par value in gold is not only no necessary element of redemption, but, as far as practicable, should be avoided. If during the period of the war the legal-tender acts operated as a bankrupt law, compelling creditors to give acquittances upon the receipt of less than the full amount of their debts, this is no reason why the law for resumption should now compel debtors at once to pay essentially more than they have contracted to pay. The adoption of such measures as will not suddenly increase the obligations of debtors, will go far to allay and disarm whatever popular opposition to resumption of specie payment may now exist, and, besides, would be but just to the debtor class. The day from which new contracts must be discharged in coin should be fixed sufficiently far in advance to give the people and the banks time to understand it and to prepare themselves for it. It is believed that not many months will be necessary for that purpose; but, to avoid the mischiefs already indicated, this day should precede the day of final resumption by a longer period. The time should not, in the opinion of the Secretary, be extended beyond three years, and might safely be made as much less as in the judgment of Congress would sufficiently protect the interest of debtors and avoid the evils of too sudden contraction.

The law should also authorize the immediate conversion of legal-tender notes into bonds bearing a low rate of interest, which, while inviting conversion, should not be so high as to appreciate the legal-tender notes rapidly, and thereby operate oppressively on the debtor class. As an additional inducement to the conversion of United States notes into these bonds at a low rate of interest, authority should be given for making them security for the circulation of national banks. The law should further provide the means for the redemption of such notes as may be presented for that purpose when the period of resumption shall have been reached. To this end, the Secretary should be authorized to make a loan not exceeding the total amount of notes remaining unconverted at the time of resumption, less the surplus revenue to be made applicable to such resumption. It is probable that the gradual and continued revival of business will so far increase the revenues that a large loan will not be required for this purpose; but it is advisable that the Secretary be authorized to make it in order to meet the contingency of a failure of sufficient surplus revenues. Such a loan should be made by issuing bonds to run for such time as the wisdom of Congress may suggest, and to be disposed of from time to time as the necessities of the case may require. In the opinion of the Secretary, these

bonds should run for a long period, and should bear interest at a rate not exceeding the lowest rate which the Government may then be paying in refunding its six per cent. securities. Any substantial or useful movement for resumption necessarily involves supplying the Treasury with increased amounts of coin, either by increased revenues or an adequate loan. The present condition of the credit of the Government, which would be further enhanced by the adoption of measures for return to a specie basis, leaves no room for doubt that a loan for such purpose would be readily taken at a low rate of interest. Measures should also be adopted requiring the banks to hold gold reserves preparatory to resumption on their part.

But the Secretary does not deem it proper to pursue the matter into further detail. If Congress shall conclude, as he earnestly hopes it will, that the time has arrived for the enactment of a law having for its object resumption of specie payments, its own wisdom will supply the necessary methods.

The act of Congress which became a law provides that the amount of United States notes outstanding and to be used as a part of the circulating medium, shall not exceed the sum of $382,000,000, and no part thereof shall be held or used as a reserve. It further provides for the repeal of the reserve required to be held by the national banks upon circulation;

For the redemption of all national-bank notes at the Treasury in legal-tender notes, for which purpose the banks are required to keep on deposit with the Treasurer 5 per cent. of their circulation; which amount is to be counted as a part of the reserve required to be held on deposits;

For the deposit by any national bank of lawful money with the Treasurer, in sums of not less than $9,000, and the withdrawal of the bonds on deposit as security for such circulating notes, provided that the amount of such bonds shall not be reduced below $50,000;

For the withdrawal of $55,000,000 from national banks in States which have received more than their proportion, and its redistribution to national banks in States which have received less than their proportion, upon an apportionment made on the basis of population and of wealth, as shown by the returns of the census of 1870, not more than $30,000,000 of which shall be withdrawn and redistributed during the fiscal year ending June 30, 1875.

Twenty-two hundred national banks have been organized since the establishment of the national banking system, under the act of February 28, 1863. Thirty-five of these banks have failed, and one hundred and thirty-seven gone into voluntary liquidation by a vote of two-thirds of the shareholders, under section 42 of the act, leaving 2,028 banks in existence on the 1st day of November, 1874. During the year, seventy-one national banks have been organized, with an authorized capital of $6,745,500. Three banks have failed and twenty have gone into voluntary liquidation.

The following table exhibits the resources and liabilities of the national banks in operation at corresponding periods for the last five years:

BANKS.	OCTOBER 8, 1870.	OCTOBER 2, 1871.	OCTOBER 3, 1872.	SEPTEMBER 12, 1873.	OCTOBER 2, 1874.
	1,615 Banks.	1,767 Banks.	1,919 Banks.	1,976 Banks.	2,004 Banks.
RESOURCES.					
Loans and discounts..............	$713,767,453	$827,089,625	$872,520,104	$940,333,304	$949,870,628
Overdrafts......................	3,160,626	3,862,585	4,677,819	3,986,812	4,524,164
United States bonds for circulation	340,857,450	364,475,800	382,046,400	388,330,400	383,254,800
United States bonds for deposits	15,381,500	28,087,500	15,479,750	14,805,000	14,691,700
United States bonds on hand....	22,323,800	17,753,650	12,142,550	8,819,850	13,313,550
Other stocks and bonds.........	23,614,721	24,517,059	23,533,152	23,714,035	27,807,827
Due from reserve agents........	66,275,699	86,578,609	80,717,071	96,184,121	83,885,127
Due from national banks........	33,948,806	43,525,362	34,486,594	41,413,680	39,695,309
Due from State banks..........	9,202,407	12,772,670	12,976,878	12,032,873	11,196,612
Real estate, furniture, and fixtures	27,470,747	30,089,784	32,276,498	34,661,823	38,112,926
Current expenses................	5,871,730	6,153,370	6,310,429	6,985,437	7,658,739
Premiums paid..................	2,491,222	5,500,890	6,546,849	7,752,844	8,876,659
Cash items.....................	12,473,107	13,984,971	14,916,784	11,433,913	12,296,417
Clearing-house exchanges.......	79,089,688	101,165,855	110,086,315	88,926,004	97,383,687
National-bank notes............	13,576,483	14,270,951	15,787,296	16,103,842	18,450,013
Fractional currency............	2,078,179	2,095,485	2,151,748	2,302,775	2,234,943
Specie.........................	18,460,011	18,252,998	10,229,737	19,868,469	21,240,945
Legal-tender notes..............	77,293,577	106,987,666	102,074,104	92,347,663	80,016,946
Three per cent. certificates......	26,330,000	7,180,000	1,555,000	....	....
U. S. certificates of deposit......	....	....	6,710,000	20,610,000	42,830,000
Clearing-house certificates.......	19,136,060	20,323,069	8,632,000	175,000	....
Redemption fund with United States Treasurer..............	....	....	....	....	20,349,950
Totals..................	$1,510,713,236	$1,730,566,899	$1,755,857,093	$1,830,627,845	$1,877,180,942
LIABILITIES.					
Capital stock..........	$430,399,301	$458,255,696	$479,629,144	$491,072,616	$493,765,121
Surplus fund...................	94,061,439	101,112,672	110,257,516	120,314,499	128,958,107
Undivided profits..............	33,608,619	42,008,714	46,623,784	54,515,132	51,484,437
National bank circulation.......	291,798,649	315,519,117	333,495,027	339,081,799	338,225,298
State bank circulation..........	2,138,548	1,921,056	1,567,143	1,188,853	964,997
Dividends unpaid..............	2,462,591	4,540,195	3,149,750	1,402,548	3,515,847
Individual deposits............	501,407,587	600,868,486	613,290,701	622,685,563	669,068,996
United States deposits.........	6,807,978	20,511,936	7,855,772	7,829,328	7,302,154
Deposits of United States disbursing officers..................	4,550,143	5,393,599	4,563,884	8,098,560	3,927,828
Due to national banks......,....	100,348,292	191,730,713	110,017,348	133,672,733	125,102,050
Due to State banks and bankers..	29,693,911	40,211,972	33,789,034	39,298,148	50,718,008
Notes and bills rediscounted.....	3,843,577	3,964,552	5,549,432	5,987,512	4,197,372
Bills payable...................	4,592,610	4,528,191	6,040,563	5,480,554	4,800,727
Totals..................	$1,510,713,236	$1,730,566,899	$1,755,857,093	$1,830,627,845	$1,877,180,942

The national-bank act authorized the issue of $300,000,000 of national-bank circulation. The act of July 12, 1870, authorized the issue of $54,000,000 of additional circulation. Of this additional circulation there was issued to November 1, 1871, $24,773,260; in the year ending November 1, 1872, $16,220,210; in the year ending November 1, 1873, $7,357,479. During the year ending November 1, 1874, there has been issued $5,817,316; and during the same year there has been withdrawn from circulation and destroyed $2,241,019—showing an actual increase of national bank circulation during the year of $3,576,297.

Two national gold banks have been organized in California during the year, with an authorized capital of $700,000. The total capital of the national gold banks, all of which are organized in the State of California, is $3,630,000, to which banks circulation has been issued amounting to $2,150,000.

The amount of legal-tender notes authorized is $382,000,000; the amount of national-bank notes, $354,000,000. The amount of legal-tender notes, under the act of June 20, 1874, cannot be reduced, but must remain continually in circulation; the amount of national-bank notes, however, may be reduced at the pleasure of the banks. If the value of the paper dollar be determined by the amount of such money in circulation, then the national-bank note is more valuable than the legal-tender note. The national-bank notes outstanding are secured by a deposit of more than $385,000,000 of United States bonds, which are at a premium of more than 12 per cent. If the United States bonds be not of sufficient value to pay the notes, the capital and surplus of the banks, amounting to $622,000,000, as well as their entire assets, are available for that purpose. The stockholders are individually liable for the full amount of their stock, in addition to the amount invested in such shares, and the United States guarantees the final payment of the notes. There are, then, absolute assets for more than three times the amount of the national-bank notes outstanding, available for the redemption of these notes, and, in addition, the contingent liability of the shareholders, and the guarantee of their final payment by the United States.

The amount of gold and silver in the country is thus estimated: According to the official reports of the Treasurer of the United States and Controller of the Currency, there were held by the Treasury and national banks at the close of the fiscal year ended June 30, 1872:

In coin....................................	$98,389,864 49
Estimated amount of coin in Pacific coast States and Territories at that time.....	20,000,000 00
And in the hands of bankers and people elsewhere...............................	10,000,000 00
Total specie, fiscal year 1872-'73.....	$128,389,864 49
Add to this two years' product of United States mines, at $70,000,000..............	140,000,000 00
Imports of coin and bullion for two years.................................	49,695,343 00
	$318,085,207 49
Deduct amount exported during the two years ended June 30, 1874..............	151,238,979 00
Total estimated stock, June 30, 1874..	$166,846,228 49

The above estimate shows a gain in specie and bullion in the last two fiscal years of $38,-456,364, and the stock of specie to be about $166,846,228.

The gold coinage at the mints during the year, including worn pieces recoined, was $50,442,690; silver coinage, $5,983,601; gold bars stamped, $31,485,818; silver bars stamped, $6,847,799.18.

The range in prices at New York for Government securities during the year 1874 has been as follows:

BONDS.	1874.		Amount Jan. 1, 1875.	
	Lowest.	Highest.	Registered.	Coupon.
6s, 1881.....................registered	115¾ July 9....	120½ May 27....	$193,257,650	
6s, 1881.................coupon	116¼ July 8....	122¼ Dec. 28....		$89,478,700
6s, 5-20's, 1862.................coupon	110¼ Nov. 4....	118⅞ April 29....	7,794,700	103,822,050
6s, 5-20's, 1864.................coupon	113 Nov. 5....	120¾ April 29....	25,998,750	32,094,050
6s, 5-20's, 1865.................coupon	114¼ Nov. 5 ...	121⅞ April 15....	33,762,900	118,771,450
6s, 5-20's, 1865, new...........coupon	114½ Jan. 3....	121⅛ Dec. 28....	57,125,250	145,537,850
6s, 5-20's, 1867.................coupon	114¼ Jan. 2....	122⅛ Dec. 30 ...	88,052,450	222,570,800
6s, 5-20's, 1868.................coupon	114 Jan. 20....	121⅛ June 22....	14,004,000	23,470,000
5s, 10-40's ....registered.. ..	109⅞ Aug. 4....	115⅛ May 22....	141,272,350	
5s, 10-40's.................coupon	111⅛ Sept. 25....	116⅜ Feb. 28....		53,294,950
5s, funded, 1881.................coupon	111 Jan. 2....	117 April 28....	195,454,800	166,243,100
6s, currency.................registered	114 Jan. 6....	119 Nov. 23....	64,623,512	

The range of securities in London was as follows:

SECURITIES.	Lowest.	Highest.
United States 6s, 5-20s, 1865, old...............................	105¼ October 16	110 February 19
United States 6s, 5-20s, 1867..	106¾ December 17	110¾ June 18
United States 5s, 10-40s..	103¼ February 16	106¼ August 1
New funded 5s..	102¾ January 15	105 May 20

The range of a few active State bonds, for the year 1874, was as follows:

SECURITIES.	1874.	
	Lowest.	Highest.
6s Tennessee, old, ex-coupon..	*52 September 21	63 June 27
6s Tennessee, new, ex-coupon..	*50 September 17	63¼ June 27
6s North Carolina, old..	18¼ August 21	31¼ November 12
6s North Carolina, new..	16 January 6	21½ March 21
6s Virginia, old..	37 November 11	42 January 30
6s Virginia, consolidated..	50 February 17	58¾ December 8
6s Virginia, deferred..	8½ September 22	13 November 10
6s South Carolina, January and July..	7 April 28	31 December 31
6s Missouri, long bonds..	90¼ January 2	99 December 7

The following remarks from the *Financial Chronicle*, relative to railroad bonds, are important:

In no department of financial affairs were transactions attended with greater interest than in the matter of railroad adjustments. In January, 1874, the total amount of railroad bonds on which interest had been passed footed up the large sum of $386,-403,668, including a considerable amount of bonds which were in default prior to the panic of 1873. In October, 1874, our statement in the *Chronicle* made the total amount $497,807,660, or about $111,000,000 larger than in January, a large part of this increase having accrued from the default of a few roads for large amounts, such as the Atlantic & Great Western for $23,000,000, the Indianapolis, Bloomington & Western for $12,000,000, the Columbus, Chicago & Indiana Central for $5,000,000, and several other roads for considerable amounts. But it should be clearly understood that the compilation in October was made without any regard to settlements with bondholders which were then pending, and which had progressed so far with many companies that a good part of their coupons had already been funded. As to the actual amount of interest overdue and un-

paid at any one time, the maximum was probably reached in July or August, 1874, and the amount has since been steadily diminished by the progress of funding arrangements, while defaults since then have been comparatively insignificant. Of all the roads which were in our lists of defaulted companies in January or October, 1874, we find that at the close of the year seventeen had been foreclosed; thirty were then in litigation; thirty-four had funding propositions, either wholly or partly accepted; thirty-seven were in a condition of "masterly inactivity," or the condition of their affairs was unknown to the public; and one company had resumed payment of its regular interest.

In the New York market it was almost impossible to place any bonds; in London, however, a very considerable amount of bonds was placed, but these were almost invariably the bonds of the soundest railroad corporations, whose financial standing was above reproach. In the latter part of the year the prices of the best class of railroad bonds advanced materially in New York, and gave indications of a renewed demand for this class of investments among home purchasers. The range of prices for a few of the leading bonds during the year was as follows:

* Range after June 27, 1874.

VOL. XIV.—20 A

BONDS.	Lowest.	Highest.
Central Pacific 1st mortgage 6s, gold	87⅛ July 27	97 December 31
Union Pacific 1st mortgage 6s, gold	81 July 15	94¾ December 31
Union Pacific land grant 7s	75 May 21	90⅜ December 30
Union Pacific income 10s (due September, 1874)	73¾ January 9	95 December 31
Erie 1st mortgage 7s	101 January 5	105 April 7
Central of New Jersey 1st mortgage 7s	102¾ February 3	110 December 1
Pittsburg, Fort Wayne & Chicago 1st mortgage 7s	103 July 22	112 December 1
Chicago, Rock Island & Pacific 1st mortgage 7s	101 January 6	109¼ December 10

The range in prices of the most active stocks sold in New York, compared as follows in the years 1874 and 1873:

STOCKS.	WHOLE YEAR, 1874.		WHOLE YEAR, 1873.	
	Lowest.	Highest.	Lowest.	Highest.
New Y. Cent. & Hud. R.	95⅞ May 19	105⅝ March 11	77⅞ November 5	106⅛ February 4
Harlem	118¾ January 7	134⅝ February 18	90 September 19	140 April 1
Erie	26 December 10	51¼ January 15	35⅝ November 7	69¼ February 4
Lake Shore	67⅞ June 19	84⅝ January 16	57¼ November 1	97¾ February 15
Wabash	18⅝ December 29	55¼ January 16	32¾ October 15	75¾ January 2
Northwest	34¾ July 15	62¼ January 9	31½ October 14	85 February 4
Northwest prefe e	51 September 10	78⅛ February 9	53 November 8	91 February 3
Rock Island	92½ June 19	109⅛ February 9	80½ October 14	117⅝ March 11
St. Paul	31¼ May 18	49¾ January 10	21½ November 1	62¼ April 21
St. Paul preferred	48 May 5	74⅞ February 9	43¾ November 7	79⅛ January 24
Atlantic & Pacific prefer'd	10¼ September 3	22 February 16	10 November 15	38⅞ January 29
Ohio & Mississippi	22⅞ June 17	33 January 10	21¼ October 14	49⅝ January 24
Central of New Jersey	98 January 3	109⅛ February 10	85 November 10	106½ June 7
Del., Lack. & Western	99 January 2	112⅜ February 10	79½ November 1	106 June 7
Hannibal & St. Joseph	22½ September 7	34¼ January 12	15 November 7	52⅛ February 7
Union Pacific	23 June 17	38¾ March 30	14¾ November 1	89½ January 4
Colorado, Chic. & I. C.	8 September 3	32⅝ March 30	16⅜ November 5	43⅞ February 11
Panama	101 April 2	118 January 9	77½ November 6	130 January 6
Western Union Telegraph	68 April 21	83½ December 10	43¼ November 1	94½ February 6
Quicksilver	22¾ April 28	36¼ November 24	18 September 30	46½ January 2
Quicksilver preferred	29 June 29	48 November 27	25 November 6	57 February 1
Pacific Mail	33⅝ December 21	51½ September 30	25 October 15	76⅞ February 7
Adams Express	92½ January 18	120 November 13	76 November 8	100¼ January 29
American Express	58½ January 2	65½ December 1	41 November 1	70¼ January 8
United States Express	60 September 28	73 February 9	41¾ October 15	82 January 6
Wells, Fargo & Co.	69½ January 5	84 November 30	56 September 30	86 January 29

The highest price of gold was 114⅛ on April 15th, and the lowest 109 on July 28th. The fluctuations were less than in previous years, and there was an absence of speculative movements. The export movement of the year was considerable, the total from New York comparing as follows with previous years:

1874	$62,458,440	1869	$32,108,448
1878	49,303,185	1868	70,841,599
1872	71,545,275	1867	51,001,948
1871	63,865,547	1866	62,553,700
1870	58,689,171		

The imports of specie at New York for the year compared as follows with previous years:

1874	$6,264,464	1870	$11.581,771
1878	18,779,929	1869	14,318,725
1872	5,547,311	1868	7,163,071
1871	8,618,290		

The foreign exchanges were undisturbed by any violent shocks, either from political or financial causes, and rates in New York for sterling bills were unusually steady, and during a large part of the year very firm. Under the present method of quoting, the specie shipping point is about 4.90½ for demand bills; and the rates reached this point for a considerable length of time in June and July, and again in November and December, leading to considerable shipments of coin. From the statement of the commerce of the United States for the fiscal year 1873–'74, it will be seen that there was an excess in the exports over imports of $57,171,246, thus placing the "balance of trade" to that extent in favor of this country. The American railroad loans placed in London footed up no inconsiderable amount, and on the other side of the account there was a return movement late in the year of United States Government bonds to this country, which was estimated by some of the most competent judges to amount to about $8,000,000.

The following statistics of local indebtedness were prepared by the Speaker of the Lower House of Congress, James G. Blaine:

There are in the United States sixteen cities having each a population exceeding 100,000, and an aggregate population of 4,500,000. Each is a city with special advantages, which cannot be taken from it; each, in the language of the day, has a large future; each has abundant wealth, and still larger prospective resources. They embrace, when taken collectively, the trade of Atlantic and Pacific, of Gulf and lake coasts, besides all the great interior rivers of the continent, and the converging traffic of thousands of miles of railway. Surely, one would think that each might bide its time and patiently await its well-assured prosperity, without being compelled to borrow largely, in some cases almost recklessly, of the future. And yet, taking these sixteen cities together, we find their municipal debts amount to $350,000,000, being $80 *per capita* for their entire population, and presenting in the aggregate an amount which, prior to our war experience, would have been considered a large burden for the nation. It would be a gross injustice, however, to leave the inference that the average debt of these cities is over $20,000,000; for, indeed, a single city, the commercial metropolis of the nation, presents a debt embracing nearly one-third of the entire amount, while several of the cities on the list have debts of comparatively insignificant proportions.

The class of cities next in size to those just referred to, those having each a population exceeding 50,000 and less than 100,000, are twelve in number—having an aggregate population of about 750,000. Their total debt does not exceed $30,000,000, which gives about $40 *per capita* for the whole list.

Taking the next class of cities, having each a population exceeding 20,000 and less than 50,000, I find there are in all some fifty-three in the United States, with a total population of something over 1,500,000. Their total debt cannot be less, I think, than $75,-000,000, or $50 *per capita*.

Interested as I have been in making these investigations, I included one more class within the scope of my inquiries, and took the cities and towns throughout the United States having populations between 10,000 and 20,000 each, a list which I found to embrace in all 105 cities and towns, whose aggregate population amounts to nearly 1,400,000, and whose aggregate debt is something over $35,000,000, or about $22 *per capita* for the whole.

Adding these four classes together it presents a table which embraces the cities and towns of the United States having over 10,000 inhabitants each—of which there are in all 186—with an aggregate population exceeding 7,000,000, and a total municipal debt of about $450,000,000.

The towns having less than 10,000 inhabitants each I have not been able to classify with the approximate accuracy of those I have given, but I feel well assured that the aggregate of these debts would reach $80,000,000—making the total municipal debt of the country about $570,000,000.

Added to these municipal debts proper, we find the county debts of the entire country amounting to about $180,000,000, and the State debts to about $390,000,000—making a grand aggregate of $1,140,-000,000 of public debt of States, counties, cities, and towns.

This sum total is nearly $300,000,000 greater than that given in the census of 1870. The addition, however, has not been made within the four succeeding years, but a part is due, I think, to incomplete returns made to the census officials. I have been at some pains, by original investigation and inquiry, to get at the aggregates of State, county, and municipal indebtedness; and while I do not assume to give details or vouch for absolute accuracy, I think the totals I have given may well be taken as approximate reliable statements. The difficulty in attaining perfect exactness of statement results from the imperfect manner in which statistics are gathered in the several States. I have found, indeed, very few States where the State officers were authorized by law to keep any thing of record in regard to debt except the direct obligations of the State. In Massachusetts, where great attention is paid to accuracy of statistics, I have been enabled to get precise information; and the entire footing of that Commonwealth, of State, county, and municipal debts, shows a grand total of $97,500,000, subject to a sinking-fund deduction of $11,000,000—leaving $86,500,000 as the net debt of that State. A very large burden, it would seem, and yet such is the wealth of the State that the entire debt does not constitute more than 4 per cent. of its valuation, and probably not 2½ per cent. of its actual wealth.

Dunn & Barlow's circular gives the mercantile failures for 1874 at 5,830, and the total number of firms reported is 650,000. The distribution of the failures is given in the following table. In 1873 the number of failures was 5,183, and the amount involved $228,499,000. The noticeable feature is, that there is a marked diminution in the amount of liabilities. Two causes are assignable for this, viz.: 1. That

the panic of 1873 caused the failure of an unusual number of large houses, thus raising very much the average amount of liabilities over all previous year; and, 2. That the volume of business had been greatly diminished during 1874, so that, when failures did occur, the liabilities were comparatively light; and further, that the houses which succumbed during the year were in a great degree a smaller class of traders than those of 1873, and than the average of those of several preceding years.

STATES.	No. of Failures.	Amount of Liabilities.
Alabama........................	48	$968,000
Arkansas.......................	12	406,000
California......................	68	2,571,000
Connecticut....................	151	2,286,000
Delaware.......................	27	578,000
District of Columbia...........	18	256,000
Florida.........................	14	293,000
Georgia........................	118	1,045,000
Illinois.........................	332	7,010,000
Indiana........................	167	2,397,000
Iowa...........................	144	2,034,000
Kansas.........................	94	988,000
Kentucky......................	167	1,879,000
Louisiana......................	99	4,429,000
Maine..........................	84	1,063,000
Maryland......................	110	1,691,000
Massachusetts.................	416	10,600,000
Michigan.......................	286	4,777,000
Minnesota.....................	60	1,290,000
Mississippi....................	66	1,555,000
Missouri.......................	175	8,061,000
Nebraska......................	42	591,000
New Hampshire................	32	266,000
New Jersey....................	146	3,854,000
New York......................	573	10,295,000
New York City................	645	32,580,000
North Carolina................	56	542,000
Ohio...........................	343	8,481,000
Pennsylvania..................	644	34,774,000
Rhode Island..................	71	1,250,000
South Carolina................	61	1,531,000
Tennessee.....................	94	1,585,000
Territories....................	67	969,000
Texas..........................	142	2,201,000
Vermont.......................	36	380,000
Virginia and West Virginia.....	111	1,514,000
Wisconsin.....................	111	2,575,000
Total......................	5,830	$155,239,000

FISHER, Rev. SAMUEL WARE, D. D., LL. D., an eminent Presbyterian clergyman, college president, and pulpit orator, born in Morristown, N. J., April 5, 1814; died at College Hill, near Cincinnati, January 18, 1874. His father was a distinguished clergyman of the Presbyterian Church, a pastor at Morristown during his boyhood. After thorough preparation he entered Yale College in 1831, and graduated with high honors in 1835. The next year he entered Princeton Theological Seminary, but after two years there he transferred himself to the Union Theological Seminary, New York City, whence he graduated in 1839. Before leaving the seminary he was called to the pastorate of the Presbyterian Church in West Bloomfield, now Montclair, N. J. He remained there three and a half years, and was then called to the Fourth Presbyterian Church in Albany in October, 1843. In his less than four years' ministry there he had achieved a reputation, as a pulpit orator, inferior to no other clergyman of his denomination in the

State. From Albany he was called in 1847 to Cincinnati, as a successor to Rev. Dr. Lyman Beecher, and for eleven years he more than made good the promise of his youth, and gave to the church of which he was pastor more than its former prestige. In July, 1858, he resigned this pastorate, to accept the presidency of Hamilton College, Clinton, N. Y. Here his scholarship, his eloquence, his untiring assiduity, and his great executive ability, infused a new life into the college, led to its more liberal endowment and to its greatly-increased efficiency. In September, 1867, finding his health impaired by his excessive labors, to which had been added the cares and anxieties which came from the civil war, and his great exertions to effect a reunion of the two branches of the Presbyterian Church, Dr. Fisher felt compelled to resign the presidency, and return to the pastorate. He accepted the call of the Westminster Presbyterian Church in Utica, and commenced his work there with much of the power and· unction which had characterized his labors at Cincinnati; but in May, 1870, he was stricken with paralysis. From the first attack he so far recovered as to be able to partially resume his duties; but a second attack, which, though apparently not affecting his mind, abridged his powers of speech and locomotion, compelled his resignation of all active duties, and he removed to Cincinnati, where his last days were spent, surrounded by his family. His death was sudden, and was the result of an apoplectic shock. Dr. Fisher, though one of the most elegant writers of our time, had published very little. Only a few sermons, orations, and occasional addresses, remain to testify to an eloquence which has rarely been surpassed in modern times. Some of these were collected, a few years before his death, into a single volume. His discourse before the A. B. C. F. M., in 1860, was one which ·none who listened to it will ever forget. Dr. Fisher received the degree of D. D. from Miami University in 1852, and that of LL. D. from the University of New York in 1860.

FLORIDA. The Legislature was in session from January 6th till February 16th. Perhaps the most important subject considered was that of amending the constitution of the State. Eleven articles of amendment were agreed upon. Before becoming a part of the constitution, the proposed amendments must be approved by a two-thirds vote of all the members elected to each branch of the Legislature which convened in January, 1875, and be subsequently ratified by the people. First in importance is that which provides for biennial sessions of the Legislature after 1877. Radical changes in the judiciary department of the government are proposed. The amendments, if adopted, will abolish the County Court as a trial-court at common law, distributing its present common-law jurisdiction to the justice and circuit courts. These changes will do away with the

costs of jurors and witnesses in those courts, which are now paid by the counties, but will increase, to some extent, this heavy item of expense in the Circuit Courts, which is paid by the State, thus reducing the expenses of the counties and increasing those of the State.

An act was passed to incorporate a company to construct a railroad from Gainesville 'to some point on the Gulf of Mexico, or some navigable tributary thereof, with further power to construct a railroad from any point on the first-named road to Key West. A company was also chartered to build a railroad from St. Augustine to Jacksonville, to be commenced within one year, and completed within three years thereafter.

To encourage the establishment of manufactories in the State it was enacted that " every person or association of persons, corporation or corporations, who shall engage in the manufacture of cotton-goods, sugar-refining, cotton-seed oil, paper, or salt, shall have so much of their property exempt from taxation as shall be used for such manufactory, including their stock of manufactured goods or raw material on hand, and all buildings and lands used by any such person, association, or corporation, for the period of five years from the establishment of any such manufactory."

The act providing a revenue for the support of common schools was amended so as to read as follows:

The Board of Public Instruction in each county shall, on or before the last Monday in June of each year, prepare an itemized statement showing the amount of money required for the maintenance of the necessary common schools of their county for the next ensuing scholastic year, and shall deliver an official copy of the same to the assessor of taxes on or before the first Monday in July following, and the said amount shall not be less than one-half of the amount received from the State by the apportionment of common-school funds, nor more than one-half of one per cent. of the assessed value of the taxable property of the county, and the assessor shall compute and the collector shall collect the said amount in like manner as other taxes are computed and collected.

An act was passed requiring the Governor "to set apart a portion of the public buildings of the State at Chattahoochee, in Gadsden County, for the purposes of an indigent lunatic asylum, to which all indigent persons who may be found to be insane, lunatic, or *non compos mentis*, by the courts of this State having jurisdiction of the subject, may be confined for safe keeping and treatment."

The Governor made a personal inspection of the public buildings at Chattahoochee, but found none of them suitable for the purposes of an insane asylum. The State is maintaining, at great expense, six of its insane at asylums outside the State, and sixteen at private houses in the State, while two are confined for safe keeping in the State-prison. Among other acts passed by the Legislature was a general law for the incorporation of railroads and canals.

An election was held on the 3d of Novem-

, ber, for Representatives in Congress and members of the State Legislature. William J. Purman, Republican, was elected to Congress in the first district, by a majority of 668 over the Democratic candidate, Mr. Henderson; and Josiah S. Walls was chosen by the Republicans in the second district, by a majority of 371 over his Democratic opponent, Mr. Finley. The total vote was as follows: First district—Purman, 10,045; Henderson, 9,377. Second district—Walls, 8,549; Finley, 8,178.

The Legislature which assembled January, 1875, was classified as follows:

PARTIES.	Senate.	House.	Joint Ballot.
Democrats.	12	28	40
Republicans	12	24	36
Democratic majority...	0	4	4

The views of the Republican party in the State may be regarded as expressed in the following resolutions adopted by the convention in the first congressional district:

Resolved, That this convention reaffirm the principles of the Republican party, as laid down by its founders at the Chicago Convention of 1860; that our faith in those principles is as strong as ever, and our confidence unbounded in their ultimate acceptance by every true patriot as best calculated to secure to each and all the blessings guaranteed by the Constitution, viz., life, liberty, and the pursuit of happiness; that we point with pride to the record of the party in the as , and hereby pledge our renewed and continued efforts for the success of the party of. progress and reform—the only party which has the courage to purge itself of all unworthy members and to rectify abuses and wrongs without fear or favor.

Resolved, That the President of the United States, Ulysses S. Grant, twice elected to the presidency by the Republican party, has faithfully upheld the standard under which he was advanced to the highest civil position in the United States. He has sustained the rights of all people, preserved good order throughout the nation, opposed all dangerous and gigantic monopolies, introduced into our national civil service greater purity, preserved a proper equilibrium between the various conflicting financial interests of the country, and, while affording American citizens every protection due to them as such, at the same time displayed the wisdom and statesmanship that saved us from foreign wars or violent disturbance at home. He has proved himself, therefore, a sagacious and patriotic President, a successful leader and administrator of the nation's affairs, and we express ourselves as unqualifiedly favorable to his renomination and reëlection to the Presidency *for a third term*

Resolved, That the Congress of the United States has equally proved itself the friend of the people, and a wise guardian of the public welfare. It has never failed to declare itself on the side of the people as against every measure and policy that was oppressive, unjust, or anti-republican. If Congress has ever erred in legislation that proved unwise, it has always evinced a disposition to heed the advice of the people and retrace its steps; wherever any public corruption has shown itself to be identified with the Republican name, it has ever struck at the evil with all its force, and purged the party of its poison. Individuals may have proved recreant, as they do in all parties, but the grand principles of the Republican party have been preserved by Congress in unassailable purity.

Resolved, That our Senators and Representatives in Congress are entitled to our cordial commenda-

tions for their faithful promotion of the best interests of the State; for establishing numerous mail facilities for the benefit of the people; for obtaining large appropriations from the United States Government for the improvement of our rivers and water-courses, and for the reconstruction of the Pensacola Navy-yard, in this manner bringing wealth into the State, giving employment to labor, and greatly adding to the general prosperity of our people.

Resolved, That we favor all prudent measures for the improvement of internal communication between the different cities and ports of our State; that we regard the building of a canal through our State, uniting the waters of the Atlantic and Gulf, as a work of national as well as State importance, and request our delegates in Congress, present and prospective, to use their best efforts to urge its importance upon the attention of our national Legislature.

Resolved, That we pledge our support to the ratification of all the amendments proposed to our State constitution, looking to the economy, purity, and greater freedom and efficiency of our State Government.

Resolved, That we are strongly in favor of and urge the immediate extension of railroad facilities through West Florida, to a direct railroad and steam communication with Mobile and New Orleans; and we also equally urge an extension of present railroad facilities through South Florida to Key West, thereby perfecting communication with Cuba. The people demand these public improvements both in West and South Florida, and we will favor all proper and well-guarded measures for their speedy construction.

Resolved, That we hereby place ourselves on record as opposed to the imposition of taxes upon the people for the payment of principal or interest of the bonds issued by the State in aid of the Jacksonville, Pensacola & Mobile Railroad Company, or any other railroad company in the State, the same having been improperly issued and the proceeds thereof misapplied; and we heartily indorse the efforts of the State administration to enforce the lieu of the State upon the railroad property, and thereby secure the return and cancellation of the said bonds by the road, and the relief of the State and people from any responsibility therefor.

Governor Ossian B. Hart died in Jacksonville, on the 18th of March, when Lieutenant-Governor M. L. Stearns became the Chief Magistrate.

The following statement exhibits the indebtedness of the State on the 1st of January, 1875:

Bonds outstanding	$1,394,867 58
Add one year's interest on $312,522.50, old bonds yet to be exchanged	20,626 48
Add six months' interest on old bonds held by School and Seminary Funds	9,960 01
Add interest due on bonds of 1871	27,286 00
Add interest due on bonds of 1873	16,833 12
	$1,469,573 19
Deduct amount in Treasury applicable to this debt	52,871 68
Total bonded debt and interest, less funds in the Treasury applicable to its reduction	$1,416,701 51
Warrants outstanding $185,646 14	
Deduct funds in Treasury applicable thereto	2,868 93
Total floating debt, less funds in Treasury applicable thereto	182,777 21
Total bonded and floating debt outstanding	$1,599,478 72
The total bonded and floating debt, January 1, 1874, was	1,620,809 27
Showing a reduction of the State debt during the past year	$21,330 55

Governor Stearns thus speaks of the finances of the State:

. It is thus highly gratifying and encouraging that, while for many years the interest remained unpaid, and the volume of the debt was annually increased, during the last two years we have not only paid all our interest promptly, but have made an actual reduction of the principal. But while the wise provisions of the law of 1873, providing for the consolidation of all the bonded debt, except the seven per cent. bonds of 1871, and those belonging to the School and Seminary Funds, are being carried faithfully into execution, and have created an interest and sinking fund sufficient to secure the prompt payment of the interest and the gradual liquidation of the principal, and while the floating debt has been reduced during the past year from $190,585.79 to $185,646.14, yet the outstanding warrants on the Treasury still remain at a large discount. And this depreciation, as shown in the Controller's report, so increases our current expenditures as to be equivalent to the payment by the State of an interest of two and a half per cent. per month on its floating debt. And yet the amount of these warrants is less than three-fourths of the State tax proper in one year. Why, then, are they so far below par? The answer is found in the fact that our current expenses annually exceed the revenue provided to meet them. It will be seen by the reports of the financial officers for the present year that while our current expenses have been $280,837.37, the receipts applicable thereto are only $254,328.58, leaving a deficiency on current account of $26,508.79, by which amount the floating debt would have been increased had not a portion of it been funded into the bonds of 1873. Had the Legislature confined the expenses within the revenue, the actual reduction of the b debt for the year, instead of $21,380.55, would have been $47,839.34.

Besides the indebtedness above described, the State has issued, pursuant to the act of the Legislature, passed in 1870, $4,000,000 bonds in aid of the Jacksonville, Pensacola & Mobile Railroad, receiving as security mortgages on the road. For the reason that the State has held this security, which has been regarded as ample protection against the bonds, they have never been considered as part of the State debt proper. The suit brought by the State in the Supreme Court of the United States for the purpose of protecting and enforcing its statutory and mortgage lien upon the railroad property has not reached a final decision, but has so far progressed as to give hope of a decision favorable to the State. On the 4th day of April, 1874, this whole property, from Jacksonville to Chattahoochee, was taken possession of by the court, and placed under the management of Major Robert Walker, as receiver. This officer is held by the court to the strictest accountability, and, under his skillful management, the credit of the road has been redeemed, and the road materially improved in every respect. The State is now receiving the benefits of the income of the road in new iron and rolling-stock, and in the improved condition of the road-bed, whereby the security of the State is enhanced, and the inducement to the holders to exchange the bonds for the security is greatly increased. It is believed that, as soon as the State shall have demonstrated the validity of its security, and its undisputed title to the property, the holders will

surrender the $4,000,000 of bonds, with accrued interest, to the State, in exchange for the property or the proceeds of its sale, thus relieving the State credit of a serious burden. .

On the 1st of October, S. B. McLin was appointed to discharge the duties of the office of Superintendent of Public Instruction, left vacant by the sudden decease of Jonathan C. Gibbs.

The school-fund now amounts to $83,736. The seminary-fund amounts to $83,736. The two seminaries are in Tallahassee and Gainesville, and are State institutions. Their object, as declared by the act of the Legislature establishing them, is "the instruction of persons, both male and female, in the art of teaching all the various branches that pertain to a good common-school education; and, next, to give instruction in the mechanic arts, in husbandry and agricultural chemistry, in the fundamental laws, and in what regards the rights and duties of citizens." Each county is entitled by law to send as many pupils to one or the other of these seminaries, free of charge, as it has representatives in the Legislature, such pupils to be selected by the Board of County Commissioners in each county. The objects of these institutions have never been carried into effect, nor have the counties availed themselves of the privilege of sending students, or taken the benefit of their scholarships. It would seem that the people of the State have forgotten their interest in, and the object of, these seminaries, and have allowed them to fall into disuse as State institutions.

FOLEY, JOHN HENRY, R. A., the most eminent of British sculptors, born in Dublin in 1818; died in London, August 28, 1874. At the age of thirteen he became a student of the Dublin Royal Society, where he obtained first prizes in the schools for modeling and architecture. He went to London at the age of sixteen, and studied sculpture at the Royal Academy, appearing first as an exhibitor in 1839, when he displayed figures representing the "Death of Abel," and "Innocence." In 1840 he produced "Ino and Bacchus," which at once rendered him famous. In 1842 he exhibited the "Houseless Wanderer," and in 1844 was chosen as one of the three sculptors to execute the statues for the new palace at Westminster, and received commissions for statues of Hampden and Selden, both of which he executed successfully. Mr. Foley, who had become in 1849 an associate of the Royal Academy, exhibited in 1851 "The Mother," and in 1854 "Egeria," commissioned by the corporation of London, and now in the Mansion House of that city. In 1856 he completed in bronze "Lord Hardinge and Charger," a group which was greatly admired by the first authorities in British art, and a duplicate of it requested for London. This was followed in 1858 by "Caractacus," modeled for the corporation of London, and in the same year the author was made a member of the Royal Academy. His diploma work from "Comus" was next executed, and henceforth his time was mainly engrossed in modeling portrait and monumental statues, the orders for which were invariably given without any effort on his part to secure them. Among the more prominent of the portrait statues he modeled were those of "Oliver Goldsmith," and "Edmund Burke," both for Dublin; "Sir Charles Barry," for the New Palace at Westminster; "Lord Herbert," for the British War-Office; "Father Matthew," for Cork; "Sir Henry Marsh," for Dublin; and "Lord Elphinstone," for Bombay. His later works have been the group personifying Asia, for the Prince Consort National Memorial, and a colossal equestrian statue of Sir James Outram, which was unveiled at Calcutta in 1864. Mr. Foley also modeled with great success a statue of Stonewall Jackson, ordered by British and Southern admirers of the Confederate general. The latest work which engaged his attention was a statue of John Stuart Mill, intended for the series of national statues which are to be placed on the Victoria Embankment, London. He was a member of the Royal Hibernian Academy, and in 1862 was chosen a corresponding member of the Belgian Academy.

FORCADE-LAROQUETTE, JEAN LOUIS DE, a French cabinet minister, and a special defender of the late Louis Napoleon, born in Paris, in 1820; died in that city, August 16, 1874. He was a half-brother of Marshal de St.-Arnaud, the zealous Bonapartist; was educated at one of the Parisian lyceums, studied law, and was admitted to the lower courts as an advocate in 1841, and in 1845 read a thesis before the Conference of Advocates, on "The Bar under Louis XIV.," which gained him a high reputation. He readily linked his fortunes with the Napoleon dynasty, and from being Master of Requests to the Council of State, in 1852, he was promoted steadily until he became Minister of Finance in 1860. He retained the latter office until November, 1861, when he was replaced by M. Fould, and assigned to other administrative duties. In 1863 he was sent to Algeria to investigate commercial questions there, and in October of the same year was appointed Vice-President of the Council of State. In January, 1867, he was recalled to the cabinet as Minister of Agriculture, Public Works, and Commerce, and conducted the International Maritime Exposition in 1868. In December of that year he was invested with the more responsible post of Minister of the Interior, and in that capacity zealously carried out the repressive measures of his imperial master, curbing the press as much as he could, as well as unblushingly manipulating the elections. Being dissatisfied with the liberal policy announced in the imperial message of July, 1869, M. Forcade-Laroquette resigned with the rest of his colleagues, but was promptly reinstated, and became a forcible defender of the empire against the democracy promulgated by Prince Napoleon. He went out of power at

the advent of the Ollivier ministry, and had not s se en been prominently before the public qu tly

FOSTER, JOHN G., Lieutenant-Colonel and Brevet Major-General U. S. A., Corps of Engineers, a brave and accomplished officer in the late civil war; born at Nashua, N. H., in 1823; died in the same city, September 2, 1874. He graduated from West Point in 1846, ranking fourth in his class; was assigned to the engineers, and went with the corps to the Mexican War. His gallant conduct at Contreras, Churubusco, and Molino del Rey, won him the brevets of first-lieutenant and captain. In the last-named action he was severely wounded. He was Assistant Professor of Engineering at West Point from 1855 to 1857, and received his commission as first-lieutenant while there. In 1858 he was assigned to duty at the fortifications in North and South Carolina, and was especially in charge of the construction and fortifying of Fort Sumter. He was commissioned captain July 1, 1860, and made brevet-major for his share in effecting the transfer of the garrison at Fort Moultrie to Fort Sumter. He was one of the garrison of Fort Sumter, and, after its surrender, was employed for some time on the fortifications of New York harbor. October 23, 1861, he was commissioned brigadier-general of volunteers, commanded a brigade in General Burnside's expedition to North Carolina, and took an active and prominent part in the capture of Roanoke Island, February 8, 1862, and of Newbern, on the 14th of March; on the recall of General Burnside in July, General Foster became commandant of that Department and of the Eighteenth Corps, and military governor of Newbern. He had been promoted to be major-general of volunteers. The force under his command was barely sufficient to hold his position, without entering on offensive warfare, but he repulsed attacks upon Southwest Creek, Kinston, White Hall, and Goldsborough. In the autumn of 1862 he was reënforced by several new regiments, and, having compelled General D. H. Hill to raise the siege of Newbern, he followed him to Washington, N. C., and compelled him to retreat from that point. On the 16th of July, 1863, he was appointed to command the Department of Virginia and North Carolina, with headquarters at Fortress Monroe. On the 13th of March, 1863, he had been promoted to be major of engineers in the regular army. He subsequently commanded the Department of the Ohio (from December 12, 1863, to February 9, 1864), and was compelled to ask to be relieved in consequence of severe injuries from the fall of his horse; from February 9 to May 5, 1864, he was on sick-leave at Baltimore; commanded the Department of the South from May 26, 1864, to February 11, 1865, coöperating efficiently with General Sherman, and preparing to assist in the reduction of Charleston under Sherman's orders, when an unhealed wound caused him such suffering that he was compelled to relinquish the command to General Gillmore. He was brevetted Brigadier and also Major-General, U. S. A., March 13, 1865; was commander of the Department of Florida from August 7, 1865, to December 5, 1866, and assigned to temporary duty in the Engineer Bureau from January to May, 1867. He was commissioned lieutenant-colonel, Corps of Engineers, in March, 1867. His subsequent service had been mainly in the Department of the Atlantic, and for more than a year previous to his death he had been at Nashua, in failing health.

FOX, Sir CHARLES, C. E., a distinguished British civil engineer, born in Derby, England, in 1810; died in London, June 16, 1874. At an early age he was articled to his brother for the medical profession, but a taste for engineering led him to devote to mechanical science every leisure moment, and the impression produced upon his mind by the opening of the Liverpool & Manchester Railway induced him to relinquish medicine and become an engineer. His first employer was Captain Ericsson. Mr. Fox struggled on as a lecturer, as a scientific assistant, and occasionally as a practical mechanist, until he was appointed by Robert Stephenson assistant-engineer to the London & Birmingham Railway Company, at the commencement of the construction of that line. He remained with the company until a year after the opening of the line, in all five years, when he joined the late Mr. Bramah in establishing the firm of Bramah, Fox & Co., the name of which, on the retirement of the former, was changed to that of Fox, Henderson & Co. Their business was railroad-building and the execution of other engineering works. His greatest triumph was the construction of the building for the Great Exhibition in Hyde Park, in 1851. The drawings for this edifice occupied Mr. Fox eighteen hours a day for seven weeks, and he received the honor of knighthood in recognition of his genius and skill. He constructed the Crystal Palace at Sydenham, and executed many extensive railway and other engineering works.

FRANCE, a republic of Europe. President, Marshal Marie Edmond Patrice Maurice de MacMahon, Duke of Magenta, elected May 24, 1873. Chief of the Cabinet, Colonel Robert; Secretary of the President, Viscount d'Harcourt; Vice-President of the Council of Ministers, at the close of the year 1873, was General Cissey. The National Assembly consists of 738 members. President, Louis Joseph Buffet.

The area of France, according to the official report on the census of 1872 (*Statistique de la France*), was 204,092 square miles.* The population, according to the census of 1872, was 36,102,921.

* The area of the several departments, as published below, agrees with the table given in the ANNUAL CYCLOPÆDIA for.1873, except for the district of Belfort and the department of Vosges. The *Statistique de la France* gives for the former 233.44 square miles (instead of 234.72), and for the latter 2268.93 (instead of 2266.17).

The table on the next page exhibits the area and population of each department, and the movement of population during the year 1871. A comparison of the population in 1872 with that of the present French territory in 1866 shows a decrease of 356,715, or of 1.2 per cent. of the total population. This decrease is exclusive of the loss which France sustained by the cession of Alsace and Lorraine to Germany. The movement of population from 1866 to 1871 was as follows:

YEARS.	Births.	Deaths.	Surplus of Births (B.), or Deaths (D.).	Percentage of Increase (I.), or Decrease (D.), of Population.
1866....	1,006,258	884,573	B. 121,685	I. 0.33
1867....	1,007,515	886,887	B. 120,628	I. 0.31
1868....	984,140	922,038	B. 62,102	I. 0.16
1869....	948,526	864,320	B. 84,206	I. 0.21
1870....	941,115	1,046,909	D. 103,394	D. 0.28
1871....	826,121	1,271,010	D. 444,815	D. 1.22

The excess of deaths over births in 1871 is greater than in any former year, and exceeded by far the expectations of French statesmen and statisticians. A comparison of the table on the next page shows that the excess of deaths appears in all departments except three, Creuse, Loire Inférieure, and Marne. The losses suffered during the war are far from accounting for this alarming fact, for the number of military persons deceased in 1870 was only 33,164, and in 1871, 61,165; figures which, though necessarily incomplete, are yet altogether without proportion to the entire mortality of the country. The decline of the French population has, however, been going on for years. The proportion of births to the total population, which, in 1827, was still 3.11 per cent., did not average, from 1848 to 1868, more than 2.62 per cent.; it was 2.57 in 1869, 2.55 in 1870, and 2.26 in 1871. While from 1817 to 1854, there was one birth to every 34.3 inhabitants, and less from 1847 to 1871, in the following proportions:

```
1847-1854..............1 birth to 37.4 inhabitants.
1854-1860..............1 birth to 37.3    "
1860-1868..............1 birth to 37.9    "
1869..............1 birth to 38.8    "
1870..............1 birth to 39.4    "
1871..............1 birth to 44.2    "
```

Considerable surprise has been caused by the remarkable increase of suicide. In 1826, when official returns on this subject were first prepared, they numbered 1,739; in 1831, they were 2,084; in 1836, 2,340; in 1839, 2,747; in 1841, 2,814; in 1845, 3,085; in 1847, 3,647; in 1852, 3,674; in 1860, 3,920; in 1869, 5,114; and in 1872, 5,275. It was feared that in 1874 they would reach 7,000. As regards Paris alone, there were 567 suicides in 1872, and 660 in 1873; while the total for 1874, it was thought, would approach 1,000.

The number of boys born considerably exceeds that of girls. From 1800 to 1860, the proportion of boys to girls was 106 to 100; from 1861 to 1868, it was 105; in 1869, 105.02; in 1870, 104.79; in 1871, 104.87. In conse-

DEPARTMENTS.	Area in Square Miles.	Population in 1866.	Population in 1872.	Births, 1871.	Deaths, 1871.	Marriages, 1871.
Ain........................	2,339	371,643	363,290	8,070	17,808	3,146
Aisne......................	2,899	565,025	559,489	11,555	16,802	3,858
Allier.....................	2,822	370,164	390,817	9,377	11,891	3,110
Alpes (Basses)	2,685	148,000	139,332	8,011	4,752	1,051
Alpes (Hautes)............	2,158	122,117	118,898	3,490	4,478	943
Alpes (Maritimes).........	1,482	198,818	199,087	5,560	6,950	1,574
Ardèche...................	2,134	387,174	380,277	10,985	12,772	3,058
Ardennes..................	2,020	326,864	320,217	6,477	9,672	2,072
Ariége....................	1,890	250,430	246,298	5,966	7,223	1,933
Aube......................	2,817	261,951	255,687	4,259	6,717	1,470
Aude......................	2,488	288,626	285,927	5,998	9,863	2,134
Aveyron...................	3,876	400,070	402,474	11,271	15,425	2,807
Belfort (territoire)........	233	56,971	56,781	1,512	2,429	465
Bouches-du-Rhône..........	1,971	547,903	554,911	14,509	19,062	3,803
Calvados..................	2,132	474,909	454,012	8,340	18,401	3,163
Cantal....................	2,217	237,994	231,867	5,995	6,418	2,054
Charente..................	2,294	378,318	367,520	7,026	15,394	3,026
Charente-Inférieure.......	2,636	479,529	465,653	8,861	20,710	3,019
Cher......................	2,779	330,613	335,392	7,928	12,357	2,354
Corrèze...................	2,265	310,843	309,746	8,987	12,156	2,895
Corsica...................	3,377	259 861	258,507	7,473	7,981	1,683
Côte-d'Or.................	3,383	382,762	374,510	7,572	13,290	2,122
Côtes-du-Nord	2,602	641,210	622,295	17,268	25,206	5,409
Creuse....................	2,150	274,057	274,663	6,898	6,662	1,677
Dordogne..................	3,545	502,673	480,141	10,953	18,575	3,762
Doubs.....................	2,019	298,073	291,251	6,548	15,295	1,851
Drôme.....................	2,518	324,231	320,417	7,723	9,460	2,466
Eure......................	2,300	394,467	377,874	6,702	11,720	2,372
Eure-et-Loir..............	2,268	290,753	282,622	5,928	9,470	1,882
Finistère.................	2,515	662,485	642,963	21,840	26,269	6,781
Gard.....................	2,253	429,747	420,131	11,437	14,347	3,058
Garonne (Haute)..........	2,429	498,777	479,362	8,076	11,852	3,165
Gers......................	2,425	296,693	284,717	4,713	10,280	2,468
Gironde...................	3,761	701,855	705,149	18,822	21,204	4,556
Hérault...................	2,393	427,245	429,878	9,312	13,951	2,888
Ille-et-Vilaine............	2,597	592,809	589,532	14,980	25,198	4,886
Indre.....................	2,694	277,360	277,693	6,442	8,866	1,948
Indre-et-Loire............	2,360	325,193	317,027	5,752	11,662	2,372
Isère.....................	3,201	581,386	575,784	13,050	18,049	4,578
Jura......................	1,928	298,477	287,634	6,735	9,008	1,768
Landes....................	3,597	306,683	300,528	6,843	10,091	1,898
Loir-et-Cher..............	2,452	275,757	268,801	5,589	10,925	1,898
Loire.....................	1,838	537,108	550,611	14,705	18,042	4,205
Loire (Haute).............	1,916	312,661	308,732	8,484	11,115	2,880
Loire (Inférieure).........	2,654	598,598	602,206	14,059	13,842	4,258
Loiret....................	2,614	357,110	353,021	8,026	12,595	2,499
Lot......................	2,013	288,919	281,404	5,825	8,571	2,077
Lot-et-Garonne............	2,067	287,692	319,369	5,296	9,443	2,363
Lozère....................	1,996	137,263	135,190	4,082	4,257	966
Maine-et-Loire............	2,750	532,325	518,471	9,944	20,191	3,749
Manche....................	2,289	573,399	544,776	11,029	23,352	4,018
Marne.....................	3,159	390,809	386,157	9,409	9,299	3,871
Marne (Haute)............	2,402	259,095	251,196	4,683	9,789	1,027
Mayenne..................	1,996	367,855	350,637	7,928	16,855	2,586
Meurthe-et-Moselle........	2,025	366,617	365,137	7,064	12,101	2,273
Meuse....................	2,406	301,853	284,725	5,187	8,833	1,837
Morbihan..................	2,695	501,084	490,853	13,605	20,172	3,745
Nièvre....................	2,632	342,773	339,017	7,699	13,152	2,270
Nord.....................	2,196	1,392,041	1,447,764	42,490	48,319	10,418
Oise......................	2,350	401,274	306,804	8,212	11,609	2,621
Orne.....................	2,351	414,618	398,250	7,029	18,976	2,722
Pas-du-Calais	2,550	749,777	761,158	20,542	24,823	5,710
Puy-de-Dôme..............	3,070	571,690	566,463	12,678	17,480	4,891
Pyrénées (Basses).........	2,945	435,486	426,700	10,330	14,443	2,516
Pyrénées (Hautes)........	1,750	240,252	235,156	4,953	6,759	1,422
Pyrénées-Orientales	1,592	189,490	191,856	5,704	6,509	1,519
Rhône....................	1,077	678,648	670,247	14,542	20,144	5,252
Saône (Haute)............	2,069	317,706	303,088	6,762	11,824	2,329
Saône-et-Loire............	3,302	600,006	598,344	14,632	21,614	4,367
Sarthe....................	2,397	463,619	446,603	8,242	20,993	3,488
Savoie....................	2,224	271,663	467,958	7,239	9,466	1,779
Savoie (Haute)............	1,667	273,768	273,027	7,067	8,329	1,908
Seine.....................	108	2,150,916	2,230,060	42,694	97,394	14,914
Seine-Inférieure...........	2,330	792,768	790,022	20,243	30,113	5,609
Seine-et-Marne............	2,215	354,400	341,490	6,889	11,192	2,053
Seine-et-Oise.............	2,164	533,727	580,180	9,716	17,328	3,451
Sèvres (Deux)............	2,317	333,155	331,243	7,381	12,675	2,514
Somme....................	2,379	578,640	557,015	11,495	18,909	4,284
Tarn.....................	2,317	355,513	352,718	8,031	11,582	2,559
Tarn-et-Garonne..........	1,436	238,969	221,610	3,996	7,045	1,554
Var......................	2,349	308,550	293,757	3,822	7,892	2,121
Vaucluse..................	1,670	266,091	263,451	6,799	7,350	1,829
Vendée...................	2,588	404,473	401,446	10,219	14,809	3,338
Vienne....................	2,691	324,527	320,558	6,984	13,329	2,333
Vienne (Haute)............	2,130	326,007	322,447	8,812	13,560	2,674
Vosges....................	2,269	397,981	392,988	8,898	14,563	2,679
Yonne....................	2,863	372,589	363,608	6,698	10,047	2,224
Total.................	204,092	36,469,836	36,102,921	826,121	1,271,010	262,476

quence, however, of the greater mortality of the male sex, the number of females always exceeded that of the males. The excess in the different census years since 1800 was as follows:

1800	725,225	1846	318,738
1806	481,725	1851	193,242
1821	868,325	1856	209,024
1831	669,033	1861	97,217
1836	619,508	1866	33,906
1841	445,382	1872	137,899

The proportion of marriages to the total population was:

1825–1828	1 to 128 inhabitants.
1829–1833	1 to 126 "
1834–1838	1 to 123 "
1839–1844	1 to 125 "
1845–1868	Varying from 143 (1847) to 118 (1858).
1869	1 to 121 inhabitants.
1870	1 to 165 "
1871	1 to 139 "

The number of illegitimate children has, since 1825, been invariably from seven to eight per cent. of all the children born. There is, however, a marked difference in the towns and in the rural communities. In the department of the Seine they constituted, in 1871, 24.50 per cent.; in the towns, by which name the French statisticians designate all the communities with more than 2,000 inhabitants, 10.87; in the rural communities, 4.39. The same proportion has substantially prevailed since 1864.

The proportion between the town population and the rural population is steadily changing in favor of the former, as will appear from the following table:

POPULATION.	1846.	1851.	1856.	1861.	1866.	1872.
	Per ct.	Per ct.	Per ct.	Per ct.	Per ct.	Per ct.
Town	24.42	25.52	27.31	28.86	30.46	31.06
Rural	75.58	74.48	72.69	71.14	69.54	68.94

It is especially the larger towns whose population rapidly increases; and while the total population of France showed, from 1866 to 1872, a remarkable decrease, the towns with upward of 10,000 increased, as the following table will exhibit:

TOWNS WITH FROM	Population. 1866.	Aggregate Population, 1872.
1, ,000 inhabitants...	992,877	1,085,430
15, ,000 "	532,653	541,520
20, ,000 "	710,207	739,234
30,000 to 40,000 "	405,681	417,576
50,000 to 115,000 "	343,244	358,491
100,000 to 200,000 "	835,845	886,756
Marseilles	785,173	808,825
Lyons	300,131	312,864
Paris	323,954	333,417
	1,825,274	1,851,792
Total	7,055,039	7,275,905

In 1869 the number of marriages was larger than it had been for many years back, with the only exception of the year 1858, when it was 1 to 118. During the year 1870, when all the young men were called into the field, it was smaller than it had ever been in any year since 1825. After the close of the war, there was at once a large increase.

The following towns, with a population of more than 30,000, showed, however, a decrease:

TOWNS.	Population in 1872.	Decrease since 1866.
Caen	41,210	854
Brest	66,272	13,575
Toulouse	124,852	2,084
Bordeaux	194,055	186
Orleans	48,976	124
Cherbourg	35,580	1,685
Lorient	34,660	2,995
Boulogne	39,700	551
Clermont-Ferrand	37,357	333
Lyons	323,417	537
Toulon	69,127	7,999
Poitiers	30,036	998
Total		31,371

With regard to nativity and nationality, the inhabitants of France were, in 1872, divided as follows:

INHABITANTS.	Number.	Per. cent.
I. French	35,362,253	97.97
1. Born in the department in which they resided at the taking of the census	30,676,943	
2. Born in other departments..	4,543,764	
3. Alsatians and Lotharingians residing in France, or having chosen the French nationality	126,243	
4. Naturalized foreigners	15,303	
II. Foreigners residing in France..	730,544	2.03

The foreigners constituted, in 1851, 1.06 of the population; in 1861, 1.33; in 1866, 1.67. Their number has therefore steadily increased since 1851.

The fluctuation in the number of foreign residents of different nationalities is shown by the following table:

NATIONALITIES.	1866.	1872.
Alsatians and Lotharingians...	......	64,803
Germans	106,606	39,361
Austro-Hungarians		5,116
English	29,556	26,003
Americans	7,223	6,859
Belgians	275,888	347,558
Dutch	16,058	17,077
Italians	99,624	112,979
Spaniards	32,656	52,954
Swiss	42,270	43,834
Russians	2,282	1,962
Poles	9,882	7,328
Scandinavians	1,226	1,058
Turks, Greeks, Roumanians...	1,654	1,173
Asiatics	......	311
Others	10,276	3,343
Unknown	19,541	9,834
Total	655,036	740,668

The Germans, owing chiefly to the hostile feelings produced against them by the war, have decreased more than one-half; though the deficiency has almost been made up by the Alsatian and Lotharingian residents, who, at the time the census was taken, had not yet chosen the French nationality. On the other hand, there has been a remarkable increase in the number of Belgians, Italians, and Spaniards.

The following table, giving the number of voters at the municipal and general elections, has a special importance in view of the efforts made by the present Government to reduce the number of voters:

DEPARTMENTS.	General Election.	Municipal Election.
Ain......................	104,088	102,029
Aisne...................	153,834	150,717
Allier...................	106,012	106,693
Alpes (Basses).........	42,832	42,389
Alpes (Hautes)	83,469	82,076
Alpes (Maritimes).....	56,231	55,725
Ardèche................	110,741	110,010
Ardennes...............	90,574	89,589
Ariége.................	72,502	72,008
Aube...................	80,891	80,110
Aude...................	89,887	87,875
Aveyron................	114,986	113,123
Belfort (territoire de)..	115,973	15,031
Bouches-du-Rhône.....	138,421	137,455
Calvados...............	127,072	124,400
Cantal.................	60,907	59,880
Charente	112,069	109,768
Charente-Inférieure....	141,396	139,582
Cher...................	95,967	94,252
Corrèze................	83,440	82,535
Corse..................	711,176	70,670
Côte-d'Or..............	115,048	113,756
Côtes-du-Nord.........	159,020	156,930
Creuse.................	75,773	75,108
Dordogne..............	141,262	138,447
Doubs..................	81,972	80,772
Drôme.................	97,715	96,897
Eure....	116,844	115,263
Eure-et-Loir...........	831,130	81,781
Finistère..............	160,263	159,408
Gard...................	134,253	132,330
Garonne (Haute)......	141,699	140,730
Gers...................	89,935	88,501
Gironde	202,015	198,373
Hérault................	137,734	135,489
Ille-et-Vilaine	154,152	151,469
Indre..................	78,140	76,902
Indre-et-Loire.........	96,677	95,517
Isère..................	163,191	161,950
Jura...................	84,610	83,434
Landes................	84,659	83,698
Loir-et-Cher...........	76,382	75,645
Loire..................	140,173	138,963
Loire (Haute).........	81,784	81,061
Loire (Inférieure).....	158,852	157,694
Loiret.................	98,973	97,887
Lot....................	85,241	84,625
Lot-et-Garonne.......	104,227	101,853
Losère.................	87,945	37,552
Maine-et-Loire........	149,114	147,585
Manche................	146,343	142,279
Marne.................	111,795	110,487
Marne (Haute)........	76,399	75,093
Mayenne	96,666	94,714
Meurthe-et-Moselle....	109,520	105,026
Meuse.................	87,286	85,915
Morbihan..............	120,202	119,290
Nièvre.................	96,109	94,714
Nord..................	829,963	326,487
Oise..................	115,070	113,441
Orne..................	116,443	115,349
Pas-de-Calais..........	204,010	201,392
Puy-de-Dôme..........	168,667	167,740
Pyrénées (Basses).....	108,263	106,908
Pyrénées (Hautes).....	65,649	65,012
Pyrénées-Orientales...	53,431	53,079
Rhône.................	166,787	185,700
Saône (Haute)........	90,536	89,834
Saône-et-Loire........	168,915	167,104
Sarthe.................	131,533	130,121
Savoie.................	68,613	67,836
Savoie (Haute)........	73,964	53,348
Seine..................	457,786	450,690
Seine-Inférieure.......	196,404	192,627
Seine-et-Marne........	99,005	97,860
Seine-et-Oise..........	145,083	143,330
Sèvres (Deux).........	98,539	97,142
Somme................	162,861	161,529
Tarn	109,992	109,082
Tarn-et-Garonne.......	73,349	72,505
Var...................	86,880	86,099
Vaucluse..............	82,696	81,814
Vendée................	113,193	110,903
Vienne................	97,305	91,804
Vienne (Haute)........	85,261	84,273
Vosges................	112,909	110,473
Yonne.................	111,221	110,210
Total............	9,992,329	9,855,705

According to recent statistics, the total area is about 125,000,000 acres. Of these, natural pastures are estimated to occupy 12,500,000 acres; vines, 5,000,000; arable land, 62,500,-000; gardens and orchards, 5,000,000; woods and forests, 20,000,000; and barren waste, 20,000,000. The acreage occupied by the vine, no greater than that of inclosed orchards and gardens, may surprise those who regard France as *par excellence* the country of the grape. The average wine production of France has been computed at 50,000,000 hectolitres, and the state finds in it resources valued at 155,-000,000 francs. In 1874 the wine-crop was supposed to be nearly fifty per cent. in excess of the average annual production. In 1862 France possessed 2,914,412 horses, against 2,882,851 in 1872. The same disproportion exists in the cattle, which were 12,733,188, against 11,284,414; and in sheep, which were 30,386,263, against 24,766,496.

The results of the census of 1872, relative to the religious denominations of the inhabitants, were as follows:

DENOMINATIONS.	Number.	PER CENT.	
		1872.	1866.
Catholics..................	35,387,703	98.02	97.48
Protestants:			
Reformed.....467,531			
Lutheran 80,117	580,757	1.60	2.23
Others..... 33,109			
Israelites.................	49,439	0.14	0.23
Other non-Christian relig-ions..................	3,071	0.01	....
Persons declaring no relig-ion or whose religion was not known..............	81,951	0.23	0.06

The separation of Alsace and Lorraine from France has largely decreased the percentage of Protestants and Israelites.

Educational statistics were for the first time included in the official census of 1866. In order to make these statistics as perfect as possible, the population was divided into three groups: 1. Children below the sixth year of age, who are supposed not to be able to either read or write; 2. Children and youths from the sixth to the twentieth year of age, the time of life during which instruction of different degrees is obtained; 3. Persons of more than twenty years of age, who may be regarded as having completed their education. The following table exhibits the general results of this special census:

PERSONS	Below 8 Years.	6 to 20 Years.	Above 20 Years
Not able to read or write.............	3,540,101	2,082,338	7,702,262
Able to read only..	292,348	1,175,125	2,305,190
Able to read and to write..........	151,595	5,458,097	13,073,057
Unknown..........	38,042	70,721	214,005
Total.........	4,022,086	8,786,281	23,294,554

If the latter class is not taken into account, we obtain the following table of percentage:

PERSONS	Over 5 Years.	6 to 20 Years.	More than 20 Years.	Upward of 6 Years.
Not able to read or write	88.85	23.89	33.37	30.77
Able to read only.....	7.33	13.48	9.99	10.94
Able to read and write	3.82	62.63	56.64	58.29

Leaving the children below six years of age aside, it appears from the table that about thirty per cent. of the population of France are unable to read and write. For the male sex alone, this proportion would be 27.41 per cent. ; for the female sex, 33.47 per cent.

The differences between the departments, as regards the statistics of illiteracy, is marked, the number of illiterates ranging from 6.9 per cent. (Doubs) to 61.8 per cent. (Haute-Vienne). The following table shows the proportion of every department:

Departments.	Per cent.	Departments.	Per cent
Doubs...............	6.9	Charente-Inférieure...	22.2
Meurthe-Moselle.....	8.3	Saône-et-Loire	32.3
Marne (Haute)........	8.4	Loiret....	32.4
Jura...................	9.8	Maine-et-Loire........	32.4
Meuse.................	9.7	Mayenne..............	32.7
Vosges............... ..	10.0	Gard	33.1
Seine.................	11.4	Loire-Inférieure......	33.1
Marne.................	11.8	Ille-et-Vilaine.........	34.6
Saône (Haute)........	11.9	Puy-de-Dôme	35.9
Seine-et-Oise.........	12.0	Herault	36.1
Aube.................	12.4	Ardèche..............	36.4
Belfort................	12.7	Nord.................	36 6
Côtes-d'Or	13.3	Sarthe.................	36.7
Alpes (Hautes)........	14.3	Sèvres (Deux)........	37.2
Rhône.................	14.5	Loir-et-Cher,..........	37.6
Orne.................	15.9	Vaucluse..............	37.6
Ardennes..............	16.4	Garonne (Haute)......	37.7
Calvados..............	16.5	Var..................	37.7
Lozère................	20.3	Lot...................	38.7
Seine-et-Marne.......	20.4	Gers..................	39.6
Isère..................	21.0	Tarn..................	40.4
Oise..................	21.8	Lot-et-Garonne......	41.5
Aveyron..............	22.0	Aude.................	41.6
Savoie (Haute)........	22.4	Tarn-et-Garonne......	42.0
Savoie................	23.2	Corse.................	42.8
Eure-et-Loir..........	23.4	Côtes-du-Nord	43.2
Cantal................	23.5	Indre-et-Loire........	43.3
Ain...................	24.1	Creuse...............	46.6
Yonne................	24.2	Nièvre................	47.4
Manche...............	25.9	Charente..............	48.4
Aisne	26.3	Vienne................	48.6
Pyrénées (Hautes).....	27.2	Pyrénées-Orientales...	49.6
Bouches-du-Rhône....	27.6	Vendée...............	50.8
Eure.................	27.8	Morbihan	52.1
Seine-Inférieure,......	28.7	Allier	52.5
Somme...............	28.9	Ariége	53.4
Pyrénées (Basses).....	28.9	Corrèze	55.8
Drôme...............	29.1	Finistère..............	56.3
Alpes (Basses)........	29.2	Indre.................	56.8
Gironde..............	29.2	Cher	57.3
Loire.................	29.5	Landes...............	57.6
Pas-de-Calais..........	29.6	Dordogne.	60.3
Alpes (Maritimes).....	31.8	Vienne (Haute)........	61.8
Loire (Haute)........	31.8		

The budget for the year 1875, voted by the National Assembly, comprised the following sources of revenue and branches of expenditures.

REVENUE.	Francs.
Direct taxes...............................	382,721,200
Special taxes, assimilated to the direct taxes..............................	20,953,494
Stamps and enregistrement................	608,498,940
Produce of forests.......:...............	38,064,680
Duties...................................	262,018,000
Indirect taxes...........'...............	968,424,000
Produce of posts..........	111,004,000
Miscellaneous receipts...................	138,281,310
Extraordinary receipts...............	43,500,000
Total.......................:...........	2,563,460,624

EXPENDITURES.	Francs.
Public debt and donations...................	1,224,199,474
Ministries:	
Ministry of Justice	33,777,473
Ministry of Foreign Affairs..............	111,255,500
Ministry of the Interior.................	05,976,049
Ministry of Finances....................	19,956,950
Ministry of Public Instruction...........	96,859,514
Ministry of Agriculture and Commerce..	17,063,040
Ministry of Public Works................	156,949,219
Ministry of War.....................	493,776,321
Ministry of the Navy....................	127,131,711
Administration of Colonies..............	81,467,831
Revenue collection........................	247,902,849
Deficits and repayments...................	19,143,900
Total................................	2,584,452,831

The public debt, according to the budget of 1873, was as follows:

DEBT.	Interest.	Capital.
Consolidated debt.........	748,303,653	49,910,366,500
Capital that may be called in	322,338,928	3,382,640,000
Dette viagère..............	122,976,162	....
Total...............	1,193,618,743	23,293,000,000

On January 1, 1873, the new army law of August 16, 1872, went into operation. Its first article enacts universal liability to military service. Every Frenchman capable of bearing arms must serve for twenty years, namely, four years in the standing army, five years in the reserve of the standing army, five years in the territorial army (Landwehr), and six years in the reserve of the territorial army. By a law of July 24, 1873, on the reorganization of the army, France is divided into eighteen districts, each of which is occupied by an army corps. One army corps, moreover, is organized in Algeria. Each of the eighteen army corps consists of two divisions of infantry, one brigade of cavalry, one brigade of artillery, one battalion of engineers, one squadron of the train, a general staff, and the subordinate staffs. The composition of the army, in time of peace, will be as follows:

Infantry (156 regiments, 505 battalions, 2,445 companies)......................................	279,986
Cavalry....................................	67,888
Artillery..................................	58,096
Engineers..................................	13,551
Train	11,486
Total.......................	441,007

To this number may be added the second division of the yearly contingent, amounting to about 60,000 men, who serve from six to twelve months, and swell the number of the army to 501,007 men. In time of war, the army will be composed as follows:

Standing army..................................	705,000
Reserve of standing army	510,000
Territorial army..............................	582,000
Reserve of territorial army	626,000
Total...........................	2,423,000

The navy, according to the budget for 1875, was composed as follows:

VESSELS.	Iron-clad.	Unarmed	Total.	Men.
Vessels fitted out	7	85	92	28,481
Vessels for service in the ports and on trial	19	43	62	
Total	26	128	154	28,481
Reserve	31	47	78	....

According to the plan for the reorganization of the navy, it is to be composed in future as follows: 12 iron-clads, first class; 12 iron-clads, second class; 20 iron-clad gunboats; 8 frigates, 8 corvettes, 38 avisos, 25 transports, 32 gunboats; and, besides, a number of school-ships, tenders, etc.

The following table exhibits the movement of French commerce from 1856 to 1872 (in francs):

YEARS.	GENERAL COMMERCE.		SPECIAL COMMERCE.		GOLD AND PRECIOUS METALS.	
	Imports.	Exports.	Imports.	Exports.	Imports.	Exports.
1872....	4,501,600,000	4,756,600,000	3,570,300,000	3,761,600,000	853,000,000	324,000,000
1871....	3,953,400,000	3,278,000,000	3,566,700,000	2,872,500,000	301,000,000	502,000,000
1870....	3,497,800,000	3,455,800,000	2,867,400,000	2,802,100,000	410,000,000	261,000,000
Annual average, 1866–1870....	3,928,100,000	3,887,100,000	3,028,800,000	2,984,700,000	733,000,000	465,000,000
1861–1865....	3,231,100,000	3,448,800,000	2,447,400,000	2,564,800,000	570,000,0.0	520,000,000
1856–1860....	2,521,100,000	2,812,800,000	1,792,700,000	2,037,900,000	701,000,000	339,000,000

The foreign countries chiefly interested in the trade of France, in the years 1871 and 1872, were the following (the value being expressed in francs):

COUNTRIES.	Imports, 1872.	Exports, 1872.
Great Britain	662,600,000	931,900,000
Belgium	440,400,000	478,900,000
Italy	375,200,000	228,800,000
Germany	211,700,000	409,600,000
Alsace-Lorraine	146,800,000	294,500,000
Switzerland	97,400,000	112,800,000
Spain	123,500,000	41,500,000
Russia	120,400,000	9,900,000
Turkey	159,400,000	14,400,000
Egypt	48,700,000	9,200,000
United States	204,800,000	332,500,000
Brazil....................	40,400,000	78,400,000
Argentine Republic.........	108,800,000	101,300,000
British India..............	101,100,000	4,600,000
Algeria	138,100,000	140,600,000

The movement of shipping, from 1870 to 1872, was as follows:

FLAG.	ENTERED.		CLEARED.	
	Vessels.	Tons.	Vessels.	Tons.
French	1,026	2,327,000	9,181	2,188,000
Foreign	19,662	4,395,000	18,375	2,986,000
Total, 1872....	29,923	6,772,000	27,556	5,174,000
" 1871....	?	6,276,000	?	3,989,000
" 1870....	?	6,582,000	?	3,979,000

The merchant navy, in 1872, was composed as follows:

PROVINCES.	Area in Square Miles.	Frenchmen.	Foreigners.	Mohammedans.	In Government Institutions.	Total.
Algiers.................................	39,120	67,008	42,181	757,908	5,854	872,951
Oran	111,831	51,729	47,483	411,874	2,456	513,492
Constantine	107,366	45,438	25,902	953,263	3,172	1,027,775
Total....................	258,217	164,175	115,516	2,123,045	11,482	2,414,418

In the column of Frenchmen are included 34,574 native Israelites. The total number of Europeans is 245,117, against 217,990 in 1866; 192,801 in 1861; 159,282 in 1856; 131,283 in 1851; 99,801 in 1845; 35,927 in 1841; 14,561 in 1836; 7,812 in 1833. The number of French-men has, ever since 1841, been about one-half of the European population, it being 16,677 in 1841; 66,050 in 1857; and 129,621 in 1872. The number of Spaniards in 1872 was 74,000. The imports of Algeria were valued, in 1872, at 199,000,000 francs, the exports at 206,000,000. The movement of shipping in the

VESSELS.	Vessels.	Tons.
Sailing-vessels of more than sixty tons..............................	4,709	902,096
Steamers of more than sixty horse-power..............................	316	240,273

According to the report of the Committee of the National Assembly on Railroads, there were, on June 1, 1873:

	Kilometres.*
In operation	19,974
In course of construction	6,647
Total	26,621

Algeria has three roads in operation: from Algiers to Oran, 420 kilometres; from Philippeville to Constantine, 86 kilometres; and the little road from Bona to the mines of Ain-Mokra, 30 kilometres.

The number of letters forwarded by the French post-office in 1873 was 359,433,000. The revenue of the department was, in 1873, 91,454,850 francs; the expenditures, for administration, 51,755,000 francs.

At the end of the year 1871 there were 46,500 kilometres of lines of telegraphs in operation, comprising 127,500 kilometres of wires. The number of telegraph-offices was about 3,800; the aggregate revenue, in 1872, 11,994,000 francs; the expenditures, 12,695,000 francs.

The area and population of Algeria, according to the census of 1872, were as follows:

same year (entrances and clearances) was as follows:

FLAG.	Vessels.	Tonnage.
French	944	128,601
Spanish	2,554	124,328
Italian	1,110	82,546
English	654	273,232

The French colonies and dependencies had, according to the latest official reports, the following area and population:

* One kilometre = 0.62 English mile.

COLONIES AND DEPENDENCIES.	Area, sq. m.	Population.
I. COLONIES.		
Asia.		
1. India: Pondichéry, Chandernager, Karikal, Mahé, Yanaon (1870)................	191.35	232,798
2. French Cochin-China	21,716.49	1,225,213
Total possessions in Asia....	21,912.94	1,488,011
Oceanica.		
1. New Caledonia and Loyalty Islands (1870)...............	7,614.51	60,804
2. Marquesas Islands	478.86	10,000
3. Clipperton Island	2.12	......
Total, Oceanica..............	8,094.09	70,804
Africa (exclusive of Algeria).		
1. Senegambia *	?	100,000
2. Réunion	969.70	212,536
3. Mayotte and Nosso Bé	195.17	21,097
4. Ste.-Marie..................	67.18	6,408
Total, Africa	1,232.05	340,041
America.		
St.-Pierre, Miquelon, etc. (1870)	......	......
Martinique (1870)..............	81.22	4,750
Guadeloupe and dependencies (1870)	381.42	154,847
French Guiana (1870)	712.44 / 46,879.77	157,705 / 21,897
Total, America..............	48,054.85	342,199
Total colonies (except Algeria)	79,294.93	2,240,555
II. DEPENDENCIES.		
Asia.—Cambodia	32,379.20	1,000,000
Oceanica.		
1. Tahiti, Moorea, Tetaacoa, Maitea (1864)	461.78	13,847
2. Tubal, Varitu, and Rapa	53.80	675
3. Tuamota Islands (79)	2,572.54	8,000
4. Gambier Islands (6)	11.48	936
Total, Oceanica..............	3,101.60	23,458
Total, dependencies..........	35,481.59	1,023,458

At the beginning of the year 1874, the Broglie cabinet found itself supported by only a feeble and wavering majority. Great trouble was caused to it by the pastoral letters issued by a number of French bishops in response to the Papal Encyclical of November 21, 1873, and denouncing directly or indirectly the German Government for its attacks upon the Catholic Church. The Emperor of Germany considered himself personally insulted by a pastoral letter issued by Bishop Plantier, of Nîmes. The Bishop of Rodez, Bourret, called the church laws which several European states had recently adopted "conspiracies of thieves," and declared that these abominable usurpations and manifest thefts would justify all attacks upon private property and all revolts against the present rulers of the states. In consequence of the remonstrances from Berlin, the Minister of Public Worship, M. de Fourtou, issued on December 26, 1873, a circular to the bishops, recommending moderation. The German Government, however, observed that the circular in no wise blamed the bishops, but merely gave them a friendly warning to be cautious on account of the difficulty of the times. It

* France has abandoned a large portion of its former possessions in Senegambia.

was impossible, therefore, for Germany to accept the circular as a reparation. The French Government yielded to the pressure brought upon it, and soon after suspended the *Univers* for two months for having published a pastoral letter of the Bishop of Périgueux, though the language of this letter was generally regarded as more moderate than that of the bishops of Rodez, Nimes, and other dioceses. The Italian Government was greatly offended by the presence at the port of Civita Vecchia of the French steamer L'Orénoque, which had been placed at the disposal of the French embassy and of the Pope, and, in consequence of its remonstrance, the French Government deemed it best to give assurances of its peaceable intentions. A passionate interpellation by General du Temple, who it was thought desired to precipitate a war with Italy, called forth from the Minister of Foreign Affairs, Duke de Decazes, on January 20, 1874, new assurances of a peaceable policy.

On January 8, 1874, the National Assembly adopted, in spite of the vigorous opposition of the ministry, a motion made by the Legitimist Franclieu, to postpone the discussion of the bill giving the Government absolute power to name the mayors in all the 36,000 communes of the country, and to take up the municipal bill first. The motion was adopted by a majority of 42 votes (268 against 226), and the ministry consequently offered its resignation, which the President, however, refused to accept, on the ground that the number of voters had not been large enough to show the opinion of the majority of the National Assembly. The majority soon confirmed the opinion of the President by giving the ministry an expression of its continuing confidence. On January 13th, M. de Kerdrel, a member of the Right, expressed the opinion that, though ministerial crises do not possess as much gravity as before the 20th of November, they are, nevertheless, injurious occurrences, and cause serious inconvenience in the administration of the country. The ministry had shown too much susceptibility. The sitting of January 8th was not numerously attended, and the Government had certainly not the majority against it. M. de Kerdrel concluded by asking the ministry for a reply such as would satisfy the Assembly and reassure the country. The Duke de Broglie in reply, said that by the vote of January 8th, the Assembly withdrew from the order of the day a bill of which the ministers demanded the immediate discussion; the ministers were bound to give in their resignation, without considering the peculiar circumstances attending the vote. The strength of the Government must reside in public opinion as well as in the Assembly. The ministry asked that the bill on the nomination of mayors should be declared urgent; because they were convinced that the measure was necessary, not because they wished to delay the introduction of the organic law which they desired, nor from party considerations, but because they were sure that the present condition of the municipalities could not continue without endangering the regular administration of the municipal districts, and impeding the exercise of the central authority. The Assembly having refused what they asked as a Government necessity, their dignity required, and their duty prescribed, that they should resign. The President, M. Buffet, then read an order of the day expressing the confidence of the Assembly in the ministry. It was signed by the Presidents of the ten bureaux, in which the Right are in the majority. M. Raoul Duval accused the ministers of being representatives of the monarchical parties. He maintained that Marshal MacMahon ought to select his ministers from among men not bound by party ties, and he proposed an order of the day expressing these views. M. Picard accused the ministry of tolerating attacks upon the republic. It ought not to allow shouts to be raised of "Long live the King!" or "Long live the Emperor!" nor permit petitions to be signed in favor of the Comte de Chambord. After another speech from the Duke de Broglie in defense of the ministry, M. Picard demanded the adoption of the order of the day pure and simple. This motion was rejected by 355 against 316 votes. The Assembly then voted in the ordinary manner upon M. de Kerdrel's motion, expressing confidence in the Government, which was adopted by 379 votes against 221. M. Delsol, a member of the Right, then moved that the mayors bill should be taken up immediately. This course was agreed to, the ministers withdrew their resignation, and on January 20th the Assembly adopted the law by 361 against 324 votes, after having voted down several amendments. The chief speech against the law was made by Louis Blanc, who declared it to be a violation of the electoral law and irreconcilable with the love for freedom, order, and country.

In view of the manifest impossibility to restore any form of monarchy at an early date, the conservative party and the large majority of the National Assembly rallied round the "Septennate" of President MacMahon as the best government attainable for the country under the existing circumstances. The President himself abandoned his usual reserve, and on February 4th, in a reply to an address from the president of a commercial court, declared his determination to preserve, uncurtailed, the powers conferred upon him for the term of seven years by the National Assembly, and to enforce on all sides a due respect for the existing constitutional laws. The Legitimists were divided on the best policy to be pursued; while some never ceased to demand the immediate restoration of Henry V., others believed that his time had not yet come. The Duke de Broglie, on many occasions, averred his desire to maintain the Septennate, but also avowed his intention to surround it with monarchical institutions. The new law on the appointment of mayors was regarded as the first step in this direction, which was soon to be followed by a curtailment of the electoral franchise and other similar measures.

The new supplementary elections for the National Assembly, which on March 1st were held in the departments of the Vaucluse and Vienne, resulted in the election of Republicans. One of the successful candidates was the old chief of the Radical party, Ledru-Rollin, who, after having lived for more than twenty years in exile and retirement, now returned for the first time to an active political life. As he was a candidate in the Vaucluse, a department reputed to be the most "red" in all France, his success was never doubted. That he did not poll as large a number of votes as his friends expected, was partly accounted for by the fact that a large section of the Republican party looked coldly upon his candidature. The Paris Liberal journals, the *Siècle*, *XIXme Siècle* and *Événement*, protested against it at first, fearing that his name, like that of M. Barodet in Paris, in 1873, might scare moderate Republicans, and encourage reaction. Another reason why M. Ledru-Rollin has scored 5,000 less votes than any Radical elected there before him was found by his friends in the existence of the reign of terror inaugurated by the prefect. It was reported that a great display of artillery and troops of the line was made in the Vaucluse to intimidate evil-minded electors, and that all the practices of the empire in support of official candidates were revived in favor of M. Ledru-Rollin's opponent, the Marquis Biliotti. Of great political importance was the election of a Republican in the Vienne, which was considered a "rural" stronghold. At the general elections of February 8, 1871, this department returned three anti-Republicans—MM. Ernoul, Murveilleux Duvignaux, and Rochethulon. When, in July, 1871, a vacancy occured, M. de Soubeyran, then a timid Bonapartist, but at all events an anti-Republican, was returned triumphantly by 32,000 votes against some scattered voices for Republicans. Now M. Lepetit, the *bâtonnier* of the Order of Advocates of Poitiers, had come forward on a decided Republican platform, backed by a letter from M. Thiers. His opponent was M. de Beauchamp, the brother-in-law of the wealthy M. de Soubeyran, who was charged with spending 200,000 francs on the election. The prefect and a number of new mayors, substituted by Government for those elected by the commune, did their utmost to support M. de Beauchamp; and yet the peasants, in a district essentially agricultural, returned M. Thiers's nominee, by 34,146 against 31,160 votes. The letter of Thiers in favor of the candidature of Lepetit made a powerful impression. The distinguished statesman warmly recommended the efforts made for establishing a moderate and lasting republic. He declared a restoration of monarchy to be impossible in view of the spirit prevailing among the masses and the split among the monarchical parties. The electors therefore would do well to enlighten the National Assembly by the election of moderate Republicans, without scaring it. The result of the election was on all sides chiefly attributed to the influence of this letter. On February 26th, Thiers again expressed his preference for the permanent establishment of a moderate republic in reply to a French delegation from New York, which in the name of a number of French residents of the United States presented him with an album. M. Thiers said: "The noble example of Washington should be a model for us all. Those who govern or may govern France should have this great model before them. They will be fortunate if they unitedly succeed in ac-

complishing the work that God gave to Washington to achieve alone." M. Thiers proceeded to point out the futility of the efforts made to restore monarchy in France, and hoped that parties would end by acknowledging their inability to carry out such projects, and leave the country to govern itself as it liked best. M. Thiers, to this end, recommended perseverance and scrupulous respect for law. He stated that he would devote to the service of France all the strength that remained to him. The Bonapartists were devided in their opinions on the Septennate. The great parliamentary leader of the party, ex-Minister Rouher, in a letter addressed to the *Ami de l'Ordre* promised to the Septennate his support, making it, however, dependent on several conditions. The Government, which cannot well do without the support of the Bonapartists, took great

LYONS.

offense at the declaration that at the right point of time only two forms of government would be face to face, the empire and the republic. Prince Napoleon, on the other hand, declared that he could not recognize the Septennate, as it was not based on universal suffrage, and that he remained a firm adherent of democratic principles. On March 16th the majority of the Prince Imperial was made the occasion of a great Bonapartist demonstration, and a much greater success attended this demonstration than a short time ago could have seemed possible. All the great personages of the party came over, numerous deputies and senators, and crowds of dismissed imperialist prefects. There were, too, a sufficient number of humbler adherents to show that imperialism has a large hold on the affections of some who do not expect to get any personal gain out of a restored empire. The Duke of Padua made

a speech to the prince in the name of the party, and the prince made a reply, which was generally commended as well suited to the occasion. He extolled the *plébescite* as the right and salvation of the country, and declared himself ready, if the name of Napoleon should, for the eighth time, proceed from the ballot-box, to assume the responsibility which the vote of the nation might impose on him. In the mean while, the prince said, the order was maintained by the sword of the Duke of Magenta, the companion of his father's glory and misfortune, whose loyalty was a guarantee that he would not give up the treasure guarded by him. The number of Frenchmen attending this demonstration was estimated at 8,000. Among the prominent men who were present were Rouher, Cassaignac, and Murat. Prince Napoleon was not present, thus indicating by his absence that the rupture between him and the family of the late Emperor was complete. The French Government deposed a few *maires* who had taken part in the demonstration, among them the Duke of Padua, but it was commonly believed that the demonstration had greatly strengthened the position and the hopes of the Bonapartists. This impression was strengthened by the glowing eulogy which Emile Ollivier, the ex-Premier of Napoleon III., made in the French Academy on the greatness of the late Emperor.

On March 27th a new and unlooked-for attempt was made by the Legitimist party to hasten the restoration of monarchy. Following up the Legitimist attack against the Septennial power, of which M. Casenove de Pradine, M. de Franclieu, and M. d'Aboville were the vanguard, M. Dahirel presented a bill enacting that, on the 1st of June, 1874, the Assembly, by a public vote, should decide between the monarchy and the republic. France, he said, was tired of the provisional. The Assembly, while pretending to be constituent, had hitherto constituted nothing, for the present patched-up state of things was no Constitution. He moved that his bill should be considered urgent. M. de Kerdrel, a fusionist, spoke proclaiming himself as good a royalist as M. Dahirel, protested that not a single hour could be subtracted from Marshal MacMahon's seven years, unless, indeed, the marshal himself chose to resign. On a division, the ministry was saved by the Left, the majority against voting the bill as urgent being 330 to 256. Some extreme Opposition deputies reproached their friends with missing an opportunity to upset the ministry, but M. Gambetta and M. Ledru-Rollin were of opinion that the Left could not for a moment sanction M. Dahirel's doctrine that the Assembly was competent to proclaim a definitive government. On the same day the report of the committee on the fortification of Paris, which recommended a large extension of the fortifications in order to make it possible to take the offensive, was adopted. M. Thiers, in a vigorous speech, which was listened to with great attention, spoke against the report. He held that the system of distant forts proposed by the committee would entail excessive expenditure and necessitate too numerous an army, and proposed that the heights nearest to the present fortifications should be fortified for the purpose of protecting Paris from bombardment. The Assembly ultimately adopted the bill as proposed by the committee, by 389 against 193 votes.

On March 28th the National Assembly adjourned to May 12th. At two supplementary elections, held on March 29th, in the department of the Gironde and the Haute-Marne, the Republicans again obtained a very marked success. In the Gironde the Republican candidate, M. Roudier, received 68,877 votes, while the Imperialist and Ministerialist candidates polled 45,079 and 21,598 respectively. In the Haute-Marne, M. Danelle Bernardin, the Re-

publican, received 23,628 votes, and M. Lespe-rut, the Ministerialist, 13,329. The figures show that in the wealthy department of the Gironde the Republican candidate had a majority of votes over the candidates of all the other parties combined, and that the Republican and the Imperialist candidates, between them, polled not far from six times the number of votes given to the representative of the Duke de Broglie. In the other department, one of those which suffered most by the war, and were only lately relieved from the German occupation, the Government hoped for a more favorable return, and was equally disappointed. Thus, after a session which had witnessed a full exposition of the ministerial policy, the Government and the majority of the Assembly were condemned from opposite sides of France.

The National Assembly reassembled on May 13th, and reëlected M. Buffet as President by 360 of 387 votes, the Left not taking part in the voting. On May 15th the Duke de Broglie proposed the bill for an Upper Chamber, to be called the Grand Council, and to be composed of 300 members. Of these 100 were to be named by the Executive power; about 150 to be elected by the departments in the proportion of one member to 200,000 voters; and cardinals and marshals of France would sit without election just as in the time of the empire. Categories of eligibilities were laid down, including retired judges, high functionaries, members of the Legion of Honor, and the highest tax-payers. The Grand Council was to have coördinate powers with the National Assembly, and moreover was to be enabled to constitute itself into a High Court of Justice to try ministers and the President of the Republic. The President of the Republic was, however, only to be responsible to it for a violation of the Constitution. The President of the Grand Council would be elected by the Grand Council itself. In the case of his death or resignation, the Grand Council would be invested with all the rights belonging to the Executive power until further order. In case of the vacancy of the Executive, the President of the Grand Council would become *ipso facto* President of the Republic *ad interim*. He must immediately convoke the National Assembly, and the two Chambers united in Congress would at once replace the President of the Republic without being bound to invest the successor of Marshal MacMahon with the same title or the same powers. On the next day, May 16th, the ministry suffered a crushing defeat upon the question of the Electoral Bill, by 381 votes against 317. M. Batbie, reporter of the Committee on the Constitutional Laws, asked the House to fix the first reading of the Electoral Bill for the following Wednesday, whereupon M. Thery, of the Right, proposed to give precedence to the Municipal Bill. M. Raudot, ministerialist, proposed a compromise; but the Duke de Broglie rose and, on the part of the ministry, insisted on the demand of the reporter of the committee, not for personal reasons, but because it recognized in it the answer to an urgent want, and a pressing appeal from the country. M. Lucien Brun said he and his friends were anxious to have the Political Electoral Bill discussed as soon as possible, but he urged the Government not to make the question of priority a cabinet question. M. de Broglie again insisted upon the importance of the vote, and the division was then taken, the result being that the ministry were in the minority. The hostile majority was composed of the different sections of the Left, with the exception of a very few Deputies of the Left Centre, of eighteen Bonapartists, almost the whole group, and more than fifty Legitimists. Immediately after the rising of the Assembly, the ministers gave in their resignation, which was accepted. Marshal MacMahon requested them to retain their portfolios until their successors should be appointed. M. Buffet and M. d'Audriffet-Pasquier both declined to undertake the formation of a ministry. M. de Goulard agreed to try his hand at forming a new cabinet, but was not successful. On May 23d a new ministry was at length constituted, consisting of the following members: General Cissey, Vice-President of the Council and Minister of War; Decazes, Minister of Foreign Affairs; Fourtou, Minister of the Interior; Magne, Minister of Finance; Callaux, Minister of Public Works; Grivart, Minister of Commerce; Camons, Minister of Public Instruction; Tailhaud, Minister of Justice; Montagnac, Minister of the Navy. The new ministry had no policy of its own; it was to avoid any conflict with the National Assembly and to oppose none of the resolutions passed by the National Assembly. It was supposed to agree with the President, especially in favoring the interests of the Church.

The result of a supplementary election held in the department of Nièvre, on May 25th, produced a more than usual excitement, as it strongly impressed the public mind on the rapid progress of Bonapartism. The department, which in October, 1873, had elected a Republican, now chose M. de Bourgoing, the chamberlain and equerry of Napoleon III., giving him 37,599 votes against 32,157 cast for the Republican candidate and 4,527 given to the Legitimist.

On June 1st the National Assembly began the discussion of the municipal electoral law. On June 8th it adopted, by 403 against 283 votes, Article I., which provides that the electoral lists have to be drawn up by a special committee, consisting of the *maire*, a delegate of the administration and a delegate of the municipal council. To Article V., which fixes the age of voters at twenty-five years, Lafayette moved an amendment, substituting twenty-one for twenty-five, and the amendment was adopted by 348 against 337 votes. On June 18th, the Assembly adopted an amendment, moved by Bardoux, which retains the method of administration at present used by the municipal councils, and rejects the system of decentralization proposed by the committee, which would add to the municipal council an equal number of payers of the highest taxes. The majority of the committee now desired to withdraw its report, but the minority at once took it up, and the Assembly, by 579 against 33 votes, adopted an amendment by Berthauld, repealing three articles of the report, which provided for the introduction of the cumulative voting system. On June 22d an amendment by the Left, that the Government may elect municipal councils, but must in that case order new elections within six months, was rejected by 366 against 311 votes. On June 28th President MacMahon, while reviewing, in the Bois de Boulogne, 50,000 troops, took occasion to define his policy with great precision and force. After praising the troops for their good appearance and their regular movements, the marshal associated the army with himself in the guardianship of order and of the public peace, saying: "This part of the mission which has been imposed upon me belongs equally to you. We will fulfill it together to the end, maintaining everywhere the authority of the law and the respect due to it." The President's order of the day was received with great applause by papers of all parties, except the Legitimists.

The Count de Chambord, on July 2d, issued a new manifesto, which, however, failed to produce the least effect, and appeared to weaken rather than to strengthen the prospects of the Legitimists. The manifesto passed over in silence the difficult question of the flag, declared that the count would follow the call of the nation, and govern with two Chambers, the second of which would be elected by the people, but that he would not allow barren political debates in the Chambers. A motion by Larochefoucauld in the National Assembly on July 7th, for the restoration of the monarchy, was promptly rejected, and the Government suspended the *Union*, by which the manifesto had been published. An order of the day proposed by Lucien Brun, which censured the suppression of the *Union*, was rejected by a large majority; but, as the Assembly, on the other hand, refused to adopt an amendment proposed by M. Paris, and supported by the Government, the ministry offered its resignation. The President refused to accept the resignation, but on July 9th addressed a message to the Assembly, in which he called for speedy action on those constitutional laws which he regarded as indispensable for the fulfillment of his Septennial powers. The ministry, on July 30th, explained the wishes of the President more fully, designating as specially necessary organic laws on the establishment of a First Chamber, and the bestowal upon the President of the right to dissolve the Second Chamber with the consent of the First. On July 15th the Constitutional Committee of Thirty laid before the National Assembly the draft of the organic laws on the Government of France. It proposed, in accordance with the wishes of the President, the erection of a First Chamber, gave the President the right to dissolve the Second Chamber, even without the consent of the First, made the President personally responsible for high-treason, while the ministers have to assume the responsibility for all acts of the Government. In case of the death or resignation of MacMahon, the Senate and Chamber of Deputies are to decide conjointly on the future form of government.

An important discussion took place on July 13th, on a motion by Casimir Perier to proclaim the republic as the definite form of government for France. The motion had, on June 15th, been declared urgent by the National Assembly, and referred to the Constitutional Committee, which now reported on it adversely. General Cissey, in the name of the Government, also declared against it; the country expected at present the organization of the powers of the President, and the Government expected that its rights be defined; in future, the country would be at liberty to dispose of its destinies. In accordance with the declaration of the Government, the Assembly rejected the motion by 374 votes against 333. A motion by Maleville, declaring the National Assembly dissolved, was also rejected by 369 against 340. On July 31st, a resolution was adopted to adjourn from August 6th to November 30th. The Minister of the Interior declared on this occasion that the Government engaged during the adjournment of the National Assembly to oppose any plot against the powers of the President. Motions for raising or suspending the state of siege where it still existed were rejected. In the standing committee, which was to represent the Assembly during the adjournment, all parties were represented except the Bonapartists.

Shortly before the adjournment, a partial modification of the ministry had taken place. The Minister of Finance, Magne, on July 15th, offered his resignation because the Assembly had rejected, by 362 against 265 votes, a motion by Goulart for doubling the salt-tax, which he warmly recommended, and because all his efforts for covering the deficit of 500,-000,000 francs by additional taxes had failed. He was followed, on July 17th, by Fourtou the Minister of the Interior, and like himself a representative of the Bonapartist party. Their places were filled by the appointment of M. Mathieu-Bodet as Minister of Finance and of General Chabaud-Latour as Minister of War. General Chabaud-Latour, who belongs to the Right Centre, is a Protestant and a friend of the Princes of Orleans, and the choice of a military man as head of the home office, was regarded as an indication of a policy of firmness on the part of the Government. M. Mathieu-Bodet occupies in the Assembly a position between the Right Centre and Left Centre, and belongs to the group of members presided over by M. Target, whose influence was decisive in the event of May 24, 1873, when M. Thiers was overthrown. All parties in the Assembly agreed that the appointment of the new Ministers of the Interior and Finance was a blow to the cause of the Bonapartists.

On August 16th the Bonapartists obtained another great victory at a supplementary election for the National Assembly in the department of Calvados. Of the 77,286 electors who voted for the Bonapartist candidate, M. le Provost de Launay received 40,794 votes; M. Aubert, Republican, 27,272; and M. de Fontette, Monarchist, 8,978. In 1872 the number of voters was 63,000. M. Paris, the deceased Republican deputy, obtained 28,000 votes; M. Fournist, Legitimist, 17,000; M. Jorel Desclosières, Orleanist, 15,000; and M. de Colbert Chapannais, Bonapartist, 3,000. A comparison of these electoral statistics shows that, while the strength of the Republicans has remained about the same, the Bonapartists have almost wholly absorbed the two other monarchical parties.

During a tour which President MacMahon made in August and September through Brittany and the northwestern provinces, he was everywhere warmly received. In his replies to the addresses with which he was welcomed, he strictly adhered to the policy which he had consistently pursued during the session of the National Assembly, and carefully avoided expressing a preference for any permanent form of government. He eagerly showed his personal devotion to the Catholic religion, without, however, giving any encouragement to the political publications of the bishops.

At a supplementary election held in the department of Marne and Loire, on September 19th, the candidate of the Republicans was elected over the monarchical candidate, in whose support all the other parties had united. The elections for the French Councils-General took place on October 4th and 11th. Of the members elected—1,436 in number—673 are Republicans, 604 Monarchists, and 158 Bonapartists. The result was, like that of nearly all the supplementary elections, favorable to the Republicans and the Bonapartists, the former gaining 30 and the Bonapartists 53 seats. Through these elections the Republicans attained a majority in 38 Councils-General and the Monarchists in 44. In three departments —namely, Aude, Ardèche, and Gard—the Republicans and Monarchists are equally divided. Among the prominent men who were not reëlected to their seats was Prince Napoleon. In consequence of the attitude assumed by him toward the Prince Imperial and the Empress, the Bonapartist members of the General-Council of Corsica, who had elected him to the presidency of the Council, were so incensed against him that they absented themselves from the April session, and a quorum could not, consequently, be obtained. At the fall election they nominated, and successfully elected against him, Prince Charles of Canino, whose father, as a member of the Roman Constituent Assembly in 1849, voted for the deposition of the Pope.

On October 18th the Orénoque was recalled from Civita Vecchia, where, ever since the month of August, 1870, she had remained at the disposal of the Pope, in "case he wished, contrary to the desire of France, to quit Italy." "The departure of the Orénoque," the *Journal Officiel* said, "implies no change in the sentiments of devotion and solicitude of France toward his Holiness." A fresh vessel will be placed at his service, but it will remain in one of the French ports of the Mediterranean. Immediately beneath this notice was an announcement that the Kleber had been ordered to leave Toulon and proceed on a special mission to Corsica.

The municipal elections, which took place in November, were even more favorable to the Republican party than the supplementary elections for the National Assembly and the elections for the Councils-General. In the large towns the Radicals met with a marked success over the candidates of the moderate Republican party, which was a remarkable feature of the electoral contest. In Marseilles the Radicals returned their candidates by a large majority, beating those recommended by M. Labadié, a well-known and violent Republican. In Lyons, thirty-four Radicals and one moderate Republican were returned almost unanimously, the Conservatives not giving themselves the trouble to vote. The last Municipal Council elected by universal suffrage in the second city of France was dissolved by M. Thiers, and replaced by a special commission, and the Conservatives of Lyons probably thought they would not have to endure the new Council for any length of time. Several Right-Centre deputies, and M. Grivart, the Minister of Commerce, were defeated, to the great delight of the opposition. No troubles worth mentioning occurred, military precautions having been adopted in dangerous localities. The Municipal Council in Paris consists of twelve Conservatives and sixty-eight Republicans; but while sixty-six of the latter were supported by the Radicals, all of them are not themselves Radical—in round numbers 180,-000 for Republican, and 78,000 for Conservative candidates. At the election of a deputy in April, 1873, M. Barodet, the Radical candidate, obtained 180,000 votes, while M. Rémusat, the moderate Republican, and Colonel Stoffel, the Bonapartist, mustered together 162,000, so that 342,000 electors in all voted.

The new session of the National Assembly met on November 30th. M. Buffet was re-elected President by 348 votes, 205 blank votes being cast. At the first balloting Martel, Benoist d'Azy, and Kerdrel, were elected Vice-

Presidents by 422,327 and 287 votes. At a second ballot, which was necessary for the election of the fourth Vice-President, the Duke Audiffret-Pasquier, of the Right Centre, was elected by 283 votes over Rampon, of the Left Centre, who received 251 votes. The members of the bureau were then drawn for by lot, amid much conversation and noise.

The message of the President was delivered on December 3d, and read by the Vice-President of the Council, General Cissey. The message states that the President during the recess had endeavored to strengthen peace and maintain order. The relations of the Government with foreign powers had become more and more friendly, and the economic condition of the country had at the same time sensibly improved. There had been an exceptionally good harvest, the prosperity of the country was increasing, and a larger revenue might be expected from existing taxation. In passing through some of the departments he had everywhere been struck with the love of order displayed, and the desire prevailing that the power he exercised should be strengthened in order that it might fulfill its mission. The House would shortly be called upon to examine this question, and he hoped that an understanding would be arrived at. He would not shrink from responsibility, nor would the intervention of his Government be wanting. He accepted power not to serve a party, but to carry out the work of social defense and national restoration, and in the accomplishment of his duty nothing would discourage him. He would remain at his post to the last day of his seven years' term, with unshaken firmness and a scrupulous respect for the laws.

An excited debate was called forth in the National Assembly by M. Jaubert's bill for freeing superior education from state control. M. Challemel-Lacour having, on December 4th, spoken against the bill and complained of the encroachments of the Catholic hierarchy, Bishop Dupanloup, of Orleans, on December 5th, in reply, reproached him with having placed Catholics outside the pale of law. The bishop asserted that the danger arose from those persons who said that the Archbishop of Paris ought to have been shot. At these words violent protestations came from the Left, and it was with difficulty the president obtained silence. M. Challemel-Lacour replied with great bitterness, and concluded by referring the personal attacks of Monsignor Dupanloup to the judgment of the honest men who sat in the Assembly, and generally to those who had any regard for the dignity of the French episcopate. M. Buffet protested against the language used by M. Challemel-Lacour when addressing a man who was one of the glories of the French episcopate. Quiet having been restored, other speakers addressed the House, and the Assembly decided, by 553 against 133 votes, that the bill should be read a second time.

The Spanish Government has ever, since the

outbreak of the Carlist war, suspected the French authorities of favoring and encouraging the Carlists. Spain repeatedly remonstrated against this conduct, and France replied that all precautions which could be required by international usage had been taken. These assurances were, however, not regarded as satisfactory in Madrid, and in October the Spanish embassador in Paris presented to the French Minister for Foreign Affairs an elaborate diplomatic note, which is in fact a pointed and detailed indictment of the conduct pursued by France toward Spain since the outbreak of the Carlist war. That some such formal accusation was pending had been conjectured from the cold and guarded language used on one side and the other by the French embassadors at Madrid and by Marshal Serrano when the embassador presented his credentials. The remonstrance which the Marquis Vega di Armijo was instructed, after full consideration, to bring under the notice of the Duke Decazes, is neither cold nor guarded. The note is couched in language which is much more direct and concise than is commonly met with in diplomatic literature. It does not confine itself to vague appeals and complaints, but challenges direct issues, specifies times and places and persons, attacks individual servants of the French Government, and demands redress of a specific kind in the most uncompromising tone. The Marquis Vega di Armijo, in protesting against the failure of the French Government to observe the obligations of neutrality toward Spain, retains a sufficient remnant of official courtesy to assume that his renewed remonstrance is rendered necessary by the default of the subordinate officers of the French Government. He reminds the Duke Decazes of the repeated engagements which had been entered into for regulating the relations of France toward the Spanish Government and the Carlists, and insists that these engagements have been broken by the direct acts or the supine and studied indifference of the prefects and lesser officials of the frontier departments of Southern France. The traffic in contraband of war goes on, it is alleged, as merrily as ever; the Carlist conspiracy is actively and openly at work in Bayonne, Perpignan, Pau, Oleran, and other populous places of the southern departments; and Carlist leaders and soldiers, with scarcely an attempt at disguise, parade streets of French towns as freely as they might the headquarters of the Pretender at Estella. The Prefect of the Lower Pyrenees is distinctly charged with permitting the passage of Carlist leaders and partisans to and fro between the headquarters of Don Carlos and Bayonne. The same functionary is charged with shutting his eyes to the traffic in contraband of war, with turning a deaf ear to the demands of the Spanish consul for the "interment" of notorious Carlist partisans, and with attempting to deal harshly with Spanish soldiers of the national armies who had been captured by the Carlists and thrust across the frontier. The conduct

of the Préfect of the Gironde is on similar grounds assailed. Finally, the Marquis Vega di Armijo charges the French Government with the breach of an "understanding"— which, though only a verbal one, was to have had, as he asserts, the force of a convention— between the French chargé d'affaires and the Spanish ministry; the former spontaneously promising and the latter accepting the assurance that all the leading Carlists, whether military or civilian, found in France should be sent to the Swiss or Belgian frontier, and that those of less mark should be forced to reënter Spain. Neither part of this engagement has, according to the Spanish embassador, been carried out by the French authorities.

The French answer to this memorandum was forwarded to the Spanish embassador on December 13th. In this communication, couched in conciliatory but firm language, the Duke Decazes confronts and discusses with precision all the allegations enumerated by the Spanish embassador against the conduct of the French authorities on the Pyrenees frontier, thus accepting the responsibility of the measures of the various governments incriminated since 1869. With regard to the chief of these allegations, such as the entry of Don Carlos into Spain, the duke finds himself able to cite the authentic testimony of the Spanish authorities, and of M. de la Vega's predecessors, who have rendered homage to the attitude of the French Government and to the zeal of its agents. He finds, moreover, in a speech by a foreign minister, an emphatic reply to the accusations which have been preferred. After this examination of the complaints put forward by the Spanish embassador, the Duke Decazes explicitly claims for the French Government the right of nominating and maintaining its agents in the plenitude of its independence and responsibility, and he expresses surprise at any indication being given by Spain on this subject. He does not consent to follow the embassador in examining the eventuality of measures which should be taken on the frontier to insure common action of the military forces of the two governments. He sets aside this suggestion, as also the example of Portugal, which seems to him opposed to it, and which he does not consider convincing. As to the reproach that France has pursued in Spanish affairs a policy contrary to the liberal sentiments of the French nation, the Duke Decazes replies that France wishes well to Spain, and desires that it may regain internal order and political security. As to the French Government, while regretting that the integrity of its conduct and the loyalty of its proceedings have not hitherto been better understood, he hopes that in future Spain will render full justice to it. The dispatch is followed by voluminous appendices, which discuss all the details of the various measures taken by the Government on the Pyrenees frontier during the last five years. An incident, not only disagreeable but humiliating to France in the history of these diplomatic negotiations with Spain, was the full information on the complicity of the French authorities with the Carlists, which the German consul at Bayonne collected and forwarded to his Government. The German did not limit his investigations to Bayonne, but, accompanied by competent guides, he made a tour of the frontier as far as Bagnères de Luchon, descending the Bidasoa afterward. He then inspected the districts where the connection was closest between the Carlists and the French. Not content with what he heard and took down in writing, the indefatigable consul purchased accoutrements, arms, ammunition, and cavalry-harness, from the stores along the frontier, where they were kept by speculators, with the knowledge of the French authorities, in readiness to equip any number of Carlists who might wish to invade Spain. He also saw at Tarbes depots of horses for their artillery and cavalry, and purchased in the French Government repositories Carlist postage-stamps, to the great consternation afterward to the venders when they found out who the purchaser was. Perhaps the most remarkable incident of the consul's tour of inspection was the interview he had with the Legitimist Marquis de Nadeaillac, Prefect of the Basses-Pyrénées. It was asked for and acceded to in writing, and proved a bitter dose to the French functionary.

An important report was, in December, presented to the National Assembly by the Minister of Marine and Colonies, upon the condition of the convicts in New Caledonia. The documents contain various topographical details relating to the Peninsula Ducos and the Isle of Pines, and gives particulars of all the convict transports dispatched between the months of May, 1872, and July, 1874, specifying the measures of sanitary precaution taken antecedently to embarkation and during the passage. It further gives a full account of the establishment of the convicts in the colony upon their arrival; tents and huts have already been prepared for them, constructed with all possible speed in the time between the Governor's notification of the notification concerning the dispatch of the convicts and their arrival, the number being estimated at 3,000 individuals; the barracks destined for the guards, for the quarters of officers and troops, and depots for provisions, as well as two ambulances for the sick, were all ready. The convicts located on the Isle of Pines were three times as numerous as those on the Peninsula Ducos, the entire body being subdivided into five groups or communes. Each group was called on to elect nine of their number, whose names were submitted to the Governor for him to select therefrom three delegates, to represent the entire group in all relations with the administration, being also charged with the duty of looking after the welfare of their comrades, presiding over the various distributions, becoming

the medium for the transmission of complaints and reclamations, and the settlement of disputes by arbitration. The functions of these delegates are by no means devoid of danger. On one occasion, owing to his zeal, one of them became the object of a savage attack, secretly planned, from which he escaped with his life only by a miracle, and for which the four assassins were executed. A deposit-bank was established, so that each convict might be enabled to place in security whatever money he possessed, and so avoid any danger which might attach to carrying a large amount on his person. All drafts upon the amount standing to a convict's credit in the bank are limited to the presumed extent of his requirements. The distribution of provisions to the convicts takes place every morning, their rations being exactly the same as those of the troops doing duty in the colony, with the exception of wine, which is only served out to those engaged on labor-tasks. Three libraries have been established: one on the Peninsula Ducos, a second on the Isle of Pines, and the third at Nouméa. Chapels have been built, where the services are conducted by three Catholic priests and one Protestant minister, attached to the convict establishment. The health of the convict colony is cared for by a staff of seven medical officers, two apothecaries, and several Sisters of St.-Joseph de Cluny, aided by a number of hospital-assistants. Under the two enactments of 1872 and 1873, the privilege of settling at the place of transportation, at the expense of the state, is granted to the families of the convicts, and the number of applications became so great that recourse had to be made to vessels of the mercantile marine for the means of transport. The first of such convoys consisted of 440 adults and 142 children. To every one of the wives of convicts a grant was made of 50 francs in money, with 25 francs additional for each child, traveling expenses to the port of embarkation, an outfit, and a free passage. On their arrival in New Caledonia the various families were provided with food and shelter until they were enabled to rejoin the convict head of the family. According to law the convicts are entitled to every liberty compatible with the measures necessary to prevent escape; but the report dwells especially on the difficulty of realizing this provision concurrently with efficient surveillance. The physical characteristics of the locality render escape next to impossible at the Isle of Pines, but it is otherwise at the Peninsula Ducos on account of the proximity of the harbor of Nouméa and the facilities of communication with the town, which is only about nine or ten miles distant. Reference is made to the escape of Henri Rochefort and his companions. Out of the whole number of those transported nearly two-fifths are old offenders and convicts. Among the 3,324 individuals transported up to January last, 1,185 had undergone 3,194 previous convictions. The Minister of Marine laments their condition of moral degradation, and states that continual efforts must be made to contend against these two chief obstacles — idleness and drunkenness. With this object it has been considered necessary to proscribe the sale, not only of spirits, but also of wine, in the canteens of the convict districts. After entering at some length into the questions which arose in relation to the provision of remunerative employment for the convicts or the alternative enforcement of task-work or "hard labor," the report concludes as follows : " Finally, two facts result clearly from the careful studies of actualities, viz. : 1. That the Peninsula Ducos is an unsuitable and badly-chosen locality for the purpose; and, 2. That the right of idleness cannot be conceded to the convicts. The evil effects of such a privilege have already been amply manifested; no such right can be deduced from the law of 1850, the authors of which never contemplated the withdrawal of the convicts from the operation of that primordial and higher law, whereby, from the Creation, all mankind are condemned to labor and to die."

In December a report was distributed in Paris, drawn up by the late M. Perrot, on the operations of what is called the Eastern Army during the war, in which Garibaldi is very roughly handled. The report says: "If Garibaldi had been a French general we should have been compelled to raise formally the question as to whether he should not have been tried by court-martial · for his conduct in having deliberately, and without fighting "— these last five words are in italics in the report — " abandoned positions which he had been ordered to defend, and having thereby occasioned the loss of a French army, and brought about a military disaster without a parallel save those of Sedan and Metz." In other words, the report lays down that when the French army, after Villersexel, was driven into Switzerland, it was Garibaldi's fault. This accusation has caused great sensation.

In March, Henri Rochefort, Paschal Grousset, the Minister of Foreign Affairs under the Commune, and some other Communists, escaped from New Caledonia, to which they had been banished. They left the island in a small boat, and after three days passed in the southern seas were picked up by an English sailing-vessel, bound for the capital of New South Wales. The Governor of New Caledonia, who was absent on a tour of inspection at the time, commenced a rigorous inquiry into the circumstances; and the French Minister of Marine, on the first report of the escape, ordered a general officer to proceed to New Caledonia, invested with the necessary powers to take the measures that might be required in so serious a case. Before his return to Europe, Rochefort paid a visit to the United States, where he gave a course of lectures.

A considerable sensation was produced in France by the escape of Marshal Bazaine from the Island of Sainte-Marguerite, near Cannes, where he was to pass the twenty years of seclusion into which President MacMahon had commuted the sentence of death pronounced against the marshal by the court-martial. His wife, who had been permitted to join, with her children, the fate of the marshal, but was not subjected to prison régime, and at liberty to walk about the island, had, in union with her brother, prepared the means of escape, for which the aid of Lieutenant-Colonel Villette, the ex-Captain Doineau, and several warders, was secured. Their case came, on September 8th and 9th, before the Correctional Tribunal of Grasse, which sentenced Villette and two warders to six months', Doineau to two months', and another warder to one month's imprisonment. Subsequently, Marshal Bazaine gave to a reporter of the Figaro the fullest details of ·his escape. A few days before, Marshal Bazaine, in a very interesting letter to the New York Herald, dated Liége, September 6th, had, for the first time, presented to the world his defense against the charges which had been brought against him. The letter is an important contribution to the history of the great Franco-German War, and severely reflects upon the members of the court-martial which found him guilty, especially upon its president, the Duke d'Aumale, as well as upon President MacMahon, who, Bazaine insists, was liable to every charge which had been preferred against him.

On the recommendation of the Minister of Commerce, a commission was appointed early in the year to examine the means of extending the French export-trade. At the first sitting of the commission, which was held in May, the Minister of Commerce delivered a speech, replying at length to the various criticisms, particularly those made by the English newspapers, upon the appointment of the commission. The minister refuted the idea that France did not produce articles which could form a staple of a great export-trade, and, in answer to the arguments of English journals, made numerous comparisons between France and England. He said facts replied triumphantly in favor of France, the exports of which, in 1873, reached a value of four milliards of francs against six and a half milliards exported by England. All branches of French manufacture participated in the export-trade. With regard to the iron-goods trade, the minister said that French· competition with England was becoming possible, and that France began to hold a good position in foreign markets. Respecting exportation to the East, the minister observed that French manufacturers could sell their produce in English colonies as elsewhere. Without doubt, the new taxes burdened labor, but they were inevitable, and did not disastrously affect production. Government had avoided augmenting the customs duties. Labor was still in a favored position in France, thanks to all the elements of wealth concentrated in the country. The working-population was daily acquiring greater aptitude, strikes were becoming less frequent, and money was abundant. Entering upon the question of the nature of the labors of the commission, the minister said the first matter before them would be the examination of the consular reports, and the means of making them more widely known. He criticised the educational system in the colleges, as rendering young men unfit for a mercantile career, contrary to the practice in England and Germany. It was necessary, therefore, to examine the means of improving the system of commercial education. These two subjects would be intrusted to two sub-committees, while a third sub-committee would examine the transport question. The minister said the reproaches made against the French transport system were exaggerated or ill-founded. The foreign systems, and particularly the American and English, were far from perfect. The minister then adverted to the question of a credit for commercial operations abroad, and laid on the table a series of questions embracing the greater part of the matters to be examined. He also presented various comparative tabular statements respecting the trade of France, England, and foreign countries, and added that the commission would institute an inquiry, in which many leading merchants would be asked to state their views verbally. At the conclusion of the minister's speech, the commission proceeded to divide its labors on the plan suggested by him.

The foreign relations of the country during the year, and the free-trade policy pursued by the present Government, were reviewed by the Duke Decazes, the Minister of Foreign Affairs, at a banquet given him at Bordeaux, in October. M. Lalande, Vice-President of the Chamber of Commerce, in proposing his health, complimented him on his consistent advocacy of free trade, and his opposition to duties on raw materials, expressing a hope that he would take every opportunity of obtaining from other countries, especially from the United States, advantages analogous to those derived by the Gironde from the English treaty of 1860. The Duke Decazes, in reply, after alluding to his connection with the province by birth, remarked that fourteen years ago he advocated economic measures, which at that time appeared to be contrary to his personal interests. It was then alleged that French colliery and metallurgical industries had every thing to fear from a broader and more liberal economic policy. He never shared that opinion, and he was glad he had not, for he now saw more clearly than ever that the widest development of free trade was the most productive means of national wealth. He remained faithful to that conviction when he endeavored to resist tendencies which he believed to be fatal, and it had since induced him to exert his best efforts to facilitate commercial and consular relations with Russia, and to renew postal relations with the United States. The latter afforded ground for a hope at no distant date of more

liberal commercial relations, which, he ventured to add, would be more advantageous for both countries. With the same convictions he had negotiated new treaties with Turkey, which would take the place of those about to expire. After stating that he was promoting French interests in La Plata and in West Africa, Japan, and Cochin-China, the duke continued: "There, as, indeed, everywhere, you ask of us liberal legislation, an effective protection, and peace. As for peace, Marshal MacMahon, that illustrious and loyal soldier, who has taken charge of France for seven years, has confided to me the special charge of it. As long as I retain his confidence and that of the Assembly, I shall not be wanting to the duties which that mission imposes on me. Peace, in order to be fruitful and to be firmly established, can only rest on bases compatible both with our dignity and our interests. It is impossible to separate the two, and that is why we have placed it under a double safeguard—the affirmation of the rights of France and of our scrupulous respect for all our international obligations. In that consists the whole secret of our foreign policy, too frequently misunderstood and so unjustly attacked, and it rests solely and absolutely on the rigorous and scrupulous execution of the treaties which bind us toward foreign powers. I shall not try at the present day—and you cannot blame this prudence—to provoke or aim at a modification of conventions which the past has bequeathed to us. I demand the strict observance of them, and I offer on my side the loyal execution of them. Is not this course dictated by our dignity and our interests? We should strangely misunderstand these serious duties if we allowed ourselves to be seduced into the abandonment of this footing. It is indeed the safeguard of France as well as the guarantee of the peace of Europe."

Much scandal and a little alarm were caused in France by the words which M. Piccon, one of the deputies from the Alpes-Maritimes, was reported to have spoken at a banquet at Nice. He was confident, he said, that Nice, the victim of Italian independence, would soon be won back by her true country. To that end he would sacrifice all the interests of himself and his family. These words raised such a storm that M. Piccon felt it needful to deny the accuracy of the report. His dignity, he added, did not permit him to be more explicit, and soon after he resigned as member of the National Assembly. It subsequently appeared that the report on the alleged secession tendencies of Nice and Savoy were gross exaggerations, and that many prominent men who were charged with favoring the secession movement, were really only in favor of a decentralizing policy which would allow Nice, like any other part of France, to adhere to its ancient provincial peculiarity.

The influence of the Catholic Church on society and on the legislation of the country appears to be on the increase. Though the Minister of Foreign Affairs could not indorse the violent attacks which the bishops and the Catholic organs made upon the Governments of Italy and Germany, but even deemed it necessary to act in opposition to their demands, and though the President appointed a Protestant as Minister of the Interior, the efforts for restoring the influence of the Church upon the masses of the people were on the whole warmly supported by the Government and the immense majority of the provincial authorities. The pilgrimages continued to assume dimensions which by far exceeded the expectations of the opponents of the Church, and, in the province of public instruction, the bishops appeared to be sure of seeing all their demands substantially complied with.

Protestantism in France has severely suffered by the cession of Alsace-Lorraine to Germany. According to the census of 1872, the Protestants now constitute only 1.60 per cent. of the total population, whereas, in 1866, they still were 2.23 per cent. One of the two Protestant Churches recognized by the state, the Lutheran, has been nearly destroyed by the loss of Alsace; the other, the Reformed, split in 1874 into two sections (see REFORMED CHURCH). The reports of the Protestant religious societies of France, made at their anniversaries in April and May, showed the year to have been generally a dull one with them. The Bible Society of France reported its expenses during the year to have been 47,000 francs. It had circulated in the same period more than 20,000 copies of the Scriptures.

On March 15th, the French Vice-Admiral Dupré concluded a new treaty with the government of Anam, in Farther India, which was ratified by the National Assembly of France on August 8th. The treaty was to put an end to the persecution of the Catholic Christians which had again taken place in Anam. It ratified the provision of the first treaty, concluded by Anam with France and Spain in 1862, by which the French and Spaniards received the free exercise of their religion, and the natives of Anam the right to embrace Christianity. The new treaty was even more favorable to France and the Christians than that of 1862, and virtually places the entire empire under the protectorate of France. In article 9 the King of Anam engages to repeal and destroy all prohibitions which formerly were issued against the Christian religion, and allows all his subjects to embrace it and exercise it. The Christians may assemble in their churches for divine worship, and they cannot be coerced into any actions which are forbidden by their religion. They shall not be subjected to any particular enumeration, and shall be admitted to all examinations and public offices. The special lists of Christians which during the last fifteen years had been prepared, shall be destroyed, and, with regard to census and taxes, the Christians shall be treat-

ed like the other subjects of the King. The former prohibition to use, orally or in writings, offensive expressions against the Christians, is renewed. The bishops and missionaries may come into the empire without hinderance, and travel in their dioceses and districts, as soon as they have a pass from the French Government of Cochin-China which has been indorsed by the Anamese Minister of Rites, or the provincial governor. They may everywhere preach the Catholic doctrines, and shall not be subjected to any special superintendence. The villagers will no longer be bound to notify the mandarins of the arrival of missionaries. The bishops, missionaries, and native priests, have the right to buy or rent lands and houses, and to establish orphan-houses, schools, hospitals, and other buildings, for religious and ecclesiastical purposes. The property which has been taken away from the Christians will be restored to them. All these provisions apply to the Spanish missionaries as well as to the French. A royal rescript was to announce to all the communes of the empire the liberty granted to the Christians, immediately after the ratification of the treaty. The party opposed to the Christians and foreigners is, however, very numerous in Anam, and soon after the conclusion of the treaty a bloody revolution was instigated by this party, which raged for several months.

General ERNEST LOUIS OCTAVE COURTET DE CISSEY, the president of the Council of Ministers in the latter half of the year 1872, is descended from an ancient noble family of Burgundy, and was born in Paris, in 1812. From 1830 to 1832 he attended the Military School of St.-Cyr, and subsequently the school of the general staff. Having been appointed officer, he went to Algeria, where he served in the war against the Kabyles. He soon became adjutant of General Trézel, and took an active part in the battles of Constantine, Mascara, and on the Isly. In 1852 he returned to France, and in 1855 he served as colonel in the Crimean War, when he in consequence of his bravery in the battle of Inkermann was appointed brigadier-general. In 1865 he was appointed as general of division at Rennes. When the war against Germany broke out in 1870, he received the command of the First Division of the Fourth Corps (Ladmirault). As such he belonged to the Army of Metz, and took a brilliant part in the battles of Borny, Rezonville, and St.-Privat. When Marshal Bazaine, on October 22d, informed his generals of his intention to capitulate, Cissey declared energetically in favor of a last attempt to force a passage through the German army. On October 25th, after the useless negotiations of General Changarnier with Prince Frederick Charles, General Cissey was sent by Bazaine to Frescaty, a castle situated under the Fort St.-Privat, in order to have an interview with General Stiehle, the chief of the general staff of the Prussian army. In these new negotiations Cissey endeavored to separate the fate of the army from that of the place, but did not succeed. In consequence of the capitulation, he was sent as prisoner-of war to Germany. At the elections of February, 1871, he was chosen as deputy of the National Assembly from the department of Ille-et-Vilaine. Having returned to France after the conclusion of the preliminary peace, he was appointed by the Government of Versailles to a command against the insurgents of Paris, where he greatly distinguished himself. On June 5th a decree of the chief of the executive power appointed him Minister of War, in place of General Le Flô, who was sent as embassador to St. Petersburg. As minister of war, Cissey labored with extraordinary energy for the reorganization of the French army, and the reforms which have been introduced there are for a large part his work. When the law to bring Marshal Bazaine before a court-martial was presented, General Cissey endeavored to procure to his former chief the privilege of demanding for himself this rigorous measure. The majority of the Assembly was any thing but pleased with this indulgence, and for a time it was believed that Cissey would have to yield his position as Minister of War to General Chanzy. In the National Assembly General Cissey took his seat at the Right Centre. On May 23, 1873, he formed a new cabinet, in which he retained, besides the presidency of the Council, the department of war.

Duke LOUIS CHARLES ELIE AMANIEN DÉCAZES, next to General Cissey the most prominent member of the cabinet appointed in May, 1874, is the son of the prominent French statesman Duke Elie Décazes. He was born on May 9, 1819, and at an early age entered the diplomatic career. The Government of Louis Philippe appointed him minister plenipotentiary and extraordinary envoy of France near the courts of Spain and Portugal. After the Revolution of 1848 he retired with his father to private life. He was in 1869 elected member of the Council-General of the Gironde, but when he was in the same year a candidate for the Corps Législatif, he was defeated by the official candidate, Chaix d'Estange. At the general election of February, 1871, he was chosen by the department of the Gironde, of which he is a native, member of the National Assembly. Like Cissey, he belonged to the party of the Right Centre. In October, 1871, he was reëlected member of the Council-General. Though a less frequent speaker than other prominent men of the Assembly, he has been one of its most influential members.

Bishop FÉLIX ANTOINE PHILIPPE DUPANLOUP, of Orleans, is the foremost champion of the interests of the Catholic Church in the National Assembly and in the country. He was born in Savoy, on January 3, 1802, studied theology at Paris, and was ordained in 1825. In 1827 he was appointed confessor to the Duke of Bordeaux, in 1828 religious instructor of the Princes of Orleans, and in 1830 almoner to the Dauphine. Having lost this position in consequence of the Revolution of July, 1830, he founded the academy of St.-Hyacinthe, and two years later was naturalized as a Frenchman. As he had achieved a great reputation both as a religious instructor and a pulpit orator, he was appointed by Archbishop Quelen Vicar-General. Under Archbishop Affre, whose appointment he had opposed, he only retained the title of Vicar-General. At the close of the year 1845, he resigned both this title and the position of Prefect of Studies in the Petit Séminaire which he had held since 1834. Having been, in 1849, appointed Bishop of Orleans, he took a prominent part in the discussion of religious, educational, and other questions. He was supposed to sympathize with Montalembert, Lacordaire, and the other leaders of the so-called liberal Catholic party, whose organ was the *Correspondant*, and he not only severely censured the course pursued by the *Univers*, the chief organ of the Ultramontane party, but even forbade its circulation in his diocese. He specially defended, against the *Univers* and Abbé Gaume's work, "Le Ver Rongeur," the reading of the pagan classics in the Church school. On the other hand, he made the utmost efforts to obtain for the Church an unlimited control of her own literary institutions. He was consulted in the framing of the law of March 15, 1850, on the reorganization of public instruction, and accepted a position as member of the Supreme Council of Public Instruction, but resigned in 1852, as he entirely disagreed with the views of Minister Tortoul. When the Vatican Council was convoked, Bishop Dupanloup did not conceal his opposition to the declaration of the doctrine of papal infallibility, and at the Council he was one of the most prominent members of the minority which declared the dogmatization of that doctrine. When, however, the Council adopted and the Pope promulgated it, he was among the first to submit. During the occupation of his episcopal city by the German army, he successfully interceded with the German authorities in favor of the mitigation of some measures adopted by the generals. Having been elected a member of the French Academy in 1854, he prevented by his influence, in 1863, the election of the radical Littré; and when the latter was, in 1871, elected in spite of his opposition, he resigned, but his resignation was not accepted. In the National Assembly, to which he was elected by his Department, he belongs to the party of the Right. As president of the committee to which was referred the new law on primary instruction prepared by the Minister of Instruction, Jules Simon, he strongly declared himself against the principle of compulsory education. Of late he has specially interested himself in the canonization of the Maid of Orleans. He has been a prolific writer on theological and educational subjects; his chief works being "De l'Education" (3 vols., 1855–'57), and "Vie de N. S. Jésus-Christ" (1872).

FREE CHURCH OF ENGLAND.

The chief features in the organization and government of the Free Church of England have been briefly stated as follows, by one of its deacons, in a published communication:

1. The constitution of the Free Church of England is defined by the deed-poll, duly enrolled in Chancery, and therefore cannot be varied.

2 and 3. The *Monthly Magazine* gives full information of what is going on.

4. The annual report gives full information of churches and ministers, with a list of the officers and governing council.

5. The Episcopacy of the Free Church of England differs slightly from the Episcopacy of the Established Church.

6. The Free Church of England acknowledges only *two* orders of ministers, viz., bishops, including presbyters, and deacons.

7. Every ordained minister in the Free Church of England who has charge of a congregation is a *bishop*, or presbyter, and is acknowledged as the bishop of that particular congregation.

8. Every layman, holding office in the church as warden or manager, is a *deacon* of the Free Church of England.

9. One of the bishops is chosen as primus or president of the whole body, otherwise his status is the same as the rest.

10. Every ordained minister is a bishop or presbyter, and becomes a bishop of a diocese when he takes the oversight and charge of any particular district.

11. Ordinations are conducted by the bishops and presbyters, the primus always presiding when present.

12. Bishops and presbyters in the Free Church of England are of equal order.

13. Confirmations are conducted by the primus or by any other bishop of the Church.

14. Ordained ministers from the Established Church or other denominations are received, if eligible, without reordination, at the annual meeting of Convocation, but they must be highly recommended, and submit to a very searching examination by the Examination and Discipline Committee, before they can be so received, and they must also be recommended by the district or diocesan meeting from which they come.

15. Both orders have equal right to be present and vote at Convocation on all matters whatsoever; the deacons (i. e., the laity holding office) outnumbering the bishops and clergy at least two to one.

16. There are at present about forty bishops or presbyters, and about one hundred deacons, constituting the Convocation meeting yearly. The Council consists of about forty members, carefully chosen, who meet monthly at Westminster and quarterly at Spa Fields, with full power to act for Convocation in all necessary matters.

17. Each of the fifty-two counties of England and Wales is a separate district.

18. These fifty-two districts are grouped into five dioceses, holding quarterly conferences, and having each a superior secretary in constant communication with the Council in London, through the principal secretary. The county secretaries are each in communication with the secretary of the district or diocese to which they respectively belong.

19. The five principal districts or diocesan secretaries are required to attend the Council in London at least four times a year.

The eleventh annual meeting of the Convocation of the Free Church of England was held in London June 23d and 24th. The bishop-president delivered an opening address on "Sacerdotalism." He then introduced the subject of the proposed union with the Reformed Episcopal Church of America, after which the following resolution, embodying the report of the committee of the Church on the subject, was adopted:

Resolved, That this Council heartily adopts the following articles of federal union between the Reformed Episcopal Church of America and the Free Church of England, humbly p a n Almighty God to bless the union of the two Churches, to the extension of his kingdom throughout the world.

Whereas, The Council of the Free Church of England addressed to the Executive Committee of the Reformed Episcopal Church a communication under date of March 10, 1874, signed by the bishop primus thereof, proposing "some closer relationship than that of mere brotherly sympathy;" and—

Whereas, The Executive Committee of the Reformed Episcopal Church had previously desired, and still desires, such close relationship: therefore, be it jointly

Resolved, That the following Articles of Federative Union be submitted by the Executive Committee of the Reformed Episcopal Church at the General Council of said Church in May next, and by the Council of the Free Church of England to the annual meeting of the Convocation of said Church in June next, for the action of the respective Churches:

ARTICLE I. As an evidence of the union existing between the Free Church of England and the Reformed Episcopal Church, a delegation of ministers and laymen may be sent annually from the Convocation to the General Council, and from the General Council to the Convocation, with the right to take part in the deliberations of said bodies respectively.

ART. II. On the consecration or ordination of bishops or other ministers in either Church, the bishops and ministers of the other Church shall be entitled to participate.

ART. III. The ministers of either of said Churches shall be entitled to officiate transiently in the congregations of the other; and also, subject to the respective regulations of said Churches, shall be eligible to a pastoral charge in either.

ART. IV. Communicants of either Church shall be received by the other on presentation of letters of dismissal.

ART. V. Divisionary or other congregations of either Church may transfer their connections to the other on such terms as may be mutually agreed upon.

ART. VI. The two Churches, recognizing the fact that they are working together in the same great cause, and on the same basis, pledge each to the other their mutual coöperation, sympathy, and support.

The annual report contained an exposition and defense of the constitution of the Church, and especially of the doctrine that there are but two orders of the Christian ministry. The reports of the several districts showed progress and continued consolidation. Five ministers were recommended and received, either by ordination, or as ministers who had been already ordained. The Secretary of Convocation was requested by resolution "to compare the constitution of the Free Church of England with that of the Reformed Episcopal Church in America, and to adopt and adapt those canons of the latter which may be found suitable and practicable as by-laws to improve and complete the organization of the former, not aiming so much at uniformity as to render the union of the two bodies easy and effectual in coöperation, and better to secure the common object for which both Churches exist; having done this, to submit the same to the standing Revision Committee, for that committee to revise and lay the result before Convocation for final approval and adoption." An effort was decided upon to adopt a prayer-book and hymnal in common with the Reformed Episcopal Church. Permission was given for the use in the mean time of the prayer-book of the Prayer-book Revision Committee, coupled with the reservation that it was "not to include the Thirty-nine Articles and the ordination service, nor the use of the Athanasian Creed." The Convocation refused its sanction to any minister becoming the pastor of any Church in which the "Hymns, Ancient and Modern," are used in public worship. Delegates were appointed to attend the General Council of the Reformed Episcopal Church in May, 1875.

A rearrangement of the diocesan districts was made, and the number of such districts was increased to seven.

FUEL, ARTIFICIAL. It is so evident that great advantages would be gained by coal-operators, and by the public generally, from the utilization of what is known as coal-dust, slack, waste, or culm, that it is to be wondered that manufactories to transform this worthless material into a marketable fuel are not erected everywhere in the mining-regions. The immense accumulations of coal-waste to be found in those regions are really a nuisance to the inhabitants and an eye-sore to the traveling public. It is generally admitted (says Mr. E. F. Loiseau, in a paper read before the Franklin Institute) that, on an average, from 40 to 50 per cent. of the entire coal production, both in America and in Europe, is converted into dust or waste. The utilization of this waste has been a problem which scientific and practical minds have tried to solve for a number of years. Partial results have been obtained, by which a certain amount of the waste of coal-mines has been utilized; and this only in Europe, where a gradual and constant increase in the cost of the natural coal has given to the manufacturers of artificial fuel a fair chance of profit; but it must be admitted that, compared with other branches of industry, the progress made in the utilization of coal-waste has been very slow. The enormous increase in the cost of coal in England, France, Germany, and Belgium, during the last three years, has, however, brought again before the public, and this time prominently, the question of utilizing the waste created everywhere that coal is handled.

Bituminous-coal dust will coke well, and it is much used for that purpose; but, the demand for coke not being in any way equal to the supply of bituminous small coal, from which it might be made, a great proportion of the latter is left underground. A small proportion of bituminous slack is used by

blacksmiths, and even in peculiar grates, for engineering purposes, but the largest part above-ground is thrown into rivers or piled up around the mines. It is estimated that the quantity of waste exceeds thirty million tons.

Although several establishments have been created in France, England, and Belgium, for the purpose of converting coal-waste into marketable fuel, that branch of industry is at present quite in its infancy. France has twenty-eight and Belgium nine manufactories of artificial fuel. In England the principal seat of these manufactories is in South Wales.

Coal-dust can be manufactured into solid lumps in two different ways: by simple compression without the addition of any cementing material, or by agglomeration with cements.

In England, Messrs. Bessemer, Rees, and Buckwell; and in France, MM. Baroulier, Evrard, and Loup, have patented different processes for the compression of bituminous coal-dust into solid lumps without cement. The coal manufactured had a great heating power, but it could not bear handling and transportation.

Bessemer, heating previously the bituminous slack until it was brought to a plastic state, forced it, by a piston, into a long tube, whose diameter was gradually reduced, and from which the compressed coal was forced in a continuous cylindrical shape. By means of a revolving knife, the fuel was cut in sections of any required length as fast as it was forced out of the tube. This process required very powerful machinery. Bessemer was compelled to reduce gradually the length of the tube, and to increase its thickness, as it very often burst. The process required a large amount of natural coal to heat the dust to a pasty mass, and, while being heated, it eliminated from the coal the greatest part of its volatile constituents. The application of Bessemer's process has long ago been abandoned.

Buckwell and Evrard compressed the bituminous waste into moulds without heating it previously. Although a powerful pressure was applied to the fuel, the product could not bear handling.

Baroulier used circular iron moulds of a certain depth, open on top and at the bottom. These moulds were filled with coal-dust, and this dust was compressed by hydraulic pressure; more coal was then added, this again compressed, and so on, until the moulds were completely filled. The process, although a real improvement on Bessemer's, had some of its defects, and the manufactured fuel could not be sold in competition with the natural coal.

These are the only serious attempts which have been made to convert bituminous coal-dust into solid fuel without cement. Rees took out an English patent for a process similar to Baroulier's.

Among the cements which have been used

to a certain extent, may be cited rosin, asphalt, petroleum, coal-tar, and its derivative fluid, and dry pitch, lime, plaster, starch, and clay.

Prof. A. S. Bickmore, in a very interesting paper on "Coal in China," read before the American Association, says that "from time immemorial, in the north of China, coal is ground to dust and mixed with clay, that it may burn more slowly."

In 1603 a pamphlet entitled "A New, Cheap, and Delicate Fire of Coal-balls," was published in London by Sir Hugh Platt. This gentleman recommended, for use in common fireplaces, a mixture of coal and clay, moulded by hand, in the shape of *balls*. He also used another mixture, which consisted of coal-dust, tanner's bark, sawdust, and cow-dung.

Another pamphlet, also published in London, in 1679, and entitled "An Excellent Invention to make a Fire," contains the following recipe:

Take three parts of the best Newcastle coal, beaten small, one part of clay: mix these well together into a mass with water; make thereof balls, which you must dry very well. This fuel is durable, sweet, not offensive by reason of the smoke or cinder as other coal-fires are, beautiful in shape, and not so costly as other fire; burns as well in a room even as charcoal.

In an article on the coal-basin of Eschweiler, M. Clèrc, a French engineer of great reputation, states that—

At Liège (Belgium) coal-dust is mixed with clay, pressed by hand in the form of balls, dried in the sun, and stored away for domestic use. That kind of fuel is there called *hochets*.

Even to this day, not only at Liège, but everywhere in Belgium, coal-dust is used in the same manner.

There exists in Belgium a certain class of working-women, who earn a scanty living by converting the coal-dust into solid fuel. They call at every house in front of which a load of coal-dust has been dumped, offering their services. These poor creatures can be seen daily in the streets, always two or three together, each one of them pushing a wheelbarrow loaded with clay, in which stands a shovel. As soon as the price is agreed upon, they go to work in earnest; the coal-dust is shoveled all around so as to form a circular bed of about one foot in thickness. From 25 to 30 per cent. of clay is diluted with water and sprinkled over the coal, which is first well mixed with the clay by means of the shovels. Then, putting on wooden shoes, they commence to trample upon the coal, turning round the coal-bed from the circumference to the centre, and back again from the centre to the circumference, following each other like ducks. When the whole surface of the coal-bed has been trampled upon twice, the mixture is turned over with the shovel, and the trampling recommences. After five or six operations of the kind have been gone through, the coal and clay have been worked to a plastic

mass. This is piled up in a heap, and, seating themselves on their wheelbarrows, these women proceed to compress the fuel in the shape of balls, by hand. These balls are then dried in the sun, after which they are ready for use.

In some parts of Germany the trampling on the coal is done by men on horseback. In the Rhine regions the mixing of the clay with coal is an affair of constant occurrence.

At Ham-sur-Sambre (Belgium), in 1859, under the direction of M. Darbois, machines, invented by M. David, a French engineer of merit, were erected for the purpose of manufacturing, by mechanical pressure, solid lumps from semi-anthracite coal-dust, mixed with 15 per cent. of clay. With these machines, lumps of cylindrical shape were pressed, also cylindrical lumps with perforations half an inch in diameter through the centre. These machines were very expensive, and their production was very limited. In 1861 they were replaced by cheaper and more productive machines, invented by Mr. Martin, from Liège (Belgium). These machines, making egg-shaped lumps, met with more favor, as the product was very similar to the lumps pressed by hand. Martin's press is still in operation at Ham-sur-Sambre.

At Tamines-sur-Sambre (Belgium), in 1862, under the direction of M. Cavenaile, the company of the "Charbonnages réunis de la Basse Sambre" erected also Martin's machines to convert the coal-dust into egg-shaped lumps, by using 18 per cent. of clay as cement. Martin's press made only one lump at a time. The feeding was very defective. This slow and very imperfect method of drying economized fuel, but required a large number of boys.

Baudry invented a drying-oven with shelves all around. It required two hours to dry the fuel. Labor being relatively cheap in Belgium, and coal selling high, no improvements have been made to diminish unnecessary handling. Notwithstanding the defects of Baudry's process, it is still applied in Belgium, the product containing 18 per cent. of clay, and not being impervious to moisture. The large percentage of clay and the fuel not being able to stand exposure to the weather are the greatest obstacles to the development of the manufacture of artificial fuel by the use of clay as a cement. Asphalt, rosin, and petroleum, as cements, have been found wanting in cohesive property, and also too expensive. Coal-tar and its derivative, fluid pitch and dry pitch, have been the most extensively used. The idea of mixing coal-dust with coal-tar originated with Peter Davey, an Englishman, who, in 1821, took out an English patent for it.

From 1821 to this day a considerable number of patents have been issued, both in this country and abroad, either for so-called new processes or for the machines to apply them.

Among the inventors who have really improved the means of manufacturing artificial fuel, by using either coal-tar, fluid pitch, or dry pitch, the names of Grant, Rathwell, Cooke, Wylam, Warlich, Dobrée, Moreau, and De Heynin, are prominent.

Fluid and dry pitch formed a good cement for bituminous and semi-bituminous coal-dust, but it did not succeed as well with anthracite and semi-anthracite waste, which is mined in South Wales and in some parts of France and Belgium. Before the cement is consumed, the bituminous artificial fuel is coked, and consequently it does not crumble in the fire. It is not the same with anthracite or lean coal-dust. When cemented with coal-tar or pitch, or any other resinous material, the cement consumes in the fire more rapidly than the coal, and the particles of coal, having lost their adhesive coating, crumble in the fire and fall through the grates without being consumed.

Resinous materials expand when burning, while clay, on the contrary, contracts progressively when submitted to elevated temperatures. Clay, used alone, would not have given a fuel impervious to moisture. It was supposed that, by mixing clay and pitch with the coal-dust, the fuel manufactured would not only be water-proof, but would remain in the fire, without crumbling, until consumed, the skrinkage of the clay compensating for the swelling of the pitch.

Among the experimenters in that direction who have really improved the manufacture of artificial fuel, are Chabannes, Sunderlandt, Stafford, Oram, Geary, Goodwin, Mohum, Sterling, Albert, Newton, Holcombe, Smith. All these attempts were unsuccessful. The presence of pitch in the fuel made it unfit for domestic use, and the clay impaired its combustible character for manufacturing purposes.

Patents were also granted to several inventors for a mixture of bituminous and of anthracite coal-dust, and coking the mixture. The first one of these patents was granted, in 1823, to John Christie and Thomas Harper, in England. The result was the same as with Bessemer, Baroulier, and others. The machinery was too expensive, and the product was not marketable.

A large number of patents have been granted in this country for artificial fuel. Most of them are modified copies of foreign patents. Dr. Joshua R. Hayes, of Winchester, Pa. (patent March 4, 1873), uses coal-dust, clay, and asphaltum ; but, although the manner in which he combines these materials is new and ingenious, the product will be liable to the same objections made against the fuel manufactured in Europe from coal-dust, clay, and pitch, by Stafford, Oram, Goodwin, Geary, and others.

The manufacture of artificial fuel, although being far from having attained the importance which it must attain in the near future, has been developed more rapidly in France and in Belgium than in England. English coal is harder than French and Belgian coal; and,

until within the last three years, the price of coal in England was so low that there was no inducement for capitalists to invest their money for the development of an industry which presented but poor prospects of good dividends. But increase after increase in the price of coal during the last three years has entirely changed the state of affairs. Large companies were organized last year, with immense capital, for the manufacture of "patent fuel" by different processes. The last one patented in England, and which has also been patented in this country, is the invention of Martin Rae, of Uphall, North Britain. It consists in mixing with coal-dust 15 per cent. of what he calls a bituminous mastic. In this process we have again a mixture of clay, coal-dust, and some other bituminous material, fluid shale-pitch.

A company was organized in May, 1873, with a capital of one million dollars, under the name of "The Diamond Fuel Company," to apply David Barker's process.

In these two processes, as well as in the old one of cementing coal-dust with pitch, or rosin, or asphalt, a large amount of natural coal is consumed, not only to dry or carbonize the product, but also to heat the cement and the coal-dust itself. If the dust was not heated, the cement would not adhere to the particles of coal. There is also the unnecessary handling in carrying the fuel to the drying-oven, and removing it when dry.

Both Martin Rae and David Barker are inventors, not only of the process, but of the machinery for its application.

The mixing-machines in Europe are almost all constructed on the same plan : they consist of vertical or horizontal cylinders, differing only in height or in length.

Although the compressing-machines used in Europe are numerous, they are all modifications of four distinct mechanical modes of applying pressure : First, by means of rollers ; second, by pistons in closed moulds ; third, by pistons in open moulds ; and fourth, by pistons pressing cylindrical lumps with a hole through the centre.

Most of the machines have also been tried to convert peat into a dense fuel. Some of them have answered the purpose very well— Milch's machine, for instance. Large peat-factories are in operation at Stalbach, Halle, Haspelmoor, and Neudstadt, in Germany, and at Montangin, in France.

I now proceed (continues Mr. Loiseau) to describe what appears to be their deficiences.

It is evident that no artificial fuel containing a resinous substance will ever be used for domestic purposes, on account of the smoke and of the bad odor. Another objection is, that such a fuel is liable to spontaneous combustion. No objection of the kind can be raised against artificial fuel cemented with clay and milk of lime.

In my process (says Mr. Loiseau) I use the

slack without heating it or drying it previously. The moisture which it contains varies with the state of the atmosphere. Therefore I am compelled to regulate the supply of lime-water accordingly. The difficulty of ascertaining the state of the materials inside the mixer suggested the idea of placing sliding doors around it. These doors facilitate the cleaning of the mixer and the removal of stones or pieces of iron which are found quite often in the coal-dust.

The pressure should be applied gradually in order to expel, as much as possible, the moisture contained in the mixture, and avoid cracks, which are the unavoidable result of a sudden pressure. An excess of compression spoils the fuel, prevents its free burning, and makes the ashes adhere to the surface of the lump, instead of falling through the grate into the ash-pan. The fuel must be sufficiently compressed to bear transportation and reasonable handling, and be still porous enough to insure free combustion. The shape of the fuel is also of great importance. Square lumps have too many sharp edges, which break off easily when the coal is handled; and the flat surfaces,

meeting very often in the fire, prevent the free access of the air. Cylindrical-shaped lumps are better, still they have sharp edges left. Round or egg-shaped lumps are evidently to be preferred. It requires less power than is required to compress square ones of the same weight, as there are no corners to fill, and, as a result, less friction. With round or egg-shaped lumps, no matter what amount of coal is piled on the fire, there is always sufficient space between the lumps to secure a good draught, and to allow a free access for a good supply of oxygen.

For these reasons I have adopted the egg-shaped form, slightly flattened, and have modified Baudry's and Martin's presses, in order to obtain more and better products.

To render the fuel impervious to moisture, instead of mixing a resinous substance with the materials, the lumps are simply dipped into a liquid composed of rosin dissolved in crude benzine. By exposure to a current of air, the benzine evaporates and leaves each lump coated with a thin film of rosin, which closes all the interstices, and renders the fuel water-proof.

G

GABLENTZ, Ludwig Karl Wilhelm, Baron von, a Field-Marshal of the Austrian Army, an Austrian soldier and diplomatist, born at Jena, June 19, 1814; died by his own hand at Zurich, Switzerland, January 29, 1874. He entered in his youth the Saxon cavalry, and served in it for many years, but previous to 1848 entered the Austrian service. He was on the staff of Radetzky in the Italian campaign of 1848, distinguished himself at Custozza, and was appointed soon after chief of staff. He took a brilliant part in the Hungarian War. After the close of this war he was employed on several political and diplomatic missions. His military promotion was somewhat rapid, though earned by his gallant conduct. He had passed through all the grades from major to major-general before 1854, when he was in command of a brigade in the army of occupation in the Danubian provinces. From this he was transferred, in 1857, to a larger command in the Lombardo-Venetian Kingdom. He fought with bravery and distinction both at Magenta and Solferino, was promoted to the command of a division on the field of battle, defended Capriana, and covered the retreat of the Austrian army. In 1863 he was made lieutenant field-marshal. He commanded the Sixth Army Corps in the invasion of Holstein in 1864, but with no great success. In the seven weeks' German War of 1866 he was in command at first of the Tenth Army Corps, and at Sadowa of the Eighth and Tenth, but met with a disastrous defeat from the second Prussian army. In July, 1869, he

was appointed commander-in-chief in Hungary, and remained there till the failure of his health, when he visited Zurich in hopes of its improvement, but, in a fit of either melancholy or mania, put an end to his life.

GEIGER, Abraham, Ph. D., a Jewish rabbi, scholar, and author, born at Frankfort-on-the-Main, May 24, 1810; died at Berlin, November 13, 1874. He received his early education from his father and elder brother, and subsequently pursued his studies at the Universities of Heidelberg and Bonn. In 1832 he was called as rabbi to the small Israelite community at Wiesbaden; in 1838 he was chosen assessor to the rabbinat at Breslau, and somewhat later elected rabbi of that flourishing community of Israelites. With a much broader culture than is usual among Jewish scholars, Dr. Geiger possessed also an independent and fearless spirit, and his publications urging the necessity of reforms and the absurdity of some of the old religious usages of the Israelites won for him in about equal numbers earnest sympathizers and violent opposers. To conciliate his opponents and to bring about harmony among the leaders of Jewish thought, he initiated a series of conferences of the rabbis, of which the first was held at Brunswick in 1844, a second at Frankfort three years later, of which he was one of the vice-presidents; and a later one at Breslau, over which he presided. The influence of these conferences upon the rabbis has been very great. Dr. Geiger had also been active as a writer both in defense of his views and on topics of general

Jewish literature. He had not yet received his doctor's degree at Bonn, when he wrote his essay, "What has Mohammed borrowed from the Jewish Religion?" which was awarded the philosophical prize of the university, and was published by order of the Philosophical Faculty. In 1835 he commenced the publication of the *Journal of Jewish Theology*, which has been from the first the ablest exponent of religious thought among the Israelite scholars of Germany. His other principal works are: "Melo Chofnajino" (1840), and "Hite Haamanim" (1847), two interesting monographs; "Studies on Moses-ben-Maimon" (Maimonides, the Jewish philosopher, theologian and legislator of the twelfth century (1850); "Concerning the Defense of the Israelites against the Attacks of Christians in the Mediæval Period," two vols. (1851–'52); "Isaac Troki, the Apologist of Judaism at the Close of the Sixteenth Century" (1853); a "Translation of the Divan of Castillan of Abul Hassan Juda ha Levi," with a commentary and a biographical notice (1817); and "A Manual of the Dialect of the Mishna" (1845). For some years past Dr. Geiger had resided in Berlin.

GEOGRAPHICAL EXPLORATIONS AND PROGRESS FOR THE YEAR 1874. The achievements in the domain of geographical science for the year 1874 bear witness to the more careful and scientific spirit which marks the exploratory enterprises of late years. The visions of wealth and the glory of conquest which have, down to the latest times, impelled adventurous spirits to strike out over untraveled ways have now but small influence upon the minds of explorers.

The unknown region lying between the colonies of South and East Australia has been crossed in two directions within the year. The seldom-visited portions of Central Asia are being made known through the efforts of recent explorers. In our own country the unexplored expanse in the Western Territories is now for the most part not only carefully examined but accurately surveyed, and the nation has been made acquainted with lands of extraordinary worth and promise. The opening of new commercial routes is now the most valuable material benefit to be looked for as a result of geographical research; and governments which are, by ancient prescription, the principal road-builders, originate many of the most important explorations and extend the aid of contributions of money and protection to others. Projects are on foot, promoted by powerful states, for the establishment of great highways through the centre of Asia in different directions, across the British possessions, and over new ocean-routes. The South American Continent has recently been brought into communication with Europe by an ocean telegraphic cable; and the plan of the Pacific cable between the United States and Japan is ripening, so that the time may soon arrive when the globe will be girdled with telegraphic

wires, and the most remote countries brought into daily and hourly intercourse. The agency of science in rendering natural wealth available as well as in demonstrating the absolute value of the knowledge of Nature and of human history, finds more and more recognition. No marine or topographical survey of any importance is conducted without the coöperation of scientific investigators. The natural history and geology of many regions, of the islands of the Pacific, of broad mountainous and remote inland tracts of Asia and Africa, of the lands which lie in the frozen Northern seas, and even plains, plateaus, and mountain-summits, are now undergoing the careful and thorough scrutiny of accomplished scientists. The hydrography of the Pacific, the courses of its currents, and the contour of its bottom, which have been heretofore but vaguely known, will henceforth be familiar, not only to our scientific men, but to the more intelligent of our officers of the naval and commercial marine, after the investigations of the Challenger and Tuscarora. The question of an open polar sea may soon be, if it is not already, determined; in any event the expeditions which are about setting out from England and Austria will bring back a fuller knowledge of the chorography and natural history of the polar regions. The next most mysterious portion of the globe, the great African Desert, may yet be traversed and all its secrets unfolded. The device employed by Rohlfs of carrying a supply of water in metallic vessels enabled him to accomplish a thirty-six days' journey through a waterless part of the Libyan waste, where the longest passage of the caravan has never exceeded seven days.

A favorable circumstance to the geographical explorer is the spread of European manners and the softening influence of the Western civilization among savage and superstitious nations. The fanatical peoples of the inner Soudan, who within a few years have slain daring travelers who ventured within their borders, received not inhospitably the courageous Dr. Nachtigal.

In this as in former years several travelers, while engaged in geographical explorations, have been overtaken by death, either from deadly malarious fevers, protracted exertions, with insufficient food, or the treachery and barbarity of the savage nations whose territory they were exploring. Dr. Stoliczka, the able geologist of the Forsyth expedition to Kashgar, died on the passage of the mountains on the 19th of June, at a point on the Shyok River, above the Lasser Pass. The death of Henry Grinnell is mentioned elsewhere (*see* GRINNELL, HENRY). Mr. Grinnell, who was the first president of the American Geographical Society, was succeeded in that office by Chief-Justice Daly, who has imparted to it a new energy. A memorable loss from the ranks of the followers of geographical pursuits was that of Captain Garnier. This young and courageous French traveler, devoted to geographical pursuits with an impetuous zeal, was born at St.-Etienne in 1839. He was educated for the navy, and when only twenty-three years of age was intrusted with the administration of Saigon, the chief post in the French establishment of Cochin-China. Divining the importance to French commerce of a knowledge of the interior of Laos or Cambodia, he supposed that the natural route lay up the Mekong Valley. A mission was sent to make these explorations under Captain Lagrée, who, as related in a previous volume of the ANNUAL CYCLOPÆDIA, died after a protracted illness on the confines of China, and was brought back to be buried by Garnier with the greatest difficulty. After the Franco-Prussian War, Lieutenant (since Captain) Garnier left France again for Cochin-China, with the object of completing his researches. Finding it impossible to reach Thibet by way of the Mekong, and not having it in his power to organize an expedition through Anam, he went to China and explored the Yang-tse-Kiang River as far as the Waterfalls. Being then appointed a commissioner to Tong-King by Admiral Dupré, Governor of Cochin-China, he endeavored to pursue discoveries in that then disturbed province. Having gained possession of the capital, Hanoi, he established quiet and order there, but met his death in leading an attack upon some still disorderly rebels, at a little distance from the city.

Dr. C. T. Beke, F. R. G. S., F. S. A., a traveler who won deserved renown by his exploration of Abyssinia, 1840-'43, in which he settled the latitude of seventy positions, and acquired the vocabularies of thirteen languages, died in London, in the seventy-fifth yaer of his age. (See BEKE, CHARLES TILSTONE). Dr. Beke was the editor of De Veer's "Three Voyages to Cathay," in the Hakluyt series, and had written largely on geographical topics.

Heinrich Baron von Maltzan, an eminent German geographer, who first distinguished himself by a daring journey to Mecca, died at Florence, February 22, 1874, while en route for the East. Baron von Maltzan had made extraordinary attainments in Oriental languages, and had also written largely and well on geographical topics.

Tyrwhitt Drake, of the English Palestine Exploration Society, died at Jerusalem, June 25th, from exposure to the malaria of the Jordan Valley.

Captain Farr, scientific member of the French mission to Burmah, died during the prosecution of explorations in the far East. He set out in company with Captain Moreau, in the spring of 1874, to explore the country between the Irrawadi and the Salwen, intending to reach Kiang-Hung on the Mekong; but, on the 11th of July, he succumbed to an attack of jungle-fever.

The Paris Geographical Society, appreciating

the success of the Antwerp Congress for geographical science of 1871, have decided to call an international congress of geographers in Paris for the 31st of March, 1875. The chairman of the Geographical Society, Vice-Admiral de la Poncière Le Noury, will preside at the congress, in connection with which there will be an exhibition of books, maps, and instruments, and collections relating to geography. One hundred and twenty questions are proposed for discussion.

CHARTOGRAPHY.—In chartography the progress of the survey in the West, and the approaching attainment of a complete map of our country, is worthy of especial notice.

A map of the Dominion of Canada, on the scale of twenty-eight miles to the inch, has been completed and recently published from the office of Crown Lands in Ontario.

A valuable map of Mexico has recently been lithographed by Dumaine, of Paris. It was drawn with great care and labor by Captain G. Noix, during the occupation of Mexico by the French troops. The investigations from which it was constructed were made by reconnoitring parties, and correspondents communicating by telegraph with the industrious engineer who plotted the map.

The map of France, which has been in progress under the direction of the War Department since 1833, is now completed, with the exception of a few sheets representing portions of the island of Corsica.

The map made by Major Lovett, under the orders of Sir F. Goldsmid, is a contribution of some value to our topographical knowledge of Persia.

One of the most elaborate maps of the Swiss Alps which has yet appeared, has been published by the English Alpine Club under the direction of R. C. Nichols. It is on a scale of about one quarter of an inch to a mile, and contains very minute details.

The maps and charts of the Coast Survey, published the past year, possess great interest, those of the Pacific coast connecting with the triangulation of Nevada, Utah, and Arizona.

A New York publishing-house has been for some years past engaged in the preparation of atlases of counties in New England, New York, and some of the Western States, from actual surveys. While these belong rather to local topography than to general chartography, they are deserving of notice from their accuracy, even in minute details, and from their beauty. Some of these counties are considerably larger than some of the Swiss cantons, and their atlases vie with those of the Swiss geographers in their perfection of detail.

BIBLIOGRAPHY.—The results of the Hayden geological and topographical survey of the Territories have hitherto been made known to the public in a variety of ways. Of the great work, nine volumes of paleontology and one of geology have been published prior to January, 1875, and also eight volumes of general reports, including the one on the geology and paleontology of Nebraska. These latter volumes contain thirteen charts, most of them representing the volcanic region of the sources of the Yellowstone and Snake Rivers. There have also been various separate publications, as—the tables of heights in the Western United States by Gannett, and the volume of meteorological observations in Utah, Idaho, and Montana, by the same; a manual of ornithology of the Northwestern Territories by Dr. Elliott Coues; a synopsis of the flora of Colorado, by Prof. Porter and J. M. Coulter; a catalogue of the photographs taken by W. H. Jackson; a supplement to the fifth annual report upon the fossil flora of the West, by L. Lesquereaux; and a synopsis of the new vertebrate animals of the Tertiary period in Colorado, by Prof. Cope. A Bulletin of the Geological and Geographical Survey of the Territories has now been commenced, which will, from time to time, communicate the results of the labors of the commission, thus preventing their being scattered through a great number of publications of various kinds. The first two numbers of the Bulletin are taken up mostly with accounts of the paleontology of the newly-explored regions by Prof. Cope. The demand for complete series of the reports of the United States Geological Survey of the Territories is so large that the first three annual reports have been ordered by the Secretary of the Interior to be reprinted. They are issued in a stout octavo volume of 261 pages.

The new geographical magazine, under the editorship of Guido Cora, bearing the title of *Cosmos*, which was started two years ago in Turin, continues in a successful career.

The able English periodical, *Ocean Highways*, has changed its form and title, but still continues to be published under the editorship of Mr. Markham. It appears monthly, under the name of *The Geographical Magazine*.

The commission of commercial geography, chosen conjointly by the French Society of Geography and the Syndical Chambers of Paris, have decided upon the establishment of a journal of commercial geography, to be called *L'Explorateur*, whose objects are to be the publication of the labors of the Commission of Commercial Geography, and also of the French and foreign geographical societies, to keep up a bulletin of the prices of commercial commodities in distant markets, and to present news relating to commercial geography, and articles illustrative of subjects connected therewith, and principally to encourage French commercial enterprise in distant countries. It will appear at least as often as once a week, in handsome form, with maps and illustrations, and is likely to be well supported.

The following works are the most noteworthy of the geographical publications of the year:

Bulletin of the United States Geological and Geographical Survey of the Territories. F. V. Hayden,

United States Geologist-in-Charge, Nos. I. and II. (Washington, 1874.)

Charles Nordhoff: Northern California, Oregon, and the Sandwich Islands. (New York, 1874.)

Dr. J. M. Toner: Dictionary of Elevations and Climatic Register of the United States; containing, in Addition to the Elevations, the Latitude, Mean Annual Temperature, and the Total Annual Rainfall of Many Localities; with a Brief Introduction on the Orographic and other Peculiarities of North America. (New York, 1874.)

Beadle: The Undeveloped West; or, Five Years in the Territories. (Philadelphia, 1874.)

Adolf Bastian: Die deutsche Expedition an der Loangoküste, nebst älteren Nachrichten über die zu erforschenden Länder. (Jena, 1874.)

Baker: Ismailia: A Narrative of the Expedition to Central Africa for the Suppression of the Slave-Trade, organized by Ismail, Khédive of Egypt. By Sir Samuel Baker, Pasha, F. R. S. 2 vols. (London, and New York, 1874.)

Livingstone: The Last Journals of Dr. Livingstone in Eastern Africa, from 1865 to his Death, continued by a Narrative of his Last Moments and Sufferings, taken down from the Mouth of his Faithful Servants Chuma and Susi. Edited by Rev. Horace Watler, F. R. G. S. (London and New York, 1874.)

Koldewey: The German Arctic Expedition in 1869-'70, and Narrative of the Wreck of the Hansa in the Ice. By Captain Koldewey, Commander of the Expedition, assisted by Members of the Scientific Staff; translated and abridged by Rev. L. Mercier, M. A., and edited by H. W. Bates, Assistant Secretary R. G. S. (London and New York, 1874.)

Captain G. S. Nares: Reports, with Abstract of Soundings and Diagrams of Ocean Temperature in North and South Atlantic Oceans, in 1873. (London. Published by the Admiralty Department, 1874.)

Albert Hastings Markham: A Whaling Cruise to Baffin's Bay and the Gulf of Boothia. (London, 1874.)

Hübner: A Ramble round the World. 1871. By Baron de Hübner. Translated by Lady Herbert. (London and New York, 1874.)

MacGahan: Campaigning on the Oxus, and the Fall of Khiva. By J. A. MacGahan, Correspondent of the *New York Herald*. (New York, 1874.)

Henry Walter Bates: The Naturalist on the River Amazons. (Boston, 1874.) A reprint of an old work.

Paul Marcoy: Travels in South America from the Atlantic to the Pacific Ocean. 2 vols. (New York, 1874.) A reprint of a work published some years since.

J. Thompson: The Straits of Malacca, Indo-China, and China, or Ten Years' Travels, Adventures, and Residence abroad; with Woodcuts from the Author's own Photographs and Sketches. (London, 1874.)

Henry Walter Bates: Warburton's Journey across Australia: an Account of the Exploring Expedition sent out by Messrs. Elder & Hughes, under the Command of Colonel Egerton Warburton, giving a Full Account of his Perilous Journey from the Centre to Roebourne, Western Australia; with Illustrations and a Map, edited with an Introductory Chapter. (London, 1874.)

Blake: Captain Tyson's Arctic Adventures; Arctic Experiences, containing Captain George E. Tyson's Wonderful Drift on the Ice-Floe, a History of the Polaris Expedition, the Cruise of the Tigress, and Rescue of the Polaris Survivors; to which is added a General Arctic Chronology; edited by E. Vale Blake, with Map and Illustrations. (London, 1874.)

Thomas J. Hutchinson: Two Years in Peru; with Exploration of its Antiquities. 2 vols. (London, 1874.)

J. L. Geiger: A Peep at Mexico, Narrative of a Journey across the Republic from the Pacific to the

Gulf, in December, 1873, and January 1874; with Maps and Photographs. (London, 1874.)

Schuyler: Turkistan, Notes of a Journey in the Russian Provinces of Central Asia and the Khanates of Bokhara and Khokand. By Eugene Schuyler, Secretary of American Legation, St. Petersburg. (London, 1874.)

H. W. Bellew: From the Indus to the Tigris, a Narrative of a Journey through the Countries of Beloochistan, Afghanistan, Khorassan, and Iran, in 1872, together with a Synoptical Grammar and Vocabulary of the Brahoe Language, and a Record of the Meteorological Observations and Altitudes on the March from the Indus to the Tigris. (London, 1874.)

Charles New: Life, Wanderings, and Labors in Eastern Africa. With an Account of the First Successful Ascent of the Equatorial Snow Mountain, Kilima Njaro, and Remarks upon East African Slavery. (London, 1874.)

Thomas Belt: The Naturalist in Nicaragua. (London, 1874.)

Captain Spalding: Khiva and Turkestan. Translated from the Russian. (London, 1874).

Ernst Marno: Reisen im Gebiete des Blauen und Weissen Nil, im Egyptischen, Soudan, und den angränzenden Negerländern in den Jahren 1869 bis 1873. (Vienna, 1874.)

We turn now to our usual review of the geographical expeditions which have been sent out or have returned during the year, beginning with—

ARCTIC EXPLORATION.—The Austro-Hungarian Arctic Expedition returned from their perilous voyage without making any important accessions to our knowledge of the polar regions. The object of the expedition was to find a northeasterly passage toward the pole from some portion of the Arctic Sea north of the coast of Siberia. The Tegetthoff was a screw-steamer of 300 tons burden. There were on board stores for three years. The crew of twenty-four men was composed of Lieutenants Weyprecht and Brosch and Ensign Orel, two engineers, fifteen selected Dalmatian sailors, Lieutenant Payer, of the Jägers, a member of the Alpine Club, with two Tyrolese mountaineers, and the surgeon, Kepesy. The vessel sailed from Bremerhaven June 13, 1872. At Nova Zembla they took leave of the two patrons of the expedition, Count Wilczek and Baron Sternberg, who came to meet them in the yacht Isbiörn, bringing stores, which they deposited in the cavity of a rock. The ships took leave of each other August 1st. For two years no news came from the explorers. During this time they were icebound in the Siberian Sea. The Tegetthoff was frozen in, in latitude 76° 30' north, within sight of Nova Zembla. The crew remained with the ship fourteen months. The mass of ice which inclosed them was steadily carried to the northward. The drift in the ice-floe was remarkable as being the first one which had ever taken a northerly direction. In the autumn of 1873 they sighted an unknown mountainous coast, which they explored from latitude 79° 54' to latitude 83°. To this they gave the name of Franz-Joseph-Land. Animal and vegetable life was very scanty. The prevailing rock was dolomite; the mountains, conical in form

and rising to the elevation of 5,000 feet, were covered with immense glaciers. In latitude 83° they sighted a headland, to which they gave the name Cape Vienna. Two tracts of land, Wilczek-Land and Zichy-Land, are separated by a wide sound—Austria Sound—which extends to the north from Cape Hansa to latitude 82°, where Rawlinson Sound forks off to the northwest. The vegetation upon the new-found territory was far poorer than that of Greenland or Nova Zembla. The only plants seen were solitary bunches of grass, a few species of saxifrage and *Silena acaxlis*, except moss, which grew in dense beds, and lichens, of which the most frequent was the *Umbilicaria arctica*. Many ice-bears were encountered by a party which explored Rawlinson Sound. In May, 1874, the ship had been raised up and warped out of shape by ice-crushes, and was no longer seaworthy; and on the 20th of that month the crew abandoned her. They were ninety-six days making their way with boats and sledges; and on the 24th of August, after sailing nine days down the coast of Nova Zembla, they were taken on board of a Russian schooner, which landed them at Vardoe, in the north of Norway.

A second Austrian arctic exploring expedition, it is said, will be started next summer. One-half of the expedition, under command of Lieutenant Payer, purpose advancing northward by way of East Greenland, and the other half, under Count Wilczek, by way of Siberia. The object of the projected expedition is to ascertain whether the newly-discovered Franz-Joseph-Land be a continent or an island.

The steamship Diana, belonging to the polar-voyager Lamont, was sent out under Captain Wiggins, for the double purpose of crossing the Sea of Kara into the Gulf of Obi, with reference to a commercial route between England and Central Asia, and of searching for the Austro-Hungarian expedition, and bringing them relief if needful. Weighing anchor the 4th of June, she passed through the Waigatch Straits, through the Gulf of Mundely and into the Gulf of Obi. From their surveys it appears that White Island (Bieloi Ostrow) is located about 60 geographical miles too far to the westward upon the chart. They met the Austrians upon their return at Hammerfest. Captain Wiggins reports that the Carian Gulf is free from ice up to the middle of October, and he knows no reason why an annual steamship connection should not take place between England and the Gulf of Obi. The Diana sailed farther to the eastward than any vessel had before reached in the Siberian Polar Sea, touching latitude 76° north, longitude 82° 30' east. They put in at Dundee harbor on their return, September 25th.

An English expedition into the arctic region is now being fitted out for extended explorations. Captain Nares, of the Challenger, has been selected to command the fleet. The chief object of the cruise is to make collections of specimens of the fauna and flora of the high latitudes. Commander A. H. Markham, of the Sultan, will also take part in the command. Captain Nares has the experience of the arctic voyage of 1852-54, in which he distinguished himself on board the Resolute. The conditions are favorable for a prosperous voyage, according to the accounts of Captain David Gray, who, making his observations from the coast of Greenland, concludes that nearly all the ice was driven out of the arctic basin last summer. The whaling-steamer Bloodhound has been purchased, and is destined to be the principal vessel of the squadron. The expedition is not to start until June, 1875. The Polaris reached a latitude of 82° 16'. Living objects were observed in the highest latitudes attained, in a not-decreasing frequency. Musk-oxen were shot in latitude 81° 38'. Flies, beetles, butterflies, and mosquitoes, were found, and seventeen different kinds of birds were killed, in latitude 82°. The English expedition will consist of about a hundred officers and men, and will be provided for a long cruise. The consideration of the non-success of the Austro-Hungarian expedition, and of the results attained by the Polaris, which induce them to choose the route of the latter vessel up Smith Sound, as the only practicable way to the pole.

THE OCEANS.—The United States steamer Tuscarora sailed from San Francisco December 20, 1873, to make soundings over a line from San Francisco to San Diego, and thence on the line of a great circle to Honolulu, to the Bonin Islands, and to Yokohama, to ascertain the most feasible route for a telegraphic cable across the Pacific Ocean. This voyage has yielded important hydrographical results, in addition to the satisfactory accomplishment of its special purpose. At 50 miles from the coast of California a depth of 2,200 fathoms was found; this was the deepest sounding made before arriving at San Diego. The ocean's bed declined on an average 90 feet to a mile to the depth of 1,900 fathoms, 115 miles out from San Diego. Thence to latitude 23° 10' north, the point of the greatest depth, 3,053 fathoms, the slope is three feet to a mile; and thence to Honolulu, a distance of 400 miles, the upward inclination averages 45 feet per mile. On the passage from Honolulu to Yokohama, six submarine mountainous elevations were crossed, with level plateaus between. The average depth was 2,450 fathoms. The course from Cape Flattery to the Aleutian Islands, passed over between October 17 and October 30, 1873, showed a rapid shoaling off Cape Flattery, from 1,500 to only 600 fathoms depth; and from that point up to the last cast, latitude 54° north, longitude 153° west, where the depth was 2,534 fathoms, there was a gradual declension of one fathom to the mile. The soundings from Yokohama to Tanaga Island showed, for 1,000 miles, depths ranging from 300 to 2,270 fathoms. A remarkable depression was found, latitude 52° 06', longitude 171° 15' east, where the depth was 4,037 fathoms.

The entire results go to corroborate the estimate of 2,500 fathoms as the average depth of the Pacific, based upon the theory of the earthquake wave. Throughout the survey careful observations were directed to the ocean-currents. The results attained strengthen the theory of ocean circulation, and supply important data for the hydrography of the Pacific Ocean. Along the shores of Kamtchatka and the Kurile Islands a counter-current was observed setting to the southwest, reaching to longitude 164° east, with a surface temperature of 49° Fahr. There they came upon the Kamtchatka current, a branch of the Japan Stream setting through Behring Strait, which is here about 350 miles in width. From 174° eastward flowed the cold Behring Strait current. From the observations of the ocean-currents the following deductions were arrived at: The Kuro Siwo, or Japan current, takes an easterly course toward the American coast, with its northern limit extending to the southern shores of Vancouver Island. The same stream passes down to the southward, in what is called the California cold current. Below this flowed an under-current, setting to the northwest, which reached the surface in latitude 50° north, and then set to the northward, along the British-American shores, from there gradually turning to the westward. In latitude 53° 30' north, longitude 157° west, the current took a southeasterly course at a depth of five fathoms; nearer the islands the current was to the southwest and close to the islands to the westward. It was conjectured that a part of the water taken to the northwest by the under-current returns to the northern branch of the Japan current in longitude 157° west, passing southward along the western shore of America as part of the surface-current, and that the part west of longitude 157° west, setting toward the southwest, passes as an under-current beneath the Japan stream. A rapid fall in temperature, from 57° Fahr. to 47°, within a few miles in the Ounimak Pass, revealed that the northwest shores of the Aleutian Islands are washed by the Behring Strait current. The northern route for a telegraph-cable, as indicated by the results of the investigations, would be 4,200 miles in length, while the southern course must be 6,000 miles in length. The difficulties of the northern course are a sudden declivity of the Aleutian Islands, as well as frequent fogs, and the cold and unfriendly climate, embarrassing to workmen in laying and repairing the cable. In the course from Cape Flattery to Atcha, in the Aleutian Islands, off Cape Flattery, the depth suddenly decreased from 1,500 to less than 600 fathoms. From that point as far as the last sounding, in latitude 54° north, longitude 153° west, there was a gradual decrease of one fathom a mile, the last depth being 235 fathoms.

The voyages of the English ship Challenger, a frigate-built steamship of about 1,500 tons, commanded by Captain G. S. Nares, R. N., have added materially to our knowledge of ocean hydrography. Her departure from England was in December, 1872. The purpose of the expedition was the investigation of the deep-sea currents and the ocean-bottom, and observations of marine animal and plant life in all parts of the world. Besides the staff of naval officers, a corps of naturalists accompanied the expedition, to pursue scientific investigations, and make collections of natural objects, under the direction of Prof. Wyville Thomson. The first voyage was across the Atlantic from Teneriffe to St. Thomas's Island. The depths increased to 3,150 fathoms at a distance of 1,150 miles from Teneriffe. In the western trough of the Atlantic the depth continued a little over 3,000 fathoms. The bottom was entirely composed of *Globigerina* ooze in the lesser depths, and red clay in the deep soundings. The red earth, which was found to cover the largest part of the ocean-bed, is, according to the theory of Prof. Thomson, the residue left after the deposits which are found unchanged in the lesser depths have been acted upon by the solvent power of carbonic acid, which accumulates in the deep waters. One of the prescribed voyages of the Challenger was to the island of Kerguelen, to decide upon a site for the observatory of the transit of Venus, and thence southward, to make observations upon the approaches to the south pole. They sailed away from Kerguelen Island, February 1, 1874, toward the antarctic ice-girdle, reaching 94° south. They passed at one point 120 miles to the southward, and at another point within six miles of the supposed position of Wilkes's Termination Laud without sighting land, thus probably determining the non-existence of the supposed antarctic continent. The antarctic icebergs, a great number of which were observed from the deck of the Challenger, did not present fantastically-jagged forms, according to the former descriptions, but were found to be smooth-topped and tabular, still preserving the snow-coverings of the glaciers, their originals. The investigations of the Challenger tend to confirm the belief in the impenetrability of the southern ice-belt. The dredgings demonstrated that the Southern Pacific is so full of life that it may be looked upon as the original birthplace of the occurring species. The marine fauna of the Southern Ocean was found to be nearly identical with that of the north. Soundings all showed a bottom of an alluvium, composed either of the shells of the *Globigerina*, which is a tiny surface animal, or of the skeletons of the *Diatomacea*, a floating alga. The process of the formation of geological strata of the future world is here so rapid that a large object falling to the bottom is speedily covered over by the ceaselessly sinking particles. The observations of the Challenger in the South Atlantic show that the drift-current which is caused by the constant westerly winds drives the waters so strongly

against the African coast, that the Agulhas current is checked in its course. A small portion mingles with the drift-current, which turns to the north upon striking against the African shore. The mean temperature of the water in the South Atlantic, to the depth of 1,500 fathoms, is 4¼° Fahr. lower than in the Northern Ocean. It seems likely that in the South as well as in the North Atlantic there is an elevation of the bottom in mid-ocean. From the Cape of Good Hope as far south as latitude 46° 16' they found no greater depth than 1,900 fathoms. The Challenger arrived at Melbourne, March 17th. In July she had again sailed on her course from the Feejee Islands to the New Hebrides and Torres Straits. In the voyage from Australia to New Zealand it was made apparent that the bottom off the southeast coast of Australia falls off suddenly, and that Australia is separated from New Zealand by a trough of 2,600 fathoms depth. The ascent from the greatest depth to the New Zealand coast is very gradual. These results disprove the theory of Peschel, that Australia, New Zealand, and New Caledonia, once formed a single continent, similar in form to Africa, a theory which the great difference in the flora and fauna of the islands had previously rendered doubtful. The dredgings produced a specimen of the sea-porcupine, genus *Porocidaris*, of which most of the species are extinct. In the deepest soundings were brought up several *Bryozoos*, a *Crangonida*, and the spicula of a *Hyalonema*.

In a survey of the Dardanelles and Bosporus by Commander Wharton, of the British naval vessel Shearwater, the existence was proved of strong under-currents setting counter to the surface-flow, which is invariably from the Black Sea into the Mediterranean.

A scientific expedition has been organized by the German Government, under the direction of Dr. Meier, for the purpose of exploring the German seas.

M. Staritzky was engaged during a number of years in investigations in the Sea of Japan and along the eastern shores of the Russian Asiatic possessions. He determined the astronomical position of thirty-eight points. By his soundings it was demonstrated that the depth of the Sea of Okhotsk is not great. The volcano of Korlak, in Kamtchatka, was found to be 11,000 feet in height.

The ship Basilisk returned to England recently, after four years spent in surveying the coasts of the British Eastern possessions. Among the results of this survey is the addition of twelve first-class harbors, several navigable rivers, and more than one hundred islands, to the chart. It has discovered a new and more direct route between Australia and China. The shores of Eastern New Guinea, hitherto unexplored, have been surveyed, and two lofty mountains discovered. On these shores dwell a copper-colored people, peaceable and intelligent, and far surpassing in intelligence the black tribes of other parts of the island. An Italian naturalist, L. M. d'Albertis, recently ascended the Arfak Mountains in New Guinea, and has departed a second time for that region, with the intention of penetrating the southern portion of the country, the parts adjacent to Torres Straits, where there are mountain-ranges of considerable altitude. The natural history of this part of New Guinea is entirely unknown.

The uninhabited and hitherto little-known Kerguelen Island, named after the French captain, Kerguelen, who visited it, as did also Cook on his first voyage, and Ross in 1841, was chosen as a station for German and English observatories of the transit of Venus, and has consequently been very thoroughly explored. It is volcanic in its character, and has a harsh and stormy climate. Remarkable basaltic columns, which had been noticed by Captain Cook, were examined. The number of vegetable species found was 150; among them 18 were phænogamous plants. Woody vegetation was totally wanting. The celebrated Kerguelen cabbage abounds in the lowlands. A range of snow-capped mountains, the highest of which is Mount Ross, with 6,000 feet altitude, traverses the island from northwest to southeast. Sea-elephants are numerous; a small variety of duck is abundant; but no land animals were found. The island is visited by American captains, who cruise for whales (which abound in its immediate vicinity), and who kill sea-elephants upon the beach.

The enterprising Italian traveler, Dr. Beccaria, has been engaged in exploring Kandari, a strange region of southeast Celebes. He was subject to constant dangers from hostile inhabitants and treacherous servants. The results of his physical and ethnologic observations are interesting; and several of the plants and animals which he met with are new to science.

The Dutch Geographical Society have concluded to send out an expedition for the exploration of the eastern coast of Sumatra. The river Jambi flows through an unknown country, which is believed to be very fruitful. Parts of Palembang, also, and the district of Korintji, remain still to be explored.

In NORTH AMERICA, in an exploration of the northern coast of Alaska, Mr. Dall discovered a glacier, three or four miles wide and twenty to thirty in length. He computed the altitude of Mount Elias, which he estimates at over 19,000 feet.

A committee of Icelanders were sent out from the Wisconsin colony to examine the Territory of Alaska, with a view to the establishment of a colony of their countrymen there. Jon Olafsson, the leader of the company, reported that Kodiak and Cook's Inlet are exceedingly well adapted for settlement. The waters they found swarming with salmon, and the temperature and productions such as would render Icelanders happy and contented.

The one-thousandth anniversary of the national existence of Iceland was celebrated in August, 1874, with great rejoicing. The King of Denmark, who is also sovereign of Iceland, was present, and with him a large number of scientific men, explorers, etc., from Europe and America. The occasion offered the opportunity, which was zealously improved, of acquiring a more accurate and exact knowledge of the geography and topography of the island.

A survey of the Canadian Dominion has been in progress since 1871, with the object of selecting a route for the projected Canadian Pacific Railway. Considerable information has been derived from the surveys respecting the character of the country, the distribution of forests, the mineral deposits, and the limits of the great river-basins.

The survey of the Adirondack region, which was ordered by the State government of New York, has been reported to the Legislature by Mr. Colvin Verplanck. The surveyors have made a much more exact triangulation of that tract than had previously been attempted. One important conclusion of the report is, that most of this region is not adapted to cultivation, and that the best uses to which the State can put it are its reservation for a State park, and such an aggregation of its abundant water-courses as to form a reservoir sufficient to supply the Hudson River and its upper affluents with a plenty of water even in the seasons of greatest drought.

From the labors of the United States Coast Survey it appears that the Jersey Flats are increasing in area, and that the tidal deposits are made upon the shores, and not, as formerly, on the extended surface.

The geological survey of Ohio, by Dr. Newberry and others, begun in 1869, and to which reference has been made in preceding volumes of the ANNUAL CYCLOPÆDIA, has been carried out with great thoroughness. One of the results of their labor was first to make known the valuable Hocking Valley or Straitsville coal, which now enters largely into commerce. The able papers of Mr. Edward King, in *Scribner's Monthly Magazine*, on the "Great South," combine with very vivid descriptions of life in the South a large amount of important geographical knowledge of the Southern States. Very interesting papers on the descriptive geography of the States of the Union have also appeared during the year in *Harper's Monthly* and in *Appletons' Journal*. Some of the articles in the last-named periodical on these subjects have been unsurpassed in interest.

Western Kansas, Western Nebraska, and portions of Iowa and Minnesota, have been subjected to a devastating visitation. Swarms of locusts overspread many counties, sweeping off the vegetation, and leaving a large part of the population without food.

Prof. Buckley, State geologist of Texas, reports that the State contains deposits of iron and coal vastly greater than had been supposed.

Salt and gypsum mines, and copper-ores, in many places, have also been found.

The survey of the Western Territories, by order of the War Department, under the direction of Lieutenant G. M. Wheeler, has for its object the mapping of the entire Territorial regions. When completed, this survey, with the Coast and Lake Surveys, will embrace the whole surface of the country. This last year there have been nine parties in the field, and their labors extended over portions of Utah, Nebraska, Colorado, New Mexico, and Arizona. A number of civilians, distinguished for their attainments in physical science, have been attached to these exploring parties. Among them were Dr. H. C. Yarrow, U. S. A., a geologist of note, whose departure in the middle of the season left Prof. Cope in charge of the geological observations; Dr. Rothrock, an experienced botanist; Mr. H. C. Henshaw, who assisted Dr. Yarrow; M. S. Severance, ethnologist; and Dr. Loew, an able analytical chemist. A pass over the main range, inferior only to the Coochetope and Tennessee Passes, was discovered in Colorado by Lieutenant Marshall. The limits of the Block, or San Francisco Forest, were approximately determined. It appears from the survey that this is the largest forest south of the 40th parallel, extending from longitude 107° to 114° west, and varying in width from thirty to one hundred miles.

The detailed portions of the survey were south of the Spanish Peaks, which lie mostly within the boundaries of New Mexico. The operations for 1874 extended over the Arkansas, Cimarron, Mora Pecos, the Rio Grande, and San Juan basins, comprising an area of 35,000 square miles. The labors of the scientists we rewarded with the discovery of large numbers of fossils, many of which were types yet strange to science. In the valley of the Rio Grande, below the Pecoris Mountains, were found the skeletons of mastodons belonging to species not occurring in the Eastern States, and the remains of protomorphic camels and horses, and animals of the Equine family, which must have once inhabited this region in droves. A singular variety of deer, which did not shed its horns, was discovered. In the northern part of the Zandia Mountains of New Mexico, Prof. Cope found the fossils of about one hundred vertebrate species, two-thirds of them mammals, and a large proportion new to science; they represent the oldest mammalian fauna of America. The largest species belonged to the genus *Bathmodon*, resembling the elephant in the form of their feet and legs, and the tapir in their heads, which were armed with powerful tusks. In these mountains the remains of human habitations were found in rows on the crests of lofty rocky upheavals, and on all the most inaccessible points of the hills. They were frequently found in ledges but a few feet wide, and looking down on one or both sides into abysses of many hun-

dred feet, or sometimes perched upon the walls of cañons in positions which were only approachable by dangerous climbing. These dwellings were often remote from water, sometimes twenty miles away.

The chemist of the expedition, Dr. Loew, analyzed the waters of all the thermal and mineral springs which were discovered during the surveys.

The maps which are being made from the late surveys are on a scale of one-eighth of an inch to a mile. The atlas, when finished, will contain maps of the entire section of the country west of the 100th meridian. The surveys will take several years yet to complete. The whole region is divided into rectangles of about 18,000 square miles each; and each map represents one of these divisions.

The surveys conducted by Prof. J. W. Powell, under the control of the Smithsonian Institution, were placed by the action of the last Congress under the direction of the Department of the Interior, and the plan of the survey has been reorganized, so that it and the geological and geographical survey of the Territories, conducted for the department for some years past by F. V. Hayden, will mutually aid and supplement one another. The latter is called the First Division and the former the Second Division of the United States Geological and Geographical Survey of the Territories. The two companies have been working this last year in neighboring Territories—Mr. Hayden's in Colorado and Mr. Powell's in Utah.

The Hayden expedition in 1873 was divided into three sections, to each of which was assigned a strip of country sixty miles wide, of which corresponded to the three sections of the Territory, the Middle Park, the South Park, and the San Luis Park. The three parties made the secondary survey, while the great primary triangulations from the prominent summits upon which their calculations were based were made independently, under the direction of J. T. Gardner.

The expedition set out from Denver on the 15th of July, 1874. It was composed of sixty men, and was divided into eight parties, three of which carried on the secondary surveying and mapping work. During 1874 they have completed the triangulation of Central Colorado, and have surveyed westward as far as the 110th meridian, comprising a tract of about 18,000 square miles of the highest land, on the average, in the United States. In the San Juan mining country over fifty mines were located. Many specimens of ores, fossils, and relics of Indian art, were forwarded to Washington. Among the most interesting discoveries were the ruins of the towns of an extinct race of Indians, and remarkable fortifications of hewn stone and mortar among the cañons. Peculiarly-glazed pottery also was found, indicating, together with the stone embankments and dwellings, a much more advanced civilization than is to be found among the surviving races of Indians. Among the altitudes measured were those of Capitol Peak, 13,800 feet; Mount Daly, 13,700 feet, a peak situate near the end of Elk Range; Snow Mass, 13,785; and Sofris, 12,800. Several others, among which are Pyramid, Gothic, Maroon, Castile, and Italia, range between 12,000 and 13,500 feet. Prof. Hayden's expedition was divided into seven parties. A photographic party, under the charge of Mr. Jackson, obtained more than two thousand negatives of the scenery and products of the Yellowstone region. In the hitherto unexplored regions of the Elk Mountains, the peaks range from 12,000 to 14,700 feet in height, and wear a constant covering of snow and ice. They are composed of granite and sedimentary rock. The mountains abound in large game, elk, antelopes, deer, and grizzly bears.

The expedition under Mr. Powell has been engaged in surveying the central and northeastern parts of Utah. The positions of the more important deposits of metals have been determined. Extensive beds of coal have been discovered. In this region also ruined towns of the ancient inhabitants were discovered in considerable numbers, in which were found hieroglyphical writings and ancient stone implements.

Other similar ruins were discovered by General James H. Simpson, on the Rio Chaco, in New Mexico; thick walls of sandstone, with thin plates of stone introduced between the blocks. The bases of the doors and windows were slabs of stone and wood. The ground-floors are divided off into narrow compartments, with low communicating openings, often not more than two and a half feet square. Some of these walls are four stories high. One of them is seven hundred feet in circumference in the interior and twenty-five feet high, while the scattered fragments around the base indicate a much greater original altitude.

The cañons of the Colorado Valley, which have been described by Major J. W. Powell, have been well explored during the surveys. Among the most remarkable are the Cataract Cañon, below the junction of the Grand and Green Rivers; the Glen Cañon, whose walls are the bright-red homogeneous sandstone of the Triassic age; the Marble Cañon, extending from the mouth of the Paria River to the mouth of the Colorado Chiquito, whose sides are of limestone, and near the foot are of a crystalline structure, which receives a beautiful polish; white, gray, slate-color, pink, brown, and saffron-colored marbles are here found, carved and fretted by the waves of the river and polished by the floods of sand which are poured over the walls during the seasons of showers, giving to the walls of the cañons, which have assumed architectural forms on a giant scale, an appearance of great beauty and grandeur. The deepest of them all is the wonderful Grand Cañon. Another singular feature of this region is the lines of bold, often vertical, precipices, hundreds or thousands of feet high, between higher and lower levels, which extend sometimes for hundreds of miles. The most remarkable are the Brown Cliffs, the southern boundary of the plateau which is cleft by the Cañon of Desolation; the Azure Cliffs, the edge of the plateau of the Gray Cañon; and the Orange Cliffs, a broken escarpment, which stretches from the foot of the Sierra la Sal across the Grand and Green Rivers, and then turns its direction toward the southwest, running parallel to the Colorado for fifty miles, and again changing its course to the southeast, ends in the Sierra la Sal, fifty or sixty miles from where it started. At the point where the Grand and Green Rivers flow together to form the Colorado, the Sierra la Sal rises up on the east, and on the other three sides the perpendicular barrier of the Orange Cliffs looms up to a dizzy height. "On every side a façade of storm-carved rocks is presented. The Indian name for this basin is *Tumpin wu-neir tu-weap*, the land of standing rocks. Buttes, towers, pinnacles, thousands and tens of thousands, of strange forms of rock, naked rock of many different colors, are here seen; so that before we had learned the Indian name we thought of calling it the Stone Forest or Painted Stone Forest; and these rocks are not fragments or piles of irregular masses, but standing forms, carved by the rain-drops from the solid massive beds."

Prof. O. C. Marsh, who has visited the extreme West annually for some years past, for the purpose of collecting geological and paleontological specimens for Yale College, has explored this last season the Bad Lands of Dakota. The remains which he met with were those of tropical animals belonging to the Miocene era, some of them entirely new species, including the hipparion and many other genera of the Equine family. Later in the season, with a few daring and courageous companions, he visited and explored the fossil district in the Black Hills region, and at great risk unearthed and brought to Omaha many tons of fossils, all of them vertebrates, and the larger portion of them mammals of many hitherto-unknown genera. These treasures, so bravely won, will make the paleontological collections of Yale College the richest in the world in fossil vertebrates.

The long-projected exploring expedition under the command of General Custer went into the region of the Black Hills during the summer. The regiment, consisting of 700 men, with 150 teamsters, cooks, and civilians, 100 army-wagons, and 650 horses, started on the march from Fort Lincoln on the 2d of July. Colonel Ludlow was the engineer of the excursion; Prof. Winchell went as the geologist, and Mr. Grinnell to study the paleontology of the regions explored. They entered the mountains from the western side, passed over the eastern and southern chains, explored a considerable part of the interior, and passed out into the plains upon the eastern side. Gypsum was found in unlimited quantities, and variegated marble, muscovite and talcose slate, suitable for whetstones, occurred in sufficient abundance, as well as iron-ore, in the southeastern parts. Gold was reported to have been found at various points upon the surface, and veins of gold-bearing quartz, it was said, were observed cropping out on the hill-sides. General Custer declares that he has seen in no portion of the United States richer pasturage or purer water than in this region. The climate of the hills is delightful; there is abundant fine timber and a sufficient quantity of arable soil to sustain a dense population. The vegetation indicated an uncommonly well-irrigated and fruitful soil. The flora is the richest and most varied of any section east of California. After ascending the Inyan Karan, a prominent peak in Wyoming, which was found to be 6,600 feet in height, they crossed a remarkably fertile valley, to which the name Floral Valley was given; it was covered with flowers of exquisite colors and perfumes, of which they counted 125 species, some of them entirely new. Harney's Peak was found to be the summit-point of the range, rising to a height of about 9,000 feet above the sea-level. The centre of the granite formations is in the southern and southeastern portions. The expedition occupied two months in their explorations. The whole route was found passable for the wagon-train.

A geyser-basin has been discovered in the eastern part of Montana, twenty-five miles southeast of Mount Washburne, which is reported to be larger than any previously-explored basin, and to contain geysers of greater force and size than any before known. One of the geysers is said to cast a volume of water 40 feet in diameter to a height of 500 feet! Mud-volcanoes, surpassing those of the Upper Yellowstone, are also said to exist at this place.

The remarkable sterile tracts called the Bad Lands, which lie along the Yellowstone and Little Missouri Rivers, are described by General Custer as having an average width of fifteen miles, stretching through the valleys of the rivers, which intersect them in the middle. They do not reach, however, to the banks of the rivers, whose immediate shores are covered with a fine growth of timber, and, in spots, with rich pasturage. The fertile strip sometimes expands to the width of miles. The line which divides the Bad Lands from the adjacent country is as plain as the shore of a stream. In some places exposed veins of coal are visible. These Bad Lands extend two hundred miles. Their appearance is a forbidding landscape, presenting a succession of hills separated by wide gorges. The Yellowstone River is found to be 550 miles in length, and navigable for 350 miles.

An expedition under Captain Jones, which explored the Yellowstone country, found the Yellowstone Lake Basin covered with pine-woods. Dr. Hilzinon discovered fish living in hot-springs whose temperature was 124° Fahr.

SOUTH AMERICA.—A telegraphic cable has been laid between Brazil and Europe, over which the first message was sent June 23, 1874.

In Peru rich saltpetre-mines have been discovered. Thomas J. Hutchinson's investigations in Peru refute the current notions of Peruvian history. The architectural and art-remains in Peru he ascribes to a period reaching far back of the Incas. Extensive guano-deposits have been found upon the southern coast of Peru. They are computed to contain about seven million tons.

In Patagonia Messrs. Moreno and Berg have explored the Rio Negro, which in the preceding year Colonel Guerries had attempted to navigate, when his boat was overturned and one of his companions murdered by the savages. Colonel Guerrics describes the country between the island Choëlechel and the Andes as very beautiful.

M. Pertuiset, in company with Captain Maguin and Viscount Bourguet da Punta Arenas, from an exploration of Terra del Fuego, report that the land presents interesting geological features; woods are infrequent, and the trees of feeble growth. Luxurious growths of grass and herbs were observed everywhere; but a scanty flora, save on the southern shore of Useless Bay, where ancient forests are standing, and thickets of laurels and fuchsias, and clumps of cinerarias, camellias, and other brilliant flowers. The natives they found very timid; they wear long hair, like the Patagonians; their food consists of fish, eggs, wild-ducks, rats, and guanacos, which they kill with arrows; their hue is a brownish white.

EUROPE.—Hon. John M. Francis, late minister to Greece, testifies to a marked progress in that country within the last generation. At the close of the Greek Revolution, Athens did not contain 1,000 souls, while now it has over 50,000 inhabitants. Its architecture will bear comparison with that of any city of its size. Other places are rapidly growing: the Piræus, the port of Athens, has a population of 12,000 to 15,000; Syra has 25,000 inhabitants; Patras, the chief depot for the currant trade, with a population of 30,000, has the largest foreign commerce of any Greek town; Zante has 20,000, and Corfu, the summer residence of the court, a larger population. There are now in operation flourishing banking, insurance, and steamship companies. The mercantile marine, in proportion to the number of inhabitants, is the largest in the world. Railroads are being rapidly constructed, and a ship-canal is to be cut across the Isthmus of Corinth. Great attention is being paid to improved methods of agriculture, a matter in which the country has always been backward. Cotton has become an important product, and 5,500,000 pounds are annually raised. The largest exportations are of Zante currants, olives, wine, and the manufactures of silk and cotton yarn.

General di Cesnola has been continuing his excavations upon the island of Cyprus. In September he struck the site of ancient Curium, the Greek Kuri, where he unearthed numerous inscriptions and remains of art.

From the new surveys of the island of Corsica several of the charts have been completed. From the recent triangulation it appears that the highest point upon the island is not Monte Rotondo, as has been supposed, but Monte Cinto. Recent excavations in Rome have resulted in the unearthing of several statues of Carrara marble and of bronze, of extraordinary beauty. One of these, a Venus, in marble, is thought to surpass in beauty that of the Medici. They are supposed to belong to the time of the Emperor Claudius.

ASIA.—The explorations in Western Asia have not been fruitless.

J. A. Paine, of the American Exploration Committee, pursued with assiduity his researches east of the Jordan, and succeeded, probably, in identifying Mount Pisgah; and in a careful exploration of the land of Gilead he came upon indications which, in his view, establish the site of Mount Gilead. He discovered ruins, supposed to be those of the town of Gaza, and determined the sites of various scriptural spots. The geology of the land of Moab has been searchingly examined by Dr. Tristram.

The explorer of the English Palestine Fund, M. Clement Ganneau, discovered significant Hebrew inscriptions between Jaffa and Jerusalem.

Maudsley, an English explorer, disinterred antique baths, an interesting ancient lime-kiln, and mosaic pavements, upon Mount Zion.

One of Dr. Beke's latest investigations was devoted to the solution of the question of the real site of Mount Sinai. He believed, and for many plausible reasons, that he had discovered its real location many miles distant from that assigned to it by Dr. Robinson and other Oriental scholars and explorers. The question is one of great difficulty, and cannot be considered as yet satisfactorily settled.

The German Exploring Expedition in ancient Phœnicia, under the direction of Dr. Sepp, excavated the Christian cathedral at Tyre, discovering the tomb of Barbarossa and the remains of early paintings, episcopal robes, and gold and silver ornaments. The pagan temple of Melkart was also uncovered.

Lieutenant Conder, of the English Palestine Survey Expedition, has reported the discovery of important ruins in the hill-country of Judea.

By the observations made during the progress of Sir Frederick Goldsmid's commission of arbitration to Seistan, in Persia, it appears that there anciently existed a great canal, whose name was Jui-Gershasp, extending fifty or sixty miles through the desert to the southwestward from Roodbár, watering the ancient capital Ram-Sheheristan, the Greek Agriaspe. The other canal, which watered the town of Zaranj,

was probably the branch which leaves Helmend at the Bend-e-Kohek; and the site of the celebrated city of Zaranj is, therefore, according to the opinion of Sir H. C. Rawlinson, to be sought among the ruins in the neighborhood of Sikoha, while Doshakh, or Jellelabad, supposed by Kinnier to be Zaranj, would be the Qurnein of the Arabs.

The Russians have actively pursued explorations of Northern and Central Asia, as well beyond as within their own borders.

M. A. Charoschin has explored the sandy plain of Kizil-Kum, which stretches between the lower Jaxartes and the Oxus. The natives affirm that the sands are drifting year by year to the south, and threaten to cover the northwestern part of Bokhara, as far as Zarafshan.

The railway to be constructed by the Russian Government through Siberia will take a circuitous route by the way of Orenburg, instead of proceeding direct from Nischnii to Troitsk.

An expedition, dispatched by the Imperial Russian Geographical Society, under the management of Colonel Tillo, for the purpose of taking a series of levels between the Aral and Caspian Seas, returned to Orenburg in November. Their computations make the level of the Sea of Aral 250 feet above the Metevi Kooltook Bay of the Caspian, or 165 feet above the ocean-level.

M. Scharnshorst, during the Russian expedition under Kaulbar to Kashgar, succeeded in determining thirteen new astronomical positions.

During the stay of the Russian troops in Khiva, partial investigations were made of the lower Amu-Daria and its delta. The Russian Government dispatched an expedition, under Colonel Stoletew, to explore the beds of the Oxus and complete the work left undone. They commenced the passage of the Aral Sea in July, 1874, charged with the duty of making complete geodetic, botanical, zoological, meteorological, and ethnographical researches. At the same time a corps of observers, organized by the Society of Naturalists, was to make researches into the natural history of the Sea of Aral, taking in, in its operations, only part of the territory traversed by the other expedition.

M. N. M. Prjewalski, under the auspices of the Imperial Russian Geographical Society, accomplished a remarkable journey into the interior of Central Asia, making his way through Koko-Nor and Northern Thibet as far as the upper course of the Yang-tse-Kiang, between September, 1872, and June, 1873. The Koko-Nor, 10,000 feet above the level of the sea, he found to be a beautiful lake; and the neighboring steppes form a rich grazing country. Ten new kinds of birds were noticed. In the south of the chain Burkhan-Buda, which forms the boundary of the cold or high land of Northern Thibet, lies an immense plateau, at an altitude of over 14,000 feet above the sea-level. In the Thibetan mountains he found everywhere great herds of yaks, gazelles, antelopes, orongos, and ados of new varieties, and mountain-sheep in herds of many hundreds. In Kansu, Koko-Nor, and Tsaidam, dwell four distinct races—Chinese, Mongols, Tangûts, and Daldüs. The latter are a peculiar race, who approach more nearly to the Mongols than to the Chinese in their character, and speak a language which is said to be a hybrid between their two tongues. The tribe of Mongols is the most degraded and repulsive offshoot of the race. The Tangûts recalled to the traveler the European Gypsies, by their thievish dispositions and other characteristics.

The diplomatic mission of Douglass Forsyth from the Indian Government to the court of Kashgar afforded a favorable opportunity to obtain geographical information of the vast region between Yarkand and Samarcand in one direction and Kashgar and China Proper in the other. In company with Forsyth were Dr. Stoliczka, who gave his life as an offering to science before their return, Colonel Warburton, Lieutenant-Colonel T. E. Gordon, and Captains Trotter and Biddulph. The great gain of the expedition consists in the trigonometrical measurements taken on the route, by which the great Indian system of triangulation was carried up to meet the Russian triangulations, so that the two systems now lap by about fifty miles. Departing from India September 19, 1873, they reached Kashgar on the 9th of December. On the 21st of May a party detached by Forsyth, in which were Captains Trotter and Biddulph and Dr. Stoliczka, under the leadership of Colonel Warburton, departed from Yengihissar for the western mountains. They reached Kila Pandsha, in Wakhan, on the 13th of April. The Emir of Kashgar did his utmost to aid the expedition, furnishing them with attendants and yaks and horses. Snow fell during the entire passage, and they were twenty days in deep snow. The Pamir they found to consist of a number of upland valleys instead of one great level steppe. The watershed between East and West Toorkistan, or the basins of the Lap and Aral Seas, is not Pamir, as has been supposed, but the Kyzilyart Plateau, which lies in the east-northeast, and has a much inferior elevation. It appears that the entire way between Khokand and India lies in the domains of the Emirs of Kashgar and Cabul. Wakhan, it appears, contains not more than a thousand inhabitants, poor in condition but of an independent nature. On the return of the expedition the geologist, Dr. Stoliczka, died while crossing the Sasser Pass. The observations of Dr. Stoliczka, made during the progress of the Forsyth embassy to Kashgar, demonstrated that the Himalayas, the Karakorum, and the Kuenlun, are, in respect to their geological character, entirely distinct from one another. The Eocene formations of the first end at Ladak, on the Indus. North of that river are found no later rocks than the Triassic; while the Kuenlun consist only of the earliest primary formations. The geological character of the Singling-Chian chain, which

runs parallel with them, is the same. The basins of Kashgar and Yarkand consist chiefly of chalk formations.

H. Fritsche made a journey in the summer of 1873 from Peking to St. Petersburg, through East Mongolia and by the way of Irkutsk and Barnaul, upon which he established the geographical position and level of fifty-nine places. The mountains are nowhere over eight thousand feet in height. Dolo-Nor, the principal town in the southeastern part of Mongolia, is a place of 30,000 inhabitants.

Lieutenant François Garnier, in the exploration in which he lost his life, found a portion of the Yang-tse-Kiang River flowing underground. This phenomenon he discovered to be so common in that country, that he was led to suppose that the parts of the rivers which are lost in the earth are as great as the visible parts. Great streams come flooding out of the sides of mountains, and again sink into chasms, to reappear at some distant point.

Baron Richthofen accomplished a successful journey in 1871-'72 from Peking, through the provinces of Shansi, Shensi, and Sze-Kuen, and made valuable additions to our knowledge of the geography, natural productions, agriculture, and trade of the regions visited. His report affords interesting information concerning the coal-mines of Chaitang, on the high-road between Singan-fu and Ching-tu-fu, on the remarkable beds of rich loam which coat the soil of nearly the whole of Northern China, and which are the cause of the great fertility which supports its enormous population. Baron Richthofen's theory of this formation is that the fine dust of decomposing rocks is precipitated over the surface by easterly, rain-bringing winds. The coal-fields of China, of which the first mine has just been opened, cover an area of 400,000 square miles. There are also unlimited supplies of iron in the empire.

AFRICA.—The discoveries of George Schweinfurth gave the chief impulse to the formation of the German African Society. Schweinfurth's travels have been published within the past year; English and French translations have also been issued, and they have been reprinted in this country. When he passed out of the Nile Basin, and, on reaching the Mbrnole, entered the land of the Nyam-Nyams, he found a territory exhibiting a great resemblance in its fauna and flora to the west coast. In the inhabitants, also, he remarked striking race-affinities with the tribes of the western side. The discoveries of Schweinfurth have been vigorously followed up by others of his countrymen, who have proved themselves, in late years, capable of the most perilous and daring explorations.

An expedition left Europe in June, 1873, under the direction of Dr. Güssfeldt, and the military command of Dr. Lohde, who, on account of ill-health, has been relieved by Major von Mechow, to follow up the discoveries of Schweinfurth and the succeeding German explorers. The Berlin African Society have also sent out a second expedition, under the management of Captain von Homeyer, which is to proceed to Canandge, on the border of Angola, and thence to endeavor to penetrate to the capital of Mnata Janivo. In March, 1874, Dr. Güssfeldt followed up the river Loango Luz, or Chilvango, as far as the junction of the Luculla and the Loango. The German expedition into the interior will start probably at the commencement of the rainy season of 1875. Prof. Bastian, setting out in June, 1873, spent three months upon the Loango coast, searching for the most favorable point of departure for the German expedition from the west coast. Upon his return he published an interesting account of his observations. The territory is divided into four kingdoms, Angoy, Kakongo, Little Loango, and Great Loango; farther inland lies the forest country, Mazûmba, which extends as far as the mountains which separate the coast from the interior. His accounts of the dwarf race, Babongo (the Obongo of Du Chaillu), and of the information that gorillas are found upon the coast, are matters of interest. Dr. Lenz set out independently to explore a portion of unknown Africa, intending to trace the course of the Gabun and Ogowai Rivers. The Okanda, the northern tributary of the Ogowai, has been traced some distance higher up by the French Marquises de Compiègne and Marche. They passed through the country of the Okatas, who live poorly, and sustain themselves chiefly upon a sweetish, doughy, wild fruit abounding in the forests, and traffic in slaves. They passed afterward through the land of the Apingis, a gentle, industrious people, who cultivate the soil and collect honey and caoutchouc. A rapacious tribe, the Oszebas, prevented their pursuing the journey to some large lakes, of which they heard many reports.

Bayard Taylor, in a visit to Egypt in the beginning of 1874, saw at Cairo two specimens of the pigmies which Schweinfurth had met with in the country of the Nyam-Nyams. Their country, called Naam or Takkatikât, lies below the equator, beyond that of the latter. It is described as a table-land, covered with low, dense thickets, in which the pigmies take refuge. They are said to prove no despicable foe to the neighboring negroes. Schweinfurth designates them under the name of Akka. They appear probably in the Abongos of Du Chaillu again; and the name itself is detected in the Bakka-bakka pigmy tribe, which Bastian observed on the Loango coast, and which was known to the Portuguese in the last century. It is possible that, as Schweinfurth supposes, commercial relations exist between the west coast and the Nyam-Nyams, and that their King Munoa draws a tribute of salt from the coast-lands. Schweinfurth found no salt in the country traversed by him. Their cannibalistic habits, the coffee-brown hue of their skins, the monthly festival with dances in the first-quar-

ter of the moon, the nocturnal orgies, the practices of wearing ox-horns, of filing their teeth to a point, and of wearing their hair in many braids, the chieftains' robes of leopard-furs, and the red-staining of their skins—all tend to strengthen the probability of the conjecture of Schweinfurth, of ethnological affinities between the Nyam-Nyams and the western nation of the Fans.

The expedition of Dr. Gerhard Rohlfs departed from Siout, in Upper Egypt, on the 17th of December, 1873, with the object of penetrating the Libyan Desert to the oasis of Kufra, which is only known by rumor, and is reported to be a large and fertile region lying in the very heart of the Libyan Desert. Accompanying Rohlfs were three noted men of science, Profs. Jordan, Zittel, and Ascherson. The expedition was provided with water-tanks of galvanized iron, and an abundant supply of provisions and equipments. The Khedive secured their safe conduct to the point of departure, and provided them with thirty-five camels, hiring sixty-five others for their use for three months. The company consisted of ninety men, all told. On the 21st of December they, having filled their tanks with fresh water and provided themselves with meat and fodder, commenced their march westward into the desert. The first plateau gradually rose in height until it was 1,000 feet above the sea-level, about 150 miles out; and then it declined again. There was no vegetation except scattered bunches of dry, tough grass. On the sixth day they came to the brink of a rocky wall, 300 feet in height, overlooking a level, sandy plain, with no signs of vegetation. Two days' journey farther brought them to the oasis of Farafrah, where they found a wretched population of about 400, composed of the fanatical sect of the Senoosee. Beyond the oasis is another sharp declivity which was found like the first to belong to the earliest Eocene period. On the way onward to the larger oasis of Dakhel, they passed for three days through a dismal waste, absolutely void of vegetation, over a broad road of pebbles, which seemed as though made by art, with sand-hills from 150 to 250 feet in height on both sides of them. The way ascended to the hard, bare plateau, and then led down again, until in a couple of days they passed through a remarkable labyrinth of fantastically-shaped, detached limestone rocks, and between two rocky chasms, the walls of one of which were 1,500 feet high. The oasis of Dakhel lay two hours' march beyond. The Egyptian governor gave them an honorable reception. The oasis, containing 1,700 inhabitants, according to Prof. Ascherson, could support ten times as many. The ancient Egyptians cultivated the whole area, and ruins of their temples and dwellings stand on places which are now barren. The gardens produce olives, grapes, apricots, and mulherries, as well as dates and oranges. Wherever the stratum of chalk which underlies the oasis is bored through, water rises to the surface in large quantity and of good quality. The travelers found no trace of the famed dry river-bed in the desert. Four days' journey beyond the oasis they reached a patch of grass and low bushes, which they took for the supposed oasis of Zerzoora. Two days farther outward brought them to an impenetrable arid waste of deep, shifting sand, with high sand-hills rising at intervals as far as they could see to the westward. The westernmost point reached was in latitude 21° 11' north, longitude 27° 40' east. They moved along the edge of this impassable desert toward the north, traversing many long strips of sand which had been driven from the main body by the wind. The thermometer was unexpectedly low, standing at from 29° to 23° Fahr. in the morning. They came in thirty-six days from their departure from the oasis of Dakhel to the oasis of Jupiter Ammon, having gone over a course of 500 miles. Their measurements proved the level here to be 200 feet below the Mediterranean. The expedition returned to Cairo on the 15th of April, having traveled over 1,700 miles in the desert.

The Royal Geographical Society, solicitous concerning the condition of Dr. Livingstone, of whom no tidings came after Stanley parted company with him, commissioned at different times Lieutenants Cameron and Grandy to seek him, the former starting from the east side and the latter from the west side of the continent. Lieutenant Cameron proceeded to Ujiji, toward the close of 1873, after meeting the messenger dispatched by the bearers of Livingstone's remains to carry the news of his death, when he succeeded in recovering the diary of Dr. Livingstone and the map of his journey to Lake Nyassa in 1866.

The last journals of David Livingstone have issued from the press, edited by Rev. H. Waller, augmented by statements taken by the editor from the lips of his two negro attendants, Susi and Chumah. These journals reveal the determined will of the resolute explorer to follow out the purpose with which his life had become identified—the discovery of the Nile-sources. In one of the entries in the journal he thus expressed himself: "Mr. Stanley used some very strong arguments in favor of my going home, recruiting my strength, getting artificial teeth, and then returning to finish my task; but my judgment said, all your friends will wish you to make a complete work of the exploration of the sources of the Nile before you return." He heard of a mound west of Lake Bangweolo, from which four rivers issued, two of which, flowing north, united to form the Lualaba. Toward this point he directed his last journey. His strength began to fail from the recurrence of a chronic disease, and under the extraordinary difficulties of the route his vital powers broke down. When no longer able to sit on his donkey he had himself borne onward upon a litter. "Nothing earthly," he

wrote, "will make me give up my work in despair." The remains of Dr. Livingstone were preserved and conveyed to Unyanyembe and thence to England in charge of the negro Jacob Wainwright, whose account of the journey has been published. On the way to Unyanyembe messengers of the party encountered Lieutenant Cameron with supplies for the relief of Livingstone. Lieutenant Cameron, on his expedition from Unyanyembe to Ujiji, pursued the Stanley route as far as Utakama, and thence took a new course more to the northward. Ujiji lies, according to his determination, in latitude 4° 58' 3" south, longitude 30° 4' 30" east. The Tanganyika Lake he found to be 275 feet above the level of the sea. This lake has later been thoroughly explored by him. Upon its western side he found the looked-for outlet, which is called Lukuga. This, he believes, flows into the Lualaba. The Lualaba itself, the Arabs report, flows into the Congo, and not, as Livingstone and Stanley supposed, into the Albert N'yanza. Lieutenant Grandy was recalled from his excursion from the west coast upon the tidings of the death of Livingstone. He supposes that the Congo has two main branches, the southern one draining Angola, and the northern one being probably the Lualaba. Lieutenant Grandy received good treatment at the hands of the chiefs. He found traces of the Portuguese occupation of Congo, and describes the natives as indolent and civilized, fond of snuff and tobacco, and addicted to the use of palm-wine. The Congo is described as one of the grandest rivers in the world, and navigable 110 miles from its mouth.

Mr. Stanley was sent out by the proprietors of the New York *Herald* and London *Telegraph* conjointly on a second expedition, to communicate for the columns of those papers information of the state of affairs upon the east coast and in the lake-region of Africa. He visited Rufigi and ascended the river to Kisu. He reported minute information concerning the course of the Rufigi and the commercial capacities of the valley.

The difficulty between the Khedive and the Sultan of Darfour has ended in the subjugation of the latter country. The trust which the Khedive reposed in Sir Samuel Baker has been transferred to Colonel Gordon, who cherishes in combination with his political objects plans for geographical researches.

Dr. Nachtigal, one of the most fearless and indefatigable of African travelers, has pursued, since 1869, a series of journeys in East Africa, through the principal districts of the eastern Sahara, the southern parts of Baghirmi, Bahr el Gasal, Fittri, and Waday, lands never before visited by Europeans who returned to give an account of their discoveries. His latest expedition to Waday, as well as those which preceded it, affords results of great value to geographers. Hearing nothing but discouragements in Tripoli and Fezzan, with the fates of Dr. Vogel and Moritz von Beurmann, who were murdered in attempting to reach Waday, before his eyes, he nevertheless set forth with undaunted courage, bearing presents to Sultan Omar of Bornou. He then pressed on to Fittri, where he presented himself as a Christian to the Sultan; afterward he was not known in his true character, pushing forward so rapidly that he could not be recognized, and was supposed by the people to be a wealthy *hadji*, or pilgrim. He approached Abeschr, the capital of Waday, with many misgivings, which were enhanced when his horses and fire-arms were taken away at the command of the Sultan. He met, however, with a friendly reception from Sultan Ali, the despotic but just and liberal ruler, who, though a zealous believer of the fanatical Moslem sect called the *Senoosee*, is not so rigorous in the exclusion of non-believers as his predecessors. Waday is inferior to Bornou in natural advantages and civilization. The laws are of the severest character. Theft and breaches of the peace are punishable with death; adulterers are executed or maimed; cowardice in battle is punished in a barbarous method. The inhabitants are brutal, quarrelsome, immoral, and drunken, intoxicating themselves daily upon a brewed drink called *melissa*. Their dwellings are of the rudest description; their domestic vessels are made out of gourd-rinds. Cattle, sheep, and goats, are raised; but milk is not used as a drink. The brutal violence of the people is held in check only by the stringent authority of the present ruler. It is only within a couple of years that the Arab merchants have dared to go about freely. Dr. Nachtigal's intention of starting immediately for Darfour was frustrated by the death of Hassim, the Sultan of that country, which put an end to all intercommunication until friendly relations were reëstablished by an envoy from his successor, Brahim, a son of Hassim. Nachtigal could learn nothing of the fate of Vogel. Beurmann had been slain by the ruler of Kanem, without the approval of Ali. Leaving Waday on the 17th of January, he traveled through a region infested by the predatory Massalit tribe. He found the eastern parts of Darfour as arid and sandy as the western side is fruitful. All the water contained in the broad river-beds lies many feet below their sandy bottoms. In Fasher he found a welcome any thing but hospitable, though letters from the Khedive had prepared the King for his coming. Journeys to Kordofan or Dongola are seldom made from here in the dry season. He left, fortunately, a short time before the marching in of the Egyptian troops; had he remained he might have fallen a victim to the vindictive rage of the superstitious populace. In Dar Hamr there are no wells, and it is necessary that the water-supply for three-quarters of the year be gathered during the rainy season in ponds and troughs, and stored in the trunks of the gigantic Adansonias. On the 10th of August Dr. Nachtigal arrived at Kordofan.

Of a number of expeditions into the vast unknown tract between the colonies of South and West Australia, two have successfully crossed the country; and now the topography of almost the entire Australian Continent may be considered pretty clearly known to the world. Ernest Giles made an attempt in 1872, and one in the following year. Gosse, in 1873, succeeded in penetrating farther up the country than had Giles, passing through a dry, sandy region, in which were found abundant grass, mulga scrub, and spinifex growths. The first successful expedition was that of Colonel Warburton, who passed overland from Adelaide to Perth. Colonel P. Egerton Warburton started out from Alice Springs on the 15th of April, 1873, with camels. The journey lasted nine months, while the party had taken only six months' supplies: they were obliged to eat the tough flesh of the camels, and suffered frequently from thirst. Before reaching the colony at Gray River, they were also in danger of starvation, having consumed all the camels except two. For the first two hundred miles along the MacDougal range there was pasturage and water; but the entire region beyond contained nothing save spinifex grass and sandy ridges. The inhabitants are exceedingly shy, and live without artificial dwellings or clothing. They subsist upon the flesh of the wallabee, the only animal of the region, and the black, hard seeds of a variety of acacia. J. Ross, an experienced bush-ranger, was sent out later by the Australian Government on a course more southerly than Warburton's. He was obliged to put back, from the failure of water. The character of the country was similar to that passed through by Warburton—an undulating table-land, with grass-plains, mulga-woods, and scattering sand-hills of considerable size.

John Forrest set out from Champion Bay in April, 1874, intending to trace the Murchison River to its source, and march thence for the telegraph-line by an easterly course. He had in his party six men with eighteen horses. They crossed through the heart of the unexplored part of the continent, keeping close to the 25th parallel, south latitude, and reached the telegraph, September 1st, having traveled over 2,000 miles. Most of the country traversed was of the poorest description; and for 600 miles the travelers had to force their way through a spinifex desert scantily supplied with water. They had several encounters with the natives. This last expedition has reduced to within narrow limits the still unexplored portion of Australia. The direct route to Perth alone remains to be traversed before the world possesses a fair knowledge of the character of inner West Australia.

GEORGIA. The annual session of the Legislature of Georgia began on the 14th of January and closed on the 26th of February. A resolution was introduced on the first day, and subsequently adopted, providing for a joint committee to receive and consider proposed amendments to the constitution. Afterward a bill was introduced providing for a convention to revise the constitution; but this, after considerable discussion, was defeated, all the Republican and colored members and many of the Democrats voting against it. Among the amendments proposed by the joint committee was one removing the capital from Atlanta to Milledgeville, which was defeated; and one, which was adopted, intended to prohibit the payment of $8,000,000 of bonds indorsed by Governor Bullock and pronounced by a former Legislature to be fraudulent. Through an ambiguous wording of the amendment, it was discovered, after the adjournment of the Legislature, that it would not accomplish the purpose intended. As it is necessary for a constitutional amendment to be adopted by two successive Legislatures and then ratified by the people before it becomes valid, an attempt was made to have an extra session called to remedy the defect; but this did not succeed, and the question of a constitutional convention to be provided for by the Legislature of 1875 was warmly agitated before the close of the year. Few of the acts of the last Legislature are of any general interest. A bill providing for a new system of popular education in place of the existing one, and requiring separate schools for white and colored children, failed to pass. Among those passed was one providing for a tax on railroad property; one repealing all provisions in railroad charters granting State aid where the companies have not already vested rights; one transferring to the Atlantic & Gulf Railroad Company three-fourths of the stock held by the State; one providing for the appointment of a State geologist; and one establishing a Department of Agriculture. The last-named creates the office of Commissioner of Agriculture, to be

MACON.

appointed by the Governor for a term of four years, at an annual salary of $2,000. He is allowed a clerk at $1,200 a year, and $10,000 in addition was appropriated to carry out the purposes of the act. Various duties of the commissioner are prescribed, calculated to disseminate information regarding the soil and products of each county of the State, the habits of destructive insects, the nature of diseases to which crops are liable, the merits of different fertilizers, and other matters affecting the agricultural interests and prosperity of the State. He is also required to obtain and distribute valuable seeds, investigate the profitableness of sheep-raising in the State, and give careful attention to irrigation and fencing.

The following resolutions were adopted unanimously in the House, and by a vote of 24 to 4 in the Senate:

Whereas, The chief object of all governments should be the protection of person and property, and that all men have an equal right to justice and to stand perfectly equal before the law; that Georgia most cheerfully accords to every individual within the borders of the State the amplest protection and security in all these rights; that there is not in our organic law, nor upon our statute-books, a single provision that militates against any class on account of race or color; that we deny the right or power of Congress, under the amended Constitution of the United States, to exercise a general municipal as well as criminal legislation over the people of Georgia; that the passage of the civil-rights bill now pending before Congress, or any other bill of like character, is an infringement upon the reserved rights of the States, and was never contemplated by the framers of that Constitution, nor of any amendment to the same; that the passage of the civil-rights bill would, in our opinion, be inexpedient, injudicious, unwise, and contrary to the wishes of both the white and colored people of this State; that we do not believe the colored people of Georgia desire mixed schools and mixed churches, or any thing which partakes of social rights; that these questions of social rights must alone be regulated by society: therefore—

Resolved, By the Senate and House of Representatives, that we most respectfully and earnestly request our national Congress not to interfere with the municipal regulations of the States by the passage of the present civil-rights bill, or any bill of like import and character, but to leave all these questions to the States, where they properly belong.

Resolved, That the Governor now forward a copy

of the foregoing preamble and resolutions to the presiding officers of each of the Houses of Congress, with a request that the same be laid before that body.

An amendment was made in the Senate and concurred in by the House, to the effect that the civil-rights bill would destroy the school-system of Georgia. Mr. De Vaux, of the Senate, made the following protest, which was spread upon the records with no signature but his own :

To the Honorable the Senate of the State of Georgia :
We, the undersigned Senators, members of your honorable body, beg leave to dissent from the views and propositions expressed in the House resolution, protesting against the passage by the national Congress of the United States of the bill commonly known as the civil-rights bill, and therefore desire to enter this our solemn protest against the same, for the following reasons, to wit:

1. Because, so long as Georgia discriminates between her citizens in any of the rights mentioned in said civil-rights bill, she does not afford "the amplest protection and security" to all, without regard to race, color, or previous condition of servitude.

2. Because we hold that the laws of Congress of the United States are the supreme law of the land, and that States have no reserved rights by which such States can abridge the privileges and immunities of citizens of the United States ; but Congress has full power under the Constitution to pass all necessary laws for the protection of its citizens, without regard to race, color, or previous condition of servitude.

3. That we deny the statement made in said resolution, to the effect that it is contrary to the wishes of the white and colored people of this State—that they do not wish the civil-rights bill enacted into law.

In April the labor of the convicts in the Penitentiary, to the number of 630, was leased, out by the Governor to various parties and at different prices, ranging from $10 to $20 a year *per capita*, under authority of an act of the Legislature. This system does not seem to be very satisfactory in its working. The escapes of convicts have been at the rate of 10 per cent. per annum of the whole number, and the deaths at the rate of 6 per cent.

A Commissioner of Agriculture was appointed under the law of February 20th, on the 26th of August, and has organized his department and gone actively to work. A State geologist has also been appointed, and began his work late in the fall. Dr. George Little, formerly a professor in the University of Mississippi, is the appointee.

The State University is reported to be in a prosperous and growing condition. The sum of $8,000 annually was appropriated to the Atlanta University by an act approved March 6th, on condition that as many colored pupils should be admitted from each county of the State as there may be members of the House of Representatives in such county, the pupils to be nominated by the representatives, so long as such appropriation lasts. The conditions were complied with, and the amount paid over this year. A common-school organization has been effected in every county of the State, and

schools are in actual operation in 125 counties. The net amount of the school-fund collected from all sources from the adoption of the present constitution to December 1, 1873, was $489,722.42. The amount collected since that date is $186,183.90, and the amount disbursed $169,071.84. The amount of poll-tax assessed in 1874, which, by an act approved February 28th, is retained in the counties for school purposes, is $199,550, of which $133,000 has been collected. There are $350,000 of school bonds in the hands of the Secretary of State, and the interest thereon from October 1, 1870, to October 1, 1874, is claimed by the School Commissioner to be due to his department.

There was a balance in the State Treasury on the 1st of January of $922,556.25, and the amount received during the year was $1,895,-116.86, making the total resources $2,817,723. The total disbursements of the year were $1,814,494.23, leaving a balance on hand on the 1st of January, 1875, of $1,003,128.88. The estimated receipts for 1875, including this surplus, amount to $2,585,628.88; expenditures, $1,499,483—which will leave a balance at the end of the year of $1,086,045.88. The reported value of taxable property for the year shows an increase of $30,000,000, a large part of which is due to the repeal of the law exempting a certain amount of property from taxation. Making due allowance for this, the actual increase is nearly $14,000,000. The funded debt of the State not yet matured on the 1st of January, 1875, was $8,105,500. The amount due thereon, principal and interest, in 1875, is $670,385. There is, besides, $269,500 of past-due bonds outstanding, which, with the unpaid interest, amounts to $323,400.

Considerable confusion still exists regarding bonds of the State claimed to be illegal, and bonds indorsed by the State, as is alleged, without due authority of law. An unsuccessful attempt has been made to obtain a settlement with Henry Clews & Co., of New York, formerly the financial agents of the State, who are accused of converting State bonds to their own use. The firm refused to furnish the Attorney-General with information regarding bonds which they had received, but not returned, unless their account against the State was first settled. This was refused, on the ground that many of the items were not accompanied by proper vouchers, and an examination of the books of the firm was not permitted. The accusation is, that some of the bonds declared invalid by the Legislature have been used by the firm for their own profit. The matter remains unsettled. The indorsement of the State upon bonds of the Macon & Brunswick Railroad was declared valid and binding by the Legislature of 1872, but the Governor claims to have discovered that a large portion of these were indorsed in violation of law, and it is probable that further legislative action will be taken. It was provided by the law of 1866 that the bonds to be indorsed by the State should not exceed $1,000,000, until an amount of capital should be subscribed and paid in equal to the amount of the indorsements. The Governor says that there is no evidence that such capital was ever subscribed and paid in, although further indorsements of the State were given. He calls for an investigation of the matter. The road is now held on behalf of the State by a receiver, and it was advertised for sale in December, but afterward withdrawn on account of the discoveries made regarding the bonds. The North & South Railroad Company having failed to pay interest on bonds indorsed by the State, the property was taken possession of by the State in April, and is still held and managed by its agent. The Memphis Branch Railroad Company, having completed and equipped five miles of its road in May, received the State's guarantee on its bonds to the amount of $34,000.

The Governor, in his message to the Legislature of 1875, has the following to say about a revision of the State constitution:

The Secretary of State has been directed to send, properly authenticated, to the Senate, where it originated, the act of the last Legislature, approved March 2, 1874, entitled "An act to amend the Constitution of the State." An examination of this act shows that it is applicable only to such indorsements of railway bonds made by the late Governor as the Legislature had "declared illegal, fraudulent, or void." A large amount of the fraudulent indorsements and bonds, issued during the late administration, are not covered by the language of the act. It is doubtful, therefore, whether the public interest would be subserved by the final adoption of the act as an amendment to the constitution. It is also questionable whether it would be competent for the Legislature so to amend the act as to include the other bonds and indorsements to which attention has just been directed. The question is thus brought before us whether, for this and other reasons, it is advisable at this time, and under existing circumstances, to call a convention for the purpose of revising and amending the constitution of the State. It is generally conceded that such a convention ought to assemble in the course of a few years. Indeed, there seems to be but little, if any, difference of opinion at to the propriety and necessity of revising the constitution; the only doubt in the public mind being as to the time when this can best be done. There are certainly many reasons why a convention should be called without unnecessary delay, and yet it must be confessed that there are other reasons, equally cogent, why, in a matter of such grave concern, the State should move with extreme caution. The peculiar condition of the State, its relations with the Federal Government, and the necessity of acting, as far as practicable, with due regard to other Southern States similarly situated with ourselves, impose upon us a grave responsibility. The people, however, have the right to decide this question for themselves, and to them the Legislature can safely remit it. When this has been done, the entire question can be discussed and determined upon its merits. I can see no reason, therefore, why the Legislature, if it see proper, may not take action during the present session, for the purpose of referring the question of assembling a convention to a vote of the people.

The subject of "direct trade" from Southern ports to those of Europe has been a good deal agitated during the year. A "Direct-Trade

Union" has been formed, and other steps taken to forward the object. A convention was held at Atlanta, in May, to which presidents of railroads and other transportation companies, mayors of cities, and presidents of boards of trade and chambers of commerce in the Southern and Western States, were invited to consider the subject of establishing a transportation line from Savannah to Liverpool to coöperate with a transportation line from the former port westward to various points on the Mississippi River and beyond. There were various reports, speeches, and resolutions, on the subject, and practical steps were taken to secure the coöperation of railroads and ship-owners in the proposed enterprise. The subject of constructing an "Atlantic & Great Western Canal," to cross the State of Georgia and reach the Mississippi River, is also agitated. There was an Agricultural Congress at Atlanta on the 4th of June, which adopted resolutions looking to the union of the cotton States in the direct-trade movement, without expressing preferences for any port. A committee of five from each State was appointed to memorialize the Legislatures on the subject of procuring statistics. The congress adjourned, to meet at Raleigh, N. C., July, 1875.

There was no election for State officers this year, and consequently no general conventions of the parties. There was an election for members of the Legislature on the 7th of October. That body now consists of 40 Democrats and 4 Republicans in the Senate, and 160 Democrats and 15 Republicans in the House of Representatives. An election for members of Congress was held on the 3d of November. In the first district Julian Herbridge, Democrat, was elected by 4,538 majority; second district, William E. Smith, Democrat, by 2,309 majority; third district, Philip Cook, Democrat, by 4,478 majority; fourth district, Henry R. Harris, Democrat, by 9,236 majority; fifth district, Milton A. Candler, Democrat, by 6,177 majority; sixth district, James H. Blount, Democrat, by 725 majority; seventh district, William H. Felton, Independent, by 82 majority; eighth district, Alexander H. Stephens, Democrat, by 6,810 majority; and ninth district, Garrett McMillen, Democrat, by 5,507 majority.

GERMANY, an empire in Europe, reëstablished January 18, 1871. The Emperor, William I., was born March 22, 1797. He is a son of King Frederick William III. of Prussia, and Queen Louisa, and was married June 11, 1829, to Augusta, daughter of the Grand-duke Charles Frederick of Saxe-Weimar. The heir-apparent, Frederick William, born October 18, 1831, has the official title of Crown-prince of the German Empire, and Crown-prince of Prussia. He was married January 25, 1858, to Victoria, Princess Royal of Great Britain and Ireland, born November 21, 1840. Offspring of the union are, three sons, Frederick William, born 1859; Henry, born 1862; Waldemar, born 1868; and four daughters, Charlotte, born 1860; Victoria, born 1866; Sophia, born 1870; Margaretha, born 1872. Imperial Chancellor (Reichskanzler), Otto, Prince von Bismarck-Schönhausen. President of the Imperial Chancery (Reichskanzler-Amt), Delbrück, Minister of State.

The following table exhibits all the states of the German Empire, the area, the population, the number of representatives of every German state in the Federal Council, and the number of deputies who represent each state in the Reichstag:

STATES.	Square Miles.	Population in 1871.	Votes in Federal Council.	Deputies to the Reichstag.
1. Prussia (including Lauenburg)	134,499	24,656,078	17	236
2. Bavaria	29,292	4,852,026	6	48
3. Saxony	5,788	2,556,244	4	23
4. Würtemberg	7,531	1,818,559	4	17
5. Baden	5,821	1,461,562	3	14
6. Hesse	2,964	852,894	3	9
7. Mecklenburg-Schwerin	5,138	501,897	2	6
8. Saxe-Weimar	1,397	286,183	1	3
9. Oldenburg	2,470	96,982	1	3
10. Mecklenburg-Strelitz	1,131	312,596	2	1
11. Brunswick	1,425	311,764	1	3
12. Saxe-Meiningen	953	187,957	1	2
13. Saxe-Altenburg	510	142,122	1	1
14. Saxe-Coburg-Gotha	760	174,339	1	2
15. Anhalt	906	203,437	1	2
16. Schwarzburg-Rudolstadt	364	75,523	1	1
17. Schwarzburg-Sondershausen	333	67,191	1	1
18. Waldeck	438	56,224	1	1
19. Reuss-Greitz (older line)	123	45,094	1	1
20. Reuss-Schleitz (younger line)	320	89,032	1	1
21. Schaumburg-Lippe	171	32,059	1	1
22. Lippe-Detmold	438	111,185	1	1
23. Lubeck	109	52,158	1	1
24. Bremen	97	122,402	1	1
25. Hamburg	158	338,974	1	3
26. Alsace-Lorraine (Reichsland)	5,903	1,549,738	1	15
German troops in France (1871)	.....	48,624	1	..
Navy in foreign waters	.....	2,054	1	..
Total	208,729	41,060,846	58	397

The Federal Council has nine standing committees: 1. For the army and fortresses; 2. For the navy; 3. For taxes, tariff, and excise; 4. For commerce; 5. For railroads, posts, and telegraphs; 6. For justice; 7. For accounts; 8. For Foreign Affairs; 9. For Alsace-Lorraine. The Emperor appoints the members of the first committee, except the member of Bavaria, and all those of the second; the members of the other committees are elected by the Federal Council. Prussia is represented in each of the committees except that of Foreign Affairs, which in 1874 consisted of the representatives of Bavaria, Würtemberg, Saxony, Baden, and Mecklenburg-Schwerin, and was presided over by the representative of Bavaria.

The members of the Reichstag are elected by universal suffrage and ballot, for the term of three years. The first Reichstag, elected in 1871, consisted of 382 members; the second, elected in 1874, and containing also 15 members for Alsace-Lorraine, of 397.

The census of 1871 showed the religious division of the population composing the German Empire as follows: Evangelical Church (under which head the census embraces the United Evangelical Church, Lutherans, and Reformed), 25,581,709; Roman Catholics, 14,867,091; Greek Catholics, 2,660; Christian sects of various denominations, 79,553; Israelites, 512,171; other forms of religion, 1,917; religious profession unknown, 15,594. The Roman Catholics constitute a majority in Alsace-Lorraine (79.7 per cent.); Bavaria (71.3 per cent.); and Baden (64.5 per cent.): they are a considerable minority in Prussia (33.5 per cent.); Würtemberg (30.4 per cent.); Hesse (27.9 per cent.); Oldenburg (22.6 per cent.); they only number from 3 to 1 per cent. in Saxe-Weimar, Bremen, Lippe, Waldeck, Brunswick, Hamburg, Saxony, Anhalt, and Schaumburg-Lippe, and less than 1 per cent. in all the other states. The Jews number 4.1 per cent. of the population in Hamburg, 3.0 per cent. in Hesse, 2.6 per cent. in Alsace-Lorraine, from 2 to 1 per cent. in Bavaria, Baden, Prussia, Waldeck, Schaumburg-Lippe, and Lubeck, and less than 1 per cent. in the other states. Of the German princes, only two are Catholics, the Kings of Bavaria and Saxony. The Old Catholics, in 1874, had about 100 congregations, containing a population of about 60,000.

The states of Germany are constitutional monarchies, with the exception of the three Hanse towns, which are democratic republics, and the two grand-duchies of Mecklenburg, where the old feudal institutions, notwithstanding the urgent demands of the population and the admonition of the German Reichstag, had, in 1874, not been abolished. In the principality of Lippe-Detmold, the constitutional government has for some years been suspended in consequence of a conflict between the government and the representatives of the people. Prussia, Bavaria, Saxony, Würtemberg, Baden, and Hesse, have Diets consisting of two Chambers; all the other states have only one Chamber. In Prussia, Bavaria, Saxony, Würtemberg, Baden, Hesse, Brunswick, Schwarzburg, Waldeck, and Schaumburg-Lippe, women can succeed after the extinction of the male line; but not in the other states.

The number of professors and students at the German universities, in 1874, was as follows:

UNIVERSITIES.	States.	Professors.	Students.
Berlin	Prussia	178	3,573
Bonn	"	99	848
Breslau	"	106	1,086
Erlangen	Bavaria	54	445
Freiburg	Baden	52	289
Giessen	Hesse	58	365
Göttingen	Prussia	108	1,018
Greifswald	"	56	540
Halle	"	93	1,040
Heidelberg	Baden	107	640
Jena	Saxe-Weimar	67	396
Kiel	Prussia	60	205
Königsberg	"	77	617
Leipsic	Saxony	113	1,160
Marburg	Prussia	34	135
Munich	Bavaria	83	600
Rostock	Mecklenburg	80	823
Strasburg	Alsace-Lorraine	62	862
Tübingen	Würtemberg		
Würzburg	Bavaria		
Total		1,487	14,642

—in all, twenty universities, of which nine are in Prussia, three in Bavaria, two in Baden, one each in Würtemberg, Hesse, Saxony, Saxe-Weimar, Mecklenburg, and Alsace-Lorraine. Sometimes the Academy of Munster, containing the two faculties of Catholic theology and philosophy, is counted among the German universities. Each university has at least four faculties: theology, philosophy, law, and medicine. In Breslau, Bonn, and Tübingen, there is a Catholic and a Protestant theological faculty; Munich, Würzburg, and Freiburg, have only a faculty of Catholic theology; the others only of Protestant theology. In Bonn and Munich, some of the professors of Catholic theology are Old Catholics. Munich, Würzburg, and Tübingen have, moreover, a faculty of political economy; and Tübingen one of natural science.

At the following universities, outside of the German Empire, the German language is exclusively or predominantly used, and in the province of literature they may be counted as German universities:

UNIVERSITIES.	Countries.	Professors.	Students.
Basel	Switzerland	65	168
Berne	"	64	316
Dorpat	Russia	65	768
Gratz	Austria	67	975
Innspruck	"	59	641
Prague	"	120	1,811
Vienna	"	226	3,813
Zurich	Switzerland	72	316
Total		738	8,808

The German Empire has 10 polytechnic institutes, namely: 2 in Berlin, 1 in Munich, 1 in Stuttgart, 1 in Carlsruhe, 1 in Dresden, 1 in Hanover, 1 in Aix-la-Chapelle, 1 in Darmstadt, 1 in Brunswick, with an aggregate of 360 teachers and 4,428 students. The num-

ber of gymnasia in 1871 was 380 (209 in Prussia, 28 in Bavaria, 17 in Saxony, 16 in Würtemberg, 13 in Baden, 6 in Hesse, 12 in the Thuringian states, 9 in Mecklenburg, 4 in Oldenburg, 5 in Brunswick, 4 in Anhalt, 7 in the other German states, exclusive of Alsace-Lorraine); of Realgymnasia 14, of pro-gymnasia and Bürgerschulen of a higher grade, 485, with an aggregate number of 177,379 students, of whom 72.5 per cent. were Protestants, 18.8 per cent. Catholics, and 8.7 per cent. Israelites.

The budget of the empire for the year 1874, as declared by law of July 4, 1873, modified by supplementary laws of February 18 and April 27, 1874, estimates revenue and expenditures each at 449,428,000 reichsmarks (1 reichsmark = 23.8 cents). Of the revenue, 67,186,000 marks are contributions paid by the particular states pro rata of population. After refunding the war loans and the loans made by the North-German Confederation for marine purposes, the debts of the German Empire consist exclusively of treasury-notes which may be issued partly for increasing the working capital, and partly for carrying through the monetary reform. The law of April 20, 1874, provides that the German States are obliged to withdraw up to July 1, 1875, all their paper-money. As a substitute for it, imperial-bank notes to the amount of 120,000,000 marks were to be issued and to be distributed on December 1, 1874, among the particular states.

At the beginning of 1874 the German army consisted of 31,830 officers, 1,329,600 men, 814,970 horses, 2,700 field-guns, and 820 siege-guns. Of these, the number of troops available for service in the field within six weeks after mobilization was (excluding the transport and staff corps) 710,130 men, with 114,850 horses, and 2,082 field-guns. The above figures do not include the fourth battalions, consisting of 3,400 officers and 152,100 men, which are to be formed in case of war, or the Landsturm to be raised under the new law, submitted to the Reichstag in 1874, and adopted early in 1875, which would bring into the field a force, by the lowest computation, of 3,718 officers and 202,500 men. The total force at the disposal of Germany in the event of a war is therefore 38,948 officers and 1,684,200 men, excluding the surgeons and the hospital corps, and not taking into account the probability that the estimated force of the Landsturm will be considerably exceeded when its members are called upon to take the field. Under the new Landsturm Bill the Emperor may summon the Landsturm without requiring the consent of the State Council. To the Emperor alone belongs the right of organizing the new force, which is to be placed under the military code, and the individual members of which may be drafted into the Landwehr in case of necessity. This means that every able-bodied man in the country is placed at the Emperor's disposal for the reënforcement of the army in time of war.

The Emperor of Germany in September visited Kiel to witness the launch of the cuirassed frigate Frederick the Great. The new vessel was built at the Government wharf at Ellerbeck, and is exactly like the Borussia, launched in November last. With a bulk of 4,118 tons and steam-engines of 5,400 horsepower, it has a cuirass of 11 inches round the turrets and centre. Its armament is to consist of four 26-centimetre guns in the turrets and two 21-centimetre guns placed fore and aft. This is the seventh iron-cased frigate of the German navy; the eighth is expected to leave the stocks early in 1875. By that time Germany will be mistress of eight iron-cased frigates, carrying 92 guns of the very heaviest calibre (mostly 400 or 500 pounders) and set in motion by engines with a total of 48,500 horsepower. In addition to these first-class ships, there are three more iron-clads of minor proportions, making up together fifteen heavy guns, and 5,400 horse-power. Twelve corvettes, with 168 heavy guns and 18,600 horsepower, attended by 24 gunboats, mustering 59 guns and 8,850 horse-power, complete the fighting array of the youthful but aspiring fleet. Of the corvettes some have twenty, others ten or fifteen guns; three of the number carrying only five, with engines of above 2,000 horsepower, being intended to act on the Alabama plan in far-off seas. The names of these vessels are the Ariadne, Louisa, and Freya. The whole German navy, including, besides the above, three sailing-frigates and three sailing-brigs, already numbers 55 ships, 425 guns, 73,768 tons, and 84,770 horse-power. About 4,000 sailors, with 1,000 marines, 500 artillerymen, and officers in proportion, were in 1874 reported in the Blue-books. Next year will witness an increase of about 2,000 in consequence of the new iron-clads being equipped for active service. The tonnage of the German ships and the size of their guns are so uncommonly great that, though few in number, they are supposed to be more than a match for any navy, those of England, Russia, and France, excepted. If England were to man her navy for war, she would require 68,000 men, of whom 22,000 would have to be enlisted for the purpose. Russia, for the like object, wants 36,000; France, 33,570; Turkey, 21,000; Spain, 14,000; Germany, 13,-000; Austria, 11,530; Italy, 11,200; Holland, 6,260; Denmark, 4,890; Norway, 3,500; Portugal, 3,300; Sweden, about 3,000. Comparing the total of the German crews with those of the other states, we find it exceeded by England, Russia, France, Turkey, and Spain. Spain does not count, so much of her forces existing only on paper; nor can Turkey's numbers be relied upon, she being to a great extent dependent upon foreign help for the effective manning and officering of her ships. Hence the German navy is in reality inferior only to the British, Russian, and French; and even this statement requires to be qualified, German vessels being much more sparingly manned

than either the Russian or the French, and 13,000 German sailors being accordingly not so very much below the strength of 36,000 Russians or 33,570 Frenchmen as the figures would seem to indicate.

The German War Department early in 1874 ordered the fortifications on the eastern frontier to be completed as soon as practicable. The plans and estimates for these works had been approved some months before, but certain modifications were subsequently decided upon. At Posen the fortifications are to be on a much larger scale than was originally contemplated, and the works at Wilhelmshaven on the landside will also be greatly extended. At Kiel, besides the fortifications of Friedrichsort, two forts will be erected at Oberjägersberg and Korügen, on the right bank of the bay of Kiel. The harbor-works of the bay were much injured by the spring tides in 1874, and steps were to be taken to protect them against inundations. The dike at Friedrichsort will be provided for this purpose with a stone front, and the dredging-works in the dock at Ellerbeck are to be pushed forward as quickly as possible. The two monitors Rhein and Mosel, built for service on the Rhine by the Weser Ship-building Company, were fully equipped. They lie very low in the water, so as to present the smallest possible surface for the aim of an enemy's guns. Two heavy guns are placed in the centre turret, and to each vessel will be attached fifty infantry soldiers besides the crew.

The Governments of Germany and Great Britain exchanged the results of new inventions and experience made in the application of torpedoes. The importance of Prof. Abel's discovery of gun-cotton applied as explosive material, has induced the German Government to introduce its manufacture on the Continent. In May, Dr. Hertz, engineer of the torpedo department of the German Imperial Navy, was deputed by his Government to study the details of the manufacturing process on the spot. The German Government, in exchange, communicated to that of Great Britain the secret of the Hertz torpedo. It was expected that the introduction of the Hertz torpedo would simplify in a very great measure the English coast-defenses, as the great number of electric cables indispensable for the English topedo, as it exists at present, would become comparatively unnecessary.

The German Admiralty, in 1874, made great efforts to improve the ship-building industry of the empire. This is to be done, not only by having a considerable number of ships-of-war built in private ship-building establishments, but also by applying almost exclusively to German manufacturers for the machinery and other articles required for naval purposes. It is hoped by this means in a few years to make the German navy quite independent of foreign countries, both as regards ship-building and its other requirements. The slight development which has taken place in the German ship-building industry during the last few years is regarded as a circumstance very prejudicial to the power of Germany at sea, and, it the Government does not succeed in obtaining all it requires for the navy from private establishments, it will create factories of its own for that purpose. This will be especially necessary for iron plates and masts, which have hitherto had to be procured from abroad.

According to the new German Constitution, the German Empire constitutes one customs and one commercial territory, with a common customs line. Hamburg and Bremen have the right to remain outside the common line of customs until they themselves demand admittance. Both have entered the customs union for a part of their territory. Besides a part of Hamburg and Bremen, a few small districts of Baden (on the frontier of Switzerland) and of Prussia do not belong to the customs union. On the other hand, the customs union comprises the entire grand-duchy of Luxemburg, and one small commune of the Tyrol.

The movement of emigration from the ports of Bremen and Hamburg was as follows:

FROM	BREMEN.		HAMBURG.		Total of both Ports.
	Emigrants.	Vessels.	Emigrants.	Vessels.	
Germany................................	48,616	} 208	69,176	117	132,417
Other states...........................	14,625				
Total 1873............................	63,241	208	69,176	117	132,417
1872............................	80,345	208	74,406	119	154,751
1871............................	60,516	203	42,224	92	102,740
1870............................	46,781	140	32,556	71	79,337
Average, 1866–1870.............	62,516	191	43,574	97	106,030
1833–1872.............	1,337,284	7,217	.....	.....	} 2,078,098
1846–1872.............	....	.....	740,874	2,564	

The aggregate emigration from Germany, from 1820 to the end of 1872, is estimated at 3,040,000, of whom about 2,630,000 went to the United States.

The German Government has taken further steps for discouraging emigration to Brazil. The provincial authorities have been instructed to point out to would-be emigrants of whom they may hear the untrustworthiness of the information circulated in Europe, and to explain what misery and ruin hundreds of Germans have been cast into by their unwise resolution to seek a better home in Santa Leopoldina, Theodoro, and other Government colonies to which settlers are invited. As a further discouragement, reference is to be made to the intention of the Brazilian Government to import coolie laborers, whose companionship the Germans are scarcely expected to appreciate.

In the following table is given the movement of shipping in the German ports for the year 1873:

STATES.	SAILING VESSELS.		STEAMERS.	
	Number.	Tons.	Number.	Tons.
Entered.				
Prussia (1872).....	56,974	4,013,228	5,426	1,381,266
Hamburg............	5,263	1,887,648	2,588	1,408,515
Bremen............	2,562	750,273	493	466,235
Lubeck............	2,844	295,216	918	152,332
Oldenburg	2,593	152,727	29	6,833
Mecklenburg......	293	86,466	107	13,501
Cleared.				
Prussia (1872).....	55,083	4,611,598	5,437	1,378,142
Hamburg............	5,344	1,904,487	2,551	1,400,357
Bremen............	2,638	768,799	448	468,053
Lubeck............	2,837	297,203	917	151,794
Oldenburg........	2,881	153,505	43	11,820
Mecklenburg....	1,003	86,889	113	14,418

The commercial navy of Germany was, in 1873, composed as follows:

STATES.	SAILING VESSELS.		STEAMERS.		Horse-power.
	No.	Tons.	No.	Tons.	
Prussia	2,061	489,890	104	25,078	7,854
Hamburg......	409	196,358	80	75,748	16,633
Bremen.........	232	177,905	37	59,715	15,571
Mecklenburg...	416	107,657	7	2,619	398
Oldenburg	432	53,374	1	20	15
Lubeck.........	45	8,541	24	4,458	1,379
North-Sea fleet.	2,394	569,843	137	139,510	33,892
Baltic fleet.....	2,101	463,882	116	28,123	7,918
German " 1873.	4,495	1,033,725	253	167,633	41,750
Total, 1872 ...	5,082	1,308,988	229	165,178	29,139
1871 ...	5,122	1,305,819	180	130,892	24,211
1870 ...	5,219	1,330,761	150	107,642	20,727

The total length of railroads of Germany (and Luxemburg) open for traffic was as follows on January 1, 1874:

STATES.	State Roads.	Private roads under State administr'n.	Private Roads.	Total Roads.
Prussia.................	4,062	2,556	7,820	14,438
Other states of Northern Germany.	....	....	964	964
Oldenburg...........	138	...	....	138
Bavaria...............	1,801	315	1,180	3,296
Saxony...............	988	100	248	1,336
Würtemberg.........	1,141	....	7	1,148
Baden.................	1,013	134	....	1,147
Hesse.................	122	....	650	772
Alsace-Lorraine.....	864	....	.....	864
Luxemburg...........	....	170	....	170
Total, Jan., 1874..	10,129	3,275	10,869	24,273

The extension of electric telegraphs is shown by the following table (in kilometres; 1 kilometre = 0.62 mile):

TELEGRAPH	Imperial.	Bavaria.	Würtemberg.	Total.
Lines........	30,643	6,864	2,312	39,819
Wires........	104,440	23,379	4,959	132,778

The postal statistics of the empire and of Bavaria and Würtemberg, which retain their own postal administration, are as follows (value expressed in marks; 1 mark = 23.8 cents):

YEARS.	Post-Offices.	Revenue.	Expenditures.	Surplus.
Imperial mail (1872)	6,001	93,372,000	82,975,000	10,397,000
Bavaria " (1871)	1,115	6,807,000	6,241,000	566,000
Würtemberg mail (1872)....................	479	10,455,000	10,053,000	402,000
Total	7,595	110,634,000	99,269,000	11,365,000

The Director-General of the German Post-Office, Herr Stephan, in a lecture on postal and telegraphic communication in Germany, stated that the number of letters posted daily in Berlin is 240,000, and that 40,000 of these are town-letters. This makes one letter for every three persons. About 86,000,000 newspapers were sent by post from Berlin alone during the past year. The number of official letters posted yearly at Berlin is 75,000,000. Of the 500,000,000 letters dispatched by the Berlin post during the past year, 15 per cent. were official, 5 per cent. were addressed to persons connected with art and science, 35 per cent. to commercial men and manufacturers, and 45 per cent. to private persons. During the same period 10,000,000 telegrams were sent from Berlin. Of these 4 per cent. were official, 1 per cent. were newspaper telegrams, and 66 per cent. related to matters connected with commerce and the Stock Exchange. It is estimated that each betrothal in the educated classes brings in to the state, on the average, a sum of 100 marks for postage and telegrams. If the 350,000 betrothals which take place in Germany yearly (including 12,000 in Berlin) were all among persons of the educated class, this alone would represent a state revenue of 10,000,000 thalers. The amount of money sent daily through the post is 12,500,000 thalers, or 900 thalers a minute; 500,000,000 letters were sent abroad from Germany last year, and the gross yearly receipts of the German Post-Office amount to 32,000,000 thalers. The total income of all the post-offices of Europe is 125,000,000 thalers, and their expenditure 100,000,000; the difference of 25,000,000 is mainly shared between England and France. These post-offices have 180,000 employés, 33,000 of whom are in England, 27,000 in France, and 60,000 in Germany. Two-thirds of the German employés are married, and last year they had 107,000 children. Of the 3,300,000,000 letters posted yearly all over the world, 490,000,000 are forwarded to their destinations by means of international conventions, of which there are nearly 1,000. A letter from Christiania addressed to Melbourne has to pass through from twenty to thirty post-offices, belonging to nine different governments, speaking seven different languages.

The first legislative period of the German Reichstag having ended in 1873, a general election for a new Reichstag was held, on January 10, 1874, in all the German states except in Alsace-Lorraine, where it was postponed until February 1st. The most remarkable feature of these elections was the large in-

crease of the Centre, or Catholic party. In the severe conflict which, during the preceding year, had been carried on between the German Governments and the heads of the Catholic Church, the people of the Catholic districts, in an overwhelming majority, sided with the Church. In the first Reichstag, the Centre had numbered 57 members; in the second, it had 102, an increase of nearly 100 per cent. The victory of the party was not limited to one or a few portions of the empire, but a clean sweep had been made of nearly every district in which the Catholic population had a majority. Thus, Silesia sent 10 Catholic deputies against 1 in 1871; the Prussian Rhine province, 27 against 20; Bavaria, 32 against 15; Würtemburg, 3 against 1. Only the grand-duchy of Baden made an exception. There, also, 2 Catholic deputies were elected instead of 1 in 1871, but as this state sends 18 deputies, and as two-thirds of the entire population are Catholic, the Catholic party was again defeated in the large majority of the Catholic districts. Besides the Catholics, the Socialists (Social-Democraten) could boast of a remarkable success. In 1871 they only elected 2 of their candidates, in January 1874, 9. Of these no less than 6 belonged to the kingdom of Saxony, where the socialist party developed a strength which greatly surprised its opponents. They not only elected more than one-fourth of the entire representation, but the votes cast for their defeated candidates in other districts were so considerable, that their aggregate vote was estimated at more than 36 per cent. of the votes cast. To the Imperial Government and its supporters the remarkable success of the two parties which preëminently were designated as "hostile to the empire" (reichsfeindlich) was a cause of deep regret and some alarm. A consolation, however, was found in the fact that the ruling party of the first Reichstag, in whose platform the consolidation of the national unity was the chief plank, the National Liberals, had also increased about 30 per cent. (from 116 to 150 members). The party of Progress (Fortschritts-partei) numbered 48 against 44 members. The number of Poles remained the same, that of the Conservatives decreased from 40 to 21, that of the Free Conservatives or German Imperial party from 38 to 25. The Liberal Imperial party, consisting chiefly of Liberals of the middle states, became entirely extinct. Northern Schleswig again sent 1 Dane, but the electoral statistics showed the Danish majority to be on the wane. Of the 15 deputies elected by the new Reichsland Alsace-Lorraine, about one-half were in full sympathy with the Catholic Centre, while the others constituted the so-called French party of protest, which went to Berlin only to protest against the incorporation of Alsace-Lorraine with Germany. More than one-half of the new Reichstag, 221 of 397, had not been members of the first, and of the 20 members of the Frankfort Parliament of 1848, who had belonged to the first Reichstag, only 11 had been reëlected.

The Reichstag was opened on February 5th by Prince Bismarck, the Emperor, though he had recovered from a serious indisposition, having been dissuaded by his physicians from being present. The speech from the throne declared that the reorganization of Germany, as it resulted from the late war, was nearly complete; that a uniform legislation had been carried through nearly all subjects which, before the establishment of the empire, were regarded as common affairs of the North-German Confederation, and that thus the task which had occupied the Reichstag during its first legislative period had been for the most part accomplished. The representatives of the new Reichsland Alsace-Lorraine, who would for the first time again form part of a German legislature, were warmly welcomed. Among the drafts to be submitted to the Reichstag, the speech mentioned in the first line a new military law which would fulfill the promise given in the imperial constitution, and, by a full development of the military strength of the empire, comply with the first duty of every commonwealth to protect the independence of its territory, and the peaceable development of its inherent spiritual and economical strength. Another law was announced on the administration of the revenue and expenditures of the empire as well as on the composition and the jurisdiction of the Court of Accounts. On the draft of the new imperial press-law, it was said that the allied governments were endeavoring to harmonize the just claims to a free expression of opinion through the press with the equally just demands which public interest makes against the abuse of this freedom. An addition to the industrial laws of the country would provide for the appointment of courts of arbitration between employers and employés, and would prevent any illegal pressure being brought upon working-men for the enforcement of strikes, and the violation of contract. Very satisfactory statements were made on the financial results of the preceding year. In conclusion, it was said that the foreign relations of the empire encouraged the hope that all governments like that of Germany were determined to secure to the world the benefit of a lasting peace. The Emperor was especially encouraged in this hope by the repeated interviews with the monarchs of other countries, and by the continuance of friendly relations with nations which, by historical traditions, are closely allied with the German people.

All the parties of the Reichstag would have united in reëlecting as President Dr. Simson, who, in December, 1873, had celebrated the twenty-fifth anniversary of his election as President of German Parliaments, who had since then filled this important place almost without interruption, and during this time had impressed all the conflicting and changing parties with the conviction that in the whole history of legislative assemblies he had few equals, both in point of ability and impartiality. He was just recovering from a long indisposition, and his medical advisers unanimously warned him against taxing his still feeble health with the burden of a position which would require the most robust constitution. A deputation which, before the opening of Parliament, was sent to him by his political friends, returned with his decided refusal to accept the presidency of the new Reichstag. As soon as it was generally known that Dr. Simson was not a candidate for reëlection, the parties, with almost equal unanimity, agreed upon the election of Herr von Forckenbeck, for many years the President of the Prussian Diet, who, like Dr. Simson, had succeeded in gaining the esteem and entire confidence of all parties. As vice-presidents were elected the Bavarian Prince of Hohenlohe-Schillingsfürst and Dr. Hänel, the former, like Forckenbeck, a sympathizer with the principles of the National Liberals, the latter a member of the party of progress. The candidates of the Centre for the position of vice-presidents, the Bavarian Baron von Aretin and Peter Reichensberger, a member of the Supreme Court of Berlin, received 85 and 81 votes. In order to shorten the time, which during the first legislative period had been consumed by taking the yeas and nays whenever they had been called for, the English system of dividing was adopted; and it was provided that hereafter, whenever it is decided to take the yeas and nays, the members of the Reichstag will leave the hall and reënter through two side-doors, the yeas through one and the nays through the other, while the secretaries, stationed near the doors, will record the numbers. The new method, popularly called "the sheep's jump," gave general satisfaction.

Some drafts submitted to the Reichstag were promptly and almost without debate disposed of. Among them were a postal convention with Brazil, a treaty of extradition with Switzerland, a bill for limiting the jurisdiction of the German consuls in Egypt, and the bills for changing some articles of the invalid law, and regulating the indemnification to be paid to communes for war services. The law concerning compulsory vaccination called forth a very long debate between the medical experts in the Reichstag, all of whom were in favor of compulsory vaccination, and some members who looked upon it as an encroachment of individual liberty. It was finally passed with an amendment of Dr. Löwe, providing for the establishment of an Imperial Health Office, which is to superintend vaccination and in general the sanitary condition of the empire. The supplementary bills for the industrial legislation of the empire, by which the Government proposed to make compulsory strikes and the violation of contracts between employers and employés criminal offenses, drew forth a very decided opposition, not only on the part of the Socialists, but also on the part of members of the party of progress like Schulze-Delitzsch, and of National Liberals like Lasker, and it was finally referred to a committee, by which it was not reported back to the Reichstag. The law concerning the introduction of an imperial paper-money (the withdrawal of the paper-money of the particular states after January 1, 1875, having been previously resolved upon) was adopted by 180 against 80 votes. Deputy Mosle (representative of the city of Bremen) again defended ingeniously, but inefficiently, his ideas concerning the uselessness and danger of every kind of paper-money. Important concessions were made to the particular states for the purpose of facilitating the withdrawal of their own notes. The bill on the Court of Accounts was not reported during this first session from the Court of Accounts.

The most important among the bills introduced by members of the Reichstag was the one concerning the introduction of civil marriage. The bill, originating with Prof. Hinschius, of the University of Berlin, and Deputy Völk, one of the leaders of the Liberal party of Bavaria, had already engaged the attention of the first Reichstag, but had not passed to the third reading. The new discussion in the second Reichstag derived a special interest from the fact that the principle of civil marriage was defended by Prof. Baumgarten, of Rostock, a Protestant theologian of the orthodox school, who, on this question, disagrees with the immense majority of the orthodox Protestant clergy of Germany, and by one of the leaders of the Old Catholic movement, Prof. Schulte, of Bonn. The bill was finally adopted by a large majority. The motion for giving to the members of the Reichstag a compensation, which had been adopted in every session of the preceding Reichstag but not yet received the sanction of the Federal Council, was renewed by Schulze-Delitzsch, and again adopted by 229 against 79 votes.

On February 16th, the fifteen representatives of Alsace-Lorraine entered the Reichstag in solemn procession, headed by the Bishops of Metz and Strasburg. On the same day they offered a resolution to take a general vote of the people of Alsace-Lorraine on their incorporation with Germany, as it had been effected without consulting them. The motion was signed by all the fifteen members, three of whom had a French name, while the first, by a singular coincidence, had the name of Teutsch. A previous motion, that those deputies of Alsace-Lorraine who were not acquainted with the German language, be allowed to address the Reichstag in French, could not be discussed, because the unanimous consent, which, according to the by-laws, is required for the immediate discussion of a motion, was not given. The speech by Deputy Teutsch in support of his motion was full of invectives against Germany, but no reply was made to it, and the motion was voted down without discussion. After Deputy Teutsch had concluded his speech, Bishop Raess, of Strasburg, took occasion to declare that he and his co-religionists (M. Teutsch being a Protestant) did not call in question the Treaty of Frankfort, which had been concluded between two great powers. This recognition by the bishop of the treaty by which Alsace-Lorraine had been united with France, called forth many protests on the part of the population of the Reichsland, which, however, were never presented to the Reichstag. After the rejection of the motion, the members constituting the French party of protest, among them the Bishop of Metz, left Berlin without, however, resigning; the others, who sympathized more with the Catholic Centre than with the French-protest party, among them Bishop Raess, of Strasburg, and the parish-priests Guerber and Winterer, remained. They, in union with members of the Centre, moved the repeal of Art. X. of the law on the administration of Alsace-Lorraine, as it curtailed the freedom of the press and of association. The motion, which called forth a vigorous speech from Prince Bismarck, was rejected by 198 against 138 votes, the minority consisting of the representatives of Alsace-Lorraine, the entire Centre, the Poles, the Federalists, and the majority of the party of progress.

The most important subjects engaging the attention of the Reichstag were, the new press law, the new military law, and the church law. On the proposed new press law the views of the Federal Council and the majority of the Reichstag were widely different, but a special committee of fourteen, to which the bill was referred, succeeded in smoothing the way for a compromise. Though the Liberals were not quite satisfied with the compromise, they regarded the bill as agreed upon as a progressive measure, and an important reform when compared with the law previously in force. The preventive confiscation of papers, in order to bring them before the tribunal, is now limited to certain settled points, as high-treason, incitement to illegal acts, or to hatred and warfare of the citizens among themselves; but in these two latter cases only when there is immediate danger of a crime or a breach of the law being committed. At the same time, the stamp-tax and the *cautionnement* to which the papers were formerly subjected, especially in Prussia, and which for twenty years hindered the healthy development of the German press, will be abolished. The law took effect on July 1, 1874.

The new military law, which demanded the

definite formation of the German army on the unchangeable basis of three years' active service, and of 400,000 men as the peace-footing of the army, threatened to bring on a serious crisis. Not only the parties generally voting against the Government, but even the National Liberals, regarded it as incompatible with constitutional government to fix forever the peace effective of the army and thus withdraw it from the control of the Reichstag. Accordingly the first clause of the bill fixing the peace effective at 401,659 men was rejected. A speech in defense of the measure, by Field-Marshal Moltke, made a sensation in Europe. He pointed out how necessary it was for every great state, and especially for Germany, to have a numerous and powerful army. He added: "What we acquired in the space of six months, we shall have to protect by force of arms for half a century. France is imitating all the German army arrangements. How, then, can we give up what our opponents are adopting? Germany is opposed to any kind of offensive action; it is her duty to act on the defensive." Count von Moltke proceeded to enumerate the measures taken by France for increasing her armaments, notwithstanding the fact that the majority of the French people were convinced of the necessity for peace. He concluded by saying: "We have become a powerful nation, but we remain a peaceable people. We require an army, but not for purposes of conquest." The prospect of a serious misunderstanding between the Government and the Reichstag caused some alarm in the country, and petitions numerously signed, even by opponents of the Government, were sent to the Reichstag, asking the latter to avoid at all events a conflict with the Government. The special committee of twenty-eight, to which the bill had been referred, adopted a compromise proposed by Herr von Bennigsen, namely, that the peace effective of 401,659 men should be voted for seven years. When the bill came up for its second reading, the Minister of War, General von Kamecke, read a statement on the part of the Government, declaring that the leading object of clause 1 of the bill was not to fix the peace effective at a certain figure forever, nor to withdraw from the Parliament its control over the budget. Its object was that in the present state of Europe the army should be maintained at the strength which was absolutely necessary for the preservation of peace and the repulse of all attacks until such time as a change in the number of men might be agreed upon between the Federal Council and the Government. In the course of the debate, Federal Commissioner General Voigts-Rheetz pointed out that the Parliament had still great scope left for exercising control over the expenditure, in the discussion which must take place upon the military estimates. Moreover, he maintained that the German army budget and the military effective were relatively lower than those of other great powers, Germany occupying, in fact, in this respect, only the third place. The German Empire required a powerful army in order to carry on a vigorous policy, and an army that was feared in order to maintain peace. For these reasons, the number of the military forces could not be brought every year into question.

Field-Marshal Count von Moltke stated that his views upon the question were unchanged. He regarded a powerful Germany in the centre of Europe as the best guarantee of peace. In presence of the shouts which had been raised for revenge, it is necessary to keep a hand upon the sword. Disarmament would mean war; but he hoped the wisdom of the French Government would avert that misfortune. Germany, in the last war, had not abused her power. She could have forced the French Government to grant all her demands, but she only exacted back the land which a restless country had formerly torn from a weak neighbor. Count von Moltke added: "We must, moreover, have full confidence in the army; we absolutely require the number of men which has been proposed, and which Herr von Bennigsen's motion admits. I believe that the peace effective should be finally and not provisionally fixed; but laws are not made forever, and I shall vote for the provisional arrangement because I believe that a patriotic Parliament at the end of the seven years will sanction that which is indispensable in the interests of the Fatherland." The House then adopted the compromise proposed by Herr Bennigsen by 224 against 146 votes. The majority of the Progressists voted with the opposition. After a third reading on April 20th, the entire law was adopted by 214 against 123 votes.

The third important measure discussed by the Reichstag was the so-called Bishops' Bill intended to prevent the legal exercise of clerical functions when the ecclesiastic has been deprived by the special tribunal instituted for this purpose. Should he profess to be still in legal possession of his functions, he can be imprisoned in a particular district or locality by the local police. If he goes further, really exercising his former functions, or resisting, in fact, the powers of the police, the central administration may deprive him of his right of citizenship, and expel him from the German territory. He has a legal remedy in being able to lay before the tribunal the bases of the charges of which he is accused. In this manner he may still be immediately imprisoned by the police; but the expulsion, with the loss of the right of citizenship, is suspended till the tribunal has decided on his appeal. The debate on the third reading of the bill lasted for three days, and was often very stormy. The Progressive party, in union with the National Liberals and the Conservatives, supported the Government, and the bill was adopted by 214 against 108 votes.

The Reichstag was closed by the Emperor on April 26th. The speech from the throne passed in review the laws voted during the past important session, and, mentioning first the Army Bill, described it as a measure guaranteeing the protection of the Fatherland and the peace of Europe. The Federal Government accepted the compromise proposed on the question in order to assure a steady development of the Constitution and obtain a basis for a general understanding in the interest of the newly-acquired national institutions. The Federal Government trusted that in this respect the country and future Parliaments would feel convinced that it was necessary to secure a durable, even maintenance of the national defensive strength, and establish a legal basis for the annual debate on the budget in order to give the requisite firmness to the constitution of the army. The Emperor thanked the House for the improvements introduced in the law affecting military invalids. He then adverted to the understanding arrived at respecting the bill for the issue of Imperial Treasury notes, a measure calculated to satisfy the commercial community. His Majesty considered the late votes of the Reichstag in furtherance and support of his policy as confirming his conviction that the Fatherland has a prosperous future before it, and that Europe will find a pledge of peace and assurance for the development of culture in the care bestowed upon the mental, moral, and material strength of Germany.

The fall session of the German Parliament was opened on October 29th by the Emperor William in person. In his speech from the throne his Majesty said that the legislative labors which awaited the members were no less important than in former sessions. Bills intended to secure unity of judicial procedure would be laid before them. Bills for completing the imperial military system would also be submitted. One of these referred to the Landsturm, and another regulated the proportion to be paid by each state for the maintenance of the army in time of peace. Measures respecting the currency would also be brought forward. For the first time the House would be called upon to coöperate in establishing a budget for Alsace and Lorraine. Owing to the resolution passed last session, bills had been drawn up by the Federal Council rendering civil marriage obligatory throughout the empire. The treaty signed at Berne, establishing a postal union, would be of great advantage. In conclusion, his Majesty spoke of the friendly relations of the empire with foreign powers, and said that the pacific intentions of his Government enabled it to disregard all unjust suspicions against its policy. The speech was received with much applause, and at its close Prince Bismarck declared the Parliament opened. President Forckenbeck was reëlected by the vote of all parties; Dr. Hänel was reëlected second Vice-President; and, instead of

Prince Hohenlohe, who had been appointed German embassador in Paris, Baron von Stauffenberg was elected first Vice-President. President Forckenbeck soon after resigned because one of his parliamentary decisions had been overruled, but, having been reëlected by a unanimous vote, consented to remain in office. In the debate on the budget of Alsace-Lorraine, the deputies from Alsace-Lorraine raised objections and opposed too high an endowment of the Strasburg University and payments for educational purposes which were made in the interest of the empire, but not of the provinces themselves. Prince Bismarck, in reply, made a speech, in which he said:

The question before us concerns the interests of the empire; it is not a question of Alsace-Lorraine. The University is to serve imperial purposes. In the well-fought war in which we had to defend our existence we conquered the provinces for the empire. It was not for Alsace-Lorraine that our soldiers shed their blood. We take our stand upon the interests of the empire and imperial policy. Alsace-Lorraine was indeed annexed on similar grounds, and not for the sake of Alsace-Lorraine's ecclesiastical interests. We have in the empire other grounds of action than those gentlemen whose past leads them to Paris, and whose present conducts them to Rome. We have to think of the empire, and for that purpose we have summoned representatives from the annexed provinces to Berlin. My views respecting an Alsace-Lorraine Parliament, which were at first too sanguine, are still entertained by me in principle, but have, nevertheless, been modified since I have become acquainted with the attitude of the Alsace-Lorraine deputies present here. Such a Parliament would lead to continual agitation, and perhaps endanger the maintenance of peace. It would be difficult to set aside such an institution if created by legislative means, and therefore that method of creating it could not be adopted. In school matters we have energetically interfered, but we shall no doubt have to take still more vigorous steps. We could not permit elements to exist in the schools which labor, I will not exactly say to make the children stupid, but yet which take care that people do not become too wise. My action in regard to Alsace-Lorraine will always be guided by the interests of the empire and its safety, and I shall not be frightened from my course by reproaches, threats, intimidation, or persuasion; but before I can decisively advance further on my course, I must be convinced that there are elements which can be trusted. We may expect better discernment from the rising generation, and we must therefore see that good schools are provided.

The discussion on the imperial budget furnished an opportunity to the Catholic deputies, Jörg and Windthorst, to attack the foreign policy of Bismarck, who replied by a severe censure of the Catholic party. The Reichstag approved of the proposition of the Federal Council, not to make any appropriation for an embassador near the Pope. Prince Bismarck, commenting upon the resolution to cancel the post of envoy to the Vatican, said:

The Pope being a purely religious chief, there was no occasion to keep a permanent political representative at his court. Things, indeed, might have been left in statu quo had not the present Pope, a true member of the Church militant, thought fit to revive the ancient struggle of the Papacy and temporal power, and more especially with the German Empire. The spirit animating the Papacy in this campaign was too well known to require comment; still, he would tell the House a story which had been long kept secret, but which, after all that had happened, had better be made public. In 1869, when the Würtemberg Government had occasion to complain of the action of the Papacy, the Würtemberg envoy at Munich was instructed to make representations; and in a conversation which passed between the envoy and the nuncio, the latter said the Roman Church was free only in America, and perhaps England and Belgium. In all other countries the Roman Church had to look to revolution as the sole means of securing her rightful position. This, then, was the view of the priestly diplomatist stationed at Munich in 1869, and formerly representing the Vatican at Paris. Well, the revolution so ardently desired by the Vatican did not come to pass, but we had the war of 1870 instead. Gentlemen, I am in possession of conclusive evidence proving that the war of 1870 was the combined work of Rome and France; that the Œcumenical Council was cut short on account of the war; and that very different votes would have been taken by the Council had the French been victorious. I know from the very best sources that the Emperor Napoleon was dragged into the war very much against his will by the Jesuitical influences rampant at his court; that he strove hard to resist these influences; that in the eleventh hour he determined to maintain peace; that he stuck to this determination for half an hour, and that he was ultimately overpowered by persons representing Rome.

Herr von Varnbüler (Würtemberg premier in 1869) then confirmed all Prince Bismarck had related of his negotiations with Rome and the statement of Monsignor Meglia. The negotiations, he said, originated in an attempt of the Pope to deprive Würtemberg students of Catholic lectures, the Vatican being of opinion that the less educated a priest, the more fitted he was for his vocation in life. Dr. Löwe, a Liberal member, who had moved that the German legation be abolished, closed the debate by reminding the House of the truth expressed by their great philosopher Fichte, when he said that the commonwealth of united Germany could be established only upon the basis of personal and intellectual liberty. The arrest of a member of the Reichstag, Majunke, led to the adoption of a resolution, moved by Hoverbeck, to request the Imperial Chancellor for an interpretation of Art. XXXI. of the Constitution, in order to prevent the arrest of members of the Reichstag during the session without the consent of the Reichstag. Prince Bismarck regarded this resolution as the expression of a want of confidence, and therefore tendered his resignation, which the Emperor, however, refused to accept. The Reichstag soon after expressed its continuing confidence in the Chancellor by a vote of 199 against 71. On December 19th, the Reichstag adjourned to January 9, 1875.

The foreign relations of Germany were on the whole of a friendly character. The language used by some French bishops and some organs of the Catholic party against the German Government, led to remonstrances in Paris, which had the desired effect. The appointment in May of Prince Hohenlohe as German embassador in Paris in place of Count Harry von Arnim, who, contrary to his instructions, had favored the plans of the Legitimists, and the appointment of the Duke de Decazes as French Minister of Foreign Affairs, greatly strengthened the hope for the continuance of friendly relations. The Emperor of Russia, in May, paid another visit to Berlin, when he gave free and emphatic expression to the feelings of sympathy which he has always felt for Germany. The report that the attitude of Germany with regard to Denmark had given great offense in St. Petersburg was explicitly denied by Prince Bismarck in the German Reichstag. In consequence of the shooting, by order of the Spanish Pretender Don Carlos, of the German captain Hermann Schmidt, who was a correspondent of German papers with the republican army, two German gunboats, the Nautilus and the Albatross, were sent from Kiel to the Spanish waters for the protection of the life and property of German subjects from the Carlists. As it was deemed too difficult to inflict a direct retaliation upon the Carlists for the outrage, Prince Bismarck had to content himself with punishing the Carlists by a recognition of the Republican Government of Spain, and by securing its recognition by all other European powers, except Russia. On December 11th and 12th the Carlists committed a new outrage against Germany by the capture of the brig Gustav, belonging to Messrs. Koch & Son of Rostock. From the account of the incident given by Herr Rudolph Sprenger, German acting consul at San Sebastian, it appears that while the crew were trying to escape the fury of the sea and enter the harbor of Guetaria, they were forced out to sea again by the Carlists firing more than two thousand rounds at them. The ship soon after ran ashore, one portion of the crew being saved by Republican boats and another falling into the hands of the Carlists, who appropriated to them everything that could be saved, private property of the crew no less than the freight. The continuance of friendly relations with Denmark seemed for a time to be threatened by the expulsion of some Danes from Northern Schleswig, but the difficulty was peaceably adjusted. Prince Bismarck, on this occasion, was again charged with entertaining the desire that Denmark itself should enter the German Federation. It is asserted positively that Prince Bismarck had submitted to the Danish King a project for entering the German Empire with the whole of his territory. In accordance with this plan, Germany would guarantee the integrity of Denmark and cede the whole of Schleswig to King Christian, in return for which the Danish fleet would become an integral part of the German fleet, and German ports would be established in the different Danish colonies. King Christian was said to have rejected these propositions. It was added that Russia felt greatly irritated on receiving this intelligence, and would never allow Germany to hold the key to the Baltic. This incident was said to have exercised great influence upon Russia's policy with regard to Spain, and to have induced the Emperor, when he received a letter from Don Carlos thanking him for not having recognized Marshal Serrano's Government, to send an immediate reply.

The views of Prince Bismarck concerning the relations between Germany and Austria were forcibly expressed in an interview which the Hungarian author and deputy, Manus Jokai, had with him at Berlin. The latter published an account of it in his Hungarian paper *Hon*, from where it passed into most of the leading newspapers of Europe without calling forth any contradiction from M. Bismarck. "It is necessary," the prince said, "that in the centre of Europe there should be a consolidated state such as the Austro-Hungarian monarchy. I was already convinced of this, as I hastened to conclude peace in 1866—a course which many of our friends did not like. The German race is destined to rule on this side of the Leitha, and the Hungarian race beyond it. The remaining races in Austro-Hungary make also good soldiers, but in administrative ability, statesmanship, intelligence, and wealth, the Germans and Hungarians are superior. All are kept together by a common history. The establishment of small states of separate nationality is impossible in the east of Europe; merely historical states are possible. For this reason the present dualistic form of government ought to be maintained in Austro-Hungary. Your history, too, is the same as that of Austria; it has become so owing to your common combats. Formerly you attacked side by side, but now you need each other for your mutual defense." The prince continued :

Some of our good friends suspect us of intending to annex the German portion of Austria. Is it really possible for any one to imagine that we are going to burden ourselves with some more priest-ridden provinces? Or are we such habitually imprudent people that we are likely to go in for conquest when we have already Alsace and Northern Schleswig on our hands? But the worst of all is that, for military reasons, which we had no right to slight, we have been obliged to appropriate a strip of French-speaking country in Lorraine. Oh, those Frenchmen! Those implacable savages! Just scratch the Parisian cook, tailor, or *perruquier*, and you will not be long in discovering the Red Indian underneath all his superficial gloss. No, we have to stand sentinel against the French, who are our mortal enemies, and we have no idea of involving ourselves in fresh troubles on the eastern frontier likewise. It would be a nice mess indeed to increase the German Empire by so many provinces bent upon pilgrimaging and that sort of thing! Besides, Vienna and Pesth are destined to become the commercial centres of the southeast ; but of what use would Vienna be to us as a mere border town? The more I think about it the more convinced I am that a German minister who should prepare to annex Austrian territory would deserve to be strung up without more ado. For myself, all I can say is this—that I should be tempted to go to war to keep the German-Austrians out of Germany rather than admit them. But in all probability Austria will enjoy a prolonged peace.

The Governments and the Diets of the small-er states continued to show themselves friendly to the progressive consolidation of German unity. Though, at the elections for the German Reichstag in Bavaria, a majority of the electoral districts had chosen deputies who were stanch opponents of Prince Bismarck and his policy, the Government acted, in all important questions, in full concord with the Central Government, and the King personally took more than one occasion to assure the chancellor of his special regard and admiration. The King of Würtemberg declared himself very emphatically in favor of national unity. When he closed, in June, the parliamentary session of his kingdom, and thanked the Diet for the zeal and devotion it had displayed in its deliberations, he dwelt upon the voting of the treaties concluded with Prussia as the most important because they were the most significant fruit of the national successes, for they were concluded for the purpose of reëstablishing the unity of Germany through the Emperor and empire. In the kingdom of Saxony, the party of progress was anxious to save as many of the sovereign rights of the states as possible, and carried, by its votes, the maintenance of a special Saxon embassy in Munich, but the suspicion that the Government of the new King would be found in open opposition to the Central Government proved unfounded. In Baden and Hesse the Governments and Diets are ardent supporters of the national unity and of the Central Government. In the grand-duchy of Mecklenburg, which is still without a constitutional form of government, a new attempt to introduce a liberal constitution was again defeated by the obstinate resistance of the knighthood. In the principality of Lippe, where, in consequence of the long conflict between the Government and the Diet, the constitutional form of government had been for some time suspended, the Liberal party declined to attend a Diet which had been called by the Government for settling the difficulty.

The conflict between the Government of Prussia and the Roman Catholic Church (*see* PRUSSIA) not only continued during the year, but more and more extended to the smaller states. The legislation of Baden is in full accordance with that of Prussia, and even anticipated that of Prussia in regulating by law the relation of the Old Catholics to the Roman Catholic Church, and acknowledging their claim to a share of the Catholic Church property. In the grand-duchy of Hesse laws for the regulation of Church affairs were prepared almost identical with those which, in 1873, were adopted in Prussia. A bishop elected by the Old Catholics was recognized as a bishop of the Catholic Church by the Governments of Prussia, Baden, and Hesse ; the Government of Bavaria, however, though in general agreeing with the other Federal Governments in the legislation on Church questions, refused the recognition of the Old Catholic bishop on the ground that it was incompatible with the

Bavarian Concordat, which, in the opinion of the Government, was still in force. The bishop of Mentz, Baron von Ketteler, one of the most influential Catholic prelates of Germany, dissuaded the Catholics from taking part in the national celebration of the victory of Sedan (September 2d); on this question, however, other prelates, like the Bishop of Passau, and the Vicar Apostolic of the kingdom of Saxony, were of a different opinion, and large numbers of priests and congregations took part in the patriotic solemnities.

The German Government professed to see in Alsace-Lorraine the beginning of a change in the public sentiment relating to its separation from France and reunion with Germany. The consideration that a continued attitude of open and fanatical hostility to the German authority could not fail to injure fatally the material interests of the province, greatly aided in the formation of an altogether new party of conciliation, whose cry is the autonomy of the province. The supporters of this accept frankly the separation from France as an accomplished fact, and direct their labors toward preventing Alsace-Lorraine from being made an integral part of any of the older German states. In fact, they desire not to be made Prussians or Bavarians, although they have become Germans against their will, and claim, therefore, a completely independent administration as the price of full reconciliation with the empire. This view is finding large acceptance with the more sober part of the well-to-do classes, which feels the struggle against the results of the late war to be hopeless. In the second half of August, all the three District Councils of Alsace-Lorraine met, and, without hesitation, took the oath of allegiance to the German Emperor. Of the twenty-five members constituting the Council of Lower Alsace, the only absentee was Dr. Schneegans, a barrister, who was excused on account of ill-health. Herr Julius Klein, a chemist, of Strasburg, and one of the leaders of the party of autonomy, was elected president. The District Council of Upper Alsace met like that of Lower Alsace, on August 17th, and all the members but one were in their places and took the oaths; among them being the Burgomasters of Mühlhausen and Colmar. At the opening of the District Council of Lorraine, twenty-six members were present. Twenty-four of these had already taken the oaths at the last session, and the oaths were subsequently administered to the two others. Two members who had been sworn were excused from attending.

On July 13th a fanatical mechanic, Kullmann, attempted to assassinate Prince Bismarck in the watering-place of Kissingen. The prince, who had just lifted his arm for a salutation, was slightly wounded, and the would-be assassin was promptly arrested. His trial before the court of assizes at Würzburg was begun on October 31st. In his examination by the president of the tribunal, Kullmann

admitted every thing brought against him, and gave his reasons for attempting the crime. He first thought of assassinating Prince Bismarck last Easter, when at Magdeburg. He purchased a pistol and went to Berlin, but watched in vain for the prince. He then went to Kissingen, but did not make the attempt on the Sunday, owing to the sacredness of the day, but waited till Monday. He aimed at the head of the prince, having heard that he wore a coat-of-mail on his breast, as in 1865. He admitted the heinousness of the crime, but justified it on the ground of the policy adopted by Prince Bismarck toward the Church. For the defense, two medical men were called, who both expressed the opinion that the accused was of weak intellect, and that hereditary influences had affected his mental and moral development. The counsel for the prosecution urged that, as Kullmann knew the magnitude of his crime and the punishment awaiting it, he must be considered a responsible agent. In reply, the counsel for the defense maintained that it was not Kullmann who was guilty, but the influences which impelled him to commit the deed. His mind, excited by Ultramontane teaching, was in an abnormal condition, and, as he was unconscious of his acts, a verdict of not guilty should be returned. The jury returned into court with a verdict of guilty, and the president sentenced the accused to fourteen years' imprisonment, and at the expiration of that time to deprivation of his civil rights for ten years. Kullmann manifested no surprise on hearing the sentence, and refused to avail himself of his right of appeal.

On October 4th Count Harry von Arnim, formerly German embassador in Paris, was arrested and conveyed to the city jail of Berlin, on the charge of having abstracted documents which he received in his official character as German embassador in Paris. Count Arnim had been recalled from Paris at the beginning of May, because he had not only openly expressed his dissent from the policy of Prince Bismarck, but even furnished to Austrian and Belgian papers articles attacking him. With regard to the documents he was charged with having abstracted, he claimed that they were confidential letters, and therefore his property. The trial began on December 9th, before the City Court of Berlin, which sentenced the count to three months' imprisonment, a decision from which both the state attorney and Count Arnim appealed. It clearly appeared from the trial that the count had hoped, in concert with the Conservative and Catholic opponents of Bismarck, to dislodge the latter from his exalted position, and to become his successor.

Max von Forckenbeck, the new President of the German Reichstag, was born at Münster, on October 21, 1821. Having studied law at the Universities of Giessen and Berlin, he was, in 1847, appointed judge at Glogau, in Silesia. In the revolutionary year of 1848 he began to take an active part in German politics as President of the Democratic Constitutional Society of Breslau. In 1849 he established himself as attorney in Elbing, Eastern Prussia. His connection with the legislative assemblies of Germany began in 1858, and has never ceased since. Being first elected for the district of Mohringen, he subsequently represented in turn the cities of Königsberg, Cologne, and Elbing. In 1866 the Chamber of Deputies elected him president, and he was at every following session of the Diet reëlected to this position until, in 1873, he was elected Burgomaster of the city of Breslau, and as such became a member of the Prussian Herrenhaus. Among the many important reports which he prepared in the name of different committees, that on the army question was especially valued. He was also elected member of the Constituent and the regular Reichstag of the North-German Confederation (Norddeutsche Bund), and of the first and second Reichstag of the German Empire. The latter, as has already been stated, elected him president by the unanimous vote of all parties. When, in the fall of 1874, he deemed it necessary to resign his position as president because the Reichstag had overruled one of his decisions, it was Deputy Windthorst, the leader of the Catholic Centre, and one of the most determined opponents of the political principles of Forckenbeck, who, in warm words of admiration, and amid the applause of all parties, moved his reëlection by acclamation, which was carried without a dissenting vote. Forckenbeck has been a prominent exponent of the principles of the National Liberals, to which party he has belonged since its formation. By birth a Catholic, Forckenbeck supports, with his political party, the Prussian laws on Church affairs, and in 1873 accepted a position as member of a new ecclesiastical court, which is to exercise the rights of the state over all the churches recognized by the state, and the establishment of which was so severely denounced by the Catholic bishops and the Catholic party.

MARTIN EDUARD SIMSON, the President of the first Reichstag of the German Empire, occupies a prominent position in the constitutional history of Germany since 1848. He was born at Königsberg, November 10, 1810, and after studying law at the Universities of Königsberg, Berlin, and Bonn, was appointed in 1831 Privatdocent and in 1843 professor at the University of Königsberg. In 1848 he was deputed by his native city to the German National Assembly, which at once elected him secretary, in September vice-president, and in December president, in place of Heinrich von Gagern, who had become prime-minister. He was reëlected president from month to month until the end of May, 1849, when he had to decline on account of severe indisposition. When in November, 1848, a conflict arose at Berlin between the Government of Prussia and

the Prussian National Assembly, Simson was commissioned by the National Assembly of Frankfort to attempt a mediation. In April, 1849, he headed the deputation of the Frankfort Assembly, which was to notify the King of Prussia of his election as German Emperor. In May, 1849, he left the Frankfort Assembly, and in August of the same year entered the second Prussian Chamber as deputy of his native city. In March, 1850, he was elected President of the Lower House of the Reichstag of Erfurt, which had been called by the King of Prussia and his allies to attempt again the union of the German states. When this project was abandoned, he reëntered the second Prussian Chamber, where he was one of the leaders of the Opposition against the policy of the ministry. Dissatisfied with the course of the Government, he declined, in 1852, a reëlection into the second Chamber, and retired from political life. In 1858, when the Prince of Prussia, as regent, formed a liberal ministry, he again accepted a mandate for the second Chamber, which in 1860 and 1861 elected him president, and in October, 1861, deputed him as its representative to the coronation of King William at Königsberg. He remained a member of the second Chamber until 1867, when he became a member of the Reichstag of the North-German Confederation. He was the permanent president of this Reichstag as well as the Customs Parliament, and in December, 1870, headed the so-called "Imperial Deputation," which expressed to King William the assent of the North-German Reichstag to the restoration of the German Empire. The first Reichstag of the restored German Empire elected him president in all of its sessions, and so high was the esteem in which he was held by all parties, that none of them ever thought of putting up a candidate against him. The reëlection as President by the second Reichstag, in 1874, he had to decline on account of failing health. His chair at the University of Königsberg he had given up in 1846, when he was appointed councillor of the so-called Tribunal of the Kingdom of Prussia. In 1860 he became vice-president, and in 1869 first president, of the Court of Appeal at Frankfort-on-the-Oder.

PRINCE CHLODWIG KARL VICTOR VON HOHENLOHE SCHILLINGSFÜRST, first Vice-President of the first German Reichstag, has long been known as a leading statesman of Bavaria. He is descended from one of the oldest princely families of Germany, and was born March 31, 1819. In 1834 he inherited, with his elder brother Victor, from the last Landgrave of Hesse-Rheinfeld-Rotenburg, the duchy of Ratibor, the principality of Corvey, the dominion of Treffurt, and other territories. In 1840 the King of Prussia conferred upon his brother Victor the title of Duke of Ratibor, and upon him that of Prince of Ratibor and Corvey. He resigned his claim to the dominion of Schillingsfürst in Bavaria in favor of his younger brother

Philip, after whose death in 1845, and in virtue of an agreement with his elder brother, Victor, concluded on October 15, 1845, he succeeded, on February 12, 1846, as Prince of Hohenlohe-Schillingsfürst, and became as such a member of the first Chamber of Bavaria. On January 1, 1867, he succeeded Baron von der Pfordten as Minister of Foreign Affairs and of the royal house, and as such declared himself to be a decided friend "of a closer union of the German states on a basis compatible with the sovereignty of the particular states." As the most prominent representative of the South-German Liberals, he was elected by the German Customs Parliament its first vice-president. On the convocation of the Vatican Council, he endeavored to bring about a coalition of European powers for preventing the proclamation of papal infallibility, but the plan failed in consequence of the opposition of France and Austria. He resigned his place in the ministry on March 8, 1870, and on the outbreak of the war was a foremost champion of the national war against France, and subsequently of the restoration of the German Empire. The first German Reichstag, in which he belonged to the Liberal Imperial party (Liberale Reichspartei), a union chiefly of South-German Liberals, elected him first vice-president by a large majority, and in 1874 he was reëlected to the same position during the first session of the second Reichstag. In May, 1874, he was appointed by the Emperor as German embassador in Paris. — His eldest brother, Victor, Duke of Ratibor, born in 1818, is also a member of the German Reichstag. Another brother, Gustav, born in 1823, is a cardinal. He was in 1873 appointed German embassador near the Pope, but not accepted by the Pope.

BARON FRANZ AUGUST SCHENCK VON STAUFFENBERG, Vice - President of the German Reichstag, the scion of an old noble family of Bavaria, was born on August 3, 1834, at Würzburg. After studying at the Universities of Würzburg and Heidelberg, he entered the service of the Bavarian Government, and was for several years state attorney. In 1866 he left the public service and entered the Bavarian House of Deputies, in which he at once became one of the leading members of the party of progress, and took an active part in all the important discussions. In November, 1873, he was elected President of the second Bavarian Chamber, and in November, 1874, first Vice-President of the German Reichstag, in the place of his friend the Prince of Hohenlohe, who had been appointed German embassador in Paris.

DR. ALBERT HÄNEL, the second Vice-President of the German Reichstag, was born on July 10, 1830, at Leipsic. After studying law at the Universities of Vienna, Leipsic, and Heidelberg, he was appointed Privatdocent at the University of Leipsic. In 1860 he became professor at Königsberg, and in 1863 at Kiel.

He has been a member of the Prussian House of Deputies since 1867 for one of the Schleswig-Holstein districts, and was also elected by Schleswig - Holstein to the North - German Reichstag, and to the first and second Reichstag of the German Empire, where he was one of the most prominent members of the party of progress. Dr. Hänel is a very prolific writer on law-questions, and was one of the chief advisers of Prince Frederick of Augustenburg when the latter pressed his claims to the succession in Schleswig-Holstein before the Federal Diet of Germany.

GRANT, ROBERT EDMUND, M. D., F. R. S., a distinguished British comparative anatomist, zoologist, professor, and author, born in Edinburgh, November 11, 1793; died in London, August 21, 1874. He was of an excellent family, and received his early education in the High School, Edinburgh, whence he proceeded to the university of that city. He entered upon his medical studies with such zeal, and distinguished himself so greatly by his devotion to anatomical and physiological investigations, that he was elected President of the Medico-Chirurgical and Royal Medical Societies of Edinburgh before he was twenty-one years of age. In May, 1814, he received his diploma as member of the Royal College of Surgeons, and a month later graduated M. D. from the University of Edinburgh. He spent the next six years in professional studies, in the universities and medical schools on the Continent, and in 1820 returned to Edinburgh and commenced the practice of his profession there. He soon commenced lecturing on comparative anatomy in Edinburgh, and his lectures were largely attended. He also contributed many valuable papers to the *Scientific Journal*. A series of papers on the "Structure and Functions of the Sponge" gained for him a high reputation. At the organization of University College, one of the institutions which grew up into the London University, he was offered the professorship of Comparative Anatomy and Zoology, and accepted it, delivering his first lecture October 23, 1828. He retained this professorship for more than forty years. He also delivered courses of lectures on the structure and classification of animals before the London Zoological Society, and in 1837 was appointed Fullerian Professor of Anatomy and Physiology in the Royal Institution of Great Britain, and for some years delivered the courses of lectures on paleontology on the Swiney foundation. He was made a Fellow of the Royal Society a few years after his removal to London, and contributed largely to its Transactions. In 1835 he commenced his great work, "Outlines of Comparative Anatomy, presenting a Sketch of the Present State of Knowledge, and of the Progress of Discovery in that Science, designed to serve as an Introduction to Animal Physiology and to the Principles of Classification in Zoology," of which the first volume was published in 1835 or

1836; but, amid the engrossing labors of his various professorships, and other literary and scientific pursuits, the subject grew to proportions too vast for him to be able to do full justice to it, and the work was never completed. In 1836 he became joint-editor, with Dr. R. B. Todd, of "The Cyclopædia of Anatomy and Physiology," and was active in other literary undertakings. Prof. Grant was an admirable scientific lecturer, a very skillful and careful anatomist, and generally an accomplished scientist. He was a member of most of the British and Continental scientific societies.

GREAT BRITAIN, or, THE UNITED KINGDOM OF GREAT BRITAIN AND IRELAND. Area, 121,115 square miles, or 77,828,829 statute acres.* Population in 1871, 31,628,338, exclusive of men in the army, navy, and merchant service abroad. Estimated population in 1874, on the basis of the registration reports of births and deaths, the same classes being excluded, 32,412,010. This is probably about 120,000 less than the actual population, and the increase is confined to England and Scotland, Ireland constantly diminishing in the number of its inhabitants. This population and area constitute but a small portion of the British Empire, which with its colonies and dependencies embraces about one-third of the surface of the globe, and nearly a fourth of its population. For a more complete statement of these, see GREAT BRITAIN, COLONIAL POSSESSIONS AND DEPENDENCIES OF. The government is a limited constitutional monarchy, consisting of the sovereign, and the Houses of Lords and Commons, without whose joint approval no legislative measure is complete, though a large discretion is left to the Executive. The executive government of Great Britain and Ireland is vested nominally in the crown, but practically in a committee of ministers, commonly called the cabinet, which has come to absorb the functions of the ancient Privy Council, as well as those of "the King in Council." The members of the cabinet, bearing the title of Right Honorable, are sworn "to advise the sovereign according to the best of their cunning and discretion," and "to help and strengthen the execution of what shall be resolved." Though not the offspring of any formal election, the cabinet is virtually appointed by Parliament, and is essentially a creature of the House of Commons, its existence being dependent on its being sustained by a majority in that body. As its acts are liable to be questioned in Parliament, and require prompt explanation, it is essential that the members of the cabinet should have seats either in the House of Lords or the Commons, where they become identified with the general policy and

acts of the Government. As the members of the House of Lords are by virtue of their rank entitled to seats in that body, there is no occasion for the members of the cabinet who are peers, to appeal to the people at their entry into the cabinet; but it is the custom, sanctified by prescription, for those cabinet officers who are members of the House of Commons, to resign their seats when they accept office, and pass, at least, through the form of a new election. Thus in the last resort, the actual ruling power in the United Kingdom, from which all government proceeds, is the House of Commons. The power of the sovereign is almost wholly nominal; whatever may be the private or personal views of the Queen on matters of public policy, she must be governed by the opinions of her ministers, and they can only remain in power so long as they sustain the views of the majority in the House of Commons. Whenever a vote expressing, either directly or indirectly, lack of confidence in the ministry, passes the House of Commons, that ministry must resign, or dissolve the session of Parliament and appeal to the people by means of an election; if in the election a majority of members of the Commons are elected who are opposed to the ministry, the Queen is obliged to call the leader of the opposition to form a new ministry, to whom the government shall be intrusted. There are indeed many privileges and vested rights belonging to the aristocracy, which make the government of the country in some sense an oligarchy; and suffrage, though much more extensive than it was fifty or even ten years since, is still far from being universal; there are also many abuses, and special burdens and wrongs, to be abolished before the Government of Great Britain can be justly considered in the largest sense a free and popular government; but, so far as the sovereign is concerned, her power is far more restricted and controlled by her ministers and Parliament than is the case in most republics. The President of the United States has much more actual power than the Queen of Great Britain; and the American Congress cannot exercise nearly as much control over his action as the House of Commons does over the Queen. This condition of affairs is mainly of modern growth. While some of the privileges and rights of the House of Commons date as far back as Magna Charta, the greater portion have been wrung from the rulers at the cost of revolutions. Large additions were made to the powers of popular government at the dethronement and execution of Charles I.; and larger still at the revolution which removed James II. from the throne. In the present century, the passage of the Reform Bill in 1832, and the enlargement of suffrage in 1868, have added much to the influence of the House of Commons; and the Irish Church Disestablishment Act, the prohibition of traffic in army commissions, and the vote by secret ballot, have materially abridged the privileges

---

* The variations in the number of statute acres in the area are not ours, but exist in the official statements made from year to year. We are unable to account for them. The difference between the statements in 1873 and 1874 was nearly 200,000 acres.

of the aristocracy. There remain, in the not distant future, the disestablishment of the English and Scottish Churches, and the curtailment of some of the remaining privileges of the aristocracy, and Great Britain will be practically the freest country in the world. Still, as was to be expected, the aristocracy cling, with an almost death-like grasp, to their immunities and privileges; and often, when these are threatened, if the ministry are weak or unwary, they manage to secure their retention by some artifice, which a little boldness would suffice to overthrow. Such an instance occurred in the defeat of the Judicature Bill in March, 1875.

The present sovereign of the United Kingdom is Her Majesty Alexandrina Victoria I. of the United Kingdom of Great Britain and Ireland, Queen, and of the Colonies and Dependencies thereof, Empress of India, Defender of the Faith; born May 24, 1819; succeeded to the throne June 20, 1837; crowned June 28, 1838; married February 10, 1840; widowed December 14, 1861. The heir-apparent to the throne is His Royal Highness Albert Edward, Prince of Wales, born November 9, 1841. The cost of the support of the royal family and its households was for the year ending March 31, 1874, as follows: " Annual grant to Her Majesty for the support of her household and of the honor and dignity of the crown of the United Kingdom," £385,000; grants to other members of the royal family out of the consolidated fund, £142,000; revenues of the Duchy of Lancaster, paid to the Queen, net amount after paying all charges, £41,000; revenues of the Duchy of Cornwall, paid to the Prince of Wales, net amount after paying all charges, £62,515, making a total of £630,515= $3,152,575. Aside from this large annual income, the royal family receive the income of the royal estates at Windsor, at Osborne, Isle of Wight, and at Balmoral, Scotland, which, as the estates are well managed, amounts to a considerable sum. The real rulers, the members of the cabinet and their subordinates and clerks, received the same year £1,933,356= $9,666,780.

The member of the cabinet who fills the position of First Lord of the Treasury, and combined with it sometimes that of Chancellor of the Exchequer, is the premier or chief of the ministry, and therefore of the cabinet; it is at his suggestion and recommendation that his colleagues are appointed; and he dispenses, with hardly an exception, the patronage of the crown. Every cabinet includes the following ten members of the administration: the First Lord of the Treasury, the Lord-Chancellor, the Lord-President of the Council, the Lord Privy Seal, the Chancellor of the Exchequer, and the five Secretaries of State. A number of other ministerial functionaries, varying from two to eight, have usually seats in the cabinet, those most frequently admitted being the Chief-Commissioner of Works and Buildings, the

Chancellor of the Duchy of Lancaster, the First Lord of the Admiralty, the President of the Board of Trade, the Vice-President of the Privy Council, the Postmaster-General, the Chief Secretary for Ireland, and the President of the Poor-Law Board. The selection usually falls upon those among the last-mentioned functionaries whose rank, talents, reputation, and political weight, render them the most useful auxiliaries, or whose services, while in opposition, may have given them the strongest claims to become members of the cabinet. It has occasionally happened that a statesman, possessing high character and influence, has accepted a seat in the cabinet without undertaking the labors and responsibilities of any particular office. Although the cabinet has been regarded for at least one hundred and sixty years as an essential part of the institutions of Great Britain, it is a singular fact that it is wholly unknown to the law. The names of the members who compose it are never officially announced; no record is kept of its resolutions or meetings, nor has its existence been recognized by any act of Parliament.

As intimated in the ANNUAL CYCLOPÆDIA for 1873, the results of the thorough canvass of his party in the House of Commons in the autumn and winter of 1873 satisfied Mr. Gladstone, the Liberal premier, that he could not command a working majority in the House at the next session, and accordingly, on the 24th of January, 1874, a dissolution of the Twentieth Parliament of the United Kingdom was announced, and writs for a new election of members of Parliament issued, the elections commencing January 31st. The returns from these elections indicated the choice of 350 "Conservatives," 242 "Liberals," and 60 "Home-Rulers." The Conservatives having thus a clear majority over all of 48, Mr. Gladstone at once resigned, and the Queen sent for Mr. Disraeli, the Conservative leader, to form a new cabinet; and on the 21st of February the following persons were installed as the new cabinet:

First Lord of the Treasury and Premier.— Right Honorable Benjamin Disraeli, born December 31, 1805; in Parliament since 1837, three times Chancellor of the Exchequer, viz., March to December, 1852; March, 1858, to June, 1859; July, 1866, to February, 1868. First Lord of the Treasury, February 25th to December 2, 1868. A full sketch of Mr. Disraeli's career will be found in the ANNUAL CYCLOPÆDIA for 1873, pp. 335, 336.

Lord High Chancellor.—Lord Cairns, formerly Sir Hugh McCalmont Cairns, born 1819, son of the late William Cairns, Esq., of Cultra, County Down, in the north of Ireland; educated at Trinity College, Dublin, graduating LL. D. in 1842; called to the Bar at the Middle Temple, London, in 1844; member of Parliament for Belfast, 1852-'66; and manifested abilities of so high an order, that Earl Derby made him Solicitor-General in 1858-'59; in 1866 he was appointed Attorney-General, and soon after Lord-Justice of Appeals, which office he held till February, 1868, when he was called into Disraeli's first cabinet as Lord High Chancellor, but resigned with his colleages, December 2, 1868. In 1867 he was elevated to the peerage as Baron Cairns of Garmoyle, and has since been the ablest debater of his party in the House of Lords.

Lord President of the Council. — Charles Henry Gordon-Lennox, Duke of Richmond, born February 27, 1818, eldest son of the fifth Duke of Richmond; educated at Westminster and Christ Church, Oxford, graduating B. A., 1839; entered the army in the Royal Horse-Guards, 1840; became captain in 1844, and was aide-de-camp to the Duke of Wellington from 1842 till 1852, and to Viscount Hardinge from 1852 till 1854. He represented West Sussex in the Conservative interest from July, 1841, till he succeeded his father as sixth Duke of Richmond, in October, 1860. The Duke was president of the Poor Law Board in 1859, and was president of the Board of Trade in Lord Derby's administration, from March, 1867, to December, 1868. He is the leader of the Conservative party in the House of Lords.

Lord Privy Seal. —James Howard Harris, Earl of Malmesbury, born in 1807, eldest son of the second Earl of Malmesbury; educated at Eton and Oriel College, Oxford, graduating B. A., 1828; member of Parliament for Wilton, June to August, 1841; succeeded to the earldom, August, 1841; Secretary of State for Foreign Affairs, February to December, 1852, and again February, 1858, to June, 1859; Lord Privy Seal July 6, 1866, to December 2, 1868.

Chancellor of the Exchequer. —Right Hon. Sir Stafford Henry Northcote, Bart., C. B.; born 1818, eldest son of H. S. Northcote, Esq.; educated at Balliol College, Oxford, graduating M. A. in 1842; called to the bar of the Inner Temple, London, 1847; member of Parliament when the latter was president of the Board of Trade, and was Financial Secretary to the Treasury from January to June, 1859. He was afterward president of the Board of Trade, in Lord Derby's third administration, in 1866, and became Secretary of State for India, March, 1867. Sir Stafford Northcote has been on good terms with both political parties in England, and was one of the commissioners appointed

HOUSES OF PARLIAMENT, LONDON.

by the Gladstone Government to negotiate the Treaty of Washington, September to October, 1871. He takes an active interest in the progress of art and education, and is author of a book entitled "Twenty Years of Financial Policy, 1842–1861," published in 1862.

Secretary of State for the Home Department.—Right Hon. Richard Assheton Cross, born 1823, son of William Cross, Esq., of Red Sear, near Preston; educated at Rugby, and at Trinity College, Cambridge; called to the Bar of the Inner Temple, 1849; M. P. for Preston, 1857 to 1862; M. P. for Southwest Lancashire, since 1868.

Secretary of State for Foreign Affairs.—Right Hon. Edward Henry Smith-Stanley, Earl of Derby, born at Knowsley Park, 1826, eldest son of the fourteenth earl; educated at Eton, and Trinity College, graduating M. A., 1848; traveled in the United States and the East Indies, 1847–1849; M. P. for Lynn-Regis, 1848–1869; made his first speech in the House in 1850, and returned to the East the next season, where he was when appointed Under-Secretary of State for Foreign Affairs in his father's ministry, February to December, 1852; Lord Palmerston offered him the post of Colonial Secretary in his cabinet in 1855, but he declined it;

he was Secretary of State for the Colonies in his father's second administration, from February to May, 1858, and Secretary of State for India, May, 1858, to June, 1859; Secretary of State for Foreign Affairs, July 6, 1866, to December 2, 1868, during which time he aided in settling the Luxemburg question, and negotiated the treaty with Reverdy Johnson, then United States minister to Great Britain, for the settlement of the Alabama claims, which the United States Senate rejected. He succeeded to the earldom in 1860.

Secretary of State for the Colonies.—Right Hon. Henry Howard Molyneux Herbert, Earl of Carnarvon, born June 24, 1831, eldest son of the third earl, educated at Eton, and Christ Church, Oxford, graduated M. A., 1855; succeeded to the earldom 1849; Under-Secretary of State for the Colonies, February, 1858, to June, 1859; Secretary of State for the Colonies, July, 1866, to March, 1867, when he resigned,

disapproving of Mr. Disraeli's Reform Bill. The earl is author of a book on the "Druses of Lebanon," and of several historical and antiquarian lectures.

Secretary of State for India.—Right Hon. Robert Arthur Talbot Gascoigne-Cecil, Marquis of Salisbury, born in 1830, eldest son of the second Marquis; educated at Eton, and Christ Church, Oxford, graduating M. A., 1853; Fellow of All-Souls' College; entered the House of Commons as Lord Robert Cecil, for Stamford, 1853, and sat for that borough till 1868; becoming meantime Viscount Cranbourne; was a contributor to the *Quarterly Review*, and attacked Mr. Disraeli as unworthy the confidence of the Conservatives; from July, 1866, to March, 1867, as Viscount Cranbourne, Secretary of State for India; resigned on account of the Reform Bill; succeeded to the marquisate in 1868.

Secretary of State for War.—Right Hon. Gathorne Hardy, born 1814; son of John Hardy,

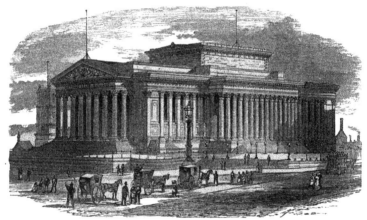

ST. GEORGE'S HALL, LIVERPOOL.

Esq., of Bradford, Yorkshire; educated at Shrewsbury, and at Oriel College, Oxford, graduating B. A., 1836; called to the bar at the Inner Temple, London, 1840; was for some years a practising barrister with a large practice; represented Leominster in Parliament, from 1856 to 1865, and Oxford University since 1865; Under-Secretary of State for the Home Department, 1858-'59; president of the Poor Law Board, July, 1866 to March, 1867; Secretary of State for the Home Department, May, 1867, to December, 1868. He is an able administrative officer, and stands high in the confidence and esteem of his party.

First Lord of the Admiralty.—Right Hon. George Ward Hunt, born in 1825; son of Rev. George Hunt, Buckhurst, Berkshire; educated at Eton, and Christ Church, Oxford, gradu-

ating M. A., 1851; called to the bar of the Inner Temple 1851; M. P. for Northamptonshire, North, since 1857; Financial Secretary to the Treasury, from 1866 to February, 1868; Chancellor of the Exchequer, February to December, 1868.

Postmaster-General.—Right Hon. Lord John James Robert Manners, born 1818, younger son of the fifth Duke of Rutland; educated at Eton, and Trinity College, Cambridge, graduating M. A., 1839; member of Parliament for Newark, 1841-'47; member of Parliament for Colchester, 1850-'57; member of Parliament for Leicestershire, North, since 1857; Commissioner of Works and Buildings, from March to December, 1852, from March, 1858, to June, 1859, and from July, 1866, to December, 1868.

The following ministerial functionaries are

not now in the cabinet, but have all, except Field-Marshal H. R. H. the Duke of Cambridge, commanding-in-chief, been appointed by Mr. Disraeli and his associates of the cabinet: *Junior Lords of the Treasury*, Viscount Mahon, Rowland Winn, Esq., Sir James D. H. Elphinstone, Bart.; *Political Secretary to the Treasury*, William Hart Dyke, Esq.; *Financial Secretary to the Treasury*, William Henry Smith, Esq.; *Junior Lords of the Admiralty*, Admiral Sir Alexander Milne, G. C. B., Vice-Admiral Sir J. W. Tarleton, K. C. B., Captain Lord Gilford, R. N., Sir Massey Lopes, Bart.; *Secretary to the Admiralty*, Hon. Algernon Fulke Egerton; *Chancellor of the Duchy of Lancaster*, Rt. Hon. Colonel Thomas E. Taylor; *President Local Government Board*, Rt. Hon. George Sclater-Booth; *Vice-President Committee of Council*, Rt. Hon. Viscount Sandon; *President Board of Trade*, Rt. Hon. Sir Charles B. Adderley; *Works and Public Buildings*, Rt. Hon. Lord Henry G. Lennox; *Attorney-General*, Sir Richard Baggallay; *Solicitor-General*, Sir John Holker; *Judge Advocate-General*, Rt. Hon. Stephen Cave.

The election and the necessity of forming a new cabinet occurred so late that the new Parliament (the twenty-first of the United Kingdom) was not assembled and constituted until March 5th, a month later than usual. At that time the only business transacted was the election of a Speaker, the choice falling on Rt. Hon. H. B. W. Brand, who had long been the "whip," or directing manager, of the Liberal party. Writs were issued for new elections of the members of the House of Commons who had accepted office, and Parliament adjourned to March 19th. At that time the Queen's speech was read, and business commenced in earnest. The previous Parliament and administration had left no immediately important legacies of vexed questions to their successors, and the session of Parliament was mainly occupied by local questions and financial measures. The report of the Chancellor of the Exchequer showed a surplus of £6,000,000= $30,000,000, to be disposed of, notwithstanding the heavy expenses of the Ashantee War, and the duty on sugar and on horses was repealed, and one penny in the pound taken off the Income tax, which now stands at two pence in the pound, on lands and tenements, on the income of occupiers of farms one penny; in Scotland and Ireland, three farthings; nurseries and market-gardens, two pence; compositions of tithes, four-sevenths of a penny; on incomes proper (Schedules C., D. and E.,) two pence per pound, incomes under £100=$500 being exempt; and incomes under £300=$1,500; of which £80=$400, are exempt. Other matters of importance were: the termination of the Ashantee War; the grant of £25,000=$125,000 to Sir Garnet Wolseley in consideration of his services in that war; a bill regulating the sale of intoxicating liquors, one altering and amending the laws relating to the appointment of

ministers to parishes in Scotland, generally known as the Patronage Bill; one for the better administration of the laws respecting the regulation of public worship; and one for the relief of the famine in India. Home-rule propositions were promptly voted down, receiving but 61 yeas to 458 nays. No acts were passed of special interest to the United States. The new Parliament has 652 members in the House of Commons, of whom 487 are from England and Wales, 60 from Scotland, and 105 from Ireland. The House of Lords consists of 492 members, of whom 4 were peers of the blood royal, 2 archbishops, 28 dukes, 32 marquises, 169 earls, 37 viscounts, 24 bishops, 195 barons, 16 Scottish representative peers, and 28 Irish representative peers. Several of the peers on the roll are minors.

The war with Ashantee, which had made considerable progress before the close of the year, was carried forward under the vigorous leadership of Sir Garnet Wolseley to successful termination in February—Coomassie, the capital of Ashantee, being captured on the 4th of that month and burned on the 6th, and King Koffee sending an embassy to sue for peace on the 13th. On their return to England in March, the troops under the command of Sir Garnet Wolseley were reviewed by the Queen in person. (*See* ASHANTEE.)

The marriage of Prince Alfred, Duke of Edinburgh, second son of the Queen, to the Grand-duchess Marie of Russia, only daughter of the Czar Alexander II., was celebrated at St. Petersburg, January 21st, and the Duke and Duchess took up their residence in England in March. The remains of Dr. Livingstone, who had died in Central Africa, May 4, 1873, were brought from Africa and buried with great ceremony in Westminster Abbey, April 18th. The decision of the British Government, to send an expedition to the north-pole, made on the 17th of November, was an event of interest to science.

Religious Statistics of the United Kingdom.— In England the Established Church is Protestant Episcopal. Its fundamental doctrines and tenets are embodied in the Thirty-nine Articles, agreed upon in convocation in 1562, and revised and finally settled in 1571. Within a few years past, there has been a constantly increasing sentiment on the part of many of the citizens of Great Britain that the union between the Established Church and state should be severed, and that the Church of England, like the dissenting bodies, should be maintained wholly on the voluntary principle. The changes which would be produced by disestablishment would be very great. The Queen is now by law the supreme (human) governor of the Church, and possesses the right, exercised through her prime-minister for the time, to nominate and in reality to appoint incumbents for all vacant archbishoprics and bishoprics, as well as to a very considerable number of deaneries, prebendaries, and canonries, which are in her gift. The patronage or advowson of private or parochial livings of the more than 12,000 parishes which now appertain to the Church of England, and which give to the incumbent the freehold of the parsonage, the glebe-lands, tithes, and other dues, is now the property of the Queen, the Lord-Chancellor, the Prince of Wales, the higher clergy, the chapters, the universities, and about 3,850 lords, gentlemen, and ladies. All these persons have a vested interest in the maintenance of the Establishment, and, as most of the older families of the peerage are included in this number, there is a very strong opposition to any movement looking to disestablishment; but, on the other hand, the Roman Catholic interest and all the dissenting interests, numbering together about half of the population, and by far the most restless and active portion, are urging it with great assiduity and pertinacity. The disestablishment or dissolution of the connection between the state and the several leading churches in Ireland, accomplished by the efforts of Mr. Gladstone in 1870–'71, was the opening wedge to a complete disestablishment throughout the United Kingdom; and the passage of the patronage bill through the Parliament of 1874, which virtually deprives the heritors of patronage in Scotland, was a measure looking toward the same end. The bishops and archbishops now have seats in the House of Lords by virtue of their offices, and the Church is in consequence of the power of patronage, to a large extent, as the army was, till within the past two or three years, a private preserve, affording comfortable positions to the younger sons and dependents of the nobility and gentry, and to the children of the higher clergy. Disestablishment means the opening of these positions to a fair competition of talent, pure character, and religious zeal, and of course it is displeasing to those who believe that long ages of custom have given them a prescriptive and exclusive right to these privileges. Till within a few years, a written assent to the Thirty-nine Articles was a necessary preliminary to a seat in the House of Commons, to a matriculation at the Universities of Oxford and Cambridge, or to the holding of any Government office; this requirement is now abolished, and the dissenters have been gradually gaining power, which they will use effectively for the overthrow of the State Church. Many, also, of the clergy and laity of the Established Church are beginning to feel that what the Church might lose in influence and patronage by disestablishment would be more than made up to her in the greater zeal, energy, and vitality, which would be infused into her membership by voluntaryism, and for that reason they look forward to it with hope rather than fear.

The Church of England had, in 1874, about 12,000 parishes, and 200 extra-parochial places, nearly 13,000 clergymen, 26 bishops, and two archbishops. She claims about 12,700,000 adherent population, but this includes between one and two millions who never enter her churches, and who can only be reckoned churchmen on the ground that they claim no affinity with any religious body. In Scotland, where the Episcopal Church is not the State Church, there are 199 clergy, and nearly the same number of parishes, but probably not more than 65,000 adherent population. The number of Roman Catholics in Great Britain is estimated at about 2,000,000. They have one archbishop, and 16 bishops, 1,697 clergymen, and 1,035 chapels. In Scotland there are three "apostolic vicariates," 228 Roman Catholic chapels, and 248 officiating clergy. There are, altogether, 146 Protestant religious denominations in Great Britain, of which a considerable number have but few adherents. The Protestant dissenters have somewhat more than 9,-000,000 of adherent population in England and Wales, and in the United Kingdom about 14,-000,000. The most numerous of these Protestant dissenters in England and Wales are the Methodists, of whom there are a number of sects, differing but slightly in doctrinal belief, but considerably in the form of church government. Their numbers in England, Wales, and Scotland were, in 1874, 3,616 ministers, 30,-978 local preachers, 12,741 chapels, 645,189 members, besides 34,186 on probation, and 1,-276,523 Sunday-school scholars. In Scotland the Established Church is Presbyterian, but has not the same degree of influence and power as the Established Church in England; the act of 1874, which takes from the heritors the right of nominating incumbents to church livings, is regarded as the death-blow to patronage in that Church and a long step toward disestablishment. The Established (Presbyterian) Church in Scotland had, in 1874, 1,250 parish churches, 1,800 ministers, 1,800 parish schools, 140,000 scholars, raised about $1,400,000 for home and missionary purposes, and has an adherent population of about 1,400,000. But the Established Church does not monopolize all the Presbyterianism even in Scotland. The Free Church of Scotland, founded in 1843 by a large secession from the Established Church, is a voluntary body, and has 954 congregations, 937 ministers, a membership of about 300,000 and an adherent population of nearly a million. It raised for home and missionary purposes in 1874, $2,555,420. The United Presbyterian Church, formed by the union of several seceding bodies, had in 1874, in Scotland, England, and Wales, 615 churches, 647 ministers, about 184,000 members, and about 650,000 adherent population. They raised for home and missionary purposes in that year $1,691,890. The Presbyterian Church in England is a smaller body, having 132 churches, 130 ministers, 24,-000 communicants, 22,000 Sunday-school scholars, and about 100,000 adherent population. There are also several other smaller Presbyterian bodies, making the Presbyterian population of Great Britain about 3,250,000.

The Independents or Congregationalists have in England, Wales, and Scotland, 2,912 churches, besides 527 churches abroad, connected with their missions, and a little more than 300,000 members. Their ministers are about 3,000, and the adherent population about 1,100,000. The Baptists had, in 1874, 3,172 chapels, 1,856 pastors, 244,416 communicants, 337,327 Sunday-school scholars, and an adherent population of nearly 1,000,000. Their contributions for missionary and benevolent purposes were $700,000.

The Calvinistic Methodists are the largest religious denomination in Wales, though but few in numbers elsewhere. They date from 1735, though not fully organized till 1810. They had, in 1874, 1,177 chapels, 798 ministers; deacons and lay-preachers, 3,610; communicants, 97,147; Sunday-school teachers and scholars, 192,253; number belonging to the congregations, 254,059; contributions to benevolent objects, $705,875. The principal of the minor denominations were the Unitarians, who had 352 chapels, and 355 ministers; the Jews, who had about 80 synagogues, 100 ministers, and numbered about 50,000; the Society of Friends, with 665 preachers, 327 meeting-houses, and 17,000 members; the Moravians, with 83 churches, 5,550 members, and 6,200 scholars; the New-Jerusalem Church (Swedenborgians), with 4,207 registered members, and 58 societies; the Christadelphians, with a little more than 5,000 members, Mormons, Irvingites, Plymouth Brethren, etc., etc.

In Ireland the distribution of religious denominations was very different from that of Great Britain. Until January, 1871, there was an Established Church (Protestant Episcopal), with its hierarchy and state institutions, but it was greatly in the minority, and allowances were made to the Roman Catholics, who were about six times as numerous as the adherents to the State Church, and also to some of the other denominations, this allowance being called *regium donum*, or "royal gift." At the time specified the Irish Church was disestablished, and these gifts and allowances both to it and the other denominations were compounded for, so as to do no wrong to the actual incumbents of parishes or the ministers of chapels. In 1871 the number returning themselves as adherents to the "Church of Ireland," or as "Protestant Episcopalians," was 683,295; at the same time 4,141,933 persons declared themselves Roman Catholics, 558,238 Presbyterians, 41,815 Methodists, 4,-485 Independents, 4,063 Baptists, 3,834 members of the Society of Friends, 258 Jews, and 19,035 as belonging to other religious persuasions. As the population of Ireland has slightly decreased since 1871, and there have been no causes to produce any very marked change in their religious beliefs, it is probable that these figures represent pretty accurately the present religious status of that island.

FINANCIAL STATISTICS OF THE UNITED KINGDOM: 1. *Revenue and Expenditure.*—The gross public revenue of the United Kingdom for the financial year ending March 31, 1874, was £77,335,656 17s. 1d.=$386,678,284.25. Of this revenue £20,339,000=$101,695,000 was from customs; £27,172,000=$135,860,000 from excise; £10,550,000=$52,750,000 from stamps; £2,324,000=$11,620,000 from land-tax and house duty; £5,691,000=$28,455,000 from income-tax; £5,792,000=$28,960,000 from the post-office; £1,210,000=$6,050,000 from the telegraph service; £375,000=$1,875,000 from the crown-lands net; and £3,882,656 17s. 1d.= $19,413,284.25 from miscellaneous sources.

The total expenditure of the Government for the same year was £76,966,510 2s. 4d.=$384,-832,550.58, leaving a surplus on the revenue of the year of $1,845,733.67, and, with the previous balance from 1873, a balance in the Exchequer of $37,214,270.68. Of this expenditure, £26,706,725 10s. 11d.=$133,533,627.62 was for the interest and management of the national debt; £1,603,084 18s.=$8,015,424.32 was for charges on the consolidated fund, including the civil list, annuities and pensions, salaries and allowances, courts of justice, and miscellaneous charges; £48,156,699,13s. 5d.= $240,783,498.22 for supply services, which included the army, the army purchase-commission, navy, miscellaneous civil, Ashantee expedition, customs, and inland revenue, postal, telegraphic, packet services, and in this year the payment of the Alabama claims to our Government. There was also a charge of £500,000=$2,500,000 for army expenses provided for by annuities.

The estimated expenditure for the year ending March 31, 1875, or what is called the "expenditure of the budget," was £72,-503,000=$362,515,000; and the estimated revenue was £77,995,000=$389,975,000. The House of Commons resolved that the estimated surplus of revenue, £5,492,000=$27,460,000 should be devoted to the following objects: Imperial contribution in aid of local taxation (poor-rates, etc.), £1,050,000=$5,250,000; reduction of income-tax from threepence to twopence in the pound, £1,500,000=$7,500,000; abolition of sugar duties, £2,000,000=$10,000,-000; abolition of duties upon horses, £480,000 =$2,400,000; leaving a balance for contingencies of £460,000=$2,300,000.

The income tax, which was established in its present form in 1842, has in the thirty-two years which had since elapsed undergone eighteen distinct changes. Beginning with 7d. in the pound, it had been raised in 1854 to 14d., and in 1855, during the war with Russia, to 16d.; dropped to 7d. in 1857, and to 5d. in 1858; in 1859 it was raised to 9d., and in 1860 to 10d. In 1861 it was reduced to 9d., and since that time had fluctuated, with almost yearly changes, between 9d. and 2d., the rate established in 1874, and which is the lowest yet fixed for the income tax. In round numbers, every penny in the pound added to this tax produces $7,500,000 to the revenue.

, The statistics for the total amount annually raised by local taxation and other local revenue, to provide for the expenditure connected with the relief of the poor, county and borough police, roads and bridges, drainage and lighting of towns, etc., are not of later date than the year ending March 31, 1872, when they were as follows: Receipts from local taxes, £26,- 444,136 = $132,220,680; other receipts, £12,- 247,192 = $61,235,960; total local revenue, £38,691,328=$193,456,640. Of this, £11,244,- 072=$56,220,360 was for poor-rates and the maintenance of the poor. The aggregate of this local taxation and revenue does not probably differ materially now from the aggregate of 1872; as, though the poor-rates have somewhat increased, other expenditures have been slightly diminished; but they show that, taken with the national revenue, the sum of £116,- 081,486 = $580,407,430 is annually raised by direct and indirect taxation in the United Kingdom, or about $17.90 per head of the population.

2. *National Debt.*—The national debt, including terminable annuities, was, on the 31st day of March, 1874, £779,283,245 = $3,896,- 416,225; and the interest charges thereon £26,706,726=$133,533,630. The principal of the debt has fluctuated greatly since 1817, when the English and Irish Exchequers were consolidated; at that time it stood at £840,- 850,491=$4,204,252,455; in 1836 it had been reduced to £787,638,616=$3,938,194,080, a reduction of nearly $266,000,000. In 1860 it had risen again to £802,190,300=$4,010,951,500. This was exclusive of about $250,000,000 of terminable annuities. So that the entire debt at that time was really about $4,261,000,000. From that date it has been constantly though slowly diminishing, till it has reached its present amount. This is equal to $120.21.5 per head of the population of the United Kingdom.

ARMY AND NAVY: 1. *Army.*—The total force of the United Kingdom during the year ending March 31, 1875, is, by vote of the House of Commons, to consist of 6,989 commissioned officers, 16,280 non-commissioned officers, trumpeters and drummers, and 105,- 725 rank and file, being a total of 128,994 men of all ranks. These are the effectives, and do not include officers on the retired lists, pensioners, militia, yeomanry-cavalry, volunteers, or riflemen. Nor does it include the British army in India, which, for the same year, amounted to 62,840 men of all ranks, a slight diminution from the previous year, while the home army shows a very material increase of about 23,000 men. The militia force provided for in 1874– '75 was 139,018; the yeomanry-cavalry, 15,378; the volunteers, which included the riflemen, 153,266; and the enrolled pensioners and army reserve force, 33,000, of whom 10,000 belonged to the first class and 23,000 to the second. There is thus preparation for a military force, in case of emergency, of 532,496 men of all

arms. The army estimates of expenditure for this force and for buildings, fortifications, supplies, and non-effective services, in 1874–'75, were £14,485,300=$72,426,500. The educational condition of the army, January 1, 1874, was as follows: Out of regiments and corps, amounting to 178,356 men, 10,724 could neither read nor write, 9,543 could read but not write, 99,910 could read and write, and 58,179 were better educated. There is now compulsory education in the army, the rule laid down in the Queen's Regulations being that every recruit is obliged to attend school until he is in possession of a fourth-class certificate of education.

2. *Navy.*—On the 1st of January, 1874, there were in commission in the British navy 112 sea-going steamers of all grades, 72 reserve steamers, and 55 sailing-vessels, making in all 239 vessels of all grades in commission. Of these only the 112 sea-going steamers were in active service, away from the home-ports or the coast-guarding service. The most efficient portion of the navy is the iron-clad fleet, which consisted, in January, 1875, of 62 vessels, including four not yet completed. A number of these are the most formidable naval vessels yet constructed by any nation. The first class, consisting of the Devastation, the Thunderer, the Fury, and the Inflexible, are iron ships, without masts, with two turrets, of from 5,600 to 8,000 indicated horse-power, and a displacement of from 9,157 to 11,165 tons, with armor-plates of twelve inches average thickness, and carrying each four 700-pounder guns in their turrets. The second class are two rams, the Rupert and Hotspur, of extraordinary power and speed, capable of crushing and destroying any armored vessels with which they may come in contact at full speed. They carry two 18-ton guns. The third class consists of nine mastless single-turret ships for coast-defense— very strong, but not adapted for long cruises. The fourth class, of five full-rigged ships, of great speed for cruising, well armored, and generally carrying seven or eight guns of 18 tons each. The fifth class consists of ten second-rate rigged ships for cruising. The sixth class, of seventeen third-rates, generally of considerable speed, but not very formidable as fighting-ships. The seventh class consists of eleven iron-clads, of small size, for coast-defense. There are also four iron unarmored frigates, of large size and great speed, with a heavy armament, twenty to twenty-six guns each, and reputed to be the swiftest vessels in the navy. The number of seamen and marines provided for the different departments of the service, in 1874–'75, was, for the fleet, 33,500 seamen and 7,000 boys, including 3,000 for training; 7,000 marines afloat and 7,000 on shore; for the coast-guard, shore-duty, officers and men, 4,300; for the Indian service, officers and men, 1,200; making a total of 60,000 men and boys in the naval service. The estimates of expenditure for the naval service for the year ending March

31, 1875, were £10,179,485=$50,897,425. This does not include the building of any new vessels except those built by contract, though it makes allowance for the completion of the few now on the stocks.

EDUCATION. 1. *Public Schools.*—There is commendable progress made in public school education in Great Britain. The latest returns are at the close of 1873, and show that in the United Kingdom there were at that time 21,114 national schools which had been inspected, having accommodations for 4,163,186 pupils, and having on their registers 3,510,926 as in attendance at some time during the year, while the average daily attendance was 2,157,-101. The total grants for the financial year 1874-'75 to public-school education were £2,577,389=$12,886,945, an advance of nearly $5,000,000 on the grant for 1872. The greater part of this progress has been in England and Wales, though, when the constantly-decreasing population of Ireland is taken into the account, it is not so far behind as it might otherwise seem. The "Act to provide for Public Elementary Education in England and Wales," passed in 1870, has done much to improve the public-school system there. That act orders that "there shall be provided for every school-district a sufficient amount of accommodation in public elementary schools available for all the children resident in such district for whose elementary education efficient and suitable provision is not otherwise made." It is enacted further, that "all children attending these public elementary schools, whose parents are unable, from poverty, to pay any thing toward their education, shall be admitted free, and the expenses so incurred be discharged from local rates." The new schools are placed in each district under "School-Boards" invested with great powers, among others that of making it compulsory upon parents to give all children between the ages of five and thirteen the advantages of education. Under this act, the public elementary schools of England and Wales had increased, in three years, from 8,986 to 11,846; the accommodations from 1,950,641 to 2,665,467, and the av-

erage attendance from 1,255,083 to 1,538,552. There was less proportional increase in Ireland, where this act was not in effect, but there was also a diminishing instead of an increasing population.

2. *Higher Education.*—In former volumes of the ANNUAL CYCLOPÆDIA a full account has been given of the universities and great endowed public schools of the United Kingdom, but these do not properly pertain to popular education. The twenty-first Report of the Science and Art Department of the Committee of Council on Education gives some particulars of interest on this subject. The number of schools for art and science at the end of 1873 was 1,182; the number of persons under instruction was 48,546. In these schools there were 4,231 different classes; there were 1,258 teachers who received aggregate salaries of £33,027=$165,135; 27,026 students came up for examination at 754 provincial and 78 metropolitan centres. The number of persons receiving instruction in art-schools was 290,176. Of these art-schools there are 988 in England and Wales, 106 in Scotland, and 302 in Ireland. They are mainly intended for the instruction of artisans and their children in the principles of practical art, and correspond to some extent to our schools of design, though the instruction is less extensive. There are also 613 night-classes, in which 20,352 students are taught, and drawing is taught in 2,074 elementary schools for the poor, to 237,733 children. The South Kensington and Bethnal Green Museums afford much instruction to those who frequent them. In 1873 the former was visited by 859,037 persons, almost 300,000 less than the previous year; and the latter by 709,472.

There are also in England and Wales thirty-four "Training Institutions," or, as we should call them, "Normal Schools," many of them very large. Of these, twenty-seven are controlled by the Church of England, two by the Wesleyans, one by the Congregationalists, and four by the British and Foreign School Society.

VITAL AND SOCIAL STATISTICS.—1. *Births, Deaths, and Marriages.*

BIRTHS, DEATHS, AND MARRIAGES.	Pop. Jan. 1, 1874.	Births in 1873.	Deaths in 1873.	Marriages in 1872.
England and Wales	23,356,414	831,809	494,003	205,460
Scotland	3,430,923	119,738	76,857	26,730
Ireland	5,337,261	144,592	97,840	26,566
Total for United Kingdom	32,124,598	1,096,139	668,700	258,756

The proportion of male to female children born in England and Wales is 104,811 to 100,-000. In Scotland, the ratio, in 1872 and 1873, was 107 boys to 100 girls. These proportions

are changed so that, at adult age, there are 100,000 women to 94,900 men.

2. *Pauperism.*—The statistics of pauperism are to January 1, 1874. They are as follows:

PAUPERS.	Number of Unions or Parishes.	Adult able-bodied or Out-door Paupers.	Other Paupers, dependents or In-door Paupers.	Total Paupers.
England and Wales	647	114,324	714,957	829,281
Scotland	886	71,537	40,459	111,996
Ireland	....	29,857	49,193	79,683
Total for United Kingdom	....	215,718	804,609	1,020,910

3. *Criminal Statistics.*—These are for the year ending January 1, 1874, but are not complete, as some of the courts do not make report of committals but only of convictions. The table shows all that are reported of the committals for trial and the convictions:

CRIMINALS.	COMMITTED FOR TRIAL.			Convicted.
	Men.	Women.	Total.	
England and Wales...........................	11,490	3,408	14,898	11,089
Scotland..	2,254	665	2,919	2,230
Ireland..	3,724	820	4,544	2,542
Total for United Kingdom	17,468	4,885	22,356	15,861

COMMERCE, NAVIGATION, EMIGRATION, ETC. 1. *Commerce.*—The imports of the United Kingdom in the year ending January 1, 1874, were £371,287,372 = $1,856,436,860. The exports of British produce for the same year were £255,164,603 = $1,275,823,015, and of foreign and colonial produce, £55,840,162 = $279,200,-810 ; making a total of exports of £311,004,765 = $1,555,023,825 ; and a total of exports and imports of £682,292,137=$3,411,460,685, or $106.14 per head of the population. The United States are the largest buyers and sellers in this vast commerce. The imports from the United States in the year 1873 were £71,471,-493 = $357,357,465, nearly one-fifth of the entire imports, and almost equal to all received from her own colonies, possessions, or dependencies. The exports to the United States were, £36,698,424 = $183,492,120, of which there was of home production, £35,574,664=$177,-873,320. This was one-seventh of the entire export to foreign countries. The other countries which deal most largely with Great Britain are, France, India, Russia, Germany, Australasia, and the Netherlands. The trade with the United States is increasing with great rapidity.

2. *Navigation.*—The total number of vessels, sailing and steam, employed in sailing from and belonging to the United Kingdom, January 1, 1874, was 21,581, with a tonnage of 5,748,-097 tons, and employing 202,239 men. Of these, 2,796 were steamers, having an aggregate tonnage of 1,690,953 tons, and employing 61,362 men. The remainder were sailing-vessels. In 1873 there were 422 sailing-vessels, with a tonnage of 89,626 tons; and 509 steamers, with a tonnage of 363,917 tons, built and registered for the first time in the United Kingdom. The entrances into British ports and clearances from them of British and foreign vessels, both sailing and steam, during the year 1873, were of British vessels 29,647,344 tons, and foreign vessels, 14,792,642 tons, making an aggregate of 44,439,986 tons.

3. *Emigration.*—In the year 1873 the whole number of emigrants who left the ports of the United Kingdom was 310,612. Of these, 37,-208 were bound for the North American colonies, 233,073 for the United States, and 26,-428 for the Australasian colonies. Of the whole number 118,190 were English, 19,541 Scotch, 72,763 Irish, 79,023 foreigners, and a small number unknown.

4. *Railways.*—On January 1, 1874, there were in the United Kingdom 16,082 miles of railway open to traffic, representing a total paid-up capital, in shares and loans, of £588,-320,308=$2,941,601,240; the total number of passengers conveyed on these railways for the year was 455,320,288, or 28,332 per mile; the total traffic receipts of the year were £55,675,-421=$278,377,105, or £3,462=$17,310 per mile. The working expenditure amounted to 53 per cent. of the total receipts, or 4 per cent. more than in the preceding year.

5. *Post and Telegraphs.*—There were in the United Kingdom in January, 1874, 12,500 post-offices, besides upward of 9,000 road and pillar letter-boxes. The number of persons employed in the Post-Office Department was 42,236 ; the number of letters delivered was 907,000,000 ; of newspapers and book-packets, 254,000,000 ; the number of money-orders issued was 15,-118,636, of the aggregate value of £25,600,069 =$128,000,345. The post-office saving-banks received during the year 2,917,698 deposits, of the aggregate amount of £7,955,740=$39,-778,700, and held January 1, 1874, deposits to the value of £21,745,442=$108,727,210 ; the post-office, life-insurance, and annuity department granted 396 life - insurance policies, amounting to £33,073=$165,365 ; 1,343 immediate annuities, amounting to £10,290= $51,450 ; and 35 deferred annuities, amounting to £583=$2,915. The gross revenue of the post-office of the United Kingdom in 1873 was £5,348,040=$26,740,200, and the cost of management £2,846,707=$14,233,535, leaving a net revenue of £2,501,333=$12,506,665. The total length of the postal telegraph-wires at that date was 107,000 ; the number of tele-graph-offices, 5,600 ; and the number of telegraphic messages sent in 1873, exclusive of press and service messages, for the whole United Kingdom, 17,294,334, of which 14,070,-993 were for England and Wales, 1,942,610 for Scotland, and 1,280,731 for Ireland.

GREAT BRITAIN, COLONIAL POSSESSIONS AND DEPENDENCIES OF.—The following table, prepared with great care from the latest authorities, and mostly from late official publications, gives the names, date of acquisition, area in square miles, population at latest census, form of government and name of ruler, revenue, expenditure, and debt of each of the colonial possessions and dependencies of Great Britain, so far as they can be ascertained:

COLONIAL POSSESSIONS AND DEPENDENCIES.	Date of Acquisition.	Area in English Square Miles.	Population.	Year of Census.	Form of Government, and Name and Title of Ruler.	Revenue.	Expenditure.	Amount of Debt.
In Europe.								
Gibraltar	1704	1¾	14,764	1871	Crown: Sir W. Fenwick Williams, G. C. B., Governor.	$240,285	$232,410	......
Channel Islands	1066	119	90,563	1871	Maj.-Gen. W. S. R. Norcott, C. B., Lieut.-Gov.			......
Isle of Man	827	227	54,042	1871	Henry Brougham Loch, C. B., Lieut.-Governor.			......
Heligoland	1814	54	1,913	1871	Lieut.-Col. H. F. B. Maxse, Governor.	20,435	20,665	......
Malta	1800	115	149,064	1871	Li.-Gen. Sir T. von Straubenzee, K. C. B., Gov.	811,415	840,310	......
In America.								
Bahamas	1629	3,021	* 39,162	1871	Represent. Inst.: Pope Hennessy, Esq., C. M. G., Gov.	270,705	259,405	$270,805
Bermudas	1609	24	12,121	1871	Maj.-Gen. J. H. Lefroy, C. B., Gov.	155,150	175,730	7,150
Canada, Dominion of	1623-1760	352,361	3,579,782	1871	Resp. G't: Rt. Hon. Earl Dufferin, K.P.K.C.B.,Gov.-Gen	0,813,469	19,174,647	105,292,556
Falkland Islands	1765	6,500	808	1871	Crown: Col. G. A. K. D'Arcy, Governor.	21,840	42,950	......
Guiana	1803	76,000	193,491	1871	James R. Longden, C. M. G., Governor.	1,809,675	1,961,735	2,374,775
Honduras	1638	13,500	24,710	1870	Maj. Robert M. Mundy, C. M. G., Lt.-Gov.	207,725	172,030	75,250
Jamaica and Turk's Island	1639-1625	6,900	510,354	1871	Sir Wm. Grey, K. C. S. I., Captain-General.	2,973,285	2,701,680	3,162,500
Leeward Islands	1626-1763	708	120,491	1871	Represent. Inst.: Hon. Geo. Berkeley, C. M. G., Gov.	495,770	538,575	344,585
Newfoundland	1583	40,200	146,536	1869	Respon. Gov't.: Col. Sir S. J. Hill, C. B., Governor.	874,575	1,026,190	1,227,775
Trinidad	1797	1,755	109,638	1871	Crown: Hon. H. Turner Irving, C. M. G., Governor.	1,407,850	1,631,410	125,000
Windward Islands	1605-1803		231,078	1871	Represent. Inst.: Rawson W. Rawson, Esq., C. B., Gov.	1,104,625	1,097,725	None.
In Africa.								
Ascension	1815	34	527	1871	Crown: Capt. J. W. East, R. N., Officer in Charge.	10,396,100	10,798,490	8,615,725
Cape of Good Hope	1806	201,000	566,156	1871	Respon. Gov't: Sir H. Barkly, Gov. & Com.-in-Chief.	86,245	89,365	
Gambia	1631		14,190	1871	Crown: C. H. Kortright, Esq., Administrator.	200,825	213,925	
Griqualand West	1660-1872	14,000	408,070	1871	Capt. G. C. Strahan, R. A., Governor.	300,000	148,000	
Gold Coast	1871	17,800	25,477	1871	Richard Southey, Esq., C. M. G., Lieut.-Gov.	306,780	296,730	4,001,000
Lagos	1861	5,000	62,021	1871	C. Cameron Lees, Esq., Administrator.	3,493,405	3,285,550	1,672,000
Mauritius	1810	708	316,042	1871	Maj.-Gen. Sir A. E. Kennedy, K. C. M. G., Gov.	902,480	664,880	
Natal	1806	11,172	223,832	1871	Rep. Inst.: Sir Benj. C. C. Pine, K. C. M. G., Lt.-Gov.	74,695	83,495	
St. Helena	1650	47	6,241	1871	Crown: Hudson Ralph Janisch, Esq., Governor.	460,515	518,140	$2,0,060
Sierra Leone	1788	463	38,936	1871				
In Asia.								
Aden	1838	5	25,490	1871	Crown: Brig.-Gen. John Schneider, Political Resident.	6,450,900	5,881,295	3,200,000
Ceylon	1796	24,454	2,405,287	1871	Represent. Inst.: Rt. Hon. W. H. Gregory, Governor.	963,570	873,405	
Hong-Kong	1843	29	124,198	1871	Crown: Sir A. E. Kennedy, K. C. M. G., C. B., Gov.			
India	1625-1849	950,919	191,307,070	1872	Rt. Hon. Lord Northbrook, G. M. S. I., Viceroy and Governor-General.	251,097,445	242,269,065	235,500,625
In Australasia.								
Labuan	1846	45	4,898	1871	Sir H. E.Bulwer, K. C. M. G., Gov. & Cons.-Gen.	84,585	35,450	
Perim	1855	7	211	1871	Brig.-Gen. J. Schneider, Governor of Aden.			
Straits Settlements	1785-1819	1,350	308,097	1871	Col. Sir Andrew Clark, C. B., Governor.	1,682,290	1,377,380	
New South Wales	1787	323,437	503,981	1871	Respon. Gov't.: Sir H. G. R. Robinson, K. C. M. G., Gov.	20,807,075	18,188,115	53,866,150
New Zealand	1814	102,000	256,260	1871	Resp. G't.: Most Hon. Marquis of Normanby, Gov., etc.	9,839,270	6,507,355	51,848,680
Queensland	1859	678,600	120,104	1871	Hon. W. W. Cairns, C. M. G., Governor.	4,961,615	4,121,350	22,729,250
South Australia	1836	760,000	185,626	1871	Anthony Musgrave, C. M. G., Governor.	3,467,210	3,301,000	11,421,000
Tasmania	1803	26,215	102,105	1871	Sir F. Aloysius Weld, Esq., Governor.	1,356,770	1,444,400	1,279,540
Victoria	1803	88,198	731,528	1871	Sir George Ferguson Bowen, G. C. M. G., Gov.	18,960,960	18,118,905	68,188,785
Western Australia	1829	978,000	24,785	1870	Wm. C. F. Robinson, C. M. G., Gov.-in-Ch.	674,155	571,345	175,000
In Polynesia.								
Fiji Islands	1874	715	200,000	1871	Protectorate: Edgar Leopold Layard, Commissioner.	120,000	130,000	

The form of government is stated after the definition given in the "Colonial Office List," under which the colonies are divided into three classes, viz.: 1. *Crown* colonies, in which the crown has the entire control of legislation, while the administration is carried on by officers under the direction of the home government; 2. Colonies possessing *Representative Institutions,* in which the crown has but a veto on legislation, but the home government retains the control of public officers; 3. Colonies possessing *Responsible Government,* in which the crown has only a veto on legislation, and the home government has no control over any public officer except its own representative. The cost of the colonial possessions to Great Britain has been gradually declining for a number of years, and does not now amount to more than $8,750,000 per annum, of which two-thirds is paid on account of nine of the possessions classed as general military and naval stations, viz., Gibraltar, Malta, Cape of Good Hope, the Mauritius, Bermuda, St. Helena, Heligoland, the Falkland Islands, and Hong-Kong.

GREECE, a kingdom of Southeastern Europe. Reigning King, George I., King of the Hellenes, born December 24, 1845, second son of the reigning King of Denmark; elected King of the Hellenes by the National Assembly at Athens, March 18 (30) 1863 ; accepted the crown June 4, 1863; declared of age by a decree of the National Assembly, June 27, 1863 ; married, October 27, 1867, to Olga, daughter of Grand-duke Constantine, of Russia, born August 22, 1851. Issue of the union are three sons and one daughter : Constantinos, Duke of Sparta, born August 2, 1868 ; George, born June 25, 1869 ; Alexandra, born August 30, 1870 ; and Nicholas, born February 2, 1872.

The area of the kingdom amounts to 19,353 square miles; the population, according to the census of 1870, to 1,457,894. The country is divided for administrative purposes into 13 nomarchies,* which are subdivided into 59 eparchies, and 351 communes; the heads of the latter, called demarchs, are chosen for a term of four years; the heads of the eparchies and nomarchies, called eparchs and nomarchs, are appointed by the King. The principal towns had, in 1871,the following population: Athens, 44,510 ; Piræus, 6,425 (in 1873 it was estimated at 10,000); Thermopolis, on the island of Syra, 20,996 ; Patras, 19,641 ; Spezzia, 9,843 ; Hydra, 9,592 ; Argos, 9,157 ; Tripolizza, 7,441 ; Zante, 17,516 ; Corfu, 15,452. According to the census of 1871, there were only 67,-941 persons who spoke another than the Greek language. Of them, 37,598 were Albanese, 1,217 Macedo-Wallachians, and 29,126 others. The number of foreign residents was 19,958, of whom 15,051 were natives of Turkey, 2,099 British, 1,539 Italians, 526 Germans, and 415 French. Nearly the entire population (1,441,-810) is connected with the Greek Oriental Church, which is governed by a permanent Holy Synod at Athens, consisting of five members, who are appointed by the King from among the bishops and other high clerical dignitaries. The Church has one metropolitan at Athens, 15 other archbishops and 16 bishops. With other Christian denominations, only 12,585 † souls are connected; most of them belong to the Roman Catholic Church, which has archbishops at Naxos and Corfu, and four bishops. All creeds are tolerated, and there is entire freedom of religious worship. The Mohammedans, of whom there were still 90,830 in 1821, have nearly all been forced out of the country.

Every child is expected to attend school from the fifth to the twelfth year of its age. Nevertheless, the attendance at the public schools is small. In 1869 the 1,141 public and private elementary schools numbered only 60,634 pupils, and, according to the reports, there were,

* The ANNUAL CYCLOPÆDIA for 1872 gives the population of every nomarchy and every eparchy for 1860 and 1870.

† The number of Roman Catholics was formerly estimated considerably higher. Neher (Kirchl. Statistik, vol. iii., 1865) gives them 29,000.

in 1870, 15 gymnasia and 144 Hellenic schools (corresponding to the German Realschulen), with 7,780 pupils, and 23 private institutions, with 1,589 pupils. The university at Athens, which has the four faculties of theology, law, medicine, and philosophy, was, in 1869, attended by 1,205 students. Of special schools, there are 1 polytechnical school at Athens, 4 theological shools of the Greek Oriental Church, 6 nautical schools, 1 agricultural school, and 1 military academy at the Piræus.

In the budget for 1873, the revenue was estimated at 35,882,000 drachmas; the expenditure at 35,897,000 drachmas; the deficit at 15,000,-000 drachmas. The actual budgets of the kingdom differ, however, widely from the budget estimates. Since the establishment of Greece as an independent kingdom, there have been few financial terms without a deficit. The funded debt of Greece amounted in July, 1872, to 337,000,000 drachmas. The floating debt, according to semi-official returns, amounted to 40,000,000 drachmas on January 1, 1870. According to other statements from Greek sources, it was above 166,000,000 drachmas. A royal ordinance, dated January 17, 1869, authorized the Minister of Finance to issue 15,000,000 drachmas of notes, with compulsory circulation.

The army of the kingdom is formed by conscription, with the general privilege to procure substitutes, which is done to a very large extent. The strength of the army on the peace footing was, in 1873, 12,397 men. The contingent for the year 1873 was 1,500 men. The official paper of the Government in February, 1874, praised the Prussian army system, and strongly recommended its adoption by Greece.

The navy, in 1871, consisted of 2 iron-clad frigates, 8 screw-steamers, and 11 sailing-vessels. It was manned by conscription from the inhabitants of the sea-coast; the number of officers and men was, in 1873, 1,078.

The general commerce in 1871 was as follows, in drachmas :

COUNTRIES.	Imports.	Exports.
Great Britain..............	33,594,000	45,499,000
Turkey....................	16,501,000	6,906,000
Austria...................	14,544,000	8,620,000
Russia....................	16,118,000	4,507,000
France....................	13,476,000	6,282,000
Italy.....................	7,624,000	1,625,000
Other countries.......,....	6,680,000	2,951,000
Total, 1871.............	108,537,000	76,383,000
" 1870.............	97,021,000	53,906,000
" 1869.............	94,880,000	62,559,000

The movement of shipping in 1870 and 1871 is shown by the following table :

ENTERED AND CLEARED.	Year.	Vessels.	Tons.
Entered.			
Ocean navigation........	1870	16,757	2,564,964
Coast	1870	94,991	2,985,520
Cleared.			
Ocean navigation........	1871	21,758	3,205,519
Coast	1871	105,612	3,960,790

The merchant navy on December 31, 1871, consisted of 6,135 vessels, of 419,350 tons; among them there were 7 steamers, of about 3,000 tons, and more than 4,000 coasting-vessels.

The first Greek railroad, which connected Athens with the port of Piræus and Phalerits, was opened in 1869, and is 12 kilometres long (1 kilom. = 0.62 m.). In 1872 the railroad from the Piræus to Lamia, which is to be in length 220 kilometres, was begun, and a charter was granted for another road, which is to connect Athens with Kalamate, a distance of 275 kilometres. A company which had obtained the right to build seven railroads in the Peloponnesus, forfeited the concession in 1874, as it had failed to comply with the contract. The aggregate length of the electric telegraph-lines is 1,600 kilometres; that of the wires, 1,800 kilometres.

On February 19th the Cabinet Deligeorgis tendered its resignation, because at the election of a President of the Chamber the candidate of the Opposition, Zaimis, had been elected by 87 votes against 71 which were given to the ministerial candidate. The resignation was accepted, and Bulgaris charged with forming a new cabinet, which consisted of the following members: Bulgaris, President and Minister of the Interior; Delijannis, Minister of Foreign Affairs; Vlassafulos, Minister of Finances; Trindetta, Minister of War; Zalonis, Minister of the Navy; Papamichailopulos, Minister of Justice; and Nicolopulos, Minister of Worship. The leaders of the Opposition, Zaimis and Kumunduros, refused to accept a place in the ministry, but appeared to be willing to support it, and induced the Chamber to disapprove, by 127 against 29 votes, of the republican programme of the deputy Lombardos.

On April 28th Bulgaris tendered his resignation, on the ground that there was no majority in the Chamber on which the ministry could rely. The King called on Zaimis, subsequently on Kumunduros, and, when both declined, on Deligeorgis, to form a new cabinet. When the latter likewise found it impossible to surmount the difficulties, Bulgaris agreed to remain in office. The political programme of Kumunduros is explained in a letter addressed by him, on the 29th of April, to the King, which a few months later was published. He demanded that in the foreign relations every thing be avoided which would be apt to undermine the friendship and the confidence between Greece and Turkey, as well as the other nations of the East, or which might throw a doubt on the gratitude of Greece toward the three protecting powers. The policy pursued by Deligeorgis since July, 1872, he regarded as injurious to the interests of the country. In home affairs, Kumunduros demanded an honest management of constitutional laws, by which the too frequent dissolutions of the Chamber would become un-

necessary. He also demanded a thorough change of the electoral law, a removal of the evils which inevitably followed a centralization of the administration, and absolute freedom in selecting the members of the cabinet. The reply from the King to this letter was as follows: "The foreign policy is one either of peace or of war; I am determined to pursue a policy of peace. I can decide nothing with regard to laws concerning which the opinion of the Chamber is not yet known. All the ministers which thus far have succeeded each other have been entirely free. This freedom of action will also exist in future within the limits prescribed by existing laws, provided that the public safety and order be disturbed neither in Athens nor in the provinces."

In order to give to the country an opportunity to express a preference for one of the four statesmen who for years have repeatedly dislodged one another as heads of the ministry, the Chamber was dissolved, and a new election took place on July 4th. The result was very favorable to Bulgaris. Among the 185 members of the Chamber, about 25 were regarded as adherents of Kumunduros, 20 as adherents of Zaimis, 10 as friends of Deligeorgis, 10 as belonging for the present to no party, and all the others as either stanch adherents of Bulgaris and the so-called court party, or as followers of Grivas, who would support any administration. The fifth party, consisting of Lombardos, whose republican sentiments had been rebuked by the preceding Chamber, and his friends, was totally extinguished, as not one of the party was reëlected. Several other prominent politicians besides Lombardos were defeated; among them Deligeorgis, Theodore Delijannis, and Trikupis. The latter was arrested for using offensive language toward the King, but soon released. The ministry was charged by its opponents with having interfered in many places with the freedom of the election. At Zante, where Lombardos enjoys an unbounded popularity, the polling-places were said to have been surrounded by soldiers, who prevented Lombardos, and all who were known to be in his favor, from casting their votes. An electoral riot of considerable magnitude occurred at Corfu. According to the Greek papers, the riot arose from some person accidentally treading upon a drunken soldier's dog. The soldier drew his sword, and struck at not only the person who had innocently made his dog yelp, but everybody else at hand. Several persons were severely wounded. The outrage was reported to the commandant of the garrison, a certain Demitrakarakos, who, instead of putting the soldier under arrest and ordering an inquiry, allowed him to go at large. The next day the soldier, taking some comrades with him, repaired to the spot where the previous scene had occurred, and began to fall upon the unarmed citizens. The latter massed together and drove the soldiers back into the citadel. Thereupon Commandant Demitraka-rakos ordered the garrison to fire upon the town. The volley killed and wounded a number of persons, among the former being the wife of Mr. Miliarossi, a medical gentleman, and an English groom. The foreign consuls took the matter up, but made no impression on the commandant, who vauntingly declared that it was he who had given the order to fire on the people. These brutal acts so exasperated public feeling against the garrison, that the townspeople threatened to pull down the Greek flag and hoist the English standard, even if they had to storm the citadel; and it was with great difficulty, and only on the no-march promising that the garrison should immediately be sent away from Corfu, that the excitement was allayed. This pledge was confirmed by the Government at Athens, and within four days from the affair not one of the garrison was left, their place being taken by troops hurriedly picked up at Patras and other stations by dispatch-boats sent to convey them. Several arrests of townspeople were subsequently made, particularly of those who raised the cry "Hurrah for the English!" and attempted to make political capital out of the broil. The election at Corfu had to be postponed for several weeks, when seven opponents and two adherents of the Government were chosen.

The Chamber met on August 6th, and, as several weeks passed without a quorum being present, they were adjourned to October. After the reassembling, the Chamber, as usual, wasted a great deal of time in the verification of the elections, after which it elected Zarkos, an adherent of the ministry, as president.

On December 12th the Chamber approved the budget for 1874. A few days later the Opposition demanded that the resolution be reversed, because 96 members had not been present. When this motion was rejected by 80 against 61 votes, the entire Opposition left the hall and presented to the King a remonstrance signed by 58 deputies. As only 90 deputies remained in their seats, the Chamber was again left without a quorum.

The election by the Holy Synod, toward the close of 1873, of the Archbishop of Corfu as Metropolitan of Attica and President of the Holy Synod, was not ratified by the Government, which suspected the archbishop of a leaning toward Russia. At a new election the Archbishop of Messania, Procopios, was chosen. The new head of the Church of Greece has the reputation of being one of the most learned men of the Greek Church. He declined to accept the election, but finally yielded to the personal entreaties of the King.

The compulsory transfer of the Laurion mines* from the Franco-Italian Society, which had rediscovered them, to a Greek company, did not prove as profitable as the Greek poli-

*See ANNUAL CYCLOPÆDIA for 1872 and 1873.

ticians had expected. Mr. Anskett, an English expert, who was consulted by the Council of Administration on the prospects of the company, stated that, unless the Government reduced by about one-half (from 51 per cent. to 30 per cent.) the tax imposed upon the company, the latter would be unable to pay a dividend of 6 per cent.

GREEK CHURCH. The population connected with the Oriental Greek Church of Russia was, in 1871, according to the "Statistical Year-book of the Russian Empire" (vol. ii., 1871), about 58,000,000, divided as follows: European Russia, 53,139,000; Poland, 30,000; Caucasia, 1,930,000; Siberia, 2,875,000; Central Asia, 131,000; Finland, 34,000. Turkey numbers about 12,000,000 inhabitants belonging to the Greek Church, of whom 4,275,000 belong to Roumania, and 1,295,000 to Servia; Austria, according to the census of 1871, 3,050,000; the kingdom of Greece, 1,440,000; Montenegro, 125,000; Germany, about 3,000. The number of Rascolniks, or sectarians, in Russia, which acknowledge the doctrinal basis of the Greek Church, but reject the liturgy of the Russian Church as corrected by Patriarch Nicon (1654), is given in the "Statistical Year-book of the Russian Empire" as 922,079 in European Russia, 4,552 in Poland, 58,876 in Caucasia, 65,505 in Siberia, and 42,443 in Central Asia. But this number embraces only those who publicly profess themselves as Rascolniks; the number of those who secretly belong to the sects is much larger. They are variously estimated at from 5,000,000 to 15,000,000. Lengenfeldt, in his recent work on Russia ("Russland im 19. Jahrhundert," Berlin, 1875), assumes their number to be about 11,000,000; while Hepworth Dixon, in his work on Russia, claims to have heard from a Russian minister that they count fully 17,000,000.

The sentiments of the Church of Russia on the question of closer relations between the Eastern and Anglican Communions is set forth in the following reply from Isidore, the President of the Holy Synod of Russia, to the Committee of the House of Bishops of the Protestant Episcopal Church in the United States:

To the Well-Beloved in Christ, and the Right Reverend Committee of the House of Bishops of the Protestant Episcopal Church in the United States of America:

Your letter addressed to His Excellency the Procurator General Count Tolstoy, having been presented by him to the consideration of the Most Holy Governing Synod of Russia, together with the report and the concurrence of the House of Bishops, approved by the House of Clerical and Lay Deputies, in reference to the establishment upon a true Catholic basis of a spiritual fraternity between the American and o*r*thodox churches, especially in the Territory of Alaska, was received by the Most Holy Synod of the Russias with the utmost pleasure, as a new proof of respect shown by the representatives of the Episcopal Church, and of their estimable purpose concerning the union of the churches. The Most Holy Synod, on their part, will make it an object of their constant care that a spirit of Christian tolerance and fraternal love and esteem, in accordance with the precepts and usages of our church, shall continue to pervade all the relations existing between the members of the Orthodox Church and those of the Protestant Episcopal Church in America, and particularly in the Territory of Alaska.

As to the hypothesis of a reciprocal participation in the solemn performance of the Sacrament of the Eucharist, the Eastern Church firmly adheres to the principles and convictions so clearly stated in the messages sent in 1723 by the orthodox patriarchs of the East, in reply to the Anglican bishops. It considers a previous agreement in faith as absolutely indispensable to the practical mutual participation in the sacraments, inasmuch as the first is the only possible groundwork or basis for the last. In order to attain this most desired end, a thorough study and investigation of the differences in the doctrine of both churches would be absolutely requisite; and, to promote this, a great principle of coöperation will undoubtedly be found in the spirit of peace and charity which animates both churches, the Orthodox as well as the American, and in those prayers for the peace of the whole world, and for the union of the holy churches of the Lord, which arise to the God of truth and mercy from the Orthodox churches, and which are most certainly shared in the American churches.

Having been authorized by the Most Holy Governing Synod, I assume the duty of presenting their answer to the House of Bishops of the American Episcopal Church, and beg you to accept the assurance of the highest esteem of your brother and coservant in Christ Jesus.   ISIDORE, First Presiding Minister of the Governing Synod of all the Russias, and Metropolitan of Novgorod and St. Petersburg.

According to an account given of the Greek Church of Turkey, by an English clergyman long familiar with Eastern Church affairs, an increased importance is now attributed to the study and the preaching of the Bible. He says:

In sermons, letters, speeches, this is the topic which is dwelt upon more frequently than I have ever before known. A new movement in this direction seems to have taken its first impulse from the sermon preached by the former Protosyncellus of the Œcumenical Patriarch, on the occasion of the enthronization of the latter. The preacher innovated (in the eyes of some offensively) by discarding compliments, and reminding the chief pastor of the dangers and the defects of the Great Church over which he was appointed to watch. "Thou canst not but see that the Word of God doth *not* dwell in us richly." That was the key-note of his strain. That preacher has been recently sent to Choritza, in Western Macedonia, as archbishop—and one good effect of this appointment has been to call forth from the organ of the Armenian Church an exclamation of delight, because a truly spiritual pastor has been appointed to tend that flock. It is to be hoped that such expressions of sympathy, besides showing a true bond of union between believers of communions unhappily still separated, may also rouse the old Armenian Church to a godly jealousy.

The Church of Greece in 1874 received a new head, by the election of the Archbishop of Messenia as Metropolitan of Attica and President of the Holy Synod (see Greece). Of other new episcopal appointments, the *Aion,* of Athens, of August 5th (17), says that "after long and careful consideration, royal decrees were day before yesterday issued, by which were designated, out of nine candidates pro-

posed by the Holy Synod, three persons to fill vacant sees. Stephen Argurides, aged about fifty-five, a select preacher, a graduate of the Rizarean School, was appointed to the See of Massenia; the Archimandrite Callinicus Terzopoulos, aged about forty-five, a graduate of the Hieratic School, to the See of Argolis; to that of Patras, Averkios Lampyres, aged fifty, for a long time past Secretary of the Holy Synod. The latter spent four years in Germany, pursuing his studies, after graduating at the Theological School of the university.

The Greek Church of the Servian nationality in the kingdom of Hungary had, in 1874, to choose as its head a new Patriarch of Carlowitz. According to the Hungarian constitution, each religious denomination of the kingdom administers its own church affairs, the legislative function being exercised by an autonomous church congress. Formerly the Servian Church Congress, which elected the patriarch, was composed of twenty-five clergymen, twenty-five military men, and twenty-five other laymen. The commissioner of the Government was generally an influential general, who, with the aid of twenty-five military members of the Congress, always knew how to secure the election of the candidate of the Government. The abolition of the military frontier, and the organization of the Greek Church of the Roumanian nationality into a separate ecclesiastical province, had caused a great change in the composition of the Church Congress, to which Article IX. of the laws of 1868 guarantees, among other autonomous rights, that of electing the patriarch. As it now consists exclusively of representatives of the Servian nationality, its actions are closely connected with the tendencies of the Servian nationality in Hungary, and were therefore watched with great eagerness. The Congress again, as in former years, consisted of seventy-five delegates, twenty-five clerical and fifty laymen. Among the latter there were this year only three military men, but on the other hand ten doctors of law, who had graduated at the Universities of Vienna and Pesth, and were the prominent leaders of the Congress. The Hungarian Government had made great efforts to prevent, at the elections for the Congress, the success of the candidates of the national Servian party, and to secure the nomination of a man of moderate views on the nationality question. As the national Servian party generally favors the extension of the rights of the Church Congress and a development of the church constitution on the broad basis of self-government, the Hungarian Government found it in its interest to ally itself closely with the hierarchical party which desires to clothe the bishops with as large powers as possible. The result of the elections was, however, unfavorable to the Hungarian Government. Of the seventy-five deputies, only three belonged to the strictly hierarchical party, ten others to a compromising middle party, while all the others were stanch partisans of the national party. The candidate of the Hungarian Government for the headship of the church was Bishop Gruitch, the administrator of the patriarchate; the court of Vienna favored the coadjutor bishop Augyelitch, the head of the clerical party; the national Servian party, in fine, was known to support Arsenius Stojkovitch, the former administrator of the patriarchate and at present Bishop of Ofen. Bishop Gruitch had, in 1848, been the greatest enemy of the Magyars, and by inflammatory speeches had stirred up the insurrection of the Servians against the Magyars. During the ministry of Bach he had to suffer much from persecution, and had to live for many years retired in a convent of Syrmia. When he finally succeeded in obtaining a diocese in Slavonia, he endeavored to atone for his national tendencies in 1848 by an excessive loyalty. His pastoral letters were chiefly remarkable for the emphatic recommendation of submissiveness to the Emperor and the lawful authorities. He found it all the easier to re-enter into friendly relations with the Hungarian Government, as he has an excellent command of the Magyar language, having been educated in a Magyar county. He has broken off all connection with the national Servian party. The coadjutor bishop Augyelitch is regarded as the best authority in all questions of the Oriental Church law. He is a determined opponent of all the innovations which the creation of an autonomous Church Congress has introduced into the administration of the parishes, of the consistories, and the eparchial assemblies. He desires to maintain the full authority of the bishops, not only in all questions strictly ecclesiastical, but also in the administration of Church property. Being thoroughly conservative in all his views, he knew how to obtain the unbounded confidence of the Vienna court. Bishop Stojkovitch is a firm and enthusiastic advocate of all the peculiar tenets of the Oriental Church, but he regards the participation of laymen in the administration of temporalities as entirely compatible with the character of the Oriental Church. He kept entirely aloof from the intrigues of the bishops and the clerical party against the authority of the Servian Church Congress, and thus gained the affection of the national party. Having been appointed administrator of the patriarchate at the death of Patriarch Mashirevitch, he gained as president of the preceding Church Congress, by the judicious exercise of his powers, universal satisfaction. In consequence of the intrigues of the clerical party against him, he was relieved from the administration of the patriarchate, although the Emperor of Austria expressed to him on this occasion his satisfaction and conferred upon him the grand-cross of the Order of Leopold. The Hungarian Government, being afraid of the popularity of Bishop Stojkovitch, endeavored to prevail upon him to decline an election even before the opening of the Con-

gress, but Stojkovitch refused to comply with this demand, unless the Emperor personally should request him to do so. The opening of this Congress was to take place at Carlowitz on July 11th, but was postponed to July 12th. The Hungarian Government had appointed as its commissioner Councillor Hueber, a German-Hungarian, and native of a Servian district of Hungary. The interest which the entire Servian nation takes in this Church Congress had brought to Carlowitz a large number of visitors from all parts of Turkish as well as Austrian Servia. On the day of opening, the administrator of the patriarchate, Bishop Gruitch, having been led by a deputation into the hall of the Congress, moved that the respects of the Congress be expressed to the royal commissioner, and that he be invited to open the Congress. When the commissioner had made his appearance, he addressed the Congress at first in the Hungarian, after that in the Servian language, and then read the royal rescript, also in both languages. The rescript designated, as the first business of the Congress, the election of a patriarch, after which the Synod would meet to dispose of several subjects referred to it, and to elect bishops for the vacant sees; subsequently the Congress would continue its transactions on church, school, and property questions. Full accounts of the proceedings of the Congress were published in a lithographed paper, specially established at Carlowitz for the purpose, and published in the German language, under the title of *Carlovitzer Correspondenz*. Immediately after the verification of the elections, the Congress proceeded to the nomination of the patriarch. In accordance with the general expectation, Bishop Stojkovitch was the first choice, sixty-three votes being cast for him and seven members abstaining from voting. The Government refused to sanction the election, the royal rescript, which is dated Ebensee, July 22d, merely stating that upon motion of the Prime-Minister of Hungary, and in agreement with the Hungarian Minister of Public Worship, and with the Government of Croatia, the royal sanction could not be given to the election of Bishop Stojkovitch. After the reading of the royal rescript, the Church Congress adopted a resolution expressing regret that, for the first time in the history of the Austro-Servians, the royal sanction had been denied to a patriarch who had been elected by a unanimous vote. The members of the Congress were at first inclined to resign in a body, as they were not willing to elect any of the other bishops of the Servian Church. At length, however, they agreed to proceed to a second election, and to cast their votes for the Metropolitan of the Greek Church of the Roumanian nation, Archbishop Ivacskovitch, who, although the head of the church of another nationality, was yet a native Servian and a personal friend of Stojkovitch. He was accordingly elected on July 31st, by fifty-six votes; the candidate of the Government, Bishop Gruitch, receiving only seven votes. The new election inspired all the more confidence, as Bishop Ivacskovitch, as head of the Church of the Roumanian nationality, had already had some experience in the administration of a similar position. Before the separation of the Church of the Roumanian from that of the Servian nationality, he had been Bishop of Arad, and, when that diocese became a part of the Roumanian Church province, he had remained its bishop; and, although of the Servian nationality, had gained the confidence of the Roumanians to such an extent that they elected him, in 1873, their metropolitan. Although the Hungarian Government was by no means pleased with the result of the second election, it deemed it best this time not to withhold its sanction, and accordingly Bishop Ivacskovitch was, on August 18th, the birthday of the Emperor, installed as Patriarch of the Servian nationality by pompous solemnities. The Synod of the Servian bishops, which could now be convoked under the presidency of the patriarch, filled the vacant sees of Temesvar and Carlstadt by the election of the priests Voinovitch and Zsiokovitch, both of whom were confirmed by the Government. The Church Congress reassembled on October 5th. The leader of the national party, Dr. Miletitch, objected to a proposition of the patriarch to invite the royal commissioner to the meetings of the Congress; the objection was, however, withdrawn, when the patriarch assured the Congress that he and not the commissioner would preside at the Congress. The commissioner laid before the Congress the report of the Episcopal Synod on the statute concerning the organization of the Church Congress, which the Hungarian Government had referred to the Episcopal Synod for its opinion. The majority of the Congress were any thing but pleased with the report of the bishops, and especially objected to their demand that not only all dogmatical, ritual, and liturgical questions should belong to the exclusive jurisdiction of the Episcopal Synod, but also all questions of church discipline. A committee of fifteen members was elected to examine the report of the bishops, and to propose to this Congress a proper course of action. While the committee was unanimous in the rejection of some demands of the bishops, it was not altogether opposed to a compromise. The leader of the compromising party, Dr. Maksimovitch, prepared a new draft of a statute for the composition of this Congress, and the Congress expressed its concurrence in the desire for a peaceable solution of the difficulties by rejecting the motion made by Dr. Miletitch to make the statute of 1871 the basis of the discussion. While the bishops demanded that the Congress should regulate the autonomy of the Church only in agreement with the Synod, thus making it dependent upon the concurrence of the Synod, the middle party conceded that the Congress should act in important questions only after hearing the opinion of the Synod. After long negotiations, in which the Hungarian Government took an active part in favor of the bishops, an agreement was attained, in virtue of which disciplinary questions, of a purely ecclesiastical character, were added to the subjects which are under the exclusive jurisdiction of the bishops. The Congress adjourned on October 26th.

The National Congress of the Greek Church of the Roumanian nation in the Kingdom of Hungary met on October 27th, at Hermannstadt, in order to elect another metropolitan and head of the Church in place of Archbishop Ivacskovitch, who had been elected by the Servian Church Congress Patriarch of Carlowitz. An important innovation in the Greek Oriental Church was the convocation by Bishop Pavel, of Szamos-Ujvar, of a diocesan synod, one-third of the members to be clerical and two-thirds lay delegates. This is believed to be the first diocesan synod of the kind in the Greek Oriental Church.

The Synod of the Greek Church of Roumania met in November, and remained in session for about six weeks. It passed a resolution to ask the Government to place the entire system of public instruction under the control of the Church. The Minister of Public Worship conceded to the bishop the right of examining and approving the school-books; but the question whether the Church was also to control the appointment of the teachers was referred to the Diet.

GREGORY, DUDLEY SANDFORD, an enterprising, useful, and philanthropic citizen of Jersey City, N. J., born in Reading, Conn., February 5, 1800; died in Jersey City, December 8, 1874. In 1808 his father removed to Albany, N. Y., and, young as he was, the boy began to look about for employment. He was at first errand-boy in the Eagle Tavern, but at the age of thirteen he had developed business abilities, which led the then State Controller to take him into that office as a clerk. He remained there fourteen years, rising to the position of chief clerk of the Canal Department, and fulfilling all trusts confided to him with such ability and integrity that the position of deputy controller was pressed upon him by Governor Marcy. He declined this, and accepted the general superintendency of Messrs. Yates and McIntire's lottery business, which was then conducted for the State, for the endowment of schools and colleges. He managed their business first as their superintendent, and after they retired as their successor, until the legal expiration of the term of the commission, a period of ten years, and then settled up the business, which took several years more. Meantime he had removed in 1834 to Jersey City, then a mere hamlet, and set himself to the work of building up this now large and wealthy suburb of New York. He became one of the "Jersey Associates," and directed their purchases of waste lands which have since

yielded such immense wealth to the association; was an efficient officer of the town and
county boards, mayor of the young city for
three successive terms, member of Congress
from 1847 to 1849, strongly pressed for United
States Senator, and Water Commissioner, Bank
Commissioner, president of the first savings-
bank of Jersey City, director at one time in sixteen different railway companies, including all
that had their *termini* in Jersey City; and
a bountiful giver to churches of all denominations, public schools, city parks, and all other
institutions and enterprises intended to benefit
his fellow-citizens. No man was better or
more favorably known to all the citizens of his
adopted city. About 1851 or 1852 Mr. Gregory
made an extended tour in Europe, and greatly
enjoyed the contrast between the more quiet
life of the Old World and the bustle, enterprise,
and push of the New.

GRINNELL, HENRY, an eminent American
merchant and philanthropist, long connected
with arctic explorations, born in New Bedford, Mass., in 1800; died in New York City,
June 30, 1874. He was of Huguenot ancestry, and the name is still preserved in a street,
a square, and an artesian well in Paris, though
with what was the original spelling—Gre-
nelle. Mr. Grinnell's early education was very
thorough; the New Bedford Academy, from
which he graduated in 1818, being one of the
best schools of that time. The same year he
came to New York and became a clerk with
Messrs. II. D. & E. B. Sewell, a large com-
mission-house in Pine Street, with whom he
remained until 1826, when, a change occurring
in the firm of Fish & Grinnell, in which his
elder brother, Joseph Grinnell, had been a
partner since 1810, he and another brother,
Moses H., joined the firm, and two years later,
Joseph Grinnell retiring, Robert B. Minturn,
Sen., entered it. The great shipping-house of
Grinnell, Minturn & Co., thus formed, transacted a safe and prosperous shipping business
for more than thirty years, never engaging in
any speculation nor departing in any way from
their legitimate department of trade. Their
credit was never for a moment in doubt, and
their business was conducted with such moderation as to leave the partners ample time for
such intellectual pursuits as they desired.
Henry Grinnell was specially interested in
geographical studies, and had always been occupied and charmed with explorations in
arctic seas, though we believe none of the
large fleet of the firm were engaged in the
whale or seal fisheries. Sir John Franklin
was one of his heroes, and when in 1850 five
years had passed since any tidings had been
received from him, Mr. Grinnell, at his own
expense, fitted out an expedition to go in search
of the lost navigator. This was the expedition
which sailed from New York in May, 1850,
under command of Lieutenant E. J. De Haven,
and in which Dr. E. K. Kane went as surgeon
and naturalist. The unknown land discovered

VOL. XIV.—25   A

in latitude 75° 24′ 21″ by this expedition was
rightly named Grinnell Land, and English and
French explorers and geographers have united
with our own in conferring that name upon it.
Mr. Grinnell's zeal was not cooled by the want
of success which attended this first expedition.
In 1853, in conjunction with George Peabody,
he expended $50,000 in fitting out the second
Franklin Expedition, which was placed in
charge of Dr. Kane, the Government bearing
the expense of manning and victualing the
Advance and Rescue, and supplying the explorers with apparatus. He gave, besides
money, his valuable time and his unwearied
efforts to the proper equipment of the expedition. He was greatly gratified with what it
accomplished, though it was less than he had
hoped. The Hayes Expedition also found in
him a liberal patron, as did the last sad but
not wholly unproductive expedition of Captain
Hall. He had great faith in Captain Hall, to
whom he believed the public were indebted
for most of what was known in regard to the
fate of Sir John Franklin and his companions.
So anxious was he for the success of the Polaris Expedition that with his approval one of
his sons came from Australia to go out in her;
but, learning from actual observation how
poorly the vessel was prepared for the work
it proposed to undertake, he pursuaded his son
to abandon the voyage. In 1852 Henry Grinnell retired from the firm of Grinnell, Minturn
& Co., and spent a considerable time in the
easy enjoyment of the fruits of his mercantile
career. After an interval of leisure he became
engaged in insurance, and since 1859 had been
connected with the Liverpool and London Insurance Company, and was for a considerable
time at the head of its interests in this country. His name has not been conspicuous in
the public eye of late years, for he took no
active part in the movements of the day outside of his favorite field. For a few years
previous to his retirement from the firm of
Grinnell, Minturn & Co., he was much interested in politics, and in 1848 was a very earnest opponent of slavery. His political opinions
afterward underwent considerable modification, and he took no part in party struggles.
A noteworthy element in his character, which
has made his name less prominent of recent
years than it would otherwise have been, was
his marked inclination for privacy and retirement. He deprecated the mention of his
name in public prints, and courteously declined to give aid in the way of information
to any who desired to make mention of his
life and services in the cause of arctic exploration in books. His decision of character and
strength of will were softened by a liberal disposition and a ready courtesy of manner.

GRISCOM, JOHN HOSKINS, M. D., an eminent American physician, humanitarian, and
author, born in New York City, August 14,
1809; died there, of disease of the brain, April
28, 1874. He was a son of the late Prof. John

Griscom, LL. D. He received his early education in the collegiate school of the Society of Friends, studied medicine with Profs. John D. Godman and Valentine Mott, and took his degree of M. D. in the University of Pennsylvania in 1832. The following year he was appointed Assistant Physician to the New York Dispensary, of which he became Physician in 1834. From 1836 to 1840 he was Professor of Chemistry in the New York College of Pharmacy, and in 1842 he was appointed City Inspector, which position he held one year, when he became Visiting Physician of New York Hospital, in which service he continued until a few years since. From 1848 to 1851 he was General Agent of the Commissioners of Emigration. He was also identified with the management of the New York Prison Association, the Juvenile Reformatory, the Home for the Friendless, the New York Sanitary Association, the Social Science Association, and the New York Association for the Advancement of Science and Art. Of the last-named association he was one of the founders, the first president, and long its most zealous and efficient member. He was through life a strict adherent of the Society of Friends. Dr. Griscom wrote much and ably on medical, sanitary, hygienic, and scientific topics. His principal published works are "Animal Mechanism and Physiology" (1839); "Sanitary Condition of the Laboring Classes of New York;" "The Uses and Abuses of Air, and the Means of the Ventilation of Buildings" (1850); "An Oration before the Academy of Medicine" (1854); "A Memoir of John Griscom, LL. D." (1859); "Essays on Prison Reform;" and numerous papers in the medical journals; and we believe he also edited an American edition of the "Life and Times of Stephen Grellét."

GUATEMALA (República de Guatemala), one of the five independent states of Central America, stretching from 13° 50' to 18° 15' north latitude, and from 88° 14' to 93° 12' west longitude. Its boundaries are: north, the Mexican State of Chiapas; east, Balize and the Caribbean Sea; south, Honduras and San Salvador; and southwest and west, the Pacific Ocean. Guatemala has as yet no written constitution, a circumstance consequent on the radical changes that have taken place there.

The territory of the republic embraces an area of 40,777 square miles; and the population, in 1873, was estimated at 1,200,000 approximately, that of the capital being set down at 45,000 in 1874. Details of the proportions of the various elements constituting the population may be found in the ANNUAL CYCLOPÆDIA for 1873, page 344.

Two attempts have been made to plant colonies in Guatemala: one at Boca Nueva, and the other at Santo Tomás, both on the Atlantic coast. None have as yet been formed on the Pacific coast. The colonists of Boca Nueva established themselves on the banks of

a branch of the Polochique, and traded with the interior by Vera Paz; those of Santo Tomás, one of the finest harbors on the Caribbean coast, proposed to open up a road to the capital by way of the department of Chiquimula, where it would be easy to take advantage of a part of the river Motagua. The natives affirm that these attempts at colonization were powerfully aided by the British minister in Guatemala. Some years ago a Belgian company took the subject up, and attracted the attention of a great number of families in Belgium, Luxemburg, South Germany, and France. Central America was then much less known than it is at present. After a considerable expenditure of time and money, the company obtained the concession of the district of Santo Tomás, but the climate proved unfavorable to European constitutions; and, besides, the bad management of the colony, the pretensions of the Government commissioner, and, above all, the difficulty of communicating quickly with the capital, presented serious obstacles to the success of the scheme. The colonists finding themselves tyrannized over by the directors, uncared for by the Government, and by agents who ought to have

protected them, and defrauded by the Belgian consul, many of them endeavored to go back to their own countries. In three months, from August to October, in the year 1844, four hundred Belgian colonists died in Santo Tomás, chiefly from neglect; for, although, by treaty between the company and the Government, the colonists were received and adopted as citizens of Guatemala, when trouble and sickness set in, the Government took no further concern about their condition.

Another cause of failure was the death of the chief agent of the company, who proposed several improvements which, if carried out, would not only have insured the prosperity of the colony, but tended to develop the general commercial interests of the republic. Among other plans which he had formed, after a due study of the topography of the region to be colonized, was that of deepening the entrance to the Rio Dulce, without which the fine port of Santo Tomás must always remain shut out from communication with the interior; while the removal of the obstruction would allow large vessels to pass in, and make the lagoon of Izabal a better port than any now existing in Central America. It would likewise render the large river Polochique serviceable as a way of communication as far as Teleman; agriculture in Vera Paz would become an important industry; land would increase in value; Livingstone would be converted into an excellent seaport; and new attractions would be offered for a numerous immigration.

But why the introduction of foreigners should be indispensable to the material development of a country with an average of thirty individuals to the square mile, may justly be regarded with wonder, while Chili, the most flourishing agricultural state in America, after the United States, has not quite nine inhabitants per square mile, and fewer natural advantages than Guatemala. The evil in the latter republic is not owing to a lack of hands, but to the improper direction of those which exist. The Indians, who constitute rather more than one-half of the population, there take the place of beasts of burden; and the only instruments they are accustomed to handle, or of which they are even aware, are the knife, the pick, the machete, and the axe; whereas, with suitable implements and machines, they would be enabled to till the ground at once more thoroughly and to greater extent; the yield of the varied products which find a genial soil in Guatemala would be increased one hundred-fold; and with adequate roads and other facilities for transporting those products to the coasts, the republic would soon have little to envy the most prosperous of the Spanish-American republics in the matter of exports.

It has been suggested that, even after the adoption of the modern labor-saving appliances for husbandry, the apportionment by families of the land allotted to the Indians would stimulate the latter to still greater activity; but if such a system were inaugurated, it would be easy to furnish each family with the necessary seeds, and render cultivation compulsory.

The President of the Republic is General Rufino Barrios; the president of the cabinet is J. M. Samayoa, Minister of War and of Public Works; the Minister of Finance is F. Alburez; of Foreign Affairs, Ramon Rosa; and of the Interior, Justice, Public Instruction, and Public Worship, M. A. Soto.

The army has been reduced to the number of men sufficient for the garrisons of the principal towns; and the militia force organized

in such a manner that, at short notice, General Barrios can have under arms a force of 10,000 men.

Thanks to several new sources of income called into existence by the Government, the public treasury has improved in a remarkable manner, as may be seen from the following statement of the finances for the year 1873:

REVENUE.

On hand from 1872	$13,000
Import duties	989,773
Spirit-tax	511,306
City contributions	29,789
Sugar-plantation tax	48,414
Other receipts ordinary	569,599
Receipts extraordinary	454,026
Total	$2,615,677

EXPENDITURES.

Army	$1,237,843
Civil administration	244,214
Pensions	600,270
Public instruction	25,662
Public works	96,312
Public worship	4,291
Foreign affairs	6,433
Subsidies	16,638
Expenditures extraordinary	30,603
Premium on exports	1,517
Municipal subsidies	35,841
Hospitals	18,715
Sociedad Económica	8,207
Mint	297,158
Post-Office	1,387
Stamp-duty	864
Gunpowder, saltpetre, etc.	1,429
Disbursements	7,818
Public debt	358,478
Reimbursements in advance	101,585
" of deposits	41,863
Sundries	38,910
Total	$2,603,538

Here, then, is a surplus of $12,139, against $13,000 in 1872, with an increased expenditure in the branch of public instruction, and an unusually large payment on account of the public debt.

According to published statistics, the Government revenue for the month of December, 1873, was $329,374.78, and the expenditure $317,215.93, leaving a surplus of $12,152.85. The revenue for May, 1874, amounted to $131,100.

The public debt on July 31, 1874, was	$4,119,784 92
On August 31	4,092,987 10
Decrease of debt	$26,797 82

The *deuda convertida* (home debt), which was at 50 per cent. two years ago, had reached 85 per cent., and the capitalists of the country were making it their principal object of investments.

The sale of spirits, in the first three months of 1874, produced the following amounts: In January, $58,508.43; February, $54,001.56; March, $60,252.68—making a total of $122,762.67.

It was decided by the Government that, instead of the Agricultural Hypothecary Bank to be created by decree of August 27, 1873, a National Bank of emission and discount should be established, with a capital of $2,000,000. The board of directors of the new bank is composed of the wealthiest and most distinguished men in the country, natives and foreigners; and the notes issued are guaranteed by the capital above mentioned, and by the national Government.

The new bank, established with the proceeds of mortmain properties, was to be opened about the 1st of July. The funds amounted to more than $2,000,000, but not more than one-half had as yet been realized. The product of the liquidations was to be paid into the bank by half-yearly installments. To begin operations, the bank counted on those for December, 1873, and June, 1874, as well as the cash already on hand, according to the law of consolidation. The opening of the bank was anxiously awaited, and great benefits were expected to accrue to commerce in general.

Notwithstanding the political disorders of recent years, the financial condition of the republic is, on the whole, comparatively prosperous, and the national credit has been sustained in Europe through very trying circumstances.

Some failures having taken place in a manner to give ground for suspicion, a decree was issued for the imprisonment of such bankrupts as could not prove their failure to be the result of unavoidable misfortune.

The value of the exports for the year 1872, and the countries to which they were sent, were as follows:

Countries.	Values.
Great Britain	$722,047 38
France	119,884 96
Germany	528,340 54
United States	904,500 55
Belgium	59,333 97
Italy	13,122 00
South America	51,521 04
Central America	126,990 20
Balize	45,969 56
Total	$2,691,710 19

The figures of this table, compared with the value of the exports for 1871, show a difference of some $55,000 in favor of the latter year; but the average for both marks a steady improvement since 1869—an improvement which was still more flattering in 1873, as is exhibited in the subjoined table of the exports for the septennium ending with that year:

Years.	Values.
1867	$1,996,405
1868	2,153,400
1869	2,497,060
1870	2,446,925
1871	2,747,784
1872	2,691,710
1873	3,363,061
Total	$17,896,345

The increase in 1873, as compared with 1872, is here seen to have been about one-third, and far in advance of the average value of the exports for the above septennial period, say $2,-556,621—this result according with the suggestion made in the ANNUAL CYCLOPÆDIA for 1873, page 345, concerning a probable marked improvement for that year.

The commodities most largely exported in 1872 were: coffee, valued at $1,669,553; cochineal, $495,880; skins, $95,416; India-rubber, $124,324.

The quantities of the principal export staples sent out of the country in 1873 were as follows:

Articles.	Quantities.
Coffee	15,050,668 pounds.
Cochineal	1,107,481 "
India-rubber	380,312 "
Lead	86,890 "
Tobacco	53,382 "
Sarsaparilla	80,873 "

Cochineal, notwithstanding the unusual abundance and excellence of the crop, was sold at such reduced prices for export that many planters have decided to follow the movement initiated in 1872 of abandoning the culture of the cochineal insect, and devoting their attention to the production of coffee.*

The yield of the dye just referred to will in all likelihood prove inferior both in quality and quantity next season, owing to extensive inundations which occurred in September in some of the chief producing districts.

Of all the products cultivated in regular plantations in Guatemala, coffee is the most important; and, notwithstanding the decline in the price of that berry in European markets of late, planters do not seem to be discouraged, but bestow more and more attention upon its culture from year to year.

The alluvial soils and deep vegetable loams of Costa Grande, not infrequently mixed with sand and volcanic *débris*, appear to be remarkably favorable to the highest development of the plant, both in respect of productiveness and the quality of the bean. The coffee-shrub thrives at almost all elevations in Central America, from the torrid coast-regions of the sea-level, where vegetation is luxuriant to rankness, up to the line of perennial cold; but it is most prolific on the sea-coast, producing all the year round, so that at any given time the same tree may present the phenomenon of fruit in every stage of growth, from the blossom to absolute maturity. This continuous fructification, which is not limited to the coffee-shrub, is owing to the showers so frequent during the dry season. In the more elevated regions the yield is smaller, but the quality is finer, when not impaired by unseasonable rains about the time of the ripening of the berry. These rains, and a growth of parasitic moss on the stems and branches of the plants, are the only dangers to be apprehended at considerable altitudes. In some parts of the republic the shrub grows exceedingly well on grounds at a height of 4,000 and even 5,000 feet above the sea-level. Northeast and northwest winds are particularly destructive to the trees, being at times so violent as to dry them up and prevent fructification for that and the following year. A coffee estate of average size contains some 100,000 trees; and of good coffee-seed, sown at the proper season—usually in September or October—and under the most favorable circumstances in every respect, not more than 75 per cent. germinates. Good plants usually

* See ANNUAL CYCLOPÆDIA for 1872, page 378.

arrive at full bearing in the sixth year; in the twelfth they are in their prime; and some continue to bear until the eighteenth or twentieth year.

The Government, at the suggestion of some sugar-planters, approved the statutes of a joint-stock company, organized for the purpose of establishing a sugar-refinery in the republic. The enterprise is to be on a large scale, and it can scarcely fail to prove successful. The new industry will also be the means of introducing many others, some of which are immediately attendant upon it, such as the manufacture of animal charcoal, which, after it has been used in the purification of the sugar, can be applied as an excellent fertilizer for the fields.

A number of India-rubber plantations have been formed of late, and this branch of cultivation bids fair to give handsome results.

Tobacco-planting, which has been attempted in various parts of the country, begins already to show signs of success.

It is reported that the chief towns are shortly to be lighted with gas, and proposals have been made for porcelain, paper, and stearine candle factories.

Rich coal-beds have been discovered near Izabal, and arrangements were about to be made for working them as soon as suitable machinery can be procured; and, in the mean time, timber-felling in the forests of Peten was to be commenced on an extensive scale, for account of the Government.

The Department of Public Works reports some progress in the matter of roads, so much needed in every direction. Work had begun on a new carriage-road, to lead northward from the capital, and which, when completed, will be eminently beneficial to the commercial interests of the eastern departments.

There is now a project on foot for the construction of a railway from Escuintla to the Pacific port of San José, the length of which, according to the report of the minister, will be 32 miles, and the total cost, at the rate of

GUATEMALA IN 1724.

$30,000 per mile, $960,000. Of this sum it is proposed to pay $768,000 in advance, and the remainder in bonds bearing interest at 6 per cent.

Judging from the good credit the republic enjoys in Europe, it was presumed that the money could be obtained there on favorable terms, viz., by issuing bonds at the rate of 70, with interest at 7 per cent. per annum, and an accumulative sinking-fund of 2 per cent. per annum, equivalent to about 11.83, or less than 12 per cent., the usual rate of interest in Guatemala.

The net proceeds of the line, calculating the exportation and importation at 10,000,000 lbs. each, exclusive of the increase of agricultural

and commercial enterprises, would give $114,-200, in which are included the yield from passengers, and one-half of the duties on imports and exports by San José, which at present are intended for the support of that end of the road. A prospectus of the line was published, and Señor Saenz de Tejada, residing in Paris, was appointed special commissioner by the Government for the negotiation of the loan. In case sufficient funds can be raised, the line will be extended to the capital.

The telegraph is fast spreading its wires through the republic; communication was established, in April, with the eastern departments; lines to the western departments were in course of construction; and on June 2d telegrams were exchanged between the capitals of Guatemala and San Salvador, through a line connecting the two cities.

Meantime the great subject of public instruction has not been neglected, although the problem of its organization so as to be in conformity with the existing Government and institutions of the country has not yet been solved. Concomitantly with the question of separation of church and state, already an accomplished fact in most of the South American states, that of placing the public schools under the exclusive direction of the civil authorities was warmly discussed in legislative circles, among the leading men of the present Liberal party, and by the official press; it being evident that the achievement of both of these reforms is regarded by President Barrios as a matter of paramount importance. This war of words, however, has not delayed action in the proper direction: the Government has determined upon the education of the people; and its efforts have already been attended with satisfactory results. Schools have been multiplied; improved text-books—many of them from the city New York—procured; and a number of teachers from the city just mentioned were engaged in the course of the year and taken to Guatemala under the immediate auspices and at the expense of the Government. About the middle of the year there were distributed throughout the republic 541 primary schools, 358 being for males, with an attendance of 14,216; and 138 for females, with 6,312 pupils on the rolls; and the aggregate expense per month for the support of these establishments was set down at $4,317.

In the schools of Escuintla there were in August last 1,077 pupils, and in September, 1,103.

The schools of both sexes in the department of Vera Paz were both numerous and successful. In July they were attended by 1,315 pupils of both sexes, and by 1,403 in August. In that of San Márcos there were 1,050 boys and 720 girls receiving primary instruction.

In examinations in geography, held at the capital, in presence of the ministers of Great Britain and the United States, the Italian chargé d'affaires, the members of the Government, and a large concourse of people, the pupils evinced a considerable degree of proficiency.

A school of medicine has been established at which lectures are given in materia medica and therapeutics, obstetrics, medical jurisprudence, and pharmacy; and a philharmonic society, under the direction of an Italian professor.

A military college was opened in Guatemala in the course of the year.

In February it was decreed by the Government that the nuns of the different convents of the capital, amounting altogether to about 140 women, should be assembled in the convent of Santa Catarina; that the inmates were freed from their vows of perpetual seclusion from the world, and were completely restored to liberty; and that conventual establishments were to be open to the visits of relatives and the inspection of the civil authorities. The ecclesiastical authorities caused to be placed at the door of the convent a notice that whoever entered without permission from the Church was, by the mere act of doing so, excommunicated. The nuns of three of the suppressed establishments petitioned the Government for a pension, and obtained a grant of $12 each per month.

The Government issued another decree prohibiting, under a fine of not less than $10 and not more than $50, priests and other clergymen from wearing the usual distinctive garments or long robes, etc., except when engaged in the performance of their sacred duties.

With monastic institutions, tithes were abolished, religious tolerance was established, and all church property decreed alienable.

In April, Mr. Magee, the British vice-consul, was unmercifully flogged in public by order of one Gonzales, commandant of the port of San José, and a native of Spain. The Government offered ample satisfaction, and the outraged man received an indemnity of $50,000. Gonzales and his accomplice were tried by court martial and sentenced, the former to five years' imprisonment and hard labor, and the other to two years, both to be dismissed in disgrace from the service of the Government.

Save the intervention of the Guatemala Government, conjointly with that of San Salvador, in the revolution in Honduras to overthrow the administration of Arias,* the republic has enjoyed perfect tranquillity both at home and abroad since August, 1873.

It is not improbable that Mexico may soon renew her claim to the district of Peten, the inhabitants of which, shortly after the establishment of independence, expressed their desire to be under the Mexican Government.

On the night of September 3d a violent earthquake occurred at Antigua, destroying a large number of houses and some of the ruins of 1773, and causing the death of some thirty-five persons,

GUIZOT, François Pierre Guillaume, one of the most remarkable of modern French statesmen, diplomatists, and historians, born at Nimes, France, October 4, 1787; died at Valricher, near Paris, September 13, 1874. He was of Huguenot ancestry, and his family numbered more than one of its members among the martyrs to the faith in the seventeenth and eighteenth centuries. His father, an eminent lawyer of Paris, perished by the guillotine during the Reign of Terror, and his mother had taken this, her only son, then but seven years old, to Geneva for his education. At Geneva, young Guizot's whole nature became permeated with the spirit and influence of John Calvin, whom he accepted as his master, not

---

* See article "Honduras," in the present volume.

only in spiritual but in intellectual and political matters, and whose principles he followed till his dying day. At a very early age he gave evidence of precocious ability, and devoted himself to the study of languages with equal zeal and success. At the age of eighteen he removed to Paris, where he became private tutor in a distinguished family. He was introduced into the literary circles of the day, and began to write for periodicals of the higher class, and finding that one of them, Le Publiciste, was suffering from the protracted illness of Mdlle. Pauline de Meulan, its editor, he very quietly made her place good by his own labors, though he had never met the lady. On her recovery, she learned the name of her generous benefactor, and in 1812 she became Madame Guizot, though fourteen years her husband's senior. During the seven years which preceded his marriage he had published several works of considerable merit, and in the year in which he was married (1812) he received the appointment of Professor of Modern History in the Sorbonne.

Upon the fall of Napoleon I., he became secretary to the Minister of the Interior, and at once attracted notice by the public documents of which he was the author. He left this office on the return of Napoleon from Elba, but, after the restoration of the Bourbons, was appointed secretary to the Minister of Justice, M. Barbi-Marbois. Other offices followed in quick succession, and he became one of the recognized leaders of the party of constitutional monarchy. His work on "Representative Government and the Present State of France" (1816), was one of the first declarations of the "Doctrinaire" school, which admitted in theory the principle of liberty, so far as was compatible with public order, though without urging its immediate realization. After the death of the Duke de Berri, Guizot again retired from office, and devoted himself entirely to literary pursuits.

In 1827 Guizot had the misfortune to lose his wife, who had been educated as a Catholic, but became a Protestant on her death-bed. She was the author of numerous valuable works of fiction, and of essays on education and the family. The following year he married a niece of Madame Guizot, who was also a writer of considerable celebrity, but who died about five years after the marriage. In 1828 Guizot was restored to his professorship in the Sorbonne, from which he had been removed during the Villèle ministry, and, in conjunction with Cousin and Villemain, delivered the brilliant courses of lectures which were attended with signal popularity, and cast a wide renown on the ancient university. These lectures were subsequently published. At this time he was returned to the Chamber of Deputies, where he took a decided stand against the Polignac ministry, and excited a vivid sensation by his vehement attack.

Upon the Revolution of 1830, Guizot drew up

the protest of the deputies, who still adhered to the King and his dynasty. He took an active part, however, in the reconstruction of the Government, opposed the claims of Lafitte, of whose cabinet he was a member, and strenuously supported the party of Casimir-Périer, with all the influence of the constitutional monarchists, of whom he was the chief. In connection with Thiers and De Broglie he formed the cabinet of 1832, under the presidency of Soult, in which he was Minister of Public Instruction. His services to his country in this capacity were very great. He prepared an excellent code of laws for promoting primary education, and attended personally to their enforcement. Had his successors been as faithful as he was in this matter, the common people of France would now be almost as well educated as the Germans. Upon the dissolution of this cabinet in 1836, after a few months passed in retirement, he resumed the same post in the Mali ministry, but soon became dissatisfied with the plans of his colleagues, and went over in disgust to the opposition.

In 1840 Guizot took the place of M. Sebastian, as minister to the court of St. James. His character was admirably suited to the English taste. His Protestant faith, his reputation as a writer, his grave manners, and his social reserve, gave him great personal success. But his policy as a diplomatist was severely criticised by French statesmen. He was recalled after a few months' service, and succeeded M. Thiers in the ministry of Foreign Affairs in the last cabinet of Louis Philippe. Here for seven years he strove with all his ability to maintain the waning fortunes of the King of the French; and while, personally, one of the purest and most upright of men, a man who, with all the avenues of fortune open to him, left office poor and without income save that derived from his books, yet, in his zeal to preserve the throne to the King, he resorted to measures which brought discredit and shame both on his royal master and himself. Never soiling his own hands with a bribe, he yet bought the venal deputies in the French Assembly, almost in open market, with the lucrative offices at his command. But his worst error, and the one which brought irreparable dishonor upon his statesmanship, was his management in regard to the Spanish marriages and the Spanish alliance. That the Duc de Montpensier (son of Louis Philippe) might not only marry an Infanta of Spain, a daughter of the vile Queen Christina, but that his chance of attaining, either in person or by his child, to the Spanish throne might be increased, the scandalous conduct of the young Queen was encouraged, and the friendship between France and England perilled, while the diplomacy of the wily statesman seemed based upon Macchiavelli's maxim, that "words were to be used to conceal thought," and that other maxim, so often reprobated by Guizot's associates, that "the end justifies the means." There was, moreover, a strange blindness in regard to the future on the part of the statesman. Already, the first mutterings of the storm which, in 1848, was to send Louis Philippe and his family once more into exile, were beginning to be heard; but Guizot heard them only with scorn. In 1844, when the voices of the opposition in the Chamber of Deputies were ringing in thunder-tones of denunciation against his course, he looked down upon them from the tribune coldly and calmly with the bitter but characteristic expression, "These insults cannot reach to the level of my contempt." But at length the deluge came, and Guizot, as well as his royal master, was well pleased to have an England to which he might escape. In a little more than a year he returned, and was defeated as a candidate for the Legislature, but sought to bring about a coalition of the two monarchical parties. For some years he employed his leisure time in writing political essays, which, first appearing in periodicals, were subsequently republished in a collected form. These, though able, do not seem to have exerted much influence on the nation, for he was not on the popular side. The on-coming years, however, brought greater calmness and discretion, and Guizot, always a diligent literary worker, returned to the vocation in which he was truly great, and in which he will be longest and best remembered. He possessed many of the qualifications for an historian, and his historical works have great merits with some defects. His style is admirable, giving evidence of great research and clear insight of his subject, a diction stately, elegant, and grand, not so vivacious as some of his compatriots, but also not so frivolous, yet always interesting and attractive. Though a Protestant of the Protestants, a life-long disciple of John Calvin, he was never a bigot, but tolerant almost to a fault; witness, in this direction, his hearty and laudatory eulogy before the French Academy of the eloquent Dominican monk, Lacordaire; and still later, his earnest defense of the temporal power of the Pope. He was, moreover, thoroughly conscientious and honest, and, if, in his careful study of any historical subject, he found facts which were not in accordance with his views or theories, he brought them out with as much clearness and distinctness as if they were wholly in his favor. With these marked merits there are some faults. His grasp of the great principles which underlie all history is weak; his dramatic power, though not wholly wanting, is far inferior to that of D'Aubigné or Bungener; his comprehension of a single act of the great historic drama is superior to his capacity to give it its fitting place and share in shaping the national character and destiny. Yet, with these defects in mind, it must be acknowledged that Guizot had few superiors among the historians of the nineteenth century. His first essay in historical writing was the translating and editing, with copious annotations, of Gibbon's

"Decline and Fall of the Roman Empire." This was published in 1812. In the following year he published his "Lives of the French Poets of the Age of Louis XIV." In 1816 appeared his first political essay, "Concerning Representative Government, and the Actual Condition of France." To the same class belonged "Concerning Conspiracy and Political Justice" (1821); "Of the Powers of Government and of the Opposition in the Actual Condition of France" (1821); an annotated edition of "Rollin's History" (1821); "History of Representative Government," 2 vols., 8vo (1821-'22); "Of Capital Punishment in Political Offenses" (1822); "An Essay on the History of France" (1823); two large collections, of papers by different authors, "On the English Revolution," with notes, in 26 vols., 8vo, and of papers relative to the "History of France since the Thirteenth Century," in 31 vols., published in 1823-'36; "History of the English Revolution from the Coronation of Charles I. to the Coronation of Charles II.," 2 vols., 8vo (1827-'28). It was while he was thus out of office and a professor in the Sorbonne, also, that M. Guizot edited the *Encyclopædia Progressive,* and founded the *Revue Française.*

To this period of his life and labors belong also the most brilliant of his works, his "Course of Modern History," in 6 vols. (1828-'30); his "General History of Civilization in Europe" (1830); and his "General History of Civilization in France," in 4 vols., (1831-'33). From 1830 to 1848, M. Guizot was almost constantly in public life, and wrote little except those masterly reports on public education which deserve to be remembered to his honor, and his "Life of Washington," which introduced to the French public the correspondence and the writings of Washington (1839-'41). During his exile in England, he wrote a stinging political essay "On Democracy in France." This was followed, in 1850, by three severe political reviews, drawing a comparison between the English Revolution and the French, of 1848, not at all to the credit of the latter.

Of his later works, since the ambition for political life had ceased to agitate him, the following are the principal: "Meditations and Rural Studies" (1851); "Love in Marriage" (1855); "William the Conqueror; Edward III. and the Bourgeois of Calais" (1855); "History of the English Republic" (1854); "Papers to preserve the History of my Own Times," 9 vols. (1858-'68); "The Church and Christian Society in 1861" (1861); "Academic Orations" (1861); "The Parliamentary History of France," a complete collection of speeches delivered in the Chamber of Deputies, from 1819 to 1848, 5 vols. (1863); "Three Generations" (1861); "Meditations on the Essence of the Christian Religion" (1864); "Meditations on the Present State of the Christian Religion" (1865); "Biographical and Literary Miscellanies" (1868); "France and Prussia responsible before Eu-

·rope" (1868); "History of France for my Grandchildren," 8 vols. (1870–'74); "History of Four Great French Christians" (1873–'74), 2 vols.

M. Guizot belonged to the Institute of France by three separate titles. He had been admitted a member of the Academy of Moral and Political Sciences (Section of History) at its reorganization in 1882; he was chosen a member of the Academy of Inscriptions and Belles-Lettres, to succeed Dacier, in 1833, and elected a member of the French Academy to succeed Count de Tracey, in 1836. He had been Grand Cross of the Legion of Honor since 1840, and held the same rank in most of the orders of the other countries of Europe. Most of his works had been translated into English, and many of them republished in this country. The more important have also been translated into nearly all the languages of Europe.

H

HAGENBACH, Karl Adolf, S. T. D., a German Protestant theologian, professor, and author; born at Basle, Switzerland, May 4, 1801, died in that city June 8, 1874. His father was an eminent naturalist and physician, at the time of his birth Professor of Anatomy and Botany in the University of Basle. The son, after obtaining his classical and academical education in the gymnasia of his native city, attended the Universities of Bonn and Berlin, to study theology. In 1823 he returned to Basle, was immediately appointed teacher-pupil in the university, soon after adjunct-professor, and in 1828 Professor of Theology in the university. In 1830 the university conferred on him the honorary degree of Doctor in Theology. He retained his professorship till his death. He was very popular as a teacher, but the greatest service which he has rendered to theology has been conferred in his numerous historical and dogmatic works. So early as 1828 he published his "Conspectus of Dogmatic History." From 1834 to 1843 his "Lectures on the Spirit and History of the Reformation" were issued in six volumes, and during the same period his "Historical Development of Evangelical Protestantism;" his "Ecclesiastical History of the Eighteenth and Nineteenth Centuries," 2 vols.; his "Treatise on Dogmatic History," in 2 vols. (1840–'41); in 1855–'56 he issued his "Lessons upon Ancient Ecclesiastical History," in 2 vols., which were translated into Dutch, English, and other languages. This was followed in 1860–'61 by "Lessons upon the Ecclesiastical History of the Middle Ages," also in 2 vols. Besides these works, Dr. Hagenbach had published, in 1833–'34, an "Encyclopædia and Methodology of the Theological Sciences," in several volumes; a collection of his "Sermons," in 4 vols. (1830–'36); "A Discourse in Memory of De Wette" (1850); a "Guide to Christian Instruction" (1850), which was enlarged in 1854 into a "Compendium of the History of Doctrines;" and an "Essay on the Introduction of the First Clergymen to the Evangelical Commune of Rheinfeld" (1856). Most of his historical works have been translated into English, and several of them have been reprinted here. Dr. Hagenbach's attainments in ecclesiastical history were hardly surpassed by those of Neander, and were not equaled by any other theologian of modern times. His works are, in their department, of very great value to the student of theology.

HANSEN, Peter Andreas, a German astronomer, born at Tondern, in the duchy of Schleswig, December 8, 1795; died in Seeberg, near Gotha, in Saxony, April 1, 1874. He studied mathematics and astronomy, and was employed in 1821 in the triangulation of the duchy of Holstein, under the direction of Schumacher, whom he also aided in his duties as director of the observatory of Altona. In 1825 he was appointed director of the Observatory of Seeberg, near Gotha, where he remained until his death. Hansen was a remarkable mathematician. He took great delight in the most difficult problems, and devoted much time to the abstruse calculations of the perturbations of the planets. He had published several of these in the *Astronomical News*, conducted by Schumacher, in the "Transactions of the Royal Astronomical Society," and of the "Royal Society of London," in the "Bulletin of the Academy of Sciences of Saxony," and in other publications. But, though preëminently a mathematician, he did not neglect other departments of astronomical science. As early as 1827 he published "Method of Observation with the Objective Micrometer of Fraunhofer;" in 1831, "Researches upon the Mutual Perturbations of Jupiter and Saturn;" in 1838, "Foundations for a New Investigation of the True Orbit traversed by the Moon;" in 1843, "Calculations of the Absolute Perturbations in Certain Ellipses of Eccentricity and of Inclination." This last formed the first part of the "Memoirs of the Observatory of Seeberg." In 1854 he prepared a memoir on the movements of the pendulum, which was crowned by the Academy of Sciences of Saxony. He had invented a new method of calculating tables of the motions of the sun and of the moon, and had expended a vast amount of labor on their construction. Olafsen, the Danish astronomer, had aided him in the first set, but the tables of the moon he had calculated alone.

HARTSUFF, Major-General George L., U. S. Army, a gallant and faithful army officer, distinguished for his services in two wars, born in Tyne, Seneca County, N. Y., May 28, 1830; died in New York City, May 16, 1874. His family removed to Michigan in his childhood, and he was appointed a cadet at West Point from that State in 1848, and graduated thence in 1852 as second brevet-lieutenant of the Fourth Artillery, and did garrison duty in New York and on the Texas frontier till 1853, when he was transferred as second-lieutenant to the Second Artillery, and ordered to Florida on topographical duty. In 1855 he was promoted to be first-lieutenant in the same regiment, and in a skirmish with the Seminoles was left for dead on the field, being pierced by three balls, one in the chest (which was never removed), and one in each leg. He dragged himself by his arms for fifteen miles through the Indian country, reached camp, and recovered. From 1856 to 1859 he was detailed as assistant instructor at West Point. He was on frontier duty at Fort Mackinac from 1859 to 1860. While stationed there he took passage on the ill-fated steamer Lady Elgin, on Lake Michigan. Four hundred persons perished, but he escaped by seizing a piece of floating timber, and was finally washed ashore. After a leave of absence in 1860 and 1861, he did garrison duty in the vicinity of Washington. In March, 1861, he was appointed brevet-captain, and assigned to duty as assistant adjutant-general, in which capacity he went with the secret expedition under command of Colonel Harvey Brown to Fort Pickens. In July, with the rank of captain, he became chief of staff of Brigadier-General Rosecrans, commanding the Department of West Virginia, and participated in the action at Carnifex Ferry, September 10, 1861, and the other battles of the campaign. He was assigned in April and May, 1862, to special duty at the War Department as assistant adjutant-general to the Secretary of War. In the latter part of May he took command of a brigade of volunteers in the field, with the First Army Corps. His brigade was in the night battle at Cedar Mountain in August, and bore itself bravely, throughout that and other actions in which it was afterward engaged. At Rappabannock Bridge his command was the only one that crossed the river, and it held the eminences south of the river, for several days, despite the almost continuous fire of the enemy. When the Army of the Potomac was retreating, his brigade formed a part of the protecting line, and, for twenty days, he was within the reach of the enemy's guns. He also bore a conspicuous part in the battles of South Mountain and Antietam, and was promoted to the rank of brevet-colonel on September 17, 1862, for gallant and meritorious services in the last-named action, when he was severely wounded. He then received leave of absence, on account of his wounds, until December 18, 1862. In the mean time he was appointed Major-General of the United States Volunteers on November 29th, and, upon his convalescence, served as member of the Board to revise Rules and Arti-

cles of War, and to prepare a code for the government of the armies in the field. From April to November, 1863, he was in command of the Twenty-third Army Corps during the operations in Kentucky and the occupation of East Tennessee. Being again incapacitated for field duty by reason of the wounds which he had received at Antietam, he was not placed on duty until July, 1864, when he served on courts-martial until January, 1865. On March 13, 1865, he was promoted to the rank of brevet brigadier-general of the United States Army for gallant services in the campaign terminating with the surrender of the insurgent army under General R. E. Lee, and was placed in command of the Bermuda front of the works for the siege of Petersburg. As Brevet Major-General of the United States Army, to which position he was promoted on the same date that he was made a brevet brigadier-general, he was afterward assigned to the command of various important posts in Virginia, until he was mustered out of the volunteer service on August 24, 1865. He afterward did duty as adjutant-general of the Department of the Gulf and of the Fifth Military District, composed of Louisiana and Texas. At the time of his retirement he occupied the position of assistant adjutant-general of the Military Division of Missouri, with headquarters in Chicago. The wounds which incapacitated him having been received when in the discharge of his duty as major-general (at Antietam), he was retired with that rank and full pay. After some time he went abroad, and interested himself in bringing American improvements in artillery to European attention. He had finally returned with the purpose of making New York his home, and had just completed his preparations for settling down to house-keeping, when he was attacked with pneumonia from becoming overheated, and the inflammation of the lungs around the cicatrix of the old wound received in Florida caused the disease to prove fatal in a very few days. He was buried at West Point at his own request.

HAVEMEYER, WILLIAM F., a prominent citizen of New York; at his death, Mayor of New York for the third time; born in New York City, February 12, 1804; died at his office, in the City-Hall of that city, November 30, 1874. He was of German ancestry, his father having emigrated to this city in 1798. He received an excellent education in the best schools of the city, and graduated from Columbia College at the age of nineteen. After his graduation he entered the sugar-refinery of his father, acquired a thorough knowledge of the business, and in 1828 succeeded to it, having a cousin as a partner. In 1842 he nominally retired from business with a handsome fortune, but retained an interest as silent partner for some years. He had always been an active politician, was a warm admirer of General Jackson, and a stanch friend to his successor. In 1844 he was a presidential elector on the Polk and Dallas ticket. In 1845 he was elected mayor of the city by a large majority, and re-elected in 1848. During his administration he was instrumental in the organization of the Board of Commissioners of Emigration and the establishment of a regular police-force. His administration was noted for economy, honesty, and a careful interest in the welfare of the city. In 1850 he declined a renomination, and the next year became President of the Bank of North America, where he served for ten years. In 1859 he was again a candidate for mayor, but was defeated by Fernando Wood. During the war he was thoroughly loyal to the Government, and urged the abolition of slavery as a war measure. Though extensively engaged in business, he found time during the few years after the war to protest most earnestly against the corruption and frauds which were rife in the city. In 1871 he became President of the Committee of Seventy —the committee which overthrew the Tweed dynasty. In the autumn of 1872 he was nominated for mayor by that committee, and elected by a small majority. He assumed office January 1, 1873, and at his death had a month more to serve. His third term was not a success. The age was too fast for him, and the greater part of his time was spent in unseemly wrangles with the aldermen and other city officers; a number of his appointments were injudicious, and an application was made to the Governor for his removal from office, a step which the Executive declined to take. Still, there was no doubt in any quarter of his honesty and integrity. In private life Mr. Havemeyer was kindly and cordial, and, though he often concealed his real benevolence under some asperity of manner, he was known to be a man of liberal and generous nature. His death was very sudden, his last illness continuing only for a few moments.

HAVEN, Rev. Joseph, D. D., LL. D., a Congregationalist clergyman, professor, and author, born in Dennis, on Cape Cod, Mass., January 4, 1816; died in Chicago, Ill., May 23, 1874. His parents having removed to Amherst, Mass., during his childhood, he was educated in Amherst Academy and Amherst College, graduating from the latter in 1835. He was for two years a teacher in the New York Institution for the Deaf and Dumb, studying theology meanwhile in the Union Theological Seminary. In 1837 he entered the Middle Class in Andover Theological Seminary, and graduated in 1839. He was ordained pastor of the Congregational Church in Ashland, Mass., in November of that year, and remained there till 1846, when he was called to the Harvard Church, Brookline, Mass., and during his four years there was also one of the editors of the *Congregationalist.* In 1850 he was invited to the chair of Mental and Moral Philosophy in Amherst College, and commenced the duties of his professorship in January, 1851. "Here he taught the Scotch phi-

losophy with a logical force and clearness worthy of the system, and with a felicity of illustration and a vein of humor that were wholly his own." In August, 1858, he resigned his professorship and accepted that of Systematic Theology in the Chicago Theological Seminary, then just organized. His labors there were very great, but they were crowned with extraordinary success. In 1870 he resigned on account of ill-health, made a tour in Europe and the East, and on his return engaged in preaching and lecturing upon ancient and modern philosophy and upon the English classics. In 1873 he became Acting-Professor of Mental and Moral Philosophy in the Chicago University, and was engaged in the duties of that office up to the time of his death. Dr. Haven was all his life a hard student, and was remarkable for the extent of his learning and the thoroughness of his scholarship. He was an admirable lecturer and an eloquent preacher. His published works, aside from many single sermons, occasional addresses, essays, and reviews, were: "Mental Philosophy, including the Intellect, Sensibilities, and Will" (1857); "Moral Philosophy, including Theoretical and Practical Ethics" (1859); "Studies in Philosophy and Theology" (1869). A work on "Systematic Divinity," completed only a few weeks before his death, has been since published. Prof. Haven received the degree of D. D. from Marietta College in 1859, from Amherst College in 1862, and that of LL. D. from Kenyon College. He was the first President of the Philosophical Society of Chicago.

HOFFMANN, Heinrich August, called "of Fallersleben," a German poet and philologist, born at Fallersleben, in Mecklenburg, April 2, 1798; died at the seat of the Duke of Ratisbon on the Rhine, January 21, 1874. His father was a merchant and burgomaster of Fallersleben, and the son was destined for a clergyman, but, after passing through the Gymnasia of Helmstädt and Brunswick, and the Universities of Göttingen and Bonn, studying theology exclusively at the former, and at the latter making the acquaintance of the brothers Grimm, he determined to devote himself to philology and German literature, under their direction. In 1820 he published an edition of the "Fragments of Otfried." Soon after, he commenced a leisurely journey along the banks of the Rhine and through Holland, collecting everywhere the poetry of the middle ages, of which so many fragments were preserved among the peasants. In the course of this journey he visited Berlin, and while there was appointed librarian to the University of Breslau, and soon after professor extraordinary, and finally full professor in the same university. For the next eighteen or nineteen years he fulfilled his duties at the university with great zeal, and published not only the middle age songs and ballads he had collected, but many of his own poems which were of such a character as to interest the common people. One of the publications (a compilation published in Hamburg in 1840–'41), entitled "Unpolitical Songs," in 2 vols., being, in spite of its title, extremely republican, called down upon the poet the displeasure of the then reigning King of Prussia, Friedrich Wilhelm IV., who in consequence dismissed him from his positions in the university in December, 1842. This only rendered Hoffmann more popular as the poet of the people. He traveled over most of Continental Europe during the next two years, studying the language and literature of the different nations. In 1845 he settled in Mecklenburg. In 1848 the hostility of the Prussian Government having relaxed, he was invited to return, and received a pension from the crown. He took no part in the revolutionary movement of that time, but pursued assiduously his literary labors. In 1854 he removed to Weimar, where he edited, in company with Schade, the "Year Book," published in that city, and in 1861 became librarian to the Duke of Ratisbon, a German nobleman with whom he remained till his death. Hoffmann's political, liberal, and bacchanalian songs are very numerous, and make him very popular in Germany, so much so that during his travels he was often received with great heartiness and enthusiasm by the people. "His poems," Longfellow observes, "are distinguished by an artless simplicity, by harmony of language, and skillful versification." The following are the principal volumes of poems, both compilations and original songs and ballads, which he published : " German Songs" (1826); "Poems," 2 vols. (1834); "Unpolitical Songs," 2 vols. (1840–'41); "Popular Songs of Silesia, with Melodies" (1842); "German Songs composed in Switzerland" (1843); "Fifty Songs for Children" (1843); "Fifty New Songs for Children" (1845); "Forty Songs for Children" (1847); "A Hundred Songs for Students" (1847); "Diavolini" (1847); "The German Popular Song-Book" (1848); "Songs of Love" (1850); "Echoes of the Country" (1850); "The Life on the Rhine" (1851); "Songs of the Soldiers" (1851); "Political Poems of the Early Times in Germany" (1843); "Songs of the German Societies (Guilds) of the Sixteenth and Seventeenth Centuries" (1844). Besides this long array of poetical works, Prof. Hoffmann had published numerous works on literature, history, and philology. The most important of these were: "*Horæ Belgicæ*," 8 vols. (1830–1852); "Materials for a History of the German Language and Literature," 2 vols. (1830–1837); "History of Religious Music in the German Church up to the Times of Luther" (1832); "*Reineke Vos*" (1834); "*Fragmenta Theotica*" (1834); "*Monumenta Elnonensia*." This contained the *Ludwigslied* discovered a short time previous at Valenciennes (1837); "Principal Characteristics of German Philology" (1836); with Haupt, "German Antiquities," 2 vols. (1835–'40); "Catalogue of Old German Manuscripts in the Imperial Library at Vienna" (1841); "Materials

for a History of German Literature," 2 vols. (1845); "Theophilus" (1853). Besides these, he had written numerous articles on philology, criticism, and literature, for the principal periodicals of Germany. His literary activity had somewhat abated in the last twenty years.

HONDURAS (República de Honduras), one of the five independent states of Central America, extending from the 13th to the 16th parallel of north latitude, and from 85° 39' to 89° 6' west longitude. It is bounded on the north by Guatemala and the gulf of its own name; on the southeast by the Caribbean Sea; on the south by Nicaragua, Fonseca Bay, and the republic of San Salvador, and on the west by the country just named and the republic of Guatemala. It embraces an area of 58,168 square miles, and the population was estimated in 1874 at 351,700, but the figures set down in the ANNUAL CYCLOPÆDIA for 1873 are probably more approximate to the truth. The number of white inhabitants does not exceed 5,000. Comayagua, the capital, has a population of about 7,500.

The President of the Republic is Señor Ponciano Leiva, elected in 1874; the Minister of the Interior and of Foreign Affairs is Señor A. Zúñiga; of Finance, Señor E. Ferrari; and of War, Señor J. López. The Bishop of Comayagua is J. F. Zepeda, appointed in 1861.

The army is composed of some 600 regular troops and about 6,000 militia.

In a country continually distracted by warfare, as is Honduras, but little attention is paid to the publication of commercial statistics. None of a reliable character have here been given since the overthrow of the Medina administration in 1872; and it is difficult, if not impossible, to arrive at even an approximate estimate of the value of the foreign commerce for the past year. It is, however, to be presumed that, if the precise state of affairs were given, a formidable diminution, rather than an increase, would be registered; for, if report be true, large numbers of laborers were diverted from agricultural concerns to fill up the ranks of the armies in the successive revolutions since the middle of 1873, and a natural consequence would be limited crops, and of course a corresponding decrease in the exports. Then the capture of Amapala, and the siege of Comayagua, the former at the end of 1873, and the latter from December of that year to the last days of the January following, did not tend to better the general condition of trade. According to Medina's report, in 1872, as above stated, the exports were of the value of $1,305,000; but it is quite probable that they did not exceed $1,000,000 in 1874.

The financial situation is disastrous. The revenue, computed in the most favorable times at not more than $4,000,000, must of necessity have fallen far short of that figure last year, owing to the depression of foreign trade, for fully one-third is derived from the customs, while another proceeds from the sale of spirits, a branch monopolized by the Government. Then the expenditure, at all times greatly in excess of the income, was considerably enhanced by the wars, and the deficit can only be made up by oppressive extraordinary taxation; for Honduras, with resources sufficient, if adequately developed, to swell the revenue to many times its hitherto usual standard, is regarded in Europe as being almost hopelessly insolvent, and can no longer, or at least until she shall have retrieved her lost reputation, resort to her time-honored remedy of borrowing.

For the present state of the national debt we cannot do better than refer to the ANNUAL CYCLOPÆDIA for 1873, page 352, since which

time no further payments have been made on account of either the foreign or the home debt. Of the home debt nothing precise is known, nor has any report thereon been published by the finance department for a considerable number of years.

It was stated in a British publication that the holders of the 5 per cent. claims to be redeemed out of the custom-house receipts of the port of Amapala were unable to obtain any satisfaction either from Señor Gutierrez, ex-President Medina's old financial agent, and now minister of Honduras at London, or from Dr. Bernhard himself.

After the foregoing statement, it would seem almost superfluous to add that the name of this

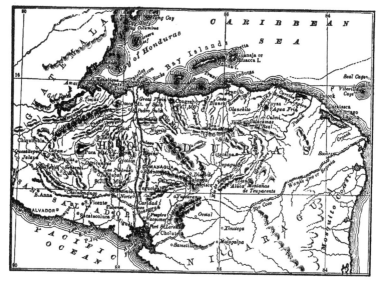

republic appeared in the same list with those of the other defaulting countries published in London in the course of the year. It was then marked as in default, in the sum of £4,972,000 since April 1, 1874.

As for the railway, which at first served as the ostensible motive for the loans of 1867, 1868, and 1870, nothing further has been done; the 56 miles opened in 1872 still represent the only finished portion of the line; and it is said that the sections yet to be completed will require an outlay of $8,000,000.

The political state of the republic is one of uninterrupted peace, and, strange as this may appear, has been so since last August. Señor Ponciano's administration is becoming daily more popular; and in the neighboring republics, even those who have heretofore been

known as the systematic detractors of every administration in Honduras, predict therefrom the consolidation of peace at no far-distant day in this the most ill-fated of the Spanish-American states, not even excepting Mexico. Señor Leiva, as mentioned in the volume for 1873, having placed himself at the head of a revolutionary movement for the avowed object of superseding Señor Arias, was proclaimed President at Choluteca, on December 16, 1873; and, thanks to the united aid of Guatemala and San Salvador, the very powers who had but some months before been instrumental in deposing Medina and setting up Arias in his stead, succeeded in taking the capital and gaining possession of the whole country by February, 1874.

Señor Leiva's proclamation was issued in November, 1873, and it sets forth some of the

more important charges against his predecessor, and the principles by which he himself
promised to be guided in reforming the Government :

PROCLAMATION.

Ponciano Leiva, citizen of the republic of Honduras, having been called to the presidency by public opinion, expressed in various ways :

Considering the notorious unpopularity and discredit into which the administration of Señor Arias
has fallen ;

That during the eighteen months of his government he has proved himself incapable of maintaining
order at home or repelling aggression from abroad,
as recent facts have shown, and as is well known to
all Central America ;

That Señor Arias, turning his back upon the noble
and generous principles proclaimed by the past revolution, has established a government which is purely personal and arbitrary ;

That the government of Señor Arias has maintained the dictatorship longer than was necessary,
without any reason of public good, and only for the
purpose of securing his election by the people ;

That he has suppressed all liberty, holding the
press under restraint, and restricting the right of
suffrage, which form the basis of all true republican
governments ;

That the most sacred civil rights, which existed
prior to and are above all legislation, have been violated in all the departments of the republic by order
of the government of Señor Arias, or with his consent ;

That military executions, proscriptions, and arbitrary imprisonments, accompanied by the most inhuman acts, and confiscation in all its forms, have
been exercised on a large scale in the republic, in the
name of democracy and liberty ;

That the anarchy into which Honduras is sunk is
the direct consequence of Señor Arias's errors and
arbitrary management ;

That it is absolutely necessary to put a stop to so
abnormal and violent a state of things to enable the
people to enjoy peace, order, and true liberty ;

That public feeling and opinion in general point to
the necessity of a change of administration ;

By the right of insurrection, proclaimed and sanctioned by all the enlightened nations of Europe and
America, declares :

1. That a new provisional government is inaugurated in the republic of Honduras.

2. In the mean time, until the cabinet is fully organized, I appoint temporarily to take charge of the
departments of Foreign Relations Government, Justice, Public Instruction, Public Works, and Public
Worship, the Licenciado Don Adolfo Zúñiga, and
for those of War and Finance, Lieutenant-General
Juan López.

3. The new government will proceed to the organization of all the branches of the public service immediately.

It may be here mentioned that freedom of
the press was not an empty promise in Señor
Leiva's initiatory proclamation, but has now
become an accomplished fact. This important
reform alone is sufficient to exalt him in public
favor far above the level of his contemporaries
guiding the destinies of the Central American
states. We should not omit to observe that,
after the capitulation of Arias in Comayagua,
he was detained a prisoner, and his predecessor, Medina, was set at liberty. Arias was
afterward sent into exile.

As a consequence of a long period of maladministration, the political and social condition
of the country on the accession of Leiva
to power was exceedingly unpromising, and
of a nature to demand the most strenuous
efforts on the part of the new President. He
found society divided into numberless factions,
all alike regardless of law and moral order;
the army almost completely broken up, the
Treasury depleted, and unsatisfactory relations
with foreign countries.

New elections were to take place, near the
end of the year, for President and for representatives of the various departments, the candidates for the executive power being Leiva
(hitherto only provisional President), Manuel
Colindre, and Ramon Midence, the last a land-
owner near Tegucigalpa, and considered by the
Guatemala press to be the real representative
of the Liberal Party. A movement, set on foot
by Señor Zúñiga, to form a party, which should
be neither Conservative nor Liberal, gave rise
to no small degree of mistrust. Such was the
state of the republic at the middle of December. In the mean time, the work of reform
had begun, and was carried on with unremitting zeal; the public-school system had received some substantial marks of attention and
encouragement; proposals were made (and
are likely to be accepted) for the introduction
of suitable school-books from the United States;
a university was to be established, and the Government manifested a desire to pay a sum of
$24,000 due to the Pacific Mail Company.

A law was promulgated defining the privileges to be enjoyed by foreigners settling in the
republic; for Honduras, in common with the
other Spanish-American states, is desirous of
seeing immigrants flock to its shores. They
will be subject to the same laws as the natives of the country; lands assigned to them
on their arrival will, after five years of uninterrupted cultivation, become their property;
they will be exempt from military duty for
ten years, save in the case of a foreign invasion, and likewise from all taxes, and will
receive patents for any mechanical invention
or improvements they may introduce. Lastly,
they will enjoy perfect liberty to exercise their
religion, though in private, if that be not the
Roman Catholic, and will have their own
cemeteries; and there will be nothing to prevent them from selling their property whenever they desire to do so, and leave the republic.

There is, nevertheless, room to doubt whether all these advantages will determine an important tide of immigration to Honduras, so
long as such superior inducements, climatic,
social, moral, and material, are offered by the
United States, Brazil, the Plate Republics, and
Australia.

It was reported in November that a convention had been agreed on between the Governments of Honduras and San Salvador for
the purpose of settling the internal affairs of
the former country and uniting to combat any
further uprising of the reactionary party.

HUNGARY, a kingdom of Europe, and one of the two main divisions of the Austro-Hungarian monarchy. (All the affairs which are common to the entire monarchy have been treated of under the head of AUSTRIA.) As the Military Frontier, which had formerly its own administration, has been wholly incorporated partly with Hungary proper and partly with Croatia and Slavonia, the lands of the Hungarian crown now consist of three large historic divisions, namely:

DIVISIONS.	Area.	Population in 1869
Hungary Proper............	87,046	11,580,397
Transylvania..............	21,217	2,115,024
Croatia and Slavonia.......	16,782	1,864,034
Total................	125,045	15,509,455

The Hungarian ministry was, in December, 1874, composed as follows: President of the Ministry, St. von Bitto, appointed March 21, 1874. 2. Minister near the King's person (ad latus), Baron Wenckheim (appointed March, 1871). 3. Minister of Finance, C. Ghyczy, March 21, 1874. 4. Minister of the Interior, Count Szapary (March 5, 1873). 5. Minister of Education and Public Worship, Dr. Augustin Tréfort (September 5, 1872). 6. Minister of Justice, Dr. Th. Pauler, formerly Professor of Jurisprudence at the University of Pesth —Minister of Education and Public Worship from March, 1871, to September 1872 (appointed Minister of Justice September 5, 1872). 7. Minister of Public Works, Count Joseph Zichy (March 21, 1874). 8. Minister of Agriculture, Industry, and Commerce, G. Bartal. 9. Minister of Croatia and Slavonia, Count Pejacsevitch (March, 1871). 10. Minister for the Defense of the Country, B. Szende von Kevesztes (March 21, 1874).

The Hungarian Diet or Reichstag consists of two Houses. The Upper House, called the Table of Magnates, was in 1873 composed of the three Austrian archdukes who have landed property in Hungary ; 31 archbishops, bishops, and other high church dignitaries of the Roman Catholic and Greek Oriental Churches; of 12 "imperial banner-bearers," 57 supreme counts (presidents of counties), 5 supreme royal judges, the count (comes) of the Transylvania Saxons, the Governor of Fiume, 3 princes, 218 counts, 80 barons, and 3 "regalists" from Transylvania. The Lower House, called the Table of Deputies, comprised in the same year 444 members, of whom 334 represented Hungary proper, 1 Fiume, 75 Transylvania, and 34 Croatia and Slavonia. The Diet meets annually, and new general elections take place every three years. The right of voting belongs to all who have received an academic education, carry on a regular business, or pay a small amount of direct taxes, as provided by the electoral law. The language of the Diet is Hungarian, which every member is required to understand; only the representatives of Croatia and Slavonia have the right to use their own language.

The public revenue of Hungary for the year 1872 amounted to $7,943,000, the expenditure to $10,904,000 ; deficit, $2,961,000. The budget estimates for 1874 showed a deficit of about $12,800,000. According to Article XXXIV. of the Hungarian Statutes of 1873, 55 per cent. of the taxes collected in Croatia and Slavonia are delivered into the common treasury of the lands of the Hungarian crown, and 45 per cent. are spent in meeting the home expenses of these countries. The total revenue of Croatia and Slavonia for 1874 was $3,240,000. To meet the interest of the common debt of the monarchy, contracted prior to 1858, Hungary pays an annual contribution of $13,630,000. Besides, Hungary has a special debt, amounting in 1874 to $275,000,000. ' The large moneyed institutions of Hungary have of late, as in cis-Leithania, increased very rapidly in number, but not so much proportionally in the amount of their capital. The following banks (all of them in Pesth) have a capital exceeding $1,000,000: Anglo-Hungarian Bank, established in 1868, $4,700,000 ; the Hungarian General Credit Bank (1867), $14,100,000 ; the Franco-Hungarian Bank (1867), $15,000,000 ; the Pesth Bank (1872), $2,350,000 ; the General Hungarian Municipal Bank (1872), $4,700,000.

The aggregate length of railways in the monarchy, open for traffic and under construction was, January 1, 1871, as follows: Open for traffic 6,280 kilometres (1 kilometre = 0.62 mile). The number of private and official letters forwarded by the post-office during the year 1873 was, 52,800,000 ; of newspapers, 23,500,000. The length of telegraph-wires, in January, 1874, was 46,780; of telegraph-lines, 13,725 kilometres. The number of telegraph-stations was 837.

At the close of the year 1873, both the country and the Diet were chiefly agitated by the wretched condition of the finances. One party expected to reëstablish an equilibrium between revenue and expenditures by reducing the expenditures, another by raising the taxes. The Diet appointed a special committee, consisting of twenty-one members, to investigate the whole subject. The Minister of Finances resigned, and for a time it was thought that an entirely new ministry would be formed. The ministerial crisis was, however, adjourned, and the president of. the cabinet provisionally assumed the department of finances.

On his return from St. Petersburg, the Emperor Francis Joseph, in March, 1874, went to Pesth, where the ministerial crisis had broken out again. The prime-minister, Szlavy, found that he could not rely on a permanent majority in the Diet, and therefore on March 8th again tendered his resignation. The Emperor personally visited the great leader of the majority, Francis Deak, and, although the aged patriot could now no more than on former occasions be prevailed upon to assume himself the task of forming a new ministry, his advice was freely given, and the support of the new cabinet by his party secured. On March 21st the reconstruction of the new cabinet was completed. Stephan von Bittó, the President of the Lower House of the Hungarian Diet, and formerly, under Lonyay, Minister of Justice, was appointed prime-minister, Ghyczy Minister of Finance, and Bartal Minister of Commerce. The other members had belonged to the Szlavy cabinet. The actual leader of the new cabinet, Ghyczy, announced on March 27th that he should aim at an improvement of the financial condition by means of a reduction of the expenditures, that he firmly adhered to the present union with Austria, and that he was in favor of adjourning other reforms until the restoration of the financial equilibrium. In place of Bittó, Bela Perczel was elected President of the Lower House. On March 28th the Diet adjourned to April 15th.

The annual meeting of the joint delegations of the Austrian and Hungarian Parliaments, which this year was held in Pesth, was opened on April 20th, and closed on May 22d. Dr. Rechbauer was elected president of the cis-Leitbau and Gorove of the trans-Leithan section. The proceedings were on the whole harmonious, and a full understanding about the common budget was reached. The prime-minister, Count Andrassy, thanked the delegations in the name of the Emperor, and President Rechbauer in response expressed a wish that the time might soon come when it would be safe to diminish the large armies.

The Diet, after reassembling on April 15th, devoted its time chiefly to the discussion of financial questions, a new electoral law, and a bill concerning the regulation of civil marriage. With regard to the latter, the prime-minister, on June 23d, asked the Lower House to postpone the discussion of the report of the committee until the fall session, as the Government intended to bring in a new bill. The request of the prime-minister was complied with by a vote of 158 against 108. In the discussion of the new electoral law so little progress was made that the Diet could not only not be closed on June 25th, as was originally intended, but when it was prorogued, on August 15th, an agreement between the two Houses had not been reached.

Among the most brilliant speeches of the session was one made in July by Tisza against Polit, the leader of the Servian national party, who had proposed the transformation of the Hungarian state into a confederation of the several nationalities, after the model of Switzerland. The Left fully agreed with the Deak party, that the unity of the Hungarian state and the ascendency of the Magyar nationality must be fully maintained.

At the beginning of September, a letter from Kossuth to Tisza was published, in which the latter was highly praised for his firmness of character, and called upon to place himself at the head of the party of independence, which aims at the severance of all the administrative ties which bind Hungary to Austria. Kossuth urged Tisza to abandon the idea of a coalition with the Deak party.

On October 19th the Banns of Croatia opened in the name of the Emperor the new Croatian University at Agram, and installed the rector. A large number of foreign universities were represented by delegates, who in their several languages welcomed the new addition to the literary institutions of Europe. The University of Agram is the third of the lands of the Hungarian crown, the two others being those of Pesth and Klausenburg, the latter of which was opened in 1872. The opening solemnities were a great Slavic demonstration against the Magyars. The Hungarian flag was entirely ignored. At the banquet not one toast was given out in honor of Hungary, while, on the other hand, all the toasts in honor of the Slavic nationality, and even a violent speech from the Slovack agitator Sassirek, met with enthusiastic applause.

The Hungarian Diet reassembled in October for its last session. The Minister of Finances, Ghyczy, found it necessary to propose a number of new taxes in order to provide for the large deficit which the budget for 1875 again presented. Although his financial schemes met with the full approval of the Emperor, they produced great excitement in the country, and the protests against them were so numerous and energetic, that at the close of the year another ministerial crisis appeared to be inevitable.

I

ICELAND, a large island in the North Atlantic Ocean, subject to the Danish crown, attracted, in 1874, unusual attention, by the solemn celebration of the millennial anniversary of the first settlement. The area, including adjacent islands, is estimated at 39,758 square miles, of which 16,243 are inhabitable. The population of Iceland, in its most flourishing period, exceeded 100,000; recent censuses give it as follows: 1864, 68,084; 1869, 69,506; 1870, 69,763; 1874, 70,900.

The long conflict between the people of Iceland and the Government of Denmark concerning the constitutional rights of the former were brought to a close on January 5, 1874, when the King of Denmark sanctioned a new constitution, which had been submitted to him by the Althing, or Legislative Assembly, of Iceland. The new constitution, which went into operation on August 1, 1874, is divided into seven parts, or chapters. The first of these, which contains thirteen paragraphs, deals with the relations between the King and Danish Government on one side, and the Legislative Assembly, or Althing, on the other. The legislative power belongs to the King and Althing, the executive power with the King alone, and the judicial power with the judges. Iceland has no voice in Danish national questions, since it is not represented in the Rigsdag at Copenhagen; consequently it bears no part of the national expenditures. The highest power in Iceland belongs to the Governor, who is appointed by the King. Should the Althing have reason to complain of the Governor, the King decides in each particular case. The Althing, called by the King, sits every other year, but only for six weeks, unless prolonged by royal consent. A special session may be called at the King's pleasure; the latter may also prorogue the Althing, but only once a year, and for four weeks at a time. The King has power to dissolve the Althing, in which case new elections shall be held within two months, and the new Assembly shall meet the following year. No decree of the Althing has the force of law without the King's consent, and, if he fail to sign a bill before the next session of the body, the bill is null and void. The minor provisions of this first chapter harmonize with these leading features.

Chapter II. relates to the constitution of the Althing. It shall consist of thirty deputies elected by the people, and six chosen by the King. The former hold office during six years, the latter retaining their places in case an Assembly should be dissolved. The Althing is divided into an Upper and a Lower House, the former composed of the six deputies appointed by the King, and six more chosen by the thirty elected members from out their own number. The Lower House is thus formed by the remaining twenty-four members of the latter class. The other clauses of this chapter relate to the filling of vacancies and the civil conditions which make a citizen of Iceland eligible to election as a member of the Althing.

Chapter III. defines the legislative functions of the two Houses and their coöperative action. The regular Althing shall meet on the first workday in July (unless the King orders otherwise), in Reikiavik. Each House has the right to introduce and pass bills; also to appoint committees for the investigation of matters of special interest, such committees having power to send for persons and papers. No tax may be imposed, altered, or removed, except by course of law. The Althing has entire control of the finances of the island, which it must regulate by a biennial budget, with the condition that the salaries of the Danish functionaries (including the six members appointed by the King) take precedence of all other expenditure. The regulations in regard to the reading of a bill three times, to returning a bill from one House to another with amendments, to a quorum of members being present, etc., are similar to the parliamentary laws of other countries, and

need not be repeated. Two-thirds of the members of either House constituting a quorum, however, it will always be possible for four of the King's deputies to prevent any legislation not agreeable to Denmark, by their simple absence.

Chapter IV. contains clauses regulating the judiciary powers.

Chapter V. provides for the state Church, the "Evangelical Lutheran," but guarantees liberty of conscience to all the inhabitants.

Chapter VI. embraces provisions relating to the freedom of the subject, the sanctity of home and private property, the freedom of labor, poor-laws, elementary education, freedom of the press, freedom of association and assembly, rights of municipal government, taxation, privileges of the nobility, which, together with their titles, are henceforth abolished.

Chapter VII., and last, provides that propositions with a view to amending or adding to the present constitution may be introduced either at a regular or an extraordinary session of the Althing. If such a proposition receive the necessary majority in both Houses, the Althing shall be dissolved forthwith and a new election ordered. If the newly-elected Althing then accepts the same proposition without amendment, and the latter then receives the royal sanction, it comes into force as part and parcel of the constitutional law.

The new constitution reconciled the people of Iceland with the Danish rule, and allayed the excitement which for several years had been threatening serious consequences. The Althing was established in 1843. Like the provincial Diets of the other parts of the Danish monarchy, the powers were only deliberative; the King being absolute monarch, who regulated the military affairs and fixed the budget without being bound to the consent of a representative Assembly. When, in 1849, Denmark was changed into a constitutional monarchy, Iceland was not consulted. The Government convoked, however, a national Assembly, to which, in 1851, the new fundamental law was submitted for approval. When the Assembly appeared to favor the change of several articles of the fundamental laws, it was dissolved even before it had taken any action. A royal rescript, of May 12, 1852, proclaimed that, for the present, the Althing would retain its former functions, and that the final relation of Iceland to the kingdom should not be changed without the consent of the former. Actually, however, the constitutional position of Iceland had been greatly changed.

From a legal point of view, the King, in all affairs concerning the entire kingdom, was dependent on the consent of the Danish Legislature, while in Iceland he remained absolute regent. Thus the Icelanders, on the one hand, had a less amount of liberty than the Danes; and, on the other hand, the Danish ministry and the Danish Diet decided on questions which concerned Iceland as well as all other parts of the monarchy. The dominant political party in Denmark demanded that Iceland, though it might retain a certain amount of provincial independence, should become an integral part of the monarchy, and send deputies to the Danish Diet at Copenhagen. On the other hand, the immense majority of the Icelanders insisted on retaining an independent legislation, and refused both to accept this fundamental law and to send deputies to the Danish Diet. They wished to be united to Denmark under one King, as Norway is with Sweden, Hungary with Austria, and Luxemburg with Holland. In addition to these constitutional difficulties, financial complications of a peculiar character had sprung up between the two countries. For many years the Icelandic budget has shown a deficit, which has had to be met by Denmark. On the part of the Icelanders it was, however, alleged that both the old domains on the islands and the episcopal property had been sold in favor of the royal treasury; that a number of funds, which had been specially intended for Iceland, had been exclusively used for Danish purposes; and that, finally, the commercial policy of Denmark had for centuries been so shaped as to enrich Danish merchants at the expense of the people of Iceland. The propositions made by the Government for settling the difficulties were not acceptable to the Althing, and in the years 1872 and 1873 the popular dissatisfaction assumed more and more threatening dimensions. One of the papers of the island proposed to invoke the intercession of foreign powers for the protection of the national rights, or secession from Denmark and annexation to some other country. In case this should be found impossible, the emigration of the entire population to America was proposed. Unexpectedly the Althing, which met on July 1, 1873, succeeded in removing the greatest obstacles which had thus far obstructed a reconciliation, and to make propositions to the Government which the royal commissary, on closing the Diet, designated as entirely satisfactory. The royal sanction given to the constitution proposed by the Althing on January 5, 1874, put an end to this long conflict.

In consequence of this reconciliation, the millennial celebration of the first settlement of the island, in August, was an occasion of universal joy. The King, accompanied by his son Waldemar and the Minister for Iceland, Klein, arrived on the island on the 30th of July, and was received with great enthusiasm. On August 1st the new constitution of Iceland was formally promulgated. As copies of it had previously reached Iceland, the people were generally acquainted with its provisions, and content to adopt it as the beginning of reform. August 2d was the first of the two days set apart for the commemorative festivities. The programme of the day consisted of services in the cathedral, a banquet in the hall of the university, and a popular festival on the hill of Austurvelli, a mile from the town. At the

service in the cathedral the "Psalm of Praise," written by Matthias Jochumsson, and composed by Sveinbjörnsson, the first musical work by a native Icelander, produced a powerful effect. At the banquet, the King expressed the hope that the new constitution, which he had brought with him, might contribute to the material prosperity of the island and the development of its people. There was great rejoicing when the King, in returning thanks for a toast to the health of the Crown Prince, announced that the latter would learn the Icelandic language. The speech made by the Minister for Iceland, Klein, also gave great satisfaction. On August 3d the King, with a large retinue, set out for the plain of the Geysers, which was reached on the next day. To the great dissatisfaction of the party, no eruption of the great geyser took place, but two eruptions of the Strokr were witnessed. On August 7th, millennial commemorative services were held in the plain of Thongvalla, when the King received addresses from a number of Scandinavian institutions and corporations. Having returned to Reikiavik, the King, on August 9th, gave a great ball, and on the next day reëmbarked for Denmark.

ILLINOIS. The first general political convention of the year was a large and enthusiastic gathering, chiefly of farmers, in Springfield, on the 10th of June. This body nominated David Gore, a Democrat, for State Treasurer, and S. E. Etter, a Republican, for State Superintendent of Public Instruction, and published the following declaration of principles:

We, the farmers, mechanics, and other citizens of Illinois, in delegate convention assembled, deeming it needful for the best interests of this State and nation that independent political action be taken by and in behalf of the producing, industrial, and other business classes, and in opposition to corporate monopolies, that are influencing, even controlling, our Legislatures, courts, and executives, and taxing and oppressing our citizens, appealing to the great fundamental principles of American liberty, and invoking the favorable judgment of our countrymen, do hereby resolve that preservation of our national life imperatively demands that every American voter should attend with care all primary nominations and elections, so as to insure the election of competent and honest men to all the offices in the Government. That the recent record of the political parties of this country is such as to forfeit the confidence and respect of the people, and that we are therefore absolved from all allegiance to them and will act no longer with them.

Resolved, That we insist on severe retrenchment, reform, and economy in all branches of our public affairs, and believe that with such economy the tax now collected from the people might be reduced at least one-half without impairing the efficiency of any branch of the public service, State or national.

Resolved, That we demand immediate reform of abuses in the civil service through which the patronage of the Government is dispensed as a reward for partisan service rather than in regard to public necessity.

Resolved, That we are in favor of improving and perfecting navigation on our lakes and rivers and water connections as soon as it can be properly done.

Resolved, That we are opposed to any further grants of public lands or loans of public credit and of national, State, or local subscriptions in aid of corporations.

Resolved, That we demand the repeal of our national banking law, and believe that the Government should issue legal-tender circulation direct from the Treasury, interchangeable for Government bonds bearing the lowest possible rate of interest.

Resolved, That we hold that patent-laws are too often made to subserve the interests of monopolists, and they should be carefully revised and restricted.

Resolved, That we are opposed to any construction of the State constitution that will justify under any pretext whatever annual instead of biennial sessions of the State Legislature.

Resolved, That existing railroad legislation in this State should be sustained and enforced until thoroughly tested before the courts. That we oppose any legislation by Congress, under plea of regulating commerce between States, which shall deprive the people of their present control and influence through State legislation, and that the claim of the railroad companies to the right to fix their freights and fares independent of the people involves the highest attribute of sovereignty, the right of a conqueror to levy contributions at will upon a subjugated people or state ; and, as this power cannot coexist with a government of the people, it must be resisted.

Resolved, That the right of the Legislature to regulate and control the railroads of the State must be vindicated, established, and maintained as an essential attribute of the State government, and that those holding the doctrine that railroad charters are contracts in the sense that they are not subject to the Legislature's supervision and control have no just appreciation of the necessary powers and rights of free government ; and we will agree to no truce, submit to no compromise, short of the complete supremacy of the State government in its right, through its Legislature, to supervise and control the railroads of the State in such a manner as the public interests may demand.

Resolved, That we condemn the practice of our public officials in receiving free passes from railroads.

Resolved, That the principle of protection as applied to duties on foreign imports is contrary to the spirit and intent of the Constitution, as it creates a privileged class, levying a tax on a large majority for the benefit of a favored few. We are therefore opposed to all duties levied with this end in view, as unjust, unequal, and we insist upon a repeal of all laws laying such duties, and that taxes shall be levied for revenue and that only.

Resolved, That this convention earnestly recommend to the independent voters of the various congressional and legislative districts and counties of the State to put in nomination at an early day and use the best efforts to elect candidates who support the principles herein enunciated.

Resolved, That the contract system practised in the construction of our public works, national, State, and municipal, has been a fruitful source of corruption and fraud, at the expense of the laboring and mechanical as well as against public interests, and such system should be revised and reformed.

Resolved, That we, the Independent Reform party of the State of Illinois, invite the people of the State, regardless of past political affiliations, to unite with us in support of the platform and ticket of this convention, and we appeal to the better judgment of all our business and professional men to lend us their aid and sympathy, remembering, as they well may, that upon our prosperity and happiness depends their success in business.

The State Convention of the Republican party assembled in Springfield, June 17th, and nominated Thomas S. Ridgway for State Treasurer, and William B. Powell for Superintendent of Public Instruction. The platform adopted was as follows

We, the delegated representatives of the Republican party of Illinois, declare the following to be substantially our political belief:

1. That emancipation and enfranchisement having been secured by the thirteenth and fifteenth amendments to the Constitution of the United States, and by appropriate legislation for their enforcement ; and equality of civil rights having been guaranteed by the fourteenth amendment, such guarantee should be enforced by appropriate statutes, so that the broad ægis of Federal power may be over black and white citizens alike.

2. That, as one of the consequences of the late civil war, about $382,000,000 of non-interest-bearing Treasury notes were issued to, and are now held by, the people as a safe and convenient currency, it would be unwise and inexpedient, in the present financial condition of the people, to attempt the immediate cancellation of any portion of such Treasury notes.

3. That the laws for the establishment of national banks having secured to the States and Territories the best system of bank circulation ever before afforded to the people, it should be no longer confided to a privileged class, but should be free to all alike, under general and equal laws, the aggregate volume of currency to be regulated by the untrammeled laws of trade.

4. That we reaffirm the declaration of the National Republican Convention of 1872, in favor of a return to specie payment at the earliest practicable day.

5. That we commend the measures which have passed the popular branch of Congress, looking to the cheapening and perfection of inter-State railway transportation, and the improvement of navigation at the mouth of the Mississippi River.

6. That we are in favor of an amendment of the Constitution of the United States providing for the election of the President and Vice-President by the direct vote of the people, without the intervention of the electoral college.

7. That the Republican party proposes to respect the rights reserved by the people to themselves, as carefully as the powers delegated by them to the State and Federal Governments ; and it will aim to secure the rights and privileges of the citizen without regard to nativity or creed ; and it is opposed to interference by law with the habits, tastes, or customs of individuals, except to suppress licentiousness or to preserve the peace and safety of the citizens of the State.

8. That while we accord to the railway companies of this State the fullest measure of property rights, we also demand for the people reasonable charges and rigid impartiality in the transportation of passengers and freight—such guarantee to be secured by appropriate State and national legislation.

Relying upon the foregoing declaration of principles and policy, and upon the broad, clear record of the Republican party during its fifteen years of State and Federal administration, we appeal once more to that silent yet conclusive tribunal, the ballot-box, confident that the people will indorse overwhelmingly the action of this representative convention.

The Democratic Convention met in Springfield on the 26th of August, and, after much discussion, agreed upon the following platform :

1. The resumption of gold and silver as the basis of currency ; the resumption of specie payments as soon as possible, without disaster to the business interests of the country, by steadily opposing inflation, and by the payment of the national indebtedness in the money of the civilized world.

2. Free commerce, and no tariff except for revenue purposes.

3. Individual liberty, and opposition to sumptuary laws.

4. Rigid restriction of the governments, both State and national, to the legitimate domain of political power, by excluding therefrom all executive and legislative intermeddling with the affairs of society, whereby monopolies are fostered, privileged classes aggrandized, and individual freedom unnecessarily and oppressively restrained.

5. The right and duty of the State to protect its citizens from extortion and unjust discrimination by chartered monopolies.

The following additional resolutions were adopted :

Whereas, The Republican party has ignored the just claims of our disabled soldiers, and violated its pledges repeatedly made, whereby thousands of these noble wards of the nation are compelled to live upon the cold charity of the world:

Resolved, That we now demand that all the pensions of our crippled soldiers shall be so increased as to shield every one of them from daily want, without compelling them to take refuge in a so-called soldiers' home.

Resolved, That the present system of pension agencies is vicious and detrimental to the interest of those it is pretending to protect, and should be thoroughly investigated by Congress.

Mr. Charles Carroll was nominated for State Treasurer, and Mr. Etter, of the Farmer's party, for Superintendent of Instruction.

The election held early in November resulted in the choice of Ridgway for Treasurer, and Etter for Superintendent of Public Instruction. The vote was as follows :

STATE TREASURER.

Thomas S. Ridgway (Republican).................. 162,974
Charles Carroll (Opposition)...................... 128,169
David Gore (Independent Republican)........... 75,580
James F. Simpson (Prohibitionist).............. 516

Total...................................... 367,239
Ridgway's plurality........................... 34,805

STATE SUPERINTENDENT OF PUBLIC INSTRUCTION.

W. B. Powell (Republican)...................... 166,984
S. M. Etter (Independent Republican Opposition) 197,490
Mrs. Potter (Prohibitionist)..................... 681
Mrs. Willing.................................. 21

Total...................................... 365,176
Etter's plurality.......................... 30,506

It will be seen that the vote for State Treasurer is over 2,000 greater than that for Superintendent of Public Instruction.

The election returns for 1872 were: For President, Grant 241,944 ; Greeley, 184,938 ; for Governor, Oglesby, 237,774 ; Koerner, 197,- 084. The Congressmen elected in 1874 were as follows :

District I.—Barney G. Caulfield........ Opposition.
"　　 II.—Carter H. Harrison..........　 "
"　　 III.—C. B. Farwell............... Republican.
"　　 IV.—S. A. Hurlbut...............　 "
"　　 V.—Horatio C. Burchard.......　 "
"　　 VI.—Thomas J. Henderson.......　 "
"　　 VII.—Alexander Campbell........ Opposition.
"　　 VIII.—Greenbury L. Fort......... Republican.
"　　 IX.—Richard H. Whiting.........　 "
"　　 X.—John C. Bagley............. Opposition.
"　　 XI.—Scott Wike.................　 "
"　　 XII.—William M. Springer........　 "
"　　 XIII.—Adlai E. Stevenson..........　 "
"　　 XIV.—Joseph G. Cannon.......... Republican.
"　　 XV.—John R. Eden................. Opposition.
"　　 XVI.—William A. J. Sparks........　 "
"　　 XVII.—William R. Morrison........　 "
"　　 XVIII.—William Hartsell...........　 "
"　　 XIX.—William B. Anderson........ Republican.

The Legislature is classified as follows :

PARTIES.	Senate.	House.	Joint Ballot.
Republicans.............	24	70	94
Democrats	24	56	80
Independents............	3	27	30
Total................	51	153	204

The election of members of the House of Representatives was held under the cumulative system of voting, which is a new feature of the constitution of 1870, intended to secure minority representation. It is provided in that instrument that " in all elections of representatives, as aforesaid, each qualified voter may cast as many votes for one candidate as there are representatives to be elected, or may distribute the same, or equal parts thereof, among the candidates, as he shall see fit ; and the candidates highest in votes shall be elected."

The total indebtedness of the State, December 1, 1874, was $1,730,972, being $329,178 less than on December 1, 1872. It is estimated that the semi-annual receipts from the Illinois Central Railroad Company, which are set apart by law for the payment of the public indebtedness, will be sufficient to meet the interest on the State indebtedness, and to pay such indebtedness as fast as it becomes due, and, on January 1, 1880, when all the outstanding obligations of the State shall have become payable and be paid, there will be a surplus of that Illinois Central Railroad Fund of over $500,000. It is believed that the bonded indebtedness of the counties, townships, cities, and towns, consisting of railroad bonds, war bonds, courthouse bonds, and bonds issued for other corporate purposes, aggregate the enormous sum of $35,000,000, compared to which the indebtedness of the State is a mere trifle.

The estimates for appropriations are : 1875, $2,920,500 ; 1876, $2,725,400 ; 1877, $2,129,- 700.

The following tables give the aggregates of the equalized assessment of property in the State, for the years 1873 and 1874 :

	Assessed Value.	Equalized.
FOR THE YEAR 1873.		
Personal property..........	$306,244,289	$292,153,289
Lands......................	645,179,647	584,476,681
Town and city lots.........	259,097,102	332,943,764
Railroads..................	123,928,479	123,928,479
Capital stock of corporat'ns	21,898,448	21,898,448
Total..................	$1,356,347,965	$1,355,401,317
FOR THE YEAR 1874.		
Personal property..........	$268,833,582	$254,259,578
Lands......................	588,073,254	526,366,032
Town and city lots.........	248,751,340	327,367,734
Railroads..................	74,848,891	74,848,891
Capital stock of corporat'ns.	11,719,216	11,719,216
Total..................	$1,192,221,283	$1,194,456,451

The assessment of personal property, lands, and town and city lots, is by local assessors, in counties, that of railroads and capital stock of corporations by the State Board of Equalization.

The following is a comparison of the assessed values of the most important of the enumerated items of personal property:

LIVE-STOCK.	1873.		1874.	
	No.	Assessed value.	No.	Assessed value.
Horses....	932,092	$48,855,005	926,573	$42,549,570
Cattle.....	2,015,819	35,776,899	2,042,327	31,928,374
Mules and Asses...	96,512	5,823,662	107,554	5,419,724
Sheep.....	1,092,194	2,135,593	1,036,831	1,676,090
Hogs......	3,560,192	11,279,790	3,452,218	8,972,402

ACRES IN CULTIVATION, ETC.	1873.	1874.
Wheat........................	2,093,308	2,558,680
Corn.........................	7,067,040	7,333,760
Oats.........................	1,817,463	1,821,693
Meadow......................	2,178,267	2,368,332
Other field products........	886,166	829,104
Inclosed in pasture.........	3,807,082	4,263,289
Orchard.....................	320,709	334,067
Woodland....	6,289,236	6,928,061

The total valuations of property, for the purposes of taxation in 1873 and 1874, were largely in excess of any previous year; these results, however, do not represent a corresponding increase in the value of property, but are attributed in a large measure to the operation of a new revenue law. The valuations returned for 1873 are believed to be about 0.65 per cent. of the cash value.

The financial transactions of the State during the past two years are shown in the following table. The balance of Revenue Fund on hand December 1, 1874, includes the 7-36 State tax, amounting to $430,466.11. Under the decision of the Supreme Court this sum could not be transferred to the Local Bond Interest Fund.

NAMES OF FUNDS.	Balances in the Treasury December 1, 1872.	Amounts received from December 1, 1872, to November 30, 1874.	Total.
Dr.			
Revenue Fund......................	$588,577 26	$5,076,229 97	$5,664,807 23
State Debt Fund...................	333,765 37	....	333,765 37
Interest Fund.....................	17,855 46	213,805 08	231,660 54
School Fund.......................	62,964 00	2,007,629 38	2,070,593 38
Illinois Central Railroad Fund....	....	827,781 96	827,781 96
Illinois River Improvement Fund...	....	188,668 34	188,668 34
Canal Redemption Fund.............	454,312 47	1,288,834 72	1,743,147 19
Unknown and Minor Heirs' Fund.....	5,485 29	187 84	5,673 13
Delinquent Land Tax Fund..........	331 06	....	331 06
Local Bond Interest Fund..........	587,485 07	2,231,755 58	2,819,240 65
Totals.......	$2,050,775 98	$11,834,892 87	$13,885,668 85

NAMES OF FUNDS.	Amounts disbursed from December 1, 1872, to November 30, 1874.	Balances in the Treasury December 1, 1874.	Total.
Cr.			
Revenue Fund......................	$4,346,947 32	$1,317,859 91	$5,664,807 23
State Debt Fund...................	333,765 37	....	333,765 37
Interest Fund.....................	231,660 54	....	231,660 54
School Fund.......................	2,029,389 65	41,203 73	2,070,593 38
Illinois Central Railroad Fund....	621,751 46	206,030 50	827,781 96
Illinois River Improvement Fund...	154,221 31	34,447 03	188,668 34
Canal Redemption Fund.............	1,743,147 19	....	1,743,147 19
Unknown and Minor Heirs' Fund.....	305 28	5,367 85	5,673 13
Delinquent Land Tax Fund..........	....	331 06	331 06
Local Bond Interest Fund	2,297,948 67	521,291 98	2,819,340 65
Totals.......	$11,759,136 79	$2,126,532 06	$13,885,668 85

Amount on hand December 1, 1872, and amount received to November 30, 1874............	$13,885,668 85
Amount paid out from December 1, 1872, to November 30, 1874............................	11,759,136 79
Total amount of all funds in the Treasury, December 1, 1874.......................	$2,126,532 06

During its adjourned session in 1874 the Legislature passed a law prohibiting all school officers from excluding, directly or indirectly, any child from school on account of color, under penalty of not less than five nor more than one hundred dollars for each offense; and "any person who shall by threats, menace, or by intimidation, prevent any colored child entitled to attend a public school in this State from attending such school, shall, upon conviction, be fined in any amount not exceeding twenty-five dollars." The school-law was further amended so as to abolish the provisional teachers' certificate. Every teacher is now required to hold a regular certificate, either of the first or second grade. It is made the duty of the county superintendent to grant, upon examination, certificates of two grades; those of the first grade shall be valid for two years, and

shall certify that the person to which such certificate is given is qualified to teach orthography, reading in English, penmanship, arithmetic, English grammar, modern geography, the elements of the natural sciences, the history of the United States, physiology, and the laws of health. Certificates of the second grade shall be valid for one year, and shall certify that the person to whom such certificate is given is qualified to teach orthography, reading in English, penmanship, arithmetic, English grammar, modern geography, and the history of the United States.

A bill providing for compulsory education was passed by the House, but defeated in the Senate. The condition of public education in the State, for the two years ending September 30th, is shown by the following statement of the Superintendent of Public Instruction:

	1873.	1874.
No. children under 21 years.	1,399,634	4,444,141
" children between 6 and 21 years.............	909,994	988,878
" school-districts........	11,361	11,285
" school-houses..........	11,323	11,434
" public free schools.....	11,648	11,646
" teachers	20,775	21,129
" pupils enrolled.........	654,309	671,775
" .days attendance	48,507,607	54,433,467
" months school...........	av. 6.59	6.80
" public high-schools....	106	116
Compensation of county superintendents...........	$104,950 65	$63,855 91
Average compensation.....	1,050 11	626 04

RECEIPTS FOR SCHOOL PURPOSES, 1873.

Balance on hand, October 1, 1872........	$1,360,118 85
Received from State	996,245 73
" interest on township funds.....	429,577 77
" district-school tax.....	5,664,585 09
" from all other sources.........	603,666 59
Total receipts.....................	$9,054,194 03
Expenditures for 1873....................	7,655,268 32
Balance.............................	$1,398,925 71

RECEIPTS FOR SCHOOL PURPOSES, 1874.

Balance on hand, October 1, 1873........	$1,398,925 71
Received from State.....................	1,021,970 74
" interest on township funds.....	551,661 28
" district-school tax.............	5,658,182 91
" from all other sources.........	661,776 15
Total receipts.....................	$9,292,516 79
Expenditures for 1874...................	7,865,682 18
Balance on hand October 1, 1874...	$1,426,834 61

COST PER SCHOLAR.	1873.	1874.
For tuition:		
Upon school-census.................	$4 90	$4 93
" enrollment...................	6 84	6 39
" average daily attendance......	12 71	12 09
For incidental expenses:		
Upon school-census.................	70	67
" enrollment...................	98	93
" average daily attendance......	1 83	1 64
For tuition and incidentals:		
Upon school-census.................	5 60	5 60
" enrollment...................	7 80	7 82
" average daily attendance......	14 54	13 73

Seventy-two per cent. of the population of school age were instructed in the public schools. A large majority of these had no other advantage of education. Eleven thousand six hundred and forty-seven schools were kept open at an average of 6$\frac{7}{8}$ months per year. These schools were maintained in 1873 at a cost of $7,655,268.32, and in 1874 of $7,865,682.18 : total $15,520,950.50. Of this amount $2,000,-000 were raised by State tax, and $13,322,768 by district-school tax, making $13,322,768— over three times the amount raised in the same time by taxation for State purposes.

The aggregate cost of the public schools is large ; yet the cost per pupil for 6$\frac{7}{8}$ months schooling each year avarages only $14.14, or $2.11 per month, showing that the system is comparatively cheap. It is the only system coextensive with the State. It opens the school-house door to every child of proper age, regardless of race or religion ; and affords him the opportunity of qualifying himself for the responsibilities and duties of the citizen.

The management of the public institutions of the State is reported to have been very satis-factory. The penitentiary is self-sustaining and requires no appropriations. The south wing of the Northern Insane Asylum at Elgin has been completed, and will be occupied as soon as the Legislature makes provision for supporting the additional inmates. This wing will accommodate 225 patients. The north wing of the Southern Insane Asylum at Auna was opened December 15, 1873, with accommodations for 140 patients. The central building will be ready for occupancy early in the summer of 1875. During the session of the Legislature a resolution of inquiry was passed by the House calling for information concerning the State institutions. In reply Rev. Frederick H. Wines, the secretary of the Board of Public Charities, gave the following interesting facts. The average number of officers and inmates of the several institutions is :

Deaf and Dumb Asylum........	34	officers,	291	inmates.
Blind Asylum....................	17	"	67	"
Feeble-Minded Institute........	28	"	85	"
Soldiers' Orphans' Home........	30	"	302	"
Elgin Insane Asylum............	54	"	190	"
Jacksonville Insane Asylum....	79	"	481	"
Normal University..............	—	"	435	"
Industrial University...........	—	"	320	"

The average number of days the institutions are open is 257, and the total number of days 1,546. The number of officers employed is 381.

Total amount of appropriations drawn during the year 1873, by the several institutions, was $710,278.93, and the amount appropriated, but not drawn, is $1,173,781.90.

The cost of operating the various institutions, including the educational, medical, mechanical, domestic, and agricultural departments for the year ending December 1, 1873, was as follows.

Deaf and Dumb Asylum..................	$28,908
Blind Asylum........................	8,542
Feeble-Minded Institute.................	8,750
Soldiers' Orphans' Home................	11,434
Elgin Insane Asylum...................	21,081
Jacksonville Insane Asylum.............	23,410
Normal University.....................	23,900
Industrial University..................	34,605

The cost, per annum, of maintaining each inmate of the different institutions, including the salaries of officers, etc., is as follows :

Jacksonville Insane Asylum.............	$159 61
Elgin Insane Asylum	207 42
Blind Asylum	212 52
Feeble-Minded Institute...............	199 49
Deaf and Dumb Asylum	201 11
Soldiers' Orphans' Home...............	153 72

This amount is exclusive of building and repairs.

The regulation by the State of passenger and freight schedules on the railroads is a topic of general interest. Several suits brought by the commissioners against railroad corporations for alleged violation of the law are still pending. One of these attracted much attention during the year. This was a suit brought by the State on the 6th of February in the Sangamon Circuit Court against the Chicago & Alton Railroad Company for extortion under the law regulating freight and fares. The suit was continued to the May term on affidavits filed by the defendants. Prior to the May term, defendants' council procured a writ of *certiorari* from the Circuit Court of the United States, under the provisions of the act of Congress of April 20, 1871, entitled "An act to enforce the provisions of the fourteenth amendment to the Constitution of the United States, and for other purposes" (commonly known as the "Ku-klux" act), commanding the transfer of the suit from the State to the Federal court. At the May term the State court, after full argument on the part of each party, declined to obey the mandate of the writ of *certiorari*, and the defendants refusing to appeal or otherwise appear, except as *amici curiæ*, the cause was tried and a judgment obtained in favor of the people for three thousand dollars and costs. Subsequently the defendants obtained a writ of error and *supersedeas* by which the cause was taken to the Supreme Court of the State, where it was pending for hearing at the January term, 1875.

At the June term of the United States Circuit Court very full arguments were submitted by counsel for the respective parties, to the full bench, consisting of Judge David Davis, of the Supreme Court of the United States, and Judges Drummond and Treat, upon the proceedings instituted in that court by the writ of *certiorari*, and a decision rendered quashing the writ and dismissing the proceedings. From this decision the defendants have taken an appeal to the Supreme Court of the United States, where it is now pending. Thus is presented the anomaly of the same case pending in the two courts at the same time.

In his message to the Legislature of 1875, Governor Beveridge discusses at length the policy of the State toward railroads. He says:

The law to prevent extortion and unjust discrimination in the rates charged for the transportation of passengers and freights on the railroads in this State, has been in force about eighteen months and the schedules prepared by the Railroad and Warehouse Commissioners, in pursuance of said law, have been in force little less than one year.

The policy of a State interfering with private enterprise, or undertaking to manage the affairs of its citizens, is controverted. This law makes no such interference, and undertakes no such management. It only seeks to correct abuses by preventing extortion and unjust discrimination. Framed in accordance with the decision of the Supreme Court, it follows the principles of the common law. It does not declare any particular act to be an unjust discrimination, but it declares certain acts to be *prima facie* evidence of unjust discrimination. It does not prescribe any rate to be charged, or declare any rate unreasonable or extortionate, but makes the schedules prepared by the commissioners *prima facie* evidence of what is a reasonable maximum rate of charges. It does not controvert a single principle of the common law, except to change the rule of evidence, and to throw the burden of proof upon the defendant, and the question whether such an act is an unjust discrimination, or such a charge is extortionate, is to be determined by a court and jury, upon the facts proved under the law.

Repeal this act, and every principle of the law remains, save that the burden of proof would be upon the plaintiff, and there would be no statutory penalties affixed to a verdict of guilty of extortion or unjust discrimination.

In deference to the law and public opinion, the railroad corporations of the State have, in the main, ceased their unjust discriminations; at least but few complaints have been heard, and few have been made to the commissioners; and on some lines the rates of charges conform nearly to the schedules prepared and published by the commissioners, and on other lines the rates have been materially lessened. Greater courtesy and a better spirit of accommodation, on the part of railroad officials and employés, have tended to create a kindlier feeling between the producing classes and the transportation lines.

Railroads have developed the resources of the State, have increased our population, have added to our wealth, have brought sections of country distant from markets into close proximity with the markets of the world, and they are indispensable to the welfare of our commercial, manufacturing, and farming interests.

No legislation should be had to embarrass railroad companies in operating their roads, to impose upon them unnecessary burdens, to cripple their energies, to prevent them from charging and collecting reasonable rates, and receiving full remuneration for proper repairs and cost of economical operation, and a reasonable compensation upon a fair valuation of their property and for the risk run.

On the other hand, they should be subject to legislative control, so far as to submit to proper police regulations, to pay their proportion of taxes, to afford safe and reasonable facilities in the transportation of persons and property, to secure economy in administration, to prohibit wasteful expenditures and corrupt management, and to prevent unjust discriminations and unreasonable or extortionate rates of charges.

Entertaining these views, I approve of the railroad legislation of the State, and of the continuance of the Board of Railroad and Warehouse Commissioners, representing the State, and standing between the people and these mammoth corporations.

The Railroad Commissioners, in pointing out the benefits to the public from the operation of the law, say that "the railroad companies seldom now, as heretofore they were in the constant habit of doing, unjustly discriminate in favor of one point on the line of their road to the detriment of another; nor do they practise to the same extent as formerly that objectionable sort of favoritism to individual shippers that has been in the past the cause of so much complaint, and was doubtless the principal, if not indeed the prime, cause of the enactment. While this law has not as yet accomplished a full reformation as to the extortion, we think it may safely be claimed that it has in a great measure put an end to unjust discrimination. It is gratifying to observe, also, that several of the roads have regulated their charges to correspond, if not exactly, very nearly, with that of the rates fixed in the schedules of the commissioners; and that the aggregate charges of all the roads in the State, taken upon the same amount of business done, are less than before the passage of the law mentioned. In the suits already named, instituted chiefly for the purpose of testing the questions in dispute, it will be observed that in every instance where the courts have passed upon the question, the law has been sustained."

The Legislature held an adjourned session,

which lasted from the early part of January till April.

INDIA, BRITISH, a vast empire in Asia, equaling in extent the continent of Europe without Russia. The area of the region in which the supremacy of England is acknowledged, is estimated at 1,558,254 square miles, with a population of 240,000,000. The population varies in density from 700 persons to the square mile in some parts of Oude and the lower provinces of Bengal to 10 in some of the hill districts. About two-fifths of the country consist of independent native states, whose chiefs acknowledge the supremacy of Great Britain, and are, to a certain extent, subject to its control. British India proper comprises the remaining three-fifths. It was in 1874 divided, for administrative purposes, into nine provinces, viz., Bengal, the Northwestern Province, the Punjab, Oude, the Central Province, British Burmah, Assam, Madras, and Bombay. Assam, which had been ceded by Burmah in 1825, formed part of the jurisdiction of the Lieutenant-Governor of Bengal until 1874, when it was made a separate province. The area and population of the nine administrative divisions were, according to the latest dates, as follows:

PROVINCES.	Area.	ADMINISTRATION.		POPULATION.		CAPITALS.	
		Divisions.	Districts.	Total.	Average per Square Mile.	Name.	Population.
Bengal......................	198,090	10	47	63,724,840	321	Calcutta.........	447,600
Northwestern Province.....	81,463	8	36	30,769,056	378	Allahabad	....
Punjab......................	103,748	10	32	17,596,752	170	Lahore	....
Oude	23,930	4	12	11,220,032	469	Lucknow.......	....
Central Province............	84,963	4	19	8,201,519	97	Nagpool......	....
British Burmah.............	88,364	3	15	2,747,148	31	Rangoon.......	....
Assam	52,000	1	11	2,926,992	60	Goalpara.......	....
Madras	139,698	8	21	31,597,872	226	Madras	397,522
Bombay.....................	124,458	3	23	16,228,774	130	Bombay.........	644,405

The following table exhibits the amount of the revenue, expenditures, imports, and exports of each one of the nine provinces during the year 1872–'73:

PROVINCES.	Revenue.	Expenditures.	Imports.	Exports.
Bengal.................................	£15,943,000	£5,422,000	£15,396,000	£24,619,000
Northwestern Province.............	5,850,000	2,084,000	....	....
Punjab.................................	3,605,000	1,587,000	....	....
Oude	1,657,000	627,000	....	....
Central Province	1,657,000	593,000	....	....
British Burmah	1,393,000	697,000	1,680,000	3,777,000
Assam.................................				
Madras.................................	8,199,000	6,045,000	2,932,000	6,347,000
Bombay.................................	9,590,000	7,391,000	10,545,000	20,587,000

In addition to these nine provinces, there are the two provinces of Mysore and Berar, which are governed on the English system, though they do not contribute to the imperial revenue. Mysore was taken possession of by the English in 1834, to put a stop to the misrule which prevailed under the late Maharajah, and will continue to be governed by them during the minority of the present young prince, whose education has been confided to an English officer. The province is under the charge of a chief commissioner, who has charge also of the little state of Coorg. Mysore and Coorg are the principal coffee-producing districts of India. Berar, which lies north of the dominions of the Nizam of Hyderabad, was placed in the hands of the English in 1853, in payment of certain arrears due to the British Government. The province forms part of the charge of the British Resident of Hyderabad. The surplus of revenue over the expenses of administration is handed over to the government of the Nizam. The area and population of Mysore, Coorg, and Berar, are as follows:

PROVINCES.	Area.	Population.
Mysore......................	27,077	5,055,412
Coorg	2,000	108,312
Berar......................	16,960	2,231,565

The native states of British India, though not constituting a part of the British dominion, are more or less under the control of the Anglo-Indian Government. Their area and population are as follows:

NATIVE STATES UNDER	Area.	Population.
Governor-General of India.........	385,396	27,716,352
Lieutenant-Governor of Bengal.....	79,156	2,139,565
Lieutenant-Governor of Northwest Provinces......................	5,890	1,284,691
Lieutenant-Governor of the Punjab.	43,877	5,086,502
Chief Commissioner of Central Provinces......................	28,399	1,095,275
Governor of Madras	31,953	2,371,033
Governor of Bombay................	72,076	6,552,170
Total native states	646,147	46,245,888

The most important of the native states is Hyderabad, with an area of about 80,000 square miles, a population of about 11,000,000, and an annual revenue of about £1,655,000. Then comes Maharajah Scindia's state of Gwalior; then Baroda and Jeypoor. The united military force of the native states is estimated at 100,000 men.

The whole number of schools in British India, in 1872 and 1873, excluding the native states and Burmah, was 40,700, giving instruction to 1,280,940 scholars, at a cost of £758,337. Government schools exist in regular gradation, from those which give the humblest elementary instruction to the highest colleges, and the ablest pupils of one grade are able to pass through the other grades by means of scholarships. Universities on the model of the London University have been established in Calcutta, Madras, and Bombay. Each province has normal schools for the training of masters.

The total revenue of India, during the financial year ending March 31, 1873, reached the sum of £50,219,489; and the expenditures amounted to £48,453,817. The three most important sources of the public revenue are land (in 1872, £21,348,669); salt (£6,165,630); and opium (£8,684,691). The heaviest items among the expenditures are the army (£11,979,-827); interest on permanent and floating debt (£2,834,764). The interest paid on the Indian debt during the year ending March 31, 1873, amounted to £4,671,699, and the total debt for loans contracted up to that date was £105,-160,127. The regular estimates for 1873-'74 place the revenue at £49,476,000. The budget estimates for 1874-'75 calculate the revenue at £48,984,000, and the ordinary expenditure at £50,372,000, of which £2,580,000 are set apart for the relief of the famine. The extraordinary expenditures for public works are estimated at £4,563,000, and the total expenditure at £54,-935,000. The surplus, excluding the extraordinary and famine relief items, is estimated at £1,192,000. The deficit, excluding the extraordinary expenditure, is £1,388,000, and including the extraordinary expenditure, £5,-951,000. It is estimated that the net famine expenditure in both years will be £6,500,000. The loans to be raised in 1874-'75 amount to £8,500,000, of which £5,000,000 will be raised by the Secretary of State for India in England; £870,000 from Gwalior and Indore for railways; the remaining £2,640,000 in India or England, as may be found convenient. There are to be no new taxes imposed in the financial year of 1874-'75.

According to the budget of 1874-'75, the army in India consisted of 6,086 English officers, 60,227 British soldiers, 3,804 volunteers, and 123,474 native soldiers; total, 193,591 men, with 13,238 horses and 394 guns. For the performance of police duties and frontier service there is a force of native police, amounting to about 190,000 men, who are mainly officered by Europeans.

On July 1, 1874, the aggregate length of railroad lines opened for public traffic was 5,872 miles, 483 miles having been added since the commencement of 1873. Among the new railways opened in 1874 was one to Hyderabad, constructed at the expense of the Nizam. The Government of India, in 1869, decided on carrying out all the new railway extensions by means of direct agency; that is, without the intervention of guaranteed companies. In June, 1874, a proposal was made by some private individuals to construct a railway on a

three-feet gauge from Rangoon to Tounghoo, in the Sittang Valley, at their own cost, if the Government would grant certain concessions. The Government of India replied that they had no intention of departing from their determination to construct all further railways by state agency, and therefore could not entertain the proposal. At the same time, they added that the facts brought forward in favor of the proposed line had established a good case for testing its merits, and a survey would be ordered in the course of the ensuing season, as soon as officers could be spared for the purpose, for the construction of a line on the metre-gauge.

The electric telegraph connects all the important places in India. The aggregate length of the telegraph-lines was 15,102 miles; total receipts, £151,261; total expenditures, £129,-562; the number of offices, 205.

The present Viceroy and Governor-General of India, Lord Thomas George Baring Northbrook, assumed his powers in May, 1872.*

The whole commerce of India, exclusive of treasure, during 1872-'73, was worth £104,-485,696, of which the foreign trade represented £83,488,056, and the coastwise trade £20,-997,640. There are no trustworthy statistics of the internal trade. The aggregate value of the merchandise exported from India, between 1835 and 1871, is estimated at £1,012,000,000, and of the imports, £583,000,000. The exports from India to China, in 1872-'73, were worth £12,074,347, of which opium took £10,-529,673.

The famine, which was anticipated at the end of the year 1873, made itself felt at the beginning of 1874. The Government was, however, prepared, and soon made energetic efforts to aid the sufferers. At a relief meeting held in January, at Calcutta, the Viceroy declared that the failure of the crops affected a population exceeding that of Great Britain, and, notwithstanding the rain, a population exceeding that of Ireland must suffer protracted and severe distress. He warmly represented the people's patience and the powerful claims which their affliction gave on their rulers, and urged that assistance should be obtained from the public. He thanked England for its sympathy. Sir George Campbell detailed the suffering of the landless classes everywhere. The promised relief has already done good; there have been no panics like those in Orissa, and the people trust to the Government. In some districts the distress assumed larger dimensions than had been anticipated. Thus, in Tirhoot, the number of persons applying at the relief-works rose from 20,000 to 100,000 within ten days. The applicants were in an emaciated condition, but preferred working to entering the poor-houses. All belonged to the laboring-classes. Three or four deaths from starvation occurred. After the spring harvest had been gathered in, a large accession of la-

---

* For a biographical notice of Lord Northbrook, see ANNUAL CYCLOPÆDIA for 1873, article INDIA.

borers flocked to the Government public works. The total number thus employed on every class of relief enterprise increased from 750,000 to 1,185,448 during a fortnight. Among these enterprises were the making of the railway which is to intersect Northern Bengal and to connect Darjeeling with the plains. They likewise included the Son Canal, the great embankments along the Gandak River, innumerable roads, and local irrigation-works, especially tanks. The saltpetre-manufacture was also used as a relief-work. Speaking generally, the special characteristics of the "relief-works" were these: They consisted for the most part of public undertakings, such as roads, tramways, a railway or a canal, which are of permanent utility, and which were either in progress at the commencement of the famine or would have hereafter been constructed in the ordinary course of things. From this point of view, the relief system may be described as a system of greatly-stimulated public works concentrated upon a single year, and executed at a high rate of wages. Their "relief aspect" consisted in the fact that, while it was endeavored to obtain a fair amount of work from the able-bodied laborers, that amount was not exacted from all. Care was taken that the weakest and the youngest on the works could earn a livelihood. In this sense they were strictly relief-works. Government undertook to find employment for the entire laboring population of Bengal from within a few miles of Calcutta to the Himalayas and the Northwestern Provinces. In only one division of this great tract—namely, the Patna division—the estimates formed by Sir Richard Temple showed symptoms of being realized. Sir Richard visited the division very carefully himself, and his forecast seems to have been an accurate one. The returns of charitable relief were equally encouraging. The system pursued embraced every man, woman, or child, who was unable, either from caste prejudices, from physical debility, or from any other cause, to earn a livelihood. The official narrative gives the fullest details as to the means employed for searching out every case of distress, and of the machinery by which it was relieved. The amount of food given to each person was from 25 to 50 per cent. greater than the amount deemed sufficient in the Orissa famine, and in many cases exceeding the quantity which the poorest class manages to go through life upon.

The aggregate number of the persons who at any time during the famine months had received relief from the Government is estimated at about 8,000,000. In October the famine was declared to be at an end. In September a resolution was issued by the Viceroy in Council announcing that a Duffla campaign on a small scale has become absolutely unavoidable, and that the commander-in-chief is to arrange all the details for moving up troops early in December to the scene of disturbance. The

objects proposed to be accomplished are the rescue of the captives carried off from British territory by the Dufflas, the infliction of a moderate amount of correction on the offending tribe, and such a display of armed force as will suffice to deter them from a repetition of the raids. Bloodshed and pillage are, as far as practicable, to be scrupulously avoided, unless the British demands are contumaciously refused. The officer in command of the force will be intrusted with full discretionary power to adopt any line of action that may insure the success of the expedition. His Excellency particularly desires it to be understood that, so long as the main object of the campaign is capable of being attained by milder measures, recourse to retaliatory acts should be abstained from. If the tribe is disposed to pay on demand a certain amount of fine which may suffice to recoup the losses of the captives, as well as to surrender the captives, this will, in his Excellency's opinion, adequately meet the requirements of the case. The expedition is to remain long enough to convince the erring Dufflas that they are not altogether beyond the reach of attack, while the opportunity afforded by this temporary occupation will be availed of to make as complete an exploration of the country as circumstances may permit. For this purpose a survey-party will be attached to the expedition. If the troops move early in the cold season, they will probably be able to return before the weather begins to prove detrimental to their health. The officer in command will be invested with supreme authority in all matters relating to the conduct of the expedition, and the civil or political officers, together with those of the survey-party, will be in all respects subordinate to him. Brigadier-General Stafford, C. B., will command the expedition.

The Government sternly warned the Guicowar of Baroda to reform the abuses pointed out by the Commission of Inquiry. The warning concluded by stating that if great improvement were not manifest by the end of 1875 the Guicowar would be deposed in the interest of his people, and for the peace and security of the empire. The effect on other native states, it was hoped, would be wholesome. In several of them abuses are becoming intolerable.

INDIANA. The assessed value of the taxable property in the State of Indiana, in 1874, was $954,857,475, an increase of more than $300,000,000 since 1872, due in part, however, to a higher standard of valuation. The assessment of railroad property was raised from $11,000,000, in 1872, to nearly $40,000,000. There was in the State Treasury, on the 1st of March, 1873, $169,633.90; the receipts from that date to October 1, 1873, the close of the fiscal year, amounted to $438,191.14; the receipts for the fiscal year ending October 1, 1874, were $893,091.97. There was raised by temporary loans, during the same period, $200,000 at 8 per cent., payable March 12, 1875; $310,000 at 7 per cent., payable April

15, 1876; and $200,000 at 8 per cent., payable December 1, 1876. Besides this, $68,584.69 was received on account of benevolent institutions, including earnings of the inmates and payments from individuals and counties. Aside from this latter sum, the total revenue was $2,410,917.01. The payments from the Treasury during this same period for revenue refunded, for ordinary expenditures, and for the benevolent institutions, amounted to $1,544,216.43. The object of the temporary loans was chiefly to provide funds for redeeming 191 old bonds issued prior to 1841, as required by act of the Legislature of December 12, 1872. Ninety-seven of these bonds have been surrendered and paid, amounting to $495,487.30. The surplus remaining in the Treasury on the 31st of October was $244,203.78. The State debt is $1,172,755.12, consisting of—

Five per cent. certificates, State stock......	$26,469 99
Two and one-half per cent. certificates, State stock...................................	3,285 13
War-loan bonds, six per cent., due 1881.....	139,000 00
Temporary loan made under Act of March 10, 1873, which I have before mentioned more in detail...........................	910,000 00
Ninety-four old bonds required to be paid by the Act of December 12, 1872..........	94,000 00
Total............................. $1,172,755 12

Besides this, the State is indebted to the school-fund to the amount of $3,904,783.22, represented by five non-negotiable bonds. The entire school-fund is as follows:

1. The amount which the State owes it, and which is evidenced by her non-negotiable bonds bearing interest at the rate of six per cent.................................	$3,904,783 21
Additions from fines and other sources.....	67,197 24
Amount held in the counties, and loaned by the auditors on mortgage security at eight per cent., and for the preservation of which the constitution makes the counties liable...............................	2,341,267 12
2. Congressional township fund, being the proceeds of the sales of the school-sections...............................	2,295,778 63
Estimated value of 13,453 acres of unsold school-lands.............................	102,293 40
Total permanent fund............. $8,711,319 40

The revenue realized during the year ending November 15, 1874, to be used in the support of schools, was as follows:

Interest on permanent fund...............	$407,839 46
Derived from school-tax...............	1,013,463 42
Unclaimed witness-fees and other sources.	72,304 96
Total...................... $1,493,597 57
To this sum is to be added the interest on the Congressional township fund..........	172,209 82
And the amount received from local taxation...................................	551,785 74

Six thousand two hundred and sixty-five dollars and four cents were not distributed, but remained in the Treasury. There was received and distributed during the year, for the support of schools, $2,211,328.13. The number of children in the State, between the ages of six and twenty-one years, is 654,364; enrolled in the schools, 489,044; average attendance, 311,272; total number of teachers, 12,655. By an act of March, 1873, $15,000 of the school revenue

is set apart for the benefit of the Normal School at Terre Haute. The total receipts of the institution for two years amounted to $29,706.85; expenditures, $39,136.38. There were enrolled during the year 804 different students; and during the past two years 187 males and 214 females have enjoyed the advantages of the school.

During the two collegiate years from June 28, 1872, to June 28, 1874, the revenues of the State University amounted to $109,800.46, of which $90,500 was appropriated from the State Treasury. The number of students in attendance in 1874 was 371, of whom 108 were connected with the medical school, 120 were pursuing the preparatory and select course, and 146 were in the literary and law departments. The college for education in "branches related to agriculture and the mechanic arts," for which the grant of land-scrip was made by Congress in 1862, was opened on the 16th of September, near Lafayette, where suitable buildings have been provided. It is called "Pardue University," on account of a large donation made to the college by John Pardue, Esq. The permanent fund derived from the sale of land-scrip and the investment of the proceeds now amounts to $356,502.92. Forty-six students were admitted at the opening of the institution.

The Soldiers' Orphans' Home, near Knightstown, contained 290 children on the 31st of October, who are provided for and educated mainly at the expense of the State. The expenditure from the State Treasury on its account for the year ending October 31, 1873, was $33,977.98; for the year ending October 31, 1874, $35,508.56. The Institution for the Blind had 113 pupils in attendance during the year ending October 31st, and the expenses for that year were $38,235.55, against $38,674.29 for the year previous. The Institute for the Deaf and Dumb, at Indianapolis, had 354 pupils during the year, and its expenses amounted to $68,960.88, against $70,584.57 in 1873. The Hospital for the Insane, located on a tract of 160 acres of land two miles west of Indianapolis, contained 474 patients on the 31st of October, 1873, and during the year following 573 were admitted and 365 discharged.. Of those discharged, 194 were considered cured, 45 improved, and 92 unimproved and incurable. The expenditures for 1873 were $209,839.47; for 1874, $195,702.52. Substantial improvements and repairs have been made to the buildings during the last two years.

In the Northern State-prison, on the 15th of December, there were 455 convicts, an increase of 85 during the year. During the two years ending with that date there was received from the income of the prison $123,200.40, while the current and ordinary expenses were $104,034.26. There has been expended on permanent improvements, during the same period, $14,060.96, and increased accommodations are now needed, as there are but 385 cells for the

455 prisoners, and insufficient shop-room for their profitable employment. The Southern Prison contained 417 convicts on the 15th of December, the average number in 1873 being 395. During the two years $39,379.26 was expended for repairs. The ordinary expenses for the same period amounted to $119,743.26, and the proceeds of prison-labor are stated at $136,314.73. The statement is somewhat confused by including in the receipts from labor a portion of $19,000 appropriated from the State Treasury, and the labor of convicts in repairing buildings, reckoned at sixty cents a day. The labor of the convicts in this institution is, for the most part, let out by contract to the Southwestern Car Company. The Reformatory Institution for Women and Girls was opened in September, 1873, and on the 1st of Decem-

STATE-HOUSE, INDIANAPOLIS.

ber, 1874, contained 93 inmates in the reformatory department and 30 in the penal department. The total expenditure for buildings and grounds has been $100,378.18. The total disbursements by the State on account of the institution have amounted to $128,255.55. The expenses for 1874 were $12,879.85. The labor of the inmates is not thus far remunerative. The annual expense of each inmate is estimated at $182, of which one-half is paid by the county sending the convict. The superintendent is Mrs. Sarah J. Smith.

The House of Refuge, located on a tract of 225 acres of land in Plainfield, contained on the 1st of December 265 inmates. The expenditure of the year amounted to $57,002.58, of which $15,582.35 was for improvements and buildings. Two buildings were erected during the year, one for a shop, and one for a family-house, which will provide for fifty boys. The value of the improvements of the year is about $25,000, of which $10,000 was derived from the work of the boys. The boys are kept at work on the farm or in the buildings a fair

share of the time, and are taught in schools, and brought generally under beneficial influences.

The State Board of Agriculture during the year caused to be erected on the Fair-grounds at Indianapolis a spacious structure for a State exposition, as a permanent means of exhibiting the products of the industries of the State. The expense was borne mainly by citizens of Indianapolis.

An ornamental iron fence has been built around the battle-ground at Tippecanoe by order of the Legislature and at the expense of the State. It cost $17,854.17, which was $6,245.83 less than the amount appropriated for the purpose.

There are nine savings-banks in the State, two at Indianapolis, two at Lafayette, and one each at Laporte, Terre Haute, Evansville, Fort Wayne, and South Bend. There are also nine banks of discount and deposit organized under State law, one each at Decatur, New Carlisle, Union City, Newcastle, Columbus, Fort Wayne, Madison, Anderson, and Portland.

The gross receipts for fire insurance during the year were $1,500,681.01 ; losses paid, $666,590.29; taxes do., $26,370.29. Gross receipts for life insurance, $1,526,544.24; losses paid, $889,240.32; taxes paid, $22,284.08.

The number of miles of railroad in the State is 3,737.12 of main track and 457.51 of side track; value of main track, $27,887,998 ; of side track, $2,699,356 ; value of rolling-stock, $9,097,842; total value, $39,740,042.

The political campaign of the year opened with a convention of farmers, which gathered at Indianapolis on the 10th of June. In the call for the convention which had been issued in April, signed by a long list of names headed by James Comstock, superintendent of the State Grange, the following language was used:

In response to the demand of the people for a reform in the conduct of public affairs, and the purification of local, State, and national politics, the undersigned, independent voters, invite and exhort the people, irrespective of party, to come together, in township, county, and district, to select delegate representatives, who shall meet in mass convention on the 10th day of June, 1874, at Indianapolis, to frame such measures and select such men as shall represent their sentiments and carry out their purposes. In the selection of such delegates, it is essential that the friends of reform guard vigilantly against the intrusion of any one not known to be in cordial sympathy with the objects of this movement. The success of this popular outbreak depends upon the exclusion of the party managers and self-seeking demagogues.

The convention was composed of about 500 delegates, representing every county in the State. A resolution was adopted assuming the name of "Independent" for the party to be organized, "as an expression of the sentiment and purposes" of the delegates, and in order to "command due recognition." There was considerable discussion and some division of sentiment as to the expediency of forming a political organization, which led to the withdrawal of several delegations, including those from the fourth, eighth, and ninth congressional districts. Finally a platform was adopted and nominations for State officers made. After a long preamble, setting forth the general principles of the organization and declaring that "our government is wholly perverted from its true design, and the sacred names democracy and republicanism are the synonyms of despotism," the platform enumerates the following as the "instrumentalities" by which these wrongs are inflicted:

1. Banking and moneyed monopolies, by which, through ruinous rates of interest, the products of human labor are concentrated in the hands of nonproducers. This is the great central source of these wrongs, in and through which all other monopolies exist and operate.

2. Consolidated railroads and other transit monopolies, whereby all industries are taxed to the last mill they will bear, for the benefit of the stockholders and stock-jobbers.

3. Manufacturing monopolies, whereby all small operators are crushed out, and the price of labor and its products are determined with mathematical certainty in the interest of the capitalists.

4. Land monopolies, by which the public domain is absorbed by a few corporations and speculators.

5. Commercial and grain monopolies, speculating and enriching their bloated corporations on human necessities.

It is thus proposed to "remedy these evils and remove their results:"

1. By abandoning the gold-basis fallacy and establishing a monetary system based on the faith and resources of this Government, in harmony with the genius of this Government and adapted to the exigencies of legitimate commerce. To this end the circulating notes of the national and State banks, as well as all local currency, to be withdrawn from circulation, and a paper currency issued by the Government, which shall be a legal tender in the payment of all debts, public and private, duties on imports included, and declared equal with gold, the lawful money of the United States; this currency or money to be interchangeable at the pleasure of the holders for Government bonds bearing a low rate of interest, say 3.65 per cent.; the Government creditors to have the privilege of taking the money or bonds at their election, reserving to Congress the right to regulate the rate of interest on the bonds and the volume of the currency, so as to effect the equitable distribution of the products of labor between money or non-producing capital and productive industry.

2. By paying the national debt in strict accordance with the laws under which it was originally contracted, gold where specifically promised, but all other forms of indebtedness, including the principal of the 5-20 bonds, should be discharged at the earliest option of the Government in the legal-tender currency of the United States, without funding it in long bonds, or in any way increasing the gold-paying and untaxed obligations of the Government.

The following resolutions are appended to these declarations, and complete the platform:

Resolved, That we are in favor of the office seeking the man, and not the man the office; that we will endeavor to select men to fill the various offices who are honest and capable, without regard to former political opinions; that we detest bribery, corruption, and fraud, in obtaining votes, either by the use of money or whiskey, and will not support any man for office known to be guilty of the same; and that we are opposed to soliciting any man to fill the same office for more than one term in succession, from the President down.

Resolved, That we uncompromisingly condemn the practice of our public officers in receiving free passes from railroad managers.

Resolved, That we denounce the action of our last Legislature, and representatives in Congress and the Senate, for the increase of taxes, fees, and salaries, and we will use all honorable means in our power to reduce the taxes, fees, and salaries of all to a reasonable basis.

Resolved, That we demand the reduction of all public expenditure, to the end that taxation may be reduced to the lowest possible limit.

Resolved, That it is contrary to the policy of good government to encourage litigation, and that the law allowing 10 per cent. on judgments and the collection of attorneys' fees off of defendant encourages litigation, favors capital, and is a source of corruption and serves no good end, therefore ought to be remedied by appropriate legislation.

Resolved, That the present assessment law of real estate imposes unequal and unjust burdens on the producing class, and favors capital and corporate wealth, and we demand its speedy amendment.

Resolved, That we demand a change in our grand-jury system, that their jurisdiction extend to felonies only.

Resolved, That no party is worthy our confidence who denies the right of the people to restrict the abuses of the liquor-traffic.

The candidates nominated for State officers were: Secretary of State, Noyes S. White, of Vigo County; Auditor of State, Ebenezer Henderson, of Morgan County; State Treasurer, Norris C. Bennett, of Steuben County; Attorney-General, James A. S. Mitchell, of Elkhart County; Judge of the Supreme Court, Horace P. Biddle, of Cass County; Superintendent of Public Instruction, Clarkson Davis, of Henry County.

Another convention was held at Indianapolis on the 12th of August, for the purpose of filling vacancies on the ticket, some of the candidates having refused to run. Messrs. Henderson and Biddle were rejected for having accepted nominations for the same offices from the Democratic Convention. There were only about 75 delegates at this convention, and the ticket finally agreed upon was: J. B. Stout for Secretary of State, T. Z. Truscott for Auditor, N. C. Bennett for Treasurer, Wm. A. Peebles for Attorney-General, and A. H. Graham for Superintendent of Public Instruction.

The Republican State Convention was held at Indianapolis on the 17th of June, and nominated by acclamation the incumbent State officers for reëlection, as follows: For Secretary of State, W. F. Curry; for Auditor, Joseph A. Wildman; for Treasurer, John B. Glover; for

Attorney-General, James C. Denny; for Judge of the Supreme Court, Andrew L. Osborn. The platform, which was unanimously adopted, was prefaced by an appeal to the past history of the party, its great achievements, and its determination to reform abuses and expose and punish fraud and corruption. Then follows the following declaration of principles:

The Republicans of Indiana, therefore, assembled in State Convention, do hereby declare—

1. Their unchangeable determination to adhere to all the fundamental principles of the Republican party in so far as the future condition of the country shall require their enforcement. As the Union remains unbroken, and the people of all sections are again bound together as brethren by a common destiny and under a common flag, we favor such measures as shall develop the material resources of every portion of it, to secure to all, of every class and condition, full protection in all just rights of person and property, to remove all acerbities of the past, and to perpetuate the nation as the model republic of the world.

2. We recognize that as the true policy of government which shall harmonize all the diversified interests and pursuits necessarily existing in a country of such vast extent as ours, and as this can be done only by so directing legislation as to secure just protection and reward to every branch of industry, we are in favor of giving precedence to those measures which shall recognize agricultural and mechanical pursuits as entitled to the amplest protection and fullest development; of putting a stop to large grants of the public domain to railroad corporations, and reserving it for settlement and cultivation; of improving the navigation of our great inland rivers; of securing cheap transportation and profitable markets for the products of agricultural and manufacturing labor; of encouraging such manufactures as shall bring the producer and consumer in the neighborhood of each other, and thus to establish mutual relations between them and those engaged in commerce and transportation; of p o e adjusting the relations between capital and labor, in order that each may receive a just and equitable share of the profits; and of holding those in the possession of corporate wealth and privileges in strict conformity to the law, so that through combined influences people of varied pursuits may be united together in the common purpose of preserving the honor of the nation and developing the immense resources of every section of the Union, and of advancing the social and mutual prosperity of all its industrial and laboring classes.

3. We are in favor of such legislation on the question of finance as shall make national banking free, and shall furnish the country with such an additional amount of currency as may be necessary to meet the wants of the agricultural, industrial, and commercial interests of the country, to be distributed between the sections according to the population of each, as is consistent with the credit and honor of the nation, and will prevent the possibility of capitalists and combinations of capital controlling the currency of the country.

4. We are in favor of such a revision of our patent-rights laws as shall destroy the oppressive monopoly incidental to the present system, and shall regulate and control the manufacture, use, and sale of patent-right articles for the benefit alike of the inventor, consumer, and manufacturer.

5. That the Republican party continues to express its gratitude to the soldiers and sailors of the republic for the patriotism, courage, and self-sacrifice with which they gave themselves to the preservation of the country during the late civil war, and it will especially recognize the services of the enlisted men by favoring extension from time to time, as the ability of the Government will admit, of the pension and bounty laws.

6. In the opinion of this convention, intemperance is an evil against which society has the right to protect itself; that our whole system of legislation, throughout all the history of our State, has asserted and maintained this right, and it cannot now be surrendered without yielding up that fundamental principle of American Government which places the power of passing laws in the hands of a majority. Therefore we are in favor of such legislation as will give a majority of the people the right to determine for themselves, in their respective towns, townships, or wards, whether the sale of intoxicating liquors, for use as a beverage, shall be permitted therein, and such as will hold the vender responsible for all damages resulting from such sales.

7. We favor the enactment of a law limiting the power of township trustees, county commissioners, and municipal authorities, to assess taxes and increase township, county, and municipal indebtedness.

8. Inasmuch as great abuses have grown up under our present system of fees and salaries, we demand such legislation as will so reduce and regulate all fees and salaries as will allow no more than a fair and just compensation for services rendered.

9. We look with pride and satisfaction upon our common-school system, and regard its munificent fund as a sacred trust to be faithfully and honestly administered, so that all the children of the State may be educated in the duties of citizenship, and thereby become better able to perpetuate our popular institutions; and whosoever shall seek to strike it down, or impair its usefulness, will meet our ceaseless and unrelenting opposition.

10. We have entire confidence in the integrity and honor of the President of the United States, and our Senators and Republican Representatives in Congress are entitled to our thanks for the zeal with which they have represented the principles of the Republican party during the present session of Congress; and the Republicans of Indiana view with especial pride and hearty approval the course of Senators Morton and Pratt, and the fidelity and ability with which they have represented the sentiments of the people of this State.

The Democratic State Convention was held at Indianapolis, on the 15th of July. Governor Thomas A. Hendricks was chosen chairman, and made an extended speech, in which he criticised the course of the Republican party, and advocated a return to specie payments, and the adoption of the license system for controlling the traffic in intoxicating liquors. The platform arraigns the Federal Administration for overthrowing the government of the State of Louisiana, and preventing the officers elected by the people from taking the positions to which they were chosen; for corrupting the sources of public justice, by squandering money to aid its party; for farming out the revenues to corrupt and unprincipled men; for appointing corrupt men to office in the District of Columbia; for recklessly squandering the money, resources, and public domain of the people, and corrupting the civil service of the country. The Republican party is declared to be responsible for these acts of the Administration, and for the "Crédit-Mobilier frauds, the enormous increase of salaries, and the Sanborn contracts." A demand is then made for "a strict construction of the Constitution and its amendments; a tariff for revenue," and a reduction of salaries.

A list of seventeen resolutions was appended to the preamble containing these matters. The following resolutions relate to national finances:

1. That we are in favor of the redemption of the five-twenty bonds in greenbacks, according to the law under which they were issued.

2. We are in favor of the repeal of the law of March, 1869, which assumed to construe the law so as to make such bonds payable exclusively in gold.

3. We are in favor of the repeal of the national banking law, and the substitution of greenbacks for the national-bank currency.

4. We are in favor of a return to specie payment as soon as the business interests of the country will permit.

5. We are in favor of such legislation from time to time as will adjust the volume of the currency to the commercial and industrial wants of the country.

The sixth resolution was as follows:

6. We are in favor of a liberal system of education for the benefit of the negro as well as the white children of Indiana, but we are opposed to the mixture of the black and white races in our public schools or other educational institutions.

The seventh condemns the civil-rights bill; the eighth pronounces the "Baxter" temperance law a failure, and demands a license act; the ninth demands legislation upon the subject of railroads and other corporations which "will effectually secure the industrial and producing interests of the country against all forms of corporate monopoly and extortion;" the tenth favors retrenchment, economy, and the reduction of taxes; the eleventh denounces as "a wanton outrage" the increase of the State tax "from five to fifteen cents on the $100," and the increase at the same time of "the valuation of property almost 50 per cent;" the twelfth calls for a restriction of county commissioners and town trustees in the matter of levying taxes and creating indebtedness; the thirteenth denounces "the practices of officers using public money as their own;" the fourteenth opposes grants of land or loans of public credit to aid railroads or other corporations. The remaining resolutions were as follows:

15. That in the formation of associations for mutual protection and improvement we recognize an effort upon the part of the industrial classes to ameliorate their condition, and heartily extend to them our sympathies and support.

16. That we are in favor of the abolition of the office of county superintendent of schools, and the repeal of the law requiring an appraisement of real estate every two years, and in favor of the restoration of the former law.

17. That we bear in grateful remembrance the sacrifices made and the services rendered by the gallant soldiers of the late war in defense of the Union, and we demand as an act of justice that the bounties of our soldiers and of their widows and orphan children shall be equalized by proper legislation.

The nominations of the convention were as follows: For Secretary of State, John E. Neff; for Auditor, Ebenezer Henderson; for Treasurer, Benjamin C. Shaw; for Attorney-General, Clarence A. Buskirk; for Superintendent of Public Instruction, James H. Smart; for Judge of the Supreme Court, Horace P. Biddle. The election occurred on the 13th of Octo-

ber, and resulted in the choice of the Democratic candidates. The total vote for Secretary of State was 347,056, of which Neff received 182,154; Curry, 164,902; and Stout, 16,283; while 2,297 were scattering. Neff's majority over Curry was 17,252; Biddle's majority over Osborn, for Judge of the Supreme Court, was 25,465. Democratic members of Congress were elected in the first, second, third, fourth, fifth, seventh, tenth, and twelfth districts, and Republican members in the sixth, eighth, ninth, eleventh, and thirteenth districts. The Legislature of 1875 consists of 23 Democrats, 22 Republicans, and 5 Independents in the Senate, and 60 Democrats, 32 Republicans, and 8 Independents in the House; making the Democratic majority 20 in the House, and 16 on a joint ballot.

A convention was held at Indianapolis on the 25th of November, for the purpose of forming a new party. There were about thirty persons present from various parts of the State, and after some discussion the following was put forth as a "basis upon which to call a preliminary national convention," to form a "new political organization":

1. It is the duty of the Government to establish a monetary system based upon the faith and resources of the nation, in harmony with the genius of this Government, and adapted to the demands of legitimate business. To this end, the circulating notes of all national and State banks, as well as all local currency, should be withdrawn from circulation, and a paper-money issued by the Government directly to the people, without the intervention of any system of banking corporation, which money shall be a legal tender in payment of all debts, public and private, duties on imports included; this money to be interchangeable, at the option of the holders, with registered Government bonds bearing a rate of interest not exceeding 3.65 per cent. per annum.

2. The interest on the present public debt, and that portion of the principal of the same which is, by the express terms of the law creating it, payable in coin, shall be so paid.

The committee reporting this "basis of union" recommended a national convention to be held at Cleveland, Ohio, on the 11th of March, 1875, "to perfect a national platform and to appoint a time and place for holding a national independent convention to nominate candidates for President and Vice-President; and all who fully indorse the foregoing basis of union shall be cordially invited to participate." The "basis of union and the recommendations" were unanimously adopted.

A decision was rendered by the Supreme Court of the State, in November, affirming the constitutionality of the law of May 13, 1869, which provides that white and colored children in the State shall be taught in separate schools. The case originated in Lawrence Township, Marion County, where a school trustee had refused admission to the schools attended by white children of three colored orphans. The guardian of these children brought suit in the County Court to compel the trustee to admit them, and it was decided in his favor. The case was then carried to the Supreme Court for review, where the decision was reversed. A long and exhaustive opinion was pronounced by Judge Buskirk, in which the constitutional bearings of the case were discussed. Regarding the limitations imposed upon the powers of the State by the thirteenth and fourteenth amendments of the Federal Constitution, the court said:

1. The State cannot in the future, while a member of the Federal Union, change her constitution so as to create or establish slavery or involuntary servitude, except as a punishment for crimes whereof the party shall have been convicted—thus protecting the new class of citizens, i. e., negroes and mulattoes, from being again reduced to slavery.

2. The State cannot deny to nor deprive a citizen of the United States, i. e., any negro or mulatto, of those national rights, privileges, or immunities, which belong to him as such citizen.

3. The State must recognize as its citizen any citizen of the United States, i. e., any negro or mulatto, who is or becomes a *bona-fide* resident therein.

4. The State must give to such, i. e., to such negro or mulatto, who is or who becomes a *bona-fide* resident therein, the same rights, privileges, and immunities, secured by her constitution and laws to her other, i. e., to her white citizens.

And speaking of the effect of the fourteenth amendment upon the rights of the negroes, the court said:

The Legislature, under our State constitution as it existed without the limitation imposed upon the sovereign power of the State by the fourteenth amendment, as hereinbefore stated, had the power to provide for the education only of the white children of the State; but, since its ratification, no system of public schools would be general, uniform, and equally open to all, which did not provide for the education of the colored children of the State. It being settled that the Legislature must provide for the education of the colored children as well as for the white children, we are required to determine whether the Legislature may classify such children, by color and race, and provide for their education in separate schools, or whether they must attend the same school, without reference to race or color. In our opinion the classification of scholars on the basis of race or color, and their education in separate schools, involve questions of domestic policy which are within the legislative discretion and control, and do not amount to an exclusion of either class. In other words, the placing of the white children of the State in one class and the negro children of the State in another class, and requiring these classes to be taught separately, provision being made for their education in the same branches, according to age, capacity, or advancement, with capable teachers, and to the extent of their *pro-rata* share in the school revenue, does not amount to a denial of equal privileges to either, nor conflict with the open character of the system required by the constitution.

The conclusion is as follows:

We are very clearly of the opinion that the act of May 13, 1869, is constitutional, and that, while it remains in force, colored children are not entitled to admission into the common schools which are provided for the education of the white children.

Judge Osborn, the only Republican on the bench, entered a qualified dissent from the views of the court, without going into any discussion of the subject.

IOWA. The biennial session of the Legislature of Iowa began at Des Moines the 11th of January, and came to a final adjournment on the 19th of March. About two weeks were spent by the House of Representatives in an attempt to elect a Speaker, there being an exactly equal division between the supporters of J. H. Gear, the candidate of the Republicans, and J. W. Dixon, the candidate of the Anti-Monopolists. About 140 ballots were taken without any material variation in the vote, but finally some of the supporters of Dixon gave way and Gear was elected. Scarcely any important legislation was effected during the session. The subject that absorbed the largest share of attention was that of the regulation of railroad transportation. Early in the session the following resolution was referred to the Committee on Railroads in the Senate:

Resolved, That the Railroad Committee be requested to report a bill or bills, if they deem proper, as soon as possible, upon the following subjects:

1. Regulating and providing for a reasonable maximum rate of freights and passenger-fare on and over the railroads of this State.

2. Prohibiting railroad companies doing business in this State from hereafter buying or holding any more real estate than is necessary to carry on the legitimate business of railroading therein, and to prohibit the consolidation of parallel or competing lines of railway in this State, and to prevent the issuing of any stock or bonds by any railway company, except the same is in good faith actually paid for in money or other valuable consideration.

3. Prohibiting railroad companies from issuing free passes or passes at a discount from the uniform rate to any person holding office as a member of the General Assembly or Judges of the Supreme Court, Circuit or District Court, Judges or State officers.

4. And prohibiting railroad companies from granting or giving to any of its officers any special privilege in carrying passengers or freight by express or otherwise over their respective lines or roads; and—

5. Taxing railroads and railroad property as the property of individuals.

These subjects were under consideration a large share of the time during the session, and a variety of bills were offered and debated, but the only act passed was one "to establish reasonable maximum rates of charges for the transportation of freight and passengers on the different railroads of this State." This fixes the maximum rate for passenger-fare at three cents a mile, and provides that the Executive Council shall, previous to the 4th day of July in each year, classify the several roads of the State, the classification to be based on the reports of earnings of roads made by their respective officers. A schedule of rates for the transportation of freight is provided for each class of roads. The reports of the officers of all railroads located in the State are required to be made during the month of January, 1875, and each succeeding January thereafter; but for the purposes of classification for the year ending July 3, 1875, it is provided that the "reports from the railroad corporations of this State for the year 1873, made pursuant to the provisions of section 1,280 of the Code," shall be used. It so happens that section 1,280 of the Code provides no penalty for failure to make reports, the only remedy being that any stockholder of the companies may bring a civil suit to compel the officers to make the report. As a matter of fact, only four of the companies actually made any report for the year 1873, and there was no basis for the required classification, so that the new law was virtually without effect during this year. With regard to the general requirements of the law, Hugh Riddle, superintendent of the Chicago & Rock Island Railroad, wrote thus to Governor Carpenter: "While this company denies the justice and constitutionality of the railroad act, it is disposed to subject it to the test of actual experiment before assailing it in the courts. Schedules have been arranged in conformity with its provisions for the transportation of persons and property between points in the State of Iowa. The officers of the company, however, are trustees charged with the management of the property of its stockholders in such manner as to secure the revenue necessary for the payment of its operating expenses, a reasonable dividend upon the stock and interest upon its bonds. While engaging in the experiment of operating upon that portion of the road in Iowa, in accordance with the schedules named in the act, it is their duty to so adjust rates applicable to inter-State commerce as to secure from the entire business of the company a reserve to which it is entitled. Inflexible schedules have uniformly been found impracticable, and we say frankly that we do not believe that the operation of this road in conformity with this one will accord with the principles that govern commerce, or that the result will be satisfactory to either the owners of the railway or to the people of the State. It is hoped, however, that some practicable good will result from submitting the act to the test of actual experience. It may contribute something toward either confirming or dispelling the new theories in regard to transportation, and bringing about a better understanding of the principles which should govern the relations existing between the owners of road property and the public. If an actual experiment shall demonstrate that the continual observance of these schedules will not result in total or partial confiscation, it may not be necessary to raise any question as to the validity of the act. Such observances must involve the permanent surrender of the revenues to which the company is entitled from the operation of its lines. A different policy will be adopted, with the view of securing such revenue, and any attempt to enforce the act as a valid law will be resisted in the proper tribunals."

The appropriation made by the General Assembly amounted to $723,170.87—the principal items being $82,500 for the pay of members, $84,000 for interest on the State debt, $125,000 for the new Capitol, $93,000 for the Hospital for the Insane at Independence, $50,000 for the relief of sufferers by the grasshopper famine in the northwestern part of the

State, $46,000 for the State University, $28,500 for the Agricultural College, $42,000 for the College for the Blind, $25,000 for the Reform School, $24,593.98 for the Penitentiary at Anamosa, $15,000 for the Institution for the Deaf and Dumb, $8,700 for the Hospital for the Insane at Mount Pleasant, and $7,300 for the Fort Madison Penitentiary.

There was an investigation ordered and carried on during the session, by a special committee, into certain charges of irregularity in the management of the Agricultural College, but it failed to establish any thing. Among the joint resolutions adopted was one requesting the Senators and Representatives of the State in Congress "to use their influence to amend the Constitution so as to elect United States Senators by a vote of the people;" one requesting the Senators and Representatives in Congress "to submit to the several State Legislatures, for their ratification, an amendment to the Constitution of the United States, providing "that no Congress shall increase the compensation of its members;" one asking members of Congress to pass a law to prevent the granting of any more lands to corporations or railroad companies; and one memorializing Congress for an increase of currency.

The first State Convention of the year was held at Des Moines on the 20th of January by the State Temperance Association. It made no political nominations, but adopted a series of resolutions, among them the following:

3. That we regard drunkenness as a dangerous form of crime; and that the venders of alcoholic beverages, and the owners of premises occupied by them, should be held to be legally accessory to and responsible for the injury and crime committed by inebriates.

4. That the only wise and efficient legislative policy in dealing with the traffic in alcoholic liquors for drinking purposes, is its absolute suppression; we therefore urge the friends of temperance throughout the State to endeavor to secure the absolute prohibition of the manufacture and sale of all intoxicating liquors as beverages; and we respectfully ask the General Assembly now in session to instruct our Senators and request our Representatives in Congress to favor the application of such prohibition to the District of Columbia and the Territories.

5. That we also ask our General Assembly to instruct our Senators and request our Representatives in Congress to favor the passage of a law prohibiting henceforth the importation of all alcoholic beverages from foreign countries.

6. That we further ask our General Assembly to instruct our Senators and request our Representatives in Congress to urge that provision be made for the appointment of a commission of inquiry concerning the traffic in intoxicating liquors as a beverage, whose duty it shall be to investigate on the legislative, criminal, scientific, economical, and other aspects of the same as related to the public welfare.

7. That we favor such a modification of our present prohibitory law as will provide for allowing at least one-half of the fines imposed for violation thereof to be paid to the prosecuting witness.

13. That the owner of the property where a liquor nuisance is maintained, and agents for the rental of the property of non-resident owners where such nuisances are maintained, should be made criminally

liable to the same extent as the venders of intoxicating liquors; and that the occupation of premises for the unlawful sale of intoxicating liquors should be made to raise a conclusive presumption of the owner's knowledge of and consent to such unlawful use.

The practice of the medical profession in prescribing alcohol for the sick was also deprecated, and the Legislature was called upon to provide for an Inebriate Asylum in the State.

The opposition to the Republican party in Iowa is organized under the name of the Anti-Monopoly party. It held its State Convention at Des Moines on the 24th of June. The candidates nominated for the State offices to be filled were as follows: Secretary of State, David Morgan, of Mahaska County; Auditor, J. M. King, of Dubuque County; Treasurer, J. M. Barnes, of Des Moines County; Attorney-General, J. H. Keatley, of Pottawattamie County; Clerk of Supreme Court, G. W. Ball, of Polk County; Supreme Court Reporter, J. M. Weart, of Buchanan County; Register of Land-Office, R. H. Roadearmel.

The following platform was adopted after some discussion on the fourth, tenth, and twelfth resolutions:

Resolved, That we, the delegated representatives of the people of Iowa, favorable to the organization of an independent political party, laying aside past differences of opinion, and earnestly uniting in a common purpose to secure needed reforms in the administration of public affairs, cordially unite in submitting these declarations:

1. That all political power is inherent in the people; that no government is worthy of preservation, or should be upheld, which does not derive its powers from the consent of the governed; that by equal and just laws the inalienable rights of life, liberty, and the pursuit of happiness shall be secured to all men without distinction of race, color, or nativity; that the maintenance of these principles is essential to the perpetuity of our republican institutions; and that to this end the Federal Constitution, with all its amendments, the rights of the States, and the union of the States, must and shall be preserved.

2. That the maintenance inviolate of the rights of the States, and especially of the right of each State to order and control its own domestic institutions according to its own judgment exclusively, is indispensable to that balance of power on which the perfection and endurance of our own political fabric depend; and that we denounce as a criminal excess of constitutional power the policy of President Grant's Administration in fostering the enormities perpetrated in certain States of the Union; in arbitrarily interfering with their local affairs; in sustaining therein the usurpations and lawless conduct of alien and irresponsible adventurers, whereby certain men have been illegally invested with official authority, and others deprived of their constitutional rights; oppressive laws enacted; burdensome taxation imposed; an immense and fictitious indebtedness created, resulting in the degradation of those States and the general impoverishment of their people.

3. That the conduct of the present Administration in its bold defiance of public sentiment and disregard of the common good; in its prodigality and wasteful extravagance; in the innumerable frauds perpetrated under its authority; in its disgraceful partiality for and reward of unworthy favorites; in its reckless and unstable financial policy; and in its incapacity to meet the vital questions of the day, and provide for the general welfare, stands without a parallel in our national history; and the highest considerations of duty require the American people,

in the exercise of their inherent sovereignty, to correct these accumulations of evil, and bring the Government back to its ancient landmarks of patriotism and economy.

4. That the faith and credit of the nation must be maintained inviolate; that the public debt, of whatever kind, should be paid in strict accordance with the law under which it was contracted; that an overissue of paper-money being at variance with the principles of a sound financial policy, the circulating medium should be based upon its redemption in specie at the earliest practical day, and its convertibility into a specie equivalent at the will of the holder; and that, subject to these restrictions, it is the duty of Congress to so provide, by appropriate legislation, that the volume of our Government currency shall at all times be adequate to the general business and convenience of the country, and be equitably distributed among the several States.

5. That tariffs and all other modes of taxation should be imposed upon the basis of revenue alone, and be so adjusted as to yield the minimum amount required for the legitimate expenditures of the Government, faithfully and economically administered; and that taxation to an extent necessary to the accumulation of a surplus revenue in the Treasury subjects the people to needless burdens, and affords a temptation to extravagance and official corruption.

6. That railroads and all other corporations for pecuniary profit should be rendered subservient to the public good; that we demand such constitutional and necessary legislation upon the subject, both State and national, as will effectually secure the industrial and producing interests of the country against all forms of corporate monopoly and extortion, and that the existing railroad legislation of this State should be faithfully enforced until experience will have demonstrated the propriety and justice of modification.

7. That while demanding that railroads be subject to legislative control, we shall discountenance any action on this subject calculated to retard the progress of railroad enterprises, or work injustice to those invaluable auxiliaries to commerce and civilization.

8. That the limitation of the presidency to one term, and the election of President and Vice-President, and United States Senators, by direct popular vote, and a thorough reform of our civil service, to the end that capacity and fidelity be made the essential qualifications for election and appointment to office, are proposed reforms which meet our hearty indorsement.

9. That we demand such a modification of the patent laws of the United States as shall destroy the monopoly now enjoyed by the manufacturers of agricultural and other implements of industry.

10. That the personal liberty and social rights of the citizens should not be abridged or controlled by legislative enactment except in so far as may be necessary to promote the peace and welfare of society.

11. That holding in grateful remembrance the soldiers and sailors who fought our battles, and by whose heroism the Union was preserved, we insist that Congress shall equalize the bounties and grant to each of them, or to his widow and children, a homestead of one hundred and sixty acres of land from the unappropriated domain of the country.

12. That we desire hereafter to be known as the Anti-Monopoly party of Iowa, and, recognizing the individual conscience of the voter as paramount to the claims of party, ask the coöperation of those only to whom this declaration of principles and the candidates nominated by this convention may commend themselves as worthy.

The Republican State Convention was held at Des Moines on the 1st of July. The following ticket was nominated: Secretary of State, Josiah T. Young, of Monroe County; Auditor of State, B. R. Sherman, of Benton

County; Treasurer of State, William Christy, of Clark County; Register of the State Land-Office, David Secor, of Winnebago County; Attorney-General, M. E. Cutts, of Mahaska County; Clerk of the Supreme Court, E. J. Holmes, of Jackson County; Reporter of the Supreme Court, John S. Runnell, of Polk County. The following platform was unanimously adopted without debate:

We, the representatives of the Republican party of the State of Iowa, in convention assembled, do adopt the following platform of principles:

Resolved: 1. That as the policy of the Republican party in relation to finance has afforded the people not only a safe, sound, and popular currency, of equal and uniform worth in every portion of our common country, but has likewise greatly improved the credit of the country at home and abroad, we point with pride to its record and accomplishments in this regard. And while reaffirming the policy announced by the party in the national conventions of 1868 and 1872, and triumphantly indorsed by the people at the polls—a policy which, while contributing to the public credit, has also enhanced the individual and collective prosperity of the American people, we favor such legislation as shall make national banking free to all, under just and equal laws, based upon the policy of specie resumption at such time as is consistent with the material and industrial interests of the country, to the end that the volume of currency may be regulated by natural laws of trade.

2. That we reaffirm the declaration of the Republican national platform of 1872 in favor of the payment by the Government of the United States of all its obligations in accordance with both the letter and the spirit of the laws under which such obligations were issued; and we declare that, in the absence of any express provision to the contrary, the obligations of the Government, when issued and placed upon the markets of the world, are payable in the world's currency, to wit, specie.

3. That, under the Constitution of the United States, Congress has power to regulate all "commerce among the several States," whether carried on by railroads or by other means, and in the exercise of that power Congress may and should so legislate as to prohibit, under suitable penalties, extortion, unjust discrimination, and other wrong and unjust conduct on the part of persons or corporations engaged in such commerce; and, by virtue of the same constitutional power, Congress may and should provide for the improvement of our great natural water-ways.

4. That the State has the power, and it is its duty, to provide by law for the regulation and control of railway transportation within its own limits, and we demand that the law of this State, passed for this purpose at the last session of the General Assembly, shall be upheld and enforced until it shall be superseded by other legislation, or held unconstitutional by the proper judicial tribunal.

5. That we feel bound to provide all appropriate legislation for the full and equal protection of all citizens, white or black, native or foreign born, in the enjoyment of all the rights guaranteed by the Constitution of the United States and the amendments thereto.

6. That the $27,000,000 reduction in the estimated General Government expenses for the coming fiscal year meets our hearty commendation, and shows that the Republican party, on questions of retrenchment and economy, is carrying out in good faith its oft-repeated pledges to the people.

7. That we are in favor of an amendment to the Constitution of the United States, providing for the election of President and Vice-President by a direct vote of the people.

8 That, while inventors should be protected in their just rights of property in their inventions, we demand such modifications of our patent laws as shall render the same more fair and equitable to consumers.

9. That the faith of the Republican party is pledged to promote the best good of the civil service of the country, and that we, as Republicans of Iowa, demand that only honest and capable men be elected or appointed to office, and that we commend the position of the party in instituting investigations of corruption in office, sparing therein neither friends nor foes.

10. That since the people may be intrusted with all questions of governmental reform, we favor the final submission to the people of the question of amending the constitution so as to extend the rights of suffrage to women, pursuant to the action of the Fifteenth General Assembly.

The State election occurred on the 13th of October, and resulted in the choice of the Republican candidates. The total vote for Secretary of State was 186,303, of which Josiah T. Young received 107,243 and David Morgan 79,060, making Young's majority 28,-183. The State officers were elected for two years, except the Clerk and Reporter of the Supreme Court, who were elected for four years. Nine members of Congress were chosen, as follows: First district, George W. McCrary, Republican; second district, John Q. Tufts, Republican; third district, L. L. Ainsworth, Anti-Monopoly; fourth district, Henry O. Pratt, Republican; fifth district, James Wilson, Republican; sixth district, Ezekiel S. Sampson, Republican; seventh district, John A. Kasson, Republican; eighth district, John W. McDill, Republican, and ninth district, Addison Oliver, Republican. The Legislature now stands, 34 Republicans, 6 Democrats, and 10 Independents, in the Senate, and 50 Republicans, 6 Democrats, 43 Independents, and one vacancy, in the House: Republican majority in the Senate 18, in the House 1, and on a joint ballot 19.

ITALY, a kingdom of Southern Europe. King, Victor Emmanuel II., born March 14, 1820; succeeded to the throne of Sardinia, on the abdication of his father, March 23, 1849; proclaimed King of Italy by vote of an Italian Parliament, March 17, 1861; married, April 12, 1842, to the Archduchess Adelaide of Austria; widower January 20, 1855.—Children of the King: 1. Heir-apparent, Humbert, Prince of Piedmont, born March 14, 1844; married, April 22, 1868, to Princess Margaretta of Genoa; offspring of the union is a son, Victor Emmanuel, Prince of Naples, born November 11, 1869. 2. Amadeo, Duke of Aosta, born May 30, 1845; King of Spain from December 4, 1870, to February 11, 1873; married, May 30, 1867, to Princess Maria della Goterna, born August 9, 1847; offspring of the union, three sons: Emmanuel, Duke of Apulia, born 1869; Victor, Duke of Turin, born 1870; Louis, born 1873. 3. Clotilde, born 1843, wife of Prince Napoleon Bonaparte. 4. Maria Pia, born 1847; wife of King Louis of Portugal.

The ministry was at the end of 1874 composed of the following members: 1. Marco Minghetti, President of the Council of Ministers, and Minister of Finance; born at Bologna, September 8, 1818; captain in the army of Sardinia, 1848–'54; deputy of Bologna to the Italian Parliament of 1860; Minister of the Interior, 1861–'62; Minister of Finance, 1862--'64; appointed Minister of Finance, and President of the Council of Ministers, July 10, 1873. 2. Ruggiero Bonghi, Minister of Public Instruction, born at Naples in 1828; appointed in 1859 a professor at the University of Pavia; in 1865 Professor of the Latin Language and Literature at the Istituto di Studii Superiori in Florence, and member of the Supreme Council of Education; in 1866 professor in the Academy of Milan; in 1871 Professor of Ancient History of Rome; member of the Italian Parliament since 1860; appointed minister, October 2, 1874. 3. Commendator Visconti-Venosta, Minister of Foreign Affairs, born 1828; Minister of Foreign Affairs, 1866–'67; appointed again, December 14, 1869. 4. Giuseppe Spaventa, appointed July 10, 1873. 5. Lieutenant-General Ricotti Magnani, Minister of

War, appointed September 8, 1870. 6. Rear-Admiral Pacoret di San-Bon, Minister of Marine, appointed September 26, 1873. 7. Giuseppe Finali, Minister of Commerce and Agriculture, appointed September 28, 1873. 8. Count Geronima Cantelli, Minister of the Interior, appointed July 10, 1873. 9. Pietro Vigliani, Minister of Justice and Ecclesiastical Affairs, appointed July 10, 1873.

The Italian Parliament consists of two Chambers, the Senate and the Chamber of Deputies.

The Council of State decides on conflicts between administrative authorities and courts, and on conflicts between the state and its creditors. President of the Council of State, L. des Ambrois de Revache, Minister of State, and senator. President of the Section of the Interior, T. Marchese Spinola; of the Section of Justice and Worship, Count de Pallieri; of Finances, J. Marchese Malaspina.

The financial accounts for the years 1872 and 1873, and the budget estimates for the year 1874, were as follows, in lire (1 lire = 19.3 cents):

ESTIMATES.	1871.	1872.	1873.	1874.
Expenditures	1,277,780,785	1,366,984,649	1,384,618,021	1,540,862,262
Receipts	1,193,548,035	1,296,598,880	1,290,785,269	1,864,147,395
Deficit	84,232,750	70,385,769	93,832,752	176,714,987

The actual disbursements have of late regularly exceeded the estimated deficits. In order to meet the alarming deficits, the Government in 1864 sold the state railways for a sum of 200,000,000 lire; in 1867 it levied the sum of 600,000,000 lire on ecclesiastical property; and in 1868 made over the state monopoly on tobacco to a French company, in consideration of 180,000,000 lire; the remainder was made up by loans.

The total debt of the kingdom amounted in January, 1873, to a nominal capital of 9,851,-731,566 lire, divided as follows:

1. Rentes, 5 per cent	$6,751,919,603
2. Rentes, 3 per cent	213,602,800
3. Perpetual rents of the Papal See	64,500,000
4. Special debts	1,315,806,856
5. Miscellaneous debts (including unpaid interest)	437,315,326
6. Floating debt:	
Bank-notes in circulation, December 31, 1873	184,407,100
Conto correntes	24,180,000
Notes of National Bank which are legal tenders	860,000,000
Total	$9,851,731,566

Elementary education is now made compulsory, but the attendance at the primary schools is still far from being satisfactory. There were, in 1872, 34,213 public, and 9,167 private elementary schools, total 43,380; the number of pupils was 1,745,467. Secondary instruction was given, in 1870, in 352 gymnasia (104 royal) and 272 technical schools; and for more advanced pupils, in 142 lyceums, 89 industrial schools and technical special schools. The number of universities was 22, of which 17

were royal, 4 (Ferrara, Perugia, Camerina, and Urbino) provincial, and 1 (the Sapienza at Rome) papal. The number of professors and students at the 17 royal universities was, in 1873, as follows:

UNIVERSITIES.	Professors.	Students and Hearers.
Bologna	58	577
Naples	73	...
Padua	65	1,121
Palermo	56	806
Pavia	45	718
Pisa	66	508
Rome	51	584
Turin	69	1,408
Cagliari	30	38
Catania	88	233
Genoa	46	460
Macerata	20	115
Messina	36	112
Modena	42	315
Parma	47	270
Sassari	31	74
Sienna	32	118
Total	805	6,397

The theological faculty has been abolished at all these universities. Bologna, Catania, Genoa, Messina, Naples, Palermo, Pavia, Pisa, Rome, Turin, and Padua, have four faculties each (law, medicine and surgery, mathematics and natural science, philosophy and literature), Cagliari, Modena, and Parma, three, and the others two. By a decree of the Minister of Public Instruction, issued in 1871, six high-schools—Naples, Pavia, Turin, Bologna, Florence, and Parma—were declared first-class universities of the kingdom.

· The results of the census as regards the religious professions of the inhabitants had not been published at the close of the year 1873. The number of Protestants was estimated at about 40,000, that of Israelites at 35,000, that of other creeds at 6,000.

According to an official return, issued by the Italian Government, March, 1870, the percentage of *analfabeti*, or totally illiterate men of the age of twenty-one, was as follows, in progressive ratio, in the various provinces of the kingdom:

Vicenza	20.37	Parma	70.66
Sondrio	25.17	Sienna	70.91
Turin	26.18	Macerata	71.19
Novara	29.89	Campobasso	71.36
Bergamo	33.13	Foggia	71.86
Leghorn	35.40	Salerno	72.25
Cuneo	35.99	Naples	73.58
Como	37.23	Arezzo	76.45
Alessandria	39.61	Lecce	76.67
Pavia	41.04	Ravenna	77.49
Brescia	41.18	Forli	77.69
Porto Maurizio	43.27	Ancona	77.71
Cremona	44.25	Sassari	77.91
Milan	49.93	Perugia	78.19
Bellano	50.92	Bari	78.56
Verona	53.54	Chieti	78.80
Genoa	54.61	Syracuse	78.91
Lucca	55.34	Messina	79.12
Treviso	55.34	Teramo	79.60
Pisa	56.72	Cagliari	79.74
Mantua	58.06	Caserta	80.00
Udine	59.96	Catanzaro	80.04
Reggio (Emilia)	61.34	Calabetta	80.34
Padua	62.66	Avellino	80.55
Venice	63.84	Pesaro	81.41
Florence	64.13	Catania	81.59
Rovigo	64.90	Palermo	81.91
Grosseto	66.16	Reggio (Calabria)	82.76
Modena	66.61	Potenza	82.23
Massa Carrara	66.67	Benevento	82.86
Bologna	67.03	Ascoli Piceno	82.49
Piacenza	68.34	Cosenza	82.99
Ferrara	68.80	Trapani	83.58
Ciquiala	70.43	Girgeuti	85.82

According to the new law, on the reorganization of the army, which was passed September 30, 1873, the liability to military service is made universal, the exception formerly allowed being reduced to an insignificant number. The annual contingent will be 100,000 men, of whom from 75,000 to 80,000 will be taken for the first class, whose term of service is three years (for the cavalry five years). The remainder enter the second class, into which the former enter at the expiration of their active service. The time of service in the second class is nineteen years; in the second and first

class together, twenty-two years. Those who enter the second class as the army of reserve, have to practise annually for forty days, and are then sent on illimited furlough, but can be called permanently under arms, at the outbreak of a war. The actual strength of the army on July 4, 1874, was as follows:

ARMY.	Officers.	Under Arms (Peace-footing).	Men on Furlough.	Total (War-footing).
Standing army	13,692	203,279	192,672	395,951
Army of reserve	918	2,328	145,676	148,004
Provincial militia	2,535	.....	279,872	279,872
Total	17,145	205,607	618,220	823,827

The navy consisted on January 1, 1874, of the following classes of vessels:

NAVY.	No.	Guns.	Tons.	Horse-power.
Men-of-War:				
Iron-clads	23	207	94,742	13,310
Screw-steamers	21	344	46,391	7,340
Wheel-steamers	17	76	15,460	4,050
Total men-of-war	61	627	156,593	24,700
Transports:				
Screw-steamers	11	22	17,209	2,516
Wheel-steamers	8	6	3,720	1,090
Total transports	19	28	20,929	3,606
Total navy	80	655	177,522	28,306

The report of the Italian Board of Customs for 1873 shows a continued forward movement of Italian commerce in its aggregate; but the equilibrium that had been established in the previous year between imports and exports, has oscillated on the side of imports. The total exports of Italy had decreased in 1873 to the amount of 25,000,000 francs, as compared with the previous year, while the total imports had increased to the amount of 45,000,000 francs. The decrease of Italian export in 1873 is fully accounted for by the trade with France alone. While France was in a state of war and disorder, there was much increased export of wine, cattle, and other products from Italy to that country, which has fallen off as France has returned to her usual condition.

The commercial navy on January 1, 1873, was composed as follows:

NAVIGATION.	KIND OF CRAFT.	Vessels.	Tons.
1. Long navigation	10,712 sailing-vessels, of 997,866 tons........ 133 steamers " 48,573 "	10,845	1,046,439
2. Port and coast service	26 tow-steamers............................ 95 pilot-boats............................ 8,589 barks............................	8,712	(?)
3. Fishing-boats	....	9,554	25,411
Total		29,111	1,071,850

The aggregate length of railroads in operation, in 1873, was 6,881 kilometres; the aggregate length of telegraph-lines is 19,837 kilometres; the length of wires 56,626.

The Italian Parliament, after an adjournment of thirty days, reassembled on January 20, 1874. On February 3d Signor Nicotera

questioned the Government respecting the dispatches published in General Della Marmora's book. Signor Visconti-Venosta, Minister for Foreign Affairs, declined on the part of the ministry all responsibility for the publication, which it was not in the power of the Government to prevent. He added: "The Government disapproves and deplores the publication of these documents, especially as it furnished a pretext for making against a friendly power accusations which can only be based on a misunderstanding, inasmuch as they fall to the ground when tested by the evidence of results. We speak in these terms, because they are the only terms consistent with truth, with the amicable relations subsisting between our Government and that of Germany, and with the solidarity of our mutual interests in the face of a party which is agitating the public mind throughout Europe, and whose conduct is especially caused and directed by its hostility toward Italy." Signor Visconti-Venosta further said he believed the published documents, though drawn up in a confidential form, must be regarded as being of a public character. The Italian laws did not contain sufficient provisions relative to the publication of official documents, but the Government at the fitting time would propose legislative measures regulating the subject. This statement was received with loud cheers. Signor Chiaves, who was a member of the Della Marmora ministry, then addressed some observations to the House, but was met by Signor Visconti-Venosta, who urged that discussions of a retrospective nature were useless, considering the grand results obtained both by Germany and Italy.

In February the liberal educational bill, which had been introduced by the Minghetti ministry, was defeated by 140 against 107 votes. The bill was of the most elaborate kind, and comprised nearly fifty clauses, providing for primary education in every parish, to be introduced at once, with compulsory attendance, and no school-fees, proper payment of the staff of teachers, means for separate religious instruction, and complete inspection. Fourteen days of the sittings of the House of Deputies were employed chiefly in discussing the proposal and the various amendments suggested, which were very numerous. But the conviction seems gradually to have come on the members that the scheme was altogether too thoroughgoing and finished for the present means of Italy, especially as regards the pecuniary payments required locally, which could not possibly be exacted from the poorer and ruder parts of the peninsula.

On March 23d, the twenty-fifth anniversary of Victor Emmanuel's accession to the throne was celebrated with the greatest demonstrations of national joy and enthusiasm. The King received at Rome, in the Quirinal Palace, deputations of the Senate and the Chamber of Deputies, of the army, of the universities and schools of science and art, and of the several provinces. The King replied to each of the addresses, and specially emphasized that he found a chief reason for the successful completion of national unity in the fact that Italy, while aspiring to the establishment of her own independence, had never forgotten to respect the independence of other nations. The rep-

resentatives of Germany, Russia, Austria, England, and France, presented letters of gratulation from their sovereigns, and the embassador of the United States read a telegram from President Grant.

On November 8th the general election for a new Italian Parliament took place. Notwithstanding the endeavors made by the ministry, the interest of the people in the elections was small, not more than fifty per cent. of the enrolled electors casting their votes. The Pope had addressed a circular letter to the bishops, in which he insisted that the clergy and the Catholics should not only abstain from voting at the forthcoming Italian elections, but also from exerting their personal influence on behalf of any of the candidates. The result was as follows: elections carried by the Right, 281; by the Left, 217; total, 498. There were 132 new deputies, who formed more than one-quarter of the Assembly. The nobility is represented in the new Parliament by eight princes, four dukes, ten marquises, fifty-three counts, and fourteen barons; that is, eighty-nine members, without counting the untitled gentry. In the opposition there are two princes, three dukes, and three marquises. Counts and barons are mostly supporters of Government. There are 125 lawyers, and only ten bankers. Among the financial men, some are simple theorists, like M. Sella. The army is represented by twenty-two generals, or superior officers, and the navy by five only There is also a certain number of retired officers. The Garibaldian army is represented by sixteen of its officers, who sit on the benches of the Left. Among the elected are seventeen journalists and twenty-four professors. Only six of the deputies are declared republicans, without counting General Garibaldi, who at a supplementary election was chosen in two electoral districts of Rome.

The opening of the Twelfth Italian Parliament by the King took place on November 21st. Victor Emmanuel was received, both in his passage through the streets from the Quirinal and in the Chamber, with applause even more enthusiastic than usual. His Majesty, in delivering the speech from the throne, after cordial words of greeting, referred first to the projected new penal code. He said: "I trust that your discussions will produce a code worthy of the science and the name of Italy. The law of commercial juries will be improved in the sense of restricting Government action. The Government will propose certain measures for the restoring of public security in those provinces where it has been gravely disturbed. In receiving them you will follow the example of the nations most advanced in civilization, and of the Parliaments most jealous of the public liberties, which fall into discredit with the people if they do not guarantee security for person and property." The other important subjects which would engage the attention of the Parliament were thus referred to: "The now military regulations have been successful, and the King is proud of his army. The work must be completed, and the national defense provided for. The navy, on which depends so large a part of our confidence for the future, will also be the care of the Legislature. Measures for the reform of taxation, especially for equalizing it, will be brought forward. This will be the beginning of a gradual reform of our system of taxation and administration, which, created at a time of difficulties and excitement, needs well-considered revision. In the mean while, we must make a halt in entering on new expenses. For those evidently necessary the Government will indicate fitting means to meet them. By following this course the balance of income and expenditure, so ardently desired by the nation, will be attained, and the attain-

ment will be the reward of sacrifices nobly borne. Thus will the regeneration of Italy, free from every stain, have this boast also—one so rare in the history of political changes—that it has never harbored the thought of not keeping faith with the public creditor. The King has pleasure in assuring the Parliament that his relations with all foreign powers are excellent. He receives with joy continual testimonies of the value attached by other nations to the friendship of Italy. This is the reward of the moderation and firmness of our conduct. Providence, which has protected us at every step, has this year given us an abundant harvest, which will be a relief to those poorer classes whose welfare is ever present to our thoughts. Let us continue, by virtue of our aims and our acts, to merit the

FLORENCE.

protection and aid of God." Great applause followed this address, and interrupted it again and again. The King spoke with a strong and clear voice, and with emphasis.

The Chamber of Deputies reëlected Signor Biancheri as President by 236 votes against 172 which were given to Depretis. The President of the Council of State, Des Ambrois de Revache, was appointed by the King President of the Senate; he suddenly died, however, a few days later.

Signor Bonghi, the Minister of Public Instruction, proposed in the new estimates an annual grant to public libraries, to be regularly allotted according, partly, to the actual use made of the library, and partly to the liberality with which the locality shall contribute for similar purposes. For 1875, the University of Naples stands at the head of the list, with a grant of £600, and then come on a descending scale those of Turin, Pavia, Padua, Rome, Genoa,

Pisa, Bologna, and lastly Catania, to which a sum of but little over £100 is allotted. Similar grants are placed on the estimates for the free national libraries of Naples, Florence, Milan, Venice, and other cities where such institutions are maintained, varying from £700 to £70, according to the case. The Italian ministry thus hope to remove a reproach hitherto made against the unity of their country, that one result of it has been to strip the local libraries of its great cities of the funds formerly allotted them by the sovereigns who have been dethroned. Provincial Italians have often cause to be proud of the rich collection of books that may be found in their chief towns; but, since the whole peninsula came under a single administration, gifts for keeping up the several libraries have been made only by chance and the good favor of the Ministry of Education.

All the political questions in Italy were cast

into the shade by the insecurity of life and property in some parts of the country. The chronic lawlessness of Sicily showed some extremely acute symptoms. In Palermo, the great Government pawnbroking establishment, the Monte di Pieta, was undermined by a regular series of engineering operations. The predatory engineers were discovered and arrested. When the day arrived for their trial, it was evident from the appearance of the streets that plans were being concerted to effect a rescue. The fact was telegraphed to the Minister of the Interior at Rome. A couple of hours brought the reply that the prisoners should be at once embarked for Northern Italy, and that the trial would take place in some town of Piedmont. Indeed, the administration of criminal justice had become hopeless in the island. On the first three days of the last Palermo assizes, not a single citizen summoned to serve as juryman had answered to the call—so completely were all quiet, respectable citizens intimidated by the *maffia*, or organized bands of Sicilian cut-purses and cut-throats. The local journalists, writing with the fear of the stiletto and revolver before their eyes, cry out against the Government for dragging free Sicilian citizens to the region of *Monte*, and declare the act to be a *coup d'état*. The town of Ravenna had in the course of the last few years acquired a terrible notoriety all through Italy. Numerous assassinations were perpetrated in open daylight, and in very few cases were the murderers brought to justice. It came to be known that there was established a secret society of assassins. The executive did not dare to interfere. Some persons, indeed, attempted to bring the assassins to trial, and, wherever they were successful, a speedy vengeance was taken. At length, one of the gang, who feared that his accomplices would regard him as a spy, and murder him, revealed the entire scheme to the prefect of a neighboring city, and the whole gang was brought to trial. In October, Mgr. Teodoli, one of the three Camerlingos of the Basilica of the Vatican, while traveling to Trisalti, near Frosinone, was captured by a band of brigands, who demanded and received a ransom of 50,000 francs. A rich proprietor of the environs of Palermo, M. Sajali, was carried off by a band of those malefactors. His brother, who is a priest, and possessor of a considerable fortune, received notice to the effect that the prisoner would be given up for a sum of 127,000 francs paid down. Reports received from Palermo stated that two or three troops of bandits were traversing the country and extorting sums of money from the rural population.

Colonel Angus Croll, chairman of the Anglo-Sicilian Giona Sulphur Company, published some correspondence which he had received from the Earl of Derby, with reference to being outraged in Sicily, respecting which he had made some representations to the noble earl. The subject was brought by the Foreign Office under the notice of the Italian Minister of the Interior, who, while promising that these complaints should receive due consideration, stated that a new organization of the service for the repression of brigandage was about to be put into execution in the whole of Sicily, by means of a considerable development of the military force, and with unity of purpose and of action. The state of Sicily, during the last three months of the year may be conjectured from the report, published in the *Military Gazette*, of the doings of the carabineers. In all Italy they arrested in three months 17,955 persons, of whom 628 were for murder, 223 attempted murder, 509 robbery with violence, 3,025 cutting and maiming, etc. Of the murders, 160 go to the account of Palermo, or the perpetrators of them were arrested by the " Legion of Palermo ; " and by the same legion were arrested 166 persons guilty of *grassazione*, robbery with violence.

General Garibaldi having become involved in financial difficulties, the directors of several Italian newspapers held a meeting, at which it was proposed to raise a sum of money which would yield an annual income of 50,000 francs, to be presented to the general as a national offering. In the Chamber of Deputies, on December 1st, several proposals were read, in favor of bestowing an annual income upon Garibaldi. Signor Minghetti agreed to a discussion of these plans, and added that the Government also desired to bring forward a bill for the same object, and would reserve its right to submit the measure to the committee. Garibaldi's difficulties arose, as was reported, from his son Riciotti, who has made a love-match in England, drawing bills upon him to pay certain expenses. The general had no means of paying these bills save by the sale of the yacht presented to him by the Duke of Sutherland, which he sent to London for sale. King Victor Emmanuel bought it for 80,000 francs, and the general intrusted a Genoese broker with the money to lodge in the bank. This broker took it into his head to take the money to America, and the general mortgaged his island of Caprera to the Naples Bank for the needful funds. The island is not nearly worth the amount advanced, and it seems that some Americans assisted the general.

The fifth General Assembly of the Free Christian Churches of Italy was held at Pisa, January 6th to 9th. Prof. Paolo de Michelis presided. The representatives of twenty-five churches were present. Among the more important subjects which came under the consideration of the Assembly were various plans for promoting and developing self-help and self-support among the churches and newly-organized societies. An address on this subject, prepared by the Rev. W. S. Alexander, of Boston (United States), was read. Prof. de Michelis, the Rev. J. R. McDougall, Signor Enrico Jahier, and Signori Gavazzi, Lagomarsino, Conti, and Bergia, were chosen as members of the Italian Committee of Evangelization for the coming year. It was decided that the committee itself should henceforth have the power of nominating foreign members, the number of whom, however, should not exceed that of the committee, or seven. Four young men had been studying during the year with Prof. de Michelis, at Pisa. One of them, Prof.

Pietro Manani, who had been formerly a priest, and spiritual director of a deaf and dumb asylum in the north of Italy, was accepted by the Assembly, and given formal recognition as an evangelist.

Dr. Luther H. Gulick has published the following statistics of Protestant churches and missionary operations in Italy :

CHURCHES IN ITALY.	Waldensian	Free Italian Church	The Brethren (Plymouthism).	English Methodist	American Methodist	English Baptist	American Baptist	Total.
Piedmont, Sardinian Kingdom, and Liguria............	10	4	19	2	..	1	1	37
Lombardo-Venetia..	8	6	5	8	1	..	1	29
Total in North Italy...............................	18	10	24	10	1	1	2	66
Emilia....	1	2	5	2	5	..	3	18
Tuscany and Island of Elba..............	5	7	2	1	1	..	..	16
The Marches, Umbria, and Comarca...................	2	4	1	2	1	..	2	13
Total in Central Italy	8	13	8	5	7	1	5	47
Neapolitan Provinces.....................	3	..	7	..	..	..	1	11
Sicily..	7	..	5	..	..	..	..	12
Total South Italy...............................	10	..	12	..	..	..	1	23
Whole total of stations......................	36	23	32	27	8	2	8	136
Whole total of out-stations..................	8	8	..	4	8	..	..	23
Communicants....................................	1,864	1,300 ?	..	1,007	447	..	204	4,822
Pastors and evangelists.........................	36	26	..	24	11	..	7	104
School-teachers	51	6	..	....	....	..	....	....
Pupils in day-schools	1,723	458	..	557	....	..	...	....
Pupils in Sabbath-schools......................	1,142	...	..	472	....	..	...	....
Pupils in night-schools........................	.....	...	..	532	....	..	...	....

J

JACKSON, Rev. ABNER, D. D., LL. D., a Protestant Episcopal clergyman, scholar, and college president, born in Washington County, Pa., November 4, 1811 ; died in Hartford, Conn., April 19, 1874. Of his early history we have no knowledge, but he entered Trinity College, Hartford, in 1833, and graduated thence with the highest honors in 1837, and was immediately appointed tutor. In 1838 he was elected Professor of Ancient Languages; in 1840 was transferred to the chair of Ethics and Metaphysics, for which he proved to be admirably qualified and which he retained eighteen years, adding to his other duties a course of lectures on chemistry. In 1858 he was elected President of Hobart College, Geneva, N. Y., and discharged the duties of that office for nine years, taking charge also of a select-school, which was a feeder of the college. In 1867 he was recalled to Trinity by his election as its president. His wide and generous culture both in literature and science, his lofty ideal of the higher Christian education, and his genial, courteous, and manly character, made him universally popular, while his rare executive ability eminently fitted him for the very difficult position of a college president. In the new field of usefulness upon which Trinity College was just entering (having sold its college-site to the city on such terms as gave it an ample endowment, and having selected a new and admirable location where it could enjoy all the advantages of both city and country, with the means of making its instructions as thorough and complete as those of any college in the United States), it could not have had a wiser and more judicious counselor or manager than President Jackson. He had visited Europe in 1873 to study the best forms of collegiate architecture, and had devoted much thought and care to the preparation for such changes as would increase in every way its efficiency and capacity for enlarged usefulness. Though an able writer and an elegant speaker, Dr. Jackson had published very little. His whole life had been so busy with the acquisition and the imparting of knowledge, that he had found little leisure for general literary labor. A few baccalaureate and other occasional addresses, sermons, and essays, and a considerable number of brilliant review articles, are all that remain to testify to his abilities.

JANIN, JULES GABRIEL, a distinguished French critic, novelist, and man of letters; born at St.-Étienne (Loire), December 24, 1804 ;

died at his chalet in Passy (Paris), June 19, 1874. He was of Hebrew parentage, and the son of a lawyer. His early education was obtained at the College of St.-Étienne, from which he proceeded to the College of Louis the Great, in Paris. He distinguished himself there by his strong opposition to the system of instruction adopted at the Restoration. Having graduated, and not desiring to study a profession, he took up his quarters in a garret in the Rue du Dragon with an octogenarian, and as a private tutor for students. But his *penchant* for journalism was too strong to be suppressed, and he soon obtained some employment on a theatrical sheet, and, his abilities attracting notice, he was called to a better position on *Figaro*, and was also sub-editor of a royalist paper, the *Quotidienne*, until the accession of the Polignac ministry in August, 1829, when he quitted the latter and cast in his lot with the moderate liberal journals. Soon after, he founded, in company with some writers of mark, the *Revue de Paris* and the *Journal des Enfants*. Shortly afterward he published his first romance, "L'Âne Mort et la Femme Guillotinée" ("The Dead Ass and the Guillotined Wife"), a quaint work, which was soon followed by his "Confession," a political and religious romance, noted for the novelty of its style. M. Janin bitterly assailed King Louis Philippe, and in 1831 published a work entitled "Barnave," wherein he narrated the recreancy of Philippe Égalité, and violently attacked the Orleans family. This work provoked an able rejoinder, but M. Janin closed the contest by making peace with the King and accepting the Cross of the Legion of Honor in 1836. He now became dramatic critic of the *Journal des Débats*, and in that capacity attained his greatest fame. His wonderful piquancy of style, his airy grace of sentiment and wit, and his dashing paradoxes of criticism, rendered his writings extremely popular, and enabled him, without fear of ridicule, to dub himself *le Prince de la Critique*. For many years he made and destroyed literary reputations, and was the leading authority of French criticism. M. Janin continued, meanwhile, writing books, and gradually produced that wonderful series of works, embracing travels, history, and romance, which display the greatest versatility, and place him in the first rank of French authors. Despite his brilliant literary career, his life was not untroubled. In 1841 he married a young and handsome heiress, and had the imprudence to give in the *Journal des Débats*, in place of the literary review, a singular article, minutely detailing his good fortune. This provoked sharp criticism, and gained him for a long time in the public journals the name of the "Married Critic." Again, in 1844, he attacked the principles and men of the Revolution, and was sharply assailed in turn by his friend, M. Félix Pyat, then editor of *La Réforme*. So irritated was the critic by this attack, that, instead of replying

in his paper to M. Pyat, he had that writer and the publisher of *La Réforme* cited before the police-court and fined for libel. After the Revolution of 1848, M. Janin withdrew from politics and devoted his attention exclusively to literary pursuits. He sought admission to the Academy, but, despite the most persistent efforts, the doors remained closed against him until 1870, when he was elected, and immediately resigned his connection with the *Journal des Débats*. He inherited shortly before his death a large fortune, and with an air of levity deplored that it came when he could no longer enjoy it. M. Janin's principal works, besides those already named, were: "Fantastic Stories," 4 vols. (1832); "New Stories," 4 vols. (1883); "Voyage of Victor Ogier in the East, etc.," 3 vols. (1834); "A Heart for Two Loves" (1837); "The Catacombs," a collection of romances, tales, etc., 6 vols. (1839); "The Nun of Toulouse," 2 vols. (1850). Of historical and descriptive works the list was larger; it embraced: "Anecdotic Tableaux of French Situations since Francis I." (1829); a cheap and popular "History of the Theatre" (1832); "A Course of Lectures on the History of Journalism in France," delivered at the Athenæum (1834); "Fontainebleau, Versailles, and Paris" (1837); "History of France," the explanatory text accompanying the "Galleries of Versailles" (1837–1843); "Versailles and its Historical Museum" (1838); "A Voyage to Italy" (1839); "The Prince Royal" (1842); "Historic, Picturesque, and Monumental Normandy" (1842–'43); "Historic Brittany," etc. (1844); "A Journey from Paris to the Sea" (1847); "The Symphonies of Winter" (1857); "A Prose Translation of Horace" (1860); "Stories from the Chalet" (1859); "A History of Dramatic Literature," 6 vols., really an analysis of his principal *feuilletons* (1858); a new edition, almost entirely rewritten, of "Barnave" (1860); "The End of a World, and a Nephew of Rameau" (1861); "The Little Blessings" (1861); "The Week of Three Thursdays" (1861); "Stories not stamped" (1862); "Blue Stories" (1863); "Poetry and Eloquence at Rome" (1863); "Béranger and his Times" (1866); "The Love of Books" (1866). He had also translated and abridged Richardson's "Clarissa Harlowe" (1846); edited with Chasles and Gautier "The Beauties of the Opera" (1844); and contributed some fragments concerning Manon Lescaut to Houssaye and Sainte-Beuve's "History of Manon Lescaut."

JAPAN, an empire in Eastern Asia. The appellation by which the Emperor is generally known in foreign countries is the ancient title of Mikado, or the Venerable. Present Mikado, Mutsu *Hito*, born at Yeddo, September 22, 1852, succeeded his father, Komei Tenno, 1867; married, December 28, 1868, to Princess Haruko, born April 17, 1850, daughter of Prince Itchidgo. The first child of the Emperor was born in 1873, but died soon after. There is no reg-

ular law of succession, and the throne generally devolves not on the son of the Mikado,
but on the eldest or the most distinguished
member of the house. It is only necessary
that the new Mikado belong to one of the four
royal families: Katzura, Arisugawa, Fushimi,
or Kannin. Of the house Katzura, only one
scion, Princess Sûmiko, born 1828, is still
alive. To the house Arisugawa belong the
Princes Takúhito (born 1812) and Tarulito
(born 1835); to the house Fushimi, Prince Sa-
danaru (born 1858); and to the house Kannin,
Prince Yassu (born 1865). The ministry consists of eight departments, namely: the Ministry of the Imperial House, of Foreign Affairs,
War, Navy, Finances and the Interior, Justice,
Public Instruction, and Ecclesiastical Affairs.
At the side of the ministry stand the Sain,
or Senate, composed of about thirty daimios,
and the Shoïn, or Council of State, of an unlimited number of members, and consulted by
the Mikado at his pleasure.—A Parliament
was formed in 1869, with deputies selected by
the provincial governments, but it was soon
dissolved, its deliberations taking no effect. A
new Parliament was to be called in the course
of the year 1875, the necessary preparations
having been completed in 1874. The empire
is divided into seventy-two Ken, or land districts, and three Fu, or residential districts,
namely: Yeddo (now officially called Tokio,
"the Capital of the East"), Osaka, and Kioto.
At the head of each of these seventy-five districts is a prefect, whose powers and attributes
are far more extensive than those of any similar functionary in Europe. There is, however,
a limit to their judicial action, for they cannot
carry into execution sentences devolving banishment or death, until they have been confirmed by the Minister of Justice.

The empire consists of the Japanese Islands,
the island of Yesso, part of the island Saghalien,
part of Kuriles, and the Liu - Khiu Islands.
The area and population of the several divisions are as follows:

DIVISIONS.	Area.	Population.
Japanese Islands	114.552	32,818,010
Yesso and Hakodadi	34.605 }	123,668
Kuriles	3.700 }	
Possessions on Saghalien	?	2,358
Liu-Khiu (Loo-choo)	2,671	166,789
Total	155,528	33,110,825

Japan proper (or the Japanese Islands) is
geographically divided into the three islands
of Niphon, the central and most important
territory; Kiusiu, "the nine provinces," the
Southwestern Island; and Shikoku, "the four
states," the Southern Island. The capital, Yeddo, or Tokio, had in 1872 a population of 779,-
361. The population of Kioto (Miaco) is 567,-
334; of Osaka, 530,885; Yokohama, 61,553;
Niegata, 32,256; Kumamotu, 300,000; Kago-
sima, 200,000; Nagasaki, 80,00; Kanasawa,
60,000. The number of foreigners in Yokohama was in 1873 about 3,000; in Hiogo, 415;

in Osaka, 103; in Nagasaki, in 1871, 193; Hakodadi, 30; Tokio, 36.

Japan has concluded treaties with the United
States (1854); Great Britain (1854); Russia
and the Netherlands (1855); France (1859);
Portugal (1860); Prussia and the Zollverein
(1861); Switzerland (1864); Italy (1866); and
Denmark (1867). Besides these states, Belgium, Austria, Peru, Sweden, and Spain, are
also represented in Japan by diplomatic agents.
By the treaties with the foreign powers, the
ports of Yokohama, Nagasaki, Niegata, Hiogo,
Osaka, Hakodadi, and the city of Yeddo, were
thrown open to foreign commerce.

The budget-estimates for the year 1873 are
contained in a report of the Commissary-General for the Administration of Finances to the
President of the Council of State, dated June
9, 1873. The revenue for 1873 is estimated at
48,700,000 ryos (1 ryo = $1.08), the expendi-
tures at 46,500,000 ryos; surplus, 2,200,000
ryos. The principal sources of revenue are
the land-tax (40,000,000 ryos), and the tax on
brandy, oil, sugar, and similar articles (2,100,-
000). The principal items of public expenditure are the pensions and indemnification of
the deposed daimios (12,600,000) and the budget of the Minister of War (8,000,000). The
budget for 1874 estimates the revenue at 58,-
473,136 yens (1 yen = $1), the expenditures at
52,804,685 yens. Of the surplus, amounting
to 5,668,451 yens, 5,000,000 are to be applied
to redeeming the paper-money; the remainder is to be added to a reserve fund, which,
at the close of 1874, amounted to 21,029,841
yens. The public debt was stated in 1874 to
be as follows:

	Yens.
Home debt (being mostly former debts of the provinces)	21,029,280
Foreign debt	15,085,592
Paper-money in circulation	96,000,000
Total	132,112,872

The imports and exports from 1871 to
1873 were as follows (value expressed in thousands of dollars):

PORTS.	1871.		1872.		1873.	
	Imports.	Exports.	Imports.	Exports.	Imp'ts.	Exp'ts.
Yokohama...	14,445	14,431	20,063	15,457	20,743	15,385
Hiogo-Osaka	1,739	2,082	4,247	5,678	6,433	3,386
Nagasaki...	1,545	2,380	1,857	2,743	1,889	2,047
Hakodadi...	16	292	23	417	83	448
Niegata......	?	......	......	?	7	1
Total....	17,745	19,189	26,189	24,295	29,105	21,217

The movement of shipping in 1873 was as
follows:

FLAGS.	YOKOHAMA.		HIOGO-OSAKA.		HAKODADI.	
	Vessels.	Tons.	Vessels.	Tons.	Vessels.	Tons.
American....	188	279.859	108	188.889	36	42,865
English....	140	104.316	82	53,862	17	4,443
French......	29	26,901	3	1,640		
German......	29	12,607	21	9,719	5	1,345
Others.......	14	7,011	22	11,944	2	523
Total....	350	427.094	236	266,054	60	49,176

An imperial edict of December 28, 1872, establishes general liability to military service. The time of service is three years. The standing army in time of peace is 35,564 men; in time of war, 50,230. The execution of the edict has already begun, but has met in several districts with considerable opposition. The navy was composed of seventeen vessels (two iron-clads), of an aggregate of seventy guns, and 2,300 horse-power; it was manned by 1,200 men.

The first railroad of Japan, from Tokio to Yokohama, was opened in November, 1872; it has a length of eighteen miles. It was at once used so much that, early in 1873, a double track had to be laid. A second railroad, from Hiogo to Osaka, of about equal length, was to be opened in the course of the year 1874.

The electric telegraph connects (since the beginning of 1873) the towns of Nagasaki, Osaka, Hiogo, Kioto, Yokohama, and Tokio, with each other, and with other countries of Asia and Europe.

A general post-office was established in February, 1873. The number of post-offices in 1872 was 1,174; the number of letters forwarded, 2,509,032. The Government has issued stamped envelopes and postal-cards.

The expedition which the Japanese Government at the close of 1873 was preparing against the savages of Formosa was put off to May, 1874. It consisted of about 3,000 men, and was under the chief command of General Saigo. Among the foreign officers accompanying it were two Americans, Cassel and Wasson. Soon after landing, the troops had an encounter with the natives, in which 48 of the latter were killed and wounded. The result of this encounter filled the natives with terror, and they fled into the mountains of the interior. The troops fortified their camp on the Langkian Bay, from which columns of 500 were sent out into the interior to search for the enemy. The expedition was chiefly directed against the Bootan tribe and its allies, in all five tribes, with only about 600 armed men. The majority of the tribes, thirteen in number, with about 1,700 armed men, who were under a common supreme chief, Tok-et-a, concluded a treaty of peace with the Japanese. These operations against the savages were continued with great vigor, and the object of the expedition, to punish them severely, was fully attained. At the same time the Japanese established forts and roads, and began the culture of silk and cotton. As China claims sovereignty over the island of Formosa, though it was admitted that the tribes of the eastern coast were actually independent, the Japanese expedition led to diplomatic complications between the Governments of China and Japan. The commander of the Japanese troops in Formosa notified the Governor-General of the Chinese province of Fo-Kien, of which Formosa is a part, that his Government, which always took a fatherly care of its subjects and

was therefore indignant at the cruelties committed by the Formosans, had sent him to confer with the Formosan chiefs in order that they might teach their subjects to behave better in future, and that the malefactors might be punished. The Governor-General, in his reply, compared the aborigines of Formosa with the savage mountaineers of several provinces of China proper, who also were actually independent, though, as their territories were fully inclosed by China, the sovereignty of the latter was undisputed. The authority of Vattel was invoked to prove the correctness of his position! In a second dispatch the Governor-General informed Saigo that he had not received any direct orders from Peking concerning the Formosan affairs. As the Japanese commander-in-chief asserted that an agreement had been arrived at between the Foreign Office at Peking and the Japanese minister, he asked for a copy of any documents relating to the agreement. In the mean time an ultimatum had been addressed by the Chinese Government to Japan to withdraw the troops from Formosa within three months. While waiting for an answer from Japan, the Chinese were making active preparations for war.

Bodies of troops were moved southward, others were under orders to be ready when called for; gunboats were taken off from the half-naval, half-commercial service in which they had been employed on the coast, and concentrated in and about the Formosan waters; the large frigate on the stocks in the arsenal at Shanghai was hurried toward completion, and the arsenal artificers were more than usually busy in manufacturing shot, shell, and torpedoes. The Chinese commissioner sent to Formosa, Shen, moreover, urged upon Li Hungchang, the Viceroy of Chich-li, the imperative necessity of at once ordering out from Europe two first-class iron-clads, and establishing telegraphic communication between Tiawan-fu, the capital of Formosa, and Foochow, on the main-land. These propositions received Li Hungchang's support in a memorial to the throne, and the initiative taken toward carrying out the second project by commissioning the manager of the Great Northern Telegraph Company to proceed to Foochow in order to lay down a wire as far as the Pagoda anchorage, the first officially authorized telegraph in China. The Japanese, on their part, strictly watched the proceedings of the Chinese. Akamats, the second in command, went to Shanghai with a serviceable frigate, the presence of which occasioned much uneasiness in the minds of the local authorities, and they made inquiries in various directions as to how far it would be practicable or prudent to request her to leave the port. Their inquietude was increased by visits which some members of the expedition made to the river-ports, where Japanese had not hitherto been seen.

The Chinese commissioner to Formosa, on his return home, was either partly or wholly repudiated by the Peking Government. His representations—at least such of them as pointed to the expediency of recognizing the correctness of the position taken by Japan—were set aside, and the attitude assumed by China grew to be so threatening that it was found expedient to send two representatives to different points to arrange for the settlement of the growing complications on a common basis. The first of these, the American General Le Gendre, the only foreigner upon whom high Japanese rank has ever been conferred, was dispatched to discuss affairs with the authorities of Fo-Kien. General Le Gendre, while in pursuance of his mission, was arrested by order of the United States officials in China, for aiding in an attack upon a power at peace with the United States, and was sent to Shanghai for trial. At Shanghai he was immediately released, but the moment for his work had passed, and he joined the later commissioner, Okubo, an official of very high station, who had been sent directly to Peking. These gentlemen arrived at Tien-tsin on the 2d of September, and reached Peking on the 10th. The first conference took place on the 13th. At this introductory interview the objects of the mission were clearly set forth.

For a few days after the commencement of the discussions, the foreign ministers gave no indication of a desire to take part in the proceedings; but soon the British minister in Peking, Mr. Wade, who appeared to be in close communication with the Chinese authorities, expressed a desire to learn from the Japanese the precise nature of their functions and the progress they were making. This information they refused to impart. The reason for the refusal was not withheld. The very first demand put forward by Okubo was an acknowledgment of the correctness of the statements made by Soyezima, former embassador at Peking, as to the denial by the Tsung li Yamen (Ministry of Foreign Affairs at Peking) of Chinese authority over the savages of Formosa, and of the propriety of the action taken by the Japanese Government on the strength of those statements. This had not been conceded, and so long as the question of veracity between the two Governments remained unsettled, the negotiations could not take such a shape as would justify the Japanese commissioners in revealing their purport. Mr. Wade confined himself to getting information from Chinese sources, and he admitted that China had not made good her claim to Formosa, although he had himself been for years fixed in the belief that the claim existed and could be substantiated. His chief concern, naturally, was in regard to English commerce, which he knew would be endangered in case of war. Under his superintendence he said that he had felt obliged, or should feel obliged, to telegraph home for armed support. When this circumstance was communicated to the chief Japanese commissioner, he is understood to have remarked that it was the best thing Mr. Wade could do. The conferences continued for nearly a month, without practical results. It was noticeable that the Chinese never once alluded to the shipwrecked Liu-Khiuans as their subjects—a point which they had endeavored to gain in some of their earlier documentary assertions. However, they steadfastly declined to admit that they had ever acknowledged the right of an outside nation to deal directly with the savages, or that Japan was justified in her course. The Japanese were ready with the defense and justification of their actions; but the Tsung li Yamen had nothing to say, beyond the endless iteration of their desire that the troops should be ordered away from Formosa. At last, on the 10th of October, an ultimatum was sent to the Chinese, in which a definite reply was demanded, in default of which the Japanese commissioners would retire. It was afterward discovered that the Emperor was absent from the capital, and that Prince Kung was in attendance upon him, so that a delay was inevitable. The imperial party returned on the 14th, and on the 15th, at noon, an answer was received, which showed a decided inclination to bring the matter to a satisfactory end. Another meeting was arranged for the 18th, at Okubo's apartments, in which the Chinese, though still expressing a desire to avoid discussing the question of their right to Southern Formosa, said they were willing to acknowledge that they had been negligent, and offered a sum of money as a compensation for the slaughter of the Liu-Khiuans. This appearing to be a step in advance, the Japanese declared their willingness to reopen the discussions; but on the 19th a note came from the Yamen, stating that a difficulty had arisen, and they could not now undertake to carry through the settlement in the way they had themselves suggested. Before any expression was given to the vexation caused by this new evasion, a plan was brought forward by an English employé of the Chinese, Mr. Hart, the Inspector-General of Customs. This gentleman appeared to hold very liberal opinions in regard to the rights of all concerned, and his representations at this juncture produced a strong impression, for on the 20th the Yamen avowed a willingness to adopt his advice, and offer a sum of money, not as an indemnity, but as a compensation for public works undertaken by the Japanese in Southern Formosa, improvements of roads and buildings of houses, and as a gratuity to the soldiers who accompanied General Saigo. They would, however, not embody the financial question in their proposed convention, but would only give a verbal promise to pay at some period after Japan should have withdrawn her soldiers from Formosa. It was urged that a written pledge of this sort would be deeply humiliating to China, and that the word of honor of the Yamen ought to be taken as sufficient. Okubo declared that he had no wish or design to humiliate China, but he could not go so far as to waive the insertion of the agreement, which must appear in plain terms. As, at another interview, which took place on October 23d, an agreement on this point could not be reached, the Japanese embassadors prepared to leave Peking for home, and on the 25th General Le Gendre did set out. Hearing of this, and of the imminent withdrawal of the remainder of the mission, Prince Kung went to the residence of Mr. Wade, and requested him to take a message to Okubo, which might have the effect of detaining him. He offered, in distinct words, the first really acceptable terms of settlement that had come from the Chinese side, and offered them in a way that, this time, left little doubt as to the sincerity of his intentions. Mr. Wade promptly consented, and visited the Japanese commissioner without delay. He stated that he was empowered to declare that there would be no objection raised against Okubo's resolution to obtain written evidence of consent to the terms proposed.

Late at night, on the 25th, Okubo informed Mr. Wade that he would listen to proposals based upon this new development, but he was determined not to consider any repetitions of the assumptions of established authority over the whole of Formosa. Nor was he disposed to confer personally with the Tsung li Yamen until he felt assured that there would be no further attempt at evasion or delay. The communications thus reopened were carried on through Mr. Wade, who courteously acted as a willing messenger, until the 31st of October, when the last and decisive interview was held. The Chinese, who formally acknowledged the right of Japan to send the expedition to Formosa, withdrew all their accusations of lack of good faith on the part of the Japanese Government, and declared themselves ready to pay 500,000 taels. All this they were fully prepared to pledge themselves to, under their hand and seal. Every stipulation should be clearly set down in the convention about to be executed. But they were still sensitive in regard to the word "indemnity," and represented with much feeling that it would leave an unpleasant impression upon their minds. They urged that the application of the money should be described as partly for the relief of the families of murdered Japanese subjects, and partly in payment for improvements in Southern Formosa, as had been previously indicated on the 20th of October. As the Japanese embassadors were willing to accept this plea, the negotiations were speedily brought to an end. The convention was drawn up and signed, and the Chinese and Japanese officers took leave of each other with the customary expressions of consideration and good-will.

The articles of the convention were as follows:

Okubo, High Commissioner Plenipotentiary of Great Japan, Councilor of State and Minister of the Interior, on the one part, and the ministers of Great Tsing (China) charged with the general superin-

tendence of foreign affairs, namely, the Prince of Kung (and nine other ministers, the names and titles of whom are given in full), on the other part—

Have agreed together upon the following articles, and hereby execute the present instrument, in proof of the arrangement determined on.

As the people of all nations have a right to protection and to immunity from wrong, it becomes the duty of each state to take its own measures to insure full protection (within itself), and it is incumbent on the state within which questions (as to protection) may occur to take its own steps for the settlement of the same.

The savage tribes of Formosa, having willfully inflicted injury upon people belonging to Japan, and Japan at first believing that responsibility rested with the said savages, dispatched a force to the spot and punished them. Now, however, Japan has distinctly agreed with China to withdraw her troops, and to conclude in three articles the following supplementary arrangement for the disposal of this question:

1. The proceedings of Japan on this occasion having originally been taken for the rightful object of protecting her people, China does not regard them as wrongful.

2. China shall pay consolation-money to the families of the distressed (or shipwrecked) people who were injured on the former occasion, and as she wishes to retain for her own use the roads, houses, and other works constructed by Japan at the said place, China first agrees to pay for the same under arrangements set forth in a separate document.

3. The whole of the correspondence relating to this question which has passed between the two nations will be withdrawn and canceled by both parties, and discussion thereon will cease forever. As to the savage tribes of the said locality, China ought, of course, to take measures for keeping them under proper control, in order that navigators may be forever protected, and never again exposed to outrage or wrong.

MEIJI, seventh year, tenth month, — day.

TUNGCHI, thirteenth year, ninth month, — day. (October, 1874.)

Countersigned by   YANAGIWARA,
          Minister Plenipotentiary of Great Japan.

SUPPLEMENTARY ARTICLE.

Okubo, High Commissioner Plenipotentiary of Great Japan, Councilor of State and Minister of the Interior, on the one part, and the ministers of Great Tsing (China) charged with the general superintendence of foreign affairs, namely, the Prince of Kung (and nine other ministers, the names and titles of whom are given in full), on the other part—

Hereby execute the following certificate of a joint agreement:

In the matter of the Formosan savages, His Excellency the British minister Wade has already at this time effected a distinct agreement with the two nations who mutually execute this day an instrument in proof of the arrangement arrived at. China agrees, in the first place, to give to the families of the distressed (or shipwrecked) Japanese who were injured on former occasions, 100,000 taels as consolation-money, and further, on the withdrawal of the Japanese troops, as China wishes to retain for her own use the roads, buildings, and other works constructed at the said place, she will pay as the cost of the same 400,000 taels. It has also been stipulated and agreed by Japan on the one hand that the withdrawal of her troops shall be completed by the twentieth day of the twelfth month of the seventh year of Meiji, and by China on the other that the whole sum shall be paid by the twelfth day of the eleventh month of the thirteenth year of Tungchi (both dates being synonymous, and answering to the 20th December, 1874). The time thus named shall not be exceeded by either party. So long as the Japanese troops are not entirely withdrawn, China will not complete the payment.

This certificate is executed in proof of the above agreement, and each party retains one copy.

Meiji, seventh year, tenth month, — day.

Tungchi, thirteenth year, ninth month, — day. (October, 1874.)

Countersigned by   YANAGIWARA,
Minister Plenipotentiary of Great Japan.

The evacuation of Formosa by the Japanese troops was completed on December 2d, and the last installment of the indemnification was paid to the Japanese embassador, Yanagiwara, before his return to Japan, on December 17th. Okubo, who had succeeded in bringing about the treaty of peace, was received in Yokohama with great demonstrations of enthusiasm, in which all classes of the population took part. The whole town was illuminated, a splendid banquet was given, and the Emperor invited the envoy to his table.

On January 14th an attempt was made upon the life of the minister Iwakara while he was returning home from a visit to the Mikado. The attack was made by a party of thirteen men, who surrounded his carriage, killed the coachman, and severely though not mortally wounded Iwakara, who, however, succeeded in making his escape. Nine of the would-be assassins were subsequently arrested and beheaded.

An attempt at another insurrection was made in February, in Saga, but, as the rebels were very insufficiently provided with arms, it was easily suppressed. Their chief, a former Minister of Justice, was arrested, and, with ten other leaders, put to death.

The number of mines which, in 1874, were worked in Japan, was as follows: gold, 82;

silver, 118; copper, 800; iron, 20; zinc, 6; lead, 52; graphite, 8; coal, 412; sulphur, 12; alum, 52; besides, there were 182 petroleum-wells.

One of the most important improvements adopted by the Japanese is the light-house system. It is in the hands of an English engineer, and of incalculable value to mariners. The bureau was organized in 1866, but did not commence active operations until 1868. At the commencement only principal points along the coast were selected for illumination, and those under the advice of American, English, and French naval officers; gradually less important points were taken up, until in 1872 there were 25 light-houses, 3 light-ships, and 11 buoys.

The gas-works in Yokohama, the first in Japan, were completed and put in use in September, 1872. They are a private enterprise, and managed by Frenchmen.

The schools of the different kens (provinces) seem to be independent of each other, and equally independent of any head. The whole number of foreigners in the employ of the educational department was, in 1873, 72, of whom 17 were Americans, 12 English, 11 French, 23 German, and 9 of other nationalities. Germans are chiefly engaged in medical schools and hospitals, and, with few exceptions, instruction in that branch of science is in their hands.

Twelve missionary societies are reported to have been laboring in Japan during 1874. The Roman Catholic societies employed fifteen missionaries, and the society of the Greek Church employed two missionaries. The following is a list of the missionaries of the Protestant societies:

MISSIONARIES.	Men.	Married Women.	Single Women.	Total.
American Board...	9	8	8	20
Presbyterian Board (American)................................	6	4	8	13
Reformed Board of Missions (American)......................	5	5	1	11
American Episcopal...	8	2	..	10
Methodist Episcopal (American)...............................	5	5	..	10
Baptist Union (American).....................................	3	3	..	6
Woman's Union Missionary Society (American)...............	..	..	5	5
Wesleyan Methodist (Canadian)...............................	2	2	..	4
Church Missionary Society (English Episcopal)..............	3	3	..	6
Society for the Propagation of the Gospel (English Episcopal)...........	2	..	..	2
Total...	43	32	12	87
These missionaries were distributed as follows:				
At Yokohama..	14	13 ·	6	33
Yeddo, now Tokio...	10	3	3	16
Osaka...	9	6	1	16
Kobe..	5	5	2	12
Nagasaki..	4	4	..	8
Awomori Ken, northern point of Niphon......................	1	1	..	2
Total...	43	32	12	87

Thirty-nine of the missionaries were registered as clergymen, and three as missionary physicians. Of the whole number of missionaries, eight were from England, and seventy-nine from America.

The native population connected with the Roman Catholic missions was, in 1873, estimated at about 14,000; with few exceptions,

they were the descendants of former Christians. The number of those who preserve the books of their Christian ancestors, and secretly adhere to (Catholic) Christianity is, however, much larger. On the island of Yesso alone their number was, in 1861, estimated at 80,000 by a former English Consul, and, for the whole of Japan, it is believed to exceed 200,000.

JONES, Owen. Mr. Owen Jones was born in 1809, in Thames Street, London. His father, Owen Jones, born at Llanvihangel Glyn y Myvyr, in Denbighshire, was distinguished as a Welsh antiquary. Making money as a furrier in Thames Street, he devoted a considerable amount of it to the collection of the remains of the literature of Wales, published as "The Myvyrian Archaiology of Wales." He also procured transcripts of Welsh poetry, extending to fifty quarto volumes, now deposited in the British Museum. When spoken of as a bard, he is called in Welsh records Owen Myvyr, from the place of his birth. Owen, the eminent son, early lost his father, and at sixteen he became the pupil of the late Mr. Lewis Vulliamy, the architect, and served with him a term of six years. In 1831 he started upon his great tour. In Greece he met Jules Goury, a French architect, and student like himself. They never afterward separated till the death of Goury. They went to Turkey, and then to Egypt. At Thebes the two architects set to work with an extraordinary enthusiasm and cleared out one of those crude brick arches which surround the Memnonium, and converted it into a comfortable residence, employing the fellaheen, and some of their boats even, to build a wall across the arch separating the kitchen from the studio, which was lighted by a large hole in the roof. From this improvised abode the two architects used to sally forth, with their Arabs carrying their ladders, boards, and implements for measuring, and return in the evening with a store of architectural knowledge derived from the surrounding remains that was quite astounding for accuracy and detail, with sometimes not a few picturesque sketches in water-color of the ruins and their present occupants. Never, seemingly, did two men work together in better harmony and success. At this time, the poems of Victor Hugo firing his imagination, he, with his friend Jules Goury, determined to go to Granada; and on arriving at the Alhambra they determined to make its beauties known to the world. The ultimate result is the "Plans, Elevations, Sections, and Details of the Alhambra." M. Goury died of cholera. Owen Jones then visited his friend's family in France, in fulfillment of a promise he had made to him, and came to England, where he commenced the reproduction of his drawings in colors and gold for publication. This was in 1836. In the following year he again visited Granada for twelve months, and then returned to London and finished the publication of the work. This was done under great difficulties. When he first came from Spain the art of printing in colors by means of stones was in its infancy. He seized the idea, obtained a press, and in an attic at his chambers in the Adelphi set to work to produce that book which, as a monument of printing alone, has never been surpassed. On its publication he spent his patrimony. On the completion of

the "Alhambra" he commenced his professional life. To keep together the few assistants he had trained to chromo-lithography he published a few works, which proved losses. About this time he married Miss Wild, herself one of a family of accomplished artists, and who survives him. He then became connected with Messrs. Longman & Co., and with Messrs. De la Rue, and made for them numbers of designs. With the latter firm, especially, he was long and largely connected. He may be said to have metamorphosed every thing in their establishment, and helped largely to give it the renown it has ever retained. He designed their playing-cards, their stamps—in fact, all that they produced. He also made designs for the great carpet-manufacturers of Glasgow. His ornamentation has generally a character similar to that of what may be called the Moorish styles, namely, the avoidance of imitation of relief. In 1842 he published "Designs for Mosaic and Tesselated Pavements." Mr. Jones was also engaged in the architectural design and superintendence of some houses. But in general architectural design, and even with the ornaments of Moorish character which he introduced, he did not at that time succeed as well as in interior decorations.

On the formation of the staff of officers for the Exhibition of 1851, Mr. Jones was named one of the "superintendents of the works;" and, when the question of design was set at rest by Paxton's blotting-paper sketch, he still retained his post, and aided in giving architectural character to the structure. As the work progressed, the problem of its decoration, a novel one was more and more discussed, and Mr. Jones's original proposals, which he stoutly supported by theory, were very freely canvassed, and became somewhat modified in the application. He, however, always maintained the propriety of adhering to the primary colors, and of using them in certain proportionate quantities in which the reflected rays are held to constitute white light, and also of using them on particular surfaces supposed to be adapted to the force of each color. There was much conflict of ideas and difficulty, but his intense desire not to lose the opportunity to impress upon the world the effect of color led him to persevere. All who saw the building will remember the harmonious whole produced. In the year 1852 one of the lectures at the Society of Arts, relative to the Exhibition, was given by Mr. Jones, and afterward published, under the title "An Attempt to define the Principles which should regulate the Employment of Color in the Decorative Arts, with a Few Words on the Necessity for an Architectural Education on the Part of the Public." Shortly afterward the Crystal Palace Company erected their building at Sydenham, and Mr. Jones was appointed "director of decorations." When the building was ready, the courts of architecture and sculpture were commenced; and the Egyptian, Greek, Roman, and Alhambra courts, and the decorative painting of the general fabric, were then completed under his directions. With reference to the system of decoration adopted by him, he was led to publish "An Apology for the Coloring of the Greek Court." St. James's Hall, designed and erected by him expressly for musical purposes, is universally recognized among musicians as one of the most satisfactory music-halls in Europe. He here first introduced a system of distributed lights by means of small, star-shaped burners, which have since been very widely used. The main object of the system is the avoidance of shadows.

In 1857 Mr. Jones, who had joined the Institute of British Architects in 1843, was awarded the royal gold medal, the gift of her Majesty the Queen to architecture. He received several other medals and recognitions from abroad, notably the diploma of honor for decorative designs at the Vienna Exhibition of 1873. The "Grammar of Ornament," his most important published work, was completed in 1856, and is recognized as a text-book throughout Europe. The facts that he has endeavored to establish in that volume are these: 1. That, whenever any style of ornament commands universal admiration, it will always be found to be in accordance with the laws which regulate the distribution of form in Nature. 2. That, however varied the manifestations in accordance with these laws, the leading ideas on which they are based are very few. 3. That the modifications and developments which have taken place from one style to another have been caused by a sudden throwing off of some fixed trammel, which set thought free for a time, till the new idea, like the old, became again fixed, to give birth in its turn to fresh inventions. 4. He endeavored to show, in the twentieth chapter, that the future progress of ornamental art may be best secured by engrafting on the experience of the past the knowledge we may obtain by a return to Nature for fresh inspiration.

"To attempt to build up theories of art, or to form a style, independently of the past," he says, "would be an act of supreme folly. It would be at once to reject the experiences and accumulated knowledge of thousands of years. On the contrary, we should regard as our inheritance all the successful labors of the past, not blindly follow them, but employing them simply as guides to find the true path."

The principles advocated in this work are:

As architecture, so all works of the decorative arts should possess fitness, proportion, harmony—the result of all which is repose.

True beauty results from that repose which the mind feels when the eye, the intellect, and the affections, are satisfied from the absence of any want.

Construction should be decorated. Decoration should never be purposely constructed. (That which is beautiful is true; that which is true must be beautiful.)

Beauty of form is produced by lines growing out one from another in gradual undulations. There are no excrescences. Nothing could be removed, and leave the design equally good or better.

The general forms being first cared for, these should be subdivided and ornamented by general lines; the intersections may then be filled in with ornament, which may again be subdivided and enriched for closer inspection.

In his introduction to the series of Moresque ornaments, Mr. Jones testifies strongly to his admiration of that style. In a succeeding volume, published some years later, he showed the beauties that could be culled from Chinese decoration; and we ought not to omit to mention, as among the earlier works of illumination, his "One Thousand and One Initial Letters," and "The Song of Songs." In the year 1866 he designed a kiosk for India, and superintended its execution in iron.

In the latter part of Owen Jones's life he was mainly occupied in the decoration of private houses, and this chiefly in connection with Messrs. Jackson & Graham. The first work of great importance was a complete series of designs for the carpets, and wall and ceiling decorations, for all the great rooms (fifteen in number) in the palace of the Viceroy of Egypt at Gesch. It was necessary that every thing should be prepared and completed in London, ready to apply on the spot, and herein his complete mastery of the principles and knowledge of the details of Arabic art shone most conspicuously in the production of fifteen series of designs, applicable as dadoes, dado-mouldings, walls, friezes, frieze-mouldings, the different sections of cornice-mouldings, and ceilings, in a style as perfect and exact as is exemplified in the tombs of the Caliphs in Old Cairo. An independent multiple, determined by the proportions of each separate saloon, was adopted throughout for all the designs for the carpets, mural and ceiling decorations. Mr. Jones regarded this, both physically and mentally, as the greatest triumph of his life. For three months, day by day, he worked not less than eighteen hours upon it. But, by far the most important and complete work in which he was associated with Messrs. Jackson & Graham, is the decoration and furniture of the London house of Mr. Alfred Morrisson, in Carlton-House Terrace. Here the woodwork of the paneling, dado, doors, architraves, and window-shutters, in the outer and inner hall, staircase, and all the rooms on the ground and first floors, is inlaid from designs by Mr. Jones, with various woods of different kinds, the colors of which were carefully selected by him with a view to perfect harmony of coloring. The walls are hung with the richest Lyons silks, all specially designed by him, and colored to harmonize with the ceilings, which may be described as perfect in the proportions of their geometrical divisions and the designs and coloring of their decorations. The chimney-pieces, too, grates, and fenders, the carpets, and the furniture, which is all marquetrie, were designed by Mr. Jones, and are in perfect keeping with each other. Unfettered by any limit with regard to cost, and working with the full confidence of Mr. Morrisson in his artistic genius, this work was a labor of love to him, and he lavished upon it all his thought and all his knowledge, with this result—that there are no accidental effects, and there are no defects, either in the association of colors or forms, or the unity of scale in the details of the different objects entering into the composition of a great harmonious whole.

K

KANSAS. The Legislature of Kansas met at Topeka on the 13th of January, and adjourned on the 11th of March, having been in actual session fifty-six days. Little legislation of general importance was effected. The Hon. James M. Harvey, who was Governor of the State from 1869 to 1873, was elected United States Senator. The State Treasurer, Josiah E. Hayes, was impeached and removed for misdemeanors in office, after a thorough examination into his administration by a legislative committee, the trial taking place at a special sitting of the Senate held for the purpose in May. A new apportionment of the State into three congressional districts was made, so that the counties of Leavenworth, Doniphan, Brown, Nemaha, Marshall, Washington, Republic, Jewell, Smith, Phillips, Norton, Graham, Rooks, Osborne, Mitchell, Cloud, Clay, Ottawa, Lincoln, Riley, Pottawatomie, Jackson, Jefferson, Atchison, Davis, and all the territory lying north of the second standard parallel, constitute the first district; the counties of Montgomery, Labette, Cherokee, Crawford, Neosho, Bourbon, Allen, Anderson, Linn, Miami, Franklin, Johnson, Douglas, and Wyandotte, constitute the second district; and all that part of the State not included in the first and second districts constitutes the third district. A joint resolution in favor of submitting to a vote of the people an amendment of the constitution, giving women the right to vote, received 48 votes to 32 against it in the House, but failed for lack of two-thirds in its favor. A bill for the regulation of the traffic in intoxicating liquors, which occupied a good deal of attention and passed in the House, was defeated in the Senate. An act was passed requiring any corporation existing under laws of the State to have its general office and its books within the State, and at least three of its directors residents of the State. A new tax bill was passed making it optional for the tax-payer to pay the whole or one-half of his tax on or before the 20th of December, and one-half on or before the 20th of June following, allowing a rebate of 5 per cent. on the half due in June, if it is paid in December, and adding a penalty of 5 per cent. to that due in December, if not paid then, 5 per cent more in March, if still unpaid, and 5 per cent. more in June. The taxation of personal property used in business was authorized to be made where the property was used, and not where the owner resided. The following act, to "secure civil rights to the citizens of the State," was passed:

Be it enacted by the Legislature of the State of Kansas:

SECTION 1. That if any of the regents or trustees of any State university, college, or other school of public instruction, or the owner or owners, agents, trustees, or managers in charge of any inn, hotel, or boarding-house; or any place of entertainment or amusement, for which a license is required by any of the municipal authorities of this State; or the owner or owners, or person or persons in charge of any steamboat, railroad, stage-coach, omnibus, street-car, or any other means of public carriage for persons or freight within the State, shall make any distinction on account of race, color, or previous condition of servitude, such person so offending shall be deemed guilty of a misdemeanor, and upon conviction thereof in any court of competent jurisdiction, shall be fined in any sum not less than ten dollars nor more than one thousand dollars; and shall also be liable to damages in any court of competent jurisdiction to the person or persons injured thereby.

SEC. 2. All fines collected under and by virtue of this act shall be paid over to the public school fund of the county in which the offense is committed.

SEC. 3. That all acts or parts of acts in conflict with this act be and the same are hereby repealed.

SEC. 4. This act shall take effect and be in force from and after its publication in the statute-book.

There was a special session of the Legislature in September, called by the Governor, to adopt some measure for the relief of destitute citizens in the western counties of the State, whose crops had been destroyed by grasshoppers. The Governor, in his message to this body, estimated the number of destitute persons at 1,500, and declared that 120,000 bushels of wheat would be required for their subsistence in addition to the corn which they had. Two relief acts were passed, one providing for the issue and sale of $73,000 of State bonds to be used in purchasing bonds of the counties in which the relief was needed; and the other authorizing these counties to issue special relief bonds. Private organizations were also formed for the aid of the destitute, and contributions were received from other parts of the country. In seventeen counties in which 158,000 acres were planted with corn, not a bushel was raised. In five of these counties an average crop of wheat, rye, oats, barley, and buckwheat, was raised, but in twelve frontier counties, with a population of 23,000, the settlements had all been made within three years, and their supplies were almost wholly destroyed. In eight counties, with 1,700 people, this was the first season after settlement, and the means of the inhabitants had been used up in building houses and putting in their first crop, which was almost totally destroyed by grasshoppers and drought.

The bonded debt of Kansas is $1,341,775, of which $703,825 has been purchased and placed to the credit of the sinking-fund, mak--

ing the net indebtedness $637,950. The receipts of the Treasury from all sources during the last fiscal year amounted to $995,102.89, and the expenditures to $976,805.82. The amount of the receipts derived directly from taxation was $690,253.59, of which $461,095.59 was for general revenue purposes, $22,988.83 for the sinking-fund, $91,715.79 for the payment of interest on the public debt, and $114,453.38 for the annual school-fund. Of the disbursements, $483,217.20 was from the general revenue - fund, $255,520.86 from the annual school-fund, $90,939.76 was invested for the permanent school-fund, $81,788.50 was for the payment of interest on the public debt, and $52,694.15 was invested in State bonds for the sinking-fund. The balance in the Treasury at the beginning of the year was $207,334.99; at the end of the year, $222,880.05. The permanent school-fund on the 30th of November amounted to $1,125,309.32, an increase of $117,163.73 during the year.

The whole number of acres of land now contained within the organized counties of this State is 35,750,400. The number of acres subject to taxation in 1874 was 16,996,746, of which 3,669,769 acres were under cultivation. The aggregate value of the land subject to taxation, as fixed by the State Board of Equalization, is $72,554,065.90; the number of town lots was 290,628, with an aggregate value of $19,238,406.22. The valuation of personal property was $22,402,769.76; valuation of railroad property, $14,721,277.92; total valuation of property, $128,906,519.80. The tax levy for general revenue purposes was four mills to the dollar, making a total tax of $515,625.23; for the sinking-fund one-fifth of a mill, raising $25,781.85; for the interest-fund four-fifths of a mill, making $103,908.28; total levy, six mills on a dollar, or $773,438.72. The number of miles of railroad in the State is 1,839, including the whole or portions of the Atchison, Topeka & Santa Fé; the Atlantic & Pacific; the Atchison & Nebraska; central branch of the Union Pacific; Kansas Central; Kansas Pacific; Kansas City & Santa Fé; Leavenworth, Lawrence & Galveston; Southern Kansas; Leavenworth, Atchison & Northwestern; Missouri River; Fort Scott & Galveston; Missouri, Kansas & Texas; Memphis, Carthage & Northwestern; Missouri River; St. Joseph & Denver City; and St. Louis, Lawrence & Washington. The value of the roads is $11,233,109.65, of the rolling-stock, $2,458,482.42; other railroad property, $1,019,585.81.

There are 4,395 school districts in the State, of which 391 were organized during the year. Over 5,000 teachers were employed, and there was an increase of 13,000 in the number of pupils attending the common schools. The State University is flourishing, and had 173 students representing twenty-three different counties of the State. The Agricultural College is sustained from the income of its endowment, which

is now about $20,000 a year. There are 34,425 acres of the endowment lands still unsold, having a value of over $218,000. That which has been disposed of brought $218,907. The industrial departments of the institution yield some revenue, $1,000 having been cleared from the farm this year. In addition to the normal schools at Emporia and Leavenworth, a new one has been opened at Concordia.

The average number of patients in the Insane Asylum during the year was 115, and the trustees report that 300 more in the State require accommodation and treatment, for which no facilities are provided. The penitentiary contained at the end of the year 425 convicts, having received 245 and discharged 160 during the year. More than two-thirds of the convicts were single men, less than one-fourth were mechanics, 48 could not read or write, and three were females.

The opposition to the Republican party in this State took the name of the Independent Reform party this year, and held its nominating convention at Topeka, on the 5th of August. The candidates nominated for State offices were: Governor, J. C. Cusey; Lieutenant-Governor, Eldred Harrington; Secretary of State, Nelson Abbott; Treasurer of State, Charles F. Koester; Auditor of State, George P. Smith; Attorney-General, J. R. Hollowell; Superintendent of Public Instruction, H. B. Norton; Associate Justice of Supreme Court, William P. Douthitt. The principles and claims of the party were set forth in the following platform:

Resolved, That we, the delegates and representatives of the people of Kansas favorable to the organization of an independent political party, laying aside past differences of opinion and earnestly uniting in a common purpose to secure needed reforms in the administration of public affairs, cordially unite in submitting these declarations:

1. That all political power is inherent in the people; that no government is worthy of preservation, or should be upheld, which does not derive its powers from the consent of the governed; and by equal and just laws, the rights of life, liberty, and the pursuit of happiness, shall be assured to all men, without distinction of race, color, or nationality; that the maintenance of these principles is essential to the perpetuity of our republican institutions, and that to this end the Federal Constitution, with all its amendments, the rights of the States, and the union of the States, must be preserved.

2. That the maintenance inviolate of the rights of the States, and especially of the right of each State to order and control its own domestic institutions according to its own judgment exclusively, is indispensable to that balance of power on which the perfection and endurance of our political fabric depends.

3. That the conduct of the present Administration, in its bold defiance of public good; in its prodigality and wasteful extravagance; in the innumerable frauds perpetrated under its authority; in its disgraceful partiality for, and reward of unworthy favorites; in its reckless and unstable financial policy; and in its incapacity to meet the vital questions of the day, and provide for the general welfare, stands without a parallel in our national history; and the highest considerations of duty require the American people, in the exercise of their inherent sovereignty, to correct the accumulation of evil, and bring the

Government back to its ancient landmarks of patriotism and economy.

4. That the faith of the nation must be retained inviolate; that the public debt, of whatever kind, should be paid in strict accordance with the law under which it was contracted.

5. That we demand the repeal of the national banking law, and that the Government shall issue a legal-tender currency direct from the Treasury, interchangeable for Government bonds bearing the lowest possible rate of interest, and which currency shall be receivable both for public and private dues.

6. That we favor the repeal of the tariff on lumber, and that the tariff on the necessities of common life be abolished or reduced to the lowest possible figure, and that the tax on incomes be restored.

7. That the act of the Legislature of Kansas of March 1, 1866, by which the 5,000 acres of land dedicated forever to the school-fund by Section 3, Article VIII. of our State constitution was divided among and appropriated to four railroad corporations, is unconstitutional and void, and this land still in right and equity belongs to the State school-fund, and the next Legislature ought to pass an act repealing the act of March 1, 1866, and directing the Attorney-General of the State to commence suit in the proper courts to cancel all patents and other conveyances made to said lands under the authority of said act.

8. That we hereby extend our sympathy to the settlers on the Osage lands and to homestead settlers whose titles are contested by railroad companies; and we hereby declare that the Reform party of Kansas will use every honest means to aid these people in their struggle for their homes.

9. That railroad corporations should be made subservient to the public good; that while we shall discountenance any action calculated to retard the progress of railroad enterprises, or work injustice to these invaluable auxiliaries to commerce and civilization, yet we demand such constitutional legislation upon this subject, both State and Federal, as will effectually secure the industrial and producing interests of the country against all forms of corporate monopoly and extortion.

10. That we denounce the passage of the act of last Congress, vesting certain powers in the courts of the District of Columbia, as an outrage tending to destroy the freedom of the press, the liberty of the citizen, and the sovereignty of the States, and we demand that our Senators and Representatives in Congress at the next session vote for its unconditional repeal.

11. That in view of the wide-spread corruption that has permeated Kansas in every department of its government since its organization as a State, we will support no man for office merely because he is the nominee of a party; but to obtain our votes, in every instance, he must possess the Jeffersonian standard of fitness—honesty, capacity, and fidelity to the Constitution.

12. The frequent cases of malfeasance in office which have been developed within the last four years upon the part of State and county officials, and the losses sustained by the people through defalcations of county treasurers, imperatively demand such legislation as will give to the tax-payer security for all funds paid into the State and county treasuries, and all interest accruing thereon, and we denounce it as an act of criminal neglect in the Legislature having failed to provide for the speedy removal of defaulting treasurers from office, and their punishment for malfeasance therein.

13. That we enter our protest against the Indian policy as now administered—subjecting as it does our citizens to brutality, and all the horrors of savage warfare.

14. That we are in favor of the election of President and Vice-President, and United States Senators, by the direct voice of the people.

The Republican State Convention was held at Topeka on the 26th of August, and nominated the following ticket: Governor, Thomas Osborn; Lieutenant-Governor, M. J. Salter; Secretary of State, T. H. Cavanaugh; Auditor, D. W. Wilder; Treasurer, Samuel Lappin; Attorney-General, A. M. F. Randolph; Superintendent of Public Instruction, John Fraser; Associate-Justice, D. M. Valentine.

The platform, which was introduced by a long preamble, rehearsing the achievements of the Republican party in the past, consisted of the following resolutions:

Resolved, That the powers of the General Government having been stretched to an unhealthy extent, to meet the crisis of civil war and reconstruction, should now be restored to their normal action; that the public debt should be reduced, not spasmodically but gradually and surely, and in a way that will not burden the industries of the country by excessive exactions; that any and all schemes of taxation devised to meet an extraordinary demand should be modified according to the dictates of the strictest principles of economy and justice; that the official prodigality, recklessness, and corruption incident to times of haste, irregularity, and convulsion, must give place to economy, stability, and honesty; and, finally, that the only test of political preferment should be capacity and integrity in the discharge of official trust; that, as the policy of the Republican party in relation to the finances has afforded the people not only a safe, sound, and popular currency, of equal and uniform worth in every portion of the Commonwealth, but has greatly improved the credit of the country, at home and abroad, we point with pride to its record and accomplishment in this regard; and while reaffirming the policy announced by the party in the National Conventions in 1868 and 1872, and triumphantly indorsed by the people at the polls—a policy which, while contributing to the public credit, has also enhanced the individual and collective prosperity of the American people—we favor such legislation as will make national banking free to all, under just and equal laws, based upon the policy of specie resumption at such time as is consistent with the material and industrial interests of the country, to the end that the volume of currency may be regulated by the natural laws of trade.

Resolved, That while all the necessary wants of the State government should be supplied by a reasonable, just, and uniform taxation, the labor and production of the Commonwealth must not be crippled by the employment and maintenance of too many office-holders. Hence it becomes the duty of the Legislature to lessen the number of officials, and make such a revision of the laws of the State as to provide for a more economical administration of our State and county affairs. We are opposed to all official gratuities under the guise of an increase of pay on salaries during official terms.

Resolved, That the peril of the Government lies not so much in high ambition as in low dishonesties, and the pressing duty of the day is to secure honesty and purity in the public service. We commend the courage of the Reform party in instituting the investigation of corruption in office, sparing neither friends nor foes, and we demand such legislation as will bring to certain punishment any officer who, being intrusted with the charge of public funds, appropriates the same to his own use or fails to properly account for them. Embezzlement is theft, and ought to be punished as such.

Resolved, That all the railroad corporations of the State are the creatures of its Legislature, and it is the duty of that body to subject them to such wise and impartial enactments as will protect the people of the State from extortion, and will secure them transportation of products, merchandise, and passengers, at reasonable rates. A revision of the patent-laws of the United States is imperatively demanded, so as to prevent a monopoly of useful inventions, and at the same time to give proper encouragement and remuneration to inventors.

Resolved, That the present peace policy of dealing with the Indians has failed to afford adequate protection to the frontier settlers, and we are in favor of transferring the Indian Bureau to the control of the War Department.

Resolved, That we commend the action of Congress in repealing the act known as the back-pay law, and favor an amendment to the national Constitution which shall forever prohibit any Congress from increasing its own compensation.

Resolved, That drunkenness is one of the greatest curses of modern society, demoralizing every thing it touches, imposing fearful burdens of taxation upon the people, a fruitful breeder of pauperism and crime, and a worker of evil and only evil continually; hence we are in favor of such legislation, both general and local, as experience shall show to be most effectual in destroying this evil.

Resolved, That we rejoice with the citizens residing on the Osage ceded lands over the late decision of the Circuit Court in their favor, and point to that decision as evidence that the rights of the people are safe in the hands of the courts.

Resolved, That the unwritten law enacted by the example of the Father of his Country, in declining a reëlection to a third presidential term, is as controlling as though it was incorporated in the national Constitution, and ought never to be violated.

Resolved, That the public lands of the United States are sacredly held for the use and benefit of the actual settlers, and we condemn and disapprove of any further grants of the public domain to railroads and other corporations.

The election took place on the 3d of November, and resulted in the choice of the Republican candidates. The total vote for Governor was 84,132, of which Osborn received 48,824, and Cusey 35,308, making the former's majority 13,516. There was a temperance candidate, W. K. Marshall, who received 2,277 votes. The majority of the Republican candidates for the other State offices was about 20,000. Two Republican and one Democratic member of Congress were chosen at the same time. The Legislature of 1875, chosen at the same election, consists of 21 Republicans, 9 Reformers, and 3 Democrats, in the Senate; and 78 Republicans, 12 Reformers, 10 Democrats, and 3 Independents, in the House, with one seat vacant on account of a tie-vote—making the Republican majority 9 in the Senate and 52 in the House, or 61 on a joint ballot.

There was considerable trouble with the Indians on the southwestern border during the summer. In June twenty-six citizens were killed in Ford, Barbour, and Comanche Counties. A portion of the militia was called into service by the Governor and sent to protect the borders, which seems to have been effectually done during the rest of the year.

KASHGAR, also called East Toorkistan, a Mohammedan empire in Central Asia, formerly a part of the Chinese Empire. A revolt of the Tunganes or Dungenes, Mohammedan inhabitants of mixed Tartar and Chinese descent, which broke out in 1863, and was followed by a rising of the Kirghiz Tartars, resulted in a few years in the expulsion of the Chinese, and the subjection of all the revolted provinces to Mohammed Yakub Beg, a military chief from Khokan. Yakub Beg has gradually consolidated his dominion, the area of which in 1874 was estimated at 570,000 square miles, with a population of about 1,000,000.

The establishment of a new state in Central Asia naturally attracted to a high degree the attention of the Governments of Great Britain and Russia, and active negotiations have been carried on by both with Yakub Beg, who at first assumed the title of Attalik-Ghaza (Head of the Warriors). After the return of a special embassy to Constantinople which sought and obtained for him the recognition of sovereign by the Sultan, he changed his former title into Ameer, and his name henceforth will be Ameer Mohammed Yakub Khan.

It may be assumed that the negotiations of both Russia and the British Government in India with Yakub Beg have generally been of a secret character, and are as yet but imperfectly known. The British Government of India in 1873 resolved to recognize Yakub Beg as sovereign, and to send Mr. David Forsyth at the head of a large and brilliant suite to Kashgar, in order to present to the new sovereign letters from the Queen of England and the Viceroy of India, and to negotiate with him a treaty of commerce. The mission arrived in Kashgar in December, 1873, and was received by Yakub Beg with the greatest marks of honor. An agreement concerning a commercial treaty was soon reached, and the treaty signed on February 2, 1874. The English Government, in this document, formally recognized Yakub Beg, his heirs and successors, as rulers of the territory of Kashgar and Yarkand. The subjects of either Government will be at liberty to enter with their goods the territory of the other, to reside there and to carry on commercial pursuits, and they will enjoy the same privileges and advantages as the subjects of the country, or of the most favored nation. These rights are granted for all times and all roads, and all limitations are excluded, except such as may be demanded by urgent political causes. The European subjects of Great Britain who enter the territory of the Ameer must be provided with regular passes. The British Government engages to admit all goods which are introduced into British India from the territory of the Ameer by way of the Himalaya passes, free of duty. On the goods imported into British India from the territory of the Ameer, no duties shall be imposed exceeding 2½ per cent. The British Government has the right of appointing a representative at the court of the Ameer, and commercial agents in all towns and places of British India where he chooses. The Ameer may appoint a representative near the Viceroy, and commercial agents in any place of British India. The British subjects have the right to buy, rent, or sell landed property, houses, or depots for goods, in the territory of the Ameer, and these buildings cannot be forcibly entered except after an understanding with the British representative, or his agents or his delegates. Civil and criminal suits between a British subject and a subject of the Ameer will be decided by a court of the Ameer, but in the presence of the English representative. If one of the two parties is a British subject, and the other the subject of another power, the cases will be decided by the courts of the Ameer, if both parties are of the Mohammedan faith; but if neither is a Mohammedan, the case will be decided by the British representative, if both parties agree; and, by the court of the Ameer, if the parties do not agree. If the British representative believes that justice has not been done in a particular case, he may bring the case to the notice of the Ameer, in order that it may be investigated by another court in the presence of the British representative or his agent. The privileges granted to British subjects are extended to the subjects of all the princes of India who are allies of the Queen of England. In a letter addressed to a friend in England, dated Kashgar, Mr. Forsyth gives the following account of the country and of its ruler Yakub Khan:

So little is known about these regions, and such wild stories have been told about the people and their ruler, that you may be surprised to hear that we find a degree of civilization much superior to any thing in India which is not directly owing to our presence there ; and there is a blessed state of security to both life and property here which people in England might envy. We have been allowed the most perfect freedom of action and motion, and go about freely when and where we like. Being thus able to mix with the peasants, and to see them occupied in their ordinary avocations, we can form a tolerably correct opinion regarding the character of the Ameer's rule. Yakub Khan is a very remarkable man, and owes his success entirely to his own personal qualities. He is a thorough autocrat, and allows no one to interfere with his authority. He looks into every thing himself, even seeing his troops paid in his esen e ; and he keeps all his subordinates in first-rate order, punishing disobedience most severely. These people are naturally in great awe of him, and the Hindostani or Afghans who came over and took service, hoping to enrich themselves by plunder, are considerably disgusted to find the peasantry protected from their grasp by the Ameer. From this class of officials stories of the Ameer's severity are only to be expected ; but instead of sympathizing with them I take it as a good sign of the healthy vigor of the Ameer's administration. Certainly the common people have cause to rejoice ; and we find the markets, which are held here at one place or another every day in the week, thronged by merry-faced men and women, who buy and barter just as if it was a market in England. Food is abundant, and even the poorest classes seem to have meat, and are warmly clad. Theft is a crime of rare occurrence, and murders are almost unknown. We have not seen much of the country yet, however, owing to the intense cold ; but when winter ceases I hope to make an extended journey. We must visit Khoten, as that is a place of note. Jade comes from the rivers which flow by that town, and silk manufactures are carried on. Cotton fabrics, too, come thence, and are exported largely to

Khokan and into Russian territory. The Russians have already established treaty relations with the Ameer, and drive a thriving trade with the Kashgarees. None of their merchants are here at present, but Russian goods are to be seen everywhere. We find on opening the packets, with Russian names outside, that in many cases the goods themselves have English marks. Comparing prices, there is no doubt that English goods sent through India can be sold at a lower figure, with profits, than the same articles fetch brought through Russia ; but as it is evident that, whether by the East or the West route, our goods do find their way here, there is no necessity for us to adopt other than a liberal policy toward Russia. I have an admirable staff of officers, who are making a very valuable collection of information of all kinds, so that my own deficiencies in this respect will not be noticed, I hope.

After the conclusion of this treaty, Mr. Forsyth remained for some time in Kashgar. The permission of the Ameer was obtained for undertaking important expeditions of exploration. The greatest feat connected with these expeditions seems to be that which was performed by Colonel Gordon and his party. When Mr. Forsyth was preparing to return, at the close of the sojourn in Yarkand, arrangements were made with the authorities for a journey to the Great Pamir Steppe. This journey was undertaken by Colonel Gordon, Captain Biddulph, Captain Trotter, and Dr. Stoliczka ; and some idea of the difficulty of the journey may be formed when it is said that this party had to march for twenty days, in deep snow, distances of twenty and twenty-five miles a day. But the journey was successfully performed ; and the Government of India expressed its thanks to these officers individually for the work accomplished by them. The Government of British India attached great importance to the result of these explorations, as its knowledge of Central Asia was greatly improved by it. Mr. Forsyth as well as Colonel Gordon returned to British India in July. The Government of India appointed, as the first British representative in Kashgar, Mr. Shaw, who had previously visited the court of the Ameer, and after his return published a work on his mission, which is still the standard authority on this country.

The negotiations of Russia with Kashgar have been kept very secret. A commercial treaty between the two countries had been concluded in 1872. Subsequently, the relations between them were reported to be less friendly, as the Russians publicly maintained that Russian caravans had been plundered by the Kashgarians. According to English accounts, Yakub Beg, after instituting a full inquiry into the allegations, claimed to have ascertained that these statements were mere inventions on the part of the leaders of the caravans, who had themselves stolen the money and goods of their employers, and then attributed the loss to imaginary Kashgarian robbers. All the documents on the subject were forwarded to Tashkend, and Yakub Beg at the same time notified the Russian Government that, although it was clear that the Kashgarians were not to blame for the losses sustained by the Russian merchants, he had given directions for compensating them, in order to keep up his friendly relations with the Russian Government. In the latter part of the year Russian accounts claimed that the relations between the two countries had again become very friendly.

Toward the close of the year 1874 the Government of China collected two armies on the frontier of Kashgar. The smaller of these armies was surrounded, about 270 miles east of Kaltcha, by detachments of Dungenes, and it was believed that it would soon disentangle itself, and then continue its march westward. A larger army was operating against the bulk of the Kashgarian army, which was commanded by Kuli Beg, a son of Yakub Khan. Kashgarian troops, on the other hand, were marching northward along the Thian-shan, against Barkul.

KAULBACH, WILHELM VON, a German historical and allegorical painter, the most eminent representative of the Düsseldorf or Cornelius School, born at Arolsen, in the principality of Waldeck, October 15, 1805; died of cholera at Munich, Bavaria, April 7, 1874. His father was a goldsmith, who also possessed considerable skill as an engraver and miniature-painter. He wished his son to become an artist, but the boy himself had no apparent liking for art, preferring literature. His childhood was sad and unhappy, and but for the misfortunes of his family, which resulted in their removal from Arolsen, his study of drawing under his father, and the falling into his hands of some engravings illustrating Schiller's dramas which he had seen acted, he might never have become a painter. But the genius for painting, once aroused, became thenceforward predominant. In 1822 his father sent him to the Academy at Düsseldorf, where he came at once under the teaching and influence of Cornelius, the director and virtual founder of what is known as the Düsseldorf School of Art. He proved a docile pupil, and acquired rapidly his master's style and ideas, yet even in his crudest early performances there was evident an originality which would not at all times submit to be bound by the conventionalities, the allegorical symbolical ideas of the Düsseldorf School. In 1825 he followed Cornelius to Munich, and there painted in fresco on the ceiling of the Odeon his first important work, "Apollo surrounded by the Muses." This was followed by allegorical representations of German rivers, painted also in fresco, on the academy walls of the Hofgarten, in 1828-'29. Three or four years before he had been sent to paint in allegorical figures the chapel of the Lunatic Asylum at Düsseldorf, and the director of the asylum, becoming interested in him, had him taken over the whole establishment. The impressions he then received would not leave him, and he made studies of them, and in 1828 painted his picture, "The Lunatic Asylum." The work

is in many respects painful and repulsive; on the faces are depicted all the dark and gloomy passions; but it is intensely real; all the figures live, and breathe, and suffer. He returned to the allegorical and mystic style in his frescoes, in the Royal Palace at Munich, from subjects found in the poems of Wieland, Klopstock, and Goethe, as well as in his sixteen mural paintings for Prince Birkenfeld, on the fable of Cupid and Psyche. In 1887 he painted "The Battle of the Huns," the subject of which was an old legend which represented that above the field of battle, on which lay the corpses of the slain Romans and Huns, their spirits again met in fierce and deadly battle. This was Kaulbach's masterpiece, and the world recognized the genius shown in it with ample plaudits. It has been admirably engraved, like nearly everything that Kaulbach has done, and the reader may easily study it for himself. Kaulbach is no colorist, and his pictures lose nothing by being engraved, so that in these severe outlines lightly shaded we get all that the master could give us in the original frescoes or in his oil-paintings. "The Battle of the Huns" was executed in sepia for Count Raczynski. It shows skill in composition, power in drawing, academic knowledge of all kinds, but better than all these proofs of learning are the rush, the fury, the concentration, that make this little patch of earth and air our world for the time we fix our eyes upon it. The following winter appeared his most charming work, the illustrations to "Reynard the Fox." This is an admirable work, not only from the thorough knowledge of animals it displays and the life and character it imparts to them, but from the deep vein of humor, the satirical power, and the profound knowledge of human character, which it evinces, and of which there are so few traces in his other works. His "Group of Bedouins" was also produced in 1888, and the first sketch of his "Destruction of Jerusalem," a colossal picture, which he finished for the Pinakothek of King Louis of Bavaria in 1846. Von Kaulbach's renown had now extended throughout Germany, and he was called to Berlin to decorate the New Museum with six grand historic compartments. "The Tower of Babel," one of the largest of his frescoes, a reproduction of his "Battle of the Huns," and of "The Destruction of Jerusalem," the colossal figures of "Moses," "Solon," "History," "Legend," etc., and a long frieze of allegorical subjects, completed five of these frescoes. The sixth and last was "The Reformation," completed in 1860. He then returned to Munich, and painted for the Pinakothek a series of frescoes representing the "History of Art since the Renaissance." The most noted of his later works was "The Epoch of the Reformation," exhibited at the Paris Exposition in 1867; but he had also painted many portraits and designed a host of illustrations of great value and interest, including a series for the Gospels, engraved both in Germany and England, and a series for the plays of Shakespeare. Herr von Kaulbach had been made a member of most of the art and scientific academies of Europe, and had received the decorations of numerous orders. He was a corresponding member of the French Institute, and had been a Chevalier of the Legion of Honor since 1855, and an officer since 1867.

KENTUCKY. The session of the Legislature of Kentucky which began on the 1st of December, 1873, continued until the 23d of February. Five hundred and ninety-six acts and twenty-five joint resolutions were adopted, nearly all of which were of a private or local character and of no general interest. Provision was made for submitting to a vote of the people at the next regular election the question of holding a convention to revise and amend the constitution of the State. The time for the meeting of the General Assembly was changed from the first Monday of December to the 31st day of December, provided that if that day falls on Sunday the session shall begin on

TRANSYLVANIA UNIVERSITY, AT LEXINGTON.

the 30th. For the first time a general law was enacted for the regulation of the sale of intoxicating liquors, but it is far from stringent in its provisions. Early in the session the Governor had, by special message, submitted a memorial from the "Blue Grass Temperance Convention" and the "Grand Lodge of Good Templars," bearing the signatures of over 147,000 citizens, praying for the passage of a bill which accompanied the memorial, for "regulating the license and sale of intoxicating drinks and liquors." The Governor did not recommend the adoption of this particular measure, but urged the importance and necessity of more stringent legislation on the subject. The act which was passed merely provides that on petition of twenty legal voters in any civil district, town, or city, in any county, the judge of

the county court shall direct an election to be held in such district or town on the question whether spirituous liquors shall be sold therein, and, if a majority of the voters vote against it, then "it shall be unlawful for any person to sell any spirituous, vinous, or malt liquors, in said district, town, or city, to any person," on penalty of a fine of not less than $25 nor more than $100. The provisions of the act do not apply to the sale by wholesale or by druggists for medicinal purposes on a physician's prescription. An act was passed establishing a State Board of Pharmacy to examine and give certificates to such persons as shall be qualified to practise as pharmacists or assistant pharmacists, and making it unlawful for any person not a "registered pharmacist, or registered assistant pharmacist in the employ of a registered pharmacist, or acting as an aid under the immediate supervision of a registered pharmacist, or a registered assistant pharmacist," to retail, compound, or dispense medicines or poisons.

Another act makes it "unlawful for any person, for reward or compensation, within the limits of this State, to practise medicine in any of its departments, or prescribe or attempt to prescribe medicine for any sick person, or perform or attempt to perform any surgical operation upon any person within said limits, who has not graduated at some chartered school of medicine in this or some foreign country, or who cannot produce a certificate of qualification from some one of the boards of examiners provided for in this act, and is not a person of good moral character." The boards of examiners are to consist of five persons in each judicial district, "practising physicians of acknowledged learning and ability," appointed by the Governor for a term of four years. The examiners are to hold annual sessions, beginning on the first Monday in June, to receive applications and examine applicants, and grant or refuse certificates of qualification to practise in medicine. Penalties by fine and imprisonment are provided for any one practising as a physician in violation of this law.

An act was approved on the last day of the session providing for a "uniform system of common schools for the colored children of this Commonwealth." A separate school-fund for the support of these schools is provided, consisting of "the present annual revenue tax of twenty-five cents, and twenty cents in addition, on each $100 in value of the taxable property owned and held by colored persons;"

a capitation tax of one dollar on each male colored person above the age of twenty-one; all taxes levied and collected on dogs owned or kept by colored persons; all State taxes on deeds, suits, or on any license, collected from colored persons; all fines, penalties, and forfeitures, collected from colored persons, except the portion allowed to attorneys of the Commonwealth; a *pro rata* share of the proceeds from any public lands given by the United States; and all sums arising from any donation, gift, grant, or devise, expressly designed to aid in the education of colored children. The revenue arising from these sources is to be distributed by the Superintendent of Public Instruction in the same manner as already provided by law. Provision is made for collecting and distributing the moneys; county school commissioners are required to divide the counties into school districts, so that no district shall contain more than 120 colored children between six and sixteen years of age; three "colored school trustees" are to be appointed in each district by the commissioner, to employ a teacher not less than three months in each year, or two months if there are not more than sixty children in the district, and to manage the schools generally; it is made unlawful for any colored child to attend a common school provided for white children, or for any white child to attend a common school provided for colored children; "no school-house erected for a colored school shall be located nearer than one mile to a school-house erected for white children, except in cities and towns, where it shall not be nearer than six hundred feet;" colored school officers and teachers are allowed to form a State association and county institutes; the State Board of Education is required to prescribe a course of study and rules of government for the colored schools; and provisions of the general school laws "deemed necessary for the government of colored common schools, not in conflict with this act, shall apply to the same, which shall be determined by the State Board of Education."

The institution formerly known as the House of Reform, and subsequently converted into the "Fourth Kentucky Lunatic Asylum" was declared to be the "Central Kentucky Lunatic Asylum," and $100,000 were appropriated to extend and improve it, one-third to be used in providing accommodation for colored lunatics, to be separate and apart from those for the white inmates. The Institution for the Education and Training of Feeble-minded Children, which had been converted into "the Third Kentucky Lunatic Asylum," was reëstablished for its original purpose, under the charge of nine commissioners, to be appointed by the Governor.

The only State officer elected at the regular election on the 3d of August was a Clerk of the Court of Appeals. The total vote was 167,-852, of which T. C. Jones, the Democratic candidate, received 114,348, or a majority of 60,-844. Ten members of Congress were elected.

In the first district A. R. Boon had a majority of 81,000 over Turner, Independent Democrat; second district, John Young Brown had a majority of 3,517 over Smith, Republican—Edward R. Weir, Independent Republican, receiving 757 votes; third district, Charles W. Milliken, Democrat, had a majority of 4,789 over Goren, Independent; fourth district, J. Proctor Knott, Democrat, had a majority of 3,581; fifth district, Edward G. Parsons, Democrat, had a majority of 5,441; sixth district, Thomas S. Jones, Democrat, had a majority of 3,127; seventh district, J. C. S. Blackburn, Democrat, had a majority of 6,253; eighth district, Milton J. Durham, Democrat, had a majority of 7,813; ninth district, John D. White, Republican, had a majority of 629; tenth district, John B. Clarke, Democrat, had a majority of 2,998. The Legislature now stands, 31 Democrats and 7 Republicans in the Senate, and 80 Democrats and 20 Republicans in the House, making the Democratic majority in the Senate 24, in the House 60 or 84 on a joint ballot. No session of the Legislature was begun in December, as that body meets biennially.

KHOKAN, or KOKAN, a country of Central Asia, one of the three great khanates of West Toorkistan, or Independent Tartary, attracted in 1874 greater attention than the other independent states of Toorkistan by the outbreak of a new civil war and the interference of the Russians. The country is bounded southwest, west, north, and northeast, by the new Russian province of Sir Darya, east and southeast by East Toorkistan, and south by the Pamir plateau and the Karateghin. The area of the khanate is, according to a map published in 1872 by the Russian Staff-General, estimated at 28,270 square miles. The population, according to the concurrent opinion of the best recent authorities, especially the Russian traveler Fedshenke, is considerably below the former estimate of 3,000,000, and is believed not to exceed 800,000. A new crisis in the history of this country appears to have come, and Russia is urged, on many sides, to put an end to the internal disorders by the annexation of the entire country.

A brief review of the reign of the present Khan, Khudayar, is necessary to understand fully the recent events. The Khan is now fifty-nine years old, and by descent a Karakirghiz, or Turk. If the time when his uncle, Musulman Kul, was his guardian (until 1849), and the period from 1857 to 1864, during which the brother of Khudayar, Mollah Khan, or rather his powerful vizier, Alim Kul, was at the head of the government, are included, his reign extends over thirty-one years. The population of Khokan is chiefly composed of the peaceable Sartes, an Iranian tribe, devoted to the arts of peace, to commerce, and industrial pursuits, and the nomadic and warlike Kiptchaks and Karakirghiz, who are of Turkish descent, and inhabit the eastern portion of Khokan. The undisputed rule of the Turkish tribes lasted from 1843 to 1849, in which latter year the Sartes obtained control of the government. They had, in 1857, again to give way to the Turks, who, amid many vicissitudes, maintained their power for about eight years until the death of their leader, Alim Kul, and the victory of the Russians. From this time the Sartes and Khudayar Khan, who fully sympathized with them, had once more absolute control of the government.

Khudayar Khan is the son of Shere Ali, who in 1841 was appointed Khan by the Kiptchaks during the conflicts with Khan Nasr Ullah of Bokhara, the father of the present Khan. In the conflict between the Turks and the Sartes, the former of whom were headed by Yussuf Ming Bashi, or rather the shrewd and energetic Musulman Kul, while the Sardes had as their leader Thade Ming Bashi, the former remained victors, and for eight years Musulman Kul, partly as prime-minister, partly as regent and sovereign, was the ruler of Khokan. During the progress of the conflict, Shere Ali sided with the Sartes; but, when the latter were totally defeated, Musulman Kul reinstated Shere Ali as ruler. Soon after the Sartes again rose in rebellion, and, during the absence of Musulman Kul, defeated Shere Ali; but their power was of short duration, as Musulman Kul suddenly appeared and fully subdued them. Instead of reinstating Shere Ali, Musulman Kul appointed the son of Shere Ali, Khudayar, at that time sixteen years old, as Khan, and remained the guardian of the young prince and the regent of the country. When the Sartes attempted another revolution, and were even favored by the ungrateful Khudayar, they were again totally defeated. Mohammed Kul was, however, unwise enough to reappoint Khudayar as Khan. The latter, to get rid of his guardian, instigated a plot for the assassination of Mohammed Kul, and, when the latter escaped and collected a small army, Khudayar totally defeated him near Ikus, at the confluence of the Marius with the Jaxartes, took him prisoner and had him put to death conjointly with 10,000 Kiptchaks. The undisputed rule of Khudayar and the Sartes lasted until 1857, when the Khan's brother, Mollah Khan, rose in rebellion at the head of the dissatisfied Turks. Khudayar soon saw himself abandoned by most of his adherents, and even his own relatives, and had to flee to the Khan of Bokhara, Nasr Ullah, who made several attempts to restore Khudayar to power, but was every time defeated. After that, Mollah Khan remained for two years in the undisturbed possession of his power; and, when he was assassinated by malcontents of his own party, his prime-minister, Alim Kul, remained at the head of the government until 1864. The attempts of Khudayar, who in the mean while had been elected ruler of Tashkend, to dislodge him from power, were fruitless; but he finally, in 1864, succumbed to the Russians, who marched an army into Bokhara and annexed

three-fourths of the khanate. Alim Kul himself lost his life under the walls of Tashkend. Khudayar Khan now succeeded in seizing again the reins of government. Following the advice of Mirza Hakim Bey, the richest merchant of Khokan, who had several times visited the fairs of Nijui-Novgorod and Poltava, he concluded to enter into negotiations with the Russians for the establishment of friendly relations. Mirza Hakim Bey was appointed plenipotentiary of Khokan, and as such took up his residence at Tashkend. He prevailed upon the Russians to conclude, on February 13, 1868, a treaty of commerce and friendship with Khokan. Khudayar appointed his brother, Sultan Marud, governor of the province of Mergulan, and his eldest son, Nassyr Eddyn Bey, also called Khan Sade, governor of the eastern provinces, with his residence at Andidjan, the centre of the Kiptchak and Karakirghiz. The son of Musulman Kul, Abu Rakhim, also called Abelurrhaman, who seemed to have forgotten the assassination of his father, lived at the court of Khudayar. The trade with Russia considerably increased, and during the winter of 1871 Khan Sade paid a visit to the Russian authorities in Tashkend, where Mirza Hakim gave in his honor a splendid banquet, at which a Russian enthusiast compared the young prince with Peter the Great. In 1873 the dissatisfaction of the Kiptchaks with the rule of Khudayar, which had never ceased, led to a conspiracy, when the Khan imposed a tax upon the wild fruit-trees of the mountains, which constitute an important article of trade for the merchants of Khokan. In consequence of the severe measures adopted by Khan Sade, and the perfidy of Khudayar, who enticed forty government Kiptchaks to his court and then had them assassinated, the Kiptchaks of the northwestern districts rose in open rebellion, and they were soon joined by the Karakirghiz in the south and the southwest. The chief of the latter, Batyr-Khan, a brother-in-law of Khudayar, was likewise assassinated in the palace of the latter. The rebellious Kiptchaks, who had established their headquarters in the town of Kara-Guldja, applied to the Russians for aid, but met with a decided refusal. During the winter of 1873–'74, the leader of the Kiptchaks, Mehemed-Emir, in the popular jargon called Mamir, shut himself up in the almost inaccessible stronghold Kara-Guldja. In 1874, according to the Russian press, this Khan had shown hostile sentiments toward Russia. Mirza Hakim, the plenipotentiary of Khokan at Tashkend, and a decided advocate of maintaining friendly relations with Russia, was deposed, and another merchant, Mir Alim Bei, became the confidential adviser of the Khan. The rebels, in the mean while, began to make considerable progress, and took the towns of Namangan and Korsan. When they, however, encroached upon territory claimed by the Russians, plundering the Jomuels, who are under Russian protection, and stealing 150 camels and four boys, the Russian authorities concluded to interfere and put an end to the insurrection. The disturbed condition of this country was thought by the Russian press to be propitious for the further extension of Russian rule.

KIRK, EDWARD NORRIS, D. D., an eminent American clergyman, author, and pulpit orator, born in New York City, August 14, 1802; died in Boston, March 27, 1874. He was of Scotch ancestry, and was educated at the New York schools and at Princeton College, whence he graduated in 1820. He next studied law for eighteen months in New York City, and then entered Princeton Theological Seminary, where he remained four years. On leaving Princeton he was employed by the American Board of Commissioners for Foreign Missions, to preach on missions to the churches. He was ordained in 1827 as assistant pastor of the Second Presbyterian Church in Albany, and in 1828 became pastor of the Fourth Presbyterian Church, which had been gathered by his labors in the great revivals in which Mr. Finney was so conspicuous. Mr. Kirk coincided with Mr. Finney's views, and in connection with Dr. Beman, of Troy, established a school of theology to train young men for service in the ministry as Evangelists. He also took a very active part with Mr. E. C. Delavan in promoting the temperance reform. In 1837, his health demanding a change, Mr. Kirk resigned his pastorate and went to Europe. He spent somewhat more than a year in Paris, where he and Dr. Baird made themselves very useful; establishing the first American Protestant religious service there, out of which grew the American Chapel, which was afterward built through his exertions, and held in his name till his death. On his return in the spring of 1839, he preached as an Evangelist in the principal cities of the country, his remarkable eloquence and his intense earnestness and faithfulness drawing thousands to hear him wherever he preached. In June, 1842, he accepted the call of the Mount Vernon Congregational Church, Boston, then just organized, to become their pastor, and remained in that relation till 1871, though in 1846 and in 1856 he spent considerable time in Europe. His last visit in 1856 was undertaken at the request of the American and Foreign Christian Union (of which he had long been an officer), to organize and erect a chapel for regular worship for American Protestants in Paris, the result of his labors there nearly twenty years before. He accomplished this work, and after a hasty visit to Palestine returned home. In 1871, in consequence of the infirmities of age and nearly complete blindness, he resigned his pastorate, though preaching occasionally. His death was caused by apoplexy. Dr. Kirk had published very many occasional sermons and addresses; three volumes of collected sermons; a series of "Lectures on Christ's Parables;" and translations of "Gaussen on Inspiraion" and of Attic's "Lectures on the Liter-

ature of the Times of Louis XIV.," besides several smaller works. He received the degree of D. D. from Amherst College in 1855.

KNAPP, Rev. JACOB, an American evangelist and revivalist, born in Central New York, in 1800; died in Rockland, Ill., March 2, 1874. His early life was passed upon a farm, but when he approached manhood he felt the necessity of a better education, especially as he believed himself called to preach. He accordingly, after a brief preparatory course, entered the Hamilton Literary and Theological Institution (now Madison University) in 1820 and remained there nearly four years. He was but a dull scholar, his early hard life on the farm having made the confinement irksome to him, or, as he himself used to say in after-life, "Hard work had made his blood too thick for any thing but failure as a student." Still there were about him even then a resistless energy, great powers of endurance, a cool self-possession, and an almost Hibernian readiness of wit. He left the institution before the completion of his full course, commenced preaching and giving vent to his overflowing energy, by managing a farm and conducting a country store at the same time. He was somewhat successful in all these pursuits, but this could not last. After two or three years of what was to him an unsatisfactory life, he passed through what he regarded as a new conversion, which led him to consecrate his life and all his powers fully to the service of God. He commenced his work as an evangelist, not knowing whence the support of his family was to come, but very soon, from small beginnings in country hamlets, he was called to the larger towns and cities, and, though at times his manners and language seemed rough, there were such earnestness, such intensity of feeling, such deep tenderness, and such genuine eloquence in his sermons and prayers, that none who listened could fail to be impressed by them. This effect was produced as surely among men of the highest culture as among the illiterate. The late President Nott, himself one of the most eloquent preachers and orators of the present century, attended his entire course of sermons in Schenectady, and took copious notes of them, and said repeatedly in public that, "as a preacher of the Gospel, Jacob Knapp was unequaled among uninspired men." "I could publish a volume of his sermons from my notes," he added, "that would be a credit to our first preachers." Mr. Knapp had held protracted religious services in almost every city and large town in the Northern States during his forty years' labors as an evangelist, and, though he had been oftentimes surrounded by howling mobs, infuriated by his vigorous denunciation of popular vices, he was never injured and never unsuccessful. Many thousands were improved in heart and life by his earnest words and prayers, and many others, in whom the change was not so thorough or enduring, were yet for the time transformed and made to have aspirations for a better life. For four or five years past his health had failed, and he had resided on his farm near Rockford, Ill. Some of his sermons have been published, and are admirable specimens of earnest appeals and inexorable logic.

KNOWLTON, Rev. MILES JUSTIN, D. D., a Baptist clergyman, missionary, Orientalist, and author, born in West Wardsboro', Vt., February 8, 1825, died in Ningpo, China, September 10, 1874. He was educated in Madison University and Hamilton Theological Seminary, N. Y., graduating from the latter in 1853, and having been ordained in his native town in October, sailed as a missionary with his wife, for Ningpo, China, December 10, 1853. He entered upon his work with great zeal, acquired the difficult language in a very short time, and so thoroughly mastered its literature and philosophy, that some time before his death an eminent native Chinese scholar said to Bishop Russell, "Teacher Knowlton is regarded by us all as the Confucius of the West." With all his cares, preaching several times a week, translating books and tracts, managing the mission

church, and teaching a theological class, it is not surprising that his health gave way; in 1862 he was obliged to return to the United States for rest and restoration. In about eighteen months he returned to his work with a constitution still vigorous and capable of great endurance, but in addition to his other duties he undertook the preparation of a work on China which he believed to be needed, and for the preparation of which he was eminently qualified.. This great labor was performed in the rare intervals of leisure (much of it taken from the hours which should have been devoted to rest) which his other engrossing duties permitted, but it is a work of extensive and profound research, and will remain as a standard authority on the customs, habits, manners, religion, and literature of the Chinese. It was published by the American Baptist Publication Society. His excessive labors had weakened his constitution so much that, when he had an attack of dysentery, about September 1st, he succumbed to it almost immediately. He received the degree of D. D. from Madison University in 1871.

L

LAIRD, JOHN, M. P., a English ship-builder and Conservative member of Parliament for Birkenhead, most widely known, both in Europe and America, as the builder of the Alabama, and other Confederate privateers; born in Greenock, Scotland, in 1805; died in Birkenhead, after a long illness, October 29, 1874. He was a son of the late William Laird, was educated at the Royal Institution, Liverpool, and in 1829, at the age of twenty-four, commenced the business of iron-ship-building and engineering, which in time grew into the great house of John Laird, Sons & Co. He retired from active participation in the business of this house in October, 1861. He was for forty years and more an active promoter of the docks and all other public works and improvements at Birkenhead; was for many years chairman of the Birkenhead Improvement Commissioners, and one of the Government Trustees of the Mersey Docks and Harbor Board. He was a deputy-lieutenant and a magistrate for Cheshire, and was first elected to Parliament in December, 1861. In politics he was a Liberal Conservative, and was decidedly opposed to the disestablishment of the Irish Church, as leading to the disestablishment of the English Church. He was, however, in favor of great reforms in the former, and the extension of its usefulness. He was also in favor of extending education among all classes, and of the exercise of economy in the naval expenditures. During our late civil war he made himself conspicuous in Parliament by his advocacy of the Confederate cause, and his incessant attacks on the United States Federal Government.

His firm built the Alabama, the Florida, the Shenandoah, and several other privateers, and numerous blockade-runners for the Confederates, and, after the Geneva arbitration, when it was found that $15,500,000 had been awarded to the United States for damages caused by these privateers, Mr. Laird became exceedingly unpopular in Great Britain. "His memory" (said one of the London papers) " will be long kept green in the budget, and he has an enduring monument in the taxation of his countrymen."

LANMAN, Rear-Admiral JOSEPH, U. S. N., a brave and highly-esteemed naval officer, forty-nine years in the service; born in Norwich, Conn., July 18, 1810; died in that city, March 13, 1874. He was appointed midshipman from Connecticut, January 1, 1825; was commissioned lieutenant in March, 1835; commander, September, 1855; captain, 1861; commodore, August 29, 1862; and rear-admiral in 1869. He commanded the frigate Minnesota in the North-Atlantic blockading squadron in 1864–'65, was in command of the second division of Porter's squadron at the two attacks on Fort Fisher, and was admiral of the South-Atlantic Squadron on the coast of Brazil, from 1869 to 1871, and on his return in May, 1872, received leave of absence, and, his health failing, retired to Norwich, where he remained till his death. His genial manners won for him the cordial respect of all his associates and acquaintances.

LEDRU-ROLLIN, ALEXANDRE AUGUSTE, originally only LEDRU, a French statesman, cabinet minister, politician, and reformer, born in Paris, February 2, 1807; died in that city,

December 31, 1874. He was the son of an eminent and wealthy physician, Dr. Jacques Philippe Ledru, and only assumed the addition *Rollin* in 1830, which belonged to his mother's family, to distinguish himself from another advocate, M. Charles Ledru, of about his own age. He was educated in the best schools in Paris, studied law at the university, passed his examination and received his diploma in 1828, and was admitted to the bar in 1830. A paper on the proclamation of martial law in Paris during the insurrection of 1832 established his ability as a lawyer, and he was employed as counsel by most of the republican conspirators who were prosecuted under Louis Philippe. In these trials he gained considerable popularity by the boldness of his style, and soon became the avowed representative of the Communist interest. In 1837 he assumed the editorship of the *Journal du Palais*, a leading law journal, and occupied this position for ten years. He also superintended the publication of several works on French jurisprudence, including a digest of decisions in the courts from 1795 to 1837, which he prefaced with an introduction on the influence of the French school on law in the nineteenth century, a history of law, of legislation, and of the teachings of eminent jurists under the Empire and the Restoration. This was subsequently extended to the period ending in 1845. He filled the position of chief editor of *Le Droit*, a daily law journal. In 1838 he purchased the position of attorney at the Court of Cassation, a position which he abandoned for politics in 1846. He had acquired a great reputation for eloquence and fearlessness in his advocacy of republican views, and in 1839 was nominated for a deputy in the National Assembly from St.-Valery-sur-Somme, but lacked 11 votes of a majority. In 1841 he was returned as a deputy from Mans, in the department of Sarthe, to fill the vacancy caused by the death of Etienne Garnier-Pages. His address to the electors, boldly avowing his republican sympathies, was made the occasion of a prosecution against him by the Government, which, in spite of the eloquent defense of Odilon-Barrot, Berryer, and Marie, sentenced him to four months' imprisonment and a fine of 3,000 francs; but this decision was annulled and the Government defeated on an appeal to the Court of Cassation. Thus ushered into the Chamber of Deputies, M. Ledru-Rollin became naturally the chief of the extreme Left, or "The Mountain," as it began to be called in allusion to the times of the earlier Revolution. But notwithstanding his extraordinary eloquence, M. Ledru-Rollin was too intensely radical to maintain cordial relations with the more moderate Republicans and Radicals of the Left, and had not sufficient tact to rally round him and retain the support of any very considerable following, and hence he was for several years a general without soldiers, and exerted but little influence in the Chamber. Outside, his radical views, his intense earnest-

ness, and his brilliant oratorical powers, as well as his devotion to the interests of the laboring-classes, made him very popular with his constituents, and caused his return at the successive elections by acclamation. In 1844 he visited Ireland, his wife being a wealthy Irish lady, and was received with great honors by the populace, though O'Connell treated him coldly. In 1845, finding that the *National*, the republican organ, was determined to oppose him, he established a new journal, *La Réforme*, and installed Flocon as editor. His social manifesto of 1845, while securing him the support of the lower ranks of society, estranged from him that of the middle classes, and his uncompromising support of the doctrine of universal suffrage displeased the monarchical opposition headed by Odilon-Barrot and others. He took a leading part in all the republican demonstrations in the provinces in 1847, and, when the revolution broke out, became for a short time its acknowledged leader, being chiefly instrumental in preventing the regency of the Duchess of Orleans from being accepted by the Chamber of Deputies, and in securing the powerful aid of Lamartine. On the organization of the Provisional Government he was one of its members, and accepted the portfolio of Minister of the Interior. But the cabinet thus improvised contained elements so incongruous that their harmonious action was impossible. Every shade of sentiment was represented, from the mild and conciliatory republicanism of Lamartine, the stalwart democracy of Berryer, and the eloquent but considerate sympathy of Ledru-Rollin for the struggling masses, to the fierce radicalism of Louis Blanc. For the moment, Ledru-Rollin was the favorite of both the *bourgeoisie* and the *ouvriers*, or working-men, and loud were the clamors that he should assume the dictatorship. But, with a patriotism worthy of all honor, he put aside promptly all such suggestions, and, though disapproving many of the measures of his colleagues in private, gave them his public sanction, in order that there might be no indications of want of harmony in the ministry, till the *bourgeoisie* came to denounce and hate him for acts which he had most heartily protested against in private. He was also held responsible for the publication of the *Bulletins de la République*, supposed at the time to be the production of George Sand. Nevertheless, by his zeal and courage, he materially assisted in maintaining tranquillity in Paris, protected Emile de Girardin from a mob, defeated the insurrectionary attempt of April 16th, and reconciled the democrats to the return of the army to the capital. In the insurrection of May 15th he aided in defeating the object of the insurgents, but courageously defended Louis Blanc and Caussidière, who were accused before the Assembly. After the insurrection of June 24th, Ledru-Rollin resumed his seat in the Assembly, and his splendid speeches in explanation of the insurrection, and against the sending of a French army into Italy, were particularly admired. In the presidential election of 1848 he received only 370,119 votes, while Louis Napoleon received 5,000,000, and Cavaignac nearly 1,500,000. His eloquent appeals in behalf of a truly republican government somewhat revived his popularity during the first part of 1849. He fraternized with the advanced republicans, and at the elections of that year was chosen by five departments. This display of popular support encouraged him to a still more hearty opposition to the Government, and especially to present himself as the defender of the Roman Republic, which had been crushed by the arms of France. On June 13th he and his adherents attempted an insurrectionary demonstration in Paris; but, before they had time to take any decisive measures, the insurgents were surrounded by troops and completely overpowered. Ledru-Rollin, after remaining concealed for about three weeks, escaped to Belgium and thence to England, whence he directed a solemn protest against the decree summoning him before the High Court of Justice. He was sentenced by default to transportation for life. In 1850 he published a notable work on the decline of England, and from time to time produced other books and pamphlets, all characterized by extreme views. He fraternized with the leading revolutionists, such as Mazzini, Kossuth, and Ruge, and in 1857 was again condemned by default to transportation for being concerned in a plot against Napoleon III. His name was excepted from the general amnesty of 1860, and he continued the unrelenting enemy of the imperial *régime*. In 1869 he was again excepted by name from the general amnesty of that year; but in 1870, during the short administration of Emile Ollivier, he was amnestied and allowed to reënter France, and on March 25th made his appearance in Paris, after an absence of more than twenty years. He was returned to the National Assembly for three departments in February, 1871, but resigned at once, having previously refused to be a candidate. He had since remained in retirement. Besides the works already named, M. Ledru-Rollin had published: "Orations and Pleadings;" "A Letter to M. de Lamartine, on the State, the Church, and Education" (1844); "On Pauperism in the Rural Districts, and the Reforms needed to abolish Mendicity;" and several pamphlets disavowing all connection with the socialists.

LITERATURE AND LITERARY PROGRESS IN 1874. According to statistical data, our literature flourished during the past year, for the Librarian of Congress reports an increase in the number of copyrights over that of the year preceding. But here, if figures do not lie, they at least convey an erroneous impression. Including school-books and ephemeral publications of all sorts, the mass of printed leaves that come legitimately under the name of books may have been larger, but

of literature proper there was a diminished amount. Yet, it is a good token that, when account is taken of the number of copies circulated, some of the best books have had a clear advantage above their inferiors. It will be found, also, in noticing the works of which an account is given in the following pages, that, though the number of important productions in the higher departments of literature is not large, yet enough will be recognized as of such superior merit that they make up in weight some part of what they lack in number.

HISTORY.—In this important department of composition, more perhaps than in any other, contributions of enduring value have been made to our literature. Mr. Bancroft's tenth volume, completing his standard "History of the United States," is worthy of the reputation won by his previous volumes. His treatment of the military operations in the Revolutionary War has occasioned no little controversy, but no room has been left to question the value of the material he has gathered to illustrate the diplomatic relations of the war, which he has used with brilliant effect. It is to be regretted that he did not select a later period for the termination of his work. A narrative covering the interval between the acknowledgment of American independence and the organization of the national government, from the materials he must have at his command, would throw light on a portion of our annals that has not been heretofore adequately explored. In "The Life and Death of John of Barneveld," Mr. Motley has furnished a valuable and deeply-interesting continuation of his historical works on the Netherlands, while he permits us to regard it as the promise of another brilliant work—a history of the Thirty Years' War. "The Old Régime in Canada," by Francis Parkman, carries forward the admirable series, in which the author is tracing the course of French exploration and attempted colonization on this continent. A work of historical importance, though autobiographical in form, in course of publication, is the "Memoirs of John Quincy Adams, comprising Portions of his Diary from 1796 to 1848," edited by Charles Francis Adams. A second volume of Vice-President Wilson's "History of the Rise and Fall of the Slave Power" covers an important portion of that epoch of our political history which was closed by the Civil War. His narrative is not specially brilliant, but is remarkable for its dispassionate treatment of a strife in which the author bore so prominent a part. To the materials for a history of the war itself, some valuable contributions have been made. "Lincoln and Seward," by ex-Secretary Welles, controversial in tone and not free from the asperity of political partisanship, yet embodies statements of fact by a competent witness that cannot well be neglected by a future historian of President Lincoln's Administration. "The Life of Rear-Admiral Andrew Hull Foote," by

Prof. Hoppin, at once commemorates an heroic character, records an important part of the operations by which the military power of the Confederacy was broken, and adds to our literary treasures one of the most charming of biographies. Of similar interest, but subordinating public to personal topics, is "Personal Reminiscences, Anecdotes, and Letters of General Robert E. Lee," by the Rev. J. William Jones, D. D. A work making no pretension to the dignity of history, but giving a clearer insight into the spirit of the Confederate soldiers than many formal histories, is the volume entitled "A Rebel's Recollections," by George Cary Eggleston. The defeated "rebel" eats no humble pie for the propitiation of the "loyal," but tells in manly fashion why and how they fought, and how they took the inevitable defeat when it came. In the department of ecclesiastical history there have appeared some works of permanent value. "The History of the Missions of the American Board of Commissioners for Foreign Missions in India," by the Rev. Dr. Anderson, for forty years Corresponding Secretary of the Board, is of the highest authority as to the facts it embodies; the venerable author, besides having access to the records of his office, interpreting them in the light of his protracted administrative experience, and bringing to their exposition a sagacious judgment and a high degree of literary culture. "The Genesis of the New England Churches," by the Rev. Dr. Leonard Bacon, is written in sympathy with the religious movement it recounts, but without bitterness toward those to whom he is antipathetic. The story he tells has been told before, but scarcely ever so well told. A work of much value in the philosophy of history is "Democracy and Monarchy in France, from the Inception of the Great Revolution to the Fall of the Second Empire," by Prof. O. K. Adams, of the University of Michigan. The publication of a new edition of the historical works of William H. Prescott, with his final revisions, gives a new lease of popularity to a series of productions which men *should* not willingly let die. We find also the following, which can be only mentioned:

Outlines of the World's History, Ancient, Mediæval and Modern, with Special Reference to the History of Civilization and the Progress of Mankind. By William Swinton, M. A., Professor in the University of California.

The Four Civilizations of the World. An Historical Retrospect. By Henry Wikoff.

Phœnicia and Israel. An Historical Essay. By Augustus S. Wilkins, M. A.

Ancient Greece, from the Earliest Times, down to the Death of Alexander. By R. F. Pennell, instructor in Phillips Exeter Academy.

A Manual of Universal Church History. By Rev. John Alzog, D. D. Translated from the German by F. J. Pabisch, D. D., and Rev. Thomas S. Byrne, of Mount St. Mary's of the West.

A Comparative History of Religions. By J. C. Moffat. Vol. II., completing the work.

The Presbyterian Church throughout the World, from the Earliest to the Latest Times, in a Series of Historical and Biographical Sketches.

History of the German Emperors and their Contemporaries. Translated from the German, and compiled from Authentic Sources, by Elizabeth Peake.

A History of Germany, from the Earliest Times. Founded on Dr. David Müller's History of the German People. By Charlton T. Lewis.

A School History of Germany, from the Earliest Period to the Establishment of the German Empire in 1871. By Bayard Taylor.

America not discovered by Columbus. An Historical Sketch of the Discovery of America by the Norsemen in the Tenth Century. By R. B. Anderson, A. M., of the University of Wisconsin. With an Appendix on the Historical, Linguistic, Literary, and Scientific Value of the Scandinavian Languages.

A History of the Origin of the Appellation "Keystone State," as applied to the Commonwealth of Pennsylvania. Together with Extracts from Many Authorities relative to the Adoption of the Declaration of Independence by the Continental Congress, etc.

The Heroism of Hannah Duston, together with the Indian Wars of New England. By Robert B. Caverly.

The History of the College of William and Mary (including the General Catalogue), from its Foundation, in 1660, to 1874.

The Secret Service in the Late War. By General L. C. Baker, Late Chief of the National Detective Police.

History of the American Ambulance in Paris. By T. W. Evans.

BIOGRAPHY.—"The Life of Thomas Jefferson," by James Parton, like others of Mr. Parton's works, but in an eminent degree, is readable. He has the art of effective selection, and of so presenting the facts which make for his purpose as to win the unsuspecting reader's confidence. At the same time he undoubtedly deserves the credit of sincerity and the full purpose of dealing fairly with his subject and with all other men. But his admiration for his hero is too great to make his representations of those who held antagonistic positions toward him altogether trustworthy. The late Chief-Justice Chase selected beforehand his biographer. He was said by some who most admired him to have been a poor judge of character, and readers of the authorized biography will think that selection an instance in proof. While Judge Waldron is undoubtedly a man worthy of the respect with which Judge Chase regarded him, the most amiable critic would find it impossible to regard his book as successful. Another account of the "Life and Public Services" of Mr. Chase, by J. W. Schuckers, his private secretary, is a much more creditable piece of work, very full on the public, and sufficiently so on the private and domestic relations, of the Chief-Justice. The life of Theodore Parker was written by Mr. Weiss in two volumes that without much literary skill, yet with great fullness, gave the thoughtful reader the means of fairly estimating their subject. But the work was too voluminous for extensive circulation, and is not likely to be republished. A more serviceable life of Parker for the general reader, more compact in plan and more attractive in style, is the volume by the Rev.

O. B. Frothingham. The Hon. John Bigelow, who had the good fortune to discover a perfect copy of Dr. Franklin's autobiography, has made up, from this and his printed correspondence and other works, a "Life of Benjamin Franklin written by himself." It has been very successfully done, and forms what may well be received as the standard popular biography. Dr. William B. Sprague, whose researches into American ecclesiastical biography are unequaled and incomparable, has put forth a "Life of Jedidiah Morse, D. D.," the father of the late Prof. Morse and Mr. Sidney E. Morse, and a man of merited distinction on his own account. The memory of an almost forgotten celebrity is pleasantly revived in the "Memoir, Letters, and a Selection from the Poems and Prose Writings of Anna Letitia Barbauld," by Grace A. Ellis. The correspondence of Miss Lucy Aikin—a niece of Mrs. Barbauld, and a lady of some literary credit— with Dr. William Ellery Channing has been liberated from its state of suppression, to which both parties had voted it, and forms a volume of biographical interest. If it cannot be said that any new developments are made of Dr. Channing's character or sentiments, still these are seen in some new lights, and show to advantage. Two characters of our Revolutionary era are recalled to notice in Mr. F. S. Drake's "Life of General Henry Knox," and a new edition of the "Memoir of the Life of Josiah Quincy, Jr., of Massachusetts, by Josiah Quincy, with Additions," edited by Eliza Susan Quincy. Also the following:

The Life of Samuel F. B. Morse, Inventor of the Recording Telegraph. By Samuel Irenæus Prime.
The Life of Edwin Forrest, with Reminiscences and Personal Recollections of the Great American Tragedian. By James Rees. With Portrait and Autographs.
Life of George Dashiell Bayard, late Captain U. S. A. and Brigadier-General of Volunteers. By Samuel J. Bayard.
The Life of Rudolph Stier, from German Sources. By John P. Lacroix.
Life and Public Services of Charles Sumner. By C. Edwards Lester.
Sketches of Illustrious Soldiers. By James Grant Wilson.
The History of a Great Mind. A Survey of the Education and Opinions of John Stuart Mill. By B. A. Hinsdale, A. M., President of Hiram College.
Life of Charles Sumner. By J. and J. D. Chaplin. With an Introduction by William Claflin, lately Governor of Massachusetts.
Life of David Crockett. By J. S. C. Abbott.
Rev. Phineas Stowe, and Bethel Work. By Rev. H. A. Cooke.
Memorial of Thomas Ewing, of Ohio.
The Life and Times of Charles Sumner; his Boyhood, Education, and Public Career. By the Rev. Elias Nason.
Reminiscences, Sketches, and Addresses, selected from my Papers during a Ministry of Forty-five Years, in Mississippi, Louisiana, and Texas. By Rev. J. R. Hutchison, D. D.
Tell it All: The Story of a Life's Experience in Mormonism. An Autobiography. By Mrs. T. B. H. Stenhouse.
A Memorial of Charles Sumner. By the City of Boston.

A History of the Character and Achievements of the so-called Christopher Columbus. By Aaron Goodrich.
Autobiography and Journal of Rev. Heman Bangs. Edited by his Daughter.
The Venerable Mayhews. By W. A. Hallock, D. D.
The Life of Horace Greeley. Including Graphic Notices of Important Historical Events, etc. By L. D. Ingersoll.
The Life and Times of Rev. George Peck, D. D.
Maria Monk's Daughter. An Autobiography. By Mrs. J. St. John Eckel.
The Life and Adventures of Rear-Admiral John Paul Jones. By John S. C. Abbott.
Lives of the Governors of Pennsylvania. With the Incidental History of the State from 1609 to 1873. By William C. Armor.

FOETRY.—Our poets have for the most part been silent, or uttered brief snatches of song. Most of the volumes worth noticing are collections of pieces heretofore published singly at intervals. Dr. Oliver Wendell Holmes has put out such a volume, entitled "Songs of Many Seasons," quite a number of them those occasional poems in which he is so adept. Mr. Whittier's collection, "Hazel-Blossoms," contains one or two poems that deserve to be ranked among the best of his recent productions. Another republication is Mr. T. B. Aldrich's "Cloth of Gold, and other Poems "— productions which will please the new friends he has made by successes in another walk of literature. "Satan: a Libretto," by Christopher Pearse Cranch, is a bold attempt (after Milton and Goethe) to form an original conception of the Evil One. More impersonal than the old Adversary of God and man, he (or it) loses in proportion the capacity to impress the imagination. Mr. Bayard Taylor has produced "The Prophet," a tragedy, which shows a good deal of power in invention and skill in construction. Mr. Longfellow has written a poem for illustration, which is noticed in another place. Mr. J. T. Trowbridge has a peculiar knack of telling—or partly telling and partly suggesting—a story in verse, which is quite effective. "The Emigrant's Story, and other Poems," includes some pieces of this sort. His "other poems" are not strikingly poetical. Nora Perry, we believe, is a new candidate for the public favor, and made a good impression by her "After the Ball, and other Poems." The following titles are noted:

The Maid of Orleans. An Historical Tragedy. By George H. Calvert.
Vers de Société. By Praed, Landor, Thackeray, Moore, Holmes, Calverley, Saxe, Locker, Dobson, and the other recent authors in this department. Selected by Charles H. Jones. With illustrated title and vignettes.
A Voyage to the Fortunate Isles, and other Poems. By S. M. B. Piatt.
Poems. By Charles Alanson Munger.
Verses of Many Days. By Wm. Osborn Stoddard.
Echoes of the Foot-Hills. By Bret Harte.
The Circassian Boy. A Poem. Translated through the German from the Russian of Lermontoff. By T. S. Conant.
Poems of Twenty Years. By Laura Winthrop Johnson.

The Captain's Story. A Poem. By Mary Ashley Townsend.
Autumn Musings. By Elizabeth Hazard.
Ralph Elmwood. A Poem. By J. Henry Vosburg.
Poems. By H. R. Hudson.
Northern Ballads. By Edward L. Anderson.
A Wild Bouquet. By Leon Claire.
The Pioneer. By William Seaton.
Atala; or, Love in a Desert. A Metrical Indian Legend. By William Watson Waldron, A. B.
Poems. By Edgar Allan Poe. With an Original Memoir. By Richard Henry Stoddard.
Thy Voyage; or, A Song of the Seas, and other Poems. By Rev. E. F. Burr, D. D

FICTION.—Considerable fertility was shown in the production of novels, and, if none of them were of the first order of excellence, several were of more than average merit. Perhaps the completest success of the year was "A Foregone Conclusion," by Mr. Howells. It, of course, possessed a very high measure of literary grace, and of delicate humor, and of felicitous description. These qualities might have been presumed, insomuch that a failure to recognize them would be felt as a reproach upon one's power of discernment, rather than an imputation on the author. But it also revealed an unsuspected command of the forces of passion. Its humor deepens to tragedy. And all the varied effects are wrought by the action of four characters with very little shifting of scenes. Noticeable also for fine literary art working to exquisite finish, is "Prudence Palfrey," by Thomas Bailey Aldrich. The plot is the least admirable feature. The trick of mystification is played too grossly, and is made to involve, in Charles Lamb's phrase, too much of the hateful incredible. "Mose Evans," by W. M. Baker, combines rich local coloring—of the South and Southwest—with freshness in the conception and freedom in the treatment of character. He draws with bold strokes, with unnecessary roughness of style, but with admirable effect on the whole. Mr. Julian Hawthorne's romance, "Idolatry," is a phenomenon — fearfully and wonderfully made. His inherited tendency to the abnormal in his plots and personalities carries him to the verge of monstrosity—the preternatural looming unnatural. The work shows great power lacking discipline. "Lord of Himself," by F. H. Underwood, is believed to be the author's first attempt in this kind. If so, it is a very successful attempt. Life in Kentucky, as it was, is well depicted, and the general management of the story is good. "The Circuit Rider," by Edward Eggleston, regarded as a picture of character and manners in what were at the era of the story the new settlements of what was then the West, is a work of more than ordinary excellence. Its weakness is a commonplace plot. "Antony Brade," by Prof. R. T. S. Lowell, is an admirable story of school-life, with such pictures of village-life in New England as show nice observation and an artist's touch. "Gunnar, a Norse Romance," by Hjalmar Hjorth Boyesen, is marked by the simplicity and earnestness, the mystery and the pensive-

VOL. XIV.—29 A

ness, that are common to Norse literature. The individuality of the writer is shown in the felicity with which he has given form to the elements of romance. Among examples of avowed moral fiction, "The Opening of a Chestnut-Burr," by the Rev. E. P. Roe, deserves a very high place. From a long list of novels and tales, including translations from foreign languages, but excluding reprints, the following are named:

Willow Brook. By the author of "The Wide, Wide World."
Pretty Mrs. Gaston, and other Stories. By John Esten Cooke.
Justin Harley. A Romance of the Old Dominion. By the same.
Alide. A Romance of Goethe's Life. By Emma Lazarus.
Fettered for Life; or, Lord and Master. A Story of To-day. By Lillie Devereux Blake.
Ninety-three. By Victor Hugo. Translated by Frank Lee Benedict.
John Andross. By Rebecca Harding Davis.
A Daughter of Bohemia. By Christian Reid.
The Italian Girl. By Mrs. Katharine Sedgwick Washburn.
Waldfried. A Novel. By Berthold Auerbach. Translated by Simon Adler Stern.
Gerda. A Novel. By Mme. Marie Sophie Schwartz. Translated from the Swedish by Selma Borg and Marie A. Brown.
Good Luck. By E. Werner. Translated from the German by Francis A. Shaw.
Broken Chains. Same author and translator.
Spring Floods. By Ivan Tourguénief. Translated by Mrs. Sophie Michell Butts.
Some Women's Hearts. By Louise Chandler Moulton.
The Vicissitudes of Bessie Fairfax. A Novel. By Holme Lee.
Hulda; or, The Deliverer. A Romance, after the German of F. Lewald. By Mrs. A. L. Wistar.
The Second Wife. A Romance, from the German of E. Marlitt. By Mrs. A. L. Wistar.
The Mysteries and Miseries of the Great Metropolis, with some Adventures in the Country; being the Disguises and Surprises of a New York Journalist. By A. P., the Amateur Vagabond.
Brockley Moor. A Novel. By J. W. L.
Tempest-Tossed. By Theodore Tilton.
The Living Link. By James De Mille.
The Lily and the Cross. A Tale of Acadie. By the same.
The Babes in the Wood: a Tragic Comedy. By the same.
Scrope; or, The Lost Library. By F. B. Perkins.
Money and Music. By Charles Barnard.
The Notary's Nose. Translated from the French of Edmond About. By Henry Holt.
The Clique of Gold. Translated from the French of Emile Garbonau. By Prof. Schele de Vere.
Toinette. A Tale of Southern Life. By Henry Churton.
Salem. A Tale of the Seventeenth Century. By D. R. Castlemon.
Losing to Win. A Novel. By Theodore Davies.
Linley Rochford. By Justin McCarthy.
South Meadows. A Tale of Long Ago. By Miss E. T. Disoaway.
Honest John Vane. A Story. By J. W. De Forest.
From my Youth Up. By Marian Harland.
His Two Wives. By Mary Clemmer Ames.
Caleb Crinkle. A Story of American Life. By Charles Carleton Cotfin.
Science in Story; or, Sammy Tubbs, the Boy-Doctor, and Sponsie, the Troublesome Monkey. By E. B. Foote, M. D.

In Six Months; or, The Two Friends. By Mary M. Meline.

Charteris. A Romance. By the same.

Phemie Frost's Experiences. By Mrs. Ann S. Stephens.

The Log of Commodore Rollingpin: His Adventures Afloat and Ashore. By John S. Carleton. Illustrated.

The Minister's Wife; or, Life in a Country Parish. The Orphan's Trials; or, Alone in the Great City. By Emerson Bennett.

Sunshine and Shadow. A Novel. By Mrs. C. J. Newby.

The Lost Model. A Romance. By Henry Hooper.

The Confessions of a Minister. Being Leaves from the Diary of the Rev. Josephus Leonhardt, D. D. Katharine Earle. By Adeline Trafton.

West Lawn, and the Rector of St. Mark's. By Mrs. Mary J. Holmes.

Not in their Set; or, In Different Circles of Society. From the German of Mary Leuzen. By M. S., translator of "By His Own Might."

Princess Isle. A Story of the Hartz Mountains. Translated from the German by an American Lady. With an Introduction by Prof. J. L. Lincoln.

His Prison Bars, and the Way of Escape. By A. A. Hopkins.

Urbané and His Friends. By the author of "Stepping Heavenward."

One Woman's Two Lovers; or, Jacqueline Thayne's Choice. By Virginia F. Townsend.

Our New Crusade. By Edward Everett Hale.

ART AND CRITICISM.—There is room for doubt of the substantial value of the study of the fine arts, as it is pursued in some of our colleges, by means of text-books and professors' lectures on the principles of art and of art-criticism, in most cases with very scanty means of illustration to the eye. It is doubtless a legitimate department of philosophy, and needs to be included in a complete exposition. And certainly the volume of academic lectures by the late Prof. Joseph Torrey, of the University of Vermont, under the title, "A Theory of Fine Art," gives a favorable impression of what a sound and highly-cultivated thinker can do in that way. His principles of criticism savor of a "school" that is a little past date, but there is enough vigorous and fresh thought to repay an attentive reading. Of literary criticism some noticeable works have appeared. Mr. Emerson has favored the public with a selection of his favorite poems, in a volume entitled "Parnassus," with some of his thoughts on the poems and the poets. "A Free Lance in the Field of Life and Letters," by Prof. William C. Wilkinson, contains critical essays on "George Eliot," Mr. Lowell (his prose and poetry), and Mr. Bryant (poems and translations), the criticism of a sort that is rare, and for the most part admirable. It is generous in praise, severe in censure, and both praise and censure supported on sound principles and justified by detailed—once or twice by almost oppressively detailed—quotations and analyses. A course of lectures before the Lowell Institute, Boston, by President Bascom, of the University of Wisconsin, on the "Philosophy of English Literature," though laboring under the disadvantage of attempting to discuss a very large subject within arbitrarily-defined limits, is

thoughtful and suggestive. Reference was made to the deficient means for prosecuting art study in our institutions of learning. It is remarkable that two translations should be almost simultaneously announced in this country and in England of a work, the author of which died nearly a century ago—"Laocoon: an Essay upon the Limits of Painting and Poetry, with Remarks illustrative of the Various Points in the History of Ancient Art," by Lessing. It is translated in this country by Ellen Frothingham. A new publication in the interest of art was projected—the reissue in this country of the "London Art Journal," with liberal additions devoted to American art, to appear from the press of D. Appleton & Co.

A Series of Studies designed and engraved after Five Paintings by Raphael. With Historical and Critical Notes, by M. T. B. Emeric-David. Twenty-four plates reproduced by the heliotype process.

Toschi's Engravings. From the Frescoes by Correggio and Parmegiano. Twenty-four Plates reproduced by the heliotype process from the "Gray Collection of Engravings," Harvard University.

The Picturesque Architecture of Switzerland. Containing Designs of Country Houses from several Swiss Cantons. By A. & E. Varin. Reproduced by the heliotype process.

Illustrations of the Book of Job. Invented and Engraved by William Blake. Twenty-two Plates reproduced by the heliotype process, with Descriptive Notes and a Sketch of the Artist's Life and Works. By Charles Eliot Norton.

The Gates of the Baptistery at Florence. By Lorenzo Ghiberti. Published by the Yale School of the Fine Arts.

On the Nile. A Series of Sketches by Augustus Hoppin.

Specimens of the Decoration and Ornamentation of the Nineteenth Century. By Liénard. Upward of 120 Designs reproduced in fac-simile by the heliotype process.

An Essay contributing to the Philosophy of Literature. By B. A. M.

A Manual of French Poetry. With Historical Introduction and Biographical Notices of the Principal Authors. By A. H. Mixer, A. M.

Brief Essays and Brevities. By George H. Calvert.

Singers and Songs of the Liberal Faith; being Selections of Hymns and other Sacred Poems of the Liberal Church in America, with Biographical Sketches of the Writers, and with Historical and Illustrative Notes. By Alfred P. Putnam.

The Poets and Poetry of England in the Nineteenth Century. By Rufus W. Griswold. Carefully revised, much enlarged, and brought down to the Present Time. By R. H. Stoddard.

PHILOSOPHY AND SCIENCE.—Philosophy, in the ancient and proper sense of the word, is now regarded as the rival rather than the partner of Science, being concerned exclusively with what are more specifically defined as intellectual and moral, in distinction from natural or physical science, and which discover their materials in the knowledge the mind has of its own operations. But they are too intimately related to be set apart from each other, and the essential harmony between them, we may hope, will in no long time be vindicated by a more comprehensive intelligence. A veteran and successful investigator in Psychology and Metaphysics, Dr. McCosh, has laid students under obligation by his volume on "The Scottish Philosophy, Biographical, Expository, Critical, from Hutcheson to Hamilton." It is not an exposition of what is known as the Scottish *school* of Philosophy, founded by Reid, and finding its last great expounder in Hamilton, but rather of what Scotland has contributed to philosophy including the schools of Hume and Hutcheson. Dr. McCosh is himself the ablest living representative of the school of Reid, which for the time has in Scotland itself no eminent expositor. The Kantian transcendental metaphysic is represented by Dr. Laurens P. Hickok, who has given us "The Logic of Reason, Universal and Eternal." We attribute to Dr. Hickok dependence on Kant for impulse, not intending to question his essential originality and independence, as no one can question his great speculative insight and power of thought. His nomenclature is his own, and requires a special study to master it. Dr. E. H. Gillett, in his "God in Human Thought," has traced the history of natural theology in ancient and modern literature to the time of Bishop Butler. An English bibliography is especially full. We pass to a far different region and atmosphere when we look into the "Outlines of Cosmic Philosophy, based on the Doctrine of Evolution, with Criticisms on the Positive Philosophy," by John Fiske, M. A., LL. B., a reverential pupil of Herbert Spencer, but having a mind of his own. The doctrine of evolution, as formulated by Spencer, is assumed by Mr. Fiske. Mr. B. P. Bowne, in his "Philosophy of Herbert Spencer, being an Examination of the First Principles of his System," criticises those principles with acuteness. "The Doctrine of Evolution: its Data, its Principles, and its Theistic Bearings," by Alexander Winchell, LL. D., Chancellor of the Syracuse University, as the title implies, finds the doctrine—which is very carefully expounded—consistent with theism. Dr. Charles Hodge, on the other hand, seeking an answer to the question, "What is Darwinism?" concludes that that form of the evolution theory is atheistic. "Strauss as a Philosophical Thinker," by H. Ulrici, translated by Dr. C. P. Krauth, deals with Strauss as a philosopher exclusively, not as a theologian, but with great vigor of criticism. Dr. Draper's "History of the Conflict between Religion and Science," though in form a history, treats of a conflict which the author regards as still in progress. His work combines the functions of the historian and the polemic, and rather marks a stage in the movement than determines a conclusion. It is able, but not conciliating. Philosophical questions and others in kindred sciences are discussed with his wonted fullness of information and freshness of style by Prof. W. D. Whitney, in a second series of "Oriental and Linguistic Studies." A new edition of the late Dr. Francis Lieber's treatise on "Civil Liberty and Self-Government," edited by Dr. T. D. Woolsey, brings afresh into notice, and under excellent auspices, a work of unequaled value in its kind, and of special value to American citizens. Dr. Woolsey has issued an improved and enlarged edition of his "Introduction to the Study of International Law," a book not intended for lawyers, but for general students. "The Earth as modified by Human Action" is the title of a new, enlarged, and revised edition of "Man and Nature," by the Hon. George P. Marsh, a work that in its original form received the highest praise both at home and in Europe.

Of works in the different departments of physical science, "The New Chemistry," by Prof. Josiah P. Cooke, Jr., of Harvard University, one of the "International Scientific Series," deserves mention as an excellent example of popularized science. "A History of North American Birds," by Spencer F. Baird, Thomas M. Brewer, and Robert Ridgway, is an important undertaking, of which two volumes on "Land Birds" have appeared. Prof. James D. Dana has published new and improved editions of his "Manual of Geology" and his "Descriptive Mineralogy," the latter almost entirely rewritten and greatly enlarged. The first volume has appeared of a work that promises to be of great interest and of scientific value, "Native Races of the Pacific States," by Herbert H. Bancroft. The volume now issued is on "Wild Tribes, their Manners and Customs." An important contribution to financial science —a branch of the greatest practical importance at the present time—is "A History of American Currency, with Chapters on English Bank Restriction and Austrian Paper Money," by Prof. William G. Sumner, of Yale College. Other works that in various degrees deserve mention are the following:

Heat as a Source of Power. With Applications of General Principles to the Construction of Steam Generators. An Introduction to the Study of Heat-Engines. By W. E. Trowbridge, Professor of Engineering in Yale College.

The Constants of Nature. Part I. Specific Gravities and Chemical Formulæ. Compiled by Frank Wigglesworth Clark, S. B. (Smithsonian Miscellaneous Collection, 255.)

Quadrature of the Circle; containing Demonstrations of the Errors of Geometry in finding the Approximations in Use. By John A. Parker.

Dictionary of Elevations and Climatic Register of the United States. Containing, in Addition to the Elevations, the Latitude, Mean Annual Temperature, and the Total Annual Rainfall of many Localities. By J. M. Toner, M. D.

Field Ornithology. Comprising a Manual of Instruction for procuring, preparing, and preserving Birds, and a Check-List of North American Birds. By Dr. Elliott Coues.

Relation of Insects to Man. By A. S. Packard, Jr.

Insects of the Plant-House. By the same.

Insects of the Pond and Stream. By the same.

Butterflies of North America. Second Series. By William H. Edwards.

The Marine Mammals of the Northwestern Coast of North America. By Charles M. Scammon.

Alcohol; its Combinations, Adulterations, and Physical Effects. By Colonel J. G. Dudley.

Earthwork Mensuration on the Prismoidal Formula. By Conway R. Howard, Civil Engineer.

Catalogue of Plants growing without Cultivation in the State of New Jersey, etc. By Oliver R. Willis, Ph. D.

The Physiology of Man. Designed to represent the Existing State of Physiological Science as applied to the Functions of the Human Body. By Austin Flint, Jr., M. D. In five vols. Vol. V.

A Collection of Tactical Studies. Translated and put together by Wyllys Lyman, Brevet-Major U.S.A.

Chapters on Political Economy. By Albert S. Bolles.

Lecture Notes on Qualitative Analysis. By Henry B. Hill, M. A., Assistant Professor of Chemistry in Harvard University.

Corals and Coral Islands. By James D. Dana, Professor in Yale College. New edition, with additional matter.

Sophisms of Protection. By the late Frédéric Bastiat. Translated from the Paris edition of 1863. With Preface by Horace White.

Eating for Strength. By M. L. Holbrook, M. D.

The Blowpipe; a Guide to its Use in the Determination of Salts and Minerals. Compiled from various Sources, by George W. Plympton, C. E., A. M., Professor in the Polytechic Institute, Brooklyn, N. Y.

A Brief Account of the Finances and Paper-Money of the Revolution. By J. W. Schuckers.

Commercial Cryptograph. A Telegraph and Double Index. Holocryptic Cipher. By J. G. Bloomer.

The Voice in Speaking. Translated from the German of E. Seiler, by W. H. Furness, D. D.

Annual Record of Science and Industry for 1873. Edited by Spencer F. Baird, with the Assistance of Eminent Men of Science.

The Science Record for 1874. A Compendium of Scientific Progress and Discovery during the Past Year. With Illustrations. Edited by Alfred E. Beach.

The Stars and the Earth ; or, Thoughts on Space, Time, and Eternity. New edition, with a New Introduction, by Thomas Hill, D. D.

Evolution and Progress. By Rev. William J. Gill.

A Brief History of Culture. By John S. Hittell.

The Moral System. With an Historical and Critical Introduction, with Special Reference to Butler's Analogy. By E. H. Gillett, D. D.

The History of the English Language. From the Teutonic Invasion of Britain to the Close of the Georgian Era. By Henry E. Shepherd, Professor in Baltimore City College.

A Grammar and Dictionary of the Language of the Hedatsa, with an Introductory Sketch of the Tribe. By William Matthews.

The Principles of Chemistry and Molecular Mechanics. By Dr. Gustavus Hinrich, Professor of Physical Science in the State University of Iowa.

The Conservation of Energy. By Balfour Stuart, LL. D. With an Appendix treating of the Vital and Mental Applications of the Doctrine.

THEOLOGY AND RELIGION.—As usual, this department of writing embraces a large proportion of the whole number of published books, and among them are to be mentioned some of superior merit. Of works in scientific and apologetic theology, of an expositional character, Dr. Horace Bushnell's volume, entitled "Forgiveness and Law, grounded in Principles interpreted by Human Analogies," is especially noticeable. It is interesting for its frank revelations of the workings of a powerful and richly-gifted mind on a most vital subject; for the ingenuity and suggestiveness of its thought;

for its sturdy, and sometimes daring independence and originality of conception. But the warmest admirers of the distinguished author must confess that his style is sometimes needlessly harsh, and it is safe to conclude, judging from the past, that many more will find food for their admiration of Dr. Bushnell than satisfaction in his conclusions. The Sermons of the Rev. Henry Norman Hudson, best known by his admirable writings on Shakespeare, will extend his reputation as a master of didactic composition. His style is that of one who has been nourished in the best of the elder English literature, the spirit of which has been thoroughly imbibed. "Religion and the State," by Alvah Hovey, D. D., carefully discusses the limits of civil action in matters of religion, and maintains that the state can properly only protect its free exercise; condemning all alliance between Church and State, and the exemption of ecclesiastical property from taxation. The same author has put forth a brief popular essay on "The State of Men after Death." A volume at once forcible in argument, and of excellent spirit and temper, is "Science and Christianity, a Series of Lectures," by the Rev. A. P. Peabody, D. D., LL. D. "Geometry and Faith ; a Fragmentary Supplement to the Ninth Bridgewater Treatise," by ex-President Thomas Hill, D. D., LL. D., appears in an enlarged edition. In a "fit audience," which must necessarily be also "few," this will be a source of great intellectual pleasure. Only a trained mathematician can do complete justice to the argument. "The Kingdom of Christ on Earth; Twelve Lectures," by the Rev. Samuel Harris, D. D., Professor in Yale College, are worthy of the larger audience to which they are offered. "David, King of Israel, his Life and its Lessons," by the Rev. William M. Taylor, D. D., is a good example of Scripture biography expounded in the light of contemporary sentiment and character. The encyclopedic commentary of Dr. Lange, translated and much enlarged under the editorial oversight of Dr. Philip Schaff, is approaching completion. The fact that so voluminous a work finds a remunerative patronage is a striking indication of the degree in which solid theological learning is appreciated. A new edition of Dr. H. M. Dexter's "Congregationalism," with much new matter, improves and perpetuates a valuable book of reference. "An Examination of the Alleged Discrepancies of the Bible," by J. W. Haley, is a defensive work, original in conception, ably executed, and in a style fitted for general perusal. Of polemic theology several noticeable works have appeared. "Infant Baptism and Infant Salvation in the Calvinistic System; a Review of Dr. Hodge's 'Systematic Theology,'" by the Rev. Charles P. Krauth, D. D., amply exhibits the author's learning and acuteness. Discussing some of the same questions, but adversely, is "Mercersburg Theology Inconsistent with Protestant and Reformed Doctrine," by B. S. Schenck, D. D. Another vigorous assault upon Dr. Hodge's system, sharp, and in parts effective, bears the expressive title, "Fetich in Theology; or Doctrinalism Twin to Ritualism," by John Miller. A contribution to a controversy still in active progress is "Eucharistic Presence, Eucharistic Sacrifice, and Eucharistic Adoration," by the Rev. Dr. Samuel Buel, Professor in the General Theological Seminary, New York; and Dr. Schaff illuminates a pending theologico-political controversy by republishing Mr. Gladstone's pamphlet on "The Vatican Decrees in their Bearing on Civil Allegiance," appending to them a History of the Vatican Council, and the texts of the Papal Syllabus and Vatican Decrees, in Latin and English. Among books of practical religion may be noticed—"Joseph Tuckerman on the Elevation of the Poor; a selection from his Reports as Minister at Large in Boston, with an Introduction, by E. E. Hale," as at once a worthy memorial of an eminent Christian philanthropist, and a manual of practical suggestion. "Strength and Beauty: Discussions for Young Men," by ex-President Mark Hopkins, D. D., a collection of insufficiently disguised sermons, in which high principles of philosophy and religion are discussed with remarkable freshness of thought and a striking, sometimes almost poetical vividness of illustration, and are applied to the conduct of life. "The Christian in the World," a prize essay, by the Rev. D. W. Faunce, has so much of unconventional good sense that, if it were not for the official announcement of the fact, it would not be suspected to have been made "to order." A book out of the heart and speaking to the heart, in a spirit of fine religious intelligence, is "Helps to a Life of Prayer," by the Rev. J. M. Manning, D. D. The "History, Essays, Orations, and other Documents of the Sixth General Conference of the Evangelical Alliance," edited by the Rev. Drs. Philip Schaff and S. Irenæus Prime, presents a series of papers, some of great ability, some merely expressive of amiable feeling, but all interesting and appropriately commemorating a memorable occasion.

Perhaps some of the works cited below by their titles, are as worthy of notice as those we have mentioned, but so much must suffice:

The Memorial Pulpit (Sermons). By the Rev. C. S. Robinson, D. D.

The Communicant's Guide, being a Directory to the Devout Receiving of the Lord's Supper. By the Rev. R. Whittingham.

A Common-Sense View of the Mode of Baptism. By the Rev. Samuel Hutchings.

A New Discussion of the Doctrine of the Trinity. By Rev. F. W. Burris. With an Introduction by Prof. Joseph Haven, D. D., LL. D.

The Safest Creed; and Twelve other Discourses of Reason. By Octavius B. Frothingham.

Holiness the Birthright of all God's Children. By Rev. J. T. Crane, D. D.

Holiness to the Lord. By Rev. Lewis R. Dunn.

A Summer Vacation. Four Sermons. By Edward E. Hale.

Heavenward; or, The Race for the Crown of Life. By Junius B. Reimensnyder.

Spina Christi; or, Musings in Holy Week. By H. Hall, D. D.

The Family Assistant; Book of Prayers for the Use of Families. To which are added Prayers for Special Occasions. By Samuel R. Fisher, D. D.

Truths for To-Day, spoken in the Past Winter. By David Swing.

Solar Hieroglyphics; or, The Emblematic Illustrations of the Revealed Doctrine of the Tri-personal Godhead which are discernible in the Solar Light. With an Introduction by J. Grier Ralston, D. D.

The Office and Duty of the Christian Pastor. By Stephen H. Tyng, D. D.

Commentary on the Gospel of Matthew. By Lyman Abbott.

Modern Skepticism: a Journey through the Land of Doubt, and back again. A Life-Story. By Joseph Barker.

Uriel; or, Some Occasional Discourses. By Joseph A. Seiss, D. D.

The Fourth Watch, and the Other Shore. By Anna Warner.

The Winter Fire. By Rose Porter.

The Secret of Christianity. By S. S. Hebbard.

The Name above Every Name. By Samuel Cutler, D. D.

On Revision of the English Version of the Bible. By Rev. Dorus Clarke.

The Earthward Pilgrimage. By M. D. Conway.

Sacred Anthology. By the same.

Prayer and the Prayer-Gauge. By Mark Hopkins, D. D.

The Catacombs of Rome. By W. H. Withrow.

Source of Salvation. A Catechism of the Jewish Religion. With an Appendix of the Confirmation Service. By Dr. Isaac Mayer.

The Bible regained, and the God of the Bible Ours. By Rev. Samuel Lee.

The Philanthropies; or, The Practical Workings of Christianity. The Gospel of Christ the only True Gospel of Humanity. By Rev. I. N. Parsons. Revised by Rev. E. N. Kirk, D. D.

The Brooklyn Council of 1874. Letter Missive, Statement, and Documents, together with an Official Phonographic Report of the Proceedings and Result of Council.

Old Wells dug out. Being a Third Series of Sermons. By T. De Witt Talmage.

Full and Complete Report of the Trial of the Rev. David Swing before the Presbytery of Chicago, for Heresy. Edited by Rev. D. S. Johnson, Stated Clerk of Presbytery, Rev. Francis L. Patton, Prosecutor, and Rev. George O. Noyes, Counsel for Accused.

Notes on the Second Plenary Council of Baltimore. By the Rev. S. Smith, D. D.

The Biblical Stand-point. Views of the Sonship of Christ, the Comforter, and the Trinity. By Asa Wilbur.

The Mode of Man's Immortality; or, The When, Where, and How, of the Future Life. By Rev. T. A. Goodwin, A. M.

Peeps at our Sunday-Schools. By Rev. Alfred Taylor.

Messiah. By Rev. William M. Willett.

Landmarks of Truth; or, Harmony of the Bible with Reason and Science. Forming a Defensive Manual of the Bible. By D. M. Evans, M. D.

The Great Conflict; Christ and Antichrist; The Church and the Apostacy; as shadowed by the Prophets and delineated in History. By A. Loomis.

Yale Lectures on Preaching. Third Series. By Henry Ward Beecher.

Gleanings. By William P. Lunt, D. D.

What is the Meaning of the Oblation in the Prayer of Consecration in the Eucharistic Service? By Robert B. Fairbairn, D. D.

Christian Theology for the People. By Willis Lord, D. D.

The Daily Service. A Book of Offices for Daily Use through all the Seasons of the Christian Year.

The Power of Grace over Acquired Habits, Special Inborn Propensities, and the Natural Appetites. By S. H. Platt, A. M.

The Church Porch. A Service-Book and Hymnal for Sunday-Schools. Compiled and edited by W. R. Huntington, D. D.

Spiritual Victory; or, Thoughts on the Higher Christian Life. By W. W. Patton, D. D.

Children and the Church; or, The Spiritual Condition, Moral Capabilities, and Church Relations of Baptized Infants. By Samuel Regester, D. D., Baltimore Conference M. E. C. S.

The baptizing of Infants defended from the Objections of Anti-Pedobaptists. By R. S. Mason, D. D.

What of the Churches and Clergy?

A Hand-book of the General Convention of the Protestant Episcopal Church, giving its History and Constitution from 1785 to 1874. By William Stevens Perry, D. D.

Sermons and Songs of the Christian Life. By Edmund H. Sears.

Christian Truth and Modern Opinion. Seven Sermons preached in New York.

Public Worship, partly responsive. Designed for any Christian Congregation. With an Introduction by the Rev. Daniel Marsh, D. D.

Hebrew History from the Death of Moses to the Close of the Scripture Narrative. By Rev. Henry Cowles, D. D.

Grace for Grace. Letters of Rev. William James.

Commentary on the Acts of the Apostles. By Thomas O. Summers, D. D., LL. D.

Expository Notes on the Book of Joshua. By Howard Crosby, D. D.

Discourses of Redemption. By Stuart Robinson, D. D.

Farmer Tompkins and his Bibles. By Willis J. Beecher, D. D., Professor in Auburn Theological Seminary.

Helps to Prayer: a Manual designed to aid Christian Believers in acquiring the Gift and in maintaining the Spirit of Prayer in the Closet, the Social Gathering, and the Public Congregation.

The King's Highway; or, The Catholic Church the Way of Salvation as revealed in the Scriptures. By the Rev. Augustine F. Hewit, of the Congregation of St. Paul.

The Modern Sunday-School. By Rev. W. H. H. Marsh.

The Christian Law of Union in Communion. By George W. Samson, D. D.

GEOGRAPHY, TRAVEL, ETC.—Several works of more than ordinary merit have appeared of this description. Mr. Henry M. Stanley, who won so much renown to his country and the *New York Herald* by his finding of Dr. Livingstone, having in a like spirit of daring enterprise assisted in two English campaigns in Africa, tells his experiences in a goodly volume entitled "Coomassie and Magdala." Another correspondent of the same journal, Mr. J. A. McGahen, describes "Campaigning on the Oxus and the Fall of Khiva," which he had personal knowledge of at the cost of great hardships and against almost insuperable difficulties. "The Land of the White Elephant; Sights and Scenes in Southeastern Asia," by Frank Vincent, Jr., is also a lively sketch of scenes and objects aside from the ordinary lines of travel. Mr. Bayard Taylor, in his volume, "Egypt and Iceland in 1874," in his Eastern journey goes over ground previously visited and described, and gives his readers the benefit of a comparison of Egypt as it now is with the

Egypt of twenty years ago. His visit to Iceland in connection with the recent Millennial Celebration has a unique interest, which communicates itself to his narrative. "Northern California, Oregon, and the Sandwich Islands," by Charles Nordhoff, has the marks of sagacious observation and vivid representation which appear in his previous work on California, and make him a favorite tourist. In purely literary merit perhaps no work of this kind during the year is superior to Mr. Charles Dudley Warner's little book, "Baddeck and That Sort of Thing"—a sort of thing which in any other hands would prove, it may be suspected, the reverse of entertaining. But his humor finds food where most minds would starve. "Syrian Home Life," compiled by Rev. Isaac Riley from materials furnished by the Rev. Henry Harris Jessup, D. D., of Beirut, Syria, is interesting as a faithful exhibition of Oriental society, from the observations of many years, under excellent opportunities, and also as showing the working of ameliorating influences. "German Universities," by Prof. James Morgan Hart, describes them from personal experience, and makes a critical and instructive comparison of the system of higher education in Germany with that of Great Britain and the United States. The following also deserve mention:

Arctic Experiences. Containing Captain George E. Tyson's Wonderful Drift on the Ice-Floe, a History of the Polaris Expedition, the Cruise of the Tigress, and Rescue of the Polaris Survivors. To which is added a General Arctic Chronology. By E. Vale Blake.

My Life on the Plains. By General G. A. Custer.

Life and Literature in the Fatherland. By John F. Hurst, D. D.

The Mormon Country. By John Codman.

Ten Days in Spain. By Kate Field.

Remains of Lost Empires: Sketches of the Ruins of Palmyra, Nineveh, Babylon, and Persepolis, with some Notes on India and the Cashmerian Himalayas. By P. V. N. Myers, A. M.

A Lawyer abroad; what to see and how to see. By Henry Day, of the Bar of New York.

Song and Scenery; or, Summer Rambles in Scotland. By James C. Moffat.

The Resources of California. By John S. Hittell. Sixth edition, rewritten.

USEFUL ARTS.—The placing of a work under this head is not, of course, a voucher that the book itself is useful:

Life under Glass. Containing Suggestions toward the Formation of Artificial Climates. By George A. Shove.

The Architectural Sketch-Book. Edited by the Portfolio Club, and comprising Designs by the most Eminent Architects of New England.

Homes, and how to make them. By E. C. Gardner.

Architecture for General Students. By Caroline Horton.

Mining Industry of the States and Territories west of the Rocky Mountains. By R. W. Raymond, Ph. D.

American Iron-Trade: Manual of the Leading Industries of the United States. Compiled and edited by Thomas Dunlap.

The Carpenter's and Builder's Assistant, and Wood-worker's Guide. By Lucius D. Gould.

Instructions on Modern American Bridge-Building, with Practical Applications and Examples, Estimates of Quantities, and Valuable Tables. By G. B. A. Tower.

A Treatise on Bracing, and its Application to Bridges and other Structures of Wood or Iron. By Robert Henry Bow, C. E.

Theory of the Strength of Materials. Illustrated by Applications to Machines and Buildings. By Francis L. Vinton, E. M., C. E.

Improvements in Steam - Engines. By John Haupt.

The Theory and Practice of the Art of Designing Cotton and Woolen Goods, from Sample. By Frederick T. Ashton, Designer.

Mechanic's Geometry: Plainly teaching the Carpenter, Joiner, Mason, Metal-plate Worker—in fact, the Artisan in any and every Branch of Industry whatsoever—the Constructive Principles of his Calling. By Robert Riddell. Illustrated by 50 plates.

Theory of Arches. By Prof. W. Allan, formerly of Washington and Lee University.

TEXT-BOOKS.—The preparation of school text-books is a branch of production in which, more than in almost any other, men "continue," as Sterne says (after Burton) "to make new books, as apothecaries make new mixtures by pouring only out of one vessel into another." A complete list of the new schoolbooks of any year, including new and modified editions, would represent a very large component of the mass of publications, especially so if measured by its commercial value. We attempt nothing of the kind. Some examples of the more valuable productions are given:

How to teach: a Manual of Methods, for a Graded Course of Instruction. By Henry Kiddle, Thomas F. Harrison, and N. A. Calkins.

Manual of the Constitution of the United States; designed for the Instruction of American Youth in the Duties, Obligations and Rights of Citizenship. By Israel Ward Andrews, D. D., President of Marietta College, O.

A Brief Exposition of the Constitution of the United States. By John S. Hart, LL. D.

An Elementary Course of Permanent Fortifications, for the Use of the Cadets of the United States Military Academy. By Prof. D. H. Mahan, LL. D. Revised and edited by Colonel J. B. Wheeler, Professor in the U. S. Military Academy.

United States Cavalry Tactics. By Brevet Major-General Emory Upton, U. S. A.

The Metric System of Weights and Measures. By J. Pickering Putnam.

Elements of Chemistry, Chemical Physics. By William Allen Miller, M. D., LL. D.

Exercises in some of the more Difficult Principles of Greek Syntax, with References to the Grammars of Crosby, Curtius, Goodwin, Hadley, Koch, and Kühner. By James R. Boise, Professor in the University of Chicago.

Demosthenes on the Crown. Edited by Rev. Arthur Holmes, A. M. Revised edition by W. S. Tyler, Professor in Amherst College.

Sallust's Conspiracy of Catiline. By J. H. Allen, W. F. Allen, and J. B. Greenough.

Cæsar's Gallic War. Four Books. By the same.

The Poems of Virgil. Vol. I., containing the Pastoral Poems and Six Books of the Æneid. By the same.

Questions on the History and Geography of Rome, suitable for Schools and Academies, and adapted to Students preparing for Harvard College. By J. F. Tufts.

The Œdipus Tyrannus of Sophocles. By John Williams White.

The Andria and Adelphi of Terence. Edited by E. P. Crowell, Professor in Amherst College.

Latin Hymns with English Notes. For Use in Schools and Colleges. By F. A. March, LL. D., Professor in Lafayette College.

The Ecclesiastical History of Eusebius. The First Book and Selections. Edited by F. A. March, LL. D. With an Introduction by A. Ballard, D. D., Professor of Christian Greek and Latin in Lafayette College, and Explanatory Notes by W. B. Owen, A. M., Adjunct Professor of Christian Greek.

An Introduction to the Study of the English Language. Grammar and Rhetoric combined. By J. Alden, LL. D.

First Steps in General History. A Suggestive Outline. By Arthur Gilman. Illustrated with Maps.

A New Treatise on the French Verbs. By Alfred Hennequin, M. A.

Handbook of the Physical Training in Schools. Adapted to Classes of all Grades and to Social and Individual Practice. By Charles J. Robinson, A. B., etc.

Electro-Astronomical Atlas. designed for Schools, Academies, etc. By Rev. J. W. Spoor, A. M.

Complete Arithmetic. By William G. Peck, LL. D.

A Grammar of the English Language, with an Analysis of the Sentence. By John S. Hart, LL. D.

Language Lessons for Beginners. By the same.

All the French Verbs at a Glance. By Etienne Lambert and Alfred Sardou.

Idiomatic Key to the French Language. By the same.

Teacher's Hand-book of Arithmetic. By Malcolm McVicar, Ph. D., LL. D.

Progressive English Exercises in Analysis, Composition and Spelling, by the Use of Symbols. By Henry W. Siglar, A. M.

A Junior Class History of the United States. By J. J. Anderson.

A Practical and Critical Grammar of the English Language. By Noble Butler.

The New French Instructor. By P. Rollin Carson.

The Complete Algebra. For Schools and Colleges. By Joseph Ficklin, Ph. D., Professor of Mathematics in the University of Missouri.

Introduction to the Teaching of Living Languages without Grammar or Dictionary. By L. Sauveur, Ph. D., LL. D.

Elements of Analytical Mechanics. By W. H. Bartlett, LL. D.

Introduction to Algebra. By Edward Olney, Professor of Mathematics in the University of Michigan.

Descriptive Astronomy. Part I. By S. E. Warren, Professor in the Massachusetts Institute of Technology.

Elements of Geometry, after Legendre; with a Selection of Geometrical Exercises, and Hints for the Solution of the Same. Part I., Plane Geometry. By Charles S. Venable, LL. D., Professor in the University of Virginia.

Plant Analysis; adapted to Gray's Botanics. By E. A. and A. C. Apgar.

The Art of reading Music. A New Method. By Laura B. Humphreys.

Outlines of Astronomy. By Arthur Searle, A. M.

Military Lessons. A Text-Book for Military Schools, Colleges, and the Militia. By W. T. Welcker, Professor in the University of California.

Reasonable Elocution. By F. Taverner Graham.

A Treatise on the Method of Government Surveying as prescribed by the United States Congress and Commissioner of the General Land-Office, with Complete Mathematical, Astronomical, and Practical Instructions for the Use of U. S. Surveyors in the Field, or Students who contemplate engaging in the Business of Public Land Surveying. By S. V. Clevenger.

LAW.—Mention should here be made of books intended not for lawyers but for the general student and the public at large. Such a book, from an author in the highest degree competent as an adviser, is "The Political, Personal, and Property Rights of a Citizen of the United States: How to exercise and how to preserve them. Together with—1. A Treatise on the Rules of Organization and Procedure in Deliberative Assemblies; 2. A Glossary of Law Terms in Common Use," by Theophilus Parsons. Another work, suitable for use as a college text-book or for general reference is ex-President Woolsey's "Introduction to the Study of International Law," of which a revised and enlarged edition, with important additions, has been published.—Omitting the regular issues of reports, the following treatises and essays may be mentioned.

The General Railroad Laws of the State of Ohio in force January 1, 1874, etc. By James A. Wilcox. Woman before the Law. By John Proffat, LL. B., of the New York Bar.

The Principles of Equity. A Treatise on the System of Justice administered in the Courts of Chancery. By George Tucker Bispham, Esq., of the Philadelphia Bar.

Reports of Cases arising under Letters-Patent for Inventions, determined in the Courts of the United States. By Samuel S. Fisher. Vol. V.

Insurance Reports, Vol. III. Reports of the Life and Accident Insurance Cases, determined in the Courts of America, England, Ireland, Scotland, and Canada, down to 1874. By Melville M. Bigelow, of the Boston Bar.

Select American Cases in the Law of Self-Defense. By L. B. Horrigan and S. D. Thompson.

The Rights of Jurors in Criminal Cases. Opinion by Hon. B. F. Thomas, with an Introduction by a Member of the Suffolk [Boston] Bar.

Digest of the Decisions of the Supreme Court of Iowa, from its Organization, in 1839, to the 35th Iowa Reports. By T. F. Withrow and E. H. Stiles. Vol. I.

The Practice at Law, in Equity, and in Special Proceedings, in all the Courts of Record in the State of New York; with Appropriate Forms. By William Wait.

A Treatise on the Law of Mechanics' Liens on Real and Personal Property. By Samuel L. Phillips.

A Treatise on the Law of Boundaries and Fences, including the Rights of Property on the Sea-Shore and in Lands on Public Rivers and other Streams, and the Law of Window-Lights. By Ransom H. Tyler.

A Digest of Decisions of the Various Courts in the United States, from the Earliest Period to the Year 1870. Comprising all the American Decisions digested in Thirty-one Volumes of the United States Digest, with Careful Revision and Important Additions. First Series, Vol. II.

On Extraordinary Legal Remedies, embracing Mandamus, Quo Warranto and Prohibition. By James L. High.

The Law of Design Patents, containing all Reported Decisions of the United States Courts and the Patent-Office in Design Cases, to 1874, with Digests and Treatise. By William E. Simonds.

Real Estate Statutes and Decisions of Illinois. Vol. I. By John B. Adams and W. J. Durham.

The Principles and Practice of Courts of Justice in England and the United States. By Conway Robinson. Vol. VII. Further on Personal Actions, as to the Grounds and Form of Defense, and the Answer to that Defense.

A Treatise of the Law of Negligence. By Francis Wharton, LL. D.

The Banker's Code: A Compilation of Laws of the State of New York relating to Incorporated, Associated, and Individual Banks, National Banks, Savings-Banks, Loan, Trust, Mortgage, Guaranty, Security and Indemnity Companies. With an Appendix, containing forms of Organization, etc. By Daniel Shaw.

A Treatise on the Rules which govern the Interpretation and Construction of Statutory and Constitutional Law. By Theodore Sedgwick. With numerous Additional Notes. By John Norton Pomeroy, LL. D.

Railway Law in Illinois. The Relations of Railroads to the People. By Frank Gilbert. With an Introduction by Governor J. M. Palmer.

A Treatise on the Probate of Wills, Settlement of Estates, etc. With Forms. By Levi North.

MEDICINE.—No discrimination is made between "schools" in the following list:

The Nature of Gunshot-Wounds of the Abdomen and their Treatment. Based on a Review of the Case of the Late James Fisk, Jr., in its Medico-Legal Aspects.

The Puerperal Diseases. Clinical Lectures delivered at Bellevue Hospital. By Fordyce Barker, M. D.

The Sphygmograph: Its Physiological and Pathological Indications. By Edgar Holden, A. M., M. D.

Treatment of Nervous and Rheumatic Affections by Static Electricity. By Dr. A. Arthius. Translated from the French by J. H. Etheridge, M. D., Professor in Rush Medical College, Chicago.

Emergencies, and how to meet them. The Etiology, Pathology, and Treatment of the Accidents, Diseases, and Cases of Poisoning which demand Prompt Action. Designed for Students and Practitioners of Medicine. By Joseph W. Howe, M. D.

Winter Homes for Invalids. An Account of the Various Localities in Europe and America suitable for Consumptives and other Invalids during the Winter Months. By the same.

Therapeutics, Materia Medica, and Toxicology. With Special References to the Application of the Physiological Action of Drugs to Clinical Medicine. By H. C. Wood, Jr., M. D.

A Manual of Toxicology. A Practical Treatise on the Properties, Modes of Action, and Means of Detection, of Poisons. By John J. Reese, M. D.

The Hygiene of the Sewing-Machine: a Brief Inquiry into the Causes of Disorders arising from the Use of Machines, with some Suggestions how they may be avoided. By a Physician.

The Ligation of the Arteries. An Operative Manual. By Dr. L. H. Farabeuf. Translated by John D. Jackson, M. D.

On Surgical Diseases of the Genito-Urinary Organs. By W. H. Van-Buren and E. L. Keyes.

Electro-Therapeutics. A Concise Manual of Medical Electricity. By D. F. Lincoln, M. D.

Essays on Conservative Medicine and Kindred Topics. By Austin Flint, M. D.

Clinical Lectures on Diseases of the Nervous System. By William A. Hammond, M. D. Reprinted, edited, and the Histories of the Cases prepared, with Notes, by T. M. B. Cross, M. D.

New-School Remedies, and their Application to the Cure of Diseases. By W. Paine, A. M., M. D.

The Breath, and the Diseases which give it a Fetid Odor. With Directions for Treatment. By J. W. Mace.

Croup in its Relations to Tracheotomy. By J. Solis Cohen, M. D.

The Encyclopædia of Pure Materia Medica. A Record of the Positive Effects of Drugs upon the Healthy Human Organism. By Timothy F. Allen,

'A. M., M. D. With Contributions from Dr. Richard Hughes, of England, Dr. C. Hering, of Philadelphia, Dr. Carroll Dunham, of New York, Dr. A. Lippe, of Philadelphia, and others.

GIFT BOOKS.—The increasing extent to which pictorial illustration is resorted to, in books that admit of it, to increase their value and attractiveness, diminishes the production of books expressly prepared for ornamentation and presentation. Of this limited and diminishing class a few of special excellence appeared. Our two most renowned poets are represented. Mr. Bryant's picturesque poem, "Among the Trees," nearly every line of which is a picture, forms the subject of a volume very beautifully illustrated. Mr. Longfellow's tender and graceful piece, "The Hanging of the Crane," a series of domestic scenes, touched with masterly art, and suffused with natural feeling, is well matched with illustrations that would tell the story without the help of the poem. "The Evangel in Verse," by Abram Coles, M. D., relates the life of Christ in verse that is genuinely poetical, and the volume is illustrated with ink photographs of paintings by celebrated artists. "Myths of the Rhine," by X. B. Saintine, translated by Prof. M. Schele de Vere, with Doré's quaint illustrations, is a unique combination, both literary and artistic. "Lotus Leaves," a volume of tales, essays, and poems, by a number of our younger literary men, "Mark Twain," Whitelaw Reid, "Nasby," John Hay, and others, with illustrations, and the following, mostly of and for the young, deserve mention: "Ballads of Beauty," edited by George M. Baker; "Little Folks in Feathers and Fur, and Others in Neither," by Olive Thorne; "Childhood Songs," by Lucy Larcom; "The Lady of Lawford, and other Christmas Stories;" and "The Children's Picture Story-Book," by Laura Loring.

JUVENILE BOOKS.—The literary pabulum provided for the young people is not in as large proportion fictitious as it has been, and some of the historical, descriptive, and didactic works offered as substitutes are of a good deal of merit. For young men on the verge of, or conscious of approaching, responsible manhood, Mr. Charles Nordhoff's "Politics for Young Americans" should be as interesting as it undeniably would be useful. "Talks with Girls," by Augusta Larned, is fresh and sensible. "Knights and Sea-Kings," edited by the Rev. S. F. Smith, D. D., is a taking account of the chivalry of the Middle Ages. "Boys and Birds," by the Rev. Sidney Dyer, introduces the one to the other in a pleasant and profitable manner. "Sights and Insights," by the Rev. Henry Warren, introduces its young readers to "knowledge by travel." In fiction and poetry, some old favorites of our young folks have continued to cater for them. For the very little ones nothing could be more delightful than the "Rhymes and Jingles" of Mrs. Mary Mapes Dodge; they are as near to the classic nonsense of Mother Goose as could

be expected in the self-conscious Nineteenth Century. The collection of "Little Songs," by Mrs. Eliza Lee Follen, discloses the authorship of some familiar pieces that have long been current. Mrs. Louise Chandler Moulton gives to the nursery "More Bedtime Stories," and the lady who writes under the name of "Susan Coolidge" shows, by her "Mischief's Thanksgiving," that her hand has not lost its cunning, nor her heart its warmth. The boys will, of course, take kindly to Mr. J. T. Trowbridge's "Fast Friends," a continuation of the "Jack Hazard" series; and to Frank R. Stockton's "What Might Have been Expected;" and to the *true* story of "Ten Days among Greek Brigands," by the Rev. H. J. Van Lennep. Prof. R. W. Raymond is as good at story-books as at mining or engineering, and has added "The Man in the Moon, and other Stories," to his previous achievements. "Heads and Tails: Studies and Stories of Pets," by Grace Greenwood, needs no commendation. A few more deserve mention:

From Four to Fourteen. By Jennie Harrison.
Mercy Gleddon's Work. By Elizabeth Stuart Phelps.
The Old Lady that lived in a Shoe. By Amanda M. Douglas.
Seven Daughters. By the same.
Running to Waste. The Story of a Tomboy. By George M. Baker.
Christmas at Cedar Hill. By Lucy Ellen Guernsey.
Lady Rosamond's Book. By the same.
Sceptres and Crowns. By the author of "The Wide Wide World."
The Flag of Truce. By the same.
Our Helen. By Sophie May.
The Schoolmaster's Stories for Boys and Girls. By Edward Eggleston.
The Young Moose-Hunters: A Backwoods-boys' Stories. By C. A. Stephens.
Antoine. The Actual Life-Story of a Boy stolen from Italy. By an ex-Consul.
John Dare; or, The Trials of Artist-Life. By C. W. Derwin.
The Fisher Boys of Pleasant Cove. By Elijah Kellogg.
Julius; or, The Street Boy out West. By Horatio Alger, Jr.
Memoir of Washington, for Boys and Girls. By Mrs. E. B. Phelps.
Captain Kidd, and the Early Buccaneers. By J. S. C. Abbott.
Roddy's Romance; A Story for Young Folks. By Helen Kendrick Johnson.
Swallow Flights. By Harriet McEwen Kimball.
The Island Home; or, The Young Castaways. By Christopher Romaunt.
Jeanie Darley; or, in the Darkness and in the Light. By the author of "Lifting the Veil," etc.
Keeping Open House. By Mary W. McLean.
Ponapé; or, Light on a Dark Shore. By Mrs. Helen S. Thompson.
Sunday Afternoons. A Book for Little People. By E. F. Burr, D. D.
The Little Princess, and other Stories, chiefly about Christmas. By "Aunt Hattie."
Take a Peep. By Paul Cobden.
Home Recreations. A Complete Manual of Tableaux and Amateur Theatricals. By William F. Gill.
Peter the Apprentice. An Historical Tale of the Reformation in England. By the author of "Faithful, but not famous."
Risen from the Ranks. By Horatio Alger, Jr.

Sunny Shores; or, Young America in Italy and Austria. By Oliver Optic [W. T. Adams].

The Life of William, Prince of Orange; or, The King and his Hostage. By Rev. T. M. Merriman.

Gipsey's Travels. By Josephine Pollard.

Brave and Bold; or, The Fortunes of a Factory-Boy. By Horatio Alger, Jr.

Sandy Cameron; or, The Way One looks at it. By the author of "Ruth Allerton."

Ralph Waring's Money. By Mrs. A. K. Dunning.

Queen Louisa of Prussia; or, Goodness in a Palace. By Catharine E. Hurst.

The Dorcas Club; or, Our Girls Afloat. By Oliver Optic.

F. Grant & Co.; or, Partnerships. A Story for Boys who "mean Business." By George L. Chany.

William Henry dramatized, by Mrs. George L. Chany, from the William Henry Books of Mrs. A. M. Diaz.

The Squire of Walton Hall; or, Sketches and Incidents from the Life of Charles Waterman, Esq., the Adventurous Traveler and Daring Naturalist.

Sowed by the Wind; or, the Poor Boy's Fortune. By Elijah Kellogg.

That Queer Girl. By Virginia F. Townsend.

His Mother's Fancy. A Story for Juveniles and Young Old Folks. By Theresa Oakey Hall.

The Giants, and Wonderful Things. By Richard Newton, D. D. .

MISCELLANEOUS.—The announcement of "The American Cyclopædia," a revision of the "New American Cyclopædia," so thorough as to make virtually a new work, excited general interest, which the character of the volumes issued has more than justified.—The volumes contributed by American authors to the "International Scientific Series" have been noticed in their appropriate connections. But the series itself is of American origin and editorship, and is as much a matter of national credit as of international interest. The publication of Dr. E. H. Clarke's "Sex in Education" has called forth an extensive polemic literature, and led to the publication, by Dr. Clarke, of a second work on the subject, entitled "The Building of a Brain." Of the replies, "Sex and Education," edited with an Introduction by Mrs. Julia Ward Howe, is critical, sifting vigorously the testimony adduced by Dr. Clarke in support of his positions. "The Education of American Girls, considered in a Series of Essays," edited by Anna C. Brackett, besides ably controverting Dr. Clarke, brings forward much valuable thought and suggestion on the subject of female education. Other works evoked by the same publication are: "No Sex in Education," by Mrs. E. B. Duffy; "Woman's Education and Health," by G. F. and A. M. Comfort, and "Critical Thoughts upon Certain Special Passages in Dr. Clarke's 'Sex in Education,'" by William B. Greene. Other noticeable books of an educational character are, a new edition of the "Records of Mr. Alcott's School," a unique specimen of pedagogy; "Helpful Thoughts for Young Men," by Dr. T. D. Woolsey; and "Gail Hamilton's" sprightly volume, "Nursery Noonings."—A work of permanent value to students of English literature is, "A Concordance to Shakespeare's Poems," by Mrs. Horace Howard Furness.—Of

miscellaneous essays, some have appeared of exceptionally good quality. Such are, "Under the Trees," by Dr. Irenæus Prime; "The World on Wheels," by B. F. Taylor; "The Schoolmaster's Trunk," by Mrs. A. M. Diaz; "John Paul's Book," the collected humors of a new popular favorite, and "The Great Conversers, and other Essays," by William Mathews. The death of Senator Sumner called forth many expressions of honor to his memory, among which the Eulogy by the Hon. Carl Shurz is preëminent. Worthy to rank with it is the Eulogy on Chief-Justice Chase, by Mr. William M. Evarts. "The Communistic Societies of the United States," by Charles Nordhoff, is valuable for its information and its suggestions. The Speeches of Josiah Quincy in Congress is a republication of a work of historical value and interest. The titles of some other works are added, without comment, though some of them deserve more distinct recognition of their merit:

Among our Sailors. By J. Gray Jewell, M. D., late U. S. Consul, Singapore. With an Appendix, containing Extracts from the Laws and Consular Regulations governing the United States Merchant Service.

The Story of a Summer; or, Journal Leaves from Chappaqua. By Cecilia Cleveland.

Woman, Love, and Marriage. By F. Saunders, author of "Salad for the Solitary" and "Social."

The Vienna Exposition and the Philadelphia Centennial Report of Charles Francis Adams, Jr., Commissioner of the State of Massachusetts to the Universal Exposition at Vienna.

Down the River; or, Practical Lessons under the Code Duello. By an Amateur. With Twelve Full-page Illustrations, by H. L. Stephens.

Epidemic Delusions. A Lecture, with Valuable Appendices, by Frederick R. Marvin.

Ancient Symbol-Worship. Influence of the Phallic Idea in the Religions of Antiquity. By Hodder M. Westropp and C. S. Wake. With an Introduction, Additional Notes, and an Appendix, by Alexander Wilder, M. D.

The Monumental City. Its Past History and Present Resources. By Geo. W. Howard. Illustrated.

Hand-book of Statistics of the United States. A Record of the Administrations and Events from the Organization of the United States Government to the Present Time. Edited by W. C. Spaulding.

The Teachings of the Ages. By A. C. Traveler.

An Encyclopædia of Freemasonry and its Kindred Sciences. By Albert S. Mackay.

Workingmen's Homes. Essays and Stories. By Edward E. Hale. With a Letter to Mr. Hale from Hon. Josiah Quincy.

A Fast Life on the Modern Highway. Being a Glance into the Railroad World from a New Point of View. By Joseph Taylor.

The Periodical Literature of the United States of America. With Index and Appendices. By E. Steiger.

Washington, Outside and Inside. By E. A. Townsend.

Our Vacations. How to go, where to go, and how to enjoy Them. By F. E. Clarke.

What I did with my Fifty Millions. By Moses Adams.

Home as it should be; with Counsel for All. By L. D. Barrows, D. D.

A Hand-book of Politics for 1874. By Edward McPherson.

Agricultural Property and Products of the United

States of America in 1840, 1850, 1860, and 1870. Arranged Geographically and by Nationalities. By Samuel B. Ruggles.

Nimrod of the Sea ; or, the American Whaleman. By William M. Davis.

An Essay on the Resumption of Specie Payments. By S. Cooper.

The Indian Question. By Francis Walker, Late United States Commissioner for Indian Affairs.

Wealth : Its Acquisition, Investment, and Use. By Franklin Wilson, D. D.

Bibliotheca Diabolica ; being a Choice Selection of the most Valuable Books relating to the Devil ; his Origin, Greatness, and Influence ; comprising the most Important Works on the Devil, Satan, Demons, Hell, Magic, etc.

Field, Cover, and Trap Shooting. By Adam H. Bogardus. Edited by Charles J. Foster.

The Sportsman's Club among the Trappers. By Harry Castlemon.

Prairie and Forest. A Description of the Game of North America, with Personal Adventures in their Pursuit. By Parker Gilmore, "Ubique."

Ten Years among the Mail-Bags ; or, Notes from the Diary of a Special Agent of the Post-Office Department. By J. H. Holbrook.

Woman and the Divine Republic. By Leo Miller.

Around the Tea-Table. By De Witt Talmage.

Unwritten History ; Life among the Modocs. By Joaquin Miller.

What a Boy ! What shall we do with Him ? What will he do for Himself? Who is to blame for the Consequences? By Julia A. Willis.

Deacons. By W. H. H. Murray.

Dress Reform : A Series of Lectures delivered in Boston. By Abba Goold Woolson.

The Ugly Girl Papers, or Hints for the Toilet.

The Finances : Panics and Specie Payments. By J. W. Schuckers.

REPRINTS AND REPUBLICATIONS. — An increasing proportion of republications are not reprints. Editions for American circulation are printed in England with the imprint of American publishers. In one way or the other English books that promise a remunerative sale are speedily put upon the market here, with what effect upon American authorship it is hardly necessary to remark. Of these republications the most numerous are novels. The works of William Black, of which "A Princess of Thule " is preëminent; of Thomas Hardy, whose " Far from the Madding Crowd " won the compliment of being suspected to be the production of "George Eliot; " of B. L. Fargeon, who succeeds Dickens—at a distant interval—as a delineator of the humbler grades of London life, and (though a Jew) in embodying the festive spirit of the Christmas season ; of Mrs. Oliphant, whose fertility of production is marvelous when the excellence of quality is considered; of Miss Mulock, the unsensational quiet of whose works would become tameness but for the engaging characters she conceives and delineates; of Wilkie Collins, who dedicates to the American people a new uniform edition of his works; of the author of "The Rose Garden," "Unawares," and (last written), "Thorpe Regis ; " of Miss Braddon, and Edmund Yates, and Jules Verne, and F. W. Robinson, and Anthony Trollope, and R. D. Blackmore, and Florence Marryat, and others, who need not be characterized, are promptly

reproduced. An attempt was made to interest the public in Sara Coleridge's fairy tale, "Phantasmion," but the present public was not much more impressible by it than that to which it was first submitted. The lady who assumes the name of "Edward Garrett" has an increasing number of admirers among serious readers, and George Macdonald among all sorts of readers except the frivolous.

Next to works of fiction come works of science. There are "Science Primers," "Half-hour Recreations in Popular Science," "Elementary Science," and "Advanced Science Series," in sizes and at prices which adapt them to wide circulation. At the other extreme is to be mentioned Herbert Spencer's "Descriptive Sociology," of which successive parts have been circulated in this country. The works of Richard A. Proctor on astronomy, "The Expanse of Heaven," "The Borderland of Science," etc., seem to be popular and successful. "Man and Apes," by St. George Mivart, of course interests the (at present) superior race represented in the title. Other important works in this department are "Problems of Life and Mind," by G. H. Lewes; "Animal Locomotion," by Pettigrew; "Responsibility in Mental Diseases," by Maudsley; "The Great Ice Age," by Geikie; "Mental Physiology," translated from the French of Dr. Ribot; "Manual of Metallurgy," by W. H. Greenwood; "The Science of Law," by Prof. Sheldon Amos; and the eighth edition, presenting the final form, of Mill's Logic.

In extent of circulation religious works vie with any others, and they are promptly laid hold of for republication, more especially as every school of religious thought in Great Britain has its representatives here. To the " Library of Philosophy and Theology," edited by Drs. Philip Schaff and H. B. Smith, has been added, by simultaneous publication in England and the United States, a translation of Van Oosterzee's "Christian Dogmatics." The "Speaker's Commentary" is regularly reproduced here under the title, "The Bible Commentary." Dr. Farrar's "Life of Christ" has had an immense circulation, considering the form of issue and the price. The Bampton Lectures of the Rev. J. G. Smith and the Rev. Stanley Leathes appeared here as soon almost as in London. "The Paraclete : an Essay on the Personality and Ministry of the Holy Ghost," published anonymously, has been authentically attributed to the Rev. Dr. Joseph Parker, author of "Ecce Deus," and, while still anonymous, attracted much attention. Other notable works were Mr. Mill's posthumously published "Three Essays of Religion; " "The State of the Blessed Dead," by the late Dean Alford; "Modern Doubt and Christian Belief," by Dr. Theodor Christlieb ; "Theology in the English Poets," by the Rev. Stopford A. Brooke; "The Silence and Voices of God, and other Sermons," by Dr. F. W. Farrar; "Dictionary of Sects, Theories, and Schools of

Thought," by John Henry Blunt, F. S. A.; the "Sermons of the Rev. Dr. R. S. Candlish;" and "The Superhuman Origin of the Bible," by Henry Rogers.

In History and Biography are to be noticed "Curtius's History of Greece," completed, with some revisions and notes belonging exclusively to the American edition; the series of volumes in "Epochs of History," edited by Edward E. Morris; the "Historical Course," edited by E. A. Freeman; "The English in Ireland in the Eighteenth Century," by J. A. Froude, completed; "History of the Jewish Nation," by E. H. Palmer; the "History of the Church," by Canon Robertson, in progress; the completion of Forster's "Life of Dickens;" "Essays in "Military Biography," by Colonel Chesney; Arnould's "Life of the First Lord Denman;" the "Autobiography and Memoirs of Dr. Guthrie;" and the "Life of Samuel Lover," by Bayle Bernard.

In Travels, Geography, etc., there have come to us such works as Sir S. Baker's "Ismaïlia," and "The Wild North Land," by Captain W. F. Butler; "The Naturalist on the River Amazon," by H. W. Bates, F. L. S.; Taine's "Tour through the Pyrenees," Victor Hugo's "Tour on the Rhine," the great work of Dr. Georg Schweinfurth, "The Heart of Africa," and the richly illustrated and picturesquely written "Travels across South America," by Paul Marcoy.

Of Poetry may be mentioned George Eliot's "The Legend of Jubal, and other Poems;" "The Poems of Schiller," translated by Edgar A. Browning; Lord Lytton's "Fables in Song;" the "Poetical Works of William Blake," edited by W. M. Rossetti; and the "Works of John Hookham Frere."

Outside these heads of classification we have received "Military and Religious Life in the Middle Ages," by Paul Lacroix, finely illustrated; "The French Humorists," by Walter Besant; "Health and Education," the last volume from the pen of the lamented Canon Kingsley; "Dorothy Wordsworth's Tour in Scotland," edited by Principal Shairp; "Manual of Mythology," by A. S. Murray; the end of the excellent series of "Ancient Classics for English Readers," the completing work being that on "The Greek Anthology," by Lord Neaves; "Chapters on Animals," by Philip Gilbert Hamerton; and several volumes of memoirs and personal reminiscence, which, under the editorship of Richard H. Stoddard, are served up "in quantities to suit purchasers" under the descriptive general title of "The Bric-à-Brac Series."

These and other works introduced from abroad, though not a part of American literature, have an important share in our literary culture, and their publication without the protection of copyright has no inconsiderable effect on our "Literary Progress." The copyright question is untouched, and likely so to continue for an indefinite time. This may be regretted, but Congress seems inaccessible to any interest that is not "inside politics" or has not "money in it."

LITERATURE, CONTINENTAL, IN 1874. The activity in Continental literature in 1874 will be seen by the following extracts from the correspondence of the London *Athenæum:*

BELGIUM. — The *Patria Belgica*, published under the direction of Prof. Van Bemmel, contains a series of highly-interesting articles devoted to the ethnography of the Belgian people, their history, their institutions, and the present organization of the country (hospitals, justice, administration, army, finance, commerce, industry, railroads, and canals), under the title of "Belgique Politique et Sociale."

Besides this there are works which deserve special mention. One of them is "Morceaux Choisis de Poëtes Belges," collected by Prof. B. van Hollebeke; the other is "L'Anthologie Belge," edited by Madame Struman Picard and Prof. Godefroid Kurth. In looking through these volumes one feels astonished at the number and the talent of the French poets of Belgium, who excite but little attention in their own country, and who are absolutely unknown in France. They are remarkable for a peculiar originality and a sturdy sense of morality, which form a strong contrast to the spirit of the present literature of France.

The prose-writers have furnished a numerous contingent. We may mention the novels of Leclercq, A. Prins, Pergameni, C. Lemonnier, X. de Reul, Émile Greyson, and Justin Grandgagnage, whose names are well known in Belgium. Octave Pirmez, whose elegant and poetical style is sometimes too diffuse and vague, has produced a new work, called "Heures de Philosophie."

A. Michiels, the brilliant and fertile art-critic, has not only issued the ninth volume of his "Histoire de la Peinture Flamande," the reputation of which is well established, but has also brought out the third edition of "L'Architecture et la Peinture en Europe du quatrième siècle jusqu'à la fin du seizième," a work which is much esteemed, and which also contains the *résumé* of the author's own ideas upon art. We must not forget to mention the work of A. Barlet upon "L'Union des Beaux-Arts avec l'Industrie," as well as the remarkable reports upon "L'Enseignement du Dessin," by Profs. De Taye and Canneel.

In the domain of history we must give the first place to the second volume of Jules Van Praet's "Essais sur l'Histoire Politique des Derniers Siècles." The first volume made a sensation both in Belgium and abroad—the present volume will do the same. It is remarked especially that the judgment he passes upon Frederick II. shows him to be a true historian, worthy to take rank among the highest names in Europe for impartiality and clearness of insight.

Among the publications of hitherto unpublished documents, the collection of "Voyages des Souverains dans le Pays-Bas," by Gachard, is worthy of notice. This work contains the travels of the Emperor Charles V., and gives some curious details, among other things, of the profusion with which the Emperor's table was served; all the animals in creation would seem to have appeared upon the board. Diegérick has published "Documents of the Sixteenth Century," taken from the archives of Ypres, a most important collection. They show the commencement and progress of the religious reformation in Flanders. Alph. Wanters, has given us the fourth volume of his excellent "Table Chronologique des Chartes et Diplômes concernant l'Histoire de Belgique." This volume comprises the thirteenth century. In an introduction, full of erudition and research, the learned archivist of Brussels clears up several obscure points of our history in the middle ages, and he treats us to much sound criticism in his disquisition upon the relative values of contemporary chroniclers.

Among the publications on judicial matters, the most important are the three new volumes of "Principes du Droit Civil," by F. Laurent, Professor at the University of Ghent (forming vols. x., xi., xii.). This work, which bears incontestable marks of learning and originality, bids fair to be one of the best books which the present century has produced on this subject.

We must not close this notice of Belgian works, written in French, without calling attention to the reorganization of the *Revue de Belgique*, which has greatly increased in its circulation. It has become the organ of different shades of Belgian Liberalism, in opposition to the two reviews, *La Revue Catholique* and the *Revue Générale*, which are the organs of the rival party.

In the present year, as in all previous ones, novelists have written the greater number of the books which have been published in 1874. The first place among them must be accorded to a remarkable work, which has made a great sensation both in Belgium and Holland, called "Ernest Staas, Advocaat," written by Tony Anton Bergmann. This book has been, like the Song of the Swan, of the most ethereal and original of Flemish prose-writers. He had already achieved a reputation as an historian and author of short, spirited, detached stories, and now "Ernest Staas" has crowned his fame in literature. The death of Anton Bergmann has left a void in the literature of the Netherlands. The "Novellen," by Rosalie and Virginie Loveling, are also remarkable works. These two sisters were, until lately, only known by their poems, full of a freshness and simplicity which remind one of the shorter pieces of Uhland and Longfellow. Their volume of stories, which are pictures of peasant-life in Flanders, is distinguished by the same literary qualities, and has achieved a great success, especially in Holland, where the public seems to have thoroughly recognized the delicacy and

good taste which are developed with charming simplicity.

Hendrik Conscience, the novelist, has not allowed his pen to be idle. Besides two stories of contemporary manners ("De Kuesvdes Harten," and "Eene Verwarde Zaak"), he has written an historical novel, called "Everard 't Serclaes," the subject of which is taken from an incident that occurred in the Brabant Communes during the fourteenth century.

In the domain of poetry, the place of honor must be given to the "Gedichten" ("Poems") of Emmanuel Hiel, which appeared in the *Bibliothèque Néerlandaise*, published in Germany by a firm well known in Leipsic, F. Brockhaus. This collection is marked by brilliant lyrical qualities; it possesses real originality of thought and profound poetic sentiment; and it is also remarkable for the wonderful richness and variety of its rhymes.

Among the literary annuals, there are two which are indissolubly linked with Flemish history and Flemish literature—one is "Le Jaarboekje," of the venerable poet F. Rens, which has appeared now for more than forty years. This year it contains the whole of the last lines written by Anton Bergmann. They describe a beautiful journey to Venice, and are called "Marietta la Bella," and were written by the poet on his death-bed. "De Studenten Almanak" ("The Almanac of the Students of Ghent") is perhaps the oldest and most curious publication of its kind. Many of the Flemish and Dutch writers have made their first appearance in its pages, for this work is open to the students of all the universities of Belgium and Holland. The Roman Catholic students of the University of Louvain, whose political and religious opinions keep them aloof from the Annual of Ghent, published an interesting volume of their own for 1874.

Dramatic literature has shown signs of life in 1874.

BOHEMIA.—Czechs are naturally proud of the fact that their nation has twice taken the lead in European thought, i. e., in the Hussite wars and in the Thirty-Years War. When the Bohemian kingdom was crushed at the calamitous battle of the White Mountain, it seemed as if the nation must disappear; but, thanks to the efforts of patriotic men, well supported in their arduous task by the nation, it was in truth remade, and this position gives a peculiar interest and stamp to the whole of Czech literature.

We turn to the productions of the expiring year, commencing with that branch to which most attention is paid in our literature. Palacky's historical work continues to appear, the latest publication being that of the second part of vol. v., containing the period of the Jagellons down to 1526. The collecting of historical materials has also found assiduous workers. The Bohemian Archives are a magnificent compilation, edited, since 1840, by Palaky', at the expense of the Bohemian Diet. This year appeared the fifth part of vol. vi. Dr. Emler, keeper of the Archives of Prague, is publishing "Fontes Rerum Bohemicarum." We have also "Reliquiæ Tabularum Terræ Regni Bohemiæ anno MDLI. igne consumptarum," "Regesta Diplomatica Bohemiæ et Moraviæ," and "Libri Citationum et Sententiarum," by Brandt, while a "History of Moravia," by B. Dudik, has reached its sixth volume. Zeleny"s "Life of Juugmanu" is an interesting account of one of the most stirring times of Bohemia. The second volume of Dr. Czupr's work on "Old Indian Lore" ("Uczeni Staroindické") contains interesting particulars on the development of the European religions.

As regards the classics, we have Prof. Niederle's "Grammar of the Greek Language," comparing it directly with the Slavonic tongue, a work valuable in preventing the necessity of studying books which treat Greek from a German point of view. The connection of the Slavonic languages, as exemplified by the old Slavonic, is well brought out by Prof. Geitler's book on the phonology of Old-Bulgarian or Church Slàv.

The Society of Bohemian Mathematicians (connected with many foreign ones) edits several periodicals, the only mathematical journals in Austria, under the direction of Prof. Studnicka and Dr. Weyr. Many publications in the area of natural science have been issued; the best known is the "Scientific Exploration of Bohemia," published by order of the Bohemian Diet, of which vol. ii., "Prodromus Floræ Bohemicæ," by Prof. L. Czelakovsky', has appeared.

The political journalism of the country has considerable influence; I may mention Czasopis Czeského Musea (Journal of the Czech Museum), published by Dr. Ember, exclusively scientific, and Osveta (Enlightenment), including novels and poetry, and edited by Vácslav Vleck, and many other more special ones, while journalism for the people, helped by compulsory education, has attained great results. The "Poesie Svetova" ("World's Poetry") is engaged in completing our translations of the best foreign authors, and the "Nadroní Bibliotheka" ("National Library"), conducted by Zakrejs, is doing the same for native literature. We have also the collection of V. Vleck's novels and tales; the poetical works of B. Janda, etc. Svatopluk Czech's poems show considerable talent, and we have also poems by Mdlle. Krasnohorská, Hejduk, and Jaroslav Goll.

DENMARK.—This year has been still less productive than 1873. Not one notable work of imagination has appeared. Some volumes of lyrics have been issued, and a number of novels and tales, none of which it is necessary to dwell upon. Bergsöe's "Rome under Pius IX." (not finished) is a large illustrated medley of descriptions. Of more interest is a small, lively volume, by an anonymous tourist, "Traits of Life in America."

In history, we have but two notable books: a large volume by C. Paludan-Müller, on "The First [Four] Kings of the Oldenburg Family," containing "outlines and thoughts" that put many things in a new light. A small volume, by General C. Hegermann-Lindencrone, on "The Year of War, 1864," contains an attack, couched in moderate terms, on the policy of the dominant "national" party, on the way in which the ministry meddled with military operations, and on the pernicious influence of the Copenhagen press.

G. Brandes's "Reaction in France," the most interesting book of the year, is vol. iii. of his "Great Currents of Literature." He and his brother, E. Brandes, in October, began a literary periodical, the Nineteenth Century, on whose prospects I cannot yet pronounce an opinion; yet signs of a coming change of "currents" are not altogether wanting. Danish literature is chiefly an offshoot of German "Romanticism," and of ideas originating in Schelling's philosophy which came in above seventy years ago, and coalesced with the "bardism" of the Klopstock school previously introduced. As the productiveness of this "current" is dying out, something must fill the void; and there is no resource except the newest European "currents," to which Brandes wants to lead his unwilling countrymen, who fear that their nationality, with all their virtue and religion, will be drowned in them.

Of H. Scharling's "Humanity and Christianity," a "philosophy of history," the concluding vol. ii. has been given to the world. The work contains sketches of non-Christian religions and of the chief Christian Churches, with remarks on ancient civilization, and a chapter on modern Humanism. How this can constitute a "philosophy of history," is not clear to me, if indeed it has ever been discovered what the "philosophy of history" really is. The book, though rich in materials, can scarcely be said to contain any thing new, but it is written in the lively, popular style characteristic of the author. He is a most orthodox Lutheran, and speaks rather contemptuously of modern researches regarding the antiquity of man, etc. R. Nielsen's "Conditions of Vigorous Volition" is one of his quasi-popular books—not those in the philosophic dialect, where not a sentence is comprehensible to common mortals, but those that are, linguistically, rather more intelligible. Yet I approach it with diffidence, expecting the common fate of being convicted of misunderstanding Nielson toto cœlo. Let me venture to state that the professor divides a human being into three parts—body, soul, spirit—so that reason belongs to the soul; and that in his system the condition of invigorating, i. e., Christianizing, the will is raising it above reason (and above the "soul") into the "spirit." Many may possibly suspect our great philosopher of having risen so far above reason as to mistake the "spirit" for one-third of the individual man, but they will, no doubt, be told to keep silence, as having themselves never risen above reason, and so being no more able to talk about the matter than the blind about color.

FRANCE.—If we look impartially at the literary results of the year now closing, we find very few original works of any real value. Let me, in the first place, direct your attention to publications connected with historical science. Reprints abound, *recueils* of articles contributed to periodicals, new and improved editions of classical authors, and that is nearly all. Your readers are aware that the French Foreign Office, adhering steadily to the custom which has prevailed for the last two centuries, had, until quite recently, closed its doors against students, even those who did not wish to transform history into a weapon for the politics of the present day. This was carrying precaution to the most absurd lengths. Better times, however, seem to be approaching; and a committee has just been organized, under the direction of M. de Vielcastel, for the purpose of revising the old rules of the Ministère des Affaires Étrangères, and placing within the reach of the public some of the treasures it contains. The merit of bringing about this improvement may justly be claimed by M. Armand Baschet, who, in a most interesting volume, has told us in detail how the "Memoirs" of Saint-Simon contain only a small portion of the documents left by that garrulous *gentilhomme* on the reign of Louis XIV. and the regency of the Duke d'Orléans. What danger can there be, as a matter of fact, in sending to the press the state papers and other documents of general importance belonging to the pre-revolutionary epoch? None in the least, if we may believe M. Geffroy and Herr von Arneth, whose three handsome and substantial octavos have rendered to the cause of history and to the reputation of the unfortunate Marie Antoinette the most signal service, by placing before us the correspondence of the Empress Maria Theresa with Count de Mercy-Argenteau, the Austrian ambassador at the court of Versailles. The influence of Spain over Continental politics reached its highest pitch about the middle of the seventeenth century; and in this chapter of modern history there are many portions which are intimately connected with the annals of our French neighbors. Such, for example, is the whole question of the matrimonial alliances, so fully analyzed by M. Perrens, in his work entitled "Les Mariages Espagnols sous le Règne de Henri IV et la Régence de Marie de Médicis." This gentleman, confining himself to an epoch with which he is thoroughly familiar, has devoted another work to the relations between the French court and the papal see. The attitude of the Ultramontanes toward the Gallican Church, the talents of the diplomatists on both sides, the importance of the theological books which arose from the conflict, and finally the serious character of the questions at stake, give exceptional value to the new volumes of M. Perrens, and lead us to wish that a writer so deeply conversant with the ecclesiastical history of his country would attempt what he himself considers so necessary, a special work on that very subject. M. d'Haussonville's "L'Église Romaine et le Premier Empire," and the book I am here noticing, are detached parts of an edifice which deserves to be raised in a careful, judicious, and impartial spirit. M. Pierre Clément's "Histoire de Colbert," finished by this *savant's* friend and *collaborateur*, M. Geffroy, is an appropriate sequel to the collection of dispatches and state papers which the great statesman issued during his long and laborous administration. It throws the greatest light upon the reign of Louis XIV., and illustrates with much detail the working of the various branches of the public service.

The Count de Paris deserves to be named for his elaborate history of the civil war in America; nor can I pass over M. Dantier's historical studies in Italy, so interesting, so beautifully written, notwithstanding their fragmentary character. The invasion of the Lombards, the reign of Theodoric, the struggles between barbarism and Christian civilization, the Normans, the *communes* of Northern Italy, the attitude of the papacy toward the empire, such are the subjects treated by M. Dantier with so much the more success because, in addition to his thorough acquaintance with printed and MS. documents, he enjoys the advantage of a long residence in Italy, and a consequent knowledge of the country. M. François Lenormant, with his wonted activity, pushes his inquiries into the most various quarters: the two volumes entitled "Les Premières Civilisations," treat of Egypt, Assyria, Phœnicia, and Chaldea; they are a series of essays originally contributed to sundry periodicals, and where a number of interesting questions connected with the history, the literature, and the religion of Eastern people are carefully discussed. In another work ("La Magie chez les Chaldéens") M. Lenormant examines the different systems of magic and incantations practised on the banks both of the Nile and of the Euphrates, thus throwing new light upon a most important side in the development of ancient mythology, and deducing from the study of comparative religion fresh arguments for the consideration of ethnologists. M. Lenormant is open to the accusation of allowing sometimes too much to mere conjecture. On the history of ancient Rome, three works of unequal importance, but each deserving a notice here, have been published during the course of the last twelve months. M. Gaston Boissier's "La Religion Romaine d'Auguste aux Antonins" is a complete and admirably drawn sketch of heathen society at an epoch when society was not yet thoroughly leavened with the spirit of Christianity.

What was the character of the reforms introduced by Augustus; how far were they successful; and to what extent did philosophy, especially that of Seneca, combined with the action of foreign religions, modify the old Roman intellectual and moral world? These questions are certainly full of interest; and the recent discoveries made by archæologists and epigraphists have accumulated a number of documents toward their solution. M. Boissier, in his two volumes, has made excellent use of all these resources, and the result is a most interesting work on the origin of Christianity. The author takes care to declare expressly that the religion of the Gospel must not be considered as a development of existing mythologies and metaphysical systems; it was to all intents and purposes an independent work, and which could not have been accomplished by other agencies. Virgil and Seneca stand forth prominently in M. Boissier's notice as representatives of Latin thought during the early empire. Tacitus, another character who comes out in bold relief, has occupied the attention of M. A. Geffroy. Under the title of "Rome et les Barbares, Études sur la Germanie de Tacite," the learned Professor of Ancient History at the Sorbonne publishes a series of lectures delivered by himself, and in which he endeavors to prove, first, that Tacitus is a very trustworthy guide as to the condition of the Teutonic world; and, secondly, that the barbarians, as they were called, really conquered Gaul during the fifth century. It is well known that, with respect to this latter point, the Abbé Dubos and Montesquieu represented with equal ability two opposite schools of historians, the former denying that a conquest had occurred, while the author of the "Esprit des Lois" maintained it. M. Geffroy takes care to show that a critic may indorse Montesquieu's ideas without adopting the singular vagaries of certain democratic writers who describe the French aristocracy as immediately descended from the German conquerors, whereas the *prolétariate* are the modern representatives of the oppressed Gauls.

The history of archæology in its various forms bears a close relationship to the topics I have just been discussing, and the reader who studies the works of M. Beulé (" Auguste et sa Famille, le Sang de Germanicus," etc.) and M. Ampère (" L'Histoire Romaine à Rome ") will soon find the interdependence of these two branches of knowledge. Besides the various *livraisons* of the *Revue Archéologique* for the year 1874, I shall mention two works which may be considered as good specimens of this class of publications : the one is Dom Guéranger's " Sainte-Cécile et la Société Romaine aux Deux Premiers Siècles," and the other the sumptuous " Mélanges d'Archéologie ". of Fathers Martin and Cahier. Written from the strongest Ultramontane stand-point, the volume on Saint Cecilia unhesitatingly adopts all the legends so thoroughly demol-

ished two hundred years ago by Tillemont, Fleury, and Mabillon. Dom Guéranger inveighs furiously against Jansenists as well as Protestants, and looks upon the " Acta Sanctorum " in the light of an unimpeachable authority; but his account of early Christian society is interesting, nevertheless, and his description of the catacombs, profusely illustrated as it is with woodcuts, will be found very valuable. The " Nouveaux Mélanges d'Archéologie " forms two quarto volumes, which treat of various questions connected with Christian art, such as *Bestiaries*, church ornamentation, relic-cases, etc. ; the drawings in it are the work of Father Martin, lately removed by the hand of death from a busy and useful career ; the letter-press, for which we are indebted to his *collaborateur*, Father Cahier, gives evidence of sound scholarship and of varied learning. Count Grimoüard de Saint-Laurent's " Guide de l'Art Chrétien " should not be forgotten ; the fifth volume, lately published, contains the iconography of the saints, and will be perused with interest even by those readers who only wish to study in the company of an amiable and intelligent guide some of the best specimens of painting and sculpture.

Among the attempts made to reconcile the claims of science with those of revelation, I must name the learned work published by M. l'Abbé Fabre d'Envieu. This gentleman starts from the supposition that the narrative contained in the first chapter of Genesis has been misunderstood, and that a better interpretation of the text would remove all the difficulties raised by destructive criticism. He then examines in detail the evidence supplied by archæology, paleontology, and geology, and endeavors to show that the theories of the present day, with which the names of Messrs. Huxley, Darwin, and Tyndall, are associated, entirely break down, because they are derived either from false data or from illogical inferences based upon true ones. The history of philosophy and of religion has suggested a certain number of memoirs, which prove that the movement inaugurated by the late M. Cousin is still going on.

The reform of public instruction in its various stages still engages the attention of thinkers who are anxious to bring about the regeneration of France. Not satisfied with writing the history of the Government which took office in September, 1871, and of describing with all the authority of an eye-witness the causes which led to the downfall of Napoleon III., M. Jules Simon devotes a thick octavo to educational subjects, and aims at drawing the University of France out of the traditional groove in which it is still slowly moving. M. Jules Simon's schemes are excellent, yet they strike me as impossible so long as the national spirit of our neighbors remains what it is. Those of your readers who relish the *esprit Gaulois*, and are fond of works of fiction, cannot do better than peruse M.

Charles Louandre's "Chefs-d'Œuvre des Conteurs Français," in three handsome volumes, corresponding to La Fontaine's predecessors, contemporaries, successors. It was quite fit that *le bonhomme* should be taken as the centre of this crowded and *piquant* group, which, beginning with the "Chanson de Roland," and finishing with Voltaire, includes some of the most characteristic specimens of French literature. M. Louandre must have had some difficulty in making a choice among hundreds of productions, the most amusing of which are not always fit to be quoted; his biographical notices, analyses, and prefaces, are beyond all praise.

I must conclude my summary with a brief notice of the principal works of fiction which have appeared during the course of the year. M. Victor Hugo's "Quatre-Vingt-Treize" stands apart, of course, more on account of the gifted author's previous celebrity than of any merit which the book itself possesses. No production of the author of "Notre Dame de Paris" can be confounded with the mass of novels which the French press incessantly pours forth; but I am bound, at the same time, to say that the wildest eccentricities in point of style, the most thorough contempt of the language, disfigure every page of the book I am now alluding to. It is not expected that I should write out here the catalogue of all the trash lately printed under the pretense of describing the features of modern society; M. de Gobineau's "Les Pleiades" stands out prominently as the best; while M. Deulin's "Contes du Roi Gambrinus" are delightful specimens of quiet humor; and M. Xavier Aubryet's "Robinsonne et Vendredine" describes, in a really original manner, the contrast between the artificial characteristics of Parisian life and the honest simplicity of a person who has never wandered in the neighborhood of the *demi-monde*.

GERMANY.—A disease which threatened to prove as injurious to German literature as the oïdium to the vine is happily dying out. Pessimistic resignation, a hypercritical contempt for the world, are no longer the only or even the favorite ideas of the poets. The Renunciation of the World which the Frankfort Buddhist, Schopenhauer, preached, and of which the natural consequence is suicide, has been given up by his Berlin successor, Hartmann. Instead of cowardly endurance and abandonment of life and action, the latter has founded his Moral Philosophy upon the full devotion of the individual personality to the world for the sake of the salvation of the world; that is, he has called to life the "positive Bejahung des Willens." The do-nothing quietism of peevish philosophers who sat in their study-chairs has given place to the strict discipline of Prussian militarism. Extraordinary successes such as Germany has won are not consistent with contemplative retirement from the world, but only with unselfish self-sacrifice in behalf of a great national or human object. The universal liability to military service, which is the secret of Prussia's strength, is the visible expression of the social requirements of this practical philosophy. The heightened national and patriotic tone which pervades most of the poems of this year is its audible echo.

Is it the result of the predominance of the politico-national tendencies of the German people that the success of the new poems of Bodenstedt is less than that of the former series which made him the favorite of the reading public? Of the first series, nearly half a hundred editions have appeared up to the present time: the second will possibly take as long to reach a second edition. The cause is not any change in the poet, who remains, in mind, as youthful as ever, but in the age, which has grown a quarter of a century older

The non-political lyric can boast, besides numbers of unknowns who must be content to remain so, many old favorites, such as Simrock, Stoeber, the ex-Hegelian and ex-Revolutionist Ruge, and the dramatist Wilbrandt. To mention merely all from whom, like the Viennese poetess Sephino von Knorr, a strain derived from the heart occasionally escapes, would take more space than can be allotted.

The dramatic crop, if we cannot boast of faultless masterpieces, has yet turned out richer, not only as regards tragedy, but also in respect to comedies and popular pieces. Thanks to its numerous courts, Germany has never been without plenty of court-theatres, or "Fathers of their Country," who, too weak to rule the world, have contented themselves with ruling on the boards which represent the world, and with being their own theatrical managers. Little theatres like Weimar, Coburg, Munich, Carlsruhe, where the rulers were at hand to give judicious advice, have reached a position of considerable influence. For instance, in Meiningen, where the Grand-duke himself took the place of responsible manager, wonderful displays of archæological dilettanteism have occurred. Since Prussia deprived the minor sovereigns of their most costly plaything, their soldiers, the princely liking for commanding and dressing people has been expended on the actors. The performances, at Berlin, of the Meiningen company, directed by the Grand-duke, have shown that, as formerly in military, so now in theatrical affairs, the essential has been sacrificed to the unessential through a spirit of pedantic discipline, and a craze for accuracy in matters of costume.

Fr. Spielhagen, the greatest artist, as far as plots go, of living German novelists, has written nothing new since his short tale "Ultimo." Auerbach's "Waldfried" and Freytag's continuation of his never-ending "Ahnen," under the separate title of "The Nest of the Hedgesparrows," are the principal works of fiction of the year. Gutzkow invented for his novels the name "Roman des Nebeneinander." Auerbach's "Waldfried" might be called a "Roman des Durcheinander," and Freytag's a "Roman des Nacheinander." In Gutzkow's "Roman Enchanter," for instance, numerous careers run parallel, yet separated, *neben einander.* In "Waldfried" the lives of the many sons, daughters, and daughters-in-law of the hero (if one may so call the narrator of the family chronicle) are so interwoven with one another, that, as a distinguished critic has remarked, one ought always to have a genealogical table in one's hand. The book is a sort of allegorical account of the history of the German people from 1848 to 1870. The honest father who writes the biographies of his children and grandchildren symbolizes the nation which in different members follows different directions, that at last, some directly, others by by-ways, even traversing the ocean, have been all led to German unity. The unpleasant form of a diary kept by a third person deprives the narrative of the charm of directness. From a certain corresponding *naïveté* of style, Auerbach was—even when in his best novel, " On the Heights," he was at his best as a literary artist—not free; and in his latest work it threatens to become an injurious mannerism.

Auerbach's heroes and heroines, though they wander to all parts of the compass, have a common father and father-in-law ; but the succeeding generations of Freytag's " Ahnen " are still more loosely united, through a half-forgotten ancestor, in the grayest antiquity. Immo, the hero of the new novel, is a descendant of Ingraban, as Ingrahan was of Ingo. Beyond this the three have no connection, except a family likeness in their names. The visible subject of the tale is the struggle between the imperial power, in the person of Henry the Holy, against the most widely-scattered little potentates, the " Hedge-sparrows," whose "nest " Henry destroys. The invisible proper hero is, as with Auerbach, the German nation, whose progress in civilization is depicted step by step. Both these remarkable works are pervaded by the political tendency of the times. Masterly description of details in Nature and life have long been the acknowledged strength of both writers. Freytag's book has the advantage that, as each portion forms a complete whole, it has a greater artistic unity in its plan. The style, too, that in Ingo resembled a loose sort of heroic Saga, is in the present installment much simpler.

While the historical novel turns history into fiction, historical inquiry turns poetry into history. The monograph on the life of the reputed Messalina of the Renaissance, Lucretia Borgia, written by F. Gregorovius, the celebrated author of the "History of the City of Rome in the Middle Ages," will disappoint all who expect an operatic romance *à la* Victor Hugo and Donizetti. That beautiful woman had the misfortune to be no better than her age ; and, as she stood on the highest pinnacle of Christendom, it is no wonder that posterity has thought her worse. Gregorovius makes it probable that she was rather the tool of

great sinners, such as Alexander VI. and Cesare Borgia, than a sinner herself; and when, by her marriage with the Duke of Ferrara, she was withdrawn from their influence and left to herself, her better nature came out. Still, at best, she makes a poor figure by the side of the great women of the Italian Renaissance—Isabella Gonzaga, Vittoria Colonna, etc. If a calumniated woman is, in Gregorovius's impartial narrative, made to appear better than she has generally been supposed to be, the opposite has happened to another lady, who has been the object both of praise and blame. The "Correspondance Secrète de Marie Thérèse et Marie Antoinette," published from the papers of the Austrian embassador, Count Mercy - Argenteau, does not, strictly speaking, belong to German literature, as it is in French, and one of the two editors, Geoffroy, is a Frenchman. But, as the other is the head of the Vienna public records, Herr von Arneth, the biographer of the great Empress, and both the illustrious correspondents were German, I may mention here this valuable contribution to the history of the times immediately preceding the Revolution. In this authentic collection of documents, the ill-starred Queen appears what her enemies all her own sister, Caroline of Naples, affirmed her to be—volatile, pleasure-loving, extravagant, indifferent to the world's opinion, and not free from dissimulation. Of the heroism which misfortune developed in her, and which has surrounded her unhappy end with the halo of martyrdom, there is no trace in these letters, which go down to the death of her mother.

Among historical works of the first importance, the " History of the German Emperors," by the learned W. Giesebrecht, and the "History of the French Revolution down to 1800," by Sybel, have advanced a stage. To a more moderate estimate of the Revolution, a movement that has hitherto been described either in a strain of panegyric or the very reverse, few historians have so effectually contributed as Sybel. "The great European crime," the partition of Poland, is put in a new light by the document published by Adolf Beer, from the Vienna, and by Max Duncker, from the Berlin Archives. The humane opposition which Maria Theresa is said to have offered to the annexation is called in question, while the statement made by Frederick the Great, in his " Memoirs," that the partition was the only way of avoiding a great European war— a statement that has hitherto been regarded as a barefaced evasion—has been confirmed in a most unexpected manner.

An extensive correspondence with the brothers Humboldt, especially with Wilhelm, that will not be inferior in value, it is said, to the celebrated correspondence of Schiller with the latter, is promised by the family for the coming year. Hermann Uhde has edited the recollections of a mediocre Weimar artist, Louise Seidler, in whom Goethe took a warm 'interest, because she submitted willingly to the somewhat dictatorial decrees of him and his friend, the well-known "Kunstmeyer," with regard to sculpture. Besides much that is worthless, these recollections contain several valuable contributions to our knowledge of art and artists at Weimar and Rome; chief among which is the information about Thorwaldsen and his wondrous domestic relations. The sculptor, who in daily life was never wiser than a child, had an Italian mistress, was engaged to an Englishwoman, and was in love with a German, and yet never made any one of them his wife. He renounced the English lady (Miss Mackenzie) because he was afraid of the vengeance of the Italian woman, while the German (an actress and a pupil of Goethe's), Fanny Caspers, of Mannheim, could not become his wife because he had promised Miss Mackenzie, when he deserted her, that he would never marry. Another member of Goethe's circle was the sister-in-law of his friend, Charlotte von Stein, Frau Sophie von Schardt, a lovable lady, who afterward turned Catholic, like her "friend," the wild author of "Luther," Zacharias Werner. The Goethe maniac, H. Düntzer, who, by-the-way, has also published the second volume of his life of Frau von Stein, has written a book about Frau von Schardt, which will interest people who are fond of literary tittle-tattle. On the whole, German *savants* have of late years made great advances toward intelligibility, and even to elegance of style, without forfeiting their most valuable qualities, completeness and conscientiousness of treatment. Historians and naturalists vie with one another in writing in a clear and sometimes even a lively and tasteful manner; while philosophy, which once had an evil name for obscurity and difficulty, is trying to follow the example. The "Natürliche Schöpfungsgeschichte" of Haeckel, the most eloquent exponent of Darwin's views in Germany, may serve as a model of popular explanation of a theory of Nature which embraces the whole of organic Nature, from the protoplasmic cell up to man himself.

The strictly philosophical books of the year are not numerous. Lotze's "Logic" and Brentano's "Psychology" show the growing influence of English philosophy. The former enlarges upon the views of Mill, the latter upon those of Prof. A. Bain and his school. Mill's "Inductive Logic," indeed, counts hardly fewer admirers in Germany than in England. His "Autobiography," like his other works, has found a translator, Th. Gomperz; while his "Auguste Comte and Positivism" has been successfully translated by a lady—Elise Gomperz.

The growing influence of the natural sciences in Germany causes Empiricism and Positivism to gain ground there, while speculation loses it. That the Germans have still, however, no wish to yield to other nations their well-grounded reputation of being the teachers in philosophy of Europe, is shown not only by the adoption of German philosophy in non-German countries, such as Italy, Russia, Spain, Holland, Belgium, Poland, Hungary, etc., but still more by collected editions and collections of philosophical writers intended for a wide circulation. Schopenhauer's complete works have been published in six volumes, under the superintendence of his indefatigable disciple, Jul. Frauenstädt. Kirchmann's "Philosophical Library" already counts some sixty volumes, and is designed to bring the principal works of all German and non-German thinkers (the latter in translations) within the reach of the people. That by the side of this activity in republication there is no lack of fresh " departures," is shown by the attempt to supplement modern Empiricism through a new *critique* of the Reason (*Ilias post Homerum !*), which A. Spir has brought out under the title of "Thought and Reality." Under the name of "Natur-Ethik," Hermann Körner has endeavored to convert moral philosophy, like the other branches of philosophy, dialectics, psychology, and anthropology, into a "Natural Science." Hartmann's "Philosophy of the Unconscious" still gives occupation to the critics, who attack it now (Knauer) from the theistic, now (Volkelt) from the pantheistic point of view, without touching on its weak point that this philosophy, although professedly based on the facts of experience, appeals to instinct and clairvoyance, which at most are facts for "Spiritualists." From philosophy to the history of civilization, the history of philosophy forms a natural bridge. Thilo's "History of Philosophy" is valuable for its terseness and the keenness of the criticism, and is also remarkable as being the first from the stand-point of the Herbartian realism, which is akin to English philosophy. The treatise of R. Zimmermann, "Kant and the Positive Philosophy," explains the relation between Comte's "Sociology" and Kant's "Philosophy of History," and corrects the account Littré has given of the latter. A not very exhaustive tract by Stadler discusses Kant's "Teleology," while another, by Cohn, is devoted to his "Theory of Cognition." Upon the whole, we may say that German philosophy, though it seemed, with its mystical tendencies toward the clouds of speculation, to have left "old, honest," somewhat skeptical Kant far behind, has returned to him its former starting-point, and, in spite of Hegel and Hartmann, seems not to have got much beyond him. In anthropology, the admirable work of F. Müller, "Ethnology," has been followed by the completion of the book begun by W. Baer, and continued by Schafhausen and F. von Hellwald—"Prehistoric Man." The political speculations of the German-Hungarian Vambéry, the man most thoroughly acquainted with Turanian relations, in his "Central Asia and the Anglo-Russian Boundary Question," especially appeal to English readers, as he espouses the English side. Statesmen who take an interest in the Oriental question, and the *rôle* that Hungary shows a disposition to play in it, will find a great deal of information in "The Magyars and other Hungarians," an able book by Franz von Löher, the historian of the Germans in North America.

Æsthetic and art can boast of a valuable and original acquisition in the clever although somewhat eccentric "Twelve Letters of an Æsthetic Heretic," under which title Karl Hillebrand, of Florence, a former contributor to the *Revue des Deux Mondes*, is concealed. Gottschall's well-known "Poetic" has reached a third edition, and Lemke's cheap "Popular Æsthetic" a fourth.

I cannot even enumerate the numberless writings which the German ecclesiastical question daily calls into existence. The theologico-political quarrel about the limits of papal and civil authority, which one imagined was extinct, has broken out with fresh violence, and one might suppose that the times of the Guelphs and the Ghibellines had begun again. Of publications which, keeping clear of the questions of the hour, attack the very foundations of the papacy, I may here mention, as the best, the "Critical Inquiries into the Roman Legend of St. Peter," by the learned evangelical theologian, R. A. Lipsius; Volkmar's lecture, "The Romish Papal Myth;" and the *critique* of the basis of the popedom, by Prof. Frohschammer, of Munich, "The Rock of St. Peter at Rome." But for the knowledge of the dogmas and constitution of the Catholic Church as they have been since the Council of Trent to the present day, the most weighty publication of the year is the "Acta Concilii Tridentini," for the first time printed in a complete form, and from the original texts in the Vatican, in two thick volumes, by the former head of the Vatican Archives, Father Theiner, whose death has since occurred. This edition was originally commenced under the direction of Pius IX., before he had fallen into the hands of the Jesuits, stopped at the instance of the society, and completed at Agram by the compiler after his banishment from Rome, under the protection of the well-known opponent, at the Council, of the dogma of the papal infallibility, the Croatian Bishop Strossmayer.

GREECE.—In history, the most important place is unquestionably due to the fifth and last volume of the "History of the Hellenic Nation," by the learned Prof. M. C. Paparigopoulos. The volume, which fills one thousand pages, presents nothing short of a picture of the civilization of Greece from the thirteenth century to the nineteenth. It is divided into three parts, the first containing the history of the Frankish rule in Greece in the thirteenth century; the second, her history under the Ottomans; and, thirdly, her efforts to attain a worthy place among the free and civilized nations of Europe. M. Paparigopoulos has the great merit of having been the first to give a comparative table of coins, and thereby shown the colossal resources of the Byzantine Empire. On the other hand, the elegant pen of Dr. D. Vikelas depicts the Byzantines under the most favorable aspect, so far as morality is concerned. I would remark, in passing, that something has always been lacking to the perfection of the Byzantines, and that is reason. Finally, our historian maintains that the politicians of the seventeeth century, known under the name of Phanariotes, entertained, in a higher degree than the Church and its clergy, the feeling of Hellenism. It is true that the Phanariotes always showed clearsightedness and patriotism, and that the men of that fraction of the nation preserved the spirit of the ancient Hellenic race, while the women preserved the ancient Hellenic type of beauty; but I do not consider it correct to say that the services rendered to the national cause by the Phanariotes equaled, or even surpassed, those of the Church and her clergy. Leake, who, for a long time to come, will be our teacher, says expressly that it was the Church that preserved the language, and with it the national union.

Besides the incomparable work of M. Paparigopoulos, there have appeared the fourth volume of the "History of the Ionian Islands" (from 1815–1829), by M. Christis; the "History of the Island of Hydra, from the Most Ancient Times down to 1821," by M. Miaulis; a new "History of the War of Independence," by M. Oeconomos; memoirs of the same war, by M. Dragoumis. They are all interesting for the documents they contain. Among geographical works, two especially deserve particular mention. The first, by M. Miliaraki, is called "The Cyclades," and contains the history and geography of those islands from the earliest period till the Frankish rule.

M. Sathas has just published, in the fourth volume of his "Library of the Middle Ages," the unpublished MS. of Michel Psellos, secretary, tutor, embassador, and minister of seven emperors in succession. By the publication of the important MS. which the industrious editor found in the National Library in Paris, the gap of one hundred years which existed in Byzantine history, between Leo Diaconos and Anna Comnena, is filled up.

A new publication of inedited Greek MSS. has been begun at Venice, under the superintendence of MM. Triantaphyllis and Grapponitis. The first part contains historical and religious writings of the Patriarch Philotheus, who lived in the thirteenth century. In the following parts, the editors propose to print only those writings of the patriarch which are immediately connected with the religion, history, and literature of Greece, properly so called.

HOLLAND. — Our diplomatic literature has been enriched this year by many works of interest. As it is impossible to enumerate all

.the writings of more than passing importance, I shall but make mention of De Bosch Kemper's "History of the Netherlands after 1830, with many hitherto Unpublished Documents;" Van Vlotin's "Middleburg Besieged and Taken, according to Original Documents;" Van der Heim's "The Archives of Antonie Heinsius, Grand-Pensionary of Holland;" G. W. Vreede's "Laurens Pieter van de Spiegel and his Contemporaries, from Letters and Other Authentic Documents," published by the Scientific Society of Zeeland; and S. Müller's "History of the Northern Company," published by the Utrecht Society of Arts and Sciences. Almost at the end of the year, Theod. Jorissen, so well versed in the so-called "patriotic" period of our history, presented our literature with another of his interesting monographs, "The Patriots of Amsterdam in 1794." No wonder that the second expedition to Acheen gave birth to an avalanche of writings on Acheen and East-Indian matters in general. The Dutch author of the splendid French work on our "Fastes Militaires," Major Gerlach, has published two interesting books, "The First Expedition to Acheen," and "Dutch East India." Prof. Veth, who knows India almost as intimately as Holland, has written "Java, Geographically, Ethnologically, and Historically Described."

More or less important contributions to topographical history have been published. Dekker, Ter Gouw, Koster, Doorninck, Kleyn, and Van Zinnicq-Bergman, respectively, have illustrated the history of Helder, Amsterdam, Groningen, Overyssel, Delshaven, and the Old Dukedom of Brabant. In this branch of knowledge Roman Catholic learning has chiefly manifested itself. I may mention Krüger's "Ecclesiastical History of the Episcopate of Breda;" Schutjes's "History of the Episcopate of Bois-le-Duc;" "Papers on the History of the Episcopate of Haarlem;" Hezenman's "Three Abbeys of the Twelfth Century: a Study on the Social Influence of Convents in the Middle Ages." Wonderful that the same respectable printing-firm publishes popular literature of this style: "Three Apparitions of Souls from Purgatory, in the Years 1527, 1856, and 1870; from Authentic Documents, and preceded by an Introduction, containing Remarkable Particularities on the Apparitions of Deceased Persons."

The principal signs of life in matters of theology are: Straatman's "Paul, the Apostle of Jesus Christ; his Life and Works, his Doctrine and Individuality: an Historical Inquiry;" "The Apocrypha; newly translated from the Greek by Dyserinck; Introduction by Dr. A. Kuenen;" Doedes's "A Materialist's (Ludwig Büchner's) Attack on the Belief in God." Mr. Kuyper, formerly a clergyman, now a member of our Second Chamber, has made a great impression by his lecture, "Calvinism: the Origin and Security of our Constitutional Liberties." In character Mr. Kuyper, a young man

of talents and eloquence, seems to be a scion of the old English Roundheads.

Our art literature has been assuming a promising appearance since the article Mr. Victor de Stuers wrote last year against Dutch vandalism and indifferentism in matters of art. It is really distressing to read the long catalogue of sins committed lately against art. Not a single poem or drama that rises above the average has appeared. Our melodious poet and masterly translator of poetry, J. J. L. ten Kate, has finished his translation of the Psalms, and begun that of Milton's "Paradise Lost," illustrated by Doré. Mrs. Bosboom-Toussaint, whose works may in many respects be compared to Sir Walter Scott's, has kept up the honor of our literature this year in "Major Frans," a lively and excellently-written novel. "The Lady of Groenerode," by Melati of Java, is also above mediocrity; and "G. van den Berg, de Jonker van Adrichem," is a book full of promise.

The finest pages of the literature of the year have once more been written by Douwes Dekker (Multatuli), in his seventh volume of "Ideas." Since the publication of his "Max Havelaar," he is generally considered one of the most remarkable writers of Europe. He displays the ardor of a true genius in his writings. His "Story of Young Walter" is a kind of autobiography, full of pathos, poetry, and most extraordinary psychological anatomy. In the latter quality it even excels "Middlemarch."

HUNGARY.—Hungarian literature in the past year has been making slow but steady progress. All who pay attention to the literary productions of the Magyars will have noticed that the researches in the field of national history and the cultivation of the vernacular occupy a preëminent place in the studies of the Hungarian *savants*. This is not at all to be wondered at. The Magyars have always looked upon their language, so essentially different in material and forms from the idioms of Europe, as the most sacred monument which their ancestors have brought with them, nearly a thousand years ago, from their distant Asiatic home.

Dr. Frakel's book on the relation of Melanchthon to the Hungarian Protestants may prove interesting, not only to the Hungarian, but the general European reader, treating, as he does, a hitherto but little-known fact, and this with an impartiality which cannot be enough praised, the author being a Catholic priest. There are not many Catholic priests in Europe who would show freedom from prejudice in a literary work of this kind, and this single fact proves sufficiently the spirit of religious toleration that prevails in Hungary. Speaking of those historical researches which throw a certain light upon events of a European importance, I will quote Mr. Alexander Szilágyi's careful studies on the reign of George Rákóczy II., which relate to the diplomatic transactions of that great Hungarian prince with the European powers of the North, and contain valuable data referring to the period before the partition of Poland, as well as the collection of his "Sketches and Essays," consisting of papers upon historical, social, and political lyrics. In speaking of other publications of a more strictly national tendency, I may mention Prof. Wenzel's monograph on "Stibor the Voyvode," Mr. Frederick Pesty's valuable contributions to the history of South Hungary, and sundry minor works resulting from the investigations made in the private archives of our noble families. In connection with history, we may mention a few publications in the branch of political science, such as "The History of European Law," by Prof. E. Hajnik ; "Hungarian Statistics," by Prof. John Humfalvi; and a "Treatise on Commercial Law," by Dr. Apáthi.

M. Jókai's never-tiring and always lively pen has produced a new novel, a most lovely picture of the Hungarian social life in the recent past, the details of which abound in those charms which made M. Jókai the favorite of this country, and indeed of civilized Europe. There are, besides M. Jókai, many other writers who tried their strength in this branch of literature, out of which I will mention M. Victor Vajda, M. Arnold Vertesi, and particularly M. Z. Beöthy, the last one a successful imitator of English novelists. Among the poetical compositions of the year I may quote, in the first place, M. John Arany's new work, which, under the form of a humoristic epos, pictures the adventures and the motley episodes in the life of a provincial actor—a composition the interest of which is much more enhanced if we know that it is a kind of autobiography of the author himself, so justly called our greatest living poet. Dramatic literature also counts a few interesting additions.

Original works referring to natural sciences have not been too numerous this year. There are, however, a few which are worth a notice. Such is "Ebb and Flood in the Bay of Fiume," by Prof. E. Stahlberger, of the Hungarian Nautical Academy. This book treats of the periodical and non-periodical movements of the sea; it is based upon careful and assiduous observations, and affords an evident proof of the author's acquaintance with his subject.

ITALY.—If the progress of a country in civilization were to be judged *only* by the literary masterpieces which it produced each year, I should be somewhat embarrassed to give a yearly account of the intellectual movement in Italy. Fortunately, this is not the case, masterpieces in literature being rather the exception than the rule in every country and in every age. New Italy is everywhere trying to found schools to lessen the number of those ignorant of the alphabet; but to be able to spell, or even to read at sight, does not include being able to understand what is read, or to love reading, nor even spending a little money to indulge the taste.

Le Monnier, the Florence publisher, has just issued, in one small and pretty volume, a selection of the best poems of the poet of Novara, Giuseppe Regaldi, the old and celebrated *improvisatore;* also a volume of poems by a distinguished Venetian poetess, Signora Erminia Fua Fusinato, in which the strength of the ideas has not diminished the sweetness and delicacy of the sentiments. At Milan there has been published the "Versi" of Michele Corinaldi, sometimes a felicitous imitator of the satiric poet Giusti.

After the poetry, I must mention the best new Italian novels which have come under my notice : "Il Piacere della Vendetta," and "Fortuna Disgraziata," written by the prolific and skillful Piedmontese novelist, Vittorio Bersezio (they are scenes of family life in Upper Italy) ; "Il Rè Prega," by F. Petrucelli della Gattina, a Neapolitan novelist, remarkable for his rich coloring, seeking for his effects in anomalous situations, and who writes after the school of sensational novels. "Contessa Matilde," by Paolo Tedeschi, an authoress of Trieste, who has taken refuge in Lombardy, gives pictures of the lives of young girls when they leave school. "Il Processo Duranti," a judicial romance, by Parmenio Bettol, of Parma, has made a sensation.

The foremost contributor to our historical literature is ever M. Adolfo Bartoli, professor at the Instituto di Studii Superiori of Florence, whose remarkable work, which is coming out in parts in Milan, is called "I Due Primi Secoli della Letteratura Italiana." In this work much new matter is introduced, and it is analyzed with critical insight.

M. Achille Monti, a Roman descendant of Vincenzo Monti, the poet, has given us an inquiry into the life of his ancestor, the aim of which is purely apologetic. Nicomede Bianchi, the Keeper of the Archives of Turin, has given us a valuable and well-written book upon "Carlo Matteucci e il suo Tempo." The Messrs. Prina Venosta and Stoppani have enriched us by their volumes of Manzoni's Biography. M. Attilio Hortis, of Trieste, has published an extremely well illustrated volume of "Scritti Inediti." Messrs. Christoforo Pasqualigo, of Venice ; Pietro Ferrato, of Padua ; Carlo Romussi, of Milan ; Domenico Carbone, of Turin ; Giosuè Carducci, professor at the University of Bologna; and the philosopher Augusto Conti, Arciconsolo of the Academia della Crusca, have all contributed illustrations of the works and life of Petrarch, on the occasion of the fifth centenary of his death.

To the departments of literary biography, and the history of philosophy, Prof. Alberto Rondani, of Parma, has contributed a volume, entitled "De Scritti d'Arte," written with boldness and good taste. Prof. Flaminio Del Seppia, a Tuscan, dwelling at Ancona, has written a book full of vigor and originality, called "I Primi Studii." Vincenzo di Giovanni, Professor of Philosophy at Palermo, and author of the excellent "Storia della Filosofia in Sicilia," has produced a volume of carefully written prose miscellanies, called "Scuola Scienza e Critica." Emmanuele Celesia, of Genoa, has written a noble and valuable work, "Storia della Pedagogia Italiana," in two volumes. Prof. Romualdo Bobba has published, at Lecce, in four volumes, "Storia della Filosofia per Rispetto alla Coscienza di Dio," that is to say, as regards metaphysics.

Linguistic studies, especially those which concern Italian dialects and inquiries into the Italian language, continue to make good progress, thanks to the admirable labors of Profs. G. I. Ascoli and Giovanni Flechia, and others of their school, which is becoming numerous, and is certainly important.

I cannot, unfortunately, chronicle the same amount of vitality in the study of the classic tongues, which are at present far too much neglected; hence, at the present moment, with the exception of some specialties, there is not throughout Italy one eminent man who is a scholar in ancient learning. Neither is the present the time to expect from Italy the solution of the great problem of the Etruscan language. Though we may not solve the mystery of the Etruscan tongue, I repeat that we turn our attention to our own living language. In a remarkable work, in two volumes, published at Milan, and written with much vigor by the Prof. Luigi Gelmetti, there may be found a *résumé* of all the questions which have recently been raised in Italy on the subject of language.

Among historical works to which special importance may be attached, and which deserve particular mention, are a new edition of two works by Cesare Cantù, "La Storia degli Italiani;" and "La Lombardia del Secolo XVII.," and, also by the same celebrated author, a very interesting and minute contemporary history, "Della Indipendenza Italiana." Cesare Cantù, who is at present the keeper of the Lombard Archives, has also established at Milan an excellent historical magazine, entitled *Archivio Storico Lombardo.*

SPAIN.—Among the great quantity of books which treat of special subjects, and which may be included within the circle of scientific publications, the best are: "Memoria sobre les Montes de Filipinas," by Vidal; "Diccionario Militar," by Almirante; "Estudio de la Poesia Heroico Popular Castellana," by Milá; and the supplement to "Los Bronces de Osuna," by Berlanga. Vidal's essay on the "Forests of the Philippine Islands" is a very interesting one, not only from the skillful way in which he treats the subject, but on account of the numerous lists of works relating to the East which accompanies this volume. The information given about the different varieties of timber to be met with on the islands, and the comparison with the timber of other colonies in those regions, are most important.

The "Diccionario Militar," by Almirante,

is a thick volume, the result of many years of study. It fills a gap in the military history of Spain. Besides the words used by the Spanish army in modern times, hundreds are given which are out of date, but which were common in Spain and Europe during the middle ages and the Renaissance.

Señor Milá's "Poesia Heroico Popular" is the best study which has yet appeared on the subject. The ballad literature of the middle ages is of interest to all Europe, and most specially when the examples are of an earlier date than the thirteenth century, either on account of the personages themselves, or the adventures which they relate, or the artistic tendencies which have influenced the poets of the time.

Señor Berlanga has published a supplement to his "Bronces de Osuna," which appeared last year. These bronzes constitute the most important discovery of Roman epigraphy in modern times; it is, therefore, necessary to call attention, not only to the *Lex Julia*, the text of which is given in these bronzes, a municipal law unknown to the present day, but also to the learned interpretations of the author.

It is a remarkable circumstance that, although the Spanish nation is supposed to have strong religious opinions, the number of modern theological works should be so small. Among the very few which have appeared this year, "Estudios Religiosos," by Father Zeferino Gonzalez, is worthy of notice; for if in some details he does not sufficiently appreciate modern scientific thought, he gives evidence, on many occasions, of a strong intelligence and courtesy when discussing the religious opinions of other authors.

Works of fiction are in Spain most popular, and have a large number of readers, but in number and literary merit bear no comparison to those which appear in England.

A book which has just been published of a more serious character, but which is written with the charm of a work of fiction, is "La Alpujarra," by Señor Alarcon. The Alpujarra is a district which is almost unknown, even to Spaniards themselves. Hardly any one crosses it, for it does not lead to any town of any commercial importance. It is situated in the province of Granada, between the southern slopes of the beautiful Sierra Nevada and the Mediterranean. The scenery is mountainous, and picturesque in the highest degree; there are hardly even any bridle-roads, and the means of locomotion are extremely difficult, even with the mules of the locality. Very few spots exist which have been more favored by nature than the fifteen or twenty miles which comprehend the width of this territory. On the summit of the sierra, in the regions of perpetual snows, the aromatic camomile and rare lichens grow; at the foot, the trees and shrubs of the north, the chestnut, oak, and pine; below are the fields of olives and vines;

beyond, the orange and lemon groves; and nearer the coast the bananas, guayabas, cotton, sugar-cane, and other tropical plants. The flowers and fruits of the Alpujarra are considered the finest of the province of Granada. Few places have witnessed so many varied and romantic events as those which have taken place there.

Dramatic works of high order have been very scarce this year—an unusual circumstance, for the average of Spanish modern dramatic literature has, up to the present time, been equal to that of other countries.

The literary societies which have been formed lately in Spain to promote the publication of manuscripts or scarce books have printed this year several interesting volumes. The "Sociedad de Bibliofilos" has published two volumes, and a third is daily expected, of "Las Campañas del Emperador Carlos V.," by Cerezeda, edited by Cruzada Villamil. No contemporary documents have appeared down to the present day concerning the history of Charles V.'s campaigns which are equal to this narrative, and it is strange that it should have remained so long unknown to students of this period.

Another society of bibliophiles, who edit their books under the name of "Libros de Antaño," has just printed a most important historical work, which, like Cerezeda's interesting account, has remained unpublished for the last three centuries. The title is "Cronica del Rey Enrico Otavo de Inglaterra." This chronicle appears to have been written by a contemporary author, whose name has not yet been certainly ascertained.

There are many points of contact between the "Cronica" and Father Rivadeneyra's "Cisma de Inglaterra, 1588." They both tell the same story, although from a different point of view. The anonymous author of the history of Henry VIII., although undoubtedly a Roman Catholic, is a partisan of the King's, although the greatest enemy of Catholicism, and praises him as much or more than English writers of the time, and in the same manner is lenient toward other historical events which appear abominable to Rivadeneyra. The notes which accompany this volume are due to the profound researches of the Marquis de Molins, and are of the greatest historical importance. The editor compares the text with Rivadeneyra's book, with documents from Simancas and other Spanish archives, and the principal English historians.

PORTUGAL.—The Government long ago proposed as a subject for an historical work, "The History, Military and Political, of Portugal, during the XVIII. and XIX. Centuries." The task was intrusted to M. Latino Coelho, and he has just published his first volume. If one formed an opinion of the book by the preface only, M. Coelho's history would be a first-class production, for the author shows a considerable knowledge of the scientific methods followed by European historians. Unfortunately, the work itself has none of the merits of the prefatory remarks, and its execution is not at all in harmony with the theory. M. Lobo d'Avila, an ex-Minister of Finance, has just issued the first volume of his "Studies on the Public Administration of Portugal." The work is divided into two parts: the one historical, in which the author reviews all the financial systems of our country since the beginning of the monarchy; the other analytical, in which he examines, in a scientific manner, all the features of our public economy down to modern days. For the early portions of the history of our finances, M. Lobo d'Avila has made no original inquiries. For the history of later times there is a great deal more information obtainable, and M. d'Avila has used his material with the skill that his knowledge and ability led the public to expect.

In novels, if we except translations from the Spanish and the French, I can hardly name three original stories.

M. Vilhena Barbosa has just issued the first volume of his "Archæological Essays," a collection of articles on various antiquarian matters that have appeared in literary journals.

RUSSIA.—Not long ago I asked the editor of one of the leading Russian journals why there had been such literary dearth in Russia during the last year. He alleged the censorship as one reason, and said that he had been unable to print the best articles which had been offered to him. That the censorship does have a certain repressive effect cannot be denied, when we remember that one of the numbers of the Messenger of Europe was stopped for some days, and two of the best articles were cut out, and that the business of two other journals was suspended for a whole month, so that a double number had finally to be published. The censorship in its desire to prevent "attacks on the existing order of things," and "the fomenting of discontent," often prevents the truth from being told, and this cannot but be detrimental to the interests of literature. At times the article or book may have nothing objectionable in itself, but be merely mal-apropos. This was the case with one of the articles above referred to, which was on Little Russia, but was considered out of place by the censorship, in consequence of some talk in the newspaper about a separative movement in the Ukraine. At the same time we must not give too much importance to the action of the censorship when we recollect that it is something to which Russian literature is accustomed, and that the greatest works of Russian writers were produced at a time when the censorship was the most severe.

Of late, Russian literature has fallen into two camps. For a long time there have been the liberal and reactionary schools in literature as well as in politics; the artistic and the realistic schools; but there are now the schools of Moscow and of St. Petersburg. Strict geographical division is, of course, impossible, as there are journals and writers in St. Petersburg that support the ideas of Moscow, though it would be difficult to say the reverse. The Moscow school is grouped round the *Russian Messenger* and the *Moscow Gazette*, or, in other words, about Mr. Katkoff; while the St. Petersburg school, embracing very different opinions and tendencies, finds its expression in the *Messenger of Europe, Annals of the Fatherland,* and *Fact* (Dyelo).

An approximately just view of the present state of Russian literature might, perhaps, be got from *Skladtchina*, a sort of literary album, which was published for the benefit of the sufferers from famine in the Government of Samara. Every prominent writer, except Count Leo Tolstoi, is here represented. At the same time it speaks badly for the literary productions of the year when I have to point to the small scraps of good writers that I find here as the best, though we are promised soon new novels by Gontcharof, Tourguénief, and Leo Tolstoi. Tourguénief did indeed about the same time publish two or three other short sketches: "Pegas," a story of his dog; "Ours," a touching episode of the French Revolution of '48; and "Punin and Barburin," the central figure of which is a republican, the action relating to the time preceding the emancipation.

In poetry the year is far worse than in fiction. Amid the pressure of reforms, of discontent, and of the pursuit of wealth, the muse is silent. The drama is represented only by a collection of the plays of Pisemsky, two feeble plays by Krylof—chiefly known as an arranger from the French—and Minaef, and "An Old Maid's Love," by Ostrofsky.

The Archæographical Commission is doing a very useful thing in publishing a carefully-collated edition of the "Lives of the Saints," one of the monuments of the Old Church literature. Pypin has been continuing his "Studies of Literary History" by an exceedingly valuable and interesting book on the critic Byelinsky, while Annenkof has completed his essays on Pushkin, and has issued them in a separate volume. Mr. Aksakof, who, since the suppression of his journal, has hardly been heard from, has just published a detailed life of his father-in-law, the poet Tutchef. Yurii Rossel, a new writer, has published an extended and carefully-written study of John Stuart Mill and his school. The only other work of a philosophical character is the "Crisis of Western Philosophy," directed as well against the positivists as against the negative school of Hartmann, by V. Solovief.

The most prominent contribution to political literature, and, in many respects, the most remarkable book of the year, is the "Essays in Political Science," edited by V. Bezobrazof, of the Academy of Sciences, the first volume of which has just appeared. It is not exactly a journal, for it is to be published from time to time as material is collected, and consists of essays on subjects relating to political and economical science by the best authorities of Russia, as well as of reviews and criticisms on books already published in Russia and abroad. The most interesting articles are "Law and Administrative Dispositions," by A. Gradofsky; "Emigration," by Prince Vasiltchikof; "The Brussels Conference," by Prof. Martens; and especially "The Russian Policy in Central Asia," by Prof. Grigorief. This last essay gives the whole history of the relations of Russia to Asia down to the accession of the Emperor Alexander, and shows that ever since Russia aspired to be a European state—that is, since the time of Peter the Great—she has been entirely without an Asiatic policy, from total ignorance and carelessness on the subject. Grigorief, with his immense knowledge of Asiatic history and life, and his practical experience as a former Governor of the Kirghis at Orenburg, could not fail to write interestingly on such a topic, and he has brought to light many facts which have been quite unknown to Russian historians.

Among the materials for history comes the first volume of the "Collection of Treaties concluded by Russia with Foreign Powers," by Prof. Martens. This volume includes the treaties made with Austria from 1648 to 1762, both in Russian and French, and contains besides an historical review of Russia's relations to Austria, with notes and introduction to all the treaties, also in French, which enhances the value of the work for foreigners.

Geographical literature is unusually rich, Central Asia naturally occupying the prominent place, owing to the recent expedition against Khiva. The official history has not yet appeared, but, besides numerous articles and sketches, Dr. Emil Schmidt has published an account of it in German, while Dr. Grimm has given us the "Impressions of a Military Surgeon," and Lerch has treated of the history and geography of the country in his "Khiva oder Kharezin," with a full discussion of the authorities.

LITERATURE, ENGLISH. As intimated in the preceding article, under the sub-title, RE-PRINTS AND REPUBLICATIONS, most of the more noticeable English books, those especially of popular interest, are promptly issued in this country. But among the mass of books that address only the British public, or that make their way more slowly across the Atlantic, are some that have a claim to at least a passing reference.

In the department of History some elaborate and valuable works have appeared. Such are, a "History of the English Institutions," by Philip Vernon Smith; "The Archæology of Rome," by J. H. Parker; "The Decline of the Roman Republic," five volumes, by George Long; "History of Greece," by G. W. Cox, not completed, but the installment that has appeared much approved; "Constitutional History of England," two volumes out, by William Stubbs; "The Scottish War of Independence," by William Burns; a volume of "The Ecclesiastical History of England," by Dr. John Stoughton; "Congregational History," by John Waddington, D. D.; "History of the Indian Administration of Lord Ellenborough," edited by Lord Colchester; "French Society from the Fronde to the Great Revolution," by Henry Barton Baker; "Early Russian History," by W. H. S. Ralston; "The Germans in France," by H. Sutherland Edwards; "A Short History of the English People," by J. R. Green—"short," but not abridged, nor superficial, nor yet dry; "Social Life in Greece, from Homer to Menander," by the Rev. J. P. Mahaffy; "History of the Inquisition," by W. H. Rule; "History of Japan," by Francis Ottiwell Adams; "Lectures on the History of Education in Prussia and in England, and on Kindred Topics," by James Donaldson, LL. D.; "History of the Creeds," by J. R. Lumly; "History of Merchant Shipping and Ancient Commerce," volumes I. and II., by W. S. Lindsay. "The Greville Memoirs," and a volume of the "Life of the Prince Consort," by Theodore Martin, published near the end of the year, are at the present writing known and read in that (it may be presumed) in every land where English is spoken. A work of permanent value is the "History of the Franco-German War, 1870–71, to the Downfall of the Empire, translated from the German Official Account at the Topographical and Statistical Department of the War Office," by Captain F. C. H. Clarke, R. A. (the authorized translation). Of this the first volume has appeared, comprising the narrative of events from the outbreak of hostilities to the battle of Gravelotte.

To these should be added several biographies that have an historical value and interest. Such are "The Life of Spencer Perceval," by Spencer Walpole; "Memoirs of his Own Time," by Henry Cockburn; "Reminiscences of Forty-three Years' Service in India," by Lieutenant-General Sir George Lawrence, edited by W. Edwards; and "Life and Times of Louisa, Queen of Prussia," by E. H. Hudson. Other biographies that may be mentioned are, the "Memoir of the Rev. William Ellis," the eminent missionary, by his Son; "Drummond of Hawthornden," by David Masson, a study in the literature of the seventeenth century, worthy of the author's painstaking research; "Mary and Charles Lamb: their Poems, Letters, and Remains," by W. C. Hazlitt—adding little to our knowledge of Charles Lamb, but much that one is glad to get of Mary Lamb; "The Life and Labors of Albany Fonblanque," a contribution to the history of recent literature; a "Memoir of Mrs. Barbauld," by A. L. LeBreton, published almost simultaneously with the appearance in Boston of the "Life," by Mrs. Ellis; "Autobiography and Memoirs of Mrs. Gilbert," formerly Ann Taylor, author with Jane Taylor of "Poems for Infant Minds," and other well-known produc-

tions; the "Life of Thomas Fuller, D. D.," a man who is worth knowing of; "Life and Character of the Rev. John Howe," by Henry Rogers; and "Henry Beyle (alias de Stendhal), a Critical and Biographical Study," by A. A. Paton.

In Philosophy and Science there have appeared, "Modern Utilitarianism," by the Rev. Prof. T. R. Birks; "Principles of Science," by W. T. Jevons; "Sensation and Intuition," by J. Sully; "Comparative Politics," by E. A. Freeman, the eminent historian; "The Philosophy of Natural Theology," by William Jackson; "Philosophy of History in Europe," vol. I., by R. Flint; "A Treatise on the Use of the Tenses in Hebrew," by S. R. Driver; "Origin and Metamorphoses of Insects," and "British Wild Flowers in Relation to Insects," by Sir John Lubbock; "Evenings at the Microscope," by P. H. Gosse; "The Birth of Chemistry," by G. F. Rodwell; "The Moon, considered as a Planet, as a World, and a Satellite," by James Nasmyth and James Carpenter; "Elements of Metallurgy," by J. Arthur Phillips; "Pathological Anatomy of the Nervous Centres," by E. L. Fox; "Treatise on Magnetism, General and Terrestrial," by Humphrey Lloyd, D. D., D. C. L.; "Polarization of Light," by W. Spottiswoode; "The Methods of Ethics," by Prof. Henry Sidgwick, an important contribution to moral philosophy; "The Origin of Creation; or, The Science of Matter and Force," by T. R. Fraser, M. D., and Andrew Dewar; "The Histology and Histo-chemistry of Man," translated from the German of Heinrich Frey, by A. E. J. Barker; "Economic Geology," by David Page; "The Logic of Style," by William Renton; "The History of Music (Art and Science) from the Earliest Records to the Fall of the Roman Empire;" and a work of science made easy and pleasant—"Tales on Political Economy," by Mrs. M. E. Fawcett.

Of Religious and Theological Books there was comparatively a large number published, though not as large as usual. The most decided sensation was made by the anonymous work "Supernatural Religion." A volume, the usefulness of which is disproportionate to its very modest dimensions, also anonymous, is entitled "Aids to the Study of German Theology." There have appeared, also, "The Teaching of the Church during the First Three Centuries in the Doctrines of the Christian Priesthood and Sacrifice," by the Rev. C. B. Drake; "Life and Epistles of Paul," by T. Lewin; "The Pastoral Epistles," by P. Fairbairn, D. D.; "Introduction to the Pauline Epistles," by Rev. P. J. Gloag; "Lectures on the Delivery and Development of Christian Doctrine," by R. Rainy, D. D.; "The Lost and Hostile Gospels," by the Rev. S. Baring-Gould; "The Mysteries of Christianity," by the Rev. T. J. Crawford; and "Hopes of the Human Race, Here and Hereafter," by Frances Power Cobbe. The best books in this department of writing appear almost simultaneously in this country and in England, and have been spoken of in another connection.

Of the abundant literature of Geography, Travel, and Exploration, the one work of world-wide interest was "The Last Journals of David Livingstone." Baron Hübner's "Ramble round the World," translated by Lady Herbert, has amused three-quarters of the globe. Besides these, we have noted "Fair Lusitania," by Lady Jackson; "Spain and the Spaniards," by N. F. Thioblin, "Azamat Batuk;" "Geography of Greece," by Rev. H. F. Tozer; "From the Indus to the Tigris," by H. H. Bellew; "Meeting the Sun; a Journey all round the World," by W. Simpson; "The Straits of Malacca, Indo-China, and China," by J. Thomson; and "Illustrations of China and its People: a Series of 200 Photographs, with Letter-press Descriptions," by the same; "Days near Rome," by A. J. C. Hare; "Two Years in Peru," by T. J. Hutchinson; and "The Amazon and Madeira Rivers," by F. Kellen.

Of works on Art, it is a coincidence worthy of note that almost at the same time that an American translation of Lessing's "Laocoon" was announced it was met by the announcement of a translation by Sir Robert Phillimore. "Our Sketching Club," by the Rev. R. St. John Tyrwhitt, has been laid in installments before the readers of an American magazine. He is also the author of the "Art-Teaching of the Primitive Church;" Mr. S. Redgrave's "Dictionary of Artists of the English School;" Mr. J. B. Atkinson's "Art Tour to the Northern Capitals of Europe," and "Historic and Monumental Rome," by C. J. Hemans, are noticed; and Mr. Ruskin finds leisure from his labors in political and social economy to utter a voice now and then upon his specialty. If illustrated works were to be added, most of the volumes of travels would claim a place also here, and a large number besides, that have not been referred to.

Fiction constitutes a large share of the literary product of England, but we find none worthy of particular notice in addition to the list of authors already given, whose works enjoy an American circulation.

Among miscellaneous works should be mentioned "Lectures on Shakespeare," translated from the German of Dr. Elze, by Dora Schmidt; "The Works of Thomas Love Peacock," edited by Lord Houghton; "Horæ Hellenicæ," by Prof. J. S. Blackie; "Hours in a Library," by Leslie Stephen; "Facts vs. Fiction: The Habits and Treatment of Animals," by the Hon. Grantley F. Berkeley; "Essays," by Richard Congreve, the representative of Comptism in England; "Scottish Rivers," by the late Sir Thomas Dick Lander, with a preface by Dr. John Brown; "Rocks ahead," by W. Rathbone Gregg; "On Compromise," by John Morley; "The Three Devils," by David Masson; "Toilers and Spinsters," by Miss Thackeray; "A Book about the Table," by J. C. Jeaffreson;

"History of Booksellers," by Henry Curwen; and the "Speeches of the Late Lord Lytton."

In the number of books published there was a falling off as compared with the year 1873, a decline accounted for by the increase in the cost of production. The whole number of new books was 3,351, classified as — theological, 478; educational, classical, and philological, 301; juvenile, 207; novels, 516; law, 71; politics and trade, 101; arts, science, and illustrated works, 421; travels and geography, 178; history and biography, 265; poetry and the drama, 223; year-books and serials in volumes, 243; medicine, 95; belles-lettres, essays, etc., 150; miscellaneous, including pamphlets, 93. The falling off in production is most marked in theology, but there is a nearly proportional increase in science and belles-lettres.

LIVERPOOL DOCK EXTENSIONS. Already much progress has been made in carrying out the great scheme of dock extension in Liverpool, projected by Mr. G. F. Lister, the dock-engineer. The new docks begun are those to be devoted to the accommodation of the steam-trade. They are to be made in the space reclaimed from the foreshore of the Mersey, between the north quay of the Canada Basin and the Seaforth shore. The area of this space is about 1,365,000 square yards, the length being about 6,200 feet, and the breadth 2,000 feet. At the front of this tract of land, and parallel with the river, a wall of enormous strength has been built, faced with granite. At the back will be formed a roadway or promenade, which may become one of the attractions of the town, and will certainly be of advantage to the inhabitants of the surrounding neighborhood, which is thickly populated. A large portion of the area thus inclosed is now being filled up; and, to prevent the encroachment of the sea, a wall has been built from Primrose Bridge down to the river-wall, a distance of nearly 2,200 feet. The foundations have been laid at the extreme westerly point of this wall, where it joins the river frontage, for a strong battery, to be constructed by the Government for the defense of the port.

The aim of the engineer has been to retain undisturbed, as far as possible, the existing arrangements and appropriation of the adjoining docks, while providing for largely-increased dock and shed accommodation for steamers of unusually large size. The width of the entrance to the Canada Basin from the river is accordingly to be increased from 250 feet to 400 feet. The area of the basin will be enlarged from seven acres to eleven acres, and form one of the principal entrances of the docks. There will be other very wide entrances in the new north dock-wall. The basin is to be excavated to a great depth, and the sill will be laid much deeper than any thing hitherto constructed on the Liverpool side of the Mersey; thus giving a depth of water at the highest state of the lowest tides during the year sufficient for the entrance of the largest steamers into the new docks, and obviating the necessity for their being loaded and unloaded in the river. In connection with this Canada Basin there will be a half-tide dock, covering an area of twenty acres, and having an aggregate quayage of 3,070 lineal feet. Northward of this will be the system of docks intended for the steam-trade. The main portion of the dock, which will extend in a northerly direction, parallel with the river, will be 1,500 feet long, by 500 feet wide, having three branches extending eastward, of the total length of 1,400 feet and a width of 300 feet. The total area of the system will be 43¼ acres, and the total quayage 10,870 lineal feet. In order to expedite the overhauling and repairs of ships a new system of hydraulic docks, invented by Mr. James Clarke, C. E., has been adopted. These docks are to be 500 feet long, and capable of receiving and raising the largest steamers. At the northwestern extremity of this dock two passages will be formed, leading into the mineral dock, which will extend for 1,600 feet in an easterly direction by a width of 500 feet toward the north. The area of this dock will be eighteen acres, and its gross quayage 3,850 lineal feet. The engineer has also planned two graving-docks on the eastern side of the half-tide basin, each 900 feet in length. Adjoining these will be another dock for repairing, 820 feet long, and 140 feet wide.

LOUISIANA. The Legislature assembled on the 5th of January, and continued in session until March. Among the most important measures passed during this period was a general law prescribing regulations for a registration of voters under the supervision of a State Registrar, a supervisor for each parish, and an assistant supervisor for each of the wards in the city of New Orleans, the appointment of these officials being vested in the Governor. Five constitutional amendments, recommended by Governor Kellogg were approved and ordered to be submitted to the people at the November election. These provided for indorsing the funding bill and the consolidated bonds issued thereunder; reducing and limiting the State debt to $15,000,000, and limiting taxation; devoting the annual revenues of the State to the expenses of the same year, prohibiting the issue of warrants in excess of the revenue; limiting the debt of the city of New Orleans, and prohibiting its further increase; and changing the day for the State election to that on which the presidential election is held.

The State Convention of the Republican party assembled in New Orleans on the 5th of August, and continued in session four days. After the nomination of Antoine Dubuclet for the office of State Treasurer, the following resolutions were adopted:

The Republican party of Louisiana, assembled in convention, in the city of New Orleans, on the 5th day of August, 1874, assumes and declares that the National Republican party is a party of positive principles and definite purposes; a party of grand achievements and a glorious history; a party of internal improvements and of material development; a party of peace and order, of liberty and law, of universal and equal rights; that it is a party capable of purifying its own organization as well as of devising reformatory measures for the public good: therefore, be it

1. *Resolved*, That its past history entitles it to future confidence, and we again reiterate our faith in and pledge ourselves to the support of the principles enunciated in its national platform, adopted at Philadelphia.

2. That we cordially indorse the liberal, enlightened, and just policy of President Grant and the national Administration, both in domestic and foreign affairs.

3. That our present State government, in the face of unparalleled difficulties, has achieved substantial reforms, and by its patient and firm adherence to the right course under an organized system of vilification and misrepresentation at home and abroad, deserves and has the unqualified approval and support of a large majority of the people of this State, of whom it is the true and lawful representative.

4. That we hereby pledge ourselves to the reduction of the expenses of the State government to the lowest possible point consistent with an efficient administration. We distinctly announce this obligation to be binding upon us, and due alike to the people of the State and to their creditors; and we specifically set forth our intention to secure a reduction of the heavy and unnecessary expenses of the assessment and collection of the revenue.

5. That duty and sound policy alike constrain us to nominate and support for office none but men of known honesty and capacity; and that men who are unmindful of the interests of the State, and whose records are a reproach to the party shall not be permitted to force themselves upon us in any capacity, under any pretense whatever.

6. That the misfortunes of war, of floods, and internal disturbances, and previous maladministration, so seriously impaired the resources of the State as to render absolutely necessary the passage by the last Legislature of the law known as the funding bill, which we approve as representing the utmost limits of our ability to pay, and more than the value received by the State for the indebtedness now outstanding; and we also declare our unqualified approval of the proposed constitutional amendments limiting the State debt to $15,000,000 and taxation to twelve and a half mills (except for school purposes), and applying the revenues of each year to the payment of the expenses of that year.

7. That the approaching general election must be a fair, peaceable, and free election, at which every legal and qualified elector shall have the opportunity to cast his ballot for such candidates as he prefers without intimidation and without illegal contrivances to deprive him of his vote; and every legal vote cast must be counted and credited as polled; and to this end such a selection of officers to take charge of registration and election should be made as will satisfy citizens of all parties that the Republican party at least does not expect or desire anything else than a fair election.

8. That we condemn the spirit of violence manifested in certain localities by the Democratic party, as being in violation of public peace and good order, and destructive of the good name and best interests of the State; the suppression of all violence is demanded by every law-abiding citizen in the State.

9. That we invoke the assistance of Congress toward the early completion of those national works, the Fort St. Philip Canal and the system of levees for the redemption and protection of the alluvial lands of the Mississippi River.

10. That we declare our belief that nothing but disaster can result from a conflict of the two races in this State, and we discountenance and condemn all

efforts to foment such a conflict, being satisfied that the true interests of both races lie in a just and harmonious adjustment of the relations of race, labor, and capital, and the united efforts of all good men to promote the common interest, and we believe that with such peace and harmony, and such united efforts, the return of a high degree of prosperity to Louisiana will not be long delayed.

11. That we a prove and indorse the civil-rights bill now pending before Congress.

12. That we sympathize with the patriotic men in Cuba who fight for liberty, and that we urge upon the national Congress the early recognition of the independence of Cuba, and hereby instruct our Representatives in Congress to use their best efforts and influence to this end.

Early in July the Democratic State Central Committee published a call for a State Convention, to assemble in New Orleans, on the 24th of August, for the purpose of nominating candidates for Congress, the Legislature, and State Treasurer. The selection of New Orleans as the place for holding the convention was unfavorably received by the Democracy of the country parishes. This feeling of dissatisfaction was specially strong in Northern Louisiana, where several papers and many prominent men united in a call for a convention to be held out of New Orleans. In consequence of

this opposition, the State Central Committee changed the place of meeting from New Orleans to Baton Rouge. The convention, therefore, assembled in Baton Rouge on the 24th of August, and nominated John C. Moncure, of Caddo, for Treasurer, and the following persons for Congress: First district, Randall Gibson; second, E. John Ellis; third, J. H. Breaux; fourth, W. M. Levy; fifth, B. F. Spencer; sixth, Joseph M. Moore. The following platform was then unanimously adopted:

We, the white people of Louisiana, embracing the Democratic party, the Conservative party, the White Man's party, the Liberal party, the Reform party, and all others opposed to the Kellogg usurpation, do solemnly resolve and declare:

1. That the government now existing in Louisiana originated in and has been maintained by force and fraud in opposition to the will of a large majority of the voters of the State, in opposition to the principles of the Constitution of the United States, and in violation of every principle of justice and liberty.

2. That the dominant faction of the Radical party in this State has, by false and fraudulent representation, inflamed the passions and prejudices of the negroes as a race against the whites, and has thereby made it necessary for the white people to unite and act together in self-defense and for the preservation of white civilization.

3. That the rights of all men under the Constitution and laws of the land must be respected and preserved inviolate, irrespective of race, color, or previous condition, but we deny that Congress can constitutionally enact laws to force the two races into social union or equality.

4. That the white people of Louisiana have no desire to deprive the colored people of any rights to which they are entitled; but we are convinced that the reforms imperatively demanded can be effected only by selecting to office white men of known capacity and integrity, and we believe that large numbers of colored persons will vote with us to secure a government which must be beneficial alike to both races.

5. That we disclaim earnestly any intention of carrying, or attempting to carry the approaching election by violence, and that charges to this effect, emanating from our Radical enemies, are without foundation, and are falsely made for the purpose of obtaining the aid of the military force of the United States, in order to overawe the people and perpetuate the existing usurpation and subvert the true principles of government.

6. That W. P. Kellogg is a mere usurper, and we denounce him as such; that his government is arbitrary, unjust, and oppressive, and that it can maintain itself only through Federal interference.

7. That the election and registration laws, under which this election is being conducted, were intended to perpetuate the usurpation by depriving the people, and especially our naturalized citizens, of an opportunity to vote, but we announce distinctly that it is the determination of the people to have a free and fair election, and to see that the result is not changed by fraud or violence.

8. That we extend to all of our race, in every clime, the right hand of fellowship and a cordial invitation to come and settle among us and unite their destinies with ours.

9. That while we are in favor of meeting punctually the payment of the legitimate debt of Louisiana, we are immovably opposed to the recognition of the dishonest and fraudulent obligations issued in the name of the State, and we pledge ourselves to make a searching investigation in the matter.

10. We advise our people to vote against the amendments to the constitution proposed by the usurping Legislature, and pledge ourselves, on the restoration of the government to honest hands, to provide for the payment of all honest indebtedness of the State.

Near the close of August great excitement was caused throughout the State by the announcement of the Coushatta tragedy. This was an affair near the town of Coushatta, in Red River Parish, which resulted in the arrest and deliberate shooting of six Republican officials; but, as in the case of every other alleged outrage, the reports were so conflicting that it is impossible to determine upon the facts with accuracy. On the one side it was alleged to have been a merciless war waged by the whites upon the blacks, while other reports attribute the origin of the difficulty to an uprising of the blacks. The account given by one side was to the effect that a party of citizens attempted to arrest a band of negroes for having shot at a white citizen, and were themselves fired upon by the negroes, one of their number being killed. The next day another difficulty occurred, in which Homer Mitchell, a Republican tax-collector, and two negroes, were charged with having fired upon Joseph Dixon and another young man, the former being mortally wounded. "On the following day," continues the account, "the whites turned out in force, capturing the white Radicals, Twitchell, Dewees, Egerton, Howell, Willis, and Holland, together with six of the most prominent negro followers. On Sunday, at their own request, the six whites were started to Shreveport under an escort of seventeen men, and while *en route* were intercepted and shot by a party not yet identified. The six negroes were set at liberty, unharmed, before the escort left Coushatta." The people of Red River Parish published an address in reference to this affair, in which, among other things, they said:

To the colored people we have to say that our action in the present instance must fully convince you of the sincerity of our repeated declarations to you that our war was only against such of you as are silly and vicious enough to combine with the horde of scallawags and carpet-baggers who, like vultures, have been preying upon our people for eight long years, and whose voracity seems to be insatiable. To all such we give fair warning.

To those who want peace and the redemption of Louisiana we guarantee ample protection in the full and free exercise of all their civil and political rights under the law, and we earnestly request you to go peaceably and quietly to work.

Some of the bad white men who have been for years inculcating vicious ideas into the minds of the colored people of Red River, and arraying them against the true interests of the country, the white people, and their own, were arrested for their complicity in a cold-blooded, murderous assassination upon our estimable fellow-citizen Joseph B. Dixon. They have tendered their resignations, and left this morning, at their own earnest prayer and request, under a guard of our best citizens, selected by themselves, to depart from the State, promising never to return.

The opposing account of this tragedy was materially different. It is in the following statement, published on the 3d of September, by Governor Kellogg, after offering a reward of $5,000 for the capture of each person implicated in the affair:

To the Public: Having felt it my duty to issue my proclamation offering a large reward for the apprehension and conviction of the murderers in the Coushatta outrage, and to the end that the law-abiding citizens of the State may fully comprehend the magnitude of the crime committed, and be induced to render more active assistance to the officers of the law, I deem it proper to make the following statements. These facts are gathered from reliable information received at the Executive Department:

On or about the 28th day of August, 1874, a body of persons belonging to a semi-military organization known as the "White League of Louisiana," assembled in the town of Coushatta, parish of Red River, in this State, for the purpose of compelling, by force of arms, the State officers of that parish to resign their positions. These officers were men of good character, most of them largely interested in planting and mercantile pursuits. They held their positions with the full consent of an admittedly large majority

of the legal voters of the parish, this being a heavily Republican parish, as admitted by their fusion returning-board. The only known objection to them was that they were of Republican principles. Frank Edgerton, the duly qualified Sheriff of the parish, in strict compliance with the laws of the State and of the United States, summoned a *posse comitatus* of citizens, white and colored, to assist him in protecting the parish officers in the exercise of their undoubted rights and duties from the threatened unlawful violence of the White League. His *posse*, consisting of sixty-five men, were overpowered by a superior force assembled from the adjacent parishes, and finally, after several colored and white men had been killed, surrendered themselves prisoners, with the explicit guarantee that their lives would be spared if the more prominent Republicans would agree to leave the parish, and those holding office would resign their positions. These stipulations, although unlawfully exacted, were complied with on the part of the Republican officials, who were then locked up in the jail for the night. The following-named persons were among those who surrendered and re-signed: Homer G. Twitchell, planter, and Tax-Collector of Red River Parish, and Deputy United States Postmaster in charge of the post-office at Coushatta; Robert A. Dewees, Supervisor of Registration, De Soto Parish; Clark Holland, merchant, and Supervisor of Registration, Red River Parish; W. T. Howell, Parish Attorney and United States Counsel; Frank S. Edgerton, Sheriff of Red River Parish, and M. E. Willis, merchant, and justice of the peace. On the following morning, Sunday, the 30th of August, these persons were bound together, two and two, and conducted by an armed guard to the McFarland plantation, just over the parish line of the Red River, within the boundaries of Bossier Parish, about forty miles east of the Texas line. There they were set upon and deliberately murdered in cold blood. On the night preceding the murder, a body of forty members of the White League of Caddo Parish, mounted and armed, left the city of Shreveport, and were seen riding in the direction of the place where the murder was subsequently committed. Their bodies were buried where they fell, without inquest or any formality whatever.

WILLIAM P. KELLOGG, Governor.

The reports of numerous outrages in Louisiana, Alabama, South Carolina, and other Southern States, having reached Washington, led to a determination on the part of the President to take measures for their suppression. For this purpose the following instructions were issued to the Secretary of War:

Long Branch, N. J., *September 2, 1874.*
To General W. W. Belknap, *Secretary of War:*

The recent atrocities in the South, particularly in Louisiana, Alabama, and South Carolina, show a disregard for law, civil rights, and personal protection, that ought not to be tolerated in any civilized government. It looks as if, unless speedily checked, matters must become worse, until life and property there will receive no protection from the local authorities until such authorities become powerless. Under such circumstances it is the duty of the Government to give aid for the protection of life and civil rights legally authorized. To this end I wish you would consult with the Attorney-General, who is well informed as to the outrages already committed and the localities where the greatest danger lies, and so order troops as to be available in case of necessity. All proceedings for the protection of the South will be under the Law Department of Government, and will be directed by the Attorney-General in accordance with the provisions of the enforcement act. No instructions need therefore be given the troops ordered in the Southern States, except as they may be transmitted from time to time on advice from the

Attorney-General, or as circumstances may determine hereafter. U. S. GRANT.

After a consultation between the Secretary of War and the Attorney-General of the United States, the following instructions, with the approval of the President, were addressed to the various United States Marshals and Attorneys in Louisiana:

DEPARTMENT OF JUSTICE, }
WASHINGTON, *September* 3, 1874. }

SIR: Outrages of various descriptions, and in some cases atrocious murders, having been committed in your district by bodies of armed men, sometimes in disguise, and with a view, it is believed, of overawing and intimidating peaceable and law-abiding citizens and depriving them of rights guaranteed to them by the Constitution and laws of the United States, your attention is directed to an act of Congress passed April 9, 1866, entitled "An act to protect all persons in the United States in their civil rights, and to furnish means for their vindication;" and to another passed April 20, 1871, entitled "An act to enforce the provisions of the fourteenth amendment to the Constitution of the United States and for other purposes;" also to one passed May 30, 1870, entitled "An act to enforce the right of citizens to vote in the several States of this Union, and for other purposes," which with their amendments make these deeds of violence and blood offenses within the jurisdiction of the General Government. I consider it my duty, in view of the circumstances, to instruct you to proceed with all possible energy and dispatch to detect, expose, arrest, and punish the perpetrators of these crimes, and to that end you are to spare no effort or necessary expense. Troops of the United States will be stationed at different and convenient points in your district for the purpose of giving you all needful aid in discharge of your official duties. You understand, of course, that no interference whatever is hereby intended with any political or party action not in violation of law, but protection to all classes of citizens, white and colored, in the free exercise of the elective franchise and the enjoyment of the other rights and privileges to which they are entitled under the Constitution and laws as citizens of the United States. These instructions are issued by authority of the President, and with the concurrence of the Secretary of War.

Very respectfully,
GEORGE W. WILLIAMS, Attorney-General.

This action on the part of the Federal Government led to the publication of the following resolutions by the Committee of Seventy:

ROOMS COMMITTEE OF SEVENTY, }
September 8, 1874. }

In view of the recent action of the Federal Government in relation to the Southern States, and considering the bearing of that action upon the State of Louisiana, be it

Resolved, That in our judgment, this action is the result of an entire misunderstanding of the real situation of affairs in this State, and, we fear, will tend to protract the unhappy condition of things out of which the evils sought to be remedied have arisen.

Resolved, That, in our opinion, the true cause of the trouble in Louisiana is to be found in the fact that the people have no confidence in the present usurping Government, which does not command their obedience, and which fails to give protection, because it is not founded upon "the consent of the governed."

Resolved, That in our opinion the immediate restoration of the State government to the hands of its legally-elected officers, from which it was wrested by Federal power, is the true remedy, and would quickly compose all our difficulties, and restore peace and good order.

Resolved, That in our opinion the only effect of this action of the Administration should be to unite the people and strengthen the determination of every true citizen to devote himself more unselfishly to the public interest, and to contribute more freely by every means in his power to the success of our cause—assured that with a clear majority, union, vigilance, and courage, must secure a victory in November.

Resolved, That in the opinion of this committee the people should refrain from all acts of violence, and should address themselves with energy to the work of organization, with the view of securing a free and impartial exercise of the elective franchise at the approaching election.

Resolved, That in the opinion of this committee the blood of every man who has been killed in this State in consequence of political strife within the past two years lies properly at the door of William Pitt Kellogg, who holds and exercises the highest office in the State, in open defiance of law and justice, and the opinion of the civilized world.

R. H. MARR, Chairman.

On Monday, the 14th of September, a mass-meeting of persons, variously estimated at from 2,000 to 5,000 in number, was held at the Clay Statue in Canal Street, New Orleans. This meeting was in response to a call previously made, and its chief objects seem to have been to protest against the Kellogg administration in general, and particularly the seizure of arms shipped to parties in New Orleans, and also to demand the immediate abdication of Governor Kellogg and the State officers under him. The meeting was called to order about eleven o'clock A. M., and, after several spirited speeches had been made, the following resolutions were adopted:

Whereas, At a general election held in Louisiana on the 4th day of November, 1872, John McEnery was elected Governor by a majority of 10,000 votes over his opponent, William P. Kellogg; and D. B. Penn Lieutenant-Governor by a majority of 15,000 over his opponent, C. C. Antoine; and

Whereas, By fraud and violence those defeated seized the Executive chair, and from time to time, by other irregular, fraudulent, and violent acts, in the face of the report of the committee of the Senate of the United States appointed to investigate the affairs of Louisiana, that the existing government of the State is a usurpation, the result of a violent abuse of judicial functions and sustained by force, W. P. Kellogg has continued himself in power to the gross wrong and outrage of the people of the State of Louisiana, and to the imminent danger of republican institutions throughout the country; and

Whereas, With a view to controlling and determining the results of the approaching election to be held in Louisiana in November next he has, under an act known as the registration act, and passed for the purpose of defeating the popular will, secured to himself and his party the power of denying registration to bona-fide citizens whose applications before the courts for a mandamus to compel the assistant supervisors to enroll and register them has been refused, the registration law indeed punishing courts if they dare to take cognizance of such appeals; and

Whereas, by false and infamous misrepresentations of the feelings and motives of our people, he has received promise of aid from the Federal Army, placed at the order of the Attorney-General of the United States, and subject to the calls of the United States Marshals, for the purpose of overawing our State, and controlling the election; and

Whereas, In the language of the call for the meeting, "one by one our dearest rights have been trampled upon, and at last, in the supreme height of its insolence, this mockery of a republican government has dared even to deny that the right so solemnly guaranteed by the very Constitution of the United States, which, in Article II. of the amendments, declares that the right of the people to keep and bear arms shall not be infringed upon: be it

Resolved, That we reaffirm solemnly the resolutions adopted by the white people of Louisiana, in convention assembled, at Baton Rouge, on the 24th of August, 1874, that the white people of Louisiana have no desire to deprive the colored people of any rights to which they are entitled ; that W. P. Kellogg is a mere usurper, and we pronounce him as such; that his government is arbitrary, unjust, and oppressive, and can only maintain itself through Federal interference; that the election and registration laws under which this election is being conducted, were intended to perpetuate usurpation by depriving the people, and especially our naturalized citizens, of an opportunity to register and vote, and therefore, in the name of the citizens of New Orleans, now in mass-meeting, and of the people of the State of Louisiana, whose franchise has been wrested from them by fraud and violence, and all of whose rights and liberties have been outraged and trampled upon, we demand of W. P. Kellogg his immediate abdication.

Resolved, That a committee of five be immediately appointed by the chairman, who shall be a member of the said committee, to wait on Mr. W. P. Kellogg, to present to him these resolutions, to demand of him an immediate answer, and report the result of such interview to this meeting.

In accordance with the last resolution, a committee of five, with Mr. R. H. Marr as chairman, called at the Executive office and requested an interview with Governor Kellogg. In the absence of that official, Henry C. Dibble, of the Governor's staff, having received the delegation and reported their errand to the Governor, returned with the following reply:

I have communicated with the Governor, and he directs me to say to you that he must decline to receive any communication from a committee appointed by the mass-meeting assembled on Canal Street. He does so, I am instructed to say, because he has definite and accurate information that there are now assembled several large bodies of armed men in different parts of the city, who are met at the call which convened the mass meeting which you represent. He regards this as a menace, and he will receive no communication under such circumstances. He furthermore directs me to say that, should the people assemble peaceably, without menace, he would deem it one of his highest duties to receive any communication from them or entertain any petition addressed to the government. I have received and answered you, gentlemen, as a member of his staff.   HENRY C. DIBBLE,
            Brigadier and Judge-Advocate-General,
                        Louisiana State Militia.

To this the committee made the following response:

We repeat that there are no armed rioters. There are no armed men on Canal Street, so far as we know. We came on a mission of peace, and we believe that if the Governor had acceded to the proposition we brought to-day—which was, to abdicate—it would have pacified the people of Louisiana, and might, or would, have prevented violence or bloodshed. So far as we are concerned, we are prepared to pledge to him no violence in person and property, and we feel in a position, on the contrary, to assure him that there should be perfect immunity to both.

Whereupon General Dibble, on the part of the Governor, replied that "while there may be no armed men on Canal Street there are armed bodies within a short distance, assembled on the same call as your mass-meeting."

The result of this interview was reported to the Canal Street meeting, which at once resorted to an appeal to arms to drive the Kellogg government from power.

In the absence of John McEnery, D. B. Penn, who had been the unsuccessful candidate for Lieutenant-Governor on the McEnery ticket in 1872, issued the following proclamation, claiming to be Lieutenant-Governor and Acting Governor, and calling upon the militia to arm and assemble:

To the People of Louisiana: For two years you have borne with patience and fortitude a great wrong. Through fraud and violence the government of your choice has been overthrown and its power usurped. Protest after protest, appeal after appeal to the President of the United States and to Congress, have failed to give you the relief you had a right, under the Constitution, to demand. The wrong has not been repaired. On the contrary, through the instrumentality of partisan judges, you are debarred from all legal remedy. Day by day taxation has been increasing, with costs and penalties amounting to the confiscation of your property, your substance squandered, your credit ruined, resulting in the failure and bankruptcy of your valued institutions. The right of suffrage is virtually taken from you by the enactment of skillfully-devised registration and election laws. The judicial branch of your government has been stricken down by the conversion of the legal *posse comitatus* of the sheriff to the use of the usurper, for the purpose of defeating the decrees of the courts, his defiance of the law leading him to use the very force for the arrest of the sheriff, while engaged in the execution of a process of the court. To these may be added a corrupt and vicious Legislature, making laws in violation of the constitution for the purpose of guarding and perpetuating their usurped authority; a metropolitan police, paid by the city, under the control of the usurper, quartered upon you to overawe and keep you in subjection. Every public right has been denied, and, as if to goad you to desperation, private arms are seized and individuals arrested. To such extremities are you drawn, that manhood revolts at any further submission. Constrained from a sense of duty, as the legally elected Lieutenant-Governor of the State, acting Governor, in the absence of Governor McEnery, I do hereby issue this, my proclamation, calling upon the militia of the State, embracing all males between the ages of eighteen and forty-five years, without regard to color or previous condition, to arm and assemble under their respective officers for the purpose of driving the usurpers from power. Given under my hand and seal, this 14th day of September, 1874.

        D. B. PENN, Lieutenant-Governor.
EXECUTIVE DEPARTMENT, STATE OF LOUISIANA.

At the same time "General Order No. 1" was issued, appointing General Frederick N. Ogden "Provisional General of the Louisiana State Militia," and ordering him "at once to assume command and organize into companies, regiments, and battalions."

As early as three o'clock large numbers of armed persons began to assemble at the appointed rendezvous in Poydras Street. Here a strong position was taken, and the neighboring streets were barricaded. About 500 Metropolitan Police in two bodies, one commanded by General Longstreet, commander of the State militia, and the other by General Badger, Chief of Police, made their appearance in Canal Street, well armed and with artillery. About four o'clock a severe contest ensued near the river end of Canal Street, between the force under General Badger and the insurgents, which resulted in the rout of the former. General Ogden reported a loss of twelve killed and thirteen wounded, several of whom subsequently died. On the other side, the killed were reported at fourteen, and the wounded variously from twenty to forty. On the following morning, the State-House was surrendered to the Penn militia, and the entire force of Metropolitan Police laid down their arms. Governor Kellogg had taken refuge in the Custom-House, and all the State and city property, armory, police-stations, arsenals, and police and fire-alarm telegraphs, etc., were seized by the insurgents. The number of militia who responded to Penn's call was about 10,000. Penn was formally inducted into office on the afternoon of the 15th, and proceeded at once to put into office those who were voted for on the McEnery ticket in 1872; also to reorganize the police force and the judiciary.

Meantime, after the *coup d'état* of the 14th, Penn sent the following dispatch to the President, requesting him to withhold Federal interference :

NEW ORLEANS, *September* 14, 1874.
To U. S. GRANT, *President of the United States :*

Hopeless of all other relief, the people of this State have taken up arms to maintain the legal authority of the persons elected by them to the government of the State against the usurpers, who have heaped upon them innumerable insults, burdens, and wrong. In so doing they are supported by the great body of the intelligent and honest people of the State. They declare their unswerving loyalty and respect for the United States Government and its officers. They war only against the usurpers, plunderers, and enemies of the people. They affirm their entire ability to maintain peace, and protect the life, liberty, and equal rights of all classes of citizens. The property and officials of the United States it shall be our special aim to defend against all assaults, and to treat with the profoundest respect and loyalty. We only ask of you to withhold any aid or protection from our enemies and the enemies of republican rights, and of the peace and liberties of the people. D. B. PENN,
Lieutenant-Governor and Acting Governor.

The action on the part of the opponents of the Kellogg government, in resorting to arms to maintain their political position, is said to have met with the most emphatic disapproval of President Grant, who expressed a determination to take the most prompt and decisive measures to restore order. Upon the receipt of an application from Governor Kellogg for aid to protect Louisiana from domestic violence, the following proclamation, ordering the insurgents to disperse within five days, was issued :

Whereas, It has been satisfactorily represented to me that turbulent and disorderly persons have com-

VOL. XIV.—31 A

bined together with force and arms, to overthrow the State government of Louisiana, and to resist the laws and constituted authorities of said State; and—

Whereas, It is provided in the Constitution of the United States that the United States shall protect every State in this Union on application of the Legislature, or the Executive when the Legislature cannot be convened, against domestic violence; and—

Whereas, It is provided in the laws of the United States that, in all cases of insurrection in any State, or of obstruction to the laws thereof, it shall be lawful for the President of the United States, on application of the Legislature of such State, or of the Executive, when the Legislature cannot be convened, to call for the militia of any other State or States, or to employ such part of the land and naval forces as shall be judged necessary for the purpose of suppressing such insurrection or causing the laws to be duly executed; and—

Whereas, The Legislature of said State is not now in session and cannot be convened in time to meet the present emergency, and the Executive of said State, under Section 4 of Article IV. of the Constitution of the United States, and the laws passed in pursuance thereof, has therefore made application to me for such part of the military force of the United States as may be necessary and adequate to protect said State and the citizens thereof against domestic violence, and to enforce the due execution of the laws; and—

Whereas, It is required that whenever it may be necessary, in the judgment of the President, to use the military force for the purpose aforesaid, he shall forthwith, by proclamation, command such insurgents to disperse and retire personally to their respective homes within a limited time :

Now, therefore, I, U. S. Grant, President of the United States, do hereby make proclamation, and command said turbulent and disorderly persons to disperse and retire peaceably to their respective abodes within five days from this date, and hereafter to submit themselves to the laws and constituted authorities of said State; and I invoke the aid and coöperation of all good citizens thereof to uphold the law and preserve the public peace.

In witness whereof I have hereunto set my hand, and caused the seal of the United States to be affixed.

Done at the city of Washington, this 15th day of September, in the year of our Lord 1874, and of the independence of the United States the ninety-eighth.
U. S. GRANT.

By the President :
HAMILTON FISH, Secretary of State.

Orders were also given for United States troops and men-of-war to proceed to New Orleans; and General Emory, in command of the United States troops, was instructed to maintain the peace, and under no circumstances to recognize the Penn government. General Emory now demanded the surrender of the State property that had been seized, and the disbanding of the insurgent forces. This demand was complied with by McEnery, who had returned to the city and assumed the functions of Governor. Whereupon the following instructions as to the surrender were issued by General Emory :

HEADQUARTERS DEPARTMENT OF THE GULF,
NEW ORLEANS, LA., *September* 17, 1874.
(Circular.)

John McEnery and D. B. Penn, styling themselves respectively Governor and Lieutenant-Governor of the State of Louisiana, having informed the department commander of their willingness, under the President's proclamation, to surrender the State property now in their p-ssession, and to disband the insurgent forces under their command, Brevet Brigadier-General J. R. Brooke, lieutenant-colonel of Third Infantry, is charged with the duty of taking possession of the arms and other State property. He will occupy the State-House, Arsenal, and other State buildings, until further orders. He is hereby appointed to command the city of New Orleans until such time as the State and city governments can be reorganized. The present police force in the city, under charge of Thomas Boylan, will remain on duty and be responsible for the good order and quiet of the city until regularly relieved.

By command of Brevet Major-General W. H. EMORY:
LUKE O'REILLY,
Captain Nineteenth Infantry, A. D. C.

On the evening of the 17th, therefore, the State Capitol and government buildings were formally surrendered by McEnery to General Brooke. In making the surrender, the former said:

GENERAL BROOKE: As the lawful and acting Governor of this State, I surrender to you, as the representative of the Government of the United States, the Capitol and remainder of the property in this city belonging to the State. This surrender is in response to a formal demand of General Emory for such surrender, or to accept as an alternative the levying of war upon our government by the military forces of the United States under his command. As I have already said to General Emory, we have neither the power nor inclination to resist the Government of the United States. Sir, I transfer to you the guardianship of the rights and liberties of the people of the State, and I trust and believe that you will g e protection to all classes of our citizens ruled and ruined by a corrupt usurpation, presided over by Mr. Kellogg. Our people could bear the wrongs, tyranny, annoyance, and insults of that usurpation no longer, and they arose in their might, swept it from existence, and installed in authority the rightful government of which I am the head. All lovers of liberty throughout the Union must admit the patriotism that aroused our people to act as one man, and throw off the yoke of this odious usurpation. I know as a soldier you have but to obey the orders of the Government of the United States, but I feel that you will temper your military control of affairs with moderation, and in all things exhibit that integrity of purpose characteristic of officers of the army. I now hand over to you, sir, the Capitol and the other property of the State under my charge.
JOHN McENERY.

The action of General Emory in appointing Colonel Brooke as the military governor of New Orleans did not meet the approval of the Government in Washington. It was there thought that the Kellogg should be recognized as the lawful government of the State until another one should be legally supplied, and that General Emory, therefore, should have named Colonel Brooke commander of the United States forces in New Orleans. The views of President Grant on this point were indicated in the following telegram to General Emory:

WAR DEPARTMENT, ADJUTANT-GENERAL'S OFFICE,
WASHINGTON, D. C., September 18, 1874.
GENERAL W. H. EMORY, New Orleans:
I am directed by the President to say that your acts to this date, so far as they have been reported and received here officially, are approved, except so far as they name Colonel Brooke to command the city of New Orleans. It would have been better to have named him commander of the United States forces in that city. The State government existing

at the time of the beginning of the present insurrectionary movement, must be recognized as the lawful State government until some other State government can be legally supplied. Upon the surrender of the insurgents you will inform Governor Kellogg of the fact, and give him the necessary support to reestablish the authority of the State government. If at the end of the five days given in the proclamation of the 15th inst. there still exists armed resistance to the authorities of the State, you will summon a surrender of the insurgents. If the surrender is not quietly submitted to, it must be enforced at all hazards. This being an insurrection against the State government of Louisiana, to aid in the suppression of which this Government has been called upon in the forms required by the Constitution and laws of Congress thereunder, it is not the province of the United States authorities to make terms with parties engaged in such insurrection.
E. D. TOWNSEND, Adjutant-General.

To this General Emory replied that he had "placed Colonel Brooke in command of the city as well as in command of the troops. Otherwise there would have been anarchy. Governor Kellogg did not and has not yet called on me for support to reëstablish the State government. His chief of police was shot down and the next in command also, and the whole force utterly dispersed and hidden away out of sight. For one of them to have attempted to stand on his beat would have been certain destruction, and even now the State authorities represented by Governor Kellogg have asked to defer taking charge for the present."

McEnery and Penn now issued an address to the people of the State, in which, after alluding to the chief events of the overthrow of the Kellogg government, they say:

We need not remind you, fellow-citizens, that at every stage of our protracted conflict with this usurpation we have constantly asserted, and maintained our assertion, that we have never intended to come in conflict with the authority or the forces of the United States; and when that has been the alternative, we have not hesitated to yield ready obedience to that authority.

Simultaneously with this, will be published the protest which we made to General Emory against this action of the Federal Government, which displaces your rightful Governor and Lieutenant-Governor, and which places the State in the possession and under the control of the military forces of the United States.

Thus, fellow-citizens, has the State of Louisiana been finally stricken down by the hand of power, and we are no longer citizens of a State, but are inhabitants merely of what was once a free State, the peer of any other in the American galaxy.

It is no disgrace to submit to power which we have not the capacity or the right to resist. It is painful to be compelled to give up our most cherished rights; but we do so with the full determination to regain them, and to have them restored by the hand by which we have been deprived of them.

It only remains for us to urge upon you to summon to your aid all your courage and fortitude, your virtue and forbearance, to enable you to submit with becoming dignity to this g ea calamity, which no act of ours or of yours could have averted. Continue to be, as you have been, law-abiding and faithful to your duty and obligations to the Government of the United States. You have just gained a great victory over your enemy, arrayed in arms against ou. Make one more sublime effort, and gain a grand victory—a 'victory over your passions and inclinations. Yield faithful, ready obedience to all legally-constituted authority, and be assured that the story of your wrongs, your long forbearance, your heroic virtues, displayed as well in your hour of triumph as in your misfortunes, will command and receive the sympathy and respect of the civilized world.

On the 18th General Emory notified Governor Kellogg, who was still at the Custom-House, that the insurgents had surrendered, and tendered "the necessary military support to reëstablish the State government." On the following morning Governor Kellogg resumed the executive functions, and published an order requiring all State officers who had been prevented during the recent troubles from performing their duties immediately to resume their official functions ; also the Board of Metropolitan Police to "assemble at once and organize the police force of New Orleans, and assume the maintenance of peace and order of the city."

General Emory now reported to Washington as follows:

HEADQUARTERS DEPARTMENT OF THE GULF, NEW ORLEANS, *September* 20, 1874.
To the Adjutant-General of the United States Army, Washington, D. C.:

Yesterday the State authorities replaced the temporary police force by the regular police force of the city. It was feared that this change might cause some disturbance, and troops were posted at various points in the city, but the night passed very quietly. I think this may be taken as an evidence that the surrender was complete and in good faith, for, by a peculiarity of the law of Louisiana, the police force of this city is organized under the State law, and under the direct control of the Governor.

W. H. EMORY,
Colonel and Brevet Major-General commanding.

Thus, within less than a week there had been civil war in the streets of New Orleans, the overthrow of the State government by armed force, and its restoration through the military power of the Federal Government. A committee representing the McEnery party now published an address, dated September 23d, to the people of the United States, in defense and explanation of the late revolutionary movement. The address asserts that "shortly after the election in November, 1872, by the alleged action of a District Judge of the United States, aided and enforced by soldiers of the Federal Government ordered from Pensacola to New Orleans for that purpose, the State-House was seized at night, a pretended Legislature, composed in great part of defeated candidates, was organized, and William Pitt Kellogg was forced upon the people of Louisiana as Governor, and C. C. Antoine as Lieutenant-Governor, both of whom were defeated by large majorities, as shown by actual count of official returns of the votes as cast." After citing certain facts and adducing arguments to show that McEnery and his associates had received a majority of the legal votes cast at the election of 1872, the address continues:

It is matter of public history that the people of Louisiana appealed to the President of the United States for relief against the usurpation set up and established by the Federal power alone, and that they were repelled with insult by the Attorney-General ; that they appealed in vain to the legislative department of the General Government for relief at two successive sessions ; that they invoked the aid of the Supreme Court of the United States to relieve them of the outrages upon their rights by an inferior Federal Judge (Durell), and that the Supreme Court found itself without jurisdiction and powerless to take cognizance of the cause.

There remained for the people of Louisiana but one hope of relief, and that a hope for partial relief only. The gubernatorial term is four years, and the present term expires in January, 1877. The State officers hold for the same term, and the Senators hold for four years, one-half being elected every two years. At the election in November, 1874, a State Treasurer, the members of the House of Representatives, and half the Senate, are to be chosen, with the addition of members of the Senate to fill such vacancies as may have occurred by deaths or otherwise, so that the most which we could have hoped to obtain by the election would have been a State Treasurer and a majority in the Legislature. The constitution of Louisiana subjects the government to impeachment, but the concurrence of two-thirds of the Senators present is requisite to the conviction. As half of the Senators hold for the same term as the Governor, the election by the opponents of the Kellogg usurpation of every member of the Senate to be chosen in November would still leave Kellogg and his colleagues in power, and the people subject to a continuation of this usurpation until the constitutional expiration of the term in January, 1877.

Partial as was the relief thus to be hoped for, the people of Louisiana determined to avail themselves of this election as the last peaceful mode of obtaining even a fragment of their rights and a voice, however feeble, in their government. In proof of this determination we refer to the proceedings of the State Convention lately held at Baton Rouge, the formation of political clubs in every ward of the city of New Orleans, of every parish in the State, and the eagerness manifested by citizens to have themselves registered as voters. The existing registration law, the passage of which by the Legislature in the form in which it has been promulgated has been questioned and is not generally believed, gives to the Supervisors of Registration supreme power, so that they may refuse to register a citizen or strike his name from the registry at their mere will and pleasure, and no court can or dare, under a penalty of a fine of $500, entertain any application to enforce the right of the voter to be registered as such.

To execute this law, Kellogg appointed as Supervisors of Registration his political adherents, many of them persons of disreputable character, and thus this tremendous po e , this machinery which has been devised and created for the especial p ose of defeating the popular will, was delegated to the mere tools and instruments of the usurper, and the result of the election was secured beyond peradventure in advance of the ceremony of casting the votes. Seeing the impossibility of obtaining a fair expression of the popular will under the uncontrolled manipulations of the usurper and his appointees, a number of citizens, representing the most respectable and influential of the population of New Orleans, called upon Mr. Kellogg and requested him to select from such names as they might furnish Supervisors of Registration to act in conjunction with those appointed by him, so that to both parties might be secured a perfectly fair election, which he had declared it to be his purpose to afford. It is almost needless to add that this request was treated with indifference, and the fraudulent registration was continued under the original appointees.

It was difficult for naturalized citizens to obtain registration, and many white persons clearly entitled to registry were refused arbitrarily, while the colored people were furnished registration papers on which, in many instances, they could vote in different wards, and colored crews of steamboats transiently visiting this port were permitted to swell the number of voters. To test the power of supervisors to refuse registration arbitrarily, a citizen clearly entitled, who had been refused, applied to Judge Hawkins, of the Superior District Court, the only court having jurisdiction to grant such writs, for a mandamus to enforce his right. The writ was refused upon the ground that the courts are specially prohibited by the registration act from interfering. Thus, the people of Louisiana are left without the hope or possibility of a fair registration or a fair election.

The origin and object of the White League were thus given by the committee:

And here it is important to say a word about a body known as the "White League," and which has been misrepresented abroad. It will be remembered that the white militia of New Orleans had been disbanded, their arms taken from them, and an exclusive negro militia organized in their stead. By an infamous by-law, the Metropolitan Police, for whose support an enormous tax is levied upon the city exclusively, had been taken from under the control of the mayor and made subject to the orders of the Governor alone. This body was used to intimidate and overawe the citizens, to guard the residences and persons of timorous officials, and to dragoon the parishes whenever any political scheme required it. The white people of the State that is stripped of every means of defense, were threatened moreover by a formidable oath-bound league of the blacks, which, under the command of cunning and unscrupulous negroes, might at any moment plunge them into what they were most anxious to avoid, "a war of races." The incessant demand for offices from the city, State, and General Governments, for which they proffered no other title than that of color; the development in their conventions of a spirit of proscription against white radicals, and even against honorable Republicans who had fought for their liberation; their increasing arrogance, which knew no bounds; their increasing dishonesty, which they regarded as a statesman-like virtue; that contemptuous scorn of all the rights of the white man, which they dared trespass upon—all these signs, as set forth in the platform of the Crescent City White League, warned us that the calamity we had long apprehended was imminent, and that we must either prepare for or perish under it. With the hope, then, as distinctly and openly declared, that a timely and proclaimed union of the whites as a race and their preparation for any emergency might arrest the threatened horrors of a social war, the White League was formed, its object being, as publicly set forth, to assist in restoring an honest and intelligent government to the State of Louisiana, and by a union with all other good citizens to maintain and defend the condition of the United States and the State, and to maintain and protect our rights and the rights of all citizens.

The immediate causes that promoted the revolution of the 14th were stated in the following terms:

Satisfied of the impossibility of securing a fair registration and election, and that it was the settled purpose of the usurper to deprive the white people of the State of Louisiana of the right to carry arms, a right secured to them by the Constitution of the United States, and in the existing state of affairs indispensable to their personal protection, a mass-meeting of the citizens of New Orleans was called to assemble on the morning of September 14th. At that meeting—the largest in numbers and most respectable in character ever collected in the streets of New Orleans—resolutions setting forth the remediless wrongs under which we suffered were adopted, and a committee of citizens was appointed to wait on William Pitt Kellogg and demand his abdication. At twelve and a half P. M., the committee waited upon Mr. Kellogg at the State-House, which had already been converted by him into an armed camp. Kellogg, however, had fled to the Custom-House, which he did not again leave until reinstated in the State-House by the Federal bayonets, and from the Custom-House returned answer, through a member of his staff, refusing to receive or treat with the committee. The committee so reported. Instantly as one man the citizens rose. In the streets and in private stores arms had been seized in open day by the police, and forcibly taken possession of and retained. The owner of a portion of the arms so seized had applied to a competent judicial tribunal, and obtained an order for their release. This order was disobeyed by the police authorities, and when the court attempted to vindicate its own dignity and the majesty of law by fine and imprisonment for contempt, W. P. Kellogg interfered and pardoned the offenders, who were immediately released. At the moment of the popular uprising a steamship lay opposite the Third Precinct Police Station, having on board arms and ammunition consigned to private individuals. A large squad of Metropolitan Police, with loaded guns and cannon pointed, prevented all access to the steamer, and the removal of the arms by those to whom they lawfully belonged; and the citizens rallying on the League, the only organized body, moved down to the levee to take possession of the property which was theirs by right of purchase. At the head of Canal Street, the Metropolitan Brigade, commanded by General Longstreet in person, intercepted and attacked. The battle thus forced upon the citizens was joined, and in a brief half-hour this prætorian band, so long a menace and a terror, was swept away, and the defeated remnants of the Kellogg usurpations, cowering fugitives from the government they had abandoned, were refugees in the Custom-House. Sheltered beneath the folds of the American flag, there they were suffered to remain unmolested. What followed has passed into history, and is matter of familiar knowledge. The lawful government of the peop e's choice, amid universal rejoicings, entered without opposition upon the discharge of its legitimate functions. Joy sat in every heart and illumined every countenance. A new era of confidence, peace, and prosperity, seemed to have dawned upon us. The wretchedness of the past was forgotten in the bright and cheering anticipations of the future. But this short-lived triumph was abruptly closed before the proclamation of the President. It bowed its head, and at the mandate of his general we laid down our arms, retired from the offices we had taken possession of and to which we were lawfully entitled, gave up the captured arsenals and stores, and so proved, as we had ever asserted, our unquestioning obedience to the General Government.

This appeal by the Conservatives was followed on the 30th of September by Governor Kellogg's address to the people of the United States, in which he aims to refute the charges made by his opponents to the effect that his administration had been corrupt and oppressive and that a majority of the legal votes in 1872 were cast in favor of McEnery. Referring to the character of the opposition to his administration, the Governor says:

Close observers of Southern politics have long been aware of a determination to overthrow Republican rule in Louisiana, strongly Republican as this State is known to be, and from the vantage-point thus gained to carry the movement into Mississippi and other Southern States in which the fourteenth and fifteenth amendments to the Constitution of the United States are still respected, and to some extent enforced. In 1868 organized violence was resorted to for this purpose, and was only defeated by the prompt action of Congress. Fraud was employed in 1872, but this also failed to achieve the desired result. In 1873 the unification dodge was tried. The colored people were promised mixed schools, employment on street-cars, and in founderies and workshops, equal rights in all bar-rooms and soda-shops, and, in short, more than the strongest advocate of civil rights had ever asked for them, on the implied condition that they would put the Democrats in office. This movement failed, and now, in 1874, all the principles of unification have been reversed, and under the organization of a white man's party an appeal has once more been made to arms.

The events of the 14th of September last are too well known to need recital. There was no honest motive, no substantial cause, to justify that misguided and disastrous movement. The sole purpose of the leaders of the insurrection was to obtain possession of the offices of the State.

Governor Kellogg then goes on to say that when the present State government came into power there were outstanding, from previous administrations, State warrants to the amount of $2,300,000 in round numbers, and bonds issued before and after the war, amounting to $21,000,000. Since his accession to office, he had signed bonds aggregating $701,000, which were authorized by acts of the Legislature passed before his official term. The outstanding floating indebtedness of $2,300,000, the Governor remarks, "left by previous administrations, has been reduced under my administration to less than $1,400,000. This reduction has been accomplished by no increase of taxation, but by an energetic collection of delinquent taxes, and an honest application of the taxes so collected to the liquidation of the past-due indebtedness of the State. The State has thus been enabled to pay under our financial management more than $900,000 of the old floating debt of the State with old assets, and the delinquent taxes now due and unpaid are sufficient, if collected and applied under the policy we have inaugurated, to pay off the balance of the old floating indebtedness." In comparing the expenditures of his administration with those under his predecessors, Governor Kellogg makes the following statement:

1. The Democratic Legislature of 1865, 1866, and 1867, composed exclusively of white men, Mr. McEnery and others of my present opponents being influential members, made appropriations of $17,-129,554, while the total taxes during the same period were $3,379,000; leaving an excess of appropriations over revenue of $13,750,554.

2. Governor Warmoth's administration made appropriations for the current State expenses, exclusive of school, levee, and interest funds, as follows: For 1868 and 1869, $2,700,000; for 1870, $2,135,920; for 1871, $3,722,969; for 1872, $1,819,856: total, $10,-378,745.

3. Governor Kellogg's administration made appropriations for current State expenses, exclusive of levee, school, and interest funds, as follows: For 1873, $1,554,255; for 1874, $1,172,124: total, $2,726,-379.

As will be seen, the saving the first year of my administration over the last year of my predecessor's was $157,213. In the second year, a still further saving was effected of $547,732. At the same rate, during the next two years, my administration will cost $5,452,758, while the administration of my predecessor for the same time cost $10,878,745, and the Democratic administration of 1865, 1866, and 1867 cost $17,129,554.

A statement made by the Auditor, of this date, now before me, shows: Bonded debt of the State January 1, 1869, $9,883,562; increase of bonded and floating debt during Governor Warmoth's administration, $14,250,685; total debt when Governor Kellogg came into office, $24,084,247; increase during Governor Kellogg's administration by the issue of bonds authorized by laws passed previously, $701,000; reduction of the debt during Governor Kellogg's administration by the redemption of past-due bonds, funding operations, and the retiring of outstanding floating obligations, $1,626,023: showing a net decrease of debt, under the Kellogg administration, of $925,023.

I respectfully commend the foregoing statement, which is, of course, easily verified, to the consideration of those Northern journals which have denounced my administration as corrupt and oppressive, and which yet profess to believe in fair play.

To recapitulate the financial result achieved under my administration:

We have in two years paid off over $900,000 of old floating indebtedness with the old assets of the State.

We have reduced the debt, by the funding bill, from $25,000,000 to $15,000,000, not to be increased until after the year 1924.

We have reduced the State taxes from 21½ mills to 14½ mills, not to be increased until after the same year.

We have provided that parish taxation shall not exceed State taxation, so that the greatest amount of taxation any one parish can be called upon to pay in any one year is 29 mills.

We have enabled the city of New Orleans to reduce taxation 5 mills.

We have largely reduced State expenditures and confined them strictly within the limits of our revenues.

We have reduced over $8,000,000 of contingent liabilities.

All this has been effected by us without aid from those who arrogantly claim to represent all the virtue and intelligence of the State, and while contending against violence within the State borders and organized vilification abroad, and while the very existence of the government was being threatened. This is the financial record of the administration which our opponents assert has been so corrupt and so oppressive as to drive the State into bankruptcy, and the people into riot.

Governor Kellogg then reviews the campaign of 1872, with the purpose of showing that a large majority of the legal voters of the State at that time voted the Republican ticket. In order to prove that the entire body of colored voters were in favor of his election, he says:

Mr. McEnery and myself were the only candidates for the governorship. We both stumped the State. I especially went into nearly every parish, making the first thorough Republican canvass ever made in Louisiana. It was well known throughout the State that I represented the Republican party and the national Administration, and that all my antecedents had been Republican. In my canvass I advocated the Republican principles pure and simple, defending the reconstruction acts of Congress, the fourteenth and fifteenth amendments and their legitimate results. On the other hand, Mr. McEnery was well known as the inflexible opponent of the colored man. It was well known that as a member of the Legislature of 1865, 1866, and 1867, he had supported the vagrant laws so obnoxious to the colored people; that he had opposed the fourteenth amendment, and had supported the several acts passed by that Legislature discriminating against the colored people; in short, that his official record had shown him capable of oppressing the colored man whenever opportunity offered, and of reducing him again to virtual slavery. This disposition, kept somewhat subdued while the Louisiana case was pending before Congress in 1873, has since cropped out in every speech which Mr. McEnery has made, and he has been, and is, one of the most consistent advocates and defenders of the white man's party, and of all the acts of violence which that organization has perpetrated. Is it likely that the colored people voted for Mr. McEnery?

In further reference to this election, which has become famous throughout the United States in consequence of the universal discussion to which it has given rise, Governor Kellogg adds:

The question as to whether Mr. McEnery or myself was elected Governor of this State is one that I have several times proposed to submit to arbitration. When the suit brought in the United States Circuit Court was still pending, I offered, through my counsel, Mr. William H. Hunt, a Southern man, and one of the foremost lawyers at the bar of this State, that the returns should be submitted to five prominent and disinterested citizens, two to be chosen by each side, and the fifth by the four, and I proposed to abide by the result of their decision; but this proposition was declined. I am prepared to show, before any competent tribunal, that a portion of the returns upon which Mr. McEnery bases his claims are forgeries manufactured in this city. I am able now to produce the judicial officer before whom a portion of the blank tally lists and returns were sworn, to be subsequently filled up, here in this city, and palmed off upon the public as the genuine returns of an election held in strong Republican parishes far distant from this city. Even Senator Carpenter, in his speech in the Senate on the 4th of March, said: "I do not think McEnery was in fact elected, though the returns show that he was." I hold myself now ready to impeach the returns relied upon by the fusion boards as altered, defaced, and, in some instances, forged outright. I charge, moreover, that the returns from Iberville, St. James, Terrebonne, St. Martin, and other Republican parishes, were thrown out by the fusion Returning Board for no other reason than because they gave myself and the Republican ticket a heavy majority. And I assert that, by the genuine returns, counting the votes actually cast, I was elected by several thousand majority, and upon this issue I am ready to stand or fall. The State constitution provides that in November next there shall be an election for Congressmen, a State Legislature, and various State and parish officers.

In the concluding portion of his address the Governor explains and defends the law under which the November election was held, and which had been vehemently denounced in the address of the Conservatives, above quoted. He says:

The present election law is substantially the law passed during the last administration in the interests of the conservative citizens of the State, but which Governor Warmoth, at the request of the fusionists, refrained from signing until after the election, in order that he might use in their behalf the

much greater powers conferred upon him by the old law, whose repeal they had previously to their alliance with him so urgently demanded. Under the old law, the law under which the fusionists conducted the last election, the ballot-boxes were removed from the polling-places to the office of the Supervisors of Election, and were counted wherever and whenever the supervisors pleased, without any adequate supervision. Under the new law the ballots must be counted openly at the po s, immediately after the election, in presence of disinterested witnesses. Under the old law the Governor appointed the supervisors, and the supervisors appointed the Commissioners of Election, who might be, and were, in fact, at the last election, all of one political party. Under the new law, the Police Judges appoint the Commissioners of Election in all the country parishes, and the commissioners must be chosen, one from each political party. Under the old law the Returning Board consisted of the Governor, Lieutenant-Governor, the Secretary of State, and two other designated persons. They had absolute control over the returns, and could alter, suppress, or reject them at will. Under the new law no State officer is a member of the Returning Board. The board consisted of five persons, elected by the Senate, one at least of the opposing political party. The returns are required to be made out in triplicate, one copy to be forwarded to the Returning Board.

The existence of many fraudulent registration papers, especially in the city of New Orleans, rendered necessary the passage of a law providing for an entirely new registration, if the election in November was to be free, as we desire it to be, from the irregularities which had characterized previous elections. Accordingly, a bill was passed by the Legislature on the last day of the session, and some time subsequently was sent to me for approval. After examining the bill, and finding it in the main a fair and just measure, marred by some defects, but still a vast improvement on the old law, which must remain in force unless I approved this bill, I announced my intention to sign and promulgate it as soon as the time came for entering upon registration. I have done so, and registration has been actively and satisfactorily progressing for the past thirty days, except when interrupted for a brief period by the insurrection of September 14th.

Desiring that there should be no possibility of doubt as to the fairness of the registration, I voluntarily offered, before the registration opened, to appoint one clerk, to be named by the opposition, in every registration-office throughout the State. At the last election we were denied all representation, both in the registration-offices and at the polls. I have more recently proposed, through the Republican State Central Committee, to agree to the appointment of an advisory board, to be composed of two Republicans and two Democrats, and an umpire to be chosen by them, with which board I declared my willingness to advise and consult in all matters relating to the appointment of registration officers, and the management of registration throughout the State. There is no just and proper safeguard that can be suggested to me which I will not be willing to throw around the conduct of the coming election.

The attempted revolution having proved a failure, and the excitement consequent upon it having somewhat subsided, the attention of both parties was now turned toward the subject of the approaching election. A conference was held between committees representing the two parties, for the purpose of agreeing upon such a system of registration and canvassing the votes as would be satisfactory to all concerned. In the negotiations, the Republican party was represented by W. P. Kellogg, S. B.

Packard, A. A. Atocha, B. F. Flanders, James Lewis, B. F. Blandin, W. G. Brown, and B. F. Joubert; and the Conservative pa t by John McEnery, D. B. Penn, B. F. Jonas, Samuel Chopin, Albert Voorhies, D. F. Kenner, O. Beard, G. W. Mott, and D. S. Cage. The result of this conference was the following agreement, which was made public on the 29th of September:

The undersigned announce the following as the result of the conference between the committees of the two political parties of the State of Louisiana:
1. The committee representing the Conservative People's party pledge themselves to cause all violence and intimidation, if any exists, to cease throughout the State, and to assist the constituted authorities in maintaining peace and insuring a strictly fair and impartial registration and election; also, to discountenance acts and threats of personal violence, and all improper influences to control the will of the electors, and render assistance and use every effort to subject to the penalties of the law all persons who may commit acts of violence or intimidation, or conspire to do the same, in order to guarantee a fair registration and election.
2. There is hereby constituted and established an Advisory Committee, composed of five members, namely: Messrs. Albert Voorhies and E. A. Burke, selected by the representatives of the Conservative People's party, and Messrs. S. B. Packard and B. F. Joubert, selected by the representatives of the Republican party, and of an umpire, namely, Dr. M. F. Bonzano, who has been jointly selected. This Advisory Committee is to supervise and carry on the registration throughout the State on behalf of all parties, to the full extent of suggesting changes in the registration officers and the manner of conducting and carrying on the registration, Governor Kellogg, in the interest of a fair and impartial registration, of his own accord pledging himself to act upon the advice and suggestions of the Advisory Committee so long as such advice and suggestions are in consonance with and permitted by the existing laws of the State.
3. It is agreed that two persons shall be named by the representatives of the Conservative People's party, who shall be elected according to law, to fill two vacancies which shall be created by resignation in the Returning Board within twenty days.
D. F. KENNER,
for the Conservative Committee of Conference,
A. A. ATOCHA,
for the Republican Committee of Conference.

The State Committee of the Democratic and Conservative party now issued an address to the people of the State, announcing the ratification of this compromise. After criticising with some acerbity the course of the party in power, they say, in reference to this agreement, that "the question of the legality of the State Government remains untouched and uncompromised; and no question of principle has been discussed, waived, or concluded. This agreement, as to details, does not operate a withdrawal of the Louisiana case from the Congress of the United States. If not fully complied with by the other party, it will only accumulate evidence of the helplessness of the efforts made by our people to have a fair and legal expression of the popular will."

The language of this address provoked a reply from Governor Kellogg, defending the course of his supporters in the recent compro-

mise negotiations. "The Republican committee," he says, "actuated by a spirit which was naturally supposed to inspire such measures of adjustment, refrained from any allusion to recent occurrences in this city and State, and abstained from any denunciation of their political opponents. In your address you take occasion to recapitulate the old charges of oppression and corruption brought against the Republican party and the present State government, notwithstanding the uncontradicted and incontrovertible statements in my published address of the 13th ultimo show that the present State government is not responsible for either the present State debt or taxation, but has reduced both, and also show that for most of the debt and taxation of both State and city the Democratic party are directly accountable."

Referring to the recent compromise, the Governor added that "I and my friends will faithfully carry out the terms of the agreement we have entered into, which I desire to remind you was strictly confined to matters of registration and election; and I trust your party, who virtually assumed the responsibility of the violence and intimidation heretofore existing in the State, will carry out your part of the agreement by suppressing the same."

During the months of September and October there was a constant state of excitement growing out of events relating to the approaching election. Rumors of political disorders were numerous; especially from the northwestern parishes came many reports alleging on the one hand that the Democrats were using their efforts to intimidate the negroes so as to prevent them from registering, and on the other that the authorities of the United States were making numerous unwarrantable arrests. Public anxiety was increased by the charge, publicly made, that the Republicans, for political purposes, had questioned the legality of the naturalizations made by the Second District Court in New Orleans. Since 1864 this tribunal had issued naturalization papers to upward of 8,000 persons, who, it was presumed, were in the Democratic ranks. The authority of this court to naturalize aliens under the acts of Congress was now questioned, and there seems to have been some diversity of opinion on this point among the leading lawyers of the State. The Democrats also publicly charged that large numbers of negroes had been fraudulently registered in New Orleans and other places.

On the 14th of October Governor Kellogg published a reply to a proposition made by McEnery to submit the election returns of 1872 to a Board of Arbitrators. Objections were made by Governor Kellogg to the form of the propositions submitted by McEnery, but the former expressed a willingness to have the returns examined by arbitrators appointed by President Grant, and to abide their decision. In concluding his letter, Governor Kellogg says: "I can now, of course, only speak for myself, but I would even now be willing that the returns, though they have been for nearly two years in the hands of the spoilers, should be submitted to the examination of three or five disinterested persons, to be appointed, say, by the President of the United States, and if, after a thorough investigation, it does not appear that I was elected, I will willingly resign. The circumstances attending the last election in this State have never yet been thoroughly and fairly investigated, nor can they be except upon the spot where the election occurred and where the proofs, *pro* and *con*, are readiest to hand. I fear nothing from an inquiry so conducted, but, on the contrary, earnestly hope that some such investigation may be had."

The Advisory Board was not destined to fulfill the useful functions of which it gave promise. On the 15th of October Dr. Bonzano, the umpire, resigned. This action was in consequence of a protest made by the two Conservative members against the decision of the umpire in the matter of certain charges against P. J. Maloney, an assistant State Supervisor of Registration; Dr. Bonzano holding that "a protest against the decision of the umpire by one-half of the board is to me an indication of the failure of his efforts to inspire this board with the confidence in his capacity, impartiality, or general fitness for the important and delicate duties called for by his position, that should warn him against persisting to remain an obstacle to the harmonious action of this board."

Representative committees of the two contending parties of the State now held a conference, having for its object the appointment of an umpire to fill the place made vacant by the resignation of Dr. Bonzano, and also the adjustment of alleged violations of the agreement creating the Advisory Board. On the part of the Republicans it was claimed that the first article of that agreement relating to the suppression of disorders had not been satisfactorily observed by the Democrats, and that powers should be given to the Advisory Board "to enforce a strict and fair adherence to the provisions of the first article of this agreement to the extent of calling upon the constituted authorities of the United States, both civil and military, and of the State through Governor Kellogg, to use such power and force as may be required" for the purpose of maintaining peace over and throughout the State, and insuring a fair registration and election. In answer to this proposition, the Democratic members of the conference submitted "as a counter-proposition that they cannot inquire into the alleged violation of the agreement by the Conservatives, or recognize the right of the Republicans to make said charges until the Republican members of the Conference Committee establish as a fact that the agreement has been complied with on their part by having qualified as agreed upon two Conservative members of the Returning Board and an um-

pire in the Advisory Board, to fill the vacancy caused by the resignation of Dr. Bonzano."

The Republican members replied that the matters contained in this counter-proposition were not within the instructions which they had received from the Republican State Central Committee, and therefore they could not act upon them. The conference now (October 20th) adjourned without having agreed upon any thing, and the functions of the Advisory Board virtually came to an end.

The law governing the November election differed in some important respects from that under which the election of 1872 was held. It was passed in 1872, but after the election of that year. Under the old law the Returning Board consisted of the Governor, Lieutenant-Governor, Secretary of State, and two other designated persons. The Returning Board under the new law comprises "five persons to be elected by the Senate from all political parties." A majority constitutes a quorum, with power to make returns; and the board is empowered to fill vacancies created by the death, resignation, or otherwise, of any of its members. Under the new law commissioners of elections are appointed by the Police Judges and must be chosen one from each political party. The returns must be made out in triplicate, and one copy forwarded to the Returning Board. The election was held on the 2d of November, and was attended with general quiet. Previous to the election United States troops had been concentrated in New Orleans, the object of their presence being explained in a general order issued from the Department of the Gulf, two days before the election, as follows: "The troops are in this city to preserve peace and order, and to prevent a conflict between armed bodies of men, and for no other purpose. They will continue to abstain from political discussions and any interference with the election. All the officers and men are required to remain in their quarters during the day of election, unless called out to prevent a conflict between armed bodies, or by orders from superior military authority."

After the election the following protest against the presence, in Louisiana, of Federal troops, was addressed to President Grant, by the Committee of Seventy:

To His Excellency U. S. GRANT, *President of the United States, Washington, D. C.:*

The Committee of Seventy have the honor to inform your Excellency that on the 2d day of this month, at a general election holden in this State, under the auspices of the Acting Governor W. P. Kellogg, the Conservative party was entirely successful, and will have in the next Legislature a clear majority upon a joint ballot. It is a well-ascertained fact that thousands of our colored fellow-citizens voted the Conservative ticket.

We address you now to make a solemn but respectful protest against the future occupation of the State by military forces, and to request their withdrawal with the return of our people to power. We can assure you that the civil law will become supreme, that its sacred obligations will be recognized both by the ruler and the ruled, and that there will be within our borders ample protection guaranteed to life and liberty. At present and for some weeks past the State-House has been garrisoned by United States soldiers, and our city has presented more the appearance of a military post than of a great commercial metropolis, while the agricultural interests of the State have been greatly hindered by the operations of a part of the army in the country parishes.

The Returning Board is to meet on the 11th of this month, for the purpose of canvassing and compiling the election returns, and will be assembled in the State-House. We cannot but consider it extremely improper that the important civil work with which that board is charged should be executed in the midst of bayonets of the Federal Government. *Inter arma silent leges.*

At the commencement of the new era which seems dawning upon our people, we wish to assure you and the people of the United States of our devotion to the principles of the Constitution and of our steadfast purpose to uphold the cause of public liberty and good government.

> J. DICKSON BRUNS,
> H. N. OGDEN,
> B. F. JONAS, } Committee.
> A. J. LEWIS,
> F. C. ZACHARIE,

It now became the duty of the Returning Board to canvass the returns of the election. For this purpose that body assembled in New Orleans early in November. Permission was given to a committee of three from each party to be present at the meetings of the board. The committee of the Democratic party at once filed a protest against the authority of the board to canvass the returns, on the grounds: " 1. That the law creating the board was unconstitutional; 2. That the law gives them judicial power which they could not possess; and, 3. Admitting it to be constitutional, its *personnel* was not according to the spirit or letter of the law."

The labors of the Returning Board were such that the results of the election were not declared until the 24th of December. This time was spent in examining the numerous cases of fraud and contested elections brought to the notice of the board. On the 23d of December the committee appointed by the Conservative and Democratic party to witness the canvassing and compiling of the returns by the Returning Board published a statement, in which they claimed that, at the election of November 2d, there had been chosen four Conservative and two Republican Congressmen, and seventy-one Conservative and thirty-seven Republican members of the Legislature; also that Moncure, the Democratic candidate for State Treasurer, had been elected by 4,851 majority. In submitting this statement to the public the committee " certify under oath that the above statement and compilation for members of the House of Representatives were compiled by us from the sworn duplicate returns in our possession, and have been by us compared with the duplicate returns in possession of the said Returning Board, and corrected thereby, and correspond to the compilation and canvass, poll by poll, and parish by parish, made by said board."

The committee then withdrew from the sessions of the board, but before doing so entered the following protest:

The undersigned committee, on behalf of the Conservative Democratic party of the State of Louisiana, beg leave to present the following final protest against the action of the board in refusing to decide upon and promulgate the returns from the parishes of Avoyelles, Bossier, Ascension, Assumption, Carroll, Concordia, Natchitoches, Red River, and St. Tammany, and against the contemplated reference of the same to the Legislature.

The protest here exhaustively reiterates in forcible terms wherein the board failed to perform its duty in relation to these parishes heretofore published, and says: " The action of this board, therefore, in so referring contested cases, as intimated by them, to the Legislature, would be unwarranted by law and unprecedented even in the shameful and disgraceful proceedings of the Lynch-Bovee Board ; nor has the illegal action of the board been confined to the improper consideration of subjects in the manner of its procedure, but its decisions seem to be guided by no other will than party interests."

In the case of the parish of De Soto the board declined to receive and canvass the duplicate original returns lodged by law with the clerk of the District Court, as it would seem for the very purpose to supply the loss of those forwarded through the Supervisor of Registration, when it was established that the latter had been fraudulently made away with by a dishonest supervisor of registration. In the case of Carroll Parish, while the fraudulent and forged returns were rejected so far as they concerned Republican candidates, they were received and counted against all Democratic candidates.

In the case of Avoyelles Parish the board went outside of the returns to canvass and allow a round majority of 150 in favor of the Republican candidate, basing its action on estimates and conjectures. In the cases of Natchitoches, St. Tammany, Red River, Assumption, and other Parishes, the returns from the polls, invariably and largely Conservative, have been rejected on insufficient, *ex parte* testimony, often contradictory in its nature, so as to give Republican majorities in parishes unquestionably Conservative. In most of these cases the Republicans have been allowed to interpolate evidence after the testimony was chosen so as not to allow its rebuttal, and the evidence filed by the Conservative Committee has been abstracted or purposely mislaid, so as not to be before the board in its deliberations. In all of these decisions the board seems to have been guided by no fixed rule of right, but has varied its action so as to promote Republican interests and defeat Conservative majorities, involving itself in a mass of contradictory and opposing rulings which offer no clew to its comprehension save the steadfast devotion to purpose of returning Republicans whether they have been elected or not. Not a single protest filed by this committee has been sustained, although it is notorious and established by irrefutable testimony that in many parishes of the State the United States army, under direction of the chairman of the Republican State Central Committee, was used on election-day to intimidate Conservative voters and drive them from the polls.

The committee now think it their duty to declare that they are reluctantly driven to the conclusion that this board as a court of elections, for such it is under the decision of the Supreme Court, has entered into a corrupt and revolutionary conspiracy with the present usurping Governor of the State, to overturn the duly-elected General Assembly of the State, and to substitute therefor one of its own creation and manufacture. For these reasons this committee feels now compelled to withdraw from further participation in the counsels and deliberations of this board. In doing so this committee deems it to be a sacred duty to the people of this State to solemnly protest against the decision of the board, as revolutionary in effect, if not in its design, of overturning the legally-elected Legislature of the people, by surrendering to a partisan minority of persons noted for the power of deciding who shall compose the majority in filling the complement required by law. The responsibility for such a step, striking at the root of our form of government, as it does, is a grave one, and such usurpation has always reacted in a terrible manner wherever it has been adopted in America, and this committee trusts that its gravity has been well weighed by your body, as it alone must bear it, as this committee can share no part of the burden by either continuing its connection with your body or lending a seeming acquiescence by its continued presence.

Having exhausted by this final protest the last means of resistance to this revolutionary decision, this committee now retires, leaving the responsibility where it belongs, to complete its duty by surrendering its trust to the constituency whom it represents, and placing before the people of the State and the Union in its proper light the action of the board and this committee, for them to pass on, as a political court of last resort, to judge the cause of Louisiana and decide the question and decree the consequence thereof. F. C. ZACHARIE,
W. R. WHITAKER,
C. CAVANAC.

On the day before the filing of the above protest, the Committee of Seventy published an address to the people of the United States, in which the Returning Board was charged with having counted out candidates legally elected. "The fact of the Conservatives having carried the election," says the address, "has been well known ever since the 5th of November, because the ballots were counted at the polls immediately, and returns made out in duplicate. Yet even now, seven weeks after the election, we are imminently threatened with being defrauded of our victory and our franchise by election returns submitted to a board of returning officers, consisting of five members, four of whom are identified with and committed to the usurping government. These men, aside from their party, have not sustained such a character before this community as to inspire us with confidence in their integrity or impartiality, or to give any hope that they will fairly and honestly compile and promulgate the returns. They have already evinced a determination to defraud the people and to defeat their will as expressed at the ballot-box. In the case of the parish of De Soto, Conservative by over 1,000 majority, the Radical election officer of the State returns placed them in the hands of a woman of the town, who offered to give them up for $1,000, and he left the State. The returning officer refused to take any steps to recover these papers. The attorneys representing the Conservatives sent to De Soto and brought down and presented duplicates of the original returns, of equal value, which had been filed with the clerk of the District Court for the parish, in pursuance of the law. These they refused to receive and consider, although in Radical parishes they had acted on secondary evidence. This is but one case of many such.

Application was made by the candidate for a mandamus to compel them to receive and compile these duplicate original returns from De Soto, to the only court competent under the existing law to grant a writ." In the address, it was claimed that the Conservatives had carried the State by at least 3,500 majority, and had elected a majority of 28 in the House of Representatives, and a majority on joint ballot in both Houses. After alleging instances of illegal action on the part of the Returning Board, the address concludes as follows:

NEW ORLEANS, *December* 22, 1874.

During the session of this board, we have seen the clerk accusing a member of frauds on election returns, and the member in return accusing the clerk; we have seen documents on the Democratic side stealthily abstracted, and the Republican cross-marked affidavit stealthily secured and acted on, the election returns themselves altered and forged in the interests of Radicals weeks after the election. There is no redress, because those to whom alone application can be made are but creatures of usurpation whose existence depends upon the continuation of Radical rule in defiance of the expressed will of the people. These returning officers have been now for seven weeks dallying with the liberties and rights of the people of an entire State, apparently waiting until an opportunity is offered for them to consummate their villainy by promulgating a Radical majority as elected to the Legislature. They hope to do this with impunity, because the State-House, where they sit, is garrisoned with Kellogg's standing army of Metropolitan Police, with several companies of the army of the United States within fifty yards, the whole force of the army and navy within call of Kellogg's whistle, sleeping on their arms, with cartridges distributed.

In this manner are we threatened with another mongrel herd of rapacious plunderers, ignorant and debauched, claiming to be Republicans, elected by Radical returning officers, and installed in the Legislature by the potential force of the army and navy of the United States, as was done in 1872. To such base uses are your soldiers put. That our people are disposed to violence, and that the rights of the black man would not be safe if the Conservative majority in Louisiana was permitted to rule, as stated by our enemies and by the President in his message, we know to be disproved by the fact that during the four days during which the elected government was in undisputed power, with a large force at its command, not a negro was hurt, not an act of violence committed, and, notwithstanding great previous provocation, not a right of any citizen violated.

Having failed in all our appeals to the justice and patriotism of the President and Congress, we now, as a last resort, appeal to the source of all power, the people of the whole country, whose moral influence we invoke, in the hope of awakening that sympathy with our wrongs and sufferings always accorded to a brave and free people struggling for liberty. In the confidence that a virtuous public sentiment may compel unprincipled men who are preying on the vitals of the State to let go their hold, we hope it may react upon the Executive and Congress, and compel them to grant us that relief which neither their sense of justice nor regard for the fundamental institutions of the country has been able to effect. We make this appeal in advance of the final consummation of a great wrong about being perpetrated upon the people, as we are positively assured of the intention of the returning officers to defraud the people of the fruits of their political victory as if the act had been already consummated. We are not clamoring for party purposes that one set of men should be substituted for another as public officials. Our repugnance to Republican rule in Louisiana is not based altogether upon the fact of its being usurpation; valued as great principles are, and grossly as they have been violated, yet it is not for that reason alone that the people of Louisiana are clamoring for relief. The people demand that those elected by them shall govern, so that they shall be relieved from the oppression, that has grown intolerable; that the taxation which has become confiscation, may be lightened; that hideous and wide-spread poverty and distrust may be removed; and that they may be permitted to live by honest industry; that an honest government, for their protection, may be substituted for systematized robbery.

For these reasons, we, the down-trodden people of once fine Louisiana, now call upon the people of the free States of America, if you would yourselves remain free and retain the right of self-government, to demand, in tones that cannot be misunderstood or disregarded, that the shackles be stricken from Louisiana, and that the power of the United States army be no longer used to keep a horde of adventurers in power. B. R. TORMAN, Chairman.

ARCH. MITCHELL,
W. C. RAYMOND, } Committee.
F. C. ZACHARIE,

ROOMS OF THE COMMITTEE OF SEVENTY,
NEW ORLEANS, *December 22, 1874.*

At a meeting held this evening the foregoing address was read and unanimously approved.

R. H. MARR, Chairman,
JOS. W. COLLINS, Secretary.

On the 24th of December Mr. Oscar Arroyo tendered his resignation as a member of the Returning Board; in doing which he said:

I am compelled to adopt the present course by the rulings of the board in the last few days, in returning to the Legislature, as elected, members who were unquestionably defeated, rulings which, to my mind, are so clearly partisan and unjust, defrauding the people of Louisiana of their chosen representatives, that my self-respect will not allow me to longer retain a seat on the board.

On the 24th of December the Returning Board completed its labors. The laws defining the duties of the board, its method of proceeding, and the principles upon which its decisions were based, are set forth in its report as follows:

NEW ORLEANS, *December 24, 1874.*

The Returning Board, in closing its labor of canvassing and compiling the vote of the State given at the election of November 2d last, states that it is only just and proper that the returning officers should give a statement of the difficulties attendant on their labors, and the principles laid down, drawn from law, to direct them in the discharge of their duties. In the first place, this election was very loosely conducted by the Commissioners of Election, so much so that not at one-tenth of the polls in the State were the forms required by law observed. The law requires that the supervisors of registration forward to the returning officers the original list of votes kept by the Commissioners of Election; second, a statement of the persons voted for, and the number of votes received by each; and, third, the tally-sheets, all of which the Commissioners of Election are required to furnish to the supervisors, and they to forward them to the returning officers. In many cases no lists of voters were kept by the commissioners, or, if there were, they were not forwarded to the Returning Board by the supervisors, and many that were forwarded to the Returning Board were not signed or sworn to, as the law

requires. In many cases there was no statement of the persons voted for, and the number of votes received by them, forwarded to the Returning Board, for the reasons that none were furnished by the Commissioners of Election to the supervisors, and many that were returned were neither signed nor sworn to, and in many cases there were no tally-sheets forwarded to the Returning Board to enable it to test the accuracy of the statement of the voter, and in some instances only tally-sheets were returned to the Returning Board, without a list of voters, or statement of votes, and they not signed or sworn to, as the law requires.

This being the case, it became necessary that the papers received from the polling-places should be carefully examined. There were over six hundred and fifty polling-places in the State, and there was a large list of candidates, so it became a very laborious duty, which occupied the board nearly a month, laboring from 11 A. M. to 4 P. M., and from 7 to 11 P. M., every day. The law requires that in such canvass and compilation the Returning Board of officers shall observe the following order: It shall compile the first statements from all polls or voting-places at which there shall have been a fair, free, and peaceable registration and election. Whenever from any poll or voting-place there has been any riot, tumult, acts of violence, intimidation, armed disturbances, bribery, or corrupt influences, which prevented or tended to prevent a fair, free, and peaceable vote of all qualified electors entitled to vote at such poll or voting-place, such returning officers shall not canvass, count, or compile a statement of votes from such poll or voting-place until statements from all other polls or voting-places shall have been canvassed and compiled. The Returning Board of officers shall then proceed to investigate the statements of riot, tumult, acts of violence, intimidation, armed disturbance, bribery, or corrupt influences, at any such poll or voting-place.

The board has followed this requirement of the law, as it was its imperative duty to do, and in examining the proceedings of the Commissioners of Election forwarded to it by the supervisors, when either of the counsel appointed by the political parties objected to the count of any polls, and laid before the board any evidence to sustain such objections, such polls were passed over and not canvassed until the board had compiled the vote from all the polls not objected to. In the progress of the examination a large number of polls were objected to, including some in twenty-seven of the parishes, and in some of these parishes all of the polls were then objected to. The grounds of objection to some of the polls were the failure of a substantial compliance with the law in conducting the election and making the returns to the supervisors; to some that the returns of the commissioners had been changed after they had been made to the supervisors; and to the far greater number that the voters had been intimidated so that they did not register or vote, or were compelled to vote differently from what they desired. Had the board decided that any thing like a strict compliance with the forms of law in holding the election and making the returns to the supervisors would be required, the effect would have been that so many of the polls would have been thrown out that there would have been no election in the State. The board then adopted a rule that when the supervisor had returned any evidence showing an election was held, although it only be a tally-sheet, unsigned or sworn to, that in the absence of fraud or intimidation it would compile the vote as shown by such evidence or document, if it may be called evidence. This decision disposed of a good many protests to the reception of polls, but when substantial forms of law had not been observed, and evidence of fraud or intimidation was produced, the failure of substantial compliance with the forms of law was considered a badge of fraud, and the poll was rejected. We believe this to be a just and reasonable rule, and the board strictly adhered to it.

In the case of Carroll, St. Helena, and St. James Parishes, where it was charged and proved that the returns made by the commissioners to the supervisors had been changed after they came into the hands of the supervisors, the board took evidence to ascertain the true state of the vote and made the compilation accordingly. The question raised against the greater number of the polls was on the charge of intimidation to prevent voters from voting and forcing them to vote against their wishes. To establish this charge a great mass of affidavits was taken, some applicable to the whole of the parishes, and some to particular po s, and a mass of counter-affidavits was also filed. The general facts proved on this point establish that about May, 1874, a military organization known as the White League was established in this State and permeated every neighborhood; that the object of this organization was to prevent colored men from voting unless they could be controlled to vote the Democratic ticket, and to prevent them from holding office; and, further, to compel the Republicans holding office under the present State government to abdicate their offices, and to prevent the Republican party in this State from organizing, with a view of concentrating their party at the late election, and expel the white Republicans from the State unless they would desist from organizing the Republican party in this State and withdraw from the active support of that party. The means taken by this White League organization to accomplish the above purposes are shown to have been by threats that, if the colored voters did not vote the Democratic ticket, they should be expelled from the plantations on which they were farming, be deprived of their crops, be excluded from renting lands hereafter or of being employed, and deprived of their rations, or credit to obtain them, and leading colored men were threatened with death if they persisted in organizing the Republican party; and white Republicans threatened with personal violence, proscription in business and socially of themselves and families, and with hanging if they persisted in organizing the party with a view to the late elections. This organization in armed bands, in many parishes in the State, carried their threats of personal violence into effect by killing some Republicans, whipping and ill-treating others, and compelled the parish officers holding office under the present State government to abdicate their offices. This was particularly the case in all the Red River parishes, most of the Têche parishes, and in the parishes between the Red and Washita Rivers.

All the above acts, resorted to by the White-League organization to carry out their purpose, were clear violations of both State and United States laws, and would subject the perpetrators of the acts to imprisonment in the penitentiary, so odious are they to the sense of the people. These acts of intimidation, which prevented a fair, free, and peaceable election in the parishes of St. Mary and Grant, were so general and overwhelming that the board felt compelled to throw out every box in these parishes, and in many other parishes where there was satisfactory p oo that intimidation had been used at designated rpofls, so as to prevent a fair, free, and peaceable election at such polls, and they were excluded from the compilation as the law requires. When the friends of a political party, such as the White-League organization is toward the Democratic party, shall clearly and generally violate the laws of the country to control an election in their interests, it is but just and proper that, when they are shown to have brought such acts to bear on an election, they should not be permitted to profit by them, and such is the intention of the law. The board, however, in this case did not exclude any

poll from compilation except on satisfactory proof that such violation had been perpetrated, and that it had the effect of intimidating a sufficient number of voters to change the result of the election. As all these acts to produce intimidation had been perpetrated in favor of the Democratic party and against the Republican party, the polls excluded from compilation generally gave majorities in favor of the Democratic party, and their exclusion from compilation reduced the vote of that party, and in some instances had the effect of returning representatives and other officers of the opposite party different from the returns made by the supervisors. This is the natural result of an illegal attempt to accomplish an object, and is no fault of the board.

The counsel of the Democratic party protested against the counting of certain polls in the parishes of Natchitoches and Bossier, on the grounds that United States troops were expected at the polls on the day of election, or did actually visit the polls on the day of election, in order to assist the United States Marshal to arrest persons charged with violations of the United States law, and that, in consequence, a great number of Democrats did not attend the polls and vote, for fear of arrest by the United States troops. Even if such facts had been fully proved as alleged, we do not see that there was any violation of the law in United States troops doing so. Certainly, a person charged with a crime against the United States law cannot say he is intimidated by the fact that the United States Marshal was trying to arrest him. It is his own fault if he is guilty, and he cannot urge his crime as protection. Persons not conscious of their guilt would not flee from the presence of a United Marshal and his posse of United States soldiers. This is preposterous, and we did not consider this a good ground of intimidation.

There were no returns of the election from the parish of De Soto by the Supervisor of Registration, as the law required. Persons interested produced the clerk of the court with such papers as were by law intrusted to him, and offered them as the returns from the parish. The board decided that they could not receive, canvass, and compile such returns. The parties in interest applied to the proper court for a mandamus to compel the board to receive the canvass and compile those returns, but upon trial the court sustained the ruling of the board. The same principle was acted upon in the Terrebonne case. There was no supervisor in the parish of Winn, the one appointed for that parish having been expelled from the parish, and an unauthorized person assumed to act. They could not recognize such lawlessness.

The board submits to the Legislature and people of this State the result of their investigation, with a consciousness that they have properly discharged their trust.   J. MADISON WELLS, President.

The results as returned by the board, excluding the returns of those polls and parishes that had been thrown out by this board, show that 69,544 votes were cast for Dubruclet, the Republican candidate for Treasurer; and 68,586 for Moncure, making the majority of the former 958. Fifty-four Republican and fifty-two Conservative members of the Legislature were returned; the election of five members was not determined, but referred to the Legislature for decision. The five constitutional amendments recommended by Governor Kellogg and approved by the Legislature were ratified beyond dispute, as it was admitted that this ratification would not be defeated by the votes of the polls and parishes which had been rejected.

When the report of the Returning Board

had been made public, Mr. McEnery published the following protest:

NEW ORLEANS, *December* 25, 1874.

The wrong just perpetrated by the Returning Board against the people of Louisiana, and which vitally threatens the safety and integrity of republican institutions in the United States, is a more crowning infamy than the action of the Lynch Returning Board, surpasses even the midnight order of Durell, and would not be submitted to by any free people.

Resistance to the national authority, represented here by a large portion of the army and a naval fleet, sustaining a usurpation, and stifling the voice of the people, has never been meditated.

JOHN McENERY.

When the returns of the Returning Board became known, there was much dissatisfaction on the part of the Conservatives. The Republicans feared that the results as announced by the Returning Board would be disputed with violence, and the indications were plain that the approaching assembling of the Legislature would not be peaceable. In view of this threatened violence, and of the fact that civil war might break out any moment, as it had done in September, the President of the United States ordered General Sheridan to make a tour of inspection through certain of the Southern States, with the view of reporting the condition of affairs there, and to assume command of the Department of the South if in his judgment it became advisable. The confidential instructions to General Sheridan, and the order to assume command, were as follows:

WAR DEPARTMENT,
WASHINGTON, D. C., *December*, 24, 1874.
To General P. H. SHERIDAN, *Chicago, Ill.*

GENERAL: The President sent for me this morning, and desires me to say to you that he wishes you to visit the States of Louisiana and Mississippi, and especially New Orleans, La., and Vicksburg and Jackson, Miss., and ascertain for yourself, and for his information, the general condition of matters in those localities. You need not confine your visit to the States of Louisiana and Mississippi, and may extend your trip to other States, Alabama, etc., if you see proper, nor need you confine your visit in the States of Louisiana and Mississippi to the places named. What the President desires is the true condition of affairs, and to receive such suggestions from you as you may deem advisable and judicious. Inclosed herewith is an order authorizing you to assume command of the Military Division of the South, or any portion of that division, should you see proper to do so. It may be possible that circumstances may arise which would render this a proper course to pursue. You can, if you desire it, see General McDowell in Louisville, and make known to him confidentially the object of your trip, but this is not required of you. Communication with him by you is left entirely to your own judgment. Of course, you can take with you such gentlemen of your staff as you wish, and it is best that the trip should appear to be one as much of pleasure as of business, for the fact of your mere presence in the localities referred to will have, it is presumed, a beneficial effect. The President thinks, and so do I, that a trip South might be agreeable to you, and that you might be able to obtain a good deal of information on the subject about which we desire to learn. You can make your return by Washington, and make a verbal report, and also inform me from time to time of your views and conclusions. Yours truly, etc.

W. W. BELKNAP, Secretary of War.

WAR DEPARTMENT,
ADJUTANT-GENERAL'S OFFICE,
WASHINGTON, D. C., *December* 24, 1874.
To Lieutenant-General P. H. SHERIDAN, *United States Army, Chicago, Ill.*

SIR: If, in the course of the inspection and investigation the Secretary of War has directed you to make in his communication of this date, you should find it necessary to assume command over the Military Division of the South, or any portion thereof, the President of the United States hereby authorizes and instructs you to take the command accordingly, and to establish your headquarters at such a point as you may deem best for the interests of the public service.

I am, sir, very respectfully, your obedient servant,
E. B. TOWNSEND, Adjutant-General.

As the time for the assembling of the Legislature drew near, the excitement increased. The Conservatives were charged with attempting to kidnap, and even threatening to assassinate Republican members of the Legislature, in order to reduce the Republican majority to a minority. A few days prior to the time of the assembling of the Legislature, A. G. Cousin, a Republican member, was arrested upon an alleged charge of embezzlement, and kept in confinement until after the meeting of the Legislature. The Republicans charged that the sole object of this proceeding was to prevent the presence of Mr. Cousin at the opening of the Legislature. The Conservatives, however, declared that the arrest was *bona fide* and for legitimate cause. Major Merrill, in command of the United States troops in the Red River District, having been instructed to be in readiness for any violence or unlawful proceedings, reported as follows upon the condition of affairs in that region:

HEADQUARTERS DISTRICT OF UPPER RED RIVER,
SHREVEPORT, LA., *December* 30, 1874.
To the Adjutant-General, Department of the Gulf.

SIR: Referring to your telegram of December 13th, directing me in certain events to be in readiness to suppress violence, and to let it be understood that I will do it, I have the honor to report that, in view of these instructions, I have been at some pains to investigate the probabilities of violence here, and the following are the facts as nearly as I can ascertain: The State Returning Board have officially announced that the candidates for office in this parish on what is known as the Radical ticket are duly and lawfully elected. The leaders of the opposing party declare that such is not the fact, and that the persons there declared elected shall not take or hold the offices. This determination appears to be well settled, and is so generally expressed and approved by a large majority of the whites, that I have no doubt it is more than an idle threat. This expression, in many instances, is accompanied by threats of violence, and even of death, to the officers if they attempt to take the offices, and I cannot doubt that such threats are very seriously made. They are only a repetition of what was at all times the open talk of the leaders before the election. Three of the officers referred to are members of the Lower House of the Legislature, and all three are now in New Orleans. The others are Parish Judge Cresswell, Sheriff Heffner, and several minor officers, the police jury, justices of the peace, and constables. There is on the part of most of them such apprehension of danger in assuming their duties that, except the Parish Judge, I do not think any of them will attempt or could be induced to take his office. The Parish

Judge is a man of courage and coolness, and I cannot tell whether he will attempt to take his office or not. I have not seen him recently, and have no definite information of his purpose. As long as any or all of these officers choose to refuse to exercise the functions of their office, I conceive I am not called upon to do any thing in the matter. My instructions cover the following points, and will be carried out:

That I recognize as legal State officials only such persons as are recognized as such by the recognized executive or judicial officers of the State; that in the legal exercise of their duties such officers must not be violently disturbed or interfered with, and if such violence occurs it shall be my duty to suppress it; and that my advice to all persons is, that if any question of right exists for any person to hold office, that such person shall be taken before the proper legal tribunals.

The leading Radicals have left. The usual worrying and harassing of negroes go on without intermission, but lately no acts of violence have come to my notice. Such acts are now confined to plundering, with or without some show of legal forms, and driving them from their homes to seek places to live elsewhere. Very respectfully your obedient servant,

LEWIS MERRILL,
Major Seventh Cavalry, commanding.

The circumstances attending the organization of the Legislature on the 4th of January constitutes one of the most memorable events in the history of the country. Different reports have given somewhat varying details of the important events of that day. Four reports, however, have been made which may be regarded as official in character, and which fully represent both sides of the controversy. One is the official report made to the Government of the United States by General Sheridan, who had arrived in New Orleans several days before the meeting of the Legislature, and assumed command at nine o'clock on the evening of the 4th. Two were prepared for presecution to Congress by committees of opposing political parties in the Louisiana House of Representatives; and the fourth was made by the members of the Congressional Committee who had visited New Orleans to investigate the condition of affairs in Louisiana, and were witnesses of the events of the 4th of January, in the Legislative hall of that State. (The last-named report will be found under the title PUBLIC DOCUMENTS.) As the matter is of the deepest current interest, and will be of importance in the future, it becomes imperative to preserve in permanent form whatever may throw light upon the proceedings of that day. The other reports above referred to are therefore here given as follows:

GENERAL SHERIDAN'S REPORT.

HEADQUARTERS MILITARY DIVISION OF THE }
MISSOURI. }
NEW ORLANS, LA., January 8, 1875. }

To Hon. W. W. BELKNAP, Sec'y of War, Washington:

I have the honor to submit the following brief report of affairs as they occurred here in the organization of the State Legislature of January 4, 1875. I was not in command of this military department until nine o'clock at night on the 4th instant, but I fully indorse, and am willing to be held responsible for, acts of the military as conservators of the public peace upon that day. During the few days in which I was in the city prior to the 4th of January, the general topic of conversation was the scenes of bloodshed that were liable to occur on that day, and I repeatedly heard threats of assassinating the Governor, and regrets expressed that he was not killed on the 14th of September last; also threats of the assassination of Republican members of the House in order to secure the election of a Democratic Speaker. I also know of the kidnapping by the banditti of Mr. Cousin, one of the members-elect of the Legislature.

In order to preserve peace, and to make the State-House safe for the peaceable assembling of the Legislature, General Emory, upon the requisition of the Governor, stationed troops in the vicinity of the building. Owing to these precautions the Legislature assembled in the State-House without any disturbance of the peace. At twelve o'clock William Vigers, the Clerk of the last House of Representatives, proceeded to call the roll, as according to law he was empowered to do. One hundred and two legally-returned members answered to their names. Of this number, fifty-two were Republicans, and fifty Democrats. Before entering the House, Mr. L. A. Wiltz had been selected in caucus as the Democratic nominee for Speaker, and Michael Hahn as the Republican nominee.

Mr. Vigers had not finished announcing the result, when one of the members, Mr. Billieu, of Lafourche, nominated Mr. L. A. Wiltz for temporary Speaker. Mr. Vigers promptly declared the motion out of order at that time, when some one put the question, and amid cheers on the Democratic side of the House Mr. Wiltz dashed on to the rostrum, pushed aside Mr. Vigers, seized the Speaker's chair and gavel, and declared himself Speaker. A protest against this arbitrary and unlawful proceeding was promply made by members of the majority, but Mr. Wiltz paid no attention to these protests, and on motion from some one on the Democratic side of the House it was declared that one Trezevant was nominated and elected Clerk of the House. Mr. Trezevant at once sprang forward and occupied the Clerk's chair amid the wildest confusion over the whole House. Mayor Wiltz then again, on another nomination from the Democratic side of the House, declared one Flood elected Sergeant-at-Arms, and ordered a certain number of assistants to be appointed. Instantly a large number of men throughout the hall, who had been admitted on various pretexts, such as reporters and members' friends and spectators, turned down the lappels of their coats, upon which were pinned blue-ribbon badges, on which were printed in gold letters the words "Assistant Sergeant-at-Arms," and the Assembly was in the possession of the minority, and the White League of Louisiana had made good its threat of seizing the House, many of the Assistant Sergeants-at-Arms being well known as captains of White-League companies in the city. Notwithstanding the suddenness of this movement the leading Republican members had not failed to protest again and again against this revolutionary action of the minority, but all to no purpose, and many of the Republicans rose and left the House in a body, together with the clerk, Mr. Vigers, who carried with him the original roll of the House as returned by the Secretary of State. The excitement was now very great, and the acting Speaker directed the Sergeant-at-Arms to prevent the egress or ingress of members or others, and several exciting scuffles in which knives and pistols were drawn, took place, and for a few moments it seemed as if bloodshed would ensue.

At this juncture Mr. Dupre, a Democratic member from Orleans Parish, moved that the military power of the General Government be invoked to preserve the peace, and that a committee be appointed to wait on General de Trobriand, the commanding officer of the United States troops stationed at the State-House, and request his assistance in clearing the lobby. The motion was adopted. A committee of five, of which Mr. Dupre was made chairman, was sent to wait upon General de Trobriand and soon returned with that officer, who was accompanied by two of his staff-officers. As General de Trobriand walked down to the Speaker's desk loud applause burst from the Democratic side of the House. General de Trobriand asked the acting Speaker if it was not possible for him to preserve order without appealing to him to preserve order as a United States Army officer. Mr. Wiltz said it was not, whereupon the general proceeded to the lobby, and, addressing a few words to the excited crowd, peace was at once restored. On motion of Mr. Dupre, Mr. Wiltz then, in the name of the General Assembly of the State of Louisiana, thanked General de Trobriand for his interference in behalf of law and order, and the general withdrew.

The Republicans had now generally withdrawn from the hall, and united in signing a petition to the Governor, stating their grievances and asking his aid, which petition, signed by fifty-two legally-returned members of the House, is in my possession.

Immediately subsequent to the action of Mr. Wiltz in ejecting the Clerk of the old House, Mr. Billieu moved that two gentlemen from the parish of De Soto, one from Winn, one from Bienville, and one from Iberia, who had not been returned by the Returning Board, be sworn in as members, and they were accordingly sworn in by Mr. Wiltz, and took their seats on the floor as members of the House. A motion was now made that the House proceed with its permanent organization, and accordingly the roll was called by Mr. Trezevant, the acting Clerk, and Wiltz was declared Speaker, and Trezevant Clerk of the House.

Acting on the protests made by the majority of the House, the Governor now requested the commanding general of the department to aid him in restoring order, and enable the legally-returned members of the House to proceed with its organization according to law. This request was reasonable, and in accordance with law. Remembering vividly the terrible massacres that took place in this city on the assembling of the Constitutional Convention in 1866, at the Mechanics' Institute, and believing that the lives of the members of the Legislature were, or would be, endangered in case an organization under the law was attempted, the posse was furnished, with the request that care should be taken that no member of the Legislature returned by the Returning Board should be ejected from the floor. This military posse performed its duty under directions from the Governor of the State, and removed from the floor of the House those persons who had been illegally seated, and who had no legal right to be there; whereupon the Democrats rose and left the House, and the remaining members proceeded to effect an organization under the State laws.

In all this turmoil, in which bloodshed was imminent, the military posse behaved with great discretion. When Mr. Wiltz, the usurping Speaker of the House, called for troops to prevent bloodshed, they were given him; when the Governor of the State called for a posse for the same purpose and to enforce the law, it was furnished also. Had this not been done, it is my firm belief that scenes of bloodshed would have ensued.

P. H. SHERIDAN, Lieutenant-General.

The following report was submitted to the Louisiana Legislature, on the 11th of January, by a Republican committee of that body, with the recommendation that it be forwarded to Congress:

To the Honorable Speaker and Members of the House of Representatives of the State of Louisiana:

GENTLEMEN: Your committee, selected to prepare a statement of revolutionary proceedings that transpired in the hall of the House of Representatives on Monday, January 4, 1875, beg leave to submit the following statement, and recommend that it be immediately forwarded to the Congress of the United States. Respectfully,

JAMES S. MATHEWS,
GEORGE DRURY,
CHARLES W. LOWELL,
W. P. SOUTHARD,
R. R. RAY.

Returns of the election held November 2, 1874, as promulgated by the proper returning officers thereof according to law, show that there were elected to the House fifty-three Republicans and fifty-three Democrats, and there were five seats for which the returning officers had made no returns, which were referred for decision of the right to hold them to the General Assembly.

The whole number of the House of Representatives is 111; a quorum is a majority of the members elected, and was, at that time, 54. A quorum, when the whole number is seated, is 56.

A few days prior to the day fixed for the meeting of the General Assembly a posse of unauthorized persons secretly kidnapped A. G. Cousin, a Republican member, and by force and violence conveyed him out of the city, under color of a pretended charge of embezzlement of $50, across Lake Pontchartrain to a distant parish, where they held him in confinement until after the day for the meeting of the General Assembly. They afterward released him, the very men who made the charge going on his bond, and acknowledging that their object in arresting and detaining him was to break a Republican majority.

Certain parties in the mean while sought, by the payment of several thousand dollars to certain Republican members, to bribe three of them to vote for the Democratic nominee for Speaker. Attempts were made to kidnap other Republican members. Public and repeated threats were made, for weeks previous to the 4th of January, of violence and assassination toward certain Republican members of the General Assembly. These threats and menaces were repeated, confirmed and indorsed by the press of the opposition throughout the State.

In consequence of information in his possession that organized violence was intended to be used to influence the organization of the House, the Governor placed the State-House under the military command of General H. J. Campbell, of the State militia, who was ordered to assist and sustain the police. Under this order, General Campbell excluded from the building, on Monday, all but officials of the State government, members of the General Assembly, and persons claiming to be members, judges, members of Congress, and members of the United States civil, military, and naval forces.

The constitutional provisions to govern the organization of the House are as follows:

ARTICLE 23. The House of Representatives shall choose its Speaker and other officers.

ART. 34. Each House of the General Assembly shall judge of the qualifications, elections, and returns of its members, but a contested election shall be determined in such a manner as may be prescribed by law.

ART. 36. Each House of the General Assembly shall keep and publish weekly a journal of its proceedings, and the yeas and nays of members on any question, and, at the desire of two of them, they shall be entered on the journal.

The law governing the organization of the House is as follows:

Section 44, Article XXVIII., approved November 30, 1872.—That it shall be the duty of the Secretary of State to transmit to the Clerk of the House of Representatives and Secretary of the Senate of the last General Assembly a list of the names of such persons as, according to the returns, shall have been elected to either branch of the General Assembly, and it shall be the duty of said Clerk and Secretary to place the names of the Representatives and Senators elect so furnished upon the roll of the House and of the Senate respectively ; and those Representatives and Senators whose names are so placed by the Clerk and Secretary respectively, in accordance with the foregoing provision, and none other, shall be competent to organize the House of Representatives or Senate. Nothing in this act shall be construed to conflict with Article XXXIV. of the constitution of the State.

At twelve o'clock M. on January 4, 1875, the State-House being surrounded by an excited crowd of several thousand persons, the members assembled in the hall of the House, and the Chief Clerk called the roll of the House. Immediately afterward, or a little before the Clerk had finished the announcement of the number of members who answered to their names, which was 102, Mr. Billieu, representative from Lafourche, moved that L. A. Wiltz, representative from Orleans, be elected temporary Speaker. The Chief Clerk replied that the legal motion was to elect a Speaker.

Mr. Billieu, paying no attention to the protest of the Clerk, proceeded hurriedly to publish his own motion, against the protest of all the Republican representatives.

The motion was put in a quick and excited manner, and not in a loud voice, and was voted for only by a portion of even the Democratic members. The negative was not put at all.

Mr. Wiltz, having previously taken a position near the Clerk's desk, as quick as thought, upon putting the motion, and without waiting for any announcement of the vote, sprang to the Speaker's desk where the Clerk was standing, seized the gavel from his hand, and pushed the Clerk violently off the stand, and declared himself temporary Speaker. Following him was W. T. Houston, first justice of the peace in the parish of Orleans, who took from his pocket a book looking like a Bible, and proceeded to go through the form of administering an oath.

Mr. Wiltz, as temporary Speaker, assumed to administer the oath to members *en masse*, against the protest of the Republican members. Some Democratic members then made a motion to elect Trezevant as Clerk. Mr. Wiltz put the motion, and declared it carried. Mr. Trezevant at once sprang forward and took the Clerk's chair. Immediately after, in a hurried and excited manner, a Mr. Flood was elected Sergeant-at-Arms upon motion by a Democratic member ; also, a motion was made from the same side of the House that a number of Assistant Sergeants-at-Arms be appointed by the Chair, which the Chair declared carried, when a large number of persons at once appeared wearing badges, on which was printed "Assistant Sergeant-at-Arms." While all the above motions were being put, the Republican members objected, and called for the yeas and nays, all of which was disregarded by the acting Speaker. Colonel Lowell, a Republican member, made the point of order that the constitution of the State allowed any two members to call for the yeas and nays on any motion. Mr. Wiltz decided the point of order not well taken. (*See* constitutional provision above.) The pretended House then proceeded, in defiance of the law, to swear in five additional Democratic members, to wit: James Brice, Jr., of Bienville ; Charles Schuler and John L. Scales, of De Soto ; C. C. Dunn, of Grant, and George A. Kelley, of Winn, by which the Democrats gave themselves a majority. The Republicans protested against this violence and lawlessness, but their protests were disregarded. The Democrats then assumed to elect a permanent chairman. Mr. Wiltz declared himself elected, and by going through the usual form, having received, as he claims, fifty-five votes, which included the five men seated in violation of law, the Republican members withdrawing and not voting, as they deemed the proceeding illegal. About the time of the withdrawal of the

Republican members of the House Mr. Wiltz gave, or caused to be given, instructions to the persons assuming to be Sergeants-at-Arms, not to allow any one to pass out of or to enter the House. Great commotion at once ensued, and quite a number of knives and revolvers were drawn and displayed in a threatening manner. Most of the Republican members had already left the room amid great confusion, when Mr. Dupre, of Orleans, a Democratic member, moved that the Speaker be requested to call on the United States troops to preserve the peace of the House. The motion prevailed, and a committee, of which Mr. Dupre was appointed chairman, was appointed to wait on General de Trobriand and request the interference of United States troops to preserve the peace. In a short time the committee returned, accompanied by General de Trobriand and staff. Upon the appearance of General de Trobriand on the floor, loud applause came from the Democratic side of the House. General de Trobriand moved to the Speaker's desk, and Mr. Wiltz stated in substance the reason for his being summoned, and informed him of the impossibility of his being able to enforce order and preserve peace. General de Trobriand, in substance, the committee being unable to get the exact words, asked Mr. Wiltz whether it was not possible for him to preserve order and keep the peace without calling on him as a United States officer. Mr. Wiltz replied that it was impossible ; that he had already instructed the Sergeant-at-Arms to do so. Then General de Trobriand took action in the matter, and quiet was restored with little trouble. Mr. Wiltz then assured General de Trobriand that his coming had prevented bloodshed, and, as your committee is reliably informed, on motion thanked him in the name of the General Assembly of Louisiana for his prompt response to the summons of the House, and the general retired. The Republican members then signed and presented the following application to the Governor, requesting that the legal members be put in possession of the hall

NEW ORLEANS, *January 4, 1875.*

To His Excellency WILLIAM P. KELLOGG, *Governor.*

DEAR SIR : The undersigned, members-elect of the House of Representatives of the General Assembly of the State, assembled at the hall of the House, in the State-House, at 12 M. this day, and answered to the call made by the Clerk. Immediately thereafter the chair was forcibly taken possession of in violation of law, and an attempt was made to organize the House contrary to law. We cannot obtain our legal rights unless the members-elect are placed in possession of the hall. Whenever the hall is cleared of all persons save the gentlemen elected we will proceed to organize. We therefore invoke your aid in placing the hall in possession of the members-elect, that we may attend to the performance of our duties. Respectfully.

Here follow the signatures of fifty-two, including the following :

I have consented to sign this document on the ground that the conservative members of the House have set a precedent by appointing a special committee to wait on General de Trobriand, who immediately appeared at the bar of the House, escorted by said special committee.

ROBERT F. GUICHARD,
Representative of St. Bernard.

This was signed by fifty-two legally-elected and returned members. In response to this application the Governor applied to the military force of the United States to assist his officers in expelling intruders and disturbers of the peace and preserving order, which assistance was rendered, and by it order was restored.

When the Republican members returned to the hall, following General de Trobriand at his request and under his protection, and attempted to follow him through the door, the Sergeant-at-Arms at the door, by order of Mr. Wiltz, closed the door in their faces and forcibly prevented them from entering, and they were not allowed to enter until the attention of General de Trobriand was called to the fact, and at his order the Republican members were admitted and the five intruders were expelled. The Democratic members, with Mr. Wiltz at their head, then withdrew, and the House proceeded to organize according to law.

STATE OF LOUISIANA,)
OFFICE OF SECRETARY OF STATE, }
NEW ORLEANS, *January* 6, 1875.)

I hereby certify that the foregoing fifty-two signatures are the genuine names of the members declared to be elected to the House of Representatives of the State of Louisiana, as certified to by the Returning Board of said State, and as by me certified to the Clerk of said House of Representatives as required by law. P. G. DESLONDE, Secretary of State.

I certify that the foregoing protest contained the genuine signatures of fifty-two members of the House of Representatives whose names are upon the list furnished me by the Secretary of State, in conformity with the law; and I further certify that all said members answered to their names at the roll-call made by me at twelve o'clock noon on Monday, the 4th day of January, 1875, being a majority of all the members present. WILLIAM VIGERS, Chief Clerk of the House of Representatives.

The memorial addressed by the Conservative members of the House to Congress was as follows:

To the Honorable the Senate and House of Representatives of the United States of America, in Congress assembled:

The House of Representatives of the State of Louisiana, duly organized in accordance with the laws of the State, would most respectfully state to your honorable bodies that, having convened in the Capitol of the State on the 4th day of January, 1875, and having organized permanently according to law, their Speaker and a majority of the members were compelled to retire by the troops of the United States; the facts being as follows:

On Monday, January 4, 1875, at twelve o'clock, M., the Clerk of the former House called the roll of members as returned by the Returning Board, to the number of one hundred and six—one hundred and eleven constituting a full House—and, after reading the certificate of the Secretary of State attached thereto, announced a quorum present; fifty-six being the number required.

Thereupon, on motion of Mr. Billieu, of Lafourche, which was carried, the Hon. L. A. Wiltz, of Orleans, took the chair as temporary Speaker. Mr. Wiltz, as Speaker, called the House to order. The oath of office was duly administered to him by Justice Houston, and thereupon the Speaker administered the oath to the returned members of the House.

A motion was then made to declare Mr. P. J. Trezevant Clerk of the House, *pro tem.*, which was carried.

A motion was next made to appoint Mr. E. Flood Sergeant-at-Arms, *pro tem.*, which was carried.

Motions and calls from both the Republican and Conservative sides for a permanent organization followed, but, great confusion prevailing, the chair refused to entertain any motion until order was somewhat restored.

The following resolution, offered by Mr. Billieu, of Lafourche, was then moved and passed:

"*Be it resolved,* That James Brice, Jr., of the parish of Bienville, Charles Schuler and John L. Scales, of the parish of De Soto, C. C. Dunn, of the parish of Grant, and George A. Kelley, of the parish of Winn, be and they are hereby declared duly elected members of this House, and as such are entitled to their

VOL. XIV.—32 A

seats, reserving to their opponents, if any, all rights of contestation."

These five, being members from the four parishes whose returns the Returning Board had neglected to promulgate and had referred to the Legislature for its decision, were then duly sworn in and took their seats.

Thereafter, motions from both Republicans and Conservatives were made for a permanent organization, and the Speaker announced the motion carried. Mr. L. A. Wiltz was nominated by the Conservatives, and Messrs. Hahn and C. W. Lowell by the Republicans. Mr. Lowell declined. The Speaker then ordered the roll to be called, which roll was the same as called by the former Clerk, Mr. Vigers (then *functus officio*), with the addition of the five names above mentioned.

The roll being called, the Clerk announced the vote as follows: L. A. Wiltz, 55 votes; M. Hahn, 2 votes; blank, 1 vote—Mr. Wiltz voting blank.

No objection or dispute was made to the count, or to the announcement of the vote. At this juncture several of the Republican members indicated a disposition to leave the hall, and a number of them retired.

Mr. Wiltz was duly sworn, and, the roll being called, the members came to the Speaker's stand and were sworn in by him, four at a time, to the number of fifty-nine, including Messrs. Baker, Drury, Hahn, Murrill, and Thomas, Republicans, who remained and participated in the proceedings after the permanent organization.

A motion was then made and carried to elect Mr. Trezevant Clerk of the House; and another motion was made and carried, electing Mr. E. Flood Sergeant-at-Arms of the House. Thus was the permanent organization of the House of Representatives effected, in accordance with the constitution of the State of Louisiana—see Articles XVII., XX., XXXIV., and XL., of Louisiana, and section 44 of act 98, of 1872—and in accordance with law and parliamentary usage. The Speaker then announced that the House was ready for business, and notices of contest of election were given.

On motion of Mr. Dupre, of Orleans, a committee of seven on elections and returns was appointed, consisting of Messrs. Dupre, Pipes, Carloss, Young, Hammond, Hahn, and Thomas. In the mean while, during the proceedings in the House, an additional number of police, with a crowd of disorderly persons, entered the lobby and engaged in menacing altercation with the Sergeant-at-Arms and his ten assistants. Finding that the Sergeants-at-Arms were contending with the mob, the Speaker endeavored to procure the attendance of additional Sergeants-at-Arms, and for this purpose addressed a note to the officials who were in possession and control of the barricaded doors of the State-House, to allow fifty citizens to be admitted for that purpose. This request, made in writing, was refused. About one o'clock, P. M., the disturbance in the lobby grew serious and a conflict was imminent.

Then, in order to avoid a collision, General de Trobriand, of the United States Army, who had some time previously entered and occupied the State-House with his soldiers, was sent for. After entering the hall he was addressed by the Speaker as follows: "General de Trobriand at the request of the members of the House of Representatives, I have sent for you to say that the House of Representatives of the State of Louisiana is organized, with myself as permanent Speaker, and to request you, if your orders will permit, to please say a few words to the unruly persons in the lobby, and thereby prevent bloodshed. I feel and know that I can maintain the dignity of the House, but it is not my wish, nor that of the members of the House, to bring on a conflict. Hence you will oblige me if you will say a few words to the lobby."

The general then retired to the lobby and spoke

to the crowd, which then dispersed, and order was restored. After this interruption, the House proceeding with its business, the Committee on Elections and Returns reported, and upon their report the following-named representatives were duly sworn in and seated as members: Messrs. John O'Quinn, of the parish of Avoyelles; J. J. Horan, A. D. Land, and Thomas R. Vaughan, of the parish of Caddo; J. Jeffries, R. L. Luckett and G. W. Stafford, of the parish of Rapides, and William F. Schwing, of the parish of Iberia.

Afterward, while the proceedings of the House were quietly progressing, about the hour of 3 o'clock, P. M., General P. R. de Trobriand, commanding the United States troops in and around the State-House, entered the hall, in uniform, his sword by his side, and accompanied by two of his staff, and by Mr. Vigers, the former Clerk of the House, and addressed Speaker Wiltz, exhibiting the documents of which the following are copies

STATE OF LOUISIANA, EXECUTIVE DEPARTMENT,
NEW ORLEANS, January 4, 1875.
General DE TROBRIAND, *commanding*:
An illegal assembly of men having taken possession of the hall of the House of Representatives, and the police not being able to dislodge them, I respectfully request that you will immediately clear the hall and State-House of all persons not returned as legal members of the House of Representatives by the Returning Board of the State. W. P. KELLOGG, Governor.

STATE OF LOUISIANA, EXECUTIVE DEPARTMENT,
NEW ORLEANS, January 4, 1875.
General DE TROBRIAND:
The Clerk of the House, who has in his possession the roll issued by the Secretary of State as the legal members of the House of Representatives, will point out to you those persons now in the hall of the House of Representatives returned by the legal Returning Board of the State. W. P. KELLOGG, Governor.

The Speaker refused to allow Mr. Vigers to read these documents, he not being Clerk of the House, and, at the request of General de Trobriand, they were read by his adjutant.

Speaker Wiltz then asked General de Trobriand: "Have you submitted these documents to General Emory?"

GENERAL DE TROBRIAND. "I have not, but I presume duplicate copies have been sent to him."

SPEAKER WILTZ. "General, I wish to say to you that since our organization we have admitted, sworn in, and seated five members from referred parishes. Are these members to be ejected?"

GENERAL DE TROBRIAND. "I am but a soldier; these are my orders. I cannot enter into the consideration of that question." The general further stated that he was under instructions to obey the orders of Governor Kellogg.

SPEAKER WILTZ. "I respect you, general, as a gentleman and soldier, and dislike to give you trouble; but I, like you, have a duty to perform, which I owe to my State, to maintain the dignity and authority of my position as Speaker of the House of Representatives. Force will have to be used before I can permit you to execute your orders."

Upon the refusal of Speaker Wiltz and Mr. Trezevant, the Clerk, to point out the persons, and the refusal of Speaker Wiltz to allow Mr. Vigers to call the roll for the purpose of identifying the members, Hugh J. Campbell and T. C. Anderson assisted General de Trobriand in identifying the members to be ejected. General de Trobriand then ordered his soldiers, fully armed and with fixed bayonets, into the hall, from the lobby, and approached the members successively, while in their seats, to wit: O'Quinn, Vaughan, Stafford, Jeffries, Luckett, Dunn, Kelley, Horan, and Land, and one by one he caused them to be taken from the hall by his soldiers, each gentleman first rising in his place and entering his solemn protest, in the name of his constituents, against the unlawful expulsion.

Thus were these gentlemen ignominiously arrested,

and despite their public protestation and their appeals to the Speaker and the House for protection, which neither could afford, were taken from their seats and forcibly ejected from the hall of the House of Representatives of the State of Louisiana, at the point of the bayonet, by the officers and soldiers of the United States Army.

General de Trobriand then proceeded to eject the Clerk, and arrested the proceedings of the Assembly, and for that purpose brought a file of soldiers to the Speaker's stand; when the Speaker arose and addressed the House as follows:

"As the legal Speaker of the House of Representatives of the State of Louisiana, I protest against the invasion of our hall by the soldiers of the United States, with loaded muskets and fixed bayonets. We have seen our brother members violently seized by force of arms and torn from us in spite of their solemn protest. We have seen a file of soldiers march up the aisle of the hall of the Representatives of Louisiana, and have protested against this in the name of a once free people.

"In the name of the down-trodden State of Louisiana, I again enter my solemn protest. Gentlemen, the chair of the Speaker of the House of Representatives of the State of Louisiana is surrounded by United States troops; the hall of the House of Representatives is in possession of armed forces, and I call upon the representatives of the State of Louisiana to retire with me from their presence."

The Speaker then left the hall, followed by all the Conservative members, the hall being left in possession of the military.

If we have dwelt thus somewhat at length upon the details of the military overthrow of a sovereign State, and her reduction to a province, it is that other States may see and know the process whereby the overthrow of their own liberties may be accomplished.

We solemnly warn the American people, jealous of their liberties, that a military power dispersing a House of Representatives in the State of Louisiana may yet serve as a precedent to shackle them and their posterity, if in the hour of trial, standing as we do to-day, amid the ruins of constitutional liberty, they leave us to our fate.

All of which is respectfully submitted.

Upon assuming command of the Department of the Gulf, General Sheridan sent the following to Washington:

HEADQRS. MILITARY DIVISION OF THE MISSOURI,
NEW ORLEANS, LA., *January 4*, 1875.
The Hon. W. W. BELKNAP, *Sec'y of War, Washington:*
It is with deep regret that I have to announce to you the existence in this State of a spirit of defiance to all lawful authority; and an insecurity of life which is hardly realized by the General Government or the country at large. The lives of citizens have become so jeopardized, that unless something is done to give protection to the people, all security usually afforded by law will be overridden. Defiance to the laws and the murder of individuals seem to be looked upon by the community here from a stand-point which gives impunity to all who choose to indulge in either, and the civil government appears powerless to punish, or even arrest. I have to-night assumed control over the Department of the Gulf.

P. H. SHERIDAN, Lieutenant-General.

On the ensuing day, General Sheridan sent to Secretary Belknap the following dispatch, suggesting that the ringleaders of the armed White League be declared banditti, and made liable to arrest:

HEADQRS. MILITARY DIVISION OF THE MISSOURI,
NEW ORLEANS, LA., *January 5*, 1875.
The Hon. W. W. BELKNAP, *Sec'y of War, Washington:*
I think the terrorism now existing in Louisiana,

Mississippi, and Arkansas, could be entirely removed, and confidence and fair dealing established, by the arrest and trial of the ringleaders of the armed White Leagues. If Congress would pass a bill declaring them banditti, they could be tried by military commission. This banditti, who murdered men here on the 14th of last September, also more recently at Vicksburg, Miss., should, in justice to law and order, and the peace and prosperity of this Southern part of the country, be punished. It is possible that, if the President would issue a proclamation declaring them banditti, that no further action need be taken, except that which would devolve upon me.

P. H. SHERIDAN, Lieut.-General U. S. Army.

The following communications also passed between General Sheridan and the Secretary of War:

WAR DEPARTMENT, }
WASHINGTON, D. C., January 6, 1875. }
Gen. P. H. SHERIDAN, *New Orleans:*
The President and all of us have full confidence in and thoroughly approve your course.

WM. W. BELKNAP, Secretary of War.

NEW ORLEANS, January 6, 1875.
The Hon. W.W. BELKNAP, *Sec'y of War, Washington:*
The city is very quiet to-day. Some of the banditti made idle threats last night that they would assassinate me, because I dared to tell the truth. I am not afraid, and will not be stopped from informing the Government that there are localities in this department where the very air has been impregnated with assassination for some years.

P. H. SHERIDAN, Lieut.-General commanding.

WASHINGTON, January 6, 1875.
To Gen. P. H. SHERIDAN, *New Orleans, La.:*
I telegraphed you hastily to-day, answering your dispatch. You seem to fear we will be misled by biased or partial statements of your acts. Be assured that the President and Cabinet confide in your wisdom, and rest in the belief that all acts of yours have been and will be judicious. This I intended to say in my brief telegram.

WM. W. BELKNAP, Secretary of War.

The events of the 4th of January, and the dispatches of General Sheridan immediately following, caused an almost unparalleled excitement throughout the country. The President was widely denounced for the part taken by the military in Louisiana, and there was a strong expression of indignation against the alleged interference with the organization of a State Legislature. Numerous indignation meetings were called in Northern cities. Several Governors addressed special messages to the Legislatures of their States, and Legislative resolutions were passed denouncing the course pursued by the Federal Government. Amid this general denunciation of the Government, there were some who claimed that the course pursued by President Grant was one of necessity, and had been the means of averting violence and bloodshed.

On the day following the eventful 4th of January, the following address was issued to the people of Louisiana by the chairman of the Committee of Seventy:

To the People of Louisiana: In the name of all that men hold dear and sacred, I implore my fellow-citizens to avoid by all means the traps which our enemies and oppressors have deliberately set for us. Our deliverance from political bondage depends upon our prudence and forbearance, and a conflict with the

soldiers or authorities would be the ruin of our hopes, a riveting of our chains. A little more of the heroism, patience, and forbearance, which have already crowned you with imperishable honor, and aroused the sympathies of the entire country in your favor, and the usurpation and misrule to which you are now subjected will have ceased, and you will be once more a free, a prosperous, and a happy people.

R. H. MARR, Chairman of the Com. of Seventy.

On the same day Mr. McEnery addressed the following to President Grant:

NEW ORLEANS, LA., January 6, 1875.
To His Excellency U. S. GRANT, *President of the United States:*
In the name of liberty and all lovers of liberty throughout the United States, I do most solemnly protest against the acts of the military forces of the United States on yesterday, in the occupation of the State-House; in the forcible ejection by the troops of members of the Legislature and the elected Speaker of the House, and the subsequent organization of the House by the direct and forcible intervention of the military. I affirm before the whole American people, that the action on the part of the military in this city yesterday is subversive of the republican institutions of this free country.

JOHN McENERY.

General Sheridan was also sharply criticised for the dispatches which he had sent to Washington. Resolutions, denying the accuracy of his statements were passed by the New Orleans Cotton Exchange and other organizations, and the following statement was published:

AN APPEAL TO THE AMERICAN PEOPLE.

To the American People:
Whereas, General Sheridan, now in command of the Division of the Missouri, under date of the 4th inst. has addressed a communication to the Hon. W. W. Belknap, Secretary of War, in which he represents the people of Louisiana at large as breathing vengeance to all lawful authority, and approving of murders and crimes; and—

Whereas, He has given to that communication full publicity:
We, the undersigned, believe it our duty to proclaim to the whole American people that these charges are unmerited, unfounded, and erroneous, and can have no other effect than that of serving the interests of corrupt politicians, who are at this moment making extreme efforts to perpetuate their power over the State of Louisiana.

N. J. PERCHE, Archbishop, New Orleans.
J. P. B. WILMER, Bishop of Louisiana.
JAMES K. GUTHEIM, Pastor Temple of Sinai.
J. C. KEENER, Bishop M. E. Church, South.
C. DOLL, Rector St. Joseph's Church.
And many others.

NEW ORLEANS, *January 5.*

General Sheridan, however, reaffirmed the statements in his first dispatches, as follows:

NEW ORLEANS, January 7, 1875.
To W. W. BELKNAP, *Secretary of War, Washington:*
Several prominent people here have for the last few days been passing resolutions and manufacturing sentimental protests for Northern political consumption. They seem to be trying to make martyrs of themselves. It cannot be done at this late day. There have been too many bleeding negro and ostracized white citizens for their statements to be believed by fair-minded people. Bishop Wilmer protests against my telegram of the 4th inst., forgetting that on Saturday last he testified under oath before the Congressional Committee that the condition of affairs was substantially as bad as reported by me. I shall soon send you a statement of the number of

murders committed in this State during the last three or four years, the perpetrators of which are still unpunished. I think the number will startle. It will be up in the thousands. The city is perfectly quiet. No trouble is apprehended.

P. H. SHERIDAN, Lieutenant-General.

NEW ORLEANS, *January* 8, 1875.
W. W. BELKNAP, *Secretary of War, Washington :*
I shall send you this evening a report of affairs as they actually occurred here on the 4th inst. My telegram to you of that date, and those of the 5th and 6th instants, are so truthful of the condition of affairs in this section, and strike so near the water-line, that ministers of the gospel and others are appealed to to keep the ship from sinking. Human life had been held too cheaply in this State for many years.

P. H. SHERIDAN, Lieutenant-General.

In support of the statements contained in his dispatches, General Sheridan, on the 10th, made the following report to the Government :

NEW ORLEANS, *January* 10, 1875—11.30 P. M.
Hon. W. W. BELKNAP, *Secretary of War, Washington :*
Since the year 1866 nearly 3,500 persons, a great majority of whom were colored men, have been killed and wounded in this State. In 1868 the official record shows that 1,884 were killed and wounded. From 1868 to the present time no official investigation has been made, and the civil authorities in all but a few cases have been unable to arrest, convict, and punish the perpetrators. Consequently there are no correct records to be consulted for information. There is ample evidence, however, to show that more than 1,200 persons have been killed and wounded during this time on account of their political sentiments. Frightful massacres have occurred in the parishes of Bossier, Caddo, Catahoula, Saint Bernard, Saint Landry, Grant, and Orleans. The general character of the massacres in the above-named parishes is so well known that it is unnecessary to describe them. The isolated cases can best be illustrated by the following instances, which I take from a mass of evidence now lying before me, of men killed on account of their political principles : In Natchitoches Parish the number of isolated cases reported is thirty-three ; in the parish of Bienville the number of men killed is thirty ; in Red River Parish the isolated cases of men killed is thirty-four ; in Winn Parish the number of isolated cases where men were killed is fifteen ; in Jackson Parish the number killed is twenty ; in Catahoula Parish the number of isolated cases reported where men were killed is fifty ; and most of the country parishes throughout the State will show a corresponding state of affairs.

The following statements will illustrate the character and kind of these outrages. On the 30th of August, 1874, in Red River Parish, six State and parish officers, named Twitchell, Divers, Holland, Howell, Edgerton, and Willis, were taken, together with four negroes, under guard to be carried out of the State, and were deliberately murdered. On the 29th of August, 1874, the White League tried, sentenced, and hanged two negroes. On the 28th of August, 1874, three negroes were shot and killed at Brownsville just before the arrival of the United States troops in the parish. Two White-Leaguers rode up to a negro cabin and called for a drink of water. When the old colored man turned to draw it they shot him in the back and killed him.

The courts were all broken up in this district and the District Judge was driven out. In the parish of Caddo, prior to the arrival of the United States troops, all of the officers at Shreveport were compelled to abdicate by the White League, which took possession of the place. Among those obliged to abdicate were Walsh, the mayor ; Rapers, the sheriff ; Wheaton, the clerk of the court ; Durant, the

recorder ; and Ferguson and Renfro, administrators. Two colored men, who had given evidence in regard to frauds committed in the parish, were compelled to flee for their lives, and reached this city last night, having been smuggled through in a cargo of cotton. In the parish of Bossier the White League have attempted to force the abdication of Judge Baker, the United States Commissioner, and the Parish Judge, together with O'Neal, the sheriff, and Walker, the clerk of the court ; and they have compelled the parish and district courts to suspend operations. Judge Baker states that the White-Leaguers notified him several times that if he became a candidate on the Republican ticket, or if he attempted to organize the Republican party, he should not live till election. They also tried to intimidate him through his family by making the same threats to his wife, and, when told by him that he was a United States Commissioner, they notified him not to attempt to exercise the functions of his office. In but few of the country parishes can it be truly said that the law is properly enforced, and in some of the parishes the judges have not been able to hold court for two years. Human life in this State is held so cheaply that when men are killed on account of political opinions the murderers are regarded rather as heroes than as criminals in the localities where they reside, and by the White League and their supporters.

An illustration of the ostracism that prevails in the State may be found in a resolution of a White-League club in the parish of De Soto, which states that they pledge themselves, " under no circumstances, after the coming election, to employ, rent land to, or in any other manner give aid, comfort, or credit to any man, white or black, who votes against the nominees of the White Man's party." Safety for individuals who express their opinion in the isolated portions of the State has existed only when that opinion was in favor of the principles and party supported by the Ku-klux and White-League organizations. Only yesterday Judge Myers, the Parish Judge of the parish of Natchitoches, called on me upon his arrival in this city, and stated that, in order to reach here alive, he was obliged to leave his home by stealth, and after nightfall, and make his way to Little Rock, Ark., and come to this city by way of Memphis. He further states that while his father was lying at the point of death, in the same village, he was unable to visit him for fear of assassination. And yet he is a native of the parish, and proscribed for his political sentiments only.

It is more than probable that, if bad government has existed in this State, it is the result of the armed organizations which have now crystallized into what is called the White League. Instead of bad government developing them, they have by their terrorism prevented to a considerable extent the collection of taxes, the holding of courts, the punishment of criminals, and vitiated public sentiment by familiarizing it with the scenes above described.

I am now engaged in compiling evidence for a detailed report upon the above subject, but it will be some time before I can obtain all the requisite data to cover the cases that have occurred throughout the State. I will also report in due time upon the same subject in the States of Arkansas and Mississippi.

P. H. SHERIDAN, Lieutenant-General.

On the 16th of January, General Sheridan sent the following communication to Washington :

NEW ORLEANS, LA., *January* 16, 1875.
To Hon. W. W. BELKNAP, *Secretary of War :*
A report has just been received from Major Merrill, at Shreveport, which is too long for telegraphic transmission, but will be sent by mail. The following is an epitome, almost in Major Merrill's own words :

The threats made before the election to drive from the community all that voted the Radical ticket are being carried out. Combinations among the whites are forming and recruiting by every form of pressure, by which all negroes who voted the Radical ticket are to be refused work or leases. All the whites not belonging to the combination are to be ostracized. Already more than 500 families, including at least 2,000 people of all ages and sexes, are wanderers, without means to go elsewhere, powerless to find other homes where they are, and on the verge of starvation in mid-winter. Theft and other crimes may result, and it is feared that the bitter feeling actually resulting from the sense of injustice received may run into one of revenge. These harmless people will gradually drift together, and the white people are not slow, as the past has shown, to set afloat inflammatory rumors of intentions of organized violence on the part of the negro, and where the revolver and mob-law are the common resort in such cases, as they usually have been here, disorders more or less extensive are sure to result if some preventive is not found for such a state of things.

P. H. SHERIDAN, Lieutenant-General.

As soon as the events of the 4th of January in New Orleans became known, the subject was brought to the attention of Congress. On the 5th of January, Senator Thurman introduced the following resolution into the Senate:

Resolved, That the President of the United States is hereby requested to inform the Senate whether any portion of the army of the United States, or any officer, officers, soldier or soldiers of such army did in any manner interfere or intermeddle with, control or seek to control the organization of the General Assembly of the State of Louisiana, or either branch thereof, on the 4th instant; and especially whether any person or persons claiming seats in either branch of said Legislature have been deprived thereof, or prevented from taking the same, by any such military force, officer or soldier; and, if such has been the case, then that the President inform the Senate by what authority such military intervention and interference have taken place.

The matter was also taken up in the House, where General Butler introduced a bill providing for a new State election to be held in Louisiana in May, under the direction of Congress. The condition of affairs in Louisiana was earnestly discussed in both Houses of Congress, but up to February no definite action had been taken.

The Senate resolution, calling upon the President for information, was passed on the 8th of January, and on the 13th the President submitted a special message to the Senate accompanied with the official documents bearing upon the subject. In this paper the President reviews the condition of affairs in Louisiana from the time immediately preceding the election of 1872; gives an account of the disorders and violence in the State, and the means used to intimidate Republican voters which had been reported to the Federal Government, and shows what demands had been made for Federal aid, and what action had been taken by the General Government pursuant thereto. The President further reminded Congress that he had long ago urged that body to take action in the premises, and repeated that recommendation in the present message, adding that until Congress relieved him from the responsi-

bility entirely, or gave him specific directions, he would feel it to be his duty to adhere to the course which he had already pursued. (This message of the President is given in full in PUBLIC DOCUMENTS.)

The documents accompanying the message were voluminous, and included many of those which have already been given in this article. The first was a letter from Governor Kellogg, dated August 19th, giving a brief statement of the condition of affairs in Louisiana, and concluding as follows:

I respectfully and earnestly suggest that if the United States troops were returned to their posts in this State such a course would have a most salutary effect, and would prevent much bloodshed and probably a formal call upon the President and a renewed agitation of the Louisiana question, which otherwise a quiet, fair election next November would forever set at rest, and fully vindicate your just policy toward us.

On the 30th of August, Marshal Packard telegraphed Attorney-General Williams a request to the Secretary of War to order a sufficient force immediately to aid in the discharge of his duties as required by law. The registration was about to begin. Large bodies of armed and mounted white men had appeared. Through fear of them the blacks would be unable to register or vote in case of a conflict, which Marshal Packard regarded as imminent.

On August 20th Governor Kellogg informed Attorney-General Williams of a gross outrage which had just been perpetrated at Coushatta. The presence of troops would go far to prevent violence and bloodshed. He said there was "an openly-avowed policy of exterminating Republicans." Information was sent to Attorney-General Williams by Marshal Packard and District-Attorney Beckwith, dated September 10th and 13th, of the proceedings of the White League, and urging the necessity for troops to prevent murder, etc. On the 14th Governor Kellogg made a requisition on the President to take measures to put down the domestic violence and insurrection then prevailing. Numerous telegrams were sent to the Attorney-General by Marshal Packard and others, asserting that armed mobs were reported all over New Orleans, and that Leaguers were much more formidable than was supposed.

The Mayor of St. Francisville telegraphed, September 19th, to the Attorney-General:

The timely arrival of Federal troops has saved the lives of unoffending Republicans. We look confidently to the loyal North for the support which they have so generously extended the weak, and hope the protection of the Government will continue until the elections are over. Life is dear to us, and we cannot risk an article so precious when surrounded by murderous White-Leaguers.

Mr. Packard, on November 1st, requested a post to be established at Natchitoches, and that General Emory be ordered to place a company of troops there. On October 12th S. B. Packard, chairman of the State Central

Committee, and Governor Kellogg, Messrs. Durell, Casey, Sypher, and Morey, addressed a telegram to Attorney-General Williams, saying:

We have authentic information that systematic violence and intimidation will be practised toward Republican voters on the day of election at three or four points in this State, and we earnestly request that General Emory be instructed to send troops to Franklin, St. Mary's Parish, Napoleonville, Assumption Parish, and Moreauville, Avoyelles Parish. Governor Kellogg will furnish transportation to those points without cost to the Government.

On December 9th Governor Kellogg telegraphed President Grant:

Information reaches me that the White League purpose making an attack upon the State-House, especially that portion occupied by the Treasurer of the State. The organization is very numerous and well armed, and the State forces now available are not sufficient to resist successfully any movement they may make. With a view of preventing such an attempt, and the bloodshed which would be likely to result, should an insurgent body gain possession of the State-House, in dispersing them, I respectfully request that a detachment of United States troops be stationed in that portion of the St. Louis Hotel which is not used for any of the State offices, where they will be readily available to prevent any such insurrectionary movement as that contemplated.

Ex-Governor Wells, President of the State Returning Board, telegraphed the President December 10th:

The members of the board are being publicly and privately threatened with violence, and an attack upon the State-House, which is likely to result in bloodshed, is also threatened. By request of the board, I respectfully ask that a detachment of troops be stationed in the State-House so that the deliberations and final action of the board may be free from intimidation and violence.

The United States Commissioner for Shreveport, A. B. Levisa, gives a full statement of the condition of affairs in North Louisiana, referring to an alleged scheme to expel from the country the Republican leaders, and then to frighten the negroes into acquiescence with their wishes; and charging that the whites were driving the freedmen from their homes, naked and penniless, to endure the severities of the winter as best they might. The negroes were cheated of their rights, and had no redress with the mixed juries of the local courts.

Next follows a telegram from Mr. Wiltz to the President, informing him of his election as Speaker of the House, and protesting against armed interference with the Legislature. General Sheridan sends to the War Department for its information a letter from Major Merrill, dated Shreveport, December 30th. He gives the facts as to the probabilities of violence there, and says:

The three Republican members declared elected to the Legislature by the Returning Board, who have gone to New Orleans to take their seats, beyond doubt could not safely return here now. Outside of the officers named above, there is no one left to do violence upon. The leading Radicals have left; the worrying and harassing of the negroes go on with little intermission, but lately no acts of violence to their person have come to my knowledge. Such acts now are confined to plundering them with or without some show of legal form, and driving them from their homes to seek places to live elsewhere. The conflict for offices, whether conducted by peaceable legal means, or violence, will stop what little legal check now exists upon crime and wrong-doing, and will greatly aggravate the condition of things, which is already serious enough. But I do not apprehend that it will result in extended disorder at present, because there is nothing left to work upon except the commoner orders, and partly because the leading White-Leaguers have gone to New Orleans.

The documents conclude with extracts from Louisiana newspapers, showing the platform of the White League and the intentions of the organization, the following serving as a specimen:

The lines must be drawn at once, before our opponents are thoroughly organized. For by this means we will prevent many milk-and-cider followers from falling into the enemy's ranks. While the White Man's party guarantees the negro all his present rights, they do not intend that white carpet-baggers and renegades shall be permitted to organize and prepare the negroes for the coming campaign. Without the assistance of these villains the negroes are totally incapable of effectually organizing themselves, and, unless they are previously excited and drilled, one-half of them will not come to the polls, and a large percentage of the remainder will vote the White Man's ticket.

On the 15th of January the special Congressional Committee which had visited New Orleans in the latter part of December, to investigate the condition of affairs in Louisiana, reported to Congress. (This report is given in full under the title PUBLIC DOCUMENTS.)

While the statements contained in it were accepted as conclusive by a large class, they were sharply criticised by some Senators in Washington. Among these were Senator Morton, who declared that the committee's opportunities had been too limited to enable them to ascertain the truth, and asserted that the committee's report to the effect that the White League was a peaceable political organization, and that there had been no intimidation of Republican voters, was specially erroneous. He also declared that the statement had been made in New Orleans to at least one member of the committee, that a conspiracy existed on the part of the Conservatives to revolutionize the State government on the 4th of January; that the object of Wiltz was to organize the House, and to connect it with the McEnery Senate; that the Legislature thus organized was to recognize the McEnery State government; and that about 20,000 fighting men were ready to respond to the call of McEnery in case their services were needed.

Immediately after the report above referred to had been submitted to Congress, another committee, comprising Representatives George F. Hoar (who had been a member of the first committee), Frye, and Wheeler, was appointed, and at once proceeded to New Orleans to investigate further the condition of affairs in Louisiana.

As soon as the Legislature was organized, Governor Kellogg submitted his message, in which he said:

You cannot be unaware that throughout a large portion of the State a condition of anarchy and violence has more or less prevailed for some time past; that the laws have been disregarded, blood has been shed, and the constituted authorities have been displaced by force. In the interest of the whole people let me beg of you to take immediate measures to secure the enforcement of that obedience to law without which no civilized community can prosper. No amount of misgovernment, no oppressive taxation, no usurpation of office, if such there be, can satisfactorily explain to the people of other communities the fact that there is less security for human life in Louisiana than in almost any other State in the Union; that grave crimes are committed and go unpunished of justice, the criminals often having the sympathy of the community; that assassination for political reasons is practised and applauded; and that, in the whole of Northwest Louisiana there is scarcely a town where a peaceful, industrious citizen from another State could openly proclaim himself a Republican and be permitted to pursue his avocation without annoyance or molestation. So long as lawlessness is known to prevail our railroads will remain unfinished, and capital and emigration will seek other fields for investment. The great need of Louisiana is peace.

The Governor reported that the total bonded and floating debt of the State, when the present administration came into office, exclusive of the amount due the fiscal agent (viz., $150,000 which has since been paid), was $23,933,407.90. The Auditor's report of December 31, 1872, states that it was increased the first year of this administration by the issue of bonds, authorized by acts passed by previous Legislatures, viz., bonds issued to the New Orleans, Mobile & Texas Railroad Company, on a section of twelve miles of completed railroad, under act No. 31 of 1870, for $125,000, and bonds issued to the North Louisiana & Texas Railroad Company, under act No. 108 of 1869, for $576,000, making a total of $24,634,407.90. The Governor said, "The issue of the last-named bonds was rendered obligatory upon me by a decision of the Supreme Court of the State." The debt has been decreased as follows:

REDUCTION OF THE BONDED DEBT.
By the redemption of past-due bonds........ $69,000 00
By exchange of $842,220 new bonds for $1,-
403,700 bonds at 60 cents on the dollar.... 561,480 00
REDUCTION OF THE FLOATING DEBT.
By retirement of old outstanding warrants.. 600,000 00
By exchange, under the funding bill, of $182,-
724.90 old warrants for $109,634.96 of consolidated bonds......................... 73,089 94

Total reduction of debt under present
administration....................... $1,303,569 94

The rate of taxation in the city of New Orleans in 1872, when the present State government came into office, was: State, including schools, 21¼ mills; city, 30 mills; total, 51¼ mills. The rate of taxation for the present year, as reduced by the measures passed by the last Legislature, is: State, including schools, 14¼ mills; city, 25 mills; total, 39¼ mills, making a reduction of the taxation of the city and State, under this administration, of 12 mills.

As the rate of parish taxation is by law limited to the rate of State taxation, and the rate of State taxation is now limited by a constitutional amendment to 14¼ mills, including schools, it follows that in no parish of the State, outside of the parish of Orleans, can a heavier tax than 29 mills be levied in any one year. In previous years the State and parish taxes in some parishes of the State reached as high as 70 mills!

One of the first duties of the Legislature was the election of a United States Senator. The choice fell upon P. B. S. Pinchbeck. On the 2d of February General Sheridan left New Orleans.

LUNALILO I. WILLIAM LUNALILO, King of the Sandwich or Hawaiian Islands, born in Hawaii, January 31, 1835; died at his palace in Honolulu, February 3, 1874. He was the sixth of the Hawaiian sovereigns, and was one of the ancient race of chiefs or kings who ruled the island of Maui before the Kamehameha dynasty was founded. He had received an excellent English education from the American missionaries, and had spent some years in the United States. He was of gigantic stature, of dignified presence, and remarkably handsome, but unfortunately had in very early life contracted habits of intemperance, manifesting themselves in occasional debauches, rather than in continuous intoxication. He had made many and honest efforts to rid himself of this degrading habit, but without complete success, and his untimely death was caused by a decline originating in a cold, the result of exposure to the night air during a protracted debauch in July, 1873. His predecessor, Kamehameha V., dying childless, there were several candidates for the vacant throne, of whom he was the most popular; and although the election of a King had never been submitted to a popular vote, and we believe, never previous to this instance, to the vote of the native Legislature, yet Prince Lunalilo, in a well-written appeal to the people of Hawaii, proposed to abide by the vote of the people, which the Legislature should afterward confirm. Of the 12,000 votes cast he received all but nineteen, which were cast for David Kalakaua (who since his death has been elected his successor), and when the Legislature assembled this election was unanimously ratified. His reign lasted not quite thirteen months, but was characterized by wisdom, moderation, and a prudent regard for popular rights. He restored the Constitution of 1854, which had been arbitrarily set aside by his predecessor, and initiated several beneficial reforms, among which were the endowment of all native-born citizens with the right of suffrage, and the division of the Legislative Assembly into two branches, one composed of elected representatives, and the other of nobles, or descendants of the old chiefs. This served to popularize the legislative branch of the government, and at the same time to perpetuate the ancient sentiment of loyalty in the island chiefs, which has suffered some diminution of late years. Though cordial and friendly to the United States, King Lunalilo had steadfastly opposed the annexation of the Sandwich Islands, either to Great Britain or the United States, and had refused his assent to a treaty of reciprocity which should include the cession of a harbor to the United States. The finances of the islands had somewhat improved under his administration.

LUTHERANS. The following are the statistics of the Evangelical Lutheran Church in the United States, as given in Kurtz's *Lutheran Almanac* for 1875:

SYNODS.	Ministers.	Churches.	Communicants.
I. DISTRICT SYNODS IN THE GENERAL COUNCIL IN AMERICA.			
1. New York Ministerium..................................	73	70	24,198
2. Synod of Pennsylvania.................................	170	344	71,785
3. Pittsburg Synod (Pennsylvania).......................	55	120	10,800
4. English District Synod of Ohio........................	26	58	5,800
5. Synod of Indiana.....................................	14	39	1,900
6. Synod of Michigan...................................	20	33	4,110
7. Swedish Augustana Synod (Northwest)................	93	211	30,127
8. Synod of Texas......................................	27	25	3,200
9· Synod of Canada.....................................	21	57	5,000
10. Holston Synod (Tennessee)...........................	11	25	2,100
Total..	510	982	158,950
II. DISTRICT SYNODS IN THE (SOUTHERN) GENERAL SYNOD OF NORTH AMERICA.			
1. Synod of Virginia...................................	27	58	3,671
2. Synod of Southwestern Virginia.......................	21	40	2,298
3. Synod of South Carolina.............................	33	45	4,911
4. Synod of Georgia....................................	11	14	1,009
5. Synod of Mississippi................................	10	12	910
Total..	101	169	12,799
III. DISTRICT SYNODS IN THE SYNODICAL CONFERENCE OF NORTH AMERICA.			
1. Joint Synod of Missouri, etc. (five districts)...........	525	670	98,000
2. Joint Synod of Ohio (three districts)..................	161	256	34,300
3. Synod of Illinois....................................	30	87	4,500
4. Synod of Wisconsin..................................	65	123	28,000
5. Synod of Minnesota..................................	25	63	5,100
6. Synod for the Norwegian Lutheran Church in America...	102	391	49,663
Total..	908	1,545	219,563
IV. DISTRICT SYNODS IN THE GENERAL SYNOD OF THE UNITED STATES OF AMERICA.			
1. Synod of New York and New Jersey...................	36	45	5,249
2. Hartwick Synod (New York).........................	35	32	4,600
3. Frankean Synod (New York).........................	24	33	3,243
4. Synod of East Pennsylvania.........................	62	86	11,675
5. Susquehanna Synod..................................	32	54	5,744
6. Synod of West Pennsylvania.........................	61	111	19,877
7. Synod of Central Pennsylvania.......................	31	85	7,589
8. Alleghany Synod (Pennsylvania)......................	48	110	8,477
9. Pittsburg Synod (Pennsylvania)......................	25	50	3,679
10. Synod of Maryland..................................	70	86	14,800
11. German Synod of Maryland..........................	10	14	4,600
12. East Ohio Synod....................................	49	83	6,400
13. Wittenberg Synod (Ohio)............................	40	48	4,810
14. Miami Synod (Ohio).................................	25	49	3,513
15. Synod of Northern Indiana...........................	29	73	3,910
16. Olive Branch Synod (Indiana)........................	16	35	1,570
17. Synod of Northern Illinois...........................	38	67	3,840
18. Synod of Southern Illinois...........................	18	28	1,350
19. Synod of Central Illinois............................	39	43	3,323
20. Synod of Iowa......................................	23	35	1,100
21. Synod of Kansas....................................	30	29	780
22. Synod of Nebraska..................................	8	20	1,200
23. Swedish Ansgari Synod..............................	10	12	700
Total..	769	1,228	117,029
OTHER SYNODS.			
1. Synod of Iowa (German).............................	109	183	13,000
2. Tennessee Synod....................................	21	68	6,500
3. Synod of North Carolina.............................	19	41	4,201
4. Evangelical Lutheran Synod in America (Eilsen's)......	22	100	6,000
5. Buffalo Synod, Grabau's (New York)...................	12	15	1,550
6. Buffalo Synod, No. 2................................	9	13	1,470
7. Concordia Synod (Virginia)..........................	5	23	1,250
8. Conference for the Norwegian Danish Lutheran Church in America......	50	195	11,000
9. Swedish Evangelical Lutheran Mission Synod (Northwest)..............	10	14	910
10. Norwegian-Danish Augustana Synod (Northwest).......................	14	43	5,650
Total..	271	695	51,531
Danish Church in America..............................	9	20	1,500
Grand total, 54 Synods..............................	2,568	4,639	561,372

Other Lutheran almanacs give different numbers, both as to the totals for the Church, and as to the numbers in the different branches. Brobst's *Lutherische Kalender* for 1875 gives:

SYNODS.	Ministers.	Churches.	Communicants.
Connected with the General Council (twelve Synods)............................	639	1,231	177,740
Connected with the Synodal Conference (six Synods)...........................	926	1,582	243,625
Concordia Synod, of Virginia, which is expected to join the Synodical Conference.........	5	24	1,295
Connected with the General Synod (twenty Synods)........................	701	1,154	106,763
Connected with the Southern General Synod (five Synods)........................	99	166	12,185
Seven Independent Synods.................	153	438	87,511
Total	2,546	4,595	559,119

The *Lutheran Church Almanac* gives :

SYNODS.	Ministers.	Churches.	Communicants.
Connected with the General Council (twelve Synods)........................	659	1,230	179,924
Connected with the Synodical Conference (eight Synods)...........	877	1,575	240,067
Connected with the General Synod (twenty-two Synods)........................	714	1,092	104,318
Connected with the General Synod South (five Synods)........................	89	163	12,222
Six Independent Synods..............................	123	394	33,015
Total..	2,462	4,454	569,549

The discrepancies regarding the number of synods included with each general body, and the number of independent synods, arise from the fact that Brobst's *Kalender* and the *Church Almanac* classify with the general bodies, to which they will belong, certain synods which have taken steps to join them, but whose accession is waiting the observance of the formal proceedings required by the constitutions of the general bodies.

YEAR.	Synods.	Ministers.	Congregat'ns	Members.
1828............	..	178	900	......
1833............	..	337	1,017	......
1845............	22	538	1,307	135,629
1860............	36	1,198	2,279	232,780
1861............	38	1,322	2,800	246,788
1862............	42	1,366	2,575	270,780
1863............	42	1,431	2,677	285,317
1864............	42	1,530	2,816	294,721
1865............	42	1,559	2,825	310,677
1866............	42	1,627	2,856	318,415
1867............	42	1,614	2,915	323,825
1868............	45	1,748	3,111	351,860
1869............	47	1,855	3,288	372,905
1870............	48	2,016	3,330	396,567
1871............	52	2,086	3,544	423,577
1872............	54	2,175	3,526	458,607
1873............	51	2,309	4,115	485,085
1874............	51	2,431	4,290	529,959
1875............	53	2,546	4,595	559,119

Kurtz's Almanac gives the following list of theological and literary institutions under the care or patronage of the Lutherans in the United States:

Theological Seminaries.—Theological Seminary of the General Synod, Gettysburg, Pa. ; Hartwick Seminary, Hartwick, N. Y. ; Theological Department of the Missionary Institute, Selinsgrove, Pa. ; Theological Department of Wittenberg College, Springfield, Ohio; Theological Department of the Swedish Mission Institute, Keokuk, Iowa ; Theological Department of the Capital University, Columbus, Ohio; Theological Seminary, Philadelphia, Pa. ; Theological Seminary of the General Synod (South), Salem, Va. ; Theological Seminary of the Missouri Synod, St. Louis, Mo. ; Theological Seminary of the German Iowa Synod, Mendota, Ill. ; Theological Department of Martin Luther College, Buffalo, N. Y. ; Augustana Seminary, Paxton, Ill. ; Augsburg Seminary, Minneapolis, Minn. ; Theological Seminary, St. Sebald, Iowa ; Theological Department of North Carolina College, Mount Pleasant, N. C.

Colleges. — Pennsylvania College, Gettysburg, Pa. ; Muhlenberg College, Allentown, Pa. ; Thiel College, Greenville, Pa. ; Wittenberg College, Springfield, Ohio ; Capital University, Columbus, Ohio ; Roanoke College, Salem, Va. ; North Carolina College, Mount Pleasant, N. C. ; Newberry College, Walhalla, S. C. ; Concordia College, Fort Wayne, Ind. ; Carthage College, Carthage, Ill. ; Augustana College, Paxton, Ill. ; College of the German Iowa Synod, Galena, Ill. ; Luther College, Decorah, Iowa ; Northwestern University, Watertown, Wis. ; Martin Luther College, Buffalo, N. Y. ; German Lutheran College, Rutersville, Texas.

Academies.—Hartwick Seminary, Hartwick, N. Y. ; St. Matthew's Academy, New York City ; Lutheran Academy, Newark, N. Y. ; Missionary Institute, Selinsgrove, Pa. ; Swedish Mission Institute, Keokuk, Iowa ; Maryland Conference Institute, Mechanicstown, Md. ; Washington Hall, .Trappe, Pa. ; Zelienople Academy, Zelienople, Pa. ; Swatara Institute, Jonestown, Pa. ; Overlea School, Catonsville, Md. ; Tableau Seminary, Emberton, Pa. ; Institute of the District Synod, Germantown, Ohio ; Preparatory School of the Missouri Synod, Springfield, Ill. ; Teachers' Seminary, Addison, Ill. ; St. Ansgar Academy, St. Peter, Minn. ; Marshall Academy, Marshall, Wis. ; Stoughton Academy, Stoughton, Wis. ; Holden Academy, Holden, Minn. ; Preparatory School, Red Wing, Minn. ; Mosheim Institute, Blue Spring, Tenn.

Female Seminaries.—Lutherville Seminary, Lutherville, Md. ; Hagerstown Seminary, Hagerstown, Md. ; Burkittsville Seminary, Burkittsville, Md.; Mount Pleasant Seminary, Mount Pleasant, N. C.; Staunton Seminary, Staunton, Va.; Female College, Marion, Va.; Young Ladies' Institute, St. Joseph's, Mo.; High School (German), St. Louis, Mo.

Kurtz's Almanac enumerates 18 English, 24 German, 1 Danish, 3 Norwegian, and 4 Swedish periodicals, as published in the interests of the Lutheran Church. Ten of these are weekly, 9 are semi-monthly, 26 are monthly, 1 is quarterly, and 4 are yearly.

Roberts's Kalender gives 19 German, 13 English, 3 Swedish, 4 Norwegian, and 1 Danish periodicals.

The *General Synod, South*, of the Evangelical Lutheran Church, met at Savannah, Ga., April 30th. Representatives were present from the Synods of South Carolina, Virginia, Southwest Virginia, and Georgia. The Rev. J. P. Smeltzer, D. D., was chosen president. A communication was received from the Corresponding Secretary of the Lutheran General Council of 1873, inclosing the action of that body in favor of holding a *Colloquium* of representatives of all the Lutheran bodies in the United States, for the discussion of the points of agreement and difference between them. It was referred to a committee. The committee returned the following report and resolutions, which were unanimously adopted:

The overture thus officially laid before us is so clear and unequivocal in its design as to allay all that suspicion with which some of us have regarded previous efforts professing a similar object. The reading of it, and the statements made by the Rev. Dr. Fry before this synod, assure us that it solely contemplates a greater unity in the one true faith of our Church, without any reference to the present general organizations as such.

A closer union between all the parts of the Lutheran Church in this land is sought not by legislation or through formal organic convention, but by a voluntary conference of those bearing the same name and holding the same confession: "That by a candid and fraternal expression of views" on points concerning which there is a difference of interpretation we may all "by the grace of God be brought to a greater unity of spirit."

Believing that such unity is highly desirable and essential to the fullest prosperity, moral power, and efficiency of the Lutheran Church on this continent, and that said *Colloquium* is neither designed nor calculated, openly or covertly, to weaken or interfere with the organic union of all the Lutheran synods in one general body—a consummation deemed by us of prime necessity in our peculiar work, and in which we should have the undisguised sympathy of the other general bodies of our Church; and being assured that nothing that may be said or done at such *Colloquium* shall in any wise bind individuals or synods with any legislative authority, but shall leave all as free to follow their own honest convictions as if they had in no way participated in it: therefore be it

Resolved, That we do most heartily approve of the holding of such *Colloquium* for the fraternal examination of our confessions in the light of God's word.

Resolved, That fervent prayer be made continually to Almighty God for that unity which is the work of the Holy Spirit.

Resolved, That a committee of five ministers and five laymen be appointed to coöperate with similar committees that may be appointed in arranging the points for friendly discussion at the proposed *Colloquium*, and the time and place of its convention.

A copy of the paper was ordered sent to the General Council. The committee of conference and arrangements, contemplated in the resolutions, was appointed. Some efforts were made for the endowment of a second professorship in the Theological Seminary. A committee was appointed to revise the Book of Worship and provide for its continued publication. The periodical, the *Lutheran Visitor*, was assumed by the synod, and an editorial committee was appointed to supervise its conduct.

The third annual convention of the *Synodical Conference of North America* was held in Pittsburg, Pa., July 15th to 21st. The Synods of Missouri, Ohio, Wisconsin, Illinois, Minnesota, and the Norwegian Synod, being all the synods in connection with this organization, were represented. The number of representative delegates was fifty-two, and as many advisory delegates were also present as swelled the number of members of the Conference to one hundred; two series of theses were discussed, one on fellowship and the other on parochial law. On the former subject, a thesis was unanimously adopted, the import of which was that whoever denies the inference legitimately drawn from the words of the confession is not a true member of the Lutheran Church, even though he does without right adhere to the Lutheran name. On the second subject several theses were adopted, the substance of which is: Parishes should be geographically limited, and have each is own territory, according to apostolical example; those persons who live within the reach of the services of an orthodox minister, but decline to use them, despise not merely a man, but the Lord; where the boundaries of different parishes meet, care for the soul and interest in the welfare of Zion must determine to which one a person must belong; parochial boundaries, being merely of human right, may be changed whenever the interests of the Church demand it. The invitation of the General Council to take part in the arrangements for a *Colloquium* occupied a considerable part of the time of the Conference. It was represented that many members would have supported a call for a free conference, but it was said they could not approve the plan of the General Council for the appointment of a committee to coöperate with the committees of other bodies accepting unreservedly the Augsburg Confession, for fear it would commit them to action implying an acknowledgment that the General Synod so accepted that confession. It was finally agreed to forego the privilege of taking part in the preliminary arrangements, and merely to declare itself willing to attend the *Colloquium* when it should be called. Action was taken toward the preparation of a series of books in the English language for churches and schools, beginning with a primer and reader for schools. A committee was appointed to superintend a mission which had been begun among the believers in St. Louis, and to inquire into the expediency of establishing a mission among the Chinese of San Francisco. This work was made a subject of the missionary collections. The immigrant missions in New York and Baltimore were commended anew to the congregations. Application was made by the Concordia Synod of Virginia to be received into the Conference. Agreeably to the provisions of the constitution, the application was referred, with the commendation of the Conference, to the synods for their separate action. A communication was received from the English brethren in Missouri, announcing their purpose to make application for admission to the Conference, although their delegate could not attend the present meeting.

The *General Council of the Evangelical Lutheran Church* met at Jamestown, N. Y., October 13th. Rev. Prof. C. P. Krauth, D. D., LL. D., was again elected president. According to a permanent custom of the Council, the first two days of the session were devoted to the discussion of Luther's "Theses on Justification," which is continued from council to council in the order of the theses. The particular thesis discussed this year was the eighteenth. The English Corresponding Secretary made a report upon the replies which had been received to the proposition of the previous General Council for holding a *Colloquium* of delegates from all the Lutheran bodies in America which receive the Augsburg Confession, at which the questions of agreement and difference between them could be discussed. The Southern General Synod had accepted the invitation. No reply had been received from the Synodical Conference, but it was known that body had discussed the subject, and, while it had declined to commit itself directly to the scheme, had left it free for any of its members, who chose to do so, to attend the *Colloquium*. The Holston Synod had reported favorably. The secretaries had learned, unofficially, of the acceptance of the North Carolina Synod. No reply had been received from the Synod of Tennessee. Pastor Grabau had replied on behalf of the Buffalo Synod (commonly called Grabau's Synod). He declined to attend the *Colloquium* on the ground that it was not necessary for his synod, because they had brought the correct interpretation of the Augsburg Confession with them from Germany forty years before. If other synods needed any discussion on this Confession, it was well enough, he thought, that they should meet. The Council expressed its gratification at the return of those bodies which had responded favorably to its proposition. The Holston Synod was admitted as an integral part of the synod, its confessional character having been examined and thoroughly commended. A good report was received from the Lutheran Immigrant Home in New York City. Its constitution had been amended by

changing the twelfth article so as to conform with the request of the General Council of 1872. The treasurer's report showed that the expenses required to fit it up had amounted, on the 1st of April, 1874, to $51,180.88. Contributions had been received for this purpose amounting to $35,150.87, leaving a debt upon the Home of $16,080.01. The further sum of $1,593.39 would be needed for fitting and maintaining the institution during the ensuing year, making the total estimated deficiency in its funds $17,623.40. The debt had been somewhat reduced since October, 1873. The celebration of the opening of the Home took place on the occasion of the anniversary of the Reformation, in 1873, when addresses were made by the Rev. Drs. Krotel and Ruperti, Pastors Dreer and Baden, and several laymen: 1,832 pilgrims had been accommodated in eleven months, and during that time no person under the protection of the Home had lost any thing or had been subjected to impositions. Poor persons had been taken care of, supported, fed, lodged, and otherwise helped. More than 200 persons had obtained employment under the auspices of the institution, six persons had been sent out as teachers, and one man had been commended and sent to the Lutheran Seminary at Mendota, Ill. The Swedish Lutheran missionary had assembled the Scandinavian immigrants in the Home every Sunday, and preached to them. The Committee on the Immigrant Mission were instructed by the Council to require the missionary appointed by them to coöperate cordially with the managers of the Immigrant Home, and to send all immigrants seeking lodging to their Home. The Committee on Home Missions had reported that they had received many calls for aid, and that they had found great destitution of the privileges of the Church in the Western States and Territories. They hoped the Council would devise measures to secure an increase of contributions for the work under its care. They had the charge of missions at Chicago and Vandalia, Ill.; Columbus, Ohio; Davenport, Iowa; and Atlanta, Ga.; also of a German mission in Morgan and the adjacent counties in Tennessee. These missions had been spiritually blessed. The Council renewed the requests which it had previously made to the district synods, that they pay to the Executive Committee of Home Missions one-third of their contributions for home-mission purposes. The Executive Committee were requested to make special appeals to the members and the churches for means, and the Vice-Presidents of the General Council were requested to bring the subject before the different synods. The Executive Committee on Foreign Missions reported their receipts for the year to have been $38,098.50, and their expenditures $40,008.96, showing an excess of $910.46 of expenditures above the receipts. This excess had been paid out of the balance on hand. The foreign mission was well established among the Telugus in India, with its principal centre at Rajahmundry.

Lutherans in France and Alsace.—Since the transfer of Alsace to Germany, the Lutheran Church in France has been reduced to two districts. The first is that of Montbéliard, which comprises five consistories. The second is that of Paris, which includes, besides the consistory of the capital, the local Councils of the Lutheran Churches of Lyons, Nice, and Algeria. The Church of Paris numbers eight full pastors, four assistants, and two vicars. Before the war there were twenty-one pastors. There are nine Lutheran churches in Paris, and a number of other places in which services are held. Lutheran churches are to be found also in five of the principal suburbs of Paris. The Lutheran Consistory of Paris has forty-two schools, which are regularly attended by 3,800 children. Ten of these schools are municipal schools, and are supported out of the public funds; the rest are sustained by contributions from the churches. Before the late war, six German schools were taught, with 400 children. The parochial schools are supported at a total expense of about 98,000 francs, or $19,600. The Lutheran population of France, according to the census of 1872, was 80,117, of whom a little more than one-half belong to the district of Montbéliard.

M. A. Racine-Brand, in the *Tablettes Historiques du Protestantisme Français*, gives the following statistical estimate of the Lutherans in France and Alsace: "Taking the census of 1866 as a basis, we find 248,045 Lutherans in the 240 parishes of the seven districts of Alsace and Montbéliard. But besides these there exists a Lutheran population of 6,655 souls outside of these parishes and districts. These members of our Church live in localities where there are Reformed but no Lutheran Churches. For all pastoral services they apply to the Reformed minister, but at the taking of every census they declare themselves as belonging to the Lutheran Church. More than this, there are Reformed Churches, one-half of whose members—and sometimes more than one-half—are Lutherans. Thus, at Guebwiller there are 887 Lutherans to 321 Reformed; at Mülhausen, 3,687 Lutherans to 8,654 Reformed."

M

MADAGASCAR, a large island and kingdom of Eastern Africa. Queen, since April 1, 1863, Ranovalomanjaka I. The area is estimated at 229,000 square miles; the population at about 5,000,000. Christianity is the religion of the Government, the prominent men of the Kovas, the ruling race, and a considerable portion of the population; the number of those who have declared their adhesion to Protestant Christianity is about 300,000; the number of Roman Catholics, about 10,000. The capital, Yananarivo, in the interior, has from 70,000 to 80,000 inhabitants. The foreign trade is chiefly carried on by English vessels from Mauritius. In 1867, 53 vessels, of an aggregate tonnage of 17,406, arrived from there, and 67 vessels of 27,064 tons went there.

The missionary work in Madagascar has been prosecuted, for the most part, under the care of the London (Congregational) Missionary Society. The Wesleyan Missionary Society at one time contemplated establishing stations in the island, and in 1821 actually assigned two missionaries to the field; they were prevented from going, however, and the society's committee afterward determined to concentrate their work upon the islands of the South Pacific, and leave Madagascar to the London Society. The operations of this society were prosecuted with great rapidity and success, till the jealousy of the heathen priests and nobles was excited, when it was opposed by persecutions of great severity and long continuance. In 1869 Queen Ranovalomanjaka I. embraced Christianity, and the persecutions were stopped. The work of the missionaries was encouraged by the Government, Christianity extended very rapidly, and is now thought to be professed or countenanced by a large proportion of the inhabitants of the island.

In the report of the London Missionary Society, made at its anniversary, May 14, 1874, the advance which had been made in this country was declared to have been, in some respects, so rapid and varied as to outstrip the power of the missionaries, with their present resources, to meet it. This, it was said, had for some time been fully recognized by the missionaries themselves, and had formed a subject of difficulty to which they had frequently invited the attention of the directors of the society. The directors had accordingly appointed the Rev. Dr. Mullens and the Rev. J. Pillaus a deputation to visit Madagascar, to review the work and consult with the missionaries respecting the best methods of meeting its needs. The deputation arrived at the capital in August, 1873. They returned to England early in the fall of 1874, and were shortly afterward formally received at a large public meeting, when they gave an account of their visit. Dr. Mullens stated that, on arriving at Madagascar, the deputation had at once proceeded to visit the mission-stations scattered all over the island. They found so many indications of real spiritual life among the native population, that their hearts were rejoiced, and moved to thankfulness for so great a blessing. It was not to be expected, they remarked, that all of the 300,000 idolaters, who had suddenly abjured heathenism by destroying their idols, would at once become matured and exemplary Christians. About 60,000 of them had been enrolled as nominal members of the Christian Church. There were, doubtless, many among these who were not ripe for membership, the same as is the case in the churches at home, but it was believed that nearly all of the 300,000 were open to receive instruction, and to be guided in their lives by the doctrines of Christianity. There were at least 25,000 real, trustworthy Christians, in whom the missionaries had entire confidence. While he was on the island, Dr. Mullens had attended the opening of a memorial church erected

on the spot where fourteen Christian missionaries were put to death in 1849. The occasion was celebrated on the twenty-fifth anniversary of that event. The deputation had been cordially received by the Queen and her husband, the prime-minister, and he believed them both to be real and earnest Christians, and extremely anxious for the progress of their people, "in all that is wise, holy, and good." They found, however, no commingling of the officers of the church and the state, and were able to deny explicitly the reports of a connection of that kind which had been circulated in England. By far the larger number of the people of the island, Dr. Mullens said, felt that the affairs of the church should be kept within the bounds of the church, and conducted entirely by its own officers.

The deputation brought home with them an illuminated address of thanks from the native

Christians to the London Missionary Society, in reply to an address from the society which they had taken out with them.

Sir Bartle Frere made an address at the anniversary of the London Missionary Society, May 14th, in the course of which he spoke of a visit which he had made to the port of Majunga, on the west coast of Madagascar. He had had no reason to expect, so far as he had been able to learn from the books and reports at his disposal, that he would meet there a single convert to Christianity. Yet he found the whole of the ruling race, all of the Kovas who were under the direction of the Queen, united in Christian worship, and acting upon Christian principles, so far as he could ascertain, in all the ordinary affairs of life. He attended religious services at two large churches in this p a e, and was, according to his account, pleased in the highest degree with the evidences of spirituality and Christian culture which were exhibited in the several features of worship. He was introduced to the leading members of this community, and formed the judgment, from their faces and from their words as they were interpreted to him, that "those men and women and children were mostly disciples of the Saviour." Sir Bartle showed that the religious activity he described had been all developed by the work of the native ministry, for no European missionary had been at this place for several years.

Besides the London Missionary Society, missionaries of a Norwegian society and of the Society of Friends are laboring in the island with considerable success. The Church Missionary Society has had a few missionaries on the eastern coast of the island, but it is understood to have determined to withdraw them, in order to avoid being involved in the proceedings of the Society for the Propagation of the Gospel. The latter society has recently appointed a bishop for Madagascar, but has as yet no missionaries there. All of the societies named, except the Society for the Propagation of the Gospel, labor in harmony and coöperation with the London Missionary Society.

A letter from the prime-minister of Madagascar to the directors of the London Missionary Society, in reply to an address from them to Queen Ranovalomanjaka, has been published in the *Missionary Chronicle*. It expressed, in the Queen's name, the utmost satisfaction with the labors of the English missionaries in Madagascar, and the hope that the kingdom of God may advance in her dominions until the joyful words shall be fulfilled, which say "They shall all know me, from the least of them unto the greatest of them, saith the Lord." It assured the society that the missionaries and teachers sent to Madagascar will continue to enjoy the Queen's protection, and be allowed full liberty to preach the Gospel, and to impart useful knowledge in accordance with the laws of the kingdom.

The following is the translation of a proclamation issued by the Queen of Madagascar, ordering the liberation of all slaves imported into the kingdom since the date of the treaty of 1865, entered into with Great Britain for the suppression of the traffic in slaves:

I, Ranovalomanjaka, by the grace of God and the will of the people, Queen of Madagascar and defender of the laws of my country, have made an agreement with my relations across the seas that there shall not be allowed to be brought into my country people from across the seas to be made slaves. And on account of this, I command that if there are any Mozambiques lately come into my country since the 7th of June, 1865, which was the year of the completion of the agreement with my relations across the seas, then they are to become "isan ny ambaniandro" (a phrase applied to the free inhabitants of Madagascar); and if they wish to dwell in this land, then they may do so, and be of the number of free people; and if they wish to return across the sea from whence they came, then they are at liberty to go. And if there are any who conceal Mozambiques lately come to be slaves, and do not set them at liberty to become "isan ny ambaniandro," according to my command, they shall be put in chains for ten years.

Says,   RANOVALOMANJAKA,
           Queen of Madagascar, etc., etc.
This is the word of Ranovalomanjaka, Queen of Madagascar.
Says,   RAINILAIARIVONY, Prime Minister and Commander-in-Chief in Madagascar.
ANTANANARIVO, October 2, 1874.

MAEDLER, JOHANN HEINRICH, a German astronomer, astronomical professor, and for twenty-five years director of the Observatory of Dorpat in Russia, born in Berlin, May 29, 1794; died in that city, March 17, 1874. He was educated at the gymnasia and the University of Berlin, and obtained about 1818 a situation as professor and one of the governing faculty of the Normal School, where he remained until 1830. He had devoted himself with great zeal to astronomical studies, and with his friend William Beer, brother of the great musical composer Meyerbeer, he made a long series of observations on the moon, from which they executed and published a large chart of the moon, in four sheets, so carefully and completely exhibiting every point of its visible surface that it remains to this day the best lunar chart published. A treatise on general selenography, in two volumes, was also prepared by them to accompany this chart. The chart and book were published in 1829-'37. In 1836 Herr Maedler was appointed to a responsible position in the Observatory of Berlin, and in 1840 called to the directorship of the new observatory at Dorpat, then just founded by the Czar Nicholas, and which at Herr Maedler's suggestion was supplied with the best and most complete instruments which money could purchase. Here he occupied himself mainly with observations relative to the movements and aberrations of the fixed stars. These observations, long continued and carefully checked, led him irresistibly to the conclusion that there was in or near the constellation Hercules a great celestial body, invisible to our sight, which he named the "Central Sun," around which the fixed stars, with their planetary

systems (our solar system among them) revolved just as the planets do around our sun. This "Central Sun" he regarded as the centre of the universe, and not improbably as the dwelling-place of the Deity. Herr Maedler published annually a volume giving a full account of the observations of the year, which he subsequently condensed into a large and interesting volume, entitled "Researches on the System of Fixed Stars." His admirable instruments enabled him to make these observations with an accuracy and precision never previously attained. In 1858 the Russian Government made him a Councillor of State. In 1865 he was compelled, in consequence of a disease of his eyes, to resign his position, and returned to Berlin. But, though almost the whole of his long life was devoted to astronomical observations, Herr Maedler did not forget the necessity of popularizing science. He published: "Popular Astronomy" (1846), of which numerous editions have been circulated; "The Existence of a Central Sun" (1846); "Elements of Mathematical and Physical Geography" (1844); "Letters on Astronomy" (1845-'47); "The Heaven of the Fixed Stars" (1858); "Total Eclipses of the Sun" (1861); and some "Memoirs" containing important calculations concerning some double stars, and two of the satellites of Saturn.

MAINE. The financial condition of the State of Maine is very favorable. At the end of the year 1873 there was a surplus in the State Treasury of $436,430.68. The receipts from all sources in 1874 amounted to $1,423,-473.70, which, with the balance above mentioned, gave $1,859,904.38 as the resources of the year. The payments from this amounted to $1,537,718.54, leaving a balance on the 31st of December of $322,185.84. The estimated receipts for 1875 are $1,753,201.84; expenditures, $1,557,560.19. The resources of the State, including cash in the Treasury, balances due on State taxes, sinking-funds, and securities in the land-office, amount to $2,940,802.26. The liabilities of the State, including $7,088,-400 of public debt, trust-funds amounting to $2,387,201.09, balances due on various accounts and for county taxes collected, are $9,959,-690.25. The public bonded debt is represented by $2,223,000 in registered, and $4,865,400 in coupon bonds. Against this is $1,514,022.80 in the sinking-fund, making the net debt $5,-574,378. The amount of the principal paid during the year was $50,000. The aggregate of payments on account of the debt, including interest premiums, maturing principal, and sinking-funds, was $679,558. In ten years nearly $7,000,000 have been paid on account of the State debt, $3,000,000 in reduction of the principal, and $4,000,000 for interest. At the present rate the remainder will be extinguished within fourteen years. The Governor, in his message to the Legislature of 1875, suggests a reduction of the assessment on account of the debt from three to two mills, and the renewal of a certain portion of the loans by the issue of bonds payable in sums of $200,000, so that sinking-funds could be done away with.

A tax on the railroads incorporated under the laws of the State, or doing business in the State, was assessed in accordance with an act of the last Legislature, as follows:

Atlantic & St. Lawrence	$30,078 84
Boston & Maine	26,342 25
Maine Central	23,416 47
Portland, Saco & Portsmouth	22,428 00
Dexter & Newport	1,189 50
Portsmouth, Great Falls & Conway	510 00
St. Croix & Penobscot	210 27
Portland Horse-Railroad	894 00

This tax, which is assessed on companies whose stock has a market value, amounts, in the aggregate, to $105,069.33. That which represents stock held in the State, about two-fifths of the whole, goes to municipalities, and the remainder to the State Treasury. One-half of this tax was payable July 1, and the rest January 1, 1875. The St. Croix & Penobscot paid the whole before it was due, the Boston & Maine paid the July installment promptly, and the officers expressed their willingness to pay the other as soon as assured that the collection of the tax was to be enforced against other corporations. The Dexter & Newton claims exemption by provisions in its charter, and the Atlantic & St. Lawrence and Maine Central claims exemption, except on its net income and above an income of ten per cent. on the cost of the roads and their appendages, and incidental expenses. The Portland, Saco & Portsmouth, and Portsmouth, Great Falls & Corning, neglected to pay the tax, without assigning any reason. The only method as yet provided to enforce payment is by civil process, which would probably involve an adjudication by the tribunal of last resort on all disputed points. The Governor recommends that provision be made for restraining the companies from prosecuting their business, after reasonable notice, until the taxes are paid. Two new railroads have been opened during the year, the Bucksport & Bangor, and the Lewiston & Auburn; and two old railroads have extended their lines, the Bangor & Piscataquis, from Guilford to Abbott, and the Somerset from Norridgewock to Madison. Ship-building has increased, but other industrial interests have been more or less depressed. On the 2d of November there were 58 savings-banks in the State, with deposits amounting in the aggregate to $31,051,-963, an increase of $1,495,439 over the amount of the previous year. The Fish-Commissioners of the State have expended $4,458 in their efforts to restock the waters of the State with fish. At the salmon-breeding works at Bucksport, 5,039,000 eggs were obtained from 590 breeders, at an expense of $2 per thousand. They are used mainly in restocking the Penobscot and Kennebec Rivers. Several ponds have also been stocked with black bass.

The educational interests of the State are gradually improving. During the last ten years the amount of money appropriated for school purposes per scholar has been doubled; the compensation of male teachers has increased fifty per cent. and that of female teachers one hundred per cent., and the term of the schools has increased ten per cent. Within that time two normal schools have been put in successful operation. The permanent school-fund has more than doubled, and is now $561,893; the amount of money distributed by the State to municipalities for common-school purposes has increased from less than $50,000 to more than $375,000, and, including the amount contributed to the free high-schools and normal schools, to more than $425,000. Of the aggregate expenditures for public schools two-fifths are now paid by the State, and three-fifths by municipalities. The free high-school system, inaugurated in 1873, has been very successful. During the year 161 towns have maintained 540 terms of free high-schools, affording instruction to 14,000 pupils, at a cost of about $100,000. The College of Agriculture and the Mechanic Arts is in a flourishing condition. It has 121 students, representing every county in the State, among them five ladies. One lady graduated at the last commencement with a rank in scholarship equal to that of any member of her class. No disadvantage of any kind has been experienced from the presence of lady students. Many interesting and valuable experiments are conducted on the farm, and practical application is continually made of the knowledge acquired.

The Insane Hospital at Augusta is in a crowded condition, and the need is felt of more ample accommodations. The number of patients at the beginning of the year was 411, of whom 205 were men and 206 women, and during the year 96 men and 93 women were admitted, and 109 men and 98 women discharged, making the number on the 30th of November 393. Of those discharged 61 were recovered, 33 improved, and 61 unimproved; 52 died during the year. The assigned causes of insanity in those admitted during the year are as follows: Ill-health, 89; intemperance, 17; domestic affliction, 16; over-exertion, 14; critical period of life, 13; puerperal, 8; masturbation, 6; disappointed affection, 6; general paralysis, 5; injury of head, 4; epilepsy, 4; loss of property, 3; paralysis, 2; decay of old age, 2; exposure to cold, 2; spiritualism, 2; religious excitement, 2; loss of friends, 2; fright, 1; suppressed discharge from ear, 1; healing of an ulcer, 1; venery, 1; sunstroke, 1; embarrassment in business, 1; excessive use of opium, 1; unknown, 35. The receipts of the institution for the year, including $34,-002.43 appropriated by the State, were $105,-192.17; the expenses, $103,917.81.

The expenses of the State-prison during the year were $30,904, which was $2,885 in excess of the earnings of the convicts. A new carriage-shop has been built during the year, at a cost of $22,000, and the prison is now in a better condition than ever before to give profitable employment to the inmates. The expenses of the Reform-School exceeded the receipts from the labor of the boys by about $14,000. The Industrial School for Girls was completed during the year, and made ready for the reception of inmates. The Home for Soldiers' Orphans receives an annual appropriation of $10,000 from the State, and has 55 children under its care.

The business of the State Land-Office has been closed up, but the abolition of the office of Land Agent, which was resolved upon by the last Legislature, can be accomplished only by an amendment of the constitution. The State has 146,000 acres of vacant public land set apart for settlement, 100,000 acres of which are mainly valuable for the lumber growing on it. There are also 9,000,000 acres of wild land owned by individuals, and 754,000 owned by the European & North American Railroad Company. The Swedish settlement in Aroostook County is reported to be in a flourishing condition. The Penobscot tribe of Indians continue to flourish under the guardianship of the State. They have three schools; one on Oldtown Island, one on Mattanawock Island, and one on Olamon Island. About $8,420 was expended for them during the year, derived from appropriations from the State, and $5,766.85 derived from leases of the shores belonging to the tribe.

The voluntary militia of the State consists of ten assigned and two unassigned companies of infantry, and one battery of artillery—in all, 918 enlisted men and 55 officers. The expense of maintaining it for the year was about $12,000.

There were 276 convictions in the Supreme Court under the prohibitory liquor law, and 41 commitments to jail; and $30,898 was collected in fines for violations of the law.

During the year, 487 divorces were granted, which shows that one in thirteen of the marriages contracted in the State is dissolved by decree of the Supreme Court. The Governor recommends an amendment of the divorce law.

The Justices of the Supreme Court, in answer to questions propounded by the Governor and Council, have given an opinion that women cannot under the constitution act as justices of the peace, or hold any office mentioned in that instrument. The Governor also recommends a change in this particular, and suggests the propriety of a commission to propose needed amendments to the constitution, which has now been in force fifty-five years.

The last session of the Legislature of Maine began on the 7th of January, and closed on the 4th of March. Of the 342 acts and 113 resolves adopted, more than two-thirds were of a special character, relating to various local interests of different towns and cities. Charters of incorporation were granted to twenty-three manufacturing companies, with an aggregate capital of $7,130,000, and thirty-seven cheese-factories, with a total capital of $370,500. An attempt to pass a general railroad law, which had been carefully prepared, and was discussed at considerable length, finally failed. A bill abolishing the death-penalty was also defeated, as well as one providing that women might vote at presidential elections, and one appropriating $100,000 for the erection of new buildings on the State-Hospital grounds for the accommodation of insane patients. Among the bills passed was one abolishing the office of Land Agent, and providing that the Governor and Council should wind up the business of the office before the close of the year; one giving any official in charge of a railroad-train or steamboat power to arrest persons gambling on such train or boat, and making the penalty for such gambling a fine of not less than $100, or imprisonment for not less than three months, or both, and affixing a penalty of $100 to any railroad corporation neglecting to post a copy of the act in every saloon and palace-car or steamboat doing business in the State; one making strict provision for the prevention of accidents on steamboats, and providing for the recovery from the owners thereof of damages not exceeding $5,000 for the loss of any life by explosion or fire. Provision was also made for the taxation of railroad companies on their share capital, and of foreign insurance companies on their premiums, and for preventing the running of passenger-trains over railroads that are in a dangerous condition. A bill was passed appropriating $12,500 for the establishment of an Industrial School for Girls at Hallowell, on condition that an equal sum be contributed by citizens for the same purpose, which was promptly done by the residents of Hallowell. One of the most important acts of the session has for its object "the better management of the Insane Hospital, the protection of its inmates, and the regulation of commitments thereto." This provides for a committee of three visitors, one of whom shall be a woman, to visit the hospital at irregular intervals of not more than one month, and without previous notice, for the purpose of ascertaining whether any of the inmates are improperly treated or wrongfully detained, and to report any instance of abuse or ill-treatment to the trustees. The visitors have power to obtain the discharge of persons wrongfully detained, and, in general, to act in behalf of the inmates to secure their rights and a redress of their wrongs. The names and addresses of the visitors are to be kept posted in every ward of the hospital, and the patients are to be allowed to write to them freely without any supervision or inspection of their letters, and the superintendent is required to furnish them with writing-materials when asked, and to see that their letters are delivered. The purpose of the committee of visitors is to act as the representatives of the patients of the hospital, and secure for them such protection of the laws as they may need but are unable to secure for themselves, thus holding the officers of the hospital to a strict responsibility.

A Woman-Suffrage Convention was held at Augusta on the 28th of January, at which the following resolutions were adopted:

Whereas, The disfranchisement of women, in addition to its palpable injustice, impairs the moral vigor of society, delays reforms, encourages a spirit of weak dependence and intellectual apathy in women and the institution of partial or oppressive social and political regulations by man;

Whereas, The women of Maine now ask for the ballot with more unanimity and earnestness than the colored people of America or the householders of England did previous to their enfranchisement;

Whereas, The natural disabilities of women as women are not wholly imaginary and certainly much more worthy of consideration than those of other proscribed classes that have at length been emancipated, including the men lately in rebellion against the Government;

Whereas, The attempt of man to conduct the Government in the present partial, one-sided, and unsymmetrical way, deliberately ignoring one-half of the mind and conscience that ought to be employed in the direction of public affairs, has resulted in so much confusion, strife, and corruption, that republican government is seriously endangered:

Resolved, That the members of this convention regard the removal of woman's political disabilities as the course which rightfully claims the precedence of other reformatory movements, and is that which is calculated to render all others possible.

Resolved, That we pledge ourselves never to cease the agitation we have begun until all unjust discriminations against woman are swept away.

Resolved, That the members of the State Legislature now in session are earnestly exhorted to grant the prayer of the hundreds of petitioners who formally appeal to them for justice.

Resolved, That the passage of an act, empowering the women of Maine to vote at presidential elections and all others in which the qualifications of the electors are not prescribed by the Constitution, would afford an opportunity for trying the experiment of woman's suffrage under circumstances that would furnish a satisfactory test of its utility, and that such an act is the least that the Legislature can honorably and in good conscience accord to its proscribed citizens.

On the same and the following days a State Temperance Convention was held at Augusta, over which Governor Dingley presided. Its principles and purposes were set forth in the following resolutions:

Resolved, That, while we rejoice and take courage in view of the great progress that has been made in the temperance movement in the past, we should not be indifferent to the fact that the traffic in and use of intoxicating liquors are prevailing to an alarming extent in our State, especially in many of our larger towns and cities. The crimes which result from this practice and the degeneracy of morals on the part of the young are truly alarming, and call for united and efficient action on the part of every man to stay the tide of evil which is sweeping over our State.

Resolved, That the reaction which is taking place is owing to the indifference and inactivity of the churches and men of position and influence, and, consequently, there is not a demand for the enforcement of the law upon the subject; neither is there that moral power in the community which would render tippling unpopular, and encourage and aid our youth in making habits of sobriety. We do believe that the change in the law, last winter, which allows of the indiscriminate manufacture and sale of domestic wine and cider, contributes largely to produce the result above alluded to.

Resolved, That we urge on the citizens of the several towns and cities of the State, irrespective of sex or parties, to immediately take action for the suppression of this evil, and we especially demand of the churches, in view of their high and holy calling, to arouse themselves to a consideration of the evils of intemperance, and that they take that action which they have the power to take to stay this mighty evil.

Resolved, That we recommend the appointment of a committee from this convention to consult with a committee already appointed by the Grand Lodge of Good Templars to request of the Legislature, now in session, so to amend the Maine law as that it shall prohibit the manufacture and sale of wine and cider for tippling purposes.

Resolved, That no motives of politics, expediency, partisan interest, or personal friendship, shall induce us to give our votes for any man for any office in the gift of the people, when that office will influence this subject, who is not a total abstainer or who will not go to the farthest verge of his constitutional power to suppress the traffic in intoxicating liquors.

Resolved, That we commend the movement now before Congress for the appointment of a commission to investigate the traffic in intoxicating liquors and the evils of intemperance in our nation, and trust that it will be favorably considered and adopted.

Resolved, That the thanks of this convention are tendered to those sheriffs and municipal officers in the State who have partially or fully enforced the law in their communities, and we recommend all temperance men to fully sustain and assist them to that end.

The Republican State Convention met at Augusta on the 18th of June. There were 516 delegates present. Nelson Dingley, Jr., of Lewiston, was unanimously renominated for Governor by acclamation. The following was adopted as the platform of the convention without discussion:

1. The Republican party should not be content with its past record, but, reiterating its former declaration of principles, should move forward to meet new issues as they arise.

2. It is a high and plain duty to return to a specie basis at the earliest practicable day, not only in compliance with legislative and party pledges, but as a step indispensable to lasting material prosperity.

3. We believe the time has come when this can be done or at least begun with less embarrassment to every branch of industry than at any future time, after resort has been made to unstable and temporary expedients to stimulate unreal prosperity and speculation on a basis other than coin as the recognized medium of exchange throughout the commercial world.

4. The Republican party of Maine approves of the action of the President in vetoing the bill known as the currency bill.

5. Our delegation in Congress are entitled to the gratitude of the people for their earnest and effectual opposition to jobbery, extravagance, and corruption, and for their efforts in behalf of an honest and economical government.

6. This convention views with lively satisfaction the increasing indications that the vast water-power of the State is being more understood and appreciated as our strongest reliance for the increase of our wealth and population, and expresses its earnest sympathy for all judicious measures which tend to encourage capital and labor to engage in manufactures in Maine as the most effective means of developing its agricultural, maritime, and commercial interests.

7. The Hon. Nelson Dingley, Jr., for the ability

and fidelity with which he is discharging his duty as Governor of Maine, giving careful personal attention to the various institutions and departments of the State, seeking equitable administration to the extent of his constitutional powers, is entitled to the confidence of his fellow-citizens, and to their cordial and united support in September for reëlection.

The following additional resolution, submitted by a delegate after the platform had been adopted, was accepted without debate :

Resolved, That we recognize not only the correctness of the principle but the importance and necessity of judicious prohibitory liquor laws, believing them to be superior to any plan of license or local option, and that the enactment, maintenance, and enforcement of such laws is a duty which we owe to the people.

The Democratic State Convention was held in Portland, on the 23d of June. There were 422 delegates present. There was some speech-making, in which the shortcomings of the Republican party were severely criticised and the prohibitory liquor law denounced. Joseph Titcomb, of Kennebunk, was nominated by acclamation as the candidate for Governor, and the following series of resolutions was adopted :

Resolved, That an inflated and irredeemable paper-currency is among the worst evils that can afflict a community. It enables cunning and unscrupulous speculators to rob producers of the fruits of their labors, and afflicts every reputable business with the peril of continual panic and disaster. We regard a currency based on specie redemption as the only one upon which the business of the country can be safely transacted, and hold that we should as rapidly as possible approximate to such a circulating medium.

Resolved, That a protective tariff is a most unjust, unequal, oppressive, and wasteful mode of raising the public revenues. It is one of the most pregnant and fruitful sources of the corruptions in administration. We, therefore, the Democracy of Maine, in convention assembled, declare for free trade, and in favor of an unfettered and unrestricted commerce.

Resolved, That the recent action of the Republican majority of the United States Senate in attempting to revive the worst features of the sedition law of John Adams's Administration, and to establish a censorship of the press of the country at the Federal capital, declares a purpose to silence all criticism of the conduct of public men, and as such demands the severest condemnation of every freeman in the land.

Resolved, That the framers of our Constitution erected a system of government, the corner-stone of which was local control of local affairs, which for nearly a century held the States in the Union as harmoniously as the planets hold their places in the heavens, and it is among the gravest offenses of the Republican party that it has wantonly overawed and prostrated the governments of several of the States.

Resolved, That the civil service of the Government should be performed by those who are found to be best qualified therefor ; and there is seen in the recent action of the Republican Congress on this subject a humiliating confession that the party in power cannot dispense with the prop afforded by public p n e .

Resolved, That the undeniable corruptions pervading all departments of the General Government are of themselves ample arguments against the continuance of the present party in power, and proof that it deserves the righteous indignation of the people.

Resolved, That in the Hon. Joseph Titcomb, of Kennebunk, our nominee for Governor, we have a statesman of eminent ability, integrity, and purity of character, whose political views are moulded after the model of the Democratic fathers of the republic, and as such we commend him to the suffrages of the electors of Maine.

The canvass for the election of Governor was a very quiet one. The election occurred on the 13th of September. The whole number of votes cast for Governor was 94,865, of which Dingley received 53,131 and Titcomb 41,734, making the former's majority 11,397. His majority in 1873 was 15,558, and that of Perham, in 1872, 17,216. Five representatives in Congress were chosen, all Republicans, as follows : First district, John H. Burleigh, by a majority of 1,470 over Bion Bradbury ; second district, Wm. P. Frye, by a majority of 2,415 over Philo Clark ; third district, James G. Blaine, by a majority of 2,830 over Edward K. O'Brien ; fourth district, Samuel F. Hersey, by a majority of 2,953 over Gorham L. Boynton ; fifth district, Eugene Hale, by a majority of 2,469 over Chas. A. Spofford. A large share of interest was taken in the election of members of the Legislature, as the duty of electing a United States Senator was to devolve on that body, and a good deal of activity was displayed by those who favored Hannibal Hamlin for reëlection, and those who were opposed to him in his own party. The Legislature, as chosen, consisted of 28 Republicans and 3 Democrats in the Senate, and 95 Republicans, 51 Democrats, and 5 Independents, in the House. A strong majority was in favor of Mr. Hamlin's reëlection.

MARYLAND. The biennial session of the General Assembly of Maryland began on the 7th of January, and came to a close on the 6th of April. One of the first acts was the election of a United States Senator, to succeed the Hon. William T. Hamilton, and to serve for the full term of six years, beginning March 4, 1875. A *viva-voce* vote was taken in each House, and the result announced next day in a joint convention of the two Houses. William Pinkney Whyte, Governor of the State, was chosen, receiving 22 votes in the Senate to 2 for R. J. Bowie, and 51 votes in the House to 8 for Washington Booth, 5 for R. J. Bowie, 4 for Lloyd Lowndes, 3 for S. Teackle Wallis, 1 for William T. Hamilton, and 1 for Frederick Stone. Governor Whyte resigned the office of Governor, his resignation to take effect on the 4th of March. The election of a Governor to fill the vacancy devolved on the General Assembly, acting in joint convention, and their choice fell on James B. Groome, a member of the House of Delegates, who received 75 votes to 18 for John E. Smith, who was the candidate of the Republican members. Mr. Groome was inaugurated on the 4th of March.

One of the most important acts of the Legislature was the passage of a new registration law. The officers of registration, who are appointed by the Governor, with advice of the Senate, for every polling-district in the State, are required to sit on the first Monday of September, and for six successive days, in Baltimore, and three days in other parts of the State, for the purpose of placing on the voting-lists the names of those entitled to vote, and removing the names of those not entitled to vote. Where legal voters have removed from one district to another, registration may be transferred by certificate. After the voting-lists have been completed, the officers of registration hold a second sitting, beginning on the first Monday in October, for the purpose of correction. The names are then arranged in books for each polling-district in alphabetical order, two copies being made, one of which is to be delivered to the sheriff, and one to the clerk of the county. The officers of registration, in determining what names to put on the lists, and what to strike off, or to refuse to insert, must be guided by the law, on evidence taken by themselves, as to the qualifications of applicants for registration, but persons who deem themselves aggrieved by the decision of the officers of registration may appeal to the judge or judges of the circuit court of the county, who may review and confirm, or reverse the action of the officers. For the purposes of this act the officers of registration have the powers of justices of the peace, to preserve order, compel the attendance of witnesses, administer oaths, etc. The voting-lists, in custody of the sheriff, are to be delivered to the judges of election in the several districts on the day prior to the election, and no person is to be allowed to vote until his name is found on the registration-list for his district, except that if he has been duly registered elsewhere, and has acquired the right to vote in a new district since the registration, he may be permitted to vote on the evidence of a certificate of his registration obtained from the county clerk. Compensation for the performance of the duties of officers of registration and penalties for neglect or refusal to comply with the provisions of the law are provided.

A new law for the regulation of the oyster-fisheries was enacted, and a Commission of Fisheries was established. The public education act was somewhat modified, but most of the changes were unimportant. The Board of Education now consists of the Governor, Principal of the Normal School, and four persons appointed by the Governor "from among the presidents and examiners of the several county boards," and the annual sum of $10,500 is appropriated for the support of the State Normal School. A new act for taxing railroad companies one-half of one per cent. on their gross receipts was passed, and more stringent provision was made for the collection of the tax on the stock of State and national banks.

The question of further legislation for the restriction of the traffic in intoxicating liquors occupied much time and attention. A new license law was prepared and discussed, as well as "an act to suppress intemperance, and to permit the voters of the city of Baltimore, and of each county in the State of Maryland, to vote on the question of granting licenses to sell intoxicating liquors," but neither of them was passed. An act was passed establishing a State Board of Health, composed of five competent physicians, having cognizance of all matters affecting the public health, on which they are required to report at each session of the Legislature. Provision was made for submitting to a vote of the people of certain suburbs of the city of Baltimore, at a special election in May, the question of annexing those districts to the city. The territory proposed to be annexed consisted of a belt one mile wide to the east and west, and two miles wide to the north of the city, all included in Baltimore County, and comprising the towns of Canton, Woodberry, and Waverley, having an area of thirty-four square miles, and a taxable value of $20,000,000. Only the people of the district to be annexed were allowed to vote on the question, and they defeated the proposition. There were over 17,000 votes cast, and the majority against annexation was 555.

A State Grange of the Patrons of Husbandry has been organized in this State, and at a meeting in Baltimore on the 7th of March made these declarations:

Whereas, The time has arrived for a declaration, on the part of the State Grange, as to her policy and mode of operation:

Resolved, That it is the sentiment of this Grange that the declaration of principles, as set forth by the National Grange at St. Louis, meets the wants of the Patrons of our State so fully, that we heartily indorse the same as our future guide of action.

Resolved, That we acknowledge the influence of woman in all great reformatory movements, and therefore most cordially invite the women of our State to assist us by joining our order in its endeavors to accomplish desired reforms.

Resolved, That we recommend to all Granges to encourage home business of all kinds, and to deal with their neighbors; but at the same time, we advise that they buy wherever the article they need can be had cheapest for the cash, and to demand such favors as cash customers are justly entitled to.

Resolved, That it is our duty, as agriculturists, to institute such means as are in our po e for the relief of the agricultural interests of the State, which are beyond a doubt at this time in a very languishing condition, and for this purpose it is necessary that the farmer be brought as near the manufacturer on the one hand, and the consumer of his products on the other, as the nature and current of the business of the country will admit.

Resolved, That we request all manufacturers and dealers in agricultural and farming implements of all kinds to discontinue the practice of demanding exorbitant pay for separate pieces or parts of such when needed for repairs.

Resolved, That the subordinate Granges be requested, from time to time, to present their views on such practical questions as affect the particular local interests of the members of our Granges in the different sections of the State, in order that the State Grange may have an intelligent understanding of the wants and wishes of our people.

A second meeting was held on the 18th of August, when the following resolutions were adopted:

Resolved, That the experience of the last five months has confirmed our faith in the good that will result from the fraternal union of farmers in the Grange.

Resolved, That we are satisfied that the presence of woman in the Grange, as an active and equal co-worker, is the strongest guarantee we have of an abiding usefulness.

Resolved, That, as Patrons, we must never forget that we are a secret order; and that upon the most inviolable secrecy and good faith depends the successful result of all our business efforts.

Resolved, That this Grange urges upon the Patrons of Husbandry, in all their efforts, to keep in view the importance of so encouraging the mill, the loom, and the anvil, as to have them everywhere near the plough, and so facilitate exchanges.

Resolved, That a library and reading-room should, wherever possible, be a feature of the subordinate Grange, and we recommend each Grange to take one or more periodicals published in the interest of the Patrons of Husbandry.

Resolved, That the Masters of the subordinate Granges are directed to carry into effect a resolution passed at the last meeting of the State Grange, that the subordinate Granges should, in the intervals between the meetings of the State Grange, mature such resolutions as will enlighten the State Grange as to what legislation is needed to advance the good of all.

There was no election for State officers this year, and consequently no general conventions of the political parties. The congressional elections occurred on the 3d of November; and resulted in the choice of Democrats in all of the six districts. In the first district, Philip F. Thomas had a majority of 2,318 out of a total vote of 22,612; in the second district, Charles B. Roberts had a majority of 2,444 out of a total of 18,920; in the third district, consisting of nine wards of Baltimore, William J. O'Brien had a majority of 4,453 out of a total of 14,121; in the fourth district, consisting of the other eleven wards of Baltimore, Thomas Swann had a majority of 5,434 out of a total of 17,054; in the fifth district, Eli J. Henkle had a majority of 1,410 out of a total of 22,314; and in the sixth district, William Walsh had a majority of 78 out of a total of 25,870. The Legislature consists of 25 Democrats, two Republicans, and one Independent, in the Senate, and 59 Democrats, 20 Republicans, and five Independents, in the House, making the Democratic majority 20 in the Senate and 34 in the House, or 54 on a joint ballot.

The total receipts of the State Treasury for the fiscal year ending September 30th, including a balance of $484,810.22 on hand at the beginning, amounted to $2,842,012.94. Of this amount, $125,000 was received from the sale of the Deaf and Dumb Asylum loan, and $268,697.50 from the Maryland Defense Loan, leaving the receipts from ordinary sources $1,963,605.22. The total disbursements for the year amounted to $2,276,906.35, of which $110,832 was invested for the Agricultural College, $125,000 was paid over to the officers of the Deaf and Dumb Asylum at Frederick, and $111,000 was paid for the Southern Maryland Railroad, leaving $1,930,074.30 for the ordinary expenses of the government, and a balance of $565,106.50 in the Treasury. The

estimated receipts for the fiscal year 1874–'75 are $2,413,539.25, including $100,000 as the proceeds of bonds issued for the State Normal School, and $260,000 for those issued for the House of Correction. The estimated expenses of the same period are $2,030,000, including $100,000 for the Normal School, and $250,000 for the House of Correction. The receipts for the year on account of the Free School fund were $71,883.07, besides a balance of $14,220.08 at the beginning of the year; the disbursements on the same account were $74,342.60. The public debt of the State at the close of the fiscal year was $11,095,019.49, of which $5,416,444.44 is sterling debt with interest payable in coin in London. The State has assets available to offset against the debt amounting to $4,469,783.26.

According to the report of the Insurance Commissioner, made December 1st, there were in the preceding January fifteen fire insurance companies chartered under laws of the State, with an aggregate capital of $2,320,068, assets $4,382,212, and liabilities, $1,007,035, and $895,049 as the income of the year; two marine insurance companies, with $331,500 capital, $585,166 of assets, $41,761 of liabilities, and $198,955 as the year's income. Of companies from other States and counties licensed to do business in Maryland, there are ninety-two fire and marine insurance companies with $30,756,795 capital, $77,421,175 of assets, $30,738,333 of liabilities, and net income for the year of $4,386,373. There are forty-two life insurance companies licensed under the laws of the State, but all incorporated in other States, with total assets of $347,677,640, liabilities to the extent of $303,717,899, and a net income of $32,142,266.

According to the last report of the Board of Education there were 123 public schools in Baltimore and 1,619 in the rest of the State, or 1,742 in all; number of pupils in Baltimore, 40,183, in the rest of the State, 90,141, or 130,324 in all. The average daily attendance in the city was 22,181, in the counties 38,636; number of teachers in Baltimore, 624; in the counties, 1,931. There are in Baltimore 15 colored schools, with 2,982 pupils, and in the rest of the State 210 colored schools with 11,189 pupils. St. John's College at Annapolis had 140 students in attendance; the Agricultural College, 130; Washington College in Kent county, 23; the State Normal School, 146. Provision has been made for new buildings for the Normal School, and the site has been selected in the city of Baltimore. The new House of Correction has been located near Jessup's Station, about 14 miles from Baltimore, but has not yet been completed.

The old Maryland Canal Company has been reincorporated, and it is proposed to complete a line of canal connecting the Chesapeake and Ohio with the Patapsco River near Baltimore, which will require 28 miles. The railroad interests of the State are flourishing, but no official statement regarding them has been made for the year 1874.

MASON, FRANCIS, D. D., F. R. A. S., a Baptist clergyman, missionary, and scientist, for nearly forty-four years resident in Burmah, born at Walingate, York, England, April 2, 1799; died at Rangoon, Burmah, March 3, 1874. His ancestors were Dissenters, and of the Baptist faith, his grandfather, Francis Mason, having been a Baptist preacher in Yorkshire, and his father, though by trade a shoemaker, yet a local preacher of the same denomination in the city of York. His early opportunities of education were somewhat meagre, being confined to the instruction afforded by the parish school, except that his parents, who were people of some culture, gave him considerable instruction. He early learned his father's trade, but while yet a lad he was seized with a passion for study, and acquired a very fair education in mathematics, geography, and English literature, under the evening instruction of a retired naval officer. He became also a somewhat fluent debater, and argued political and social questions in which mechanics in England were then very much interested, with such skill as to draw the approval of his fellow-workmen. In 1818 he came to the United States to seek his fortune. Landing first at Philadelphia, he spent the next five or six years in a sort of wandering life, visiting all the larger Western and Southwestern cities and spending a few months in each, working at his trade, and acquiring a knowledge both of men and books. At this time, his religious views, though unsettled, were skeptical, and he was trying very hard to be at least a deist. In the spring of 1824 he sailed from New Orleans for Boston, and went thence to Randolph, Mass., to work at his trade. Here he came under new and better influences, and, while his intellect was active, and he thirsted for knowledge, his moral nature began to develop. In December, 1825, he married a lady of Randolph, and through her efforts and those of other friends, and the critical study of "Butler's Analogy," he very soon became convinced of the truth of Christianity, and professed conversion, and united with the Baptist Church. It was not long before he felt it to be his duty to preach the gospel which had been to him such good news; and in October, 1827, he was licensed to preach, and soon after entered Newton Theological Seminary, where he soon proved himself a thorough and brilliant scholar, and developed a facility in the acquisition of languages which was a marked characteristic of his subsequent life. His wife died in 1828, but, before he had completed his course at Newton, he had decided to become a missionary, and in May, 1830, he received ordination, married a second wife, and sailed for Burmah under appointment from the American Baptist Missionary Board. He landed in Maulmain in November, 1830, and a few months later removed to Tavoy to become the helper

and successor of Rev. Mr. Boardman, who was dying of pulmonary disease. He remained at Tavoy about twenty-two years, his missionary work being mostly among the different tribes of Karens, though he was very familiar with the Burmese language as well as the Pali and Sanscrit, and could, upon occasion, converse or preach in most of the languages of Farther India. Among the Karens, he reduced two of their dialects, the Sgan-Karen and the Pwo-Karen, to writing, and translated the Scriptures into both, besides making some progress with a third, the Byhai-Karen; conducted a seminary for the education of native preachers and teachers, and superintended the general work of the Mission for a considerable period; and, with a view to making his translations of the Karen Scriptures more intelligible and accurate, commenced making collections of notes and facts concerning the fauna, flora, minerals, and ethnology of Burmah. By the most rigid and systematic division of his time, he was enabled, with his remarkably vigorous constitution, and his unflagging industry, to accomplish all that he undertook. On the publication of his first work, "Tenasserim; or the Fauna, Flora, Minerals, and Nations of British Burmah and Pegu," in 1852, he was elected a member of the Royal Asiatic Society, and the highest commendation bestowed upon his labors, which received the warm approval of the most eminent scientists of Europe and Asia. In 1853 he removed to Toungoo, a new field, and one of great missionary promise. The next year he was compelled, on account of his health and other considerations, to revisit England and America, and in both countries was warmly welcomed, both by scientists and friends of missions. He was made a corresponding member of several of the European scientific societies, and of the American Oriental Society, the Boston Natural History Society, and the New York Lyceum of Natural History. He returned to his work in 1856, and his always busy life became still more busy. His labors in translation and theological instruction were diversified by his investigations in all departments of natural history, which he called his "recreations." He also prepared a Pali grammar, with chrestomathy and vocabulary, and an edition in the Pali language of Kachchayano's grammar, besides translations from Burmese, Pali, and Sanscrit. These grammars are standard works, and have the sanction and approval of both the Royal Asiatic and the Oriental Society. In 1860 he published his "Burmah; its People and Natural Productions; or, Notes on the Nations, Fauna, Flora, and Minerals of Tenasserim, Pegu, and Burmah," etc., a stout octavo of 930 pages. This was based on his previous work, but mostly rewritten and greatly enlarged. He enumerated and described over 500 species of birds found in Burmah, about 120 species of mammals, about 200 species of fishes, and proportional numbers of the other

natural orders of animals. He gave full accounts of nine tribes of Karens, and of five or
six races of the Burmese family of nations,
with extended vocabularies of the languages
of each, and a vast amount of information concerning the religion, habits, manners, and civilization of these different nations, all or nearly all gathered from personal observations.
The India Government were so much pleased
with this work that they purchased the greater
part of the edition, and in 1872–'73 paid Dr.
Mason's expenses to Northern Burmah, which
required some further explorations; and proposed to pay him a liberal sum for its revision,
and for the copyright of a new edition, and
to defray his expenses to and from Calcutta,
and while remaining there to superintend the
printing of the work, assuming also all the
expense of its publication. Of this work, the
greatest of English botanists said that "Dr.
Francis Mason had made the most valuable
additions to the flora and fauna of Burmah of
any man of modern times." It was characteristic of Dr. Mason that, finding a difficulty in
getting the edition of 1860 printed according
to his ideas at Rangoon, he learned the printer's art when past sixty years of age, and set up
the greater part of the work himself, and produced the most creditable piece of book-print-
ing that had ever been done in Burmah. Besides the works already mentioned, he had
prepared the first book published in the Karen
language, "The Sayings of the Elders," and
subsequently a small work on pathology and
materia medica for his students, in one of the
Karen dialects, having studied medicine for
the purpose; and had published in English:
"Report of the Tavoy Mission Society;" "Life
of Ko-Tha-Byu, the Karen Apostle;" "Memoir of Mrs. Helen M. Mason" (1847); and
"Memoir of Sau Quala" (1850). He had also
contributed largely to the *Missionary Magazine*, to the Transactions of the Royal Asiatic
Society, and for several years edited the *Morning Star*, a Karen monthly, which was published in both the Sgau and Pwo dialects.

MASSACHUSETTS. The session of the
Massachusetts Legislature for 1874 began on
the 8th of January, and ended on the 30th
of June. Scarcely had the session opened
when a large number of petitions were received, asking that a resolution adopted by
the Legislature in 1872, which had been construed as censuring Senator Charles Sumner for introducing a bill in the United States
Senate providing that "the names of battles
with fellow-citizens shall not be continued in
the Army Register, or placed on the regimental colors of the United States," be rescinded.
Most of the petitions read as follows, and were
unanimously signed:

*To the Honorable Senate and House of Representatives
of Massachusetts:*

Whereas, At the extra session of the Legislature
of 1872 of this Commonwealth, called for the sole
and exclusive purpose of alleviating a great public

calamity, a resolution virtually censuring one of the
representatives of the State, in the Senate of the
Union, was offered and adopted:

Therefore, we, the undersigned, citizens of Massachusetts, with a jealous regard to the honor and good
name of the State, and with a proud and grateful
appreciation of the character and public services of
Charles Sumner, respectfully but earnestly ask your
honorable body to rescind and annul the resolution
aforesaid, passed by the Legislature of Massachusetts on the 18th of December, 1872.

A resolution rescinding the resolution of
1872 was promptly offered, and after long debates was adopted in both branches. The
vote in the Senate was 26 in favor of the rescinding resolution, and 7 against it; in the
House 119 voted in favor of it, and 49 against
it, and 69 members were absent when the vote
was taken. A few weeks after this, Senator
Sumner died, and the duty of choosing his successor devolved upon the Legislature. There
was a long contest extending over several
weeks, and involving many ballots before the
matter was decided. The Republican members were divided in their preference, the
two leading candidates being Henry L. Dawes,
and Ebenezer Rockwood Hoar, while the Democrats voted for Benjamin R. Curtis. Finally
a compromise was effected, in accordance with
which the Republicans were generally united
on William B. Washburn, then Governor of
the State, and elected him. The last two ballots taken show approximately the position of
the members during the long contest, and precisely their position on the final vote. The
last ballot but one was as follows:

Whole number of votes...................... 265
Necessary to a choice......................... 133
  E. R. Hoar................................... 75
  Henry L. Dawes............................. 72
  B. R. Curtis.................................. 69
  N. P. Banks.................................. 12
  Charles F. Adams........................... 19
  William B. Washburn....................... 18
  Scattering................................... 8

The last and decisive ballot was as follows:

Whole number of votes....................... 267
Necessary to a choice......................... 134
  William B. Washburn....................... 149
  Benjamin R. Curtis.......................... 64
  Henry L. Dawes............................. 26
  Charles F. Adams........................... 17
  N. P. Banks.................................. 4
  Scattering................................... 7

Governor Washburn resigned the Executive
chair to Lieutenant-Governor Talbot on the
30th of April. The important subjects of
legislation which occupied by far the largest
share of attention were the regulation of the
hours of labor in manufacturing establishments,
the repeal of the laws prohibiting the sale
of intoxicating liquors and establishing a State
constabulary to enforce the same, and the
management of the railroad-line through the
Hoosac Tunnel. On the first subject there
were several different bills introduced, and various substitutes and amendments offered and
discussed at great length. A bill was finally
passed limiting the hours of labor for minors
under eighteen years of age, and for women,
in the manufacturing establishments of the

State, to ten hours per day, and providing penalties by fine for violations of the act.

The question of abolishing the State constabulary occupied the time of a special committee on the subject for some weeks. Public hearings were given, and a large amount of testimony taken as to the efficiency and value of the force. Finally an act was reported repealing the constabulary law, and authorizing the Governor to assume command of the municipal police forces within the State on special emergencies. After considerable discussion and various modifications in its details the bill passed both Houses, but was returned to the Senate unsigned, with the Governor's objections, on the 2d of June. The main grounds given for his disapproval were that the constabulary force was of great value in preserving order and assisting in the execution of the laws in different parts of the State, that its place could not be efficiently taken by the local police forces. So far as its use in enforcing the prohibitory law was concerned, the Governor said:

By the terms of the act which brought it into being, the constabulary is specially, but not exclusively, charged with the enforcement of the law concerning the traffic in intoxicating liquors. Is its abolition sought because it enforces this law too much? Surely this cannot be true. Such an admission would be equivalent to a charge that the makers of the prohibitory law trifled with public morality in its enactment. Why does it remain upon our statute-books if not for enforcement to the best of our ability? Perhaps it will be said that the constabulary is abolished because it enforces the prohibitory law too little? But is this a valid reason for sweeping it out of existence? Ought we not the rather to devise means for making it more efficient? If the combined efforts of our State police and our municipal police are not equal to so thorough an enforcement of this law as is desired, shall we gain anything by abolishing the State police and remitting its enforcement to the municipal police alone?

Desirous as we all are that order and morality may be promoted in our Commonwealth, and believing as I do that, on the whole, we are making progress toward good ends, I am not able to see that we can yet dispense with any of the agencies calculated to conserve these ends. We are still under the painful necessity of maintaining penal and reformatory institutions, and that vacant rooms may be found in them is not because we are without criminals. Why should we throw away so valuable a weapon as the State police has proved to be in the conflict against crime? In my judgment, the continuance of the force is advisable, whatever liquor law we have upon our statute-books. Furthermore, its continuance, without decrease of power in any direction, seems to me of the highest importance on grounds wholly irrespective of the liquor question; and I am not aware that any considerable portion of our law-abiding citizens have manifested a desire to divest the Executive Department of the power "to preserve the public peace and enforce the laws" that it has been accustomed to exercise through the constabulary office.

The Senate immediately passed the bill over the Governor's veto, but in the House a two-thirds vote could not be obtained. Shortly after this another act, originating in the House, and having the same object in view, but obviating the principal objection put forth by the Governor, was passed and sent to the Executive for his approval. This was returned on the 19th of June to the branch of the Legislature in which it originated, with the Governor's objection. This act provided for a State detective force of thirty-one officers used for the purpose of bringing criminals to justice, and aiding in the general enforcement of the law. The Governor objected that the functions of the detective and the constable were combined, while they should be separated, and that the force was too large for the one purpose, and too small for the other. He then spoke of the value and efficiency of the constabulary, and the reason for continuing it in existence. Without speaking directly of the enforcement of the prohibitory law, the Governor used this language:

I am not aware that there is any general demand for the abolition of the present State police on the part of my fellow-citizens who respect the laws upon our statute-books and wish to see them enforced. So far as their voice reaches me, it is for the elevation and improvement of the force. That there may be inefficient or corrupt men in it, while a thing to be deplored and rectified as fast as possible, is no more than can be said of every police in the civilized world. Because many kinds of vice flaunt unblushingly and unpunished in our large cities, and officers are occasionally found derelict or corrupt, would it be considered wise to abolish municipal police altogether, and trust the safety and security of these communities to the old-fashioned constabulary, annually elected at the ballot-box? Because we cannot enforce our criminal laws with omniscient impartiality against all offenders, shall we cease to enforce them as best we can with the agencies at our command?

An attempt to pass this act over the veto failed. A bill was afterward passed and signed abolishing the Board of State Police Commissioners, and giving the appointment of the chief of the force directly to the Governor and Council.

Meantime the subject of replacing the prohibitory law with a license act had been occupying a large share of attention. Extensive committee hearings had been given on the subject, and arguments and testimony from interested parties listened to at great length. Several different license bills were introduced and discussed, and one of them, after numerous amendments and modifications, was passed under the title, "An act regulating the sale of spirituous or intoxicating liquors." This was returned to the House of Representatives on the 27th of June, with the Governor's objections. He spoke of the evils of intemperance, and the efforts that had been made to check them, and undertook to show that the license system had not been successful as an agency of reform, while the prohibitory policy had been productive of various good results. With regard to the results of the law he said:

I am aware that it is said intemperance increases under our prohibitory law; that the sale of intoxicants is as great as it would be under a license law. But I call your attention to the absence here of the flaunting and attractive bar-rooms that spread their snares to capture the thoughtless and easily tempted in cities where licenses prevail; to the constantly-growing sense of disfavor with which the liquor traffic is regarded by the community generally, and to the powerful, systematic, and unrelenting activity of those interested in it to break down the law and the officers who try to enforce it. Here is evidence that the statute does impose an effective and crippling restraint from which relief is sought in the elastic and easily-evolved province of license. Even if some sincere friends of temperance prefer a stringent license law to a prohibitory system, there can be no denial that the men who have money and business at stake in this contest are the most ardent and urgent advocates of license, and I cannot doubt that they understand themselves and calculate shrewdly the advantage they will gain. * * *

Nor is the argument at all conclusive to my mind that we should not retain upon our statute-books a law that is in advance of public opinion on this subject. Law is in one sense a guide-board, pointing out the course of conduct which, if followed, will secure the greatest degree of good, and happiness, and safety for all. Therefore it must often be largely ideal in its character, and frequently in advance of the general conduct of those subject to it, that it may be an instructor and elevator, and thus a source of restriction and punishment. To a law committing the Commonwealth of Massachusetts to a public acknowledgment that the sale of intoxicating liquors as a beverage is necessary and desirable, I cannot on my conscience give assent. It seems to me that the only safe and sound position for a Christian community to take in regard to this matter is that of absolute and unqualified opposition to the traffic.

The vote on the motion that the bill pass, notwithstanding the Governor's objections, was 110 to 93, and it failed to pass for want of a two-thirds vote in its favor.

The formidable question of the whole session was the means to be used for utilizing the Hoosac Tunnel to the best advantage. Two committee reports were made on the subject. The majority of the committee submitted a bill providing for the appointment of five trustees to form a body corporate under the name of the Trustees of the Boston Hoosac Tunnel & Western Railroad, to control and manage the line on behalf of the State. The trustees were to be vested in trust with the rights of the State in the Troy & Greenfield Railroad, the Hoosac Tunnel and the Southern Vermont Railroad, and to negotiate with the Troy & Boston, Vermont & Massachusetts, and Fitchburg Railroads, with a view to the consolidation of the lines under a common ownership and management. All the details of the business were minutely provided for. Another plan was submitted by a minority of the committee, and various others were proposed from time to time in the Legislature, but it was found impossible, after long discussions and complicated changes and amendments, to come to an agreement on any one of them. Finally the subject was disposed of by referring it to "five competent and discreet persons as corporators," to be appointed by the Governor, with the advice and consent of the Council, "who shall examine and report to the next Legislature a plan for the utilization of the Troy & Greenfield Railroad and Hoosac Tunnel, and for the organization and perfection of one or more continuous consolidated lines of railroad from Boston to the Hudson River by way of the Hoosac Tunnel, with a view of promoting the establishment of one or more competing lines of railroad to the West." The corporators were required in their report to furnish "full and specific information" on the following points:

1. What combination, or consolidations, or running arrangements, can be made by and between the Commonwealth, as owner of the Hoosac Tunnel, and Troy & Greenfield Railroad, and any other railroad corporation of this State, with a view to organizing a through railroad route between Boston and Lake Ontario or the West.

2. What connections or arrangements can be made between the Hoosac Tunnel and the Troy & Greenfield Railroad and any persons or corporations without the Commonwealth, with a view to establishing such through route, and the terms and conditions on which the same can be effected.

3. To ascertain what legal rights have been reserved at any time to the Commonwealth in respect to taking possession of the roads of any corporation connecting with the said Hoosac Tunnel and Troy & Greenfield Railroad, and through what process and at what probable cost such rights could be exercised.

4. On what terms the railroads connecting with the Hoosac Tunnel and Troy & Greenfield Railroad, as a through line from Boston to the West, could be purchased or leased by the Commonwealth.

5. What contracts have been entered into between the Commonwealth and corporations operating any roads connected with said Hoosac Tunnel and Troy & Greenfield Railroad, together with their opinions, as to the purport, value, and binding effect of such contracts.

6. In addition to the foregoing, the said commissioners shall further give such other information and offer such suggestions and recommendations in regard to the management, development, or disposition, to be made of such railroad and tunnel as they may deem expedient and for the interest of the Commonwealth.

7. They shall, immediately after their appointment, proceed to examine the different railroad routes between the Troy & Greenfield Railroad and Lake Ontario, for the purpose of recommending the best through route or routes for transporting the products of the West to the seaboard, in the interests of the citizens of the Commonwealth.

As usual, a large number of petitions were received asking for the right of suffrage for women. These were referred to a committee who gave hearings on the subject and listened to all that advocates or opponents of the proposed change had to say. After six weeks devoted to the subject, a majority of the committee reported to the Senate a resolution providing that the word "male" should be stricken from the sections in the constitution relating to the right of suffrage. This report was signed by eight members of the committee, while three united in a minority report arguing against the change.

The Senate rejected the resolution submitted, by a vote of 19 against it to 14 for it.

An important act, affecting the rights of husband and wife, was passed as follows:

Section 1. A married woman may convey her shares in corporations, and lease and convey her real property, and make contracts oral and written, sealed and unsealed, in the same manner as if she were sole, and all work and labor performed by her for others than her husband and children shall, unless there is an express agreement on her part to the contrary, be presumed to be on her separate account; but her separate conveyance of real estate shall be subject to her husband's contingent interest therein, and nothing in this act shall authorize a married woman to convey property to, or make contracts with her husband.

Sec. 2. When a deed of land is made to a married woman, and at the same time she mortgages the same to the grantor to secure the payment of the whole or any part of the purchase-money, or to a third party to obtain the whole or any part of such purchase-money, the seizing of such married woman shall not give her husband any estate by the courtesy as against such mortgage.

Sec. 3. A married woman may sue and be sued in the same manner and to the same extent as if she were sole, but nothing herein contained shall authorize suits between husband and wife.

Sec. 4. A married woman may be an executrix, administratrix, guardian, or trustee, and bind herself and the estate she represents without her husband joining in any conveyance or instrument whatever, and be bound in the same manner and with the same effect in all respects as if she were sole.

Sec. 5. The first section of chapter four hundred and nine of the acts of the year eighteen hundred and sixty-nine, and chapter one hundred and sixty-five of the acts of the year eighteen hundred and sixty-three, are hereby repealed.

Sec. 6. Nothing in this act shall impair the validity of any ante-nuptial or post-nuptial settlement.

Among the miscellaneous business of the session was the incorporation of the new town of Rockland, formed from a portion of Abington. A long hearing was given by a committee to a proposition to provide for better care of the insane by a bill similar to that passed by the Legislature of Maine, but nothing was accomplished on the subject.

The political campaign of the year was one of unusual interest. Governor Talbot's veto of the bills repealing the prohibitory liquor law and the State constabulary act created a strong opposition to him on the part of those of the Republican party who were hostile to those measures, and made him the special exponent of the prohibitory policy. He was talked of as a candidate for Governor by the prohibitory element long before the time came for holding the State Conventions, and those in favor of a license law or an essential modification of the existing statutes warmly opposed the movement for his nomination. Thus the liquor question was forced into prominence as the principal issue of the canvass. The Democratic Convention was held first, and expressed itself clearly and explicitly on the question of prohibition or license, and put forward a candidate whose known moderation and high character were calculated to win off many of the disaffected Republicans. The convention took place at Worcester on the 9th of September, and was characterized by general harmony and good feeling. Speeches were made in which the weaknesses and shortcomings of the opposing party were freely criticised, and the reforms that might be effected through a restoration of the Democrats to

power commented upon. The 306 cities and towns of the State were represented by 1,543 delegates. No sooner was the organization of the assembly completed than the Hon. George M. Stearns moved that the Hon. William Gaston, of Boston, be declared the nominee of the convention for Governor, by acclamation. The motion was put and responded to by every man in the convention rising to his feet and giving three cheers. William M. Smith, of Springfield, was then nominated for Lieutenant-Governor, by acclamation. The ticket was completed by a committee, whose report was adopted by the convention without opposition, as follows: For Secretary of State, B. F. Mills, of Williamstown; for Treasurer and Receiver, General Nathan Clark, of Lynn; for Attorney-General, Waldo Coburn, of Dedham; for Auditor, O. Osgood Morse, of Newburyport. The platform, which was adopted by a rising vote and three cheers, was as follows:

The Democrats of Massachusetts, in convention assembled, hereby make the following declaration of principles:

1. Unwavering devotion and fidelity to the Constitution of the United States as the only guarantee of safety and tranquillity to the Union; equal political rights for all races, colors and conditions of men to this end, and to secure perfect harmony and reconciliation, by which only the Union can be maintained; we openly denounce any and all Federal interference with popular elections in every State, and we heartily declaim the conduct of those who, under any pretense or guise, disgrace themselves and their country by lawless acts of violence against the colored race in the Southern States, as also those carpet-baggers who have for years past eaten up the substance of the people whom they have oppressed and deceived.

2. The speedy resumption of specie payments is alike demanded by honor and recognized by all the civilized nations of the world as the only sound and healthy basis of currency.

3. Firm and unswerving opposition to sumptuary laws as founded on coercion and prohibition, the two agencies of despotism and arbitrary power, and we especially oppose the so-called prohibition law and its accessories as impotent for good, and powerful for evil, alike to private and public morals.

4. A stringent, judicious, and efficacious law for the restriction and regulation of the sale of intoxicating liquors, impartially and faithfully enforced, is the only practical, legal restraint against the evils of intemperance.

5. A proper respect for the will of the people as expressed through their representatives, as opposed to Executive interference and arbitrary power.

6. A vigorous reform in State affairs; a reduction of expenses and strict economy; the abolition of all useless and unnecessary rings and commissions, including the State constabulary; and a return of the old and true principle of the administration of the government by general laws, and its constituted executive and ministerial agents and officers held to the strictest accountability.

7. To foster with care the interest of labor, the bases of material prosperity, and of the industrial classes on whose moral and intellectual condition must ever depend the character and success of popular political institutions.

8. We commend to the cordial support of the voters of the Commonwealth the Hon. William Gaston, of Boston, our candidate for Governor; the Hon. William L. Smith, of Springfield, our candidate for Lieutenant-Governor, and the other candidates for

State offices this day nominated. We know and admire their integrity and capacity, and no one need fear that they will repudiate the platform on which they have been nominated.

The only show of discord or division of sentiment appeared in the election of a State Central Committee, there being some opposition to the plan of nominating this body by a committee appointed by the chair, and then voting on the report of this committee. Those who opposed this plan desired that the delegation from each congressional district should choose the member of the State Central Committee from that district, and that the members at large should be chosen by the full convention. The method by nomination of a committee, however, prevailed.

The Republican Convention was held at Worcester, on the 7th of October. The delegates had been very generally selected with special reference to their favoring or opposing the nomination of Mr. Talbot, though strong efforts had been made to secure unity of sentiment by sinking this issue out of the canvass. When the delegates came together on the night before the convention, it was found that a large majority of them were in favor of Mr. Talbot's nomination, and, in order to avoid any serious division, and all discussion on the next day, it was arranged that he should be nominated as promptly as possible, and all mention of the prohibition issue avoided in the platform. The Hon. Henry L. Dawes was chosen chairman of the convention, and made a conciliatory speech, dwelling on the importance of the continued ascendency of the Republican party and the necessity for union and harmony. A ballot was then taken for a candidate for Governor. The number of votes cast was 1,042, of which 755 were for Thomas Talbot, 198 for George B. Loring, 51 for Charles Devens, Jr., 20 for John E. Sandford, 16 for Benjamin F. Butler, 1 for E. R. Hoar, and 1 for Henry L. Dawes. On motion of Alexander H. Rice, of Boston, a viva-voce vote was taken on making the nomination unanimous, and declared carried, though it was by no means unanimously supported. A ballot was taken on the nomination for Lieutenant-Governor, which resulted in the selection of Horatio Knight, of Easthampton, also a pronounced prohibitionist. He received 643 votes out of 1,012, and a motion to make the nomination unanimous prevailed. Before the result of this ballot had been declared, the other candidates were nominated by acclamation as follows: For Secretary of State, Oliver Warner, of Northampton; for Attorney-General, Charles R. Train, of Boston; for Auditor, Charles Endicott, of Canton; for Treasurer, Charles Adams, Jr., of North Brookfield.

The platform adopted was as follows:

The Republicans of Massachusetts, proud of the historic record of their party, reaffirm their devotion to the great principles of justice upon which it was founded, and they pledge their best and constant endeavors to the maintenance of those principles in the future. Be it therefore resolved ·

1. That a sound currency is indispensable to national prosperity, and that to this end the nation must make its demand promises to pay equal in gold, which is the recognized standard of value in the whole civilized world; that it is further the duty of Congress to adopt such measures as shall safely and speedily lead to this equalization of value; and no inflation of the currency by adding to the Government issues should be permitted.

2. That Massachusetts has seen with abhorrence the attempt, through banded leagues, to deprive whole classes of our population of their constitutional prerogatives; and, as the amplest protection of the individual in his civil rights and privileges is the first duty of the national Government, therefore, as Republicans, reaffirming our unshaken faith in fundamental rights and the exact equality of all citizens before the law, we express our gratitude to the President of the United States for his prompt interference against an effort at usurpation over a recognized State government, and for his determined opposition towards all movements and combinations seeking to abridge, limit, or restrain the rights of any portion of the American people.

3. That the Republican party of Massachusetts demands and will require of all persons holding office, whether State, national, or municipal, an administration of government which shall conform to the highest standard of honesty, integrity, and economy, to the end that the public indebtedness may be honorably and speedily paid, and the burden of taxation lightened.

4. That the record of the Republican party of Massachusetts is a sufficient guarantee of its continued sympathy with that legislation which will promote the best interests of labor and tend to the moral and intellectual elevation of all persons engaged in industrial pursuits.

5. That the Republican party has proved itself under all circumstances the party of progress and reform; that it has shown itself ready and prompt to correct all abuses and bring its own servants to strict account for unfaithfulness in official conduct; that it denounces all laws and practices that open a way for corruption in the public service, and that it will demand of all its servants that their official position shall never be made subservient to their personal aggrandizement.

6. That in the nomination of the Hon. Thomas Talbot as Chief Magistrate of this Commonwealth, this convention expresses its appreciation of the character and ability of a distinguished public servant, and relying upon his administrative experience, his personal purity and sterling integrity, we feel confident of his triumphant election by our loyal and law-abiding people; and we heartily commend him and the other nominees of this convention to the suffrages of our fellow-citizens.

The following resolution, which had been offered early in the convention, and referred to the Committee on Resolutions, but had been ignored by that committee, was brought up by the original mover before the close of the convention, and was adopted:

Resolved, That, to protect the rights of all law-abiding citizens at the Republican caucuses held for the choice of delegates to the State Convention, the ballot and the check-list should be used, provided as many as five voters shall demand the same; and, in case of refusal to comply with the request, the remonstrants may call another caucus and proceed to elect delegates to represent their ward or town, and act in such convention.

The election occurred on the 3d of November, and resulted in the choice of Mr. Gaston for Governor, but to all the other State offices the Republican candidates were chosen. The total vote for Governor was 185,720, of which Gaston received 96,376, and Talbot 89,344, making the majority of the former 7,032. The majority of Knight for Lieutenant-Governor, was 12,013; of Warner for Secretary of State, 22,489; of Adams for Treasurer, 21,842; of Endicott for Auditor, 22,788; and of Train for Attorney-General, 22,576. The Legislature chosen on the same day consists of 24 Republicans, 15 Democrats, and 1 independent in the Senate; and 155 Republicans, 79 Democrats, and 6 independents in the House—making the Republican majority 8 in the Senate, 70 in the House, and 78 on a joint ballot. A majority is understood to be in favor of modifying the liquor laws.

The congressional elections excited scarcely less interest than that for State officers. For some years the entire representation had been Republican, but divisions and dissatisfaction raised the probability of a change in that respect. In the first, second, third, fifth, sixth, eighth, and ninth districts, the Republicans nominated the old Representatives, viz., James Buffinton, Benjamin W. Harris, Henry L. Pierce, Daniel W. Gooch, Benjamin F. Butler, John M. S. Williams, and George F. Hoar. In the fourth there was considerable division in the party, but Rufus S. Frost was nominated; in the seventh James C. Ayer, of Lowell; in the tenth Charles A. Stevens, and in the eleventh Henry Alexander. Against these candidates were the following Democrats: First district, Louis Lapham; second, Edward Avery; third, Benjamin Dean; fourth, Josiah G. Abbott; sixth, Charles P. Thompson; seventh, John K. Tarbox; eighth, William W. Warren; ninth, Eli Thayer; tenth, Henry C. Hill; eleventh, Chester W. Chapin. In the fifth district, Nathaniel P. Banks, formerly a Republican, and in the presidential campaign of 1872 a Liberal Republican, ran as an independent candidate, and was accepted by the Democrats. In the tenth district, Prof. Julius H. Seelye, of Amherst College, was taken up by some of the Republicans as their candidate, without a formal nomination, and as a protest against the caucus system of making nominations. The aggregate votes for the regular Republican candidates was 87,599, for the opposition candidates 94,177. Of the Republicans, Buffinton, Harris, Pierce, Frost, and Hoar, were elected. Of the opposition, Banks, Thompson, Tarbox, Warren, Seelye, and Chapin, were elected. Banks's majority over Gooch was 6,175; Thompson's over Butler, 969; Tarbox's over Ayer, 1,564; Warren's over Williams, 724; Seelye's plurality over Stevens 420, over Hill 4,299; Chapin's majority over Alexander, 5,737. Charles A. Stevens was elected in the tenth district at a special election early in January, 1875, to fill the vacancy in the Forty-third Congress caused by the death of Alvah Crocker.

At the election in November, 1873, four women were chosen on the School Committee of Boston, to serve during the year 1874. On the organization of the committee in January, seats were refused to these women, on the ground that they were not legally qualified, this action being based on an opinion of the City Solicitor. Protests were made and indignation meetings held, but the committee refused to recede from their action. The matter was taken up in the Legislature, which was then in session, and a bill introduced declaring women not disqualified to act on school committees. The question was first submitted to the Judges of the Supreme Court, whether there was any constitutional objection to the passage of such a bill. An opinion was rendered in April, to the effect that there was no such objection, the constitution being silent on the subject of women having the right by common law to hold that office. Miss Lucia Peabody, one of the women who had been elected and refused admission to her place, then brought a suit in the Supreme Court asking for a mandamus compelling the committee to admit her to the seat which she claimed. The court dismissed her petition in June, on the ground that it had no jurisdiction in the matter, the authority of the School Committee to decide on the qualifications, election, and return of its members being exclusive and not subject to revision by any court. The act was then passed in the Legislature on the last day of the session, declaring that sex was no disqualification for the office of school committee. The committee did not, however, take any further action in the matter during the year, and the seats remained vacant. At the election of this year (1874) seven women were elected on the same committee, and no objection made to their admission.

On the 16th of May a disastrous flood occurred in the county of Hampshire, caused by the breaking away of the dam which confined a large reservoir in the upper part of the town of Williamsburg. This reservoir contained a reserve water-supply for the factories on Mill River in the villages of Williamsburg, Skinnerville, and Haydenville, in the township of Williamsburg, and Leeds and Florence, in Northampton, and covered 124 acres, with an average depth of 24 feet. It was three miles above the village of Williamsburg, on a level about 300 feet higher, and contained about 1,000,000,000 gallons of water. At about 7½ o'clock in the morning the dam was discovered to be giving way, and, before warning could be sufficiently spread in the villages below, an enormous flood rushed down the valley carrying every thing before it. A large part of the village of Williamsburg was destroyed, including a button-factory, woolen-mill, saw and grist mill, and several dwelling-houses. The silk-mill at Skinnerville, together with some 15 dwellings, was swept away. At Haydenville the extensive brass-works of Hayden, Gere & Co., were entirely destroyed, and several dwelling dashed to pieces. The village of Leeds was almost entirely destroyed, including the Honobuck silk-factory, and considerable damage was done in Florence and Northampton, though the flood lost most of its force on the broad meadows above Florence. The valley was strewed with the *débris* of the destroyed villages and covered with desolation. The pecuniary loss amounted to about $1,500,000, and nearly 200 lives were lost in the four villages. The destitution and suffering which might have followed were averted by timely relief from different parts of the State and from other sections of the country. A coroner's inquest was held at Northampton to ascertain the cause of the disaster, and a verdict was rendered on the 3d of July. In this the breaking away of the dam is said to have been the natural and inevitable result of the great and manifest delinquency of the several parties who were concerned in originating, planning, constructing, and approving for use the said dam and reservoir, not excepting the Legislature itself under whose authority the reservoir company acquired its chartered privileges. The proprietors of the dam are charged with having consulted far less for the safety and security of the lives and property of the inhabitants below the dam than for reducing the cost of construction to the minimum figure. The jurors expressed the opinion that there was no engineering connected with the work which does not reflect equal discredit on the party employing and the party employed. The contractors are declared to have been guilty of great and manifest delinquency in executing the work required of them even under the specifications as drafted. The county commissioners who examined and accepted the reservoir dam come in for their share of blame for a superficial discharge of a most important duty.

The State debt has been increased $987,400 during the year, loans to the amount of $1,519,400 having been negotiated on account of the Troy & Greenfield Railroad, the harbor improvement, and the Danvers Lunatic Asylum, and $532,000 having been paid on maturing obligations. The following statement shows the amount and character of the funded debt, January 1, 1875:

Aggregate funded debt, January 1, 1874......		$28,477,804
Scrip issued during the year:		
Troy & Greenfield Railroad loan.....	$469,400	
Harbor Improvement loan..........	400,000	
Danvers Lunatic Hospital loan......	650,000	
		1,519,400
		$29,997,204
Paid during the year:		
State-House Enlargement loan.......	$100,000	
Almshouse loan.....................	49,000	
Union Fund loan....................	290,000	
Taunton Lunatic Hospital loan.......	93,000	
		532,000
Present funded debt....................		$29,465,204
Classification of the debt:		
Railroad loans.....................	$14,971,016	
War loans..........................	12,936,188	
Ordinary loans.....................	1,558,006	
		$29,465,204

Twenty-one thousand dollars of debt, already matured, has not yet been called for. There will mature during the year 1875: of the harbor improvement loan, $230,000, and of the Union fund loan, $420,000; in all, $650,000, the payment of which is amply provided for. The sinking-funds amount to $10,989,595.16, nearly all of which sum is productive. These funds, together with unsold Back Bay lands in Boston, estimated at $1,800,000, the South Boston flats, believed to be of large value, and some other property (all of which are, by existing laws, pledged to the sinking-funds), will, with perhaps the exception of the Troy & Greenfield Railroad loan and the Danvers Lunatic Hospital loan, be sufficient, with their accruing accumulations, for the redemption of the entire outstanding debt at its maturity.

The receipts of the Treasury for the year amounted to $14,251,320; expenditures, $11,777,464. The taxable property of the State is valued at $2,164,398,548, an increase of $77,048,533 over the valuation of 1873. The increase of taxable property in the last ten years is $1,098,966,429.. The estimated ordinary expenses for 1875 are $5,214,550, receipts $3,568,983, leaving a deficit of $1,645,566.

The work of the contractors for the completion of the Hoosac Tunnel has been finished, and the tunnel surrendered to the State. The entire amount of the contract was for $4,594,268, but a deduction of $36,547.54 was made on account of certain deficiencies. The amount paid previous to the completion of the work was $4,101,705.60, and the balance of $456,014.82 was paid on the 22d of December. The contractors presented a claim of $70,404.53 for extra work, $27,115.47 of which was allowed and paid. The total cost of the tunnel, to January 1, 1875, is $12,973,822.31. The corporations appointed under the act of the last Legislature, in making their report, propose a plan for utilizing the tunnel. It provides for the appointment of four directors of the Boston, Hoosac Tunnel & Western Railroad Company, to whom shall be transferred the rights and property of the State in the Southern Vermont Railroad, the Troy & Greenfield Railroad, and the Hoosac Tunnel. It further provides that the directors shall, as soon as possible, "proceed to negotiate with the corporations owning or operating railroads forming parts of a through railroad line between a point or points in Eastern Massachusetts and points in the eastern part of the State of New York by way of the Hoosac Tunnel, with a view to the early consolidation of such roads under one management." The directors are authorized to consolidate the properties and franchises under their charge with those of the other corporations, subject to the ratification of the Governor and Council and of the stockholders of the private corporations, the consolidated corporation to be known as the Boston, Hoosac Tunnel & Western Railroad

Company, and to be under the control of eleven directors, five being those appointed on behalf of the State, five chosen by the stockholders of the consolidated corporation, and the eleventh to be the president of the company, *ex officio*, who is to be elected by the ten directors before mentioned.

The receipts of the railroads of the State for the year amount to $34,632,482. The amount of freight handled was 12,014,812 tons, and the number of passengers carried 42,480,494. The number of accidents was very small, and but one person was killed and seven injured, except as the result of their own carelessness or indiscretion. The experiment favoring cheap trains for laborers, from Boston to Lynn on the Eastern Railroad, has proved very successful. These trains run to Boston in the morning and out at night, and the fare is placed at the uniform rate of five cents for the whole or any part of the distance. The receipts were $19.28 per trip, and the cost of running $14.14 per trip. The increase in receipts over the previous year, which was the first of the enterprise, was 42 per cent.

There are 4,000 insane persons in the State. Those cared for in public institutions are distributed as follows: At Worcester, 485; at Taunton, 508; at Northampton, 475; at Somerville, 150; at South Boston, 206; at Tewkesbury, 319; at Ipswich, 61. The asylums are all crowded, and there are many lunatics in the workhouses and private institutions. The number of prisoners in the penal and reformatory institutions of the State is 4,000. The number of paupers maintained by the Commonwealth is 2,700. The number of town and city poor fully supported is 6,100; partly supported, 25,000. There are nine institutions belonging to and sustained wholly by the State for the care of paupers, criminals, and insane persons. These are under the charge of a State Board of Charities, and are as follows: For paupers, the State Almshouse at Tewkesbury, the State Workhouse at Bridgewater, and the State Primary School at Monson; for the insane, the hospitals at Worcester, Taunton, and Northampton; for criminals, the State-prison at Charlestown, the State Reform School at Westboro', and the State Industrial School at Lancaster. The actual cost of sustaining these institutions for the year, after deducting the earnings of the State-prison, is $464,000. There was expended directly for charitable purposes by the State, outside of the institutions, $192,486; for State and to local or private institutions, $470,000. The cities and towns take care of their local poor in various ways. During the year, 217 almshouses were used by the towns in which they are located, while the remaining 123 towns mostly kept their poor in private families, though twelve of them made occasional use of the almshouses of other towns. The reported value of almshouse property is $2,622,336, viz.: land and buildings, $2,080,602, and personal property, $541,734. The

average cost of full support is found to be $3.05 per week, and was given to 4,057 persons in 1874, being 209 more than in 1873; 17,768 persons were partially supported during the same time, being an excess of 7,188 over the corresponding number for 1873. An increase of 5,000 in the number of "tramps" is recorded. In the three reformatories, an average number of about 850 children was maintained last year, and the whole number of deaths was but twelve, or one in seventy.

Nothing has yet been done about the construction of a new State-prison and a prison for women, which was authorized in 1873, except a report from the commissioners in favor of the project, and recommending the location of the new prison at Concord, and the sale of the old one.

The State militia now consists of 406 officers, and 6,042 enlisted men. The expense of supporting for the year was $181,565.98, besides $195,000 appropriated for new uniforms.

The Fish Commissioners have caused fishways to be built in several streams, and have made much progress in restocking the waters of the State. The number of shad-spawn taken at North Andover last year was 6,249,000; hatched and turned in above Lowell, 1,950,000; above Lawrence dam, 800,000; sent to Neponset, R. I., 550,000. At South Hadley, 3,016 shad were taken, and 44,556,000 spawn. The average from each shad taken at South Hadley was 22,691 spawn. Of those taken at South Hadley, 2,300,000 were put in the Connecticut at Bellows Falls and Smith's Ferry, and places between. The artificial hatching of trout has been very successfully carried on. Of salmon-spawn, 280,000 have been received and hatched with a loss of less than eight per cent. Of land-locked salmon, 5,500 spawn were hatched and distributed; and of 200,000 Sacramento salmon-spawn, presented to the State, only 7,000 were hatched.

There are fifty-four mutual fire-insurance companies in the State, with cash assets of $4,903,508, and eleven mutual marine and fire insurance companies, with a guarantee fund of $2,050,000, and gross assets amounting to $4,868,277, besides twenty-one joint-stock insurance companies, with a cash capital of $4,867,000. There are also numerous companies from other States doing business in this State. The grand total of capital represented in the insurance business is $65,844,270, much the larger portion belonging to companies out of the State.

There are now 178 savings-banks in the State, of which five were organized during the year. One was closed for lack of business. The total number of depositors was 702,099; aggregate amount of deposits, $217,452,120; average to each account, $309.71.

There are sixty railroad corporations doing business in the State, with 2,418 miles of main line and branches, 657 miles of siding, and 626 miles of double track. Three companies operate roads built on the narrow-gauge plan. The average cost per mile of the railroads of the State is $56,888.62, exclusive of equipment, which has cost $7,701 per mile. The entire system of the State is represented in $165,-624,136.72 of securities, of which $117,066,-798.07 is stock, and $48,557,338.65 is debt. There was an increase of debt of $11,000,000 during the year. The total earnings of the year were $34,632,488.54, a falling off of eight-tenths of one per cent. represented by a decrease of $1,155,900 in receipts from freight, and an increase of $527,381 from passengers. The total net increase was $10,703,301.70, or six and four-tenths per cent. on the permanent investment. Of the sixty corporations, twenty-nine paid dividends ranging from one to ten per cent., averaging nine per cent. on the stock of the dividend-paying roads.

The number of children in the State between five and fifteen years of age is 292,481, of whom 210,248 attended the public schools. According to a report of the deputy-constables on the labor of children in factories, there are 60,000 children in the State growing up in ignorance, and receiving no benefit whatever from the schools.

McFARLAND, Right Rev. FRANCIS PAT-RICK, D. D., a Roman Catholic Bishop of the Diocese of Hartford, born in Franklin, Pa., April 6, 1819 ; died in Hartford, Conn., October 12, 1874. He received his early education at a private academy in his native town taught by Rev. Father Clark, S. J., and passed thence to Mt. St. Mary's Seminary, at Emmittsburg, Md., where he finished his studies, and was subsequently professor. He was ordained priest in St. Patrick's Cathedral, New York City, by the late Archbishop Hughes, May 18, 1845, and for the next year was a professor in St. John's College, Fordham, N. Y. After three months' service as assistant priest at St. Joseph's Church, New York, he was appointed in the beginning of 1847 pastor of the Catholic church in Water-town, N. Y., and in 1851 was transferred to St. John's Church, at Utica, N. Y., where he remained till his elevation to the episcopate in 1858. He was consecrated Bishop of Hartford, March 14, 1858, by Archbishop Hughes, and his episcopal residence was at Providence until 1872, when the diocese was divided, and Bishop McFarland came to Hartford. His labors were abundant and he was very successful in ministering to the prosperity of his diocese. A studious, dignified, yet very zealous prelate, his death was a great loss to the Catholic Church, not only in his own diocese, but throughout the United States.

McLEOD, Rev. JOHN NIEL, D. D., a distinguished clergyman and theological professor in the Reformed Presbyterian Church, born in New York City, October 11, 1806 ; died there April 27, 1874. His father, a native of the island of Mull, but a graduate of Union College, had been for more than thirty years a prominent minister of the Reformed Presbyterian

Church in New York, and the organizer of the American Colonization Society. The son, after a very thorough training in the best schools of New York City, graduated with high honors from Columbia College in 1826, studied theology with his father, and in 1828 was ordained as an assistant to his father. On the death of his father, in 1832, he was elected his successor, and installed January 14, 1833. He was for many years the stated clerk of the General Synod of the Reformed Presbyterian Church, and a professor in the Theological Seminary of that Church at Philadelphia. He was a member of the Committee on Versions of the American Bible Society, and was for many years perhaps the most conspicuous among those leaders of the Reformed Presbyterian Church who were unwilling to unite with the other branches of the Scottish Church, in the United Presbyterian Church, as constituted in 1858, or with the Presbyterians of the General Assembly, on account of minor doctrinal differences, and such points of practice as the singing of Rouse's version of the Psalms only (as they believe that, in religious worship, it was wrong to use any hymns which were not inspired productions), the right of membership with Freemasons or Odd-Fellows, etc. He was prominent in procuring the infliction of the discipline of the Church upon Mr. George W. Stuart, of Philadelphia, for singing hymns in a Union meeting, and once or twice, in late years, was also conspicuous in some of the litigations growing out of questions of church-property in the congregation to which Mr. Stuart belonged. Dr. McLeod was always a man of large influence in his denomination, and highly esteemed by those who knew him best. Though a vigorous and able writer, Dr. McLeod had published but little ; some addresses, sermons, and devotional essays and discussions, are all that are extant from his pen.

MENNONITES. The Mennonite *Board of Guardians* are a committee who were appointed at the beginning of 1874, with the consent of members of several Mennonite Conferences, as a central body to receive funds and afford help to Mennonites in Russia who wished to emigrate to the United States, but were not able to pay their passage. The purpose of the board was to pay the passage of as many emigrants as circumstances would permit from Hamburg to the United States, but not to defray their expenses from their homes in Russia to Hamburg. Nevertheless, it stationed an agent at Hamburg, who obtained from the European railroads advantages in the reduction of fares and the provision of more convenient means of transportation, by which the progress of the emigrants was considerably facilitated from the time they crossed the Russian lines. It made contracts with one of the lines of steamers to bring over all emigrants at reduced rates, and stationed an agent at Castle Garden, in New York, to attend to their wants on reaching this country, and provide for their comfortable and cheap conveyance to their future homes. It became recognized as an authorized aid committee in America and Germany, and by the brotherhood in Russia.

The Board of Guardians reported in October, 1874, that it had furnished passages for about 70 families without means, at an expense of about $11,000, and that, including those who had paid their own expenses, about 200 families had come over under its care. Including those families who had come under other agencies, 851 families had arrived in America in 1874. Forty families had come in 1873; adding these, the total extent of the immigration so far had been nearly 900 families, which were distributed principally in five different settlements, as follows: In Manitoba, 230 families; in Dakota Territory, 200 families; in Minnesota, 15 families; in Nebraska, 80 families; in Kansas, 315 families. Eighty families were reported as distributed among the churches in the more Eastern States. Those families were estimated, after examination of the passenger-lists, to consist on the average of about five members each. Upon this basis, the actual number of persons in the different settlements was computed to be: In Manitoba, 1,150; in Dakota, 1,000; in Minnesota, 75; in Nebraska, 400; in Kansas, 1,575; in other places, 300: total, 4,500. A report from another source gave to the board the number of families settled in Manitoba to be 271, and of persons, 1,400. Three hundred families were yet expected to arrive before the end of the year, making the total immigration for 1873 and 1874 nearly 1,200 families. The board were informed from credible sources that about 1,000 families were making preparations to emigrate from Russia in 1875. The board had received requests for aid more than it could answer without increased contributions. Applications had been made to it also by colonists for help in beginning their settlements. This, however, was not within the purpose for which the board was organized. It had not been able, therefore, to give the help asked for out of its own funds, but had endeavored to obtain means through special contributions. The Aid Committee in Canada had opened a subscription to obtain $20,000 to be lent to the Bergthaler Church in Manitoba, on interest, for eight years. This scheme was meeting with a 'air degree of success. A conference of all the .ocal and branch aid committees of the Church was recommended, in which the brethren from Russia now in this country should be represented, to consider the plans for future action.

MERIVALE, HERMAN, C. B., an English publicist, professor, and Under-Secretary of State, born in Barton Place, Devon, England, in 1806; died in London, February 8, 1874. He was of a family distinguished in literature, his father being known as a legal writer, and his brother, Rev. Charles Merivale, as the eminent historian. He was educated at Harrow, and at Trinity College, Oxford, graduating B. A.

from the latter in 1827, with first-class honors, and was elected Fellow of Balliol College. He was called to the bar at the Inner Temple in 1832, and, having a strong predilection for politico-economical studies, so distinguished himself in that direction, that in 1837 he was appointed Drummond Professor of Political Economy in the University of Oxford, and held that pos on for eleven years. During this period many of his lectures on special topics of political economy were published, and deservedly rank among the ablest contributions to that science. Among these we may specify: "Five Lectures on the Principles of a Legislative Provision for the Poor in Ireland" (1838); "Lectures on Colonization and Colonies" (2 vols., 8vo, 1841). In 1848 he was appointed permanent Under-Secretary of State for the Colonies, and some years later permanent Under-Secretary of State for India. In 1859 he was created a Civil Companion of the Order of the Bath. His work on "Colonization and the Colonies" was revised and enlarged in 1860, and is now regarded as the standard authority on that subject. In 1865 he published "Historical Studies."

METALS. *Mechanical Puddling.* — When machinery was first introduced as a substitute for hand-labor in the puddling process, the expensive transformations it made necessary in existing establishments proved a great obstacle to its general employment. M. Pernot, a French engineer, has met this difficulty by applying machinery to the old style of furnace in a way that requires but slight and comparatively inexpensive changes, and with greatly-improved results. The most important feature of his invention is thus described:

M. Pernot takes the common circular puddling-ladle, and causes it to turn round the inclined axle in such a manner that half the bowl emerges from the molten iron in the furnace. The portion of the bowl above the metal comes in contact with the flame, becomes oxidized, and, passing round amid the iron, produces the action of refining; while the rotation, either by attraction or centrifugal force, causes the iron to mount upon this inclined plane in thin layers, and thus develops enormously the surface exposed to oxidation. These effects combined produce far more perfect puddling than can be obtained by hand-labor, and, especially, more regular. On this principle a furnace has been set to work by MM. Petin and Gaudet. The bowl is mounted on a small cast-iron carriage, which rotates with it, and which enables it to be drawn out of the furnace when repairs are required. The movement is given by means of a toothed wheel and pinion, and a small horse is at present employed for the purpose, but a motor is now being planned which will have a cylinder 0.150 metres in diameter, with 0.250 stroke, and a speed of 100 to 150 revolutions per minute, the puddler to revolve at the rate of five or six turns.

The head and door of the furnace remain the same, so that at the end of the operation the bloom can be divided as in the old furnaces. Consequently the same hammers and all the accessories remain unchanged.

In this furnace, in its present enlarged form, charges of 18 cwt. of fine iron (900 kilogrammes), i. e. obtained from charcoal pig, viz., 22 cwt. of ordinary iron made from common pig, are obtained at each operation. The waste amounts to about 37 per cent. based on a production of 90 tons of fine iron. The consumption of fuel is from 22 to 24 cwt. (from 1,100 to 1,200 kilogrammes). The cost of. production, compared with that of the ordinary furnaces, shows in favor of the new system the economy of at least 32s. (40 francs) per ton. The puddling process of M. Pernot is now a thoroughly practical one; it is no longer an experiment; it is a real mode of manufacture by which can be obtained with certainty all the different products which are expected from a puddling-furnace. The advantages of the new system of furnace are the following: Increase in product, as no doubt can be entertained that it will soon double the production as obtained now with a Siemens-Martin furnace; decrease of nearly one-half in the consumption of fuel; decrease in the same proportion of the working and general expenses, etc.; the repairs of arches and other parts of the furnace are very easily and rapidly made and, finally, this process can be applied as easily by the small producer as by the large one, doing away altogther with those gigantic machines which characterize the Bessemer process. A small firm may have its one furnace limited to the production of its wants, and a large company may put up several of them. Its first cost is very small; it requires no special workmen to attend to it; it keeps itself in good order; and, although no precise estimate of the cost of its production has been made, it must be comparatively very small. The operation is always under control and easily altered in one way or other, according to circumstances, which is in itself a real advantage over the Bessemer process. The homogeneousness of the steel is insured in consequence of the perfect stirring produced by the rotatory motion, which gives it a decided superiority over the Martin process; and stirring by hand is avoided, and no wire or tools are to be taken into account. The process can be applied to either small or large iron-works.

Effects of Cold on Iron and Steel. — *Iron* publishes an account of a long series of experiments on this interesting question lately made by Mr. J. P. Joule, with results which appear to confirm those obtained by Spence some years ago. The most striking of these experiments are described as follows:

1. A mixture of snow and sea-salt having been placed upon a table, iron and steel wires were stretched in such a manner that a portion of their length was engaged in the freezing mixture, while the rest was free from it; in each case the wires experimented upon broke outside the cold mixture, the temperature of which was 12° C.

2. Twelve needles of good quality, about 3 inches long, and $\frac{1}{16}$ inch. in diameter, were fixed firmly by their two ends at two inches distance from each other; a wire was then fastened by one of its ends to the middle of each needle, and attached at the other end to a machine for measuring the power of springs. The machine was then set in action until each needle broke. Six of the needles taken at hazard were tried at the temperature of +13° C., and the six others in a freezing mixture, which reduced their temperature to —11° 11′ C.; in the former case, five of the needles broke with forces varying from 1.134 to 1.842 kilogrammes, the sixth bearing 1.701 without breaking; in the latter case, five broke under forces varying from 1.184 to 2.041 kilogrammes, while the sixth bore a strain 1.701 without breaking. The result is curious, the lowest breaking point being identical in the two cases, while the highest occurred when cold was applied. Comparing the totals, the averages are as follows: At ordinary temperature, 1.637; at —11° 11′, 1.801 kilogrammes. M. Joule had previously tried the elasti-

city of all the needles, and could find no difference between them.

3. It having been stated that the violent action to which a railway-wheel tire is exposed resembled an active power rather than mere pressure, and, further, that cast-iron was supposed to be more affected by cold than wrought-iron or steel, M. Joule made an experiment of a different kind. He procured a number of cast-iron nails, $1\frac{1}{4}$ inch long, and about $\frac{1}{4}$ inch diameter in the middle, and having selected those of which the weights were as nearly as possible the same, he arranged each nail in such a way that a cutting-hammer, weighing 5$\frac{1}{4}$ lbs., fell from a fixed height on the middle of the nail, which was supported at each end. In order that the test should be as sure as possible, the nails were taken at hazard, and the trials with the cold nails alternated with those at the ordinary temperature. The nails were chilled by being plunged in a freezing mixture, and were struck with the hammer within five seconds of being taken out. Twelve series of these nails were experimented on, each series comprising sixteen nails, those which were not broken being added to the following lot. The results were as follows: Three series were tried at the ordinary temperature, being +2° 22′ C., the cold being increased from —12° 22′ to —16° 67′, and the fall of the cutting-bit from twenty to thirty inches, and only one of the cold nails broken. In the fourth case, the temperatures being the same, but the fall increased to thirty-five inches, two cold and one of the other nails were broken. In the fifth experiment, the fall being 30$\frac{1}{4}$ inches, one of each eight nails was broken. In the sixth, the cold was increased to 17° 78′. with the same ordinary temperature, and the same fall of the cutter, and one of each eight again broken. In the seventh, the fall was raised to nearly forty inches, when only one of the cold nails was broken. In the next two experiments, the ordinary temperature was —4° 40′, and artificial cold, 16° 67′; when, with a fall of fifty-nine inches, two cold and one other nails were broken; and, with a fall of seventy-five inches, three of each. Ten of the same nails were then tried at the same temperatures, with a fall of eighty-five inches, when two cold and one other nails were broken. The six remaining nails were then tried, three at the temperature of +4° 44′, and three at 16° 11′, with a fall of ninety-eight inches, two only of the cold nails and three of the others being broken. Finally, an experiment was tried with fresh nails, twelve of which had been kept for four hours at a temperature of —16° 11′, the ordinary temperature being +5°, and the fall seventy inches, the result being the breakage of seven of the frozen and eight of the other nails. Total broken—twenty-two of the frozen nails and nineteen of the others.

Taking the whole of the above experiments into consideration, M. Joule arrives at the conclusion that frost or lowering of temperature does not render cast-iron, wrought-iron, or steel, more liable to break, and that the accidents which happen on railways arise from the negligence of the companies in not submitting their wheels, axles, and all the other parts of their rolling-stock, to practical and sufficient test before using them in the service of the line.

Silicon in Pig-Iron. — In a paper on the condition in which silicon exists in pig-iron, Mr. C. Handfield Morton holds that this element is chemically combined with the iron, and not, as claimed by many, in a state of mechanical admixture. The author states that he was induced to make a few experiments upon this subject, by noticing that silica was obtained in the insoluble residue when pig-iron containing a large quantity of silicon was dissolved by dilute sulphuric acid, *in vacuo*, instead of silicon, which must have been expected as the result of the decomposition of the pig-iron under these conditions. This fact appeared to clearly point out that the theory of silicon being *intimately mixed* with pig-iron was untenable, at least as regarded this particular pig, which was a No. 1 Bessemer iron, containing 4.012 per cent. of silicon, and was therefore not at all unlikely to contain silicon in admixture, if tho element ever occurred in pig-iron in such a condition. As far as he was aware, no experiments had been made with the object of proving that silicon existed in a state of combination in pig-iron, although he believed it was the generally received opinion that such was the case. He had therefore made a considerable number of experiments with the view of ascertaining how far this conclusion was correct. After detailing the various experiments to prove his theory, he went on to say that from these results it must fairly be concluded that the silicon contained in pig-iron did not exist in a state of mechanical mixture, but existed combined with a portion of the iron as a silicide of iron, in the same manner that carbon existed as a carbide of iron, only differing from carbon in so far that it did not exist in a graphitoidal form in pig-iron. If the pig-iron used had contained any uncombined silicon it would have been found in the insoluble residue from the experiments with Nordhausen sulphuric acid and hydrofluoric acid, as it was insoluble in even the lesser acid, after being strongly heated; and as an uncombined silicon must have been heated intensely in the blast-furnace, there could be little doubt that, as a rule, pig-iron did not contain any uncombined silicon. In conclusion, it must fairly be considered, from various experiments he had made, that silicon was not contained in pig-iron in a state of mechanical mixture (except, perhaps, under peculiar circumstances), but as a chemical constituent.

Extraction of Iron from Pyrites Refuse.— In the manufacture of sulphuric acid from iron pyrites a large amount of refuse, containing a high percentage of iron, has hitherto gone to waste, owing to the difficulty of separating the metal from the sulphur which remains. Some experiments, with a view to the extraction of the iron in available shape, have lately been made by Dr. Hoffmann, who claims to have reached a successful result. His experiments were made with the pyrites from the Meggen mines in Germany, the source of supply for nearly all the German manufactories of sulphuric acid. The residuum of sulphur, always in considerable quantity, renders the iron nearly useless for any practical purposes. The efforts of chemists have been directed toward removing the sulphur completely from the refuse, and that could be done by long-continued heating, along with abundant introduction of air. Dr. Hoffmann has repeated these experiments under the most favorable conditions, but he has always found that the sulphur is peculiarly

difficult to remove from the refuse of the Meggen pyrites, much more so than elsewhere. He concluded that the composition must be quite different; and, submitting the substance to chemical analysis, he found in it, besides sulphur, iron, selenium, arsenic, lead, mercury, and thallium, considerable quantities of zinc in the form of zinc-blende; various specimens contained over 6 per cent. zinc. The presence of this metal explains the difficulty of expelling the last traces of sulphur. By lixiviation the zinc is got rid of, and the refuse afterward falls down into a fine powder, which, however, still contains lumps that appear to have been little affected by the previous roasting. These lumps hold large quantities of sulphur, and have, therefore, to be removed, which is done by sifting, when the powdery portion is ready for the separation of the iron in the ordinary way.

Strength of Iron increased by Strain.—In the course of some experiments on the tensile strength of iron made by Prof. Thurston during the past year, in Washington, it was observed that when subjected to heavy strain, even to the point of apparent weakening, and then allowed to rest for a time, iron not only regained its original strength, but actually became stronger than before strain was applied. Attention was called to this fact in the following way: A piece of iron was being subjected to tensile strain by means of an eye welded to each end of the piece. When the limit of strength was apparently reached, and a sensible contraction of the circumference indicated that the piece was about to break, the weld holding one of the eyes gave way, and caused a postponement of the test until the next day, the eye having, in the mean time, been welded on again. On renewing the test the iron, instead of parting at the weakened spot, as was expected, sustained an additional strain of 20,000 pounds, and then parted at the other end, where no signs of weakness had before been observed. The weakened part had thus actually gained in strength during its period of rest. This remarkable result was confirmed by subsequent experiments. And it was also shown that the longer the rest after strain the greater was the increase of strength.

Restoration of Burned Steel.—The following simple process for the restoration of burned steel is described in *Iron* by Mr. J. L. Davies, Swansea; Wales. A mixture consisting of one part by weight of the residue of paraffine-stills with four parts by weight of resin-oil, is the preparation employed. The burned steel is first heated red hot and then plunged into this fluid, where it is allowed to remain for a few seconds; it is then reheated and cooled in the ordinary way. Experience in the use of this preparation will quickly enable persons to give any desired temper to their tools, and they may be made especially hard by heating them red hot, dipping into the liquid, and then reheating to a slightly white heat, and immediately afterward cooling in pure water.

Preservation of Iron.—Several methods for preventing the rust or corrosion of iron surfaces have been published during the year. Mr. R. A. Fisher, of San Francisco, offers the following as not only an excellent means of preventing the wasting away of iron and steel by corrosion, oxidation, and other similar causes, but as specially adapted to the prevention of incrustation in water *tuyères* and steam-boilers. His method is to bring in direct contact with any iron or steel surfaces exposed to the action of any natural water, or aqueous, saline, or other solution, some metal or metallic alloy that is more easily oxidized, corroded, or eroded, than either iron or steel, and which also forms an oxide insoluble in water. The metals which may be used for this purpose, either separately or in combination, are, according to the inventor, aluminium, antimony, cadmium, lead, magnesium, mercury, tin, and zinc.

M. Stanislas L. Delatot, a chemist of Paris, originates an improvement in the manufacture of iron and steel, by the combination of nickel or cobalt, separately, or as a mixture of the two, in definite proportions, with iron or steel; the effect of which is stated to be that the iron or steel is thereby rendered inoxidizable, i. e., proof against deterioration by rust through exposure to moisture, atmospheric or other oxidizing influences. Cast-iron, so treated, is capable of conversion into wrought-iron and steel, by means of the ordinary and well-known processes, producing an excellent quality of metal.

A composition for coating the surfaces of metals, in order to prevent oxidation, has been patented in Florence, and is highly recommended. This is composed of quartz, of a suitable "solvent," such as carbonate of potash, and metallic oxides, such as oxide of lead or oxide of cobalt, in equal proportions, the selection of the oxide being made according to the color to be given to the composition; and the other components also vary according to the metals to be operated upon and the quality of the composition or varnish required. These ingredients are first reduced to fine powder, water is added so as to form a mixture of the consistence of paste, of which a layer is applied with a brush on the surface of the articles (previously cleaned and dried) to be varnished or protected, and, this done, they are exposed to the open air to dry. The articles are afterward placed in cast-iron or fire-brick muffles, and heated, in kilns of suitable construction, to 800° C. The heat acting on the mixture of silica and metallic oxides causes their combination, at the same time fixing them firmly on the surface of the metals. On being gently cooled and taken out, the metal is covered with a polished silicate or glass, which is said to resist the impact of hard bodies without scaling or cracking. This composition is applicable to many metals, but more especially and with the greatest advantages to cast and wrought iron, which by this means may, through their low price, be employed for many articles now made of copper and tin. Iron thus treated becomes coated with a silicate of iron, and may be exposed in very damp places, and even immersed in water, without undergoing any oxidation. It is suggested that this process may be employed for protecting ships' armor-plating, and other iron used in ships.

Spongy Iron as a Water-Purifier.—During the past year Prof. Gustav Bischoff, of Glasgow, has been studying the properties of spongy iron with a view to its employment as a water-purifier. He finds—1. That spongy iron decomposes water—even distilled water—which has been previously boiled; 2. It reduces nitric acid to ammonia; 3. It is capable of decomposing nitrogenous organic matter, and reduces considerably the amount of organic carbon in water filtered through it; 4. A minute but almost constant quantity of the iron is dissolved by the carbonic acid present in the water when it passes through the filter, ferrous carbonate being formed. This, however, is soon oxidized and precipitated; 5. The purification of water increases slightly for some five or six hours after the filtration through spongy iron has been completed; 6. If the iron is prevented from dissolving by adding to the water before filtration a minute quantity of sodium carbonate, its purifying action on the water is considerably diminished; 7. The purifying influence exerted by spongy iron on water containing organic matter is more energetic in hot weather than in winter, when the temperature of the water is frequently below the point at which fermentation almost entirely ceases. The author says:

These facts appear to confirm my opinion, expressed on former occasions, that the action of spongy iron on impure water is twofold—namely, chemical and mechanical. The chemical action must be found in its decomposition of water, to which is probably owing, in part at least, the decomposition of nitrites and nitrates, and the direct combination of nascent hydrogen with the nitrogen, to form ammonia. The readiest explanation for the decomposition of water is the intimate contact between electro-positive and electro-negative bodies, such as metallic iron and carbon, or even metallic iron and any ferric-oxide which has escaped reduction; and it may be well supposed that, consequent to the galvanic current thus produced, the atmospheric oxygen dissolved in water is ozonized, and caused to act as a powerful oxidizing agent. I am driven to this conclusion from the results of a large number of analyses made before and after filtration through spongy iron, which, notwithstanding the fact of the reduction of nitrates and nitrites, also clearly indicates an oxidizing action shown by the increase of nitrates after filtration. This increase is mostly considerable—up to twice the original quantity—while sometimes there is also a decrease.

Prof. Bischoff further states that water impregnated with lead is thoroughly purified by filtration through spongy iron. A sample of water containing 0.175 grains of lead to the gallon was passed through one of these filters, and its purity afterward tested. In the filtered water no trace of coloring could be seen, and even after concentration to $\frac{1}{50}$ of its volume, the presence of lead could not be detected. This result was to be expected from the well-known fact that lead salts are precipitated by metallic iron, and that spongy iron is a much more energetic precipitant than iron in other forms. This property, too, is an important and welcome addition to the employment of spongy iron for purifying water

Although applicable to the purification of water on an extended scale, as shown by the experiments of one of the London water companies, the author thinks that spongy iron will be found most effective and economical in small filters designed for domestic use. On this point, which is one of great practical importance, he says:

I would prefer to see it used in small domestic filters, and in this case, if such a filter were to contain one gallon by volume of spongy iron (or 10 lbs. to 12 lbs. by weight), a yield of 2,000 gallons of purified water with an undiminished action of the spongy iron would more approach a practical result. Supposing ten gallons of water a day for cooking and drinking, such a domestic filter would, as far as the action of the spongy iron is concerned, purify as energetically after 200 days as on the first day; so that, doing away with all hypothesis, it would certainly not require a renewal under less than six months of constant use, and at a cost of hardly one shilling. Of course, in such domestic filters, the filtration can be made much slower in order to effect a more complete purification than would be practicable for water companies. I should think that one gallon in half an hour, or even in an hour, is a sufficient speed for domestic filters.

Improved Tin-Dressing Machinery.—In a paper on this subject, read before the London Society of Engineers, Mr. S. Cox called attention to the following as the most important improvements that have of late years been made in tin-dressing machinery. Shool's atmospheric stamps for crushing the ore were first mentioned, and their advantages over the old system pointed out. Briefly these were stated to be: 1. A greater length of stroke, by which the weight of the heads is reduced from 5 cwt. to 3¾ cwt.; 2. A greater speed, the relative velocities being respectively 150 and 60 blows per minute; 3. The additional momentum produced by the compressed air and the power thus afforded of regulating the length of the stroke. The Propeller Knife Buddle recently introduced at Restronguet Steam Tin-Works, as well as Collom's Patent Jigger, were then described. The last machine consists of hutches with fine wire sieves placed upon the top, the sieves being covered with a layer of coarse ore and the machine being kept full of water under pressure. Each hutch is in connection with a trunk in which a piston fits loosely and works with a short vertical stroke. At each stroke the water is forced through the sieves, and partially floats the tin-stuff, the return-stroke allowing the heavier particles of tin to subside.

The author stated it to be a very important point with both of these machines to first separate the ore into various degrees of coarseness, and for that purpose a machine known as Cox's Separator was proposed to be employed. In this machine a column of water ascending in a conical hopper meets with descending tin-stuff, which is supplied from the stamps. The flow of water is regulated so as only to allow the coarser particles to fall, the lighter ones being carried by the water into a second machine of the same kind with a less strong flow of water. An additional washing action is produced by supplying the water through a perforated case, and the upward flow of the water is regulated by means of a hollow cone which fits into the bottom of the hopper, and round the top of which quarter-inch holes are drilled in a horizontal direction. An active agitation is kept up by the water passing through the holes, and meeting the ascending column of water at right angles.

Mr. Cox then described Stephens's Pulverizer, in which, by means of strips of wood placed in slots in the covering plate, the rotating action of the water is turned into a jigging one, thus carrying the pulverized ore through the covering plate, whence it is conveyed away by launders.

Nickel and Cobalt Ores.—The following notes on the nickel and cobalt ores of foreign countries are published in *Iron*. The ores of nickel and cobalt are found in almost all parts of the world where other minerals exist, but those which yield the chief supply of these metals abroad, are found in Norway, Sweden, and Hungary. The mineral from which nickel is derived in Sweden and Norway is an iron pyrite, which is in most cases magnetic, but is nearly free from cobalt. These ores are exceedingly poor, never containing more than 3 per cent. of nickel. In some cases they are worked when yielding only 1 per cent. of the metal. The nickel-ores are found abundantly in Hungary, where the nickel is always in association with cobalt. The ore generally contains 15 per cent. of the former metal, and 5 per cent. of the latter. This is a very valuable mineral, and the mines have been worked profitably for the last thirty or forty years. The ore is composed of an arsenical mundic, highly impregnated with the more valuable metals, and in this respect differs from the Norwegian and Swedish ores, insomuch that the latter contain little or no arsenic, and appear simply as sulphides.

Precipitation of Copper with Tin-Scrap.— Prof. T. Sterry Hunt has patented an improved method for the precipitation of metallic copper from solution by the employment of tin-scrap:

This invention consists in using tin-plate scrap or waste for the precipitation of copper from the solutions obtained in the various wet processes of copper extraction, and in saving in the operation the adhering tin. The copper solution must contain at the same time protochloride of copper (otherwise called cupric chloride) and sulphate of soda, or some other base. Such solutions are obtained from sulphuretted copper-ores, which have been calcined with common salt, as in the Longmaid or Henderson process, or when similar ores after roasting are digested with chlorides of iron or other chlorides, as, for example, in the Hunt and Douglas patent process. In case, however, the solutions of copper to be precipitated contain no chlorides, a portion of common salt is added, and in case they contain no sulphates, a portion of sulphate of soda or other soluble sulphate is added. In either case, these salts may equal the amount of copper present. Such solutions, containing both chlorides and sulphates, especially if heated, as is usual in copper precipitation, very quickly dissolve the tin from tinned iron when this is immersed therein, and at once let it fall again as an insoluble hydrated oxide of tin, which may be readily drawn off while suspended in the liquid, and collected by subsidence in proper tanks, to be subsequently treated by methods known to chemists, such as dissolving in hydrochloric acid and precipitating by metallic zinc, by reduction in the dry way, or by conversion into stannate of soda. The scrap-iron thus freed from tin is then employed in the ordinary way to precipitate the dissolved copper, as metallic or cement copper, from the solutions described. The copper solution, holding the suspended oxide of tin, may be drawn off at once from the iron to the settling-tank, and a fresh solution added; or the precipitation of the copper may be carried on without interruption in the first solution till this is exhausted, and the oxide of tin afterward separated from the metallic copper by taking advantage of the greater lightness and the more finely-divided state of the former. Should it be desirable to remove the tin from the iron plate without causing an immediate precipitation of copper thereon, this may be effected by mixing a solution of perchloride, or other persalt of iron, with the copper solution.

New Method of welding Copper.—Improvements in the operation of welding copper have been introduced by a Baltimore firm (Messrs. Rehbein, Roberts & Brocchus). The two pieces of copper to be united having previously been prepared, so that the surfaces form a lap or other suitable joint, prepared borax (biborate of soda) is applied on and between the surfaces of the joint, which are heated and hammered. The borax is prepared by being heated until all the water of crystallization has evaporated, when the residuum is pulverized for use. After being hammered while hot, the joint is further heated to a white heat, and sprinkled over with a chloride, magnesic, sodic (common salt), or other equivalent compound, suitable for the exclusion of the oxygen, and then finally welded, or during the welding operation a stream of chlorine gas may be directed upon the heated copper joint.

Purification of Lead by Steam.—This process, as described in *Iron*, serves as a substitute for stirring the molten lead either by hand or by steam-machinery. The apparatus employed in the steam system consists of an upper and lower boiler, each with its own furnace: the former, for the melting of the lead and separating the silver, will contain about nine or ten tons; and the lower, which is for the crystallization, from fifteen to sixteen tons. A stage, erected around the lower boiler, allows the workmen to watch the operation and remove the oxides. The metal is run from the upper to the lower vessel through tubes fitted with friction-valves moved by means of a lever; and in order to prevent the lead from penetrating into the steamway-pipe a valve-cock is adopted.

The lead, having been melted in the upper boiler, is skimmed and run off into the lower one, and at that moment a small jet of steam is let in to effect the mixture of the crystals of the previous operation with the lead in fusion. A small stream of water, thrown upon the surface of the lead at the commencement of the operation, facilitates the formation of the crystals. The steam is introduced from a boiler close at hand, under the pressure of three atmospheres, which are opened alternately every bottom of the lower boiler, and is distributed uniformly by means of a horizontal disk of cast-iron placed over the nozzle of the steampipe in the centre of the lower part of the boiler. The boiler is fitted with a cover in segments, which are opened alternately every five or six minutes, when a workman detaches such lead as has been flung by the action of the escaping steam against the upper sides of the boiler and adhered there. Beneath the lower boiler are two small supplementary furnaces, which bring up the discharge-tubes to the proper temperature, and are lighted just previous to the drawing off. The steam causes a violent and continued boiling of the whole mass of metal in fusion most favorable to the separation of the silver from the lead and the purification of the latter. The above action is chiefly mechanical, but a sensible chemical effect is also perceived, for the lead undergoes a refining action independent of that which results from its fusion at a dull-red heat previous to crystallization, so much so that all previous refining is dispensed with in the case of moderately hard lead, though not when the metal is very hard.

If the chemical action of the steam were *nil* the purity of the lead produced without previous refining could only be attributed to the series of partial refinings to which the lead is submitted by the fact of a great number of remeltings at a dull-red heat; but a fact which tends to show that the steam exercises a chemical action is, that the oxides which are produced are first yellowish and earthy, but, as the operation proceeds, become black and heavily charged with copper, a circumstance which is not produced in the boilers of the ordinary system in spite of the most vigorous stirring. Toward the end of the operation, while the steam is still in action, in the liquid portion in which are concentrated the silver, copper, antimony, and arsenic, the lead is found to have been deprived of the copper which it contained. The antimony is gradually eliminated by the oxidation caused by the air during the remeltings; soft lead gives even more oxide than hard lead containing more antimony, which proves that the latter oxidizes first and preserves the lead from oxidation.

The lead produced by the steam method is perfectly soft, and, besides a suppression of a special operation of refining, the employment of steam offers many advantages, as the saving of the cost of previous purification, reduction of oxidation of the lead, and consequently of waste. The economy of time and labor is due to the rapidity of the operation, the smaller number of hands required, while better workmen are necessary in the old system than in the present, and also more space.

When the lead to be dealt with contains not more than one-half per cent. of antimony, it may be operated upon by the new system directly, and the purification becomes reduced to that of the rich dross, and the expense to about one-fifth of that by the ordinary mode. In the case of lead which contains a larger amount of antimony, previous purification is necessary, but this operation need not be carried so far as in the ordinary process; it may be arrested when only half per cent. of antimony remains in the lead. The arsenic having the greatest tendency to take the place of the silver, it has been proposed to effect the purification by means of soda.

Assay of Lead.—Mr. F. Maxwell Lyte publishes the following in the *Chemical News* as a convenient method for the assay of lead-ores, particularly when, as is often the case, the lead to be estimated is mixed as sulphate with the matrix insoluble in acid: "I dissolve the sulphate or chloride, as the case may be, in acetate of ammonium, make the solution as neutral as possible, and estimate the lead by a standard solution of bichromate (a half decinormal solution answers well) with a nitrate-of-silver indicator." This process, according to the author, shortens labor, enables the insoluble matrix to be weighed direct after drying, and gives accurate results.

Quicksilver.—The *Scientific and Mining Press* describes an improved apparatus for the condensation of quicksilver-fumes, the invention of Messrs. J. B. Randol and Ferdinand Feidler, of California. Having discovered that the condensation of mercurial fumes is very much facilitated when they are brought in contact with the inside of a glass plate the outside of which is exposed to the external air, they make the sides of their condensing-chambers largely of glass. Otherwise the surfaces with which the fumes come in contact are of wood, this being much more durable than metal under the action of the fumes, and leaving the quicksilver in a cleaner state. The use of water for cooling is entirely dispensed with, as the glass performs that service in a more satisfactory manner. The above are the distinguishing features of the invention, which for cheapness, durability, and efficiency of working, is said to be much superior to the appliances in common use.

The same journal describes a new process for purifying quicksilver from the extraneous matters with which it becomes associated in the condensing-chambers. The blast or draught which draws off the mercurial fumes into and through the condensers from the furnace where the ore is roasted also carries with it a mechanical mixture of fine dirt, particles of unconsumed carbon, some ash, some undecomposed cinnabar, and various other impurities and minute particles of the metal. This combination of matter is deposited in the condensers in a condition resembling lamp-black or paste, it having become moistened by the steam introduced from the fuel and ore, and, as a consequence, it becomes intermixed with the quicksilver. The quicksilver, thus contaminated, is placed in an iron tank, to which water heated to the required degree is added, and the substance intimately mixed. Wood-ashes or other suitable alkalies are added for the purpose of still further cleaning the quicksilver, which is then drawn off into another vessel. When the soot and ashes are put into the tank, the hot water is shut off. A man mixes the soot, ashes, and hot water thoroughly with a shovel, and thus separates the soot from the metal, allowing the quicksilver to pass off clear and pure.

Origin of Gold-Nuggets.—It having been alleged, on the basis of experiment, that grains of gold may be made to grow to the size of "pieces" in solutions of auric chloride by the addition of a small quantity of organic matter, the deposition being similar to that which takes place in operations of electro-plating, and that in this we have an explanation of the formation of gold-nuggets in Nature, Prof. Skey, analyst to the Geological Survey of New Zealand, took up the subject, and in a series of careful experiments has failed to find any confirmation for the statement. His experiments were briefly as follows:

1. 0.1315 gramme of gold, hammered thin and bent to a curved disk of such a size as to expose about half a square inch of superficies, was placed in a glass vessel containing two ounces of a solution of auric chloride of a strength equal to half a grain of gold per ounce. For reducing agents small pieces of cork and wood were sunk by glass attachments to the bottom of the vessel in close proximity to the disk of gold.

The vessel was then closed, put in a darkened place, and suffered to remain at rest until all the gold present in solution had been reduced, a process occupying in this case a period of time equal to rather more than two months.

The gold disk was then carefully examined and weighed. It had a small quantity of very finely granular gold loosely adherent to it, and apparently equally disposed over its surface.

With the whole of this loose gold attached, the disk only increased in weight 0.0005 of a gramme, or $\frac{1}{74}$ of its weight (a rate of increase that would require about forty-four years to double the size of the disk), consequently only about the $\frac{1}{10}$ part of the total amount of gold present in solution had deposited upon the disk, the remainder having deposited away from it, and this was seen to have indiscriminately attached itself to every surface which had contact with the auriferous solution, whether the bottom or sides of the vessel, the glass attachments, or even the surface of the liquid having contact only with the atmosphere.

In reference to the minute quantity deposited upon the gold disk, it was found by numerical calculation that the proportion was certainly not more, relatively to the surface of the disk, than that which the remainder of the gold bore to the extent of the surfaces upon which it had affixed itself.

2. The same experiment repeated, but vessel and contents not darkened. Same results as before.

3. Gold solution reduced to half its strength, and time of total deposition extended to four months. Diffused sunlight admitted.

4. Soluble organic matter used in place of wood; sunlight excluded. Time of total deposition of gold two months.

No discernible difference in results upon point in question to those obtained in experiment No. 1.

So far, therefore, as is shown by these results, gold reduced from solution of its chloride by aid of such kinds of organic matter as cork or wood does not in the manner of its deposition exhibit such a notable selective power for metallic gold as the description of Mr. Daintree's results would lead us to suppose. It does not, indeed, show any such selective process at all, that is, to a greater extent than can be attributed to the action of surfaces generally regardless of their nature; and, in support of this, I believe I am correct in stating that the whole sum of our experiences (omitting those of Mr. Daintree) is directly against this theory, as to the rapid and marked deposition of gold on gold in the manner stated; indeed, so far as I am aware, we only produce by these means fine incoherent powder—minute crystals or films of exceeding thinness—nothing nuggety. We get a certain size of grain or crystal, or a certain thickness of film, which our efforts have hitherto failed to enlarge.

Gold Assays.—A committee appointed by the British Association for the Advancement of Science, to investigate the subject of gold assays, report some interesting facts concerning the accuracy of the results obtained in the commercial process. The committee instituted a series of experiments for the purpose of discovering to what extent the weight of pieces of pure gold and of alloys of known composition would be affected by submitting them to the process of assaying, and consequently how far the results of assay operations were trustworthy. These results showed that the maximum error was only 0.001 per cent. of the original weight of the assay piece, and consequently that the results obtained by assaying gold, represented the composition of the portion of metal under examination to the $\frac{1}{10000}$ part, a fact which would doubtless appear remarkable to all who were accustomed to the ordinary methods of quantitative analysis. The committee were not unmindful that, although it was possible to attain this high degree of accuracy, it was nevertheless well known that a comparison of the assay reports of different analyses as to the composition of the same might often disclose discrepancies of $\frac{1}{10000}$ parts. Portions of metal from nineteen gold ingots were assayed by the assistant assayer, and were then sent to five other assayers, each of whom furnished an independent report. The discrepancies in their reports varied from $\frac{1}{12000}$ parts to one part of fine gold in 1,000 of the alloy, or an average deviation of $\frac{1}{10000}$ parts.

Alloys.—An alloy of copper, lead, tin, and zinc, the invention of Mr. J. E. Jacoby, of Hamburg-on-the-Heights, Germany, designed for the reduction of friction in the working parts of machinery, is highly spoken of. The proportions of the different metals entering into its composition are: copper, varying from 70 to 73 per cent.; lead, from 15 to 20 per cent.; tin, from 9 to 11 per cent.; and zinc, in very small proportions, from 1 down to 00.5, or $\frac{1}{5}$ per cent.

A new form of phosphor-bronze, intended for the same purpose as the above, has been introduced by Dr. Kunzel, one of the original discoverers of that now celebrated alloy. The subjoined description is given in *Iron*:

When phosphor-bronze is combined with a certain fixed proportion of lead, the phosphorized triple alloy, when cast into a bar or bearing, segregates into two distinct alloys, one of which is hard and tough phosphor-bronze, containing but little lead, and the other a much softer alloy, consisting chiefly of lead, with a small proportion of tin and traces of copper. The latter alloy is almost white, and, when the casting is fractured, it will be found nearly equally diffused through it; the phosphor-bronze alloy forming, as it were, a species of metallic sponge, all of whose cavities are occupied by the soft metal alloy segregated from it. This phenomenon of the segregation into two or more alloys of combinations of copper with tin and zinc has long been known, and from the fact that such separation is generally massive, and not equable throughout the mass, it has been a source of great annoyance to the founder. Dr. Kunzel, however, seems to have succeeded in causing the segregation to take place in uniform distribution throughout the casting, and has taken advantage of the properties of the product which he obtains in this manner, to construct therefrom bearings of railway and other machinery.

A new white metal has just been invented by M. Delatot, with the object of replacing those at present in use at a much less cost. The composition of the metal is as follows: Pure red copper, eighty parts; oxide of manganese, two parts; zinc, eighteen parts; phosphate of chalk, one part. The mixing is effected thus: To the melted copper is added the oxide of manganese in very small quantities at a time. When the oxide of manganese is dissolved in the copper, the phosphate of chalk is added similarly in small quantities. After this reduction has lasted about half an hour, the scoria which floats on the metallic bath must be skimmed off and then the zinc added, about ten minutes before running the metal. This will give a white hard metal, equal to gun-metal in tenacity and resistance, and superior in obviating friction, and can be made at a less cost. In order to accelerate the fusion of the oxide of manganese, a flux may be made of the following composition: half part of fluoride of calcium, half part of borate of soda, and one part of charcoal.

A metallic alloy, claimed to approach more closely the appearance and properties of silver than any heretofore produced, is also described in *Iron*:

The new alloy is a compound of copper, nickel, tin, zinc, cobalt, and iron. The following proportions are said to produce a very white metal, perfectly imitating silver: copper, 71.00 parts; nickel, 16.00; cobalt, 1.75; tin, 2.50; iron, 1.75; zinc, 7.00. A small portion of aluminium, say about 1.5 per cent., may be added. The manufacture is, as might be expected, from the alleged fact of the alloy possessing the specific gravity of silver, rather peculiar. "The first step is to alloy the nickel with its own weight of the copper, and add zinc, in the proportion of six parts to ten of copper. The nickel alloy, the iron, the rest of the copper, the cobalt in the form of black oxide, and charcoal, are then placed together in a plumbago crucible, which is covered over with charcoal, and exposed to a great heat. When the whole is melted, the heat is allowed to subside gradually, and the alloy of zinc and copper is added when the temperature is just sufficient to melt it. This done, the crucible is taken from the fire, and its contents stirred with a hazel-stick. The tin is next added, first being wrapped in paper and then dropped into the crucible. The alloy is again stirred, and finally poured into the mould; it is then ready to be rolled and wrought just like silver. A great portion of the zinc is volatilized in the act of fusion, so that a very little remains in the alloy." The superiority of this metal is said to depend principally on the cobalt, to which is due its peculiar argentine lustre.

Ornamentation of Metals.—Metals can be easily colored by forming on their surface a film of sulphide, which is deposited by placing the article to be colored in some solution containing sulphur. In a few minutes brass or gun-metal articles can be given the color of gold, of copper, of carmine, dark red, bright blue, pale blue, or pinky white, according to the thickness of the coat, which depends on the length of time the metal remains in the solution used. The colors possess a very good lustre, and if the articles to be colored have been previously well cleaned by means of acids and alkalies, they adhere so firmly that they may be polished without injury.

To prepare the solution, dissolve 1½ ounce of hyposulphite of soda in 1 pound of water, and add 1½ ounce of acetate of lead dissolved in ½ pound of water. When this clear solution is heated to from 100° to 210° Fahr., it decomposes slowly, and precipitates sulphide of lead in brown flakes. If some metal or article to be colored is now present, a part of the sulphide of lead is deposited thereon, and, according to the thickness of the deposited sulphide of lead, the above colors are produced. To produce an even coloring the articles must be evenly heated. Iron treated with this solution takes a steel-blue color; zinc, a brown color; in the case of copper objects, the gold-color does not at first appear; lead and zinc are entirely indifferent.

If, instead of the acetate of lead, an equal weight of sulphuric acid is added to the hyposulphite of soda, and the process carried on as before, the brass is covered with a very beautiful red, which is followed by a green (which is not in the first-mentioned scale of colors), and changes finally to a splendid brown, with green and red iris-glitter. This last is a very durable coating, and may find special attention in manufactures, especially as some of the others are not very permanent.

Very beautiful marble designs can be produced by using a lead solution thickened with gum-tragacanth, on brass which has been heated to 210° Fahr., and is afterward treated by the usual solution of sulphide of lead. The solution may be used several times.

Much time and attention have been devoted by Prof. Kick, of Prague, to the subject of etching iron with acids. After many experiments with the different acids and some other etching solutions, Prof. Kick found that a mixture of equal parts of hydrochloric acid and water with a drop of chloride of antimony to every quart of the mixture was the best etching solution. Some kinds of iron showed what is called a passive state, acids not acting upon it until this condition has been destroyed by heating, and then the surfaces seemed quick to rust; but the action of the chloride in the solution appears to arrest this tendency. The smooth surface to be etched is surrounded with a ridge of wax, and the acid is poured into the disk thus formed. At a temperature of 55° to 65° Fahr. the action soon begins, as shown by the gas evolved; in winter the etching is poor. The time required is from one to two hours, but the etching should go on until the texture is visible. Every half-hour the acid can be poured off without removing the wax, the carbon rinsed off, and the surface examined. If too much chloride of antimony is added to the acid, a black precipitate will soon form, which can easily be distinguished from the carbon. When the etching is finished, the wax rim is removed, the iron washed, first in water containing a little alkali, then in clean water, brushed, dried, and varnished. If in a few hours it begins to rust, the varnish should be removed with turpentine, which will also take off the rust, and then varnish again.

The appearance of different kinds of iron when etched is essentially as follows: Soft or sinewy wrought-iron of excellent quality is attacked so equally by the acid, and so little carbon is separated, even after several hours' action, that the surface remains bright and smooth. Fine-grained iron acts the same; the surface is still smoother, but a little darker. Coarse-grained and cold-short iron is attacked much more violently by acid than the above. In ten minutes, especially with the latter, the surface is black. After thirty minutes a black slime can be washed off, and the surface will remain black in spite of repeated washings, and exhibits numerous little holes. Certain parts of the iron are usually eaten deeper, while others, although black and porous, offer more resistance. By allowing the acid to act for an hour or so, then washing, drying, and polishing with a file, a distinct picture is obtained. Malleable cast-iron rusts more easily than wrought-iron, and it is interesting to know that the action of acids is also violent, the surface being attacked more vigorously. Gray pig-iron acts like steel; the etched surfaces have quite a uniform gray color. In puddled steel the color, after etching and washing, is gray, with quite a uniform shade, and the lines are scarcely visible. Cement steel has a very similar appearance, the lines being very weak. In Bessemer and cast-steel the etched surfaces are of a perfectly uniform gray color, with few, if any, uneven places. The softer the steel the lighter the color

On etching, the finest hair-like fractures are rendered prominent. A piece of steel which looked perfect before etching, afterward exhibited a hair-like fracture throughout its whole length. When different kinds of iron are mixed, the acid attacks that for which it has the greater affinity, while the other is less acted upon than if it were alone. Etching is exceedingly valuable to all who deal largely in iron, as it enables them to determine with comparative accuracy the method of preparing the iron, as in the case of rails, etc., as well as the kinds employed.

Iron can be plated or coated with silver or gold by a direct process, i. e., without the use of copper as an auxiliary, according to the present custom of electro-platers. As an essential preliminary, the iron must previously be alloyed with nickel and manganese; the iron being melted and then mixed with those metals in the proportion of 12 lbs. nickel and half a pound of manganese to 1,000 lbs. of iron. Such mangano-nickelized iron may then be silvered or gilt in baths of suitable solutions; it is first hand-rubbed and immersed in a lime-bath, containing 1 lb. of slaked lime for every 100 lbs. or pints of water, and is thence transferred at once to the plating-bath, which is prepared as follows: For gilding, 100 lbs. or pints of water, 4½ lbs. bicarbonate of soda, 1½ lb. pyrophosphate of soda, 1 oz. cyanide of sodium, 2 drops hydrocyanic acid, and ¼ oz. neutral chloride of gold: for silvering, to the same quantity of water add 2 lbs. bicarbonate of soda, 6 oz. cyanide of potassium or of sodium, 10 drops of hydrocyanic acid, and 2 oz. of neutral nitrate or chloride of silver.

METHODISTS. The *Methodist Almanac* for 1875 gives the following general summary, compiled from authentic sources, of the Methodist churches in the United States and in the world:

CHURCHES.	Itinerant Ministers.	Local Preachers.	Lay Members.
Episcopal Methodist Churches in the United States:			
Methodist Episcopal Church..	10,845	12,796	1,563,521
Methodist Episcopal Church South..............................	3,371	5,344	667,685
Colored Methodist Episcopal Church..........................	635	683	67,888
African Methodist Episcopal Church...........................	600	1,300	200,000
African Methodist Episcopal Zion Church....................	694	1,416	164,000
Evangelical Association..	737	476	90,249
United Brethren in Christ...	967	742	120,445
Total.....	17,749	22,667	2,873,998
Non-Episcopal Methodist Churches:			
Methodist Church...	624	300	65,000
Methodist Protestant Church....................................	423	250	65,000
American Wesleyan Church......................................	250	190	20,000
Free Methodist Church..	90	80	6,000
Primitive Methodist Church.....................................	20	25	2,000
Total.....	1,407	1,845	158,000
Total Methodists in the United States.........................	19,156	24,512	3,031,988
Throughout the World:			
Methodists in the United States................................	19,156	24,512	3,031,988
Wesleyans in Great Britain......................................	1,715	13,720	376,489
Irish Wesleyan Church..	152	760	20,740
French Wesleyan Church...	28	96	2,012
Australian Wesleyan Church....................................	348	1,438	66,686
Primitive Methodist Church.....................................	1,020	14,833	164,660
New Connection Church..	210	1,270	33,563
United Methodist Free Church..................................	358	3,361	66,909
Bible Christian Church...	244	1,747	26,878
British Wesleyan Reform Union................................	365	148	8,109
Methodist Church of Canada....................................	1,004	1,027	102,887
Methodist Episcopal Church in Canada......................	236	214	22,641
Grand total.....	24,866	63,131	3,923,512

I. METHODIST EPISCOPAL CHURCH.—The annual minutes of the conferences for 1874 give the details of the statistics of this Church (see table on next page).

The statistics of the West Texas Conference, after the number of traveling preachers, are included with those of the Texas Conference. The traveling preachers are classified as follows: On trial, 1,383; in full - connection, 7,733; superannuary, 679; superannuated, 1,060. The number of local preachers is given at 12,581; number of Sunday-schools, 18,628; of officers and teachers in the same, 200,492; of Sunday-school scholars, 1,363,870. The number of baptisms during the year was: of children, 58,911; of adults, 71,915. The number of churches is 15,010; probable value of the same, $69,288,815. Number of parsonages, 4,893¾; probable value, $9,604,230. The contributions for benevolent purposes were: For conference claimants, $159,881.54; Missionary Society (from churches, $424,267.03, from Sunday - schools, $187,687.51), $611,954.54; Woman's Foreign Missionary Society, $55,-406.26; Church extension, $83,347.52; Tract Society, $19,840.09; Sunday - school Union, $20,196.61; Freedmen's Aid Society, $37,-029.65; education, $23,754.68.

CONFERENCES.	Traveling Preachers.	Members.	Proba-tioners.	Total.
Alabama	81	9,761	1,114	10,908
Arkansas	86	4,582	864	4,896
Baltimore	193	28,005	4,259	32,264
California	133	7,392	1,779	9,171
Central German	114	10,381	1,135	11,516
Central Illinois	249	24,181	1,998	26,179
Central New York	282	29,003	3,127	32,130
Central Ohio	156	21,705	1,649	23,854
Central Pennsylvania	217	29,480	7,862	37,342
Chicago German	62	4,552	902	5,454
Cincinnati	172	33,352	2,542	35,894
Colorado	20	1,720	369	2,089
Delaware	52	10,678	1,156	11,834
Des Moines	142	16,394	1,866	18,260
Detroit	246	20,731	2,376	23,107
East German	44	2,884	537	3,421
East Maine	97	8,280	2,310	10,590
East Oregon and Washington	18	1,100	269	1,369
Erie	823	34,900	3,128	38,028
Florida	31	1,870	596	2,466
Georgia	99	11,168	3,950	15,118
Germany and Switzerl'd	74	7,022	1,899	8,921
Holston	100	21,397	3,057	24,454
Illinois	248	36,140	3,361	39,501
India	46	876	691	1,567
Indiana	141	29,072	3,862	32,934
Iowa	129	18,971	1,318	20,289
Kansas	108	9,101	2,975	12,136
Kentucky	93	15,704	3,458	19,162
Lexington	60	6,739	1,657	8,396
Liberia	19	1,892	140	2,032
Louisiana	74	9,043	2,694	11,737
Maine	138	11,328	2,012	13,340
Michigan	225	23,205	3,297	26,592
Minnesota	141	10,880	1,798	12,678
Mississippi	121	26,446	3,897	30,343
Missouri	124	14,609	4,057	18,666
Nebraska	89	7,444	1,249	8,693
Nevada	17	411	85	496
Newark	208	29,993	6,337	36,330
New England	264	26,296	3,860	30,156
New Hampshire	127	12,273	2,135	14,408
New Jersey	175	29,278	5,823	35,101
New York	273	38,447	5,863	44,310
New York East	236	36,841	5,421	42,262
North Carolina	37	7,803	1,328	9,131
Northern New York	233	21,657	4,395	26,052
North Indiana	170	25,080	6,804	31,884
North Ohio	163	20,651	1,343	21,994
Northwest German	69	4,137	891	5,028
Northwest Indiana	152	28,085	2,045	25,060
Northwest Iowa	62	3,403	898	4,301
Ohio	184	36,694	3,141	39,835
Oregon	61	3,012	713	3,725
Philadelphia	237	35,978	7,689	43,667
Pittsburg	298	51,438	11,467	62,905
Providence	181	17,904	3,022	20,926
Rock River	228	23,116	2,035	25,151
Rocky Mountain	18	516	178	694
South Carolina	92	25,608	5,068	30,676
Southeastern Indiana	120	24,028	1,849	25,877
Southern German	16	438	73	511
Southern Illinois	160	22,732	3,094	25,826
South Kansas	90	9,226	3,495	12,721
Southwest German	118	8,806	1,227	10,033
St. Louis	136	13,841	2,652	16,493
Tennessee	92	9,895	1,643	11,538
Texas	77	15,014	2,881	17,895
Troy	254	29,550	5,058	34,608
Upper Iowa	191	17,427	1,874	19,301
Vermont	130	9,832	1,549	11,381
Virginia	60	5,240	1,167	6,477
Washington	106	23,160	3,042	26,202
Western New York	231	18,142	1,755	19,897
West Texas	61	...	...	...
West Virginia	158	23,830	6,025	29,855
West Wisconsin	130	11,178	1,309	12,487
Wilmington	124	22,312	4,314	26,626
Wisconsin	188	13,642	1,569	15,211
Wyoming	205	23,187	4,686	27,873
Missions outside of Conference	...	8,057	3,389	11,446
Total	10,854	1,345,089	218,432	1,563,521
Total in 1873	10,571	1,288,704	175,328	1,464,027

The organization of separate conferences, to include the German-speaking churches in the United States, was begun in 1864. There were, in 1874, six such conferences. The following table exhibits the relative condition of the German churches in 1864 and 1874, and their growth in ten years:

CHURCHES.	1864.	1874.
Traveling preachers	233	471
Local preachers	224	378
Members in full connection and on probation	22,088	36,183
Churches	244	552
Parsonages	130	254
Value of church property	$579,446	$2,380,590
Sunday-schools	410	647
Officers and teachers	3,002	6,448
Scholars	19,229	32,011
Benevolent Contributions.		
For missions	$14,791 28	$22,053 51
For church extension	...	$18,637 08
For the Tract Society	$701 72	$845 68
For worn-out preachers	$1,505 74	$3,979 67
For the Sunday-school Union	$529 94	$760 30

Adding the statistics of the Methodist Episcopal churches in Germany (Germany and Switzerland Conference), the whole strength of German Methodism is shown to be seven conferences, 534 traveling preachers, 426 local preachers, 45,099 members, and 43,673 Sunday-school scholars.

The annual meeting of the General Missionary Committee was held November 11th. The treasurer reported the receipts to the 31st of October to have been $675,080.32, showing a decrease from the previous year of $5,756.32. The decrease was not regarded as excessive, provided the great financial stringency which had marked the year be taken into consideration. The disbursements had been: On account of foreign missions, $243,607.75 ; of domestic missions, $409,249.03 ; of incidental, office, and other expenses, $50,998.48 : total, $703,-855.26. A balance of $13,288.86 remained in the treasury on the 1st of November. The debt of the Society was stated to be $115,000. The following appropriations were made for 1875:

I. To FOREIGN MISSIONS (INCLUDING THE COST OF EXCHANGE):

1. Africa (Liberia)	$9,000 00
2. South America	9,000 00
3. China (three mission districts)	49,854 00
4. Germany and Switzerland	29,380 00
5. Scandinavian (Denmark, Norway, and Sweden)	61,200 00
6. India (India Conference, and Bombay and Bengal)	76,819 20
7. Bulgaria	9,600 00
8. Italy	15,600 00
9. Mexico	22,200 00
10. Japan	51,300 00
Total foreign missions	$303,853 20

II. MISSIONS IN TERRITORIES OF THE UNITED STATES TO BE ADMITTED AS FOREIGN MISSIONS:

1. Arizona	$3,000 00
2. New Mexico	8,000 00
Total	$11,000 00

III. Domestic Missions:

1. Welsh missions......................	$150 00
2. Scandinavian missions................	16,200 00
3. German missions....................	42,125 00
4. Chinese missions....................	7,500 00
Total for foreign population in the United States....................	$65,975 00
6. Indian missions......................	$3,500 00
7. American domestic missions..........	249,525 00
IV. For Miscellaneous Purposes.........	73,006 00
V. For the Liquidation of the Debt....	115,000 00
Grand total........................	$821,353 20

The annual report of the Missionary Society furnishes the following summary of the statistics of the missions for 1874:

FOREIGN MISSIONS.	American Missionaries and Assistants.	Native Preachers.	Members.	Probationers.
Africa	1	19	1,392	140
South American..........	8	*..	*.....	*...
East China (Foo-Chow)...	14	67	1,085	640
Central China (Kin-Kiang)	10	3	25	26
North China (Peking).....	13	5	14	16
Germany and Switzerland.	2	109	7,022	1,899
Denmark..................	2	9	388	229
Norway....................	4	16	1,597	291
Sweden....................	6	88	2,971	1,546
India......................	44	43	928	734
Bombay and Bengal.......	15	*..	*.....	*...
Bulgaria..................	2	6	50	7
Italy......................	2	12	600	...
Japan.....................	10	..	2	6
Mexico	9	8	.....	...
Total..................	145	385	16,570	5,534

Twenty-three missionaries of the Women's Foreign Missionary Society are included in the column of American missionaries and assistant missionaries. They were distributed as follows: In South America, 2; in East China, 3; in Central China, 3; in North China, 2; in India, 9; in Japan, 1; in Mexico, 3. The number of teachers was 1,785, distributed as follows: In Central China, 3; in North China, 3; in Germany and Switzerland, 1,051; in Denmark, 61; in Norway, 168; in Sweden, 292; in India, 204. Number of churches, 135; probable value of the same, $588,802.99. Number of parsonages, 78; probable value, $91,495. Amount of missionary collections, $3,967.46; of other benevolent contributions, $56,945.72. Number of Sunday-schools, 420; of scholars in the same, 22,940. Number of day-schools, 259; of scholars, 8,960.

DOMESTIC MISSIONS—FOR-EIGN POPULATION.	Missionaries.	Local Preachers.	Members.	Probationers.
Welsh	2	6	118	.....
German....................	201	129	9,761	1,805
Scandinavian..............	42	63	4,678	781
Chinese...................	2	..	18	.....
American Indian..........	10	23	1,166	380
Total.................	257	221	15,741	2,966

The number of churches connected with these missions was 295; probable value of the same, $750,875. Number of parsonages, 139;

* No returns.

probable value, $160,490. Amount of missionary collections, $9,305.41.

MISSIONS IN THE TERRITORIES.	Missionaries.	Local Preachers.	Members.	Probationers.
Arizona	3	1	13	8
New Mexico.........	10	4	124	7
Total..............	13	5	137	15
Total missionaries...	415	....	....	....

The seventh annual meeting of the *Freedmen's Aid Society of the Methodist Episcopal Church* was held at Cincinnati, Ohio, December 29th. The corresponding secretary reported the receipts for the year to have been $55,134.98, showing an average contribution of four cents by each member of the Church. Complaints were made of the smallness of the sum. The plans of the Society for the year had been based upon estimates that the contributions would reach $100,000. It had been embarrassed by the failure to realize that amount, and involved in debts amounting to $17,778. Quite $100,000 would be required to liquidate its debts and carry on its operations for the ensuing year. The Society had helped to establish and support the following institutions: Central Tennessee College, Nashville, Tenn.; Shaw University, Holly Springs, Miss.; Claflin University and Baker Institute, Orangeburg, S. C.; Clark University and Theological Seminary, Atlanta, Ga.; Haven Normal School, Waynesboro', Ga; Baldwin Seminary, Baldwin, La.; New Orleans University and Thomson Biblical Institute, New Orleans, La.; Rust Biblical and Normal Institute, Huntsville, Ala.; Richmond Normal School, Richmond, Va.; Centenary Biblical Institute, Baltimore, Md.; Wiley University, Marshall, Texas; Cookman Institute, Jacksonville, Florida; Bennett Seminary, Greensboro', N. C.

It had also aided in the support of schools taught by the ministers of the Church in connection with their mission-work. Three thousand pupils had been enrolled in all the schools, of whom 1,000 were preparing to be teachers or preachers.

The ninth anniversary meeting of the *Board of Church Extension* was held November 12th. The receipts for the year were reported to have been: By balance from the previous year, $1,321.71; on general account, $75,546.59; on loan-fund account, $19,931.80: total, $96,800.10. The disbursements had been: On general account, $64,046.25; on loan-fund account, $17,475.90: total, $96,800.10. A net balance remained, after deducting the amount of drafts due, of $9,146.79. The board had, however, made grants not yet paid, amounting to $12,275. If these should be required immediately, the existing cash balances would be overdrawn to the amount of $3,128.21.

During the nine years of its active work, ending November 1, 1874, the board had collected and disbursed $804,763.94, of which $200,541.03 belonged to the loan-fund. Of the money lent from the loan-fund, $33,385.85 had been returned to the treasury and relent to other churches. The board had helped, in all, 1,385 churches. Appropriations for 1875 were authorized to the amount of $144,050, and the same amount was asked from the Conferences in the shape of contributions.

At the annual meeting of the *Book Committee*, held in the city of New York, Febru-

ary 10th and 11th, the aggregate amount of the sales of the two publishing-houses in New York and Cincinnati, for 1874, was reported to have been $1,552,048.50.

II. METHODIST EPISCOPAL CHURCH SOUTH.—The following are the statistics of the Methodist Episcopal Church South, as they are given in the general minutes of the Conferences, published in March, 1874:

CONFERENCES.	Traveling Preachers.	Superannuated Preachers.	Local Preachers.	White Members.	Colored Members.	Indian Members.	Total Ministers and Members.
1. Baltimore	173	9	100	23,451	63	.....	23,796
2. Virginia	160	10	181	44,574	599	37	45,561
3. Western Virginia	61	1	93	11,657	18	.....	11,830
4. Holston	145	7	291	38,205	171	129	38,948
5. North Carolina	144	10	295	48,912	465	.....	49,756
6. South Carolina	143	10	118	36,432	645	.....	37,348
7. North Georgia	156	18	416	47,696	140	.....	48,426
8. South Georgia	118	20	230	26,335	...	.....	26,698
9. Florida	46	7	80	7,167	20	.....	7,320
10. Alabama	120	16	216	27,751	104	.....	28,207
11. North Alabama	111	7	328	29,052	58	.....	29,556
12. Louisiana	75	9	91	12,585	179	.....	12,889
13. Mississippi	113	11	166	19,656	...	.....	19,945
14. North Mississippi	125	12	219	25,900	...	.....	26,149
15. Memphis	120	10	282	20,964	...	.....	30,376
16. Tennessee	174	6	340	39,645	22	.....	40,187
17. Kentucky	101	6	119	19,502	129	.....	19,857
18. Louisville	122	4	201	29,052	47	.....	29,426
19. St. Louis	45	6	104	9,863	3	.....	10,021
20. West St. Louis	82	6	127	13,937	20	.....	14,172
21. Missouri	120	6	120	22,963	...	.....	23,209
22. Western	44	..	80	2,993	...	.....	3,067
23. Indian Mission	17	3	78	221	477	4,613	5,404
24. Arkansas	55	1	150	11,119	22	.....	11,347
25. White River	53	1	95	10,294	7	.....	10,450
26. Little Rock	70	6	168	14,827	8	.....	15,079
27. Trinity	77	10	183	14,953	...	.....	15,223
28. East Texas	46	2	107	9,082	...	.....	9,237
29. Texas	61	7	84	6,400	191	.....	6,743
30. Northwest Texas	89	6	210	14,051	...	.....	14,356
31. West Texas	36	5	44	3,859	37	.....	2,981
32. Los Angeles	19	..	15	769	...	.....	803
33. Pacific	46	3	57	3,316	4	.....	3,426
34. Columbia	13	..	18	1,054	...	.....	1,085
35. Illinois	52	2	67	5,507	...	.....	5,628
China Mission	..	..	3	83	...	.....	86
Bishops	8	..	...	......	...	.....	8
Total in 1873	3,134	237	5,344	659,677	3,429	4,779	676,600
Total in 1872	3,013	219	5,134	637,526	3,557	4,710	654,159
Increase	121	18	210	22,151	....	69	22,441
Decrease	...	...	...	......	128	....	......

The total number of infants baptized during the year was given at 22,755; number of adults baptized, 37,454. Number of Sunday-schools, 7,019; teachers in the same, 48,530; scholars, 321,572. Total amount of collections in the churches for conference claimants, $64,013.70; collections for missions, $96,644.31.

The agent of the Publishing-House at Nashville, Tenn., reported to the General Conference that the concern possessed assets to the amount of $533,577.92, of which $220,597.55 consisted of real estate; and that its liabilities amounted to $219,540.81, leaving an unincumbered balance in its favor of $314,037.11. The clear value of the assets of the house had increased $37,920.78 since the 1st of July, 1873. The following comparative statement was made of the value of the property, after deducting all liabilities, year by year, since 1870:

July 1, 1870	$188,352 45	July 1, 1873	$276,117 41
July 1, 1871	216,517 55	April 1, 1874	314,037 13
July 1, 1872	229,736 78		

This shows an increase in value, in less than four years, of $125,684.66.

The General Conference authorized the book agent, with the Book Committee, to negotiate for the transfer of the property of the Southwestern Book and Publishing Company, at St. Louis, to the Southern Methodist Publishing-House, provided it can be made without damage to the publishing interests of the Church, and without increasing the debts and liabilities of the Publishing-House.

Reports were made to the General Conference, of the condition of sixty-one educational institutions. Many of the reports were incomplete in regard to the value of property and funds, and the number of their students, so that the aggregate of values could not fairly be given. Of the institutions, one (the Southern University, Greensboro', Ala.,) was designated as a university; 48 were classed as colleges, eight as high-schools, two as academic schools, one as a collegiate school, and one as a boarding-school. Thirty-two of them were recorded as "female" colleges or institutes. The corner-stone of the Vanderbilt University was laid at Nashville, Tenn., April 29th, by Bishop Paine. On the occasion a letter was read from Mr. Cornelius Vanderbilt, offering $100,000 in addition to his former gifts to the institution. With this amount, an endowment fund was secured of $300,000, exclusive of the value of the grounds and buildings.

The *Board of Missions* submitted to the General Conference a statement of their operations during the preceding four years, from which it appeared that their receipts had been: from general contributions, $346,411.37; for the extinguishment of the old debt, $34,563.68; by donations and bequests, $13,492.42; making a total of $394,476.77; and that their home and office expenses had amounted to $14,339.92. During the same period 14,985 conversions had taken place, and 8,733 adult persons and 4,258 infants had been baptized.

The seventh *General Conference* of the Methodist Episcopal Church South met at Louisville, Ky., May 1st. The bishops presided daily in turn. An address was presented by the bishops, in which the condition and progress of the Church during the preceding four years were reviewed, and suggestions were offered for the consideration of the Conference. The results of the missionary organization, especially in reference to the foreign fields, had not been satisfactory. Some provision was recommended by which the interests of the domestic and foreign fields could be so adjusted as to avoid a conflict in the public mind with reference to their respective claims. Great progress had been made in church-building, not only as to the number of houses, but also as to the style of architecture, accommodation, and provisions for comfort at all seasons. A slow but steady improvement had also taken place in financial plans. The district conferences were represented as working well and doing good, but the Church conferences were regarded as having failed to accomplish the objects for which they were instituted. The publishing-house had been destroyed by fire since the preceding General Conference, but had been rebuilt and improved, and was prospering, notwithstanding the panic, with largely-increasing sales of its standard publications. The subject of education, in all its branches, was especially commended to consideration. The right training of children, the literature of the Sunday-school system, and denominational education, were presented as subjects of increasing importance. The adjustment of a complete system of education, from the district school to the university, under the care of the Church, was mentioned as one of the objects which should be held in view.

The bishops also submitted a report of the organization of the Colored Methodist Episcopal Church which had been effected under their superintendency, and in accordance with the acts of the General Conferences of 1866 and 1870. The newly-organized Church had now 4 bishops, 15 annual conferences, 607 traveling preachers, 518 local preachers, 74,799 members, 535 Sunday-schools, and a monthly paper which was self-sustaining. An address from the bishops of the Colored Methodist Episcopal Church accompanied the report. It expressed thankfulness to the Church South for the provision it had made for its colored members, and the belief that "it is best for both white and colored to have separate schools." The Church was suffering more from the want of "a better-informed ministry than from any other cause, and was engaged in efforts to raise means to erect an institution for the training of ministers. It was pledged to do all in its power to educate and Christianize the colored race; and hopes were expressed that before many years it would be able to send educated missionaries to Africa.

The Conference approved the organization of this Church, commended it to the confidence and Christian affection of its members, "and to all Christians of every name," and also commended its efforts to establish an institution of learning "to the friends of the colored people everywhere."

A fraternal address was received from the British Wesleyan Conference. It was the first act of official recognition which that body had given to the Methodist Episcopal Church South. This fact was mentioned and explained in the opening paragraphs of the address.

The address then gave an account of the condition and operations of the Wesleyan Methodist Connection in Great Britain, and concluded with the words: "We shall rejoice to hear of your welfare, and to receive, either by deputation or otherwise, information as to your affairs."

A reply was adopted by the Conference in which the past attitude of the Church in respect to other Christian bodies, and the circumstances attending the opening of fraternal relations, were referred to.

The Rev. Albert S. Hunt, D. D., the Rev. Charles H. Fowler, D. D., and General Clinton B. Fisk, had been appointed by the General Conference of the Methodist Episcopal Church which met in 1872, to convey fraternal greetings to the General Conference of the Methodist Episcopal Church South. The object of the appointment was declared in the resolution under which it was made to be "to place ourselves" (the Northern Church) "in the truly paternal relation toward our Southern brethren which the sentiments of our people demand, and to prepare the way for the opening of formal fraternity with them." The delegates were received Friday, May 8th, and spoke with reference to the establishment of fraternal relations. They expressed spiritual fellowship and sympathy with the Southern Church, reviewed the many matters of history and faith which the two Churches had in common, spoke of their substantial oneness in doctrine, polity, and usage, and referred to the time which had elapsed since the division occurred as having removed the most active causes of difference, and with them the most formidable obstacles to the establishment of fellowship. The addresses were received with favor, and were referred, together with the general subject of fraternal relations with the Methodist Episcopal Church, to a committee of nine persons, who were directed to prepare a suitable response. Before the committee had an opportunity to report, the following resolution was unanimously adopted:

Whereas, The message of love and brotherly kindness from the Methodist Episcopal Church has been cordially received, and has been referred to a committee of nine, who, in due time will formally and fraternally reply thereto:

Resolved, That we regret that the distinguished messengers sent by that Church cannot remain to await the presentation and reception of that report; but, understanding that they leave us to-day, we are unwilling that they should return home without carrying with them the knowledge of our appreciation of their Christian, courteous, and fraternal bearing among us, and our wishes and prayers for their future happiness and prosperity.

The response was reported by the committee May 22d, and was adopted on the following day, after full discussion and slight amendment. After speaking of the pleasure with which the visit and addresses of the Northern delegates had been received, it said: " We are called upon by the terms of the action of their General Conference to consider measures necessary ' to prepare the way for the opening of formal fraternity.' Every transaction and utterance of our past history pledges us to regard favorably and to meet promptly this initial response to our long-expressed desire." It then gave a review of the past action of the Church South in this direction. The General Conference of 1846 delegated Dr. Lovick Pierce to visit the Northern General Conference in 1848, and tender to that body its Christian regards and salutations. He was met by a resolution declaring the existence of "serious questions and difficulties between the two bodies," and declining to enter into fraternal relations. He replied with an address to the Northern General Conference, in which he said that the Church South could never renew the offer of fraternal relations, but that the proposition could be renewed at any time by the Northern Church. The General Conference (South) of 1850 also declared, by resolution, that it could never renew the offer it had made, but that it would at all times entertain any proposition coming from the Methodist Episcopal Church, whether by written communication or by delegation, having for its object friendly relations, "and predicated on the rights granted to us by the plan of separation, adopted in New York in 1844." In May, 1869, the bishops of the Methodist Episcopal Church invited the bishops of the Church South to confer with them as to "the propriety, practicability, and

method of reunion." The Southern bishops declined to consider this subject, but invited attention to the cultivation of fraternal relations, and suggested the removal of causes of strife. The Northern bishops having, in their communication, spoken of the Church South as having separated from the Methodist Episcopal Church, the Southern bishops replied to this point:

Allow us, in all kindness, brethren, to remind you, and to keep the important fact of history prominent, that we separated from you in no sense in which you did not separate from us. The separation was by compact and mutual; and nearer approaches to each other can be conducted, with hope of a successful issue, only on this basis.

A deputation from the Northern Church visited the General Conference (South) of 1870, proposing to treat with it, in the name of the Methodist Episcopal Church, on the subject of union, but they were not commissioned by their General Conference, and could not act authoritatively. Their communication was received, however. The General Conference (South), in reply, approved the action taken by the bishops the year before, and expressed its judgment that even had the commission been clothed with authority in the premises, the true interest of the Church of Christ would require the maintenance of a separate and distinct organization, but uttered the desire that the day might soon come when proper Christian sentiments and fraternal relations between the two branches of the Church should be permanently established. The address continued:

Thus stood the case when the distinguished delegates of the Methodist Episcopal Church, duly authorized by their General Conference of 1872, brought us their fraternal greetings. We hail them with pleasure, and embrace the opportunity at length afforded us of entering into negotiations to secure tranquillity and fellowship to our alienated communions upon a permanent basis, and alike honorable to all.

We deem it proper for the attainment of the object sought to guard against all misapprehension. Organic union is not involved in fraternity. In our view of the subject, the reasons for the separate existence of these two branches of Methodism are such as to make corporate union undesirable and impracticable. The events and experiences of the last thirty years have confirmed us in the conviction that such a consummation is demanded by neither reason nor charity. We believe that each Church can do its work and fulfil its mission most effectively by maintaining an independent organization. The causes which led to the division in 1844, upon a plan of separation mutually agreed upon, have not disappeared. Some of them exist in their original form and force, and others have been modified but not diminished.

The first cause mentioned was the size of the connection, and the extent of the territory covered by it.

Another cause of division was, that the two Churches differed in regard to the powers of the General Conference. On this point it was said:

It will be remembered that the last formal deliverance of the Southern representatives, in the united General Conference, was a protest against the power claimed for and exercised by that highest judicatory of the Church. The Northern members, who were a controlling majority, claimed for it prerogatives which seemed to us both dangerous and unconstitutional. In their view the General Conference is supreme. Although restricted in the exercises of its power by a constitution, it is the judge of the restrictions, and is thus practically unlimited. In our view, the General Conference is a body of limited powers. It cannot absorb the functions of other and coördinate branches of the Church government, and there are methods by which all constitutional questions may be brought to a satisfactory issue. Each Church still maintains its own construction of these fundamental questions. They are not theoretical merely, but very practical in their bearing. Were the two Methodisms organically united, it would lead to serious collision, and expose the minority to harassing legislation, if not to oppression.

The existence of slavery in the Southern States furnished an occasion, with its connected questions, fruitful of disturbance. The position of Southern Methodists on that subject was held to have been scriptural. The address continued:

Our opinions have undergone no change. We held ourselves in readiness to carry the gospel to the bond and to the free. Missions to the slaves constituted a large part of our work. Many of our ministers labored in this field, and much of our means was expended on it. These labors were eminently owned of God. At the beginning of the late war, a quarter of a million of negroes were in the communion of our Church, and thousands of their children were receiving catechetical instruction. The societies organized in the Southern States during the last ten years by our Northern brethren, and the members which swell their statistics, are made up largely of those who in slavery had been converted by our instrumentality.

The Church South had now, without abandoning this work, adapted its methods to the changed condition of the colored members, and at their own request had set them off into an independent ecclesiastical body. The Northern brethren had pursued a different plan, and had organized mixed conferences, mixed congregations, and mixed schools. "We do not ask them," says the address, "to adopt our plan. We could not adopt theirs."

But, while the General Conference (South) was clear and final in its declarations against the union of the two Methodisms, it welcomed measures looking to the removal of obstacles in the way of unity and peace, the existence of which obstacles was generally known. No adjustment could be considered by it that ignored the plan of separation of 1844. By that plan the Southern Church held all its church-houses, cemeteries, school-buildings, and other property, which had been acquired before the division. Under it, it had claimed and recovered its portion of the common fund in the Book Concerns at New York and Cincinnati. The question of its validity had been taken by the Northern Church to the Supreme Court of the United States, and affirmed by that tribunal without a dissenting voice. However others might regard that instrument, it was too important in its application to the

status and security of the Church South to be lightly esteemed by it.

If it should be said that its provisions touching territorial limits have been violated by both parties, we have this to say: We are ready to confer with our Northern brethren on that point. A joint commission having this feature of the compact under revision might reach a solution mutually satisfactory.

The address continued:

Measures preparatory to formal fraternity would be defective that leave out of view questions in dispute between the Methodist Episcopal Church and ourselves. These questions relate to the course pursued by some of their accredited agents while prosecuting their work in the South, and to property which has been taken and held by them to this day against our protest and remonstrance. Although feeling ourselves sorely aggrieved in these things, we stand ready to meet our brethren of the Methodist Episcopal Church in the spirit of Christian candor, and to compose all differences upon the principles of justice and equity. * * *

The report concluded with the following resolutions, which were adopted along with it:

Resolved, That this General Conference has received with pleasure the fraternal greetings of the Methodist Episcopal Church, conveyed to us by their delegates, and that our College of Bishops be and are hereby authorized to appoint a delegation, consisting of two ministers and one layman, to bear our Christian salutations to their next ensuing General Conference.

Resolved, That, in order to remove all obstacles to formal fraternity between the two Churches, our College of Bishops is authorized to appoint a commission, consisting of three ministers and two laymen, to meet a similar commission authorized by the General Conference of the Methodist Episcopal Church, and to adjust all existing difficulties.

The following resolutions, bearing on the same subject, were also adopted just before the adjournment of the General Conference:

Whereas, The discussions and votes of this Conference on the subject of fraternal relations with the Methodist Episcopal Church, and its cognate subjects, present the appearance of essential differences which do not exist: therefore—

Resolved, That upon the subject of fraternal relations with the Methodist Episcopal Church, upon a proper basis, this Conference is a unit.

Resolved, That we are also a unit upon the propriety of appointing a commission, empowered to meet a like commission from the Methodist Episcopal Church, to settle all questions of difficulty between us, and that such settlement is essential to complete fraternity.

Resolved, That the only points of difference between us on this whole subject are the best methods of accomplishing this desired end.

Fraternal greetings were exchanged with the General Conference of the Methodist Protestant Church, in session at Lynchburg, Va. The Rev. Alexander Clark was received and spoke in behalf of the Methodist Church.

A new constitution was adopted for the organization of missions. The Board of Missions, to which is given the charge of the foreign missions, and of all others not provided for by the Annual Conferences, was made to consist of a president, vice-president, secretary, and seventeen managers, to be elected quadrennially by the General Conference, bishops to be *ex officio* members. It was authorized to appropriate money to defray the expenses of its work, and incidental expenses; to provide for the support of superannuated missionaries, and the widows and orphans of missionaries not provided for by any Annual Conferences; to build houses for worship, for schools, and for missionaries; and was directed to make reports of its operations to the General Conference, etc.

The following clause, giving a veto-power to the bishops, having been approved by the requisite majority in the Annual Conference, was incorporated into the Discipline:

When any rule, or regulation, is adopted by the General Conference, which, in the opinion of the bishops, is unconstitutional, the bishops may present to the Conference which passed such rule or regulation their objections thereto, with their reasons, in writing; and if then the General Conference shall, by a two-thirds vote, adhere to its action on said rule or regulation, it shall then take the course prescribed for altering a restricted rule, and if thus passed upon affirmatively, the bishops shall announce that such rule, or regulation, takes effect from that time.

A provision was added to the Discipline for the support of the widows and orphan children of deceased bishops. The election of superintendents of Sunday-schools was vested in the Quarterly Conference, on the nomination of the preacher in charge. An amendment to the general rule in relation to the use of intoxicating liquors was adopted for submission to the Annual Conferences, by which, if it is approved, members will be required to avoid "drunkenness, or drinking spirituous liquors, unless in cases of necessity."

The bishops were requested to address a pastoral letter to the people, bringing prominently before them the pastoral worship of the Church, explaining the action of the General Conference of 1866 respecting class-meetings; emphasizing the obligation to read the Scriptures; deprecating the increasing indulgence in such divisions "as cannot be taken in the name of the Lord Jesus;" and expressing disapprobation of "operatic performances in our churches, which drown the sense of our hymns, and utterly destroy congregational singing."

III. COLORED METHODIST EPISCOPAL CHURCH IN AMERICA.—The report of this Church, made in May, 1874, showed it to have fifteen Annual Conferences, 607 traveling preachers, 518 local preachers, 74,719 members, 535 Sunday-schools, 1,102 Sunday-school teachers, and 49,955 Sunday-school scholars.

The *General Conference* of the Colored Methodist Episcopal Church in America, met at Louisville, Ky., August 5th. The bishops presented an address reviewing the condition of the Church. Many recommended that as few changes as possible be made in the Book of Discipline. They invited serious attention to the affairs of the Book Concern. It had been established at Memphis, Tenn., by the previous General Conference, but had not been successfully operated there. The Book Committee had adjudged it necessary to remove it to Louisville, Ky., and had so removed it. It has since been successful, has paid its way, and returned some dividends.

The bishops had been appointed at the last session of the General Conference a committee to mature a plan of education. They reported that the Tennessee and Kentucky Conferences had bought a lot in Louisville for the purpose of establishing a school, and had invited the other conferences to join them. Steps had been taken toward erecting a building. The General Conference resolved that this contemplated school be made the central university of the Church, and that all the Annual Conferences be requested to give it their aid and patronage. Measures were also adopted looking to the establishment of a school for the education of young women.

Action was taken to further the prosecution of mission-work, and the hope was expressed that in the course of the next ten years the Church might be able to send missionaries to Africa. For the present the mission-work of the Church is confined to the home field. The publication of a monthly Sunday-school paper was determined upon.

A fundamental principle was adopted at the organization of this Church, that none but persons of the colored or negro race should be members of it. A resolution was offered at the present Conference to modify this rule, so as to permit the admission of others (Indians were particularly contemplated), but it was almost unanimously rejected.

The Conference was visited by a deputation representing the Louisville District Conference of the Methodist Episcopal Church South. A resolution of thanks was voted the District Conference "for this expression of their love," in which was also embodied the expression of gratitude to the Church South for its action in organizing and setting apart the colored Church, and of the desire and wish of the General Conference for the perpetuation of friendly relations with the members of that Church, "as Christians and the people of God." The following resolution on fraternal relations with other churches was adopted:

Resolved, That a committee on fraternal greeting be appointed by this Conference; that, should any Christian Church offer fraternal relations, said committee is also authorized to effect the same; that the committee is also authorized, if any other Church should offer a union with our Church, to effect that union with them, without relinquishing any of the rights or principles of our Church.

IV. METHODIST PROTESTANT CHURCH.—Statistical reports were made to the General Conference of this Church, in May, 1874, from twelve conferences, as follows: Number of ministers, 500; of members, 40,122; value of church property, $999,065. No reports were received from eight conferences.

The *General Conference* of the Methodist Protestant Church met at Lynchburg, Va., May 1st. The Rev. L. W. Bates, D. D., of Baltimore, was chosen president. The most important business transacted by this body related to the subject of reunion with the Methodist Church. The Rev. Alexander Clark and the Rev. Alexander Robinson were present, as fraternal delegates from that Church, and delivered addresses expressing their own desire for reunion, and the belief that it was favored by the preachers and members of their denomination. They also presented a letter from the Hon. Francis H. Pierpont, President of the last General Conference of the Methodist Church, expressing similar views.

The following action was taken on the subject:

Whereas, This General Conference is satisfied that there is a growing desire on the part of the membership of the Methodist Protestant Church to hold a General Convention to take into consideration certain changes in the constitution of the Church: therefore—

Resolved, That we recommend the Annual Conferences composing the Methodist Protestant Church to unite unanimously in a call for a General Convention, for the purpose of effecting such changes in the second, tenth, and fourteenth articles of the constitution of the Methodist Protestant Church as may be deemed by said convention necessary; together with such alterations in all other articles of the constitution and Book of Discipline as they may judge proper.

Resolved, That said convention shall meet at Ahingdon, Va., on the first Friday in May, 1878.

Resolved, That a commission of nine persons be appointed by this General Conference to confer with any like commission from any Methodist body in America, who may signify a desire to confer with them upon the subject of union with the Methodist Protestant Church, and especially with a commission of nine to be appointed by the General Conference of the Methodist Church, which has made overtures to us for a reunion.

Further, "believing it to be the desire of the members of the Methodist Church to effect a union of the Methodist Protestant Churches upon terms which shall be alike agreeable and honorable to each, and to submit the terms of union to the General Convention," the Conference provided for the immediate appointment of the commission, to consist of ministers and laymen. It was constituted as follows: From Maryland, L. W. Bates, S. B. Southerland, O. Hammond; from West Virginia, E. F. Westfall, U. V. Chichester; from North Carolina, R. H. Wills, S. Simpson; from Virginia, M. F. Peoples, M. D.; from Tennessee, B. F. Duggan, M. D. A fraternal messenger was received from the Methodist Episcopal Church, and a fraternal communication from the General Conference of the Methodist Episcopal Church South, in session at Louisville, Ky.

Those sections of the Discipline which authorized the order of deacons, and prescribed a form for the ordination of deacons, were stricken out. Provision was made that the General Conference may appoint ministers as presidents, professors, or agents in educational institutions, as editors or agents of religious periodicals and newspapers, or as chaplains, without such appointments changing the rela-

tions of the appointees to their Annual Conferences. A rule was made that "Sabbath-school superintendents shall be elected by the teachers and officers of the school, subject, however, to the confirmation of the Church." A resolution was adopted declaring the "manufacture, sale, and use of intoxicating liquors as a beverage, or the lending of one's influence, by signature or otherwise, in the procurement of any license to sell alcoholic beverages," to be, in the opinion of the General Conference, "manifestly in opposition to the teachings of God's word." A reorganization of the Book Concern, and of the method of conducting its business, was effected. A report on education was adopted which urged the duty of encouraging popular education as necessary to the success of a representative Church, and declared the importance of educating ministers, and of establishing denominational institutions of learning. Yadkin College, North Carolina, the West Virginia Institute, and Western Maryland College, were represented favorably. The theological department of the latter institution was recommended to the patronage of the entire Church. The enlargement of the same institution as a central university was also advised. An offer was received from the trustees of Bowdon College, Georgia, to transfer their institution to the Church.

V. PRIMITIVE METHODISTS.—The following is a summary of the statistics of the Primitive Methodist churches in the United States: *Eastern Conference.*—Number of circuits, 17; of members approved, 977; of probationers, 239; whole number of members, 1,216; number of traveling preachers, 16; of local preachers, 88; of class-leaders, 72; of churches, 23; of other preaching-places, 21; of Sunday-schools, 27; of scholars in the same, 2,134; of Sunday-school teachers, 428; value of church property, $100,404.49; amount of debt on the same, $28,593.70; amount collected during the year for missions, $733.74; income of the contingent fund (for the conference year), $111.59.

Western Conference.—Number of circuits and missions, 19; of members approved, 1,534; of probationers, 130; whole number of members, 1,664; number of traveling preachers, 16; of local preachers, 86; of class-leaders, 83; of churches, 37; of other preaching-places, 42; of parsonages, 11; of Sunday-schools, 45; of scholars in the same, 2,781; of Sunday-school teachers, 481; value of church property, $67,444.89; amount of collections during the year for missions, $1,098.50; for the superannuated preachers' fund, $145.57; for the conference fund, $54.49; for the Bible cause, $38.25. The total amount of salaries paid to ministers was $8,395.35. The whole number of approved members and probationers in the two Conferences is 2,880.

The *Eastern Conference* met at Mount Carmel, Northumberland county, Pa., May 13th. Charles Spurr was elected president. The following test for membership in the churches was adopted: "Profession of religion, attendance at class-meetings according to discipline, or regular attendance on means of grace; and to be supporters of the cause of God." The Conference resolved that in future the salary of a minister in full connection should be *not less* than $630 a year; and that circuits able to pay more without injury to connectional funds be requested to do so. Strong resolutions were adopted in favor of the temperance movement. The *Western Conference* met in its thirtieth session at Dodgeville, Wis., May 21st. The Rev. J. Sharp was chosen president. New rules were enacted in regard to the new constitution of the Conference and lay delegation, to the following effect: "1. That all existing regulations on delegates to the Conferences be repealed; 2. That in future the Annual Conference shall be composed of the connectional officers, of all the traveling preachers in good standing and in full work, and one lay delegate from each charge, who shall be selected at the third quarterly meeting. Circuits (not missions) having one hundred members, or more, may send two lay delegates." Action was taken requiring preachers and quarterly meetings building churches to have the property properly secured to connectional uses. Resolutions were adopted condemning intemperance and the use of tobacco.

VI. FREE METHODIST CHURCH.—The *General Conference* of the Free Methodist Church met at Albion, N. Y., in October. The general superintendent, in an address at the opening of the session, described the progress which had been made in the work of the Church during the preceding four years. New fields had been opened in the South, and in these, as well as in the North and West, the Church was making considerable advances, and was represented as exerting a powerful influence. The General Conference having secured an act of incorporation, the Rev. Joseph Travis, the Rev. J. E. Terrill, O. P. Rogers, and J. L. Ward, were elected a Board of Trustees. A general missionary board was organized, to have its central office in New York City. It is to consist of the superintendents of the Church, two ministers, and two laymen. The course of study for ministers was revised and improved. The Conference decided to elect two general superintendents, the Rev. B. T. Roberts, of the General Conference, New York, and the Rev. E. P. Hart, of Michigan, were chosen to that office. Two new conferences, the Wisconsin and the Iowa Conferences, were organized. The Illinois Conference was made to embrace the entire State of Illinois, and the city and vicinity of St. Louis, Mo.

VII. WESLEYAN METHODIST CHURCH IN CANADA AND EASTERN BRITISH AMERICA.—The report on *Sunday-schools* submitted to the Wesleyan Conference of Canada showed that there were 1,002 such schools, with 9,617 teachers, and 71,583 scholars. The receipts of the children's fund were reported to have been $24,-

144, and the payments on account of it $23,-977. The income of the superannuation fund was given at $27,627; of the contingent fund, $7,479. The missionary fund had increased upward of $6,000. The cash-sales of the Book Concern had increased during the year $5,000, and its assets exceeded all liabilities $55,276.

The financial prospects of the *university* were represented to be in a very promising condition. The agent had obtained $31,000 of subscriptions since the preceding Conference; the debt had been reduced to $8,412.25, and a bequest and a gift of $10,000 each had been made to the endowment fund.

The fifty-first annual session of the *Conference of the Wesleyan Methodist Church in Canada* was held at Hamilton, beginning June 3d. The Rev. S. D. Rice, D. D., presided. Returns were made as follows of the vote of the quarterly meetings upon the questions submitted to them concerning the division of the Conference into Annual Conferences, confederation with the Conference of Eastern British America, and union with the Methodist New Connection. The number of quarterly meetings entitled to vote was 418, of which 280 were required to make up the two-thirds majority necessary to carry the proposed changes into effect. They had voted, concerning confederation with the Conference of Eastern British America, 370 yeas, 2 nays; concerning union with the Methodist New Connection, 360 yeas, 12 nays; concerning the surrender of the veto-power, hitherto possessed by the quarterly meetings, and the acceptance by the laity of representation in the General Conference instead thereof, 339 yeas, 33 nays; on a change in the constitution, proposed to take effect if union should be effected, 341 yeas, 31 nays; on a change of the constitution of the Canadian Conference, proposed to take effect if union should not be carried, 305 yeas, 67 nays. The president stated that official instructions had been received from the Conference of Eastern British America that all the propositions submitted in connection with the plans of union had been accepted almost unanimously. A deputation was received from the Conference of the Methodist New Connection, who asked the consent of the Conference to an alteration which that body desired to have made in the 23d section of the Articles of Union. As originally adopted, the section in question read: "Any act of the General Conference affecting the rights and privileges of the Annual Conference shall become law only when it secures a majority of two-thirds of the members of the General Conference, who may vote thereon, and also a majority of the members of the several ensuing Annual Conferences who may be present and vote thereon."

The Conference of the New Connection asked that the latter clause be omitted, and in its stead there be inserted: "Provided also that such act be not disapproved of by a majority of the next ensuing Annual Conferences." The Conference accepted the proposed modification.

It was determined to hold the General Conference in Toronto, in September. The three Annual Conferences, into which the Wesleyan body in America has been divided, met for organization immediately after the adjournment of the Conference. Sixty-three lay delegates were for the first time admitted as members to the Conference, and took part in its proceedings.

The *Wesleyan Methodist Conference of Eastern British America* met at Charlottetown, Prince Edward Island. Reports were presented of the votes of the Quarterly Boards upon the questions submitted to them regarding the proposed union with the Conferences of Canada and of the New Connection, and the adoption of lay representation. On each section the vote was, yeas 125, nays 3. Three boards had declined to vote. The modification of the plan of union, which was asked by the Conference of the New Connection, was agreed to, and the union was declared carried. The Nova Scotia Conference was organized July 3d.

VIII. METHODIST NEW CONNECTION IN CANADA.—The forty-sixth annual *Conference of the Methodist New Connection in Canada* met at Milton, May 20th. The Rev. D. Savage was chosen president. The Executive Committee presented a report giving the returns of the votes of the Quarterly Boards, which met in November, 1873, on the question of union with the Wesleyan Conference, and also a number of communications which had passed between them and the Missionary Committee of the Parent Conference in England. The English Committee had endeavored to defeat the union movement, and to that end sent over messengers to present its views to the Canadian Churches. The Executive Committee had objected to this action, and protested against it as a violation of an agreement which had been entered into between the representatives of the English and Canadian Conferences, that no attempt should be made to influence the decision of the quarterly meetings until they should have opportunity to record their votes on the subject. The report of the votes showed that fifty-six quarterly meetings had declared in favor of union with the Wesleyan Conference, and nineteen against it. The subject was then referred to a committee "to consider the connectional situation," composed of representatives of the union and the anti-union parties. This committee agreed upon the following report as a final settlement of the differences on the subject existing within the Connection, and it was cordially adopted, with one opposing vote:

Whereas, A majority of the quarterly meetings have adopted the basis of the proposed union submitted by our last Conference:

Resolved, That this Conference hereby ratifies and adopts the basis of union, provided that our interpretation of the twenty-third clause in the basis of union be approved by the Wesleyan Conference,

viz.: Any act of the General Conference affecting the rights and privileges of the Annual Conferences shall become law only when it secures a majority of two-thirds of the members of the General Conference who may be present and vote thereon: provided, also, that such act be not disapproved of by a majority of the next ensuing Annual Conference; also, that a respectful statement, by deputation or otherwise, of the whole case be submitted to the English Conference: also that a deputation be appointed to the next Wesleyan Conference, soliciting their approval of our interpretation of said twenty-third clause.

In accordance with this resolution, a deputation was sent to the Wesleyan Conference to ask its approval of the proposed change in the Articles of Union, and a memorial was prepared to be sent to the English Conference. An extra meeting of the Conference was appointed to be held at Milton, in August, to consider the action that might be taken by the Wesleyan and English Conferences on the questions submitted to them.

Resolutions were adopted in favor of total abstinence from the use of intoxicating liquors, and of a prohibitory liquor law; also against the use of tobacco.

The Conference met a second time, pursuant to adjournment, at Milton, August 12th, to hear the reports of the deputations who had been appointed to visit the English Conference and the Wesleyan Conference of Canada. The deputation to the English Conference reported verbally that they had been well received, and that the Conference had given its consent to the severance of the Canadian branch of the Connection from the parent body and its union with the Wesleyan Conference. The deputation to the Wesleyan Conference reported that that Conference had readily accepted the amendment, or new construction, which the New Connection had suggested to be made to the articles of union. The following resolution was then unanimously adopted:

Whereas, This Conference, at its former session, held in Milton on May 23, 1874, did agree to adopt the basis of union, on condition that the Wesleyan Conference of Canada, the Wesleyan Conference of Eastern British America, and the Methodist New Connection Conference of England would accept our declaration of union, with the interpretation of clause 23 in the basis then agreed to; and whereas these conditions have since been fulfilled by all the contracting parties, this Conference hereby declares its final acceptance of the terms of union between the Wesleyan Methodist Church of Canada and the Methodist New Connection Church of Canada, all necessary legal provisions to be determined by the General Conference of the United Wesleyan Methodist Church of Canada.

Another resolution, which was passed, recognized the services which the English New Connection had through many years rendered to their Canadian mission, and the liberality with which they had sustained it. Delegates were elected to the General Conference of the United Wesleyan Methodist Church of Canada, after which a final adjournment was made.

IX. METHODIST CHURCH OF CANADA.—The results of the latest estimates of the number of ministers and members of the three bodies which have united in the Methodist Church of Canada are embodied in the following table :

CHURCHES.	Ministers.	Members.	Probationers.
Wesleyan Methodist Church in Canada........................	695	69,212	4,489
Wesleyan Methodist Church in Eastern British America....	204	17,580	3,370
Methodist New Connection Church in Canada............	119	7,587	275
Total	1,018	94,389	8,134

The *first General Conference of the United Wesleyan Methodist Church of Canada* met in the Metropolitan Wesleyan Methodist Church, Toronto, September 16, 1874. The Hon. L. A. Wilmot, ex-Governor of New Brunswick, was chosen chairman *pro tem.* Subsequently, the Rev. Dr. Edgerton Ryerson was elected President of the General Conference for four years. It was decided that persons who had been elected as alternative delegates should be admitted as members. On the third day of the session a resolution constituting the Conference was adopted.

At a subsequent stage of the proceedings it was decided that the name of the Church should be THE METHODIST CHURCH OF CANADA. A General Conference seal was adopted, to have upon it the words, "The General Conference of the Methodist Church of Canada. The best of all is God is with us." The Rev. Mr. Robinson, who was present as the representative of the English Conference of the Methodist New Connection, addressed the Conference, and expressed the acquiescence of that body in the union.

The attention of the Conference was mainly directed to the adjustment of the connectional interests and enterprises, hitherto distributed among three distinct conferences, so as to conform them to the changed conditions resultant upon consolidation. The constitution, boundaries, and functions of the six Annual Conferences were defined. Three of these conferences, the Toronto, Montreal, and London Conferences, are in the Provinces of Ontario and Quebec; and three, the New Brunswick and Prince Edward Island, the Nova Scotia, and the Newfoundland conferences, are in the Eastern Provinces. The Annual Conferences were left with all the rights, powers, and privileges they already possessed, except such as had been vested in the General Conference, including those of choosing their presidents, secretaries, and chairmen of districts by ballot, from among their own members, of examining ministerial characters, and of stationing ministers. Provision was made for the adjustment, for the present, of the boundaries of the circuits of the former Wesleyan and New Connection Conferences where they may overlap each other. The missionary committee were

authorized to take the income arising from the New Connection Missionary Society, and, considering the independent circuits as domestic missions, to make equitable grants to them. Provisions were also made for effecting the permanent adjustment of the boundaries of circuits ; for the disposal of surplus Church property ; and for the consolidation of the funds of the Wesleyan and New Connection Churches. Plans were devised for adjusting the relations of the General Conference to the educational institutions of the Connection. These consisted of one university, five colleges, and numerous academies. An Educational Society was recommended ; an Educational Institute for the French Canadians in the Province of Quebec was proposed. It was stated that the colleges and schools at present in operation required to maintain them fifteen thousand dollars a year more than their present income. A scheme was adopted to regulate the tenure of Church property, and a standing committee was appointed to carry out its provisions.

A constitution was adopted for a General Conference Missionary Society, membership in which should be determined by subscriptions of four dollars a year and upward. Existing missionary societies were recognized as auxiliaries, and provision was made for district and Annual Conference societies. The income of the Missionary Society for the current year was reported to have been $150,000. The Book Committee was constituted, to consist of thirty-seven ministerial and lay members, to be selected proportionately from the several Annual Conferences. It is to be divided into Eastern and Western sections, which will meet yearly, and it will itself meet as a whole at the time and place of holding the next General Conference, and make a full report of its doings. The book and printing establishments at Toronto and Halifax were ordered continued, and action was taken toward establishing an agency at Montreal. A committee was appointed to revise and prepare the materials for a new hymn-book for the use of the denomination, and submit the results of its work to the next General Conference. The salaries of unmarried ministers were fixed at three hundred dollars a year, and the minimum stipend of married ministers at seven hundred and fifty dollars a year, including house-rent and all other costs. The Conference was visited by fraternal delegates from several other Methodist Churches in Canada and the United States, and from the British Wesleyan and New Connection Conferences. It adopted addresses and appointed fraternal delegates to the General Conferences of the Methodist Episcopal Churches in Canada and the United States, of the Methodist Episcopal Church South, of the Methodist New Connection in England, of the Primitive Methodist Church in Canada, and of the British Wesleyan Connection.

Au address was also adopted to Lord Dufferin, Governor-General of Canada.

X. METHODIST EPISCOPAL CHURCH IN CANADA.—The reports of the three Conferences of this Church show a total of 438 churches, 236 traveling preachers, and 22,641 members. The number of parsonages is given at 134. The total value of churches and parsonages is estimated to be $800,550. The entire receipts for missions in 1874 were $13,304.15, or $913.33 more than the receipts for the previous year.

The *General Conference of the Methodist Episcopal Church in Canada* met at Napance, Ontario, August 26th. Bishop Richardson presided. It was decided that the first business in order should be the election of an additional bishop. The Rev. John Morrison Reid, D. D., one of the missionary secretaries of the Methodist Episcopal Church in the United States, was chosen to that office. He declined to accept, and a second election was held. The Rev. A. Carman, D. D., President of Albért College, was chosen, and, accepting, was ordained bishop.

Provision was made for the admission of lay delegates to the Conference.

The following new rule was adopted to govern the appointment of presiding elders: "That each Annual Conference shall elect two members from each district, by and with whose consent the bishop shall appoint the presiding elders."

Provision was made respecting the appointment of a layman to the office of book-agent, in case the Conference or the Book Committee should be disposed to make it. The committee who had been appointed by the previous General Conference, four years before, on the subject of Methodist union, made a report relating the steps which they had taken in negotiating with the other Methodist bodies of the Dominion, and announcing their failure up to the present sime to accomplish the object sought. They spoke of the union which had been effected between the Wesleyan and the New Connection Methodists, and recommended the appointment of a committee to confer with other Methodist bodies on the subject. A committee was accordingly appointed, to consider and formulate a basis of union "with the Methodists of the Dominion, or of the Continent, or any branch or section thereof." The committee consists of the bishop, the secretary of the Conference (Rev. Michael Benson), Thomas Webster, J. Gardiner, T. B. Brown, S. Morrison, W. Pirritte, S. M. Thomas, D. Wilson, J. H. Andrews, and J. C. Huffman.

A deputation was appointed to convey the greeting of the Conference to the first General Conference of the United Wesleyan Methodist Church of Canada, which was to meet in Toronto on the 16th of September. A constitution was adopted for the Missionary Society of the Methodist Episcopal Church in Canada, and trustees were appointed to secure the incorporation of such a society.

XI. PRIMITIVE METHODIST CHURCH IN CANADA.—This Church had, in 1874, 89 ministers, 5,618 members, and 1,163 probationers.

The *Conference of the Primitive Methodist Connection in Canada* met at Toronto, June 5th. The Rev. S. Antliff presided. A message was received from the English Conference, announcing that that body had made a grant of five thousand dollars to the Canadian work. The Conference decided to undertake to establish a special fund for the purpose of opening a mission at once in Manitoba, and to instruct the Missionary Committee to open such a mission as soon as a guarantee fund of five hundred dollars for each of the next five years should have been secured. A meeting was immediately held in the interest of the proposed mission, at which the whole sum required as a condition for its establishment was secured.

XII. BIBLE CHRISTIAN CHURCH IN CANADA.—This Church was estimated to have in Canada, in 1874, 72 ministers and 5,700 members.

The *Twentieth Conference of the Bible Christian Church in Canada* met in London, June 4th. The Rev. William Hooper was elected President. The following items relating to the state of the connection were reported: Increase—itinerant preachers, 5; churches, 8; other places of worship, 4; admitted during the year, 530; deaths, 8; on trial, 433; approved members, 137; in church-fellowship, 570. Decrease—local preachers, 21; removals, 128. The entire value of the church property was reported to be $306,379, against which were debts to the amount of $61,272, leaving a value over incumbrances of $245,106. Of this amount, at least $175,000 was said to have been accumulated within the preceding ten years. The churches provided accommodation for 28,542 persons. The attendance upon worship was good. The report on Sunday-schools showed the number of scholars to be 8,542, and of teachers 1,126.

Other Methodist churches in Canada are: *The British Methodist Episcopal Church* (African), 47 ministers, 2,800 members; and *The Independent Methodist Church*, 7 ministers, 500 members.

XIII. WESLEYAN METHODIST CONNECTION.—The chief ecclesiastical court of this Church is, by the Rev. John Wesley's Deed of Declaration, enrolled in Chancery and dated February 28, 1784, defined to be "The Yearly Conference of the People called Methodists," and to consist of "Preachers and Expounders of God's Holy Word, commonly called Methodist Preachers." The number of members forming this Conference is one hundred, but, besides these, there are present at its meetings other ministers, authorized by their district meetings to attend.

The *Conference of the Wesleyan Methodist Connection* met at Camborne, Cornwall, July 29th. The preliminary meetings of the Committee of Review began Friday, July 24th.

The Committee on *General Education* reported the number of day-schools under local committees to be 886; number of day-schools not under local committees, 20; number of scholars, 178,717, an increase from the previous year of 7,845; average attendance upon the day-schools, 116,332; number of Sunday-schools, 5,787; of teachers and officers in the same, 110,123, showing an increase from the previous year of 1,667; number of scholars, 688,986, showing an increase of 22,220. *Increase of the Schools:* Amount of "children's pence" during the year, £71,743; amount of Government annual grants, £66,518; received from subscriptions, etc., £22,452; total income, £160,173, or £13,126 more than the income of the previous year.

The *Chapel Committee* reported that they had sanctioned during the year 385 erections and enlargements, by which nearly 2,000 additional sittings were provided at a cost of £337,000. The total amount that had been expended during the year upon erections and the reduction of debts was £378,000. The sum of £320,000 had been contributed for these purposes, or £80,000 more than had been received the year before. There were now 5,712 chapels, with 1,503,797 sittings, an increase of 1,430 chapels and 518,075 sittings since 1851.

The Rev. William Morley Punshon, LL. D., was elected President of the Conference.

A plan was adopted for the organization of a connectional Sunday-school union.

Regulations were adopted in regard to local preaching, having in view the encouragement and assistance of suitable men in preparing for this sphere of work, and the raising of the standard of qualification.

A concentration of the system of education at the New Kingswood and the Woodhouse Grove Schools was determined upon.

A committee had been appointed by the previous Conference to consider the course which should be taken in reference to persons not members of the society who may desire to receive the Lord's Supper at the hands of connectional ministers. The number of persons of this class was found to be increasing rapidly, and it was considered desirable to adopt some plan of action to bring them under pastoral influence and induce them to become members. The committee made a report recommending the following regulations to be observed toward such persons: "1. They should in the first instance be seen by one of the ministers resident in the circuit, and conversed with as to their spiritual condition. 2. They should be met or pastorally visited by one of the ministers periodically, at least once a quarter. 3. The names of all such persons should be recorded in a proper book, to be kept by one of the ministers. 4. Communicants' tickets should be given to such persons by one of the ministers quarterly. The list of such communicants kept by any minister should be handed to his successor. 6. No such communicant shall be eligible to be a member of the leaders' or quarterly meeting." A seventh rule authorized the leader to withhold tickets in the case of any communicant against whose character and conduct any reasonable objection should be entertained. The recommendation of the committee was sent to the district meetings for their action.

The following is the summary of the statistics of the British and subordinate and affiliated Conferences of this body, as officially published in connection with the minutes of the British Conference for 1874:

CONFERENCES.	Members.	On Trial.	Ministers.	On Trial.	Supernumeraries.
I. BRITISH CONFERENCE:					
Great Britain	351,645	24,794	1,315	221	226
Ireland and Irish Missions	20,040	828	137	23	23
Foreign Missions	73,700	7,279	243 *	113 *	8 *
II. FRENCH CONFERENCE	1,857	155	23 †	1 †	3 †
III. AUSTRALASIAN CONFERENCE	60,571	6,885	299	61	23
Total	507,813	39,941	2,017	419	283

The numbers of ministers in connection with the Conferences of Canada and Eastern British America, which have heretofore been given in connection with the general summaries, are omitted from the present one, the connection of those Conferences with the British Conference having been dissolved.

The *Irish Wesleyan Conference* is subordinate to the British Conference, and its returns as to numbers and the condition of the funds are included in the statistical reports of the latter body. A separation of the accounts was made in 1873, so far as they concerned the auxiliary fund for worn-out ministers and widows, and the sum of £20,000 was allotted to the Irish Conference as an offset to the claims its members had on the general fund. At the

meeting of the Conference in 1874 the sum of £10,000 was added to this amount by subscriptions from the Irish laity. During the year ending in June, 1874, £9,133 were raised for the home mission and contingent fund, and £9,372 were expended on its account; the receipts of the General Educational Committee were £1,550, and their expenditures £1,449.

The *Irish Conference* met at Dublin, June 8th. The Rev. George T. Pecks presided. A committee had been appointed by the Conference of 1873, to meet a committee of the Primitive Wesleyan Methodist Conference, with reference to bringing the two Churches into closer

* Exclusive of missionaries in Ireland.
† The French ministers who are employed in the Channel Islands district are *not* included in these returns.

relations, and ultimate union. The committee reported that they had had several meetings during the year, with satisfactory results. The principal question to be adjusted was that of representation of the laity in the Conference. In the Primitive Wesleyan Church the laity participate equally with the ministers in legislation, and in all proceedings affecting the general interest of the Church. In the Wesleyan Church, the laymen have no part in the Conference itself, but are only permitted to act on the preparatory committees, through which they may recommend legislation, but cannot otherwise govern it. The subject was carefully discussed by the Conference, and a resolution was adopted, "that the prayer of the memorialists should be granted." The Primitive Wesleyan Methodist Conference met at Dublin at the same time with this body. During the session its members were invited to breakfast with the members of the Wesleyan Conference. The best means of extending the salvation of the gospel in Ireland was discussed on the occasion. The proposed union of the two Churches was referred to, but no business was done relative to it, because it was understood that further negotiation should be suspended until the introduction of lay representation into the Irish Conference should be secured.

The anniversary of the *Wesleyan Missionary Society* was held in London, May 4th. The receipts of the society for the year were reported to have been: "Home receipts," £122,-092 7s. 1d.; Foreign receipts (from affiliated conferences and the mission districts), £45,902 14s. 7d.: total, £167,995 1s. 8d. The expenditures had been: General expenditures, including the cost of the Canton and Hankow Missions, and of the missions in Italy and Spain, £154,818 3s. 5d.; for payment of the balance on the mission premises in Paris, £4,778 11s. 2d.; for Rome and Naples, £6,861 12s. 10d.: total, £166,458 7s. 5d.

XIV. METHODIST NEW CONNECTION.—The returns of the members in connection of this denomination, made to the Conference in June, showed a decrease (exclusive of Canada) of 133 members, and an increase of 485 probationers. The amount of collections and subscriptions during the year for the Chapel Fund was reported to have been £698 7s. 9d. Chapel debts, on trust estates, had been paid off, to the amount of upward of £18,000. More than £12,000 had been contributed toward the erection and enlargement of chapels and schools. The increase of the Home Mission Fund, for the year, was reported to have been £1,661 18s. 1d.; the expenditures had been £1,591 7s. 8d. The debt of the fund had been slightly reduced, and was now £404. The total receipts of the year for foreign and colonial missions had been £7,220 6s. 5d., showing a net increase of £1,653 15s. 6d. over the receipts of the previous year. A balance remained over the expenditures of £2,924 17s.

The seventy-eighth Annual Conference of the Methodist New Connection met at Hanley June 15th. The Rev. W. Wilshaw was chosen President. The most important feature of the proceedings related to the request of the Canadian Conference for permission to consummate its projected union with the conferences of the Wesleyan Methodist Church in Canada.

Resolutions were received from several quarterly meetings asking the Conference to consider whether such an alteration in the test of Church-membership could not be safely made as would enable the leaders' meetings of the several societies to recognize and return as members, not only those who meet in class, but all pious persons who stately worship and communicate with them. The question was remitted to the quarterly meetings, with the request that they transmit an expression of their views to the annual committee, to be by them classified and presented to the next Conference.

XV. PRIMITIVE METHODIST CONNECTION.—The following statistics of the Primitive Methodist Connection, including the missions and the colonies, were reported to the Conference, June 3d: Members, 164,660, an increase of 4,002 from 1873; traveling preachers, 1,020; local preachers, 14,838; class-leaders, 9,961; connectional chapels, 3,826; other preaching-places, 2,571; Sunday-schools, 3,536; teachers in the same, 49,887; Sunday-school scholars, 306,333. A later report from the Canada Conference, received after the regular returns were made up, swelled the total increase of members to 4,114. Increase was shown in all the other particulars, except that of class-leaders.

The total value of connectional property was estimated at not less than £1,597,574. Ninety-nine new chapels had been built during the year, at a cost of £87,000. The total increase from chapels was £195,554; sittings were provided for 715,289 persons, but two-thirds of them were not occupied. The debts on chapels had been reduced to the extent of £42,000.

The fifty-fifth Annual Conference of the Primitive Methodist Connection was held at Hull, beginning June 12th. The Rev. W. Rowe was chosen President. The most important topic considered related to the invitation of ministers to stations.

The thirty-first anniversary of the *Primitive Methodist Missionary Society* was held in London, April 28th. The report reviewed in succession the home missions, the colonial stations, and the foreign missions. It showed progress and success in all departments of the work.

UNITED METHODIST FREE CHURCHES.—The statistics of the United Methodist Free Churches for 1874 are as follows: In Great Britain, members, 61,259; persons on trial for membership, 5,650; increase, 581; in the foreign stations, members, 6,112; persons on trial, 545; totals; itinerant ministers, 334; supernumeraries, 24; local preachers, 3,361; class-leaders, 4,312; members, 67,371; on trial, 6,195; removals, 5,960; withdrawals, 2,936; deaths, 1,070; chapels, 1,311; other preaching-rooms, 262; chapels built during the year, 40; chapels enlarged, 10.

The *Chapel Committee* reported to the Annual Assembly that 86 chapels had been built or enlarged, and 13 school-rooms built at a total cost of £62,740, of which £34,920 had been received.

Reports were made to the Annual Assembly of the condition of other benevolent funds as follows: Beneficent and superannuation funds, total amount of capital, £19,576; increase during the year, £1,315.—Children's fund: income, £1,549 10s. 5d.; disbursements, £1,540 4s. 4d. Theological Institute: income, £871 18s. 2d.

The receipts of the Book-Room for business done were reported to have been £6,059, from which a benefit had been derived of £1,125.

The *Annual Assembly* of the United Methodist Free Churches met at Newcastle-on-Tyne, July 29th. The Rev. Joseph Garside was chosen President.

The anniversary of the *Missionary Society* of the United Methodist Free Churches was held in London, April 28th. The Lord-Mayor of London presided. The report of the treasurer showed the receipts of the society for the year to have been: from home resources, £9,501 14s. 10d.; from foreign local contributions, £5,046 19s. 7d.: total, £14,548 14s. 5d. This amount showed an increase of £625 4s. over the receipts of the previous year.

XVII. WESLEYAN REFORM UNION.—The following is a summary of the statistics of the churches of the Wesleyan Reform Union: number of chapels and preaching-places, 256; of preachers, 500; of preachers on trial, 85; of ministers, 16; of leaders, 502; of members, 7,687; of members on trial, 422; of Sunday-schools, 181; of Sunday-school teachers, 3,128; of scholars in Sunday-schools, 18,615; of day-schools, 4.

XVIII. BIBLE CHRISTIANS.—The statistics of this denomination are as follows: Number of itinerant preachers, 272; of local preachers, 1,747; of chapels, 873; of members, 35,690; of persons on trial for membership, 1,132; of Sunday-school teachers, 9,529; of Sunday-school scholars, 49,407. These returns show a considerable increase in all the departments.

MEXICO (ESTADOS UNIDOS DE MÉJICO, Aztec, *Mexitli*), a federal republic occupying the southwestern portion of the North American Continent, comprised between latitude 15° and 32° 27' north, and longitude 86° 34' and 117° west. Its boundaries are: North, by the United States (California, Arizona, New Mexico, and Texas); east by the Gulf of Mexico, the Caribbean Sea, and Balize; south by Guatemala; and south and west by the Pacific Ocean.

The present territorial division of the republic is into twenty-seven States, one Federal District, and one Territory, which, with their areas, population (in 1871), and capitals are as follows:

STATES.	Area in sq. m.	Population.	Capitals.
Aguas Calientes...	2,216	140,630	Aguas Calientes.
Campeachy........	26,083	80,366	Campeachy.
Chiapas...........	16,760	193,987	Chiapas.
Chihuahua........	105,295	179,971	Chihuahua.
Coahuila..........	98,397	98,397	Saltillo.
Colima...........	2,892	63,333	Colima.
Durango..........	42,643	185,077	Durango.
Guanajuato.......	11,180	874,043	Guanajuato.
Guerrero.........	24,226	300,029	Guerrero.
Hidalgo...... ...	8,480	404,207	Pachuca.
Jalisco...........	48,697	924,580	Guadalajara.
Mexico...........	9,598	650,663	Toluca.
Michoacan........	21,609	618,240	Morelia.
Morelos..........	1,808	150,384	Cuernavaca.
Nuevo Leon.......	14,863	174,000	Monterey.
Oajaca...........	27,389	646,725	Oajaca.
Puebla...........	9,598	697,788	Puebla.
Querétaro........	3,429	153,286	Querétaro.
San Luis Potosi...	28,689	476,500	San Luis Potosi.
Sinaloa..........	25,927	163,095	Culiacau.
Sonora...........	81,022	109,388	Ures.
Tabasco..........	12,716	83,707	San Juan Bautista
Tamaulipas.......	28,659	108,778	Cuidad Victoria.
Tlaxcala..........	1,498	121,665	Tlaxcala.
Vera Cruz........	27,433	459,962	Vera Cruz.
Yucatan..........	32,658	422,365	Mérida.
Zacatecas........	26,585	397,945	Zacatecas.
Federal District...	85	275,996	Mexico.
Lower California (Territory)......	59,033	21,645	La Paz.
Total..........	702,990	9,169,707	

More recent tables, compiled from returns sent in by State Governors, carry the number of inhabitants up to 9,400,000; but it is to be presumed that these figures are too high, owing to an exaggerated estimate of the population of some of the States. The population of the republic is made up nearly thus: About 6,000,-000 Indians of unmixed blood, nearly one-half of whom are nomadic savage tribes of the mountainous districts of the north; about 500,000 whites or creoles, chiefly descended from the early Spanish colonists; perhaps 25,000 Africans or hybrids possessing some negro blood, whether mixed with the European or the Indian element; and mestizoes or half-breeds derived from the union of the whites and Indians. Of the Indians there are 25 tribes, speaking as many different tongues, and nearly 150 dialects.

The city of Mexico, the capital, has an estimated population of 250,000.

The President of Mexico is Señor Don Sebastian Lerdo de Tejada, elected November 21, 1872; the Minister of the Interior, Señor Don C. G. Perez; the Minister of Foreign Affairs, Señor Don José Maria Lafragua; of Finance, Señor Don Francisco Mejia; of War, General of Division Ignacio Mejia; of Justice, Public Instruction, and Public Worship, Señor Don J. D. Covarrubias; and of Public Works, Señor Don Blas Balcárcel.

The Treasurer-General of the republic is Señor Don Manuel Izaguirre; the President of the Supreme Court of Justice (whose office is equivalent to that of Vice-President of the Republic) is General Porfirio Diaz; and the Postmaster-General is Señor Don Pedro Garay y Garay.

The Mexican minister plenipotentiary to the United States is Señor Don Ignacio Mariscal;

and the Mexican consul-general at New York, Dr. Juan N. Navarro.

The financial position of the republic for the fiscal year 1872–'73 is set forth in the following tables:

Here follow comparative tables of the national revenue for the two years 1871–'72 and 1872–'73:

REVENUE.	1871-'72.	1872-'73.
Customs receipts......	$9,265,609 68	$9,076,709 74
Divers contri-) Fed. butions.... }district.	1,192,796 78	1,741,622 91
Customs.....	488,016 45	471,228 75
Stamped paper.........	2,217,274 60	1,734,894 54
Nationalized property.	895,261 65	505,438 58
Mint...................	239,481 58	159,484 13
Public-instruction fund	78,050 36	65,864 11
Carriage-tax..........	10,235 79	7,078 68
Post-Office............	474,819 10	265,440 22
Sundries...............	617,445 81	284,586 27
Arrears................	47,694 87	22,078 27
Totals..........	$15,046,756 67	$14,333,926 50

The expenditures were as follows:

EXPENDITURES.	1871-'72.	1872-'73.
Legislative............	$630,195 82	$964,912 32
Executive.............	28,088 70	41,965 23
Supreme Court........	41,754 37	63,905 98
Circuit Courts........	27,942 10	39,843 63
District "	105,443 32	135,549 30
Ministry of Foreign Relations	110,810 49	137,675 93
Ministry of the Interior	1,359,220 67	1,323,429 77
" of Justice......	557,105 12	778,878 30
" of Finance......	1,963,947 01	2,390,581 48
" of War and Navy.	7,624,282 82	7,427,891 60
" of Public Works.	1,719,418 76	1,243,628 71
Public debt............	275,188 27	432,894 16
Balance from preceding year	218,216 87	254,969 73
Reserve fund..........	79,600 30	1,136,394 13
Provisional branches...	2,450,629 81	3,648,176 20
Sundries...............	1,054,838 38	909,647 42
Totals	$18,246,714 81	$20,939,363 89

From the foregoing tables it would appear that there was a surplus of $51,629; but both revenue and expenditures for the year referred to were from three to four millions below those for the year 1871–'72. The estimated expenditures for 1873–'74 were $23,956,421.

In the report of the Minister of Finance the foreign debt of the country is mentioned as follows:

To Great Britain............................	$63,498,130
To Convention..............................	4,351,348
To Spain...................................	7,400,000
To Padre Moran............................	800,000
To American citizens, as per claims adjusted by the mixed commission.................	401,685
Total..............................	$76,452,163

The foregoing amount of national indebtedment is, as calculated by Minister F. Mejia, equivalent to $8.48 for each inhabitant of the republic.

In a list of defaulting states, published in London, in the course of 1874, with the title "Black Sheep," Mexico figured thus:

Public loans issued in England..	£16,106,450
Deferred bonds.................	434,450
Presumed outstanding amount of British convention debt....	834,856
	£16,375,756=$81,878,780

The Minister of Finance made, on March 6, 1874, the following report to Mr. Foster, United States minister to Mexico, concerning Mexican bonds sold in the United States, and mainly held by American citizens: 1. Of the bonds amounting to $2,950,000, issued in San Cárlos de Tamaulipas on July 4, 1865, by General Carbajal, there remain unfunded $1,438,050, in 6,368 bonds, as follows:

695 bonds, letter L, of $ 50 each..........	$34,750
3,583 " " C, of $100 "	358,300
2,090 " " D, of $500 "	1,045,000
6,368 bonds, of the value of..................	$1,438,050

2. Of the $10,000,000 in bonds issued by General Sanches Ochoa in San Francisco, on July 1, 1865, there remain unfunded $500,000; and these, according to the memoranda existing in the Treasury, are in the possession of Messrs. Eugene Kelly & Co., of New York, who hold them by order of the New York Supreme Court. The numbers of the bonds corresponding to the said $500,000 are not specified, inasmuch as no information can be obtained of the numeration of the bonds lost at sea on board the steamer Nevada, in May, 1868, and representing a value of $3,750,000, nor of that of the bonds now in the hands of Kelly & Co., as above mentioned.

There were in 1873 eleven mints in the republic: Durango, Guadalajara, Oajaca, Culiacan, Hermosillo, and Alamos, under the supervision of the central Government, and Mexico, Guanajuato, Zacatecas, San Luis Potosi, and Chihuahua, rented by private individals. The aggregate coinage at all of them in 1872 was $20,374,554, of which $19,686,434 was silver.

An interesting item of Mexican statistics is that of the total coinage in the country from the time of the conquest down to 1873; it is as follows:

Colonial period....................	$2,151,581,958
Period of independence...........	793,773,655
Total......................	$2,945,355,613

The value of the precious metals from the Mexican mines from the conquest to 1826 was: from 1521 to 1802, $2,027,952,000; from 1803 to 1810, $161,000,000; and from 1810 to 1826, $180,000,000: total, $2,368,952,000. The quantity of silver annually extracted is estimated at 500 tons, and that of gold at a ton and a half. Almost one-half of the total yield is derived from the great mining-districts of Guanajuato, Zacatecas, and Catorce, which form a group between latitude 21° and 24° north. Guanajuato alone furnishes every year about 180 tons, nearly one-sixth of all the silver annually produced in America. The whole of the gold and silver extracted from the mines of Mexico up to 1840 is estimated at $4,200,000,000. The seven principal mines of San Luis Potosi alone produced in 1868 silver to the value of $2,176,890.26. The annual yield during the decade of 1858–'67, judging from the coinage in the nine principal mints, averaged $17,500,000, which would be increased by the probable yield of the Sonora mines to upward of $78,-000,000, and by the value of the contraband portion to about $20,000,000. The State of Sinaloa is said to be literally covered with silver-mines, the foreign property in which is distributed as follows : American, $2,000,000 ; Spanish, $1,450,000 ; English, $250,000 ; and German, $50,000. Mexicans there work so many mines on so small a scale, that accurate statistics concerning them cannot be obtained. Scientific explorers, who visited the Sinaloa mines in 1872, reported that those on the Pacific slope would be the great source of the supply of silver for the next century. In 1870 there were in Oajaca 83 silver and 40 gold mines ; in Sonora, 444, chiefly yielding gold, besides 583 in which, although very productive, the works were suspended.

Lower California is justly celebrated for the large number and superior quality of its pearls. The fisheries of the *Avicula margaritifera*, or pearl-oyster, are carried on all along the gulf-coasts of the Californian peninsula, and have long been highly productive. In the year 1870 there were gathered 10,200 quintals of shells, worth $25,500, yielding pearls to the value of $62,000 ; making a total yield of $87,-500. The number of divers employed was 581, regularly occupied from April to October, inclusive. In 1873 the value of the shells obtained by 636 divers was $112,030, and of the pearls, $64,300.

Notwithstanding that mercury occurs in Chihuahua and elsewhere, that article, now so extensively used in the amalgamation process, is for the most part imported, and at enhanced prices. The value of the landed property of Mexico is set down as follows in an official report for the year 1873 : municipal, $147,819,-162.20 ; rural, $173,641,176.81 ; total, $340,-891,403.17. The Minister of Finance remarks, however, that triple that amount ($1,022,374,-200.57) would more nearly approximate the truth.

It is difficult to present an accurate statement of the foreign commerce, for systematic smuggling is so prevalent at all the ports that the official returns can never be regarded as correct. The figures representing all the imports, and those for bullion in the exports, may safely be doubled.

The articles most largely exported are silver and gold coin, silver and copper ore, cochineal, indigo, and other dye-stuffs, coffee, vanilla-beans, hides, timber, cabinet-woods, Sisal hemp, ixtle, etc. ; and the imports consist mainly of cotton, linen, woolen, and silk fabrics, iron, wrought and unwrought, machinery, hardware, provisions, etc.

Coffee is a compartively new article of export for Mexico ; before 1869 none was sent out of the country, and indeed very little was cultivated. It has now become more important than all the other commodities sent from certain States, Vera Cruz, for instance, as will be seen in the table of exports from that State and port

below. A similar increase is noticeable in the exportation of vanilla-beans, of which one single shipment to France two or three years ago was of the value of $400,000. The coffee of Colima, with an annual yield of some 50,000 lbs., is by many esteemed equal in quality to that of Mocha ; and that grown in Vera Cruz, particularly in Jalapa, Cordoba, and Orizaba, is likewise much sought after.

The great cacao centre is Oajaca, where its three yearly crops render its culture the most profitable in the State. The tobaccos of Tabasco and Vera Cruz are quite equal to the finest of Cuba ; large quantities are manufactured in the State of Vera Cruz, especially into cigars ; but the exportation thereof is still limited, for there seems to be some defect in the process of curing and manufacturing which impairs the quality of the cigar.

There are in Mexico fifty-nine classified species of medicinal plants, and some of these form important branches of export trade, especially jalap, the annual shipments of which at the beginning of the present century were over 170,000,000 lbs. Of this drug the United States alone took $10,000 worth in 1873.

Agriculture is assiduously but extremely laboriously carried on by the natives, who here, more than elsewhere in Spanish America, persist in using the implements handed down to them by their forefathers, to the almost absolute exclusion of efficient modern appliances for husbandry.

One of the chief cultivated products is maize, of which three and even four abundant crops are obtained annually in many districts, and which thrives in all parts of the country. Wheat gives an increase of about sixtyfold, and rice about forty-six. The annual value of the food-crops in the republic may be estimated at some $58,000,000, and that of all agricultural products at $110,000,-000.

Tortoise-shell, from the coasts of Yucatan and Guerrero, is annually exported to the amount of about $20,000.

The value of the exports to Great Britain for the six years, 1868–'73, was as follows :

Years.	Value.	Years.	Value.
1868	$1,753,320	1871	$1,986,620
1869	1,752,850	1872	2,317,620
1870	1,499,065	1873	

The imports from the same source in the period just referred to were :

Years.	Value.	Years.	Value.
1868	$4,242,940	1871	$5,345,065
1869	3,158,620	1872	4,315,930
1870	4,554,410	1873	

The total value of the exports to all countries in the year ending September 30, 1873, was estimated at $25,500,000 ; and that of the imports at $28,500,000. It is here seen that the balance of trade is uniformly against Mexico, and chiefly so with respect to Great Britain ; and, for the reason already hinted of the prevalence of smuggling, it is even greater than the difference between the foregoing figures for the imports and exports would suggest.

In the year ending June 30, 1870, specie was shipped as follows:

Silver subject to duty............	$15,605,585 37½
Silver free of duty,.	729,922 00
Gold............	1,145,506 65
Total.....................	$17,479,014 02½

The annexed table shows the relative proportion of imports from different countries:

COUNTRIES.	Value.	COUNTRIES.	Value.
Great Britain..	$13,000,000	Italy..........	$200,000
United States..	5,000,000	Ecuador	150,000
France..........	5,000,000	Guatemala...	50,000
Germany.........	2,000,000	Colombia	40,000
Spain..........	1,500,000	Chili..........	40,000
Cuba............	1,500,000	Venezuela....	30,000
China..........	1,000,000		
Belgium........	500,000	Total.....	$30,010,000

The duties collected in the year ending June 30, 1870, amounted to $17,303,945.45, of which $8,274.572 were received at maritime, and $9,029,373.24 at frontier custom-houses.

The exports from the Yucatan peninsula consist mainly of Sisal hemp, of which 4,231,055 lbs., of the value of $270,814,061, were shipped from Progreso (the port for Merida) in the year ending September 30, 1873.

The total value of the exports from Yucatan in the year just mentioned, and the destination of the articles, are set forth in the subjoined table:

Countries.	Value.
United States	$326,012 16
Cuba	165,496 14
England	10,375 00
France............................	5,518 00
Total.........................	$507,401 30

The value and sources of the imports into Yucatan during the same year were thus:

Countries.	Value.
United States......................	$236,993 73
England............................	107,758 00
Cuba..............................	44,381 49
Germany...........................	12,778 00
France............................	11,592 00
Balize	1,012 00
Total.........................	$414,515 22

According to the latest official report, published in November, 1873, the shipping movements at all the ports of the republic, in 1870, were as follows:.

ENTERED.			CLEARED.		
FLAG.	Vessels.	Tons.	FLAG.	Vessels	Tons.
Mexican....	2,155	108,641	Mexican....	2,140	100,008
British......	163	75,461	British......	177	84,514
Spanish ...	45	11,494	Spanish ...	42	7,898
French......	116	47,685	French	110	48,073
Prussian....	62	18,234	Prussian....	66	10,959
U. States...	328	386,176	U. States...	327	378,710
Dutch........	19	4,157	Dutch......	22	3,959
Norwegian..	25	7,905	Norwegian..	23	6,894
Danish......	16	3,996	Danish	13	8,571
Others......	21	5,492	Others......	21	5,965
Total.....	2,950	669,061	Total.....	2,941	659,551

Of the number of vessels entered, 362 were steamers, and of those cleared, 378. One

French and two British lines of steamers ply regularly between St. Nazaire, Southampton, Liverpool, and the Gulf ports of Vera Cruz and Tampico, touching at Havana, St. Thomas, Martinique, and Santander. The British steamers frequently call at New Orleans. An American line plies between New York and the principal Gulf ports every 20 days, calling at Havana and New Orleans, receiving a subsidy of $2,200 per round trip from the Mexican Government. Regular communication is kept up between Acapulco and Panama and the intermediate ports of Mexico and Central America, and between Acapulco and San Francisco and the intermediate ports of Manzanillo, Mazatlan, and Cape San Lucas, by two American lines, one of which has a subsidy of $2,500 per round trip, and the other $2,000 monthly from the Mexican Government. In 1872 there were 5,740 arrivals at, and 5,095 departures from, Mexican ports. The Mexican merchant navy comprises 1,029 craft of all sizes, 357 of which are sea-going or large coasting vessels. The railways of the republic are as follows:

Mexico to Vera Cruz......................	264½	miles.
Branch, Apizaco to Puebla........	29½	"
Mexico to Tlalpam......................	15½	"
Vera Cruz (La Zamorana) to Medellin......	11	"
Mexico to Guadalupe...................	4½	"
* Mexico to Tacubaya and Popotla.........	8½	"
* Mexico to Atzcapozalco	6½	"
* Vera Cruz to Puebla via Jalapa †.........	25	"
Total................................	363½	miles.

The traffic on the Mexico & Vera Cruz Railway amounts to about 240,000 passengers and 184,000 tons of freight per annum; the receipts are about $2,500,000, and the running expenses average 60 per cent. of the receipts. The line between Mexico and Atzcapozalco is to be extended to Cuautillan and Toluca. There is a line of horse-cars from Matamoras to Paso de Santa Cruz. Among numerous projected lines may be mentioned one from Tuxpan on the Gulf to a port on the Pacific, passing by Mexico; one from Puebla to Matamoros; and one from Mexico north to El Paso, to communicate with the United States railway system.

In May, 1873, a contract was made between the Government and Mr. Edward Lee Plumb, representative of the International Railway Company of Texas, for the construction of some railway lines in the republic; but that contract was revoked during the following session of Congress; and a new one, by order of President Lerdo, made with a company purporting to be Mexican in its organization and interests, but the majority of whose members are in fact foreigners. This new contract was approved by Congress, but the measure elicited bitter comments on the part of the public press, and was the subject of warm debate in the House. Señor Guzman defended the policy of the Executive, and attempted to demonstrate the inexpediency of linking the railway

---

* Horse cars.   † Completed to Tolomé.

systems of Mexico and the United States, urging that such a step would be likely to facilitate another invasion from the latter; but Señor Cañedo, a deputy of considerable distinction, and well acquainted with American affairs, commended American skill and enterprise, and the policy of preferring Americans as constructors of Mexican railways. The Mexican company, however, having failed to file at the time fixed therefor—April 30, 1874—a bond for the faithful execution of their contract, the President declared the concession forfeited; the organization of the company was formally dissolved; and the Congress was adjourned on May 31st, without granting any new concession. So the subject of new railways in the republic was once more, and indefinitely, postponed.

The reason assigned for the non-compliance of the company with the terms of the concession was the impossibility to negotiate the requisite loans in Europe.

There are twenty-four regular lines of diligences established between the principal towns of the republic. Merchandise is mostly carried by mules at an immense expenditure of time and money. The lack of good roads in a country whose topographical structure deprives it of navigable rivers, seriously retards its material development and prosperity. Large sums were appropriated in 1873 for new highways, and for repairs on such as already exist. A net-work of telegraph-wires, 4,345 miles in length, in 1874 embraced all the States but Chihuahua, Sonora, and Chiapas, and 655 miles more were in process of construction. The Central Government owns 1,575 miles of the line, and State governments 605 miles.

The army comprises 22,387 men, viz.: 15,407 foot, 5,140 horse, 1,463 artillery, and 377 coastguards and invalids. The estimated total expenditure for the War Department in 1872–'73 was $10,252,522.32, which would include an extraordinary appropriation of $2,628,239.50.

Public instruction is in a comparatively prosperous condition; the number of schools is steadily increasing, through the liberal appropriations of the central and the various state governments for the development of the system, and the coöperation of private individuals. The following institutes in the city of Mexico are supported by the Central Government: an advanced school for girls, preparatory school, and schools of law, medicine, agriculture, engineering, fine arts, commerce, and arts and trades; besides which there were in 1873 in the whole Federal District 338 schools of all grades, 103 being for females, and the total attendance being 22,407, of whom 8,773 are females.

Among these schools were twelve under the jurisdiction of the Lancasterian company, six under that of the Benevolent Society, the schools of the Foundling Hospital and other charitable institutions, private schools to the number of 100, and three for adults, with 248 pupils, 148 of whom were females. In the other States there were 3,532 public schools, of which 3,498 were male primary, and 29 male grammar-schools; the total attendance of all of them was 165,864, of whom 19,594 were females. The number of public schools for adults was 28, with 935 male and 76 female pupils; and that of the literary institutes 15, with 2,493 students.

The first session of the seventh Congress terminated on January 21, 1874. We here transcribe the more important portions of the President's message to that body before its adjournment:

Citizen Deputies: In the first period of our sessions you have considered subjects of great importance, which you have decided to the advantage of the republic. The long-pending treaties which the Executive celebrated with the King of Italy, concerning commerce and extradition, have been approved by Congress, and will soon be ratified in order to go into operation as a law of the Union. The friendly relations which fortunately exist between the two countries will be thereby rendered more intimate.

The great work which cost such bloody sacrifices, the laws of reform,* having definitively received constitutional sanction, now form an integral part of our institutions. This act, of the highest importance for the Mexican people, will ever be a title of glory for the seventh constitutional Congress.

The intelligent discussion which has continued during your session upon some other reforms in the fundamental compact gives reason to hope that they may soon be terminated, aiding not only to perfect our system, but also to further develop the practice of liberal principles. Congress having scrutinized the popular election of magistrates of the Supreme Court of Justice, the highest tribunal of the Union, to which the laws concede such high attributes, has been duly completed. The judicial organization in Lower California was insufficient for the vast extent of its territory, causing real damage to public interests. This evil has been remedied by the action of Congress, in establishing the new tribunals found necessary for so noble an object.

The subsidy granted to the steamship line between Vera Cruz and New York having been renewed by Congress, this important means of communication will continue to exist, and will afford new advantages to commerce, and greater facilities for the movement of passengers between the extreme and intermediate points of that interesting line.

A new line of steamers between Vera Cruz and Havana, which is to touch at several ports of the Gulf, having also been subsidized by another decree, this line will efficiently serve to stimulate our mercantile relations with the island of Cuba and the exportation of our valuable national products.

The modifications made in the law of real-estate contributions have remedied defects shown by experience. Some disadvantages for the tax-payer have thus been abolished without damage to our fiscal interests. The admitted propriety of extending to a greater number of localities the benefits of the telegraph inspired Congress with the resolution of establishing new telegraphic lines from Michoacan to Guadalajara and the ports of Manzanillo and San Blas, as also from San Luis to Zacatecas and Durango. The utility of these measures is unquestionable, as is also that of the decree for the canalization between the lagoons of Chijol and Tamiahua, in the State of Vera Cruz. These communications will develop an important trade. Among other beneficent measures taken by Congress, that relating to a road

* Separation of Church and State.

to Comanja, to facilitate the extraction of the abundant products of its iron-mines, deserves notice, as also the power given the Executive to transfer to another company the concession for a railroad between Puebla and Matamoras Izúcar, so important for that rich district.

The period granted to the company which proposes to establish interoceanic communication across the Isthmus of Tehuantepec having been extended for a year, there is a new hope of the realization of so highly-interesting a project, and one recognized as such by all the governments of the republic.

The settlement of the new tariffs for the railway from Mexico to Vera Cruz has been one of the principal subjects to which Congress has devoted its intelligent attention. If in this important matter all that could be desired was not accomplished, there was at least obtained all that was possible for the purpose of stimulating the exportation of our products.

The revenue-cutters to be purchased, in virtue of the decision of Congress, will be very useful for the maintenance of order in our ports and the due protection of our fiscal interests. The conflict between the powers of the State of Coahuila reached a point which rendered the intervention of the Federal authority indispensable. We may hope for much under the auspices of the peace happily maintained throughout the nation. We cherish flattering hopes that public order will not be disturbed, resting upon the good sense of the Mexican people, and its well-known desire to devote itself to social progress.

On March 2d a number of persons murdered the Rev. J. L. Stephens, an American citizen and missionary, at Guadalajara. Prompt measures were taken by the authorities for the arrest and punishment of the criminals. Up to April 15th seven of these had been tried and sentenced to death, and more than a dozen others of the accomplices were awaiting trial. Those first condemned appealed to the Supreme Court.

President Lerdo, at an audience which he granted to the Protestant missionaries resident in the capital, declared his determination to make every endeavor in his power to the end that the guilty should receive condign punishment, to protect the missionaries in the free exercise of their labors, and to maintain religious toleration in all parts of the republic.

MICHELET, JULES, a French historian, polemic and essayist, a member of the Institute of France, born in Paris, August 21, 1798; died in that city, February 10, 1874. He was the son of a printer employed by the French Republic to print the government *assignats* or bonds, and was intended at first for his father's vocation, but his parents, seeing his fondness for study, at great sacrifices maintained him in the Collége Charlemagne, where, under the tuition of MM. Villemain and Le Clerc, he distinguished himself and graduated with high honors. In 1821, after an unusually sharp competition, he was called to the professorship of History in the Collége Rollin, where he taught also the ancient languages and philosophy until 1826. His first work, "Synchronic Charts of Modern History," was published in 1825, and his translation of Vico's History in 1826, and as a result he received the appointment of Master of Conferences at the Normal

School. The Revolution of 1830 having been successful, he was appointed by Louis Philippe chief of the historical section of the Archives of the Kingdom, and soon after, M. Guizot, finding himself unable on account of his official duties to continue his lectures on history at the Sorbonne, appointed Michelet as his substitute, and the King assigned to him the place of instructor in history to his daughter, the Princess Clémentine. In 1838 M. Michelet succeeded Daunou as Professor of Morals and History in the College of France, and Count Reinhard as a member of the Academy of Moral Sciences in the Institute of France. The previous year the first volume of his "History of France" appeared. In his new professorship M. Michelet soon became an active propagandist of democratic ideas, and a formidable opponent of the Jesuits, against whom he evoked the bitterest animosity. Aided by M. Quinet, he published in 1843, "The Jesuits;" in 1844, "Concerning the Priest, the Wife and the Family;" and in 1846, "Concerning the People." In 1847 he published the first volume of his "History of the Revolution." In 1848, after the revolution of that year, he was nominated as a deputy to the National Assembly, but declined to be a candidate, on the ground of the necessity for devoting himself to the work of completing his projected histories. He continued to give to his lectures at the College of France the character of democratic propagandism, which they had previously maintained, till his course was closed by the government of Louis Napoleon, in March, 1851. Refusing to take the oath to the empire, after the *coup d'état*, M. Michelet lost his place at the Archives Office, and thenceforth devoted himself exclusively to literary pursuits. While continuing his historical labors, he indulged himself at intervals in the preparation of a series of essays marked by an exquisite beauty of style, a grace of imagination, and in some of them an evil suggestiveness of sentiment covered by the most dainty phrases, of which his previous career and writings had given no promise. These works were "The Bird" (1856); "The Insect" (1857); "Love" (1858); "The Wife" (1859); "The Sea" (1861); "The Sorceress" (1862)— this was seized and destroyed in France, but was published in large editions in Brussels; and "The Mountain" (1868). Of these books it may be said with truth that the two, "Love" and "The Wife," have been, by the beauty of their style, and the insidious poison of their free-love doctrines, among the most mischievous productions of the century. During this period M. Michelet also brought out three more polemic volumes, viz.: "Poland Martyred" (1863); "The Bible of Humanity" (1864); and "Our Son," a plea for compulsory education (1869). M. Michelet, however, based his claims to immortality as an author on his historical works, which, though inferior in style and dignity to those of Thiers and Guizot, were yet possessed of the merits of precision and accuracy. The following are their titles: "History of France," 16 vols., 8vo (1837-1867); this work closes with Louis XVI.'s dethronement; "Introduction to Universal History" (1840); "A Compend of Modern History," a text-book (1833); "A Compend of the History of France up to the French Revolution" (1838); "The Origin of French Laws sought in the Symbols and Formulas of Universal Law" (1837); "History of the French Revolution," 7 vols. 8vo (1847-1853); "The Women of the Revolution" (1854); "Principles of the Philosophy of History," drawn in part from Vico's "*Scienza Nuova*," 2 vols. 8vo (1831); a translation of "The Memoirs of Luther," 2 vols. 8vo (1835); and some compilations, many review articles and contributions to the "*Encyclopédie des Gens du Monde*," to the *Comptes Rendus* of the Academy of Moral Sciences, etc., etc.

MICHIGAN. At the general election held on the 3d of November, the vote for Governor was as follows, including the vote of Manitou and Presque Isle Counties, not received at the office of the Secretary of State in time for the official canvass:

For John J. Bagley, Republican.......... 111,611
For Henry Chamberlain, Democrat....... 105,704
For Charles K. Carpenter, Prohibition... 3,937

Total........................... 221,252

Majority for Bagley over Chamberlain, 5,897; over both Chamberlain and Carpenter, 1,930.

The following persons, all Republicans, were chosen to the several State offices named: Lieutenant-Governor, Henry H. Holt, over Frederick Hall, Dem., Thomas A. Granger, Pro., and Jerome W. Turner, Reform. Secretary of State, Ebenezer G. D. Holden, over George H. House, Dem., and Samuel W. Baker, Pro. State Treasurer, William B. McCreery, over Joseph M. Sterling, Dem., and James I. Mead, Pro. Auditor-General, Ralph Ely over John L. Evans, Dem., Joseph Newman, Pro., and Frederick M. Holloway, Reform. Commissioner of State Land-Office, Leverett A. Clapp over Chauncey W. Greene, Dem., and Thomas S. Skinner, Pro. Superintendent of Public Instruction, Daniel B. Briggs over Duane Doty, Dem., and John Evans, Pro. Attorney-General, Andrew J. Smith over Martin V. Montgomery, Dem., Albert Williams, Pro., and Charles S. May, Reform. Member of State Board of Education, Edward Rexford over Edward W. Andrews, Dem., John D. Lewis, Pro., and Carroll S. Frazer, Reform.

The Legislature chosen at the same election may be politically classified as follows: Senate—Republicans, 18; Democrats, 14. House —Republicans, 53; Democrats, 47. Republican majority on joint ballot, 10.

The vote for Representatives in Congress in the several districts was as follows: First— Moses W. Field, Rep., 8,892; Alpheus S. Williams, Dem., 10,848; John Russell, Pro., 48. Second—Henry Waldron, Rep., 14,611; John J. Robison, Dem. (including 979 returned for

Robinson), 14,059. Third—George Willard, Rep., 13,372; Fidus Livermore, Dem., 12,174; D. P. Sagendorph, Pro., 941. Fourth—Julius C. Burrows, Rep., 12,278; Allen Potter, Dem. and Reform, 13,317; imperfect, 9. Fifth— William B. Williams, Rep., 13,370; Mark D. Wilber, Dem. and Reform, 12,212; James A. McKay, Pro., 360. Sixth—Josiah W. Begole, Rep., 16,122; George H. Durand, Dem., 17,- 758; Erastus O. Harrington, Pro., 902. Seventh—Omar D. Conger, Rep., 10,185; Enos M. Goodrich, Dem., 8,203; Henry Fish, Pro., 167. Eighth—Nathan B. Bradley, Rep., 10,- 258; Geo. F. Lewis, Dem., 9,979; imperfect, 85. Ninth—Jay A. Hubbell, Rep., 12,877; Henry D. Noble (informally nominated), 3,460. Scattering, 690—a Democratic gain of three members.

At the same election the amended or revised constitution of the State, reported by the Constitutional Commission of 1873, and amended and submitted by an extra session of the Legislature, held in March 1874, was voted upon, the result being, for its ratification, 39,285; against, 124,039. The question of woman suffrage was submitted and voted upon separately, the vote being, for woman suffrage, 40,077; against woman suffrage, 135,957.

The political platforms of the year were as follows: Republican—adopted by convention held at Lansing, August 26, 1874:

We, the delegated representatives of the Republican party in Michigan, assembled in convention in the twentieth anniversary year of its organization, appear before the people of the State and of the Union after the uninterrupted exercise by that party of all the responsibilities of power during its entire existence, offering no apologies, deprecating no criticism, invoking no charity in the construction of its acts, but challenging a faithful scrutiny of its record through every vicissitude of war and peace, and the candid judgment of all just men.

In no spirit of vainglory, but in simple deference to historic truth, we assert that, since the Republican party raised its banner in 1854, it has never failed, under trials more severe than have beset the history of any other party since the organization of the Government, to stand in the advance line of human and national progress. During the turbulent years before the war, throughout the war, and in the unprecedented perplexities which succeeded, it has forfeited none of its pledges to humanity, to its sister States, nor to the interests of our own citizens. It has promised the protection of good laws and a faithful administration of them. It has legislated wisely for the development of our abundant resources. It has been liberal in the encouragement of learning, and bountiful in providing for the unfortunate. It has persistently cultivated a better civilization, and there is no malignant hand that can point to any of its legislation which may be used to make men worse. At the same time it has been prudent and economical in its expenditure; has kept down taxation; has been and is steadily reducing the public indebtedness, and the financial credit of the State, under its management, is of the highest standard in all the commercial cities of the world.

We shall regard it as good reason for acceding to the statement of our opponents that "the mission of the Republican party is ended," when we are pointed to a political organization more beneficent in its aims, or more devoted or comprehensive in its patriotism; but, as long as it leads all other parties as it has done in the past, and still does, in the advancement of goo work, in the investigation of grievances, and indthe redress of wrongs, we can discover no reason for surrendering the reins of power into the hands of a party whose last public service was to drag the country into civil war, to disgrace its financial credit, and to leave the Government on the very brink of dissolution, and which made its last effort to regain the confidence of the people under the lead of its life-long enemy in the most brazen, barefaced, and shameless coalition ever known in the history of parties, formed solely and avowedly on the basis of "spoils" alone.

Upon the financial record of the Republican party alike in the nation and in the State, we confidently challenge comparison with any other party which ever held power in either, pointing with just pride to the great and steadily increasing reduction of the national debt, and the improvement of the national credit, accompanied by an equally remarkable reduction of taxation and of expenditure in administering the Government. With all this our national interests and general prosperity have enormously increased, and our citizens are better clothed, better fed, and better paid for their labor than any other people in the world. In this State the State Republican management has secured the same blessings of light taxation, economical administration, and rapidly-diminishing debt, while our State institutions have been literally built up until they have become the pride of the people; education, public morals, and the various branches of industry, have been fostered, crime has been repressed, suffering alleviated, and the unfortunate provided for; large and important improvements have been projected and are in process of completion, and every State interest has been generously yet economically cared for, with such scrupulous honesty in every department of the State government, that even partisan calumny dare not bring a specific accusation against any.

We fully appreciate the extraordinary character of the financial difficulties through which the country has recently passed, and regard it as inevitable that able and patriotic representatives should have differed, like their constituencies, as to what were proper remedies in circumstances wherein they were without specific precedents for guidance. We indorse as wise and timely the measure finally agreed upon by Congress between conflicting interests and opposing theories.

While we recognize in the greenbacks and national-bank notes a circulating medium far superior to any paper currency heretofore existing in the United States, saving as it does to the people, directly and indirectly, many millions of dollars annually over the old State-bank system in exchange and discount, we demand that in all financial legislation Congress shall keep steadily in view the resumption of specie payment, to the end that at the earliest day practicable the promises to pay of the Government may be equivalent to coin in like amounts throughout the commercial world.

We believe that banking, under a well-guarded national system, should be free, the volume and locality of issue being regulated by the business law of demand; and we denounce repudiation in every form or degree; holding the pledged faith of the Government sacred and inviolable in both letter and spirit.

We would not forget the claims of the colored people of the South to the nation's fostering care and protection. Wrested from their masters' control, with freedom conferred upon them by the Government as a war-measure and in aid of the Union cause, given the elective franchise as means not alone of protection to themselves, but of protection to the nation, it is now the high duty of the Government, from which it cannot shrink without incurring and deserving the execration of mankind for all time, to protect them in the rights and privileges of their enforced citizenship. Their ignorance is not their fault. Errors of theory and mistakes in conduct are but the legitimate fruits of their former enslaved condition. The Government assumed the responsibility for evils resulting from these when it clothed them with the full rights and privileges of citizens.

We appeal to the national Government, as the good name and fair fame of the nation are dear to it, to protect these people in their civil and political rights, and in their persons, property, and homes, and to provide and secure them in the enjoyment of all educational advantages and privileges.

Democratic—adopted by a convention of 400 delegates, held at Kalamazoo on the 10th of September:

Resolved, That we arraign the party in power for its unexampled extravagance and corruption, and for its unconstitutional and dangerous usurpation of power not delegated to the Federal Government, and we demand an honest, and economical, and just administration of the national offices.

We demand an immediate abandonment of all efforts to rule the States for corrupt party purposes by an infamous alliance of carpet-baggers, scalawags, and bayonets. We demand the adequate punishment of all men guilty of corruption and embezzlement in office. We demand an immediate repeal of the law increasing salaries, and of the infamous "gag law," by which the party in power seeks to muzzle a free press.

Denouncing its wholesale appropriation of the public domain, the Credit Mobilier, and other corrupt corporations, we demand of the Government a careful reservation of the remaining public lands for the use and benefit of the Union soldier and sailor, and of the actual settler.

We demand a repeal of the legal-tender act, to take effect not later than July 4, 1876, a specie basis, and free banks with a secured currency.

We demand a tariff for revenue only, free from the unjust discriminations that raise little or no revenue, create monopolies, unnecessarily increase the cost of living, and encourage corrupt legislation, and we demand the payment of all forms of the national debt, in coin or its equivalent, when due, and an equal and just distribution of the taxes and imposts required to raise the needed revenue.

Resolved, That in the management of our State affairs we demand prudence in the creation of taxes, honesty and economy in the expenditures of money; that we condemn the management of our State finances, for the reasons: first, that with a large balance in the Treasury, tax-payers in these times should be, but are not, relieved of any of their annual burden; second, that this large balance is loaned to the pets of a political ring, for which no adequate security is required, while, if it should be lost, the bond of the State Treasurer is quite too small to protect the State; third, that, the books and accounts of the State Treasurer being public, the Legislature has refused to permit them to be thoroughly examined by the representatives of the people; the State Treasurer has refused to report to the Legislature the location and condition of the million of money in his hands, but above all that the political majority of the Legislature has tolerated this refusal, all which are facts well calculated to excite serious fears for the safety of our money.

Resolved, That we are in favor of amending our State constitution at the earliest time possible, so that the Legislature may have power to regulate the liquor-traffic.

Resolved, That, when the State, impelled by a public necessity, confers corporate powers to secure a public benefit, such powers must be held subject to just laws judicially interpreted, a sound public policy that protects alike the rights and interests of the State, the people, and the corporation.

Resolved, That the railroad and industrial interests of our State should be identical and reciprocal, and that we have a right to such legislation as will secure reasonable and uniform rates of freight.

A new party, christened the "National Reform Party," was organized at Lansing, August 6th. A nominating convention was held at Jackson on the 9th of September, and a ticket nominated which was partially adopted by the Democrats, the next day. The candidates not adopted and not withdrawn received a vote ranging from 2,287 to 7,000. The platform put forth by this party was:

Believing that it will be impossible to secure such reforms of administration and changes of policy as will restore the honesty and economy of the early days of the republic through either of the political parties heretofore trusted with power; tired of shuffling financial experiments and false standards of value; and deeming the encroachments of Federal authority upon the powers for a long time exercised exclusively by the States prejudicial to our liberties, we will perfect our organization as a National Reform party, and present candidates upon the following platform:

1. Reduction of the number and diminution of the power of offices under the national Government.

2. A reduction of salaries paid, to such an extent that no fund for political purposes can be raised by assessments upon office-holders, and that no office shall be sought on account of its emoluments.

3. Political opinion should be neither a reason for an appointment to office nor a ground for removal therefrom; but frequent changes should be made to secure purity of administration.

4. A prohibition of recommendations or solicitations for office by any Senator or Representative in Congress, and the election of all local and Federal office-holders by the people.

5. A speedy return to hard money as the only standard of value.

6. All banking, State or national, should be made free.

7. A tariff for revenue and an equitable system of taxation, which shall cause all classes of property and every species of capital to bear its just proportion of the burdens of the Government.

The school statistics for the year, compiled from official reports in the office of the Superintendent of Public Instruction, are as follows: Number of townships reporting, 955; of districts, 5,571; new districts organized, 118. Number of children between the ages of five and twenty years, 436,694; between the ages of eight and fourteen, 186,714; number that attended school during the year, 327,506. Number of private or select schools, 166; pupils attending same, 5,845. Number of volumes in district libraries, 120,577; increase for year, 10,315; paid for books, $12,962. Number of volumes in township libraries, 49,872; increase for year, 4,521; paid for books, $5,576.68. Voted for libraries at spring election, $1,449.05; fines and penalties received from county treasurers for libraries, $18,393.41. Stone school-houses, 81; brick, 682; frame, 4,390; log, 549; furnishing seats for 407,072 pupils. Value of school-houses and lots, $8,912,698. Graded schools, 327. Visits by county superintendents, 7,288; by directors, 14,927. Number of meetings held by school inspectors, 1,733; paid (or due) inspectors for services for fiscal year

ending September 7th, $5,776.42. Qualified teachers employed—males, 3,156; females, 9,120. Aggregate months taught—by males, 14,061; by females, 43,573. Wages paid teachers—males, $737,471; females, $1,179,540.11. Average wages per month—males, $5,245; females, $2,701. School-moneys on hand at beginning of fiscal year, $576,056.03. Receipts for year: from two-mill tax, $466,086.05; from primary school-fund, $205,480.14; from tuition of non-resident scholars, $37,311.26; from district taxes for all purposes, $2,393,604.73; from all other sources, $410,288.13. Total resources for year, $4,107,583.78. Expenditures for year: paid teachers, $1,905,363.71; paid for buildings and repairs, $536,307.28; on bonded indebtedness, $384,954.41; for all other purposes, $600,901.48. Total expenditures, $3,423,922.45. Amount on hand at close of fiscal year, $683,661.33. Bonded debts of districts, $1,734,890.29; other indebtedness, $115,873.90; total, $1,850,764.19.

The number of students attending the State Normal School in 1874, 550. Salaries paid instructors, $19,205; other expenditures, $7,113.71: total, $26,318.71. Receipts: from the State Treasury, $25,000; tuition, $1,942; other sources, $1,412.40; total, $28,354.40. The total amount of the Normal School (endowment or trust) fund held by the State is $69,363.54, at 7 per cent.

Number of students in the Agricultural College, 121; graduated during the year, 21. The permanent fund of the college is now $212,986.16, of which $107,879.14 is held in trust by the State, and $105,107.02 is due for lands sold, both amounts drawing 7 per cent. interest from the State. September 30, 1874, the unsold lands of the college were 169,793.56 acres. The college has received and expended since its foundation to September 30, 1874: from State appropriations, $418,977.18; from State for interest on lands sold, $36,664.84; from sales of lands donated by State, $37,166.43: total, $492,808.45. Value of personal property and real estate belonging to college, $209,038. Running expenses for eighteen years, $283,770.45, or an average annual expenditure of a fraction over $15,765. Whole number of graduates of college, 85. Salaries paid professors and instructors in 1874, exclusive of house-rent, $14,850; to gardeners, foremen, and laborers, $6,000, exclusive of board.

Number of students in the university, 1,183. Degrees conferred — Bachelor of Laws, 126 (two females); Doctor of Medicine, 71 (nine females); Bachelor of Arts, 35 (four females); Bachelor of Philosophy, 13 (two females); Bachelor of Science, 18 (one female); Civil Engineer, 13; Pharmaceutical Chemist, 20 (two females); Master of Science, 2; Master of Arts, 20 (one female). Amount of university fund, $542,768.24. Value of buildings and other property, $457,500.

In May of this year a census of the State was taken, as required by the constitution. A tabular statement of population, compared with the United States census of 1870, is appended:

COUNTIES.	United States, 1870.	State, 1874.
Alcona	696	1,214
Allegan	32,105	32,381
Alpena	2,756	4,807
Antrim	1,985	3,240
Barry	22,199	22,051
Bay	15,900	24,832
Benzie	2,184	2,663
Berrien	35,104	35,029
Branch	26,226	25,726
Calhoun	36,569	35,655
Cass	21,094	20,525
Charlevoix	1,724	3,360
Cheboygan	2,196	3,070
Chippewa	1,689	2,170
Clare	366	1,854
Clinton	22,845	23,661
Delta	2,542	* 4,571
Eaton	25,171	26,907
Emmet	1,211	1,272
Genesee	33,900	34,568
Grand Traverse	4,443	5,349
Gratiot	11,810	13,886
Hillsdale	31,684	31,566
Houghton	13,879	19,080
Huron	9,040	* 10,922
Ingham	25,268	29,193
Ionia	27,681	28,376
Iosco	3,163	4,782
Isabella	4,113	6,059
Jackson	36,047	37,988
Kalamazoo	32,054	31,848
Kalkaska	424	1,259
Kent	50,403	62,671
Keweenaw	4,205	5,415
Lake	548	1,813
Lapeer	21,345	25,140
Leelanaw	4,576	5,031
Lenawee	45,595	46,084
Livingston	19,336	20,329
Mackinac	1,716	1,496
Macomb	27,616	28,865
Manistee	6,074	8,471
Manitou	801	* 657
Marquette	15,093	21,946
Mason	3,263	5,361
Mecosta	5,642	9,132
Menominee	1,791	3,490
Midland	3,285	5,306
Missaukee	130	606
Monroe	27,483	* 27,838
Montcalm	13,629	20,815
Muskegon	14,894	19,375
Newaygo	7,204	8,758
Oakland	40,867	38,082
Oceana	7,222	8,360
Ontonagon	2,845	2,406
Osceola	2,093	6,216
Ottawa	26,651	29,929
Presque Isle	355	1,615
Saginaw	39,097	48,409
Sanilac	14,562	16,292
Schoolcraft	*	1,290
Shiawassee	20,858	21,773
St. Clair	36,661	40,688
St. Joseph	26,275	25,906
Tuscola	13,714	16,998
Van Buren	28,829	29,156
Washtenaw	41,434	38,728
Wayne	119,038	144,903
Wexford	650	3,011
Unorganized	82	....
Total	1,184,089	1,330,111

The following is given in the *Northwestern Mining Journal*, as an approximate statement of copper-mining in the Upper Peninsula:

* One ward of the city of Monroe, the town of Masonville, Delta County, Caseville, Huron County, and three islands of Manitou County, failed to make returns in time to be included in the above table. Their estimated population would increase the above aggregate about 3,500.

YEAR.	Ore, Tons.	Ingots, Tons.	Value.
To 1858	18,954	13,955	$9,000,500
1858	4,100	3,500	1,886,000
1859	4,200	3,500	1,890,000
1860	6,000	4,800	2,610,000
1861	7,500	6,000	3,387,500
1862	9,962	8,000	3,402,000
1863	8,548	6,500	4,420,000
1864	8,472	6,500	6,110,000
1865	10,791	7,000	5,145,000
1866	10,376	7,000	4,760,000
1867	11,735	8,200	4,140,000
1868	13,049	9,985	4,592,000
1869	15,288	12,200	5,868,000
1870	16,183	12,946	5,696,240
1871	16,071	12,857	6,171,860
1872	15,166	12·132	7,774,720
1873	18,688	14,910	8,200,500
1874	21,729	17,383	7,996,180
Total	206,761	167,368	$92,500,000

The assessments levied for the year aggregated $1,022,000, and the dividends $1,940,000. The latter were paid by four companies. The Marquette *Mining Journal* states the production of iron for the year at 935,488 tons ore, 90,494 tons pig, total value, $7,592,811; total production from 1856 to 1874 inclusive, 7,648,281 tons.

The capital of the national banks of the State is $10,202,200.

The cost of Michigan railroads is given at $141,582,400, with a debt at the beginning of the year of $90,414,846. These totals are arrived at by apportioning the cost and debt of those which extend into other States, according to the length in each State.

The Commissioners of State Fisheries did a large business during the year in distributing fish among the interior waters. More than 1,500,000 young white-fish were distributed among upward of 200 lakes, and large quantities of Atlantic, land-locked, and California salmon and shad. An establishment for hatching spawn has been located at Crystal Springs, Jackson County.

In the manufacture of salt there was a large increase, the quantity inspected being 1,026,979 barrels, as against 823,346 in 1873. The inspection of salt is classed as fine, packer's, solar, and number 2. Of refuse salt no notice is taken. Number of companies engaged in the business, 68; wells, 104; capital employed, $2,024,500; men employed, 2,426. The stock on hand at the close of the year was somewhat less than at the beginning, showing a healthy and steady demand for the product. Of the amount shipped from the Saginaw Valley, more than one-half went to Chicago.

The manufacture of lumber progressed steadily and with considerable activity through the year, though under great embarrassments in consequence of the general stagnation of trade in the country, which rendered resort to unusual credits necessary. The amount manufactured probably fell but little, if at all, below that of the preceding year.

In the last days of the term of office of Commissioner Edmonds, who was Land-Commissioner for 1871-'72, a large quantity of State lands was conveyed to various parties in violation of law and at inadequate prices. Mr. Byron D. Ball, the Attorney-General, falling sick, resigned his office early in this year, and Isaac Marston, of Bay City, being appointed to succeed him, commenced proceedings to recover the lands, and was successful in every instance, so that the State lost nothing by the irregularities in the Land-Commissioner's office. The Legislature of 1873 made provision for a new Insane Asylum, to be located in the eastern part of the State. Commissioners were appointed to make the location, who selected Pontiac as the place, and land was procured for the erection of the necessary buildings. Another commission, under legislative authority, selected Ionia as the location for a State House of Correction.

A short session of the Legislature was held in March, for the purpose mainly of passing upon the proposed revision of the constitution. A few acts were passed, but not of general interest.

The following statistics are abstracted from the report of the Inspectors of the State-prison for the year ending September 30, 1874: convicts in the prison, September 30, 1873, 655; received during the year (including 3 recaptured), 313; discharged during year, by expiration of sentence, 228; by commutation, 3; by reversal of sentence, 5; pardoned, 13; died, 7; escaped, 9: total, 265. Leaving in prison, 703. Average daily number, 687.1; average daily increase, 70.7. Crimes for which convicts were received during year; against persons, 65, including—assault with intent to kill, 5; to commit rape, 4; to rob, 4; adultery, 4; bigamy, 4; incest, 4; larceny from person, 11; murder, second degree, 5; manslaughter, 9; murder, 4; polygamy, 3; prostitution and concubinage, 4; rape, 4; against property, 245; including—arson, 3; burglary, 34; burglary and larceny, 8; embezzlement, 1; false pretenses, 13; forgery, 7; larcenies, 159; malicious mischief, 8; passing counterfeit United States Treasury notes, 1;

THE CAPITOL, AT LANSING

robbery, 9; robbing United States post-office, 1; uttering and publishing forged instruments, 1. Of the sentences, 2 were for life; 1 for 20 years; 8 for 10 years and under 20; 46 for 5 years and under 10 years; 232 for 1 year and under 5 years; and 24 for less than 1 year. Average sentence, 2 years and 10 months, excluding life-prisoners. The ages of the convicts were: from 16 to 21, 80; from 21 to 30, 138; from 30 to 40, 58; from 50 to 60, 7; from 60 to 70, 4; from 70 to 80, 1.

Nationality: Belgium, 4; Denmark, 2; England, 6; Germany, 17; Holland, 5; Ireland, 18; Norway, 3; Ontario (Prov.), 44; Russia, 1; Scotland, 1; Sweden, 2; Switzerland, 1; Michigan, 34; other United States, 172: 161

could read, write, and cipher; 68 read and write; 51 read only; and 30 classed as illiterate: 185 were single; 10 widowers; 105 married, and 10 married and separated: 115 temperate; 132 occasional drinkers, and 63 intemperate. First convictions, 205; second, 40; third, 35; fourth, 30. White, 259; black, 41; mulatto, 10. Disbursements—for rations, $32,780.88; for other purposes, except buildings and repairs, $56,319.92; for buildings and repairs, $3,311.79: total, $92,412.59. Income from convict-labor, $94,027.47; fugitive convicts, $561; United States convicts, $2,627.-49; visitors, $2,015; team-work, $1,105.00; barber-shop, $142.90; other sources, $5,624,-68: total, $106,103.54. Whole number of convicts in prison, from 1839 to 1874 inclusive, 5,018; number of solitary life-convicts (for murder in first degree), from 1848 to 1874, inclusive, 68.

Number of inmates in State Reform-School at beginning of the fiscal year, 222; admitted during year, 109; discharged, 88; inmates September 30, 1874, 243; increase, 21. Whole number received since opening of school in 1856, 1,512. Of committals for the year, 79 were for larceny, 3 for grand larceny, 5 for burglary, 4 for burglary and larceny, 7 for assault and battery, 8 for vagrancy, 1 for false pretenses, and 2 returned: 97 were white, and 22 colored; 81 natives of the United States, and 28 of foreign birth; average age, 13 years and 3½ months.

The Board of Supervision of Charitable, Penal, Pauper, and Reformatory Institutions give the following statistics of the persons who received, in some manner, public aid or support in the State during the year ending September 30th:

DETROIT.

INSTITUTIONS.	Males.	Females.	Total.	Average.
In the county poor-houses...	Sex not	given.	4,532	1,642
Temporarily relieved outside of poor-houses.......................	Sex not	given.	26,362	72
State Public School..	112	47	159	105
Asylum for the Insane..	324	301	625	424
Institution for Deaf and Dumb, and the Blind......................	135	108	243	184
Harper Hospital, Detroit...	51	....	51	8
State-prison.	966	2	968	687
Detroit House of Correction...	2,256	580	2,836	450
Reform-School..	331	....	331	228
County jails..	7,286	685	7,971	251
Total...	11,461	1,723	44,078	4,046

Of the number in prisons, it is estimated that 2,500 were first in jails, and were therefore included twice in these figures.

The entire number of persons in the State wholly supported at the public charge, on the 30th day of September, 1874, in establishments organized and administered by public authority, was as follows:

INSTITUTIONS.	Males.	Females.	Total.
In the poor-houses..	Sex not	given.	1,642
State Public School...	107	43	150
Asylum for the Insane..	208	193	401
Institution for Deaf and Dumb, and the Blind......................	108	87	195
State-prison..	701	2	703
Detroit House of Correction...	372	123	495
Reform-School..	243	...	243
County jails..	Sex not	given.	270
Totals...	1,789	448	4,099

The total cost of fully supporting all the paupers in the several poor-houses of the State, for the year ending September 30, 1874, was... $167,177 46
The total sum expended for temporary relief outside the poor-houses, including medical attendance was.. 188,338 67
The total sum paid for transportation of paupers was... 10,395 74
Total cost of paupers maintained in poor-houses, and of those receiving "out-door relief" and transportation, was.. $360,911 87

Brought forward.. $360,911 87
The total sum paid by State for care of insane in asylum was $17,500; of which $3,500 was
paid for arrearages of 1873, leaving.. $14,000 00
The total sum paid by the several counties for care of insane in asylum was................... 75,258 86
The total sum paid by individuals, for care of insane, was... 23,739 86
The total sum received from all other sources was.. 486 52
Total cost of the insane was... 113,485 24
The total cost of pupils maintained in the institution for the education of the deaf and dumb,
and the blind, was.. $45,898 86
The total cost of supporting the children in the State Public School for neglected and de-
pendent children was... 7,807 75
The total cost of maintaining boys at the Reform-School was $39,002.11, less $10,875.96 re-
ceived from labor of boys.. 28,126 15
Total cost of pupils supported in institutions for mutes and blind, and in reformatories, was.......... 80,827 26
Total cost of maintaining disabled soldiers at Harper Hospital... 2,592 40
The sums received for labor of convicts in State-prison, for admission of visitors to prison,
and for property sold, amount to $107,013.72; while the total expense for running the
prison amounts to $96,758.58; leaving a revenue, over all expenses, for the support of the
prisoners, of $10,215.14.
The total sum paid by counties for keeping prisoners in the Detroit House of Correction was $18,630 34
The total sum paid by the several counties of the State for maintaining prisoners in jail was 55,010 87
Total cost of maintaining prisoners, exclusive of their earnings.. 73,641 21
Grand total of all expenditures for public dependents, exclusive of sums paid for grounds,
buildings, and repairs, for the year closing September 30, 1874.. $631,457 98

The following is the estimated value of the grounds, buildings, etc., occupied and used by the State, or some department thereof, for charitable or correctional purposes :

CHARITABLE PURPOSES.

County poor-house............................	$705,663 04
State Public School..........................	101,938 98
Asylum for the Insane.......................	589,859 22
Institution for Deaf and Dumb, and the Blind....................................	429,689 94

CORRECTIONAL PURPOSES.

State-prison..................................	474,000 45
Detroit House of Correction................	450,000 00
Reform-School..............................	238,155 00
County jails..................................	400,060 00
	$3,388,806 63

Gross receipts to September 30, 1874................................... $2,211,165 73
Balance in Treasury October 1, 1873.................................. 854,718 44

Total in Treasury during fiscal year................................. $3,065,879 17
Disbursements during fiscal year.................................... 1,995,604 85

Balance at close of fiscal year..................................... $1,070,274 32

Excess of receipts over disbursements............................... $915,560 88

Gross receipts to State Treasury.................................... $2,211,165 73
Which includes price of swamp-land expended in the construction of swamp-land State
roads—not cash....................................... $166,257 21
And amount of refundings and reimbursements................. 14,872 63
                                                                        181,129 53

Leaving for net cash receipts....................................... $2,030,035 90
The cash receipts which form no part of the State revenue amount to.... 421,090 74

Giving for net cash general revenue receipts........................ $1,608,945 16

The net cash revenue receipts were :

From direct taxes........................	$1,004,168 82
From specific taxes.......................	459,820 83
From trust-funds.........................	55,508 51
	$1,519,498 16
Miscellaneous sources....................	89,447 00
	$1,608,945 16

The gross disbursements for the fiscal year were........................ $1,995,604 85
The swamp-land warrant expenditures.............. $166,257 21
Refundings and reimbursements..................... 14,872 62
                                                                        181,129 83

Giving for net cash disbursements................................... $1,814,475 02
The disbursements from non-revenue receipts......................... 415,619 13

Leaving for net disbursements from general revenue receipts......... $1,398,855 89

The State bonded indebtedness, September 30, 1873..................... $1,733,292 78
There has been redeemed during the year............................. 145,157 14

Leaving outstanding September 30, 1874.............................. $1,588,135 64
Credit balance of two-million loan sinking-fund..................... 563,865 87

Debt in excess of sinking-fund...................................... $1,024,269 77

If to $631,457.98, the sum before stated as the grand total of all expenditure for the public dependents, we add interest for the year on the estimated value of the grounds, buildings, and personal property used and occupied for this purpose as aforesaid, being $237,216.46, we swell the grand total expended during the year, for public dependents, to the sum of $868,674.44, or about $20.89 to each individual so dependent.

Retiring Auditor-General William Humphrey gives the following summary of the fiscal operations of the State Treasury for the year closing September 30, 1874:

MINNESOTA. The most important measures passed by the Legislature, which was in session during the early part of the year, were a tax law and "an act creating a Board of Railroad Commissioners, defining their duties and providing for the establishment of maximum rates for the transportation of passengers and freight upon the railroads of this State, and to prevent extortion and unjust discrimination of railroad corporations or their employés, and to prescribe a mode of procedure and rules of evidence in relation thereto."

The commissioners were required to make for each company in the State before the 1st of August "a schedule of reasonable maximum rates of charges, for any and all distances, for the transportation of freight of all kinds and quantities, and passengers and cars on each of said railroads, as well as reasonable maximum rates for receiving, handling, and delivering freights and cars received by them for transportation."

Further powers and duties of the commissioners are defined as follows:

Such commissioners shall, on or before the first day of December in each year, and oftener if required by the Governor so to do, make a report to the Governor of their doings for the preceding year, containing such facts, statements, and explanations, as will disclose the actual workings of the system of railroad transportation in its bearings upon the business of the State, and such suggestions in relation thereto as may to them seem appropriate. They shall also, at such times as the Governor may direct, examine any particular subject relative to the condition and management of such railroads, and report to him in writing their opinion thereon, with the reasons therefor.

Said Board of Railroad Commissioners shall have power to employ railroad experts, to examine the property, books, records, accounts, papers, and proceedings of all railroad companies; to issue subpœnas for the attendance of witnesses, and to administer oaths, and take testimony; and the attendance of witnesses and production of evidence may be enforced as now provided for by law in causes before referees, and any court or officer authorized by law to issue subpœnas shall, whenever requested by said Board of Commissioners, issue subpœnas requiring the parties therein named to appear before such Board of Railroad Commissioners and testify, and any disobedience of such subpœna, or refusal to appear and testify thereunto, shall be regarded as a contempt of the court issuing the same, and punished by said court as a contempt.

Whenever it shall come to the knowledge of said Board of Commissioners, or they shall have reason to believe, that the laws of this State have been or are being violated by any railroad corporations, they shall, whenever in their judgment the public interest shall require, cause to be prosecuted all corporations or persons guilty of such violations, and to this end require the assistance of the Attorney-General, or any county attorney or other county officer as may be needed to institute or prosecute any or all such proceedings.

The political campaign of this year had reference to the election of a Chief and Associate Justice of the Supreme Court, and members of Congress. The Republican State Convention assembled in Minneapolis early in September, for the purpose of making judicial nominations. The resolutions adopted favored the judi-

cious enforcement of all laws for the protection of all classes of citizens of both North and South, and the whole country, against the perils of a new insurrection and a new rebellion; the preservation of public faith; the reduction of the public debt; the preservation of a sound currency against any ruinous inflation that may be inspired by speculative interests; the earliest possible return to specie payment consistent with the just rights of both the debtor and creditor classes; constant vigilance in hunting out and exposing to public condemnation delinquent officials and corruption in office, regardless of party interests and party relations; the opening up of new and cheaper channels of communication by water between the granaries of the West and the markets of the East; and, finally, approving the action of Governor Davis in relation to the prosecution of the persons charged by the report of the State Committee with defrauding the school-fund.

The Democratic State Convention met in St. Paul on the 23d of September, and adopted the following platform:

Whereas, The special occasion which brought the Republican party into being has long since ceased to exist, and there is not now, and has not been for years, any central animating principle or purpose in that party, except the cohesive principle of public plunder and the settled purpose to retain power by any means and at all hazards; and—

Whereas, To perpetuate its hold upon office, that party has formed alliance with the capital and organized monopolies of the country, and together they purpose to run the Federal and State governments in the interests of the favored classes, by exempting them from all burdens and restraints, and casting the whole crushing weight of onerous taxation upon the masses of the people: therefore, we, representatives of the people of the State of Minnesota, who demand a reform in the administration of our Federal Government, having assembled without regard to former parties and former partisan distinction, hereby proclaim the following platform of principles:

We declare the condition of the Southern States to be largely due to the corrupt rule of carpet-bag politicians, who have plundered and impoverished the people, intensified prejudices of race, and driven communities to the verge of civil war. Knowing that this state of affairs has been developed during the Administration of President Grant and been fostered by the course of the Republican party; and despairing of relief except through a radical change of policy, we demand—

1. The maintenance of a just and impartial policy toward the people of the South, whereby both races will be protected in all their rights; the expulsion of the thieves, and perfect equality before the law for all persons without regard to race, color, or political opinion.

2. A return to gold and silver as a basis of the currency of the country, and resumption of specie payments as soon as public interests will allow.

3. A tariff for revenue only consistent with an honest administration; none for protection; no government partnership with protected monopolies.

4. Home rule to limit and localize most zealously the few powers intrusted to public servants, municipal, State, and Federal. No centralization.

5. Equal and exact justice to all men. No partial legislation; no partial taxation.

6. A free press. No gag-laws.

7. Free men; uniform exercise of the laws. No sumptuary laws.

8. Official accountability enforced by better civil

and criminal remedies. No private use of public funds by public officers.

9. Chartered corporations by State always supervisable by the State in the interest of the people.

10. The party in power is responsible for the administration of the government while in power.

Resolved, That the nomination by the Republicans of a noted salary-grabber in the first congressional district, of an apologist and defender of that outrage in the second, and of one of the most unscrupulous congressional lobbyists in the third, shows the utter hollowness of all Republican promises of reform.

Resolved, That the startling exposures of corruption in the offices of the State Treasurer and Auditor, concealed through so many years of Republican administration, cause just alarm to all good citizens, and demonstrate anew the impossibility of reform within the Republican organization.

The election, held on the 3d of November, resulted in a Republican success. S. J. R. McMillan, Republican, was elected Chief-Justice by a majority of 10,492 over his Democratic opponent, Wescott Wilkin. The former received 51,607 votes, and the latter 41,115. Republicans were elected to Congress in each of the three congressional districts, viz., Mark H. Dunnell in the first, Horace B. Strait in the second, and William S. King in the third. The Legislature is classified as follows:

PARTIES.	Senate.	House.	Joint Ballot.
Republicans	21	54	75
Democrats	18	48	66
Independents	2	4	6
Republican majority...	1	2	3

In the early part of the year facts came to light which indicated that, by official corruption extending over several years, in the Auditor's department, the State had lost large sums of money. The official against whom these charges were made was Charles McIlrath, who had been State Auditor from January, 1864, to January, 1873, having been elected for three successive terms of three years each. During this period Mr. McIlrath was also *ex officio* Commissioner of the State Land-Office, and had the general supervision of all lands belonging to the State, of those in which the State had an interest, and of those held in trust by the State. Of the class last named were large tracts of land held by the State in trust for the University of Minnesota, for other educational purposes, and for internal improvements. The law provided for the sale of the timber on these lands, and for the payment of the proceeds into the State Treasury. The charge brought against Mr. McIlrath was, that he had not only neglected to collect the full amount of money actually due the State from this source, but had neglected to pay into the Treasury large sums of what he had collected. In February, 1874, a committee of three was appointed by the Legislature to investigate the affairs and management of the office of State Auditor. This committee was authorized to sit during the adjournment, and was directed to make its final report to the Governor. This report was filed with the Governor, September

4, 1874, and showed that the late State Auditor had received, on account of timber cut on the State lands, $77,041.13 more than he had paid the State Treasurer; that his management of certain stumpage transactions in Kandiyohi County, and of certain lands in Hennepin County, had resulted in a loss to the State of the further sum of $12,518.04; that the examiners appointed by the late State Auditor to report to him the quantities of timber cut on the State lands had made a systematic business of defrauding the State for pecuniary considerations, by reporting the quantity cut as less than the actual quantity, leaving the unreported quantities as the subject of spoliation by those whose duty it was to protect the interests of the State in these matters.

It was also shown by the report that the quantities cut were, by collusion between the claimants of the logs and the examiners, so under-estimated that, allowing for all that the State received, and all that its officers received and did not pay over, the State has been defrauded of large sums of money.

The committee conclude their report as follows:

One of the most astonishing developments of this investigation has been the utter lack of material in the Auditor's office from which your committee could obtain information, or even a clew regarding transactions involving thousands of dollars. In place of a clear exhibit upon the pages of the books of the office of important transactions, we find in some instances loose memoranda giving indefinite information of an ambiguous character; and in many cases involving matters of great consequence, nothing whatever can be found in the office in any manner referring to them. The labors of your committee would have been greatly lessened if they could have had access to any authentic record of the transactions referred to, but the almost entire absence of data in the Auditor's or Land Commissioner's offices upon which to base our investigations, has imposed upon us a vast amount of labor in obtaining the information from other sources.

Under the instruction of the Governor the Attorney-General at once brought suit against the ex-Auditor for the recovery of $94,641. When the inquiry arose as to what remedy the State had to indemnify itself for the losses sustained, the surprising fact was developed that Mr. McIlrath had executed no official bond at the beginning of or during his last term, and therefore there were no sureties to proceed against.

The financial transactions of the State are summarily presented in the following exhibit:

Total receipts during the fiscal year ending November 29, 1873	$1,331,210 87
Total disbursements	1,148,059 96
Leaving a general balance of	$183,150 91

The acknowledged bonded debt of the State December 1, 1874, amounted to $480,000, which has been contracted since 1867, chiefly for the erection of buildings for State institutions.

There are, however, bonds amounting to $2,275,000 outstanding against the State, the validity of which has been disputed. These bonds were issued in 1858, and lent to railroad companies upon the authority of an amendment to the constitution made in that year. Soon after receiving them the companies, as is alleged, failed to comply with the conditions upon which the bonds were granted, and payment was refused by the State. In 1860 another amendment to the constitution was adopted "expunging" the amendment of 1858, and providing that "no law levying a tax or making other provisions for the payment of principal or interest of the bonds denominated Minnesota State railroad bonds shall take effect or be in force until such law shall have been submitted to a vote of the people of the State and adopted by a majority of the electors of the State voting upon the same." Before this amendment was adopted the mortgages held by the State had been purchased and the mortgaged railroads bought by the government at nominal prices. In May, 1871, a popular vote was taken on a proposition for settlement by arbitration of these claims, when 21,499 votes were cast against and 9,293 in favor of the proposition, the total vote being less than half the average vote of the State.

The effect of the operation of the new tax law requiring property to be assessed at its cost value, has been to increase the total value of assessed taxable property from $112,035,561 in 1873 to $217,427,211 in 1874. In the former year 13,277,823 acres of land, exclusive of town and city lots, were valued with buildings at $57,211,460; town and city real estate, $30,285,861; personal property, $24,538,240. In 1874 the assessed property included lands and buildings valued at $113,410,620; real estate in cities and towns, $58,994,793; personal property, $45,021,798. The total tax levied in 1873 amounted to five mills, but a levy of 2$\frac{88}{100}$ mills on the valuation of 1874 will be sufficient to raise a revenue to meet the current expenses of the State.

As yet Minnesota does not hold a high rank as a manufacturing State, the people being more extensively engaged in agriculture. It has, however, a most important element for great industrial prosperity in the abundant water-power afforded by its numerous streams. It has been estimated that about 100,000 horse-power could be utilized during the daytime throughout the entire year, at the Falls of St. Anthony in the Mississippi near Minneapolis, while the St. Croix Falls, in the St. Croix River, are only second to St. Anthony Falls in hydraulic power. The total number of manufacturing establishments reported by the census of 1870 was 2,270, having 246 steam-engines of 7,085 horse-power, and 434 water-wheels of 13,054 horse-power, and employing 11,290 hands, of whom 10,892 were males above sixteen, 259 females above fifteen, and 139 youth. The capital invested amounted to $11,993,729; wages, $4,052,837; materials, $13,842,902; products, $23,110,700. The most important industries are given in the following statement:

INDUSTRIES.	No. of Establishments.	No. of Hands.	Capital.	Products.
Blacksmithing........	310	630	$255,511	$628,923
Boots and shoes.......	172	526	223,589	653,165
Carpenter'g and building.................	223	676	104,860	1,067,203
Carriages and wagons.	102	444	358,168	549,568
Cars, freight and passenger...............	1	79	170,000	783,800
Cooperage............	62	338	136,020	457,338
Grist-mill products...	216	790	2,900,015	7,534,575
Furniture............	85	393	302,550	448,772
Liquors, malt.........	65	225	450,550	388,555
Lumber, planed.......	13	58	143,400	239,642
" sawed........	207	2,952	3,311,140	4,299,162
Machinery, railroad repairing.............	4	456	253,021	788,074
Machinery, steam-engines and boilers....	8	233	220,000	336,482
Printing and publishing newspapers......	20	241	267,000	343,304
Saddlery and harness.	93	259	165,475	354,259
Sash, doors and blinds.	27	264	263,133	357,616
Tin, copper, and sheet-iron ware..........	78	231	161,685	348,696

The vast pine-forests of Minnesota constitute an important source of wealth. It is estimated that about one-third of the State is lumbered land. On the head-waters of the various tributaries of the extreme Upper Mississippi and St. Croix Rivers is an extensive "pine-region" comprising an estimated area of 21,000 square miles. Vast forests are also found on the shore of Lake Superior, and on the Red River and its tributaries. The annual cutting and sawing of logs affords extensive employment for men and capital; 164,743,150 feet of logs were reported to have been scaled in the North Mississippi district in 1873, including 161,880,670 feet at Minneapolis, while 33,000,000 feet were estimated to have been sawed but not scaled. The total number of feet scaled in the St. Croix district was 147,618,147; sawed and not scaled, 8,338,976; sawed and scaled, 94,229. In the Duluth district the number of feet scaled amounted 6,147,988. In the St. Croix district the manufactured lumber was reported at 74,-063,976 feet, besides 19,200,000 shingles, and 19,477,850 lath. Minnesota has unusual commercial advantages, having within its limits three great navigable water systems, which are connected with the railroad system of the State, and afford continuous channels of communication with Hudson Bay, the Atlantic Ocean, and the Gulf of Mexico. The Mississippi is navigable to St. Paul about 225 days in the year. The completion of the Northern Pacific Railroad, which has its eastern terminus at Duluth, on Lake Superior, and is now (1875) in operation to Bismarck, in Dakota, 450 miles, will give the State direct communication with the Pacific. This road, which joins the lake and the Red River water systems, is to be connected with the other railroads of Minnesota and the Mississippi River by three lines of railroad at the eastern, central, and western portions of the State. The Lake Superior and Mississippi Railroad joins St. Paul at the head of navigation on the Mississippi River, and Duluth, at the head of Lake

Superior; while the former city will have direct connection with the Northern Pacific Railroad by the two divisions of the St. Paul & Pacific, which are now in process of construction, extending from St. Anthony to Brainerd, and the other from St. Cloud to St. Vincent, on the northwestern border of the State, a distance of 315 miles, crossing the Northern Pacific at Glyndon, 13 miles east of the Red River. This road is now in operation from St. Cloud to Melrose, 85 miles from St. Vincent; it is to be continued to Fort Garry, in the province of Manitoba, 61 miles from the Minnesota border. The State also has connection with the Union Pacific Railroad by means of the St. Paul & Sioux City and Sioux City & St. Paul Railroads. Furthermore, the completion of the contemplated improvements in the Fox and Wisconsin Rivers will give to Minnesota a continuous water-channel from the Mississippi River to Lake Michigan. In Minnesota a grant of six sections per mile of the public lands was made to aid in the construction of railroads, which was increased to ten sections per mile in 1865. Thus not less than 13,-200,000 acres of land, or more than one-fourth of the entire area of the State, have been granted to railroad corporations, either by the General Government or that of the State. These grants comprise 11,250,000 acres by Congress and 1,950,000 by the State; and 5,515,007 acres

have already been conveyed to the companies. The railroad companies in the State organized under special charters are required to pay to the State, in lieu of all other taxes, 1 per cent. of their gross earnings for the first three years, 2 per cent. during the next seven years, and 3 per cent. thereafter. Other railroad companies can acquire the same privileges by complying with the provisions of the law. The gross earnings of the companies subject to this law in 1872 were reported at $5,999,518, on which the tax amounted to $106,876. The gross earnings during the year ending September 1, 1873, were $5,536,104, including $1,-385,272 from passengers and $3,811,603 from freight. The total expenses of all the companies amounted to $4,140,885. A commissioner is appointed by the State, whose duty is to report to the Legislature annually concerning the finances, business, and general condition of every railroad company in the State. Minnesota had 31 miles of railroad in 1863, 298 in 1866, and 1,092 in 1870. In 1874 there were 1,821 miles of main track and branches, exclusive of side-track, etc. The railroads completed in the State, and their termini, in 1874, with the capital stock issued, the latter items being reported by the State Commissioners, for the year ending September 1, 1873, and the number of acres of land granted by Congress, are shown in the following statement:

NAME OF CORPORATION.	TERMINI.	Miles completed in the State in 1874.	Total length between terminal when different from the preceding.	Capital stock issued as reported by State Commissioners, Sept. 1, 1873.	Acres of land granted by Congress.
Chicago, Dubuque & Minnesota.......	Dubuque, Iowa, and La Crescent.	24	118	$426,215	....
Chicago, Milwaukee & St. Paul.......	....	...	...	3,152,000	....
Via La Crosse......................	Milwaukee, Wis., and St. Paul..	130	324	....	....
" Prairie du Chien..............	" "	127	405	....	....
Branches......................... }	Mendota and Minneapolis....	9	...	....	....
	Mason City, Iowa, and Austin....	10	40	....	....
Leased (Hastings & Dakota)..........	Hastings and Glencoe...........	75	...	750,000	500,000
Lake Superior & Mississippi..........	St. Paul and Duluth...........	156	...	5,125'000	430,854
Leased { Stillwater & St. Paul........	White Bear and Stillwater.......	13	...	400,000	....
{ Minneapolis & Duluth	White Bear and Minneapolis....	14	...	200,000	....
{ Minneapolis & St. Louis....	Minneapolis and Sioux City Junc.	28	...	92,000	....
Northern Pacific....................	Duluth and Puget Sound.......	254	1,800	18,239,300	2,918,400
St. Paul & Pacific...:..............	St. Paul and Breckenridge.......	217	...	500,000	1,248,688
Branch.....................	St. Anthony and Brainerd.......	75	125	1,468,800	940,000
St. Vincent extension...............	St. Cloud and St. Vincent......	85	315	....	2,000,000
St. Paul & Sioux City..............	St. Paul and St. James..........	122	...	1,851,500	850,000
St. Paul, Stillwater & Taylor's Falls..:	Near St. Paul and Stillwater....	18	...	277,500	....
Sioux City & St. Paul..............	Sioux City, Iowa, and St. James.	66	143	1,515,780	....
Southern Minnesota.................	Grand Crossing and Winnebago.	108	...	3,825,000	450,000
West Wisconsin....................	St. Paul and Elroy, Wis.......	4	197	....	....
Winona & St. Peter.............	Winona and Lake Kampeska,Dak.	288	326	400,000	710,000
Total.............................		1,821	....	....	....

Among the many natural advantages with which this State is endowed is the remarkable convergence of the shores of Lake Superior at its western end, forming a harbor of great extent and perfect safety. These advantages are shared by the State of Wisconsin. The efforts of the people to utilize their harbor facilities—efforts which the terminus of two railroads in this State at that point and the existence of the most important city on that lake have rendered imperative—were impeded in their inception by some embarrass-

ments- which were fairly and legally surmounted.

A brief statement of facts is necessary to an understanding of the present condition of this important interest. In 1870, the city of Duluth began to excavate a ship-canal across Minnesota Point, near its base. While this work was in progress the United States commenced a suit in the Federal courts to restrain the prosecution of the improvement, on the ground, among others, that such a canal, when opened, would tend to deflect the current of the St. Louis River from its outlet, and thereby injure the natural harbor. A temporary injunction was obtained, and the matter then became the subject of negotiations between the promoters of the improvement and the proper authorities of the United States. These negotiations resulted in an arrangement whereby the city was permitted to go on and construct the canal, upon giving a bond in the penal sum of $100,000, conditional that the city should build a dike below the canal from Rice's Point to Minnesota Point. This bond was given. The dike was built and the canal completed. It is two hundred and fifty feet wide and deep enough to float any vesssel on the lakes. It is and has been since its construction the entrepot of nearly all the commerce transacted at the western extremity of Lake Superior. It gives safe ingress to the Bay of Superior, which is dangerous of access through its natural and tortuous outlet.

Since the adjustment of the issues between the United States and the city, the collection district of Duluth has been established and Duluth made its port of entry. Appropriations for the improvement of its harbor have been made by Congress and expended.

The State of Wisconsin, however, deems itself aggrieved by these improvements, and has therefore recently exhibited in the Supreme Court of the United States its bill of complaint against the city of Duluth and the Northern Pacific Railroad Company in which the decree of that tribunal is prayed that the defendants be perpetually enjoined from keeping open or maintaining the canal and also required to fill it up. The paramount interests of Minnesota in this suit have led the Governor to take such steps as will protect the rights of the State.

MISSISSIPPI. The condition of affairs in this State, during the latter part of the year, attracted general attention throughout the country.

On the 7th of December a serious conflict occurred in Vicksburg between the whites and blacks, which resulted in great loss of life, and caused wide-spread alarm. About five o'clock on the morning of that day (Monday) the alarm was given that armed negroes, with hostile intent, were approaching the city from several directions. The white citizens at once armed and organized in companies. At nine o'clock a general alarm was given, and a detachment of city troops marched out of Grove Street, and, near Point Lookout, just outside the city limits, met a body of 200 negroes. A conflict at once ensued, and the negroes were soon put to rout, with a loss of six killed, several wounded, and some taken prisoners. About the same time, an engagement was in progress between a force of citizens, who had been sent out on the Jackson road on the northeast side, and a body of negroes who, as reported, were intrenched in the old Federal breastworks, just west of the monument where Pemberton surrendered. The

conflict here lasted an hour, and was the most sanguinary of the day. The infantry in front engaged the negroes, while the cavalry charged their flanks. The negroes fled in wild disorder. Their losses were reported at twenty killed and wounded. Only one white man was reported killed. While these two engagements were in progress, three companies of citizens, having met about 250 negroes in Cherry Street, charged on them, and routed them with small loss. At other points the negroes were dispersed by cavalry, and by noon the "war" was over. Great excitement prevailed in the city during the day, and business was entirely suspended; but on the following day quiet and order were restored. The reported losses comprise three white citizens killed and three wounded; while of the negroes about seventy-five were killed and wounded, and thirty or forty taken prisoners.

The causes that led to this unfortunate affair, and the events preceding it, have been reported very differently by the opposing parties. It is impossible to determine with accuracy the exact facts and the true condition of affairs. It becomes important, therefore, to give both sides a hearing in making up the record.

First will be given the substance of the statement published on the 12th of December, and signed by many citizens of Vicksburg. This recites that, in 1873, T. W. Cardoza was clerk of the Circuit and G. W. Davenport of the Chancery Court of Warren County. In November of that year, Peter Crosby was elected sheriff, and G. W. Walton, C. Axelson, W. B. Lewis, Oscar Speed, and Henry Hunt, as members of the Board of Supervisors of Warren County. All of the above-named officers were Republicans, and all but Axelson were colored. In October, 1873, Cardoza was elected State Superintendent of Education, when Governor Ames appointed A. W. Dorsey, a colored Republican, to the office of Circuit Clerk, made vacant by Cardoza's resignation. This act, on the part of the Governor, was characterized as " a gross usurpation of power, inasmuch as our statutes plainly declare that such vacancies shall be filled by election." In August, 1874, Dorsey was arrested on the charge of issuing forged witness-certificates, and committed to jail, whence he was released on bail. He then resigned his office. The vacancy thus created was filled by an appointment made by Governor Ames. The investigation of Dorsey's frauds led to the discovery of similar ones in the case of his predecessor, T. W. Cardoza. At the same time, George W. Davenport, being ex officio Clerk of the Board of Supervisors, was charged with the issue of fraudulent county warrants for money. For the offenses above stated the grand-jury, composed of ten blacks and seven whites, found bills of indictment against Dorsey, Cardoza, and Davenport. Pending this investigation by the grand-jury, the books of the County Treasury and other valuable records were taken from the court-house, which it appears was in the charge of Sheriff Crosby. As tax-collector, Sheriff Crosby was required to give bond, with good securities, in the sum of $81,000, besides $20,000 as sheriff. During the summer of 1874 it was charged that the official bonds, given by Crosby and approved by the Board of Supervisors, were almost worthless. He was, therefore, required to give new bonds. "On the day when Crosby appeared to tender new bonds," says the Citizens' Address, "the petitioning tax-payers being present, the board refused to pass upon the new bonds, and announced that their action would be postponed until the next morning. On the evening of the same day they met stealthily and informally, and accepted the new bonds which were notoriously insufficient and almost worthless, the sureties thereon being for the most part public officials residing in different parts of the State, and colored men of small or no means residing in this county. Moreover, after this action, at least eight of the sureties of the new bonds applied to the board by written communications to be relieved as such sureties, and although two members of the board twice called meetings to take action in the matter, no quorum could be obtained, and it was well known that neither illness nor disability prevented the attendance of the other members. It was generally believed that the failure to act was due to the influence of Crosby and the indicted officials who were interested in keeping him in office. After this, Crosby, on the 7th day of November, 1874, published a card in the *Vicksburg Times*, stating that he would not further attempt to give his bonds, and would hold his office until ousted by a judgment of the Supreme Court. In this state of affairs, all confidence in the integrity and competency of these officials being destroyed, a mass-meeting of tax-payers of the county was held in Vicksburg on Wednesday, December 2, 1874 (this date is important), at which a committee was appointed to wait upon Crosby and Davenport and the Board of Supervisors, and demand their resignations. This committee found only Crosby and Davenport, by whom they were informed that they would give their answers in half an hour. Failing to receive their answers within this time, the tax-payers proceeded in a body to the court-house to repeat their demand. There they found Crosby only, who, upon demand made (unaccompanied by any threats or exhibition of violence), placed his resignation in their hands. Davenport had in the mean time absconded, and has not since been seen in the county."

Two days after the holding of this meeting, the following proclamation was issued by Governor Ames:

EXECUTIVE OFFICE, STATE OF MISSISSIPPI,
JACKSON, MISS., *December* 4, 1874.

Whereas, Positive information having been received by me that riotous and disorderly persons

have combined togther with force and arms, and by threats and intimidation have expelled from his office the legally-elected Sheriff of Warren County, and do now resist the execution by him of the laws of the State; and—

Whereas, said riotous and disorderly persons have combined together with force and arms, and made threats against other county officials whereby said county officials were compelled to flee for their lives; and—

Whereas, The State courts were in full force and vigor, and competent to punish any of such officials, if dishonest, until said courts were paralyzed by the action of such unlawful assemblage; and—

Whereas, Such threats and intimidation have been directed exclusively against colored officials; and—

Whereas, It is satisfactorily presented to me that the object of said riotous and disorderly action is to deprive colored men of their civil and political rights because of their color; and—

Whereas, It is provided by the Constitution and laws of the United States that the protection of the laws shall not be denied to any citizen because of race or color; and—

Whereas, It is the duty of the Governor of the State to use all his powers to execute the laws, and to suppress riots and insurrections, as provided in the State constitution: now, therefore—

I, Adelbert Ames, Governor of the State of Mississippi, do hereby make proclamation and command said riotous and disorderly persons to disperse and retire peaceably to their respective abodes, and hereafter submit to the legally-constituted authorities of the State, and I invoke the aid and coöperation of all good citizens to uphold the laws, and preserve the public peace.

By the Governor:
JAMES HILL, Secretary of State.

Governor Ames's proclamation was followed on the next day by an address from the tax-payers of Warren County, signed by Judge Warren Cowan, chairman of the convention. This declares that Governor Ames's proclamation is false in representation, and made upon "the *ex-parte* statements of corrupt partisan office-holders, forgers, embezzlers of public funds, and thieves;" and further, that Governor Ames had "directed an ignorant negro, recently from the work-house of the city of Vicksburg, to be prepared with arms and men to endeavor to intimidate the tax-payers of this city and county, and thereby bring on a conflict of races." After protesting against the light in which the tax-payers were placed by Governor Ames, and declaring that they had assembled in a lawful and peaceful manner, the proclamation continues:

1. Having been satisfied that said officials of the county were stealing and plundering our substance.

2. That they had combined together and with other officials to prevent each other's punishment, and perpetuate their unlawful and criminal courses.

3.. The execution of the law was intrusted to these officials, and they had persistently refused to execute it, but had by their acts and assertions defied and insulted our people, already groaning under unjust, unnecessary, and oppressive taxation.

4. The sheriff of this county, who has the custody of the court-house, has, through his negligence and carelessness, permitted the destruction of the county records, which furnished testimony of the guilt of the Chancery Clerk and others.

5. The sheriff was about to collect the taxes of the State and county, to an amount exceeding $100,000, and had failed notoriously to give a bond according

to law, and had, by the aid of members of the Board of Supervisors, evaded the requirements of the law, by having a worthless bond approved.

6. The tax-payers having failed, after repeated efforts, to have the law enforced, and being aware that it would be impossible to convict the criminals as long as the sheriff had the power to pack the juries, and being satisfied that he would so pack them to procure the acquittal of his friends and fellows in crime and corruption, the mass-meeting of tax-payers determined, in a deliberate, firm, but peaceful manner, to adjourn to the court-house, where they had a perfect right to go, and firmly insist upon the resignation of the sheriff, the Chancery Clerk, and other obnoxious officials. This they did, and the sheriff resigned.

7. That no violence was offered to the said sheriff, but he was told repeatedly that his resignation was all the people wanted. No weapons of any description were used or exhibited, and the sheriff remained in the Court-House Square unmolested.

8. The Chancery Clerk and coroner fled on the approach of the tax-payers, and no one had an opportunity to threaten or injure them.

9. The tax-payers, long ere the issuance of said proclamation of said Ames, dispersed to their respective abodes, and their only desire is that the laws shall be executed; that the records shall not be subjected to mutilation and destruction by being placed in the custody of criminals and thieves, who are wholly unreliable and irresponsible. In view of all these facts, we desire to say that the charge of interfering with the rights of the colored people on account of their color or race is particularly and especially false. Relying upon the judgment of an impartial, honest, brave, and sympathetic people, we submit our case.

The Citizens' Address continues as follows :

Contemporaneously with this proclamation of Governor Ames, a printed handbill, over the signature of Peter Crosby, appeared upon the streets of Vicksburg, and was extensively circulated among the colored people of the county, in which the tax-payers were denounced as a " mob " of " ruffians," " barbarians," and " political banditti," and which, in highly inflammatory language, called upon his friends to support him. This handbill, Crosby has since stated, was prepared for him by a colored Republican in the office of the Secretary of State at Jackson.

On the day after its appearance in Vicksburg, Crosby published a card in the newspapers of the city, stating that his object in publishing the said handbill was " not to direct abusive language against anybody, but to set himself right before the people, to whom he owed every thing, and that he did not see it before publication." This proclamation of Governor Ames and the handbill of Crosby appeared on Saturday, December 5th. About the same time, O. S. Lee, aide-de-camp to Governor Ames, and A. G. Packer, his adjutant-general of militia, appeared in Vicksburg—upon what business it is not certainly known. But it is known, from a statement made by O. S. Lee, aide-de-camp, to two of our prominent citizens, that P. C. Hall, a colored captain of militia, of violent temper and bad character, received orders from Governor Ames to hold his company of militia in readiness, which orders were not transmitted to him through Brigadier-General Furlong, who is the commander of this militia district, and who is an ex-Federal officer and a Republican. It is also known that no orders were given to any other militia company.

Determined to exhaust every possible means of protection afforded by the law, and ignorant of the violent measures contemplated by Crosby and his confederates, the tax-payers, on the evening of Sunday, December 6th, prepared and presented to Hon. E. Hill, the Republican chancellor of this district, a bill of equity praying that Crosby might be required to execute sufficient bonds within a time to be fixed, and that in the mean while he be enjoined from exercising the functions of the office of sheriff and tax-collector.

The chancellor prepared the order granting the injunction at his house on Sunday night, and would have delivered it to the attorneys who prepared the bill, on the following morning, to be served, had not events happened which made it useless to prosecute that remedy any further. Pending the injunction, had it been permitted the citizens to follow that course, it would have been the duty of the Judge of the Circuit Court, then in session, also a Republican, to appoint some responsible person sheriff *pro tempore*, and it was confidently believed that in this way our principal troubles would have been peaceably and permanently removed. While the consultation was being held with Chancellor Hill, A. G. Packer, Governor Ames's adjutant-general, and Crosby, came in together, and Crosby was informed that it was rumored that the negroes of the county would attempt to invade the city upon the following morning. He disclaimed any knowledge upon the subject, but said that he had the power to disperse them, though he saw no objection to their coming if they desired. Upon this he was earnestly besought by Chancellor Hill and the citizens present to send out orders to them that night to return to their homes, since if they made such an attempt much blood would be shed. Crosby promised to do so. Nevertheless, early on the next morning positive information was received that armed negroes from the country were marching on Vicksburg in large numbers.

Our citizens, thus suddenly aroused to a sense of their great danger, hastily armed and took positions on the roads in the suburbs of the city. They came in conflict with three separate bodies of armed negroes numbering from two to four hundred each, on three different roads, and defeated and repulsed each body. It is estimated that from fifty to one hundred negroes were killed and wounded, and about thirty were captured, all of whom, except four of the leaders, have been released and permitted to go to their homes.

Early on Monday Crosby was arrested, and has been, since then, strongly guarded to protect him from the vengeance of men of his own color, who say that he instigated them to attempt the invasion of the city, and hold him responsible for all the blood of his own race which was shed in this conflict, as well as from any violence which might be attempted by any of our citizens who have lost friends in repelling this assault upon our city.

On Tuesday afternoon, when it was supposed that all fighting was over, a party of our citizens, while engaged in burying a friend who had been slain in the conflict, was fired on from an ambush by a body of armed negroes, and one of their number was killed. Since then the Mayor of Vicksburg has organized a special police force, and under its surveillance peace and quiet have been completely restored, and our people have resumed their usual vocations.

The version of these difficulties given by Governor Ames is materially different from that above recorded. According to his statement, the troubles in Vicksburg were but the natural outgrowth of the violence of the preceding election in August, and were for political purposes. Says Governor Ames:

The White Leagues at one time, and the Tax-payers' League at another, have been for some time through their committees examining the books and papers of the county officials. They (the leaguers), it is said, forced themselves on the grand-jury, and after a lengthy session found indictments against but one official, a colored man by the name of Davenport.

MISSISSIPPI. 571

This information relative to the action of the grand-jury I received from the foreman of said jury and the leaguers. No charge was made against the official conduct of Sheriff Crosby. I know that he has made his settlements to date. They anticipated—so said the foreman of the grand-jury referred to—that the county would be defrauded because Crosby's bond was not sufficient. Here let me say, Republican officials who have to give bonds are constantly being attacked through them and embarrassed beyond measure, yet the number of defaulters in the State during the year have been more numerous among Democratic officials and for a greater amount, so say all our reports, than among Republican officials. The leaguers pretend to say that the petit jury will be packed to acquit Davenport and two ex-county officials against whom indictments have been found. So far as I know—so far as I could learn from the foreman of the grand-jury—the indictment against Davenport, and the pretended fear of packed juries, were the only cause of the present usurpations and bloodshed in that city. After a meeting of the so-called tax-payers, a committee waited on Crosby and demanded his resignation. Crosby declined to resign, and asked what charges had been preferred against him. The chairman of the committee stated they were only instructed to ask his immediate resignation. Afterward a mob of some six hundred waited on him, and he resigned to save his life—so he has stated to me. The other officials to be waited on made their escape or secreted themselves.

The Circuit Court was in session, and the judge, being deprived of his sheriff, came down from the bench and was going to leave the room, but (so I am informed by an eye-witness) was forced to return to it and adjourn the court to a given day.

The following is a note received by me from the judge:

To His Excellency Governor Ames:

It becomes my duty to inform you that an organized mob composed of several hundred armed men have this evening taken forcible possession of the court-house and jail of this county, and forced most of the county officers to resign or flee to the country for protection. The mob are in possession of the records of the offices, and threaten violence to any one who does not recognize their authority. My court is in session, but I am powerless and cannot execute the law. Relief must be furnished from abroad in the way of military by the State or General Government, and that quickly, to prevent general riot and loss of life. Very respectfully, GEORGE E. BROWN, Judge Fifteenth Judicial District.

Thus anarchy prevailed. Then came the question, Shall the United States be called upon, or shall the State attempt to maintain its authority and laws? For obvious reasons the President should not be appealed to until the State authorities had acted. Saturday Sheriff Crosby returned to Vicksburg. My adjutant-general went the same day. The city was then full of armed men, many having gone there from other towns and from Louisiana.

The colored men had an understanding to aid Crosby in his effort to regain possession of his office, and started from various parts of the county Monday morning. Early that morning Crosby was seized by the mob. One of the leading men of a body of men going to Crosby's aid, one Owen, saw him and received his orders countermanding those previously given, and ordering him to desist from further efforts in his behalf. Under a flag of truce Owen returned to his friends, and was reporting his interview with Crosby when the White-Leaguers voted to assault Owen's party, and at once advanced on them and opened fire. It is reported that a few of Owen's men had arms, and at once broke and ran. Then the slaughter began. It is said and believed that some sixty or eighty colored men were killed. The same old story—negroes killed by the score, none of their opponents hurt, and still the negro to blame. It is reported to me that unarmed negroes on cotton-bales, going to town, were killed. Also

men were killed elsewhere without any arms in their possession.

Immediately after the troubles in Vicksburg Governor Ames issued a proclamation, which, after reciting that rioters had by threats and intimidation expelled the sheriff of Warren County, that they had made threats against other county officials, compelling them to flee for their lives, and that the laws were resisted, concluded as follows:

I, Adelbert Ames, Governor of the State of Mississippi, do hereby make proclamation and command said rioters and disorderly persons to disperse and retire peaceably to their respective abodes, and hereafter submit to the legally constituted authorities of the State, and I evoke the aid and coöperation of all good citizens to uphold the laws and preserve peace.   ADELBERT AMES, Governor.
JAMES HILL, Secretary of State.

Upon receipt of this, Mayor O'Leary, of Vicksburg, issued a proclamation, which, after repeating the charges and statements of the Governor, concluded as follows:

Now, I, Richard O'Leary, Mayor of the city of Vicksburg, do hereby make my proclamation, reciting what is known to every citizen of Vicksburg, of every party, color, denomination, and condition of life, that there has been no riotous assemblage in this city; that what seems to have given rise to the uncalled-for proclamation of his Excellency was a quiet and orderly meeting of the owners and tax-payers of the city and county, who, without arms and violence, requested the resignation of irresponsible officials from the office of sheriff and chancery clerk of this county, who had failed to execute bonds as required by law; that the city government of Vicksburg is amply able to preserve the peace and quiet of said city under all circumstances; that the laws of the city and of the State of Mississippi have been threatened, and the recitals in the Governor's proclamation tending to produce a contrary impression are meretricious and mendacious, and unjust to the last degree: I therefore warn all persons to be guarded, to preserve good order and respect for law; and whereas said proclamation has excited the citizens of the county, and that I have this moment received information that armed bodies of colored men have organized and are now marching on the city, I call upon all good citizens to observe the laws of the land, and I warn all such unlawful assemblages and armed bodies of men to disperse and retire to their homes; and, for the preservation of law and order in the city, I hereby command all good citizens to hold themselves in readiness to report at any call I may make upon them for the purpose of enforcing this proclamation.
                              R. O'LEARY, Mayor.
VICKSBURG, December 7, 1874.

Later in the day the mayor put forth a second proclamation, as follows:

Citizens: Be quiet and discreet but firm. Your dearest interests are at stake. All keepers of bar-rooms and liquor-dealers are hereby ordered to close their places of business, and permit no drinking upon or about their premises until to-morrow at 12 M. By order of   R. O'LEARY, Mayor.
Monday, December 7, 1874.

On the 8th of December the following proclamation was issued by the Governor for convening an extra session of the Legislature on the 17th of December:

Whereas, The lawfully-constituted officers of Warren County are prevented from discharging their official duties by an armed insurrection, notwithstanding and in defiance of my proclamation on the 4th instant:

Now, therefore, I, Adelbert Ames, Governor of the State of Mississippi, by virtue of the authority vested in me by the seventh section of the fifth article of the Constitution of the State of Mississippi, do issue this my proclamation convening in extra session the Legislature of the State of Mississippi, at the Capitol, in the city of Jackson, at 12 o'clock, meridian, on Thursday, the 17th day of December, A. D. 1874.

In testimony whereof, I have hereunto set my hand and caused the Great Seal of the State of Mississippi to be affixed this 8th day of December, A. D. 1874.

ADELBERT AMES.

By the Governor:

JAMES HILL, Secretary of State.

Pursuant to this summons, the Legislature assembled in Jackson, on the 17th of December. In reviewing the subject which the Legislature had been convened to consider, Governor Ames said:

To-day, in Warren County, the laws and authority of the State are set at defiance. Although there is not in that county a single militia officer, they have organized companies and regiments, officered by men who pretend to act by authority of the State, exercising all the functions of an independent sovereignty, even so far as to search the homes of citizens of different political faith to take from them their arms, incarcerate them in jail, compelling legally-elected officials to resign their offices, and, above all, putting citizens to death, without even the formalities of law.

Officials and prominent men holding political views different from the insurgents, have been compelled to flee, and the Judges of the State courts, though one of those courts was in session, were forced to escape under cover of night that they might not fall a sacrifice to the mob.

It is pretended that their acts of bloodshed were a necessity; that men were fighting for their homes, their families, and their firesides. But how inadequate the plea when we know that those who went to the city of Vicksburg from Warren County, as many did, left their homes, their families, and their firesides, absolutely unprotected, in the midst of a large population of the very class they were engaged in shooting down! Had they believed there was danger they would not, they could not, have abandoned them; for had those they pretended to fear the purpose to destroy, they could have done so without opposition.

By armed men riding through the county, this persecuted class have been maltreated and intimidated till a perfect reign of terror prevails. Such has been, and is, the condition of affairs in Warren County.

What is the real or pretended cause therefor? A recent grand-jury indicted one official, two ex-officials (clerks of the courts), and the sheriff's bonds are claimed to be insufficient and invalid. It is also asserted that another cause of action was a fear, real or imaginary, that the petit jury for the trial of these indicted persons might be organized to acquit.

These are proclaimed as the causes for the attempted expulsion of these officials from office, the interruption of the State courts, the violations of the laws, and defiance of the authority of the State.

No single legal remedy has been exhausted. The petit jury had not been organized. The sheriff could have been restrained from continuing to act as sheriff and tax-collector until he should comply with the requirements of the law with regard to his bonds by injunction, upon application to any one of the thirty-three Chancellors and Circuit Judges of the State, or any one of the Supreme Court Judges. And, upon proper showing to the Chancellor, could have been required to give new bonds, either as sheriff or tax-collector, or both. Yet not the first step was taken to remedy any grievance by such injunction, nor by such application to the Chancellor.

The subject was at once taken up by the Legislature, and on the following day, the 18th, the subjoined majority report was adopted:

Whereas, It is provided in the Constitution of the United States, article IV., section 4, that the United States shall guarantee to every State in the Union protection to each State against domestic violence, on application of the Legislature of that State; and—

Whereas, In the county of Warren, in the State of Mississippi, several of the legally elected and acting officers of said county, including the sheriff thereof, by force and violence on the part of lawless persons, have been compelled to abandon, and have been prevented from exercising the duties of their respective offices; and the public property, including the court-house, the jail, together with the prisoners lawfully confined therein, and the public records of said county, have been taken possession of by like force and violence, and are still held by such lawless and unauthorized persons, contrary to and in defiance of the laws of said State; and—

Whereas, In consequence of such illegal and violent acts, as aforesaid, many of the peaceable citizens of said county have been killed, and a large number, through fear of violence, have been compelled to abandon their homes and families, and forced to seek protection by flight and concealment, and are still unable to peaceably return to and occupy their respective abodes; and—

Whereas, Certain lawless, armed, and riotous persons, in flagrant violation of the Constitution and laws of the United States, and of the State of Mississippi, have made illegal searches of the private houses and persons of citizens of said county of Warren, have also imprisoned and held for a number of days many of the citizens of said county, including public officers, without any legal authority and process of law whatever; and—

Whereas, A large number of armed men from adjacent States have invaded the State of Mississippi in aid of such lawless and riotous persons and acts therein, and others have signified their willingness to assist such lawless and riotous persons whenever called upon; and—

Whereas, The courts of the country have been paralyzed to such extent that they cannot be held, and thus rendered incapable to suppress such violence and to enforce the laws; and—

Whereas, The chief Executive of the State has no sufficient force at his command, by calling out the militia, nor other adequate power, to suppress such domestic violence, to execute the laws, and to guarantee full protection to all citizens, irrespective of race, color, or condition, without causing a conflict of races, and thereby endangering life and property to an alarming extent: therefore—

Resolved, That the Senate of the State of Mississippi (the House of Representatives concurring), That the President of the United States be and is hereby called upon, and urgently requested, by use of the military power at his command, to suppress such domestic violence, to restore peace and order, in this State, and to guarantee to all citizens the equal and impartial enjoyment of their constitutional and legal rights. Be it further

Resolved, That his Excellency the Governor of this State be and is hereby authorized and requested to transmit, forthwith, the foregoing resolutions, properly attested, to his Excellency the President of the United States.

At the same time the following minority report was submitted:

We, the undersigned members of the joint committee to whom was referred the Governor's message, feel constrained to dissent *in toto* from that part of the report of the majority of this committee, wherein a call is made upon the United States Government for troops. And upon this subject present this minority report:

Having duly and fully considered the extraordinary message of his Excellency, and deliberated upon the statements therein contained and the unfortunate disturbances discussed, we can see no just cause for the action recommended. So far as we have been able to ascertain from reliable sources, this is in brief a history of the recent troubles in the vicinity of Vicksburg:

The county officials at Vicksburg were charged with embezzlement, forgeries, and defalcations in office, and some of them had been duly indicted for their offenses, and the sheriff, who is *ex-officio* tax-collector, had been found exercising the functions of his office without having first given the bond required by law. Tax-payers, aggravated by their many grievances, had repeatedly demanded of him that he should comply with the law in this particular, and had again and again appealed to the constituted authorities to require him to do so. Their appeals were disregarded, and their remonstrances were vain. They also had learned that the records of their courts were being mutilated for the purpose of protecting corrupt officials.

In their extremity, a number of them repaired to the court-house and demanded of these irresponsible officials a surrender of their trust.

That this may have been technically wrong may be conceded; yet can it be said that when the people, in moral justice, at least, required at the hands of these officers a compliance of the provisions of the law, or a vacation of their offices illegally held, that it is an excuse for these men, thus deposed, to summon their clans in the night-time, and without notice march upon the city?

Up to this time there had been no violence and bloodshed, and no more of threat or intimidation than could reasonably have been expected from a community thus excited, wronged, and outraged.

Had the Governor, at this juncture, with a due regard for the right of all, and as chief Executive of the whole people, gone to Vicksburg, and diligently inquired into the complaints upon the one hand, and the alleged wrongs upon the other, and shown a determination to have the laws faithfully and fairly executed, without partiality or prejudice, we are of the opinion that no collision would have taken place, and no blood been shed; but, instead thereof, a proclamation was issued which had a tendency only to fan the flame and intensify the passions.

We cannot fail to call attention to the fact that one of these very complained-of officers had been installed in office by the Governor, after the Senate had refused to confirm him, upon the express ground of a want of power of the Governor to make the appointment—thus overriding all parties and all constitutional restraints in exercising what he deemed his prerogatives, and thereby depriving the people of one of their constitutional and inalienable rights.

In this condition of affairs what could the citizens of Vicksburg be expected to do? An armed host was marching upon their city from every direction—their houses and firesides were about to be invaded—their wives and children were in danger, and no matter what was the original cause, could they stand idly by and see every thing near and dear to them thus endangered? Was it not the prompting of self-preservation; nay, more, the protection of their families, that required them to repel the attack at all hazards and at any cost?

There is one strange and inexplicable thing connected with this message, and that is, that while the Governor can denounce in severe and unmeasured terms the action of the tax-payers, he utters no word of reflection upon the officers; his anathemas are all

hurled at the white citizens, and their grievances, whatever they may be, are no extenuation or excuse with him.

We further dissent from the statement made in the preamble and resolutions of the majority, for this reason, that it assumes as true the very charges against the citizens of Vicksburg which are by them asked to be investigated.

Whatever there may have been, there certainly is now no domestic violence to suppress, and no necessity for United States troops for any purpose, unless it be to aid in carrying special election ordered there for the 31st inst. The question for us should be, what is best for the State? and not how to maintain the supremacy of any party. We cannot hope for peace and prosperity until the people are left to control their own local affairs, free from Federal interference.

An address to the people of the United States was also signed by forty-nine Conservative members of the Legislature to vindicate their action in dissenting from the majority in calling on the President for troops, and in order to preserve the good name and fame of the people of the State from the alleged calumnious charges made by the Governor, and indorsed by the Legislature.

On the 21st of December the following proclamation was issued by President Grant:

Whereas, It is provided in the Constitution of the United States that the United States shall protect every State in the Union on the application of the Legislature, or the Executive, when the Legislature cannot be convened, against domestic violence; and—

Whereas, It is provided by the laws of the United States that, in all cases of insurrection in any State, or of obstruction of the laws thereof, it shall be lawful for the President of the United States, on application of the Legislature of such States, or of the Executive, when the Legislature cannot be convened, to call forth the militia of any other State or States, or to employ such part of the land and naval force as may be judged necessary for the purpose of suppressing such insurrection, or of causing the laws to be duly executed; and—

Whereas, The Legislature of the State of Mississippi, now in session, have represented to me in a concurrent resolution of that body several of the legally-elected officers of Warren County, in said State, are prevented from executing the duties of their respective offices by force and violence; that the public buildings and records of said county have been taken possession of, and are now held by lawless and unauthorized persons; that many peaceable citizens of said county have been compelled to abandon and remain away from their homes and families; that illegal and riotous seizures and imprisonments have been made by lawless persons; and, further, that a large number of armed men from adjacent States have invaded Mississippi, to aid such lawless persons, and are still ready to give them such aid; and, whereas, it is further represented, as aforesaid, by said Legislature, that the courts of said county cannot be held, and that the Governor of said State has no sufficient force at his command to execute the laws thereof in said county, and suppress said violence without causing a conflict of races, and endangering life and property to an alarming extent; and—

Whereas, Said Legislature, as aforesaid, have made application to me for such part of the military force of the United States as may be necessary and adequate to protect said State and citizens thereof against the domestic violence hereinbefore mentioned, and to enforce the due execution of the laws; and—

Whereas, The laws of the United States require

that, whenever it may be necessary, in the judgment of the President, to use military force for the purposes aforesaid, he shall forthwith, by proclamation, command such insurgents to disperse and retire peaceably to their respective abodes, within a limited time: now—

Therefore, I, Ulysses S. Grant, President of the United States, do hereby command said disorderly and turbulent persons to disperse and retire peaceably to their respective abodes within five days from the date hereof, and that they refrain from forcible resistance to the laws, and submit themselves peaceably to the lawful authorities of said county and State.

In witness whereof, I have hereunto set my hand and caused the seal of the United States to be affixed.

Done at the city of Washington, this twenty-first day of December, in the year of our Lord one thousand eight hundred and seventy-four, and of the independence of the United States the ninety-ninth.

U. S. GRANT.

By the President:
HAMILTON FISH, Secretary of State.

The condition of affairs above described led to the appointment of a Congressional Investigating Committee, composed of Messrs. Conger, Speer, O'Brien, and Williams, who proceeded to Vicksburg, and, after taking testimony there, went to Jackson. The committee was engaged in these duties at the close of the year.

The committee appointed by Governor Ames to investigate the condition of the State Treasury, reported the following financial transactions for the year:

RECEIPTS.

Uncurrent funds, in sealed box, consisting of Confederate, cotton, and other notes..	$795,936 48
School-funds, currency......................	66,865 56
Coupons paid, canceled, and not audited, because series not complete..............	46,410 00
United States currency, Teachers' Fund....	5,148 40
Bond Tax and General Fund, United States currency..................................	29,197 47
Certificates of indebtedness	74,269 00
Currency in drawer.........................	156 80
Balance, January 20, 1874...................	900,352 05
Receipts to November 30, 1874.	1,321,845 57
" from that date to December 9, 1874.	27,636 76
Total..........................	$2,255,824 38

DISBURSEMENTS.

From January 30 to November 30, 1874.....	$1,231,049 67
" November 30 to December 9, 1874.....	7,091 00
Total................................	$1,238,140 67
Balance, accounted for........................	1,017,683 71

The Legislature, in session in the early part of the year, did not adjourn until April. One of the most important measures passed was the funding bill. This provides that when warrants for $50 or a multiple thereof are presented, the Treasurer shall take up and cancel the same, and issue therefor a bond or bonds, bearing the date of the January or July preceding the issuance and bearing eight per cent. interest, payable semi-annually in currency. Six series of bonds of $250,000 each are to be issued, and a special tax of three-fourths of one mill on a dollar will be levied each year till and including 1881, and an additional tax of one and three-fourths mill on a dollar is to be levied in 1876 and subsequent years up to and including 1881, or until the interest and principal are paid.

Section 9 of the law of 1872, to fund the floating debt of the State, was amended so as to provide that the special tax of one and a half mill therein levied, to pay the principal and interest of certain bonds, should be collected in full only for the years 1874 and 1875, and should be reduced to one-half of one mill for the year 1876, after which no tax should be collected under the provisions of said section for the successive years therein provided.

The act in relation to the State Board of Equalization provides that it shall be composed of the Lieutenant-Governor, Secretary of State, Auditor, Treasurer, Attorney-General, and Superintendent of Education. The Governor is an *ex-officio* member, and the action of the board must receive his approval before taking effect. The duties of the board are prescribed as follows:

1. They shall add to the aggregate value of the realty or personalty, or both, of the property of every county which they believe to be valued below its true value in money, such per centum in each case as will raise the same to its true value in money.

2. They shall deduct from the aggregate valuation of the realty and personalty of the property of every county which they believe to be valued above its true value in money, such per centum as will, in each case, reduce the same to its true value in money.

3. If they believe that right and justice require the valuation of the realty and personalty of the property of any town or towns in any county, or the realty and personalty of such county not in towns, to be raised, or to be reduced without raising or reducing it in the same ratio, they may in every such case add to or take from the valuation of any one or more of such towns, or of property not in towns, such per centum as they believe will raise or reduce the same to its true value in money.

4. They shall not reduce the aggregate value of all the property of the State as returned by the county assessors.

5. Said board shall keep a full record of their proceedings and orders, and four members of said board shall constitute a quorum for the transaction of business.

The valuation of property, according to the United States censuses, has been as follows:

YEARS.	ASSESSED VALUE.			True Value of Real and Personal.
	Real Estate.	Personal Estate.	Total.	
1850...	....	....	....	$228,951,130
1860...	$157,836,737	$351,636,175	$509,472,912	607,324,911
1870...	118,278,460	59,000,430	177,278,890	209,197,845

The diminution in the value of personal property is chiefly due to the emancipation of the slaves.

The State debt, January 1, 1874, amounted to $3,558,629.24, viz.: Due school-funds, $1,157,415.69; certificates of debt, $294,150; Auditor's warrants, $1,083,682.57; bonds, $634,650; interest on bonds, $73,436; interest on insurance deposits, $15,294.98. Of the bonds, $100,000 were payable on January 1, 1874, 1875, and 1876; $150,000 on January 1, 1875 and 1876; and $34,650 on January 1, 1877. This statement of the debt does not include bonds to the amount of $7,000,000, of which the principal and interest have remained unpaid since 1842. The State institutions are the Penitentiary, Blind Institute, Institute for the Deaf and Dumb, and Lunatic Asylum, situated at Jackson. The Penitentiary contains 200 cells, and is inadequate for the accommodation of the prisoners. The convicts are partly employed within the walls in manufactures, and partly leased to persons who employ them on public works in different parts of the State.

Mississippi's foreign trade is indirect, and almost entirely through New Orleans and Mobile. Cotton and lumber are the chief exports. The coasting and river trade is large. The coasting-trade is chiefly directed to Mobile and New Orleans, while the Mississippi River trade centres in the latter, and that of the Tombigbee in Mobile. The railroads terminating at these two ports and at Memphis are also large car-

riers of merchandise. There are three customs districts: Natchez, Pearl River (port of entry, Shieldsborough), and Vicksburg. The direct foreign trade and the coasting-trade are centred entirely in the district of Pearl River. The value of foreign commerce for the year ending June 30, 1874, was $233,400, almost entirely exports, including 13,293,000 feet of boards, 529,000 shingles, and 191,563 cubic feet of timber. The number of entrances in the foreign trade was 93, of 22,523 tons; clearances, 94, of 20,249 tons; entrances in the coastwise trade, 68, of 12,048 tons; clearances, 96, of 21,382 tons.

In 1844 there were 26 miles of railroads in the State; in 1854, 222; in 1864, 862. The statistics of the different lines for 1874 are contained in the following table:

RAILROADS.	TERMINI.	Miles in Operation in the State.	Distance between Terminal, Miles.
Alabama & Chattanooga............................	Chattanooga, Tenn., and Meridian..........	18	295
Memphis & Charleston...........................	Memphis, Tenn., and Stevenson, Ala.........	88	272
Mississippi & Tennessee.........................	Memphis, Tenn., and Grenada................	85	100
Mississippi Central *............................	Canton and Cairo, Ill......................	183	350
Mobile & Ohio.................................. {	Columbus, Ky., and Mobile, Ala.............	266	472
	Muldon and Aberdeen........................	6½	9½
Branches .... {	Artesia and Columbus.......................	14½	14½
	" and Starkville........................	11	11
New Orleans, Jackson & Great Northern *....	New Orleans, La., and Canton..............	118	206
Branch..	Durant via Kosciusko and Aberdeen.........	39	...
New Orleans, Mobile & Texas.................	New Orleans, La., and Mobile, Ala..........	77	180
Ripley..	Middleton, Tenn., on Memphis & Charleston Railroad, and Ripley.................	23	26
Vicksburg & Meridian..........................	Vicksburg and Meridian....................	140	140
West Feliciana.................................	Woodville and Bayou Sara, La...............	7½	27
Total........................		1.035½	

The following lines are in progress: The Natchez, Jackson & Columbus Railroad, from Natchez to Columbus (180 miles); Vicksburg & Nashville, from Vicksburg to Nashville, Tenn. (380 miles), with a branch from Grenada to the Mississippi River, opposite Eunice, Ark. (90 miles); Selma, Marion & Memphis, from Selma, Ala., to Memphis, Tenn. (280 miles); Mississippi Valley & Ship Island, from Vicksburg to Mississippi City (210 miles); and Vicksburg & Brunswick, from Eufaula, Ala., to Meridian (225 miles).—There are no national banks in Mississippi. In 1874 there were six savings-banks, with an aggregate capital of about $300,000, and five banks of deposit, incorporated under State law, with an aggregate capital of about $550,000. One of each class also does an insurance business. At the close of 1873, 21 insurance companies of other States and countries were doing business in the State.

MISSOURI. The special session of the Missouri Legislature, which began on the 6th of January, ended on the 29th of March. It was called mainly for the purpose of having a new revenue law enacted, and provision made for refunding the State bonds that came due in 1874 and 1875; but the revenue bill failed altogether, and no attention was given to the State debt until the very last day of the ses-

* Consolidated as the New Orleans, St. Louis & Chicago Railroad.

sion, and then it was necessary for the Auditor to call attention to the matter. The necessary bill was framed, introduced, and passed through both branches in three hours; while the session of three months, called mainly for this business, and costing the State $250,000, had been devoted to matters of general legislation. The refunding act provides for the issue of $1,000,000 in new bonds, payable in twenty years, with interest at six per cent., payable semi-annually. These were to be issued from time to time on requisition of the Fund Commissioners, as the proceeds were needed to pay maturing bonds of the State, and were to be applied to that use only. An act was passed making a new division of the State into thirty-four senatorial districts. After a good deal of discussion, and a strong opposition, an act was passed providing for submitting to a vote of the people at the election in November the question of holding a convention to revise the constitution of the State. An attempt was made to carry through a bill providing that the State should assume the debts of the counties, and fund the same in bonds of the Commonwealth. This occupied a good deal of time, but was finally defeated. An important change was made in the school law. The township boards were abolished, and the office of county commissioners created. The people are empowered to vote a tax at their annual school-meeting to extend the school beyond four months, provided the levy does not exceed one per cent. on the taxable property of the district. Loans to aid in the erection of school-houses were also authorized. The principal feature of the law is the change from town to county supervisors, and leaving the direct control with the local district authorities. An act was passed providing for the punishment of bribery at elections. The following are its principal provisions:

SECTION 1. Every person who shall give any money or other valuable consideration to any person whomsoever, for the purpose of securing the services of such person as a canvasser or electioneerer, in any election held under or in pursuance of the laws of this State, or of any town or city duly incorporated under the laws of this State, and every person who shall give to another any money or other valuable thing to be used in paying for vinous, spirituous, or fermented liquors, to be given away or treated or which may have been given away or treated at any election or during the canvass preceding any such election, shall be deemed guilty of a misdemeanor, and on conviction thereof shall be punished by a fine, not less than five hundred dollars, nor more than five thousand dollars, or by imprisonment in the county jail not less than six nor more than twelve months, or by both such fine and imprisonment.

SEC. 2. If any person shall receive any money or other property or other valuable thing whatever, to influence such person in his vote in any election held under the laws of this State, or of any incorporated town or city, or to be used by such person for the purpose of influencing or controlling, or in any manner affecting any such election, or to be used for any electioneering purposes whatever, such person shall be deemed guilty of a misdemeanor, and upon conviction thereof shall be fined in a sum of not less than five hundred dollars nor more than one thousand dollars, or by imprisonment in the county jail not less than six months nor more than one year, or by both such fine and imprisonment.

SEC. 3. If any person convicted under the provisions of this act shall have been a candidate for any office at the election at which he committed the offense for which he was convicted, he shall, in addition to the penalties prescribed in this act, be ineligible to such office, and if he was elected at such election, his conviction as aforesaid shall vacate his office, and the same shall be filled in the manner provided by law.

A special message of the Governor, dated March 23d, revealed a state of lawlessness in certain districts of the State which the authorities were unable to suppress. He said

Your present session is rapidly drawing to a close, and I am sorry to say that up to the present time you have not deemed it expedient or necessary to make any provision enabling the Executive to enforce the criminal law and have the outlaws and murderers who are bringing disgrace upon the State and the law into contempt arrested and brought to trial and punishment. So far as the ordinary councils are concerned the machinery provided by your predecessors for the enforcement of the laws is ample, but you, in common with the people of the State, are aware of the fact that certain bands of outlaws, in their disregard of all legal and social obligations, have been for years past and still are among us, robbing and murdering with impunity, and defying the local officers residing in their vicinities where their crimes are committed. Those desperadoes one day enter and rob a bank and in cold blood shoot down the cashier. Next they visit an agricultural fair in one of the richest and most populous counties of the State, and, almost in the midst of thousands of men, women, and children, rob the safe containing the treasure of the association, shoot a young woman, and make good their escape. Soon again we hear of them in adjoining sister States, robbing and murdering. Anon, they reveal their presence in Missouri, enter a town containing a population of hundreds, rob a bank, and shoot one of its officers. Soon afterward they stop a railroad-train, pass through all the cars, rob the passengers, apply their pistols to the heads of the mail and express agents, and, under the threat of instant death if they refuse, force them to open their safes and place their valuable contents in their hands. Only a few weeks intervene until we hear of them at the hour of one o'clock in the morning, with a prisoner in their possession, forcing the keepers of a public ferry across the Missouri River to transport them from the north to the south side of the stream, and the following morning their prisoner of the preceding night is found a corpse in the public road, riddled by their murderous bullets. Ten days does not intervene until they are found in pursuit of the officers of the law in St. Clair County, and the next news is that they have killed the deputy-sheriff of the county, and wounded, perhaps mortally, a detective who was with him.

The Governor asked that power be placed in his hands to bring these criminals to justice. An act immediately passed the Senate providing for a secret-service force for the arrest of outlaws, but it was defeated in the House; whereupon the Governor sent another message, giving the facts concerning the lawless proceedings of a desperado named William Monks, and his followers, who defied the officers of the law, and produced a reign of terror in Howell County. No further action was taken, however, by the Legislature.

The State debt of Missouri, on the 1st of January, 1875, was $17,735,000, and the amount of annual interest on it $1,074,590. During the two years preceding, $1,412,000 of the bonded debt of the State had been paid, but $400,000 of new bonds had been issued; so that the net reduction was $1,012,000. During the year 1875 $1,428,000 of the debt matures, $3,907,000 in 1876, and $701,000 in 1877. Under an act of last March to audit and adjust the war debt of the State, 19,961 claims, amounting to $4,844,362, have been presented. Of these, 7,554 were allowed, and certificates issued for them to the amount of $2,382,132. The Governor, in his message to the Legislature of 1875, expresses the belief that these claims are just, and should be paid by the United States. He declared that the State was under no legal or moral obligation to pay them, and that the act of the Legislature providing for their adjustment was passed with the express understanding that no liability of the State was implied in it.

The annual meeting of the State Grange of the Patrons of Husbandry was held at Booneville, beginning on the 18th of February, and continuing four days. The time was taken up mainly with reports and discussions, and the sentiment of the organization was expressed in the following series of resolutions:

1. That the State Grange of Missouri adopt and reiterate the declaration of principles laid down by the National Grange at its late session at St. Louis.

2. That, as cultivators of the soil, we have been too long governed and controlled by the great moneyed power of the land, and by the rings and combinations which are in league against us, simply because we are ignorant of our own strength, or have not exerted that strength for our own defense, or have wasted it in wrangling with each other.

3. That as retrenchment and reform is our motto as Patrons, we should begin at home, and while we demand, as we have a right to, that our legislators and rulers shall be economical in the expenditure of the pu_l o money, let us not be prodigal in the expenditure of our private means. While we condemn the extravagance of public officials and complain of the wrongs inflicted upon us by those whom we have intrusted with power, let us not still further wrong ourselves and our families by living above our income, thus sacrificing peace, comfort, and independence, at the shrine of a fashion and show.

4. That we invite the hearty support and coöperation of our sisters of the order in our reformatory movement; that woman's true position is the God-given and divinely-sanctioned one of helpmeet to man; therefore her place is by his side. Hers is a high and noble position, and if rightly improved will rear to her memory monuments more durable than marble, and leave an inheritance to those that will come after more to be prized than wealth or honor.

5. That in a republican government all power is vested in the hands of the people, and that in ours a majority of the people belong to the producing or farming classes. Yet the power and strength of that class have been used by a less numerous and more unscrupulous class for the advancement of their own selfish purposes. That, although this is not a political organization, and especially ignores political or partisan questions, yet we call upon our representatives in Congress and the State Legislature to listen to the appeal of more than 100,000 Patrons in the State of Missouri to economize the resources of the Government, and stop the current of extravagance and corruption which has borne us to the very verge of ruin.

The opposition to the Democratic party in the political canvass of the year was consolidated under the name of the People's party. The Democratic State Convention was held at Jefferson City, on the 26th and 27th of August. The first day was taken up chiefly with discussions. On the second day the nominations were made and the platform adopted. On the first ballot for a candidate for Governor, General F. M. Cockrell received the largest number of votes, but on the fourth ballot Chas. H. Hardin was nominated. The other nominations were Colonel Norman J. Colman for Lieutenant-Governor, Michael K. McGrath for Secretary of State, Thos. Holliday for Auditor, J. W. Mercer for Treasurer, J. A. Hockaday for Attorney-General, Geo. M. Deiger Register of Lands, R. D. Shannar Superintendent of Schools, Warwick Hough Judge of the Supreme Court, and Wm. B. Naptin Judge of Supreme Court for the short term. The platform, which was unanimously adopted, was as follows:

The representatives of the Democratic party of the State of Missouri, in convention assembled, point with justifiable pride to the two years of record of a Democratic administration, during which time nearly $1,500,000 of the State debt have been discharged without an increase in taxation—the result of strict economy in all branches of the public service.

We desire our fellow-citizens to note that the pledges upon which, in 1872, we were again intrusted with power, have been observed in the reduction of the expenses of the government to an amount in excess of $300,000 per annum, with an assurance of a still greater reduction in the future through the curtailment of the fees of public officers, State and county; a careful revision of the law relating to the cost of criminal trials; and a change in the penitentiary system, by which it has been made a self-supporting institution instead of an annual burden upon the Treasury to the extent of nearly $200,000.

We call attention also, with gratification, to the addition of over $50,000,000 to the taxable wealth of the State, by a judicious assessment of the railroad property within its borders, wherefrom an annual income of $250,000 will be derived—thus lessening the burdens of taxation by a just and equal distribution of them.

Believing that we thus, by our acts, justified the confidence of the people when they intrusted us with power, and also profoundly convinced that every reasonable demand in the way of reform and retrenchment can be best effected by the Democratic party, we cordially invite the coöperation and support of all classes of our citizens who agree with us in those objects, irrespective of their former political associations.

We favor now, as in the past, a strict construction of the Constitution of the United States, and especially of that article which provides that the powers not delegated to the United States by the Constitution, nor prohibited by it to the States, are reserved to the States respectively or to the people.

Resolved, That we arraign the national Republican Administration as having proved false to the true principles of government and to the Constitution, in the revival of the worst features of the sedition law, by the passage of an act known as the Poland libel law, and as disclosed in the shameful Crédit Mobilier and revenue moiety frauds, and we denounce as especially unworthy of confidence every man, Democrat or Republican, who voted for the equally flagrant increase of congressional and presidential salaries.

Resolved, That we are opposed to the passage of the civil rights bill, believing it to be uncalled for by the blacks, and grossly unjust to the whites—sure to work great injury to the cause of education throughout the nation, and possibly lead to a dangerous conflict between the two races. While thus declaring, we announce ourselves in favor of a liberal system of education for the benefit of the negro, as well as the white children of Missouri, but are opposed to the mingling of the white and black races in our public schools or other educational institutions.

Resolved, That beyond guaranteeing to each State a republican form of government, neither the President nor Congress has the slightest right or justification for interfering with their domestic concerns, and that the personally irresponsible, wasteful, and anarchical rule in South Carolina, Louisiana, and other Southern States, by which republican institutions have been brought into general disrepute, is the natural result of a violation of this fundamental article of the Democratic creed.

Resolved, That the public debt should be paid in exact accordance with the contract whereby it was created; that any thing less would be repudiation, and that any thing more would be an unjustifiable abuse of power by Congress, in the interests of the bondholder and to the detriment of every other class. That the 5-20 bonds, authorized by the act of February, 1862, and succeeding acts, are distinctly by their terms made payable in legal-tender notes, or greenbacks, and that the act of March 18, 1869, whereby Congress solemnly pledged the faith of the United States to a coin redemption, was an utterly unjustifiable usurpation of power.

Resolved, That, while not conceding the right of

the Government to issue and maintain a national paper currency, if this policy is to be persisted in, we favor a repeal of the national banking law, and the substitution of greenbacks, to the extent of the national-bank currency, thereby providing for an immediate corresponding redemption of our bonded indebtedness, and the saving of $24,000,000 of interest annually to an overtaxed people.

Resolved, That the evils necessarily attendant upon an irredeemable paper currency should be removed by a removal of the cause; and that, as a first and, we believe, the only necessary step to such a result, the legal-tender notes of the United States, in addition to being receivable in payment of all debts and demands of every kind due to the United States, and to individuals, should also be made receivable for duties on imports.

Resolved, That railroads and all other corporations created for gain or profit should be rendered subservient to the public good; that we demand such legislation upon the subject, both State and national, as will effectually secure the industrial and producing interests of the country against all forms of corporate monopoly and exaction.

Resolved, That we denounce the present tariff as having been concocted alone in the interest of Eastern manufacturers, and in lieu of it we recommend a tariff for revenue only, that will be just to all sections of the country.

Resolved, That while the West is heavily burdened to sustain the manufacturers of the East, a sum of upward of $100,000,000 is annually collected from us in the shape of a revenue tax on distilled and fermented spirits, the product of our grain; and on tobacco, which by another unjust provision of the same law the producers are prohibited from selling in the best markets; we therefore demand in a spirit of justice that this law be repealed so that we may thereby be relieved from this unjust and partial system of taxation.

Resolved That the Democratic party of Missouri will elevate to office no man upon whose personal or political integrity there rests even a well-founded suspicion; that honesty and capability are the requisites for all candidates, and that the officer who forgets that he is simply the servant of the people, and seeks his own aggrandizement at the public expense, is personally dishonored and should be denounced by all honest men without reference to party ties or past affiliation.

The Reform, or People's party, which was made up chiefly of Republicans, held its State Convention at Jefferson City, on the 3d and 4th of September. The following platform was put forth as embodying the principles and purposes of the party:

We, non-partisan citizens and voters of the State of Missouri, in view of the evils which we have been suffering from disorder and partisan ring rule, deem it necessary for the best interests of the State that the people thereof should take the management of their affairs into their own hands, and therefore assemble in convention independent of all old party organizations. A long and painful experience has taught us that the custom of selecting State and local officers upon national issues which have nothing to do with State and local affairs has served to confuse the minds of the people with regard to the State and local questions to be decided by such election, and has thus become one of the chief causes of reckless partisanship and corruption in public affairs, and we believe it is time that the people should conduct their government in all its branches upon strict business principles, and should choose State officers relative to fitness for their respective duties and questions of State policy alone. This State needs order, a faithful enforcement of law, that capital and immigration may be invited, and that industry may

prosper. We demand the suppression of lawlessness, and mob violence; fearless execution of the law without regard to public feeling in particular localities. All law-abiding citizens must be treated with equal justice, and be made to feel that all their rights and legitimate interests are fully protected by a government of law. All proscription on account of former differences must be suppressed, that the industrious immigrant may again be attracted to this State. Every dollar derived from the use of public moneys belongs to the people. Every officer intrusted with public funds should pledge himself as the Treasurer nominated by this convention stands pledged, to account to the Treasury for all interest received from the moneys of the people. We are in favor of the passage of such laws as will provide such care in the disposition of the moneys of the State as will yield to the tax-payer the revenue derived therefrom. Honesty is the best policy for the people in their corporate capacity, as for individuals. No government, national, State, or local, can serve the interest of the people without strict fidelity to every honorable obligation. We are opposed to any further increase of the public debt of the State.

We are opposed to all combinations which tend to increase the cost of transportation beyond a fair remuneration to the carrier. We believe that all railroad corporations being the creatures of the legislative power, it is the duty of the legislative branch of the government to subject them to such wise and impartial enactments as will protect the people from extortion without impairing the rights or usefulness of such corporations.

The safety and permanence of our free institutions depend upon the intelligence of the people, and we are therefore in favor of our public-school system under the same principles as now, and are determined to protect and improve it by all the appliances of culture and intelligence, so that every child may have the advantages of an education. We believe that the maintenance of the inviolability of the school-fund beyond the reach of constitutional majorities or corrupt officers or mercenary speculators is one of the most sacred duties of the State government, not only as a basis of intelligent self-government, and the best safeguard to the public peace and good order, but as an inducement to industrious and intelligent immigration.

Frequent sessions of the Legislature are productive only of confusion in our laws and largely increase the burdens upon the tax-payers of the State by means of the unnecessary and wasteful appropriations and expenditures entailing thereto. Therefore we are in favor of a constitutional revision requiring a session only once in four years, unless in cases of emergency, in which event the Governor may convene a special session.

We cordially invite all good citizens of this State to unite with us in the election of State officers pledged to the maintenance and enforcement of these principles.

Resolved, That any further contraction of the national currency would be detrimental to the producing class, and we therefore oppose any step in that direction. We recommend to the people of the several congressional districts to elect members of Congress who will have constantly in view the true interests of the producers of the West, the improvement of the water-routes of the country and other means of transportation to the seaboard, the reduction of taxes, and the adjustment of duties on imports to a revenue basis; the speediest feasible safe reduction; cancelment of the interest-bearing debt, the abolition of the monopoly features of our banking system, with as early a return to specie payment as can be effected without disaster.

Major William Gentry was unanimously nominated by acclamation for the office of Governor. The other candidates were as follows:

For Lieutenant-Governor, Samuel W. Headlee; for Secretary of State, William R. Leflet; for Auditor, Ewen C. Hale; for Treasurer, John H. Fisse; for Attorney-General, Daniel S. Twitchell; for Register of Lands, Colby T. Quisenberry; for Superintendent of Schools, John Monteith; for Judge of the Supreme Court, Samuel Ensworth; for Judge of Supreme Court, short term, Peter E. Bland.

The election took place on the 3d of November, and resulted in the success of the Democratic ticket. The total vote for Governor was 261,670, of which Hardin received 149,566, and Gentry 112,104, making the former's majority 37,462. The majorities for the Democratic candidates for other offices varied from 37,676 for Mr. Colman, for Lieutenant-Governor, to 47,247 for Mr. Hoyt for Judge of the Supreme Court. At the same election thirteen members of Congress were chosen, all of whom were Democrats. Seven of the thirteen were members of the Forty-third Congress. The Legislature of 1875 consists of 28 Democrats and 6 Republicans in the Senate, and 91 Democrats and 40 Republicans in the House, making the Democratic majority 22 in the Senate, 51 in the House, and 73 on a joint ballot. The question of calling a convention to revise the constitution of the State was also submitted to a vote of the people at this election, and was decided in the affirmative by a majority of only 283 out of a total vote of 222,315. In accordance with this decision, the Governor ordered an election for delegates to the proposed convention, to take place on the 26th of January, 1875.

CHARLES H. HARDIN, who was elected Governor of Missouri on the 3d of November, and inaugurated January 12, 1875, was born in Columbia, Boone County, in 1820, whence he moved to Fulton in 1843, and began the practice of law. He was elected attorney of the third judicial district in 1848, and held the office four years. He was first elected to the lower branch of the Legislature in 1852, and served several times therein. In 1855 he was one of the commissioners appointed to revise the State laws. In 1860 he was chosen to the State Senate, and was chairman of the Judiciary Committee. He voted against the secession of the State from the Union, and in 1862 left the Legislature, and retired to his farm in Audrain County. At the close of the war he had resumed the practice of law, and was living near the town of Mexico. In 1872 he was an unsuccessful candidate for Circuit Judge, but was elected to the State Senate again, and was a member of that body when chosen Governor. A female college, near Mexico, bears Mr. Hardin's name, having been endowed by him with real estate valued at $30,000.

The past year has seen the completion of the great bridge over the Mississippi River at St. Louis. A brief statement of this magnificent work was given in the volume for 1873. It was constructed for the Illinois & St. Louis Bridge Company, of which Charles K. Dick-

son, of St. Louis, is president; Robert Lennox Kennedy, of New York, vice-president; James H. Britton, treasurer. A large amount of the stock is held in England. It is the most costly bridge in this country. The construction has been directed from the beginning by Captain James B. Eads. The bridge has three spans, each formed with four ribbed arches, made of cast-steel. The centre span is 520 feet, and the side ones 500 feet each in the clear. The four arches forming these spans consist each of an upper and lower curved rib, extending from pier to pier, and an horizontal system of bracing extends between these ribs, for the purpose of securing the arches in their relative distances from each other. The two centre arches of each span are 13 feet 9½ inches. apart from centre to centre, and the upper member of one arch is secured to the lower one of the other by a system of diagonal bracing. The roadways are formed by transverse iron beams 12 inches in depth, suitably separated. From the opposite ends of the iron beams, forming the roadways, a double system of diagonal, horizontal iron bracing binds the whole together. The original estimate contemplated an extreme width of 50 feet for the bridge, but this was afterward increased to 54 feet 2 inches for several reasons. The upper roadway is 34 feet wide between the foot-walks. The latter are 8 feet in width. The railway-passages below the carriage-way are each 14 feet 6 inches in the clear, and 18 feet high. The railways are carried over the wharves on each side of the river on 5 stone arches, each 26 feet wide, and are inclosed throughout the distance by a cut-stone arcade of 20 arches, supporting the upper roadway. They are then carried on brick arches into the tunnel on Third Street. On the Illinois shore the railways reach the level of the East St. Louis railways by a descending grade of 1¼ foot in 100 for a distance of 3,000 feet. The carriage-road at the eastern end descends with a grade of 4 feet in 100, and on the Missouri side the grade is nearly level. Its strength is so enormous that, if the bridge was loaded with people from one end to the other, the arches would only be taxed to the extent of less than one-sixth of the ultimate strength of the steel of which they are constructed. The piers and abutments were designed with a view to sustain either span when thus loaded, even if the others were entirely unloaded, and to sustain either span entire if, from any cause, the adjoining ones should be destroyed. The arches were designed with a similar end in view. The three arches are capable of sustaining 28,972 tons before giving way; so that it will be seen that the bridge could sustain a vastly greater load than could possibly be placed upon it. The greater part of the stone composing the masonry is a firm magnesian limestone, yellowish in color, and was taken from the quarries at Grafton, Illinois. This material was used only under water. From two feet below low-water mark to two feet above high-water mark the exterior of the piers, including those on the wharves and abutments, is of the best quality of granite. Above the granite the exterior is entirely of cut sandstone. A granite course, eight feet in thickness, is laid through the channel-piers and in the abutments, to receive the heavy cast-iron plates against which the ends of the arches rest. The bridge accommodates two double tracks of steam-railways, foot-walks, street-railways, and all styles of vehicles, none of which interfere with the others, nor can the bridge interfere with navigation.

The formal test was made July 2d. Two trains of locomotives, weighing 560 tons altogether, fourteen in all, were moved out abreast, and simultaneously over each one of the three spans. The deflection of the middle span was

BRIDGE OVER THE MISSOURI AT ST. LOUIS.

3½ inches; of each side span, 3 inches. The two trains moving abreast upon each arch was the severest possible test to produce distortion of the curve of each arch. Ten locomotives were then coupled together, and these were run over each track on each side of each arch of the entire bridge, covering the entire track of each span, and throwing the whole weight of the train, 400 tons, on one side of each span. This test was applied to each side of the bridge, and produced the severest twisting strain to which each arch can be subjected. The vertical deflection produced by this test on the centre span was 2½ inches. The locomotives thus coupled were run at a speed of ten miles an hour. The local traffic on the upper road-way of the bridge was uninterrupted during the progress of the tests. The instruments failed to detect any side-motion whatever during the test.

MONTANA. The tribal Indians of Montana, according to the report of the United States Commissioner of Indian Affairs for 1874, numbered 22,486, as follows:

TRIBES.	Number.
Flatheads	471
Pend d'Oreilles	1,026
Kootenays	332
Mountain Crows	3,000
River Crows	1,200
Blackfeet	1,500
Bloods	1,500
Pieguns	2,450
Santee and Sisseton Sioux	1,163
Yanktonais Sioux	2,266
Uncpapa Sioux	1,420
Uncpatina Sioux	460
Assiniboins	4,698
Gros Ventres	1,000

The Flatheads, Pend d'Oreilles, and Kootenays, have a reservation of 1,433,600 acres in the valley of Jocko River, a tributary of the Flathead, near Flathead Lake, but most of the Flatheads have hitherto resided in the valley of the Bitter-Root River, and refused to remove to the reservation. The Crows have a reservation bounded west and north by the Yellowstone River, east by the 107th meridian, and south by Wyoming. The other tribes have had assigned to them the region north of the Marias and Missouri Rivers. The Blackfeet never and the Bloods seldom visit their agency, roaming most of the time north of the British line. Besides those above enumerated, there are some roving Sioux not belonging to any agency.

The most important industry of Montana is mining. The precious metals, found in the metamorphic rocks, are abundant, Montana having been second only to California in the production of gold. The placer-diggings are chiefly on the tributaries of the Hell-Gate, Big Blackfoot, Madison, and Jefferson Rivers, on the Missouri and its tributaries, from the junction of the three forks to the mouth of Smith's River, and on the bars of the Upper Yellowstone. The principal quartz-mines are near Argenta, Bannock, Helena, Highland in Deer Lodge County, and Virginia City. Much attention is now given to silver and copper. These metals exist 'in conjunction with each other and with gold, and sometimes separately. Silver is chiefly found on Flint and Silver-Bow Creeks, affluents of Hell-Gate River; Alder and Ram's-Horn Gulches of Stinking-Water River; Ten-Mile Creek, near Helena; and on Rattlesnake Creek, a tributary of Beaver-Head River. Copper predominates on Beaver Creek, near Jefferson City, Jefferson County; on a branch of Silver-Bow Creek, near Butte City, Deer-Lodge County; and at the source of Musselshell River.

Gold was first discovered on Gold Creek, a branch of the Hell-Gate, in 1852, but no mining took place until the autumn of 1861. The first quartz-mill was erected in the beginning of 1863. The bullion-product of the Territory has been as follows:

YEARS.	Product.	YEARS.	Product.
1862	$500,000	1870	$9,100,000
1863	8,000,000	1871	8,050,000
1864	18.000,000	1872	6,073,339
1865	11,500,000	1873	5,178,047
1866	16,500,000	1874	4,300,000
1867	12,000,000		
1868	15,000,000	Total	$120,901,386
1869	9,000,000		

Of the product in 1872, $351,944, and in 1873, $176,500, was silver. The deposits of gold from the Territory at the United States Mints and assay-offices, to June 31, 1874, amounted to $36,640,618; of silver, $304,361. There are no railroads in Montana, but the Northern Pacific is to cross the Territory from east to west. The principal towns have telegraphic communication with the East and the Pacific coast. There are five national banks, with an aggregate capital of $350,000. The value of property for purposes of taxation, in 1873, was $9,803,745; and the taxation for Territorial purposes, $39,214. The receipts into the Territorial Treasury for the year ending December 1, 1873, including $643 on hand at the beginning of the year, were $66,517; disbursements, $65,792: balance, $725. The net Territorial debt, January 1, 1874, amounted to $128,762, a decrease during the previous year of $13,786; $92,283 of this amount was in bonds bearing twelve per cent. interest.

The seat of government heretofore has been Virginia City; but in 1875 Helena, with a population in 1870 of 3,106, became the capital.

MONTEBELLO, NAPOLEON LANNES, Duc de, a French diplomatist, senator, peer, and at one time cabinet minister, born in Paris, July 30, 1801; died in that city, July 20, 1874. He was a son of Marshal Lannes, and was made a peer of France by Louis XVIII. in 1815, in consideration of his father's services. In 1833 he was sent on a diplomatic mission to the court of Copenhagen, and three years afterward was made embassador to Switzerland. In 1838 he represented his country at Naples; a year later he became a member of the French cabinet as Minister of Foreign Affairs, but soon afterward he returned to his former post in Italy. He became Minister of Marine in 1847, and, while holding that position, he pronounced against the enfranchisement of slaves in the colonies. The February Revolution caused his fall from power. Under the imperial dynasty, in 1858, he went as embassador to St. Petersburg, and in 1864 he was made senator. He had been Grand Cross of the Legion of Honor since 1844, and had received orders of merit from most of the sovereigns of Europe.

MORAVIANS. The statistics of the American Province of the Moravian Church, December 31, 1874, furnish the following totals:

Northern District, 60 churches; number of communicants, 7,527; of non-communicants over thirteen years of age, 1,385; of children, 4,511; total number of members, 13,423; number of Sunday-school scholars, 6,078; of officers and teachers in Sunday-schools, 755. The total increase of members from the previous year was 556.

Southern District, 13 churches; number of communicants, 1,178; of non-communicants over thirteen years of age, 187; of children, 520; total number of members, 1,885; number of Sunday-school scholars, 622; of officers and teachers in Sunday-schools, 81. Increase of members from the previous year, 15.

Total for the entire Province, 73 churches; number of communicants, 8,705; of non-communicants over thirteen years of age, 1,572; of children, 5,031; of members of all classes, 15,308; of Sunday-school scholars, 6,700; of officers and teachers in Sunday-schools, 836.

The annual report of the Unity Elders' Conference for 1874 contained, as usual, a review of the affairs of the whole Church during the year. Two changes in the membership of the Conference had taken place. A vacancy caused by the death of Bishop Clemens had been filled by the election of the Rev. W. F. Beckler, of the South-African Mission; another vacancy, caused by the retirement of E. N. Hahn, was filled by the choice of Eugene T. Groche, of Sarepta. The congregations constituting the Bohemian Mission had progressed steadily and quietly. Their legal recognition was considered only a question of time. The chapel of the rebuilt orphan-house at Rothwasser was dedicated on the 6th of December. The new congregations in Switzerland had given evidence of their satisfaction with their present relation to the Brethren's Church. In the British Province an important Provincial Synod was held at Fairfield from June 29th to July 8th. The mission department of the Unity Elders' Conference was represented by two delegates. Three Home-Mission congregations had been received into full connection with the Church. An attempt to instruct in the principles of the Moravian Church, and revive an organized congregation of Germans in the city of Manchester, had failed, although the work was undertaken on the solicitation of the pastor of the congregation. Four new congregations had been organized in the Northern District of the American Province, at Zoar and Laketown in Minnesota, Gerah in Wisconsin, and Urichsville in Ohio. Bishop Emil A. de Schweinitz had been consecrated in the Southern District. The educational work of the Church had been carried on in all the three provinces with unabated interest, and generally with success. A question of considerable importance had arisen in the German Province in relation to the practical working of the new school-laws. Two conferences on this and other subjects connected with educational interests had been held, one at Nisky and the other at Montmirail. A normal school for women teachers had been established at Gradau. The Diaspora work of the German Province had been prosecuted without the occurrence of any events to call for especial remark. The mission-work had been prosecuted with encouragement at some points, in the face of difficulties at others. The congregation at Lichtenau, in Greenland, celebrated its centennial anniversary in July, and that at Friedrichsthal its semi-centennial in the same month. Disturbances had interrupted the peace of the congregation at Okak, in Labrador, but they had been quieted after much difficulty. A new church of the Indian congregation, in the Cherokee Nation, was dedicated on the 14th of June. The people in the West Indian congregations had been impoverished by drought, and the work of the missions had suffered in consequence. A new church was dedicated at Bethel, St. Kitts. The congregation at Gracehill, Antigua, celebrated its centennial anniversary on the 2d of August. The mission at Surinam had substantially passed through the difficulties incident upon the completion of the emancipation of the negroes, and had so far escaped material harm. A new church was dedicated at Maripastoon, September 13th. The mission of the Mosquito coast had suffered by the destruction of two mission-ships. The congregation of Elim, in the South-African Mission, celebrated its semi-centennial anniversary in August. The work in the South-African field had been increased by the establishment of an additional station, and one outstation. The mission in Australia had been blessed with spiritual prosperity and progress in the schools, but reported no great increase in numbers. The missionaries in the Himalaya Mountains were laboring hopefully. Two of them had made extensive journeys through the country, distributing the Scriptures and conversing with the natives when opportunity offered. It was observed that the work in this field is one which requires time and great patience.

MORRIS, Right Rev. Thomas A., D. D., Senior Bishop of the Methodist Episcopal Church, born near Charleston, Kanawha County, West Va., April 28, 1794; died at his residence, Springfield, Ohio, September 2, 1874. When he was about ten years old, his family removed to Cabell County, West Va., then a comparatively wild and uninhabited region, where, however, he had the advantage of an excellent school established at the county-seat; and when he was about seventeen years of age he became deputy-clerk under an older brother, who was the clerk of the county. His health in youth was very delicate and precarious, but the hardships of a pioneer life, and of agricultural pursuits in a new country, inured him to toils and perils, and gave his constitution greater vigor. His family were members of the Baptist Church, and he had imbibed some prejudices against the Methodists, which, however, were removed by attendance at their meetings during a great

revival in 1873, and by his personal acquaintance with Rev. David Young, one of the pioneer Methodist preachers of that region, and soon after presiding elder of the Muskingum District, which included Northwestern Virginia. He had been greatly impressed by Mr. Young's sermons, and in August, 1813, was baptized by him, and received as a probationer in the Methodist Church. He was soon requested to lead a class, to hold prayer-meetings, and on the 2d of April, 1814, was licensed to preach by his friend Young, and assigned a place as junior preacher in a circuit. At the age of twenty-two Mr. Young's junior preacher was admitted on trial by the Ohio Conference, and his itinerant ministry in the West, which was very extensive and successful, lasted until 1834. During the first seven years of his regular ministry he suffered greatly from ill-health, being afflicted with a complication of diseases, and finally suffering from paralysis of the left hand, foot, and eye. The life which he so largely led in the open air, and the constant exercise on horseback, at length restored his health. He was ordained a deacon by Bishop George, and afterward as an elder by Bishop Roberts, and he preached with power and effect in the three States of Ohio, Kentucky, and Tennessee. In 1834 he was appointed the first editor of the *Western Christian Advocate*, which was started at Cincinnati on the 2d of May in that year. He filled the position with credit until 1836, when he was chosen a bishop by the General Conference. In 1841 the degree of D. D. was conferred upon him by McKendree College, Illinois. He discharged the duties of his bishopric with laborious fidelity, with singular ability, and marked success. In the antislavery controversy, and those concerning the questions of secession and the War for the Union, he did much to mould opinion in the Church. His rare gifts as a singer helped to sustain the zeal of the meetings in which he took part. In person, Bishop Morris was short and rotund, with a ruddy complexion, and a lofty and intellectual brow. He had only published a volume of essays, biographical and historical sketches, and notes of travel, about 1851; a volume of sermons of exceptional popularity, and several single biographical discourses and essays.

MUSIC BY TELEGRAPH. Mr. Elisha Gray, of Chicago, a gentleman well known in the electric-telegraph world as a maker and inventor, has succeeded in perfecting an instrument which will convey sound by electricity over an unbroken current of extraordinary length, that is, without the aid of automatic repeaters. In the ordinary transmission of messages over the telegraph-wires to points at long distances, a message is generally repeated by automatic working instruments about every 500 miles, in order to renew the current of electricity. Mr. Gray has already transmitted sounds which are distinctly audible at the receiving-point, over an unbroken circuit of

2,400 miles. This is, more properly speaking, a discovery, not an invention. The invention merely consists in adapting certain appliances to the discovery for the purposes of its practical illustration. Music played on a small melodeon, or piano key-board, transmitted through an unbroken circuit of 2,400 miles, is reproduced on a violin attached to the receiving end of the wire. Mr. Gray played "Hail Columbia," "The Star-spangled Banner," "God save the Queen," "Yankee Doodle," and other well-known airs, and they were unmistakably repeated, note for note, on the violin which lay on a table near at hand. The apparatus by means of which this extraordinary feat in telegraphy is accomplished, has been named by Mr. Gray the telephone, or an instrument designed for the purpose of transmitting sound to a distance. It consists of three general parts: first, the transmitting instrument; second, the conducting wire, running to a distant point; and third, the apparatus for receiving the sound at that distant point. The transmitting apparatus consists of a key-board having a number of electro-magnets corresponding with the number of keys on the board, to which are attached vibrating tongues or reeds, tuned to a musical scale. Any one of these tongues can be separately set in motion by depressing the key corresponding to it. Thus a tune may be played by manipulating the keys in the same way as those of an ordinary piano or melodeon. The music, produced entirely by electricity, of these notes is so distinctly audible in the next room that, in spite of much talking, there is no difficulty in determining what tune the manipulator is playing. To this transmitting instrument the conducting wire is attached, the other end being attached to the receiving apparatus, which

may be any thing that is sonorous so long as it is in some degree a conductor of electricity. A violin with a thin strip of metal stretched between the strings at a point where the bridge of the instrument is ordinarily placed, will, on receiving the sound transmitted through the conducting wire from the piano, give out a tone very similar in quality to that of a violin. If, then, the metallic strip is electrically connected with a wire say 500 or 1,000 miles long, which has its distant end properly connected with the transmitting instrument, any one at the receiving end can distinctly hear, without the aid of electro-magnetism, the tune or air which is being played 500 or 1,000 miles away from him, if he properly manipulate the receiving apparatus. The length of the wire connecting the transmitting with the receiving apparatus may be one mile or 10,000 miles, provided that the isolation is sufficiently good to prevent the escape of the electric current before it reaches its destination. In fact, there seems no limit to the distance to which sound, of any desired pitch, may be thus conveyed with from two to five cells of battery, all the conditions being proper. The quality or timbre of the tones depends upon the character of the receiving apparatus, which may be a violin prepared as described above, a tin hoop, with foil-paper heads stretched over it, after the fashion of a baby's rattle, a nickel five-cent piece, an old oyster-can, and a thousand other things. A sound, sufficiently loud to read Morse telegraphic characters, made by interrupting, with the common telegraphic key, one sustained note, has been obtained, under favorable circumstances, at the receiving end of the wire without any more scientific sounding apparatus than that of a piece of common tissue-paper.

N

NAVY OF THE UNITED STATES. At the end of 1874 the Navy consisted of 168 vessels, with 1,254 guns. Of this number twenty-six have sail-power only, of which only five can be put to practical use at sea as store-ships, transports, or surveying-vessels.

The steam-navy consists of 137 vessels, of which twenty-five are tugs, used with one or two exceptions for yard purposes; thirty-seven are armored vessels, and ten are torpedo-boats, leaving seventy-three steam-vessels originally of a class adapted for cruising, of 94,830 tons, and carrying 902 guns, including howitzers.

Of the iron-clad or armored vessels, sixteen are of a class and in condition for actual and efficient service; four others, of the class of powerful double-turreted monitors, are undergoing repair, and the fifth is well worth the same attention; but the remainder may be counted as really useless for any active and efficient purpose. Four of the largest of them, designed

and commenced during the war, have never been launched, and consist, in fact, only of their wooden frames, still on the stocks, and their incomplete plating and machinery stored at the navy-yards, though their names and designed dimensions appear on the Navy list; and the remaining twelve, of the class known as light-draught monitors, not able to carry their turrets, guns, and munitions of war, are valuable only as old material. Of the seventy-three steam cruising-vessels, five, of over 2,000 tons each, have remained on the stocks since the war, never having been launched, and are not estimated to be worth the cost of completion; seven are condemned and laid up in ordinary as unfit for further use; three others with condemned machinery; and forty-one are in commission for various duty. Of the remaining seventeen, two are laid up ready for service, seven are repairing at the various navy-yards, and eight are building under special appropriations of Congress. Thus it will be seen that one-half of the steam-navy adapted to cruising is in commission and in actual service.

An act, passed by Congress in June, 1874, to encourage the establishment of public marine-schools, authorized and directed the Secretary of the Navy to furnish on certain conditions, on the application of the Governor of the State, a suitable vessel, with all her apparel, charts, books, and instruments of navigation, provided they could be spared without detriment to the naval service, to be used for the benefit of any nautical school or college having a nautical branch established at any of the ports of New York, Boston, Philadelphia, Baltimore, Norfolk, and San Francisco. The act further authorized the detail of proper officers of the navy as superintendents or instructors of such schools. Pursuant to this provision, training-ships have been supplied to New York and California.

Secretary Robeson recommends that the Hydrographic Office, which is so important to the maritime interests of the country, should receive from Congress such support as will place it on a footing with the most important of such institutions abroad, and to enable it to furnish to our naval and commercial marine the charts, books, and information required in the navigation of the waters of the globe. Before the establishment of the United States Hydrographic Office in 1866, the navigators of this country were almost entirely dependent upon the hydrographic labors of England — their charts, books, and nautical information were all imported—the United States being thus dependent on a foreign country for the means of navigating its vessels and tracing their paths on the ocean. Since that date the commerce of this country has been supplied by the United States Office with hydrographic information for which there is a constant demand.

At the close of 1873 two vessels of the Navy, the Portsmouth and the Narragansett, were engaged on surveys in the Pacific Ocean. The latter was engaged in the survey of the coasts and Gulf of Lower California, the charts of which are now in course of publication. The Portsmouth was withdrawn from the survey.

In the surveys of the great channels of commerce, this country, with the exception of a few isolated expeditions, has done but little, and has been indebted for hydrographic information almost entirely to England and France. The North-Pacific Ocean is in a measure considered an American ocean, and the accurate establishment of the innumerable and comparatively unknown dangers becomes a pressing duty of the nation claiming the preponderance in these waters. The annual list of vessels lost (numbering 1,465 in 1872) always contains a large number the fate of which is unknown, and there is great probability that many have been wrecked on dangers not at all shown or imperfectly located on charts. This applies especially to the Pacific. Serious er-

rors are also known to exist in all charts of the coasts of the republics bordering the Gulf of Mexico and the Caribbean Sea.

A running survey of the gulf-coast of Mexico has been made by the United States steamer Fortune, Lieutenant-Commander Green, under the supervision of the Bureau of Navigation, which has very materially changed the delineation of the coast as heretofore laid down, and has disclosed new and important shoals. This work should be extended at least to the boundary of Brazil. At the present day our knowledge of the hydrography of many of the islands of the West Indies is very imperfect, and the correct positions of many of them by no means established with accuracy. An expedition for the determination of longitudes in the West Indies, by means of the electric cable, was organized by the Hydrographic Office, under the Bureau of Navigation. Owing to adverse occurrences, this expedition was necessarily detained, but left the United States near the close of the year, under the command of Lieutenant-Commander Green, for the prosecution of this work.

During 1874 the United States steamer Tuscarora, Commander George E. Belknap, was employed in taking deep-sea soundings in the North-Pacific Ocean, for the purpose of ascertaining a practicable route for a submarine cable between the United States and Japan. The northern and southern routes between these countries have been examined by running lines of soundings. The line on the former route commenced at Cape Flattery, touched the Aleutian Islands, skirted the coasts of the Kurile Islands, and terminated at Yokohama, Japan. On the latter route the line commenced at San Diego, California, touched the Hawaiian and the Bonin Islands, and terminated also at Yokohama. Besides these lines of soundings, others were run on and off shore between Cape Flattery and San Diego, for the purpose of determining the continental outline or the commencement of the ocean-bed proper.

The reports of Commander Belknap have been collated at the Hydrographic Office, and are in course of publication.

The number and yearly amount of pensions of the Navy on the rolls November 1, 1874, were as follows:

CLASS.	On the Rolls November 1, 1874.	Yearly Amount of Pensions on the Rolls November 1, 1874.	Amount paid for Pensions during the fiscal Year ending June 30, 1874.
Navy invalids......	1,601	$171,350	$174,185 00
Navy widows and others	1,814	290,558	367,511 04
Total..........	3,415	$461,908	$541,696 04

The appropriations applicable to the fiscal year ending June 30, 1874, including the unexpended balance of the appropriations for the building of new sloops, and the special appropriations to reimburse the bureaus for their extraordinary expenditures during the threatened complications with Spain, amounted in the aggregate to $27,147,857.68, and the actual expenditures for the same period, to wit, from July 1, 1873, to June 30, 1874, from these appropriations, amounted to $26,254,155.82, or about $900,000 less than the whole amount. The appropriations made available for the current year, commencing July 1, 1874, amount in the aggregate to $19,273,731.27. The amount of these appropriations for the current year, drawn for the five months since July 1st, and up to the 1st of December, 1874, is $11,854,-446.87, which, reduced by the amount refunded during the period, and that remaining in the hands of the paymasters and agents of the Government, will leave a little less than $9,000,000 as the sum actually expended from the current appropriations during the five working summer months.

The estimates for the ensuing year aggregate $19,096,567.

The Secretary reports the Navy to be "in a better condition of effective and permanent strength than it has been for years." He also reports "the fighting force of our Navy in good and effective condition." During the past two years the whole fleet of single-turreted monitors has been thoroughly overhauled and repaired, their sides raised up, their rotten wooden beams and decks replaced by iron, and their turrets and machinery put in complete order, so that they are now efficient to their utmost capacity, and ready to go to sea at any time as soon as crews can be put on board and organized. These, with the Dictator and Roanoke, also in good order, make a fleet of sixteen iron-clads, powerful for any naval purpose which does not require long voyages, or great speed. Two powerful iron torpedo-vessels have also been completed, and are ready for service, fully equipped with this most powerful weapon of modern warfare. Four of the powerful double-turreted monitors, viz., the Terror, the Miantonomah, the Monadnock, and the Amphitrite (by far the most formidable vessels ever in our Navy), are also undergoing repairs. The eight new sloops specially authorized, and built entirely of live-oak or iron, are about ready to be added to the cruising navy, and seven other vessels have been thoroughly repaired with like durable material, and supplied with new and improved machinery, so as to be in all respects equal to new ships of their class. Thus have been added fifteen new and active ships to the cruising navy, to take the places of those vessels which are worn out and must be relieved. Most of the powerful wooden ships of the first class were also put in condition at the time of the threatened difficulties with Spain.

Admiral Porter, however, in his annual report to the Secretary of the Navy, dated November 6, 1874, argues that the Navy is in poor condition for war, being greatly inferior to the navies of other countries. He says:

We have now but six monitors fit for service out of the forty-eight which appear on the Navy register. Twenty were long ago condemned as unfit for service.

The available monitors formed part of our West India fleet, which lately assembled; but they would have been of little use in a fleet fight on account of their want of speed. Their turrets and hulls could not resist the heavy rifled projectiles now in use, and they cannot raise their turrets from their seats in a sea-way, for the water would rush in and deluge their holds.

These monitors were built during the late war for a specific purpose, which they amply fulfilled—viz., to operate in smooth water against fortifications and for the defense of harbors. For such service they proved themselves admirably adapted, and their turrets and hulls, well marked with heavy shot, which did no harm, showed that they were practically invulnerable at that time. Possessing the heaviest ordnance then known, they were a match for any single ship afloat; but since they were built ten and eleven inch plates have been easily perforated by the eleven-inch rifle.

Either of the above-mentioned guns could perforate the turrets of any of our monitors, while the vessels from which they were fired could remain at a distance where our smooth-bore guns could do them no harm.

If such guns could so easily demolish the turrets of our monitors, what chance would the latter have against a ship like the Inflexible, now building in England? She is of 11,095 tons displacement, 8,000 indicated horse-power, is to be driven at a speed of fourteen knots by twin-screws, and it is understood she is to mount four 8-ton guns, throwing shot of about 1,600 pounds weight. It is very evident that such a ship, with her 24-inch iron plates, would receive no damage from one of our monitors, except at very close quarters.

Thus you will see that these monitors, with their present batteries, speed, and armor, are in no respect a match for the new style of iron-clads, with their powerful rifled guns; and it was apparent to myself and to every officer of the West India fleet who had studied the subject, that the monitors would have been of little avail if brought in contact with the foreign vessels in Cuban waters.

In showing that in respect to its Navy the United States is unprepared for war, Admiral Porter says:

We have never had a settled policy with regard to the class of vessels we should build, and I beg leave to suggest a system, which, if adhered to, will soon place us in a very respectable condition, enable us to defend our coasts, and do great damage to our enemies.

Mines planted in channels will not prevent an enemy from shutting up New York at both ends, if he is superior to us in iron-clads. It is, therefore, imperatively necessary that we should at once provide for building annually so many tons of monitors —say 5,000 tons for the present—until we have thirty first-class monster rams of great speed, armed with monster guns, in addition to our present force, and at least fifty iron torpedo-boats of not less than 100 tons, of good speed. The latter should be hauled up under cover, fitted with all the modern improvements, and kept for an occasion, while hundreds of others could be improvised in a short time after the commencement of a war.

This is partly the system pursued by Great Britain. She builds 20,000 tons of naval vessels annually, and finds it the cheapest way of averting war and protecting and increasing her commerce, which has doubled since 1865, while ours has dwindled away exactly one-half.

On the 20th of January, 1875, President Grant sent to Congress a special message, calling attention to the condition of the armament of our fortifications and the absolute necessity for immediate provision by Congress for the procurement of heavy cannon. The large expenditures required to supply the number of guns for our forts is the strongest argument that can be adduced for a liberal annual appropriation for their gradual accumulation. In time of war such preparations cannot be made; cannon cannot be purchased in open market, nor manufactured at short notice; they must be the product of years of experienced labor.

The President recommends an appropriation of $250,000 for utilizing the 1,294 ten-inch Rodman smooth-bore guns by converting them into 8-inch rifles capable of piercing seven inches of iron. He adds:

While convinced of the economy and necessity of these conversions, the determination of the best and most economical method of providing guns of still larger calibre should no longer be delayed. The experience of other nations, based on the new conditions of defense brought prominently forward by the introduction of iron-clads into every navy afloat, demands heavier metal, and rifle-guns of not less than 12 inches in calibre. These enormous masses, hurling a shot of 700 pounds, can alone meet many of the requirements of the national defenses. They must be provided, and experiments on a large scale can alone give the data necessary for the determination of the question. A suitable proving-ground, with all the facilities and conveniences referred to by the Chief of Ordnance, with a liberal annual appropriation, is an undoubted necessity. The guns now ready for trial cannot be experimented without funds, and the estimate of $250,000 for the purpose is deemed reasonable, and is strongly recommended. The constant appeals for legislation on the armament of fortifications ought no longer to be disregarded, if Congress desires in peace to prepare the important material without which the future must inevitably lead to disaster. This subject is submitted with the hope that the consideration it deserves may be given it at the present session.

NEBRASKA. The increase in population during the past two years has been unparalleled in this State: the number of inhabitants, now at least 300,000, has doubled within this time. New settlers have been drawn for the most part toward western portions of the State, attracted by the cheapness and fertility of the lands. The educational and commercial status has improved commensurately with the growth of the population. The agricultural welfare which this richly-favored country has hitherto experienced has been grievously disturbed in the past year by the drought and the grasshopper devastation; but the ready aid, which the older and more prospered communities have extended to the ravaged districts, has averted suffering, and prevented the abandonment of the outer settlements.

The Republican State Convention met at Omaha, September 2d, and nominated Silas Garber for Governor, Lorenzo Crounse for Congressman, Bruno Tyschuk for Secretary of State, J. C. McBride for Treasurer, and General George H. Roberts for Attorney-General. The following platform was adopted:

Whereas, The Republican party has allied itself to the liberty-loving masses of the world, and made a record which invites scrutiny and challenges history for a parallel:

Resolved, 1. That honest practical labor should be protected and receive its just reward.

2. We earnestly desire that the credit of the country should be firmly maintained in order that the commercial and industrial interests of the country may not suffer injury or a fluctuation of values, by impairing in any degree the confidence which now prevails in regard to the circulating medium, which we hope soon will be based on a metallic currency.

3. We believe that banking should be free under a well-guarded national system, and counsel economy and reform in all departments of the public service, and a reduction of the public debt, as rapidly as may be without imposing burdens on the industries of the country.

4. We demand a rigid accountability in the discharge of the duty of all office-holders, State or national.

5. While appreciating the advantages derived from them, we demand that the railroads be subservient to public good, and proclaim our determination to resist by lawful means the efforts to extort exorbitant tolls.

6. We favor equally-imposed taxation, and demand State and national legislation to compel the railroads to pay the same proportion as individuals.

7. We recognize the power of the General Government to regulate commerce between the States, and recommend that the Government establish and operate a double-track railroad from the Missouri River to the Atlantic.

8. We favor the passage of Crounse's railroad land-tax bill.

9. We favor an amendment to the Constitution of the United States, providing for the election of the President, Vice-President, and all other Federal officials, by a direct vote.

10. We decidedly oppose a third term for the President.

11. We declare the Quaker Indian policy a failure, and recommend the transfer of the management of the Indians to the War Department.

12. We favor a reapportionment of the State representation through the enactment of a new constitution, and favor the submission to a direct vote of the people of the questions of prohibition, local option, and license.

13. We approve of the action of Congress in the passage of the civil-rights bill, and demand its enforcement in the Southern States, but disapprove all unconstitutional legislation for the cure of disorders of society or evils prevailing in our land.

The 14th and 15th invite immigration, and express an unwavering determination to stand by the great principles of the Republican party.

The Independents held their convention at Lincoln, on the 9th of September, nominating J. F. Gardner for Governor, Major James W. Davis for Congress, and M. Cummings for State Treasurer. Their platform was as follows.

1. That we, delegated representatives of the people of the State of Nebraska, favorable to the organization of an independent political party, laying aside past differences of opinion, and earnestly uniting in a common purpose to secure needed reforms in the administration of public affairs, cordially unite in submitting these declarations: That all political power is inherent in the people; that no government is worthy of preservation or should be upheld which does not derive power from the consent of the governed by equal and just laws; that the inestimable right of life, liberty, and the pursuit of happi-

ness, should be secured to all men without distinction of race, color, or nationality; that maintenance of principles is essential to the prosperity of republican institutions, and that to this end the Federal Constitution, with all amendments, and the rights of States and the union of States, must and shall be preserved.

2. That we favor the restoration of gold and silver as the basis of currency, and a resumption of specie payment at the earliest practicable day without injury to the business interests of the country, and we strenuously demand that the faith and credit of the nation be maintained inviolate, and that all existing public debts shall be liquidated under and in pursuance of the laws by which said debts originally were created; that, until such time as the Government shall find it practicable to resume specie payment, we favor a system of currency based upon the credit of the nation issued by the Government directly to the people.

3. We oppose all combinations and devices of whatever character that tend to increase the cost of transportation beyond a fair remuneration to the carriers, and we demand the exercise of all constitutional rights to remedy the existing evils, and to prevent their occurrence in future.

4. That we are opposed to further land-grants, subsidies to steamships, or any or all donations of bonds, either State, municipal, or national, to aid public enterprises.

5. That we are in favor of a tariff for revenue only.

6. That we favor a constitutional amendment by which the President, Vice-President, and Senators of the United States should be elected by the direct vote of the people.

7. That we favor the strictest and most rigid economy in all public affairs involving the expenditure of the people's money, and hold that salaries of public officers should be in proportion to the income of the masses of the people.

8. That taxes in this State in many localities are beyond endurance. Their magnitude is a blight on prosperity, by impoverishing the people and in retarding settlement; and in view of these facts our various candidates for office are hereby instructed to use all the power within the scope of their official duties to prevent any increase in such burdens, and are also pledged to reduce the taxes as far as possible by cutting off extravagant and useless expenditures.

9. That our candidate for Governor is hereby pledged to the people to veto in all cases those jobs that, under the pretense of subserving the public interests, are mean schemes of individual gain.

10. That we oppose such legislation as grants royal privileges to capital, by the exercise of which labor is crushed and illegally defrauded of its legitimate profits. We hold it to be grossly unjust that bounties should be paid to wealth, while the labor which produces it is manacled by legislative enactments, the result of political intrigue and corruption.

11. That we ask such legislation, State and national, as shall effectually secure the industrial and agricultural interests from the odious exactions and wrongful discrimination of corrupt power.

12. That we are in favor of an equitable uniform license law.

13. That we hereby pledge ourselves to abide by and carry out, in their spirit and essence, the principles herein set forth to the end that official corruption may be checked, and that the State and National governments may ultimately be remitted to the keeping of those who regard their public duties as sacred trusts to administer in the interest of the whole people.

14. That we favor revision of the homestead laws, so that the present unlawful charges by United States officials may be abated, and endless inconvenience and expense avoided.

15. That we favor a memorial, by the proper authority, to Congress for the passage of an act for the relief of the homesteaders resident in the district visited by grasshoppers, similar in its provisions to the Minnesota bill.

16. That inter-State commerce should be regulated by Congress, and that railroad-pools—such as are entered into by the Burlington & Missouri River, of Iowa; Chicago & Northwestern; Chicago, Rock Island & Pacific; Kansas City, St. Joseph & Council Bluffs Railroads—should be prohibited, so that competition may be encouraged in the interest of cheap transportation.

17. That we hold in grateful remembrance the services of the Union soldiers, and ask for the passage of an equalization bill of bounties, and most favorable legislation for their interests in the homestead laws.

The Democratic nominations were: Colonel J. W. Savage for Congress; A. Tuxbury for Governor; John A. Sherty for Secretary of State; Robert Jordon for State Treasurer; and Montgomery Lancaster for Attorney-General.

The platform declared for the resumption of specie value as a basis of currency; for individual liberty, and opposition to sumptuary laws; for free commerce; for the duty of the State to protect citizens from extortion and unjust discrimination by chartered monopolists; and the compulsion of railroads to pay the like taxes with individual citizens.

The Republicans carried the State elections, in accordance with whose platform the constitution of the State is to be reconstructed; also their candidate, Crounse, was elected to Congress.

From the report of the State Treasurer, on the 30th of November, 1874, the total receipts for the preceding two years were $1,567,691.69: $198,287.65, balance in the treasury, December 1, 1872, and $1,469,404.04, later receipts, up to date of report. The total disbursements were $1,433,152.28, leaving a balance of $134,539.41. After the date of the report, an appropriation of $184,000 was made for the temporary school fund.

The total per cent. levy for all State purposes, for the year 1874, was 6¼ mills on the dollar, and should realize the following revenue:

General fund, 2½ mills	$200.995 77
Sinking-fund, 1 mill	79,864 77
School-fund, 2 mills	161.507 89
Penitentiary-fund, ½ mill	40,376 99
University-fund, ¼ mill	20,188 41
Total	$502,933 83

The total delinquent taxes due in the State, as shown by the Auditor's books, are $599,460.47. The total property valuation in the State, as returned to the Auditor, for 1874, was $81,218,-813.42, from which is deducted $464,769.25 valuation, exempt from taxation by reason of tree-planting, as provided by law, leaving the net total valuation, for taxable purposes, $80,-754,044.17. The total amount of assessable property, however, is estimated at as much as $300,000,000.

There are now outstanding evidences of State indebtedness the permanent investment of the common-school fund, general fund warrants, $184,119.67, and certificate of State indebtedness for a former investment under authority of law, $158,837.67; total State investment in school-fund, $342,957.34, drawing ten per cent. interest.

Besides this permanent fund, certificates of indebtedness for some $35,000 have been issued for the building of the State penitentiary, which, owing to arrearage in tax payments, have not been drawn in again. The State warrants are taken at par. The State has had, up to the present year, no bonded debt. The entire local indebtedness is nearly $4,500,000.

The State University contains, in its literary and agricultural departments, above one hundred students. The yearly expenses are about $20,000. The Agricultural College, in connection with the university, has been started within the year, with 320 acres of land, purchased from the proceeds of the sale of saline lands vested by the gift of the Government in the university. A number of students have entered upon the course of instruction in agricultural economy.

The educational interests of Nebraska have been furthered with intelligent zeal. Deliberative meetings of teachers have, at various times, taken place, and improvements in instruction have been favored by the public, and advanced by the government. The total number of pupils at the close of the year 1872 was 51,123; at the close of 1874, 72,991, showing an increase in the two years of 21,868. The total amount of school-money apportioned by the Superintendent for the years 1871 and 1872 was somewhat over $370,000. The past two years the total amount apportioned was nearly $100,000 of an increase. At the close of the year 1872 there were 1,512 qualified teachers in the State. The reports for 1873 and 1874 show 2,200. In the same time the number of school-houses has increased from 538, valued at about $700,000, to 1,345, of $1,300,000 estimated value. The normal school, for which $49,500 has been expended in improvements, has a faculty of nine professors and an attendance of 210 students. The expenses of its management are about $10,000 annually.

In October a State Fair was held in Omaha, which evinced decided attention among stock-raisers to the introduction of improved races of cattle, and made good the great reputation of the State for horticultural products.

The mercantile activity of Omaha has exceeded that of all past years. The smelting-works in the city have reduced 7,000 tons of bullion, and separated 2,000 tons of ore, producing $1,350,000 worth of gold and silver, and lead to the value of $800,000. The manufacture of linseed-oil, of beer and spirits, etc., has considerably increased. Many new buildings have been built within the twelvemonth.

Suits have been instituted, in the name of the State, against the Sioux City & Pacific and Omaha & Northwestern Railroads, for the recovery of 44,943 acres from the first, and 36,017 acres from the second, of internal-improvement lands alleged to have been illegally conveyed to these corporations.

The distressful famine brought on by drought and the ravages of locusts affected chiefly the new counties, and the frontier lands. The inhabitants of Howard, Valley, Greeley, Taylor, and Sherman Counties, were stripped of their corn-crop, their principal support, and in a great measure of their wheat-crop also. About half the farmers of this region, having a population of about 1,500, were left in destitution. A number of prominent citizens of the State met together on the 18th of September, at the request of the Governor, and organized a society for relief, which took the name "Nebraska Relief and Aid Society," under the chairmanship of General E. O. C. Ord. At the end of the year the amount of the donations received was $68,080, of which the sum of $37,280 was in cash, and $30,800 in goods. The railroads granted free transportation for all commodities sent for the succor of the impoverished communities. The people of Nebraska, and of many portions of the country, extended prompt assistance. The War Department aided them with clothing. The Patrons of Husbandry of Nebraska formed a relief society, and other branches of that organization have likewise lent their aid. By the action of Congress, extension of time has been given homesteaders, and a cash appropriation of $30,000 has been made, with which to purchase seeds the coming spring. The corn-crop has been, in the least injured districts, not more than half as great as in ordinary years. Root-crops have also been much shorter than common. The fruit-yield, though inferior in quality, has been greater than ever before.

NETHERLANDS, THE, a country in Europe. King, William III., born February 19, 1817; succeeded his father, March 17, 1849; heirs-apparent to the throne: sons—1. William, Prince of Orange, born September 4, 1840, admiral-lieutenant in the navy; 2. Alexander, born May 25, 1851, lieutenant in the navy; brother of the King, Henry, born June 13, 1820. The area of the kingdom is 12,679 square miles. The population of the several provinces was, according to an official statement of December, 1873, as follows:

PROVINCES.	Population, 1871.	Population, 1873.
Drenthe	106,713	109,454
Friesland	300,257	307,390
Gelderland	436,029	441,086
Groningen	228,882	232,789
Limburg	225,352	227,469
Brabant	435,141	443,045
North Holland	591,338	610,990
South Holland	700,318	731,464
Overyssel	256,681	260,533
Zealand	181,531	182,355
Utrecht	175,037	179,465
Total	3,637,279	3,716,002

With regard to religion, the population was, on the 1st of December, 1869, composed as follows:

PROVINCES.	PROTESTANTS.		CATHOLICS.		ISRAELITES.	OTHER SECTS.
	Total.	Per Cent.	Total.	Per Cent.		
Drenthe..........................	97,533	92.3	5,578	5.2	2,339	187
Friesland.........................	265,496	90.9	24,045	8.2	2,173	670
Gelderland........................	288,464	62.0	159,274	36.8	4,745	210
Groningen.........................	204,715	90.8	15,798	7.0	4,526	202
Limburg..........................	8,734	1.7	218,702	97.7	1,370	15
Brabant...........................	40,711	11.6	277,188	87.9	1,961	62
North Holland.....................	382,607	66.3	160,699	27.8	32,953	1,177
South Holland.....................	508,082	78.8	166,342	24.6	12,152	1,728
Overyssel.........................	174,656	68.7	75,422	29.7	3,768	205
Zealand	130,557	73.5	45,048	25.9	504	460
Utrecht...........................	107,756	62.1	64,143	37.0	1,512	145
Total.....................	2,193,281	61.3	1,313,064	36.7	68,003	5,161

The following towns had, on December 1, 1873, more than 20,000 inhabitants:

Cities.	Population.	Cities.	Population.
Amsterdam........	281,944	Leeuwarden......	26,500
Rotterdam.........	125,893	Dortrecht..........	25,577
Hague.............	94,895	Tilburg............	24,345
Utrecht...........	63,140	Herzogenbusch......	24,162
Leyden............	39,869	Delft..............	23,000
Groningen.........	39,284	Nimeguen..........	22,721
Arnheim..........	35,192	Zwolle............	21,310
Haarlem..........	32,758	Helder.............	20,778
Maestricht........	28,483	Schiedam..........	20,104

The area of the Dutch colonies in the East Indies is estimated at 615,000 square miles. The population was, in 1872, as follows:

Colonies.	Population.	Colonies.	Population.
Java and Madura.	17,298,200	Western Borneo..	365,881
Western Sumatra.	1,620,979	Celebes..........	349,756
Bencoolen.......	140,126	Menado..........	514,483
Lampong........	112,271	Moluccas { Ternate..	97,402
Palembang......	573,697	Islands. { Amboyna.	233,668
Riouw...........	76,869	{ Banda..	200,000
Banca...........	62,216	Timor, 1863......	860,000
Billiton..........	26,160	Bali and Lombok.	200,000
South and Eastern Borneo.........	869,763	Total........	24,301,411

The foreign population of these colonies included 12,902 Europeans in the army; 36,494 other Europeans (28,003 in Java and Madura); 1,324 descendants of Europeans; 291,224 Chinese; 13,903 Arabs; and 25,912 Hindoos.

The budget for the year 1874 estimates the expenditures at 100,244,000 florins; the revenue at 93,742,000 florins; the deficit at 6,502,000, which was to be provisionally covered by the issue of bank-notes. At the commencement of 1874 the national debt was represented by a capital of 937,020,000 florins, divided as follows:

DIVISION OF DEBT.	Capital.	Interest.
Debt bearing interest at the rate of 2½ per cent........	$638,988,000	$15,975,000
Debt bearing interest at the rate of 3 per cent........	92,682,000	2,781,000
Debt bearing interest at the rate of 3½ per cent........	12,121,000	427,000
Debt bearing interest at the rate of 4 per cent........	183,279,000	7,332,000
Debt bearing no interest....	10,000,000	....
Terminable annuities and sinking-fund..............	....	9,457,035
Total..................	$937,020,000	$27,101,000

In the session of 1873, the States-General passed an act to increase the annual sum set aside as a sinking-fund for the redemption of the national debt, namely, 1,900,000 florins, by 7,000,000 florins, and thus redeem a total amount of 8,900,000 florins within the year. The entire reduction of the national debt, in the twenty-two years from 1850 to 1872, amounted to 275,016,112 florins. In the budget of the East India colonies the revenues are estimated at 123,598,000 florins; the expenditures at 113,054,000 florins; surplus, 10,544,000 florins. The colonies have no longer any public debt, as it has been transferred to the home government.

The army of the Netherlands in Europe consisted, in 1874, of 2,057 officers and 60,014 men; the East Indian army numbered 27,659 men, inclusive of 1,213 officers.

The navy, on January 1, 1874, consisted of 84 steamers, with 565 guns, and 16 sailing-vessels, with 108 guns: total, 100 vessels and 673 guns.

The merchant navy, on December 31, 1872, consisted of 1,731 vessels, of 438,031 tons. The aggregate length of railroads in operation was, on January 1, 1874, 1,538 kilometres (1 kilometre equals 0.62 of an English mile). The aggregate length of the state telegraph-lines, in January, 1874, was 3,277 kilometres; the aggregate length of the wires, 11,738 kilometres.

The imports and exports in 1872 were valued as follows (value expressed in florins):

COUNTRY.	Imports.	Exports.
Netherlands................	549,747,000	449,853,000
Java......................	67,454,000	34,608,000
West Indian colonies.......	599,000	322,000
Guinea....................	26,000	197,000
Total.................	617,827,000	484,980,000
Transit...................	....	188,996,000
Grand total	617,827,000	484,980,000

The movement of shipping, in 1872, was as follows:

SHIPPING.	LOADED.		IN BALLAST.		TOTAL.	
	Vessels.	Tons.	Vessels.	Tons.	Vessels.	Tons.
Entered, total	8,426	2,897,606	336	70,798	8,762	2,968,404
Entered, steamers.......................	3,521	1,702,140	75	56,378	3,596	1,758,518
Cleared, total...........................	4,481	1,601,872	4,284	1,427,774	8,765	3,029,646
Cleared, steamers	2,561	1,213,535	1,004	574,650	3,565	1,788,185

The commander of the second Dutch expedition against the Sultan of Acheen,* General Van Swieten, completed the landing of his army about December 11th. It was effected under the protection of his marine guns, which without difficulty demolished the enemy's intrenchments on the coast. The second expedition consisted of about 9,500 European troops and 3,000 coolies. The artillery numbered nearly 700 men and about 75 cannon, exclusive of a number of smaller pieces of ordnance and two mitrailleurs. The vessels carried 58 pieces of ordnance, and were manned by about 1,300 men. As the best place for landing, a point east of the Acheen River had been chosen, a selection which was subsequently proved to be very fortunate. The cholera and other epidemics began to decimate the troops, and it was principally the coolies who fearfully suffered from the Beriberi disease, which is only found among the natives of Sumatra. Soon after his landing, Van Swieten issued a proclamation to the Sultan and the people of Acheen. To the latter the free exercise of the Mohammedan religion, the security of their property, and freedom of trade, were guaranteed. To the Sultan the integrity of his territory was promised, in case he was willing to conclude a treaty of peace ; in case he should refuse this, General Van Swieten threatened that he had enough cannon to destroy the Kraton, and that he would not leave Acheen before a treaty should be concluded. The Sultan was at the same time admonished to treat Dutch prisoners humanely, Van Swieten promising in return that all Achinese who might fall into his hands would be treated in the same way. A Malay, by the name of Wedikyo, who was found willing to take the letter to the Sultan, was put to death by the Achinese ; his two companions succeeded in making their escape. Four Achinese captives, who had been set free by Van Swieten, were likewise put to death by order of the most fanatical. Achinese commander, Panglima Polim, because they had not tried, while brought before the Dutch general, to murder him. The first object of the Dutch was the occupation of the Misigit, a fortified mosque, which formed an advance work of the chief fortress of the Achinese, the Kraton. A reconnoissance which was begun on December 25, 1873, led to a severe engagement, which ended in the successful storming of the Misigit. The Achinese made a most desperate and determined resistance, and the Dutch troops suffered a loss of seventeen killed and 197 wounded. The newly-organized ambulances, which on this occasion were used for the first time, proved to be excellent. . The Misigit was at once strongly fortified, to serve as a base of operations against the Kraton. In view of this desperate resistance and the dauntless bravery of the Achinese, General Van Swieten abandoned the hope of a speedy termination of the war, and sent for the reserve which he

* See ANNUAL CYCLOPÆDIA for 1873, article Acheen.

had left at Padang. The Sultan of Acheen, however, did not regard the Kraton as sufficiently safe, and left it for the interior of the kingdom. The fire of the Kraton became from day to day fainter, and on January 24th the Dutch found out that the Achinese had secretly left their great fortress, which was at once occupied by the Dutch. The closing scene is thus described by a correspondent, who says:

During the night the enemy for many hours kept up an incessant fire on the Dutch encampment, which was scattered along more than half the circumference of the Kraton—a fire heavier than usual, which seemed to presage a night-attack. Toward the morning the fire gradually died off. Early on the next morning, the Second Battalion made a reconnoitring expedition south of the Kraton, and also the Fourteenth, which latter kept nearer to the place. A German gentleman, agent of the Red Cross Society, accompanied by a corporal of the Fourteenth Battalion and a medical officer, approached close to the outer defenses of the fortress, and, to their surprise, noticed that all was silent within. Managing, after some delay, to effect an entrance, they found themselves the sole living human beings within the Kraton. Speedily they were followed by two companies of the corporal's (or Fourteenth) Battalion, and the Dutch flag soon replaced that of Acheen. The German gentleman's name is Bulstenslowen—a connection of Prince Bismarck's—and to him must be conceded the venturesome but successful idea of penetrating into the Kraton almost alone and unaided. During the night the enemy, under cover of darkness and the din of their cannonade, successfully managed to defy the observation of the troops, and, fearing to become totally surrounded, marched off toward the interior with bag and baggage unmolested. Their baggage cannot have been much ; but, at any rate, they left very little, almost nothing, behind them, the personal effects of natives being any thing but bulky, and their few valuables readily disposable on their persons. In the Kraton were found hundreds of dead Achinese, many emaciated, and their faces blue and distorted, showing that they, as well as the Dutch, had suffered fearfully from that still raging plague at Acheen—cholera. Some eighty cannon, mostly old, and of the carronade class, were found within its walls.

The same officer gives the following description of the Kraton :

It is not one building, or series of buildings, as imagined by many, but consists of a camp of scattered houses, placed here and there in the midst of an almost uncultivated jungle, the whole surrounded by a ditch, double wall, and three rows of "bamboo-douri," which consists of the piled-up and interlaced thorny branches and stems of a "prickly bamboo" and giant cactus. The outermost row of "bamboo-douri" was nearest to us—so high that it overtopped the walls of the Kraton, and hid them from our sight. Small gaps or holes were left here and there, to enable the enemy to fire through. Next to this was a broad ditch full of water, then a wall, next another line of prickly bamboo, the second wall within this again being backed up by an innermost lining of this almost impermeable brushwood defense. The walls are twenty feet high in places, and six to ten feet thick. They are made of hard-baked mud, and are of very recent construction—the defenses having been made since the April expedition. Traverses, case-mates, etc., are properly provided, and show much skill in their construction. The houses within the walls, not excepting the King's Palace—so called —are very poor, and were quite empty. Many were riddled by our shells, the palace not having escaped —indeed, one grenade is said to have passed through the Sultan's bed and bedroom-floor.

The Dutch fleet, which since the failure of the first expedition had blockaded the coast of Acheen and thus cut off its trade with Penang, in the British Strait Settlements, the chief market of Acheen, had in the mean while punished Pedir, one of the vassal states of Acheen, the Rajah of which was the father-in-law of the Sultan of Acheen, and supported the latter by his whole army. Several places on the coast of Pedir were bombarded, and a Pedirese powder-magazine was blown up; on the other hand, a projected expedition into the interior had to be abandoned by the marine troops. Most of the coast states recognized, after the fall of the Kraton, in rapid succession the sovereignty of the Netherlands. On January 31, 1874, General Van Swieten addressed a proclamation to all the vassal states of Acheen, in which he notified them that the Sultan had died of cholera, that the Kraton had been occupied by Dutch troops, and that the country, by right of conquest, had become a possession of the Netherlands. They were therefore called upon to declare their submission, in which case the blockade of their coasts would be raised and they would be left in possession of their territories. On February 18th three men-of-war were dispatched to visit the eastern, northern, and western coasts of Sumatra, to make the proclamation generally known. Some of the rajahs at once declared their submission; others hesitated; but the number of those who recognized the sovereignty of the Netherlands steadily increased. From the interior it was reported that the grand-nephew of the Sultan had been elected ruler of Acheen, that this new ruler was only nine years of age, and that a regency, consisting of four members, had been appointed to carry on his government during his minority.

The conquest of the Kraton radically changed the designs of the Netherlandish Government with regard to Acheen. The Governor-General of the Netherlandish possessions in India, in a telegram to the Government at the Hague, expressed his decided conviction that the conclusion of another treaty with Acheen would be useless, as it would never be observed, and the best policy would be to annex Acheen to the Netherlandish possessions. The Government of the Netherlands sanctioned the policy proposed by the Governor-General, and accordingly the proclamation taken out by the three war-steamers demanded from the rajahs submission to the rule of the Netherlands. In the interior of the country the fanatical Panglima Polim, and the influential Imam Longbattah, organized a combined resistance to a further advance of the Dutch; but General Van Swieten had no intention whatever of continuing an aggressive war. His plan, on the contrary, was to defend the territory conquered, to encourage the commerce of the natives with the Dutch, and to coerce the native chiefs into submission by enforcing the blockade, which deprived them of the pepper-trade of Penang, their principal source of income.

General Van Swieten regarded the second expedition to Acheen as successfully finished by the occupation of the Kraton, and he accordingly proposed to the Governor-General to leave in Acheen a military force sufficient to protect the new conquests and to recall the remainder of the army to Java. The plan was approved, and General Van Swieten, on April 25th and 26th, embarked for Java, while Colonel Pel, with 2,800 men, remained in Acheen.

Public opinion in the Netherlands as well as in the colonies was, however, greatly divided in regard to the policy pursued by General Van Swieten and the Governor-General of Netherlandish India, and with regard to the permanent results to be expected from it. The most violent attacks were made by a number of papers belonging to the Conservative party upon General Van Swieten, and some went so far as to represent his expedition as a failure. In reply to these attacks, General Van Swieten, in an elaborate letter addressed to General Knoof, one of the most prominent military authorities of the Netherlands, reviewed the whole history of the expedition, and showed that the results already attained exceeded the original expectations, and the success of the second expedition would stand a comparison with almost any war in the Asiatic colonies of the European powers.

According to an official report published by the Dutch Government in November, 1874, the loss of the first expedition against Acheen was seventy-five wounded and seven dead; that of the second, 2,042 dead, of whom 607 died of the cholera. The number of wounded is not stated. The total amount of war expenditures was up to that time 23,614,000 florins.

The Dutch Chambers reassembled on February 29th. Among the laws adopted was one on the fortification of the country, which aims at concentrating all the works of defense around Amsterdam and the neighboring districts, leaving seven of the eleven provinces, in case of war, without any defense. Another law forbids the employment of children of less than twelve years for hired labor. On June 22d the Minister of the Interior notified the Second Chamber that the cabinet had tendered its resignation, because the Second Chamber, by 39 against 32 votes, had rejected the first article of the bill on lowering the electoral census.

On May 12th the Netherlands celebrated the 25th anniversary of the King's accession to the throne. Several foreign princes, among them the Emperor of Russia, personally visited the King on the occasion. The Burgomaster of Amsterdam, in the name of the country, presented the King with the amount of a national subscription, which the King announced would be devoted to a fund for invalids, and for the veterans of the army and navy.

The ministerial crisis, which began in June

by the resignation of the ministry, was terminated on August 26th by the official appointment of a new ministry, consisting of the following members: Heemskerk, Interior and presidency of the Council; Van Lynden, Justice; Van Goltstein, Colonies; Van der Heim, Finances; Van der Does de Willebois, Foreign Affairs; General Wertzel, War; Taalman Kip, Navy. The Minister of Foreign Affairs is a prominent Catholic, and was formerly Governor of the province of Limburg. Heemskerk, Van Heim, and Goltstein, belong to the Conservative party; Van Lynden is a champion of Protestant orthodoxy; Wertzel was formerly member of a Liberal ministry.

A new session of the States-General was opened by the King on September 21st. The King referred to the cordial manner in which the jubilee of his accession was celebrated. He said that relations with foreign powers were very friendly. From a financial point of view the state was prosperous, and he had also to announce that the crops were satisfactory. The King recommended that great public works should be undertaken or prepared, and mentioned specially the drainage of a portion of the Zuyder Zee. His Majesty stated that a scheme for partial revision of the penal code had been drawn up, and he recommended that serious attention should be given to the education laws with a view to consider what modifications were necessary. The news from Acheen gave reason to anticipate that prudence and perseverance will triumph over the resistance of the enemy. In conclusion, his Majesty praised the army and navy in the East Indies, and said that the condition of the colonies was satisfactory.

At the discussion of the colonial budget for 1875, the Colonial Minister announced that immediately after entering upon his office he had instructed the Governor-General of British India to prepare for the abolition of slavery in Sumatra and Celebes. In consequence of this announcement, a motion by a Liberal deputy for the abolition of slavery in the two colonies mentioned was withdrawn. The minister declared that he would substantially pursue the same policy which had been pursued by his Liberal predecessor; the only difference was, that he intended to advance more slowly.

The Minister of Finance, in laying the budget estimates for 1875 before the Chambers, said that the total expenditure would be 110,000,000 florins, which would be 10,000,000 in excess of that of 1874. The cause of this increase was the augmentation in various items of the national expenditure—namely, in foreign missions, great public works at the naval ports, the extension of the state railway system, pilotage, and the national defense. The total amount of revenue was estimated at about 103,000,000 florins; thus the deficit in the budget would probably be about 7,000,000. This deficit, however, judging by the results obtained in the last few years, will be covered by the surplus arising from the Indian revenue and the continuous increase of the ordinary receipts. The minister proposes to make no change in the present system of taxation, and he dwelt upon the favorable result of the returns from the Dutch Indies and from the ordinary taxes. As a sign of the increasing prosperity of the country, the minister said: "We have been able to provide for all our wants, even the war in Sumatra, without having recourse to extraordinary measures, which is a good augury for the future."

The relations of Acheen with the Netherlands and other European countries are of old date; the dealings of Holland with this state date from 1599, when a part of the crews of two Dutch vessels, attempting to open a trade, were treacherously captured and held in bond, one of the commanders, Frederick Houtman, being among the sufferers. They were released, after some negotiation, two years later, about which time English vessels visited the Sultan, and Admiral Sir James Lancaster was publicly entertained by the reigning monarch. The Portuguese were at that period already the owners of the Malacca Peninsula, and the chief enemies of the Sultan, and for generations afterward it seems to have been the policy of this Mohammedan power to play off one set of infidels against another. It was with Dutch aid that the armies of Sultan Isané, in 1641, drove the Portuguese out of Malacca altogether, after a series of expeditions and counter-expeditions extending over many years. The present internal feud between the sovereign and "the native party," which refuses to submit to the Dutch army, is even more ancient than the foreign policy of the kingdom. The reigning house has always been fanatic in adherence to the faith of Islam, and has supported purity of religion as a proper pendant to the absolute autocracy sought by it; while the great chiefs have equally claimed support on their side from the mass of the people on the ground of their leniency toward the old superstitions. This politico-religious schism has in fact been going on ever since Sultan Moghayet set his subjects the example of conversion about the year 1510.

The special envoy from Acheen to the Sultan of Turkey, who was to induce the Porte to recognize the Mussulman state as a vassal state of Turkey, returned early in 1874 from Constantinople, without having attained his object. The Porte did not dare to assume the responsibility involved in assenting to the overthrow of the Achinese, and the envoy was not received at all by the Sultan.

At the close of the year 1874, it appeared, from official statements relative to the Achinese war, that a third campaign was to be entered upon (in 1875), with the object of gaining the heights surrounding the Kraton. Four battalions and six companies were secretly concentrated by the Indo-Dutch Government on the narrow belt of coast in Acheen which is occupied by the Dutch troops. The total force assembled on the coast would then consist of seven and a quarter battalions of infantry, and a few companies of artillery and engineers, making about 6,000 men in all; but only one-half of them would be available for active operations, as the occupied districts will have to be strongly garrisoned. The new expedition was to be placed under the command of Colonel Pel, who held the post of commander-in-chief and civil commissioner in Acheen after the return of General Van Swieten.

NEVADA. Silver-mines constitute Nevada's greatest source of wealth. They exist in nearly every section of the State. The richest deposit of silver in the State, if not in the world, is the Comstock lode, on the east side of Mount Davidson, in Storey County, and partly under the towns of Virginia and Gold Hill. Its area contains about one-third in value of gold, and two-thirds of silver. The lode has a general north and south course, and an east dip, and has been traced on the surface 27,000 feet. It has been actually explored for 19,000 feet, and within this space the principal mines are situated. It has been opened to a depth of 2,000 feet. A tunnel, known as the Sutro Tunnel, is in progress, designed to drain the mines, and otherwise facilitate operations on the lode. It commences at a point one and a half mile from Carson River, and three and a half miles below Dayton, and runs northwest to the Savage Mine, a distance of 20,178 feet, where its depth will be 1,922 feet. At the close of 1874 it had reached a distance of 8,250 feet, and was progressing at the rate of seven feet a day. Next to those of the Comstock lode, the most productive silver-mines are in the region near Eureka, in the east central portion of the State, and in the Ely district, near Pioche, Lincoln County, in the southeast. The White Pine region, in the eastern part of the State, which, after the discovery of the mines, in 1868, was the scene of great excitement, now yields comparatively small returns. The bullion product of the State since the opening of the mines, according to R. W. Raymond, United States Commissioner of Mining, has been as follows:

YEARS.	ENTIRE PRODUCT OF THE STATE.			Separate Product of the Comstock Lode.
	Gold.	Silver.	Total.	
1861....	$600,000	$1,400,000	$2,000,000	$1,500,000
1862....	2,500,000	4,500,000	6,500,000	6,000,000
1863....	4,000,000	8,500,000	12,500,000	12,000,000
1864....	5,000,000	11,000,000	16,000,000	14,500,000
1865....	4,750,000	11,250,000	16,000,000	14,500,000
1866....	4,000,000	9,000,000	13,000,000	12,000,000
1867....	4,500,000	11,500,000	16,000,000	13,000,000
1868....	2,800,000	10,500,000	13,300,000	8,500,000
1869....	2,500,000	11,500,000	14,000,000	7,550,000
1870....	2,800,000	13,200,000	16,000,000	8,500,000
1871....	3,780,000	18,700,000	22,480,000	11,350,000
1872....	6,000,000	19,550,000	25,550,000	14,000,000
1873....	10,000,000	25,250,000	35,250,000	22,000,000
Aggregate	$52,730,000	$155,850,000	$208,580,000	$146,000,000

The reported production of bullion in 1874 was $35,457,233, nearly all of which was silver. The value of the bullion product of Nevada since 1871 has exceeded that of California. The United States census of 1870 (admitted to be incomplete) returns 139 mines, having 44 steam-engines of 2,780 horse-power, and two water-wheels of 50 horse-power; hands employed, 2,866 (809 above and 2,057 below ground); capital invested, $32,253,400; wages paid during the year, $2,900,872; value of materials used, $1,636,865; of products, $11,166,452. Of the mines, 91 were quartz-mines of silver; 46 quartz-mines of gold and silver; 1 copper, and 1 lead. The number of quartz-crushing-mills in 1872, according to the report of the State mineralogist, was 162; number of smelting-furnaces, 16; number of stamps, 1,904; daily capacity in tons, 5,183. These numbers include those idle as well as those in operation. The amount of bullion from Nevada deposited at the United States mints and assay-offices to June 30, 1873, was $10,401,717.37, of which $9,261,649.43 was silver, and $1,140,067.94 gold.

A mint was established at Carson City in 1870. The deposits of gold and silver bullion during the years ending December 31st, has been as follows:

YEARS.	Gold.	Silver.
1870...................	$213,131 59	$57,219 54
1871...................	2,500,950 44	2,967,997 47
1872...................	4,891,135 97	4,042,513 11
1873...................	3,784,121 20	3,879,041 92
1874...................	2,704,148 66	3,162,245 15
Total.............	$14,093,487 86	$14,109,017 19

At the close of the year, great excitement prevailed in consequence of the discovery of a vein of silver in the Comstock lode, of which the value was estimated by experts as high as $1,500,000,000. This great bonanza was supposed to be from 1,000 to 1,200 feet in length, and about 600 feet in depth. The ore was reported to average not less than $200 per ton, while much of it would yield $500 per ton; and specimens were found of which the value was far in excess of that sum. The great bonanza is thus described by an expert, under date of January 9, 1875:

At last the great "bulge," the true heart of the world-famous Comstock silver-lode, would seem to have been reached. As far as explored, it lies in the Consolidated Virginia, California, and Ophir claims. In all three of these mines have been developed marvelously rich bodies—wonderful masses of sulphuret and chloride ores. We have said "bodies," but there is in reality but one body—one immense bonanza, chimney, or whatever·else we may choose to call it—one huge mass of ore extending all the way from the Consolidated Virginia through the California into the Ophir, and no one knows how much farther; nor does any one know much of its height or width, and nothing at all of its depth. As to its length we know something definite, namely, that it extends 400 feet through the Consolidated Virginia, and undoubtedly traverses the entire·length (600 feet) of the California, as it has been discovered in the Ophir mine, which adjoins the California on the north. How far it extends into the Ophir ground, time and the honest miner can alone determine. It is conceded, however, that the ore body cannot be less than 1,200 feet in length. The great fissure in which this large bonanza of ore rests appears to have expanded at this particular point in the course of the vein in order to form for it a cradle suited to its giant proportions. Measuring across from the true " west country " rock to the true " east country " rock, the distance is from 1,000 to 1,200 feet. The space between the east and west country rock is the fissure in which lies the body of ore, which of late has so startled and bewildered all of the "experts" and the whole "mining world" of the Pacific coast. The great fissure is filled with what our mining men call " vein-matter," or gangue, a mixture of quartz, clay, or porphyry. Here, in the midst of this vein-matter or gangue, which fills the vast fissure from side to side, has formed and is now found the huge mass of ore which runs through the three mines mentioned above. The California cross-cut is not in the California ground, but is fourteen feet south of that company's south line. It is here, in this drift, that the wonderfully rich ore, of which so much has of late been said, was found. The ore is moderately rich where it was first cut by the drift, but it rapidly grows richer, and within a few feet it becomes a mass of glittering sulphurets and pale-green chloride ore. The drift has now penetrated this mass of ore—a part of the great whole—a distance of about twenty-five feet. Look where you may—at the bottom, the top, or the sides of the drift—it is everywhere the same. This ore yields an average assay of $600 per ton! It would be an easy matter to get samples of ore in this drift that would assay far up into the thousands; indeed, in taking a sample the trouble would be to avoid getting hold of this very rich ore. This is the famous drift which seems to tell the story of the fabulous wealth lying near at hand in the California.

Later advices represent the above accounts to have been exaggerated; but what are the true nature and value of the newly-discovered mines is not accurately known.

The total receipts into the State Treasury during the year ending December 31, 1874, amounted to $570,277, of which $527,547.64 was in coin, and $42,729.26 in currency. The chief sources of revenue were as follows :

Property tax	$275,369
Tax on proceeds of mines	163,114
State poll-tax	25,196
Gaming licenses	16,756
Fines	2,562
State-prison	21,701
Sales of State lands	42,480

The total expenditures amounted to $641,-856, including $629,833 specie and $12,023 currency. The following were the most important items:

Salaries and contingencies of Executive Department	$61,012
Salaries and contingencies of Judicial Department	25,876
State Library	2,601
Support of State-prison, including salaries of warden and deputy	64,090
Charitable purposes	38,478
Including for State Orphans' Home	12,121
" " Support of Indigent Insane	25,429
" " Deaf Mutes and Blind	927
State Capitol	15,464
Support of schools	30,510
Interest on State bonds	64,304
Purchase of United States gold bonds for investment	271,783
Construction of new prison at Reno	50,601
State University	1,479
Miscellaneous purposes	15,652

The balance in the Treasury, December 31st, was $518,712, of which $489,177 was coin and $29,540 currency. The State debt at that date amounted to $733,528, viz. : 10 per cent. bonds, due April 1, 1881, $160,000 ; 9¼ per cent. bonds, due March 1, 1882, $120,000 ; 9½ per cent. bonds, due March 1, 1887, $380,000 ; outstanding warrants, $73,528. The assets were as follows : State bonds belonging to school-fund, $104,000 ; United States bonds belonging to school-fund, $146,000 ; United States bonds belonging to sinking-fund, $100,000 ; United States bonds belonging to University-fund, $10,000 ; balance in Treasury, $518,717 : total, $878,717.

The assessed value of. property for 1874, according to the report of the Controller, was : real estate, $14,125,578 ; personal estate, $12,-504,701 : total, $26,630,279. The State tax ($1.25 on $100) amounted to $332,878 ; county tax, $562,555 : total tax on property, $895,-433. Besides this, a State tax is levied on the proceeds of mines, at the same rate as the State tax on property. A poll-tax of $4, one-half for State and one-half for county purposes, is also levied on each male resident between twenty-one and sixty years of age.

At the November election, L. R. Bradley (Democrat) was elected Governor by a majority of 2,585 over his Republican opponent, Hazlett. The total vote was 18,093, of which Bradley received 10,339, and Hazlett 7,754. William Woodburn (Republican) was elected to Congress by a majority of 750 over Adrian Ellis (Democrat), the vote being : Woodburn, 9,317 ; Ellis, 8,567. The Legislature for 1875–'76 is classified as follows :

PARTIES.	Senate.	House.	Joint Ballot.
Republicans	17	31	48
Democrats	7	16	23
Independents	1	3	4
Republican majority	9	12	21

The present State government is as follows : Governor, Louis R. Bradley, Democrat ; Lieutenant-Governor, Jewett Adams, Democrat ; Attorney-General, John R. Kittrell, Democrat ; Secretary of State, James D. Minor, Republican ; Controller, W. W. Hobart, Republican ; Treasurer, Jerry Schooling, Democrat ; Surveyor-General, John Day, Republican ; State Mineralogist, H. R. Whitehall, Republican ; Superintendent of Public Instruction, S. P. Kelley, Republican.

NEW HAMPSHIRE. The Republican party of this State met in general convention at Concord, on the 7th of January, 1874, for the purpose of nominating their candidates for the offices of Governor and Railroad Commissioner. Six hundred and eighty-six delegates from all parts of the State attended the meeting. The result of the nominations was as follows : For Governor, Charles H. Bell, of Exeter, received 262, and Luther McCutchins, of New London, 320, votes, whereupon the latter was declared nominated, and his nomination was made unanimous. Mr. McCutchins is a farmer, and in this competition represented the farming interest of New Hampshire, as he himself declared in his address to the convention, accepting the nomination.

For Railroad Commissioner, the whole number of votes was 458, of which 245 were given to G. P. Conn, of Concord, and the rest unequally distributed among seven competitors. He was declared nominated.

The following platform was unanimously adopted by the convention :

Whereas, The Republican party sprang into existence as the ally of liberty, justice, and integrity, in their contest with the slave power and the Democratic party, it has battled manfully and triumphantly to preserve the Union, to crush rebellion, to emancipate and enfranchise, and to establish the foundation of the republic on the eternal principles of unity, equality, and freedom. Emerging from the chaos of civil war, through the valor and sacrifice of our citizen soldiery, the Republican party has restored the straying States to their orbits. It has established peace, justice, and tranquillity ; it has secured indemnity from England through arbitration, and reparation from Spain through a just and prompt demand ; it has paid more than $300,000,000 of the public debt, reduced taxation, and held the Republic steadily on its onward and upward course : therefore—

Resolved, That while we recall with pride the noble origin, the heroic career, and the beneficent achievements of the Republican party, we regret and condemn the want of fidelity which has characterized a few of those whom it trusted with place and power.

Resolved, That the bill providing for back pay and increase of salaries, passed by the Forty-second Congress, was a violation of the pledge of economy contained in the Philadelphia platform, renewed by the press and on the stump throughout the presidential campaign, and reaffirmed after the reëlection of President Grant.

Resolved, That we call upon our Senators and Representatives to vote for the unconditional repeal of the so-called salary act of the Forty-second Congress, and to use their influence and votes to reestablish all salaries, including the salary of the President of the United States, at the old scale, so far as the Constitution will admit.

Resolved, That in view of the prevailing industrial and financial depression, we call upon our Senators and Representatives, who have profited by the back pay voted by the Forty-second Congress, to make restitution to the Government, which they have helped to embarrass.

Resolved, That we heartily commend the efforts of the House of Representatives, seconded by every department of the national Administration, to retrench expenditures and reduce appropriations for the civil, military, and naval service, and that no additional burdens by way of taxation should be laid upon the business, labor, and consumption of the people until every effort has been exhausted to bring the expenses of the Government within its present and prospective means ; and that, if a resort to such taxation becomes necessary, in order to meet the obligations of the Government, we believe it should be laid, as far as practicable, upon objects of luxury which do not enter into the daily use and comfort of the people, and upon those traffics especially which are deleterious in their influence to the health, morals, and happiness of mankind.

Resolved, That we earnestly invite the coöperation of the Republican party of the other States in the united and determined effort to preserve the organization from reproach from any quarter, so that it may continue to occupy the proud position of being the party of the people, for the people, and by the people.

Resolved, That we deplore the prevalence of intemperance as one of the most alarming evils of our land, producing most of the ignorance, pauperism, vice, and crime, which burden us with debt and shame; that we rejoice in the growth of a deep and earnest moral sentiment in behalf of temperance principles ; that we believe the work of temperance reform cannot be successfully prosecuted without a more thorough appeal to moral suasion than has been employed for the last few years ; and that we indorse the unanimous action of our last Legislature for the maintenance of the present temperance legislation of the State.

Resolved, That agricultural pursuits are the basis of all material prosperity, and best calculated to foster those habits which conduce to the highest welfare of a State ; that we hail with gratification the advances making in the science of agriculture, and the evidences of awakening interest in it as a pursuit in our State ; that the Republican party will welcome the healthy influences which the tillers of the soil always bring to their councils, and accord to them their full and legitimate weight in government; and that we pledge our utmost efforts to redress any grievances and unjust discriminations under which the farming interests suffer, to deny special privileges, and to give to all classes of men equal and exact justice.

Resolved, That we deprecate the growing tendency to special legislation, both in the State and national Legislatures, as a prolific source of abuse, consuming time which should be devoted to general business, and tending to prodigality, corruption, and the aggrandizement of individual and corporate monopolies at the expense of the people; and that we urge upon our members of Congress to use all their influence for a reform of this increasing evil. We also approve without reserve of President Grant's recommendation for an amendment of the organic law so as to protect the country from the abuse of loading down appropriation bills with plundering schemes and other objectionable legislation in the shape of riders and amendments in the closing hours of the sessions of Congress.

Resolved, That as in a republic there should be no privileged classes, and the burdens of government should be equally borne, we protest against any revival of the abuses of the franking privilege, and will hail the day when free passes, favoritism, and all unjust discriminations, shall be eliminated from railway management, and a corresponding reduction made in fares and freights to the whole people.

Resolved, That we call upon Congress to pave the way by early and wise legislation for such improvements in our banking system, and for as speedy a return to specie payments, as will be most beneficial to the great industrial and commercial interests of the country.

Resolved, That we demand such a revision of the laws creating and governing savings-banks as shall lead to the investment of their funds in undoubted securities and real estate within New Hampshire, and the total separation of their management from other banking institutions, to the end that their funds may be securely invested, our towns and villages built up, and our mechanics and working-men encouraged to provide homes and farms for themselves.

Resolved, That we call upon the next Legislature to make a thorough revision of the laws relating to taxation and valuation, so that taxation shall be just and equal, and no unjust burden be imposed on the earnings of labor.

Resolved, That we point with pride to the auspicious results of Republican rule in the State of New Hampshire—a faithful and efficient administration of law, a healthy growth and development of our varied industrial interest, economy in expenditures, honesty among officials unmarred by a single example of corruption or defalcation by the custodians of public funds, moderate taxation, prompt provision for all public obligations, and a steady decrease of the State and municipal debts; and that we confidently appeal to the voters to continue in power a party which has given such substantial proofs of honesty of purpose and watchful care for the rights and interests of the people.

Resolved, That we commend Luther McCutchins, our candidate for Governor, and Granville P. Conn, our candidate for Railroad Commissioner, as citizens of capacity and integrity, and we pledge them our united, hearty, and triumphant support.

The Democrats held their State Convention at Concord, on the 8th of January. The organization had scarcely been completed when, without waiting for the report of the Committee on Credentials, a delegate moved " to proceed to ballot for a candidate for Governor ; " which motion, notwithstanding opposition, was carried and acted upon. The ballot was to be considered informal. The whole number of votes was 650, almost all of which were distributed among three of the five candidates proposed, Albert R. Hatch, of Portsmouth, having received 143 votes; Hiram R. Roberts, of Rollingsford, 230; and James A. Weston, of Manchester, 240. This result caused great excitement, and it was agreed to take a formal ballot, the delegates voting by counties. The result of the first ballot proved decisive, as, the whole number of votes being then 632, Mr. Hatch received 51 votes, Mr. Roberts 252, and Mr. Weston 323, who was declared nominated, and his nomination made unanimous.

Alvah Sulloway received the nomination for Railroad Commissioner.

The following resolutions were then adopted by the convention:

We, the Democratic Republican party of the State of New Hampshire, in convention assembled, hereby affirm, in the language of the seventh article of our Bill of Rights, that the people of the State have the sole and exclusive right of governing themselves as a free, sovereign, independent State, and do and forever hereafter shall exercise and enjoy every power, jurisdiction, an right pertaining thereto which is not or may not hereafter be by them expressly delegated to the United States of America in Congress assembled : therefore—

Resolved, 1. That we are in favor of the union of the States and the rights of the States as declared and defined by the Constitution of the United States.

2. That we are in favor of retrenchment, reform, and economy in the expenditures of all the governments of the people, whether national, State, or municipal.

3. That, while we are in favor of all just and equal taxation necessary to sustain our Government and public institutions, we are opposed to all unjust and unequal systems of taxation which tend to favor one class at the expense of other classes of the people.

4. That the public domain of the United States is the property of the people, and should be preserved for the people as a refuge to which they can flee from the oppression of capital, and that we condemn the policy of giving the same to railroad corporations or other corporate bodies for the benefit of the few and not for the people.

5. That the veto of the President, given him in the Constitution, was intended to be used for the protection of the rights of the people, and that we regret that that great conservative power has never been used by the present incumbent of that high office for the purposes for which it was intended, when so many opportunities have been presented for its use by the action of Congress during the existence of the present Administration.

6. That this convention offers its adherence to the Cincinnati-Baltimore platform of 1872, and cordially invites the coöperation, without regard to former political associations, of those voters of the State who desire reform in the administration of public affairs.

7. That the present national Administration by its devotion to personal and partisan interests, its utter disregard of constitutional obligations, by its reckless mismanagement of the national finances, by its interference with the local self-government of the people, by its support of all manner of corrupt jobs and speculations, by its nominations of notoriously incompetent and corrupt men to the highest offices in its gift, and its blundering and unstatesmanlike direction of our foreign affairs, has justly brought upon itself the condemnation and contempt of the American people.

8. That the law increasing the salaries of the President and other officers of the Government was wholly without justification, and we demand its unqualified repeal, and we will support no man for political office who voted for the bill or is not in favor of such repeal.

9. That the Democracy of New Hampshire are opposed to all monopolies which operate for the special benefit of privileged persons or classes, and to all combinations or corporations made to effect purposes hostile to the best interests of the people; that they are opposed to the use of money by corporate bodies to influence elections and the legislation of the State; but they are not opposed to the corporations established for the promotion of legitimate interests and the public good, while their operations are confined within the limits of their chartered privileges and to the objects and purposes of their creation.

10. That we recognize the grievances of which the farmers and other producing classes complain. The national Government has unnecessarily depreciated their property by crowding its own land upon the market in advance of any natural demand. It has imposed onerous taxes in the interest of monopolies upon nearly all of the goods they consume, while it protects them in nothing; it exempts billions of money from taxation, leaving the burden it ought to bear to fall with aggravated weight upon them; and the political effect of local laws is equally unjust, inasmuch as the farmer has no disguise for his little wealth, while property in other forms escapes taxation altogether, or bears no just proportion of the burdens according to prospective value.

11. That we are in favor of more stringent laws in relation to the investment of deposits by savings-banks, so that the savings of those in moderate circumstances which may be intrusted to their care shall be more securely invested, and used so far as practicable in developing and enlarging the resources and business interests of all sections of the State.

12. That the practical effects of rigid sumptuary laws at all times, in all places, have been to generate disregard of law among both officials and peoples, and to change the form without lessening the extent of the evils they seek to remedy, and that the deductions of reason as well as the lessons of experience suggest that a judicious license law, which may be made prohibitory by local option, will yield better results than the present law, which is partially and unfairly enforced or wholly ignored as the caprice of men or parties may dictate.

13. That we extend our hearty congratulations to

our brethren of the West for the signal victories they have achieved in behalf of an honest and equal administration of the Government, and we cordially invite all men, without regard to past political designations, to unite with us in an honest and great effort to emulate their noble example and achieve a victory not in the interest of any party, but in the name and in behalf of a common country.

14. That we will use our most earnest efforts to secure the election of the candidates this day nominated.

The New Hampshire State Temperance Union held its annual State Convention at Concord on the 18th of December, 1873. There was a good attendance, every important section of the State being represented. A large number of ladies were present, and admitted as delegates. From the reports read to the meeting by the recording secretary and the treasurer, this organization appears to be in a prosperous condition; and the president, in a short address, congratulated the Union upon the success that had attended its operations during the past year.

The following preambles and resolutions were adopted by the convention:

Whereas, The evil of intemperance still exists in our land, desolating homes, crushing hearts, creating pauperism, engendering crime, ruining health, and blighting the intellectual and moral natures of all who yield to its influence; and—

Whereas, The State Temperance Union thus organize to oppose, by moral and intellectual means, this great and alarming evil: therefore, be it

Resolved, That the first year's work of our organization has been quite as successful as could reasonably be expected, and fully convinces us that we are laboring in the right way, and strengthens the conviction that success in our work largely depends upon—1. The organization of reform clubs wherever practicable; 2. The formation of county and town temperance unions, auxiliary to the State Union; 3. The organization of churches and Sabbath-schools into temperance societies; 4. Cordial coöperation with all the temperance organizations in their work; 5. The circulation of the pledge among all classes of people; and, 6. Special effort to interest the young in the principles and practice of total abstinence. We base our hopes of ultimate success largely on the education of the masses in the direction in which we are working, being fully persuaded that a deep and earnest popular sentiment in behalf of temperance principles is absolutely essential to the successful prosecution of our work, and that without this enlightened sentiment we cannot reasonably hope for the triumph of the temperance cause.

Resolved, That temperance is a cardinal virtue, the rigid practice of which is enjoined on all who aim to reach the highest self-culture, and to confer the greatest amount of good upon society.

Resolved, That inasmuch as total abstinence alone insures safety to the moderate drinker no less than to the reformed inebriate, we urge its practice on every one, both as a safeguard to himself, and as an example to others; and we enjoin on temperance men everywhere the paramount importance of teaching and practising this principle by circulating the pledge, and exhorting to its faithful maintenance.

Resolved, That the formation of temperance leagues in various parts of our State by earnest and devoted women is one of the hopeful signs of the times, and we welcome them to the ranks of organized temperance workers, assuring them of our sympathy and hearty good-will.

Resolved, That when the temperance cause is lifted out of the arena of party politics as a distinctive work and taken up by the churches as a moral and religious duty we will see greater results than can reasonably be hoped for under existing circumstances. We regard it as a duty, that every temperance man owes himself and society to vote only for such men as most nearly represent his principles and the welfare of the country. In view of this fact we call upon the political parties to place in nomination only such as we can consistently and honorably support; men who, both by precept and practice, are true to the principles that underlie the temperance reform.

Resolved, That we do again pledge ourselves to labor for obtaining from every person his or her signature to the pledge; that we as citizens will give our sympathy and aid to the mayors and aldermen of our cities and to the selectmen of our towns as they fulfil the oaths of their office in the legal suppression of the traffic which is one great hinderance to morality and religion in our State.

Resolved, That we are unqualifiedly opposed to all schemes looking to the repeal of the prohibitory law and substitution of license in any form in its stead. We adhere unswervingly to the belief that the traffic in intoxicating liquors is a crime, and as such has no right to demand the protection of law. While believing that men are amenable to moral suasion in greater degree than to any other reformatory principle, yet we recognize the fact that legal as well as moral means are essential in carrying on our work. Let, then, our motto be, "Moral suasion for the tempted; moral and legal suasion for the tempter; moral suasion for the drunkard; moral and legal suasion for the drunkard-maker."

Resolved, That while we point with much satisfaction to the work we have already accomplished in the cause of moral reform, we ask our brethren abroad to consider it merely an earnest of what we hope to accomplish in the future, and that we confidently look forward to the time when the benign cause of temperance will be held as high above all mere partisanship as are the tenets of Christian churches, believing that, when that exalted position is reached and held, we shall have every assurance of final victory over intemperance.

Resolved, That the labors of our State Agent, Mr. Francis Murphy, have been so greatly prospered as to occasion in our hearts deep feelings of gratitude to God for the blessings vouchsafed to our cause through his instrumentality, and whether he longer continues with us or removes to other fields of labor, we most cordially indorse him as a true, earnest, and consistent temperance man, a friend to all who need sympathy and help in their efforts to free themselves from the terrible thraldom of intemperance."

The temperance candidates for the offices of Governor and Railroad Commissioner were John Blackmer and David Heald.

There was no election of Governor or Railroad Commissioner by the people. For Governor, the whole number of votes cast was 71,893, of which John Blackmer had 2,097, Luther McCutchins 34,143, and James A. Weston 35,608—necessary for a choice being 35,942. For Railroad Commissioner, whole number of votes cast, 71,752, of which David Heald had 2,107; Granville P. Conn, 34,186; Alvah W. Sulloway, 35,482—necessary for a choice being 35,887.

At the district elections, also, four of the twelve Senators and three of the five Councilors were not elected.

The election of all these officers devolved on the Legislature, which assembled on June 3d. The final results of the ballotings were as follows: For Governor, James A. Weston 182;

Luther McCutchins, 151. For Railroad Commissioner, Alvah W. Sulloway, 181; Granville P. Conn, 153. For Secretary of State, William Butterfield, 185; Benjamin F. Prescott, 158; for State Treasurer, Josiah C. Dearborn, 180; Solon A. Carter, 158. For State Printer, Charles C. Pearson, 180; Edward A. Jenks, 154. For Commissary-General, Tobias D. Foss, 180; Charles F. Montgomery, 157.

The finances of the State appear to be sound and satisfactory. The debt on June 1, 1874, was as follows: Liabilities, $4,102,166.49; assets in the Treasury, $275,576.47: net indebtedness, $3,826,599.02. On June 1, 1873, it had been: Liabilities $4,191,965.48; assets in the Treasury, $59,805.04: net indebtedness, $4,-142,160.44—showing the reduction during the last fiscal year to have been $315,561.42.

The State debt is funded, and will mature within thirty-one years in about equal installments.

The total revenue of the State during the same year amounted to $740,062.24; of which $600,000 were collected from the State tax, the remaining $140,062.24 from all other sources. The amount of the public expenditures, ordinary and extraordinary, was $434,491.32, including $250,798.77 paid as interest on the public debt. Of the excess of revenue over expenditure a large portion was paid for reducing the principal of the debt; the rest was cash on hand.

From carefully-prepared estimates, based upon an economical administration of the government, it is apparent that an annual State tax of $400,000 for a few years, with the income from other sources, will be adequate to meet the current expenses of the State, together with her obligations as they mature, and leave a handsome margin besides.

There is only one bank of discount in New Hampshire doing business by State authority; while there are forty-six national banks and private banking-houses in successful operation. The number of savings-banks in the State is sixty-four, their deposits amounting to the aggregate to $28,829,376.83; which is an increase of nearly $367,000 over last year's deposits. The whole number of depositors owning the money kept in these banks is 92,788. Three of these banks were chartered and organized last year.

Public instruction for the education of youth is commendably attended to by both the local government and the people. There are nearly 4,000 schools maintained in New Hampshire, and the Normal School designed to prepare thoroughly trained and educated teachers for them is in successful operation.

The changing and in many towns greatly reduced population has left a very small number of pupils for the public schools, and in some there are none.

The charitable and benevolent institutions are well cared and provided for. In the New Hampshire Asylum for the Insane, on April 30, 1874, there remained 281 patients, their average number in the whole year, ending that day, having been 268. The average number of the inmates of the asylum, including the employés of every description connected with the institution, is about 300: 138 indigent patients were more or less aided during the year. The most indigent were aided to the extent of half the cost of their board, the regular price of which is $5 a week for each patient, medical attendance included.

The receipts of the institution from all sources during the year, amounted to $86,580.01; its expenses to $84,871.46; leaving a surplus of above $1,700 in the treasury.

The legacies and donations to the New Hampshire Asylum for the Insane during the time elapsed from its establishment to April 30, 1874, amount in the aggregate to $244,179.95. The asylum is possessed of a farm containing 125 acres, well stocked, and producing, besides what comes from the kitchen-garden, a variety of crops, among which, in 1874, have been "900 bushels of potatoes, 200 bushels of corn in the ear, 80 tons of hay, 20 of corn-fodder, and 18 of straw."

The inmates of the New Hampshire Penitentiary at the beginning of June, 1874, were more numerous than ordinarily, which seems to have been regarded as beneficial to the State, Governor Weston saying, in his message to the Legislature: "By the reports of the warden and the committee of the Council on the State-prison, it will be seen that its affairs are in a prosperous condition, particularly those pertaining to its finances. There is now a much larger number of convicts in this institution than usual, and hence a proportionally larger income, as the State receives a *per diem* compensation from the contractor for all the convicts who are able to attend the work assigned them. The net receipts for the past year are $10,611.61, which, added to previous earnings, makes a balance in favor of the prison of more than $30,000. This is principally invested in the bonds of the State."

The Reform-School for the correction and education of wayward boys is in successful operation, and kept under excellent discipline.

The geological survey of New Hampshire, which has been going on since 1869, will be completed in 1874, and the first volume of the final report be ready for distribution in July, 1874, the second and last volume within a year thereafter. The entire work will occupy some 1,400 pages, illustrated by numerous plates, and accompanied by an atlas. The cost of the printing alone, including plates and maps, is estimated at $10,000.

The legislative body were in session about five weeks, till the 10th of July. Numerous acts of public interest were passed. Among the most important laws of a general character was that relating to the judiciary, under the title "An act to abolish the present judiciary system, and establishing a new one," going into operation in August. The general purport of the change introduced by this act, and the range of the jurisdiction belonging to the new courts established by it, appear from the first three sections, as follows:

Section 1. From and after the time when this act takes effect, instead of the Supreme Judicial Court heretofore existing, there shall be established in this State a Superior Court of Judicature, consisting of one chief and two associate justices, to be appointed and commissioned as prescribed by the constitution; also a Circuit Court, to consist of one chief and two associate justices, to be appointed and commissioned in the same manner.

Section 2. Said Circuit Court and the justices thereof shall have jurisdiction of all actions, appeals, process and matters and things whatsoever, both civil and criminal, now provided by law to be entered at or done, and which may be entered at or done, at the trial terms of said Supreme Judicial Court, and also concurrent jurisdiction with the justices of the Superior Court of Judicature of all matters and things which may now be done by any of the justices of said Supreme Judicial Court in vacation.

Section 3. Said Superior Court of Judicature and the justices thereof shall have jurisdiction of all other writs, process, appeals, and matters and things whatsoever, of which said Supreme Judicial Court now has jurisdiction, and also full power and authority to do any act in vacation which the justices of said Supreme Judicial Court or any one of them may now do. * * *

The greatest importance was also attached to the legislative action on the bill "to authorize the Nashua & Lowell and the Boston & Lowell Railroad Companies to unite and become one corporation," which was repeatedly and warmly debated. When first put to the vote, on July 7th, the bill was lost, but a motion to reconsider that vote having been, after further debate, carried in the Lower House by 175 yeas to 132 nays, the bill was put to the vote again on the 9th, and passed—yeas 169, nays 149. The Senate passed it on the same day.

The bill entitled "To restrain the sale and use of intoxicating liquors in the State," which was considered one of the most important subjects acted upon by the Legislature during this session, was, after warm and excited debate, finally defeated. Though favored by a large number of members, its passage met with such decided opposition on the part of others who were most friendly to the cause of temperance, but maintained that this bill, notwithstanding the words of its title were apparently in favor of prohibition, was introduced, and its passage strenuously advocated, in the interest of liquor-dealers. After a long contest the vote was taken, on July 9th, and the bill was rejected: yeas 137, nays 155.

In compliance with the terms of the act establishing the new judiciary system, which took effect in August, 1874, the Governor and Council appointed the six judges constituting the two new courts, as follows: For the Superior Court: Chief-Justice Samuel Newell Bell, of Manchester; Associate Justices, William Spencer Ladd, of Lancaster, and Francis A. Faulkner, of Keene. (Mr. Bell graduated

from Dartmouth College in the class of 1847; had represented New Hampshire in the Federal Legislature at Washington as a member of the Lower House in the Forty-second Congress, and, besides being a lawyer, is regarded to be a railroad business-man, being president of the Suncook Valley Railroad, and a Director in the Concord & Boston and Concord & Montreal Railroads. Mr. Ladd also graduated from Dartmouth College in the class of 1855, and for several years has served on the bench of the old court to the acceptance of the bar generally. Mr. Faulkner is a lawyer of about fifty years of age, and enjoys a distinguished reputation in his profession.) For the Circuit Court: Chief-Justice William Lawrence Foster, of Concord; Associate Justices, Ellery A. Hibbard, of Laconia, and John S. H. Frink, of Greenland. (Mr. Foster is a native of Westminster, Vermont, and has been on the bench of the old court for many years, in which office he has proved himself an able and popular judge. Mr. Hibbard, born in St. Johnsbury, Vermont, in 1826, has been a Representative from New Hampshire at Washington during the Forty-second Congress, and soon after the completion of his term was appointed to fill a seat on the bench of the old court. Mr. Frink is a prominent lawyer in the county where he resides. Mr. Faulkner, in the Superior Court, and Mr. Foster, in the Circuit Court, are Republicans.)

NEW JERSEY. The Legislature, which assembled early in January, continued in session till the 27th of March. Very little of the legislation was of general interest. Several amendments to the State constitution, reported by the constitutional commission, were agreed upon. Pursuant to the present constitution, these amendments came before the Legislature of 1875 for approval or rejection, in whole or in part. Those concurred in by the members of that body will be submitted to the people for ratification or rejection, at a special election to be held for that purpose within four months after the dissolution of the Legislature.

The provisions of the amendments of general interest which were agreed upon may be briefly summarized as follows: No county, city, borough, town, or village, shall give any money or property, or loan its money or credit, to any individual or corporation, or own any stock or bonds in any association or corporation. In the article on the right of suffrage the word "white" is stricken out, and, in order to put an end to all question on woman suffrage, the word "male," expunged by the constitutional commission, is restored. In time of war, no elector in the service of the State or national Government, in the army or navy, shall be deprived of his vote by reason of absence from his election-district, and the Legislature shall provide the manner in which the vote of such absent elector shall be received. The Legislature may pass laws to deprive persons guilty of the crime of bribery, of whatever kind, of the right of suffrage. Members of the Legislature shall be elected on the first Tuesday in November, and they shall receive $500 annually during the time for which they are elected, and no other allowance or emolument, for any other purpose whatever, shall be allowed them. No law shall be revived or amended by reference to its title only, but the act revived or the section amended shall be inserted at length. in the bill. No general law shall embrace any provision of a private, special, or local character. No act shall be passed which shall provide that any existing law, or any part thereof, shall be made or deemed a part of the act; nor shall any act be passed which enacts that any existing law, or any part thereof, shall be applicable, except by inserting it in such act. The Legislature shall provide for the maintenance and support of a thorough and efficient system of free public schools for the instruction of all the children of the State between the ages of five and eighteen years. The assent of three-fifths of the members of each House of the Legislature shall be required for the passage of every law for granting, continuing, altering, amending, or renewing charters for banks or similar corporations; and all such charters shall be limited to twenty years.

The Legislature shall not pass private, local, or special laws, regulating the internal affairs of towns and counties, appointing local offices or commissions to regulate municipal affairs, impaneling grand or petit jurors, or granting to any corporation, association, or individual, any exclusive privilege whatever, but may pass general laws providing for all such cases. Property shall be assessed for taxes under general laws, and by uniform rules, according to its true value. If any bill passed by the Legislature and presented to the Governor contain several items of appropriation of money, the Governor may object to one or more of such items while approving other portions of the bill. The Governor of the State shall not be elected by the Legislature to any office during the term for which he shall have been elected Governor. Judges of the inferior Court of Common Pleas shall be appointed by the Governor. The State Treasurer shall hold office three years. The keeper of the State-prison is to be nominated by the Governor. Sheriffs and coroners shall be elected for three years, and sheriffs shall annually renew their bonds. No county shall be divided, or have any part taken from it, unless a majority of the people of the county so consent. An elector must be a resident of the district in which he lives for thirty days prior to an election before he can vote. No member of the Legislature shall, during his term, be nominated or appointed by the Governor or the Legislature to any civil office in the State which shall have been created, or its emoluments increased, during the time for which he was elected. No act of the Legislature shall limit the amount to be recovered for

injuries resulting in death, or for injuries to person or property. No act shall prescribe limitation of time within which suits may be brought against corporations for injuries to person or property, or for other causes, different from that fixed by the general laws. No trust funds shall be invested in the bonds or stock of any private corporation, unless such investment be authorized by the person creating the trust. The Legislature may establish a court or courts with original jurisdiction over all cases of condemnation of lands and assessments for improvements. There shall not be more than two justices of the inferior Court of Common Pleas in any county in the State. Not more than two justices of the peace shall be elected in a township, nor more than one in a city ward, and the Legislature shall prescribe by law the qualifications necessary for such justices to possess, and also provide for the summary suspension of justices of the peace for misconduct in office. No amendment to the charter of any municipal corporation shall be received by the Legislature after thirty days from the first day of the meeting thereof, public notice of which must be previously given. No act of the Legislature shall take effect until the 4th day of July next after its passage, unless by a vote of two-thirds of both Houses.

By act approved March 27, 1874, the Legislature authorized and directed the sale of the famous iron war-vessel known as the Stevens Battery, which has been in the course of construction since 1843, and which was originally designed by R. L. and E. A. Stevens, and left, by the will of the latter, to the State of New Jersey. The present dimensions of the vessel are: Length, 400 feet; beam, 45 feet; depth, 24½ feet; boilers, 10 feet; engines, 4 feet; maximum horse-power, 6,000. The battery was nearly rebuilt by General George B. McClellan. About $2,500,000 has been expended upon the vessel, and it is estimated that about $300,000 more will be necessary to complete it as a war-vessel, or $200,000 as a merchant-vessel.

The vessel having been offered for sale, the bids were opened November 2d, when it was found that the highest sum absolutely offered was $105,000. A conditional offer of $145,000, however, was made by the United States Secretary of the Navy, subject to the approval of Congress, and their appropriation for the purchase. An arrangement was thereupon made with the highest absolute bidder, by which his offer will be held in abeyance, in order to afford the United States sufficient time within which to secure the vessel.

The Republican State Convention was held in Trenton, on the 27th of August, when George A. Halsey was unanimously nominated as candidate for Governor. The resolutions adopted are as follows:

Resolved, That the Republicans of New Jersey, in entering upon a local contest for the political control of the State, at a time midway between two national elections, deem it unnecessary to advert to national questions, further than to declare:

1. That we approve and will continue to uphold the principles upon which the Republican party was founded, and which, during fourteen years of ascendency in the national Government, have resulted in the preservation of the Union; in the extinction of slavery; in the reorganization of all the States; in securing equal political rights to all citizens; in the maintenance of the national credit; in the diminution of the public debt; in the reduction of taxes; in the honorable adjustment of foreign complications; in the advancement of the nation in power and dignity abroad and prosperity at home; and in courageous efforts to expose official delinquencies and promote integrity in public trusts.

2. That President Grant, who has borne so large a part in producing these results by his skill in war and his wisdom in administration, deserves our unabated confidence.

3. That we are in favor of such national legislation as will maintain inflexibly the faith of the Government to its creditors, and secure the speedy resumption of specie payments.

Resolved, That, while not unmindful of the good of the whole country, we feel at liberty in this purely State contest to maintain especially the interests of New Jersey, to remember her peculiar position between two great manufacturing and commercial States in the path of our vast national traffic, to be justly proud of her mineral and agricultural wealth, her commercial facilities, her great system of railroads, and her important manufacturing interests, and to be watchful against any form of national legislation and any theories of political economy which shall tend to lessen her advantages, to cripple her industries, or diminish her sources of wealth; and therefore we are in favor of such a tariff and such equal internal taxation as will afford protection to domestic manufactures and best promote and encourage the industrial interests of the State. And for the same reasons we are in favor of the establishment of a port of entry at Jersey City, in order to secure to New Jersey the just advantage of her unrivaled harbors, and to facilitate the flow of commerce in its natural channel through her territory.

Resolved, That in regard to State affairs we commend and will pursue the measures and policy adopted by the Republican party during its control of the State government, viz.:

1. The general railroad system and the consequent diminution of corrupting influences in legislation.

2. The judicious amendment of the State constitution.

3. The generous support of our system of public education.

4. The wise management and liberal extension of our public institutions for penal, sanitary, and charitable purposes.

5. And the general promotion of the varied industries of the State so far as they lie within the sphere of State control.

The Democracy assembled in State Convention in Trenton on the 15th of September, nominated Joseph D. Bedle for Governor, and agreed upon the following platform of principles, reported by ex-Governor Randolph from the Committee on Resolutions:

The Democracy of New Jersey, in convention assembled, make the following declaration of principles:

1. Rigid restriction of the Government, both State and national, to the powers of government expressly granted or necessarily implied by the Constitution.

2. Favoring equal political rights for all, and condemning all acts of violence and lawlessness that infringe upon the rights of any, they protest against Federal interference in popular elections; denounce

as a crime against free government the open and secret support which the present Federal Administration has given to notorious adventurers and plunderers, who have forced themselves upon the people of States impoverished by war and weakened in resources by repeated calamities.

3. The restoration of gold and silver as the only true basis of the currency of the country. The prompt resumption of specie payments, and the payment of all national indebtedness in the money recognized by the civilized world.

4. Recognizing the necessity of a tariff for revenue by which the legitimate expenditures of the Government may be assisted, we advocate a true revenue reform that will secure to labor both steadiness and compensation, by equitable and judicious tariff laws.

5. Opposition to the civil-rights bill as detrimental to the cause of education, fatal to the true interests of the race in whose interest it is ostensibly required. The daily evidence is with us, of the uselessness of attempting to compel by law that which is repelled by Nature. The attempt so to do adds meanness to folly, in attempting to force upon a defenceless people that which we refuse to do ourselves. Born of vindictive partisanship, intended for humiliation, the passage and enforcement of the civil-rights bill would foment the worst passions of both races, give pretext for constant Federal interference, and indefinitely delay the return of peace and prosperity.

6. That the attempt of the Grant party as represented by the majority in Congress, led by Senator Frelinghuysen of this State, to establish a new sedition law, and to subject the press of the country to a new censorship and new forms of punishment to be administered in the interest of the tenants of power through the local magistrates of the District of Columbia, constitutes a grave outrage upon both the spirit and the letter of the Constitution; and we demand the immediate and unconditional repeal of such legislation.

7. Opposition to the government of municipalities by legislative commissions. We favor a system of general laws by which all corporate power is rendered equally accessible and responsible.

8. Condemnation of prominent Federal officials and the inaction of leading Administration organs and speakers that have rendered the third-term question a live issue before the people. We oppose a third term for any presidential candidate, no matter what his political associations.

9. Recognizing in labor the true basis of a nation's wealth and prosperity, and recognizing its right to obtain full and equitable remuneration, we extend to our fellow-citizens now out of employment our sincere sympathies.

10. That the assumption by the Republican Convention of credit for the passage of the General Railroad Law is as imprudent as it is false, this measure so destructive of monopoly having been originated and sustained in both branches of the Legislature by distinguished Democrats.

11. That corporations are created by the State for the public benefit, and their reasonable profits being secured, they shall be held by law to an exact, prompt, and faithful performance of their duty to the public.

12. That the illegal issue of paper promises in forced payment of wages is an unjustifiable imposition upon the laboring-man, and tends to a monopoly of trade—and the laboring-man should be left free to purchase when and where he deems proper.

In addition to the declaration of principles the Democracy of New Jersey assert:

That Republican administrations are no longer entitled to the confidence and support of the people, because—

They have wantonly violated the pledges upon which they came into power, and failed to adhere to their professed principles.

They have claimed, without regard to facts, to have alone preserved the union of the States; sustained the national credit; extinguished slavery; when, but for the Democracy of the country and its men and means, every Republican administration would have miserably failed.

They have been so wasteful of the public revenues, so extravagant in expenditure, and so lenient to defalcations, that the public debt remains to-day a terrible and dangerous burden, and taxation an onerous weight.

They have had the power to permanently settle the financial question, but have failed to do so, and are responsible for the wide-spread stagnation in business which to-day threatens bankruptcy and ruin to our people; labor is poorly paid, or without employment, and the promised "golden era" proves a delusion.

They have failed to make our name respected abroad; our flag has been insulted, and a miserable naval farce made to stand instead of the prompt vindication required by our people; our citizens have been executed by foreign powers, without color of law or trial by jury, and no reparation has been obtained for the outrage.

They have had official corruption presented to them in every form, and committed by all grades of Federal officers, executive, judicial, and legislative, and, notwithstanding the universal judgment of the people in condemnation, not a single instance of note, of exemplary punishment, has been made by Republican authority.

They endanger republican institutions by endorsing the Administration of a President whose power is being used for his indefinite reëlection to the chief magistracy.

They have used the military power of the country to intimidate voters at the polls, have forced aliens and strangers of vile character to the highest offices of many States, and by the same illegal power have practically protected them while robbing defenseless people. Federal judges have issued illegal orders in support of outrage, and remain to-day unpunished and unimpeached.

They have put in office at the Federal capital, as managers of District affairs, a set of men whose robberies in brief time have never been excelled in boldness or amount. Yet the chief of this notorious gang, in defiance of decent respect for public opinion, was renominated to office by the President of the United States.

By complacent assumptions of superior patriotism, integrity, and intelligence, the Republican party of New Jersey have invoked public criticism, and we stand ready before the people of the State to make good our charges against them in general and in detail.

The election held in November resulted in the choice of the Democratic candidate for Governor, Mr. Bedle, by a majority of 13,-233 votes, he having received 97,283 votes, while 84,050 were cast for Mr. Halsey. The vote for Governor aggregated 181,333. being 12,291 greater than that cast for President in 1872, and 22,588 greater than the gubernatorial vote of 1871. The majority for President Grant in 1872 was 14,810; for Parker, Democratic candidate for Governor in 1871, 5,979. The following Congressmen were elected in 1874:

Dist. I.—Clement H. Sinnickson.......... Republican.
"   II.—Samuel A. Dobbins............. "
"   III.—Miles Ross...................... Democrat.
"   IV.—Robert Hamilton.............. "
"   V.—Augustus W. Cutter............. "
"   VI.—Frederick H. Teese............. "
"   VII.—Augustus A. Hardenberg........ "

The Legislature of 1875 is classified as follows:

PARTIES.	Senate.	House.	Joint Ballot.
Democrats........	8	41	49
Republicans.......	13	19	32
Democratic maj.	5*	22	17

The Democrats, therefore, have a majority of 22 in the House, and 17 on joint ballot, while the Republicans have a majority of 5 in the Senate.

The receipts and disbursements of the several funds during the year ending October 31, 1874, were as follows:

FUNDS.	Receipts.	Disbursements.
Agricultural College fund..	$6,960 00	$6,960 00
Library-fund	3,550 00	1.211 87
War-fund	283,884 55	286,247 25
School-fund(including State school-tax)...............	1,363,547 20	1,352,431 00
State-fund...................	1,707,141 68	1,618,416 54
In bank, November 1, 1873.	173,043 54	....
Total..................	$3,538,126 97	$3,265,266 16

Amount in bank to credit of all the funds, October 31, 1874, $272,860.81.

The Controller estimates the expenditures for 1875 at $1,400,000, exclusive of the two-mill tax for schools. The revenue (excluding the State school tax) is estimated at $1,610,000, including $680,000 from usual sources, and $930,000 from taxes which go into State and war funds.

The war debt amounts to about $2,500,000. It is represented by bonds of which about $100,000 fall due annually. The payment of principal and interest is met by tax and the income of the sinking-fund. The investments of the sinking-fund amount to a little over $1,300,000. The war debt will be reduced to the same amount as the sinking-fund in about twelve years without resorting to additional taxation. The amount drawn from the taxes to pay the war debt will diminish with each successive year. The tax levy for the purposes of both the State and war funds is only one and a half mills.

The value of taxable property as returned from the several counties for 1874 was $619,-057,903, being an increase of $10,929,762 over that of the previous year.

New Jersey has no institution for the education of its deaf and dumb, blind or feebleminded; but about $40,000 are annually expended by the State for their support in the institutions of other States. The establishment of State institutions for these classes has been strongly urged. There are two institutions for the care of the insane. The Lunatic Asylum, in Trenton, was opened in 1868, since which time 4,588 have been under treatment, of whom about 3,000 have been discharged as recovered or improved. At the close of 1874 the asylum contained 655 patients, of whom 106 were supported by friends. The maintenance of the

_____
* Republican majority.

insane in this institution during the year cost the State a little over $42,000. About $31,000 were received for private patients, and the balance of the receipts, amounting to a little less than $170,000, came from the counties. The State also paid for care of the insane, to the authorities of three counties in which asylums have been established, $11,624. About three miles from Morristown one of the largest and best-arranged institutions for the insane in the country is approaching completion. It will probably be ready for occupying on or before January 1, 1876, and with site and equipments will cost about $2,000,000. The grounds embrace 416 acres. The entire length of the building is 1,243 feet, and the depth, from the front of the main centre to the rear of the extreme wing, 542 feet. The wings on the right and left of the centre building are three stories high, except those at the extreme ends, which are two stories. It is built principally of light granite, quarried on the grounds, in ornamental style, and will accommodate about 1,000 patients. ·

Prior to 1870, $60,000 was annually appropriated by the Legislature for the maintenance of convicts in the State-prison in Trenton; but since that time the institution has been a source of income to the State. The receipts of the prison during the year ending October 31st amounted to $104,041.98, of which $101,813.71 was received for the labor of convicts on contracts. The cost of maintaining the convicts was $58,807.05, not including the salaries of officers or the amount expended by the Board of Inspectors, prior to March 3d, for repairs and improvements. Of the net gain of the prison ($45,234), $30,000 was paid into the State Treasury, making, with two former payments, $80,000 that has been realized from this source in three years. The number of prisoners October 31st was 653.

The State Reform School for Juvenile Delinquents is at Jamesburg. The number of boys

INSANE ASYLUM, MORRISTOWN.

at the close of 1874 was 184. The total number during the year was 235. They are chiefly employed in making chairs and stools, and in farm-labor.

The State Industrial School for Girls has a farm of 80 acres near Trenton. Since the opening of the school in 1872, 40 girls have been received, of whom 19 were remaining at the close of 1874.

A home for disabled soldiers is supported by the State in Newark, in which 1,365 beneficiaries were cared for in 1874; the number remaining at the close of the year was 344.

The Soldiers' Children's Home in Trenton, also a State institution, had at the close of 1874 155 children, of whom 96 were boys and 54 girls.

Prior to April, 1871, New Jersey had no free-school system, but its schools were then made free. The tax for school purposes is now assessed and collected by the State in-

stead of the townships, and the funds are apportioned among the different districts according to the school population. Every district is required to maintain a school for at least nine months in the year, or forfeit its share of the apportionment. The permanent school fund amounts to $857,426. The amount of the income from this fund that is devoted to schools is determined by the Legislature, and is now $35,000 annually; the remainder of the income goes to increase the principal. In 1871 the State gave to the free-school fund the proceeds of sales and rentals of all riparian lands lying between high and low water marks, and chiefly in and near the harbor of New York on the New Jersey shore. These lands will add to this fund not less than $5,000,000, and possibly $10,000,000. The sources and amount of the funds for the support of the schools for the year ending August 31, 1874, were: 1. The two-mill State tax, which amounted to

$1,225,592; 2. Additional State appropriation, including the income of the school-fund, $100,-000; 3. Interest of the surplus revenue, $31,-573; 4. Township tax, $23,834; 5. District and city tax for teachers' salaries, $311,161: Total, $1,691,160, besides $613,238 derived from district and city taxation for building and repairing school-houses. The more immediate supervision of the schools is vested in a State Superintendent and county superintendents, all of whom are appointed by the State Board of Education. County superintendents are authorized to hold examinations and grant certificates to teachers. A law forbidding corporal punishment in schools was enacted in 1867. The condition of the public schools for the year ending August 31, 1874, is shown in the following statement:

Number of school districts	1,369
" " buildings	1,493
" " departments	2,835
Capacity of public schools	155,152
Number of unsectarian private schools	253
" of sectarian private schools	101
" of persons between 5 and 18 years old	298,000
" enrolled in public schools (63 per cent.)	186,392
Average attendance (52 per cent.)	96,224
Attendance upon private schools (12 per cent.)	86,527
Number not attending school (25 per cent.)	71,895
Average time schools kept open	9 mos. 12 days.
Number of male teachers in public schools	960
Average wages per month	$65 77
Number of female teachers	2,256
Average wages	$38 00
Total amount appropriated for schools	$2,304,398
Total amount for maintaining schools	$1,691,160
Valuation of school property	$6,000,732
Average annual cost of education per pupil according to school population	$5 67
According to average attendance	$17 57

In several of the manufacturing cities and towns evening-schools are maintained for adults and others unable to attend the day-schools. There is a State institution in Trenton for training teachers, comprising a Normal School and a Model School. There are two courses of study in the former, one of two and one of three years. During the year ending July 1, 1874, there were 12 instructors and 269 pupils in the Normal, and 17 instructors and 443 pupils in the Model School. The Farnham School, at Beverly, which is aided by the State, serves as a preparatory institution for the Normal School. Since 1871 the State has supported a free-library system in the public schools by extending aid to such districts as raise funds for this purpose; nearly 400 free school-libraries have been established and receive annual aid from the State.

The commissioners appointed by the Legislature of 1874 to examine into the sanitary needs of the State, into the deficiencies of existing laws as to the securement of vital statistics, the abatement of nuisances, or whatever concerns the prevention or mitigation of disease, have made an exhaustive report on the subjects referred to them. The committee was composed of Ezra M. Hunt, of Metuchin (chairman); James R. Mercein, of Jersey City; Samuel Lilly, of Lambertville; George H. Cook, of New Brunswick; William Elmer, Jr.,

of Trenton; and Lewis W. Oakley, of Elizabeth. The committee recommend the passage of a law establishing a State Board of Health and Vital Statistics, similar to those in Massachusetts and Michigan. The duties of this board are stated in the following recommendation:

The board shall take cognizance of the interests of health and life among the citizens of this State. They shall make sanitary investigations and inquiries in respect to the people, the causes of disease, and especially of epidemics and the sources of mortality, and the effects of localities, employments, conditions, and circumstances on the public health; and they shall gather such information in respect to these matters as they may deem proper for diffusion among the people. They shall also make inquiries and reports in reference to disease affecting animals, and the methods of prevention. They shall convene on the call of any two members, and appoint a chairman, who shall call meetings as often as every three months, or when requested to do so by two members of the board. They shall, in the month of December, make report to the Governor of their investigations and opinions during the year ending December 1st, with such suggestions, as to legislative action, as they may deem necessary.

JOSEPH D. BEDLE, the present Governor of New Jersey, was born in Monmouth County, in that State, in 1830. Having been admitted to the bar, he became prosecuting-attorney of the county. When Governor Parker was first elected, he appointed Mr. Bedle Circuit Judge, and in 1873 reappointed him to that position for seven years. In that year he was prominently named for Chancellor, but the choice fell upon Mr. Runyon.

NEW YORK. The Legislature continued in session till April 30th. The measure of most general interest passed was perhaps the bill for compulsory education, which, notwithstanding considerable opposition, became a law May 11th, to take effect January 1, 1875. It requires all parents, and those who have the care of children between the ages of eight and fourteen years, to see that they are instructed in spelling, reading, writing, English grammar, geography, and arithmetic, at least fourteen weeks in each year, either at school or at home, unless the physical or mental condition of the child may render such instruction inexpedient or impracticable.

Eight of the fourteen weeks' attendance at school must be consecutive. Any person neglecting to comply with this requirement is liable to a fine of one dollar for the first offense. For each succeeding violation, after having been properly notified, the offender shall pay five dollars for every week, not exceeding thirteen in any year, during which he shall fail to comply with the law. The fines thus collected are to be devoted to school purposes.

No person shall employ any child under the age of fourteen years to labor in any business during school-hours, unless the child has been instructed, either at school or at home, for at least fourteen of the fifty-two weeks next preceding the year in which such child shall be employed. The child must also furnish a written certificate of having received such instruction. The penalty for violating this provision is fifty dollars for every offense.

In every school district the trustees are required in September and February to examine into the situation of the children employed in all manufacturing establishments; and manufacturers must furnish a correct list of all children between the ages of eight and fourteen years employed.

Trustees are required to furnish text-books when the parents or guardians are unable to do so. If the parent or guardian is unable to compel the child to attend school, and shall so state in writing, the child shall be dealt with as an habitual truant.

Boards of instruction and trustees, in cities, school districts, etc., are authorized and directed to make all needful provisions and regulations concerning habitual truants, and children between the ages of eight and fourteen years, found wandering about the streets during school-hours, having no lawful occupation or business, and growing up in ignorance; and to provide for their instruction and confinement, when necessary, subject to the approval of the Justices of the Supreme Court of the district.

The statistics of the common schools for the year ending September 30, 1874, are as follows:

Total receipts, including balance on hand September, 30, 1873	$11,944,023 26
Total expenditures	$10,779,779 61
Amount paid for teachers' wages	$7,559,090 59
" " " school-houses, repairs, furniture, etc	$1,721,282 64
Estimated value of school-houses and sites	$28,714,736 00
Total number of school-houses	11,775
Number of school districts, exclusive of cities	11,299
Teachers employed at the same time for the full legal term of school	18,554
Teachers employed during any portion of the year	29,683
Children attending public schools	1,039,097
Persons attending normal schools	6,568
Children of school age in private schools	133,610
Volumes in school district libraries	835,882
Persons in the State between five and twenty-one years of age	1,591,874

There are in the State 22 literary colleges, 10 medical colleges, and 240 academies and

COLUMBIA COLLEGE, NEW YORK CITY.

academical departments of union schools. Special schools of law, of medicine, and of science, are connected with several of the colleges.

The academies of New York are regarded as a part of the system of public instruction. These, as well as most of the colleges and medical schools, are subject to the visitation of the Board of Regents of the University, a corporate body created in 1787, with power to incorporate colleges and academies, and to require from them reports as to their studies, finances, instructors, pupils, etc. It comprises nineteen members elected for life by joint ballot of the Legislature on nomination of the Governor, besides the Governor, Lieutenant-Governor, Secretary of State, and Superintendent of Public Instruction, who are members ex officio. The regents make annual reports to the Legislature. Academies are incorporated on condition that a certain amount of funds is raised by private contribution. The property and funds of the academy must be vested in trustees, and used only for public academic instruction. These trustees are amenable to the Legislature and the courts, and are required to make annual reports to the regents. From 1838 to 1872 $40,000 derived from the literary and United States deposit funds was annually distributed among the academies according to the number of pupils passing an examination held by the regents. In the latter year an additional appropriation of $125,000 was made for this purpose. Besides this, about $18,000 is annually distributed to the academies for instruction of teachers. Academic departments of union schools are admitted to the benefits of these appropriations on the same terms as academies. About 200 academies and academical departments annually report to the regents. In 1874 these contained about 30,000 pupils and nearly 12,000 teachers.

The State Library in both its departments has been enlarged by the application of all the means at the disposal of the trustees. The Law Library contains about 26,000 volumes, and the General Library about 68,000, including many rare and valuable works.

The total funded debt of the State, on the 30th of September, 1873, was $36,530,406. On September 30, 1874, it amounted to $30,-199,456, classified as follows:

General fund	$3,988,526
Contingent	68,000
Canal	10,230,430
Bounty	15,912,500
Total	$30,199,456

The actual reduction of the State debt during the fiscal year, by cancellation of matured stocks and $4,902,500 of bounty loan 7s of 1877, purchased for the bounty debt sinking-fund, during the year, was $5,1025,950.

The following statement shows the amount of the State debt on the 30th of September, 1874, after deducting the unapplied balances of the sinking-funds at that date:

FUNDS.	Debt on September 30, 1874.	Balances of Sinking-Funds on September 30, 1874.	Balance of Debt after applying Sinking-Funds.
Gen'l fund	$3,988,526 40	$4,142,693 84	....
Contingent	68,000 00	52,823 49	$35,176 51
Canal	10,230,430 00	1,561.018 99	8,669,411 01
Bounty	15,912,500 00	7,125.288 20	8,787,221 80
Total	$30,199,456 40	$12,861,814 52	$17,491,809 32

The State debt on September 30, 1873, after deducting the unapplied balances of the sinking-funds, amounted to	$21,141,379 34
On September 30, 1874, to	17,491,800 32
The contributions to the sinking-funds during the year being	$3,649,570 02
While the actual reduction of the debt by cancellation is	$6,024,950 00

Of the canal debt, under section 1 of Article V. of the constitution, $1,106,420 matured January 1, 1874, and was redeemed from the

CORNELL UNIVERSITY, ITHACA.

sinking-fund moneys set apart for that purpose. Of the principal of the canal debt, contracted under section 3 of Article VII., $1,974,-600 fell due November 1, 1873, and $2,099,000 October 1, 1874; and funds were provided for the redemption of both sums in coin by borrowing on the credit of the sinking-fund.

The receipts into the Treasury on account of all the funds, except the canal and common-school funds, for the year ending September 30, 1874, amounted to $26,465,370.43, and the expenditures to $19,636,308.36, leaving a balance of $6,829,062.07 at the close of the year. The available balance was $6,494,781.44, the difference being made up by the defalcation in the State Treasury in 1873 of $304,957.91, and the sum of $29,222.72, being an old balance due from the Bank of Sing Sing.

The expenditures from the public Treasury for educational purposes, during the last fiscal year, amounted to $3,278,858.66, of which $2,-662,032.98 were the proceeds of a direct tax of 1¼ mill for common schools. The purposes for which these expenditures were made were as follows:

Academies, for dividends	$171,611 74
Academies, for instruction of common-school teachers	15,877 00
Common-school dividends	297,996 98
Cornell University	30,000 00
Indian schools	2,924 56
Normal schools	3,333 98
School commissioners' salaries	90,982 42
School-tax, 1¼ mill	2,662,082 98
Elmira Female College	3,500 00
Total	$3,278,858 66

During the same period the State paid $338,-852.07 for the support of certain dependent classes, viz.: Deaf and dumb, $120,810.94; blind, $82,307.06; insane, $102,234.07; idiotic, $33,500. These amounts do not include the large sums appropriated for building-purposes to the institutions which have been in progress during the year.

All the charitable, eleemosynary, correctional, and reformatory institutions of the

State, except prisons, whether receiving State aid or maintained by municipalities or otherwise, are subject to the inspection of the State Board of Charities, composed of eleven members appointed by the Governor, with the consent of the Senate, besides the Lieutenant-Governor, Secretary of State, Controller, Attorney-General, and State Commissioners in Lunacy, all of whom serve without pay. The board reports annually to the Legislature concerning the various institutions visited by them, which embrace the State, local, incorporated, and private charities for the insane, blind, deaf and dumb, idiots, inebriates, juvenile delinquents, orphans, paupers, etc. There are five State institutions for the treatment of the insane, of which the oldest is the lunatic asylum in Utica, opened in 1843, and having accommodations for about 600. Acute cases are chiefly treated here, while the chronic insane are received in the Willard Asylum, opened at Ovid, Seneca County, in 1869, which, with projected improvements, will accommodate 1,000. The Hudson River Hospital for the Insane in Poughkeepsie, the State Asylum in Buffalo, and the Homœopathic Asylum in Middletown, are State institutions not yet completed. The estimated cost of each of the two former is $3,000,000; when completed, each will accommodate about 600 patients. The institution at Middletown is smaller. On September 30, 1874, there were about 1,719 inmates, 590 being in the Utica asylum, 879 in the Willard, 212 in that at Poughkeepsie, and 38 in that at Middletown. There is also a State institution on Ward's Island, New York City, for insane immigrants.

The prison system of New York comprises three State-prisons, six county penitentiaries, two State and eleven local reformatories, besides county jails, city prisons, etc. The general supervision of the prisons is vested by the constitution in three inspectors elected for three years. All prison-officers are appointed by the inspectors. Cigars, shoes, harness and saddlery hardware, tools, machinery, and axles, are made at Auburn and Sing Sing, while in the latter a large number of convicts are employed in the marble and lime works. In the Clinton prison, at Dannemora, the manufacture of iron, nails, etc., from ore mined on the premises, is the chief employment of the convicts. All the industries are managed by contract in Auburn, all but stone-cutting in Sing Sing, and none in Clinton prison. No one of the prisons is self-sustaining; in all instruction is afforded to convicts, and all have libraries. The condition of these institutions for the year ending September 30, 1874, was as follows:

PRISONS.	Auburn.	Clinton.	Sing Sing.
Number of cells..........	1,292	538	1,200
Capacity for inmates.....	1,300	...	2,508
In prison Sept. 30, 1874..	1,202	552	1,306
Advances from State Treasury............	$233,167	$337,678	$360,054
Earnings.................	$101,910	$153,473	$124,009
Excess of expenditures..	$131,157	$184,205	$236,045

Including $26,231 miscellaneous expenditures not distributed, the entire excess of expenditures was reported at $588,537. This, however, is reduced by stock on hand, permanent improvements, and unpaid accounts of the previous year, amounting to $68,358 in favor of Auburn, $225,748 of Clinton, and $163,370 of Sing Sing. With these deductions, the real excess of expenditures over earnings becomes $131,060. The expense of maintaining each convict is from $3 to $4 a week in excess of the income. The prisons are full, and a greater capacity is needed. The six penitentiaries are situated in Buffalo, Syracuse, Brooklyn, Rochester, Albany and New York (Blackwell's Island). In the three first named, trades are taught to the inmates, and evening schools are held. The State has no share in the management of these institutions, which are under the control of the counties where situated; but State prisoners are confined in them. The total number of prisoners in the penitentiaries at the beginning of 1874 was 5,940.

The excess of advances from the Treasury on account of the State-prisons over receipts from earnings, for a series of years, has been as follows:

1867..............	$366,875	1871..............	$470,309
1868..............	512,547	1872..............	465,881
1869..............	595,774	1873..............	297,289
1870..............	451,304	1874..............	588,537

The expense of permanent improvements during the last fiscal year, the value of stock on hand, and the amount due for sales and convict-labor, September 30, 1874, were as follows:

PRISONS.	Value of Permanent Improvements.	Value of Stock on Hand Sept. 30, 1874.	Debts due for Stock sold and Convict Labor Sept. 30, 1874.	Total.
Auburn...	$40,740 16	$8,972 45	$18,645 80	$68,358 41
Clinton..	34,203 28	160,119 51	31,425 62	225,748 41
Sing Sing.	52,209 00	19,058 69	92,111 10	163,369 79
Total...	$127,143 44	$188,150 65	$142,182 52	$457,476 61

The statute requires real and personal estate to be assessed for taxation "at the full and true value thereof," but it is maintained by high authority that not more than one-third in value of the property liable to taxation is placed upon the assessment-rolls. The entire valuation of taxable property has increased from $1,500,999,877 in 1864 to $2,169,307,873 in 1874; and the State tax, including the school tax, from $7,880,249 in 1864 to $15,727,482 in 1874. The valuation of 1874 included $1,750,698,918 of real and $418,608,955 of personal estate. The rate of the State tax for 1874 was 7¼ mills, viz.: schools, 1¼; general purposes, 1¼; general purposes (deficiency), $\frac{1.9}{10}$; bounty debt, 2; new Capitol, ¼; asylums and reformatories, $\frac{8}{10}$; canal floating debt, $\frac{5}{10}$; new work on canals and extra repairs, ¼; for payment of awards by canal appraisers and commissioners, and certain certificates of indebtedness, $\frac{8}{10}$; academies and union schools, $\frac{1}{10}$. Of the above 2 mills are for ordinary expenditures.

The above tax of 7¼ mills on the present valuation will yield $15,727,482.08.

Exclusive of extraordinary work on the canals, and work on the new Capitol and other public buildings, the following rate will be necessary for the ensuing fiscal year:

	Mills.
For general fund	1¾
For schools	1¼
For bounty-loan	2
For floating canal debt, chapter 271, laws of 1859,	0¼
Total	5

The National Guard of the State consists of eight divisions, containing nineteen brigades, composed of one regiment and nine separate troops of cavalry, one battalion and ten batteries of artillery, thirty regiments and thirteen battalions of infantry. Total, officers, non-commissioned officers, musicians, and privates (three brigades estimated), 20,532.

For thirty years following 1818 the laws of New York restricted the banking business to companies or institutions chartered by special law. This was followed by the "free-banking" system, which was based on the deposit of securities with redemption at a fixed rate of discount. State and savings banks are required to report to the Superintendent of the Banking Department, the former quarterly, and the latter semi-annually. Three examiners are constantly passing through the State, inspecting banks. The Superintendent reports annually to the Legislature. In October, 1873, eighty banks were doing business under the laws of the State. The amount of circulation outstanding, including that of the forty-one incorporated banks, and of banking associations and individual bankers, was $1,400,116, of which $656,240 was secured. In October, 1874, the number of State banks was eighty-one. Their condition, September 13th, as compared with that of the preceding year, was as follows:

Capital	$26,958,890	$26,336,290
Loans and discounts	71,073,544	66,485,729
Due depositors	70,738,491	62,471,306
Total resources	116,536,734	111,180,300

The diminution in capital during the year is small, while the shrinkage in deposits, and in loans and discounts, is considerable. This reduction is regarded as an exponent of the contraction in the volume of business since the panic of 1873.

The number of national banks on November 1, 1874, was 276, with a paid-in capital of $108,339,691; bonds on deposit, $64,963,050; outstanding circulation, $59,299,049. The circulation per capita was $13.53; ratio of circulation to the wealth of the State, 9 per cent.; to bank capital, 54.7. The total number of savings-banks on January 1, 1874, was 155, with 822,642 depositors, and deposits aggregating $285,520,085; average to each depositor, $340.12; resources, $307,589,730; liabilities, $285,140,778; surplus assets, $21,448,952. Insurance companies are subject to rigid inspection by the Superintendent of the Insurance Department, who reports annually to the Legislature.

The canals of New York are an important feature in its commercial facilities. The Erie Canal, connecting Lake Erie with the Hudson River, affords a continuous water-channel through which the produce of the Western States and Canada may reach the port of New York; while the several canals traversing the State from north to south supply transportation facilities to the interior of New York and Pennsylvania. The canals and navigable feeders owned by the State aggregate 857 miles in length, and the river and other improvements which have been completed increase the length of the artificial system of navigable waters to 907 miles. This does not include the several lakes which are used as a part of the canal system. The total cost of constructing and repairing these canals and improvements has been $73,440,894, while the net profit to the State arising from their operation to September 30, 1872, was $60,880,632. The general superintendence of the canals is vested in three commissioners, elected for three years, who have charge of the construction of new and the repairs of old canals. The State Engineer and Surveyor inspects the canals and performs other duties, while the Canal Board, composed of the above-mentioned officers and the Commissioners of the Canal Fund, fix the rates of toll, appoint officers, etc. The amounts of freight transported on all the State canals during 1873 was 6,364,782 tons, valued at $191,715,500, including products of the forest valued at $18,657,838; agricultural products, $60,194,909; manufactures, $5,979,656; merchandise, $76,173,336, and other articles, $30,715. The total quantity of freight carried by the canals was more than half as great as that transported by the Erie and New York Central Railroads. The amount of freight brought to the Hudson River by the Erie and Champlain Canals was 3,376,649 tons, valued at $97,869,497; 1,740,628 tons of freight, worth $73,260,034, were brought by canal-boats directly to New York. The number of boats arrived at and cleared from New York, Albany, and Troy, was 33,608. Until 1875 the Legislature was prohibited by the constitution from selling or leasing any of the State canals; but in that year an amendment was adopted removing the restriction except in the case of the Erie, Oswego, Champlain, and Cayuga and Seneca Canals. Besides the State canals there are belonging to corporations the Delaware & Hudson Canal, connecting Roundout with Honesdale, Pa., 108 miles, of which 87 are in New York; and the Junction Canal, which extends from Elmira to the Pennsylvania State line, 18 miles. In the following table are given details of the canals owned and operated by the State, including their termini, their length in miles, total cost of construction, the financial results of their operation, and the aggregate income and expenditures for three years.

NAME OF CANAL.	TERMINI.		Length in Miles.	Total Cost of Construction to September 30, 1874.	Financial Result of operating from 1846 to September 30, 1874.		Aggregate Income and Expense for Three Years ending September 30, 1874.	
	From	To			Profit.	Loss.	Income.	Exp'ditures.
Black River............	Rome........	Lyon's Falls..	85	$3,417,880	....	$850,148	$32,418	$294,716
Feeder................	Boonville...	Head of Reservoir	12	....	....	....	....	....
Cayuga & Seneca.......	Montezuma..	Geneva	21	1,702,675	$49,690	....	59,675	156,102
Cayuga Inlet......	Cayuga Lake.	Ithaca........	2	9,968	2,375	....	1,196	418
Champlain.............	West Troy...	Whitehall....	66	*	....	....	427,666	1,730,898
Glen's Falls feeder...	....	....	12					
Pond above Troy dam.	....	....	3					
Chenango..:.........	Utica	Hinghamton..	97	4,542,107	....	1,182,292	14,416	588,911
Chemung..............	Watkins......	Elmira........	23	1,643,141	....	1,300,795	10,699	212,908
Feeder.............	Horseheads..	Knoxville....	16					
Crooked Lake........	Dresden......	Penn Yan....	8	403,698	....	297,091	....	36,856
Erie, including 4½ miles navigable feeders...	Buffalo	Albany.......	355	† 50,412,710	† 65,118,933	....	8,143,536	5,079,063
Genesee Valley.......	Rochester...	Mill Grove...	113	6,433,842	....	1,566,016	61,583	464,315
Danville branch......	Shakers......	Dansville.....	11					
Oneida Lake..........	Higgins......	Oneida Lake..	7	441,239	....	43,581	....	34,425
Oswego...............	Syracuse....	Oswego......	38	4,172,503	692,904	....	249,344	669,787
Baldwinsville Canal & Improvement	....	Jack's Reefs.	12	29,489	....	17,243	....	214
Oneida River Improvement..............	Oswego Canal.	Oneida Lake.	20	237,151	167,338	....	1,756	....
Seneca River towing-path................	Baldwinsville.	Mud Lock....	6	1,488	6,469	....	445	....
			857	$73,440,894	$66,037,801	$5,157,168	....	....

Although the gross income from all the canals of the State for the last fiscal year is less than that of the preceding year, the exhibit of the income and expenses shows a gratifying result. The gross receipts of the last year were $2,921,721.74—for the year 1873 they were $3,021,528.78—being a decrease or a deficiency for 1874, as compared with 1873, of $99,806.04; but the income in excess of all disbursements for the past year is $225,364.44, while for the year 1873 the disbursements exceeded the income by $176,023.99, showing an actual increase in the revenue from this source for the past fiscal year over that of 1873 of $404,388.53.

In Onondaga County are the most extensive salt-works in the United States. They are owned and managed by the State, which derived from this source in 1874 a net revenue of $10,341. The works in operation have an annual productive capacity of about 10,700,000 bushels. The amount of salt inspected in 1874 was 6,594,191 bushels, being 1,364,981 bushels less than the amount inspected during the previous year.

The political campaign this year was of more than usual importance. It was opened with the assembling of the Prohibition Convention in Auburn on the 23d of June. The call which had been issued by the Executive Committee in May invited " all persons in the State of New York who oppose the licensing of the *liquor-traffic*—the manufacture, sale, and use of alcoholic liquors as a beverage—who are willing to unite upon one common platform for the prohibition of the same, through national, State, and municipal legislation, to meet in convention to nominate State officers, and to transact such other business as may properly come before the convention."

The convention organized with C. C. Leigh as president, when it appeared that twenty-five counties were represented, some of which had delegations numbering from ten to twenty. The platform adopted was as follows:

Resolved, first, That we more than ever are persuaded that the legal prohibition of the manufacture and sale of ardent spirits for beverage purposes is the only effectual remedy for the unparalleled evils resulting from their use.

Resolved, That we are as firmly persuaded that such a remedy can only be secured through a separate political party; that while equally competent to deal with all other public questions, we shall make prohibition the paramount aim of its organization, and to that conclusion we are impelled, among others, by the following reasons:

1. Of two great parties we have the Democracy, which neither pretends nor could with justice pretend to favor repressive interference with rum interests.

2. That while the Republican party has claimed to be a party of great moral ideas and a true friend of temperance, it has forfeited all right to be recognized as such.

3. It has had possession through its Governor and two successive Legislatures of the State administration for nearly the whole of the past two years, with the full power to grant anti-liquor legislation if it had been disposed to do so.

4. It came into power fully committed to one measure of prohibition, by pledge, which it first violated and has since failed to redeem.

5. It has refused to submit to be voted upon by the people an amendment to the constitution as to the prohibition of the rum-traffic as asked for by the leading temperance organizations.

6. It has, at the instigation of the liquor-sellers, so interfered with and modified the law of the excise in existence when it came into power, so far as the civil penalties go, as to give a practical free trade in rum in our larger cities, and remove the principal restriction upon traffic upon the Sabbath-day.

7. It has put upon the statute-book a law unprecedented in its support of the rum interest; an act incorporating a wine and spirit traders' society, of the United States, as thereby it has given the highest legal sanction and protection to the rum-traffic, and conferred upon those openly and actively engaged therein the most extraordinary privileges and

* Included in Erie.　　† Including Champlain.

powers, including those belonging to the courts of justice and directly affecting the liberty of the citizen as well as the authority of money in controlling and corrupting legislation.

8. It has refused to remove or modify obnoxious statutes of its enacting, when protested against and appealed to for that purpose by the temperance people, treating their petitions and drafts of bills with undisguised indifference and contempt.

9. It has shown itself, by its entire administration of public affairs, to be a friend of the rum-dealers, and chiefly concerned in the securing of their support.

Resolved, That for the reasons assigned in the foregoing resolutions, we approve the establishment of a distinct prohibition party in the State of New York, and thereby declare our abiding purpose, and persist in its maintenance until, with God's help, we put the State into the hands of well-known, publicly-pledged prohibitionists.

Resolved, That we are unalterably committed to an amendment to the constitution of the State, forbidding the manufacture and sale of alcoholic beverages within its limits.

Resolved, That while we hold it to be equally the duty and interest of both sexes to work for rum's overthrow, we cannot refrain from grateful commendation of those women who have set an example of devoting all the powers and influence they possessed, an example which we regret there are so many of the other sex to applaud and so few to imitate: and we would call upon the temperance women of the land to continue their efforts, and especially until such time as they will be endowed with the same legal privileges as their fellows, to employ all their influence and power with husbands, fathers, and others who have the ballot, that it may be used on the side of sobriety and good order.

Resolved, That a State Central Committee be nominated by a committee named by county delegations.

Resolved, That we hail with devout thankfulness to God the great uprising among the women of our land to put away the liquor nuisance from among us, and that we renew our pledge to put the ballot into the hands of women when we shall have power to do so, thus enabling them to vote as well as pray against the giant curse of the world.

A State ticket was then nominated, as follows: Governor, Myron H. Clark; Lieutenant-Governor, J. L. Bagg, of Onondaga; Judge of the Court of Appeals, Horace V. Howland, of Cayuga; Canal Commissioner, Daniel Walford; State-prison Inspector, Ira Bell, of St. Lawrence.

In the same city, on the same day, fifty temperance Republicans from various sections of the State assembled upon invitation of B. E. Hale, of Brooklyn, to consider the expediency of renominating Governor Dix. David Dicker, of Chemung, presided, with Judge William H. Van Cott, of Westchester, as vice-president. Among the resolutions passed were the following:

Resolved, That the unanimous passage by the Republican State Convention of resolutions indorsing the principles and policy of prohibition inspired additional hope for the triumph of the cause, and secured to the party for several years almost the entire temperance vote of the State; that we have supported in good faith and earnestly General John A. Dix as candidate for Governor, believing that, standing squarely upon the platform of his party, he would justify the confidence of temperance men by his official acts.

Resolved, That by his veto of the local prohibition bill in the interest of the liquor-traffic, Governor

John A. Dix forfeited all claims upon the support of the friends of temperance and of the Christian Sabbath, and that the Republican party by renominating him for reëlection will deliberately assume the responsibility of that act and detach from its support thousands of earnest men who have been among its most faithful adherents. We therefore, as Republicans and as temperance men, solemnly protest against such renomination as in violation of good faith, and endangering the integrity and success of the party.

These elicited a warm discussion, but when it was understood that their main object was to influence the nominations of the Republican State convention, they were passed with only two dissenting voices.

The Liberal Republicans assembled in State Convention in Albany, on the 9th day of September, and passed resolutions, but made no nominations. Charles E. Hughes, of Washington County, was made chairman. Two hundred and twenty-eight delegates were in attendance. The resolutions, which were unanimously adopted, were as follows:

Resolved, That the Liberal Republicans of the State of New York stand for the defense of constitutional liberty, for the right of local self-government, for the restriction of delegated power, for strict accountability on the part of public officers, for the restoration of the constitutional currency, and for the protection of the rights and interests of the masses of the people.

Resolved, That the Administration of President Grant has failed to fulfill the reasonable expectations of the people; that it has pursued a vacillating and imbecile financial policy which has plunged the business of the country into disaster and bankruptcy; that it has invaded the rights of sovereign States by imposing upon them Governors by means of the bayonet whom the people had rejected at the ballot-box; that it has employed spies and informers to plunder our merchants and establish a system of terrorism, paralyzing enterprise; that it has conspired with corrupt men and monopolies to prey upon the community, and has kept in existence in the District of Columbia an infamous being, in whose thefts, although carefully screened by their confederates in Congress, high officers of the Government have been proved to be participators.

Resolved, That "the liberty of the press is essential to the security of freedom;" that the sedition law of 1798, "abridging the freedom of speech and the press," was an infraction of the Constitution which a justly exasperated nation resented by exiling forever from power the party responsible for its enactment; that the Poland-Frelinghuysen bill of 1874, under which an immediate attempt was made to procure the indictment of an obnoxious editor, is a measure of like character, involving even greater peril to our liberties, "depriving us in many cases of the benefit of trial by jury," and transporting the citizen away from his home and from witnesses by whom his innocence might be established, to a distant place "to be tried for pretended offenses;" that its precedent is to be sought in the tyrannical acts of the King of Great Britain as enumerated in the Declaration of Independence, and that its enactment can only be effectively met by expelling from power both the men and the party guilty of the treason.

Resolved, That while we believe that sound policy requires that no President should be reëlected, we further declare our uncompromising hostility to every pretension toward perpetuating power in the hands of the same person beyond a second term. Such a pretension deserves and should receive the indignant condemnation of the people, who should demand of any party respecting their votes an explicit declaration against the claims of any man to become President of the United States for a third term, or against the conduct of any man tolerating the use by others of his name for such a candidacy.

Resolved, That the return of the country to a specie basis is an object of paramount importance; that as the great purpose of money is to serve as the medium of exchange, a national integrity demands a speedy return to the common standard of the world; and that the business interests of the country require that a free banking system should be established.

Resolved, That the acts of Congress providing for supervision of elections are oppressive, and should be amended or repealed.

Resolved, That experience demonstrates the injustice of governing the cities of the State by legislative commissions, and we advocate the restoration to them of the right of self-government.

After passing the above resolutions, the convention adjourned, to meet again in Albany on the 20th of September. At this session there was an earnest discussion upon the expediency of indorsing the Syracuse ticket, but it was finally decided to declare in favor of neither the Republican nor the Democratic nominations, and the convention adjourned, after passing the following resolution:

Resolved, That this convention deem it unwise to make nominations for State officers; but adhering to the integrity of the Liberal Republican organization, and the principles which it represents, we recommend to the Liberal Republicans and other independent electors of the State that they support for office men only of approved honesty, and who most fitly represent the principles enunciated at the organization of the party at Cincinnati, and subsequently reaffirmed at State Conventions, and who also stand committed by the action of the convention which placed them in nomination against a third presidential term and the centralization of power at the seat of the Federal Government.

The Democratic State Convention was held in Syracuse, on the 16th and 17th of September, with General Lester B. Faulkner, of Livingston, as president. The resolutions, reported by ex-Governor Horatio Seymour, were as follows:

The Democratic party of New York pledge themselves anew to the principles set forth in their platform, adopted last year at Utica, approved by the votes of the people of the Empire State, and indorsed by the Democrats of Illinois, Michigan, Maine, and other States of the Union:

1. Gold and silver the only legal tender; no currency inconvertible with coin.

2. Steady steps toward specie payment. No steps backward.

3. Honest payment of the public debt in coin; sacred preservation of the public faith.

4. Revenue reform; Federal taxation for revenue only; no Government partnership with protected monopolies.

5. Home rule to limit and localize most jealously the few powers intrusted to public servants—municipal, State, and Federal. No centralization.

6. Equal and exact justice to all men. No partial legislation. No partial taxation.

7. A free press. No gag-laws.

8. Free men. A uniform exercise of laws. No sumptuary laws.

9. Official accountability, enforced by better civil and criminal remedies. No private use of public funds by public officers.

10. Corporations chartered by the State always

supervisable by the State, in the interests of the people.

11. The party in power responsible for all legislation while in power.

12. The presidency a public trust, not a private perquisite. No third term.

13. Economy in public expense, that labor may be lightly burdened.

The Democrats of New York, in convention assembled, recognizing the independence and the patriotism of the Liberal Republicans, who, preferring principles to party, shall unite with them in opposing the present State and national administrations, commend to their support and the approval of all honest and independent persons the foregoing platform and the nominees of the convention.

The leading claimants before this convention for the gubernatorial nomination were Samuel J. Tilden and Amasa J. Parker, the former receiving 252 votes, and the latter 126. The ticket put in nomination comprised, besides Mr. Tilden for Governor, William Dorsheimer for Lieutenant-Governor, Adin Thayer for Canal Commissioner, George Wagener for Inspector of State-prisons, and Theodore Miller for Associate Judge of the Court of Appeals.

The Republican State Convention met in Syracuse, on the 23d of September, and organized with E. D. Morgan as president. The proceedings were attended with great enthusiasm, speeches being made by Theodore M. Pomeroy, ex-Governor Morgan, General Woodford, Senator Conkling, and others. Governor Dix was renominated by acclamation for the office of Chief Magistrate, and General John C. Robinson for that of Lieutenant-Governor. Alexander Barkley was renominated for Canal Commissioner, Thomas Kirkpatrick for State-prison Inspector, and Alexander S. Johnson for Judge of the Court of Appeals. The following platform was adopted:

The Republicans of New York, in convention assembled, adopt the following resolutions:

1. That the Republicans of New York reaffirm the principles so often approved by the people, and point to the past achievements of their party as a pledge that it is equal to every new requirement.

2. That we demand obedience to the laws and the full protection of every citizen in the enjoyment of his rights against the assaults of Ku-klux assassins and White-League revolutionists, who are encouraged by every Democratic success. This protection to be given by the States, if they can and will; but, if the States fail, by the General Government, in strict conformity with the Constitution and the laws.

3. That an armed attempt to subvert the recognized government of a State is revolution, and revolution must be suppressed and the supremacy of the law maintained at every cost.

4. That the public faith must be preserved inviolate, and the public debt be paid in coin.

5. That we oppose any inflation of the paper currency, and indorse the President's veto of the inflation act; and we are in favor of a return to specie payments, and of such action on the part of the Government as will speedily secure that result.

6. That taxation, whether national or State, whether direct or indirect, should be kept at the lowest practical point permitted by economical administration and the requirements of the public credit, and should be so adjusted as to be least burdensome to all classes.

7. That the Administration of President Grant

has been true to its pledges, and distinguished by achievements in domestic and foreign policy unsurpassed in the history of the country.

8. That the administration of Governor Dix, in its purity, dignity, and wisdom, has fulfilled the highest expectations of the people, and we point especially to the management of the State finances as showing the wide difference between Republican and Democratic rule, which Democratic rule was such in its profligacy as not only to consume all the heavy taxes paid by the overburdened people, but also to take $6,500,000 from the sacred deposit of the sinking-fund. This the Republican administration has now made good, and has increased the sinking-fund from $1,000,000 to more than $15,000,000, thus relieving the people of that indebtedness.

The election was held on November 3d, and resulted in a Democratic victory. The official vote, as declared by the State Board of Canvassers, was as follows:

Governor.

Whole number of votes cast	794,959
For Samuel J. Tilden	416,391
" John A. Dix	366,074
" Myron H. Clark	11,768
Plurality for Tilden	50,317
Majority "	38,549

Lieutenant-Governor.

Whole number of votes cast	793,707
For William Dorsheimer	416,714
" John C. Robinson	365,226
" James L. Bagg	11,310
Plurality for Dorsheimer	51,488
Majority "	39,978

Canal Commissioner.

Whole number of votes cast	794,009
For Adin Thayer	417,023
" Alexander Barkley	565,244
" Daniel Walford	11,328
Plurality for Thayer	51,779
Majority "	40,551

Inspector of State-Prisons.

Whole number of votes cast	792,778
For George Wagener	415,253
" Thomas Kirkpatrick	365,734
" Ira Bell	11,344
Plurality for Wagener	49,519
Majority "	38,175

Associate Judge of the Court of Appeals.

Whole number of votes cast	777,254
For Theodore Miller	406,553
" Alexander S. Johnson	360,760
" Horace V. Howland	9,587
Plurality for Miller	45,793
Majority "	36,256

Theodore Miller received 3,619 votes in Sullivan County for "Judge of the Court of Appeals." No such office being known to the constitution, these votes were rejected.

The total vote for Governor in 1872 was 838,151, of which John A. Dix, the candidate of the Republicans, received 445,801, and Francis Kernan 392,350; the majority of the former, 53,451. The vote on the various constitutional amendments was as follows:

Art. II.—Suffrage and Bribery.

Whole number of votes	534,673
For	357,635
Against	177,033
Majority for	180,602

Art. III., Part 1.—Legislature and its Organization.

Whole number of votes	531,936
For	325,904
Against	206,029
Majority for	119,875

Art. III., Part 2.—Powers and Forms of Legislature.

Whole number of votes	533,363
For	435,313
Against	98,050
Majority for	337,263

Art. IV.—Governor and Lieutenant-Governor, their Powers and Duties.

Whole number of votes	532,325
For	333,197
Against	196,125
Majority for	139,072

Art. VII.—Finance and Canals.

Whole number of votes	532,332
For	428,190
Against	104,139
Majority for	324,051

Art. VIII., Part 1.—Corporations, Local Liabilities and Appropriations.

Whole number of votes	532,180
For	337,821
Against	194,355
Majority for	143,655

Art. VIII., Part 2.—State Appropriation.

Whole number of votes	531,287
For	336,237
Against	195,047
Majority for	141,190

Art. X.—Relative to Compensation for Certain Officers.

Whole number of votes	530,484
For	335,548
Against	194,933
Majority for	140,615

Art. XII.—Oath of Office.

Whole number of votes	531,882
For	352,514
Against	179,365
Majority for	173,149

Art. XV.—Official Corruption.

Whole number of votes	529,619
For	351,693
Against	177,923
Majority for	173,770

Art. XVI.—Time for Amendments to take Effect.

Whole number of votes	532,796
For	446,883
Against	85,758
Majority for	361,125

The members of Congress elected are—

District		
I.—Henry B. Metcalf	Democrat.	
II.—John G. Schumaker	"	
III.—Simeon B. Chittenden	"	
IV.—Archibald M. Bliss	"	
V.—Edwin R. Meade	"	
VI.—Samuel S. Cox	"	
VII.—Smith Ely, Jr	"	
VIII.—Elijah Ward	"	
IX.—Fernando Wood	"	
X.—Abram S. Hewitt	"	
XI.—Benjamin A. Willis	"	
XII.—N. Holmes Odell	"	
XIII.—John O. Whitehouse	"	
XIV.—George M. Beebe	"	
XV.—John H. Bagley, Jr	"	
XVI.—Charles H. Adams	Republican.	
XVII.—Martin J. Townsend	"	
XVIII.—Andrew Williams	"	
XIX.—William A. Wheeler	"	
XX.—Henry H. Hathorn	"	
XXI.—Samuel F. Miller	"	
XXII.—George A. Bagley	"	
XXIII.—Scott Lord	Democrat.	
XXIV.—William H. Baker	Republican.	
XXV.—Elias W. Leavenworth	"	
XXVI.—Clinton D. MacDougall	"	
XXVII.—Elbridge G. Lapham	"	
XXVIII.—Thomas C. Platt	"	
XXIX.—Charles C. B. Walker	Democrat.	
XXX.—John M. Davy	Republican.	
XXXI.—George G. Hoskins	"	
XXXII.—Lyman K. Bass	"	
XXXIII.—Augustus F. Allen	Democrat.	

The General Assembly comprises 75 Democrats and 53 Republicans in the House, and 18 Republicans, 12 Democrats, and 2 Independents in the Senate. The Senators were elected in 1873.

In the city of New York, 87,623 votes were cast for Tilden for Governor, 44,871 for Dix, and 160 for Clark, making the majority of the first-named 42,752. For Associate Judge of the Court of Appeals, Miller received 87,797, and Johnson 43,992; Miller's majority, 43,805. The vote for mayor was as follows:

William H. Wickham, Tammany.......... 70,071
Salem H. Wales, Republican.............. 36,953
Oswald Ottendorfer, Independent......... 24,225

William H. Wickham, therefore, received 33,118 votes more than Wales, 45,845 more than Ottendorfer, and 8,892 more than both.

Patrick H. Jones, the successful candidate for Register, received 71,107 votes; while his opponent, Mr. Hayes, the Tammany candidate, received 59,460, making the majority of the former 11,647.

The seven members of Congress elected by New York City (Districts V., VI., VII., VIII., IX., X., and XI.) are all Democrats.

The State government for 1875 is constituted as follows, the names of Republicans being in italics:

Governor, Samuel J. Tilden; Lieutenant-Governor, William Dorsheimer; Secretary of State, Diedrich Willers, Jr.; Controller, *Nelson K. Hopkins;* Treasurer, Thomas Raines; Attorney-General, Daniel Pratt; State Engineer and Surveyor, S. H. Sweet; Canal Commissioners, Adin Thayer, James Jackson, Jr., *Reuben W. Stroud.*

All of the above-named officials, except the Governor, constitute the Canal Board.

The Board of Commissioners of the Canal Fund consists of the Lieutenant-Governor, Secretary of State, *Controller,* Treasurer, and Attorney-General.

The Board of Commissioners of the Land-Office consists of the same, with the addition of the State Engineer and Surveyor, and Speaker of the Assembly.

The Board of Trustees of the Capitol consists of the Governor, Lieutenant-Governor, Speaker of the Assembly, Secretary of State, *Controller,* Treasurer, and Attorney-General.

The Board of Trustees of the State Hall consists of the same, with the addition of the State Engineer and Surveyor.

Inspectors of State-prisons, George Wagener, *Moses K. Platt, Ezra Graves;* Auditor of Canal Department, *Francis S. Thayer;* Superintendent of Bank Department, *De Witt C. Ellis;* Superintendent of Insurance Department, *Orlow W. Chapman;* Superintendent of Public Instruction, *Neil Gilmour;* Canal Appraisers, *Thaddeus C. Davis, Vivius W. Smith, Charles G. Meyers;* State Assessors, *John S. Fowler, James A. Briggs, Sterling G. Hadley.*

Court of Appeals.—Chief Judge, Sandford E. Church; Associate Judges, William F. Al-

len, Martin Grover, Charles A. Rapallo, *Charles J. Folger, Charles Andrews,* Theodore Miller.

The amendments to the constitution, ratified by the people at the election of this year, make important changes in the supreme law of the State. In addition to the qualifications of electors mentioned in section 1 of Article II. of the constitution, the amendment requires the voter to have resided for thirty days in the election district where he offers to vote. The property qualifications of colored voters are abolished, thus removing all distinction between white and colored citizens at the polls. The following stringent regulations concerning bribery at elections were introduced into the second section of this article:

Section 2. No person shall receive, expect or offer to receive, or pay, or promise to pay, contribute, offer, or promise to contribute to another, to be paid or used, any money, or other valuable thing as a compensation or reward for the giving or withholding a vote at an election, or who shall make any promise to influence the giving or withholding any such vote, or who shall make or become directly or indirectly interested in any bet or wager depending upon the result of any election, shall vote at such election; and upon challenge for such cause, the person so challenged, before the officers authorized for that purpose shall receive his vote, shall swear or affirm before such officers that he has not received or offered, does not expect to receive, has not paid, offered or promised to pay, contributed, offered or promised to contribute to another, to be paid or used, any money or other valuable thing as a compensation or reward for the giving or withholding a vote at such election, and has not made any promise to influence the giving or withholding of any such vote, nor made or become directly or indirectly interested in any bet or wager depending upon the result of such election. The Legislature, at the session thereof next after the adoption of this section, shall, and from time to time thereafter may, enact laws excluding from the right of suffrage all persons convicted of bribery or of any infamous crime.

By the amended Article III. the pay of each member of the Legislature is fixed at $1,500 per annum, besides one dollar for every ten miles traveled in going to and returning from the capital once in each session. The limit of one hundred days to the sessions is abolished. The following new sections, restricting the powers of the Legislature in regard to special legislation, were added to this article:

Sec. 17. No act shall be passed which shall provide that any existing law, or any part thereof, shall be made or deemed a part of said act, or which shall enact that any existing law, or any part thereof, shall be applicable, except by inserting it in such act.

Sec. 18. The Legislature shall not pass a private or local bill in any of the following cases:

Changing the name of persons.

Laying out, opening, altering, working, or discontinuing highways or alleys, or for draining swamps or other low lands.

Locating or changing county-seats.

Providing for changes of venue in civil or criminal cases.

Incorporating villages.

Providing for the election of members of Boards of Supervisors.

Selecting, drawing, summoning, or impaneling grand or petit jurors.

Regulating the rate of interest on money.

The opening and conducting of elections or designating places of voting.

Creating, increasing or decreasing fees, percentage or allowance of public officers, during the term for which said officers are elected or appointed.

Granting to any corporation, association, or individual the right to lay down railroad-tracks.

Granting to any private corporation, association, or individual any exclusive privilege, immunity, or franchise whatever.

Providing for building bridges and chartering companies for such purposes, except on the Hudson River below Waterford, and on the East River, or over the waters forming a part of the boundaries of the State.

The Legislature shall pass general laws, providing for the cases enumerated in this section, and for all other cases which in its judgment may be provided for by general laws. But no law should authorize the construction or operation of a street railroad except upon the condition that the consent of the owners of one-half in value the property bounded on, and the consent also of the local authorities having the control of that portion of a street or highway upon which it is proposed to construct or operate such railroad, be first obtained, or in case the consent of such property-owners cannot be obtained, the general term of the Supreme Court, in the district in which it is proposed to be constructed, may, upon application, appoint three commissioners, who shall determine, after a hearing of all parties interested, whether such railroad ought to be constructed or operated, and their determination, confirmed by the court, may be taken in lieu of the consent of the property-owners.

Sec. 19. The Legislature shall neither audit nor allow any private claim or account against the State, but may appropriate money to pay such claims as shall have been audited and allowed according to law.

Sec. 20. Every law which imposes, continues, or revives a tax shall distinctly state the tax and the object to which it is to be applied, and it shall not be sufficient to refer to any other law to fix such tax or object.

Sec. 21. On the final passage, in either House of the Legislature, of any act which imposes, continues, or revives a tax, or creates a debt or charge, or makes, continues, or revives any appropriation of public or trust money or property, or releases, discharges, or commutes any claim or demand of the State, the question shall be taken by yeas and nays, which shall be duly entered upon the journals, and three-fifths of all the members elected to either House shall, in all such cases, be necessary to constitute a quorum therein.

Sec. 22. There shall be in the several counties, except in cities whose boundaries are the same as those of the county, a Board of Supervisors, to be composed of such members, and elected in such manner, and for such period, as are, or may be, provided by law. In any such city the duties and powers of a Board of Supervisors may be devolved upon the Common Council or Board of Aldermen thereof.

Section 17 of said article is hereby made section 23 of the proposed amendment, and is amended so as to read as follows:

Sec. 23. The Legislature shall, by general laws, confer upon the Boards of Supervisors of the several counties of the State such further powers of local legislation and administration as the Legislature may from time to time deem expedient.

Sec. 24. The Legislature shall not, nor shall the common council of any city nor any board of supervisors, grant any extra compensation to any public officer, servant, agent, or contractor.

Sec. 25. Sections 17 and 18 of this article shall not apply to any bill, or the amendments to any bill, which shall be reported to the Legislature by commissioners who have been appointed pursuant to law to revise the statutes.

Article IV., as amended, changes the official term of the Governor and Lieutenant-Governor from two to three years; fixes the annual salary of the former at $10,000 and the use of a furnished residence, and that of the latter at $5,000; provides that a two-thirds vote of all the members elected to each branch of the Legislature shall be necessary to pass an act over the Governor's veto; that no bill shall become a law after the adjournment of the Legislature unless approved by the Governor within thirty days; and that the Governor may veto particular items in an appropriation bill without vetoing the entire bill. As Governor Tilden was elected under the old constitution, his term will expire in 1876.

Section 8 of Article VII. is amended by adding that "no extra compensation shall be made to any contractor, but if, from any unforeseen cause, the terms of any contract shall prove to be unjust and oppressive, the Canal Board may, upon the application of the contractor, cancel such contract."

The restriction imposed upon the Legislature, preventing the sale or other disposition of the State canals, was removed, except in the case of the Erie, Oswego, Champlain, and Cayuga and Seneca canals. These must remain the property of the State and under its management forever. The expenditures for collections, superintendence, ordinary and extraordinary repairs on these canals, must not exceed in any year their gross receipts. All funds that may be derived from the lease, sale, or other disposition of any canal, must be applied in payment of the debt for which the canal revenues are pledged. The following sections (§§ 13 and 14) were added to this article in place of sections 13 and 14, which were transferred and inserted as sections 21 and 22 of Article III.

Sec. 13. The sinking-funds provided for the payment of interest and the extinguishment of the principal of the debts of the State shall be separately kept and safely invested, and neither of them shall be appropriated or used in any manner other than for the specific purpose for which it shall have been provided.

Sec. 14. Neither the Legislature, Canal Board, Canal Appraisers, nor any person or persons acting in behalf of the State, shall audit, allow, or pay any claim which, as between citizens of the State, would be barred by lapse of time. The limitation of existing claims shall begin to run from the adoption of this section; but this provision shall not be construed to revive claims already barred by existing statutes, nor to repeal any statute fixing the time within which claims shall be presented or allowed, nor shall it extend to any claims duly presented within the time allowed by law, and prosecuted with due diligence from the time of such presentment. But if the claimant shall be under legal disability, the claim may be presented within two years after such disability is removed.

The amended section 4 of Article VIII. requires the Legislature, by general law, to conform all charters of savings-banks or institutions for savings, to a uniformity of powers, rights, and liabilities, and that all charters hereafter granted for such corporations shall be made to conform to such general law. And it is provided that no such corporation shall have any capital stock, nor shall the trustees thereof, or any of them, have any interest whatever, direct or indirect, in the profits of such corporation; and no director or trustee of any such bank or institution shall be interested in any loan or use of any money or property of such bank or institution for savings. The Legislature is prohibited from passing any act granting any special charter for banking purposes; but corporations or associations may be formed for such purposes under general laws. The following new sections are added:

Sec. 10. Neither the credit nor the money of the State shall be given or loaned to or in aid of any association, corporation, or private undertaking. This section shall not, however, prevent the Legislature from making such provision for the education and support of the blind, the deaf and dumb, and juvenile delinquents, as to it may seem proper. Nor shall it apply to any fund or property now held, or which may hereafter be held, by the State for educational purposes.

Sec. 11. No county, city, town, or village shall hereafter give any money or property, or loan its money or credit, to or in aid of any individual, association, or corporation, or become, directly or indirectly, the owner of stock in or bonds of any association or corporation, nor shall any such county, city, town, or village be allowed to incur any indebtedness, except for county, city, town, or village purposes. This action shall not prevent such county, city, town, or village from making such provision for the aid or support of its poor as may be authorized by law.

An additional section was made to Article X., providing that "no officer whose salary is fixed by the constitution shall receive any additional compensation. Each of the other State officers named in the constitution shall, during his continuance in office, receive a compensation, to be fixed by law, which shall not be increased or diminished during the term for which he shall have been elected or appointed; nor shall he receive to his use any fees or perquisites of office or other compensation."

Besides the ordinary oath prescribed in section 1 of Article XII. for members of the Legislature (and all officers, executive and judicial, except such inferior officers as may be exempted by law), all such officers who have been chosen at any election are required to take the following oath or affirmation: "And I do further solemnly swear (or affirm) that I have not, directly or indirectly, paid, offered, or promised to pay, contributed, or offered or promised to contribute, any money or other valuable thing as a consideration or reward for the giving or withholding a vote at the election at which I was elected to said office, and have not made any promise to influence the giving or withholding any such vote," and no other oath, declaration, or test shall be required as a qualification for any office of public trust.

The constitution was further amended by adding the following new articles:

ARTICLE XV., Section 1. Any person holding office under the laws of this State, who, except in payment of his legal salary, fees, or perquisites, shall receive or consent to receive, directly or indirectly, any thing of value or of personal advantage, or the promise thereof, for performing or omitting to perform any official act, or with the express or implied understanding that his official action or omission to act is to be in any degree influenced thereby, shall be deemed guilty of a felony. This section shall not affect the validity of any existing statute in relation to the offense of bribery.

Sec. 2. Any person who shall offer or promise a bribe to any officer, if it shall be received, shall be deemed guilty of a felony and liable to punishment, except as herein provided. No person offering a bribe shall, upon any prosecution of the officer for receiving such bribe, be privileged from testifying in relation thereto, and he shall not be liable to civil or criminal prosecution therefor, if he shall testify to giving or offering of such bribe. Any person who shall offer or promise a bribe, if it be rejected by the officer to whom it is tendered, shall be deemed guilty of an attempt to bribe, which is hereby declared to be a felony.

Sec. 3. Any person charged with receiving a bribe, or with offering or promising a bribe, shall be permitted to testify in his own behalf in any civil or criminal prosecution therefor.

Sec. 4. Any district attorney who shall fail faithfully to prosecute a person charged with the violation in his county of any provision of this article which may come to his knowledge, shall be removed from office by the Governor, after a due notice and an opportunity of being heard in his defense. The expenses which shall be incurred by any county in investigating and prosecuting any charge of bribery, or attempting to bribe any person holding office under the laws of this State, within such county, or of receiving bribes by any such person in said county, shall be a charge against the State, and their payment by the State shall be provided for by law.

ARTICLE XVI., Section 1. All amendments to the constitution shall be in force from and including the first day of January succeeding the election at which the same were adopted, except when otherwise provided by such amendment.

An important decision was rendered in June by the Court of Appeals, in what is known as the "Ring suits," brought in the name of the people of the State against James H. Ingersoll and others, for the recovery of certain moneys, "alleged to have been obtained by the respondent and the other persons named in the complaint, his associates and confederates, by false and fraudulent means and devices." The crucial question was whether the State or the county of New York had the right to bring the action. This question was presented by demurrer in the case of W. M. Tweed, one of the defendants, but the demurrer was overruled at the trial by the Special Term, and this decision was affirmed by the General Term, thus upholding the right of the people of the State to maintain the action. This result was acquiesced in by Tweed, who answered over, and the action stood for trial upon the issues of fact joined. Subsequently, upon the motion of Ingersoll, about one-third of the complaint was, by order of another judge, stricken out as "irrelevant and redundant," the court holding that the allegations were not essential either to the right of the plaintiffs or the liability of the defendants, in respect to the cause of action stated. To the complaint thus modified, Ingersoll demurred upon the ground that the plaintiffs (the people of the State) had no standing in court, or right to maintain the action; and the lower courts decided in his favor.

Thus two conflicting decisions have been given, one affirming, and the other denying the right of the State to sue.

No opinion was expressed by the Court of Appeals concerning the allegations and statements stricken out as above mentioned. Nor did the appeal involve the right of the State to maintain an action against the Auditors for malfeasance in office, or any person occupying an official position, and who has been faithless in his trust. The vital issue was as to the ownership of the money; and the court being of opinion that the money belonged to the county and not to the State, held that the right of action was in the former, and not in the latter, and therefore affirmed the ruling of the lower courts.

A State topographical and trigonometrical survey of from 3,000 to 5,000 square miles of the Adirondack region has been in progress for several years under Verplanck Colvin. The reports already published present many facts not before known. The positions and altitudes of hundreds of mountains, lakes, and other features, were determined, many of which had not been indicated on any map. The heights of many well-known peaks, heretofore estimated, were ascertained with accuracy for the

first time, the highest two in the State, Mount Marcy and Mount McIntyre, being 5,402 feet, and 5,201 feet. Mount Haystack and Mount Skylight, which have heretofore escaped the attention of surveyors, were found to rank third and fourth in height, the former being 5,006 feet high, and the latter nearly, if not quite, 5,000 feet. Among others measured for the first time, and having an altitude of nearly 5,000 feet, are Gothic and Basin Mountains. Among those the height of which had been over-estimated, are Mount Dix, found to be 4,916 feet; Mount Seward, 4,384; and Mount Santanoni, 4,644. Mr. Colvin reports the existence in this region of the moose, though nearly extinct, and of the beaver in one or two localities. The bear, panther, and wolf, are still abundant, and afford a livelihood to some trappers who kill them for fur or State bounty. The common deer are plentiful in some sections, and almost wanting in others. Mr. Colvin places the lake-sources of the Hudson River in the lakelets known as Tear of the Clouds, or Summit Water, and Moss Pool, near Mount Marcy, and shows that the watershed of the Adirondacks chiefly supplies the canals and rivers of the State.

There still remain small portions in all probability never trodden by man, but along the streams and lakes navigable by canoe. The accessible portions of this region are now famous resorts for camping and hunting parties in summer, and a class of men termed guides has arisen who obtain a livelihood in their mingled avocations of boatmen, huntsmen, fishermen, and cooks, for the party they guide. With the increase of travel has come an increase of cost, and men who would once accompany a party will now only guide for one person, obtaining from $2.50 to $3.00 a day, with board

and expenses. The expense of carrying boats overland by team at certain points (a few dollars) must also be borne by the tourist. A Commission of State Parks, appointed by the Legislature, have reported in favor of setting apart as a State park from 600 to 3,000 square miles of the high mountain-region of the Adirondacks, embracing Mount Marcy and all the great peaks; the chief objects being to preserve the forests for their beneficial climatic effects, moderating the spring freshets in the Hudson by sheltering the snow from the heat of the sun, shielding the sources of this river from evaporation, and affording a healthful pleasure-ground for the people of the State. The establishment of this park is beginning to attract earnest attention from the leading men of the State, not only on account of the pleasure it may afford to the people, but also for reasons of political economy.

SCENE IN THE ADIRONDACK REGION.

SAMUEL J. TILDEN, the present Governor of New York, was born in New Lebanon, Columbia County, N. Y., in 1814, where his grandfather, John Tilden, settled in 1790, and where his father, Elam Tilden, was a farmer and merchant. In 1837 young Tilden entered Yale College, but did not graduate. He completed his collegiate course at the University of New York, and was subsequently admitted to the bar. In 1846 he was a member of the Assembly from New York; he was also a member of the Constitutional Convention, and served on the Committee on Canals and Finance. In 1860 he exerted himself to avert the civil war, and during the war sustained the Administration. He became chairman of the Democratic State Committee in 1866, and was a leading member of the Constitutional Convention of

1867, serving with distinction on the Finance Committee.

For several years past Mr. Tilden has been an indefatigable laborer in the cause of judicial and political reform in the city of New York. He was active in the organization of the Bar Association of the city, which has for its object the correction of judicial abuses.

When the contest was waged against the city officials who were charged with defrauding the city treasury of many millions of dollars, Mr. Tilden rendered invaluable services to the cause of reform by his famous analysis of the accounts of the Broadway Bank, showing conclusively how the alleged culprits had shared their spoils, and furnishing legal proof for their conviction. In 1872, Mr. Tilden was again elected to the General Assembly, where he continued his exertions in the cause of reform. In politics Mr. Tilden has always been a Democrat.

Soon after the organization of the Legislature, in 1875, FRANCIS KERNAN was elected to the United States Senate for six years, from March 4, 1875, to succeed Hon. Reuben E. Fenton. Mr. Kernan was born in Wayne, Steuben County, N. Y., January 14, 1816. After graduating from Georgetown College in the District of Columbia, he studied law in the office of Joshua A. Spencer, and subsequently became his partner. He was Reporter of the Court of Appeals from 1854 to 1857, and in 1860 was elected to the Assembly from a district which the previous year had elected a Republican by a large majority. In 1862 he was elected to Congress, where he rendered valuable service as a member of the Judiciary Committee. He was a member of the Constitutional Convention in 1867, and of the Constitutional Commission, whose work was ratified at the election of 1874. In 1872 he was the unsuccessful candidate of the Democrats and Liberal Republicans for Governor. In politics, Mr. Kernan has always been a Democrat; in religion, a Catholic. He possesses, in a preëminent degree, all the qualifications essential to the discharge of the duties of the high position to which he has been elected; and his election gives general satisfaction. His efforts in behalf of the public schools of the State have identified his name with that cause. He holds a high rank as a jurist and a statesman, and is described as "very forcible in debate and argument, being clear and concise in his statements, logical and direct in reaching conclusions, pointed and pertinent in illustration, chaste and strong in diction, attractive in manner, and commanding in presence."

NICARAGUA (REPÚBLICA DE NICARAGUA), a republic of Central America, situated between Costa Rica and Honduras, and the shores of which are bathed by the Caribbean Sea on the east and by the Pacific Ocean on the west. It comprises an area of 39,000 square miles, and has a population of 350,000.

By the terms of the existing constitution, promulgated on August 19, 1858, after the filibuster war, the country is under a popular representative government. The power is divided into three branches—legislative, executive, and judicial. The legislative power is vested in a Senate and a Chamber of Deputies, the first composed of two members for each of the seven departments of the republic, and elected for a term of six years; and the second of one representative from each of the four common districts, and two from each of the seven head-districts of departments: in all, eighteen deputies, their term of office being four years.

The legislative period embraces two years, and commences on the 1st of January. Two-thirds of the senators are changed at a time, and one-half of the deputies. Every senator must be a native of Nicaragua, or of Central America, and have resided ten years in the republic, and possess landed property equal to an income of $2,000 per annum, be a layman, and not less than thirty years of age.

The only indispensable requirements for a deputy are five years' residence in the republic, if born in any part of the territory of Central America, and to have completed twenty-five years of age.

The executive power is vested in a President, aided by a number of ministers, to be determined by law. Of these there are at present four. The presidential period is four years, and no one can be reëlected to that office.

The judicial power is divided into two sections, one of which resides in Leon and the other in Granada. They are composed of four magistrates each, and appeals may be made from either one to the other.

The magistrates are elected for four years each; and one-half of the members of each section is changed during each legislative period. They are elected by the Congress.

The first constitutional Congress was inaugurated on January 1, 1859; and the first constitutional on March 1st of the same year. Since then there have been eight uninterrupted congressional, and four presidential periods. The first two presidential periods were embraced by the administration of General Tomás Martinez; the third, by that of General Fernando Guzman; and the fourth, by that of Señor Don Vicente Quadra, to end on March 1, 1875.

The members of the Quadra cabinet were as follows: Minister of Foreign Affairs, Public Instruction, Agriculture, and Commerce, Señor Don Anselmo H. Rivas; of the Interior, Justice, and Ecclesiastical Affairs, Dr. Francisco Barberena; of War, Marine, Police, and Public Works, Licentiate Isidoro Lopez; and of Finance, Dr. Teodoro Delgadillo.

The outgoing administration is the only one in Nicaraguan annals throughout the whole course of which peace has been preserved, with the single exception of the first presidential period, inaugurated with the common consent of the various parties which had been exhausted by a three-years war that began in May, 1854, and terminated in the expulsion of the filibusters in June, 1857. The *junta gubernativa*, composed of Generals Martinez and Jerez, was then intrusted with the reorganization of the country.

During the last period of peace the interests of agriculture, commerce, and public instruction, have been considerably developed. In the departments of Leon and Chinandega the sugar-cane has been more extensively cultivated than ever before; and the same may be said of coffee and indigo in Granada and Rivas. The wealth of Matagalpa, Chontales, and Nueva Segovia, chiefly consists of cattle; and in the last two there is a mining-district of considerable importance.

The zealous activity with which public and private enterprises have been carried forward is particularly noticeable in the improvements in many of the towns throughout the country, those made in Leon and Granada being mentioned among the most considerable. A school has been founded in Rivas, under the direction of Dr. (formerly General) Máximo Jerez. In Leon have been established two schools for males, under the auspices of Señores José Victor Valle and Alfredo Alvarado; and one for females by Señorita Emilia Dawson. But, of all the educational establishments, that most worthy of especial mention is the *Colegio de Granada*, with professors from Europe, magnificent furniture and appointments, the whole expenditures for which were met by the citizens themselves.

It is officially reported that the condition of the national Treasury has undergone a favorable change under the recent reforms in its administration; and that the revenue derived from the sources enumerated below has been so considerably in advance of that obtained in former years as to be sufficient to cover all the expenditures, without leaving any arrears, and to admit of a certain appropriation on account of the national debt.

SOURCES OF REVENUE—CUSTOMS.

Tax on slaughtered cattle.
Domestic spirits, ⎫
Gunpowder,   ⎪
Tobacco,   ⎬ Monopolies.
Salt,   ⎪
Imported spirits.   ⎭
Printed laws.
Fines.
Uncultivated lands.
Post-Office.

The first four branches are the most productive.

During the years 1872, 1873, and 1874, three exploring expeditions were sent from the United States to examine the isthmus, and ascertain the most suitable route for an interoceanic canal. The result of the surveys was, in each case, favorable to Nicaragua, owing to the peculiar facilities presented by its territory, level in the main, and the vast repository of water situated between the two oceans, and sufficient to feed thirty canals.

It may here be added that, in the opinion of M. Lesseps, the successful engineer of the Suez Canal, no one of the American isthmuses admits of the problem being solved in the same way as on the African isthmus; that is to say, without weirs. The interoceanic canal must be a large one, with weirs, and with no small number of them; hence the indispensable necessity of an inexhaustible supply of water, such as could alone be afforded by the Lake of Nicaragua. It was long supposed that the San Juan River was navigable from the lake to its embouchure at Greytown, and consequently that, to complete the transisthmian water-route, it was only necessary to cut the narrow neck—some eighteen miles—on the other side, from the lake to the Pacific. In

view of this theory, numerous surveys of the narrow neck have been made since the first half of the sixteenth century: one for the Spanish Government, in 1781, by Manuel Galista; and again, in 1838, by a Mr. Baily, for the Central-American Government. But it is not generally known that, between 1842 and 1844, a survey was made at the instance of Prince Louis Napoleon, afterward Napoleon III., and then a captive in the castle of Ham. The Government of Central America decreed, on January 8, 1846, that the cut should be called "Canal Napoleon de Nicaragua." Louis, after his flight to England in the same year, gave publicity to his plans, laying down the very line reverted to by the American surveyors in 1872.

Nicaragua offers a salubrious climate, abundance of building-materials, and robust and willing hands to undertake the work within her borders.

On October 4, 1874, was elected the new President, who is to enter upon his functions on March 1st of the present year. After a lengthy and obstinate struggle, the Republican party triumphed in the person of their candidate, Señor Don Pedro Joaquin Chamorro, distinguished for the active part he took in the defense of his country against the filibusters, and again in the rebellion of 1869. A proof of his popularity, and of the spontaneity of the suffrage tendered to him, is afforded by the fact of his absence in Europe at the commencement, and almost up to the close, of the electioneering campaign.

NORTH CAROLINA. The Legislature of this State adjourned on the 16th of February, and assembled again on the 16th of November. Chief among the acts passed during the session, in the early part of the year, was one providing for the local prohibition of spirituous liquors. By this law it is made "the duty of the county commissioners of any county, upon petition of one-fourth of the qualified voters of any township in their respective counties, to order an election to be held on the first Monday in May in every year, to ascertain whether or not spirituous liquors shall or may be sold in said township or townships." If a majority of the votes cast are in favor of prohibition, "it shall not be lawful for the county commissioners to license the sale of spirituous liquors, or for any person to sell any spirituous liquors within such township for one year next after any such election; and, if any person so prohibited shall sell any spirituous liquors within such township, such person offending shall be deemed guilty of a misdemeanor, and on conviction of such offense shall be fined not exceeding fifty dollars, or imprisoned not exceeding one month." But if a majority of the votes are cast in favor of license, then spirituous liquors may be sold in such township as now provided by law, and not otherwise.

This act, however, does not affect localities in which the sale of spirituous liquors is prohibited by law.

An act was also passed making it unlawful for any dealer to sell intoxicating liquors to minors.

The "election law," passed by the General Assembly at this session, ordered an election to be held on the first Thursday in August, 1874, and every two years thereafter, for members of Congress, members of the Legislature, and certain county officers; also for the choice of six Superior Court Judges, on that day, and every eight years thereafter. The act further provides for the holding of an election on the first Thursday in August, 1876, and every four years thereafter, for Governor, Lieutenant-Governor, Secretary of State, Auditor, Treasurer, Superintendent of Public Instruction, and Attorney-General. On the same day, and every eight years thereafter, five Supreme Court and six Superior Court Judges are to be elected.

North Carolina is represented in Congress as follows:

Senate.—M. W. Ransom, Democrat; A. S. Merrimon, Democrat.

House of Representatives.—First district, Jesse J. Yates, Democrat; second district, John A. Hyman, Republican; third district, A. M. Waddell, Democrat; fourth district, Joseph J. Davis, Democrat; fifth district, A. M. Scales, Democrat; sixth district, Thomas S. Ashe, Democrat; seventh district, William M. Robins, Democrat; eighth district, R. B. Vance, Democrat.

The General Assembly is classified as follows:

PARTIES.	Senate.	House.	Joint Ballot.
Democrats	37	82	119
Republicans.......	11	34	45
Independents	2	2	4
Democratic maj...	24	46	70

The total vote cast for Superintendent of Public Instruction was 182,812, of which Stephen D. Pool, Democrat, received 98,217, and his Republican opponent, Mr. Purnell, 84,595. The election throughout the State showed large Democratic gains. A congratulatory address to the people of the State was issued by the Executive Committee of the Conservative Democratic party, in which the results of the election and their causes were thus given:

Notwithstanding the overwhelming defeat you sustained in the last presidential election, you now carry the State, electing the Superintendent of Public Instruction by nearly 12,000 majority, gain five Superior Court Judges, elect nine Solicitors, have more than two-thirds in the General Assembly, and send to Congress a Conservative member from each district except one, where we largely reduced the majority against us.

It is true that in this contest you are not unmindful of the record of the Republican party, consisting of so many grievous evils, among which we may enumerate:

1. The great corruption that existed among the leaders of that party.

2. The fraudulent misuse of legislative power to fasten on our people a large and oppressive public debt still unprovided for.

3. The sacrifice of the State's interest in nearly all her public works.

4. The protection of our system of internal improvements.

5. The corruption, imbecility, and malpractices of many ministers of the law, who turned our courts into engines of oppression and mocked at justice, disgracing the high places heretofore adorned by the most illustrious names in the history of our State.

6. The denial to some of our citizens of many of their dearest and most sacred rights, the free use of unlawful means to carry elections, and other invasions of the liberties of the people.

Yet the chief issue presented in the canvass was one recently forced on us by our political adversaries, namely, that arising from the civil-rights bill, a measure fraught with the most direful consequences to all of our people, and especially to the laboring-classes, being calculated to arouse the worst passions of the two races, to destroy the peaceful and even friendly relations existing between them, and to inaugurate an era of strife and commotion which would be destructive of our present prosperity. Its adoption would destroy the common schools of our State, so much needed in a country whose government must rest on the virtue and intelligence of the people, and where all men are invested with the elective franchise; while its social features are violative of the dearest rights of freemen, and in direct conflict with the principles of local self-government declared in the Constitution of the United States.

On the 17th of July Governor Tod R. Caldwell died at Hillsboro', whither he had gone to attend to the interests of the State at the annual meeting of the stockholders of the North Carolina Railroad Company. He was succeeded as chief magistrate by Lieutenant-Governor Curtis H. Brogden. In his message to the Legislature in November, Governor Brogden spoke of the late Executive in the following language: "He was a man of noble and generous impulses, of unsullied virtue, and stern integrity. His loss to the State was a great public calamity, and his name and memory will be long and affectionately cherished by his friends and countrymen. Ever faithful to the calls of duty, he passed through the numerous responsibilities and trials imposed upon him without a stain upon his integrity as a public servant, his honor as a man, or his character as a citizen. He was candid and conscientious, sincere and just. He loved his State with the affection of a true son, and, as his life was crowned with honors, may his memory be crowned with fame!"

On the 1st of October the educational fund showed a balance of $8,322 and the public fund $225,702. The receipts of the educational fund for the year ending September 30, 1874, were $44,384, and disbursements $56,029. The receipts of the public fund amounted to $667,114, and the disbursements to $451,339.

The State debt is a subject of grave importance to the people of North Carolina, as it is already large and rapidly increasing by the accumulation of interest. On the 1st of October the debt was reported as follows:

1. Bonds issued before the war, called "old bonds"	$8,372,000 00
Interest unpaid on same	3,006,175 00
Total	$11,379,075 00
2. Bonds issued since the war, but under acts passed before the war	$2,297,000 00
Interest unpaid on same	791,910 00
Total	$3,088,910 00
3. Bonds issued during the war for internal improvement purposes	$1,128,000 00
Interest unpaid on same	586,590 00
Total	$1,714,590 00
4. Bonds issued since the war for funding interest and matured bonds as follows:	
Under funding act of 1866	$2,472,200 00
Interest unpaid on same	814,136 00
Total	$3,286,336 00
Under funding act of 1868	$1,702,900 00
Interest unpaid on same	614,904 00
Total	$2,317,804 00
Total for funding	$5,604,140 00
5. Bonds issued since the war under ordinances and acts passed since the war, not special tax	$1,622,045 00
Interest unpaid on same	577,157 53
Total	$2,199,202 53
6. Bonds commonly called "special tax"	$11,407,000 00
Interest unpaid on same	3,528,930 00
Total	$14,935,930 00
Total bonds and interest not special tax	$23,985,918 05
Total debt, including special tax, bonds, and interest	$38,921,848 05

In calling the attention of the Legislature to the importance of this subject, Governor Brogden said:

The people cannot pay the annual interest that accrues on the entire debt, in addition to the ordinary expenses of the State government; and the question arises as to the best mode and manner of its adjustment.

Various plans have been suggested in relation to this subject, but in matters of business two or more parties are necessary to a contract, and to give it any validity it must have the assent of both.

I earnestly recommend to your careful attention and consideration the adjustment of the State debt, because it is filled with the fate of future consequences which may ultimately redound to the honor and good name or the shame or humiliation of the State. We have great cause for honest pride in her past history, her present position, and future prospects, and may it never be truly said that her patriotic and honest sons quietly submitted to any unjust imputation or stain upon her character for integrity and fidelity.

The financial question was one of the most important that claimed the attention of the Legislature upon its assembling, and bills relating to the State debt were early introduced. In the House of Representatives a bill was introduced providing for a new State debt, to be called the consolidated debt, and a tax levy to pay the interest on it and a reserve for a sinking-fund. It then declares all bonds issued under legislation before the war as of equal validity, and also includes the bonds issued under the funding-acts of 1866 and 1868, as they were for interest on the first-class or old bonds. It then provides that the

Treasurer shall issue the new bonds to the holders of this first-class or old bonds at 33⅓ per cent. on the principal, or, in other words, give one bond for three old ones, with the past-due interest attached. All other bonds are ignored. It then authorizes the North Carolina Railroad Company to buy the construction bonds, so called, and gives that company the right to buy the stock of the State for the company, and turns over all right of the State to representation by proxy or directors in the company to the private stockholders, with a proviso that the State may, within ten years, purchase that interest again by paying the cost and six per cent. interest.

Another section provides for the purchase, by the public Treasurer, of the Western North Carolina Railroad, if the same can be done at the sale, for $800,000, payable in State bonds, with ten years to run, interest guaranteed; and it provides for the appointment, by the Governor, of five commissioners, with the concurrence of the Senate, who shall hold and operate and complete the Western North Carolina Railroad with convicts.

The interest of the State in the North Carolina Railroad is of prime importance to the people. The public faith of the State is pledged for the redemption of the bonds issued to construct the road, and that all of the stock held by the State in the company, and any dividends or profits arising therefrom, shall be applied to the payment of the interest accruing on such bonds. For several years the dividends arising from the State stock have been paid into the public Treasury, and applied to the general expenses of the State government. A suit having been brought in the United States Circuit Court by Anthony Swazey, and other bond-holders, to have the dividends applied to the payment of interest on the construction bonds, a receiver was appointed, in June, 1871, to collect the dividends. These dividends, as far as received, have been applied to the payment of interest; but, as they were not sufficient for that purpose, application was also made to the same court for a decree for a sale of the State stock to pay past-due interest. A decree was accordingly rendered by the court at the June term, 1874, to the effect that, if the State fails to provide for payment of the interest due up to the 1st day of April, 1875, the stock may be sold.

If that decree is carried into effect it will thwart and defeat the main purposes of the "act to amend the charter of the North Carolina Railroad Company, and for other purposes therein mentioned," ratified the 10th day of February, 1874, commonly called "the consolidation bill," providing for a continuous line of railroad from Morehead City, on the Atlantic ocean, through almost the entire length of North Carolina, a distance of more than 500 miles, connecting the seaports with the great West and the Mississippi Valley: 440 miles have already been completed, and a large amount of tunneling in the Blue Ridge, and grading done on the seventy miles not yet finished to Paint Rock.

The State has appealed from the decree of the District Court to the Supreme Court of the United States, and it is hoped that the late decision in favor of the sale of the stock held by the State in the North Carolina Railroad may be reversed. But, if it should be confirmed, the probability is, that the main objects of the consolidation bill will be defeated, and the people of Western North Carolina, who have been so long deprived of the immense benefits and advantages of railroad facilities, will have to suffer still longer for want of those important veins and arteries of trade and commerce which so greatly promote the prosperity and wealth of the country.

On the 11th of September, 1871, the North Carolina Railroad and all its property was leased to the Richmond & Danville Railroad Company, for a term of thirty years, for a rent of $260,000 per annum, payable on the 1st days of July and January of each year. The Richmond & Danville Company is also bound by the lease to pay any tax imposed on said Railroad, not to exceed $10,000 per annum. The rent has been paid regularly thus far, and the money applied to the payment of interest on the construction bonds, in accordance with a decree of the United States Court.

The sum necessary to be raised by the present General Assembly to pay the past-due interest on the construction bonds, and thus save the stock of the State from sale under the decree of the United States Circuit Court, will probably amount to more than $200,000.

Another road destined to have an important influence on the prosperity of the State is the Western North Carolina. Most of the road is already completed; but, in consequence of a portion being unfinished, the State is unable to reap any of the advantages of this great through line.

The Eastern Division of the Western North Carolina Railroad extends from Salisbury to the French Broad River, near Asheville, and has been completed and in operation for sev-

eral years from Salisbury to Old Fort, in McDowell County, a distance of 115 miles, and cost $6,000,000, $4,000,000 of which was paid by the State, and $2,000,000 by individuals.

The Western Division extends from near Asheville down the French Broad River to the Tennessee line at Paint Rock, some few miles below the Warm Springs, in Madison County.

Old Fort is 25 miles from Morgantown, and 24 miles from the French Broad River. This 24 miles includes the mountain-section and all the tunnels, three small ones and one large one at the top of the mountain. The small tunnels were nearly completed, when the work was suspended, and the large one, through solid rock, nearly half finished. The large tunnel is about 1,600 feet in length, 700 feet of which is complete, and some 900 to finish. The entire tunneling yet to do in all four of the tunnels is a little more than a fourth of a mile, and a very large proportion of the grading between Old Fort to the top of the mountain is done, and considerable grading has also been done from the mountain to the French Broad River. The company, previous to the war, had surveyed and located the section from the French Broad River to the Tennessee line, near Ducktown, a distance of 135 miles from Asheville, at the estimated cost of over $5,000,000, and had located the road from the French Broad River down that river to Paint Rock on the Tennessee line, 44 miles from Asheville.

The Western North Carolina road has been under mortgage since 1867, and suit is now pending in the Circuit Court of the United States for the Western District of North Carolina, for the sale of said road, and it is understood that the North Carolina Railroad Company have made arrangements with the creditors of the Western North Carolina road to purchase it whenever it is sold, as without that the consolidation act will be a failure. And, by reason of objections to that act, applications have been pending in the State and Federal Courts for injunctions and orders to restrain the North Carolina Railroad Company from purchasing the Western North Carolina Railroad.

O

OBITUARIES, AMERICAN. *Jan.* 1.—SWEET, General BENJAMIN J., Deputy Commissioner of Internal Revenue, a gallant officer in the late war; died in Washington, D. C., aged 41 years. In August, 1862, he aided in organizing the Twenty-first Wisconsin Infantry, of which regiment he became colonel, and soon after rendered effective service at Chaplin Hills. By some mistake the regiment was ordered to a position too far in advance of the main line, where the men were under the fire both of the Union troops and the Confederates. Many lives were lost, and among the wounded was

Colonel Sweet, who was so disabled that he was thenceforth unfitted for field-duty. Upon his recovery he was placed in command of Camp Douglas, near Chicago, where by his energetic measures he repressed the revolt contemplated by the prisoners at that place on the evening prior to the presidential election of 1864. He discharged the duties of his last official position with honor and integrity, winning the respect and confidence of all who had official or personal relations with him.

Jan. 2.—PARKER, JAMES, a famous railroad-conductor; died at Springfield, Mass., aged 58

years. He was a native of Hollis, N. H., and in 1833 entered upon his career as stage-driver. In 1836 he became agent for Burt & Billings's stage-line between Worcester and Springfield, holding that position until the opening of the Western Railroad, when he was taken into the new service of transporting passengers and freight, having had charge of the first train of cars from Boston to Springfield in 1839. Upon his resignation of his position as conductor he was appointed superintendent of the sleeping-cars between Boston and New York, and in 1872 was made superintendent of all the sleeping, parlor, passenger, and baggage cars of all the trains between the two cities. In 1871 and 1873 Mr. Parker was elected a member of the Massachusetts House of Representatives. He was very fond of antiquarian studies, and was made a member of the Massachusetts Historical and Genealogical Society in 1862.

Jan. 6.—BAYLOR, RICHARD E. B., LL. D., a political leader and philanthropist, born in Alabama (about 1797), of an influential family, who after receiving a good education entered the ministry in the Baptist denomination, and in 1829 was elected to Congress. At the expiration of his term he declined a reëlection, and about 1840 removed to Texas, where he acquired a large amount of land and an ample property in the vicinity of Independence, Washington County. He was for twenty-five years a Judge of the District Court in Texas. Judge Baylor founded Baylor University at Independence, giving it 700 acres of land and some money. One of the counties of Texas was also named after him.

Jan. 7.—LOWELL, Mrs. A. CABOT, a well-known teacher and writer for children; died at Cambridge, Mass. She was a native of Boston, Mass. Her principal works were, "Theory of Teaching" (1841); "Edward's First Lesson in Grammar" (1843); "Gleanings from the Poets" (1843); "Edward's First Lessons in Geometry" (1844); "Olympic Games" (1845); "Outlines of Astronomy" (1850); "Letters to Madame Pulsky" (1852); "Thoughts on the Education of Girls" (1853); and "Seed Grain for Thought and Discussion," 2 vols. (1856).

Jan. 7.—THOMPSON, Hon. JOHN B., former Lieutenant-Governor of Kentucky; died at Harrisonburg, Ky., aged 64 years. He was a native of that State, from which he was chosen as a Whig Representative to Congress, serving from 1841 to 1843, and again from 1847 to 1851. In 1853 he was elected to the U. S. Senate for the long term, and served on the Committees on Private Land Claims and on Pensions.

Jan. 8.—EASTMAN, SANFORD, M. D., an eminent physician, surgeon, and medical professor; died at Riverside, San Bernardino County, Cal., aged 53 years. He was born in Lodi, Seneca County, N. Y., graduated from Amherst College in 1841, spent a few years in teaching and agricultural pursuits, and, having turned his attention to the study of medicine, graduated from the Medical Department of the University of Buffalo in February, 1851. Entering upon the practice of his profession in Buffalo, he was in 1858 appointed to the professorship of Anatomy in the Medical Department of the University of Buffalo, to which was added in 1867 that of Clinical Surgery, which position he held with honor to himself until his resignation in 1870. He was also surgeon to the Hospital of the Sisters of Charity, and surgeon to the Buffalo General Hospital, to which he gave his services without compensation. From 1861 to 1867 he was the health-officer of the city, and in 1871 was appointed by Governor Hoffman a member of the Board of State Charities. Later in the same year he removed to California for the benefit of his impaired health, continuing his practice to some extent until a short time previous to his death. Dr. Eastman was an able physician, a skillful surgeon, and a superior lecturer, while his philanthropy led him to give more than half his services to the poor and helpless.

Jan. 14.—STILLWELL, Hon. THOMAS N., minister to Venezuela during President Johnson's Administration; was killed at Anderson, Ind. He was President of the First National Bank in that town, and some difficulty growing out of a business transaction led to a rencontre with John E. Corwin, by whom he was shot and instantly killed.

Jan. 15.—PELL, DUNCAN C., a well-known and enterprising merchant of New York; died in Newport, R. I., aged 68 years.

Jan. 16.—STEARNS, Rev. JOHN G., a venerable Baptist clergyman and author, born in New Hampshire, 1795, a member of the first class in the Hamilton Literary and Theological Institution (now Madison University), ordained in 1821, and for fifty years a preacher in Central New York; author of "The Primitive Church;" "Immortality of the Soul;" "Calvinism and Arminianism;" and "Free-Masonry," an antimasonic work which had a very large sale; died in Clinton, N. Y.

Jan. 17.—SPARROW, Rev. WILLIAM, D. D., an eminent Episcopal clergyman, and professor, Dean of the Faculty of the General Theological Seminary of the Protestant Episcopal Church, near Alexandria, Va., for the last thirty-three years; died very suddenly at the First National Bank in Alexandria, aged 73 years. Dr. Sparrow was eminent for his scholarship, his thorough Biblical learning, and his remarkable piety and devotion.

Jan. 19.—STRÖBELS, FRIEDRICH, a distinguished musician of German birth, but long resident in this country, a musical composer of fair ability; died at Greensborough, N. C.

Jan. 21.—LAUNITZ, ROBERT E., an American sculptor, born in Russia, but came to this country in infancy, his father, whose name he bore, being eminent as a sculptor and having emigrated to the United States in 1830. Mr. Launitz studied art under his father's tuition, and became distinguished for his monuments, statues, and groups, a number of which adorn Greenwood Cemetery. He was also the sculptor, or designer, of several of the soldiers' monuments in different sections of the country, and aided his father both in the design and execution of the statue and monument to General Thomas at Troy, N. Y. He was killed by a railroad collision in Harlem Tunnel.

Jan. 22.—RICH, THOMAS B., a venerable and estimable citizen of New York City, for many years engaged in the manufacture of chemical and medical drugs and preparations, the first to introduce into the American market carbolic acid and its various compounds, and for thirty years past the faithful and efficient treasurer of the Board of Foreign Missions of the Associate Reformed and United Presbyterian Churches—a work of great labor and responsibility, and at times involving large advances, and which he performed during the whole time without any remuneration. He was a native of New York City, and died there, aged 80 years.

Jan. 25.—HOLTON, Prof. ISAAC FARWELL, a Presbyterian clergyman, a botanist, chemist, professor, and journalist, born in Westminster, Vt., August 30, 1812; prepared for college at South Berwick, Me., and Amherst Academy, Amherst, Mass.; graduated from Amherst College in 1836, having taught his way through college; graduated from Union Theological Seminary in 1839, and was licensed to preach the same year. In 1840 he went to Illinois as a home missionary, and during the next five years, besides preaching, was instructor in Greek and natural history in the "Mission Institute" near Quincy, Ill., and was afterward principal of a school near Natchez, Miss.; from 1848 to 1852 professor in the New York College of Pharmacy; in 1853 and 1854 lecturer in chemistry and natural history to the College of New Jersey; in 1855-'56 was traveling in New Granada, and studying its flora, and on his return for two years Professor of Chemistry and Natural History in Middlebury College, Vt., acting as pastor of the Congregational Church in Meredith Bridge, N. H., the while. In 1857 he brought out his work, "New Granada; Twenty Months in the Andes," and soon after went to Illinois, where he remained in the pastorate for five years, not having received ordination until 1860. Coming East in 1864, he engaged in literary labor, and in 1865 became one of the editorial staff of the *Boston Recorder*, and was one of the editors of the *Boston Daily News* from its establishment, besides doing much other literary work. He was also, at the time of his death, clerk of the State Senate Committee on Elections. His death was the result of heart-disease, and occurred at his residence in Everett, Mass., in the 62d year of his age.

Jan. 28.—ALRICKS, HERMAN, an eminent lawyer, antiquarian, and historical writer, a descendant of the oldest Dutch family in Pennsylvania; died in Harrisburg, Pa. He ranked among the most distinguished lawyers of his State both for his professional learning and his wide general attainments, and was, withal, a man of the most sterling integrity. No man in the State had so thorough a knowledge of the history of Pennsylvania, both as a colony and an independent State.

Jan. —.—RUNNELS, ex-Governor HARRISON GRAY, a political leader and politician of Texas, being a member of the Legislature of that State, elected Governor in 1857 over General Sam Houston, and held office from 1857 to 1859; died in Texas. He was an active supporter of the Confederacy, and after the war retired to private life.

Jan. —.—RUOFF, CHARLES, a German machinist, a native of Wurtemberg, who settled in Philadelphia in 1822, and from that time was actively engaged in the manufacture of iron-work. He invented a machine for cutting grooves in cannon and gun-barrels similar to that which was afterward patented by Sir William Armstrong. He died in Philadelphia, aged 76 years.

Feb. 1.—COBLEIGH, Rev. N. E., a Methodist clergyman and journalist; died in Atlanta, Ga. He was formerly a resident of Boston, Mass., where he was one of the editors of *Zion's Herald*, and at the time of his death was editing the Atlanta *Methodist Advocate*.

Feb. 2.—DODGE, NATHANIEL S., an American author; died in Boston, aged 64 years. He was a very voluminous contributor to newspapers and magazines, and wrote useful and entertaining articles. He saw some service as an army quartermaster, and was afterward a clerk in one of the departments at Washington. At the time of his death he was president of the "Papyrus Club," an organization of literary men in Boston. He was the author of "Stories of a Grandfather about American History."

Feb. 2.—LOUIS, JACOB, an old soldier of Napoleon; died in New York City, aged 107 years. He fought in the battles of Leipsic, Cairo, Alexandria, Austerlitz, Moscow, and Waterloo, receiving in these engagements nineteen wounds, nearly all in the right leg. He came to this country in 1847, and married his last wife when he was eighty-one years of age.

Feb. 3.—MILLS, Mrs. C. R., wife of Rev. C. R. Mills, Presbyterian missionary at Tungchow, China; died there. She was formerly from Buffalo, N. Y., where she was married in 1857, and immediately entered upon her missionary work. After about fourteen years of service, she returned with her husband on a visit to this country, and had resumed her labors at Tungchow only two or three years since.

Feb. 4.—VAN ALEN, JAMES I., an eminent New York merchant; died at Fort Washington, in the 86th year of his age. He entered upon his business career about 1811, and might be called one of the founders of the commercial prosperity of New York, ranking among the merchant-princes. His noble personal appearance, united to the rarest gentleness and polish of the old-school manner, made his presence always noteworthy.

Feb. 5.—CONKLING, ALFRED, jurist, diplomatist, and a legal writer; died in Utica, N. Y., aged 85 years. He was born in East Hampton, Suffolk County, N. Y., October 12, 1789; graduated from Union College, studied law, and was admitted to the bar in 1812; was district attorney for Montgomery County three years, and was elected a Representative from New York to the Seventeenth Congress. He then settled in Albany, and in 1825 was appointed by President John Quincy Adams Judge of the U. S. District Court for the Northern District of New York, which office he held until 1850, when President Fillmore appointed him minister to Mexico. On his return from that mission he settled at Genesee, N. Y., devoting himself mainly to literary pursuits. While upon the bench, he wrote two law-books, viz., "Conkling's Treatise" and "Conkling's Admiralty." In 1867 he published a work on "The Powers of the Executive Department of the United States."

Feb. 7.—GERARD, JAMES W., a prominent lawyer and public benefactor of New York City; died there, aged 80 years. He was born in New York City, and was of Huguenot descent. He graduated at an early age from Columbia College with high honors, and studied law under the late George Griffin; throughout a long life he maintained a high rank in his profession, taking his place among the ablest members of the New York bar, and being offered more than once a position on the bench. He was one of the founders of the House of Refuge, and one of its most zealous friends through life. He had been for many years deeply interested in the improvement of the police force, and was instrumental in causing their adoption of a uniform. But his most constant and earnest efforts had been directed to the improvement of the public schools of the city. He was for many years school-inspector, and was constantly on the watch to devise measures for the benefit of popular education.

Feb. 8.—PORTER, JOHN, an eminent jurist and political leader, of Auburn, N. Y., a native of Hadley, Mass., and a graduate from Williams College in 1810; died at Auburn, aged 83 years. After graduation he removed to Auburn, where he studied law in the office of Governor Throop, but afterward entered the office of Bleecker & Sedgwick in Albany. In 1815 he became the law-partner of Governor Throop. In 1828 he was appointed Surrogate of Cayuga County, and held the office for eight years. From 1836 to 1843 he was actively engaged in his profession. From 1843 to 1847 he was a member of the State Senate, which then sat also as a Court of Errors, and manifested great abilities as a jurist in the cases which came under review. He was for many years a political leader in his section, and was

much esteemed and honored for the purity and integrity of his character.

Feb. 9.—MILLER, HENRY, M. D., a physician, medical writer, and professor; died in Louisville, Ky., aged 73 years. He had been for many years connected, as a professor, with medical colleges at Washington, D. C., Cincinnati, and Louisville, and at the time of his death was president of Louisville Medical College. He had also written largely on medicine, the following being his most important medical treatises: "Human Parturition," 8vo (1849); "The Principles and Practice of Obstetrics," 8vo (1858); and numerous papers, essays, and memoirs, in the medical journals.

Feb. 9.—WALTERS, Commander JOHN, U. S. Navy; died at Baltimore, Md., aged 43 years. He was a native of Michigan, and appointed from that State as a midshipman February 12, 1846. He was a gallant and brave officer during the late war, and fought his way up to a commander's position in April, 1867. In 1868 he was in command of the Cyane (third rate), but in 1870 was assigned to the receiving-ship Potomac. His home had been in Baltimore for several years.

Feb. 17.—WAKEFIELD, JOHN LUMAN, M. D., an eminent physician; died at Shakopee, Minn., aged 51 years. He was born in Winsted, Conn., graduated from Yale College in the class of 1847, studied medicine, and returning to his native town practised his profession until 1849, when he went to California. There he continued in practice until 1854, when he was severely attacked with the cholera, and upon partial recovery and a visit home settled in Shakopee, Minnesota, for the sake of his health. In 1861 he was appointed physician to the Upper Agency for the Sioux Indians, and was there at the time of the massacre of August 18, 1862, when he succeeded in escaping, while his wife and children were captured. After their release in October, he settled at St. Paul, being stationed at Fort Snelling, in medical charge of the friendly Indians. In 1863, after a brief visit to Missouri in the same capacity, he resigned his appointment, and returned to Shakopee, where he was a practising physician until his death.

Feb. 22.—JONES, Rev. ALEXANDER, D. D., an eminent Episcopal clergyman, long settled in Virginia, and afterward in Perth Amboy, N. J. He was born in Charleston, S. C., in 1796; and died at Perth Amboy, aged 78 years. He graduated from Brown University in 1814, was ordained a priest in 1818, was rector of an Episcopal Church in Charlestown, Va., for twenty-seven years, and was called thence to Richmond, Va., where he was rector of St. Paul's for about six years. He then sought a parish farther north and became rector of St. Peter's at Perth Amboy in 1851, where he was highly esteemed and honored. In 1871, after twenty years' service, he resigned in consequence of failing health, but resided at Perth Amboy till his death. In 1844 he received the degree of D. D. from Kenyon College.

Feb. 22.—PORTER, SAMUEL, one of the pioneer promoters of the magnetic telegraph, born in Geneva, N. Y.; died in Albion, N. Y., aged 55 years. He was in early life a clerk in the office of the New York *Observer*, and thus became acquainted with Prof. Morse and interested in his telegraphic experiments. In 1844 he entered upon the business of building lines of telegraph with Morse, Ezra Cornell, and others, aiding in the construction of the line from Baltimore to New York, and then from New York to Albany and Buffalo. He then on his own account built and opened the line from Buffalo to Toronto, stretching the first line across the Niagara River in 1846, and the first line that extended the wires across the St. Lawrence into Montreal. He originated and built the first marine line between New York City and Sandy Hook, in 1853, and since that time had built competing lines on important routes in the West and East. His great enterprise and energy broke down his health and caused his early death.

Feb. 23.—SMITH, HENRY, a noted politician and political leader in New York City, President of the Board of Police Commissioners, and a member of the Board of Health; died in New York City, in the 54th year of his age. He was born in Amsterdam, N. Y., and was the son of a farmer. He began life early as a canal-boat driver, and before reaching his majority had added to this a shop in Fultonville, in which he kept groceries and canal-stores. He was subsequently employed as an agent of the Albany Merchants' line of canal-boats. He did so well that he was induced, about 1843 or 1844, to come to New York as the agent for the Fultonville line of canal-boats. He filled this position for several years and purchased an interest in the line. By his efforts he built up an extensive forwarding and commission business. He was subsequently connected with Abram Van Santvoord in running a line of tow-boats, and afterward with Albert Van Santvoord in the same business. Van Santvoord and he built the handsome steamboats Chauncey Vibbard and Drew, and organized a day line to Albany. For twenty-five years Mr. Smith had been one of the most active politicians in his party, and for the last eight or ten one of the most influential political leaders in the State. He was very popular with the working-classes, and was on several occasions elected over his opponents in a district politically against him. He was not, however, so desirous of office as of power and influence. He had been for four years a councilman, four years an alderman, and a supervisor for seven years, till that board was abolished. From 1868 till his death he was a police commissioner, for two years treasurer and for four president of the board, and *ex officio* a member of the Board of Health. In all the district, county, State, and national

Republican Conventions he was present and generally a delegate, and a member of the District and State Executive Committees. He was President of the Bowling Green and National Savings-Banks, both of which failed in 1871, but does not seem to have been personally responsible for their bad management, which, indeed, he tried to rectify, to his own heavy loss.

Feb. 24.—BUFFUM, JOSEPH, an eminent citizen of Westmoreland, N. H., a member of the Sixteenth Congress; died at Westmoreland, N. H., in the 90th year of his age. He was born at Fitchburg, Mass., and graduated from Dartmouth College in 1807. He studied law and was admitted to the bar at Keene, N. H., and practised law there till 1819, when he was elected to Congress from that district. He served but a single term, and then returned to Keene, and removed to Westmoreland, where for more than fifty years he devoted himself to agricultural pursuits. He was a man of fine intellect and sterling integrity.

Feb. 26.—MILLSON, JOHN S., an eminent lawyer, formerly member of Congress from Eastern Virginia; died at Norfolk, Va. He was born in that city, October 1, 1808, studied law, and was elected a Representative from his State in the Thirty-first Congress, which position he held by reëlections until 1860, serving as a member of the Committees on Commerce and Ways and Means, and of the Special Committee of Thirty-three on the rebellious States. In 1844 and 1849 he was also a presidential elector.

Feb. 26.—PERLEY, IRA, LL. D., an eminent jurist, ex-Chief-Justice of New Hampshire, died at Concord, N. H., aged 75 years. He was born in Boxford, Mass., graduated from Dartmouth College with high honor in 1822, remained as tutor two years, and, having studied law, was admitted to the bar at Guilford, N. H., in 1827. He entered upon the practice of his profession at Hanover, where he was five years treasurer of the college, and in 1834 removed to Concord, where he soon won a high reputation as a lawyer. In July, 1850, he accepted the appointment of an Associate Justice of the Superior Court; resigned that position in 1852; in 1855 was made Chief-Justice of the Supreme Judicial Court; resigned in 1859, in order to resume practice, and in 1864 accepted the latter position again, holding it until 1869, when his age disqualified him for the office. Judge Perley ranked high as a jurist, was an accomplished scholar in science and literature, and, although not a politician, served two years as a Republican Representative from Concord in the State Legislature. In 1852 Dartmouth College conferred upon him the honorary degree of Doctor of Laws.

Feb. —.—BEATON, Mrs., a centenarian, died in Southampton County, Va., aged 104 years.

Feb. —.—KITCHEN, Miss BECKY, a centenarian, died in Southampton County, Va., aged 120 years.

March 2.—HALL, NATHAN K., Judge of the U. S. District Court for the Northern District of New York; died at Buffalo, N. Y., aged 64 years. He was born in Marcellus, Onondaga County, N. Y., March, 1810, studied law in the office of Millard Fillmore (afterward President), whose partner in practice he became in 1832, held different administrative and judicial offices in his native State, and was a Representative in Congress from 1847 to 1849. On Mr. Fillmore's accession to the presidency, in 1850, he was appointed to the office of Postmaster-General, the responsible duties of which position he performed with strict integrity and honor, never allowing himself to be influenced by unworthy or partisan motives. In 1852, on the retirement of Judge Conkling from the bench of the U. S. Court, Judge Hall was appointed his successor. Coming to this position in the maturity of his powers, he devoted himself with patient industry, a conscience void of all offense, and an earnest desire to be found faithful to his great responsibilities, to his new duties. No one of the U. S. District Court judges won a higher reputation for legal knowledge, sterling integrity, and judicial ability, than Judge Hall.

March 2.—HAWKINS, Mrs. MARY ANNE, widow of Charles W. Hawkins, a devoted and philanthropic Christian woman; died in Brooklyn, N. Y., aged 66 years. Her attention was called early to the condition of children and youth, and especially of young girls, who were morally imperilled, and without home or friends who could protect them from falling into vice. She possessed great executive ability, and was earnest, persevering, and self-denying, in her labors in their behalf. She was one of the founders of the American Female Guardian Society, and it was largely through her efforts that the present commodious and eminently useful "Home for the Friendless" was erected, furnished, and liberally endowed. She was almost from the first President of the Female Guardian Society and editor of the *Advocate and Guardian*, and though for many years she had been an invalid, confined to her couch and easy-chair, and much of the time suffering severe pain, she was so wise in counsel, so clear-headed and able in planning and carrying out measures for the society's advancement, that she was retained in the presidency till her death. Few women have been so signally useful.

March 2.—STEPHENS, Rev. JOHN L., a missionary of the American Board in Mexico, was murdered by a mob at Ahualulco, Mexico, aged 27 years. He was a native of Swansea, Wales, and came in early childhood to America; was educated in California, graduated from the Theological Seminary of the Pacific, and while pursuing his studies taught a night-school of Chinese, into which some native Mexicans found their way. Becoming deeply interested in the latter, he sought an appointment as missionary to Mexico, was ordained in Sep-

tember, 1872, and soon after left for the field of labor. Having been prospered in his work at Guadalajara, he courageously proceeded to Ahualulco, where he fell a sacrifice to his missionary ardor.

March 3.—BURRALL, WILLIAM PORTER, a prominent railroad officer; died in Hartford, Conn., aged 68 years. He was born at Canaan, Conn., graduated from Yale College in the class of 1826; studied law in Salisbury, and the Litchfield Law School, and was admitted to the bar of Litchfield County in April, 1829. He practised law in his native town until October, 1839, when he was chosen president of the Housatonic Railroad Company, just organized, and removed to Bridgeport, Conn. This office he held for the period of fifteen years, when he resigned in consequence of the pressure of other engagements. He was also connected with the New York & New Haven Railroad during its construction and the earlier years of its operation; was treasurer, and afterward president, of the Illinois Central Railroad, vice-president, and afterward president, of the Hartford & New Haven Railroad, and was finally vice-president of the New York, New Haven & Hartford Railroad upon the consolidation of those companies. In 1859 he removed to Salisbury, and subsequently represented that town several times in the General Assembly, and had also been a member of the State Senate.

March 3.—FOWLER, ROBERT, a leading merchant and politician in Baltimore; died there. He held the office of State Treasurer from 1862 to 1870, and was a member of the present Maryland House of Delegates. During the war he was a strong Unionist, and as a business-man he was largely identified with the commercial interests of the State.

March 3.—RITCHIE, Captain DAVID, U. S. Revenue Marine Service; died on Long Island, aged 38 years. He was a gallant officer, and rendered good service at the Metis disaster in saving nineteen of the passengers from drowning, for which he received the thanks of Congress.

March 11.—BONDI, Rev. J. D. D., a Hebrew rabbi, scholar, and editor; died in New York City, aged 70 years. He was born at Dresden, Saxony, in 1804, and came to this country about 1854. Since 1865 he had been editor of the *Hebrew Leader*. He was also the author of several controversial works.

March 13.—GARDNER, HIRAM, a New York jurist; died at his residence in Lockport, N. Y. He was one of the earliest settlers of that town. He was elected to the Assembly for Niagara County in 1836. In 1847 he was elected County Judge, and in 1868 he was reappointed to the same court by Governor Fenton, in place of Judge Laurent, who had been appointed to the Supreme Court. He was also elected Canal Commissioner in 1868.

March 13.—SHARPS, CHRISTIAN, inventor of the famous Sharps rifle; died at Vernon,

Conn., aged 63 years. He was a native of New Jersey, of German or Swedish ancestry, and early developed remarkable ingenuity in every department of mechanical invention. He made himself thoroughly familiar with every branch of the machinist's art, and whatever he attempted to invent he always perfected and made a success — for somebody; though not 'usually for himself. He was best known by the rifle which bears his name, and which twenty years of experience have proved to be the most simple, admirable, and practically efficient and serviceable army-gun ever invented, and also one of the most valuable for large game on the Plains. He removed to Hartford in 1854 to superintend the manufacture of this rifle, and subsequently invented several other fire-arms of great value, and scores of articles and machines for other purposes than war and bloodshed. He was an enthusiastic sportsman, and had fitted up at Vernon an establishment for the propagation of trout. His death occurred from a sudden and severe hæmorrhage from the lungs.

March 17.—JONES, J. PRINGLE, a Pennsylvania jurist; died at Reading, Pa. He was for some years president judge of the Circuit Court in the Reading district.

March 18.—HART, OSSIAN B., Governor of the State of Florida; died at his residence in Jacksonville, Fla. He was of Northern birth, but had resided for some years in Florida. He was appointed Associate Justice of the Supreme Court of Florida by Governor Reed in 1868, and in November, 1872, was elected Governor, receiving a majority of 1,599 votes over the Democratic candidate. He entered upon his duties in January, 1873, and in his first message urged the Legislature to improve the election laws and adopt a sound financial policy.

March 18.—VERREN, Rev. ANTOINE, D. D., a French Protestant Episcopal clergyman, for forty-five years rector of the Church du St. Esprit, New York City; died there in the 73d year of his age. He was born in the city of Marseilles, in France, in 1801, received his early education at Marseilles, and completed it at the Theological College at Geneva. In 1825 he was ordained as a minister of the gospel in Switzerland, and shortly afterward obtained a cure at Ferney, on the banks of Lake Geneva, and celebrated throughout the world as having been the residence of Voltaire. In the year 1829 he came to New York. When he first arrived, the French church was situated in Pine Street, near where the Sub-Treasury at present stands. Subsequently a handsome edifice was built in Franklin Street in 1835, but which, after being twice burned, was sold, and, with the money received, the present church in Twenty-second Street, near Fifth Avenue, was erected in the year 1857.

March 19.—COLGROVE, BELA H., M. D., one of the most eminent physicians and surgeons in Western New York; died in Sardinia,

N. Y., aged 77 years. He was born in Coventry, R. I., in 1797. He supported himself by teaching while acquiring both his classical and professional education; attended lectures in the New Haven Medical School, the University of·Pennsylvania, and the College of Physicians and Surgeons, New York City, graduating M. D. from the latter. He·commenced practice in Sardinia in 1820, and his remarkable abilities, both as a physician and surgeon, his assiduous and thorough investigation, and his untiring industry, soon gave him a reputation far beyond the bounds of his village or town. For nearly fifty years he was recognized as the leading surgeon and physician in Western New York or Northwestern Pennsylvania. His manifold gifts, both as a speaker and writer, led to repeated attempts to draw him away from his profession into politics or literature, but he uniformly refused to leave his professional duties. His entire freedom from all petty jealousies, and his cordiality toward every struggling physician, won him hosts of friends, in the profession as well as out of it.

March 19.—SHIMEALL, Rev. RICHARD C., a Presbyterian clergyman and author; died in New York City, aged 71 years. He was born in New York, in 1803, graduated from Columbia College in 1821, and from the General Protestant Episcopal Theological Seminary in 1824; was ordained priest the same year, and commenced his labors as rector of St. Jude's Protestant Episcopal Church, formed through his zealous efforts. He continued with St. Jude's for ten years, receiving no compensation for his services. Some years later he transferred his membership to the Reformed (Dutch) Church, and still later joined the New York Presbytery. He had been pastor of several important churches. Mr. Shimeall was a very profound Biblical scholar; his knowledge of the Greek and Oriental languages was both thorough and critical. He had adopted many years since substantially the views of the English Millennarians—Cumming, Bickersteth, and others—and most of his numerous works were upon subjects connected with the prophecies and their interpretation. The following are his principal works: "Age of the World as it is founded on Sacred Records" (1842); "The End of Prelacy," 8vo (about 1845); "Illuminated Scriptural Chart;" "Our Bible Chronology, Historic and·Prophetic. First Series," royal 8vo (1859); "Christ's Second Coming: is it Pre-Millennial or Post-Millennial?" 8vo (1865); "Political Economy of Prophecy, with Special Reference to the History of the Church" (1866). We believe a second series of "Biblical Chronology," and one or two of the other works, were published in 1871-'73.

March 22.—DENT, LOUIS, a lawyer and politician—a brother of Mrs. Grant, wife of President Grant; died in Washington, D. C., aged 52 years. He was born in St. Louis, in 1822, and received a liberal education in that city.

He subsequently studied law, and went to California about 1849 or '50, where he married, engaged in business, and was for some years a judge in one of the courts. In 1862 he returned to St. Louis, and from 1863 to 1867 was extensively engaged in cotton-planting in Mississippi and Louisiana, where he rented large plantations. He then came to Washington and practised law with success. After President Grant's first election he returned to Mississippi, where in 1869 he was nominated for Governor by the National Union Republicans and supported by the Democrats. He was, however, badly beaten by Mr. Alcorn, the regular Republican candidate, who received twice as many votes as he. Soon after he withdrew from politics, and, again making his home in Washington, engaged in a general practice of law there. In December, 1873, he embraced the Roman Catholic faith, and during his protracted illness was attended by Rev. Dr. White, of St. Matthew's Roman Catholic Church.

March 23.—DUNNING, Rev. EDWARD OSBORNE, a Congregationalist clergyman and archæologist; died in New Haven, Conn., aged 64 years. He graduated from Yale College in 1832, and from the Yale Divinity School in 1835, and was settled as a pastor, in Rome and in Canajoharie, N. Y., till 1846. He then accepted an appointment from the American Bible Society as their agent in the Southern States, in which he continued till the late civil war, when he became a chaplain in the army and was stationed at Cumberland, Md., but returned to his work after the war. He had become very much interested years ago in exploring ancient mounds in various parts of the South, and continued his explorations till a few months before his death.

March 24.—TRACY, Rev. JOSEPH, D. D., a Congregationalist clergyman, journalist, and author; died at Beverly, Mass., in the 80th year of his age. He was born in Hartford, Vt., November 3, 1794, graduated from Dartmouth College in 1814, and after a theological course entered the ministry. He was pastor at Thetford and West Fairlee, Vt., from 1821 to 1829, and subsequently for some years in his native town, Hartford, Vt. Thence he removed to Windsor, Vt., to edit the *Vermont Chronicle*, where he continued five years, and then went to Boston as editor of the *Boston Recorder*, being also a contributor to the *New York Observer*, *Journal of Commerce*, etc. He was appointed, a year or two later, New England Secretary of the American Colonization Society. He published: "Three Last Things;" "History of the American Board;" "The Great Awakening" (1842); and "Memorial of the Colonization Society continued" (1867).

March 27.—HARRISON, JOSEPH, an eminent mechanical engineer, born in Philadelphia, in 1810; died there, aged 64 years. Having mastered engineering science, he was one of the first builders of locomotive-engines in this country; and, his reputation becoming established, he was invited by the Czar to St. Petersburg, where he established extensive machine-shops, and derived large profits from contracts with the Russian Government. He had erected several costly buildings in Philadelphia, and had collected a large and very choice gallery of paintings at his residence.

March 29.—BARTLETT, HOMER, a prominent manufacturer and philanthropist, of Massachusetts; born in Granby, Conn., in July, 1795; died in Boston, aged 79 years. He graduated from Williams College in 1818, studied law, was admitted to the bar, and commenced practice in Williamstown; removed to Ware, Mass., in 1824, and soon after became cashier of a bank there, but resigned in 1832, to become connected with manufacturing. In 1837 he removed to Lowell, and became manager of one of the manufacturing companies there, and in 1860 removed to Boston, where he spent the last fourteen years of his life. He was twice a member of the Massachusetts Legislature, and once a presidential elector. In 1854 he was a member of the Governor's Council. He had taken a deep interest in the struggle in regard to the removal of Williams College to Northampton, in 1818–'21, and was a trustee of the college from 1858 to 1869. He left it $4,500 in his will.

March 31.—HIRST, HENRY B., a poet and magazine writer, of Philadelphia; died in that city, aged 61 years. He was born in Philadelphia, August 23, 1813; in his youth engaged in mercantile pursuits, but finally studied law, and was admitted to the bar in 1843. He had at that time published several poems in *Graham's Magazine*, which were very popular. In 1845 his first collected volume of poems was published in Boston, under the title of "The Coming of the Mammoth: the Funeral of Time, and Other Poems." In 1848 was published his "Endymion: a Tale of Greece," in four cantos. This was a classic story, varied from the old Greek legend, and was written, the author said, before he had perused the poems of Keats. In 1849 he published another volume of poems, which included a romance entitled the "Penance of Roland," based on an incident in the days of knighthood and rigorous penalties. The volume also contained the ballad "Florence," and verses descriptive of a "robin's life."

March —.—VAN TASSELL, Mrs., a missionary among the Ottawa Indians and subsequently a physician; died in Maumee City, Ohio, aged 89 years. She commenced her medical education when she was fifty-eight years old; attended medical lectures in New York City, and was said to have been the first woman ever admitted to the full course of medical lectures in this country. After qualifying herself for practice, she spent several years as a medical practitioner in Memphis, Tenn.

April 1.—MARSH, Rev. SAMUEL, a venerable and able Congregationalist clergyman, born at

Danville, Vt., July 3, 1796; died at Underhill Flats, Vt., in the 78th year of his age. His father was a farmer, and he remained on the farm, receiving only the scanty educational opportunities afforded in a new and scattered population till he was eighteen years of age. In the winter and spring of 1815 he studied with the clergyman of his native parish, and the autumn of that year walked to Andover, Mass., 160 miles, to enter Phillips Academy. In 1817 he entered Dartmouth College, and graduated thence with honor in 1821, and in 1824 completed his theological course at Andover Theological Seminary. He was ordained in 1825, and was a home missionary in Vermont for two years, and was then called to the pastorate of a Presbyterian Church in Mooers, N. Y., and four years later to a church in Beekmantown, N. Y. His subsequent labors for a period of nearly forty years were connected with Congregational churches in Vermont. He had resided at Underhill Flats, Vt., since June, 1851. In 1827 he originated and carried into active and successful operation what is known as "the American system of colportage," which has since been employed with such excellent results by the American Tract Society, American Sunday-School Union, and other religious societies. He was noted for many years as an able polemic and public debater, and had repeated public controversies with Universalists, Unitarians, and others. He was a very profound Biblical scholar, his knowledge of both Greek and Hebrew being remarkably thorough; he was also a clear, vigorous, and logical writer, as his published works testify. His "Uncle Ned: or Exact Conformity to God in his Word," had an extensive circulation, and his essays and sermons on temperance and antislavery were very popular. He had written in the latter years of his life nearly one thousand Biblical hymns, some of which had been published.

April 5.—EDMONDS, JOHN WORTH, an able New York jurist, born in Hudson, N. Y., March 13, 1799; died in New York City, aged 75 years. He was of patriot stock, his father having been an officer in the Revolutionary army. He was fitted for college in Hudson, and graduated from Union College in 1816, studied law and was admitted to the bar in 1819, and commenced practice in Hudson in 1820. He remained there about fifteen years, a part of which time he held the office of Recorder. Previous to his receiving this appointment from Governor De Witt Clinton, he held various positions in the State militia, rising to the rank of colonel. He also represented Columbia County in the Legislature, both in the Senate and Assembly, and did much to improve, by legislation, the condition of working-men. After leaving the Legislature he went on a Government mission to the Indians, and while living among them learned several Indian languages. Late in 1837 he came to New York City, and began practice as a lawyer, soon securing a high reputation among his associates.

During 1843 he was appointed State-prison Inspector, and founded the prison association for ameliorating the condition of convicted criminals. By his exertions corporal punishment was removed, and a series of rewards for good conduct were instituted. He also adopted measures for enabling discharged criminals to gain an honest livelihood. From 1845 to 1853 he occupied the positions of Circuit Judge, Judge of the Supreme Court, and Judge of the Court of Appeals. In 1853 he retired from the bench on account of his having declared a religious belief in spiritualism. His attachment to this doctrine was so strong that for several years he devoted a large part of his time to the investigation of its phenomena, and became himself a "medium," and in 1854–'55 published a work entitled "Spiritualism," in 2 vols. 8vo, recounting what he had seen, and aiming to harmonize the doctrine with Divine revelation. During this period, however, he did not neglect his professional business, though it had seriously fallen off. His legal ability was unquestioned. For many years he was a public defender and firm advocate of the spiritualistic doctrine, but latterly had taken no active part in the movement, though he never expressed any doubt of the correctness of his belief.

April 9.—WOOD, Rev. HENRY, D. D., U. S. Navy, a Congregationalist clergyman, journalist, and since 1856 a chaplain in the navy; died in Philadelphia, aged 78 years. He was a native of New Hampshire, and learned the printer's trade at Concord, but subsequently fitted for college, and graduated from Dartmouth College in 1822. In 1823 he was appointed tutor, and in 1825 studied theology and was settled as pastor of a Congregational church at Haverhill, Mass., and subsequently became pastor of the College Church at Hanover. He owned and edited the *Congregational Journal* for some years, and, soon after the accession of his friend Mr. Pierce to the presidency, was appointed consul to Syria, and, on his return from that post in 1856, was offered a chaplaincy in the navy. Since 1862 he had been on the retired list, but had most of the time performed shore duty. He had been at one time, we believe, in early life, Professor of the Latin and Greek Languages and Literature in Hampden Sydney College, and from that college he received in 1867 the degree of D. D.

April 11.—BREVOORT, HENRY, a venerable and distinguished citizen of New York; died at Rye, Westchester County, N. Y., aged 83 years. He was descended from the old Holland Dutch stock, and inherited a large landed estate in the vicinity of Forty-ninth Street and the East River, as well as other property. He removed, in early life, to Yonkers, but returned to New York and was a member of the Common Council for many years. In 1852 he removed to Rye, where he resided till his death. One of his daughters married Charles Astor Bristed.

April 11.—STORMS, General HENRY, a political leader and prominent military officer of New York City; died at Tarrytown, N. Y., aged 79 years. He was an alderman in 1825, and for many years after; a member of the Tammany Society, was a cavalry officer and commandant of a cavalry regiment in 1824, and acted as General Lafayette's escort, receiving him at Castle Garden, and attending him to Putnam Hill. He became, a few years later, brigadier-general in the First Division of the N. G. N. Y., and retained that position for twenty years. He was Commissary-General of the State in 1842, and Inspector of State-prisons for several years. A few years since he removed to Tarrytown, where he had been prominent in religious matters.

April 13.—BOGARDUS, JAMES, an American scientist and inventor, born in Catskill, N. Y., March 14, 1800; died in New York City, aged 74 years. He possessed in an eminent degree an inventive genius. After receiving an ordinary English education in his native town, he was apprenticed to a watch-maker at the age of fourteen years, and soon became a skillful die-sinker and engraver. His first invention was an eight-day three-wheeled chronometer clock, for which he received the highest premium at the first fair of the American Institute. He next invented an eight-day clock, with three wheels and a segment of a wheel, which struck the hours, and, without dial-wheels, marked the hours, minutes, and seconds. In 1828 he invented the "ring-flier," for cotton-spinning, now in general use; in 1829 an eccentric mill, which differs from all other mills, the grinding-stones or plates running the same way with nearly equal speed; in 1831 an engraving-machine, which cut the steel die for the gold medal of the American Institute, and engraved many beautiful medallions; and another machine for transferring bank-note plates. In 1832 he invented and patented a dry gas-metre, and for this received the gold medal from the American Institute; he improved it in 1836, by giving a rotary motion to the machinery, thereby overcoming the difficulties which had appeared in the original meter. Being in England in 1836, and noticing in the newspaper a challenge to produce an engraving from the head of Ariadne (a medal in very high relief), he accepted it and produced a medallic-engraving machine, which not only made a perfect fac-simile of the head of Ariadne, but from the same medal engraved comic distortions of the face. This machine engraved a portrait of the Queen, dedicated to herself by her own request; one of Sir Robert Peel, and of several other distinguished persons. He contracted with a company in London to construct a machine for engine-turning which not only copied all kinds of machine-engraving, but engraved what the machine itself could not again imitate; and a machine for transferring bank-note plates, and other work. In 1839 a reward was offered by the English Government for the best plan for manufacturing postage-stamps, and out of twenty-six hundred applicants his plan was one of those to which a prize was awarded. After visiting France and Italy, Mr. Bogardus returned to New York in 1840. He invented a machine for pressing glass, another for shirring India-rubber fabrics, and for cutting India-rubber in fine threads. He also made an important improvement in the drilling-machine, and improved and adapted the eccentric mills for a great variety of purposes. In 1848 he invented and patented a planetary horse-power and a dynamometer for measuring the speed and power of machinery while in motion. In 1847 he put in execution his long-cherished idea of iron buildings, by constructing his factory in New York entirely of iron. This building, five stories high and ninety feet in length, was the first cast-iron building erected in the United States. He subsequently went largely into the business of erecting iron warehouses. A pyrometer which he invented is remarkable for delicacy and accuracy; simply breathing on the object, or a touch of the finger, is instantly responded to by the dial-pointer. Like several other of his inventions, no description of it has yet found its way into print.

April 13.—TAYLOR, EMMONS, an eminent lawyer of Wisconsin, born in Rupert, Vt., June 26, 1828; died in Portage, Wis., aged 46 years. He was a graduate from Williams College, in the class of 1847, studied law in Granville, N. Y., and was admitted to the Washington County (N. Y.) bar. In 1857 he removed to Portage, Wis., and became the partner of Hon. S. S. Dixon, now Chief-Justice of Wisconsin. He soon attained eminence in his profession, and at his death was regarded as the ablest advocate before a jury in the State. He was greatly esteemed by all who knew him.

April 14.—CLARK, HENRY S., a politician and political leader in North Carolina; died at Tarboro', N. C., aged about 65 years. He was born in Beaufort County, N. C., received a good education, studied law, was a member of the State Legislature 1834-'36, State Solicitor 1842-'45, and member of Congress from 1845 to 1847. He was for a time acting Governor of the State.

April 14.—WARREN, JOSIAH, an eccentric but benevolent reformer and author; died in Boston, Mass., aged 75 years. His views on the organization of society were very peculiar. He took an active part in Robert Owen's communistic experiments at New Harmony, Ind., during the two years of 1825 and 1826, but he was so discouraged by the failure of that enterprise that he was on the point of abandoning any further attempt in that direction, when, as he has said in his book, "a new train of thought seemed to throw a sudden flash of light upon our past errors, and to show plainly the path to be pursued." He abandoned the idea of maintaining a communal system of society, and sought to attain the same ends through individual sovereignty. He held that the proper reward of labor was a like amount of labor. "If I am a bricklayer, and need the services of a physician," said he, "an hour of my work in bricklaying is the proper recompense to be given the physician for an hour of his services. In other words, the cost, measured in time, of any thing, is the limit ot price." Mr. Warren carried this singular notion into practical effect by establishing what was known as the "time-store" in Cincinnati, which he conducted with fair success for two years, he giving and receiving labor-notes in transactions with his customers. He propounded his theories in a work entitled the "True Civilization," and elicited the commendation of John Stuart Mill for some of his views. Until increasing age and infirmity rendered it impossible, Mr. Warren was frequently seen at labor-reform meetings, and often engaged in discussions on these themes.

April 16.—Croxton, Brigadier and Brevet Major-General John Thomas, U. S. Volunteers, an American lawyer, soldier, and diplomatist, born in Bourbon County, Ky., November 20, 1837; died at La Paz, Bolivia, in the 37th year of his age. He graduated from Yale College in 1857, studied law with Hon. James F. Robinson, of Georgetown, Ky., and was admitted to the bar in September, 1858, and, after a few years of teaching in Mississippi, began practice in Paris, Ky., in August, 1859. Two years later he was active in the movement for raising Union troops in Kentucky, and went to the front in June, 1861, as lieutenant-colonel of the Fourth Kentucky Infantry. In March, 1862, he succeeded to the command of the regiment, and received his commission as brigadier-general of volunteers (in which capacity he had acted for some time) in August, 1864, for his previous gallant conduct at Chickamauga. Soon after he was brevetted major-general. He had a large share in the perils and heroism of the battles of Sherman's army, and at the close of the war was put in command of the Military District of Southwest Georgia, with headquarters at Macon. He remained there till December, 1865, when he resigned his commission and returned to Kentucky, where, after reviewing his studies, he resumed the practice of law, residing on his farm near Paris. Two or three years later he took an active part in establishing the *Louisville Commercial*, as a Republican journal. His exposure during the war and subsequent overwork had greatly impaired his health, and he visited Colorado early in 1873, in the hope of gaining relief. While there the position of United States minister to Bolivia was tendered to him and accepted, in the expectation of benefit to his health from it; but it was too late. He died at La Paz about six months after his arrival there.

April 20.—Bailey, Alexander H., a political leader and jurist, of Oneida County, N. Y., member of Congress, and, at his death, Judge of the Oneida County Court; died at Rome,

N. Y., aged 57 years. He was born at Minisink, Orange County, N. Y., in 1817, and graduated from Princeton College in 1838. He practised law several years, and in 1849 was elected a member of Assembly. He held the office of Judge in Greene County from 1851 to 1855, and was a member of the State Senate from 1861 to 1864. Mr. Bailey succeeded Roscoe Conkling as member of Congress for the twenty-first district when the latter was elected to the United States Senate in 1867, and served in all two terms. He was a County Judge in Oneida County at the time of his death. Mr. Bailey was a Republican, but voted against the impeachment of President Johnson when in Congress.

April 20.—Milligan, Hon. Samuel, Associate Judge of the U. S. Court of Claims; died in Washington, D. C. He was a native of Greenville, Tenn., where he had been a prominent lawyer and a highly-esteemed citizen for many years. He was appointed to the Court of Claims by his old friend President Johnson in 1868.

April 23.—Slicer, Rev. Henry, D. D., a venerable and eloquent Methodist clergyman and author, born at Annapolis, Md., in 1801; died in Baltimore, Md., aged 73 years. He was of English and Scotch descent, and his father was an officer in the War of 1812. He received a good academical education, but was apprenticed to a firm of furniture-painters in Baltimore in 1816, and remained with them till 1821. He joined the Methodist Episcopal Church in 1817, and was diligent in study and active in religious duties throughout his apprenticeship, studying theology during the last two years of it with Bishop Emory. He was licensed to preach in 1821, and appointed to the Harford Circuit, joining the Conference in full connection in 1822. In 1823 he was appointed to the Redstone Circuit, a part of which lay west of the Alleghanies, and involved much hardship. In 1824 he was transferred to the Navy-yard, Washington, and his subsequent appointments were mostly in Eastern Maryland and Virginia. In 1832 he was appointed presiding elder of the Potomac District, and in 1837 elected chaplain of the United States Senate, and twice reëlected. He was stationed at Carlisle, Pa., in 1846, and was again elected chaplain of the Senate, and held the office till 1850. In the following thirteen years he was stationed at Baltimore and Frederick City, was yet again chaplain of the Senate, and was for eight years presiding elder. From 1862 to 1870 he was chaplain of the Seamen's Union Bethel of Baltimore. In 1870 he was again presiding elder of the Baltimore District, though he had been almost fifty years in the ministry. He had been a member of seven of the Quadrennial General Conferences. Throughout his whole life he had abstained strictly from alcoholic liquors and tobacco. He was a very able writer. In 1835 he published an "Appeal on Christian

Baptism," and the next year "A Further Appeal," which went through five or six editions. While chaplain of the Senate the first time, he preached and published in 1838 a notable discourse against dueling, occasioned by the duel fought near Washington between Mr. Graves, of Kentucky, and Mr. Cilley, of Maine, in which the latter was killed. Dr. Slicer's argument was read extensively, and aided powerfully the passage of the act making duels illegal. He received the degree of D. D. from Dickinson College, Carlisle, Pa., in 1860.

April 25.—WALKER, S. L., one of the earliest experimenters in photography in this country, and for many years successful; died in Poughkeepsie, at the age of about 80 years.

April 30.—STRONG, OLIVER SMITH, a well-known philanthropist of New York City; died at the residence of his son-in-law, in Yonkers, N. Y., aged 68 years. From early youth he had been active in all philanthropic measures. He was a director of the Society for the Reformation of Juvenile Delinquents while yet a young man, and for many years its president, and thus the general manager of all matters pertaining to the House of Refuge. The present prosperous condition of that vast charity is largely the result of Mr. Strong's untiring industry and energy. He was also one of the most active and efficient directors of the New York Institution for the Deaf and Dumb. He had made himself thoroughly familiar with the whole subject of deaf-mute education, and, by his earnest efforts before the Legislature, succeeded in procuring for them such aid as to secure their moral and mental elevation. In other departments of philanthropy he was also active and laborious.

May 1.—HEARTT, JONAS C., former Mayor of Troy, N. Y.; died there, aged 81 years. In 1851 he was Speaker of the Assembly.

May 2.—DEMAREST, Rev. WILLIAM, a clergyman of the "True Reformed Dutch Church;" died in New York City, aged 74 years. He was a man of very pronounced and positive opinions, and, when, some years ago, he found, as he believed, that the Reformed (Dutch) Church had departed from some doctrines which he considered essential, he withdrew, and formed with three or four others "The True Reformed Dutch Church." The new denomination did not increase in numbers; but the pure and blameless life of its chief apostle secured for him the respect and esteem of those who did not wholly agree with his views.

May 3.—HALL, Brigadier-General WILLIAM, "New York National Guard;" died in New York City, aged 78 years. He was born in Sparta, N. Y., May 13, 1796. He served in the War of 1812. In his youthful days he commanded the Eighth Regiment of the National Guards, and afterward was elected brigadier-general of the Third Brigade, serving for several years. In 1821 he entered the music-publishing business, which he continued until his death. On the occasion of the "Astor Place

Riots," he commanded the brigade of militia ordered out by the Governor for their suppression, and by his coolness and courage saved the lives of many innocent spectators, while he speedily dispersed the mob. About the year 1863 he retired from the active command of the brigade. During the terms of Governors Fish and King, General Hall was a State Senator.

May 4.—GREEN, Rev. BERIAH, an active and zealous reformer; died at Whitestown, N. Y., aged 80 years. He was a native of New York State; graduated from Middlebury College, Vt., in 1819, and studied for the ministry, with the intention of joining the Presbyterians; but early in life he formulated a creed of his own, differing in many particulars from those of the religious denominations around him. In 1824 he commenced preaching in Brandon, Vt., in 1829 removed to Kennebunk, Me., and in the following year to Hudson, O., accepting the professorship of Sacred Literature in the Western Reserve College. His uncompromising attitude of opposition to slavery, however, rendered his stay there short, and three years later he became president of Oneida Institute. From this time until his death he was a fast friend and zealous coworker with Gerrit Smith, who survived him but a few months. In 1834 he took part in the formation of the American Antislavery Society in Philadelphia, having been chosen president of the convention. His closing address on that occasion was one of great eloquence and fervor. As a speaker and public teacher, whether in the pulpit or on the platform, he possessed marked and rare ability. His language was direct, sinewy, and forcible, his words fitly chosen, and every sentence pervaded with earnestness. He was also an earnest temperance advocate and a zealous promoter of public education. He founded a Manual-Labor School, which was afterward merged into the Whitestown Seminary. At the time of his death he was addressing the Board of Excise in the Town Hall in deprecation of the granting of licenses for the sale of intoxicating drinks, and, after speaking a few moments, died almost instantly. Mr. Green wrote but little for the press; aside from some essays, anniversary addresses, etc., he had only published two volumes, "Miscellanies" and "Sermons and Discourses."

May 4.—MORRIS, EDWARD, a New Jersey journalist and author; died in Burlington, N. J. He was a native of Massachusetts, but long resided in New Jersey, where he had an excellent and profitable market and fruit garden. He was for many years editor and publisher of the *Trenton Gazette*, Trenton, N. J., and was the author of a brilliant and popular little work entitled "Ten Acres Enough," and a larger but not so successful volume, "How to get a Farm."

May 7.—HECKER, JOHN, a wealthy and benevolent citizen of New York; died in that city, aged 62 years. He was of German ancestry, and born in New York, in 1812. In 1835 he opened a large bakery in Rutgers Street, and soon obtained sufficient trade to form the basis of the fortune which he subsequently acquired. In 1842, in connection with his brother, George V. Hecker, he erected the Croton Mills, and carried on the business under the name of Hecker & Brother. In 1850 he was tendered the congressional nomination by the Free-Soil party. In 1857 he distributed large quantities of bread to the poor, repeating this act of charity several winters subsequently; and, at the outbreak of the war, sent a number of cooks to Washington at his own expense, to provide proper food for the soldiers; but, as the Government could not make their services available, they returned to New York. In 1864 he was chosen Inspector of Public Schools, retaining that office until his death. The subject of popular education engrossed much of his attention, and he was the author of a volume entitled "Scientific Basis of Education," which had some circulation among educators in this and other States. At one time he edited the *Churchman*, in which he advanced some very peculiar and impracticable ideas. One of his brothers, after a somewhat varied experience, became one of the Paulist fathers in the Roman Catholic Church; but the subject of this sketch, though a very High Churchman, never showed a disposition to leave the Anglican Church.

May 10.—MARVIN, Rev. E. P., D. D., a Congregationalist clergyman and editor; died in Wellesley, Mass., aged 55 years. He was a native of Seneca County, N. Y. He was for some years editor of the *Boston Recorder*, and, after its absorption in the *Congregationalist*, was also the proprietor. Subsequently he was managing editor of the *Boston Daily News*. He was a man of extensive culture, and was a vigorous writer.

May 11.—PALMER, CORTLANDT, a prominent merchant, railroad president, and real-estate owner, of New York City; died there, aged 74 years. He was a native of Stonington, Conn., and in early boyhood removed to New York, to seek his livelihood. Manfully refusing the proffered assistance of his father, he entered the hardware-store of his brother, in Maiden Lane, a penniless boy, and, when nearly twenty-one years of age, borrowed the necessary capital for entering upon business on his own account. His industry and tact won for him unusual success, enabling him in a short time to pay off his indebtedness and rapidly rise in both wealth and influence. The panic of 1837 proved disastrous to his business firm; but, with his usual forethought, he invested his little capital left from the wreck in real estate well located in the city, and also some tracts of land in the West, to which he added from time to time, until, at his death, his property amounted to several millions. Mr. Palmer was a director and one of the founders of the Safe Deposit Company, and at one time was president of the Stonington Railroad Company. He

was also one of the commissioners for appraising the real estate owned by the city of New York.

May 12.—BLANCHARD, ALBERT C., a prominent Western banker and financier; died in Brookfield, Mass., aged 66 years. He was born in Brookfield in 1808, and entered upon his business-life as a clerk in Springfield. After a few years of faithful service, he removed to the West to engage in business for himself, and finally settled in Richmond, Ind., where the greater part of his life was spent. His financial ability being soon recognized, he was, in 1835, chosen president of the Richmond branch of the State Bank of Indiana, holding that position for a period of twenty years, when the charter expired. When the Bank of the State of Indiana was chartered, he became connected with it, and was always influential in its general management; his influence in financial matters extending throughout the State. He was also one of the pioneers in private banking in the West, establishing, in connection with some others, the Citizens' Bank in 1853, one of the first institutions of its kind in the State.

May 12.—BUCHANAN, FRANKLIN, Admiral, C. S. N., formerly an officer in the United States Navy; died in Talbot County, Md., aged 74 years. He was of Scotch descent, and was born in Baltimore, September 17, 1800, entered the navy as a midshipman, June 28, 1815, served some years at sea, and before reaching the age of twenty-one years served as acting-lieutenant on a cruise to India. In July, 1826, he was in command of the frigate Baltimore, built for the Emperor of Brazil, Lieutenant Buchanan having been ordered to carry her to Rio Janeiro. Upon his return he sailed in the Pacific, part of the time being attached to the Peacock. In 1841 he was promoted to a commander, having charge of the Mississippi, and afterward of the Vincennes. In 1845 he was selected by the Secretary of the Navy for the responsible duty of organizing the Naval Academy in Annapolis. The same year he opened the school as its first superintendent, but in 1847 relinquished the position for the command of the Germantown, in which he took part in the Mexican War, participating in the capture of Vera Cruz and other well-known engagements. In 1852 he commanded the Susquehanna, flagship of Commodore Perry's Japan expedition, which opened China and Japan to the commerce of the world. Having been promoted to be captain, he was in 1859 ordered to the command of the Washington Navy-yard, which position he resigned in April, 1861, and in May, 1861, resigned his commission, which was not accepted, and he was dismissed, to date from April 22d. In September, 1861, he entered the Confederate service as captain. He commanded the Virginia in the attack upon the Federal fleet in Hampton Roads, when the Cumberland was sunk, and the Congress blown up. In this action he was severely wounded, and as a reward was promoted to full admiral and senior officer of the Confederate navy. Subsequently, he was placed in command of the naval defenses of Mobile, and there superintended the construction of the iron-clad ram Tennessee. In August, 1864, he was in command of the Tennessee during the action with the Union fleet in Mobile Bay. He was again wounded, and taken prisoner of war, but was exchanged the February following. Since the war, Admiral Buchanan was for a time president of the Maryland Agricultural College, and afterward was for a few months an agent for a St. Louis life-insurance company.

May 15.—HOYT, EDWIN, a prominent and greatly - esteemed merchant of New York, senior partner of Hoyt, Sprague & Co.; died in that city, aged 70 years. He was born in Stamford, Conn., May 15, 1804, and at the age of nineteen removed to New York to enter upon a clerkship in a dry-goods establishment. In less than a year he commenced business upon his own account, in which he was greatly prospered, and in 1858 the great and well-known firm of Hoyt, Sprague & Co. was formed. Mr. Hoyt was a man of sterling honesty and indomitable energy and perseverance. He was a director of the Manhattan Bank for thirty years, and of the Fourth National Bank since its establishment. He was also a director of the New York Life and Trust Company, and of the National Fire Insurance Company.

May 17.—ROBERTSON, GEORGE, an eminent Kentucky jurist, born in Mercer County, Ky., November 18, 1790; died at Lexington, Ky., in the 84th year of his age. He was educated at Transylvania University, studied law, and was admitted to the bar in 1809. He was a member of Congress from 1817 to 1821; subsequently a member of the State Legislature, and Speaker of the House for four sessions, ending with 1827. In 1828 he was Secretary of State, and the same year chosen Judge of the Court of Appeals, and in 1829 commissioned Chief-Justice of Kentucky. In 1843 he resigned this position, and in 1845 resumed the practice of law in Lexington. For twenty-three years he was Professor of Law in Transylvania University. He was repeatedly tendered diplomatic appointments, such as the mission to Colombia, and that to Peru, as well as other high official positions, but in every instance declined them.

May 20.—DYER, Brigadier and Brevet Major-General ALEXANDER B., U. S. A., Chief of Ordnance since 1864, a brave and meritorious army officer; died in Washington, D. C., aged 57 years. He was born in Virginia, in 1817, graduated from West Point in 1837, served in the artillery at Fortress Monroe, Va., in the Florida War, in 1837–'38, and on ordnance duty at various arsenals 1838–1846; was Chief of Ordnance of the army invading New Mexico, from 1846 to 1848; was engaged at Cañada, Taos, and at Santa Cruz de Rosales, Mex-

ico, receiving the brevets of first-lieutenant and captain for his gallant conduct in these two battles. He was on ordnance duty and in command of various arsenals from 1848 to 1861, and a member of the Ordnance Board in 1859. In 1861 he was appointed to the command of the Springfield Armory, and remained in that position till 1864, greatly extending the manufacture of small-arms demanded for the army; from 1860 to 1863 he was a member of the Ordnance Board, and in 1864 was appointed Chief of Ordnance, and placed in charge of the Ordnance Bureau at Washington, with the rank of brigadier-general in the Regular Army. In March, 1865, he was brevetted Major-General, U. S. A., for faithful, meritorious and distinguished services. For a year previous to his death he had been in bad health.

May 21.—BENNETT, Rev. ALVIN, a venerable and useful Baptist clergyman; died at Freetown, N. Y., aged 91 years. He was born in Mansfield, Conn., in 1783, and, though a sickly and feeble child, developed vigor as he approached manhood, and, having received a good academical education, entered the ministry in 1806, and continued to preach very acceptably for sixty-seven years. He was a pastor at Munson and Wilbraham, Mass., for twenty-six years, and thenceforward preferred to be a stated supply. In 1853 he removed to Central New York, and spent the last twenty-one years of his life in Cortland County, preaching regularly until he had completed his ninetieth year. He was an able preacher, a sound reasoner, very clear in his expositions of doctrine, and greatly beloved in private life.

May 21.—DOOLITTLE, CHARLES HUTCHINS, a New York jurist, one of the Judges of the Supreme Court of the State of New York; lost overboard at sea on his way to Europe, aged 58 years. He was born in Herkimer, N. Y., February 19, 1816, fitted for college at Fairfield Seminary, New York, and graduated from Amherst College in 1836. He studied law at Little Falls and Utica, N. Y., and was admitted to the bar in 1839. For thirty years he practised law in Utica, and had attained a very high rank in his profession among the very able and distinguished members of the Oneida County bar. In 1869 he was elected by a large majority a Judge of the Supreme Court for the Fifth Judicial District, and maintained his high reputation to the close of his life. His judicial abilities were of the highest order, and but for his untimely death he would have undoubtedly attained to the highest position on the bench. His voyage to Europe was undertaken for the improvement of his health, which had become seriously impaired by his judicial labors, and he was lost overboard on the second day out.

May 21.—STEARNS, WILLIAM F., an enterprising and wealthy merchant, formerly engaged in the East India trade, and for some years resident in Bombay; died at Orange, N. J., aged 39 years. He was a son of President Stearns, of Amherst College, and a gentleman of the highest character and standing. While in Bombay he was at the head of the eminent house of Stearns, Hobart & Co., and on his return to the United States he established a house in New York for the same class of trade. He rendered great services to the American Board of Foreign Missions during the late war in managing their foreign exchanges for the salaries and expenditures of their missionaries in the East; built a beautiful chapel for Amherst College, and, as the personal friend and correspondent of Dr. Livingstone, aided largely in fitting out his last expedition.

May 22.—EVANS, Prof. EVAN WILLIAM, a distinguished scholar and college professor; died at Ithaca, N. Y., aged 47 years. He was born near Swansea, in Wales, and, his parents having emigrated to the United States when he was a child, he received his early education in Bradford County, Pa., and graduated from Yale College in 1851. He studied theology for a year at New Haven, and then became principal of Delaware Literary Institute at Franklin, N. Y. In 1855 he was recalled to Yale College as a tutor, but in 1857 was appointed Professor of Natural Philosophy and Astronomy in Marietta College, Ohio, where he remained till 1864. He then occupied himself for three years in mining engineering, and spent one year in European travel. He was the first professor appointed in Cornell University, and occupied the chair of Mathematics in that institution till 1872. His health failing, he resigned, went South for a few months, and returned to Ithaca, where he died of consumption. He bore the reputation of being the best Celtic scholar in this country.

May 22. — WILLIAMS, WILLIAM GRAVES, a Presbyterian clergyman and professor; died in Leavenworth, Kansas, in the 68th year of his age. He was born in Goshen, Mass., November 2, 1806, fitted for college at Sanderson Academy, Ashfield, and graduated from Amherst College in 1834. A large part of his life was spent in teaching, thirteen years at Richmond and Salem, Va.; five years more in St. Mary's, Athens, and Decatur, Ga.; from 1852 to 1862 he was Professor of Natural Sciences, and vice-president of La Grange College, Alabama; from 1862 to 1864 in the service of the U. S. Christian Commission; from September, 1864, to July 27, 1865, a hospital chaplain, stationed at Memphis, and the next year at the General U. S. Hospital and Military Prison at St. John's, Ark. From February, 1867, to his death, he was a resident of Kansas, first as pastor at Marysville, and principal of the Public Graded School there, and subsequently as chaplain of the Home for Friendless Women, at Leavenworth. While teaching in Virginia he studied law, and was admitted to the bar in 1841, but subsequently devoted his leisure hours to theological studies under Drs. Plumer and Hoge,

and was ordained in Georgia in 1848. He was an eminent scholar and a successful teacher.

May 23.—HOMANS, I. SMITH, Sr., a New York publicist, editor of the *Bankers' Magazine* and *Bankers' Almanac*, and author of several works on banking and finance; died in New York City, aged 67 years. He had formerly been a banker, and wrote on financial matters with decided ability.

May 23. — MELLISH, DAVID B., an active politician and member of Congress from New York City; died at the Government Asylum for the Insane, in Washington, aged 43 years. He was born in Oxford, Mass., January 2, 1831, received a common-school and academic education, learned the printing business at the office of the *Worcester* (Mass.) *Spy*, and taught school in Massachusetts, Maryland, and Pennsylvania. He was a proof-reader in New York two years, and while so engaged acquired Pitman's phonographic system of verbatim reporting. In 1860 and 1861 Mr. Mellish was one of the general news and short-hand reporters of the *Tribune*, and was afterward official stenographer to the Metropolitan and subsequently to the Municipal Board of Police in New York City, nearly ten years, meanwhile contributing articles to the press. In 1871 Mr. Mellish was appointed Assistant Appraiser of the port of New York, and held that position until elected in November, 1872, to the Forty-third Congress, receiving a plurality of 773 votes. Mr. Mellish was for a long time a member of the Republican Central Committee, and a prominent supporter of the party in the Seventeenth Assembly District. In the House of Representatives he was a member of the Committee on Invalid Pensions, and took an active interest in the recent legislation on the finances. Mr. Mellish was of a kind, cheerful disposition, and popular among his political associates.

May 23.—NEWTON, WILLOUGHBY, a prominent agriculturist, political leader, and member of Congress from Virginia; died in Westmoreland County, Va., aged about 75 years. He was an active Whig politician from the origin of the Whig party, a member of the Virginia Legislature for many years, and member of Congress from 1843 to 1845. He was also during many years an officer, and for several years president, of the Virginia Agricultural Society, and efficient in developing the agricultural resources of the State.

May 25.—CARLISLE, RICHARD RISLEY, better known as "Professor Risley," a famous performer of feats of strength, agility, and skill; died in the lunatic department of the Blockley Almshouse, in Philadelphia, aged 60 years. He had run a singularly successful career, his exhibitions being really wonderful, and bringing in large sums of money; but when he relied upon the help of others to interest the public his fortune deserted him, and finally, after repeated and heavy losses, poverty, insanity, and death came. He was born in Salem, N.

J., and at an early age showed a taste for a public exhibition of his powers as a gymnast in a traveling circus, in which he was announced as "Prof. Richard Risley, athlete, and performer on the flute," a title which he retained through life. In 1838 he made his first appearance in Philadelphia, at Welsh's Circus. He trained his two sons, John and Harry, while yet very young, to perform with him, and the "Risley family" became famous and rich. An engagement at Drury Lane, and other theatres in London, in 1845, and a performance before Prince Albert and the Queen, at Windsor Castle, made the professor still more popular. After receiving badges and presents from the Queen, he and his boys went to France, and then to St. Petersburg. Here he distinguished himself as a marksman with the rifle, winning sixteen rifles as prizes. In the Russian capital he also excelled all his competitors in skating. He returned to London, and at a dinner given to him wagered that he was the best shot, the toughest wrestler, the longest jumper, the farthest thrower of the hammer, and the finest billiard-player in the city. His boast was on the next day shown not to be an idle one, for, though London's best sporting-men came out against him, he hit the bull's eye with the rifle a majority of times, vanquished the wrestler, made a standing jump of thirteen feet one inch, and gave the London hammer-thrower ten feet and beat him fifteen inches. But the wager in regard to the billiard-match seems to have been the first step in the downward course from the summit of his fame and wealth. The well-known English billiard-champion, Roberts, was pitted against him, and he lost. He at once came to this country, sought out our best American billiard-player, Andrew Stark, and carried him back to match him against his antagonist, Roberts, for heavy wagers, all of which he lost, amounting to $30,000. He returned to this country, bought a fine place near Chester, Pa., and sent his sons to college. But his former active life had unfitted him for that of a country gentleman, and he again took to the theatrical business, and in its prosecution finally spent his whole fortune. The importation of the Roussel Sisters and ballet from France, and other European actors, met with considerable loss. In 1848 he visited Japan, and secured, for performance in this country, at a cost of $100,000, the first royal Japanese troupe of acrobats and wrestlers. Every attempt to return to public favor failed, and in 1870 his last venture was made with some English actors, who deserted him and left him to pay all expenses.

May 26.—ANTHONY, CHARLES L., a New York merchant, manufacturer, and underwriter, a native of Providence, R. I.; died in New York City, in the 55th year of his age. He had been largely engaged in the manufacture and sale of woolen goods, at first in the firm of Anthony, Whittemore & Clark, and after-

ward of Anthony & Hale, and was also a special partner with Whittemore, Peet, Post & Co., a member of the Chamber of Commerce, a director of the New York Life Insurance Company, the Fourth National Bank, and the Guardian Fire Insurance Company; a member of the Union League and Knickerbocker Clubs.

May 30.—FLEMING, General ROBERT, a leading lawyer of Lycoming County, Pa.; died at Williamsport, Pa., aged about 80 years. He was the senior member of the Lycoming bar, and had been a State Senator and a member of the Constitutional Convention of 1837–'38.

May 30.—SPRAGUE, HAVILAH MOWRY, M.D., an able and successful physician of New York; died at Fordham, N. Y., aged 39 years. He was born in Scotland, Conn., July 4, 1835, fitted for college at West Killingly Academy, graduated from Amherst College in 1858 and from the University Medical College, New York, in 1861. He became by examination a junior walker in the New York Hospital in the winter of 1861, but he resigned this position at the breaking out of the civil war and became an assistant surgeon in the Regular Army, passing No. 2 in a long list of successful applicants. He distinguished himself on the field of battle, under General Lyon, by his coolness in operating under fire. After this Dr. Sprague had charge of a hospital on the Mississippi River, connected with General Grant's army, and at Fort Schuyler. He resigned his position in the army at the close of the war, and entered private practice at West Farms, and subsequently at Fordham. He was also physician to the "Home for Invalids," at West Farms, from 1866 to 1870, and, from 1869 to his death, attending-physician of the "Home of Rest for Consumptives," at Tremont, N. Y. Dr. Sprague was no ordinary man. He had greatly endeared himself to the community in which he lived, and the profession in New York mourned him as a gifted, accomplished, and worthy associate.

May 31.—JAUDON, SAMUEL, a distinguished banker and financier; died in Philadelphia, aged 80 years. He was the cashier of the United States Bank in 1832, and under his management it attained great prosperity and influence. After the removal of the deposits he established the United States Bank of Pennsylvania, and went to London to represent its interests there. His reputation for financial ability was very great for many years. After the failure of this bank, in 1845, he returned to the United States, and had since lived in retirement.

May 31.—PEARSON, ISAAC GREEN, an eminent merchant and underwriter of New York; died in New York City, aged 87 years. He was born in Boston, but came to New York in early life, and was for many years in business in South Street. He was the first secretary of the Merchants' Exchange, a prominent member of the Chamber of Commerce, one of the founders and a life-long director of the Mutual Life Insurance Company, vice-president of the Relief Fire Insurance Company, and active in all business matters.

June 4.—MENDENHALL, GEORGE, M. D., an eminent physician, professor, and philanthropist; died in Cincinnati, Ohio, aged 60 years. He was born in Sharon, Pa., in 1814, of Quaker parentage, studied medicine under Dr. Benjamin Stanton, at Salem, Ohio, and was so proficient as to receive his diploma in Philadelphia before he had attained the age of twenty-one. In 1843 he settled in Cincinnati, where he henceforth resided, enjoying in due time extensive practice, and holding the first rank in his profession. He became noted especially for his success in obstetrics, and was successively professor of that branch of medical science at the Miami and Ohio Medical Colleges. Dr. Mendenhall was a Fellow of the Royal Obstetrical Society of England, and was president of the National Medical Association of this country. Dr. Mendenhall was a man of great benevolence and philanthropy, and at the organization of the Sanitary Commission, at the commencement of the late civil war, he was one of the "associates," and president of the Cincinnati branch of the Commission. In this capacity he rendered great and valuable services to the work of the Commission, and, seconded by the energetic and judicious assistance of his estimable wife, who was president of the Ladies' Soldiers' Aid Society of that city, he made the Cincinnati branch one of the most efficient auxiliaries of the Commission. After the close of the war the attention of Dr. and Mrs. Mendenhall was attracted to other philanthropic work in the city of their adoption, and their charitable labors will be long remembered.

June 12.—McNAUGHTON, JAMES, M. D., an eminent physician and medical professor; died in Paris, France, aged 78 years. He was of Scotch descent, and born in Perthshire, Scotland, in 1796. He was prepared for the university at Kenmure College, and graduated from the medical department of the University of Edinburgh in 1816. The following year he came to this country and entered upon the practice of his profession in Albany, N. Y. Subsequently he was chosen professor in the Medical College of Fairfield, Herkimer County, N. Y., which position he held for a period of twenty years. In 1840 he was elected Professor of the Theory and Practice of Medicine in the Albany Medical College, where he remained until his death. During his connection with this latter institution it is stated that he never missed one week of lectures, so thoroughly devoted was he to his work, and at the time of his death he was the oldest teacher of medicine living, having lectured for fifty-three years, and delivered seventy courses of lectures. Dr. McNaughton served for a time as president of the Albany County Medical Society, was a governor of the medical department of Union University, and president of the medical and

surgical staff of the Albany Hospital. He was traveling in Europe with his family and had reached the railroad depot in Paris, preparatory to starting for Geneva, Switzerland, when he was taken with faintness and survived but a few hours.

June 18.—McKIM, JAMES MILLER, a Presbyterian clergyman and famous antislavery leader; died at West Orange, N. J., aged 64 years. He was born in 1810, studied at Dickinson College, Pa., and Princeton College, N. J., and entered the ministry as pastor of a church at Womelsdorf, N. J., in 1835. A few years previous, a copy of Garrison's "Thoughts on Colonization" fell into his hands, the perusal of which made him an abolitionist. He served as a delegate in the convention which formed the Antislavery Society, and from that time the objects of his ministry and of the Society became inseparable. In October, 1836, he left the pulpit to devote all his time and energies to the cause of emancipation, accepting a lecturing agency under the auspices of the Society. In the summer of 1834 he delivered addresses in Pennsylvania, and although often subjected to obloquy, and even danger from personal violence, he knew no fear, neither was his zeal in any degree abated. His theological views having undergone some change, he was led to sever his connection with the Presbyterian Church and its ministry, and in 1840 removed to Philadelphia and became the publishing agent of the Pennsylvania Antislavery Society. His principal duties, at first, were the management of the *Pennsylvania Freeman*, which he also edited for a short time, after the retirement of John G. Whittier. His duties were subsequently much enlarged, and his position changed to that of corresponding secretary of the Society, in which capacity he acted for a quarter of a century as a general manager of the affairs of the Society, taking an active part in the national as well as local antislavery work. The *Pennsylvania Freeman* was consolidated with the *National Anti-slavery Standard* in 1854, subsequently to which time he acted as a correspondent of the latter journal. Mr. McKim's position and labors brought him in constant contact with the operations of the "underground railroad," and he was frequently connected with the slave cases which came before the courts, especially after the passage of the Fugitive-slave Law of 1851. In the winter of 1862, immediately after the capture of Port Royal, he procured the calling of a public meeting of the citizens of Philadelphia, to consider and provide for the wants of the 10,000 slaves who had been suddenly liberated. One of the results of this meeting was the organization of the Philadelphia Port Royal Relief Committee. By request he visited the Sea Islands, accompanied by his daughter, and on his return made a report which served his associates as a basis of operations, and which was republished extensively in this country and abroad. He continued his labors, however, became an earnest advocate of the enlistment of colored troops, and as a member of the Union League aided in the establishment of Camp William Penn, and the recruitment there of eleven regiments. In November, 1863, the Port Royal Relief Committee was enlarged into the Pennsylvania Freedmen's Relief Association, and Mr. McKim was made its corresponding secretary. In this capacity he traveled extensively, and worked laboriously in the effort to establish schools at the South, and organize public sentiment at the North for their support. He was connected from 1865 to 1869 with the American Freedman's Union Commission, and labored earnestly to promote general and impartial education at the South. In July, 1869, the Commission having accomplished all that seemed possible at the time, it decided unanimously, on Mr. McKim's motion, to disband. Mr. McKim then retired to private life, his health being greatly impaired, and passed the remainder of his days in repose.

June 13.—PARRIS, VIRGIL D., formerly acting-Governor of Maine, member of Congress, and connected with the Treasury Department; died in Kittery, Me. He was born in Maine, educated for the law, and in 1831 was Assistant Secretary for the State Senate. From 1833 to 1839 he was a member of the Legislature of his State; was a Representative in Congress from 1838 to 1841; a State Senator in 1842 and 1843; U. S. Marshal for Maine from 1844 to 1848; U. S. Special Mail Agent from 1853 to 1856; and subsequently held the office of Naval Store-keeper at Kittery, Me. When in the State Senate he was president *pro temp.*, and for a short time Acting-Governor of the State.

June 13.—STUDLEY, HIRAM, one of the original founders of Studley's Baggage Express; died in New York City, aged 59 years. About 1848 a brother, Warren Studley, started the first Baggage Express of New York, and, the speculation proving a good one, he induced his brother Hiram to come on from Boston, and together they started Studley's Express in Canal Street, near Broadway. Subsequently they obtained the exclusive privilege of conveying the baggage of passengers by the New Haven and Harlem Railroads. After the death of Warren Studley the business was sold out to Dodd, but was continued under the old name. Subsequently Hiram opened a livery-stable in the upper part of the city. He was a man of strict integrity and personal popularity.

June 14. — WALKER, RICHARD WILDE, a prominent political leader in Alabama; died in Huntsville, aged 51 years. In 1855 he was Speaker of the House of Representatives of Alabama, Judge of the Supreme Court from 1859 to 1863, and Confederate Senator from his State from 1863 to 1865. He was a man of extensive legal attainments, of wide political knowledge, and of most unblemished character.

June 15.—JACK, Captain CHARLES EDWARD, of the U. S. Navy-yard, Brooklyn; died in

East New York, aged 43 years. He was a son of the late Colonel E. Jack, a prominent Brooklyn lawyer. Previous to the war he was the mate of a merchant-vessel plying between Liverpool and New York. At the opening of the conflict he enlisted in the navy as ensign, speedily rising to the position of master's mate. He was attached to Admiral Porter's squadron, and took part in the bombardment of Forts Jackson and St. Philip, and in the taking of New Orleans. At the close of the war he re-entered the merchant service, in which he remained till 1872, when he was appointed Captain of the Watch at the Brooklyn Navy-yard.

June 16. — DICKINSON, EDWARD, LL. D., member of Congress from Massachusetts; died in Boston, aged 71 years. He was the son of the Hon. Samuel Fowler Dickinson, one of the founders of Amherst College, and was born in that town, January 1, 1803. From Amherst Academy he entered Yale College in his sophomore year, and graduated in the class of 1823; studied law for two years with his father, and after one year in the Law School in Northampton, opened in 1826 an office in Amherst, where he continued in practice until his death. As early as 1835 he was elected Treasurer of Amherst College, and held that office until a few months previous to his death, when he resigned, and was succeeded by his son. In 1838 and 1839, and again in 1874, he was chosen a member of the Massachusetts Assembly, and in 1842 and 1843 of the State Senate. In 1846 and 1847 he was one of the Governor's Council, and from 1853 to 1855 a Representative in Congress. Having been elected to the State Legislature in 1873, for the main purpose of securing to the town the advantages of the Massachusetts Central Railroad, he prepared and delivered an able speech in the interests of that railroad in connection with the Hoosac Tunnel, and died on the evening of that day.

June 16.—LEE, Colonel JAMES, a New York merchant; died in that city, aged 79 years. He was of Scottish birth, and engaged mainly in the Scotch trade. For many years he was connected with the Society Library, and it was mainly through his instrumentality that the Washington Monument, in Union Square, was erected.

June 17. — BUTLER, FRANCIS, an eminent scholar and author, who, from his love for the canine race, had become a dog-trainer and fancier; died in Brooklyn, of hydrophobia, aged 64 years. He was a native of England, and his education was of a superior order. He was an accomplished linguist, and had been connected with several educational institutions as a Professor of Languages, and was also the author of a work upon French and German literature. Some years since he went into the business of training, and buying and selling dogs of the choicest breeds, his ability in controlling and taming them being remarkable; and a work on "Dog-Training," which he published, is regarded as a standard authority on the subject. He was a genial, courteous gentleman, and his death, from the bite of a dog which he had but recently undertaken to treat, was a great loss to the community. ,

June 17.—STEVENSON, Major ——, a Confederate officer, General Forrest's chief quartermaster during the war, and since, collector of Internal Revenue for Northern Mississippi ; died at Holly Springs, Miss.

June 17.—WATROUS, JOHN CHARLES, late U. S. District Judge for the Eastern District of Texas; died at Baltimore, aged 68 years. Judge Watrous was born at Colchester, Conn., in 1806. He was the son of Dr. John Watrous, an eminent physician, State Senator, and Lieutenant-Governor of Connecticut. The son was fitted for college at Bacon Academy, Colchester, and graduated from Union College in 1828. He afterward studied law, and settled in Tennessee, and subsequently in Alabama, where he attained a high reputation for his legal knowledge and his judicial ability. He emigrated to Texas about 1842, and was Attorney-General of the Republic of Texas. In 1849 or 1850 he was appointed, by President Taylor, District Judge of the Eastern District of Texas. During the next ten years he had become known as one of the ablest judges in the South; but an effort was made by some of his enemies and among the number the late General Sam Houston, to procure his impeachment before the U. S. Senate. He was tried on their charges of impeachment, and triumphantly acquitted. During the war he was not suffered to act as a judge, as he was a strong Unionist; but on the proclamation of peace he resumed his seat, and presided with great ability over the District Court until the close of 1869, when he was disabled by paralysis, and resigned, removing to Baltimore, and, so far as his infirm health would permit, resuming the practice of his profession. During the war he lost heavily by his fidelity to the national cause.

June 18.—BABCOCK, JAMES F., a Connecticut journalist and political leader; died in New Haven, Conn., aged 65 years. He was a native of Southeastern Connecticut, or Rhode Island, but entered the journalistic ranks at an early age, and in 1830, at the age of twenty-one years, became editor of the *New Haven Palladium*, at that time a weekly paper, but which very soon began to issue a daily edition also. He continued to be the editor of that paper for thirty-one years, and being an active Whig, and an energetic speaker and manager as well as a vigorous writer, he soon became the Warwick of his party in the State. Apparently not desirous of office for himself, he controlled the party nominations for many years, and, though hostile to the Free-Soil party at its inception, he finally gave it a hearty welcome in 1854, in his brilliant and long-remembered leader, headed, "Give us your hand, Honest John Boyd." He retained his prestige with the Republican party for some years, took an active part in furthering the national cause during

the war, and, shortly after his resignation as editor of the *Palladium*, was appointed, by President Lincoln, Collector of the Port of New Haven. He retained that office under President Johnson, whose policy he supported ; but, after the rupture between the President and the Republicans, Mr. Babcock acted with the Democratic party, and was nominated by them for Congress, in the second district, after an angry and excited contest, but was defeated by Mr. S. W. Kellogg, the Republican nominee. He was nominated and elected by the Democrats to the State Legislature in 1873, and was appointed, by Governor Ingersoll, chairman of the Labor Commission while a member of that body. The Legislature of 1874 elected him Judge of the Police Court of New Haven, and he had entered upon his duties a few days before his death.

June 19.—AUDUBON, Mrs. LUCY BAKEWELL, widow of the late John J. Audubon; died at the residence of her sister-in-law, in Kellyville, Ky., aged 88 years. She was born in England, of an excellent family, and came to America with her father when not more than twelve years of age. They settled on the Schuylkill River, near Philadelphia, Mr. Bakewell's estate joining that of young Audubon. A friendship sprang up between the two families, and in April, 1808, Lucy Bakewell, then, twenty-two years of age, became the wife of John J. Audubon. She left her father's house at once with her husband, and began a remarkable and eventful career, by a journey through Pennsylvania to Pittsburg, and down the Ohio River in a flat-boat to Louisville. From that time onward, for more than thirty years, she had no permanent home, yet her spirits never flagged, weariness never produced discontent, isolation from friends never chilled the warmth of her affections, nor did the independent life to which she was compelled produce selfishness and misanthropy. She had given her heart with her hand to her husband, and she identified herself entirely with his pursuits, his interests, and his hopes. She accompanied him in his wanderings, encouraged him in trials, and, when misfortune overtook him, she bent to the task of relieving him with an active intellect and a strong will. In order to obtain money to educate their children and leave him free to pursue his studies in natural history, she took a place as governess in a family in New Orleans, and afterward in Natchez. When her husband was anxious to go to Europe, in order to perfect himself in the use of oil-colors, and could not for lack of funds, she established a family-school at Bayou Sara, and earned the needful money while she also educated her own children. When, in the face of many obstacles, and contrary to the advice of his friends who regarded him as a madman, Audubon decided to pursue ornithology as a profession, his wife determined that his genius should have the opportunity which it craved. She gave him not only words of encouragement, but devoted several thousand dollars which she had earned by teaching, to help forward the publication of his drawings and insure his success. Twice she went with her husband upon his voyages to England, and traveled with him while he obtained subscribers to his great work. For years she bore the pain of long separation patiently, stimulating his enthusiasm by her letters, while she provided for their children by her labors, and rejoiced in the triumph which she had aided him to achieve without a thought of the struggles and privations which it had cost her. And when the keen eye that had caught so quickly each shade of the plumage of birds grew dim, and the dexterous fingers could no longer ply the pencil, when "silent, patient sorrow filled a broken heart," and paralysis had weakened body and mind, then for years, in the beautiful home which their mutual efforts had provided, his wife read to him and walked with him, she nursed and tended him with untiring faithfulness and Christian serenity till the last moment of recognition and departure came together. After the death of her husband, Madame Audubon did not sink into inactivity and despondency. She interested herself in the children for whose training she had done so much, and gave to children's children the benefit of a regular and systematic education. Her days were filled with active efforts for the good of others, and no rust dimmed the mind to which intellectual activity had become a constant delight. She loved to read, to study, and to teach; she knew how to gain the attention of the young, and to fix knowledge in their minds. "If I can hold the mind of a child to a subject for five minutes, he will never forget what I teach him," she once remarked; and acting upon this principle she was as successful at threescore and ten years in imparting knowledge as she had been in early life when she taught in Louisiana. Madame Audubon interested herself in all that pertained to the welfare of the neighborhood where she lived. Although it was not without a pang that she saw her sylvan home invaded by the growth of the city, and all old associations broken up, she did not treat those who came to live near her as strangers. She had a large and generous heart, and with her husband always exercised a liberal hospitality, and a hearty kindness toward all. The poor had reason to bless her bounty, and the rich were her debtors for courtesies and attentions which they could not claim, but which she freely gave. Madame Audubon had none of that petty pride which sometimes stains a great name, and which so often shows the low birth of ostentatious millionaires. In prosperity and adversity she was equally sincere and humble, a friend to all worthy people; a woman respected for her strong character and loved for her genuine and warm heart. The death of her husband was at length followed by the death of both of her sons, who had been the

collaborators and traveling companions of their father, the fortune which had rewarded their mutual efforts was reduced by unfortunate investments, and many trials and burdens pressed upon her declining years; but she met her trials without shrinking and bore her burdens patiently. Cheered by the society of the intelligent and the good, with undiminished fondness for intellectual pursuits, and still surrounded by descendants who honored and loved her, she occupied her time in preparing a biography of her husband, which is at once a noble tribute to his memory and a monument of her own literary ability and industry. It is a most fascinating volume, and one which no one who reads it can fail to prize and enjoy. The last years of Audubon's life had been saddened by the loss of sight, and partial blindness now cut her off from reading. But as she had been eyes to the blind, so now a granddaughter with filial affection supplied her loss of sight, and read to her for hours from books of travel and valuable literature, with daily portions of the word of God. It had always been her wish to die without long illness, and the wish was granted. Taken ill Monday June 16th, she was at rest on Thursday. So gently did she fall asleep that her granddaughter hardly knew that she was dying till she ceased to breathe.

June 20.—CHENEY, CHARLES, one of the brothers of the great American silk manufacturing firm of Cheney Brothers; died at his home in South Manchester, Conn., aged 70 years. He was born in what is now South Manchester, Conn., in 1804, and was the third of the eight sons of Mr. George Cheney. Five of these eight brothers still survive, all remarkable for artistic taste and love of the beautiful, as well as for their concord and harmony in all their enterprises and in their relations to each other and to their workmen. Charles Cheney went to Tolland as clerk in a store when he was about fourteen, and before he was of age migrated to Providence and engaged in mercantile business on his own account, having Solomon Pitkin for a partner. In 1836 or 1837 he removed to Ohio, and established himself as a farmer at Mount Healthy, near Cincinnati, where he remained about eleven years, and during that period became strongly interested in the antislavery movement. About the time of his removal to Ohio, Mr. Ward Cheney and some of the other brothers had started a small silk-factory at their old home in South Manchester. They had many obstacles to contend with, and the factory was suspended after three or four years, but was revived again in 1841, and with somewhat better success, and in 1847 Charles Cheney joined his brothers in the undertaking. During the next twenty-seven years, till his death, the brothers worked with the utmost harmony in building up, by slow but sure steps, the great industry, which, with its mills at South Manchester and Hartford, is now one of the most conspicuous of American manufactures. The

model manufacturing village of South Manchester, built up entirely by these brothers, a
"rural paradise for workmen," as it has been
well called, with its cottage homes, its churches,
public halls, schools, and libraries, is a nobler
monument to their practical benevolence, their
intense faith in human brotherhood, and their
attachment to those who for a generation have
been their faithful employés, than pillar, statue,
or storied pile, since it has developed their rare
culture, their sweet charity and philanthropy,
and has offered a practical example of the harmony which may exist between employers and
workmen. Here all the brothers had their
homes, and they sought to surround them with
artistic beauty and with the sweet atmosphere
of affection and sympathy. In all these movements of business, artistic taste, or philanthropy, Charles Cheney shared most heartily with
his brothers, every thing being done by the harmonious concurrence of all. It fell to his lot
in the management of their business to spend
a considerable portion of his time in Hartford,
where they had also extensive manufactures;
and he came to be considered as in some sort
a citizen of that city; and one of its most eloquent and accomplished writers said of him, at
his death: "He was in the best sense a public
man, without being an office-holder (except for
a term or two in the Legislature), and in fact
always shrinking from any public display. He
took the warmest interest in political affairs,
especially in the moral questions, and his name
and purse were always at the service of the
cause of humanity. He was an abolitionist
when it was singular to be one, and, in all the
drama of the war and the preparation for it, he
was one of the wise whose counsel was sought,
one of the liberal to whom appeal was never
made in vain. Whenever aid was sought for
any thing worthy, the name of Charles Cheney
was sure to be one of the first thought of. He
was full of charity and toleration for all men."

June 20.—DERBY, GEORGE, M.D., an eminent
sanitarian, secretary of the Massachusetts State
Board of Health since January, 1866; died in
Boston, aged 55 years. He was a native of Salem, born in 1819, and entered Harvard College
in 1834, but in consequence of ill health left in
1836. He was subsequently admitted to a
degree. He graduated from Harvard Medical
School as M. D. in 1843, and after a short time
commenced the practice of his profession in
Boston, giving great attention to sanitary science. He had acquired a fine practice and a
high reputation by his writings on sanitary subjects in the sixteen or seventeen years which
followed, when in September, 1861, he volunteered and was commissioned surgeon of the
Twenty-third Regiment Massachusetts Volunteers. His services not only to that regiment,
but to the health and sanitary condition of the
army, were exceedingly valuable, and the Government recognized them by commissioning
him, even after his health had compelled him to
leave the army, as surgeon of volunteers, with

brevet rank of lieutenant-colonel. On his return home he at once set about the creation of
a State Board of Health, and notwithstanding
many adverse influences he succeeded in effecting its organization in 1865, and had acted as
its secretary since January, 1866. His eight
registration reports were full of interest, and
exceeded in ability any documents of the kind
ever published. In 1871 he was appointed
Professor of Hygiene in Harvard College, and
held that position till his death.

June 20.—MADDIN, Rev. THOMAS, D. D.,
an eminent and venerable clergyman of the
Methodist Episcopal Church, South; died in
Nashville, Tenn., after a brief illness, at the age
of 80 years.

June 20.—MORSE, Colonel HENRY BAGG, U.
S. Volunteers, a gallant soldier of the late war,
and subsequently Circuit Judge in Arkansas;
died at Eaton, N. Y., aged 38 years. He
was born in Eaton, July 2, 1836, received a
good academical education, and assisted his
father in his large farming and manufacturing
enterprises. In 1862 he was authorized by
Governor Morgan to raise a company for the
Chenango and Madison regiment, and by the
13th of August, had enlisted one hundred and
thirty men. He was commissioned captain
at once and promoted in three weeks to be
major and lieutenant-colonel. His regiment
was sent to the Department of the Gulf. Here
he soon distinguished himself for bravery and
military ability; he was active at Bisland and
Cedar Creek; led the assault on Port Hudson,
June 14, 1863, where he was severely wounded,
and subsequently was in command, at Sabine
Cross-Roads, of a brigade; and for his gallant
conduct there was brevetted brigadier-general.
He was also one of the Board of Prison Inspectors for the Department of the Gulf at New
Orleans, and acting chief-quartermaster of the
Nineteenth Army Corps during the latter part
of his term of service. At the close of the war
he studied law for two years in the office of
Pratt, Mitchell & Brown, of Syracuse. Going
thence to Arkansas, he arrived there during
the time that State was under martial law.
He held the office of revenue collector, and,
upon the organization of the State government,
he was appointed Probate Judge, and afterward Circuit Judge, which office he held for
nearly six years, and was much commended
by the papers of that State for his fairness and
ability. His health failing, he returned to his
friends in Eaton in the summer of 1873, and
remained until March, 1874. He reached Arkansas in the heat of the Brooks-Baxter excitement, and took an active part, as heretofore, in State matters, being chairman of the
Jefferson County Republican Committee, but
his strength was too greatly taxed, and he was
compelled to return North again, reaching
home on the 3d instant, to learn the sudden
death of his mother, and very soon to follow
her.

June 21.—JACOBY, Rev. L. S., a German

Methodist clergyman, journalist, presiding elder, and author, of Jewish extraction; died at St. Louis, in the 61st year of his age. He was born in Old Strelitz, Mecklenburg, October 21, 1813. His parents were of Levitical and priestly descent, highly intelligent, and of most affectionate disposition. His early education was very thorough, especially in the ancient languages. In 1835 he united with the Lutheran Church, and, having studied medicine, came to the United States in 1839, and settled as a physician in Cincinnati, but after a time devoted himself to teaching. In the beginning of 1841 he united with the Methodist Episcopal Church, and almost immediately entered the ministry. In August of that year he was sent by Bishop Morris to St. Louis, to establish the first German Methodist mission. His success was very great, and in 1849, at his own request, he was sent by the Missionary Board to Bremen, to found a mission there. Here he labored incessantly, filling the various positions of pastor, presiding elder, editor, publishing agent, and superintendent, and all with the greatest success, for the space of twenty-two years. Early in 1872 he returned to the United States, and was stationed in St. Louis. In 1873 he was made presiding elder of the St. Louis District; but his health soon began to fail, and from January, 1874, to his death he was a great but very patient sufferer. He had published numerous tracts, sermons, and essays, both in German and English.

June 29.—PERKINS, HENRY A., an eminent banker and financier of Hartford, Conn., for more than forty years president of the Hartford Bank; died in that city. In all matters of practical finance Mr. Perkins was regarded as the highest authority in his city or State.

June 29. — WARREN, CHARLES HENRY, a prominent jurist and railroad-officer of Massachusetts; died in Plymouth, Mass., in the 76th year of his age. He was born in Plymouth, September 29, 1798. He fitted for college at Sandwich Academy, and graduated from Harvard College in 1817. He studied law in Plymouth, was admitted to the bar in 1819, and, after practising there a year, removed to New Bedford. There he was United States District Attorney for the Southern District of Massachusetts, 1832 to 1839; Judge of the Court of Common Pleas, 1839 to 1844. He removed to Boston in the latter year, and practised his profession till 1846, when he was elected president of the Boston & Providence Railroad, which office he held till 1867, when he retired to Plymouth, where he passed the closing years of his life.

June —.—PARMELEE, THEODORE N., a venerable editor, correspondent, and author; died at Branford, Conn., aged 70 years. He had been editor of the old *Middlesex* (Conn.) *Gazette*, Washington correspondent of the *New York Herald*, in the days of Van Buren, and later in life an editor of the *Buffalo Commercial*. Being clever, affable, and sagacious, he

became a favorite with the leading men of his time, and during the Tyler Administration was on intimate terms at the White House. His "Recollections of an Old Stager," contributed during recent years to the magazines, were deemed entertaining, the author's mind being well stored with the political history of the country anterior to the war. Mr. Parmelee was the confidential friend and secretary of the late Dean Richmond, and enjoyed the esteem of many leading men.

July 1.—UPTON, GEORGE BRUCE, a distinguished manufacturer and shipping-merchant of Boston, born in Eastport, Me., October 11, 1804; died in Boston, at the age of 70 years. Losing his father when he was but a year old, young Upton's childhood and youth were spent in Billerica, Mass. In the excellent academy there he had nearly fitted for Harvard College, when, at the age of fourteen, he decided to go into business, in preference to taking a collegiate course. He spent nearly three years in Boston, and then went as confidential clerk to a dry-goods house in Nantucket, in which, at the age of twenty-one, he became a partner. The new firm built ships, engaged in the sperm-whale fishery, manufactured oils and candles, and carried on a large and thriving business till 1845, when Mr. Upton, being satisfied that the trade of Nantucket had reached and passed its culminating point, decided to go elsewhere and enter upon those extended business operations for which he was so well adapted. While in Nantucket he had been twice a member of the General Court and three times State Senator. He removed first to Manchester, N. H., and established the Manchester Print-Works, and the next year took up his residence in Boston. In that city he was treasurer for eight years of the Michigan Central Railroad, and was largely engaged in commerce, building numerous clipper-ships for the California and Pacific trade, entered into the banking business, and, forming no partnerships, took upon his own shoulders an amount of business which few men could have transacted without breaking down; yet, so perfect was his system and so completely was he master of all his business, that he was never hurried or worried, and always found ample time for rest and recreation. He was very active and patriotic during the war, and, though long past the age of military service, kept a substitute in the army, contributed largely for bounties to recruits, aided in all efforts for the relief of sick and wounded soldiers, and did all in his power toward bringing the piratical cruisers of the ocean to destruction. He was warmly in favor of reconstruction, but protested most vigorously and ably against the Clarendon-Johnson Treaty in regard to the Alabama; and, when Earl Russell sought to traverse the averments of that petition of "the stern republican, Upton," Mr. Upton replied in an "open letter to Earl Russell," which effectually nullified the statesman's criticisms. At the great fire of 1872 in Boston, Mr. Upton, though a heavy loser, was the first to organize measures of relief for the other sufferers, and contributed largely to the fund for this purpose. His death was caused by internal cancer.

July 7.—MYERS, Lieutenant-Colonel and Brevet Brigadier-General FREDERICK, U. S. A., Deputy Quartermaster-General of the Department of Arizona; died at Santa Fé, New Mexico, aged 49 years. General Myers was a native of Connecticut, and appointed from that State to the Military Academy at West Point in 1841. He graduated in 1846, and the same year was commissioned second-lieutenant of the Fifth Infantry, and entered into service immediately in the Mexican War, and for good conduct was promoted to a first-lieutenancy in October, 1848. He served with his regiment on frontier duty in Texas till January 1, 1855, when he was made quartermaster of his regiment, and in August, 1856, promoted to the rank of captain on the staff and assistant-quartermaster in New Mexico. He served in that Territory, in Oregon and Washington Territory, till the summer of 1861, when he was recalled to the East, and from September, 1861, to April, 1862, was engaged in organizing the Ohio Volunteers; and from that time till the close of the war was on active duty as chief-quartermaster and deputy chief-quartermaster in the Department of the Rappahannock, in the Third Army Corps, in the Army of the Potomac; and from April 1, 1863, to February 1, 1865, in the Department of the Northwest, and subsequently in the Military Division and the Department of Missouri to October 1, 1865. During this period he had been promoted to the staff rank of major and lieutenant-colonel, and on the 13th of March, 1855, had been brevetted lieutenant-colonel, colonel, and brigadier-general U. S. A., for faithful and meritorious services. Since October, 1865, he had been engaged in settling quartermasters' accounts at St. Louis, on a board of examination at Washington for several months, on a tour of inspection of military posts in the Department of Missouri for two months, as quartermaster at headquarters of the Department of Missouri, on special duty at Chicago, and subsequently as deputy quartermaster-general of the Department of Arizona.

July 8.—COWDIN, Colonel ROBERT, First Regiment Massachusetts State militia, a brave officer of Massachusetts troops in the late war, who in June, 1861, marched his regiment through Baltimore to Washington, and distinguished himself at the battle of Blackburn's Ford, in July of that year, by his coolness and fearlessness. He was well known and greatly esteemed by all parties in Boston.

July 8.—RANDALL, Captain HENRY, a veteran steamship commander and inventor; died in New York City, aged 72 years. He was born at Berlin, N. Y., in 1802, and from a boy exhibited a great fondness for the sea, and a decided talent for navigation. He became a seaman, and rapidly advanced from an obscure position on shipboard to a high rank, and, while yet a young man, became the commander of the steamboat Empire, then plying on Lake Erie. A few years later he was placed in command of the steamship Northerner, one of the first steamers ever dispatched from New York to the Pacific coast. He was afterward a resident of New York City, and in 1850 became commander of the steamship Yankee Blade, in the California trade. He at length settled in California, where he remained several years. He again appeared in New York, and soon afterward obtained a patent for his invention of four-wheeled steamers. He never carried into execution this dream of his life, though during the few months previous to his death he was more zealous than ever before in perfecting his invention. He obtained from the New York Legislature, in 1873, a charter for a steamship company whose vessels were to be built on the plan which he had patented. Considerable success had attended his efforts in the formation of this company, though it was still far from an organization. He was a man of strict integrity and much energy and decision of character, and had great business talent.

July 11.—CALDWELL, TOD R., Governor of North Carolina, and long a prominent political leader in that State; died at Hillsboro, N. C., aged about 56 years. He was born in Morganton, Burke County, N. C.; graduated from the University of North Carolina in 1840; studied law, and was admitted to the Burke County bar in 1842, and the same year was elected to the State Legislature from Burke County, and continued there till 1844. He then devoted himself to his profession very closely for several years, but in 1850 was elected State Senator, and had been in public life most of the time since. After the close of the war he was a member of the Reconstruction Committee and president of the Western N. C. Railroad, and in 1868 was elected Lieutenant-Governor on the same ticket with W. W. Holden, who was chosen Governor. After the impeachment of Holden and his removal from office in March, 1871, Lieutenant-Governor Caldwell became Governor. In August, 1872, he was elected Governor over Judge and U. S. Senator Merrimon, by 1,882 majority, after a most exciting and hotly-contested election. His administration had given general satisfaction, and the confidence of the people of the State in his honesty, integrity, and sound judgment was very strong. His death was sudden, and resulted from disease of the kidneys.

July 12.—HILLYER, Brigadier-General WILLIAM SILLIMAN, U. S. Vols., an officer of volunteers on General Grant's staff during the late war, and previously a lawyer in St. Louis; died in Washington, D. C., aged 43 years. He was practising law in St. Louis in 1859, and perhaps some years earlier, and had become intimate with the then ex-Captain Grant, and recommended him for the office of county engineer of St. Louis County. Very soon after General Grant was commissioned as brigadier-general he offered Mr. Hillyer a place on his staff, and during the Tennessee and Vicksburg campaigns he rose to the rank of brigadier-general, receiving his commission in July, 1863. After the close of the war, President Grant appointed General Hillyer to be revenue agent in New York City. He held this office for a short time only, and began the practice of the law there. His success in a legal way was not very great, as he was naturally a politician, and devoted most of his time to political pursuits. In the spring of 1874 he was nominated by the President as general appraiser in the Custom-House, in place of Judge Hogeboom, but his unfitness for this position was so obvious to those who knew him best, that a general demurrer was raised by the press, and the nomination was withdrawn. General Hillyer was the last surviving member of General Grant's original staff.

July 16.—HOLT, PHILETUS H., a wealthy flour-merchant and patriotic citizen of New York City; died there, aged 71 years. He was born in New Bedford, Mass., but was brought to New York by his parents in his childhood, and, after receiving an excellent education, went into the flour-business with his father, and continued in it till his death. He was an enthusiast in military matters, and was active in encouraging the Seventh Regiment, N. Y. N. G., to attain its excellence in drill and discipline. He spent his money on it without stint, and contributed liberally toward its expenses at the beginning of the war.

July 17.— GOODRICH, Rev. WILLIAM H., D. D., an eminent Presbyterian clergyman, scholar, and writer; died at Lausanne, Switzerland, in the 50th year of his age. His father, the late Prof. Chauncey A. Goodrich, D. D., was eminent alike as a theologian and lexicographer. Dr. W. H. Goodrich was born in New Haven, in 1825, fitted for college in the Hopkins Grammar-School, and under his father's direction graduated from Yale College with high honors in 1843, studied theology in the Yale Divinity School, and from 1847 to 1848 was a tutor in Yale College. He then went to Europe, where he remained for nearly two years, and in 1850 was ordained pastor of the Congregational Church in Bristol, Conn., where he remained four years, when he accepted a call to the pastorate of the Presbyterian Church in Binghamton, N. Y., and in 1858 was called to become pastor of the First Presbyterian Church in Cleveland, where he remained until 1872, when his arduous labors having overtasked his strength he went to Europe for his health, retaining his pastoral connection. But his health did not improve, and he longed to return, and was only restrained from coming by the decided opposition of his physicians, and he finally sank and died in Switzerland. Dr. Goodrich was an able and

brilliant writer, an eloquent and instructive preacher, and one of the best pastors in the country. His people were very strongly attached to him. He had published some miscellaneous sermons and addresses, many review articles, and several religious essays, and was a frequent contributor to the religious press. He received the degree of D. D. from Western Reserve College in 1864.

July 18.—EATON, GEORGE N., a prominent merchant and promoter of education in Baltimore; died in Europe, where he had been traveling for his health, aged 62 years. Although an energetic business-man, he had been a hard student, and, while self educated, was a man of wide and generous culture. He had taken a deep interest in the promotion of the public schools of Baltimore. In 1854 he was elected a member of the Board of School Commissioners, in which body he remained eleven years, nine of which he was its president. In 1865 Harvard University conferred on him the degree of Master of Arts, in recognition of his services in the cause of education. These services received further recognition in 1865, when the late George Peabody appointed Mr. Eaton one of the trustees of the Peabody Educational Fund for the Southern States. He was for many years a director and for a time vice-president of the Board of Trade, and a director in the Union Bank, the Savings-Bank of Baltimore, and of the Maryland Institute for the Instruction of the Blind.

July 18.—WINSLOW, JAMES, a New York banker, senior partner of the great banking-house of Winslow, Lanier & Co.; died in New York City, in the 60th year of his age. He was born in Albany, and passed his earlier business-years in the hardware-store of Erastus Corning, in that city. Subsequently he came to New York, and entered the firm of Winslow, Lanier & Co., which had been established by his father. From modest proportions the business grew until the firm was considered one of the best in the street. Mr. Winslow had been identified also with national banking interests, and at the time of his death was vice-president of the Third National Bank. His youngest son was a member of the scientific corps sent out by the Government in the Swatara to observe the transit of Venus.

July 19.—HARDING, Brigadier-General ABNER O., U. S. Volunteers, a lawyer, soldier, railroad-builder, and member of Congress; died at Monmouth, Warren County, Ill., aged 67 years. He was born in East Hampton, Middlesex County, Conn., February 10, 1807, and was educated chiefly at Hamilton Academy, in Oneida County, N. Y. After practising law in Oneida County for some time, he removed to Illinois. In that State he continued to practise law for fifteen years, and to manage farms for twenty-five years. In 1848 he was a member of the convention which framed the constitution under which Illinois was governed from 1848 to 1870. He also served in the State Legislature in 1848-'49, and 1850. During the ten years preceding the rebellion he was engaged in railway enterprises. In 1862 he enlisted as a private in the Eighty-third Illinois Infantry, and rose to the rank of colonel. For bravery at Fort Donelson he was raised to a brigadier-generalship, and in 1863 had command at Murfreesboro', Tenn. In 1864 he was elected a Representative in the Thirty-ninth Congress, and was a member of the Committees on Manufactures and Militia. In 1866 he was reëlected to the Fortieth Congress, from what was then the fourth district, and served on the Committees on the Union Prisoners, Claims, and Militia. General Harding early entered with zeal into the construction of railroads in Central Illinois, and was one of the master-spirits in projecting and building the Peoria & Oquawka Railroad, now a part of the Chicago, Burlington & Quincy combination. He is supposed to have left a fortune of $2,000,000, no small part of which he amassed in railroad enterprises. Some years before his death he endowed a "Harding Professorship" in Monmouth College.

July 20.—QUINBY, JAMES M., a distinguished citizen of Newark, N. J.; died there, aged 69 years. He had been mayor of the city, State Senator, and had held other positions of honor and trust. He was widely known and esteemed not only in Newark, but throughout the South, with which he had long had business connections.

July 22.—FREEMAN, Captain FORTUNATUS, a noted sea-captain of remarkable energy and fertility of resources, a native of Yarmouth, England; died in New York City. Coming to the United States young, he first commanded vessels sailing from Baltimore. Subsequently he was commander of the sailing-ships Sea, Marmion, Resolute, Guy Mannering, and Silas Wright, all of which sailed from New York. When captain of the Sea, he took over the last presidential message ever carried by a sailing-vessel, and made then the fastest time ever made in a transatlantic passage by a sailing-vessel. He was commander of the steamers Colorado and Minnesota, and distinguished himself when the latter took fire in mid-ocean. The flames were overcome after twelve hours of heroic exertion.

July 25.—POTTER, HORATIO, Jr., First-Lieutenant and Adjutant Seventeenth United States Infantry, U. S. A., Captain and Brevet Major of Volunteers, a gallant officer in the late war, son of Bishop Potter; died in New York City, aged 33 years. He was born in Albany, in 1841, and was intended for the law. He entered Columbia College in 1860, but left in 1861, enlisted in the Seventh Regiment, N. Y. N. G., and marched with it to Washington in April, 1861. On his return, he received a commission as second-lieutenant in the Seventh New York Artillery. To enter active service,

he exchanged and obtained position on the staff of General R. B. Potter, who commanded the Second Division of the Ninth Army Corps. He served throughout the campaign, and took part in all the engagements with that corps. He was made a first-lieutenant on April 1, 1864, and a captain on June 12, 1865. At the assault on Petersburg he distinguished himself by bravery and daring, and was brevetted major. After the war he obtained a commission as second-lieutenant in the Seventeenth United States Infantry, and served with that regiment two years in Texas. Later the regiment was sent to Dakota, where Lieutenant Potter was engaged in several expeditions against the Indians. In September, 1867, he was made a first-lieutenant, and in December, 1870, was promoted to the position of adjutant of his regiment. His death was caused by hæmorrhage from the lungs.

July 26.—HARRIOTT, JOHN V., an able and accomplished underwriter and a very active philanthropist in all religious benevolent enterprises; died in Brooklyn, N. Y., aged 50 years. Mr. Harriott was born in New York City, November 1, 1824, and educated in the public schools there; he had been connected with the Firemen's Insurance Company for more than thirty years, and was for twelve years the president of the company, and an active member of the Board of Underwriters. He had been for many years an officer and superintendent of Sunday-schools, and was very hearty in his support of all important religious enterprises.

July 26. — SHAW, Commodore THOMPSON DARRAH, U. S. Navy, a brave and efficient naval officer; died at Germantown, Pa., aged 75 years. He was a native of Pennsylvania, and entered the navy May 28, 1820; was commissioned a lieutenant, May 17, 1828. In 1827 he was on duty on the frigate Macedonian, with the Brazilian Squadron, and again, in 1833-'4, saw service in Brazilian waters, on the sloop-of-war Lexington. His next active duty was on the frigate Constellation, in the Pacific, in 1840. Subsequent to that date he was on duty at the Baltimore and Philadelphia rendezvous, and with the Bureau of Construction. In 1855 he was in command of the sloop-of-war Falmouth, of the Home Squadron, and during the early period of the late war commanded the steamer Montgomery, of the Western Gulf Blockading Squadron. His last cruise expired in February, 1862. On July 16, 1862, he was commissioned a commodore on the retired list, but subsequent to that date was on special duty in Philadelphia for a short time in 1864-'65.

July 27.—HEWITT, MAHLON T., an enterprising and energetic citizen of New York and Brooklyn, remarkable for the extent and sagacity of his philanthropic labors; died in Brooklyn, aged 66 years. He had been foremost in numerous public enterprises, was president of the Freedmen's Savings-Bank; and afterward of the Oriental Savings-Bank, was active in Sunday-school efforts, and was noted for his strict integrity and uprightness in all business matters.

July 27.—SHEEHAN, JAMES M., a lawyer, antiquarian, book-collector, and scholar, born in Ireland, and educated there, but for twenty-five years a resident of New York City; died there, aged 48 years. He was an accomplished classical scholar, and had a special fondness for collecting rare books and manuscripts relative to his native country. His library of valuable Irish and Anglo-Irish books and manuscripts was said to be the most complete in in this country.

July 31. — VAN TRUMP, PHILADELPHUS, a journalist, lawyer, judge, and M. C. of Ohio; died in Cincinnati, aged 64. He was born in Lancaster, Ohio, in 1810, where he learned the art of printing, and edited a newspaper for several years. In 1838 he was admitted to the bar, becoming the law-partner of H. F. Staubery, with whom he studied law. Mr. Van Trump was a Whig, and was a member of the Baltimore Convention of 1852, which nominated General Scott for President. After being three times nominated for the Supreme Court, he was elected in 1862 a Judge of the Court of Common Pleas. In 1866 he resigned that office, and was elected on the Democratic ticket to Congress in the twelfth district. In the House of Representatives he served on the Committees on the Pacific Railroad and on Manufactures.

Aug. 2.—SOUTHWORTH, Rev. TERTIUS DUNNING, a Presbyterian clergyman and author; died at Bridgewater, N. Y., in the 74th year of his age. He was born in Rome, N. Y., educated at Whitesboro' Academy, Hamilton College, and Auburn and Andover Theological Seminaries, graduating from Hamilton in 1827, and from Andover in 1829 or '30. He preached for a time at Sauquoit, Oneida County, N. Y., then for four years at Claremont, N. H.; and in 1838 was installed as successor of the celebrated Dr. Nathaniel Emmons at Franklin, Mass., where he remained eleven years. In 1850 he resigned, and was for the next nine years a stated supply, his health being impaired. In 1859 he moved to Pleasant Prairie, Wis., where he preached for nine years, and then came back to Bridgewater, N. Y., the home of his childhood, where in failing health and great suffering he spent the last six years of his life. Mr. Southworth was an able and eloquent writer, as his published sermons and addresses, and especially his funeral discourse on Rev. Dr. Emmons's death, abundantly testify.

Aug. 3. — HASKIN, Lieutenant-Colonel and Brevet Brigadier-General JOSEPH A., U. S. A., a brave and gallant officer of the Mexican and late civil wars, a graduate from West Point in 1839; died at Oswego, N. Y., aged about 57 years. He was born in New York, and appointed from that State to the Military Academy, and entered the army as second-lieutenant of the First Artillery. He was on duty in Maine during the "disputed frontier" controversy, from 1840 to 1845, afterward in Florida and Louisiana, and during the Mexican War took part in all the battles under General Scott, losing an arm at the storming of Chapultepec; was subsequently in garrison and fortress duty, on the frontiers and elsewhere, becoming captain in the First Artillery, in 1851; was compelled to surrender Baton Rouge Arsenal to a vastly superior force of insurgents in the winter of 1861; served during the civil war, in Washington, at Key West; in command of the northern defenses of Washington, 1862–1864; as Chief of Artillery in the Department of Washington from 1864–1866; and subsequently at different fortresses, having been promoted to be major in 1862, lieutenant-colonel of staff the same year, and lieutenant-colonel First Artillery in 1866, and brevet colonel and brevet brigadier-general, March 13, 1865. He was retired in 1872, and had since resided mostly at Oswego.

Aug. 3.—SPALDING, Rev. H. H., a Presbyterian clergyman and missionary of the American Board among the Indians of the Northwest coast; died at Lapwai, Idaho, aged 70 years. He was born near Prattsburg, N. Y., in 1804, and, amid intense poverty and innumerable obstacles, fought his way to and through Western Reserve College, and Lane Theological Seminary, and in 1836 was appointed by the A. B. C. F. M. missionary to the Nez Percés Indians, and crossed the continent with his wife amid great hardships the same year, establishing himself on the Lapwai River, while his associate, Rev. Dr. Whitman, settled in the Walla Walla Valley. They remained in the field till November, 1847, when, through the influence of Jesuit missionaries connected with the Hudson's Bay Company, Whitman and all those attached to his post in the Lapwai Valley were massacred by the Indians, and Spalding and his family at Lapwai, ninety miles distant, were in great jeopardy, and were finally obliged to escape to the Willamette Valley. There he remained for about fourteen years, laboring zealously among the Indians who could be reached from that point, and making use of the translations of the Scriptures in the Nez Percés language, which he had reduced to writing, and in which he had printed portions of the Scriptures. In 1862 he reëntered his work on the Lapwai, and remained for several years, till he was recalled to the East, to lay before the Government the facts relative to the massacre, which had been misrepresented, and to give evidence of the great services which Dr. Whitman and himself had rendered to the Government. This accomplished, he returned to his missionary work, this time under the direction of the Presbyterian Board of Missions, and remained in the country of the Nez Percés and Spokans in Northwestern Idaho and Northeastern Washington Territories till his death. His labors among these tribes had been very successful; several thousands had been civilized and brought to lead industrious lives, and over one thousand became professedly Christians.

Aug. 4.—FAULKNER, Colonel S. C., a prominent citizen of Little Rock, Ark., well known as a journalist and humorous writer; died in that city, aged 71 years. He was the author of the "Arkansas Traveller," and other sketches exhibiting the broad, rollicking humor of the Southwest.

Aug. 8.—BOLLES, Rev. AUGUSTUS, a Baptist clergyman and journalist; died at Montville, Conn., aged 97 years and seven months. He was born in Ashford, Conn., in January, 1777; was a brother of the late Rev. Samuel Bolles, D. D., and the late Matthew Bolles, Esq., an eminent banker of Boston. He entered the ministry of the Baptist Church about the beginning of the present century, was prominent in the founding of the Connecticut Baptist State Convention, and from 1830 to 1838 was the editor of the *Christian Secretary*, the organ of the denomination in Connecticut. He subsequently spent some years in Illinois, but returned in 1843 or 1844 to Connecticut, and passed the remainder of his life in Colchester and Montville, Conn. He was a man of fine intellect, and wide general culture.

Aug. 8.—BRIGGS, AMOS, a prominent citizen, manufacturer, and former State Senator, of Schaghticoke, N. Y.; died at Newport, R. I., in the 80th year of his age. He was born in East Greenwich, R. I., in 1795, and removed to Schaghticoke in 1820. He had done much to build up the town, by his energy, enterprise, self-reliance, and public spirit. He had been engaged in manufacturing there for more than fifty years, and had been throughout the whole period a trusted counselor, a wise and judicious manager, and a kind friend to his fellow-citizens. He had been often elevated to responsible positions by his townsmen, and had more than once represented his district in the State Senate. He had also been prominent and active in religious matters in the town.

Aug. 8.—GOULD, JOHN STANTON, an active and intelligent farmer, reformer, and philanthropist of Columbia County, N. Y.; died at Hudson, N. Y., of congestion of the lungs, in the 64th year of his age. He was a member of the Society of Friends, and had received a very thorough education, and had been in physical sciences, and was well known as an industrious student, and popular essayist and lecturer on scientific subjects. He had an admirably conducted farm in Columbia County, and took an active part in agricultural improvement, being for several years president of the State Agricultural Society, in which position he was very efficient. He was an earnest temperance advocate, and though in earlier years a Whig, and a member of the Assembly from that party in 1846, and subsequently acting generally with the Republicans, he held his temperance principles above party allegiance, and had been recognized as a pro-

hibitionist. He was very much in earnest, also, on the subject of prison reform, and was for many years one of the directors and executive officers of the New York Prison Association.

Aug. 9.—SMITH, THOMAS U., a prominent merchant and banker of New York City; died there, at the age of 60 years. He was a native of Centre Island, Oyster Bay, L. I., born July 2, 1814. He entered into business-life in New York City early, and became a member of the firm of Henrys, Smith & Townsend, while yet a young man, remaining in the firm till their failure in 1861. He then connected himself with the firm of Robert L. Maitland & Co., with which he remained until he was elected president of the Mercantile Trust Company. He had been for many years a trustee of Princeton College and of the Princeton Theological Seminary, to which he was a liberal benefactor, and had been elder of the Fifth Avenue Presbyterian Church since 1845. In 1859, when the Equitable Life Insurance Company was organized, he was chosen a director, which position he retained until his death. He was considered a man of strict integrity, possessed a wide business capacity, and had been very successful since his failure, before the late civil war.

Aug. 11.—NASH, ALANSON, an eminent admiralty lawyer of New York City; died there, aged 67 years. He was a native of Vermont, and came to New York City in 1828, and studied law in the office of John A. Morrill. His greatest ambition seems to have been to make himself thoroughly master of the whole subject of maritime law, and for this purpose he acquired all the languages, ancient and modern, which had any treatises on the subject. He became an authority on all questions of maritime jurisprudence, but practised only as a counselor.

Aug. 13.—BAIRD, Rev. WILLIAM S., a clergyman of the Methodist Episcopal Church, South, and for some years past the editor of the *Baltimore Episcopal Methodist*, their leading organ; died on his way to Baltimore from some of the Virginia Springs. He was widely known and highly esteemed.

Aug. 15.—FISHER, Colonel SAMUEL S., an able and distinguished patent solicitor and lawyer, of Cincinnati; drowned in the Susquehanna River, in Luzerne County, Pa. He was a member of a family eminent for talent, being a grandson of the late Rev. Samuel Fisher, of Bordentown, N. J., a nephew of the late Rev. S. W. Fisher, D. D., LL. D., the eloquent president of Hamilton College, and others of less note. He had been for many years engaged in the managing of patent causes, and had the reputation of being one of the ablest patent lawyers in this country. In 1869 he was appointed, by President Grant, Commissioner of the Patent-Office, but resigned early in 1872, to devote his attention wholly to private business. In the summer of 1873 he had spent some months in Switzerland, and in 1874 was following the

Susquehanna up toward its source, and exhibiting its beautiful and wonderful scenery to his son, when they were both drowned in its waters.

Aug. 16. — DICKINSON, Rev. RICHARD W., D. D., an eminent Presbyterian clergyman and author; died in Fordham, N. Y., in the 70th year of his age. He was a native of New Jersey, graduated from Yale College in 1823, and from Princeton Theological Seminary in 1826; was ordained in New York City in 1827, preached for some time in Philadelphia, and was installed pastor at Lancaster, Pa., in 1829. After some years of faithful labor there, he was called to the Market Street Church in New York, and subsequently he became pastor of the Bowery and Canal Street Church. Impaired health compelled him to resign this charge, and he then resided at Fordham, and performed pastoral duties at Inwood, on the upper part of Manhattan Island. For some years past he had been unable to act as pastor, but had devoted much time to literary pursuits, and was a frequent contributor to religious periodicals and reviews. He had published several volumes on religious subjects, which gave evidence of his marked ability as a writer.

Aug. 17.—CHASE, Rev. B. A., a Methodist clergyman, a member of the Providence Methodist Episcopal Conference; died in Cumberland, R. I. He was a native of Maine, and chaplain of the Fourth Maine Regiment during the late civil war.

Aug. 19. — HARPER, JOHN, a well-known horse-breeder and owner of numerous racing-horses; died at Midway, Ky. He had for many years taken an active interest in all matters connected with the turf, and acquired a considerable part of his large fortune by raising superior horses. He was the owner of the celebrated racer Longfellow.

Aug. 21.—SPRING, MARCUS, a well-known reformer, business-man, and teacher; died at Englewood, Perth Amboy, N. J., aged 64 years. He was born in New York, in 1810, and began business in that city as a commission-merchant in 1831. Not long after, his brother died, leaving a badly-complicated and heavily-indebted estate. Mr. Spring at once assumed the debts of his brother, and began paying them; and after thirty years of arduous labor succeeded in liquidating every dollar of them, and his brothers' creditors testified their appreciation of his disinterestedness by presenting him with a massive silver pitcher, suitably inscribed. He became identified with the antislavery movement in 1836, and married a daughter of Arnold Buffum, the first president of the American Antislavery Society. He had frequently visited Europe, and accompanied Margaret Fuller (afterward Countess d'Ossoli) when she wrote her famous letters to the *New York Tribune*. He was long associated with the late Horace Greeley in coöperative movements, and was named by him as an executor in one of his wills. At one time he was president of the Resolute Insurance Company, and had been officially connected with several insurance companies and banks. During the late war he founded a military academy, known as the Eagleswood Military Academy, and which during six years educated many fine soldiers and business-men. He lost $100,000 by the Chicago fire in 1871, and that and more recent business troubles hastened his death.

Aug. 24.—PRIME, Mrs. JULIA ANN (*Germaine*), widow of the late Rev. Dr. N. S. Prime, and mother of Rev. Drs. S. Irenæus and Edward D. G. Prime, and of William C. Prime, Esq.; died at White Plains, N. Y., aged nearly 86 years. She was born in Sag Harbor, N. Y., January 31, 1789, received an excellent education, married Rev. Nathaniel S. Prime in 1808, and reared a family of seven children, of whom five are living, and all have attained distinction. She was a lady of great force of character, combined with remarkable gentleness, purity, and dignity.

Aug. 25.—GAVIT, JOHN E., president of the American Bank Note Company; died at Stockbridge, Mass., in the 58th year of his age. He was a native of New York City, received a good public-school education, and engaged early in life in steel-engraving in Albany, where he resided until, in 1858, he united his business in that city with the American Bank Note Company, which he had assisted in organizing. In 1866 he was elected president of the latter, and retained that position until his death. Mr. Gavit was formerly secretary of the American Institute, and took an active interest in the progress of science, being acquainted with many leading inventors. He was president of the Microscopical Society of this city, and was an earnest promoter of the branch of science which it was formed to develop. He had made many friends by his genial manners and zeal for the diffusion of knowledge.

Aug. 26.—BLOT, Prof. PIERRE, a distinguished cook and teacher of the culinary art, on which he had written with great ability; died in Jersey City, N. J., aged about 56 years. He occupied for several years, in New York City, the prominence acquired in the same line by Soyer in London. Making the culinary art his special study, he practised it with great earnestness and success. He aimed at popularizing good cookery and effecting economy in the preparation of food. Several articles were contributed by him to the press, in which he imparted practical information and discountenanced the consumption of such game and fish as were out of season. He wrote a book on cookery, and also lectured on that subject, and established one or two schools of instruction in the art. Prof. Blot engaged in business enterprises in Brooklyn and New York, partly with the view of carrying into effect his views on the preparation of food.

Aug. 27.—HAMMOND, ABRAM A., a distinguished citizen, lawyer, judge, and Governor, of Indiana; died in Denver, Colorado, aged 60 years. He was born in Brattleboro, Vt., in March, 1814, but removed to Indiana in youth, and having been admitted to the bar in Brookville, Ind., in 1835, commenced the practice of his profession at Greenfield, Hancock County, Ind. He soon attained distinction as an attorney, and in 1840 removed to Columbus, Ind., where he remained till 1846, when with his partner he removed to Indianapolis, and the next year to Cincinnati. Dissatisfied with that city, they returned to Indianapolis, and in 1850 Mr. Hammond was appointed the first Judge of the Marion County Court of Common Pleas, and gave great satisfaction in that position. In 1852 he resigned, and went to California as the law-partner of the celebrated Rufus Lockwood, but in 1854 returned to Indiana, and settled in Terre Haute. In 1856 he was elected Lieutenant-Governor, and, on the death of Governor Willard in 1860, became Governor. His health commenced failing soon after, and for nearly fourteen years he had been a great sufferer from rheumatism and asthma; he had visited Denver in the vain hope of relief.

Sept. 2. — ORLANDINI, AGATHA GAYNOR STATES, an operatic singer and prima donna, better known by her stage name as "Madame Agatha States;" died in New York City, of pleurisy. Her maiden name was Agatha Gaynor, and she was a native of Dublin, but came in childhood with her parents to the United States, and settled in San Francisco. Evincing fine talents as a vocalist, she was sent to Italy, where she completed her musical education, and made her *début* in opera. After achieving fair success in Europe, she came to the United States, and was favorably received in the Academy of Music in New York, and subsequently sang in the principal cities of this country, as well as in South America and Australia. She had married when quite young a Mr. States, who occasioned her much annoyance by his boisterous conduct and his intemperate habits, leading eventually to some painful scenes in the police courts, and to her procuring a divorce from him. About two years before her death she married the baritone Signor Orlandini. She returned to San Francisco from Australia, in the early summer of 1874, and while coming from San Francisco to New York contracted the pleurisy of which she died.

Sept. 6. — CONWAY, FREDERICK B., a well-known actor and theatrical manager, born in Clifton, England, February 10, 1819; died in Manchester, Mass., in the 55th year of his age. He early developed a taste for the stage, and had won a fair position in his profession in England, when he came to this country in August, 1850, and soon formed an attachment for Edwin Forrest, in most of whose favorite pieces he played the second part, being *Iago* to his *Othello*, *De Mauprat* to his *Richelieu*, etc. After the death of his first wife, Mr. Conway

married, in May, 1852, Miss Sarah Crooker, then as now a leading actress, and sister to Mrs. D. P. Bowers, and the two thenceforward acted together in the Metropolitan and other theatres. In 1859 they were engaged to open Pike's Opera-House in Cincinnati with a first-class company, Mr. Conway to be stage-manager and leading actor; but the engagement was not a profitable one, and they returned East. In 1861 they visited England, and filled a short engagement at Sadler's Wells Theatre, London. On their return they became star-actors, and made an extensive and profitable tour. In 1864 Mrs. Conway leased the Park Theatre in Brooklyn, and subsequently the new Brooklyn Theatre, in which for nine years Mr. Conway played leading parts, seldom appearing at any other theatres. Though naturally somewhat pompous and magniloquent in speech and manner, as became one who had had a long training under Forrest, Mr. Conway was a good actor, with a fine personal appearance and a commanding delivery. In private life he was much esteemed. He died of disease of the heart.

Sept. 8. — BUMSTED, WILLIAM H., a noted local politician of Jersey City, and one of its most enterprising citizens; died there, aged 39 years. He was born in Norfolk County, England, July 16, 1835, and emigrated with his parents to this country in 1836, and had resided thenceforward till his death in Jersey City. Between the ages of fourteen and twenty-four he had served four years' apprenticeship to the furniture-business, three to civil engineering, and three to the mason's trade. At the age of twenty-four he went into business for himself in the firm of Bumsted & Robertson, in which capacity he did much for the permanent improvement of Jersey City. While South Bergen was a separate city, he was for several times one of its aldermen. After its consolidation with Jersey City he was chosen to represent it in the city government, and was conspicuous in the management of its financial matters. When the Board of Works was organized, he was appointed a member, and remained so until the board was indicted for some technical irregularities, for which he and his associates were sentenced to a term of nine months in the State-prison. He was pardoned before the expiration of his term, since which time he had remained in private life. He was a shrewd politician, and was at one time chairman of the Republican County Executive Committee of Hudson County. He left a fortune of more than a million dollars, accumulated during the past ten years.

Sept. 10. — EDGERTON, BELA, a venerable citizen of Fort Wayne, Ind., who had in early and middle life been active in the politics of New York; died in Fort Wayne, aged 87 years. He was born in Franklin, Conn., September 28, 1787, was fitted for college in his native town by Rev. Dr. Samuel Nott, brother of the late President Nott, and graduated from Middlebury College, Vt., in 1809. He was a classical teacher, for several years after his graduation, in Vergennes, Vt., and Plattsburg, N. Y.; volunteered at the latter place in the War of 1812, and took part in the battle of Plattsburg, September 11, 1814. After the war he was admitted to the bar, having previously studied law, and practised his profession in Clinton County, N. Y., till 1839. In 1826, 1827, and 1828, Mr. Edgerton was a member of the New York Legislature, at a period when it numbered among its members the ablest men in the State, most of whom attained national fame in after years. Among these he was recognized as a peer of the best, and had much to do with shaping the legislation of the State. Though an ardent friend of Daniel D. Tompkins, and of course an anti-Clintonian, he reported on the day after De Witt Clinton's funeral, as chairman of a special committee, a bill to give the children of Clinton, who had died poor, a sum, nominally in payment of unexpired salaries, of about $10,000, and defended his report in a very able and eloquent speech. He originated many other important bills which have passed into the statutes as permanent laws. Declining further political preferment, Mr. Edgerton continued in the practice of his profession till his removal to Hicksville, Ohio, in 1839, when he engaged in farming. Some years later, after the death of his wife, he resided in the family of his eldest son, and subsequently removed with him to Fort Wayne, Ind., where he died.

Sept. 14.—VANDERVOORT, CHARLES, Grand-Master of the Independent Order of Odd-Fellows of the State of New York; died at Harlem, N. Y., aged 54 years. He had been a prominent member of the Order for many years, and was elected Grand-Master in 1872.

Sept. 18.—FRANKLIN, Commander CHARLES L., U. S. N., a gallant young naval officer, distinguished in the late civil war; died at Pensacola, of yellow fever, aged about 36 years. He was a native of Ohio, and entered the Naval Academy in 1854. After graduation, he was assigned to duty on the Mediterranean Squadron in 1860, and in the summer of 1861 returned and took part in the naval movements of the war, being present at the capture of Forts Hatteras and Clark, and in 1864-'65 at the two attacks on Fort Fisher. His zeal and efficiency caused his rapid promotion, and in April, 1872, he was commissioned commander.

Sept. 19.—MACCAFERRI, Signor, a noted operatic tenor; died in New York City, aged 52 years. He came to this country in 1858, and was actively engaged in operatic pursuits until 1871. Since that time he had been giving concerts with a company through the South and West.

Sept. 20.—STEVENS, A. S., a venerable citizen of Attica, Wyoming County, N. Y.; died there, aged about 80 years. He had resided in Attica fifty-two years; was sheriff of old Genesee County (from which Wyoming County was taken) in 1830, and some years later Judge of

the Court of Common Pleas for the county. He was one of the founders of the Union School at Attica, and for many years president of its Board of Trustees.

Sept. 22.—WILLIS, Rev. NATHAN ELLIOT, a Congregationalist clergyman and teacher, killed by a railroad accident on the route to Marion, Ala. His age was about 35 years. He was a graduate from Amherst College in 1862, and after his graduation was for several years a teacher in the English High-School, Boston. He was ordained and settled, in 1870, at Bridgewater, Mass., but for a year previous to his death had been acting as an agent of the American Missionary Association at Marion, Ala., and was bringing his wife and son thither when he was killed.

Sept. 26.—LEE, Right Rev. HENRY WASHINGTON, D. D., LL. D., late Bishop of the Protestant Episcopal Diocese of Iowa; born in Hamden, Conn., July 29, 1815; died at Davenport, Iowa, September 26, 1874. He was fitted for college at the Cheshire Academy, and graduated from Trinity College in 1835, and from the General Theological Seminary in New York in 1838, and received deacon's orders the same year. He was assistant minister for some time in New York, and was chosen rector of St. Luke's, Rochester, in 1843. He was greatly esteemed and beloved by his parishioners, and, on his elevation to the bishopric, was consecrated, October 18, 1854, in the church of which he had been for eleven years rector. He had been an efficient and hard-working bishop for twenty years, and, under his labors, the Church in Iowa had grown and become a very efficient body. His death was the result of a fall on the stairs of his house in Davenport, which was followed by gangrene and eventually death, with extreme suffering. He was universally esteemed and beloved. He received the honorary degree of D. D. from Trinity College, and that of LL. D. from the University of Cambridge, England, at the time of the Pan-Anglican Council.

Sept. 27.—BUCKHOUT, ISAAC CRAIG, C. E., an able and energetic American civil-engineer; died at White Plains, N. Y., in the 44th year of his age. He was born in 1831, on the old Gouverneur Morris estate, of which his father was manager. During his boyhood he showed a great love for study, and at an early age chose the profession of engineer. After leaving school in 1848, he was employed on the Harlem Railroad as a rodman under Allen Campbell, who was afterward president of the road. Here he attracted the attention of his employers by his intelligence and quickness. Later he was employed in surveying in Paterson, N. J., under the direction of Colonel J. W. Allen, civil-engineer, and then became engineer and superintendent of the water-works of that city. Returning to New York he obtained the position of City Surveyor, and associated himself with Mr. Southard. He resumed his connection with the Harlem Railroad Company, and superintended the construction of the old viaduct over the Harlem Flats and bridge over the Harlem River in 1858. In 1857 he was engineer of the company, and in 1863 he was made superintendent. He designed the Grand Central Depot, as well as the improvement on Fourth Avenue. When the charter for that work was granted, the Legislature appointed a board of four engineers, one of whom was Mr. Buckhout, and the members elected him as the superintendent. When Mr. Vanderbilt obtained the charter for building an underground railroad to the City Hall, Mr. Buckhout made the plan which received the approval of all the other engineers, and was declared the best submitted. He also designed the plan for the underground railroad in Brooklyn, which was also adopted. Mr. Buckhout was a personal friend of Horace Greeley, and superintended the improvements about Mr. Greeley's residence at Chappaqua. About two years ago he was requested to make a plan for a depot at St. Louis. This plan, when completed, was declared to be the best one submitted, and adopted, and it was reported that an offer was made to him by the officers of the road to take charge of the building and the road. Mr. Buckhout was also in charge of the improvement at Sixtieth Street and North River, where an elevator is being constructed for the Hudson River Railroad Company. Here he exposed himself to the damp, standing for hours on the marshy ground, and it is supposed that he contracted a malarial fever; his constitution was undermined, and he returned home with an acute attack of inflammatory rheumatism and pneumonia, which changed into typhoid fever, of which he died. As an engineer Mr. Buckhout was a man of great practical and theoretical ability, his advice being often sought by other engineers. As an employé he was skillful, energetic, persevering, indefatigable, and careful in details. He was invaluable to the directors of the road, who frankly say that they do not know how to replace him. Toward his subordinates he was kind and even affectionate. Every one who was employed by him will mourn the loss of a personal friend.

Sept. 27.—Hows, John A., a young artist and journalist of remarkable ability; died in New York City, of consumption, aged 43 years. He was a son of the late Prof. John W. S. Hows, and a graduate of Columbia College. On leaving college he studied a short time for the ministry in the Protestant Episcopal Church, but subsequently studied law in the office of Dennis McMahon. He was at one time associate editor of *The Churchman,* and of *The Home Journal* during the editorship of that paper by the late N. P. Willis and George P. Morris. He finally adopted art as a profession, studying with Messrs. Greatorex, A. D. Shattuck, and the late James H. Cafferty. The first important picture exhibited by him at the National Academy was entitled "Vanitas Vanitatum." He was elected an associate of that institution, and contributed to its exhibitions. His chief prominence in the art-world was achieved by his drawings upon wood. Among the books illustrated by him exclusively were "A Forest Hymn," "In the Woods," "Forest Pictures in the Adirondacks," "A Christmas Carol," and Coxe's "Christian Ballads." He had also contributed to *Appletons' Journal* and *The Aldine,* for which he had nearly completed, at the time of his death, an interesting series of pictures of Pennsylvania scenery.

Sept. 28.—Ganson, John, an eminent lawyer and political leader in Buffalo; died there, in his 57th year. He was a native of Le Roy, Genesee County, where he received a good education. After graduating from Harvard College, in 1839, he studied law and was admitted to the bar. Finding after some time that the field for advancement was too limited in his native county, he removed about thirty years ago to Buffalo, and immediately resumed the practice of law in that city, his first legal partner in Buffalo being the Hon. Elbridge G. Spaulding, and his second Judge James M. Smith. Both firms acquired an extensive reputation, and were for many years solicitors to the Central Railroad. In 1861 Mr. Ganson was elected State Senator on the Democratic ticket, and in 1862 was elected to Congress, receiving 3,415 more votes than Mr. Spaulding, his opponent and former partner. At the expiration of his term Mr. Ganson declined to be again a candidate, and devoted himself sedulously to his profession, of which he was very fond, and in which his abilities were of a very high order. He was, against his wishes, elected to the State Senate again in 1871, and was in 1874 proposed by the party in the western part of the State as their candidate for Governor. His death was very sudden, occurring in his carriage while being conveyed from the Superior Court room to his house.

Sept. 30.—Brewer, Gardner, one of the wealthiest and most liberal of the Boston merchants; died at his beautiful villa in Newport, R. I., aged 68 years. He was the son of a Boston merchant in the West Indian trade. After attaining his majority, he was for some time engaged in the distillery business, but afterward turned his attention to the dry-goods trade, and founded the house of Gardner, Brewer & Co., which represents some of the largest mills in New England, and has branches in New York and Philadelphia. In this business, by accurate method combined with great sagacity, he accumulated a fortune which is estimated at several millions of dollars. Mr. Brewer at one time took an active part in politics as a Republican. He was also a strong protectionist, and showed great interest in the industrial development of the country. He used his large wealth liberally for the public good, and a few years ago gave to the city of Boston a beautiful fountain, which stands in the angle of Boston Common between Beacon and Park Streets. Last summer Mr. Brewer superintended the completion of one of the finest buildings in Boston, erected on the site of the firm's old warehouse, which was destroyed at the great Boston fire. His city residence, built on the site of the house of John Hancock, is one of the most elegant dwellings in Boston.

Sept. —.—GLENN, JOSEPH, a journalist and newspaper publisher of Cincinnati, for many years one of the principal proprietors of the *Cincinnati Gazette;* died in that city, aged about 60 years. It was through his capital and personal management that it was converted from a blanket-sheet into one of the ablest of the Western newspapers. He was a man of winning personal traits, and of scrupulous integrity. Although connected for nearly half his mature life with newspapers, he wrote comparatively little, but the matter he did furnish was always marked by strong sense, exceeding care as to details both of fact and style, and a quaint humor, which often sent fragments from his work for months through the press of the country.

Sept. —.—HARRISON, BAZEL, a pioneer settler of Michigan, and largely connected with its early history; died at Prairie Ronde, Mich., aged 104 years. He was many years ago a judge of one of the first courts of the State or Territory. He retained his faculties and vigor to the last, and was present at the Pioneers' Reunion at Schoolcraft, in 1874. He was long supposed to have been the "Bee-Hunter" of Cooper's novel of that title, but this is now said to be a mistake.

Sept. —.—HEATH, Captain BYRON S., a skillful railroad engineer from Chester, O., but employed by the Peruvian Government in laying out and building railways in that country; died at the summit of the Oroya Railway, which is nearly 14,000 feet above the sea, from the effects of the rarefied atmosphere.

Sept. —.—SADLIER, OLIVER, a Catholic publisher, bookseller, and one of the proprietors of the New York *Tablet;* died in New York City, aged 51 years. He was one of the partners in the firm of D. & J. Sadlier & Co., and was a man of culture and refinement.

Oct. 2.—WOOLSEY, Commodore MELANCHTHON B., U. S. N., a gallant officer of the United States Navy; died of yellow fever at Pensacola, Fla., aged 57 years. He was born in New York City, August 11, 1817, entered the naval service as midshipman December 24, 1832; was promoted to be lieutenant July 16, 1847; commander, July 16, 1862; captain, July 25, 1866; and commodore in 1871. While commanding the steamer Ellen, of the South-Atlantic Squadron, he took part in the engagement at the Wapper Creek battery, May 30, 1862; at Secessionville Creek, June 1, 1862; and coöperated with the army in the attempt to carry James Island by assault, June 3, 1862. On the 28th of June, 1863, he was engaged in the steamer Princess Royal, of the Western

Gulf Squadron, in defense of Donaldson, and Fort Butler, La., against the Confederates under Generals Green and Taylor, and repulsed them with a loss. Since the war he had been on active duty, and was in command at the Pensacola Navy-yard, where he fell a victim to yellow fever.

Oct. 3.—BISNET, JOE, a well-known interpreter and guide with the Cheyennes and Arapahoes, who had long been a prominent actor in Indian councils and treaties, and was noted for his fearlessness in interpreting to the commissioners and Indians exactly what either said to the other, however distasteful the language might be; died at Fort Laramie, from the effects of a pistol-shot wound received in a brawl near the fort, six years before.

Oct. 3.—PORTER, Mrs. MEHITABLE M., a venerable and accomplished lady of Farmington, Conn., the widow of the late Rev. Noah Porter, D. D., of that place, and mother of President Porter, of Yale College; died in Farmington, aged 88 years. She had been, during the many years of her husband's ministry, his faithful and efficient helper, and to her her distinguished son owes much of his extraordinary powers. She was so gentle, yet so dignified in her manners, as to be greatly loved and honored by all who knew her. She retained to the close of life, in large measure, the possession of her intellectual faculties, which were of a superior order.

Oct. 5.—LAMAR, GAZAWAY B., a merchant and banker of Savannah and New York, prominent in the late civil war; died in New York City, aged 76 years. He was born in Georgia, in 1798, and was engaged in business for many years in Savannah. He had a narrow escape from death in the shipwreck of the steamer Pulaski, in which several members of his family were lost. He was at that time a large slaveholder, and became a religious man, it is said, through the conversation of one of his slaves. In 1845 he removed to Brooklyn, N. Y., and engaged in business in New York, being very active also as a ruling elder in the First Presbyterian Church, Brooklyn. He was very successful in business, and in 1860, and for some years previous, was president of the Bank of the Republic, in New York. His sympathies were strongly enlisted on the Southern side, and in the winter of 1860–'61 he shipped large quantities of arms to Georgia in anticipation of the war. He also accepted the position of financial agent of the Confederate Government, and in that capacity procured the printing in New York of their notes and bonds. Soon after the actual commencement of hostilities he went to Savannah, and was largely concerned in cotton speculations and blockade-running during the war. He lost in the service his only son, Colonel Charles A. L. Lamar, who was killed in 1865. Soon after the occupation of Savannah he was arrested by order of the Secretary of War, and confined in the Old Capitol Prison at Washington. A few months after his release he was tried at Savannah by a military commission for attempted bribery of Government officers, and was sentenced to several years' imprisonment, and a very large fine, but the sentence was remitted by President Johnson. This prosecution led to counter-suits by him against the Government in the New York district. In private life Mr. Lamar was a generous, liberal, whole-hearted man, ardent in his friendships, exemplary in his character, and ready to every good word and work. That he should have erred in his estimate of the war, its causes and consequences, is greatly to be regretted, but his position in this matter was the legitimate result of his love for his native State, and his intense though mistaken attachment to Southern institutions and policy.

Oct. 7.—EDDY, Rev. THOMAS M., D. D., a Methodist clergyman, journalist, and author; born in Hamilton County, N. Y., September 7, 1823; died in New York City, October 7, 1874. He was educated in the Classical Seminary at Greensboro', Ind., joined the Indiana Conference as a circuit-preacher in 1842, received appointments within the bounds of that conference till 1853, when he acted as agent of the American Bible Society for a year, and was then elected presiding elder of the Indianapolis district. In 1856 he was appointed, by the Quadrennial Annual Conference, editor of the *Northwestern Christian Advocate*, at Chicago, and entered at once upon his duties. He was continued in this post, which he filled with marked ability, for twelve years, but in 1868 returned to the pastorate, being in charge of the Charles Street Methodist Episcopal Church in Baltimore. At the close of that service he was assigned to the Metropolitan Methodist Episcopal Church in Washington, was a member of the General Conference of 1872, and was by that body elected one of the corresponding secretaries of the Missionary Society. The duties of this new field involved an excess of labor, especially in the visitation of conferences. On his return from a protracted and very fatiguing journey about the 1st of October, 1874, Dr. Eddy was attacked with bilious fever, from which he did not recover. Though a copious and brilliant writer for the press, Dr. Eddy had published but little in a permanent form. His " History of Illinois during the Civil War," published in 1867 (2 vols. 8vo), was creditable alike to his patriotism and his intellectual ability. He had also published a few small books, occasional sermons, etc.

Oct. 12.—PERKINS, JOHN, a New York publisher, for many years at the head of the school-book publication department of the house of D. Appleton & Co.; died in New York City, of apoplexy, aged 51 years. He was a native of Cooperstown, N. Y., and a brother of the eminent mathematician, Prof. George R. Perkins, in whose series of mathematical works he was greatly interested. He retired from his connection with Messrs. Appleton in 1871.

Oct. 14.—KELLER, CHARLES M., an eminent patent-lawyer of the firm of Keller & Blake, of New York City; died at his country residence, Millburn, N. J., aged 64 years. He was born in Southern France, but came to this country when a child. He was employed in the old Patent-Office, and in 1836 he framed and secured the passage of the act upon which the American system of patent-law is founded. He also prepared the amendments to that act passed in 1839. He afterward came to this city and rose to the first rank in the practice of patent-law. He took part in nearly every important case of that kind in this country.

Oct. 16.—WELLBORN, Rev. MARSHALL J., a Baptist clergyman of Georgia, and previously to his entering the ministry an eminent lawyer, circuit judge, and member of Congress; died in Columbus, Ga., in the 68th year of his age. Educated at Mercer University and possessing talents of the highest order, he early became one of the ablest lawyers of the Georgia bar. About 1840 he was elected Judge of the Circuit Court in the Columbus Circuit, and in 1848, when Hon. Alfred Iverson was transferred from the national House of Representatives to the U. S. Senate, Judge Wellborn was elected his successor from the Columbus district. After serving one term in Congress he returned to his profession, and in 1858 commenced a religious life, uniting with the Baptist Church in Columbus. In 1864 he abandoned his legal profession and entered the ministry. Possessing an ample fortune, he refused the call of any of the wealthy city churches to which his eloquence and ability would have made him very welcome, and took charge of some poor and dependent churches around Columbus, which he served with great zeal but almost entirely without money compensation. He was meantime a most bountious giver to the poor and to all objects of Christian benevolence.

Oct. 17. — SHURTLEFF, NATHANIEL BRADSTREET, M. D., A. A. S., an American physician, naturalist, antiquary, and author; Mayor of Boston 1868-'70; died in that city, of paralysis, aged 64 years. He was born in Boston, June 29, 1810, graduated from Harvard College in 1831, and from the Medical Department in 1834. He devoted much of his time to literary and scientific pursuits after receiving his medical degree, though he could at any time have commanded a large practice. Among his published works were: "Epitome of Phrenology" (1835); "Perpetual Calendar for Old and New Style" (1848); "Passengers of the May Flower in 1620" (1849); "Brief Notice of William Shurtleff, of Marshfield" (1850); "Genealogy of the Leverett Family" (1850); "Thunder and Lightning and Deaths in Marshfield in 1658 and 1666" (1850); "Records of Massachusetts Bay," 1628-'86," 6 vols., 4to; "Topographical Description of Boston," 8vo (1871); and, with David Pulsifer, edited "Records of New Plymouth," 12 vols., 4to. Dr.

Shurtleff possessed an ample fortune, and was very liberal. He endowed a college at Alton, Ill., which took its name of Shurtleff College from its benefactor.

Oct. 18.—SHEDDAN, Rev. SAMUEL S., D. D., an eminent Presbyterian clergyman and teacher; died in Rahway, N. J., aged 64 years. He was born in Northumberland County, Pa., September 13, 1810, graduated from Jefferson College, Pa., in 1882, and from Princeton Theological Seminary in 1834, was ordained in 1835, passed the first fifteen years of his ministerial life at Williamsport, Muncey, and Warrior Run, teaching most of the time, as well as maintaining his position as a preacher and pastor. In 1852 he was called to the pastorate of the First Presbyterian Church in Rahway, N. J., where he remained till his death—twenty-two years and a half. He was a man of fine abilities and considerable eloquence. He received the degree of D. D. from Columbia College, New York City, in 1864.

Oct. 19.—STEVENS, JOHN AUSTIN, a leading merchant and banker of New York, for twenty-seven years president of the Bank of Commerce, and long secretary of the Chamber of Commerce, and president of the Merchants' Exchange; died in New York City, in the 80th year of his age. He was a son of General Ebenezer Stevens, an artillery - officer of the Revolution, and a brother of the eminent surgeon Alexander H. Stevens. He was born in New York City, January 22, 1795, graduated from Yale College in 1813, and with one of his brothers became partner in his father's business in 1818. He was president of the Merchants' Exchange from its organization, and for many years secretary of the Chamber of Commerce, his son succeeding him in that office. He was president of the Bank of Commerce from its organization in 1839 until 1866, when he resigned. He was chairman of the Committee of Banks of New York, Boston, and Philadelphia, which met in August, 1861, and decided to take $50,000,000 of the Government 7.30 loan; $30,000,000 of this was assigned to New York, $15,000,000 to Boston, and $5,000,000 to Philadelphia; but, as Boston declined to take more than $10,000,000, at Mr. Stevens's suggestion New York took $35,-000,000, greatly to her advantage subsequently. During the late civil war Mr. Stevens was an able, faithful, and far-seeing adviser of the Government in all financial matters.

Oct. 20.—MONTGOMERY, Rev. HENRY EGLINTON, D. D., an accomplished, hard-working, and remarkably successful clergyman of the Protestant Episcopal Church, rector of the Church of the Incarnation in New York City; died there, aged nearly 54 years. He was born at Eglinton, near Tivoli, N. Y., December 9, 1820, and was the son of the late John C. Montgomery, Postmaster of Philadelphia in 1841. Dr. Montgomery graduated from the University of Pennsylvania in 1839, studied law for two years, traveled in Europe, and then continued his studies in Nashota Theological Seminary, Wis., for two years, and completed his theological course in the General Episcopal Theological Seminary in New York City. He was ordained by Bishop Alonzo Potter, and in 1846 assumed charge of All Saints' Church of Philadelphia, then a small organization. His labors were very successful, the church-membership rapidly increased, and the pas or became highly respected and beloved. tAt the expiration of nine years he received and accepted a call to the Church of the Incarnation, of New York City, which was an offshoot from and dependent upon Grace Church, and which worshiped in the edifice at the corner of Madison Avenue and Twenty-eighth Street. During the earlier years of his ministry in New York he was able to separate his church from Grace Church, and so efficient and satisfactory was his work, that in 1864 the new church-building at Madison Avenue and Thirty-fifth Street was erected. The church is now reputed to be one of the wealthiest and most influential in the city. Dr. Montgomery received his degree of D. D. from the University of Pennsylvania. He was a man of acknowledged ability, large *physique*, and of more than ordinary endurance. He was always a hard worker; he had no assistant in his ministry, and besides the constant demands upon his strength made by a growing church, he had for years been a prominent member of nearly all the missionary and home societies for the advancement of the gospel. His death was unquestionably the result of overwork in his parish, in which he employed more hours of the day and night than even his strong constitution could endure. He was recognized as a Low Churchman and was strongly opposed to ritualism.

Oct. 21.—DENNY, THOMAS, an eminent New York merchant and banker; died in New York City, aged 70 years. He was the son of a distinguished manufacturer in Leicester, Mass., and was born in 1804. He graduated from Harvard College, with high honors, in 1823, studied law in Boston under Hon. Bradford Sumner, was admitted to the bar, but soon removed to New York and engaged in mercantile pursuits as an importer of goods in the French trade, but in 1846 withdrew from it to enter upon the business of a banker and broker. In 1852 he became a member of the Stock Exchange, and in 1858 formed the existing banking-house of Thomas Denny & Co., which has always maintained a very high reputation. Mr. Denny retained his early literary tastes throughout his life, and added to them a deep interest in the promotion of education and in every department of philanthropic and Christian effort. He was school trustee in the Fifteenth Ward, an active promoter of the College of the City of New York, and of the Free School for Girls, in Twelfth Street, New York City. He was one of the founders of the Society for improving the Condition of the Poor;

a director of the New York Juvenile Asylum, trustee of the Society for the Relief of the Ruptured and Crippled, one of the managers of the City Mission, an elder in the Presbyterian Church, and, withal, a man of singular sweetness and purity of life, one of the few whose life was a benediction and whose death was more than a private calamity.

Oct. 23.—FLANIGAN, HARRIS, Governor of Arkansas during the war; died at his residence in Arkadelphia, Ark. He was one of the leading members of the last Constitutional Convention of the State.

Oct. 23.—INMAN, WILLIAM, Commodore U. S. Navy, a gallant and deserving naval officer, sixty-two years in the service; died in Philadelphia, aged about 77 years. He was born in Utica, N. Y., entered the navy as midshipman January 1, 1812; was promoted to be lieutenant, April 1, 1818; commander, May 24, 1838; captain, June 2, 1850; commodore (on the retired list), July 10, 1862. He served on the lakes during the War of 1812, commanded one of two boats which captured a pirate-vessel of three guns on the coast of Cuba, in 1823; commanded the steamer Michigan on the lakes in 1845; commanded the steam-frigate Susquehanna, of the East India squadron, in 1851; and the squadron on the coast of Africa from 1859 to 1861. At the time of his death he was the senior officer of his rank on the retired list.

Oct. 23.—PAYNE, Right Rev. JOHN, D. D., late Missionary Bishop of the Protestant Episcopal Church in Cape Palmas, Africa; died at his residence in Westmoreland County, Va., of paralysis, aged about 63 years. He was a native of Virginia, educated at William and Mary College and at the Fairfax Theological Seminary; for some years rector of St. Paul's Church, Alexandria, and was consecrated Bishop of Cape Palmas, in that church, July 11, 1851. On the 21st of October, 1871, having returned from Africa and his health being seriously impaired, he resigned his jurisdiction, and had remained in his early home until his death.

Oct. 23.—PENDERGRAST, Commander AUSTIN, U. S. Navy, a gallant naval officer, twenty-six years in the service; died in Philadelphia, aged about 45 years. He was born in Kentucky, was the son of Captain Garrett J. Pendergrast, who died in 1862. He entered the navy in October, 1848, and was active in the service during the late civil war, being promoted to be lieutenant-commander in 1862, and commander in 1867. He was engaged in the unfortunate action at Galveston Bay, but his conduct on that occasion reflected no dishonor on him or the other officers of the command.

Oct. 25.—KERNOT, HENRY, a well-known dealer in books in New York City, born in London, October 20, 1806; died in New York City, aged 68 years. He was of Huguenot ancestry, received a good education, and was apprenticed to Treuttel & Würtz, German

booksellers and publishers in London. Before his apprenticeship expired both members of the firm died, and he entered another London house, where he soon became manager. Several years later he removed to Dublin, where he was charged with the completion of the different departments of the library of Trinity College, a duty which required extensive bibliographical knowledge. In 1836 he came to America. Soon after his arrival he obtained a situation with Wiley & Putnam, booksellers, in Broadway. After remaining with them several years he engaged in business on his own account. Not meeting with success, he abandoned the attempt. Then he was with Appleton & Co. for several years. When the firm of Mohun & Ebbs was established he found employment with them, and remained there till 1868, when he went into house of Scribner and Co. In his manner of life he was quiet and unostentatious. He was remarkable for his knowledge of books. He was probably as well informed, especially in regard to old books, as any man in the country, and his extensive knowledge was always at his command and readily used for the advantage of others. He had compiled numerous catalogues *raisonnée*, which showed his thorough acquaintance with the contents as well as the titles of books. A few months before his death he had published a "Bibliotheca Diabolica," or carefully arranged descriptive catalogue of works relative to the devil, comprising over 500 titles, and since its publication he had been laboring to make it as nearly absolutely perfect as possible in a second edition, and had collected about 800 more titles for that purpose.

Oct. 29.—ANTHON, JOHN H., an able lawyer and philanthropist of New York City; died at Cooperstown, N. J., aged about 45 years. He was a member of the Anthon family, of which so many members have attained distinction in law, classics, and theology, a graduate from Columbia College, and a student of law under General Authon. He soon acquired a large practice, but took especial pains to defend the poor, the friendless, and the unfortunate. He was for many years an active and useful officer of the New York Prison Association, a zealous member of the Citizens' Association, and so thoroughly identified with the People's Reform Party that he was their candidate for mayor. He had been for years very influential in the Masonic Order, and was Grand-Master of the Order in New York State in 1871 and 1872. His health having become impaired, he visited Europe in 1873, and on his return, in the early summer of 1874, went to Cooperstown, where he remained till his death.

Oct. 31.—SANDFORD, Rev. MILES, D. D., a Baptist clergyman, journalist, and author; died in Salem, N. J., of apoplexy, in the 59th year of his age. He was born in Litchfield, Conn., February 13, 1816, removed to Ohio in 1832, and, after suitable preparation, entered the ministry in the Methodist Episcopal Church in 1886, and was highly esteemed as a preacher and pastor till April, 1840, when he formally announced his withdrawal from the Methodists, and gave back his ordination-papers to the presiding elder. In the same month he united with the Baptist Church, and in August, 1840, was ordained as a Baptist minister. He was subsequently pastor at Pontiac, Mich., from 1840 to 1843; edited the *Michigan Christian Herald* from 1843 to 1845; was pastor of the First Baptist Church, Chicago, from 1845 to 1847; at East Boston and at Gloucester, Mass., from 1847 to 1853; and from 1853 to 1871 at North Adams, Mass. After a year's service of the American Bible Union, undertaken to restore his failing health, he again became pastor, at Salem, N. J., where he remained till his death. He was an active, energetic man, of great ability and endurance, and most winning manners, yet of very positive convictions. He was a zealous temperance man at North Adams, and carried his town with him in favor of prohibition; he was also a strong Unionist, and served as chaplain during the early part of the war. Few men have been more universally loved and esteemed than was Dr. Sandford. At the news of his death, the town of North Adams was in mourning, though he had been three years absent from them. He had published several occasional sermons and small volumes of a religious character. He received the degree of D. D. from Madison University in 1869.

Nov. 2.—PALMER, Mrs. PHŒBE, wife of Walter C. Palmer, M. D., a woman of remarkable piety and energy, an evangelist and missionary, and author of several works on the subjects of Holiness, Entire Sanctification, and the Higher Life; died in New York City, in the 67th year of her age. Possessing an ample fortune, and with every temptation to a life of fashion and aimless enjoyment, she chose rather a life of active religious effort and of serious labor for the conversion of others. Beginning as a Bible-class teacher in the Allen Street Methodist Episcopal Church in 1832 or 1833, she had with each successive year devoted herself more exclusively to religious work, and had, as she believed, experienced the blessing of entire consecration to the service of God. Many years ago she opened a meeting on Tuesdays at her own house, for the assembling of Christians of every denomination, and this meeting was not omitted for any cause. If she and her husband (who sympathized fully in her views) were absent, the meetings still went on, usually presided over by some clergyman, but, when she was present, often addressed by her. She had the gift of direct, forceful speech, and of great concentration on a few leading truths. She and her husband had traveled extensively as evangelists, traversing every part of the United States and Canada, and spending four years in Great Britain and Ireland, among the Primitive Methodists, New Connection, and

Wesleyans. In twelve weeks of this time, while they were laboring in the north of England, 3,444 members were added to the churches, and during their stay abroad between 15,000 and 20,000 professed conversion through their labors. Mrs. Palmer had written several works on her favorite themes, which have had a large circulation; the most important were "The Way of Holiness" (1854), often reprinted in England and America; "Faith and its Effects" (1856); "Devotion to God," many editions (1857, *et seq.*); "The Useful Disciple, or, A Narrative of Mrs. Mary Gardner" (1857); "Pioneer Experience" (1868); "The Altar and Sacrifice" (1870). The last named had a very large circulation, and provoked much controversy; but she adhered to the views there expressed till her death. She had been also a frequent contributor to *The Guide to Holiness*, a monthly periodical, as well as to the other papers of the Methodist Church.

Nov. 6.—SCOTT, Captain DUNLAP, an officer in the Confederate army, lawyer, political leader, and legislator; died at Rome, Ga., in the 44th year of his age. He was born in Madison County, Ga., June 20, 1831; was educated at the University of Georgia, moved to Floyd County in 1858, studied law, and was admitted to the bar at Rome in 1860. He was from the first an ardent secessionist, and entered the Confederate service as a lieutenant in the Eighth Georgia Infantry; in which he afterward became captain, and served till the close of the war. Returning to Rome in 1865, he resumed the practice of his profession, in which he was very successful, took an active part in politics, was elected to represent Floyd County in the Legislature in 1868, and was from the first an influential and prominent member, and at the second session the acknowledged leader of the Democratic minority. He waged a fierce warfare against Governor Bullock and the plunderers of the State, and, though he refused a reëlection, yet, by the death of his elected successor, he was compelled to serve, and was chosen by a large majority. He had been very active in ferreting out and defeating the frauds which were attempted by the State officials, and his sudden death was greatly lamented.

Nov. 9.—HEAD, Colonel JOHN W., member-elect of the Forty-fourth Congress from the fourth congressional district of Tennessee; died in Gallatin, Tenn., aged 55 years. He was educated for the law, and had won great distinction as a jurist, and in 1855 or thereabouts was elected Attorney-General, and Reporter of the Supreme Court of the State, which offices he filled with great acceptance for several years. He was colonel of a Confederate regiment during the war, and at its close resumed the practice of his profession, in which he regained his former distinction. He had been elected to Congress only six days before his death.

Nov. 13.—HASKELL, DANIEL N., a Boston journalist, editor of the Boston *Transcript;* died in Boston, of pneumonia, aged 57 years. He was born in Newburyport, Mass., January 1, 1818, received a good academic education, was apprenticed in Boston, afterward entered the fancy-goods trade, but was a constant writer for the press, and in 1853 became editor of the *Transcript*, and remained its editor till his death. Mr. Haskell was from early manhood an industrious student, his taste being for historical research. He wrote with vigor and plainness, paying little regard to the graces of composition, but devoting special care to accuracy and clearness. His imagination rarely found expression in poetic sentiment, and he never professed to be familiar with the refinements of art. His rare common-sense, quickness of judgment, and aptitude for journalism, enabled him to attain prominence as an editor and conduct successfully one of the leading evening papers of Boston. In old Whig times Mr. Haskell took an active part in politics, but was always indifferent to official honors, the only public position he ever held being that of councilman for three years during the mayoralties of John C. Bigelow and Benjamin Seaver. He was in latter years a supporter of the liberal antislavery wing of the Whig party, merging thence into the Republican ranks.

Nov. 14.—BILLINGS, HAMMATT, a celebrated artist and architect, of Boston; died there. He possessed exquisite taste as a designer, and his reputation extended over the whole country. He was successful alike in making designs for a pictorial work or a book-cover and in the most stately monumental or architectural subjects. The Pilgrim monument at Plymouth was built from his designs, as was also the case of the great organ in Music Hall, Boston, and many churches and public buildings in other cities.

Nov. 16.—MAY, Mrs. LEWIS, *née* KING, a Jewish lady of great refinement and culture, well known in New York City and elsewhere for her many works of charity; died suddenly in that city, in the 46th year of her age. Her husband was a banker, and president of the Temple Emanuel. At the time of her death Mrs. May was vice-president of the Ladies' Auxiliary Society of the Mount Sinai Hospital, and a director in the Hebrew Home and many other charitable societies.

Nov. 17.—ENO, WILLIAM, an eminent lawyer of Dutchess County, N. Y.; died at Pine Plains, Dutchess County, aged 74 years. He was a prominent member of the Dutchess bar for forty years, and conducted a large practice. He was a member of the Legislature in the year 1836, and district attorney two terms for Dutchess County at a time when the office was filled by appointment by the Supreme Court Justices. Soon after the adoption of the constitution of 1846, his name was mentioned by his brethren of the bar for the office of Supreme Court Justice, but he refused the nomination, preferring the retirement of his farm.

Nov. 18.—STUART, JOSEPH, a New York banker, of the firm of J. & J. Stuart; died of apoplexy, in New York City, aged 71 years. He was born November 25, 1803, in the County Armagh, Ireland. He emigrated to this country in 1827, and in the following year established the existing dry-goods firm of Stuart Brothers in Philadelphia, in connection with his brothers John and David, now heads of Manchester and Liverpool banking and mercantile houses. Shortly after, the Philadelphia house was joined by the two other brothers of the Stuart family, George H., the distinguished philanthropist, and president of the United States Christian Commission, and James. Mr. Stuart removed to New York in 1833, and took charge of the dry-goods house of J. & J. Stuart, which was founded in 1831, and continued until 1851, when the character of the business was changed to that of banking. His reputation as a financier and business-man was very high. He was a trustee of the Emigrants' Savings-Institution, a director and vice-president of the National Mercantile Bank, and was connected with several insurance and other companies. He was also largely interested in most of the benevolent institutions of the day, and his house were the bankers through whom the Presbyterian Board of Foreign Missions effected their foreign money transactions.

Nov. 19.—QUACKENBOSS, HEMAN J., a veteran legislator of New York; died at Lansingburg, N. Y., in the 85th year of his age. In early life a tanner, he conducted his business with such energy, intelligence, and integrity, as to secure himself a competency and a good name. In 1825 he was a member of the Assembly from Delaware County; in 1830 he represented Greene County in the same body. In 1831 he was elected Senator from the Greene and Delaware district, and after serving there for four years was elected to the Assembly again from New York in 1835. Some years afterward he removed to Michigan, where he was twice elected judge, and on his return to New York, in 1853 or 1854, withdrew from business and from public life.

Nov. 20.—BUTTS, ISAAC, a wealthy citizen and journalist of Rochester, N. Y.; died there. He was for many years editor of the *Rochester Union*, a Democratic journal of that city, and author of a pamphlet on the national finances.

Nov. 22.—BARCLAY, J. T., M. D., a former missionary at Jerusalem, and long a resident there, an author, and since 1871 a professor in Bethany College, W. Va.; died there, aged 67 years. He was born in Hanover Court-House, Va., in 1807, but resided for many years in Philadelphia, where he studied medicine. He went as a missionary to Jerusalem, we believe, under the patronage of the "Christian Connection" or the "Disciples," about 1850, and remained in that capacity three and a half years, when he resigned his connection with the Missionary Board, and devoted some time to a very careful exploration of Jerusalem.

Returning to the United States, he prepared a very elaborate and valuable work, entitled "The City of the Great King; or, Jerusalem as it was, as it is, and as it is to be." In 1858 he returned with his family to Jerusalem, and resided there till 1870, acting for some time as U. S. consul at Jerusalem. One of his sons was for some years U. S. consul at Beirût, and a son-in-law U. S. consul at Larnika, Cyprus. Shortly after Dr. Barclay's return to the United States, he revised very thoroughly his "Map of Jerusalem and its Environs," originally published in 1856, and in 1871 accepted an appointment as professor in Bethany College.

Nov. 25.—CAMPBELL, SHERWOOD COAN (the Campbell was a stage name, the real name being Sherwood Coan), a distinguished baritone singer; died in Chicago, aged about 44 years. He was born in New Haven, Conn., about 1830, was apprenticed to the trade of carriage-making, which he left at the age of eighteen, to join the Campbell Minstrels, from whom he borrowed the name by which he was afterward known. He subsequently joined the Christy and Bryant Minstrel companies, and spent some of the best years of his life in the negro minstrel business. But his musical gifts were of too high an order to be employed in this pursuit, and he was induced by Mr. L. F. Harrison to become a concert-singer, and soon passed to the English operatic stage, of which he became one of the brightest ornaments in a short time. He sang in the chief cities of America with Fanny Stockton, with Rose Cook, Zelda Harrison, Caroline Richings, and Madame Parepa-Rosa, as leading ladies, and everywhere accompanied by the eminent tenor, William Castle, and wherever he sang he won the admiration and regard of the public. He went to England with the Rosas, and there attracted great attention. He had joined Miss Kellogg's English Opera Company, and was to have appeared first at Chicago, but was attacked with dropsy, the result of a liver-affection, from which he had suffered for some years. His voice was a magnificent low baritone, sweet, mellow, sympathetic, firm and powerful, and by thorough training was almost faultless. His style was utterly free from affectation, simple, easy, and always pleasing.

Nov. 26. — DENNETT, JOHN RICHARD, an American journalist, publicist, and professor; died at Westborough, Mass., of consumption, in the 37th year of his age. He was a native of New Brunswick, but had resided in the United States from his boyhood. He graduated from Harvard College with honors in 1862, and was class poet at commencement. Going South, Mr. Dennett became manager of a plantation on the Sea Islands, then under military control, and acted in that capacity till the end of the war, when he traveled through the Southern States, contributing a series of able and interesting letters to *The Nation* on the condition and prospects of that section. Returning from this tour Mr. Dennett entered the office of *The Nation* as one of its editorial staff, and retained that position till his death. Besides being a regular contributor to *The Nation*, Mr. Dennett was from 1870 to 1872 Assistant Professor of Rhetoric to Prof. Child at Harvard, and discharged with great credit the duties of that honorable position, which ill-health caused him to resign. He wrote ably and forcibly on political and social subjects, but acquired marked distinction in the field of literary criticism by the evidence which his reviews afforded of extensive reading, keenness of judgment, and subtile analysis.

Nov. 27.—HERBERT, Mrs. MARY A. (RANNEY), an accomplished and successful teacher in Brooklyn, a daughter of the late Lieutenant-Governor Ranney, of Vermont; died in Brooklyn. She was born in Townshend, Vt., received a very superior education, which, added to her remarkable mental endowments, qualified her eminently for her life-work as a teacher, which she commenced at the early age of sixteen. She was connected with the Brooklyn Heights Seminary until the death of its principal, Prof. Gray, and subsequently with Miss Harrison established a school at Remsen and Clinton Streets, which was very popular. Latterly she had been associated with Miss Newton in Henry Street. She was remarkably successful, and greatly beloved as a teacher.

Nov 28.—ALVORD, CORYDON A., a well-known and celebrated printer of New York City; died at his residence in Hartford, Conn., aged 61½ years. He was a native of Winchester, Litchfield County, Conn., learned the printer's trade in Hartford, removed to New York City in 1845, and by careful and diligent practice and study acquired a reputation, as a printer of illustrated books, second to that of no man in America. His establishment in Vandewater Street was one of the most extensive in the country, and he acquired a handsome fortune there, which was subsequently lost through the misdeeds of others. He retired from business in 1871, and had since resided in Hartford, devoting much attention to the local history of Hartford and Winchester.

Nov. 28.—DODD, Colonel JOSEPH, a former contractor for mail-delivery and transportation, long an attaché of the New York Post-Office, and one of the founders of Dodd's Express; died in Jersey City, aged 84 years.

Nov. 28.—LABOR, GEORGE, a venerable citizen of Stroudsburg, Pa.; died there at the well-authenticated age of 113 years.

Nov. 28.—STURGES, JONATHAN, an eminent and leading merchant and philanthropist of New York City, nearly fifty years in business; died at his residence there, in the 73d year of his age. The best brief sketch of the career of this excellent man is to be found in the following extracts from the minutes entered upon the records of the Chamber of Commerce, of which he was a distinguished member. It is from the pen of A. A. Low, Esq., a former president of the Chamber: "Mr. Sturges was born at Southport, Conn., March 24, 1802, entered the service of R. & L. Reed, grocers, in Front Street, in 1821, and became a partner in 1828, when the firm name was changed to Reed & Sturges, and it so continued till 1843. It was then changed to Sturges, Bennet & Co., and again in 1865 to Sturges, Arnold & Co. In 1868 Mr. Sturges retired from active business with an ample fortune and a reputation for probity and honor which is better than earthly riches. He had come to be regarded as the foremost man in the tea and coffee trade, which he had followed for so many years, and was recognized as a wise counseler and a warm and steadfast friend. The good example which he lived doubtless did much to impart to the whole body of traders, of which his house was a conspicuous member, that character for integrity and upright dealing which it has always borne, which it still maintains. The following extract from the letter addressed to him by his brother merchants on December 30, 1867, when he was about to retire from the firm with which he had been so long connected, exhibits the feeling that prompted them in their invitation to meet them at dinner: 'Your life among us of nearly half a century, in the same locality in Front Street, we can only say has been such as commends itself to every one, both old and young, who regards that which is true and noble in mercantile character.' Mr. Sturges was a promoter of many important undertakings, as well as an able coadjutor in all, and in the discharge of his various and responsible duties he was always governed by rectitude of purpose and an unswerving fidelity to his trust. Good sense and a sound judgment were the distinguishing characteristics of his great work in all corporate bodies. As one of the founders and directors of the Bank of Commerce, as director and acting-president of the Illinois Central Railroad, as one of the proprietors and directors of the New Haven Railroad Company, and as vice-president of this Association, he was widely known and held in high regard. Nor was it in the walks of business, in the counting-room, and in the Exchange, that he was chiefly honored and beloved. He was a recognized patron of art. In the Church he manifested the virtues of the Christian; in society, the unostentatious attributes of a gentleman; in the service of his country, the devoted zeal of a true patriot; as a citizen, the love of the philanthropist, never forgetting his obligations to the poor, the sick, and the crippled, but extending to all the benefactions of a warm heart and of an open hand. The homage we paid the good man when living, we desire to perpetuate in hallowed memories; and to this end we inscribe on our minutes the sentiments that are graven on our hearts—of gratitude for this life of uncommon beauty, of sincere sorrow for our own great loss, and of our sympathy for the family of the bereaved."

Nov. 29.—BUCHANAN, WILLIAM JEFFERSON,

a lawyer, Confederate officer, and *littérateur*, of Baltimore; died in that city, aged 42 years. He was the oldest son of Hon. James M. Buchanan, U. S. minister to Denmark from 1858 to 1861; he graduated from Princeton College in 1853, studied law, and was admitted to the Baltimore bar, where he practised till his father's appointment to Denmark, when he accompanied him as secretary of legation. At the commencement of the late civil war he went south and joined the First Maryland Artillery as a private. Narrowly escaping death from an attack of typhoid fever, on his recovery he entered the secret service of the Confederacy, and was intrusted with delicate and dangerous duties on both sides of the Atlantic. While thus in the Confederate service, he wrote and published two pamphlets, "Maryland's Hope," and "Maryland's Crisis," which attracted considerable attention. He was a brilliant and logical writer, and after the war was for a time correspondent of the *New York Herald* and *New York Tribune*, as well as some of the magazines. His death was occasioned by congestion of the spine, and he had been a great sufferer for many months.

Nov. 29.—TALBOT, CHARLES N., a distinguished merchant of New York City, in the China trade for many years; died in New York City, aged 72 years. He was a grandson of Commodore Talbot. When a very young man he went to China, where, some years later, he became a member of the house of Olyphant & Co. in China. Upon his return to this country he became a member of the American firm of Talbot, Olyphant & Co., a connection which he retained until 1849, when he retired from business. Since that time he had been especially active in charitable works in New York City. As a business man Mr. Talbot attained to much success, was given to no display, but adhered through life to the strict business principles which he laid down for himself in his youth. He was noted among his associates for his great purity of character, integrity of purpose, and careful business habits, and in his later life he carried all these qualities into his labors of benevolence.

Nov. —.—BULLOCK, ANDREW D., M. D., printer, preacher, journalist, and physician; died in Wyoming Territory, aged about 56 years. He learned the printer's trade in his boyhood, and worked at the case for some time; he was then educated for the ministry in the Baptist Church, and preached acceptably to Baptist congregations in Leighton, Palmer, and other places in Massachusetts. He next entered the editorial profession, and was on the editorial staff of the Fall River *News*, the Springfield *Union*, and the Fishkill (N. Y.) *Recorder;* dissatisfied with journalism, he studied medicine at Pittsfield, Mass., graduated M. D., and practised medicine for several years in Rhode Island, whence he emigrated three or four years since to Wyoming Territory.

Dec. 1. — LINECOCUM, GIDEON, M. D., a

learned and accomplished but somewhat eccentric physician and scientist; died in Brenham, Washington County, Texas, aged 83 years. He was a native of Georgia, of Scotch ancestry, and in 1812 was a member of General Floyd's brigade of dragoons. Though actively engaged in the practice of his profession for many years, he very early gained a reputation as an accurate, painstaking, and skillful observer in natural science. He devoted his leisure for fourteen years to the study of the habits of the red ant, and his monograph on that subject is said to be as interesting as Huber's on the bee. He was a member of the leading scientific societies in this country and Europe, and was a frequent and valued correspondent of the Baron von Humboldt, Prof. Liebig, Charles Darwin, and other distinguished scientists abroad. He had contributed numerous articles of importance to the "Transactions" of the natural history societies, the *Journal of the Franklin Institute*, and the Smithsonian "Reports." One of his eccentricities was said to be, that every Christmas morning, at daylight, for fifty-three years, he stood in the door of his house, barefoot and in his night-clothes, and played the Scotch air of "Killiecrankie" on a fiddle made specially for him in Paris in 1820.

Dec. 1. — TYLER, Lieutenant - Colonel and Brevet Major-General ROBERT O., U. S. Army, Chief of the Second Military District of the Department of the Atlantic, a gallant officer in the late civil war, born in New York City, about 1832, but a resident of Hartford, Conn., from boyhood. He graduated from the Hartford High School in 1849, and immediately entered the Military Academy at West Point, whence he graduated in 1853 as brevet second-lieutenant of artillery, and in December following received his commission as second-lieutenant of the Third Artillery. He was on frontier duty for several years, and in September, 1856, had been promoted to a first-lieutenancy. He was mustered out of the volunteer service January 15, 1866; and on August 17th of that year was appointed chief-quarter-master of the Department of the South, having the full rank of lieutenant-colonel. At the battle of Cold Harbor he was severely wounded in the leg, and it is related of him that, as a surgeon was about to amputate the limb, he drew a pistol and threatened to shoot any one who should attempt amputation. He saved his limb thereby, though he suffered much from the wound, and was made permanently lame. After his assignment to the South, with headquarters in Louisville, in 1866, he went to San Francisco, and then made a voyage around the world, on completing which, he was ordered to New York, and last year was assigned to duty in Boston, where he died of neuralgia of the heart.

Dec. 2. — COWLES, EDWARD PITKIN, an eminent New York jurist, who was for two terms one of the Judges of the Supreme Court of New York; died at Chicago, Ill., on his way homeward from California, from gangrene, following a slight injury of the foot, in the 60th year of his age. He was born at Cannan, Litchfield County, Conn., in January, 1815. He graduated from Yale College in 1836, and almost immediately afterward began the study of law in Hudson, Columbia County, N. Y., with Killian Miller, and afterward studied under the direction of Ambrose L. Jordan. In 1839 he was admitted to the bar, and entered into practice at Hudson, with his brother, the late Colonel Cowles, of the One Hundred and Twenty-eighth New York Volunteers, who was killed at Port Hudson. He continued in practice at Hudson for some years, and came to New York in 1853. He was soon after appointed Judge of the Supreme Court by Governor Clark, and, at the end of his first term, was reappointed to fill a vacancy created by the death of Judge Morris. His first appointment was made without solicitation on his part or that of his friends, and was entirely unasked for. On leaving the Supreme Court, he engaged in private practice with Chief-Justice Barbour, afterward of the Superior Court, and had since that time enjoyed a large counsel business.

Dec. 6. — KIMBALL, Rev. JOSEPH, D. D., an able and eloquent clergyman of the Reformed (Dutch) Church; died at Newburg, N. Y., of apoplexy, in the 55th year of his age. Dr. Kimball was born in Newburg, August 17, 1820, graduated from Union College in 1839, and was ordained to the ministry from the Seminary of the Associate Reformed Church, in 1844. He was first settled as pastor of the Presbyterian Church of Hamptonburg, Orange County, and was afterward settled at Brock-port, N. Y., and at Fishkill, N. Y. In 1865 he accepted a call to the pastorate of the First Reformed Church of Brooklyn, and remained in that position until the time of his death. He received the degree of D. D. in 1871.

Dec. 10. — COLAHAN, STEPHEN J., a young but brilliant political leader of Brooklyn, N. Y.; died in that city of albuminuria, aged 33 years. At the time of his death he was Clerk of the City Court and Assemblyman-elect from the seventh Assembly district. He had served one term in the Legislature, was a member of the State Constitutional Convention of 1867, and the Democratic candidate for Congress from his district in 1872.

Dec. 10. — MARSHALL, THOMAS W., a young landscape and *genre* painter of great promise; died in Brooklyn, N. Y., in the 24th year of his age. Though his opportunities for art-study had been limited and his training desultory, he had produced some very beautiful landscapes and interiors. His "A Late Afternoon in the Forest at Keene Flats, Adirondacks," his "L'Abbaye de Villiers," and his "Interior at Barbison, France," were among his best. He was a member of the American Society of Painters in Water-Colors.

Dec. 11. — CATE, ASA P., a New Hampshire

politician and political leader, a member of the State Senate in 1843 or 1844, Democratic candidate for Governor in 1858, 1859, and 1860, and for many years Judge of Probate; died in Concord, N. H.

Dec. 13. — ROBERTS, Mrs. CAROLINE D. (SMITH), wife of Marshall O. Roberts, Esq., of New York; died in London, Eng. She was a daughter of the late Normand Smith, Jr., of Hartford, Conn., was highly educated, and carried to her prominent and exalted position, as the wife of a great merchant, the graces of a well-cultivated and remarkable intellect, a sweet and winning manner, an ardent yet unobtrusive piety, great executive ability, and a benevolent, philanthropic disposition, which enabled her to devise wise measures for the relief of the poor and unfortunate, as well as to give liberally for their help. Mrs. Roberts was the acknowledged, though never the self-appointed, leader in many of the organizations for the aid of the suffering.

Dec. 13.—SILL, Rev. FREDERICK W., an Episcopal clergyman, rector for sixteen years of St. Ambrose Church, and a most active and devoted philanthropist, the friend of the poor, the miserable, and the unfortunate; died in New York City, aged 62 years.

Dec. 13.—UMBSCHEIDEN, FRANZ, a German scholar, revolutionist, and journalist, a resident of the United States since 1852; died at Newark, N. J., in his 54th year. He was born in Gruenstadt, Rhenish Bavaria; was educated at the Universities of Heidelberg and Munich, studying law and political economy at both. In 1848 he plunged into the revolution, traveling and making inflammatory speeches. His oration over the sanguinary death of Robert Blum was so revolutionary in its tone, that he was compelled to flee to France. When the revolution broke out in Rhenish Bavaria he returned, took an active part in it, and was made major and adjutant on the staff of General Blenker. He was present at the occupation of Worms and the storming of the fortress of Landau. He was subsequently made a civil commissioner with Dr. Greiner, who recently died in Newark. He then went to Baden under General Sigel, and when the latter was defeated he went to Switzerland. During his absence he was tried and sentenced to death. In Switzerland he became a private tutor, and was expelled in April, 1852, to appease Louis Napoleon. In May, 1852, he came to Newark, and resumed the occupation of teaching. In the Fremont campaign he joined the Republican party, and in 1859 he coöperated with the Democrats. In 1860 he became local editor of the *New York Staats Zeitung*, which position he filled till 1864, when he returned to Newark and started the *Newark Volksmann*. In 1867 he took the editorial chair of the *New Jersey Demokrat*, and from 1869 to 1871 he edited the *Volksmann*.

Dec. 22.—TILGHMAN, General TENCH, an influential citizen of Talbot County, Md., a graduate from West Point in 1832; died in Baltimore, aged 65 years. On his graduation from West Point, he was made second-lieutenant in the Fourth Artillery. He resigned in November, 1833. He returned to Maryland, and took charge of his farm at Oxford, Md., from 1834 to 1861, being inspector, brigadier-general, and major-general of the Maryland militia, Commissioner of Public Works from 1841 to 1851, superintendent of the military department of the Maryland Military Academy at Oxford, Md., 1847–'57; was U. S. consul at Mayagues, Porto Rico, W. I., 1849–'50; collector of customs for Oxford, Md., 1857–'60; president of National Agricultural Society, 1858–'60, and of the Maryland & Delaware Railroad Company, 1855–'61. He took part with the Confederates in the late civil war, but was not, we believe, in any important action.

Dec. 24.—CHASE, Mrs. ANN, wife of the Hon. Franklin Chase, late U. S. consul-general at Tampico, Mex.; died in Brooklyn, N. Y., aged 65 years. She was a woman of remarkable bravery and executive ability; born in the north of Ireland in 1809, emigrated to this country in 1818, and acquired a good general and mercantile education to assist her brother in his business. In 1832, with her brother, she removed to New Orleans, and thence, in August, 1834, to Tampico, where she became acquainted with Mr. Chase, to whom she was married in 1836. In 1846, during the Mexican War, on account of his official character as U. S. consul, Mr. Chase was compelled to leave the city of Tampico, but, with his concurrence, Mrs. Chase remained to protect the Government property, the records of the consulate, and the interests of the American people. In his absence an infuriated mob attempted to tear down the flag that floated over her residence, whereupon Mrs. Chase ascended to the house-top, and declared that no one should touch that flag except over her dead body. With revolver in hand, she defied them. That flag had such priceless value in her memory that she never parted with it, and her husband draped her casket in its folds when her remains awaited removal to the final resting-place. When Mr. Chase left Tampico, in 1846, he confided to his wife all his plans, and authorized her to use his fortune for their consummation. So successfully did this brave lady carry them out, that she communicated with Commodore Conner, then commanding the United States fleet in the Gulf of Mexico, and the city of Tampico through her instrumentality was surprised and taken by the American forces without expenditure of life or treasure. The letters written to Mr. Buchanan, then Secretary of State, detailing her plans, created a conviction in his mind of the capture of the city before its consummation. In honor of Mrs. Chase's agency in this important event, and as a token of their appreciation of her heroism, the army named the fortress of the city Fort Ann, and the ladies of

New Orleans presented to her a service of plate. Mrs. Chase remained in Tampico as her residence until 1871, when her husband resigned his position and took up his abode in Brooklyn. During the many years of her residence in Tampico, Mrs. Chase dispensed with great liberality a gracious hospitality to all Americans who visited that city in naval, military, or civil life. Upon her last voyage home to the United States a little child stumbled and fell down the hatchway of the steamer. With characteristic bravery and forgetfulness of self, Mrs. Chase sprang to the rescue, and succeeded in saving the life of the child—as events proved, at the expense of her own, for she then received an injury, disregarded by her at the time, which produced cancer of the breast, of which she died. Although her sufferings were intense, she never murmured, and, when informed that an operation had become necessary, she said she was ready, and, refusing anæsthetics, submitted without flinching, although the operation was unusually prolonged.

Dec. 26.—BYERLY, D. C., a New Orleans journalist, and former Confederate officer, shot in a rencontre with ex-Governor Warmoth in New Orleans, and died there in his 48th year. He was by profession a printer, and came to New Orleans at the age of eighteen, where he was employed on several journals. He was foreman of the old *Commercial Bulletin* from 1856 to 1861, and then went into the Confederate army as a lieutenant. He fought the war through, and at Atlanta was four times wounded. After the war, he was clerk of the Third District Court for two terms, until 1872; in February, 1874, he became business manager and one of the principal owners of the *New Orleans Bulletin*, of which he was also one of the editors. He was strongly in sympathy with the White League movement, and had considerable political influence in his party.

Dec. 26.—CROCKER, Colonel ALVAH, a large manufacturer, railroad-manager, and member of Congress from the tenth Massachusetts district; died at Fitchburg, Mass., aged 73 years. He was born at Leominster, in 1801, and at eight years of age was placed in a factory. He acquired a fair education, and engaged in the manufacture of paper at Franklin, N. H., but in 1823 removed to Fitchburg, and from small beginnings became eventually the most extensive paper-manufacturer in the Union. He was a member of the Massachusetts Assembly in 1836, 1842, and 1843, and also served two terms in the State Senate. In 1871 he was elected to fill Governor Washburn's unexpired term in Congress, and was subsequently reëlected by a large majority. He was a persistent advocate of the Hoosac Tunnel project, and was identified with the railroad interests of Northern Massachusetts.

Dec. 27.—GOETZ, MORITZ, a journalist and teacher, of German birth, but resident in the United States since 1855; committed suicide

from want, in New York City. He was a native of Coblentz, Germany, highly educated, and when he first came to the United States was employed on a Baltimore paper. In 1861 he became one of the editors of the *New York Staats Zeitung*, and in 1867 associate-editor of the *New-Yorker Journal*. Being very near-sighted, he was run over by a street-car, and his leg fractured. The *Journal* supported him during the long sickness which followed, and after his recovery, his sight failing, he relinquished newspaper-work, and gave private instruction in the languages; but after a time his pupils failed him, and he was without employment and without money, and in desperation took his own life.

Dec. 27.—RUSSELL, JOHN, an extensive cutlery-manufacturer, of Fitchburg; died at Greenfield, Mass., aged 77 years. He was born in Greenfield, in 1797, removed to Georgia in 1816, was in business there till 1830, when he returned, and in 1831 commenced the manufacture of cutlery at Fitchburg, importing English mechanics, and expending large sums for machinery. Eventually the firm arrived at such excellence that their cutlery took its place of the English, and importation of that class of goods virtually ceased.

Dec. 28.—CAMPBELL, Rev. ALFRED E., D. D., an eminent Presbyterian clergyman, a brother of Judge W. W. Campbell, and for a number of years Secretary of the American and Foreign Christian Union; died at Castleton, Rensselaer County, N. Y., aged 72 years. He was born in Cherry Valley, N. Y., in January, 1802, graduated from Union College in 1820, in the same class with W. H. Seward, Tayler Lewis, Chancellor Kent, Dr. L. P. Hickok, and others. He studied theology and entered the Presbyterian ministry, preaching successively at Palmyra, Ithaca, etc., and finally becoming pastor of the Spring Street Church, in New York. From this pastorate he went to the secretaryship of the American and Foreign Christian Union, which he resigned in 1873, and returned to his country home at Castleton.

Dec. 29.—SMITH, Major-General MORGAN L., U. S. Vols., a gallant and meritorious officer in the Mexican and late civil war, former United States consul at Honolulu; died at Jersey City, N. J., of congestion of the lungs, aged 56 years. He was born in Oswego County, N. Y., and when yet young left his father's house and enlisted in the army as a private soldier. He was in most of the battles of the Mexican War, and was made sergeant for his bravery. After that war he returned to New York, and was in business there and in the West for a number of years. At the commencement of the late civil war he offered to raise a regiment of men from Illinois and Missouri, composed of men who would never retreat nor abandon the field under any circumstances. The regiment was formed, and, in the words of a Confederate general, "they fought like devils, and they never knew when they were whipped." At the capture of Fort Donelson Colonel Smith led his regiment in a gallant charge, and was made a brigadier-general. His brother, Giles A. Smith, commanded a brigade at the same time. In front of Vicksburg, at the battle of Shiloh, before Chattanooga, and in most of the battles in the Southwest, General Smith served with distinguished gallantry under General Grant, who repeatedly recognized his valor and bravery. When General Grant was called to Washington, General Smith reported to General Sherman, under whom he marched with his command to the sea. On that march he distinguished himself, and was made a major-general, and given the command of a division. After the movement in front of Atlanta, which compelled the surrender of that place, General Sherman, in referring to General Smith, used the following words: "He is one of the bravest men in action I ever knew." During one of his battles General Smith was struck with a Minié-ball in the back, just above the hip-bone. The ball penetrated to the bone, a piece of which was removed before the bullet could be extracted. Although he was terribly wounded, after a few months he presented himself for duty again, but was denied the command of his division, as it was evident that he was too enfeebled to perform the duties. General Sherman offered him the command of any post he might name, and he chose Memphis, Tenn. He was provided with an order to take command of that post, but when he arrived there he found his friend General Cadwallader C. Washburn in command, and forbore showing him the order for his deposition. General Smith passed on to Vicksburg, and took command there. While at Vicksburg he ordered a court-martial on thirteen negroes charged with murdering a family of white people. The negroes were convicted and executed by his order. This put an end to similar outrages in that region. After the close of the war General Smith was appointed United States consul at Honolulu. He subsequently declined the Governorship of Colorado, and acted as counsel for the collection of claims. At the time of his death he was connected with the Clephane Brick Company, of Washington, and supervised the erection of buildings by the company.

Dec. 31.—VARNUM, JOSEPH B., a prominent and influential citizen of New York City, several times a member of the State Legislature, and always identified with its best interests; died in Astoria, L. L, in the 57th year of his age. He was born in Washington, Conn., in 1818, of Revolutionary stock, graduated from Yale College in 1838, studied law but did not seek admission to the bar until 1849. He was a member of the Legislature in 1845, 1849, 1851, and 1857, and in one of these terms he was Speaker of the House. . He was at one time a candidate for Congress from his district, but failed of an election. He was a member

of the Common Council and of the Committee of Seventy, and an influential member of the Union League Club, and connected with most of the movements in New York City leading to the advancement of literature and art.

OHIO. The Sixty-first General Assembly organized January 5th, and adjourned April 20th until December. It had a strong Democratic majority in each branch. In his inaugural address, Governor Allen urged the reduction of taxes and appropriations. During the first session the General Assembly passed one hundred and twenty-five general laws, the most notable of which were a number of laws changing the control of the several benevolent, reformatory, and punitive institutions of the State. On the 1st of December the General Assembly reassembled, and continued in session until the holidays. In his address at the opening of the adjourned session, Governor Allen made a brief review of the affairs of the State during the year, and renewed the recommendations of his inaugural address that expenses should be cut down to the lowest practicable limit. Full reports from all the departments of the State government, showing the exact condition of affairs, were afterward submitted to the General Assembly.

The following is a brief summary of the present financial condition of the State:

On the 15th day of November, 1873, the public funded debt of the State was...... $8,211,062 10

The redemptions during the year were—

Loan of 1870..................	$128,980 00
Loan of 1875..................	92,700 00
Loan of 1881..................	1,176 80
Total......................	222,856 80

Outstanding November 15, 1874..... . $7,988,205 30

Of this amount $22,365 had ceased to draw interest, having been called in for redemption; so that the interest-bearing funded debt is $7,965,840.30.

The local indebtedness of the State on the 1st day of September, 1874, was as follows:

Debts of counties.......................	$3,482,575 62
Debts of townships, including debts created by boards of education other than for separate school districts............	329,339 08
Debts of cities (first and second class)....	15,899,112 83
Debts of incorporated villages..........	884,355 18
Debts of school districts (special)......:..	1,290,624 65
Total.........................	$21,886,007 86

Meigs County not reported.

The amount of reimbursable debt, therefore, is—

State........................	$7,988 205 30
Local.......................	21,886,007 86
Total.............................	$29,874,212 66
Irreducible debt...........................	4,122,991 86
Aggregate debts in Ohio (State, local, and trust funds)...................	$33,997,204 52

The local indebtedness in this statement is reckoned to September 1, 1874, and the State debt to November 15, 1874.

The balance in the State Treasury on the 15th day of November, 1873, was........	$129,586 42
The receipts, including transfers of $125,-956.51, for the fiscal year ending November 15, 1874, were......................	5,894,745 67
Amount of funds in Treas'y for the yr,	$6,024,332 09
The disbursements, including transfers, during the year have been..............	5,211,934 90
Balance in the Treasury Nov. 15, 1874.	$812,397 19

The taxes levied in 1873, collectible in 1874, were—

State taxes.............................	$5,477,859 25
County and local.........................	20,653,498 98
Delinquencies and forfeitures............	843,106 75
Total.................................	$26,474,459 98

The taxes levied in 1874, collectible in 1875, are—

State taxes............	$5,050,367 42
County and local taxes....................	21,786,829 35
Delinquencies and forfeitures............	777,532 39
Total.................................	$27,614,729 16

The taxable valuations in Ohio, as shown by the grand duplicate of 1874, are—

Real estate in cities, towns, and villages	$354,849,199 00
Real estate not in cities, towns, nor villages...................................	697,408,537 00
Personal property	528,121,588 00
Total.............................	$1,580,379,824 00
Which is an increase over the grand duplicate of 1873 of............	$13,104,685 00

This increase arises as follows :

On real estate in cities, towns, and villages	$11,900,999 00
On personal property.....................	2,610,880 00
Total increase.......................	$14,511,879 00
Reduction in valuation of real estate not in cities, towns, nor villages	1,407,194 00
Net increase.........................	$13,104,685 00

Considering the general stagnation of business during the year, this exhibit is a remarkable indication of the rapid development of the material resources of the State.

The report of the Secretary of State, based on the returns collected by the township assessors showing the crop statistics of 1873 and part of 1874, presents the following facts :

The acreage of wheat for 1873 was 1,742,756, being 131,539 acres more than in 1872. The yield was 21,974,385 bushels, showing an increase of 3,886,721 bushels. Not only were the acreage and total yield much larger, but the yield was also more than a bushel and one-third per acre greater in 1873 than in 1872.

The number of acres planted to corn was 2,400,295, and the yield 81,598,328 bushels, as against 2,520,253 bushels in 1872, and a yield of 103,053,234. There was thus a decrease of breadth planted to corn, and a more than proportionate decrease of crop raised.

Of oats there were 791,927 acres sown in 1873, as against 971,494 acres in 1872, with a yield of 20,401,158 bushels against 25,825,742 bushels. The acreage of rye was 30,408, against 25,166 acres the year previous, and a crop of 291,829 bushels, against 295,843 bushels. Barley was sown to the extent of 49,872 acres, against 72,483 acres in 1872, and the

yield was 1,074,906 bushels, against 1,528,266 bushels. The acreage of buckwheat was 21,-047, against 34,882 acres in 1872, and the crop 217,004 bushels, against 206,807 bushels.

The total breadth planted to all kinds of grain in 1873 was 5,036,305 acres, against 5,235,495 acres in 1872. The total crop raised in 1873 was 125,557,700 bushels, against 140,-057,556 bushels in 1872.

The extent of meadow in 1873 was 1,315,157 acres, while in 1872 it was 1,322,387. The number of tons of hay saved in 1873 was 1,302,164, and in 1872, 1,270,779. The decrease in the acreage of timothy meadows in the State, which has been going on for several years, still continues. The highest point reached was in 1867, when the breadth of meadow was 1,586,704 acres ; from that it has gone down by regular degrees to the present figure of 1,315,157 acres.

In clover 651,158 acres yielded 568,048 tons of hay, and 205,944 bushels of seed, with 64,-089 acres ploughed under for manure. The figures for 1872 were 549,557 acres sown, 493,171 tons of hay produced, 308,903 bushels of seed saved, and 51,552 acres ploughed under for manure.

The flax statistics show a great decrease in acreage and yield, the number of acres cultivated being 43,650, against 72,078 in 1872, the seed raised in 1873 being 167,510 bushels, and pounds of fibre saved being 5,070,788, against 457,379 bushels of seed and 9,060,588 pounds of fibre the preceding year.

There was a great falling off in potatoes also. The number of acres was 78,199, against 105,896 acres in 1872, and the yield 5,966,316 bushels, against 7,832,297 bushels.

Tobacco had a smaller acreage and a much larger yield, 43,850 acres producing 39,572,558 pounds, against 34,900,996 pounds from 46,227 acres in 1872. This was much the largest crop of tobacco raised in the State for nine years.

In dairy products there was a decrease in the amount of butter and an increase in cheese, the pounds of butter produced being 43,533,-865, and of cheese 36,668,530, against 45,413,-066 pounds of butter and 34,403,857 pounds of cheese in 1872. There has been a steady increase in the production of cheese for several years, the total for 1873 being in excess of that for any previous year, and double that for some years within the present decade, while the yield of butter is a little under the average for the previous three years.

The acreage of sorghum was much less in 1873 than in 1872, being 9,426 acres, against 12,932 acres, but the yield of sugar was much greater, being 52,242 pounds, against 34,599 pounds. There was a falling off in syrup, being but 676,918 gallons, against 968,130 gallons. The acreage of sorghum is steadily decreasing.

The number of pounds of maple-sugar made in the season of 1874 was 2,150,072, and the gallons of maple syrup 376,348.

The number of acres planted to vineyard in 1873 was 818, and in 1872 it was 941. The whole number of acres in the vineyards in 1873 was 19,649. The number of pounds of grapes gathered in that year was 6,607,653, against 10,016,427 pounds in 1872. The gallons of wine pressed in 1873 numbered 208,289, and in 1872 the number of gallons was 425,923.

The orchard-crop showed a material falling off from the figures of 1872. The number of acres reported in orchard was 385,829, against 391,550 acres the previous year. The yield was 11,343,431 bushels of apples in 1873, and 21,632,475 acres in 1872; 94,516 bushels of peaches, against 405,619 bushels in 1872; 80,-033 bushels of pears, against 153,968 bushels in 1872. The apple-crop was not much below the usual crop, that of 1872 being exceptionally larger, but the peach-crop of 1873 was an almost total failure as compared with a succession of previous years.

The sweet-potato acreage in 1873 was 2,692 acres, and the yield 170,370 bushels; in 1872 it was 3,026 and 215,032 bushels.

The statistics of land owned in 1873 show 8,117,830 acres under cultivation, 4,855,425 acres in pasture, 4,085,969 acres of wood-land, and 541,022 acres lying waste, making a total of acres owned 20,708,322.

The clip of wool reported was 17,175,465 pounds, against 17,536,209 pounds in 1872. The returns show 180,906 dogs to be registered in the State. The number of sheep killed by dogs in 1873 was 35,440, and 35,124 injured, making an aggregate of injury to sheep by dogs $157,094.75. The total loss in 1872 was $160,841.75. The total loss from dogs sustained by the owners of sheep in the State for the past four years is $638,930.

The number of horses listed for taxation in 1874 was 729,303; value, $45,932,368; average value, $62.94. This in an increase of 4,701 in number and a decrease of $1,280,131 in aggregate value, and of $2.22 average value.

The number of mules reported in 1874 was 25,345; they were valued at $1,778,181; average value, $70.15.

The number of cattle reported in 1874 was 1,673,864; value, $27,917,537; average value, $16.67. There was a decrease from previous report of 91,467 in number, and $1,532,411 in value.

The number of sheep in 1874 was 4,333,868; value, $10,452,067; average value, $2.41. Compared with the previous year, there was a decrease of 262,996 in the number, of $1,258,340 in value, and of fourteen cents in the average value.

The number of hogs in 1874 was 1,915,220; value, $6,152,875; average value, $3.21. This was a falling off from 1873 of 173,093 in number, and of $573,722 in value, and an increase of ninety-eight cents in the average value.

The banking capital of the State, as reported April 12, 1874, by the county auditors, was thus classified: 165 national banks, with a capital of $29,195,024; 21 banks incorporated under act of February 24, 1845, with a capital of $658,666; 82 savings-banks incorporated under act of February 26, 1873, with a capital of $1,879,324: 190 private banks, with a capital of $8,502,414; making the total number of banks 408, and total capital $40,235,428.

The general financial depression has been felt by the railroad interest of the State more than by any other interest. But few new lines have been projected, and several roads that would have been built under more favorable circumstances have been temporarily abandoned. The Baltimore, Pittsburg & Chicago Company has completed one hundred and ten miles of new track during the year; the Painesville & Youngstown Company has completed thirty-nine miles of narrow-gauge track; the Marietta, Pittsburg & Cleveland Company has completed nineteen miles of new track; the Lake Erie & Louisville Company has completed eight miles; the Toledo and Maumee Company has completed seven miles; the Mansfield, Coldwater & Lake Michigan Company has completed twenty-seven miles; the Baltimore Short Line Company has completed thirty miles; and the Cincinnati & Whitewater Valley Company has completed two miles. This makes a total of nearly two hundred and forty-five miles of new track.

The reports made by the county recorders show that 19,441 new buildings, valued at $12,293,365, were erected within the year ending April 30, 1874, being a decrease of 809 in the number erected, and an increase of $170,000 in value, as compared with the report for the previous year.

The number of deeds recorded during the year was 80,731; leases recorded, 2,846; mortgages recorded, 50,101; money secured by mortgages, $62,003,951; mortgages other than railroad mortgages canceled, 26,437; amount of money released by same, $32,846,268.

The Assessors report in the State, on the second Monday of April, 1874: deaf and dumb, 1,039; blind, 870; insane, 1,347; idiotic, 1,271; total, 4,527.

In the year ending March 31, 1874, there were sent to the Reform Farm at Lancaster 174 boys, and to the school at White Sulphur Springs 25 girls, as reported by the probate judges. There was an increase in number, as compared with the previous year, of 49 boys, and a decrease of 38 girls.

The number of persons supported in the county infirmaries, as reported to the county auditors for the year ending March 31, 1874, was 4,066, and the number of dependent persons otherwise supported by the counties, 1,935; total, 6,001. Compared with 1873, there was a decrease of 371 in the number in infirmaries, and an increase of 413 in the number of paupers otherwise supported.

The returns of vital statistics for the year ending March 31, 1874, are given as shown above:

Number of marriages (couples)..................... 26,678
Number of births, 31,686 males; 29,546 females; 322
  sex not stated; total.......................... 61,553
Number of deaths, 15,114 males; 13,800 females;
  total... 28,414
Excess of births over deaths, or natural increase
  of population.................................. 33,139
Daily average number of births.................. 169
    "   "   of deaths................... 78
    "   natural increase 91
Proportion of males to 100 females born........... 107
    "   "   to 100 "   died........... 114

The following results, prepared from the reports of county auditors and coroners for the year ending June 30, 1874, shows the occurrence of 89 homicides, 156 suicides, 511 deaths by accidents, and 164 from causes unknown —a total of 920 deaths. There were 107 deaths reported as caused by intemperance. Number of inquests held, 698.

The reports of the clerks of the Courts of Common Pleas for the year ending June 30, 1874, show 942 suits for divorce pending at the beginning of the year, 1,742 brought within the year, 1,618 decided, and 1,066 pending at the close of the year. Of the cases decided, 1,159 divorces, 800 on application of the wife, and 359 on application of the husband, were granted; 66 suits were decided against the plaintiff, and 386 were dismissed.

Reports from the probate courts show that 2,854 persons were naturalized in eighty-seven counties in Ohio in the year ending March 31, 1874, being a decrease of 4,317 as compared with the number reported the previous year.

The reports of the clerks of the Courts of Common Pleas for the year ending June 30, 1874, show that 1,628 indictments were pending at the beginning of the year against 1,669 persons, for all classes of crimes; 7,818 indictments were found against 6,041 persons, and 5,132 indictments against 4,652 persons were disposed of, leaving 4,314 indictments against 3,058 persons pending at the close of the year. A comparison with the numbers reported the previous year shows an increase of 4,093 in the number of indictments found, and of 2,123 in the number of persons included. The increase is mostly for offenses against the liquor law.

The following is a summary of the school statistics of Ohio for the year ending August 31, 1874:

Number of primary schools................. 14,356
Number of high-schools........ 412
Number of teachers in primary schools..... 21,664
Number of teachers in high-schools........ 711
Number of scholars enrolled in primary
  schools 683,644
Number of scholars enrolled in high-schools, 24,299
Amount paid teachers in primary schools.. $4,196,406 20
Amount paid teachers in high-schools...... $408,101 25
Amount paid for sites and buildings........ $1,472,100 95
Amount paid for fuel and other contingent
  expenses................................ $1,328,462 00
Amount paid on bonds and interest........ $516,603 20
Making the total amount paid.............. $8,072,157 65
Total enumeration of youth, six to twenty-
  one years of age........................ 988,180
Average amount paid for all school pur-
  poses for each youth enumerated........ $8 16
Number of universities and colleges....... 36
Number of academies, normal schools, etc.. 44
Number of schools of theology............. 12
Number of schools of law.................. 3
Number of schools of medicine............. 11

The Democratic State Convention was held at Columbus, August 26, presided over by Hon. Thomas Ewing. The following ticket was put in nomination: For Secretary of State, William Bell, Jr.; State School Commissioner, C. S. Smart; Supreme Judge, J. W. Gilmore; Clerk of Supreme Court, Arnold Green; member of the Board of Public Works, Martin Schelder. The following platform was adopted:

The Democratic party of Ohio adheres to its ancient principles of securing equal rights and exact justice to all men, and to all the States and communities of the American people, maintaining the independence of the coördinate departments of the Government, the legislative, the executive, and the judicial; condemning all encroachments of either upon the functions of the others, and resisting every attempt to usurp any of the powers reserved by the Constitution to the States respectively, and to the people. Therefore—

Resolved, That a sound currency is indispensable to the welfare of a country, that its volume should be regulated by the necessities of business, and that all laws that interfere with such natural regulation are vicious in principle and detrimental in their effects. We are in favor of such an increase of the circulating medium as the business interests of the country may from time to time require.

2. That sound policy and justice require that not less than one-half of the customs duties should be payable in the legal-tender notes of the United States, commonly called greenbacks.

3. That the power of the national banks to issue and loan their notes upon interest is a power to draw interest on their debts, while the people pay interest on what they owe. That this special and unequal privilege ought not to exist unless it is manifest that in no other way can a sound paper currency be supplied. Believing that a better system can be devised, and one that will be free from unjust privileges, we are in favor of abolishing the franchise of the national banks to issue a paper currency, as soon as the same can safely and prudently be done, and that the notes so withdrawn by the banks be replaced by the Government with legal-tender currency.

4. That the Democracy of Ohio reiterate their declaration that the 5-20 bonds, by the letter and the spirit of the law, and the general understanding of the community, were payable in legal-tender notes, and the act of March, 1869, which pledged the faith of the nation to their payment in coin, was an unnecessary and wicked sacrifice of the interests of the tax-paying laborers for the benefit of the non-tax-paying bond-holders.

5. That without equality of taxation there cannot be equality of rights; and the exemption of the public bonds from bearing their due proportion in supporting the Federal Government and maintaining the law is unwise and unjust.

6. That we are the friends of all the industries of the country, whether agricultural, mechanical, or commercial, and, believing that these industries thrive best when no unequal privilege is conferred by law upon one over another, we are therefore opposed to the unjust and oppressive features of the existing tariff laws, insist on their repeal or modification, and that a revenue tariff shall be substituted for them.

7. We are opposed to all combinations and devices of whatever character, that tend to increase the cost of transportation beyond a fair remuneration to the carrier, and we demand the exercise of all constitutional powers to remedy existing evils in this respect, and to prevent their occurrence in the future.

8. We are opposed to excessive taxation, the deadly foe, as all experience proves, to every industry, and we insist upon strict economy in every

department of the Government, Federal or State, county or municipal.

9. We are opposed to grants of the public domain to railroad corporations, and we rejoice at the fact that the determined opposition of Democratic Senators and Representatives in Congress, and the unequivocal condemnation of the people, have put a stop to a scheme of legislation that but lately threatened to bestow upon great corporations, comparatively few in number, the whole body of the public lands. We favor the policy that looks to the ownership of these lands by actual settlers, and therefore approve the principle of the homestead settlement law.

10. That freedom of the press is essential to the preservation of the public liberty, and we denounce the attempts made by the radicals at the last session of Congress, to subject the proprietors of the principal newspapers of the United States to indictment and trial in Washington City for alleged libel, as efforts to revive and embody in legislation the spirit of the gag and sedition laws of the elder Adams's Administration, which were overthrown, as it is hoped, forever, by the election of Thomas Jefferson.

11. That, while we admit the equality of all persons before the law, we protest against the attempt being made by the radicals in Congress to enforce social equality by unconstitutional pains and penalties, and we call the attention of the voters of Ohio to the fact that, although our Supreme Court unanimously decided that our statute, which provides for separate schools for white and colored children, is a constitutional law, and this judgment is supported by recent judgments of the Supreme Court of the United States, yet the civil-rights bill, so called, which passed the Senate at its last session, and is now pending in the House of Representatives, seeks to overthrow our statute, and in disregard and defiance of it to compel mixed schools in Ohio, by the infliction of severe criminal punishment and civil penalties upon all who resist that unconstitutional attempt.

12. That we have seen with alarm and regret the advocacy in influential quarters of the election of the President of the United States for a period beyond that to which the traditions and usages of the country have almost given the sanction of a fundamental law; that such election would be a long stride on the road to practical monarchy and personal despotism, and we are decidedly in favor of establishing the one-term principle by an amendment of the Constitution.

13. We favor the submission to the people, by the General Assembly, of an amendment to the Constitution authorizing the passage of a license law.

14. That with this declaration of our principles and policy, we arraign the leaders of the Republican party for their extravagant expenditures and profligate waste of the people's money; for their oppressive, unjust, and defective system of taxation, finance, and currency; for their continued tyranny and cruelty to the Southern States of the Union; for their squandering of the public funds; for their continuance of incompetent and corrupt men in office, at home and abroad; and for their general mismanagement of the Government; and we cordially invite all men, without regard to past party associations, to coöperate with us in expelling them from power, and in securing such an administration of public affairs as characterized the purer and better days of the republic.

The Republican State Convention was held at Columbus, September 2d, the presiding officer being U. S. Senator John Sherman. The following ticket was placed in nomination: For Secretary of State, A. T. Wikoff, of Adams County; Supreme Judge, long term, Luther Day, of Portage County; Supreme

Judge, short term, in place of Judge Walter F. Stone, resigned, W. W. Johnson, of Lawrence County; School Commissioner, Thomas W. Harvey, of Lake County; Clerk of Supreme Court, Rodney Foos, of Clinton County; member of Board of Public Works, Stephen R. Hosmer, of Muskingum County. The following platform of principles was adopted:

Resolved, 1. That we reaffirm the principles and policy of the Republican party, as announced by its National Conventions. That we are proud of its history and great services, and we especially commend the vigor and force by which it maintained the Union, abolished slavery, and secured equal civil and political rights to all citizens. We demand that these rights be enforced by appropriate legislation, so that all citizens shall have the equal protection of the law, and be secure in the equal enjoyment of their rights. We demand of our public agents fidelity to their principles, the honest execution of the pledges made to the people, purity, integrity, and economy in the discharge of their official duties, and the prompt and fearless examination and punishment of those who violate any of their obligations.

2. That we favor a tariff for revenue, with such incidental protection as may foster and encourage American industry.

3. That we denounce all forms of open or covert repudiation, and declare that justice and the public faith alike demand that the debt of the United States be paid in accordance with the letter and spirit of the laws under which it was created, as declared in the act of Congress of March 18, 1869; and it is the duty of the National Government to adopt such measures as shall gradually but certainly restore our paper money to a specie standard without shock to the business interests of the country.

4. That, when the currency shall have been restored to a specie value, banking should be made free, so that the circulating medium may expand or contract, according to the demands of commerce and trade.

5. That the Democratic party, by its uniform opposition to the improvement of our harbors, and our great national water-courses, has shown itself incompetent to deal with the vitally important question of cheap transportation and all internal improvements; that the cheap and prompt transportation of the products of industry should be promoted by the national and State Governments by appropriate legislation.

6. That we heartily indorse the present Republican Congress in repealing the law increasing official salaries; in reducing expenses by more than $20,000,000; in successfully resisting all "jobs;" in abolishing the extravagant government of the District of Columbia, and in reforming abuses generally; whereby the Republican party is proved to be worthy of the continued support of the people.

7. That the recent outrages and murders in the South, of which unoffending colored citizens have been the victims, committed in pursuance of the avowed purpose of maintaining an exclusive "white man's government," demand and hereby receive the indignant condemnation of the Republicans of Ohio.

8. That the restraint of intemperance and its causes, to the full extent of the legislative, judicial, and police powers of the State, and the forfeiture of public trust for intoxication, are demanded by the moral and material welfare of society and the State.

9. We deprecate the action of the present General Assembly in reorganizing the punitive and benevolent institutions of the State for merely partisan and political purposes, as tending inevitably to the impairment of their efficiency and usefulness.

The Prohibitionists also placed a ticket in the field, as follows: For Secretary of State, John R. Buchtel; Judge of Supreme Court, full term, G. T. Stewart; Judge of Supreme Court, short term, S. E. Adams; Clerk of Supreme Court, S. B. Foster; State Commissioner of Common Schools, P. M. Weddell; member of Board of Public Works, Enoch G. Collins. The election was held October 13th, and resulted in the election of all the Democratic candidates. The official count was as follows:

Secretary of State.
William Bell, Jr., Democrat...................... 238,406
Allen T. Wikoff, Republican...................... 221,304
John R. Buchtel, Prohibition...................... 7,815

Judge of Supreme Court (Full Term).
W. J. Gilmore, Democrat...................... 237,556
Luther Day, Republican 221,701
G. T. Stewart, Prohibition...................... 7,711

Judge of Supreme Court (to fill Vacancy).
George Rex, Democrat...................... 238,307
W. W. Johnson, Republican...................... 221,182
S. E. Adams, Prohibition...................... 6,278

Clerk of Supreme Court.
Arnold Green, Democrat...................... 238,089
Rodney Foos, Republican...................... 221,581
S. B. Foster, Prohibition...................... 7,831

State Commissioner of Common Schools.
C. S. Smart, Democrat...................... 237,044
Thomas W. Harvey, Republican...................... 221,821
P. M. Weddell, Prohibition...................... 7,714

Member Board of Public Works.
Martin Schelder, Democrat...................... 238,106
S. R. Hosmer, Republican...................... 220,625
Enoch G. Collins, Prohibition...................... 7,776

The total vote cast was 467,425, against 448,-878 the year before. There was a large increase in both the Republican and Democratic votes, and a falling off of 2,463 in the Prohibition vote.

Elections for members of the Forty-fourth Congress were held on the same day. Prohibition candidates were put in nomination in some districts. The following was the result:

First District.—Milton Sayler, Dem., 11,566; J. K. Green, Rep., 7,250. Sayler's maj., 4,314.

Second District.—H. P. Banning, Dem., 10,-852; Job E. Stevenson, Rep., 9,317. Banning's maj., 1,535.

Third District.—J. S. Savage, Dem., 12,972; J. Q. Smith, Rep., 11,810; L. T. Cook, Pro., 33. Savage's plu., 1,162.

Fourth District.—John A. MacMahon, Dem., 15,411; Lewis B. Gunckle, Rep., 14,312; W. A. Campbell, Pro., 216. MacMahon's plu., 1,099.

Fifth District.—A. V. Rice, Dem., 13,477; R. K. Lytle, Rep., 8,279; D. J. Callen, Pro., 22. Rice's plu., 5,198.

Sixth District.—Frank H. Hurd, Dem., 13,-108; A. M. Pratt, Rep., 11,271; J. Granger, Pro., 875. Hurd's plu., 1,837.

Seventh District.—L. T. Neal, Dem., 11,333; T. W. Gordon, Rep., 9,108. Neal's maj., 2,225.

Eighth District.—J. E. Pearson, Dem, 10,-378; William Lawrence, Rep., 10,756; W. J. Sullivan, Pro., 994. Lawrence's plu., 378.

Ninth District—E. F. Poppleton, Dem., 11,-627; J. W. Robinson, Rep., 11,199; M. Harrod, Pro., 1,045. Poppleton's plu., 428.

Tenth District.—G. E. Seney, Dem., 13,619; O. Foster, Rep., 13,778; W. G. Mead, Pro., 289. Foster's plu., 159.

Eleventh District.—J. L. Vance, Dem., 12,-437; II. S. Bundy, Rep., 10,496; D. Locke, Pro., 239. Vance's plu., 1,941.

Twelfth District.—A. T. Walling, Dem., 13,-580; D. Taylor, Jr., Rep., 9,667; H. A. Thompson, Pro., 888. Walling's plu., 3,913.

Thirteenth District.—M. I. Southard, Dem., 13,602; J. H. Barnhill, Rep., 9,651; H. Gertner, Pro., 292. Southard's plu., 3,951.

Fourteenth District.—J. B. Cowan, Dem., 12,-394; W. W. Armstrong, Rep., 7,214; M. Deal, Pro., 399. Cowan's plu., 5,180.

Fifteenth District.—W. H. Oldham, Dem., 10,656; N. H. Van Vorhes, Rep., 11,755; A. Alderman, Pro., 363. Van Vorhes's plu., 1,099.

Sixteenth District.—H. Boyles, Dem., 10,861; L. Danford, Rep., 12,097; J. Day, Pro., 35. Danford's plu., 1,236.

Seventeenth District.—D. M. Wilson, Dem., 10,837; L. D. Woodworth, Rep., 11,113; L. Paine, Pro., 445. Woodworth's plu., 276.

Eighteenth District.—J. K. McBride, Dem., 10,095; J. Monroe, Rep., 12,229; H. F. Miller, Pro., 105. Monroe's plu., 2,134.

Nineteenth District.—D. B. Words, Dem., 6,245; J. A. Garfield, Rep., 12,591; R. H. Hurlburt, Ind., 3,427; J. Price, Pro., 391. Garfield's plu., 6,346.

Twentieth District.—H. B. Payne, Dem., 13,849; R. C. Parsons, Rep., 11,330; W. D. Godman, Pro., 364. Payne's plu., 2,519.

Thirteen Democrats and seven Republicans were elected to take the place of thirteen Republicans and seven Democrats. A special election was held in the twelfth district to fill the vacancy in the Forty-third Congress, caused by the resignation of H. J. Jewett, Dem. W. E. Finck, Dem., received 14,090 votes, against 9,301 for D. Taylor, Jr., Rep., and 361 for H. A. Thompson, Pro.

The Constitutional Convention which organized at Columbus, May 14, 1873, and, after adjourning August 8th, reassembled at Cincinnati, December 2d of that year, concluded its labors by agreeing upon a constitution, May 14th, which was to be submitted to the popular vote August 18th. Shortly after the opening of the adjourned session the presiding officer, M. R. Waite, was appointed Chief-Justice of the Supreme Court of the United States, and Rufus King was elected president of the convention. Numerous changes were contemplated by the proposed constitution. The most important of these were the making State elections biennial, instead of annual; prohibiting any person interested in a contract or unadjusted claim against the State having a seat in the General Assembly; changing the compensation of legislators from a *per diem* to annual salary; providing for annual sessions; giving the Governor a qualified veto-power; placing limitations on the passage of appropriation bills; making radical alterations in the organization of the judiciary; striking the word "white" from the elective-franchise article; permitting women to be elected to any school-offices except that of State Commissioner of Schools; removing the power of appointing the directors of public institutions from the Governor to the General Assembly; limiting the power of communities to incur debts; changing somewhat the militia system so far as concerns the appointment of officers; making all counties and townships bodies corporate; changing the compensation of county officials from fees to fixed salaries; restricting the taxing power of municipal corporations; introducing minority representation into the management of all private corporations; making stringent regulations in the interests of the stock-holders and the public as to the management of railroad companies; changing and enlarging the taxing powers of the General Assembly; making a new basis for legislative apportionment and representation; introducing in the election of State Senators and Representatives the principle of minority representation by the cumulative vote; permitting women to be appointed to any (except an elective) office, and providing greater security to miners. In addition to the main body of the amended constitution, three propositions were to be submitted separately: 1. *Minority Representation.*—In every election for Judges of the Supreme and Circuit Courts, where three or more are to be chosen of the same court, and for the same term of service, no elector shall vote for a greater number of candidates than a majority of the judges of such court and term then to be chosen. 2. *Railroad Aid.*—This permitted the General Assembly, by general laws, to authorize any township, city, or incorporated village, to aid any railroad company in the construction of its road within the State, subjected to certain recited restrictions. 3. *Traffic in Intoxicating Liquors.*—This was an alternative proposition, providing either that license to traffic in spirituous, vinous, or malt liquors, under such regulations and limitations as shall be prescribed by law, may be granted—but this section shall not prevent the General Assembly from passing laws to restrict such traffic, and to compensate injuries resulting therefrom—or that no license to traffic in intoxicating liquors shall be granted; but the General Assembly may, by law, restrain or prohibit such traffic, or provide against evils resulting therefrom.

The vote was taken August 18th, and the new constitution and all the separate propositions were lost by a heavy adverse majority. The official count was as follows:

New Constitution.—For, 102,885; against, 250,169: majority against, 147,284.

Minority Representation. — For, 73,615; against, 259,415: majority against, 185,800.

Railroad Aid.—For, 45,416; against, 296,-658: majority against, 251,242.

License.—For, 172,252; against, 179,538: majority against, 7,286.

The State Grange of the Patrons of Husbandry met at Xenia, February 18th, being the first annual meeting after the organization of the Grange. The first Grange was organized in Ohio in 1872, Stark County having the precedence. The growth was very slow for a time, but, at the annual meeting, 517 subordinate Granges were reported organized within the twelvemonth, making the total number over 600, with 30,000 members.

The year 1874 is remarkable in the annals of Ohio as that of the women's temperance crusade, which began in the closing days of 1873, at Washington Court-House, and during the early part of 1874 swept like a wave of excitement over nearly the entire State. The women marched in procession through the streets, singing and praying in the saloons where admitted, and on the sidewalks when excluded. A large number of saloons were closed, and in some villages the liquor-traffic was suspended for a time. Ultimately a reaction set in, disturbances occurred at Cincinnati, Cleveland, and Columbus, which led to the enforcement of the municipal laws against obstructing the streets; the controversy was carried into the elections, with unfavorable results to the temperance movement, and by the close of the year the excitement had mostly subsided.

OREGON. The Legislature was in session from September 14th to October 23d. During this brief session the most important legislation had reference to retrenchment and economy in public expenditures, and to securing additional railroad facilities for the State.

The receipts into the State Treasury during the two years ending September 1, 1874, were $628,775; disbursements $663,193; balance in the Treasury September 1, 1874, $188,179.

The current expenses for the two years ending September 1, 1876, were estimated at $553,-350, viz.: legislative expenses, $30,000; salaries of executive officers, $15,000; salaries of judges, etc., $36,600; salaries, etc., of various officers, $40,000; penitentiary, $80,000; Insane Asylum, $120,000; conveyance of convicts and insane, $15,000 each; public printing and binding, $26,000; Agricultural College, $19,-000; keeping and tuition of mutes, $10,000; support of poor, $5,000; Orphans' Aid Society, $3,000; miscellaneous, $48,750. The total amount of taxes levied in 1873 for State purposes was $238,482.57, of which $222,701.57 (55 cents on $100) was on property and $15,-781 on polls. The equalized value of property for purposes of taxation in 1874 was $45,688,-924.94, including land (3,489,394 acres), $22,-220,381.40; live-stock, $8,116,841; property of corporations, $2,283,296.49. The actual value is estimated by the Secretary of State at from $100,000,000 to $450,000,000. The total debt on September 1, 1874, was $596,256, of which $247,247 was in bonds bearing interest at 7 per cent., and $349,000 in warrants bearing interest at 10 per cent.

The public schools of Oregon are well supported. The Board of Education consists of the Governor, Secretary of State, and Superintendent of Public Instruction. There are county superintendents of common schools, elected by the people for two years, and boards of district officers. The following statistics, incomplete, owing to the failure of some districts to report wholly or in part, are from the report of the Superintendent of Public Instruction for 1873–'74:

Number of districts.............................	680
Persons of school age, four to twenty years (21,519 males and 19,379 females)..........	40,898
Pupils enrolled in public schools (11,138 males and 9,542 females)..................	20,680
Average attendance.........................	15,169
Persons of school age attending private schools.............................	2,926
Persons of school age attending no school...	10,711
Number of public schools (518 of ordinary and 12 of advanced grade)...............	530
Number of teachers employed during the year.....................................	860
Largest number employed at one time.......	581
Average monthly salaries of teachers, males..	$45 92
" " " females..	$34 46
Average length of public schools.............1.52 quarter.	
Number of districts having six months' school or more..................................	288
Number of private schools (43 primary, 21 academic, and 6 collegiate)...............	70
Number of public school-houses..............	555
Value of school property.....................	$332,764 84

The schools of advanced grade include those in which most of the pupils pursue the higher branches; in many of those of ordinary grade, probably 100, some of the higher English branches are taught. The total receipts for public-school purposes during the year amounted to $204,760.13, viz.: from district tax, $47,243.04; from State apportionment, $31,589.37; from county apportionment, $87,573.39; from rate-bills and subscriptions, $34,671.45; from other sources, $3,682.61. The expenditures were $215,107.12, of which $157,102.90 was for teachers' wages, $46,608.96 for erection of school-houses, and $11,395.26 for incidental expenses. The "irreducible school-fund," the income of which is apportioned among the different districts, amounted to about $50,000. Among the principal and most urgent needs of the school system of Oregon are the following:

1. A sufficient increase of school-funds to enable every district in the State to maintain a *free school* for six months or longer during each year.

2. Some means by which a larger and more regular attendance upon public schools may be secured.

3. Better facilities for training teachers and fitting them for their calling.

The State has six colleges and universities, viz.: Tualatin College, at Forest Grove; Willamette University, at Salem; McMinnville College, at McMinnville; Christian College, at Monmouth; Philomath College, at Philomath; and Corvallis College, at Corvallis. The State Agricultural College, endowed with the congressional land-grant of 90,000 acres, was organized as a department of Corvallis College in 1872. It has a farm connected with it, and receives an annual grant of $5,000 from the State. Grounds have been selected and buildings erected for the University of Oregon, near Eugene City, but the institution has not yet been opened.

The penitentiary is at Portland, where a new building of brick has been recently erected. The convicts are employed chiefly in brickmaking, but also on the farm, in the construction of public buildings, and in various manufactures. The number of convicts September 1, 1874, was 113. The expenditures on account of the penitentiary, for the two years preceding that date, amounted to $86,127; deducting supplies on hand, permanent improvements, etc., the actual expenditures are stated at $69,822. The earnings of the prison for the same period are reported at $76,026, showing an excess of earnings over expenditures of $6,204.

The political campaign opened toward the latter part of March by the meeting of the Democratic State Convention in Albany. The session lasted two days. The nominations embraced L. F. Grover for Governor, S. F. Chadwick for Secretary of State, A. H. Brown for Treasurer, M. V. Brown for State Printer, Rev. E. J. Dawne for Superintendent of Public Instruction, and T. A. La Dow for Congress. The platform adopted was as follows

1. We declare our unfaltering devotion to the Constitution of the United States and to the Union of the States thereby established, and we affirm that the people of the several States have the sole and exclusive right of governing themselves as free, sovereign and independent States, subject only to the limitation of the Constitution, and that all powers not therein expressly granted to the National Government are reserved to the States respectively, and we deny the right of the Federal Government, through the treaty power, to permanently domicile Mongolians within any State without the consent of the Legislature thereof.

2. We affirm that the greatest danger with which we are now threatened is the corruption and extravagance which exist in high official places, and we do declare as the cardinal principle of our future political action, that retrenchment, economy, and reform, are imperatively demanded in all the governments of the people, Federal as well as State and municipal, and we here proclaim ourselves the uncompromising foes of the salary-grab law, ring politicians, and land-monopolists, whoever they may be and wherever they may be found, whether they are in office or out; and we appeal to honest men everywhere, without regard to past political affiliations, to join us in branding, as they deserve, these corrupt leeches on the body politic, and assist us to purge official stations of their unwholesome and baneful presence.

3. The present Federal Administration, by its utter inability to comprehend the dignity or responsibilities of the duties with which it is charged, by its devotion to personal and partisan interests, by its weak and inconsistent management of the national finances, by its unwarrantable interference with the local self-government of the people, by its support of the corrupt governments which it has imposed by its power upon several States of the Union, by its complicity with corrupt practices and scandals in various quarters, and by its appointment of notoriously incompetent men to high official position, has justly brought upon itself the condemnation of the American people.

4. That the persistent interference by Federal offi-

cials in local elections, and the use of large sums of money to defeat the voice of the people through the ballot-box, deserve and receive our severest condemnation.

5. That corporations are the creations of law; their franchise and privileges are granted to subserve the public interests, and when these are used not to subserve the objects of their creation, but for purposes of oppression and extortion, we declare it to be the right and duty of the Legislature to regulate and control such corporations.

6. That we favor speedy return to specie payments; just and equal taxation for support of Federal and State Governments; and that we are opposed to all discrimination in the assessments of Federal revenue for the purposes of protection.

7. That the free navigation and improvement of the Columbia River, the construction of a breakwater at Port Orford, the improvement of the Coquille and Willamette Rivers, and the construction of the Portland, Dalles & Salt Lake Railroad, are improvements demanded by the commercial interests of this State, and that the Federal Government ought by all proper means to assist these measures; that we are in favor of the bill now before Congress, generally known as the Portland, Dalles & Salt Lake Railroad bill; and we also favor the early completion of the Oregon & California Railroad to the southern boundary of the State.

8. That we disapprove all measures in the interests of capitalists and monopolists against labor, believing that distinctions, if distinctions be made, should be in favor of the laboring class, who constitute the mass of our citizens, the producers of the wealth and prosperity of our country. We therefore approve of the declared principles and sympathize with the avowed object of the organization known as the Patrons of Husbandry, and with those of all other orders having for their object retrenchment and reform in public affairs, and the social advancement of the people; that we are opposed to a monopoly in the publication and sale of books used in the common schools of this State, and we are in favor of amending the existing laws in relation to such, so as take away from the publishers of the Pacific Coast Series of readers and spellers the special privileges in relation thereto which they now enjoy.

9. That the act relating to the fees of sheriffs and clerks ought to be so amended, either by making such offices salaried, or by so reducing the fees now attached to the same, as shall make the compensation received by such officers a fair remuneration and nothing more for the services required of them. That the constitution be so amended that all printing for the State, after the expiration of the term of the State Printer in office when such amendment is passed, shall be provided for by letting the same to the lowest responsible bidder. That we are in favor of the Litigant act.

10. That the only legitimate object of government is the protection of its citizens in their lives, liberty, and property, and the pursuit of happiness; that to accomplish this end direct means only should be resorted to; that the good resulting from a departure from this rule is temporary, the evil lasting. We are, therefore, opposed to the State engaging in the purchase, leasing, or speculating in property of any kind, except such only as is necessary for conducting the ordinary functions of the government.

11. That we favor the immediate construction of a good and serviceable wagon-road along the south bank of the Columbia River, from the mouth of the Sandy River to the Dalles.

12. That the compensation of all officers should be only such as will be a just remuneration for their services.

13. *Resolved*, That we are in favor of congressional aid for the construction of the Portland,

Dalles & Salt Lake Railroad, and also for continuing the Oregon Central Railroad, from St. Joseph to Junction City.

Resolved, That we are in favor of free trade and direct taxation.

The Republican State Convention assembled in Salem on the 8th of April, and nominated Richard Williams for Representative in Congress, Judge J. C. Tolman for Governor, C. M. Foster for Secretary of State, D. G. Clark for Treasurer, E. M. Waite for State Printer, and L. L. Rowland for Superintendent of Public Instruction.

The following resolutions were adopted:

Resolved, 1. The Republican party of the State of Oregon, in convention assembled, declare that the end of government is to secure equal and exact justice to all its citizens with as little infringement as possible upon individual freedom; that the government of the people by the people and for the people, interpreted and foreshadowed by the Declaration of Independence, is the true American idea; that this idea can only be realized by the election of honest and capable men to public office, and by conducting public affairs with strict prudence and in accordance with the sound and approved maxims of business and political economy.

2. That party organizations are useful and necessary, but that, while we are proud of the birth and history of the Republican party, we recognize no such allegiance to political associations as shall prevent our fair and candid criticism of the acts of all public men, and that every case of negligence, wastefulness, or dishonesty, on the part of those having control of public money, ought to be promptly investigated and severely punished, without fear or favor; that we expect of our State legislators and State officers the strictest integrity and economy, the largest possible relief from the burden of taxation, the maintenance of public education, the preservation of the purity and freedom of the ballot-box, the enforcement of such laws as will secure to all entitled to suffrage the right to its exercise, and such as will at the same time exclude all fraudulent voting.

3. That we insist upon the right and duty of the State to control every franchise of whatever kind it grants; and while we do not wish that any injustice shall be done to the individual or corporation investing capital or industry in enterprises of this kind, we yet demand that no franchise shall be granted which is prejudicial to the public, in which the rights and interests of the State and the people are not carefully and fully guarded.

4. That while we recognize the full right of every citizen to express and act upon his convictions upon all questions of public or State interest, no person holding a Federal or State office has the right to seek to influence the action of his subordinates by exciting their fears of loss of place if their opinions or actions shall differ from his own; and that we are opposed to all interference or participation by them in the conventions of the people for the nomination of their candidates for office.

5. That we are desirous of political reform, and for honest economy and purity in all official administration. That to secure this is the duty of every citizen; that to this end every good man should feel bound to participate in politics, and to make an end of bad men forcing their election by securing a party nomination. That we believe there are as good men in the Republican party as out of it, and only the best men should be nominated for office, and only such are entitled to receive the support of the people.

6. That we sympathize with every movement to secure for agriculture and labor their due influence, interest, and rights, and the Republican party will be their ally in every just effort to attain that end.

7. That the interests of this State demand in its commercial relations with the other States of the Union, both present and prospective, and will warrant, a liberal expenditure on the part of our national Government in the improvement of our harbors and of our river channels, and it is the true policy of our people that they should be so represented in Congress as shall the most effectively secure this result.

8. That true economy in the management of public lands of the United States, as well as the settlement of our vast domain and the development of its resources, demands liberal grants of the public lands to aid in the construction of railroads and other public works, with such limitations and restrictions as will secure the ultimate sale to actual settlers.

9. That we are in favor of congressional aid to the Portland, Dalles & Salt Lake Railroad; for the improvement of the Columbia River at the Dalles and Cascades; to aid the extension of the Oregon Central Railroad from St. Joseph, through the counties of Polk and Benton, to its junction with the Oregon & California Railroad, and the improvement of the Willamette River.

10. That we favor congressional aid for the construction of a wagon-road from some point in Rogue River Valley to the nearest practicable point on the coast, and that we favor the immediate construction of a good and serviceable wagon-road along the south bank of the Columbia River, from the mouth of Sandy to the Dalles.

11. That we are opposed to the purchase or leasing, by this State, of the canal and locks at the falls of the Willamette River.

12. That we demand the repeal of the litigant law, Portland police bill, the unconstitutional acts increasing the emoluments and salaries of State and judicial officers, the acts increasing the fees of clerks and sheriffs, and the modification of the school-laws so as to relieve the people of the school-book monopoly.

13. That we are in favor of the speedy payment in full of all just claims of citizens and volunteers, for supplies furnished and services rendered in the suppression of Indian hostilities in Southern Oregon in the years 1872 and 1873.

14. That we are in favor of such legislation to regulate the sale of intoxicating liquors as will restrain the abuses growing out of indiscriminate license, and operate as a needful check upon the growing evils of intemperance.

15. That we are in favor of opening Wallowa Valley to settlement.

The Independent State Convention was held in Salem, on the 15th of April. The nominations were: T. W. Davenport for Congress, T. F. Campbell for Governor, J. H. Douthitt for Secretary of State, D. Beach for Treasurer, Wm. M. Hand for State Printer, and M. M. Oglesby for Superintendent of Public Instruction. The following were the resolutions:

Resolved, 1. That extravagance and corruption have become so prevalent in the administration of the affairs of this State and nation as to burden the people with taxes that are not necessary to good government, make politics a trade, and debauch the morals of society; that there is no ground to hope for a remedy for these evils through the agency of the two political parties that have heretofore ruled the country, and that the welfare of the people demands that every citizen, laying aside all party prejudices, and differences of opinion upon immaterial points, unite in selecting for the public service men who will exert themselves to secure public economy, retrenchment, and reduction of taxation in every practicable way.

2. That we view with alarm the reckless course of

the State and national governments in the multiplication of officers beyond the requirements of the public service, many of whom, while receiving salaries from the public Treasury, are devoting themselves to their private pursuits. And we demand that officers paid do give their time exclusively to the service for which they are appointed.

3. That we favor the adoption, by the national and State government, of all reasonable measures of securing cheap transportation; and to this end we favor liberal aid from the General Government for the opening and improvement of our harbors and rivers, for the construction of the Portland, Dalles & Salt Lake Railroad, the completion of the Oregon & California Railway to the southern line of the State, and the extension of the Oregon Central Railway to Junction City. That the interests of the State demand the completion of the Oregon Central Railway to Astoria; that we favor such aid as may be consistent with prudence and public economy, for the construction of roads across our mountain-chains. And we favor the immediate construction of a wagon-road along the south bank of the Columbia River, from the mouth of Sandy to the Dalles.

4. That all property rights, individual and corporate, should be subject to law; that we would give all proper aid, encouragement, and protection to corporations, companies, or persons engaged in transportation, commerce, or any other legitimate pursuit; but we would hold all subject to law; and we demand that the rates of freight and fare on railways within the State be fixed by the Legislature of the State, and on inter-State railways, by Congress.

5. That we demand a return to the salaries fixed by the constitution for State officers, and we condemn all the schemes that have been devised to increase such salaries by indirection. That the compensation of all officers should be only such as would pay them fairly for the services they perform; that county clerks and sheriffs should have salaries fixed by law according to their services; that the law increasing their fees should be repealed, and a law enacted providing reasonable fees to be charged by them in cases where private parties alone are concerned, such fees to be paid by officers into the County Treasury. That we demand the passage of a law to protect the public against unreasonable charges for the State printing.

6. That we favor a liberal system of public schools, but we condemn the act creating a monopoly in the sale of school-books, and demand its repeal.

7. That we demand the repeal of the Litigant printing law.

8. That we demand equal rights for all citizens, and accord special privileges to none.

9. That the interests of the people demand competition in the transportation of freights to and from our seaboard; that we are opposed to the purchase or leasing by the State of the canals and locks at the falls of the Willamette, but would hold both the State and the Lock Company to a strict compliance with their existing contract.

10. That we especially condemn those acts of the Legislature that have enabled speculators to obtain the public lands of the State in large tracts, to the exclusion of poor men and men of moderate means, who would take them for homes.

11. That the removal of a faithful and competent officer merely because of his political opinions is a gross abuse of power. That the use of the appointing power to reward politicians for services in conventions and elections is no less corrupt than any other species of bribery. That the removal of faithful public officers for the conscientious performance of their duties is an outrage upon good government.

12. That personal character is the proper criterion by which to judge of the fitness of men for public position, and it is dangerous business to men of disreputable private character.

13. That the General Government should pay all

the expenses, losses, and damages necessarily arising from its course of dealing with the Indians; and we demand that our fellow-citizens in Eastern and Southern Oregon be indemnified by the Government for their losses and damages in the Modoc War.

14. That we are in favor of such legislation on the subject of the liquor-traffic as will allow each precinct to decide by a vote of the citizens thereof whether liquor shall be sold in that precinct or not, and which shall make the venders of intoxicating drinks responsible for damages which may be done by the abuse of that privilege where sale is permitted.

15. That the uprising of the agricultural classes, and their organization into a compact society for mutual protection against the extortions of oppressive monopolies, commends itself to the favor of every just mind, and cannot but result in ultimate good to the whole people.

Early in May a State Temperance Convention was held in Portland, and the following resolutions were adopted:

Whereas, The Temperance party of the State of Oregon, in convention assembled, declare that the purpose of government is to secure equal and exact justice to all its citizens, the protection of the weak against the attacks and inroads of the base and strong; and as this is most signally and continually defeated by intemperance in all its forms: therefore,

Resolved, 1. That we most emphatically affirm our full belief in the principles of total abstinence from all intoxicating beverages as affording the only basis for any permanently successful temperance movement.

2. That we, with all our might, and by every lawful means, will try to induce our congressional and legislative bodies to enact laws prohibiting the importation, manufacture, or traffic in intoxicating beverages; and that no party nor candidate for public office shall be supported by us at the ballot-box, or otherwise, who will not use all their influence to carry out the spirit of this resolution.

3. That we regard the public-school system as grand in conception, and vital to the life and honor of our country, and we desire such a change in our common-school law as will give at least six months' free-school instruction each year, in every school district in our State.

4. That we are in favor of a liberal expenditure on the part of our national Government in the improvement of our harbor and river channels.

5. That we favor aid from Congress to the Portland, Dalles & Salt Lake Railroad, and in the extension of the Oregon Central Railroad through to its junction with the Oregon & California Railroad.

6. That we demand the repeal of the litigant law, and all laws increasing the salaries of State, judicial, and county officers.

7. That we are opposed to the purchase or leasing of the locks at the Willamette Falls by the State.

8. That we invite the hearty coöperation of the noble and earnest women of our State in the cause of temperance, until, by the power of the ballot, we may the more effectually banish the curse of intemperance from our land.

9. That it is the sense of this State Temperance Convention that it is important to the interests of our cause that we organize by electing a Congressman, and State and district officers, to be supported at the coming June election.

It was decided that the candidates to be presented by the friends of temperance should be selected, as far as possible, from those put forth by the other parties. The following nominations were then made: For Congress, T. W. Davenport; Governor, J. C. Tolman; Secretary of State, S. F. Chadwick; State Treasurer,

D. G. Clark; State Printer, Enoch Turner; Superintendent of Public Instruction, L. L. Rowland.

The total vote for Governor at the election held on the first Monday in June was as follows: Grover (Democrat), 9,713; Tolman (Republican), 9,163; Campbell (Independent), 6,532: total vote, 25,408. The total vote for Governor in 1870 was 22,821, of which Grover received 11,726, and Palmer (Republican) 11,095. In 1872, 11,819 votes were cast in favor of Grant for President, and 7,730 for Greeley. The vote for Congressman in 1874 was: George A. La Dow (Democrat), 9,642; Richard Williams (Republican), 9,340; T. W. Davenport (Independent), 6,350. The vote for other State officers was as follows:

Secretary of State.

S. F. Chadwick, Democrat	10,977
C. M. Foster, Republican	8,603
J. H. Douhitt, Independent	5,783

Treasurer.

A. H. Brown, Democrat	10,228
D. G. Clark, Republican	9,043
Demas Beach, Independent	6,132

State Printer.

Martin V. Brown, Democrat	10,301
E. M. Waite, Republican	9,078
William Hana, Independent	5,781

Superintendent of Public Instruction.

L. L. Rowland, Democrat	9,730
E. J. Dawne, Republican	9,690
M. M. Oglesby, Independent	5,657

The Legislature is constituted as follows:

PARTIES.	Senate.	House.	Joint Ballot.
Democrats	13	90	28
Independents	6	23	29
Republicans	11	17	28
Total	30	60	90

The question of woman's suffrage has received no little public attention during the year. The annual convention of the State Woman's Suffrage Association was held in Portland, on the 14th and 15th of February, when the following resolutions were adopted:

Whereas, The Government of the United States is based upon masculine superiority instead of the inherent rights of human beings, regardless of sex, thereby causing much dissatisfaction among the taxed but unrepresented citizens of the non-voting class, who feel aggrieved because of the political disabilities to which they are forced to submit: therefore—

Resolved, That the first duty of the voters of the nation is to inaugurate such legislation as may be necessary to endow the disenfranchised half of the people with all the rights, privileges, and immunities of citizens, such as can only accrue to any people through personal representation.

Resolved, That the motto of the Association, copied from the war-cry of our forefathers, is, and shall be till the victory is won, "Taxation without representation is tyranny."

An effort was made to secure the passage of a law by the Legislature, at its autumn session, securing to women the right to vote, but the measure was defeated.

The salmon-fisheries of the Columbia are becoming of such importance as to demand the attention of the Legislature. Four years ago the product of these fisheries was of comparatively little importance; but in 1873 it approximated $1,000,000 in export value, and during the season of 1874 exceeded $1,500,000. There are now thirteen canning establishments on the Lower Columbia, extending from Rainier to Astoria. There are 300 boats engaged in the fishing on this river, employing 600 men, or two men to a boat—one to manage the boat and the other to attend to the net. These men are paid 25 cents for every fish they catch, making the wages paid to these 600 men for the four months' fishing $250,000, less about $50,000 for nets, leaving an average of $333 for each man. In the thirteen canning establishments there are 2,000 men employed in all the departments, earning daily $2,500, including night-work and other extra time, making $250,000 paid for wages during the 100 days comprising the fishing-season—from April to July inclusive.

The process of canning is more or less interesting, and shows the value of the proper division of labor. In catching the fish, two men are required to a boat. Another receives the fish at the wharf and counts them. A boy places the fish on the splitter's table; the splitter, who is generally a strong, active man, holds a large, sharp knife, and with ten cuts removes seven fins, head, tail, opens the fish and disembowels it. A competent man will handle from 100 to 120 in an hour, or from 1,000 to 1,200 in ten hours. A man then washes the fish, scrapes it, and transfers it to another for a further washing and scraping, so that all the blood and slime possible may be removed before cutting. He then puts the fish on the cutter's table. The cutter places the fish in a frame, and with a circular knife of six blades cuts the fish with one stroke into six pieces, each piece the size of the depth of the can. With one motion he transfers these pieces to the opposite side of the table, where another man with an ordinary knife subdivides them into about twelve pieces and puts them into a vat of strong brine. Another man subjects them to a second process of a similar

kind, with the object of removing all impurities; he then, with a strainer, places them on a table, where the watery parts are drained off, and the fish are ready for canning. A man with a barrow conveys the pieces to the canner's table; another puts a small quantity of brine or salt in each can; another fills the can with fish (one or two pounds, as the case may be); another removes any slime about the mouth of the can; another puts on the lid; another solders it; another conveys it to the bath-room for cooking. Five men and the superintendent are employed in this department, which is one of the most important. The cans are placed on trays and boiled in kettles for two hours, then taken out and tested, to ascertain that they are air-tight; then boiled for two hours more; then dipped in lye to remove all oily substances from the cans; then washed with cold water by means of a hose; then removed to the store-room, where another man dips them in a preparation that protects the can from rust; another person puts on the label; another puts them in the case, and another nails it up, when it is ready for shipment.

The salmon has seldom frequented the waters of the Upper Willamette River, not being able to pass the falls at Oregon City. It was anticipated that the salmon would pass to the Upper Willamette through the canal and locks lately constructed at those falls for the purpose of navigation; but it is ascertained that the fish will not follow slack-water channels, and consequently will not present itself at the gates of these locks. Yet the Upper Willamette River, on account of its smooth and pure waters, and its milder temperature, is thought by the observant to be the best home for young fish of all the tributaries of the Columbia. If the salmon could pass the falls of the Willamette without injury, the result would be a great blessing to the people of the Willamette Valley, as well as a great addition to the spawning-grounds tributary to the Columbia fisheries. The Governor recommends the appointment of a commission to investigate the subject, and report to the Legislature the best plan for protecting and promoting this important industry.

P

PARAGUAY (República del Paraguay), a country of South America, extending from latitude 21° 27' to 27° 30' south, and from longitude 54° 21' to 58° 40' west. Its boundaries are: on the north and northeast, Brazil; on the southeast, south, and southwest, the Argentine Republic, and on the northwest, Bolivia; and it embraces an area variously estimated at from 57,000 to 90,000 square miles, exclusive of the triangular section of the Gran Chaco lying mainly between the two rivers Paraguay and Bermejo, and the 22d parallel,

one portion of which is claimed by Bolivia and the remainder by the Argentine Republic. The area was much more considerable before the war of 1865–'70, at the termination of which Paraguay ceded, as a war-indemnity, to Brazil, some thousand square miles. The limits of the country were then fixed, by the terms of the treaty of March 26, 1872, as follows: "The bed of the Paraná River from the mouth of the Iguazú (latitude 25° 30' south) to the Salto Grande (latitude 24° 7'). From these falls the line runs (about due west) along the highest divide of the Sierra de Maracayú to the termination of the latter; thence, as nearly as possible, in a straight line northward along the highest ground to the Sierra de Amambay, following the highest divide of that sierra to the principal source of the Apa, and along the bed of that river (westward) to its junction with the Paraguay. All the streams flowing north and east belong to Brazil, and those south and west to Paraguay."

The republic was here constrained to abandon the very portion of her territory which was so long coveted by her imperial neighbor, and the northern limit of which was the mouth of the Rio Blanco, 80 miles above the *embouchure* of the Apa. The computations of the population are generally as discordant as those of the area, ranging from 100,000 to 1,300,000. The latest census (before the five years' war), regarded as tolerably accurate, was that ordered by Dr. Francia in 1840, the returns of which gave 220,000. By the natural rate of increase, that number would be doubled by 1865, in which year the population would be 440,-000; but the losses in the subsequent war may be reckoned at half the total number of inhabitants—170,000 males by battle and disease (chiefly the latter), and 50,000 women and children by famine and exposure in the forests; so that the census-returns of January 1, 1873, were probably correct, viz., 221,079. Of this number, 28,746 were males, and 106,-254 females, over fifteen years of age; and the remainder, 86,079, of both sexes under that age. The average proportion of male to female births is very nearly as eight to nine. The inhabitants are chiefly Indians (Guaranis and a few other tribes); the language of that people is principally spoken throughout the republic. The few hundred white natives preserve their blood tolerably pure by intermingling or by alliance with Europeans, and are mainly grouped in or around Asuncion, the capital. Next to the Indians, the most numerous element is the mulatto or hybrid, from the union of the early Spanish settlers and the Indian women, and further modified by the Mamalucas from São Paulo, in Southern Brazil, and by the introduction of African slaves. Pure-blooded Africans are, however, now in comparatively small numbers. In 1873 there were 2,300 foreign residents, made up of Italians, Germans, English, Austrians, Dutch, and Swiss.

By the terms of the new constitution, promulgated on November 25, 1870, and for the most part based upon that of the Argentine Republic, which in turn resembles that of the United States, the legislative authority resides in a Congress composed of a Senate and a Chamber of Deputies; and the executive authority in a President elected for a term of six years, with a non-active Vice-President, and a cabinet of five ministers; the departments of these latter being severally those of the Interior, Foreign Affairs, Finance, Public Worship and Public Instruction, and War and the Navy. Señor Don Bautista Gil has been President of Paraguay since October, 1874.

There is no bank or other credit institution in the country. The national revenue, which, in 1863, amounted to $4,275,000, did not exceed $412,-000 in 1873, the chief sources from which it is derived being the custom-house, yielding in the year last mentioned $348,000 for imports, and $70,500 for exports; rents of state property, licenses, etc. The estimated expenditures for 1874 were $341,805.

Previous to 1865, Paraguay was exceptional among South American states, in that she had no national debt; on the contrary, she possessed a large surplus income; but, at the present time the republic is almost hopelessly insolvent, her name having figured side by side with those of other bankrupt states in a list published in a London financial journal in the second half of 1874, and according to which she was in default $2,903,000 since April of that year; hence, her total indebtedness to Great Britain—principal and interest of a loan contracted in 1871—is no less than $14,518,500. But to this sum are to be added her liabilities arising out of stipulations consequent upon the issue of the late war, and by virtue of which she owes $177,000,000 to Brazil, the Argentine Republic, and Uruguay, in the following proportions: $150,000,000 to the first, $26,250,-000 to the second, and $750,000 to the third. Hence her total foreign debt is, at the present time, $191,518,500. There is, likewise, a home debt, the amount of which has not transpired.

Public instruction has of late been the subject of more serious attention than at any period since the days of the Jesuits. Indeed, Paraguay had in 1861 as many public primary schools, in proportion to her population, as the most advanced Spanish-American states; instruction was then made compulsory and gratuitous, and the justices of the peace were required to aid in carrying out that measure. Grammar-schools were few; of higher instruction there was only such as the masters of a single establishment in the capital could dispense. But well-directed and determined efforts have, since the end of the war, been successful in extending primary education. In the budget for 1874 is observed an appropriation of $34,860 for schools. The total value of the books imported during the decade ending in 1865 was but $3,299.

The Roman Catholic is the religion of the state, but all sects are tolerated.

The present strength of the army is about 2,000 men, comprising two regiments of cavalry, two battalions of infantry, and a regiment of artillery. The estimated expenditure for the War Department for 1874 was set down at $98,918. Manufactures are few, and include coarse cotton and woolen fabrics, utensils made of wood, hides, cigars, preparations of gums and resinous substances, the distillation of liquors from the sugar-cane and the *algaroba*, sugar, molasses, and ropes and cordage. Agricultural implements are rude and primitive. There were constructed at the arsenal of Asuncion, in the three years 1861–'63, seven mail-steamers to ply to Montevideo.

During the second Lopez administration (1862–'70), commerce was hampered in various ways, such as government monopolies and other abuses, which rendered freedom of trade unknown in the republic; and the chief staples of export were purchased by the dictator's agents. Nevertheless, and in spite of the natural difficulties in the way of transporting merchandise to the sea from this land-locked state, the commerce of Paraguay had considerably increased during the decade following the downfall of Rosas, the Argentine dictator, and the consequent opening of the river-traffic.

PAREPA-ROSA, EUPHROSYNE, the most accomplished vocalist and operatic singer of the present century, born in Edinburgh in 1839; died in London, January 22, 1874. Her father was a Wallachian nobleman, Baron Georgiades de Boyesku, of Bucharest. Her mother, *née* Seguin, was the daughter of Edward Seguin, Sen., and sister of the famous basso and composer of that name. The sudden death of the baron, just after the birth of Euphrosyne, left his widow, at the age of twenty-one years, in poverty; and she soon after adopted the lyric stage as a profession for her own support and that of her infant daughter, and early commenced training her to the same pursuit. The child was endowed with genius of a high order; but she was also patient and persevering. She made rapid progress in her musical studies—so rapid as to astonish her teachers; and, meanwhile, she had acquired a thorough mastery of five languages, English, Italian, French, German, and Spanish. At the age of sixteen she made her *début* in one of the Italian cities, and attained a marked and promising success. Within the next two years she had appeared with constantly-increasing applause at Naples, Genoa, Rome, Florence, Madrid, and Lisbon, and even the sternest musical critics of those cities were enraptured by her wonderful voice, her perfect training, and her admirable simplicity of manners and of performance. In 1857 she made her first appearance in London, in "Il Puritani," in the same company with Ronconi, Gardoni, and Tagliafico. From the beginning she was a great favorite with the British public. In 1863 she married Captain Carvill, an officer in the East Indian service, a man of brilliant talents and great promise, and highly connected. The fortune of the young couple was about $125,000; but the gallant captain developed such a passion for speculation, that he sunk the whole of it in a few months in Peruvian mining shares, and, after seven months of married life, sailed for Lima, to look after his mining property, where he died in April, 1865. Their infant child being

dead, the young widow returned to the lyric stage, to repair her shattered fortunes and divert her mind from her domestic griefs. In the latter part of August, 1866, she came to the United States, making her *début* in New York in Mr. H. L. Bateman's company, of which the violinist, Carl Rosa, and the cornet-player, Levy, were also members. Her first appearance was in concert; but, during her stay in the United States, she achieved high honors both in oratorio and opera, in most of the principal cities of the republic. In 1867 she became the wife of Carl Rosa, with whom she lived a most happy and affectionate life till her untimely death. Her domestic life was singularly free from unpleasant passages; she was not lacking in dignity or energy, but she was always amiable, gentle, and thoughtful for the comfort and happiness of others. Her rank in the musical world was of the highest, and rested upon solid merits. She possessed one of the most exquisite voices ever heard upon the stage. It had all good qualities. Its compass was magnificent; it reached the lowest notes of the soprano register, and ran up with ease to F in alt, or perhaps a little higher; and in all this great extent there was not an imperfect tone; every sound was deliciously sweet, and pure, and full; the most acute critic could detect no flaw, no weakness, no difference of quality. In volume it was absolutely phenomenal. It filled the Boston Coliseum of 1869, where it rang out above the roar of cannon and the shouting of the monster chorus. Its whispers were heard through the largest opera-houses, and its clarion tones electrified us, in triumphant songs like Händel's "Let the Bright Seraphim," as no voice ever did before, as no voice ever will again. So perfect was the beauty of this glorious voice, that it used to touch the feelings merely by its rare purity and strength, quite apart from any sentiment which might lie in the music. Voice, however, was not the secret of her power. She had reached the very pinnacle of art, for she had learned to despise mere opportunities for vocal display, to discard vulgar embellishments and *tours de force*, and to esteem that the noblest style of singing which was the simplest and most natural. How many years of hard work and intelligent study were needed before this perfect culture was complete the public never suspected. When she stood before them, so quiet, so easy, so unaffected, the song seemed to flow from her lips without an effort, and without premeditation. She sang as if she could not help it. Music had no difficulties for her. With a physical strength equal to the most unparalleled demands, and a technical education which had long ago triumphed over the most serious problems of art, the exercise of her marvelous gift became a sort of second nature. Song for her was as easy as speech. The versatility for which she has been so much praised was in part the result of high culture and in part a natural endowment. She won her first victories and her last on the Italian operatic stage. When she came to America in 1866, she charmed the whole country with modern English ballads, and no one else has ever given those little inartistic songs so pleasant a character. She turned to the long-neglected music of Händel, and, filled with the spirit of the grand old master, poured forth the mighty music of "The Messiah" and "Samson" with a majesty and glory of which America had no previous conception. Passing from this to English opera, she gave it a character it had never enjoyed before, either here or abroad, and greatly increased the probability of its becoming permanently established here. During the last two years of her stay in the United States, she had sung mostly in opera, her husband being the manager of the operatic season. She followed the English opera with a brilliant series of Italian operas, including "Norma," "The Barber of Seville," "Il Trovatore," "Martha," etc. After leaving the United States in 1872, she sang in opera in London, and visited Egypt, where she received the most triumphant honors. She had returned to London, and her husband had engaged Drury Lane for a series of English operas, and where she was to have presented Wagner's "Lohengrin" for the first time to an English audience, herself assuming the magnificent and exacting rôle of Elsa; but her sudden death prevented the accomplishment of her plans. Her greatest achievement, after all, and her truest glory, was that she honored her profession alike in her work and her life. She opened the minds of the multitude to new conceptions of art. She discovered to them unsuspected beauties. She elevated and refined their taste. She taught them to despise vulgarity, and false pretense, and affectation; to appreciate whatever is pure, and dignified, and conscientious; to hate the cheap devices of the show-man. In six years she advanced the musical taste and knowledge of America by the measure of a whole generation. What Theodore Thomas has done with the orchestra she did with the oratorio, the opera, and the ballad. Her influence will last all the longer from the fact that she was taken away before her great powers had shown any evidence of decay.

PENNSYLVANIA. The public debt of Pennsylvania on the 30th of November amounted to $24,568,635.57, including $196,751.36 of unfunded liabilities. During the year preceding, $1,230,186.57 of the State debt had been redeemed. The sinking-fund contains $9,000,-000 of bonds of the Pennsylvania Railroad Company and the Alleghany Valley Railroad Company. By the constitution of the State, the proceeds of the sale of public works, and, by an act of the last Legislature, the tax on the capital stock of corporations, are assigned to the sinking-fund, to be applied only to the payment of loans and of interest on the debt. There was a balance in the Treasury at the beginning of the

fiscal year, December 1, 1873, of $1,825,151.24, and the receipts of the year amounted to $5,871,968.27, making $7,697,119.51 the total resources. The disbursements of the year amounted to $6,642,567.86, leaving a surplus on the 30th of November of $1,054,551.65. The revenues diminished from $7,076,723.20 in 1873 to $5,871,968.27, in consequence of the repeal of the taxes on the gross receipts of railroads, and the net earnings of industrial and other corporations, and the tax on cattle and farming-implements. While the revenues were thus reduced by over $1,200,000, the expenses were increased by about $500,000, in consequence of changes made necessary by the new constitution.

There are in the State 199 national banks, with an aggregate capital of about $52,000,000, and 117 savings-institutions, with a capital of $8,370,168.85. The deposits in the latter during the year amounted to over $23,000,000.

The Fish Commissioners of the State during the year placed in the streams running into the sea 376,000 California and 137,000 Kennebec salmon; 85,000 salmon-trout were distributed in different bodies of water favorable to them, and 3,000,000 shad were hatched and turned into the Susquehanna.

There are 145 railroad companies some portion of whose lines are within the State of Pennsylvania. The latest official report covers the year 1873. This shows the following facts: Length of main lines of road, 6,655 miles, of which 4,257 miles are in the State; length of double track, 1,819 miles; length of sidings, 2,218 miles; length of branch roads owned, 1,597; miles laid with steel rails, 1,976; capital stock paid in, $476,701,873; funded debt, $378,590,370; floating debt, $37,601,157; cost of road and equipment, $621,312,048; value of real estate held by the companies exclusive of roadway, $25,821,727; number of engines, 4,054; number of first-class passenger-cars, 1,773; second-class cars, 257; baggage, mail, and express cars, 757; freight-cars, 58,744; coal, fuel, and tank cars, 79,438. The net earnings of the roads for the year were, $52,788,075. The total receipts were, $147,995,214; total expenses, $95,207,139. The accidents of the year involved the killing of 27 passengers, and the injuring of 166; the killing of 254 employés, and the injuring of 665; and the killing of 295 other persons, and the injuring of 281; or the killing of 576 persons in all, and the injuring of 1,112. Fully one-third of the roads included in this statement are beyond the limits of the State, and statistics are not given applying to those roads and parts of roads wholly within the State.

The first session of the Legislature under the new constitution began on the 6th of January, and continued until the 15th of May. Much of the legislation was such as was necessary to make the laws conform to the changes in the constitution. The State was apportioned into new senatorial and representative districts, and the number of Senators fixed at 50, and representatives at 201. Representatives are to be chosen biennially for a term of two years, and one-half of the Senate every two years for a term of four years. A new election law was passed providing for the registration of legal voters and the conduct of elections. The registration is made by the assessors, who at the same time make assessments for taxes on those not already assessed. The elections are to be conducted by judges and inspectors, who are appointed by the judges of the county courts, but overseers of election may also be appointed in any election district on the petition of five citizens setting forth that it is necessary in order to secure a fair election. These overseers must be two in number, one from each political party, who shall supervise the proceedings of the election-officers, and make a report thereon to the Court of Common Pleas of the county.

Every ballot cast must be numbered in the order in which it was received, and the same number is placed opposite the name of the person voting. Any person whose name is not on the registration list may vote on satisfactory proof to the election-officers that he has a legal right to do so in the district in which he claims the right, but he must produce at least one witness who shall testify under oath to the facts necessary for his qualification. The right to vote of any person whose name is upon the list may be challenged at the polls by any qualified voter of the same district, whereupon proof of the right of suffrage of the person so challenged shall be made and passed upon by the Election Board, and the vote received or rejected according to the evidence. The polls must close at seven o'clock P. M., and the votes be immediately counted and returns made out in triplicate. The result shall also be announced

HARRISBURG, FROM THE WEST BANK OF THE SUSQUEHANNA.

to the citizens present and posted in writing on the door of the "election-house." The triplicate returns must be sealed in the presence of the officers and taken to the prothonotary of the county. One copy of the returns is to be placed on file for public inspection, one delivered to the Judges of the Court of Common Pleas, and the other sealed up in the box with the ballots. The returns for the entire county are to be opened and computed in the Court of Common Pleas. The county returns must be transmitted to the Secretary of the Commonwealth by the county commissioners. Provision is made for compensation to election-officers, and punishment for neglect of duty or violation of the law.

An act providing that all children over the age of six years should be admitted to the common schools of the State "without regard to color," and that colored children should "enjoy all the rights and privileges of said schools now allowed or which hereafter may be allowed to white children," was introduced in the Senate and passed by a strict party vote of 20 Republicans to 11 Democrats. At the same time a bill was introduced in the House of Representatives making attendance on the common schools compulsory. These measures were intended to make the laws of the State conform to the civil-rights bill then pending in Congress, and, when that bill failed to pass, they were abandoned without becoming law. Among the other measures of the session was one providing for a geological survey of the State. This authorized the appointment by the Governor of a board of ten scientific and practical men to serve without compensation, who should select the State geologist and superintend the survey. An appropriation of $85,000 per year was made to carry on the work, which is to be completed in three years. The appointments under this act were made, and a competent geologist was selected in June. The work of the survey began in September and extended before the close of the year to an examination of the iron-ores and slate-quarries of York, Adams, Lehigh, and Northampton Counties, the fossil iron-ores of the Juniata Valley, the bituminous coal-basins of Clearfield and Jefferson Counties, and the oil-regions of Vanango County. A museum of minerals is to be collected at Harrisburg, as one of the results of the survey.

The State Convention of the Republican party was held at Harrisburg on the 19th of August, and the following nominations were made: for Judge of the Supreme Court, Edward M. Paxon, of Philadelphia; for Lieutenant-Governor, A. G. Olmsted, of Potter County; for Auditor-General, Harrison Allen, of Warren County; for Secretary of Internal Affairs, Robert B. Beath, of Schuylkill County. The platform, which was unanimously adopted, opened with approval of the State and national administrations under Republican control, and condemnation of the conduct of the Democratic party. Then followed these resolutions relating to State affairs:

2. The Republicans of Pennsylvania having been the first to demand a change in the constitution that would abolish special legislation and all its attendant evils, and the necessary legislation for the call of a constitutional convention for that purpose having emanated from them, we are justified in rejoicing to-day over the accomplishment of that great reform and over the delivery of the State from the evil consequences of the old system.

3. The movement for the formation of the new constitution having been made by the Republican party, and carried to completion under its auspices, the task of putting into operation the machinery of the new fundamental law belongs to it of right, and the duty it involves will be, as it has been, faithfully performed by it.

4. Inasmuch as great abuses have grown up in this State under our present system of fees as a compensation for county officers, we demand such legislation as will substitute adequate salaries for fees, and such as will allow no more than a fair and just compensation for services rendered.

5. We look with pride and satisfaction upon our common-school system, which has grown up under the fostering care of the State, and as it is now munificently endowed by the annual appropriation from the State, secured to it by the constitution, the State is bound to see that all her children are duly educated under it in the duties of citizenship; that they may thereby become better able to enjoy and perpetuate our popular institutions.

The following resolutions relate to matters of national policy:

6. We recognize that as the true policy of government which shall harmonize all the diversified interests and pursuits necessarily existing in a country of such vast extent as ours, and this can be done only by directing legislation so as to secure just protection and reward to every branch of industry. We are in favor of giving precedence to those measures which shall recognize agricultural, mining, manufacturing, and mechanical pursuits as entitled to the amplest protection and fullest development; of putting a stop to large grants of the public domain to railroad corporations and reserving it for set-

tlement and cultivation; of improving the navigation of our great inland rivers, and securing cheap transportation and profitable markets for the products of agricultural and manufacturing labor; of encouraging such manufactures as shall bring the producer and consumer in the neighborhood of each other, and thus establish mutual relations between them and those engaged in commerce and transportation; of properly adjusting the relations between capital and labor in order that they may receive a just and equitable share of the profits, and of holding those in the possession of corporate wealth and privileges in strict conformity to the law, so that through combined influences people of varied pursuits may be united together in the common purpose of preserving the honor of the nation and developing the immense resources of every section of the Union and of advancing the social and mutual prosperity of all its industrial and laboring classes.

7. The paralysis which has fallen upon the manufacturing industry of the country within the past year is a fresh evidence of the necessity of that protection to our manufacturing interests for which the Republicans of Pennsylvania have always fought. The reduction of the tariff, accompanied as it was by largely-increased importations, not only helped to bring on the panic, but has rendered recovery from it more difficult, as well as lamentably slow.

8. The attempt made just prior to the adjournment of Congress to establish free-trade through the agency of the reciprocity treaty with Canada, demands the severest condemnation. It was an effort to accomplish through the treaty-making power alone that which belongs properly and of right to the popular branch of the Government, and to put redress out of the people's reach for twenty-one years to come. The control over the subject of the national revenue was placed by the Constitution in the hands of the immediate representatives of the people, and we protest against any scheme to take it out of their hands by means of a treaty which the people cannot abrogate or repeal.

9. The frantic efforts now being made by the Democratic party to bring on a war of races in the South, with the design of depriving a portion of its citizens of the rights which belong to them, show that the mission of the Republican party has not ended, and that its further continuance is necessary to secure equally to every citizen the rights which belong to all.

10. Emancipation and enfranchisement having been secured by the adoption of the thirteenth and fifteenth amendments to the Constitution of the United States, and by the necessary legislation for their enforcement, and equality of civil rights having been guaranteed by the fourteenth amendment, it is the imperative duty of Congress to see that such guarantee is enforced by appropriate statutes.

11. The establishment of the national-bank system having secured to the people of the entire nation the best system of bank currency ever before offered to them, the privileges of that system should be no longer confined to a privileged class, but should be free to all under general and equal laws, the aggregate volume of the currency to be regulated by the necessities of the people and the recognized laws of trade.

12. We reaffirm the declaration of the National Republican Convention of 1872 in favor of a return to specie payments at the earliest practicable day.

13. That the Republican party continue to remember with gratitude the soldiers and sailors of the republic for the patriotism, courage, and self-sacrifice with which they gave themselves to the preservation of the country in the late civil war.

Other resolutions presented Governor John F. Hartranft as a candidate for nomination to the presidency in 1876; directed that the candidates and the president of the convention appoint the chairman of the State Committee; and called for a hearty support of the Centennial Exposition. A resolution pledging support to President Grant "in the event of his being a candidate for a third term" was voted down.

The Democratic Convention took place at Pittsburg, on the 26th of August. The nominations were as follows: for Judge of the Supreme Court, Warren J. Woodward, of Berks County; for Lieutenant-Governor, John Latta, of Westmoreland County; for Auditor-General, Justus F. Temple, of Greene County; for Secretary of Internal Affairs, General Wm. McCandless, of Philadelphia. The following platform was adopted:

The Democracy of Pennsylvania, in convention assembled, do declare: That the Republican party, since its accession to power, has violated the Federal Constitution and degraded the judiciary; prostrated industry; plundered the people; usurped power; loaned the Government credit to corporations without constitutional sanction; fostered corporations to the detriment of the agricultural interests of the country; introduced frauds and corruption into the departments of the Government and among its office-holders, and failed to dismiss them when exposed and convicted; appointed spies and informers to oppress the business interests of the country; increased its taxation till labor can hardly live, business prosper, trade and commerce earn their fair rewards, or manufacturers continue their operations; overawed and ignored the civil power and set the military up as the exponent of the laws; invaded and subverted the sovereign rights of States; revived the sedition laws, and by Federal legislation attempted to destroy the liberty of the press; dominated the white by the negro race in some States, and by its proposed civil-rights bill made a war of races imminent. Therefore, charging these offenses to the Republican party, we call on all honest and upright citizens to redress them by so voting in November as to produce a change and expel their authors and abettors from all places of public trust and confidence.

Resolved, That the following are among the leading principles of our political belief:

1. That the present prostration of the industrial and commercial interests of the country has been brought about by the unwise legislation of the Republican party, and that prosperity can only be restored by a change in the administration of government.

2. That we are opposed to governmental grants of public lands to corporations, as tending to general corruption and demoralization of the public service.

3. That we favor an honest and economical government, lopping off every needless expense, a reduction of the number of office-holders, the abolition of the fee system, local and national, and the return to the moderate living and plain customs of former days.

4. That we cherish a grateful remembrance of our brave soldiers and sailors, and will give a prompt recognition of every just claim in their behalf, or that of their widows and orphans.

5. That a steady effort should be made to bring Government notes to par with gold, and to secure a return to specie payment at the earliest possible period that resumption can be effected with safety.

6. That we denounce the civil-rights bill of the last Congress, believing its passage to be a gross invasion of the right of the States to control their domestic concerns in their own way, and that it would result in incalculable evil to both the white and the negro races.

7. That while we recognize to the fullest and broadest extent that it is the duty of the State to secure to all the blessings of education, and hence that our public-school system should be generously sustained, we emphatically declare against the establishment of mixed schools by law, in which white and black children shall be compulsorily associated, believing as we do that the interests of the two races will be best served by training the children in separate schools.

8. That the leaders of the Republican party, having opposed the present constitution of this State, inviting the Supreme Court to proclaim in advance of the vote for its ratification partisan objections to its provisions, selecting to preside over its late State Convention one who refused to sign the constitution as adopted, and nominating for State officers avowed opponents of the instrument, cannot deny the hostile attitude on their part to constitutional reform, and deceive people with false pretenses in regard to their future policy.

The State election, in accordance with the provision of the new constitution, occurred on the 3d of November instead of the second Tuesday of October, as in former years. The Democratic candidates were elected. The total vote for Lieutenant-Governor was 549,711, of which Latta received 277,195 and Olmsted 272,516, making the majority of the former 4,679. Benjamin Rush Bradford, Temperance candidate, received 4,632 votes. Both Woodward and Paxson were elected Judges of the Supreme Court under the new constitution. Twenty-seven members of Congress were chosen at the same election, of whom 17 were Democrats and 10 Republicans. The new Legislature consists of 20 Democrats and 10 Republicans in the Senate, and 110 Democrats, 89 Republicans, and two Independents in the House; giving the Republicans 10 majority in the Senate, and the Democrats 19 in the House.

An occasion arose on the 28th of March for the use of the military in enforcing the laws at Susquehanna Depot. The employés in the shops of the Erie Railway at that place struck for their pay, which was two months in arrears, and took possession of the road, refusing to permit the trains to run until they were paid. The sheriff was unable to subdue the rioters, and called on the Governor for assistance. Troops were sent, under General E. S. Osborn, to assist the sheriff in preserving the peace and securing to the railroad company the control of its property. This action promptly brought the strikers to terms, and the difficulty was amicably settled. To a protest of some of the citizens of Susquehanna Depot against military interference, Governor Hartranft made this reply:

HARRISBURG, March 29, 1874.

W. J. FALKENBURG, Burgess, Susquehanna Depot:

As an individual I may sympathize with your people in their misfortune in not receiving prompt payment of their dues; but, as the chief Executive of this State, I cannot allow creditors, however meritorious their claims may be, to forcibly seize property of their debtors and hold it without due process of law. Much less can I allow them to take and hold illegal possession of a great highway and punish the innocent public, either as passengers or transporters, for the default of a corporation with which they have no concern. Whenever the laws of this Commonwealth shall pro   e that the employés of a railroad may suspend all traffic upon it until their wages are paid I will asquiesce, but I cannot do so while the law refuses to contemplate any such remedy. My duty is not to make the laws, or to criticise them, but to execute them, and that duty I must discharge without fear or favor. General Osborn is the officer in command. I have implicit confidence in his impartiality, firmness, and discretion. I have ordered him to confer with the sheriff of your county, who is its proper peace-officer. If the laws are not set at defiance, the sheriff will so inform General Osborn. If they are set at defiance, General Osborn has been ordered to enforce obedience to them. If unfortunate consequences follow, the responsibility must rest with those who endeavor to redress their wrongs by violence, in contempt of the laws of their country, and of the officers whose sworn duty it is to take care that they be faithfully executed.

J. F. HARTRANFT.

A prolonged conflict between Italian and native miners, at the Armstrong mines in Westmoreland County, occurred in the latter part of the year, in which violence and lawlessness were displayed on both sides. Four Italians were killed and several wounded, but no action was taken by the local authorities to prevent or punish these riotous outbreaks. The Governor called the attention of the Legislature to the matter at the opening of the session of 1875.

PERSIA, a country of Asia. Reigning sovereign, Nassr-ed-Din, Shah of Persia, born September 4, 1829, eldest son of Shah Mohammed; succeeded to the throne at the death of his father, September 10, 1848. Children of the Shah: Muzaffer-ed-Din, heir-apparent, born in 1850; Djilal-ed-Dauleh, born in 1853. The present sovereign is the fourth of the dynasty of the Khadjars, which fully secured the rule over the country in 1794. It is within the power of the Persian monarchs to leave the crown, with disregard to the national heir, to any member of the family.

The area of Persia is estimated at 636,000 square miles. The population is about 5,000,-000. The vast majority of the inhabitants of Persia are Mohammedans. The Armenian population is estimated at 4,660 families, or 26,035 souls; the Nestorians, including both Protestants and persons who have joined the Roman Catholic Church (Chaldees about 3,-500 souls, and 600 families), respectively at 4,100 families, or 25,000 souls; the Jews at 16,000 souls; the Guebers or Parsees at 1,200 families, or 7,190 souls. The new sect of the Babis, which was founded about forty years ago, is believed to have a very large number of adherents, notwithstanding the cruel persecution to which it has been subjected. The Gregorian Armenians have an archbishop at Ispahan, who resides in the suburb Djulfah; and another archbishop at Tabreez; the United Armenians have an episcopal see in Ispahan, which was established by Pius IX. The Nestorians have two metropolitans and two bishops. The Chaldees, or United Nestorians, have an archbishop at Kerkuk, and a bishop at Salmas. The aggregate number of United Armenians and Nestorians is from 7,000 to 8,000.

The Protestant missions among the Nestorians of Persia were begun by the American Board of Commissioners of Foreign Missions in 1834, at Oroomiah. In 1871 they were transferred to the Presbyterian Board. According to the annual report of the board for 1874, there were in Persia three stations, 70 out-stations and places where there was regular preaching; 54 native pastors and preachers; 95 teachers, and 70 village schools, with 1,124 scholars. There are 17 organized churches, with a membership of 767, and their contributions exceed $800 a year. The press has issued 110,000 volumes and 21,250,000 pages. The female seminary had 32 pupils. The male seminary, which has been closed for some time, will be reopened. A school for Mohammedan girls was reported to be in a flourishing condition.

The country is divided into twenty provinces, each of which is administered by a beglerbeg, or civil and military governor. The governors of the large provinces mostly reside in the capital. The provinces are subdivided into districts, superintended by a hakem, or lieutenant-governor, whose chief duty is the collection of revenue. The towns are governed by an elective ketkhodah, or magistrate; the villages by a muhuleh, who administers justice, and serves as an organ of intercommunication between the people and the Government.

The standing army of Persia comprises 18,000 infantry, 10,000 irregular cavalry, 1,500 artillery, and 500 regular cavalry: total, 30,000 men.

The imports of Persia are estimated at $12,-240,000; the exports at $7,200,000. The chief articles of import are cotton-goods from England; the chief exports, silk, opium, and cotton. The Shah of Persia has a larger wealth of precious stones than any other monarch of the globe. His strong-box consists of a small room, twenty feet by fourteen, reached by a steep stair, and entered through a very small door. Here, spread upon carpets, lie jewels valued at £7,000,000 sterling. Chief among them is the Kaianian crown, shaped like a flower-pot, and topped by an uncut ruby as large as a hen's-egg, and supposed to have come from Siam. Near the crown are two lamb-skin caps, adorned with splendid aigrettes of diamonds, and before them lie trays of pearl, ruby, and emerald necklaces, and hundreds of rings. Mr. Eastwick, who examined the whole, states that in addition to these are gauntlets and belts covered with pearls and diamonds, and conspicuous among them the Kaianian belt, about a foot deep, weighing perhaps eighteen pounds, and one complete mass of pearls, diamonds, emeralds, and rubies. One or two scabbards of swords are said to be worth a quarter of a million each. There is also the finest turquoise in the world, three or four inches long, and without a flaw. There is also an emerald as big as a walnut, covered with the names of kings who have possessed it. The ancient Persians prized the emerald above all gems, and particularly those from Egypt. Their goblets decorated with these stones were copied by the Romans. The Shah also possesses a pearl worth £60,000. But the most attractive of all the Persian stones is the turquoise, which is inlaid by the native lapidaries with designs and inscriptions with great effect and expertness.

The year 1874 opened in Persia under very unfavorable auspices. Mirza Hussein Khan, the leader of the reformatory party, and, in the opinion of the Europeans in Teheran, the most enlightened statesman Persia has ever had, had been deposed from his place as first minister. The contract with Baron Reuter for the construction of railroads and telegraphs, and the introduction of other improvements, had been broken by the Persian Government. New complications with Turkey threatened another war. Soon, however, the situation appeared again to improve. A letter from Teheran to the *Augsburger Allgemeine Zeitung*, dated February 24, 1874, says:

Political affairs in Persia are improving, the country is again entering on the path of progress, and there is every prospect of a new policy being maintained for some time to come. The relations with Turkey have also greatly improved. At the beginning of the month a rupture between the two leading states of Islam was far from improbable, while now both sides are striving to find a peaceful means of arranging their differences. The chief cause of dispute was the commercial jurisdiction with regard to Persian subjects in Turkey, and the application of the Turkish laws to insolvent Persian traders in that country. An understanding has at length been arrived at between the two Governments on this point, thanks chiefly to the efforts of the Minister of Foreign Affairs, Mirza Hussein Khan, who is the ruling spirit of the whole cabinet. It is considered highly probable that the new year (which in Persia falls on the 21st of March) will bring some changes in the ministry. Mirza Hussein Khan will, it is said, again assume the functions of Grand-Vizier, and his brother, Yahia Khan, will succeed him as Minister of Foreign Affairs. Yahia Khan is well known in Europe; he is the ideal of a Persian gentleman, and would be thoroughly qualified for the post of Foreign Minister. Mirza Hussein Khan has ordered several roads to be constructed; one of these will go from Teheran to the Araxes, and be the future channel of Persian trade with the Caucasus, the Black Sea, and Tiflis. An engineer has already gone out to superintend the works, which are to be completed in the course of the summer. A second road is to be made to Rescht, and a third will connect the capital with Shahabdulazim, and thence be carried to Khoum and Ispahan. As soon as these roads are finished, a regular line of coaches (carioles) will run upon them. The minister has also adopted some severe measures for enforcing the payment of arrear taxes, many towns not having paid any thing to the state since the Shah left on his European tour. The princes, who are the irreconcilable enemies of all progress, have been removed from the capital, and appointed governors of provinces.

A letter from Teheran, dated July 23d, states that the Shah had conferred upon Mirza Hussein Khan the title of Sepezelarazam, one of the highest titles of Persia, and that Mirza Hussein Khan continued to be Minister of Foreign Affairs and of War, and had charge of the larger portion of interior affairs. When the Persian army began to show signs of disaffection in consequence of the non-payment of its wages, Mirza Hussein Khan himself advanced the money to pay it. In order to reorganize the Persian army, a Danish officer, M. de Lessoë, was appointed, who was to begin with organizing a regiment of engineers according to European models.

On the other hand, the Mohammedan priests persisted in arousing the people against the reforms. A letter from Trebizond, dated September 3d, says:

The intelligent policy pursued by Mirza Hussein Khan is evidently too far in advance of popular ideas in Persia to do much good for the present. The Mirza's influence has prevailed to such an extent at court, that the Shah was actually induced to grant his loving subjects a charter conferring upon them a number of privileges hitherto unknown in Persia, and calculated to protect them against the extortions of the clergy and the oppression of the rich. Unluckily for the people, however, the clergy were beforehand with the Grand-Vizier, and, before he could issue his charter, they had succeeded in persuading everybody that the promised privileges would never in reality exist, and that, on the contrary, the charter was directed against the poor, and would in the end only aggravate their position. Popular credulity easily succumbed to these insinuations, and the appearance of the charter, or *Tanzimat*, was greeted with riots. The latest news is, that the people still refuse to have the charter; and that the *musteik*, or supreme head of the clergy, has been summoned from his country residence to Teheran, to account for the rebellious behavior of the peasantry. Judging from these reports, the conflicts between the liberal lay party, represented by Mirza Hussein, and the ecclesiastical party under the *musteik*, will soon become hot and thick, and the struggle will then be interesting to watch.

PERU (REPÚBLICA DEL PERÚ), an independent state of South America, comprised between Ecuador on the north, Brazil and Bolivia on the east, the latter republic on the south, and the Pacific Ocean on the west. It has an area, according to the majority of geographers, of 500,000 square miles, -and is divided into sixteen departments, and two provinces, one littoral and one constitutional; the aggregate population of all of which, according to official statements based upon the census returns of 1862, is somewhat under 2,500,000.*

The following changes have taken place in the cabinet since the publication of the volume for 1873: President of the Council and Minister of Justice, Señor Don T. E. Sanchez; Señor Don Y. de la Riva Agüero is in charge of the portfolio of Foreign Affairs alone; the Minister of War is General N. Freyre; and the Minister of Finance, Señor Don Z. Z. Elguera.

No more perfect idea can be gathered of the material development of this (after Mexico, perhaps) the richest of all the Spanish-American

* For minute details of population and other statistics, *see* ANNUAL CYCLOPÆDIA for 1873.

states, and now ranking among the most prosperous, since the beginning of President Pardo's administration—no more perfect idea, we say, is to be obtained from any other source than from the message delivered by that statesman at the inauguration of Congress, on August 28, 1874, and of which we here transcribe the more important portions:

In young countries like ours, where we are accustomed to accomplish in a few years what elsewhere has been the labor of centuries, a period of peace is equivalent to a term of advances realized; and a new legislature offers every hope of the satisfaction of new wants, and of renewed strength for the achievement of new conquests in our onward march toward perfection.

It is my pleasing duty to inform you that Peru is at peace with all nations; that she has carefully cultivated and extended her relations with them by new treaties, and especially by consular, postal, and extradition treaties with some of them.

An unfortunate incident, which, as you are already aware, occurred to one of our merchant-vessels on the coast of Japan, gave rise to the necessity of sending a minister to the Government of that country to sue for due reparation. Our demands were graciously granted; our flag was saluted for the first time in those distant waters; and the most amicable relations have been established between the two countries.

Our envoys to the East are at present in Peking; and it is to be hoped that they will obtain the sanction of the emigration of Chinese colonists to our shores, upon the reasonable and liberal basis so justly demanded by public opinion, as well within as without the republic of Peru.

The boundary commission appointed in 1871 to carry out the terms of the treaty of 1851 with Brazil, in reference to a part of the boundary-line with that empire, have terminated their important labors; hence the only portion now remaining to be fixed is that to the north and east of the head-waters of the Javari, for which no provision was made in the treaty alluded to.

LIMA.

The Government does not abandon the idea of an American Congress, nor the hope that it may meet to unite still more closely the bonds of union between the nations of this continent.

Peace has been maintained within our borders, spite of unremitting efforts to disturb it; and that, too, at a time when, by the establishment of absolute liberty, various pernicious elements have been unfettered, and when new popular institutions, whose efficacy became apparent from the first, have been the only safeguard of constitutional order. The history of this period demonstrates that the really solid and durable basis of pure peace lies in the citizens themselves, and shows the government that the surest method to preserve tranquillity is. not to lose the people's confidence. Thus, under the new order of things, the opposition has been gradually brought to see the beneficent effects of free institutions, and, renouncing with shame the weapons of rebellion, have learned to appeal to the legal mode of attack. This triumph is also apparent in the public press.

The various municipal councils throughout the republic are performing their functions, save in a very few provinces. That the inauguration thereof should be attended with difficulty is but natural. A new

municipal decree has bestowed upon those councils the necessary powers and faculties for self-administration; and in most cases the efforts have been in this first year very satisfactory. The provincial bodies, made up from the ranks of the provincial councils, though more numerously constituted and vested with higher powers, work with great regularity. The district and department councils are entirely new corps; nor is it a matter of wonder that their organization should be somewhat slow. I am happy to be able to inform you that the department councils Piura and Huancavélica have particularly distinguished themselves by zeal and intelligence displayed in the branches of administration confided to their charge. Experience has shown the municipal laws to be defective in many respects; but any premature attempt at reform might prove unadvisable. Time will doubtless lead to the discovery of still greater defects; but in the mean time we shall have learned to draw a line of distinction between the actual imperfection of the laws and ministerial incompetency.

The police department has been entirely reorganized, and a much better system adopted, without any additional expenditure. Experience, the gradual improvement in the class of men employed in that service, and the coöperation of the inhabitants, who have taken part in the new police regulations, will render the advantages already derived from the new system more and more manifest every day. But before a complete reform has been made in the administration of justice in criminal affairs, little real good can be expected from police reforms.

The corps of civil-engineers has also been reconstructed upon a new basis; the ministry have called into service the majority of the Peruvian engineers, and a number of foreigners besides, all familiar with mining operations, and their assistants are youths chosen, after a rigorous examination, from among the students in the College of Sciences. The establishment of a new School of Mines has, with our extended railway system, become an obvious necessity, and steps have already been taken toward its accomplishment.

The national printing-office has been completely refitted, preparatory to the putting into press Señor Raimondi's illustrated work on Peru, to be published with an atlas, by order of the Government.

A contract has been made for the placing Payta in telegraphic communication with Panama; and it is hoped that, spite of some obstacles raised by the Government of Colombia, this project of linking Peru to the great telegraphic net-work of the world will in due time be consummated. The laying of another cable southward of Chili and the Argentine Republic is likewise contemplated, and this line, when completed, cannot fail to promote the mutual interests of the three states joined together.

A Board of Immigration has been organized, mainly composed of distinguished foreign residents in our country, interested at once in its welfare and that of the strangers who disembark upon our shores. The association, although with very limited means at its command, has already given proofs of its efficacy, in earnest of the good results fairly to be expected from its efforts. The Government, well aware of the many social and political advantages to be derived from an extended immigration, will shortly sue for your sanction for the introduction of 50,000 immigrants; but the accomplishment of the project on so extended a scale must of necessity depend upon the liberality of your appropriations for the purpose.

Primary instruction requires two elements for its reform: liberal and regular appropriations, and a larger and more competent corps of teachers. It is the opinion of the Government that the municipal councils should be permitted to make the school-tax obligatory. Rules for primary instruction have been fixed by decree; education has been rendered compulsory in so far as the branches obtainable in all the schools throughout the republic are concerned, and the establishment of higher schools in each department has been authorized. The requirements of grammar-school instruction have likewise been attended to, in order to abolish preparatory courses in the universities, and admission to these has been confined to such as are quite prepared to enter upon university studies. A number of competent teachers have been engaged in Europe, and the services of many more still will be engaged; and arrangements are likewise on foot for the establishment of suitable normal schools. The departmental councils are authorized to institute correctional agricultural schools for uneducated children, to be supported out of certain branches of the ordinary contributions, a portion of those outstanding in Puno and Arequipa having been granted for the purpose.

In finances we have had to overcome many obstacles, a great monetary crisis having weighed upon the country for the last two years. The sufferings resulting therefrom are commonly attributed rather to the remedies adopted for the mitigation of the evil than to the excesses which gave rise to it. The most absorbing subject of attention for me has been

the depression in the bonds of the national debt, mainly owing to the fact that the financial agents were obliged to sell at the end of that year, and the continual and exaggerated reports of political disorders in the interior, and above all to the doubts suggested as to the sufficiency of the guano deposits to meet the interest and sinking-fund of our home debt, both of which have, however, been attended to with that punctuality ever characteristic of Peru.

Again, a special survey in the southern deposits has proved the existence of guano in sufficient quantities to meet all our obligations, after the exhaustion of the northern beds. The most convenient mode of shipment for this guano is at present under consideration, and the examination of still other deposits steadily carried forward.

During the year 1873 no less than 782,906 soles* were paid out of the proceeds of the guano-beds, on account of our European debt of 1872; 1,469,287.74 were applied on account of the home debt in the same year, out of the national revenue; and on July 1st of the present year (1874) the Peruvian-Chilian debt to the United States was liquidated out of the proceeds of the guano sold in that country.

The expenditures for the last year amounted to 17,389,100.62 soles, of which 1,505,114.33 soles represent the floating debt for the same period. The budget for that year amounted to 23,511,407.95 soles.

Despite the financial troubles, public works have not been interrupted. Within the two years last past, 370 miles of railway have been constructed; rails have been laid over a distance of 523 miles; and forty-three tunnels, of a total length of 3 miles, have been opened.† Barely 25 miles remain to be completed on the Oroya line.

Steam navigation has been regularly established on Lake Titicaca, almost on the crest of the Andes; and, after seven years of unremitting labor, the thorough exploration of our eastern rivers has been terminated.

The army, though small, is undergoing a slow but efficient process of reorganization, and the future soldiers of the republic will find education within their reach in the Military College and schools already in satisfactory operation. The National Guard has done excellent service whenever the preservation of order has called them into requisition. A measure as indispensable for the army as for the public is that of a reform in the regulations concerning retired officers and their widows, for the unsettled condition in which the present law leaves such a large number of officers always awaiting appointment renders their existence precarious, and not unfrequently gives rise to disturbance. The reverse is the case with our naval officers, whose attainments cause them to be so eagerly sought after by private companies, that special regulations are necessary to secure their services to the state. New naval schools have been opened in the course of the past year.

Such are briefly the subjects which more especially engaged the attention of the Government for the last two years, though the requirements of the country and my own wishes might have extended much further. Whatever has been done has mainly tended to eradicate the obstacles of the past, and sow the seed of future prosperity. It is not always given the laborer to reap the fruit of his toil; but, although the vanity of the commander may not be satisfied, the conscience of the statesman is at rest; and what is the vanity of one individual as compared to the welfare of a nation?

PORTUGAL, a kingdom in Southwestern Europe. King, Louis I., born October 31, 1838; succeeded his brother, King Pedro V., Novem-

---

* Equal to about 90 cents.

† For the details of railways in Peru, see the ANNUAL CYCLOPÆDIA for 1873.

ber 11, 1861; married October 6, 1862, to Pia, youngest daughter of King Victor Emmanuel of Italy. Issue of the union are two sons: Carlos, born September 28, 1863, and Alfonso, born July 31, 1865. The King has a civil list of 365,000 milreis (1 milreis = $1.08), but returns annually 55,000 milreis to be used for general purposes.

Portugal is divided into six provinces, the area and population of which, according to official calculations made in 1871, were as follows:

PROVINCES.	Area.	Population in 1871.
Minho.	2,807.47	971,001
Tras-os-Montos.	4,287.84	365,833
Beira.	9,244.56	1,294,282
Estremadura.	6,872.94	889,691
Alemtejo	9,416.14	331,341
Algarve	1,872.64	188,422
Total.	34,501.59	3,990,570
Azores Islands.	996.48	258,933
Madeira Islands.	314.65	118,379
Total provinces and islands..	35,812.72	4,367,882

The foreign possessions of Portugal are as follows:

POSSESSIONS IN AFRICA AND ASIA.	Area.	Population in 1871.
1. POSSESSIONS IN AFRICA:		
Cape Verde Islands (nine inhabited), 1872.	1,650.25	76,003
In Senegambia (Bissao, etc), 1843.	35,866.75	8,500
Islands of St. Thomas and Principe, 1871.	454.12	23,681
Ajuda.	13.60	700
Angola, Benguela, Mossamedes, 1865.	312,531.85	2,000,000
Mozambique, Sofala, etc.	382,692.06	300,000
2. POSSESSIONS IN ASIA:		
Goa, Salcete, Bardez, etc., 1864	1,458.48	474,234
Damao, 1866.	155.62	40,980
Dia, 1864.	2.76	12,303
Indian Archipelago.	5,527.77	250,000
In China (Macao), 1871.	11.90	71,739
Total possessions.	740,365.16	3,258,140

The following were the gross sums of the budget estimates for the financial year 1874-'75 (value expressed in contos and milreis : 1 conto = 1,000 milreis ; 1 milreis = $1.08 ; 5,652 : 260 means 5,652 contos and 260 milreis) :

REVENUE.

1. Direct taxes.	5,652,260
2. Register.	2,304,700
3. Indirect taxes.	11,213,000
4. National domain.	2,384,240
5. Deduction from civil list and salaries.	282,100
6. Interest on bonds in public exchequer.	441,770
	22,278,070

EXPENDITURE.

1. Interest on home and foreign debt.	10,570,428
2. Ministry of Finance.	2,881,195
3. Ministry of Foreign Affairs.	248,249
4. Ministry of the Interior.	1,904,591
5. Ministry of Worship and Justice.	536,061
6. Ministry of War.	3,406,873
7. Ministry of the Navy and Colonies.	1,101,424
8. Ministry of Public Works.	1,291,873
Total, ordinary.	21,940,694
Total, extraordinary (chiefly construction of roads).	1,337,900
	23,278,594

The budget of the colonies for the year 1871-'72 was as follows:

COLONIES.	Revenue.	Expenditure.	Surplus.
	Milreis.	Milreis.	Milreis.
Cape Verde Islands.	214,569	1,831,336	6,284
St. Thomas and Principe	97,086	96,296	791
Angola.	542,234	542,165	69
Mozambique.	247,713	247,368	345
India.	467,783	433,294	34,488
Macao and Timor.	374,236	303,927	70,309
Total.	1,943,620	1,831,336	112,286

The public debt of Portugal dates from the year 1796, when the first loan of 4,000,000 milreis was raised. In 1835 it amounted to 55,000,000 milreis; in 1872, to 349,000,000. The interest on the public debt has frequently remained unpaid; and portions of the public debt have at various periods been repudiated.

The movement of shipping in 1871 was as follows:

FLAG.	ENTERED.		CLEARED.
	Total.	Steamers.	
Portuguese:			
Sea-going vessels.	706	64	778
Coast vessels.	5,319	480	4,330
Foreign.	4,033	1,360	3,962
Total.	10,058	1,904	9,070

The commercial navy of Portugal consisted, in 1873, of 432 vessels, of a total burden of 108,351 tons. The total length of railways in operation was, at the close of 1873, 842 kilometres. The number of post-offices, in 1872, was 599, and the number of telegraph-offices, in 1874, 129. The aggregate length of telegraph-lines was 3,111, and of telegraph-wires, 5,725 kilometres.

The military system is based on the law of June 23, 1864, which has been modified by several decrees of the year 1868, as well as by a decree of October 4, 1869. The strength of the army, on July 31, 1874, on the peace footing, was 34,559 men, inclusive of 1,993 officers, and 70,680 on the war footing.

The navy of Portugal was, in 1874, composed of 39 vessels (23 steamers and 16 sailing-vessels), with 153 guns. It is officered by one vice-admiral, five rear-admirals, and thirty-one captains, and manned by 3,493 sailors and marines. The Portuguese Government, in 1874, resolved to make important additions to its naval power. The Cortes voted a sum of £370,000 for the construction of new ships-of-war, and Captain Testa, a distinguished officer of the Portuguese Navy, was instructed to proceed directly to England and obtain the fullest information on the various types of vessels now building for the English Admiralty. The Government finally resolved to build two powerful corvettes, designed to carry six large guns, at a high rate of speed, to be constructed on the system known as composite, and to be something like the new English ships Cormorant and Osprey. Three gunboats, similar in all respects to those most lately built for the English Government; one iron transport-ship, designed to carry easily five hundred soldiers in addition to the crew; and a large iron-plated frigate, were likewise ordered to be built in England.

The trade of Portugal, in the years 1870 and 1871, was as follows:

DATE.	Imports.	Exports.
1870........	25,240,000 Milreis.	20,290,000 Milreis.
1871........	27,160,000 "	21,360,000 "

More than half the import and export trade of Portugal has hitherto been carried on with Great Britain. There are signs that this state of things will not last much longer. England declines to modify her alcoholic scale, so as to permit the commoner Portuguese wines to be imported under the 1s. per gallon duty. This greatly displeases the Portuguese; and they retaliate by refusing to admit England to the benefits of the treaties of commerce recently signed with France, Germany, Austro-Hungary, Italy, and Spain. The result is, that England is being driven out of Portuguese markets. According to a statement in a recent consular report, an article which costs in England 5s. pays 5s. duty, while the same article, costing 6s. in France or Germany, pays only 2s. 6d. duty. The French and German merchants have thus an immense advantage. Englishmen in Portugal bitterly complain of their treatment. The Anglo-Portuguese Treaty of 1842 contained a most-favored nation clause, and when the British Treaty of Commerce with France was signed, Portugal was freely admitted, as the above-mentioned consular report points out, to every advantage conferred on France.

On January 2, 1874, the Portuguese Cortes were opened by the King. In the course of his speech from the throne his Majesty expressed the hope that the Minister of Finance

LISBON.

would be able to balance the public revenue and expenditure. He thanked the British and German Governments for the supply of arms they had furnished in the course of the year to Portugal to enable her to complete her armaments. In conclusion, he congratulated the Chambers upon the tranquil and prosperous condition of the country, and also stated that its relations with the foreign powers were excellent.

On April 10th Dom Osorio, in the Senate, called the attention of the ministry to the fact that the Ultramontanes in Portugal were enlisting recruits for Don Carlos. In reply, it was stated that the Government was well acquainted with what was going on, and was on the point of adopting appropriate measures.

Troops were subsequently sent to the frontier to guard against any violation of the Portuguese territory by the Carlists, who nevertheless were reported to receive aid from their sympathizers in Portugal.

The Cortes, in August, voted the maintenance of the dotation granted to the Infante Dom Augusto, only brother of the King (born November 4, 1847). There were only eight dissentient votes. This was regarded as a demonstration in favor both of monarchy and of the present dynasty.

PRESBYTERIANS. I. Presbyterian Church in the United States of America (Northern).—The following are the general statistics of this Church, as reported to the General Assembly in May, 1874:

SYNODS.	Presbyteries.	Ministers.	Churches.	Communicants.
Albany	5	137	126	16,966
Atlantic	6	41	99	7,924
Baltimore	4	122	123	13,440
Central New York	5	182	167	19,962
China	7	48	21	928
Cincinnati	4	162	157	18,955
Cleveland	4	134	164	18,808
Colorado	4	33	35	1,184
Columbus	5	121	167	14,636
Erie	6	164	225	26,633
Geneva	5	123	99	12,737
Harrisburg	4	143	173	19,657
Illinois, Central	4	161	181	15,326
Illinois, North	4	162	146	14,035
Illinois, South	3	112	155	9,236
India	5	88	17	538
Indiana, North	4	101	143	11,095
Indiana, South	4	114	158	14,834
Iowa, North	4	93	135	6,625
Iowa, South	7	133	240	11,646
Kansas	5	112	168	6,490
Kentucky	3	53	80	5,415
Long Island	3	101	73	14,311
Michigan	6	134	156	13,034
Minnesota	5	89	124	5,335
Missouri	6	127	205	9,885
New Jersey	9	352	254	39,419
New York	5	329	169	34,639
Pacific	6	110	105	6,382
Philadelphia	8	380	284	44,335
Pittsburg	5	157	189	22,812
Tennessee	4	37	58	3,676
Toledo	4	73	99	8,837
Western New York	6	167	135	18,960
Wisconsin	5	108	116	6,951
Total	174	4,597	4,946	495,634

The *General Assembly* of the Presbyterian Church in the United States of America met at St. Louis, Mo., May 21st. The Rev. Samuel J. Wilson, of Pittsburg, Pa., was chosen moderator. Several days were spent in discussing schemes for consolidating the boards of the Church. The boards, or central committees charged with managing the benevolent enterprises of the Church, were nine in number, and were thought to be inconveniently many. A plan was adopted which differed in its most important features from both reports. It provided: I. That the Board of Foreign Missions continue as it was already constituted. II. That the work of the Board of Home Missions be divided into two departments, that of Home Missions, and that of Sustentation, but that it have but one treasurer; that the claims of each of these departments be presented to the churches for a separate collection, and that each collection be applicable to its own department exclusively; that the Home Board be ordered so to alter its rules as to adopt and operate the sustentation scheme in all cases to which it may apply; that the Churches now or hereafter connected with the Home Board be required to come under the scheme of sustentation as soon as they are able; that no Church be continued under the Home Mission department for a period of more than five years, unless for special reasons satisfactory to its presbytery; and that every Church aided by the Home Board contribute annually to each cause for which collections are recommended by the Assembly. The pecuniary obligations of the Committee of Sustentation were transferred to the Board of Home Missions, to be paid by them out of funds contributed for that purpose. III. That the Committee on Freedmen be continued for five years, and be conducted with the view of merging its work at the end of that time with that of the Board of Home Missions. IV. That the Board of Church Erection be continued as at present. V. That the Board of Publication be continued, but with its missionary department separately constituted; that it be the duty of this department to disseminate the publications of the board by gifts to ministers and needy churches, and by sale through its appointees, who shall be called missionaries of the Board of Publication; that the missionary department be also given, in connection with the presbyteries, supervision of the whole Sunday-school work of the Church; and that its accounts be kept distinct from the other accounts of the Board of Publication, and collections be taken in the churches for it. VI. That the Board of Education and the Committee of the Relief Fund remain as they were already constituted, except that they shall employ but one treasurer, who shall also be treasurer of the Board of Trustees of the General Assembly. In view of the changes effected by the adoption of this plan, the Standing Committee of Benevolence and Finance was ordered to be discontinued, while the grateful acknowledgment of the Assembly was given to it for the work it had done. The number of boards is reduced by the operation of this plan to seven, but eight collections are taken. A deputation attended the Assembly as the representatives of a conference which had recently been held by a few Presbyterians connected with the Old-School Synod of Missouri, commonly called the "Declaration and Testimony Synod," and presented a paper which had been adopted by that body. It contained a statement of facts, a definition of the position of the conference on certain questions of doctrine and church government, and an implied request for the Assembly to explain its position on the same questions. The Assembly, by a unanimous vote, adopted the following answer:

Resolved, That this Assembly cordially accept this overture as exhibiting the principles of the Presbyterian Church in the United States of America, and consider all actions of the Church in the past, if any, which may have been done contrary to these principles, to be null and void.

The committee that had been appointed by the preceding General Assembly to confer with a committee of the Cumberland Presbyterian Church on the subject of union reported the proceedings of the conference which was held at Nashville, Tenn., February 25th and 26th, and were continued. The committee appointed by the preceding General Assembly to confer with a committee from the General Synod of the Reformed Church in America reported that the two committees had met in New York, and that, after a conference, they had come to the conclusion that closer union was desirable, and had discovered no reason why it should not be brought about. They believed, however, that it should not be pressed to a conclusion, but should take place by general consent of each Church, and were not prepared to recommend any scheme of union. The committee appointed to confer with a committee of the United Presbyterian Church had not obtained communication with that body, and were continued. The committee appointed at the previous General Assembly to consider the subject of a federation of all Presbyterian bodies reported that they had held a meeting in New York City, during the Conference of the Evangelical Alliance, in October, 1873, at which influential members of the Presbyterian Churches of the United States, the Dominion of Canada, and several countries of Europe, were present; that they found the idea of the proposed federal union, and of a pure Presbyterian convention with that end in view, cordially approved; and that they had prepared a circular letter and sent it to thirty-five Presbyterian bodies in Europe and America, inviting them to appoint committees, by whom the details of a general convention might be settled. They recommended the appointment of a committee to correspond with other committees on the subject. Their action was approved, and their recommendation was adopted.

II. PRESBYTERIAN CHURCH IN THE UNITED STATES (SOUTHERN).—The following is a comparative summary of the statistical reports of this Church for 1873 and 1874 :

SUMMARY.	1873.	1874.
Synods..............................	11	12
Presbyteries.........................	57	64
Ministers and licentiates..............	938	1,056
Candidates for the ministry...........	209	199
Number of churches..................	1,585	1,764
Licensures..........................	42	63
Ordinations.........................	31	45
Installations........................	61	65
Pastoral relations dissolved..........	41	85
Churches organized..................	55	49
Churches dissolved..................	7	10
Ministers received from other denominations........................	4	5
Ministers dismissed to other denominations.............................	....	8
Members added on examination.......	5,369	7,129
Members added on certificate.........	2,876	8,429
Whole number of communicants......	93,903	105,956
Churches not reporting (exclusive of Synod of Missouri).................	84	78
Adults baptized.....................	1,535	2,017
Infants baptized.....................	3,756	4,249
Children in Sabbath-schools..........	54,710	60,293

The *General Assembly* of the Presbyterian Church in the United States met at Columbus, Miss., May 21st. The Rev. J. L. Girardeau, D. D., of Charleston, S. C., was chosen moderator. Commissioners were present from the presbyteries of the Synod of Missouri, commonly called the "Declaration and Testimony" Synod. They were received with a resolution of congratulation on the consummation of the reunion of which their presence was taken as a sign, and their names were at once enrolled

on the list of members. Several questions concerning the relations of the Southern Presbyterian Church with other Christian bodies were discussed and acted upon. The paper adopted by the Northern General Assembly of 1873, with other documents bearing upon the subject regarding its relations with the Southern Church, was laid before the General Assembly early in the session, and referred to a special committee. The committee made a report reciting the previous transactions of the two General Assemblies in respect to the opening of fraternal relations, and proposed the following answer to the overture of the Northern Assembly. It was adopted:

But now, in reference to this renewed proposal already referred to, this Assembly does hereby again agree to appoint a committee consisting of three ministers and two elders, whose duty it shall be to meet with the committee appointed by the Northern General Assembly at such time and place as may be designated by the chairmen of the committees, and enter into full conference concerning the removal of these causes which have heretofore prevented fraternal relations between the two Churches.

Inasmuch, however, as it appears that the instructions given to its committee by our Assembly of 1870 were made a ground of objections by the other party, this Assembly, with a sincere desire "to follow the things which make for peace, and things wherewith one may edify another," yields to the wishes of the Northern Assembly in this particular, and appoints its committee without any special instructions, only requiring that the result of the conference shall be reported to our next General Assembly for its judgment thereon.

In order to prevent misapprehension, whether on the part of our own people or of others, as to the purport and scope of any negotiations which may arise from the step here taken, the Assembly feels that it is due to itself and to candor to state explicitly that an organic union with the Northern Assembly is not contemplated in this action, it being our deliberate conviction that the agitation of that subject would tend to retard and not to promote the formation of those "closer fraternal relations" which we understand the communications now before us to propose. But, on the other hand, the Assembly as explicitly declares the readiness and desire of our Church, both of our judicatories in their official capacity, and of our people in their social Christian intercourse, to welcome to full and equal fellowship with ourselves, in the privileges of the gospel and labors for the extension of our Redeemer's kingdom, all those who, holding the same great principles of evangelical doctrine and ecclesiastical polity which we hold, are willing to cast in their lot with us by entering our communion.

A separate report was submitted by one member of the committee declining official intercourse for the present. Afterward a protest signed by twenty-three members of the Assembly was presented against its action in appointing a committee of conference, and was spread upon the record without answer.

The committee appointed by the previous General Assembly to confer with a committee of the General Synod of the Reformed Church in America, respecting the establishment of closer relations between the two denominations, reported the results of the conference and the plan of coöperation which had been agreed upon by the two committees. [The plan is given under its appropriate head in another part of this article.] The Assembly "heartily adopted" the plan entire, except as to the number of delegates contemplated in it, "as the basis of an 'intimate coöperative alliance,' such as is therein set forth; of a union not (for the present at least) organic, but nevertheless a union, real and practical; one which it is believed will, under the Divine blessing, prove to be 'comfortable and useful' to the two bodies." Corresponding members were appointed to meet the General Synod of the Reformed Church at its ensuing session in June, should that body also adopt the plan of coöperation.

III. UNITED PRESBYTERIAN CHURCH OF NORTH AMERICA.—The following is a summary of the statistics of this Church, as they were reported to the General Assembly for 1874:

Synods	8
Total presbyteries	56
Ministers	595
Congregations	776
Sabbath-schools	625
Contributions	$853,298

HOME MISSIONS.

Churches and stations receiving aid 1873-'74	182
Ministers and licentiates under appointment	105
Appropriations for 1874-'75	$40,775

FOREIGN MISSIONS.

General missions	4
Mission-stations	23
Missionaries in active service	37
Churches	21
Communicants	635
Mission-schools	22
Pupils in schools	2,358
Native helpers	80
Native ordained ministers	3
Native licentiates	1
Preparing for the ministry	12
Appropriation for the year	$73,440
Expenses for past year	$54,964

INSTITUTIONS.

Theological seminaries	5
Students in attendance	86
Colleges	2
Total students in attendance	521

PROPERTY.

Seminaries	$225,000
Colleges	250,000
Churches (estimated)	5,000,000
Parsonages	200,000
Total	$5,675,000

The sixteenth *General Assembly* of the United Presbyterian Church of North America met at Monmouth, Ill., May 27th. The Rev. J. G. Brown, D. D., of Pittsburg, Pa., was chosen moderator. A favorable report was made regarding the prospects for a closer association with the Associate Reformed Synod of the South. The Rev. E. E. Boyce, corresponding delegate from that body, spoke of the desire of the synod to join the United Presbyterians in their foreign mission work; and their general sympathy with them in faith. The Assembly, by resolution, expressed its desire and hope that the two bodies should be brought into organic union "as soon as the providence of God shall indicate that the time has come for it." Delegates were appointed to attend the next meeting of the Associate Reformed Synod, and were instructed "to act as Divine Providence shall direct with regard to the propriety of proposing or acceding to the appointment of a committee by the Assembly to confer with a similar committee appointed by the synod on the whole subject of coöperation or organic union."

The proposition for calling a council of Presbyterian Churches was heartily approved of. A committee were appointed to confer with the committees who may be appointed by other Presbyterian bodies on the subject, but under directions that, while doing all they can to secure the particular objects for which the council is to be called, they should do nothing to compromise the peculiar principles and practices for the maintenance of which the United Presbyterian Church believed itself called upon "in Providence and by the head of the Church" to maintain a separate ecclesiastical organization.

IV. CUMBERLAND PRESBYTERIAN CHURCH.— The statistics of the Cumberland Presbyterian Church are very incomplete, a large number of the presbyteries having failed to report. The following estimates give an approximate representation of the condition of the Church: Number of communicants (including estimates from presbyteries from which no reports were received), 99,832; number of ministers, 1,219; amount of contributions for all purposes, $482,490; average salary of pastors, $143.71. Another statement gives the following details: Number of ordained ministers, 1,173; of licentiates, 265; of candidates for the ministry, 216; of congregations, 2,116; of elders, 6,114; of deacons, 1,648; of baptisms (adult and infant), 5,718; of additions by profession, 7,565; of additions by letter, 2,295. Funds and contributions: Income, $95,123; income of Sunday-schools, $44,684; money for home missions, $12,462; for foreign missions, $1,798; for education, $17,587; for publication, $671; for church building and repairing, $148,903; for presbyterial purposes, $5,528; for pastors' salaries and support, $168,578; for miscellaneous purposes, $22,071; for charity, $8,781.

The forty-fourth *General Assembly* of the Cumberland Presbyterian Church met at Springfield, Mo., May 21st. The Rev. J. O. Blake, D. D., of Nashville, Tenn., was chosen moderator. The clerk announced that two presbyteries had been organized during the year. The Committee on Organic Union with the Presbyterian Church in the United States of America presented a report of their action. It embodied the record of the proceedings of the joint meeting of the committees of the Cumberland Presbyterian Church and of the Presbyterian Church (Northern), which was held at Nashville, Tenn., February 25th, and a plea for the continuance of the negotiations and for the careful consideration of the subject of union. The Assembly acted adversely on the subject, and passed, by a large majority, the following resolution:

Resolved, That the report of the committee on the subject of union with the Presbyterian Church of the United States of America be published with the minutes of this General Assembly; and, it appearing from said report that the committee on the part of the Presbyterian Church neither accepted the proposition made to it by our committee as a basis of organic union, nor proposed any other in lieu thereof, for the acceptance of our committee, this General Assembly, therefore, without expressing any opinion upon the plan of union proposed, deems it inexpedient at present to continue said conference; and said committee is hereby discharged.

Assent was given to the proposition for holding a General Council of Presbyterian Churches, and a committee of five members was appointed, to confer with similar committees from other Presbyterian assemblies, in order to arrange for such a council.

Jefferson, Texas, was designated as the place for holding the next meeting of the General Assembly.

The Rev. Mr. Johnson was received by the General Assembly as a delegate from the *Colored Cumberland Presbyterian Church*, and gave an account of the organization and condition of that body. Under cover of the action taken by the General Assembly of the Cumberland Presbyterian Church of 1869, colored ministers had been from time to time set apart to the whole work of the ministry, to labor among their own people. These ministers had formed themselves into presbyteries and synods, and on the 1st day of May, 1874, commissioners from various presbyteries had met in Nashville, Tenn., and formed a General Assembly. The official title of this body is the "General Assembly, colored, of the Cumberland Presbyterian Church in the United States of America." There were under the control of this body seven presbyteries, viz., those of Huntsville, Elk Creek, Farmington, and Hiwassee, constituting the Synod of Tennessee; and those of New Hopewell, New Middleton, and Springfield, constituting the Synod of Kentucky.

This Colored Church was estimated to number in its communion 47 ordained ministers, 46 licentiates, 30 candidates, and 3,000 communicants. The value of its church property was about $5,000. In reference to the scheme for a Federal Union of Presbyterian Churches, the synod adopted a resolution "recognizing the unity of the Church through her living head, and the propriety of Christians coöperating in every proper way for the extension of Christ's kingdom," and appointed a committee to confer with committees from other churches, "in order to ascertain more fully what is proposed in the communication from the General Assembly of the Reunited Presbyterian Church, and report to the next General Synod."

V. PRESBYTERIAN CHURCHES IN BRITISH NORTH AMERICA.—The following table shows the number of ministers and communicants in the Presbyterian Churches of Canada and the Eastern Provinces which have adopted the basis of union of the *Presbyterian Church of British North America:*

CHURCHES.	Minis- ters.	Commu- nicants.
Canada Presbyterian Church...............	329	49,315
Presbyterian Church in Canada, in connection with the Church of Scotland...	122	17,247
Presbyterian Church of the Lower Provinces....................................	124	18,082
Presbyterian Church of the Maritime Provinces, in connection with the Church of Scotland...................	31	4,622
Total.............................	606	89,266

The *General Assembly* of the Canada Presbyterian Church met at Ottawa, June 2d. The Rev. Thomas McPherson was chosen moderator. A resolution was adopted approving the proposition for holding a general council of Presbyterians, and a committee was appointed to meet or correspond with the committees from other Presbyterian denominations on the subject. The attention of the Assembly was given chiefly to the consideration of the question of union with the Presbyterian Church in Canada, in connection with the Church of Scotland and the Presbyterian Churches of the Lower and Maritime Provinces. Report was made of the vote of the presbyteries, sessions, and congregations, on the basis of union sent down by the previous General Assembly, as follows:

Fourteen synods had approved *simpliciter* of the basis; five presbyteries had technically disapproved (three absolutely, and two with modifications).

One hundred and forty-four sessions had approved the basis and resolutions; one had given a qualified approval; six had approved the basis only; and eighty-five had disapproved.

One hundred and sixty-eight congregations had approved *simpliciter;* eight had approved of the basis only; eighty-eight had disapproved, and one had given a qualified approval.

After consideration of the reports and discussion, the Assembly decided to propose a modification of the preamble of the basis of union, and the removal of the fourth article of the basis (which refers to the relations of the United Church with other branches of the Church of Christ) from its original position in the basis to a place among the resolutions. Some changes were also desired in the resolutions. The Synod of the Presbyterian Church in connection of the Church of Scotland, which was in session at the same time in Ottawa, was invited to meet with the General Assembly and discuss the proposed modifications of the basis and resolutions. An agreement was reached. The modified plan was formally adopted by the General Assembly, and was ordered to be sent down to the presbyteries, in terms of the barrier act, and also to the sessions and congregations, with instructions to report them to an adjourned meeting of the General Assembly, to be held in Toronto on the first Tuesday in November.

At the adjourned session returns were received and compared from nineteen presbyteries, 226 sessions, and 238 congregations. All of the presbyteries had approved the result. Two hundred and sixteen sessions had approved it; nine sessions had disapproved it. Only one session, however, had disapproved the result generally; the dissent of the others applied only to the resolution on modes of worship. Two hundred and thirty-one congregations had approved the result *simpliciter*, one had disapproved it generally, and six had expressed dissent to the resolution on the modes of worship. The following resolution was then adopted:

The General Assembly, finding from the returns to the remit, containing the preamble, basis, and resolutions on the subject of union, that all the nineteen presbyteries of the Church have approved of the remit—of 226 sessions 217 have approved *simpliciter*, eight with dissent from one of the resolutions, and only one has disapproved; and that of 238 congregations 231 have approved *simpliciter*, six with dissent from one of the resolutions, and only one has disapproved — does now adopt the said preamble, basis, and resolutions as the articles of union between the four negotiating Churches, viz.: the Presbyterian Church of Canada in connection with the Church of Scotland, the Canada Presbyterian Church, the Presbyterian Church of the Lower Provinces, and the Presbyterian Church of the Maritime Provinces in connection with the Church of Scotland; and does resolve to consummate the union on the ground of these articles at the close of the Supreme Court of this Church in June next, in the event of the other Churches agreeing to this basis; and further, the General Assembly, in coming to this resolution, does express its thanksgiving to the God of all wisdom and grace, who has guided the Church to this harmonious termination of the negotiations carried on for several years, and its fervent prayer that the union about to be consummated may, by his rich blessings, be made eminently conducive to the advancement of the cause and kingdom of the Lord Jesus Christ in this and other lands.

The vote upon this resolution was: ministers, yeas 69, of whom 4 voted *cum nota*, nays 2; elders, yeas 41, nays none. A number of members who voted yea were permitted to record the fact that they could not approve the resolution relating to modes of worship.

The *Synod* of the Presbyterian Church in Canada in connection with the Church of Scotland met in Ottawa, June 2d. The number of ministers on the roll was stated to be 114. The Rev. Mr. Rennie, of Chatham, Ont., was chosen moderator. The attention of the Synod was chiefly given to the consideration of the subject of union with the Canada Presbyterian Church and the Presbyterian Churches of the Lower and Maritime Provinces. The statement of the returns of the votes of the presbyteries, kirk sessions, and congregations, on the remit on union, sent down by the Synod of 1873, showed that 9 presbyteries, 83 kirk sessions, and 197 congregations, had approved the basis *simpliciter;* 1 presbytery, 4 kirk sessions, and 6 congregations, had approved of it with modifications or reservations; and 3 kirk sessions and 3 congregations had approved of parts and disapproved of other parts; while 14 kirk sessions and 12 congregations had disapproved of it *simpliciter;* and 1 kirk session had dis-

approved of it with modifications. The Synod declared, in view of the report, that it considered itself fully justified by the returns to adhere to its former resolutions in favor of union, and to take steps toward the consummation of that object. It ordered a committee appointed to consider all matters on which legislation might be required, and to take all competent measures for obtaining such legislation. In order, however, to obtain a more unanimous consent of the smaller courts to the union, it consented to change the resolution in reference to the disposal of the temporalities fund in such a way as to meet objections which had been urged against it. The General Assembly of the Canada Presbyterian Church having asked for some modifications in the plan of union, a conference of the two bodies was held on the 9th of June. An amended scheme was agreed upon, to be submitted to the presbyteries, sessions, and congregations of both bodies. An adjourned meeting of the Synod was appointed for the 3d of November, to receive the reports of the action of the lower courts on the amended basis. The Committee on Legislation were instructed to prepare drafts of such measures as they might deem necessary to the proper consummation of the union, and lay them before this meeting.

At the adjourned session returns were presented from 8 presbyteries, 92 sessions, and 110 congregations. Three presbyteries, 46 sessions, and 45 congregations, had made no reports. The 8 presbyteries had voted in favor of the adoption of the basis. Of the sessions, 80 had voted in favor of it, and 12 against it; and of the congregations, 95 had voted yea and 10 nay. Under the terms of the barrier act those bodies which had not made returns could be counted as acceding to the remit. Taking the votes as returned directly, and adding to them the voices of other presbyteries, sessions, and congregations, as they had been expressed at the previous meeting of the Synod, the vote would stand: presbyteries, 11, or the whole number, yea; sessions, 102 yea, 16 nay, 20 not heard from; congregations, 120 yea, 13 nay, 17 not heard from. The following resolution was adopted by a vote of 68 to 17:

The Synod, having heard the report of the committee appointed to examine the returns to the Synod's unit on union, do now adopt the preamble, basis, and resolutions as the articles of union between the four negotiating Churches, viz.: the Canada Presbyterian Church, the Presbyterian Church of Canada in connection with the Church of Scotland, the Presbyterian Church of the Maritime Provinces in connection with the Church of Scotland, and the Presbyterian Church of the Lower Provinces, do now resolve to consummate the union on the ground of these articles after the next meeting of this Synod, in June, 1875, provided the necessary legislation with regard to church property shall have been consummated at that time.

PRESBYTERIAN CHURCH OF THE LOWER PROVINCES.—The statistical reports of this body give returns from 131 out of 139 congregations. In these the total number of adherents is given at 74,461; of families, 18,870; of churches, 240; of communicants, 18,082; amount of stipends promised, $70,301; amount of stipends paid, $68,400. Total amount of funds raised, $168,818.

The *Synod* of the Presbyterian Church of the Lower Provinces met at Halifax, N. S., June 30th. The Rev. P. G. McGregor was chosen moderator.

The basis of union agreed upon by the two Presbyterian Churches of Canada, and designed to include also the two of the Lower Provinces, was accepted by a unanimous vote of the Synod. The Synod met again in adjourned session at New Glasgow, N. S. The returns from the presbyteries showed that they had all voted in favor of union and of the proposed basis. Three congregations had recorded their exceptions to one of the resolutions appended to the basis; but no objection had been made to the basis itself, or to the union. A resolution to take whatever steps were necessary to carry out the union was unanimously adopted.

Synod of the Church of Scotland in the Maritime Provinces.—This body includes about forty ministers. The Synod met at Halifax, N. S., May 30th. The basis proposed for the union of the two Presbyterian Churches of Canada with the two of the Eastern Provinces into one body was accepted by the vote of a very large majority of the body.

The Synod met again in adjourned session later in the year at New Glasgow, N. S. All the presbyteries except that of Pictou were reported to have voted in favor of the proposed union with the other Presbyterian Churches and of the offered basis; eleven congregations in the Presbytery of Pictou opposed the union on the ground that they feared the *status* of the ministers of the Synod might be prejudiced by its adoption. A resolution in favor of the union upon the proposed basis was adopted by a vote of 26 affirmative to 7 negative.

The following is the basis of union, with the resolutions, as finally approved by all the parties to the measure:

The Presbyterian Church of Canada in connection with the Church of Scotland, the Canada Presbyterian Church, the Church of the Maritime Provinces in connection with the Church of Scotland, and the Presbyterian Church of the Lower Provinces, holding the same doctrine, government, and discipline, believing that it would be for the glory of God and advancement of the cause of Christ that they should unite, and thus form one Presbyterian Church in the Dominion, independent of all other Churches in its jurisdiction, and under authority of Christ alone, the head of his Church, and head over all things to the Church, agree to unite on the following basis, to be subscribed by the moderators of the respective presbyteries in their name and under their behalf.

Basis.—1. The Scriptures of the Old and New Testaments, being the Word of God, are the only infallible rule of faith and manners.

2. The Westminster Confession of Faith shall form the subordinate standard of this Church; the larger and shorter Catechisms shall be adopted by the Church, and appointed to be used for the instruction of the people, it being distinctly understood that nothing contained in the aforesaid Confession or Catechisms regarding the power and duty of the civil magistrate shall be held to sanction any principles or views inconsistent with full liberty of conscience in matters of religion.

3. The government and worship of this Church shall be in accordance with the recognized principles and practice of the Presbyterian Churches, as laid down generally in the form of Presbyterian Church Government, and in the Directory for the Public Worship of God.

The aforesaid Churches further agree to the following resolutions:

Relations to other Churches.—1. This Church cherishes Christian affection toward the whole Church of God, and desires to hold fraternal intercourse with it in its several branches as opportunity offers.

2. This Church shall, under such terms and regulations as may from time to time be agreed on, receive ministers and probationers from other Churches, and especially from Churches holding the same doctrine, government, and discipline, with itself.

Modes of Worship.—With regard to modes of worship, the practice presently followed by congregations shall be allowed, and further action in connection therewith shall be left to the legislation of the United Church.

Fund for Widows and Orphans of Ministers.—Steps shall be taken at the first meeting of the General Assembly of the United Church for the equitable establishment and administration of an efficient fund for the benefit of the widows and orphans of ministers.

Collegiate Institutions.—The aforesaid Churches shall enter the union with the theological and literary institutions which they now have, and application shall be made to Parliament for such legislation as shall bring Queen's University and Knox College, the Presbyterian College at Montreal, Morrin College, and the Theological Hall at Halifax, into relations to the United Church, similar to those which they now hold to their respective Churches, and to preserve their corporate existence, government, and functions, on terms and conditions like those under which they now rest; but the United Church shall not be required to elect trustees for an art department in any of the colleges above named.

Legislation with Regard to Right of Property.—Such legislation shall be sought as shall preser e undisturbed all right of property now belonging to congregations and corporate bodies, and at the same time not interfere with freedom of action on the part of corporate bodies, which may find it to be expedient to discontinue wholly or partially their separate existence.

Home and Foreign Missionary Operations.—The United Church will partially take up and prosecute the Home and Foreign Missionary and benevolent operations of the several Churches according to their respective claims, and with regard to the practical work of the Church and the promotion of its schemes, while the General Assembly shall have the supervision and control of the work of the Church; yet the United Church shall have due regard to such arrangements, through the synod and local committees, as shall tend most effectually to unite in Christian love and sympathy the sections of the Church, and at the same time to draw forth the resources and energies of the people in behalf of the work of Christ in the Dominion and throughout the world.

Government Grants to Denominational Colleges.—In the United Church the fullest forbearence shall be allowed as to any difference of opinion which may exist respecting the question of state grants to educational establishments of a denominational character.

Bills giving legal sanction to the measures necessary to complete the union were passed by the Legislative Council of the Province of Quebec in February, 1875.

VI. ESTABLISHED CHURCH OF SCOTLAND.—
At the meeting of the General Assembly of the
Established Church of Scotland reports of
general religious statistics were made from 706
parishes of Scotland, in which the numbers of
persons attached to the different communions
were given as follows: Established Church,
679,488; Free Church, 272,104; United Presbyterian, 106,134; other Presbyterians, 11,-
455; unclassified Presbyterians, 37,067; Episcopalians, 21,152; Roman Catholics, 86,708;
miscellaneous, 49,275; "no church," 91,107.

The *General Assembly* of the Established
Church of Scotland met in Edinburgh, May
21st. The Rev. Dr. Trail, Professor of Divinity
in the University of Aberdeen, was elected moderator. A committee was appointed to consider the bearing of the question of pluralities.

The *Commission* of the Church of Scotland
met at Edinburgh, November 18th. The Rev.
Dr. Trail presided. The committee on union
with other Churches presented the following
report, which was adopted:

The Committee on Union with other Churches,
bearing in mind their remit from the General Assembly, which expresses "their hearty willingness
and desire to take all possible steps, consistently
with the principles on which this Church is founded,
to promote the reunion of Churches having a common
origin, adhering to the same confession of faith, and
the same system of government and worship;" and
being satisfied that the spiritual welfare of the whole
country is intimately bound up with the successful
prosecution of the object which has been remitted to
them, resolve to recommend that the General Assembly should, without further delay, formally approach the other Presbyterian Churches in Scotland,
with a view to union. They are of opinion that, in
order to the accomplishment of this great object, the
Church of Scotland should be prepared to consider
any basis of union which is consistent with its historic principles; and in making this recommendation, they express the earnest hope that such overtures on the part of the Church will be met in a spirit
of brotherly kindness and conciliation; and their
sincere prayer is, that, by the blessing of the great
Head of the Church and the guidance of his Holy
Spirit, a way may be opened up to the reunion of
the Churches, and the removal of those obstacles
which now so seriously impede the success of evan-
gelistic operations at home and abroad.

VII. FREE CHURCH OF SCOTLAND.—The entire revenue of the Free Church of Scotland,
from all sources, for the year ending in May,
1874, was reported at the meeting of the General Assembly to have been £511,000. The total contributions to the sustentation fund were
£152,112 8s. 4d., being £15,789 8s. 6d. more
than contributed during the previous year.

The *General Assembly* of the Free Church
of Scotland met at Edinburgh, May 21st. The
Rev. Dr. Robert Stuart, of Leghorn, Italy, was
elected moderator. One of the first questions
which demanded attention was concerning the
eligibility of brewers to offices in the Church.
The congregation at Inverness had elected a
Mr. George Black, a brewer, a ruling elder.
Mr. Black's character was not questioned, but
his appointment was objected to by twelve
members, on the ground that his business was
wrong, and should disqualify him for holding

the office. The session, to whom the objection
was submitted, declared that they had no
jurisdiction over the question, and resolved to
proceed with the ordination of Mr. Black. The
case was then carried up to the presbytery,
by whom the judgment of the session was affirmed. An appeal was taken to the Synod
of Moray, and was dismissed by it. Another
appeal was taken to the General Assembly.
It was dismissed, on the ground that there was
no law of the Church forbidding such appointments as the one in question.

A resolution was also adopted, by a vote of
295 to 98, declaring that "the Assembly believe that disestablishment, effected in an equitable manner, would be conducive to the efficiency of the Churches themselves, as well as to
the general good of the community." The Assembly approved of the General Council of
Presbyterian Churches, proposed by American
Presbyterian ministers, and appointed a committee to meet with the committees of other
Presbyterian bodies, and report to the next
General Assembly.

The country had been the scene, during the
previous winter and spring, of a remarkable
religious awakening, promoted under the labors
of Messrs. D. L. Moody and Ira D. Sankey, two
American lay evangelists. A "deliverance"
was adopted by the Assembly, recognizing this
movement as an answer to prayer, and an encouragement to ask and expect still greater
blessings; and the presbyteries were instructed
to confer, at an early day, on the subject, and
concerning the steps best fitted to extend the
movement.

The *Commission* of the General Assembly
of the Free Church of Scotland met at Edinburgh, November 18th. A report was presented
from the Synod of the Reformed Presbyterian
Church for the appointment of a committee to
confer with a committee of their body, on the
subject of the union of the Reformed and Free
Churches. The committee was appointed.

VIII. UNITED PRESBYTERIAN CHURCH (*Great
Britain*).—The following is a summary of the
statistics of the United Presbyterian Church in
Great Britain, as they were reported to the
Synod in May, 1874: Number of Churches,
611; of communicants, 184,033; Sunday attendance on worship, 207,172; number of
elders included in the sessions of the Church,
4,592; of missionaries, Bible-women, and catechists, 173; of Sunday-school teachers, 10,-
963; of Sunday-school scholars, 84,754. The
increase in the number of members during the
year was 1,223, and was 161 less than the increase of the previous year. This amount of
increase was not regarded as satisfactory, inasmuch as it did not correspond proportionally
with the steady increase of population.

The *Synod* of the United Presbyterian
Church met in Edinburgh, May 11th. The Rev.
Dr. Andrew Thomson, of the Broughton Place
Church, Edinburgh, was elected moderator.
The most important subject before the Synod
was the question of the union between the

United Presbyterian Churches in England and the English Presbyterian Church, which had been agreed upon by both parties conditionally upon the consent of the Synod being given to it. A resolution was passed by a vote of 174 to 178, declaring that "the Synod judge it unwise and unsafe to press the scheme on their congregations in England, and agree to suspend for a time negotiations for an immediate union." Dr. Cairns, who had offered a motion committing the Synod to the acceptance of the scheme of union, which was rejected, entered his dissent to this action. The Synod declared anew its desire for union with the Reformed Presbyterian Church, and reappointed its committee to confer on the subject of an incorporating union with that body, and "to watch over the interests of Christian union among the Churches of the land."

IX. FEDERAL UNION OF THE PRESBYTERIAN CHURCHES. — The following report upon this subject, prepared by a general committee representing various Churches of the Presbyterian family, was laid before all the General Assemblies and General Synods of the several Presbyterian Churches in the United States and Great Britain in 1874, and acted upon by them. It is referred to in the reports of the proceedings of these bodies as the plan of Presbyterian Confederation, or the scheme of an Œcumenical Council of Presbyterian Churches:

To the Churches of Christ, organized on Presbyterian Principles, throughout the World:

Churches of the Presbyterian family are found, though under a variety of names, in Europe, in America, in Australia, and in the mission-fields of Asia and Africa. If these could be regarded as one communion, they would constitute, perhaps, the largest Protestant Church in the world. But, at present, they are united by no visible bond, either of fellowship or of work. Of late, however, it has occurred simultaneously to a number of minds in different countries that those who hold to the Presbyterian form of Church government may, in perfect consistency with their well-known and general interest in all the branches of the Church Universal, inquire for some way of coming into formal communion with each other, and of promoting great causes by joint action.

It is not proposed to form an organic union of all the Presbyterian Churches throughout the world. It is evident that one General Assembly could not regulate, with advantage, the internal economy of Churches in such widely-separated countries as Switzerland, Germany, France, England, Scotland, Ireland, Wales, Australia, United States, and Canada. Great injury might arise from any attempt to interfere with these different Churches in the management of their own affairs; for all ecclesiastical history shows that serious dangers are to be apprehended from the establishment of any central power, which would be almost sure to interfere with the liberty of local Churches and of individuals. Some denominations, moreover, have grand historical recollections which they wish to cherish; and some regard it as their duty to bear a testimony on behalf of truths which others seem to them to overlook. In these circumstances, the Churches will not be asked to merge their separate existence in one large organization, but, retaining their self-government, to meet with the other members of the Presbyterian family to consult for the good of the Church at large, and for the glory of God.

In order that a Church be entitled to join this union, it should hold to the Presbyterian form of government, and have a creed in accordance with the *consensus* of the Reformed Churches. No new creed or formulary of any kind is contemplated.

Several formal steps have been taken with the view of effecting this Presbyterian union. The subject was specially brought before the great meeting held in Philadelphia in 1862, to celebrate the tercentenary of the Scottish Reformation. The General Assembly of 1873 of the Presbyterian Church in the United States of America unanimously adopted resolutions in favor of an Œcumenical Council of Presbyterian Churches, and appointed a committee to have its resolutions carried into effect. In the same year the General Assembly of the Presbyterian Church of Ireland passed a series of like resolutions; and it is ready to join with other Churches in seeking the same great end.

Having respect to this concurrent expression of feeling, the Committee of the General Assembly of the Presbyterian Church in the United States of America availed themselves of the presence of so many Presbyterian ministers and elders at the Conference of the Evangelical Alliance in New York, in 1873, to hold a meeting for a comparison of views on this subject. The meeting was held on October 6th. About one hundred and fifty persons attended, coming from various Presbyterian denominations in widely distant countries; from the principal Presbyterian Churches in the United States and the Dominion of Canada, from England, Scotland, Wales, and Ireland; from Italy and Germany. The utmost cordiality was shown at the meeting, and the following resolutions were adopted unanimously:

1. That whereas the General Assembly of the Presbyterian Church in the United States of America, and the General Assembly of the Presbyterian Church of Ireland, at their last meetings passed resolutions in favor of an Œcumenical Council of Presbyterian Churches, we, providentially brought together at this time, and belonging to various branches of the Presbyterian family, cordially sympathize with these movements toward a General Council of the Presbyterian Churches in various lands.

2. That the following gentlemen be a committee to correspond with individuals and organized bodies in order to ascertain the feeling of Presbyterians in regard to such Federal Council, and to take such measures as may in their judgment promote this object.

3. That this committee be authorized to coöperate, as far as possible, with the General Assembly of the Presbyterian Church in Ireland, and with the committee of the General Assembly of the Presbyterian Church in the United States of America.

The committee thus appointed have a deep sense of the responsibility laid on them. While they believe that the cause is good, and that there is sufficient popular opinion in its behalf to secure, with the blessing of Almighty God, its ultimate success, they fear lest they should take any step that might injure so noble an undertaking. They, therefore, desire to begin and carry on all their measures under the guidance of the wisdom that is from above. All that they propose at present is to ask, as they now do, every Presbyterian organization in the world:

1. To express in a formal manner its approval of the object; and—

2. To appoint a committee to meet or correspond with committees from other Presbyterian denominations, for the purpose of arranging for a meeting or convention of representatives to be appointed by the denominations, which meeting may effect an organization, and determine its character and practical modes of action.

Meanwhile they solicit attention to the following benefits, which, by the grace of God, may be expected to flow from the proposed union:

1. It would exhibit before the world the substantial unity, quite consistent with minor diversities, of the one great family of Presbyterian Churches.

2. It would greatly tend to hold up and strengthen

weak and struggling Churches, by showing that they are members of a large body. The Protestant Churches of the Continent of Europe, for example, feel the great need of sympathy and support from Churches more favorably situated.

3. It would enable Churches which are not inclined to organic union to manifest their belief in the unity of the Church, and to fraternize with those whom they love, while they still hold to their distinctive testimony.

4. Each Presbyterian Church would become acquainted with the constitution and work of sister Churches, and their interest in each other would be proportionally increased. Some might be led in this way to see in other Churches excellences which they would choose to adopt.

5. The Churches may thus be led to combine in behalf of the truth, and against prevalent errors; as, for instance, to defend the obligations of the Sabbath, to resist the insidious efforts of the papacy, especially in the matter of education, and to withstand infidelity in its various forms.

6. Without interfering with the free action of the Churches, this Council might distribute judiciously the evangelical work in the great field " which is the world:" allocating a sphere to each, discouraging the planting of two congregations where one might serve, or the establishment of two missions at one place, while hundreds of other places have none. In this way the resources of the Church would be husbanded, and her energies concentrated on great enterprises.

7. It would demonstrate to the Christian world these great facts in the working of the Presbyterian system: That, by its reasonable polity, it consists with every form of civil government; that, by the simplicity of its usages, it is adapted to all the varying conditions of the Church upon earth; and that, by its equal distance from license and arrogance, it is best prepared to recognize the kinship of all believers.

8. It would manifest the proportions and power of the Presbyterian Churches, and thus offer effectual resistance to the exclusive pretensions of prelacy and ritualism in all their forms.

9. From such a council, hallowed and quickened by the Redeemer's presence, there might proceed, as from a heart, new impulses of spiritual life, bringing every member of the Church into close fellowship with his Divine Master, into deeper affection for his brethren for his Master's sake, and into more entire consecration of all his powers to the Master's work.

HOWARD CROSBY, D. D., LL. D.,
Chancellor New York University, N. Y.
J. W. DAWSON,
Principal Macgill College, Montreal, Can.
WILLIAM PAXTON, D. D.,
New York, Presbyterian Church, U. S. A.
H. D. GANSE,
New York, Reformed Church in America.
HOWELL POWELL,
New York, Welsh Presbyterian Church.
H. L. GRANDLIENERE,
New York, French Evangelical Church.
JOHN HALL, D. D.,
New York, Presbyterian Church, U. S. A.
DAVID GREGG,
New York, Reformed Presbyterian Church.
WILLIAM ORMISTON, D. D.,
New York, Reformed Church in America.
J. H. A. BOMBERGER, D. D.,
Lancaster, Pa., Reformed Church in the U. S.
JAMES MURRAY, D. D.,
Modr. Pres. Ch. of Lower Provinces of B. N. A.
G. D. MATTHEWS,
New York, United Presbyterian Church, Sec'y.
JAMES McCOSH, D. D., LL. D.,
President of the College of New Jersey, Princeton, N. J., Chairman.
NEW YORK, 1874.

The committees appointed by the General Courts of the various Presbyterian and Reformed Churches in the United States and Canada which had approved of the scheme for the Federal Union of Presbyterian Churches to confer upon that subject met for consultation in the city of New York, December 3d. The committees were constituted as follows:

From the Presbyterian Church in the United States of America: the Rev. Dr. Howard Crosby, New York; Rev. Dr. William M. Paxton, New York; Rev. Dr. James McCosh, Princeton, N. J.; Rev. William J. Roberts, Elizabeth, N. J.; Rev. William P. Burd, Philadelphia, Pa.; Rev. Thomas H. Robinson, Harrisburg, Pa.; Elder Charles A. Drake, Washington, D. C.; Elder William F. Lee, New York.

From the Synod of the Reformed Presbyterian Church: the Rev. Dr. J. R. W. Sloane, Alleghany City, Pa.

From the General Synod of the Reformed Presbyterian Church: the Rev. Dr. David Steele, Philadelphia, Pa., and Elder Alexander Woods, New York.

From the United Presbyterian Church in North America: the Rev. Dr. D. R. Kerr, Pittsburg, Pa.; Rev. Dr. Alexander Young, Parnassus, Pa.; Rev. Dr. J. B. Dale, Philadelphia, Pa.; Rev. Dr. J. C. Cooper, Alleghany, Pa.

From the Welsh Calvinistic Methodist Church of the United States (Presbyterian): the Rev. Dr. William Roberts, of Hyde Park, Pa.; Rev. Dr. M. A. Ellis, Bangor, Pa.

From the Reformed Church in America: the Rev. Dr. Hutton, and Rev. Dr. A. P. Van Gieson, Poughkeepsie, N. Y.; and Rev. Dr. Philip Petty, New Palz, N. Y.

From the Presbyterian Church in Canada, the Rev. Mr. McPherson, of Stratford.

The Presbyterian Church in the United States and the Associate Reformed Synod of the South had declined to appoint committees. The General Synod of the Reformed Church in the United States held no meeting in 1874, and was therefore not officially represented. The Cumberland Presbyterian Church also was not represented. The regular meeting of the committees was held in private. The Rev. Dr. A. P. Van Gieson, of Poughkeepsie, N. Y., presided. A series of resolutions, embodying the outline of a plan of Federative Union, was presented by the Rev. Dr. James McCosh, of Princeton, N. J. It was adopted after being subjected to a friendly discussion, and receiving some amendments. It was made public at a meeting held in the evening of the same day. It is as follows:

Resolved, That, in the opinion of the Churches represented at this meeting, it is desirable to form a confederation of the Reformed Churches holding to the Presbyterian system, in order to manifest the substantial unity of these Churches, and to combine them in the accomplishment of the great work committed to them by Christ, the Head of the Church.

2. While furnishing to the Presbyterian Churches a means of entering into closer fellowship with one

another, this Confederation is not meant to separate them in any way from other Churches which hold by Christ, the Head, with which Churches it will always be ready to coöperate.

3. This Confederation does not propose to form or adopt a new Confession of Faith, but will require every Church proposing to join it to submit its creed, and will admit only the Churches whose creed is in conformity with the *consensus* of the Reformed Churches.

4. It shall not interfere with the internal order and discipline of a Church.

5. It shall hold from time to time a General Council composed of representatives of all the Churches constituting the Confederation.

6. The representatives of this Council shall always consist of an equal number of ministers and elders.

7. The General Council shall take up only such subjects as have been committed to the Church by her great Head.

8. The General Council shall seek to guide public sentiment aright in various countries by papers read, by addresses delivered, by information collected in order to publication, by the exposition of sound scriptural principles, and defenses of the truth.

9. The decisions come to by the Council shall be laid before the several Churches, and be entitled to receive from them a respectful, prayerful, and careful consideration. It will labor to promote the unity and harmony of the Churches.

10. It will ever rejoice to support weak and struggling Churches which have to carry on their operations amid infidel or anti-Christian opposition.

11. It will defend by all lawful means those who in any country are persecuted for conscience' sake. It will strive to procure for the Churches that freedom of government and of action which Christ has given to his Church. It will employ all moral means so to distribute the missionary work in the foreign field as to secure that missionary enterprises do not interfere with or hinder each other, that missionaries be sent to every nation, and our Lord's command fulfilled by the Gospel's being preached to every creature.

12. This Confederation will encourage the Churches to combined effort to provide for the religious wants of great cities and other destitute portions of the home field.

13. It will press upon all the Churches the imperative duty of securing the adequate instruction of the young in the Scriptures of the Old and New Testaments.

14. It will make every effort to preserve the Sabbath as a divine institution, fitted to convey so many blessings, temporal and spiritual.

15. It will endeavor to combine the Churches in their efforts to suppress intemperance, and the other great prevailing vices of the age, and generally to promote the moral improvement and elevation of mankind.

16. It will aim to foster among Christians systematic beneficence for the furtherance of Christian objects.

17. It will make systematic efforts to meet prevailing forms of infidelity all over the world.

18. It will seek to combine the Protestant Churches in opposing the errors and inroads of Romanism.

19. In order to organize the Federation, a committee shall be appointed to correspond with the committees of the British Churches throughout the world holding the Presbyterian system.

20. This committee, in correspondence with the committees of the British Churches, shall call a preparatory meeting of the committees of all the Churches joining in the Confederation, to be held in London or elsewhere, in the year 1875.

21. This preparatory meeting is expected to agree upon, and circulate in proof, a constitution of the Confederation, to be laid before a General Council

of the Federal Churches, to be held, if possible, in the year 1876.

22. This preparatory meeting shall agree upon a provisional plan of representation, i. e., upon the number of deputies to be sent by each Church to the first General Council.

A meeting of committees of the British Presbyterian Churches was held in Edinburgh, in November, for the discussion of the same subject. Their conclusions were also favorable to the scheme. A meeting has been appointed to be held in London, July 21, 1875, to which have been invited delegates from all Presbyterian Churches in Great Britain, America, the Continent of Europe, the British colonies, and elsewhere.

The Rev. Samuel Jennings Wilson, D. D., Moderator of the Northern General Assembly in the United States, was born in Washington County, Pa., and was at the time of his election fifty-five years of age. He was graduated at Washington College in 1852, and at the Western Theological Seminary in 1855. He is pastor of the Sixth Presbyterian Church, in Philadelphia, and Professor of Church History in the Western Theological Seminary. He gained a literary reputation through his tercentenary oration on John Knox, which was first delivered in Philadelphia, in 1872, and which has been since repeated in several of the large cities. Dr. Wilson had been a member of a General Assembly but once before, in 1859.

The Rev. J. L. Girardeau, D. D., Moderator of the Southern General Assembly in the United States, has been for many years pastor of the Zion Colored Presbyterian Church, of Charleston, S. C. At the time the proposition for the organization of separate Colored Churches was under discussion in the Assembly, Dr. Girardeau said that when his attention was first directed to the subject of foreign missions, he had determined to give his life to the heathen in his own country. After the adjournment of the Assembly the Zion Church decided to accept a separate organization, as provided by the Assembly's plan for the formation of colored presbyteries. This action was understood to require the retirement of Dr. Girardeau from the pastorate of the Church, as it was expected that they would be served by a minister of their own color.

PROCTER, BRYAN WALLER ("BARRY CORNWALL"), an English poet, born in Wiltshire, in 1787; died in London, October 5, 1874. His family was in comfortable circumstances, and he was educated at Harrow School, where he had Byron and Sir Robert Peel for schoolfellows. He was for some time in a solicitor's office in Calne, Wiltshire, but, as a gentleman of fortune, was in no haste to enter a profession. Eventually, however, he studied law in London, and was called to the bar at Gray's Inn in 1831. Not long after he was appointed a commissioner in lunacy, a lucrative office, which he held until 1861, when he resigned, and John Forster, the political essayist, was appointed his successor. But long before his admission to the bar he had acquired some distinction as a poet by his graceful contributions to the periodical literature of the time. In 1819 these were collected into a volume under the title of "Dramatic Scenes and other Poems," the purpose of which was declared by the author to be to try the effect of a more natural style than that which had for a long time prevailed in dramatic literature. This volume was very favorably received, Charles Lamb, Hazlitt, and other critics, speaking of it in terms of high praise. In 1820 he published two other volumes, "A Sicilian Story, with Diego de Mantilla, and other Poems," and "Marcian Colonna, an Italian Tale, with Three Dramatic Sketches, and other Poems," both of which were commended in the *Edinburgh Review* and *Blackwood's Magazine*, which, however, treated some of his subsequent works with great severity. These, like all his works, were written under the pen-name of "Barry Cornwall." They were characterized, like most of his poems, by a fine fancy, a beautiful diction, and an intense sympathy and purity of heart. His other works were: "Mirandola, a Tragedy" (1821); "Poetical Works," 3 vols., 12mo (1822); "The Flood of Thessaly, the Girl of Provence, and other Poems" (1823); "Effigies Poeticæ; or, the Portraits of British Poets, illustrated by Notes, Biographical, Critical, and Poetical" (1824); "English Songs and other Small Poems" (1831)—enlarged editions of this were published in 1832, 1844, and 1851; "Life of Edmund Kean,". 2 vols. (1835); "Essays and Tales in Prose," 2 vols. (1851); "Charles Lamb: a Memoir" (1866). Mr. Procter also edited, with memoirs of his life and writings, an edition of the works of Ben Jonson, published in 1838; a "Memoir and Essay on the Genius of Shakspeare," prefixed to an edition of the complete works of that poet. He was credited, also, with the authorship of the Trade Songs published in *All the Year Round* in 1859, and many miscellaneous contributions to annuals, etc. He will be longest remembered for his graceful lyric poems, which entitle him to a high place among English poets of the second rank. His daughter, Adelaide Anne Procter, who died in 1864, was a very fine lyric poet.

PROTESTANT EPISCOPAL CHURCH. The first *Church Congress* of members of the Protestant Episcopal Church in the United States was held in the city of New York, October 6th, 7th, and 8th. It was called several weeks previously, upon the recommendation of a committee, the members of which, to use substantially their own language, represented very diverse styles of thought "within the limits of a true and admitted Church comprehensiveness." The plan of the Congress was modeled after that of the English Church Congress, and its object was to furnish the opportunity for a more full and free discussion of the questions pertaining to the life and workings of

the Church than could be given in its regularly constituted conventions. The bishop of the diocese in which the Congress was held (Bishop Potter, of New York) was invited to preside, but he declined. The Rev. Alexander H. Vinton, D. D., was then chosen to preside. Dr. Vinton also made the opening address at the meeting of the Congress. The first topic for discussion was "The Limits of Legislation as to Doctrine and Ritual." Papers were read upon it by the Rev. John Cotton Smith, D. D., the Rev. Hugh Miller Thompson, D. D., and the Rev. C. W. Andrews, D. D., and brief addresses were made upon it by the Rev. B. S. Huntington, the Rev. E. A. Washburn, D. D., and Bishop Whipple, of Minnesota. The second topic was "Clerical Education." Papers were read upon it by the Rev. Edwin Harwood, D. D., and the Rev. Samuel Buel, D. D.; and it was discussed in addresses by Bishop Clark, of Rhode Island, the Rev. George H. Norton, D. D., the Rev. Dr. Richards, the Rev. P. B. Morgan, the Rev. Hugh Miller Thompson, D. D., and Bishop Whipple, of Minnesota. Previously to the discussion of the third topic, a paper was read by the Rev. W. D. Wilson, D. D., on "The Mutual Christian Obligations of Capital and Labor." The third stated topic for consideration was "The Relation of our Church to other Christian Bodies." Papers were read upon this subject by the Rev. E. A. Washburn, D. D., and the Rev. E. C. Porter, of Wisconsin; and it was discussed in addresses by the Rev. C. G. Currie, the Rev. Samuel Osgood, D. D., LL. D., and Bishop Whipple. Greetings were exchanged by telegraph with the English Church Congress, which was in session at the same time at Brighton.

The Committee on the State of the Church reported to the General Convention that ten bishops had died during the preceding three years, as follows: The Rt. Revs. Charles Pettit McIlvaine, Ohio, March 12, 1873; Manton Eastburn, Massachusetts, September 11, 1872; George Upfold, Indiana, August 26, 1872; Henry John Whitehouse, Illinois; John Payne (retired), Africa, October 23, 1874; Thomas F. Davis, South Carolina, December 2, 1871; Henry W. Lee, Iowa, September 6, 1874; George M. Randall, Colorado, September 28, 1873; William E. Armitage, Wisconsin; John G. Auer, Cape Palmas, Africa.

The same committee reported that, during the same period, seven additions had been made to the line of bishops, as follows: The Rt. Revs. Mark Anthony De Wolfe Howe, D. D., Central Pennsylvania, 1871; William Hobart Hare, D. D., Niobrara, 1873; John Gottlieb Auer, D. D., Africa, 1873; Benjamin H. Paddock, D. D., Massachusetts, 1873; Theodore B. Lyman, D. D., Assistant, South Carolina, 1873; John F. Spaulding, D. D., Colorado, 1874; Edward R. Welles, D. D., Wisconsin, 1874.

The statistics of this Church were, according to the *Church Almanac* for 1875, as follows:

DIOCESES AND MISSIONS.	Clergy.	Parishes.	Communicants.	Contributions for Missionary and Church Purposes.
Alabama	33	41	8,652	$62,184 85
Albany	111	117	10,000	....
Arkansas	...	...	......	......
California	60	43	2,879	......
Central New York	108	105	10,053	219,450 32
Cent'l Pennsylvania	83	87	5,863	166,852 62
Connecticut	173	149	17,129	603,918 77
Delaware	25	31	1,802	37,421 53
Easton	26	33	2,154	46,012 94
Florida	14	16	784	20,000 00
Georgia	33	37	4,009	72,051 67
Illinois	91	101	6,785	149,812 97
Indiana	39	42	3,210	75,439 40
Iowa	44	57	2,991	75,648 48
Kansas	25	30	1,011	......
Kentucky	41	39	3,927	......
Long Island	89	87	11,792	547,971 21
Louisiana	31	44	4,351	93,017 77
Maine	28	21	1,944	45,062 15
Maryland	153	131	16,442	340,020 00
Massachusetts	130	101	12,492	511,446 35
Michigan	80	90	8,791	239,776 58
Minnesota	56	46	3,659	91,335 82
Mississippi	29	49	1,818	25,518 21
Missouri	43	44	4,735	146,982 81
Nebraska	25	26	1,294	18,467 84
New Hampshire	23	23	1,575	18,093 24
New Jersey	144	129	12,116	440,589 10
New York	313	190	28,834	933,408 01
North Carolina	56	81	3,923	56,093 81
Ohio	112	119	11,599	205,682 99
Pennsylvania	174	120	20,690	826,329 78
Pittsburg	52	57	4,114	150,065 93
Rhode Island	41	41	5,307	152,049 93
South Carolina	48	67	3,970	75,586 80
Tennessee	33	33	2,495	38,987 77
Texas	34	36	2,567	53,096 34
Vermont	29	40	2,901	......
Virginia	152	...	11,831	105,512 52
Western New York	100	113	10,676	......
Wisconsin	82	61	4,735	131,487 94
Oregon and Washington	17	17	708	20,010 78
Dakota	7	...	153	......
Colorado, Wyoming, and New Mexico	23	17	635	5,235 82
Montana, Idaho, and Utah	8	8	402	18,389 04
Niobrara	10	...	......	......
Nevada and Arizona	10	9	269	32,377 18
Western Africa	10	...	269	......
China and Japan	17	...	193	......
Europe	6	...	......	......

The following is a general statistical summary of the Church:

Dioceses	43
Missionary jurisdictions	13
Bishops	50
Priests and deacons	3,085
Whole number of clergy	3,140
Parishes, about	2,750
Ordinations—deacons (in 28 dioceses and 4 mission jurisdictions)	127
Priests (in 24 dioceses)	102
Total (in 33 dioceses and 1 mission jurisdiction)	229
Candidates for deacons' order (in 26 dioceses and 4 mission jurisdictions)	203
Churches consecrated (in 20 dioceses and 1 mission jurisdiction)	54
Baptism—total (in 36 dioceses and 7 mission jurisdictions)	41,999
Confirmations (in 38 dioceses and 6 mission jurisdictions)	26,888
Communicants—Number reported in 40 dioceses and 7 mission jurisdictions	273,551
Marriages (in 36 dioceses and 7 mission jurisdictions)	10,713
Sunday-school teachers (in 36 dioceses and 4 mission jurisdictions)	23,007
Scholars (in 38 dioceses and 5 mission jurisdictions)	225,733
Contributions (in 38 dioceses and 7 mission jurisdictions)	$6,851,983 27

The *Triennial General Convention* of the Protestant Episcopal Church in the United States met in the city of New York, October 7th. The opening sermon was preached by the Rt. Rev. Dr. Selwyn, Lord Bishop of Lichfield, England. The House of Deputies was organized by the election of the Rev. James Craik, D. D., of Kentucky, president at the preceding General Convention, as president, and of the Rev. Dr. William Stevens Perry as secretary. The Lord Bishop of Lichfield, the Bishop of Montreal, and Metropolitan of Canada, the Lords Bishops of Kingston, W. I., and of Quebec, and several other foreign clergymen, were introduced to the Convention, and were invited to attend upon its sessions. A telegram was received from the Bishop of Chichester, conveying the greetings of the Church Congress of the Church of England, in session at Brighton, to which a suitable response was voted. The Bishop of Lichfield, previous to addressing the Convention upon his introduction to it, presented addresses from the archdeaconries of Staffordshire, Derbyshire, and Shropshire. He also offered an invitation on behalf of the Archbishop of Canterbury to the Convention to take part in the holding of a second Pan-Anglican Synod, representing all the branches of the Anglican and Episcopal Churches, for consultation upon questions and interests common to them all. The following resolution was adopted as the answer of the Convention to this invitation:

Whereas, In the address of the Right Rev. the Lord Bishop of Lichfield, made to this House on the occasion of his formal presentation on the 9th instant, as well as in the address of the Most Rev. the Metropolitan of Canada and the Bishops of Kingston and Quebec upon the same occasion, reference was made to the probable reassembling of a Lambeth Conference at an early day, including an intimation that an expression of the sentiment of this Church upon the subject might possibly facilitate the convening of the second session of this Conference: therefore—

Resolved, That all exchange of greetings, all evidence of the existence of the unity of the Spirit in the bond of peace between the Church of England and the Protestant Episcopal Church in America, whether by bishops in conference or otherwise, are especially welcome to this Church.

The convention were informed that a joint committee had been appointed by the Provincial Synod of Canada to confer with a similar committee of the Church in the United States, on the best measures to promote intercommunion and fellowship between the sister Churches. A committee of three bishops, three presbyters, and three laymen, was appointed to confer with the Canadian committee on the subject named. This committee held a conference with the delegation from Canada, made a report of it to the convention, and was continued until the next General Convention.

The convention was called upon to pass upon the ratification of the election of the Rev. Edward R. Welles, D. D., as the Bishop of Wisconsin, and the Rev. George F. Seymour, D. D., as Bishop of Illinois, they having been chosen by Diocesan Conventions of those dioceses within the year. The committee, to whom the cases of the two bishops-elect were referred, reported in favor of confirming the action of the Diocesan Conventions in both cases. Several memorials were presented against the confirmation of Dr. Seymour, alleging that he entertained or tolerated ritualistic views, and that he had permitted ritualism to be advocated in the General Theological Seminary, in which he was a professor.

Preparatory to entering upon the consideration of the cases of the bishops-elect, the House of Deputies adopted a rule that " whenever the election or confirmation of a bishop is under consideration, this House shall sit with closed doors." The questions involved in the case of Dr. Seymour were discussed for several days in secret session. The vote was then taken by dioceses upon the report of the committee on the consecration of bishops, approving the testimonials of Dr. Seymour, and resulted as follows:

CLERICAL VOTE.—Dioceses represented, 41·
Yea.—Albany, California, Central New York, Easton, Georgia, Illinois, Indiana, Iowa, Long Island, Maine, Michigan, Minnesota, Mississippi, Missouri, New Hampshire, New York, Vermont, Western New York, Wisconsin—19.
Nay.—Connecticut, Delaware, Florida, Kansas, Kentucky, Louisiana, Maryland, Ohio, Pennsylvania, Virginia—10.
Divided.—Alabama, Arkansas, Central Pennsylvania, Massachusetts, Nebraska, New Jersey, North Carolina, Pittsburg, Rhode Island, South Carolina, Tennessee, Texas—12.

LAY VOTE.—Dioceses represented, 40.
Yea.—Alabama, Albany, Illinois, Maine, Maryland, Michigan, Mississippi, Missouri, Nebraska, New Jersey, New York, North Carolina, Vermont—13.
Nay.—California, Delaware, Florida, Georgia, Indiana, Iowa, Kansas, Kentucky, Long Island, Minnesota, New Hampshire, Ohio, Pennsylvania, Rhode Island, South Carolina, Virginia, Western New York, Wisconsin—18.
Divided.—Central New York, Central Pennsylvania, Connecticut, Easton, Louisiana, Massachusetts, Pittsburg, Tennessee, Texas—9.

Failing to receive the approval of the majority of all the dioceses voting, the report of the committee was rejected, and the election of Dr. Seymour was not confirmed. It will be seen, however, by the following recapitulation of the individual votes of Deputies, that while Dr. Seymour was opposed by a majority of the lay deputies, he was sustained by a majority of the clergy, and by a small majority on the combined vote:

RECAPITULATION.

VOTE.	Yeas.	Nays.	Absent.	Total.
Clerical	89	71	4	164
Lay	56	69	39	164
Total	145	140	43	328

The election of Dr. Wells as Bishop of Wisconsin was approved without objection.

Several memorials and resolutions were presented, asking legislation to restrain the excess of ritual. The subject was broadly discussed in both the House of Bishops and the House of Deputies, and the following canon upon the subject was agreed upon by the two Houses, and enacted:

The following addititional section is to be added to Canon 20 of Title I., as follows:

Section 2. If any bishop have reason to believe, or if complaint be made to him in writing by two or more of his presbyters that within his jurisdiction ceremonies or practices not ordained or authorized in the Book of Common Prayer, and setting forth or symbolizing erroneous or doubtful doctrines, have been introduced by any minister during the celebration of the Holy Communion (such as—
a. The elevation of the Elements in the Holy Communion in such manner as to expose them to the view of the people as objects toward which adoration is to be made.
b. Any act of adoration of or toward the Elements in the Holy Communion, such as bowings, prostrations, or genuflections; and—
c. All other like acts not authorized by the Rubrics of the Book of Common Prayer)—
It shall be the duty of such bishop to summon the Standing Committee as his council of advice, and with them to investigate the matter.

[2.] If, after investigation, it shall appear to the bishop and Standing Committee that ceremonies or practices, not ordained or authorized as aforesaid, and setting forth or symbolizing erroneous or doubtful doctrines, have in fact been introduced as aforesaid, it shall be the duty of the bishop, by instrument of writing under his hand, to admonish the minister so offending to discontinue such practices or ceremonies; and if the minister shall disregard such admonition, it shall be the duty of the Standing Committee to cause him to be tried for a breach of his ordination vow:
Provided, That nothing herein contained shall prevent the presentment, trial, and punishment of any minister under the provisions of section 1, Canon 2, Title II., of the Digest.

[3.] In all investigations under the provisions of this canon, the minister whose acts or practices are the subject-matter of the investigation shall be notified, and have opportunity to be heard in his defense. The charges preferred and the findings of the bishop and Standing Committee shall be in writing; and a record shall be kept of the proceedings in the case.

Petitions were offered, one of which was signed by 501 clergymen, asking such alterations to be made in the phraseology of the baptismal office as would permit the clergyman to use or omit the words in that service which were considered to imply a recognition of the doctrine of baptismal regeneration. No definite action was taken on the subject.

Petitions were presented from ten dioceses asking that measures be taken to secure "for use in divine worship "an English version of the Creed, commonly called the Nicene, as conformable as may be to the original text." The petitioners sought particularly the omission of the "filioque" clause. The convention took no action on this subject. The committee to whom it was referred reported that the Church ought not to enter upon the consideration of such a proposition till the revision sought can be effected "in some united council of all those autonomous Churches using this rite, and in communion with this Church and th Church of England."

The following rule was passed, as an amendment of Canon 8 of Title II., providing for the case of the abandonment of the communion of the Church by a bishop

If any bishop shall, without availing himself of the provisions of section 16 of Canon 13 of Title I., abandon the communion of this Church, it shall be the duty of the Standing Committee of the diocese of said bishop to make certificate of the fact to the presiding bishop, together with a statement of the acts or declarations which prove such abandonment, which certificate shall be recorded by the presiding bishop; and the presiding bishop, with the consent of the three bishops next in seniority, may then suspend said bishop from the exercise of his office and ministry, until such time as the House of Bishops shall consent or refuse to consent to his disposition, and in case the bishop so abandoning the communion of the Church be the senior bishop, the bishop next in order of seniority shall be deemed to be and shall act as the presiding bishop under this canon.

Notice shall then be given to said bishop by the bishop receiving the certificate that unless he shall within six months make declaration that the facts alleged in said certificate are false, he will be deposed from the ministry.

And if such declaration be not made within six months as aforesaid, it shall be the duty of the presiding bishop to convene the House of Bishops, and if a majority of the whole number of bishops entitled at the time to seats in the House of Bishops, shall at such meeting give their consent, the said presiding bishop, or the senior bishop present, shall proceed to depose from the ministry the bishop so certified as abandoning, and to pronounce and record in the presence of two or more bishops, that he has been so deposed: *Provided*, nevertheless, that if the bishop so certified as abandoning, shall transmit to the presiding bishop a retraction of the acts or declarations constituting his offense, the bishop may at his discretion abstain from any further proceedings.

With regard to the case of the abandonment of the communion of the Church by a minister, the first section of Canon 6 of Title II. was amended so as to read:

Section 1. If any presbyter or deacon shall, without availing himself of the provisions of Canon 5 of this title, abandon the communion of this Church, either by an open renunciation of the doctrine, discipline, or worship of this Church, or by a formal admission into any religious body not in communion with the same, or in any other way, it shall be the duty of the Standing Committee of the diocese to make certificate of the fact to the bishop of the diocese, or, if there be no bishop, to the bishop of an adjacent diocese; which certificate shall be recorded, and shall be taken and deemed by the ecclesiastical authority as equivalent to a renunciation of the ministry by the minister himself: and the said bishop may then proceed to suspend for six months the presbyter or deacon so certified as abandoning the communion of this Church. Notice shall be given to the said minister, by the said bishop receiving the certificate, that unless he shall, within six months, make declaration that the facts alleged in said certificate are false, he will be deposed from the ministry of this Church.

The following new canon was enacted in reference to Church-music:

Section 1. The selections of the Psalms in metre, and hymns which are set forth by authority, and anthems in the words of Holy Scripture, are allowed to be sung in all congregations of this Church before and after morning and evening prayers, and also before and after sermons at the discretion of the minister, whose duty it shall be by standing directions, or from time to time, to appoint such authorized psalms, hymns, or anthems, as are to be sung. *Sec.* 2. It shall be the duty of every minister of the Church, with such assistance as he may see fit to employ from persons skilled in music, to give order concerning the tunes to be sung at any time in his Church; and it shall be his duty to suppress all light and unseemly music, and all indecency and irreverence in the performance, by which vain and ungodly persons profane the service of the sanctuary.

That clause of Article IV. of the constitution which prescribes the conditions under which a bishop may officiate in another diocese than his own, was amended by omitting the last seven words—" by any Church destitute of a bishop " —and substituting for them the words "in another diocese by the ecclesiastical authority thereof," so that the whole article should read:

ARTICLE IV. The bishop or bishops in every diocese shall be chosen agreeably to such rules as shall be fixed by the convention of that diocese; and every bishop of this Church shall confine the exercise of his episcopal office to his proper diocese, unless requested to ordain, or confirm, or perform, any other act of the episcopal office, in another diocese by the ecclesiastical authority thereof.

In the regulations concerning missionary dioceses, an amendatory provison was made that the bishop shall yearly appoint two presbyters and two laymen, communicants of the Church, resident within his missionary jurisdiction, to perform the duties of a standing committee for such jurisdiction; but that no such missionary standing committee should have power to give or refuse assent to the consecration of a bishop.

Additional provision was made in the regulations concerning the division of dioceses, that, "whenever a diocese is divided into two or more dioceses, any professor in a theological seminary therein, which is governed by trustees from every part of such original diocese, may select to which of said dioceses he shall belong, and shall not be obliged to obtain and present the above-mentioned letters of transfer."

In the case of the organization of new dioceses, the rule was amended so as to provide that if there is no bishop who can call the Primary Convention in pursuance to the regulations previously described, "then the duty of calling such convention for the purpose of organizing, and the duty of fixing the time and place of its meeting shall be vested in the Standing Committee of the diocese within the limits of which the new one is erected, or the Standing Committee of the oldest of the dioceses by the junction of which, or parts of which, the new diocese may be formed. And such Standing Committee shall make such call immediately after the ratification of a division by the General Convention."

Amendatory legislation was also adopted regarding the ordination of ministers to officiate in foreign Churches in missions by bishops having jurisdiction over the same; with reference to the preparation and presentation of reports of statistics, and the condition of the funds of the Church and its benevolent associations within the several dioceses; and to the trial of clergymen who may be charged with misconduct or canonical irregularities in other dioceses than those to which they are attached.

The following resolutions were adopted with respect to communication with the Russo-Greek Church:

Resolved, That this General Convention has great satisfaction in learning the courteous and brotherly tenor of the letters received from the Most Reverend Anthimus, Patriarch of Constantinople; Sophronius, Patriarch of Alexandria; Hierothius, Patriarch of Antioch; Isidore, president of the Holy Governing Synod of Russia; and Theophilus, Metropolitan of Athens, president of the Holy Synod of Greece, in answer to the communication of the action of the last General Convention, through the Joint Committee, as now reported.

Resolved, That we regard the establishment of full and free reciprocal relations of Christian brotherhood between the great Eastern Churches and our own Communion as daily growing in importance and in hopefulness, and heartily pray the Great Head of the Church that His Spirit may so rule in all our Councils as to remove all hinderances which the pride, prejudice, or error of human frailty may present to hinder its consummation.

Resolved, That we desire the continuance and increased frequency of friendly correspondence with our brethren of the Holy Orthodox Eastern Church, in the assured confidence that on either part there will be the fullest recognition of all feelings and rights which might be imperiled by undue or inconsiderate interference.

The Joint Committee appointed at the previous General Convention, to consider the expediency of reviving the primitive order of deaconesses, reported a canon in favor of the order, and unanimously recommended its passage.

The proposed canon was referred to a joint committee, consisting of three bishops, three clerical and three lay deputies, who are to report to the next General Convention.

The formation of new dioceses was authorized in Ohio, New Jersey, Wisconsin, and Michigan. Two missionary districts were constituted out of parts of the Diocese of Texas, to be known respectively as the Missionary Districts of Northern and of Western Texas. The Rev. Alexander Charles Garrett, D. D., of Nebraska, was appointed Missionary Bishop of Northern Texas, and the Rev. Robert W. B. Elliott, of Georgia, Missionary Bishop of Western Texas. The Missionary District of Northern California was constituted out of a part of the Diocese of California, and the Rev. John H. D. Wingfield, of Virginia, was appointed its bishop. The Territories of New Mexico and Arizona were detached from the jurisdiction of the Missionary Bishops of Colorado and Nevada, to which they had respectively belonged, and were constituted the jurisdiction of another missionary bishop. The Rev. William F. Adams, of Louisiana, was chosen bishop of the new jurisdiction. Japan was constituted a separate missionary district, and its supervision was assigned to the Rt. Rev. Channing Moore Williams, D. D.,

present Missionary Bishop of China and Japan, with the title of Missionary Bishop of Yeddo. China was also constituted a separate missionary district, and the Rev. William Pendleton Orrick, of Michigan, was appointed its bishop, who was designated as Missionary Bishop of Shanghai. A missionary diocese was constituted in Hayti, and the Rev. J. Theodore Hally, D. D., was appointed its bishop.

Upon the division of the Diocese of New Jersey, Bishop Odenheimer elected the new diocese (comprising the northern part of the State) as his jurisdiction. A special session of the Diocese of New Jersey was called to meet at Burlington, November 12th. At this meeting, the Rev. John Scarborough, D. D., rector of Trinity Church, Pittsburg, Pa., was chosen bishop.

The primary convention of the new diocese, in the same State, met at Newark at the same time (November 12th), under the presidency of Bishop Odenheimer. It decided upon the name of the Diocese of Northern New Jersey.

A special convention of the Diocese of Kentucky met at Louisville, November 11th, to elect an assistant bishop in place of Bishop Cummins, withdrawn from the Church and deposed. The Rev. Thomas U. Dudley, D. D., of Baltimore, was chosen.

The primary convention of the new diocese to be formed by the division of the Diocese of Michigan, met at Grand Rapids, December 2d. It chose the name of the Diocese of Western Michigan. The Rev. George D. Gillespie was elected bishop.

The primary convention of the new diocese to be formed out of the Diocese of the Ohio was appointed to be held at Columbus, January 13th. Bishop Bedell, Bishop of Ohio, made choice of the Northern Diocese as his diocese. It retains the name of the Diocese of Ohio.

Bishop Henry W. Lee, of Iowa, died on the 6th of September, 1874. The diocesan convention, called to elect his successor, chose the Rev. Henry C. Potter, D. D., of New York. He declined the election, and the convention then chose the Rev. W. R. Huntington, O. T. D., of Worcester, Mass., who accepted and was duly consecrated bishop.

The Rt. Rev. George D. Cummins, Assistant Bishop of Kentucky, on the 10th of November, 1873, resigned the office of bishop in the Protestant Episcopal Church, and announced his intention to withdraw from the Church, and transfer his work and office to another sphere of labor. He afterward engaged in the work of the organization of the Reformed Episcopal Church. Proceedings were duly instituted against him, in conformity with the canons, for abandoning the communion of the Church. On the expiration of the six months required by the rules, sentence of deposition from the ministry of the Church, and from all the rights, privileges, powers, and dignities pertaining to the office of bishop in the same, was pronounced against him in June, 1874.

The sentence of deposition was signed by six bishops.

PRUSSIA, a kingdom of Europe, forming part of the German Empire. King, William I., German Emperor and King of Prussia (see GERMANY). The following table exhibits the area of the provinces into which the kingdom is divided, according to the latest official accounts, as well as their population and their religious statistics : *

PROVINCES.	Square Miles.	Population in 1871.	Evangelical.	Catholic.	Anrihian hects.	Jews.
Prussia	24,116	3,137,545	2,202,913	874,579	18,952	41,057
Brandenburg	15,408	2,863,529	2,730,242	86,047	5,541	47,484
Pomerania	11,630	1,431,633	1,397,467	10,858	4,266	18,036
Posen	11,179	1,583,843	511,292	4,009,491	1,065	61,962
Silesia	15,556	3,707,167	1,760,841	1,896,136	8,960	46,629
Saxony	9,746	2,103,174	1,966,896	126,735	8,813	5,917
Sleswick-Holstein	6,766	995,873	984,972	6,144	1,015	3,729
Hanover	14,857	1,963,618	1,713,711	233,809	3,264	12,799
Westphalia	7,799	1,775,175	806,464	949,118	2,334	17,245
Hesse-Nassau	6,188	1,400,370	988,041	371,786	3,802	36,390
Rhine Province	10,416	3,579,347	906,867	2,628,173	5,834	38,423
Hohenzollern	441	65,558	1,766	63,051	30	711
Soldiers not in the country	.....	35,355	29,038	6,163	7	147
Marines and sailors	.....	2,054	1,914	137	1	2
Kingdom of Prussia	134,047	24,643,941	15,991,724	8,268,177	53,994	325,551
Duchy of Lauenburg	454	49,546	49,391	132	9	14
Grand total	134,501	24,693,487	16,041,115	8,268,309	54,003	325,565

Among the Christian sects, there were 1,565 Greek Catholics, 20,011 dissenters, 14,-052 Mennonites, 9,375 Baptists, 2,531 Free Religionists, 1,370 German Catholics, 384 Christian Catholics, 874 Anglicans, 1,357 Apostolic Catholics, 987 Free Congregationalists, 600 Methodists, 68 Presbyterians, 254 Irvingites, and 592 others. Besides these, there were also 17 Mohammedans, 13 Gypsies, 81 Buddhists, 1 Fire-worshipper, 1 Chinese, 14 pagans, 6 Mormons, 1 Rationalist, and of 4,410 inhabitants the religion was unknown. The Old Catholics are recognized by the Government as a division of the Roman Catholic Church, and their bishop receives an annual salary of 16,000 thalers.

The non-German population of Prussia comprises :

NATIONALITIES.	In the Provinces of	Number.	Percentage
Lithuanians	Prussia	146,800	0.6
Poles	Silesia, Posen, Prussia, and Pomerania.	2,432,000	10.1
Czechs	Silesia	50,000	0.2
Wends	Brandenburg and Silesia	33,000	0.4
Walloons	Rhine Province	10,400	....
Danes	Sleswick-Holstein	145,000	0.6
Others		80,000	0.1

Of these, only the Poles and the Danes constitute a compact majority in some of the electoral districts, and are represented in the Diet by deputies who desire an ultimate separation of their nationalities from Prussia and from Germany. The Poles constitute, in the district of Oppeln, 60.1 per cent. of the population ; in Posen, 59.3 ; in Bromberg, 46.9 ; in Marienwerder, 37.8 ; in Dantzic, 27.3 ; in Gumbinnen, 21.9 ; in Königsberg, 17.1 ; in Breslau, 4.3 ; and in Köslin, 0.7.

According to the budget for the year 1874, the revenue and expenditures were as follows (value expressed in marks ; 1 mark = 23 cents) :

REVENUE.

	Marks.
Ministry of Finances	379,726,298
Ministry of Commerce	268,644,579
Ministry of State	443,700
Ministry of Justice	42,525,000
Ministry of the Interior	3,764,803
Ministry of Agriculture	3,401,655
Ministry of Education and Ecclesiastical Affairs	767,016
Total	698,274,051

EXPENDITURES.

I. ORDINARY EXPENDITURES :

	Marks.
Costs of administration	261,599,619
Charges on consolidated debt	66,180,530
Administrative expenditures	268,514,094
Total ordinary expenditures	596,244,243
II. EXTRAORDINARY EXPENDITURES	102,029,808
Total of all expenditures	698,274,051

The public debt, according to the budget of 1874, was as follows :

I. INTEREST-BEARING DEBT :

	Marks.		Marks.
1. Of the old provinces	817,987,206		
2. Of the new provinces	146,950,878		
3. Floating debt	27,900,000		
			992,888,144
II. RENTES			28,500,000
III. DEBT BEARING NO INTEREST			60,044,163
Total			1,081,382,307

According to the budget of 1873, the total debt was 1,317,888,534 marks, showing a reduction of the debt within one year of 236,-506,227 marks. In 1874, out of the total sum of 1,087,000,000 marks, 450,000,000 were devoted exclusively to the construction of railways, and interest thereon is paid out of the profits of the state lines, with the yearly-increasing dividends.

The attention of the Prussian Diet, which was in session at the beginning of the year 1874, was chiefly engrossed by the conflict between the state Government and the heads of the Catholic Church. The majority of the

* For a list of the administrative districts into which the provinces are divided, with the area, Protestant, Catholic, and Jewish population of each, see ANNUAL CYCLOPÆDIA for 1873.

House was in this question in full accord with the Government—the Catholic party, as the "Centre," being generally only supported by the Poles, the Socialists, and a few ultra-conservative Protestants. On January 23d the Diet adopted the law concerning the introduction of civil marriage, by 284 against 95 votes. The Herrenhaus adopted the law on February 20th by 99 against 51 votes. Several amendments, proposed by the Herrenhaus, were consented to by the Lower House, on February 24th.

An inquiry which the Government was said to have instituted into the politics of the Roman Catholic elementary teachers in a certain district of the Rhine Province led to violent attacks upon the Imperial Chancellor by several members of the Catholic party, specially by its leader, Herr von Mallinkrodt. He said:

The Rhine country was one of the most patriotic provinces, and the elementary teachers there had a right to cherish Ultramontane politics, even though appointed and salaried by Government. What must be the feelings of these devoted patriots on finding themselves coerced by the cabinet? Was not the cabinet presided over by a statesman who, when preparing for the Austrian War, told the Italian General Govone that he did not object to give Rhineland up altogether to France as a sop thrown to Cerberus?

To this charge Prince Bismarck replied in a set speech, during which he said:

I find myself compelled to declare that the statement of Herr von Mallinkrodt with reference to an alleged transaction between General Govone and myself is an infamous lie. Of course, it is not Herr von Mallinkrodt who told the lie. Of course, he repeated only a falsehood invented by some one else. However, as the story has been invented with *malice prepense*, it might perhaps have been expected that Herr von Mallinkrodt would have reflected twice before fathering it. I have never allowed any one to hope that I should be able to bring myself to consent to the cession of a single village or a single acre of land. The fiction circulated at my expense is a downright and daring lie, got up to blacken my reputation in the eyes of my countrymen. Once upon this subject, I should like to say a few words on an incident which occurred at a previous sitting, when I was unfortunately absent. A gentleman belonging to the same party as Herr von Mallinkrodt chose to attack me as a statesman. He, too, did so in connection with foreign politics, censuring my conduct most severely. May I perhaps suggest to the gentleman opposite that, as a member of a Government which they will be the last to deny is a divinely appointed institution, I have some claim to decent treatment at their hands? May I lay claim to this privilege, if not in domestic, at least in foreign affairs? Do they not really perceive that they are acting an unhandsome part in calumniating me, in connection with matters calculated to attract the particular attention of other countries? Are they not conversant with a certain proverb referring to the bird who fouls his own nest? Surely, if I am to believe that the pious gentlemen opposite are more especially engaged in the defense of truth, religion, and Christianity than others, I must beg of them to be a little more cautious in repeating all manner of stories, derived by them from questionable sources. I am led to offer these remarks by Herr von Schorlemer's accusations. His first accusation was comparatively mild. He began by charging me with contradicting myself. He said I had formerly acknowledged the necessity of respecting the dogma

of infallibility, a dogma accepted by millions of Roman Catholics; and he asserted, further, that I was now acting contrary to my first intentions and promises. The one is true; the other is not. Even now, I acknowledge it as my duty to respect the dogmas of the Catholic Church as dogmas, and I never have interfered with anybody for believing in them. But, if the Infallibility dogma is so interpreted as to lead to the establishment of an ecclesiastical *imperium in imperio*, if it occasions the setting aside of the laws of this country, because unapproved by the Vatican, I am naturally driven to assert the legitimate supremacy of the state. We Protestants are under the conviction that this kingdom of Prussia ought not to be ruled by the Pope, and we demand that you, the Ultramontane section of the Roman Catholics, respect our convictions as we do yours. Unfortunately, however, you are accustomed to complain of oppression whenever not permitted to lord it over others.

He added that he would have much to do to refute all that was said and written against him in every country, and not the least in Germany. He was proud of being the most hated man among all his contemporaries. The accusations drawn from La Marmora's book were founded on dispatches privately written by an envoy, and without the corresponding Prussian documents, which alone might set them in their proper light. The fact was, that had he chosen to concede to France the smallest portion of German territory, even a mere village, or something which would have cast a stain on Germany's honor, he could have obtained the largest concessions from the Emperor Napoleon. But he refused to do so, and at last preferred a dangerous war. He had acquired the habit of treating all these insinuations and slanders with supreme contempt.

The proposition of the Government to give to the Old Catholic bishop a salary of 16,000 thalers was on January 30th approved by the usual majority.

The Diet adjourned on February 26th to the close of April, when it resumed the discussion of the new ecclesiastical laws, specially that on the administration of vacant bishoprics. In the course of the discussion, Dr. Falk, the Minister of Public Worship, made a speech, in which he stated that no difference of opinion existed between him and the leaders of German policy with regard to the course to be pursued in dealing with the Church. He added that he had good reasons for stating that the Roman Curia had manifested willingness to make advances to Switzerland on condition that Prussia should be left alone to struggle with the Papacy. The minister mentioned that other letters had been addressed by the Pope to foreign princes besides the one written last August to the Emperor of Germany. Replying to the Ultramontane Deputy Herr von Malinkrodt, Dr. Falk said he knew nothing of any letter from the Pope to the Emperor William other than that sent in August last. The Lower House adopted the bill by a large majority. In the Herrenhaus, the Protestant nobility strongly opposed the law, which, however, received nearly a two-thirds majority, being adopted by

81 against 46 votes. A supplement to the law on the education of clergymen was likewise adopted by both Houses. From the report of the Minister of Finances, made on April 28th, it appeared that the financial administration of the kingdom is very successful. During the year 1873 there had been a surplus of 21,000,000 thalers, of which 12,000,000 were derived from the administration of mines, 2,000,000 from the forests, and 2,800,000 from the indirect taxes.

The Diet was closed on May 22d.

The bishops and priests of the Roman Catholic Church remained almost unanimous in their resistance to the new Church laws, which, in 1873, had been adopted by the Diet and approved by the Government. In addition to the Archbishop of Posen, the Archbishop of Cologne, and the Bishops of Treves and Paderborn, were imprisoned in the course of the year; the two former were, however, set free again before the end of the year. In addition to these bishops, a large number of priests were imprisoned for non-compliance with the Church laws, and a still larger number were deprived of their salaries. The severest sentence was on April 15th pronounced by the Ecclesiastical Court of Berlin against Archbishop Ledochowski, who, on account of his persistence in non-compliance with the state laws, was deprived of his see, in conformity with the provisions of the law of May, 1873. As the chapters of the archdiocese at Posen and Gnesen refused to elect an administrator of the vacant diocese, on the ground that Ledochowski was considered by them the only lawful archbishop, the Government appointed a civil officer as administrator of the Church property.

Contrary to the expectations of the Government, the lower clergy were almost unanimous in openly and emphatically supporting the policy pursued by the bishops. Only in a few isolated cases the priests submitted or even invoked the state laws against the bishops. The Ecclesiastical Court of Berlin, at its first session in January, had before it the complaint of a chaplain who had been removed, as he thought, illegally, from his office by the Bishop of Paderborn. The court decided that the act of the bishop was null and void. At Xions, in the province of Posen, a public disturbance arose out of a similar case. The living being vacant, the patron appointed a priest named Kubeczack; but the dean, on whom the function devolves during the imprisonment of the bishop, refused to institute him. Kubeczack repaired to his post, but the dean and vicar refused to hand over the key of the church. The building was accordingly forced open, as also the chest containing the church books. At the beginning of the service on Sunday, a mob, mostly consisting of peasants, entered the church, seized on the crucifixes and images, which they carried round, and insulted the new incumbent. The military had to be sent for from Schrimm to restore order.

Though the resistance of the Catholic bishops, the lower clergy, and the laity, to the new church law proved to be much more formidable than had been anticipated, the Government remained unyielding in its policy, and even announced that in 1875 laws still more stringent would be proposed to the Diet to carry out its designs.

Dr. ADALBERT FALK, the chief representative, next to Prince Bismarck, of the policy now pursued with regard to the Catholic Church by the Prussian Government, is the Minister of Public Education and Ecclesiastical Affairs, He was born on August 10, 1827, studied from 1844 to 1847 at the University of Berlin, and entered the service of the Prussian state in 1847. From 1850 to 1862 he was in succession state attorney at Breslau, Lyck, and Berlin; from 1862 to 1868 councillor of the Court of Appeals at Glogau. In 1871 he received the title of Geheimer Oberjustizrath, and in 1872 he was appointed minister. From 1854 to 1861 he was a member of the Prussian House of Deputies; in 1867 he was elected member of the North-German Reichstag, and in 1873 of the second Reichstag of the empire. At the new election of a Prussian House of Deputies no less than seven districts elected him their representative. In 1871 he was for a time one of the representatives of Prussia in the Federal Council. The first important bill introduced by him aimed at extending the control of the state Government over the educational institutions, including the theological schools. The bill was enthusiastically supported by all the Liberal parties of the Prussian Diet, disliked by a large portion of the Protestant clergy of orthodox views, and violently opposed by the Catholic bishops and the Catholic party.

Dr. RUDOLPH FRIEDENTHAL.—The ministry of Agriculture, which for some time had been vacant and provisionally been administered by the Minister of Commerce, was, in September, filled by the appointment of Dr. Friedenthal, a prominent member of the Conservative Reichspartei in the German Reichstag. The appointment, which had been recommended to the King by all members of the ministry, was hailed by papers of all parties with the unreserved and most cordial recognition of his eminent services Born on September 15, 1827, he studied law at the Universities of Breslau, Heidelberg, and Berlin, and had, from 1850 to 1854, been employed in the service of the Government. He left the state service in order to devote himself wholly to agricultural and industrial pursuits, in which he met with eminent success. Since 1857 he has been an active influential, and universally respected member of the Parliament of Prussia and Germany, and in 1873 he was elected vice-president of the Prussian House of Deputies. Even before accepting the office of minister, Dr. Friedenthal disposed of his large commercial establishments at Breslau, Pesth, and Trieste.

PUBLIC DOCUMENTS. *Message of President* GRANT, *at the commencement of the second session of the Forty-third Congress, December 7, 1874.*

To the Senate and House of Representatives:

Since the convening of Congress, one year ago, the nation has undergone a prostration in business and industries such as has not been witnessed with us for many years. Speculation as to the causes for this prostration might be indulged in without profit, because as many theories would be advanced as there would be independent writers—those who expressed their own views, without borrowing—upon the subject. Without indulging in theories as to the cause of this prostration, therefore, I will call your attention only to the fact, and to some plain questions as to which it would seem there should be no disagreement.

During this prostration two essential elements of prosperity have been most abundant; labor and capital. Both have been largely unemployed. Where security has been undoubted, capital has been attainable at very moderate rates. Where labor has been wanted, it has been found in abundance, at cheap rates compared with what—of necessaries and comforts of life—could be purchased with the wages demanded. Two great elements of prosperity, therefore, have not been denied us. A third might be added: our soil and climate are unequaled, within the limits of any contiguous territory under one nationality, for its variety of products to feed and clothe a people, and in the amount of surplus to spare to feed less favored peoples. Therefore, with these facts in view, it seems to me that wise statesmanship, at this session of Congress, would dictate legislation ignoring the past; directing in proper channels these great elements of prosperity to any people. Debt, debt abroad, is the only element that can—with always a sound currency—enter into our affairs to cause any continued depression in the industries and prosperity of our people.

A great conflict for national existence made necessary, for temporary purposes, the raising of large sums of money from whatever source attainable. It made it necessary, in the wisdom of Congress—and I do not doubt their wisdom in the premises, regarding the necessity of the times—to devise a system of national currency, which it proved to be impossible to keep on a par with the recognized currency of the civilized world. This begot a spirit of speculation, involving an extravagance and luxury not required for the happiness or prosperity of a people, and involving, both directly and indirectly, foreign indebtedness. The currency being of fluctuating value, and therefore unsafe to hold for legitimate transactions requiring money, became a subject of speculation within itself. These two causes, however, have involved us in a foreign indebtedness, contracted in good faith by borrower and lender, which should be paid in coin, and according to the bond agreed upon when the debt was contracted—gold or its equivalent. The good faith of the Government cannot be violated toward creditors without national disgrace. But our commerce should be encouraged; American ship-building and carrying capacity increased; foreign markets sought for products of the soil and manufactories, to the end that we may be able to pay these debts. Where a new market can be created for the sale of our products, either of the soil, the mine, or the manufactory, a new means is discovered of utilizing our idle capital and labor to the advantage of the whole people. But, in my judgment, the first step toward accomplishing this object is to secure a currency of fixed, stable value ; a currency, good wherever civilization reigns; one which, if it becomes superabundant with one people, will find a market with some other; a currency which has as its basis the labor necessary to produce it, which will give to it its value. Gold and

silver are now the recognized medium of exchange the civilized world over; and to this we should return with the least practicable delay. In view of the pledges of the American Congress when our present legal-tender system was adopted, and debt contracted, there should be no delay—certainly no unnecessary delay—in fixing, by legislation, a method by which we will return to specie. To the accomplishment of this end I invite your special attention. I believe firmly that there can be no prosperous and permanent revival of business and industries until a policy is adopted—with legislation to carry it out—looking to a return to a specie basis. It is easy to conceive that the debtor and speculative classes may think it of value to them to make so-called money abundant until they can throw a portion of their burdens upon others. But even these, I believe, would be disappointed in the result if a course should be pursued which will keep in doubt the value of the legal-tender medium of exchange. A revival of productive industry is needed by all classes; by none more than the holders of property, of whatever sort, with debts to liquidate from realization upon its sale. But admitting that these two classes of citizens are to be benefited by expansion, would it be honest to give it? Would not the general loss be too great to justify such relief? Would it not be just as honest and prudent to authorize each debtor to issue his own legal tenders to the extent of his liabilities? Than to do this would it not be safer—for fear of over-issues by unscrupulous creditors—to say that all debt obligations are obliterated in the United States, and now we commence anew, each possessing all he has at the time free from incumbrance? These propositions are too absurd to be entertained for a moment by thinking or honest people. Yet every delay in preparation for final resumption partakes of this dishonesty, and is only less in degree as the hope is held out that a convenient season will at last arrive for the good work of redeeming our pledges to commence. It will never come, in my opinion, except by positive action by Congress, or by national disasters which will destroy, for a time at least, the credit of the individual and the States at large. A sound currency might be reached by total bankruptcy and discredit of the integrity of the nation and of individuals. I believe it is in the power of Congress at this session to devise such legislation as will renew confidence, revive all the industries, start us on a career of prosperity to last for many years, and to save the credit of the nation and of the people. Steps toward the return to a specie basis are the great requisites to this devoutly to be sought for end. There are others which I may touch upon hereafter.

A nation dealing in a currency below that of specie in value labors under two great disadvantages: First, having no use for the world's acknowledged medium of exchange, gold and silver, these are driven out of the country because there is no need for their use; second, the medium of exchange in use being of a fluctuating value—for, after all, it is only worth just what it will purchase of gold and silver; metals having an intrinsic value just in proportion to the honest labor it takes to produce them—a larger margin must be allowed for profit by the manufacturer and producer. It is months from the date of production to the date of realization. Interest upon capital must be charged, and risk of fluctuation in the value of that which is to be received in payment added. Hence, high prices, acting as a protection to the foreign producer, who receives nothing in exchange for the products of his skill and labor, except a currency good, at a stable value, the world over. It seems to me that nothing is clearer than that the greater part of the burden of existing prostration, for the want of a sound financial system, falls upon the working-man, who must after all produce the wealth, and the salaried man, who superintends and conducts business. The burden falls upon them in two ways, by the deprivation of employment and by the decreased purchasing-power of their salaries. It is the duty of Congress to devise the method of correcting the evils which are acknowledged to exist, and not mine. But I will venture to suggest two or three things which seem to me as absolutely necessary to a return to specie payments, the first great requisite in a return to prosper t . The legal-tender clause to the law authorizing the issue of currency by the national Government should be repealed, to take effect as to all contracts entered into after a day fixed in the repealing act; not to apply, however, to payments of salaries by Government, or for other expenditures now provided by law to be paid in currency in the interval pending between repeal and final resumption. Provision should be made by which the Secretary of the Treasury can obtain gold as it may become necessary from time to time from the date when specie redemption commences. To this might and should be added a revenue sufficiently in excess of expenses to insure an accumulation of gold in the Treasury to sustain permanent redemption.

I commend this subject to your careful consideration, believing that a favorable solution is attainable, and, if reached by this Congress, that the present and future generations will ever gratefully remember it as their deliverer from a thraldom of evil and disgrace.

With resumption, free banking may be authorized with safety, giving the same full protection to bill-holders which they have under existing laws. Indeed, I would regard free banking as essential. It would give proper elasticity to the currency. As more currency should be required for the transaction of legitimate business, new banks would be started, and, in turn, banks would wind up their business when it was found that there was a superabundance of currency. The experience and judgment of the people can best decide just how much currency is required for the transaction of the business of the country. It is unsafe to leave the settlement of this question to Congress, the Secretary of the Treasury, or the Executive. Congress should make the regulation under which banks may exist, but should not make banking a monopoly by limiting the amount of redeemable paper currency that shall be authorized. Such importance do I attach to this subject, and so earnestly do I commend it to your attention, that I give it prominence by introducing it at the beginning of this message.

During the past year nothing has occurred to disturb the general friendly and cordial relations of the United States with other powers.

The correspondence submitted herewith between this Government and its diplomatic representatives, as also with the representatives of other countries, shows a satisfactory condition of all questions between the United States and the most of those countries, and with few exceptions, to which reference is hereafter made, the absence of any points of difference to be adjusted.

The notice directed by the resolution of Congress of June 17, 1874, to be given to terminate the convention of July 17, 1853, between the United States and Belgium, has been given, and the treaty will accordingly terminate on the 1st day of July, 1875. The convention secured to certain Belgian vessels entering the ports of the United States exceptional privileges which are not accorded to our own vessels. Other features of the convention have proved satisfactory, and have tended to the cultivation of mutually beneficial commercial intercourse and friendly relations between the two countries. I hope that negotiations which have been invited will result in the celebration of another treaty which may tend to the interests of both countries.

Our relations with China continue to be friendly. During the past year the fear of hostilities between China and Japan, growing out of the landing of an armed force upon the island of Formosa by the latter, has occasioned uneasiness. It is earnestly hoped, however, that the difficulties arising from this cause will be adjusted, and that the advance of civilization in these empires may not be retarded by a state of war. In consequence of the part taken by certain citizens of the United States in this expedition, our representatives in those countries have been instructed to impress upon the Governments of China and Japan the firm intention of this country to maintain strict neutrality in the event of hostilities, and to carefully prevent any infraction of law on the part of our citizens.

In connection with this subject I call the attention of Congress to a generally-conceded fact—that the great proportion of the Chinese immigrants who come to our shores do not come voluntarily to make their homes with us and their labor productive of general prosperity, but come under contracts with headmen who own them almost absolutely. In a worse form does this apply to Chinese women. Hardly a perceptible percentage of them perform any honorable labor, but they are brought for shameful purposes, to the disgrace of the communities where settled and to the great demoralization of the youth of those localities. If this evil practice can be legislated against, it will be my pleasure as well as duty to enforce any regulation to secure so disirable an end.

It is hoped that negotiations between the Government of Japan and the treaty powers, looking to the further opening of the empire, and to the removal of various restrictions upon trade and travel, may soon produce the results desired, which cannot fail to inure to the benefit of all the parties. Having on previous occasions submitted to the consideration of Congress the propriety of the release of the Japanese Government from the further payment of the indemnity under the convention of October 22, 1864, and as no action had been taken thereon, it became my duty to regard the obligations of the convention as in force; and, as the other powers interested had received their portion of the indemnity in full, the minister of the United States in Japan has, in behalf of this Government, received the remainder of the amount due to the United States under the convention of Simonoseki. I submit the propriety of applying the income of a part if not of the whole of this fund to the education in the Japanese language of a number of young men to be under obligations to serve the Government for a specified time as interpreters at the legation and the consulates in Japan. A limited number of Japanese youths might at the same time be educated in our own vernacular, and mutual benefits would result to both Governments. The importance of having our own citizens competent, and familiar with the language of Japan, to act as interpreters and in other capacities connected with the legation and the consulates in that country, cannot readily be over-estimated.

The amount awarded to the Government of Great Britain by the mixed commission organized under the provisions of the Treaty of Washington in settlement of the claims of British subjects arising from acts committed April 13, 1861, and April 9, 1865, became payable, under the terms of the treaty, within the past year, and was paid upon the 21st day of September, 1874. In this connection, I renew my recommendation, made at the opening of the last session of Congress, that a special court be created to hear and determine all claims of aliens against the United States arising from acts committed against their persons or property during the insurrection. It appears equitable that opportunity should be offered to citizens of other states to present their claims, as well as to those British subjects whose claims were not admissible under the late commission, to the early decision of some competent tribunal. To this end, I recommend the necessary legislation to organize a court to dispose of all claims of aliens of the nature referred to, in an equitable and satisfactory manner, and to relieve Congress and the Departments from the consideration of these questions.

The legislation necessary to extend to the colony of Newfoundland certain articles of the Treaty of Washington of the 8th day of May, 1871, having been had, a protocol to that effect was signed in behalf of the United States and of Great Britain, on the 28th day of May last, and was duly proclaimed on the following day. A copy of the proclamation is submitted herewith.

A copy of the report of the commissioner appointed under the act of March 19, 1872, for surveying and marking the boundary between the United States and the British possessions, from the Lake of the Woods to the summit of the Rocky Mountains, is herewith transmitted. I am happy to announce that the field-work of the commission has been completed, and the entire line, from the northwest corner of the Lake of the Woods to the summit of the Rocky Mountains, has been run and marked upon the surface of the earth. It is believed that the amount remaining unexpended of the appropriation made at the last session of Congress will be sufficient to complete the office-work. I recommend that the authority of Congress be given to the use of the unexpended balance of the appropriation in the completion of the work of the commission in making its report and preparing the necessary maps.

The court known as the Court of Commissioners of Alabama Claims, created by an act of Congress of the last session, has organized and commenced its work, and it is to be hoped that the claims admissible under the provisions of the act may be speedily ascertained and paid.

It has been deemed advisable to exercise the discretion conferred upon the Executive at the last session, by accepting the conditions required by the Government of Turkey for the privilege of allowing citizens of the United States to hold real estate in the former country, and by assenting to a certain change in the jurisdiction of courts in the latter. A copy of the proclamation upon these subjects is herewith communicated.

There has been no material change in our relations with the independent states of this hemisphere which were formerly under the dominion of Spain. Marauding on the frontiers, between Mexico and Texas, still frequently takes place despite the vigilance of the civil and military authorities in that quarter. The difficulty of checking such trespasses along the course of a river of such length as the Rio Grande, and so often fordable, is obvious. It is hoped that the efforts of this Government will be seconded by those of Mexico to the effectual suppression of these acts of wrong.

From a report upon the condition of the business before the American and Mexican Joint Claims Commission, made by the agent on the part of the United States, and dated October 28, 1874, it appears that of the 1,017 claims filed on the part of citizens of the United States, 483 had been finally decided, and 75 were in the hands of the umpire, leaving 462 to be disposed of; and of the 998 claims filed against the United States, 726 had been finally decided; one was before the umpire, and 271 remained to be disposed of. Since the date of such report other claims have been disposed of, reducing somewhat the number still pending; and others have been passed upon by the arbitrators. It has become apparent, in view of these figures, and of the fact that the work devolving on the umpire is particularly laborious, that the commission will be unable to dispose of the entire number of claims pending prior to the 1st day of February, 1875—the date fixed for its expiration. Negotiations are pending looking to the securing of the results of the decisions which have been reached, and to a further extension of the commission for a limited time, which it is confidently hoped will suffice to bring all the business now before it to a final close.

The strife in the Argentine Republic is to be deplored, both on account of the parties thereto and from the probable effects on the interests of those engaged in the trade to that quarter, of whom the United States are among the principal. As yet, so far as I am aware, there has been no violation of our neutrality rights, which, as well as our duties in that respect, it shall be my endeavor to maintain and observe.

It is with regret I announce that no further payment has been received from the Government of Venezuela on account of awards in favor of citizens of the United States. Hopes have been entertained that if that republic could escape both foreign and civil war for a few years its great natural resources would enable it to honor its obligations. Though it is now understood to be at peace with other countries, a serious insurrection is reported to be in progress in an important region of that republic. This may be taken advantage of as another reason to delay the payment of the dues of our citizens.

The deplorable strife in Cuba continues without any marked change in the relative advantages of the contending forces. This insurrection continues, but Spain has gained no superiority. Six years of strife give to the insurrection a significance which cannot be denied. Its duration and the tenacity of its adherence, together with the absence of manifested power of suppression on the part of Spain, cannot be controverted, and may make some positive steps on the part of other powers a matter of self-necessity. I had confidently hoped, at this time, to be able to announce the arrangement of some of the important questions between this Government and that of Spain, but the negotiations have been protracted. The unhappy intestine dissensions of Spain command our profound sympathy, and must be accepted as perhaps a cause of some delay. An early settlement, in part at least, of the questions between the Governments is hoped. In the mean time, awaiting the results of immediately pending negotiations, I defer a further and fuller communication on the subject of the relations of this country and Spain.

I have again to call the attention of Congress to the unsatisfactory condition of the existing laws with reference to expatriation and the election of nationality. Formerly, amid conflicting opinions and decisions, it was difficult to exactly determine how far the doctrine of perpetual allegiance was applicable to citizens of the United States. Congress by the act of the 27th of July, 1868, asserted the abstract right of expatriation as a fundamental principle of this Government. Notwithstanding such assertion, and the necessity of frequent application of the principle, no legislation has been had defining what acts or formalities shall work expatriation, or when a citizen shall be deemed to have renounced or to have lost his citizenship. The importance of such definition is obvious. The representatives of the United States in foreign countries are continually called upon to lend their aid and the protection of the United State to persons concerning the good faith or the reality of whose citizenship there is at least great question. In some cases the provisions of the treaties furnish some guide; in others, it seems left to the person claiming the benefits of citizenship, while living in a foreign country, contributing in no manner to the per ormance of the duties of a citizen of the United States, and without intention at any time to return and undertake those duties, to use the claims to citizenship of the United States simply as a shield from the performance of the obligations of a citizen elsewhere.

The status of children born of American parents residing in a foreign country, of American women who have married aliens, of American citizens residing abroad where such question is not regulated by treaty, are all sources of frequent difficulty and discussion. Legislation on these and similar questions, and particularly defining when and under what circumstances expatriation can be accomplished or is to be presumed, is especially needed. In this connection I earnestly call the attention of Congress to the difficulties arising from fraudulent naturalization.

The United States wisely, freely, and liberally offers its citizenship to all who may come in good faith to reside within its limits on their complying with certain prescribed reasonable and simple formalities and conditions. Among the highest duties of the Government is that to afford firm, sufficient, and equal protection to all its citizens, whether native-born or naturalized. Care should be taken that a right, carrying with it such support from the Government, should not be fraudulently obtained, and should be bestowed only upon full proof of a compliance with the law; and yet frequent instances are brought to the attention of the Government of illegal and fraudulent naturalization and of the unauthorized use of certificates thus improperly obtained. In some cases the fraudulent character of the naturalization has appeared upon the face of the certificate itself; in others examination discloses that the holder had not complied with the law; and in others certificates have been obtained where the persons holding them not only were not entitled to be naturalized, but had not even been within the United States at the time of the pretended naturalization. Instances of each of these classes of fraud are discovered at our legations, where the certificates of naturalization are presented, either for the purpose of obtaining passports, or in demanding the protection of the legation. When the fraud is apparent on the face of such certificates, they are taken up by the representatives of the Government and forwarded to the Department of State. But even then the record of the court in which the fraudulent naturalization occurred remains, and duplicate certificates are readily obtainable. Upon the presentation of these for the issue of passports, or in demanding protection of the Government, the fraud sometimes escapes notice, and such certificates are not infrequently used in transactions of business to the deception and injury of innocent parties. Without placing any additional obstacles in the way of the obtainment of citizenship by the worthy and well-intentioned foreigner who comes in good faith to cast his lot with ours, I earnestly recommend further legislation to punish fraudulent naturalization, and to secure the ready cancellation of the record of every naturalization made in fraud.

Since my last annual message the exchange has been made of the ratification of treaties of extradition with Belgium, Ecuador, Peru, and Salvador; also of a treaty of commerce and navigation with Peru, and one of commerce and consular privileges with Salvador; all of which have been duly proclaimed, as has also a declaration with Russia with reference to trade-marks.

The report of the Secretary of the Treasury, which, by law, is made directly to Congress, and forms no part of this message, will show the receipts and expenditures of the Government for the last fiscal year; the amount received from each source of revenue, and the amount paid out for each of the departments of Government. It will be observed from this report that the amount of receipts over expenditures has been but $2,344,882.30 for the fiscal year ending June 30, 1874, and that for the current fiscal year the estimated receipts over expenditures will not much exceed nine millions of dollars. In view of the large national debt existing, and the obligation to add one per cent. per annum to the sinking-fund, a sum amounting now to over $34,000,000 per annum, I submit whether revenues should not be increased or expenditures diminished to reach this amount of surplus. Not to provide for the sinking-fund is a partial failure to comply with the contracts and obligations of the Government. At the last session of Congress a very considerable reduction was made in rates of taxation, and in the number of articles submitted to taxation; the question may well be asked whether or not, in some instances, unwisely. In connection with this subject, too, I venture the opinion that the means of collecting the revenue, especially from imports, have been so embarrassed by legislation as to make it questionable whether or not large amounts are not lost by failure to collect, to the direct loss of the Treasury and to the prejudice of the interests of honest importers and tax-payers.

The Secretary of the Treasury in his report favors legislation looking to an early return to specie payments, thus supporting views previously expressed in this message. He also recommends economy in appropriations; calls attention to the loss of revenue from repealing the tax on tea and coffee, without benefit to the consumer; recommends an increase of ten cents a gallon on whiskey; and, further, that no modification be made in the banking and currency bill passed at the last session of Congress, unless modification should become necessary by reason of the adoption of measures of returning to specie payments. In these recommendations I cordially join.

I would suggest to Congress the propriety of readjusting the tariff so as to increase the revenue, and, at the same time, decrease the number of articles upon which duties are levied. Those articles which enter into our manufactures, and are not produced at home, it seems to me should be entered free. Those articles of manufacture which we produce a constituent part of, but do not produce the whole, that part which we do not produce should enter free also. I will instance fine wool, dyes, etc. These articles must be imported to form a part of the manufacture of the higher grades of woolen goods. Chemicals used as dyes, compounded in medicines, and used in various ways in manufactures, come under this class. The introduction, free of duty, of such wools as we do not produce would stimulate the manufacture of goods requiring the use of those we do produce, and, therefore, would be a benefit to home production. There are many articles entering into "home manufactures" which we do not produce ourselves, the tariff upon which increases the cost of producing the manufactured article. All corrections in this regard are in the direction of bringing labor and capital in harmony with each other, and of supplying one of the elements of prosperity so much needed.

The report of the Secretary of War, herewith attached, and forming a part of this message, gives all the information concerning the operations, wants, and necessities of the Army, and contains many suggestions and recommendations which I commend to your special attention.

There is no class of Government employés who are harder worked than the Army—officers and men; none who perform their tasks more cheerfully and efficiently, and under circumstances of greater privations and hardships.

Legislation is desirable to render more efficient this branch of the public service. All the recommendations of the Secretary of War I regard as judicious, and I especially commend to your attention the following: The consolidation of Government arsenals; the restoration of mileage to officers traveling under orders; the exemption of money received from the sale of subsistence stores from being covered into the Treasury; the use of appropriations for the purchase of subsistence stores without waiting for the beginning of the fiscal year for which the appropriation is made; for additional appropriations for the collection of torpedo material; for increased appropriations for the manufacture of arms; for relieving the various States from indebtedness for arms charged to them during the rebellion; for dropping officers from the rolls of the Army without trial for the offense of drawing pay more than once for the same period; for the discouragement of the plan to pay soldiers by checks; and for the establishment of a professorship of Rhetoric and English Literature at West Point. The reasons for these recommendations are obvious, and are set forth sufficiently in the reports attached. I also recommend that the status of the staff corps of the Army be fixed—where this has not already been done—so that promotions may be made and vacancies filled as they occur in each grade when reduced below the number to be fixed by law. The necessity for such legislation is specially felt now in the Pay Department. The number of officers in that department is below the number adequate to the performance of the duties required of them by law.

The efficiency of the Navy has been largely increased during the last year. Under the impulse of the foreign complications which threatened us at the commencement of the last session of Congress, most of our efficient wooden ships were put in condition for immediate service, and the repairs of our iron-clad fleet were pushed with the utmost vigor. The result is that most of these are now in an effective state, and need only to be manned and put in commission to go at once into service.

Some of the new sloops authorized by Congress are already in commission, and most of the remainder are launched and wait only the completion of their machinery to enable them to take their places as part of our effective force.

Two iron torpedo-ships have been completed during the last year, and four of our large double-turreted iron-clads are now undergoing repairs. When these are finished, everything that is useful of our Navy, as now authorized, will be in condition for service, and, with the advance in the science of torpedo warfare, the American Navy, comparatively small as it is, will be found at any time powerful for the purposes of a peaceful nation.

Much has been accomplished during the year in aid of science and to increase the sum of general knowledge and further the interests of commerce and civilization. Extensive and much-needed soundings have been made for hydrographic purposes and to fix the proper routes of ocean-telegraphs. Further surveys of the great Isthmus have been undertaken and completed, and two vessels of the Navy are now employed, in conjunction with those of England, France, Germany, and Russia, in observations connected with the transit of Venus, so useful and interesting to the scientific world.

The estimates for this branch of the public service do not differ materially from those of last year, those for the general support of the service being somewhat less, and those for permanent improvements at the various stations rather larger than the corresponding estimate made a year ago. The regular maintenance and a steady increase in the efficiency of this most important arm, in proportion to the growth of our maritime intercourse and interests, are recommended to the attention of Congress.

The use of the Navy in time of peace might be further utilized by a direct authorization of the employment of naval vessels in explorations and surveys of the supposed navigable waters of other nationalities on this continent; specially the tributaries of the two great rivers of South America, the Oronoco and the Amazon. Nothing prevents, under existing laws, such exploration, except that expenditures must be made in such expeditions beyond those usually provided for in the appropriations. The field designated is unquestionably one of interest and one capable of large development of commerical interest advantageous to the peoples reached, and to those who may establish relations with them.

Education of the people entitled to exercise the right of franchise I regard essential to general prosperity everywhere, and especially so in republics, where birth, education, or previous condition, does not enter into account in giving suffrage. Next to the public school, the post-office is the great agent of education over our vast territory; the rapidity with which new sections are being settled, thus increasing the carrying of mails in a more rapid ratio than the increase of receipts, is not alarming. The report of the Postmaster-General, herewith attached, shows that there was an increase of revenue in his department in 1873 over the previous year of $1,674,411, and an increase of cost of carrying the mails and paying employés of $3,041,468.91. The report of the Post-

master-General gives interesting statistics of his department, and compares them with the corresponding statistics of a year ago, showing a growth in every branch of the department.

A postal convention has been concluded with New South Wales, an exchange of postal cards established with Switzerland, and negotiations pending for several years past with France have been terminated in a convention with that country, which went into effect last August.

An international postal congress was convened in Berne, Switzerland, in September last, at which the United States was represented by an officer of the Post-Office Department of much experience and of qualification for the position. A convention for the establishment of an international postal union was agreed upon and signed by the delegates of the countries represented, subject to the approval of the proper authorities of those countries.

I respectfully direct your attention to the report of the Postmaster-General, and to his suggestion in regard to an equitable, adjustment of the question of compensation to railroads for carrying the mails.

Your attention will be drawn to the unsettled condition of affairs in some of the Southern States.

On the 14th of September last, the Governor of Louisiana called upon me, as provided by the Constitution and laws of the United States, to aid in suppressing domestic violence in that State. This call was made in view of a proclamation issued on that day by D. B. Penn, claiming that he was elected Lieutenant-Governor in 1872, and calling upon the militia of the State to arm, assemble, and drive from power the usurpers, as he designated the officers of the State government. On the next day I issued my proclamation commanding the insurgents to disperse within five days from the date thereof, and subsequently learned that on that day they had taken forcible possession of the State-House. Steps were taken by me to support the existing and recognized State government; but before the expiration of the five days the insurrectionary movement was practically abandoned, and the officers of the State government, with some minor exceptions, resumed their powers and duties. Considering that the present State administration of Louisiana has been the only government in that State for nearly two years; that it has been tacitly acknowledged and acquiesced in as such by Congress, and more than once expressly recognized by me, I regarded it as my clear duty, when legally called upon for that purpose, to prevent its overthrow by an armed mob under pretense of fraud and irregularity in the election of 1872. I have heretofore called the attention of Congress to this subject, stating t at, on account of the frauds and forgeries committed at said election, and because it appears that the returns thereof were never legally canvassed, it was impossible to tell thereby who were chosen; but, from the best sources of information at my command, I have always believed that the present State officers received a majority of the legal votes actually cast at that election. I repeat what I said in my special message of February 23, 1873, that in the event of no action by Congress I must continue to recognize the government heretofore recognized by me.

I regret to say that, with preparations for the late election, decided indications appeared in some localities in the Southern States of a determination, by acts of violence and intimidation, to deprive citizens of the freedom of the ballot, because of their political opinions. Bands of men, masked and armed, make their appearance; White Leagues and other societies were formed; large quantities of arms and ammunition were imported and distributed to these organizations; military drills, with menacing demonstrations, were held; and, with all these, murders enough were committed to spread terror among those whose political action was to be suppressed, if possible, by these intolerant and criminal proceedings. In some places colored laborers were compelled to vote according to the wishes of their employers, under threats of discharge if they acted otherwise; and there are too many instances in which, when these threats were disregarded, they were remorselessly executed by those who made them. I understand that the fifteenth amendment to the Constitution was made to prevent this and a like state of things, and the act of May 31, 1870, with amendments, was passed to enforce its provisions, the object of both being to guarantee to all citizens the right to vote and to protect them in the free enjoyment of that right. Enjoined by the Constitution "to take care that the laws be faithfully executed," and convinced by undoubted evidence that violations of said act had been committed, and that a wide-spread and flagrant disregard of it was contemplated, the proper officers were instructed to prosecute the offenders, and troops were stationed at convenient points to aid these officers, if necessary, in the performance of their official duties. Complaints are made of this interference by Federal authority; but if said amendment and act do not provide for such interference under the circumstances as above stated, then they are without meaning, force, or effect, and the whole scheme of colored enfranchisement is worse than mockery, and little better than a crime. Possibly Congress may find it due to truth and justice to ascertain, by means of a committee, whether the alleged wrongs to colored citizens for political purposes are real, or the reports thereof were manufactured for the occasion.

The whole number of troops in the States of Louisiana, Alabama, Georgia, Florida, South Carolina, North Carolina, Kentucky, Tennessee, Arkansas, Mississippi, Maryland, and Virginia, at the time of the election was four thousand and eighty-two. This embraces the garrisons of all the forts from the Delaware to the Gulf of Mexico.

Another trouble has arisen in Arkansas. Article XIII. of the constitution of that State (which was adopted in 1868, and upon the approval of which by Congress the State was restored to representation as one of the States of the Union) provides in effect that, before any amendments proposed to this constitution shall become a part thereof, they shall be passed by two successive Assemblies, and then submitted to and ratified by a majority of the electors of the State voting thereon. On the 11th of May, 1874, the Governor convened an extra session of the General Assembly of the State, which, on the 18th of the same month, passed an act providing for a convention to frame a new constitution. Pursuant to this act, and at an election held on the 30th of June, 1874, the convention was approved, and delegates were chosen thereto, who assembled on the 14th of last July and framed a new constitution, the schedule of which provided for the election of an entire new set of State officers in a manner contrary to the then existing election laws of the State. On the 13th of October, 1874, this constitution, as therein provided, was submitted to the people for their approval or rejection, and according to the election-returns was approved by a large majority of those qualified to vote thereon, and at the same election persons were chosen to fill all the State, county, and township offices. The Governor elected in 1872 for the term of four years turned over his office to the Governor chosen under the new constitution; whereupon the Lieutenant-Governor, also elected in 1872 for a term of four years, claiming to act as Governor, and alleging that said proceedings by which the new constitution was made and a new set of officers elected were unconstitutional, illegal, and void, called upon me, as provided in section 4, Article IV. of the Constitution, to protect the State against domestic violence. As Congress is now investigating the political affairs of Arkansas, I have declined to interfere.

The whole subject of Executive interference with the affairs of a State is repugnant to public opinion, to the feeling of those who, from their official capacity, must be used in such interposition, and to him or those who must direct. Unless most clearly on the side of law, such interference becomes a crime; with the law to support it, it is condemned without a hearing. I desire, therefore, that all necessity for Executive direction in local affairs may become unnecessary and obsolete. I invite the attention, not of Congress, but of the people of the United States, to the causes and effects of these unhappy questions. Is there not a disposition on one side to magnify wrongs and outrages, and on the other side to belittle them or justify them? If public opinion could be directed to a correct survey of what is, and to rebuking wrong, and aiding the proper authorities in punishing it, a better state of feeling would be inculcated, and the sooner we would have that peace which would leave the States free indeed to regulate their own domestic affairs. I believe on the part of our citizens of the Southern States—the better part of them—there is a disposition to be law-abiding, and to do no violence either to individuals or to the laws existing. But do they do right in ignoring the existence of violence and bloodshed in resistance to constituted authority? I sympathize with their prostrate condition, and would do all in my power to relieve them; acknowledging that in some instances they have had most trying governments to live under, and very oppressive ones in the way of taxation for nominal improvements, not giving benefits equal to the hardships imposed; but, can they proclaim themselves entirely irresponsible for this condition? They cannot. Violence has been rampant in some localities, and has either been justified or denied by those who could have prevented it. The theory is even raised that there is to be no further interference on the part of the General Government to protect citizens within a State where the State authorities fail to give protection. This is a great mistake. While I remain Executive all the laws of Congress, and the provisions of the Constitution, including the recent amendments added thereto, will be enforced with rigor, but with regret that they should have added one jot or tittle to Executive duties or powers. Let there be fairness in the discussion of Southern questions, the advocates of both, or all political parties, giving honest, truthful reports of occurrences, condemning the wrong and upholding the right, and soon all will be well. Under existing conditions the negro votes the Republican ticket because he knows his friends are of that party. Many a good citizen votes the opposite, not because he agrees with the great principles of state which separate parties, but because, generally, he is opposed to negro rule. This is a most delusive cry. Treat the negro as a citizen and a voter—as he is and must remain—and soon parties will be divided, not on the color line, but on principle. Then we shall have no complaint of sectional interference.

The report of the Attorney-General contains valuable recommendations relating to the administration of justice in the courts of the United States, to which I invite your attention.

I respectfully suggest to Congress the propriety of increasing the number of judicial districts in the United States to eleven, the present number being nine, and the creation of two additional judgeships. The territory to be traversed by the circuit judges is so great, and the business of the courts so steadily increasing, that it is growing more and more impossible for them to keep up with the business requiring their attention. Whether this would involve the necessity of adding two more Justices of the Supreme Court to the present number I submit to the judgment of Congress.

The attention of Congress is invited to the report of the Secretary of the Interior, and to the legislation asked for by him. The domestic interests of the people are more intimately connected with this department than with either of the other departments of Government. Its duties have been added to from time to time until they have become so onerous that without the most perfect system and order it will be impossible for any Secretary of the Interior to keep trace of all official transactions having his sanction and done in his name, and for which he is held personally responsible.

The policy adopted for the management of Indian affairs, known as the peace policy, has been adhered to with most beneficial results. It is confidently hoped that a few years more will relieve our frontiers from danger of Indian depredations.

I commend the recommendation of the Secretary for the extension of the homestead laws to the Indians, and for some sort of territorial government for the Indian Territory. A great majority of the Indians occupying this Territory are believed yet to be incapable of maintaining their rights against the more civilized and enlightened white man. Any territorial form of government given them, therefore, should protect them in their homes and property for a period of at least twenty years, and before its final adoption should be ratified by a majority of those affected.

The report of the Secretary of the Interior, herewith attached, gives much interesting statistical information, which I abstain from giving an abstract of, but refer you to the report itself.

The act of Congress providing the oath which pensioners must subscribe to before drawing their pensions cuts off from this bounty a few survivors of the War of 1812 residing in the Southern States. I recommend the restoration of this bounty to all such. The number of persons whose names would thus be restored to the list of pensioners is not large. They are all old persons who could have taken no part in the rebellion, and the services for which they were awarded pensions were in defense of the whole country.

The report of the Commissioner of Agriculture, herewith, contains suggestions of much interest to the general public, and refers to the approaching Centennial and the part his department is ready to take in it. I feel that the nation at large is interested in having this Exposition a success, and commend to Congress such action as will secure a greater general interest in it. Already many foreign nations have signified their intention to be represented at it, and it may be expected that every civilized nation will be represented.

The rules adopted to improve the civil service of the Government have been adhered to as closely as has been practicable with the opposition with which they meet. The effect, I believe, has been beneficial on the whole, and has tended to the elevation of the service. But it is impracticable to maintain them without the direct and positive support of Congress. Generally the support which this reform receives is from those who give it their support only to find fault when the rules are apparently departed from. Removals from office without preferring charges against parties removed are frequently cited as departures from the rules adopted, and the citing of those against whom charges are made, by irresponsible persons and without good grounds, is also often condemned as a violation of them. Under these circumstances, therefore, I announce that, if Congress adjourns without positive legislation on the subject of "civil-service reform," I will regard such action as a disapproval of the system, and will abandon it, except so far as to require examinations for certain appointees, to determine their fitness. Competitive examinations will be abandoned.

The gentlemen who have given their services without compensation, as members of the board to devise rules and regulations for the government of the civil service of the country, have shown much zeal and earnestness in their work, and to them, as well as to myself, it will be a source of mortification if it is to be thrown away. But I repeat that it is impossible to carry this system to a successful issue without general approval and assistance, and positive law to support it.

I have stated that three elements of prosperity to the nation, capital, labor, skilled and unskilled, and products of the soil, still remain with us. To direct the employment of these is a problem deserving the most serious attention of Congress. If employment can be given to all the labor offering itself, prosperity necessarily follows. I have expressed the opinion, and repeat it, that the first requisite to the accomplishment of this end is the substitution of a sound currency in place of one of a fluctuating value. This secured, there are many interests that might be fostered, to the great profit of both labor and capital. How to induce capital to employ labor is the question. The subject of cheap transportation has occupied the attention of Congress. Much new light on this question will without doubt be given by the committee appointed by the last Congress to investigate and report upon this subject.

A revival of ship-building, and particularly of iron-steamship-building, is of vast importance to our national prosperity. The United States is now paying over $100,000,000 per annum for freights and passage on foreign ships—to be carried abroad and expended in the employment and support of other peoples—beyond a fair percentage of what should go to foreign vessels, estimating on the tonnage and travel of each respectively. It is to be regretted that this disparity in the carrying-trade exists, and to correct it I would be willing to see a great departure from the usual course of Government in supporting what might usually be termed private enterprise. I would not suggest as a remedy direct subsidy to American steamship-lines, but I would suggest the direct offer of ample compensation for carrying the mails between Atlantic seaboard cities and the Continent on American-owned and American-built steamers, and would extend this liberality to vessels carrying the mails to South American states and to Central America and Mexico, and would pursue the same policy from our Pacific seaports to foreign seaports on the Pacific. It might be demanded that vessels built for this service should come up to a standard fixed by legislation, in tonnage, speed, and all other qualities, looking to the possibility of Government requiring them at some time for war purposes. The right also of taking possession of them in such emergency should be guarded.

I offer these suggestions, believing them worthy of consideration, in all seriousness, affecting all sections and all interests alike. If any thing better can be done to direct the country into a course of general prosperity, no one will be more ready than I to second the plan.

Forwarded herewith will be found the report of the commissioners appointed under an act of Congress approved June 20, 1874, to wind up the affairs of the District government. It will be seen from the report that the net debt of the District of Columbia, less securities on hand and available, is:

Bonded debt issued prior to July 1, 1874... $8,883,940 43
3.65 bonds, act of Congress June 20, 1874... 2,088,168 73
Certificates of the Board of Audit.......... 4,770,558 45
                                              _____
                                              $15,742,667 61

Less special-improvement assessments (chargeable to private property) in excess of any demand against such assessments.................. $1,614,054 37
Less Chesapeake & Ohio Canal bonds...................... 75,000 00
And Washington & Alexandria Railroad bonds............ 59,000 00

In the hands of the commissioners of the sinking-fund $1,748,054 37

Leaving actual debt less said assets...... $13,994,613 24

In addition to this there are claims preferred against the government of the District, amounting, in the estimated aggregate reported by the Board of Audit, to $3,147,787.48, of which the greater part will probably be rejected. This sum can with no more propriety be included in the debt account of the District government than can the thousands of claims against the General Government be included as a portion of the national debt. But the aggregate sum thus stated includes something more than the funded debt chargeable exclusively to the District of Columbia. The act of Congress of June 20, 1874, contemplates an apportionment between the United States Government and the District of Columbia, in respect of the payment of the principal and interest of the 3.65 bonds. Therefore, in computing with precision the bonded debt of the District, the aggregate sums above stated as respects 3.65 bonds now issued, the outstanding certificates of the Board of Audit, and the unadjusted claims pending before that board, should be reduced to the extent of the amount to be apportioned to the United States Government in the manner indicated in the act of Congress of June 20, 1874.

I especially invite your attention to the recommendations of the commissioners of the sinking-fund relative to the ambiguity of the act of June 20, 1874; the interest on the District bonds, and the consolidation of the indebtedness of the District.

I feel much indebted to the gentlemen who consented to leave their private affairs and come from a distance to attend to the business of this District, and for the able and satisfactory manner in which it has been conducted. I am sure their services will be equally appreciated by the entire country.

It will be seen from the accompanying full report of the Board of Health that the sanitary condition of the District is very satisfactory.

In my opinion the District of Columbia should be regarded as the grounds of the national capital, in which the entire people are interested. I do not allude to this to urge generous appropriations to the District, but to draw the attention of Congress, in framing a law for the government of the District, to the magnificent scale on which the city was planned by the founders of the Government; the manner in which, for ornamental purposes, the reservations, streets, and avenues were laid out; and the proportion of the property actually possessed by the General Government. I think the proportion of the expenses of the government and improvements to be borne by the General Government, the cities of Washington and Georgetown and the county, should be carefully and equitably defined.

In accordance with section 3, act approved June 23, 1874, I appointed a board to make a survey of the mouth of the Mississippi River with a view to determine the best method of obtaining and maintaining a depth of water sufficient for the purposes of commerce, etc.; and in accordance with an act entitled "An act to provide for the appointment of a commission of engineers to investigate and report a permanent plan for the reclamation of the alluvial basin of the Mississippi River subject to inundation," I appointed a commission of engineers. Neither board has yet completed its labors. When their reports are received they will be forwarded to Congress without delay.

U. S. GRANT.

───── ● ─────

The Transportation Question.

In the Senate, on December 4, 1873, the following select Committee on Transportation Routes to the Seaboard was appointed: Messrs. Windom, Sherman, Conkling, West, Conover, Mitchel, Norwood, Davis, and Johnston.

On April 24th, Mr. Windom said:

I ask the consent of the Senate to present the report of the Select Committee on Transportation Routes to the Seaboard.

The President *pro tempore:* The report will be received.

Mr. Windom: Mr. President, in submitting this report, I deem it my duty to state, as briefly as the nature of the subject will permit, the conclusions and recommendations of the committee, and some of the leading facts and considerations upon which they are based. Whenever convenient I shall take the liberty of employing without further acknowledgment the language of the report. It is perhaps unnecessary to say that an investigation covering a field so broad, embracing interests so vast and complex, and involving an examination of details almost infinite in variety and number, requires more than a single vacation, and that the pressure of business during the session of the Senate has afforded but little opportunity for the preparation of a report commensurate with the importance of the questions involved. The committee do not pretend to have treated the subject exhaustively.

In Great Britain parliamentary committees and commissions have been engaged upon the same subjects for more than thirty years, and yet even in that country, comparatively so small in geographical extent, with only 15,000 miles of railway, and with a Parliament of unlimited powers, the problems of cheap transportation and go ernmental regulation of railways are still unsolved. v

In the State of Massachusetts a most able and untiring commission, headed by Mr. Charles Francis Adams, Jr., have devoted five or six years to a similar investigation, and yet they by no means consider the subject exhausted.

It was hardly to be expected, therefore, that a committee who were charged with the duty of investigating and reporting upon a transportation system embracing 70,000 miles of railway and more than 80,000 miles of water-routes could, within the limited time at their command, do full justice to all of the important questions involved.

The following is a brief *résumé* of the principal subjects which have especially commanded the attention of the committee, and which with others are embraced in their report:

1. The annual average price of wheat and corn during the five years 1868 to 1872, inclusive, at Chicago and Milwaukee and at points west of these cities; at Buffalo, Montreal, New York, St. Louis, New Orleans, and Liverpool.

2. The quantity of grain recived and shipped from all the lake-ports and ports on the Ohio and Mississippi Rivers, and ports on the Atlantic and Gulf coasts.

3. The total shipments of grain to the States on the Atlantic seaboard; the quantity distributed between the western and eastern borders of these States; the total quantity consumed in the New England States; the Atlantic States south of New England; and the total quantity exported; also the quantity of grain shipped to the Gulf States, and the quantity exported from these States; the quantity exported to Canada and also from the Pacific coast to foreign countries.

4. The shipments of grain from the West by the lakes and St. Lawrence River; by the Lakes, Erie Canal, and Hudson River; by the lakes to the east end of Lake Erie; thence by rail toward the seaboard; and by the "all-rail" lines from lake-ports and interior points in the West, to the East and to the South; and the quantity shipped southward by the Mississippi River.

5. The average annual freight-charges from point to point are presented as follows: From points on the Mississippi River to Chicago and Milwaukee; Chicago to Buffalo; Chicago to Montreal by lake and St. Lawrence River, and by rail; Chicago to New York by lake and canal, by lake and rail, and by rail; St. Louis to New Orleans; New Orleans to Liverpool, New York to Liverpool, and Montreal to Liverpool. These averages have been deduced from computations based upon the quantity shipped and the average rates which prevailed each month.

6. Great Britain being the principal grain-importing country, very full information in regard to the sources of her supply, the quantity received from each country for thirteen years, the rates of freight from each country to England for a period of ten years, and the average prices in the English markets of wheat and

corn imported from each country during the period of thirteen years. This information has been obtained from the British reports on trade and navigation, and from data furnished especially for the committee by the British Board of Trade through the United States consuls at London and Liverpool.

7. Some general facts are presented in regard to the commerce of the Pacific coast.

One of the most important branches of the work commanding the attention of the committee has been that of the improvement and construction of water lines of transport. The lines which the committee have personally examined and most carefully investigated are:

1. The proposed Caughnawaga and Lake Champlain route, from the river St. Lawrence to New York.
2. The Oswego & Oneida Canal route, from Oswego to New York.
3. The Erie Canal route, from Buffalo to New York.
4. The James River & Kanawha Canal, or central water-line, from Richmond to the Ohio River.
5. The Atlantic & Great Western Canal, from the Tennessee River to Savannah, Georgia.
6. The proposed ship-canal across the peninsula of Florida.
7. The improvement of the Ohio River.
8. The improvement of the Mississippi above the Falls of St. Anthony; between St. Paul and St. Louis; and between St. Louis and New Orleans.
9. The Fort St. Philip Canal, and other plans for improving the mouth of the Mississippi River.
10. The Wisconsin and Fox Rivers improvement.
11. The Illinois & Hennepin Canal.
12. The Niagara Ship-canal.

In addition to these routes the committee have obtained information in regard to the canals of Pennsylvania, and the Chesapeake & Ohio Canal.

The inquiries of the committee in regard to railroads have embraced among other subjects the following:

Combinations between different lines; the consolidation or amalgamation of lines; fast freight-lines; the issuing of stocks not representing money paid in for construction, a device commonly known as "stock-watering" or capitalization of net earnings; competition between railroads and water-lines; the relative cheapness of the various methods of transportation; the regulation or control of existing railroads by States and by the national Government, involving the questions as to the limitation of the powers of Congress under the commercial clause of the Constitution; the construction of one or more double-track freight-railroads by the Government, to be operated by the Government, or leased to parties who shall operate such road or roads, subject to Government control; and the chartering of freight-railroads to be constructed and managed by private corporations, such roads to receive aid from the Government and to submit to governmental regulation with regard to their rates of freight and the facilities which they shall afford.

A thorough elucidation of these topics involves a study of railway abuses in all their various phases, and the whole question of the economy of transport by rail and by water.

In entering upon the investigation directed by the resolution of the Senate, the committee were fully impressed with the importance and difficulties of their work, and they have assiduously devoted themselves to its discharge. The absence of official information concerning the transportation interests of the country has added to their embarrassments. Perhaps the most extraordinary feature of our governmental policy, touching the vast internal commerce of the nation, is the apparent indifference and neglect with which it has been treated. Careful statistics have been prepared of our foreign commerce, while those appertaining to the much greater interests of internal trade seem to have been almost wholly, and in some cases intentionally, ignored. No officer of the Government

has ever been charged with the duty of collecting information on this subject, and the legislator who would inform himself concerning the nature, extent, value, or necessities of our internal commerce, or of its relations to our foreign trade, must patiently grope his way through the statistics of individual Boards of Trade, Chambers of Commerce, and transportation companies. Even the census reports, which purport to contain an inventory of the property and business of the people, and which in some matters descend to the minutest details, are silent with regard to the billions of dollars represented by railways, ships, and other instruments of internal transportation, and to the much greater values of commodities annually moved by them.

We have no means of estimating accurately the magnitude of our internal trade; but its colossal proportions may be inferred from two or three known facts. The value of commodities moved by the railroads in 1872 is estimated at over $10,000,000,000, and their gross receipts reached the enormous sum of $473,241,055. The commerce of the cities of the Ohio River alone has been carefully estimated at over $1,600,000,000 per annum. Some conception of the immense trade carried on upon the Northern lakes may be formed from the fact that during the entire season of navigation, in 1872, an average of one vessel every nine minutes, day and night, passed Fort Gratiot light-house, near Port Huron. It is probably safe to say that the value of our internal commerce is ten times greater than our trade with all foreign nations, and that the amount annually paid for transportation is more than double the entire revenues of the Government.

The indifference which has hitherto prevailed on this subject may be partially accounted for by the fact that great moral questions, exciting political issues, and a terrible struggle for the maintenance of national unity, have engrossed the public mind. All of these questions being now happily settled or in process of speedy adjustment, other issues, relating to the material welfare of the people, and the enhancement of national wealth and power, force themselves into recognition. Among those questions none are more important, and none more thoroughly absorb public attention, than that which it has been the duty of the committee to consider.

Cheap and ample facilities for the interchange of commodities between the widely separated sections of our country, and with foreign nations, constitute the prime conditions of national progress and prosperity. By reason of the failure of existing systems of transportation to fully meet these conditions, commerce is impeded, agriculture languishes, labor is inadequately rewarded, food is unnecessarily taxed, exportations are diminished, and nearly all the most important business interests of the country are depressed. Hence the most important problem now pressing for solution is, "*How shall cheaper and better facilities for transportation be provided?*"

PROPOSED REMEDIES.

For the accomplishment of this object various measures have been suggested, all of which are embraced in one or more of the following general propositions, namely:

1. Competition between railways and its promotion, by additional lines without regulation.
2. Direct congressional regulation of railway transportation, under the power to regulate commerce among the several States.
3. Indirect regulation, and promotion of competition through the agency of one or more lines of railway, to be owned or controlled by the Government.
4. The improvement of natural water-ways, and the construction of artificial channels of water communication.

Earnestly endeavoring to solve the problem intrusted to them, the committee have given to each of these propositions the most careful attention. At the threshold of their inquiry they were confronted by questions touching the nature, extent, and application of the national power to regulate commerce among the several States, and as to the practicability of so exercising it as to effect the desired object.

In the discussion of that power they have intentionally omitted all considerations of the danger of its exercise. Whatever those dangers may be, they address themselves to the sound discretion of Congress, in view of its responsibility to the people, but do not in the slightest degree affect the inquiry as to the existence of the power itself. To argue that because a governmental power may be abused it therefore does not exist, is to contradict facts patent in the constitution of every civilized nation. It would in fact be impossible to construct a government that could maintain its own existence, without giving it powers which may be used to the injury of the people, and even to its own ruin. Take, for instance, the war powers of our own Government. Congress may to-morrow, without any cause whatever, declare war against all the nations of the earth, and yet no one will argue that, because of this liability to abuse, the power to declare war does not exist.

The power to lay and collect taxes may be used to the injury of the people in many ways, but no one doubts its existence. So of many of the other acknowledged powers of the Government. The wise and illustrious men who embodied in our Constitution the element of free government were careful to delegate to Congress all powers essential to the existence and progress of a great nation; but at the same time they provided an ample safeguard against the abuse of such powers by making those to whom they were intrusted directly responsible to the people. In fact, the theory upon which they constructed our Government was that the people themselves exercise the powers granted, through their special agents appointed for that purpose; and this being not only the theory but practical effect of the Constitution, there was less danger in conferring power on Congress than upon the legislative department of any other nation.

"Where there is a doubt as to whether a certain power has been granted, the inquiry very naturally and properly arises, is it unusual in its character and unknown in other governments?" If so, the keenest scrutiny will be invited and the most satisfactory demonstration of its existence will be required. "But if, on the contrary, it be a power which every government in Christendom is admitted to possess, which has always been exercised by every government hitherto existing, a power essential to the progress of civilization, without which agriculture must be depressed and commerce and trade must be impeded and intercourse obstructed, then the inquirer will approach the investigation in a different spirit. While he will still require satisfactory evidence, he will be prepared to give a favorable ear to what may be adduced to establish the fact of such a power having been granted." There can be no doubt to which class of powers the one under discussion belongs.

It being conceded that certain powers over interstate commerce are delegated to Congress by the Constitution, the inquiry is not what powers *ought* to have been granted, but *what are the nature, extent, and application of the powers actually delegated?*

In the discussion of this question the report maintains the following propositions:

1. That the powers of Congress, whatever they may be, are derived *directly* from *the people of the several States, and not from the States themselves.*

2. That prior to the adoption of the Constitution the powers now possessed by the General Government constituted a part of the *supreme sovereignty* which resided *in the people* of the several States; and that the sovereignty of the people of the States over commerce was absolute, excepting only as it was limited by the Articles of Confederation.

3. That whatever *elements* and *attributes* of *sovereignty* appertained to these powers when they exist-

ed *in the people of the several States were transferred* to the General Government *with the powers themselves* by the Constitution, and that they now exist in Congress as fully and completely as they formerly did in the people of the States, subject only to the express limitations of the Constitution.

4. That the grant of powers to Congress is an investment of power for the general advantage, in the hands of agents selected for that purpose, and hence they are not to be construed strictly and against the existence of the power, but according to the natural and obvious meaning of the language of the Constitution, taken in connection with the purposes for which they were conferred.

5. That every important word in the clauses which confer the "*power to regulate commerce among the several States,*" and to "make all laws, which shall be necessary and proper for carrying it into execution," has received legislative, executive, and judicial construction, and that under such construction the power of Congress to regulate interstate transportation by railroads, and to *aid* and *facilitate* commerce, is clearly established.

6. That, in the exercise of its specific powers, Congress is authorized under the grant of auxiliary powers, to employ such *means* as are *appropriate* and plainly *adapted* to their execution, and is not confined to means which are *indispensably necessary:* and that the courts will not inquire into the *degree* of *necessity* of any particular means that may be adopted.

7. In the selection of *means* by which interstate commerce shall be regulated, Congress, in its discretion and under its responsibility to the people—1. May prescribe the rules by which the *instrument, vehicles,* and *agents* engaged in *transporting* commodities from one State into or through another shall be governed, whether such transportation is by land or by water; 2. It may appropriate money for the construction of railways or canals, when the same shall be necessary for the regulation of commerce; 3. It may incorporate a company with authority to construct them; 4. It may exercise the right of eminent domain within a State in order to provide for the construction of such railways or canals; or, 5. It may, in the exercise of the right of eminent domain, take for the public use, paying just compensation therefor, any existing railway or canal owned by private persons or corporations.

These propost ons are discussed at length in the report of the committee, and the decisions of the courts from which they are deduced are there cited. I will, therefore, content myself for the present with the statement of conclusions, deferring until some future occasion the discussion of constitutional questions. Believing that the powers of the General Government are ample to provide any or all of the measures of relief indicated in the four general divisions of remedies just mentioned, I proceed to consider the practicability and probable results attainable by each.

1. COMPETITION BETWEEN RAILWAYS, AND ITS PROMOTION BY ADDITIONAL LINES.

In order to understand the nature, extent, and value of unregulated railway competition, I have carefully studied the history of railway combinations and consolidations in other countries, and find that however diverse the principles of government under which their systems have grown up, or the regulations which have been imposed by law, actual and effective competition between railways is unknown. Combination is the natural law of their development. Competition, which is so powerful a regulator in other commercial affairs, will not suffice to regulate railways unless it be itself regulated by some power higher than the motives of self-interest which govern railway managers.

In Great Britain, Parliament, with unlimited powers, having struggled in vain for forty years against amalgamation, has ceased to look for relief in voluntary competition. The actual effects of railway competition in that country, and the greater combinations and more powerful monopolies which it ultimately induced, have disheartened those who regarded it as the panacea for railway evils and abuses, and it is said that the present tendency of the public is toward state ownership as the only effectual remedy. The late parliamentary commission, after an exhaustive investigation of the whole subject, conclude their review of the history of railway amalgamation with the statement—

That while committees and commissioners carefully chosen have for the last thirty years clung to one form of competition after another, it has nevertheless become more and more evident that competition must fail to do for railways what it does for ordinary trade and that no means have yet been found by which competition can be permanently maintained. * * * It may be taken as a general rule that there is now no active competition between different railways in the matter of rates and fares. Whenever different companies run between the same places they arrange their prices. * * * And if a new railway should ever be started with the promise of lower rates, it is sure, after a short time, to arrange with its original rivals on a system of equal charges.

The experience of our own country accords with that of Great Britain in this regard.

The theory here, as in England, has always been that the transportation business, like other commercial affairs, would regulate itself on the principle of competition. On this theory our railroad system has attained its present gigantic proportions. Believing that additional lines would create and stimulate competition and thereby reduce rates, towns, cities, counties, and States have made haste to burden themselves with debt in order to secure the coveted boon. The General Government having never interfered, and until recently the States having made but little effort to control or direct it, the system has developed itself under the influence of the natural laws which govern that kind of business. Hence the tendencies and results evolved by the operation of those laws, if carefully studied by the light of the experience of other countries, will enable us to form an opinion as to what may be anticipated from railway competition in the future, if left to regulate itself by the ordinary laws of trade. That there is effective competition in the matter of charges at many points cannot be doubted, that the same natural laws which have destroyed it in other countries are vigorously at work here, and will ultimately produce the same results, is also obvious. The history of railway combinations in Europe, and especially in Great Britain, discloses the fact that during the period of development, and while each corporation was struggling to appropriate to its exclusive control as large a district of country as possible, competition was very sharp. When, by the consolidation of separate links, through trunk-lines were formed between the principal centres of population and trade, competition at once sprang up between those points. But self-interest very soon suggested to the competing companies that, as the traffic must be divided, it was desirable to divide its profits between themselves rather than with the public. The result was an agreement as to rates and an end of competition. Having become strong and rich, the trunk-lines began the work of extending their power by the construction of branches and the absorption of weaker lines extending into the adjacent districts. Then followed a great struggle for territorial dominion, during which sharp and active competition reappeared at numerous points in the contested districts. Its duration and vigor were measured chiefly by the relative strength of the giants contending for the prize, but the ultimate result was seldom long delayed, and never doubtful. By purchase, lease, arrangement of rates, or some other of the numerous forms of combination and consolidation, one point after another disappeared from the competing list, and finally the disputed territory passed under the exclusive control of one of the contestants. The same motives and influences which operated in Great Britain are rapidly producing similar results in this country.

" Existing competition, whatever may be its extent and value, is gradually disappearing from the trunk lines, and is found mainly at points in the outlying districts from which these roads draw their support. The contest between the great companies for territorial dominion is still progressing in our country, and the struggle for control of the trade of some of the common termini, and points of intersection of branch lines and feeders owned and operated by them, is apparent in the reduced charges which prevail at these places. The number of such competing points is, however, constantly diminishing as each of the great corporations absorbs, one after another, the inferior lines which have served as allies to its rival. Thus every additional absorption defines with constantly increasing precision the territorial boundaries of the district which is certainly and rapidly passing under its exclusive domination. The wide extent of our country and the colossal proportions of our railway system (equaling one-half of the railway mileage of the globe) require a longer time for complete development than in some of the states of Europe, and hence the influences which induce competition will extend through a longer period, but the ultimate result will probably be the same. And when the natural tendencies of corporate power working through railway organization shall have wrought out their inevitable conclusions, the magnitude of our combinations will probably be in proportion to the extent of the field in which they operate.

In illustration of the statement that competition has already substantially disappeared from the main trunk-lines, take those which centre in Chicago, from the East—the Pennsylvania line, running to New York and Philadelphia; the Lake Shore & Michigan Southern, running in connection with the Erie and New York Central; and the Michigan Central Railway, in connection with the last two, and also the Grand Trunk. These lines all have agents at Chicago, who meet together and agree on prices for eastern-bound freight ; and the prices established by such agreement bind the eastern roads. Agents at the eastern termini meet in convention and agree upon the charges for western-bound freights.

The evidence taken by the committee shows that the principle upon which rates are adjusted on these lines is not what the services are actually worth, but " What are the rates charged by the water-lines ?" and " What will the property bear, in view of its movement to market ?" During the winter months, when there is no water competition, the charges are usually so high as to prevent a large proportion of the crops which accumulate in the cities of Chicago and Milwaukee from going forward to market, and hence they remain in store awaiting reductions to be caused by the opening of water-routes. On the 1st of January, 1872, there were in store in Chicago and Milwaukee 2,516,597 bushels of wheat, and during the months of January, February, and March, there were received at those ports 1,578,790 bushels. Of this total quantity in store and received, amounting to 4,095,487 bushels, only 286,000, or about 7 per cent., were shipped by rail during those three months. The quantity of corn received and in store at Chicago during the months of January, February, and March, of that year amounted to 8,898,236 bushels, of which only 1,702,905, or 19½ per cent., were shipped by rail before the 1st of April. In the month of April, when the water competition began to be felt, the railways carried 462,570 bushels of wheat, as against a total of 286,000 in the preceding three months. The effect of this competition on the movement of corn was to send forward in April 1,018,271, against an aggregate of 1,702,905 bushels moved in January, February, and March.

The suggestive fact presented by these statistics is that, while only 1,988,905 bushels of wheat and corn were moved by rail during the three months named, in the month of April, when the approaching water competition began to exert its influence, the reduction of rail-rates induced 1,480,841 bushels to go forward by the railroads. Hence, if the farmers of the West were compelled to rely upon railway competition for the movement of their crops, they would be unable to reach the Eastern markets.

An impression has prevailed that during the winter months all the rail-lines from Chicago to the East are choked with the surplus products of the West, but the above facts seem to demonstrate that the companies prefer not to move them at all, rather than to do it at rates which those products will bear.

The two great companies which largely control the traffic of Wisconsin and Minnesota—the Chicago & Northwestern, and the Milwaukee & St. Paul—afford another illustration of the value and extent of railway competition when regulated by its own laws. Towns and cities favored with a line belonging to, or controlled by, one of these companies have contributed liberally to aid in the construction of a second, which should be in the interest of the other company. For several years, while those great corporations have been extending their branches and absorbing weaker lines, competition has, at times, been active at certain places, but the territory which each can hope to control being now pretty well defined, an agreement as to rates has been made, and the people are alarmed by rumors, but too well founded, of a contemplated arrangement for pooling receipts. Thus the people of the great wheat-growing region of the continent, after having hoped and struggled for years for reduced rates through competition, and after having in many cases imposed upon themselves grievous burdens of taxation for that purpose, now find that, instead of bringing into the field a competitor, they have not only doubled the power with which they have to contend, but they have quartered upon themselves a new and expensive organization which must be supported from the products of their toil.

The history of railway management in every State of the Union, and throughout the civilized world, proves that competition invariably ends in combination. Hence the well-known aphorism, "Where combination is possible, competition is impossible."

In view of these facts, it is probable that additional railway lines, under corporate control, will materially reduce the cost of transportation?

What reason have we to suppose that the same principles of combination which govern existing lines will not control the new ones? If, as already shown, competition with the water-routes and "the highest charge the commodity will bear" now rule the rates, have we any guarantee that they will not do so on the additional lines? In fact, every new line from the Mississippi to the Atlantic Ocean will add from seventy-five to one hundred million dollars to the capital on which the transportation business of the country must pay five to seven million dollars annual interest, in addition to the cost of maintaining the new organization. Will not this afford an irresistible inducement to combine with existing companies, in order to make the largest possible profits out of the business to be performed? Is there any thing in experience, or in the known principles of railway management, which teaches us to hope that the new competing line would not at once participate in the councils of its rivals and be governed by their policy?

For these reasons, and others stated in the report of the committee, they have come to the conclusion that no substantial reduction in the cost of transportation is to be anticipated from unregulated competition between existing railways, nor in competition to be induced by authorizing the construction of additional lines, if they are to be under private management and control.

Let us therefore consider the second remedy proposed, namely:

2. DIRECT REGULATION BY ACT OF CONGRESS.

Railway regulation, though untried by Congress, is by no means a novel experiment in the States, or in other countries. It has many earnest advocates, who seem to regard it as a certain and effectual remedy for high charges—a panacea for all the ills of our present systems of transportation. In the discussion of this branch of the subject, I wish it distinctly understood that the considerations which apply to the vast system of railways in the United States do not apply with the same force to the smaller number of roads and the less diverse conditions existing in a single State. The regulation of railway rates and fares, by law, is one of the most difficult problems ever presented to the Legislature of a State; but when extended to a great nation, composed of many independent sovereign States, having within their limits over thirteen hundred different railways, and embracing every conceivable variety of conditions and circumstances, the problem becomes one of much greater difficulty.

I have no doubt of the power of Congress to regulate interstate commerce, when carried on by railroads constituting continuous lines between two or more States. Under the power to regulate commerce among the several States, I believe Congress may prescribe the rules by which the *instruments*, *agents*, and *vehicles* engaged in such commerce shall be governed; and that it may prevent undue impositions by corporations of one State upon the commerce of other States; and, in the maintenance of commercial equality among the States, it may prescribe a rule of charges for interstate commerce. Otherwise it would be in the power of the State of New York, extending as she does from Canada to the ocean, to authorize her railway companies to impose such charges as would virtually place an embargo upon the trade between New England and the West. That she probably will not do so is no answer to the argument. The question is not what will the State of New York *permit* in this regard, but what are the commercial *rights* of the States, and by what power are those rights to be guaranteed? Were the illustrious men who framed our Constitution so incompetent for their high duty as to have created an instrument which leaves it in the power of any one State to cripple and destroy the commerce of another? Is it conceivable that such a blunder could have been committed in view of the fact that "the *design* and *object* of *that power* (the power to regulate commerce), as evinced in the history of the Constitution, *was to establish a perfect equality among the several States as to commercial rights, and to prevent unjust and invidious distinctions which local jealousies or local and partial interests might be disposed to introduce and maintain?*" (14 Howard's Reports, page 574.) But if the power to prevent unjust and invidious distinctions exist, how is it to be exercised if any one State may create corporations with unlimited power to levy tribute at pleasure, and without control, upon the commerce of other States?

Take another case in illustration of this position. For five months each year there is practically no means of transportation for a large section of the country but by railroads. Illinois and Kentucky extend from the lakes on the north, around to the Alleghany Mountains at the east, thus rendering it impossible for the products of those States lying west and south of them to reach a market without passing through their limits.

Now, suppose those two States have granted to all the railroad companies within their jurisdiction the right to charge such rates as they please for transportation, and that those roads have become parts of the great through lines of transportation between the States to the west of them and the Atlantic seaboard. Suppose, further, that, in a season of short crops in the East and in Europe, the managers of those roads combine, purchase a large quantity of breadstuffs, ship them to the East, and, having them safely stored in New York and other Eastern cities, put up the tariff for transportation so high as to prevent the products of other States from going forward. Can any one doubt that in such a case it would be not only right, but the sacred duty of Congress, to interfere by prescribing needful rules and regulations for the conduct of this traffic through those States? If the power does not reside in Congress, it is nowhere. The aggrieved States could do nothing, and the people of one-half the Union might starve, while the other half with overflowing granaries would be denied the privilege of feeding them. It is true this is a strong case, but its circumstances would change no principle of the Constitution; its hardships and aggravations would create no new powers. If the power be in the Constitution, it exists at all times. If it exist for the purpose of relieving the people of the States in the aggravated case supposed, it exists for all purposes connected with interstate commerce. The circumstances do not call it into life, though they may demonstrate the necessity for its existence and the policy of its exercise.

Assuming, for the present, that the power of Congress is ample to regulate rates and fares on railroads engaged in interstate commerce, let us briefly inquire as to the practicability and expediency of its exercise; the extent to which with our present limited information on the subject it may be safely exerted, and the results probably attainable thereby.

In several of our own States, and in nearly all the countries of Europe, legislative regulation of rates and fares has been tried in almost every form, but I have yet to learn that such experiments have resulted in a material reduction of charges.

In England, to whose railway system ours corresponds more closely than to that of any other nation, the subject of regulation has been discussed for more than a third of a century, and experimented upon by Parliament in almost every conceivable form. Commenting on these experiments, the Massachusetts Railway Commissioners say:

Nowhere has the system of special legislation been more persistently followed, and nothing, it may be added, could have been more complete than its failure. As the result of forty years' experience, reviewed in the recent elaborate report of the joint committee on amalgamation of railways, it may be said that the English legislation has neither accomplished any thing it sought to bring about, nor prevented any thing which it sought to hinder.

In Ohio, where the system of direct regulation has been tried for several years, the Railway Commissioner, in his report for 1873, says:

It is unnecessary here to reiterate the experience of Ohio, or the results of the numerous and persistent efforts of her Legislature to fix upon some practical and equitable law governing this matter. The report of this office for 1869 gives a list of nine distinct rates authorized by law for the transportation of passengers and freight. The several acts since passed, and labored attempts each session to devise some system by which rates can be justly regulated by law, have failed, as in the past, to accomplish the object desired.

In his report for 1870 the Commissioner says:

There is not a railroad in the State, whether operated under a special charter or the general law, upon which the laws regulating rates are not in some way violated nearly every time a regular passenger, a freight, or mixed train, passes over it.

The railway commission of Massachusetts, after a thorough investigation of this subject, embracing the railway systems of foreign countries, and the various attempts at regulation in the United States, pronounce legislative regulation of rates and fare impracticable, and recommend "*the control and regulation of the whole, through the ownership and management of a part.*"

The parliamentary committee of 1872, after elaborately reviewing the various modes of railway regulation that have been proposed and tried in Great Britain, many of which compared with those on which reliance seems to be placed in this country, state their conclusions, drawn from forty years' experience, as follows:

"*Equal mileage rates*" they pronounce "impracticable."

"*Rates to be fixed by relation to cost and profit on capital*" they dismiss, because "attended with difficulties which are practically insuperable."

"*Immediate reduction of rates*," they say, "would be merely a temporary remedy, for the reason that a change which will give the company ample profit to-day may, through increased economy, or other cause, be excessive to-morrow."

"*Periodical revision of rates*" is declared to be "inexpedient and impracticable."

"*Absolute limitation of dividends*" is pronounced "impossible and undesirable."

"*Divisions of profit beyond a certain limit between companies and the public*" they reject, because attended with "insuperable difficulties."

"*Maxima rates*," they say, "will effect but little, if any, reduction, because the actual legal maxima are rarely charged in the case of goods, as is evident from the existence of *special rates;* and in the case of passengers, the present action of the companies in carrying third-class passengers at parliamentary fares by all their trains shows how impossible it is for Parliament, or any other authority, to determine a scale of maximum charges which shall continue to be fair and liberal to the public under changes of time and circumstances."

Each and all of these modes of regulation have their advocates in this country who confidently rely upon them to reduce the cost of transportation. Let us examine them with reference to the practicability and expediency of their adoption by Congress. I assume that a general law of Congress regulating railway transportation, to be successful in the accomplishment of the desired object, must operate fairly and justly upon all, and that, while it protects the public from undue exactions, it must also guard the equitable and just rights of stockholders who have honestly invested their money in railroads. Any thing short of this would shock the sense of justice and fair play which distinguishes the American people, and hence would prove a failure.

1. *Equal mileage rates.*—The reasons upon which this form of regulation is pronounced "impracticable" in England apply with much greater force in the United States.

Our roads are much longer. Their circumstances and condition are less uniform. The difference in cost of construction and expense of working different sections of the same road is greater. There is less uniformity in the amount of business on different roads, and on different sections of the same road. A rate that would ruin one road costing $100,000 per mile would be excessive on another that cost only $25,000 per mile, if the amount of business on each be the same. On the other hand, the more expensive road could, with a sufficiently large amount of business, make a profit at rates which would be ruinous on the cheaper one with a small amount of business. And, even on the same road, a rate that would be excessive on one section would not pay the running expenses on another section. It would be manifestly unjust to require local freights passing over a given number of miles, costing $1,000,000, to pay the same rate per mile that other local freights pay for carriage over a like distance, on the same road, which cost $5,000,000. Distance, also, is an important element in the economy of railway transportation, but it is not the only one, nor is it in fact always the most important element. Extortionate charges for short distances, and unjust discriminations against certain points, afford good ground for complaint, and doubtless demand a remedy, but that remedy, to be effective, must be based upon sound principles. It is a fact susceptible of the clearest demonstration, that it actually costs more per mile to transport a short distance than a long one; and this principle has received universal recognition by railway managers. In Belgium, where, through state management, the cheapest and in many respects the best railroad system in existence has been developed, the charges on fourth-class goods are graded according to distance, as follows:

Charge per ton per mile in 1868, including terminals, on Belgian Railways.

	Cents.
15 miles	2.54
31 miles	1.86
46 miles	1.66
62 miles	1.38
77 miles	1.18
93 miles	1.02
108 miles	.92
124 miles	.86
139 miles	.80
155 miles	.74

A similar decrease in rates in proportion to increase of distance prevails in every country in Europe, and I may add on every road in the United States.

The enforcement of equal mileage rates, instead of bringing relief to the producers in the distant interior of the continent, would add very largely to their present burdens. The average charges for transporting all freights on the leading trunk lines between Chicago and New York, in 1872, was about 1¼ cent per ton per mile, which on a bushel of wheat would amount to about 44 cents. The actual average charge by rail, per bushel, was 33¼ cents. Hence, an equal mileage rate on those lines, if adjusted upon the basis of their average charges, would have reduced the value of the 213,000,000 bushels of wheat and corn moved that year about 10 cents per bushel, amounting to an aggregate loss to the producers of $21,000,000, with no compensating gain to the consumers. And as the price of wheat and corn at the West, as well that part which remains at home as that which is sent abroad, is fixed by the market price in Liverpool, less the cost of transportation, the loss to the Northwestern States on the entire crop of that year, estimated at over 900,000,000 bushels, would have amounted to the enormous sum of $90,-000,000. Such a law, if permanently enforced, would, by the reduction of 10 cents per bushel on the value of the cereal crop of the Northwest, reduce the value of the farms in that section by an amount which would build and equip all the trunk-lines of railroad from Chicago to New York.

Not only would an equal mileage rate, if applied to the whole country, impose additional burdens on those sections most in need of relief, but it would tend to destroy whatever of competition now exists. This fact is demonstrated by the operation of the *pro rata* law of the State of Illinois. At many points in that State the people have contributed largely to aid the construction of a second road for the purpose of securing competition. The two roads are not the same length. But the law says that both shall charge the same rate per mile. The longer one, being compelled to charge more to the common point of destination, is of course driven out of competition, and the shorter one takes a monopoly of the business. The people who have contributed to build competing roads thus find themselves taxed to pay the cost of transportation for others who have been less enterprising. A general *pro rata* law applied to the whole country would indefin'tely multiply such evil results at competing points, without any compensating benefits at other places. The non-competing points would not be benefited, for, if by reason of low rates, at the point of competition, a largely-increased traffic should be created, from which the company could make a small profit, it would be enabled, to the extent of such profit, to reduce the rates at the intermediate point.

2. "*Rate to be fixed by relation to cost and profit on capital.*"—If the difficulties of this mode of regulation are found to be "practically insuperable" in Great Britain with fifteen thousand miles of railway, what shall be said of the United States with their seventy thousand miles? In order to establish intelligently a

rule of charges based upon cost and profit, we must investigate thoroughly the circumstances and conditions of every one of the thirteen hundred roads. We must know all about each individual road, its original cost, how much of its capital is real and how much fictitious; how much was actually paid on its stock, and what proportion of the profits charged to capital account should have been charged to expenses. Having completed this detailed investigation, which would necessarily involve an examination and readjustment of the accounts of the company from its organization, we next turn our attention to its profits. In order to adjust charges to profits by a general rule of law, we must know what the actual profits are now, and what they will be in the future. This requires a knowledge of its grades and curvatures; the cost of fuel, supplies, and other items of working expenses; the amount of business it now does, and what it will continue to do; the economy or extravagance with which it will be managed; the condition and character of its construction and equipment; how long its iron, ties, and rolling-stock will last, and what it will cost to replace them; the storms of winter and the floods of summer it will probably encounter; and, finally, the losses which will result from accidents of all kinds. This completed, we must study carefully the nature of its traffic, so as to know what relation the various classes of goods bear to each other in cost of transportation; what charge each class will bear without injury to the business interests of the country, and how much the expense of carrying a ton of silk goods twenty-five miles per hour exceeds that of carrying a ton of corn ten miles per hour.

When we have thus informed ourselves with reasonable accuracy in regard to all these details, and many more that might be named, we will be prepared to commence the investigation of the next road on the list, and so on through the 1,300. By the time we have completed the investigation, the changed conditions and circumstances of the roads, and the rapid changes in the business of the country, will render a reëxamination imperatively necessary.

3. "*Immediate reduction of rates and fares.*"—In addition to the fact that this would be only a "temporary remedy," it involves all the difficulties mentioned under the last proposition; for, if the reduced rates are to stand the test of practical experiment, they must be just and reasonable, and hence all the circumstances and conditions of each road must be understood in order to establish a standard of reduction.

4. "*Periodical revision of rates.*"—Stating their reasons for the conclusion that this method of regulation is "inexpedient and impracticable," the parliamentary committee from whose report I have quoted say:

How is it to be performed, and by whom? If it is to be purely arbitrary, if no rule is to be laid down to guide the revisers, the power of revision will amount to a power to confiscate the property of the companies. It is not likely that Parliament would attempt the exercise of any such power itself, still less that it would confer such a power on any subordinate authority.

Assuming for the present that Congress would attempt the exercise of a power from which the Parliament of England shrinks, let us inquire how such revision of rates can be made in this country. Shall it be done by Congress itself, or by some tribunal acting under its authority? Surely not the latter, for the power of Congress over the subject is only a delegated power, which it cannot delegate to another. The revision must, therefore, be made by Congress itself, if at all. It is said in the English reports that "the rates in the case of all the great companies are numbered by millions." In this country each of the 1,300 roads has its through rates to every station on its own line, and to every station on the lines with which it connects, its scores of special rates, and its numerous classifications of goods. A bill which should enumerate them all, if such a bill could be framed, could hardly be read through during the session, and, if read, not one member in a dozen would be the wiser. If Congress should undertake the periodical revision of rates on the 70,000 miles of railroad in the United States, it must remain in constant session and devote its attention exclusively to this work.

5. "*Absolute limitation of dividends.*"—"This form of proposed regulation assumes that the passenger and shipper will receive, in the shape of reduced fares and charges, whatever excess of profits may remain after paying to the shareholder the limit allowed by law." It involves the power of revision, and the necessity for accurate and detailed information, referred to under the forms of regulation already discussed, and hence, in its practical application, would encounter many, if not all, of the difficulties therein mentioned. In England it is pronounced "impossible and undesirable." "Impossible," because it involves the necessity of judging "what rates will enable the company to make the given dividend on a given capital," and of determining "what are the proper expenses of the companies and what economies they can practise." These are declared to be "matters which require the knowledge, skill, and experience of the managers themselves, and any attempt on the part of any government department to do it for them is impossible, unless the agents of the government were to undertake an amount of interference with the internal concerns of the companies which is neither desirable nor practicable." "Undesirable," because it would encourage extravagance, stock-watering, and corruption.

The assumption that what is withheld from the shareholders would be available for reduction of rates is declared to be a "fallacy, because the company, having no interest in making more than the fixed rate of profit, will have every inducement to use up the surplus in needless expenditure." "The result, therefore, of limiting the dividends of companies would be to deprive them, monopolists as they are, or will be, of the ordinary motives for efficiency or economy, and to impose upon government or Parliament an impracticable task, the result of which must be either to delude the public by giving a formal and groundless sanction to the schemes of the companies, or to take out of their hands the management of their own affairs."

The reasons thus forcibly presented against an absolute limitation of dividend are quite as applicable to the railroad system of America as to that of England. It is surely undesirable to increase the present extravagance and waste in railway management. It would be an easy matter for railway managers to keep their dividends within the prescribed limits, without a decrease of rates, by increasing their own compensation, by special contracts for the enrichment of favorites, and by other means but too well known. If the dividend could not extend beyond a certain fixed amount, it would be to the interest of the company to do only enough business to produce that sum, and hence if the movement of 1,000,000 tons at two cents per ton per mile, or of 2,000,000 tons at one cent per ton per mile, would produce the profit limited to the company, the lesser amount of work would be preferred. The direct inducement, therefore, would be to increase the price and diminish the traffic, thereby giving to the public an inferior service at an enhanced cost. It is apparent, also, that another result would be to stimulate stock-watering, which has already become so offensive to the public, and which has so largely increased the cost of transportation; for, if the shareholder can receive only a certain fixed dividend on the amount of his capital, he will not be slow in finding some plausible excuse for increasing his stock.

One of the chief motives for the practice of stock inflations which prevails on some of our leading roads is the fear of offending public sentiment by an exhibit of actual profits. When public sentiment shall have crystallized into a law of absolute limitation, may we

not expect to see this evil aggravated to an extent even more alarming than at present?

Such a limitation of dividends would also tend to discourage the construction of new and competing roads in localities where they are needed, for capital will not readily seek investment where the profits are limited, unless it be accompanied with a guarantee which no one proposes to give. This is illustrated by the fact that a bond of the New York Central Railroad, which guarantees 6 per cent., is worth as much in the market as its stock on the expectation of 8 per cent.

A law of Congress establishing this form of regulation would, even if practicable, afford no relief, but, on the other hand, it would result in a withdrawal of every inducement to economy; in increased expenditures and waste; in enhanced prices for inferior service; in an additional stimulus to the reprehensible practice of stock-watering, and in special contracts, jobbery, and favoritism.

6. "*Division of profits beyond a certain limit between the companies and the public.*"—This is a modification of the last-named proposition, and is designed to avoid some of the difficulties and objections therein suggested. The theory upon which it proceeds is, that a certain limit being fixed the excess should be divided between the companies and the public, one portion being added to the dividend and the remainder being applied to the reduction of charges. It is true, this method would partially obviate the objection urged against an absolute limitation of dividend, because, in proportion to the amount which might be added to the profits of the company, an inducement to economy would exist. But other difficulties, which in Great Britain are declared to be "insuperable," would remain. It would involve the obnoxious task of selecting special traffic and special rates for reduction, and of deciding what should be the amount or description of any particular reductions, and in whose favor they should be made. A regulation of this kind was once adopted in England, but it never went into effect. It has been tried in France, but, on account of the difficulty of selecting rates and classifications of goods on which to apply it, the reduction has been abandoned, and one-half the surplus profit is paid into the national treasury. There is, therefore, but little encouragement to try the experiment in this country, where, by reason of the larger number of our roads, and the greater diversity of conditions and of traffic, as well as the instinctive aversion of our people to meddlesome governmental interference in private affairs, vastly greater difficulties would be encountered than in France or England.

7. "*Maximum rates.*"—It is doubtless entirely practicable for State Legislatures to establish *maxima* rates which will afford a remedy for local extortions and discriminations; and it is possible that in certain cases such rates may be established by act of Congress with beneficial results. But it is difficult to see how a general law of Congress, establishing *maxima* rates, can be framed that will materially *cheapen* the cost of transport on existing lines of railway between the interior of the continent and the seaboard. The intelligent enactment of such a law would require an investigation of all the facts, circumstances, and conditions mentioned under the propositions just discussed, and hence would involve the difficulties there in suggested.

A commission with authority to establish *maxima* rates, subject to revision by the courts, has been suggested as the means of avoiding the difficulty last stated. But Congress acts only under delegated powers, and a serious constitutional question arises whether it can delegate its powers to another tribunal. I believe it is a well-settled principle of law that an agent cannot, without the authority of his principal, delegate his powers to another agent; else such subagent may again delegate them, and so on without limit. Assuming, however, that no constitutional difficulties exist, the expediency of clothing the President with power to appoint commissioners authorized to establish rates that will increase or diminish the dividends on over $3,000,000,000 of railway capital is seriously questioned. If there is any truth in the oft-repeated assertions that railway companies already exercise a corrupting influence over legislative bodies, what may we expect when the powers which now belong to Congress shall be transferred to a commission whose duties will require them to decide what profits shall be made upon this immense capital?

In the words of Mr. Charles Francis Adams, Jr., I ask, "Is it consistent with ideas of common-sense, is it within the bounds of reason, to suppose that the man who owns will not do his best to control the man who regulates?" The immense money power with which such a commission would have to contend may be appreciated from the fact that in 1873 the gross receipts of the railways of the United States amounted to over $473,000,000. The proposed commission is to have discretionary power to increase or diminish this enormous revenue. Five per cent. reduction would cost the companies over $20,000,000. Five per cent. increase would enable them to place ten millions "where it would do the most good," and to make as much more by the operation. I am inclined to think much that is said about the use of money by railway corporations, in influencing legislation, is born of the imagination, or perhaps of the spirit of calumny which disgraces the period in which we live. But I confess that, so long as poor human nature remains unchanged, I hesitate to expose it to temptations so powerful as would be encountered by such a commission. Especially do I hesitate to place the interests of the public in the hands of men who are to be subjected to such temptations.

Nor am I inclined to confer on any executive officer of the Government power so unlimited as the appointment of such a commission would give.

But granting that the commission be honestly appointed, and composed of men whose integrity shall bid defiance to temptation, can substantial benefits, in the matter of reduced charges, be reasonably anticipated from their action? *Maxima* rates, whether established by Congress or by a commission, must be high enough to pay the actual cost of transportation and leave a margin large enough to provide a fair return for capital honestly invested, and to cover all contingencies. The actual average charge on all cereals moved by the trunk lines of railway between Chicago and New York in 1872 was less than 12 mills per ton per mile. The evidence taken by the Committee on Transportation shows that the average cost of movement, exclusive of interest and dividends, was from 8 to 9 mills per ton per mile. Assuming the cost to be 8½ mills there would be left for the payment of interest and dividends 3½ mills. The number of tons carried one mile on the Pennsylvania Railroad in 1872 was 1,190,052,-975, which, at 3½ mills, gives $4,165,185. The actual cost of the road, with its equipment, was something over $42,000,000; hence, if the same rates had been charged on all the tonnage moved, the margin between the actual cost of movement and the actual average charges that year would have paid a little less than 10 per cent. on the cost of the road. Is it probable that either Congress, or a commission, could have established a maximum rate with less margin above actual cost than the rates which were in fact imposed? In practice the *maxima* rates established by law in England, France, and Germany, are seldom charged. The parliamentary committee of 1872 say:

Legal *maxima* rates afford little protection to the public, since they are always fixed so high that it is, or becomes sooner or later, the interest of the companies to carry at lower rates. The same thing is true of terminal charges. The circumstances are so various and so constantly changing that any legal *maxima* which might now be fixed would probably be above the charges now actually made, certainly far above those which will hereafter be made. Indeed, attempts made in 1861 and 1866 to fix a maximum for terminals broke down, because the

only maximum that could be agreed upon was so much beyond the charge then actually made to coal-owners that the coal-owners feared it would lead to a rise in that charge.

Captain H. W. Tyler, in his report to the secretary of the railway department, Board of Trade, says:

The attempt to limit rates and fares by the principle of fixing a maximum has almost always failed in practice, and is almost always likely to fail, for the simple reason that the parliamentary committees and authorities by whom such limits are decided cannot do otherwise than allow some margin between the actual probable rate, so far as they can forecast it, and the maximum rate; and cannot foresee the contingencies of competition, of increase in quantities, of facilities, or economy in working, or of alteration in commercial conditions which may occur in the course of years after such limits have been arranged by them.

The practical results, in the matter of charges attained under the various systems of management and governmental regulation, are shown by the following comparative statement. Great Britain may represent the system of direct governmental regulation without financial aid; France, the system of financial aid with the most rigid surveillance and regulation; Belgium, the system of indirect regulation of the whole through state ownership and management of a part, and entire non-interference with the private corporations except in matters of safety and police. The charges per ton per mile on fourth-class goods on the leading railways in each country and under each system, for the distance stated, are as follows:

GREAT BRITAIN.	Cents.
On the London & Southwestern and London & Northwestern Railways, for 192 miles, per ton per mile	3.16
On the Great Northern Railway, for 155 miles, per ton per mile	4.4
On the Great Northern, London, Chatham & Dover Railways, for 198 miles, per ton per mile	4.5
On the Great Northern, Northeastern, North British, and Highland Railways, for 594 miles, per ton per mile	1.98
FRANCE.	
On the line between Paris and Orleans, for all distances over 186 miles, per ton per mile	1.74
BELGIUM.	
On the Belgium state railways, for all distances over 155 miles, per ton per mile	.74

From this statement it will be seen that the experience of other countries affords little encouragement to seek reduced railway charges through direct Government regulation. The rates both in England and France, where legislative regulation has been most freely practised, are higher than even in this country upon roads doing a large amount of business. The remarkably low rates in Belgium furnish a powerful argument in favor of state ownership, and also in confirmation of the principle that *cheap* transportation is to be obtained only through *competition* under governmental control.

If the experience of other nations is worth any thing as a guide to the solution of the difficult and important problem under discussion, it proves that the adoption by Congress of any one of the seven methods of regulation just mentioned would be to delude the public with false hopes, without accomplishing the end sought.

I believe that a rule of *maxima* charges may be established by the States which will prevent local extortions and discriminations, and also that in certain cases Congress may impose such a regulation with advantage to the public; but I am compelled to say that, in my judgment, *cheap* transportation is not to be secured by such congressional legislation. And, as the adoption of ill-advised measures will only tend to postpone the accomplishment of the desired object, it becomes important to consider well our action before entering upon experiments, the uniform failure of which is demonstrated by the experience of all other nations

There are, however, certain measures which may be adopted with great advantage to the public interest, among which the following may be mentioned :

1. *Publication of rates.*—This mode of regulation proceeds upon the not unreasonable theory that the moral restraints of public opinion will have a salutary effect upon the companies, and that such publicity will tend to insure stability and certainty to the business of transportation, and to remove the discontent and suspicion of the public. And further, it is believed that a company dealing honestly and fairly should court publicity, and challenge criticism, by giving to the public every possible facility for obtaining information regarding its charges and its reasons for making them.

It is proposed as a remedy for the evils of unjust discrimination against one locality in favor of another, or in favor of one description of trade at the expense of another; for the prevention of higher rates for a short distance than for a longer one, and of uncertainty and favoritism by means of special contracts, rebates, drawbacks, and the thousand and one other means by which a rich and powerful company may by the secret adjustment of rates impose upon the public, and render fluctuating and precarious the business transactions of those who are compelled to use its line.

On this subject a singular unanimity prevails in nearly all the countries of Europe ; France, Prussia, Austria, Sweden, and Belgium, all regard it as important and insist upon its enforcement. In nearly all of those countries hand-books are published giving all the particulars regarding distance, classification, rates, special tariffs, etc. There is no doubt that a valuable reform in railway management may be attained by requiring such publication in this country, especially if it be accompanied, as in several European countries, with a provision prohibiting an increase of rates without reasonable public notice.

As many of the causes of complaint arise from fluctuations, discriminations, and favoritism at and between points entirely within a State, the remedy for such abuses must be applied by the State Legislature, if at all.

But there is a large class of cases in which interstate traffic is alone concerned, for which the remedy is in the hands of Congress.

2. *Railway companies should be compelled to receipt for quantity and to account for the same at its point of destination.*—The enforcement of a regulation of this kind upon all railway companies and freight-line organizations, employed in transporting cereals from one State into another, would remedy an evil of no small magnitude, and one which falls peculiarly within the scope of national power. The evidence taken by the committee shows that the "shortage" on a car-load of grain transported from Chicago to New York varies from ¼ to 10 per cent.; 1 to 3 per cent being not uncommon. Assuming the average shortage to be 2 per cent., it amounts to a loss of 3 cents per bushel on wheat, when the market price in New York is $1.50 ; a loss that falls wholly on the shipper from the Western point. And as the Western buyer knows by experience that the usual loss is from 1 to 3 per cent., and sometimes as high as 10 per cent., he will buy on a margin large enough to cover the greatest probable deficit. Hence the producer has to bear a loss even larger than the actual shortage. It may be said that a law compelling the carrier to receipt and account for quantity would render necessary an increased charge for transportation. This is doubted for two reasons: First, because the water lines now account for quantity ; and as the railways fix their prices in competition with the water-routes, they cannot, during the season of navigation, increase their prices. Second, the evidence taken by the committee shows that the rule of railway charges is, "How much will the article bear ?" and, as they usually put on *all it will bear,* when not in competition with water, it is likely that the effect of such a law would be

to compel them to exercise greater care, instead of increasing the rate. But, even if it should cause an increase of charges, the producer would then lose only the actual increased rate, instead of the undefined margin between 1 and 10 per cent. A congressional regulation of this kind would be peculiarly applicable to freight-lines which are organized for the express purpose of carrying on interstate traffic.

3. *Railway companies, freight-lines, and other common carriers engaged in interstate commerce should be prohibited from discriminating between persons or places ;* and especially those engaged in carrying freights from one State into another, whose lines touch at any river or lake port, should be prohibited from discriminating against such port. One of the serious evils now complained of is that by an unfair adjustment of charges the public is denied the advantages of the cheaper transportation afforded by water-routes, and in many cases the business of such river-ports is seriously impaired by reason of such discriminations. The remedy for this evil is largely within the power of the States. For instance, freights starting from the interior of Iowa for the East are exclusively under the jurisdiction of that State until they cross the Mississippi River, and any unjust discriminations against river towns within her borders must be corrected, if at all, by the authorities of that State. But freights from Nebraska, destined for the East, which pass through the State of Iowa, must be regulated in this regard, if at all, by the General Government. It is, in my judgment, clearly within the power of Congress to remedy unjust discriminations in the case last mentioned, and in all others involving a passage through two or more States.

Other matters in which congressional regulation would probably effect beneficial results are discussed in the report I have submitted, and will be referred to in the "summary of conclusions and recommendations" to which I will presently refer.

While I am thoroughly convinced that the relief required in the matter of *cheap* and *ample* commercial facilities is not to be obtained by any form of direct congressional regulation of rates and fares, I am equally well assured that many of the evils and abuses incident to our present systems of transportation may be remedied by this means. Hence it is, in my judgment, of the utmost importance that some means should be adopted for procuring accurate information on which intelligent action may be based. The Constitution having confided to the General Government the regulation of interstate commerce, it becomes a matter of great public concern that Congress be fully advised upon the subject.

I am therefore in favor of the establishment of a Bureau of Commerce in one of the Executive Departments of the Government, which shall be charged with the duty of collecting full and detailed information on the subject of internal commerce to be annually laid before Congress, and to this end such Bureau should have authority, under regulations to be prescribed by the head of the Department, to require sworn returns to be made by all railways and other common carriers engaged in transporting persons or commodities from one State into or through another.

I will say, in passing from this branch of the subject, that in my judgment the public service would be greatly benefited by the organization of a new Department, to be called the "Department of Industry," the head of which should have equal rank and emoluments with other cabinet officers, and be charged with the supervision and care of the agricultural, commercial, manufacturing, and mining interests of the country, in so far as the same have been confided to the national Government by the Constitution. In every other commercial nation these great interests are intrusted to the care of one or more ministers of cabinet rank, who study their necessities, their relations to each other, and the best means for their promotion and encouragement. France has ten departments, one of which has charge of the interests of "agriculture, commerce, and public works." Great Britain has thirteen cabinet ministers, one of whom is "president of the Board of Trade," and another is "president of the Board of Public Works." Duties which in England are considered of sufficient importance to require the services of two cabinet officers are in this country confided to subordinates and clerks, or wholly neglected.

It is true that under the limited powers of our Government such a Department would exercise less control than in European nations, but its usefulness in promoting the great industrial interests of the people, on which the prosperity of the country depends, would be incalculable. The organization of a Department of Industry has not, however, been recommended by the committee, and I will therefore defer its further discussion until some future occasion.

Believing that competition among railways, when governed by private interests, is wholly unreliable and utterly inefficient, that direct congressional regulation of rates and fares may cure certain evils and abuses, but will never provide such commercial facilities as the necessities and best interests of the country demand, let us inquire, by what means may they be obtained?

I answer, *they are to be obtained only through competition under governmental control, and operating through cheaper means of transport than are now provided; and such cheaper means of transport can only be provided by the construction of double-track freight railways, or by the improvement and creation of water-routes.*

The solution of the problem of *cheap* transportation is therefore narrowed down to the consideration of these alternative propositions, namely: freight railways under governmental control, or water-routes open to free competition.

III. INDIRECT REGULATION BY MEANS OF ONE OR MORE DOUBLE-TRACK FREIGHT RAILWAYS TO BE OWNED OR CONTROLLED BY THE GOVERNMENT.

In the report submitted the committee have discussed at considerable length the merits and advantages of a double-track freight railway between the Mississippi River and New York City, and have come to the conclusion that such a railway honestly constructed and operated, and performing an amount of business reasonably to be anticipated, could pay all expenses together with a fair return on its cost, at rates for transportation of fourth-class freights not exceeding 7½ mills per ton per mile. At this rate a ton of wheat could be carried from the Mississippi River to New York for about $8.25, or at the rate of 25 cents per bushel. The average cost during the last five years by rail has been about $16.50 per ton, or at the rate of about 50 cents per bushel. All the data on which this conclusion is based will be found in full in the evidence and report submitted by the committee. The construction of such a line would doubtless be of incalculable benefit to a large section of the country, but other sections would be entitled to equal consideration, and if one such road should be built at Government expense, fair dealing toward those sections not directly benefited would require the construction of at least two additional lines, costing in the aggregate from two hundred and fifty to three hundred million dollars. The heavy expenditure required, and other considerations of a political and economic character mentioned in the report, have induced the committee to content themselves with a statement of the probable advantages to be derived from such improvements, without making any recommendations on the subject, excepting in so far as they have suggested railway portages, to connect natural water-routes, where canals may be considered impracticable, or where it is believed that comparatively short freight railways will do the work more cheaply than it can be done by water.

This brings me to the consideration of the alternative measure above stated, namely:

IV. "THE IMPROVEMENT AND CREATION OF WATER-ROUTES."

A careful and thorough investigation of the relative merits of water and rail transportation, both in Europe and in this country, has convinced me that for all cheap, heavy, and bulky articles, where cost is a more important element than time, water affords the cheapest and best known means of transport. In making this comparison, and in the conclusions deduced therefrom, I shall rely wholly upon testimony drawn from actual operations by water and by rail. The verdict of commerce itself, pronounced upon various routes and under diverse circumstances, is recorded in the following facts:

On the through line from the Ohio River to Boston, composed of the Baltimore & Ohio Railroad and the Boston Steamship Company, the earnings were divided as four to one in favor of water, counting the actual distances operated by each.

On the line between Baltimore and New York, consisting of railway, canal, and open water, and involving payment of tolls on the canal, the earnings were prorated by allowing the vessels 125 miles for an actual distance of 230 miles—making nearly two to one in favor of water.

The Erie Railway Company and the steamers from New York to Boston have a prorating arrangement equivalent to three to one in favor of water.

From Parkersburg and Cincinnati the arrangement between the railway and river steamers allows the latter for 250 miles by water as the equivalent of 125 miles by rail, being two to one in favor of the river.

The arrangements between the Erie Railway Company and the lake-steamers is that the railway shall furnish terminal facilities at Buffalo and Dunkirk, and the steamer-lines terminal facilities at Milwaukee and Chicago; and the actual distance of 1,000 miles is prorated at 212 miles, making nearly five to one in favor of the lake.

The Central Vermont Railway and the Northern Transportation Company (steamer-line) constitute a through line from Chicago to Boston and other places in New England. The distance by water is 1,365 miles, and the distances by rail average about 500 miles. The earnings are divided equally, being nearly three to one in favor of water. This comparison is the more valuable, because the officers of the railway company own a controlling interest in the stock of the steamship company, and hence may be supposed to divide according to actual cost of service. Mr. Diefendorf, agent of the steamboat company, testified that this division of earnings "is predicated upon the cost of transportation,"

The Chesapeake & Ohio Railway prorates with vessels on the Ohio River upon the basis of two to one in favor of the river.

The gross earnings on the through line from Chicago to New Orleans, *via* the Illinois Central Railway to Cairo (365 miles), and thence by the Mississippi River to New Orleans (1,050 miles), are divided, three-fifths to the railroad and two-fifths to the river; making, on the charge of $7 per ton from New Orleans to Chicago, 27 mills per ton per mile for the river, and 11.5 mills per ton per mile by the railroad, or over five to one in favor of the Mississippi River, against the current.

From the Kanawha coal-mines to Huntington, West Virginia, the distance by rail is 67 miles, and the minimum charge for transporting coal 75 cents per ton; from the same coal-mines, to Cincinnati, by the Ohio River, the distance is 275 miles, and the charge per ton for coal transportation is 50 cents; being at the rate of nearly 2 mills per ton per mile by river, and 11.2 mills per ton per mile by rail; nearly six to one in favor of the river. The river rates include the return of the boats to the coal-mines.

From Pittsburg to New Orleans, *via* the Ohio and Mississippi Rivers, 2,400 miles, coal is transported during high water for $1.60 per ton, or at the rate of ⅜ of 1 mill per ton per mile. This is done in barges, and in very large quantities.

The New Orleans Chamber of Commerce furnished to the committee a detailed statement of the actual expenses of a tow-boat with five barges (each barge of 1,500 tons' capacity), from St. Louis to New Orleans (1,250 miles), from which it appears that the expense was ₇⁄₈ of 1 mill per ton per mile, or at the rate of 5¼ mills per bushel of wheat for the entire distance. Also a statement of the actual expenses of the steamer John F. Tolle, 1,650 tons' capacity, value $65,000, showing a cost per ton per mile of 3.47 mills, or at the rate of 1⅞ cent per bushel of wheat for the whole distance. Neither of the last two cases includes any profit to the carrier or interest on the cost of vessels.

The average cost of freight from Cincinnati to New Orleans by water is stated by a joint committee of the Board of Trade and Chamber of Commerce of the former city to be 3¼ mills per ton per mile. The same average charge exists from Louisville to New Orleans. Even on the Tennessee River, which is hardly navigable for want of proper improvements, the charge between Knoxville and Chattanooga is only about 6 mills per ton per mile.

The following comparison between the Erie Canal and competing railways summarizes a portion of the benefits conferred upon the country by the former: From 1854 to 1864 the total number of tons moved one mile by the New York Central Railway, was 2,132,073,612, and by the Erie Railway 2,587,274,914 tons; by the New York canals 8,175,803,085 tons; and the average charges of the Central Railway were 2.6 cents, Erie Railway 2.22 cents, and the canals .91 cent per ton per mile. Had the freights which were carried by canal for the ten years been carried by rail, the additional freight charges would have amounted to $122,637,045.97.

Hon. Joseph Utley, president of the Illinois & Michigan Canal, furnishes the committee with the data from which the following comparison of charges is made.

Comparative charges for the transport of grain to Chicago by rail, from points 100 miles distant on five different railroads:

Average charge per 100 pounds for 100 miles.

	Cents.
Chicago, Rock Island & Pacific	8
Chicago, Burlington & Quincy	14
Chicago & Northwestern	13
Chicago & Alton	12
Illinois Central	16

The first-named road is the only one affected by water competition.

Perhaps the most unsatisfactory and defective kind of navigation known is that of the Ohio canals, from which arguments have been adduced against artificial water-ways. But even the Ohio canals, only forty feet wide, four feet deep, partially filled with mud, and capable of passing vessels of only 65 tons' burden, are by no means an entire failure. True, they do not compensate the lessees who operate them, nor do they pay dividends to the State; but they do, to a very considerable extent, hold the railways in check and regulate their charges. Hon. Benjamin Eggleston, who has been connected with those canals in various ways for thirty years, testified before the committee that the opening of those very inefficient canals reduces railway rates from twenty-five to fifteen cents per hundred between Cincinnati and Toledo. He adds that the canals would long since have been controlled by the railways, but for the fact that they belong to the State of Ohio, and by law the lessees are prohibited from increasing tolls. The practical effect of nearly all the canals in this country, however small and defective, has been to regulate and reduce railway charges. Where they are susceptible of being worked at all, they exercise a potential competition, which always prevents exorbitant rail charges, and thereby indirectly confer upon the public the benefits of reduced cost of transport.

Many other illustrations on this point may be found in the evidence submitted with the report of the committee; but these, taken from all parts of the country and from all kinds of water-carriage—by ocean, lake, river, and canal—will suffice to show the relative economy of the two modes of transportation for heavy and cheap commodities, and to indicate the means by which cheap transportation may be secured.

The experience of other countries accords with our own upon the relative cheapness of water and rail transport, and the effective competition between them. In England various parliamentary committees, after seeking in vain for means of obtaining competition among railways, report that they can find no practical means of securing that end, and that the only effectual and reliable competition which can be expected is between railways and artificial water-lines. In France, where competition has always been discountenanced, it has been found necessary, in some cases, in order to prevent it, to authorize the railways to purchase the canals. Throughout the commercial world the unvarying testimony of practical results is that water is the natural competitor and only effective regulator of railway transportation.

In view of these facts, and particularly of the beneficial results produced by competition afforded by the great northern water-route; of the verdict of commerce itself as expressed in the prorating arrangements between railways and water-lines; and of the reduced rates caused by even the most inefficient artificial water-channels (such as the Ohio canals), the conclusion is that for all coarse, cheap, and heavy commodities, water is much the cheapest known means of transport; and that for long distances, in which a large proportion of the value of a commodity is consumed by the cost of carriage, water-channels will always be an element of prime importance in any successful solution of the transportation question.

The president of the Pennsylvania Railroad Company, in his recent report, pronounces canals "a failure," and assures his stockholders that they "have nothing to fear from this threatened rivalry." It is quite certain he did not always entertain that opinion; for the canals of Pennsylvania, 360 miles, have been purchased or leased by his company, either to prevent their competition, or because they can carry cheaper than the railroad. Some of them have since been improved at large expense, and even those which run parallel with the Pennsylvania Railway are now operated by it. That company can hardly be accused of the blunder of sustaining an effete mode of transportation.

The efforts which have been made by the New York Central Company to obtain control of the Erie Canal are also indicative of the estimate which railway managers place upon these "failures."

The Philadelphia & Reading Railroad Company transports freight (principally iron, coal, and other minerals) at less cost per ton per mile than any other railroad in the United States, yet this company also operates two canals.

It is true that canals of small size, which do not connect natural navigable waters, or which have not the facilities for transporting a large amount of heavy freights, have failed to be remunerative to their owners; a few canals badly located have been abandoned, but it is also true that hundreds of miles of unremunerative railroads have been built in this country, and millions of dollars have been lost to those who embarked in their construction.

I now beg leave to present to the Senate, in the language of the report, a brief

SUMMARY OF THE CONCLUSIONS AND RECOMMENDATIONS OF THE COMMITTEE.

First. One of the most important problems demanding solution at the hands of the American statesman is, by what means shall cheap and ample facilities be provided for the interchange of commodities between the different sections of our widely-extended country.

Second. In the selection of means for the accomplishment of this object, Congress may, in its discretion and under its responsibility to the people, prescribe the rules and regulations by which the instruments, vehicles, and agencies, employed in transporting persons or commodities from one State into or through another State shall be governed, whether such transportation be by land or by water.

Third. The power "to regulate commerce" includes the power to *aid* and *facilitate* it by the employment of such means as may be appropriate and plainly adapted to that end; and hence Congress may, in its discretion, improve or create channels of commerce on land or by water.

Fourth. A remedy for some of the defects and abuses which prevail under existing systems of transportation may be provided through direct congressional regulation; but, for reasons stated at length in the report, it is seriously doubted if facilities sufficiently *cheap* and *ample* to meet the just and reasonable requirements of commerce can ever be obtained by this method.

Fifth. The attempt to regulate the business of transportation by general congressional enactments, establishing rates and fares on 1,300 railways, aggregating nearly one-half the railway mileage of the world, and embracing an almost infinite variety of circumstances and conditions, requires more definite and detailed information than is now in the possession of Congress or of your committee. Believing that any ill-advised measures in this direction would tend to postpone indefinitely the attainment of the desired object—cheap transportation—the committee deem it expedient to confine their recommendations in this regard to such measures only as may be enacted with entire safety, reserving other matters of legislation for further inquiry and consideration. They therefore recommend for present action the following:

1. That all railway companies, freight lines, and other common carriers, engaged in transporting passengers or freights from one State into or through another, be required, under proper penalties, to make publication, at every point of shipment from one State to another, of their rates and fares, embracing all the particulars regarding distance, classifications, rates, special tariffs, drawbacks, etc., and that they be prohibited from increasing such rates above the limit named in the publication without reasonable notice to the public, to be prescribed by law.

2. That combinations and consolidations with parallel or competing lines are evils of such magnitude as to demand prompt and vigorous measures for their prevention.

3. That all railway companies, freight lines, and other common carriers, employed in transporting grain from one State into or through another, should be required, under proper regulations and penalties to be provided by law, to receipt for *quantity* and to account for the same at its destination.

4. That all railway companies and freight organizations receiving freights in one State to be delivered in another, and whose lines touch at any river or lake port, be prohibited from charging more to or from such port than for any greater distance on the same line.*

5. Stock inflations, generally known as "stock-waterings," are wholly indefensible; but the remedy for this evil seems to fall peculiarly within the province of the States which have created the corporations from which such inflations proceed. The evil is believed to be of such magnitude as to require prompt

* This provision, it is believed, will prevent the discriminations now practised against such ports, and will enable States which are separated from water-lines by intervening States to reach such lines at reasonable cost. Congress has no power to regulate commerce wholly within a State, and hence States bordering upon such water-lines will regulate the rates to ports within their own territory.

and efficient State action for its prevention, and to justify any measures that may be proper and within the range of national authority.

6. It is believed by the committee that great good would result from the passage of State laws prohibiting officers of railway companies from owning or holding, directly or indirectly, any interest in any "*non-cooperative* freight line" or car company operated upon the railroad with which they are connected in such official capacity.

7. For the pu po e of procuring and laying before Congress and the country such complete and reliable information concerning the business of transportation and the wants of commerce as will enable Congress to legislate intelligently upon the subject, it is recommended that a Bureau of Commerce, in one of the Executive Departments of the Government, be charged with the duty of collecting and reporting to Congress information concerning our internal trade and commerce, and be clothed with authority of law, under regulations to be prescribed by the head of such Department, to require each and every railway and other transportation company, engaged in interstate transportation, to make a report, under oath of the proper officer of such company, at least once each year, which report should embrace, among other facts, the following, namely: 1. The rates and fares charged from all points of shipment on its line in one State to all points of destination in another State, including classifications and distances, and all drawbacks, deductions, and discriminations; 2. A full and detailed statement of receipts and expenditures, including the compensation paid to officers, agents, and employés of the company; 3. The amount of stock and bonds issued, the price at which they were sold, and the disposition made of the funds received from such sale; 4. The amount and value of commodities transported during the year, as nearly as the same can be ascertained, together with such other facts as may be required by the head of such Bureau, under the authority of law.

Sixth. Though the existence of the Federal power to regulate commerce, to the extent maintained in this report, is believed to be essential to the maintenance of perfect equality among the States as to commercial rights; to the prevention of unjust and invidious distinctions which local jealousies or interests might be disposed to introduce; to the proper restraints of consolidated corporate power, and to the correction of many of its existing evils, yet your committee are unanimously of the opinion that the problem of *cheap* transportation is to be solved through *competition*, as hereinafter stated, rather than by direct congressional regulation of existing lines.

Seventh. *Competition*, which is to secure and maintain *cheap* transportation, must embrace two essential conditions: 1. It must be controlled by a power with which combination will be impossible; 2. It must operate through cheaper and more ample channels of commerce than are now provided.

Eighth. Railway competition, when regulated by its own laws, will not effect the object; because it exists only to a very limited extent in certain localities; it is always unreliable and inefficient; and it invariably ends in combination. Hence additional railway lines, under the control of private corporations, will afford no substantial relief, because self-interest will inevitably lead them into combination with existing lines.

Ninth. The only means of securing and maintaining reliable and effective competition between railways is through national or State ownership, or control, of one or more lines, which, being unable to enter into combinations, will serve as regulators of other lines.

Tenth. One or more double-track freight railways, honestly and thoroughly constructed, owned or controlled by the Government, and operated at a low rate of speed, would doubtless be able to carry at much less cost than can be done under the present system of operating fast and slow trains on the same road; and, being incapable of entering into combinations, would no doubt serve as a very valuable regulator of all existing railroads within the range of their influence.

Eleventh. The uniform testimony deduced from practical results in this country, and throughout the commercial world, is, that water-routes, when properly located, not only afford the cheapest and best known means of transport for all heavy, bulky, and cheap commodities, but that they are also the natural competitors and most effective regulators of railway transportation.

Twelfth. The above facts and conclusions, together with the remarkable physical adaptation of our country for cheap and ample water communications, point unerringly to the improvement of our great natural water-ways, and their connection by canals, or by short freight-railway portages under control of the Government, as the obvious and certain solution of the problem of *cheap* transportation.

After a most careful consideration of the merits of various proposed improvements, taking into account the cost, practicability, and probable advantages of each, *the committee have come to the unanimous conclusion*, that the following are the most feasible and advantageous channels of commerce to be created or improved by the national Government, in case Congress shall act upon this subject, namely:

First. The Mississippi River.

Second. A continuous water-line of adequate capacity from the Mississippi River to the city of New York, *via* the northern lakes.

Third. A route adequate to the wants of commerce, through the central tier of States, from the Mississippi River, *via* the Ohio and Kanawha Rivers, to a point in West Virginia, and thence by canal and slack-water, or by a freight railway, to tide-water.

Fourth. A route from the Mississippi River, *via* the Ohio and Tennessee Rivers, to a point in Alabama or Tennessee, and thence by canal and slack-water, or by a freight railway, to the ocean.

In the discussion of these four existing and proposed channels of commerce we shall, for the sake of brevity, designate them respectively the "Mississippi route," "Northern route," "Central route," and "Southern route."

THE MISSISSIPPI ROUTE.

The improvements necessary on the Mississippi route are:

First. The opening of the mouth of the river, so as to permit the free passage of vessels drawing 28 feet. Estimated cost, $10,000,000.

Second. The construction of reservoirs at the sources of the river (if upon a careful survey they shall be deemed practicable). Estimated cost, $114,000.

Third. Improvements upon a system to be provided by the War Department at all intermediate points, so as to give from 3 to 5 feet navigation above the Falls of St. Anthony; from 4½ to 6 feet from that point to St. Louis; and from 8 to 10 feet from St. Louis to New Orleans, at the lowest stages of water. Estimated cost, $5,000,000.

The total cost of the Mississippi improvements may, we think, be safely estimated at $16,000,000.

THE NORTHERN ROUTE.

The improvements suggested on this route are:

First. The Fox and Wisconsin River improvement, by which five feet of navigation will be secured, during the entire season, from the Mississippi River to Green Bay, thereby affording the shortest and cheapest connection between the centres of wheat production and the Eastern markets, and a continuous water-channel from all points on the Mississippi River and its tributaries to the Atlantic Ocean. Estimated cost, $3,000,000.

Second. The construction of the Hennepin Canal (65 miles long) from a point on the Mississippi River, near Rock Island, to the Illinois River, at Hennepin, thereby affording the shortest and cheapest route

from the largest areas of corn production to the East, and a connection by water between the river system of the West, the Northern lakes, and the Atlantic Ocean. Estimated cost, $4,000,000.

Third. The enlargement and improvement, with the concurrence of the State of New York, of one or more of the three water-routes from the lakes to New York City, namely: the Erie Canal from Buffalo to Albany; or the Erie Canal from Oswego to Albany; or the Champlain Canal from Lake Champlain to deep water on the Hudson River, including such connection as may be effected with the coöperation of the British Provinces between Lake Champlain and the St. Lawrence River. Estimated cost, $12,000,000.

Total cost of Northern route from the Mississippi River to New York City, $12,000,000.

The enlargement of the Welland Canal, now in progress, with the construction of the Caughnawaga Canal and the proposed enlargement of the Champlain Canal, will enable vessels of 1,000 tons to pass from Western lake-ports to ports in Vermont and to New York City. The Erie Canal, enlarged as proposed, will pass vessels of about 700 tons.

The necessary improvement of the connection between Lakes Superior and Huron, and between Lakes Huron and Erie, should also be pressed to a speedy completion.

THE CENTRAL ROUTE.

The plan of improvement for this route contemplates:

First. The radical improvement of the Ohio River from Cairo to Pittsburg, so as to give 6 to 7 feet of navigation at low water. Estimated cost, $22,000,000.

Second. The improvement of the Kanawha River from its mouth to Great Falls, so as to give six feet of navigation at all seasons. Estimated cost, including reservoirs, $3,000,000.

Third. A connection by canal or by a freight railway from the Ohio River or Kanawha River, near Charleston by the shortest and most practicable route through West Virginia, to tide-water in Virginia; the question as between the canal and freight railway to be decided after the completion of careful surveys and estimates. If by canal and slack-water, the estimated cost is $55,000,000; if by a freight railway, the cost would probably not exceed $25,000,000.

The total expenditure necessary for the improvement of the Ohio and Kanawha Rivers is estimated at $25,000,000. The amount necessary to complete the connection of the Ohio with tide-water depends upon the nature of the improvement, as above stated.

THE SOUTHERN ROUTE.

The plan suggested by the committee for the Southern route contemplates:

First. The improvement of the Tennessee River from its mouth to Knoxville, so as to give three feet of navigation at lowest stages of water. Estimated cost, $5,000,000.

Second. A communication by canal, or freight railway, from some convenient point on the Tennessee River in Alabama or Tennessee, by the shortest and most practicable route, to the Atlantic Ocean. The railway, if constructed, will be about 430 miles long; the question as between the canal and railway to be decided after a careful survey and estimate of both shall have been completed. If by canal, the cost will be about $35,000,000; if by railway, probably about $30,000,000. All of these routes are considered at length in the report of the committee, and the advantages, cost, and practicability of each, are fully discussed.

SURVEYS RECOMMENDED.

Large portions of all of the above routes have been surveyed and careful estimates prepared by the War Department. It is recommended that appropriations be made at the present session of Congress for completing the surveys of the entire system of improvements proposed, in order to determine accurately the cost of each route and to enable the Government to enter at once upon the work, if the same shall be deemed practicable and expedient, after such surveys shall have been completed.

In presenting this general plan of improvements, the committee wish it to be distinctly understood that the ordinary annual appropriations for other important works in aid of commerce should not be omitted.

AGGREGATE COST.

The cost of the entire improvement will depend upon the decision to be hereafter made between the canals and the freight-railway portages on the Central and Southern routes. If the canals be constructed, the total cost will be about $155,000,000. If the railways be chosen, the total cost will be about $120,000,000.

An expenditure of from $20,000,000 to $25,000,000 per annum will be required for six years, when the whole work can be completed. The resulting benefits will for all time annually pay more than the entire cost.

In view of the fact that private companies invariably combine with each other against the public, it is recommended that no aid be given to any route to be owned or controlled by private corporations, but that the four great channels of commerce suggested shall be improved, created, and owned by the Government, and stand as permanent and effective competitors with each other and with all the railways which may be within the range of their influence.

The committee believe that the water-routes suggested should constitute free highways of commerce, subject only to such tolls as may be necessary for maintenance and repairs. If, however, Congress shall deem it expedient to require them to provide interest on the cost of construction, and the means for ultimate redemption of the principal, the whole improvements will involve only a loan of Government credit.

NATIONAL CHARACTER OF THE WORK.

By reference to the map of the United States it will be seen that the completion of the system of improvements proposed will provide four great competing commercial lines from the centre of the continent to the Atlantic seaboard and the Gulf of Mexico. It will also be observed by reference to the crop-maps, republished with the report, that all of these routes lead directly from or through the greatest areas of production to those sections which constitute the greatest areas of consumption, thus dividing their benefits equitably between producers and consumers, and contributing to the development and prosperity of the whole country. The Great Architect of the continent seems to have located its rivers and lakes with express reference to the commercial necessities of the industrious millions who now and hereafter shall occupy it. The plan of improvements suggested by the committee merely follows the lines so clearly indicated by his hand.

The proposed improvements are so located as to distribute their benefits with great equality among all the States east of the Rocky Mountains. Twenty-one of those States are situated directly on one or more of said routes; two States, Kansas and Nebraska, are so situated as to enjoy the full benefits of reduced cost of transportation from the Mississippi River by all of the proposed lines. Eleven States, namely, Maine, New Hampshire, Massachusetts, Connecticut, Rhode Island, Delaware, Maryland, New Jersey, North Carolina, Florida, and Texas, nearly all of which consume largely the food of the West, and most of which are to a great extent dependent upon the West for a market for their manufactures and other products, are directly connected by the waters of the ocean with their several termini. The proposed improvements will, therefore, connect by the cheapest known means of transport every one of the thirty-four States east of the Rocky Mountains with all the others, and but one State in the Union

will be without water connection with the whole world. The accomplishment of so great a result, by an expenditure of money comparatively so small, illustrates the wonderful provisions of Nature for cheap commercial facilities on this continent.

These four great channels of commerce under public control, and hence unable to combine with each other or with existing lines of transport, will, by the power of competition, held in check all the railways radiating from the interior to the seaboard, and by affording cheap and ample means of communication will solve the problem of cheap transportation. If local railways discriminate against them, it will be in the power of the States whose boundaries they touch to prescribe regulations for the correction of such discriminations. A law of Congress prohibiting discriminations against river or lake ports will enable the other States not directly upon any of said lines to reach them at reasonable rates. The committee submit that no plan of public improvement could be more eminently national in its character, nor diffuse its benefits more generally and equitably, than the one proposed, and they believe that the entire system of improvements indicated should be considered and acted upon as a whole.

I will now state more specifically, and as concisely as possible, the benefits and advantages anticipated from each route, and from the combined effects of the whole system when completed.

BENEFITS AND ADVANTAGES ANTICIPATED FROM THE NORTHERN ROUTE.

In the section of the report devoted to the Fox and Wisconsin River improvement and the Hennepin Canal, the committee have shown that by these improvements the cost of transport between the Mississippi River and the lakes can certainly be reduced an average of 10 cents per bushel, from all points west of the river, north of the parallel of Quincy, Illinois. This will include the whole of Minnesota, Iowa, and Nebraska, and a large part of Dakota, Kansas, and Missouri.

The following table, based upon the actual average railway charges in 1872, and upon an assumed charge of 6 mills per ton per mile down the Mississippi River and through the Fox and Wisconsin River improvement and 8 mills per ton per mile up the Mississippi, shows the saving that may be effected by the contemplated improvement from Prairie du Chien to Green Bay.

Table showing the actual cost of transportation by rail to Chicago, and the estimated cost (upon the above basis) by the Fox and Wisconsin improvement from the river-ports named to Green Bay.

FROM—	Actual cost per bushel of Chicago by rail.	Estimated cost per bushel of Chicago to Green Bay via the Fox and Wisconsin improvement and the Mississippi River.	Saving by the improvement.
	Cents.	Cents.	Cents.
St. Paul	19.3	8.7	10.6
Winona	18.4	6.5	11.9
La Crosse	18.4	5.9	12.5
Prairie du Chien	18.4	4.8	13.6
Dubuque	17	5.1	11.9
Savannah	18	7.5	10.5
Fulton	17.5	7.9	9.6
Rock Island	15	8.8	6.2
Burlington	12	11.5	.5
Average	17.1	7.4	9.7

The rates estimated are higher than those which usually prevail upon similar water-routes — nearly double the average rates from Cincinnati and Louisville to New Orleans; and yet the average saving shown from all the ports named is 9.7 cents per bushel; from all of Minnesota and Northern Iowa ports the saving will amount to 12 cents per bushel.

Estimating the reduction to be effected by the Hennepin Canal upon the same basis, namely, 6 mills per ton per mile *down* the Mississippi, 8 mills *up* the river, and at one cent per ton per mile through the canals to Chicago, the saving is shown by the following table:

Table showing the actual cost of transport by rail to Chicago in 1872, and the estimated cost from the ports named by the proposed water-route.

FROM—	Actual average rail-rates per bushel.	Assumed water-rates per bushel.	Water-rates less than rail-rates.
	Cents.	Cents.	Cents.
St. Paul to Chicago......	19.3	12.7	6.6
Winona to Chicago......	18.4	10.5	7.9
La Crosse to Chicago.....	18.4	9.9	8.5
Prairie du Chien to Chicago..................	18.4	8.8	9.6
Dunleith to Chicago.....	17.0	7.8	9.2
Savannah to Chicago....	18.0	6.3	11.7
Fulton to Chicago........	17.5	6.2	13.3
Rock Island to Chicago..	15.0	5.8	9.2
Burlington, Iowa, to Chicago..................	12.0	7.6	4.4
Average............	17.1	8.4 .	8.7

If the river charges be estimated at the rates which actually prevail on the Mississippi during high water, or at the average rate charged from St. Louis to New Orleans, the average saving would be about 9½ cents per bushel. With the Mississippi improved and the use of steam on the canal, I have no doubt the reduction will average at least 10 cents per bushel from all the river points named, and that competition of the canal will largely reduce the railway rates as far south as St. Louis. It is therefore safe to say that the construction of those two improvements will reduce the charges from all points on the Mississippi River above Quincy, Illinois, from the present average of 17 cents to 7 cents per bushel.

It is believed, by those who are best informed on the subject, that the enlargement of the New York canals so as to pass boats of 600 to 1,000 tons will reduce the cost of transportation on that part of the line 50 per cent. The effect of the former enlargement of the Erie Canal was to reduce the cost of transportation one-half, and, as the proposed improvement will more than treble its capacity, and permit the passage of boats of 690 tons instead of 210 tons as at present, there seems to be no reasonable doubt that the anticipated reduction will be accomplished. The establishment of reciprocal trade relations with the Dominion of Canada, which shall induce the construction of the Caughnawaga Canal (if such an arrangement can be made), and which will encourage Canadian ship-masters to compete for the carrying trade on the lakes, will also materially cheapen the cost of transport to New England. The evidence taken by the committee fully justifies the opinion that by the enlargement of the New York Canals, the construction of the Caughnawaga Canal, and the use of the enlarged Canadian canals, the cost of transport from Chicago to Burlington, Vermont, and to New York City, will not exceed from 12 to 15 cents per bushel, making the entire cost from the Mississippi River to Burlington, Vermont, or to New York, not more than 22 cents per bushel, against the present cost of 43.6 cents by water and 50¼ cents by rail. We may, therefore, reasonably estimate that by the proposed improvements upon this route a saving can be effected of 20 cents per bushel, or $6.70 per ton, on all the vast tonnage moved between that river and the East.

BENEFITS AND ADVANTAGES ANTICIPATED FROM THE CENTRAL ROUTE.

Assuming a charge of 4 mills per ton per mile on the Mississippi River and on the improved Ohio and Kanawha Rivers, a charge of 8 mills per ton per mile on the James River and Kanawha Canal, and 6 mills

per ton per mile on the slack-water improvement, the following statement will represent the cost of transport from Cairo, Illinois, to Richmond, Virginia, by the central water-line:

Cairo to Great Falls of the Kanawha, 790 miles, 4 mills per ton per mile...........................	$3 06
From Great Falls to Richmond, the distance (equating each lock at one-half mile of canal) is 509 miles, of which 348 is canal (equated), and 161 is slack-water:	
Canal, 348 miles, at 8 mills per ton per mile.......	2 78
Slack-water, 161 miles, at 6 mills per ton per mile.	99
Total per ton for entire distance.............	$6 80

Equal to 20.4 cents per bushel of sixty pounds.

If the freight railway from the Kanawha to tide-water be adopted, instead of the canal and slack-water improvement, the cost of transport from the Ohio River to the ocean will, it is believed, be substantially the same as above stated.

The Central route would be closed by ice only about thirty days each year, and hence it would be an active competitor with all the railways from the Mississippi River to the Atlantic, at times when competition is now suspended, by reason of frost, on the northern water-route. The effect of such a regulator of railway charges would be to greatly reduce the present winter rates, and, by the constant competition it would maintain, to compel uniformly low charges on all rail and water-lines from the interior to the Eastern and Southern seaboard. Its advantages would be greatest, however, to the central tier of States. Four of the largest interior cities of the continent—St. Louis, Cincinnati, Louisville, and Pittsburg—are situated directly upon it. The trade of these cities, together with the other towns and cities on the Ohio River, is now far in excess of our entire foreign commerce. A vast area of the richest agricultural and mineral country in the world is directly tributary to it, and only awaits reasonable facilities for transportation to develop a commerce the magnitude of which it is difficult now to conceive.

It is due to this route to say that the estimated cost of transport is fully 50 per cent. higher than the figures relied upon by its special advocates. The committee have adopted them from superabundant caution, preferring to understate, rather than to risk an exaggeration of its advantages.

The evidence taken by the committee shows that the average charges on the Ohio and Mississippi are only 3½ to 4½ mills per ton per mile, and in some cases only 2 mills. The estimated cost for the Central route is lower than has been assumed for the Fox and Wisconsin improvement, or for the Hennepin Canal, the reason for which is that the season of navigation will be much longer, and hence vessels can be more constantly employed.

The saving to be anticipated from the Mississippi River to Richmond, Virginia, as against the present water-route to New York, estimated upon the basis just stated, is 23 cents per bushel, and against the all-rail route about 30 cents per bushel.

BENEFITS AND ADVANTAGES ANTICIPATED FROM THE SOUTHERN ROUTE.

Assuming the same rate of charges as in the estimate just made for the Central route, namely, 4 mills per ton per mile on open river, 6 mills per ton per mile on slack-water navigation, and 8 mills per ton per mile per canal, the following will represent the cost of transport by this route from Cairo to the ocean:

Open river, 980 miles, 4 mills per ton per mile.....	$3 92
Slack-water, 70 miles, 6 mills per ton per mile.....	42
Canal, 325 miles, 8 mills per ton per mile.........	2 60
Total per ton for entire distance.............	$6 94

Equal to 20.8 cents per bushel of 60 pounds.

It is believed that a freight railway from the vicinity of Guntersville, Alabama, or Chattanooga, Tennessee, would enable this route to accomplish very nearly the same results. This route will never be obstructed by ice, and hence will afford unfailing competition throughout the year. Its greatest advantages, however, will be found not so much in furnishing a highway of commerce to the seaboard, as in opening up a valuable connection between the grain-growing States of the West and the cotton plantations of the South, whereby each section will have the full benefit of those crops for which its soil and climate are best adapted. It will connect with various Southern rivers, penetrating a very large portion of the cotton districts of the South. It is believed that eventually inland navigation will be obtained at small expense along the coast of South Carolina, Georgia, and Florida, connecting with the rivers in those States which flow into the ocean. By this route the centre of the cotton-producing districts can be reached from the centre of the corn area, at a cost not exceeding 15 to 18 cents per bushel; and hence, in addition to the creation of a new competing avenue to the sea, the home market for food that will be developed, and the increased production of cotton that will be induced, will vastly more than compensate for the entire cost.

The same remark should be made with reference to this line as with regard to the Central route, namely, that the estimated cost of movement is much in excess of what is expected by its special friends and advocates. It will be observed that the saving to be effected on through-freights to the seaboard is about the same as by the Central water-line.

BENEFITS AND ADVANTAGES ANTICIPATED FROM THE MISSISSIPPI RIVER IMPROVEMENTS.

The evidence submitted with the report justifies the conclusion that, upon the completion of the entire improvement of the Mississippi River, wheat and corn can be transported from Minnesota, Iowa, Wisconsin, Illinois, Indiana, Missouri, and other States above Cairo, to New Orleans, for an average of 12 cents per bushel, and that the cost from St. Paul will not exceed 17 cents. The average rate from New Orleans to Liverpool in 1872 was about 27 cents (currency), which can be reduced, as shown by the evidence submitted to the committee, to 18 or 20 cents by the improvement at the mouth of the river. Estimating the cost from St. Paul to New Orleans at 17 cents, the two transfers at St. Louis and New Orleans at one cent each, and the charge from New Orleans to Liverpool at 20 cents, the total from St. Paul to Liverpool will be 39 cents per bushel. The charge, in 1872, from St. Paul to Liverpool, including transfers and terminals at Chicago, Buffalo, and New York, by the cheapest route, averaged 67.5 cents per bushel. The saving to be effected by the improvements of this route may, therefore, be estimated at 28 cents per bushel from St. Paul to Liverpool, with the proportionate reduction from all other points on the river.

COMBINED BENEFITS AND ADVANTAGES OF THE PROPOSED SYSTEM OF IMPROVEMENTS.

In view of the benefits and advantages to be derived from each of the four proposed routes, and from their combined effects when in constant competition with each other and with the railroad system of the country, it is entirely safe to say that the completion of the system of improvements suggested will effect a permanent reduction of 50 per cent. in the cost of transporting fourth-class freights from the valley of the Mississippi to the seaboard, and that the cost of carrying a bushel of wheat or corn to the markets of the East, and of the world, will be reduced at least 20 to 25 cents per bushel below the present railway charges, and that a similar reduction will be effected on return-freights.

The actual movement of grain to the Eastern and Southern markets in 1872, as shown by the carefully-prepared statistics submitted with this report, amounted to about 213,000,000 bushels. An average saving of 20 cents per bushel on the surplus moved

that year would have amounted to over $42,000,000. But for the fact that large quantities of corn were unable to find a market, on account of the high transportation charges, the amount moved would have been very much greater. Hence, in addition to the saving in transportation above named, a benefit perhaps equally great would have been conferred upon the producer in affording him a market for his surplus products.

To this must be added the enhanced value which such reduction would give to the improved lands of the West, amounting, in the eight Northwestern States of Indiana, Illinois, Iowa, Minnesota, Wisconsin, Missouri, Kansas, and Nebraska, in 1870, to 55,-841,000 acres. Estimating the productive capacity of these lands at an average of only 20 bushels per acre (the average of corn, oats, etc., being, in fact, very much greater), an addition of only 10 cents per bushel (one-half the estimated saving) to the value of the cereals those States are capable of producing, would give a net profit of $2 per acre, which is the equivalent of ten per cent. interest on a capital of $20, and hence equal to an increase in the value of lands to that extent. Twenty dollars per acre added to the value of improved lands, in those States, would exceed an aggregate of $11,000,000,000. This calculation assumes that one half of the reduction inures to the benefit of the consumer and the other half to the producer.

Add to all this the increased value of farms in other States, the increased value of unimproved lands, the enhanced value of cotton-plantations, the benefits to accrue from reduced cost of movement of the products of the mine, the foundery, the factory, the workshop, and of the thousands of other commodities demanding cheaper transportation, and some conception may be formed of the vast additions to be made to our national wealth and prosperity by the system of improvements under consideration. In comparison with the great benefits and advantages reasonably to be anticipated, their cost is utterly insignificant.

The probable effect of such reduction in the cost of internal transportation upon our exports and foreign balances of trade is also worthy of the most careful consideration. America and Russia are the great food-producing nations of the world. Great Britain is the principal market. For many years America and Russia have been active competitors for the supply of that market. Until recently the farmers of the West have had the advantage of the wheat-producers on the Don and the Volga; but a few years ago Russia inaugurated a system of internal improvements by which the cost of transporting her products from the interior to the seaboard is greatly reduced. The result is shown by the importations of wheat into the United Kingdom during two periods of five years each.

Imports of wheat from Russia and America into the United Kingdom from 1860 to 1864, compared with the imports from 1868 to 1872.

1860 to 1864 inclusive.		1868 to 1872 inclusive.	
FROM—	Wheat.	FROM—	Wheat.
	Bushels.		Bushels.
Russia.........	47,376,809	Russia.........	117,967,022
United States..	127,047,126	United States..	116,462,380

An *increase*, during the latter period as compared with the former, of 70,590,213 bushels from Russia, and a *decrease* of 10,584,746 from the United States.

The cheaper mode of handling grain by elevators has not yet been adopted by Russia, but doubtless will be very soon. When this shall be done, and her wise system of internal improvements, which have already turned the wavering balances in favor of our great competitor, shall be completed, she will be able to drive us from the markets of the world, unless wiser counsels shall guide our statesmanship than have hitherto prevailed. In fact, as the increased size of ocean-vessels is constantly decreasing the cost of ocean transport, and our wheat-fields are yearly receding farther westward from the lakes, it is not impossible that when she shall have driven us from the markets of Europe she will become our active competitor in Boston and Portland, if cheaper means of internal transport be not provided. The value of American wheat in the British markets is about 7 cents per bushel over the average from all other countries, and about 5 cents per bushel above that imported from Russia. With this advantage in our favor, and with a reduction of 20 cents per bushel in the cost of internal transport, we might successfully demand the right to supply the markets of the world with food.

Our cotton exports are quite as unsatisfactory as the exports of other agricultural products. High transportation charges from the grain-fields of the Northwest to the cotton-fields of the South have compelled the planter to devote his cotton-lands to the production of wheat and corn, for which they are by nature unsuited, thereby reducing the product of cotton and diminishing the market for grain. The effect upon our cotton exportations is shown by the following statement:

Receipts of cotton in Great Britain in 1860, *compared with* 1872.

1860.		1872.	
FROM—	Cotton.	FROM—	Cotton.
	Pounds.		Pounds.
United States..	1,115,890,608	United States..	625,600,080
All other countries.........	275,048,144	All other countries.........	783,237,392

The cotton exports of the United States have fallen off nearly 50 per cent., while other countries have gained nearly 300 per cent. This is doubtless largely due to the war, which stimulated the production of cotton in India, but it is also attributable to a great extent to the causes just mentioned, and to the system of internal improvements inaugurated by Great Britain in India, for the express purpose of rendering herself independent of us for the supply of cotton. *Every cent unnecessarily added to the cost of transportation is to that extent a protection to the cotton-planters of India and the food-producers of Russia, against the farmers of the West and the cotton-planters of the South.*

The murmurs of discontent which come from the overburdened West, the demand for cheaper food heard from the laboring-classes at the East and from the plantations of the South, and the rapid falling off of our principal articles of export, all indicate the imperative necessity for cheaper means of internal communication. If we would assure our imperiled position in the markets of the world, reinstate our credit abroad, restore confidence and prosperity at home, and provide for a return to specie pa men , let us develop our unequaled resources and stimulate our industries by a judicious system of internal improvements.

A reference to the expenditures of our Government since the adoption of the Constitution will show that in some matters we have been sufficiently liberal, but in appropriations for the benefit of commerce and for the development of our vast resources most parsimonious. For public buildings, including those in the District of Columbia, and custom-houses, post-offices, and court-houses in other parts of the country, we have expended over $62,000,000; while for the improvement of the twenty thousand miles of Western rivers, through which should flow the life-currents of the nation, we have appropriated only $11,438,300. For the improvements of these great avenues of trade, which were designed by Nature to afford the cheapest and most ample commercial facilities for the teeming millions who inhabit the richest country on earth, we have expended an average of $133,100 per annum; while for public buildings we have appropriated an average of over $750,000 a year. Is it not high time

that all expenditures not absolutely necessary be suspended, and that the imperative necessities of the country receive attention?

Louisiana.

THE following special message of President Grant was sent to the United States Senate on January 13, 1875. As it treats of events which took place in Louisiana in December, 1874, etc., it is inserted here as a part of the history of 1874.

To the Senate of the United States:

I have the honor to make the following answer to a Senate resolution of the 8th inst., asking for information as to any interference by any military officer or any part of the Army of the United States with the organization or proceedings of the General Assembly of the State of Louisiana, or either branch thereof, and also inquiring in regard to the existence of armed organizations in that State hostile to the government thereof, and intent on overturning such government by force. To say that lawlessness, turbulence, and bloodshed have characterized the political affairs of that State since its reorganization under the Reconstruction acts, is only to repeat what has become well known as a part of its unhappy history; but it may be proper here to refer to the election of 1868, by which the Republican vote of the State, through fraud and violence, was reduced to a few thousands, and the bloody riots of 1866, 1867, and 1868, to show that the disorders there are not due to any recent causes or to any late action of the Federal authorities.

Preparatory to the election of 1872, a shameful and undisguised conspiracy was formed to carry that election against the Republicans without regard to law or right, and to that end the most glaring frauds and forgeries were committed in the returns, after many colored citizens had been denied registration and others deterred by fear from casting their ballots. When the time came for a final canvass of the votes, in view of the foregoing facts, William P. Kellogg, the Republican candidate for Governor, brought suit upon the equity side of the United States Circuit Court for Louisiana, and against Warmoth and others, who had obtained possession of the returns of the election; representing that several thousand voters of the State had been deprived of the elective franchise on account of their color, and praying that steps might be taken to have said votes counted, and for general relief. To enable the court to inquire as to the truth of these allegations a temporary restraining order was issued against the defendants, which was at once wholly disregarded and treated with contempt by those to whom it was directed. These proceedings have been widely denounced as an unwarrantable interference by the Federal Judiciary with the election of State officers, but it is to be remembered that by the fifteenth amendment to the Constitution of the United States the political equality of colored citizens is secured, and under the second section of that amendment, providing that Congress shall have power to enforce its provisions by appropriate legislation, an act was passed on the 31st of May, 1870, and amended in 1871, the object of which was to prevent the denial or abridgment of suffrage to citizens on account of race, color, or previous condition of servitude; and it has been held by all the Federal judges before whom the question has arisen, including Justice Strong of the Supreme Court, that the protection afforded by this amendment and these acts extends to State as well as to other elections. That it is the duty of the Federal courts to enforce the provisions of the Constitution of the United States, and the laws passed in pursuance thereof, is too clear for controversy.

Section 15 of said act, after numerous provisions therein to prevent an evasion of the fifteenth amendment, provides that the jurisdiction of the United

States shall extend to all cases in law or equity arising under the provisions of said act and of the act amendatory thereof. Congress seems to have contemplated equitable as well as legal proceedings to prevent the denial of suffrage to colored citizens, and it may be safely asserted that if Kellogg's bill in the above-named case did not present a case for the equitable interposition of the court, that no such case can arise under the act. That the courts of the United States have the right to interfere in various ways with State elections so as to maintain political equality and rights therein, irrespective of race or color, is comparatively a new and to some seems to be a startling idea, but it results as clearly from the fifteenth amendment to the Constitution and the acts that have been passed to enforce that amendment, as the abrogation of State laws upholding slavery results from the thirteenth amendment to the Constitution. While the jurisdiction of the court in the case of Kellogg *vs.* Warmoth and others is clear to my mind, it seems that some of the orders made by the judge in that and the kindred case of Antoine are illegal. But, while they are so held and considered, it is not to be forgotten that the mandate of this court had been contemptuously defied, and they were made while wild scenes of anarchy were sweeping away all restraint of law and order. Doubtless the judge of this court made grave mistakes, but the law allows the Chancellor great latitude, not only in punishing those who contemn his orders and injunctions, but in preventing the consummation of the wrong which he has judicially forbidden. Whatever may be said or thought of those matters, it was only made known to me that the process of the United States court was resisted, and as said act specially provides for the use of the army and navy when necessary to enforce judicial process arising thereunder, I considered it my duty to see that such process was executed according to the judgment of the court. Resulting from these proceedings through various controversies and complications, a State administration was organized, with William P. Kellogg as Governor, which, in the discharge of my duty, under Section 4, Article IV., of the Constitution, I have recognized as the government of the State. It has been bitterly and persistently alleged that Kellogg was not elected. Whether he was or not is not altogether certain, nor is it any more certain that his competitor, McEnery, was chosen. The election was a gigantic fraud, and there are no reliable returns of its result. Kellogg obtained possession of the office, and, in my opinion, has more right to it than his competitor.

On the 20th of February, 1873, the Committee on Privileges and Elections of the Senate made a report, in which they say they were satisfied by testimony that the manipulation of the election machinery by Warmoth and others was equivalent to 20,000 votes, and they add that to recognize the McEnery government would be recognizing a government based upon fraud, in defiance of the wishes and intentions of the voters of the State. Assuming the correctness of the statements in this report, and they seem to have been generally accepted by the country, the great crime in Louisiana, about which so much has been said, is, that one is holding the office of Governor who was cheated out of 20,000 votes, against one whose title to the office is undoubtedly based on fraud, and in defiance of the wishes and intentions of the voters of the State. Misinformed and misjudging as to the nature and extent of this report, the supporters of McEnery proceeded to displace by force in some counties of the State the appointees of Governor Kellogg; and on the 13th of April, in an effort of that kind, a butchery of citizens was committed at Colfax, which, in blood-thirstiness and barbarity, is hardly surpassed by any acts of savage warfare. To put this matter beyond controversy, I quote from the charge of Judge Woods of the United States Circuit Court to the jury, in the case of the United States against Cruikshank and others, at New Orleans, in

March, 1874. He said: "In the case on trial there are many facts not in controversy. I proceed to state some of them in presence and hearing of counsel on both sides, and if I state as a conceded fact any matter that is disputed they can correct me." After stating the origin of the difficulty, which grew out of an attempt of white persons to drive the parish judge and sheriff, appointees of Kellogg, from office, and their attempted protection by colored persons, which led to some fighting, in which a number of negroes were killed, the judge says: "Most of those who were not killed were taken prisoners." Fifteen or sixteen of the blacks had lifted the boards and taken refuge under the floor of the court-house. They were all captured. About thirty-seven men were taken prisoners. The number is not definitely fixed. They were kept under guard until dark. They were led out two by two and shot. Most of the men were shot dead; a few were wounded, not mortally, and by pretending to be dead were afterward during the night able to make their escape. Among them was the Levi Nelson named in the indictment. The dead bodies of the negroes killed in this affair were left unburied until Tuesday, April 15th, when they were buried by a deputy marshal and an officer of militia from New Orleans. These persons found fifty-nine dead bodies. They showed pistol-shot wounds, the great majority in the head and most of them in the back of the head. In addition to the fifty-nine dead bodies found, some charred remains were discovered near the court-house, six dead bodies found under a warehouse, all shot in the head but one or two, which were shot in the breast. The only white men injured from the beginning of these troubles to their close were Hadnot and Harris. The court-house and its contents were entirely consumed. There is no evidence that any one in the crowd of whites bore any lawful warrant for the arrest of any of the blacks. There is no evidence that either Nash or Cazabat, after the affair, ever demanded their offices to which they had set up claim, but the Register continued to act as parish j ge and Shaw as sheriff. These are the facts in the case, as I understand them to be admitted. To hold the people of Louisiana generally responsible for these atrocities would not be just; but it is a lamentable fact that insuperable obstructions were thrown in the way of punishing these murderers, and the so-called Conservative papers of the State not only justified the massacre, but denounced as Federal tyranny and despotism the attempt of the United States officers to bring them to justice. Fierce denunciations rung through the country about office-holding and election matters in Louisiana, while every one of the Colfax miscreants goes unwhipped of justice, and no way can be found in this boasted land of civilization and Christianity to punish the perpetrators of this bloody and monstrous crime. Not unlike this was the massacre in August last. Several Northern young men of capital and enterprise had started the little and flourishing town of Coushatta. Some of them were Republicans and office-holders under Kellogg. They were, therefore, doomed to death. Six of them were seized and carried away from their homes and murdered in cold blood. No one has been punished, and the Conservative press of the State denounced all efforts to that end, and boldly justified the crime.

Many murders of a like character have been committed in individual cases which cannot here be detailed; for example: T. S. Crawford, Judge of the Parish, and the District Attorney of the Twelfth Judicial District of the State, on their way to court, were shot from their horses by men in ambush on the 8th of October, 1873; and the widow of the former, in a communication to the Department of Justice, tells a piteous tale of the persecutions of her husband because he was a Union man, and of the efforts made to screen those who had committed a crime which, to use her own language, "left two widows and nine orphans." To say that the murder of a negro or a white Republican is not considered a crime in Louisiana, would probably be unjust to a great part of the people; but it is true that a great number of such murders have been committed and no one has been punished therefor, and manifestly show that the spirit of hatred and violence is stronger than law.

Representations were made to me that the presence of troops in Louisiana was unnecessary and irritating to the people, and that there was no danger of public disturbance if they were taken away. Consequently, early in last summer, the troops were all withdrawn from the State, with the exception of a small garrison at New Orleans barracks. It was claimed that a comparative state of quiet had supervened. Political excitement as to Louisiana affairs seemed to be dying out, but the November election was approaching, and it was necessary for party purposes that the flame should be rekindled. Accordingly, on the 14th of September, D. Penn, claiming that he was elected Lieutenant-Governor in 1872, issued an inflammatory proclamation, calling upon the militia of the State to arm, assemble, and to drive from power the "usurpers," as he designated the officers of the State. The White Leagues, armed and ready for the conflict, promptly responded. On the same day the Governor made a formal requisition upon me, pursuant to the act of 1795, and section 4, Article IV., of the Constitution, to aid in suppressing domestic violence. On the next day I issued my proclamation, commanding the insurgents to disperse within five days from the date thereof; but before the proclamation was published in New Orleans, the organized and armed forces, recognizing a usurping Governor, had taken forcible possession of the State-House and temporarily subverted the government. Twenty or more people were killed, including a number of the police of the city. The streets of the city were stained with blood. All that was desired in the way of excitement had been accomplished, and, in view of the steps taken to repress it, the revolution was apparently, though it is believed not really, abandoned, and the cry of Federal usurpation and tyranny was renewed with redoubled energy. Troops had been sent to the State under this requisition of the Governor, and, as other disturbances seemed imminent, they were allowed to remain to render the Executive such aid as might become necessary to enforce the laws of the State and repress the continued violence which seemed inevitable the moment the Federal support should be withdrawn. Prior to and with a view to the late election in Louisiana, white men associated themselves together in armed bodies called White Leagues, and at the same time threats were made in the Democratic journals of the State that the election should be carried against the Republicans at all hazards, which very naturally greatly alarmed the colored voters. By section 8 of the act of February 8, 1871, it is made the duty of United States marshals and their deputies, at the polls where votes are cast for representatives in Congress, to keep the peace and prevent any violations of the, so-called Enforcement Acts, and other offenses against the laws of the United States; and upon a requisition of the Marshal of Louisiana, and in view of said armed organizations and other portentous circumstances, I caused detachments of troops to be stationed in various localities in the State to aid him in the performance of his official duties.

That there was intimidation of Republican voters at the election, notwithstanding these precautions, admits of no doubt. The following are specimens: On the 14th of October eighty persons signed and published the following at Shreveport:

We, the undersigned merchants of the city of Shreveport, in obedience to a request of the Shreveport Campaign Club, agree to use every endeavor to get our employés to vote the People's ticket at the ensuing election, and in the event of their refusal so to do, or in case they vote the Radical ticket, to refuse to employ them at the expiration of their present contracts.

On the same day another large body of persons

published, in the same place, a paper in which they used the following language:

We, the undersigned merchants of the city of Shreveport, alive to the great importance of securing good and honest government to the State, do agree and pledge ourselves not to advance any supplies or money to any planter the coming year who will give employment or rent lands to laborers who vote the Radical ticket in the coming election.

I have no information of the proceedings of the Returning Board for said election which may not be found in its report which has been published, but it is a matter of public information that a great part of the time taken to canvass the votes was consumed by the arguments of lawyers, several of whom represented each party before the board. I have no evidence that the proceedings of this board were not in accordance with the law under which they acted. Whether in excluding from their count certain returns they were right or wrong is a question that depends upon the evidence they had before them. But it is very clear that the law gives them the power, if they choose to exercise it, of deciding that way, and prima facie the persons whom they return as elected are entitled to the offices for which they were candidates. Respecting the alleged interference by the military with the organization of the Legislature of Louisiana on the 4th inst., I have no knowledge or information which has not been received by me since that time and published. My first intimation was from the papers of the morning of the 5th of January. I did not know that any such thing was anticipated, and no orders or suggestions were ever given to any military officer in that State upon that subject p io to the occurrence. I am well aware that any military interference by the officers or troops of the United States with the organization of a State Legislature or any of its proceedings, or with any civil department of the government, is repugnant to our ideas of government. I can conceive of no case not involving rebellion or insurrection where such interference by authority of the General Government ought to be permitted or can be justified. But there are circumstances connected with the late legislative imbroglio in Louisiana which seem to exempt the military from any intentional wrong in the matter, knowing that they had been placed in Louisiana to prevent domestic violence and aid in the enforcement of the State laws. The officers and troops of the United States may well have supposed that it was their duty to act when called upon by the Governor for that purpose. Each branch of the Legislative Assembly is the judge of the election and qualifications of its own members, but if a mob or a body of unauthorized persons seize and hold the legislative hall in a tumultuous and riotous manner, and so prevent any organization by those legally returned as elected, it might become the duty of the State Executive to interpose, if requested by a majority of the members-elect, to suppress the disturbance, and enable the persons elected to organize the House. Any exercise of this power would only be justifiable under most extraordinary circumstances, and it would then be the duty of the constabulary, or, if necessary, the military force of the State, to act; but with reference to Louisiana it is to be borne in mind that any attempt by the Governor to use the police force of that State at this time would have undoubtedly precipitated a bloody conflict with the White League, as it did on the 14th of September. There is no doubt but that the presence of the United States troops upon the occasion prevented bloodshed and the loss of life. Both parties appear to have relied upon them as conservators of the public peace.

The first call was made by the Democrats to remove persons obnoxious to them from the legislative hall, and the second was from the Republicans to remove persons who had usurped seats in the Legislature without legal certificates entitling them to seats, and in sufficient numbers to change the majority. Nobody was disturbed by the military who had a legal right at that time to occupy a seat in the Legislature. That the Democratic minority of the House undertook to seize its organization by fraud and violence; that in this attempt they trampled under foot law; that they undertook to make persons not returned as elected members, so as to create a majority; that they acted under a preconcerted plan, and under false pretenses introduced into the hall a body of men to support their pretensions, by force if necessary; and that conflict, disorder, and riotous proceedings followed, are facts that seem to be well established, and I am credibly informed that these violent proceedings were a part of a premeditated plan to have the House organized in this way, reorganize what has been called the McEnery Senate, then to depose Governor Kellogg and so revolutionize the State government.

Whether it was wrong for the Governor, at the request of the majority of the members returned as elected to the House, to use such means as were in his power to defeat these lawless and revolutionary proceedings, is, perhaps, a debatable question, but it is quite certain that there would have been no trouble if those who now complain of illegal interference had allowed the House to be organized in a lawful and regular manner. When those who inaugurate disorder and anarchy disavow such proceedings, it will be time enough to condemn those who, by such means as they have, prevent the success of their lawless and desperate schemes. Lieutenant-General Sheridan was requested by me to go to Louisiana to observe and report the situation there, and, if in his opinion necessary, to assume the command, which he did on the 4th instant, after the legislative disturbances had occurred—at 9 o'clock p. m.—a number of hours after the disturbance. No party motives or prejudices can reasonably be imputed to him; but, honestly convinced by what he has seen and heard there, he has characterized the leaders of the White-Leaguers in severe terms, and suggested summary modes of procedure against them, which, though they cannot be adopted, would, if legal, soon put an end to the troubles and disorders in that State. General Sheridan was looking at facts, and possibly not thinking of proceedings which would be the only proper ones to pursue in a time of peace, and thought more of the utterly lawless condition of society surrounding him at the time of his dispatch, and of what would prove a sure remedy. He never proposed to do an illegal act, nor expressed a determination to proceed beyond what the law in the future might authorize for the punishment of the atrocities which have been committed, and the commission of which cannot be denied. It is a deplorable fact that political crimes and murder have been committed in Louisiana which have gone unpunished, and which have been justified or apologized for, which must rest as a reproach upon the State and country long after the present generation has passed away.

I have no desire to have United States troops interfere in the domestic concerns of Louisiana or any other State. On the 9th of December last Governor Kellogg te e a e to me his apprehension that the White Leaguer intended to make another attack upon the State-House, to which, on the same day, I made the following answer, since which no communication has been sent to him:

Your dispatch of this date just received. It is exceedingly unpalatable to use troops in anticipation of dangers. Let the State authorities be right, and then proceed with their duties without apprehension of danger. If they are then molested, the question will be determined whether the United States is able to maintain law and order within its limits or not.

I have deplored the necessity which seemed to make it my duty, under the Constitution and laws, to direct such interference. I have always refused, except where it seemed to be my imperative duty, to act in such a manner under the Constitution and laws of the United States. I have repeatedly and earnestly entreated the people of the South to live together in peace and obey the laws, and nothing would give me greater pleasure than to see reconciliation and tranquillity everywhere prevail, and thereby remove all necessity for the presence of troops among them. I regret, however, to say that this state of things does not exist, nor does its existence seem to be desired in some localities, and as to those it may be proper for me to say that to the extent that Congress has conferred power on me to prevent it, neither Ku-klux Klans, White Leagues, nor any other association using arms and violence to execute their unlawful purposes, can be permitted in that way to govern any part of this country. Nor can I see with indifference Union men or Republicans ostracized, persecuted, and murdered on account of their opinions, as they now are in some localities. I have heretofore urged the case of Louisiana upon the attention of Congress, and I cannot but think that its inaction has produced great evil.

To summarize: In September last an armed organized body of men in the support of candidates who had been put in nomination for the offices of Governor and Lieutenant-Governor at the November election in 1872, and who had been declared not elected by the board of canvassers recognized by all the courts to which the question had been submitted, undertook to subvert and overthrow the State government that had been recognized to me in accordance with previous precedents. The recognized Governor was driven from the State-House, and but for his finding shelter in the United States Custom-House in the capital of the State of which he was Governor, it is scarcely to be doubted that he would have been killed. From the State-House, before he had been driven to the Custom-House, a call was made in accordance with the fourth section of the fourth article of the Constitution of the United States for the aid of the General Government to suppress domestic violence. Under those circumstances, and in accordance with my sworn duties, my proclamation of the 15th of September, 1874, was issued. This served to reinstate Governor Kellogg to his position nominally; but it cannot be claimed that the insurgents have to this day surrendered to the State authorities the arms belonging to the State, or that they have in any sense disarmed. On the contrary, it is known that the same armed organizations that existed on the 14th of September, 1874, in opposition to the recognized State government, still retain their organization, equipments, and commanders, and can be called out at any hour to resist the State government. Under these circumstances the same military force has been continued in Louisiana as was sent there under the first call, and under the same general instructions. I repeat, that the task assumed by the troops is not a pleasant one to them; that the army is not composed of lawyers capable of judging at a moment's notice of just how far they can go in the maintenance of law and order; and that it was impossible to give specific instructions providing for all possible contingencies that might arise. The troops were bound to act upon the judgment of the commanding officer upon each sudden contingency that arose, or wait instructions which could only reach them after the threatened wrongs had been committed which they were called on to prevent. It should be recollected, too, that upon my recognition of the Kellogg government I reported the fact, with the grounds of recognition, to Congress, and asked that body to take action in the matter; otherwise I should regard their silence as an acquiescence in my course. No action has been taken by that body, and I have maintained the position then marked out. If error has been committed by the army in these matters, it has always been on the side of the preservation of good order, the maintenance of the law, and the protection of life. Their bearing reflects credit upon the soldiers, and if wrong has resulted the blame is with the turbulent elements surrounding them. I now earnestly ask that such action be taken by Congress as to leave my duties perfectly clear in dealing with the affairs of Louisiana, giving assurance at the same time that whatever may be done by that body in the premises will be executed according to the spirit and letter of the law, without fear or favor.

I herewith transmit documents containing more specific information as to the subject-matter of the resolution. U. S. GRANT.

EXECUTIVE MANSION, *January* 13, 1875.

The documents accompanying the message are voluminous. The first is a letter from Governor Kellogg, dated August 19, 1874, addressed to President Grant at Long Branch, in which Governor Kellogg regrets to have to trouble him again about Louisiana affairs, but the exceptional circumstances, and the importance of the issues involved, render it necessary he should make a brief statement of the situation, which he proceeds to do, premising that Louisiana is now the last State in the Southwest, except Mississippi, that remains true to the Republican party. He concludes by saying:

I respectfully and earnestly suggest that if the United States troops were returned to their posts in this State such a course would have a most salutary effect, and would prevent much bloodshed and probably a formal call upon the President and a renewed agitation of the Louisiana question, which otherwise a quiet, fair election next November would forever set at rest, and fully vindicate your just policy toward us.

Marshal Packard, on August 30, 1874, telegraphed Attorney-General Williams a request to the Secretary of War to order a sufficient force immediately to aid in the discharge of his duties as required by law. The registration was about to begin. Large bodies of armed and mounted white men had appeared. Through fear of them the blacks would be unable to register or vote in case of a conflict, which Marshal Packard regarded as imminent. On August 30th, Governor Kellogg informed Attorney-General Williams of a gross outrage which had just been perpetrated at Coushatta. The presence of troops would go far to prevent violence and bloodshed. He said there was "an openly-avowed policy of exterminating Republicans." Information was sent to Attorney-General Williams by Marshal Packard and District-Attorney Beckwith, dated September 10th and 13th, of the proceedings of the White League, and urging the necessity for troops to prevent murder, etc. On the 14th Governor Kellogg made a requisition on the President to take measures to put down the domestic violence and insurrection then prevailing. Numerous telegrams were sent to the Attorney-General by Marshal Packard and others, asserting that armed mobs were reported all over New Orleans, and that Leaguers were much more formidable than was supposed, etc.

The Mayor of St. Francisville telegraphed, September 19th, to the Attorney-General:

The timely arrival of Federal troops has saved the lives of unoffending Republicans. We look confidently to the loyal North for the support which they have so generously extended to the weak, and hope the protection of the Government will continue until the elections are over. Life is dear to us, and we cannot risk an article so precious when surrounded by murderous White-Leaguers.

Mr. Packard, on November 1st, requested a post to be established at Natchitoches, and that General Emory be ordered to place a company of troops there. On October 19th, S. B. Packard, chairman of the State Central Committee, and Governor Kellogg, Messrs. Durell, Casey, Sypher, and Morey, addressed a telegram to Attorney-General Williams, saying:

We have authentic information that systematic violence and intimidation will be practised toward Republican voters on the day of election at three or four points in this State, and we earnestly request that General Emory be instructed to send troops to Franklin, St. Mary's Parish, Napoleonville, Assumption Parish, Moreauville, Avoyalles Parish. Governor Kellogg will furnish transportation to those points without cost to the Government.

On December 9th, Governor Kellogg telegraphed President Grant:

Information reaches me that the White League purpose making an attack upon the State-House, especially that portion occupied by the Treasurer of the State. The organization is very numerous and well armed, and the State forces now available are not sufficient to resist successfully any movement they may make. With a view of preventing such an attempt, and the bloodshed which would be likely to result should an insurgent body gain possession of the State-House in dispersing them, I respectfully request that a detachment of United States troops be stationed in that portion of the St. Louis Hotel which is not used for any of the State offices, where they will be readily available to prevent any such insurrectionary movement as that contemplated.

Ex-Governor Wells, president of the State Returning Board, telegraphed the President December 10th:

The members of the board are being publicly and privately threatened with violence, and an attack upon the State-House, which is likely to result in bloodshed, is also threatened. By request of the board, I respectfully ask that a detachment of troops be stationed in the State-House so that the deliberations and final action of the board may be free from intimidation and violence.

The United States Commissioner for Shreveport, A. B. Levisa, gives a full statement of the condition of affairs in Northern Louisiana, referring to an alleged scheme to expel from the country the Republican leaders, and then to frighten the negroes into acquiescence with their wishes; and charging that the whites were driving the freedmen from their homes, naked and penniless, to endure the severities of the winter as best they might. The negroes were cheated of their rights, and had no redress with the mixed juries of the local courts. The following was communicated confidentially to General Sheridan:

WAR DEPARTMENT, WASHINGTON, D. C., }
December 24, 1874. }

To General P. H. SHERIDAN, *Chicago, Ill.*

GENERAL: The President sent for me this morning, and desires me to say to you that he wishes you to visit the States of Louisiana and Mississippi, and especially New Orleans, La., and Vicksburg and Jackson, Miss., and ascertain for yourself, and for his information, the general condition of matters in those localities. You need not confine your visit to the States of Louisiana and Mississippi, and may extend your trip to other States—Alabama, etc., if you see proper; nor need you confine your visit in the States of Louisiana and Mississippi to the places named.

What the President desires is the true condition of affairs, and to receive such suggestions from you as you may deem advisable and judicious. Inclosed herewith is an order authorizing you to assume command of the Military Division of the South, or of any portion of that division, should you see proper to do so. It may be possible that circumstances may arise which would render this a proper course to pursue. You can, if you desire it, see General McDowell in Louisville, and make known to him confidentially the object of your trip, but this is not required of you. Communication with him by you is left entirely to your own judgment. Of course you can take with you such gentlemen of your staff as you wish, and it is best that the trip should appear to be one as much of pleasure as of business, for the fact of your mere presence in the localities referred to will have, it is presumed, a beneficial effect. The President thinks, and so do I, that a trip South might be agreeable to you, and that you might be able to obtain a good deal of information on the subject about which we desire to learn. You can make your return by Washington and make a verbal report, and also inform me from time to time of your views and conclusions. Yours truly, etc.,

W. W. BELKNAP, Secretary of War.

WAR DEPARTMENT, ADJUTANT-GENERAL'S OFFICE, }
WASHINGTON, December 24, 1874. }
To Lieutenant-General P. H. SHERIDAN, *United States Army, Chicago, Ill.*

SIR: If, in the course of the inspection and investigation the Secretary of War has directed you to make in his communication of this date, you should find it necessary to assume command over the Military Division of the South or any portion thereof, the President of the United States hereby authorizes and instructs you to take the command accordingly, and to establish your headquarters at such a point as you may deem best for the interests of the public service. I am, sir, very respectfully, your obedient servant,

E. D. TOWNSEND, Adjutant-General.

A copy of the above letter was furnished General McDowell, commanding the Military Division of the South, on January 5, 1875:

[*Telegram.*]

HEADQUARTERS, MILITARY DIVISION OF THE MIS- }
SOURI, CHICAGO, ILL., *December 26, 1874.* }
To General W. W. BELKNAP, *Washington, D. C.:*
Your letter has been received all right.

P. H. SHERIDAN, Lieutenant-General.

HEADQUARTERS, ARMY OF THE UNITED STATES, }
ST. LOUIS, *December 30, 1874.* }
GENERAL: I have the honor to acknowledge the receipt of your confidential communication of December 26th, with inclosures. Your obedient servant,

W. T. SHERMAN, General.
To W. W. BELKNAP, *Sec'y of War, Washington, D. C.*

Next follows a telegram of Mr. Wiltz's to the President, informing him of his election as Speaker of the House, and protesting against armed interference with the Legislature. Next appear the telegrams of Sheridan, dated January 5, 1875, addressed to the Secretary of War, relating to terrorism, banditti, etc. General Sheridan sends to the War Department for its information a letter from Major Merrill, dated Shreveport, December 30th. He gives the facts as to the probabilities of violence there, and says:

The three Republican members declared elected to the Legislature by the Returning Board, who have gone to New Orleans to take their seats, beyond doubt could not safely return here now. Outside of the officers named above there is no one left to do violence upon. The leading Radicals have left; the worrying and harassing of the negroes goes on with little intermission, but lately no acts of violence to their persons have come to my knowledge. Such acts now are confined to plundering them with or without some show of legal form, and driving them from their homes to seek places to live elsewhere. The conflict for offices, whether conducted by peaceable legal means, or violence, will stop what little legal check now exists upon crime and wrong-doing, and will greatly aggravate the condition of things, which is already serious enough. But I do not apprehend that it will result in extended disorder at present, because there is nothing left to work upon except the commoner orders, and partly because the leading White-Leaguers have gone to New Orleans.

The telegrams of General Sheridan to the Secretary of War, and those from the latter to the former, appear in the correspondence, and also the following telegram:

NEW ORLEANS, *January 10, 1875—11.30 P. M.*
The Hon. W. W. BELKNAP, *Secretary of War, Washington, D. C.:*

Since the year 1866, nearly 3,500 persons, a great majority of whom were colored men, have been killed and wounded in this State. In 1868 the official record shows that 1,884 were killed and wounded. From 1868 to the present time, no official investigation has been made, and the civil authorities in all but a few cases have been unable to arrest, convict, and punish the perpetrators. Consequently there are no convict records to be consulted for information. There is ample evidence, however, to show that more than 1,200 persons have been killed and wounded during this time, on account of their political sentiments. Frightful massacres have occurred in the parishes of Bossier, Caddo, Catahoula, St. Bernard, St. Landry, Grant, and Orleans. The general character of the massacres in the above-named parishes is so well known, that it is unnecessary to describe them. The isolated cases can be best illustrated by the following instances, which I take from a mass of evidence now lying before me of men killed on account of their political principles:

In Natchitoches Parish, the number of isolated cases reported is 33; in the parish of Bienville the number of men killed is 30; in Red River Parish the isolated cases of men killed are 34; in Winn Parish the number of isolated cases where men were killed is 15; in Jackson Parish the number killed is 20; in Catahoula Parish the number of isolated cases reported where men were killed is 50, and most of the country parishes throughout the State will show a corresponding state of affairs. The following statements will illustrate the character and kind of these outrages. On the 30th of August, 1874, in Red River Parish, six State and parish officers, named Twitchell, Divers, Holland, Howell, Edgerton, and Willis, were taken, together with the four negroes under guard, to be carried out of the State, and were deliberately murdered. On the 29th of August, 1874, the White League tried, sentenced, and hanged two negroes. On the 28th of August, 1874, three negroes were shot and killed at Brownsville, just before the arrival of the United States troops in the parish. Two White-Leaguers rode up to a negro cabin and called for a drink of water. When the old colored man turned to draw it they shot him in the back and killed him. The courts were all broken up in the district, and the district judge driven out. In the parish of Caddo, prior to the arrival of the United States troops, all of the officers at Shreveport were compelled to abdicate by the White League, which took possession of the place. Among those obliged to abdicate were Walsh, the mayor; Rapirs, the sheriff; Wheaton, the clerk of the courts; Durant, the recorder; and Ferguson and Reufro, administrators. Two colored men who had given evidence in regard to frauds committed in the parish were compelled to flee for their lives, and reached this city last night, having been smuggled through in a cargo of cotton. In the parish of Bossier, the White League have attempted to force the abdication of Judge Baker, the United States Commissioner, and the parish Judge, together with O'Neal, the sheriff, and Walker, the clerk of the court; and they have compelled the Parish and District Courts to suspend operations. Judge Baker states that the White-Leaguers notified to him several times that if he became a candidate on the Republican ticket, or if he attempted to organize the Republican party, he should not live until election. They also tried to intimidate him through his family by making the same threats to his wife; and when told by him that he was a United States Commissioner, they notified him not to attempt to exercise the functions of his office.

In but few of the country parishes can it be truly said that the law is properly enforced; and in some of the parishes the judges have not been able to hold court for two years. Human life in this State is held so cheaply that when men are killed on account of political opinions the murderers are regarded rather as heroes than as criminals in the parishes where they reside, and by the White League and their supporters. An illustration of the ostracism that prevails in the State may be found in a resolution of a White League club in the parish of De Soto, which states that they pledge themselves "under no circumstances, after the coming election, to employ, rent land to, or in any other manner give aid, comfort, or credit to any man, white or black, who votes against the nominees of the white man's party." Safety for individuals who express their opinion in the isolated portions of this State has existed only when that opinion was in favor of the principles and party supported by the Ku-klux and White-League organizations. Only yesterday Judge Myers, the Parish Judge of the parish of Natchitoches, called on me upon his arrival in this city, and stated that in order to reach here alive he was obliged to leave his house by stealth and after nightfall, and make his way to Little Rock, Ark., and come to this city by way of Memphis. He further states, that while his father was lying at the point of death in the same village he was unable to visit him for fear of assassination, and yet he is a native of the parish, and is proscribed for his political sentiments only. It is more than probable that if bad government has existed in this State, it is the result of the armed organizations which have now crystallized into what is called the White League. Instead of bad government developing them, they have by their terrorism prevented to a considerable extent the collection of taxes, the holding of courts, the punishment of criminals, and vitiated public sentiment by familiarizing it with the scenes above described.

I am now engaged in compiling evidence for a detailed report upon the above subject, but it will be some time before I can obtain all the requisite data to cover the cases that have occurred throughout the State. I will also report in due time upon the same subject in the States of Arkansas and Mississippi.

P. H. SHERIDAN, Lieutenant-General.

To W. W. BELKNAP, *Sec'y of War, Washington, D. C.:*

Several prominent people have for the last few days been passing resolutions and manufacturing sensational protests for Northern political consumption. They seem to be trying to make martyrs of themselves. It cannot be done at this late day. There have been too many bleeding negroes and ostracized white citizens for their statements to be believed by fair-minded people. Bishop Wilmer protests against my telegram of the 4th inst., forgetting that on Satur-

day last he testified under oath, before the Congressional Committee, that the condition of affairs here was substantially as bad as reported by me. I will soon send you a statement of the number of murders committed in this State during the last three or four years, the perpetrators of which are still unpunished. I think that the number will startle you. It will be up in the thousands. The city is perfectly quiet. No trouble is apprehended.

P. H. SHERIDAN, Lieutenant-General, U. S. A.

General Sheridan sends a communication to the Secretary of War, with no signature, as illustrating the action in Louisiana in kidnapping a member-elect of the Legislature. Next follows Sheridan's telegram to the Secretary of War, dated January 8th, submitting a report of the affairs as they occurred in the organization of the State Legislature. The documents conclude with extracts from Louisiana newspapers, showing the platform of the White League and the intentions of the organization, the following serving as a specimen:

The lines must be drawn at once, before our opponents are thoroughly organized. For by this means we will prevent many milk-and-cider followers from falling into the enemy's ranks. While the white man's party guarantee the negro all of his present rights, they do not intend that white carpet-baggers and renegades shall be permitted to organize, and prepare the negroes for the coming campaign. Without the assistance of these villains the negroes are totally incapable of effectually organizing themselves, and unless they are previously excited and drilled, one-half of them will not come to the polls, and a large percentage of the remainder will vote the white man's ticket.

ACTION OF THE CONGRESSIONAL COMMITTEE.

The Congressional Investigating Committee presented the following report on affairs in Louisiana to the House of Representatives on January 14, 1875.—Representative George F. Hoar, in behalf of the special committee on that portion of the President's message relative to the condition of the South, reported as follows:

In pursuance of the order of the full committee, of December 22d, a special committee of three visited New Orleans and proceeded with an investigation, the result of which they report to the general committee, as follows:

REPORT OF THE SUB-COMMITTEE.

In pursuance of the order of the general committee of December 22d, the undersigned visited New Orleans, and there proceeded with all diligence to the examination directed by the committee. During the eight days they remained there they were attended throughout their sessions, which were public, by the counsel of the Republican and Conservative State Committees. In that period they examined over ninety-five witnesses, besides taking a large amount of documentary evidence, amounting in all, it is estimated, to more than 1,500 printed pages. In view of the exigency that now exists in the affairs of that State and of the delay of weeks which must elapse before that testimony can be written out and printed, your committee has determined to state the conclusions at which they arrived, so far as they are unanimous in reaching their conclusions. The committee undertook no investigation of the election of 1872. Much evidence has already been taken by other committees of Congress upon that question, and the time allowed both for their action and for the session of Congress seemed to be too short to call for their then entering on that investigation. They announced this conclusion; and that, therefore, they would first proceed to an examination of the acts of the Returning Board of the State in respect of the late election, and then to an inquiry in reference to the White League. The law provides that the board shall consist of five persons, "representing all parties." It consisted at the opening of their last session of five Republicans, upon the resignation of one of whom (General Longstreet), Mr. Arroyo, a Conservative, was taken to fill the vacancy. After protesting against the action of the board, in secret session, Mr. Arroyo resigned, before the conclusion of the labors of the board, and his place was not filled, so that, as your committee think, the law as to the constitution of the board was not complied with. The election laws of Louisiana provide for a Supervisor of Registration, who appoints his own deputies for each ward in New Orleans, and for one Supervisor of Registration for each parish in the State. The officers were all appointed by Governor Kellogg. In addition to these supervisors, the police jurors, the local authorities of the parishes, appointed three Commissioners of Election for each poll in the parish, and there were also two United States supervisors appointed by the District Judge of the United States for each poll. The law further provided that in case of such violence, intimidation, or corruption at or near either poll, either during registration or election, preventing a fair, free, peaceable and full vote, the Commissioners of Election, if the occurrence was on election day, the Supervisors of Registration, if on the day of registration, should make a full verified statement of the occurrence, forward the same with and annexed to the returns; and further provided that when the Returning Board, in canvassing the returns, should come to any poll where the returns were accompanied by such a protest, they should not canvass, count, or compile the statement of voters from such poll until the statements from all other polls had been canvassed and compiled. The Conservative counsel objected that the board on reaching the returns from such protested polls read and became informed of those returns before laying them aside to take up the other polls. They insisted that the purpose of the law was to prevent the commissioners from knowing what the results at the polls protested against were, in order that when they came to examine the polls protested against they might do so without being biased by knowing what was the result returned; and they objected that in these cases of protest the board had proceeded to read the returns, add up, and compile them, and then defer their determination of the case until after having acquired knowledge of how the returns protested against would affect the elections. On the other hand, the Republican counsel insisted that such a course was impracticable; that the object of the law in deferring any determination of the results of the polls protested against until the returns from the other polls were canvassed, was merely to enable the board to ascertain whether the result of the disputed returns would affect the election, however decided, so that if they would not the board might be spared the labor of considering this protest. Your committee have not found it necessary to come to any determination upon that question.

The election embraced but one State office. The chief struggle was over the election of members of the State Legislature and parish officers, and in those elections local and personal considerations as well as national and State politics entered.

The returns by the Commissioners of Election, compiled and forwarded by the Supervisors of Registration, gave the Conservatives a majority of 29 members out of a total of 111 members. In only three instances were there any protests accompanying the returns. The Returning Board was in session for many weeks. As finally announced, their findings gave, as Governor Kellogg reckoned it, 53 members to the Republicans, and 50 members to

the Democrats, of whom, however, one was regarded as not a staying Democrat. The board made no decision as to the remaining five seats. The public sittings of the Returning Board were attended by the counsel of the Republican and Conservative State Committees. Objections were received from the counsel of the respective parties to the returns from different polls. The objecting party was generally allowed to produce evidence to support the objection, and the other party to reply by affidavits. A day was fixed when these proofs were to be closed. After these public sessions the board went into private, or, as they were called, executive sessions, where the proofs and matters in dispute were discussed, and a decision arrived at. The minutes of the board are very meagre. They contain little more than a record of its meeting, going into executive session, and its adjourning, and some formal public orders. They contain no minutes whatever of the proceedings in executive session, and furnish, therefore, little light upon the findings of the board. The Parish of Rapides chose three members to the Legislature. The returns elected all three Conservatives. When the proofs closed the only paper filed with the Returning Board was the affidavit of the United States Supervisor that the election was in all respects full, fair, and free. It was not known in the parish that any contest existed against those members. They left their homes and proceeded to New Orleans, to be present at the opening of the Legislature, no intimation of contesting their seats or objection to their election having been given by their opponents. At one of their last sessions, the Returning Board declared all the Republican members elected from that parish. When the papers of the Returning Board were produced before your committee there was found among them an affidavit by Mr. Wells, the president of the board, declaring that intimidation had existed at certain polls in that parish, and that the returns from those polls should, therefore, be rejected. The counsel for the Democratic Committee testified that they had no opportunity to contradict the statements of this paper; that they had never seen or known of it before, and that upon an examination of the papers before the board, when the proofs closed, it was not among them. The counsel for the Republican Committee reserved the right to make explanation upon this point, but offered none. The affidavit was dated —— day of December, 1874. It appeared that Governor Wells was not himself in the parish on the day of the election, and though at the opening of their first session your committee declared their intention to examine into the action of the Returning Board, Governor Wells never came forward as a witness. At the close of our proceedings leave was asked that his deposition might be given in. This we declined, and Mr. Wells was invited to appear before the committee, but he never came. Leave was also given for taking his testimony by a commissioner, if he declined to appear; but this was not availed of. Your committee are, therefore, constrained to declare that the action of the Returning Board in the rejection of these returns in the parish of Rapides, and giving the seats for that parish to the Republican candidates, was arbitrary, unfair, and without warrant of law.

If the committee were to go behind the papers before the board and consider the alleged charge of intimidation upon the proofs before the committee, their finding would necessarily be the same. It was asserted in Governor Wells's affidavit that the McEnery officials had usurped the offices of the parish, and thereby intimidated voters. Immediately after September 14th, when the Kellogg authorities in New Orleans were put out by the Penn authorities, certain changes took place in some of the parishes. When the news from New Orleans reached those parishes, the McEnery officers demanded their places of the Kellogg officials; they were at once given up. When the Federal Government interfered and unseated the McEnery authorities, the Kellogg officials demanded and received back their places, but some time seems to have elapsed before the Kellogg officials took their places back. Indeed, the McEnery Register of Deeds was still acting as such when your committee were in New Orleans, the Kellogg Register never having come to reclaim the place, which was said to be worth nothing now. In Rapides Parish the Kellogg clerk was Mr. Wells's son, who, having yielded his place to the McEnery competitor in September, does not appear to have reclaimed it, and he was accordingly sent for after the election to come from his residence, some miles distant, to sign the returns of the elections, which he did. Your committee are at a loss to see in their action any intimidation of Mr. Wells, still less of the electors of the parish. It so happens that this parish was taken as a sample parish of intimidation, many witnesses from which of both parties were examined with reference to it. They show beyond question that there was a free, full, fair, and peaceable election and registration there; there was no evidence of any intimidation of voters practised on the day of election, although it was asserted that intimidation of colored men before the election had been effected by threats of refusal to employ them, or to discharge them if they voted the Republican ticket. No evidence, either of discharge or of refusal to employ, was produced. Certain witnesses, themselves every one office-holders, testified generally to such action; but hardly any one was able to specify a single instance in which he heard any employer threaten to discharge any voter, or knew of any employé being so threatened or discharged. Not one single colored man throughout the entire parish was produced to testify, either to such a threat, or to the execution of such a purpose, whether before or after the election.

The action of the Returning Board in the parish of Rapides alone changed the political complexion of the Lower House, and their action in the other parishes was equally objectionable; for instance, in Iberia Parish, it was claimed before your committee that the vote of poll No. 1 in that parish had been rejected on account of intimidation, but the papers produced by the clerk of the board showed no such proof whatever. One of the counsel, Mr. Ray, produced some affidavits which he declared had been submitted to the board by another of the counsel, General Campbell. The Conservative counsel insisted that these papers had never been before the board, when opportunity was given the Republican counsel to show that the paper had been submitted; but the testimony offered for that purpose by them so far, however, from establishing that fact, established the reverse. It was then asserted that the returns were rejected because the accounts of the election were not delivered to the Supervisor of Registration within twenty-four hours after the close of the election, which was six o'clock on the 3d day of November, whereas it appeared that, both in the morning and afternoon of the 3d of November, search was made for this Supervisor of Registration for that parish in order to deliver to him these returns, and he was not to be found until after six o'clock, but that as soon as he could be found on the evening of that day they were offered to him, and again reoffered the next morning, but were refused to be received. Yet this same Supervisor of Registration, who received other Republican returns, after he had refused to receive these Conservative ones, on the ground that they were too late, and the Returning Board, although it had held, as to other polls in the State, that the returns were not to be rejected merely because they were sent too late, rejected the returns from this poll, and thereby changed the representation of the parish from Conservative to Republican. So in the parish of De Soto, the returns showed a Conservative elected by over 1,000 majority. It was alleged that the Supervisor of Registration had brought the returns to New Orleans, and had left them with a woman of bad character, who offered to produce them on payment of $1,000. The Conservative Committee took legal

proceedings to compel their production, but the court held that it had no jurisdiction to that end. They then caused to be produced before the board the duplicates of those returns from the office of the Secretary of State, together with the tally-sheets, poll-lists, etc., filed there according to law. These duplicates correspond exactly with the alleged result of the compiled returns which the said woman had produced; and of these alleged facts undisputed proof was submitted to the board. Nevertheless the board refused to count that vote for the parish. So in Winn Parish, where 404 Conservative and 164 Republican votes were cast, upon a verbal protest that the registrar of elections was not properly qualified—of which the only proof was that he had failed to forward his oath of office to the Secretary of State—although there was no pretense that the election was not a fair representation of the will of the people, the whole vote of the parish was rejected, and the case referred to the Legislature. So in Terre Bonne Parish, where there was a Conservative majority, it was proved that the Commissioners of Election, through misapprehension of their duties, inclosed all the returns in the ballot-boxes, and deposited them with the clerk of the court, with whom the law required the boxes to be left. The judge of the court thereupon issued a mandamus commanding the clerk to take the returns from the boxes and forward them to the Secretary of State, which was done. Nevertheless, the board rejected the returns from these polls, thereby giving the parish to the Republicans, with the result of choosing a Republican Senator, two Republican members of the Legislature, and the Republican parish-officers.

Without now referring to other instances, we are constrained to declare that the action of the Returning Board on the whole was arbitrary, unjust, and in our opinion illegal; and that this arbitrary, unjust, and illegal action alone prevented the return of a majority of the Conservative members to the Lower House. Upon the general subject of the state of affairs in the South, and as to whether the alleged wrongs to colored citizens for political offenses are real, or were asserted without due foundation, your committee took such proof as the opportunity offered. Both parties agreed upon four parishes as samples of the condition of affairs in that respect in the State. Of these, owing to the impossibility of procuring witnesses from the locality in time, your committee were obliged to confine their especial examination to two parishes. They received all the testimony that was offered, and in addition they received all the testimony that was then on hand in New Orleans, offered by either party, as to the condition of affairs in other parts of the State. As a whole, they are constrained to say that the intention charged is not borne out by the facts before us. No general intimidation of Republican voters was established. No colored man was produced who had been threatened or assaulted by any Conservative because of political opinion, or discharged from employment or refused employment. Of all those who testified to intimidation, there was hardly any one who of his own knowledge could specify a reliable instance of such acts, and of the white men who were produced to testify generally on such subjects very nearly all, if not every single one, was the holder of an office. Throughout the rural districts of the State the number of white Republicans are very few; it hardly extends beyond those holding office and those connected with them. No witnesses, we believe, succeeded in naming in any parish five Republicans who supported the Kellogg government who were not themselves office-holders or related to office-holders, or those having official employment. On the other hand, applications to the United States Commissioners in the various parishes, not only for alleged crimes, but because of alleged threats of discharge and non-employment, or other interference with political preference, were frequent. Upon these applications warrants were often issued and white citizens arrested and bound over for trial.

In many localities the Federal troops were detained for service under the marshals and deputy-marshals, and not only made many arrests immediately before the election, but the reports that they were coming to particular neighborhoods about the time of the election, for the purpose of making such arrests, served, as the Conservatives claimed, to intimidate and sometimes even to produce a stampede among the white voters. How differently the two parties look upon the same fact will appear from the testimony of Mr. Riddle. He was a United States Commissioner in the parish of Iberia. Shortly before the election, upon the application of colored persons, he issued a large number of warrants. He considered it his duty, upon the arrest of the persons charged, to require bail from sureties who possessed landed estates within the parish, certified to by the assessor of the parish to be of sufficient value, and of which the title was approved by the Register of Deeds. This rule necessarily produced delay in procuring bail for the persons arrested, and he was waited on in one case by a procession of citizens, who offered him a bond signed by every man in the procession. This he regarded as in derision of his proceedings, and refused to receive the bond. He was called as a witness to prove the intimidation that existed in that parish. He had himself no knowledge of any act of the kind except this procession, which he thought was calculated to intimidate the colored voters. He had no idea that the arrests made upon his warrants and the proceedings under them had any effect in interfering with the Conservative voters. On the other hand, the Conservatives in that neighborhood thought about this just the reverse. Indeed, the reports of the military officers in command of the forces of the United States in the country, though generally indicating a condition of quiet and order, take sometimes an entirely different view of the situation. On the other hand, it was in evidence that the blacks who sought to act with the Conservative party were, on their part, sometimes exposed to enmity and abuse. In the interior one colored man was shot for making a Conservative speech, and in New Orleans it appeared from the testimony that colored men who sought to coöperate with the Conservatives were subject to so much abuse from the police and otherwise that an association of lawyers volunteered to protect them, but with little effect.

The general condition of affairs in the State of Louisiana seems to be as follows: The conviction has been general among the whites since 1872 that the Kellogg government was a usurpation. This conviction among them has been strengthened by the acts of the Kellogg Legislature abolishing existing courts and judges and substituting others presided over by judges appointed by Kellogg, having extraordinary and exclusive jurisdiction over political questions. By changes in the law centralizing in the Governor every form of political control, including the suspension of elections; by continuing the Returning Board with absolute power over the returns of elections; by the extraordinary provisions enacted for the trial of titles and claims to office; by the conversion of the police force, maintained at the expense of the city of New Orleans, into an armed brigade of State militia, subject to the command of the Governor; by the creation, in some places, of monopolies in markets, gas-making, water-works, and ferries, cleaning vaults, removing filth, and doing work as wharfingers; by the abolition of courts with election judges, and the substitution of other courts with judges, appointed by Kellogg, in evasion of the constitution of the State; by enactments punishing criminally all persons who attempted to fill official positions unless returned by the Returning Board; by unlimited appropriations for the payment of militia expenses, and for the payment of legislative warrants, vouchers, and checks issued during the years 1870 to 1872; by laws declaring that no person, in arrears for taxes after default published shall bring any suit in any court of

the State, or be allowed to be a witness in his own behalf; measures which, when coupled with the extraordinary burdens of taxation, have served to vest, in the language of Governor Kellogg's counsel, "a degree of power in the Governor of a State scarcely exercised by any sovereign in the world." With this conviction is a general want of confidence in the integrity of the existing State and local officials, a want of confidence equally in their persons and in their *personnel*, which is accompanied by the paralyzation of business and destruction of values. The most hopeful witness produced by the Kellogg party, while he declared that business was in a sounder condition than ever before, because there was less credit, has since declared that there was no prosperity. The securities of the State have fallen, in two years, from 70 or 80 to 25, of the city of New Orleans from 80 or 90 to 30 or 40; while the fall in bank-shares, railroad-shares, city and other corporate companies, has in a degree corresponded.

Throughout the rural districts of the State the negroes reared in habits of reliance upon their masters for support, and a community in which the members are always ready to divide the necessaries of life with each other, not regarding such action as very evil, and having immunity from punishment from the nature of the local officials, had come to filching and stealing fruit, vegetables, and poultry so generally, as Bishop Wilmer stated without contradiction from any source, that the raising of these articles had to be entirely abandoned, to the great distress of the white people; while, within the parishes as well as in New Orleans, the taxation had been carried almost literally to the extent of confiscation. In New Orleans the assessors are paid a commission on the amount appraised, and houses and stores are to be had there for the taxes. In Natchitoches Parish the taxation reached about 8 per cent of the assessed value on property. In many parishes all the white Republicans and all the office-holders belong to a single family. There are five of the Greens in office in Lincoln Parish, and there are seven of the Boults in office in the parish of Natchitoches. As the people saw taxation increase and prosperity diminish, as they grew poor while the officials grew rich, they became naturally sore. That they loved their rulers cannot be pretended. The Kellogg government claims to have reduced taxation. This has been effected in part by establishing a board to fund the debt of the State, at 60 per cent. of its face value. This measure aroused great hostility, not so much because of the reduction of its acknowledged debt, as because it gave to the Funding Board, whose powers seem to be absolute and without review, discretionary authority to admit to be funded some $6,000,000 of debt alleged to be fraudulent, so that under the guise of reducing the acknowledged debt it gave opportunity to swell the fraudulent debt against the State. This nominal reduction of the State taxes has been accompanied by a provision that the parish tax shall not exceed the State. But parishes have, notwithstanding, created liabilities. Judgments having been received on them, the courts have directed taxes to be levied for their payment, and thus the actual taxes have been carried far beyond the authorized rates. Rings have been formed in parishes composed of the parish officers, their relatives, and of coöperating Democrats, who would buy up these obligations, put them in judgment, and cause them to be enforced, to the great distress of the neighborhood —a distress so great that the sales of lands for taxes have become almost absolutely impossible. But the reduction of wages, the non-fulfillment of personal or political pledges, the malfeasance of home and local officials, disputes among the leading colored persons, in other localities, of the loss and embezzlement in some cases of the school-funds, and the failure of the Freedmen's Bank—all combined to divide the views of colored voters during the late campaign. An effort was accordingly made by the Conservatives to

acquire a part of the negro vote. With that view it
was sought in many quarters to propitiate them.

The frequent arrests by the United States marshals
for intimidation or threats of non-employment, and
the apprehension that was felt that the Returning
Board would count out their men if an excuse for
such a course were offered, all combined, especially
after September 14th, to put the Conservatives on
their good behavior, and the result was, that in November, 1874, the people of the State of Louisiana did
fairly have a free, peaceable, and full registration and
election, in which a clear Conservative majority was
elected to the Lower House of the Legislature, of
which majority the Conservatives were deprived by
the unjust, illegal, and arbitrary action of the Returning Board. That there were turbulent spirits cannot
be denied. Those returned to office by the Returning Board, in violation of the wishes of the people,
are especially odious. In one instance the editor of
the *Shreveport News*, in anticipation of the frustra-
tion by the Returning Board of the will of the people,
openly declared that the only remedy was "to kill
the usurpers," and declared this to be the sentiment
of the Conservatives of his section of the State; but,
beyond a newspaper editor or two, no declaration even
of that sort was brought to our own notice, although
it was admitted on all hands that the white people of
the whole State felt greatly outraged by the action
of the Returning Board. Indeed, it is conceded by
all parties that the Kellogg government is only upheld by the Federal military. Withdraw the military,
and that government will go down. This was true
before the 4th of January, as well as now. Governor
Kellogg says this is owing to the doubt that Congress
has permitted about the legality of his government.
The Conservatives say that this is not only because
his government is illegal, but because it has been
abusive and corrupt.

In this connection we refer to the White League
mentioned in the message of the President. In the
last campaign in Louisiana the opposition was composed of various elements—Democrats, Reformers,
dissatisfied Republicans, Liberal Republicans, old
Whigs—and in order to induce the coöperation of all,
some of whom refused to unite with an organization
called Democrats, they took the name of "The
People's party," called in some localities "The Conservative party," in others "The White Man's party,"
in others "The White League;" and had ordinary
political clubs under these names throughout the
rural districts, which were ordinary political clubs,
and nothing more—neither secret, nor armed, nor
otherwise different from usual political organizations.
These must not, however, be confounded, from the
similarity of names, with the "White League of the
City of New Orleans." That league is an organization comprised of different clubs, numbering in all between 2,500 and 2,800—the members of which have provided arms for themselves, and with or without arms
engage in military drill. They have no uniform, and
the arms are the property of the individuals and not
of the organizations. They comprise a large number
of reputable citizens, and of property-holders in New
Orleans. Their purpose they declare to be simply
protection, a necessity occasioned by the existence of
leagues among the blacks, of the hostility with which
the Kellogg government arrayed the black against
the white race, of the want of security to peaceable
citizens and their families, which existed for those reasons, and because also of the peculiar formation of the
police brigade. On the other hand, the Republicans
assert that this is an armed body of volunteers existing for the purpose of intimidating the blacks and
overthrowing the Kellogg government. That it had
any considerable relations outside of the city of New
Orleans, or that it was intended in any way to interfere with the rights of the colored citizens, did not
appear; nor, on the other hand, did it appear that
there was any extensive secret league among the blacks
of any kind. That the White League would readily

coöperate in any feasible scheme for overthrowing
the Kellogg government, your committee do not
doubt; so will substantially all the white citizens of
Louisiana. Such organizations may be dangerous
and are very rarely to be justified. The affair of
September 14th is an illustration of this. The members of the White League had purchased arms. The
police had seized these arms without process of law,
taking them forcibly from the merchants who had
sold and from the members who had bought them.
A consignment of arms was to arrive by the steamer
Mississippi. The members of the League were called
out, on the morning of the 14th, to go and take them
in a body. The police undertook to seize the arms.
The two bodies came into collision on the wharf, and
several persons were killed and wounded. There
were then hardly any Federal troops in New Orleans,
and the disintegration of the Kellogg party was
such that before night Penn and his associates had
only to take possession of the Executive offices without
a struggle. The movement was everywhere quietly
accepted by the whites throughout the State until
the Federal Government interfered, when Penn and
his associates at once surrendered. If Louisiana was
a country by itself, McEnery and his associates would
at once be installed in power, but the Conservatives
of Louisiana do not propose to fight the Federal
Government. They submit, not because they want
to, but because they must; not because they proclaim
any enmity against the flag, not because free labor
has not been found practicable, not because of any
hostility to the colored people because they are
colored, but because they regard themselves as defrauded out of the election of 1872; and yet more,
out of the last election, and because they think their
State government has been to the last degree destructive and corrupt. Indeed, in our judgment, the
substantial citizens of the State will submit to any
fair determination of the question of the late election,
or to any thing by which they can secure a firm and
good government. What they seek is peace and an
opportunity for prosperity. To that end they will
support any form of government that will afford them
just protection; in their distress they have got beyond any mere question of political party.

After your committee had announced their intention not to investigate the election of 1872, they received a letter from Governor Kellogg, expressing a
desire that they should investigate that subject; later
they received a letter from McEnery and Penn and
associates, proposing to submit their claims to the
State offices, to the committee as arbitrators. In
view of the assurance that a like submission was desired on the part of Messrs. Kellogg and Antoine and
their associates, the committee addressed a letter to
each of these gentlemen, desiring to know explicitly
whether each one would submit to the determination
of the committee, and if they found he was not duly
elected he would resign his office, or all claim to the
office, and would not enter upon it during the term
for which he claimed to have been elected. To this communication they received a reply from Mr. McEnery
and those associated with him, assenting to the submission; and in the course of his examination before
the committee, Governor Kellogg expressed the same
intention, and his opinion that those associated with
him ought to consent to the arrangement. His formal reply has been received since our return, and we
see by the public press that Mr. Antoine has expressed
his willingness to accede to the arrangement.

As to the proceedings on the 4th of January, about
which the committee desired a statement, we now
add that your sub-committee, on the invitation of
the Democratic Conservative Committee of the State
of Louisiana, visited the hall of the House of Representatives, and witnessed the convening of the Louisiana House of Representatives, Mr. Potter refusing
to go inside the bar, remained outside, while Messrs.
Foster and Phelps were seated inside and near to the
Speaker's chair. Mr. Potter remained only until

Wiltz was elected Speaker, and states nothing as to what subsequently occurred. Mr. Foster retained perhaps an hour, and Mr. Phelps remained about an hour longer, until he learned that the military were about to enter under Governor Kellogg's orders. The doings in the State-House on the 4th of January, as seen by the committee or subsequently in evidence, were substantially as follows:

At twelve o'clock, noon, William Vigers, the Clerk of the last House, called the Assembly to order and proceeded to call the roll of members, as made up from the returns of the Returning Board. This roll contained the names of 106 members, classed by Governor Kellogg as 53 Republicans and 53 Democrats. But it is claimed that one of the Democrats was not a staying Democrat. The Republicans claimed that one of their members, Mr. A. G. Cousin, had been kidnapped and forcibly taken to a distant parish to prevent his presence at the organization of the House. Your committee were about to investigate this charge, when in public session, it was claimed by the Democratic counsel and admitted by the Republican counsel that the arrest was under legal process and by the hands of the sheriff. It was further claimed, and not denied, that the privilege of his office did not shield him from arrest. The charge was embezzlement. The full House would contain 111 members, of which 56 would be a quorum. On the first call of the roll, 102 answered to their names. It is claimed by the Republicans, and we believe conceded by the Democrats, that 50 of these answering to their names were Democrats, and 52 were Republicans. The instant the Clerk finished the roll-call, several members rose to their feet, but the floor was successfully held by Mr. Billieu, who said that he nominated L. A. Wiltz as temporary chairman. The Clerk suggested that the legal motion was to elect a Speaker. Mr. Billieu, himself, paying no attention to the Clerk, proceeded hurriedly to put his own motion, which was received by loud yeas followed by loud nays, and declared it carried. Mr. Wiltz sprung instantly to the platform, took from the Clerk the gavel, was quickly sworn in by Justice Houston, who followed him to the platform, and then rapped the House, which during this time had been in great confusion, into a temporary quiet. Mr. Wiltz, as temporary chairman, administered the oath to the members en masse, who rose to receive it. Some member made a motion to elect Mr. Trezevant Clerk. Mr. Wiltz put the motion and declared it carried. Trezevant at once came forward and took the Clerk's chair.

Immediately after, and with the same haste, Mr. Flood was elected Sergeant-at-Arms, and at once, whether on motion or not your committee do not remember, a number of assistant Sergeants-at-Arms were appointed, who promptly appeared, wearing badges on which was printed, "Assistant Sergeant-at-Arms." While the above-mentioned motions were being put, numbers objected and called for the yeas and nays, all of which was disregarded and pronounced out of order by the acting chairman. Colonel Lowell, a Republican, made the point of order that the constitution of the State allowed any two members to call for the yeas and nays on any motion, but the temporary chairman decided the point not well taken until a motion for permanent organization was made.

Next, a motion to go into election for a permanent organization was offered, and declared premature. Against this ruling the Republicans protested. A motion to seat the Democratic members alleged to be elected in the four parishes, whose election was referred to the Legislature, was immediately made and carried. During this stage there was much disorder. The Republican members protested, but their protests were disregarded. These gentlemen then appeared and were sworn in. A motion to adjourn was then put and declared lost. Mr. Lowell (Republican) then moved that the House proceed to a permanent organization, and that the vote be taken upon the roll of the Returning Board. This motion was declared

lost, Mr. Lowell protesting. Mr. Matthews (Republican) then nominated Mr. Lowell as temporary chairman, and put the motion amid great confusion and disorder, and declared it passed. Mr. Lowell declined to serve. The House then proceeded to elect a Speaker; the roll was called by Clerk Trezevant, who reported 55 votes for Wiltz, 2 for Hahn, and 1 (Mr. Wiltz's own) blank. This result was ascertained by the Clerk by simply keeping a tally of the members voting as they answered to their names; no roll of members voting was kept, neither were tellers ordered, or any such other means employed than calling the roll to ascertain the number voting. This vote includes the five members who had been sworn in to fill vacancies; during the roll-call, when Mr. Hahn's name was called, he rose and asked to be excused from voting, and to be allowed to state his reasons. Objection was made, and then the Speaker pro tem. asked for unanimous consent to his explanation: consent was given, and Mr. Hahn spoke at some length. After the announcement by the Clerk of the vote, Mr. Wiltz was sworn in as Speaker, and proceeded to swear in others present so far as they came forward to be sworn. Those thus sworn in were said to number 60 in all, made up of 50 Conservatives and 5 Republicans who were returned by the Returning Board, and the 5 Democratic members who had just been admitted.

Outside of the bar of the legislative hall in the State-House there were a large number of police, supported by the Federal troops. No person was permitted to enter the State-House except through the orders of Governor Kellogg. Within the bar of the House were permitted only the gentlemen returned by the Returning Board, and the Clerk and Sergeant-at-Arms of the former Legislature, ten persons allowed to the Conservatives as messengers, who suddenly became their assistant Sergeants-at-Arms, and a few other persons, such as were admitted by courtesy to the floor. Without the bar in the public part of the hall stood the contestants and other persons admitted; they numbered by actual count 127. Besides these the door of the hall was kept by 27 police. Wiltz maintained control of the Assembly until some time after he was chosen Speaker. When the Republicans undertook to withdraw from the hall, Mr. Wiltz gave instructions to the Sergeants-at-Arms not to allow any one to pass out or enter the hall. Then the disturbance without the bar at once increased, and pistols were displayed, when, at this juncture, a Conservative member moved that the Speaker be requested to ask Colonel de Trobriand to preserve order. A committee was appointed to wait on Colonel de Trobriand and request his compliance. Colonel de Trobriand came to the bar, unaccompanied, except by one aide, whom he left there, and then alone approached the Speaker. The Speaker requested him to ask for order in the lobby. Colonel de Trobriand did so, and order was then restored. The Speaker thanked him in the name of the House for his courtesy, and he withdrew. The action of the body proceeded for an hour or so without interruption, during which time a committee on contested seats was appointed, minor officers elected, and debate had; but no message was sent to the Senate or to the Governor notifying them that the House was organized and ready to proceed to business; when, at length, Colonel de Trobriand returned and stated he had orders to remove the five members sworn in who had not been returned by the Returning Board; and, after the protest and resistance of Mr. Wiltz and the persons referred to, and after General Campbell had been sent for to point them out, they were removed by the United States soldiers. Mr. Wiltz then left the chair, as Mr. Vigers, to organize the House, began to call the roll made out by the Returning Board; and two Democratic members had answered to their names, when Mr. Wiltz interrupted the Clerk, and called upon the Conservative members to refuse to answer and to leave the hall. The interruption over, Mr. Vigers began anew his roll-call, and obtained only fifty responses, but as the two Democratic members had just before answered on the roll-call, which was interrupted, he assumed it right to announce that 54 members had answered to their names.

Those who remained after Mr. Wiltz and his friends withdrew, elected Hahn Speaker by acclamation and proceeded to the business of the Legislature. There was no subsequent roll-call by which the number of those members whose names were returned by the Returning Board, and who still remained present at these deliberations, could be determined. Your committee have not been able to agree upon any recom-

mendation; but upon the situation in Louisiana, as it appeared before us, we are all agreed.

CHARLES FOSTER,
WM. WALTER PHELPS,
January 14, 1875.   CLARKSON A. POTTER.

The evidence upon which the sub-committee base their conclusions is not yet being written out. It will be submitted hereafter, if it shall be deemed desirable.

The committee themselves voted to adopt the report, and also to report the same to the House, with the recommendation that the same be printed and recommitted.   For the committee:
GEORGE F. HOAR, Chairman.

Q

QUETELET, LAMBERT ADOLPHE JACQUES, a Belgian astronomer and statistician; born in Ghent, February 22, 1796; died at Brussels, February 16, 1874.   He developed from early childhood a remarkable aptitude for mathematical studies, and at the age of eighteen, having completed his university course, he was appointed Professor of Mathematics in the College of Ghent, and, five years later, was called to the same professorship in the Athenæum of Brussels.   In 1824 King William sent him to Paris, to complete his astronomical studies, and in 1826 he reported from that city a plan, which had met the approval of the learned astronomers of Paris, for an observatory at Brussels, which was commenced that year, and with the construction and direction of which he was charged.   He remained its director till his death.   From 1827 to 1829 he visited the observatories of England, Scotland, Germany, Switzerland, and Italy, and, his observatory being completed, settled himself to his life-work.   He employed his leisure moments in the preparation of statistical and astronomical works, of which he published a large number.   In 1841 he was appointed President of the Central Commission of Statistics.   In 1820 he had been elected a member of the Royal Academy of Belgium, and not long afterward was chosen its perpetual secretary.   He was a corresponding member of the French Institute, in the departments of Moral

and Political Sciences, and a member of most of the scientific societies and orders of the Continental states.   He had published: "Elementary Astronomy" (1826); revised and enlarged as "The Elements of Astronomy" in 1847; "Statistical Researches on the Kingdom of the Netherlands" (1830); "Plan of a Law for Public Instruction in Belgium" (1832); "Researches on the Births and Deaths and the Population of Belgium" (1832); "Criminal Statistics of Belgium" (1832); "On the Influence of the Seasons on the Mortality at Different Ages" (1838); "Letters addressed to the Duke of Saxe Coburg and Gotha, on the Application of the Theory of Probabilities to the Moral and Political Sciences (1846); "On the Social System and the Laws which govern it" (1848); "On Moral Statistics and the Principles which ought to form their Basis" (1848); "Annual Reports of the Royal Observatory of Brussels," 4to volumes (1833–1866); "History of Mathematical and Physical Sciences among the Belgians" (1865); "International Statistics" (with M. Heuschling), 4to (1865); "Mathematical and Physical Sciences among the Belgians at the Beginning of the Nineteenth Century" (1866); "Meteorology of Belgium compared with that of the Globe" (1867).   He had also furnished numerous papers and memoirs for the "Belgian Physical and Mathematical Correspondence," for the "Annals of the Observatory," etc., etc.

R

RAILWAY BRIDGE.   A bridge of novel construction, for the passage of railway-trains without hindering the navigation of the river, has been built for the Milwaukee & St. Paul Railroad at Prairie Du Chien, Wis.   The bridge is constructed on piles driven into the bed of the river, over which rests a single railroad track.   The length of the bridge is 7,200 feet.   There are two pontoon draws.   The one over the eastern channel consists of three pontoons, connected lengthwise firmly, and representing a distance of 396 feet.   The draw over the western channel consists of but one pontoon,

408 feet long, breadth of 28 feet, height of 4½ feet, and draught of 11 inches.   When trains are passing over, the draught of both draws increases to about 18 inches.   The varying height of the planes between the pile-bridge and the pontoons is overcome by aprons, or movable tracks, which are adjusted by means of powerful screws and movable blocks.   The connection between the ends of these aprons and the track on the bridge is a simple device, counterbalanced by equal weights, so that one man clamps and unclamps the end of the pontoon when swung into or out of position.   The

opening of each draw is effected by a small engine, with the current, in one minute, and the closing, against it, in three minutes. The direction of the current strikes the eastern draw at an angle of 75° 30′ and the western at an angle of 55°, thus leaving a clear space of 383 feet for the former channel and 334 feet for the latter, besides permitting the surface current to flow past the pontoons without expending its full force on them. It is commended on all hands by the pilots and river-men as not interfering with navigation. In relation to the passage of trains it is proved to afford greater security than ordinary drawbridges, for the pontoon is capable of floating a weight six times greater than that of the heaviest trains, and there is no danger of accident from the breaking of overstrained spans. It affords facilities for the passage of 1,000 cars a day, the average number being now about 300. The cost of the entire structure and its appurtenances is one-sixth of that of the most inexpensive bridge across the river, and one-fifteenth of the lowest estimates for constructing an iron drawbridge at the same point.

REFORMED CHURCHES. I. REFORMED CHURCH IN AMERICA.—The following is a summary of the statistical reports of this Church made to the General Synod at its annual meeting, June 3, 1874:

CLASSES.	Churches.	Ministers.	Communicants.
Albany	17	18	2,880
Arcot	17	9	731
Bergen	14	17	2,001
South Classis, of Bergen	11	11	1,492
Cayuga	12	10	1,274
Grand River	11	9	1,664
Geneva	19	17	2,098
Greene	10	10	1,397
Holland	16	14	9,019
Hudson	10	13	1,725
Illinois	20	21	1,936
Kingston	13	10	2,041
North Classis, of Long Island..	18	21	2,866
South Classis, of Long Island..	15	20	8,417
Michigan	9	10	542
Monmouth	8	11	1,125
Montgomery	23	16	1,920
Newark	11	15	2,077
New Brunswick	10	17	2,164
New York	19	29	4,582
South Classis, of New York...	6	11	1,259
Orange	25	24	3,535
Paramus	20	18	2,462
Passaic	13	17	1,856
Philadelphia	15	15	3,006
Poughkeepsie	11	17	2,136
Raritan	16	19	2,903
Rensselaer	13	12	1,895
Saratoga	16	14	1,504
Schenectady	12	15	2,304
Schoharie	12	11	928
Ulster	13	16	1,843
Westchester	14	18	1,714
Wisconsin	20	15	1,909
Total	489	520	69,149

The number of families connected with the Church is given at 43,099; number of catechumens, 22,764; number of Sunday-schools, 629; number of scholars in the same, 64,164; number of adult baptisms during the year, 951; number of infant baptisms, 4,378; number of candidates for the ministry, 9; amount of contributions for religious and benevolent purposes, $276,404; contributions for congregational purposes, $931,256.

The *General Synod* of the Reformed Church in America met at Poughkeepsie, N. Y., June 3d. The Rev. Goyn Talmage was chosen president. The committee appointed by the previous General Synod to take into consideration the whole subject of union, whether federal or organic, with other Presbyterian and Reformed Churches, presented a report of the conferences which they had held with the Committee of the Presbyterian Church in the United States of America (Northern), in the city of New York, January 15th and May 14th, and the conclusions which they had reached. It expressed the conviction that a closer union between the two denominations was desirable, particularly as regarded the interests of the missionary work in the newer parts of the country. It suggested that coöperation once begun in this department might in the end be advantageously extended to other branches of work, and ultimately, perhaps, result in the union of the Churches themselves. "A matter so large and so delicate as the union of these independent and historic Churches should in no way," the report continued, "be pressed to a conclusion, but should come about, if at all, as the result of the deliberate, well-informed, and general choice of the members of the two Churches." It was therefore considered premature to propose at this time any scheme of union in any form. Reference was made in the report to the distinct characteristics, historical relations, and denominational trusts and institutions of the two Churches, the adjustment of which would have to be carefully studied and guarded. A minority report was presented which advised the dismissal of all thought of organic union, but recommended the continuance of conferences for a revision and clearer understanding of the articles of correspondence, "with a view to obviate rivalry and promote coöperation in the field of domestic missions."

The following action was taken upon the subject of the reports, after which the consideration of the reports was indefinitely postponed, while the reports themselves were ordered to be printed in an appendix to the proceedings of the Synod:

Whereas, This Synod is constrained to believe that our Church is not prepared to effect an organic union with the Presbyterian Church of North America: therefore—

Resolved, That on this ground we must decline the appointment of a committee to continue the conference held so pleasantly with the committee appointed by the General Assembly of the Presbyterian Church.

Resolved, That in deferring action on this subject till the indications of Divine Providence shall have shown our Church ready for such movements as may lead to union, if that time shall ever come, we take special care to express our affection for and our confidence in the Presbyterian Church, which has, in a manner so courteous and honorable to ourselves, made overtures to us on this subject.

Resolved, That our delegate to the General Assembly of the Presbyterian Church in North America be instructed to lay before that esteemed body a proposition to appoint a committee to meet with a committee of the Synod of our Church to revise our articles of correspondence, with a view of giving practical expression to the close relations of our respective churches in sentiment and polity, as well as to secure better coöperation for the work given us as sister branches of the Church of Christ.

The recommendations of the same committee in relation to the Southern Presbyterian and German Reformed Churches were adopted as follows:

Resolved, That the Synod continue its Committee of Conference, to confer, in accordance with its present action, with the Presbyterian Assembly (South), and the Reformed Church in the United States (German).

The following resolution was also adopted:

Resolved, That while this Synod has declined to continue conference with the General Assembly of the Northern Presbyterian Church, on the basis of the report of the Committee of Conference, it directs its Committee of Conference, which it has now voted to continue, to confer with the Committee of the General Assembly (North) with regard to any correspondence with that Assembly, within the limits of the arrangements already made with the Southern Assembly.

The committee appointed to confer with a committee of the Southern Presbyterian General Assembly reported the proceedings of the joint meeting of the two committees which was held in the city of New York, February 27th, with the plan of coöperation which they had agreed upon.

In reference to this subject, the Synod

Resolved, That the aforesaid plan be, and the same is hereby, adopted entire (except as to the number of delegates by this Synod), as the basis of an intimate coöperative alliance such as is therein set forth; a union not organic, but nevertheless a union real and practicable, and one which it is believed will, under the Divine blessing, prove to be comfortable and useful to the two bodies that at length are happily brought into effective concert, and which, it is hoped, will redound to the honor and glory of the Great Head of the Church. And, in accordance therewith, the General Synod will now appoint one minister and one elder, with alternates, as corresponding members, to meet said General Assembly at its next annual session.

The Rev. H. D. Ganse and Elder Jonathan Sturges were, in accordance with this resolution, appointed primarii, and the Rev. Dr. J. Elmendorf and Elder S. R. W. Heath alternates. The following resolution was also adopted, bearing upon the same subject:

Resolved, That in accordance with the provisions of the plan, the various questions relating to the details of coöperation are referred to our Boards of Education, Publication, Foreign Missions, and Domestic Missions, respectively, who shall report as soon as practicable to this Committee of Conference, hereby reappointed, and that the committee shall consider and digest the information so obtained, with a view to continue the conference to such an end as shall be most to the glory of God and the interests of both denominations.

In response to an invitation to take part in the proposed Œcumenical Council of Presbyterian Churches (designated as Churches holding by the Westminster Standard), and to appoint a committee to correspond or confer with other committees on the subject, a committee of five persons was appointed, "to represent the Synod in arranging the time, place, and manner, of holding such a council."

The following action was taken for opening a correspondence with the Reformed Episcopal Church:

Resolved, That this Synod expresses cordial sympathy with the efforts of the Reformed Episcopal Church to establish and perpetuate pure and spiritual worship, and recognizes with pleasure the ministry and membership of that Church as forming with ourselves, and all our brethren of Christ's household, a part of the true Church of God upon earth.

Resolved, That, to express this feeling more strongly, the Synod will appoint, at this session, a delegate to convey to the Convention of the Reformed Episcopal Church our Christian salutations, and that our delegates suggest the expediency of an annual correspondence by delegates between that Convention and this Synod.

The committee who had been engaged in the revision of the Liturgy made a report of their work. The Synod approved so much of the Liturgy reported by them as is not inconsistent with or forbidden by the constitution, and gave permission to use the same, providing, however, that its action should not be construed as sanctioning any change in the baptismal form, or in the form for the administration of the Lord's Supper.

Thirty-one of the thirty-four classes made return of their action on the adoption of the revised constitution. Nineteen classes had voted in favor of adoption, and eight against. A clause separately submitted, in reference to the requirement of the presence of a deputation on certain occasions, was lost. A section requiring certain questions as to the preaching on the Heidelburg Catechism was retained. Twenty-two classes had voted in favor of the order of worship, and five against it. The new constitution, excepting the rejected articles, was declared to be in force from the day of the final adjournment of the Synod.

In regard to the Union Church in Yokohama, Japan, and to a proposition for an alliance of the Presbyterian and Reformed missions in India, the Synod

Resolved, That the resolution of 1864, in reference to the churches at Amoy, as far as the principle therein stated is applicable to this, be adopted, in regard to the Church of our Lord Jesus Christ in apan.

J *Resolved*, That the General Synod, from the slight information it possesses in regard to the Presbyterial Confederation in India, refers the matter of alliance, on the part of our brethren on that field, to their discretion, permitting such alliance in so far as it shall not conflict with their nearer relations to our own boards.

II. REFORMED CHURCH IN THE UNITED STATES. — *The Almanac for the Reformed Church in the United States*, published by the Reformed Church Publication Board, Phila-

delphia, gives the following statistics of the Church :

SYNODS.	Classes.	Ministers.	Congregations.	Members.	Unconfirmed Members.
United States........	9	192	427	64,129	32,914
Ohio.................	10	144	398	28,083	12,778
Northwest..........	8	109	179	12,717	10,877
Pittsburg............	6	60	133	10,276	8,936
Potomac.............	5	92	248	25,587	16,744
Total...........	38	597	1.325	135,702	82,249

Number of baptisms, 13,509; of confirmations, 7,790; of Sunday-schools, 1,187; of scholars in the same, 69,132; of students for the ministry, 67. Amount of benevolent contributions, $86,238.45.

Eleven English and five German papers are published in the interest of this Church. Four of them are weekly, two are published every other week, two are semi-monthly, seven are monthly, and one is quarterly.

The literary and theological institutions of the Church are as follows: Franklin and Marshall College, Lancaster, Pa.; Heidelburg College, Tiffin, Ohio; Catawba College, Newtown, N. C.; Mercersburg College, Mercersburg, Pa.; Clarion Collegiate Institute, Rimersburg, Pa.; Palatinate College, Meyerstown, Pa.; Greensburg Female Collegiate Institute, Greensburg, Pa.; Ursinus College, Collegeville, Montgomery County, Pa.; Calvin Institute, Cleveland, Ohio; Blairstown Academy, Blairstown, Iowa; Shelby College, Shelbyville, Ill.; Eastern Theological Seminary, Lancaster, Pa.; Western Theological Seminary, Tiffin, Ohio; Mission House, Howard's Grove, Wis.; Allentown Female College, Allentown, Pa.; St. John's Select School, Knoxville, Md.

The committees appointed by the Synods of the Reformed Church in the United States and the Reformed Church in America, to consider the expediency of organic union between the two bodies, met for consultation with each other at Philadelphia, November 18th. The Rev. Dr. Ganse, of the Reformed Church in America, and the Rev. Dr. Gerhardt, of the Reformed Church in the United States, were chosen joint chairmen of the meeting. A brief discussion took place on the tenets and forms of worship of the two denominations, after which the two committees held separate sessions in order to mature, if possible, some plan for union. A second joint session was held, at which the differences in ritual and doctrine between the denominations were subjected to a full discussion. These proved to be more important than it had been thought they would be; the representatives of the Reformed Church in America did not feel that they could admit the advanced ritualism to which a part of the Reformed Church in the United States professed to be attached, while the representatives of the latter body were not ready to recommend the reception of the Belgic Confession

and the Canons of the Synod of Dort, which the Reformed Church in America holds as of equal validity with the Heidelberg Confession. The subject was referred to a sub-committee of three from each denomination, with a view to their embodying the conclusions of the whole joint committee in a report. This committee brought back the following report, which was adopted, to be laid before the General Synods of the two Churches as the result of the conference:

The Committees of Conference appointed by the General Synods of the Reformed Church in the United States and the Reformed Church in America met in Philadelphia on the morning of November 18, 1874, and spent in joint sessions the greater part of that and the succeeding day. After a very free and brotherly interchange of information concerning the organization, symbols, doctrinal sentiments, and usages of the two denominations, the Committees agreed upon the following statement of the results of their conference:

1. Such large and obvious elements of likeness and sympathy as exist between the two bodies seem to point very plainly to some ultimate union between them. They are almost identical in name, as in origin and in early history. Their ecclesiastical organization and nomenclature of consistory, classes, synod, and general synod, are substantially the same. One venerable symbol, the Heidelberg Catechism, is held in common by the two denominations. The body of doctrine which either Church derives from this common symbol, of necessity has close and fundamental resemblances. The committees have found, moreover, a perfect unity of method and spirit in the devotional acts which they have performed together, and their whole interview has reminded them of the essential unity of their work of caring for those Continental Christians of the Reformed faith who are so widely distributed over the newer parts of our country. With these and similar points of contact between the two bodies, the committees cannot believe that they will abide apart.

2. The committees have further found, with gratification, that some elements of seeming difference between their two denominations have, upon fuller information concerning them, lost much of their apparent importance. In particular, the usage of confirmation prevails in the Reformed Church in the United States, and is unknown in the Reformed Church in North America, but, as it is interpreted in the constitution of the first-named Church, it is plain that it may fully consist with the principles and methods by which the other Church admits her baptized youth to full communion. It does not appear, therefore, that the continuance of that usage on one side, or the abstinence from it on the other, ought to be a decisive obstacle to union. The observance of festal religious days in the Reformed Church in the United States, though very general, is not enjoined, and therefore stands upon the same footing with the same observance as it prevails, though to a less extent, in the Reformed Church in America. Even such divergences as may exist in the matter of liturgical services, so long as they might not be seen to turn upon important differences of doctrinal belief, might be harmoniously adjusted. The committee, indeed, have little doubt that all the minor elements of difference which have grown up in the two Churches during their separate life could either be softened or accumulated in a cordial and intelligent attempt to bring these Reformed Churches under a single banner.

3. The committees, however, are constrained to say that some other obstacles to union seem to be of a less manageable character. The most patent of these lies in the fact that while both of these denom-

inations accept the Heidelberg Catechism, the Reformed Church in America adds to this symbol the Belgic Confession and the canons of the Synod of Dort. In order, therefore, to an organic union of the two bodies, the one or the other would be compelled to make a material change in its doctrinal standards. Since neither committee feels prepared to advise its Synod to make so important a concession, they can only agree in making a frank statement of this difficulty, in the hope that time and the best wisdom of the two denominations, and, above all, the Providence of God, may direct to its final solution. In addition to this, the probable fact that a body made up of these two denominations would include important differences in doctrinal views and ecclesiastical feeling, has appeared during the conference. These obstacles seem to preclude any further present negotiations in the direction of organic union. The committees, in conclusion, are fully persuaded that although their interview has developed no plan or distinct prospect of the organic union of their two churches, a real advance toward that most desirable result has been made in the frank and friendly conference which has now been held. The difficulty of merging denominations so old and so well established could not be expected to be small. It is something gained to be able to see at what point the obstacles are greatest. Not less valuable is that cultivation of brotherly acquaintance, esteem, and sympathy, which the conference has greatly furthered. The ultimate issue of their interview, the committee intrust to Christ, the one Head of the Universal Church, in the faith that He has kindled in these sister denominations the desire of union, and that He will not suffer the desire to fail.

A motion was then made that the General Synods of the two Churches be recommended to direct their Boards of Missions to ascertain if coöperation in the work of home and foreign missions would be practicable, but it was voted down. The committees then adjourned.

REFORMED EPISCOPAL CHURCH. The second General Council of the Reformed Episcopal Church met in the city of New York, May 13th. Seventeen clerical delegates, including the two bishops, and nineteen lay delegates, were present. Eight churches were represented. A telegram of congratulation was received from the Committee of the Free Church of England. The Standing Committee on Canons and on Revision of the Prayer Book, appointed at the meeting of the Council in December, 1873, presented their report. They had held six stated and six adjourned meetings, and had prepared a Constitution and Canons, and made certain revisions of the liturgy and offices, all of which were submitted for the action of the Council. The Constitution consists of fifteen articles. It defines the membership of the General Council to consist of bishops and presbyters with lay delegates, who shall be members of the congregations which they represent, and shall be chosen in the proportion of one delegate for every fifty members. The right of the bishops to sit in a separate house is denied. The bishop chosen president of a General Council is made presiding bishop of the Church for the next ensuing year. The General Council is given the right of defining the duties of the bishops, but it is provided that "any bishop may perform any act of the episcopal office in any church in

communion with this." Ministers, on ordination, are required to make a declaration of belief in the Holy Scriptures of the Old and New Testaments as the word of God, and containing all things necessary to salvation, and to promise to conform to the doctrine, discipline, and worship of the Reformed Episcopal Church, so long as they continue ministers of it. The article on decorations, rituals, and other adjuncts of the service, directs that "nothing calculated to teach, either directly or symbolically, that the Christian ministry possesses a sacerdotal character, or that the Lord's Supper is a sacrifice, shall ever be allowed in this Church. Nor shall any communion-table be constructed in the form of an altar, but shall be plain, and supported on an open framework."

The canons were for the most part adopted in the form in which they were reported by the Standing Committee. That in relation to wardens and vestrymen was made to direct that "the wardens and deputies shall be chosen from among the communicants, and, when practicable, the vestrymen also; in any case, the wardens, vestrymen, and deputies, shall be men of unimpeachable moral character." The canon on marriage and divorce, which is an exact transcript of the Protestant Episcopal canon, was referred to the Committee on Canons, to be reported upon at the next meeting of the General Council.

In the morning service an addition was made to the sentences introductory to worship, of the passage: "God is a Spirit; and those who worship Him must worship Him in spirit and in truth." The Confession, the prayers, the Venite, the Gloria in Excelsis, the Gloria Patri, the Te Deum, the Jubilate Deo, and the Benedictus, with their respective rubrics, were accepted. The words "he descended into hell" were omitted from the Apostles' Creed, but the rubric referring to this creed was so amended as to permit them to be used by those who desire to do so. Thus amended, the rubric was made to read: "Then shall be said the Apostles' Creed, by the minister and the people, standing. And any minister may insert the words, He descended into hell; or may, instead of them, use the words, He descended into the place of departed spirits, which are considered words of the same meaning in the Creed." The punctuation of the final paragraph of the Creed was changed so as to read as follows: "I believe in the Holy Ghost; the Holy Catholic Church—The Communion of Saints; The forgiveness of sins; The resurrection of the Body; And the Life Everlasting, Amen;" it being intended, by substitution of a dash for a semi-colon, to indicate that the words, The communion of Saints should be understood as defining and explaining the words, The Holy Catholic Church. The Nicene Creed was inserted with the following words appended to it: "[Note.—By 'One Catholic and Apostolic Church' is signified 'The Blessed Company of all faithful people ; ' and by ' One Baptism for the remission of sins, the Baptism of the Holy Ghost.']" The Declaration of Absolution was changed into a simple prayer for forgiveness made by the minister, still kneeling, as in the public confession. A rubric was attached to the prayer for those in authority, directing that it may be omitted when the Litany is used, and the prayer was amended so as to read, " Most heartily we beseech thee with thy favor to behold and bless the President of these United States, and all in authority, legislative, judicial, and executive," etc. The prayer for Congress was bracketed, to show that it is to be used only during the sessions of Congress. The Litany was adopted without change. The amendments made to the Morning Service were also adopted as to the corresponding parts of the Evening Service. The expression " Pardon and absolve," in the prayer for forgiveness, was changed to " pardon and accept." The alternate Evening Service was shortened. The Psalter in the Prayer Book of 1783, with the addition of the ten selections of psalms, as in the Protestant Episcopal Prayer Book, was adopted, with the provision, however, that the ten selections should be made to conform to the translation of Psalms as in King James's Bible. The Collects, Epistles, and Gospels of the Protestant Episcopal Prayer Book from the first Sunday in Advent to the twenty-fifth Sunday after Trinity, were adopted, but those for the Saints' days were excluded. The notice with reference to the invitation to the communion-table was amended so as to direct the use, by the minister, of the following or a similar form : " Our fellow-Christians of other branches of Christ's Church, and all who love our Divine Lord and Saviour Jesus Christ in sincerity, are affectionately invited to the Lord's table." The exhortation was amended so as to begin, " Dearly beloved in the Lord, ye who mind to come to this holy table of the Lord, must consider how St. Paul exhorted all persons to examine themselves," etc., the words " so is the danger great if we receive the same unworthily " were stricken out. The following form was prescribed for administering the elements : " Then shall the minister first receive the communion himself, and proceed to deliver the same to the ministers assisting, and after that to the people. And before delivering the bread, he shall say to all the communicants around the table : ' The body of our Lord Jesus Christ, which was given for you, preserve your bodies and souls unto everlasting life,' and when he delivereth the bread he shall say : ' Take and eat this bread in remembrance that Christ died for thee, and feed on Him in thy heart, by faith, with thanksgiving.' " The rubric and formula before delivering the cup were changed so as to correspond in style with that for the delivering of the bread. A rubric was adopted directing that " in conducting this service, except when kneeling, the minister

shall face the people, and at no time shall his back be turned to the congregation ; " and a note was appended, declaring that " the act and prayers of consecration do not change the elements, but merely set them apart for a holy use, and the reception of the elements in a kneeling posture is not an act of adoration."

In the order for the administration of baptism for infants, all references to confirmation and regeneration were stricken out, and the words " sanctification of water to the mystical washing away of sin " were omitted. A rule was adopted that, " in the event of neither of the parents of the child being a communicant, the child must be presented by at least one person who is a communicant of the Reformed or some other church." The reference to the signing of the cross on the child's forehead was omitted from the formula of baptism, but a note was added to the formula, permitting the making of the sign when the parents desire it. The formula and note are as follows : " Then shall the minister say : ' We receive this child into the congregation of Christ's flock ' [Note.—Here the minister may make the sign of the cross upon the child's forehead, if it is desired, and add, ' and do sign him with the sign of the cross, and pray,' etc.] ; ' and pray that hereafter he shall not be ashamed to confess the faith of Christ crucified, but manfully fight under his banner against sin, the world, and the devil, and continue Christ's faithful soldier and servant unto his life's end.' "

The question of the dedication of infants, and the preparation of a service suitable for such a purpose, was referred to the Committee on Doctrine and Worship. The " order of administration of baptism to adults " was considerably shortened. In the address to the persons to be baptized, the words of the old form, " desiring to receive holy baptism," were changed to " desiring to be baptized." In the rubric preceding the formula of baptism was substituted : " Then shall the minister take each person to be baptized by the right hand, and shall ask the witnesses the name, and then shall dip him into the water, or pour water upon him," etc.

A rubric was added to the confirmation service, declaring that " the administration of the order of confirmation is confined to the bishop, not as of divine right, but as a very ancient and desirable form of church usage." The references to the " bishop confirming " were stricken out from the service itself, and the applicant is represented therein as being " desirous of confirming his baptismal covenant." The handing of the ring to the minister was omitted from the marriage-service ; also the passage, " with all my worldly goods I thee endow ; " and the reference in the prayer to the married life of Isaac and Rebecca. The words " man and wife " were changed to " husband and wife." Several passages from the New Testament were added to the opening versicles in the order for the burial of the dead, and an additional lesson, from the gospel of St. John, describing the raising of Lazarus, was provided. The minister was also empowered to introduce any other passage of Scripture suited to the occasion. The use was allowed of a hymn and prayer in the "form for visitation of the sick," but the words, "the Catholic Church," in the prayer, were changed to "Thy Church." In order to provide more appropriately for the case of persons whose lives have been immoral or irreligious, the committal service was changed so as to read:

Forasmuch as it has pleased Almighty God, in his wise providence, to take out of this world the soul of our deceased brother, we therefore commit his body to the ground, earth to earth, ashes to ashes, dust to dust, awaiting the general resurrection on the last day and the appearing of our Lord Jesus Christ, at whose second coming in glorious majesty, to judge the world, the earth and the sea shall give up their dead, and the corruptible bodies of those who sleep in him shall be changed, and made like unto his glorious body, according to the mighty working whereby he is able to subdue all things unto himself.

The rubric preceding the words, "I heard a voice from heaven," etc., was made to read, "then may be said," instead of "then shall be said;" and provision was made that after that passage should be read, in case of the burial of a child, the words from St. Mark's gospel: "And the Lord Jesus Christ said, Suffer little children to come unto me, and forbid them not, for of such is the kingdom of heaven." To the "prayers and thanksgivings upon several occasions" were added a prayer for a person or persons traveling by land, and thanksgiving for a safe return from a journey and for deliverance from peril. The collect for Good Friday, as it appears in the Mission-Book of the Reformed Episcopal Church, was substituted for the form in the Protestant Episcopal Prayer Book. The title, "Form of ordaining Presbyters," was adopted instead of the form styled in the old Prayer Book, "The form and manner of ordaining priests." In this form the bishop, instead of "Right Reverend Father in God," is addressed as "Reverend brother in Christ." In the address of the bishop relative to the candidates, those present at the ordination, before whom it is delivered, are styled "brethren," instead of "good people;" and the words, "any impediment or notable crime, or any other reason," after the words, "if there be any of you who knoweth," were changed to, "any sufficient reason for which any of them ought not to be received." The words in the questions relative to the ministry of the doctrine and sacraments were changed from, "as this church has received the same according to the commandments of God," to, "As this church has set forth the same according to the teachings of the Holy Scriptures." The words "within your cures" are omitted. The requisition of obedience to bishops and other chief ministers is also left out. The prayer beginning "Receive the Holy Ghost," said in

connection with the laying on of hands, was changed so as to read: "Take thou authority to execute the office of a Presbyter in the Church of God, now committed unto thee, and be thou a faithful dispenser of the Word of God and of his holy ordinances. In the name of the Father, and of the Son, and of the Holy Ghost. Amen." All references to the laying on of hands were struck out, and the word sacraments was changed to ordinances. The power given to the minister to preach and administer the sacraments was left unrestricted, the words "in the congregations where thou shalt be lawfully appointed thereunto" in the old form having been struck out. In the office for the ordination of deacons, the power to baptize and administer the communion was not given. The "consecration" was substituted for the "ordination" of bishops. The order for the consecration of churches was changed so that the service may be performed without the presence of a bishop. In the order for the installation of pastors all that refers to the submissiveness of the laity to ministerial authority was excluded. The word "altar" was also omitted, and the words "Holy Church Universal" were substituted for "Holy Apostolic Church." A new office was adopted for the public reception of presbyters.

A plan of coöperation with the Free Church of England was adopted. It had been previously approved by the Committee of the Free Church. It provides that delegates be sent annually from the Convocation of the Free Church to the General Council, and from the General Council to the Convocation, with the right to take part in the deliberations of said bodies respectively; that the bishops and ministers of either church be allowed to participate in the consecration or ordination of bishops or ministers in the other church; that the ministers of either church shall be entitled to officiate transiently in the congregations of the other, and also to be eligible to a pastoral charge in either; that communicants of either church be received in the other on presentation of letters of dismissal; that congregations of either church may transfer their connection to the other; and that they pledge, each to the other, mutual coöperation, sympathy, and support. Bishop Cummins and Colonel J. B. Aycrigg were appointed delegates to attend the next Convocation of the Free Church of England, and the Rev. Walter Windemeyer and Mr. James H. Morgan alternates.

Before the General Council adjourned a sufficient sum of money was subscribed to pay, with the subscriptions expected from the regular congregations, the entire expenses of the church for one year, including the support of bishops and several missionaries, the publication of the Prayer Book, and incidental expenses.

According to a statement made by Bishop Cheney, in a sermon preached in December, 1874, the Reformed Episcopal Church had, at the close of one year after its organization, forty ministers, thirty-six churches, and upward of 8,000 communicants.

RHODE ISLAND. The adjourned session of the Rhode Island Legislature, which begun at Providence, on the 20th of January, continued until the 8d of April. A large number of acts were passed, but few of them have any general interest. Provision was made for dividing the town of North Providence, and annexing one portion to the city of Providence, and another portion to the town of Pawtucket, subject to the approval of the people concerned, to be ascertained by a vote on the question at the next election.

The law for the regulation of the traffic in intoxicating liquors was amended and made more stringent, but no special means were adopted for its enforcement. A joint special committee was also raised to sit during the recess, to consider the subject of intemperance, and report at the next session.

An act for the relief of convicts and their families, and convicts in the State-prison, which was passed, authorizes the inspectors of the State-prison to pay to convicts at the time of their discharge a sum of money not exceeding one-tenth of their earnings while in prison. In case a convict has been incapacitated for labor by sickness, he may receive a sum not exceeding one-tenth of the average compensation of convict-labor for the time of his sickness; but in all cases the inspectors may at their discretion pay the money to which a convict may be entitled under this act to his family during his imprisonment, instead of to him at his discharge.

The subject of granting the right of suffrage to women was referred to a special committee, together with all petitions, remonstrances and other communications relating to that matter. This committee made a report on the 3d of March, in which they argued at considerable length in favor of granting the privilege. After giving the oft-repeated reasons why women should be allowed to vote, this committee said:

And so every consideration impels us to the decision from which we see no escape. We rebelled from the mother-country to establish the truth of the proposition that taxation without representation is tyranny. Yet women are not allowed to represent their property. They should have the right that they may protect it. Women are the natural guardians and educators of children, and therefore should be members of school committees. Women best know the necessities of women, and therefore should be eligible as overseers of the poor, asylums, and hospitals. Women have as much at stake as men in all questions of social reform, and therefore should have equal facilities for assisting in framing and seeing to the execution of laws on such subjects. Women have equal right with men to the highest attainable wages, subject only to the law of supply and demand. This right they have not, so long as they are debarred by social prejudice, custom, and law, from competing equally with men for all positions they may choose to try to fill. The common law of England gave foreigners the right to claim that half the jury should be foreigners, yet women are compelled to submit to trial by men only, no matter

what motives of delicacy may prompt them to prefer a trial by women. It is a fundamental rule of equity, that all persons shall be tried by their peers. Yet women are tried by a male jury and male judges. To sum up: women are subject to law, and therefore should have the power to assist in framing laws and in their execution. If, as so often asserted, women are inferior to men, then the law should discriminate in their favor instead of against them. But, being their equals, women should be subject to all the duties and liabilities of men, and should be free to enjoy all their rights and privileges.

With the report was submitted the following resolution:

Resolved, a majority of all the members elected to each House of the General Assembly concurring herein, That the following article be proposed as an amendment to the constitution of the State, and that the Secretary of State cause the same to be published, and printed copies thereof to be distributed in the manner provided in Article XII. of the constitution.

ARTICLE.—Men and women, politically and legally, shall be entitled to equal rights and privileges, and shall be subject to equal duties and liabilities.

The subject was taken up in the House, and the resolution was adopted by a vote of 44 to 17, but it did not receive the sanction of the Senate.

The principal interest in the political campaign of the spring attached to the composition of the Legislature, in view of the fact that a successor to the Hon. William Sprague in the United States Senate was to be chosen, and some decided action was looked for on the subject of regulating or prohibiting the sale of intoxicating liquors. The first State Convention was held by the prohibitionists in the State-House at Providence, on the 26th of February. Immediately after the organization, a motion that the convention proceed to nominate a "distinct, separate, teetotal prohibition ticket for State officers" was carried, and the following nominations were made: For Governor, Henry Howard; for Lieutenant-Governor, W. F. Sayles; for Secretary of State, Joshua M. Addeman; for Attorney-General, Edwin Metcalf; for Treasurer, Henry Goffe.

A State Central Committee was chosen, consisting of two members from Providence County, and one each from the other four counties of the State. Several other members were afterward added to the committee. The following was adopted as the platform of the convention:

Resolved, That the progress of the cause of temperance, in the past fifty years of its history, is sufficient evidence that it is under the guidance of a Divine Providence—with its blessing we may expect a final victory.

Resolved, That while we recognize the prime importance of earnest work in educating the people up to the practice of total abstinence, we hold it to be the duty of the State to aid this work by enacting and enforcing prohibition.

Resolved, That we hold it to be the duty of Congress to prohibit the sale of alcoholic liquors to be used as a beverage in the District of Columbia and in the Territories.

Resolved, That we will put forth all reasonable efforts to secure the election of the ticket this day put in nomination.

Resolved, That we recommend to the consideration

of the State Executive Committee the publication of a daily campaign paper sustaining the principles and candidates of this convention.

The following was adopted after some warm discussion, as an independent resolution expressing the sentiments of the convention:

Resolved, That we heartily commend the faithful Christian efforts of the women of the West, which have been so eminently successful in inducing the dealers in intoxicating liquors to abandon the traffic.

The Republican State Convention was held in Representatives' Hall, Providence, on the 11th of March, and was in session just one hour. No platform was adopted, and all the nominations were made by acclamation, the ticket being as follows: For Governor, Henry Howard; for Lieutenant-Governor, Charles C. Van Zandt; for Secretary of State, Joshua M. Addeman; for Attorney-General, Willard Sayles; for General Treasurer, Samuel Clark.

The Democratic Convention met at Providence, on the 23d, and neither adopted a platform nor a ticket of candidates. After an organization had been effected, and a State Central Committee chosen, a motion was made to proceed to an informal ballot for a candidate for Governor, whereupon Mr. William B. Beach, of Providence, said the first question to be considered was, whether or not it was advisable to put a ticket in the field at this time. He had, after mature deliberation, come to the conclusion that it was not best to make a nomination at this time. "If we had a newspaper," he said, "so that we could reach the voters in this State, and they be notified that we had a ticket in the field, I should be in favor of making a nomination. There are reasons, plentier than blackberries ever were, why we should have a ticket and an organization in this State. I know there is corruption in high places, and I look forward to a time when we can come into power again and put a stop to it. There is a Kilkenny-cat fight going on among the ranks of the Republican party, for which I am glad. God give them speed to scratch each other's eyes out! There are general dissatisfaction and demoralization in their ranks, among themselves; but I don't know that we can aid that any by making a nomination to-day. I hope, by the time we want to make a presidential nomination, there will not only be a Democratic organ in this State, but that we shall have been punished enough, that the Democrats of this State will have been humiliated enough; that two dollars and a half won't be sufficient to buy a Democratic vote, or to keep a Democrat away from an election. I should like to have a general expression of opinion of the members of the convention as to whether it is, at this time, good policy to make a nomination." After some further discussion it was voted, 40 to 19, to indefinitely postpone the nominations, and the convention adjourned.

The election took place on the 1st of April. The official report of the result, made to the

Legislature at the May session, showed that 14,101 votes were cast for Governor, of which Henry Howard received 12,335, Lyman Pearce 1,589, and 177 were scattering: making Howard's majority over all others 10,569. The whole number of votes cast for Lieutenant-Governor was 14,181, of which Charles C. Van Zandt received 7,710, Wm. F. Sayles 6,348, and 123 were scattering; Van Zandt's majority, 1,239. Addeman received 12,492 votes for Secretary of State, a majority of 11,492; Willard Sayles received 12,552 for Attorney-General, a majority of 10,937; and Samuel Clark 8,495, and Henry Goff 5,447 for Treasurer. Benjamin T. Eames, Republican, was elected to Congress from the Eastern District by a vote of 2,842, against 824 for Wm. B. Beach, Democrat; in the Western District, Latimer W. Ballou, Republican, was elected by a vote of 2,362, against 1,235 for Daniel Rodman, Democrat. The Legislature consists of 26 Republicans and 10 Democrats in the Senate, and 59 Republicans and 13 Democrats in the House; making the Republican majority 16 in the Senate, 46 in the House, and 62 on a joint ballot. Three women were elected upon the school committee of the city of Providence.

The annexation of one portion of North Providence to the city of Providence, and of another to Pawtucket, was ratified in those places by large majorities. About 15,000 was added to the population of Providence by this action.

The regular session of the new Legislature began at Newport on the 26th of May, when the customary parade, and other ceremonies connected with the inauguration of the new government, took place. After a few days of the session at Newport, the sittings were transferred to Providence, and continued there until the 25th of June, when an adjournment was taken to the third Tuesday of January, 1875. A part of the business of the session was to choose a United States Senator to succeed the Hon. Wm. Sprague, but twenty-one ballots were taken, beginning with the 10th of June, and continuing from time to time until the day of adjournment, without reaching any result. The votes were taken in joint convention of the two Houses, called in this State the Grand Committee; and on the first ballot there were 107 votes cast, of which 39 were for Ambrose E. Burnside, 24 for Nathan F. Dixon, 13 for Amos C. Barstow, 10 for Henry Howard, 10 for Charles S. Bradley, 6 for Wm. P. Sheffield, 3 for Thomas A. Jenckes, 1 for Charles Hart, and 1 for Wm. W. Hoppin. No important variations appeared in the number of votes for the leading candidates from time to time, and on the twenty-first ballot Burnside received 42, Dixon 26, Barstow 19, Sheffield 7, Howard 5, and Jenckes 4.

The most important subject of legislation during the session was that of restraining the traffic in intoxicating liquors. A new and more stringent bill on the subject was passed, prohibiting any person to "manufacture or sell, or suffer to be manufactured or sold, by any person, except for the purpose of exportation; or keep or suffer to be kept on his premises or possessions, or under his charge, for the purpose of sale, within this State, any ale, wine, rum, or other strong or malt liquors, or any mixed liquors, a part of which is ale, wine, rum, or other strong or malt liquors, unless as is hereinafter provided.".

The only authority given for selling the liquors here enumerated is granted to persons authorized and licensed to sell medicines and poisons, and they can sell them "for medicinal, artistic, and mechanical purposes only, and not to be drunk on the premises of the seller."

No sale is allowed to a minor, "without a written request from his or her parent or guardian, or a physician's prescription, or to a person of known intemperate habits." Any person authorized to sell medicines and poisons, who shall violate this act, is subject to a fine of not less than $100 nor more than $500, and deprived of his privileges as a pharmacist. Any person not authorized by this act to sell liquors, who shall do so, is made subject to both fine and imprisonment, and "liable for all injuries which such purchaser may commit while in a state of intoxication, arising, in whole or in part, from drinking the liquors sold as aforesaid, in an action of the case in favor of the person injured." "An act in amendment of and in addition to" this, provides that "sales of liquor for medicinal purposes, under authority of section 8 of said last-named act, shall be made only upon and in accordance with a written prescription or prescriptions from a medical practitioner, and sales of liquor for mechanical or artistic purposes shall be made only upon receipt of a written statement, signed by the party purchasing, of the use to which the same is to be applied: *Provided*, That neither said act nor this section shall be construed to prevent the sale by registered pharmacists and others of flavoring extracts and essences similar to those heretofore in common use, nor by such pharmacists the sale of wine for sacramental purposes, and of articles enumerated in section two of said acts, to physicians and pharmacists." Any person obtaining liquor on false statements regarding the use for which it is intended is made subject to a fine of from $50 to $100.

For the purpose of securing the enforcement of the several measures prohibiting the sale of intoxicating liquors, "an act in relation to the preservation of the public peace," better known as the "Constabulary Act," was passed. This provides that the Governor shall appoint a State Constable, who shall appoint not more than seven deputies, to be approved by the Governor, who shall give bonds in $10,000 each for the restoration of any property that may be seized. Any person injured by a breach of the bond may bring an action thereon in the name of the General Treasurer for his own use. The Constable and deputies are appointed for one year, but are removable at the pleasure of the Governor. The powers and duties of the State constables are thus defined:

Section 8. The State Constable and his deputies shall have and exercise all the common law and statutory power of constables, except the service of civil process, and also all the powers given to special constables or State police by the General Statutes, concurrently with such officers, and also all powers given to sheriffs, chiefs of police, or other officers, relating to the inspection or assay of liquors, and their powers shall extend throughout the State.

Sec. 9. It shall be the duty of the constables of the several towns and cities of the State, city marshals, chiefs of police, and all other police-officers, to aid the State Constable and his deputies in the discharge of their duties, whenever reasonably notified and called upon for that purpose.

Sec. 10. The State Constable and his several deputies, in the due execution of their offices, are empowered to command all necessary aid and assistance in the execution of their said offices; and, if any person, when so required, shall refuse or neglect to give such aid and assistance, he shall be fined not exceeding twenty dollars.

While their powers are thus made general, the purpose of calling them into existence was to secure the enforcement of the prohibitory liquor law.

A petition was received from the Executive Committee of the Rhode Island Woman Suffrage Association, which, after speaking of the importance of keeping the idea of reformation prominently in view in the management of penal institutions, and the need of the special qualifications of women for the purpose, submitted the following bill for consideration:

The Board of State Charities and Corrections shall hereafter consist of twelve persons—two men and two women from the county of Providence, and one man and one woman from each of the other counties.

The members of the present board shall respectively hold their offices for the terms for which they were appointed, and men shall continue to be appointed their successors in the manner now provided by law.

In addition thereto, the Governor, with the advice and consent of the Senate, shall appoint six women to be members of the board, one of whom shall hold office for six years, one for five years, one for four years, one for three years, one for two years, and one for one year, from the — day of —, and shall, in like manner, annually, on the — day of —, appoint one woman to such office, who shall hold office for six years, unless sooner removed.

This was referred to a special committee, with instructions to report thereon at the next session of the General Assembly.

The State constabulary force was organized and began operations on the 15th of August. From that time to the 1st of January, 1875, 421 prosecutions were instituted by them, of which 108 were for maintaining liquor nuisances, 208 for selling liquor, 75 for keeping liquor for sale, and others for various offenses against the general laws of the State. Thirty-two seizures of liquors were made, amounting in all to 3,272 gallons, valued at something over $4,000. The amount of fines accruing to the State from suits pending at the close of the year was $11,120, at the lowest rate of fine imposed by law. With regard to the work of the constabulary force, the Governor said, in his message of January, 1875: "Having the opportunity of observing to some extent the interior working of the department, and painfully aware of the obstacles persistently placed in its way, I am surprised that a force of only eight men should have accomplished in so short a time so great an amount of work, and, I may also add, so great an amount of good. I unhesitatingly place upon record the commendation which these men have earned from the State, by their honest, energetic, and fearless discharge of duty."

There was in the State Treasury, the 1st of May, the beginning of the fiscal year, a balance of $294,306.08; and the receipts from that time to December 1st amounted to $255,395.74. The expenditures for the same period were $282,854.98, which left in the Treasury, December 1st, $266,846.84. The bonded debt of the State is as follows:

Bonds of Oct. 1, 1861, payable 1881	$500 00
" Sept. 1, 1862, " 1882	994,000 00
" April 1, 1863, " 1883	200,000 00
" July 1, 1863, " 1893	631,000 00
" Aug. 1, 1864, " 1894	738,000 00
Total	$2,563,500 00

The bonds are held at a premium, and, as the act authorizing their purchase before maturity requires that they shall be bought at a price not exceeding the par value, no reduction of the debt was made during the year.

The school-system of Rhode Island is one of the most efficient in the country. The number of children between the ages of five and fifteen in the State is 43,800. Of these, 39,401 attended school at least one day during the year ending April 30, 1874. The average number belonging to the schools was 30,165, the aggregate attendance 24,434. The number of schools was 732, an average of 13 over the previous year; the average length of schools was 8 months and 19 days; number of teachers employed, 805, an increase of 47. The average compensation per month of male teachers was $83.65, an increase of $7.95; average compensation per month of female teachers, $43.86, an increase of $1.89. There were 52 evening-schools, with an aggregate length of 13¼ weeks, in which the number of different pupils enrolled was 6,083, and the average attendance 2,930. The entire receipts from all sources throughout the State, for school purposes, were $745,769.60; expenditures, $690,851.53.

Some important changes were made at the State Farm during the year. The old workhouse was remodeled and converted into an almshouse, at a cost of $7,669.85. The new Workhouse and House of Correction was completed, and the buildings of the Insane Asylum were put in repair. On the 1st of January there were in the Workhouse and House of

Correction 190 men and 67 women; during the year, 333 men and 145 women were committed; 37 escaped men were returned, 334 men and 152 women were discharged, 81 men and 2 women escaped, 3 men and 1 woman died, and at the end of the new year 142 men and 57 women remained in the institution. The inmates are employed about the farm and buildings, and in making baskets and seating chairs. The Asylum for the Incurable Insane contained 78 men and 79 women at the beginning of the year; 28 men and 22 women were received, and 10 men and 14 women discharged, during the year, 4 escaped, 2 escaped inmates were returned, and 9 died. The Almshouse was opened on the 1st of August. From that date to January 1, 1875, 64 men, 72 women, 31 boys, and 29 girls, were received, including 2 boys and 5 girls born in the establishment; 8 men, 19 women, 13 boys, and 7 girls, were discharged; 3 men, 4 women, and 1 girl, died; and at the end of the year 53 men, 49 women, 18 boys, and 21 girls, 141 inmates in all, remained. Work has begun on the new State-prison, and the inmates of the Workhouse are employed upon it to some advantage. The cost of supporting the institutions on the State Farm, under the direction of the Board of State Charities and Correction, for the year, was $100,954.11; the estimates for 1875 are $112,000.

There are 37 institutions for savings in the State, with 98,359 depositors, having an average of $495.85 on deposit. The total amount of deposits is $48,771,501.86; increase over previous year, $2,154,318.83. The total resources and liabilities of the savings-banks amount to $50,540,703.19.

There are seven stock-insurance companies chartered by the General Assembly of the State, with a paid-up capital of $1,300,000; gross assets, $2,110,428; liabilities, $587,054; surplus, $1,523,394. Besides, there are 35 companies of other States and 15 of foreign countries, doing business in Rhode Island. There are also 16 mutual companies with State charters, and 7 from other States.

The Rhode Island militia force consists of 44 general and staff officers, 36 cavalry, 53 artillery, and 220 infantry officers, under commission; and 221 enlisted men in the cavalry, 282 in the artillery, and 1,972 in the infantry; making a total of 2,799 men. The entire enrolled militia, comprising all persons between the ages of eighteen and forty-five, liable to service under the United States laws, numbers 34,263.

RINEHART, WILLIAM H., an American sculptor of rare genius, born in Carroll (near Frederick) County, Md., in 1827; died at Rome, Italy, October 28, 1874. His father was a farmer, and gave him a good common-school education, and he worked on the farm, and in a marble-quarry which had been discovered on it, till he came of age. Developing a remarkable aptitude for carving in stone, he then went to Baltimore to acquire the stone-cutter's trade, and there was employed till 1854, having meantime displayed genius of a high order in his sculptures in monuments, mantles, etc. During this period he had carved directly from the block, without modeling, several small portrait busts, of great excellence; a statuette of a negro cutting stone, in black marble; a finely-chiseled bouquet; a group after Teniers's "Smokers;" and many other small pieces. In 1854 he went to Italy, and pursued the study of his art at Florence for two years, with very scanty means and under great privations. He returned in 1856, very poor, but bringing with him the two reliefs of "Night" and "Morning," which soon attracted attention and brought him many orders. He modeled at this time two caryatides, which are now the supporters of the great clock of the House of Representatives; a head of Moses, intended for the Capitol; and completed the bronze doors of the Capitol, which Crawford had left unfinished at his death. In 1858 Mr. Rinehart returned to Italy, and thenceforward made Rome his home, except one or two excursions to the North of Europe, and two visits to the United States in 1860 and 1873. During this time he produced the works of art which have established his reputation; among them the bronze doors of the Capitol at Washington, the statuettes on the clock of the House of Representatives, the statue of the fountain at the General Post-Office, the colossal bronze statue of Chief-Justice Taney, at Annapolis; a number of ideal figures in marble—"Clytie" (owned by the Peabody Institute, Baltimore), probably his best work; "Hero;" "Antigone;" "Endymion;" the "Woman of Samaria;" the "Christ" and the "Angel of the Resurrection," both in Loudoun Park; and many portrait busts. Mr. Rinehart returned to Baltimore in the autumn of 1873, to superintend the erection of the Taney statue. He went back to Rome in the spring of the following year, taking with him a large number of orders, only a few of which he lived to fulfill. His last finished work—a companion figure to his famous "Clytie"—was "Atalanta." Early last summer his failing health compelled him to abandon his work and seek relaxation among the mountains of Switzerland. But he derived no benefit from his sojourn there, and in October he was taken back to his studio in Rome, where a few days later he died. He left by will the greater part of his estate to be applied for art uses.

ROMAN CATHOLIC CHURCH. The pontificate of Pius IX., already far advanced in history, was continued through the year 1874. No important bull or encyclical addressed to the whole Church recognizing his authority was issued till the close of the year, when, on the 24th of December, he issued the following Encyclical, announcing the Jubilee of the year

1875, but without the accustomed ceremonies at the Porta Santa:

ENCYCLICAL LETTER OF POPE PIUS IX., ANNOUNCING A JUBILEE.

To all the Patriarchs, Primates, Archbishops, Bishops, and other Ordinaries of Places having Grace and Communion with the Apostolic See, and to all Faithful Christians.

VENERABLE BROTHERS AND BELOVED SONS, HEALTH AND APOSTOLICAL BENEDICTION: Moved not only by the grave calamities of the Church and of this century, but also by the necessity of imploring Divine aid, we have never omitted in the time of our pontificate to arouse the Christian people, in order that they might strive to appease the majesty of God and merit celestial clemency by holy habits of life, by works of penitence, and by pious and dutiful continuance in prayer. To this end we have, with apostolic liberality, several times opened to the faithful the spiritual treasures of the indulgences in order that, animated thereby to true penitence and purged by the sacrament of reconciliation from the stains of sin, they might be able to approach the throne of grace with more confidence, and be worthy of their prayers being benignantly received by God. This also, as at other times, we especially considered our duty to fulfill on the occasion of the Œcumenical Vatican Council, in order that the very grave work undertaken for the benefit of the Universal Church might at the same time, by the prayers of the whole Church, be furthered in the sight of the Almighty; and, although the celebration of the same Council remained suspended, through the calamities of the times, we nevertheless declared and made known for the good of the faithful people that the indulgence to follow it in the form of a jubilee, promulgated on that occasion, continued, as it still remains, in all its force, firmness, and vigor.

IN PEACEFUL TIMES.

Nevertheless, the course of these sorrowful times still continuing, behold the commencement of the seventy-fifth year after the eighteenth century of the Christian era—the year, that is to say, which marks that sacred space of time which the holy custom of our elders and the ordinations of the pontiffs our predecessors consecrated to the celebration of the Universal Jubilee. With what respect and religious feeling the year of the Jubilee was observed when the tranquil times of the Church permitted them to celebrate it with every solemnity, both ancient and recent historical monuments testify, for it was always looked upon as the year of salutary expiation by the whole Christian people, as the year of redemption and of grace, of the remission of sins and of the indulgence, in which they assembled from all the world in this our *alma* city and seat of Peter, and all the faithful, aroused to works of piety, offered for the health of souls most abundant aids of reconciliation and of grace. What a pious and holy solemnity was seen in this our century when, the Jubilee of the year 1825 having been intimated by Leo XII. of blessed memory, our predecessor, this benefit was received by the Christian people with so much fervor that the said Pontiff could rejoice in having seen during the whole course of the year a never-interrupted concourse of pilgrims in this city, and through which was marvelously manifested the splendor of religion, piety, faith, love, and all the virtues. O that such were was to-day our condition, and the condition of civil and sacred things, as to permit us happily to celebrate, according to the ancient rites and customs which our elders used to observe, that solemnity of the great Jubilee, which, occurring as it did in the year 1850, of this century, it was necessary to omit because of the mournful circumstances of the times! But those grave causes which at that time impeded us from intimating the Jubilee, so far from having ceased, have instead—God so permitting it—increased daily. Nevertheless, observing the many evils which afflict the Church, the many efforts of her enemies directed to tear the faith of Christ from souls, to corrupt her sound doctrines, and to propagate the poison of impiety; so many scandals which present themselves everywhere to true believers, the depravity of manners so widely spread, and the infamous emancipation from divine and human duties so amply diffused, so fecund of ruin, and which tends to destroy all sense of rectitude in the souls of men; and considering that in such a flood of evils still more should we endeavor, in accordance with our apostolic duty, that faith, religion, and piety, should be fortified and awakened, that the spirit of prayer be fomented and increased, that the fallen be aroused to penitence of heart and to the mending of their ways, that the sins which merit the wrath of God be redeemed by holy works, all fruits to the obtaining of which the celebration of the great Jubilee is principally directed — we thought that it was not our duty to permit that on this occasion the Christian people should be deprived of this salutary benefit, observing that form which is permitted by the condition of the times, in order that thus comforted in the spirit they may walk in the way of righteousness with greater alacrity, and, purged from sins, more easily and more richly merit the divine propitiation and pardon.

A CALL TO THE CHURCH MILITANT.

Let, then, the Universal Church Militant of Christ receive our utterances, with which we intimate, announce, and promulgate the great and universal Jubilee during the whole of the coming year 1875, for reason of which we, suspending and declaring suspended at our good will and pleasure, and of this Apostolic See, the indulgence above mentioned, conceded in form of Jubilee for the occasion of the Vatican Council, open in all its amplitude that celestial treasure which, formed by the merits, sufferings, and virtue of the Lord Christ and of His Virgin mother, and of all the saints, was intrusted by the Author of human salvation to our dispensation. In the mean time, relying upon the mercy of God and on the authority of His blessed apostles Peter and Paul, by virtue of that supreme power of binding and loosing which God willed to be conferred upon us, however unworthy—to all and every one of the faithful of Christ, whether living in this our *alma* city, or who shall be about to come to it; as well as to all those existing outside the said city, in whatever part of the world, and who are in the grace of, and in obedience to, the Apostolic See, and who, having truly repented, confessed, and communicated once a day for fifteen days, continuous or interrupted, natural or ecclesiastic, to be computed, that is, from the first vespers of one day until the full evening twilight of the day following, shall, as regards the first, visit the basilicas of the Saints Peter and Paul, of St. John Lateran, and of Santa Maria Maggiore, in Rome; and, as regards the second their principal or cathedral church and other three churches of the same city and place, or of the suburbs of the same, to be designated by the ordinaries of the places, or by their vicars, or by others by order of the same, after this our letter shall have come to their notice, and shall there offer up humble prayers to the Lord, according to our intention, for the prosperity and exaltation of the Catholic Church and of this Apostolic See, for the extirpation of heresies, for the conversion of all erring, for the peace and unity of all Christian people—we concede and mercifully bestow in the Lord that once in the course of the year above mentioned may be obtained the full indulgence of the year of Jubilee and full remission and pardon for all their sins; which indulgence we concede may be applied by "means of suffrage," and be available for those souls which, united to God by charity, shall have left this world.

RULES AND DISCIPLINE.

In virtue, also, of this our present letter, we concede that the travelers by sea or by land who, as soon as they shall have returned to their homes, or shall have reached a fixed dwelling-place, completed the work above described, and visited as many times the cathedral, principal or parochial church of the place of their domicile or dwelling, can and shall be able to obtain the same indulgence. Likewise, we concede, in virtue of this our present letter, to the above-mentioned ordinaries of the places, that they may, according to their prudent counsel, dispense solely as regards the visits, the oblate nuns, the girls and women living in the cloisters of monasteries or in other pious or religious houses or communities, as well as anchorites, and hermits, and other persons, whoever they may be, whether laymen, ecclesiastics, or regulars, existing in prison or in captivity, or affected by some infirmity of body, or prevented by any other impediment which makes it an absolute impossibility for them to perform the said visits; to children, also, not yet admitted to first communion, we concede that they may also dispense from the prescribed communion, prescribing to them, all and every one, be it to themselves, be it by means of their superiors or regular prelates, or by means of prudent confessors, other works of piety, charity, and religion, in place of the visits or of the sacramental communion which should be fulfilled by the same; and, with regard also to chapters and congregations, whether secular or religious, to companies, confraternities, universities, which shall processionally visit the above-named churches, we concede that they may reduce the prescribed visits to a lesser number; and also to the said nuns and their novices we concede that they can to this effect select any one among the confessors, approved by the actual ordinary of the place where their monastery is situated, to hear the confessions of the nuns; and to all and every one of the other faithful of both sexes, whether lay or ecclesiastic, and to the regulars of whatever order, congregation, and institute, which has yet to be specially named, we concede license and faculty that they may to the same effect select whatever priestly confessor, whether secular or regular, of whatever different order or institute, and at the same time approved for hearing confessions of secular persons by the actual ordinaries in the cities, dioceses, and territories, where they will have to hear the said confessions; by those confessors, within the period of the above-mentioned year, those men and women who sincerely and seriously have undertaken to obtain the benefit of the present Jubilee, and, with this intention of benefiting by it, and to complete the other works necessary to do so, shall approach them to make their confessions, for this time and only *in foro conscientiæ* can absolve them from excommunication, suspension, and other ecclesiastical sentences, and censures threatened and inflicted *a jure vel ab homine*, for whatever cause even reserved to the ordinaries of the places and to us, or to the Apostolic See, and which otherwise, in whatever concession, however ample, would not be understood as conceded.

Equally may the same confessors absolve the above-named penitents from all the sins and excesses, however serious and enormous they may be, as has been said, reserved to the said ordinaries and to us, or to the Apostolic See, enjoined to them as a salutary penitence, and other things to be enjoined by right; as also they shall be able to commute into other pious and salutary works whatsoever vow, even sworn and reserved to the Apostolic See (excepting, however, vows of chastity, of religion, and of obligation, which may have been accepted by a third person, or which may be to the prejudice of a third person, not to say the penal vows, which are called preservatives from sin, unless the commutation may not be judged such, as that, not less than the first material of the vow, it may prevent the commission of sin); and, finally, with the same authority and fullness of apostolic benignity, we concede and permit that they may dispense such penitents, even among the regulars constituted in sacred orders, from secret irregularity in the exercise of the said orders, and to ascend to the other superiors, contracted solely through violation of censures.

We do not intend, however, in force of these presents, to dispense from whatsoever other irregularity —whether public or secret, whether wanting or known—or from whatsoever other incapacity or inability, in whatsoever way contracted, or to grant any faculty for dispensing from the same, or to rehabilitate and restore into the primal state even *in foro conscientia;* nor yet do we intend to derogate from the constitution, with the opportune declarations given forth by Benedict XIV., of blessed memory, our predecessor, which begins, "*Sacramentum pænitentiæ,*" dated the 1st of June, in the year 1741, the first of his pontificate. Neither, finally, do we intend that these same, our letters, can or ought to benefit those who by us and by the Apostolic See, or by whatsoever other prelate or ecclesiastical judge, may have been by name excommunicated, suspended, interdicted, or declared fallen under other sentences or censures, or publicly denounced, unless within the limit of the present year they may not have satisfied or come to an arrangement where needful with the others. For the rest, if any, having the intention of gaining this Jubilee, after having commenced the fulfillment of the prescribed works, overtaken by death, shall not be able to accomplish the prescribed number of visits, we, desiring to fill up the measure of their pious and ready intention, will that the said persons, truly penitent, confessed and communicated, may participate in the aforesaid indulgence and remission in the same manner as if they had in the prescribed days really visited the aforesaid churches. If any, however, after obtaining on the strength of these presents the absolution from the censures or the commutations of their vows or the aforesaid dispensations, shall change that serious and sincere intention otherwise necessary to benefit by this jubilee, and thereby fail to complete the works necessary to gain it, although by this same they can scarcely consider themselves blameless, we, nevertheless, decree and declare valid the absolutions, commutations, and dispensations, obtained with the aforesaid dispositions. We also will and decree that these present letters be fully valid and effective, and have and obtain their plenary effect wherever they are published and put in execution by the local ordinaries, and that they be of use to all the faithful of Christ who remain in the grace and obedience of the Apostolic See, and who are either living in the several jurisdictions or have just reached them on their journeys by land or sea; notwithstanding the constitutions about not granting indulgences *ad instar* and the other apostolic constitutions, and the constitutions, ordinances, and the general or special reservations of absolutions, relaxations, and dispensations, decreed in general, provincial, and synodal councils, as well as the statutes, laws, customs, and uses, of every mendicant or military order, congregation, or institution, even though confirmed by oath, or apostolic approval, or any other kind of ratification, as well as privileges, pardons, and letters apostolic, granted to the same, especially those in which the professors of any order, congregation, or institution, are expressly prohibited from confessing themselves outside their own community. With regard to which things, all and singular, although for their complete repeal, a special, specific, express, and individual mention should be made of them and of their whole tenor, or some special form should be made—nevertheless, we, holding as though their full tenor were inserted, and such form were most accurately adhered to, for this occasion and only for the above-indicated purpose, repeal them fully, as we repeal every thing else to contrary effect.

While thus by the apostolic office which we exercise, and through the solicitude with which we are bound to embrace the whole flock of Christ, we propose the salutary opportunity of obtaining remission and grace, we cannot abstain from beseeching and adjuring by the name of Jesus Christ our Lord, the Prince of Pastors, all the patriarchs, primates, archbishops, bishops, and other local ordinaries, prelates, and those who are legitimately exercising the office or the ordinary jurisdiction of the above said bishops and prelates in their stead, who maintain grace and communion with the Apostolic See, that they announce so great a benefit to the people committed to their charge, and that they give all diligence in order that all the faithful, being reconciled to God by penance, may turn to the gain and profit of their souls the grace of the Jubilee. Therefore, your first care, venerable brethren, after having implored with public prayers the divine clemency to fill the minds and hearts of all with His light and grace, shall be to direct, by means of timely instruction and admonition, the Christian people to perceive the fruit of the Jubilee, so that they may understand accurately what are the force and the nature of the Christian Jubilee for the profit and advantage of souls in which with a spiritual reason are abundantly fulfilled by virtue of the Lord Christ those benefits, which among the Jewish people were promised by the law on the return of every fiftieth year, and so that they may be still sufficiently instructed with regard to the force of indulgences, and of all those things which ought to be performed for the fruitful confession of sins, and for the holy receiving of the sacrament of the eucharist. Because then-not only the example but the whole work of the ecclesiastical ministry is necessary in order that the fruits of the desired holiness may be had among the people, do not omit, venerable brethren, to excite the zeal of your priests, willingly and readily to exercise their ministry particularly in this time of salvation; for which and for the common good, it will certainly conduce much, when it can be done, if they, preceding the Christian people with the example of piety and religion, will, by means of spiritual exercises, renew the spirit of their holy calling, so that they may employ themselves more usefully and salutarily in the discharge of their own offices and in the sacred missions to be directed to the people according to the order and method prescribed by you. Since, therefore, at the present time so many are the evils which need to be repaired and the benefits which need to be sought, drawing the sword of the spirit, which is the Word of God, give every heed that your people be led to detest the immense sin of blasphemy, the violation of which nothing at the present time is too sacred to escape, and that they be led to know and fulfill their duties about the holy observance of the festival days and about the laws of fasting and abstinence to be observed according to the prescription of the Church of God, and this to avoid those punishments which the contempt of such things has called down upon the earth. So likewise let your anxious zeal watch constantly over the maintenance of discipline among the clergy and securing the right ordering of the clergyman, and in every possible way give assistance to the youth around you, who are placed in so many dangers and who are subjected to so many great perils. You certainly are not ignorant. This kind of evil was so bitterly sad for the heart of the Divine Redeemer himself as to cause him to utter against the authors of the same these words: "Whosoever shall offend one of these little children that believe in me, it were better for him that a millstone were hanged about his neck and he were cast into the sea" (St. Mark ix. 41). Nothing then is more worthy of the time of the Holy Jubilee than being unweariedly occupied in every work of charity; this, then, also shall be the duty of your zeal, venerable brethren, the adding of stimulus, so that the poor may be relieved, sins may be redeemed with alms, the benefits of which are shown to be so numerous in Holy Scripture; and that the fruit of love may be greater and more lasting, shall be very opportune if the funds supplied by charity are directed to aid or establish those pious institutions which at the present time are considered most conducive to the well-being of souls and bodies. If to obtain these benefits your minds and efforts are united, it cannot fail but that the kingdom of Christ and His righteousness shall receive great increase, and that in this acceptable time and in these days of salvation the divine clemency shall pour upon the sons of love a great abundance of heavenly gifts.

To you, finally, all ye sons of the Catholic Church, we direct our discourse, and you, each and all, we exhort with paternal affection so to make use of this opportunity of the Jubilee to obtain pardon as the sincere pursuit of your salvation requires of you. If at all times it is necessary—now more especially is it so—most beloved sons, to cleanse the conscience from dead works, to offer the sacrifices of righteousness, to bring forth fruits meet for repentance and to sow in tears that you may reap in joy. The Divine Majesty sufficiently shows what he requires from us, while now, for a long time, through our depravity, we are laboring under His threatenings and under the inspiration of the spirit of His anger. In truth, "men are accustomed when they are suffering under a too hard necessity, to send embassadors to neighboring nations to receive some aid. We, as is better, send an embassy to God himself;" from Him we implore aid, to Him we turn with all our hearts, with prayers, and fastings, and alms. For, "the nearer we are to God the further shall our enemies be driven from us" (S. Maxim., Hom. xci.). But do ye chiefly hear the apostolic voice because we are embassadors of Christ. Ye who labor and are heavy laden, and who, departing from the path of salvation, are oppressed by the yoke of depraved desires, and by the slavery of the devil, do not despise the riches of the goodness and patience and long-suffering of God, and while there is opened out before you so easy and broad a way for the obtaining of pardon, do not, by your obstinacy, render yourselves inexcusable before the Divine Judge, and lay up for yourselves a treasure of wrath in the day of wrath, and of the revelation of the just judgment of God. Return, therefore, sinners, be reconciled to God; the world passeth away, and the lust thereof; cast off the works of darkness, put on the armor of light; cease so to be the enemies of your own souls, so that you may at the last merit peace in this world, and in the world to come the eternal rewards of the just. These are our desires, these things we will not cease to ask from the most merciful Lord, and these same benefits—all the sons of the Catholic Church being united to us in this society of prayer—we trust we can obtain accumulatively from the Father of Mercies. Meanwhile, for the successful and salutary fruit of this holy work, let the auspicious omen of all grace and heavenly gift be the apostolic benediction, which from our inmost heart we affectionately grant in the Lord to you all, venerable brethren, and to you beloved children, as many as are numbered within the Catholic Church.

Given in Rome, near St. Peter's, the 24th of December, of the year 1874, and twenty-ninth of our pontificate. POPE PIUS IX.

A document purporting to be a brief of Pius IX., regulating the next papal election, was issued in Germany, but proved to be spurious, and was disavowed at Rome. The question of the coming election was, however, taken up by the German Government in its relations with that of Italy. During the year the Pope, in answer to various delegations, pronounced a number of allocutions, all bearing on the actual condition of the Church in Italy and throughout the world. On the 17th of June, in reply to an address from Cardinal Patrizi, Dean of the Sacred College, on the occasion of the twenty-ninth anniversary of his election, Pius IX. delivered the following allocution, bearing on attempts made to bring about terms between the Holy See and the Italian Government:

As afflictions grow greater, as contradictions and the infernal rage against the Church of Jesus Christ and against the Holy See increase, so also there increase in this Sacred College its firmness and constancy in sustaining the rights of the Spouse of Jesus Christ and the seat of His Vicar. The words spoken by his Eminence, the Cardinal Dean, prove that with the growth of evil there corresponds the growth of your efforts and of your labors to combat it. And it should be so, because it is your duty to share with me in the administration and the government of the universal Church. In fact, at this moment, while the Church is so maltreated and persecuted, we see flowing to Rome demands for instruction, for counsel, and for decisions. The congregations are more frequented, and it appears that the Catholic world more than ever has its eyes fixed upon the centre of unity and this chair of truth, that it may receive from it light to guide it in the midst of the terrible storms that agitate it. And, since it has pleased God to permit me to begin the twenty-ninth year of my pontificate, this occasion appears to me opportune to renew certain acts which cannot long be neglected, so as not to lead into error men of good faith, and not to give any pretext to the enemy to offer in opposition customs and prescriptions. Then, in the presence of this august assembly which surrounds me, I repeat the most solemn protests against the usurpation of the temporal dominions of the Holy See, against the spoliation of the religious orders, and, in fine, against all the sacrilegious acts committed by the enemies of the Church of Jesus Christ. In renewing these protestations I have, besides, a motive suggested by an extraordinary circumstance. A little time ago some people addressed me, as well viva voce as by writing, certain desires tending to establish a rapprochement between us and the new-comers. The last letter, which is still upon my table, is written with much calmness and respect. They tell me in it that, being the Vicar of a God of peace, I ought to pardon all the enemies of the Church, and remove the excommunications with which I have loaded their consciences.

And observe here that the revolutionaries are of two kinds—one has imagined and brought to its term the revolution; the other has adhered to it while dreaming of happiness, of progress, and of some unknown earthly paradise, without seeing that they would reap tribulations, torments, and a thousand miseries. The first, obstinate in their hearts, are the Pharaohs of our age; hard as the millstone; an act of the greatest goodness would not soften them. The second (to whom belong those who speak to me in a low voice and who write to me with sentiments of moderation), seeing that the earthly paradise has vanished, that to wealth, to riches, to the prosperity of which they dreamed, there has succeeded a deluge of evils, with taxes and enormous oppressions, experience stings of conscience for having coöperated in producing this state of things, and they appeal to my "sentiments of peace." But what peace can I have with them? They experience stings! And for what good? Saul experienced them also when, wounded to death, and to be delivered from them, he prayed the Amalekite soldier to kill him. "Stand over me and slay me, since distress overwhelms me." And the soldier dared to kill him, and took away from him that little life which remained to him, for which he was mortally punished by David. And what do they aim at? That the Pope will become for them an Amalekite soldier, or that the Pope should imitate the suicide of the unhappy Saul? Oh, insensate counsels! If the Amalekite did not escape the chastisement of David, could the Vicar of the Eternal Bishop of our souls escape the chastisement of God? They ask for peace; they ask for a truce; they ask, I say, for a *modus vivendi!* And is a *modus vivendi* (a way of living) possible with an adversary who is continually armed with a *modus nocendi* (way of hurting), with a *modus auferendi* (a way of stealing), with a *modus destruendi* (way of destroying), with a *modus occidendi* (a way of killing)? Can the calm ever be reconciled with the tempest which bellows and rises up, beating down every thing, tearing up the roots and destroying all that it finds in its way?

What shall we do, then, venerable brethren, we to whom it has been said, "*Statis in domo Dei, et in atriis domus Dei nostri*" (you stand in the house of God and the halls of the house of God)? We shall be united with the Episcopate which in Germany, in Brazil, and in all the Church gives luminous proofs of constancy and firmness. We will unite ourselves to it and to all the souls dear to our Lord, and we shall be constant in prayer, demanding patience and courage to combat our enemies; but not with sword in hand, for Jesus Christ combats with the Cross, and the Cross will be our arm, and we shall supplicate God for them, never conforming ourselves to their principles, but condemning the poltroons who repeat, in their cowardice, "What will you do? How will you do it?" an imbecile question worthy of the worms of the earth, but not of men. Courage, then. Blessed Mary, whose feast we celebrate to-day under the title of *Auxilium Christianorum*, inspires us. The 24th of May, destined for this feast, has been occupied this year by the feast of the Holy Spirit, the Spouse of Mary. Let this coincidence augment our confidence. As Mary has protected one Pius, who crushed the pride of the Turks; as she protected another Pius to crush a great imperial pride; so at this hour she protects the least Pius and his see, attacked by a thousand different enemies. And as she has conquered *apud Echinadas Insulas* (at the Islands of Ægina), as she has conquered *apud Savonam* (at Savona), the morning of a new victory will come *apud Sanctum Petrum* (at St. Peter's).

May God bless me, His unworthy Vicar, and you, my collaborators, in the administration of His Church. And may He, by this benediction, plunge our hearts in the fire of His love. May the same benediction descend upon the episcopate, the religious orders, and especially upon the poor religious, so ill-treated and oppressed. May it descend upon families, upon fathers and mothers—in fine, upon everybody. And may it be the pledge of the eternal benediction which God will give us at our departure from this life! *Benedictio Dei, etc.*

The Italian Government continued the confiscation of ecclesiastical property. On the 4th of January, thirty-two convents were seized in Rome, and property belonging to the Roman churches and even to the Propaganda, given by Catholics of all countries for the purpose of supporting foreign missions, were seized and sold. According to statistics officially given between October 26, 1867, and July 31, 1874, 102,019 pieces of property were seized and sold, producing $93,430,942. The vestments, church-plate, office books, libraries, also seized, were valued at about $3,000,000. In the province of Rome 4,054 ecclesiastical institutions have been seized.

The demonstrations made on the anniversary of the Pope led to arrests, and the severe punishment, extending to years, of some who shouted "*Viva Pio Nono!*" The removal of the stations and cross from the Colosseum was followed by the prohibition of all praying there, and the arrest of the Belgian Countess Steinlein, and other foreign ladies. A Catholic Congress met at Venice in June, which sent an address to the Pope. The clergy were not, however, generally molested in their functions, except in some cases like that of Bishop Rota, who was imprisoned in September for language used in a pastoral letter.

In Prussia and the German Empire the enforcement of the Falk laws was steadily continued. The Pope, on the 3d of November, 1873, had addressed to the Archbishop of Gnesen and Posen the following, encouraging him in the course he had taken:

REV. BROTHER—Greeting, Apostolic blessings. If at any time it has been God's pleasure to show to men that the fabric of the Church is of Divine building, and that on that account all attacks directed against it by the powers of hell and the malice of man must be in vain, surely it is now, reverend brother, while this truth is forced upon the sight even of those who do not wish to see it, for He has permitted all to conspire for the destruction of the Church. We see contempt, calumny, laws and temporal superiority arrayed against it, the effect of resolutions long formed brought to realization by protracted labor and developed by the most exasperated sect, which has almost everywhere secured supreme power. Its professors are designated rebels; its bishops are condemned by lay courts as agitators, persecuted with fines, deprived of their offices and expelled the country. The spiritual orders are prohibited, the clergy is gagged, and, by arbitrary measures, prevented from exercising its office. Education of youth in the spirit of the Church is forbidden, in order that, on the one hand, the population may not be confirmed in the principles of religion, and that, on the other, the hope may vanish of able and faithful servants of the altar being trained up. In order to undermine the glory of God, the property dedicated to God is robbed; even the chief helmsman of the Church is kept in bondage in order that, though utterly despoiled, he may not govern the Church with freedom according to his powers. All this, reverend brother, makes your heart bleed, but it likewise rends our own; for, though we are grieved at the heavy portion of woe meted out specially to you—so heavy that by the weight of our persecutions your health has been endangered—we see on the other hand, and beyond this, the evil spreading over the whole of Europe to its full length and breadth, and, moreover, over other continents likewise.

Nevertheless, the very magnitude of the evil and the uncommon breadth of the diffusion give the sure hope that deliverance is close at hand; for if God at a former time, when He desired to save the world, permitted so many devilish perversities that even His own Son was not spared, we have cause to infer that the same God is now, by the unbridled efforts of hell, preparing the generally eventual regeneration, and for a triumph of the Church, at this moment deprived of all human assistance, and that by the visible manifestation of His power He will compel even the proudest hearts into obedience. Furthermore, reverend brother, you make the tokens of your love the dearer to us the more you are afflicted with troubles, and magnanimously sacrifice every thing, even life itself, to the execution of your office; and the more resolutely and stanch you fight for the Church the more does our desire gain in intensity that you may be quickly restored to all the more complete health.

The gifts from your diocesans which you have forwarded to us forced us to admire their fervent love, but have at the same time occasioned a certain regret because these alms are offered by those who are themselves hemmed in on all sides by severe tribulation. Receive, therefore, the assurance of the deep gratitude of our heart, you as well as your clergy and your people, on behalf of whom we pray fervently to God that He may give them the same spirit which He has given their pastor, and like perseverance in the hour of peril in which they find themselves. May God grant them and you that unfailing unanimity which annihilates and exhausts all the power of the adversaries, in order thus to provide a fresh victory for the just cause and fresh glory for the Church. Meanwhile, as herald of the grace of God, and in proof of our particular attachment, we pronounce upon you and both your archdioceses our apostolic blessing.

Given at Rome, at St. Peter's, November 3, 1873, the twenty-eighth of our reign.   PIUS P. P. IX.

On the 24th of November, President Gunther cited the archbishop to resign his episcopal dignity within a week, or in default thereof to appear before the Royal Tribunal of Ecclesiastical Affairs at Berlin. He replied the next day in a spirited letter, denying the competency of the civil power to depose him from a purely ecclesiastical office, or the justice of making the conscientious discharge of his duty a crime against the state. He as well as several other bishops had been repeatedly fined, each act of episcopal jurisdiction being regarded a new offense, but, as the seizure of property had failed to intimidate them, he was now prosecuted for appointing a priest named Anton Arndt to the parish of Felehne without leave of the Government officials. Declining to appear before the Royal District Court, criminal division, he was condemned to imprisonment, and on February 3d sent to Ostrowo, a town on the Olabock. The remaining archbishops and bishops then issued a circular letter, in which, looking forward to the possible removal of all the Catholic bishops and priests, they exhort all to fidelity and courage. The Bishop of Treves and the Archbishop of Cologne were arrested in March, and priests in all parts of the country were imprisoned. On the 15th of April, Archbishop Ledochowski, though actually in prison, was tried before the Ecclesiastical Tribunal in Berlin, condemned for not appearing, and deprived of his see. The Bishop of Paderborn was also imprisoned, refusing a subscription made up to pay his fines. A new law, supplemental to the Falk law, provided that all church officials who at the direction of any bishop, unrecognized by the state, or deposed by the state, or at the direction of any person acting for such bishop, in opposition to the law, shall carry out any ecclesiastical functions, will be fined one hundred thalers, or undergo a year's imprisonment. And, if, in the fulfillment of such a commission, they shall perform any episcopal duties, they shall be imprisoned from six months to two years. Provision was also made, requiring Catholics to elect new bishops and priests to

replace any who should be deposed by the state and in default the church property was to be seized. The Catholic chapter of Posen having, on the 19th of June, refused to elect a capitular vicar or recognize the see as vacant, an administration of the diocese was appointed by government. A Catholic congress met at Mayence in June, but its protests and those of the bishops were disregarded. The Government even prosecuted and on July 20th punished thirty-six noble ladies who had sent an address of sympathy to the Bishop of Münster. The attempt to assassinate Bismarck tended to make the Government more rigorous, and the police on the 1st of November attempted to arrest a priest while saying mass at Treves. This led to a conflict in the church between the police and the people, in which blood was shed. The movements led, as usually happens, to accessions to the Church assailed, the chief convert to the Catholic Church in Germany being the Queen-dowager of Bavaria, in September.

Early in the year Austria showed a disposition to adopt an ecclesiastical policy similar to that of Prussia, reviving the theories of Joseph II. This drew from Pius IX. the following Encyclical:

DEAR SONS AND VENERABLE BRETHREN, HEALTH AND APOSTOLIC BENEDICTION: Scarcely had we, in our letter of November 24th last, announced to the Catholic world the serious persecution which has been inaugurated against the Church in Prussia and in Switzerland, than a fresh source of anxiety was prepared for us by the news of other acts of injustice, menacing this Church, which may well, like its Divine Spouse, utter this complaint, "You have added to the pains of my wounds." These instances give us all the more anxiety as they are committed by the Government of the Austrian people, which, in the most glorious period of Christian history, fought so valiantly for the Catholic faith, in the closest alliance with this Apostolic See.

It is true that a few years back certain decrees were published in that monarchy which are diametrically opposed to the most sacred rights of the Church and of the treaties solemnly concluded, and which we, conformably with our duty, condemned and declared invalid in our allocution of June 22, 1868, addressed to our venerable brothers, the cardinals of the Holy Roman Church. But now new laws have been presented for the deliberation and approval of the Reichsrath, which tend openly to lead the Church into the most pernicious condition of servility, and to place her entirely at the mercy of the secular power, which is contrary to the divine arrangement of our Lord Jesus Christ. For the Creator and Redeemer of the human race has founded the Church most assuredly, as His visible kingdom upon earth; He has not only endowed it with the supernatural gifts of an infallible teaching for the propagation of holy doctrines, with a holy priesthood for the performance of divine services and the sanctification of souls by the sacrifice and the sacraments, but He has also given it full power to create laws and to judge and exercise a salutary constraint in all things relating to the true end of the kingdom of God upon earth. But this supernatural power of ecclesiastical government, based on the teachings of Jesus Christ, is entirely distinct and independent of the secular authority. This kingdom of God on earth is a kingdom of a perfect society which rules and governs itself, according to its own laws and its right, by its own chiefs, who watch over it so as to give an account of souls, not to secular sovereigns, but to the Prince of Pastors—to Jesus Christ, who instituted pastors and doctors, who, in their spiritual administration, are subject to no secular power. Just as it is the duty of the hierarchy to govern, so also is it the duty of the faithful, according to the admonition of the apostle, to obey and to submit to them; and therefore it is that the Catholic people have a sacred right which ought not to be interfered with by the civil power in its sacred duty of following the discipline and laws of the Church.

You recognize with us, dear sons and venerable brothers, that the laws debated to-day in the Austrian Reichsrath contain and manifest a serious violation of this divine constitution of the Church, and an intolerable subversion of the rights of the Apostolic See, of the holy canons, and of the entire Catholic people.

In effect, by virtue of these laws, the Church of Christ, in almost all its relations and acts relative to the direction of the faithful, is judged and considered completely subordinate and subjected to the superior power of the secular authorities, and this is very openly expressed and, so to say, spoken of as a principle in the document which explains the full object and sense of the laws in question. It is also expressly declared that the secular government, in virtue of its unlimited power, possesses the right of making laws on ecclesiastical subjects just as it has on those purely secular, and to overlook and dominate the Church just as if it were a mere human institution within the empire.

By this the secular government arrogates to itself the right of judgment and teaching over the constitution and rights of the Catholic Church, as well as over its exalted administration, which it exercises of itself, partly by its laws and acts, and partly by different ecclesiastical persons.

Hence it follows that this will and power of the civil government usurp the place of the religious power, which was established by divine ordination for the direction of the Church and edification of the body of Christ. Against such a usurpation of the sanctuary the great Ambrose rightly says: "They say that every thing is permitted to Cæsar, and that all things belong to him." I answer: "Do not imagine that thou possessest an imperial right over the things consecrated to God. Do not exalt thyself, but be subject to God." He has written: "What is God's is God's, and what Cæsar's, Cæsar's." To the Emperor belong the palaces, the priests, the churches.

As regards these laws which have been preceded by an exposition of their object, they are in reality of the same nature and kind as those of Prussia, and prepare for the Church in Austria the same misfortune, although they appear at first sight to be more moderate when compared with the Prussian laws.

We do not care to examine in detail each article of these laws, but we cannot pass in silence the cruel insult which by the presentation of such laws has been offered to us and to this Apostolic See, as well as to yourselves, dear sons and dear brethren, and to the entire Catholic people of the empire.

The contract which was concluded in 1855 between ourselves and the illustrious Emperor, and was confirmed by this Catholic sovereign by the most solemn promises and promulgated throughout the entire empire, is now presented to the Chamber of Deputies, with the declaration that it is completely without force and annulled, and this without any previous negotiation with the Apostolic See, and moreover with a public contempt of our most just representations. Could such a thing ever have happened at a time when public faith had still some value? But now, in this sad epoch, it is not only undertaken but completed. Against this public violation of the Concordat we protest once more, before you, well-beloved sons and venerable brothers.

We reprove all the more this outrage inflicted upon the Church, as the cause and pretext of this rupture of the Concordat and of other laws which were attached to it are insidiously rested upon the definition of the teachings of faith published and confirmed by the Œcumenical Council of the Vatican; and they have spoken of these Catholic dogmas in an impious manner and styled them new fashioned, and changes made in the articles of faith and in the constitution of the Church.

There may be in the Empire of Austria some persons who have renounced the Catholic faith on account of these unworthy inventions; but its illustrious monarch and the whole imperial household preserve and confess it, as do also the vast majority of the people, and it is to this people that these laws, founded on such inventions, are to be given. Therefore, without our knowledge and will, they have torn the convention which we had concluded with the noble Emperor in the interest of the salvation of souls and the advantage of the state. A new form of right has been invented, and they have attributed to the civil government a new power, so that it can interfere in all ecclesiastical matters, and so that it can ordain and arrange the affairs of the Church as it thinks fit.

With the projected laws they have been able to bind the Church with heavy chains and to paralyze her action and her inviolable liberty, which she must ever possess for the government of the faithful, the religious guidance of the people, and even of the clergy, to help the progress of Christian life toward evangelical perfection, in the administration and even possession of property. They introduce perversion in discipline, they favor apostacy, and the union and conspiracy of the sects against the true dogmas of Christianity are actually protected and assisted by laws.

In truth, a great task would fall to our lot if we had to mention the nature and number of the evils which we should have to fear as soon as the laws are in operation; but, dear sons and venerable brothers, they cannot either deceive us or escape your wisdom, for really all the ecclesiastical functions and benefices, and even the exercise of pastoral duties, are so entirely subjected to the civil power, that the ecclesiastical superiors, supposing that they would submit to the new laws—which is far from being possible—would ultimately not be able to administer their dioceses (for which they have a strict account to render to God) according to the salutary rules of the Church, but they would be obliged to exercise this direction and to restrain it according to the will and pleasure of the head of the state.

Again, what are we to expect from those laws that bear the heading in consideration of the religious communities? Their fatal intent and hostile meaning are so evident that all easily perceive that they are destined to prepare the way for the ruin and extinction of the religious orders. The loss of temporal property is so great that it is scarcely to be distinguished from a public sale and confiscation. The Government will place the property in question under its authority after the passing of these laws, and will arrogate to itself the right and power of dividing it, of letting it out, and of reducing it by taxation to such an extent that the miserable result and benefit which will remain over can scarcely be considered by the Church as honorable, but rather as a mockery and a mere cloak to cover the injustice.

As the laws discussed by the Chamber of Deputies of the Austrian Reichsrath are worded in this sense, and based upon the principles which we have exposed, you can clearly see, dear sons and venerable brothers, the actual dangers which menace the flock placed under your charge and vigilance. The unity and peace of the Church are notably at stake, and they only wish to deprive her of that liberty which St. Thomas of Canterbury well called "the soul of the Church, without which she has no life, and without which she has no strength to fight against those who seek to possess by inheritance the sanctuary of God."

This phrase has been explained by another invincible defender of the same liberty, St. Anselm, in the following terms: "God loves nothing in the world so much as the liberty of the Church. Let those who care less to serve the Church than to dominate her consider themselves the enemies of God. God wishes His spouse, the Church, to be free, and not a slave."

Therefore we call upon you and seek to inflame your pastoral vigilance and the zeal which animates you for the welfare of the house of God, so that you may do your best to remove the danger which is approaching. Take great courage to sustain the fight worthily, for it is a combat which is in every sense worthy of your virtue. We feel certain that you will display neither less courage nor strength than our other honorable brethren who elsewhere, amid the most bitter trials, having become in the midst of contempt and persecution a spectacle, endure with joy, for the liberty of the Church, not only the loss of their goods, but even in chains sustain the combat of grief. But our hopes are not all placed on your own strength, but on God. This matter concerns Him, who by His infallible Word advises and teaches us, "In the world you will be persecuted, but have confidence; I have conquered the world."

We, therefore, who by virtue of our Apostolic charge, in which the grace of God strengthens our weakness, have been placed at the head as guide in this cruel warfare against the Church, we repeat and praise the words of the Saint of Canterbury, who thus expresses himself in words which admirably suit our times: "The war which the enemies of God wage against us is a war between themselves and the Almighty." Therefore, we only desire of them what the Eternal God when He made Himself flesh left to the Church as His eternal legacy.

Uplift your hearts, therefore, with us in faith and in love of Christ, for the protection of the Church, and come to the help of your fellow-men, with the authority and the wisdom which you share, for no good will befall them as long as the Church is deprived of liberty. We have confidence in you—all the more because the cause of God is at stake. In that which concerns us it is certain that we should prefer, much rather, to suffer temporal ills than assume the trials of a disgraceful servitude. For the issue of this struggle has for posterity this significance—that the Church will be eternally afflicted. May God preserve us from this, or else that she enjoy an eternal liberty! But as you will have to direct your efforts to prevent the dangers which menace the Church, by your authority and by your wisdom, you will readily acknowledge that nothing would be more opportune or useful than that you should examine in common council the proper means whereby to attain this object. While they are attacking the Church, it is your duty to protect the faithful; but the wall of defense will be all the more sure, and the defense itself all the stronger, the more unanimous and united your efforts are, and the more carefully and zealously studied and arranged the means you employ to master the situation. We exhort you to unite yourselves as much as possible, and to fix, after common deliberation, a sure and approved line of conduct, which will permit you, conformably with the duties your position imposes on you, to combat in common accord the evils which menace the Church, and to protect her with all your energy. Our exhortation is necessary in order that we may not appear to have neglected our duty in such an important matter, but we are convinced that even without the exhortation you would have done your duty. Further, we have not abandoned the hope that God will withdraw these existing evils, and what encourages us thus to hope is the devotion and faith of our well-beloved son in Christ, the

Emperor and King, Francis Joseph, whom we have pressingly adjured, in a letter addressed to him this day, never to allow that in his vast empire the Church be subjected to an ignominious servitude and his Catholic subjects to great afflictions.

But as the number of assailants of the Church is great, as each assault is eminently dangerous, you can at least persevere without fear. May He deign to guide your decisions and sustain you by His strength and all-powerful protection, so that you may decide happily and realize all that may help the glory of His name and the welfare of souls! As a sign of this divine protection and of our particular love we impart to each of you, dear sons and venerable brothers, as also to the clergy and the faithful under your charge, our Apostolic benediction.

Given at Rome, near St. Peter's, March 7, 1874, and in the twenty-eighth year of our pontificate.

PIUS P. P. IX.

A general meeting of Catholics opposed to the proposed bills was held at Vienna, March 19th–24th; and the Austrian episcopate presented to the Upper House of the Reichsrath a dignified memorandum embodying their objections. The Pope, to avert the threatened abolition of the Concordat, also, April 29th, addressed a letter to the Austrian cardinals. The strong opposition evinced prevented the full execution of the project.

In Switzerland, however, the position of the Catholic clergy and people was extremely hard. The Government had broken off all intercourse with Rome, deposed bishops, made the clergy elective, and had thus thrown many of the churches into the hands of a few of those who recognized the Old Catholic movement. The seizure of Notre-Dame de Vorbourg and of Mariastein was severely felt. The Catholic congregations, where their pastors had not been driven out, worshiped in any temporary shelter they could find, but their priests were not recognized and their marriages considered null and void. They were constantly punished for officiating or attending the sick. Before the close of the year scarcely a priest was left in the cantons of Geneva and Berne. The new constitution gave the General Government complete authority in all religious matters, "so that," says the London Spectator, "the Confederation can, in fact, prohibit the Roman Catholic religion, if it pleases."

The Russian Government had placed an administrator of the United Greek rite over the Ruthenian Catholics in the district of Chelm. Early in the year the Russian rite was forced into the churches, and the resistance of the peasantry drew upon them the vengeance of the troops. Forty were shot down at Daelow. Their priests are in exile or in prison; the administrator and deans appointed by Government belong to the Russian Church, so that they are left without any clergy, but prefer death to a change of faith. The Pope, June 27th, issued an Encyclical, disproving of the alterations in the liturgy sought to be forced upon the Ruthenians.

In England a movement was made, supported by the episcopate, for establishing a university or college for higher studies, the object of which was developed in a synodal letter, August 11th. It was organized with Monsignor Capel as rector, and a faculty numbering several distinguished men. The agitations relating to the Catholic Church on the Continent were felt in England. Lord John Russell wrote to the Emperor of Germany, sympathizing warmly with the Falk laws, and in his reply the Emperor appealed for the moral support of England. At a later date Gladstone, in a very skillful pamphlet, attacked the Vatican Decrees as making loyalty to the state impossible for a Catholic. This drew replies from Archbishop Manning, Dr. Newman, Capel, and others, to all of whom he replied in a second pamphlet. The discussion was read by thousands in England and America, showing a general interest in the position of Catholics and their relation to the state.

In the East there were also troubles. Among the United Armenians in the Turkish Empire, a party arose similar to the Old Catholics. The Turkish Government sided with them, and adjudged to them all the churches of the Armenian Catholics. In 1866 Hassoun, Patriarch of Constantinople, was elected also Patriarch of Cilicia, uniting in his person the two patriarchates of the empire; and the Pope, by a bull Reversurus, extended to Cilicia the electoral system of Constantinople. During the Vatican Council and the absence of Hassoun in attendance upon it, Ohan Kupelian was elected patriarch by some discontented Armenians. He was recognized by the Porte, which exiled Patriarch Hassoun in 1872. The delivery of the Cathedral of Trebizond, and the Church of St. Saviour, June 20, 1874, to the adherents of Kupelian, only 2,000 out of 100,000, called out a protest from the French, Russian, English, Austrian, American, and Italian embassadors, but the Turkish Government did not recede.

Remarkable progress is claimed for the Roman Catholic Church in India, especially in Ceylon; but in the Empire of Anam a terrible persecution took place. On the 24th of February an army attacked the Christian villages of Trunlam, Movink, Bantach, and a multitude of others, burning the villages and massacring most of the people. Three priests and twenty missionary students were slain, 300 villages ravaged, 70,000 Christians dispersed, slain on the spot, or subsequently beheaded or forced to seek refuge in the mountains, where many perished. Two hundred churches and ten convents were destroyed, the total loss of the Anamite Christians amounting to $3,000,000.

In America the revival of pilgrimages in Europe led to an American pilgrimage to Lourdes and Rome, which sailed from New York in May. A Provincial Council was held at San Francisco April 26th, and the bishops of the province addressed a letter of sympathy to Archbishop Ledochowski. A local pilgrimage was made to Whitemarsh, in Maryland, just a place of devotion. The position of Catholics in public schools and public institutions was agitated in several parts. At Rochester, N. Y.,

the authorities of the Western House of Refuge, November 29th, on the advice of learned counsel, decided that Catholic inmates should be free to attend the worship and religious instructions of their own Church; but the Legislature of New Jersey (March 28th) refused to grant a like freedom in similar institutions in that State. The assignment of the Indian tribes to religious bodies had deprived Catholic Indians in various parts of their missionaries, and appeals were made to the Government by the Osages and by the Catholic clergy of Oregon in behalf of the Catholic Indians in that State. A case arose in Vermont which also excited attention. One hundred and twenty pupils in the public school at Brattleboro were absent to attend mass on Corpus Christi, a feast of obligation in the Catholic Church. For this they were expelled from the school, and a judge held the expulsion legal.

The Catholic Church in the United States, at the close of 1874, had 7 archbishops, 53 bishops, 4,873 priests, 4,731 churches, 1,902 chapels and stations, 68 colleges, 1,444 parish schools, 14 academies, 302 asylums and hospitals, and claimed a Catholic population of more than 6,000,000.

In New Brunswick a new school law was resisted by the Catholics as unjust and illegal; but it was steadily enforced. They had maintained schools of their own, and refused to pay the tax for non-Catholic schools; but the property of the bishop was seized and sold, and one priest, Rev. Mr. Michaud, imprisoned October 17th. At a subsequent period the excitement led to acts of violence.

Brazil continued the course begun in 1873. Although Bishop Oliveira claimed that under the law (No. 809) of August 18, 1851, bishops could be prosecuted in the civil courts only in causes that were not purely spiritual, he was arrested in January, and taken to the arsenal in Pernambuco, from which he was conveyed to Rio Janeiro. He was brought to trial on the 18th of February for refusing to remove the interdict laid by him on certain religious confraternities for declining to expel members who belonged to Masonic lodges. One of the judges, known to be favorable to the bishop, was challenged by the crown. The bishop refused to plead, but two volunteer counsel were heard in his defense, and on the 21st the bishop was found guilty under the 96th Article of the Criminal Code, two judges dissenting, and he was sentenced to four years' imprisonment with hard labor. Bishop Macedo, of Pará, was subsequently tried and condemned to four years' imprisonment in the island of Cobras. When the troubles began, the Brazilian Government dispatched Baron Penedo to Rome, as was officially stated, "to try to induce the Pope to avoid encouraging the bishops in their disobedience." Baron Penedo had presented a note to Cardinal Antonelli, October 29, 1873, maintaining that the rules of the confraternities did not exclude Masons, and that the decrees of the Popes condemning Freemasons had not received the *beneplacitum* of the Brazilian Government. To this Cardinal Antonelli replied:

The undersigned, Cardinal Secretary of State of his Holiness, has received the memorandum remitted to him by your Excellency with your prized note of the 29th of October last, and, after having examined with mature attention the contents of the document, has fulfilled the duty of promptly bringing to the knowledge of the Holy Father a circumstantial relation of them. His Holiness, warmly deploring the conflict in Brazil between the ecclesiastical and the civil powers, the causes and circumstances giving rise to it, and the unhappy consequences which have resulted or may result from it, has seen with much satisfaction that the Imperial Government, in deference to the supreme chief of the Church, and in proof of adhesion to the Catholic religion, has directed itself to the Holy See, invoking its authority to put an end to the lamentable conflict, and declaring at the same time that it desires to maintain between the two powers the good harmony so necessary for the prosperity of the Church and state. Wherefore, the Holy Father, justly appreciating the step taken toward the Holy See by the Imperial Government, and also the sentiments it has expressed, and having presented the reply given by his Holiness on the 29th of May of the current year to Monsignor the Bishop of Olinda and Pernambuco, is disposed to adopt those means which, in his high wisdom and his paternal benevolence toward the Brazilian Catholics, he will judge opportune to terminate the deplorable conflict. He hopes, however, that the Imperial Government will contribute to the removal of all the obstacles which might delay the prompt restoration of the desired concord, and will in this way assist the benignant measures of the Holy See.

The undersigned cardinal judges it superfluous, when bringing the above to the knowledge of your Excellency, to make any observation upon what the memorandum says in respect to the *beneplacitum* to which some governments subject the decrees of councils, the apostolic letters, and every other ecclesiastical constitution, and also in respect to the appeal to the crown, it being well known what are the principles professed by the Holy See upon the one and the other.

The undersigned cardinal profits, therefore, by this opportunity to reiterate to your Excellency the assurances of his distinguished consideration.

ANTONELLI.

Baron DE PENEDO, etc., etc.

The negotiations continued, but the Brazilian Government did not satisfy the Pope that the bishops had gone beyond the line of their duty. The attitude of Brazil, in appealing to an authority whose competence it denied and whose decrees it declared null, was anomalous. The Pope sustained the bishops by two briefs:

To our Venerable Brother Antonio, Bishop of Belem and Pará, Pius IX. Pope. Venerable Brother, Health and Apostolic Benediction: From intelligence that has reached here we learn with much satisfaction the various circumstances connected with the struggles now going on between the Brazilian Episcopate and Freemasonry, so greatly misrepresented by the person who came as a representative to us on the subject, and whose bad faith has been still further demonstrated by his subsequent acts. We, therefore, confirm all we wrote in May last to our Venerable Brother, the Bishop of Olinda, who is proving himself so worthy of his charge. And still further, we have seen absolutely nothing in your conduct against the sacred canons, but, on the contrary, we have observed that you have acted

wisely and prudently in every thing. It is unnecessary for us to give you any commands; but we exhort you, in this trying persecution everywhere waged against the Church by the Freemasons, always to display the same firmness, and never to allow yourself to waver either before the threats of the mighty, nor through a fear of spoliation, exile, imprisonment, or other trials; because all afflictions are to the Christian, who suffers like Jesus Christ, so many crowns of glory. They manifest no less than they strengthen in the eyes of the faithful the authority of the bishop, and increase their faith more than any counsel or cares whatsoever. In a word, just as in the infancy of the Church they overcame idolatry, so will they overthrow Freemasonry, together with the multitude of abominable errors growing out of it, and they will reëstablish the practice of our religion in all its integrity. These afflictions, doubtless, appear to surpass the strength of human infirmity, but we can do every thing in Him who strengthens us, and in whose name we combat. We earnestly implore, therefore, His all-powerful aid for you, for the illustrious and most worthy Bishop of Olinda and for your venerable brethren; and at the same time, as an earnest of heavenly gifts, and as an evidence of our special good-will, we most affectionately bestow upon you, Venerable Brother, upon them and upon your whole diocese, our Apostolic Benediction.

Given at Rome, near St. Peter's, on the 18th of May, 1874, and the twenty-ninth of our pontificate.

PIUS IX., POPE.

The brief to the Bishop of Olinda was similar in tone, heartily approved of his course, and hoped for his speedy liberation. The imprisonment of the Bishop of Olinda and laws bearing on the question led in November to an outbreak of the people in Parahyba do Norte, which required the calling out of troops.

In Venezuela President Guzman Blanco had, on the Prussian plan, deposed the Archbishop of Carácas, and ordered a new election, after banishing Mgr. Sylvester Guebara di Lyra, the archbishop, and some of his suffragans and clergy. Congress then passed an act, appointed a new archbishop, suppressed convents, established civil marriages, and recognized marriages of the clergy. Against these acts the archbishop addressed a protest to Congress, April 10, 1874. Peru likewise showed hostility to institutions of the Catholic Church.

In Chili acts were also passed, imposing penalties for obedience to decrees from Rome, which led to a protest from the Chilian hierarchy on the 5th of October. Ecuador, on the contrary, endeavored to act in harmony with the Catholic Church.

Mexico pursued the course of hostility to the Catholic Church begun previously, and, toward the close of the year, expelled the Sisters of Charity and all priests of foreign birth. The Government also encouraged Protestant missionaries from the United States, and their preaching and publications excited an indignation and animosity in the lower orders which led to deplorable scenes. One missionary was murdered, and an attack by a mob on a private Catholic chapel, seized by the Government and given to an American missionary, resulted in the death of several persons at Acapulco.

Among the eminent Catholics who died during the year were Cardinals Tarquini and Antoniacci, recently promoted; Cardinal Barnabo (February 24th), who had long been prefect of the Propaganda, in which position he was succeeded by Cardinal Franchi; Mgr. Mérode; Brother Philippe (January 8th), Superior of the Brothers of the Christian Schools; Very Rev. J. B. Etienne, Superior of the Priests of the Mission and of the Sisters of Charity; Herr von Mallinkrodt, leader of the German Catholics; Madame Josephine Gretz (January 4th), Superior-General of the Ladies of the Sacred Heart; and the Oratorian, Augustine Theiner, historian and antiquary (August 9th), who had, however, become suspected during the Vatican Council, and, as appeared clearly after his death, was in full harmony and concert with the Old Catholic movement.

The Old Catholics in Germany and Switzerland held a strange position. Though excommunicated by the Pope, and by Catholics held to be no longer Catholics, they still claimed to be Catholics, and in Germany were recognized as still belonging to the Catholic Church, and their bishop as a Catholic bishop, in spite of his irregular election and his consecration by a bishop not of the Catholic Church. In Switzerland the Government recognized them as Catholics, and did not recognize the Catholics or their clergy as such. Yet, the Old Catholic body in Germany had a distinct national organization, independent of all control, and as such held a synod at Bonn, consisting of Bishop Reinkens, 28 clerical and 57 lay members. To retain their character as Catholics, they did not, with Loyson, reject the celibacy of the clergy, or the use of Latin; but their action on the sacraments of penance and of matrimony was at variance with the doctrine and discipline of the Catholic Church. According to an official statement made in the Prussian Parliament, the whole number of Old Catholics in Prussia, including all the families of members, was 17,028; and in Bavaria, Baden, and other German states, they were estimated at as many more; and the number of priests, 31.

RUSSIA (Empire of all the Russias), an empire in Europe and Asia. Emperor, Alexander II., born April 17 (April 29, new style), 1818; succeeded his father, February 18 (March 2), 1855; crowned at Moscow, August 26 (September 7), 1856. Sons of the Emperor: 1. Heir-apparent, Grand-duke Alexander, born February 26 (March 10), 1845; married November 4, 1866, to Maria Dagmar (born November 26, 1847), daughter of King Christian IX., of Denmark. (Offspring of the union are two sons: Nicholas, born May 6, 1868; and George, born April 28, 1871.) 2. Grand-duke Vladimir, born April 10, 1847. 3. Grand-duke Alexis, born January 2, 1850. 5. Grand-Duke Paul, born September 1, 1860.

The area and population of the great divisions of the Russian Empire were, according to the latest dates, as follows:

PROVINCES.	Sq. Miles.	Population.	Year.
1. European Russia........ Former kingdom of Poland.................	1,867,057 49,159	63,056,234 6,225,618	1867 1874
2. Finland..................	142,253	1,832,188	1872
3. Caucasus..:.............	172,797	5,200,000	1871
4. Siberia.................	6,277,846	3,327,027	1867
5. Central Asia..........		3,014,320	1873
Total.................	8,509,112	83,260,000	

European Russia, inclusive of the former kingdom of Poland, is divided into sixty governments, the area and population (in 1867) of which are given in the ANNUAL CYCLOPÆDIA for 1872.

The following cities of Russia have a population upward of 100,000 inhabitants:

St. Petersburg. (1869)..667,026 | Odessa.... (1873)..162,814
Moscow....... (1871)..611,970 | Kishinev.. (1867)..108,043
Warsaw....... (1873)..279,502 | Riga....... (1867)..102,043

The official estimate of revenue and expenditure for the year 1874, as sanctioned by the Emperor, is as follows: revenue, 539,851,656 rubles; expenditure, 536,683,836 rubles: surplus, 3,167,820 rubles.

The public debt of Russia, on January 1, 1873, amounted to 2,277,081,564 rubles.

The new law on the reorganization of the Russian army was proclaimed by an imperial ukase, dated January 1 (January 13), 1874. The armed force of this empire consists of the standing army and the landwehr; the latter has to serve only in times of war. The standing army consists of land and naval troops. The land army comprises: 1. The regular army, which is to be kept complete by annual recruiting. 2. Of the reserve, formed of men who are furloughed until they are called upon to serve their time. 3. Of Cossack troops, formed of other tribes. The landwehr embraces the entire male population capable of bearing arms and not belonging to the standing army, from the twentieth to the fortieth year of age. It is divided into two sections, one of which, containing the younger men, may be employed to complete the standing army. In times of peace the army will, as before, consist of about 750,000 men; in times of war, the force at the disposal of the Government would at present be about 1,520,000 in European Russia and in the Caucasus, with about 300,000 horses. While the new law established the principle of universal liability to military service, it reserved to the Government the power of determining annually how many of the able-bodied men who have attained the proper age are to be actually selected for military service. Assuming all those obliged to serve to be actually draughted into the army, the prospect would be an alarming one indeed. If the 40,000,000 Germans under the ban of universal conscription easily supply 130,000 recruits a year, 70,000,000 Russians, when subject to the same régime, will yield a total of 227,000. This is exactly twice the number of the recruits enlisted at the old average rate of four in each thousand males. Again, each man under the new law being obliged to hold himself in readiness for active service through a period of fifteen years, this, after the first fifteen years are over, and ever after, would place a force of 3,405,000 men at the disposal of the Czar. Deducting those who die, or are invalided, there still remains the fearful figure of something like 3,000,000 soldiers. Or, if the Government have not the money and necessary number of officers to carry out the law to its full extent, there will still be 2,000,000.

The following particulars on the condition of the Russian Navy in 1874 are given by a Russian naval journal:

The total number of ships-of-war in Russian waters is 225; 29 of which are iron-clads, and they carry 921 guns. Their total burden amounts to 172,401 tons, and their steam-power is 37,978 horses. The *personnel* consists of 1,305 officers (including 81 admirals), 513 pilots, 210 artillery engineers, 145 marine engineers, 545 mechanical engineers, 56 marine architects, 297 admiralty officials, 260 surgeons, 480 civil officials, and 24,500 subordinates of various ranks. The ships are distributed as follows: In the Baltic there are 27 iron-clads and 110 unarmored steamers, 70 of which do not carry guns, and the rest have about 200 guns in all. The same number of guns are to be placed on the iron-clads, four of which are still in course of construction. The Black Sea fleet consists of two iron-clads and 29 unarmored steamers. The iron-clads are armed with four guns, and the other steamers, except four which do not carry guns, with 45. In the Caspian there are 29 unarmored steamers, one of which is in course of construction, and nine are without guns; the rest have 45 guns in all. The Siberian flotilla consists of 23 steamers, seven of which carry 36 guns between them; and the Aral flotilla has six small steamers, five of which are armed with 13 guns. In the White Sea there are three ships-of-war with four guns. The educational department of the Russian Admiralty comprises a naval school for 265 pupils at St. Petersburg, a scientific-school for 220 pupils, a training-school for 400 boys, and a writing-school for 150 sailors at Cronstadt; and a midshipmen's school, a ship-building school, and a school for sailors' daughters at Nicolaieff. A sum of 442,951 rubles for the expenses of these schools is included in the budget of 1874.

The movement of commerce in the years 1871 and 1872 was as follows:

I. WITH EUROPE, ETC.

COUNTRIES.	IMPORTS.		EXPORTS.	
	1871.	1872.	1871.	1872.
Germany	162,717	171,328	74,911	77,319
Great Britain	97,284	120,067	171,778	143,306
France	12,405	18,899	33,978	22,331
Austro - Hungarian Monarchy	16,748	23,786	18,860	19,559
Turkey	11,578	18,709	10,190	6,028
Belgium	4,916	5,251	9,542	6,907
Netherlands	6,173	5,388	14,834	7,487
Italy	10,456	12,773	8,429	8,950
Spain	1,484	548	378	109
Sweden and Norway	4,167	4,423	4,963	5,442
Denmark	363	404	2,607	6,802
Greece	3,767	2,411	1,857	1,235
Roumania	3,444	4,092	2,428	2,868
Portugal	612	435	658	570
United States	16,970	12,295	865	1,078
Other countries	3,243	12,878	1,490	1,532
Total	356,227	413,678	352,758	311,553

II. WITH ASIA, ETC.

COUNTRIES.	IMPORTS.		EXPORTS.	
	1871.	1872.	1871.	1872.
Turkey	5,446	6,275	3,469	3,552
China	6,524	8,015	3,482	2,825
Persia	3,949	4,925	1,429	1,693
Other countries	10	20	523	1,262
Total	15,929	19,235	8,903	9,332

The movement of shipping in 1872 is exhibited in the following table:

PORTS.	ENTERED.			CLEARED.		
	Laden.	Ballast.	Total.	Laden.	Ballast.	Total.
Baltic Sea	4,100	1,610	5,710	5,271	372	5,643
White Sea	328	383	711	739	2	741
Black Sea	1,634	2,016	3,650	2,921	739	3,660
Total, 1872	6,062	4,009	10,071	8,931	1,113	10,044
" 1871	6,264	5,992	12,256	10,952	1,220	12,172

The merchant navy, in 1874, was composed of 2,504 vessels, of an aggregate burden of 260,292 lasts, among which there were 227 steamers. Included in this number are 826 vessels of Finland, of 123,336 lasts.

The length of railroads in operation on January 1, 1874, amounted to 16,800 kilometres. At the close of the year 1872 the telegraph-lines in operation had an aggregate length of 72,084 kilometres, while the length of wire was 145,856 kilometres.

An imperial ukase, dated March 9 (new style 21), 1874, regulates the administration of the "Transcaspian Territory."

This new Russian acquisition comprises the whole of the country between the khanates of Khiva and Bokhara and the Caspian Sea. It extends northward as far as Mertvy Tultuk, southward to the Atrek (which is to be the Russo-Persian frontier), eastward to the borders of the khanate of Khiva, and westward to the Caspian, including the islands of Kulaly, Sviatoi, etc. The governor of the new territory is to be subordinate in all things to the commander-in-chief of the Caucasus, and his headquarters will be at Krasnovodsk. There will also be a sub-district, with Alexandrovsk as its capital. The governor will be assisted in his administrative duties by a physician, an engineer, a topographer, and interpreters, and a physician will also be attached to his deputy at Alexandrovsk. The Russian population in the new territory will be governed according to the general laws of the empire, but special regulations are laid down for the native population. The latter are to be divided into larger and smaller communities severally called "volosts" and "auls."

The treaty between Russia and Bokhara, concluded on October 10, 1873,[*] did not, as was at first announced, turn over to Bokhara the whole of the territory ceded by Khiva to Russia, but only a few isolated patches of pasture-land on the right bank of the Amu. The real oasis on that side of the river which is north of Meschekli remained in the possession and was organized into the circle (province) of Amu Darya, which is subordinate to the Governor-General of Russian Toorkistan.

[*] *See* ANNUAL CYCLOPÆDIA for 1873, article "Russia."

The marriage of the only daughter of the Emperor, the Grand-duchess Marie Alexandrovna, born October 17, 1853, with Alfred, Duke of Edinburgh, second son of Queen Victoria of Great Britain, took place on January 23, 1874. There were two marriage ceremonies, one in conformity with the custom of the Eastern Church, and one of the Anglican. The Russian ceremony, which is very long, occupied about two hours; when it was over, the pair passed from the Russian church to the Alexander Hall, close by, where the shorter ceremony was performed by Dean Stanley, assisted by the Rev. Arthur S. Thompson, the resident clergyman, who was formerly a pupil of the dean at Oxford. The two ceremonies took place under one roof, and the interval between them was but short. The marriage ceremonies were followed at four o'clock by a great wedding banquet. The celebration of the marriage was attended by the Prince and Princess of Wales, Prince Arthur of Great Britain, and the crown-prince and the crown-princess of the German Empire. Enthusiastic demonstrations in honor of the marriage took place in all parts of the empire. In most of the governments the nobility gave valuable wedding-presents; in many of the large towns the municipal corporations did the same; and large sums had been collected for the purpose of endowing educational and charitable institutes, to bear the name of the Duke or the Duchess of Edinburgh. Before the duke returned with his bride to England, St. Petersburg was visited, on February 13th, by the Emperor of Austria. At the festivities which were given in his honor, the Emperor as well as the Czar bore public testimony to the friendly relations now existing between these two Governments as well as with Germany and Great Britain. The same assurance was repeatedly given during the visits which the Czar in May, June, and July, made to Germany and England. He started for his journey on May 1st, going first to Stuttgart, where he was present at the marriage of his niece, the Grand-duchess Vera; thence he proceeded to England, and lastly to Ems, where he took the waters with the German Emperor. His return to Russia took place early in July.

Owing to the good understanding established between the courts of St. Petersburg and Vienna, the Russian Government gave orders for the discontinuance of the fortification works in progress at Dubno and Ossovieco, begun some time ago with much display and expense. The reason officially stated was financial considerations, but the true reason was sought for abroad in the better understanding established between the two courts. The new fortifications are situated near the Austrian frontier.

The intimate relations between the Governments of Russia and Germany remained undisturbed, although many papers of both countries tried, on two different occasions, to spread a belief in a serious disagreement having taken place. When the reports about negotiations between Germany and Denmark, concerning the retrocession of Schleswig to Denmark and the entrance of the entire Danish kingdom into the German Empire was under discussion, the *Golos* of St. Petersburg, and many other Russian papers, had articles strongly advocating the continuance of Danish independence. "So long," an article of the *Golos* says, "as the entrance to the Baltic is in the hands of Denmark, it is practically a free and open sea. Should Germany command the Sound, the Baltic would virtually become German property. Such an important change Europe does not wish, and will not allow. German statesmen ought to know that even the raising of this question is dangerous to the peace of Europe." German papers, on the other hand, which were unfriendly to the policy pursued by Prince Bismarck, attributed a grave significance to the refusal of the Russian Government to recognize the Government of the Spanish Republic, when most of the European Governments followed Germany in this question, and to a personal letter addressed by the Czar to Don Carlos. The Governments of both Germany and Russia officially denied, however, that the friendly relations existing between them had in the least been affected.

In Asiatic politics the rival interests of Russia and England are too antagonistic to be permanently affected by the new tie of relationship connecting the sovereign families. Though no unpleasant complications of any kind arose during the year, it was not doubted that each power, at more than one point, endeavored to counteract the influence of the other. (*See* AFGHANISTAN, and KASHGAR.) At the close of the year it was feared that the warlike preparations made by China for the reconquest of Kashgar might lead to difficulties between China and Russia.

An invitation was issued from Russia to the other powers of Europe to send delegates to an International Conference, which was to consult on the best means to mitigate the horrors of war. The invitation was generally accepted, though with considerable reluctance by England, and the conference was held in August, at Brussels (*see* BELGIUM).

The emigration of Tartars from the Crimea, which has been going on for some years, still continued in 1874, and the efforts made by the authorities to prevent it proved quite fruitless. The emigrants decided beforehand where they were to embark, and they then proceeded in such numbers, by small boats, to the Turkish ships, which lay waiting for them, that the Russian coast-guardsmen could do nothing against them. It would be easy to put an end to the exodus with a single Russian cruiser; but the Government did not seem disposed to adopt this course, and it was inferred that the Government did not care about retaining a population which, on account of its religion, could never be amalgamated with the Russian nationality. From an agricultural point of view, however, this emigration *en masse* is a great evil.

Besides the Tartars who emigrate to Turkey, Russia is losing a large number of Mennonites, who have arranged an emigration to the United States of America, as the Russian Government is unwilling to exempt them from military service, to which they have religious objections. (*See* MENNONITES.)

Field-Marshal Count Berg, for many years the Governor of the former kingdom of Poland, died on January 18th, and was buried with full military honors, the funeral services being attended by the Emperor, the Czarevitch, and several of the Grand-dukes. In his place, Adjutant-General Kotzebue, Governor of New Russia and Bessarabia, was appointed commander-in-chief and governor-general at Warsaw. Perfect quiet prevailed in Poland throughout the year. At the beginning of October an international agricultural exhibi-

tion at Warsaw, which was to have remained open till the 27th, was suddenly closed by the police. This measure was attributed to the discovery that the Polish nobility from Posen, who attended it in strong force, took no interest in the exhibition itself, but found in it an opportunity of displaying their disaffection toward Prussia.

The breach between Poles and Russians was once more widened by a church movement among the United Greeks of Poland, which, after having long been planned, began at the close of the year to take definite shape. A number of congregations, headed by their priests, declared their secession from the communion of the Roman Catholic Church, and their desire to join the state Church of Russia. According to Polish accounts, the Russian Government had had recourse to the most outrageous acts of cruelty to coerce priests and congregations into this move, which, according to the Russians, was, on the contrary, entirely voluntary.

S

SANDWICH ISLANDS, or HAWAIIAN ISLANDS, a group of islands situated in the Pacific Ocean, and governed by a king. Area, 7,629 square miles; population in 1872, 56,897, of whom 49,044 were natives, 889 Americans, 1,938 Chinese, 2,539 Europeans, and 1,485 of mixed descent. The capital, Honolulu, had, in 1872, 14,852 inhabitants. King, Kalukaua I., son of Kapaakeen, born November 16, 1836; elected King February 12, 1874. The Government is a constitutional monarchy, the present constitution having been proclaimed by King Kamehameha V. on August 20, 1864. For the discussion of important questions, the King must convoke a secret council, consisting of the ministers, the governors of the principal islands, of the chancellor of the kingdom, and of sixteen members, one-half of whom are selected from natives, and one-half from naturalized foreigners. The revenue for the period from April 1, 1872, to March 31, 1874, amounted to $1,136,524, the expenditure to $1,192,512. The public debt on March 31, 1874, was $355,050. The total imports in 1873 amounted to $1,849,-000; the exports to $2,128,000; the vessels entering the port of Honolulu consisted of 106 commercial vessels, tonnage 62,089, and 63 whalers.

The population of the Sandwich Islands continued to decrease rapidly. In 1779 Captain Cook placed it at 400,000.; in 1823 it was estimated by American missionaries at only 142,000. According to the official censuses, taken at different periods, the population decreased from 1832 to 1872 as follows: In 1832, 130,315; in 1836, 108,579; in 1850, 84,164; in 1853, 73,138; in 1860, 69,800; in 1864, 69,800; in 1866, 58,765; in 1872, 56,891. Captain Vancouver, who visited the islands fifteen

years after Cook, thought the latter over-estimated the number of inhabitants. On the other hand, however, there are important reasons to assume that Cook's estimate is entitled to be thought correct.

On November 17th the King, with a large suite, embarked on board the American frigate Benicia, to pay a visit to the United States. A month before, commissioners had been sent to Washington, to arrange with the Government of the United States a treaty of reciprocity. During the absence of the King, Prince Leleiohoku acted as regent. The King arrived at San Francisco on December 4th. The President, who had been informed by telegraph of the arrival of the King, replied, in the same way, that he anticipated with great pleasure the opportunity of a special greeting, and assured his Highness of the sincere friendship which, in common with the people of the United States, he felt for his Royal Highness. The King reached Washington on December 12th, where he was formally presented to the President on the 15th, and welcomed by Congress on the 18th. The King subsequently visited New York, Boston, and other cities of the Eastern States.

The total membership of the Protestant Churches in 1873 was 12,283, the large majority of whom are Congregationalist. The first Protestant missionaries arrived in the islands from America, in 1820. The whole number of persons admitted to the Hawaiian Protestant Churches from that time to the end of 1875 was 67,792. A French Catholic mission was established in Honolulu in 1827. In 1829 the Government directed the Catholic priests to close their chapels, but in 1839 it was prevailed upon by the influence of France to declare the Catholic religion free to all. According to the official census of 1853, there were in the islands 11,401 Catholics, by the side of 36,840 Protestants and 2,778 Mormons. In 1874 Catholic missionaries in the Sandwich Islands claimed a Catholic population of 24,-000, while of the remainder, according to their statements, 23,000 belonged to the "several sects of Methodists, Anglicans, and Mormons," and the others were pagans. The Sandwich Islands were made a vicariate apostolic in 1846. The number of churches in 1874 was about 60.

King Lunalilo I. died February 12, 1874. Leaving, like most of his predecessors, no heirs, the choice of a new sovereign fell, by the terms of the Hawaiian Constitution, to the Legislative Assembly, and two candidates were put forward—Queen Emma, well known both in England and the United States, who was supported by the foreign party, and was looked upon as the candidate favored by the English; and David Kalukaua, representative of the national party, and also regarded as the American candidate. The death of Lunalilo, the late King, occurred just after the biennial election for delegates to the Legislative Assembly; when, for the first time in the history of the kingdom, the successful candidates, with a single exception, were natives, using the cry of "Hawaii for the Hawaiians!" The most prominent of these native members, the before-mentioned David Kalukaua, had been Lunalilo's rival at the previous election to the throne, and now came forward again. A proclamation was at the same time issued by Queen Emma, widow of Kamehameha V., by whose influence the mission of the Anglican Church was established at Honolulu, and who now, in declaring herself a candidate for the sovereignty, called "her loyal people" to rally round her.

But, as the day for the Legislative Assembly to proceed to the election approached, it occurred to thoughtful and intellectual observers that if Emma was elected the kingdom would have "Church and state united, and the throng of evils and expenses which such a union would bring with it;" and, finally, American sympathies were, as a rule, on the side of Kalukaua, and English sympathies on that of Queen Emma. The votes of the Assembly went in favor of Kalukaua.

In October the cabinet resigned, and the King appointed W. L. Green, Minister of Foreign Affairs; W. L. Mochonera, Minister of the Interior; J. S. Walker, Minister of Finances, and R. H. Stanley, Attorney-General; besides, W. P. Nood, W. C. Parker, and W. J. Smith were appointed Councilors of State and J. K. Boyd, Chamberlain.

The Hawaiian Legislature, which closed its sessions in September, passed, among others, laws for promoting immigration, for a better irrigation of the country, for the conclusion of a new treaty of reciprocity with the United States, for contributing to the laying of a cable from California to Japan, and for contracting a loan of $1,000,000.

SMITH, GERRIT, an American philanthropist, reformer, and statesman, born in Utica, N. Y., March 6, 1797; died in New York City, December 28, 1874. He was the second son of Peter Smith, at one time a partner of John Jacob Astor in the fur-trade, and subsequently the largest landholder in New York. Gerrit was educated at Hamilton College, Clinton, N. Y., graduating in 1818 with the highest honors of his class, and the same year married the daughter of Rev. Azel Backus, D. D., the president of the college. She lived less than a year. When he attained his majority his father presented to him as a birthday gift, a deed of the entire town of Florence, in Oneida County. During his college course he gained a high reputation both as a student and an orator, and he retained it amid all his cares and his manifold business. He studied law and was admitted to the bar, that he might the better manage the vast interests confided to his care, and also that he might be able to aid the poor and the unfortunate. As soon as he left college, and perhaps even before, he was employed in the management of his father's immense landed estates, buying and selling, and so satisfactory was his management that very soon his father gave the entire business into his hands, and made him, though the younger son, the executor of his will. He was a model business-man; systematic, prompt, and exact. He was inflexibly honest and trustworthy: it is related of him that in 1837, finding himself greatly embarrassed by the impossibility of making collections, and in danger of being compelled to sacrifice his valuable property, he applied to his father's and his own friend, John Jacob Astor, for a loan of $250,000, giving his verbal promise to execute mortgages on certain tracts of land as security for its repayment. For the only time in his life the cautious old merchant paid over to him, on his verbal promise, the sum for which he asked, and required no memorandum even of the transaction. Mr. Smith, on his return to Peterboro', immediately executed the mortgages and had them recorded, but through the negligence of the county clerk the papers were pigeon-holed, forgotten, and not forwarded; and it was not till six months later that Mr. Astor wrote, saying he thought it was time the mortgages were sent on. But while thus judicious in his purchases of land, the conviction had been for years fastening itself upon Mr. Smith's mind that landed monopoly was a wrong to the landless. In 1842, the owner of large tracts of land in forty-two out of the sixty (fifty-nine at that time) counties of the State, he proceeded to give away 200,000 acres, mostly in parcels of about fifty acres, to deserving poor white and black men in these various counties, and in many cases aiding them in erecting cheap but comfortable houses on their little farms. He required them to live on their lands, not usually a difficult condition. In distributing these lands he had in every case a committee selected of those who resided near his property. A small portion of this land was bestowed on institutions of learning and charity, such as the Orphan Asylum at Oswego, which he founded and maintained, Hamilton College, etc., etc. At a later period (about 1857) he established a farming region in Essex County for colored people, and presented John Brown, of Ossawatomie, with a farm there, that he might teach the colored men how to till their land in a northern clime. His gifts of land as well as of money were continued through his life, so that at his death he retained scarcely an eighth of his original magnificent estate. But vast as was his property, it did not wholly occupy his time or his strength. By the very constitution of his mind he was a philanthropist and a reformer. His second marriage, which took place about 1824, was to a Miss Fitzhugh, of Maryland, whose father was a slave-holder; Mrs. Smith survived her husband but two months. By this marriage he was brought into contact and acquaintance with American slavery, and at once he sought some method of ameliorating its evils. At first he believed he had found this in the plans of the Colonization Society, and as early as 1825 he became a member of that organization, and in 1826 or 1827 one of its officers. He contributed largely to its funds, and for several years hoped for much benefit to the African race from its measures, but he withdrew from it in 1835, and thenceforward identified himself with the voting portion of the antislavery party. To this cause he gave largely, and was known everywhere as the most pronounced, though perhaps the most genial, of its advocates. His attachment to the cause of temperance was hardly less ardent—certainly not less permanent. He was also a vigorous opponent of the use of tobacco, and published and circulated tracts against it. He was a strong advocate of peace, heartily labored for the emancipation of woman from the legal disabilities which formerly enthralled her, in the holding of property etc., and eventually included suffrage in the catalogue of her rights. He sought most earnestly for reform in the management of prisons and houses of detention, and aided largely in the establishment of juvenile reformatories. He promoted education, in the public school, the academy, and the college, giving largely both in lands and money to all grades of schools. To Hamilton College, his *alma mater*, he *gave* liberal donations of lands, and, on two occasions, $10,000 in money; and to several of the Western institutions nearly as much. To hospitals orphan asylums, homes for the aged and feeble, insane asylums, churches, libraries, etc., his bounty was unceasing in its flow, and generous and often munificent in its amount. His charities bestowed during his life were more than eight times the

amount of property he left at death, and yet his estate was inventoried at over a million dollars.

As a politician and statesman Mr. Smith's course was for most of his life influenced by his reformatory views, though in early life he was very active as an anti-mason. In 1852 many of the voters of Madison and Oswego Counties of both parties united in inviting him to accept a nomination for Congress. The Whigs and Democrats had each nominated a candidate, but Mr. Smith was elected over both. Mr. Smith remained in Congress only through the first or long session, his health being somewhat infirm, and he anxious to return, untrammeled by office, to his labors in the cause of reform. While in Congress he was active, and advocated, almost single-handed, his views on slavery, temperance, homesteads, the reciprocity treaty, and the Nebraska bill. In 1859 his previous intimacy with John Brown, of Ossawatomie, and the fact that he had given him, as he gave to almost all who applied to him, pecuniary aid, led to severe denunciations of Mr. Smith as being implicated with Brown in the Harper's Ferry affair. As a matter of fact, though knowing Brown's plans only in part, Mr. Smith had earnestly sought to dissuade him from them, and had never given them his sanction or aid. During the war Mr. Smith rendered good service to the Union by his writings, his eloquence, his personal influence, and his money. During the period of reconstruction he pleaded earnestly for reconciliation, but evinced distrust of the Southern politicians, and was uncompromising in his demands for the civil equality of the colored race. When a young man, Mr. Smith became connected with the Presbyterian Church, and in later years the church in Peterboro' was greatly dependent upon him. About 1850 his views on religious subjects, as he himself phrased it, were "modified, enlarged, and changed." His new belief found form in the religion of Nature, or what he called "Rationalism." Mr. Smith's hospitality at Peterboro' was literally baronial. A score of guests was not unusual at his table, and every room in his house was filled for weeks at a time by persons not connected with him by blood or marriage, a majority of them self-invited. The black man and the white were equal guests at his board, and their visits were never shortened or hurried by the generous host. Mr. Smith was a ready and somewhat voluminous writer; but many of his publications, having accomplished an ephemeral purpose, have been so thoroughly lost that their titles cannot now be recalled. Of his more important works the following are the principal: "Speeches in Congress" (1856); "Sermons and Speeches by Gerrit Smith" (1861); "The Theologies" (1866); "Nature's Theology" (1867); "Letter from Gerrit Smith to Albert Barnes" (1868); and a pamphlet on the question of the Bible in schools (1873).

SOUTH CAROLINA. The Legislature of this State closed its session of 1873-'74 by final adjournment on the 17th of March, having continued sitting for about five months. About 270 acts and joint resolutions were passed during that time, more than two-thirds of which are special laws. Among the acts and resolutions of a public character are the following:

Two joint resolutions proposing amendments to the constitution of the State, to be voted upon by the people at the general election next following; the object of one of them being " to insert a clause in the organic law forbidding the increase of the debts of counties, cities, and towns;" of the other, "to limit to two years the term of the offices of the Secretary of State, Controller-General, State Treasurer, Attorney-General, and State Superintendent of Public Instruction."

" An act to repeal section 4 of an act entitled ' An act to relieve the State of South Carolina of all liability for its guarantee of the bonds of the Blue Ridge Railroad Company, by providing for the securing and destruction of the same,'" was approved March 2, 1872.

" An act to reduce the volume of the public debt, and provide for the payment of the same," commonly called " The Funding Bill," seems to be most noteworthy among the laws enacted during the session of 1873-'74, on account of its import as well as its present and prospective consequences. The act enumerates all the outstanding State bonds issued, under the acts of 1838 and afterward till March 1, 1870, inclusive, amounting to $8,427,844.51, and the certificates of stock issued under the acts of 1838 and successive years down to March 23, 1869, and one issued under act of 1794, amounting in the aggregate to $1,438,-782.84, both classes making a total of $9,866,-627.35; recognizes them as valid State obligations for one-half their nominal value; and provides for the funding of their amount thus reduced, and canceling the old certificates of stocks and bonds by giving new ones upon their being surrendered to the State at that rate. It provides also for the funding of the interest accrued upon the said bonds and stocks for about three years up to January 1, 1874; which, added to the principal, makes the nominal debt of the State $11,480,033.91, and the actual, as reduced and funded, $5,740,016.95.

The act mentions another class of outstanding State bonds, called " conversion bonds," amounting to $5,965,000, and these it wholly rejects as not valid State obligations, enacting as follows: " That the bonds known as conversion bonds, amounting to $5,965,000, and which were put upon the market without any authority of law, be, and the same are hereby declared to be, absolutely null and void."

The act provides that the new certificates of stocks and bonds shall bear upon their face the words " Consolidation Certificates of Stock," or " Consolidation Bonds;" shall also bear upon their faces the declaration that the

payment of the interest and the redemption of the principal are secured by the levy of an annual tax of two mills on the dollar on all the taxable property of the State, which declaration shall be considered a contract between the State and every holder of the said bonds and stocks.

It provides also that the principal of the debt, as reduced, shall be payable within twenty years, reckoned from the 1st of January, 1874; and in the mean time bear six per cent. interest, payable semi-annually, on the 1st of January and the 1st of July, at the State Treasury, and at a place in New York to be designated by the Financial Board; that the new issue of bonds and certificates of stock shall be of convenient denominations, but of uniform design and appearance; shall be dated January 1, 1874; the first coupon shall be payable July 1, 1874, and all coupons shall be receivable for all taxes during the year in which they mature, except the tax for the public schools; and that the said bonds and certificates of stock shall be exchangeable the one for the other.

The act designates the State officers who shall issue, sign, and countersign the new certificates of stocks and bonds; pledges the faith, funds, and credit of the State solemnly to the punctual payment of the interest and principal at their stated times, respectively, and that a fund shall be provided for that purpose.

In the second month of the session the following concurrent resolution was adopted by the General Assembly concerning the affairs of the Bank of the State, and acted upon:

Whereas, It is reported that the assets of the Bank of the State are in an unsatisfactory condition, and that the receiver thereof has not made the report required of him by order of the court; and whereas the holders of a large portion of the State debt have a first lien upon the assets of said bank, which would be satisfied by a prompt administration of its affairs, now delayed from some unforeseen cause: therefore, be it

Resolved by the House of Representatives, the Senate concurring, That a committee of five on the part of the House of Representatives, and five on the part of the Senate, be appointed with authority to thoroughly investigate the condition of the Bank of the State, and to send for persons and papers, and ordered to report to the General Assembly at the earliest practicable moment the condition of the said bank.

The committee appointed to perform the duty specified in the foregoing resolution began their work on the 23d of December, 1873, and attended to it in Columbia and Charleston, where the bank is located, for two months, with but little success, owing to their inability to obtain the information required of those who had successively managed the affairs of the bank, or been connected with it in any capacity, and especially of one among the receivers in whose hands the assets of the bank had lately been placed.

The only fact ascertained through the labors of this committee seems to be the gradual and remarkably great diminution of the bank's assets through those in whose hands they were successively placed since the late war. The bank was incorporated in 1812, under an act "to establish a bank on behalf and for the benefit of the State." On September 30, 1860, it had a working capital of $7,260,-612.29, its assets being regarded then as unquestionably good. By its operations and investments during the war, the bank lost above $3,700,000, the statement of its president, dated October 1, 1866, showing its assets on September 30th of that year to have been $3,500,-000, which he considered as good. In April, 1869, the assets of the bank were taken out of the hands of its former officers and placed in the hands of a receiver. From his report it appears that the assets of the bank at this time were less than $800,000, or less than one-fourth of their amount in October, 1866.

The State and county taxes levied on property in South Carolina seem to have been so large of late years that a great number of property-owners could not pay them. It is stated, on the authority of official records, that during the year 1874, in the county of Charleston alone, more than 2,900 pieces of real estate were forfeited to the State because of the inability of their owners to pay the taxes imposed on them; and that in nineteen counties, taken together, 93,293 acres of land, equal to 146 square miles, have been sold for unpaid taxes during the current year, and 343,971 acres, equal to 547 square miles more, have been forfeited to the State, and are now held by her, for the same reason.

A large number of tax-payers, several years ago, organized themselves into a body for the purpose of protecting their common interests. At a meeting of the president and the Executive Committee of this Tax-payers' Union at Charleston, on January 13, 1874, the following preamble and resolutions were unanimously adopted:

Whereas, The Convention of the Tax-payers of the State of South Carolina held in May, 1871, with a view to the protection of the rights of the citizens, adjourned, subject to be reassembled on the call of its president and Executive Committee; and—

Whereas, The necessities of the times, and a due regard for the common welfare of all interests and classes, require that the tax-payers of the State should again meet for counsel: therefore,

Resolved, That the Tax-payers' Convention of this State be summoned and requested to reassemble in the city of Columbia, on Tuesday, the 17th day of February ensuing, at twelve o'clock, meridian.

Resolved, That for the purpose of enlarging the said convention, the tax-payers of the State of South Carolina who are opposed to the frauds and corruptions which prevail, and who are in favor of honest government, with exact and equal justice to all, are requested to meet at the county-seats of their respective counties, on the first Monday of February, ensuing, and then and there elect or appoint additional delegates, equal to the representation of each county in the House of Representatives of the General Assembly, to represent them in the Tax-payers' Convention of the State, with a view to the security of right and the prevention of wrong.

The convention met and was largely attended, delegates being present from all sections of the State; among them some white and black Republicans.

The Committee on Increased Taxation reported the following resolutions, as an appeal to the State Legislature for a remedy to the evil complained of:

Resolved, That in this State taxation has reached the last point of endurance, and that the tax-payers cannot continue to bear the excessive burdens imposed upon them.

Resolved, That the most efficient steps be taken for organizing in every county, township, and precinct in the State a Tax-payers' Union, to membership in which each tax-payer shall be eligible, the object of which shall be the reduction of taxation to the legitimate amount necessary for the administration of the government and the honest expenditure of the money raised thereby.

Resolved, That, among its duties, the Tax-payers' Union shall keep watch upon the acts of the State and county officers, and shall promote all proper legal measures for repressing and punishing fraud, extravagance, and malpractice.

Resolved, That this convention hereby request the General Assembly that they will amend, simplify, and abridge the tax laws of the State, especially that they will so amend the law as to secure a fair and equal assessment of property, and to enable any citizen who has been over-assessed to apply to the courts for redress before he is forced to pay the tax.

The Legislature so far acted upon this appeal in regard to taxation as to pass an act to amend and reduce all the previously enacted laws concerning taxation into one act, and to provide for a reassessment of the real property of the State.

An unexampled criminal suit was instituted in 1874 before one of the courts of South Carolina by the State against her Governor; the indictment making no mention of his official capacity as Governor, but designating him only by his name, Franklin J. Moses, Jr., yet arraigning him for offenses which he committed while he was Governor, because he was Governor, and which he could not have committed if he had not been the Governor. The matter was argued by counsel on both sides before Judge R. F. Graham, of the First Judicial Circuit, who decided it on June 8, 1874. The decision, beginning with a statement of the case, is as follows: "The question which the court is now called on to decide arises upon a motion made by the solicitor for a bench-warrant for the arrest of Franklin J. Moses, Jr., and upon a motion made by the counsel for Franklin J. Moses, Jr., one of the above-named defendants, to strike the case, as to said defendant, from the docket, on the general ground that this court has no jurisdiction at the present time to try the said defendant." From the constitution of the State, and reasoning from analogy, there being no legal authorities directly bearing on the case in hand, which is unprecedented, Judge Graham holds "that until after impeachment the Governor is not liable to indictment and trial in the courts of the State." He reviews and answers the points made in the solicitor's argument, declares the indictment idle as well as void, and concludes his decision with the words: "It is now, therefore, ordered and adjudged that the indictment, as to Franklin J. Moses, Jr., be quashed, and the case, as to him, be struck from the docket."

The political campaign of 1874 in South Carolina was almost exclusively confined within the Republican party, yet unusually active and excited. A large body of the party, having refused to accept the nominations of candidates for Governor and Lieutenant-Governor, nominated others. The State Convention was held at Columbia, on September 8th. It was numerously attended, and continued in session six days, and its proceedings seem to have been exceedingly stormy and discordant. For the office of Governor, three candidates were put in nomination: Daniel H. Chamberlain, John T. Green, and J. Winnsmith. The result of the first ballot decided the contest, as, the whole number of votes cast being 122, Mr. Winnsmith received ten votes, Mr. Green forty, Mr. Chamberlain seventy-two. Mr. Chamberlain was declared nominated. For the office of Lieutenant-Governor R. H. Gleaves, colored, the present incumbent, was renominated. The convention adopted the following platform:

1. It reaffirms adhesion to the principles of the National Republican Convention, at Philadelphia, in 1872, as embodying the true ideas of American progress.

2. It maintains the authority of the General Government to interfere for the preservation of domestic tranquillity in the several States, and acknowledges with gratitude the interposition in this State.

3. It deprecates lawlessness in any form; condemns turbulent agitation in any place; deplores violence, intimidation, or obstruction of personal or political rights by any party; demands a universal respect and consideration of the elective franchise in the hands of the weakest; and declares it shall hold all men enemies to equal rights who interfere with or deny a free and lawful exercise of the ballot to any citizen of whatever party-creed.

4. It pledges to continue scrupulously to enact and enforce the financial reforms promised two years ago, and in a large measure fulfilled. In proof of which it points to the following laws, viz.: the law to levy a specific tax, the law to reduce the volume of public debt, the law to regulate the number of attachés, the law to regulate public printing, the law to regulate the disbursement of the public funds, and the law to regulate assessments.

5. It pledges to reduce the public expenses within the public revenue, and to secure the enactment of a law requiring officers who disburse moneys to give to the public monthly statements of all receipts and expenditures derivable from a moderate assessment and tax rate.

6. It earnestly entreats Congress to pass the civil-rights bill, which is absolutely essential to enforce the constitutional guarantee of equal rights for all American citizens.

7. It pledges to maintain the settlement of the public debt as made last winter, and reject all claims against which there is a suspicion.

8. It holds that all franchises granted by the State should be subservient to the public good, the charges for travel and freight equitable and uniform, and no unjust discriminations should be made between through and local travel and freights.

9. It advocates such modification of the present system of taxation as will prove of the largest advantage to the agricultural interests, and promises the most earnest endeavors to the enactment of such laws, and to the encouragement of such means as will most speedily develop the resources, and build up the manufacturing and industrial prosperity of South Carolina, and the construction of such new railroads as will give the largest and cheapest facilities to all citizens.

10. It pledges protection in the truest sense to the property of the State, and to such wise, just, and humane laws as will perfect the education and elevation of the laboring-classes.

11. That, with a full faith in the justice of these principles, acknowledging the errors in the past, but feeling confident of the ability and determination to correct them, we appeal to all true Republicans to unite in bearing our candidate to victory, and we pledge to carry out in a practical administration of the government every principle inscribed upon the standard, in the interest of the whole people of the State.

Not many hours after the adjournment, a large number of the delegates, being utterly opposed to the nominees, met together and resolved to form themselves, with others of the same sentiment, into a separate independent Republican body, and appointed an Executive Committee of six, who immediately commenced work, and a few days after published an address to the Republican voters of South Carolina, in which, after stating the reasons of their repudiating the action of the Columbia Convention, they invite their fellow-Republicans in the several counties of the State to elect delegates to an Independent Republican Convention to be held at Charleston, on Friday, October 2d, at 12 M., to nominate independent Republican candidates for the offices of Governor and Lieutenant-Governor.

The new movement spread widely from the beginning, and found great favor among the Republicans throughout the State.

During the session of the Republican Convention at Columbia, the County Unions of Tax-payers in South Carolina, pursuant to a call previously published, met in that city on September 10th, "for the purpose of organizing a State Union," which was soon done, and the following resolution was adopted:

Resolved, That the Executive Committee of the State Tax Union be authorized and empowered, in the exercise of their discretion, to recommend to the citizens of the State in favor of honest and good government, to send delegates to a convention to assemble in Columbia, on such a day as shall be fixed by the Executive Committee, to consider the necessity of making nominations for the State officers to be elected at the approaching election.

No nominations were made by the Tax-payers' organization.

The Independent Republicans met in convention at Charleston, on October 2d. The proceedings of the convention were characterized by singular harmony in sentiment, determination of purpose, and enthusiasm. The final result of its work was as follows: John T. Green, of Sumter, was nominated for Governor, and Martin R. Delany, of Charleston, for Lieutenant-Governor. Mr. Delany is a full-blooded negro, above sixty years of age, and seems to deservedly enjoy the esteem and confidence of blacks and whites. Both of the nominees briefly addressed the meeting.

As to platform, the Independent Republican Convention adopted the identical one which had been adopted by the Republican Convention at Columbia in September, as given on a preceding page.

The following resolutions were adopted by the convention shortly before its final adjournment:

Resolved, That the Independent Republican movement is not hostile to the domination of the Republican party in South Carolina, but is designed to maintain its integrity against the corrupt "rings" which control it, and at the same time protect the common interests of the whole people of the State.

Resolved, That while maintaining the integrity of the Republican party in South Carolina, we cordially invite the whole people of the State to support the nominees of this convention as the only means of preserving their common interests—especially requesting the Conservatives that, having persistently declared that their desire was only for good government, without regard to partisan politics, they will now attest the sincerity of their declarations by marching with us, shoulder to shoulder, for the triumphant election of Green and Delany, and the certain redemption of the State from the corrupt "rings" which have disgraced the Republican party, and trampled upon the interests of Republicans and Conservatives alike.

On October 8th the Conservatives of South Carolina, in accordance with the call previously issued, assembled in State Convention at Columbia, for the purpose of considering the advisability of making nominations of candidates for State offices. The body was composed of eighty-five delegates, representing all the counties in the State, except four. Simpson Bobo, of Spartanburg, presided over the meeting, both as chairman before its permanent organization was effected, and as president afterward.

The final result of the deliberations of the convention was, that the Conservative party of South Carolina should nominate at this time no candidates of their own, but support those nominated by the Independent Republican Convention at Charleston a few days before. The following resolutions were adopted:

Whereas, The Republican party, being in the majority in this State, is responsible for its government, and the Conservative citizens of the State having declared that if the Republicans would nominate for Governor and Lieutenant-Governor men of their own party, of honesty, character, intellect, and competence, the Conservatives would refrain from opposition to them;

And, *whereas*, the regular Nominating Convention of the Republican party have nominated for Governor and Lieutenant-Governor men whose antecedents show them to be unworthy of confidence, and whose success will insure the continuance of the corruption, dishonesty, and party tyranny, which have prostrated the State;

And, *whereas*, the Independent wing of the Republican party has declared its intention to reform the government of the State, and in pursuance of this intention has made nominations of men whose antecedents entitle them to confidence in their integrity and honesty, for which nominations they have asked the support of the Conservative voters of the State;

And, *whereas*, we recognize that, in the present condition of the State, the necessity of checking corruption and procuring honest officials is paramount to all questions of party politics or affiliations, and believing the opportunity afforded us of securing such reform will be in the success of the nominees of the Independent Republican party:

Resolved, That it is the sense of this convention, called to consider the necessity of making nominations for State officers in the approaching elections, that no nominations for Governor or Lieutenant-Governor in the approaching election be made by the Conservative citizens of the State.

Resolved, That in the opinion of this convention the Conservative citizens will best promote their interest and the welfare of the State by giving their support to the candidates for Governor and Lieutenant-Governor nominated by the Independent Republican party.

Resolved, That we adopt as the platform of the Conservative party of South Carolina, "Honesty and economy in the administration of the State government."

The election resulted in the choice of the Republican nominees for Governor and Lieutenant-Governor, by considerable majorities over the Independent Republican. The whole number of votes cast in the State at this election was the largest polled since 1868. For Governor it was 149,217, of which Mr. Chamberlain received 80,403, Mr. Green 68,814. For Lieutenant-Governor it was 144,341, of which Mr. Gleaves had 80,073, Mr. Delany 64,248.

In the next General Assembly the Republicans have a small majority in the Senate, and an about equally small minority in the House of Representatives. In the last General Assembly the proportions were: In the Senate—Republicans 25, Conservatives 8; in the Lower House—Republicans 101, Conservatives 23.

The result of the elections in the congressional districts for Congressmen was as follows: First district, J. H. Rainey, Republican, received 14,370 votes, Samuel Lee, Independent Republican, 13,563; second district, C. W. Buttz, Republican, 14,204, E. W. M. Mackey, Independent Republican, 16,742; third district, S. L. Hoge, Republican, 16,431, S. McGowan, Conservative, 12,873; fourth district, A. S. Wallace, Republican, 16,452, J. B. Kershaw, Conservative, 14,455; fifth district, Robert Smalls, Republican, 17,752, J. P. M. Epping, Independent Republican, 4,461.

In the third district, an election was held to fill the seat of R. B. Elliot, who had resigned. L. C. Carpenter was elected to the place without opposition.

The amendments to the State constitution were approved by a majority of the people. Upon their being ratified by a two-thirds vote of the next Legislature, they will become a part of the constitution.

DANIEL HENRY CHAMBERLAIN, the Governor-elect of South Carolina, is a native of the State of Massachusetts, and a graduate of Yale College. He pursued his studies at the Cambridge Law School with distinction. Upon the outbreak of the late civil war he received a commission in the Fifth Massachusetts (colored) Cavalry, with which he served till the end. In 1865 he settled himself in South Carolina, and seems to have taken an active part in the political agitations which followed in that as in the other Southern States; was elected a member of the convention called to form a new State constitution for South Carolina; and in the administration of the government organized under the new constitution he has held the office of Attorney-General till the end of 1872. From that time to September, 1874, when he was nominated as the Republican candidate for Governor of South Carolina, he attended to the practice of his profession as a lawyer.

The General Assembly met at Columbia at the end of November, 1874. Upon the organization of the House of Representatives, R. B. Elliot was elected Speaker.

Governor Chamberlain states that the valuations of property for assessment made previous to the present year "have been, to a great extent, unjust and oppressive;" averring "that property has borne a valuation almost arbitrary when different localities or separate pieces of similar property are compared, and excessive in amount when tested by any reasonable standard of value."

A new assessment of the real property in the State, the fourth since 1868, was made last year. From reliable information given him in reference to the result of the work, the Governor estimates that "the aggregate valuation of all the property in the State under this assessment will fall from $30,000,000 to $40,-000,000 below the aggregate of the previous amount."

The deficiencies of the fiscal year ending October 31, 1874, were $472,619.54; and those of the next preceding year, $540,328.

By authority of the Legislature, State obligations, called "certificates of indebtedness," were issued last year by the State Treasurer to the amount of $231,996, and he was directed to issue about $340,000 more of them. The right of the General Assembly to authorize such issues was contested in the Supreme Court of the State, from which the cases were carried, on a writ of error, to the Supreme Court of the United States, where they are now pending.

The provisions of the funding act passed at the previous session, reducing certain State bonds and certificates of stocks to one-half of their nominal value, and wholly rejecting the conversion bonds, as has before been related, Governor Chamberlain regards as a final settlement, and expresses his belief that "no party, nor even any man, will hereafter dare to interpose an objection to the prompt discharge of the new obligations of the State." This settlement seems also to have been recognized as final by the people of the State generally, and in particular by both of the political parties during the late canvas in the State,

they having expressly pledged themselves to maintain it. Within the five months elapsed since the funding act was put in operation, above $2,000,000 of the old bonds and stocks have been surrendered to the State by their holders, and exchanged for the new ones, as provided by the act.

The common-school system for the education of youth seems to have made for several years past a considerable progress. "The number of free common schools within the State in 1870 was 769; in 1873 it was 2,017. The number of pupils in attendance in 1870 was 30,448; in 1873 it was 83,753.' The number of teachers employed in 1869 was 754; in 1873 it was 2,310." The aggregate number of persons of school-age, between six and sixteen years, in South Carolina, is 230,102; so that about one-third only of the school-population attended school in 1873. The amount expended by the State for the free schools within the year ending October 31, 1874, was $298,-440.91.

The financial condition of the State of South Carolina, as appears from the report of her Treasurer, for the year ending October 31, 1874, submitted to the General Assembly in December, may be briefly stated as follows:

```
Bonded debt.......................$9,540,750 28
Floating debt.................:......  2,679,292 75
Contingent liabilities...............  4,797,608 20
                                      _____
   Total..........  ................$17,017,651 23
```

The public receipts from all sources during the same year amounted to $1,718,766.41; and the expenditures to $1,592,075.04; leaving a surplus of $126,691.37 on hand in the Treasury.

SPAIN, a kingdom of Southern Europe. King, Alfonso XII., born November 28, 1857, proclaimed King December 30, 1874. Spain is divided into forty-nine provinces (for the area and population of which see the volume for 1873). The area and population of the foreign colonies were, according to the latest dates, as follows:

COLONIES.	Area—Square Miles.	Population.
1. AMERICA :		
Cuba......................	45,883	1,400,000
Porto Rico.................	3,596	625,000
Total....................	49,479	2,025,000
2. ASIA AND OCEANICA :		
Philippines................	65,908	6,000,000
Carolines and Palaos.......	916	28,000
Marianas................	417	5,610
Total....................	67,241	6,033,600
3. AFRICA :		
The Guinea Islands........	489	35,000
Total Spanish colonies...	117,209	8,098,610

In the budget for 1872–'73, the revenue was estimated at 588,000,000 pesetas (1 peseta = 19.3 cents); the expenditures at 627,000,000 pesetas; the deficit at 39,000,000 pesetas. The public debt amounted, in May, 1873, to 7,830,-150,000 pesetas.

The army of Spain was reorganized in 1868, after the model of that of France. Since then the laws on the organization of the army have been repeatedly modified, and further changes were expected. The force in Spain was to number about 216,000 men. The army in Cuba consisted of about 60,000 men, namely, 54,400 active army, 4,000 reserve, 1,500 militia. The army in Porto Rico consisted of 9,400 men; that in the Philippines, of 9,000. Total number of troops in the colonies, 78,106. For military purposes, the kingdom is divided into five districts, or "capitanias generales," at the head of each of which stands a captain-general, with the rank of field-marshal.

The fleet, in 1874, was composed as follows:

NAVY.	Guns.	Horse-power.
Vessels of the First Class.		
7 iron-clads	145	5,900
10 screw-frigates	431	5,380
3 wheel-steamers......................	48	1,500
Vessels of the Second Class.		
10 wheel-steamers	48	3,130
9 screw-steamers......................	30	1,800
2 transports.........................	..	600
Vessels of the Third Class.		
20 screw-steamers.....................	45	2,100
54 gunboats...........................	54	2,160
10 wheel-steamers	20	4,000
4 wheel-steamers	..	540
Vessels not classified.		
2 steamers............................	6	1,000
1 monitor.............................	3	260
132	830	25,370

Of sailing-vessels, there were one frigate (28 guns), two corvettes, one transport, two pontoons. The navy was manned, in 1872, by 9,700 sailors and 5,000 marines, and commanded by 2,344 naval officers and 144 marine officers.

The following table exhibits the trade of Spain during the years 1868 and 1869; the value being expressed in reals (one real = 4.8 cents):

YEAR.	IMPORTS. Value of Total Trade.	VALUE OF TRADE WITH AMERICA. Spanish Flag.	Foreign Flag.
1868....	2,296,000,000	313,000,000	64,000,000
1869....	1,769,000,000	282,000,000	91,000,000

The merchant navy in 1873 consisted of 3,069 sea-going vessels, of 678,886 tons, of which 2,867, of 540,211 tons, were sailing-vessels, and 202, of 138,675 tons, were steamers.

The aggregate length of the railroads in operation amounted, on January 1, 1874, to 5,426 kilometres (1 kilometre = 0.62 m.); the aggregate length of the telegraph-lines, on January 1, 1871, to 11,754 kilometres.

The new year opened with another *coup d'état*. On January 2d the session of the Cortes was reopened, and the President of the Republic, Señor Castelar, read his message, expressing himself favorably on the situation of the country. The message was received coldly by all parts of the House, except when an allusion to Cartagena provoked murmurs from the Left, and counter-cheers when Señor Olias, of the Right, moved a vote of thanks to the Government. A member of the left, Santamaria, moved the "previous question." President Castelar declared that the Government would immediately resign if the previous question were taken into consideration. Señor Salmeron, the President of the Cortes, bitterly upbraided Señor Castelar for this course, as endangering public order. Castelar retorted that the Government still held itself responsible for public order, and renewed the threat of resignation. Santamaria withdrew the motion, amid loud cries of "Vote! vote!" At seven the House adjourned. It met again at eleven. In reply to a new attack upon the policy of the Government by Salmeron, Castelar declared the Government policy republican in the best sense, though not democratic and socialistic. His alliance with the Radicals was necessary for protection against the Intransigentes, who destroyed republicanism by provoking reaction. He declared that, with the present Cortes, all government was impossible, and that no ministry could last eight days. The vote of thanks was nevertheless lost by 120 against 100. Castelar then presented the resignation of the cabinet, and the sitting was suspended to form a new ministry. Palanca was elected President. Suddenly the Captain-General of Madrid, General Pavia, entered the Cortes with a strong military force, and sent his aide-de-camp to inform the President of the Cortes that it must disperse. For five minutes there were loud cries and protests, General Soceas and others threatening resistance, but the officers answered that the troops would fire if the deputies did not immediately retire. At this instant two shots were fired in the air by the soldiers. The House then broke up immediately in great confusion. No resistance was made by any one, consequently there was no bloodshed and no attempt at arrest. All the deputies were allowed to go quietly home. General Pavia had seized the Home-Office in order to get the control of the telegraph. He next strongly occupied with troops and artillery all the principal points, especially the Calle Toledo, the Belleville of Madrid. He rode round the town himself, inspecting the arrangements, which were so thorough that the Intransigentes had no chance of a successful resistance. An order was issued that all but the new national militia were immediately to give up their arms on pain of prosecution. The *cafés* and shops were at first shut, but many afterward reopened. The day was fine, and there were large crowds in the streets. There was naturally much excitement, but little alarm. The municipal authorities of Saragossa, Barcelona, and Valencia, made an attempt to oppose the new Government, but the troops succeeded without much difficulty in crushing the movement.

It was generally known that, though the *coup d'état* had been carried through by General Pavia, Marshal Serrano was the instigator and real leader of this movement. Immediately after the dispersion of the Cortes, General Pavia summoned the most eminent men of all parties —excepting the Intransigentes and the Carlists —as well as the principal members of Señor Castelar's cabinet, in order to form a new ministry. General Pavia himself, however, declined to be a member. The new ministry was formed under the presidency of Marshal Serrano, as chief of the Executive power of the Republic. It was composed as follows: Sagasta, Minister of Foreign Affairs; Zavala, Minister of War; Figuerola, Minister of Justice; Becerra, Minister of Agriculture; Echegarray, Minister of Finance; Garcia Ruiz, Minister of the Interior; Topete, Minister of Marine. While the majority of the members of the new cabinet had during the reign of King Amadeo belonged to one of the monarchical parties, the Minister of the Interior, Garcia Ruiz, is the most prominent representative of a centralized republic, and in his journal he praised the *coup d'état* as a victory of the centralized over the federal republic, and as a salvation of the nation from the dangerous illusions of the Federalists. On the 5th Señor Martos was appointed Minister of Justice in place of Figuerola, who resigned, and Señor Mosquera Minister of Commerce. Castelar not only declined to have any thing to do with the new Government, but issued an address to the Spanish nation in which he says: "I protest with all the energy of my soul against the brutal act of violence committed against the Constituent Cortes by the Captain-General of Madrid. My conscience will not permit me to associate with demagogues, but on the other hand my conscience and my honor keep me aloof from the state of things just created by the force of bayonets." Several deputies belonging to the majority adhered to the protest made by Señor Castelar. The new ministry, in its turn, addressed a long manifesto to the nation, explaining the events of the 3d. It says that the same parties now placed in power made the revolution of 1868, and the constitution of 1869. They neither condemn nor destroy their previous work—the voluntary abdication of the monarch, and the proclamation of the republic, only destroyed one of its clauses. They will not consent that this work, which has thus been modified, should be changed in its essence. The Government will oppose both absolutism and anarchy. A decree was also issued dissolving the Cortes, and announcing that the Government would convoke the ordinary Cortes when the maintenance of order was secured, and universal suffrage could be freely exercised.

Only a few days later, on January 12th, the last stronghold of the Intransigentes, Cartagena, fell into the hands of the Government. Its surrender had been certain for some time.

On January 11th the Junta, which had before resisted all entreaties addressed to it in the name of humanity, itself sent commissioners into the besiegers' lines. But by that time the Madrid Government felt that it had required too many sacrifices of the army and Spain to consent to terms which would have been willingly granted four months before, in order to spare life. Besides, the offer had not been made until Cartagena was visibly within the the compass of the besiegers' means of attack. Thus all stipulations were refused. The insurgents were to have until noon on January 12th to surrender, and pardon was promised to all who should surrender with arms in their hands, save only the members of the Junta. This answer appears to have determined the leaders of the insurrection to separate their cause from that of a city which could be of no further use to them; and they took their departure very speedily on board the Numancia, and the city on the afternoon of January 12th was occupied by General Domingues. The fugitives on board the Numancia, Contreras, Galves, the members of the Junta, and other fugitives, ultimately disembarked at Oran, in Algeria, and delivered themselves up to the French authorities. They alleged that Cartagena surrendered through the treachery of the commander of the principal fort, a charge which was fully confirmed by later reports. The town was found to have suffered severely, though not so much as had been supposed, except near the Madrid Gate, where the damage was very great. Scarcely one house had escaped untouched, and some were riddled with shells; two houses had been thrown down and the street pavement ploughed up. Immense damage had been done by the recent explosion of the powder-magazine, where over 200 persons were said to have been killed. The walls near the Madrid Gate had suffered much, but there was nothing approaching to a breach. A few guns had burst, but most were in their places. The forts appear to have received little injury, the Atalaya Fort so little as to confirm the suspicion that it was surrendered by treachery. No guns were dismounted or spiked. The entry of the troops was effected very quietly and without bloodshed, except the shooting of eight men who tried to escape.

The capture of Cartagena enabled the Government to concentrate all its forces against the Carlists, who in December, 1873, and during the first weeks of the new year, had been eminently successful. The attempt of General Moriones to relieve Bilbao, the capital of the Basque provinces, had been a wretched failure, and on January 8th the troops of Don Carlos began the siege of the fortress in form. Portugalete, near Bilbao, was captured by the Carlists on January 22d. General Moriones collected all the available forces of the Government, and, being strengthened by the Republican troops set free by the fall of Cartagena, marched to the relief of Bilbao, and for the first time during the war there seemed a chance of a fair trial of strength between the two armies. But once more he was to receive a severe check. On February 21st, the preparations for the siege of Bilbao being terminated, Don Carlos left Durango, a town some miles to the southeast, and took up his quarters at Baracaldo, on the north side of Bilbao, at a short distance from the mouth of the river where the Republican squadron was stationed. The next day the Carlists began shelling the city. According to one of the dispatches, they had 1,500 shells and an abundant supply

of powder—perhaps not material enough for a prolonged and vigorous siege, but formidable against such a town as they attacked. Bilbao had kept them at bay since the beginning of the war, but now its safety must depend on the energy of the Republican commander in the field. General Moriones had advanced a week before as far as Somorrostro, and every day it was expected in Madrid that he would attack the enemy. About the time when the fire on Bilbao opened, he telegraphed to the Government that he was ready to advance, but had been prevented by the bad weather. His

ROYAL PALACE, MADRID.

forces were variously estimated at from 20,000 to 30,000 men, but there can be little doubt that he commanded the most powerful force which has been at the disposition of any General since the abdication of King Amadeo and the disorganization of the regular army. Moriones advanced against the Carlists, and attacked them on the 24th in their lines at San Pedro; but the troops, after crossing the bridge of San Pedro, were encountered by a bayonet-charge of the Carlists, and, after suffering a loss of about 800 men, he was obliged to fall back on his position at Somorrostro. He telegraphed that he was able to maintain himself there, and to keep up his communication with Castro-Urdiales and Santander. But he demanded new reënforcements, and also desired that another general should be sent to command the Republican forces. The Carlists were highly elated at their new success, and their prospects at this time appeared all the more hopeful as considerable progress had also been made in other quarters. Tolosa was in their hands, and, in Catalonia, Vich and Manresa had been taken; General Nouvitas had been defeated by them at Olot, and had himself been captured. In the provinces of Aragon, Valencia,

and Murcia, they numbered about 20,000 infantry, 1,000 cavalry, and 12 cannon. In the two Castiles and in Estremadura the movement was also gaining ground. Don Carlos appointed governor-generals for all the provinces, even for those in which there were as yet no organized forces of his partisans. The siege of Bilbao, which had been opened on February 22d, was vigorously pushed, and from that day to March 4th about 2,600 bombs were thrown into this town. The conservatives of the besieged town were willing to capitulate, but the volunteers, the middle and lower classes, were utterly opposed to any negotiations concerning surrender.

Under these circumstances, Marshal Serrano deemed it best to assume himself the chief command. He appointed, on February 27th, Señor Zabala prime-minister, retaining only the title of chief of the executive power, and placed himself at the head of the army. From March 25th to 27th severe encounters took place between the two armies. The Republicans made some progress, but the key to the Carlist position, the church of San Pedro Abanto, they could not take, the Carlists making a desperate resistance. On the Republican side, General Loma was wounded, and also Primo de Rivera; Brigadier Prillo was killed. The troops lost at the least 1,500 in the three days; the Carlists must have lost about 1,000. Serrano was in the thick of the fight throughout the day, and Admiral Topete had a bullet through his coat.

Soon after these indecisive engagements, Serrano and Topete left for Madrid, where dissensions had broken out among the ministers, which Serrano succeeded in terminating. Don Carlos, on the other hand, organized a complete government, appointing General Elio Minister of War, Admiral Vinalet Minister of Foreign Affairs, and Count Pinal Minister of Home Affairs and Finance. His army, in the northern provinces, consisted of the six divisions of Navarre, of Guipuzcoa, Biscay, Alava, Castile, and Santander.

Having returned to the army, which had received large reënforcements, Serrano again assumed the offensive, but, instead of assaulting the impregnable heights of Somorrostro only in front, decided simultaneously to develop flank and direct attacks. The plan of operations was that of Marshal Concha, who, with the divisions of Echague, Martinez Campos, and Reyes, constituting a corps of about 15,000 effective combatants, was to advance by Valmaseda; while Serrano himself, with about 20,000 men, was to engage the Carlists in front, and to press them if he saw an opportunity of doing so. On the 29th Serrano's right opened communications with Concha's left, and the cannonade was opened against San Pedro de Abanto, and, as had been anticipated, was but feebly answered. On the 30th Concha succeeded in taking the heights of Valmaseda, and the cannonade of Pedro de Abanto by Serrano, and the bombardment of Portugalete by the fleet, were kept up with vigor. On the 1st of May, Concha continuing to gain ground on the right, the Carlists abandoned their positions at Monte Abanto and Santo Juliano, which were immediately occupied by Serrano's, troops. Marshal Concha redeemed his pledge to relieve Bilbao on the anniversary of Dos de Mayo, the great national festival of Spain. He made his triumphal entry, Marshal Serrano having chivalrously waived his claim to enter first. The entry of the troops was a very fine spectacle. The inhabitants turned out in their best attire to give an enthusiastic welcome to their deliverers. Cannon fired salutes, the church-bells rang, and flags of all hues and the national colors were conspicuous. Serrano returned to Madrid, where he met with an enthusiastic reception. In Madrid, in the mean while, a new crisis had declared itself at the Council of Ministers. Señor Martos maintained the necessity of continuing the policy of conciliation, while several other ministers wished to place certain restrictions upon that policy. On May 13th, after much discussion and difficulty, another new Spanish cabinet was formed, composed as follows: General Zabala, President of the Council and Minister of War; Señor Sagasta, Minister of the Interior; Señor Ulloa, Minister of Foreign Affairs; Señor Camacho, Minister of Finance; Señor Alonso Martinez, Minister of Justice; Señor Alonso Colmenares, Minister of Public Works; Señor Ortiz, Minister of Colonies; Señor Rodriguez Arias, Minister of Marine. The new ministers entered office with the suspicion of anti-republicanism very freely cast upon them, and their advent produced great alarm in the real Republican camp. Señor Castelar still refused to emerge from his retirement, and his action in this respect, in spite of the direct solicitation of Serrano and other leading men, not a little tended to produce the above solution. The more excitable and timid of his followers predicted the speedy proclamation of the monarchy of Prince Alfonso or that of the Duchess of Montpensier. The ultra-Reds began already to talk of a rising. The Radicals did not know how to find invectives bitter enough to hurl at Serrano for his decision. The Alfonsists were delighted, as they considered the ultimate triumph of their cause only a question of time, which was brought nearer by the presence of Sagasta as the leading spirit in the new cabinet. The Sagastinos were in ecstasies of joy.

On May 15th the new ministry issued a manifesto to the nation expressing regret that it was still unable to convoke the representatives of the people, and calling on all the liberal parties to support the Government. It also appointed Marshal Concha commander-in-chief of the Northern Army. The available strength of the entire Republican army was at this time stated to be about 120,000 infantry and 10,000 cavalry. Marshal Concha had with him 38,000 men and 87 guns. The military operations during May were of no special importance. At the beginning of June the brother of Don Carlos, Don Alfonso, crossed the Ebro, at the head of about 12,000 troops, in order to carry the war into Valencia and the heart of Spain; but he was totally defeated in the battle at Alcora, in which also the Infante, Don Enrique, was killed. General Concha used nearly the whole of May and June to prepare for a grand attack upon the fortified position of the Carlists at Estella. The result of the movement was very different from what the Government confidently expected. Not only did the Carlists, when attacked on June 27th and the two following days, make a desperate resistance and maintain their position, but Marshal Concha himself lost his life. The bloodthirsty Carlist general, Antonio Dorregaray, ordered every tenth man of the captives and all the officers to be shot. Among those put to death was the German Captain Schmidt, who accompanied the army as correspondent of German papers, and was shot under the pretext that he was a spy. The Carlist commander-in-chief of Biscay, Horaechea, ordered all the Liberals of the district of Zornaza to be imprisoned, and one Liberal to be shot for every cannon-shot fired by a Government steamer upon the towns and villages of the coast. Don Carlos, from his headquarters at Morentin, issued on July 16th a manifesto to the Spanish nation, defining the policy which, as King of Spain, he would pursue, and promising especially that he would reëstablish the authority and the influence of the Catholic religion. The Government of Madrid declared, on July 31st, all the provinces in a state of siege, clothed the captain-generals with extraordinary powers, established in all the provinces permanent military commissions, and ordered the property of the Carlists to be confiscated, in order to prevent it from being used for continuing the war, and in order to indemnify from it all persons who had been injured by the war, especially the families of the killed soldiers. In the mean while the Carlists had obtained some remarkable successes on the seat of war. On July 15th they even entered the town of Cuenca, in Castile, which, however, they had again to evacuate on July 20th. In Catalonia, the Carlist chief Saballs occupied a few places between Barcelona and Montserrat, and caused 160 captured soldiers to be shot at Olot, a fate which soon after was shared by 250 other captives, belonging to the corps of General Nouvilas. In Navarre the Carlists took the town of La Guardia, but this victory was more than neutralized by a great victory which General Moriones gained over them at Oteiza, southwest of Pampeluna. The cruelties committed by the Carlists, especially the shooting of Captain Schmidt, induced the Government of Germany to recognize the Republican government of General Serrano, and the example of Germany was almost immediately followed by Italy, Belgium, France, and England. Only Russia declined to take the same step. From France, the Spanish Government, aided by the diplomatic influence of Germany, obtained a promise that the frontier would be strictly watched, and due care be taken to prevent reënforcements to be sent to the Carlists. The latter captured the border-fortress of Urgel, but were unable to take Puigcerda, and even suffered, near this town, a severe defeat. The Government of Madrid, in order to make a decisive attack upon Estella, ordered another levy of 60,000 men. The commander of the Northern Army and prime-minister, Zabala, resigned both positions, as he was too outspoken in favor of the restoration of monarchy under Alfonso, the son of Isabella, and he was succeeded as general-in-chief by General Laserna, and as prime-minister by Sagasta.

The military operations during the last months of the year were destitute of any interest. The commander-in-chief of the Government troops, Laserna, had sent General Loma by sea to San Sebastian, in order to raise the siege of Irun. Loma was successful in this mission, though his success remained without further results. The Carlists retired, but they were not pursued by the Government troops.

More harm was done to the Carlist cause by the dissensions among the Carlist generals. General Dorregaray, in October, resigned the chief command of the Carlist troops, and went to France; according to Carlist reports, in consequence of ill-health, but, according to the Republicans, in consequence of difficulties with Don Carlos. That Cabrera, the most famous of the military champions of the Carlist cause, had openly fallen out with the Pretender, was generally known. Reports were even rife of serious mutinies in the Carlist camps, and of attempts against the life of Don Carlos. Nevertheless, the Carlists, at the end of the year 1874, had lost but little of their territory; and although Serrano, at the beginning of December, went once more himself to the scene of war, the army of the Government appeared to be inactive, or, at most, to prepare very slowly for another aggressive movement.

The year closed with another *coup d'état*, which, though it had long been planned, surprised the world by its sudden and unexpected execution. In the last days of December two battalions of General Martinez Campos pronounced, at Murviedro, in favor of Prince Alfonso, the son of ex-Queen Isabella; the garrison of Madrid and the fleet followed; the same news was received from the Armies of the North and the Centre; and thus the Spanish Republic was overthrown, and the Bourbons were restored to one of the many thrones from which they have been, since 1848, expelled. At the first news of the *pronunciamiento*, the prime-minister, Sagasta, and the Captain-General of Madrid, Primo de Rivera, appeared to be desirous to put down the movement. Sagasta issued an energetic manifesto against the troops, and the captain-general had several prominent Alfonsists arrested, among them Canovas de Castillos, who, as long ago as August 22, 1873, had been authorized by Alfonso to assume the government in his name. But when the Armies of the North and the Centre declared in favor of Alfonso, Sagasta, Primo de Rivera, and Serrano, hastened to recognize the new order of things, and Canovas de Castillos assumed, in the name of Prince Alfonso, the reins of government.

The struggle of the Cubans for their independence was not abandoned in 1874, but it attracted little attention. Near the close of February, Carlos Manuel Cespedes, ex-President of the Republic of Cuba, was betrayed into the hands of the Spanish authorities, by whose orders he was shot.

ST. GOTHARD TUNNEL. This great engineering enterprise is making steady advancement; and it is expected that its progress will be more rapid as the work approaches completion. At the close of June, 1874, the contractors had completed nearly one-seventh of the whole distance. The tunnel is being constructed for an international association of capitalists, known as the St. Gothard Company, which was founded October 10, 1871.

The capital was at first fixed at 102,000,000 francs, or £4,080,000. Of this, £1,360,000 was raised by shares, and the remaining £2,-720,000 by bonds. The International Association consisted of three groups: that of Germany, which found 34,000,000 francs; that of Italy, which supplied 34,000,000 francs; and that of Switzerland, which furnished the remaining third. The groups consisted solely of bankers and finance companies, and among the names may be found the houses of Rothschild, Oppenheim, etc. The final formation of the St. Gothard Company was completed in December, 1871. The primary surveys had, however, been made by M. Gelpke as early as 1869. The final staking out of the ground—a work of great difficulty, as may be imagined when we state that no fewer than fifteen stations were required, many of them in situations all but inaccessible—was satisfactorily accomplished. The work was begun at both ends, and the lines met with an error of but four inches in the middle, which we regard as a triumph of trigonometrical surveying, bearing in mind the difficulties to be overcome. It was finally decided that the dimensions of the tunnel should be nearly identical with those of the Mont Cenis Tunnel. The height to the crown of the arch is to be 6 metres, or 19.68 feet; maximum width, 8 metres, or 26.24 feet; and minimum width, 24.93 feet. Various systems of construction are adopted, according to the nature of the ground. The works were let by contract to M. Favre, of Geneva, in the summer of 1872. Seven tenders were received. Of these, two were withdrawn; a third did not supply satisfactory information as to the system of construction the contractor proposed to adopt; and of the remaining four, two were struck off the list. Only two competitors remained—M. Favre and the Italian Company of Public Works; but the latter required nine years to make the tunnel, and M. Favre only eight, and whereas the Italian Company would only forfeit the caution money—£320,000—if the work was not complete in eleven years, M. Favre consented to pay it over at the end of nine years. Again, the Italian Company wanted about half a million sterling more than M. Favre. The work began in June, 1872, at Gö-schenen, and at Airolo on the 1st of July in the same year. The rock to be pierced consists at the Göschenen end for the most part of a hard granitic gneiss, much fissured, but free from water. At the Airolo end, gravel, sand, and pebbles, were first met with, and then yellow limestone. Gypsum, talc, and mica-schist, were also found; finally a dolomite. This did not last, however, and at about 286 feet from the end a bed of schist was pierced, which discharged torrents of water, and was only traversed with the utmost difficulty. The work is carried on by drilling holes by machinery worked by compressed air, and exploding charges of dynamite in these holes. In the beginning the drills were worked by temporary steam-engines which

supplied the compressed air required. But now three turbines, worked by a fall of 279 feet, erected at Göschenen, drive the compressors. These work to 600-horse power. At Airolo three other turbines, each work under a head of 541 feet, to 210-horse power. Each turbine actuated three Colladon compressers, supplying per minute 2,258 cubic feet of air at seven atmospheres. Thus, in all, at least 1,200-horse power can be brought to bear on the works.

The tunnel starts from Airolo, on the southern, or Italian side, and runs to Göschenen, on the northern, or Swiss side of the Alps. The line was set out by M. O. Gelpke, C. E. No direct measurements could be obtained, but the possible error in length amounts to only about two feet either way. The tunnel is approached at the Göschenen end by a rising grade of 1 in 40, on a line made from Altorf, on the Lake of Lucerne, by way of the valley of the Reuss. Just outside the tunnel is a short bit of level. The line then rises at the rate of 1 in 171.8 to a point not far from the centre of the tunnel, where another short piece of level will connect the rising grade with one falling to Airolo at the rate of 1 in 1,000. Then comes a short length of level on a line now in course of construction from Airola to Bellinzona, which will establish communication with the Ticino Valley. The road will be double through the tunnel and perfectly straight, with the exception of a curve 15 chains radius and 475.73 feet long, near the southern, or Italian end. The total length of the tunnel proper, not including the cuttings at either end, will be 14,900 metres, or nine miles 455 yards—a length greater than that of the Mont Cenis Tunnel by about 1.4 mile. The highest portion will be 3,781 feet above the level of the sea. To assist the ventilation it is proposed to construct a shaft at Andermatt, which will be about 340 yards deep, and will enter the tunnel about 3½ kilometres, or 2.17 miles, from the Göschenen end. According to the report issued by the Federal Council at the end of 1874, the gallery driven on the north side of the tunnel at Göschenen had been advanced 1,771 yards, and on the southern end at Airolo 1,455 yards. Only 95 yards of the vaulting had been finished on the north side; on the south side 357 yards of the tunnel had been vaulted. On the north side the rock bored had been principally hard granite. The moisture was inconsiderable. About 1,740 yards from the opening, the tunnel passed under the bed of the river Reuss at a depth of 262 yards. The boring of the gallery proceeds regularly at the rate of about three yards per day, that distance being accomplished by the aid of six of Ferroux's machines. On the south side, at Airolo, the gallery runs almost constantly through hornblende, difficult to pierce and of a very tenacious nature. The great influx of water was met with at a depth of 1,402 yards, amounting to two litres per second. In this working, seven of Dubois &

François's machines are used with the daily average progress above recorded. Boring operations had to be suspended during the whole of December on account of the want of ventilation, caused by the fall of the waters of the Tremola. Snow and ice also hindered the operations very much. Up to the 12th of December three of Someiller's machines had been in use for widening the tunnel; from that date four of McKean's machines began working. In several places boring operations were also carried on by hand. For the railways in the Ticino Valley in connection with the tunnel, over 660,000 cubic feet of earth had been cleared away; the total number of workmen employed there at the present time is on the average 2,952, and on the whole St. Gothard Railway 4,914.

SUMNER, CHARLES, LL. D., S. P. A. S., etc., an American statesman, scholar, and author, born in Boston, Mass., January 6, 1811; died in Washington, D. C., March 11, 1874. He was the son of Charles Pinkney Sumner, of Boston, and was educated at the Boston Latin School and at Harvard College, graduating from the latter in 1830. He commenced the study of law under Mr. Justice Story. He was admitted to the bar in Worcester in 1834, but began in Boston the practice which soon surpassed that of any other young lawyer there. He was not long after made Reporter of the United States Circuit Court, and published three volumes of Judge Story's decisions, at the same time editing the *American Jurist*. During the first three winters following his entrance into the profession, he lectured before the Law School in the absence of Judge Story and Prof. Greenleaf, and with so much success, that he was urged to take a professor's chair. Several years before he had edited, with great ability and discrimination, "A Treatise on the Practice of the Courts of Admiralty in Civil Causes of Maritime Jurisdiction," by Andrew Dunlap; a work undertaken in consequence of the illness of Mr. Dunlap. In 1837 he went to Europe, and remained there three years, visiting the highest courts, and both Houses of Parliament. In France and Germany he made the acquaintance of the most eminent jurists, publicists, and distinguished scientists. While in Paris, he wrote, at the request of our minister, General Cass, a paper in defense of our northeastern boundary claims, which attracted great attention both in Europe and America. In 1840 he resumed the practice of his profession. In 1843 he was again made lecturer at the Law School, and in 1844–'46 published, with numerous biographical sketches and explanatory notes, "Vesey's Reports," in twenty volumes. On July 4, 1845, he pronounced, before the authorities of the city of Boston, an oration entitled "The True Grandeur of Nations." It was an eloquent defense of peace. Before the close of the year, he spoke ably and eloquently against the Mexican War and against the pro-slavery inter-

ests which were urging it; and in 1846, in an address before the Whig Convention on the "Antislavery Duties of the Whig Party," he announced his uncompromising hostility to slavery. In 1848 Mr. Sumner abandoned the Whigs, and went over to the Free-Soilers; Mr. Webster, after having sustained the fugitive-slave law, resigned his seat in the Senate for one in the cabinet; and in 1851, after a long and fierce struggle, Sumner was elected his successor. He was almost alone in the Senate, and the tactics of his adversaries were, never to allow him to gain the floor, so that it was nearly nine months after he had taken his seat in the Senate, and then only by seizing an opportunity when they were off their guard, that he was able to make a speech on the subject nearest his heart. That speech has become historical under the title, "Freedom National, Slavery Sectional." Thenceforward, in the Senate and out of it, he was known and welcomed as the most eloquent and efficient of the opponents of slavery. He spoke at Plymouth Rock in August, 1853; at the Republican Convention of Massachusetts, in September, 1854; in the Metropolitan Theatre in New York, in May, 1855; and at Fanueil Hall in November of the same year: and each time with great boldness and fervor, on different phases of the great subject. In the Senate he opposed the repeal of the Missouri Compromise. In May, 1856, he delivered his great speech in the Senate, "The Crime against Kansas," occupying two days; and its uncompromising spirit, and its severity, led to his being assaulted in his seat in the Senate-chamber, by Preston S. Brooks, a member of Congress from South Carolina, two days later, the circumstances of which are well known. The injuries he received were severe, so that he was disabled from public duties for nearly four years; and from its effects he never fully recovered. He took his seat again in the Senate in the spring of 1860, and in the early summer delivered a speech entitled "The Barbarism of Slavery," in which he referred to the assault in no vindictive or even pointed terms. He labored actively in the presidential campaign of 1860 for the election of Lincoln and Hamlin. In the winter of 1860–'61 he was firm in his opposition to any concessions to the South, as alike foolish and wicked.

At the commencement of the next session of Congress, in the summer of 1861, he became chairman of the Senate Committee on Foreign Relations. Mr. Sumner was often accused of being radical, ultra, and bitter; but in all the years of the war, he was, according to the testimony of those best qualified to judge, and who were themselves never accused of radicalism, the most cautious, prudent, and judicious of counselors, and more than once was instrumental in averting war with Great Britain or France when it appeared imminent. In other measures appertaining to home affairs, he was not less active and useful. The thirteenth constitutional amendment, if not originated by him, received his hearty support, and was carried by his influence. He was also prompt in his advocacy of reconstructive measures, and in the manifestation of a kindly spirit toward the South. He was a decided enemy to the "policy" of President Johnson, and was active in his impeachment trial. He voted for President Grant at his first election, though he was not particularly active in the canvas. His speech on the Alabama claims was vehemently denounced abroad, but its principles were those on which the arbitrators subsequently acted, and to which the British Government gave its reluctant sanction. In December, 1870, he opposed with great ability and some vehemence the project of President Grant for the annexation of the Dominican Republic, and caused its defeat. The President, at the opening of the next Congress, signified his desire to his friends that Mr. Sumner should be removed from the chairmanship of the Committee on Foreign Relations, and Senator Cameron was put in his place. In February, 1872, he made one of his finest efforts on the question of an investigation of the sales of ordnance made by the United States during the Franco-German War. This speech was said even by those most bitterly opposed to him to have been the ablest of his whole senatorial career; but his health was breaking down from the long-continued mental strain, and the old malady which had resulted from the assault upon him returned immediately after the delivery of this speech, and his physician ordered him to abstain from all mental labor for the remainder of the session. He absented himself for some weeks, but he could not wholly refrain from taking part in the contest which was coming. The supplementary civil-rights bill, a measure he had much at heart, was after a severe struggle passed in the Senate, but failed to receive the necessary two-thirds vote in the House. On May 31, 1872, he delivered a long and carefully-prepared speech vindicating his course, and arraigning the President for the alleged misuse of the appointing power. The condition of his health making it necessary for him to go to Europe about the 1st of June, whence he did not return till late in November, he took no part in the presidential campaign of 1872, and declined the nomination for Governor of Massachusetts, which was tendered him. His influence was thrown in favor of Horace Greeley. On taking his seat again in the Senate, in December, 1872, he introduced a resolution providing that the names of battles with fellow-citizens shall not be continued in the Army Register, or placed in the regimental colors of the United States. This resolution excited the indignation of some bitter partisans, and a resolution was offered in the Massachusetts Legislature to censure Senator Sumner for an attempt to degrade the loyal soldiery of the nation and their grand achievements by this proposal.

This resolution of censure was passed, but the Legislature of 1874 made haste to rescind it, and before his last illness the news reached Washington that Massachusetts had struck from her legislative records her first and only censure of him. During the short session of 1872-'73, as well as the early portion of that of 1873-'74, Mr. Sumner seldom mingled in debate. More than once he was alarmingly ill from angina pectoris, and he was compelled to content himself with passing as far as he was able the measures in which he was specially interested. During the whole winter of 1873-'74 he was an invalid, and constantly under the care of a physician, but was generally in his place in the Senate. The fatal attack of angina commenced on the afternoon of Tuesday, March 10th, but with no considerable severity till after 6 P. M. For the next twenty hours his suffering was intense and almost constant, and he died at 2.47 P. M. of Wednesday, March 11th.

In person Mr. Sumner was tall, well formed, and commanding. His voice was remarkably melodious, and his action in speaking graceful as well as animated. His mind was not only marked by the highest characteristics of ability, it was stored with a rich array of elegant and useful knowledge. He was equally at home in the modern and the ancient classics, and could quote from either with singular readiness and accuracy; and, in addition to a very retentive memory, he was gifted with strong imaginative powers. To the most elegant accomplishments he added the sternest purity of purpose. That he sometimes erred from the very intensity of his convictions, his best friends will admit, but no man could accuse him justly of any mean, low, or personal motive in his action. His hands were clean from bribes.

Mr. Sumner had been a somewhat voluminous writer, though every thing from his pen was very carefully prepared, and touched, and retouched, till it satisfied his fastidious taste. Among his smaller works were: "The Scholar, the Jurist, the Artist, the Philanthropist" (1846); "Fame and Glory" (1847); "White Slavery in the Barbary States" (1847); "Law of Human Progress" (1848); "Finger Point from Plymouth Rock" (1853); "Landmark of Freedom" (1854); "The Antislavery Enterprise" (1855); "Position and Duties of the Merchant" (1855); "Our Foreign Relations" (1863); "The Case of the Florida" (1864); "The Provisions of the Declaration of Independence" (1865); "Eulogy on Abraham Lincoln" (1865); "The National Security and the National Faith" (1865); "Our Claims on England" (1869). A collection of his speeches, in two volumes, was published in 1850; his more recent speeches and addresses were published in 1856, and a collection of his entire works which was in progress at his death, has since been published, with a memoir by Charles A. Phelps, LL. D., in 12 vols., 8vo.

SWEDEN AND NORWAY, two kingdoms of Northern Europe, united under the same dynasty. King, Oscar II., born January 21, 1829; succeeded to the throne at the death of his brother, Charles XV., September 18, 1872; married June 6, 1857, to Sophia, born July 9, 1836, daughter of the late Duke Wilhelm of Nassau. Oldest son: Gustavus, heir-apparent, Duke of Wermland, born June 16, 1858.

The executive authority is in the hands of the King, who acts under the advice of a Council of State, composed of ten members, of whom two have the title of State Ministers, and eight that of Councillors of State; of the latter five are chiefs of departments. At the close of 1873, the Swedish Council of State was composed of the following members: 1. The Minister of State and Justice, E. H. de Carleson, appointed May 4, 1874, appointed Minister of Justice, June 3, 1870; 2. Minister of State and Foreign Affairs, Major-General Oscar M. de Björnstjerna, appointed Minister of Foreign Affairs, December 17, 1872; 3. C. J. Berg, appointed June 4, 1868; 4. Chief of the Department of the Navy, Major-General Baron Brader Abraham Leijonhufvud, appointed January 14, 1870; 5. Chief of the Department of Ecclesiastical Affairs, Dr. G. Wennerberg, appointed June 3, 1870; 6. Chief of the Department of the Interior, Dr. P. A. Bergström, appointed June 3, 1870; 7. Baron C. J. O. Alströmer, appointed June 15, 1870; 8. Chief of the Department of War, Major-General Erik Oscar Weidenhielm, appointed December 5, 1871; 9. Dr. J. H. Lovén (June 5, 1874); 10. Chief of the Department of Finance, J. G. N. S. Baron Akerhielm, appointed September 28, 1874.

In Norway the King exercises his authority through a Council of State, composed of one Minister of State and nine Councilors. Two of the councilors, together with the minister, form a delegation of the Council of State, residing at Stockholm, near the King.

The area of Sweden is 170,591 square miles; population, in 1873, 4,297,972.*

The emigration, from 1851 to 1860, numbered 16,900 persons; from 1861 to 1870, 122,447; in 1868, 27,024; in 1869, 39,064; in 1870, 20,003; in 1871, 17,458; in 1872, 15,912; in 1873, 13,580.

The following towns, in 1873, had a population of more than 10,000 inhabitants: Stockholm, 147,249; Göteborg, 61,599; Malmö, 28,325; Norrköping, 25,982; Carlscrona, 16,586; Gefle, 16,265; Upsala, 12,086; Jönköping, 12,138; Lund, 11,408.

In the budget for 1875 the revenue was estimated at 99,249,939 crowns; the expenditures at 99,249,939 crowns. The public debt, at the end of 1873, amounted to 122,080,000 riksdalers.

The total strength of the armed forces was, in September, 1873, as follows:

* For the area and population of the several läns into which the country is divided see ANNUAL CYCLOPÆDIA for 1873.

ARMY.	Guard.	Line.	Beväring Conscrip'n Troops.	Total.
Infantry...............	1,800	25,200	72,578	99,578
Militia of Gothland...	.....	....	8,511	8,511
Cavalry................	440	4,740	3,974	9,154
Artillery (234 guns)....	.... .	4,673	3,311	7,984
Engineers	.....	972	1,052	2,024
Military train.........	.....	.....	5,524	5,524
Total.............	2,240	35,585	94,950	132,775

The navy, which was entirely reorganized in 1866–'67, consisted, at the beginning of 1874, of 37 steamers, 8 sailing-vessels, 88 galleys: total, 133 vessels, of 455 guns. At the end of 1873, the navy was officered by two rear-admirals, six commanders, 20 commanding-captains, 43 captains, and 43 lieutenants. The principal port is that of Carlscrona, on the Baltic.

The imports and exports, in 1872 and 1871, were as follows (expressed in thousands of crowns):

YEAR.	Imports.	Exports.
1872............................	216,360	199,815
1871............................	169,179	161,028

The movement of shipping was, in 1872, as follows:

FLAG.	ARRIVALS.		CLEARANCES.	
	Loaded Vessels.	Lasts.*	Loaded Vessels.	Lasts.*
Swedish	3,650	117,272	7,492	216,547
Norwegian.............	813	37,744	2,750	237,056
Foreign...............	2,276	117,504	4,666	260,429
Total.............	6,739	272,520	14,908	714,032

* 1 Swedish last = 3.27 tons.

The commercial navy of Sweden numbered, in 1871, 3,878 vessels, of 130,267 lasts. The number of vessels registered for the foreign trade was 1,783, of a total burden of 102,328 lasts.

The aggregate length of railroads in operation, in August, 1874, was 2,638.9 kilometres; of those in course of construction, 2,807 kilometres (1 kilometre = 0.62 mile). The number of post-offices in 1872 was 546. The revenue amounted to 2,716,050 riksdalers; the expenditures to 2,291,318 riksdalers. The aggregate length of the state telegraph-lines was 7,057 kilometres; and of telegraph-wires, 14,943 kilometres.

The area of Norway is 122,280 square miles. The population was, in 1872, estimated at 1,763,000. The following towns had, in 1870, a population of more than 10,000 inhabitants: Christiania, 66,657 (in 1872 about 70,000, and with the suburbs 80,000); Bergen, 30,252; Drontheim, 20,858; Havanger, 16,053; Drammen, 15,458; Christiansand, 11,468. The budget for the period ending June 30, 1874, estimates the revenue and expenditure at 5,455,704 specie dalers each (1 specie daler = $1.11). The public debt at the end of August, 1873, had become reduced to 6,876,000 specie dalers. On

January 1, 1872, the troops of the line numbered 18,000 men, the reserve forces 19,000, and the landvaern 11,000. The naval force, in 1872, consisted of 21 vessels (4 iron-clads), with an armament of 172 guns. The imports, in 1871, amounted to 26,788,000 specie dalers; in 1872, to 34,928,000. The exports, in 1871, to 20,189,000 specie dalers; in 1872, to 26,768,000.

The movement of shipping, in 1872, was as follows:

SHIPPING.	Vessels.	Lasts.
Arrivals....................	13,029	806,206
Clearances.................	13,863	889,259

The commercial navy, at the end of 1873, consisted of 7,447 vessels, of a total burden of 592,997 commercial lasts (1 last = 2.1 tons). The aggregate length of railroads in operation at the end of 1873 was 502 kilometres; the aggregate length of telegraph-lines, 6,238 kilometres; of wires, 9,643 kilometres.

The Swedish Diet was opened by the King on January 19th. In his opening speech, while speaking of the foreign relations of Sweden, the King laid special stress on the visit of the Crown-prince of Germany, as a proof of the friendly connections of Sweden and Germany. On closing the Diet, May 22d, the King referred with special satisfaction to the passage of the new law on commercial navigation, and to the increased appropriations for educational purposes.

SWITZERLAND, a republic of Central Europe, consisting of twenty-two cantons, three of which are divided each into two independent half-cantons. The supreme legislative and executive authority is vested in a Parliament of two Chambers, the Ständerath, or State Council, and the Nationalrath, or National Council. The first is composed of forty-four members, two for each canton. The Nationalrath consists of 135 representatives of the Swiss people, chosen in direct election, at the rate of one deputy for every 20,000 souls. Both Chambers united are called the Federal Assembly, and as such represent the supreme Government of the republic. The chief executive authority is deputed to a Federal Council, consisting of seven members, elected for three years by the Federal Assembly. The President and Vice-President of the Federal Council, who are the first magistrates of the republic, are elected by the Federal Assembly for the term of one year, and are not reëligible till after the expiration of another year. The President of the Federal Council for the year 1874 was K. Schenck, of the canton of Bern; Vice-President, Dr. E. Welti, of the canton of Aargau. President of the National Council for the session of the Federal Assembly, beginning in June, 1874, K. Feer Herzog, of the canton of Aargau; Vice-President, L. Ruchonnet, of the canton of Vaud. President of the State Council, A. Köchlin, of the canton of Basel; Vice-President, J. K. P. Morel, of the canton of St.-Gall.

Area of Switzerland, 15,992 square miles. Population, according to the census of 1870, 2,669,147, of whom 1,566,347 (58.7 per cent.) were Evangelical; 1,084,369 (40.6 per cent.) Catholics; 11,485 members of Christian sects, and 6,996 Jews.

The total revenue of the Confederation in the year 1873 amounted to 34,843,168 francs; the expenditures to 33,618,325 francs. The budget for 1874 estimated the revenue at 37,061,000 francs; the expenditures at 37,071,000 francs. The liabilities of the republic amounted, in 1873, to 29,288,181; as a set-off against which there is Federal property amounting to 29,487,829 francs.

The strength and organization of the armed forces of Switzerland were as follows, at the end of 1873.

TROOPS.	Bundesauszug.	Reserve.	Landwehr.	Total.
Staff...................	......	......	......	841
Infantry...............	66,649	39,078	54,334	160,061
Riflemen..............	6,001	3,864	4,616	13,918
Cavalry...............	1,913	1,086	1,571	4,570
Artillery..............	8,262	5,350	4,643	18,255
Engineers.............	1,245	1,059	474	3,047
Administrative troops.	299	129	74	502
Total...............	84,369	50,069	65,981	201,257

The aggregate length of Swiss railways, in 1874, was 1,573 kilometres; that of telegraph-lines, in 1873, 5,843 kilometres; of wires, 14,169 kilometres.

The revision of the Federal Constitution which, in 1873, had been made by the Federal Council,* was submitted to a popular vote on April 19, 1874. The new revision strengthens the authority of the central Government in matters military, legal, and especially ecclesiastical. The control of the Confederation over the army has hitherto been, more especially as far as the line is concerned, of the loosest and feeblest kind; and the cantons look with keen jealousy on any infringement of their existing power to manage their own contingent of the Federal army. But it is evident that the victories of Germany, due in chief measure to the homogeneous organization, have impressed the more thoughtful of the Swiss people with the untrustworthiness of disjointed and segregated battalions in time of war, and more especially in the event of a sudden emergency. The partial assimilation of the law, which varies almost inconceivably in the various cantons, is another main object of the revision, and every thing has been done by those who were intrusted with drawing it up to avoid exciting unnecessary opposition. It would be impossible at once to pass a uniform code of laws for the entire Confederation, and it is intended only to provide for the gradual introduction of the more urgent reforms, in a style likely to be acceptable to the cantons which are

---

* See ANNUAL CYCLOPÆDIA for 1873, article SWITZERLAND

thus asked to surrender a portion of their old customs. Finally, the innovations in the relations between the Catholic Church and the cantonal governments are of a sweeping kind, and will place the Roman Catholic Church in Switzerland in a yet more subject state than that to which it is being reduced in Germany. Hence the vote of the Catholic party was given undividedly against the revision. Save as regards ecclesiastical affairs, the present revision was much less ambitious than its rejected predecessor; and this fact no doubt accounts for the striking contrast between the present and the previous *plebiscitum:* while the latter was, in 1872, adverse to revision by a majority of about 4,000, the people this time approved revision by about a two-thirds majority. The proportion of those voting for the revision to the total number of voters, in the several cantons, was as follows:

	Per cent.		Per cent.
Schaffhausen	96.7	St.-Gall	57.0
Neufchâtel	92.9	Grisons	53.4
Zurich	84.6	Zug	39.6
Basel (country)	86.6	Lucerne	3.83
Basel (city)	84.4	Ticino	83.4
Thurgau	82.9	Nidwalden	18.9
Appenzell, Out.Rhodes	82.9	Freyburg	18.8
Bern	77.3	Schwytz	17.5
Geneva	77.3	Obwalden	17.2
Glarus	75.8	Valais	15.7
Soleure	65.1	Appenzell, In. Rhodes	14.3
Aargau	65.1	Uri	7.9
Vaud	58.7		

The popular vote on the revised Constitution, as well as the election of new Grand Councils in a number of cantons, shows that, on the whole, the policy of the Federal authorities in church questions, as well as the extension of the jurisdiction of the central Government, was only, as heretofore, opposed by the Catholic cantons of Lucerne, Zug, Schwytz, Uri, Unterwalden, Freyburg, Valais, and the

LUCERNE.

half-canton of Appenzell (Inner Rhodes). The only addition to this phalanx was the canton of Ticino, which, though wholly Catholic, had for more than thirty years, during all the conflicts of the Federal Government and the Catholic bishops, sided with the former. The government of the canton cast again its vote in favor of the revision, but the large majority of the people voted against it. Many other indications showed that the long ascendency of the Liberal party in this canton had been undermined, and thus foreshadowed the complete overthrow of the Liberal party, which took place at the new election of a Grand Council at the beginning of 1875.

The conflict between the Federal authorities and the majority of the cantons on the one hand, and the heads of the Catholic Church on the other, continued throughout the year 1874. The Papal nuncio and the bishops sent, in Jan-

uary, 1874, notes to the Federal Council, protesting against the proposed suppression of the Papal nunciature to Switzerland,[*] but the Federal Council resolved to lay them on the table, and the Papal nuncio, having received his passports, departed on February 9th. The Grand Councils of Bern, Geneva, St.-Gall, and others, continued to encourage the Old Catholics, who remained in possession of nearly all the Catholic churches in the canton of Bern, and in addition received a faculty of (Old) Catholic theology in connection with the University of Bern. The progress of the Old Catholic movement among the Catholic population appears, however, not to have been considerable, and at the close of the year the organization had not been completed by the election of a bishop.

* See ANNUAL CYCLOPÆDIA for 1873.

In June the National Assembly elected the city of Lausanne, in the canton of Vaud, as the seat of the Federal Court (Bundesgericht). The new Federal Court, which is to serve from 1875 to 1878, was elected in October; it consists of the following members: Dr. Blumer, of the canton of Glarus, President; Roguin, of Vaud, Vice-President; Morel, of St-Gall; Anderwert, of Thurgau; Pictet, of Geneva; Niggder, of Bern; Stamm, of Schaffhausen.

The International Postal Congress met in the city of Bern, on September 15th, and elected Federal-Councilor Borel its president. The invitations to this Congress had been issued by the Government of Germany, and all the invited states, twenty-one in number, had sent

delegates. The states represented were: Germany, Switzerland, Austro-Hungarian Monarchy, Belgium, Denmark, Egypt, Spain, United States of North America, France, Great Britain, Greece, Italy, Luxemburg, Norway, Netherlands, Portugal, Roumania, Russia, Servia, Sweden, and Turkey. The Congress agreed upon the introduction of uniform rates throughout the territory of the states belonging to the Postal Union, and the total abolition of transit postage. The city of Bern was elected the seat of the International Postal Bureau. It was resolved to hold the next Congress in 1875, in Paris. The Congress closed its session on October 9th, the treaty having been agreed to and signed by the representatives of all the

LAUSANNE.

states except the one of France, who had not yet received instructions from his Government.

Among the most important bills adopted by the Federal Assembly in its fall session was the new army bill. The main questions to be settled were: In how many days can the militiaman be made effective, and how many must be insisted on afterward for his periodical drills? Fifty-two days had been asked for by the Government for the training of infantry recruits, and this period had been declared by the Assembly of the cantonal military societies lately held at Olten to be acceptable only as the minimum. However, the House Committee of the Deputies on the bill resolved to reduce it by a week, and they succeeded by a majority of ten votes after a sharp debate, so that the future training will be for forty-

five days only. As to the drilling practice, or repetition, there was by no means the same striking divergency of opinion. It is true that the Government, in Colonel Welti's project, had asked for ten days in every year for the first eight years, while the committee preferred sixteen every second year. But the Olten meeting had received with favor this proposed modification since it was announced, and it was therefore accepted on behalf of the Executive by Colonel Welti as accordant with sound military views, and so adopted almost unanimously. The one remaining point of great general interest was the clause, which was agreed to, directing the cantons to take care that all the male youth between the school and recruit ages shall get fifteen afternoon drills annually, of course without arms.

T

TELEGRAPHIC PROGRESS. A remarkable improvement in telegraphy seems to have been discovered simultaneously in Bavaria and in the United States. The German inventor is Herr Hencker, of Munich, and his "Electromagnetic Copying Apparatus," as he calls it, has been already secured by a Frankfort banking firm. This apparatus, it is said, without the aid of a telegraphist, can transmit writing in different languages, signatures, portraits, plans, etc., to any distance, with perfect resemblance to the original in all points. Among other exploits of this wonderful invention it telegraphed the opening speech of the Singers' Festival, which took place lately, as printed, surrounded by garlands of oak and laurel ; also bills of exchange, Government dispatches in cipher, messages in Greek and Hebrew letters, an arrest-warrant with portrait of the person "wanted," and a map as used by generals in time of war, with the intended movements of the troops marked out upon it. An impression of the object, writing, drawing, etc., is taken in a prepared ink on a sort of silver paper, which is rolled on a revolving cylinder and forwarded to its destination without further visible aid ! The American rival is Mr. Edison. His discovery relates to that form of apparatus known as the automatic or chemical telegraph, in which signals are made and recorded by causing the electricity to pass through paper, the latter being saturated with a chemical substance which changes in color when the current acts. In the ordinary working of this form of telegraph the electricity is sent over the line-wire by a key, in the usual manner, and passes through a pen, stylus, or lever, which has no movement, but simply rests upon the paper, the latter being moved by a weight or clock-work. No magnet and armature are used. The salient feature in Mr. Edison's present discovery is the production of motion and of sound by the pen or stylus, without the intervention of a magnet and armature.

TENNESSEE. The movements of the political parties in this State were carried on with unusual energy and excitement during the year.

The colored people met in State Convention at Nashville, on the 28th of April. Delegations from about twenty counties, situated in different sections of the State, attended. A number of colored speakers addressed the convention, animated apparently by unfriendly feelings toward the whites, even Republicans. They charged the laws of the State with unjust discriminations against their race, and urged the negroes not to support, by their votes, the nominee of whatever party who would not pledge himself to advocate their cause, and aid them in securing the attainment of the full measure of their rights as citizens of the United States, politically and socially. They claimed, in a special manner, the right of admission on equal terms with the whites to all public places of whatever nature ; insisting chiefly on their children being admitted and taught in the public schools, not separately, but with the white children in the same schools.

A series of resolutions was adopted asking for the passage of the "civil-rights bill" before Congress, equal privileges with whites in all educational institutions, etc., and pledging the convention to raise sufficient funds to secure able counsel to obtain the release of one of their color who had married a white woman against the law of the State, and had been sent to prison.

The Democrats assembled in State Convention at Nashville, on August 19th. Before proceeding to action, a resolution for determining the result of the ballot by a two-thirds vote was offered, and, notwithstanding opposition, adoped by a vote of above four yeas to one nay.

Eleven candidates for the office of Governor were put in nomination, and fourteen ballots taken on them, without decisive result; the number of competitors, by the successive withdrawal of names, steadily decreasing as the number of ballots increased. At the fourteenth ballot there remained two competitors only—James D. Porter, of Henry County, and James E. Bailey, of Montgomery—but neither of them received a sufficiency of votes. The whole number then cast was 948, of which Mr. Bailey received 359 votes, Mr. Porter 589; necessary to a choice, 632. It being then midnight, the name of Mr. Bailey was withdrawn, and a motion made that "James D. Porter be declared the unanimous choice of the convention." The motion was put to the vote, and carried amid great enthusiasm without a dissenting voice. The following platform was unanimously adopted :

The representatives of the Democratic and Conservative party of Tennessee, in convention assembled, most cordially invite all good and true men, who desire to increase the prosperity of the people of the State, and preserve her honor untarnished, to unite with us in carrying out the following principles, to wit:

1. That all honest labor should be protected, and receive its just reward.

2. That the burden of government should be borne by the whole property of the country ; that all assessments of taxes should be equal, uniform, and just, and no improper discrimination should be made against any species of property.

3. That we favor a strict construction of the Constitution of the United States, and insist that no power should be exercised by the General Government that is not clearly delegated or clearly implied in the necessary exercise of the powers so delegated.

4. That we oppose all monopolies, rings, and combinations formed for the oppression of the people;

that we are for the abolition of all useless and unnecessary offices; for the proper reduction of all excessive salaries; for the most rigid economy in the administration of the State government; for all necessary reforms in the law so as to make its execution speedy, just, and certain; that we will hold the collectors of revenue to a strict accountability in the collection and application of said revenue; that we deplore the existence of all indebtedness, Federal, State, county, and municipal, and demand that no more taxes shall be laid upon the people than shall be found to be essentially necessary for the support of the State government administered on principles of the most rigid economy, and for the payment of its just debts and obligations, and the preservation of its credit and honor untarnished, and therefore are opposed to an increase of taxation.

5. That we favor the abolition of the present odious national banking system and the payment of the bonds of the Government by issuance of its non-bearing-interest notes according to the contract expressed and implied at the time of the creation of such obligation, and a repeal of the present oppressive Federal tariff, and the enactment of a law solely with a view to the collection of the necessary revenue.

6. That we denounce all legislation that seeks to interfere with the individual right of the citizen to select his own associates, and particularly what is known as the supplementary civil-rights bill pending before the Federal Congress, as a palpable violation of the Constitution, intended to vex, harass, oppress, and degrade the people of the Southern States, and productive of untold social and political evils to both races, and which we should resist by all legal and constitutional means in our power.

The Republicans held their State Convention at Chattanooga, on the 16th of September, white and colored delegates being in attendance. A disagreement on important matters manifested itself between the representatives of the two races; the white delegates being against nominating any candidate for Governor, and against the civil-rights bill; the colored advocating and insisting upon both points, chiefly upon their civil rights. In reference to this they intimated that the white Republicans, who were not in favor of the civil-rights bill, should leave the party. They seem to have subsequently relented somewhat in regard to certain parts understood as included within the meaning of that bill, declaring that "they did not care for mixed schools or social equality," but insisted upon their right of getting equal accommodations with the whites in hotels, cars, steamboats, and other public places. Between the members of the Committee on Platform, also, a long debate took place, with the result that the members of opposite views finally agreed to a sort of compromise, whose terms are set down in the third paragraph of the following platform, reported from the said committee and adopted by the convention:

The Republicans of Tennessee, in State Convention assembled, make the following declaration of principles:

1. We reaffirm the platform of principles set forth by the National Republican Convention of the Republican party in the year 1872, and commend it to the favorable consideration of the voters of Tennessee.

2. That the system of national currency founded by the Republican party has proved the best ever devised for the purpose intended, and while we would favor no violent change which might be oppressive to either the debtor or creditor class, we would recommend a system of free national banking, based upon a safe plan for redemption, and a return to specie payment at the earliest practicable period consistent with a sufficient supply of currency to meet the reasonable wants of business.

3. We are in favor of the full and equal enjoyments of accommodations, advantages, rights, and privileges, by all citizens and other persons within the jurisdiction of the United States, without regard to race, creed, or color, and at the same time we deem it unnecessary and unwise to attempt, by congressional legislation, or otherwise, to compel, as between such races, creeds, or colors, the joint exercise of such accommodations, advantages, rights, or privileges. But we recognize the principle, which is older than our Constitution, that every man's house is his castle, and that, under our Government, every citizen, white or black, has the right to bear arms in conformity to law, and to express his opinions without interference or molestation.

4. We favor the calling, by the next Legislature, of a Constitutional Convention for the following purposes: 1. To reform our present cumbersome and expensive judicial system; 2. To do away with useless offices, and with the great abuses which have grown up under our present unwise system of fees and salaries, and to make such other useful alterations in the present organic law as will tend to lessen the expenses and advance the interests of the State.

5. That we are opposed to the payment of the "new issue" of the Bank of Tennessee; that we favor the payment of the public debt, both State and national; that we alike are opposed to the iniquitous funding-bill passed by the late Democratic Legislature, and to the present assessment law, because of its unjust and inquisitorial provisions, and we demand a thorough reform in our present mode of assessing property, and collecting it.

6. That, as an enlightened public opinion is the only safeguard of civil and religious liberty, we favor, by the means of free schools, the education of every child within the limits of the State of Tennessee.

7. That the opening of our great rivers and water-courses, especially the mouth of the Mississippi and the navigable streams of Tennessee, being of the utmost importance to the development of our country, we ask that such appropriations may be made from time to time, by the General Government, as will accomplish this result.

8. That we denounce the administration of Governor John C. Brown, in its inefficiency in enforcing the laws and protecting life and property; in its fraudulent disposition of the property of the State; in its corrupt lease of the penitentiary; and in its many shortcomings and general mismanagement, as unworthy of the great State of Tennessee, and as disastrous in the extreme to the best interests of her citizens.

9. That we earnestly appeal to all citizens of Tennessee, whatever their past political associations, who revere the sacred majesty of the law and the dignity of the Commonwealth, to aid the Republican party in an effort to restore tranquillity within her borders, to invite immigration, and uphold the material interests of our people.

Horace Maynard was nominated by acclamation as the candidate of the Republican party for Governor.

The result of the election, on November 3d, was the success of the Democratic candidates, with few exceptions. The whole number of votes polled for Governor was about 158,904, of which 103,061 were cast for the Democratic nominee, 55,843 for the Republican; thus giving Mr. Porter a majority of 47,218 over Mr.

Maynard. A third candidate for Governor, B. F. C. Brooks, as the Working-men's nominee, received 192 votes. In 1872, the aggregate number of votes polled for Governor was 181,789, which were less unequally distributed; the majority of Mr. Brown over Mr. Freeman having been 13,589.

The state of parties in the Legislature is as follows: In the Senate—Democrats, 23; Republicans, 2; in the House of Representatives —Democrats, 70; Republicans, 5.

The following are the names of the successful candidates for Congress: From the first district, William McFarland, of Hamblin; second district, Thornburg; third district, George D. Dibrell, of White; fourth district, John W. Head, of Sumner; fifth district, John M. Bright, of Lincoln; sixth district, John F. House, of Montgomery; seventh district, W. C. Whitthorne, of Maury; eighth district, J. D. C. Atkins, of Henry; ninth district, W. P. Caldwell, of Weakley; tenth district, H. Casey Young, of Shelby. Nine are Democrats, and one is a Republican.

John W. Head having died, Samuel M. Fite was elected to the vacancy.

Serious disturbances of the public peace, and deeds of blood, have been of frequent occurrence in Tennessee during the year 1874— the effect of hostile feelings, reciprocally entertained by the white population of the State, or a considerable portion of it, and the blacks, against each other. Among such deeds was that of sixteen negroes forcibly taken out of the Trenton Jail, and shot down on the public road by a large body of disguised men, early in the morning of August 26th. The apparent cause of the misdeed was that, on the night of August 22d, an armed band of thirty or forty negroes discharged their guns upon two white men on horseback at a short distance from Pickettsville, in Gibson County, and continued shooting at them even after they had abandoned their horses and sought safety by flight through a corn-field. The occurrence, related by the two men who took refuge in that town, created the most intense excitement and alarm not only in the white population at Pickettsville, the male portion of which armed themselves and continued in the street all night to guard the place against the constantly-apprehended attacks upon it, but also in all the neigbboring towns, whose local magistrates and prominent citizens hastened to Pickettsville, both to offer assistance, and concert measures together for the common defense. The juridical hearing being ended, the accused were bound over by the justices of the peace, and, in default of the required bail, committed. They were placed under the charge of the town-marshal and two constables, who, with a guard of above forty men, escorted the prisoners to the jail of Trenton, the county-seat of Gibson, and some ten miles distant from Pickettsville, there to await their trial.

At about two o'clock in the morning of August 26th, a large body of disguised, fully-armed horsemen rode into the town of Trenton, surrounded the jail, and, calling out the jailer and sheriff on duty, demanded the keys of the negro prisoners' cells. Upon the absolute and several times repeated refusal of those officers to comply with that request, the horsemen declared that they would have the prisoners without the use of keys by pulling the jail-building down, and made preparations for commencing work at it. Those officers then delivered the keys under protest of compulsion and violence. Part of the band then took the sixteen prisoners out of their cells, tied them in couples with cords, and, having placed them in their midst, left the town by the Huntington road. Having gone scarcely half a mile from Trenton, the band halted and shot six of the prisoners down on that road; then continued their march some two miles farther up the river-bottom, when they halted again and shot the remaining ten prisoners, leaving the bodies of these also lying where they fell on the road.

On being informed of so remarkable an occurrence, Governor Brown issued a proclamation, offering a reward of $500, the largest sum which the law allowed him to offer, for the detection and apprehension of those jail-breakers and murderers, "the reward to be paid upon final conviction."

On August 29th the Governor issued a proclamation, addressed to the officers and citizens of all classes in the State, wherein he says that, without their strenuous coöperation, he is unable for want of means to suppress the lawlessness prevailing in Tennessee; and points out the duties incumbent on each of them respectively, and which they are expected faithfully to comply with for the realization of that purpose.

A short time after the Trenton prisoners' massacre, one of the band of masked horsemen who committed the deed, a youth scarcely seventeen years of age, moved by repentance, or the desire of escaping punishment, turned State's evidence and revealed all he knew of that criminal transaction, at which he was present from beginning to end, and about the persons who composed the band. This he said to have been formed of two companies, representing the whole neighborhood, and numbering thirty and thirty-eight mounted men respectively, who, according to previous appointment, met together at a certain place five miles from Trenton, at nine o'clock in the evening of August 25th, thence to proceed to the town's jail after midnight. He was three different times before the grand-jury in order to make his statements; and his revelations probably contributed more than any thing else to the capture of many of his accomplices. A number of them were arrested and held in custody by the State's authorities to be tried before her courts.

The financial condition of the State, as exhibited in the report of the Controller of the Treasury, for the two years from January 1, 1873, to the date of the report, December 19, 1874, is as follows:

Recognized bonded indebtedness of the State, $22,908,400; assets held in her favor against this bond account, $3,817,895.25; leaving the excess of liabilities at $19,090,504.75.

The floating debt is $1,035,540.49, against which there are assets amounting to $2,255,704.25. The outstanding Treasury warrants have been reduced since January 1, 1873, from $476,834.72 to $283,290.49; though warrants to the amount of $998,158.93 were in the mean while issued for the payment of the interest on the school-fund, the State debt, and other public expenses.

The loan account also had been reduced since May 1, 1873, from $343,053.30 to $65,000. Most of the loans embraced in this account bore ten per cent. interest.

The total taxable property of the State in 1873 was $308,089,738, being an increase over 1872 of $34,215,480. The four counties of Davidson, Hamilton, Jefferson, and Roane, have made no report of taxable property for 1874. Estimating the probable amount in those four counties, the total taxable property for 1874 is $289,533,560, being an increase over 1872 of $16,659,307, and a decrease from 1873 of $18,556,173.

The balance due for the year 1874, added to the delinquency from revenue due prior to January 1, 1874, makes the total amount due from non-collected taxes $1,828,333.44.

The educational interest in Tennessee appears to be in a prosperous condition. The law is absolutely impartial in its provisions as affecting the white and colored populations of the State, enacting that " the public schools shall be free to all persons between the ages of six and eighteen years, residing within the school district ; " with the only distinction between the two races that " the white and colored persons shall not be taught in the same school, but in separate schools, under the same general regulations as to management, usefulness, and efficiency." And as colored children of school-age are counted alike with the whites in the apportionment of school-moneys, and are entitled to pursue the same studies, so are the adult colored people eligible as teachers, school directors, county superintendents, and State Superintendents, in the same manner as they are eligible to the civil offices of the State or Federal Government. The whole number of children of school-age in the State then was 418,185. Of this number, representing the aggregate of children of school-age in Tennessee, about 102,000 were colored. Of these, some 37,000, or about 36 per cent., attended the public schools. Since the present school system went into effect, 745 schools have been organized throughout the State for the instruction of colored children. Of the

white scholastic population a little over 50 per cent. attended school.

From the report of the Commissioner of Education, wherein the gifts of individuals to educational institutions of all the States in the Union are collected and classified, it appears that the gifts received by the educational institutions of Tennessee, during the year 1873, amounted in the aggregate to $654,350, distributed among them as follows:

Union University, Murfreesboro	$13,000
Fisk University, Nashville	20,000
Vanderbilt University, Nashville	511,300
King College, Bristol	14,000
Hiwassee College, near Sweetwater	500
East Tennessee Wesleyan University, Athens	250
Central University, Knoxville	50,000
Cumberland University, Lebanon	20,000
Maryville College, Maryville	2,700
Christian Brothers' College, Memphis	5,000
Washington Female College, Washington	2,500
Theological Dept. Central College, Nashville	100
Tennessee School for the Blind, Nashville	15,000
Total	$654,350

The Tennessee Hospital for the Insane, the Blind School, and the Deaf and Dumb School, are in a very satisfactory condition. Since January 1, 1873, the average number of patients accommodated in the Hospital for the Insane " has exceeded that of any former biennial term," and the number in its charge at the close of the year was " greater than at the date of any previous report."

An act was passed by the last General Assembly, approved March 20, 1873, providing for the establishment of two additional Hospitals for the Insane, one in East the other in West Tennessee. After careful examination of various sites, the new hospital for East Tennessee was located, in 1874, near to the city of Knoxville, and its building is now in progress of construction. The endeavors to locate also the West Tennessee Insane Asylum have proved unsuccessful.

In the State-prison of Tennessee, at the end of 1874, there were 963 convicts under confinement, of whom 380 were whites and 583 negroes. The Governor of the State avers that, before the emancipation of slaves, the colored convicts in the penitentiary never numbered more than fifteen or twenty, and that the large increase in the number of penitentiary inmates is to be attributed in no sense to an increase of crime, but that "it is the result of a more efficient administration of the criminal law, aided by an improved and more healthy state of public sentiment."

There are now in the prison 59 convicts of the age of sixteen years and under ; 275 of the age of twenty years and under ; and 316 from sixteen to twenty-one years old, inclusive; notwithstanding a number have been pardoned simply on account of their youth.

TEXAS. One of the most important questions before the people of this State relates to the needed revision of the State constitution. According to Governor Coke, the present constitution is in many essential particulars an extremely defective instrument, and a barrier to many reforms desired by the people. "In its incongruous, repugnant, and heterogeneous provisions, are faithfully reflected the extraordinary character of the Assembly, and the disordered times which produced it. Necessity forced it on the people of Texas, and held it on them until the first meeting of their honorable bodies. Prudence and policy prompted submission to it from then until this time. No reason exists now for longer submitting to it. The causes which one year ago rendered it imprudent to call together a constitutional convention have ceased to exist, and the time and temper of the people are propitious for the work of constructing a new constitution. We no longer fear Federal interference; we are not hampered with financial embarrassment; the popular mind is free from passion or excitement, and views the great questions to be solved through no discolored medium; and last, but not least, for twelve months past the thinking men of the State have been studying and investigating the subjects to be dealt with in framing a constitution, and are now prepared to act."

The Governor, therefore, recommended that the Legislature provide for assembling, at the earliest practicable day, a convention for revising the constitution.

The entire public debt of the State, January 1, 1875, not including about $800,000 due to trust-funds of her own creation, the obligations of which are in the vaults of the Treasury, was $4,012,421. Of this amount there is unbonded $976,988. Deducting the amount of the floating debt from the aggregate debt, the balance, $3,035,433, is the amount of the State's outstanding bonded debt. The increase in the public debt since January, 1874, is represented by bonds and certificates to the revolutionary veterans, amounting to $899,389. The remainder is due to school-teachers for services in 1873. The estimated deficiencies for 1875 amount to $332,574, and to this must be added the cost of the session of the Legislature in that year, and the anticipated constitutional convention.

The number of convicts in the penitentiary is believed to be greater than in any other State. In the prison-buildings at Huntsville, as at present constructed, there are about 278 cells. A new building is in process of construction, which will furnish 125 additional cells. There are 676 convicts at labor within the walls of the prison, being an average of nearly three to each cell, leaving 777 who are employed outside. Of the latter, 255 are employed on the various railroads, and the remainder are engaged in cultivating plantations, making brick, etc.

The report of the Commissioner of the General Land-Office shows that, during the year ending September 1, 1874, there were issued 3,339 patents, of all classes, embracing in the aggregate 1,787,397 acres of land. During the

same time 7,890 new files, of all kinds, covering 6,319,754 acres of land, were made. Of these, 5,349, covering 5,427,675 acres, were made with railroad scrip; 1,608, covering 249,923 acres, were made under the preëmption laws, and the remainder with miscellaneous certificates of scrip. The estimated number of acres of land in the State is 175,594,560.

In accordance with the act of April 10, 1874, a battalion of six companies of seventy-five men each, comprising the usual company officers, was, on the 4th of June last, organized, and, under command of Major John B. Jones, took the field for the defense of the Indian frontier. The threatening and hostile attitude of the various tribes of wild Indians, at that time, in the judgment of the Executive, justified the fear that the entire force would be immediately needed for active defensive operations. The decisive and energetic campaign conducted by the forces of the United States stationed in Texas, together with the presence of this battalion on the frontier, constantly scouting the whole line, from Red River to the head-waters of the Nueces, under the eye and personal supervision of Major Jones, it is believed, saved the outer settlements of Texas from devastation by the Indians. Thus protected, however, the frontier has suffered very little during the past year, and the people are now more hopeful and encouraged, and the prospects for immigration and advancing the settlements are better than for many years. In addition to this, the battalion has cleared the frontier of many desperate and lawless characters, and given valuable aid, when greatly needed, to the local authorities in maintaining law and good order.

The production and movement of cotton in this State during the past two seasons have been as follows:

COTTON.	1873-'74.	1872-'78.
Exported from Galveston, Indianola, etc.:	Bales.	Bales.
To foreign ports, except Mexico	273,404	209,441
To Mexico	979	997
To coastwise ports	115,046	133,804
Stock at close of year	4,505	4,889
Total	393,934	348,631
Deduct:		
Received from New Orleans	....	487
Stock at beginning of year	4,889	4,694
Total product for year	389,045	343,450

Included in the production of 1872-'73 are 1,100 bales of sea-island, and in that of 1873-'74, 920 bales.

An election for Congressmen was held in November, and resulted in the choice of Democrats in all the districts, as follows: First district, J. H. Reagan; second district, D. B. Culberson; third district, J. W. Throckmorton; fourth district, Roger Q. Mills; fifth district, John Hancock; sixth district, Gustave Schleicher.

The present State government comprises: Richard Coke, Governor; Richard Hubbard,

Lieutenant-Governor; A. J. Dorn, Treasurer; Stephen H. Darden, Controller; J. J. Groos, Commissioner of the Land-Office; and O. N. Hollingsworth, Superintendent of Public Instruction. All of these are Democrats. The Legislature is classified as follows:

PARTIES.	Senate.	House.	Joint Ballot.
Democrats	26	79	105
Republicans.............	4	11	15
Democratic majority...	22	68	90

The second city of Texas (Galveston being the first) in population and importance is Houston, which is situated at the head of tide-water on Buffalo Bayou, 45 miles above its mouth, in Galveston Bay, 46 miles northwest of Galveston, and 150 miles east-southeast of Austin; population in 1860, 4,845; in 1870, 9,382, of whom 3,691 were colored; in 1874, estimated by the local authorities at 20,000. It is built on the left bank of the bayou, which is spanned by several bridges, the principal ones being of iron, and embraces an area of nine square miles. The City-Hall and Market-House, of brick, just finished at a cost of $400,000, is 272 feet long by 146 feet wide, and has two towers, 14 by 21 feet, and

114 feet high. It contains a hall, 70 by 110 feet, fitted up for public entertainments, and capable of seating 1,800 persons. The Masonic Temple is a handsome structure, costing $200,000. The principal hotel, the largest in the State, has accommodations for 500 guests. The city is lighted with gas, and is easily drained. The construction of street-railroads and grading of streets are in progress. Houston is the centre of the railroad system of the State, and attracts the trade of the surrounding country, which is rich in grazing and agricultural products. There are six diverging lines: the Houston & Texas Central; the Houston & Great Northern & International; Houston Tap & Brazoria; Galveston, Houston, & Henderson; New Orleans & Texas; and Buffalo Bayou, Brazos & Colorado. The bayou opposite the city has a depth of five feet, but, owing to bars in Galveston Bay, vessels drawing more than four feet cannot reach this point. Improvements are in progress by the United States Government, and an incorporated company, which will render Houston accessible by vessels drawing nine feet. The navigation of the bayou is mainly controlled by the Houston Direct Navigation Company, which has a capital

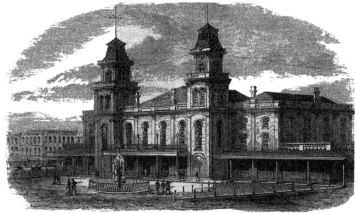

MARKET AND CITY HALL, HOUSTON.

of $300,000, and owns six steamers, four tugs, and twenty-four barges. The whole number of vessels regularly engaged in the trade of the bayou in 1872 was 71, viz.: steamers, 10; tugs, 6; barges, 30; schooners, mostly employed in the lumber-trade with the Sabine, Louisiana, and Florida coasts, 25. An extensive lumber-trade is also carried on by flat-boats with the bayous emptying into Buffalo Bayou and San Jacinto River. The principal business, however, is manufacturing, in which Houston surpasses all other places in the State. The chief establishments, besides the extensive ma-

chine-shops of the railroads, are 2 cotton-factories, 4 iron and brass founderies, 8 car-factories, 4 planing-mills and wood-works, 5 manufactories of furniture, 2 of soap, 1 of cement-pipe, 1 of bone-dust, 5 of sheet-iron and tin-works, 5 carriage and wagon works, 1 beef-packing and ice-manufacturing establishment, and 7 brick-yards. There are three nurseries, two fire and marine insurance companies, a cotton-press company, two national banks with a capital of $200,000, and a State bank with $500,000 capital. The valuation of property in 1873 was $7,669,625. The State fair is held here annually. The city contains 14 public schools, which in 1872 had 26 teachers and 1,228 pupils; two public libraries with about 3,000 volumes; three daily and six weekly newspapers; two monthly periodicals; and 12 churches. Houston was settled in 1836, and in 1837 was temporarily the seat of government.

TURKEY, an empire in Eastern Europe, Western Asia, and Northern Africa. Reigning sovereign, Sultan Abdul-Aziz, born February 9, 1830; succeeded to the throne at the death of his elder brother, Sultan Abdul-Medjid, June 25, 1861. Sons of the Sultan: 1. Yussuf Izzedin Effendi; born October 9, 1857; 2. Mahmoud Djemol Eddin Effendi, born November 20, 1862; 3. Mehemed Selim Effendi, born October 8, 1866; 4. Abdul-Medjid, born June 27, 1868.

The area and population of Turkey are variously estimated. At the beginning of 1874 they were given as follows:

COUNTRIES.	Sq. Miles.	Population.
1. Turkey proper in Europe........	139,990	8,397,529
2. Vassal states in Europe (Roumania and Servia)	68,527	5,340,000
3. Possessions and vassal states in Africa.......................	1,049,214	11,550,000
4. Possessions in Asia............	944,104	13,186,000
Total..................	1,996,835	38,973,529

In December, 1874, the annexation of Darfur to Egypt largely added to the area and population of one of the vassal states in Africa. If the incorporation is permanent, the area of the empire will amount to about 2,230,000 square miles, and the population to more than 46,000,000.

Constantinople is believed to have 400,000 to 500,000 inhabitants, of whom 110,000 belong to the Asiatic portion; Adrianople, 100,-000 to 150,000; Salonica, 50,000; Gallipoli, 50,-000; Philippopolis, 50,000; Serayervo, 46,000; Sofia, 22,000. Of the towns in Asiatic Turkey, Smyrna has 150,000; Damascus, 120,000; Beyroot, 100,000; Broussa, 100,000; Erzeroom, 100,000; Aleppo, 100,000; Bagdad, 40,000; Jerusalem, 25,000.

For the year ending February 28, 1875, the revenues were estimated at 4,961,484 purses, the expenditures at 5,026,916. The debt in 1874 was estimated at 4,325,100,000 francs. In the course of the year 1874 the floating debt was largely increased; but it is now to be wholly consolidated. A law of September 20, 1874, authorizes the Minister of Finance to enter a new debt of 44,000,000 Turkish pounds (1,000,-000,000 francs) into the Great Book. Of this sum, 36,300,000 pounds are devoted to the extinction of floating liabilities; the remainder is deposited with the new Imperial Ottoman Bank, to secure advances.

According to a law of June 22, 1869, and later decrees, the reorganization of the army is to be completed in 1878. It is to consist of 700,000 men, divided into the active army (about 150,000 men), the first reserve (70,000

men), the second reserve, and the sedentary army (corresponding to the German Landsturm). The irregular troops are calculated to consist of—1. Kavas, or gendarmes on foot; seymens, or mounted gendarmes and country militia as soubechis, 30,000; 2. Tartars of Dobrodja and Asia Minor, 5,000; 3. Hungarian or Polish volunteers, 2,000; Moslem volunteers, 50,000; total of irregulars, 87,000. The war-vessels, in 1873, consisted of 21 iron-clads (4 frigates, 5 corvettes, 6 monitors, and 6 galleys) and 99 transports. The navy was manned by 30,000 sailors and 4,000 marine troops.

The commercial marine is estimated at about 200,000 tons. The chief port of Turkey is that of Constantinople. The movement of shipping in the Suleina mouth of the Danube was, from 1869 to 1871, as follows:

SHIPPING.	1869.	1870.	1871.
Vessels..................	2,881	2,511	2,254
Tons....................	676,960	600,970	549,720

The aggregate length of railroads, in April, 1874, was 1,334 kilometres (1 kilometre = 0.62 mile) in European Turkey, and 274 in Asia Minor.

The Turkish dependency of Roumania was in 1873 governed by Prince Charles I., son of the late Prince Charles of Hohenzollern-Sigmaringen. Prince Charles was born April 20, 1839; elected Prince of Roumania, May 10, 1866; married November 15, 1869, to Elizabeth, Princess of Neuwied. The state ministry was in 1874 composed as follows: Presidency and Interior, Catargi (appointed 1871); Finance, Mavrogeni (1871); War, Floresco (1871); Foreign Affairs, Boëresco (1873); Justice, Lahovary (1873); Agriculture, Commerce, and Public Works, Cantacuzene (December, 1873); Public Instruction and Worship, Maïoresco (1874). The Senate consists of 78 members, the Chamber of Deputies of 157 members, of whom 82 are for Wallachia and 75 for Moldavia; area, 16,817 square miles; population in 1871, about 4,500,000. About 85.5 per cent. of the total population belong to the Roumania nationality, and about 92.4 per cent. to the Greek Oriental Church. In the budget of the year 1875 the revenue was estimated at 91,441,418 francs, and the expenditures at 97,149,552 francs; the public debt in 1874 amounted to about 210,000,000 francs. The imports, in 1871, were valued at 89,700,000 francs; in 1872, at 84;917,000 francs; the exports, in 1871, at 172,500,000 francs; in 1872, at 158,925,000 francs. In 1874 the length of the railroads in operation was 965 kilometres; that of the telegraph-lines, 3,420; that of wires, 6,089 kilometres.

The military force is divided into four classes: 1. The standing army with its reserves; 2. The territorial army with its reserves; 3. The militia; 4. The national guard in the towns and the people in the rural districts. The territorial army which is subject to be mobilized and concentrated for manœuvres or other service, consists of eight regiments of infantry called *dorobanzi;* eight regiments of cavalry, called *calarashi;* and one battery of artillery for each of the thirty-three districts into which the country is divided. The militia consists of two classes: one embracing the men from twenty-one to twenty-nine years who have not been drawn for the standing or territorial army; the second the men from twenty-nine to thirty-seven years who have completed their service in either of these two armies. The national guard and the masses include the men from thirty-seven to forty-six years of age. According to the budget of 1875, the standing army embraced 1,103 officers, and 18,271 men; the *dorobanzi,* 411 officers, 31,980 men; the *calarashi,* 160 officers, 10,706 men; total of standing and territorial armies, 62,631 officers and men, with 14,573 horses.

The present ruler of *Servia,* the other dependency of Turkey in Europe, Milan Obrenovitch IV., was born 1855, and succeeded to the throne by the election of the Servian National Assembly, after the assassination of his uncle, Prince Michael Obrenovitch, June, 1868; was crowned at Belgrade, and assumed the government, August 22, 1872. The legislative authority is exercised by two bodies, the Senate and the Skuptchina, or House of Representatives. The Senate consists of seventeen members, nominated by the people, and is permanently in session. The Skuptchina is composed of delegates chosen by the people at the rate of one deputy to every 2,000 electors. According to the budget for the years 1874–'75, the revenue was 35,035,000 "tax-piasters" (1 piaster = 4 cents), and the expenditure at 35,031,983 piasters. The area of Servia is 16,817 square miles; population in 1872, 1,338,505; of whom about 5,000 are Mohammedans, 1,500 Jews, 360 Protestants, 3,500 Roman Catholics, and the remainder members of the Orthodox Greek Church. The capital, Belgrade, had in 1871 a population of 27,589. The army, actually under arms, consists of about 4,000 men; with the exception of 200 cavalry and a small artillery corps, all infantry. The strength of the militia is estimated at about 79,000 men. The imports were valued in 1872 at 32,000,000 francs, the exports at 30,900,000 francs. There were in 1873 not yet any railroads in Servia; but the construction of a road from Belgrade to Alexinatz was begun; the aggregate length of the telegraph-lines was, in 1873, 602 miles.

The Grand-Vizier, Mehemed Rushdi Pasha, had to resign in February, because he had allowed the French embassador, Count Vogué, to address the Sultan directly in behalf of the Papal party in the United Armenian Church. In compliance with the remonstrances of France, the Hassunists (Papal party of the Armenian Church) were allowed to form a separate civil community, and to elect their own representative near the Porte. A com-

mittee was appointed by the Government to decide on the property of the Armenian Church, and the majority of the committee declared in favor of the anti-Hassun party.

Several districts in Asia Minor, especially the neighborhood of Angora and Cæsarea, severely suffered in the latter part of the year from a famine. In the town of Angora, 3,000 persons were reported in December as being dependent for their daily bread upon charity. Fourteen villages in the district, whose population previous to the famine was 7,200, lost more than 2,000 by death and 1,400 by emigration. In the city of Cæsarea, 200 families were being assisted, at Talas about 1,130 persons, including Greeks, Moslems, and Armenians. The population of the village of Ahali, which two or three years ago was about 1,100, has been reduced by the famine to 500.

In May, Prince Milan, of Servia, paid a visit to the Sultan, at Constantinople. This act of homage to his suzerain was regarded in Servia, as well as in Constantinople, as an event of considerable political importance. The National Servian party, which subordinates every thing to its desire for the establishment of an independent Servian empire, felt greatly humiliated by this step, in which it saw, on the part of the prince and his advisers, a marked change in policy, not at all favorable to their own special views.

The Skuptchina (National Assembly) of Servia was opened on November 22d. Prince Milan, in his opening address, laid special stress on the honorable reception which he had met with in Constantinople, Vienna, and Paris, and recommended to the Legislature liberal amendments to the state constitution. The Government also announced a bill for the establishment of a National Bank. The Skuptchina met not, as usual, in Krajugevatz, but in Belgrade. In discussing the address, by which the Skuptchina was to answer the speech from the throne, one member used so violent expressions against the head of the state, that he was for one month excluded from the Assembly. The draft of the address which was recommended by the committee was so warlike against Turkey, that the ministry declared the address would not be accepted by the prince. In compliance with the demand of the ministry, the Skuptchina rejected the proposed address, but only by a majority of three. The ministers, therefore, offered their resignation, and a new cabinet was formed by the Minister of the Interior, Zumitsh. The new ministry declared, however, that it would adhere to a peaceable policy, like its predecessors, and the majority of the Assembly deemed it best for the present to express their confidence in the Government.

Roumania has taken another important step toward establishing its complete independence. The autumn manœuvres of the Mòldo-Wallachian army, laughed at in 1872, but which attracted some attention a year later, again took place, in 1874, in the neighborhood of Bucharest, in the presence of the military commissioners of the principal governments of Europe. The Austrian, Russian, and other Governments, informed the Porte that their interests on the Danube are far too important to admit of their being interfered with by exaggerated pretensions of suzerainty on the Bosporus, and that treaties or conventions are about to be negotiated directly with the Roumanian Government. The Porte instructed its embassadors at St. Petersburg, Berlin, and Vienna, that the Treaty of Paris must be maintained, and, if violated in this case, reference to the signatory powers would follow; but, if the Roumanian Government would submit the case to the Porte, a satisfactory compromise might be arrived at to meet the peculiar commercial necessities of the principalities.

The new communal law, adopted by the Roumanian Legislature in February, gives to the Government the right to appoint the mayors.

The session of the Roumanian Chambers was opened on November 27th by Prince Charles. The speech from the throne referred to the good understanding existing between the Government and the representatives of the people, to the friendly relations to foreign countries, the progress of the military organization, the increased revenue from railroads, and the good condition of the finances. Bills were announced on the reorganization of the jury, on the reform of the civil law, on recruitment, on the administration of mines and forests, and on public education. Prince Demeter Ghika was almost unanimously elected President of the Chamber of Deputies. The Government had a majority in each Chamber.

A serious complication between Turkey and Montenegro arose from the massacre of seventeen Montenegrins by the Turkish populace of Podgoritza, a small Turkish town near the frontier, which, on market-days, is visited by many Montenegrins. A wealthy and influential Mohammedan, Jussuf, having been killed on October 19th by a Christian, Ivanov, the report that the murderer was a Montenegrin was sufficient to arouse the populace against the Montenegrins, and to lead to a general attack upon them, during which seventeen lost their lives and many more were wounded. According to the Montenegrins, the murderer was not at all a Montenegrin, but a subject of Turkey. The Prince of Montenegro demanded from the Porte the appointment of a mixed commission to investigate the matter, to which the Turkish Government agreed. On the other hand, Turkey declined to comply with the request of the Russian and German embassadors, that the foreign powers should also be represented in this commission. The matter was not yet fully settled at the close of the year 1874, though thirty-two Turks, who were implicated in the massacre, had been sentenced to twenty years' imprisonment.

A complication between Turkey and England, which had arisen in 1873, was amicably settled at the beginning of 1874. From the official correspondence on this subject, published by the English Government, it appears that the territory of Yemen having been brought more immediately under Turkish authority, the Porte claimed rights of sovereignty over the Sultan of Lahadj, who immediately appealed to the British Government for protection. Thereupon Lord Granville telegraphed to Sir Henry Elliot, directing him to inform the Porte that any hostile operations against Arab chiefs calculated to disturb the position of England at Aden would create a bad impression both in England and India. Lahadj lies within fifteen miles of Aden, and its chief, or sultan, as he styles himself, receives a monthly salary from the British Government for supplying Aden with food and keeping roads open. Being ally and stipendiary of England, and never having paid tribute to the Porte, he refused submission, even when the Turkish Government, giving weight to Sir Henry Elliot's representation, agreed that it should be purely nominal. This refusal placed the Porte in a delicate position. On the one hand, it wished to avoid all action calculated to give umbrage to England; on the other, immediate abandonment of the claim to exercise sovereignty over Lahadj would be regarded as a sign of weakness by other tribes meditating revolt. This dilemma naturally led to lengthy correspondence between the Turkish and English Governments, and it was not until nearly a year after the complication first arose that the matter was finally settled by the withdrawal of Turkish troops from the threatened attack on Lahadj.

In August, two treaties were signed at Constantinople between the Ottoman Government and that of the United States—one having reference to the extradition of criminals, and the other to the naturalization of the subjects of either power in the dominions of the other. In the treaty of naturalization the Ottoman Government has for the first time recognized the principle that Ottoman subjects, naturalized according to American law, become *de facto* American subjects, and America reciprocates, the whole arrangement being in accordance with "the first principles of international law." The extradition treaty is considered to be of great value to the Ottoman Government, whose extensive transactions with America for the supply of arms render it indispensable for the protection of national interests that the arm of Turkish law should be able to reach across the Atlantic. It is supposed that this is the first instance on record of any treaties with foreign powers in which Turkey has not conceded more than she received. Simultaneously, a protocol was signed on behalf of the United States Government relating to the tenure of landed property by foreign subjects, to which that Government has not until now adhered.

The Sultan, after having for a long time endeavored to change the order of succession, has at length abandoned this design, and through the good offices of the Sheik-ul-Islam and Sir Henry Elliot, the English embassador, has been reconciled to his nephew, Prince Mourad Effendi, the legal heir to the throne. The Sultan solemnly swore on the Koran to respect the legal rights of his nephew; and Prince Mourad also promised that Prince Yussuf-Izzeddin, oldest son of the Sultan, should retain his rank of generalissimo, and that the other sons of the Sultan should keep their appanages, the high offices of state they hold, and their own palaces.

U

UNITARIANS.

I. UNITARIANS IN THE UNITED STATES.—The forty-ninth annual meeting of the *American Unitarian Association* was held in Boston, May 26th. The Treasurer reported the amount of contributions received during the past year to have been $37,698.02. The subject of the principle which ought to be observed in preparing the list of Unitarian ministers to be published in the *Year Book of the Unitarian Congregational Churches*, formed one of the most prominent topics of discussion before the Association. The following resolution was adopted on the subject:

Inasmuch as the term Unitarian, as used in the title of this Association, and in its publications, has always been held to carry a distinctively Christian meaning—our Unitarian ministers being held and regarded by us as public teachers of the Christian religion—and as the action of the Assistant Secretary, sustained by the Executive Committee, in omitting from the catalogue the name of a minister who says he is no longer a Christian, has been in harmony with the common usage of the term among us: therefore—

Resolved, That the said action be now and hereby is approved and ratified.

The *National Conference of Unitarian and other Christian Churches* in the United States met, for its sixth biennial session, at Saratoga, N. Y., September 15th. The Hon. E. Rockwood Hoar, of Massachusetts, presided. The Council of Ten presented a report of their proceedings since the previous National Conference, and of the condition of the several interests of which they had the care. A larger number of societies of the Unitarian body had been invited to the Conference than ever before. The discussion of general religious and social questions occupied a prominent place in the proceedings of the Conference. Papers were read in this department as follows: On "The Causes and Cure of Intemperance," by the Rev. J. H. Heywood, of Louisville, Ky.; on "The Morality of Prohibitory Liquor Laws," by William B. Weeden, of Providence, R. I.; on "The Merits and Results of the Voluntary System in Church Organization and Work," by the Rev. Charles G. Ames, of Germantown, Pa.; on "The Relations between Religious and Modern Scientific Thought," by the Rev. S. R. Calthrop, of Syracuse, N. Y.; on "The Causes of Crime," by the Rev. A. Woodbury, of Providence, R. I.; and on the "Punishment of Criminals," by the Rev. J. F. Moors, of Greenfield, Mass.

II. GERMAN ASSOCIATIONS OF LIBERAL CHRISTIANS IN THE UNITED STATES.—1. The Protestant Union of Liberal Christian Churches in North America was established at Cincinnati in 1863. It includes congregations in Ohio, Pennsylvania, West Virginia, Texas, New Jersey, and Indiana. The Conference meets once a year. It is stated that the Union has suffered considerably from internal dissensions and religious indifference. It has now but twelve churches connected with it.

2. The Union of Independent Evangelical Protestant German Churches in the West was organized in 1869, mostly by ministers from the Protestant Union mentioned above. It resembles the Protestant Union in its tendencies, and maintains a friendly intercourse with it, but is regarded as being more radical in its views. It has fourteen churches, the greater number of which are in Illinois and Minnesota.

UNITED BRETHREN.

The following are the statistics of the Church of the United Brethren in Christ, as given in the *United Brethren Almanac* for 1875:

CONFERENCES.	Organized Churches.	Number of Ministers.	Number of Members.
Alleghany	150	49	5,759
Auglaize	164	55	5,649
Central Illinois	88	42	2,611
California	19	16	296
Cascade	12	7	207
Colorado	9	8	205
Dakota	14	9	274
East Pennsylvania	76	60	4,196
East German	119	41	3,594
East Des Moines	78	38	1,973
Erie	110	63	2,325
Fox River	53	15	538
Illinois	97	50	3,349
Iowa	111	78	3,956
Indiana	138	62	6,151
Kansas	120	60	2,173
Lower Wabash	138	76	5,457
Miami	77	55	5,154
Muskingum	78	37	3,654
Minnesota	25	14	663
Missouri	111	56	2,121
Michigan	167	59	3,180
North Ohio	111	51	3,806
Oregon	89	17	611
Ohio German	46	29	1,539
Ontario	36	16	1,045
Osage	95	40	1,899
Nebraska	84	33	1,305
Pennsylvania	141	63	6,864
Parkersburg	182	51	5,880
Rock River	67	51	1,810
Scioto	207	82	8,942
Sandusky	191	92	7,124
St. Joseph	135	75	4,695
Southern Illinois	15	9	522
Tennessee	18	7	560
Upper Wabash	117	55	4,220
Virginia	152	56	5,831
West Des Moines	85	40	1,932
White River	114	76	5,693
Western Reserve	98	61	3,381
Wisconsin	69	29	1,695
Germany	3	2	150
Total	3,959	1,886	131,859

The number of members was 4,298 larger than the number which was reported in 1873. The bishops of the United Brethren Church are: The Rev. J. J. Glossbrenner, Churchville, Augusta County, Va.; the Rev. David Edwards, D. D., Baltimore, Md.; the Rev. Jonathan Weaver, Dayton, Ohio; and the Rev. John Dickson, Decatur, Ill.

The general publishing-house of the United Brethren in Christ is established at Dayton, Ohio. The aggregate circulation of the periodicals published by this Church, on the 1st of July, 1874, was 181,500 copies. The educational institutions of the United Brethren Church are: Otterbein University, Westerville, Ohio; Hartsville University, Hartsville, Ind.; Westfield College, Westfield, Ill.; Lebanon Valley College, Annville, Pa.; Lane University, Lecompton, Kansas; Western College, Western, Iowa; Philomath College, Philomath, Oregon; and the Union Biblical Seminary, Ohio.

UNITED STATES. Some changes were made in the cabinet of President Grant during the year. The resignation of Mr. Richardson, as Secretary of the Treasury, was accepted, and the vacancy filled by the acceptance of BENJAMIN H. BRISTOW, on June 4th. Mr. Bristow was born in Elkton, Todd County, Ky., in 1833. He became a prominent lawyer in the State, and in 1861 entered the Union army, as a major of the Twenty-fifth Kentucky, was at the battles of Fort Donelson and Shiloh, at the latter of which he was wounded. He was appointed United States District Attorney about the close of the war. When the office of Solicitor-General was created he was appointed its first incumbent, organized the office, and, during the absence of the Attorney-General, performed his duties and filled his place in cabinet meetings. The ability he displayed in this office increased his reputation at Washington. After two years' service he resigned, to attend to his private affairs.

On June 24th the Postmaster-General, John A. J. Creswell, resigned, and the vacancy was filled by the appointment and acceptance of MARSHALL JEWELL, of Connecticut. Mr. Jewell was born in Winchester, N. H., October 24, 1825. In 1847 he moved to Hartford and worked for two years in his father's currier-shop. He then relinquished the business and learned the art of telegraphing, and, being an expert operator, was engaged in the office in Rochester, N. Y., from which place he went to Ohio, and afterward to Columbia, Tenn. After the election of General Taylor to the presidency, Mr. Jewell, who was a warm supporter of the Whig nominee, removed to Jackson, Miss., and was subsequently elected general superintendent of the telegraph line between Nashville and New Orleans. He returned to New York in 1849, and the following year entered into partnership with his father in the tanning and belting business. He visited Europe in 1859 and 1860, and in 1865 again went to Europe, extending his travels to Egypt and the Holy Land. Mr. Jewell has always been in sympathy with the Republican party. Although comparatively unknown as a politician, he was elected Governor of Connecticut in 1869, and in 1871 he was again elected to the same position, and reëlected the following year, thus serving for three terms. On the 20th of May, 1873, the President nominated Governor Jewell to succeed James L. Orr as minister to Russia, and in this office he exhibited marked ability.

One of the most important acts of the last Congress was the adoption of the revision of the United States Statutes. The first commission for this purpose was appointed in 1866, and consisted of Caleb Cushing, William Johnson, of Ohio, and Charles P. James, of the District of Columbia. Little progress was made by them, and after the expiration of the term of their appointment—three years—they retired. In May, 1870, Congress passed an act reviving the commission, and Benjamin Vaughn Abbott, Charles P. James, and V. M. Barringer, were appointed the commissioners, who have completed the work. After it was reported by the commission it was referred to the Congressional Committee on the Revision of the Laws, and was by them and by Mr. Thomas J. Durant, of Washington, who was employed by the committee, subjected to a careful review. After coming from the hands of the committee the revision was patiently gone over in both Houses, and was finally adopted about two weeks before the adjournment. This revision contains the Statute Law of the United States down to the present year, and embraces within the limits of two volumes the contents of seventeen octavo volumes.

The decision of the Supreme Court of the United States in the "Slaughter-house" cases at New Orleans, is stated in the volume of this work for 1873. In the recent case of Bartemeyer vs. the State of Iowa, decided by the same court, Justices Field and Bradley took occasion to restate the grounds of their dissent from the opinion of a majority of the court in the Slaughter-house cases, in order to correct some apparent misapprehension of their views as to the fourteenth amendment. Mr. Justice Field says that the judges who dissented in those cases, never contended that the fourteenth amendment interferes, in any respect, with the police power of the State, but that, on the contrary, "they recognized the power of the State in its fullest extent, observing that it embraced all regulations affecting the health, good order, morals, peace and safety of society; that all sorts of restrictions and burdens were imposed under it, and that, when these were not in conflict with any constitutional prohibition or fundamental principles, they could not be successfully assailed in a judicial tribunal. But they said that, under the pretense of prescribing a police regulation, the State could not be permitted to encroach upon any of the just rights of the citizen, which the Constitution intended to guard against abridgment; and because, in their opinion, the act of Louisiana, then under consideration, went far beyond the province of a police regulation, and created an oppressive and odious monopoly, thus directly impairing the common rights of the citizens of the State, they dissented from the judgment of the court. * * * It was because the act of Louisiana transcended the limits of police regulation, and asserted a power in the State, to farm out the ordinary avocations of life, that dissent was made to the judgment of the court sustaining the validity of the act." The judge continues: "The amendment was not, as held in the opinion of the majority, primarily intended to confer citizenship on the negro race. It had a much broader purpose; it was intended to justify legislation, extending the protection of the national Government over the common rights of *all* citizens of the United States, and thus obviate objections to the legislation, adopted for the protection of the emancipated race. It was intended to make it possible for *all* persons, which necessarily included those of every race and color, to live in peace and security wherever the jurisdiction of the nation reached. It therefore recognized, if it did not create, a national citizenship, and made all persons citizens, except those who preferred to remain under the protection of a foreign government, and declared that their privileges and immunities, which embrace the fundamental rights belonging to citizens of all free governments, should not be abridged by any State. This national citizenship is primary and not secondary. It clothes its possessor, or would do so if not shorn of its efficiency by construction, with the right, when his privileges and immunities are invaded by partial and discriminating legislation, to appeal from his State to his nation, and gives him the assurance that, for his protection, he can invoke the whole power of the Government." The views of Mr. Justice Bradley were to the same effect, and were concurred in by Mr. Justice Swayne.

An important decision was rendered in the early part of the year by Mr. Justice Bradley, of the Supreme Court of the United States, in which were considered the powers of Congress in legislating to enforce the provisions of the thirteenth, fourteenth, and fifteenth constitutional amendments. The consideration of the question grew out of the conflict between certain white and black persons at Colfax in Grant Parish, La., in 1873, an account of which is contained in the President's message on Louisiana affairs, given under the title PUBLIC DOCUMENTS in this volume. In this affair a number of negroes were killed, and an indictment was found against certain white persons, charging them with conspiring to injure, oppress, intimidate, and otherwise to deprive colored citizens of their rights, and with murders, while engaged in this conspiracy. For

this proceeding, ninety-eight white men were indicted under the Ku-klux act, of whom nine were brought to trial in the United States Circuit Court. The first trial resulted in a disagreement of the jury, and the second in a conviction of the accused. A motion in arrest of judgment was then made before Judge Bradley, of the United States Supreme Court, and Judge Wood, who presided at the trial when the prisoners were convicted.

In an elaborate opinion, in which the indictments were held to be illegal, Mr. Justice Bradley remarked that the law was firmly established, that Congress has power to enforce by appropriate legislation every right and privilege given or guaranteed by the Constitution. Those acknowledged rights and privileges of the citizens which form a part of his political inheritance, must be protected and enforced by the State; and when any of these rights and privileges are secured in the Federal Constitution only by a declaration that the State or the United States shall not violate or abridge them, it is at once understood that they are not created or conferred by the Constitution, but are only guaranteed against impairment by the State or the United States.

The thirteenth amendment declares that neither slavery nor involuntary servitude, except as a punishment for crime, shall exist within the United States, and that Congress shall have power to enforce this article by appropriate legislation. This clothes Congress with the power to pass laws for the prosecution and punishment of those who deprive or attempt to deprive any person of the rights thus conferred, or hinder him in the exercise thereof.

The effect of the fifteenth amendment is next considered, under which the law in question was primarily framed. This amendment, although its terms have a general application to all persons, was intended for the benefit of the colored race, by securing to them the right to vote. But in the opinion of the court "it does not confer the right to vote. That is the prerogative of the State laws. It only confers a right not to be excluded from voting by reason of race, color, or previous condition of servitude, and this is all the right that Congress can enforce. It confers upon citizens of the African race the same right to vote as white citizens possess. It makes them equal. This is the whole scope of the amendment. The powers of Congress, therefore, are confined within this scope." The amendment does not confer upon Congress any power to regulate elections, or the right of voting where it did not have that power before, except in the particular matter specified. It does, however, confer upon Congress the right of enforcing the prohibition imposed against excluding citizens of the United States on account of race, color, or previous condition of servitude.

The real difficulty in the present case was to determine whether the amendment had given to Congress any power to legislate except to furnish redress in cases where the States violate the amendment. On this point the court inclined to the opinion that Congress has the power to secure that right, not only as against the unfriendly operation of State laws, but against outrage, violence, and combinations on the part of individuals, irrespective of the State laws.

The question was then considered, whether the fourteenth amendment empowered Congress to pass laws for directly enforcing all privileges and immunities of citizens of the United States, by original proceedings in the courts of the United States. Justice Bradley was of opinion that the manner of enforcing the provisions of this amendment depends upon the character of the privilege or immunity in question. If simply prohibitory of governmental action, there will be nothing to enforce until such action is undertaken. On the other hand, when the provision is violated by the passage of an obnoxious law, such law is clearly void, and all acts done under it will be trespasses. The legislation required from Congress, therefore, is such as will provide a preventive or compensatory remedy or due punishment for such trespasses, and appeals from the State courts to the United States courts in cases that come up for consideration. In the opinion of Justice Bradley, therefore, the indictment was fatally defective. Judge Wood, however, affirmed its validity. A certificate of division was therefore made, and the case sent up to the Supreme Court of the United States.

The number of civil suits to which the United States was a party, that were pending on July 1st, was 6,854. During the year previous to that date 3,058 civil suits were terminated. The aggregate amount of judgments in favor of the United States in these suits was $2,021,724, and the amount actually realized in these judgments during the last fiscal year was $867,192. Six thousand and eighteen criminal cases were terminated during the year, 202 of these being under the customs laws, in which there were 147 convictions, 8 acquittals, and 47 discontinuances; 3,291 under the internal revenue laws, in which there were 1,641 convictions, 392 acquittals, and 1,258 discontinuances; 251 under the Post-Office laws, in which there were 168 convictions, 25 acquittals, and 58 discontinuances; 966 under the enforcement acts, in which there were 102 convictions, 92 acquittals, and 772 discontinuances; one under the naturalization laws, in which there was a conviction; 37 for embezzlement, in which there were 11 convictions, 4 acquittals, and 22 discontinuances; 1,270 were miscellaneous prosecutions, in which there were 553 convictions, 224 acquittals, and 493 discontinuances.

The state of affairs in Alabama, Arkansas, South Carolina, and Louisiana, was regarded by the Federal Government as very unsettled during a portion of the year. With the approval of the President, the following circular was issued to the United States Attorneys and Marshals, after a consultation between Secretaries Bristow and Belknap and Attorney-General Williams:

DEPARTMENT OF JUSTICE,
WASHINGTON, September 3, 1874.

SIR: Outrages of various descriptions, and in some cases atrocious murders, have been committed in your district by bodies of armed men, sometimes in disguise, and with a view, it is believed, of overawing and intimidating peaceable and law-abiding citizens, and depriving them of the rights guaranteed to them by the Constitution and laws of the United States. Your attention is directed to an act of Congress passed April 9, 1866, entitled "An act to protect all persons in the United States in their civil rights, and to furnish means for their vindication," and to another passed April 20, 1871, entitled "An act to enforce the provisions of the fourteenth amendment to the Constitution of the United States and for other purposes;" also to one passed May 6, 1870, entitled "An act to enforce the rights of the citizens of the United States by vote in the several States of this union and for other purposes," which, with their amendments, make these deeds of violence and blood within the jurisdiction of the General Government. I consider it my duty, in view of these circumstances, to proceed with all possible energy and dispatch to detect, expose, arrest and punish the perpetrators of these crimes, and to that end you are to spare no effort or necessary expense. Troops of the United States will be stationed at sufficient and convenient points in your district for the purpose of giving you all needful aid in the discharge of your official duties. You understand, of course, that no interference whatever is hereby intended with any political or party action not in violation of the law, but protection to all classes of citizens, white and colored, in the free exercise of the elective franchise and the enjoyment of the other rights and privileges to which they are entitled, under the Constitution and laws, as citizens of the United States. These instructions are issued by authority of the President, and with the concurrence of the Secretary of War. Very respectfully,

GEORGE H. WILLIAMS, Attorney-General.

At the same time the following letter from President Grant was made public:

LONG BRANCH, N. J., September 3, 1874.
General W. W. BELKNAP, Secretary of War:

Recent atrocities in the South, particularly in Louisiana, Alabama, and South Carolina, show a disregard for law, civil rights, and personal protection, that ought not to be tolerated in any civilized government. It looks as if, unless speedily checked, matters must become worse until life and property there will receive no protection from the local authorities —until such authority becomes powerless. Under such circumstances, it is the duty of the Government to give all aid for the protection of life and civil rights legally authorized to this end. I wish you would consult with the Attorney-General, who is well informed as to the outrages already committed and the localities where the greatest danger lies, and so order the troops as to be available in case of necessity. All the proceedings for the protection of the South will be under the law department of the Government, and will be directed by the Attorney-General, in accordance with the provisions of the enforcement act. No instructions need, therefore, be given the troops ordered into the Southern States, except as they may be transmitted from time to time on advice from the Attorney-General, or as circumstances may determine hereafter.

(Signed) U. S. GRANT.

As to the disturbances in the States above mentioned, the reader is referred to the details of the affairs in these States under the title of the States respectively. In the proceedings of Congress will be found the discussions relating more particularly to Louisiana; and among Public Documents will be found the messages of the President relating to the same State.

Several conventions, of a more or less national character, were held during the year; but the results which followed their action were small, and entitle the proceedings only to a brief statement.

A convention of delegates from the reconstructed States assembled at Chattanooga on October 13th, and organized by the selection of Lewis E. Parsons, of Alabama, as President. Vice-Presidents, L. D. Evans, Texas; A. E. Barber, Louisiana; John N. Sarher, Arkansas; Tennis H. Little, Mississippi; David Woodruff, Alabama; Jefferson Long, Georgia; T. W. Osborne, Florida; J. T. Wilder, Tennessee; L. N. Shoemaker, Virginia. Secretaries, George W. Paschal, Jr., Texas; H. W. Lewis, Mississippi; J. A. Emerson, Arkansas. The following letter from the Republican Congressional Executive Committee was read before the convention:

To —— ——, *Delegate to the Chattanooga Convention.*

SIR: Considerate men, who have given the subject attention, regard the movement for a convention of Southern Republicans as of very great importance to the section of country to be represented. They believe that if calm and considerate counsels prevail, and the delegates come together possessed of the facts bearing upon the condition of the Southern communities, and lay them before the country in an authentic and concise form, an impression will be made which may favorably affect the judgment of the well-disposed in every section. At this convention the record should be fully and honestly made up, showing all the hinderances to material, moral, and intellectual progress with which the Republicans have had to contend, what progress has been made, and whether in the States and sections where Democracy has control any of the great interests of society have prospered more, and which, if any, have been depressed; also whether persons or property have been more or less secure, and the reasons therefor, whichever the fact may be; outrages of all classes should be carefully reported, whether resulting in crime or extending only to intimidation. The spirit and purpose of the action of the legislative, judicial, and executive departments should be reviewed. All, in fact, that tends to disorder, lawlessness, or oppression, may well be considered upon. The whole record thus honestly and fairly made up, the considerate judgment of the American people may be safely invoked. To the sincere and thoughtful statesmen who will assemble on this occasion, these suggestions are believed to be entirely unnecessary. But, lest some should deem them unwarranted, I here state that they are suggestions only, and that they are submitted with great diffidence, but with the sincere hope that they may to some extent aid in securing careful preparation for the work of the convention, and a full attendance upon its sittings.

J. M. EDMUNDS, Secretary.

October 13, 1874.

A lengthy address on the state of affairs in the Southern States was reported by Senator West, of Louisiana, and unanimously adopted, after which, and the adoption of some unimportant resolutions, the convention adjourned.

The Cheap Transportation Convention assembled in Richmond, Va., on December 1st, and adjourned on the 4th. Numerous important and valuable papers on the general subject were read, and all the substitutes for the report of the Committee on Water Routes from the West were finally withdrawn, and a compromise resolution unanimously adopted, recognizing, in addition to the lines of transportation recommended by the United States Senate Committee on Transportation (*see* PUBLIC DOCUMENTS), the proposed Rock Island & Hennepin Canal in Illinois, connecting the Mississippi with the Illinois River and canal, and the chain of water to the seaboard, as a project of great merit; and urging upon Congress the necessity of the speedy construction of the work. Resolutions, showing the necessity of cheap transportation to improve the finances, were also adopted.

The committee on resolutions reported a digest of all the resolutions previously passed on the subject of cheap transportation, in the form of a memorial to Congress, together with a petition to the New York Legislature for the reduction of tolls on the Erie Canal to the lowest possible rates, and recommendations to Congress to build a ship-yard in the East, and a steamboat-yard in the West, all of which were adopted.

Josiah Quincy, of Massachusetts, was re-elected president, with a large number of persons for vice-presidents.

A National Grange Convention was held in St. Louis, on February 11th. As this is an organization of farmers, independent of politics, it is unnecessary to present here the entire declaration of their principles. The fifth resolution was as follows:

We emphatically and sincerely assert the oft-repeated truth taught in our organic law, that the Grange, national, State, or subordinate, is not a political or party organization. No Grange, if true to its obligations, can discuss political or religious questions, nor call political conventions, nor nominate candidates, nor even discuss their merits in its meetings. Yet the principles we teach underlie all true politics, all true statesmanship, and if properly carried out will tend to purify the whole political atmosphere of our country, for we seek the greatest good to the greatest number; but we must always bear it in mind that no one by becoming a Grange-member gives up that inalienable right and duty which belong to every American citizen to take a proper interest in the politics of his country. On the contrary, it is right for every member to do all in his power legitimately to influence for good the action of any political party to which he belongs. It is his duty to do all he can in his own party to put down bribery, corruption, and trickery; to see that none but competent, faithful, and honest men, who will unflinchingly stand by our industrial interests, are nominated for all positions of trust, and to have carried out the principles which should always characterize every Grange-member; that the office should seek the man, not the man the office. We acknowledge the broad principles that difference of opinion is not crime, and hold that progress toward truth is made by differences of opinion, while the fault lies in the bitterness of controversy. We desire a proper equality, equity, and fairness, protection of the weak, restraint upon the strong, in short, justly-distributed burdens and justly-distributed power. These are American ideas, the very essence of American independence, and to advocate the contrary is unworthy of the sons and daughters of an American Republic. We cherish the belief that sectionalism is, and of right should be, dead and buried with the past. Our work is for the present and the future of our agricultural brotherhood and its purposes. We shall recognize no North, no South, no East, no West. It is reserved by every person, as his right, as a freeman, to affiliate with any party that will best carry out his principles.

A Women's National Temperance Convention assembled in Cleveland on November 19th. Its organization resulted from the women's crusade movement, and was intended to embrace and concentrate all the bands of women, in all parts of the country, who desire to bring to the work the kind of effort which the crusade inaugurated, viz., persistent prayer, personal appeal to drunkards and drunkard-makers, and social influence. Sixteen States were represented by accredited delegates, and the crowded sessions of the three days' convention were presided over by Mrs. Jennie F. Milling, of Bloomington, Ill. The president, in her opening remarks, drew attention to the fact that this was a distinctively religious movement, and one which demanded full consecration to and trust in Almighty God.

The fifth national convention representing persons desiring to secure a religious amendment of the Constitution of the United States assembled at Pittsburg, Pa., on February 3d. Felix R. Brunot, of Pittsburg, was reëlected President. Some other conventions were held, but they were chiefly of local importance and limited in their results.

Within a few years fish-culture has become very extensive in the United States. In 1873 the subject was presented to Congress and favorably acted upon; the result being an appropriation of $15,000 "for the introduction of shad into the waters of the Pacific States, the Gulf States, and the Mississippi Valley, and of salmon, white-fish, and other useful food-fishes into the waters of the United States to which they are best adapted," for the fiscal year of 1872–'73, with a supplementary appropriation of $10,000 for the same year, having special reference to the propagation of shad. A further appropriation of $17,500 was subsequently made for the same object during the fiscal year of 1873–'74. This action on the part of the United States was the natural culmination of what had already been done by many of the States, accelerated by the action of the American Fish Culturists' Association.

The financial question was the most important one before the country during the year. It was extensively discussed in the debates of Congress. (See CONGRESS, U. S., and the article FINANCES OF THE UNITED STATES.) Under the expectation of the passage by Congress of the bill known as the "civil-rights" bill, much

apprehension was excited in the Southern States relative to the public schools, which the bill originally contemplated to make "mixed" schools, containing both white and black children. The bill was amended. For the relations of the United States with foreign countries, see the article DIPLOMATIC CORRESPONDENCE. The preparations for the celebration in Philadelphia of the hundredth anniversary of the independence of the United States were greatly accelerated during the year by the action of public bodies and States.

UNIVERSALISTS. The *Universalist Register* for 1875 furnishes the following statistics of the Universalist churches in the United States:

STATES, ETC.	Parishes.	Churches.	Church-Members.	Ministers.
Alabama	12	9	224	8
Arkansas	..	2	40	1
California	..	1	44	2
Colorado	..	..	....	2
Canada	20	7	383	8
Connecticut	17	12	752	21
District of Columbia	1	1	53	3
Florida	..	1	47	2
Georgia	10	6	173	12
Illinois	69	49	2,776	48
Indiana	52	46	2,334	24
Iowa	43	24	785	29
Kansas	11	9	146	10
Kentucky	6	4	275	5
Louisiana *	....	..	....	..
Maryland	3	2	153	3
Maine	87	32	1 242	41
Massachusetts	104	75	5,020	192
Michigan	40	22	817	30
Minnesota	25	7	335	9
Missouri	20	16	406	10
Nebraska	..	1	16	2
New Hampshire	26	15	585	17
New Jersey	8	6	250	7
New York	127	89	4,390	100
North Carolina	..	3	80	5
Ohio	111	98	4,445	60
Oregon	..	6	183	4
Pennsylvania	37	28	2,447	22
Rhode Island	6	4	549	8
South Carolina	..	1	22	2
Tennessee	..	1	7	..
Texas	..	..	....	6
Vermont	63	27	1,485	32
Virginia †	....	..	....	..
West Virginia	11	2	55	3
Wisconsin	26	18	486	21
Total	935	624	30,905	674

The *General Convention* of Universalists in the United States met in the city of New York, September 15th. The Hon. Olney Arnold, of Rhode Island, was chosen President. The reports of the Treasurer and the Board of Trustees showed the Murray Centenary Fund to have reached the amount of $120,901.10. The General Secretary had attended the State Conventions of Missouri, Indiana, Massachusetts, Kansas, Pennsylvania, Ohio, Minnesota, Rhode Island, New Hampshire, Maine, Illinois, and Iowa, and had been led, by what he observed at these meetings, to take a hopeful view of the missionary work in the United States.

---

* One meeting-house is reported in this State, and the value of church property is given at $40,000.

† One meeting-house; value of church property, $5,000.

URUGUAY (República de la Banda Oriental del Uruguay), or Banda Oriental, an independent state of South America, extending from latitude 30° to 33° 55' south, and from longitude 52° 40' to 58° west. The boundaries of the republic are: on the north, the Brazilian province of Rio Grande do Sul; on the east, the South Atlantic Ocean; on the south, the Rio de la Plata; and on the west, the Argentine province of Entre Rios.

The President, since March 1, 1873, is Señor Don José Ellauri; and his cabinet is composed of the following members: Minister of Foreign Affairs, Dr. G. Perez Gomar; of the Interior, including Justice, Agriculture and Public Works, Public Instruction, and Public Worship, Dr. S. Alvarez; of Finances, Señor Don J. Peñalva; and of War and the Navy, Señor Don E. Fonda. Although Engineer José M. Reyes estimated the area of the republic at more than 84,000 square miles,* a more recent report sets it down at 63,322 square miles. The territorial division is into thirteen departments, and six ports are enumerated at which ocean and coasting craft find fair facilities for loading and discharging cargoes. The means of intercourse with Brazil and Europe are numerous, and not exposed to such interruptions as have frequently, within the last few years especially, trammeled the commercial intercourse with the Argentine Republic, whose ports are often closed for months at a time during the visitation of epidemics at Montevideo. Six British mail-steamers call monthly at the latter port, and five others, not belonging to lines under government contract, carry the mails, besides four French, three Italian, one Anglo-Belgian, and two Brazilian mail-packets. A line of mail-schooners, owned by the Falkland Island Company, carry on the service in eight annual trips between Montevideo and the Falkland Islands.

The value of the exports, which are statistically shown to have steadily increased since 1870, was $16,550,000 in 1873, against $15,490,000 in 1872, $13,330,000 in 1871, and $12,780,000 in 1870. At least one-half of these sums were represented by the single article of hides. With the addition of the goods exported by contraband, to avoid the oppressive export duties, it is computed that the total value of the shipments from the country would not fall short of $25,000,000.

The imports, comprising almost every kind of manufactured goods, machinery, etc., are likewise growing in value, having been as follows for the years above expressed: 1873, $19,420,000; 1872, $18,860,000; 1871, $14,860,000; and 1870, $15,000,000.

The extent of land under cultivation is increasing from year to year, and it is affirmed that the cereal productions have more than doubled within the last decade, spite of the great lack of hands to till the ground, and the consequent enhanced price of labor. Reapers are not unfrequently paid as much as $2 per diem, and boarded. Recent experiments in cotton-culture in the northern districts have proved successful; and flax and tobacco would here find a genial soil.

The horned cattle in the country in 1874 were computed at 7,200,000 head; that of sheep, at 20,000,000; and the quantity of wool shipped each year, at 14,464,000 pounds. Railway interests are receiving all the attention compatible with the hampered condition of the national Treasury; it was reported that the Central Uruguayan line would by the end of the year be open to public traffic as far as Florida, seventy-two miles north of the capital, Montevideo. A branch of that line will communicate with the port of Colonia, on the estuary of the River Plate, and the work on the northwestern line, from Salto on the Uruguay River, to the frontier of Brazil, has been prosecuted with unusual energy. A line from Montevideo eastward is also in course of preparation, and several other concessions have been obtained for lines which, with those above referred to, will establish a net-work of railways to all points of the republic. Four lines of horse-cars lead from Montevideo to the environs; and the enterprise of deepening the harbor of the capital is carried on without interruption.

The number of vessels entered at Montevideo in 1873 was 1,818, with an aggregate of 907,328 tons; and that of the clearances was 1,839, the aggregate tonnage being 924,070. The national revenue, as estimated in the budget for 1874, was $6,756,009; and the expenditures, $6,568,077.

The customs, the main source of the revenue, yielded, in 1873, $6,478,209. The national debt is about $42,000,000, or a little less than $100 per head for each inhabitant.

V

VERMONT. The financial condition of Vermont is very favorable. On the 1st of August, 1872, there was in the Treasury a balance of $178,179.14, besides $184,551.02 belonging to the sinking-fund. During the year following the receipts amounted to $566,504.08, including $4,386.80 received from Senator J. S. Morrill,

being the amount of his "back pay," and $7,836.74 received for interest on balances. Thus the entire amount credited to the Treasury for the year ending July 31, 1873, was $869,034.24. Against this payments were made amounting to $526,410.65, leaving a balance of $101,851.02 to the sinking-fund, and $240,772.57 cash in the Treasury. Beginning the accounts of the next year with these two items, and adding the receipts from various sources, amounting to $460,380.26, including $6,328.98 received from military stores sold, we have a credit of $803,003.85 for the year ending July 31, 1874. The payments of the same year, including installments on the funded debt, amounted to $397,188.20, and the balances on the 1st of August were $37,932.36 belonging to the sinking-fund, and $367,883.29 surplus cash. The payments on the funded debt, for the year ending July 31st, were as follows:

Registered loan of 1874	$16.500 00
Registered loan of 1876	2.500 00
Coupon bonds of 1874	20.000 00
Coupon bonds of 1876	26,000 00
Coupon bonds of 1878	6,000 00
Total	$71,000 00

The remaining liabilities of the State are the following:

Due towns, United States surplus fund	$11,519 96
Due on soldiers' accounts	13,424 46
Due on outstanding checks	1,886 06
Due on funded debt:	
Bonds due December 1, 1874	$50,500 00
Bonds due December 1, 1876	110,500 00
Bonds due December 1, 1878	65,500 00
	226,500 00
Due Agricultural College fund, June 1, 1890	135,500 00
Total	$388,830 48

Against this are to be placed $5,671.44 due on the tax of 1873, and the cash in the Treasury, amounting to $405,815.65, making the total assets $411,487.09, or $22,656.61 in excess of the liabilities. Of the liabilities $194,000 is in outstanding coupon bonds—payable,

December 1, 1874	$50,500 00
December 1, 1876	109,500 00
December 1, 1878	34,000 00
Total	$194,000 00

—and $168,000 is in outstanding "certificates of registered loan" issued under the act of 1867 and the act of 1870, which sum includes the Agricultural College fund. These certificates are payable—

December 1, 1876	$1,000 00
December 1, 1878	31,500 00
June 1, 1890, Agricultural College fund	135.500 00
Total	$168,000 00

The State Reform-School, located at Waterbury, was totally destroyed by fire on the 12th of December. The property was valued at $60,000. The institution was established in November, 1865, and first opened for the reception of juvenile delinquents in June, 1866. There was a farm of 133 acres, and a chairshop and mill connected with it. The number of inmates on the 31st of July was 145, and the number committed during the year preceding was 41. The earnings of the boys for the year ending August 1st were $8,598.42. The current expenses for two years were $26,563.83. The average expense of each boy to the State for the last year, after deducting his earnings, was $85.27.

An extra session of the Legislature was immediately called, which met at the Capitol in January, 1875, and passed several acts relating to the Reform-School. A sum "not exceeding $30,000" was appropriated for the purpose of erecting and fitting up new buildings for the institution, but the location was changed from Waterbury to Vergennes, where the Governor was authorized to purchase the grounds and buildings known as the Champlain Arsenal, at a cost not to exceed $11,000, and additional land at a cost not to exceed $8,000. The property at Waterbury, and such as cannot be profitably used at Vergennes, are to be sold, and the proceeds carried into the Treasury. A second act provides for the transfer of the pupils to the new buildings as soon as they are ready, and declares that the proceeds of the sale of property at Waterbury or Vergennes shall be for the benefit of the Reform-School. A third act provides for the admission of girls not less than ten years of age, nor more than fifteen, on the same terms and for the same offenses as boys, but requires a complete separation of the two sexes in the buildings, "except for educational and religious instruction, and such recreation as may be allowed by the trustees and superintendent at their discretion." Other acts have reference to the legal proceedings in cases where the penalty is a committal to the Reform-School, make unimportant changes in the regulations of the school, and provide for the payment of the extra expense occasioned by the fire at Waterbury. An act was also passed providing for an enlargement of the State-prison, and appropriating $12,500 for the expenses thereof.

The Republican State Convention was held at Burlington, on the 17th of June, and consisted of 658 delegates, one for each city and town, and one for every 100 votes cast for the Republican candidate for Governor in 1872. The nominations made were as follows: For Governor, Judge Asahel Peck, of Jericho; for Lieutenant-Governor, Lyman G. Hinckley, of Chelsea; for State Treasurer, John A. Page, of Montpelier. The platform of the convention, which was adopted without opposition, was as follows:

Resolved, That the Republicans of Vermont again affirm their adhesion to the declaration of the principles and policy of the national Republican party, made in its last national Convention.

Resolved, That the events of the national campaign of 1872, and the history of public affairs since, have fully justified our party in its action, and have clearly shown that now, as heretofore, it can be relied upon to maintain and preserve the great results of the overthrow of the rebellion, in giving and securing equal rights to all citizens; in spreading the principles of real republicanism and just government; in making labor everywhere honorable; in protecting the people against reaction in aid of the principles of the "lost cause" and its friends; and in guarding, now and in the future, the Treasury of the nation from being depleted by claims for losses incurred in the rebellion.

Resolved, That while we hail with joy every step toward permanent peace and obedience to law in the States lately in rebellion, and pledge ourselves to aid in promoting the welfare and happiness of the people thereof, we do not mean to forget that the cause of the Union and its noble defenders is sacred, and ought to be steadily and publicly kept in view, as the polestar of the future progress of the republic.

Resolved, That we express our full approval of the Administration of the President of our choice, and congratulate him and our party that it is able and willing to punish wrongs and rectify abuses, wherever found; and that it does not, like former Administrations of our adversaries, cover up or palliate the shortcomings of any of the public servants.

Resolved, That we stand by the oft-repeated and cardinal doctrine of our party, that a currency always redeemable in coin is the only true and safe one for the honesty and welfare of the community, as it is for the honor and good name of the nation; that we condemn all steps, direct or indirect, in any other direction than toward early resumption; and that we earnestly thank the President for his steadfast and active support of these principles by the exercise of his constitutional powers.

Resolved, That the tax and tariff laws ought to be so framed as to aid in the promotion and protection of American industry.

Resolved, That we favor all proper and prudent measures for the improvement of internal communication between the different parts of our common country, and especially in opening to a larger commerce the line of water communication created by Nature between the Northwest and the Atlantic, through the Great Lakes, and the valley of Lake Champlain.

Resolved, That we will give the ticket this day nominated our earnest and hearty support.

The Democratic State Convention assembled at Montpelier, on the 25th of June, and nominated W. H. H. Bingham, of Stow, for Governor; Henry Chase, of Lyndon, for Lieutenant-Governor; and Otis Chamberlain, of Pomfret, for Treasurer. The following platform was unanimously adopted:

Resolved, That we renew our devotion to the Democratic party and its principles, and we invite all citizens to unite with us in an effort to restore the principles of this party to the government of the country.

Resolved, That the present prohibitory law is undemocratic, and has proved injurious to the cause of temperance and good order, and that we favor its unconditional repeal and the adoption of a stringent license law.

Resolved, That we hail with joy the prospect of an early, speedy completion of the Caughnawaga Canal, whereby Lake Champlain will be the reservoir for the surplus productions of the Great West, and an outlet for the trade and commerce between the interior and the seaboard, and beneficial alike to the farmer, manufacturer, producer, and consumer, by an increase of transportation facilities and consequently more direct and friendly relations, and cheap transit of property.

Resolved, That the ticket this day nominated shall be supported by us, and we advise all good citizens to help us in electing it, and giving good government to the State.

The election took place on the 1st of September, and resulted in the election of the Republican candidates, though by majorities considerably reduced from those of the preceding State election. The total vote for Governor was 46,839, of which Peck received 33,-582 and Bingham 13,257, making the former's majority 20,325. The congressional canvass excited unusual interest. In the first district, Charles W. Willard, who had already served

some years in Congress and made a good record, was defeated by a political combination in the Republican nominating convention, and Colonel Charles H. Joyce was made the candidate. The latter was elected over Heaton, Democratic, by 7,041 majority. In the second district, Judge Luke P. Poland, whose record in Congress was not satisfactory to a large portion of his own party, secured the regular nomination, and the consequence was, that a second Republican nomination was made, Dudley C. Dennison being the candidate. At the same time C. W. Davenport ran as a Democratic candidate, and John B. Mead, Independent. The result was no election, Poland having fewer votes than Dennison and no candidate having a majority. A special election was ordered, and held on the 3d of November, Poland and Dennison both being candidates again. The latter was elected by 2,685 majority. In the third district, George W. Hendee was reëlected without opposition in his own party, and received 5,397 majority over Edwards, Democrat.

The regular biennial session of the Legislature opened at Montpelier on the 7th of October, and continued until November 24th. During that time, eighty-eight statutes and one joint resolution received the approval of the Governor. The question which received the largest share of attention was that of modifying the law relating to the sale of intoxicating liquors. The existing statute was a strict prohibitory law. A license act was introduced early in the session, but did not meet with favor from any considerable portion of the members. The result of the agitation on the subject, however, was several modifications of the old law. The most important of these was the following:

Whenever any person by reason of intoxication shall commit or cause any injury upon the person or property of any other individual, any person who by himself, his clerk or servant, shall have unlawfully sold or furnished any pa of the liquor causing such intoxication, shall be liable to the party injured for all damage occasioned by the injury so done, to be recovered in the same form of action as such intoxicated person would be liable to; and both such parties may be joined in the same action, and in case of the death or disability of any person, either from the injury received as herein specified, or in consequence of intoxication from the use of liquors unlawfully furnished as aforesaid, any person who shall be in any manner dependent on such injured person for means of support, or any party on whom shall be injured person may be dependent, may recover from the person unlawfully selling or furnishing any such liquor, as aforesaid, all damage or loss sustained in consequence of such injury, in any court having jurisdiction in such cases; and coverture or infancy shall be no bar to proceedings for recovery in any case arising under this act, and no person shall be disqualified as a witness, by reason of the marriage relation in any proceeding under this act.

Several acts were passed relating to the matter of public education. One of these abolished the Board of Education, and created the office of State Superintendent of Education. The Superintendent is to be elected by the

Legislature at each biennial session, and receive a salary of $1,500 a year, besides having all the direct expenses involved in the performance of his duties paid by the State. He is required to devote his whole time in promoting the highest educational interests of the State, and visit every part thereof during each year, deliver lectures upon the subject of education; confer with town superintendents, visit schools in connection with them, and furnish each of them blank forms for collecting school statistics. He is also required to hold a teachers' institute in any county on application of twenty-five teachers therein. Town superintendents make their reports to him each year on or before the 10th of April, and he must make a full report to the Legislature on the first day of each biennial session. Another act provides for the appointment of teachers and the conduct of examinations, etc., in the normal schools, of which there is one in each of the three congressional districts. Still another defines the duties of town superintendents, and another provides for the division of public money among school districts. An act providing for a strict supervision of the insurance business, another providing for the taxation of the real estate of railroads, and several intended to secure a more efficient provision for the insane poor, were among the other legislative acts of the session. The amount appropriated for the support of the government was $980,000 for two years.

On the 20th of October, George F. Edmunds was reëlected to the United States Senate, receiving the vote of every Senator but two, one of whom was absent, while the other voted for Edward J. Phelps, and a majority of 97 in the House, out of a total vote of 257.

VIRGINIA. The most important matter considered by the people of Virginia during the past year related to the financial condition of the State. A joint resolution was passed by the Legislature, and approved April 30, 1874, providing for the holding of a conference in Richmond, on the 10th of November, between the Governor and Treasurer, on behalf of the State and the creditors of the Commonwealth. The object of the conference was "to effect such exact and authentic understanding of the resources and liabilities of Virginia, and to consider such propositions for final agreement between the parties interested, as will afford the best attainable security for the rights and interests both of public creditors and the Commonwealth." The meeting was held at the time and place indicated, when an elaborate review of the recent financial history of the State was presented by Governor Kemper. The Governor attributed the present unsatisfactory state of the finances to the effect of the funding bill of 1871. He says:

The passage of the act of the 30th of March, 1871, commonly called the funding bill; the circumstances attending its passage; the exposition then made to the world of the resources of this State by those who stood forth as its organs and representatives: these

are the causes of all the subsequent misunderstandings and of all the criminations under which the State has suffered and now suffers. They are causes which have inflicted equal injury upon all parties concerned in the debt and the credit of the State. When the incontestable facts are disclosed to you, they will be found to constitute a stupendous and disastrous mistake which you are bound to know in order to protect your own interests. They are the origin and seat of the disease which this conference seeks to remedy.

The funding bill became a law when nearly all the experienced public men of the State had been shut out from participation in its government. They were practically disfranchised by measures resulting from the late war. Those who legislated for Virginia were generally new men, unused to public affairs, and called suddenly to the control of the most important and intricate financial and other interests. I testify that many of those who voted for the funding bill were patriotic and incorruptible men, who acted on the purest convictions.

At the time of passing this measure the whole indebtedness of the former Commonwealth amounted to $45,718,119.73. One-third of this amount was set apart for future settlement with West Virginia; the balance, $30,478,746.49, was assumed as the debt proper of Virginia, and provision was made for at once funding that amount in bonds, with tax-paying coupons, and bearing annual interest at the rate of six per centum—excepting sterling debt. The funding bill unconditionally pledged the State to pay full interest on the new bonds to the extent to which creditors should accept them. The annual interest on the whole of the debt proper thus proposed to be funded was $1,810,540.73, which, added to the amount yearly expended for the support of government and of public schools, to wit, $1,528,295.84, made it necessary to raise an annual State revenue of $3,338,836.57 in addition to the local taxation before mentioned. But the result proved that so far from taxation at the rate of forty cents on the one hundred dollars sufficing to support the government and pay six per cent. interest on the original debt of $45,718,119.73, an addition of 25 per centum to that rate of taxation fell far short of enabling the government to pay two-thirds of the interest on two-thirds of the debt. The increased rate of taxation has fallen short of enabling the government to pay full interest on two-thirds of the original debt, by an average annual deficiency of $1,062,578.05. If full interest had been hitherto paid on the debt intended to be assumed by the funding bill, no more than a balance of $465,717.79 of the annual State revenue would have been left in the Treasury; of that balance, $371,998.56 would have been absorbed by the mandatory provision of the constitution in favor of public schools, so that only $93,719.23 would have been left annually for defraying all the expenses of supporting the government.

When a new Legislature had been elected by the people, with special reference to the funding-bill legislation of the previous Assembly, and when its members were convened in December, 1871, they found themselves confronted with appalling financial entanglements which threatened to speedily stop the wheels of the government. The work of issuing the new funded bonds had been rapidly progressing, and influences were being exerted to hasten and urge it forward. It was evident that, if two-thirds of the original debt should be funded in bonds with tax-paying coupons, the coupons would annually absorb the bulk of the State revenues, and the government would be left without the means to preserve its existence. Thereupon the funding act was so modified as to prevent the further issuing of bonds with coupons receivable for taxes, and to provide for funding the residue of the debt in like bonds, but with coupons not receivable for taxes.

But, before this legislation took effect, $17,-

281,100 of the debt had been funded in coupon bonds with tax-paying coupons, and the further sum of $2,957,915.80 had been funded in registered bonds and fractional certificates, which are convertible at the option of the holder into coupon bonds with tax-paying coupons; making $20,239,015.80 in all, funded under the provisions of the original funding act upon which the annual interest is or may become demandable on tax-paying coupons.

The following statement of taxation in Virginia, under State laws, for the fiscal year 1872–'73, the latest for which returns of local taxation have been received, has been made by Governor Kemper:

State revenue derived from taxation.........$2,421,945 41	
Amount of reported county, township, road, and local school levies....................	2,217,538 49
Amount of unreported county, township, road, and local school levies, as estimated by the Auditor of Public Accounts........	282,461 51
Costs of collection, retained by tax collectors, etc...................................	172,318 09
Total of taxes paid, under State laws, for one year...............................	$5,094,263 60

During the same year the United States Government collected in Virginia, in the shape of internal revenue taxes, $7,310,015.56; and assuming, says the same authority, what is far short of the truth, that the money directly and indirectly drawn from the people of Virginia by United States tariff taxation is in the proportion of the population of the State to that of the whole country, it is shown that Virginia pays, by reason of the national customs laws, the further sum of $5,976,401.95, making a total in one year of $18,388,681.01. And yet the total of fairly-assessed taxable values in the State is but $336,686,433.23.

The Legislature of 1874 passed a new tax bill, which promises to yield greater revenues in future. In many particulars it enlarges the subjects and increases the rates of previous taxation. This increased taxation is considered as onerous as the people of the State can endure in their present impoverished condition. As above stated, it requires $1,528,295.84 annually to pay the ordinary expenses of the government, and the constitutional requisition in favor of the public schools. It is hoped and believed, by the friends of the new tax law, that it will probably yield that amount, and the further sum of $1,200,000 annually. This surplus would pay full interest on two-thirds of the new funded debt, or four per cent. on the whole. And this is supposed to be the utmost that the State can pay to its creditors under existing circumstances.

The committee of bondholders to whom was referred the communication made by the Governor, reported that they were "of the opinion that, notwithstanding the reduced and impoverished condition of Virginia in her taxable valuables, and various industries, taxation sufficient to pay the necessary expenses of the State government, including the proper main-

tenance of the public schools, as provided for by the State constitution, and the payment of four per cent. interest on her funded and two-thirds of her unfunded debt, can be levied without serious damage or inconvenience to the people of the State; that, to secure this end, your committee are of the opinion that an arrangement may be effected by which large numbers of holders of the bonds can be induced to surrender the tax-receivable coupons as they fall due, and receive the two per cent. payable on the debt semi-annually." This, in the opinion of the committee, can be largely effected by legislation providing for the prompt payment of four per cent. interest, as it falls due, at points accessible and convenient to the bondholder. This legislation, it was believed, would result in retiring seventy-five or eighty per cent. of the tax-receivable coupons on the payment of the four per cent. interest, and that only the coupons from bonds held in Virginia would be used in payment of taxes. The following resolutions recommended by the committee were unanimously adopted by the conference:

Resolved, That the State ought to provide, by appropriate legislation, by permanently setting apart a specific portion of its accruing revenue, for the prompt payment of two per cent. interest semi-annually at London, New York, and Baltimore, and the Treasury of the State, and the issue of certificates for the unpaid interest, payable at the pleasure of the State at any time within ten years; and if not paid in ten years then such certificates ought to be fundable in four per cent. bonds.

Resolved, That the State ought to resume payment of full six per cent. interest at the earliest practicable moment.

The State government of Virginia in 1874 was as follows: Governor, James L. Kemper; Lieutenant-Governor, Robert E. Wilbers; Attorney-General, Raleigh T. Daniel; Secretary of the Commonwealth, James McDonald; Treasurer, R. T. M. Hunter; Auditors, William F. Taylor and Asa Rogers; Superintendent of Public Instruction, W. H. Ruffner; Register of the Land-Office, Samuel H. Boykin. All are Conservatives.

The Legislature is composed as follows:

PARTIES.	Senate.	House.	Joint Ballot.
Conservatives.....	33	99	132
Republicans.......	9	33	42
Conserv. majority	24	66	90

The congressional election of 1874 resulted in the choice of the following Representatives:

Dist.	I.—Beverly B. Douglas...........	Conservative.
"	II.—John Goode, Jr..............	"
"	III.—Gilbert C. Walner............	"
"	IV.—William H. H. Stowell........	Administra'n.
"	V.—George C. Cabell..............	Conservative.
"	VI.—John R. Tucker..............	"
"	VII.—John T. Harris..............	"
"	VIII.—Eppa Hunton..............	"
"	IX.—William Terry..............	"

The constitutional amendment abolishing the township system was ratified by a majority vote of 26,516.

W

WEST VIRGINIA. The total receipts into the Treasury during the year ending September 30, 1874, amounted to $695,951, and the disbursements to $657,183, leaving a balance in the Treasury at that date of $282,364. This includes balance of the general school-fund, $224,524; balance of school-fund, $22,882; balance of fund for general purposes, $30,904; and balance of building-fund, $4,352. In the balance of $30,604, applicable to general purposes, is included $18,470 borrowed for the use of the State, and not yet paid. Governor Jacob recommends an appropriation for the payment of this sum. "The foregoing statement," says that official, "shows the healthy condition of our finances; all the demands upon the Treasury have been met, and a substantial balance left to carry over to the present fiscal year. The last Legislature failed to impose the five-cents tax, heretofore known as the hospital or building tax, and consequently the

revenue for the present year will be considerably reduced. I estimate this reduction at $60,-000 in round numbers, consequently the appropriations for this fiscal year must necessarily be less than heretofore, for, even if it should be your pleasure to restore this tax, it can only avail for the next fiscal year. This is greatly to be regretted, for at least two of the public institutions need liberal appropriations for construction purposes. I recommend that this building tax be renewed for one year."

The question of the removal of the State capital has been prominently agitated during the year, and will doubtless be acted upon by the Legislature of 1875. The present capital, Charleston, is far from the centre of the State, and is difficult of access to a large portion of the people. Early in June a State Convention of delegates to consider this subject was held in Grafton. C. M. Bishop, having been chosen as the president, remarked that "the wheels of

HARPER'S FERRY.

prosperity are now clogged by the lack of a proper and permanent location of the State capital. The seat of government is not where the people want it, and, if a popular vote were had upon the question, an overwhelming majority would pronounce in favor of removal. Charleston is difficult of access to two-thirds if not three-fourths of the people of the State, and it is not uncommon for delegates going to Charleston to be compelled to pass through portions of three States before reaching the capital of their own."

The views of the Convention on this subject are set forth in the following resolutions, which were adopted:

We, the representatives of the people of West Virginia, in convention assembled, recognizing the importance of securing the location of our State capital at some point that shall be accessible to the people, and believing that its present location is detrimental to our best interests on account of its remoteness and inaccessibility, would recommend to the people of the State for their consideration the following resolutions:

Resolved, That we favor the removal of the State capital from Charleston to some more accessible point.

Resolved, That the question of the removal of our State capital has for its object solely the general convenience and accommodation of the people; that it has no political significance, but is demanded by a large majority of the people of this State, without regard to party or political creed; and that we will oppose with an unrelenting opposition any scheme of political aspirants that shall have for its object the bargain or sale of this question for present or future political preferment.

Resolved, That we recommend to the political parties of the State that this matter be made a subject of consideration in political primary meetings, and that all candidates for the Legislature be requested to pledge themselves unqualifiedly in favor of removal.

Resolved, That in taking this position upon this question, we are animated by no feeling of hostility to the people of Charleston, but are actuated solely by what we conceive to be the true interests and welfare of the whole State.

Resolved, That the following gentlemen be appointed by this convention an Executive Committee, for the purpose of carrying out the sentiments embodied in these resolutions, and their presentation to the people of the State.

In accordance with the last resolution, a large number of prominent citizens were appointed as committee-men.

A new railroad, called the Wheeling & Lake Erie Railroad, is in process of construction between Wheeling and Toledo. A junction with the Atlantic & Southeastern Railway is spoken of, and coöperation of the two roads from the point of junction to the Ohio River. Little support has been derived from the citizens of Wheeling.

An act of the Legislature, passed February 6, 1864, authorizing boards of supervisors to borrow money to pay bounties to soldiers, was decided in the Circuit Court of Wetzel County, by Judge C. S. Lewis, to be in violation of a clause in the constitution to the effect that "no law shall embrace more than one object, which shall be expressed in its title." The title of the act in question runs thus: "To provide for the relief of the families of soldiers," which, the court held, does not imply the provision of bounties for the soldiers themselves.

Several Normal Institutes, supported by the Peabody fund, held in different parts of the State during the summer, were attended by the experienced and progressive educators of West Virginia. The sessions lasted from ten days to two weeks, and the results were helpful and promising.

The present Legislature, composed of 68 Democrats, 16 Republicans, and 5 Independents, will be called upon to decide the question of the removal of the capital, and to choose a Senator. The foremost candidates for the senatorship are Henry S. Walker; the public printer; J. N. Camden, who has been twice candidate for the governorship; and J. C. Faulkner, ex-minister to France, and Confederate officer during the war.

It is the opinion of many leading citizens that a geological survey of West Virginia is needed, and will have an important influence in promoting the industrial and commercial prosperity of the State. In presenting this subject to the consideration of the Legislature in January, 1875, Governor Jacob said:

Our valuable mineral deposits are becoming widely known; they have attracted the attention of some

of the leading capitalists of other States, and also of England, many of whom have visited the State with a view of investment. But unfortunately, when they come, we have comparatively little authentic information to communicate to them. Our people are, in the main, ignorant of our true resources, and this sometimes leads to an exaggeration of their extent, or, on the other hand, to a depreciation of their value. Some of our more enterprising citizens have had local investigations and examinations made, but these, even when made by men of the highest scientific character, are neither so reliable nor so satisfactory as a general survey. We need a general examination of our geological strata and mineral formations; when this has been done, local investigations can be made intelligently and with advantage. I therefore think it would be highly conducive to the public interests to have a general geological survey made under State authority.

WHELAN, Right Rev. RICHARD VINCENT, D. D., Roman Catholic Bishop of the Diocese of Wheeling, West Va., born in Baltimore, January 29, 1809; died in that city, July 7, 1874. He entered Mount St. Mary's College, Emmettsburg, Md., when ten or eleven years of age, and remained there eight or nine years, being Prefect of Studies the latter part of the time. He was then sent to the Seminary of St.-Sulpice, Paris, for his theological and philosophical course, and graduated with high honors in 1831, being ordained priest at Versailles the same year. He was employed, on his return to the United States, as professor at St. Mary's College, till 1835, when he was assigned, by the Archbishop of Baltimore, to the missions at Harper's Ferry, Martinsburg, etc. His labors were so zealous and successful that, in 1840, he was appointed by the Pope Bishop of Richmond, and consecrated March, 1841. In 1850 the diocese was divided, and he chose the western or Wheeling diocese, and resided thenceforward in that city. He was very active in promoting the educational interests of the Church, and had built up a seminary for young ladies and a convent at Mount de Chantal, near Wheeling, which has attained a very high reputation. He was a lithe, active man, of great energy, and one of the most self-sacrificing, zealous, and hard-working prelates in the country. He opposed, in the Vatican Council, the promulgation of the dogma of papal infallibility, but gave in his adhesion to it promptly when it was promulgated.

WHITEHOUSE, Right Rev. HENRY JOHN, D. D., LL. D., D. C. L., Bishop of the Protestant Episcopal Diocese of Illinois, born in New York City, August 19, 1803; died August 10, 1874. He graduated from Columbia College in 1821, and from the General Episcopal Theological Seminary, New York, in 1824, receiving deacon's orders the same year, and priest's orders in 1827, and ministered to a parish in Reading, Pa., for about three years. He was then called to the rectorship of St. Luke's, Rochester, and remained there, greatly esteemed by all Christian denominations, till 1844, a period of fifteen years. He was next rector of St. Thomas's Church, New York City, till 1851, when he was elected Assistant

Bishop of Illinois, and, on the death of Bishop Chase, became bishop, September 20, 1852. Here he soon became a rigid constructionist, very conservative and exceedingly High Church in his doctrines, and was drawn into some bitter controversies in his diocese in consequence. Bishop Whitehouse visited England in 1867, and preached the opening sermon before the Pan-Anglican Council held at Lambeth Palace. During his visit he was treated with marked attention, and received degrees from both the Oxford and Cambridge Universities. He was an accomplished scholar, an eloquent preacher, and earnest defender of his Church. He discharged efficiently his episcopal duties, claiming no exemption because of his advanced years. His views were accorded great weight in the Council of Bishops, and generally favored conservatism.

WHITNEY, ASA, an American inventor, engineer, manufacturer, and philanthropist, born in Townsend, Mass., December 1, 1791; died in Philadelphia, June 4, 1874. His early education was scanty, but every opportunity was diligently improved. He learned the blacksmith's trade, then became a machinist, worked for several years in Swanzey, N. H., Brattleboro, Vt., and Brownville, Jefferson County, N. Y., in the production of cotton-mill and saw-mill machinery, and at the latter place owned and ran for a time a cotton-mill. In 1831 he became master-machinist, and in 1833 Superintendent of the Mohawk & Hudson Railroad, and remained in the latter position, except for one year, till the close of 1839, when he resigned, and the next year was elected Canal Commissioner of New York. In 1842 he removed to Philadelphia, and was the partner of the celebrated M. W. Baldwin, in the manufacture of locomotives, until 1846, when he withdrew, to start the manufacture of car-wheels on a new plan of annealing which he had invented. He commenced this in 1847, and carried it on till his death, his sons being associated with him. His works were so extensive that, for many years, he has made 75,000 to 80,000 car-wheels per annum, using 12,000 tons of the best-selected iron, and 4,000 to 5,000 tons of coal, and employing 200 to 250 men. His car-wheels are acknowledged to be the best made. He was, in 1846, President of the Morris Canal Company, and invented a series of inclined planes for their boats to pass elevations, the motive-power of which was derived from turbine wheels driven by the waste-water of the canal. In 1859 he was President of the Reading Railroad, and his management of it was very successful. By his will he bequeathed $50,000 to found a professorship of Dynamical Engineering in the University of Pennsylvania, and $37,500 to other local benevolent objects.

WISCONSIN. The railway companies whose lines traverse this State in every direction have for many years been complained of by her people, who charged them with unjust discriminations and exorbitantly high rates for the transportation of passengers and merchandise. The charters covering the whole length of these lines within the borders of Wisconsin, except for the road running from Milwaukee to Prairie du Chien, which was chartered by acts of her Territorial Government in 1847 and 1848, have been granted to the respective companies by acts of her Legislature under the present constitution, which was adopted by her as a State in 1848, and which contains the following provision:

Corporations may be formed under general laws, but shall not be created by a special act, except for municipal purposes and in cases where, in the judgment of the Legislature, the objects of the corporations cannot be attained under general laws. All general laws, or special acts, enacted under the provisions of this section, may be altered or repealed by the Legislature at any time after their passage. (Art. XI., Section 1.)

The complaints of the people seem to have remained unheeded by the railway companies concerned, to whose notice they were repeatedly brought. On March 11, 1874, the Legislature enacted a law respecting these roads, entitled "An act relating to railroad, express and telegraph companies in the State of Wisconsin, classifying railroads and freights, limiting and fixing the compensation to be charged for the transportation of freights and passengers, and providing for the appointment of Railroad Commissioners."

The act distributes all the railways operating within the State into three classes—A, B, and C: the first including "all the railroads in Wisconsin now owned, operated, managed, or leased, either by the Milwaukee & St. Paul Railroad Company, the Chicago & Northwestern Railroad Company, or the Western Union Railway Company;" the second, "all the railroads, or parts of railroads, owned, operated, managed, or leased, by the Wisconsin Central Railway Company, and the Green Bay & Minnesota Railway Company;" the third, "all the other railroads, or parts of railroads, in the State." It then fixes the maximum rates which each of the roads, or their classes, are severally allowed to charge for the transportation of passengers and merchandise. These rates, whose difference is said to have been regulated by taking into consideration the character of the country run upon, and the amount of business transacted by the railroads respectively, are as follows:

With regard to passengers, the compensation per mile for the transportation of any person, with ordinary baggage not exceeding one hundred pounds, is fixed at three cents for class A, three and a half cents for class B, and four cents for class C. For children of the age of twelve years and under, one-half of the said rates, respectively, is allowed. As to freights, the act distributes merchandise into four general classes, and subdivides it into seven special classes, which latter are therein enumerated in a detailed schedule, with their respective rates affixed. According to the quality. of the merchandise, the rates of freight are reckoned by weights of one hundred pounds, by barrels, or car-loads, and calculated in a steadily decreasing scale, in proportion as the distance run increases; the distance itself being considered as divided into lengths of twenty-five and thirteen miles. The rates fixed for the transportation of merchandise, included within any of the seven special classes, are applicable only to the railroad companies named above. All the other roads are allowed to charge for it the same rates which were in force on June 1, 1873, and no more. As to merchandise comprised within the four general classes, all of the railroads in the State, without distinction, are permitted to charge for its transportation the same rates which they did charge for it on June 1, 1873, and no more.

In order to realize the purpose intended, and secure compliance with its provisions, the act establishes a Board of Railroad Commissioners, to be appointed by the Governor. Every evasion, or violation of the provisions of the act, is declared to be a misdemeanor. The penalty for each offense is a fine not exceeding $200; in addition to which the in-

STATE-HOUSE, MADISON.

jured party has the right to recover from the offending company three times the amount taken from him in excess of the legal rates, as fixed by the act.

A resolution was adopted by the Legislature on the 12th of March, directing the Secretary of State not to publish the act of the 11th of that month until the 28th day of April next ensuing, when it should immediately go into operation. In the State of Wisconsin no general law is in force till after its publication.

On the same day on which this law was published, April 28th, the President of the Chicago, Milwaukee & St. Paul Railroad Company, in the name and behalf of the corporation which he represented, addressed to the Governor a communication, officially, to inform him of the resolution taken by that body concerning the operations of the road in reference to the provisions of the said act, stating as follows: "The Board of Directors have caused this act to be carefully examined and considered by our own counsel, and by some of the most eminent jurists in the land, and after such examination they are unanimous in their opinion that it is unconstitutional and void. The Board of Directors are trustees of this property, and are bound faithfully to discharge their trust, and to the best of their ability protect it from spoliation and ruin. They have sought the advice of able counsel, and after mature consideration believe it their duty to disregard so much of said law as attempts arbitrarily to fix rates of compensation for freight and passengers."

Another communication of a like import was sent to the Governor by the President of the Chicago & Northwestern Railroad Company. Both of these communications their respective writers caused to be filed in the office of the Executive Department of the State of Wisconsin, on April 29th.

Upon this, Governor Taylor issued his proclamation, declaring that the law must be obeyed.

A lawsuit against the State of Wisconsin, with reference to the laws regulating railroads, was instituted in June, 1874, when, in the United States Circuit Court at Madison, a bill was filed in behalf of a number of bondholders of the Chicago & Northwestern Railway Company, citizens of Europe, and other States, praying for an injunction to enforce their equitable rights, and to restrain the Railroad Commissioners of the State from enforcing the law of March 11, 1874, to prevent action which might result in serious injury to the plaintiffs. Judge Davis, of the Supreme Court of the United States, Judge Drummond, of the United States Circuit Court, and Judge Hopkins, of the United States District Court for the Western District, convened at Madison, to determine upon the case. Numerous and highly-reputed counsel of Wisconsin, Chicago, and New York, among them two ex-Chief-Justices of the Supreme Courts of Wisconsin and Illinois, appeared for either side, and fully argued the matter during the first three days of July. The court decided it unanimously against the plaintiffs on the 4th, when Judge Drummond delivered the decision, his two colleagues fully concurring in it.

Upon the delivery of the decision, Justice Davis, of the Supreme Court of the United States, read a short address, in which, considering the gravity of the questions involved in this litigation, and that the court of last resort would ultimately have to pass upon them, he suggested harmony of action on the part of both complainants and defendants as necessary to obtain a speedy decision, and that it would be better for the defendants to have prosecutions for penalties suspended while this litigation was in progress. He concluded, saying: "These prosecutions are not required to settle rights; are attended with great expense; and, if enforced while an effort is being made to test the validity of this legislation, must cause serious irritation, and cannot be, as it seems to us, productive of any good results."

Prior to the time when the decision was rendered, the Attorney-General for the State had commenced proceedings in the Supreme Court of Wisconsin on a writ of *quo warranto*, for the forfeiture of the charters of the Chicago, Milwaukee & St. Paul, and the Chicago & Northwestern Railroad Companies, because of their violating the State law of March 11, 1874. And on the 8th of July he also filed, in the same Supreme Court, a bill in equity, complaining for the State that the two Railroad Companies above named did persistently violate the law of March 11, 1874, and asking that these companies be enjoined to obey the said law so far as the United States Circuit Court, by their late decision, had pronounced it valid.

A copy of this bill, with a notice that the attorneys for the State would ask for a hearing on the 14th of July for an injunction, was served upon the officers of the railways complained of.

The matter came to a hearing on the 4th of August, when the same counsel who, in the previous July, had appeared before the United States Circuit Court for the State and for the Chicago & Northwestern Railway Company, respectively, came now before the Supreme Court of the State, with the addition of one more on each side; their number being further increased by four on the part of the Chicago, Milwaukee & St. Paul Railway Company, who made common cause with the Chicago & Northwestern. They argued the case in all its aspects and at great length, the argument having occupied the sittings eight successive days, at the end of which it was closed, and the case submitted to the court for judgment. The court pronounced it on the 15th of September, and it was adverse to the railway companies. The decision, which was delivered on that day by Chief-Justice Ryan, is a lengthy document, as it is comprehensive, answering also the points raised by the counsel for the railway companies in detail. From a synopsis of the principal points decided, prepared by the Chief-Justice himself, we here subjoin the following conclusions:

It is not material here whether the defendants had an election to accept or reject the alteration of their charters by Chapter 273. They were bound to obey the statute, or to discontinue their operations as corporate bodies. In either case, they had no right to conduct their operations in defiance of public law. Chapter 273, of 1874, so far as its provisions are before the court in these cases, is a valid amendment of the special charters of the defendants, granted by the State. * * * The motions of the Attorney-General must be granted; and the writs issue as to all the roads of the Chicago & Northwestern Railway Company, and all of the roads of the Chicago, Milwaukee & St. Paul Railway Company, except the railroad from Milwaukee to Prairie du Chien, built under the territorial charter of 1847–'48. But, before the writs issue, the Attorney-General must file in these causes his official stipulation not to prosecute the defendants as for forfeiture of their charters for any violations of Chapter 273, charged in these informations, before the 1st day of October next; that time being allowed by the court to the defendants to arrange their rates of toll under Chapter 273.

In consequence of this decision, the President of the Chicago, Milwaukee & St. Paul Railroad Company addressed to Governor Taylor an official communication, dated September 28, 1874, notifying him of the company's conditional acquiescence in it.

The President of the Chicago & Northwestern Railway Company had previously expressed his intention to work the road in accordance with the provisions of the said law until repealed or amended.

The controverted law has been in practical operation since the 1st day of October, 1874.

The political contest, ending in the election

of November 3, 1874, was conducted in Wisconsin with remarkable energy by the Republicans and their antagonists, whom they designated by the general name of "Reformers," including, it seems, Democrats and Grangers, whatever the political opinions of the latter might have been.

The result of the election for Congressmen was five Republicans and three Reformers, as follows: First district, Charles G. Williams, Republican, 12,568; Fratt, Reformer, 9,532; second district, Lucien B. Caswell, Republican, 11,676; Cook, Reformer, 11,423; third district, Henry S. Magoon, Republican, 11,- 535; Thompson, Reformer, 10,343; fourth district, Ludington, Independent, 9,545; William P. Lynde, Reformer, 12,049; fifth district, Hiram Barber, Republican, 9,889; S. D. Burchard, Reformer, 15,784; sixth district, Alanson M. Kimball, Republican, 14,783; Bouck, Reformer, 14,641; seventh district, Jeremiah M. Rusk, Republican, 13,634; Fulton, Reformer, 10,196; eighth district, Alexander S. McDill, Republican, 9,444; Cate, Reformer, 9,446.

The whole number of votes polled throughout the State at the November election in 1874, as classified by congressional districts, amounted to 186,435; of which 93,411 were cast for Reform, and 93,024 for Republican nominees. In 1873 it was 147,823, of which 81,199 were cast for Reform, and 66,224 for Republican candidates.

The members of the Legislature elected in November, 1874, will stand in regard to politics as follows: In the Senate—Republicans 17, Reformers 15, Independent 1; in the House of Representatives—Republicans 64, Reformers 35, Independent 1; showing a Republican majority over Reformers and Independent combined of 1 in the Senate, 28 in the Lower House, and 29 on joint ballot. In the House of Representatives of the previous Legislature, the Reformers had a majority of about 20 over the Republicans.

The total amount of taxable property, personal and real estate, in the State, for the year 1874, was $346,476,464, showing an increase of $5,856,212 over its amount in 1873.

The education of youth is well provided for in Wisconsin, and her public schools, including the university, the Agricultural College, and the normal schools, are in successful operation, and largely attended. The school-age is by law between four and twenty years.

The various charitable institutions of the State are commendably cared for and under excellent management, realizing the purposes for which they were respectively established.

WYMAN, JEFFRIES, M. D., an eminent anatomist, regarded as the highest authority in comparative and general anatomy in America, born at Chelmsford, near Lowell, Mass., August 11, 1814; died at Bethlehem, N. H., September 4, 1874. He graduated from Harvard College in 1833, and from the Harvard Medical School in 1837. He next visited Europe, and, during a two years' stay, studied medicine in the hospitals of Paris, and natural history in the *Jardin des Plantes*. From 1843 to 1847 he was Professor of Anatomy in the Hampden-Sidney Medical College at Richmond, Va., and from 1847 to his death Horsey Professor of Anatomy in Harvard University, and Professor of Comparative Anatomy in the Lawrence Scientific School. In 1839 he had been appointed Curator of the Lowell Institute, and in 1841 delivered his first course of lectures there. These were not published, but a second course, delivered in 1849, were. He had long been a member and officer of the Boston Society of Natural History, and was from 1856 to 1857 its president. He had also been President of the American Association for the Advancement of Science, and a member of the American Academy of Arts and Sciences, and of the National Academy of Sciences. In 1866 he became Curator and one of the trustees of the Peabody Museum of Archæology and Ethnology, and had made it a magnificent success. His essay "On the Nervous System of the *Rana Pipiens*, or Bull-Frog," published by the Smithsonian Institution, is one of the most remarkable anatomical monographs ever written; and his other numerous papers had given him the highest reputation abroad, though his extreme modesty kept him from being so widely appreciated as he deserved.

INDEX OF SUBJECTS.

INDEX OF CONTENTS.